ESV Expository Commentary

VOL. I

Genesis–Numbers

EDITORS

Iain M. Duguid
James M. Hamilton Jr.
Jay Sklar

EXPOSITORY
Commentary

VOL. I
———
Genesis–Numbers

Genesis
Iain M. Duguid

Leviticus
Christine Palmer

Exodus
Jay Sklar

Numbers
Ronald Bergey

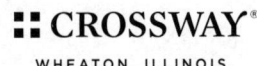

ESV Expository Commentary, Volume 1: Genesis–Numbers

© 2025 by Crossway

Published by Crossway
    1300 Crescent Street
    Wheaton, Illinois 60187

All rights reserved. No part of this publication may be reproduced, stored in a retrieval system, or transmitted in any form by any means, electronic, mechanical, photocopy, recording, or otherwise, without the prior permission of the publisher, except as provided for by USA copyright law. Crossway® is a registered trademark in the United States of America.

Cover design: Jordan Singer

First printing 2025

Printed in China

Unless otherwise indicated, Scripture quotations are from the ESV® Bible (The Holy Bible, English Standard Version®), © 2001 by Crossway, a publishing ministry of Good News Publishers. Used by permission. All rights reserved. The ESV text may not be quoted in any publication made available to the public by a Creative Commons license. The ESV may not be translated in whole or in part into any other language.

Scripture quotations marked AT are the author's translation.

The Scripture quotation marked CEV is from the *Contemporary English Version*. Copyright © 1995 by American Bible Society.

Scripture quotations marked CSB are from *The Christian Standard Bible*®. Copyright © 2017 by Holman Bible Publishers. Used by permission.

The Scripture quotation marked ICB is from The Holy Bible, International Children's Bible®. Copyright © 1986, 1988, 1999, 2015 by Thomas Nelson. Used by permission.

Scripture quotations marked JPS are from the Jewish Publication Society's 1917 English translation of the Hebrew Bible.

Scripture quotations marked KJV are from the *King James Version* of the Bible.

Scripture quotations marked NASB are from *The New American Standard Bible*®. Copyright © The Lockman Foundation 1960, 1962, 1963, 1968, 1971, 1972, 1973, 1975, 1977, 1995, 2020. Used by permission.

The Scripture quotation marked NEB is from the *New English Bible*. Copyright © 1961, 1970 by Cambridge University Press and Oxford University Press. All rights reserved.

Scripture quotations marked NET are from *The NET Bible*®. Copyright © 2017 by Biblical Studies Press, L.L.C. https://netbible.com. All rights reserved.

Scripture quotations marked NIV are taken from *The Holy Bible, New International Version*®, NIV®. Copyright © 1973, 1978, 1984, 2011 by Biblica, Inc.™ Used by permission. All rights reserved worldwide.

Scripture quotations marked NJPS are from *Tanakh: The Holy Scriptures: The New JPS Translation according to the Traditional Hebrew Text*. Copyright © 1985 by the Jewish Publication Society. Used by permission.

Scripture quotations marked NLT is from *The Holy Bible, New Living Translation*. Copyright © 1996, 2004, 2015. Used by permission of Tyndale House Publishers, Inc., Wheaton, IL, 60189. All rights reserved.

Scripture quotations marked NRSV are from *The New Revised Standard Version*. Copyright © 1989 by the Division of Christian Education of the National Council of the Churches of Christ in the U.S.A. Published by Thomas Nelson, Inc. Used by permission of the National Council of the Churches of Christ in the U.S.A.

There are also brief citations of the *New American Bible* (NAB) and the *Revised Standard Version* (RSV).

All emphases in Scripture quotations have been added by the authors.

Hardcover ISBN: 978-1-4335-4628-0

Crossway is a publishing ministry of Good News Publishers.

RRDS			33	32	31	30	29	28	27	26	25
15	14	13	12	11	10	9	8	7	6	5	4	3	2	1

CONTENTS

Tables 7

Figures 9

Preface to the ESV Expository Commentary 11

Contributors 13

Abbreviations 15

Genesis 21	Leviticus 817
Iain M. Duguid	*Christine Palmer*
Exodus 435	Numbers 1055
Jay Sklar	*Ronald Bergey*

Scripture Index 1336

TABLES

Exodus

2.1: Responding to Skepticism about Exodus's Historicity 443

2.2: The Lord's Promises and Faithfulness in Genesis and Exodus 449

2.3: The Lord's Awareness and Action in Exodus 3 479

2.4: Parallels between First Nine Strikes 515

2.5: Thematic Parallels in Exodus 15–17 565

2.6: Three Approaches to Exodus 21:22–25 650

2.7: Parallelism in Exodus 22:8 and 22:11 658

2.8: The Lord's Holy Times 683

2.9: Comparison of a Palace, Mount Sinai, and the Tabernacle: Three Zones and Who May Enter Them 693

2.10: The Making of the Tabernacle Components 808

2.11: Parallels between the Lord's Coming Down on Sinai and the Tabernacle 812

2.12: Parallels between Tabernacle Account and Creation Account 814

Leviticus

3.1: Offenders and Offerings 860

3.2: Offering, Portions, and Remains 878

3.3: Commands and Motives in Leviticus 11:41–45 921

3.4: The Skin-Diseased Person and the High Priest 933

3.5: The Decalogue in Leviticus 19 982

3.6: Priestly and Animal Blemishes 1007

3.7: Redemption Prices 1049

Numbers

4.1: Inclusio in Numbers 1:1–46 1086

4.2: Gershon, Kohath, and Merari in Numbers 3:21–37 1104

4.3: Covers and Transportation for the Sacred Furnishings 1110

4.4: Connections between Numbers 5:5–10 and Leviticus 6:1–7 1118

4.5: New Generation Compared to Exodus Generation 1233

4.6: Blessing Motif Introduced in Numbers 22 1243

4.7: Main Theme throughout Numbers 23–24 1252

FIGURES

Numbers

4.1: "Standard" (Hb. *degel*) Positions around the Tabernacle (T) Compass Points 1095

PREFACE
TO THE ESV EXPOSITORY COMMENTARY

The Bible pulsates with life, and the Spirit conveys the electrifying power of Scripture to those who lay hold of it by faith, ingest it, and live by it. God has revealed himself in the Bible, which makes the words of Scripture sweeter than honey, more precious than gold, and more valuable than all riches. These are the words of life, and the Lord has entrusted them to his church, for the sake of the world.

He has also provided the church with teachers to explain and make clear what the Word of God means and how it applies to each generation. We pray that all serious students of God's Word, both those who seek to teach others and those who pursue study for their own personal growth in godliness, will be served by the ESV Expository Commentary. Our goal has been to provide a clear, crisp, and Christ-centered explanation of the biblical text. All Scripture speaks of Christ (Luke 24:27), and we have sought to show how each biblical book helps us to see the "light of the knowledge of the glory of God in the face of Jesus Christ" (2 Cor. 4:6).

To that end, each contributor has been asked to provide commentary that is:

- *exegetically sound*—self-consciously submissive to the flow of thought and lines of reasoning discernible in the biblical text;
- *biblically theological*—reading the Bible as diverse yet bearing an overarching unity, narrating a single storyline of redemption culminating in Christ;
- *globally aware*—aimed as much as possible at a global audience, in line with Crossway's mission to provide the Bible and theologically responsible resources to as many people around the world as possible;
- *broadly reformed*—standing in the historical stream of the Reformation, affirming that salvation is by grace alone, through faith alone, in Christ alone, taught in Scripture alone, for God's glory alone; holding high a big God with big grace for big sinners;
- *doctrinally conversant*—fluent in theological discourse; drawing appropriate brief connections to matters of historical or current theological importance;
- *pastorally useful*—transparently and reverently "sitting under the text"; avoiding lengthy grammatical/syntactical discussions;
- *application-minded*—building brief but consistent bridges into contemporary living in both Western and non-Western contexts (being aware of the globally diverse contexts toward which these volumes are aimed);

- *efficient in expression*—economical in its use of words; not a word-by-word analysis but a crisply moving exposition.

In terms of Bible translation, the ESV is the base translation used by the authors in their notes, but the authors were expected to consult the text in the original languages when doing their exposition and were not required to agree with every decision made by the ESV translators.

As civilizations crumble, God's Word stands. And we stand on it. The great truths of Scripture speak across space and time, and we aim to herald them in a way that will be globally applicable.

May God bless the study of his Word, and may he smile on this attempt to expound it.

—The Publisher and Editors

CONTRIBUTORS

Editors

IAIN M. DUGUID
PhD, University of Cambridge
Professor of Old Testament, Westminster Theological Seminary

JAMES M. HAMILTON JR.
PhD, The Southern Baptist Theological Seminary
Professor of Biblical Theology, The Southern Baptist Theological Seminary;
Preaching Pastor, Kenwood Baptist Church, Louisville

JAY SKLAR
PhD, University of Gloucestershire
Professor of Old Testament, Covenant Theological Seminary

Authors

IAIN M. DUGUID
PhD, University of Cambridge
Professor of Old Testament, Westminster Theological Seminary
(*Genesis*)

JAY SKLAR
PhD, University of Gloucestershire
Professor of Old Testament, Covenant Theological Seminary
(*Exodus*)

CHRISTINE PALMER
PhD, Hebrew Union College
Adjunct Professor of Old Testament, Gordon-Conwell Theological Seminary
(*Leviticus*)

RONALD BERGEY
PhD, Dropsie University
La Faculté Jean Calvin
(*Numbers*)

ABBREVIATIONS

General

AT	Author's Translation		masc.	masculine
c.	circa, about, around		mg.	marginal reading
cf.	confer, compare, see		MT	Masoretic Text
ch(s).	chapter(s)		n.	noun
ed(s).	editor(s), edited by, edition		NT	New Testament
			OT	Old Testament
e.g.	for example		pl.	plural
esp.	especially		r.	reigned
et al.	and others		repr.	reprinted
etc.	and so on		rev.	revised (by)
fem.	feminine		sg.	singular
ff.	and following		SP	Samaritan Pentateuch
g	gram		Syr.	Syriac
Gk.	Greek		trans.	translator, translated by
Hb.	Hebrew		v., vv.	verse(s)
i.e.	that is		vb.	verb
kg	kilogram		vol(s).	volumes
km	kilometer		vs.	versus
lit.	literal, literally		Vulg.	Vulgate
LXX	Septuagint			

Bibliographic

- 1QM   Milḥamah *or* War Scroll
- AB   Anchor Bible
- ABD   *Anchor Bible Dictionary*. Edited by David Noel Freedman. 6 vols. New York: Doubleday, 1992.
- ACCS   Ancient Christian Commentary on Scripture

ANEP	*The Ancient Near East in Pictures Relating to the Old Testament*. 2nd ed. Edited by James B. Pritchard. Princeton: Princeton University Press, 1994.
ANET	*Ancient Near Eastern Texts Relating to the Old Testament*. Edited by James B. Pritchard. 3rd ed. Princeton: Princeton University Press, 1969.
ApOTC	Apollos Old Testament Commentary
AYB	Anchor Yale Bible
BA	*Biblical Archaeologist*
BAR	*Biblical Archaeology Review*
BASOR	*Bulletin of the American Schools of Oriental Research*
BBR	*Bulletin for Biblical Research*
BBRSup	*Bulletin for Biblical Research, Supplements*
BDB	Brown, Francis, S. R. Driver, and Charles A. Briggs. *A Hebrew and English Lexicon of the Old Testament*.
BHS	*Biblia Hebraica Stuttgartensia*. Edited by Karl Elliger and Wilhelm Rudolph. Deutsche Bibelgesellschaft, 1983.
BJS	Brown Judaic Studies
BR	*Biblical Research*
BSac	*Bibliotheca Sacra*
BSC	Bible Student's Commentary
BST	The Bible Speaks Today
BZAW	Beihefte zur Zeitschrift für die alttestamentliche Wissenschaft
CAD	*The Assyrian Dictionary of the Oriental Institute of the University of Chicago*. Chicago: The Oriental Institute of the University of Chicago, 1956–2006.
CBC	Cambridge Bible Commentary
CD	Cairo Genizah Copy of the Damascus Document
CDCH	*The Concise Dictionary of Classical Hebrew*. Edited by David J. A. Clines. Sheffield, UK: Sheffield Phoenix Press, 2009.
CHALOT	*A Concise Hebrew and Aramaic Lexicon of the OT*. Edited by William L. Holladay. Grand Rapids, MI: Eerdmans, 1971.
ConC	Concordia Commentary
COS	*The Context of Scripture*. Edited by William W. Hallo. 3 vols. Leiden: Brill, 1997–2002.
DCH	*Dictionary of Classical Hebrew*. Edited by David J. A. Clines. 9 vols. Sheffield: Sheffield Phoenix Press, 1993–2014.

DOTP	*Dictionary of the Old Testament: Pentateuch*. Edited by T. Desmond Alexander and David W. Baker. Downers Grove, IL: IVP Academic, 2003.
EBC	Expositor's Bible Commentary
ESVEC	ESV Expository Commentary
ExpTim	*Expository Times*
FAT	Forschungen zum Alten Testament
FOTL	Forms of the Old Testament Library
GKC	*Gesenius' Hebrew Grammar*. Edited by Emil Kautzsch. Translated by Arthur E. Cowley. 2nd ed. Oxford: Clarendon, 1910.
HALOT	*The Hebrew and Aramaic Lexicon of the Old Testament*. Ludwig Koehler, Walter Baumgartner, and Johann J. Stamm. Translated and edited under the supervision of Mervyn E. J. Richardson. 5 vols. Leiden: Brill, 1994–2000.
HBT	*Horizons in Biblical Theology*
HC	Heidelberg Catechism
HCOT	Historical Commentary on the Old Testament
HSM	Harvard Semitic Monographs
IBHS	*An Introduction to Biblical Hebrew Syntax*. Bruce K. Waltke and Michael O'Connor. Winona Lake, IN: Eisenbrauns, 1990.
ICC	International Critical Commentary
IDBSup	*Interpreter's Dictionary of the Bible: Supplementary Volume*. Edited by Keith Crim. Nashville: Abingdon, 1976.
ISBE	*International Standard Bible Encyclopedia*. Edited by Geoffrey W. Bromiley. 4 vols. Grand Rapids, MI: Eerdmans, 1979–1998.
ITC	International Theological Commentary
JANES	*Journal of the Ancient Near Eastern Society*
JAOS	*Journal of the American Oriental Society*
JBL	*Journal of Biblical Literature*
JETS	*Journal of the Evangelical Theological Society*
JJS	*Journal of Jewish Studies*
Joüon	Joüon, Paul. *A Grammar of Biblical Hebrew*. Translated and revised by T. Muraoka. 2 vols. Rome: Pontifical Biblical Institute, 1991.
JPSTC	The JPS Torah Commentary
JSJ	*Journal for the Study of Judaism in the Persian, Hellenistic, and Roman Periods*
JSOT	*Journal for the Study of the Old Testament*

JSOTSup	Journal for the Study of the Old Testament Supplement Series
LAI	Library of Ancient Israel
LHBOTS	The Library of Hebrew Bible/Old Testament Studies
NAC	New American Commentary
NCBC	New Century Bible Commentary
NICNT	New International Commentary on the New Testament
NICOT	New International Commentary on the Old Testament
NIDOTTE	*New International Dictionary of Old Testament Theology and Exegesis.* Edited by Willem A. VanGemeren. 5 vols. Grand Rapids: Zondervan, 1997.
NIVAC	The NIV Application Commentary
OTG	Old Testament Guides
OTL	Old Testament Library
PTW	Preaching the Word
RB	*Revue biblique*
RCS	Reformation Commentary on Scripture
RRef	*La revue réformée*
SJLA	Studies in Judaism in Late Antiquity
SOTSMS	Society for Old Testament Study Monograph Series
TLOT	*Theological Lexicon of the Old Testament.* Edited by Ernst Jenni, with assistance from Claus Westermann. Translated by Mark E. Biddle. 3 vols. Peabody, MA: Hendrickson, 1997.
TNTC	Tyndale New Testament Commentaries
TOTC	Tyndale Old Testament Commentaries
TTC	Teach the Text Commentary
TynBul	*Tyndale Bulletin*
VT	*Vetus Testamentum*
VTSup	Supplements to Vetus Testamentum
WBC	Word Biblical Commentary
WEC	Wycliffe Exegetical Commentary
WLC	Westminster Larger Catechism
WSC	Westminster Shorter Catechism
WTJ	*Westminster Theological Journal*
WUNT	Wissenschaftliche Untersuchungen zum Neuen Testament
ZAW	*Zeitschrift für die alttestamentliche Wissenschaft*
ZECOT	Zondervan Exegetical Commentary on the Old Testament

ZIBBC Zondervan Illustrated Bible Backgrounds Commentary
ZPED *Zondervan Pictorial Encyclopedia of the Bible.* Edited by Merrill C. Tenney. 5 vols. Grand Rapids, MI: Zondervan, 1975.

Books of the Bible

Gen.	Genesis	Obad.	Obadiah
Ex.	Exodus	Jonah	Jonah
Lev.	Leviticus	Mic.	Micah
Num.	Numbers	Nah.	Nahum
Deut.	Deuteronomy	Hab.	Habakkuk
Josh.	Joshua	Zeph.	Zephaniah
Judg.	Judges	Hag.	Haggai
Ruth	Ruth	Zech.	Zechariah
1 Sam.	1 Samuel	Mal.	Malachi
2 Sam.	2 Samuel	Matt.	Matthew
1 Kings	1 Kings	Mark	Mark
2 Kings	2 Kings	Luke	Luke
1 Chron.	1 Chronicles	John	John
2 Chron.	2 Chronicles	Acts	Acts
Ezra	Ezra	Rom.	Romans
Neh.	Nehemiah	1 Cor.	1 Corinthians
Est.	Esther	2 Cor.	2 Corinthians
Job	Job	Gal.	Galatians
Ps., Pss.	Psalms	Eph.	Ephesians
Prov.	Proverbs	Phil.	Philippians
Eccles.	Ecclesiastes	Col.	Colossians
Song	Song of Solomon	1 Thess.	1 Thessalonians
Isa.	Isaiah	2 Thess.	2 Thessalonians
Jer.	Jeremiah	1 Tim.	1 Timothy
Lam.	Lamentations	2 Tim.	2 Timothy
Ezek.	Ezekiel	Titus	Titus
Dan.	Daniel	Philem.	Philemon
Hos.	Hosea	Heb.	Hebrews
Joel	Joel	James	James
Amos	Amos	1 Pet.	1 Peter

2 Pet.	2 Peter	3 John	3 John
1 John	1 John	Jude	Jude
2 John	2 John	Rev.	Revelation

Apocrypha and Other Noncanonical Sources Cited

2 Macc.	2 Maccabees
Sir.	Sirach/Ecclesiasticus

GENESIS

Iain M. Duguid

INTRODUCTION TO
GENESIS

Overview

The book of Genesis is foundational to the whole Bible, so much so that Bible translators around the world often translate this book first before turning to the rest of Scripture. Without the book of Genesis we cannot properly understand who this God is who has taken flesh and redeemed us in the person of Jesus Christ. The book introduces us to Israel's God, the Lord, who is the sole creator God of the whole universe (Genesis 1–3). In the beginning, before the world existed, there was God. He has made everything that exists, including time, and he reigns sovereignly over all things and all history. Genesis explains the nature of the universe, the relationship of good and evil, the place of humanity in the world, and God's good purposes for creation. The book also shows us Israel's place among the nations: Israel is the heir of God's unique calling and promises, which are designed to bring blessing to the whole world (Gen. 12:1–3). Moreover, Genesis shows how these promises are slowly worked out in the lives of the patriarchs, bringing them closer to what God had promised, despite the patriarchs' repeated sin and rebellion. These promises leave them looking forward in faith to a greater, heavenly inheritance that we share with them in Christ (Genesis 12–50).

The opening chapters of the book, Genesis 1–11, constitute the divinely authorized origin story. Everyone lives his or her life on the basis of an origin story of some kind or other. We know something of other ancient Near Eastern origin stories, such as the Enuma Elish and the Atrahasis Epic; these are so different from modern conceptions of origins that sometimes we may be tempted to think that we have no similar accounts. In reality, however, it is not possible to function without some account of the nature of reality, the nature of mankind and its place within the cosmos, and the purpose and goal of the universe (or lack thereof). A vague version of the theory of evolution serves that purpose for many people in the modern world, though in the West people are often inclined to borrow elements that lean on the Genesis account to defend particular views they wish to hold, such as opposition to racism or the supreme value of human life, for which their origin story provides no rational basis.

Of course, origin stories do not need to be true for people to build their worldviews upon them, but only true origin stories can provide solid foundations for our beliefs. The biblical claim to present the true story of the origins of the universe is uncompromising and provides a firm basis for our understanding of creation and our place within it. To the extent to which our ideas of origins deviate from those revealed in Genesis 1–11, they will be built upon sand rather than solid rock. That is not to say that Genesis 1–3 provides a full scientific portrayal of the origin of the universe; it does not. That is not its purpose. However, its portrayal of origins is truthful and accurate and undergirds its answers to life's essential questions.

It is sometimes suggested that premodern people, including the original readers of Genesis, did not ask questions about the truthfulness of their origin stories; it was sufficient that the stories be compelling. This is, of course, nonsense. Ancient people were not stupid. The test proposed by Elijah on Mount Carmel in 1 Kings 18 is a basic scientific experiment under controlled conditions designed to determine which deity—the Lord or Baal—is actually able to do what the Baal myths claim concerning him: that, as the storm god, he could deliver fire from heaven (as well as rain). The people understand clearly the test Elijah proposes, and they recognize the significance of the Lord's victory over Baal on that day. Clever myths are not enough; truth matters (cf. 2 Pet. 1:16).

The opening chapters of Genesis also deal with foundational questions about the origin of evil in the world. Why do we live in a world in which things fall apart, people die (often tragically), and other people commit grotesque and reprehensible acts? These questions demand answers from all of us. Genesis roots our experience of the existence of evil in the fall of Adam and Eve, recounted in Genesis 3: the universe is not an eternal dualistic balance of good and evil, as some religions teach. Neither is it simply a place where everyone starts out good and chooses for oneself the good path or an evil one. Evil is within all of us, as a result of our descent from Adam; as a result, we all die (cf. Genesis 5). Even a worldwide flood is unable to cleanse that inner evil with which we all struggle (Genesis 6–8). All nations on earth may be part of one great, big related family (Genesis 10), but it is a family that by nature is united in its commitment to seeking to live without reference to its Creator (11:1–9). From the beginning, however, God has been committed to his promise to redeem humanity through a descendant of Eve (3:15). Decline and fall cannot be the end of the story.

At the end of Genesis 11, therefore, a pivotal change comes in the storyline of Genesis, with the call of Abram to go from Mesopotamia to the land that the Lord would show him, which is soon revealed to be Canaan. In place of the fivefold curse pronounced upon sin in Genesis 3–11 we see in Genesis 12 a fivefold promise of blessing, not merely for Abram and Sarai but for the whole world (cf. Section Overview of 12:1–9). They will have abundant offspring, who will possess the land and provide a blessing for all nations. Yet initially that promise seems impossible to fulfill: it takes twenty-five years and numerous missteps before Abraham and Sarah have a single child of their own (Genesis 21). Abraham's commitment to the promise is then tested when the Lord commands him to offer Isaac as a sacrifice, though the drama is resolved by the Lord's affirming Abraham's faith and by his providing a ram as a sacrifice so that Isaac's life can be spared and the promise reconfirmed (Genesis 22).

The book of Genesis follows the next three generations of the patriarchs: Isaac, Jacob, and Jacob's twelve sons (Genesis 23–50). In each generation the Lord sovereignly chooses the line through which the promise descends: Isaac, not Ishmael; Jacob, not Esau; all twelve of Jacob's sons. The narrative makes clear that this is not a matter of choosing the best and leaving the rest; in particular, Jacob is not chosen because he is a better human being than Esau, a reality underlined by the fact that the Lord's choice takes place prior to the twins' birth, while both are still in the womb (Genesis 25).

God's design for Jacob's offspring is that they should become a "company of peoples" (*qehal 'ammim*, "worshiping community of peoples"; Gen. 28:3; 48:4). The Hebrew word *qahal* is often used for sacred assemblies (Deut. 4:10; 9:10; etc.), and in most of the OT it is rendered in the LXX as *ekklesia*.[1] It is thus not too strong to say that Israel's sons are called to be a "church of peoples," yet the initial history of Joseph and his brothers suggests that this calling is unlikely to be realized. Joseph's brothers are incensed by the favoritism shown to him by his father, as well as by the divinely inspired dreams that show their bowing down before Joseph, and so they conspire to kill him (Genesis 37). In the end they decide not to follow through with this plan but, in order to make some money out of Joseph, to sell him down to Egypt as a slave instead (37:25–28). Yet their evil plan is designed by God to bring about good (50:20), as God miraculously makes Joseph ruler of all Egypt alongside Pharaoh, with the God-given insight to foresee through Pharaoh's dreams the coming of a terrible famine (Genesis 41). The result is the salvation of Jacob and his family as well as of the Egyptians, which leads to the whole family's going down to sojourn in Egypt for a while (Genesis 46), as the Lord earlier told Abraham (cf. 15:13).

This sequence of events not only provides food for Jacob's family amid the famine but also moves the sons of Israel into place for the next part of the Lord's plan, which will involve their mistreatment in Egypt and ultimate exodus from there (Exodus 1–15; cf. Gen. 15:13–14). In the meantime the book of Genesis closes with the deaths of Jacob and Joseph, who each testifies in his own way to his faith in the promise of the land of Canaan, even while living outside it. Jacob makes Joseph take his body back to Canaan upon his death and bury him in the family tomb at Machpelah alongside Abraham and Isaac (Gen. 50:1–13). Joseph, on the other hand, gives instructions for his body to be embalmed and buried in a coffin so that, when the Israelites go up from Egypt, his bones can share in their exodus (50:24–26).

At the end of Genesis the stage is thus set for the book of Exodus that follows. Indeed, the whole Pentateuch (Genesis—Deuteronomy) forms a coherent narrative that unfolds the story begun in Genesis. Ultimately, of course, the story will not end until Revelation 22, when the promise of Genesis 3:15 finds its full outworking in

---

[1] Though not in Genesis, where the Greek translator prefers *synagōgē*; cf. comment on 27:41–28:5.

the redemption of all those who have become children of God through the death and resurrection of the seed of the woman and second Adam, Jesus Christ.

Title and Author

In this instance the Hebrew and Greek names for the book are both fitting. The Hebrew title, *bereshit* ("In the beginning"), points to the function of the book as an origin story, not merely for Israel but for the entire world. Meanwhile, the Greek title, *genesis*, alludes both to the role of the book as an origin story and (in the plural form, *geneseis*) to the *toledot* ("family history") formula that structures the whole book (cf. comment on 2:4–7). This is not a collection of ancient myths and legends but an origin story that tells the family history of God's chosen people.

Traditionally, the author of Genesis has been held to be Moses, largely because the book is tightly integrated with the rest of the Pentateuch, which addresses the chosen family—now become a nation—as it is about to enter the land. That traditional ascription has been widely challenged in scholarly circles, which have often doubted that a single person could have produced such a wide-ranging and complex piece of literature as the Pentateuch, encompassing narratives, poetry, laws, and so on. It has also been questioned whether the Pentateuch could have been *written* at such an early period of history and whether many of the laws were relevant for the period in question. Scholars have sometimes endeavored to separate out different sources (often termed "J," "E," "D," and "P"), each of which purportedly contributed to the whole at different times and with different interests.

These challenges remind us of the complexity of questions of authorship in antiquity, especially of a document as complicated (and unique) as the Pentateuch. It is unlikely that no memory of Israel's family story or the origins of the universe existed in Israel prior to Moses, and, whereas the book of Exodus describes events contemporaneous to Moses, the events of Genesis all precede the time of Moses by hundreds of years. At the same time, Moses was himself brought up as the adopted child of an Egyptian princess (Ex. 2:1–10) and thus likely schooled in a wide range of ancient Near Eastern literature, including various origin stories.

We need not therefore suppose that everything in Genesis was composed by Moses *de novo*; under the inspiration of God, he would likely have been using and interacting with a wide variety of preexisting literature. The opening chapters of Genesis form a clear polemic against other ancient Near Eastern creation accounts and also provide a positive statement of the true nature of things, as we would expect. Moses likely had access to a variety of records, written and oral, concerning the early history of the Abrahamic families. The laws that Moses ordained for his people in the remainder of the Pentateuch probably drew on, as well as challenged, other ancient Near Eastern standards of justice. Yet Moses' pen was guided throughout by the inspiration of the Holy Spirit. There is a remarkable coherence to the entire Pentateuch—and within it to the book of Genesis—that would be hard to account for if it were the result of a series of mergers and edits by multiple rather clumsy hands with conflicting beliefs and interests over centuries of transmission. Many of the supposed "doublets" and "contradictions" from which these theories flow can be better accounted for by a closer study of the literary artistry of the author.

There are a few places at which minor editorial changes have been made to make the work more accessible to later generations, such as the identification of 'Dan' as the city where Abram pursued Lot's kidnappers (Gen. 14:14). Dan did not acquire that name until the time of the Judges. Likewise, the final chapter of Deuteronomy, recording the death of Moses and the lack of a prophet like him since that time (Deut. 34:10–12), must also postdate the time of Moses. Such oddities are few and far between, however, and there is no reason to doubt the traditional attribution of the Pentateuch (and thus of Genesis) to Moses himself.

Date and Occasion

If the author of Genesis is in fact Moses, the time of writing would be during Israel's wilderness wanderings, after the exodus (Exodus 14) and prior to the entry into the Promised Land under Joshua (Joshua 1–11). Depending on the date of the exodus, which is variously placed in the fifteenth or thirteenth century BC, Genesis would be dated to roughly the same time period. While there is nothing corresponding to the Pentateuch in the literature of the time, there are parallels to many of the component parts—origin stories, family sagas, laws, epic poetry, and so on. Indeed, since no people has ever existed without origin stories and laws of some kind or another, if we did not have the Pentateuch we would have to postulate the existence of many separate similar materials, whether in oral or written form. Israel's unique constitution as a "people of the book" and the central place of Moses as lawgiver and author (e.g., Josh. 1:13; 1 Kings 2:3) are hard to account for if Moses in fact wrote little or nothing.

As a new nation, Israel had its relationship with God sealed at Mount Sinai in the form of a covenant (Exodus 19–24). However, that was far from the beginning of its interactions with this God, who had revealed himself much earlier as the God of Abraham, Isaac, and Jacob (Ex. 3:6). That backstory was of vital importance to Israel's self-identity, as well as its understanding of that covenant relationship. The Sinai covenant was not an entirely new and different covenant but a further development of the covenant God had made with Abraham in Genesis 15, sealed with the sign of circumcision in Genesis 17. In addition the people of Israel needed to understand who they were as human beings in relationship to God, in relationship to other human beings, and in relationship to the world God had created. As those created in the image of God, they had rights and responsibilities (Gen. 1:26–28). In Abraham they had been called to be blessed and to be a blessing to all peoples on earth (12:1–3). And, like Abraham and Sarah, they too were called to look forward to the promised seed of the woman, who would bruise the serpent's head and restore all creation to its destiny (3:15).

One small detail highlights the original setting of Genesis during the wilderness wanderings: the identity of Egypt as a place of tempting fruitfulness

(12:10–20; 13:10). It is not coincidental that Hagar, who is repeatedly called "the Egyptian" (16:3; 21:9; 25:12), is fertile, while the wife of promise, Sarah, is barren. Nor is it coincidental that the property Lot chooses outside the Land of Promise is "like the land of Egypt" (13:10), while the Promised Land is repeatedly wracked with famine. This theme would have resonated with Israel in the wilderness, as the people were constantly tempted to look back to Egypt with longing as the place of food and fertility (Num. 11:5; 14:3). Moses repeatedly reminds his hearers that the "Egyptian option," while outwardly looking attractive, never constitutes the pathway to blessing.[2]

Genre and Literary Features

The Pentateuch as a whole comprises a dizzying array of different genres and perhaps should be seen as a unique example of its own genre. So too Genesis includes an array of origin stories, historical narratives, and genealogies, as well as a smattering of laws and explanations of laws (e.g., Gen. 9:6; 32:32). Origin stories are distinct from historical narratives not because they are necessarily nonhistorical but because their focus is on providing an explanation of reality, both natural and supernatural. Thus the narratives in Genesis 1–11 have global implications that stretch forward through time in a way that the narratives in Genesis 12–50 do not.

One of the distinctive features of the biblical origin story is its profound historical rootedness, in contrast to similar ancient Near Eastern accounts, which are not directly connected to present-day history in the same way. The events described do not take place in a galaxy far, far away but in the same world we inhabit, to people to whom the first hearers were directly related. Indeed, a common function of linear genealogies is to establish a vital relationship between the first and last members of the listing,[3] and that purpose certainly applies to many of the Genesis linear genealogies. Certain positions in linear genealogies may be particularly significant, especially the seventh, tenth, and twelfth generations. Segmented genealogies, on the other hand, primarily define family connections—"insiders" and "outsiders" for the purposes of particular definitions of family. For example, the table of nations in Genesis 10 defines all humanity as part of the Adamic family—a very inclusive definition in a world that included those ready to deny the full humanity of outsiders, or "barbarians." On the other hand, the table also distinguishes within that larger family three smaller groupings that are singled out for a closer or more distant relationship with the line of promise.

The largest part of Genesis—and indeed its overall genre—is historical narrative. As Meir Sternberg has pointed out, biblical narratives have three driving impulses: history, ideology (or perhaps "theology"), and literary artistry.[4] That is,

---

[2] Cf. Iain M. Duguid, "Hagar the Egyptian: A Note on the Allure of Egypt in the Abraham Cycle," *WTJ* 56 (1994): 419–421.
[3] Cf. Robert R. Wilson, *Genealogy and History in the Biblical World* (New Haven, CT: Yale University Press, 1977), 9.
[4] Meir K. Sternberg, *The Poetics of Biblical Narrative: Ideological Reading and the Drama of Scripture* (Bloomington, IN: Indiana University Press, 1985), 41–48.

these stories can be appreciated for their literary skill and beauty, but they have always been intended to convey a message to their hearers, and they are also rooted and grounded in historical events. Of these three, history is foundational: it would have mattered to an ancient audience, as it should to a modern audience, whether these events actually happened as described.[5] Yet, at the same time, because these stories are important parts of God's story, these real events convey vital lessons to readers about ourselves, our world, and our God (1 Cor. 10:11). Moreover, these stories are so vital for us to understand that they not only *may* be but *must* be recounted with great literary skill and attention to detail. To be boring or trite in speaking of such events and such a God would be a sin in its own right.[6]

Theology of Genesis and the Relationship to the Rest of the Bible and to Christ

Insofar as it is an origin story, the book of Genesis has a strong polemic note to it, proclaiming a different perspective on who God is, how he created the world, who humans and animals are, and the purpose for which we exist. Since it proclaims itself to be the revelation of the only true God, who made all things in heaven and on earth and for whom and by whom all things exist, it cannot stand as merely one perspective among many; either it must be accepted as true and therefore allowed to govern our worldview in all of its different dimensions, or it must be rejected as false in favor of some other origin story, ancient or modern. The book of Genesis does not explicitly cite alternative origin stories; it simply lays out its own story, but it does so in many respects in conscious disagreement with the origin stories of Israel's neighbors, with their multiple competing gods, fundamentally chaotic worlds, and low view of humanity. In the same way, the book of Genesis does not have to mention modern humanistic worldviews in order to challenge them at the most fundamental level.

DOCTRINE OF GOD AND CREATION

In contradiction to ancient Near Eastern worldviews, the Genesis creation account involves only one God, who goes by the generic title "God" and the covenantal name "Yahweh" ("the LORD"). The two names are (unusually for Scripture) juxtaposed as "the LORD God" in Genesis 2–3 in order to make clear that the one God who created the heavens and the earth is Israel's God, the one who delivered them from the land of Egypt. What is more, in the Genesis account there is no conflict involved in the creation of the world. Unlike in other Near Eastern creation stories, there are no battles against the forces of chaos. Instead there is simply the serene ordering of space and time via God's word. This God has no rivals and faces no threats to his authority. He is good, and so is the world that he creates, which he blesses and fills with the potential for life to multiply (Gen. 1:28–31).

---
[5] See Peter's warning in the NT about the danger of "cleverly devised myths" (2 Pet. 1:16), as well as Paul's contrast between "the truth" and "myths" (2 Tim. 4:4).
[6] As Martyn Lloyd-Jones remarked, "How can a man be dull when he is handling such themes? I would say that a 'dull preacher' is a contradiction in terms; if he is dull, he is not a preacher. He may stand in a pulpit and talk, but he is certainly not a preacher." Lloyd-Jones, *Preaching and Preachers* (Grand Rapids, MI: Zondervan, 2012), 100–101.

Yet, even though the world as created in the beginning is good, it is not eternal. It has a beginning: there was a time when creation was not. What is more, it has a goal: the Sabbath pattern built into the world by God, with a day of rest at the end of the creation week, is intended to point mankind forward from the beginning to the fulfillment of creation's purpose (2:1–4). Unlike some other ancient worldviews, creation is not an ever-repeating cycle of life; it came from somewhere and is going somewhere as well.

DOCTRINE OF HUMANITY

Other ancient Near Eastern origin stories assign a low place to humanity in general, and an even lower place to women. According to an Assyrian proverb, "Man is the shadow of a god, a slave is the shadow of a man; but the king is like the (very) image of a god."[7] Kings may perhaps be related to the gods, but ordinary people are not—still less slaves and women. In contrast, the biblical account relates how all human beings—Jew and Gentile, male and female, slave and free—are created in God's image, with an inherent dignity that comes with that status (1:26–28). Our status is not based on our functional competencies (the fact that we are reasoning, relational, and religious creatures) but is ontological: we are made in the image of God, no matter how poor, weak, or incapacitated we may be. Yet there is also an order in human relationships: even prior to the fall Eve is created to be Adam's helper, corresponding to him and completing him (2:18–24). The original couple are not identical and interchangeable but complementary in their differences.

In the Genesis account human beings are like the animals in being created on the sixth day but unlike them in being created in the image of God, inbreathed with God's very breath, in the language of Genesis 2:7. We are called to rule over the lower aspects of creation as God's representatives—not harshly or in an exploitative way but by imitating the rule of our heavenly Father, whose reign is a blessing to all creation. It is significant that it is as the image of God that mankind is assigned dominion over the world (1:26).

Since we are made in the image of God, we are also crafted to be revelation receivers; we are designed for a personal relationship with God in a way that other aspects of creation are not. The sun and moon may declare God's glory by obeying his laws (Ps. 19:1–4), but human beings are designed to glorify God and enjoy him in a unique way. For this reason God places the first humans in a sanctuary-garden, where they might enjoy his presence and glorify him through their happy obedience (cf. 3:8).

DOCTRINE OF SIN

One of the ways in which God communicates with Adam and Eve is to give to Adam his law (2:16–17). This law is not burdensome; indeed, it begins with a command to eat freely from all the trees of the garden (save one)! Yet, when the serpent questions the intent behind this law, impugning God's kindness and goodness,

---

[7] ANET, 425.

Eve breaks the law by eating the forbidden fruit and then gives some to Adam, who is with her (3:1–6). The order of creation is turned upside down, with catastrophic consequences not only for Adam and Eve but for the entire created order. Humanity now groans under a curse, affecting men and women at their deepest levels, and creation groans alongside them (Rom. 8:19–23). Far from becoming like God, as the serpent claimed (Gen. 3:5), human rebellion leads to the entry of death into the world (Rom. 5:12).

THE DOCTRINE OF JUDGMENT AND REDEMPTION

The first doctrine that the serpent denies is God's ability to judge rebels. God had said, "In the day that you eat of [the tree of the knowledge of good and evil] you shall surely die" (Gen. 2:17), whereas the serpent boldly claims, "You will not surely die" (3:4). But Satan, whom the serpent represents (Rev. 12:9), has been a "murderer from the beginning" (John 8:44), and God is more than capable of judging his wayward creation (Gen. 18:25). What is perhaps more surprising, however, is the Lord's desire to redeem fallen humans. As Exodus 34:6–7 makes clear, the Lord is the judge of the guilty but also full of compassion and mercy, abounding in steadfast love (Hb. *khesed*) and faithfulness. His grace is revealed immediately in the garden, as the sentence of death is delayed and a promise made of an ultimate transformation of the curse of the fall upon creation through the coming of the seed of the woman (Gen. 3:15). Sin will not have ultimate dominion over humanity (Rom. 6:14). These themes of judgment and redemption are reprised at the time of the flood, when all humanity turns aside to sin except for one man—Noah, whose righteousness redeems his family in the face of a worldwide outpouring of divine wrath (Genesis 6–8). Yet Noah and his family are themselves sinners, and there is no hope for ultimate deliverance through a mere man (cf. Genesis 9). The promises of God are reiterated on this side of the flood, but the problem of sin remains as challenging as ever.

THE DOCTRINE OF CHRIST

That promise of blessing through the seed of the woman would not be the result of human effort, no matter how lofty. The attempt by the builders of Babel to storm heaven's gates through their splendid tower accomplishes nothing but further judgment upon themselves (11:1–9). Hope for humanity will come only from God, and it does so in his calling of Abram and Sarai to go from Ur of the Chaldeans and sojourn in a backwater province called Canaan (11:27–12:3). Through them and their offspring God will restore blessing to all nations. Yet the faith of Abram and Sarai is deeply tested, first as they must wait for a son, and then as they almost see that son offered back to God as a sacrifice (Genesis 22). But on the mountain God instead provides a lamb as a figure showing ahead of time how he will win blessing for the world.

Through Abraham, Isaac, and Jacob God gradually builds up the nucleus of what will become a great nation, Israel, which will be called to become a worshiping "company of peoples" (Gen. 28:3), a "kingdom of priests" (Ex. 19:6). Yet the sins of the patriarchs are visible to all: it is clear that God does not choose them because they are better than those whom God passes over. Eventually God will use the enslavement of Joseph by his own brothers and their selling him to slave traders in order to save their lives and protect them in a great famine. What they mean for evil, God means for good (Gen. 50:20). Yet at the end of Genesis the promises of offspring, land, and blessing are merely beginning to unfold. It is clear that, if the hope of Abraham, Isaac, and Jacob is only for this world, they are of all men most to be pitied (1 Cor. 15:19). But in fact their faith shines out through even their deaths and burials; by faith they look forward after death to receiving a city with foundations that God will build (Heb. 11:10).

That is where the story ends in Genesis—but only so that it can be picked up again and resolved throughout the rest of Scripture. The people who go down to Egypt as a place of protection find it transformed into a place of bondage, just as God had told Abraham (Gen. 15:13). As promised, however, God brings them out of Egypt with a mighty arm in the exodus and leads them into possession of the land of Canaan (cf. Joshua 1–12). Like post-flood humanity, post-exodus Israel continues to be as sinful as its forefathers, wracked with grumbling and unbelief (cf. the book of Numbers). The Lord provides godly leaders, yet the people rebel against them, either during the leader's reign or after his death. It gradually became clear through the OT that Israel itself is not the answer to the world's problems.

What is needed is the promised seed of the woman, a new Adam and new Israel who will triumph where the first Adam and first Israel fail. That promised seed of the woman is Jesus Christ, God himself taking on humanity in order to redeem his creation. The lamb that God provides to take Isaac's place in Genesis 22 foreshadows the Lamb of God, come to take away the sin of the world (John 1:29) through his own death and resurrection. This good news is now preached not merely to Israel but to the ends of the earth (Acts 1:8). The God of judgment and mercy has triumphed in Christ and will one day complete the transformation of this cursed world into a "new heavens and a new earth" at Christ's return (2 Pet. 3:13). Then we will be restored to the kind of face-to-face intimacy with God that Adam and Eve enjoyed—only better, because there will be no risk of losing it due to sin. We are even now a new creation in Christ (2 Cor. 5:17), God's beloved children, upon whom the fullness of his blessing rests (Eph. 1:3–14).

Preaching from the Book of Genesis and Interpretive Challenges

Preaching from Genesis, as from any book of the Bible, should focus our eyes on the sufferings of Christ and the glories to follow (Luke 24:26, 46–47). The Scriptures are never intended simply to provide historical information and moral guidance, though they certainly contain both of those. The origin stories at the beginning of Genesis are intended to counter alternative ancient and modern origin stories (including the evolutionary narrative prevalent in our own time) rather than to give a full scientific account of origins. Of course, the historical veracity of the biblical origin story matters, but it is easy to get sidetracked onto such matters to the point that the focus of the narrative itself becomes obscured. It may be better to schedule another opportunity outside a worship service to explore such apologetic issues at the appropriate depth, where people can ask their questions and receive good answers.[8] Preaching a text should focus on the point of the text itself rather than addressing ancillary matters, no matter how relevant to one's culture.

The length of the book of Genesis poses a different kind of challenge. The outline below breaks the text into approximately sixty literary units, which, if preached consecutively, would normally require fifteen to eighteen months, allowing for a few Sundays devoted to other topics. Even that pace requires moving through passages fairly quickly, often dealing with a chapter of narrative at a time, and such a series may be felt to be too long for a contemporary audience. However, it could easily be broken into four sections: Genesis 1–11 (Origins), 12–25 (Abraham), 26–36 (Isaac and Jacob), and 37–50 (Joseph).[9] This would allow other series to be interspersed with Genesis for a more balanced diet over, say, a three- or four-year period. Of course, some literary units probably do not merit an entire sermon in their own right (e.g., the family history of Ishmael in 25:12–18), while other literary units stretch over as much as three chapters (e.g., Genesis 43–45) and may require more than one sermon. In general, however, sermons ought to roughly match a literary unit in order to ensure that the point of the sermon matches the point of that unit. Shorter preaching units lend themselves to taking a minor point out of context and elevating it to become the main point.

The earlier assertion that the central focus of each text in Genesis is "the sufferings of Christ and the glories that will follow" (sometimes called a "Christ-centered" or "redemptive-historical" approach to preaching) raises the question of application. To what extent may we (must we?) use the human characters of the text to derive moral lessons for our hearers? Some preachers shy away almost completely from such application, for fear of moralism.[10] Yet, while teaching "life lessons" may not be the primary purpose of Scripture, the OT and NT point out that there are at least some insights that we ought to glean from those who have preceded us in our earthly pilgrimages. Isaiah 51:2 holds up Abraham and Sarah as positive models of faith for a later generation,[11] while the writer to the Hebrews warns against sharing the unbelief of the wilderness generation

---

[8] Helpful resources include, among many others, Iain M. Duguid, *Thinking about Science, Faith, and Origins: A (Very) Short Introduction* (Glenside, PA: St. Colme's Press, 2019); Vern Poythress, *Redeeming Science: A God-Centered Approach* (Wheaton, IL: Crossway, 2006).
[9] E.g., Iain M. Duguid, *Living in the Gap between Promise and Reality: The Gospel according to Abraham*, 2nd ed. (Phillipsburg, NJ: P&R, 2015); *Living in the Grip of Relentless Grace: The Gospel according to Isaac and Jacob*, 2nd ed. (Phillipsburg, NJ: P&R, 2015); Iain M. Duguid and Matthew P. Harmon, *Living in the Light of Inextinguishable Hope* (Phillipsburg, NJ: P&R, 2013).
[10] Cf. Sidney Greidanus, *Sola Scriptura: Problems and Principles in Preaching Historical Texts* (1970; repr., Eugene, OR: Wipf & Stock). His later works, including *Preaching Christ from Genesis: Foundations for Expository Sermons* (Grand Rapids, MI: Eerdmans, 2007) are notably light on application and critical of the applicatory efforts of others (e.g., *Preaching Christ from Genesis*, 378).
[11] Compare John 8:39, where Jesus assumes that we can identify at least some of Abraham's works that we should imitate. However, Ezekiel 33:24 demonstrates how easy it is to draw the wrong lesson from such efforts!

(Heb. 3:7–19). Paul goes so far as to say, "These things took place as examples for us" (1 Cor. 10:6–11). The Scriptures are *more* than moral instruction, to be sure, but not less.

Indeed, this is typically how stories work. Leland Ryken puts it like this: "Heroic narrative springs from one of the most ancient and persistent impulses of literary art, namely, the desire to embody accepted norms of thought and action in the story of a protagonist whose destiny is regarded as being representative or exemplary. The true hero expresses an accepted social or moral norm."[12] Of course, the biblical account is not merely "heroic narrative"; it is part of the unfolding revelation of God's plan of salvation, which often progresses in spite of, rather than because of, the actions of the "hero." What is more, the correct lessons to infer from the behavior of biblical characters are not always straightforward. They text is rarely divided neatly into "heroes" and "villains," and the narrator often sets characters' behavior before us without overt moral comment. Sometimes, in narratives as in real life, we must interpret a character's complex behavior in the light of the larger trajectory of his life and the narrative as a whole. Not every action is easy to interpret, and there will be times when good expositors will disagree about the interpretation of a character.

To give a concrete example, I take quite a negative view of the character of Lot in Genesis, based on his downward trajectory throughout the narrative from the moment he leaves Abraham and sets off toward Sodom (Genesis 13–19) until he ends up living a degraded life in a cave, deceived and abused by his daughters (19:30–38). Yet 2 Peter 2:7 calls him "righteous Lot," so other commentators have taken a more positive view of his actions. To be sure, the presupposition of the text is that Lot is "righteous"; the conversation between Abraham and the Lord in Genesis 18:23–33 concerns how to deliver the righteous from the coming judgment, and Lot and his immediate family are the only ones rescued. However, "righteous" people behave in all sorts of ungodly ways in Genesis, and the message is perhaps that even very compromised and hesitant sinners may be saved by God's grace. Often the message of a biblical narrative is not "Be like this biblical hero" but rather "Don't be like him or her; instead, be thankful that God's grace in Christ extends to sinners like us, who all too often fail in the same way, and strive out of gratitude for the gospel to live in a manner that is worthy of the grace you have received."

This brings us to see how we may preach Christ from all the Scriptures, not merely from passages with an "obvious" connection, such as Genesis 3:15 or 49:8–12. In reality, every biblical passage challenges our thinking and behavior and exposes our hearts in some way or another. As sinners we do not treat those around us as made in the image of God (Genesis 1), we do not resist Satan's siren call to trust our eyes over God's Word (Genesis 3), we use our technology and sexuality to make a reputation for ourselves rather than to glorify God (Genesis 4), and so on. Every passage of Scripture is thus "law" in a sense, in that it convicts

---

12 Leland Ryken, *The Literature of the Bible* (Grand Rapids, MI: Zondervan, 1980), 45.

us of our sin and is designed to drive us to see our need of Christ as believers and unbelievers.

Moralistic preaching short-circuits that process by presenting our own righteousness as the answer to our sin, as if the Scripture simply provides us with examples of people we should either imitate or shun. Our salvation and our sanctification depend on ourselves and our effort in this schema. But the gospel points us instead to Christ's righteousness as the answer to our sin, whether we are unbelievers who need to come to Christ for salvation or believers who need to go back to Christ in gratitude for his perfect obedience in our place. Christ-centered preaching does not place another brick in the believer's backpack, crushing him with yet more guilt, but instead joyfully brings him back to see the perfect righteousness of Christ in his place. Its goal is thus thoroughly doxological, leaving our hearts motivated to love and praise God.[13]

Preaching that avoids application altogether, on the other hand, tends to act as though the law of the passage no longer has any relevance for us as believers. Yet, if the law is holy and good (Rom. 7:12), then it should still be "a lamp to [our] feet and a light to [our] path" (Ps. 119:105). God has "delivered us from the domain of darkness" (Col. 1:13) and has begun a good work in us that he will bring to "completion at the day of Jesus Christ" (Phil. 1:6). As a result, the believer should find himself asking, "How do I live a life of grateful obedience to this God who has loved me so overwhelmingly? What difference should this passage make in my life on Monday morning?" The wise preacher will help to answer those questions via skilled application.

Such application requires a proper understanding of the unfolding of redemptive history. Obedience for Abraham did not look identical to obedience for Joshua, or David, or Jesus, or Paul; the Bible does not merely give us "timeless truths." Of course, some of God's laws remain unchanged throughout history: you shall not kill; you shall not steal; you shall not commit adultery; and so on (Ex. 20:1–17). These laws have traditionally been called "moral laws." Others relate to the ceremonies and sacrifices designed to point forward specifically to the coming of Christ and are therefore no longer in operation—what are often called "ceremonial laws." Still other OT laws are designed to provide specific application of God's wisdom to Israel's situation in the land of Canaan under the Sinai covenant, such as the law forbidding harvesting all the way to the edge of one's fields, in order to make provision for the able-bodied poor (Lev. 19:9–10). These laws do not bind us directly but have a more generalized application to the different specifics of our society; these are commonly called "civil laws."[14] Any preaching from the OT must consider into which of these three categories the "law of the passage" fits. Yet any and all of these categories will in some way point us to Christ as the remedy for our sin through his suffering and death and as the provider of our righteousness through his own perfect and holy keeping of this law.

---

13 Thomas Chalmers, "The Expulsive Power of a New Affection," in *Sermons and Discourses* (New York: Robert Carter & Brothers, 1877) 2.271–277.
14 On this cf. Iain M. Duguid, *Is Jesus in the Old Testament?* (Phillipsburg, NJ: P&R, 2013).

Outline

I. Prologue: The Creation of the Heavens and the Earth (1:1–2:3)
   A. Introductory Summary Statement (1:1)
   B. Pre-creation Situation (1:2)
   C. Narrative of Creation (1:3–31)
   D. Concluding Summary Statement (2:1)
   E. Epilogue/Climax: Sabbath Rest (2:2–3)
II. The Family History of the Heavens and the Earth (2:4–4:26)
   A. Adam and Eve in the Garden (2:4–25)
   B. The Fall (3:1–24)
   C. Cain and Abel (4:1–26)
III. The Family History of Adam (5:1–6:8)
   A. From Adam to Noah (5:1–32)
   B. The Spread of Wickedness (6:1–8)
IV. The Family History of Noah (6:9–9:29)
   A. Announcement of Judgment and Salvation (6:9–22)
   B. God's Judgment Descends (7:1–24)
   C. God Remembers Noah (8:1–14)
   D. Celebrating Salvation (8:15–22)
   E. A New Beginning (9:1–17)
   F. Blessing and Curse on the Next Generation (9:18–29)
V. The Family History of Noah's Sons (10:1–11:9)
   A. The Table of Nations (10:1–32)
   B. The Tower of Babylon (11:1–9)
VI. The Family History of Shem (11:10–26)
VII. The Family History of Terah (11:27–25:11)
   A. Introducing Abram and Sarai (11:27–32)
   B. The Call of Abram (12:1–3)
   C. Abram Traverses the Land (12:4–9)
   D. Abram in Egypt (12:10–13:4)
   E. Abram and Lot Separate (13:5–18)
   F. A Tale of Two Kings (14:1–24)
   G. Abram Believed God (15:1–21)
   H. Abram and Hagar (16:1–16)
   I. The Lord Renews Covenant with Abra(ha)m (17:1–27)
   J. The Friend of God (18:1–33)
   K. The Destruction of Sodom and the Rescue of Lot (19:1–38)
   L. Abraham and Abimelech (20:1–18)
   M. The Birth of Isaac (21:1–7)
   N. Hagar and Ishmael Sent Away (21:8–21)
   O. Peace with Abimelech (21:22–34)
   P. The Binding of Isaac (22:1–19)
   Q. The Family of Nahor (22:20–24)

    R. The Death and Burial of Sarah (23:1–20)
    S. A Bride for Isaac (24:1–67)
    T. The Death of Abraham (25:1–11)
VIII. The Family History of Ishmael (25:12–18)
  IX. The Family History of Isaac (25:19–35:29)
    A. Introducing Esau and Jacob (25:19–34)
    B. Another Famine and Its Consequences (26:1–35)
    C. Jacob Steals the Blessing (27:1–28:9)
    D. The House of God (28:10–22)
    E. The Woman at the Well (29:1–14)
    F. The Deceiver Deceived (29:15–30)
    G. The Battle for Love (29:31–30:24)
    H. The Battle for Jacob's Wages (30:25–43)
    I. Turning for Home (31:1–55)
    J. Wrestling with God (32:1–32)
    K. Meeting Esau (33:1–20)
    L. Trouble at Shechem (34:1–31)
    M. Return to Bethel (35:1–29)
   X. The Family History of Esau (36:1–43)
  XI. The Family History of Jacob (37:1–50:26)
    A. Joseph's Dreams (37:1–11)
    B. The Brothers Sell Joseph (37:12–36)
    C. Judah and Tamar (38:1–30)
    D. Joseph and Potiphar (39:1–23)
    E. The Cupbearer's and Baker's Dreams (40:1–23)
    F. A World Turned Upside Down (41:1–57)
    G. Joseph's Brothers Seek Grain (42:1–38)
    H. Restoring Shalom (43:1–34)
    I. Joseph Reconciles with His Brothers (44:1–45:15)
    J. The Lord's Blessing in Egypt (45:16–46:34)
    K. Israel in Egypt (47:1–31)
    L. Jacob Blesses Ephraim and Manasseh (48:1–22)
    M. Mixed Blessings (49:1–27)
    N. Death Is Not the End (49:28–50:26)

GENESIS 1:1–2:3

1 In the beginning, God created the heavens and the earth. ² The earth was without form and void, and darkness was over the face of the deep. And the Spirit of God was hovering over the face of the waters.

³ And God said, "Let there be light," and there was light. ⁴ And God saw that the light was good. And God separated the light from the darkness. ⁵ God called the light Day, and the darkness he called Night. And there was evening and there was morning, the first day.

⁶ And God said, "Let there be an expanse[1] in the midst of the waters, and let it separate the waters from the waters." ⁷ And God made[2] the expanse and separated the waters that were under the expanse from the waters that were above the expanse. And it was so. ⁸ And God called the expanse Heaven.[3] And there was evening and there was morning, the second day.

⁹ And God said, "Let the waters under the heavens be gathered together into one place, and let the dry land appear." And it was so. ¹⁰ God called the dry land Earth,[4] and the waters that were gathered together he called Seas. And God saw that it was good.

¹¹ And God said, "Let the earth sprout vegetation, plants[5] yielding seed, and fruit trees bearing fruit in which is their seed, each according to its kind, on the earth." And it was so. ¹² The earth brought forth vegetation, plants yielding seed according to their own kinds, and trees bearing fruit in which is their seed, each according to its kind. And God saw that it was good. ¹³ And there was evening and there was morning, the third day.

¹⁴ And God said, "Let there be lights in the expanse of the heavens to separate the day from the night. And let them be for signs and for seasons,[6] and for days and years, ¹⁵ and let them be lights in the expanse of the heavens to give light upon the earth." And it was so. ¹⁶ And God made the two great lights—the greater light to rule the day and the lesser light to rule the night—and the stars. ¹⁷ And God set them in the expanse of the heavens to give light on the earth, ¹⁸ to rule over the day and over the night, and to separate the light from the darkness. And God saw that it was good. ¹⁹ And there was evening and there was morning, the fourth day.

²⁰ And God said, "Let the waters swarm with swarms of living creatures, and let birds[7] fly above the earth across the expanse of the heavens." ²¹ So God created the great sea creatures and every living creature that moves, with which the waters swarm, according to their kinds, and every winged bird according to its kind. And God saw that it was good. ²² And God blessed them, saying, "Be fruitful and multiply and fill the waters in the seas, and let birds multiply on the earth." ²³ And there was evening and there was morning, the fifth day.

²⁴ And God said, "Let the earth bring forth living creatures according to their kinds—livestock and creeping things and beasts of the earth according to their kinds." And it was so. ²⁵ And God made the beasts of the earth according to their kinds and the livestock according to their kinds, and

everything that creeps on the ground according to its kind. And God saw that it was good.

²⁶ Then God said, "Let us make man[8] in our image, after our likeness. And let them have dominion over the fish of the sea and over the birds of the heavens and over the livestock and over all the earth and over every creeping thing that creeps on the earth."

²⁷ So God created man in his own image,
    in the image of God he created him;
    male and female he created them.

²⁸ And God blessed them. And God said to them, "Be fruitful and multiply and fill the earth and subdue it, and have dominion over the fish of the sea and over the birds of the heavens and over every living thing that moves on the earth." ²⁹ And God said, "Behold, I have given you every plant yielding seed that is on the face of all the earth, and every tree with seed in its fruit. You shall have them for food. ³⁰ And to every beast of the earth and to every bird of the heavens and to everything that creeps on the earth, everything that has the breath of life, I have given every green plant for food." And it was so. ³¹ And God saw everything that he had made, and behold, it was very good. And there was evening and there was morning, the sixth day.

2 Thus the heavens and the earth were finished, and all the host of them. ² And on the seventh day God finished his work that he had done, and he rested on the seventh day from all his work that he had done. ³ So God blessed the seventh day and made it holy, because on it God rested from all his work that he had done in creation.

[1] Or *a canopy*; also verses 7, 8, 14, 15, 17, 20 [2] Or *fashioned*; also verse 16 [3] Or *Sky*; also verses 9, 14, 15, 17, 20, 26, 28, 30; 2:1 [4] Or *Land*; also verses 11, 12, 22, 24, 25, 26, 28, 30; 2:1 [5] Or *small plants*; also verses 12, 29 [6] Or *appointed times* [7] Or *flying things*; see Leviticus 11:19–20 [8] The Hebrew word for *man (adam)* is the generic term for mankind and becomes the proper name *Adam*

Section Overview

The book of Genesis is a book of beginnings, as the first word (Hb. *bereshit*, "In the beginning") suggests. Indeed, that first word is the Hebrew title for the book. The subject of the opening sentence is the subject of the entire passage and, we might add, the entire Bible: God. The object of the opening sentence, the heavens and the earth—creation, in other words—is the object of the entire passage. At the outset the Bible makes clear that there is one universal God, that he created all things, and that he himself is quite distinct from the world he has created. The origin of the world tells us a great deal about its nature and destiny in seed form and therefore much about who we are as human beings and that for which we have been designed. We ourselves are not gods, defining our own identity and living for our own glory; we are creatures, made in the image of our Creator in order to glorify and enjoy him forever.

Every story in the world thus begins with Genesis 1 and unfolds against the foundational backdrop that this chapter paints. One story runs from the beginning of Genesis through to the end of Genesis, which begins in a garden-sanctuary but ends in a grave in Egypt. Yet it is not without hope: Joseph's bones are buried in a portable coffin (Gen. 50:24–26) so that, when (not if) the exodus occurs, he may posthumously join in the journey to the Promised Land alongside his people. That storyline finds its fulfillment in the book of Deuteronomy, which recounts Israel's deliverance out of Egypt and to the brink of the Promised Land.

Another storyline that begins with Genesis 1:1 runs connectedly through to the end of 2 Kings, when Israel's possession of the Promised Land is brought to an end by her sin, and the people find themselves in exile in Babylon. A third story that begins with Genesis ends with the book of Malachi (or 2 Chronicles, if one follows the Hebrew ordering of the OT), with Israel's having returned from exile to rebuild the ruins in the land of Judah. But all these stories are incomplete. The full account of the world that God creates runs all the way to the end of the book of Revelation, whereupon the lost paradise of Eden is replaced with a fully restored new Jerusalem and the original heavens and earth are transcended by a new heavens and new earth, now inhabited forever by multitudes of people, not just from Israel but from every tribe, nation, and language—all those who are Abraham's spiritual children through faith in Christ (cf. Romans 4).

The creation of the world is described in two distinct accounts, Genesis 1:1–2:3 and Genesis 2:4–25. Each of these accounts has its own focus and distinct contribution, just as each of the four Gospel accounts gives its own picture of Jesus—the differences between them are not contradictory but complementary. In the opening account (Gen. 1:1–2:3) the focus is on the creation of the whole universe by an utterly transcendent God (*'elohim*), who has neither peers nor rivals but establishes the world exactly as he pleases through his sovereign Word. That creation finds its focus and pinnacle in humanity, made in God's image as male and female, created for a special role ruling over the other animals, not just living among them (1:26–28), and in the Sabbath, the seventh day of divine and human rest (2:2–3).

In Genesis 2:4–25 the lens zooms in to examine more closely the creation of Adam and Eve, their location in the garden-sanctuary God makes for them, and their special roles and relationship. In this section God appears under his covenant name, Yahweh ("the LORD"), by which he later reveals himself to Moses and delivers his people from Egypt. In Genesis 3 the two names are brought together in the composite *yahweh 'elohim* ("the LORD God") in order to guard against any misunderstanding in a polytheistic environment that there might be two different creator gods, Yahweh and Elohim. The theme of this entire opening section is "It was good" (seven times in Genesis 1). In the beginning God orders and makes a universe of vast scope and minute detail that is good in every aspect, and he sets humanity to rule over it under his authority so that they might eventually enter into his rest.

Section Outline

    I. Prologue: The Creation of the Heavens and the Earth (1:1–2:3)
        A. Introductory Summary Statement (1:1)
        B. Pre-creation Situation (1:2)

C. Narrative of Creation (1:3–31)
D. Concluding Summary Statement (2:1)
E. Epilogue/Climax: Sabbath Rest (2:2–3)

Comment

1:1 The book of Genesis opens with an introductory statement that sums up God's great work in history: "In the beginning, God created the heavens and the earth."[15] This summary statement covers the whole of what follows in Genesis 1 and is balanced by the summary completion statement in Genesis 2:1: "Thus the heavens and the earth were finished, and all the host of them."

The Hebrew word "create" (*bara'*) generally implies a finished product, not merely the manufacture of raw materials.[16] So when Genesis 1:1 tells us that God created the heavens and the earth, it does not mean (as some have thought) that he creates the raw materials in verse 1, out of which he then proceeds to create the cosmos in the remainder of the chapter (perhaps after a lengthy gap of time). "Created" describes the end of the process, not the various stages in that process.

The word *bara'* by itself does not necessarily imply creation *ex nihilo* (cf. Ps. 51:10), and indeed it is used synonymously with *'asah* ("to make") in Genesis 1. However, it is always used, when God is its subject, to describe the origin of things that he alone can manufacture. What is more, the combination "heaven and earth" functions as a merism, so together these terms include everything that exists, implying that *ex nihilo* doctrine.

What this means is that "In the beginning" in Genesis 1:1 refers not to a time prior to creation but rather to the initial six days of creation, as a summary heading; the rest of the chapter lays out the development of God's initial purpose in the ordering of space and time.

1:2 Having begun with a universal focus ("the heavens and the earth"), the creation account immediately focuses on the center of God's purpose, which is the earth. Its initial state is *tohu vabohu* ("without form and void"), a rhyming pair in Hebrew that is hard to translate. *Tohu* often refers to the wilderness or wasteland (cf. Deut. 32:10; Isa. 34:11), and the combination with *bohu* is used in Isaiah 34:11 and Jeremiah 4:23 in judgment passages, where formerly habitable land is rendered uninhabitable. The reference here is thus not so much to a primordial chaos, as older scholars argued, but to a wilderness that is unsuitable for life ("desolate and empty") yet transformed into a perfect environment.[17] The unusual dual combination *tohu vabohu* alludes to the two-phase creation project, God's forming the environments in days 1–3 and filling those environments with occupants in days 4–6.

---

[15] Some have argued the alternative translation, "When God began to create the heavens and the earth, the earth was unformed and void" (NJPS) on the basis of an alleged similarity to ancient Near Eastern creation stories, such as the Enuma Elish. However, these similarities have been overstated, and all the ancient versions (along with John 1:1, and probably Mark 1:1 as well) presuppose the traditional understanding; Kenneth A. Mathews, *Genesis 1–11:26*, NAC (Nashville: B&H, 1996), 137–138.
[16] Cf. Psalm 51:10, where David asks the Lord to "create" a new heart in him, or Isaiah 4:5, where the Lord will "create" a pillar of cloud and fire over Mount Zion.
[17] David T. Tsumura, *Creation and Destruction* (Winona Lake, IN: Eisenbrauns, 2005), 33–35.

The deep sea and darkness were the most inhospitable conditions to life for the Israelite, so "darkness . . . over the face of the deep" describes a wilderness that must necessarily be devoid of life. Yet even this scene is not hopeless, because over it all is the Spirit of God, hovering like an eagle over its chicks (cf. Deut. 32:10–11). Without God the scene would be one of total, hopeless desolation, but when God is present—whether in a universe or in the life of an individual—he brings life, order, and hope. Even the most inhospitable conditions cannot prevent him from establishing life in a world of beauty, splendor, and majesty—the best of all possible worlds. In Genesis 1 the darkness and the sea are the elements from which the cosmos takes shape, but in the new creation described in Revelation 21 even these are gone: "I saw a new heaven and a new earth, for the first heaven and the first earth had passed away, and the sea was no more" (Rev. 21:1); "Its gates will never be shut by day—and there will be no night there" (Rev. 21:25).

The phrase "Spirit of God" (*ruakh 'elohim*) could also be rendered "wind of God" or "mighty wind," which draws our attention to the parallel situation at the height of Noah's flood (Gen. 8:1). Then too darkness was upon the face of the deep: water was everywhere and every living soul perished, except for the few occupants of the ark. But when God remembered Noah and sent his *ruakh* over the waters, he once again brought life and hope out of a wilderness world.

1:3–5 Having described the inhospitable pre-creation state in verse 2, Genesis 1 goes on to report the process of creation by the word of God. It is described as taking place over six days, each of which has the same basic structure. The day begins with an *announcement*: "And God said." God's will is expressed through his all-powerful word. Following the announcement comes a *commandment* ("Let there be") and a *report* ("And so God made . . . and he separated"). The report is followed by *naming*, as God not only brings the universe into existence but defines its essential nature. God names only the basic ecosystems, the static life-support systems; the animals, in contrast, he brings to Adam, the first man, for him to name as an act of subordinate authority under God's rule (2:19–20). Finally, there is an *evaluation* ("And it was good") and the whole is placed within a sequential, *temporal framework* ("There was evening and there was morning"). The latter is an essential element of the creation narrative since it demonstrates that in creation God is ordering not merely cosmic space but time as well. In contrast to ancient views of history that were cyclical or essentially timeless, the biblical understanding of history is linear, proceeding from an origin point ("the beginning") and moving toward an ending point, as anticipated by the Sabbath rest that is the goal of the original creation week.

In addition to the repeated themes within the days, there are also patterns that run across the days. For instance, the six days subdivide into two sets of three days. In the first three days, with four creative words (each beginning with "And God said") God creates the spaces and life-support systems of the universe:

(1) light (one word; 1:3–5)
(2) sky and waters (one word; vv. 6–8)
(3) land and seas; vegetation (two words; vv. 9–10, 11–13).

In the first three days God replaces an inhospitable wilderness with an inhabitable universe. Then in the next three days, again with four creative words, God creates various moving creatures to fill these spaces:

(4) sun, moon, and stars (one word; vv. 14–19)
(5) fish and birds (one word; vv. 20–23)
(6) various beasts; humans (two words; vv. 24–25, 26–27).

In these last three days God replaces emptiness with fullness. The sun, moon, and stars on day four correspond to the light on day one; the fish and birds in day five correspond to the seas and skies in day two; and the beasts and man in day six correspond to the land and vegetation on day three. In each triad the creative work moves from the heavens to the water to the earth. Each triad ends with two creative words on the last day and with the earth's bringing something forth.

This structure is designed to call attention to the sixth day, which is the chronological and literary climax: the report of the sixth day takes up twice as much space as any other day. Not only that, but God breaks into poetry over the man he has created (v. 27); for the first time a day is deemed not simply good but "very good." This, the sixth day, with the creation of man, is the high point of the story so far, to be surpassed only by the seventh day and the cosmic rest it anticipates.

In keeping with the structure described earlier, the first day revolves around the creation of light and its separation from darkness (vv. 3–4). God is not said here to create darkness (though cf. Isa. 45:7), perhaps because darkness is perceived as a negative entity rather a positive one. Separation is a key concept in Genesis 1, flowing from the idea of there being a proper place for everything, with boundaries determined by God. A collapse in the boundaries between the distinct realms of light and darkness would be a sign of God's returning cosmos to chaos as an act of ultimate judgment (e.g., Zech. 14:6–7).

Light and darkness are thus imagined not in modern scientific terms as the presence or absence of electromagnetic radiation but rather as two distinct realms: a realm of light and a realm of darkness, each of which will receive its proper inhabitants on day four. These realms are given their names, "Day" and "Night," by God in an act of sovereign determination. The privilege of naming someone or something was a sign of power in the ancient world; for example, an Egyptian pharaoh renames Eliakim as "Jehoiakim" before placing him on the throne of Judah in place of his deposed brother (2 Kings 23:34). God is not sovereign merely over humans, on occasions giving them new names (cf. Genesis 17); he rules even over the foundational structures of the universe, such as day and night. His authority is finally evident in the new name that will be given to "the one who conquers" in Revelation 2:17.

By beginning his work with the creation of day and night God starts out by ordering time as well as space, a theme underlined by the refrain that divides the creative acts: "There was evening and there was morning, the [number] day" (Gen. 1:5, 8, 13, etc.). Much ink has been spilled on the question of whether the days are normal, representational, or analogical. These questions are important, and each reader should be convinced in his or her own mind.[18] However, it is worth remembering that these questions would have been unlikely to occur to the original readers, or most readers throughout the history of the church, so the meaning of the passage should be able to be established without recourse to this discussion.

1:6–8 The second day begins with the creation of a *raqia'* ("expanse"; KJV: "firmament"). This word is hard to translate into English; the underlying Hebrew verb means to beat out metal (Isa. 40:19), though most uses of the noun refer back to the creational context. It seems plausible that the underlying metaphor depicts the bright sky as a metal mirror[19] that God has hammered out and set in place (Job 37:18), but the poetic image should not be pressed too strongly. Robert Alter suggests "vault," like a vaulted ceiling, which seems as good a concept as any.[20]

More importantly, the spreading out of the *raqia'* represents a mighty act of God's incomparable power, as well as establishing a fundamental division between the heavenly realm and the earthly (cf. Ezek. 1:22). The *raqia'* is part of the heavenly realm and may thus be named "the heavens," in contrast to the earth. It is also an element of the water cycle, dividing the waters above, from which the rain and dew descend, and the waters below, which include rivers as well as seas and the subterranean deeps (Gen. 1:6–8). As a result, God is sovereign over the provision of the life-giving elements of dew and rain, as well as the chaotic seas (cf. Psalm 29).

1:9–13 On the third day two creative words are spoken by God. His first word gathers the waters under the heavens, so that dry ground can appear (Gen. 1:9), which is then named "Earth" (v. 10; or "land"). After this the land is commanded to bring forth vegetation, which it does: each plant has within it the seed necessary to propagate itself according to its own kind (v. 12), stressing again the orderly universe that the Lord has created. This is the first occurrence of the word "seed," which will have a prominent role to play later in Genesis: like the plants, humans too carry seed, and each generation will reproduce the image of the father in the children. The distinction of different "kinds" of animals anticipates the later Levitical laws against mixing species (Lev. 19:19)—God's order for creation is to be respected.

Although the earth "brings forth" the plants, this is in no way conceived as a naturalistic process; these elements too are part of what God has made (cf. Gen. 1:24–25, where the animals that the earth brings forth are "made" by God). The lesson for an agricultural community is obvious: God makes the ground fruitful,

---

[18] Those who are interested in thinking more deeply about the relationship of science and origins may find help from the author's short ebook *Thinking about Science* or the fuller treatment by Vern Poythress, *Redeeming Science*.
[19] E.g., the descriptions of the (cloudless) sky as being "like iron" in Leviticus 26:19.
[20] Robert Alter, *The Five Books of Moses* (New York: Norton, 2004), 17.

not the pagan deities. Vegetation belongs in the first triad of days because it does not move, unlike the various elements of the second triad.[21]

1:14–19 On day four the second triad of days begins, as the spaces created in the first triad receive their occupants. Day and night were created on day one, and, correspondingly, God creates the sun, moon, and stars on day four (v. 16). Their purpose is also assigned: to distinguish between day and night; to distinguish between seasons, months, and years; and to act as signs, as well as the more obvious function of imparting light to the earth (vv. 14–15). The announcement in verses 14–15 is fulfilled in reverse order in verses 17–18, placing the focus on the creative act itself in verse 16.

The function of these heavenly bodies is carefully limited to providing services to those on earth. Though they have the honor of "rule" over day and night (v. 18), they have no independent status as deities, as they do in other ancient Near Eastern creation accounts. Indeed, the sun and moon are not even called by name in Genesis 1 but are denoted as "the greater light" and "the lesser light" (v. 16). The stars, which were conceived by many in antiquity as controlling human destinies and whose creation comes before the moon and the sun in the Enuma Elish, are almost an afterthought at the end of verse 16. Although the heavenly lights are good and useful to humanity, there is nothing in their nature that deserves worship or praise. Indeed, part of their function is to remind humans of the appropriate time to worship their Creator: *mo'adim* in verse 14, which the ESV renders "seasons," generally has religious festivals in view (cf. Lev. 23:2). The stars also serve as a testimony to the Lord's power and authority (cf. Ps. 19:1–6).

1:20–23 On day two the skies were formed first, followed by the seas, whereas on day five the skies and seas are populated in reverse order. The seas are filled with smaller, "swarms of living creatures" (Hb. *sherets*), which conjures up an image of abundant schools of fish (Gen. 1:20). The seas are also the home of "great sea creatures" (*tanninim*); these sea monsters, like Leviathan (cf. Job 41; Ps. 74:14), feature in cosmic battles in other ancient creation narratives, but in the biblical account they are merely one more of God's obedient creatures (Ps. 148:7).[22] There is no intense battle against chaos in Genesis 1, out of which the earth finally emerges. Rather there is the simple, repeated, unruffled combination "And God said . . . and it was so."

The skies are likewise filled with birds or, more precisely, "flying things" (cf. ESV mg.)—*'op* is a broader term than *zippor* ("bird"), encompassing insects and bats as well (cf. Lev. 11:19–20). All these are "living creatures" (*nepesh hakhayyah*; Gen. 1:21); like the beasts and humans, they are to be fruitful and multiply under God's

---

21 Mathews, *Genesis 1–11:26*, 152.
22 For *tannin* in Ugaritic literature cf. M. K. Wakeman, *God's Battle with the Monster: A Study in Biblical Imagery* (Leiden: Brill, 1973), 79. It is hard to find a suitable English word to translate the concept with suitably threatening connotation; when we think of "great sea creatures," we immediately think of whales, which we do not generally find particularly threatening, or perhaps sharks, which are dangerous but only as a natural threat. The supernaturally threatening connotations of the *tanninim*, like Behemoth and Leviathan in Job, tend to get obscured.

blessing in their proper place, in the waters of the seas and upon the earth (v. 22). The Levitical laws will later divide animals, birds, and insects into the categories of "clean" and "unclean," but these divisions are not there in the beginning: at the outset of creation all creatures are "good." They are "blessed" with the ability to procreate, a key linkage between the original creation and God's new order that will be established in Noah (9:1, 7), and ultimately in Abram in Genesis 12:1–3.

1:24–31 The sixth day parallels the third in that both record two creative words of God ("And God said"). On the third day the land appeared and brought forth vegetation, while on the sixth day the land brings forth animals and vegetation is assigned to them as food. As noted earlier, the sixth day is the literary and chronological climax of creation thus far, with the longest description of any of the days. The living creatures are brought forth from the earth and reproduce after their own kind, as was the case with vegetation (cf. 1:11–12). However, they acquire a special honor in being brought into existence on the same day as humanity, and, along with humanity, they are given the plants and trees as food (vv. 29–30).

The formation of humanity in the image of God is the climax of the sixth day, and with it of the entire creation week. Humans are the only part of creation addressed directly by God, setting them apart from all other creatures. The concept of all humanity, male and female, slave and free, as being made equally in the image of God was radically countercultural in the ancient Near East. A proverb dated to the reign of the Assyrian king Esarhaddon (r. 681–669 BC) claims, "Man is the shadow of a god, a slave is the shadow of a man; but the king is like the (very) image of a god."[23] Women did not merit a mention in the proverb, being ranked even lower than slaves! In the Bible, however, women are fully equal to men in status, even though the sexes are assigned different roles in Genesis 2. This passage also shows that our gender as male or female is an essential feature of God's design from the beginning, not a mere social construct that can be reconfigured in a multitude of ways according to one's desires or feelings.

The importance of the decision to make mankind is underlined by the unusual act of self-deliberation preceding it: "Let us make man in our image" (v. 26).[24] This plural is not merely an address to the heavenly council. No such body appears in this passage (unlike in Isa. 6:8, where the plural may perhaps have that force), for reasons that should be obvious: nothing can distract from the relentless monotheism of the creative process. There is no divine or angelic being but God, the Lord, involved in creating the world (cf. Isa. 40:14). Humans are made not in the image of angels but in the image of God himself. There is not yet here a full revelation of the Trinity, but later biblical revelation fills out that doctrine, showing us God's creation by the Word (Jesus; cf. John 1:1–14), through the work of the Spirit (Gen. 1:2). In that regard it is intriguing that it is as "male and female" that humanity is made in God's image, hinting at the relational dimension at the heart of the

---

23 *ANET*, 425.
24 Cf. Claus Westermann, *Genesis 1–11: A Continental Commentary*, trans. J. J. Scullion (Minneapolis: Fortress, 1994), 145.

Trinity as a differentiated unity. But no earthly analog can ultimately explain the mystery of the Trinity.

Genesis 1 does not unpack all that is involved in being made in the image of God. But this text is a striking affirmation for the OT, which is so resistant to any attempt to image God in worship in any form—human or nonhuman (Ex. 20:4).[25] In context, the emphasis on man's ruling over the lower creation as a vassal king fits the ancient Near Eastern emphasis on the relationship between image and kingship. There are a nobility and a rule assigned to humanity by being made in God's image, as well as the implication of the possibility of a relationship with the God who made us sufficiently like him that we could come to know him. Theologians have organized a number of attributes under this theme—rationality, morality, goodness, and so on—and have sometimes sought to distinguish between "image" (Hb. *tselem*) and "likeness" (*demut*). However, in Genesis these seem to be broadly synonymous terms, as is common in Hebrew poetry, and both image and likeness continue in man after the fall (Gen. 9:6; James 3:9), though damaged through sin and in need of renovation. Although God has no body, even our physical bodies reflect something of the nature of God: our ears reflect his power of hearing, and our arms image his power to save (cf. Deut. 26:8; Ps. 94:9). Since we are inscribed with God's image, we belong to him and owe him our service (cf. Matt. 22:20–21).

Having made humanity in his image, God then blesses them, turning his face toward them in favor (Num. 6:24–26) and endowing them with the gifts of fruitfulness and life (Gen. 1:28). Together as male and female they are to fill the earth with their offspring and subdue it—not in an oppressive way but by organizing it productively and beautifully so that its varied aspects cohere in form and function. In the beginning the animals and birds have no fear of humanity or each other, just as it will be in the new heavens and new earth (cf. Isa. 65:25).

As a final act of blessing, God provides food for humans and animals, assigning them plants and fruit as their food (Gen. 1:29–30). This does not necessarily mean that all creatures were vegetarians before the fall, any more than it means that humans could have eaten grass. The point is that God has made a world in which everything necessary for human and animal flourishing has been provided. The original inhabitants of the world God has made lack for nothing, so much so that at the end of the creative process God can survey the universe he has made and declare it "very good" (v. 31).

2:1–3 It might seem, now that the creative work is done, that the initial episode is over—hence the ending of chapter 1. The heavens and the earth (days 1–3) and all their inhabitants (days 4–6) are now in place (Gen. 2:1). However, the author adds a crucial seventh day to the week, recording the fact that on it God rests from all his labors (v. 2). Since God never gets tired or weary, this cannot be a rest for his own sake but makes sense only as a model for humanity, made in his image, to follow. Other cultures in antiquity had significant cycles of seven days, but the concept of

---

25 Walter Brueggemann, *Genesis*, Interpretation (Louisville: John Knox Press, 1982), 32.

breaking up time into a series of seven-day weeks seems to be original to the OT.[26] A seven-day system cuts across all natural rhythms that may be derived from the sun and moon (such as years and months) and therefore becomes a means for Israel to subordinate its time to God's rule. It is a weekly reminder that God made the universe without our help and that the universe can continue on without us. Six days of labor culminating in a seventh day of rest points humanity forward, even before the fall, from the work of this world to the ultimate rest for which humanity has been created. The original world, good though it was, was never intended to be humanity's final destination. God created time as well as space, and his intention from the very beginning was to bring both to an ultimate conclusion in Christ.

Response

Origin stories, like the one in Genesis 1:1–2:3, are designed to define the nature of the world and the relationships that exist within it. Who am I as a human being? How do I relate to God/the gods? How am I like or unlike the animals? What defines my purpose in life? Every culture, ancient or modern, that has ever existed has its own answers to these questions, which define our understanding of the reality around us. As a result, the biblical worldview is necessarily polemical, insofar as its origin story provides different answers to these questions than other worldviews do. In its ancient context it described a world made by one sovereign, all-powerful God—the same God, we learn in Genesis 2, who under the name Yahweh will make a covenant with Israel's forefathers and ultimately bring them out of the land of Egypt. In the biblical worldview there is no equally powerful force of chaos constantly threatening to undo the cosmos if the proper rituals are not performed by humans. There is no heavenly conflict between different gods with different agendas, some of whom may be for humanity but most of whom do not care about us. The only God makes everything good in the beginning.

To apply the insights of this passage in a modern context, we must ask about the modern answers to these questions. Many around us believe an origin story based (loosely)[27] on evolutionary ideas, in which there is no god (and therefore no being to whom humans are ultimately accountable). Reality around us is the result of a series of random chance events with no ultimate arbiter of truth; we therefore define for ourselves who we are and how we relate to other humans and animals, including foundational concepts such as the nature of gender or marriage. There is still some carryover of ideas from a more broadly Christian conception, such as the uniqueness of human beings, but these ideals are swiftly ebbing since they lack any proper foundation in a secular origin narrative.

---

26 Cf. Ilaria Bultrighini and Sacha Stern, "The Seven-Day Week in the Roman Empire: Origins, Standardization and Diffusion," in *The Origins of Calendars from the Roman Empire to the Later Middle Ages*, ed. S. Stern (Leiden: Brill, 2021), 11. The authors are, however, incorrect in claiming that no event in the OT is recorded as taking place on the Sabbath: it is true that events are normally dated with reference to day and month, but several texts record historical events as taking place on a Sabbath, such as 2 Kings 11:5–9 and Nehemiah 13:15–21, demonstrating that at least in Jerusalem the practice was familiar at an early point of Israel's history.

27 I say "loosely" because in my experience most people, whether Christians or non-Christians, cannot accurately represent the current scientific theory of evolution. Nonetheless, its broad principles and the worldview that stems from adopting it as an origin story have become deeply embedded in our culture.

The biblical account provides the foundation for our understanding of racial and sexual equality, since both men and women are made in the image of God, without reference to a particular tribe or ethnicity (cf. Genesis 10). This provides an inherent value for persons based simply on their humanity, without regard to physical or mental capacities. That much sounds appealing to the modern world, especially since there is no similar basis for these concepts in the secular origin narrative.

However, the biblical origin story also calls us to submit to the Lord's rule over our lives, not least in the shape of a weekly Sabbath rest—something that is much less attractive to our culture. Although the OT ceremonial aspects of the Sabbath have passed away (Col. 2:16), the Sabbath as a foundational principle of life was made for man (and creation) at the outset of all things and therefore it is *prima facie* likely to be a persistent obligation and blessing (Heb. 4:1–13). The biblical origin story is not just a metaphorical (or mythical) account but rather an understanding of reality rooted in actual history. The story that begins in Genesis 1:1 continues on in unbroken fashion down to the lives of the patriarchs and the history of Israel as a nation. In this it is quite unlike other ancient Near Eastern creation narratives.

There was, however, another clear lesson for the generation to which Moses was writing. They found themselves in a literal desert, surrounded by *tohu vabohu* everywhere they looked. But even such unpromising conditions could not stand between them and their possession of the Land of Promise if God was on their side and his Spirit was hovering over them (cf. Deut. 32:10–12). That is a timeless lesson for God's people. Like the people of Isaiah's day, we often find ourselves walking in deep darkness and hopelessness (Isa. 9:2). We too need the life-giving light of the Lord's favor to shine upon us, bringing us deliverance from the darkness and chaos of our sin-entangled lives. As the apostle Paul reminds us, the same God who commanded the light to shine in the darkness in the beginning now shines his light in our hearts as well, enabling us to recognize the glory of God shining in the face of Jesus Christ (2 Cor. 4:6). Our God will one day re-create his good world in all its intricate details as an eternal home for his redeemed people, and he invites us to share that inheritance through faith in Christ.

GENESIS 2:4–25

4 These are the generations
of the heavens and the earth when they were created,
in the day that the Lord God made the earth and the heavens.

5 When no bush of the field[1] was yet in the land[2] and no small plant of the field had yet sprung up—for the Lord God had not caused it to rain on the land, and there was no man to work the ground, 6 and a mist[3] was

going up from the land and was watering the whole face of the ground— [7] then the LORD God formed the man of dust from the ground and breathed into his nostrils the breath of life, and the man became a living creature. [8] And the LORD God planted a garden in Eden, in the east, and there he put the man whom he had formed. [9] And out of the ground the LORD God made to spring up every tree that is pleasant to the sight and good for food. The tree of life was in the midst of the garden, and the tree of the knowledge of good and evil.

[10] A river flowed out of Eden to water the garden, and there it divided and became four rivers. [11] The name of the first is the Pishon. It is the one that flowed around the whole land of Havilah, where there is gold. [12] And the gold of that land is good; bdellium and onyx stone are there. [13] The name of the second river is the Gihon. It is the one that flowed around the whole land of Cush. [14] And the name of the third river is the Tigris, which flows east of Assyria.[4] And the fourth river is the Euphrates.

[15] The LORD God took the man and put him in the garden of Eden to work it and keep it. [16] And the LORD God commanded the man, saying, "You may surely eat of every tree of the garden, [17] but of the tree of the knowledge of good and evil you shall not eat, for in the day that you eat[5] of it you shall surely die."

[18] Then the LORD God said, "It is not good that the man should be alone; I will make him a helper fit for[6] him." [19] Now out of the ground the LORD God had formed[7] every beast of the field and every bird of the heavens and brought them to the man to see what he would call them. And whatever the man called every living creature, that was its name. [20] The man gave names to all livestock and to the birds of the heavens and to every beast of the field. But for Adam[8] there was not found a helper fit for him. [21] So the LORD God caused a deep sleep to fall upon the man, and while he slept took one of his ribs and closed up its place with flesh. [22] And the rib that the LORD God had taken from the man he made[9] into a woman and brought her to the man. [23] Then the man said,

> "This at last is bone of my bones
>   and flesh of my flesh;
> she shall be called Woman,
>   because she was taken out of Man."[10]

[24] Therefore a man shall leave his father and his mother and hold fast to his wife, and they shall become one flesh. [25] And the man and his wife were both naked and were not ashamed.

[1] Or *open country* [2] Or *earth*; also verse 6 [3] Or *spring* [4] Or *Asshur* [5] Or *when you eat* [6] Or *corresponding to*; also verse 20 [7] Or *And out of the ground the* LORD *God formed* [8] Or *the man* [9] Hebrew *built* [10] The Hebrew words for *woman* (*ishshah*) and *man* (*ish*) sound alike

Section Overview

The majority of the book of Genesis is structured by ten *toledot* formulae (cf. comment on 2:4–7) scattered throughout the book. These formulae divide up the narrative into sections of varying sizes and significance but highlight the fact that Genesis is a connected family history—indeed, the title "Genesis" comes from the Greek translation of this word in the LXX. Genesis 1:1–2:3 stands outside this literary structure, forming a prologue to the larger account, or, in musical terms, the overture to the symphony. Genesis 2:4 marks the first of these *toledot* formulae. This chapter covers ground parallel to Genesis 1 but focuses on the "things generated" by the heavens and the earth, especially the first humans, Adam and Eve. As in Genesis 1, the main actor in Genesis 2 is God—or more precisely "the LORD God" (*yhwh 'elohim*). He is the one who forms the man (2:7), plants the garden (v. 8), sovereignly places the man in the garden (v. 15), assigns him his tasks there (vv. 15, 16), notices his potential for loneliness (v. 18), and provides him with a bride (vv. 21–22).

As is Genesis 1:1–2:3, Genesis 2:4–25 is an origin story, a defining narrative that intends to shape its readers' understanding of the nature of reality. In this case the focus is on God's creation of a garden-sanctuary for the first couple and their disparate roles in God's design for marriage. As in Genesis 1, the key thought is that God creates all things good for humans—the single "not good" element, Adam's aloneness (Gen. 2:18), being swiftly rectified. This consistent picture makes all the more jarring the claims of the serpent in Genesis 3 that the Lord God does not have mankind's best interests at heart.

Section Outline

II. The Family History of the Heavens and the Earth (2:4–4:26)
    A. Adam and Eve in the Garden (2:4–2:25)

Comment

2:4–7 The Hebrew word *toledot* ("generations"; or "family history"[28]) comes from a root that means "to generate" or "to father a child"; the formula "These are the generations of X" typically introduces the history of X's offspring. Some scholars have argued that this is a closing rather than an opening formula, which would then include Genesis 1:1–2:3 in the larger structure of Genesis but at the cost of excluding 37:3–50:26.[29] It is clear, however, from the use of the formula elsewhere that it introduces the section that follows (cf. Num. 3:1; Ruth 4:18), and that makes the best sense in Genesis as well.

Here the creator God is identified as *yahweh 'elohim* ("the LORD God"), an unusual title that occurs more frequently in Genesis 2–3 than it does in the entirety of the rest of the OT. The reason for this change in title is not due to different source material, one with a different name for God (as many critical scholars claim). Rather it is an emphatic way in which the author can identify the transcendent God who created the universe in chapter 1 with the covenant deity, Yahweh, who led his people out of Egypt, while making it clear that there is only one God. In a pantheistic context great care would be necessary to avoid the misconception that a High God, Elohim, had made the world but then delegated the task of creating

---

28 This translation is preferred by Gordon Wenham, *Genesis 1–15*, WBC (Waco, TX: Word, 1987), 55.
29 The theory was advanced originally by P. J. Wiseman, *New Discoveries in Babylonia about Genesis* (London: Marshall, Morgan, and Scott, 1936), 47–60. For a fuller refutation cf. Victor P. Hamilton, *Genesis 1–17*, NICOT (Grand Rapids, MI: Eerdmans, 1990), 8–10.

insignificant humanity to a lesser deity, Yahweh. No! In Israel's world there is only one God, and Yahweh is his name (cf. Deut. 6:4).

Having offered a chronological account of creation in Genesis 1, marked by repeated temporal notices, the author makes a more thematic presentation in Genesis 2. He starts by observing a twofold lack at a specific point in the creative process. Certain kinds of plants[30] had not yet been made because there was not yet a regular water source to support them, nor yet a human to cultivate them (Gen. 2:5). That twofold lack is no sooner introduced into the storyline than the Lord answers it by creating a water source and a caregiver. First he establishes a "mist" (or perhaps better a "raincloud") to provide rain,[31] and then he makes a man from the dust of the earth to care for these plants (vv. 6–7). This establishes a connection between humans (*'adam*) and the cultivation of the ground (*'adamah*; v. 5) that will be developed later in the garden (v. 15). The main point, however, is the immediate provision by the Lord of anything that is lacking, so that creation might be good for humanity. After the intervention of sin, however, the twin blessings of tilling the ground and God's provision of rain will also have a dark side, as humans are condemned to till the cursed soil and God pours out rain in overwhelming quantities in the flood.

The creation process is described in very concrete terms, with the first man being formed out of the dust from the ground and inbreathed with the very breath of God himself (v. 7)—a uniquely personal mode of creation[32] in comparison to the rest of the animals, which were brought forth by the earth (1:24). In the creation of humanity the Lord "forms" (*yatzar*) the man, as a potter (*yotser*) might shape a piece of clay, an image highlighting the Lord's absolute sovereignty over human beings (cf. Jer. 18:6; Rom. 9:20). Man's origin in the dust highlights his fragility (Ps. 103:14), yet the Bible holds out no vision of humanity's ultimately transcending the body and existing on a purely spiritual plane. Rather it envisages a bodily resurrection in which the earthly body is transformed into a heavenly one (cf. 1 Cor. 15:35–49).

2:8–17 Not content with making a good world for mankind, the Lord takes the man he has made and places him in a garden (Gen. 2:8), a place of special fruitfulness in a fruitful world—a kind of Most Holy Place in a holy land.[33] In the ancient Near East, temples generally faced east, toward the rising sun. So also the access to the garden of Eden is from the east, a fact demonstrated by the location of the guardian cherubim in Genesis 3:24.[34] Technically the garden is "in Eden," suggesting that the name Eden was attached to the larger area around the garden that

---

30 "Bush of the field" and "plant of the field" seem to be more restrictive categories than the general "vegetation" that the earth brings forth on day three (Gen. 1:11–12). The latter seems self-propagating, while the former explicitly require human cultivation (2:5). Cf. U. Cassuto, *A Commentary on the Book of Genesis* (Jerusalem: Magnes Press, 1961), 1.102; Mark D. Futato, "Because It Had Rained: A Study of Gen 2:5–7 with Implications for Gen 2:4–25 and Gen 1:1–2:3," *WTJ* 60 (1998): 3–4.
31 Cf. Futato, "Because It Had Rained," 6–8.
32 "*Breathed* is warmly personal, with the face-to-face intimacy of a kiss and the significance that this was giving as well as making; and self-giving at that"; F. D. Kidner, *Genesis*, TOTC (Downers Grove, IL: InterVarsity Press, 1967), 60.
33 M. G. Kline, *Kingdom Prologue: Genesis Foundations for a Covenantal Worldview* (Overland Park, KS: Two Age Press, 2000), 47–49.
34 Cassuto, *Genesis*, 1.174.

was also a place a special abundance (2:11–14). Gold and onyx are associated with the high priestly breastplate in Exodus 28:20 and Ezekiel 28:13, while bdellium is associated elsewhere with the color of the manna from heaven (Num. 11:7).

The garden of Eden is set upon a mountain. This location is implicit in Genesis 2:10, where the four rivers flow out of the garden to all four points of the compass, and becomes explicit in Ezekiel 28:13–14, where Eden is called the mountain of God. Mountains in the Bible, as elsewhere in the ancient Near East, symbolize God's connection with man. Mount Sinai is where Moses receives his great revelation from God (Exodus 32–34). Ezekiel's picture of a restored temple in Ezekiel 40 is located on a high mountain, and so too is the new Jerusalem in Revelation 21:10. It is no coincidence that Jesus' transfiguration and ascension take place on mountains. The Bible is full of mountaintop experiences with God—and such is the case with Eden.

Out of this "garden on the mount" flow four rivers that impart blessing to the whole world. Two of these rivers are easily identifiable, the Tigris and the Euphrates, the chief rivers of Mesopotamia. The other two, the Pishon and the Gihon, remain enigmatic. Even the identifiers "Cush" and "Havilah" do not necessarily provide greater clarity, since several places are named Cush in the Bible, and Havilah remains indeterminate. Perhaps that is the point: the geography of Eden cannot be straightforwardly mapped onto the world as we know it, but neither is it in an imaginary location.

Clearly the garden is well watered, without the need for irrigation, which was so prevalent and necessary in much of the ancient Near East. Yet there is more to the "river of life" that flows from Eden than merely the provision of water. It is the flowing source of life for the whole earth. The image of a life-giving stream flowing from the sanctuary is ubiquitous in Scripture, from here to the closing chapter of Revelation, which features a similar river that flows outward from the throne of God and the Lamb to nourish the tree of life, whose fruit appears every month and whose leaves are for the healing of the nations (Rev. 22:1–2). The motif of the river of life is attested also in mythological literature of the ancient Near East, while the tree of life is itself a feature typical of sanctuaries, in the form of a literal sacred tree or a symbolic representation of such a tree.[35]

If Eden is thus a sanctuary, it sheds light on the task assigned to the man, to "work" (Hb. *'abad*) and "keep" it (*shamar*; "take care"). When these two phrases occur together in the OT, they normally refer to priestly work, especially the work of guarding from profane intrusion the sphere of that which is sacred.[36] In short, Adam should have been keeping his eye open for serpents that contradicted the word of God and crushing them on sight. After all, that is what God promises that his seed, the new Adam, will do when he comes (Gen. 3:15).

---

[35] Gordon Wenham, "Sanctuary Symbolism in the Garden of Eden Story," in *I Studied Inscriptions from Before the Flood: Ancient Near Eastern Literary and Linguistic Approaches to Genesis 1–11*, ed. R. S. Hess and D. T. Tsumura (Winona Lake, IN: Eisenbrauns, 1994), 401. Wenham cites Carol Meyers's observation that the later temple menorah is itself a stylized tree of life.

[36] Note especially Numbers 3:7, where the Levitical task is summed up by these verbs; cf. Wenham, "Sanctuary Symbolism," 401; Kline, *Kingdom Prologue*, 85.

In 2:16–17 Adam receives his instructions (*torah*, we might say, to utilize the later terminology). He is commanded first to eat freely of all the trees of the garden—the law begins by enjoining the enjoyment of the good world he has been given (v. 16). Only after this positive command to delight in *all* the attractive trees of the garden (cf. v. 9) is the restriction imposed that he may not eat of the tree of the knowledge of good and evil. In this way an element of conditionality is imposed upon mankind's existence in the garden. Will they submit to their Creator's definition of "good" and "evil"—ordaining which trees are "good" to eat and which would be "evil" to eat—or will they seek autonomously to determine for themselves that which constitutes good and evil? To eat defiantly from the tree of the knowledge of good and evil would be to make a claim of absolute moral authority, a prerogative the Bible reserves for God alone.

As God's priest, it is Adam's task to teach this *torah* to Eve. In regard to the trees of the garden he is to teach her to "distinguish between the holy and the common, and between the unclean and the clean" (Lev. 10:10, 11), so that both might live and not die (the Hebrew is a strong imperative of the infinitive absolute, followed by the cognate verb: "You shall *surely* die"). The one who is faithful in keeping *torah* will "live," a term describing not merely physical life but the fullness of relationship with the Great King that flows from obedience. Death, on the other hand, means estrangement from both God and the covenant community. To be cut off from God's people is to be "dead" even while physically still alive, for in such a case one would be separated from the source of life, which in the garden is symbolized concretely in the form of the tree of life.

2:18–25 Into this original world of universal sweetness and light a discordant note enters at Genesis 2:18: The Lord God remarks, "It is not good that the man should be alone." Thus far everything has been "good" (six times in Genesis 1) or "very good" (a climactic 7th pronouncement), but now there is not merely something lacking in goodness (Hb. *'en tob*) but something that is positively *not* good (*lo' tob*).[37] Man is not meant to be a solitary creature: he needs a "helper corresponding to him" (2:18; cf. ESV mg.).

As is often the case when the Bible describes a particularly challenging situation, an initial insufficient solution is presented before the final answer is provided.[38] First the Lord brings to Adam all the animals that he has (previously)[39] made so that Adam can name them—a sign of his lordship over them as God's visible representative on earth. But no suitable helper for Adam is found among them (v. 20). The animals are created for man's enjoyment and blessing, but they are no substitute for human society. The purpose of placing man in the midst of this zoo is not so that God could determine by trial and error whether Adam

---

37 Cf. Bruce Waltke with Cathi Fredericks, *Genesis* (Grand Rapids, MI: Zondervan, 2001), 88.
38 Compare Ezekiel 37:1–11, where the dry bones are first brought together but are still lifeless until God breathes his spirit into them, or Mark 8:22–25, where Jesus heals the blind man in two distinct stages.
39 We noted earlier that Genesis 2 does not present a chronological account. The *vav*-consecutive imperfect here can easily be understood as a past perfect; cf. Bruce Waltke and Michael O'Connor, *An Introduction to Biblical Hebrew Syntax* (Winona Lake, IN: Eisenbrauns, 1990), 33.2.3a.

could be happy living with an armadillo or a zebra; God knew already that he was not going to squander his greatest creation on an unappreciative audience.[40] However, it is necessary for the man to feel his aloneness and to understand that it is not good for him to be alone. Rabbinic commentators imagine all the animals bounding up to Adam in pairs to be named, underlining his solitary state.[41] The Trinitarian God does not intend his created image to dwell alone. Man is built for marriage—and so, of course, is woman (cf. Prov. 18:22).

To provide for this need in man God creates woman. Unlike with the creation of man, Eve is not formed from the dust of the ground but "built" from one of Adam's ribs to emphasize their close connection. As Matthew Henry puts it, "Eve was not taken out of Adam's head to top him, neither out of his feet to be trampled on by him, but out of his side to be equal with him, under his arm to be protected by him, and near his heart to be loved by him."[42] The Lord first places Adam under a very "deep sleep" (*tardemah*; Gen. 2:21), a word found often in the context of dreams and visions and almost always divinely induced (cf. Gen. 15:12; 1 Sam. 26:12).[43] God then brings the woman to the man, playing the role of the father of the bride (or the attendant at a Jewish wedding), whose job it is to present the bride to the groom.[44]

The woman is perfectly designed to be a "helper corresponding to" the man (ESV mg. on Gen. 2:18). Eve is man's equal in being—created in the image of God, just as man is (1:27). God creates for the man not a "helper like him" (*'ezer kamohu*) but a "helper corresponding to" him (*'ezer kenegdo*). There is no suggestion of inferiority in this title, for God himself can be called our helper (e.g., Ps. 33:20). Rather the focus is on complementarity: like two pieces of a jigsaw puzzle, men and women are designed to fit together perfectly, completing each other precisely because they are not the same but have different roles.

When Adam is presented with God's answer to his need, he breaks into the first recorded human poetry:[45] "Yes! This is it! Bone of my bone and flesh of my flesh" (Gen. 2:23 AT).[46] Adam also names her "Woman," just as he named the animals, as an act of authority (v. 23; cf. v. 19). Yet that authority is softened by the passive voice of the verb, "She shall be called," and the acknowledgement in the form of her name that she is from him, made of the same stuff (*'ishah* from *'ish*).

Just as Genesis 1 climaxes in the Sabbath, a day of rest with lasting significance for all humanity, so chapter 2 climaxes in the union of Eve and Adam, a model for

---

40 Cf. Peter Martyr Vermigli, *In Primum Librum Mosis* (1569), 12r: "The animals weren't brought before Adam as if God wanted to find out whether some suitable helper for the man might be found among them. The Lord perfectly well knew that one would not be discovered, but he brought the animals so that his gift would be welcomed by *Adam* all the more, lest he happen to think that there was no need for the creation of woman, because something could have been discovered among the animals as suitable for him as the woman was. God wanted Adam to learn for himself that no such helper was to be found." Cited in John L. Thompson, ed., *Genesis 1–11*, RCS (Downers Grove, IL: InterVarsity Press, 2012), 97.
41 Genesis Rabbah 17:5, cited in Wenham, *Genesis 1–15*, 68.
42 Matthew Henry, *Commentary on the Whole Bible*, 6 vols. (Peabody, MA: Hendrickson, 1991), 1:16. Henry here is developing an idea found already in Thomas Aquinas, *Summa Theologiae*, 1a, 92, 3c.
43 Nahum M. Sarna, *Genesis*, JPS Torah (Philadelphia: Jewish Publication Society, 2001), 22.
44 Gerhard von Rad, *Genesis*, rev. ed., OTL (Philadelphia: Westminster Press, 1973), 84.
45 Robert Alter (*Five Books of Moses*, 22) points out that the first recorded human speech does not come until after God has created a fellow human with whom to converse.
46 Hebrew identifies "flesh and bone" as the key kinship ingredients rather than "flesh and blood" (cf. 29:14).

marriage for all human societies. Even the most holy people in the OT, the high priest and the Nazirite, are allowed to marry. Marriage is holy; it is life as God intended. Indeed, the marriage relationship is assigned priority even over relationships within the husband's family of origin: the husband is commanded to leave his father and mother—the very ones whom he is told to honor in the fifth commandment (cf. Ex. 20:12)—and cleave to his wife in a unique one-flesh relationship (Gen. 2:24). Since in most cases in antiquity sons did not leave the physical household of their parents, this "leaving" must be metaphorical, giving preference and honor to his wife over long-lasting and deeply rooted family ties. There was no need for a similar instruction to brides, since the wife usually moved in with her new in-laws.

However, this absolute statement of the goodness and priority of marriage is qualified in the NT. There is a spiritual gift of celibacy; some are gifted not to marry so that they can be free to serve God (Matt. 19:11), while there may be times when even wives must be counted as secondary in pursuit of God's kingdom (Luke 14:26). Paul makes a remarkable statement in 1 Corinthians 7:1: "It is good for a man not to marry" (ICB), which he then goes on to explain as being due to the particular challenges of the present situation in Corinth (cf. 1 Cor. 7:29–35). In a fallen world there may be some circumstances in which singleness is better, as Paul's own example illustrates (cf. 1 Cor. 7:8). But singleness is not in itself a higher, more spiritual state than marriage, as the monks and nuns thought in the Middle Ages. Although Jesus himself was not married while he lived here on earth, he has a bride prepared for him, his church. The usual state for human beings to desire and pursue is marriage.

Profound though the parent-child bond is, only the bond of marriage involves becoming "one flesh." This has in view far more than sexual intercourse, though certainly not less than that. Intercourse is indeed designed by God to create and sustain deep bonds of relationship, which is why sexual relations outside of marriage are so deeply damaging (1 Cor. 6:16). Just as the prohibition on eating from the tree of the knowledge of good and evil is preceded by the command to eat freely of all the other trees of the garden (Gen. 2:16–17), so also the command "You shall not commit adultery" (Ex. 20:14) is preceded by the celebration of unashamed sexuality within marriage (Gen. 2:24–25). Similarly, the prohibition on homosexual activity and relationships (e.g., Lev. 20:13) is preceded by the foundational and defining marriage between a man and a woman, two distinct and different genders joined in one flesh (Matt. 19:5–6). They were naked before one another, with nothing to hide because neither was seeking an advantage over the other. As long as they were both agreed that the Lord was their king and that they would mutually submit to the roles he had defined for them, there was nothing over which to fight. It is only after they decide to strive after divine status and throw off the Lord's yoke that conflict—and therefore concealment and shame—becomes inevitable (Gen. 3:7).

Response

Genesis 1–2 lays the foundation and sets the trajectory for understanding the cosmos properly, whenever and wherever we live. The world and everything in it was created by God and belongs to him. Humans are not merely animals but transcend them in their composition and calling. We were made to worship God together, coming into his presence with praise, glorifying and enjoying our Creator. And marriage is a sacred joining of one man and one woman in an unbreakable relationship intended to result in offspring ("filling the earth"; 1:28) and mutual encouragement ("a helper corresponding to him"; ESV mg. on 2:18). If Genesis 1 is lofty and poetic prose, stressing the transcendence of almighty God, then Genesis 2 paints a more personal and intimate picture of the Lord's interactions with the world, especially with humanity. Israel's God (and ours) is both the high and holy God who inhabits eternity and also the God who stoops down to dwell with the humble and contrite in spirit (Isa. 57:15).

This passage has wide-ranging implications for understanding our place in the world. Created in the world to have dominion over it, the first man was immediately taken out of the wider world and placed directly in the divine presence and in divine service. This is how the creation mandate was intended to be exercised: man was to control the world not primarily by immersing himself in the tasks of ordering it but by "seek[ing] first the kingdom of God" (Matt. 6:33). If Adam was relating rightly to his Creator, then he would necessarily respond rightly to creation. This includes the male-female relationship. As with his dominion within wider creation, the man is given the obligation of seeking to understand the nature of the marriage relationship as well as the duty to maintain it first of all by exercising a God-centered life (1 Pet. 3:7).

Eve's task of helping Adam certainly includes the chief end for which he is made: glorifying and enjoying God in the garden-sanctuary within which they are placed. It is not possible to worship and glorify God to the fullest extent on one's own or in company with a Labrador retriever! Human fellowship is required. The first couple's freedom and privilege are enormous: they are given a home in the most beautiful part of the most perfect world, living in the presence of God himself, constantly enjoying the smile of his blessing. The only limitation on their freedom is the command not to eat of the tree of the knowledge of good and evil (Gen. 2:17), hardly an onerous restriction in a garden filled with other good trees to enjoy (vv. 8–9).

Of course, we no longer live in Eden. Nakedness is no longer unaccompanied by shame, and marriage sometimes ends in divorce. With the fall in Genesis 3 everything has changed. Our world is cursed because of human sin, which mars the natural order as well as complicating our relationships with God, with other humans (especially our spouses), and with the created order. The "good" trajectory launched in Genesis 1–2 has turned tragically "evil" through the entry of sin. But God's plan from the beginning included a new creation, in which he would redeem a people for himself in Christ—a people who would become the spotless bride of Christ, clothed in his righteousness, and would inhabit a new creation, of which they themselves would be part. God's goal for humanity is not merely union with one another in marriage but the deeper reality that marriage exists to image: the union between Christ and his church (Eph. 5:32). This goal can be accomplished only through Christ's self-sacrifice for his bride, which now becomes the inspiration and model for Christian husbands (Eph. 5:25–27), while Christian wives are called to submit to their husbands as the church submits to Christ (Eph. 5:24).

GENESIS 3

3 Now the serpent was more crafty than any other beast of the field that the Lord God had made.

He said to the woman, "Did God actually say, 'You[1] shall not eat of any tree in the garden'?" [2] And the woman said to the serpent, "We may eat of the fruit of the trees in the garden, [3] but God said, 'You shall not eat of the fruit of the tree that is in the midst of the garden, neither shall you touch it, lest you die.'" [4] But the serpent said to the woman, "You will not surely die. [5] For God knows that when you eat of it your eyes will be opened, and you will be like God, knowing good and evil." [6] So when the woman saw that the tree was good for food, and that it was a delight to the eyes, and that the tree was to be desired to make one wise,[2] she took of its fruit and ate, and she also gave some to her husband who was with her, and he ate. [7] Then the eyes of both were opened, and they knew that they were naked. And they sewed fig leaves together and made themselves loincloths.

[8] And they heard the sound of the Lord God walking in the garden in the cool[3] of the day, and the man and his wife hid themselves from the presence of the Lord God among the trees of the garden. [9] But the Lord God called to the man and said to him, "Where are you?"[4] [10] And he said, "I heard the sound of you in the garden, and I was afraid, because I was naked, and I hid myself." [11] He said, "Who told you that you were naked? Have you eaten of the tree of which I commanded you not to eat?" [12] The man said, "The woman whom you gave to be with me, she gave me fruit of the tree, and I ate." [13] Then the Lord God said to the woman, "What is this that you have done?" The woman said, "The serpent deceived me, and I ate."

[14] The Lord God said to the serpent,

> "Because you have done this,
>   cursed are you above all livestock
>   and above all beasts of the field;
> on your belly you shall go,
>   and dust you shall eat
>   all the days of your life.
> [15] I will put enmity between you and the woman,
>   and between your offspring[5] and her offspring;
> he shall bruise your head,
>   and you shall bruise his heel."

¹⁶ To the woman he said,

> "I will surely multiply your pain in childbearing;
>   in pain you shall bring forth children.
> Your desire shall be for[6] your husband,
>   and he shall rule over you."

¹⁷ And to Adam he said,

> "Because you have listened to the voice of your wife
>   and have eaten of the tree
> of which I commanded you,
>   'You shall not eat of it,'
> cursed is the ground because of you;
>   in pain you shall eat of it all the days of your life;
> ¹⁸ thorns and thistles it shall bring forth for you;
>   and you shall eat the plants of the field.
> ¹⁹ By the sweat of your face
>   you shall eat bread,
> till you return to the ground,
>   for out of it you were taken;
> for you are dust,
>   and to dust you shall return."

²⁰ The man called his wife's name Eve, because she was the mother of all living.[7] ²¹ And the LORD God made for Adam and for his wife garments of skins and clothed them.

²² Then the LORD God said, "Behold, the man has become like one of us in knowing good and evil. Now, lest he reach out his hand and take also of the tree of life and eat, and live forever—" ²³ therefore the LORD God sent him out from the garden of Eden to work the ground from which he was taken. ²⁴ He drove out the man, and at the east of the garden of Eden he placed the cherubim and a flaming sword that turned every way to guard the way to the tree of life.

[1] In Hebrew *you* is plural in verses 1–5 [2] Or *to give insight* [3] Hebrew *wind* [4] In Hebrew *you* is singular in verses 9 and 11 [5] Hebrew *seed*; so throughout Genesis [6] Or *to*, or *toward*, or *against* (see 4:7) [7] *Eve* sounds like the Hebrew for *life-giver* and resembles the word for *living*

Section Overview

In Genesis 1–2 we saw God create a good and perfect world. The one thing that was not good, man's being alone, was swiftly and perfectly put right. The first man and woman lived in a world in which there was no excuse for sin. Genesis 3 is therefore shocking in its introduction of sin and evil into this world: we move from a perfect world into a broken and dysfunctional one in the space of a few verses. Some theologians are reluctant to speak of a "fall" since the Bible does not use that terminology explicitly. But it is hard to think of a better term for the injury inflicted on all subsequent humanity by Adam and Eve's original sin—a sin that affects not only themselves but all subsequent offspring (1 Cor. 15:22).

As it records the fact and the consequences of that first sin, it is striking that Genesis 3 does not tell us *why* man sins. Ultimately, there is no reason for sin.[47] If there were a "why" behind sin, then in some measure we might claim that sin is not completely our fault; it is (at least in part) the product of our genetics or our environment. Yet Adam and Eve can blame neither of these things. In showing the fundamental irrationality of the very first sin (and all subsequent sins) the Bible reveals us as we really are: without excuse.

Section Outline

    II. The Family History of the Heavens and the Earth (2:4–4:26) . . .
        B. The Fall (3:1–24)

Comment

3:1–5 Genesis 3 begins with a disjunctive construction (*vav* + nonverb), separating what follows from what precedes grammatically, just as the chapter will separate "life before" from "life after" in a comprehensive way. We are introduced to a new character, "the serpent." This character is not a god; he is merely one of the creatures that the Lord God has made, albeit potentially dangerous in being "more crafty" ("shrewder")[48] than all other creatures (Gen. 3:1). We are not told the serpent's backstory here. Indeed, the entire Bible says very little about Satan's origins, except to affirm that he has been created by God and is subject to his control—he is "God's devil,"[49] as it were, and, wicked though he is, Satan cannot do anything beyond God's permission (cf. Job 1–2). The form chosen by the serpent is not arbitrary; Leviticus classifies animals in terms of clean and unclean—for a variety of reasons, some connected with eating habits, some with means of locomotion—and snakes are in the unclean category (Lev. 11:42). The serpent's writhing motion on the ground, which is connected to this episode (cf. Gen. 3:14), makes it an appropriate anti-God image.[50]

The serpent speaks to the woman—a surprising turn of events, given our experience of the world. Yet the woman's experience of life is much more limited at this point, perhaps especially with the "beasts of the field," who live outside the garden. The serpent clearly targets the woman since she did not hear the prohibition in Genesis 2:16–17 directly from the mouth of God. Yet the man evidently is also present with her throughout the entire encounter (3:6). There is a reversal of

---

[47] Claus Westermann, *Genesis: A Practical Commentary*, trans. D. Green (Grand Rapids, MI: Eerdmans, 1987), 22.
[48] It is hard to translate *'arum* into English, since most potential equivalents either have a positive connotation ("wise") or a negative one ("crafty"), while *'arum* can be either. It is a positive attribute in Proverbs 12:23 but negative in Job 15:5. "Shrewd" (NET) is perhaps the best morally neutral equivalent, allowing the reader to experience the same moral ambiguity in encountering the serpent that Eve experiences—though that ambiguity is swiftly dispelled once the serpent opens his mouth.
[49] The appellation is often attributed to Martin Luther, though it is not clear that he ever said those exact words. He did, however, say similar things, such as "The devil must serve us with the very thing with which he plans to injure us; for God is such a great Master that He is able to turn even the wickedness of the devil into good." Cf. Ewald Plass, *What Luther Says* (St. Louis: Concordia, 1959), 401–402.
[50] Serpents were also prominent in the worship and mythological symbolism of many ancient Near Eastern cultures, not least Egypt, from which Moses' audience had recently emerged. Cf. K. R. Joines, *Serpent Symbolism in the Old Testament* (Haddonfield, NJ: Haddonfield House, 1974).

the proper ordering of creation from man-woman-beast to beast-woman-man in this chapter. This theme is highlighted by the chiastic structure of the passage in terms of the characters interacting in each scene, which begins with disordered relationships in scenes A and B and ends with those relationships' being properly reordered after the divine intervention.

   (A) The serpent and the woman (vv. 1–5); the man is silently present (v. 6)
      (B) The woman and "her man" (vv. 6–7)
         (C) God and the man (vv. 8–12); the woman is silently present
            (D) God and the woman (v. 13)
               (E) God and the serpent (vv. 14–15)
            (D') God and the woman (v. 16)
         (C') God and the man (vv. 17–19)
      (B') The man and "his woman" (v. 20)
(A') God and the man (vv. 21–24)

As is typical of Satan, the serpent uses the things God has created good for his own wicked purposes. He begins with a question that misrepresents God's words: "Did God actually say, 'You shall not eat of any tree in the garden'?" (v. 1). Far from saying "You shall not eat of any tree in the garden," what God actually said was, "You may surely eat of every tree of the garden" (2:16), with a single exception. Eve's response is initially accurate—though omitting the intensification of God's command ("You may *surely* eat")—but she adds a clause to God's words that make the prohibition regarding the tree of life sound petty and legalistic. According to her, God told them not merely to avoid eating from the tree of the knowledge of good and evil but not even to touch it,[51] lest they die (3:3). Again Eve omits the intensification of the original command ("You shall surely die").

The serpent not only misquotes God; he goes on to contradict him. God had said, "Of the tree of the knowledge of good and evil you shall not eat, for in the day that you eat of it you shall surely die" (2:17). Satan says to Eve, however, "You will not surely die" (3:4). His inclusion of the intensification that Eve omitted evinces firsthand knowledge of the truth, even as he twists it to serve his own purposes. The shrewdness of the serpent is evident further in the fact that he never directly tells Eve to eat from the tree; he simply proposes a different exegesis of the key biblical text and then allows her to draw her own desired conclusion. Eve also follows the serpent in referring to the deity generically as "God" rather than by his more relational covenant name, "the LORD." The greater the distance that exists between humans and the deity, the easier it is for them to believe that God does not have their best interests at heart.

After the serpent denies the doctrine of judgment ("You will not surely die"; v. 4), the doctrine of divine providence is the next target of the serpent's attack. Far from acknowledging God's working all things together for Eve's good (Rom.

---

51 The (imagined) prohibition on touching the tree aligns it with the (real) prohibition on touching the mountain of Sinai under pain of death in Exodus 19:12.

8:28), the serpent claims that God is seeking to protect the uniqueness of his divine status, which would be imperiled if the humans ate from the tree of the knowledge of good and evil and became like him (Gen. 3:5). The irony of the man and woman's believing this claim is deeply tragic, for God had created them in his very image for rulership over an entire creation designed for their good. Nevertheless, this is the same heresy that we routinely believe any time we choose to sin rather than to obey the Lord's fatherly commands to us.

The serpent claims not only that Adam and Eve (the verb is plural) will not die but that they will have their eyes opened, acquiring godlike knowledge and status (vv. 4–5). But the serpent is trading in characteristic half-truths. Adam and Eve do not die immediately, though their fullness of life in God's presence is immediately lost. Moreover, while their eyes are opened with a new kind of knowledge, this knowledge brings shame and conflict rather than status and power (vv. 7–13).

3:6–7 In light of the serpent's words the woman looks at the tree of the knowledge of good and evil in a new way, considering it to be "good for food," "a delight to the eyes," and desirable "to make one wise" (v. 6). Even before she takes the fruit she is already beginning to form her own evaluations independently of God's word.[52] In reality, every tree that God had made was "good for food" and "pleasant to the sight" (cf. 2:9), but now she sets her heart on the forbidden tree. The wisdom offered by eating from that tree is certainly not God's wisdom, for the beginning of that wisdom is the fear of the Lord (Prov. 9:10). The fear of the Lord would have kept her from eating from the tree. Eve's "logic" thus deconstructs itself, as our reasoning in favor of sin always does. But it is enough to tempt her to take and eat the fruit from the forbidden tree, hoping for a new kind of knowledge that would give her autonomy from her creator. Christian art since at least the Middle Ages has pictured the fruit as an apple, likely based on the fact that in Latin the word for "apple" and for "evil" is the same (*malum*). The type of fruit is unspecified in the Genesis account, however, and it was unlikely to have been an apple, since those were not introduced to Israel until significantly later.[53]

It is at this point that we learn that Adam has evidently been with Eve throughout the entire encounter (Gen. 3:6), apparently without contributing a single word to a conversation in which God's words to him have been misquoted, maligned, and denied by both the serpent and his own wife. Instead of being Adam's helper, Eve is leading him astray, and he has done nothing to challenge her. Before the fruit is even touched Adam fails in his God-appointed priestly task as guardian of the sanctuary and teacher of *torah*. Adam's sinful abdication of his responsibility throughout the encounter is highlighted at this point by his being named "her husband" (v. 6; "her man"). Sin always subverts God's ordering of the world. However, the chapter is not devoid of hope. In the corresponding chiastic section B' (cf. structure above), when order is restored after God's intervention, their relationship

---

[52] John H. Sailhamer, *The Pentateuch as Narrative: A Biblical-Theological Commentary* (Grand Rapids, MI: Zondervan, 1992), 104.
[53] Cf. Othmar Keel, *Song of Songs: A Continental Commentary*, trans. F. J. Gaiser (Minneapolis: Fortress, 1994), 82.

is once more "the man and his woman" (v. 20; ESV: "his wife") as Adam resumes a leadership role by naming his wife "Eve" in response to God's word of promise.

Immediately after Adam and Eve sin the consequences of that sin begin to become apparent: "The eyes of both were opened, and they knew that they were naked" (v. 7). Their nakedness had not bothered them previously because they had had nothing to hide. Because they had been content to accept their assigned place in the divine order, there had been nothing over which to fight. But now that they have declared themselves to be as gods, everything is in flux. Once they have rejected the created order, they seek to establish their own order, which inevitably means conflict with one another, a striving for the dominant position. In that struggle, knowledge is power. No longer could they be completely open with one another, because the other person might use that openness against the spouse. As a result, they begin to cover up and hide from one another with ineffectual and uncomfortable loincloths made from fig leaves in a desperate attempt to regain the safety they had experienced prior to the fall (v. 7). In a tragicomic scene, after Adam and Eve's declaration of cosmic war on the creator of the universe, the highest priority on their to-do list is to sew fig leaves together to hide from one another.

Adam and Eve do not die immediately, in the sense that their life is not at once extinguished. Otherwise the Lord's purposes of redemption could not be completed. However, in the Bible death is the reverse of life, not of existence. Adam and Eve's experience of life in its fullness is immediately greatly diminished as their sin exposes them to shame and fear. The serpent had claimed that, if they disobeyed God, they would experience freedom and power; in actuality their sin brings bondage and helplessness. They discover the hard way that Satan is the real hard taskmaster, not God.

3:8–13 The futility of Adam and Eve's attempt to "be like God" is rapidly exposed when the Lord makes known his presence in the garden. It was apparently customary for the Lord to "walk to and fro"[54] in the garden on a daily basis. The difficult phrase "With respect to the wind/Spirit of the day" (Hb. *leruakh hayyom*; v. 8) is understood by most as a temporal description, following the LXX, which translates it "in the afternoon" (*to deilinon*). This would thus be a reference to the time of day when the afternoon breeze picks up, making it a pleasant time for a walk: "At the breezy time of day" (NET).[55] When Adam and Eve heard the sound of God's arrival, they immediately recognized the inadequacy of their flimsy coverings and ran to hide in the trees, as if the created world could conceal them from the one who had made all things.

Like a parent confronting a naughty child, the Lord calls out a question that gently invites the man to reveal himself: "Where are you?" (v. 9). Unlike the serpent,

---

54 The form of *halak* here likely has an iterative force, "walking to and fro" (cf. *IBHS*, 26.1.2).
55 Jeffrey Niehaus, "In the Wind of the Storm: Another Look at Genesis III 8," *VT* 44 (1994): 263–267, has interpreted the phrase in a more threatening fashion as describing the manner of the Lord's approach ("with respect to the wind of the storm"), but that seems contextually and grammatically unlikely. Niehaus builds on an earlier suggestion by Meredith Kline, *Images of the Spirit* (1980; repr., Eugene, OR: Wipf & Stock, 1999), 102–115, but Kline was comprehensively refuted by Christopher Grundke, "A Tempest in a Teapot: Genesis III 8 Again," *VT* 51 (2001): 548–551.

who inverted the proper order by approaching the woman, God begins his questioning with the man (the pronoun is singular). Adam immediately emerges from hiding and answers not only God's question but the unspoken question behind it as well (i.e., "Why are you hiding?"): "I heard the sound of you[56] in the garden, and I was afraid, because I was naked, and I hid myself" (v. 10).

Adam's response reveals not only his location to God; it also reveals the nature of his problem. Adam does not come to God humbly confessing his sin and seeking forgiveness. Rather, he laments the consequences of that sin as if it were an unfortunate natural disaster for which he was not responsible. He is afraid of the Lord, but only when it is too late. Earlier, the fear of the Lord might have kept him from sin, but not fearing the Lord at the right time led to an overpowering fear of God later. Adam's refusal to receive God's wisdom leaves him with nothing to receive from God but his judgment.

Adam also laments his nakedness before God (v. 10). That had never been an embarrassment to Adam and Eve before. God had made them, after all, and he was not unfamiliar with the shape of their bodies! But now, with the coming of sin into the world, Adam and Eve have a powerful urge to hide from God. That relationship, once so unhindered, is now shattered in pieces. Adam immediately realizes that his fig leaves are an inadequate covering. They might have been sufficient to keep out his wife's threatening gaze, but not that of the all-seeing God.

The Lord continues his interrogation: "Who told you that you were naked? Have you eaten of the tree of which I commanded you not to eat?" (v. 11). Again, these are questions not seeking to elicit information but rather aimed at giving Adam the opportunity to make a confession. No one needed to tell Adam that he was naked; his own guilty conscience is sufficient to cause his shame. However, Adam's answer to God's questions is less about taking responsibility for his action than it is about placing the responsibility elsewhere: "The woman whom you gave to be with me, she gave me fruit of the tree, and I ate" (v. 12). In Hebrew the sentence starts with the subject rather than the verb, highlighting the woman's role in the transgression. Next, Adam blames God for giving the woman to him—the Lord gave him the woman, and she gave him the fruit, as if he were entirely passive throughout the process.[57] Then he returns to blaming the woman (the feminine pronoun is emphatic: "*She* gave me"), and it is only with the very last word of the sentence that Adam utters anything close to a confession ("and I ate"; one word in Hebrew).

Then God turns to the woman, asking her: "What is this that you have done?" (v. 13), opening the door for her to admit her responsibility. However, she too seeks to blame someone else: "The serpent deceived me." Once again it is only with the final word of her sentence that she made the same one-word confession ("and I ate"). The catastrophic effects of that first sin are already evident in the blame-shifting and evasion that have become humanity's modus operandi. Instead of

---

[56] Sadly, "I heard the sound of you" could also mean "I obeyed you" (= "I listened to your voice"), the exact opposite of what had happened here; cf. Sarna, *Genesis*, 26.
[57] Alter, *Five Books of Moses*, 25.

being "naked and . . . not ashamed" (2:25), they are now inadequately clothed and deeply ashamed.

3:14–19 Having heard Adam and Eve's worthless defense, God pronounces his gracious sentence. He does not ask the serpent to explain his behavior: he is not permitted to speak. The Lord could justly destroy humanity outright on the spot. However, God's sentence is remedial, not retributive. God will be the judge, notwithstanding the serpent's denial, but he is not the harsh master Satan had portrayed him to be. The order of judgment parallels the proper order of creation, first addressing the lower order, then the woman, and then the man.

God begins by judging the serpent.[58] In a larger narrative marked out by a focus on God's blessing, this is the first occurrence of the word "cursed" (Hb. *'arur*; v. 14). As in English, the relative clause normally comes after the main clause; putting it first here highlights its importance in giving the reason for the curse, which has just cause and is not a capricious act on God's part. The serpent that has been distinguished from the rest of creation by its shrewdness will now be distinguished by the judgment it experiences, which will bring it low. Just as the serpent's offense involved eating, so too does God's judgment curse. To "lick the dust" expresses abject humiliation and defeat, as when someone is prostrated before his conqueror (cf. Ps. 72:9; Mic. 7:17); the equivalent English idiom is to "bite the dust."[59] This is the opposite of triumphing with head held high. Satan's moment of triumph will be short lived.

Not only will Satan be brought low, but his apparent victory in ensnaring the pinnacle of creation will be short lived: the Lord will place enmity between the serpent and the woman, and between their offspring[60] as well (Gen. 3:15). This accounts for the continuing need for subterfuge on the part of Satan; very few of his followers are out-and-out Satanists, for he has nothing within himself to attract people. To overcome man's God-given enmity Satan must pretend to be something he is not, to deceive and seduce people into a continued rebellion against God. Yet there is no question about the outcome of this multigenerational conflict. Ultimately, though he may wound the seed of the woman, the serpent will be kicked in the teeth and defeated by the seed of the very race he has just brought down.

This is not merely an etiological story about people's fear and loathing of snakes; it has a singular conflict in view, the struggle between the second Adam, who is the ultimate promised seed of the woman, and the ancient Serpent (cf. Rom. 5:19; Rev. 12:9). Not coincidentally, the issue of "seed" is prominent in the rest of Genesis (cf. Gen. 4:25; 12:7), as humans look forward to the coming promised seed and the salvation he will bring. However, Genesis also reveals a fundamental

---

[58] Although judgment is pronounced upon the serpent, and snakes depict the outworking of that judgment curse, it is clear that the real target of God's curse is the spiritual enemy behind the serpent, whose ultimate downfall is prophesied in these verses.
[59] Greidanus, *Preaching Christ from Genesis*, 81.
[60] Lit., "seed" (Hb. *zera'*), a word that can be a collective or a singular. Here both are in view: the enmity between the woman and the serpent will be a continuing reality until the coming of the final seed of the woman who will triumph definitively over the serpent.

division within humanity from this point onward, which finds expression in the conflict between the line of promise and a line of children of the devil (John 8:44), a conflict that leads to the murder of Abel by Cain (Genesis 4).

In spite of this continual opposition the curse on the serpent in Genesis 3:15 is at the same time the first proclamation of the gospel, the promise that through this seed of the woman God will restore humanity to his side and thus reverse the effects of the curse upon creation. In light of the forthcoming judgment upon the woman it is striking that the victory is assigned to the seed of the woman. The victor will not merely be a second Adam; he will also vindicate Eve.

God next judges the woman (Gen. 3:16). His judgments on the first couple strike at the heart of what it means to be a man and woman, respectively. Thus, because men and women are not the same, neither are their judgments.[61] The woman's judgment strikes primarily at her relationships, especially motherhood and marriage. Eve was designed for one-fleshness with her husband, but now that one-fleshness will be dogged by problems—on both sides. To begin with, the woman will desire to dominate her husband; when God says, "Your desire shall be toward[62] your husband," the Hebrew word for "desire" (*teshuqah*) is the same rare word used in Genesis 4 to describe the relationship between sin and Cain. Some have interpreted *teshuqah* as sexual desire, on the basis of the other use of this word in Song of Solomon 7:10; however, the usage in Genesis 4:7 is more relevant, not merely because it is adjacent and by the same author but because the same combination of *teshuqah* and *mashal* recurs. There sin is depicted as a wild animal, crouching outside the door of Cain's heart, waiting to overpower Cain unless he masters (*mashal*) it. So too here the woman will constantly be in danger of repeating her disruption of the created order in relationships, while for his part the man will seek to dominate her. Now "he shall rule over" her harshly (Gen. 3:16), rather than with the sensitive, servant leadership pose he was intended to have in the beginning (cf. discussion of Genesis 2 above, though the creational order between men and women lies on the surface of Genesis 3 as well, as we have seen).[63]

The fall also affects a woman's natural desire to be a mother. Now, even though the bearing of children is the means through which salvation comes, the process itself is inseparably linked with pain and anguish. As Kenneth Mathews puts it, "By this unexpected twist the vehicle of her vindication (i.e., labor) trumpets her need for the deliverance she bears (cf. 1 Cor. 11:12). Painful childbirth signals hope but also serves as a perpetual reminder of sin and the woman's part in it."[64] Moreover,

---

61 So Geerhardus Vos, *Biblical Theology* (Grand Rapids, MI: Eerdmans, 1948), 44: "The woman is condemned to suffer in what constitutes her nature as woman."
62 The ESV has "for" in the main text and "to, or toward, or against" in the marginal note. It is not so much that the woman and the husband will desire different things ("against") or that she will desire her husband sexually (though it has that sense in the more distant parallel text, Song 7:10) but that she will desire to dominate him and make him conform to her own wishes. This is the meaning in the more immediate parallel passage of Genesis 4:7, in which sin is pictured as a wild animal about to pounce on Cain: sin desires to possess Cain and govern his behavior.
63 Waltke, *Genesis*, 94; contra Ada Besançon Spencer, *Beyond the Curse: Women Called to Ministry* (Nashville: Nelson, 1985), 39–42; Gilbert Bilezikian, *Beyond Sex Roles: A Guide for the Study of Female Roles in the Bible* (Grand Rapids, MI: Baker, 1985), 56–58, who argue that submission is a result of the fall, not part of the creation order.
64 Mathews, *Genesis 1–11:26*, 250.

the initial suffering associated with childbirth is simply a miniature depiction of the suffering that goes with being a mother in a fallen world. One of Eve's sons, Abel, will be brutally and senselessly murdered; the murderer will be her own firstborn, Cain (Genesis 4; cf. Mary's experience in Luke 2:34–35). It is not easy being a mother in a fallen world.

Nor is it always easy to *become* a mother in a fallen world. With God's blessing and command that mankind should be fruitful and multiply, conception ought to have been easy (Gen. 1:27). But the fall changes that. God's challenge to a woman he is about to use in a special way is often seen in precisely the area of her fertility. Sarah (Gen. 11:30), Hannah (1 Samuel 1), and Elizabeth, mother of John the Baptist (Luke 1:7), are among many who face this challenge as a preparation for roles of remarkable importance in God's plan.

God's judgment upon the man likewise strikes at the heart of what it means to be a man, namely, in the realm of his work. Man was designed to work the garden in Eden and take care of it (Gen. 2:15). Now, however, his labor will lead to sweat and anxiety, not joy. Work will no longer be fulfilling and satisfying, as it was intended to be in the beginning; instead, it will be laborious and frustrating toil (cf. Eccles. 1:3; Ps. 90:9–12). Our labor-filled days are turned to sorrow, frustration, and pain. Both men and women are condemned to pain in the deepest area of their identity.

The man is also rebuked because he abdicates his leadership role in the marriage and "listened to the voice of your wife" (Gen. 3:17). The same problem recurs in Genesis 16:2: there Abram "listened to the voice of Sarai" and took Hagar as a concubine.[65] This does not mean it is always wrong for a man to listen to his wife— Abraham is specifically instructed by God to listen to Sarah in Genesis 21:12. But a proper creational order is to be observed in that relationship.

The ultimate judgment on both men and women is death (3:19). This is the complete refutation of the serpent's lie. He had claimed, "You will be like God"— the one who never dies (cf. v. 5). Instead death lies at the heart of the curses on both the woman and the man. Death leads to great pain in relationships. One day, if the Lord tarries, we shall all have to say goodbye to those we love. And death relativizes the joys and sorrows of our work, for one day we shall leave that behind as well if the Lord does not first return. Final judgment on humanity may have been postponed, but it has not been abolished. From dust we are, and to dust we shall return (cf. Ps. 90:3–6).

3:20–24 The proper reordering of male-female relationships is reiterated in Adam's immediate response to God's word of judgment and hope: "The man called his wife's name Eve" (Gen. 3:20). From "the woman and her man" (cf. v. 6) we have returned to "the man and his woman," so to speak. The name Adam gives his wife (Hb. *khavvah*, "Eve") is a play on the verb "to live" (*khayyah*) and reflects not only his recognition that there will be a continued existence for himself and Eve but also his

---

[65] The similarity between the two episodes is highlighted because in both instances the woman "takes" and "gives" something to her husband (Gen. 3:6; 16:3).

faith that through Eve God's promise of restored blessing will ultimately be established (cf. v. 15). Through Eve's seed God will ensure that his final word on humanity is "life" and not the "death" that Adam and Eve have merited because of their sins.

God also provides more effective coverings for Adam and Eve's nakedness[66] in the form of tunics of animal skin (v. 21). Older scholars often derived an atoning significance from this provision of God, in which animals lose their lives in order to cover the effects of human sin;[67] however, that seems to be deriving the right doctrine from the wrong text. In the passage there is no mention of God's killing the animals, let alone of their foreshadowing a sacrificial ritual. Rather the focus is on the fact that God provides an effective covering for Adam and Eve's shame, replacing the inadequate works of their own hands (the fig leaves) with something much better. To be sure, the theme of clothing as a metaphor for redemption does appear later in the Bible (e.g., Zechariah 3), and that theme may certainly be seen foreshadowed here, but this verse does not directly connect Adam and Eve's clothing with the need for blood sacrifices. The focus is far more on God's continued providential care for his children in covering their shame, even after the fall (cf. Matt. 6:28–30).

At the same time, Adam and Eve's sin has immediate and tragic consequences, as they are driven out of the garden (Gen. 3:22–24). Because[68] the man has aspired to become like God in knowledge, he must not now be allowed to "take" and "eat" from the tree of life in a repetition of his rebellion involving the tree of knowledge. Once again the headship of Adam is acknowledged, and he is held responsible for the sin that has caused humanity's expulsion. It is not entirely clear from the text whether Adam and Eve have previously been permitted to eat the fruit of the tree of life; it is not included in the prohibition of 2:17. However, a key consequence of their sin is a loss of access to the Lord's presence, which the tree of life concretely represents. The wages of their sin is indeed death (Rom. 6:23).

From now on they will have to work the ground outside the garden, which, while still good, is now under God's curse and will yield its fruit only in response to strenuous labor (cf. Gen. 3:17–19; the phrase "sweat of your face" is literally the more vivid "sweat of your nose"). Toiling in the dust from which he had been taken will be a constant reminder to Adam of his mortality, since that same dust will be his

---

66 The genitive in "garments of skin" (Hb. *kotnot 'or*) is generally understood as a genitive of material, that is, the tunics were made from animal skin. However, it is also possible to interpret this phrase as reflecting purpose ("tunics for the skin"), which would leave the material from which they were manufactured unspecified. Compare Nehemiah 7:70, where the *kotnot kohanim* are tunics for the use of the priests, not tunics made from priests. Cf. Genesis Rabbah 20:12 and Sotah 14a for early examples of this understanding (cited by Sarna, *Genesis*, 29). However in Leviticus 16:4 a *ketonet-bad* is a linen tunic, so either understanding is possible.
67 So Matthew Henry: "It is supposed that they were slain, not for food, but for sacrifice, to typify the great sacrifice, which, in the latter end of the world, should be offered once for all. Thus the first thing that died was a sacrifice, or Christ in a figure" (*Commentary on the Whole Bible*, 1.34). In contrast, John Calvin thought the clothing made of skins simply represented a suitably humble form of attire for humans after the fall, and he uses it to make application that Christians should adopt a "frugal and unexpensive mode of dress"; *Commentaries on the First Book of Moses, Called Genesis*, trans. J. King (Grand Rapids, MI: Eerdmans, 1948), 1.182. Geerhardus Vos (*Biblical Theology*, 156–157) observes: "It must be admitted . . . that the Pentateuch contains no record of the institution of sacrifice either as to its expiatory or as to its consecratory aspect. Some profess to find it in Gen. 3:21. The covering provided by God from the simple skins of animals would have carried the implication that animal life is necessary for covering sin. Against this speaks the fact that the word used for this act of God is not the technical term used in the law for the covering of sin by sacrifice. It is a word signifying 'to clothe,' a term never employed in the law for the expiation of sin."
68 Understanding *hen* as supplying the reason for the decision that follows; cf. *IBHS*, 40.2.1c.

final resting place (v. 23). Meanwhile, the entrance to the garden of Eden—and with it to the presence of God—is closed, guarded by cherubim, along with a flaming sword (v. 24). The cherubim are stationed on the east side of the garden because that is where the entrance is, as with the tabernacle. As composite creatures the cherubim sum up and unite the highest forms of all creation (cf. Ezek. 1:5; 10:15) and are the fearsome guardians assigned to guard (*shamar*) God's holiness. They will not fail to protect the sanctity of the garden, as Adam has failed (Gen. 2:15). No longer will access into the presence of the Lord be easy and untroubled for humanity, as it once was. For now the doorway into the Most Holy Place has been firmly closed in their faces, and mankind is left to make its own way "east of the garden of Eden."

Response

The fall is one of the key events in redemptive history, a tragedy that explains the brokenness of the world in which we find ourselves living. Every religion—and every person—has to wrestle with the big question of why bad things happen, not just to the wicked but to the innocent as well. Some religions, such as those of Israel's ancient neighbors, solve the problem by imagining multiple deities locked in a perpetual conflict, with humanity as an unfortunate bystander. Others imagine a God who tries his best but is not powerful enough to avert all evil, especially given human free will.

The Bible gives us a different answer. Evil and suffering in this world are a result of the failure of our first parents to resist temptation. Because of their sin, all people now are born with a bent toward sin that they cannot fully resist, even if they wished to do so. Creation itself is under God's curse because of human sin, which results in innumerable natural disasters and sicknesses (Rom. 8:20–23). Yet none of this is outside God's control, any more than individual human decisions are. Without being the author of sin, God ultimately controls it and directs it for his glory and the good of those who love him and are called according to his purpose (Rom. 8:28). Thus the fall, tragic as it is, becomes the context in which we hear the first promise of the gospel, in Genesis 3:15. The rest of Scripture is in many ways the sovereign working out of God's fulfillment of that promise in Christ. The obedience of the second Adam transcends the disobedience of the first Adam. The death that enters the world through Adam and Eve's sin is overcome by life and hope in the second Adam, Jesus Christ (1 Cor. 15:22).

Indeed, we can sketch the main flow of the history of the world in four movements: creation, fall, redemption, and consummation. Each of these represents a different experience for mankind: as created before the fall, it was possible for humans to sin, but also possible for them to resist it (man was *posse peccare*—able to sin). After the fall our natural state is one in which it is not possible for us not to sin (*non posse non peccare*)—we may choose to sin in differing ways, but we are all living for our own glory, not our Creator's. Redemption makes it possible for us not to sin (*posse non peccare*), although we are still deeply stained with sin's legacy (Romans 7; 2 Cor. 5:17). At the consummation God will finish the sanctifying work he has begun in us, and we will no longer be able to sin (*non posse peccare*), which will be true freedom (Phil. 1:6).[69]

To be sure, we must be careful not to confuse the categories of the *historia salutis* (the history of salvation) with those of the *ordo salutis* (the order of salvation): many saints were regenerated by the Spirit and saved in the OT, long before the coming of the Christ in whom they placed their trust by faith (John 8:56). However, as a way of categorizing the broad sweep of redemptive history, these categories seem helpful. The next several chapters of Genesis will work out the implications of life outside the garden, under God's curse. It is a very different world from the one in which Adam and Eve first lived, and without a proper understanding of the fall many aspects of this broken world are impossible to explain.

In addition to this primary focus of the chapter on the fall, we find a number of secondary themes as well, as might be expected in an origin story. The foundational differences and nonreversible relationship between men and women lie at the heart of the narrative. The fall occurs through a reversal of the male-female relationship, an order that God restores when he intervenes by addressing the man first. This pre-fall order underlies the rest of Scripture's teaching about the proper roles of men and women, including in the church. Many scholars have gone astray by attempting to interpret Paul's teaching about women's roles in the church in 1 Corinthians and 1 Timothy in a vacuum, or against the background of Second Temple Judaism, rather than seeing it as rooted and grounded in creation, a plain connection that Paul makes explicit in 1 Timothy 2:12–15.

GENESIS 4

4 Now Adam knew Eve his wife, and she conceived and bore Cain, saying, "I have gotten[1] a man with the help of the Lord." ²And again, she bore his brother Abel. Now Abel was a keeper of sheep, and Cain a worker of the ground. ³In the course of time Cain brought to the Lord an offering of the fruit of the ground, ⁴and Abel also brought of the firstborn of his flock and of their fat portions. And the Lord had regard for Abel and his offering, ⁵but for Cain and his offering he had no regard. So Cain was very angry, and his face fell. ⁶The Lord said to Cain, "Why are you angry, and why has your face fallen? ⁷If you do well, will you not be accepted?[2] And if you do not do well, sin is crouching at the door. Its desire is for[3] you, and you must rule over it."

⁸Cain spoke to Abel his brother.[4] And when they were in the field, Cain rose up against his brother Abel and killed him. ⁹Then the Lord said to Cain, "Where is Abel your brother?" He said, "I do not know; am I my

---

69 These four categories were originally advanced by Augustine. Perhaps the fullest development of this idea is in Thomas Boston, *Human Nature in the Fourfold State* (repr., Edinburgh: Banner of Truth, 1964).

brother's keeper?" ¹⁰ And the LORD said, "What have you done? The voice of your brother's blood is crying to me from the ground. ¹¹ And now you are cursed from the ground, which has opened its mouth to receive your brother's blood from your hand. ¹² When you work the ground, it shall no longer yield to you its strength. You shall be a fugitive and a wanderer on the earth." ¹³ Cain said to the LORD, "My punishment is greater than I can bear.⁵ ¹⁴ Behold, you have driven me today away from the ground, and from your face I shall be hidden. I shall be a fugitive and a wanderer on the earth, and whoever finds me will kill me." ¹⁵ Then the LORD said to him, "Not so! If anyone kills Cain, vengeance shall be taken on him sevenfold." And the LORD put a mark on Cain, lest any who found him should attack him. ¹⁶ Then Cain went away from the presence of the LORD and settled in the land of Nod,⁶ east of Eden.

¹⁷ Cain knew his wife, and she conceived and bore Enoch. When he built a city, he called the name of the city after the name of his son, Enoch. ¹⁸ To Enoch was born Irad, and Irad fathered Mehujael, and Mehujael fathered Methushael, and Methushael fathered Lamech. ¹⁹ And Lamech took two wives. The name of the one was Adah, and the name of the other Zillah. ²⁰ Adah bore Jabal; he was the father of those who dwell in tents and have livestock. ²¹ His brother's name was Jubal; he was the father of all those who play the lyre and pipe. ²² Zillah also bore Tubal-cain; he was the forger of all instruments of bronze and iron. The sister of Tubal-cain was Naamah.

²³ Lamech said to his wives:

"Adah and Zillah, hear my voice;
    you wives of Lamech, listen to what I say:
I have killed a man for wounding me,
    a young man for striking me.
²⁴ If Cain's revenge is sevenfold,
    then Lamech's is seventy-sevenfold."

²⁵ And Adam knew his wife again, and she bore a son and called his name Seth, for she said, "God has appointed⁷ for me another offspring instead of Abel, for Cain killed him." ²⁶ To Seth also a son was born, and he called his name Enosh. At that time people began to call upon the name of the LORD.

¹ *Cain* sounds like the Hebrew for *gotten* ² Hebrew *will there not be a lifting up* [of your face]? ³ Or *to*, or *toward*, or *against* (see 3:16) ⁴ Hebrew; Samaritan, Septuagint, Syriac, Vulgate add *Let us go out to the field* ⁵ Or *My guilt is too great to bear* ⁶ *Nod* means *wandering* ⁷ *Seth* sounds like the Hebrew for *he appointed*

Section Overview

In the beginning everything in creation is good. The fall, however, changes everything, bringing sin and death into a previously untarnished world. The dramatic nature of that change is nowhere clearer than in Genesis 4, in which we hear of the first human death, which is the result not of old age or a natural disaster but of murder. Having heard the curse pronounced and sin judged in theory, we now see the effects of sin starting to work themselves out in reality. The formula "God said . . . and it was so" is not limited to Genesis 1 but stretches throughout Scripture, now with devastating results.

In Genesis 3 Adam and Eve had to be talked into sin by the subtlety of the serpent (cf. Gen. 3:1–6), whereas in Genesis 4 Cain will not be talked out of sin by the direct intervention of God himself (4:6–7). Yet God's longsuffering grace is shown even to Cain, allowing human history and culture to develop and flourish (vv. 19–22), albeit in rebellion against God, which reaches a climax in the celebration of gratuitous violence by the seventh of Cain's line, Lamech (vv. 23–24). Nevertheless, the Lord provides a replacement seed for Adam and Eve in the person of Seth to carry on the line of promise (v. 25). This line has neither the technology nor artistic prowess or cities that come from the line of Cain, but it has something far better: hearts that call upon the name of the Lord (v. 26).

Section Outline

    II. The Family History of the Heavens and the Earth (2:4–4:26) . . .
        C. Cain and Abel (4:1–26)

Comment

4:1–5 The chapter starts on a positive note. Adam has sexual relations[70] with Eve, and she gives birth to two sons, fulfilling her role as "the mother of all living" (3:20). Women were often involved in the naming process in the OT (cf. Gen. 29:32–30:24; 38:4–5; Judg. 13:24; 1 Sam. 1:20), though men also named their children (cf. Gen. 21:3; 38:3; Ex. 2:22). The firstborn child she names "Cain" (Gen. 4:1; Hb. *qayin*) because, she says, "I have gotten [*qanah*, "acquired, created"] a man with the help of the Lord." The woman who was herself taken from the man (cf. 2:23) has now produced a man herself.

The reason given for Cain's name suggests great rejoicing at his arrival, which is natural given that he was the first human to arrive in this way. Does Eve think that this son is perhaps the promised seed of Genesis 3:15? He is, after all, the oldest son, who follows in his father's footsteps as a cultivator of the ground (4:2), and Eve attributes his arrival to "the help of the Lord" (v. 1).[71] Eve calls this little baby a "man" (*'ish*), like the man, Adam, from whom she herself was taken (2:22), suggesting his potential to be a second Adam, reversing the effects of the fall.[72] Certainly her words are an expression of faith in the promise of God, even if she does not yet understand how long the redemptive process will take.

Abel's name, on the other hand, sounds like "worthless, vanity" (*hebel*; the same word used frequently in Ecclesiastes, rendered "vanity"; e.g., Eccles. 1:2). There is no special rejoicing recorded over his birth, nor mention of the Lord's help. The text simply says, "And again, she bore his brother[73] Abel" (Gen. 4:2). To the casual

---

[70] Literally, "Adam knew his wife"; *yada'* is far from being merely an intellectual exercise but can have overtones of a special relationship (e.g., Amos 3:2); cf. Waltke, *Genesis*, 96.
[71] Literally she simply says, "I have acquired a man with the Lord." Martin Luther rendered this "a man of the Lord," seeing this as Eve's belief that Cain would be the promised seed. Cf. "Lectures on Genesis 1–5," *The Works of Martin Luther*, trans. J. Pelikan (St. Louis: Concordia, 1958), 1.242.
[72] Greidanus, *Preaching Christ from Genesis*, 92.
[73] The word "brother" occurs seven times in the Cain and Abel narrative, always with a possessive suffix, "your" or "his," of which Cain is always the subject. This feature underlines the fact that Cain later denies, which is that he has a duty of care for his brother.

observer Abel seems the disadvantaged one as the younger brother. After all, if the promised seed of the woman has already arrived in Cain, what need is there for Abel?

Each brother pursues a different calling. Cain, like Adam, works the ground (v. 2; cf. 3:23), while Abel keeps flocks of sheep (or perhaps goats; Hb. *tson* can refer to either animal). Their respective callings form the backdrop for the conflict that ensues. At some unspecified point of time[74] the brothers bring offerings to present to the Lord from their respective produce, with Cain bringing a grain offering and Abel offering a lamb (4:3–4). We are not told where they bring these sacrifices; since there is no sanctuary in Genesis 4–11, they may simply present them on a suitable rock. But God reverses the natural order and accepts the offering of the younger brother, Abel, while refusing the offering of the older brother, Cain. Perhaps fire descended from heaven on Abel's offering indicating God's favor, while Cain's was untouched (as in 1 Kings 18:38; 2 Chron. 7:1).[75]

The reason God accepts Abel's sacrifice while refusing Cain's has been much debated. Some interpreters suggest that it is because Abel offers a blood sacrifice while Cain's sacrifice is of grain.[76] They point out that the Bible insists that "without the shedding of blood there is no forgiveness of sins" (Heb. 9:22). But that understanding fails to recognize that both offerings are specifically described as being *minkhot*, "tribute offerings" (Gen. 4:4–5).[77] According to the law of Moses, a *minkhah* would very often be a grain offering—and this is how the ESV often translates the word (cf. Lev. 2:11). That is because the aim of the *minkhah* is *not* to seek forgiveness of sins but rather to acknowledge someone as overlord by bringing him a gift or, more precisely, tribute. In 1 Samuel 10:27, when Saul has been crowned king over Israel, it is reported that certain people "brought him no present [*minkhah*]." These troublemakers are reluctant to recognize Saul as their king, and they show it in their lack of tribute offerings.

So then, the offerings Cain and Abel bring to God are tribute offerings, acknowledging him as their king. But Abel, we are told, brings the very best that he has (some "of the firstborn of his flock and of their fat portions"; Gen. 4:4), whereas Cain brings "an offering of the fruit of the ground" (v. 3).[78] There is a difference in heart attitude between Cain and Abel, expressed in the quality of the sacrifices they offer: it is not simply Abel's sacrifice that God favors but Abel (v. 4).[79] To put

---

74 The Hebrew word *yammim* often seems to indicate a period of about a year (cf. Lev. 25:29; 2 Sam. 14:26; Jer. 13:6); so Wenham, *Genesis 1–15*, 103.
75 Cf. Sarna, *Genesis*, 33.
76 E.g., James Montgomery Boice, *Genesis*, 3 vols. (Grand Rapids, MI: Zondervan, 1982), 1:201.
77 Kidner, *Genesis*, 80.
78 So B. K. Waltke, "Cain and His Offering," *WTJ* 48 (1986): 363–372; Sarna, *Genesis*, 32. Cf. Franz Delitzsch, *A New Commentary on Genesis*, 2 vols (Edinburgh: T&T Clark, 1889), 1:69. Greidanus points out the absence of any mention of "firstfruits" in describing Cain's offering (*Preaching Christ from Genesis*, 93).
79 G. Herion thinks that Cain's problem is that he offered the fruit of the soil (Hb. *'adamah*), which has been cursed; "Why God Rejected Cain's Offering: The Obvious Answer," in *Fortunate the Eyes That See*, ed. A. Beck (Grand Rapids, MI: Eerdmans, 1995), 52–65. However, God told Adam to continue working the soil (Gen. 3:19), and Cain was simply following in his father's footsteps, which must have mitigated the curse at least to some extent. It is not clear why the fruit of the soil would be inappropriate to offer to God in the days of Cain yet be required as an offering to God as part of the Mosaic order, or for that matter how animal offerings would escape the general curse on the ground that resulted from the fall.

it another way, the writer to the Hebrews tells us that Abel's sacrifice is offered in faith (Heb. 11:4). He offers a better sacrifice because he believes in God's promise that one day there will be a Redeemer, and so gives of his very best, while, in contrast, Cain has no love for God; he is simply going through the motions of religion.

Cain's reaction to God's refusing his offering is significant: he becomes very angry (Gen. 4:5). "His face fell" indicates a feeling of rejection; acceptance is sometimes described as a person's having his face lifted (cf. ESV mg. on v. 7; Job 11:15). Cain does not ask himself the question "Why did God not accept my offering?" He simply explodes with rage, as if God has no right to determine which offerings are acceptable and which are not—or which offerers are acceptable and which are not. Like his parents, he wants to decide for himself what constitutes good and evil when it comes to making offerings to God. He believes that God should gratefully receive whatever is given to him.

4:6–8 In the midst of Cain's rebellion God gives him a second chance: he comes to Cain directly and asks, "Why are you angry, and why has your face fallen? If you do well, will you not be accepted? And if you do not do well, sin is crouching at the door. Its desire is toward[80] you, but you must rule over it" (Gen. 4:6–7). Once again, as in the garden, God approaches humans with questions designed to spark self-reflection. Rather than being angry with Abel (and with God), Cain should examine his own heart. If he had offered his sacrifice with the right spirit, his sacrifice—and he—would also have been accepted. The doorway to life through a relationship with God is still open to him.

However, the Lord also warns Cain of the danger facing him. Sin is depicted as a wild animal poised and ready to spring on the unwary Cain (v. 7; cf. 1 Pet. 5:8). This is the first time in Genesis that "sin" has been named, and it appears not merely as a wrong action on Cain's part but as a powerful force that desires to take over his life. The parallelism of Genesis 4:7 and 3:16 is instructive: sin now fills the woman's position in the equation. Through the fall mankind has now become "one flesh" with sin; like a nagging wife, it will not go away. Yet there is still time for Cain to recognize the danger, repent with godly sorrow, and resist sin's power. The original mandate for man to have dominion over creation (1:26) has now become the struggle for man to have dominion over himself. To quote Romans 6:12, "Let not sin therefore reign in your mortal body, to make you obey its passions."

As noted earlier, the progress of sin's power is evident in Cain's refusal to listen even to a direct appeal from God. He submits to sin's power, and the results are fatal for his brother. He invites Abel out into the field,[81] and there he kills him (Gen. 4:8). In the OT violent crimes committed in the field are regarded as premeditated, since they take place where there would be no witnesses to respond to

---

80 Again, following the footnote rather than the main text, as in 3:16; cf. comment on 3:14–19.
81 The MT, which simply has "Cain said to Abel his brother," is awkward (Gen. 4:8; ESV smooths it in English by rendering "Cain said" as "Cain spoke"). Normally, "said to" is followed by the content of that conversation (e.g., Gen. 1:28; 3:1; etc.). Here the LXX fills in the lacuna with "Let us go out into the open country," which may represent the original text, omitted in error by the MT, or may simply be an attempt on the part of the Greek translator to smooth an obviously difficult text.

cries for help.[82] The deadly seriousness of sin is on full display. Anyone tempted to dismiss the original sin as a victimless crime, an offense against God rather than man, must recognize that breaking the earlier commandments inevitably ends with breaking the latter ones as well.

4:9–16 God then comes to Cain, as he had earlier come to Adam, and confronts him with a question inviting confession of his sin: "Where is Abel your brother?" (v. 9). Even though Adam made excuses for his actions, at least he finally told the truth and confessed his sin, as did Eve (cf. 3:12–13). Cain does neither. He first lies to God, saying, "I do not know," and then attempts to evade his own responsibility for Abel, asking, "Am I my brother's keeper?" (4:9). Having failed in its appointed task as the guardian (Hb. *shomer*; 2:15) of God's sanctuary, now mankind shrugs off its responsibility as the guardian (*shomer*; 4:9) of one's brother. But Cain's pretense of innocence could hardly deceive the all-knowing God, who responds, "What have you done? The voice of your brother's blood[83] is crying to me from the ground" (v. 10). Alienated from the ground, which previously he had worked, Cain will from now on be a wanderer upon the face of the earth (v. 12). He will become a man without a place, an outcast from God's presence, alienated from the ground from which his food comes and from his fellow man. Whereas Adam was indirectly cursed through the ground that he worked (3:17), the curse on Cain is direct and personal: "You are cursed" (4:11). The doctrine of judgment, denied by the serpent (3:4), is nonetheless real. Only the blood of Jesus, which cries out for grace rather than justice, can redeem those under the wrath of God (cf. Heb. 12:29).

There is no sign of penitence in Cain's response to God—only anger and fear at the fate awaiting him (Gen. 4:13–14). He laments the forthcoming absence of God's face (v. 14), yet he had done nothing to cultivate that relationship earlier by offering proper sacrifices from a broken and contrite heart or by resisting the pull of sin. Yet in his grace God does not allow judgment to take its immediate course. He puts a mark of his protection on Cain (v. 15)[84] to keep him safe in a dangerous world, showing far more compassion on Cain than Cain had shown to his brother. Even the unbelieving murderer is to be afforded protection from revenge and anarchy and allowed to live out the full number of his days on earth. Cast out from the vicinity of Eden, Cain goes farther and further from God, away to the east, to the land whose very name means "wandering" (*nod*; v. 16)—an expression of Cain's deep lostness.

4:17–24 In a sad parody of the optimistic beginning of Genesis 4 we are told that Cain "knew" his wife, who bears him a son. The son's name is "Enoch" (Hb. *khanok*; v. 17), which comes from a verb meaning "to dedicate," usually at the outset of a

---

82 Wenham, *Genesis 1–15*, 106.
83 The word "blood" here is plural (Hb. *damim*), as is often the case when describing bloodshed, as if to reflect the blood spatter caused by violent acts.
84 More precisely *'ot* means "a sign." Elsewhere in Genesis it is always a sign of a covenant relationship. Here it is less than that but nonetheless marks out Cain as remaining under God's direct protection despite his sin.

project (cf. Deut. 20:5; 1 Kings 8:63).[85] There is nothing in the text to suggest that this Enoch is dedicated to the Lord in any way, however, and he serves primarily as a foil for the later Enoch, from the line of Seth, who will truly embody the meaning of his name (Gen. 5:18–22).

Since Cain has no center for his society in God, he founds a city to provide that center, forming an imitation of the sacred community that has been lost through his sin against his brother. There is already here an anticipatory contrast with Abraham: Cain seeks an earthly city, desiring to make a name for himself by founding a civilization and pursuing immortality through naming a city after his son (4:17). Abraham, however, is promised both offspring and a great name by God (12:2) yet spends his earthly lifetime as a wanderer here on earth, looking for a city yet to come, "whose designer and builder is God" (Heb. 11:10). From the outset there is a profound contrast between earth-centered religion and heaven-centered religion, between the true covenant community and the noncovenant imitation community.

The city is in a profound sense Cain's natural territory; it is archetypally the place where no one is his brother's keeper. Yet God's grace can redeem even the city; the place that in Genesis 1–11 is the home of Cain's descendants and the builders of the Tower of Babel becomes in Revelation 21 the new Jerusalem, where God dwells with his people, where we know God and are fully known by him, and where we live in intimate and untroubled fellowship with our brothers and sisters.

Intriguingly, advances in farming, in the arts, and in engineering are ascribed to Cain's line (Gen. 4:20–22).[86] The city concentrates human talent and insight, encouraging progress and development, even in a fallen world. Jabal is called the father of the nomadic shepherding lifestyle (v. 20), while his brother, Jubal, is the originator of musical instruments (v. 21). Their half-brother, Tubal-cain, originates metalwork of various kinds,[87] while his sister, Naamah ("Pleasant"), earns a rare genealogical mention for a woman in Genesis, though we are not informed of any particular innovations on her part. The point is clear: Cain's line is advanced in power, wealth, luxury, and artistic accomplishment—and likely beauty as well.

At the same time that the line of Cain contributes all these advances to mankind, it also declines rapidly in morals, as exemplified in Lamech, the seventh in Cain's line. In addition to being the place of technological, artistic, and educational opportunities, the city is a place of moral decay from the beginning. It is Lamech who transgresses God's design for marriage between one man and one woman through the introduction of polygamy (v. 23). It is Lamech who has access to the technology necessary to make deadly weapons and the vicious ruthlessness to

---

85 The same verb is used in Proverbs 22:6, where our English translations usually render it "train up a child," though the idea of setting a child apart for the way he should follow is likely also present there.
86 This contrasts sharply with other ancient Near Eastern creation accounts, which generally attribute such advances to specific gods.
87 The forging of bronze and iron came later; the Hebrew word *latish* means "to hammer, sharpen," which would have been some of the earliest methods of forming meteoric iron and naturally outcropping bronze into something useful. It has been suggested that his unusual double name thus represents "Sharpener-smith." Cf. Richard S. Hess, *Studies in the Personal Names of Genesis 1–11* (Winona Lake, IN: Eisenbrauns, 2009), 127.

use them. What is more, Lamech composes the first poetry since the fall, in order to glorify to his wives an act of gratuitous violence he commits—killing a *child* (*yeled*) for merely hurting Lamech (v. 23). In the process he turns God's gracious withholding of punishment on Cain into the justification for his own outrageous personal vindictiveness, promising seventy-seven-fold judgment upon those who cross him (v. 24), thereby becoming the father of all genres of music that glorify sex and violence. The seventh of Cain's line has developed the full measure of sin's destructiveness. In diametric contrast Jesus teaches a model of seventy-seven-fold forgiveness of those who wrong us (Matt. 18:21–22).

Cain's house comprehensively turns its back on God. His descendants are still living busy, productive lives, taking the gifts God has given them and using those gifts to build their own kingdoms and to establish their own forms of security and significance. They completely invest themselves in the progress and the pursuits of this world, and their course is determinedly set to the east of Eden. Despite this, however, they cannot escape the fulfilling of God's purposes of the creation mandate, and their inventions and discoveries, intended to serve their own glory, will nonetheless help the progress of civilization under God's sovereign plan.

4:25–26 God is not finished with humanity. In place of Abel God raises up another son to Adam and Eve, through whom his promise will ultimately bear fruit. The end of the chapter brings us full circle to the beginning, as "Adam knew his wife again, and she bore a son and called his name Seth" ("appointed"; Gen. 4:25). In this line lies the hope of the world. Seth is not simply appointed to be a replacement child for Abel. In naming him Seth Eve sees far more in him than that. She says, "God has appointed for me another seed [ESV: "offspring"], instead of Abel, for Cain killed him" (v. 25). Eve recognizes that the true hope of the world lies not in the rich, the powerful, the educated, or the artistic influencers—not in the descendants of Cain, in other words, for all their vaunted achievements—but in the seed of the woman, which was promised in Genesis 3:15. As long as that line survives, there is hope of salvation.

In contrast to the line of Cain, which is steadily increasing in decadence and immorality, the line of Seth preserves true religion, calling on the name of the Lord (Gen. 4:26).[88] There is no pomp or circumstance in its worship; it seems to be simple and unadorned prayer and praise, presumably along with heartfelt sacrifices similar to the ones offered by Abel, acknowledging the Lord as God. It may look like

---

88 In the book of Genesis it appears that the patriarchs worship Yahweh by name, even though in Exodus the divine name appears to be a new revelation (Ex. 6:3). One possibility is that they knew the name Yahweh but not yet its significance and meaning as the God who brought his people out of the land of Egypt. Another possibility, however, is that Moses has deliberately included the name Yahweh anachronistically into the patriarchal narratives, much like we might talk about Jesus' appearing to Abraham in the OT, to make it abundantly clear that "the God of the Fathers" worshiped by the patriarchs is the same God as the one who brought Israel out of Egypt. A couple of lines of evidence support this theory. One involves passages in which it appears that an original reference to *'el* or *'elohim* in a narrative has been replaced by a reference to Yahweh. So in Genesis 16 the narrator regularly references "the Lord," but Hagar refers only to *'el* ("God"), and she names her son "Ishmael" ("God heard"), not Shemaiah ("the Lord heard"). Similarly in the Pentateuchal narratives there are many Israelite names that include "El" or "Shaddai" as a theophoric element but none with "Yah." For a fuller discussion of the issues cf. R. W. L. Moberly, *The Old Testament of the Old Testament: Patriarchal Narratives and Mosaic Yahwism* (Minneapolis: Fortress, 1992), 5–104.

nothing compared to the great City of Man, founded and developed by Cain's line. The true remnant seems pitiably small and backward in comparison. It is probably significant that Seth names his son "Enosh," which means something like "mere man" (e.g., 2 Chron. 14:11; Job 7:17). Seth is under no illusions about the weakness of his family line. But God's strength is made perfect in human weakness (2 Cor. 12:9). In God's own time he will bring the treasures and insights of all civilizations into the heavenly city, the new Jerusalem (Rev. 21:26). Technology and the arts can ultimately be redeemed because God is the ultimate source of all knowledge, insight, and beauty. On the last day even the spiritual descendants of Cain must bow their knees and confess that the seed of the line of Seth, Jesus Christ himself, is the Lord of all, to the glory of God the Father (Phil. 2:10).

Response

The story of Cain and Abel challenges all of us in terms of our worship. It is not enough to make offerings to God, not even to the true God, if they come from a heart that lacks faith and love for God. In this regard it is striking that most people ask "Why was Cain's sacrifice rejected?" instead of "Why was Abel's accepted?" Those two questions reveal two contrasting approaches to God: the approach of self-justification versus the approach of humble dependence upon divine grace. Self-justification expects God to be obligated to receive whatever we choose to offer, no matter how sketchily we go through the motions of presenting it. Grace realizes that even our best offerings are not adequate to present to a holy God, and it marvels that he would be pleased to receive such poor gifts as we have to offer, even though they be our very best.

Of course, the reality is that all of us offer deeply tainted worship to God, even as Christians. Our minds wander, our bodies fidget, and our hearts are given over to other idols, even as we are physically there, offering a half-hearted song and perhaps some money that we can easily spare. We should be profoundly thankful for Jesus, who came as a wholehearted worshiper, the fulfillment of David's cry in Psalm 69, "Zeal for your house has consumed me" (Ps. 69:9; cited in John 2:17). Unlike our half-hearted worship, which so easily spills over into indifference or anger toward our brothers and sisters, his worship led him to the cross, where the temple of his body was destroyed for us (John 2:19). His blood, shed for us on the cross, cries out for mercy and acceptance by the Father toward all those who are in him, cleansing us from all our sins, including our dysfunctional worship (Heb. 12:24).

Who, though, is my brother? We are often overly enamored of the powerful and influential, those who control the world of technology and the arts, even though they bear the marks of Cain's spiritual parentage rather than that of the line of promise. In our modern culture we are sometimes also overly enamored of cities, thinking that through them we can gain power to reach the wider culture with the gospel. The desire for influence and power often penetrates the church in our age, especially in more affluent countries. Yet the call to follow Jesus is often a call to leave the city, the place of worldly influence, and go outside its gates to the place of suffering and of the cross, the place of simple, heartfelt, dependent worship by men and women calling on the name of the Lord. As the writer to the Hebrews reminds us,

> Jesus also suffered outside the gate in order to sanctify the people through his own blood. Therefore let us go to him outside the camp and bear the reproach he endured. For here we have no lasting city, but we seek the city that is to come. Through him then let us continually offer up a sacrifice of praise to God, that is, the fruit of lips that acknowledge his name. (Heb. 13:12–15)

Of course, the poor, the weak, and the needy can be found in many places, and cities need the gospel too. Yet those who live in cities are not more precious to God than those who live in suburbs or rural towns and villages.

GENESIS 5

5 This is the book of the generations of Adam. When God created man, he made him in the likeness of God. ² Male and female he created them, and he blessed them and named them Man[1] when they were created. ³ When Adam had lived 130 years, he fathered a son in his own likeness, after his image, and named him Seth. ⁴ The days of Adam after he fathered Seth were 800 years; and he had other sons and daughters. ⁵ Thus all the days that Adam lived were 930 years, and he died.

⁶ When Seth had lived 105 years, he fathered Enosh. ⁷ Seth lived after he fathered Enosh 807 years and had other sons and daughters. ⁸ Thus all the days of Seth were 912 years, and he died.

⁹ When Enosh had lived 90 years, he fathered Kenan. ¹⁰ Enosh lived after he fathered Kenan 815 years and had other sons and daughters. ¹¹ Thus all the days of Enosh were 905 years, and he died.

¹² When Kenan had lived 70 years, he fathered Mahalalel. ¹³ Kenan lived after he fathered Mahalalel 840 years and had other sons and daughters. ¹⁴ Thus all the days of Kenan were 910 years, and he died.

¹⁵ When Mahalalel had lived 65 years, he fathered Jared. ¹⁶ Mahalalel lived after he fathered Jared 830 years and had other sons and daughters. ¹⁷ Thus all the days of Mahalalel were 895 years, and he died.

¹⁸ When Jared had lived 162 years, he fathered Enoch. ¹⁹ Jared lived after he fathered Enoch 800 years and had other sons and daughters. ²⁰ Thus all the days of Jared were 962 years, and he died.

²¹ When Enoch had lived 65 years, he fathered Methuselah. ²² Enoch walked with God[2] after he fathered Methuselah 300 years and had other sons and daughters. ²³ Thus all the days of Enoch were 365 years. ²⁴ Enoch walked with God, and he was not,[3] for God took him.

²⁵ When Methuselah had lived 187 years, he fathered Lamech. ²⁶ Methuselah lived after he fathered Lamech 782 years and had other sons and daughters. ²⁷ Thus all the days of Methuselah were 969 years, and he died.

²⁸ When Lamech had lived 182 years, he fathered a son ²⁹ and called his name Noah, saying, "Out of the ground that the LORD has cursed, this one shall bring us relief⁴ from our work and from the painful toil of our hands." ³⁰ Lamech lived after he fathered Noah 595 years and had other sons and daughters. ³¹ Thus all the days of Lamech were 777 years, and he died.

³² After Noah was 500 years old, Noah fathered Shem, Ham, and Japheth.

¹ Hebrew *adam* ² Septuagint *pleased God*; also verse 24 ³ Septuagint *was not found* ⁴ *Noah* sounds like the Hebrew for *rest*

Section Overview

Genesis 5 provides an interlude after the breathtaking march of sin in Genesis 3–4. It comprises a linear genealogy for the line of Seth, from the beginning (Adam) to the time of the flood (Noah). The genealogy shows the line of Seth as it obediently fulfills the creation mandate and continues the line from which the promise of Genesis 3:15 will ultimately find its fulfillment. A remarkable feature of this genealogy is the prominence of dates and of death. A normal genealogical structure consists of identifying father-son relationships over multiple generations, often with relevant mininarratives inserted where appropriate (e.g., Genesis 36). Here, however, the (remarkable) ages achieved by the patriarchs at their deaths are an additional feature, along with the repeated refrain "and he died" (nine times in Genesis 5, with the age and notice of the death of the 10th generation, Noah, deferred to 9:29).

This repeated formula highlights the unique position of Enoch, in the seventh generation, whose culminating age is given without a death notice: "He was not, for God took him" (Gen. 5:24). The contrast to the line of Cain is striking: the seventh[89] in the line of Adam through Cain was Lamech, the depths of depravity (4:19–24), while the seventh in the line of Adam through Seth, Enoch, walks with God—a phrase indicating a special intimacy with God and a life of piety—and then he is not, for the Lord takes him (5:24). The only other OT character to avoid death in this way is Elijah, whom God takes to heaven in a chariot of fire (2 Kings 2:11–12).

The genealogy climaxes in the tenth generation with the birth of Noah, whose name means "relief" (Gen. 5:29). His father has high hopes that in him the promised rest from laboring over the cursed ground might finally be achieved. But the peace of Genesis 5 is merely the calm before the storm. Noah is not the promised seed of the woman, though he will have an important role to play in maintaining humanity's hope. Many generations must yet pass before the coming of the promised and eagerly anticipated Christ, but that hope is faithfully preserved by the line of Seth.

---

89 All these sequences adopt the biblical practice of counting the generations inclusively.

Section Outline

    III. The Family History of Adam (5:1–6:8)

        A. From Adam to Noah (5:1–32)

Comment

5:1–5 The chapter begins with the main structuring device in Genesis, the *toledot* formula (cf. comment on 2:4–7). Here it introduces the "family history," or the "account of the offspring," of Adam and specifically the line of Seth. The focus of chapter 4 was the line of Cain and its advancements of technology, civilization, and the arts, in contrast to which the line of Seth received only a very brief mention in connection with true worship (4:26). Now the focus shifts to the elect line, though there is no mention of any similar cultural achievements on its part. It is often assumed that this chapter was borrowed from an earlier source;[90] this is plausible, since genealogies by their very nature tend to have an independent existence, preserving remembrance of the family line. However, a more interesting question asks why Moses chose to incorporate this genealogy here and what function it serves within the wider narrative. (Note esp. the tight connections to 1:26–28 and 4:25–26, connecting this section with the prologue, 1:1–2:3, and the first *toledot*, 2:4–4:26.) The genealogy is not a random insertion at this point in the story; rather it serves to underline the historical nature of the narratives surrounding it. These events did not take place "in a galaxy far, far away" or in some timeless heavenly realm of the gods but in real time and space that are connected directly through these genealogies down to the world of Moses' first readers.

    The passage begins with a reprise of 1:26–28, focusing specifically on humanity's relationship to God and omitting all the aspects of the original that had to do with its lordship over creation. Humans were made in the likeness of God—both male and female—and named by him. What is more, they existed under his blessing in the beginning (5:1–2). This reprise both introduces and forms a contrast with what follows. Just as humans were made in the image of God and named by him, so too Adam had a son in his own likeness, whom he named Seth (v. 3). In a fallen world conception and safe delivery cannot be taken for granted; both are a blessing from God (cf. Ps. 127:3–5) in light of the judgment on the woman in Genesis 3:16. If Seth is in Adam's likeness, and Adam is in God's likeness, then this implies that all subsequent humans are also in the likeness of God, even after the fall.[91] God's creation of and naming of mankind form a pattern that the line of Seth will imitate. The story of Cain and Abel does not need to be repeated here; Cain is not included in the line of promise because of his sin, and Abel has been replaced by Seth (4:25).

    An unusual feature of the genealogy in Genesis 5 is the cataloging of the ages of the primeval figures, both when each fathers his first child and when each dies.

---

90 In this case it is uniquely called "the book [*sefer*] of the family history," indicating that it reflects a written record, not just an oral tradition; cf. Wenham, *Genesis 1–15*, 125–126.
91 It is in this sense that Luke 3:38 can call Adam the "son of God."

The figures for both these events are high throughout the genealogy—Adam, for example, fathers his first child at 130 years old and then lives to be 930 (Gen. 5:3–5). Ancient people were as familiar with normal lifespans as modern people are (cf. Ps. 90:10), yet their memory was that people lived to far greater ages in the period prior to the flood. In the providence of God this would, of course, have permitted far more rapid population growth (note the repeated refrain "And he had other sons and daughters"; Gen. 5:4, 7, 10, etc.), enabling much of the earth to be occupied within only a few generations. It also suggests that the full effects of the curse had not yet taken hold; it is not until the time of the flood that normal human life expectancy is reduced to less than 120 years (cf. 6:3). Yet the curse is still in effect upon humanity, as may be seen by the repeated refrain "And he died" (5:5, 8, 11).

In most cases nothing is recorded in the genealogy about the lives of these early humans beyond their birth, having and naming children, living out their days, and death. The message of Psalm 90—the one biblical psalm by Moses—is that humans are like the grass that springs up in the morning and is swept away by the evening, because we pass our days under the wrath of God; our time is soon gone and we return to the dust from which we were taken (Ps. 90:3–10). Genesis 5 communicates the same message in the form of a genealogy; even the longest human life is largely empty and devoid of substance. Although we may fill the earth with children made in our own image, sooner or later we will die and return to the ground from which we were taken. This is true not merely of the line of Cain, the non-elect line; it is the fate also of the elect line of promise. Calling on the name of the Lord (Gen. 4:26) does not exempt the family from the trials and challenges of living in a world in which (almost) every life ends in death. Yet we should not miss the significance of the fact that each of these otherwise unknown people has his own part to play in passing on the line of promise.

5:6–24 This repeated cycle of birth, fathering a son, living a long (but essentially empty) life, and then dying makes the story of Enoch distinct. Just as Lamech is the seventh from Adam in the line of Cain (Gen. 4:19–24), so Enoch is the seventh from Adam in the line of Seth. But whereas Lamech is noted for the height of his iniquity, introducing polygamy and celebrating gratuitous violence with his poetry, Enoch is marked out because he "walked with God" (5:24). Although he fathers his first child at age 65 (a relatively normal age in the genealogy; cf. v. 15), Enoch lives to be a mere 365 years old, by far the youngest of the preflood patriarchs, less than half the lifetime of his grandson (also named Lamech), who at 777 years is the shortest-lived of the antediluvian patriarchs. This clearly challenges the idea that a long life is an unmitigated blessing from God: in this case the patriarch who walks most closely with God lives the shortest life before God takes him (5:24).[92]

---

[92] The Hebrew clause for "He was not" is used elsewhere to describe unexpected deaths (Gen. 37:30; Ps. 37:10), so by itself it does not imply that Enoch did not die. However, as Hebrews 11:5 deduces, the similarity

It is sometimes suggested that the idea of individual resurrection is a late concept in the Hebrew Bible, appearing first in books such as Daniel (e.g., 12:2–3). This may be true if one is looking for explicit references to bodily resurrection; however, the whole fabric of the Hebrew Bible rests on the reality of life after death (or more precisely in Enoch's case, "life after life"). Jesus, of course, points this out to the Sadducees when he reminds them of the simple formula "I am the God of Abraham, Isaac, and Jacob," which, he argues, presupposes the reality of the resurrection, since the Lord is the God not of the dead but the living (Matt. 22:32). He could just as easily have pointed to the experience of Enoch. If life in this world is all there is, then the one who walks with God should live here longer than others. What is more, if there is nothing beyond this life, what could it mean for God to "take Enoch" (Gen. 5:24) or for the later patriarchs to be "gathered to [their] people" (e.g., Gen. 49:29)? If Abraham had no expectation of a resurrection, why did it matter for him to be buried in a plot of the Promised Land that he owned (cf. Genesis 23)? As the writer to the Hebrews correctly discerns, everything in Genesis rests on the substratum of a hope of life beyond this life, a hope that finds its firstfruits, as it were, in the experience of Enoch.

When we are told that Enoch walked (Hb. *hithallek*) with God, we are immediately reminded of God's walking around in the garden, which he apparently did regularly with Adam and Eve, which uses exactly the same form of the verb (cf. comment on 3:8–13). Similar terminology is later used to describe the Lord's presence in the midst of his people in the wilderness by means of the tabernacle (Deut. 23:14). This is the language of keeping company with and sharing intimate fellowship with someone, not merely marching together along the same road (cf. 1 Sam. 25:15). The same virtue will be ascribed to Noah in Genesis 6:9: in contrast to the wicked and perverse generation surrounding him, Noah walks with God. However, whereas for Enoch the outcome of his walking with God is to be caught up to live with God "early," as it were, thus avoiding many of the trials and pains that accompany life in a fallen and cursed world, for Noah the fruit of his walking with God is that the Lord preserves him through those trials and pains as he endures and survives the flood. God has more than one way of dealing with his faithful servants.

5:25–32 The last three generations in the ten-generation sequence from Adam to Noah include the longest-lived patriarch of all, Methuselah, whose son, Lamech—not to be confused with the Lamech in the line of Cain[93]—is the shortest lived of the patriarchs to live out a full life and die. Methuselah lives 969 years, while his son lives a mere 777 years. Yet, like most of the other antediluvian patriarchs, neither of them does anything more significant than having children to carry on the line of promise.

---

of the language about Enoch to the experience of Elijah in 2 Kings 2:11–12 suggests something more than that Enoch simply suffered a tragic accident.

[93] The fact that both lines have an Enoch and a Lamech invites the reader to compare and contrast the characters with identical names; the Enoch and Lamech in Seth's line are quite different from those in Cain's.

This reality is emphasized by the explanation of the name given to Lamech's son, Noah. Thus far there has been no explanation given for any name since the time of Cain and Seth (cf. Gen. 4:1, 25). This should caution us against the attempts of some popular commentators to draw imaginative significance out of the sequence of names in Seth's line; to do so is at best to interpret the passage in a direction entirely unintended by the original author, while at worst some of the proposed etymologies are extremely tortured in such an interpretation. The passage itself largely uses these names as markers of the passage of the generations, while the line of promise keeps alive hope that God would in due time send the appointed seed.

This hope is expressed concretely by Noah's father, Lamech, who names him "relief" (Hb. *noakh*; 5:29),[94] saying, "This one will bring us relief [*yenakhamenu*] from the agonizing labor of our hands, caused by the ground the LORD has cursed" (v. 29 CSB).[95] The reference to the "agonizing labor of our hands" and the curse on the ground clearly alludes to God's judgment upon Adam in 3:17, so the hope of Noah providing relief must be a reference to the promise of Genesis 3:15. Surely, now that Adam had died,[96] it is time for God to provide relief to his people through the promised seed of the woman? But, though Noah will carry humanity safely through the judgment of the flood, it is not yet time for the people to enter their rest. That seed will take many more generations to arrive.

Noah is marked out in one other way from the other generations in the genealogy. Each of the other patriarchs has a single named son who carries on the line of promise and multiple other sons and daughters who disappear from the picture. Are we to assume that they virtually all assimilate to the line of Cain, so that the elect line remains just that—a line, with almost no branches? That may be the case, if Noah's generation is in any way representative: Noah walks alone with God, surrounded by a wicked and rebellious generation (cf. 6:9–12). Yet unlike his ancestors Noah has three named sons—Shem, Ham, and Japheth—through whom there will be a new beginning for humanity. He has to wait a long time for those sons, even by antediluvian standards: Noah's first son is born when he is six hundred, which explains why there are no grandchildren on the ark and hints at a lengthy period of barrenness for Noah and his wife, a theme that will become prominent later in Genesis.

It will not take long before the line of promise returns to being a single thread, however, passed down through the line of Seth to Terah, then to Abraham and to

---

[94] Strictly speaking, Noah's name comes from *nuakh* ("rest") rather than *nakham* ("to give relief"), so this is a play on words rather than a precise etymology of Noah's name.

[95] Following the RSV, the ESV here takes the final clause "Out of the ground that the LORD has cursed" and makes it an initial clause, so that now it is Noah who is taken from the cursed ground, like Adam, rather than understanding the phrase as referring to the relief Noah would provide from the difficult labor caused by the curse on the ground.

[96] According to the chronology of the MT Noah would have been the first generation born after the death of Adam. Some have suggested that the genealogy may be telescoped, with some generations omitted to achieve the ten-generation schema, as Matthew's Gospel does with its three-part fourteen-generation genealogy of Jesus (cf. Matt. 1:17). However, the fathers' ages at the birth of each firstborn suggest that it is perhaps intended to be taken more literally.

Isaac. It will not branch into a segmented genealogy again until the time of Jacob, whose twelve sons will together form the nation of Israel. But the remaining offspring of Shem, Ham, and Japheth will have important roles to play in establishing the various nations of Israel's world (cf. Genesis 10).

Response

According to Romans 6:23 "The wages of sin is death," an assertion that Genesis 5 thoroughly confirms. Tracing the line of promise from Adam to Noah, we see that each of the patriarchs dies in turn. Being in the image of their father Adam means that they all die, just as he did. Yet the chapter's emphasis on universal death is the background, not the focus. Two characters introduced here demonstrate the possibility of a different future. The first is Enoch, who walks with God and then is not, for God takes him. The writer to the Hebrews asserts that by his faith Enoch is miraculously exempted from the normal human ending of life (Heb. 11:5). In that regard he is somewhat like those who will still be alive at the return of Christ: "We shall not all sleep, but we shall all be changed" (1 Cor. 15:51).

Enoch models for us what the godly life looks like: walking with God. For Enoch that presumably means obeying what he knows about God's law, which is in some measure written on his heart, but it also means more than that: living a relationship of faith in the God who has made him and called him to himself. The reward for Enoch's life of obedience is not length of days but a shorter time here on this broken planet, the sooner to enter heavenly fellowship with God. As the missionary martyr Jim Elliot put it, "He is no fool who gives up what he cannot keep to gain what he cannot lose."[97] In that regard Enoch points forward to his Savior, Jesus, who lived a far shorter life than his and walked with God even more consistently, to the point of drinking the cup of God's wrath in order to redeem the line of Seth from its sins.

The other pointer of hope is Noah, another man who, we will later be told, "walked with God" (Gen. 6:9). Unlike Enoch, Noah is not delivered from the trials and sufferings of this world but enabled to endure them by God's grace. In that regard Noah also points us to Jesus, the one who brought true relief and rest from our burden of sin through his death and resurrection. Noah and Enoch finish their days in faith and hope, looking forward to the promised seed of the woman (3:15). We may now look back on that promised seed and find strengthening for our own faith and hope in a dark and perverse world. In him we are offered rest in all its fullness (Matt. 11:28–30).

---

[97] *The Journals of Jim Elliot* (Old Tappan, NJ: Revell, 1978), 174.

GENESIS 6:1–8

6 When man began to multiply on the face of the land and daughters were born to them, ² the sons of God saw that the daughters of man were attractive. And they took as their wives any they chose. ³ Then the LORD said, "My Spirit shall not abide in¹ man forever, for he is flesh: his days shall be 120 years." ⁴ The Nephilim² were on the earth in those days, and also afterward, when the sons of God came in to the daughters of man and they bore children to them. These were the mighty men who were of old, the men of renown.

⁵ The LORD saw that the wickedness of man was great in the earth, and that every intention of the thoughts of his heart was only evil continually. ⁶ And the LORD regretted that he had made man on the earth, and it grieved him to his heart. ⁷ So the LORD said, "I will blot out man whom I have created from the face of the land, man and animals and creeping things and birds of the heavens, for I am sorry that I have made them." ⁸ But Noah found favor in the eyes of the LORD.

¹ Or *My Spirit shall not contend with* ² Or *giants*

Section Overview

Chapter 5 presented a peaceful interlude between the increasing wickedness of the line of Cain, in the person of Lamech (Gen. 4:19–24), and the even more widespread wickedness of Genesis 6. Now, as we return to the world outside the confines of the elect line, we discover that the peace of Genesis 5 was merely the calm before the storm. The spread of wickedness picks up with the mysterious transgression of 6:1–4, as the "sons of God" go in to the "daughters of men." Until this point sin has been committed only by specific individuals; now for the first time it involves whole classes of people.

Nor does sin stop there; it eventually engulfs an entire generation, so that *every* thought of the *whole* world is *only* evil *all* the time (Gen. 6:5). God's response is to decree the destruction of the created order (v. 7). But one man stands out from the crowd: Noah alone is righteous (v. 9), and so through him God determines to preserve alive a people for himself, along with the various kinds of animals that would otherwise be destroyed in the flood. Through Noah and his sons mankind will have a future, so that the Lord's promise to bruise the head of the serpent through a seed of the woman could ultimately find its fulfillment (cf. 3:15).

Section Outline

III. The Family History of Adam (5:1–6:8) . . .
    B. The Spread of Wickedness (6:1–8)

Comment

6:1–4 The timing of this episode is introduced in rather vague terms: "When man began to multiply on the face of the land and daughters were born to them" (6:1). However, from what follows it appears that these events occur during the lifetime of Noah. At this time "the sons of God *saw* that the daughters of man were attractive [Hb. "good"]. And they *took* as their wives any they chose" (v. 2). The language of seeing and taking something perceived to be good echoes the first temptation in Genesis 3:6, so it is clear that this action represents a significant sin on the part of the "sons of God." But who are the "sons of God" and the "daughters of man," and why is their intermarriage sinful?

Three views of the identity of these groups have been argued, with the first two explanations both finding support since the earliest interpreters.[98] The first view suggests that the "sons of God" are the descendants of the line of Seth, with the "daughters of man" being the descendants of Cain.[99] The second view interprets the "sons of God" as (demonic) spirit beings, who engage in sexual intercourse with human women ("daughters of man"). Justin Martyr (AD 100–160) wrote, "God, when He had made the whole world, and subjected things earthly to man, . . . committed the care of men and of all things under heaven to angels whom He appointed over them. But the angels transgressed this appointment, and were captivated by love of women, and begat children who are those that are called demons."[100] Meanwhile, a third view identifies the "sons of God" as kings, who in many ancient Near Eastern societies claimed divine status for themselves as "sons of the gods." These kings had the power of life and death over their subjects, and on this interpretation the stress in 6:2 lies on the rulers' taking on "any [of the daughters of men] they chose." These kings seize whatever women they wish for their harems—marrying not just one woman, as God intended (2:24), but as many as they choose. Whereas Lamech first broke God's pattern for marriage by having two wives (4:19), these kings multiply that sin many times over by multiplying for themselves wives.[101]

Each of these views has able exponents and is defensible, though each has its own problems. The greatest challenge for the first view is that nowhere else in the OT are human beings described as the "sons of God"; on the contrary, the term consistently designates angelic beings (cf. Job 1:6; 38:7; and probably Deut. 32:8).[102] In addition, "daughters of man" in verse 2 seems obviously related to the daughters born to men in verse 1, which does not seem to limit them to a particular subgroup (i.e., the daughters of the line of Cain).[103] Moreover, some NT passages seem to reference

---

[98] On the early interpretation of this passage cf. Robert C. Newman, "The Ancient Exegesis of Genesis 6:2, 4," *Grace Theological Journal* 5 (1984): 13–36.
[99] This view is held by, among others, Augustine, *City of God*, 15.22–23; John Calvin, *Genesis* (1554; repr., Edinburgh: Banner of Truth Trust, 1992), 1.238; Robert S. Candlish, *Studies in Genesis* (repr., Grand Rapids, MI: Kregel, 1979), 123–124; Mathews, *Genesis 1–11:26*, 324–331.
[100] Justin Martyr, *Apology* 2.5 (cited in Newman, "Ancient Exegesis of Genesis 6:2, 4," 21–22).
[101] For this view cf. Meredith G. Kline, "Divine Kingship and Genesis 6:1–4," *WTJ* 24 (1962): 187–204; so also Waltke, *Genesis*, 116–117.
[102] Deuteronomy 32:8 has text-critical difficulties, but the reading "sons of God" rather than "sons of Israel" seems probable. Cf. Michael S. Heiser, "Deuteronomy 32:8 and the Sons of God," *BSac* 158 (2001): 52–74.
[103] It is possible to adapt the first view to take "daughters of men" globally as covering *all* women, not just the daughters of the line of Cain. On this understanding the sons of Seth were not deliberately marrying

the involvement of spiritual beings in these events. For example, Jude 6–7 speaks of angels' leaving their proper home and sinning in a way similar to the sin of Sodom and Gomorrah in pursuing "strange flesh."[104] Similarly, 1 Peter 3:19–20 references the proclamation of the gospel to spirits who were disobedient in the time of Noah.

The main challenge for the second view is the question of whether angels are capable of producing offspring through intercourse with humans (cf. Matt. 22:30). John Calvin says the angelic view "is abundantly refuted by its own absurdity; and it is surprising that learned men should formerly have been fascinated by ravings so gross and prodigious,"[105] though it must be said that ancient audiences did not find the idea as obviously absurd as Calvin did. Moreover, Genesis says remarkably little about the world of angelic beings, good or bad; on the contrary, it is focused much more closely on human sin and its consequences.[106] Indeed, the transgression in Genesis 6 (whatever it may be) seems to result in a specific judgment that comes upon humanity, not on angelic beings.

The third view offers a potential explanation for the use of the language of "sons of God" to describe humans but does not necessarily provide a much better alternative overall. In general, ancient Near Eastern kings as individuals may have styled themselves as "son of the gods," but there is little evidence for the use of "sons of the gods" as a collective term for kings or rulers. There seems little interest in the political organization of the ancient city-states in Genesis 4, which references farming, music, and technology as advances belonging to the line of Cain but says nothing at all explicitly about kingship.

It is hard to establish with any certainty which of these interpretations is to be preferred. However, a significant contextual consideration is the fact that the contrast between the lines of Cain and of Seth forms the larger backdrop against which this episode occurs. Indeed, Genesis 6:1–8 is itself incorporated into the larger genealogy of Seth that starts in chapter 5 and concludes in 9:29.[107] On this view the passage provides an explanation of why the two families do not result in large numbers of people in the category of "righteous" and "wicked." Because so many of the sons of the line of Seth intermarry indiscriminately, the result is an almost complete loss of the righteous line.

What is more, it is also true that, even though the OT does not elsewhere use "sons of God" to describe God's people, the idea is not entirely foreign to the passage. In Genesis 5:1–3 image and sonship are intimately connected: Adam is made in God's image, and he passes that image on to his children through Seth. If Adam is thus, by virtue of bearing his image, God's son (Luke 3:38), and Seth is explicitly made in the image of Adam (Gen. 5:3), could not Seth and his line rightly be called "sons of God"?[108]

---

outside the line of promise but were carelessly marrying whichever women they chose, without reference to their origins. Cf. Mathews, *Genesis 1–11:26*, 330.
104 It is worth noting that Jude also cites elsewhere from *1 Enoch*, which clearly adopts the supernatural being view; cf. Newman, "Ancient Exegesis of Genesis 6:2, 4," 16, 28–29.
105 Calvin, *Genesis*, 1.238.
106 Cf. Vos, *Biblical Theology*, 48.
107 Cf. Mathews, *Genesis 1–11:26*, 329.
108 It is striking that in Genesis 5 it is explicitly *Seth* who bears Adam's image, not Cain. Moreover, all the other uses of *bene-'elohim* occur outside the Pentateuch (with the possible exception of Deuteronomy 32:8).

Finally, elsewhere in the Bible Satan's three primary modes of attack on God's people take the form of deception, persecution, and seduction,[109] and it could be argued that the same modus operandi is evident already in the opening chapters of Genesis: deceiving Eve (Genesis 3), martyring Abel (ch. 4), and now seducing the line of promise (6:1–4). These considerations, taken together, persuade me that the interpretation that understands the sin as being the wrongful mixing of the lines of Seth and the line of Cain is correct, though the alternative views each has its strengths.

Whichever interpretation is adopted, what is abundantly clear is that as man multiplies and fills the earth—evidence itself of God's blessing (Gen. 1:28)—sin multiplies also. The sin of these verses forms an evil parody of the creation mandate: these beings, who aspire to be in the image of God, seek to fill the earth with their offspring as God has commanded, but they go about it in the wrong way, abusing the marriage relationship to serve their corrupt desires and seeking to make a name for themselves, following the pattern of Cain (6:4; cf. 4:17).

In this pursuit they are unsuccessful, as is the case for every act of human rebellion in Genesis. God judges the "sons of God," and their sin results in curse and destruction rather than the blessing and prosperity that was sought. Just as indiscriminate eating in Genesis 3 resulted in death, so too indiscriminate marriage that transgresses the boundaries set by God results in death. In contrast to the lengthy lives of the antediluvian patriarchs in Genesis 5, human life will be limited to a mere 120 years.[110] The reason given ("For he is flesh"; 6:3) could describe human mortality or corruption. In fact, both are likely in view: human mortality is the result of human corruption, and the expansion in corruption in these verses will be matched by a decrease in human lifespan. The divine breath/spirit gives life to humanity, and, when it is withdrawn, the result is death (cf. Gen. 2:7; Pss. 104:29; 146:4; Ezek. 37:10).

The judgment of Genesis 6:3 logically separates verses 1–2 from verses 4–5, though they are linked by the renewed mention of the sons of God and the daughters of man in verse 4. The result is a chiastic structure that focuses our attention on the judgment curse that falls on humanity:

(A) Humanity multiplies on the face of the earth (v. 1)
   (B) Sin increases: the sons of God and daughters of men transgress (v. 2)
      (C) Judgment declared upon humanity (v. 3)
   (B') Sin increases: the Nephilim and mighty men transgress (v. 4)
(A') Human wickedness grows great in the earth (v. 5)

The significance of this observation is to note that the sin in verse 4, while contemporaneous with that of verse 2 ("When the sons of God came in to the daughters

---

109 Deception (2 Cor. 11:14; Rev. 12:9); persecution (1 Pet. 5:8; Rev. 2:10); seduction (2 Cor. 11:2–3; Rev. 19:2).
110 On the translation issues of Genesis 6:3 cf. Mathews, *Genesis 1–11:26*, 332–335. This is obviously not an absolute limitation of age, since Abraham lives to be 175 (Gen. 25:7), but after this point very few people exceed that number.

of man and they bore children to them"),[111] is not necessarily identical to it. In other words, the Nephilim and the mighty men are not necessarily the offspring of the sons of God and daughters of men, as is often assumed by the interpretation that sees the sons of God as angelic beings.[112] Genesis 6:4 simply asserts that the Nephilim ("fallen ones," cf. CSB mg.) were also present during these corrupt days, as well as later on. It does not tell us anything about the Nephilim, assuming that readers are already familiar with these people.

The only other explicit reference in the Bible to the Nephilim is at Numbers 13:33, where the scouts claim that the fearsomely large Anakim that they encountered were "of" (*min*) the Nephilim. This Hebrew construction could mean that the Anakim were "descended from" the Nephilim, though that raises questions about how the Nephilim could have survived the flood.[113] More likely the point of the comparison is that the Anakites shared the characteristics of the Nephilim of old, not that they were actually related to them. In that case, Numbers 13 gives us a window into what the original audience of Genesis thought the Nephilim were like: tall and strong, fearsome and invincible in battle.

Given this, it makes sense to identify the Nephilim as the antecedent of the pronoun in the last part of Genesis 6:4: "they" would then refer to the Nephilim rather than to the children of the illicit unions described immediately before, so that the Nephilim would be the "mighty men" ("warriors"; *gibborim*) and the "men of renown" (or "men of name"). In that capacity the Nephilim represent a different manifestation of the growth of sin, namely, self-promoting violence rather than sexuality. Their sin lies in seeking to make a name for themselves through their military conquests rather than humbly calling on the name of the Lord, as the line of Seth had done (cf. 4:26). Not coincidentally, Lamech celebrated his deviancy in both his sexuality and his fame-seeking violence in 4:19–24; likewise the universal spread of sin in Genesis 6 demonstrated in both these areas. Yet, as the concentric structure emphasizes, what counts ultimately is not human striving but God's action, here in judgment (and later in making a name for his chosen one, Abraham; cf. 12:2).

6:5–8 Verse 5 summarizes the culmination of man's downward spiral into sin that has been unfolding since Genesis 3. Seven times in Genesis 1 we read, "God saw ... and it was good"; now, however, what the Lord sees is the great wickedness of mankind (6:5). It has become so comprehensive that for almost everyone "*every* intention of the thoughts of his heart was *only* evil *continually*" (v. 5). Theologians often stress the fact that the doctrine of total depravity does not mean that people are as wicked as they could possibly be; it is simply that every aspect of their thinking and doing is tainted with sin. However, the world of Noah's day was

---

111 We may note the similarity to the temporal clause in Genesis 6:1 ("When man began to multiply on the face of the land and daughters were born to them") as supporting the interpretation of this phrase in verse 4 as temporal rather than causal.
112 A connection that is likely behind the LXX translation, *gigantes* ("giants"), which was then followed by the KJV.
113 The Talmud suggests the unlikely possibility that one of them clung to the outside of the ark!

closer to the former, with unbridled sexual expression and gratuitous violence on all sides.

God is not an "unmoved mover" who coldly surveys the destruction of his good world without caring. The Scriptures can speak of God's "regretting" that he had made humanity, of how the situation "grieved him to his heart" (v. 6). Of course, we must remember that our speech about God is always analogical; he no more literally "regrets" and "grieves" than he has a literal heart or mouth. A God who transcends time cannot "regret" an action in exactly the same way humans do, for he knows the end from the beginning and plans every event perfectly. Yet, because we are made in the image of God, this language can communicate something important to us. Even though God does not have emotions, our emotions nonetheless help us to understand something important about God, just as, even though God does not have a mouth, when the Scriptures speak of the "mouth of the Lord" we understand something of his nature as a speaking God. So we may meaningfully speak of God's care and compassion for the world he has made and of his grief over the damage sin causes to it and the people it contains.

And God is not merely a helpless bystander, watching the chaos and evil of the world unfolding while wringing his hands and wishing he could do something. He is the God who created this world out of nothing, and he can return it to nothing at any time he chooses. He will judge wickedness, as he warned Adam in 2:17, and, though he is "merciful and gracious, slow to anger, and abounding in steadfast love and faithfulness, keeping steadfast love for thousands, forgiving iniquity and transgression and sin," he is also the God who "will by no means clear the guilty" (Ex. 34:6–7). As a result, judgment will come upon all flesh, both human and animal, blotting them out from the face of the land and the heavens. The comprehensiveness of the destruction is highlighted by the repetition of language from Genesis 1 ("man and animals and creeping things and birds of the heavens"; Gen. 6:7; cf. 1:20, 24). The sweeping spread of sin in Genesis 3–6 is matched by sweeping judgment on the whole world, proving that the wages of sin is indeed death (Rom. 6:23).

Yet in the midst of the blackest description of human sin a shaft of light still shines: "Noah found favor in the eyes of the LORD" (Gen. 6:8). A single individual who walks with the Lord (v. 9) can have an impact far beyond what might be expected. Noah's faith and faithfulness will be the means by which the Lord preserves the human race and moves forward his purposes for creation. In the midst of the coming destruction of the flood a holy remnant will be preserved and kept safe by God.

Response

Many people naively believe that humans are, in their heart of hearts, fundamentally good. They may be misguided or misled into sin, but, if they really followed their best instincts, they would end up in a good place. Rabbinic Judaism, for example, teaches that within each of us there is not one *yetser* ("inclination"; cf. Gen.

6:5) but two, struggling for control; one is good and one is evil. What we need to do is to fight hard to control the evil *yetser* and to support the good *yetser*.[114] If that is the case, then what humanity needs is not a savior but merely a helper, or a life coach—someone who will show us the right way and give an inspiring example for us to follow. Christianity, however, insists that there is only one *yetser* naturally present in our hearts, the evil one. This is the doctrine that theologians call total depravity. Or, as Paul puts it in his letter to the Ephesians,

> You were dead in the trespasses and sins in which you once walked, following the course of this world, following the prince of the power of the air, the spirit that is now at work in the sons of disobedience—among whom we all once lived in the passions of our flesh, carrying out the desires of the body and the mind, and were by nature children of wrath, like the rest of mankind. (Eph. 2:1–3)

Genesis 6:1–8 shows us the same doctrine in OT garb. The natural tendency of humanity without God is to fill the world with sin. Sin always blurs the lines between things that God created to be separate, and believers are regularly tempted to compromise their distinctive identity and join themselves to unbelievers. The temptation to intermarriage with people who do not share our values is perennial (cf. 2 Cor. 6:14), but it inevitably ends badly. If the center and focus of our individual worlds is so far apart, how can those worlds be joined together as one? Either our love for the other person will draw us away from a life centered on God, or a life centered on God will draw us away from the other person.

In addition to unbridled sexuality, pervasive and gratuitous violence remains a problem. If we are not finding our identity in Christ, we will tend to find our "name" in other things, and we will bite, destroy, and kill in order to achieve and protect the status we desire (cf. James 4:2). It is doubtful that the modern world is really any better than the world of Noah's day. The flood did not accomplish a fundamental change in the hearts of men and women (cf. Gen. 8:21)—nor was it intended to do so.

Yet, instead of sending another flood to destroy the present world order, God sent his own Son to redeem it. He is the one who most of all found favor in the Lord's sight (Matt. 3:17) and in whose life was no hint of sin. Through Jesus' death and resurrection God put to death our evil and sin and now makes us a new creation (2 Cor. 5:17). The evil of the world that surrounds us will not endure forever but will finally be judged and destroyed—yet we who ourselves are so deeply stained with our sin are even now called "sons of God" (Rom. 8:14) and look forward with the remainder of creation to its full and final renovation (Rom. 8:19–21).

---

[114] Cf. P. W. van der Horst, *Jews and Christians in Their Graeco-Roman Context*, WUNT 196 (Tübingen: Mohr Siebeck, 2006), 61.

GENESIS 6:9–22

⁹ These are the generations of Noah. Noah was a righteous man, blameless in his generation. Noah walked with God. ¹⁰ And Noah had three sons, Shem, Ham, and Japheth.
¹¹ Now the earth was corrupt in God's sight, and the earth was filled with violence. ¹² And God saw the earth, and behold, it was corrupt, for all flesh had corrupted their way on the earth. ¹³ And God said to Noah, "I have determined to make an end of all flesh,[1] for the earth is filled with violence through them. Behold, I will destroy them with the earth. ¹⁴ Make yourself an ark of gopher wood.[2] Make rooms in the ark, and cover it inside and out with pitch. ¹⁵ This is how you are to make it: the length of the ark 300 cubits,[3] its breadth 50 cubits, and its height 30 cubits. ¹⁶ Make a roof[4] for the ark, and finish it to a cubit above, and set the door of the ark in its side. Make it with lower, second, and third decks. ¹⁷ For behold, I will bring a flood of waters upon the earth to destroy all flesh in which is the breath of life under heaven. Everything that is on the earth shall die. ¹⁸ But I will establish my covenant with you, and you shall come into the ark, you, your sons, your wife, and your sons' wives with you. ¹⁹ And of every living thing of all flesh, you shall bring two of every sort into the ark to keep them alive with you. They shall be male and female. ²⁰ Of the birds according to their kinds, and of the animals according to their kinds, of every creeping thing of the ground, according to its kind, two of every sort shall come in to you to keep them alive. ²¹ Also take with you every sort of food that is eaten, and store it up. It shall serve as food for you and for them." ²² Noah did this; he did all that God commanded him.

[1] Hebrew *The end of all flesh has come before me* [2] Transliterated from Hebrew; the identity of this tree is uncertain [3] A *cubit* was about 18 inches or 45 centimeters [4] Or *skylight*

Section Overview

One of the distinctive features of Israel's God is his propensity to announce ahead of time his great works, both of salvation and of judgment. As Amos 3:7 says,

> The Lord GOD does nothing
>   without revealing his secret
>   to his servants the prophets. (cf. Gen. 18:17)

Unlike the gods of the ancient Near East, who were capricious and acted on a whim, the Lord has a purpose and plan from the beginning that he will carry out, for his own glory and for the good of his people. These two things are connected: as God announces his works ahead of time, humans may acknowledge that these are the Lord's work, not merely random chance events. When the work is one of judgment, people may have the opportunity to repent and be saved out of the coming judgment; when it is one of salvation, people may have their faith in God's power and goodness increased.

Israel will have its own formative moment of judgment and salvation involving water at the exodus, when God drowns the Egyptians at the Red Sea and brings his people safely through (cf. Exodus 12–14). But even that mighty work is only a faint echo of the flood, when God brings watery judgment on almost the whole world, delivering only one family through that trial.

Other ancient Near Eastern societies had their own flood narratives, with similarities and differences to the biblical account.[115] This is as one would expect, as memories of such a catastrophic ancient historical event would have tended to be preserved, in forms that cohered with and revealed a culture's worldview. The differences between the stories are often more significant than the similarities, since they highlight the uniqueness of Israel's (inspired) version. For example, the boat that Utnapishtim—the Noah figure in the Gilgamesh epic—is instructed to build is a perfect cube; this is the ideal form for a sacred place in the ancient Near East (compare the Most Holy Place of the tabernacle and the temple) but hardly ideal for an actual boat. In comparison Noah's ark, although massive, is more nautically appropriate.

In the Akkadian Atrahasis epic[116] the cause of the flood is human overpopulation, which leads to the gods' being troubled by noise pollution, while in the biblical account it is caused by human sin. Moreover, in the Akkadian account it is an accident that any humans survive, due to differences of opinion among the gods, while the gods themselves are terrified by the forces they have unleashed, cowering before them like dogs. However, it is just as well for the gods that Utnapishtim survives, since they are dependent upon the sacrifices offered by humans for their food, and so they gather like hungry flies around Utnapishtim's altar. These accounts have a very different worldview than that of the biblical picture, which shows a single God who sovereignly executes his plan of judgment and salvation by unleashing the mighty forces of nature according to his will and to accomplish his own purposes.

Section Outline
IV. The Family History of Noah (6:9–9:29)
    A. Announcement of Judgment and Salvation (6:9–22)

Comment

6:9–12 The *toledot* formula ("These are the generations of"; cf. comment on 2:4–7) introduces the third major section in the book of Genesis, which will concern Noah and his offspring, Shem, Ham, and Japheth.[117] Their story begins with a reprise

---

115 The best known is part of the Epic of Gilgamesh, an Akkadian saga from the eighteenth century BC. Cf. *ANET*, 93–95.
116 Atrahasis was written down during the mid-seventeenth century BC but clearly represents a much older oral tradition; cf. *ANET*, 512–517.
117 The standard formula is "Shem, Ham, and Japheth," even though Ham is the youngest son (cf. 9:24). This may be due to grouping the monosyllabic names before the disyllabic.

of the immediately preceding verses. "Noah found favor in the eyes of the LORD" (6:8) is unpacked in terms of Noah's behavior that has led to such acceptance before God. In contrast to the universal wickedness surrounding him (vv. 1–5) Noah is a righteous man (Hb. *tsaddiq*; v. 9), a term with roots in legal texts that recognize someone as being "in the right."[118] He is also "blameless" (*tamim*), a word that has to do with wholeness and integrity. Sacrificial animals that are *tamim* are "without blemish" (Lev. 1:3); so too people with this quality are morally pure and upright.

These two attributes of righteousness and integrity summarize Noah's ethical behavior, but he also "walked with God," a phrase describing relational intimacy (cf. comment on 5:6–24 [at v. 24]). Noah is thus a man of outstanding character, all the more so in contrast to "his generation" (*dorotav*),[119] which is evil to the core. Second Peter 2:5 infers from the distinction between Noah and his contemporaries that Noah must have preached to those around him, without seeing any turn and repent. Noah's exemplary reputation leads to his being cited as an example of righteousness elsewhere in the Bible (e.g., Ezek. 14:14; Heb. 11:7). Noah is not perfect, of course, but like Abraham after him he walks consistently before God by faith (Gen. 15:6).

As the first man born after the death of Adam (according to the chronology of ch. 5), Noah becomes a kind of second Adam figure, a new father for the entire human race.[120] Like the first Adam, Noah has three named sons, one of whom proves to be reprobate. Shem, Ham, and Japheth are introduced here, repeated from 5:32, since they will have a major part to play in the later story, but no evaluation is yet given of their character, unlike with Noah (6:9) and the remainder of their contemporaries (v. 5). Their salvation from the destruction of the flood rests not upon their own righteousness but on Noah's, their faithful covenant head.

The indictment against humanity is repeated in order to make it clear that the Lord's judgment is just and righteous: the earth (*ha'arets*) had been corrupted (*shakhat*, used three times in vv. 11–12) and filled with violence by humanity. The Hebrew *ha'arets* can, of course, be translated as "the land" rather than "the earth," and some have therefore argued for a limited flood, covering only a small portion of the earth; however, the global nature of the spread of sin described in these verses suggests the flood is at least as widespread as the spread of humanity at this point. "All flesh" has corrupted the earth (v. 12), and the only solution is for God to make an end to all flesh because of the violence it has spread throughout the earth (v. 13), as demonstrated by the behavior of Lamech (4:19–24) and the Nephilim (6:4). "Violence" (*khamas*) is the opposite of "justice" (*mishpat*), the situation that provides the ideal circumstances for human flourishing (cf. Job 19:7).

---

118 Westermann, *Genesis: A Practical Commentary*, 54. Genesis 6 is the first time that the concepts of "righteous" (Hb. *tsaddiq*) and "wicked" (*ra'ah*) occur in the Bible, though the text assumes that its readers already understand the concepts.

119 The plural "generations" is unexpected and is not reflected in the ESV. It may reflect the fact that, at six hundred years in length, Noah's life spans several generations of contemporaries. It is not the same word translated "generations" by the ESV earlier in the verse; that was *toledot*.

120 This emphasis on the unity of the entire human race rooted in common ancestry, prominent in the biblical account, is absent from the ancient Near Eastern flood stories, in which a significant number of unrelated people survive the flood in the boat with Utnapishtim.

These sins are committed "in God's sight" (Gen. 6:11) rather than being concealed in secret. It is natural to hide our sins (Isa. 29:15; Heb. 4:13), but to sin openly and brazenly in this way is almost challenging the Lord to act—a challenge he is ready and willing to meet. "God saw" does not mean merely a casual observation; as judge, he examines the facts and then issues a just sentence. Mankind has corrupted the perfect world it has been given, so the judgment of the destruction of its world is merely turning man over to the fate he richly deserves.

6:13–22 Although God threatened to make a complete end of the earth and all its human occupants because of its corruption, it was not yet time for that final destruction (cf. 2 Pet. 3:5–13). Noah and his family will be preserved, and, because they are not sinless—not even Noah—with them will be carried the seeds of sin that will reflower on the far side of destruction. Only a complete new creation will finally achieve God's ultimate goal of creating a holy people prepared to walk with him in a sin-free environment.

In the meantime Noah is instructed to make himself an "ark" (Hb. *tebah*);[121] Noah is also informed of the reasons for the Lord's decision, which shows that God's action is neither hasty nor capricious. He has waited ten generations of increasing corruption before acting to bring judgment upon the world. The word "ark" is probably a loanword from Egyptian, where it means a chest or even a coffin,[122] with the latter sense being particularly fitting for a vehicle designed to take its occupants through a symbolic death and resurrection. The Hebrew word is used only of Noah's ark and of the container in which Moses is placed as a baby for his equally risky water adventure (Ex. 2:3).[123] Noah is given very precise instructions by the Lord for the materials and manufacture of the ark, a procedure seen more commonly in the ancient world when a deity instructs a king about the plans for building a sanctuary.[124] That precision is fitting, for constructing this boat is an equally sacred endeavor.

The ark is to be 450 feet [135 m] long by 75 feet [23 m] wide and 45 feet [14 m] high, made of "gopher wood," which is simply a transliteration of the Hebrew word *gofer*. The term occurs only here, and so it is uncertain what kind of wood is intended, though an etymological connection is possible to "cypress," a coniferous wood used widely in ancient shipbuilding. The three floors of the ark are each to have an unspecified number of "rooms" (*qannim*, "nests"), presumably to provide separate quarters for the various animals. The ark is to have a roof, necessary to keep the rainfall off, though it seems to have an opening of 18 inches [46 cm] all around under the roofline.[125]

In spite of God's decree to destroy every living thing under heaven[126] through the flood[127] (Gen. 6:17), he will establish his covenant with Noah (v. 18). When a

---

121 This should not be confused with "ark of the covenant," which uses a quite different Hebrew word (*'aron*).
122 Mathews, *Genesis 1–11:26*, 364.
123 This unique parallel is particularly striking if Moses is indeed the author of Genesis; cf. Ronald Youngblood, *The Book of Genesis: An Introductory Commentary* (Grand Rapids, MI: Baker, 1992), 89.
124 Compare the instructions given to King Gudea of Lagash for the temple of Ningirsu in *ANET*, 268.
125 Cf. Wenham, *Genesis 1–15*, 173–174.
126 This could be taken as a merely phenomenological description, but it is most naturally understood as speaking of a global judgment; cf. Mathews, *Genesis 1–11:26*, 365.
127 The Hebrew word translated "flood" (*mabbul*) is used only here in the flood narrative and in Psalm 29:10, underlining the uniqueness of this event.

new covenant was made in the ancient Near East, the terminology was usually to "cut" (*karat*) a covenant, reflecting the self-imprecatory oath taken by the parties passing between two dismembered animals, asking the gods to make them like those animals if they broke their word (cf. 15:9–18). In this case, however, the Lord speaks of "confirming" (*heqim*; cf. Gen. 17:7, 9, 21) his covenant with Noah, which may reflect a reference to the covenant originally made with creation.[128] In this case God is covenanting to keep Noah and his family safe within the ark, along with two of every kind of animal, bird, and creeping creature according to their kinds (6:20; cf. 1:24–26), along with their necessary food (6:21; cf. 1:29). The extensive reuse of terminology from Genesis 1 stresses the fact that this mission is nothing less than a new start for creation.

The chapter closes with an affirmation of Noah's obedience (6:22). This might seem superfluous, given the earlier description of Noah's righteousness and integrity, but such notices of precise conformity ("As God/the LORD commanded him") are common throughout the Pentateuch (Ex. 7:6, 10, 20, etc.). Exact obedience to the Lord's commands is of vital importance, especially when constructing a sacred object such as the ark, notwithstanding God's covenanted promise of blessing. It is the appropriate response of gratitude to the Lord's grace extended to Noah and his family.

Response

There were (broadly speaking) two kinds of covenants in the ancient world: (1) suzerainty treaties, in which a great king (a suzerain) entered into a relationship with a lesser king (a vassal), promising protection and reward in return for future obedience to the specified terms of the covenant, and (2) covenants of grant, which were unconditional promises of favor, often based on past acts of faithfulness.[129] The Sinai covenant is often classified as belonging to the former category, while the Noahic covenant, like the Abrahamic and Davidic covenants, is generally regarded as being more like a covenant of grant. That is, it reflects a reward for Noah's past history of serving and walking with God and is not dependent upon his future obedience.

These distinctions are helpful in focusing our attention on some crucial differences between different biblical covenants. Yet covenants—even of the suzerainty variety—always have an inherently gracious quality in that there is nothing forcing the great king into making this commitment to the vassal. Moreover, covenants of grant may sound entirely unconditional, but that does not mean that future obedience is unimportant if the grant is to be maintained.[130] God owes

---

[128] The Hebrew word "covenant" (*berit*) is not used in the creation account; however, many of the features of a covenant are present there, and the strong recollections of creation in these verses suggest that a connection is being made. Cf. W. J. Dumbrell, *Covenant and Creation: A Theology of the Old Testament Covenants* (Grand Rapids, MI: Baker, 1993), 15–26.
[129] Moshe Weinfeld, "The Covenant of Grant in the Old Testament and in the Ancient Near East," *JAOS* 90 (1970): 184–203.
[130] Bruce K. Waltke, "The Phenomenon of Conditionality within Unconditional Covenants," in *Israel's Apostasy and Restoration: Essays in Honor of Roland K. Harrison*, ed. A. Gileadi (Grand Rapids, MI: Baker, 1988), 123–139.

Noah nothing in return for his years of walking with him, which is simply what humanity owes God, and God could equally easily have preserved Noah by taking him out of the world, as with Enoch. Yet through this covenant God promises that he will preserve not only Noah's life but the lives of his family as well. His righteousness brings blessings not only to himself but to his entire household, as is typical of biblical covenants.

It is in this way that the passage points us forward to Christ. The Father has made a covenant with the Son that, through the righteousness of Christ, salvation will come to all those who are in him. Jesus has fulfilled the conditions of the covenant through his perfect righteousness of life and his self-offering as the blameless Lamb of God, whose death atones for our sins. In him God accomplishes the complete new creation that the flood was never able to establish, pouring out his Spirit on believers and their children (Acts 2:39). To paraphrase the writer to the Hebrews, the blood and water that flows from Jesus' side on the cross speaks a better word than that of the water that fell from heaven in Noah's days (Heb. 12:24). We who have benefitted from this new covenant should respond as Noah did, with gratitude-infused obedience to all that God has commanded us through his Word.

GENESIS 7

7 Then the Lord said to Noah, "Go into the ark, you and all your household, for I have seen that you are righteous before me in this generation. 2 Take with you seven pairs of all clean animals,¹ the male and his mate, and a pair of the animals that are not clean, the male and his mate, 3 and seven pairs² of the birds of the heavens also, male and female, to keep their offspring alive on the face of all the earth. 4 For in seven days I will send rain on the earth forty days and forty nights, and every living thing³ that I have made I will blot out from the face of the ground." 5 And Noah did all that the Lord had commanded him.

6 Noah was six hundred years old when the flood of waters came upon the earth. 7 And Noah and his sons and his wife and his sons' wives with him went into the ark to escape the waters of the flood. 8 Of clean animals, and of animals that are not clean, and of birds, and of everything that creeps on the ground, 9 two and two, male and female, went into the ark with Noah, as God had commanded Noah. 10 And after seven days the waters of the flood came upon the earth.

11 In the six hundredth year of Noah's life, in the second month, on the seventeenth day of the month, on that day all the fountains of the great deep burst forth, and the windows of the heavens were opened. 12 And rain fell upon the earth forty days and forty nights. 13 On the very same day Noah and his sons, Shem and Ham and Japheth, and Noah's wife and the three wives of his sons with them entered the ark, 14 they and every

beast, according to its kind, and all the livestock according to their kinds, and every creeping thing that creeps on the earth, according to its kind, and every bird, according to its kind, every winged creature. ¹⁵ They went into the ark with Noah, two and two of all flesh in which there was the breath of life. ¹⁶ And those that entered, male and female of all flesh, went in as God had commanded him. And the LORD shut him in.

¹⁷ The flood continued forty days on the earth. The waters increased and bore up the ark, and it rose high above the earth. ¹⁸ The waters prevailed and increased greatly on the earth, and the ark floated on the face of the waters. ¹⁹ And the waters prevailed so mightily on the earth that all the high mountains under the whole heaven were covered. ²⁰ The waters prevailed above the mountains, covering them fifteen cubits⁴ deep. ²¹ And all flesh died that moved on the earth, birds, livestock, beasts, all swarming creatures that swarm on the earth, and all mankind. ²² Everything on the dry land in whose nostrils was the breath of life died. ²³ He blotted out every living thing that was on the face of the ground, man and animals and creeping things and birds of the heavens. They were blotted out from the earth. Only Noah was left, and those who were with him in the ark. ²⁴ And the waters prevailed on the earth 150 days.

¹ Or *seven of each kind of clean animal* ² Or *seven of each kind* ³ Hebrew *all existence*; also verse 23 ⁴ A *cubit* was about 18 inches or 45 centimeters

Section Overview

Genesis 6 gives us very few details about the process of building the ark. There is no mention of what Noah's neighbors think or of the construction challenges and cost overruns that typically accompany such a massive project. God tells Noah to build an ark, and he does—just as, at creation in Genesis 1, God spoke the word and it was so.[131] Now, in Genesis 7, it is time to gather the animals and enter the completed ark, for the judgment rains are about to fall. The lives of Noah and his family depend upon their trusting God's word and entering their coffin-shaped boat, dying to the world, as it were, while believing that God's promise to protect them will keep them safe. So it transpires: judgment falls upon the world around them, but they are kept safe in the midst of the storm, just as God has promised. God judges the wicked while preserving the lives of those who trust in him.

Section Outline

IV. The Family History of Noah (6:9–9:29) . . .
    B. God's Judgment Descends (7:1–24)

Comment

7:1–5 Noah is not left to calculate the time of God's coming judgment by watching for signs; instead, God tells him when it is time to enter[132] the ark and exactly how the judgment will transpire. Noah is also instructed to take his household

---

[131] The same pattern will be repeated in the calling and response of Abraham in Genesis 12: God calls and a person responds by faith.
[132] The key Hebrew verb *bo'* ("enter") occurs seven times in this chapter.

with him. His family members are included in this act of salvation explicitly on the basis of Noah's by-faith righteousness, not their own. The Hebrew is emphatic: "Go into the ark, you and all your household, for I have seen that you [singular] are righteous" (7:1). God's "seeing" of Noah's righteousness is the equivalent of his "reckoning" Abraham to be righteous in 15:6. It also contrasts with God's "seeing" the extensive wickedness of the world in which Noah lives (cf. 6:5, 12). Noah's righteousness not only serves as the foundation for his family's salvation but also underlines the condemnation of the rest of his generation for its wickedness. When Lot is told to flee from the judgment coming upon Sodom, he finds it hard to persuade his household to join him (19:12–14), but Noah has no similar difficulties in recruiting his family for this much more challenging mission.

Noah had earlier been told to gather one pair of every kind of animal and bird (Gen. 6:19); God now adds the stipulation that seven pairs of clean animals must be brought along, along with seven pairs of birds (7:2–3). The reason for this is not explicitly stated, but presumably it is to allow for the possibility of offering sacrifices after the flood without wiping out an entire species in the process. This does not necessarily require Noah to be aware of the full Levitical laws of clean and unclean animals (cf. Leviticus 11); he simply needs to be aware of which animals might legitimately be offered as sacrifices and which are not "kosher" for that purpose.[133]

The number seven is prominent in the flood account, echoing the seven days of the original creation (Gen. 1:1–2:3). In addition to the seven pairs of clean animals and birds, there is a seven-day delay before the rain comes (7:4, 10) in order for the collection process to be completed. Another sacred number, forty, is also prominent in the forty days and nights during which the rain falls, wiping out every living creature from the face of the earth (v. 4). The period of forty days is often associated with periods of testing and trial in the Bible—for example, Moses' forty days and nights at Mount Sinai (Ex. 24:18), the spies' forty days in the Promised Land (Num. 13:25), Goliath's taunting Israel for forty days (1 Sam. 17:16), and Jesus' testing in the wilderness for forty days (Luke 4:2).[134] Once again we are informed explicitly of Noah's obedience to the Lord's commands, underlining his righteousness (Gen. 7:5).

7:6–10 And it is so: having heard God's word announcing to Noah what will happen, we see these same events unfolding exactly as God has said. The repetition may seem cumbersome to modern readers, but it drives home the point effectively. This is no random or out of control process that God has unleashed (unlike the flood brought about by the gods in the Gilgamesh epic) but rather a measured and controlled process of judgment. What God has created, he has the power and the authority to destroy (v. 4; cf. Jer. 18:4). Noah follows the Lord's instructions with precision, and, when the appointed day of judgment arrives, so too does the flood.

---

133 Sarna, *Genesis*, 54.
134 John Currid, *A Study Commentary on Genesis, Volume 1: Genesis 1:1–25:18* (Darlington, UK: Evangelical Press, 2003), 192.

7:11–16 For a third time we hear more or less the same facts related, each time with a little more detail, stressing just how precisely the events follow the divinely ordained pattern. The date of the flood, the seventeenth day of the second month (Gen. 7:11),[135] is significant precisely for its insignificance: it is not the day of any major festival or celebration. There is no ultimatum given to humanity that slowly ticks down to zero; rather, at a moment no one anticipates time finally runs out for this evil generation and the day of God's terrible judgment begins. The implications for the Lord's future judgments are unmistakable: no one knows the hour or the day (or the month or the year) of the end of all things.

The source of the water is described phenomenologically in terms of an opening of the fountains of the deep and the windows of heaven (v. 11).[136] In other words, the waters that had been separated and ordered by God on days two and three of creation in order to form the dry land are now reunited, so that the dry land once again disappears into the great deep (Hb. *tehom*; cf. 1:2, 6–9). The hospitable world the Lord built for man returns to a wilderness state, "without form and void" (*tohu vabohu*; cf. 1:2). For three chapters humanity has been sinfully striving to erase the lines of separation God had drawn; it is therefore a fitting judgment when the Lord removes the lines of separation upon which life itself rests.

From an Israelite perspective there would be a certain irony in the Lord's bringing destruction by opening wide the windows of heaven and pouring out rain, since in Israel the problem was usually the reverse—a drought caused by the Lord's closing the windows of heaven in judgment upon Israel (cf. Deut. 11:17; Mal. 3:10). The Lord is sovereign over the rain as a means both of blessing and of curse, a theme underlined by the use of the verb *hamtir* ("to rain down"; Gen. 7:4), which can be used equally of curse or of blessing (curse: Gen. 19:24; Ex. 9:23; blessing: Ex. 16:4; Amos 4:7).

Those who enter the ark are described as having the "breath of life" (Gen. 7:15). Soon they will be the only ones left on the earth who still have this breath, since all others will be blotted out. The difference between the two groups is simple: those inside the ark will live because of their relationship to Noah, with whom God has covenanted, while all those outside the ark will die because they lack such a saving relationship. It is not explicit in Genesis, but 1 Peter implies that, in spite of a climate of unrestrained sexuality all around them, Noah and his family remain committed to monogamy, so that the human contingent on the ark comprises only eight people (1 Pet. 3:20).[137] The description of the embarkation onto the ark is very detailed in some ways but equally sparing in others. Unlike Utnapishtim, who takes all his gold and silver onto his boat with him,[138] Noah and his family's possessions go unmentioned. There is no mention of other people's seeking

---

[135] There is debate among the rabbis as to whether this reflects a fall or a spring new year and thus whether the flood occurred in April or in October according to our reckoning. Multiple calendars were in use in the ancient world, and in Israel at different times. In either case the specificity of the date underlines the historical reality of the event being described—this is no timeless myth.
[136] Any attempt to reconstruct a "Hebrew cosmology" from texts like these, whose purpose is very different, is likely to end up with a misleading picture with very little connection to the thought processes of ancient readers.
[137] Kidner, *Genesis*, 97. This fits with the emphasis on the animals' going onto the ark in pairs; even in the animal kingdom (Gen. 7:9) monogamy is presented as the norm!
[138] *ANET*, 94.

admission to the ark and being turned away; only those who have been called by God and have faith in God's word would want to enter this coffin-shaped refuge. But there is no other sanctuary in which to seek shelter from the judgment to come.

One added detail is the fact that "the LORD shut [Noah] in" (Gen. 7:16). Noah built the ark and collected the animals, as he had been commanded to do, but the final act in the process, safely sealing him into the ark, is God's.[139] This ensures that the safety of those on board rests not in the effectiveness of Noah's marine engineering or navigational skills but in the hands of God. They can relax, confident that the God who has sealed them safely on board will watch over them every moment of their voyage until their ship comes safely to dry land.

7:17–24 Forty days of torrential rain, along with the outpouring of subterranean springs, is more than sufficient to complete the task of blotting out every living creature from the face of the earth (vv. 17–21). The rising floodwaters are marked literarily by a repetitive style, piling sentence upon sentence as the waters gradually prevail over the earth, then cover the mountains, then finally cover the mountains by a significant amount, 15 cubits (roughly 27 feet [8 m]; v. 20), which would provide plenty of clearance for the ark, with its total height of 30 cubits. The floodwaters then remain high for a total of 150 days (v. 24).[140] Eight times in verses 19–23 the word "all" appears, stressing the comprehensiveness of the global destruction. Only Noah is left alive, along with those with him in the ark (v. 23). Nothing outside the ark could survive such a deluge; it all dies (v. 22), fulfilling God's judgment upon Adam and all those made in his image (cf. Genesis 5).

Response

Since the beginning the serpent has sought to deny the doctrine of divine judgment (Gen. 3:4) and has had considerable success in sowing doubt into human minds (cf. Mal. 2:17). Even believers sometimes struggle to believe that evil will have its proper day in court and that the righteous will be vindicated (cf. Ps. 73:2–14). Throughout history, however, the Lord has given us clear lessons of his judgment, of which the flood is perhaps the most prominent. Does God see the wicked? Is he able to judge them? Can he preserve the righteous in the midst of that sweeping judgment upon sin? The flood narrative answers all those questions with a resounding "Yes!" God sees; God judges; God preserves a righteous remnant[141] alive.

The implications of these realities are clear. Those who do not know God live their lives in the face of clear and present danger. Just as no one knew ahead of time exactly when the flood would come, so no one knows when Christ will return to bring the final day of judgment (cf. Matt. 24:36–39, which explicitly draws a comparison to the days of Noah). As a result, we should strive constantly to be

---

[139] This forms a stark contrast to the Gilgamesh epic, in which Utnapishtim seals the entrance to his own boat and also employs the services of experienced sailors; cf. *ANET*, 94.
[140] It appears that the 150 days includes the forty days of actual rain. On the chronology of the flood cf. Hamilton, *Genesis 1–17*, 298.
[141] "Noah was left" (Hb. *vayisha'ar noakh*; 7:23) uses the key verb (*sha'ar*) that is used later to describe the preservation of a righteous remnant through the exile.

ready for the Lord's return (Matt. 24:44). Now is the time to make one's peace with God, before the judgment draws nigh.

In addition to a warning to unbelievers, however, this passage provides a comfort for believers that "the Lord knows how to rescue the godly from trials, and to keep the unrighteous under punishment until the day of judgment" (2 Pet. 2:9; again explicitly referencing the flood—cf. 2:5). Believers too wonder about God's deferred justice in a wicked world, but the flood shows us that justice is not always delayed and will not be deferred forever. At the same time, the Lord is able to keep safe in that coming judgment those with whom he has covenanted (Gen. 6:18). As we follow his commandments faithfully—however strange that obedience may look to a watching world—the Lord will seal us safely into the ark that preserves our lives from the deluge of his wrath.

For us as Christians the fulfillment of that theme is found in Christ himself. Christ is the righteous covenant-keeper in whom we, like Noah's family, find undeserved safety. Faith in Christ calls us to die to the world around us, just as the inhabitants of the ark voluntarily entered their coffin-shaped vehicle of salvation. We are called to trust not in our ability to pilot the vessel of our lives—for the ark had neither sails nor rudder—but in the God who has sealed us into the vessel that he will guide safely into the harbor of heaven. Through a final act of cataclysmic judgment God will bring about his new heavens and new earth, where righteousness reigns (2 Pet. 3:13), and we will be free from the sin and wickedness that currently still afflicts us all.

GENESIS 8

8 But God remembered Noah and all the beasts and all the livestock that were with him in the ark. And God made a wind blow over the earth, and the waters subsided. ² The fountains of the deep and the windows of the heavens were closed, the rain from the heavens was restrained, ³ and the waters receded from the earth continually. At the end of 150 days the waters had abated, ⁴ and in the seventh month, on the seventeenth day of the month, the ark came to rest on the mountains of Ararat. ⁵ And the waters continued to abate until the tenth month; in the tenth month, on the first day of the month, the tops of the mountains were seen.

⁶ At the end of forty days Noah opened the window of the ark that he had made ⁷ and sent forth a raven. It went to and fro until the waters were dried up from the earth. ⁸ Then he sent forth a dove from him, to see if the waters had subsided from the face of the ground. ⁹ But the dove found no place to set her foot, and she returned to him to the ark, for the waters were still on the face of the whole earth. So he put out his hand and took her and brought her into the ark with him. ¹⁰ He waited another seven

days, and again he sent forth the dove out of the ark. ¹¹ And the dove came back to him in the evening, and behold, in her mouth was a freshly plucked olive leaf. So Noah knew that the waters had subsided from the earth. ¹² Then he waited another seven days and sent forth the dove, and she did not return to him anymore.

¹³ In the six hundred and first year, in the first month, the first day of the month, the waters were dried from off the earth. And Noah removed the covering of the ark and looked, and behold, the face of the ground was dry. ¹⁴ In the second month, on the twenty-seventh day of the month, the earth had dried out. ¹⁵ Then God said to Noah, ¹⁶ "Go out from the ark, you and your wife, and your sons and your sons' wives with you. ¹⁷ Bring out with you every living thing that is with you of all flesh—birds and animals and every creeping thing that creeps on the earth—that they may swarm on the earth, and be fruitful and multiply on the earth." ¹⁸ So Noah went out, and his sons and his wife and his sons' wives with him. ¹⁹ Every beast, every creeping thing, and every bird, everything that moves on the earth, went out by families from the ark.

²⁰ Then Noah built an altar to the LORD and took some of every clean animal and some of every clean bird and offered burnt offerings on the altar. ²¹ And when the LORD smelled the pleasing aroma, the LORD said in his heart, "I will never again curse¹ the ground because of man, for the intention of man's heart is evil from his youth. Neither will I ever again strike down every living creature as I have done. ²² While the earth remains, seedtime and harvest, cold and heat, summer and winter, day and night, shall not cease."

¹ Or *dishonor*

Section Overview

Many scholars have suggested that the flood narrative is structured as a large-scale chiasm.¹⁴² The proposals vary in their details, but everyone agrees that Genesis 8:1 represents the central turning point: "But God remembered Noah." God is just as much in control of the aftermath of the flood as he was over its causes. The same God who brought the rain now closes up the fountains of the deep and the floodgates of heaven and sends a wind to dry up the earth (vv. 1–2). The resemblance to creation, at which God's Spirit/wind (Hb. *ruakh*) was hovering over the waters, deliberately paints this action as an act of recreation, once again separating the waters and returning them to their allotted boundaries so that the dry ground may appear and the world may again be populated by people and animals. God is sovereign over salvation as well as over judgment.

Section Outline

IV. The Family History of Noah (6:9–9:29) . . .
  C. God Remembers Noah (8:1–14)
  D. Celebrating Salvation (8:15–22)

---

142 E.g., Gordon J. Wenham, "The Coherence of the Flood Narrative," *VT* 28 (1978): 336–348; Yehuda T. Radday, "Chiasmus in Hebrew Biblical Narrative," in *Chiasmus in Antiquity: Structure, Analysis, Exegesis*, ed. John W. Welch (Provo, UT: Research Press, 1981), 99–100.

Comment

8:1–5 "But God remembered Noah" highlights this verse as the turning point in the flood narrative. Up to this point God has been bringing destruction upon the earth; from here onward he begins to restore what he has destroyed. Yet grammatically speaking the *vav*-consecutive imperfect form is more commonly conjunctive than disjunctive, so we might as easily translate "And God remembered Noah" (KJV; NJPS). Furthermore, speaking of God's remembering Noah does mean he forgot Noah for the duration of the rains and then suddenly recalled him to mind and so began to dry up the flood. Rather, throughout this whole period of destruction and restoration God has remembered Noah and watched over him and his ark, keeping its occupants safe from all harm. "Remembering" in Hebrew is always more than a mental activity; it includes the appropriate actions that flow from such knowledge. Hence the term is used often to describe the behavior that follows from a prior commitment, such as a covenant. To "remember a covenant" is to keep its conditions and fulfill its obligations, while to "forget" it is to disobey it (Ex. 2:24; 6:5).

God's re-creative work begins just as his creative work did,[143] with his sending a Spirit/wind (Hb. *ruakh*) upon the face of the chaotic waters (Gen. 8:1; cf. 1:2). Just as the work of destruction was no mere natural process but God's work, so too the restoration process rests on God's decision and follows his exact timeline. The twin sources of the water for the flood, the fountains of the deep and the windows of heaven, are closed up (8:2; cf. 7:11)—the rain ceases and the earth begins to dry out. The 150 days the water takes to dry up (8:3) equal the 150 days the rain "prevailed on the earth" (7:24), so that the ark comes to rest five months after the rain began (five thirty-day months equal 150 days), on the seventeenth day of the seventh month (8:4; cf. 7:11). The seventh month of the Jewish calendar would later include the Feast of Booths, when the Israelites would camp out for a week to remember the wilderness wanderings and look forward to their heavenly inheritance (Lev. 23:24–43), making this date a fitting one for the ark's wilderness wanderings to end and for it to find rest (*vattanakh*; Gen. 8:4). This is probably not the "rest" for which Noah's father, Lamech, named him (*nuakh*; 5:29 ESV mg.), but it is a fitting play on his name.

Ararat, upon whose mountains the ark finishes its journey, is usually identified with Urartu, a region in northern Mesopotamia now part of Turkey. The modern-day Mount Ararat came to be associated with Noah only in the eleventh or twelfth century AD, however. There is no biblical record of any subsequent interest in this region; it did not form a place of pilgrimage for God's people, perhaps in part because of the significant distance involved and the uncertainty of its exact location. However, even Mount Sinai was not generally considered a place of religious interest in biblical times after Israel departed from its sojourn there.[144] There was

---

[143] His deliverance of Israel from Egypt through the Red Sea at the Exodus follows a similar pattern (Ex. 14:21).

[144] The exception is Elijah's journey there in 1 Kings 19, when he is called to recreate Moses' experience on the mountain, which seems to leave him entirely unmoved. (His response in 1 Kings 19:14, after the theophany, is identical to that in 1 Kings 19:10, prior to the Lord's appearing.)

only one place worthy of pilgrimage for God's people, and that was the place where God chose to place his name: Jerusalem.

8:6–13 Even though the ark finds its rest, the occupants must wait a considerable time before it is safe to leave the ark. It is another two and a half months before the tops of the mountains become visible (8:5); the lengthy process of renovation is striking in contrast to the rapid process of creation in Genesis 1. Indeed, waiting is a key theme of this section (vv. 10, 12). Forty days pass before Noah sends out a raven; it fails to return, presumably satisfied with the endless supplies of carrion for it to eat. Then he sends out a dove three times, at weekly intervals, with different results each time. The first time the dove comes back with nothing, having found no place to alight (v. 9); the second time it comes back with a fresh olive twig in its mouth, a sign of hope that the trees are growing above the remaining waters (v. 11); the third time it does not return, presumably because it now finds the earth to be habitable (v. 12).

The significance of the raven and the dove lies in the fact that they are opposites: the raven is an unclean bird, while the dove is not only a clean bird but one suitable for sacrifice. The raven's self-sufficient attitude is suggestive; it does not return to the ark but forges its own path in the new world independently, while the dove meekly returns repeatedly to Noah until it has conveyed to him the message that all is safe. The combined impact of the raven and the dove is ominous, however, suggesting that, though the world Noah is inheriting is new, the old sinful tendencies have not been entirely wiped out by the flood (cf. v. 21).

Finally, on the first day of Noah's 601st year in this world, it is time to open the roof of the ark and survey the scene (v. 13). The first day of a year was considered an auspicious day for a major religious undertaking such as consecrating or reconsecrating a sacred building (e.g., Ex. 40:2; 2 Chron. 29:17), so it seems a fitting day to start afresh in the new world God has given Noah and his family. The face of the ground, from which the Lord had determined to blot out every living creature (Gen. 7:4, 23), is finally dry (8:13).

8:14–19 Even then, with the face of the ground "dry," it is still not time to leave the ark. That awaits the twenty-seventh day of the second month, when "the earth had dried out" (v. 14). The difference between the two dates suggests the time needed for the surface water to disappear and the ground to dry out sufficiently enough to allow Noah and his family to walk on it. More importantly, however, it seems that Noah is waiting for divine sanction to leave the ark. Just as God had told Noah when it was time for him and his menagerie to enter the ark (7:1–4), so Noah must wait until God tells him it is time to leave (8:15–17). The parallels are striking: just as Noah was told to enter the ark with his wife, his sons, and their wives, now he must leave with the same people. The birds, animals, and creeping things that he took in with him must now be brought out by him, so that they may once again be fruitful and multiply on the earth (v. 17; cf. 1:22). And it is so. Noah obeys this commandment too, as detailed in 8:18–19—verses that seem to underline the fact that not one creature is missing out of all those Noah had brought with him onto the ark. The God who shut Noah into the ark has remembered him and his cargo and brought them safely through the watery trial to a new beginning on the other side.

8:20–22 The first action Noah takes upon emerging from the ark is to build an altar and offer sacrifices (v. 20). Open-air altars could be simple affairs, not requiring a priest to tend them, as a sanctuary would. For that reason these are commonly where the patriarchs offer their sacrifices (e.g., Gen. 12:7, 8; 13:18). This offering is not a *minkhah*, a tribute offering, such as Cain and Abel offered (4:3, 4), but rather a whole burnt offering (Hb. *'olah*; lit., "ascending offering"), the first explicit atoning sacrifice to be recorded.[145] The whole burnt offering stands in place of the person offering it, who identifies it as representing him by laying hands on the animal (i.e., by leaning on it).[146] It is a ransom payment given to God, frequently with a strong undertone of atonement and substitution (e.g., Lev. 1:4).[147] Here the clean animals and birds suffer the judgment of death that Noah and his family have escaped by grace. The deaths of those animals and birds substitute for redeemed humanity, as it stands represented in Noah and his family.

Particularly striking is the impact this sacrifice is said to have on God: he smells the pleasing smoke of the "ascending offering" and is pacified by it (Gen. 8:21). There is another play on Noah's name here: the Hebrew for "pleasing" (*nikhoakh*) sounds similar to Noah's name (*noakh*)—it is a "rest-giving" aroma. We even hear God's inmost thoughts: because of Noah's sacrifice, never again will the Lord bring a flood of similar magnitude upon the earth—even though[148] the nature of mankind has not changed. Nor will God add to the curse that already exists on the ground (though neither is the curse on the ground lifted, as human experience makes all too clear). The power to bring delight to God's wounded heart resides not in the sacrifices themselves but in that to which they point: the atoning work of Christ, which provides lasting hope even for deeply broken and sinful people like us (Heb. 10:4–10).

Noah's sacrifice is a faithful response to the deliverance he has received, thanking God and seeking atonement for his own sins and those of his family. God receives that offering, just as he received Abel's offering earlier (cf. Gen. 4:4), and he commits himself to preserving the fundamental distinctions that keep the world in balance, "seedtime and harvest, cold and heat, summer and winter, day and night" (8:22)—distinctions that had been dissolved in the flood. God also

---

145 As we saw in Genesis 3–4, many traditional commentators have inferred an atoning significance from the animals slaughtered to provide tunics for Adam and Eve (Gen. 3:21) and from Abel's *minkhah* (4:4), but neither of these is explicitly an atoning offering in the text.
146 Cf. Gordon Wenham, *Leviticus*, NICOT (Grand Rapids, MI: Eerdmans, 1979), 63.
147 P. P. Jenson, "The Levitical Sacrificial System," in *Sacrifice in the Bible*, ed. R. T. Beckwith and M. J. Selman (Grand Rapids, MI: Baker, 1995), 28.
148 ESV translates the Hebrew *ki* as "for," which makes man's essentially unchanged evil *yetser* ("intention"; cf. 6:5) the reason that God will not again flood the world. It seems more likely that this is a concessive *ki* ("even though"; cf. CSB; NIV; NET); the reason for refraining from continual acts of judgment upon the world is rooted in God's sovereign purpose to redeem a people for himself in Christ, rather than the recalcitrance of humanity. For *ki* as concessive cf. Geoffrey Khan, ed., *Encyclopedia of Hebrew Language and Linguistics* (Leiden: Brill, 2013), 1.538–539.

blesses Noah and his renewed covenant with him (cf. 9:9); in this way Noah and God continue to walk together (cf. 6:9).

Response

The flood's work of judgment is complete by the end of Genesis 7, but Noah's work of faithful perseverance is far from done. God could have instantly dried out the land, just as he did in creation (1:9), but instead he chose to leave Noah and his family in the confined quarters of the ark for many more months. Yet, unlike Israel, who rapidly turned to grumbling when forced to remain in the wilderness, Noah and his family apparently wait patiently. Even after the dry ground appears they wait longer for God to give the word to leave the ark. Peter draws the conclusion from the ark narrative that we should also be patient as we wait for the return of the Lord, not accusing the Lord of slowness but recognizing his longsuffering with sinful humanity (cf. 2 Pet. 3:6–9).

Like Noah, we should live righteous and holy lives, walking with God through whatever trials we may face, remembering that the Lord is as sovereign over each of our situations as he was over Noah's experience. If he asks us to go through difficult and tragic circumstances, the Lord will personally seal the door for us too, keeping us safe through the midst of the storm (Isa. 43:2). When the Lord finally determines our time of trial to be over, he will cause the floodwaters to subside around us and call us out of our refuge, having worked in us an endurance and patience that we could not have learned any other way.

Ultimately, Noah's flood was a dress rehearsal for the final cataclysmic destruction of the world, which will complete God's work of a new creation in which righteousness dwells. On that day the inclination of our hearts will be no longer constantly toward evil but only toward good, all the time (2 Pet. 3:12–13). We will be safe on that day, if we are Christians, through faith in Christ, who offered the perfect and unblemished sacrifice on the cross for our sin and the sins of all his people (1 John 2:2). When the Father beholds the suffering of his Son, his wrath is satisfied and his love is kindled, first toward Jesus and then toward all those who are in him. For the sake of Christ he will not execute further judgment upon us, because Jesus has taken it all in our place as the atoning Lamb of God (John 1:29). So on that great day our sins will be fully forgiven and our hearts cleansed, and we too will be able to walk with God in the new Jerusalem that God will bring down from heaven as our eternal home (Rev. 21:2–5).

GENESIS 9

9 And God blessed Noah and his sons and said to them, "Be fruitful and multiply and fill the earth. ² The fear of you and the dread of you shall be upon every beast of the earth and upon every bird of the heavens, upon everything that creeps on the ground and all the fish of the sea. Into your hand they are delivered. ³ Every moving thing that lives shall be food for you. And as I gave you the green plants, I give you everything. ⁴ But you shall not eat flesh with its life, that is, its blood. ⁵ And for your lifeblood I will require a reckoning: from every beast I will require it and from man. From his fellow man I will require a reckoning for the life of man.

⁶ "Whoever sheds the blood of man,
    by man shall his blood be shed,
for God made man in his own image.

⁷ And you,¹ be fruitful and multiply, increase greatly on the earth and multiply in it."

⁸ Then God said to Noah and to his sons with him, ⁹ "Behold, I establish my covenant with you and your offspring after you, ¹⁰ and with every living creature that is with you, the birds, the livestock, and every beast of the earth with you, as many as came out of the ark; it is for every beast of the earth. ¹¹ I establish my covenant with you, that never again shall all flesh be cut off by the waters of the flood, and never again shall there be a flood to destroy the earth." ¹² And God said, "This is the sign of the covenant that I make between me and you and every living creature that is with you, for all future generations: ¹³ I have set my bow in the cloud, and it shall be a sign of the covenant between me and the earth. ¹⁴ When I bring clouds over the earth and the bow is seen in the clouds, ¹⁵ I will remember my covenant that is between me and you and every living creature of all flesh. And the waters shall never again become a flood to destroy all flesh. ¹⁶ When the bow is in the clouds, I will see it and remember the everlasting covenant between God and every living creature of all flesh that is on the earth." ¹⁷ God said to Noah, "This is the sign of the covenant that I have established between me and all flesh that is on the earth."

¹⁸ The sons of Noah who went forth from the ark were Shem, Ham, and Japheth. (Ham was the father of Canaan.) ¹⁹ These three were the sons of Noah, and from these the people of the whole earth were dispersed.²

²⁰ Noah began to be a man of the soil, and he planted a vineyard.³ ²¹ He drank of the wine and became drunk and lay uncovered in his tent. ²² And Ham, the father of Canaan, saw the nakedness of his father and told his two brothers outside. ²³ Then Shem and Japheth took a garment, laid it on both their shoulders, and walked backward and covered the nakedness of their father. Their faces were turned backward, and they did not see their father's nakedness. ²⁴ When Noah awoke from his wine and knew what his youngest son had done to him, ²⁵ he said,

> "Cursed be Canaan;
>   a servant of servants shall he be to his brothers."

²⁶ He also said,

> "Blessed be the LORD, the God of Shem;
>   and let Canaan be his servant.
> ²⁷ May God enlarge Japheth,⁴
>   and let him dwell in the tents of Shem,
>   and let Canaan be his servant."

²⁸ After the flood Noah lived 350 years. ²⁹ All the days of Noah were 950 years, and he died.

¹ In Hebrew *you* is plural ² Or *from these the whole earth was populated* ³ Or *Noah, a man of the soil, was the first to plant a vineyard* ⁴ *Japheth* sounds like the Hebrew for *enlarge*

Section Overview

Surviving the flood was just the beginning for Noah and his family. Now that they have emerged from the ark, they face the massive task of rebuilding and repopulating the world. Just as the original creation had been followed by a commissioning and a blessing for the first humans, so too this re-creation will be recommissioned and re-blessed by God. In some ways the world will be the same as it had always been, while in other ways it will be quite different. Noah and his family need reassurance that humanity will not be wiped out repeatedly every ten generations or so, something that seemed eminently plausible given the fact that human nature had not been transformed by the cataclysm (cf. Gen. 8:21). The reassurance comes in the form of a renewal of the covenant between God and Noah, with a new sign of God's commitment to humanity in the shape of the rainbow.

Just as the original creation was swiftly followed by a fall, so too this re-creation of the world is marked by Noah's fall into drunkenness. The man who had walked blamelessly with God for six hundred years gets drunk shortly after his new beginning (9:21). Just as Noah's righteousness had implications for his children, so too does his sin. Shem and Japheth seek to preserve their father's dignity, but Ham leaves him exposed to ridicule (vv. 22–23). As a result of this failure to honor his father properly, Ham, and especially his son Canaan, receive a divine curse (vv. 25–27). Divine election is once again choosing its own pathway as God determines who is blessed and who is cursed. Finally, the chapter closes with the deferred ending of Seth's genealogy in chapter 5 as it records the days of Noah's life and his death (v. 28).

Section Outline

    IV. The Family History of Noah (6:9–9:29) . . .
        E. A New Beginning (9:1–17)
        F. Blessing and Curse on the Next Generation (9:18–29)

Comment

9:1–7 Just as God blessed Adam and Eve and the original creation with the command "Be fruitful and multiply and fill the earth" (1:28), so now that blessing is repeated for Noah and his family (9:1). In some of ancient Near Eastern flood accounts, such as the Atrahasis epic, human overpopulation and noise pollution were the reasons that the gods sent the flood in the first place. As a result, after the flood the gods imposed barrenness, miscarriages, and singleness on mankind to prevent a recurrence of the problem.[149] Utnapishtim, the Noah figure, was rewarded with eternal life and removed from the challenges of everyday survival. Israel's God, on the other hand, is profoundly pro-life and in favor of human flourishing; he calls the gift of children a blessing to be celebrated, not a nuisance to be avoided (Ps. 127:3–4; cf. Matt. 19:14). Noah's own sons and grandchildren are a particular blessing since it is through one of them that the promised seed of the woman must come (Gen. 3:15). God also calls his representatives to get their hands dirty in the task of culture building rather than separating themselves in safe ghettos, away from the problems of everyday life.

However, whereas Adam and Eve had been granted uncomplicated dominion over the lower orders of creation (1:28) in a world in which there was not yet any fear, from now on the animals and birds will fear humans (9:2). These creatures will now learn the need to keep their distance from people, which is ironic and sad since they have so recently survived the flood thanks to contact with Noah and his family. However, that same fear will keep Noah and his descendants safer from potential attacks by wild animals. Creation looks forward longingly to the day when that distance will be closed and friendship between humanity and wild animals—even potentially dangerous ones—will finally be restored (cf. Isa. 11:6–9; Mark 1:13).

One reason for that fear among the animals and birds is the fact that from now on animals, birds, and fish will serve as food for humans (Gen. 9:3). Previously, it appears, humans (and perhaps animals) ate a primarily vegetarian diet (cf. 1:29–30), though it should be noted that those verses describe the pre-fall state of the world. Abel's offering (and indeed the provision of clothing for humanity; 3:21; 4:4) suggests that meat was not entirely off the menu prior to the flood. Nonetheless, here God's permission for man to eat a broad diet is made explicit (9:3).

One single restriction is applied to potential food sources: humans must not eat "flesh with its life, that is, [the] blood" (v. 4). It is striking that there is no reference here to clean and unclean animals; this distinction awaits the Mosaic covenant, although the principle that only certain animals may be sacrificed is already known to Noah (cf. 7:2; 8:20). Nor is it simply blood that is prohibited as food but "flesh with its life." This suggests that the symbolic role of blood as representing the vitality of the animal is significant; partaking of that fresh blood is thought of not simply as tasty or nutritious but explicitly as a way of

---
[149] ANET, 104.

absorbing that life-essence. The consumption of blood formed part of certain religious rituals in the ancient world, which is one reason the consumption of blood is utterly forbidden in the Pentateuch.[150] The blood, representing the life, belongs to God alone, since he gave it in the first place, and it is to be returned to God by pouring out the blood either on an altar or on the ground (cf. Lev. 1:5; Deut. 12:16). This principle lies behind accepting the blood of each sacrificial animal as representing its life.

If the life of animals is to be treated with respect by regarding their blood as requiring special treatment, how much more special is the blood of a human being? The shedding of human blood requires an accounting, whether by an animal or by another person (Gen. 9:5). In the case of domestic animals that causes a human death, they are to be put to death (cf. Ex. 21:28); it is plausible that wild animals that killed a person would also have been hunted down, although there is no explicit record of such. Ultimately, whether or not the animal is found and put to death, God himself is the judge who will call that animal to account.

The same principle is true in the case of human murder:[151] justice for the dead person requires a commensurate payment with the life of the guilty party. The chiastic structure of the sentence underlines the appropriateness of the judgment: "Whoever sheds the blood of man, by man shall his blood be shed" (Gen. 9:6). Murder is an assault on the image of God in man, and therefore a form of sacrilege, as well as being an assault on one's brother ("fellow man," 9:5, is in Hb. "his brother," recalling Cain's murder of Abel). It is a crime not merely against a fellow human being, or even against society, but against God, which means that God is a plaintiff in every murder case, demanding an accounting from the guilty party. Capital punishment, rightly administered,[152] is pro-life, inasmuch as it acknowledges the value of the life that has been taken. Given the explosion of violence immediately prior to the flood and the fact that humanity at its core has not been changed, these verses address a foundational element in a just society. The section is then rounded off with an inclusio that repeats the opening command: "Be fruitful and multiply," which is the opposite of murdering one's brother.

9:8–17 God previously established his covenant with Noah in Genesis 6:18 (cf. comment on 6:13–22), though few details were given at that point. The word "covenant" (Hb. *berit*) occurs seven times in 9:8–17, highlighting its centrality in this passage. God here reestablishes his covenant with Noah and his sons, as well as with the rest of creation, with explicit application for the future. This universal aspect of the covenant with Noah as being a covenant with all creation distinguishes it from subsequent biblical covenants made only "with you and your seed/offspring" (e.g., 17:7). Although different covenants focus on different

---

150 Sarna, *Genesis*, 60.
151 The OT law code distinguished clearly between murder and manslaughter. Murder required the death penalty, without the possibility of paying a ransom (Num. 35:31). Manslaughter, on the other hand, was punished by internal exile to one of the Levitical cities for the lifetime of the high priest (Num. 35:22–25).
152 It is appropriate to acknowledge that human court systems do not always administer the death penalty fairly, with wealthy murderers who can afford good lawyers sometimes avoiding it while poorer murderers remain liable.

aspects of life, they are all part of the single eternal covenant (*berit 'olam*; 9:16; cf. Heb. 13:20) between God and man.

Ancient Near Eastern covenants were always sovereignly decreed by the suzerain, and God's covenants are no exception: it is God's covenant, and he determines with whom he will enter covenant and the terms of that covenant. The human responsibility is simply to submit and accept those terms and conditions or suffer the consequences. In this case, unlike the Sinai covenant, there are no conditions imposed on humanity; God is solemnly and unilaterally binding himself never[153] to repeat the judgment of the flood and destroy the earth once more.

It is customary for biblical covenants to have signs attached to them; for example, the Abrahamic covenant has the sign of circumcision (Gen. 17:11). These signs serve as visible and tangible reminders to the parties of the agreement that has been made (cf. Rom. 4:11). In this case the sign is that the Lord has hung his bow (*qeshet*) in the sky as a symbol that it is no longer drawn and pointed toward humanity in judgment (Gen. 9:12–17). In a similar manner, in the Babylonian creation narrative, after the conflict between the gods, Marduk's bow was hung in the sky, although in that case as a constellation of stars rather than as a rainbow.[154] In Noah's case the rainbow becomes a perpetual symbol of peace that is all the more relevant because it occurs in the context of storm clouds that remind observers of the power of God's wrath (cf. Ezek. 1:28). It is not necessary to suppose that the rainbow was a new element in the world after the flood, just as circumcision was not a newly invented ritual when Abraham was instructed to use it as a sign, nor were Israelite sacrifices unknown to their neighbors; God frequently takes up existing elements of human cultures (placed there sovereignly by his own direction) and invests them with new, redemptive significance.[155] What is significant is that this is a sign that only God can put in place, unlike signs such as circumcision, baptism, or the Lord's Supper, highlighting the fact that it is God alone who is bound by this covenant.

The rainbow is thus not merely a comforting reminder to humanity of God's promise; it is a reminder to the Lord himself (Gen. 9:15). This is not because God could forget something. Rather, it represents God's commitment to act according to all that he has promised in the covenant. The need for such a memorial is a regular testimony to man that God would be perfectly justified in once again bringing comprehensive judgment upon the world, since human wickedness continues unchecked (8:21), but he tempers his judgment with mercy—for now. The day will come, of course, when he will consume the heavens and the earth in a mighty conflagration that will usher in the fullness of new creation (cf. 2 Pet. 3:7).

9:18–29 The text now shifts in focus from Noah to his sons, preparing the way for the table of nations in Genesis 10, which will define the relationships between the various nations of Israel's world. Shem, Ham, and Japheth have been named

---

[153] The combination *lo' kol* indicates a comprehensive negation, as in 3:1; cf. Currid, *Genesis 1:1–25:18*, 220.
[154] *ANET*, 69.
[155] Cf. Mathews, *Genesis 1–11:26*, 411.

as Noah's sons several times before (Gen. 5:32; 6:10; 7:13), but here they become individual actors in the story for the first time. They are described as "the sons of Noah who went forth from the ark" (9:18), which highlights their mutual experience of salvation and as the ones from whom the whole earth will be repopulated. Ham is also described as the father of Canaan, preparing for the curse that is to come upon the latter because of Ham's sin (v. 18; cf. v. 25). As the ancestor of the inhabitants of the land later promised to Abraham, Ham is of special interest to Moses' original audience. Often in biblical narratives a character's first actions are of pivotal importance for establishing his nature (e.g., Gen. 25:27), and this is certainly true of Canaan, whose origins are corrupt and cursed.

If Noah is a second Adam in being the father of all the living, he is like Adam in other ways as well, not all good. Like Adam, he works the soil (2:15; 9:20), sins (3:6; 9:21) and is ashamed of his nakedness (3:8; 9:21). This underscores God's remark in 8:21 regarding the unchanged evil intent of man's heart. The sin of both bears bitter fruit in the next generations, with Cain killing Abel (4:8) and Ham's son Canaan being condemned to slavery for his father's sin (9:27). This is the last notice of Noah's life, even though he lives for another 350 years (9:28), and it is a sad epitaph for a man who has walked with God for 600 years (7:6).

With the flood behind him, Noah begins to work the soil by planting a vineyard (9:20), just as God planted a garden in Eden (2:8). When he drinks of the wine he has produced, however, he becomes intoxicated and lies exposed in his tent (9:21). There is nothing to suggest that he is the first person ever to engage in viniculture, or that the results of his drinking could not have been predicted. His drunkenness is shameful enough, but it is compounded by his uncovering himself in his tent.

The focus of the narrative is not on Noah's sin, however, but on that of Ham, who sees the "nakedness of his father" and subsequently tells his brothers about it (v. 22). Attempts have been made to explain Ham's sin as some form of physical or sexual abuse of Noah, through the observation that in Leviticus 18:7 "to uncover the nakedness of your father" is a euphemism for sexual intercourse with the person's mother.[156] However, this euphemism is used only of heterosexual sins, especially incest, which is not in view here; the book of Genesis tends to use a different euphemism ("to know") for homosexual rape (Gen. 19:5). Moreover, the obscure phrase in 9:22 is immediately clarified by the following verse, in which Ham's brothers do the exact opposite of what Ham has done by covering up their father with a garment while deliberately "not seeing" his nakedness by walking backward (9:23). This suggests a more literal understanding of the nature of Ham's sin. It is enough that, instead of "covering over" his father's private shame, Ham chooses to publicize it further by announcing it to his brothers (cf. Prov. 20:19 for a warning about "uncovering" secrets). Shem and Japheth, on the other hand, honor their father (Ex. 20:12), even in his dishonorable state, restoring his modesty by covering his nakedness, just as God had done for Adam and Eve (Gen. 3:21).

---

[156] Wenham, *Genesis 1–15*, 200. The idea of some form of sexual abuse against Noah dates back to the rabbis; cf. Sarna, *Genesis*, 66.

When Noah awakes from his binge and discovers what has happened, he pronounces a blessing and curse upon his children in response to their actions—a blessing and curse that will have an impact not only on them but on their children and their descendants in a lasting way. Just as Noah's sons have been blessed because of Noah's faithfulness, so too Shem and Japheth's lineage will be blessed by their honoring of their father, while Ham's sons, especially Canaan, his youngest, will be cursed because of his parental disrespect. Ham is the youngest of Noah's sons, and often in Genesis the younger son is favored by God, but not in this case. This is not a blanket curse on all Ham's offspring (although it has sometimes been read tendentiously in that way); it is a specific curse on Canaan, the youngest son of Noah's youngest son. Because his father, Ham, failed to honor his own father, Noah, Canaan will receive the opposite of long life in the land (cf. Ex. 20:12): a life of servitude under the descendants of Shem and Japheth.[157] To modern readers a curse on someone who has not personally participated in a sin may seem unfair, but of course the same is true of blessings: God deals corporately with families, not simply individuals.[158] Moreover, God's curse falls not on an "innocent" victim but on one whose sins would have been well known to the original readers. This judgment is completed when the Israelites conquer the Promised Land in Joshua's days and has no further aspect yet to be fulfilled.

In contrast to the curse upon Canaan, the blessings upon Shem and Japheth are much more indirect. Indeed, the blessing on Shem is really a blessing of Shem's God, the Lord (Gen. 9:26), while Japheth's blessing is that as he increases[159] he should dwell in the tents of Shem, sharing fellowship with the brother upon whom the Lord's primary blessing lies (v. 27). This implies that God will be Shem's God in a unique way, such that Japheth will find blessing only in identifying with the line of his brother, an idea that will be developed further as the book of Genesis unfolds.

Indeed, the entire mininarrative has a longer perspective. God chooses for blessing whom he will, younger or older son, and no one can argue with his choices. Shem's and Japheth's behavior are identical, yet their blessings are different: God has chosen the line of Seth to be the line of promise, so the calling for the descendants of Japheth is to identify with the promised seed of the Sethite line. This is a promise that finds almost no fulfillment in the course of the OT, though it is anticipated in Isaiah 66:19–20. However, it is fulfilled richly in the NT, as the gospel comes to the Japhetite world of the Mediterranean in the book of Acts—and even to the descendants of Ham.[160] Yet by the same token God's election is not arbitrary. The judgment that is coming upon the Canaanites in the days of Joshua is related to their father's sin of disrespect, a sin that finds full flower in the Canaanite opposition to the descendants of the line of Shem (and Abraham). Those whom God has chosen for blessing come and place their hope in

---

157 "His brother" (Gen. 9:25) refers not to Ham's other sons but more broadly to his relatives.
158 Cf. Vos, *Biblical Theology*, 57.
159 "May he increase" (Hb. *yaft*) is a play on Japheth's own name (*yefet*).
160 Cf. Kidner, *Genesis*, 111.

the line of promise that God has provided, whereas those who are reprobate will never come to him—and so face a future of judgment and curse. It is not a case of the "innocent" descendants of Ham being denied the opportunity to repent and believe. There are no innocent descendants of Noah, and the sin of the inhabitants of Canaan is the primary reason for their subjugation and expulsion from the land (Gen. 15:16; 1 Kings 21:26).

The passage closes by completing the genealogy of the line of Seth, interrupted at the end of chapter 5 to include the flood narrative (Gen. 9:28–29). This reminds us that the issue of the two seeds is still with us even after the flood. Not all those who come from Noah will share his faith, and the distribution between believers and unbelievers is not a random distribution. God generally works by calling families, working for the most part through that structure. In this case the line of hope will descend through the line of Shem, whose name means "name" or "renown"; God is the one who gives this renown, not human exploits (6:4).

Response

The ugly reality of the continuing sin of humanity, highlighted in Genesis 8:21, casts its long shadow over the whole of this chapter. What should be a joyful recommissioning, in which humanity and animals alike are commanded to be fruitful and multiply and fill the earth (Gen. 9:1), is overshadowed by fear: the fear the animals now have of humans, and the fearful reality that humans will continue to kill their brothers, just as Cain killed Abel (9:6; cf. 4:8). The theme climaxes in Noah's drunkenness, which leads to Ham's sin toward his father and the curse that thereby descends on Ham's descendant, Canaan, and his offspring. Sin is an indelible stain on the human condition as a result of Adam's fall. Even though God singled out one man and his family for redemption, a man who alone in his generation walked with God in righteousness, nothing has fundamentally changed in the heart of man. What can prevent yet another destructive outpouring of God's judgment that this time might wipe out the entirety of the human race?

The answer is God's covenant, which in this chapter is signified by the rainbow, representing the light of God's favor that continues to shine through the deep storm clouds of his wrath (9:13). The sign is necessary because of the continuing sin of mankind that constantly cries out for judgment. Yet God commits himself to hang up his battle bow and shine his favor on Noah and (some of) his descendants through the line of Seth. God has not forgotten his promise to bruise the head of the serpent and return humanity to his side through the seed of the woman (3:15). Renewing his covenant with Noah is a renewal of that commitment.

However, though the covenant is renewed here with Noah, its foundation cannot be Noah's personal righteousness. Even though Noah was uniquely righteous in his own generation—one of only two people in the Bible who "walked with God" (6:9)—if the covenant rested on Noah's righteousness it would have been rapidly undermined by his fall into drunkenness. God alone can provide the righteous head whose obedience provides us with the perfect righteousness we need in order to stand forever in the sunlight of God's favor; he did so in the person of Jesus, to whom Noah was looking forward by faith ahead of time. At the cross of Christ the wrath of God and his favor met just as they did in the rainbow; the dark clouds of God's wrath were poured out on Jesus in our place so that we might live forever in the light of the Father's smile. Jesus' lifeblood was shed unjustly by men and yet became the means by which our lives are redeemed. Through his curse we receive blessing forever.

GENESIS 10

10 These are the generations of the sons of Noah, Shem, Ham, and Japheth. Sons were born to them after the flood.
² The sons of Japheth: Gomer, Magog, Madai, Javan, Tubal, Meshech, and Tiras. ³ The sons of Gomer: Ashkenaz, Riphath, and Togarmah. ⁴ The sons of Javan: Elishah, Tarshish, Kittim, and Dodanim. ⁵ From these the coastland peoples spread in their lands, each with his own language, by their clans, in their nations.
⁶ The sons of Ham: Cush, Egypt, Put, and Canaan. ⁷ The sons of Cush: Seba, Havilah, Sabtah, Raamah, and Sabteca. The sons of Raamah: Sheba and Dedan. ⁸ Cush fathered Nimrod; he was the first on earth to be a mighty man.¹ ⁹ He was a mighty hunter before the Lord. Therefore it is said, "Like Nimrod a mighty hunter before the Lord." ¹⁰ The beginning of his kingdom was Babel, Erech, Accad, and Calneh, in the land of Shinar. ¹¹ From that land he went into Assyria and built Nineveh, Rehoboth-Ir, Calah, and ¹² Resen between Nineveh and Calah; that is the great city. ¹³ Egypt fathered Ludim, Anamim, Lehabim, Naphtuhim, ¹⁴ Pathrusim, Casluhim (from whom² the Philistines came), and Caphtorim.
¹⁵ Canaan fathered Sidon his firstborn and Heth, ¹⁶ and the Jebusites, the Amorites, the Girgashites, ¹⁷ the Hivites, the Arkites, the Sinites, ¹⁸ the Arvadites, the Zemarites, and the Hamathites. Afterward the clans of the Canaanites dispersed. ¹⁹ And the territory of the Canaanites extended from Sidon in the direction of Gerar as far as Gaza, and in the direction of Sodom, Gomorrah, Admah, and Zeboiim, as far as Lasha. ²⁰ These are the sons of Ham, by their clans, their languages, their lands, and their nations.
²¹ To Shem also, the father of all the children of Eber, the elder brother of Japheth,³ children were born. ²² The sons of Shem: Elam, Asshur, Arpachshad, Lud, and Aram. ²³ The sons of Aram: Uz, Hul, Gether, and Mash. ²⁴ Arpachshad fathered Shelah; and Shelah fathered Eber. ²⁵ To Eber were born two sons: the name of the one was Peleg,⁴ for in his days the earth was divided, and his brother's name was Joktan. ²⁶ Joktan fathered Almodad, Sheleph, Hazarmaveth, Jerah, ²⁷ Hadoram, Uzal, Diklah, ²⁸ Obal, Abimael, Sheba, ²⁹ Ophir, Havilah, and Jobab; all these were the sons of Joktan. ³⁰ The territory in which they lived extended from Mesha in the

direction of Sephar to the hill country of the east. ³¹ These are the sons of Shem, by their clans, their languages, their lands, and their nations.

³² These are the clans of the sons of Noah, according to their genealogies, in their nations, and from these the nations spread abroad on the earth after the flood.

¹ Or *he began to be a mighty man on the earth* ² Or *from where* ³ Or *the brother of Japheth the elder* ⁴ *Peleg* means *division*

Section Overview

Genealogies are not most people's favorite part of reading the Bible. It is hard for us to make sense out of a list of names, most of which we know little or nothing about. Yet genealogies were important in the ancient world as a kind of road map indicating the connections between people. These connections could reach back through time, as is the case for linear genealogies such as the one in Genesis 5.[161] In these genealogies, though there may be some small details introduced about people along the way, the most important links in the chain are the first and the last, who are linked together firmly by descent. So in Genesis 5 the primary focus is on the link between Noah and Seth, highlighting the line through whom the promise would descend. Noah is the heir of that great promise, not just a random righteous person selected by God for salvation.

Segmented genealogies like the one in Genesis 10, on the other hand, serve to group and distinguish families horizontally (though there is often a vertical element as well). This is the kind of genealogy one uses to decide whom to invite to a family reunion. Generally, someone does not reach out to everyone in the world who happens to share his last name. Rather, such a person might go back a generation or two and then forward and sideways to invite all his cousins. The further back one goes, the larger the reunion, with more people being counted as family. At the same time, other individuals will be excluded from that particular definition of the family, being included in someone else's family instead.

In this way Genesis 10 locates Israel among the seventy[162] nations that are identified at this point in history. Other nations also descended from Shem are relatively close family to the descendants of Abraham (even though not Israelites themselves). Meanwhile, others are less close relatives, being descended from Japheth or Ham. With them Israel has less to do. This listing of the origins of nations reverberates elsewhere in the OT as history plays itself out, showing that God has planned out everything from the earliest days of his world.[163] It also identifies the entire human race as members of one family, despite their diversity. It is hard to date this table, though a careful analysis of which nations are absent and which are present suggests a date somewhere in the second millennium BC.[164]

---

[161] On the distinction between linear and segmented genealogies cf. Wilson, *Genealogy and History in the Biblical World*, 9.
[162] Excluding Nimrod, who is listed as an individual, not the father of a nation. Seventy is a number of completeness—like seven, only on a larger scale (cf. Gen. 46:27; Luke 10:1).
[163] As in Ezekiel 38, e.g., where Genesis 10 is clearly the source for a comprehensive list of enemies from all four points of the compass who will be gathered against the Lord's renewed people for one final battle.
[164] Daniel I. Block, "The Table of Nations," *ISBE*, 4:712.

Section Outline

V. The Family History of Noah's Sons (10:1–11:9)
   A. The Table of Nations (10:1–32)

Comment

10:1–5 This passage begins a new section according to the *toledot* formula: "These are the generations of . . ." (Gen. 10:1; cf. comment on 2:4–7). In this case the *toledot* outlines the family history of Noah's sons—that is, the various lines that come from Shem, Ham, and Japheth. Their descendants are all born after the flood (10:1), since there were only eight people on the ark: Noah, Shem, Ham, Japheth, and their respective wives (1 Pet. 3:20). The genealogy does not begin with Shem, even though he is the oldest (cf. Gen. 10:21); as the line of promise, his line is held back so that it can lead into the story of Abraham. Instead the genealogy starts with Japheth, the second son.[165] As a segmented genealogy, its purpose is to express relative kinship between nations and peoples and to define who is "not far from the kingdom of God" (the Shemite line; cf. Mark 12:34) in contrast to those who are more distant (the lines of Japheth and Ham). At the same time, there is no bar preventing anyone from coming as an individual and being added to God's kingdom, and Isaiah anticipates the day when both Japhethite and Hamite nations will come flocking to Israel's God (Isa. 19:21–23; 66:19–20).

The Japhethite family seems to have settled in a wide sweep from the Aegean Sea in the west to the area north of the Caspian Sea in the east, on the most distant horizon of Israelite vision. There is an awareness that many of these different groups have their own distinct languages, which anticipates the result of the Tower of Babel in Genesis 11.

Of the seven sons and seven grandsons of Japheth it is possible to identify many of these people groups from other ancient sources. Gomer (Gen. 10:2) represents the warlike *gimirrai*, who originated in the Crimea but were pushed southward across the Caucasus by the Scythians at the end of the eighth century BC.[166] Magog is similarly in "the uttermost parts of the north" in Ezekiel 38:6, which need not refer to anywhere further north than the nations surrounding it in Genesis 10. The Madai are more familiar to most Bible readers as the Medes (cf. Esther and Daniel). Javan represents the Ionian Greeks and later became a term more generally used for the inhabitants of Greece. Tubal and Meshech likely refer to the *Tabal* and *Mushku* peoples of central and eastern Anatolia, who appear in cuneiform texts from the first half of the first millennium BC,[167] while Tiras may perhaps be related to the Etruscans.[168]

---

[165] Even though the standard formula is "Shem, Ham, and Japheth," Ham is the youngest son according to Genesis 9:24.
[166] Edwin M. Yamauchi, *Foes from the Northern Frontier: Invading Hordes from the Russian Steppes* (Grand Rapids, MI: Baker, 1982), 51.
[167] Edwin M. Yamauchi, "Meshech, Tubal, and Company: A Review Article," *JETS* 19 (1976): 243–245.
[168] Wenham, *Genesis 1–15*, 217.

To match the seven sons of Japheth seven grandsons are also listed, from the lines of Gomer and Javan. Gomer's offspring are located in Asia Minor: Ashkenaz represents the Scythians, who lived between the Black Sea and the Caspian Sea; Togarmah is known in Assyrian as *Tilgarimmu*, located in Armenia;[169] while Riphath ("Diphath" in 1 Chron. 1:6 ESV mg.) is otherwise unknown. Meanwhile, Javan's offspring occupy coastal areas and islands of the Mediterranean: Cyprus ("Elishah" = Alashiya from Egyptian and cuneiform texts of the 2nd millennium; also "the Kittim" = inhabitants of Kition/Larnaca), Spain ("Tarshish" = Tartessus?), and Dardenia or Rhodes ("Dodim" or "Rodim"; 1 Chron. 1:7).[170]

These names are not to be thought of as an exhaustive survey of the people groups of the area; the text suggests that others—the "coastland peoples" (Gen. 10:5)—will also come from them. But the names and groupings demonstrate some real knowledge and understanding of the geography and history of the Mediterranean world.

10:6–20 After Japheth's sons come the sons of Noah's youngest son, Ham (v. 6). These are focused in a wide sweep to the south and west of the Mediterranean. Four sons are attributed to Ham: Cush (Upper Egypt), Egypt (more precisely Lower Egypt), Put (Libya), and Canaan, who was introduced in the previous chapter. Links between Egypt and the Canaanite city-states prior to Israel's conquest are well attested.[171] The identification of Canaan in both biblical and ancient sources fluctuates between a people and a geographical location.

Cush's genealogy goes two generations deep (seven descendants in all, encompassing a number of people groups known from the Arabian peninsula). The peoples who occupied places such as Seba and Sheba were very wealthy during biblical times due to their control of trade routes from Africa and further afield at a time when oceangoing ships were a very limited and unreliable form of transport.

Mizraim (Egypt) also has seven descendants, who become the focus in verses 13–14. The identities of most of these peoples is uncertain, though several have an Egyptian or North African connection. The Ludim are associated with Cush and Put in Jeremiah 46:9 and Ezekiel 30:5, while the Pathrusim are connected with Pathros ("Southland" in Egyptian and therefore another word for Upper Egypt). The Caphtorim (Akkadian *kaptaru*) originated in Crete but spread from there to colonize various coastal areas of the Mediterranean (Deut. 2:23), which explains their identification with the Philistines, or "Sea Peoples" (cf. Jer. 47:4; Amos 9:7).[172]

---

169 Stephen L. Cook, *Ezekiel 38–48* (New Haven, CT: Yale University Press, 2018), 75.
170 Hamilton, *Genesis 1–17*, 334.
171 Mathews, *Genesis 1–11:26*, 445.
172 The exact origin and history of the Philistines is complex and disputed. Generally they are associated with the "Sea Peoples" who migrated in the twelfth century BC to the coastal areas adjoining Israel, where they quickly became a significant problem for Israel from the time of the later Judges onward. On this view references to the Philistines in Genesis (cf. Gen. 21:32; 26:1) are often thought to be anachronisms. Yet it is possible that there were earlier migrations of people who called themselves *pilishtim*, from either Crete or Egypt, whose name was taken over by the later invaders. Genesis 10:14 attributes the origins of the Philistines not to the Caphtorim (unlike Amos and Jeremiah) but to the otherwise unknown Casluhim. Perhaps the two groups were related. There is much that remains unknown about this period of history.

Meanwhile, Canaan is attributed no fewer than eleven offspring (Gen. 10:15–19), highlighting their importance from an Israelite perspective. Sidon is attributed firstborn position (v. 15), with no mention of Tyre, which later becomes a more significant city, attesting to the antiquity of the listing. The Sidonians are later usually distinguished from Canaanites (e.g., Josh. 13:4), though their lands are adjoining. The Hittites (sometimes "sons of Heth"; Gen. 23:3 ESV mg.) are a smaller tribal group resident within Canaan, not the much larger Hittite empire of Asia Minor and northern Syria.[173] The Jebusites, Amorites, Girgashites, and Hivites, along with the Hethites, were all peoples living in the land at the time of Joshua's conquest, though this exact combination does not occur anywhere else (Josh. 3:10 is perhaps the closest). The Arkites, Sinites, Arvadites, Zemarites, and Hamathites (Gen. 10:17–18) do not appear in the conquest narrative, however, perhaps because these were coastal and border towns that remained outside Israelite control.

The importance of the land of Canaan to this genealogy is shown by a brief mention of its borders (v. 19). This description is not as detailed as the later borders defined in Numbers 34:2–12 or Ezekiel 47:15–20, simply comprising a brief delineation of the limits on the western side (from north to south, from Sidon to Gaza) and then on the eastern side (from south to north, from Sodom and Gomorrah to the unknown Lasha).[174] Some have suggested that these borders broadly match those of the Egyptian province that emerged following a treaty between the Egyptian Pharaoh Ramses II and the Hittite King Hattusilis III (c. 1280 BC).[175]

In the middle of the passage the focus shifts to Nimrod, who is assigned the parentage of many of Israel's later enemies in Mesopotamia, especially Assyria and Babylon (Gen. 10:10–12). It is not coincidental that the chief opponents of the line of promise are found among the descendants of Ham, the cursed youngest child of Noah. Nimrod is unusual in the entire list in that his importance is as an individual rather than as a people group, though he founds a number of key cities. He also uniquely receives a brief biographical sketch, describing characteristics that he is undoubtedly assumed to pass on to the cities that he founds.

Nimrod is described as a "mighty man" (Hb. *gibbor*; v. 8), that is, a warrior, and a "mighty hunter [*gibbor tsaid*] before the LORD" (v. 9). These two images immediately conjure up visions of the portrayals of Assyrian kings and gods in their monumental reliefs, such as those from Sennacherib's palace at Nineveh, now housed at the British Museum.[176] Both kings and gods are portrayed as hunting lions and bulls, as well as engaged in warfare, so Nimrod certainly epitomizes the later Assyrian

---

173 Andrew Steinmann, *Genesis*, TOTC (Downers Grove, IL: InterVarsity Press, 2019), 127.
174 Lasha is usually located in the Dead Sea area, not far from Sodom and Gomorrah; however, that leaves the border incomplete, covering only two sides of the territory, rather than four, as all the other border definitions do. That would be remedied if Lasha were located somewhere in the northeast of Canaan. However, despite attempts to emend Lasha to Laish, such a conclusion remains speculative.
175 Sarna, *Genesis*, 77.
176 Cf. Mary Katherine Y. H. Hom, "A Mighty Hunter before YHWH: Genesis 10:9 and the Moral-Theological Evaluation of Nimrod," *VT* 60 (2010): 68.

and Babylonian image of masculine power. Whether Nimrod can be identified with a known figure from Babylonian history, either human or divine,[177] is much more uncertain; his attributes were not restricted to any one individual but were widespread throughout that society. In this he resembles the "men of renown" in Genesis 6:4—hardly a positive comparison.

The description of Nimrod as a mighty hunter "before the LORD" (10:9) is particularly challenging to interpret. Some have taken it as positive affirmation of Nimrod, while others render it in the opposite direction—"a mighty hunter against the Lord," an interpretation influentially advanced by Augustine.[178] Although the etymology of Nimrod's name is not explored in the text, it could easily be read as "Let us rebel," which would fit with the links between his account, the subsequent narrative of the Tower of Babel (11:1–9), and the general role of Babylon throughout the biblical text.[179] Yet even his rebellion is "before the Lord," under his oversight and control rather than that of the gods of Assyria and Babylon.[180]

Nimrod's kingdom begins in the land of Shinar, a place associated invariably with idolatry and false worship in the Bible (cf. Isa. 11:11; Dan. 1:2), where he founds the cities of Babylon (Babel), Uruk (Erech), Akkad, and Calneh (Gen. 10:10); from there he moves on to found Nineveh, Rehoboth-Ir, Kalkhu (Calah), and Resen; the description "the great city" recalls the similar description of Nineveh (and its environs?) in Jonah 1:2. Nimrod is thus credited with establishing the heartland of the later Assyrian and Babylonian empires, places that will later be associated with infamy from an Israelite perspective. Indeed, the dark shadow of Mesopotamian aggression is already being felt in Canaan as early as Genesis 14, following the pattern that Nimrod first sets for those aggressors.

10:21–32 Lastly we come to the line of promise, the descendants of Shem. This is why his genealogy has been saved until last, even though he is the firstborn (Gen. 10:21). Shem is described as the father of all those descended from Eber (v. 21). There is an obvious connection between the name Eber (Hb. *'eber*) and the people group "the Hebrews" (*'ibrim*), the term outsiders typically used to identify Israelites (Gen. 14:13; 39:14; Jonah 1:9).[181] In Genesis 10, however, Eber is the father of many more descendants than simply Israelites, and the term "Hebrew" may originally have denoted a wider referent than merely the Israelites.

The word *'eber* can mean "region beyond," especially in terms of rivers (cf. Gen. 50:10; Num. 21:13); in Akkadian sources the land to the west of the Euphrates was called *'eber nari*, often with reference to Syria,[182] which plausibly explains the name. Attempts have often been made to connect the title "Hebrew" with the *Habiru*, a

---

177 *HALOT* suggests a possible connection with the Assyrian god Ninurtu or the king Tukulti-Ninurtu (1235–1138 BC), but any resemblance is very tentative. As Sarna (*Genesis*, 73) points out in a classic understatement, "It is not easy, however, to connect the name Nimrod with Tukulti-Ninurtu."
178 Augustine, *City of God*, 16.4.
179 Waltke, *Genesis*, 168–169.
180 Hom, "Mighty Hunter before YHWH," 66.
181 Von Rad, *Genesis*, 362.
182 Sarna, *Genesis*, 78.

wandering group of rebels and mercenaries who appear in various ancient Near Eastern sources throughout the second millennium BC, but these attempts have not been compelling.

Unlike the genealogies of Japheth and Ham, which are wide but no more than a couple of generations deep, the genealogy of Shem traces multiple generations, although (of necessity) incompletely. Shem's five sons are the foundation for the family, including well-known peoples such as the Elamites, the Assyrians, and the Arameans (Gen. 10:22). Later narratives indicate a particularly close relationship between Abraham's family and certain Arameans, even though they are not especially close in the genealogy (cf. Gen. 25:20; 28:5).[183]

Arpachshad is the son of Shem through whom the promise will descend, in spite of his curiously non-Hebrew sounding name (10:24).[184] The latter part of the name may be linked with the "Chaldeans" (*kasdim*), who occupied part of Babylon and came to dominate it in the days of Nabopolassar, father of Nebuchadnezzar. In the context of the genealogy, however, his role is simply to father Shelah, who fathers Eber (cf. above on "Hebrew"), who is himself the father of Peleg (v. 25). Unusually for a person forming a link in the chain of a linear genealogy, Peleg is given a biographical note that—like the earlier description of Nimrod—anticipates the Tower of Babel in 11:1–9: "In his days the earth was divided" (10:25).[185]

As the line of promise, Peleg's line will not be picked up until later, after the Tower of Babel narrative (Gen. 11:18). Instead the present genealogy focuses on the non-elect line, through Joktan. The descendants of Joktan, where they can be identified, belong to southwest Arabia,[186] an unexpected place to find Semitic connections. Ophir was famous for its gold (1 Kings 9:28), as was neighboring Havilah (Gen. 10:29; cf. 2:11). The extensive listing of sons, many representing unidentifiable places and people groups, highlights the importance of Joktan (and thus also Peleg) as the generation in which there is a decisive parting of the ways (10:25). These are Israel's "separated kinsmen," but the emphasis is more on "separated" than on "kinsmen."

This point is drilled home by the conclusion of this part of the genealogy in verse 32: "From these the nations spread abroad on the earth after the flood." The line of promise is extending down through the generations, even as mankind is fruitful and multiplies from a single family into a massive family of nations according to God's command (9:1). Yet as the example of Nimrod shows—soon to be reinforced by the narrative of the Tower of Babel—that expansion and spreading out may often be driven by a violent and rebellious spirit.

Response

The purpose of the table of nations is twofold. First, it identifies all the nations and ethnic groups on earth as being descended from Noah and his wife. In this

---

[183] Uz, a son of Aram (Gen. 10:23), presumably gives his name to the region where Job lives (Job 1:1).
[184] Sarna suggests a link with Hurrian names, which often begin with *Arip-* (*Genesis*, 78).
[185] There is a wordplay here on the similarly sounding "divided" (*niflega*) and Peleg (*peleg*).
[186] Waltke, *Genesis*, 183.

sense all human beings everywhere are brothers and sisters, part of the same family, all together made in the image of God, whether Jew or Greek, male or female, king or slave. This emphasis provides a profound basis to confront the xenophobia, sexism, and class distinctions that were rife in ancient times, as they are in our own.

Yet on top of that fundamental unity is a fundamental distinction that divine election brings. Only one of Noah's sons is the bearer of the line of promise: Shem. And only one family from Shem will continue that line until it finds its immediate focus in Abraham (11:26). That divine election is preserved precisely in the distinction of Abraham and his offspring from all other families on earth, which is why genealogies connecting God's people to their ancestral families subsequently become so important to the Israelite community (cf. Josh. 22:14; 1 Chronicles 1–9; Ezra 10:16). The other nations will find blessing only through submitting themselves to Abraham and his seed (Gen. 12:1–3; Acts 3:25).

Ultimately it is in Christ that "there is neither Jew nor Greek, there is neither slave nor free, there is no male and female, for you are all one in Christ Jesus" (Gal. 3:28). Along with kosher food, the need for genealogies that identify a kosher ethnicity have been done away with, for Abraham's descendants are those who share his faith in Christ, not simply those who come from him physically (Rom. 4:16).

This fundamental division in humanity—ultimately, into those who have faith in Christ and those who do not—is alluded to in the reference to the division in the time of Peleg (Gen. 10:25), a division that comes to the fore in the Tower of Babel narrative that follows (11:1–9). There the city founded by Nimrod demonstrates its penchant for false worship. Babel's worship seeks to create an artificial unity based on human religiosity without regard to the true God, a worship that elevates man and seeks to make a name for itself, rather than humbly seeking God and glorifying his name. That quest for blessing by that path is inevitably fruitless, since only the true God has the power to bless his people.

GENESIS 11:1–9

11 Now the whole earth had one language and the same words. ² And as people migrated from the east, they found a plain in the land of Shinar and settled there. ³ And they said to one another, "Come, let us make bricks, and burn them thoroughly." And they had brick for stone, and bitumen for mortar. ⁴ Then they said, "Come, let us build ourselves a city and a tower with its top in the heavens, and let us make a name for ourselves, lest we be dispersed over the face of the whole earth." ⁵ And the LORD came down to see the city and the tower, which the children of man

had built. ⁶ And the Lord said, "Behold, they are one people, and they have all one language, and this is only the beginning of what they will do. And nothing that they propose to do will now be impossible for them. ⁷ Come, let us go down and there confuse their language, so that they may not understand one another's speech." ⁸ So the Lord dispersed them from there over the face of all the earth, and they left off building the city. ⁹ Therefore its name was called Babel, because there the Lord confused¹ the language of all the earth. And from there the Lord dispersed them over the face of all the earth.

¹ *Babel* sounds like the Hebrew for *confused*

Section Overview

The story of the Tower of Babel[187] is familiar from children's story Bibles, but it often comes without context. This is another part of the story of the city founded by Nimrod, famous for his hunting prowess, a man whose very name suggests "rebellion" against God (Hb. *marad*; Gen. 10:8–10). The Tower of Babylon is also the culminating episode in the downward spiral that is Genesis 4–11, in which humanity receives the ultimate judgment. The flood of Noah's day may have affected everyone alive at that moment, but it did not have a lasting impact upon subsequent humanity, whereas the judgment upon Babylon, which results in the confusion of human languages, continues to plague us until today. As in Noah's generation, it is not the sin of a single individual that is the problem but rather a sin involving "the whole earth" (five times in these verses: 11:1, 4, 8, 9 [2x]).

Section Outline

V. The Family History of Noah's Sons (10:1–11:9) . . .

  B. The Tower of Babylon (11:1–9)

Comment

11:1–4 The narrative does not begin by identifying the precise location of these events—that information is held back to the end of the story. Nor is a precise date given. Rather, as in Genesis 6:1, a general circumstance forms the introduction: the earth has a single language and vocabulary ("the same words"; Gen. 11:1), and indeed at this point humans are still traveling together as a single group.

As they journey, humanity moves eastward,[188] which is not a positive direction of travel in Genesis. The garden of Eden itself is "in the east" (2:8). Yet when the man and woman are driven from the presence of the Lord, they settle in a land on

---

[187] "Babel" is simply the Hebrew name for Babylon, and there is no obvious reason, apart from tradition, to use a different identifier in our English translations in Genesis 10:10 and in 11:9 than we do elsewhere in our Bibles. The LXX translates it as "Babylon" in 10:10 and "Confusion" in 11:9, while the Vulgate has "Babylon" in 10:10 and "Babel" in 11:9, perhaps also to try to bring out the wordplay in the Hebrew. However, the wordplay is lost on English readers, and the result has been to lose the connection between Genesis 11 and Babylon, which would have been immediately obvious to Hebrew readers.

[188] The Hebrew *miqqedem*, here rendered "from the east," can also mean "in the east" (Gen. 2:8) or "on the east" (12:8). Genesis 13:11 is a particularly close parallel, where Lot journeys eastward from the Promised Land (using the same verb, *nasaʿ*).

the east side of the garden (3:24). When Cain is sent to wander, he settles in the land of Nod, a land "east of Eden" (4:16). Similarly, when Lot separates from Abraham in chapter 13 and follows his eyes into a land "like the garden of the LORD," the place where he heads is "east" (Hb. *miqqedem*) from the Promised Land (13:11). As John Sailhamer puts it, "In the Genesis narratives, when people go 'east' they leave the land of blessing (Eden and the Promised Land) and go to a land where their greatest hopes will turn to ruin (Babylon and Sodom)."[189]

Moreover, the wanderers end up settling on a plain (*biqʿah*) in Shinar, or Babylonia (Gen. 11:2; cf. Dan. 1:2). It is not coincidental that Nebuchadnezzar will later erect his massive golden statue on a similar plain (*biqʿah*) in the province of Babylon—the flat land of Babylonia is the archetypal home of idolatry (Zech. 5:5–11), the antithesis of the high mountains where the Lord is to be worshiped (cf. Ezek. 40:2).[190] Mountains in the Bible, as elsewhere in the ancient Near East, symbolize God's connection with man,[191] which is precisely the rationale driving the building of the Babylonian tower.

There in Shinar mankind works together[192] to harness the latest technological advancements in material science (bricks and pitch) and build himself a city and accompanying tower. The combination of moving eastward and building a city, alongside a fascination with technology, aligns these people with the history of Cain's line, not Seth's (Gen. 4:16–22).[193] The communal building of a city is very unusual in the ancient Near East, where the founding of cities and the building of sanctuaries is usually attributed to kings or other powerful individuals. Moreover, in general deities would send instructions to the king to build them a sanctuary, specifying the materials as well as the location. In the case of the Lord's temple in Jerusalem it is to be made out of naturally occurring (or more precisely God-made) materials such as stone and wood, rather than the products of human hands, such as bricks or bitumen (1 Kings 6:7, 18).[194] It is therefore striking that the inhabitants of Babel feel bold enough to build their own access point to heaven without prior authorization, constructed out of the best bricks they could manufacture (Gen. 11:3).

The clue to the builders' intentions lies in the name they give to their city: *Bab-ilu*, which means "The gate of the gods." They are also open about their purpose for building it, which is to make a name for themselves and not be scattered throughout the earth (v. 4), in contrast to what God had commanded in his earlier blessing (9:1). To achieve these goals they build not only a city but also a "tower," or ziggurat—a stepped pyramid functioning as an artifi-

---

189 Sailhamer, *Pentateuch as Narrative*, 134.
190 Compare Isaiah's anticipation of the eschatological exaltation of the temple mount in Jerusalem to become the highest of the mountains, from where *torah* would flow to all nations (Isa. 2:2–4). This contrasts with the "valley" or "plain" (Hb. *biqaʿh*) of the exiles in Ezekiel 37:1, where the prophet sees the ground covered with the skeletal remains of God's people.
191 Richard J. Clifford, *The Cosmic Mountain in Canaan and the Old Testament*, HSM 4 (Cambridge, MA: Harvard University Press, 1972).
192 This is the first use in Genesis of the idiom "each with his neighbor," stressing the communal nature of this project.
193 Cf. Waltke, *Genesis*, 177.
194 Wenham, *Genesis 1–15*, 239.

cial mountain.[195] Since they live in a flat area, there are no naturally occurring mountaintops on which to worship, and so, as with the brick and pitch, they decide to create their own.

What the Babylonians are doing is constructing a counterfeit Eden, the place where God visited with man in the garden. Babylonian technology attempts to imitate Eden by building the tower as a man-made mountain "with its top the heavens" (11:4). It could also be thought of as a convenient staircase for the gods to come down and visit the earth (cf. 28:17). The Babylonians believe that their "gate of God" could bypass the cherubim and the flaming sword preventing humanity's return to the garden (3:24).

This city with its tower is intended to serve as a center for their society. But it is striking what is *not* said about the builders of Babel: there is no mention of calling on the name of the Lord, as the Sethites did (4:26). There is no attempt to offer up acceptable sacrifices, as Abel did (4:4). The builders of Babylon do not want to be dependent upon God. Rather, they want to return to Eden through their own efforts and technological innovations, bypassing God's route.

11:5–9 If the goal of the builders of Babel is to make their own way back to God, they fail miserably. They plan a tower so big that it will reach heaven—but the result is so small that God must come down to see it (v. 5).[196] They vastly overestimate their own resources and vastly underestimate the scale of the task they have set for themselves. The builders of Babel said, "Come, let us make bricks … come, let us build" (vv. 3–4), but God's "Come" is the decisive word. God simply says "Come, let us[197] go down and there confuse their language" (v. 7), and it happens. Just as God had once said, "Let us make man in our image" (1:26), and out of the dust sprang Adam, so also here God simply speaks the word and judgment falls.

God is not threatened or troubled by these human attempts to storm his residence; he is more amused at the impertinence of such a foolish enterprise (cf. Ps. 2:4). There is more than a hint of sarcasm in God's "Nothing that they propose to do will now be impossible for them" (Gen. 11:6), since they have clearly failed to achieve their more limited goals. They are, after all, merely *bene-ha'adam*, the children of Adam (v. 5), mortal ones, in contrast to the all-powerful deity.[198] Man may propose, but ultimately only God disposes—and here he will dispose of even a potential threat by scattering man and dividing his languages.

The centrality of God in the passage is highlighted by its chiastic structure, which focuses on verse 5 as the key turning point in the passage:

---

195 John Walton, *Genesis*, NIVAC (Grand Rapids, MI: Zondervan, 2001), 372–374.
196 Wenham, *Genesis 1–15*, xlviii–xlix.
197 As in Genesis 1:26, the plural here could be understood as a plural of self-deliberation, even if it also contains a hint of the triune nature of God that will be fully revealed later.
198 The term *ben-'adam* (lit., "son of man") is often viewed exclusively through the lens of its use in Daniel 7:13, where one "like a son of man" comes riding on the clouds in glory. However, the most common use of the term is in Ezekiel, where it highlights the prophet's weakness in comparison to the glory of God. As a mere human, he could not even stand up in God's presence without the empowering work of the Spirit (cf. Ezek. 2:1–2). It is this dual usage—as a weak human and yet also an exalted godlike being—that makes it such a perfect title for Jesus to adopt for himself on his earthly mission of humiliation and exaltation.

(A) "the whole world had one language" (v. 1)
  (B) "there" (v. 2)
    (C) "each other" (v. 3)
      (D) "come, let us make bricks" (v. 3)
        (E) "come, let us build ourselves" (v. 4)
          (F) "a city, with a tower" (v. 4)
            (G) "the Lord came down" (v. 5)
          (F') "the city and the tower" (v. 5)
        (E') "that the men were building" (v. 5)
      (D') "come, let us ... confuse" (v. 7)
    (C') "each other" (v. 7)
  (B') "from there" (v. 8)
(A') "the language of the whole world" (v. 9)[199]

When God comes down to investigate and to judge, everything changes. The builders of Babel built their city "lest [they] be dispersed" (v. 4); God scatters them anyway (v. 8). They sought to make a name for themselves, finding security and significance through the work of their hands (v. 4); God makes their name a laughingstock. He sees to it that they will be remembered down through history not for what they achieve but for what they fail to do. Finally, what they seek to build is what Babel means: the gate of God. What they actually built is what Babel sounds like: *balal*, which literally means "confusion" or, as we might render it in English, "Blah, blah, blah." Finally, we should not miss the polemic against Babylonian ideology here: the Babylonians proclaimed that their city was as old as the earth itself, having been established by the gods and then rebuilt after their flood.[200] The biblical text, however, affirms Babylon as a relatively latecomer to the world, established by mere mortals (*bene-ha'adam*; 11:5),[201] who fail utterly in their designs.

Response

This narrative wraps up Genesis' account of prehistory: sin has reached its widest limit with a united attempt on mankind's part to reenter God's presence by storm, to establish the glory of man through ingenious use of technology. The attempt to gain fame and a lasting center for human society that define its relationship with God on its own terms not only fails but is woefully inadequate. Man's "massive" tower is so small that God must come down even to see it, and man's attempt to entrench himself ends with his being not only scattered physically but divided in his speech, so that humanity can never again work together on such an ambitious project, a judgment whose bitter fruits reach down to the present day. United humanity gave its best effort to finding its own way back to God but failed. What hope is there now for a divided world desperately seeking God in all the wrong

---
199 Mathews, *Genesis 1–11:26*, 468.
200 ANET, 60.
201 Allen P. Ross, *Creation and Blessing: A Guide to the Study and Exposition of Genesis* (Grand Rapids, MI: Baker, 1997), 246.

ways and places? Why would any individual think that he could now reach God through his own insight and wisdom? If there is to be hope for a new relationship between God and Noah's offspring, it will come not through human initiative's stretching upward but by God's coming down to meet us where we are.

This hope of a God-given pathway of salvation is the unfolding message of the rest of the Scriptures. It begins in Genesis 12, with God's coming down and calling Abram—who originally is living not very far from Babylon—and promising to give him a great name and make him a great nation, through whom blessing will come to all the scattered nations of the earth (Gen. 12:1–3). God's answer to a scattered and divided world is to raise up a united people, a worshiping community of nations (Hb. *qehal 'ammim*; 28:3), bound together in their covenant commitment to God and their mutual calling to be a blessing to the world.

The staircase to heaven that God shows Jacob at Bethel (Gen. 28:12) is his answer to the confusion and chaos of Babel, a new way of access to God that finds its fulfillment in Christ (John 1:51). In Christ God will reveal himself to men and women from many nations, giving them new life in him and calling them into his kingdom. The day of Pentecost marks the beginning of this work of undoing the effects of Babel, as people from all over the diaspora each hear the gospel in their own tongue (Acts 2:7–11). The rest of the book of Acts maps out the spread of the gospel to the "end of the earth" (Acts 1:8). But the ultimate fulfillment of the promise is found in the multitude from every tribe and language and people and nation who together will serve God forever in a renewed and restored earth (Rev. 5:9, 10), while Babylon will be cast down and destroyed forever (Rev. 18:2–3; 21–22).

GENESIS 11:10–32

¹⁰ These are the generations of Shem. When Shem was 100 years old, he fathered Arpachshad two years after the flood. ¹¹ And Shem lived after he fathered Arpachshad 500 years and had other sons and daughters.

¹² When Arpachshad had lived 35 years, he fathered Shelah. ¹³ And Arpachshad lived after he fathered Shelah 403 years and had other sons and daughters.

¹⁴ When Shelah had lived 30 years, he fathered Eber. ¹⁵ And Shelah lived after he fathered Eber 403 years and had other sons and daughters.

¹⁶ When Eber had lived 34 years, he fathered Peleg. ¹⁷ And Eber lived after he fathered Peleg 430 years and had other sons and daughters.

¹⁸ When Peleg had lived 30 years, he fathered Reu. ¹⁹ And Peleg lived after he fathered Reu 209 years and had other sons and daughters.

²⁰ When Reu had lived 32 years, he fathered Serug. ²¹ And Reu lived after he fathered Serug 207 years and had other sons and daughters.

²²When Serug had lived 30 years, he fathered Nahor. ²³And Serug lived after he fathered Nahor 200 years and had other sons and daughters. ²⁴When Nahor had lived 29 years, he fathered Terah. ²⁵And Nahor lived after he fathered Terah 119 years and had other sons and daughters. ²⁶When Terah had lived 70 years, he fathered Abram, Nahor, and Haran.

²⁷Now these are the generations of Terah. Terah fathered Abram, Nahor, and Haran; and Haran fathered Lot. ²⁸Haran died in the presence of his father Terah in the land of his kindred, in Ur of the Chaldeans. ²⁹And Abram and Nahor took wives. The name of Abram's wife was Sarai, and the name of Nahor's wife, Milcah, the daughter of Haran the father of Milcah and Iscah. ³⁰Now Sarai was barren; she had no child.

³¹Terah took Abram his son and Lot the son of Haran, his grandson, and Sarai his daughter-in-law, his son Abram's wife, and they went forth together from Ur of the Chaldeans to go into the land of Canaan, but when they came to Haran, they settled there. ³²The days of Terah were 205 years, and Terah died in Haran.

Section Overview

The genealogy of Genesis 10 was a segmented genealogy, designed to explore and express kinship within wider families; in contrast, the genealogy of Genesis 11:10–26 is a linear genealogy, like that of Genesis 5, designed to express connection between its starting and ending points. The starting point is Shem, the son of Noah who has already been identified as bearing the line of blessing (9:26–27); the end point is Abram, who will shortly receive the promise of land and offspring, along with bearing blessing for all nations (12:1–3).

These linear genealogies, when taken together, connect the work of creation in the persons of Adam and Eve to the historical context of Israel's ancestors, communicating a message about the fundamentally historical nature of reality. The events we experience are not an endless cycle, in which the same things happen over and over without resolution, as the ancient Stoics held—even though it may sometimes feel as though that were the case (Eccles. 1:5–10). Rather, history is an unfolding story, with a beginning, a middle, and an end. These events are connected, for history is itself nothing other than the outworking of God's plan to fulfill his promise to redeem a people for himself. Indeed, the didactic nature of stories, with all their literary artistry, rests fundamentally on their rootedness in history and in God's sovereignty as the divine storyteller.[202]

The section divides into two parts: a ten-generation genealogy from Shem to Abraham (Gen. 11:10–26) and the background to Abram and Sarai's story (vv. 27–32). The ten-generation pattern matches that in Genesis 5, where the ten generations link Seth and Noah; here they connect Shem with Abram. Meanwhile, the second section has only eight names, including the otherwise unknown Iscah, leaving the reader anticipating the ninth and tenth names, Ishmael and Isaac.[203]

---

[202] On the relationship of literary artistry, history, and ideology (theological message) cf. Sternberg, *Poetics of Biblical Narrative*, 41–48.
[203] Sailhamer, *Pentateuch as Narrative*, 137.

But, since Sarai is barren, a potential crisis is brewing: What will happen to the line of promise if the wife is unable to have children (v. 30)? The answer to that question will drive much of the next section of Genesis.

Section Outline
  VI. The Family History of Shem (11:10–26)
  VII. The Family History of Terah (11:27–25:11)
     A. Introducing Abram and Sarai (11:27–32)

Comment

11:10–26 The genealogy of Seth is introduced with the *toledot* formula, the major structuring device in Genesis (cf. comment on 2:4–7), which marks it out as important and distinct from what precedes it. Its linear form is quite different in genre from the segmented genealogies of Japheth and Ham (cf. Genesis 10). The interest in Japheth and Ham lies purely in identifying the connections and distinctions between the nations that come from them and hardly extends more than two or three generations deep. Meanwhile, the interest in Shem's offspring is linear, listing just one descendant in each generation but covering at least ten generations.[204] The resemblance to chapter 5 is heightened by the text's mentioning the patriarch's age at the birth of his first child, how long he lived after his first child, and the fact that he subsequently had other sons and daughters. In both genealogies (and unlike ch. 10), those other sons and daughters are not named in order to avoid any distraction from the single-minded focus on the line of promise. Missing are any expository notes about the life of the patriarch, such as the comments on Enoch (5:22–24), as well as the ubiquitous conclusion "And he died," preparing the reader for the more positive turn in the narrative. The lifespans of the patriarchs are also notably shorter than those before the flood.

With the tenth generation, that of Abram, the genealogy breaks the usual pattern in order to highlight the significance of this generation. Just as Noah had three named sons, one of whom was chosen for blessing, so too Abram's father, Terah, has three named sons: Abram, Nahor, and Haran (11:26). In Terah's case the announcement of the length of his life after the birth of his first child is delayed until the final verse of the chapter, verse 32. In addition his death is recorded, as with the patriarchs in Genesis 5, and his place of death is noted as being in Haran. This serves to bind this genealogy to the genealogy of chapter 5 as a coherent and consecutive connection between Seth, the replacement "seed" (4:25), and Abram, as well as with the events that follow as God calls Abram to leave his homeland and go to the land of Canaan (12:1–3). Joshua 24:2 identifies Terah explicitly as a worshiper of other gods, so it is not surprising that several members of his family either bear names or are associated with places connected with the worship of the moon.[205]

---

[204] Such linear genealogies are sometimes abbreviated, with one or more generations passed over in silence. Their omission is not important, provided the other links in the chain are still in place.
[205] Sarna, *Genesis*, 85.

11:27–32 After a relatively short section on the *toledot* (family history) of Shem, a new *toledot* formula (cf. comment on 2:4–7) introduces the family history of Terah. This is the sixth of eleven *toledot* formulae in the book of Genesis, highlighting the central role of Abraham in the storyline. As is commonly the case, this *toledot* focuses on the next generation after the person named (Terah): the story of Abram, Nahor, and Haran (11:27), though primarily Abram. As earlier in Genesis, the author deals quickly with the non-elect lines before moving on to focus on the elect line. Haran's only role in the narrative is to have a son,[206] Lot (v. 27), who will feature significantly in the chapters that follow, after which Haran dies early and is buried in the ancestral home, Ur of the Chaldeans. Haran's death leaves Lot free to travel with his uncle Abram.

The location of Ur and its relationship to the Chaldeans have prompted much discussion. At least two locations for Ur have been proposed: a location in southern Mesopotamia identified with the well-known city of Uru[207] and an unknown northern location, perhaps named after the southern city and closer to Haran. The southern city of Uru was of great importance during the time of Abram, but the Chaldeans did not become a recognized force in Babylonian history until much later, during the reign of Ashurnasirpal II or III (883–859 BC).[208] It is possible, if the southern location is preferred, that calling Ur "of the Chaldeans" is a later addition to make explicit the connection between Abraham's origins and subsequent Israelite history: both left southern Mesopotamia in response to God's call to (re)inhabit the land of Canaan.[209] However, the first mention of the Chaldeans in the cuneiform texts refers to them as coming from elsewhere, which presupposes that they existed prior to that date in a different location, perhaps for a long time.[210] It is possible that they were present at an earlier time in the region to the south of Babylon or that their existence was further north, where they also had a city called Ur.[211] There is not enough evidence to be certain of the exact geographical location of Ur at this time, but the fact that the text explicitly links it with the Chaldeans (also in 15:7; Neh. 9:7) should not be dismissed too hastily.

Both Abram and Nahor marry. In Nahor's case it is explicit that he marries his niece, his brother Haran's daughter, but Sarai's origins are left unclear for now, to allow for a later revelation that Sarai is Abram's half-sister (Gen. 20:12). We are also told that Sarai experiences the ultimate tragedy in the ancient (and much of the modern) world: she is barren (11:30). The point is then repeated for emphasis: she has no child. This is an aspect of the curse upon the woman in Genesis 3:16,

---

206 The fact that the Hiphil of *yalad* is used here rather than the Qal is sometimes used to divide this material up according to its literary sources, with J using the Qal and P the Hiphil; cf. J. A. Emerton, "The Source Analysis of Gen XI 27–32," *VT* 42 (1992): 43. This analysis misses the fact that linear genealogies (e.g., Genesis 5; Ruth 4) generally use the Hiphil, while segmented or compound genealogies prefer the Qal (e.g., Genesis 10; 22:20–24). So here, with the focus on the father-son relationship, the Hiphil is to be expected.
207 E.g., Emerton, "Source Analysis of Gen XI 27–32," 40.
208 William D. Barrick, "'Ur of The Chaldeans' (Gen 11:28–31): A Model for Dealing with Difficult Texts," *The Master's Seminary Journal* 20 (2009): 15.
209 John H. Sailhamer, *Genesis*, in *The Expositor's Bible Commentary*, 12 vols., ed. Frank E. Gaebelein (Grand Rapids, MI: Zondervan, 1990): 2:110.
210 Note the evidence from ancient historians adduced in Robert Dick Wilson, *Studies in the Book of Daniel* (1917–1918; repr., Grand Rapids, MI: Baker, 1927), 1.329–334.
211 Cf. A. R. Millard, "Where was Abraham's Ur? The Case for the Babylonian City," *BAR* 27 (2001): 52–57.

where judgment is rendered upon the whole process of childbirth; barrenness could be considered grounds for divorce in the ancient world.[212] Yet in the Bible God chooses to use barrenness as a training ground for faith for many women whom he will use in a special way: alongside Sarai, other barren women for whom God provides children include Rebekah (25:21), Rachel (29:31), Samson's mother (Judg. 13:2), Hannah (1 Sam. 1:2), and Elizabeth (Luke 1:7).

Prior to God's speaking to Abram about his future, Abram has already begun to move toward Canaan: his father, Terah, initiates the journey, along with Abram and Sarai and Lot, Abram's nephew (Gen. 11:31). No reason is given as to what prompts this desire to leave one of the biggest and most advanced population centers of the ancient world, Ur, and go to a backwater territory like Canaan, though this is a period of history in which many people are migrating for a variety of reasons. The Elamites will destroy Ur around 1950 BC, so that may perhaps have something to do with it, or it could simply have to do with more general issues of overpopulation or a poor economy.

However, Terah does not complete the journey to Canaan. Instead, when the family comes to Haran[213] in northern Mesopotamia, a journey of about 550 miles [900 km] from Ur, it halts and settles down there (v. 31). Nevertheless, the idea of migration has been planted in Abram's mind: God is preparing him for the challenging call that he will shortly receive, beginning the process of separating him from his ties to his family of origin and his native land. Ultimately it is not Terah but the Lord who brings Abram out of Ur to bring him to Canaan (15:7). We are not told when Nahor moves from Ur to the area around Haran, but, since he is settled there in 24:10, he may also have traveled there with his father.

Here ends the story of Terah, and the stage is set to move from prehistory into history with the decisive event that changes the direction of the entire story: the calling of Abram. Terah belongs to the previous epoch, and so the end of his story returns to the classic genealogical style of Genesis 5, recording the length of his days and the fact that he dies short of the land that will be promised to Abram and, as far as we know, with little or no knowledge of the true and living God (cf. Josh. 24:2). His destiny is to be "not far" from the kingdom of God (Mark 12:34); the Lord will later describe himself as the "God of Abraham, Isaac, and Jacob" but never as the "God of Terah."

Response

We often pass over the prequel to Abram's story in our hurry to get to God's promise of blessing in the beginning of Genesis 12. However, the literary marker at 11:27, "These are the generations of Terah," shows that this is where the story of Abram properly begins. God's dealings with Abram do not begin with him as a seventy-five-year-old about to set out on a journey to Canaan. By bringing Abram's

---

[212] Cf. Code of Hammurabi, law 138 (*ANET*, 172).
[213] In English the name of Terah's son and the name of the Mesopotamian city are identical, but they have a different first letter in Hebrew: the son is *haran* while the city is *kharan*.

father—who, as far as we know, remains an idol worshiper his whole life—out of Ur and up to Haran, God is preparing Abram for a much more important move yet to come, planting in Abram's mind the idea of going to Canaan. Through this experience of moving once from home and family in Ur God is preparing him so that, when the call comes, he is ready.

Of course, Terah is not picked at random, either. The genealogy of Genesis 11:10–26 shows us that Terah comes from the line of Shem, the son of Noah, and that Abram is the tenth descendant of Noah, who was the tenth descendant of Seth. Through Abram a new deliverance will be set in motion, with far greater impact even than Noah's ark, not merely preserving mankind alive but ultimately providing them with a savior. The "name" (Hb. *shem*) that the builders of Babel thought to make for themselves is already present in the divinely chosen genealogy.

Abram is born and grows up in a hotbed of idolatry in Ur, and his family is not immune from its temptations. In Joshua 24:2 we read, "Long ago, your fathers lived beyond the Euphrates, Terah, the father of Abraham and of Nahor; and they served other gods." But God will not give up on rebellious humanity. With Abram the time comes for the next phase in the history of redemption. Although Abram may be unaware of the ways in which God has prepared him for his task, everything is ready.

Sarai is also being prepared in the traditional school of hard knocks for women: barrenness. Not to be able to have children in a society in which a woman's value is measured by her fertility is a bitter blow indeed. Sarai likely sheds many bitter tears over her inability to bear children. But, paradoxically, her inability in this area is a crucial part of God's preparation of her for her role in his plan. In order for her to be the mother of the child of promise it is necessary for her to be unable to bear children *without* the direct intervention of God.

God is also at work in our lives, preparing us for the tasks he has prepared for us. As was the case for Abram and Sarai, that process of preparation may be incomprehensible to us, and also very painful, yet God knows exactly how to use trials and dislocations to accomplish good fruit in our lives for him (cf. James 1:2–4). Our calling may be much more modest than Abram and Sarai's, but God has a purpose for each one of us and for every difficulty and loss we experience.

GENESIS 12:1–9

12 Now the Lord said[1] to Abram, "Go from your country[2] and your kindred and your father's house to the land that I will show you. ²And I will make of you a great nation, and I will bless you and make your name great, so that you will be a blessing. ³I will bless those who bless you, and him who dishonors you I will curse, and in you all the families of the earth shall be blessed."[3]

⁴So Abram went, as the Lord had told him, and Lot went with him. Abram was seventy-five years old when he departed from Haran. ⁵And Abram took Sarai his wife, and Lot his brother's son, and all their possessions that they had gathered, and the people that they had acquired in Haran, and they set out to go to the land of Canaan. When they came to the land of Canaan, ⁶Abram passed through the land to the place at Shechem, to the oak[4] of Moreh. At that time the Canaanites were in the land. ⁷Then the Lord appeared to Abram and said, "To your offspring I will give this land." So he built there an altar to the Lord, who had appeared to him. ⁸From there he moved to the hill country on the east of Bethel and pitched his tent, with Bethel on the west and Ai on the east. And there he built an altar to the Lord and called upon the name of the Lord. ⁹And Abram journeyed on, still going toward the Negeb.

[1] Or *had said* [2] Or *land* [3] Or *by you all the families of the earth shall bless themselves* [4] Or *terebinth*

Section Overview

The genealogy in Genesis 11 introduced Abram as a key character in the narrative, the tenth generation from Shem, just as Noah was the tenth generation from Seth. Genesis 12 marks the transition from prehistory, in which events that are clearly intended to be understood as part of a connected and unfolding series nonetheless tend to be of universal significance for all humanity, to something closer to what we understand as regular history, events that are easier to locate in time and space and our own lived experience.

What is more, the call of Abram represents nothing short of a new beginning for mankind. In the first eleven chapters of Genesis the narrator shows us the slow, steady, shocking spread of sin from its origin in the garden of Eden to its culmination in the Tower of Babylon. Five times in these chapters God's solemn curse is pronounced upon the created order, replacing the original blessing upon life in the garden: God curses the serpent (3:14–15); the ground from which the man and the woman are made (3:17); Cain, because he murders his brother (4:11); the earth for the wickedness of society (8:21); and Canaan, because of the sin of his father, Ham (9:25). Now, however, God begins the process of re-creating for himself a people by pronouncing a fivefold blessing upon Abram.[214] God will turn Abram into a living model of what blessing should look like. What the builders of the Tower of Babel sought to do on their own behalf but failed to accomplish—to establish a lasting city and make a name for themselves—God will do for Abram, making him into a numerous people and granting him a land in which to dwell, thereby making his name great. Through his obedience Abram will bring blessing to the whole world so that "In you all the families of the earth shall be blessed" (12:3).

In response to this great and glorious promise Abram steps out in faith, along with his wife, Sarai, his nephew Lot, and all those with them (vv. 4–5). He arrives in the land promised him by God, the land of Canaan, and moves through it from north to south, building altars and worshiping at key locations—claiming it for his God, as it were (vv. 5–9). Although the presence of the Canaanites in the land is noted (v. 6), their existence poses no explicit challenge to the promise. Rather, we see Abram responding to the word of God in faith and worship, exactly as he ought.

Section Outline

VII. The Family History of Terah (11:27–25:11) . . .
    B. The Call of Abram (12:1–3)
    C. Abram Traverses the Land (12:4–9)

Comment

12:1–3 There was no mention of the Lord in Genesis 11:27–32, even though his fingerprints were all over the events that transpired. Now, though, the Lord speaks directly to Abram, just as he had earlier spoken to Adam and Eve (chs. 2–3), Cain (4:6–15), and Noah (6:13–9:17). His words are a command that would be especially challenging in an ancient context: Abram is to leave his country, his wider relations ("kindred"; Hb. *moledet*), and his nearer relations—his "father's house" (12:1), including his father, Terah, who will live in Haran for another sixty years (11:32). Nothing is specified about this land to which he is headed, except that the Lord will show it to him (12:1). Abram has already left the land of his kindred, Ur of the Chaldeans (11:28–31), with the goal of traveling to Canaan but has stopped at Haran, which could still be considered "home turf" for Abram since it remains the home of his immediate family (cf. 24:4). Many would make the journey regularly from Haran to Ur and back again. Now, though, the Lord is calling Abram to complete the journey into the unknown that he began earlier.

In light of this command the Lord promises to make Abram into a great nation (12:2), which implies numerous descendants—a remarkable promise to a seventy-five-year-old man with a barren wife. In contrast to God's original command to

---

[214] Wenham, *Genesis 1–15*, li. Kenneth Mathews points out the confluence of a series of motifs from Genesis 1–11 in Genesis 12:1–3: land/country, bless/curse, seed, nation/family, name; cf. *Genesis 11:27–50:26*, NAC (Nashville: B&H, 2005), 104.

creation to be fruitful and multiply (1:22), which simply required the creatures to fulfill the potential with which the Lord had endowed them through his blessing, this promise will require a special work of God to complete. It therefore is an enormous step of faith on the part of Abram (and Sarai) to believe this incredible word (cf. Isa. 51:2). The promises of a land and of a nation are integrally related: without descendants, Abram's ownership of territory would be fleeting, while a nation without a land would be homeless and subject to oppression, as Israel will experience in Egypt prior to the exodus.

The Lord also promises to bless Abram (Gen. 12:2), a promise that would normally include material prosperity as well as numerous offspring. This will be the first aspect of the blessing to be realized, as God multiplies Abram's possessions when he returns from Egypt at the end of this chapter. The provision of an heir will take considerably longer. The Lord will see that Abram's "name," or reputation, is made great, a concern of the builders of Babel (11:4) and of the Nephilim in 6:4. In fact, the Lord will change Abram's name to Abraham ("father of nations") and make him the spiritual ancestor of those from all nations who have faith in God (17:5; cf. Rom. 4:16–17).

Abram will also be a blessing to others (Gen. 12:2). That is, when others want to bless someone, they will invoke Abram as a model of what blessing looks like: "May the Lord make you like Abram" (cf. 48:20; Ruth 4:11). This general promise is unpacked in what follows. As Abram is the chosen representative of the deity, people's attitude to Abram will define the Lord's response to them. Those who bless Abram, treating him with respect and favor, will receive blessing from the Lord, while those who dishonor him will be placed under divine curse (Gen. 12:3), resulting in their dishonor or even death. Abram and Sarai will thus be under the Lord's direct and personal protection. It is ironic that this protection is most evident in the episodes in which Abram doubts God's ability to take care of him (vv. 10–20; 20:1–18).

In Hebrew "Those who bless you" is plural, while "Him who dishonors you" is singular, perhaps suggesting that many more will belong to the former category than the latter one.[215] This sense is reinforced by the concluding clause "In you all the families of the earth shall be blessed."[216] The goal of Abram's calling is to bring salvation to the peoples of the earth, not merely judgment—though those who despise Abram and his offspring will surely find themselves under God's wrath. This calling for Israel to be a light to the Gentiles recurs throughout the OT, especially in the prophet Isaiah, where it becomes the mission of God's servant (cf. Isa. 49:6). This enigmatic servant at first seems to be Israel as a nation (e.g., Isa. 41:8–9), but it is clear that even after the return from exile Israel is in no fit state to fulfill this calling. Its mission will devolve to the true seed of Abraham, the true Israel and true servant of the Lord, Jesus, who through his suffering, death,

---

215 Sarna, *Genesis*, 89.
216 Some commentators take this as a reflexive verb rather than a passive ("All peoples will bless themselves by you"), seeing Abraham as a model of blessing rather than the channel of it. However, this would merely repeat what was said earlier, so a passive sense of the verb seems more likely here.

and resurrection will bring salvation not only to ethnic Israel but to the ends of the earth (cf. Acts 1:8; 3:25–26). In this way people from all tribes and nations will indeed find blessing for themselves in Abraham and his offspring (Rev. 7:9–10).

12:4–9 In the beginning of all things God spoke and his word was immediately fulfilled (Genesis 1). So too here in this momentous new beginning for humanity God says "Go!" and Abram goes, even though he does not yet know where he is going. This is the archetypal response of faith that will (in large measure) characterize Abram's life. His nephew, Lot, also goes with him. As we shall see, while he travels with Abram, sharing his faith, Lot is also blessed, just as Genesis 12:2 anticipated. Once he leaves Abram and strikes out on his own, however, Lot's story takes on a different and more negative trajectory.

The text also reiterates Abram's age, seventy-five years, which by itself does not preclude his having offspring (his own father, Terah, had been seventy when Abram was born; Gen. 11:26) but certainly highlights the fragility of that hope. The next twenty-five years will be spent waiting for the fulfillment of the promise. More serious still, Abram takes with him his wife, Sarai, whom we have already been told is barren (12:5; cf. 11:30). Nothing short of the Lord's help could solve their need and fulfill God's promise. Lot is no substitute for a child of Abram and Sarai's own, as we shall see.

The promise of a land for his offspring is also challenged by the revelation that Abram is headed for Canaan (12:5). This is not an empty territory, waiting to be inhabited, but the historical home of the Canaanites and Amorites, among others (cf. v. 6; 15:16). This raises the question that will not be resolved until later in the Pentateuch concerning how this land will become Israel's, though, since the inhabitants have already been declared to be under God's curse, the outcome of the conflict is not in question (9:25).

Abram does not leave Haran empty handed, however. He begins his journey with the possessions and people he acquired while in Haran (12:5). These "people" may be what we call "servants" or "slaves," though ancient working patterns and relationships could be quite different from modern slavery. One of these "people" acquired by Abram is undoubtedly Eliezer, described in 15:2 as "heir of my house," who stands to inherit Abraham's estate if he dies childless. Others undoubtedly have much more menial roles but are still regarded as part of the larger household over whom Abram has authority and for whom he also bears responsibility.

Once he arrives in the land of Canaan Abram traverses it from north to south, stopping at three significant locations: Shechem, Bethel/Ai, and the Negeb (12:6–9). Jacob will also visit each of these places when he returns to the land after his sojourn in Paddan-aram (cf. 33:18; 35:6, 27), and they are each the site of important events during the conquest under Joshua. In the first two of these places, at the oak of Moreh[217] at Shechem and in the area between Bethel and Ai, Abram builds

---

217 Great trees were often used as cultic sites by the Canaanites. Yet the text is clear that, though Abram may worship the Lord in the same place where the Canaanites worshiped their gods, they are not worshiping the same deity; Abram erects his own altar from scratch.

altars and offers sacrifices to the Lord, symbolically claiming ownership of this land for his God and renewing his own commitment to serve him (12:7–8). It is significant that, though God had called Abram to go to the land of Canaan while he was still living in Ur, the Lord does not appear to him until he has arrived within the boundaries of the Promised Land, at Shechem (vv. 6–7). It is in response to this revelation that Abram builds his first altar and calls on the name of the Lord, fulfilling the customary pattern of worship in the Bible: God speaks and humans respond, a pattern that the builders of Babel willfully rejected in seeking to enter heaven without reference to heaven's God (cf. 11:1–9).

Response

Great promises make great demands on our faith. God does not come to Abram and ask him what he wants out of life. If he had, Abram's requests would probably have been much more modest—a son, perhaps, rather than a nation; a manageable piece of property on which to settle down rather than an entire land; positive relationships with his neighbors and their respect rather than a great name and being regarded as a blessing by the nations. Yet our God promises the unimaginable—"more abundantly than all that we ask or think," in Paul's language (Eph. 3:20)—and he more than delivers on his promises.

At the same time, God's big promises are often at least partially delayed, as Abram experiences. There is a significant gap between what God promises and what he sees with his eyes all around him. We often have a similar experience when we step out in faith: things do not immediately fall into place for us. This is not an accident but part of God's plan to grow Abram (and us) in our faith. Abram's faith in God's promises will be repeatedly tested by God's sovereign orchestration of circumstances. Sometimes Abram demonstrates great faith, while at other times he falls short. But God is always faithful to his promises, even when Abram is unfaithful (cf. 2 Tim. 2:13).

Yet, though Abram and Sarai are excellent models of faith for us (Isa. 51:2), they are not our saviors. They point forward to their ultimate offspring, Jesus Christ, who for the joy set before him left a far greater homeland, his Father's house in heaven, and came to earth to bring us this blessing. Like Abram, he did so on the strength of God's promise (cf. Ps. 2:8–9). His faith never wavered, even under the greatest trials, culminating in the cross—a faith that was vindicated in his resurrection from the dead. Abram received a great name and was a blessing to those who blessed him, while those who cursed him were cursed. But Christ has received "the name that is above every name," that "at the name of Jesus every knee should bow" (Phil. 2:9–10). He has now inherited a glorious homeland, where he awaits the arrival of his people—men and women from every tribe, nation, and tongue, all those who by faith have trusted in his righteousness for their salvation. Every blessing that Abraham anticipated by faith is wrapped up in Christ and is inherited by us through our own faith in him (Eph. 1:3–12).

GENESIS 12:10–13:4

¹⁰ Now there was a famine in the land. So Abram went down to Egypt to sojourn there, for the famine was severe in the land. ¹¹ When he was about to enter Egypt, he said to Sarai his wife, "I know that you are a woman beautiful in appearance, ¹² and when the Egyptians see you, they will say, 'This is his wife.' Then they will kill me, but they will let you live. ¹³ Say you are my sister, that it may go well with me because of you, and that my life may be spared for your sake." ¹⁴ When Abram entered Egypt, the Egyptians saw that the woman was very beautiful. ¹⁵ And when the princes of Pharaoh saw her, they praised her to Pharaoh. And the woman was taken into Pharaoh's house. ¹⁶ And for her sake he dealt well with Abram; and he had sheep, oxen, male donkeys, male servants, female servants, female donkeys, and camels.

¹⁷ But the LORD afflicted Pharaoh and his house with great plagues because of Sarai, Abram's wife. ¹⁸ So Pharaoh called Abram and said, "What is this you have done to me? Why did you not tell me that she was your wife? ¹⁹ Why did you say, 'She is my sister,' so that I took her for my wife? Now then, here is your wife; take her, and go." ²⁰ And Pharaoh gave men orders concerning him, and they sent him away with his wife and all that he had.

13 So Abram went up from Egypt, he and his wife and all that he had, and Lot with him, into the Negeb.

² Now Abram was very rich in livestock, in silver, and in gold. ³ And he journeyed on from the Negeb as far as Bethel to the place where his tent had been at the beginning, between Bethel and Ai, ⁴ to the place where he had made an altar at the first. And there Abram called upon the name of the LORD.

Section Overview

Genesis 12 began with great promises of blessing and a response of simple obedience. Yet the rest of the chapter shows how complicated the blessed life can be in a cursed world. Before Abram can even begin to establish himself in this "land flowing with milk and honey" (Ex. 3:8), a famine in the land sends him fleeing down to the more bountiful resources of Egypt in order to survive (Gen. 12:10). In the process, fear drives Abram to deception, pretending that Sarai is his sister and not his wife, a strategy that results in a kind of antifulfillment of the promise of Genesis 12:1–3: Abram is out of the land, his wife is taken into Pharaoh's harem, threatening the prospect of offspring, and his presence brings curse on Pharaoh instead of the blessing he is supposed to represent to the nations.

God will not let his plans be thwarted, however. He intervenes not only to rescue Abram from his own folly and sin but also to deliver him from Egypt and bring him back to the Promised Land with even greater possessions than before (vv. 17–20). In the process this episode foreshadows Israel's later journey down to Egypt, sojourning there and returning, once again laden with Egyptian plunder.[218] Just as God takes care of Abram, protecting him from external dangers and his own sinful compromises, bringing him back to the Land of Promise, so also the Lord will later provide for Israel as well.

Section Outline

VII. The Family History of Terah (11:27–25:11) . . .
    D. Abram in Egypt (12:10–13:4)

Comment

12:10–20 The apparent plenty and fertility of Egypt in comparison to the famine of the Promised Land is a repeated theme in Genesis, one that would have resonated with the original audience in the wilderness (as well as many other later Israelite readers), who were constantly tempted to return to Egypt (cf. Num. 11:4–6).[219] The relative geography of the two regions readily explains the phenomenon: the land of Canaan was dependent upon unreliable seasonal rainfall from the Mediterranean for its fertility, while Egypt's abundance was supplied by the more reliable resource of the Nile, whose annual inundation based on rains in the Ethiopian highlands was a regular occurrence. It is therefore striking that the Lord chooses to call Abram to possess the land of Canaan rather than the land of Egypt as his inheritance, a backwater country on the major land bridge between Asia and Africa without reliable water supplies.[220] These features will later require Israel to exhibit constant dependence upon God for her survival, and the Lord similarly put Abram's faith to the test at a very early stage by means of a severe famine.

Significantly, Abram does not seem to consult God in this difficult circumstance,[221] in contrast to Jacob's inquiry of the Lord in 46:1–4. Rather, he follows the "commonsense" approach of going down to Egypt in search of food. He views it as a temporary move, to be sure—he is going to "sojourn" (Hb. *gur*) there for a while and then return (12:10). However, this temporary status far away from kinfolk and friends leaves him in a vulnerable situation, with few legal protections.

As a result, one fear-driven choice on Abram's part is swiftly followed by another: persuading Sarai to identify as his sister rather than his wife, lest he be murdered in order to take her as a wife for an Egyptian (v. 11). Sarai *is* his half-sister (v. 11), and his fear is not entirely without cause, since there are cases in the OT of kings' eliminating husbands in order to marry their wives (cf. 2 Samuel 11). However, Abram's actions are now being driven by his fears, not by his faith: the promises of the living God have been forgotten under the pressure of difficult circumstances.

---

218 See the striking verbal and thematic parallels adduced in Sailhamer, *Pentateuch as Narrative*, 142.
219 Cf. Iain M. Duguid, "Hagar the Egyptian, A Note on the Allure of Egypt in the Abraham Cycle," *WTJ* 56 (1994): 419–421.
220 In a similar complaint the former Israeli prime minister Golda Meir once lamented the fact that Moses brought Israel to the one place in the Middle East that had no oil.
221 Cf. Kidner, *Genesis*, 126.

The reasonableness of Abram's fears becomes clear once his retinue arrives in Egypt. The Egyptians notice Sarai's attractiveness and "praised her to Pharaoh," who takes her into his harem (Gen. 12:15). This is the first biblical reference to the title *Pharaoh*, which is never modified by a personal name, much to the frustration of scholars who would like to synchronize the biblical account with Egyptian history. It appears that Abram's strategy for dealing with the situation is succeeding, at least superficially; not only is he still alive, but he prospers greatly as the brother of Pharaoh's newest wife, gaining an abundance of servants and animals, including camels, which are quite rare in this time period.[222] Yet this material prosperity hardly compensates for Abram's sense of having completely derailed God's plan, leaving the Promised Land, losing his wife and therefore the prospect of children, and becoming a curse rather than a blessing to those around him. There is therefore a heavy irony in the statement "He dealt well with Abram" (v. 16).

Of course, God's plans are not so easily threatened by human sin. As he does later in the time of Moses, the Lord brings great plagues upon Pharaoh, so that Pharaoh sends Abram away to return to the land of Canaan (v. 20), with Sarai and his now greatly enlarged possessions of livestock, silver, and gold (13:2). Yet Abram is left silent, without anything to say in his own defense in his audience with Pharaoh, who appears as the entirely innocent and wronged party in this encounter (12:18–19).

13:1–4 The opening verses of Genesis 13 show Abram systematically reversing his tracks from the previous chapter. The spiritual geography matches the physical geography: having gone *down* to Egypt in Genesis 12:10, now he goes *up* to return to the Promised Land (13:1). He first returns to the Negeb in the southern part of Judah (v. 1), which is where he was when he made the wrong decision to go down to Egypt (12:9). From there he makes a further pilgrimage to Bethel (13:3), to the place where he had pitched his tent earlier and had built an altar (12:8). There he once again calls on the name of the Lord, just as he had on the earlier occasion (13:4; cf. 12:8). It is clear that this is a journey of repentance and renewed faith, retracing his steps and trusting God to provide for him from now on within the Promised Land. Like later Israel when coming out of Egypt, the goal of Abraham's exodus is the worship of the Lord who had promised the land to him.

Response

If in the opening part of chapter 12 Abram is a model of faith to be emulated, in the latter part of the chapter he is a reminder of how quickly the strongest faith

---

222 Early OT references to camels are often viewed as anachronistic additions by a late editor, since domesticated camels were not in widespread use in Israel until the mid- to late-tenth century BC, when they appear as part of the Sinai copper-mining industry. However, earlier references to camels in the OT generally show them in the service of long-distance caravans (e.g., Gen. 37:25) or desert-dwelling tribesmen (Judg. 6:5) down until the time of the later reign of David (e.g., 1 Chron. 27:30), which is in a similar time frame to the copper-mining evidence. The exception is Abram, but the text is clear that these unusual animals come from Egypt, which has a long history of camel domestication. These beasts are still available for use by Abram's servant in Genesis 24, while Jacob acquires a number of camels in Paddan-aram (cf. Gen. 31:17; 32:7), but the exotic beasts are nowhere depicted in common use in Israel during these early times.

can falter in the face of life's difficulties. It is clear that God's wonderful plan for the life of his people often includes trials and difficulties, not merely blessing and prosperity—otherwise how would we ever grow in our faith? It is also clear that even the "heroes" of the biblical text regularly fail and fall short of God's perfect standard. Before we judge Abram too harshly, we should consider how quickly our own faith crumbles in the face of sickness, adversity, and loss, which tempt us to turn away from trusting God and instead to seek to rely on seemingly more solid earthly refuges, such as Egypt represented to OT Israel.

Yet the narrative does not end with Abram's being cast off for his lack of faith. Instead, God orchestrates events in such a way as to bring him back to the path of obedience he left behind him. There is a doorway of repentance and renewal open to Abram, as he turns his face back toward God and returns to the altar at Bethel, where he previously called on the name of the Lord. The same door is always open to us when we sin and wander astray. God is the good Father, who stands with arms open wide to welcome home the prodigal son (cf. Luke 15:20), even though our rebellion is equally without cause and without excuse.

This pathway of repentance is open to us because of what the altar at Bethel signifies, which is the sacrifice offered to atone for our many sins. The death and resurrection of Christ atone for our failure and faithlessness, and we are now clothed in his constant faithfulness, which enables us to stand before the Father as his beloved children. Because of the grace of this Father, we should run along the pathway of repentance that leads us to the cross whenever we find ourselves to have sinned again, knowing that he will receive us and restore us to his favor and blessing.

GENESIS 13:5–18

⁵ And Lot, who went with Abram, also had flocks and herds and tents, ⁶ so that the land could not support both of them dwelling together; for their possessions were so great that they could not dwell together, ⁷ and there was strife between the herdsmen of Abram's livestock and the herdsmen of Lot's livestock. At that time the Canaanites and the Perizzites were dwelling in the land.

⁸ Then Abram said to Lot, "Let there be no strife between you and me, and between your herdsmen and my herdsmen, for we are kinsmen.¹ ⁹ Is not the whole land before you? Separate yourself from me. If you take the left hand, then I will go to the right, or if you take the right hand, then I will go to the left." ¹⁰ And Lot lifted up his eyes and saw that the Jordan Valley was well watered everywhere like the garden of the LORD, like the land of Egypt, in the direction of Zoar. (This was before the LORD destroyed Sodom and Gomorrah.) ¹¹ So Lot chose for himself all the Jordan Valley, and Lot journeyed east. Thus they separated from each

other. ¹²Abram settled in the land of Canaan, while Lot settled among the cities of the valley and moved his tent as far as Sodom. ¹³Now the men of Sodom were wicked, great sinners against the LORD.

¹⁴The LORD said to Abram, after Lot had separated from him, "Lift up your eyes and look from the place where you are, northward and southward and eastward and westward, ¹⁵for all the land that you see I will give to you and to your offspring forever. ¹⁶I will make your offspring as the dust of the earth, so that if one can count the dust of the earth, your offspring also can be counted. ¹⁷Arise, walk through the length and the breadth of the land, for I will give it to you." ¹⁸So Abram moved his tent and came and settled by the oaks² of Mamre, which are at Hebron, and there he built an altar to the LORD.

¹Hebrew *we are men, brothers* ²Or *terebinths*

Section Overview

The Lord had promised to provide Abram with an heir, but before that can happen several potential "heir substitutes" have to be eliminated from possible consideration. Abram's nephew, Lot, is one of these. He has traveled with Abram from Haran, after the death of his own father, and prospered alongside Abram as an immediate example of the promise of Genesis 12:3 working its way out. As long as Lot stays with Abram, his fortunes are assured. Yet in this chapter Lot makes the catastrophic decision to part from Abram and strike out on his own, choosing what seems like the best location to prosper, even though it is outside the land promised to Abram and means separating from the presence of the one upon whom God's blessing rests (13:10). He does not know—though he will discover later to his cost—that the inhabitants of the area he has chosen are wicked in the eyes of the Lord (v. 13). The land that looked so good to his eyes turns out to be anything but the best option.

Lot's story serves a purpose in the narrative on the individual level, exposing the danger of choosing with our eyes rather than following our faith, but he is also important as the ancestor of the Moabites and the Ammonites (19:37–38), who will be Israel's neighbors once she enters the land under Joshua. They are therefore Israel's close relatives after the flesh, and their stories would continue to be intertwined with Israel's down through history, but they are not part of the people upon whom the Lord has placed his name.

Section Outline

VII. The Family History of Terah (11:27–25:11) . . .
    E. Abram and Lot Separate (13:5–18)

Comment

13:5–7 Lot was reintroduced into the storyline at Genesis 13:1, which recounts the return from Egypt. This prepares for his importance in the rest of the chapter, although it is also significant that he participates without becoming an heir to Israel's inheritance. In that regard his story parallels that of the "rabble" (Hb. *hasafsuf*; Num. 11:4) that accompanies Israel later on its exodus.[223] It is possible to travel for a while with the people of God without ever truly being part of them.

During his time with Abram Lot prospers greatly, which in a seminomadic context means an abundance of flocks (sheep and goats), herds (cattle), and tents (Gen. 13:5). This is a fulfillment of God's promised blessing in Genesis 12:2: as long as Lot accompanies Abram, he is blessed abundantly and prospers greatly. Yet prosperity can be as challenging as adversity, and the combined abundance of Abram and Lot leads to pressure on the available grazing land and conflict between their herdsmen over scarce resources (13:6). This is an ominous note with regard to the Promised Land—how will it support Israel if it cannot support two seminomadic families? However, the tension is explained by a note: "At that time the Canaanites and the Perizzites were dwelling in the land" (v. 7). It is their presence that limits the available resources; once the Israelites drive them out of the land under Joshua, there will be sufficient resources for all. Of course, if Israel fails to drive the Canaanites and Perizzites out of the land comprehensively, as will prove to be the case, the story will be different (cf. Judges 1).

13:8–13 To resolve the conflict Abram makes a remarkable offer. Although he is the senior member of the alliance and the one to whom God has promised the entire land, he will cede part of the land to Lot—and, what is more, Lot can choose for himself which part of the land he desires, either the right or the left, that is, north or south as they look eastward over the plain of the Jordan from the heights near Bethel (Gen. 13:8–9). Abram proposes this division in order to avoid strife ("For we are men, brothers"; ESV mg. on v. 8), a striking description given the frequently unbrotherly actions of literal brothers elsewhere in Genesis. It is also striking that the word "strife" (Hb. *meribah*; v. 8) is the same word used elsewhere for Israel's incessant complaining against the Lord in the wilderness (e.g., Ex. 17:7),[224] which suggests an ungrateful attitude on Lot's part.

Many Westerners misunderstand this offer and fail to see the offensiveness of Lot's response. It is customary in negotiations in many parts of the world for something to be offered as a gift that politeness demands the recipient to decline. An example of this kind of negotiation may be seen in Genesis 23, where Ephron the Hittite appears to offer to give Abraham the burial site he has requested before a purchase price of 400 shekels of silver is finally negotiated. Ephron would have been shocked and offended if Abraham had accepted the land as a gift! So too here, readers from non-Western countries often recognize the inappropriateness of Lot's eager acceptance of Abram's offer. As the younger family member, he should politely refuse the offer and either insist on staying together or insist that Abram make the first choice as the older one in the relationship.

---

223 Sailhamer, *Pentateuch as Narrative*, 142.
224 Sarna, *Genesis*, 98.

Even more profoundly, since God's blessing rests upon those who honor Abram (cf. Gen. 12:3), Lot should insist on remaining with Abram on those grounds alone. He has prospered alongside Abram already, and surely some arrangement could be found that would enable them to live together in harmony, even if it limited their potential for wealth and possessions.

Yet Lot's decision making is not driven by such spiritual considerations. Instead he "lifted up his eyes and saw that the Jordan Valley was well watered everywhere" (13:10). As noted earlier, intermittent rainfall is a common cause of famine in Israel, so a reliable water supply is a significant asset. As Eve did in the garden (3:6) and the sons of God did prior to the flood (6:2), Lot sees something attractive and pursues it, with similarly catastrophic results. After the Lord's destruction of Sodom and Gomorrah (13:10; cf. ch. 19) the land is no longer such an attractive place to settle. The small settlement of Zoar is mentioned (13:10) because it represents the southern limit of the plain of the Jordan; it will reappear later in Lot's story (14:2, 8; 19:22–23).

The Jordan Valley is described as being "like the garden of the LORD, like the land of Egypt" (Gen. 13:10). This may sound like a good place to choose to settle down, since the garden of the Lord was beautiful and Egypt was the place where there was no famine. Yet this superficially delightful description carries with it ominous undertones of spiritual danger. It was in the garden of the Lord that Lot's first ancestors, Adam and Eve, were tempted by the serpent and fell into sin (3:6). As did the builders of the Tower of Babel (11:1–9), Lot thinks to bypass the cherubim guarding the way back to God's presence and to enjoy the benefits of a place resembling the garden of the Lord without the inconvenience of having to trust in the Lord of the garden.

Describing the land chosen by Lot as being "like the land of Egypt" (Gen. 13:10) further reinforces the image of physical prosperity combined with spiritual danger. Abram and Lot have only just returned from Egypt, where they prospered materially at the cost of endangering God's promise. It appears that Lot would be quite happy to return there. The danger of this attitude should not have been lost on the original readers of this account in the time of Moses, who had themselves just emerged from captivity in Egypt and experienced its continuing attraction as well.[225] Finally, to get to this land Lot journeys "east" (13:11), an ominous direction of travel in Genesis (cf. 3:24; 4:16; 11:2).[226]

Genesis 13:10 adds parenthetically, "This was before the LORD destroyed Sodom and Gomorrah." The fate of Sodom and Gomorrah have not yet been sealed, although their sin is already a well-known feature of their city (cf. 13:13). In choosing with his eyes and neglecting a fuller exploration of the facts, Lot entrusts his life to a dangerously flawed sense. The land that Lot is choosing for himself[227] is on the edge of the land promised to Abraham, if not actually outside

---

225 Duguid, "Hagar the Egyptian," 419–421.
226 Sailhamer, *Pentateuch as Narrative*, 134.
227 "Lot chose for himself" in Genesis 13:11 contrasts sharply with God's word to Abram, "I will give to you," in verse 15.

it (cf. v. 12), and he chooses to live with wicked sinners, under God's curse, rather than with Abram, the bearer of the Lord's blessing. It is no surprise that Lot's life begins to follow a downward trajectory from this moment onward after the two of them separate (v. 11).

Once Lot begins on this path of compromise he progresses smoothly along it. He may have started out living "as far as Sodom" (v. 12), but before long he is living "*in* Sodom" (14:12). Later Lot is to be found "sitting in the gate of Sodom" (19:1), which suggests that he holds a position of honor and respect among the citizens of Sodom, and his daughters are pledged to marry inhabitants of the city (19:14). At that point Lot's destiny and that of Sodom are intertwined, and only a personal intervention by the Lord could deliver him from Sodom's destruction (cf. Genesis 19). Lot may seem to have triumphed in this exchange, receiving "all the Jordan Valley" (13:11), but in reality he is the loser in terms of everything that really matters.[228]

13:14–18 The real winner in this division of the land is Abram, who continues in faith, trusting that God can provide for him within the Land of Promise. In return he receives a renewed blessing from the Lord. The one who refuses to live by sight is now told to lift up his eyes[229] and look in all directions—north, south, east, and west (v. 14). Instead of limiting himself to the land on the left or the right (v. 9), or even the apparently best of the land, all the land that he can see is to be his, and his offspring will become as numerous as the dust of the earth (vv. 14–16). This represents a substantial expansion of the Lord's promise to Abram in 12:7, which had merely mentioned offspring and land. Now, even though he has just separated himself from the last remaining member of his father's house, he is told that his offspring will be as innumerable as the dust of the earth and that his offspring will possess the whole land forever (13:15–16). For this promise to be fulfilled God will have to give him an heir and a family line.

In contrast to Lot, who settles down quickly with the inhabitants of Sodom, Abram continues his nomadic travels, walking to and fro throughout the land (v. 17), exploring the goodness of God's gift to him. Abram will never receive the full ownership of that property while he lives here on earth. At the time of his death all that Abram owns is a field containing a cave with two small burial plots for himself and his wife—significantly, in Hebron, where he ends this chapter (v. 18). If Abram's hope is in earthly property, then it must be said that God fails him. As the apostle Paul puts it, "If in Christ we have hope in this life only, we

---

228 Second Peter 2:7 calls him "righteous Lot" and suggests that he became troubled by the wickedness around him in Sodom. Moreover, the discussion between Abraham and the Lord in Genesis 18 about not sweeping away the righteous with the wicked in judgment suggests that Lot is among those considered righteous even while living in Sodom. But righteous people can nonetheless get caught up in all sorts of ungodly and sinful behavior that ruins their lives and the lives of others around them.

229 The command to Abram to lift up his eyes includes the Hebrew particle *na'*, which is often termed the "particle of entreaty" (Joüon §105c) but which more precisely marks the command as being a logical consequence of the previous statement or the general situation; T. O. Lambdin, *Introduction to Biblical Hebrew* (New York: Scribners, 1971), 170. It occurs only four times when God speaks to a human; in each case God is asking the person to believe something incomprehensible (Gen. 13:14; 15:5; 22:2; Ex. 11:2; cf. Hamilton, *Genesis 1–17*, 394).

are of all people most to be pitied" (1 Cor. 15:19). Yet Abram is looking for a city with foundations, which God himself will build (Heb. 11:10), so his hopes are not disappointed.

Abram's spiritual hopes are summed up by the conclusion to the chapter. After surveying the land and settling at Hebron, in the center of Judah, Abram builds an altar there to the Lord (Gen. 13:18). In this way the entire section is bracketed by worship (cf. v. 4), the appropriate response of faith to God's promises. To borrow from the language of a later chapter, "[Abram] believed the LORD, and he counted it to him as righteousness" (15:6).

Response

Lot chooses with his eyes and takes the apparently easy prosperity offered to him in the fertile Jordan Valley next to Sodom and Gomorrah. From a worldly perspective this seems the sensible choice, but it is a decision Lot will live to regret. Turning his back on the Land of Promise also means turning his back on the one in whom blessing resides, Abram, and ultimately Abram's offspring, Jesus Christ.

In a similar encounter the devil takes Jesus up onto a very high mountain and shows him all the kingdoms of the world and their splendor, promising to give them all to Jesus if he would just bow down and worship him (Matt. 4:8–9). Yet, knowing the emptiness of Satan's promises, Jesus refuses this offer, quoting Scripture back at Satan: "It is written, 'You shall worship the Lord your God and him only shall you serve'" (Matt. 4:10). As Abraham's offspring and heir, Jesus will indeed inherit all the kingdoms of this world as the Father's gift (cf. Psalm 2)— but only by following the painful pathway of faithful suffering all the way to the cross. Whatever the cost, Jesus is committed to a life of worship and trust in his heavenly Father for the sake of the joy set before him (Heb. 12:2), knowing that his inheritance is secure.

As a result, we are called to turn our backs on the pathway of worldly compromise, even when it promises us a life of ease and security. As Lot discovers to his cost, even in this world compromise does not always pay, and in the light of eternity it is a foolhardy bargain. Far better to step out in faith, believing God and trusting him to deliver the good things he has promised us in Christ, even though it means following Christ along the road of suffering and trials.

GENESIS 14

14 In the days of Amraphel king of Shinar, Arioch king of Ellasar, Chedorlaomer king of Elam, and Tidal king of Goiim, ² these kings made war with Bera king of Sodom, Birsha king of Gomorrah, Shinab king of Admah, Shemeber king of Zeboiim, and the king of Bela (that is, Zoar). ³ And all these joined forces in the Valley of Siddim (that is, the Salt Sea). ⁴ Twelve years they had served Chedorlaomer, but in the thirteenth year they rebelled. ⁵ In the fourteenth year Chedorlaomer and the kings who were with him came and defeated the Rephaim in Ashteroth-karnaim, the Zuzim in Ham, the Emim in Shaveh-kiriathaim, ⁶ and the Horites in their hill country of Seir as far as El-paran on the border of the wilderness. ⁷ Then they turned back and came to En-mishpat (that is, Kadesh) and defeated all the country of the Amalekites, and also the Amorites who were dwelling in Hazazon-tamar.

⁸ Then the king of Sodom, the king of Gomorrah, the king of Admah, the king of Zeboiim, and the king of Bela (that is, Zoar) went out, and they joined battle in the Valley of Siddim ⁹ with Chedorlaomer king of Elam, Tidal king of Goiim, Amraphel king of Shinar, and Arioch king of Ellasar, four kings against five. ¹⁰ Now the Valley of Siddim was full of bitumen pits, and as the kings of Sodom and Gomorrah fled, some fell into them, and the rest fled to the hill country. ¹¹ So the enemy took all the possessions of Sodom and Gomorrah, and all their provisions, and went their way. ¹² They also took Lot, the son of Abram's brother, who was dwelling in Sodom, and his possessions, and went their way.

¹³ Then one who had escaped came and told Abram the Hebrew, who was living by the oaks[1] of Mamre the Amorite, brother of Eshcol and of Aner. These were allies of Abram. ¹⁴ When Abram heard that his kinsman had been taken captive, he led forth his trained men, born in his house, 318 of them, and went in pursuit as far as Dan. ¹⁵ And he divided his forces against them by night, he and his servants, and defeated them and pursued them to Hobah, north of Damascus. ¹⁶ Then he brought back all the possessions, and also brought back his kinsman Lot with his possessions, and the women and the people.

¹⁷ After his return from the defeat of Chedorlaomer and the kings who were with him, the king of Sodom went out to meet him at the Valley of Shaveh (that is, the King's Valley). ¹⁸ And Melchizedek king of Salem brought out bread and wine. (He was priest of God Most High.) ¹⁹ And he blessed him and said,

> "Blessed be Abram by God Most High,
>   Possessor[2] of heaven and earth;
> ²⁰ and blessed be God Most High,
>   who has delivered your enemies into your hand!"

And Abram gave him a tenth of everything. ²¹ And the king of Sodom said to Abram, "Give me the persons, but take the goods for yourself." ²² But Abram said to the king of Sodom, "I have lifted my hand³ to the Lord, God Most High, Possessor of heaven and earth, ²³ that I would not take a thread or a sandal strap or anything that is yours, lest you should say, 'I have made Abram rich.' ²⁴ I will take nothing but what the young men have eaten, and the share of the men who went with me. Let Aner, Eshcol, and Mamre take their share."

¹ Or *terebinths* ² Or *Creator*; also verse 22 ³ Or *I have taken a solemn oath*

Section Overview

In Genesis 12 Abram and Lot's personal story interacted with one of the great empires of the day as they journeyed down to Egypt to avoid a famine in the land of Canaan (12:10). The Lord protected and provided for them despite their unbelief in going down there and Abram's deception concerning Sarai. In Genesis 14 Abram and Lot encounter the alternative great danger that could befall occupants of the land of Canaan: military invasion and exile, in this case by the other great world empire, based in Mesopotamia. Once again, however, God protects his people from all harm.

In between Genesis 12 and 14 Lot had separated himself from Abram and gone to live near Sodom, a city of great wickedness (13:13). And now, because of his close proximity to Sodom, Lot is swept up in their military defeat and carried away with the exiles from that city (14:12). Since Lot had chosen to abandon Abram and make his own way, Abram could easily have left Lot to his deserved fate. Instead, Abram pursues the Mesopotamian army at great personal risk and retrieves Lot along with the other captives from Sodom, returning them to their homes.

On Abram's return he is met by two contrasting figures. One of these, the king of Sodom, treats Abram as a mercenary, brusquely asking for the return of his people but ceding rights over the property to Abram (Gen. 14:21). The other, Melchizedek, king of Salem, comes out as priest of God Most High to bless Abram and give thanks for his victory with a celebratory meal of bread and wine (vv. 18–20). It is clear which of these two is a kindred spirit to Abram. There is no mention in the conclusion of what happens to Lot. We might perhaps have expected this experience to have drawn Lot to repent and return to dwell with his uncle Abram, in whose presence blessing resides. Instead, as we discover later (cf. ch. 19), Lot returns to Sodom and becomes even more entrenched in its godless and wicked society.

Section Outline

VII. The Family History of Terah (11:27–25:11) . . .
    F. A Tale of Two Kings (14:1–24)

Comment

14:1–12 The beginning of Genesis 14 includes an abrupt change in style, with verses 1–11 closely mirroring the style of the annals of ancient Near Eastern kings.

The cycle of the subjection of a people, followed by rebellion, followed by the great king's crushing defeat of his enemies and their resubjection to him, was a common one in the ancient world. This need not necessarily mean that these verses come from a different source;[230] rather, this may simply be the author's way of communicating the nature of the conflict he is describing: a mighty empire bent on imposing its authority and steamrollering local opposition. The kingdoms represented here form a major alliance of empires, underlining the risk Abram takes in confronting them, even if the actual army involved may be more of a raiding party than a full-scale assault. It also reminds us that the narratives of the patriarchs intersect with the real world of ancient history, even if we cannot precisely identify from external sources the names mentioned here.

The Mesopotamian alliance is led by Chedorlaomer of Elam (v. 4),[231] supported by the kings of Shinar (i.e., the area around Babylon; cf. 11:2) and two unknown locations, Elassar and Goiim. On the opposing side is a local alliance of five small cities around the Dead Sea: Sodom, Gomorrah, Admah, Zeboiim, and Bela/Zoar (14:2). It is an unequal struggle, and the five cities of the plain are reduced to vassal status, which would require them to pay annual tribute and accept other obligations to serve their overlord. They continue in this state of subjection for twelve years but then rebel in the thirteenth year (v. 4). Often such revolts would be triggered by changes in leadership or in response to another perceived weakness on the part of the great king, requiring him to send an army if he wanted to reestablish his hegemony. Since the Mesopotamian alliance is a considerable distance away, it takes time for news of the revolt to travel and additional time to put together a fighting force, so campaigning does not commence until the fourteenth year of the subjugation.

It is clear that the rebellion is much more widespread than the involvement of merely five cities of the plain, and so the Mesopotamian army deals first with a series of other threats: the Rephaim, the Zuzim, the Emim, and the Horites (vv. 5–6). These peoples are listed in order from north to south along the King's Highway, the main road south through the land east of the Jordan that any army from the east would follow on its way into Israel. And one can imagine the mounting concern as news arrives of the successive fall of these cities. None of these tribal groups is individually particularly significant, but their mention underlines the power and commitment of the invaders: no one who challenges their power will escape.

Finally they arrive on the doorstep of the cities of the plain after defeating the more significant forces of the Amalekites at Kadesh and the Amorites at Hazazon-tamar (En-gedi; Gen. 14:7; cf. 2 Chron. 20:2). The outcome of the battle close to the Dead Sea with the five local kings and their small forces is predictable: the

---

[230] It is true, however, that there is a significant confluence of unique features in this text, such as rare words and unique titles for God (cf. Sarna, *Genesis*, 101–102), which might suggest an independent origin for this account. It would later have been incorporated into the larger narrative by Moses under the inspiration of God.
[231] It is not immediately clear why Amraphel, king of Babylon, is mentioned first, though it may be a deliberate choice to foreground the Babylonian contingent. The ability of Abram's God to scatter and defeat the Babylonians is an important theme in the early chapters of Genesis.

kings of Sodom and Gomorrah are defeated, and many of their men flee to hide in the hill country, while others fall (or perhaps throw themselves) into the bitumen pits dotting the area (Gen. 14:10). The cities are left defenseless, to be looted and pillaged by the invaders. The remaining inhabitants will be enslaved, their possessions stolen.

Thus far there seems to be no connection between these events and Abram, but that changes with the mention of Lot in Genesis 14:12. Lot does not seem to have been directly involved in the fighting, but, as someone allied to the inhabitants of Sodom, he and his household are also enslaved and their possessions stolen. It seems that the end of his story will be an ignominious life of bondage in faraway Mesopotamia, an apt punishment for his selfish grasping of what looked like the best of the land when separating from Abram in Genesis 13. However, Lot is Abram's relative, as verses 12–14 remind us, and Abram will not leave him to his fate.

14:13–16 A fugitive brings the news to Abram, who is still living where he had been at the end of chapter 13, by the oaks of Mamre at Hebron (14:13; cf. 13:18), a distance of 20–30 miles [32–48 km] over very rough terrain. Abram is here uniquely called "Abram the Hebrew," a description normally applied to Israelites by outsiders or used by Israelites to identify themselves to outsiders (cf. Gen. 39:14; Ex. 1:15).[232] We also discover that Abram has formed an alliance with some of the local people, who, as Amorites, would have their own reasons for resisting the Mesopotamian alliance (cf. Gen. 14:7). Yet the motivating factor for Abram's unexpected military action is not a generalized desire to protect the land from invaders but a very specific concern to rescue his kinsman, Lot (v. 14). In response to Lot's capture and forced exile Abram mobilizes a significant part of his household: 318 fighting men (v. 14). Those "born in his house" as servants would generally be regarded as more reliable than those enslaved as adults or paid to serve.[233] This force is a significant body for one man to put into the field but is tiny compared to the resources that could be mustered by the Mesopotamian alliance. Yet Abram pursues the victorious army as far as the northern border of Israel, which will later be marked by the city of Dan (v. 14).[234] Abram is putting into practice the principle articulated many years later by Saul's son Jonathan: "Nothing can hinder the LORD from saving by many or by few" (1 Sam. 14:6).

At Dan, Abram follows a time-tested strategy of smaller forces taking on much larger armies, dividing his company into groups and attacking the enemy encampment at night, counting on creating confusion and fear in the darkness (Gen. 14:15; cf. Judges 7). The strategy is a success, and the Mesopotamian alliance is routed, with Abram pursuing the remnants of their force a considerable distance, as far as the unknown location of Hobah (Gen. 14:15), which is north of

---

232 Von Rad, *Genesis*, 362.
233 Wenham, *Genesis 1–15*, 314.
234 The city was not named "Dan" until the time of the judges (cf. Judg. 18:29); in Abram's time it was called Laish. If we assume Mosaic authorship of Genesis, this must represent a later editorial clarification, much as we might refer to the Romans as having a settlement in London rather than in Londinium.

Damascus and thus well outside what would later constitute the Promised Land. Having seen off the invaders, Abram returns home to the southern part of Israel, bringing with him all the captives and spoil that the Mesopotamian alliance had carried off, including Lot (v. 16).

In this passage Abram is depicted as though he were the king of the land promised to him, risking his own life in warfare to deliver his people from bondage to foreign enemies. This is quite different from the way in which Abram is portrayed elsewhere in Genesis, but the point is not so much Abram's boldness and military might as it is the Lord's protection and support, which enable Abram—and others who are later called to follow in his footsteps—to triumph by faith over adversaries far mightier than they. A striking example of this pattern is found in the person of King Jehoshaphat in 2 Chronicles 20, whose faith-filled conflict with an overwhelming enemy is explicitly connected with Genesis 14 by the mention in both texts of Hazazon-Tamar, a location mentioned nowhere else in the Bible (2 Chron. 20:2; cf. Gen. 14:7).

14:17–24 Upon his return Abram is faced with a much more subtle struggle that tests his faith in the Lord's power and provision. It comes in the approach of two kings, Melchizedek, king of Salem, and the unnamed king of Sodom, who both come to meet him in a location named "the King's Valley" (vv. 17–18). These two kings form a study in contrasts. Melchizedek's name means "king of righteousness," and the name of his city means "peace";[235] he approaches Abram as the priest of God Most High, offering Abram the priestly elements of life, bread and wine, pronouncing a gracious blessing upon him, and praising God for Abram's victory (vv. 19–20). In consequence Abram gives him a tithe of the spoils of battle[236] as an acknowledgement of God's role in the victory (v. 20)—an explicit acknowledgment that Melchizedek's "God Most High" (Hb. 'El 'Elyon) is the same God whom Abram serves. The title "Most High" ('elyon) or "God Most High" ('El 'Elyon) recurs a number of times in the OT, especially in the Psalms and Daniel. On the other hand, the title "Possessor [or Creator][237] of heaven and earth" (qoneh shamayim va'arets) occurs only in this passage. Abram makes the identification explicit when he calls him "The LORD, God Most High" in his response to the king of Sodom (14:22).

The king of Sodom, on the other hand, rules over a territory justly notorious for its wickedness (13:13). He "went out" (vayyetse'; 14:17) to meet Abram, a verb that often implies a confrontation of some kind.[238] His words to Abram are terse and rude, offering no thanks to Abram for his actions nor praise to God for the victory (v. 21). Rather, he assumes that Abram is a man like himself, motivated chiefly by

---

235 It is generally accepted that Salem here refers to what will later become Jerusalem, grounding that city's history in a profound connection to the patriarchs (cf. Ps. 76:2).
236 A one-off voluntary tithe of the profits of a venture as an acknowledgement of God's blessing is quite distinct from the required annual tithe of agricultural produce imposed on Israel under the Mosaic covenant as an acknowledgment of the Lord's ownership of the land. Cf. Iain M. Duguid, *Should Christians Tithe? Excelling in the Grace of Giving* (Glenside, PA: St. Colme's Press, 2018).
237 In Ugaritic *qny* is used of *El* as creator. So too the LXX translates the Hebrew as "Creator" (*hos ektisen*).
238 Sarna, *Genesis*, 109. The king of Sodom comes out to Abram empty handed, bringing nothing but an attitude, whereas Melchizedek brings a gift of bread and wine.

the desire for personal gain (v. 21). In response Abram calls on the Most High God as his witness that he will take nothing of the spoil recovered by Sodom—not even the most worthless items, a thread or the strap of a sandal. He marks the solemnity of the oath by formally swearing with an uplifted hand (v. 22). His Amorite allies are not bound by his oath and are entitled to their share, which is part of the blessing due to those who have aligned themselves with Abram (cf. 12:2–3), but no one will be able to credit the looting of Sodom with making Abram rich. His trust for his financial provision rests entirely in the Lord's fulfilling his promise to bless him, just as his trust for safety in battle had done.

Response

In a chapter in which we see Abram's acting as though he were already the king of the land that God had promised him, going out in faith at great personal risk to ensure the safety of his undeserving kinsman, Lot, we also see the mysterious figure of Melchizedek towering over Abram. Although God has declared that there is blessing to be found in Abram, here is another worshiper of El Elyon who is even greater than Abram. In the NT the book of Hebrews picks up this idea, mediated by the promise to David as the then-king of Jerusalem of a future priest-king after the order of Melchizedek (Ps. 110:4), a promise that the writer of Hebrews sees fulfilled in the coming of Christ. He highlights three specific points of comparison between Melchizedek and Jesus.

First, both men exercise a priesthood established on the basis not of their heredity but rather of their office. Unlike the Levitical priesthood, for which the appropriate lineage was of critical importance, Melchizedek is a priest simply because he is king of Salem. Similarly, Jesus is likewise a priest not because of his heredity—he does not come from the priestly tribe of Levi—but rather because he is ordained by God into the promised priesthood of Melchizedek (Heb. 6:20).

Second, both men exercise an "eternal" priesthood. That is, there is no mention in the Bible of Melchizedek's having, or needing, any predecessor or successor (Heb. 7:3). His priestly office, so far as the Bible is concerned, is completely fulfilled in this single encounter. For the Levitical priesthood, however, there is a great deal of concern in the OT to ensure the provision of a proper succession. Sacrifices had to be offered continually, and so new generations of Levitical priests were constantly needed to fulfill that calling. Jesus' ministry, however, like Melchizedek's, is completed in a once-for-all sacrifice (Heb. 7:27). What is more, having been raised from the dead, Jesus is personally able to intercede for his people perpetually.

Third, both men exercise a superior priesthood. Abram acknowledges Melchizedek's superiority when he gives him a tithe and receives from him a blessing—since the greater always blesses the lesser, not vice versa (Heb. 7:4–7). This acknowledgement is particularly striking because elsewhere Abram acts as the priest for his own family, building his own altars and offering his own sacrifices. Here, uniquely, he publicly acknowledges the priesthood of another. In a sense we might say Levi, though yet unborn, also submits to Melchizedek in the person of his ancestor and recognizes the superiority of his priesthood (Heb. 7:9–10). In these ways Jesus, the priest after the order of Melchizedek, holds a priesthood superior to the Levitical one.

This is good news, because all of us are more like Lot in this story than like Abram. We too have wandered astray from the pathway of blessing through our own sinful choices and found ourselves in desperate bondage to our sins and transgressions, unable to free ourselves. However, we need a far greater deliverance than that provided by Abram for Lot. Abram rescued Lot and brought him back to where he had been before—but then Lot simply renewed his pursuit of this world's pleasures in Sodom. Abram could not give Lot what he most needed: a new heart and a new spirit that would bring him to repentance and real change. Through the sacrifice offered for us by our true priest-king, Jesus Christ, however, we can be made into new creations and given a heart that, like Abram's, is turned toward God in repentance and faith.

GENESIS 15

15 After these things the word of the Lord came to Abram in a vision: "Fear not, Abram, I am your shield; your reward shall be very great." 2 But Abram said, "O Lord God, what will you give me, for I continue[1] childless, and the heir of my house is Eliezer of Damascus?" 3 And Abram said, "Behold, you have given me no offspring, and a member of my household will be my heir." 4 And behold, the word of the Lord came to him: "This man shall not be your heir; your very own son[2] shall be your heir." 5 And he brought him outside and said, "Look toward heaven, and number the stars, if you are able to number them." Then he said to him, "So shall your offspring be." 6 And he believed the Lord, and he counted it to him as righteousness.

7 And he said to him, "I am the Lord who brought you out from Ur of the Chaldeans to give you this land to possess." 8 But he said, "O Lord God, how am I to know that I shall possess it?" 9 He said to him, "Bring me a heifer three years old, a female goat three years old, a ram three years old, a turtledove, and a young pigeon." 10 And he brought him all these, cut them in half, and laid each half over against the other. But he did not cut the birds in half. 11 And when birds of prey came down on the carcasses, Abram drove them away.

12 As the sun was going down, a deep sleep fell on Abram. And behold, dreadful and great darkness fell upon him. 13 Then the Lord said to Abram, "Know for certain that your offspring will be sojourners in a land that is not theirs and will be servants there, and they will be afflicted for four hundred years. 14 But I will bring judgment on the nation that they serve, and afterward they shall come out with great possessions. 15 As for you, you shall go to your fathers in peace; you shall be buried in a good

old age. ⁱ⁶And they shall come back here in the fourth generation, for the iniquity of the Amorites is not yet complete."

¹⁷When the sun had gone down and it was dark, behold, a smoking fire pot and a flaming torch passed between these pieces. ¹⁸On that day the LORD made a covenant with Abram, saying, "To your offspring I give³ this land, from the river of Egypt to the great river, the river Euphrates, ¹⁹the land of the Kenites, the Kenizzites, the Kadmonites, ²⁰the Hittites, the Perizzites, the Rephaim, ²¹the Amorites, the Canaanites, the Girgashites and the Jebusites."

¹ Or *I shall die* ² Hebrew *what will come out of your own loins* ³ Or *have given*

Section Overview

After Abram's refusal of the king of Sodom's grudging offer of wealth at the end of the previous chapter Genesis 15 opens with the Lord's promise of protection and reward to Abram (v. 1). Certainly the Lord has demonstrated his faithfulness to Abram in both these areas over the preceding chapters, protecting him from the dangers of Egypt and the Mesopotamian alliance (chs. 12; 14), as well as greatly expanding his flocks and herds (13:6). Yet the two central elements of the Lord's promise to Abraham, offspring and land, seem as far away from fulfillment as ever. In Genesis 15 the Lord appears to Abram and confirms by means of a covenant ceremony his commitment to give both these blessings to him. The focus of verses 1–5 is on posterity, while verses 7–21 focus on the promise of land, leaving verse 6 as the crucial hinge holding the chapter together:[239] Abram's faith in God's promise, counted to him as righteousness. This verse sums up the central thrust of Abram's story: he is a man of faith who takes God at his word and lives his life on the basis of it—not perfectly, as we shall see again in Genesis 16, but consistently. In this way he anticipates the coming of Jesus, the one in whom all of God's covenant commitments will be definitively fulfilled.

Section Outline

VII. The Family History of Terah (11:27–25:11)...
    G. Abram Believed God (15:1–21)

Comment

15:1–6 The Lord appears to Abram in a vision (v. 1), the first reference to such an event in the Bible. Abram is called a prophet in Genesis 20:7, and this chapter contains information about the Lord's future plans, concerning not just Abram personally but the future of the nation that will come from him. Even though this revelation is termed a "vision," the verbal content of the revelation is more important than what, if anything, the prophet actually sees. Thus we are told that "the word of the LORD came to Abram" (15:1, 4)—the standard form for a prophetic revelation (e.g., Jer. 1:2) but the only use of the form in Genesis.

---

[239] Sarna, *Genesis*, 111.

The initial vision takes place at night (Gen. 15:5) and seems to continue until the end of the following day (v. 12), unless two distinct visions have been combined. Both sections begin with an "I am" statement by the Lord, marking out the structure of the passage: "I am your shield; your reward shall be very great" (v. 1);[240] "I am the LORD who brought you out from Ur of the Chaldeans to give you this land to possess" (v. 7).

It is very common when the Lord or an angelic figure appears to someone in the Bible for the first words communicated to be "Fear not" (v. 1). It is an overwhelming experience to encounter God in this way, and so words of reassurance are in order. However, in this context these words are far more than pro forma. Fear is connected closely to unbelief (cf. Matt. 25:25), and Abram has clearly been concerned about the continuing lack of an heir, despite God's promise to make him into a great nation (Gen. 15:2; cf. 13:16–17). In the absence of a son God's promises could easily ring hollow and start to create doubt in Abram's mind.

God's promise to be a shield to his followers is common in the Psalter (cf. Pss. 3:3; 18:2; etc.) and forms a concrete image to support the imperative "Fear not." The further assurance "Your reward shall be very great" emphasizes the Lord's provision for as well as his protection of Abram, both of which have been in the forefront of the preceding chapters. Yet these assurances leave unaddressed the great promises of offspring and land that the Lord has also made to Abram, and as a prophet Abram boldly confronts the Lord, seeking clarification about his lack of offspring to serve as an heir. As things stand, his heir would be Eliezer of Damascus, a servant in his household, not a member of his family (Gen. 15:2–3). This is the only explicit reference to Eliezer, though it is plausible that he is the servant sent to find a wife for Isaac in Genesis 24. It was common in the ancient Near East for childless couples to adopt a servant to fill the role of a son in providing for them in old age, in return for becoming their heir. Once such an adoption had been completed, however, it could not be revoked, so it appears that Abram has not yet formally adopted Eliezer.[241]

The Lord in turn reiterates his promise that he will give Abram a seed from his own body ("your very own son"; v. 4), not just an adoptive heir. He will provide not merely a single heir to inherit Abram's possessions but an abundantly numerous family of descendants. The Lord illustrates this truth by taking Abram outside and showing him the stars: just as the stars are uncountable, so also will Abram's offspring be (vv. 4–5). Yet the vision of the innumerable multitude of heaven is also intended to remind Abram that the one who called these stars into existence could surely also raise up a son for him, even if it were beyond all human hope and help. As the prophet Jeremiah puts it, "Ah, Lord GOD![242] It is you who have

---

[240] The Hebrew could also be translated "[I am] your very great reward" (KJV; NIV). This would make the Lord himself Abram's reward, which is certainly a biblical concept (e.g., Ps. 73:25); however, the precise terminology of "reward" (or "wages"; *sakar*) is used more often with God as the giver (e.g., Ruth 2:12; Ps. 58:11) and can be used of the gift of offspring, which becomes the focus as this passage unfolds (Ps. 127:3).
[241] Cf. Wenham, *Genesis 1–15*, 329.
[242] Jeremiah uses the same title for God as Abram does, "Lord GOD" (Hb. *'adonai yahweh*), a title that stresses the servant-master relationship of the prophet with the deity. This title is rare in Genesis but common in the prophets, providing another way in which Abram foreshadows them (cf. Gen. 20:7).

made the heavens and the earth by your great power and by your outstretched arm! Nothing is too hard for you" (Jer. 32:17).

It is worth noticing that there is no fundamental change in Abram's circumstances at this point. The Lord has not yet provided a son for him. Even the promise is not exactly new; in chapter 13 the Lord promised to give Abram offspring as numerous as the dust of the earth, a similarly immeasurable quantity (Gen. 13:16). Yet on the basis of the bare word of promise Abram believes God (15:6), just as he had when he left Haran, trusting that the Lord would certainly do what he had said. This is the posture of faith in its most dependent form, and God acknowledges it, reckoning it as righteousness for Abram. That is, Abram's continuing faith in God's promise forms the basis on which the Lord will enter into covenant with him later in the chapter, a covenant whose fulfillment rests entirely in God's hands, not Abram's (cf. below). The order of events is important: The Lord promises. Abram believes the Lord's promise. His faith is vindicated in the Lord's ratification of the covenant between them. Abram's salvation is thus "by faith" and not by works every bit as much as the salvation of Christians is (cf. Eph. 2:8–10).

15:7–16 The second interaction between Abram and the Lord follows a similar statement-question format. The Lord reminds Abram that he was the one who had brought Abram all the way from Ur of the Chaldeans in order to give him this land of Canaan (cf. Gen. 12:7). The phrasing anticipates the opening of the Decalogue in Exodus 20:2: "I am the LORD your God, who brought you out of the land of Egypt," which invites a comparison of this covenant with the Sinai one. In both cases the Lord's past faithfulness is the starting point for the covenant about to be enacted.

Once again Abram points out that the promise remains yet unfulfilled; what assurance could Abram have to be sure of the Lord's commitment to this promise (Gen. 15:8)? It is clear that faith—even deep and genuine faith—does not eliminate profound questions. On the contrary it provides the relational context in which believers can ask their deepest questions to God. In the first interaction the Lord simply showed Abram the night sky in response to his question, but his response in this second section is to invite Abram to a covenant-making ceremony, in which the Lord will underline the full depth of his commitment to fulfilling his promises to Abram and, through him, to all humanity.

First, Abram is told to gather a representative selection of sacrificial animals and cut them in two: a three-year-old (i.e., fully grown) young cow, a similar female goat and ram, a turtle dove, and a young pigeon (v. 9). Although these are animals regularly offered as sacrifices in the later Israelite cult, here they are not sacrificed, for there is no altar and no instructions concerning their blood. Rather they are killed and cut in two, except for the two birds, which are simply killed, perhaps because of their small size (v. 10; cf. Lev. 1:17).

The significance of this action is not explained in the text since it was well known to its original audience. At the conclusion of some ancient Near Eastern covenant ceremonies it was the practice for both of parties to pass between the pieces of slaughtered animals as an oath of self-malediction. In effect the participants would be saying, "If I break the terms of this covenant, may I become like these animals." Thus one of the Sefire treaties from around 750 BC declares,

> As this wax is consumed by fire, thus Matti'el shall be consumed by fire. As this bow and these arrows are broken, thus Inurta and Hadad [the two gods guaranteeing the covenant] shall break the bow of Matti'el and the bow of his nobles. As a man of wax is blinded, thus Matti'el shall be blinded. As this calf is cut up, thus Matti'el and his nobles shall be cut up.[243]

Given the symbolic importance of this action, the birds of prey that immediately threaten to consume the animals before the covenant is consummated likely speak of the difficulties and dangers that will surround Abram's offspring as they travel to Egypt (cf. Gen. 15:13).[244] The setting sun and the arrival of thick darkness (v. 12) also add to the threatening and fear-inducing atmosphere of the scene. The Lord proclaims Israel's forthcoming fate in three distinct stages: going down to Egypt, being enslaved, and then being afflicted (v. 13). This would be followed by a corresponding three-stage liberation process: judgment on their afflicters, freedom and deliverance from Egypt, and return to the land (vv. 14–16). The period of exile will be four hundred years (v. 13; Ex. 12:40 records it more precisely as 430), which corresponds approximately to the "four generations" of verse 16 if "generation" (Hb. *dor*) here stands for an entire lifetime.[245]

The Lord's sovereignty over history is on full display here. There is no question as to how Israel's future will unfold: the Lord is as sovereign over its suffering and exile from the land as he is over the time of its return to the land. Moreover, that timing is interlinked with the completion of the sin of the Amorites (Gen. 15:16), which provides the moral basis for the conquest under Joshua. The actions of the Lord's enemies are as under his control as those of his servants are, and even the sinful acts of human beings cannot do anything other than his good purposes (50:20). Only the Lord can do such things; no other god can compare (cf. Isa. 44:6–8).

As for Abram himself, his own departure will be peaceful, after a long life (Gen. 15:15). He will experience God's goodness and see the beginnings of the fulfillment of the promise in the shape of Isaac. When Abram dies, he will go to his fathers (v. 15), a statement that necessarily implies a concept of some form of life beyond death. But the fullness of God's promise to him will remain unfulfilled in this life. Abram must recognize that the land he is seeking is a heavenly country, not an earthly one. God has already demonstrated his goodness to Abram, and he

---

[243] ANET, 660.
[244] Mathews, *Genesis 11:27–50:26*, 172.
[245] Kidner, *Genesis*, 136.

will continue to do so throughout his lifetime. Yet the chief and crowning blessing of his life awaits him on the other side of the grave.

15:17–21 Abram had fallen into a deep sleep at sunset (v. 12). Once it is fully dark, God's verbal revelation that the promised offspring would indeed inherit the land of Canaan, though only after a lengthy period of suffering in a faraway country, is accompanied by a dramatic sign driving home the Lord's personal commitment to the promise. Abram sees a smoking firepot and flaming torch pass between the pieces (v. 17). The smoke and fire represent God himself in a way that clearly anticipates the pillar of cloud and fire that will lead Israel out of Egypt (Ex. 13:21), as well as the Lord's self-revelation to Moses at Mount Sinai (Ex. 19:18). As noted earlier, the general pattern in covenant making was for both parties to pass between the pieces of the animals, symbolizing a self-imprecatory oath, yet here only one of the parties passed between the pieces: the Lord. Clearly this is a unilateral covenant, in which the Lord is taking upon himself full responsibility to fulfill the promises of seed and land confirmed to Abram in this chapter. Abram's only responsibility is to place his faith in God's promise and to trust him to fulfill it.

This is a pivotal moment for mankind and especially for Israel. The solemnity of the occasion is underlined by the phrase "on that day" and the note that God is making (or "cutting") a covenant with Abram (Gen. 15:18). The same God who will later give his people the law on Sinai is declaring four hundred years earlier that he alone will be responsible for fulfilling his commitment to Abram and his offspring. Grace comes first, before the law, over which it has ultimate priority. As a result, our salvation is by grace through faith from beginning to end (cf. Galatians 3).

Yet what could it mean for the ever-living God to pledge himself to be torn apart like those animals, rather than letting his covenant with Abram fail in its purpose? It must seem like a metaphor to Abram, a pledge of the impossible as an assurance of God's determined purpose. Yet in the gospel the figure becomes an outrageous reality: the eternal, immortal God takes on human nature and tastes death in the place of the covenant-breaking children of Abram. On the cross God takes upon himself the full burden of making the covenant effective, despite our weakness, sin, and failure. In Jesus God himself bears the punishment of being almost literally torn apart by the whips, the thorns, the nails, and the spear for our sins, so that he could be faithful to his promise to be our God and that we might be his people through simple faith in him.

To Abram the Lord makes the unbreakable commitment to fulfill his promise to give Abram the land of Canaan—and more. In this case the boundaries allotted to the land stretch from the "river of Egypt" (Hb. *nahar mitsrayim*) to "the great river, the river Euphrates" (Gen. 15:18). The former landmark is sometimes identified with the "Wadi of Egypt" (*nakhal mitsrayim*), which represents the traditional southwestern boundary of the land (e.g., Num. 34:5).[246] However, since the latter landmark—the Euphrates—is far beyond the normal boundaries of Israel, it may

---

[246] So Hamilton, *Genesis 1–17*, 438.

be that this boundary also reaches into Egyptian territory, perhaps as far as the eastern arm of the Nile delta. Certainly, the land described here is never controlled and inhabited by Israel, not even at the height of the Solomonic empire, which suggests that the Lord is already directing Abram's eyes beyond mere real estate in the middle east to what the Promised Land has always represented: an eternal heavenly dwelling with God (Heb. 11:10).

At the time of the original audience, as in Abram's day, this land was still occupied by no fewer than ten[247] different tribal groupings: the Kenites, the Kenizzites, the Kadmonites, the Hittites, the Perizzites, the Rephaim, the Amorites, the Canaanites, the Girgashites, and the Jebusites (Gen. 15:19–21). Israel's commission under Joshua, trusting in the Lord's promise, was to drive these tribes out on the basis of their sin (v. 16)—just as Abram had trusted the Lord to do the impossible four hundred years before them.

Response

Old Testament saints were saved in exactly the same way that NT saints are, through faith in Christ. They anticipated the coming of Christ ahead of time and trusted God to fulfill his promises (John 8:56); we look back with the benefit of hindsight and trust in the reality. The Mosaic law, given to Israel by God at Mount Sinai, was never intended to be an alternative method of salvation. It could never have supplanted the promise of the Abrahamic covenant that our salvation is by grace, through faith in God's work of salvation (Galatians 3). Nor are the Abrahamic and Mosaic covenants in ultimate tension with each other, as though the Abrahamic covenant were a covenant of grace alone while the Mosaic covenant was purely legal. The God who covenants with Abram under the form of a smoking firepot and flaming torch is the same God who reveals himself in fire and cloud on Mount Sinai, while the animals that are cut in two by Abram are the same as those sacrificed in the Levitical order.

How then do these covenants relate to one another? First comes the Abrahamic covenant with its emphasis on God's sovereign choice and gracious promise to Abram, to which he responds by faith. That faith then shows itself as a living reality in a life lived in accordance with God's character, as it has been revealed to Abram, out of gratitude for the promise (e.g., Gen. 17:1; cf. James 2:21–23). The Sinai covenant works out in far greater detail what obedience to God looks like for Israel as she lives in the Promised Land.

Yet the Abrahamic covenant is a constant reminder to Israel not to treat the law as a means of self-salvation. Salvation is of the Lord from beginning to end,

---

[247] In different places the Bible makes various listings of the tribes living in Canaan, with the number ranging from two (Gen. 13:7) to twelve (10:15–18). The ten listed here probably imply a complete set; the Kenites, Kenizzites, Kadmonites, and Rephaim are not included in other lists, whereas the Hivites are omitted here. Perhaps some of these tribal groups migrate in the intervening period; at least some of the Kenites and Kenizzites seem to ally themselves to Israel prior to the conquest (cf. Judg. 1:16; 1 Sam. 15:6; Num. 32:12). The absence of the Philistines, Ammonites, and Moabites suggests the antiquity of the list, prior to the actual historical realities faced by Israel as a historical entity in the latter part of the second millennium BC (cf. Wenham, *Genesis 1–15*, 333–334).

and it requires the Lord to take on flesh and dwell among us as the new Israel, the one who keeps the terms of the Sinai covenant perfectly. In that way he merits our salvation and clothes us in his righteousness while at the same time giving himself up to experience the curse of covenant breaking on our behalf (2 Cor. 5:21). This is how the demands of the law have been fully satisfied and we may be saved by faith alone, through grace alone, to the glory of God alone (Eph. 2:8–10).

GENESIS 16

16 Now Sarai, Abram's wife, had borne him no children. She had a female Egyptian servant whose name was Hagar. ²And Sarai said to Abram, "Behold now, the Lord has prevented me from bearing children. Go in to my servant; it may be that I shall obtain children¹ by her." And Abram listened to the voice of Sarai. ³So, after Abram had lived ten years in the land of Canaan, Sarai, Abram's wife, took Hagar the Egyptian, her servant, and gave her to Abram her husband as a wife. ⁴And he went in to Hagar, and she conceived. And when she saw that she had conceived, she looked with contempt on her mistress.² ⁵And Sarai said to Abram, "May the wrong done to me be on you! I gave my servant to your embrace, and when she saw that she had conceived, she looked on me with contempt. May the Lord judge between you and me!" ⁶But Abram said to Sarai, "Behold, your servant is in your power; do to her as you please." Then Sarai dealt harshly with her, and she fled from her.

⁷The angel of the Lord found her by a spring of water in the wilderness, the spring on the way to Shur. ⁸And he said, "Hagar, servant of Sarai, where have you come from and where are you going?" She said, "I am fleeing from my mistress Sarai." ⁹The angel of the Lord said to her, "Return to your mistress and submit to her." ¹⁰The angel of the Lord also said to her, "I will surely multiply your offspring so that they cannot be numbered for multitude." ¹¹And the angel of the Lord said to her,

> "Behold, you are pregnant
>   and shall bear a son.
> You shall call his name Ishmael,³
>   because the Lord has listened to your affliction.
> ¹² He shall be a wild donkey of a man,
>   his hand against everyone
>   and everyone's hand against him,
> and he shall dwell over against all his kinsmen."

¹³So she called the name of the Lord who spoke to her, "You are a God of seeing,"⁴ for she said, "Truly here I have seen him who looks after me."⁵ ¹⁴Therefore the well was called Beer-lahai-roi;⁶ it lies between Kadesh and Bered.

¹⁵ And Hagar bore Abram a son, and Abram called the name of his son, whom Hagar bore, Ishmael. ¹⁶ Abram was eighty-six years old when Hagar bore Ishmael to Abram.

¹ Hebrew *be built up*, which sounds like the Hebrew for *children* ² Hebrew *her mistress was dishonorable in her eyes*; similarly in verse 5 ³ *Ishmael* means *God hears* ⁴ Or *You are a God who sees me* ⁵ Hebrew *Have I really seen him here who sees me?* or *Would I have looked here for the one who sees me?* ⁶ *Beer-lahai-roi* means *the well of the Living One who sees me*

Section Overview

In Genesis 13–15 Abram is portrayed as a man of faith and obedience, trusting God and following him, even amid doubts and difficulties. Genesis 16 shows that he remains a fallible sinner, able to make significant mistakes that will continue to haunt him (and his descendants after him) for many years. He has been promised an heir that will come from his own body (Gen. 15:4), but ten years have now passed since God brought him to Canaan and made him the original promise (16:4). So when his wife, Sarai, suggests following an ancient custom whereby a husband might take his wife's maidservant as a subordinate wife in order to have children by her, Abram agrees to the idea. It might seem like a reasonable way to help God fulfill the promise, but the result is an unmitigated disaster. Abram blames Sarai, Sarai is cruel to Hagar, and Hagar responds by running away.

However, the angel of the Lord appears to Hagar in her hour of need, encouraging her to go back to Abram and Sarai and endure the mistreatment in order to receive the blessing that still adheres to the chosen family despite its sin (v. 9). Her child, Ishmael, although not part of the chosen line, will nonetheless be multiplied into a nation and thrive with God's help (v. 10). His family will continue to be at odds with Abram's descendants, however, highlighting the limits to its blessing. Worldly prosperity is not the same thing as membership in the kingdom of God.

Section Outline

VII. The Family History of Terah (11:27–25:11) . . .
    H. Abram and Hagar (16:1–16)

Comment

16:1–6 This chapter opens with a reminder of Sarai's childless status (v. 1). Normally in the Bible this would be a signal that God is about to do something to redress the situation. In this case, however, the intervention comes from Sarai herself, not God. Sarai has an Egyptian slave named Hagar, presumably acquired during Abram and Sarai's sojourn in Egypt (cf. 12:16). Her Egyptian status is not a random detail but part of an ongoing motif in the narrative contrasting the attractiveness and fertility of Egypt with the apparent fruitlessness of the Promised Land. Thus Egypt provides food when there is a famine in Canaan (12:10); Lot chooses the visually most attractive destination, even though it is outside the Promised Land, because it is "like the land of Egypt" (13:10); and here Hagar the

Egyptian maidservant is instantly fertile while her mistress, the heir of God's promise, is barren. This motif warns the original audience against the temptation to trust in the apparent bountifulness of Egypt when they find themselves in times of difficulty (cf. Num. 11:5).[248]

Sarai suggests that Abram should take Hagar as his concubine and have children through her (Gen. 16:2). This practice is well attested throughout the ancient Near East,[249] and the children of such unions were normally considered full members of the family, inheriting alongside children born to the primary couple (cf. Genesis 30).[250] It was also regarded in some situations as a potential treatment for infertility, with the child born to the maidservant somehow inducing a similar effect for the wife. Many of the ancient Near Eastern laws concerning the practice have to do with regulating the relational problems that would predictably arise: the maidservant's elevating herself to equality with the wife, the maidservant's being mistreated by the wife, questions regarding the maidservant's being sent away or not, and so on. Genesis 16 could serve as a sociological case study of the reason behind such laws.

Sarai blames the Lord for her lack of conception (16:2). Her frustration is palpable, and of course God is indeed ultimately sovereign over the opening or closing of the womb, but instead of laying out her fears and concerns before the Lord, as Abram did in 15:2, she confronts her husband. She commands him to have sexual relations with her maidservant, Hagar, in hopes of Hagar's having children that will be reckoned as belonging to Sarai (cf. 30:3). Abram in turn "listened to the voice" of Sarai, his wife, and does as she asks (16:2). Listening to one's wife is not always problematic in Genesis; later the Lord commands Abraham to listen to Sarah's voice and send Hagar and Ishmael away (21:12). However, Adam is earlier rebuked for listening to the voice of his wife (3:17), so the reader is forewarned that this failure of leadership (and reversal of gender roles) will likely not turn out well for Abram. In another echo of the fall narrative, Sarai "took" Hagar and "gave" her to Abram (16:3; cf. 3:6).

In this case Sarai's plan works exactly as anticipated. Abram sleeps with Hagar, who becomes pregnant (Gen. 16:4). However, having conceived, Hagar then becomes proud and looks down on her mistress, an outcome foreseen in the Code of Hammurabi.[251] Her resentment of her mistress is perhaps not surprising; Sarai never speaks directly to her in this chapter, and both Abram and Sarai treat her more like an object than a person. Yet Hagar is not blameless in this matter; verse 4 tells us that Hagar "looked with contempt [*qalal*] on her mistress"—the same word used in Genesis 12:3, where blessing is promised to those who bless

---

248 Duguid, "Hagar the Egyptian," 419–421.
249 Cf. Tikva Frymer-Kemsky, "Patriarchal Family Relationships and Near Eastern Law," *BA* 44 (1981): 211–212.
250 However, although Jacob's children with the maidservants became the ancestors of full tribes in Israel, the lesser status of those tribes is evident in the arrangement of the camp of Israel, where the tribes that come from the offspring of the maidservants receive less favorable positions. Cf. Iain M. Duguid, *Numbers*, PTW (Wheaton, IL: Crossway, 2006), 41–43.
251 Section 146. Cf. *ANET*, 172.

Abram but a curse is pronounced on those who despise (*qalal*) him. Sure enough, Hagar's disdain of Sarai ends up with her wandering in the wilderness.

Sarai in turn responds with anger against both Hagar and Abram, blaming him for her idea. She even boldly enlists the Lord as judge between them, confident that he will support her as the wronged party (16:5). Abram, meanwhile, abdicates his responsibility as leader in the home, just as Adam had done before him. He washes his hands of the whole matter, leaving Hagar to be abused by Sarai to the point that she feels she has no choice but to run away (v. 6)—an extremely desperate measure for a pregnant servant girl without resources or protection of any kind.[252]

16:7–12 Yet, despite her own sins and the sinful mistreatment of Hagar by Abram and Sarai, the Lord has not forgotten Hagar. His concern naturally extends to the poor and needy, the disadvantaged and helpless, even though there is nothing to suggest that Hagar knows the Lord or calls out for help to him in any way. She is carrying Abram's child and, on that basis at least, receives the Lord's care in the shape of an angelic messenger,[253] the angel of the Lord (Gen. 16:7). He encounters Hagar on the way to Shur, which is itself on the road to Egypt, her homeland (cf. 1 Sam. 15:7). She is beside a spring, a natural place to rest on a journey. However, there may also be a wordplay here: *'ayin* can mean "eye" as well as "spring," and so it is a fitting place for the Lord to "see" her (Gen. 16:13).

As with Adam and Eve, the angel of the Lord asks a question designed to elicit a confession: "Hagar, servant of Sarai, where have you come from and where are you going?" (16:8; cf. 3:9, 11, 13). Since the angel addresses her by name, it is clear that he already knows her story, but he induces her to admit, "I am fleeing from my mistress Sarai" (16:8). The angel responds with a command and a promise. The command is that Hagar should go back to Sarai and submit to her mistreatment (v. 9). It would be better for her to be in the house of blessing, even under such circumstances, than to go back to Egypt in peace and abundance. If she returns to Sarai, the Lord will bless her child on an Abrahamic scale: the Lord will ensure that her offspring will be too numerous to count (16:10; cf. 15:5). Hagar is also informed that her child will be a son, and she is commanded to call him Ishmael, which means "God heard," because the Lord has heard her cry of affliction.[254] This is the first time in the biblical text that a positive promise is made directly to a

---

[252] The irony should not be missed that Sarai mistreated (Hb. *'anah*) an Egyptian, just as the Israelites will later be mistreated in Egypt (*'anah*; cf. 15:13).

[253] The Hebrew word *malakh* can refer to human messengers as well as angelic ones (cf. Hag. 1:13; Mal. 2:7), but there is no reason to assume that this is not a heavenly messenger, even if his appearance in this instance is human. The angel speaks for God as his emissary, and Hagar responds directly to God, believing that she has seen him (Gen. 16:13). This has led many commentators to identify the angel of the Lord as a manifestation of God himself, perhaps even the preincarnate Christ, which is plausible. However, authorized messengers can speak in the name of the one who sends them and can receive communications for him—and characters in biblical narratives do not always assess situations accurately—so certainty is not possible.

[254] It is curious that he is not named "Shemaiah" ("the Lord heard"); similarly in Genesis 6:13 Hagar calls *the Lord* who speaks with her "You are *a God* of seeing." In fact, prior to the exodus, there are no names in the account that clearly have Yahweh as the theophoric element; all of them incorporate "El" or "Shaddai." This suggests to some scholars that the name Yahweh was not actually revealed explicitly to the patriarchs (in line with Ex. 6:2–3); under the inspiration of God, however, Moses has made clear what was true all along—that the God of the patriarchs is the God Israel had now come to know as Yahweh. Cf. ESV mg. on Genesis 4:25–26.

woman, while the divine instruction concerning Ishmael's name is a mark of the Lord's interest in Ishmael and his future.

The Lord's care and protection for Hagar and Ishmael are all the more remarkable because these two will not ultimately be part of God's people. Yet the Lord's care for these outsiders is also profoundly encouraging to his own people. If the Lord takes such personal care of Hagar and Ishmael in their time of need in the wilderness, how much more will he take care of his own people when they are in distress?

In fact, the parallel is very apt. Hagar's cry of affliction heard by the Lord (Gen. 16:11) explicitly parallels Israel's cry amid the bondage of Egypt (Ex. 3:7). Sarai's oppression of her Egyptian maid forms a miniature picture in reverse of the suffering and oppression Israel will later undergo in Egypt. But the similarities between Hagar's situation and that of the Israelites only highlights the difference between the commands that the Lord gives each of them. God will say to Pharaoh, "Let my people go!" (Ex. 5:1), but he says to Hagar, "Return to your mistress and submit to her" (Gen. 16:9). One must find freedom by leaving the house of bondage, while the other will find freedom only by reentering the house of bondage. Hagar is sent back simply because there is no blessing to be found apart from Abram and his seed. Painful though the path of submission may be, there is no other way for Hagar to receive the blessing of God.

However, Hagar's blessing will come at a long-lasting cost for Israel. Her son, Ishmael, will be a "wild donkey of a man" (v. 12), that is, someone not bound by normal social conventions. He will live outside society in the wilderness, "close to" or "in hostility to"—the Hebrew *'al-peney* can mean either[255]—his brothers (v. 12). As we might put it, Ishmael will constantly be in his brothers' faces. His hostility to Isaac will eventually cause him and Hagar to be sent away from the Abrahamic family (21:9–13).

As an "also-son" like Esau, in R. Syrén's terminology, Ishmael will father an "also-people," whose existence as legitimate offspring of Abram will be part of Abram's legacy of blessing.[256] Yet their continuing bitter opposition to Israel will confirm and display their non-elect status. They will receive a measure of common-grace blessing via their relationship with Abram but not the special-grace blessing that comes only to the true heirs of Abram, who share his faith. Of course, the same could be said for many of Abram's physical descendants in Israel.

16:13–16 Hagar responds to this revelation of God with obedient faith. She identifies God as *El ro'i*, the "God of seeing" (v. 13).[257] In seeing the angel she believes that she has actually seen the one who has been watching out for her, and so thenceforth the spring at which the encounter takes place is called "Beer-lahai-roi" ("the well of

---
255 Kidner, *Genesis*, 138.
256 R. Syrén, *The Forsaken First-Born: A Study of a Recurrent Motif in the Patriarchal Narratives*, JSOTSup 133 (Sheffield: Sheffield Academic Press, 1993), 144.
257 As pointed in the MT. With a different pointing, matching the vocalization at the end of Genesis 16:13 and in the name of the well in verse 14, it means "the God who sees me" (so NIV, NET, NLT). However, the MT pointing should probably be preserved here as the more difficult reading.

the Living One who sees me," ESV mg. on v. 14; cf. 24:62; 25:11). She then returns home to Abram and Sarai, despite Sarai's mistreatment, and there bears Abram's son, whom Abram names "Ishmael," just as the Lord had commanded (16:15). At this point, eleven years after Abram's initial call, he is eighty-six years old. He will still be waiting for a child by Sarah thirteen years later, which is where the following chapter picks up the narrative.

Response

The great heroes and heroines of the biblical story are profoundly sinful people, capable of going from the heights of faith in one chapter to the depths of unbelief in the next—as are all of us. Abram is saved not by the strength of his faith but by the strength and grace of the God in whom his faith rests. Like Abram, we too face situations in life in which we are tempted to doubt the reality of God's promises, especially when their fulfillment is delayed. As the proverb says, "Hope deferred makes the heart sick" (Prov. 13:12). In such situations it is easy to persuade ourselves that God needs our help to accomplish his purposes. Yet, as Abram discovers, human wisdom rarely solves a problem and often massively increases it. The family of God can be a deeply dysfunctional place as people hurt and abuse one another while all the time being convinced that they are pursuing the will of God. Abram and Sarai need to learn that, when God calls us to wait, the proper response is . . . to wait. This remains true even when the time of waiting grows long.

It will help us as we wait to ponder the lesson Hagar learns while attempting to flee the messiness of her life with the family of God. She meets the living God, who is looking out for her. Often we forget that God is living and active in our lives. If we do not see him at work, we assume he is not there, and so we take matters into our own hands. Alternatively, we forget that God cares for us. When our hopes and dreams are delayed, we begin to think that God does not see what is happening or have any concern for our well-being. But our God is still *El lahai roi*, the Living One who sees and provides for us.

The proof of this care comes in the person of Christ. In Christ God entered this broken world and experienced firsthand what it is like to be abused by the very people who claimed to be serving God. He endured great suffering, even to the point of death, at the hands of those who considered themselves to be Abraham and Sarah's heirs so that he could provide hope for a lost and wandering world. Through Jesus' death and resurrection those who were once outsiders to the promise, like Hagar, have now been brought near to God. The gospel has a place for the descendants of Ishmael as well as for the descendants of Abram if they come to share Abram's faith in the Lord. What is more, the gospel reminds us that God is sovereign over all our sufferings, which he will use to bring glory to himself and to grow us up into the image of his Son. This hope will sustain us through the many long and dark stretches of our earthly pilgrimage to our heavenly home.

GENESIS 17

17 When Abram was ninety-nine years old the LORD appeared to Abram and said to him, "I am God Almighty;¹ walk before me, and be blameless, ²that I may make my covenant between me and you, and may multiply you greatly." ³Then Abram fell on his face. And God said to him, ⁴"Behold, my covenant is with you, and you shall be the father of a multitude of nations. ⁵No longer shall your name be called Abram,² but your name shall be Abraham,³ for I have made you the father of a multitude of nations. ⁶I will make you exceedingly fruitful, and I will make you into nations, and kings shall come from you. ⁷And I will establish my covenant between me and you and your offspring after you throughout their generations for an everlasting covenant, to be God to you and to your offspring after you. ⁸And I will give to you and to your offspring after you the land of your sojournings, all the land of Canaan, for an everlasting possession, and I will be their God."

⁹And God said to Abraham, "As for you, you shall keep my covenant, you and your offspring after you throughout their generations. ¹⁰This is my covenant, which you shall keep, between me and you and your offspring after you: Every male among you shall be circumcised. ¹¹You shall be circumcised in the flesh of your foreskins, and it shall be a sign of the covenant between me and you. ¹²He who is eight days old among you shall be circumcised. Every male throughout your generations, whether born in your house or bought with your money from any foreigner who is not of your offspring, ¹³both he who is born in your house and he who is bought with your money, shall surely be circumcised. So shall my covenant be in your flesh an everlasting covenant. ¹⁴Any uncircumcised male who is not circumcised in the flesh of his foreskin shall be cut off from his people; he has broken my covenant."

¹⁵And God said to Abraham, "As for Sarai your wife, you shall not call her name Sarai, but Sarah⁴ shall be her name. ¹⁶I will bless her, and moreover, I will give⁵ you a son by her. I will bless her, and she shall become nations; kings of peoples shall come from her." ¹⁷Then Abraham fell on his face and laughed and said to himself, "Shall a child be born to a man who is a hundred years old? Shall Sarah, who is ninety years old, bear a child?" ¹⁸And Abraham said to God, "Oh that Ishmael might live before you!" ¹⁹God said, "No, but Sarah your wife shall bear you a son, and you shall call his name Isaac.⁶ I will establish my covenant with him as an everlasting covenant for his offspring after him. ²⁰As for Ishmael, I have heard you; behold, I have blessed him and will make him fruitful and multiply him greatly. He shall father twelve princes, and I will make him into a great nation. ²¹But I will establish my covenant with Isaac, whom Sarah shall bear to you at this time next year."

²²When he had finished talking with him, God went up from Abraham. ²³Then Abraham took Ishmael his son and all those born in his house or bought with his money, every male among the men of Abraham's house,

and he circumcised the flesh of their foreskins that very day, as God had said to him. ²⁴ Abraham was ninety-nine years old when he was circumcised in the flesh of his foreskin. ²⁵ And Ishmael his son was thirteen years old when he was circumcised in the flesh of his foreskin. ²⁶ That very day Abraham and his son Ishmael were circumcised. ²⁷ And all the men of his house, those born in the house and those bought with money from a foreigner, were circumcised with him.

¹ Hebrew *El Shaddai* ² *Abram* means *exalted father* ³ *Abraham* means *father of a multitude* ⁴ *Sarai* and *Sarah* mean *princess* ⁵ Hebrew *have given* ⁶ *Isaac* means *he laughs*

Section Overview

After Abram and Sarai's failure in Genesis 16, it must have been a long thirteen years of waiting before the events of Genesis 17 occurred. Abram and Sarai had sought their own solution to the problem of Sarai's barrenness with disastrous results. The status of Ishmael is still lacking clarity: He is Abram's son, but is he the child of promise? If not, whence will this promised child come? Many questions remain, requiring Abram and Sarai to fall back once again on their faith in the God who does the impossible. Finally the Lord appears to Abram again, reiterating his commitment to him and to the promise he has made him, a lasting covenant that will now be confirmed through the sign of circumcision, applied to Abram and his (male) offspring. This sign will separate them from the nations around them and mark them out as belonging to the Lord in a unique way, reminding them of the Lord's promise to them and their children.

Section Outline

VII. The Family History of Terah (11:27–25:11) . . .
    I. The Lord Renews Covenant with Abra(ha)m (17:1–27)

Comment

17:1–8 At the end of chapter 16, when Hagar gave birth to Ishmael, Abram was eighty-six years old; at the beginning of this chapter he is ninety-nine. The narrator does not routinely mention Abram's age, so the gap here is significant. Abram has been waiting a long time, not just thirteen years since Ishmael's birth but twenty-four years since the original promise, when he was seventy-five (12:4).

Now the Lord appears to Abram in order to renew the covenant he had made in Genesis 15. We see both similarities and differences between the two events. The promise of land and offspring remain the same, although it is becoming gradually more detailed. However, in the covenant encounter in Genesis 15 Abram was entirely passive—even asleep (cf. Gen. 15:12)—whereas in Genesis 17 he is given instructions that must be followed precisely if he and his offspring are not to be cut off (cf. 17:14). Sometimes theologians have made overly sharp distinctions between conditional covenants, such as the Sinai covenant—which is often compared to ancient Near Eastern suzerainty treaties—and unconditional covenants such as the Abrahamic and Davidic covenants, which are in turn compared to ancient Near Eastern covenants of grant.[258] However, there seem to be elements of both conditionality and unconditionality within all biblical covenants, which implies a more complex relationship between the parties.[259] OT covenants have differences of emphasis, to be sure: the Sinai covenant is much more condition-oriented, while the Abrahamic and Davidic covenants emphasize the gracious aspect of the relationship. However, each covenant must be taken in turn and related to the unfolding narrative of biblical covenants, which find their climax in the new covenant, in which Christ fulfills all the covenants' conditions so that we might experience their blessings entirely by grace.

A covenant is at its heart a vehicle for relationship, and so it begins with an identification of the parties. In this case the Lord identifies himself as "God Almighty" (Hb. *El Shaddai*; v. 1), an archaic title that appears primarily in the Pentateuch and in poetic forms. Most of the biblical names that incorporate "Shaddai" as a theophoric element are also early. The derivation and meaning of the name are extremely obscure; the rendering "God Almighty" is probably as good as any. Abram is commanded by El Shaddai to "walk before me, and be blameless" (v. 1; also of Noah in 6:9), a stipulation that implies not perfection but rather faithfulness within a relationship. In Akkadian to "walk before a king" has a corresponding meaning of personal commitment and loyalty.[260] Abram's recorded behavior in this narrative thus far qualifies as "blameless," though far from perfect.

Abram's response is to fall down before the Lord (Gen. 17:3), a fitting response of submission to the Lord's words. Once again the unilateral nature of the covenant comes to the fore: the Lord has decided to make the covenant with Abram and set the terms and conditions of the covenant. Abram's part is simply to submit himself to those conditions. This sets the tone for any view of the relationship between God and humanity that has covenant at its heart, as the biblical view does; it naturally elevates God as sovereign initiator and determiner of the nature of the relationship, of which man is the humble recipient. This is not a relationship in which the two parties negotiate the terms as equals but one in which "I will take you to be my people, and I will be your God" (Ex. 6:7).

It is striking that in nine of the thirteen times that this chapter uses the word *covenant* the Lord calls it "*my* covenant" (Gen. 17:2, 4, 7, 9, 10, 13, 14, 19, 21). Since it is the Lord's covenant, it is only fitting that he initiates the relationship and sets the terms. He even dictates the one will be the heir of the covenant in the next generation. God promises that Ishmael will be blessed in many ways and will receive the sign of the covenant in circumcision, but the promise of covenant blessing rests ultimately with Isaac, not Ishmael. This is not because Isaac will respond properly

---

258 Indeed, some have sharply distinguished between God's covenant with Abram in Genesis 15 and this covenant in Genesis 17. Yet Nehemiah 9:7–8 clearly views the elements of both chapters as part of the same covenant.
259 Cf. Waltke, "Phenomenon of Conditionality within Unconditional Covenants," 123–139. Even here, while Abraham is required to circumcise himself and his household, the Lord promises, "I will multiply you," in contrast to the earlier commands "Be fruitful and multiply," emphasizing the decisive divine role in accomplishing this blessing. Cf. Gordon Wenham, *Genesis 16–50*, WBC (Waco, TX: Thomas Nelson, 1994), 22.
260 Hamilton, *Genesis 1–17*, 461.

to God's invitation while Ishmael refuses it. On the contrary, Isaac has not even been born yet, and Ishmael is as yet only a boy. But God sovereignly chooses Isaac to be the heir of his promise, not Ishmael (cf. Rom. 9:7–9). Salvation is of divine election from the beginning, which is God's right, since this is his covenant.

God continues to sketch out the scope of his plans for Abram; he will be the father not only of one nation, as promised earlier, but of many nations (Gen. 17:4; cf. 12:2). This refers immediately to the nations that will come from Ishmael and Esau, as well as Israel (cf. Genesis 25; 36), but it also has in view the spiritual heirs of Abraham through faith in Christ, who come from many different nations rather than all being Abraham's physical descendants (Rom. 4:11–12). In view of this enlarging of the promise the Lord renames Abram ("Exalted Father"; cf. ESV mg.) as Abraham ("Father of a Multitude Nations";[261] cf. ESV mg. on Gen. 17:5).

This too is an expression of the Lord's sovereignty and control over Abraham. It was not uncommon when a covenant was made in the ancient world for the great king to give a new name to the lesser king. In 2 Kings 23:34, for example, Pharaoh renames Eliakim as Jehoiakim before placing him as a puppet on the Judean throne. To rename someone is to exert power over the most fundamental aspect of his personality, especially in the ancient world, where names were viewed as expressions of someone's identity in a far more powerful way than in contemporary society.

Previously, God had promised to give Abraham offspring, but now Abraham is promised that he will be very fruitful (Gen. 17:6). The command to be fruitful occurred at creation and after the flood (Gen. 1:22, 28; 8:17; 9:1, 7), lending the establishment of this covenant relationship with Abraham and his offspring overtones of a new creation. Abraham will become a father not only to nations but to kings as well, the highest form of organizational leadership in the ancient world.

This covenant will be established not only between God and Abraham but with his offspring after him as well (17:7). Since the Hebrew word for offspring (*zeraʿ*) is singular, this leaves open the question as to whether the covenant will be made with all Abraham's descendants or with a singular seed yet to come. The answer, in a profound sense, is both. On the one hand, the Lord promises to be God to all Abraham's offspring (v. 7), which is why they are to be marked out with the covenant sign of circumcision. Given the facts that salvation is by divine election and that similar promises are not made to other nations, this is no small privilege. Yet, in light of the promised offspring of the woman in Genesis 3:15 through whom God would accomplish his salvation, the covenant also has a singular goal in mind: the one seed of Abraham, through whom salvation will come to the whole world (cf. Gal. 3:16). It is as we are united to this particular offspring of Abraham by faith that Jews and Gentiles become God's children and enter a new relationship with him.

---

[261] This meaning is not transparent in Hebrew and represents more of a folk etymology than a scientific derivation. Ibn Ezra suggested a consonantal abbreviation deriving *ABRHM* from *ABiR* + *Hamon* + *goyiM*. Cf. Sarna, *Genesis*, 124.

The final part of the promise, which is now also explicitly made to Abraham and his offspring, is possession of the land of Canaan forever (Gen. 17:8). Given that this comes after the Lord's declaration in Genesis 15 that Abraham's descendants will be slaves in another land for four hundred years (15:13), this does not preclude temporary periods when the land will not belong to them. Indeed, they will have to wait until after this exile in Egypt to inherit the land, and, even after they conquer it, they will be required to spend one week each year in temporary accommodations during the Feast of Booths (Lev. 23:42–43). This practice will be to remind them both of their past wilderness wanderings and that their ownership of Canaan will always be typological of a greater inheritance, a heavenly city (Heb. 11:10).

The greatest privilege of all, however, is the Lord's commitment to be Abraham's God and the God of his offspring after him, a commitment so important that it is stated twice (Gen. 17:7, 8). Modern people might not find this commitment surprising or significant since we are used to the idea that we can choose to serve whichever deity meets our needs. On our view, humans choose their gods, not vice versa. We imagine, "Of course the Lord will be our God if we choose to follow him: he should be grateful for our decision." However, this was not the way in which people thought in antiquity. Gods were often closely associated with territories, so to move from one place to another meant entering the realm of a different god, and there was no guarantee that the new god would show you favor. Moreover, if the God of the Bible—the eternal, sovereign, omniscient, all-powerful God—exists, he must necessarily be the one who chooses his followers, not vice versa. As a result, a commitment from this God not only to be our God but to allow our children to serve him as well is an inestimable privilege. And, in light of Abraham's failures in chapter 16, the promise that the Lord would be his God and the God of his children after him is a treasure of great price.

17:9–14 Biblical covenants often had signs attached to them (e.g., the rainbow in Gen. 9:12–17), in this case the sign is circumcision. In making a covenant with Abraham the Lord has committed himself to a relationship with him, and real relationships always have a profound impact on our lives. The Lord has made his commitment in the implied "As for me" of 17:4, and now it is Abraham's turn in the "As for you" of verse 9. For Abraham and his offspring to "keep the covenant" that the Lord has sovereignly made with them means accepting a mark on their bodies symbolic of that life-changing commitment to follow the Lord.

Circumcision is not a random act of mutilation;[262] rather, it is a covenant sign that involves cutting, just like the cutting of the animals in Genesis 15. There, the curse of the broken covenant was symbolized by animal carcasses, starkly demon-

---

[262] At least in Israel's case. Israel was not unique in practicing circumcision in the ancient world; it was the meaning that the Lord imparted to the practice that was significant, not the practice itself. In most of the nearby cultures that practiced circumcision it was a rite of passage associated with puberty and becoming a man. For Israel, however, it was practiced at the earliest possible moment as a sign of the fact that all Israelites belonged to the Lord as his distinctive people. The eighth day was likely specifically chosen as the day following the first seven days of the baby's life, corresponding to the seven days of creation (Sarna, *Genesis*, 125).

strating the destruction that would come upon the covenant breaker. God himself passed alone between the pieces, symbolizing the fact that he himself would pay for any breach of the covenant. In Genesis 17, however, the sign of judgment is applied to Abraham's organ of reproduction. This is the source of the hoped-for promised seed and also the organ of Abraham's failure with Hagar. Turning the sign into the reality of curse would merely mean applying the knife a little more extensively, cutting off Abraham's seed. If Abraham (or his descendants) failed to keep the covenant by not being circumcised, his seed would be cut off.[263]

The practice of "cutting off" (Hb. *karet*) people from the covenant community is prescribed for a variety of significant sins (e.g., Lev. 20:1–6). It is not always clear whether this has in view a divine sanction of death, a human sanction of execution, or the sanction of expulsion from the community. In context, to be cut off from the community of faith was itself a form of death, since the person was excluded from the only place where life and blessing were to be found. Whether or not that led to a person's immediate physical death was a secondary consideration.

This mark is to be applied not merely to Abraham and his children; it is applied also to servants or slaves (Gen. 17:13). They too share in the inestimable privilege of belonging to the people whom the Lord has chosen to be his, with all the blessings that come with that status (cf. Ps. 33:12). This principle illuminates the pattern of household baptisms in the NT, where the sign of the new covenant, baptism, is applied also to family members and servants on the basis of the faith of the head of the household (e.g., Acts 16:15).

17:15–22 Sarai's name is also changed to Sarah, though no significance is attached to this change, unlike that from Abram to Abraham. Both Sarai and Sarah are versions of "Princess," a fitting name for the future mother of kings (Gen. 17:15). Sometimes the mere fact of the name change, and the power that it demonstrates, is more important than the content. So, when the Egyptians change Eliakim's name (meaning "God has established") to Jehoiakim ("the Lord has established," 2 Kings 23:34), they hardly alter its meaning but vividly demonstrate their authority. In this case Sarah's name change reflects a fundamental change that the Lord is bringing about in her status. She will no longer be barren Sarai; now, as Sarah, she will finally bear Abraham's promised son (Gen. 17:16). It is through her that Abraham's offspring will become nations, and from her kings will come (cf. vv. 5–6).

This promise seems to Abraham too good to be true; he falls on his face and laughs (v. 17). This is a laugh of happy incredulity rather than unbelief (cf. Rom. 4:19–21). He believes God but at the same time struggles to put that belief together with the facts in front of him: his own age of nearly one hundred and Sarah's age of almost ninety. He seeks to redirect the Lord to a more feasible proposition, that Ishmael, the son he has already had with Hagar, might receive the Lord's blessing and become the child through whom these promises might be fulfilled (Gen.

---

[263] Cf. Hamilton, *Genesis 1–17*, 473.

17:18). But, when God insists on his original plan, Abraham does not protest further; he already knows too well the Lord's ability to do the unimaginable.

The Lord specifies a name for the promised child, emphasizing the certainty of the promise; the child will be called "Isaac" (Hb. *yitskhaq*; v. 19), derived from the Hebrew word "to laugh" (*tsakhaq*), and he will be born the very next year (v. 21). When he is born, Isaac will bring laughter of delight to his parents in place of their doubtful laughter at his promise (21:6). He is the one through whom the promise of an eternal covenant will descend, not Ishmael (17:19). Ishmael will indeed be richly blessed with the things this world values, fathering twelve princes[264] as a reflection of Jacob's twelve sons (cf. 25:12–16) and becoming a mighty nation (17:20). But he has no special place in God's plan to bless the world through Abraham and his seed—in those terms he is a dead-end line. The son of the slave woman will not ultimately inherit the promise alongside Isaac (cf. Gal. 4:30). It is God's sovereign right to choose who will be blessed and how, in terms both of the good things of this world and of the glories of the world to come. These blessings are not necessarily connected; those rich in eternal blessings are often poor and despised, while those like Ishmael may have possessions and power yet be strangers to a personal relationship with God.

17:23–27 As will become a common pattern in the Pentateuch, the giving of a divine command is followed immediately by a record of compliance. Abraham immediately has himself circumcised, along with Ishmael and all those born in his house or bought with his money (Gen. 17:23). It does not matter whether they are old (Abraham is ninety-nine), or young (Ishmael is thirteen), slave or free—all are included in this painful privilege of being marked out as belonging to the Lord in a unique way. There is no delay in his obedience—it takes place that very same day (v. 26). Abram's faith in God leads him to obey the Lord's word to him unquestioningly, thereby demonstrating the living reality of that faith (cf. James 2:22–23).

Response

God's renewal of his covenant is a testimony to his faithfulness, even when Abraham fails to "walk before [him], and be blameless" (Gen. 17:1). Because of the Lord's unilateral commitment to the covenant displayed in Genesis 15, even Abraham's sin and failure cannot destroy the Lord's purpose of salvation. The promise to Abraham and his offspring must be fulfilled. This does not mean that Abraham can remain unchanged by his relationship with God, however. The unconditional covenant that the Lord makes with Abraham includes demands that will demonstrate Abraham's positive response to the covenant. These include the sacrament of circumcision, by which the covenant is signed and sealed to him and to his offspring, and the name change that will be a daily reminder of his (and Sarah's) new identity in relationship to the Sovereign Lord. When a great king

---

[264] There may be an implied contrast in that "princes" come from Ishmael's line while "kings" come from Abraham's line through Isaac (cf. Gen. 17:6).

comes and offers to establish a covenant, one has only two choices: to accept the covenant relationship on his terms and receive its benefits or else refuse it and face the consequences.

Applying the sign of circumcision is a bloody process, symbolizing the cutting off of the promised seed of Abraham. When Isaac, the child of promise, is finally born, the symbolic judgment of circumcision almost becomes a reality. Abraham is instructed to take Isaac up onto a mountain, bind him on an altar, and offer him as a sacrifice (Gen. 22:2). As Abraham stands with his knife stretched above his beloved son, a voice from heaven stays his hand (v. 12). A ram takes the place of Abraham's seed on the altar (v. 13), a substitute that points forward to the cross, where Jesus Christ, the seed of Abraham, takes upon himself the curse of the covenant in all its awful fullness. There Jesus bears the reality of judgment for covenant breaking to which circumcision points.

With Jesus' death on the cross, the blood that circumcision foreshadows has been shed. Circumcision is thus no longer necessary; as Paul says, what counts is not circumcision or uncircumcision but faith in Christ expressing itself through love (Gal. 5:6). Yet we are not left without a sign under the new covenant: now the rite of initiation into the covenant community is the sign of baptism. Thus Paul can say in Colossians 2:11–12, "In him also you were circumcised with a circumcision made without hands, by putting off the body of the flesh, by the circumcision of Christ, having been buried with him in baptism, in which you were also raised with him through faith in the powerful working of God, who raised him from the dead." The true circumcision that we receive as Christians is baptism into the name of Christ and putting our faith in him. As is fitting for the sign of the new, richer covenant relationship, it is a more expansive sign that is now applied to men and women alike, not merely to men.

Yet, when God chose Abraham, he also chose his children. As a result, Abraham was to circumcise his children to show them that they were part of the covenant people. They belonged to the one true God and were to submit to him in a covenant relationship. That circumcision did not in itself save them. Ishmael was circumcised on the same day that Abraham was (Gen. 17:26), yet he showed no evidence of a heart renewed by grace. Although he bore the sign of the covenant, he was not ultimately part of God's covenant people. As Genesis 17:19–20 makes clear, although God's blessing rested on Ishmael and his descendants, his covenant was with Isaac and his descendants. In a similar way, circumcision pointed Israel's children to the Sovereign God who alone could save them. If they trusted in him, as their father Abraham did, they would find a refuge in him. But if they refused that God and rebelled against him, they would be cut off from the presence of God, just as Ishmael was.

GENESIS 18

18 And the LORD appeared to him by the oaks[1] of Mamre, as he sat at the door of his tent in the heat of the day. **2** He lifted up his eyes and looked, and behold, three men were standing in front of him. When he saw them, he ran from the tent door to meet them and bowed himself to the earth **3** and said, "O Lord,[2] if I have found favor in your sight, do not pass by your servant. **4** Let a little water be brought, and wash your feet, and rest yourselves under the tree, **5** while I bring a morsel of bread, that you may refresh yourselves, and after that you may pass on—since you have come to your servant." So they said, "Do as you have said." **6** And Abraham went quickly into the tent to Sarah and said, "Quick! Three seahs[3] of fine flour! Knead it, and make cakes." **7** And Abraham ran to the herd and took a calf, tender and good, and gave it to a young man, who prepared it quickly. **8** Then he took curds and milk and the calf that he had prepared, and set it before them. And he stood by them under the tree while they ate.

9 They said to him, "Where is Sarah your wife?" And he said, "She is in the tent." **10** The LORD said, "I will surely return to you about this time next year, and Sarah your wife shall have a son." And Sarah was listening at the tent door behind him. **11** Now Abraham and Sarah were old, advanced in years. The way of women had ceased to be with Sarah. **12** So Sarah laughed to herself, saying, "After I am worn out, and my lord is old, shall I have pleasure?" **13** The LORD said to Abraham, "Why did Sarah laugh and say, 'Shall I indeed bear a child, now that I am old?' **14** Is anything too hard[4] for the LORD? At the appointed time I will return to you, about this time next year, and Sarah shall have a son." **15** But Sarah denied it,[5] saying, "I did not laugh," for she was afraid. He said, "No, but you did laugh."

16 Then the men set out from there, and they looked down toward Sodom. And Abraham went with them to set them on their way. **17** The LORD said, "Shall I hide from Abraham what I am about to do, **18** seeing that Abraham shall surely become a great and mighty nation, and all the nations of the earth shall be blessed in him? **19** For I have chosen[6] him, that he may command his children and his household after him to keep the way of the LORD by doing righteousness and justice, so that the LORD may bring to Abraham what he has promised him." **20** Then the LORD said, "Because the outcry against Sodom and Gomorrah is great and their sin is very grave, **21** I will go down to see whether they have done altogether[7] according to the outcry that has come to me. And if not, I will know."

22 So the men turned from there and went toward Sodom, but Abraham still stood before the LORD. **23** Then Abraham drew near and said, "Will you indeed sweep away the righteous with the wicked? **24** Suppose there are fifty righteous within the city. Will you then sweep away the place and not spare it for the fifty righteous who are in it? **25** Far be it from you to do such a thing, to put the righteous to death with the wicked, so that the righteous fare as the wicked! Far be that from you! Shall not the Judge of all the earth do what is just?" ²⁶ And the LORD said, "If I find at Sodom fifty righteous in the city, I will spare the whole place for their sake."

²⁷ Abraham answered and said, "Behold, I have undertaken to speak to the Lord, I who am but dust and ashes. ²⁸ Suppose five of the fifty righteous are lacking. Will you destroy the whole city for lack of five?" And he said, "I will not destroy it if I find forty-five there." ²⁹ Again he spoke to him and said, "Suppose forty are found there." He answered, "For the sake of forty I will not do it." ³⁰ Then he said, "Oh let not the Lord be angry, and I will speak. Suppose thirty are found there." He answered, "I will not do it, if I find thirty there." ³¹ He said, "Behold, I have undertaken to speak to the Lord. Suppose twenty are found there." He answered, "For the sake of twenty I will not destroy it." ³² Then he said, "Oh let not the Lord be angry, and I will speak again but this once. Suppose ten are found there." He answered, "For the sake of ten I will not destroy it." ³³ And the LORD went his way, when he had finished speaking to Abraham, and Abraham returned to his place.

¹ Or *terebinths* ² Or *My lord* ³ A *seah* was about 7.7 quarts or 7.3 liters ⁴ Or *wonderful* ⁵ Or *acted falsely*
⁶ Hebrew *known* ⁷ Or *they deserve destruction*; Hebrew *they have made a complete end*

Section Overview

Abraham is the only person in the OT to receive the title "friend of God" (2 Chron. 20:7; Isa. 41:8). Even though the Lord spoke to Moses "as a man speaks to his friend" (Ex. 33:11), Moses is never explicitly called "God's friend," only "God's servant" (1 Chron. 6:49). Abraham thus has a unique relationship with the Lord, as illustrated in Genesis 18. The Lord visits Abraham and shares a meal with him (Gen. 18:8), after which he confirms the promise of a son for Abraham and Sarah (v. 10) and reveals to him the coming fate of Sodom (vv. 17–21). A friend is someone to whom another opens his heart, who knows not just what someone is doing but why. Abraham, the friend of God, is the man to whom God opens his heart and with whom he shares his inmost thoughts in a unique way. Abraham intercedes with the Lord for the city of Sodom, that it might be spared if even ten righteous men may be found within it (v. 32). However, Sodom's subsequent fate shows the comprehensive nature of its wickedness, since no such righteous quorum exists (Genesis 19). The Lord can deliver Lot out of Sodom, but the doom of the city is assured because of its many sins, and even the intercession of someone as righteous and close to God as Abraham is cannot rescue it (cf. Ezek. 14:13–23).

Section Outline

VII. The Family History of Terah (11:27–25:11) . . .
    J. The Friend of God (18:1–33)

Comment

18:1–8 The chapter opens by the oaks of Mamre, at Hebron, where Abraham has been sojourning for a while (v. 1; cf. 13:18; 14:13). While there, one day Abraham looks up and sees three figures coming out of the shimmering heat of the midday.

Although there are three of them, and they appear in human form, one of the three is clearly their leader, while the other two are his attendants.[265] The text alternates between singular and plural, reflecting this imbalance in authority. The latter two figures will be sent to Sodom to investigate and at that point be identified as "angels" (19:1). The exact time of their arrival at Abraham's tent is not specified, as is typical of texts from a time before clocks became ubiquitous. However, the noontime heat means that this is not a pleasant time for travel in that area, and it would be common for travelers to seek some kind of shelter in which to rest before going on with their journey as the day cooled. The impression that the narrative gives is that they appear suddenly, right in front of Abraham (18:2). Perhaps surprisingly for people on a lengthy journey, there is no mention of any beasts of burden (contrast Judg. 19:19–21, a passage with strong links to Genesis 19). All these elements combine to suggest the unusual nature of these visitors.

Abraham runs to greet the men and make them welcome, persuading them to break their journey with him, as any good ancient Near Eastern host would. The text repeatedly stresses the depth and extent of Abraham's hospitality. He runs to them and humbly prostrates himself before them (18:2). He speaks with deeply deferential language, persuading them to stay and rest under the shade of a nearby tree while a servant washes away the dust of the journey from their feet (vv. 3–5). Abraham hurries into the tent to inform Sarah, runs to fetch a tender young calf, and serves a meal of royal richness, with meat, bread, and goat milk (v. 7). Three seahs is an enormous amount of flour (v. 6), perhaps as much as six gallons, and Abraham specifies that it must be the highest grade of flour! The meal that Abraham presents is far more elaborate than the "morsel of bread" that he had offered them, involving the preparation and serving of an abundance of tasty foods.[266]

Abraham's generous and respectful welcome to his heavenly visitors can be both compared and contrasted with the experience awaiting the angels in Sodom in the following chapter. Lot too is sitting down at an entrance when they arrive (19:1); he too offers them water to wash their feet and food to eat, though his provision of unleavened bread cannot match Abraham's extravagant welcome (19:2–3). But the key difference comes in what occurs thereafter: Abraham's invitation ushers his guests into a place of safety, comfort, and provision, while Lot's invitation brings them into a place of danger and disrepute. Sodom's "welcome" is the antithesis of Abraham's hospitality.

Although the readers are informed immediately that this is a divine visitation, it is not clear at what point the true identity of these visitors becomes clear to Abraham. It seems likely that Abraham understands the significance of this event quite early, as he addresses one of them as "My Lord," marked in English with a capital L, which implies God and is not merely the form of polite address

---

265 Sarna, *Genesis*, 128.
266 Waltke, *Genesis*, 267.

to a stranger.[267] This may help to explain Abraham's outrageously extravagant hospitality and his deferential posture of remaining standing like a servant while his guests sit down and eat (18:8).

18:9–15 The first item on the visitors' agenda is to confirm the promise of a child to Abraham and Sarah (v. 10). In Genesis 17 the promise had been conveyed to Abraham, causing him to laugh and request that Ishmael fill that role (17:16–20). Is it possible that he has not relayed the substance of that conversation to Sarah, fearing to raise her hopes only for them to be cruelly disappointed? Or perhaps he has told her but she has refused to believe him. The Lord's words rebuking the unbelief in Sarah's laughter might support the latter view (18:13–14). She has come to doubt that the Lord would fulfill his promise, as if this promise were unbelievable, beyond even the unparalleled power of the Lord. But God does not need her faith in order to do the unthinkable and give her a child. Whatever the reason for her unbelief, the visitors are determined that this time Sarah herself should hear the good news.

As is customary in that culture, the men have eaten privately, apart from the women, and they ask after Sarah's location—which, of course, the Lord has known all along, just as he knew Adam's location while he hid in the garden (3:9). Even if Abraham has not already guessed the identity of his mysterious visitors, it becomes clear when the leader makes a promise to Abraham that only the Lord can carry out: "I will surely return to you about this time next year, and Sarah your wife shall have a son" (18:10). A powerful king might promise to give land and riches to his favorites, but only God is able to guarantee offspring, because he alone holds the power of conception in his hands. Nothing is too difficult for the Lord (v. 14).

What is more, this stranger knows everything; he demonstrates his omniscience by uncovering Sarah's secret laughter of doubt. While Sarah thinks she is safely concealed in the inner part of the tent, observing everything without being observed, this stranger knows her most private thoughts (vv. 12–13). He even knows exactly when this child of promise will be born—in about a year (v. 10; cf. 17:21), something no one but the Lord could know. The miraculous nature of the birth is underlined by the fact that Sarah has ceased her menstrual cycle (18:11; cf. 31:35). It is no surprise, then, that this mysterious visitor is identified explicitly as the Lord (18:13).

Sarah not only laughs in unbelief but also lies about having done so (v. 15). She is afraid, a common enough response when we are confronted with our sin by humans, let alone by God himself. But her fear is misplaced. The God who said "Fear not" to Abraham (15:1) is a kind and gracious God, to whom we may confess our fears and our sins and be forgiven for them (1 John 1:9).

---

[267] This distinction assumes the correctness of the MT pointing, which uses *'adonay* for address to God ("My Lord") and *'adoniy* ("My lord") for respectful address to human superiors (e.g., Gen. 23:6). In 19:2, 18 Lot uses a unique plural form of the deferential address *'adonay* (with a *patakh* rather than a *qamets*; "my lords"), suggesting that he lacks Abraham's immediate insight into their identity. While Lot may have "entertained angels unawares" (Heb. 13:2), it does not appear that the same can be said for Abraham. Cf. Sailhamer, *Pentateuch as Narrative*, 163.

Throughout their encounter the Lord treats Abraham as his personal friend. He shares an intimate meal with him. This is a unique privilege for Abraham. It is the only case prior to the incarnation in which the Lord eats food set before him. On many other occasions the Lord appears to people and they offer him food (e.g., Judg. 6:17–21) or eat in his presence (Ex. 24:11). However, on those occasions the Lord does not eat, though he sometimes turns the food into a sacrifice. But with Abraham he sits down and eats with him as part of their special relationship.

18:16–21 This special relationship of friendship extends beyond the shared meal. As the three men set out, presumably as the day has begun to cool a little, Abraham accompanies them to make sure they find the right road to their destination, Sodom (Gen. 18:16). As they travel, we are given a brief insight into the Lord's inmost thoughts in the form of a rhetorical question that provides the rationale for the discussion to follow. Elsewhere the Lord reveals his purposes ahead of time to his servants the prophets as a means of vindicating his actions (cf. Amos 3:7); here he reveals his thoughts to Abraham as his "chosen"[268] channel of blessing to the nations (Gen. 18:18; cf. 12:1–3). However, whereas the Lord often reveals his purposes ahead of time to Israel through his prophets in order to allow time for the preaching of repentance, in this case no repentance is possible. The time for judgment has come, as it will later in Israel's own history; there is no more time for repentance. However, the revelation to Abraham will allow him to intercede on behalf of Sodom.

Since Abraham will become the father of a mighty nation, through whom blessing will come to the world, it is also necessary for him to understand the Lord's retributive justice and his mercy, which are about to be displayed in his judgment upon Sodom. In this way he will be able to teach his children and his household to follow the way of the Lord after he is gone, pursuing righteousness and justice, the antithesis of the wicked behavior of the men of Sodom (18:20; cf. 13:13). Righteousness and justice (Hb. *tsedeq umishpat*) are essential characteristics of the Lord himself (cf. Pss. 33:5; 89:14) and are to be pursued by his followers as well (Prov. 2:9; 21:3). Otherwise, if they reject that pathway and pursue the lifestyle of the men of Sodom, they may face a similar fate, and the Lord's promised blessing might be thwarted (Gen. 18:19). Of course, such an outcome is unthinkable; the Lord's promised blessing cannot fail to come to fruition. However, the Lord ordains the means to accomplish the end as well as the end itself. Abraham's faithful instruction will be the means of directing his descendants in the Lord's righteous and gracious character and purposes ("the way of the LORD"; v. 19). Election can never be divorced from its goal, which is that the Lord would create a holy nation, set apart to serve him in righteousness and justice (Ex. 19:6; Eph. 1:4).

In contrast to the righteousness (*tsedaqah*; Gen. 18:19) to which the Lord calls Abraham and his descendants, Sodom is characterized by a "cry" (*tse'aqah*; v. 21)—

---

[268] The word for "chosen" in Genesis 18:19 is literally "known" (*yada'*) rather than the more common word in Deuteronomy, *bakhar* ("to choose"). "I have known him" emphasizes the relational goal of God's election: "I will be your God and you will be my people."

or, as we might say, an "outcry" to the Lord. This is the cry of the powerless and oppressed who have no advocate to speak for them except the Lord (Deut. 15:9; Job 34:28; Ps. 9:12). The Lord has heard their cry and seen the "great" and "very grave" sin of Sodom and Gomorrah, terminology echoing the description of the world of Noah's day (Gen. 6:5) and calling for a similar act of comprehensive judgment. This suggests that the sin of Sodom is not limited to (though is certainly not less than) the attempted homosexual rape of Genesis 19 but includes many other acts of social injustice as well (cf. Ezek. 16:49). As a just judge, the Lord does not rely on hearsay or secondhand testimony; before he delivers his sentence he is determined to investigate the situation thoroughly by sending his own representatives to visit Sodom and report to him (Gen. 18:21; cf. 11:5).

18:22–33 While the two angels go on ahead to investigate the state of affairs in Sodom, Abraham remains with the Lord and seeks to intercede on the city's behalf. Other prophets intercede on behalf of God's own people, but Abraham intercedes on behalf of wicked foreigners.[269] In his petition Abraham does not claim any merit or standing of his own before God as the reason his requests should be granted. He humbly recognizes that he has none; even though he is God's friend, he is but "dust and ashes" in the presence of his great Creator (18:27). Whereas in his high priestly prayer Jesus refers to his own authority and glory in the presence of the Father (John 17:2, 5), Abraham appeals simply to God's just character: "Shall not the Judge of all the earth do what is just?" (Gen. 18:25).

Although Abraham expresses his concern that the Lord should not sweep away the righteous with the wicked, he is not simply worried that a few good people might get caught up in the fall of Sodom. That injustice could be prevented by removing the righteous from the scene of the destruction, as eventually occurs with Lot and his family (19:15–22).[270] Moreover, the righteous do suffer alongside the wicked in both "natural" and man-made disasters all too often. Rather, Abraham's hope rests in the possible leavening influence of the righteous on the wider community. As long as a sufficient number of righteous people remain in Sodom, the possibility of the conversion of the wicked and the restoration of the city remains open. As in the parable of the wheat and the weeds (Matt. 13:24–30), Abraham's concern is that a premature destruction of the city might root out the Lord's harvest.

It seems likely that this is why Abraham stops his intercession at ten righteous men (Gen. 18:32). He argues the Lord down from a minimum of fifty righteous men to ten but then stops. Ten men is the number later laid down in Judaism as the minimum necessary to form a synagogue, a holy community shining the light

---

[269] Mathews, *Genesis 11:27–50:26*, 226. The contrast with Jonah is striking: Jonah is commanded by the Lord to preach to the Ninevites on account of the city's wickedness that had come up to the Lord, but he shows none of Abraham's compassion and concern for them.

[270] This passage may be part of the reason 2 Peter 2:7 asserts that Lot is counted among the "righteous" even though his behavior and trajectory in the Genesis account are sadly headed in the opposite direction. It is a valuable reminder that the righteous can at times live very conflicted lives, since we are saved by our faith and not our works. Even King David could be capable of adultery and murder yet nonetheless counted among the righteous.

in the midst of darkness. Of course, a city can be so far gone that, even if the most righteous of people were to dwell in its midst, they could not save it. In Ezekiel's time even the presence of such luminaries as Noah, Daniel, and Job would not have saved Jerusalem (Ezek. 14:12–23). As Zvi Adar summarizes,

> So long as there are righteous men, the wicked may be pardoned in the hope that good will eventually prevail. In the absence of any righteous man, mercy shown to the wicked would only encourage and reinforce their wickedness.[271]

If even Sodom, for all its wickedness, need not have been destroyed had only ten righteous men been found in it, how much more hope is there for our contemporary cities? Sadly, though, here not even such a basic quorum of righteousness is to be found in Sodom, and so after Abraham and the Lord go their separate ways the fate of Sodom is sealed (Gen. 18:33). Yet the reader is assured that in judging Sodom the Judge of all the earth indeed does what is right, demonstrating the righteousness and justice that embody his way (cf. v. 19). The same will be true of his final judgment on the last day.

Response

Most religions depict their god as either transcendent or immanent; he is either an accessible friend to humans or the exalted and distant judge of all the earth. The Bible presents a God who is both.[272] He stops to visit Abraham in his tent, seeking to reassure him and his doubting wife that he has not forgotten his promise of a child. In fact, the time for that promise is imminent and will come within the year. Such a specific promise is an even greater test of Abraham and Sarah's faith than a more generic word, as it sets their hopes on an impossible event that must soon come to pass. No wonder Sarah struggles to believe and then denies her unbelief. When we struggle to believe, we should bring our doubts to God as questions, as Abraham does in Genesis 15:2, rather than laughing in unbelief like Sarah and then pretending we did not laugh. Yet God's grace is sufficient for our weak faith and our doubts (cf. Mark 9:24; John 20:27), since what counts is the mighty God in whom our faith rests, not the strength of our faith itself.

A modern reader who enters a conversation about God regarding his impending judgments might approach it very differently than Abraham did. In our day many are confident in their own ability to critique the Judge of all the earth rather than adopting Abraham's deferential and cautious language. In C. S. Lewis's image, we are eager to arraign God to appear in the dock of our courtroom rather than recognizing that we belong in the dock of his court.[273] We might lecture God on the social causes of evil or the injustice of corporate acts of judgment involving

---
271 Zvi Adar, *The Book of Genesis: An Introduction to the Biblical World* (Jerusalem: Magnes, 1990), 80.
272 Cf. Vos, *Biblical Theology*, 73.
273 C. S. Lewis, *God in the Dock: Essays on Theology and Ethics* (Grand Rapids, MI: Eerdmans, 2014), 263–268.

whole cities. For many, sin has become merely an alternative lifestyle choice rather than an offense before a holy God.

Instead we should humbly intercede for the broken and sin-polluted cities that surround us and for the many lost souls that they contain. As Abraham did, we should rest our case on God's righteousness, confident that the Judge of all the earth will do what is right. As Abraham looked out at the cup of wrath about to be poured out on Sodom and Gomorrah, it was as though he prayed, "Father, if it be possible, let this cup pass from them; give more time for them to repent; yet not my will but thine be done" (cf. Luke 22:42).

Ultimately, the only way for a just judge to save the ungodly is for him to drink the cup of wrath they have merited. Jesus Christ, Abraham's greater descendant, did not simply intercede on behalf of his unrighteous people; he himself took the judgment we deserved—even if we once shared Sodom's defining sins (cf. 1 Cor. 6:9–11). Abraham's intercession for Sodom was not wasted; even though Sodom itself was destroyed, God remembered Abraham and rescued Lot and his daughters out of the city (Gen. 19:29). How much more may we be certain that the high priestly intercession of Jesus will be effective for us! God remembers the sacrifice of Jesus on the cross, and, as a result, he is rescuing an uncountable host of humanity from the fiery wrath to come. What is more, in Jesus Christ the creator God calls us all his friends (John 15:14–15), friends who have been given insight into the lost and broken world around us so that we too can pray effectively for its salvation.

GENESIS 19

19 The two angels came to Sodom in the evening, and Lot was sitting in the gate of Sodom. When Lot saw them, he rose to meet them and bowed himself with his face to the earth **2** and said, "My lords, please turn aside to your servant's house and spend the night and wash your feet. Then you may rise up early and go on your way." They said, "No; we will spend the night in the town square." **3** But he pressed them strongly; so they turned aside to him and entered his house. And he made them a feast and baked unleavened bread, and they ate.
  4 But before they lay down, the men of the city, the men of Sodom, both young and old, all the people to the last man, surrounded the house. **5** And they called to Lot, "Where are the men who came to you tonight? Bring them out to us, that we may know them." **6** Lot went out to the men at the entrance, shut the door after him, **7** and said, "I beg you, my brothers, do not act so wickedly. **8** Behold, I have two daughters who have not known any man. Let me bring them out to you, and do to them as you please. Only do nothing to these men, for they have come under the shelter of my roof." **9** But they said, "Stand back!" And they said, "This fellow came to sojourn, and he has become the judge! Now we will deal

worse with you than with them." Then they pressed hard against the man Lot, and drew near to break the door down. ¹⁰ But the men reached out their hands and brought Lot into the house with them and shut the door. ¹¹ And they struck with blindness the men who were at the entrance of the house, both small and great, so that they wore themselves out groping for the door.

¹² Then the men said to Lot, "Have you anyone else here? Sons-in-law, sons, daughters, or anyone you have in the city, bring them out of the place. ¹³ For we are about to destroy this place, because the outcry against its people has become great before the LORD, and the LORD has sent us to destroy it." ¹⁴ So Lot went out and said to his sons-in-law, who were to marry his daughters, "Up! Get out of this place, for the LORD is about to destroy the city." But he seemed to his sons-in-law to be jesting.

¹⁵ As morning dawned, the angels urged Lot, saying, "Up! Take your wife and your two daughters who are here, lest you be swept away in the punishment of the city." ¹⁶ But he lingered. So the men seized him and his wife and his two daughters by the hand, the LORD being merciful to him, and they brought him out and set him outside the city. ¹⁷ And as they brought them out, one said, "Escape for your life. Do not look back or stop anywhere in the valley. Escape to the hills, lest you be swept away." ¹⁸ And Lot said to them, "Oh, no, my lords. ¹⁹ Behold, your servant has found favor in your sight, and you have shown me great kindness in saving my life. But I cannot escape to the hills, lest the disaster overtake me and I die. ²⁰ Behold, this city is near enough to flee to, and it is a little one. Let me escape there—is it not a little one?—and my life will be saved!" ²¹ He said to him, "Behold, I grant you this favor also, that I will not overthrow the city of which you have spoken. ²² Escape there quickly, for I can do nothing till you arrive there." Therefore the name of the city was called Zoar.¹

²³ The sun had risen on the earth when Lot came to Zoar. ²⁴ Then the LORD rained on Sodom and Gomorrah sulfur and fire from the LORD out of heaven. ²⁵ And he overthrew those cities, and all the valley, and all the inhabitants of the cities, and what grew on the ground. ²⁶ But Lot's wife, behind him, looked back, and she became a pillar of salt.

²⁷ And Abraham went early in the morning to the place where he had stood before the LORD. ²⁸ And he looked down toward Sodom and Gomorrah and toward all the land of the valley, and he looked and, behold, the smoke of the land went up like the smoke of a furnace.

²⁹ So it was that, when God destroyed the cities of the valley, God remembered Abraham and sent Lot out of the midst of the overthrow when he overthrew the cities in which Lot had lived.

³⁰ Now Lot went up out of Zoar and lived in the hills with his two daughters, for he was afraid to live in Zoar. So he lived in a cave with his two daughters. ³¹ And the firstborn said to the younger, "Our father is old, and there is not a man on earth to come in to us after the manner of all the earth. ³² Come, let us make our father drink wine, and we will lie with him, that we may preserve offspring from our father." ³³ So they made their father drink wine that night. And the firstborn went in and lay with her father. He did not know when she lay down or when she arose.

³⁴ The next day, the firstborn said to the younger, "Behold, I lay last night with my father. Let us make him drink wine tonight also. Then you go in and lie with him, that we may preserve offspring from our

father." ³⁵ So they made their father drink wine that night also. And the younger arose and lay with him, and he did not know when she lay down or when she arose. ³⁶ Thus both the daughters of Lot became pregnant by their father. ³⁷ The firstborn bore a son and called his name Moab.² He is the father of the Moabites to this day. ³⁸ The younger also bore a son and called his name Ben-ammi.³ He is the father of the Ammonites to this day.

¹ *Zoar* means *little* ² *Moab* sounds like the Hebrew for *from father* ³ *Ben-ammi* means *son of my people*

Section Overview

The previous chapter ended without a resolution. Abraham and the Lord separated, and each went his own way after Abraham had interceded with God on behalf of Sodom, bargaining his way down to the sparing of the "city"[274] if only ten righteous people could be found within it (Gen. 18:32). The Lord confirmed that he would do as Abraham had asked but did not promise to spare the city outright. The question of whether there were that many righteous people in Sodom had still to be answered—and the two angels were already on their way to investigate the city (18:21–22).

It does not take them long to uncover the truth. Upon arriving in the town square they immediately meet Lot, who presses them to spend the night at his house, mirroring Abraham's hospitality (Gen. 19:1–2; cf. 18:2–5). But later that night, while the angels are at Lot's house, all the men of the city, apparently without exception, surround the house and demand that the strangers be brought out to them to be raped (19:4–5). From then on the doom of Sodom is certain.

The angels strike the men of Sodom with blindness (Gen. 19:11) and urge Lot to flee with his entire family (v. 12). His future sons-in-law think he is joking (v. 14), while his wife looks longingly backward while she flees and shares Sodom's awful fate, leaving Lot alone with his two daughters (v. 26). Overcome by fear, Lot ends up living in a cave in the hills (v. 30). In that isolated situation Lot's two daughters get him drunk and lie with him out of desperation in order to produce offspring, becoming in the process the ancestresses of Moab and Ammon (vv. 37–38).

Sodom's destruction and Lot's (partial) rescue has more than mere historical interest. The broader background of the fall of Sodom is the universal wickedness of humanity, which began with the fall in Genesis 3 and continued as the cause of the flood in Genesis 6. It is not just the inhabitants of Sodom who "were wicked, great sinners against the LORD" (13:13). From Adam and Eve onward all the people whom God created to know him have rebelled (cf. 8:21), raising the question of whether (and how) we too may be saved from the destruction to come.

Section Outline

VII. The Family History of Terah (11:27–25:11) . . .

    K. The Destruction of Sodom and the Rescue of Lot (19:1–38)

---

[274] It is common to translate *'ir* as "city" (Gen. 18:28) even though in many cases the settlements being described were tiny, with populations of a few hundred people—by our standards little more than villages.

Comment

19:1–3 The two men who accompanied the Lord on his visit to Abraham are now identified as "angels" (Hb. *mal'akim*). The Hebrew word can be used of both human and angelic messengers, focusing attention on their task as agents of their master. In this case they are not bringing a message to the inhabitants of Sodom; rather, they have been sent to investigate whether the outcry the Lord had heard was accurate (18:20–21). In light of Abraham's negotiation with the Lord, presumably they are now tasked also with determining whether there are at least ten righteous people in the city. Significantly, they arrive in Sodom at dusk, as the darkness is deepening (19:1); the angels and Lot will leave the city before sunrise (v. 23). The contrast between the bright sunlight of Abraham's noontime encounter with the Lord and the black night of Sodom is emblematic of the two entirely contrasting communities.

As soon as the angels arrive in Sodom, they meet Lot, sitting in the city gate (v. 1). Ancient city gates had rooms within them, forming the place where the elders and decision makers of the city would sit (cf. Ruth 4:1–4). Lot's presence at the city gate shows that he is now an honored member of the community in Sodom. He has come to regard the men of Sodom as his "brothers" (Gen. 19:7), while his daughters are engaged to be married to men of the city (v. 14). His transition from envious outsider in Genesis 13 to settled man of substance with a house of his own in Sodom is complete, yet significant compromises must have marked his rise in the community. It is not possible to live comfortably in a place of such wickedness as Sodom without compromise.

But even while he compromises, the spark of Lot's faith is not utterly extinguished. He is called "righteous" in the NT because he apparently grieves over the wickedness that he sees around him (cf. 2 Pet. 2:7–8). Genesis 19 also implies that Lot must be considered among the righteous, since he is rescued (Gen. 19:29), and Abraham's intercession was on behalf of the righteous.[275] Lot never totally identifies with the world in which he lives, but at the same time he is unwilling to leave it behind. Derek Kidner calls him "the righteous man without the pilgrim spirit."[276]

This concern for righteousness, however muted, is seen in Lot's immediate reaction to meeting the angels, which is to show them hospitality; like Abraham, he gets up to meet the men and prostrates himself before them, addressing them in deferential terms and offering them lodging for the night and water to wash the dust of their journey from their feet (Gen. 19:1–2; see 18:2–5). When they make to decline Lot's offer, instead desiring to spend the night in the city square, he continues to press them strongly—so much so that the reader begins to suspect that all is not well in Sodom (19:3) if spending the night in the town square is unsafe for travelers. That concern may also lie behind his encouragement for them to get on their way early in the morning, before the inhabitants of Sodom become aware

---

[275] Sailhamer, *Pentateuch as Narrative*, 172.
[276] Kidner, *Genesis*, 133.

of their presence.[277] The two men finally accept his offer, and he makes for them a "feast" (*mishteh*). The only food specified at Lot's feast, however, is unleavened bread (19:3), which pales in comparison to the genuinely outrageous meal that Abraham had served them earlier the same day, with cakes made of fine flour, a tender young calf, curds, and milk (18:6–8).[278]

19:4–11 This peaceful scene of domestic comfort is soon shattered as an angry mob gathers outside Lot's house (19:4). This mob comprises the whole male population of Sodom, an entirety stressed by repetition in the Hebrew, which reads, "The men of the city, the men of Sodom, both young and old, all the people to the last man, surrounded the house." This is the definitive answer to the question in chapter 18 about the number of righteous men within Sodom: zero (with the exception of Lot himself). They call on Lot to violate the cultural standards of hospitality and surrender the men he is hosting so that the mob can "know" them, in the sense of sexual intercourse (19:5).[279] This is not a consensual homosexual relationship, though such encounters are also clearly forbidden in the OT and NT (Lev. 20:13; 1 Cor. 6:9–11), but rather homosexual rape—an expression of power and humiliation rather than lust.

Lot goes out to speak to the men of Sodom, addressing them as "brothers" and pleading with them not to act wickedly (Gen. 19:7). However, his "solution" to the situation is every bit as wicked as theirs: he proposes bringing out his two betrothed daughters for the mob to do with as it pleases (v. 8). This is a mark of how seriously ancient people took the responsibility to protect guests who had come under their roof, though ancient audiences would have found the idea of Lot's turning his daughters over to a mob as abhorrent as modern people do. Many ancient law codes required the death penalty for violating a betrothed woman.[280] Lot's sensibilities have clearly been impacted negatively by his time in Sodom; he is concerned more to maintain his artificial relationship with the men of Sodom as his brothers than to defend his own daughters.

Lot's proposal falls on deaf ears, as the mob ridicules Lot as a "sojourner" rather than recognizing the status of "brother" he has just claimed. They threaten to abuse him as well as the two visitors if he prevents their access to the house, and they move in to try to break down the door (v. 9). They resist the idea that Lot will be their judge (v. 9), though in reality they have a far more fearsome authority to fear, the "Judge of all the earth" (cf. 18:25). Lot deems their behavior "wicked" (Hb. *r'*; 19:7), and they threaten to treat him more wickedly than the two men (*r'*; v. 9; "deal worse"). Only the timely intervention of the two angels rescues Lot, as they blind the nearest group of men and draw Lot back into the house (vv. 10–11).[281]

---

277 Sarna, *Genesis*, 135.
278 Mathews, *Genesis 11:27–50:26*, 234.
279 Some scholars have attempted to deny the sexual sense of *yada'* ("to know") here; e.g., M. Morschauser, "'Hospitality,' Hostiles and Hostages: On the Legal Background to Genesis 19.1–9," *JSOT* 27 (2003): 461–485. However, Lot's response of offering his two virgin daughters as substitutes hardly makes sense on any other reading.
280 E.g., Code of Hammurabi §130, in *ANET*, 171.
281 The Hb. *sanverim* is used only of divinely induced blindness, here and at 2 Kings 6:18.

By miraculously closing the eyes of their attackers the two men open Lot's eyes to their true angelic identity.

19:12–14 Just as corporate judgment is about to fall upon Sodom, so is there the possibility of salvation for any who identifies with Lot—and thus with his wider family, including Abraham. This includes not merely blood relatives but in-laws: just as Noah's daughters-in-law were delivered alongside his sons (Gen. 7:7), so too an offer of salvation is extended to the two young men to whom his daughters are betrothed. If the earlier language describing those surrounding Lot's house was as comprehensive as it sounded, then these men must have been part of the assault group (19:4), but, even if they were somehow excluded, they reveal their true nature by thinking that Lot must surely be joking rather than serious (v. 14). A desperate last-minute appeal in the dead of night will not convince them, perhaps because Lot has never spoken to them before about God or about divine judgment. The doctrine of divine judgment is perhaps the hardest doctrine for fallen men and women to believe and has been a primary focus of Satan's assaults since the beginning (3:4). Even when the men are warned of the impending arrival of final judgment upon Sodom, Lot's words seem like an idle tale to them, and so they perish along with their city (19:14).

Despite their disbelief the decree of judgment has already been delivered: the facts of the case have been thoroughly explored by the Judge of all the earth, and Sodom has proved itself guilty as charged. The iniquity of the Amorites might not yet be full (cf. Gen. 15:16), but the sins of the Sodomites are more than sufficient to warrant their total elimination (19:13). Nothing more can be done to save the city or its inhabitants; it is time for Lot and his family to wipe Sodom's dust off their feet and leave the city to its fate (cf. Matt. 10:14–15).

19:15–26 It is not easy for Lot to leave Sodom, even after hearing its imminent destruction announced. It entails leaving his house and possessions, all the worldly goods that he has labored for, and so Lot lingers as long as possible (v. 16). As morning finally dawns on the darkened city of Sodom, the angels take Lot and his family by the hand and virtually drag them outside the city, telling him to flee to the hills lest they be swept away in Sodom's downfall (vv. 16–17). The family must not stop, or even look back (v. 17).

Even then Lot still lingers, paralyzed by fear, claiming that he could not possibly flee to the mountains and asking for the small city of Zoar to be saved as a refuge within running distance (v. 20). As a result, prior to Sodom's destruction at the hands of a righteous and just God, that same God offers yet another demonstration of his unfathomable grace. He holds back his entire timetable of destruction on Sodom so that he can save poor, compromised Lot and with him the little town of Zoar. For the sake of Abraham and his intercession on Lot's behalf, Lot is not destroyed (cf. v. 29).

The Lord no sooner provides a refuge for Lot than the threatened destruction falls on Sodom and Gomorrah in the shape of "sulfur and fire from . . . heaven"—

or perhaps "burning sulfur" if we take this as a hendiadys (Gen. 19:24). This is no mere accident of nature but the Lord of nature's summoning the created order to do his bidding, as he will do with the plagues of Egypt.[282] The destruction of Sodom and Gomorrah and their inhabitants, along with the surrounding area and its vegetation, is complete; the cities are "overthrown" (Hb. *hapak*, "overturned"), a word that the rest of the OT associates repeatedly with this destruction (cf. Deut. 29:23).[283]

Tragically, Lot's wife is caught up in the destruction, as she fails to heed the angel's warning and instead looks longingly backward (Gen. 19:26). The word translated "looked" (*nabat*) does not mean a casual glance but suggests an intense gaze; her heart and affections are still bound up in Sodom, and so she shares the fate of the rest of the inhabitants.[284] That "she became a pillar of salt" implies that she is overcome where she stands and is buried in a salty deposit that would remain a recognizable landmark. This highlights the fact that being outwardly part of the community that God has marked out for salvation will not save us if we do not combine that membership with faith (cf. Heb. 3:7–19). The Lord can do to his own people what he did to Sodom and Gomorrah if they share the latter's wickedness (cf. Deut. 29:23).

19:27–29 From the destruction of Sodom and the narrow escape of Lot the text returns to Abraham's vantage point. Early the next morning he goes back up to the place of intercession to see what has happened to Sodom and Gomorrah (19:27). Perhaps he is hoping for a last-minute miracle of repentance, as will happen to Nineveh in Jonah's day (Jonah 3). One look at the rising cloud of dense, black smoke, however, gives Abraham the answer (Gen. 19:28). The Judge of all the earth has done what is just and destroyed the cities (cf. 18:25). Yet Abraham's intercession for Sodom has not been wasted. It is on account of God's remembering Abraham, just as he remembered Noah in 8:1, that God has rescued Lot out of the midst of the destruction despite his sinfully compromised lifestyle. The final judgment of the wicked is not incompatible with the gracious deliverance of sinners on account of the intercession of a righteous mediator on their behalf.

19:30–38 The aftermath of Lot's story continues his tragic downward trajectory. Although he has sought safety in the town of Zoar and been assured of it by the angel (19:20–21), he is afraid to stay there for long and ends up living in a cave in

---

[282] A recent multiauthored paper reviews the evidence that a "cosmic airburst" with a thousand times the energy of the Hiroshima atomic bomb destroyed a Middle Bronze Age city just northeast of the Dead Sea in 1650 BC. While we cannot be certain that the event described was the one recounted in the Bible, it demonstrates the potential of a catastrophe similar in nature and scale to that which destroyed Sodom. Cf. Ted E. Bunch et al., "A Tunguska-Sized Airburst Destroyed Tall el-Hammam, a Middle Bronze Age City in the Jordan Valley near the Dead Sea," *Nature* 11:18632 (2021): 1–64, www.nature.com/articles/s41598-021-97778-3.pdf, accessed December 21, 2021.

[283] Ironically, the Lord's message to Nineveh through Jonah is that the city will be "overthrown" (Hb. *hapak*; Jonah 3:4). Jonah hopes for a "Sodom-like" act of destruction for Nineveh, but in his case the city is "turned upside down" with repentance, removing the need for her destruction.

[284] It is possible that she herself was from Sodom, since there is no mention of Lot's wife earlier in the text (Waltke, *Genesis*, 279), but, given the age of Lot's daughters, it is perhaps more likely that her heart had simply been ensnared by the worldly attractions of life in Sodom.

the hill country, completely isolated from wider society, with only his daughters for company (v. 30). So much for his earlier choice of the land that looked "like the garden of the LORD, like the land of Egypt" (13:10)!

Because of the absence of any potential husband to provide Lot's daughters with children, and thus with meaning in life, they hatch a plan worthy of the inhabitants of Sodom in order to get themselves pregnant: they will get their father sufficiently drunk and then sleep with him in turn as a means of continuing the family (19:31–33). There is a certain irony in this plan; Lot was willing to sacrifice their virginity without consulting them in order to achieve his own purposes earlier (v. 8), and now they use him sexually to achieve their own purposes without his knowledge. The heightened echoes of Noah's disgrace in Genesis 9:21 are obvious, even if that incident did not involve sexual misconduct, as this episode does.

The result of the sordid plan is the birth of the ancestors of two of Israel's neighboring nations, Moab and Ammon (vv. 37–38). Their incestuous origins means that Moabites and Ammonites cannot normally be added to the Israelite assembly (Deut. 23:2–3). However, gracious exceptions are made: King David himself comes from Moabite ancestry through Ruth, giving hope to those who would normally be excluded from God's family (Ruth 4:13–22).

Response

The judgment of Sodom and Gomorrah is emblematic of both the later judgment that falls on the land of Canaan in the time of Joshua and the final destruction that will accompany the end of the world. In each case a period of extended divine patience is followed by uncompromising judgment upon sin. The Lord waits so long in his graciousness that people begin to think that he cannot judge, but, when he does come in judgment, it is so decisive that it seems as though he cannot show mercy.[285] This is not the sudden anger of an irritable temper, easily inflamed but equally easily pacified. This is deliberate, measured wrath following a full investigation of the facts of the case. There can be no last-minute appeals or reprieves, for there is no higher court to whom appeal can be made, and no pertinent facts have been overlooked in reaching the verdict. So it was with Sodom and Gomorrah, and so it shall be at the end of history. Jesus specifically compares those final days to the destruction of Sodom in Luke 17:28–30:

> Likewise, just as it was in the days of Lot—they were eating and drinking, buying and selling, planting and building, but on the day when Lot went out from Sodom, fire and sulfur rained from heaven and destroyed them all—so will it be on the day when the Son of Man is revealed.

On that day judgment will fall without mercy on the ungodly. But in the present there is a little place of refuge to be found for us, just as there was for Lot. Lot was not saved by his own wisdom or righteousness. Rather, he was saved by God's

---

285 Cf. Candlish, *Studies in Genesis*, 327.

providing a place of refuge for him to hide from the destruction on all sides. So it is also for us. We too are saved not by our own goodness or wisdom but by taking refuge in Jesus Christ. There is no other hiding place, no other safe refuge from the final outpouring of the wrath of God against sin.

In OT and NT alike God is depicted as both just and gracious. How is it possible for him to be both? The answer is found at the cross. There God's wrath and justice are satisfied as God judges sin comprehensively, putting to death the sinless Son of God for all the sins committed by his people. There too God's grace is equally on display as mercy is offered freely to all who would come to Jesus Christ in repentance and faith, trusting in his goodness and not their own. At the cross perfect justice meets perfect mercy, establishing our salvation and leaving the unrepentant utterly without excuse.

GENESIS 20

20 From there Abraham journeyed toward the territory of the Negeb and lived between Kadesh and Shur; and he sojourned in Gerar. ² And Abraham said of Sarah his wife, "She is my sister." And Abimelech king of Gerar sent and took Sarah. ³ But God came to Abimelech in a dream by night and said to him, "Behold, you are a dead man because of the woman whom you have taken, for she is a man's wife." ⁴ Now Abimelech had not approached her. So he said, "Lord, will you kill an innocent people? ⁵ Did he not himself say to me, 'She is my sister'? And she herself said, 'He is my brother.' In the integrity of my heart and the innocence of my hands I have done this." ⁶ Then God said to him in the dream, "Yes, I know that you have done this in the integrity of your heart, and it was I who kept you from sinning against me. Therefore I did not let you touch her. ⁷ Now then, return the man's wife, for he is a prophet, so that he will pray for you, and you shall live. But if you do not return her, know that you shall surely die, you and all who are yours."

⁸ So Abimelech rose early in the morning and called all his servants and told them all these things. And the men were very much afraid. ⁹ Then Abimelech called Abraham and said to him, "What have you done to us? And how have I sinned against you, that you have brought on me and my kingdom a great sin? You have done to me things that ought not to be done." ¹⁰ And Abimelech said to Abraham, "What did you see, that you did this thing?" ¹¹ Abraham said, "I did it because I thought, 'There is no fear of God at all in this place, and they will kill me because of my wife.' ¹² Besides, she is indeed my sister, the daughter of my father though not the daughter of my mother, and she became my wife. ¹³ And when God caused me to wander from my father's house, I said to her, 'This is the kindness you must do me: at every place to which we come, say of me, "He is my brother."'"

¹⁴ Then Abimelech took sheep and oxen, and male servants and female servants, and gave them to Abraham, and returned Sarah his wife to him. ¹⁵ And Abimelech said, "Behold, my land is before you; dwell where it pleases you." ¹⁶ To Sarah he said, "Behold, I have given your brother a thousand pieces of silver. It is a sign of your innocence in the eyes of all[1] who are with you, and before everyone you are vindicated." ¹⁷ Then Abraham prayed to God, and God healed Abimelech, and also healed his wife and female slaves so that they bore children. ¹⁸ For the LORD had closed all the wombs of the house of Abimelech because of Sarah, Abraham's wife.

[1] Hebrew *It is a covering of eyes for all*

Section Overview

Genesis 20 opens with Abraham on the move again and repeating the sin of pretending that Sarah is merely his sister and not also his wife (Gen. 20:2). This is sometimes imagined to be merely a variant telling of the earlier episode when Abram went down to Egypt (12:11–20), but we see significant differences between the two events. Those who know and work with people understand that sins are rarely random but rather tend to fall into standard patterns, reflecting our own personal heart idolatries. Those who are inclined to be fearful do not suddenly stop being fearful simply because the situation resolved itself on a previous occasion. It is entirely plausible that under the pressure of a new situation Abraham adopts an old pattern of sin as a defense mechanism, even though the outcome is predictable. Indeed, 20:13 reveals this to have been Abraham's default approach to new environments. Once again God must intervene to deliver Abraham from the consequences of his sin and restore him to a position from which the Lord's promise to him can finally be accomplished. This is the final hurdle to be crossed before the promised child can be given to Abraham and Sarah.

This passage also explicitly calls Abraham a "prophet" (v. 7), not because he has a direct revelation from God for Abimelech but because he will intercede for him. Intercession is a key part of a prophet's calling,[286] as may be seen from the exceptional restriction placed on Ezekiel, preventing him from interceding for his people (Ezek. 3:26).[287] Here Abraham eventually fulfills his calling to be a blessing to the nations (Gen. 12:3) despite his earlier missteps.

Section Outline

VII. The Family History of Terah (11:27–25:11) . . .

    L. Abraham and Abimelech (20:1–18)

---

[286] A. B. Rhodes, "Israel's Prophets as Intercessors," in *Scripture in History and Theology: Essays in Honor of J. C. Rylaarsdam*, ed. A. L. Merill and T. W. Overholt, Pittsburgh Theological Monograph Series 17 (Pittsburgh: Pickwick, 1977), 107–128. Abraham is also depicted in prophetic terms in Genesis 15 (cf. comment on 15:1–6).
[287] The Hb. *'ish mokiakh* in Ezekiel 3:26 generally describes a mediator between two parties in a legal case (e.g., Job 9:33) and thus has in view a restriction of the prophet's ability to intercede for Israel; cf. Robert R. Wilson, "An Interpretation of Ezekiel's Dumbness," *VT* 22 (1972): 99–101.

Comment

20:1–2 In contrast to Lot, who had settled down to a life of compromise with the inhabitants of the land (before his comfortable lifestyle fell apart), Abraham is still a sojourner in the Promised Land, moving from place to place (v. 1). This mode of living is not without its dangers. As Abraham wanders around without the protection of a clan structure or an overlord, the possibility of exploitation or even death at the hands of those in whose land he is living is always present, especially when he moves into a new area. In Genesis 20:1 Abraham travels farther south and west than before, into the region of the Negeb, between Kadesh and Shur, on the edge of Egypt (cf. 25:18), before finally ending up in Gerar, a little to the north, where there would be good grazing for his flocks and a ready market for his products. He is now wandering on the outer fringes of the Promised Land, which seems to be a place of danger for the patriarchs.

As in chapter 12, Abraham persuades Sarah to pose as merely his sister, with similar results: Abimelech, the king of Gerar, sends for Sarah to become part of his harem (Gen. 20:2). "Abimelech" ("The [divine] king is my father") is perhaps a title rather than a personal name, as there will be another king called Abimelech in Gerar in Isaac's days (26:1), while King Achish is given this title in the superscription to Psalm 34.[288] It is possible that Sarah's beauty is the driving force behind the proposed relationship even at her advanced age, as in 12:14, though it could also be that the primary attraction for Abimelech lies in being able to cement a connection with Abraham, incorporating Abraham's wealth into the coffers of the city.[289]

20:3–8 Dreams play a significant role in Genesis as a means of the Lord's revelation to people both within and outside the covenant community. They were viewed as significant communications from the gods more widely throughout the ancient Near East. Later, "dreams and visions" will be part of the Lord's revelation by the Spirit through his prophets (Num. 12:6; cf. Joel 2:28), though these are regarded as inherently less clear than the revelation via Moses (i.e., the Pentateuch), which is "face to face" or, more literally, "mouth to mouth" (Num. 12:8).

In this case, unlike dreams that take the form of symbolic events and require an interpreter, the dream has verbal content: the Lord sentences Abimelech to death for possession of another man's wife (Gen. 20:3). Abimelech protests his innocence, claiming that he had no knowledge of her status and had not consummated the relationship. To bring judgment upon Abimelech and his people on account of these innocent actions would be unjust (v. 4). Abimelech affirms the integrity of his heart[290] and the innocence of his hands (v. 5). He addresses God as "Lord" (Hb. *'adonai*; v. 4) rather than Yahweh since he does not worship the same God as Abraham.

---
[288] Kidner, *Genesis*, 148.
[289] Sarna, *Genesis*, 141.
[290] Hb. "With an integrated heart" (*tam lebab*), the opposite of what James calls "double-mindedness" (James 1:8; cf. Ps. 119:113).

The Lord responds by affirming his own sovereign role in keeping Abimelech from sin: the integrity of his heart would have counted for nothing without the Lord's protecting hand (v. 6). Had Abimelech sinned, that transgression would have been against the Lord, not just against Abraham (v. 6). Nor does his personal integrity excuse Abimelech entirely: ignorance is not a watertight excuse under the law. In addition to returning Sarah to Abraham, Abimelech must ask Abraham to pray for him so that he might live (v. 7). If Abimelech fails to return Sarah to Abraham, he will incur the divine death penalty, not just for himself but also for his people, for whom he is responsible as covenant head. When Abimelech awakes in the morning and recounts these things to his servants, the people are understandably afraid (v. 8).

As a prophet (v. 7), Abraham has direct access to God, and therefore his intercession is particularly powerful; in this case it would result in Abimelech's forgiveness. This is the first time the word "prophet" (*nabi'*) occurs in the Bible, but Abraham's prophetic calling has already been evident, notably in chapter 18, where the Lord had taken Abraham into his confidence and Abraham had interceded for Sodom, as well as in chapter 15, where Abraham had received "the word of the LORD" (15:1).

20:9–18 Without wasting time Abimelech summons Abraham, asking how he has sinned against Abraham that Abraham has brought upon him and his people this "great sin" (Hb. *khata'ah gedolah*; v. 9). The language of "great sin" refers to adultery in Akkadian and Egyptian legal documents and elsewhere in the Bible to spiritual adultery, that is, idolatry (e.g., Ex. 32:21).[291]

Abraham's rationale for his deception is that he thought there was no fear of God in this place (Gen. 20:11). As it turns out, Abimelech clearly does fear God, as is apparent from his response to the dream.[292] What is equally clear is that in that moment Abraham himself is not fearing God—for, if he feared God, whom else would he have to fear (cf. Ps. 27:1)? Had Abraham feared God, he would have obeyed him and trusted God to take care of him in whatever way he saw fit. Instead, Abraham fears Abimelech more than he fears the Lord and as a result has slipped back into his old sinful patterns.

The rest of Abraham's speech is pure defensiveness, seeking to justify his sin on the grounds that Sarah really is his (half-)sister and that this is a settled pattern of deception for them. Neither of these claims helps Abraham's case in the least. Moreover, Abraham declares that it is in fact God's fault, as it all began "when God caused me to wander from my father's house" (Gen. 20:13)—and in fact his words could be rendered "When the gods caused me to wander," since the verb is plural.[293] When talking to Abimelech, Abraham makes his divine call to go to the Promised Land sound like nothing more than the aimless wandering of a homeless refugee. Instead of witnessing to Abimelech about God's enduring faithfulness to him over the past twenty-five years, Abraham talks like one pagan

---

[291] Victor P. Hamilton, *Genesis 18–50*, NICOT (Grand Rapids, MI: Eerdmans, 1995), 67.
[292] Wenham, *Genesis 16–50*, 72.
[293] Hamilton, *Genesis 18–50*, 65.

to another. Given the opportunity to speak about God's persistent goodness to him despite his own failures, Abrahams speaks as though his future lies in the hands of blind fate.

Once again Abraham's fears prove unjustified; indeed, the Lord showers him with additional abundance in the form of gifts from Abimelech of livestock, people, and a vast amount of silver, just as Pharaoh had done earlier (v. 14; cf. 12:16). And Abraham may choose to settle wherever he wishes in Abimelech's kingdom (20:15). In the meantime he prays for Abimelech and his people, and the women are once again able to have children, just as the Lord had said, as he reopens their wombs (vv. 17–18). The irony of Abraham's being able simply to pray and watch the Lord open the wombs of many women all around him, while his own wife's womb remains barren, can hardly be lost on Abraham and Sarah. How heartbreaking it would be to see fertility return to Abimelech's household while they still await the Lord's promised child! However, they do not have much longer to wait before their prayers will finally be answered and Sarah will be able to conceive. God's promise will be fulfilled in his own time.

Response

Abraham feared people more than he feared God—even after so many years of walking by faith before the Lord. He idolized his own safety and, in pursuit of that, was willing to give up Sarah's safety and the way of obedience to the Lord. Yet the God whom he had failed to trust for his safety nonetheless protected both of them, bringing them out of the dangers facing them. The Lord enabled Abraham to be a blessing to Abimelech, praying for him and seeing the judgment lifted that had been placed upon his household, so that the women could once again have children.

This truth is both humbling and encouraging. It is a humbling reminder that we too, even after many years of walking with the Lord, will only ever make small beginnings on the road to righteousness. Our besetting idolatries continue to exert a strong hold over us, and "experience" is often simply the name we give to the ability to recognize our sins as we commit them all over again. Yet this truth is also encouraging, for the Lord does not give up on Abraham despite his weakness, defensiveness, and sin. The Lord will not let him go until he has done what he promised for him, and he will use Abraham's many failures to humble him and deepen his grip on the Lord's grace.

One of the ways in which God matures all his followers is by showing us, and others, our sin. Often this will be embarrassing for us, even humiliating, especially if we are in positions of Christian leadership. But in this way he gives us an opportunity to repent publicly and to speak plainly to others about the gospel, which is the only hope for sinners like us. Jesus loves us when we are bad, as well as when we are good, and our public sins give us ample opportunity to reflect on and to testify to that amazing fact. We never grow beyond our need of the gospel, and our remaining sins make that reality abundantly clear to all.

GENESIS 21

21 The Lord visited Sarah as he had said, and the Lord did to Sarah as he had promised. **2** And Sarah conceived and bore Abraham a son in his old age at the time of which God had spoken to him. **3** Abraham called the name of his son who was born to him, whom Sarah bore him, Isaac.[1] **4** And Abraham circumcised his son Isaac when he was eight days old, as God had commanded him. **5** Abraham was a hundred years old when his son Isaac was born to him. **6** And Sarah said, "God has made laughter for me; everyone who hears will laugh over me." **7** And she said, "Who would have said to Abraham that Sarah would nurse children? Yet I have borne him a son in his old age."

8 And the child grew and was weaned. And Abraham made a great feast on the day that Isaac was weaned. **9** But Sarah saw the son of Hagar the Egyptian, whom she had borne to Abraham, laughing.[2] **10** So she said to Abraham, "Cast out this slave woman with her son, for the son of this slave woman shall not be heir with my son Isaac." **11** And the thing was very displeasing to Abraham on account of his son. **12** But God said to Abraham, "Be not displeased because of the boy and because of your slave woman. Whatever Sarah says to you, do as she tells you, for through Isaac shall your offspring be named. **13** And I will make a nation of the son of the slave woman also, because he is your offspring." **14** So Abraham rose early in the morning and took bread and a skin of water and gave it to Hagar, putting it on her shoulder, along with the child, and sent her away. And she departed and wandered in the wilderness of Beersheba.

15 When the water in the skin was gone, she put the child under one of the bushes. **16** Then she went and sat down opposite him a good way off, about the distance of a bowshot, for she said, "Let me not look on the death of the child." And as she sat opposite him, she lifted up her voice and wept. **17** And God heard the voice of the boy, and the angel of God called to Hagar from heaven and said to her, "What troubles you, Hagar? Fear not, for God has heard the voice of the boy where he is. **18** Up! Lift up the boy, and hold him fast with your hand, for I will make him into a great nation." **19** Then God opened her eyes, and she saw a well of water. And she went and filled the skin with water and gave the boy a drink. **20** And God was with the boy, and he grew up. He lived in the wilderness and became an expert with the bow. **21** He lived in the wilderness of Paran, and his mother took a wife for him from the land of Egypt.

22 At that time Abimelech and Phicol the commander of his army said to Abraham, "God is with you in all that you do. **23** Now therefore swear to me here by God that you will not deal falsely with me or with my descendants or with my posterity, but as I have dealt kindly with you, so you will deal with me and with the land where you have sojourned." **24** And Abraham said, "I will swear."

²⁵ When Abraham reproved Abimelech about a well of water that Abimelech's servants had seized, ²⁶ Abimelech said, "I do not know who has done this thing; you did not tell me, and I have not heard of it until today." ²⁷ So Abraham took sheep and oxen and gave them to Abimelech, and the two men made a covenant. ²⁸ Abraham set seven ewe lambs of the flock apart. ²⁹ And Abimelech said to Abraham, "What is the meaning of these seven ewe lambs that you have set apart?" ³⁰ He said, "These seven ewe lambs you will take from my hand, that this³ may be a witness for me that I dug this well." ³¹ Therefore that place was called Beersheba,⁴ because there both of them swore an oath. ³² So they made a covenant at Beersheba. Then Abimelech and Phicol the commander of his army rose up and returned to the land of the Philistines. ³³ Abraham planted a tamarisk tree in Beersheba and called there on the name of the LORD, the Everlasting God. ³⁴ And Abraham sojourned many days in the land of the Philistines.

¹ *Isaac* means *he laughs* ² Possibly *laughing in mockery* ³ Or *you* ⁴ *Beersheba* means *well of seven* or *well of the oath*

Section Overview

Abraham and Sarah have been waiting a very long time for the birth of their promised son, Isaac. Their road has taken many twists and turns, but finally the promised day comes and Isaac is born, bringing laughter to his parents, as his name suggests (Gen. 21:6). But not everyone's laughter is in celebration of the new child; Sarah sees Ishmael laughing with scorn at the celebration of Isaac's weaning (vv. 8–9). He is mocking Isaac and, with him, God's promise to Abraham and Sarah. To Ishmael the excitement surrounding the birth of Isaac is all a big joke.

In consequence Sarah insists that Ishmael and Hagar be cast out of the house (Gen. 21:10). Abraham is reluctant to see them go, because Ishmael is, after all, his son, but the Lord supports Sarah's demand (v. 12). Ishmael has his own future, but it is through Isaac that the promise will come (v. 12). As long as Ishmael is still present, Abraham has a "Plan B" that means not having to commit fully to Isaac as the child of promise. For the test of Genesis 22 to have its full force, Abraham must let Ishmael go. Meanwhile, God protects Ishmael and Hagar as they pursue their own path.

In sharp contrast to Ishmael's mockery of Isaac, which leads to his being cast out of Abraham's family, the latter part of Genesis 21 returns our attention to Abimelech, the Philistine king of Gerar (vv. 22–34). Abimelech's earlier encounter with Abraham had evidently made a strong impression on him, for he comes to Abraham and seeks to establish a lasting covenant with him and his descendants (v. 23). The pagan king recognizes the hand of God at work in Abraham, and he seeks to ensure an end to falsehood from Abraham toward him and his descendants (v. 23). This is an implicit rebuke of Abraham for his previous actions, yet Abimelech now wishes to move forward into an amicable future, making a covenant with Abraham and ensuring a future of peace between them.

Section Outline

VII. The Family History of Terah (11:27–25:11) . . .
    M. The Birth of Isaac (21:1–7)
    N. Hagar and Ishmael Sent Away (21:8–21)
    O. Peace with Abimelech (21:22–34)

Comment

21:1–7 The most important aspect of the birth of Isaac is that it is "as the LORD had said/as the LORD had promised" (v. 1). That promise has been in process for twenty-five years, and finally it is delivered.[294] If it is true, as we have seen in Abraham and Sarah's story, that "hope deferred makes the heart sick," then it is equally true that "a desire fulfilled is a tree of life" (Prov. 13:12). That is, when God grants us the temporal answer to one of our prayers, it points us forward to the final answer of all our prayers in the new heavens and the new earth, when our access to the tree of life will finally be restored (cf. Rev. 22:14). This general principle is especially true in this case, as the child of promise will be the father of the line through whom the promised seed of the woman will come, who will finally defeat the serpent and restore humanity's relationship with God (cf. Gen. 3:15). The long-awaited son, Isaac, comes according to God's promise, at the time of which God had spoken (21:1–2). In response, Abraham gives him the name God had specified, Isaac (21:3; cf. 17:19), and circumcises him on the eighth day, just as God had commanded (21:4; cf. 17:12–13).

It is no hardship for Abraham and Sarah to give their son the name Isaac ("laughter"); rather, it accurately represents their emotional state in response to this awesome gift. Sarah remarks, "God has made laughter for me; everyone who hears will laugh over me" (Gen. 21:6). Had it been written by then, Abraham and Sarah might have sung,

> Then our mouth was filled with laughter,
>   and our tongue with shouts of joy;
> then they said among the nations,
>   "The LORD has done great things for them." (Ps. 126:2)

Few events in the Bible, apart from the birth of Jesus, have been so anticipated. Yet to most people around Abraham and Sarah the event must seem utterly insignificant: a little baby is born to an elderly nomad—unusual, perhaps, but hardly earth shattering (Gen. 21:7). Only the eye of faith could see in Isaac the fulfillment of God's promise.

21:8–21 Sarah's "Everyone who hears will laugh over me" (v. 6) is understandable; it is how people should respond to the joyous news. Ishmael's response to

---

[294] "The LORD visited" (Hb. *paqad*) implies direct divine intervention in human affairs, which can be positive (Ruth 1:6; 1 Sam. 2:21) or negative (Isa. 29:6). A similar English concept might be "take care of," which can have either a positive sense ("His mother took care of him") or a negative one ("The mafia hitman took care of him").

the new arrival is very different, however, mocking rather than celebrating the child's presence. Isaac's arrival displaces Ishmael from his central position in the household, a shift reflected in the use of names in the chapter: "Isaac" occurs six times in verses 1–12, while Ishmael is never referred to by name; his is the "son of Hagar the Egyptian" (v. 9), the son of the slave woman (vv. 10, 13), "her son" (v. 10), "the boy" (v. 12), and "the child" (vv. 14–16), even though to Abraham he is still "his son" (vv. 11, 13). In contrast, Sarah refers to Isaac as "her son," which renders inevitable the conflict between Sarah and Hagar.

Matters come to a head at the feast given by Abraham to celebrate Isaac's weaning, which would normally take place around age two or three. During the feast Ishmael laughs at Isaac (v. 9); while this expression can denote harmless merriment (e.g., Zech. 8:5), it more commonly has mockery in view (e.g., Gen. 39:14). In the NT Paul interprets Ishmael's actions as a form of persecution (Gal. 4:29). Taking this attitude to the promised seed of Abraham puts him in the category of those under a curse rather than a blessing in Genesis 12:3. Since Hagar and Ishmael have no interest in the true inheritance of Abraham, they have no place in his household.

It is to Abraham's credit that he finds the situation distressing; Ishmael is, after all, his son (Gen. 21:11). But the Lord supports Sarah at this point. Whereas in Genesis 16:2 Abraham was wrong to listen to his wife, in this situation he should listen to her (21:12). This shows that godly feminine submission in marriage should not be construed as the wife's always giving in to her husband. Sarah is commended as the prime model of godly womanhood for precisely her submissiveness (1 Pet. 3:5–6), yet there are times when she strongly expresses an opinion contrary to Abraham's. For the sake of the promise Abraham must commit himself fully to Isaac (Gen. 21:12). Neither natural concern for the welfare of those whom he loves nor tentativeness on his part can be allowed to hold him back. God has promised to take care of Hagar and Ishmael (vv. 12–13), and Abraham must place his trust in that promise. So Abraham gets up early, provides Hagar and Ishmael with what resources he can, and sends them on their way (v. 14).

Separated from Abraham and his family, Hagar and Ishmael are extremely vulnerable as they wander in the wilderness. At first it seems as though their story will end in tragedy as they get lost and run out of water, finding themselves in imminent danger of death. Their situation is so desperate that Hagar puts the weakened Ishmael under a bush and retreats "a good way off"[295] so that she will not have to watch her son die.[296] But the Lord is still watching over Hagar and Ishmael, just as he had promised Abraham, and, when they cry out for help, he hears and answers them from heaven,[297] showing Hagar a well from which she can

---

[295] Also described as "the distance of a bowshot," which is an ironic measure, given Ishmael's subsequent career as an archer (Gen. 21:20).
[296] A casual reader might think that Ishmael is still a small boy at this point, but he must be about sixteen (cf. Gen. 16:6; 21:5). Although Ishmael is described as a *yeled* ("child") in relation to his mother (vv. 14–16), God refers to him as a *na'ar* ("young man"; vv. 17–20). The two terms are overlapping synonyms, covering the entire range from childhood to early manhood (Gen. 4:23; 1 Kings 12:8).
[297] This voice from heaven, rescuing Abraham's oldest son, Ishmael, from death, foreshadows the voice from heaven in the next chapter, rescuing Isaac, Abraham's younger son (cf. Gen. 22:11). Hagar is shown a well, which saves her son's life, while Abraham is shown a ram in a thicket, which will likewise save his son.

get water to sustain them (v. 19). Ishmael's name ("God heard") is once again fitting, just as it described Hagar's previous experience in the wilderness (cf. 16:11). This experience should also have encouraged the original audience, who were themselves wandering in the wilderness and often in need of water (cf. Exodus 17); if the Lord provided for Hagar and Ishmael's needs because of his promise to make Ishmael into a great nation (Gen. 21:18), how much more could he be trusted to provide for Isaac's descendants?

Hagar and Ishmael are provided for physically, enabling them to survive this initial trial. From here they seem to prosper in material terms, albeit living in the desert of Paran (v. 21).[298] Spiritually speaking, however, their condition is not so good. Ishmael grows up to be an archer (cf. Isa. 21:17), but more importantly his mother arranges for him to marry an Egyptian (Gen. 21:21). This contrasts to the great lengths to which Abraham goes to secure a suitable wife for Isaac from among his own kinfolk (Genesis 24). Since throughout the Abraham narrative Egypt represents the temptation to abandon the Promised Land, this choice is very revealing. Hagar (and Ishmael) has no interest in the spiritual inheritance that she might have received from Abraham, and so for Ishmael an Egyptian wife is perfectly adequate.

21:22–34 Around the same time as these events Abimelech reaches out to Abraham, seeking to make a covenant with him (21:22).[299] It is a sign of Abimelech's respect for Abraham that he travels to Beersheba to meet with Abraham rather than summoning him to Gerar. The episode is linked to the preceding one not merely by the time designation but by the reference to Beersheba: the well that Hagar was shown by the Lord (v. 19) is in the same area as a well that Abraham had dug and now concerning which he and Abimelech make a covenant (vv. 30–31). It might even have been the same well, in which case Abraham would once again have been the source of life and blessing for Hagar and Ishmael, even after they had left his household.

In any event, Abimelech comes to Abraham because he recognizes that "God was with him," that is, that God's hand of blessing rests upon Abraham (v. 22). As a result, Abimelech wants Abraham to swear an oath not to deal falsely with him or his descendants and to return the same loyalty and faithfulness (Hb. *khesed*)[300] to him that he had earlier shown to Abraham (v. 23). Before that can happen, however, Abraham has a matter of his own to raise. Abimelech's men have seized a well that Abraham had dug (v. 25); he wishes to see this injustice resolved. Water is a vitally precious commodity for herdsmen in the very dry climate of the Negeb.

Both general and particular concerns are addressed in what follows. Abraham gives sheep and cattle to Abimelech, mirroring Abimelech's earlier gift to him

---

298 Paran sounds like *pere'* ("wild donkey"), which is how the Lord described Ishmael earlier (cf. 16:12).
299 A similar event is recorded with Isaac in Genesis 26:26, also involving an Abimelech and an army commander named Phicol. These may have been family names handed down through the generations.
300 *Khesed* (ESV: "dealt kindly"; elsewhere often "loving-kindness") in this context means acting appropriately in a relationship, showing loyalty and faithfulness. It is the opposite of "dealing falsely" (*shaqar*) in the earlier part of the verse.

after the issue with Sarah (Gen. 21:27; cf. 20:14), and together they make a general treaty. Then Abraham sets aside another seven lambs from his flock as "witnesses"; in accepting them as a gift Abimelech is publicly recognizing Abraham's specific claim to have dug the disputed well (21:28–30). The agreement is memorialized by the planting of a tamarisk tree and by the name given to that place: Beersheba, which means "well of seven" or "well of the oath." Abraham also worships God there, under the name "the Everlasting God" (*'El 'Olam*; 21:33; cf. Isa. 9:6). As a result of the covenant made on that day, Abraham and the Philistines are able to live happily together—if not forever after, at least for a long time (Gen. 21:34).[301] This positive resolution of their differences is further evidence that the Lord is with Abraham, making his neighbors eager to pursue peace with him (Gen. 21:22; cf. Prov. 16:7). Beersheba will remain a base of operations for both Abraham and Isaac, though in Jacob's time the family's center of gravity will move further north.

The name under which Abraham worships God is a reminder that it is God's covenant with him that is of prime importance, a relationship in which God will indeed show him and his descendants *khesed* forever, just as he has promised. The end of the chapter thus connects with its beginning, where God proved his *khesed* with Abraham by finally giving him the promised son, Isaac. It also prepares for the next chapter, where Abraham's faith in God's *khesed* will be put to the ultimate test through the near sacrifice of Isaac at God's command.

Response

Hagar and Ishmael experience the blessing of life within the household of Abraham only as long as they show appropriate respect to God and his promises. When Ishmael disrespects Isaac, it is time for them to leave, with implications likely to be negative. Even though the Lord provides for them in the wilderness, their trajectory is away from Israel's God and not toward him.

The apostle Paul picks up the imagery of this chapter in Galatians 4:21–31, where he uses the story as the basis for an allegory. The servant woman, Hagar, stands for those who depend on their own efforts to please God. They are in bondage to the law, and their standing before God is therefore inevitably temporary and precarious. Sarah, on the other hand, stands for those living by faith on the basis of the gospel. Such people are trusting not in their own righteousness but in the righteousness of Jesus Christ, credited by God to their account. They are the children of the promise. Theirs is a liberty that Hagar could never know. Such people enjoy a permanent relationship with God, for they are not merely tolerated but approved.

Hagar and Ishmael must have always lived under the threat of being sent away. They had no established status in Abraham's household, and so their presence there was always insecure. One careless action could, and ultimately did, cost them their place in the household. So it is also for those who rely on their good

---

301 On the Philistines cf. comment on 10:6–20.

works. They can never have assurance of their salvation because they can never be sure they have done enough to please God. But Isaac's place in the household, along with that of Sarah, is secure. They are family, and so they belong. They are the objects of God's promise and can never be cast away. Likewise, those who rely on Jesus will never be cast away by God, for we are his adopted children, to whom the inheritance belongs by right. As John puts it, "To all who did receive [Jesus], who believed in his name, he gave the right to become children of God, who were born, not of blood nor of the will of the flesh nor of the will of man, but of God" (John 1:12–13). It is striking that in Paul's use of Genesis 21 identification with Ishmael or Isaac has nothing to do with Jewish heritage; Jews who depend on the law become Ishmael, while Gentiles who trust in God through faith become the true Israel of God. It is in our relationship to Christ that we become part of the true Israel, not through human ancestry.

In his interaction with Abraham, Abimelech provides a model of how the kings of the earth should act toward God's people. Even though Abimelech is identified with the Philistines, the later enemies of Israel in the days of Saul and David, he humbly entreats Abraham for a covenant bond, and the result is mutual blessing for both men. Like the wise rulers of Psalm 2:10–12, Abimelech makes his peace with the Lord and the Lord's anointed by respecting and dealing faithfully with Abraham. In the process Abraham fulfills his calling to be a blessing to the nations (cf. Gen. 12:3). Indeed, Abraham discovers that the very land about which he had said, "There is no fear of God at all in this place" (20:11), turns out to be a land where, by God's grace, he can dwell at peace for a long time. This is not Abraham's heavenly home, but it is a pleasant oasis along his journey.

GENESIS 22:1–19

22 After these things God tested Abraham and said to him, "Abraham!" And he said, "Here I am." ²He said, "Take your son, your only son Isaac, whom you love, and go to the land of Moriah, and offer him there as a burnt offering on one of the mountains of which I shall tell you." ³So Abraham rose early in the morning, saddled his donkey, and took two of his young men with him, and his son Isaac. And he cut the wood for the burnt offering and arose and went to the place of which God had told him. ⁴On the third day Abraham lifted up his eyes and saw the place from afar. ⁵Then Abraham said to his young men, "Stay here with the donkey; I and the boy¹ will go over there and worship and come again to you." ⁶And Abraham took the wood of the burnt offering and laid it on Isaac his son. And he took in his hand the fire and the knife. So they went both of them together. ⁷And Isaac said to his father Abraham, "My father!" And he said, "Here I am, my son." He said,

"Behold, the fire and the wood, but where is the lamb for a burnt offering?" ⁸ Abraham said, "God will provide for himself the lamb for a burnt offering, my son." So they went both of them together.

⁹ When they came to the place of which God had told him, Abraham built the altar there and laid the wood in order and bound Isaac his son and laid him on the altar, on top of the wood. ¹⁰ Then Abraham reached out his hand and took the knife to slaughter his son. ¹¹ But the angel of the LORD called to him from heaven and said, "Abraham, Abraham!" And he said, "Here I am." ¹² He said, "Do not lay your hand on the boy or do anything to him, for now I know that you fear God, seeing you have not withheld your son, your only son, from me." ¹³ And Abraham lifted up his eyes and looked, and behold, behind him was a ram, caught in a thicket by his horns. And Abraham went and took the ram and offered it up as a burnt offering instead of his son. ¹⁴ So Abraham called the name of that place, "The LORD will provide";² as it is said to this day, "On the mount of the LORD it shall be provided."³

¹⁵ And the angel of the LORD called to Abraham a second time from heaven ¹⁶ and said, "By myself I have sworn, declares the LORD, because you have done this and have not withheld your son, your only son, ¹⁷ I will surely bless you, and I will surely multiply your offspring as the stars of heaven and as the sand that is on the seashore. And your offspring shall possess the gate of his⁴ enemies, ¹⁸ and in your offspring shall all the nations of the earth be blessed, because you have obeyed my voice." ¹⁹ So Abraham returned to his young men, and they arose and went together to Beersheba. And Abraham lived at Beersheba.

¹ Or *young man*; also verse 12 ² Or *will see* ³ Or *he will be seen* ⁴ Or *their*

Section Overview

The binding and near sacrifice of Isaac holds a central place in both Jewish and Christian theology. It is the ultimate test of Abraham's faith: Can he trust God's promise that his descendants will be numbered through Isaac (17:19–21) while at the same time obeying God's mysterious command to sacrifice him (22:2)? The readers are informed at the outset of the chapter that this is a test for Abraham (v. 1), lest they imagine that the Lord is a God who demands child sacrifices, but of course it is vital to the integrity of the test that Abraham himself be kept in the dark. Once again Abraham believes God, and it is reckoned to him as righteousness (15:6).

Yet the ultimate lesson to be drawn from this encounter is not about the strength of Abraham's faith; otherwise the mountain would subsequently have been named "Abraham passed the test." Rather, the point being driven home is that the Lord provides a ram to take the place of Abraham's son as a sacrifice, enabling the boy to live. As a result the mountain is named "The LORD will provide" (22:14). This name highlights the fact that the episode was never meant to be complete in itself. It points forward to Jesus, the ultimate Lamb of God, whose death will take away the sin of the world (John 1:29). When Jesus claims that Abraham saw ahead of time the coming of Jesus (John 8:56), it is likely this passage that he has in mind.

Section Outline

VII. The Family History of Terah (11:27–25:11) ...
    P. The Binding of Isaac (22:1–19)

Comment

22:1–2 This narrative is loosely connected to the previous chapter by the introduction "After these things" (v. 1). Enough time has passed for Isaac to become a young man (Hb. *na'ar*; vv. 5, 12), which typically covers a range from about five to seventeen years of age, so Isaac would be old enough to walk up a mountain carrying a significant load of wood (v. 6). It is, however, significant that these events follow those of Genesis 21, because there God prevailed upon a reluctant Abraham to send away Hagar and Ishmael (21:11–12). This means that there is no alternative son of Abraham who could step into Isaac's shoes if anything happens to him and thus provide an alternative means of the Lord's fulfilling his promise. In a time and place where child mortality was rife, the lack of another heir is itself a significant step of faith for Abraham. But in what follows the Lord will put Abraham's faith to the ultimate test by commanding him to offer Isaac as a whole burnt offering (22:2).

Although humans may not put God to the test (Num. 14:22; Deut. 6:16), the Lord regularly tests his people (Ex. 15:25; 20:20). This is not because the Lord is seeking additional information from the outcome of these tests, since the Lord knows all things (Matt. 10:29). Rather the Lord's testing more closely resembles a refiner's fire, which tests a material in order to demonstrate its true nature as gold or dross (Deut. 13:3). Abraham's faith is publicly demonstrated and purified, as he discovers once again in his situation of greatest need that the Lord will indeed provide a substitute to die for Isaac—and ultimately for Abraham as well.

Abraham's attitude of humble obedience is immediately demonstrated: when the Lord calls his name, he immediately responds, "Here I am," indicating a posture of willing submission (Gen. 22:1; cf. 37:13; 1 Sam. 3:4–8; Isa. 6:8). He cannot imagine what the Lord's command will be: in the space of three short imperatives—"Take ... go ... offer him" (Gen. 22:2)—Abraham's whole world comes crashing down around him. The Lord emphasizes the nature of the sacrifice: Isaac is his only son—there is no other to take his place—and his beloved son (v. 2),[302] the one for whom he had waited, longed, and prayed over so many years. It thus appears that Abraham will have to sacrifice not only his own son but also all his hopes and dreams, since the fulfillment of God's promises are so tightly bound up in the person of Isaac.

Specifically, Abraham is to go to the region of Moriah (v. 2), an area not previously mentioned in the narrative but, as it transpires, about three days journey away (v. 4), in the region of Jerusalem (2 Chron. 3:1). In an ironic echo of his original call, which was to go to an unspecified country that the Lord would show him

---

[302] This is the first use of the word "love" (Hb. *'ahab*) in the Bible.

(Gen. 12:1),[303] Abraham is now to go to an unspecified mountain of which the Lord will tell him (22:2). Once again Abraham is being pressed into bare, empty-handed faith that trusts the Lord to provide the impossible.

Mountains are often places of encounter with God in the Bible (cf. comment on 2:8–17), though the altars that Abraham has built in the Promised Land to this point have not been on particularly elevated locations (12:7–8; 13:18), perhaps to avoid the overtones of Canaanite high places. In this case the solemnity of the endeavor is reinforced by its location on a mountain—indeed, the same one upon which Solomon's temple will ultimately be built (cf. 2 Chron. 3:1).

22:3–8 In Genesis 21:14 Abraham rose early when faced with the unpleasant task of saying goodbye to Hagar and Ishmael. Now he once again rises early to begin this journey of difficult obedience. No conversation with Sarah is recorded, leaving it open as to whether she is informed of what is about to happen.[304] The narrator records all the little details of Abraham's preparation: he saddles the donkey, gathers the servants, and cuts the wood necessary for the sacrifice (Gen. 22:3). When the Lord told Abraham that he was about to judge Sodom and Gomorrah, Abraham had argued with God at length, interceding for those wicked cities (18:23–33). Here, though, Abraham's only word in response to the Lord is *hinneni* (Hb. "Here I am"). God speaks and Abraham obeys, just as he had those long years earlier in leaving Haran.

On the third day[305] Abraham arrives at the place indicated by God,[306] leaving the servants and the donkey while he and Isaac go ahead alone (Gen. 22:5). Abraham's words to his servants may indicate a level of confidence that God will miraculously restore Isaac's life: "I and the boy will go over there and worship and come again to you" (v. 5), although it would have seemed odd to phrase it any other way. Moreover, when Isaac inquires about the absence of a lamb, Abraham assures him, "God will provide for himself the lamb for a burnt offering, my son" (v. 8). But, should there be no miracle, Abraham is willing to carry through his obedience to the utmost. He may reason that the God who has given him Isaac can raise the dead (Heb. 11:19), but he has no direct promise from God to that effect.

As Abraham and Isaac climb the mountain alone, they now must carry the implements necessary for the sacrifice that will take place at the top. The task is poignantly divided between them, with Abraham carrying the dangerous items (the knife and the fire) and Isaac the wood. The mutuality of their journey is stressed by the narrator, who twice describes their going along together (Gen. 22:6, 8). All of this highlights and heightens the pathos of the intervening conversation. The

---

[303] The language of "Go forth" (Hb. *lek leka*) occurs only in Genesis 12:1; 22:2, with these two episodes bracketing the main body of the Abraham narrative; cf. Sarna, *Genesis*, 150.
[304] Josephus suggests that he does not tell her (*Antiquities* 1.12.2).
[305] In the Bible many important events take three days, especially when involving a journey (cf. Ex. 3:18; Jonah 3:3). This may perhaps be a stock term for a lengthy journey, which would answer the objection that the 60 miles (97 km) or so of rough terrain from Beersheba to Jerusalem would take longer than three days to traverse.
[306] The statement "Abraham lifted up his eyes and saw" links the revelation of the place of sacrifice (Gen. 22:4) with the revelation of the substitute lamb (v. 13).

closeness of their family relationship is repeatedly stressed, as we are told that Isaac addresses Abraham as "My father" (*'abi*), to which Abraham responds, "Here I am, my son" (*hinneni beni*, v. 7; cf. v. 1). The relational terms "father" and "son" occur no fewer than thirteen times in verses 1–16. Isaac then asks a question revealing his own ignorance of the key fact to which the readers know the painful answer: "Behold, the fire and the wood, but where is the lamb for the burnt offering?" (v. 7). Abraham's answer is truer than he can know at this point: "God will provide for himself the lamb . . . , my son" (v. 8). The word "provide" is a form of the verb "to see," so we could translate his answer as "God will see to the lamb." This recalls Genesis 16, where God proved himself to be *'El-ro'i*, the God who sees, in rescuing Hagar (16:13), implying Abraham's hope of a similar intervention here to rescue Abraham's only son.

22:9–14 When Abraham and Isaac arrive at the appointed location atop Mount Moriah, Abraham once again builds an altar, as he has done before (cf. Gen. 12:7–8; 13:18). Only this time, instead of placing a sheep or bull on the altar, he takes his own son and binds him to the altar (22:9). Normally a sacrifice would be slaughtered before being placed on the altar, but Isaac takes his place on the altar alive—a living sacrifice, we might say (cf. Rom. 12:1). He is bound, which is not part of the normal sacrificial ritual (since the animal was normally already dead) but a process requiring Isaac to be fully aware of what is about to happen, rather than being killed unawares.[307] It appears that Isaac is fully cooperative, since he is presumably stronger and faster than Abraham.

The narrative slows down as the climax is reached, with Abraham stretching out his hand for the knife with which he must strike the fatal blow and slaughter his only son (Gen. 22:10).[308] He had taken a knife to his son at the time of his circumcision (21:4); now it seems he must complete the symbolic act of judgment. At the very last moment, however, a voice from heaven intervenes, sparing Isaac. The angel of the Lord calls, "Abraham, Abraham!" with the repetition adding intensity to the address (22:11; cf. 1 Sam. 3:10; Acts 9:4), while Abraham's response is the same submissive "Here I am" with which he responded earlier in the chapter (22:11; cf. v. 1).

On this occasion the angel of the Lord speaks "from heaven," the place of God's presence, as when God was about to deliver Hagar (Gen. 21:17). Abraham's hand, which already holds the fateful knife, must not be stretched out against the boy to harm him in any way (22:12). The test is complete: Abraham has demonstrated his faith in God through his willingness even to offer up his only son at his command (v. 12). "Now I know" should not be taken as implying that God previously lacked this knowledge about Abraham, any more than he lacked knowledge about the true state of affairs in Sodom (cf. 18:21). God is omniscient and eternal, knowing the end from the beginning (Isa. 46:9–10). Rather, the test has served as a public

---

[307] Cf. Wenham, *Genesis 16–50*, 109. The word "bind" (Hb. *'aqad*) occurs nowhere else in the OT.
[308] The Hebrew verb *shakhat* ("slaughter") is often used of killing sacrifices, including the Passover lamb (cf. Ex. 12:21; Lev. 3:2; 2 Chron. 35:6).

demonstration of the depth of Abraham's faith for the sake of the watching world, human and angelic.[309] The lasting impact of the lesson is underscored by the contemporary saying about the mountain of the Lord ("to this day"; Gen. 22:14).[310]

Continuing the theme of seeing that runs through this chapter, "Abraham lifted up his eyes and looked" (Hb. *ra'ah*), seeing a ram caught by its horns in a thicket and recognizing it as God's provision of a sacrifice in place of (*takhat*) his son (v. 13). The principle of substitutionary atonement at the heart of the later Levitical system of sacrifice could hardly be conveyed in clearer terms: the animal is substituted for Isaac as a whole burnt offering, and its death obviates the need for him to die. The Lord has indeed provided ("seen to," also from *ra'ah*) a lamb for the sacrifice, just as Abraham had trusted that he would (v. 8), and so the place is named "the LORD will provide" (or "the Lord will see to it," *yhwh yir'eh*).[311] The "mount of the Lord/mountain of God" is elsewhere normally Sinai (Num. 10:33; Ex. 3:1; 18:5; 1 Kings 19:8), though the term can refer to Zion (Isa. 2:3; Zech. 8:3) and even Eden (Ezek. 28:14, 16).

22:15–19 A second word from heaven confirms the Lord's blessing upon Abraham (Gen. 22:16–18). In an unusual act of affirmation the Lord swears by himself (v. 16; Heb. 6:13–14) to fulfill his promise to Abraham of blessing and numerous offspring. The intensification in the promise is evident in the infinitive absolute + cognate verb structure ("I will surely bless you"; Gen. 22:17), as well as the doubling of the metaphor, adding the imagery of sand on the seashore to the previous imagery of the stars of heaven (cf. 15:5).

Another new element is added to the blessing in the shape of promise of military victory: to "possess the gate of his enemies" (22:17) means to have captured their cities and taken administrative control over them. Most important, however, is the reiteration of the original promise: that in Abraham's seed all the nations of the earth will be blessed (22:18; cf. 12:1–3). This promise is particularly poignant since the blessing will come to the world through a divine reenactment of this scene on Mount Moriah, yet one in which the Father will not spare his only Son, whom he loves. All this is possible because of Abraham's obedience (22:18), which in turn highlights the importance of the obedience of his ultimate offspring, Jesus, whose righteousness is now credited to us, just as our sin is imputed to him (2 Cor. 5:21).

The episode closes with Abraham and Isaac's journeying together back down the mountain, rejoining the servants and returning to Beersheba (Gen. 22:19). The relationship of father and son is not disturbed by the Lord's testing and perhaps is even strengthened and deepened. Certainly Abraham models for his son what

---

[309] Job was likewise put to the test by God, with his trust in God being finally vindicated before the angelic hosts as well as before his friends.
[310] The narrator often adds "to this day" in Genesis (e.g., 19:37–38; 26:33; etc.). This is not a precise time marker but an implication that the practice or name remained in place over a lengthy period of time, down to his own time.
[311] Strictly speaking, the altar is given this name, not the mountain (cf. Judg. 6:24 for another example of naming an altar with a specific attribute of the deity). Given the significance of the event, however, it is not surprising that the name carries over to the mountain more generally.

the fear of the Lord looks like: an absolute commitment to obey the Lord's word, no matter what the consequences might appear to be.

Response

According to Jesus, Abraham had a unique insight into the way of salvation that God would establish through Jesus Christ (John 8:56). Genesis 22 was surely pivotal in that understanding, as Abraham learned that God was the one who would provide the sacrificial lamb to suffer and die in our place for our sins. This lesson had already been played out in the lives of the first readers of this story, the generation that had gone into the wilderness with Moses. They too had seen their own beloved firstborn sons spared by the blood of the Passover lambs they had slaughtered, while the destroying angel struck down all the firstborn of Egypt (cf. Exodus 12). Subsequent generations of Abraham's offspring would reenact the key elements of the storyline each time they brought their own lambs to the temple in Jerusalem, which was itself built on Mount Moriah (2 Chron. 3:1), not far from the place of this encounter between God and Abraham. As each sheep was slaughtered as a substitutionary atonement for sin, God's people were reminded of God's grace and mercy to them.

But all these numerous OT sacrifices were merely pictures of the ultimate reality, when God himself reenacted this scene on another mountain not far away, the mountain of Calvary (or Golgotha; Matt. 27:33). There God the Father himself filled the role of Abraham, bringing his Son, his only Son, the one whom he loved (Matt. 17:5), and laying him on the altar. Jesus Christ became both the willing Son and the willing sacrifice; he was, as John the Baptist put it, "the Lamb of God, who takes away the sin of the world" (John 1:29), or, in the language of Isaiah, the sheep who before his shearers was silent (Isa. 53:7).

In this reenactment, however, there was no angelic voice from heaven at the crucial instant that said, "Stay your hand." There was only the spreading darkness of God's curse surrounding the cross and centering upon the mangled and twisted body of the dead Son. There was no substitute for Jesus, because he himself had come to be the substitute for us. The spotless Lamb was slain for our transgressions; his wounds were for our unbelief; his scars were for our sins (Isa. 53:4–6).

Jesus himself has already forged the path through the ultimate test of his faith and obedience. In the garden of Gethsemane two roads presented themselves to him. The soldiers had not yet come; his disciples around him slept (Matt. 26:36–46). Jesus could still have chosen to decline the cup and call down the angelic hosts in righteous judgment on sinful man, or he could have remained faithful to his calling and drunk the bitter cup of obedience. He trod the painful path up the hill, carrying his cross, as Isaac bore the wood for his own sacrificial pyre (Gen. 22:6). Jesus allowed himself to be nailed to the cross, silently acquiescing, just as Isaac allowed himself to be bound to the altar without a word. He looked up to heaven and saw the knife in the Father's hand poised above him, all the while knowing that for him there would be no last-minute reprieve. Jesus had to drink the cup of God's wrath to its dregs if God's sworn promise of blessing to Abraham and his descendants was to become a reality. So the knife descended; the cup was drained. That was the cost of our redemption.

Yet, just as Abraham's willing obedience demonstrated clearly his love for God, so too the Father's willingness to take his Son's obedience all the way to the agonies on the cross demonstrated the depth and reality of his love for us, beyond a shadow of a doubt. It was not just the Son who suffered for our sin on the cross; the Father also paid a profound cost for our sin as he laid it all on his beloved Son, bringing down the knife of his righteous judgment upon his Son's defenseless head. As Paul puts it, "He who did not spare his own Son but gave him up for us all, how will he not also with him graciously give us all things?" (Rom. 8:32).

GENESIS 22:20–23:20

[20] Now after these things it was told to Abraham, "Behold, Milcah also has borne children to your brother Nahor: [21] Uz his firstborn, Buz his brother, Kemuel the father of Aram, [22] Chesed, Hazo, Pildash, Jidlaph, and Bethuel." [23] (Bethuel fathered Rebekah.) These eight Milcah bore to Nahor, Abraham's brother. [24] Moreover, his concubine, whose name was Reumah, bore Tebah, Gaham, Tahash, and Maacah.

23 Sarah lived 127 years; these were the years of the life of Sarah. [2] And Sarah died at Kiriath-arba (that is, Hebron) in the land of Canaan, and Abraham went in to mourn for Sarah and to weep for her. [3] And Abraham rose up from before his dead and said to the Hittites,[1] [4] "I am a sojourner and foreigner among you; give me property among you for a burying place, that I may bury my dead out of my sight." [5] The Hittites answered Abraham, [6] "Hear us, my lord; you are a prince of God[2] among us. Bury your dead in the choicest of our tombs. None of us will withhold from you his tomb to hinder you from burying your dead." [7] Abraham rose and bowed to the Hittites, the people of the land. [8] And he said to them, "If you are willing that I should bury my dead out of my sight, hear me and entreat for me Ephron the son of Zohar, [9] that he may give me the cave of Machpelah, which he owns; it is at the end of his field. For the full price let him give it to me in your presence as property for a burying place."

[10] Now Ephron was sitting among the Hittites, and Ephron the Hittite answered Abraham in the hearing of the Hittites, of all who went in at the gate of his city, [11] "No, my lord, hear me: I give you the field, and I give you the cave that is in it. In the sight of the sons of my people I give it to you. Bury your dead." [12] Then Abraham bowed down before the people of the land. [13] And he said to Ephron in the hearing of the people of the land, "But if you will, hear me: I give the price of the field. Accept it from me, that I may bury my dead there." [14] Ephron answered Abraham, [15] "My lord, listen to me: a piece of land worth four hundred shekels[3] of silver,

what is that between you and me? Bury your dead." ¹⁶ Abraham listened to Ephron, and Abraham weighed out for Ephron the silver that he had named in the hearing of the Hittites, four hundred shekels of silver, according to the weights current among the merchants.

¹⁷ So the field of Ephron in Machpelah, which was to the east of Mamre, the field with the cave that was in it and all the trees that were in the field, throughout its whole area, was made over ¹⁸ to Abraham as a possession in the presence of the Hittites, before all who went in at the gate of his city. ¹⁹ After this, Abraham buried Sarah his wife in the cave of the field of Machpelah east of Mamre (that is, Hebron) in the land of Canaan. ²⁰ The field and the cave that is in it were made over to Abraham as property for a burying place by the Hittites.

¹ Hebrew *sons of Heth*; also verses 5, 7, 10, 16, 18, 20 ² Or *a mighty prince* ³ A *shekel* was about 2/5 ounce or 11 grams

Section Overview

Abraham's story began with a prologue (11:27–32), leading up to his call to go from Ur to the land God would show him (12:1), and it ends with an epilogue (22:20–25:11), following his call to go and sacrifice his son in the place that God would tell him (22:2). The epilogue returns to the beginning to pick up the story of Abraham's brother Nahor, who in contrast to Abraham had a wife who was very fertile (vv. 20–24). Then it moves on to record briefly the death of Sarah (23:1–2) and then in much more detail the purchase of a burial plot within the borders of the Promised Land (vv. 3–20). The latter is significant because it demonstrates the partial realization of the promise to Abraham and Sarah of the possession of the land (12:7). In death Sarah achieves something she never attained in life: ownership of property. It is a tiny plot, and its function as a burial ground demonstrates the fact that the fulfillment of the promise lies beyond this world, but its symbolic significance is enormous. Just as one son, Isaac, is the down payment on the promise of offspring like the stars of the sky, so too one small field is the down payment on the entire land, representing and foreshadowing the complete fulfillment of the promise.

Section Outline

VII. The Family History of Terah (11:27–25:11) . . .
    Q. The Family of Nahor (22:20–24)
    R. The Death and Burial of Sarah (23:1–20)

Comment

22:20–24 The account of Nahor's family belongs here as part of the larger *toledot* of Terah (cf. Gen. 11:27). As noted above, the listing of his offspring takes us back in time, contrasting Sarah's barrenness with the eminent fertility of Nahor's wife and his concubine—between them Milcah and Reumah produce no fewer than twelve heirs for Nahor, without any miraculous divine intervention (22:20–22).

However, this account also looks forward by introducing Nahor's granddaughter Rebekah, who will become the wife of Isaac (cf. ch. 24); the report mentioned here is important in informing Abraham of his wider family's growth and prosperity, which leads him to send his servant to those relatives in search of a suitable wife for his son. The promise of blessing to the nations (22:18) will come not only through Abraham and Isaac but also through Nahor and Rebekah. Since Milcah, Nahor's wife, is the daughter of Abraham's brother Haran, all three branches of Terah's line have a part to play in the story.

Included in Nahor's family is Kemuel, who is credited with being the founder of Aram (v. 21). Aram will play an important role in Israel's future as the location of Jacob's twenty-year sojourn (31:18–21), as well as subsequently becoming one of Israel's staunch enemies. Uz, the firstborn son, shares his name with the land where Job lives, though it is uncertain whether there is a connection to that figure of unknown lineage.

23:1–2 A good death, in biblical terms, is one that comes after a full life, surrounded by family and friends and at peace, followed by a decent burial in one's own land (cf. Gen. 25:8–10).[312] Measured by these categories, Sarah's death qualifies as a good death (23:1). She is 127 years old, with a husband and a son; she does not die in a tragic accident or at a young age. Her importance to the biblical account is made clear by the fact that she is the only woman in the Bible whose age at death is mentioned. She dies in Kiriath-arba, the city that will later be renamed Hebron, in the land of Canaan, the land that God had promised to give to her and Abraham (v. 2).

Yet there is something profoundly tragic even about the best of deaths in this broken world. Death is not a natural part of living but a result of the divine curse that has come into the world through sin (3:19). So it is fitting that Abraham goes in to mourn and weep for Sarah (23:2). They have endured many things together, sometimes working well together and at other times in conflict, but always together. Death often results in a sense of deep sadness and loss on the part of those left behind.

23:3–20 Yet the death of Sarah and Abraham's subsequent mourning for her are not the central focus of the chapter. A key part of the good death—burial in one's own land—must still be accomplished. Despite the Lord's promise to give the land of Canaan to Abraham and Sarah, they still own precisely none of it. As a result, Abraham goes to the Hittites, among whom he is dwelling, to request the purchase of a suitable piece of land to serve this purpose (v. 3). The Hittites here are not to be confused with the Hittite empire of Syria but are a smaller local group, the "sons of Heth."[313] The tension in the story comes from the fact that as a "sojourner and foreigner" among the inhabitants of the land Abraham has few rights, and in

---

312 This is why the climax of Ruth's self-sacrificial commitment to Naomi is not "Your God will be my God" but "Where you die I will die, and there will I be buried" (Ruth 1:16–17).
313 Cf. Sarna, *Genesis*, 395. The Hittites in Genesis have distinctively Semitic names. There may nevertheless have been some links between the groups, since distinctively Hittite pottery has been found at Megiddo, dating

general property was not for sale in the ancient world; it was inherited from one's family. The bonds between a family and its land were deep and often inviolable, unless in exceptional circumstances (cf. 1 Kings 21). Why should anyone sell his family patrimony to a mere sojourner?

Initially the Hittites offer to allow Abraham temporary use of any of their tombs (Gen. 23:6). These tombs were likely caves cut in the rock that could be used multiple times. Normally they would be used for members of only one particular family, so it is a mark of deep respect that the Hittites make this offer. They regard Abraham as a "prince of God," or perhaps a "mighty prince," among them (cf. KJV; NASB 1995; the phrase need not have a religious sense[314]). Essentially they are inviting him to identify his family with their community in the most permanent way possible.

Abraham cannot accept their generous offer. He is not about to give up his status as a "sojourner and foreigner" in their midst, living in their world but not of it; that is God's calling to him. That which Abraham wants to purchase from them is something more lasting than a temporary tomb; he is seeking to buy a piece of property that will serve as an 'akhuzzat qeber, a permanent burial site (vv. 4, 9, 20). The Hebrew 'akhuzzah carries with it the idea of land as a permanent inheritance, passed down from one member of the family to the next.[315] Abraham does not want simply a temporary repository for Sarah's bones; he wants a place that will belong to him and his family permanently, a little piece of the Promised Land that will finally be his. Nonetheless, since the Hittites have agreed in principle to allow him to bury his dead on their land, discussions can now proceed further.

The whole negotiation is carried out with the utmost courtesy and deference, as would have been customary in that culture. It is conducted as between equals who seek to outdo each other in extravagant displays of respect. Abraham therefore bows to the Hittites, who are called the "people of the land" ('am ha'arets). This term can be used to denote either the whole population or, perhaps more likely here, a smaller group of elders and other leaders in the community who must witness and approve any property transfer that will take place (cf. Ruth 4:1–9).[316]

At this point Abraham introduces his request, which is that Ephron the Hittite sell him the cave of Machpelah at the end of his field at full price as a permanent burial place (Gen. 23:8–9; 'akhuzzat qeber). This is an invitation to Ephron to name his price, but customary politeness requires Ephron first to offer it to Abraham free of charge (v. 11). Even if this is a serious offer—and most commentators doubt so (cf. 2 Sam. 24:18–25 for a similar negotiation)—a gift would not meet Abraham's need, since it could be revoked or disputed at some point in the future.[317] So Abraham asks Ephron again to name his price. There is a catch, however; in his

---

from around 1650 BC. For arguments in favor of a stronger connection between the groups cf. Hamilton, *Genesis 18–50*, 127.
314 *'Elohim* or *'el* can be used in a superlative sense (cf. Ps. 80:10; Jonah 3:3).
315 Sarna, *Genesis*, 158.
316 E.g., Jeremiah 1:18. On the *'am ha'arets* cf. Iain M. Duguid, *Ezekiel and the Leaders of Israel* (Leiden: Brill, 1992), 119–121.
317 R. Westbrook, "Purchase of the Cave of Machpelah," *Israel Law Review* 6 (1971): 30–31.

"free" offer Ephron linked together the field and the cave (Gen. 23:11), so now Abraham requests the price for both the field and the cave (v. 13), not merely the cave for which he originally asked.

Ephron's price may well be astronomical—400 hundred shekels of silver,[318] more than a year's wages for a normal worker—though it is hard to be sure what the going rate for such a property was at that time. His audacious request remains cloaked in the most profound politeness: "What is that between you and me?" (v. 15). He probably expects Abraham to make a counteroffer, haggling for a better price, but Abraham does not want anyone to be able to claim that he has somehow cheated Ephron out of the property. He is willing to pay the full asking price in order to establish the clearest possible title to the property in question, and he weighs out the money in front of witnesses so there can be no questions later (v. 16).

In this way Abraham acquires the cave of Machpelah along with the field and all the trees in it,[319] to become a permanent burial site for the family and its first foothold of ownership in the Promised Land. Sarah will be the first occupant to rest there (v. 19), but she will be joined later by Abraham, Isaac, and Jacob, as well as by Rebekah and Leah (49:31). Their bodies are all committed to the earth there, in hope of the heavenly fulfillment of the promise of the land, which they never see completed in their own lifetimes. As John Calvin puts it, "While they themselves were silent and speechless, the sepulchre cried aloud, that death formed no obstacle to their entering on the possession of it."[320]

Response

Throughout his entire life Abraham is a "sojourner and foreigner" in the land promised to him by God (23:4). He never settles down and owns property, apart from the field mentioned in this chapter as a burial ground. As Christians, we too are called to be "sojourners and foreigners" in this world; we are *paroikous kai parepidēmous*, as the apostle Peter reminds us in 1 Peter 2:11, using exactly the same words as the Greek translation of Genesis 23:4. Thinking about ourselves as temporary residents in this way should radically impact the way in which we think about our lives and our possessions, as well as the meaning of death and what lies beyond it.

This purchase of property makes no sense for a wandering nomad, except as a statement of Abraham's faith that one day God's promise would be fulfilled and the entire Promised Land would be his.[321] In faith he trusts God to deliver on his promise, and so, instead of taking Sarah's body back to their ancestral home in Haran, he buries her in the land of Canaan. Abraham himself will later be buried on this same spot (25:9), as also Isaac, Rebekah, Jacob, and Leah will be (49:29–32).

---

[318] Coinage was not invented until long after this time, so the shekels in question would have represented a weight, a little under half an ounce each.
[319] Reference to the trees on a property was a regular feature of Hittite property records, presumably indicating that it was possible to buy a property with or without including them.
[320] Calvin, *Genesis*, 1.579.
[321] Compare Jeremiah's purchase of property in the occupied land of Judah, right before the fall of Jerusalem, as a statement of faith that there was a future for God's people beyond the exile (Jer. 32:6–25).

To Abraham and his descendants the field of Machpelah represents the firstfruits of the Promised Land. Even as he mourns his wife Abraham believes that death is not the end of the story. Rather it is the doorway through which one enters into the full measure of one's future *'akhuzzah*, the glorious inheritance that God has prepared for those who love him and are called according to his purpose (Rom. 8:28–30).

Jesus knows what it is to live as a sojourner and foreigner on earth better than anyone else, because he is the only person who ever entered this planet with experience of life in another world. He came to this earth from a place where he was literally the center of the universe, yet on entering the world he humbled himself and took the form of a servant. Instead of surrounding himself with this world's goods, he said, "Foxes have holes, and birds of the air have nests, but the Son of Man has nowhere to lay his head" (Matt. 8:20). When he died, his only possession was the single garment he wore. This world was truly not his home.

What is more, Jesus faced a worse death than Sarah or Abraham—or any of us. Physically, he endured the agonizing sufferings of the cross; spiritually, he bore the torment of God's wrath against our sin, an eternity of pain distilled into six short hours of darkness and dread. In death he had no family tomb to be buried in, only a borrowed cave that a stranger had provided for him. Of course, Jesus did not need to own a grave, because his tenancy in the tomb would be a mere three days before he rose from the dead, the true firstfruits of God's promise of life to all who trust in him. His earthly body, sown in weakness and pain, was now raised as a new heavenly body, incorruptible, glorious, and majestic.

Through his death and resurrection Jesus absorbed the sting of death, which is sin, and now he gives us the remarkable promise that we too shall one day exchange our earthly bodies, with all their weakness, suffering, pain, and tears, for glorious heavenly bodies bearing his likeness. Death has been swallowed up in victory, ushering us into the glorious inheritance that God has promised all his saints. As surely as the little piece of property that Abraham purchased was a down payment on the entire Promised Land, so too the resurrection of Christ is the down payment assuring us that the same God who raised Jesus Christ from the dead will also raise our mortal bodies into newness of life in his presence (Rom. 8:11).

GENESIS 24

24 Now Abraham was old, well advanced in years. And the Lord had blessed Abraham in all things. ² And Abraham said to his servant, the oldest of his household, who had charge of all that he had, "Put your hand under my thigh, ³ that I may make you swear by the Lord, the God of heaven and God of the earth, that you will not take a wife for my son from the daughters of the Canaanites, among whom I dwell, ⁴ but will go to my country and to my kindred, and take a wife for my son Isaac." ⁵ The servant said to him, "Perhaps the woman may not be willing to follow me to this land. Must I then take your son back to the land from which you came?" ⁶ Abraham said to him, "See to it that you do not take my son back there. ⁷ The LORD, the God of heaven, who took me from my father's house and from the land of my kindred, and who spoke to me and swore to me, 'To your offspring I will give this land,' he will send his angel before you, and you shall take a wife for my son from there. ⁸ But if the woman is not willing to follow you, then you will be free from this oath of mine; only you must not take my son back there." ⁹ So the servant put his hand under the thigh of Abraham his master and swore to him concerning this matter.

¹⁰ Then the servant took ten of his master's camels and departed, taking all sorts of choice gifts from his master; and he arose and went to Mesopotamia¹ to the city of Nahor. ¹¹ And he made the camels kneel down outside the city by the well of water at the time of evening, the time when women go out to draw water. ¹² And he said, "O LORD, God of my master Abraham, please grant me success today and show steadfast love to my master Abraham. ¹³ Behold, I am standing by the spring of water, and the daughters of the men of the city are coming out to draw water. ¹⁴ Let the young woman to whom I shall say, 'Please let down your jar that I may drink,' and who shall say, 'Drink, and I will water your camels'—let her be the one whom you have appointed for your servant Isaac. By this² I shall know that you have shown steadfast love to my master."

¹⁵ Before he had finished speaking, behold, Rebekah, who was born to Bethuel the son of Milcah, the wife of Nahor, Abraham's brother, came out with her water jar on her shoulder. ¹⁶ The young woman was very attractive in appearance, a maiden³ whom no man had known. She went down to the spring and filled her jar and came up. ¹⁷ Then the servant ran to meet her and said, "Please give me a little water to drink from your jar." ¹⁸ She said, "Drink, my lord." And she quickly let down her jar upon her hand and gave him a drink. ¹⁹ When she had finished giving him a drink, she said, "I will draw water for your camels also, until they have finished drinking." ²⁰ So she quickly emptied her jar into the trough and ran again to the well to draw water, and she drew for all his camels. ²¹ The man gazed at her in silence to learn whether the LORD had prospered his journey or not.

²² When the camels had finished drinking, the man took a gold ring weighing a half shekel,⁴ and two bracelets for her arms weighing ten gold shekels, ²³ and said, "Please tell me whose daughter you are. Is there room in your father's house for us to spend the night?" ²⁴ She said to him, "I am the daughter of Bethuel the son of Milcah, whom she bore to Nahor." ²⁵ She added, "We have plenty of both straw and fodder, and room to spend the night." ²⁶ The man bowed his head and worshiped the LORD ²⁷ and said, "Blessed be the LORD, the God of my master Abraham, who has not forsaken his steadfast love and his faithfulness toward my master. As for me, the LORD has led me in the way to the house of my master's kinsmen." ²⁸ Then the young woman ran and told her mother's household about these things.

²⁹ Rebekah had a brother whose name was Laban. Laban ran out toward the man, to the spring. ³⁰ As soon as he saw the ring and the bracelets on his sister's arms, and heard the words of Rebekah his sister, "Thus the man spoke to me," he went to the man. And behold, he was standing by

the camels at the spring. **31** He said, "Come in, O blessed of the Lord. Why do you stand outside? For I have prepared the house and a place for the camels." **32** So the man came to the house and unharnessed the camels, and gave straw and fodder to the camels, and there was water to wash his feet and the feet of the men who were with him. **33** Then food was set before him to eat. But he said, "I will not eat until I have said what I have to say." He said, "Speak on."

34 So he said, "I am Abraham's servant. **35** The Lord has greatly blessed my master, and he has become great. He has given him flocks and herds, silver and gold, male servants and female servants, camels and donkeys. **36** And Sarah my master's wife bore a son to my master when she was old, and to him he has given all that he has. **37** My master made me swear, saying, 'You shall not take a wife for my son from the daughters of the Canaanites, in whose land I dwell, **38** but you shall go to my father's house and to my clan and take a wife for my son.' **39** I said to my master, 'Perhaps the woman will not follow me.' **40** But he said to me, 'The Lord, before whom I have walked, will send his angel with you and prosper your way. You shall take a wife for my son from my clan and from my father's house. **41** Then you will be free from my oath, when you come to my clan. And if they will not give her to you, you will be free from my oath.'

42 "I came today to the spring and said, 'O Lord, the God of my master Abraham, if now you are prospering the way that I go, **43** behold, I am standing by the spring of water. Let the virgin who comes out to draw water, to whom I shall say, "Please give me a little water from your jar to drink," **44** and who will say to me, "Drink, and I will draw for your camels also," let her be the woman whom the Lord has appointed for my master's son.'

45 "Before I had finished speaking in my heart, behold, Rebekah came out with her water jar on her shoulder, and she went down to the spring and drew water. I said to her, 'Please let me drink.' **46** She quickly let down her jar from her shoulder and said, 'Drink, and I will give your camels drink also.' So I drank, and she gave the camels drink also. **47** Then I asked her, 'Whose daughter are you?' She said, 'The daughter of Bethuel, Nahor's son, whom Milcah bore to him.' So I put the ring on her nose and the bracelets on her arms. **48** Then I bowed my head and worshiped the Lord and blessed the Lord, the God of my master Abraham, who had led me by the right way[5] to take the daughter of my master's kinsman for his son. **49** Now then, if you are going to show steadfast love and faithfulness to my master, tell me; and if not, tell me, that I may turn to the right hand or to the left."

50 Then Laban and Bethuel answered and said, "The thing has come from the Lord; we cannot speak to you bad or good. **51** Behold, Rebekah is before you; take her and go, and let her be the wife of your master's son, as the Lord has spoken."

52 When Abraham's servant heard their words, he bowed himself to the earth before the Lord. **53** And the servant brought out jewelry of silver and of gold, and garments, and gave them to Rebekah. He also gave to her brother and to her mother costly ornaments. **54** And he and the men who were with him ate and drank, and they spent the night there. When they arose in the morning, he said, "Send me away to my master." **55** Her brother and her mother said, "Let the young woman remain with us a while, at least ten days; after that she may go." **56** But he said to them, "Do not delay me, since the Lord has prospered my way. Send me away that I may go to my master." **57** They said, "Let us call the young woman and ask her." **58** And they called Rebekah and said to her, "Will you go with this man?" She said, "I will go." ⁵⁹ So they sent away Rebekah their sister and her nurse, and Abraham's servant and his men. ⁶⁰ And they blessed Rebekah and said to her,

> "Our sister, may you become
>   thousands of ten thousands,
> and may your offspring possess
>   the gate of those who hate him!"⁶

⁶¹ Then Rebekah and her young women arose and rode on the camels and followed the man. Thus the servant took Rebekah and went his way. ⁶² Now Isaac had returned from Beer-lahai-roi and was dwelling in the Negeb. ⁶³ And Isaac went out to meditate in the field toward evening. And he lifted up his eyes and saw, and behold, there were camels coming. ⁶⁴ And Rebekah lifted up her eyes, and when she saw Isaac, she dismounted from the camel ⁶⁵ and said to the servant, "Who is that man, walking in the field to meet us?" The servant said, "It is my master." So she took her veil and covered herself. ⁶⁶ And the servant told Isaac all the things that he had done. ⁶⁷ Then Isaac brought her into the tent of Sarah his mother and took Rebekah, and she became his wife, and he loved her. So Isaac was comforted after his mother's death.

¹ Hebrew *Aram-naharaim* ² Or *By her* ³ Or *a woman of marriageable age* ⁴ A *shekel* was about 2/5 ounce or 11 grams ⁵ Or *faithfully* ⁶ Or *hate them*

Section Overview

Genesis 24 is part of the transitional material that rounds out Abraham's story and introduces that of Isaac. A key part of that transition is finding for Isaac a suitable wife who by faith will share his life journey. The patriarchal narratives of Abraham, Isaac, and Jacob are significantly also about the patriarch's wives in a way that is unusual in ancient—and even biblical—literature. Job's wife, for example, has little role to play in the story except to admonish her husband to "curse God and die" (Job 2:9) and to bear his children. The wives of Moses, Joshua, and Samuel barely appear in their accounts. Yet Sarah, Rebekah, Rachel, and Leah each has an important role in the narrative as founding mothers in the faith.

The acquisition of a wife is thus an important part of the story. The wrong wife can have a significant negative effect. Lot's wife identifies too much with Sodom and pays the price (Gen. 19:26). Ishmael's wife comes from Egypt, confirming his path away from the family of promise (21:21). Esau multiplies wives of the wrong sort, including one from Ishmael's family (26:34; 28:9). Judah marries a Canaanite woman as part of his distancing himself from Jacob's family (38:2). Jacob's wives come from the right family but are foisted on him through a trick of precisely the same kind he had perpetrated on his dead father (29:18–28).

Amid all this marital chaos the story of Rebekah's introduction into the family of promise shines with a peculiar kind of beauty. Abraham sends his servant to seek a woman of faith for his son (24:1–7), and the servant pursues his quest with deep faith of his own, bathing the process with prayer and being led by the Lord to precisely the right woman (vv. 12–21). Rebekah herself immediately leaves her home and family by faith to go from her native land and live in the country the Lord had promised her new husband (v. 58).[322] She is thus the perfectly matched bride for Isaac as he continues to live as a sojourner and a foreigner, trusting the Lord to provide for all their future needs.

Section Outline

    VII. The Family History of Terah (11:27–25:11) . . .
          S. A Bride for Isaac (24:1–67)

Comment

24:1–9 The episode recounted here occurs shortly after Sarah's death (cf. Gen. 24:67), by which time Abraham is about 138 years old, which certainly counts as being "well advanced in years" (v. 1). Likely it is his wife's death that focuses Abraham's attention on the need for Isaac to acquire a wife. The Lord's promise of innumerable offspring could not be fulfilled without Isaac's getting married and supplying an heir. In that culture marriage was the primary responsibility not of the man and woman concerned but of their families. It would presumably have been straightforward enough for Abraham to locate a wife for Isaac from the Hittites among whom he was dwelling as a sojourner and foreigner (23:4); through God's blessing Abraham was wealthy (24:1), and his only son would have seemed an attractive match. That would be the route taken by Esau in the next generation (26:34).

Alternatively, Abraham could have journeyed back to Paddan-aram himself with the boy to search for a suitable bride. Yet it appears that his previous travels outside the Promised Land (e.g., Gen. 12:10–20) have convinced him of the folly of leaving the land that God has promised to give him. Those efforts to find human solutions to his problems have created more difficulties than they have removed. So Abraham devises a plan that allows him to remain with Isaac while sending a trusted representative to seek a suitable wife (24:3–4). If the Lord blesses the plan, the problem will be solved. If not, Abraham will trust the Lord to resolve it in his own way and time (vv. 5–8).

The trusted representative is described simply as "the oldest of his household, who had charge of all that he had" (v. 2). It is plausible that this is Eliezer of Damascus (cf. 15:2), the member of Abraham's household who would have inherited had Abraham produced no offspring, but it is impossible to know for sure. Certainly he is a man who has walked with Abraham for a long time and shares his deep faith in the Lord. Abraham summons this man and makes him swear an oath by the Lord—not merely the more generic title "the God of heaven and the God of the earth"[323]—that he will not take a wife for Isaac from the Canaanite women but will go and find one

---

322 Sarna (*Genesis*, 161) points out the fact that the key verb *halak* ("to go") that summoned Abraham from his native land in Genesis 12:1 is used of Rebekah no fewer than seven times in this chapter.
323 The title "The God of heaven and the God of earth" is significant, since Abraham is predicating his acting at a distance from the land of Canaan. Unlike the Canaanite gods, who were typically thought to have only local sway, Abraham's God rules over the whole earth.

from Abraham's own family (24:3–4). The solemnity of the oath is reinforced by the symbolic gesture of placing his hand under Abraham's "thigh" (Hb. *yarek*; v. 2; cf. 47:29), which seems likely to be a euphemism for the genitals (cf. 46:26; Ex. 1:5; Judg. 8:30, where offspring come from a person's *yarek*),[324] though the exact significance of this gesture remains obscure. The content of the oath is that the servant will under no circumstances permit Isaac to marry a Canaanite woman (Gen. 24:3), nor will he take Isaac back to Abraham's family or land of origin (v. 6). Rather he must find a wife from there who is willing to come and join Isaac in the Land of Promise.

The reason for not taking a wife from the Canaanites is not mere prejudice on Abraham's part. The current residents of the land are consistently portrayed as deeply sinful people whom it is the Lord's purpose to dispossess through a holy people that he will create (cf. Gen. 13:13; 15:16; etc.). It is not that Abraham's family is sin-free, any more than Abraham himself is. Rather, it has been chosen by God to provide the foundation of this new people through the Lord's grace. Isaac, as the chosen son of the promise, therefore needs a wife who is equally chosen by God to be the bearer of the promise. Genesis 24:6–9 contains Abraham's final recorded words: a clear confession of faith in God's power and ability to provide the right wife for Isaac, just as he will fulfill his promise to give Isaac the land. The two promises of land and offspring are ultimately inseparable: a people needs somewhere to live, while a land needs occupants.

24:10–14 The servant goes on his way taking ten camels, which might have been a very unusual sight in those days,[325] along with gifts to provide evidence of Abraham's prosperity, and he journeys back from Canaan to Mesopotamia,[326] to the "city of Nahor," which is not just the place where Nahor himself lives but a city (or village) bearing his name (v. 10). Given Abraham's awareness of the growth of Nahor's family (22:20–24), this is the obvious place to go in looking for a family member suitable for marriage.

If someone were seeking to meet women in antiquity, a well was the ideal place to go (cf. Gen. 29:9–11; Ex. 2:15; John 4:6–7). Carrying water was women's work and would typically involve trips to the well at least twice a day, in the morning and the evening. Wells were also places where one could glean information, such as the whereabouts and welfare of Nahor's family (cf. Gen. 29:4–6). Abraham's servant does not leave the encounter to chance, however. He prays that the Lord would grant him success in his search and thereby show "steadfast love" (Hb. *khesed*) to Abraham (24:12). *Khesed* often describes behavior that is fitting in a covenant context, so it is plausible that the servant specifically has in mind the fulfillment of the Lord's promise to Abraham of offspring through Isaac (21:12).

---

324 Currid, *Genesis 1:1–25:18*, 412.
325 Cf. comment on 12:10–20.
326 Literally, *'aram nakharaim*, which occurs elsewhere only at Deuteronomy 23:4; Judges 3:8; 1 Chronicles 19:6; Psalm 60:1. "Mesopotamia" follows the LXX in reading the second word as a dual, "two rivers" (i.e., the land between the Tigris and the Euphrates), rather than as "within the river," that is, the area surrounded on three sides by the Euphrates—which would be in the kingdom of Mitanni, as references from Egyptian and Tel Amarna sources make clear. This is further north and west than Mesopotamia proper. Cf. Sarna, *Genesis*, 163. This is the same area called "Paddan-aram" in Genesis 25:20 and elsewhere.

The servant proposes a test whereby he will be able to identify the Lord's choice of a wife for Isaac: when he approaches and asks for a drink, she will not only grant his request but offer to water his camels also (24:14). This is the first recorded prayer for guidance by an individual in Scripture. Superficially, this may look similar to Gideon's fleece that he laid out before the Lord as a sign, asking first that the fleece would be wet with dew in the morning and the ground around it dry, and then (as confirmation) that the fleece would be dry and the ground wet (Judg. 6:36–40). However, the differences are as profound as the similarities: Gideon's sign requires a supernatural work of God, while Abraham's servant proposes a test of character, looking for a woman with a generous and hospitable spirit (cf. Prov. 31:10–31). It requires someone who is willing to go the extra mile in ministering to a stranger. After all, a few ounces of water would satisfy the thirst of Abraham's servant, but his ten camels could consume many gallons of water, all of which the woman would have to draw from the well by hand.

24:15–28 The prayer of Abraham's servant is answered almost before he has finished praying it: Rebekah arrives at the well carrying her water jar (Gen. 24:15). She fits all the usual requirements for a good wife: she is a young woman (Hb. *na'arah*) who is not yet married and still under the authority of her father (*betulah*), and is a virgin ("Whom no man had known"; v. 16).[327] As a bonus, Rebekah is described as being "very attractive" (v. 16). What is more, she passes the character test with flying colors, offering to water the servant's camels as well as providing him with the water he requests for himself (vv. 18–19), a task that clearly takes some time (v. 20).

One more question remains to be answered. Abraham's servant asks Rebekah to what family she belongs (v. 23), and he receives the welcome news that she is part of Abraham's wider family: the daughter of Bethuel, the son of Nahor and Milcah (v. 24). The specification of Bethuel's mother is important, because Nahor also had children through a concubine (cf. 22:20–24). Only then does the servant permit himself a sigh of relief and of praise: "Blessed be the LORD, the God of my master Abraham, who has not forsaken his steadfast love and his faithfulness toward my master. As for me, the LORD has led me in the way to the house of my master's kinsmen" (24:27).[328] For Isaac God has provided not merely a lamb but now also the perfect wife. Abraham's faith in God's provision is fully justified.

---

[327] People sometimes claim that the Hebrew word *betulah* means "virgin," but the regular use of the clause "Whom no man had known" and similar circumlocutions show that there is no exact equivalent word in Hebrew. Rather, three words operate in the same broad semantic field: *na'arah*, *betulah*, and *'almah*, all of which occur in Genesis 24. A *na'arah* ("young woman") is the female equivalent of *na'ar* ("young man") and primarily defines a person's age and gender, though it can also indicate a person's status as a servant. A *betulah* is a woman who is not yet married and therefore still lives under the authority of her father, not a husband. An *'almah* is a young woman who has reached the age of sexual maturity and is thus ready to be married. In Genesis 24 Rebekah is first identified as a *na'arah* (v. 16), someone who fits broadly into the category of people Abraham's servant is seeking. But that term might also be used of married women and younger girls, neither of which would suit. So it is necessary that he determine that she is also a *betulah* (v. 16) and an *'almah* (v. 43), as well as a person of good character ("Whom no man had known"), before he concludes she is the right one for Isaac. Cf. Mathews, *Genesis 11:27–50:26*, 333.

[328] We might perhaps say, "The Lord led me straight to the house of my master's kinsmen." Cf. E. A. Speiser, *Genesis*, AB (New York: Doubleday, 1964), 180.

In verses 22–25 it appears that Abraham's servant adorns Rebekah with gifts prior to learning her family, while in verse 47, in the servant's reporting of events to Laban, the order is reversed and the servant confirms her family before giving her the gifts. The latter order would seem more logical; however, it may be that the servant is so awed and impressed by the apparently immediate answer to his prayer from the Lord that he gives Rebekah the gifts first, believing by faith that she is indeed the one even before she confirms her family. His subsequent prayer of thanksgiving would then be an affirmation that his faith has not been misplaced and that Rebekah's appearing is indeed due to the Lord's *khesed* ("faithful love") to Abraham.

The jewelry with which Abraham's servant adorns Rebekah is of significant value: the gold ring weighs a *beqa'*, a weight equivalent to half a shekel or one-fifth of an ounce (6 g), while the bracelets weigh ten shekels, or about 4 ounces (113 g) (Gen. 24:22). Verse 47 clarifies that the ring in question is a nose ring, not a ring for a finger or ear. These are extravagant gifts, far out of proportion to the service that Rebekah has rendered him, which must immediately have raised questions about his intentions. He has also asked about the possibility of accommodation for the night, and so Rebekah runs home to share the news with her mother's household, apparently leaving Abraham's servant by the well (v. 28; cf. v. 30). Calling it "her mother's house" contrasts it with Isaac's mother's tent (v. 67), where she will live at the end of this chapter, and also underlines the near invisibility of her father, Bethuel, throughout the encounter.

24:29–48 At this point Laban, Rebekah's brother, appears on the scene. Having seen his sister arrive home adorned with unexpected jewelry, he goes to investigate (vv. 29–30). The fact that Laban undertakes this role rather than Rebekah's father, Bethuel, who is absent throughout this interaction apart from a brief mention in verse 50, suggests that Bethuel is likely elderly and frail. Laban seems more impressed by the gift than Rebekah was, which hints at the greed that he will demonstrate later in the story.[329] Laban's name ("White one") has been connected with the moon cult, along with the names of others of Abraham's family of origin (Terah, Sarai, Milcah), which fits with the perspective of Joshua 24:2, 14, that Abraham's ancestors worshiped other gods. However, Laban addresses Abraham's servant in Yahwistic terms ("blessed of the LORD"; Gen. 24:31) and warmly invites him into the house to receive the hospitality he has requested for himself and his camels.

Abraham's servant himself takes care of getting the camels settled in their temporary accommodations (Gen. 24:32), perhaps because Laban's servants are unsure of how to care for these exotic beasts. Water is also provided for Abraham's servant and his attendants so that they can wash their feet and refresh themselves after their long journey (v. 32). However, before he settles down to eat with Laban, the

---

[329] It is very common for an OT character to reveal on his first appearance characteristics that will define him in the later narrative. Abraham's first act is to step out in faith (Gen. 12:4), Jacob and Esau struggle in the womb (25:22), and Samson sees a Philistine woman and wants to marry her (Judg. 14:1–2).

servant wants to unburden himself of his commission so that he will not receive Laban's hospitality under false pretenses (v. 33). He recounts the whole story, giving the Lord credit for blessing Abraham and Sarah with great wealth—flocks and herds, silver and gold, male servants and female servants, camels and donkeys—as well as one son, who stands to inherit the entire estate after Abraham's death (v. 35). The importance of what has transpired, and especially the Lord's part in the whole endeavor from beginning to end in directing him to Rebekah, is highlighted by the fact that the narrator repeats the entire story, almost word for word, rather than summarizing it. The effect on the reader, as well as on Laban, is to highlight the inevitability that Rebekah is indeed the one set apart by the Lord for this unique calling to be the wife of Isaac.

24:49–61 As Abraham's servant's retelling of events catches up with the present, the narrative tension rises, leading to the crucial question: Are Rebekah and her family willing to entrust her to this stranger to be taken to a faraway country and married to an unknown man, albeit one in her wider family? Abraham's servant puts as much pressure on Laban as he can, implying that agreement is owed to Abraham as an act of *khesed* ("steadfast love") and faithfulness (v. 49). Nevertheless, he acknowledges that Laban would be within his rights to refuse, in which case the servant would need to move on and try elsewhere, though the vagueness of his options ("turn to the right hand or the left") reveals that he has no immediate alternative plan. It is possible that there are other daughters of Rebekah's age in Nahor's wider family, but in that case the prayer that Abraham's servant prayed at the well would have been not so much unanswered as misleadingly answered by the Lord.

The reader can scarcely avoid agreeing with Laban and Bethuel's assessment: "The thing has come from the LORD; we cannot speak to you bad or good" (v. 50).[330] The transaction is approved, and it is agreed that Rebekah will return with Abraham's servant to become Isaac's wife (v. 51). The relief experienced by Abraham's servant is palpable: when he hears their words of agreement, he bows low before the Lord, giving thanks for the divine guidance and sovereignty that have so evidently superintended the whole process from the moment he first arrived in Paddan-aram (v. 52). He then brings out rich gifts for Rebekah, as well as for her family, to celebrate the forthcoming union and fulfill the bride-price (v. 53). Then they eat and drink together to seal the relationship (v. 54).

The only complication in negotiations come over the timing of Rebekah's departure (vv. 54–59). Abraham's servant is understandably eager to get back on the road to his master and celebrate the Lord's goodness (v. 54). After all, Abraham is old, and it is far from certain how much longer he will live (v. 1). But leaving Laban's household is not simple; hospitality demands that certain protocols be

---

[330] As noted earlier, this is Bethuel's only contribution to events, which suggests that he is old and largely incapacitated. He is not even listed as a recipient of gifts in verse 53. In his absence Laban takes the lead in everything, yet in the approval of an offer of marriage for his daughter Bethuel's agreement nonetheless matters, even if it is only in token form.

followed (cf. 31:27), particularly since his departure entails Rebekah's leaving her home forever. Laban seeks to detain him from going for a while, perhaps ten days or so (24:55; lit., "days or ten"; *yamim 'o 'asor*). In the end, when Abraham's servant presses them, they put the question to Rebekah herself, allowing her to speak her own commitment of faith to accompany the visitor to his distant home. Her response is simple, just one word in Hebrew: *'elek* ("I will go!" v. 58).

Rebekah leaves Paddan-aram accompanied by her former nurse (v. 59) and an unspecified number of female servants, reflecting her social status (v. 61). Having been with her from childhood, the nurse would be almost a second mother to Rebekah and could be her chaperone as well as friend. Rebekah's family sends her on her way with a blessing that echoes the Lord's own blessing on Abraham:

> May you become
>   thousands of ten thousands,
> and may your offspring possess
>   the gates of those that hate him! (v. 60; cf. 22:17)

This is an expression of their faith and hers that God has called Isaac and Rebekah to be the channels of the promised Abrahamic blessing to the world.

24:62–67 The story closes with an account of Isaac and Rebekah's first meeting. Isaac and Abraham are continuing their nomadic existence as "sojourners and foreigners," moving from place to place with their flocks and herds, and are now in the Negeb, having visited Beer-lahai-roi, a well in that same region (24:62; cf. 16:14). It is fitting that he has been at a place named after the Lord's watching over his people while that same providential care has been orchestrating the selection of his wife.

Their encounter takes place while Isaac is outside in the evening "meditating" (Hb. *suakh*; Gen. 24:63). This Hebrew word is obscure; some have suggested that it simply means walking, while others have connected it to a similar word for talking (*siakh*) and hence with "meditation" (Ps. 104:34). However, in most cases in which the verb is used of talking to God it has to do with complaining or bemoaning one's situation (e.g., Pss. 55:3; 64:2) rather than pondering the existence and attributes of God—a sense that would also fit here. If so, perhaps Rebekah's arrival is quite literally the answer to Isaac's prayers. It is worth noting the fact that her arrival "comforted" Isaac, a verb describing relief from the circumstances that cause *siakh*.[331]

Isaac and Rebekah both "lifted up their eyes and saw" (Gen. 24:63–64), suggesting a simultaneous event. Rebekah dismounts from her camel in order to meet Isaac face to face rather than looking down on him from a great height, and she puts on her veil (v. 65). Women did not generally go around veiled in the ancient world; otherwise she would have already been wearing her veil. Veils were used for a variety of reasons in the ancient Near East but were associated particularly

---

[331] Cf. G. Vall, "What Was Isaac Doing in the Field (Genesis XXIV 63)?" *VT* 44 (1994): 521.

with betrothal and weddings.[332] Indeed, the Akkadian word *kallatu* (Hb. *kalla*, "bride"; Song 4:11, 12; 5:1) is connected etymologically to *kullulu*, which means "to veil." The veil was not simply a form of concealment in an ancient context; it often served as a pledge and sign of an exclusive relationship. So too here Rebekah's veiling identifies her as Isaac's bride.

The narrative concludes with Isaac's marrying Rebekah and installing her as the "first lady" of the family by bringing her into the tent formerly belonging to his mother (Gen. 24:67). Although this is an arranged marriage, it is by no means a cold and formal relationship—it has, after all, been arranged by God himself! Isaac loves Rebekah and finds comfort in her after his mother's death (v. 67), a wonderful testimony to the closeness of their friendship.

Response

Back in Genesis 22 Abraham showed that his heart was settled on one fundamental biblical principle: "The LORD will provide" (22:14). Here in Genesis 24 the Lord provides a wife for Isaac, just as he once provided a ram in a thicket for him. In this chapter Abraham's elderly servant is his proxy,[333] acting with exactly the same faith as his master's and seeing it rewarded with guidance to exactly the right young woman for Isaac. It is striking that it is not her beauty that makes her the one, though she is indeed beautiful (24:16). It is her godly character as a willing servant of strangers (vv. 19–20)—and above all the deep faith that leads her boldly to leave her family and kindred and go to a land that she has never known (v. 58), just as Abraham did so many years before (12:1–4)—that makes her so.

Those who are seeking a spouse should look for similar attributes: godly character and shared faith in Christ. Not coincidentally, these are the virtues exhibited by the godly wife in Proverbs 31:10–31. Beauty is a bonus, not an essential, since the fear of the Lord has a beauty of its own (Prov. 31:30). The result of such shared values ought to be a marriage in which love and comfort abound. Where such a spouse is to be found, no special sign from God should be necessary to indicate the fittingness of the match. Ordinary wisdom ought to suffice.

Rebekah is also a model of our calling as Christians. She came into Abraham's family as an outsider in some respects, choosing to join in their journey of faith, counting on the extension of God's promises to her also, who previously had been far off (geographically at least) from the promise. Yet in God's grace the promises are made to her as well (Acts 2:39), and she is incorporated into the family of blessing by faith.

Yet Rebekah's primary role in the story is not simply to be our model; it is to be the mother of the seed of Abraham, a link in the chain that will culminate in the coming of Jesus to deliver his people from their sins (Matt. 1:21). Without God's provision of a savior ultimately all the blessings he gives Abraham and Sarah, as

---

[332] K. Van der Toorn, "The Significance of the Veil in the Ancient Near East," in *Pomegranates and Golden Bells: Festschrift for J. Milgrom*, ed. D. P. Wright (Winona Lake, IN: Eisenbrauns, 1995), 330–336.
[333] Cf. L. Teugels, "The Anonymous Matchmaker: An Enquiry into the Characterization of the Servant of Abraham in Genesis 24," *JSOT* 65 (1995): 13–23.

well as Isaac and Rebekah, would be in vain. They would be people to be pitied, leaving a secure home life to become sojourners and foreigners in a land not their own. It is Christ's incarnation, death, resurrection, and ascension that give profound meaning to Rebekah's step of faith, as he himself becomes the pioneer and perfecter of that faith (Heb. 12:2), bringing all his people safely to their heavenly home.

GENESIS 25:1–18

25 Abraham took another wife, whose name was Keturah. ²She bore him Zimran, Jokshan, Medan, Midian, Ishbak, and Shuah. ³Jokshan fathered Sheba and Dedan. The sons of Dedan were Asshurim, Letushim, and Leummim. ⁴The sons of Midian were Ephah, Epher, Hanoch, Abida, and Eldaah. All these were the children of Keturah. ⁵Abraham gave all he had to Isaac. ⁶But to the sons of his concubines Abraham gave gifts, and while he was still living he sent them away from his son Isaac, eastward to the east country.

⁷These are the days of the years of Abraham's life, 175 years. ⁸Abraham breathed his last and died in a good old age, an old man and full of years, and was gathered to his people. ⁹Isaac and Ishmael his sons buried him in the cave of Machpelah, in the field of Ephron the son of Zohar the Hittite, east of Mamre, ¹⁰the field that Abraham purchased from the Hittites. There Abraham was buried, with Sarah his wife. ¹¹After the death of Abraham, God blessed Isaac his son. And Isaac settled at Beer-lahai-roi.

¹²These are the generations of Ishmael, Abraham's son, whom Hagar the Egyptian, Sarah's servant, bore to Abraham. ¹³These are the names of the sons of Ishmael, named in the order of their birth: Nebaioth, the firstborn of Ishmael; and Kedar, Adbeel, Mibsam, ¹⁴Mishma, Dumah, Massa, ¹⁵Hadad, Tema, Jetur, Naphish, and Kedemah. ¹⁶These are the sons of Ishmael and these are their names, by their villages and by their encampments, twelve princes according to their tribes. ¹⁷(These are the years of the life of Ishmael: 137 years. He breathed his last and died, and was gathered to his people.) ¹⁸They settled from Havilah to Shur, which is opposite Egypt in the direction of Assyria. He settled[1] over against all his kinsmen.

[1] Hebrew *fell*

Section Overview

Genesis 24 already began to shift the focus from Abraham to Isaac as the central character of the narrative. In the beginning of the chapter, when Abraham's servant refers to "my master," he means Abraham (Gen. 24:12), but by the end of the chapter the same title is applied to Isaac (24:65). Abraham's absence from the scene on his servant's return is particularly striking; it is to Isaac that the man recounts all his adventures in fulfilling Abraham's instructions (24:66). The reader might assume that perhaps Abraham dies during the trip were it not for the fact that the record of his death follows in the subsequent chapter. The chronology, moreover, requires Abraham to remain alive for another thirty-five years after Isaac's marriage (25:7, 20).

The marriage to Keturah described here probably occurs much earlier, while Sarah is still alive (1 Chron. 1:32 calls Keturah Abraham's "concubine"; cf. Gen. 25:6). After all, Abraham described himself as too old to have children many years earlier (17:17). Keturah is included in the narrative at this point to underline the point that Abraham is indeed the father of many nations, just as God had promised (17:5).

Yet, although Abraham has other children apart from Isaac, Isaac is the only one that really matters, the child of God's promise. Abraham's other children receive gifts from him, but, like Ishmael, they do not remain with Abraham; during his lifetime he sends them away (Gen. 25:6), just as he did with Ishmael, so that Isaac alone will inherit (25:5; cf. 24:36). We are not told when Abraham sends his other sons away, but plausibly it is shortly after the time of Isaac's birth, when Hagar and Ishmael are dismissed (cf. 21:12–14), so that by the time of chapter 22 Isaac is indeed Abraham's only son (22:2).

When Abraham dies, his is also a "good death," just as Sarah's had been, "old ... and full of years" (Gen. 25:7–8; cf. 23:1–2). His death brings about a temporary reconciliation between Isaac and Ishmael for the funeral, when the sons come together to see Abraham buried on the small piece of Canaan that he owned, the cave of Machpelah (25:9; cf. ch. 23). Thereafter, however, their ways diverge once more. Isaac is blessed by God and returns to his former residence at Beer-lahai-roi (25:11), the "Well of the God Who Sees Me"—the very place where God had earlier taken care of Ishmael. Meanwhile, Ishmael's subsequent history is told by means of his own *toledot* (family history) sequence, which takes the form of a genealogy. Ishmael has many sons without apparent difficulty (in contrast to Isaac and Rebekah's long wait for children; v. 21) and is blessed by God in many ways. Yet the summary of his story is contained in the end of the genealogy: his descendants settle nearer to Egypt than the Promised Land and live "over against" their brothers (v. 18; cf. 16:12). They spend their whole lives "not far from the kingdom of God" (Mark 12:34) but remain outsiders to it, in tragic opposition to the ones through whom alone God's richest blessings can be found. In a section that recounts the story of all Abraham's other sons, Isaac's uniqueness is clear.

Section Outline

 VII. The Family History of Terah (11:27–25:11) ...
   T. The Death of Abraham (25:1–11)
 VIII. The Family History of Ishmael (25:12–18)

Comment

25:1–6 The final episode of Abraham's story highlights the various ways in which God fulfills his promises to the patriarch. God had promised Abraham that he would have many descendants (13:16; 15:5; 17:2; 22:17) and would be the father of many nations (17:4). That promise is fulfilled not simply through Isaac and Ishmael but also through Abraham's children by Keturah, listed in the first four verses of Genesis 25. It seems that there is no special divine intervention required for the birth of these children, as there was not for the birth of Ishmael, which reinforces the idea that the marriage to Keturah occurred earlier, before the birth of Isaac.

Most of the nations that come from these offspring are located in the Arabian Peninsula and connected with the spice trade, which is fitting, since their mother's name, Keturah, has been connected to spices and incense.[334] They are clearly counted as part of the Abrahamic family, but, while these are children of Abraham in the physical sense, only Isaac is the child of promise. As a result, he alone inherits Abraham's estate (v. 5), along with the promises made by God to his father (26:3–5). Abraham loves and provides for all his children (25:6), but there is no confusion in his mind about God's promise. He does not try to pass it on to a different child, as Isaac will (cf. Genesis 27), nor seek a share of the inheritance for others of his children, as he sought earlier for Ishmael (17:17; 21:10–11). Rather he trusts the God who had said, "Through Isaac shall your offspring be named" (21:12). Acting upon that faith, he makes provision for his other children—who are linked with Ishmael as the children of his concubines (25:6)—and sends them away, just as he sent away Ishmael (cf. 21:12–14).

It is significant that many of these tribal groups, such as the Midianites, will be subsequently hostile to the Israelites when they come out of Egypt under Moses (cf. Num. 22:4–7) and after the conquest (cf. Judges 6). Though descended from Abraham, they do not share in his spiritual blessings because, like Ishmael, they choose to live "over against all his kinsmen" (Gen. 25:18). Sheba and Dedan—if these are the same groups as later—are singled out for judgment in the prophets for their opposition to Judah at the time of the Babylonian exile (Jer. 25:23; 49:8). The offspring of Asshurim are not to be confused with the Assyrians; they are a distinct group (mentioned also in Numbers 24:22, 24; Ps. 83:8) located close to Egypt (cf. Gen. 25:18).[335] What links all these diverse groups is their opposition to Israel (cf. Ps. 83:8–9). It is not enough to be Abraham's offspring physically if this is not combined with Abraham's faith. The "not sons" end up being sent away to the east (Gen. 25:6), as when Adam and Eve were expelled from the garden (3:23–24).

25:7–11 Abraham himself lives a long and full life under God's blessing, just as Sarah had, dwelling in the land of Canaan for a full century (cf. 12:4). His death is in line with what God had promised long before: "As for you, you shall go to your fathers in peace; you shall be buried in a good old age" (15:15). Here we read that Abraham is indeed gathered to his people in a "good old age" (25:8). This means more than simply joining his ancestors in the family grave, since in Abraham's case the grave site is a new one, occupied only by Sarah. Rather, it contains at least a hint

---

334 Steinmann, *Genesis*, 243.
335 Hamilton, *Genesis 18–50*, 166.

of a continued existence, without which the main point of this chapter—God's faithfulness to fulfill his promises to Abraham—would fall rather flat.

Abraham's subsequent funeral is marked by precisely the peace and harmony promised in Genesis 15. His sons Isaac and Ishmael bury their differences long enough to bury their father together in the cave of Machpelah, where Abraham had earlier buried Sarah (Gen. 25:9–10). The rest of their lives will be marked by the "in your face" hostility prophesied by the angel of the Lord in Genesis 16:12, which will be passed down to succeeding generations of their children (25:18). For this brief moment, however, their enmity is forgotten as they join together in the peaceful burial of their father. Here is a man in whose life many promises of God have indeed been fulfilled.

Of course, this documentation of promises fulfilled also highlights those promises that have not yet been fulfilled. God had promised to give Abraham the entire land of Canaan, and thus far he only owns a small field as a burial site, including the cave of Machpelah. The conclusion of Abraham's story has an "already and not yet" feel to it, with a clear acknowledgement of what God has done to bless him together with a vivid awareness that so much more still remains to be fulfilled.

25:12–18 Ishmael receives his own *toledot* (family history), a title that highlights the function of the term as an introduction of whatever follows rather than a colophon ending that which precedes it.[336] It details the story of the subsequent generations, in this case those who come from Ishmael. Ishmael is identified as a son of Abraham, but he is also the son of Hagar the Egyptian, Sarah's maidservant (v. 12). These two identities presuppose the reader's familiarity with the story so far and represent the outworking of Ishmael's family as part of that same story. Although the subject of the chapter ostensibly shifts from Abraham to Ishmael, the underlying theme is unchanged: God's faithfulness to Abraham.

Ishmael's prosperity and numerous progeny is therefore presented as a fulfillment of God's promises to Hagar and to Abraham that Ishmael would father twelve princes and become a great nation (16:10; 17:20). The twelve sons of Ishmael are listed in 25:13–15, and the fact is recorded that they all become princes. We are informed that Ishmael himself lives to a good age, and, when he dies, he too is "gathered to his people" (v. 17). Assuming this is not simply a stock euphemism for death, this conclusion to Ishmael's story raises the question regarding to which people he is gathered. Is his final destiny to be with the family of faith, represented by his father, Abraham, or with the family of unbelief, where he spends most of his life? Out of that mixed parentage, who are Ishmael's true people? The trajectory of his offspring, who choose to dwell in the vicinity of Egypt, is not encouraging. What is more, the last word on Ishmael confirms the prophecy of Genesis 16:10–12, that he would live "over against all his kinsmen" (v. 18). To be an enemy of Abraham's seed is to place oneself under the curse of Abraham's God (12:1–3).

---

336 Cf. comment on 2:4–7.

Response

This passage is about the promises of God, fulfilled and unfulfilled. God has been faithful to Abraham throughout his life, and he is faithful to him in his death. He is faithful also to Abraham's other children in fulfilling his promises of worldly blessing to them. Yet they miss out on the richest blessing of all, which is transmitted through Isaac alone. For Ishmael and the sons of Keturah to join in those blessings, they would need to align themselves with Isaac, something that in most cases never happens.

Abraham, like Sarah, dies in possession of no more of the Promised Land than he needs for his burial. He dies in faith, having not yet received the fullness of God's promise. His faith stands as a challenge to the Israelites under Moses as they are about to enter the Promised Land, which they are called to possess by faith. Abraham's faith likewise stands as a challenge to many subsequent generations of Israelites, showing that there is more to God's promise than the possession of a particular piece of real estate that they never quite seem able to occupy fully.

Abraham's faith also stands as a challenge to us. We have received even greater and more precious promises than Abraham did. Indeed, we have received nothing less than the promised Holy Spirit, poured out upon us and our children, upon all types of people and all classes of society, in a way of which the OT saints and prophets could only dream (Acts 2:17, 38–39). Yet we too know what it is to see in part, to know in part, to experience in part (cf. 1 Cor. 13:9). Even the fullness of the Holy Spirit that we have received is simply a down payment on the inheritance that we will one day receive (Eph. 1:14). Like Abraham, we too must live by faith and die by faith, receiving only in part that which God has promised.

By faith the Christian recognizes a reality beyond this present reality, a story that transcends history. He or she knows by faith that the painful reality that we see all around us will one day pass away. It will be replaced by a world in which God will dwell with his people, in which he will wipe away every tear from their eyes, and in which there will be no more death or mourning or crying or pain (Rev. 21:3–4). Then we shall see God face to face, and all doubt and fear will finally be gone. As Augustine puts it, "There we shall rest and see, see and love, love and praise. Behold what shall be in the end and shall not end."[337]

---

[337] Augustine, *City of God*, 22.30.

GENESIS 25:19–34

ⁱ⁹ These are the generations of Isaac, Abraham's son: Abraham fathered Isaac, ²⁰ and Isaac was forty years old when he took Rebekah, the daughter of Bethuel the Aramean of Paddan-aram, the sister of Laban the Aramean, to be his wife. ²¹ And Isaac prayed to the LORD for his wife, because she was barren. And the LORD granted his prayer, and Rebekah his wife conceived. ²² The children struggled together within her, and she said, "If it is thus, why is this happening to me?"[1] So she went to inquire of the LORD. ²³ And the LORD said to her,

"Two nations are in your womb,
    and two peoples from within you[2] shall be divided;
the one shall be stronger than the other,
    the older shall serve the younger."

²⁴ When her days to give birth were completed, behold, there were twins in her womb. ²⁵ The first came out red, all his body like a hairy cloak, so they called his name Esau. ²⁶ Afterward his brother came out with his hand holding Esau's heel, so his name was called Jacob.[3] Isaac was sixty years old when she bore them.

²⁷ When the boys grew up, Esau was a skillful hunter, a man of the field, while Jacob was a quiet man, dwelling in tents. ²⁸ Isaac loved Esau because he ate of his game, but Rebekah loved Jacob.

²⁹ Once when Jacob was cooking stew, Esau came in from the field, and he was exhausted. ³⁰ And Esau said to Jacob, "Let me eat some of that red stew, for I am exhausted!" (Therefore his name was called Edom.[4]) ³¹ Jacob said, "Sell me your birthright now." ³² Esau said, "I am about to die; of what use is a birthright to me?" ³³ Jacob said, "Swear to me now." So he swore to him and sold his birthright to Jacob. ³⁴ Then Jacob gave Esau bread and lentil stew, and he ate and drank and rose and went his way. Thus Esau despised his birthright.

[1] Or *why do I live?* [2] Or *from birth* [3] *Jacob* means *He takes by the heel*, or *He cheats* [4] *Edom* sounds like the Hebrew for *red*

Section Overview

The previous thirteen chapters of Genesis have been dominated by the figure of Abraham, whose family history (Hb. *toledot*) was introduced in Genesis 11:27. Now with Abraham's death and burial in the Promised Land (Gen. 25:1–18) his story has come to an end, and a new section is signaled with a new *toledot*, that of Isaac (v. 19). As is normally the case in Genesis, this family-history marker introduces the story of the subsequent generation (cf. comment on 2:4–7). In a significant deviation from the previous pattern of linear genealogies Isaac and Rebekah have twins—yet those twins are polar opposites of one other. From before their birth Jacob and Esau are engaged in conflict, a conflict that will continue throughout their lives. What is at stake is nothing less than the birthright, the spiritual inheritance of God's promises to Abraham.

From before Jacob's birth God chooses him to be the recipient of those divine promises, so that it might be clear that election is a gift of divine grace, not a result of human merit (Rom. 9:14–16). Even though both children come from the same parents and are born almost contemporaneously, the humanly disfavored younger son will inherit the promises rather than the firstborn (Gen. 25:23). It will rapidly become clear that the firstborn has no interest in the spiritual inheritance he has been denied; Esau is content to barter his birthright for a bowl of stew (vv. 31–33), so he can hardly accuse God of unfairness. Jacob, meanwhile, is not content to wait for God to give him what he has promised. Jacob will scheme and plot to try to steal the birthright from his elder brother. Election does not convey immediate sanctification; indeed, God chooses the ungodly to receive his grace (Rom. 4:5). Yet his grace will not be without effect in Jacob's life; unlike Esau, who remains worldly minded throughout his life, Jacob will grow through his trials and suffering into a person who appreciates the gift of grace he has been given.

Section Outline

 IX. The Family History of Isaac (25:19–35:29)
    A. Introducing Esau and Jacob (25:19–34)

Comment

25:19–21 Isaac's history is relatively brief in Genesis, highlighting the fact that the book is in no sense a modern biography. Isaac's struggles, such as they are, are largely the same as his father's, as we shall see reiterated in Genesis 26. As a result, his relevance is primarily as a demonstration of the Lord's continued faithfulness to the next generation, a point that requires relatively little elaboration. The narrative of Jacob and Esau, however, is much more complex and will be unfolded in far greater detail. This transition is marked in the standard way in the book of Genesis, by means of the *toledot* formula ("generations"; cf. comment on 2:4–7). In this case Isaac's descent as the heir of Abraham (and Sarah) is highlighted by the additional, formally redundant notice that "Abraham fathered Isaac."[338] In contrast, in 25:12 Ishmael's descent was explicitly derived from "Hagar the Egyptian, Sarah's servant."

One aspect of similarity between Isaac and his father, Abraham, lies in the fact that they both have barren wives (Gen. 11:30; 25:21), a reality that once again threatens the fulfillment of God's promise to Abraham of numerous descendants. Sarah's barrenness formed a major motif in the Abraham narrative, with its resolution taking no less than ten chapters of the narrative (twenty-five years in real

---

[338] Hamilton, *Genesis 18–50*, 175.

time), as well as a major subplot involving Hagar and Ishmael (Genesis 16–21). Rebekah's barrenness, on the other hand, is no sooner mentioned than it is reported as resolved: Rebekah is barren; Isaac prays for her; Rebekah conceives (25:21).

Although Rebekah is not beyond normal childbearing years, her pregnancy is nonetheless an answer to many prayers. The issue is resolved rapidly only in a literary sense. From the details of the text it is clear that Rebekah's barrenness lasts almost twenty years (cf. vv. 20, 26). Yet the only significant action that takes place during these twenty years is Isaac's prayer for Rebekah. It appears that Isaac has learned from Abraham and Sarah's experience and trusts that, even though he does not see an immediate answer to his prayers, God will nonetheless answer his prayers and fulfill in his own time all that he has promised. As a result, the Genesis narrative simply highlights the prayer and the Lord's answer, rather than the significant waiting period in between.

25:22–23 Rebekah's pregnancy is hardly problem-free, however. The two children are already engaged in conflict before birth, attempting to crush one another (form of *ratsats*)[339] in her womb (v. 22). This internal conflict is so great that Rebekah seeks an explanation from the Lord (v. 22). Her question ("If it is thus, why is this happening to me?") is very difficult in Hebrew, reading literally, "If thus, why this I/me?" The Syriac adds an explicit reference to "living" ("Why do I live?"; cf. NRSV), but the ESV is equally plausible in reading the question as reflecting her attitude. Twins were often thought to be portentous in the ancient world, and violently struggling twins even more so, raising the question of the significance of this struggle.

It is not clear precisely how Rebekah inquires of the Lord. Later Israelites might find answers through a priest, perhaps by means of the Urim and Thummim (Ex. 28:30; 1 Sam. 28:6; cf. Hannah's encounter with Eli in 1 Sam. 1:10), or through a prophet (Ezek. 20:1). With the exception of Melchizedek (Gen. 14:18–20) there is no mention of priestly service by anyone outside the patriarchal family. Since Abraham served as a prophet in interceding for Abimelech (20:7), and Isaac has already interceded on behalf of his wife (25:21), it seems most likely that Isaac himself serves as the intermediary with the Lord in this matter as well,[340] seeking and receiving an oracle about the two children on Rebekah's behalf.

The response from the Lord shows that this conflict is significant in instructing Isaac and Rebekah about the nature of their children. Thus, even though the oracle is addressed to Rebekah, it is of relevance to both parents. The two boys represent two peoples or nations, highlighting the fact that Esau and Jacob together represent a fulfillment of God's earlier promise to bring many nations from the line of Abraham (17:4–5). However, just as Abraham and Lot could not live together in peace (13:9, 11, 14), nor Isaac and Ishmael (21:10), so too Jacob and Esau will be

---

[339] *Ratsats* is a violent word in most contexts; cf. John D. Currid, *A Study Commentary on Genesis, Volume 2: Genesis 25:19–50:26* (Darlington, UK: Evangelical Press, 2004), 13.
[340] Claus Westermann, *Genesis 12–36: A Continental Commentary*, trans. J. J. Scullion (Minneapolis: Fortress, 1995), 412. Hamilton (*Genesis 18–50*, 177), however, argues that Rebekah seeks the Lord directly, without an intermediary.

divided, with the older son (Esau) being subjugated by the younger (Jacob). God's promise will descend through the line he himself has chosen, according to the pathway he has chosen, not through a descent established by human categories, such as that of the firstborn son. In this way election is all of grace and not at all by merit (Rom. 9:14–16). Jacob's victory over Esau is the result not of his morally dubious trickery but of prior divine choice—a choice that applies not merely to the two individuals concerned but to the nations that will come from them as well (cf. Mal. 1:1–5).

This theme of conflict between brothers is not a departure at this point in Genesis. A similar struggle takes place between Cain and Abel in Genesis 4; there too the younger child is the one favored by God. This motif continues throughout the book of Genesis, that of a constant pattern of rivalry and discord within the family, flowing from election. Those whom God has not chosen, or those who are living out of step with God, are always at war with those whom God has chosen, even when they grow up within the same household.

25:24–26 In due course the two boys are born, and from birth onward they are easily distinguishable. Esau, the firstborn, comes out of the womb ruddy in appearance and covered with body hair.[341] Although a ruddy complexion was often regarded as a positive feature (cf. Song 5:10), excessive hairiness was generally associated with boorish and uncouth behavior in the ancient Near East.[342] These features are also associated with a nickname for Esau, "Edom" ("Red"; cf. Gen. 25:30), and the name of the principal mountain in Edom's territory, Mount Seir ("Hairy").

Jacob, meanwhile, is born grasping his brother's heel, as though seeking to trip up Esau in order to get out of the womb first (Gen. 25:26; cf. Hos. 12:3). This posture is linked to his name, since "heel" (Hb. *'aqeb*) sounds like "Jacob" (*ya'aqob*), though the actual derivation of the name is more properly from the verb *'aqab*, which means "to protect."[343] The brothers' names are significant precursors of their subsequent history, as so often in biblical narratives. Edom ("Red") points forward to the red stew for which Esau will barter his birthright (Gen. 25:30), while Seir ("Hairy") foreshadows Jacob's use of animal skins to impersonate his brother and steal his blessing (27:11, 15); these become the means by which Jacob successfully trips up his brother and forges ahead of him in the race for the birthright and the blessing.

Since Isaac is sixty years old at the birth of the Esau and Jacob (25:26) and Abraham was one hundred years old at the birth of Isaac, Abraham would still be alive when the twins are born (cf. v. 7). Although the biblical text does not mention their interactions, it must have been a great comfort to Abraham to see the birth of the next generation and the continuation of God's promises through them.

---

341 The ESV translation of "red" might be understood as referring to Esau's hair, though such a hair coloring would not be usual in this ethnic group. The same word is used to describe David in 1 Samuel 16:12; 17:42, where the ESV renders it "ruddy."
342 Sarna (*Genesis*, 180) draws a parallel with Enkidu, the archetypal wild man in the Gilgamesh epic.
343 Westermann, *Genesis: A Practical Commentary*, 183.

25:27–28 In the light of the oracle's declaration that "the older shall serve the younger," Isaac and Rebekah should have trained the boys to fulfill their callings. Esau should have been prepared for his need to find a blessing in Jacob and particularly in Jacob's descendant through whom salvation would come. Jacob should have been prepared for his role as godly ancestor of the Messiah, recognizing in humility that he had been given a high calling not because of his greatness but through God's choosing. Unfortunately, instead of being trained for God's calling, however, the boys are allowed to develop in their own ways.

Esau is a natural hunter who loves the outdoor life, as presaged by his ruddy complexion from birth (v. 27; cf. v. 25). Jacob, on the other hand, is described with the ambiguous Hebrew word *tam* (v. 27), which the English translations usually render as "quiet." This term normally means "whole" or "complete," with positive overtones describing a person of physical beauty or high moral character. It describes someone whose desires and actions are thoroughly unified, as in the English word *integrity*. In Jacob's case, however, his single-mindedness will lead him in a far less positive direction, as we shall see. Unlike with his brother, Esau, Jacob's natural habitat is the tent, not the field. Once again there is a certain ambiguity in this description. It could describe his occupation as a (civilized) nomadic shepherd rather than a rough-and-ready hunter like his brother. But in what follows Jacob's perpetual presence in the tent will also be crucial to his efforts to rob his brother of his birthright and his blessing. Because of Jacob's preference for staying at home, he is able to be in the right place at the right time to pursue his single-minded schemes.

The differing respective aptitudes of the two boys lead to favoritism within the family: Isaac values the fruits of Esau's hunting abilities and the tasty food they provide, while Rebekah favors Jacob, who is never far from the tents that are her domain (v. 28). In time, however, the sin of Isaac and Rebekah in playing favorites will be fittingly returned on their own heads: Isaac will be deceived by his passion for wild game, while Rebekah will find her stay-at-home son propelled far away from her.

25:29–34 The boys' respective aptitudes form the backdrop for the next scene. Esau has been out in the fields hunting and comes home famished (v. 29; Hb. *'ayef* can mean faint from hunger or tiredness, hence "exhausted"). Meanwhile, Jacob has been hanging around the tent, cooking a stew,[344] most likely of lentils, given its color—an ironic occupation, given Esau's famed ability to provide meat for his father (v. 28). Esau requests a portion of Jacob's food, albeit in a rather rough manner; literally we might translate, "Let me stuff my face[345] with the red stuff, this red stuff, for I am starving" (v. 30). The color of the stew aligns with Esau's own color at birth and the name of the nation that will come from him: Edom.

---

[344] The verb used for Jacob's cooking (Hb. *zid*) is more normally used for presumptuous or rebellious actions, which hints that Jacob's motives have been questionable from the outset. Cf. Gary V. Smith, "*zid*," NIDOTTE, 1.1094.

[345] The rare verb *la'at* is later used of animals' eating rather than people's; Alter notes the unusually coarse representation of Esau's speech as a whole (*Five Books of Moses*, 131).

In itself Esau's request seems fairly simple, one that in most families would receive a positive answer: "Of course, brother! Sit down and let me serve you a bowl. What would you like to drink?" But this is no ordinary family, as seen in Jacob's response: "Sell me your birthright now" (v. 31). Jacob has evidently been looking for an opportunity to acquire the birthright of the firstborn, which the oracle has already promised him (cf. v. 23). He is not content to await God's provision but wants to gain the favored position through his own cleverness. Meanwhile, Esau should on no account be willing to trade the valuable right to be the heir of the blessing that God has promised should descend through Isaac's line.

However, Esau regards the right of inheritance as of less value than a bowl of lentil stew, claiming that, since he is about to die of hunger, the birthright will be of no use to him (v. 32). The deal is sealed with Jacob's requiring a formal oath on Esau's part (v. 33), so that he cannot change his mind later when he is no longer quite so hungry. Meanwhile, Esau quickly downs his food and leaves; the sequence of four *vav*-consecutive verbs in rapid succession in the Hebrew matches the speed with which Esau eats, drinks, gets up, and goes on his way again. This thoughtless action on Esau's part is not merely an aberration; it reveals his heart. He despises his birthright (v. 34), selling it for a pittance and subsequently giving the deal no further thought. This episode also demonstrates the fact that God's election of Jacob to inherit the promise and his correlative passing over of Esau do not rob Esau of anything he values; on the contrary, what Esau loses means nothing to him. It is not surprising that Hebrews 12:16 highlights Esau as the classic example of an unholy person. Yet at the same time Jacob's actions are hardly noble; he treats God's promised blessing to Abraham as something that might be bargained for, bought and sold for a pittance. Neither brother comes out of this episode with any credit.

Response

The biblical doctrine of election seems abstract at best to many Christians, if not a doctrine that implies unfairness on God's part. Why should God condemn people just because he has not chosen them? Genesis 25 points us to a fuller understanding of election, beginning with the question of fairness. Jacob is not chosen for his spirituality or moral character, nor is Esau rejected for his failings, since the choice is made in the womb, before they have the chance to develop in either of these directions. In fact, as rapidly becomes clear, Jacob is no better than Esau. The question is therefore not "Why does God reject innocent Esau?"; it is "Why does God choose guilty Jacob?" Ultimately, there is no answer to this beyond the freedom of divine choice. Since no human being deserves to receive God's favor, as all are polluted by the effects of the fall, God is under no obligation to choose anyone for a relationship with him. That he does so is part of his mercy, and he has the absolute right to show mercy to whomever he wishes (Ex. 33:19; Rom. 9:15).

The practical value of election ought to be to free us from the kind of insecurity that drives Jacob to cheat, steal, and lie his way into a birthright and a blessing that has already been promised to him by God. This is a lesson that Jacob, like many of us, is slow to learn. If God has chosen us for himself, then nothing in all creation can separate us from the fulfillment of his loving purposes for us (Rom. 8:38–39). Since we are chosen by God not because of our merit but because of his love, there is nothing we can do to undo that choice. This is a very comforting reminder for Israel much later in its history, as the exiles return to the land after the catastrophe of Babylonian exile. Because God has chosen Jacob, they can be confident that he will rebuild their city and their community after the exile, while the fate of Edom will have no such positive outcome (Mal. 1:1–5). As the rest of Malachi shows, the doctrine of election is not a recipe for licentious living; on the contrary, knowing that God has loved and chosen us in spite of ourselves gives us the boldness to face up to the reality of our sins and to look to him for our cleansing, as well as the incentive to pursue greater faithfulness to him in the future.

God chooses the weak to shame the strong. He chooses the powerless, who know that they have no righteousness of their own in which to boast—not those who think themselves able to earn their own way to heaven. Our salvation depends on the fact that God chose us first, out of pure grace, long before we chose him. Indeed, left to ourselves, we would never have chosen him. Because our salvation depends on God's choice, not our obedience, there is no room for human boasting but only humble praise of his incomparable mercy.

GENESIS 26

26 Now there was a famine in the land, besides the former famine that was in the days of Abraham. And Isaac went to Gerar to Abimelech king of the Philistines. ²And the LORD appeared to him and said, "Do not go down to Egypt; dwell in the land of which I shall tell you. ³Sojourn in this land, and I will be with you and will bless you, for to you and to your offspring I will give all these lands, and I will establish the oath that I swore to Abraham your father. ⁴I will multiply your offspring as the stars of heaven and will give to your offspring all these lands. And in your offspring all the nations of the earth shall be blessed, ⁵because Abraham obeyed my voice and kept my charge, my commandments, my statutes, and my laws."

⁶So Isaac settled in Gerar. ⁷When the men of the place asked him about his wife, he said, "She is my sister," for he feared to say, "My wife," thinking, "lest the men of the place should kill me because of Rebekah," because she was attractive in appearance. ⁸When he had been there a long time, Abimelech king of the Philistines looked out of a window and saw Isaac laughing with¹ Rebekah his wife. ⁹So Abimelech called Isaac and said, "Behold, she is your wife. How then could you say, 'She is my sister'?" Isaac said to him, "Because I thought, 'Lest I die because of her.'"
¹⁰Abimelech said, "What is this you have done to us? One of the people

might easily have lain with your wife, and you would have brought guilt upon us." **11** So Abimelech warned all the people, saying, "Whoever touches this man or his wife shall surely be put to death."

12 And Isaac sowed in that land and reaped in the same year a hundredfold. The LORD blessed him, **13** and the man became rich, and gained more and more until he became very wealthy. **14** He had possessions of flocks and herds and many servants, so that the Philistines envied him. **15** (Now the Philistines had stopped and filled with earth all the wells that his father's servants had dug in the days of Abraham his father.) **16** And Abimelech said to Isaac, "Go away from us, for you are much mightier than we."

17 So Isaac departed from there and encamped in the Valley of Gerar and settled there. **18** And Isaac dug again the wells of water that had been dug in the days of Abraham his father, which the Philistines had stopped after the death of Abraham. And he gave them the names that his father had given them. **19** But when Isaac's servants dug in the valley and found there a well of spring water, **20** the herdsmen of Gerar quarreled with Isaac's herdsmen, saying, "The water is ours." So he called the name of the well Esek,[2] because they contended with him. **21** Then they dug another well, and they quarreled over that also, so he called its name Sitnah.[3] **22** And he moved from there and dug another well, and they did not quarrel over it. So he called its name Rehoboth,[4] saying, "For now the LORD has made room for us, and we shall be fruitful in the land."

23 From there he went up to Beersheba. **24** And the LORD appeared to him the same night and said, "I am the God of Abraham your father. Fear not, for I am with you and will bless you and multiply your offspring for my servant Abraham's sake." **25** So he built an altar there and called upon the name of the LORD and pitched his tent there. And there Isaac's servants dug a well.

26 When Abimelech went to him from Gerar with Ahuzzath his adviser and Phicol the commander of his army, **27** Isaac said to them, "Why have you come to me, seeing that you hate me and have sent me away from you?" **28** They said, "We see plainly that the LORD has been with you. So we said, let there be a sworn pact between us, between you and us, and let us make a covenant with you, **29** that you will do us no harm, just as we have not touched you and have done to you nothing but good and have sent you away in peace. You are now the blessed of the LORD." **30** So he made them a feast, and they ate and drank. **31** In the morning they rose early and exchanged oaths. And Isaac sent them on their way, and they departed from him in peace. **32** That same day Isaac's servants came and told him about the well that they had dug and said to him, "We have found water." **33** He called it Shibah;[5] therefore the name of the city is Beersheba to this day.

34 When Esau was forty years old, he took Judith the daughter of Beeri the Hittite to be his wife, and Basemath the daughter of Elon the Hittite, **35** and they made life bitter[6] for Isaac and Rebekah.

[1] Hebrew may suggest an intimate relationship [2] *Esek* means *contention* [3] *Sitnah* means *enmity* [4] *Rehoboth* means *broad places*, or *room* [5] *Shibah* sounds like the Hebrew for *oath* [6] Hebrew *they were bitterness of spirit*

Section Overview

We noted earlier the similarities (and differences) between the experiences of Isaac and Abraham. Both have barren wives, who require divine intervention to resolve their situations (Gen. 11:30; 25:21). In addition, both face a time when the Promised Land proves to be similarly barren through famine, leading to the temptation to go down to Egypt. Isaac receives a direct word from God that keeps him from going down to Egypt (26:2–5), as his father did (12:10), but he nonetheless still falls into the same sinful pattern of pretending that his wife is his sister—as Abraham did twice, latterly in Gerar, the same place where Isaac is sojourning at this point (20:1; 26:1). Both stories of interactions with the Philistines end with quarreling over water supplies and then the making of a covenant at Beersheba as the Philistines observe the reality of the Lord's presence with Abraham and Isaac (21:22–34; 26:18–35).

Critics often assume that these stories are simply variant accounts of the same events, but such an assumption ignores the literary function of such type-scenes. The reader is intended to set the stories side by side and compare and contrast them, paying particular attention to repeated themes and divergent details. For example, in the Abraham narrative both episodes threaten the promise of seed, since Sarah appears lost into the harem of a pagan ruler, whereas in Isaac's case the promised seed has already been born. In both the Abrahamic episodes God intervenes supernaturally to reveal the truth and to pressure the pagan ruler to restore Sarah to Abraham, whereas in Isaac's case Abimelech makes the discovery by chance, as it were, and needs no chiding to restore Rebekah. Meanwhile, the quarreling over water supplies in Isaac's story is triggered by jealousy on the part of the Philistines, which must be resolved before the larger story arc can find its resolution. Each of these stories ends with the patriarch's receiving the Lord's rich blessing, which enables him to bless his Gentile neighbors as well, insofar as his neighbors approach him with appropriate respect, just as promised in 12:2–3.

The episode with Isaac and Abimelech is thus in no sense a mere repetition of what has gone before. Its significance lies in the fact that the Abrahamic blessing has now been visibly passed on to the next generation in all its fullness, despite Isaac's repetition of the sins of the previous generation. This passing on of the torch would be a message of considerable importance to the original audience to whom Moses is writing, who are themselves the second generation during the wilderness wanderings.

Section Outline

IX. The Family History of Isaac (25:19–35:29) . . .

    B. Another Famine and Its Consequences (26:1–35)

Comment

26:1–6 The notice of a famine in the Promised Land is always ominous (v. 1; cf. 12:10). The narrator highlights the connection to the earlier famines in Abraham's days to ensure that it is not overlooked. Unlike the famines that Israel suffers due to drought after the conquest of the land, there is no hint here of any connection between a sin on the part of God's people and an absence of rainfall (cf. Deut. 28:22; 1 Kings 17:1)—the Sinai covenant, with its blessings and curses, is not yet in effect. The topography of the land of Canaan makes the southern region, where Isaac lives, particularly vulnerable to a lack of rainfall since it receives relatively little precipitation even during normal times. Egypt, on the other hand, receives most of its water from the Ethiopian Highlands via the Nile, whose supply is considerably more consistent. It is not coincidental that the Lord calls his people out of Egypt to live in a land where they will constantly be dependent upon him for their fertility and will thus have to exercise constant faith in his provision.

The reason for Isaac's initial move to Gerar from Beer-lahai-roi is not specified further (Gen. 26:1; cf. 25:11). As a royal city, Gerar would likely have storehouses, and Isaac may expect his father's covenant relationship with Abimelech (the father or grandfather of the monarch of that name in Abraham's time)[346] to give Isaac a favorable reception. It is also possible that, being closer to the coast, Gerar may receive a little more rain than Beer-lahai-roi. Moreover, if supplies prove insufficient, it would be straightforward for Isaac to journey from there down the coast road to Egypt (cf. Ex. 13:17).

However, the Lord intervenes and appears to Isaac, forbidding him to complete the journey to Egypt (Gen. 26:2). Instead, like Abraham before him, Isaac is to dwell in the land that the Lord will tell him about (v. 2; cf. 12:1). There the Lord will bless him and fulfill the oath made to Abraham, namely, to multiply his offspring like the stars of heaven (15:5) and to give them that land to dwell in (13:15–17) so that they might be a blessing to all nations of the earth (12:3). The only new element is the promise "I will be with you" (26:3), though a similar concept may be suggested by "My covenant is with you" (17:4). This word serves as an explicit promise of protection at a time when Isaac has no rights or formal status in Gerar, where he is a "sojourner" (Hb. *gur*; 26:3). To stay in Gerar at such a time requires Isaac to show the same faith in the promise that his father, Abraham, had. Just as Abraham's faith led him to precise obedience to the Lord's commandments and statutes (v. 5), so Isaac must trust and obey. And that is exactly what he does (v. 6).

26:7–11 However, there are limits to Isaac's trust in the Lord; just as Abraham had done, he pretends that his wife is his sister (v. 7). His motivation is exactly the same as Abraham's: fear that, if the men of the place think she is his wife, they will arrange a convenient accident for him in order to allow one of them to marry her (v. 7). It is certainly ironic that Isaac is unwilling to trust his life to the same God who provided a lamb to take his place on Mount Moriah (22:14), as though the God who has just promised to be with him (26:3) might prove unable to protect him against the Philistines.

The fact that the deception is not uncovered for a long time (v. 8), and yet no one tries to marry Rebekah, underlines how misguided is Isaac's fear. Finally, the

---

[346] More than seventy-five years have passed since the events of chapter 20, as that chapter was before the birth of Isaac, when Abraham was not quite one hundred, and this chapter is after the death of Abraham, recorded in Genesis 25:7. Since the name Abimelech means "My [divine] father is king," it may be a regnal name adopted by successive Philistine monarchs (cf. Psalm 34 title; 1 Sam. 21:11–15; Mathews, *Genesis 11:27–50:26*, 402). John Currid notes the presence of a dagesh in the spelling of the second Abimelech's name as a Masoretic indicator that different people are in view (*Genesis 25:19–50:26*, 24). On the supposed anachronism of the reference to "the Philistines" cf. comment on 10:6–20.

true state of affairs is revealed when Abimelech is surprised[347] to see Isaac fooling around with his wife (v. 8).[348] When Abimelech demands an explanation, Isaac's answer is revealing: "Because *I* thought, 'Lest *I* die because of her'" (v. 9). The pronouns indicate the problem: Isaac is thinking only of himself, not of the damage his actions might do to others. As Abimelech points out, his actions risks bringing guilt on others—and indeed on the whole community—by deceiving them about Rebekah's married status (v. 10).

Like his namesake before him, Abimelech responds by issuing a protective decree over Isaac and Rebekah, proving once again that the fear of God may sometimes be encountered in unexpected places (v. 11; cf. 20:8–11). No one might "touch" (Hb. *naga'*; a word that covers sexual as well as more general assault) Isaac and Rebekah; though they are sojourners, they are under royal protection. The Lord is indeed with Isaac, just as much in this episode, where no direct intervention by the Lord is required, as he was in Abraham's experience, when the Lord confronted Abimelech directly. However, in due time the family pattern of deception will come home to roost, as Isaac will himself be deceived by his own wife and son (Genesis 27).

26:12–22 The Lord's blessing is not limited to protecting Isaac from the dangers of living in Gerar. Isaac also sows and reaps abundantly (26:12)—"a hundredfold," which need not be taken literally but is a shorthand for maximal fruitfulness (cf. Matt. 13:8). To flourish so abundantly in a strange land in the midst of a time of drought—and as a pastoralist turning his hand for the first time to the art of raising—could only reflect the hand of the Lord upon him. Isaac becomes rich and multiplies his flocks and servants, as Abraham had before him (Gen. 12:16).

However, such an accumulation of wealth—especially in the form of flocks, herds, and humans—almost inevitably leads to tension with Isaac's neighbors, the Philistines (Gen. 26:13–14). They envy him and, as with Abraham and Lot in Genesis 13, find themselves competing with him over limited water resources. To discourage other seminomadic herdsmen, the Philistines have stopped up with earth all the wells that Abraham's servants had dug during their time in the region (v. 15). Filling the wells with earth would not ruin them, but it does mean they will have to be redug, a significant increase in effort for the herdsmen. Isaac and his herdsmen move away from Gerar itself into the Valley of Gerar, but the disputes over water rights continue, with respect both to the reclaimed older wells, whose names Isaac reassigns as an assertion of ownership, and to two new wells dug by Isaac's own men (vv. 18–21). It is not until Isaac moves further away, to a place he names "Rehoboth" ("Room"), that he finally finds water over which no one else claims rights (v. 22). Isaac attributes this providence to the Lord's "making room" (Hb. *hirkhib*) for his family to be fruitful and prosperous (v. 22).

---

[347] The Hebrew word *hinneh* (sometimes translated in the ESV as "Behold") often introduces a note of surprise; cf. Christo H. J. Van der Merwe, Jackie A, Naudé, and Jan H. Kroeze, *A Biblical Hebrew Reference Grammar* (Sheffield: Sheffield Academic Press, 1999), §44.3.4.1.

[348] The Hebrew verb *shakhaq* ("laughing") hints here and elsewhere at sexual intimacy (cf. ESV mg.; cf. Gen. 39:14; Ex. 32:6). The verb is similar to the root of Isaac's own name, so one could say that Abimelech saw Isaac "Isaacing." His behavior revealed his own true identity as a deceiver as well as Rebekah's identity as his wife.

26:23–25 Nevertheless, Isaac does not stay permanently at Rehoboth but moves on to Beersheba, 19 miles (30 km) to the northeast, where Abraham had spent many years after his own stay in Philistine country (21:31–33). There the Lord appears to Isaac and confirms that his covenant promises made to Abraham will continue to be fulfilled in Isaac (26:24). Isaac's sin and failure in Gerar do not negate the Lord's promise; the Lord will bless him and multiply his seed for Abraham's sake. That is, God will continue to fulfill the promise that "through Isaac shall your offspring be named" (21:12). The mandate of God for man in the beginning was to be fruitful and fill the land (1:28); now Isaac declares that the Lord has given his new humanity a place where that word may be fulfilled.

Isaac responds to the theophany by building an altar at Beersheba and calling on the name of the Lord (26:25), just as his father, Abraham, had done earlier upon his initial entry into the land (12:7). This repetition reiterates the theme of Isaac's following in his father's footsteps that pervades the narrative ("your/his father" occurs no fewer than five times in this chapter). Like his father, Isaac also digs (or perhaps redigs) a well there (26:25).

It is at Beersheba that the Lord identifies himself to Isaac as "the God of Abraham your father" (v. 24), the first time this title is used. The Lord was not the God of Abraham's father, Terah, who was an idol worshiper (cf. Josh. 24:2);[349] a new bond had been established between the Lord and Abraham in Abram's call to leave Ur and go to Canaan, a bond that was definitive for their relationship from that time forward: the Lord *is* the God of Abraham (and, subsequently, of Isaac and of Jacob/Israel) in a unique way, quite distinct from his relationship to any other individual or people group.

26:26–33 After all this conflict between their herdsmen, Abimelech comes to make a covenant with Isaac at Beersheba, the very same place where his ancestor had made a similar covenant with Abraham (Gen. 26:26–29; cf. 21:22–24). He brings with him his top "adviser,"[350] Ahuzzath, and his military chief, Phicol,[351] making it clear that this is an official covenant between two peoples rather than a personal compact between individuals. Isaac is surprised at the visit, given the strained relations that had led Abimelech to expel him from his territory, but Abimelech explains the motivation in terms of the Lord's obvious blessing on Isaac (26:28). Rather than risk having a clan of Isaac's magnitude on his doorstep that might choose to ally itself with any potential foe, Abimelech seeks a "sworn treaty" (Hb. *'alah*; i.e., an oath enforced with self-imprecatory curses, which would be enforced by the gods in the case of any unfaithfulness) that Isaac will do them no harm (v. 29). Isaac might raise an eyebrow at Abimelech's claim that he has "done to you

---

349 In Genesis 31:53 Laban swears an oath in the name of the God of Abraham as well as by the god of Nahor, the god of their father (two distinct deities, as the plural verb shows), but Isaac swears only by the Fear of Isaac, the Lord. Cf. comment on 31:36–55.
350 Or "his friend"; "the king's friend" was a recognized office in the ancient Near East (1 Kings 4:5; cf. Sarna, *Genesis*, 187).
351 Like Abimelech, Phicol may be a family name passed down from father to son, as this is unlikely to be the same individual as in 21:22.

nothing but good and have sent you away in peace" (v. 29), but he nonetheless swears the oath, and they confirm the covenant by sharing a meal (v. 30).

As with Abraham's earlier covenant with the king of Gerar, the real significance of this encounter is as a fulfillment of Genesis 12:3. The nations are coming to Abraham and his offspring, recognizing the Lord's blessing upon them and seeking a blessing for themselves through relationship with them. There is peace to be found in relationship with Abraham and his offspring, a peace that foreshadows and points to the peace to be found in relationship with the ultimate son of Abraham, Jesus Christ.

The blessing of God on Isaac (and upon his pact with Abimelech) is seen in the discovery by Isaac's servants of water on the very same day (26:32). The resulting well is called "Shiba," which sounds like the Hebrew verb "to swear" (v. 33). This second naming of Beersheba ("Well of the oath") reinforces the primary thrust of the chapter, which is to show how Isaac's life recapitulates that of his father, Abraham (v. 33; cf. 21:31).[352]

26:34–35 If Isaac is reliving Abraham's experience, Esau seems determined to relive Ishmael's. Like Ishmael, he marries outside the covenant community, though in his case he takes a Hittite wife rather than an Egyptian one (26:34; cf. 21:21).[353] He does so at forty years of age, the exact age of Isaac when Abraham sent his servant to Paddan-aram to find a wife of faith for him (Genesis 24; cf. 25:20). The extraordinary care that Abraham took to ensure that Isaac would find a spiritually suitable bride is of no importance to Esau. Even worse, Esau emulates Lamech in marrying multiple wives (4:19), apparently without the mitigation of the first wife's barrenness, and he takes on the responsibility of arranging his own marriages rather than waiting for his parents to contract a marriage for him. His wives may have attractive names, Judith ("praise") and Basemath ("fragrance"), but their pagan values make the lives of Isaac and Rebekah bitter (26:35). Esau is Isaac's son physically, but the profound spiritual differences between the two men are all the more evident in a chapter that so strongly highlights the remarkable similarities between Isaac and Abraham.

Response

As noted earlier, the primary focus of the narrative is on Isaac's reliving the story of his illustrious father, Abraham, and experiencing God's blessing upon him, thus confirming the covenant with Abraham. This would have been very relevant for Moses' first audience, who were themselves the second generation in the wilderness. They had not seen firsthand the great works of God during the exodus, but they needed to trust that the Lord would nonetheless be with them as they sought to enter the Promised Land. That lesson continues to be relevant to all of us: the God of our forefathers will continue to be with us as he has promised, granting us the blessing of peace for the sake of the true seed of Abraham, Jesus Christ.

---

352 It is not surprising to find two namings of Beersheba, since it is Isaac's practice to give wells the same name as his father (Gen. 26:18). On the tight literary connections between the two episodes cf. Sarna, *Genesis*, 188.
353 On the Hittites cf. comment on 10:6–20.

To be sure, not all of us are children of Abraham via physical descent. The covenant Isaac makes with Abimelech and Phicol shows how those who are not physical heirs of the promise may nonetheless share in the peace the Lord gives as they come to Abraham's seed and enter into relationship with him. This is exactly what Genesis 12:2–3 anticipates: that those who are children of Abraham by faith may be included in the Lord's plan of blessing for the world. Yet even a righteous lifestyle will not always result in trouble-free relationships with those around us. The other side of Paul's admonition to live at peace with our neighbors whenever possible (Rom. 12:17–18) is his sobering caution to Timothy: "All who desire to live a godly life in Christ Jesus will be persecuted" (2 Tim. 3:12). Even in the midst of persecution our peace, gentleness, and patience may still point people to our God.

At the same time, not all those who are physically descended from Abraham are true heirs of the promise. Esau demonstrated his lack of interest in his birthright at the end of the previous chapter, and in this chapter he continues to show his true spiritual colors in his marriages to two Hittite women. Esau would rather attach himself to this world and enjoy its advantages than keep himself distinct as part of the holy people of God. Likewise, Christians may find themselves tempted to intermarry with those who do not share their faith, in contravention of God's call on their lives (cf. 2 Cor. 6:14–18).

Ultimately, our hope does not rest in the strength of our faith, or in how faithfully we follow God's law—important though that is. Our hope does not rest in Isaac, who is revealed in this chapter as a deeply flawed son of Abraham, a man who shares in his father's sins as well as in his faith. Our hope rests in Jesus Christ, the only son of Abraham who is utterly without fault. In his case the nations did not seek him out to sign a nonaggression pact for mutual blessing. On the contrary, the nations conspired together with his own people to put him to death on a cross (Acts 4:27). Yet it was God's sovereign purpose that through Jesus' death on the cross he would bring his chosen ones to himself and thus unite Jews and Gentiles together into one body as heirs of the promises first given to Abraham (Acts 4:27–28).

GENESIS 27:1–28:9

27 When Isaac was old and his eyes were dim so that he could not see, he called Esau his older son and said to him, "My son"; and he answered, "Here I am." ² He said, "Behold, I am old; I do not know the day of my death. ³ Now then, take your weapons, your quiver and your bow, and go out to the field and hunt game for me, ⁴ and prepare for me delicious food, such as I love, and bring it to me so that I may eat, that my soul may bless you before I die."

⁵ Now Rebekah was listening when Isaac spoke to his son Esau. So when Esau went to the field to hunt for game and bring it, ⁶ Rebekah said to her son Jacob, "I heard your father speak to your brother Esau, ⁷ 'Bring me game and prepare for me delicious food, that I may eat it and bless you before the Lord before I die.' ⁸ Now therefore, my son, obey my voice as I command you. ⁹ Go to the flock and bring me two good young goats, so that I may prepare from them delicious food for your father, such as he loves. ¹⁰ And you shall bring it to your father to eat, so that he may bless you before he dies." ¹¹ But Jacob said to Rebekah his mother, "Behold, my brother Esau is a hairy man, and I am a smooth man. ¹² Perhaps my father will feel me, and I shall seem to be mocking him and bring a curse upon myself and not a blessing." ¹³ His mother said to him, "Let your curse be on me, my son; only obey my voice, and go, bring them to me."

¹⁴ So he went and took them and brought them to his mother, and his mother prepared delicious food, such as his father loved. ¹⁵ Then Rebekah took the best garments of Esau her older son, which were with her in the house, and put them on Jacob her younger son. ¹⁶ And the skins of the young goats she put on his hands and on the smooth part of his neck. ¹⁷ And she put the delicious food and the bread, which she had prepared, into the hand of her son Jacob.

¹⁸ So he went in to his father and said, "My father." And he said, "Here I am. Who are you, my son?" ¹⁹ Jacob said to his father, "I am Esau your firstborn. I have done as you told me; now sit up and eat of my game, that your soul may bless me." ²⁰ But Isaac said to his son, "How is it that you have found it so quickly, my son?" He answered, "Because the Lord your God granted me success." ²¹ Then Isaac said to Jacob, "Please come near, that I may feel you, my son, to know whether you are really my son Esau or not." ²² So Jacob went near to Isaac his father, who felt him and said, "The voice is Jacob's voice, but the hands are the hands of Esau." ²³ And he did not recognize him, because his hands were hairy like his brother Esau's hands. So he blessed him. ²⁴ He said, "Are you really my son Esau?" He answered, "I am." ²⁵ Then he said, "Bring it near to me, that I may eat of my son's game and bless you." So he brought it near to him, and he ate; and he brought him wine, and he drank.

²⁶ Then his father Isaac said to him, "Come near and kiss me, my son." ²⁷ So he came near and kissed him. And Isaac smelled the smell of his garments and blessed him and said,

"See, the smell of my son
　　is as the smell of a field that the Lord has blessed!
²⁸　May God give you of the dew of heaven
　　and of the fatness of the earth
　　and plenty of grain and wine.
²⁹　Let peoples serve you,
　　and nations bow down to you.
　Be lord over your brothers,
　　and may your mother's sons bow down to you.
　Cursed be everyone who curses you,
　　and blessed be everyone who blesses you!"

³⁰ As soon as Isaac had finished blessing Jacob, when Jacob had scarcely gone out from the presence of Isaac his father, Esau his brother came in from his hunting. ³¹ He also prepared delicious food and brought it to his

father. And he said to his father, "Let my father arise and eat of his son's game, that you may bless me." ³² His father Isaac said to him, "Who are you?" He answered, "I am your son, your firstborn, Esau." ³³ Then Isaac trembled very violently and said, "Who was it then that hunted game and brought it to me, and I ate it all before you came, and I have blessed him? Yes, and he shall be blessed." ³⁴ As soon as Esau heard the words of his father, he cried out with an exceedingly great and bitter cry and said to his father, "Bless me, even me also, O my father!" ³⁵ But he said, "Your brother came deceitfully, and he has taken away your blessing." ³⁶ Esau said, "Is he not rightly named Jacob?[1] For he has cheated me these two times. He took away my birthright, and behold, now he has taken away my blessing." Then he said, "Have you not reserved a blessing for me?" ³⁷ Isaac answered and said to Esau, "Behold, I have made him lord over you, and all his brothers I have given to him for servants, and with grain and wine I have sustained him. What then can I do for you, my son?" ³⁸ Esau said to his father, "Have you but one blessing, my father? Bless me, even me also, O my father." And Esau lifted up his voice and wept.

³⁹ Then Isaac his father answered and said to him:

"Behold, away from[2] the fatness of the earth shall your dwelling be,
    and away from[3] the dew of heaven on high.
⁴⁰ By your sword you shall live,
    and you shall serve your brother;
but when you grow restless
    you shall break his yoke from your neck."

⁴¹ Now Esau hated Jacob because of the blessing with which his father had blessed him, and Esau said to himself, "The days of mourning for my father are approaching; then I will kill my brother Jacob." ⁴² But the words of Esau her older son were told to Rebekah. So she sent and called Jacob her younger son and said to him, "Behold, your brother Esau comforts himself about you by planning to kill you. ⁴³ Now therefore, my son, obey my voice. Arise, flee to Laban my brother in Haran ⁴⁴ and stay with him a while, until your brother's fury turns away— ⁴⁵ until your brother's anger turns away from you, and he forgets what you have done to him. Then I will send and bring you from there. Why should I be bereft of you both in one day?"

⁴⁶ Then Rebekah said to Isaac, "I loathe my life because of the Hittite women.[4] If Jacob marries one of the Hittite women like these, one of the women of the land, what good will my life be to me?"

28 Then Isaac called Jacob and blessed him and directed him, "You must not take a wife from the Canaanite women. ² Arise, go to Paddan-aram to the house of Bethuel your mother's father, and take as your wife from there one of the daughters of Laban your mother's brother. ³ God Almighty[5] bless you and make you fruitful and multiply you, that you may become a company of peoples. ⁴ May he give the blessing of Abraham to you and to your offspring with you, that you may take possession of the land of your sojournings that God gave to Abraham!" ⁵ Thus Isaac sent Jacob away. And he went to Paddan-aram, to Laban, the son of Bethuel the Aramean, the brother of Rebekah, Jacob's and Esau's mother.

⁶ Now Esau saw that Isaac had blessed Jacob and sent him away to Paddan-aram to take a wife from there, and that as he blessed him he directed him, "You must not take a wife from the Canaanite women," ⁷ and

that Jacob had obeyed his father and his mother and gone to Paddan-aram. ⁸So when Esau saw that the Canaanite women did not please Isaac his father, ⁹Esau went to Ishmael and took as his wife, besides the wives he had, Mahalath the daughter of Ishmael, Abraham's son, the sister of Nebaioth.

¹*Jacob* means *He takes by the heel*, or *He cheats* ²Or *Behold, of* ³Or *and of* ⁴Hebrew *daughters of Heth* ⁵Hebrew *El Shaddai*

Section Overview

Jacob was promised the Abrahamic blessing while still in the womb (25:23), just as Abram was promised offspring and a land before leaving Ur of the Chaldeans (12:2). However, both men found it hard to wait over a lengthy period for what God had promised to give them, and both fell into the temptation to attempt to seize through their own efforts what God had promised (chs. 16; 27). Indeed, both found that the source of such temptation came from within their own families: in Abraham's case from his wife, Sarah (16:2), and in Jacob's case from his mother, Rebekah (27:6–10). Both found that these "shortcuts" resulted in years of pain and family brokenness. Trusting God is hard, but failing to trust God is even harder.

At the core of this chapter is a family in which each member is going his own way, without reference to God. Isaac seeks to pass on the family blessing to the eldest son, his personal favorite, Esau, while Rebekah endeavors to ensure it will go to the youngest, her favorite, Jacob. Rebekah has God's oracle to support her (25:23), but the method she chooses is the opposite of godly honesty. Esau does not care about the spiritual dimensions of his birthright, which he earlier had been willing to trade away for a mess of pottage (25:29–34). Meanwhile, Jacob's only concern over his mother's plan is his fear that the deception might be discovered by his father and earn a curse rather than a blessing (27:11). It is clear that God can accomplish his holy purposes by using not merely unholy people but even the unholy actions of those he has chosen.[354]

The narrative comprises contrasting scenes that highlight the transition that takes place within it. The blessing story begins and ends with a scene involving Isaac and Esau, in which the blessing is promised and ultimately not delivered (vv. 1–4, 30–40). In between are scenes involving first Rebekah and Jacob (vv. 5–17) and then Isaac and Jacob (vv. 18–29), in which Jacob literarily and literally supplants Esau. Finally, after a scene involving all four members of the family (vv. 41–46), in another scene between Isaac and Jacob the latter finally receives his father's blessing honestly, without further dissembling (28:1–5).

Section Outline

IX. The Family History of Isaac (25:19–35:29) ...
    C. Jacob Steals the Blessing (27:1–28:9)

---

[354] It is poignant to contrast the simplicity with which Jacob passes on the primary blessing to Joseph's younger son, Ephraim, rather than the older, Manasseh (Gen. 48:13–20). In that case there is no deception but a simple recognition of, and submission to, the divine will; cf. Kidner, *Genesis*, 166.

Comment

27:1–4 The previous chapter ended on the observation that Esau's intermarriage with two Hittite women made life bitter for Isaac and Rebekah (26:35). However, Esau's blatant disregard for his spiritual heritage does not prevent Isaac from seeking to pass on the family blessing to him,[355] despite the divine oracle given at Esau and Jacob's birth (27:4; 25:23). The family patterns of favoritism, which were set early (25:28), continue in force: Esau is referred to repeatedly as "his [Isaac's] son" (27:1, 5, 20, 21, 24, 26, 27, 32), while Jacob is "her [Rebekah's] son" (vv. 6, 17). However, the narrator carefully avoids the term "firstborn" for Esau (cf. vv. 15, 42), which might carry overtones of the birthright he has already despised.[356]

Esau's ability to hunt and bring home wild game (Gen. 25:27) remains a factor in his father's preference for him: he is commissioned to go and hunt meat for a special meal at which Isaac will pass on to him the family blessing (27:3–4). Such an important event ought to involve a public ceremony before the whole household, so the fact that Isaac wants to keep it quiet suggests he is well aware that he is deviating from the words of the oracle that identified Jacob as the divinely chosen heir of the promise. Just as Esau had been willing to trade his birthright for a bowl of stew, Isaac is willing to transgress the Lord's revealed will for a portion of food. Isaac is by this point at least one hundred years old (cf. 25:26; 26:34), and his eyesight is gone, a fact that will become crucial in the narrative that follows. It is not uncommon in the Bible for a lack of physical sight to go along with diminished spiritual insight, as seems to be the case here (e.g., 1 Sam. 3:1–2; for the reverse cf. Matt. 20:30–34).[357]

27:5–10 Rebekah, meanwhile, is listening in to the conversation between Isaac and "his son, Esau" (Gen. 27:5), and she quickly forms a plan in favor of "her son, Jacob" (v. 6). Rebekah is quite sure that she can prepare food for her husband from young goats that are to hand that will be just as tasty as Esau's famous game stew and thus forestall the blessing's being passed on to Esau in favor of Jacob (vv. 9–10; cf. v. 4).[358] She is clear that this is not merely a personal blessing that is to be passed on but the Lord's promised blessing ("before the LORD"; v. 7).[359] Since Jacob is hanging around the tents as usual (cf. 25:27), he is on hand to assist with the deception. Esau is referred to as Jacob's "brother," a term that occurs thirteen times in this chapter, recalling the conflict between Cain and Abel in Genesis 4.

Rebekah's instructions to her son are not a suggestion but a command: three times she tells Jacob, "Obey my voice" (Gen. 27:8, 13, 43). The third time will be the instruction to leave home to save his life, which are Rebekah's last recorded

---

[355] Literally, "That my soul [*nepesh*] may bless you" (Gen. 27:4, 19, 25, 31), indicating a transfer from the depths of Isaac's identity to his son's.
[356] Sarna, *Genesis*, 190.
[357] Mathews, *Genesis 11:27–50:26*, 427.
[358] Derek Kidner writes, "Rebekah had not the slightest doubt that she could reproduce Esau's gastronomic masterpiece—had she often smarted under this?—in a fraction of Esau's time" (*Genesis*, 167).
[359] Rebekah's inclusion of the phrase highlights its omission by Isaac; he does *not* use the divine name, Yahweh, in the entire chapter, except in a passing reference to the smell of Esau's clothing as being like "a field that the LORD has blessed" (Gen. 27:27). When he gives the actual blessing, Isaac uses the generic title "God" (v. 28).

words to Jacob. She is the instigator and driver of this deception, though Jacob is a more than willing participant in the scheme.

27:11–17 Jacob does foresee one problem with his mother's plan: the difference between the two brothers in their hirsuteness. Esau is very hairy (Hb. *saʿir*; v. 11; cf. 25:25), while Jacob is "smooth" (*khalaq*). The latter term can be used of verbal slipperiness as well as physical smoothness (Prov. 5:3; 26:28) and thus is a fitting descriptor of Jacob morally as well as physically. It is worth noting that Jacob's scruple concerns not the moral appropriateness of the plan but merely its practicality. If his father were to touch him, something that would inevitably occur as part of a blessing ceremony even if Isaac did not use touch as a substitute for his defective vision, surely he would notice the difference between the sons and call down a curse rather than a blessing upon Jacob?

Yet Rebekah swiftly reassures Jacob on this point, offering to take upon herself the curse if such should be necessary (Gen. 27:13). In many respects she does indeed share in the judgment that follows, as she is separated from her favorite son for the rest of her life. In any case, Jacob is instructed to gather the necessary materials to make the tasty food required for the deception of his father, and he promptly obeys (vv. 13–14). Meanwhile, Rebekah gives Jacob Esau's best clothes, along with goatskins to cover the lack of hair on Jacob's arms and neck so that the smooth brother could impersonate the hairy one (vv. 15–16), and sends Jacob in to his father with the tasty food she has made (v. 17).

27:18–29 It is one thing to make all the preparations for the deception; it is quite another to carry it off successfully. As soon as Jacob enters his father's tent and says, "My father," using the same address of trust Isaac had used to his own father on Mount Moriah (Gen. 22:7), Isaac responds, "Here I am. Who are you, my son?" (27:18). This is not a conventional greeting,[360] suggesting some uncertainty in Isaac's mind over the identity of the person who has entered. Jacob's response is a barefaced lie: "I am Esau your firstborn. I have done as you told me; now sit up and eat of my game, that your soul may bless me" (v. 19). The title of "firstborn," which the narrator has carefully withheld from Esau, is claimed by Jacob, underscoring his claim to receive the blessing. When Isaac voices his suspicion that his son has been away only a short time,[361] Jacob doubles down on his deception, boldly invoking the name of the Lord in support of his lie: "The LORD your God granted me success" (v. 20).

Not only can Isaac's weakened sight not tell the brothers apart; his other senses also let him down. When he summons Jacob to come near him so that he can touch him, as Jacob feared he would do, Isaac is deceived by Jacob's disguise (v. 22). His taste buds cannot discern a difference between the food his wife has prepared, made from domesticated goats, and Esau's wild-game stew (v. 25). Even his sense

---

[360] Though this is similar to how Naomi greets Ruth in the first light of dawn (Ruth 3:16), which can be rendered woodenly, "Who are you, my daughter?"
[361] In Hebrew the form of Isaac's question expresses surprise; cf. *IBHS*, 312, 326.

of smell is fooled by the scent of Esau's clothes in which Jacob is dressed (v. 27). Only Isaac's hearing tells him the truth, as he recognizes the voice speaking to him as the voice of Jacob (v. 22).[362] But in the face of the evidence of his other senses Isaac disbelieves his own ears.

The result is that Isaac is completely deceived by Jacob—betrayed by a kiss (27:26–27)—and he grants Jacob the Abrahamic blessing that he seeks. Isaac invokes over him abundant fruitfulness: the regular supply of morning dew that is critical in that climate to raising crops (Deut. 33:13),[363] as well as the fatness of the earth and abundant grain and new wine (Gen. 27:28). "New wine" (Hb. *tirosh*) is the freshly pressed, as yet unfermented grape juice that is the agricultural product of a good harvest and therefore commonly referred to in ascriptions of blessing (e.g., Hos. 2:9; Ps. 4:8), whereas "wine" (*yayin*) refers to the fermented product that people actually drank (Gen. 14:18; Lev. 10:9).

Isaac also blesses Jacob with lordship over peoples and nations, as well as over his brothers (Gen. 27:29). If Isaac were actually blessing Esau, as he so fondly imagines, this blessing would be directly contrary to the oracle Rebekah received before the twins' birth. Instead, Isaac speaks more truly than he knows; the Lord's purposes for blessing cannot be prevented by any human stratagems, as the prophet Balaam will later acknowledge (Num. 23:19–21; 24:9). Finally, Isaac passes on to his son the climactic blessing that God had promised Abraham: "Cursed be everyone who curses you, and blessed be everyone who blesses you!" (Gen. 27:29; cf. 12:3).

27:30–40 Jacob's deception has always run the risk of being interrupted, and the text stresses how close to disaster he comes. It is "as soon as Isaac had finished blessing Jacob" and "Jacob had scarcely gone out from the presence of Isaac his father" that Esau comes in from his hunting (v. 30). He then swiftly prepares his father's favorite meal and brings it into him, expecting to receive the blessing (v. 31). When he goes in, his father asks the same question he had asked Jacob in verse 18 ("Who are you?") and receives the same reply, "I am your son, your firstborn, Esau" (v. 32; cf. v. 18). Isaac must immediately guess the truth, since he earlier thought he recognized Jacob's voice, but he trembles violently and asks in effect, "Who was it who brought me food earlier and received my blessing?" (v. 33). To his credit Isaac does not try to undo what has been done, acknowledging, "He shall be blessed" (v. 33). He recognizes that the Lord's oracle has been fulfilled, even though he has tried his best to circumvent it, and he will not try a second time to thwart God. Jacob may have come deceitfully, but he has successfully acquired the blessing.

Esau is angry at the loss of his blessing, which he links to the loss of his birthright as two acts of deception on Jacob's part (Gen. 27:36; cf. 25:31–34). In reality, there was no deception in the bargain over the birthright; Esau had simply regarded it as of no account. Now the blessing (Hb. *berakah*) has gone the way of the

---

[362] Gordon Wenham (*Genesis 16–50*, 208) points out that, in contrast to his longer earlier responses, Jacob's reply after hearing his father wonder about his voice is restricted to a single Hebrew word, *'ani* ("I am"; Gen. 27:24), as if he is concerned that his voice might betray him.
[363] Waltke, *Genesis*, 379.

birthright (*bekorah*) he had earlier despised (27:36). When Esau seeks an additional blessing from Isaac, all his father can promise is this:

> Behold, away from the fatness of the earth shall your dwelling be,
> and away from the dew of heaven on high.
> By your sword you shall live,
> and you shall serve your brother;
> but when you grow restless
> you shall break his yoke from your neck. (vv. 39–40)

This is the exact opposite of the blessing conferred on Jacob (vv. 28–29). Whereas Jacob had been promised the earth's richest blessing and lordship over other nations as the source of blessing to other people, Esau will have neither prosperity, lordship, nor blessing (v. 39). He will live by violence and be subject to his brother (v. 40). What is more, Esau will reject even the blessing that he might have found for himself in submitting to Jacob and acknowledging him as the bearer of the line of promise. To break the yoke of the one chosen by God is to choose the way of curse over the way of blessing (cf. Ps. 2:3). Down throughout Israel's history Edom is characteristically opposed to Israel, the archetypal enemy of God's people (cf. Ezekiel 35).

27:41–28:5 Jacob and Rebekah's plot may have succeeded in achieving the blessing for Jacob, but only at the cost of further poisoning family relationships. Esau hates Jacob for stealing the blessing, and he plots to kill Jacob after their father dies (27:41). When Rebekah hears this, she realizes that the only way to protect Jacob from his brother is to send him away to her brother, Laban, in Paddan-aram (v. 43). Otherwise she might lose both husband and son in very short succession (v. 45). In time, she hopes, Esau's anger will be mitigated and Jacob will be able to come home—as indeed proves to be the case (27:44; cf. Genesis 33). However, that day is much further away than Rebekah hopes, and by that point she will be dead.

It is a mark of the depth of the brokenness of the family that Rebekah evidently cannot even tell her husband the real reason for Jacob's departure. Instead she appears to use Esau's marriages to the Hittite women as a pretext to send Jacob to Paddan-aram to find a wife from among her people (27:46). It is left to Isaac to put this venture in specifically spiritual terms, telling Jacob, "You must not take a wife from the Canaanite women" (28:1). This echoes Abraham's command to his servant when he was sent to Paddan-aram to find a wife for Isaac from there (cf. 24:3). However, Isaac passes over Abraham's command that his son should under no circumstances go back there (24:6). Jacob will have to go into exile from the Land of Promise for a period of time.

That is merely to be a temporary stay, however, as Isaac's blessing on Jacob makes clear. This time it is given legitimately in the name of God Almighty (*'El Shaddai*), the title under which the Lord revealed himself to Abraham in 17:1. He asks that God would bless Jacob and make him fruitful and multiply him, mirroring the original blessing upon mankind at creation that was reiterated after the flood (1:28; cf. 9:1).

A new element is added to the promise that Abraham would be the father of many nations: now that grouping is designated a *qahal* of peoples (28:3). The importance of this promise may be seen from the fact that it is reiterated to Jacob by God himself in 35:11, and Jacob refers to it as an essential part of the blessing he has received from God in 48:4. The predominant Greek word used to translate *qahal* in the LXX is *ekklesia*,[364] which the NT picks up as the key term to denote the church. Jacob's offspring will be an "assembly" (AT) of peoples, a term focusing on the *reason* for their coming together. As Edmund Clowney explains,

> The Old Testament assembly [*qahal*] is defined by the great covenant assembly at Sinai. It is extended in the major assemblies for covenant renewal and in the festival assemblies three times a year. In assembly the people stand before their covenant Lord. They are not a tribe, defined genealogically, but a holy nation bound together by the word of God in the presence of God.[365]

In other words this promise that Jacob's descendants will be a *qehal 'ammim* is the first anticipation of Israel's nature as the original church of God, a dedicated people called to worship a holy God. As Clowney points out, this promise finds its immediate fulfillment in Israel as the *qehal yhwh* gathered for worship at Mount Sinai (Deut. 9:10; 10:4; 18:16; etc.).

The call for Jacob to return to the Promised Land after his stay in Paddan-aram comes at the end of the blessing, which asks that Jacob and his offspring would "take possession of the land of your sojournings that God gave to Abraham!" (Gen. 28:4). However successful he might become in Paddan-aram, Jacob is never to forget his calling to inherit the Abrahamic promise, which is bound up with that particular piece of real estate known as the Promised Land. These are the words ringing in Jacob's ears as he leaves to go and visit his uncle, Laban (v. 5).

28:6–9 The narrative closes by returning to Esau in order to demonstrate that he has learned nothing through the whole process.[366] Seeing that Jacob has been sent off to Paddan-aram to get a non-Canaanite wife (vv. 6–7), Esau proceeds to compound his earlier polygamy by adding a third wife (v. 9). Although she comes from the Abrahamic line, she is the daughter of Ishmael and thus still outside the line of promise (v. 9). The similarities with Jacob's next move (also marrying the daughter of an uncle) highlight the fundamental differences. Although Esau has lost the blessing through Jacob's trickery, he has no spiritual interest in the Abrahamic promise, just as he had earlier despised his birthright. What he lost was something he did not value, not an inheritance that rightfully should have been his.

---

[364] Though it is not used in Genesis, where the translator prefers *synagōgē*.
[365] Edmund P. Clowney, "The Politics of the Kingdom," *WTJ* 41 (1979): 300–301.
[366] The two accounts of Esau's marriages form an inclusio around the whole episode, spotlighting Esau's spiritual insensitivity; cf. Currid, *Genesis 25:19–50:26*, 65.

Response

Genesis 27 paints a tragic picture of a family at war with itself. No one comes out of this chapter with any credit, and the "life lessons" are mostly negative ones. Yet Isaac, for all his sinful motivation in seeking to pass the blessing on to his favorite son, is still commended in Hebrews 11:20 for his faith in blessing Jacob. That may seem strange, since Isaac sought to counteract the revealed will of God and bless his other son. Yet, although Isaac's faith was mistaken in its direction, it was well founded in its heart. Isaac believed God's word that one day the promise given to Abraham would bear fruit in the lives of his descendants; it is in those terms that he gave his blessing.

That was no small faith on Isaac's part, especially when you consider how little progress toward that goal had been made in his lifetime. Many years had passed since the death of Abraham, and to human eyes Isaac seemed as far from possessing the promised blessing as his father had been. In light of the promise of numerous descendants, two children in place of one is not much progress, especially when one of them has no interest in the spiritual dimensions of the promise. The land was as firmly under the control of the Philistines and Canaanites as ever. However, although the visible horizon was empty, Isaac still had his spiritual eyes fixed firmly on the city to come, and so he blessed Jacob by faith.

Yet the negative lessons of this passage are perhaps stronger. Once again in Genesis, we see the real and devastating consequences of human sin. Sin does not pay, even when it gives what you thought you wanted. The sins of all the participants in this drama would come back to haunt this family for the rest of their lives, especially Rebekah and Jacob. Rebekah's plan might have won the blessing for her favorite son, but it also resulted in his exile from their home forever. As far as we know, Rebekah never saw Jacob again after his enforced departure from the family. What is more, Jacob might have been blessed by his father with every material blessing, but he soon found himself leaving home with nothing other than the clothes he wore and the staff he carried. It would be a long, hard road before Isaac's words of blessing over Jacob saw any fulfillment. In the meantime, Jacob would find out from his own experience what it was like to be deceived, and he would return a humbled, chastened man.

Despite sin upon sin by the patriarchs—and the bitter fruits that such sin brought in its wake—God's purposes to bless his people were nonetheless secure. God would bring his promised Redeemer, not from a perfect family but from a long line of sinners. This Redeemer was also to be found dressed in clothes that were not his, but in the case of Jesus the clothing he wore at the climactic moment of his life was not the stolen finery of Esau but a purple robe on loan from the Roman soldiers (Mark 15:17–18), followed by a shroud borrowed from Joseph of Arimathea (Matt. 27:57–59). Jesus took that path not in order to steal someone else's blessing for himself but rather to take upon himself our curse. In the most remarkable reversal of all Jesus graciously says to us what Rebekah rashly said to her son: "Let your curse be on me" (Gen. 27:13).

The words Rebekah said so carelessly Jesus said to us knowing the full depths of what he was saying. The curse that you and I earn for ourselves every day by our many sins was laid upon him, so that the Father's blessing that was rightfully his might be given to us, his undeserving people. Jesus wore the shroud of the cursed death that we deserved so that we might be clothed lawfully in our elder brother's garments, the spotless robes of Christ's righteousness, and be welcomed to receive the Father's blessing as his beloved children.

GENESIS 28:10–22

¹⁰ Jacob left Beersheba and went toward Haran. ¹¹ And he came to a certain place and stayed there that night, because the sun had set. Taking one of the stones of the place, he put it under his head and lay down in that place to sleep. ¹² And he dreamed, and behold, there was a ladder[1] set up on the earth, and the top of it reached to heaven. And behold, the angels of God were ascending and descending on it! ¹³ And behold, the Lord stood above it[2] and said, "I am the Lord, the God of Abraham your father and the God of Isaac. The land on which you lie I will give to you and to your offspring. ¹⁴ Your offspring shall be like the dust of the earth, and you shall spread abroad to the west and to the east and to the north and to the south, and in you and your offspring shall all the families of the earth be blessed. ¹⁵ Behold, I am with you and will keep you wherever you go, and will bring you back to this land. For I will not leave you until I have done what I have promised you." ¹⁶ Then Jacob awoke from his sleep and said, "Surely the Lord is in this place, and I did not know it." ¹⁷ And he was afraid and said, "How awesome is this place! This is none other than the house of God, and this is the gate of heaven."

¹⁸ So early in the morning Jacob took the stone that he had put under his head and set it up for a pillar and poured oil on the top of it. ¹⁹ He called the name of that place Bethel,[3] but the name of the city was Luz at the first. ²⁰ Then Jacob made a vow, saying, "If God will be with me and will keep me in this way that I go, and will give me bread to eat and clothing to wear, ²¹ so that I come again to my father's house in peace, then the Lord shall be my God, ²² and this stone, which I have set up for a pillar, shall be God's house. And of all that you give me I will give a full tenth to you."

[1] Or *a flight of steps* [2] Or *beside him* [3] *Bethel* means *the house of God*

Section Overview

Once again human strategies to gain the promised blessing lead to the exact opposite result. Just as Abraham's attempt to acquire the promised child through Hagar led instead to lasting dissension, so also Jacob's deception of his father leads to his being forced to leave the land now promised to him. Instead of the abundance anticipated in his father's blessing, Jacob goes with only what he can carry, headed out to find refuge with his uncle Laban—a man who will prove to be every bit as deceptive and "smooth" as Jacob himself (cf. 27:11). Jacob will spend many years outside the Promised Land, in exile from what had been promised. Yet his journey to Paddan-aram is interrupted by an unexpected appearing of God, who will also meet him on his return journey (28:9–22; 32:1–2; 24–31). Jacob's time outside the land is thus bracketed with these encounters, in both of which angels play a prominent part (28:12; 32:1–2), representing the Lord's presence with and protection of Jacob in the intervening period. It is not insignificant that as Jacob leaves the land the sun is setting on him, while on his return daybreak is at hand (28:11; 32:31).

The point of these encounters is for the Lord to meet Jacob at his lowest point. The Lord reassures him that he will be with Jacob while he is away from the land and will ultimately fulfill what he has promised to do for him by bringing him back to the land. Just as Abraham's sin with Hagar could not derail the Lord's purpose, so too Jacob's sin will not prevent the Lord's blessing him. This point would hardly be lost on Moses' original audience, the second generation in the wilderness, which has just spent forty years wandering in the wilderness because of the previous generation's sin. The Lord has been with them during that period and will now fulfill for them the promise of the land—the exact same promise reiterated to Jacob at Bethel.

Section Outline

IX. The Family History of Isaac (25:19–35:29) . . .
    D. The House of God (28:10–22)

Comment

28:10–15 Jacob begins his journey from Beersheba, in the south of the country, and heads off to Haran (v. 10), a journey of around 500 miles (800 km), paralleling the journey that Abraham's servant had taken some sixty years earlier seeking a wife for Isaac. The parallels between the two quests invite comparisons that will be especially striking in the next chapter. Here the most obvious contrast is that Abraham's servant had an entire entourage supporting him, including ten camels and lavish gifts to support his cause (24:10), while Jacob travels alone, with virtually nothing in his hands (32:10).

Ancient travelers would often seek refuge in a walled city overnight, where they might receive hospitality, although that had risks of its own (cf. Genesis 19). Sometimes choice or necessity might result in the traveler's spending the night in the open country, as is the case for Jacob in the vicinity of what will later become Bethel. At this point it is simply a "certain place" (Hb. *maqom*; Gen. 28:11).[367] The

---

[367] The Hebrew word *maqom* is often used for sites of special religious significance, though it can simply mean an ordinary location; cf. R. de Vaux, *Ancient Israel: Social and Religious Institutions* (New York: McGraw-Hill,

sun sinks relatively rapidly in those latitudes, and further travel after sundown would be impossible. This leaves Jacob to make the best of his uncomfortable surroundings, with nothing but a stone for a pillow (v. 11). There is no indication that Jacob anticipates or seeks this dream through some kind of religious ritual. On the contrary, the *hinneh* in verse 12 ("he dreamed, and *behold*") is a typical expression of surprise.[368]

Certainly the content of the dream is surprising: Jacob sees a stone staircase (*sullam*) set up on the ground with its top (*ro'sh*) reaching the heavens (v. 12). The object is traditionally called a "ladder" but is far more likely "a stepped ramp, a series of rising stones"[369] (cf. ESV mg., "flight of steps"). This rendering highlights the comparison and contrast between events at Babel (*bab-ilu*; "the gate of the gods") and Bethel ("the house of God"). At Babel humans built a ziggurat, a step-pyramid temple, conceived as essentially a similar kind of stone stairway "with its top [*ro'sh*] in the heavens" (11:4). It was made of materials designed by human ingenuity—bricks and bitumen—with the goal of accomplishing fame and security for its builders.

In stark contrast, Jacob's stairway is unsought, unexpected, and undeserved. He does not make it (or climb it, contra the popular children's song). Like Abraham in Genesis 15, he is simply the passive recipient of divine revelation. At a time when Jacob surely imagines himself far away from God, being driven from his home on account of his sin, the staircase is alive with angels ascending and descending (28:12), representing God's knowledge of affairs on earth and his constant provision for and protection of his people. The access to God—and the blessings that such access would entail—that the builders of Babel sought unsuccessfully is promised to Jacob as a free gift.

At the top of the staircase stands the Lord,[370] who confirms the bestowal of the Abrahamic blessing upon him (28:13). This is now the third time that Jacob has heard the blessing pronounced: the first two times were by his father, Isaac, initially through deception (27:28–29) and then legitimately (28:3–4). However, it carries significant added weight to hear these words directly from the Lord, confirming beyond any possible doubt the divine bestowal of the blessing promised to him in utero (25:23).

What God promises Jacob is the fullness of the covenant made with Abraham, which was itself God's answer to the events at Babel. It is no coincidence that Genesis 12, with its promise to Abraham of a name and blessing for the nations, follows right after Genesis 11 and the failure of the builders' efforts to make a name for themselves and gain their own security. Here the Lord promises Jacob the land

---

1961), 279. At Bethel Jacob experiences for himself the double meaning of *maqom*. He may think of it simply as a "place" to spend the night, but he discovers that it is indeed a "sacred place."
368 Van der Merwe, *Biblical Hebrew Reference Grammar* §44.3.4.1.
369 S.v. סֻלָּם, HALOT, 2.757. The word occurs only here in the OT. It would be hard to envisage multiple angels ascending and descending on a ladder, whereas significant traffic could use a substantial stairway.
370 As the ESV mg. points out, it is possible to translate the Hebrew as describing the Lord's standing beside Jacob, implying that he has descended the ladder to be with Jacob. However, given the presence of the angels who are ascending and descending on the ladder, it makes most sense to see the Lord at the top of the ladder, with angels acting as intermediaries between God and man.

on all sides of Bethel, which is near one of the places where Abraham had camped and built an altar in his first tour of the Promised Land (28:13; cf. 12:8). Along with the land Jacob is promised offspring as numerous as the dust of the earth (28:14; cf. 13:16), who will spread out throughout the earth—another contrast to the inhabitants of Babel, who sought to remain concentrated at a single spot.[371] Through Jacob's offspring all nations of the earth will be blessed (28:14; cf. 12:3; 18:18; 22:18). The Lord also promises to be with Jacob, as he had promised Isaac (26:24)—and not just while he is within the boundaries of the Promised Land but "wherever" he goes (28:15). This promise includes bringing him safely back into the land, a prospect that must seem very distant to Jacob at this point.

Clearly, Jacob contributes nothing to this relationship; indeed, he has nothing to offer. God comes to bless Jacob at his lowest point in order that it might be seen clearly that all is of grace—unmerited, undeserved favor—and not of human effort or skill. Indeed, it is a double misnomer to call the stairway to heaven "Jacob's ladder," for Jacob has no part in building or traversing it. Rather it is God's stairway, the sovereign means by which he reaffirms the constancy of his loving care for his chosen but sinful child.

28:16–19 On awakening from his dream, Jacob realizes the momentousness of what has occurred: the Lord is present in that place (v. 16). To stumble into the presence of a deity unawares is potentially dangerous, since the ground might be holy and to be treated with special reverence (cf. Ex. 3:5). To trespass on holy space, even inadvertently, could be fatal (Ex. 19:12–13), so to be there is "awesome" (Hb. *nora'*, "fear inspiring"; Gen. 28:17). The place where he has spent the night is the "house of God" (*beth-'el*); it, not Babel, is the true "gate of heaven" (v. 17).

Jacob's response is not limited to surprise and fear. He responds also with worship, setting up a *matsebah*, a standing stone, as a permanent reminder and witness of God's appearing to him, dedicating it by pouring oil upon it (v. 18). *Matsebot* were used by both Canaanites and Israelites for religious purposes, and Israel is commanded to destroy Canaanite *matsebot* in Leviticus 26:1; Deuteronomy 16:22. However, they have a legitimate place in Israelite worship in memorializing places significant in redemptive history, as Exodus 24:4; Isaiah 19:19 make clear.

In this case the stone pillar (*matsebah*) is itself a miniature depiction of the vision, a symbol of the staircase that God had set up (*mutstsab*; Gen. 28:12). So Jacob pours oil "on its head" (*'al ro'shah*), recalling the source from which his blessings flowed—the "head" of the staircase in heaven (v. 12).[372] He also gives the place its name, "Bethel," which was used proleptically in Genesis 12:6. The narrator notes also the Canaanite name of Luz (28:19), which links it to its later history, recorded in Judges 1:23–26.

28:20–22 Jacob also makes a vow at Bethel that echoes exactly God's promise to him in Genesis 28:15. If God will indeed be with him and keep him, supplying him with the necessities of life, food, and clothing and bringing him safely back to his

---
371 Mathews, *Genesis 11:27–50:26*, 451.
372 Jan P. Fokkelman, *Narrative Art in Genesis* (Assen: Van Gorcum, 1975), 66–67.

father's house in peace (*beshalem*)—the very opposite of the state in which he left it—then the Lord will be his God (v. 21). The location marked by the stone pillar will be regarded as a sanctuary, "God's house" (a "house of God"),[373] and he will offer a tithe (one tenth) of everything he receives in between as an acknowledgement that the Lord is the source of all his blessings, just as the dream has promised (v. 22).[374] Indeed, when God finally fulfills all those promises many years later and brings Jacob back to the land safely (*shalem*; 33:18), Jacob returns to this place in order to worship (35:6–15). He builds an altar (35:7), on which he presumably offers sacrifices to fulfill his vow. He also restores the stone pillar and hears God renew the promise of blessing to him and his family (35:9–14).

Response

The primary significance of Genesis 28, as we have seen, lies in its role in reversing the story of the Tower of Babel in Genesis 11. There humans, working in their own strength and with their own materials, sought to create an access point back into heaven in order to make a name for themselves and a united focal point for their society. They failed abjectly; their "gate of the gods" (Hb. *Bab-ilu*) was so small that the Lord had to come down to see what they were doing. He then judged them by scattering them and cursed them by dividing their speech (11:6–9).

Now at Bethel the Lord reverses the earlier judgment upon mankind at Babel. Bethel, not Babel, reveals the true gate of heaven as the Lord himself opens a stairway for angelic traffic from heaven to earth and back again (28:12). What humans could never do for themselves, even working together in perfect harmony, God does in the life of undeserving Jacob, the child of a thoroughly divided family. God's answer to the tragic dividedness of the post-Babel world is the community of peoples that he will establish through Jacob, the forefather of Israel (28:13). In relationship with Jacob's seed the nations of the world will find for themselves the blessing of unity and access to God for which they long but could never achieve for themselves.

The fulfillment of the promise is not realized until the coming of Jesus, the true son of Jacob and the true Israel. When Jesus speaks to Nathanael in John 1:51, he tells Nathanael that he will see heaven opened and angels ascending and descending upon the Son of Man (John 1:51). The reference to Jacob's dream at Bethel is unmistakable. Jesus himself is the true stairway to heaven, the only way to God. His coming is the only means by which fellowship and friendship between God and man can be reestablished. In him alone we find the security and significance for our lives that the builders of Babel sought in vain from their tower. It is through Jesus' death and resurrection alone that God in his grace comes to bless scheming scoundrels like Jacob, and like us, so that we can be called the people of God.

---

373 The pillar is not itself the house of the deity; cf. Westermann, *Genesis 12–36*, 456.

374 This vow to offer a tenth of the results of a specific project is similar to Abraham's tithe to Melchizedek in Genesis 14:20 but quite distinct from the annual tithe of agricultural produce, which the Lord imposes on Israel in recognition of his ownership of the land of Canaan (cf. Deut. 14:22–29). On the question of the continuing obligation to tithe cf. comment on 14:17–24.

This new relationship with God spills over into a new relationship with other people as well. We go from being mere fellow travelers through life who manipulate and exploit others for what we think we can get from them to forming part of a new, united community in Christ. This is what Jesus prays for in his high priestly prayer in John 17:21: that his followers would be one even as he and the Father are one—a single people of God, bound together in an intimate spiritual unity. What is more, in Jesus the boundaries of the community of peoples, the true Israel of God, now extend more broadly than the physical descendants of Jacob to take in those from all nations who by faith are the spiritual descendants of Abraham. By faith in Christ the Gentiles are now incorporated into the one new people of God, becoming the children of God and heirs of the promised blessing (Rom. 4:11–12). God's ear is now attentive to their prayers, and his angels are sent to watch over them, so that no danger or trial could separate them from the Father's personal care or attention.

Jacob's response to the unexpected grace he receives is worship and a vow of self-commitment to the God who has committed himself to him. How much more should we respond in grateful thanksgiving to the Lord, offering our bodies as living sacrifices to him (Rom. 12:1–2), in return for the far more astounding mercy we have received in Christ!

GENESIS 29:1–14

29 Then Jacob went on his journey and came to the land of the people of the east. ²As he looked, he saw a well in the field, and behold, three flocks of sheep lying beside it, for out of that well the flocks were watered. The stone on the well's mouth was large, ³and when all the flocks were gathered there, the shepherds would roll the stone from the mouth of the well and water the sheep, and put the stone back in its place over the mouth of the well.

⁴Jacob said to them, "My brothers, where do you come from?" They said, "We are from Haran." ⁵He said to them, "Do you know Laban the son of Nahor?" They said, "We know him." ⁶He said to them, "Is it well with him?" They said, "It is well; and see, Rachel his daughter is coming with the sheep!" ⁷He said, "Behold, it is still high day; it is not time for the livestock to be gathered together. Water the sheep and go, pasture them." ⁸But they said, "We cannot until all the flocks are gathered together and the stone is rolled from the mouth of the well; then we water the sheep."

⁹While he was still speaking with them, Rachel came with her father's sheep, for she was a shepherdess. ¹⁰Now as soon as Jacob saw Rachel the daughter of Laban his mother's brother, and the sheep of Laban his mother's brother, Jacob came near and rolled the stone from the well's mouth and watered the flock of Laban his mother's brother. ¹¹Then Jacob kissed

Rachel and wept aloud. **12** And Jacob told Rachel that he was her father's kinsman, and that he was Rebekah's son, and she ran and told her father.

13 As soon as Laban heard the news about Jacob, his sister's son, he ran to meet him and embraced him and kissed him and brought him to his house. Jacob told Laban all these things, **14** and Laban said to him, "Surely you are my bone and my flesh!" And he stayed with him a month.

Section Overview

One of the features of the narrative style of Genesis is the presentation of parallel episodes that invite the reader to compare and contrast. We have already observed this tendency with the three wife-sister episodes (Gen. 12:11–20; 20:2–14; 26:7–11), and the first half of Genesis 29 gives us the opportunity to lay the encounter between Jacob and a woman at a well alongside the similar episode involving Abraham's servant (Genesis 24).[375] Both texts involve a man on a quest to find a wife, and the events may even occur at the same well. Both men are ultimately successful in their quest to find a wife, and both women are beautiful.

Yet the differences between the narratives are of more significance than the similarities. Abraham's servant came equipped with everything necessary for success, yet he stopped to pray and seek the Lord's guidance before he came to the well. There he sought a sign of the Lord's will involving a test of the young woman's character—would she be willing to serve a stranger by watering his camels, which was no small task? Jacob, on the other hand, has nothing to offer the potential bride he seeks, yet there is no word of any prayer's crossing his lips. He is determined to prove himself worthy by watering the woman's flock, and he gives no consideration to the woman's character—it is enough for him that she is beautiful. Taken together, the two episodes are thus far more revealing of the character of Abraham's servant and of Jacob than either episode would be by itself.

Section Outline

IX. The Family History of Isaac (25:19–35:29) . . .
    E. The Woman at the Well (29:1–14)

Comment

29:1–3 After his vision of God at Bethel Jacob continues his journey to Paddan-aram,[376] here simply called "the land of the people of the east" (v. 1). "The people of the east" is a very general phrase in the OT, ranging from groups in the Transjordan associated with the Midianites and Ammonites (Judg. 7:2; 8:10) to those in Mesopotamia more generally (Job 1:3). Here it underscores the fact that Jacob's journey takes him eastward, away from the Promised Land—not a positive direction in Genesis.[377]

---

[375] Alter, *Art of Biblical Narrative*, 51–57.
[376] Hb. "He lifted up his feet," a unique combination with unclear meaning. Most likely it suggests setting out on his journey with renewed purpose. At the very least it highlights again the difference between Jacob's journey on foot and the parallel pathway of Abraham's servant, riding comfortably mounted on a camel (Gen. 24:10).
[377] Hamilton, *Genesis 18–50*, 252.

On his arrival Jacob sees a well in a field (i.e., outside any settlement); the mouth of the well is blocked by a large stone, and three flocks of sheep are lying beside it (Gen. 29:2). The surprising nature of the scene (cf. the repetition of *hinneh*, v. 2; "saw," "behold") is explained by the shepherds' regular routine of waiting until they are all gathered before rolling the stone away and then back again (v. 3). Each of these seemingly trivial elements will be important to the narrative that follows.

29:4–8 Jacob then engages the shepherds in conversation, seeking information. Once he discovers that they are from Haran, the home city of Laban, Jacob asks them about Laban's *shalom*, his well-being (v. 6). Given the difficulties of communication over distance in these days, Jacob's knowledge of Laban's situation could be significantly out of date—but no, they assure him, Laban's *shalom* is fine. Of course, Jacob's presence will soon disrupt Laban's *shalom*! Not only do the shepherds know Laban, but almost immediately Rachel, Laban's daughter, appears with his sheep (v. 6).

Jacob's immediate response—which is bold for a stranger from out of town—is to rebuke the shepherds for their laziness (vv. 7–8). The area immediately around the well would have little for the sheep to eat, so every minute spent there, beyond what is necessary for them to water the sheep, is unprofitable. The time would be better spent by the shepherds' leading their flocks out in various directions to find pasture. A large part of an ancient shepherd's life would be spent searching out pasture for his flock, especially as the dry season wore on and the flock would have to go further and into more rugged areas to find hidden pockets of grass. But that would mean individual shepherds' wrestling the large stone away from the mouth of the well and back again by themselves, and these shepherds apparently prefer an easier life—they are "hireling shepherds" instead of "good shepherds" (John 10:12–13; cf. Zechariah 11).

29:9–12 In contrast to those lazy shepherds, who would rather sit around than serve their flocks, Jacob single-handedly rolls away the stone from the mouth of the well and proceeds to water Rachel's flocks (Gen. 29:10). Although in comparison with Esau Jacob may have been a homebody, preferring the tents to the open fields (25:27), he is not work-shy. His action is triggered by first seeing Rachel (29:10). The reader is not informed until verse 17 that Rachel is beautiful, but Jacob sees it immediately, and so, as well as watering Laban's sheep, he kisses Rachel (v. 11).[378] These may seem to be utterly unrelated actions, but their parallel nature is clear in the Hebrew, in which the words "he watered" and "he kissed" contain the same consonants (*vayyashq/vayyishaq*).[379] One might almost say that his mouth waters equally at the sight of Laban's daughter and at the sight of his flocks. The focus

---

378 The most natural interpretation of the Hebrew suggests that Jacob kisses Rachel *before* telling her that they are related. It is possible that Genesis 29:12 is a circumstantial clause ("Now Jacob had told Rachel . . ."; cf. NIV), but in that case one would more commonly expect an initial *vav* conjunction with a noun rather than the *vav*-consecutive imperfect. Cf. *IBHS*, 31.2, 33.2.3.

379 Sarna, *Genesis*, 202, suggests that this is the only instance in the biblical narrative of a man's kissing a woman who is neither his mother nor his wife. However, Song 8:1 assumes that brothers' kissing sisters in public was normal behavior in that culture.

of the next few chapters will be to show how Jacob succeeds in stealing both from Laban.

For her part Rachel is described as a "shepherdess" (*ro'ah*; v. 9), the only woman described by that term in Scripture. Shepherding was a tough job in those days, as Jacob notes in Genesis 31:38–40, and therefore it was normally seen as a male role.[380] Rachel is probably overjoyed at the prospect of someone else to take her place in the fields. It is ironic that Jacob, the brother more at home in the tents than out in the fields (25:27), is drawn to Rachel, the sister employed out in the fields, rather than Leah, the one who seems to have remained at home.

As noted earlier, there is a striking contrast between our first glimpse of Rachel and our first glimpse of Rebekah. Both have similar encounters at the well that lead to their marriages, and both are outstandingly beautiful (Gen. 24:16; 29:17). However, Abraham's servant was not convinced of divine guidance simply by means of Rebekah's good looks. He had prayed that the Lord would show him the wife for Isaac by a test of character—a willingness to serve him by watering his camels. Even after he saw that she was beautiful, he waited to see whether she would fulfill the test; only then did he know that she was the one the Lord had chosen for his master's son (24:21). Everything Abraham's servant did on the entire journey, from start to finish, was bathed in prayer and conducted in the name of the Lord.

In contrast, while Jacob may have adequately demonstrated his physical strength to Rachel, he knows next to nothing about her apart from her good looks before he decides that he wants her to be his bride. He waters her animals and serves her, not vice versa. As Proverbs 31:30 reminds us, looks alone are a dangerously deceptive basis on which to choose a bride. There is no word of prayer on Jacob's lips for divine guidance, or even any indication that such guidance is what he desires. Rachel is his choice, and he intends to earn her by his own works, not by grace.

29:13–14 The same contrast between Abraham's servant and Jacob persists in the conversations of the two men with Laban. In Genesis 24 Abraham's servant repeatedly invoked the name of the Lord, praising God for leading him to his master's relatives, asserting that his master's wealth was a gift from God, and claiming that the Lord's guidance had led him to Laban and Rebekah. Abraham's servant was the kind of man who made everyone around him think in God-centered categories. Having heard the whole story, Bethuel and Laban had little choice but to say in response, "The thing has come from the LORD; we cannot speak to you bad or good. Behold, Rebekah is before you; take her and go, and let her be the wife of your master's son, as the LORD has spoken" (24:50–51).

In the same situation Jacob tells Laban "all these things" (29:13). The text is enigmatic as to precisely what "things" Jacob tells Laban. Presumably Jacob does

---

[380] Jethro's daughters are also assigned to water his flocks (Ex. 2:16–19), but this is clearly a less than ideal situation, since it appears they are regularly driven away by the male shepherds and forced to wait at the end of the line (Ex. 2:17–18). When Moses comes to their aid, Jethro immediately hires him to replace them, marrying him to one of his daughters (Ex. 2:21).

not give Laban a full account of his deceit in stealing the birthright and blessing from Esau—although, if he does, there would be a certain ironic appropriateness to Laban's response to him, "Surely you are my bone and my flesh!" (v. 14). He is indeed carved from the same material as Laban, as subsequent events will richly demonstrate. However, the name of the Lord is as conspicuously absent from Jacob's lips as it was conspicuously present on the lips of Abraham's servant. Neither does Laban talk about the Lord. In contrast to the send-off of Rebekah, which was a clear declaration of faith in the God who works all things together for good, the agreement that will be made between Jacob and Laban is simply a business deal. Laban will ask Jacob to name his wages, and he does: one daughter for seven years' hard labor (v. 18).

Kisses play an important part in this narrative. Jacob deceives his father with a kiss (27:26–27) and greets Rachel with a kiss before being welcomed into Laban's family with a kiss (29:13). However, having deceived Jacob as comprehensively as Jacob deceived Isaac, Laban will eventually have to pursue his daughters and grandchildren in order to kiss them goodbye as they return to the Promised Land with Jacob (31:28, 55). One might have expected Laban's identification of Jacob as his family ("my bone and my flesh"; 29:14) to lead to Jacob's preferential treatment by Laban, but in fact Laban seeks to exploit that relationship remorselessly in what follows.

Response

Although Jacob is the heir of the Abrahamic blessing and thus the Lord's chosen channel of blessing to the whole world as well as the recipient of the Lord's promise of protection and blessing (Gen. 28:13–17), he acts as though he were an orphan, alone in the world without resources or recourse to anything or anyone outside himself. This was understandable at the beginning of chapter 28, but after the events at Bethel things should have been different. By faith he could have introduced himself to Laban as the bearer of the Abrahamic promise. He could have boldly asked for Rachel to be given to him without a bride-price so that together they might return to the Promised Land immediately to build a family for God's glory there. If he had approached the situation in prayer, on the basis of who he was by God's grace, much of the subsequent conflict and sin might perhaps have been avoided. But, instead of living his life in the light of the blessing of Bethel, Jacob trusts in himself and his own ability to negotiate a deal with Laban—and he pays a steep price for that decision.

We too are the heirs of rich promises in Christ. We have a heavenly Father who has blessed us with every blessing in Christ (Eph. 1:3) and promised to work all things together for good for those who love him and are called according to his purpose (Rom. 8:28)—yet how often do we too behave like spiritual orphans, dependent on ourselves and our own wisdom for our safety and prosperity in this world? If we remembered God's promises of care and provision for us, we might pray more and fret less amid the challenging and confusing circumstances of our lives. We could speak more clearly to others about what God has done for us, and we might draw them toward this God who welcomes them to come to him through faith in Christ.

GENESIS 29:15–30

¹⁵ Then Laban said to Jacob, "Because you are my kinsman, should you therefore serve me for nothing? Tell me, what shall your wages be?" ¹⁶ Now Laban had two daughters. The name of the older was Leah, and the name of the younger was Rachel. ¹⁷ Leah's eyes were weak,[1] but Rachel was beautiful in form and appearance. ¹⁸ Jacob loved Rachel. And he said, "I will serve you seven years for your younger daughter Rachel." ¹⁹ Laban said, "It is better that I give her to you than that I should give her to any other man; stay with me." ²⁰ So Jacob served seven years for Rachel, and they seemed to him but a few days because of the love he had for her.
²¹ Then Jacob said to Laban, "Give me my wife that I may go in to her, for my time is completed." ²² So Laban gathered together all the people of the place and made a feast. ²³ But in the evening he took his daughter Leah and brought her to Jacob, and he went in to her. ²⁴ (Laban gave[2] his female servant Zilpah to his daughter Leah to be her servant.) ²⁵ And in the morning, behold, it was Leah! And Jacob said to Laban, "What is this you have done to me? Did I not serve with you for Rachel? Why then have you deceived me?" ²⁶ Laban said, "It is not so done in our country, to give the younger before the firstborn. ²⁷ Complete the week of this one, and we will give you the other also in return for serving me another seven years." ²⁸ Jacob did so, and completed her week. Then Laban gave him his daughter Rachel to be his wife. ²⁹ (Laban gave his female servant Bilhah to his daughter Rachel to be her servant.) ³⁰ So Jacob went in to Rachel also, and he loved Rachel more than Leah, and served Laban for another seven years.

[1] Or *soft* [2] Or *had given*; also verse 29

Section Overview

Laban called Jacob "my bone and my flesh" (29:14), and that turns out to be true in more ways than one. Not only are the two men physically related, but they share a similar ability to deceive others in pursuit of their own self-interest. Jacob took advantage of his father's blindness and pretended to be Esau in order to receive the blessing that Isaac had intended for his eldest son. Meanwhile, Laban will take advantage of the darkness of the marital tent to substitute Leah for her sister and thus squeeze an additional seven years of unpaid labor from his relative.

Even though both deceptions are "successful," neither man really prospers through his deception. Jacob is forced to leave his home and family to flee for his life (27:43), while Laban's deception sows the seeds of discord in his own family that leads ultimately to both his daughters' abandoning him and leaving Paddan-aram with Jacob (31:14–16). In hiding the household gods she has stolen, Rachel will prove herself to be every bit as tricky as her father (31:34–35). That same deceptive streak will emerge in the next generation as well (37:31–32). Yet, despite these ongoing patterns of sin, God's sovereign purposes continue to advance. His choice of Jacob over Esau is not thwarted by Jacob's sin, and the Lord will ensure that Laban's sin not only does not profit him but will be the means by which the Lord's promise to Jacob of abundant offspring and prosperity will come to pass. Our sin may have significant negative consequences in our lives, but it does not prevent God from accomplishing his goal of blessing the world.

Section Outline
> IX. The Family History of Isaac (25:19–35:29) ...
>> F. The Deceiver Deceived (29:15–30)

Comment

29:15–20 Abraham's servant came seeking a bride for Isaac from a position of strength, bearing rich gifts and the promise of financial security for Rebekah (24:36–51). Jacob has none of these advantages; he arrives as a penniless wanderer whose only asset is his work ethic. He has shown that he is not afraid of hard work (29:10), and, after a month of living with the family, he has already demonstrated his usefulness to Laban. So Laban introduces the idea of paying him wages to stay—a theme that will dominate the next several chapters, as Laban persistently promises one thing and then seeks to give Jacob something far less. Since Jacob is a relative, not a slave or a hired worker (v. 15), the usual rules of compensation do not apply, leaving a gray area for Laban to exploit.

Before Laban's question to Jacob about suitable wages can be answered, some additional background information is required, namely, the complicating presence of another (older) daughter of Laban. Normally Hebrew refers to wives and daughters as "first," "second," and so on (4:19; Ruth 1:4; Job 42:14),[381] but here the language of "older" and "younger" is used to recall the struggle between Esau and Jacob (Gen. 25:23). In this case also "the older shall serve the younger." The derivation of Leah's name is uncertain, though it may be related to an Akkadian word meaning "cow," while Rachel's name means "ewe."[382]

Both daughters are described in terms of their physical appearance. Rachel is "beautiful in form and appearance" (Gen. 29:17), recalling Sarah, who was also "beautiful in appearance" in 12:11 (cf. Rebekah in 24:16); Leah's eyes, however, are *rakkot*, a Hebrew word whose meaning is obscure. English translations have ranged from "weak" (ESV) or "no sparkle" (NLT) to "lovely" (NJB), while some have opted for the more multivalent "tender" (KJV). Commentators have suggested an even

---
[381] Mathews, *Genesis 11:27–50:26*, 467.
[382] Waltke, *Genesis*, 405.

wider selection of choices, including "young looking"[383] and "pale in color."[384] What is abundantly clear, however, is the contrast between Rachel and Leah, who has (at best) one good feature, her eyes, while the rest of her appearance is no match for Rachel, or has (at worst) a significant bad feature in contrast to Rachel's uniform beauty.[385] The eyes were a defining part of ancient beauty standards, as the Song of Solomon makes clear, especially in a culture where, even if a woman was not normally fully veiled (cf. comment on 24:62–67), much of her anatomy would be modestly covered.

The difference in the girls' appearance explains the subsequent sentence: "Jacob loved Rachel" (29:18). Unlike her aunt, whom Abraham's servant chose on the basis of her character, Rachel is chosen for her beauty. As a penniless sojourner, Jacob has no way to pay Laban any bride-price for her, but he can offer his services as a hired worker to Laban. Seven years of constant labor is no small commitment to make on Jacob's part, yet the text notes how the time will fly by in his eyes because of his love for Rachel (v. 20). Even after one month living with Laban Jacob understands the importance of having a proper contract for the agreement, so he specifies clearly to Laban which of his daughters he is working for: "Your younger daughter Rachel" (v. 18). And Laban seems to agree to his terms apparently without demur, desiring to keep her (and Jacob) in the family, where they could both continue to serve him, rather than marrying her to another family, where she would be gone from his household into another. Even though Laban does not formally adopt Jacob, this is clearly an advantageous arrangement for him in many different ways. Jacob may think that at the end of the seven years he can leave with Rachel; subsequent events will prove that such a plan is not so easy to carry through. What is more, a sharp lawyer would have pointed out that Laban nowhere actually explicitly committed himself to anything.

29:21–30 After the seven years are completed Jacob is naturally eager to consummate the relationship (v. 21). Laban in turn makes ready all the arrangements for a wedding feast, as though following the agreed plan—but at the crucial moment he brings in Leah and substitutes her for her younger sister, so that Jacob is deceived (v. 23). Laban's deception of Jacob is a case of a punishment that fits the crime. The words that Jacob says to Laban—"Why then have you deceived me?" (v. 25)—could just as well have been directed at Jacob by his own father, Isaac. Laban's response, "It is not so done in our country, to give the younger before the firstborn," is an explicit rebuke. In his place, Jacob may have supplanted his elder brother—Esau, the firstborn—but Jacob is no longer in his country. He is a sojourner now, without rights or recourse, completely at the mercy of his uncle. Even the way in which Jacob is deceived would be achingly familiar to him. Jacob first fed his father a celebratory meal, then took advantage of the old man's blindness; so too, Jacob is

---

[383] Hamilton, *Genesis 18–50*, 259.
[384] Von Rad, *Genesis*, 286.
[385] Cf. Alter, *Five Books of Moses*, 154: "There is no way of confidently deciding whether the word indicates some sort of impairment ('weak' eyes or perhaps odd-looking eyes) or rather suggests that Leah has sweet eyes that are her one asset of appearance, in contrast to her beautiful sister."

wined and dined by Laban before being deceived in the dark. As it turns out, it is not the "weakness" of Leah's eyes that is the problem but rather the inability of Jacob's eyes to discern who is in the tent with him that causes his mistake. At the crucial moment he is just as blind as Isaac had been. In the morning, when it is too late, it all becomes painfully clear to him, just as Isaac had an epiphany when Esau came in. There in the bed beside him is Leah!

Laban, of course, has prepared a solution to the problem: in order to acquire Rachel, Jacob can serve him for another seven years, although at least this time he will receive payment up front (v. 27). In this way Laban will retain the ongoing services of both daughters, as well as trapping his son-in-law within his family for a further seven years. Laban evidently does not care about the relational carnage that his plan will bring about, condemning his two daughters to a competitive marriage in which only one is loved by her husband,[386] not to mention the cost to his own relationship with Jacob. But then, Jacob had put equally little thought into the relational damage wrought by his deception of Isaac and stealing the blessing.

Along with two wives Jacob also acquires their two maidservants, Zilpah and Bilhah respectively (vv. 24, 29). If Leah and Rachel are treated like pawns in a larger game by Laban, Zilpah and Bilhah are doubly taken advantage of, treated as chattel not merely by Laban but by their mistresses as well—though little else would be expected, given their status as "maidservants" (Hb. *shifkhot*). They will subsequently become relevant as "proxy wives" in the competition to win Jacob's affections, presenting him with children (cf. 30:4–13). However, the bitterness of the battle that ensues is undoubtedly driven by one fundamental fact: "Jacob ... loved Rachel more than Leah" (29:30). The favoritism that has torn Jacob's own family apart will now be perpetuated in the next generation.

Response

Jacob can hardly complain about the treatment he receives at the hands of Laban, given how closely it mirrors his own deception of Isaac. The deceiver has been deceived! Nevertheless, he surely must ponder how far away his life is from the blessings promised to him at Bethel (Gen. 28:13–15). Instead of possessing the Land of Promise, with abundant offspring through whom blessing would come to all the families of the earth, after the first seven years with Laban he has nothing to show for his labors except two wives who cannot get along with each other (or him, it will subsequently transpire), no children, and a commitment to spend *another* seven years working for free for the man who has deceived him. It must seem more like an antifulfillment of the promise.

Yet God is nonetheless at work through this fractious family, whose inner conflict will be used by him to multiply Jacob's offspring. The hope of the world is not Jacob. On the contrary, spreading circles of deceit and confusion flow out from Jacob. But God will take this schemer and transform him through various

---

[386] Leviticus 18:18 forbids a man from marrying a sister of his wife during her lifetime because of the likelihood of rivalry, a provision also found more widely in the ancient Near East (cf. *ANET*, 196).

challenging providences until he is a showcase of God's grace. In due time the Lord will bring him back to the Promised Land, humbled and changed by his time away—though not yet completely sanctified, by any means. None of these frustrating circumstances will be wasted; each has a purpose in God's providence.

The hope of the world is on display in another encounter between a man and a woman at another well, many centuries later. There, at a well named for Jacob (John 4:5), Jesus meets a Samaritan woman whose notorious lifestyle makes even Jacob seem like a holy man (John 4:17–18). She has sought blessing through relationships with men and has been passed from one to the next, to the point where she has had five husbands and is now with a man to whom she is not even married, a lifestyle that has left her with deep shame.

As he had done for Jacob in Genesis 28, God meets her in the midst of her brokenness. Jesus offers her "living water," a gift that would well up into eternal life in her soul (John 4:13–14). "Living water" matches the LXX translation of the Hebrew term for the water produced from the sacrifice of the red heifer in Numbers 19: water that purifies everyone it touches—but only at the cost of the defilement of the one who prepares it (Num. 19:17–22). Jesus is offering this woman cleansing from her life of sin, a welcome into the family of the Father, who is continually seeking those who will bow before him in spirit and in truth (John 4:24). He himself will pay the cost of her cleansing at the cross, where he will be "made . . . to be sin" for her (2 Cor. 5:21). The result of that conversation is life for the woman and for many of her townsfolk, as the blessing promised to Jacob finds its fulfillment in Jesus.

GENESIS 29:31–30:24

³¹ When the LORD saw that Leah was hated, he opened her womb, but Rachel was barren. ³² And Leah conceived and bore a son, and she called his name Reuben,[1] for she said, "Because the LORD has looked upon my affliction; for now my husband will love me." ³³ She conceived again and bore a son, and said, "Because the LORD has heard that I am hated, he has given me this son also." And she called his name Simeon.[2] ³⁴ Again she conceived and bore a son, and said, "Now this time my husband will be attached to me, because I have borne him three sons." Therefore his name was called Levi.[3] ³⁵ And she conceived again and bore a son, and said, "This time I will praise the LORD." Therefore she called his name Judah.[4] Then she ceased bearing.

30 When Rachel saw that she bore Jacob no children, she envied her sister. She said to Jacob, "Give me children, or I shall die!" ² Jacob's anger was kindled against Rachel, and he said, "Am I in the place of God, who has withheld from you the fruit of the womb?" ³ Then she said, "Here is my servant Bilhah; go in to her, so that she may give birth on my

behalf,⁵ that even I may have children⁶ through her." ⁴ So she gave him her servant Bilhah as a wife, and Jacob went in to her. ⁵ And Bilhah conceived and bore Jacob a son. ⁶ Then Rachel said, "God has judged me, and has also heard my voice and given me a son." Therefore she called his name Dan.⁷ ⁷ Rachel's servant Bilhah conceived again and bore Jacob a second son. ⁸ Then Rachel said, "With mighty wrestlings⁸ I have wrestled with my sister and have prevailed." So she called his name Naphtali.⁹

⁹ When Leah saw that she had ceased bearing children, she took her servant Zilpah and gave her to Jacob as a wife. ¹⁰ Then Leah's servant Zilpah bore Jacob a son. ¹¹ And Leah said, "Good fortune has come!" so she called his name Gad.¹⁰ ¹² Leah's servant Zilpah bore Jacob a second son. ¹³ And Leah said, "Happy am I! For women have called me happy." So she called his name Asher.¹¹

¹⁴ In the days of wheat harvest Reuben went and found mandrakes in the field and brought them to his mother Leah. Then Rachel said to Leah, "Please give me some of your son's mandrakes." ¹⁵ But she said to her, "Is it a small matter that you have taken away my husband? Would you take away my son's mandrakes also?" Rachel said, "Then he may lie with you tonight in exchange for your son's mandrakes." ¹⁶ When Jacob came from the field in the evening, Leah went out to meet him and said, "You must come in to me, for I have hired you with my son's mandrakes." So he lay with her that night. ¹⁷ And God listened to Leah, and she conceived and bore Jacob a fifth son. ¹⁸ Leah said, "God has given me my wages because I gave my servant to my husband." So she called his name Issachar.¹²

¹⁹ And Leah conceived again, and she bore Jacob a sixth son. ²⁰ Then Leah said, "God has endowed me with a good endowment; now my husband will honor me, because I have borne him six sons." So she called his name Zebulun.¹³ ²¹ Afterward she bore a daughter and called her name Dinah.

²² Then God remembered Rachel, and God listened to her and opened her womb. ²³ She conceived and bore a son and said, "God has taken away my reproach." ²⁴ And she called his name Joseph,¹⁴ saying, "May the LORD add to me another son!"

¹ *Reuben* means *See, a son* ² *Simeon* sounds like the Hebrew for *heard* ³ *Levi* sounds like the Hebrew for *attached* ⁴ *Judah* sounds like the Hebrew for *praise* ⁵ Hebrew *on my knees* ⁶ Hebrew *be built up*, which sounds like the Hebrew for *children* ⁷ *Dan* sounds like the Hebrew for *judged* ⁸ Hebrew *With wrestlings of God* ⁹ *Naphtali* sounds like the Hebrew for *wrestling* ¹⁰ *Gad* sounds like the Hebrew for *good fortune* ¹¹ *Asher* sounds like the Hebrew for *happy* ¹² *Issachar* sounds like the Hebrew for *wages*, or *hire* ¹³ *Zebulun* sounds like the Hebrew for *honor* ¹⁴ *Joseph* means *May he add*, and sounds like the Hebrew for *taken away*

Section Overview

It should be no surprise to anyone that Jacob's new marriages has troubles, but these troubles are exacerbated by Rachel's barrenness (29:31). The wives of the previous patriarchs, Sarah and Rebekah, had also been barren, but without the complication of a sister-wife who had no such disability. Yet the Lord will use the sisterly rivalry to multiply the size of Jacob's family, so that he has twelve sons—not yet "offspring... like the dust of the earth" (28:14), but a significant step in that direction compared to the one or two sons of the previous generations.

The narrative is not merely interested in documenting the growth of Jacob's family, however. Indeed, Jacob is in the background of this episode, while Leah and

Rachel are in the foreground. Their conflict over children—directly and through the children of their maidservants—is played out in detail, with their inner thoughts being revealed by the names they give to their offspring. These provide a window into Rachel and Leah's hearts (and their idolatries) as they struggle not merely for Jacob's affections but for the right to become the mother of the seed of promise, as anticipated in Genesis 3:15.

Section Outline

IX. The Family History of Isaac (25:19–35:29) . . .
    G. The Battle for Love (29:31–30:24)

Comment

29:31–35 The narrative opens by attributing Leah's fertility to the Lord, while Rachel remains barren (v. 31). In Genesis 16 the Lord "saw" Hagar's situation of need (16:13) and gave her conception; so too here with Leah. Although the Lord is expressly said to have opened Leah's womb, he is not said to have closed Rachel's; rather, without the Lord's direct intervention barrenness is a natural condition.[387] The Lord's action is specifically attributed to his seeing that Leah was "hated" (Hb. *senu'ah*; 29:31). This Hebrew word can have a broad semantic range, from "unloved" and "despised" all the way through to "hated," each of which in English can serve as an antonym of "loved"—and each of which represents an extremely negative outcome in marriage. The Hebrew word also has legal connotations highlighting the insecurity of Leah's position in Jacob's household. Leah is the unfavored wife, who in that culture could be mistreated, cast off, or divorced.

The word has strong emotional connotations as well; there is no doubting the sting that Leah feels, as verse 32 makes clear. Given the circumstances of their marriage, it is not surprising that Jacob resents her, and it is hard to believe that there was not some level of complicity in Jacob's deception on her part. He likely also blames her for his seven extra years of unpaid servitude to Laban. That leaves her in an extremely difficult situation.

Leah thinks that her fertility might win her husband's favor, especially since Rachel is barren. When she delivers a son, she names him Reuben, whose meaning she derives via a pun: "See! A son" (*re'eh ben*). Sons were especially highly valued in the ancient world, so with Reuben's birth Leah thinks she might finally win her husband's love: "Because the LORD has looked upon my affliction; for now my husband will love me" (v. 32). In these words Leah's pain comes to expression, yet these words also reveal the idolatry gripping Leah's heart. She views the Lord as a useful means to winning what is really important to her—Jacob's affections—not as the one who in and of himself supplies all the meaning in her life. This is the essence of idolatry.

The same idolatrous orientation is present in Leah's naming of her second and third sons, Simeon and Levi. The name Simeon means "heard," and she affirms

---

[387] Compare Genesis 30:2, where Jacob describes God's action as "withholding the fruit of the womb."

with her lips that the Lord has heard of her unloved status and responded to her with this gift (Gen. 29:33). Yet it is evident that the fact that the Lord has seen and heard her misery counts for little if there is no similar seeing and hearing on the part of Jacob. In the same vein, Levi means "attached"; the verbal root is used in the OT to describe converts who attach themselves to Israel, becoming part of God's people (e.g., Isa. 56:6). But the one to whom Leah really longs to be attached is her husband,[388] not the Lord, and she is sure that now—finally—he will pay attention to her (Gen. 29:34). Surely three sons are enough—the same number fathered by Adam, Noah, and Terah.[389] Yet Jacob is still coldhearted toward her, and Leah's idolatry remains frustratingly unsatisfied.

It is not until Leah's fourth son, Judah ("praise"; v. 35), that Leah's attention finally shifts from Jacob to the Lord, as she says, "This time I will praise the LORD." It seems that she has become resigned to her status as a perpetual second-class citizen in her marriage and is finally seeking comfort from the only one who can truly give it to her, the Lord. The Lord has dealt faithfully with her, granting her these four sons, and he deserves her praise whether or not Jacob ever loves her. It is at this point she stops bearing children, perhaps because, having acquired four sons, Jacob is no longer attentive to her sexually. According to Genesis 30:14–16, once Jacob's attention is restored to Leah, she once again begins to bear children.[390]

30:1–8 Leah's children may not bring her the favor of her husband, but they certainly incur the wrath of her sister. Rachel is envious of her sister (the same Hb. verb, *qana'*, is translated "jealous" in Gen. 37:11 regarding Joseph's brothers), which is a natural response in the situation. What is not so natural is her demand of Jacob: "Give me children, or I shall die!" (30:1). Disappointment, sorrow, and grief are appropriate when a cherished desire goes unmet; as Proverbs 13:12 reflects, "Hope deferred makes the heart sick." Rachel's response that life without children is not worth living reveals an inordinate desire in her heart, however; having children has become her primary goal in life. Without that, Jacob's love—and the Lord's—is not enough.

In fact it is Rachel's rivalry with her sister, not her barrenness itself, that makes her childless situation so unbearable. Sarah and Rebekah were barren for far longer than Rachel has been, yet without showing any of her bitterness. They, however, did not have the same kind of household rivalry to contend with, which made their pain more manageable.

Jacob's response is far from compassionate. Instead of praying for Rachel to conceive, as Isaac did for his wife (25:21), he responds to Rachel's anger with anger of his own: "Am I in the place of God, who has withheld from you the fruit of the womb?" (30:2). Rather than taking any personal responsibility for the difficult family situation or coming alongside her in her pain, he blames God for her dif-

---

[388] She uses the language of "my husband" five times (Gen. 29:32, 34; 30:15, 18, 20), highlighting the conflict between her and Rachel over Jacob's affections. Cf. Mathews, *Genesis 11:27–50:26*, 480.
[389] Mathews, *Genesis 11:27–50:26*, 480.
[390] Alter, *Five Books of Moses*, 157.

ficulty. Although what he says is theological truth, it is not delivered kindly or out of love (cf. Eph. 4:15).

In her desperation Rachel offers her maidservant, Bilhah, to her husband—though this is more of a demand than a request (Gen. 30:3). Even though this strategy caused such havoc when employed by Abraham and Sarah (16:1–2), Rachel deems it her only option. Any children that result from this union will legally be hers (30:3),[391] enabling her to fight back against her sister. "So that she may give birth on my behalf" (v. 3) is in Hebrew "That she may bear upon my knees"; this may refer to a formal ceremony in which the newborn baby was placed on someone else's knees as a symbol of legitimation as that person's child and heir (cf. Gen. 48:12; 50:23).[392]

Through Bilhah Rachel does indeed receive two children she can call her own, Dan and Naphtali. The names she gives to these boys show that Rachel regards their birth as positive proof that God approves of her choice of means. Dan means "He has judged/vindicated," a statement of her belief that Dan's birth means the vindication by God of her strategy (30:6), while Naphtali's name ("my struggle," v. 8) is a claim to have triumphed in her titanic struggle with her sister.[393] The narrator ascribes no direct role to God in these births, however, as he did with several of the other births in this account (cf. 29:31; 30:17). Rachel's claims to have received divine help are left unsupported. It is, however, notable that Rachel nowhere asserts that these children will or should gain the attention of her husband, as Leah does. Perhaps she is more confident of her husband's affections than her sister is. In fact each sister possesses what the other sister desires: Leah has children but feels empty without Jacob's love, whereas Rachel has Jacob's love but feels unfulfilled without children.

30:9–21 Each of the movements in this narrative begins with someone's seeing something. First, "The LORD saw" (29:31), then "Rachel saw" (30:1), and now "Leah saw" (v. 9). Stung by the recognition of the facts that she has stopped bearing children and that her sister is gaining on her, Leah adopts the same strategy her sister has chosen. She sends her servant, Zilpah, in to Jacob (v. 9). She too sees this strategy succeed, as Leah bears Jacob two more sons who can be counted on her side of the equation. These she names Gad ("good fortune," v. 11)[394] and Asher ("to be envied," v. 13),[395] claiming that their births are proof that God's favor rests upon

---

[391] Cf. comment on 16:1–6.
[392] Sarna (*Genesis*, 207) considers this phrase to be euphemistic language, connecting "knees" to sexual organs. This is plausible, but taking a child into one's lap is such a natural gesture for a parent that the procedure may not need so subtle an explanation (cf. Ruth 4:16).
[393] Hebrew *naftuley 'elohim* (Gen. 30:8) is ambiguous and could be translated as "my wrestlings with God" (CSB) or "mighty wrestlings" (ESV, NASB 1995), taking *'elohim* as a superlative (as in 23:6). There is at least a certain irony in Rachel's claiming to have triumphed in her "wrestlings with God" two chapters earlier than her husband's similar encounter with the deity; although the word for "wrestling" used there is quite different, both humans are said to "prevail" (*yakol*; 30:8; 32:28). Cf. Wenham, *Genesis 16–50*, 248–249.
[394] Gad was the name of a pagan god of fortune in the ancient Near East (cf. Isa. 65:11) that was widely incorporated into personal names. It is not clear that Leah is appealing to this god, however, and Hebrew seals have been discovered with the name "Gadyahu," which would mean something like "May Yahweh grant good fortune." Cf. Sarna, *Genesis*, 208.
[395] Asher comes from the same root as *'ashre* ("blessed," Ps. 1:1, e.g.). There are two Hebrew words for "blessed," *'ashre* and *baruk*. The latter verb is only ever used with God as the active subject and refers to being filled with

her. Once again, however, the narrator says nothing about God's direct involvement in either of these conceptions.

At this early period of biblical history it is common to date events by agricultural seasons rather than by months; the wheat harvest would occur during May (v. 14). Although Laban and Jacob are primarily pastoralists, raising sheep and goats, it was common for such people to engage in seasonal field-based agricultural activity as well. Mandrakes were used widely for a variety of medicinal purposes but were especially prized as fertility aids, to the point that the Greek goddess of love, Aphrodite, was called "the Lady of the Mandrake."[396]

When Leah's son Reuben goes out into the fields and finds some mandrakes, therefore, the find is significant (v. 14). As Leah's oldest son, Reuben has much to gain from any improvement in his mother's status in the household, so he takes the plants home for his mother's use. Word of his find spreads quickly, however, and it is not long before Rachel is in the tent, requesting a share of the mandrakes. Not surprisingly, Leah is reluctant to part with her valuable commodity, especially to her chief rival. But Rachel persists until her sister agrees to trade the mandrakes for a night with Jacob (v. 15)—a deal that suggests Leah's recent "infertility" has had as much to do with lack of access to her husband as anything else.

By now the sisters' bitter rivalry has cheapened the marital relationship to the point that Jacob's one-flesh intimacy with his wife has become a commodity to be bartered. The word used in Rachel's offer (Hb. *shakab*, "He may lie with you"; v. 15) is generally used of immoral relationships rather than marital intimacy (e.g., 19:32; 34:2; 39:7). Jacob is again reaping what he sowed when he sought to wrest the birthright from Esau in exchange for a bowl of soup. Now he is the one being traded for an item of food.[397]

Ironically, however, it is the sister who gives up the artificial fertility aid that becomes pregnant (30:17). This is because the Lord alone, not mandrakes, has the power to open the womb. God hears Leah's cries (v. 17) and in response grants her two more sons of her own, Issachar ("wages," v. 18)[398] and Zebulun ("honor," v. 20). Yet these gifts of God's kindness are misinterpreted by Leah. The reason she gives for Issachar's name is that God has rewarded her for her idolatrous shortcut of presenting her maidservant to her husband. Even worse, with the naming of Zebulun Leah returns to her original idolatrous starting point. "Now my husband will honor me, because I have borne him six sons," she says (v. 20). She also bears Jacob a daughter, Dinah (v. 21), who is mentioned briefly in passing because of her significance later in the story (cf. Genesis 34). However, it is clear that daughters do not count for much in the emotional calculus of Jacob's family. They are incidental rather than central to a woman's efforts to demonstrate her worth and value.

---

the potential for life and fruitfulness (e.g., Gen. 1:28). The former is used more widely to describe someone in an enviable situation in life. The English word "happy" often has an emotional content describing a person's feelings that is absent from the Hebrew, although someone occupying that state of life might normally be expected to feel content.
396 Sarna, *Genesis*, 209. The Hebrew name, *duda'im*, sounds like the word for sexual embraces, *dodim* (cf. Song 7:13–14).
397 Sailhamer, *Pentateuch as Narrative*, 195.
398 There is a play here on the word "hired" in Genesis 30:16.

30:22–24 Finally God remembers Rachel, hearing her cries and opening her womb (30:22). It is not, of course, as though God had been deaf to Rachel earlier. However, she needed to recognize that Jacob could not provide her with a son (v. 1), nor could the mandrakes (v. 14). Only the Lord could open her womb and cause her to bear a son. And indeed, the Lord has compassion on her need and emptiness and gives her a child. Having a son of her own takes away Rachel's disgrace (v. 23), though there is no evidence that it weakens her competitive spirit with her sister. As well as a thanksgiving to God for mercies received, Joseph's name is a request to the Lord for another son (v. 24; cf. v. 1). Rachel is still dissatisfied with God's gracious provision, though at least her request now seems to be directed to the right person—to the Lord, rather than to her husband. The use of the Lord's name in 30:24 provides a neat inclusio with 29:31, bracketing the birth accounts and reminding the reader that it is the Lord who provides and withholds conception.[399]

The language of God's remembering someone generally points to a decisive act on his part, as at the turning point of the flood in Genesis 8:1. When the time is right, God intervenes decisively not just in Rachel's life but in the lives of his people, and the result is the birth of Joseph, the child who ultimately will be used by God to save the lives of all his brothers—despite their best efforts to murder him (cf. Genesis 37). Joseph's birth also brings about a decisive change in Jacob's own thinking. It is striking that it is only after *Rachel* gives birth to a son that Jacob's thoughts finally turn homeward (30:25).[400] He already has ten sons by his other wife and concubines, but in Jacob's mind none of them really count. For Jacob, Joseph is always the child of promise for whom he has been waiting all these years. All Jacob's hopes revolve around him, which is why, when he later thinks Joseph to be dead, his grief is utterly inconsolable (37:34–35). The result of this attitude will later be a repetition of the kind of destructive favoritism that has so scarred and broken his own family of origin.

Response

Genesis 29:31 is a classic study in idolatry.[401] Leah and Rachel bind up their value in their identities in their roles of wife and mother: to fail in either is to become a worthless person, lacking in significance and security. This perspective is understandable, given the limitations on women's roles in antiquity. Children were necessary to provide for a person in old age (cf. Ruth 4:15) and, especially in a competitive marriage, the primary means for the wife to contribute to the family's fortunes.

In this family those normal desires turn into inordinate ones, whereby the two women are driven into wrathful outbursts and self-destructive behavior in pursuit of the blessing of their idols. To imagine that adding two more concubines into a strained marriage would add to domestic peace and harmony is the definition of

---

[399] Currid, *Genesis 25:19–50:26*, 94.
[400] Wenham, *Genesis 16-50*, 248.
[401] Cf. Timothy J. Keller, "The Girl Nobody Wanted," in *Heralds of the King: Christ-Centered Sermons in the Tradition of Edmund P. Clowney*, ed. Dennis E. Johnson (Wheaton, IL: Crossway, 2009), 53–72.

insanity, while trading a husband's favors for mandrakes shows a low regard for the sanctity of the marriage bed. The names given to the various children allow us to peer inside the hearts of the women and to see how they imagine they are experiencing God's favor and blessing, even though their actions are entirely contrary to his Word.

However, although human sin and rivalry have been driving the action in the narrative at one level, at another level God has been accomplishing his purpose of making Jacob the father of a multitude of sons (cf. Gen. 28:14). Would Jacob have had twelve sons if he had married only Rachel and not been tricked into marrying Leah first? Or if Rachel and Leah had enjoyed a beautiful sisterly friendship rather than a bitter rivalry? God's plan for the Abrahamic blessing is that its channel would broaden out so that, instead of a single chosen son, all Jacob's sons would be included in the new people of God, of whom he would be the father (cf. 28:3). God is making Jacob into a company of peoples, and the sordid scheming of his wives will be the providential means by which God will accomplish his purpose of granting Jacob many sons.

Of course, many things might have been easier for the family if from the outset Leah and Rachel had worked together harmoniously in pursuit of God's glory. Idolatry causes real pain and suffering, devastating relationships and families. But God's plans are in no way jeopardized by Leah and Rachel's stubborn, self-serving strategizing. On the contrary, it is precisely through their sin that the Lord achieves his good purposes. What they mean for evil, the Lord means for good (50:20).

The ultimate answer for our sin is not to be found among any of Leah's or Rachel's children. It is to be found only in another name, the ultimate offspring of Jacob, the true Israelite, Jesus. He is God's one and only Son, who earns the name the angel assigns to him: "You shall call his name Jesus, for he will save his people from their sins" (Matt. 1:21). As Peter declares in Acts 4:12, this name is the only name given to mankind whereby we may be saved. He is the one who brings hope to the hopeless, rest to the weary, and new life to the lost—even to those, like Leah and Rachel, who are hopelessly lost in their idolatries.

GENESIS 30:25–43

²⁵ As soon as Rachel had borne Joseph, Jacob said to Laban, "Send me away, that I may go to my own home and country. ²⁶ Give me my wives and my children for whom I have served you, that I may go, for you know the service that I have given you." ²⁷ But Laban said to him, "If I have found favor in your sight, I have learned by divination that¹ the LORD has blessed me because of you. ²⁸ Name your wages, and I will give it." ²⁹ Jacob said to him, "You yourself know how I have served you, and

how your livestock has fared with me. ³⁰ For you had little before I came, and it has increased abundantly, and the LORD has blessed you wherever I turned. But now when shall I provide for my own household also?" ³¹ He said, "What shall I give you?" Jacob said, "You shall not give me anything. If you will do this for me, I will again pasture your flock and keep it: ³² let me pass through all your flock today, removing from it every speckled and spotted sheep and every black lamb, and the spotted and speckled among the goats, and they shall be my wages. ³³ So my honesty will answer for me later, when you come to look into my wages with you. Every one that is not speckled and spotted among the goats and black among the lambs, if found with me, shall be counted stolen." ³⁴ Laban said, "Good! Let it be as you have said." ³⁵ But that day Laban removed the male goats that were striped and spotted, and all the female goats that were speckled and spotted, every one that had white on it, and every lamb that was black, and put them in the charge of his sons. ³⁶ And he set a distance of three days' journey between himself and Jacob, and Jacob pastured the rest of Laban's flock.

³⁷ Then Jacob took fresh sticks of poplar and almond and plane trees, and peeled white streaks in them, exposing the white of the sticks. ³⁸ He set the sticks that he had peeled in front of the flocks in the troughs, that is, the watering places, where the flocks came to drink. And since they bred when they came to drink, ³⁹ the flocks bred in front of the sticks and so the flocks brought forth striped, speckled, and spotted. ⁴⁰ And Jacob separated the lambs and set the faces of the flocks toward the striped and all the black in the flock of Laban. He put his own droves apart and did not put them with Laban's flock. ⁴¹ Whenever the stronger of the flock were breeding, Jacob would lay the sticks in the troughs before the eyes of the flock, that they might breed among the sticks, ⁴² but for the feebler of the flock he would not lay them there. So the feebler would be Laban's, and the stronger Jacob's. ⁴³ Thus the man increased greatly and had large flocks, female servants and male servants, and camels and donkeys.

¹ Or *have become rich and*

Section Overview

Jacob was in the background and largely passive in the previous passage, which focused on the point of view of his wives. Now that Rachel has a son, however, Jacob starts to think about returning home to the Promised Land (30:25). Laban is less than eager to see them go, not so much because of any emotional attachment to his daughters but due to his shrewd financial assessment that he has profited from Jacob's presence with him (v. 27). Jacob is a hard worker, and fourteen years of labor in return for two of Laban's daughters has been a good deal for Laban, yet he also recognizes God's hand of blessing upon him for Jacob's sake. As a result, he seeks to persuade Jacob to stay with him (v. 28).

Having worked with Laban for a while, Jacob is wary of entering into an agreement with him, but he can see the advantages of a mutually beneficial contract that is clear, fair, and easily policed. That is what Jacob thinks he is getting when he arranges to receive all the spotted or speckled sheep and goats in the flock (v. 32), with Laban retaining the (presumably much larger) remainder. However, Laban has no intention of playing fair, and he separates from his flocks all the sheep and goats that might be expected to have offspring that would fit the description of Jacob's share, putting them three days' journey away (v. 35). He must chuckle to think of himself as pulling the wool over Jacob's eyes one more time. Yet the Lord has other ideas, and he blesses an unconventional breeding strategy that Jacob adopts, which leaves him with the strongest and best of the flocks, outsmarting his uncle (vv. 37–43). As a result, not only does Jacob receive a fair return for his many years of faithful service to Laban, but an irrevocable breach is also created between Jacob and Laban, so that Jacob follows through on his intention to leave Paddan-aram and return to Canaan (cf. 31:1).

Section Outline

IX. The Family History of Isaac (25:19–35:29) . . .
    H. The Battle for Jacob's Wages (30:25–43)

Comment

30:25–28 As noted earlier, it is "as soon as" (Hb. *ka'asher*) Rachel bears her first son that Jacob's mind turns to returning to his homeland. This is very revealing of Jacob's thoughts about the way in which God's promise to him of a land and offspring (Gen. 28:13–15) would be fulfilled. First, he knows that the land in question will be the land of Canaan, which the Lord promised to Abraham ("my own home and country"; 30:25).[402] Even after Jacob has lived there for fourteen years and married into Laban's family, Paddan-aram is not home. Jacob is merely a sojourner there (cf. 32:4).

Second, Jacob clearly anticipates that his offspring will be numbered through Joseph and not through his other sons, in the same way that the blessing descended from Abraham to Isaac and from Isaac to himself—thus excluding Ishmael and Esau. He has not yet grasped the significance of his father's blessing, which prayed that he would become a "company [or "assembly"] of peoples" (*qahal 'ammim*; 28:3)—which finds its fulfillment in the inclusion of all twelve of his sons in the line of promise. Indeed, *the* seed of promise descends from Jacob not through Joseph but through Judah, one of unloved Leah's sons.

The way in which Jacob makes his request of Laban highlights the power dynamics at play. Jacob asks in very formal terms to be dismissed from Laban's service and sent home (cf. 1 Kings 11:21). He uses the word "serve" or "service" twice, identifying his wife and children as the wages he has earned over the previous fourteen years. Laban holds all the power, and he is eager not to let Jacob slip away so easily. His language to Jacob is equally formal and surprisingly deferential ("If I have found

---

[402] This phrase is sometimes rendered as a hendiadys (NIV: "my own homeland") or as virtual synonyms (ESV: "my own home and country"). However, we should not miss the possibility that two distinct movements are in view, first going to "my place" (*maqomi*)—that is, visiting the sanctuary (*maqom*) at Bethel to which Jacob had vowed to return—and then subsequently settling in "my land" (*'artzi*). Cf. Mathews, *Genesis 11:27–50:26*, 495.

favor in your sight";[403] Gen. 30:27; cf. 50:4), and he acknowledges that the Lord has blessed him because of Jacob (30:27). Yet Laban's language is rarely straightforward; though he uses the Lord's name as the source of his blessing, he also attributed his insight to divination (*nakhash*; v. 27),[404] a practice forbidden to Israel (Lev. 19:26). This by itself should leave the reader uneasy. Is Laban taking the Lord's name in vain? Moreover, when did this supposed act of divination take place? If Laban had divined this truth earlier, why is he only mentioning it now—and why had he not sought to compensate Jacob better earlier? It is plausible that Laban is simply fabricating this insight in a bid to retain Jacob's services. Nothing he says can be trusted.

The normal expectation is that an indentured servant who has completed his full contract faithfully, as Jacob has, might expect some additional compensation and not simply be turned away with nothing ("empty handed"; cf. Deut. 15:13–14; Jacob uses the same language in Gen. 31:38–42).[405] But here Laban offers nothing to Jacob except the invitation to stay with him for a further period of time. "Name your wages, and I will give it" (30:28) sounds like the height of generosity, but, as Jacob knows only too well, Laban is not to be trusted when it comes to making deals (cf. 29:15).

30:29–34 In his response to Laban Jacob stresses the second-person pronoun, "You *yourself* know,"[406] in such a way as to suggest that he thinks that divination ought hardly to have been necessary for Laban to discern Jacob's value. Common sense should have told Laban that Jacob was more than worthy of his keep, yet he is also careful to attribute the benefit to the Lord's presence, not merely his own hard work. Nevertheless, beyond his two wives and their children Jacob has gained nothing personally out of his Herculean labors in caring for Laban's livestock. When will he get a chance to look after his own family interests (Hb. *bethi*, "my own household"; 30:30)?[407]

Laban then reiterates his earlier offer: "What shall I give you?" (v. 31). Perhaps mindful of Laban's last "gift" to him (Leah instead of Rachel), Jacob responds sharply: "You shall not give me anything" (v. 31). Rather, he prefers to be able to keep a portion of the increase of the flock in return for his shepherding duties—wages rather than a "gift" (v. 33). Jacob has clearly thought through the possibility of this kind of offer ahead of time. His proposal to Laban is straightforward enough in its broad outlines, if also difficult enough to unravel in all its details, keeping generations of commentators arguing. In essence Jacob requests all the unusually

---

[403] The sentence is incomplete, lacking the expected request that might follow these words: "Please stay with me longer." Some have speculated that Laban is blindsided by Jacob's request and that the incomplete sentence shows him fumbling for the right words. Cf. von Rad, *Genesis*, 295.

[404] Hamilton appeals to an Akkadian root to translate this verb as "I have grown rich" rather than "I have learned by divination," on the grounds that divination concerns the knowledge of the future, not the past (*Genesis 18–50*, 282). However, Genesis 44:15 (where Hamilton is content to translate the same root as having to do with divination) envisages an exactly parallel situation, where through divination Joseph is able to discern something hidden about the past, namely, who stole his cup.

[405] Sarna, *Genesis*, 211.

[406] The pronoun *'atah*, which is formally redundant, is fronted before the verb for emphasis.

[407] The repeated use of the first-person pronoun in these verses, which is emphatic in Genesis 30:20, suggests that Jacob is fully focused on himself as the sole means of providing for his family's needs. His dependence upon the Lord as his provider is not mentioned here, though it is the focus of Genesis 31:5–13.

colored animals in the flock—the black sheep and speckled and spotted sheep and goats,[408] which would naturally be a small proportion of the whole—while Laban can have the rest. This looks like an eminently fair deal; statistically speaking, a roughly consistent percentage of the flock would have these characteristics and thus belong to Jacob. If the flock gets bigger, both will benefit. If it gets smaller, both will suffer. The different coloration will make it easy to divide the flock and identify each man's share without dispute or argument. Any subsequent inspection can vindicate Jacob's "honesty" (*tsidqati*; Hb. "my righteousness"; v. 33).

Jacob may be offering the contract in good faith, but Laban's eagerness to seal the deal should raise his suspicions. Laban begins his response with two particles, *hen* and *lu*, expressing his eagerness to "let it be as you have said" (v. 34). Unfortunately for Jacob, Laban has no intention of keeping his own word. He has his own idea of how to ensure that, once again, Jacob will end up serving him for nothing.

30:35–43 Laban puts his nefarious plan into action immediately, removing all animals from his flocks that fit the description Jacob has specified and putting them in a separate flock watched over by his sons (v. 35).[409] In this way he will rob Jacob not only of his present share of the flock but the likelihood of any significant future share, since it is basic biology that striped and spotted animals are more likely to have offspring with matching coloration than solid-colored animals. He puts his sons' flocks at three days' distance from the main flock so that there can be no possibility of accidental interbreeding.[410] It seems he has thought of everything, and Jacob will be outwitted yet again.

Jacob is not so easily defeated, however. He responds with a complex strategy of his own involving strange practices with branches and selective breeding (30:37–42). The idea behind this is the ancient one that a mother's experiences during pregnancy could have an imprint on the baby.[411] So exposing a mother to a constant vision of striped or blotched materials might increase the likelihood of her having striped or blotched offspring. Some older commentators claimed a scientific method behind all this,[412] or that God revealed the process to Jacob in a dream.[413] However, this is based on a misreading of Genesis 31:8–12. Nowhere in that passage does it refer to Jacob's strategy with the branches; rather, what Jacob sees in his dream is that all the goats mating with his flock are speckled

---

408 See the discussion of the various colors in Athalya Brenner, *Colour Terms in the Old Testament* (JSOTSup; Sheffield: University of Sheffield Press, 1983), 121–123, 166.
409 Mention of "every one that had white on it" sounds odd in English, since white was not mentioned in Jacob's list. But in Hebrew there is a wordplay there: since the word for "white" is *laban*, like Laban's name, any that have white on them obviously belong to him (at least in his own mind). Cf. Currid, *Genesis 25:19–50:26*, 100.
410 "Three day's journey" is a common distance in the OT (Ex. 3:18; Num. 10:33; 33:8); it may not always represent a literal number but rather an approximation for a substantial distance. Cf. A. Hurvitz, *A Linguistic Study of the Relationship Between the Priestly Source and the Book of Ezekiel* (Paris: Gabalda, 1982), 94n19.
411 John Calvin comments, "It is well known, that the sight of objects by the female has great effect on the form of the foetus" (Calvin, *Commentary on the Book of Genesis*, 2.156).
412 "This artifice was founded upon a fact frequently noticed, particularly in the case of sheep, that whatever fixes their attention in copulation is marked upon the young" (Delitzsch, *Genesis*, 1:293). This idea continued to be supported by John Skinner in the early twentieth century: *A Critical and Exegetical Commentary on Genesis*, rev. ed. (New York: Scribner's, 1925), 393. For a different, more modern, explanation of the science cf. Scott B. Noegel, "Sex, Sticks and the Trickster in Gen. 30:31–43," *JANES* 25 (1997): 7–17.
413 Sarna, *Genesis*, 212; Calvin, *Commentary on the Book of Genesis*, 2.155–156.

or multicolored.[414] In other words, the Lord ensures the increase of his flock, a process that has nothing to do with anything Jacob does involving superstitious breeding techniques!

As with the mandrakes in the previous passage, there is more superstition than science behind Jacob's ploy.[415] Jacob neither prays nor requests help from God; he believes he can defeat Laban through his own cleverness. It is not until the Lord sends him the dream that he relates in the following chapter how he has come to see that every blessing is from the Lord, not from his own ingenuity. One way or another, however, the outcome of the scheming and counter-scheming is that Jacob grows rich at Laban's expense. Thanks to God's intervention on Jacob's behalf—which becomes explicit in the following chapter but ought to have been expected by all parties based on their earlier interchange (cf. 30:27, 30)—Laban has been outmaneuvered at his own game. The two things that attracted Jacob's attention when he first arrived in Paddan-aram twenty years earlier, Rachel and the flocks, have after a long and convoluted struggle finally become his.

Jacob's wealth is not limited to sheep or goats. The final verse of the chapter summarizes Jacob's situation, linking his prosperity to that of his father and, especially, his grandfather, including servants and maidservants, camels and donkeys (30:43; cf. 12:16; 24:35; 26:13).[416] He now "increased greatly," just as anticipated in God's blessing in 28:14. The blessing that Laban experienced from the Lord earlier for his sake (cf. 30:30) has been transferred to Jacob: Laban now decreases so that Jacob might increase.

Response

Jacob's faith is still very limited at this point in the story. There is no prayer or trusting in God to provide for him in the face of his exploitative uncle's attempts to defraud him yet again. Instead there is a reliance on a superstitious strategy as a means to counter Laban's greater power. But God does not wait for us to have enough faith before he acts. He continues to bless Jacob in spite of himself. He has chosen Jacob and is preparing everything for him to return home, just as he promised. Having given him abundant offspring, now God will provide richly for his financial needs as well. In the process the Lord also ensures a definitive breach in relationship between Laban and Jacob that will motivate Jacob to follow through on his earlier plan to return home, six years after he originally planned to do so (cf. Gen. 31:38). Only later will Jacob recognize that God has been at work in all his circumstances behind the scenes, working all things together for his good and to accomplish the Lord's plans for him.

The lesson for us is obvious. God works in our lives, not only in the moments when we can muster up strong faith but in our times of weakness and lack of

---

414 Genesis Rabbah 73.10 appears to take the dream literally, imagining that "ministering angels" transported animals from Laban's flock to Jacob's in order to provide breeding males with the right characteristics to produce the required offspring. But the Lord is not subject to the conventional rules of genetics; he is completely sovereign over the produce of the womb, whether human or animal.

415 Sailhamer, *Pentateuch as Narrative*, 196.

416 On camels cf. comment on 12:10–20.

trust in him. The "all things" that must work together for the good of those whom God loves and has called according to his purpose (Rom. 8:28) really do include all things—not just the things that see us operating at our best. Christ's strong hold on us never weakens, even when our grip on him is at its weakest (John 10:28). He will keep us safely in his grasp until he has brought us into the full inheritance he has prepared for us.

GENESIS 31

31 Now Jacob heard that the sons of Laban were saying, "Jacob has taken all that was our father's, and from what was our father's he has gained all this wealth." ²And Jacob saw that Laban did not regard him with favor as before. ³Then the Lord said to Jacob, "Return to the land of your fathers and to your kindred, and I will be with you."

⁴So Jacob sent and called Rachel and Leah into the field where his flock was ⁵and said to them, "I see that your father does not regard me with favor as he did before. But the God of my father has been with me. ⁶You know that I have served your father with all my strength, ⁷yet your father has cheated me and changed my wages ten times. But God did not permit him to harm me. ⁸If he said, 'The spotted shall be your wages,' then all the flock bore spotted; and if he said, 'The striped shall be your wages,' then all the flock bore striped. ⁹Thus God has taken away the livestock of your father and given them to me. ¹⁰In the breeding season of the flock I lifted up my eyes and saw in a dream that the goats that mated with the flock were striped, spotted, and mottled. ¹¹Then the angel of God said to me in the dream, 'Jacob,' and I said, 'Here I am!' ¹²And he said, 'Lift up your eyes and see, all the goats that mate with the flock are striped, spotted, and mottled, for I have seen all that Laban is doing to you. ¹³I am the God of Bethel, where you anointed a pillar and made a vow to me. Now arise, go out from this land and return to the land of your kindred.'" ¹⁴Then Rachel and Leah answered and said to him, "Is there any portion or inheritance left to us in our father's house? ¹⁵Are we not regarded by him as foreigners? For he has sold us, and he has indeed devoured our money. ¹⁶All the wealth that God has taken away from our father belongs to us and to our children. Now then, whatever God has said to you, do."

¹⁷So Jacob arose and set his sons and his wives on camels. ¹⁸He drove away all his livestock, all his property that he had gained, the livestock in his possession that he had acquired in Paddan-aram, to go to the land of Canaan to his father Isaac. ¹⁹Laban had gone to shear his sheep, and Rachel stole her father's household gods. ²⁰And Jacob tricked[1] Laban the Aramean, by not telling him that he intended to flee. ²¹He fled with all that he had and arose and crossed the Euphrates,[2] and set his face toward the hill country of Gilead.

²²When it was told Laban on the third day that Jacob had fled, ²³he took his kinsmen with him and pursued him for seven days and followed

close after him into the hill country of Gilead. ²⁴ But God came to Laban the Aramean in a dream by night and said to him, "Be careful not to say anything to Jacob, either good or bad."

²⁵ And Laban overtook Jacob. Now Jacob had pitched his tent in the hill country, and Laban with his kinsmen pitched tents in the hill country of Gilead. ²⁶ And Laban said to Jacob, "What have you done, that you have tricked me and driven away my daughters like captives of the sword? ²⁷ Why did you flee secretly and trick me, and did not tell me, so that I might have sent you away with mirth and songs, with tambourine and lyre? ²⁸ And why did you not permit me to kiss my sons and my daughters farewell? Now you have done foolishly. ²⁹ It is in my power to do you harm. But the God of your³ father spoke to me last night, saying, 'Be careful not to say anything to Jacob, either good or bad.' ³⁰ And now you have gone away because you longed greatly for your father's house, but why did you steal my gods?" ³¹ Jacob answered and said to Laban, "Because I was afraid, for I thought that you would take your daughters from me by force. ³² Anyone with whom you find your gods shall not live. In the presence of our kinsmen point out what I have that is yours, and take it." Now Jacob did not know that Rachel had stolen them.

³³ So Laban went into Jacob's tent and into Leah's tent and into the tent of the two female servants, but he did not find them. And he went out of Leah's tent and entered Rachel's. ³⁴ Now Rachel had taken the household gods and put them in the camel's saddle and sat on them. Laban felt all about the tent, but did not find them. ³⁵ And she said to her father, "Let not my lord be angry that I cannot rise before you, for the way of women is upon me." So he searched but did not find the household gods.

³⁶ Then Jacob became angry and berated Laban. Jacob said to Laban, "What is my offense? What is my sin, that you have hotly pursued me? ³⁷ For you have felt through all my goods; what have you found of all your household goods? Set it here before my kinsmen and your kinsmen, that they may decide between us two. ³⁸ These twenty years I have been with you. Your ewes and your female goats have not miscarried, and I have not eaten the rams of your flocks. ³⁹ What was torn by wild beasts I did not bring to you. I bore the loss of it myself. From my hand you required it, whether stolen by day or stolen by night. ⁴⁰ There I was: by day the heat consumed me, and the cold by night, and my sleep fled from my eyes. ⁴¹ These twenty years I have been in your house. I served you fourteen years for your two daughters, and six years for your flock, and you have changed my wages ten times. ⁴² If the God of my father, the God of Abraham and the Fear of Isaac, had not been on my side, surely now you would have sent me away empty-handed. God saw my affliction and the labor of my hands and rebuked you last night."

⁴³ Then Laban answered and said to Jacob, "The daughters are my daughters, the children are my children, the flocks are my flocks, and all that you see is mine. But what can I do this day for these my daughters or for their children whom they have borne? ⁴⁴ Come now, let us make a covenant, you and I. And let it be a witness between you and me." ⁴⁵ So Jacob took a stone and set it up as a pillar. ⁴⁶ And Jacob said to his kinsmen, "Gather stones." And they took stones and made a heap, and they ate there by the heap. ⁴⁷ Laban called it Jegar-sahadutha,⁴ but Jacob called it Galeed.⁵ ⁴⁸ Laban said, "This heap is a witness between you and me today." Therefore he named it Galeed, ⁴⁹ and Mizpah,⁶ for he said, "The LORD

watch between you and me, when we are out of one another's sight. ⁵⁰ If you oppress my daughters, or if you take wives besides my daughters, although no one is with us, see, God is witness between you and me."

⁵¹ Then Laban said to Jacob, "See this heap and the pillar, which I have set between you and me. ⁵² This heap is a witness, and the pillar is a witness, that I will not pass over this heap to you, and you will not pass over this heap and this pillar to me, to do harm. ⁵³ The God of Abraham and the God of Nahor, the God of their father, judge between us." So Jacob swore by the Fear of his father Isaac, ⁵⁴ and Jacob offered a sacrifice in the hill country and called his kinsmen to eat bread. They ate bread and spent the night in the hill country.

⁵⁵ ⁷ Early in the morning Laban arose and kissed his grandchildren and his daughters and blessed them. Then Laban departed and returned home.

¹ Hebrew *stole the heart of*; also verses 26, 27 ² Hebrew *the River* ³ The Hebrew for *your* is plural here ⁴ Aramaic *the heap of witness* ⁵ Hebrew *the heap of witness* ⁶ *Mizpah* means *watchpost* ⁷ Ch 32:1 in Hebrew

Section Overview

It took Abraham's servant a few days to arrive in Paddan-aram, acquire a wife for his master's son, and leave (cf. Genesis 24). It takes Jacob twenty years to accomplish the same feat (Gen. 31:38). In part this is because Abraham's servant had resources that Jacob lacks, putting him in a position of strength from which to negotiate with Laban. However, this is also due to his faith and prayer, neither of which has so far been much in evidence in Jacob's life. Jacob tackles life with confidence in his own ability to work hard and outwit his opponents in order to achieve the goals he desires.

But God is at work, both through Jacob's circumstances and within his heart, to begin a process of change within him. Externally, Jacob's trickery may have succeeded in making him wealthy, but, unsurprisingly, it sours relationships with Laban and his sons. He has always been a sojourner in a foreign land, but now that the climate toward him has turned frostier he begins to turn his thoughts once again to the prospect of returning home. Internally, the change in Jacob is visible as he freely acknowledged the Lord's role in protecting and providing for him thus far ("God did not permit him to harm me"; v. 7). To be sure, Jacob is not yet ready to leave Laban in a straightforward and honest manner, but he is ready to leave and step out in faith, taking on the various challenges awaiting him on the long road home.

Section Outline

IX. The Family History of Isaac (25:19–35:29) . . .
    I. Turning for Home (31:1–55)

Comment

31:1–3 It can hardly be surprising to Jacob that "Laban did not regard him with favor as before" (v. 2; Hb. "His face was not toward him"). Deceit always leaves a sour residue behind—even when someone "wins," everyone loses. Laban had been eager to retain Jacob's services when he observed the Lord's blessing him on Jacob's account (30:27), but when he and his sons see Jacob's prospering at their expense (31:1),[417] the advantages of Jacob's continued presence suddenly become far less obvious. Family members have been murdered for far less in the pages of Genesis (cf. ch. 4), and as a sojourner (*ger*; 32:4) Jacob has few rights and almost no protection from wider society. A convenient "accident" could easily be arranged for him, much as Joseph's brothers later plan for him (cf. ch. 37).

As a result, when God speaks to Jacob, calling him to return home to the "land of his fathers"[418] and promising him his continued presence and protection (31:3; cf. 28:15), Jacob is ready to leave. If everything had gone well between him and Laban, Jacob might never have left Paddan-aram. But when his life circumstances become difficult, he starts to think about a different future—and through these difficulties the Lord speaks to him to redirect his steps. No matter how much Laban's attitude toward Jacob might have changed, the Lord's remains unchanged.

31:4–16 Jacob invites his wives, Rachel and Leah, to meet him out in the field (31:4), where they will not be overheard. Bilhah and Zilpah, the two maidservants, are not invited; as concubines, it is assumed that they will go with their mistresses. The field is where "his flock" lies, a fact that implicitly contrasts them with Laban's flock and underlines the choice that must be made: Are Rachel and Leah with Jacob or with their father?

Jacob lays before Rachel and Leah the realities of their situation, highlighting the fact that the choice is not simply between Laban and Jacob but between Laban and Jacob and his God.[419] Their father's favor has turned away from Jacob, and his fortunes have diminished, but the favor of Jacob's God remains upon him (v. 5). Although Jacob has served their father faithfully, their father had not dealt fairly with Jacob—on the contrary, he has repeatedly sought to cheat Jacob (v. 7). Yet Jacob's God has been with him and protected him from harm at Laban's hands (v. 7). However many times Laban has written and rewritten the contract, the Lord has made sure that the outcome nevertheless favors Jacob, and the part of the flock designated as Jacob's has prospered while Laban's share has decreased. It is not clear whether we should take this language literally, as implying that the agreement with Laban and Jacob has gone through multiple iterations over the six years it has been in force, or whether Jacob is being hyperbolic in referring to Laban's untrustworthiness. Either way, the point is clear: the more Laban has sought to rob Jacob, the more the Lord has blessed Jacob and enhanced his wealth.

In Jacob's description of his success there is no mention of his own strategy with the tree branches (cf. 30:37–42). It appears that the dream Jacob received

---

[417] "Sons" in this context is perhaps not limited to Laban's immediate family but could include his wider kinship group. However, the passage poses a neat contrast between Laban's sons, who side with him, and his daughters, who abandon family loyalty to go with Jacob.
[418] That is, not simply the land where his ancestors happened to live, but the land promised to Abraham and Isaac by the Lord.
[419] Jacob calls him "the God of my father" (Gen. 31:5), connecting God's blessings on Jacob with the Abrahamic promise.

has finally gotten across the fundamental point that his prosperity rests in God and God alone, not on his own clever strategies. God is the one who has given him abundant flocks, not his knowledge (real or imagined) of animal husbandry. In his dream *all* the breeding flock were of the multicolored variety belonging to him, and so it is no wonder that the proportion of the flock belonging to him has steadily increased. God has seen Laban's trickery (31:12) and is vindicating Jacob's fundamental honesty in dealing with his father-in-law (30:33). In the process God is also fulfilling the promise he had made to Jacob at Bethel to protect and provide for him (31:13; cf. 28:18–22).

Rachel and Leah, for once operating together rather than as rivals, opt to stay with Jacob, although it has to be said that their motivation for the decision seems to be based more on financial calculation than on any romantic attachment. Here there is no declaration of undying love and commitment, such as we see from Ruth to Naomi (Ruth 1:16–17). Rather, the women simply see no future for themselves with their father, who has treated them like commodities, selling them to Jacob in return for fourteen years of his labor and then consuming the proceeds, leaving nothing for them to inherit from him (Gen. 31:14–16). If God has taken their inheritance from Laban and given it to Jacob, they might as well stay with him (v. 16). Although Jacob wins their vote, they do not sound as though they think the match their father arranged for them was exactly the catch of the century—merely the lesser of two evils. However, they are willing to leave their home and family and venture out with him, wherever his God is calling him to go, which is no small act of faith on their part. They renounce their loyalty to their father in favor of loyalty to Jacob.

31:17–21 Jacob owes Laban nothing. He has faithfully fulfilled the terms of their agreement, albeit with some defensive breeding practices to counter Laban's outright attempt to exploit him. Yet instead of going to Laban and announcing his departure publicly he tries to slip away like a fugitive while Laban is away shearing his sheep (v. 19).[420] This is understandable, perhaps, given the power imbalance between the two men and the bad feeling between Jacob and Laban's kinsmen, but it reflects a lack of trust in God's promise of protection for him. It is a further episode of deceit in a relationship marked out by that characteristic from the beginning (v. 20).

Having arrived in Paddan-aram empty handed, Jacob leaves weighed down with offspring and possessions. The extent of his acquisitions is underlined by the fact that he can afford to mount his wives and family on camels, which were rare and exotic beasts of burden in those days.[421] In addition to showcasing Jacob's wealth, the camels' ornate saddles later provide the opportunity for Rachel to conceal her purloined goods (cf. v. 34).

Thus far in the narrative the primary role of deceiver has been occupied by the menfolk, Jacob and Laban (though it should not be forgotten that Rebekah was the driver of Isaac's deception by Jacob in ch. 27). Now, however, Rachel reveals

---

[420] Sheep shearing was a lengthy operation involving all the men of the household and so provided a clear window during which Jacob could slip away unnoticed.
[421] On camels cf. comment on 12:10–20.

herself to be her father's daughter, stealing her "father's household gods" (Hb. *terafim*; 31:19). She probably rationalizes it as recompense for the bride price her father had consumed (v. 15), but the narrator is quite clear that this constitutes theft. The *terafim* were small household idols representing the deities who were expected to protect and provide for matters of daily domestic importance ("my gods"; v. 30).[422] These were the gods expected to "give us this day our daily bread," as it were. The name *terafim* may actually be a contemptuous way of referring to them by the biblical authors, as they do elsewhere with *gillulim* and *shikkutsim* (2 Kings 23:24), perhaps calling them "impotent things" or "decaying things."[423] The Bible knows that such idols are nonentities, without power either to bless or to curse.

Rachel perhaps steals the *terafim* not simply because of their monetary value. *Terafim* are often associated with divination in the biblical text (e.g., 1 Sam. 15:23), and it is possible that Rachel thinks their loss will hamper their father's ability to pursue them. Some commentators note the role that possession of the family *terafim* played in inheritance claims in the ancient world,[424] but this motivation seems less likely, since Jacob's family is comprehensively cutting ties with Laban and can hardly have imagined that they would share in his inheritance after his death. It is more likely that Rachel thinks the *terafim* themselves represent the inheritance that she deserves, in payment for her bride price.

Rachel is not the only person to have stolen something. The verb *ganab* is used no fewer than eight times in this chapter (Gen. 31:19, 20, 26, 27, 30, 32, 39 [2x]; in fact, nine times if one includes 30:33), in comparison to only two other uses in the book (40:15; 44:8). In addition to several references to literal theft, the term also occurs in an unusual idiom, in which Jacob "stole the heart of Laban the Aramean" (31:20, 26, 27 [without *leb*]). This is often translated contextually as something like "tricked" (ESV) or "deceived" (CSB), in light of the explanatory clause "By not telling him that he intended to flee." Several commentators note the similarity in sounds between *leb* ("heart") and Laban, as well as *ramah* ("deceived"; see Gen. 29:25) to Aramean.[425] Apart from this chapter, the idiom occurs only at 2 Samuel 15:6, where it refers to Absalom's stealing the affections of Israel away from David. That suggests that the choice of idiom here might refer to Jacob's success in stealing the affections of the daughters of Laban, which is a central concern in what follows. Jacob's method of secret flight is becoming habitual (cf. Gen. 27:43), but now Rebekah's command "Arise, flee" has been reversed: "Jacob fled ... and he arose" (31:21).[426] Jacob is on his way back home, a journey that starts with crossing a river, the Euphrates (v. 21; *hannahar*, "the River"; cf. ESV mg.) and ends with crossing another river, the Jabbok, in 32:22.[427]

---

422 Although on occasions they could be near life-size, as 1 Samuel 19:13 demonstrates. On the nature and function of the *terafim* cf. M. Greenberg, "Another Look at Rachel's Theft of the Teraphim," *JBL* 81 (1962): 239–248.
423 Waltke, *Genesis*, 427.
424 E.g., Kidner, *Genesis*, 176.
425 E.g., Hamilton, *Genesis 18–50*, 296.
426 Sarna, *Genesis*, 216.
427 Although there is nothing miraculous in either of Jacob's water crossings, the liminal role of these events parallels Israel's passage through the Red Sea into the wilderness and its exit from the wilderness by passing through the Jordan River.

31:22–35 Jacob's deception gives him a three-day head start over Laban (31:22) but does not prevent the kind of confrontation Jacob fears; it only delays it. Laban's pursuit surrounded by his kinsmen has overtones of a semimilitary operation or hostage-retrieval scenario (cf. 14:14–16). Given the difference of pace of travel between Jacob, with his flocks and family, and a lightly armed military detachment, it was always inevitable that Laban would catch up with Jacob sooner or later. The numbers of days are likely representative, since the distance between Paddan-aram and Gilead is around 400 miles (650 km), far further than Jacob could cover in ten days with his flocks of sheep.[428]

However, before Laban overtakes Jacob, God comes to Laban in a dream to warn him to tread carefully when encountering Jacob (the Hb. could be rendered "Be careful not to say anything to Jacob, good or bad"; 31:24; cf. 24:50). Dreams play an important role in Genesis as a means of communication between God and humanity. Jacob himself experienced a pivotal dream at Bethel in chapter 28, as well as another dream confirming God's protection of him against Laban's schemes earlier in this chapter (31:11), while Joseph's destiny will likewise be revealed in two dreams in chapter 37. However, the Lord can also use dreams to reveal himself to outsiders to the covenant, such as Abimelech (20:3), Pharoah's servants (ch. 40), and Pharoah himself (ch. 41). Dreams can serve to reveal aspects of the future, but they can also function as warnings to humans against particular courses of action, and it is the latter aspect that is in view here. It suggests that Laban did in fact have harm against Jacob in mind when he set out on his pursuit, but the divine intervention prevents him from such an outcome.

Despite the divine warning regarding his speech, Laban's tone of voice is decidedly aggrieved, suggesting that Jacob has essentially kidnapped his daughters by force (31:25). While he is undoubtedly correct that the proper protocol would have been for Jacob to be sent off by his uncle in style, with feasting and celebration, as with Abraham's servant (24:54–61),[429] there is little indication that such a departure would have been possible for Jacob. It is rather ironic for the man who has repeatedly deceived and defrauded his nephew to complain that Jacob has now done the same to him. Indeed, Laban's language leaves the impression that only God's warning is keeping him from harming Jacob. Even the portrayal of the two groups encamped in separate locations facing each other is more like that of warring armies than like that of a warm family reunion.[430]

Laban then moves on to the subject of his stolen gods (31:30). Jacob might well have responded that any gods worthy of worship would be powerful enough to prevent themselves from being misappropriated (cf. Isa. 44:9–20). Instead, however, he responds with aggrieved innocence. Unaware of Rachel's theft of the

---

[428] Sarna, *Genesis*, 217. Sarna suggests 6 miles (10 km) a day as a realistic rate of travel under these circumstances. It is possible, however, that the seven days refers to the speed with which Laban and his lightly burdened force cover the ground (Alter, *Five Books of Moses*, 170).
[429] The two passages are linked further by Laban's recognizing in each situation that, because this is from the Lord, he cannot speak anything good or bad (Gen. 24:50; cf. 31:24).
[430] Even the unusual verb used for pitching tents (Hb. *taka'*) has military connotations the other time it is used for such an activity (Jer. 6:3). Cf. Hamilton, *Genesis 18–50*, 300.

terafim, Jacob says, "Anyone with whom you find your gods shall not live" (Gen. 31:32; see a similar self-imprecation in Isa. 44:9). This raises the narrative tension considerably for the reader as Laban and his kinsmen search Jacob's camp, going from tent to tent until they finally close in on Rachel's (Gen. 31:33). However, our concern is misplaced. Rachel is craftier than both Jacob and Laban. She hides the idols in a camel's saddle, which doubles as a kind of ornate seat, and then reclines on them (v. 34).

To prevent Laban and his allies from searching in the crucial place, Rachel claims she cannot get up because the "way of women" is upon her (v. 35)—that is, that she is menstruating (cf. Gen. 18:11). This not only provides a convenient excuse for protecting the hiding place but (if true) is doubly insulting to Laban's deities, since menstruation would render a woman temporarily unclean (cf. Lev. 15:19–24)—an impurity that would be transmitted to everything she sat on, including the *terafim*. Rachel's excuse is sufficient to throw her father off the trail; the daughter who was the victim of her father's deceit many years earlier now returns the favor. But, although the idols remain safely undiscovered, Jacob's curse is nonetheless tragically prophetic. Within a few months Rachel will be dead, expiring in the course of giving birth to Benjamin (Gen. 35:16–19). The stolen household idols bring her nothing but trouble.

31:36–55 Now it is Jacob's turn to speak. Since Laban has searched the entire camp and found no stolen goods—though not because nothing had been stolen!—Jacob remonstrates with him over all the ways in which Laban took advantage of him during their time together. He served Laban faithfully for twenty years, fourteen for his daughters and six for his flocks, and during that time Laban repeatedly changed the terms of his employment (31:41). Meanwhile, Jacob's service as shepherd in Laban's employ had been entirely exemplary.[431] Normally in the ancient Near East a shepherd was not liable for incidental losses to the flock, such as by wild animals, provided he could prove the manner of the animal's death.[432] However, Laban had demanded Jacob reimburse him for any such losses, day or night, whatever the cause (v. 39). Unless his God had protected and provided for him, Jacob would have left Laban's service empty handed.

Laban's truculent response sounds like that of a naughty schoolboy caught in the act. He insists that Jacob's wives and flocks are still his but acknowledges that in the face of God's intervention on Jacob's side there is nothing he can do about the situation (v. 43). As a result, Laban proposes a covenant between the two. So Jacob sets up a *matsebah*, a standing stone, as a permanent reminder of their agreement, with a larger cairn of stones beside it (vv. 45–46), and they ratify the covenant with a meal together beside the stones (v. 46). Jacob commits himself not to mistreat his wives, Laban's daughters, nor to take other wives before them, and they both commit themselves not to pass that place in order to harm the other person. The

---

[431] Westermann (*Genesis 12–36*, 221) comments, "Jacob's summary of his labors helps us understand what the New Testament metaphor of the good shepherd is meant to express."
[432] Cf. Code of Hammurabi §266 (*ANET*, 177).

making of this covenant marks a change in their relationship. Laban and Jacob are no longer employer and employee, patron and client, but are now two equals, almost the representatives of two nations.[433]

Yet there is something uneven about the way in which the covenant is formulated, a difference highlighted in the fact that they name the memorial cairn the same thing in two different languages: Laban calls it Jegar-sahadutha, while Jacob calls it Galeed, both words meaning "heap of witness" in Aramaic and Hebrew, respectively.[434] Laban frames their covenant in the form of his religious understanding, swearing by the God (or gods) of Abraham *and* the God (or gods) of Nahor (Gen. 31:53; cf. Josh. 24:2). Laban thinks of these authorities as distinct and plural gods, as the plural verb form in the Hebrew shows.[435] Jacob, however, takes his oath in the name of the Fear of his father Isaac (Gen. 31:53),[436] the God of his experience at Bethel, the same God who had been watching over him throughout his time with Laban (v. 42). This God is a fear-inducing God—hence the appropriateness of the name "the Fear of Isaac." He is a deity capable of demanding the sacrifice of a beloved only son. Jacob's awareness of his God is a far more personal experience than that of his uncle Laban.

The peaceful separation of the two parties, despite the underlying tensions, is a mark of the Lord at work, as was the case in Genesis 21; 26. Laban arises early in the morning, kisses his daughters and grandchildren (but apparently not Jacob, in contrast to his arrival in 29:13), and departs back to his home (31:55). Jacob is now likewise headed back to his home, with his father-in-law's blessing (v. 55), which subtly highlights the challenge that will face him on his return to a land still occupied by his brother, Esau, whose blessing and birthright he earlier stole.

Response

It was God's time for Jacob to leave Laban and go back to the Promised Land, but the manner of leaving was pure Jacob: that is, it was governed by the fear of man rather than by the fear of God (even the God he himself called "the Fear of Isaac"; v. 42). Jacob could have left Paddan-aram with his head held high; he certainly had nothing to apologize for, having behaved responsibly throughout his relationship with Laban, as he made clear when his uncle finally caught up with him. However,

---

[433] Though, as Hamilton points out, Jacob says only two Hebrew words in this entire covenant-ratification process ("Gather stones"; Gen. 31:46), and these are said to his kinsmen, not to Laban. Laban is the one who initiates the pact and describes in detail that to which is being agreed. Having said his piece in verses 36–42, Jacob apparently has nothing more to say to his father-in-law (*Genesis 18–50*, 314).

[434] The heap of stones was also named Mizpah ("watchtower") by Laban, underlining his request that the Lord would watch over the enforcement of their agreement when they were no longer together (Gen. 31:49).

[435] The SP and LXX have a singular verb, which reflects a tendency to smooth the text's awkwardness by identifying the gods of the two parties with one another. On this cf. Edward J. Young, "The God of the Fathers," *WTJ* 3 (1940): 34.

[436] The patriarchs, in keeping with some other ancient Near Eastern texts, refer regularly to the Lord as "the God of the Father." The formula "The God of your father" is never used by Abraham because in the person of Abraham a distinctly new relationship had begun: God was not the God of Terah in the way he became Abraham's God. It was with Abraham that God first entered into covenant to be his God and the God of his descendants after him (Gen. 17:7). As a result, the title "the God of Abraham" was used first in divine address to Isaac in 26:24. Likewise, the title "the God of Isaac" appears when God addresses Jacob at Bethel (Gen. 28:13), and the title "the God of Jacob" does not appear until Exodus 3:6. Thereafter "the God of Abraham, Isaac, and Jacob" is ubiquitous throughout the OT, alongside "the God of [the people] Israel."

he did not trust the Lord to protect him and his family from Laban, and so he sought to sneak away undetected. In this case, Jacob's stratagem did not work; he still had to have that difficult encounter with his father-in-law, yet in the end it turned out to be much less threatening than he had anticipated, because the Lord had gone ahead of him in the matter. So too we are often inclined to place our trust in clever and deceptive strategies to keep ourselves safe in dangerous situations rather than relying on the Lord to protect us.

Rachel added to the complications of Jacob's situation by stealing the *terafim*. This evidenced a lack of trust in the Lord to provide for her. She did not need to steal these gods in order to provide for her needs; the Lord had already provided for her many times over and would continue to do so. During the journey the idols became so much useless and dangerous baggage, as Laban pursued the family looking for them (Gen. 31:30–32). Later they probably ended up with the other idols, unceremoniously buried by the oak at Shechem like the trash that they were (35:2–4). Not only did these gods do nothing for Rachel, but Jacob's imprecatory oath ("Anyone with whom you find your gods shall not live"; 31:32) would be fulfilled in her subsequent death in childbirth (35:19). How often do we, like Rachel, lack trust in God and so resort to trusting in our idols to meet our needs, even though they cannot help us but often become a great hindrance to our souls?

That is why we need a God whom we love for his grace as much as we fear him for his awesome magnificence and holiness. This is the God whose grace was abundantly evident in his faithful love to Jacob and Rachel (and Leah!), who were far from devoting their lives completely and utterly to the Lord. He is the God whose grace is similarly evident in our lives, as he continues his slow, sanctifying work in us, even though we persist in carrying our own personal household idols around everywhere we go.

Unlike Jacob, who went out into the wilderness with nothing and became rich there through God's blessing, the Lord Jesus left behind the glories of heaven and for our sakes went out into this sin-stricken world with nothing. Instead of trying to save himself through deceptive words, Jesus at the cross took upon himself the wrath of God and the curse we deserved for our idolatry, deceit, and trickery. At Calvary God sacrificed his one beloved Son so that lost wanderers like Jacob and Rachel—and you and me—might be forgiven and might enjoy life in all its fullness.

GENESIS 32

32 Jacob went on his way, and the angels of God met him. ² And when Jacob saw them he said, "This is God's camp!" So he called the name of that place Mahanaim.¹

³ And Jacob sent² messengers before him to Esau his brother in the land of Seir, the country of Edom, ⁴ instructing them, "Thus you shall say to my lord Esau: Thus says your servant Jacob, 'I have sojourned with Laban and stayed until now. ⁵ I have oxen, donkeys, flocks, male servants, and female servants. I have sent to tell my lord, in order that I may find favor in your sight.'"

⁶ And the messengers returned to Jacob, saying, "We came to your brother Esau, and he is coming to meet you, and there are four hundred men with him." ⁷ Then Jacob was greatly afraid and distressed. He divided the people who were with him, and the flocks and herds and camels, into two camps, ⁸ thinking, "If Esau comes to the one camp and attacks it, then the camp that is left will escape."

⁹ And Jacob said, "O God of my father Abraham and God of my father Isaac, O LORD who said to me, 'Return to your country and to your kindred, that I may do you good,' ¹⁰ I am not worthy of the least of all the deeds of steadfast love and all the faithfulness that you have shown to your servant, for with only my staff I crossed this Jordan, and now I have become two camps. ¹¹ Please deliver me from the hand of my brother, from the hand of Esau, for I fear him, that he may come and attack me, the mothers with the children. ¹² But you said, 'I will surely do you good, and make your offspring as the sand of the sea, which cannot be numbered for multitude.'"

¹³ So he stayed there that night, and from what he had with him he took a present for his brother Esau, ¹⁴ two hundred female goats and twenty male goats, two hundred ewes and twenty rams, ¹⁵ thirty milking camels and their calves, forty cows and ten bulls, twenty female donkeys and ten male donkeys. ¹⁶ These he handed over to his servants, every drove by itself, and said to his servants, "Pass on ahead of me and put a space between drove and drove." ¹⁷ He instructed the first, "When Esau my brother meets you and asks you, 'To whom do you belong? Where are you going? And whose are these ahead of you?' ¹⁸ then you shall say, 'They belong to your servant Jacob. They are a present sent to my lord Esau. And moreover, he is behind us.'" ¹⁹ He likewise instructed the second and the third and all who followed the droves, "You shall say the same thing to Esau when you find him, ²⁰ and you shall say, 'Moreover, your servant Jacob is behind us.'" For he thought, "I may appease him³ with the present that goes ahead of me, and afterward I shall see his face. Perhaps he will accept me."⁴ ²¹ So the present passed on ahead of him, and he himself stayed that night in the camp.

²² The same night he arose and took his two wives, his two female servants, and his eleven children,⁵ and crossed the ford of the Jabbok. ²³ He took them and sent them across the stream, and everything else that he

had. ²⁴ And Jacob was left alone. And a man wrestled with him until the breaking of the day. ²⁵ When the man saw that he did not prevail against Jacob, he touched his hip socket, and Jacob's hip was put out of joint as he wrestled with him. ²⁶ Then he said, "Let me go, for the day has broken." But Jacob said, "I will not let you go unless you bless me." ²⁷ And he said to him, "What is your name?" And he said, "Jacob." ²⁸ Then he said, "Your name shall no longer be called Jacob, but Israel,⁶ for you have striven with God and with men, and have prevailed." ²⁹ Then Jacob asked him, "Please tell me your name." But he said, "Why is it that you ask my name?" And there he blessed him. ³⁰ So Jacob called the name of the place Peniel,⁷ saying, "For I have seen God face to face, and yet my life has been delivered." ³¹ The sun rose upon him as he passed Penuel, limping because of his hip. ³² Therefore to this day the people of Israel do not eat the sinew of the thigh that is on the hip socket, because he touched the socket of Jacob's hip on the sinew of the thigh.

¹ *Mahanaim* means *two camps* ² Or *had sent* ³ Hebrew *appease his face* ⁴ Hebrew *he will lift my face* ⁵ Or *sons* ⁶ *Israel* means *He strives with God*, or *God strives* ⁷ *Peniel* means *the face of God*

Section Overview

When Jacob turned his thoughts toward home, he knew he would have to surmount several potential hurdles. Prominent in his thinking would have been the challenge of safely extricating himself and his family from the clutches of Laban, a task negotiated successfully in chapter 31. He would also have been thinking ahead to the challenges of meeting his brother, Esau, once again, as is clear from the way Jacob organizes his family for the journey. Esau had been breathing murderous threats against Jacob when he left Canaan (27:41) That encounter awaits in chapter 33.

Genesis 32, however, is taken up by the conflict that Jacob almost certainly did not foresee but which is actually far more critical to the success of his return to the Promised Land than either of the other encounters. Ultimately it is not the blessing of Laban or Esau that will determine Jacob's destiny but the Lord's blessing. Jacob has spent much of his life wrestling with the wrong people, in pursuit of the blessing he was promised as a gift before he was even born (25:23), but in Genesis 32 Jacob will wrestle with God himself. Remarkably, Jacob will prevail in that encounter—not through superior strength or guile but simply by clinging to God and refusing to let him go. It is this persistent commitment to seek blessing from God alone that earns him the new name Israel, which will be the definitive identity of the people who will come from his offspring.

Section Outline

IX. The Family History of Isaac (25:19–35:29) . . .
    J. Wrestling with God (32:1–32)

Comment

32:1–2 As he goes on his journey back home, having put Paddan-aram in the rearview mirror, Jacob is immediately encouraged by an enigmatic meeting with angels (v. 1). We are not told that the angels bring him anything or provide for him in any way, so it seems likely that their presence represents the Lord's protection of him on his journey. God's angels are always present to guard and protect his own, whether we see them or not (cf. 2 Kings 6:15–17). As the psalmist puts it, "The angel of the LORD encamps around those who fear him, and delivers them" (Ps. 34:7). In this instance, however, the Lord opens Jacob's eyes to enable him to see the angelic host keeping guard over him. They had been prepared to protect him against Laban, and they stand ready to guard him from Esau as well.[437]

Jacob names the place of his encounter with the angels Mahanaim ("Two camps") in recognition of the event. In the Hebrew numerous verbal connections link Jacob's experience at Mahanaim to his former vision of the Lord and the stone staircase at Bethel (Genesis 28).[438] His wilderness years outside the Land of Promise are thus bracketed by these two visions of angels, a drawing back of the veil that has enabled Jacob to recognize God's unseen presence with him throughout the intervening period (cf. 31:5). Here is not only the camp of Jacob but the camp of God as well (32:2). This assurance would have been particularly meaningful to the original readers of Genesis, accustomed as they were to camping in the wilderness, by reminding them that the angels of God accompanied them too on every step of their own journey to the Promised Land.

32:3–6 Jacob now prepares to meet with his brother, Esau,[439] who by this time is living near Mount Seir in the area that will become known as Edom,[440] to the east of the Jordan (v. 3). It would be possible for Jacob to return to the Land of Promise without meeting Esau, since the road from Paddan-aram to Canaan does not run through Edom, but to his credit Jacob as a top priority seeks to set things right in that relationship. He therefore sends messengers ahead of him to Esau with instructions to tell Esau that (1) Jacob has been staying with Laban up until this point (and therefore setting things right with Esau is his first priority on his return to Canaan) and (2) he has prospered during his stay with Laban (and thus will not be a burden to Esau in any way; vv. 4–5). It is notable that when giving the inventory of his possessions Jacob omits mention of his camels, the rarest and most valuable of his items.

The messengers that Jacob sends to his brother correspond to God's messengers that he received earlier (v. 3; in Hb. the word for "messenger" and "angel" is the same: Hb. *mal'ak*). They go bearing gifts and a carefully crafted message of repentance. Jacob describes himself as "your servant" and Esau as "my lord" (v. 4). He thus voluntarily reclaims the position of subordinate younger brother, which he had

---

[437] Westermann, *Genesis 12–36*, 225.
[438] See the verbal correspondences laid out in Mathews, *Genesis 11:27–50:26*, 547.
[439] The text stresses the fact the Esau is Jacob's brother, recalling Jacob's deception of their father in Genesis 27:23, 30.
[440] Sarna (*Genesis*, 224) points out that all three words, "Seir," "country" (*sadeh*), and "Edom" (Gen. 32:3), evoke memories of Esau: he is hairy (*sa'ir*), a man of the fields (*sadeh*), and red (*'adom*) in his complexion. Edom—outside the Promised Land—is Esau's natural habitat, as it were.

schemed and worked so hard to get out from in his earlier life. Jacob's only desire is to find favor in Esau's sight and for their fraternal relationship to be restored (v. 5).

However, Esau's initial response is more threatening than encouraging. The messengers return with the news that Esau is coming out to meet Jacob with four hundred men (v. 6). This is far more than what would be necessary to form a welcoming committee and sounds more like a small army. (For comparison, Abraham took 318 armed men with him to take on the mighty armies of the four kings in Gen. 14:14; cf. David's force of 400 men in 1 Sam. 22:2.)[441] This force would be more than large enough to wreak havoc on Jacob's flocks and family.

32:7–12 Jacob's response of fear is understandable under the circumstances. His faith in God's calling to return to the land is being put to the test. He has the resources, humanly speaking, to make his way elsewhere in the world and to avoid a threatening encounter with Esau. It is a mark of his trust in the Lord, however, bolstered by his earlier vision of the angelic host surrounding his camp, that he continues on his course to return to the Promised Land. He also devises a plan to protect his family and resources by dividing them into two distinct camps, so that, if one is attacked, the other might still escape (vv. 7–8).

More significantly, however, Jacob prays (v. 9). This is the first time in the narrative that we have seen Jacob praying rather than relying on clever strategies.[442] Jacob's prayer begins with an affirmation of God's past faithfulness to his promises (v. 9), the kind of recitation of God's history of goodness that is common in Psalms.[443] He acknowledges that God has fulfilled everything he had said he would do for Jacob in Genesis 28, using the plural of *khesed* as an intensifier to describe the "deeds of steadfast love" that the Lord has shown him (32:10). At the same time Jacob also proclaims his personal unworthiness of God's favor (v. 10). It is hardly a coincidence that Jacob proclaims himself to be God's servant for the first time on the same day he declares himself to be Esau's servant. Jacob has come to see that in God's program growing greater means becoming smaller (cf. Mark 9:35). Jacob is growing in his humility and his dependence upon God.

As a result, the essence of Jacob's plea to God in his prayer is for God to continue to fulfill his promises to him, and before him to Abraham (Gen. 32:12). He acknowledges his own fear of Esau, who could attack Jacob along with his wives and children (v. 11). Yet these are the same children whom God had promised Abraham to make as numerous as the sand of the sea (v. 12; cf. 22:17), and thus they merit his protection.

32:13–23 After spending another night at Mahanaim under the protection of God's angels, Jacob sends a caravan of gifts ahead of him (32:13–21). These gifts are designated *minkhah*, a word that means "homage" or "tribute,"[444] offerings made by an

---

[441] Alter, *Five Books of Moses*, 177.
[442] Jan P. Fokkelman, "Genesis," in *The Literary Guide to the Bible*, ed. Robert Alter and Frank Kermode (Cambridge, MA: Harvard University Press, 1987), 50.
[443] Westermann, *Genesis 12–36*, 226.
[444] S.v. מִנְחָה, *HALOT*, 2.601, A3 ("homage") and A5 ("tribute").

inferior to a superior. The catalog of Jacob's gifts is overwhelming: herds of goats and sheep and expensive camels and donkeys,[445] underlining the depth of Jacob's self-humiliation and his desire to make up for the blessing he had stolen. Then, after all these gifts have been received by Esau—in wave upon wave of generosity—Jacob will come last, hoping to receive Esau's favor (v. 20). The brother who previously fought for first place is finally content to be last.

The implication of the gifts is to be reinforced by the explicit instructions given by Jacob to his servants. Each of them is to say to Esau that his offering is a gift from *your servant* Jacob to *my lord* Esau (v. 18). In this way Jacob hopes to turn aside Esau's wrath and thus be able to see his face (v. 20)—not just to meet him but to be received before him with favor. The language is religious in nature, similar in vocabulary and form to that used in seeking favor and acceptance from a deity by means of sacrifice (cf. Ex. 32:30). It is easy to see the repetition of "face" in Hebrew; Jacob hopes to "cover Esau's face" with his gift so that Esau might "lift up Jacob's face" and enable Jacob to "see Esau's face."[446] Of course, as it transpires, the "face" Jacob really needs to see is God's—an encounter that will occur later in this chapter.

Meanwhile, Jacob sends his wives, his children,[447] and his flocks over the Jabbok River, one of the major tributaries of the Jordan, while he remains alone on the other side (Gen. 32:21–23). It is unclear precisely why he does this. Perhaps Jacob thinks that if Esau encounters the women and children before encountering Jacob he might be more sympathetic, or perhaps it as an act of cowardice on Jacob's part. John Currid suggests that Jacob actually sends the family back across the Jabbok from south to north, putting Jacob alone between his family and Esau's men,[448] though that would seem to reverse the geographical logic of the passage. Sarna's suggestion that Jacob intends to minimize the time between the gifts' arriving with Esau and the family's following them seems more likely.[449] His own remaining behind seems to be motivated by a desire to spend time in prayer with God prior to meeting Esau.

32:24–32 As so often, the biblical text reports an extraordinary event in very prosaic terms. While Jacob is alone—presumably in prayer—a man comes and assaults him, not merely striking him with one or two blows but wrestling with him for hours, until daybreak (v. 24). What is in view here is a monumental struggle for Jacob, a struggle he cannot win but which he is determined not to lose. The power of Jacob's opponent is evident from the easy way in which he dislocates Jacob's hip when he chooses to do so (v. 25). Clearly this man could kill Jacob if he chose to do so. Yet even when the struggle cripples Jacob's hip and Jacob can do no more than cling to his adversary, he does just that and will not let him go until he

---

[445] It is notable that, whereas the sheep, donkeys, and cows all include male and female specimens, the camels are all female (with their calves; 32:15). This would have prevented Esau from developing his own self-sustaining herd of camels, thus maintaining their rarity value.
[446] Hamilton, *Genesis 18–50*, 326.
[447] Eleven sons are mentioned, since Benjamin is not born and Dinah (along with other daughters, perhaps) does not count in the dynastic line.
[448] Currid, *Genesis 25:19–50:26*, 133.
[449] Sarna, *Genesis*, 226.

receives from him a blessing (v. 26). Finally, when the day is breaking, Jacob receives the blessing he seeks—and along with the blessing a new name: "Israel," "for you have striven with God and with men, and have prevailed" (v. 28).[450]

All Jacob's life thus far has been spent struggling with men, especially Esau and Laban, in an attempt to prevail over them and win the blessing. Yet everything Jacob has attained has been received not because of his struggles but because the Lord has been with him. Now in this climactic encounter Jacob wrestles with God and not man, and he prevails not by overthrowing his opponent—an impossible task—but simply by clinging to him in his wounded state and refusing to let go. Jacob has finally realized that God—and God alone—is the one with whom he has needed to wrestle in order to receive his blessing.

That transformation in Jacob is marked by the new name, Israel (v. 28). The original etymology and meaning of this name are obscure,[451] but in context the name is taken to indicate a shift from man to God as the opponent of Jacob's striving. What is particularly striking about this name change is that his new name is not a variant or an extension of his previous name, as with Abram/Abraham and Sarai/Sarah, but rather a total transformation of his identity. His lifelong attempt to gain the promised blessing by ingenuity and striving rather than by grace must now be abandoned. However, perhaps because that sanctifying transformation is partial in all of us in this life, Jacob's name change is still only partial. Unlike Abraham and Sarah, who, once given their new names, never revert to their old ones, Jacob is from now on both Jacob *and* Israel. The biblical text alternates between the two designations for the patriarch, not because it comes to us from two different sources, as scholars have sometimes argued, but because Jacob/Israel has two warring natures. God's transforming work is established in principle in this man's life, as the new name declares, but it will take a lifetime for that principle to work itself out in fullness. As long as "Israel" lives here on earth, part of him will still always be "Jacob."

It is significant that the crucial encounter with God climaxes at daybreak, just as the encounter at Bethel began at sunset. The intervening period, while Jacob has been out of the Land of Promise, has been one long night. God has been with Jacob to protect and bless him, but now he will be with Jacob in a new way as the dawn breaks on his renewed sojourn in the land. A new day is quite literally dawning for Jacob—and in him for all humanity.

Jacob obtains what he had sought from this encounter, as he sees God face to face and receives God's blessing. Yet in this instance meeting with God leads not to peace and healing for Jacob but rather to an enduring, painful crippling of his hip. Jacob will forever bear in his body the marks of this excruciating yet grace-filled encounter, in which to survive and to cling to the Lord was to triumph. Thereafter

---

450 It is striking that Jacob does not receive an answer to his inquiry about the Lord's name, unlike Moses at the burning bush (Ex. 3:13–14), and Jacob's own new name, Israel, is built around the divine appellation El. This plausibly fits with the theory that the divine name Yahweh was not actually revealed until the time of the exodus. Cf. comment on 4:25–26.

451 Cf. Sarna, *Genesis*, 404. Names of this pattern would normally be taken to mean something like "God strives [for him]" or "Let God strive [for him]" (cf. the meaning of Jerubbaal ["Let Baal contend"] in Judges 6:32).

his descendants memorialize Jacob's encounter by not eating the meat attached to the socket of the hip as a permanent reminder of this reality (v. 32).

Response

Jacob's painful wrestling with God points us clearly to the cross. Having completed his wrestling with man throughout his earthly life, Jesus Christ wrestled with God on our behalf so that grace and blessing might flow to his people. He wrestled with the difficult and painful will of God in the garden, crying out, "If it be possible, let this cup pass from me" (Matt. 26:39). He wrestled with the holy and fearsome wrath of God on the cross in that awful moment when he cried out, "My God, my God, why have you forsaken me?" (Matt. 27:46). The outcome of his wrestling was not merely a crippled hip; he was wounded and bruised for us, he was flogged and crucified, burdened with the whole weight of our transgressions. But in the midst of that painful trial Jesus clung to God and would not let him go unless he received a blessing—not for himself but for us, his people. Through Jesus' faithful clinging to the Father he has prevailed over sin and death and, risen from the dead, has been given the name above every name.

Jesus is the true Israel, with no Jacob mixed in; he is the one who has in fullness struggled with God and man and has overcome. As we are united to Christ, we in turn are given a new name as Christians and become part of the Israel of God (Gal. 6:16). As we do so, we are called to participate in Christ's struggles and suffering as well as in his victory, overcoming the world through our faith (1 John 5:4). Jesus struggled on the cross not so that we might never have to struggle but so that our struggles might conform us into his image (Phil. 3:10–11).

In our struggles and suffering we are taught to abandon our self-dependence and look to the cross, clinging to God alone for blessing. When we fear God, we have nothing else to fear. When we cling to him with all our strength, we will find that he will not let us go. Even when we feel too weak to cling to him and too fearful to hold on to him a second longer, we still find that his strong arms are encircling us in his love and that the Good Shepherd will not let us go. His strength is not empowered by our strength; rather, it is made perfect in our weakness (2 Cor. 12:9).

What is more, we too are called regularly to memorialize Christ's great battle on our behalf in our eating of the Lord's Supper. There we remember Christ's wrestling on the cross. When we eat the bread, we remember the tearing apart of his body for us. When we drink the cup, we recall the shedding of his blood for our transgressions. There we cling to God and ask him to fulfill his promises to us and in us. At the table our souls are fed once again with God's assurance that, no matter what difficulties may face us in this life, the love of God has chosen us for blessing in Christ, and he will not let us go.

GENESIS 33

33 And Jacob lifted up his eyes and looked, and behold, Esau was coming, and four hundred men with him. So he divided the children among Leah and Rachel and the two female servants. ² And he put the servants with their children in front, then Leah with her children, and Rachel and Joseph last of all. ³ He himself went on before them, bowing himself to the ground seven times, until he came near to his brother.

⁴ But Esau ran to meet him and embraced him and fell on his neck and kissed him, and they wept. ⁵ And when Esau lifted up his eyes and saw the women and children, he said, "Who are these with you?" Jacob said, "The children whom God has graciously given your servant." ⁶ Then the servants drew near, they and their children, and bowed down. ⁷ Leah likewise and her children drew near and bowed down. And last Joseph and Rachel drew near, and they bowed down. ⁸ Esau said, "What do you mean by all this company[1] that I met?" Jacob answered, "To find favor in the sight of my lord." ⁹ But Esau said, "I have enough, my brother; keep what you have for yourself." ¹⁰ Jacob said, "No, please, if I have found favor in your sight, then accept my present from my hand. For I have seen your face, which is like seeing the face of God, and you have accepted me. ¹¹ Please accept my blessing that is brought to you, because God has dealt graciously with me, and because I have enough." Thus he urged him, and he took it.

¹² Then Esau said, "Let us journey on our way, and I will go ahead of[2] you." ¹³ But Jacob said to him, "My lord knows that the children are frail, and that the nursing flocks and herds are a care to me. If they are driven hard for one day, all the flocks will die. ¹⁴ Let my lord pass on ahead of his servant, and I will lead on slowly, at the pace of the livestock that are ahead of me and at the pace of the children, until I come to my lord in Seir."

¹⁵ So Esau said, "Let me leave with you some of the people who are with me." But he said, "What need is there? Let me find favor in the sight of my lord." ¹⁶ So Esau returned that day on his way to Seir. ¹⁷ But Jacob journeyed to Succoth, and built himself a house and made booths for his livestock. Therefore the name of the place is called Succoth.[3]

¹⁸ And Jacob came safely[4] to the city of Shechem, which is in the land of Canaan, on his way from Paddan-aram, and he camped before the city. ¹⁹ And from the sons of Hamor, Shechem's father, he bought for a hundred pieces of money[5] the piece of land on which he had pitched his tent. ²⁰ There he erected an altar and called it El-Elohe-Israel.[6]

[1] Hebrew *camp* [2] Or *along with* [3] *Succoth* means *booths* [4] Or *peacefully* [5] Hebrew *a hundred qesitah*; a unit of money of uncertain value [6] *El-Elohe-Israel* means *God, the God of Israel*

Section Overview

Jacob has dreaded meeting his brother, Esau, and with good reason. The last time Jacob met him, Esau was threatening to kill him (27:41), and the last news he had was that Esau was approaching with four hundred men (32:6). Yet, when the meeting between the brothers actually occurs, it is rather anticlimactic. This is due in part to the fact that Jacob has just met with God (32:24–29); after such an encounter, any human meeting would necessarily be anticlimactic. But it is due also to the Lord's preparing the way for Jacob. Jacob's fears of an unfriendly welcome turn out to be unfounded, and indeed he has to deal with the opposite problem: an invitation to live with Esau (33:12–16), which would mean settling once again outside the borders of the Land of Promise.

Apart from the outcome of the meeting between the two brothers, the encounter is interesting primarily for what it reveals about how their hearts have changed or remained the same over the intervening twenty years. Both have prospered in worldly goods in the meantime, but, while Jacob is quick to attribute his prosperity to the Lord (v. 11), Esau makes no such connection (v. 9). Jacob has clearly grown spiritually through all the challenges he has faced, while Esau—whose path through life seems to have been relatively plain sailing in comparison—has remained the same, completely lacking in any spiritual interest or discernment. Esau may have lost the Abrahamic blessing to his younger brother through God's choice (25:23), but he does not seem to have felt its absence. As long as Esau has worldly prosperity, that is sufficient for him.

Section Outline

IX. The Family History of Isaac (25:19–35:29) . . .
   K. Meeting Esau (33:1–20)

Comment

33:1–3 Jacob's wrestling match with God is scarcely over before his brother Esau is upon him, with his threatening company of four hundred men (v. 1). Fearing the worst, Jacob splits up his caravan into different groups, so that, if some are attacked, the others might have a chance to escape. Significantly, he puts the maidservants and their children at the front, in the most dangerous position, followed by Leah and her children, with his favorites Rachel and Joseph at the rear, where the prospect of escape would be highest (v. 2).[452] He himself, however, goes first of all, in the position of greatest danger, prostrating himself to the ground seven times, indicating his complete abasement before his brother (v. 3).[453] Previously, he had sought to grasp the right to be lord over his brother (25:23), taking for himself his father's blessing ("Be lord over your brothers, and may your mother's sons bow down to you"; 27:29), but now he is the one bowing before his brother.

33:4–11 The hostility that Jacob had feared does not materialize. On the contrary Esau runs to meet him—in contrast to Jacob's awkward limp—and embraces

---

452 Mathews, *Genesis 11:27–50:26*, 566. Joseph is the only named child in this arrangement, highlighting his position as favorite. He is also the only child mentioned by name in Genesis 33:7.
453 Sarna (*Genesis*, 229) notes references to seven-fold prostration before Pharaoh in the Amarna letters, written from vassal kings of Canaanite city-states to Pharaoh, most likely in the fourteenth century BC.

him, falling on Jacob's neck and kissing him in a tumbling sequence of verbs that stresses the rapidity of the actions (33:4; cf. 29:13, as well as the return of the prodigal son in Luke 15:20).[454] In place of the wrestling and bitter conflict that had characterized Jacob and Esau's earlier relationship there is now hugging and joyful weeping. The deception of Isaac that had led to the rift between the brothers in the first place was sealed with a kiss (Gen. 27:26), and so too is the brothers' final reconciliation. In certain previous encounters that might have been expected to be hostile the Lord had explicitly intervened to ensure that they were at least civil (20:3; 31:24), and a similar work may be involved here, though none is explicitly described. However, the change in Esau's heart is far more comprehensive, as he gives Jacob an effusive welcome.

Esau then "lifted up his eyes" (33:5), just as Jacob had done earlier (v. 1), seeing Jacob's wives and children approaching, along with his flocks, which leads Esau to ask who these people are and why Jacob has sent the many flocks ahead of his party. Both questions give Jacob the opportunity to testify to the effects of God's grace in his life. They are "the children whom God has graciously given" (v. 5), and the goal of the gifts is "to find favor in the sight of my lord" (v. 8). Jacob credits the Lord with all that he has acquired and once again positions himself in the inferior position relative to Esau. He likens seeing Esau's face and being received by him to "seeing the face of God" (v. 10), a comparison that is particularly weighty in light of the events of the previous chapter. On the one hand, meeting Esau has been the goal of his endeavors; Jacob wants more than anything else in this world to be in a right relationship with the one whom he had earlier so wronged. It is as desirable as seeing the face of God. On the other hand, however, seeing the face of God is an extremely dangerous business. Not many people see God and live, so in 32:30 Jacob had exclaimed in amazement, "I have seen God face to face, and yet my life has been delivered." Jacob was willing to take that risk to restore the relationship with his brother. He even calls the gifts "my blessing" (33:11),[455] which highlights his desire to make restitution for the blessing he stole from Esau.

Yet if God's name is repeatedly on Jacob's lips in this encounter (vv. 5, 10, 11), God is never mentioned by Esau. Esau acknowledges that he too has plenty (v. 9), but there is no gratitude or acknowledgement of divine provision. In Esau's mind the loss of divine blessing has made little or no difference in his life. He has an abundance of the world's goods, and that is enough for him. Yet, when Jacob continues to press him, Esau accepts the gifts Jacob has offered as a confirmation of their new relationship of friendship.[456] Although Jacob repeatedly addresses his

---

[454] Hamilton, *Genesis 18–50*, 344.
[455] In describing God's abundant provision for his needs Jacob carefully speaks of God's gracious gift rather than of God's blessing (Gen. 33:5), which he stole from his brother. Jacob first calls his own gift to his brother "tribute" (Hb. *minkhah*), such as an inferior owes to a superior (33:10). Only after this does Jacob specifically call that which he is giving his brother a "blessing" (*berakah*; 33:11). Cf. Westermann, *Genesis 12–36*, 233.
[456] The formal refusal of Jacob's offer in Genesis 33:9 is to be understood as a standard part of ancient Near Eastern culture, where a gift must initially be refused before it can be accepted (cf. the interaction between Abraham and the Hittites in Genesis 23; cf. Sarna, *Genesis*, 230).

brother deferentially as "my lord," Esau in his response names Jacob "my brother" (v. 9)—not merely as a statement of fact but at last as a term of endearment.

33:12–17 Esau's enmity toward his brother has been so overcome that he proposes that Jacob journey with him to Mount Seir in Edom (v. 12; cf. vv. 14–16). However, that is outside the Promised Land, and Jacob had earlier vowed to return to Bethel (28:19–22). Jacob does not seem strong enough in his convictions at this point to be honest with Esau about his intentions, however. As a result, he dissembles, claiming (truthfully) that his children and flocks require him to travel at a much slower pace than Esau and his men, so Esau should go ahead of him and allow Jacob to follow him to Seir (33:14). When Esau offers to leave some of his men with Jacob to travel with him for protection, Jacob also begs off (v. 15).

Meanwhile, as Esau makes his way south to his home in distant Seir, Jacob travels only as far as Succoth, in the Jordan Valley, where he settles for a while— long enough to build a house and the shelters for his cattle from which Succoth ("Shelters") receives its name (vv. 16–17).[457] Although Jacob has achieved a reconciliation with his brother, the difference in their worldviews is such that they cannot live side by side.

33:18–20 Although Succoth will later be reckoned as part of the Promised Land in the territory of Gad (Josh. 13:27), it is still east of the Jordan and thus not part of the land of Canaan proper. As a result, Jacob's journey home is not complete until he leaves Succoth and travels on to Shechem, which we are explicitly told "is in the land of Canaan" (Gen. 33:18). Only then, when Jacob has arrived back in the land "in peace" (Hb. *shalem*), is the Lord's promise in 28:15 complete (cf. 28:21; *beshalem*, "in peace").

Yet it is here at Shechem that Jacob's journey stops, with the tragic consequences that are recounted in the next chapter. Instead of proceeding back to Bethel to fulfill his vow to the Lord (28:20–22), Jacob camps in front of the city of Shechem and purchases a piece of ground from the inhabitants of the city, the sons of Hamor, for one hundred *qesitah* (ESV: "pieces of money"; 33:19).[458] There he settles down and builds an altar, naming it for "El, the God of Israel" (v. 20; cf. ESV mg.).

Although Jacob was right not to join forces with his brother, Esau, and journey to Seir, his sojourns at both Succoth and Shechem represent a falling short of full obedience. Building a house (*beth*) at Succoth contrasts sharply with traveling to God's house at *Beth-El*, while buying a piece of property at Shechem from the Canaanite inhabitants of the land is the opposite of receiving it as the Lord's gift. It suggests that Jacob is in danger of being assimilated into the existing population,

---

[457] Though Succoth is west of Peniel rather than south, it is quite likely that Esau would travel through it and then go south down the Jordan Valley, leading some commentators to believe that Jacob originally intended to go and visit Esau later. However, Jacob's next move to Shechem makes it likely that he had no such intention.
[458] A *qesitah* cannot be a coin, since coinage was a much later invention, so it is presumably a weight, though the amount of silver or gold in question is uncertain. The exact price would have been important in records of property purchases and sales in order to confirm the authenticity of the transaction.

a danger that becomes prominent in Genesis 34. Bethel is a mere twenty miles further than Shechem, but it will take a family tragedy to get Jacob to travel the final leg of his journey and fulfill his vow to the Lord.

But if Jacob builds his altar to God in the wrong place, at least he gives it the right name: "El-Elohe-Israel" (Gen. 33:20). In so doing he confesses that El,[459] the Great Creator God whom he met at Bethel ("the house of El") and with whom he wrestled at Peniel ("the face of El"), is not merely the God of his fathers ("the God of Abraham and the Fear of Isaac"; 31:42) but is his own personal God also. This represents a new confession on the part of Jacob, a mark of his growing spiritual insight and understanding, even though he is still falling short of full obedience to God. There is no record of any sacrifice that takes place at this installation, and it may well serve more as a memorial marker than as an altar as such. The unusual verb *natsab* ("set up") rather that *banah* ("built") supports this idea and further links this action with the events at Bethel in chapter 28.[460]

Response

Genesis 33 shows us how the doctrine of election works out in practice. It is not as though Esau desperately wanted to be the chosen son and God harshly turned him away. On the contrary, left to himself, Esau showed absolutely no interest in God or in the spiritual side of divine blessing. He gave God no credit for the blessings he had received and was entirely content to live his life without reference to God. Regret is not the same thing as contrition and repentance (cf. Heb. 12:17). Equally, although Jacob was God's chosen heir, he was not instantly sanctified. To be sure, God's grace has an effect in his life that is clearly visible in this chapter; he is penitent over his sins against his brother and seeks to make amends insofar as he can. He also clearly credits God for the blessings he has received, and he is returning to the Promised Land by faith. Yet at the same time he is guilty of favoritism, protecting Rachel and Joseph over the rest of his family. He also lies to Esau about his future plans and settles down short of fulfilling his vow to return to Bethel and offer sacrifices to the Lord.

This is why we all, like Jacob, need a perfect savior. Our lives as believers should evidence significant growth in obedience to God, but we will always fall short of God's holy standard of perfection. Our obedience can never be good enough, even on our best days. But the perfect righteousness of Christ is always good enough to measure up, and it is this righteousness, credited to us as a free gift, that makes all God's chosen ones acceptable in his sight. It is God's grace that saves us, grasped by simple faith and not our works, so that there is no room for boasting in the Christian life (Eph. 2:8–10).

---

[459] This is not to suggest that Jacob is worshiping the Canaanite deity El, who is quite different in character and attributes from the God of Israel. The terminology El is merely a generic title, "God," that can apply to the true God or to pagan counterfeits.
[460] Hamilton, *Genesis 18–50*, 349.

GENESIS 34

34 Now Dinah the daughter of Leah, whom she had borne to Jacob, went out to see the women of the land. ² And when Shechem the son of Hamor the Hivite, the prince of the land, saw her, he seized her and lay with her and humiliated her. ³ And his soul was drawn to Dinah the daughter of Jacob. He loved the young woman and spoke tenderly to her. ⁴ So Shechem spoke to his father Hamor, saying, "Get me this girl for my wife."

⁵ Now Jacob heard that he had defiled his daughter Dinah. But his sons were with his livestock in the field, so Jacob held his peace until they came. ⁶ And Hamor the father of Shechem went out to Jacob to speak with him. ⁷ The sons of Jacob had come in from the field as soon as they heard of it, and the men were indignant and very angry, because he had done an outrageous thing in Israel by lying with Jacob's daughter, for such a thing must not be done.

⁸ But Hamor spoke with them, saying, "The soul of my son Shechem longs for your[1] daughter. Please give her to him to be his wife. ⁹ Make marriages with us. Give your daughters to us, and take our daughters for yourselves. ¹⁰ You shall dwell with us, and the land shall be open to you. Dwell and trade in it, and get property in it." ¹¹ Shechem also said to her father and to her brothers, "Let me find favor in your eyes, and whatever you say to me I will give. ¹² Ask me for as great a bride-price[2] and gift as you will, and I will give whatever you say to me. Only give me the young woman to be my wife."

¹³ The sons of Jacob answered Shechem and his father Hamor deceitfully, because he had defiled their sister Dinah. ¹⁴ They said to them, "We cannot do this thing, to give our sister to one who is uncircumcised, for that would be a disgrace to us. ¹⁵ Only on this condition will we agree with you—that you will become as we are by every male among you being circumcised. ¹⁶ Then we will give our daughters to you, and we will take your daughters to ourselves, and we will dwell with you and become one people. ¹⁷ But if you will not listen to us and be circumcised, then we will take our daughter, and we will be gone."

¹⁸ Their words pleased Hamor and Hamor's son Shechem. ¹⁹ And the young man did not delay to do the thing, because he delighted in Jacob's daughter. Now he was the most honored of all his father's house. ²⁰ So Hamor and his son Shechem came to the gate of their city and spoke to the men of their city, saying, ²¹ "These men are at peace with us; let them dwell in the land and trade in it, for behold, the land is large enough for them. Let us take their daughters as wives, and let us give them our daughters. ²² Only on this condition will the men agree to dwell with us to become one people—when every male among us is circumcised as they are circumcised. ²³ Will not their livestock, their property and all their beasts be ours? Only let us agree with them, and they will dwell with us." ²⁴ And all who

went out of the gate of his city listened to Hamor and his son Shechem, and every male was circumcised, all who went out of the gate of his city. ²⁵ On the third day, when they were sore, two of the sons of Jacob, Simeon and Levi, Dinah's brothers, took their swords and came against the city while it felt secure and killed all the males. ²⁶ They killed Hamor and his son Shechem with the sword and took Dinah out of Shechem's house and went away. ²⁷ The sons of Jacob came upon the slain and plundered the city, because they had defiled their sister. ²⁸ They took their flocks and their herds, their donkeys, and whatever was in the city and in the field. ²⁹ All their wealth, all their little ones and their wives, all that was in the houses, they captured and plundered.

³⁰ Then Jacob said to Simeon and Levi, "You have brought trouble on me by making me stink to the inhabitants of the land, the Canaanites and the Perizzites. My numbers are few, and if they gather themselves against me and attack me, I shall be destroyed, both I and my household." ³¹ But they said, "Should he treat our sister like a prostitute?"

¹ The Hebrew for *your* is plural here ² Or *engagement present*

Section Overview

When he left Bethel in Genesis 28, Jacob vowed that, if the Lord brought him safely home, he would return there and offer sacrifices of thanksgiving. Yet on his return to the Promised Land Jacob stops short of Bethel, at Shechem, where he purchases property and seems ready to settle down (33:18–20). Although Jacob is not living in the city of Shechem, his lifestyle seems to be in contrast to Abraham and Isaac's nomadic sojourning existence, and it sets up himself and his family for what occurs next. Jacob's daughter, Dinah, goes to visit some of the women of the land (34:1), and the encounter leads to her being sexually assaulted by a man named Shechem, son of the local chieftain (v. 2). Shechem seeks to make amends by marrying her (v. 4), a pathway that could lead to the complete assimilation of Jacob's family into the local population.

Jacob himself does not immediately respond to this outrage, since his sons are out in the field (v. 5)—and, when they return, they take the lead. They deceive the inhabitants of the city into being circumcised, and then Simeon and Levi slaughter them all while they are still suffering the aftereffects (v. 25). Jacob is angry at this outcome, not because of the moral implications but because of the potential for reprisals from the local population (v. 30). It is a sad chapter that concludes with an unanswered question: "Should he treat our sister like a prostitute?" (v. 31). The answer is, of course, "No!" But neither should Simeon and Levi have used their faith to deceive people and put them to the sword. The whole sorry episode could have been avoided if Jacob had maintained an appropriate distance from the people of the land in the first place.

Section Outline

IX. The Family History of Isaac (25:19–35:29) . . .

    L. Trouble at Shechem (34:1–31)

Comment

34:1–7 In addition to his sons Jacob has at least one daughter by Leah, named Dinah (v. 1; cf. 30:21). Dinah goes out to see the "women of the land," that is, the young women who live in Shechem. The *vav*-consecutive imperfect construction suggests this may be a single visit rather than a recurring habit, but one visit is all it takes. We are not told what prompts this visit; presumably she is curious to meet other young people of her own age. As her father, Jacob should have anticipated the potential for trouble and protected her from herself. Instead, Jacob is absent or passive in this process, as he is throughout this entire chapter. He is not involved in the choices his daughter makes, and, as a result, this seemingly innocent act of curiosity ends in disaster.

Instead of seeing the women of the land, however, Dinah is seen by one of the men of the land, Shechem, the son of the ruler of the city (34:2). Just as in the first sin of Adam and Eve (3:6), so here "seeing" leads quickly to desiring and taking the forbidden fruit; the language is similar also to Genesis 6, in which the sons of God see and take the daughters of men in marriage (6:2). Shechem takes Dinah and lies with her and violates her, a sequence of three verbs whose rapid succession mirrors the rapidity of the events they describe. "Humiliated" (34:2; or, "violated") can cover a variety of sexual sins, from rape (2 Sam. 13:14–15) to willing premarital sex on the part of the woman (Deut. 22:28–29); what all such encounters have in common is that the man, as the primary actor, shames the woman and her family. Here it appears that Shechem takes her by force.[461]

Often such a sexual encounter would be followed by the rejection of the young woman, as in the case of Amnon and Tamar (cf. 2 Sam. 13:14–15). Yet Shechem becomes emotionally attached to the girl and speaks kindly to her (Gen. 34:3 could be rendered "He spoke to the heart of the young woman"),[462] even asking his father to seek her hand in marriage on his behalf (v. 4). Shechem's proposal of marriage to a girl he has just raped may seem bizarre to us, with our modern views of courtship and marriage. What self-respecting woman would be willing to undertake a relationship under those circumstances? However, in a culture in which marriage provided the only means of security for a woman, Dinah would have been regarded as "damaged goods." Even a marriage contracted under such an initial cloud would be viewed as superior to the alternative of being left forever in the socially perilous position of an aging single woman.

Shechem's proposal shows that at least he wants to make some kind of reparation for his actions, in a manner that his society recognizes (cf. Deut. 22:28–29). Yet, on the other hand, Shechem's tone with his father is as peremptory as his previous actions (Gen. 34:4); as the crown prince of the city, he seems to regard himself as entitled to take whatever he wants for himself. When he asks his father to get her

---

[461] Mathews, *Genesis 11:27–50:26*, 592.
[462] "He spoke to her heart" does not imply romantic speech (*pace* NET and some commentators). Such an assumption imports western notions of the heart into the idiom. Instead the language implies kind and gentle words, often in a context in which they are unexpected. The same idiom is used of Joseph's words to his brothers in 50:21.

for him, she is simply "this girl" (Hb. *yeldah* suggests she is still quite young at this point); her name is of no account to him (v. 4).

When Jacob hears of Dinah's defilement, he fails to respond outwardly to the news; instead, he waits passively until his sons return from the fields (v. 5). In part this delay makes sense, given the weakness of his position. However, as the chapter unfolds it is clear that this is not merely a wise pause on Jacob's part to wait for reinforcements before acting but rather flows from a greater desire for peace than honor.[463] One wonders whether Jacob would have responded more forcefully if Dinah had been Rachel's daughter rather than Leah's.

Jacob's lack of reaction to Dinah's defilement contrasts strongly to the reaction of his sons, who are filled with great fury at the offense against their sister. They come in from the fields as soon as they hear the news (v. 7).[464] Such a thing is disgraceful and ought not be done in (or against) Israel, they say (v. 7).[465] In fact, Shechem's act is an offense not only against the law codes of Israel (not yet written down at this point) but against most of the law codes of the ancient Near East. Yet Jacob and his family are still a seminomadic family with no citizenship in the community. It is not immediately clear what power they have to enforce punishment, especially on a prince of a city-state.

34:8–12 The aftermath of Shechem's sin begins to unfold when Hamor, the father of Shechem, arrives with a formal marriage proposal (v. 8). There is no explicit admission of Shechem's sin, though it is perhaps hinted at in the offer of an enhanced bride-price in verse 12. Hamor stresses his son's genuine affection for Dinah ("The soul of my son . . . longs for your[466] daughter"; v. 8), and his offer extends far beyond a simple marriage proposal; it is the offer of union as a single community. The Israelites and the Shechemites would live together as one people,[467] intermarrying and sharing a common destiny. The language that in Genesis 13:9 was the precursor to the division of two families ("Is not the whole land before you?") here becomes the precursor to the potential union of two families ("The land shall be open to you"; 34:10). Not only would the Israelites become part of the Shechemite community, but they would in this way inherit the Promised Land. Significantly, the verb used in 34:10, *'akhaz* ("acquire property"), is related to the word for "possession" in God's promise of the land to Abraham as an eternal inheritance in 17:8 (*'akhuzzah*). In other words, Hamor is offering Jacob a shortcut to receive as a gift from a Canaanite (cf. 14:21–23) the inheritance that God has promised him.

---

[463] Kidner, *Genesis*, 184.
[464] As Sternberg (*Poetics of Biblical Narrative*, 448) points out, "The phrasing of verse 7 (with the agentless 'when they heard') brings into doubt whether he [Jacob] even summoned them from the field for an emergency meeting."
[465] To do an "outrageous thing in Israel" later becomes a set formula for an action so disgraceful that the honor of the community demands action against the offender (e.g., Deut. 22:21; Josh. 7:15; Judg. 19:23–24; 20:6, 10; 2 Sam. 13:12; Jer. 29:23). Here it is used somewhat anachronistically, though it perhaps indicates the beginnings of a sense among the brothers of their identity as a people—called by their father's name "Israel"—who are to embody an ethic distinct and different from that of the surrounding peoples (Kidner, *Genesis*, 184).
[466] The Hebrew is plural here, acknowledging the "paternal" interest of Dinah's brothers in her welfare.
[467] Sailhamer (*Pentateuch as Narrative*, 200) points out that the previous reference in Genesis to becoming "one people" involved the inhabitants of Babel (Gen. 11:6), which underlines the contrary nature of what is proposed to God's way of uniting people together.

Shechem himself then approaches Jacob and Dinah's brothers and asks that he might find favor in their eyes and make appropriate restitution for his offense (Gen. 34:11–12). That was the right response according to ancient Near Eastern law codes, which, along with the Bible (Ex. 22:16–17; Deut. 22:29), specified that the offender should pay an enhanced bride-price for his actions.[468] The fact that such forgiveness and favor is exactly what Jacob had sought and received from Esau (Gen. 33:10) would add weight to his words.

In the light of the larger story Jacob and his sons cannot be bought off with Hamor's offer, however. The land is to be received not through intermarriage with its inhabitants but through God's gift. Shechem's sin against Dinah and the honor of her family could perhaps be forgiven and friendly relationships restored, as with Esau, but Jacob's family can no more join into a single people with Shechem than they could have with Esau. Their calling is to be a distinct community—Israel—separated from those dwelling in the land, whom they will ultimately drive out for their accumulated sin. Israel and his family should therefore decline Shechem's advances courteously, explaining clearly the reasons for their decision and inviting Shechem to become a worshiper of their God and be incorporated into his people by faith. Although God's people were not to intermarry with pagans, the door was always open for pagans to leave their prior allegiances and become part of God's people, as the examples of Rahab (Joshua 2) and Ruth later demonstrate.

34:13–19 What actually happens is something quite different. Jacob's sons take charge of the negotiations, leaving him still silent (Gen. 34:13). But instead of offering a plain and straightforward response, they answer deceitfully. Just as Jacob deceived (Hb. *bemirmah*; 27:35) his father in order to steal his brother's birthright, so now Jacob's sons deceive (*bemirmah*; 34:13) Hamor in order to massacre the unsuspecting citizens of Shechem. They have learned well from their father. Their initial response is true enough: "We cannot do this thing, to give our sister to one who is uncircumcised, for that would be a disgrace to us" (v. 14). But, instead of calling Shechem and its inhabitants to faith in the God of Israel as a prerequisite for marriage,[469] they ask merely for an external change: every male member of the community should submit to the covenant sign of circumcision, thus becoming like Israel.

The practice of circumcision was not unique to Israel; some other ancient Near Eastern cultures also practiced it, typically as a rite of puberty. It was what the sign meant as a marker to Israel of its call to be a holy people, dedicated to the Lord, that mattered, not the bare sign in itself. There is a distinct irony in applying the painful sign of circumcision to the part of Shechem's anatomy directly involved in his sin with Dinah![470] However, Shechem participates eagerly, not because he is enamored of Israel's God but simply because he is enamored of Dinah (v. 19). Indeed, he is as quick to be circumcised as he was to defile Dinah in the first place.

---

468 Sarna, *Genesis*, 234.
469 Although they echo the language of the Abrahamic covenant, "You shall circumcise every male" (Gen. 34:15; cf. 17:10, 12), their intent is the exact opposite of the covenant sign.
470 Sarna, *Genesis*, 236.

34:20–24 Shechem must still convince the rest of the male inhabitants of the city to undergo the painful ritual, so he gathers them to the gate of the city, the place where important community decisions were made by the elders (v. 20).[471] It helps his cause that he is the most honored son of his family (v. 19). But the most convincing argument involves the economics of the proposal. Intermarriage would result in the assimilation of Jacob's significant flocks and herds into the possessions of Shechem (v. 23); Hamor conveniently omits to mention the right to acquire property in Shechem that he has offered to Jacob's family (cf. v. 10).[472] The only condition is this family's trifling religious quirk of circumcision, a mere formality that need not affect their lives in any way (v. 22). Perhaps the greatest irony is Shechem's statement that Jacob and his family "are at peace with us" (Hb. *shelemim hem*; v. 21), which shows how utterly he has been deceived by Jacob's sons. In the previous chapter Jacob arrived at Shechem in peace (*shalem*; 33:18), but the result of his coming will be anything but peace for the inhabitants of the city.

Neither side takes seriously the preciousness of the covenant sign of circumcision. That is what might be expected of pagans, but it is a sad commentary on the spiritual state of Jacob and his family. They use the religious form of circumcision to give themselves an unfair advantage, so that Simeon and Levi can more easily massacre the unsuspecting inhabitants of Shechem. Circumcision is supposed to be a mark of Israel's covenant separation from the nations; here, however, Israel offers to become one nation with the Canaanites, not on condition that the Canaanites share their faith but merely on condition that they share Israel's religious practices.

34:25–31 On the third day, while the men of the city are still recovering, Simeon and Levi—Leah's sons and thus Dinah's full brothers—take advantage of the situation to massacre the unsuspecting inhabitants (34:25). They killed not only the guilty party, Shechem, and his father, Hamor, but all the men of the city, who are faultless in the matter (vv. 25–26). While the other sons of Jacob do not participate directly in the massacre, they join in plundering the city and its surrounding fields and carrying off the women and children (vv. 27–29).[473] The hypocrisy is staggering. Jacob's sons are outraged at the defilement Shechem commits against Dinah but not at all concerned at the defilement they inflict on themselves by stripping the corpses (v. 27). They are angry that Shechem took Dinah, but along with the flocks, herds, donkeys, and other wealth of Shechem they take the women and children (v. 29).[474] Shechem's initial sin of forcibly taking one woman is returned in kind but in multiplied form. Certainly, the Israelites demonstrate that they are in no way morally better than the previous inhabitants of the Promised Land.

---

471 In this case the decision is ratified by "all who went out of the gate of his city" (Gen. 34:24), which may be a description of all the men of an age subject to military conscription (Alter, *Five Books of Moses*, 192).
472 Sarna, *Genesis*, 237. Sarna sees this as deceptive on the part of Hamor, but it may simply be the omission of something that seems irrelevant. Mathews takes a more positive view (*Genesis 11:27–50:26*, 604).
473 Since the combination of "city" with "field" is already a comprehensive merism for everything, it is possible that the specification "All that was in their house" (Hb. *bayit*; Gen. 34:29; ESV treats as a collective, "in the houses") actually refers to the temple of Baal-Berith, for which the city is later well known (Judg. 9:4; cf. Currid, *Genesis 25:19–50:26*, 156).
474 The key verb *laqakh* ("take") occurs no fewer than nine times in this chapter.

Meanwhile, when Jacob becomes aware of his sons' actions, there is no word of condemnation for their sin; he is as passive now as he was when he learned of Shechem's earlier transgression (v. 30; cf. v. 5). All he says is, "You have brought trouble on me by making me stink to the inhabitants of the land, the Canaanites and the Perizzites. My numbers are few, and if they gather themselves against me and attack me, I shall be destroyed, both I and my household" (v. 30). The pronouns *I*, *me*, and *my* occur no fewer than eight times in this one verse, showing that Jacob's sole concern is for his own welfare, not for justice or for the offense such sin causes to a holy God.

It is the brothers who raise the ethical question in their own defense: "Should he treat our sister like a prostitute?" (v. 31). This question is where the chapter ends, with Jacob once again silenced. It is true that Shechem's sin has set these events in motion, and a case could perhaps be made that Shechem himself should have been executed for his offense. Yet this justification for the elimination of an entire city ignores all Shechem's efforts at reconciliation and restitution. Is the sin of one man, for which he attempts to make some restitution, however inadequate, a sufficient reason for the extermination of a community? The brothers have not been appointed as agents of divine judgment, as later Israel would be in the conquest of Canaan.[475] Indeed, their harsh treatment of Shechem is the exact opposite of the forgiveness and welcome they received from Esau, despite Jacob's history of sin against him.

Jacob will eventually declare judgment upon Simeon and Levi when it comes time to give his family his final blessing in Genesis 49. It will then be clear that he has not forgotten their behavior at Shechem, and he pronounces God's punishment upon them for their crime (49:5–7). But justice delayed often serves to embolden the offenders (Eccles. 8:11). It is obvious that Jacob's control over his own sons is slipping, which will have devastating consequences, first for those around him and finally for his own family as the story unfolds.

Response

The trouble at Shechem does not begin with Shechem's abuse of Dinah. Before that, Dinah went out to see the local women (Gen. 34:1), an unwise step against which Jacob should have warned her. Even before that, though, it began with Jacob's settling down near Shechem and purchasing land there—giving the Shechemites the clear impression that he was ready to assimilate into their community—when he should have gone all the way to Bethel to fulfill his earlier vow to the Lord. A failure to follow full obedience followed by an unwise decision sets in motion the rest of the sorry story, which ends up with a woman abused and a city destroyed. Small sins can easily lead to larger ones, as well as to painful and difficult circumstances, of which we may find it hard to see a way out.

The justification given by Simeon and Levi for their bloodthirsty behavior is the rhetorical question with which the chapter ends: "Should he treat our sister like a prostitute?" (v. 31), to which the obvious answer is "No!" But how should

---

475 The contrast with the destruction of Sodom and Gomorrah is instructive; that sin involved all the men of the city (Gen. 19:4) and was executed by the divine Judge, without human intermediaries.

they have dealt with Shechem's sin? It is clear in Jacob's curse on Simeon and Levi in Genesis 49:5–7 that their decision to slaughter the sinner (and everyone else in the vicinity) was not the right answer. But neither is Jacob's answer of pretending that nothing has happened, lest his own peace be disturbed. Some evil deserves the death penalty, even on a human level, and we may appropriately be glad when such justice is meted out. God not only restrains evil in this world, but he also appoints governing authorities to bear the sword and act as agents of his judgment, as Paul reminds us in Romans 13—even if all their judgments are flawed and their power to judge is limited and fallible. In addition the Bible tells us that a final day of judgment is coming, when all evil will be appropriately judged by God himself. No one will ever truly get away with his or her evil actions.

Yet that raises the question about our own evil. Are we as outraged with our own sin as we are with the abuses recorded in this chapter of Scripture? Do we acknowledge that we all deserve the death penalty for the sins of our hearts (cf. Matt. 5:22), even if we have not followed through on those evil desires in our actions? Like Jacob, we may have stood by and allowed sins in our family or community to go unchecked, or, like Simeon and Levi, we may have lashed out unjustly against the sinners in front of us.

What we need is an intervention from God that acknowledges the vileness of the evil we have suffered from others and that we ourselves inflict on others, while still leaving room for our repentance and forgiveness. That is precisely what God has provided for us at the cross. The wages of sin is death, and it must be paid (Rom. 6:23). The cross reminds us that evil is a serious business for which there is literally hell to pay. Yet at the cross Jesus endured that hell for all the sins of his people. Instead of the people's dying for the sins of their prince, as happened at Shechem, the King of kings has died for the sins of his people. No one is beyond reach of such a great redemption. The God of Israel is mighty to forgive all our sins and receive us into his presence, through the death of the Lamb of God, Jesus Christ.

GENESIS 35

35 God said to Jacob, "Arise, go up to Bethel and dwell there. Make an altar there to the God who appeared to you when you fled from your brother Esau." ² So Jacob said to his household and to all who were with him, "Put away the foreign gods that are among you and purify yourselves and change your garments. ³ Then let us arise and go up to Bethel, so that I may make there an altar to the God who answers me in the day of my distress and has been with me wherever I have gone." ⁴ So they gave to Jacob all the foreign gods that they had, and the rings that were in their ears. Jacob hid them under the terebinth tree that was near Shechem.

⁵And as they journeyed, a terror from God fell upon the cities that were around them, so that they did not pursue the sons of Jacob. ⁶And Jacob came to Luz (that is, Bethel), which is in the land of Canaan, he and all the people who were with him, ⁷and there he built an altar and called the place El-bethel,¹ because there God had revealed himself to him when he fled from his brother. ⁸And Deborah, Rebekah's nurse, died, and she was buried under an oak below Bethel. So he called its name Allon-bacuth.²

⁹God appeared³ to Jacob again, when he came from Paddan-aram, and blessed him. ¹⁰And God said to him, "Your name is Jacob; no longer shall your name be called Jacob, but Israel shall be your name." So he called his name Israel. ¹¹And God said to him, "I am God Almighty:⁴ be fruitful and multiply. A nation and a company of nations shall come from you, and kings shall come from your own body.⁵ ¹²The land that I gave to Abraham and Isaac I will give to you, and I will give the land to your offspring after you." ¹³Then God went up from him in the place where he had spoken with him. ¹⁴And Jacob set up a pillar in the place where he had spoken with him, a pillar of stone. He poured out a drink offering on it and poured oil on it. ¹⁵So Jacob called the name of the place where God had spoken with him Bethel.

¹⁶Then they journeyed from Bethel. When they were still some distance⁶ from Ephrath, Rachel went into labor, and she had hard labor. ¹⁷And when her labor was at its hardest, the midwife said to her, "Do not fear, for you have another son." ¹⁸And as her soul was departing (for she was dying), she called his name Ben-oni;⁷ but his father called him Benjamin.⁸ ¹⁹So Rachel died, and she was buried on the way to Ephrath (that is, Bethlehem), ²⁰and Jacob set up a pillar over her tomb. It is the pillar of Rachel's tomb, which is there to this day. ²¹Israel journeyed on and pitched his tent beyond the tower of Eder.

²²While Israel lived in that land, Reuben went and lay with Bilhah his father's concubine. And Israel heard of it.

Now the sons of Jacob were twelve. ²³The sons of Leah: Reuben (Jacob's firstborn), Simeon, Levi, Judah, Issachar, and Zebulun. ²⁴The sons of Rachel: Joseph and Benjamin. ²⁵The sons of Bilhah, Rachel's servant: Dan and Naphtali. ²⁶The sons of Zilpah, Leah's servant: Gad and Asher. These were the sons of Jacob who were born to him in Paddan-aram.

²⁷And Jacob came to his father Isaac at Mamre, or Kiriath-arba (that is, Hebron), where Abraham and Isaac had sojourned. ²⁸Now the days of Isaac were 180 years. ²⁹And Isaac breathed his last, and he died and was gathered to his people, old and full of days. And his sons Esau and Jacob buried him.

¹ *El-bethel* means *God of Bethel* ² *Allon-bacuth* means *oak of weeping* ³ Or *had appeared* ⁴ Hebrew *El Shaddai* ⁵ Hebrew *from your loins* ⁶ Or *about two hours' distance* ⁷ *Ben-oni* could mean *son of my sorrow*, or *son of my strength* ⁸ *Benjamin* means *son of the right hand*

Section Overview

Genesis 35 is the conclusion of the *toledot* of Isaac, which has focused on the life of Jacob. It ends not with Jacob's death—which is not reported until the end of Genesis—but with his return to Bethel, completing the vow he made in Genesis 28, and then with the death of his father, Isaac. With Jacob's return to Bethel, his return to the Promised Land is complete. God's name was completely absent from Genesis 34, as Jacob and his sons did whatever was right in their own eyes, with predictably disastrous results. God is active and central once again throughout the narrative in Genesis 35, as Jacob moves back toward full obedience.

Jacob's own renewed pursuit of God leads him to a renewed desire to shepherd his family faithfully, calling on them to put away their foreign gods and to purify themselves in preparation for worshiping God at Bethel (Gen. 35:2). There Jacob receives a renewed promise from God and a reiteration of his new name, Israel (vv. 9–13). Although Jacob's life has not been consistently transformed, and indeed he frequently falls back into old habits, this chapter shows us that God's commitment to him and his call on Jacob's life have not waned, despite Jacob's many failures. God's gifts and calling are irrevocable (cf. Rom. 11:29).

Section Outline

IX. The Family History of Isaac (25:19–35:29) . . .
    M. Return to Bethel (35:1–29)

Comment

35:1–8 Jacob's return to Bethel—like his original return to the Promised Land—comes at the explicit encouragement of God, who commands him to return there and build an altar (Gen. 35:1).[476] In both cases God's word comes to Jacob after events have made it uncomfortable for him to remain where he is, first with Laban (31:1–2) and then at Shechem (34:30). In place of the altar he built to El-Elohe-Israel at Shechem (33:20) Jacob is commanded to build an altar to El-Bethel—the God who appeared to him at Bethel when he was escaping from Esau and who has been with him to protect him and bless him ever since (28:19–22; 31:11–13).

In contrast to his earlier passivity in leading his family (cf. Genesis 34) Jacob now confronts his household about its "foreign gods" (Gen. 35:2; Hb. *'elohe-hannekar*), a term that includes Laban's *terafim* that Rachel brought with her (31:19) but is not limited to those idols. It is clear that Jacob has known of these objects but has previously said nothing about them. Now, however, it is time for them to be brought out and buried like the nonentities that they are, which is done at the terebinth tree near Shechem (35:4). These idols' inability to predict or prevent such a fate for themselves only highlights still further the impotence of these "gods." Yet they are not merely powerless; they are unnecessary, for the blessings of health and prosperity that they are supposedly able to give are exactly the blessings that the Lord himself has promised Jacob—and has repeatedly demonstrated his power to deliver. Israel's religion can never be a both-and, embracing the worship of the Lord and of idols: it is an either-or, a choice that lies at the heart of the opening section of the Ten Commandments in Exodus 20:3–5.

---

[476] The command "Go up to Bethel" is both physical and spiritual, with Bethel being located about a thousand feet higher than Shechem. Cf. Waltke, *Genesis*, 472.

Jacob also tells his household members to purify themselves and change their garments in preparation for the journey. After the repeated theme of defilement in the previous chapter, now the time has come for purification. We are not told what such purification rites look like, though the later Levitical laws perhaps give some clues (e.g., Num. 31:19–24). Although the word "holy" and its cognates do not occur in Genesis (apart from Gen. 2:3), the idea of God's holiness is nonetheless understood and implicit. Cleansing and preparation are necessary before humans can stand in the presence of the Lord, and the symbolic significance of clothing as representative of a person's spiritual state runs throughout the Bible (e.g., Zechariah 3; Eph. 4:24). Along with putting off the old, sin-stained garments of the former way of life, faithful members of God's people must put on new habits of devotion and obedience.

Jacob describes the God of Bethel as the God who answers him in the day of his distress and who has been with him wherever he has gone (Gen. 35:3). This reflects God's promise in 28:15 and Jacob's own experience in the intervening years (cf. 31:5). The last time Jacob was at Bethel he had been fleeing (*barakh*; 35:7); this time he is there to be blessed (*barak*; v. 9).[477] God's faithfulness to his promises necessitates Jacob's fulfilling his own vow to return to Bethel to build an altar and make appropriate sacrifices there (28:20–22).

Along with the foreign gods Jacob's household also surrenders its earrings (35:4). In the ancient world earrings were sometimes worn as amulets, invoking the protection of pagan deities over the wearer;[478] in some cases these earrings were refashioned into pagan cult objects (Ex. 32:2–3; Judg. 8:26–27), though they were also used in the construction of the tabernacle (Ex. 35:22) or for other legitimate purposes (e.g., Job 42:11). The disposal of such unclean objects via burial is unique in the OT; destruction by fire is the normal procedure, and an unusual Hebrew verb is used for the burial process (*taman*), lest the disposal be construed as some kind of honorific religious rite. The careful specification of the burial site as the "terebinth at Shechem" invites connections with the altar built by Abraham at the "terebinth of Moreh" (Gen. 12:6–7), as well as significant later events that transpire beside this same tree (Josh. 24:26; Judg. 9:6).

Jacob had feared reprisals from other local communities in the aftermath of events at Shechem (Gen. 34:30). However, just as the Lord had protected him from Laban and Esau, so too the Lord protects Jacob and his household against the Canaanites, causing a "terror" (*khittat*; 35:5) to fall on the surrounding cities, which prevents their pursuing Jacob and his sons. As a result he is able to journey to Bethel without interference and finally to fulfill his vow. The site is referred to by its earlier name, Luz (28:19), and the point is made that at this point Bethel is still in the land of Canaan—the land promised to the patriarchs by God but as yet not possessed by them. Jacob's altar-building is thus not merely an act of thanksgiving for the Lord's past faithfulness but a sign of his faith in the promises of God that are yet to be fulfilled.

---

477 Hamilton, *Genesis 18–50*, 380.
478 Sarna, *Genesis*, 240.

Yet Jacob's repentance and faith that issue in new obedience do not protect him from the pains and sorrows of life. As Jacob arrives at the holy place he buries his mother's faithful nurse, Deborah (35:8). And as he leaves this place he buries his beloved wife, Rachel (v. 19). The journey to and from the house of God at Bethel is thus bracketed by two gravestones, reminding us of the ubiquitous presence of death in this world, the result of the curse on Adam and Eve's sin (3:19).

35:9–15 At Bethel God appears to Jacob once more and renews his covenant with him (35:9–13). God reminds him of the transforming new name, Israel, given to him at Peniel (32:28). This name is a permanent reminder of God's ongoing work in his life. At Bethel God also pronounces his blessing upon Jacob in the same words that his father, Isaac, had used in his blessing so many years before: "Be fruitful and multiply" (35:11; cf. 28:3). Yet now a new element is added to the blessing, picked up from God's blessing to Abraham: "Kings shall come from your own body" (35:11; cf. 17:16). In place of Jacob's ill-fated efforts to buy a piece of the Promised Land for himself at Shechem (33:19) God confirms that he will give it to him and his descendants as a gift.

God's transforming work of blessing is not limited to turning Jacob into Israel: it will also take in Jacob's family. His family has thus far been a model of strife and discord, yet God announces that from him will come a "company [or "community"] of nations" (Hb. *qehal-'ammim*), just as Isaac had requested for him in Genesis 28:3. As we saw in chapter 28, it is not too strong to translate this phrase as "church of nations"—a covenant community of God's people, bound together in spiritual unity. The blessings promised to all nations through the original blessing on Abraham (12:2–3) thus come to his spiritual heirs as they are incorporated into the new community of spiritual Israel, the church, a people who are one in Christ. However, as the story unfolds the tension between the two primary sons—Joseph (from the favored wife, Rachel) and Judah (from the unfavored wife, Leah)—will continue, leaving to be resolved the question as to which line will carry forward the messianic promise.

Jacob's completion of his earlier vow upon this return to Bethel is marked by the erecting of a stone pillar (*matsebah*; 35:14; cf. 28:18) and its anointing with oil, just as Jacob did earlier, symbolizing the divine blessing he has received over the intervening years. In thanksgiving to God—and perhaps marking a rededication of the pillar, if it is the same stone set up earlier—this time he also pours out a drink offering to God.[479] It is not clear whether this is a representative part of the fulfillment of his vow to offer a tithe of everything received in the meantime or a (rather inadequate) substitute for it. The former seems more probable. Just as Jacob's renaming as Israel is confirmed in this chapter, so too the renaming of the location from its pagan identity of Luz to its true identity as Bethel is reiterated (35:15; cf. 28:19). This new name anticipates the capture and renaming of the city by the Benjaminites in the days of the judges (Judg. 1:23–26).

---

[479] Cf. Sarna, *Genesis*, 242.

35:16–20 After departing from Bethel, Rachel goes into labor with her second and Jacob's twelfth and final son. The labor is hard, but the midwife gives her the news that is supposed to cheer any woman facing difficult circumstances: "You have another son!" (Gen. 35:17; cf. 1 Sam. 4:20).[480] As she lies dying, Rachel names her son Ben-Oni (cf. ESV mg. on Gen. 35:18: "son of my sorrow"), but Jacob gives him the more positive name Benjamin ("son of the right hand"). The right hand is the position of power and influence (Ps. 110:1). Having recently been renamed himself, Jacob knows well the power of a name and longs for a good future for his last son. Rachel's earlier words to Jacob, "Give me children, or I shall die!" (Gen. 30:1), were strangely prophetic of her sad end, while her early death also fulfills Jacob's unwitting curse in 31:32: "Anyone with whom you find your goods shall not live."

The text records Rachel's burial not far from Ephrath (Bethlehem), where Jacob sets up a pillar over her tomb (35:20). So soon after the pillar set up at Bethel, it is impossible to miss the poignant symbolism: one pillar represents God's faithfulness and blessing upon Jacob, while the other emblematizes the sad losses of life in this fallen world. God's presence with Jacob does not prevent his experiencing the latter as well as the former.

35:21–29 The period of Jacob's life after Shechem is marked by a continued movement from place to place. After his disastrously failed attempt at settling down and integrating with the people of the land at Shechem Jacob adopts the sojourning life modeled for him by Abraham and Isaac (v. 27). The location of the tower of Edah (v. 21) is unknown to us, though presumably it lies somewhere between Bethlehem and Hebron.[481] Its significance here is in Reuben's reprehensible behavior of lying with Bilhah, his father's concubine (v. 22). Such an act is not merely a sexual sin but represents a potential leadership challenge by Reuben against his father (cf. 2 Sam. 16:21).[482] Jacob is aware of this sin of Reuben, but no response is recorded at the time, which seems to mark a return to the passivity of Genesis 34, where Simeon and Levi's sin went unchecked by their father. Reuben's sin is not forgotten, however; it earns him a curse rather than a blessing in Jacob's final words (cf. 49:3–4). Along with that of Simeon and Levi (49:5–7), Reuben's sin means that Leah's first three sons have now all disqualified themselves, clearing the way for Leah's fourth son, Judah, to become preeminent.

All twelve of Jacob's sons are included in God's promises, however, and so they are listed together here (Gen. 35:23–26). We find a variety of different orderings of the twelve sons in the Pentateuch (cf., e.g., the different arrangements in Num. 1:5–15 and 2:3–31, the latter of which takes the judgments of Genesis 49 into account), but in each case the mother's identity outweighs strict birth order. A son's sins may have a lasting impact on the status of the tribe descended from him, but none is excluded from the community. God's gracious calling transcends

---

[480] Hamilton, *Genesis 18–50*, 384.
[481] Mathews, *Genesis 11:27–50:26*, 627.
[482] Hamilton, *Genesis 18–50*, 387.

the impact of human sin. Moreover, though all of them (apart from Benjamin) are born outside the land of Canaan, they are all heirs together of God's promise of the land.

When Jacob left Bethel in Genesis 28, he defined the successful completion of his journey as "com[ing] again to my father's house in peace" (28:21), so it is fitting that the conclusion of this section of Genesis records his peaceful return to visit Isaac at Hebron (35:27), where his father has continued to sojourn all the years Jacob has been gone. Isaac passes away at the age of 180 (v. 28), the third death to be recorded in this chapter.[483] His death is a "good" death, "old and full of days" (v. 29; cf. 25:8), and he is "gathered to his people"—an idiom that strongly suggests a continuing existence of some kind beyond the grave, both for those who are heirs of God's promise (Abraham, 25:8; Jacob, 49:33; Aaron, Num. 20:24; Moses, Deut. 32:50) and for those who are not (Ishmael, Gen. 25:17).[484] These connections highlight the similarities between Isaac's death and that of his father, Abraham; just as their lives mirrored each other, so too do their deaths. The earlier reconciliation between Jacob and Esau also continues in force, as they are involved together in burying their father, an ending that seemed unlikely earlier in the story. It is not stated explicitly here, but Isaac is buried at the cave of Machpelah, where Abraham and Sarah were also buried (cf. 49:31).

Response

Prior to his return to Bethel Jacob issues a call to purity to his family, a call extended to each of us in Psalm 24:3–6:

> Who shall ascend the hill of the LORD?
>   And who shall stand in his holy place?
> He who has clean hands and a pure heart,
>   who does not lift up his soul to what is false
>   and does not swear deceitfully.
> He will receive blessing from the LORD
>   and righteousness from the God of his salvation.
> Such is the generation of those who seek him,
>   who seek the face of the God of Jacob.

The connections between this passage and the Jacob narrative go far beyond the mention of the "God of Jacob."[485] The psalm describes a person who does not swear "deceitfully" (Hb. *mirmah*; Ps. 24:4), a key word in Jacob's story (cf. Gen. 27:35; 29:25; 34:13). Such a person is able to stand in God's holy place (*maqom*), as Jacob did at

---

[483] Isaac's death rounds out his *toledot* but is not strictly chronological; it appears that he actually lives until some years after the disappearance of Joseph, recorded in Genesis 37. Certainly he lives much longer than he himself anticipated in Genesis 27, when he thought himself ready to die soon. Cf. Sarna, *Genesis*, 246, for the calculations.
[484] Cf. Kidner, *Genesis*, 161. The phrase is unique to the Pentateuch and is nowhere else used of death.
[485] In Hebrew the words "God of" are lacking; the text reads "who seek your face—Jacob." Most assume that a reference to the deity has fallen out here, but it instead may be a rather abrupt invitation to compare the blessed man in the psalm with Jacob, who did not fit the pattern of clean hands, pure heart, and undivided loyalties but nonetheless sought the face of God and received his blessing.

Bethel (28:11), and seek God's face, replicating Jacob's encounter with God at Peniel (32:30). He will receive God's blessing, the goal of all Jacob's striving.

Yet, as the passage makes clear, to receive God's blessing does not mean a life free from sorrow or sadness. Jacob loses three people to death in the space of a few verses: Rebekah's nurse, Deborah (35:8); his beloved wife, Rachel (v. 18); and his father, Isaac (v. 29). Moreover, he experiences the heartache of seeing his firstborn son commit adultery with his concubine Bilhah (v. 22). Sin and sorrow remain part of our experience throughout this life.

It is precisely through those acts of sin, however, that the spotlight falls on Judah as the one through whom the blessing will descend. Judah is certainly not free from sin himself (far from it—cf. Genesis 38!), but he is God's chosen vessel through whom the promised line of kings will come (49:10). Yet ultimately the blessing of seeing God's face comes to us not merely through a human descendant of Jacob's line but through the God of Jacob himself as he takes on human flesh. Only in this way is it possible for the entrance requirements of Psalm 24 to be satisfied: it is in Christ that we receive the clean hands, pure heart, and undivided loyalties that we need. Neither Jacob nor his sons could meet those requirements, and neither can we—but Christ can and has done so for us. It is his righteousness reckoned to him by faith that enables Abraham to be justified before God (Gen. 15:6), and that same faith unites us to Christ also, enabling even Gentiles like ourselves to be incorporated into the people of promise and to share in Jacob's spiritual inheritance: a heavenly home in God's presence (Heb. 11:10–16).

GENESIS 36

36 These are the generations of Esau (that is, Edom). ²Esau took his wives from the Canaanites: Adah the daughter of Elon the Hittite, Oholibamah the daughter of Anah the daughter¹ of Zibeon the Hivite, ³and Basemath, Ishmael's daughter, the sister of Nebaioth. ⁴And Adah bore to Esau, Eliphaz; Basemath bore Reuel; ⁵and Oholibamah bore Jeush, Jalam, and Korah. These are the sons of Esau who were born to him in the land of Canaan.

⁶Then Esau took his wives, his sons, his daughters, and all the members of his household, his livestock, all his beasts, and all his property that he had acquired in the land of Canaan. He went into a land away from his brother Jacob. ⁷For their possessions were too great for them to dwell together. The land of their sojournings could not support them because of their livestock. ⁸So Esau settled in the hill country of Seir. (Esau is Edom.)

⁹These are the generations of Esau the father of the Edomites in the hill country of Seir. ¹⁰These are the names of Esau's sons: Eliphaz the son of Adah the wife of Esau, Reuel the son of Basemath the wife of Esau. ¹¹The

sons of Eliphaz were Teman, Omar, Zepho, Gatam, and Kenaz. ¹²(Timna was a concubine of Eliphaz, Esau's son; she bore Amalek to Eliphaz.) These are the sons of Adah, Esau's wife. ¹³ These are the sons of Reuel: Nahath, Zerah, Shammah, and Mizzah. These are the sons of Basemath, Esau's wife. ¹⁴ These are the sons of Oholibamah the daughter of Anah the daughter of Zibeon, Esau's wife: she bore to Esau Jeush, Jalam, and Korah.

¹⁵ These are the chiefs of the sons of Esau. The sons of Eliphaz the firstborn of Esau: the chiefs Teman, Omar, Zepho, Kenaz, ¹⁶ Korah, Gatam, and Amalek; these are the chiefs of Eliphaz in the land of Edom; these are the sons of Adah. ¹⁷ These are the sons of Reuel, Esau's son: the chiefs Nahath, Zerah, Shammah, and Mizzah; these are the chiefs of Reuel in the land of Edom; these are the sons of Basemath, Esau's wife. ¹⁸ These are the sons of Oholibamah, Esau's wife: the chiefs Jeush, Jalam, and Korah; these are the chiefs born of Oholibamah the daughter of Anah, Esau's wife. ¹⁹ These are the sons of Esau (that is, Edom), and these are their chiefs.

²⁰ These are the sons of Seir the Horite, the inhabitants of the land: Lotan, Shobal, Zibeon, Anah, ²¹ Dishon, Ezer, and Dishan; these are the chiefs of the Horites, the sons of Seir in the land of Edom. ²² The sons of Lotan were Hori and Hemam; and Lotan's sister was Timna. ²³ These are the sons of Shobal: Alvan, Manahath, Ebal, Shepho, and Onam. ²⁴ These are the sons of Zibeon: Aiah and Anah; he is the Anah who found the hot springs in the wilderness, as he pastured the donkeys of Zibeon his father. ²⁵ These are the children of Anah: Dishon and Oholibamah the daughter of Anah. ²⁶ These are the sons of Dishon: Hemdan, Eshban, Ithran, and Cheran. ²⁷ These are the sons of Ezer: Bilhan, Zaavan, and Akan. ²⁸ These are the sons of Dishan: Uz and Aran. ²⁹ These are the chiefs of the Horites: the chiefs Lotan, Shobal, Zibeon, Anah, ³⁰ Dishon, Ezer, and Dishan; these are the chiefs of the Horites, chief by chief in the land of Seir.

³¹ These are the kings who reigned in the land of Edom, before any king reigned over the Israelites. ³² Bela the son of Beor reigned in Edom, the name of his city being Dinhabah. ³³ Bela died, and Jobab the son of Zerah of Bozrah reigned in his place. ³⁴ Jobab died, and Husham of the land of the Temanites reigned in his place. ³⁵ Husham died, and Hadad the son of Bedad, who defeated Midian in the country of Moab, reigned in his place, the name of his city being Avith. ³⁶ Hadad died, and Samlah of Masrekah reigned in his place. ³⁷ Samlah died, and Shaul of Rehoboth on the Euphrates² reigned in his place. ³⁸ Shaul died, and Baal-hanan the son of Achbor reigned in his place. ³⁹ Baal-hanan the son of Achbor died, and Hadar reigned in his place, the name of his city being Pau; his wife's name was Mehetabel, the daughter of Matred, daughter of Mezahab.

⁴⁰ These are the names of the chiefs of Esau, according to their clans and their dwelling places, by their names: the chiefs Timna, Alvah, Jetheth, ⁴¹ Oholibamah, Elah, Pinon, ⁴² Kenaz, Teman, Mibzar, ⁴³ Magdiel, and Iram; these are the chiefs of Edom (that is, Esau, the father of Edom), according to their dwelling places in the land of their possession.

¹ Hebrew; Samaritan, Septuagint, Syriac *son*; also verse 14 ² Hebrew *the River*

Section Overview

Just as the family history of Ishmael was briefly included to round out the *toledot* of Abraham (Gen. 25:12–18), so too the family history of Esau rounds out the *toledot* of Isaac (Genesis 36). In both cases the portrayal highlights the blessings that come from being related to the Abrahamic line, even when one is not the child of promise. Both Ishmael and Esau prosper and multiply greatly in terms both of offspring and of influence, becoming the ancestors of significant peoples with whom the nation of Israel will have to reckon. In Genesis 36 this focus is highlighted by the repeated refrain "Esau (that is, Edom)" (vv. 1, 8, 19, 43). This positive portrayal of Esau's development leaves open the door for his descendants to join themselves to Israel by faith (Deut. 23:7) as representatives of the wider call for Gentiles to be included in God's kingdom (cf. Acts 15:17),[486] though it has to be said that in terms of Israel's later history Edom is more often viewed as the archetypal opponent of Israel (e.g., Ezekiel 35–36; Mal. 1:2–5).

Section Outline

X. The Family History of Esau (36:1–43)

Comment

36:1–5 The *toledot* formula always introduces the story of the next generation, those whom the eponymous ancestor "brought forth" (Hb. *yalad*).[487] This is now the ninth of the ten formulae that structure the book of Genesis. The *toledot* of Esau is relatively short compared to that of Isaac, which it follows, reflecting the fact that Esau's offspring represent a side branch of the family line. But his story is not ignored; though he is not the chosen son of Isaac, through whom the promise will descend, he is nonetheless a son of Isaac, and the Lord's blessing rests upon him.

Esau's story is introduced with the reminder of his choice of wives from among the Canaanites rather than from the Abrahamic family (cf. Gen. 26:34). This demonstrated a lack of spiritual discernment and of valuing the call to be a distinct people, a shortcoming unremedied by his adding a wife from the line of Ishmael to his collection (28:9). Just as Jacob's sons were ordered with reference to their mothers (35:23–26), so too are Esau's offspring (36:4–5). Whereas Jacob's children (except Benjamin) were "born to him in Paddan-aram," Esau's children were Canaanite in both birth and heredity (v. 5).[488]

The names assigned to Esau's wives differ here from those mentioned earlier: Adah the daughter of Elon the Hittite;[489] Oholibamah the (grand)daughter of Zibeon the Hivite;[490] and Basemath, the daughter of Ishmael (Gen. 36:2–3)—as opposed to Judith the daughter of Beeri the Hittite, Basemath the daughter of Elon the Hittite (26:34), and Mahalath the daughter of Ishmael (28:9). There is no reason to assume that conflicting traditions have been conflated here, as some

---

486 Sailhamer, *Pentateuch as Narrative*, 204–205.
487 On the *toledot* formula cf. comment on 2:4–7.
488 Whereas Esau's third wife is distinguished as being Ishmaelite rather than Canaanite in Genesis 28:9, here she is lumped in as being essentially Canaanite, like Esau's other wives (36:2).
489 On the Hittites cf. comment on 10:6–20.
490 The name of the intervening generation is listed as Anah, with the Hebrew calling her Zibeon's daughter (Gen. 36:2), while the other ancient versions call her Zibeon's son. The Hebrew is the harder reading, since sons are more commonly included in genealogies than daughters, but no great weight rests on the choice of translation.

commentators do. Since women as well as men sometimes had multiple names in the ancient world, it is likely that Adah = Basemath (the daughter of Elon), and Mahalath = Basemath (the daughter of Ishmael). Meanwhile, neither list is necessarily comprehensive; if Judith had no sons, there would be no reason to mention here, while the three wives listed earlier were only the wives that Esau had married prior to Jacob's departure from home. Oholibamah may well have been a later addition to his family.[491] From these three women (out of four wives in total), Esau had five sons, as well as daughters whose names are not listed (36:4, 6). This is significantly fewer than Jacob's twelve sons, though many more than Abraham or Isaac produced.

36:6–8 Having listed Esau's wives and offspring, the narrative recounts his move to Mount Seir (v. 8). Esau took with him his people and his possessions, both of which were acquired "in the land of Canaan" (v. 6), which underlines the fact that his destination was outside the land of Canaan—the Land of Promise—and "away from his brother Jacob" (v. 6; cf. 27:39). The separation of Jacob and Esau is described in similar terms to that of Abraham and Lot, as it was due to the inability of the land to support their livestock together (36:7; cf. 13:6), even though Esau had already settled at Seir before Jacob's return home (32:3) and later invited Jacob to join him there (33:12–14). This comparison highlights the fact that Esau, like Lot before him, voluntarily chose to settle outside the land, where he stayed—unlike Jacob, who, after a temporary sojourn outside the land, returned there as heir to the promise.

36:9–19 The first section of the chapter ends with a version of the formula "Esau (that is Edom)" (36:8), which highlights the twofold nature of the account, focusing on Esau the person (vv. 1–8) and on Edom the tribe (vv. 9–43). The new section is also marked by an unusual repetition of the *toledot* formula (v. 9; cf. v. 1). The story of Edom begins with the next generation, the children of Esau's children. These are also categorized in terms of Esau's wives and are described as "chiefs" (Hb. *'allufim*; v. 19). The word likely originated as the leader of an *'elef* (lit., "a thousand," a military unit that may in practice have often been much smaller; Num. 31:5).[492] Thus these men were likely founders and heads of various clans within Edom.

36:20–30 Next the genealogy of the native inhabitants of Seir are listed, with whom the descendants of Esau intermarried. These are described as "Horites" after Seir's grandson, Hori (v. 20). Horites are often linked with the Hurrians, a non-Semitic people who were widely distributed through the ancient Near East at this time. However, this particular group of Horites are not so easily connected with the Hurrians and may well have been a separate people; the name may be connected to "cave dweller" (cf. 1 Sam. 14:11).[493] As with Esau, after the sons are listed the account itemizes the chieftains (or "clans"; cf. comment above).

---

491 Cf. Currid, *Genesis 25:19–50:26*, 176.
492 S.v. אֶלֶף, *HALOT*, 1.59. Currid argues that the word should be translated "clan" rather than "chieftain" (*Genesis 25:19–50:26*, 178), which highlights the fact that there is a fine line between the originator of the clan and the clan named for him.
493 Mathews, *Genesis 11:27–50:26*, 653.

36:31–43 The list of Edomite kings follows eight successive generations, with a consistent formula. The comment at the end of verse 31 ("Before any king reigned over the Israelites") is probably a later editorial note, though the expectation of Israelite kings has already been raised (35:11), so it could simply be an anticipation of that promised outcome. After these eight generations of Edomite kings Israel gained the ascendancy over Edom for much of the subsequent period.

In many respects the Edomite story recounted here is a variant of Israel's own story ahead of time: Edom too conquered the "land of their possession" (Hb. *'erets 'akhuzzah*, Gen. 36:43; cf. Deut. 2:12; Josh. 22:4) and established a society run by kings. However, their land was outside the promised boundaries of Israel's land, and they possessed their land by intermarriage with the native peoples rather than by conquest. The differences in Edom's experience compared to Israel's are thus ultimately more significant that the similarities, and of course the end of their story will be very different, as Malachi 1:2–5 makes clear. Although divine election does not result in a smoother pathway through life for Israel than for Edom—if anything, it does the reverse—ultimately it makes all the difference in the world. God's choosing is the foundation upon which redemption is possible after sin and judgment; the Lord will not abandon the people he has elected.

> Blessed is the nation whose God is the LORD,
> the people whom he has chosen as his heritage! (Ps. 33:12)

Response

Esau and Edom prosper significantly as part of God's blessing upon Abraham and his offspring. The result is a self-sufficient and sophisticated society, dwelling comfortably in a land they can call their own, something toward which Moses' first hearers were still aspiring after many years of wandering. They might well have been tempted to envy Edom's situation. Yet Edom's blessings are limited to worldly prosperity, and their conquest of Seir comes as much through intermarriage as it does through military triumph. Nor will Edom's independence and prosperity endure forever. God's plan for their future ends in destruction (Mal. 1:2–5).

There is ultimately only one way to receive the fullness of the Abrahamic blessing and avoid the destiny of destruction. That is to share in the faith of Abraham, by which we become Abraham's spiritual children, heirs with him of the promise of salvation. It is through his seed, Jesus Christ, that salvation comes to all, both descendants of Jacob and descendants of Edom alike. There is no distinction between them: "All have sinned and fall short of the glory of God" (Rom. 3:23), and all may be saved through trust in the righteousness of Christ, through whom we have peace with God (Rom. 5:1). There is no other name given to us by whom we may be saved (Acts 4:12).

GENESIS 37:1–11

37 Jacob lived in the land of his father's sojournings, in the land of Canaan.

² These are the generations of Jacob.

Joseph, being seventeen years old, was pasturing the flock with his brothers. He was a boy with the sons of Bilhah and Zilpah, his father's wives. And Joseph brought a bad report of them to their father. ³ Now Israel loved Joseph more than any other of his sons, because he was the son of his old age. And he made him a robe of many colors.[1] ⁴ But when his brothers saw that their father loved him more than all his brothers, they hated him and could not speak peacefully to him.

⁵ Now Joseph had a dream, and when he told it to his brothers they hated him even more. ⁶ He said to them, "Hear this dream that I have dreamed: ⁷ Behold, we were binding sheaves in the field, and behold, my sheaf arose and stood upright. And behold, your sheaves gathered around it and bowed down to my sheaf." ⁸ His brothers said to him, "Are you indeed to reign over us? Or are you indeed to rule over us?" So they hated him even more for his dreams and for his words.

⁹ Then he dreamed another dream and told it to his brothers and said, "Behold, I have dreamed another dream. Behold, the sun, the moon, and eleven stars were bowing down to me." ¹⁰ But when he told it to his father and to his brothers, his father rebuked him and said to him, "What is this dream that you have dreamed? Shall I and your mother and your brothers indeed come to bow ourselves to the ground before you?" ¹¹ And his brothers were jealous of him, but his father kept the saying in mind.

[1] See Septuagint, Vulgate; or (with Syriac) *a robe with long sleeves*. The meaning of the Hebrew is uncertain; also verses 23, 32

Section Overview

Family relationships have been strained throughout the book of Genesis, with tension between brothers going all the way back to Cain and Abel (cf. ch. 4). As the spotlight shifts from Jacob to the next generation, the family's disharmony is plain for all to see. The word "brother" occurs no fewer than twenty-one times in this chapter, but the brothers are far from being the harmonious "company of nations" that the Lord has promised (cf. 35:11). Joseph irritates his brothers by bringing "a bad report" against them (37:2) and by announcing dreams that depict him as the God-ordained head of the family (vv. 5–10). Meanwhile, his father exacerbates the situation by gifting him an ornate robe that prevents his partaking in the mundane work of shepherding (vv. 3–4). Toxic favoritism roiled Jacob's own childhood, but he seems to be oblivious to its impact on his own children.

Yet none of these events lies outside of God's control, sinful though they are. What humans mean for evil, God means for good (50:20). He will work all these things for his people's salvation and blessing when a great famine comes, and ultimately he will restore and heal these broken family relationships. None of Joseph's sufferings will be wasted in the providence of God. Not only will Joseph be transformed by his experiences, but so will his brothers, especially Judah.

The *toledot* of Jacob has a clear chiastic structure that focuses our attention on Joseph's testing and unveiling of himself to his brothers in Genesis 44–45, as follows:

(A) Joseph the Dreamer (37:2–11)
  (B) Jacob Mourns the "Death" of Joseph (37:12–36)
    (C) Judah and Tamar (38:1–30)
      (D) Joseph's Enslavement in Egypt (39:1–23)
        (E) Joseph, Savior of Egypt (40:1–41:57)
          (F) Journeys of Brothers to Egypt (42:1–43:34)
            (G) Joseph Tests the Brothers (44:1–34)
            (G') Joseph Reveals His identity (45:1–28)
          (F') Journey of Family to Egypt (46:1–27)
        (E') Joseph, Savior of Family (46:28–47:12)
      (D') Joseph's Enslavement of the Egyptians (47:13–31)
    (C') Jacob Favors Joseph and Judah (48:1–49:28)
  (B') Joseph Mourns the Death of Jacob (49:29–50:14)
(A') Joseph the Provider (50:15–26)[494]

Section Outline

XI. The Family History of Jacob (37:1–50:26)
  A. Joseph's Dreams (37:1–11)

Comment

37:1–2 Genesis 37:1 is a transitional verse, connecting the preceding account of Esau and his descendants to the account that follows about Jacob and his sons. It contrasts Jacob with Esau: while Esau lives a settled life on Mount Seir, outside the land, Jacob follows the pattern of his father (and grandfather) as a sojourner within the Land of Promise (cf. 35:27). It also establishes that the events that follow are not a judgment upon Jacob for his failures; at this point he is faithfully fulfilling his calling.

The story proper begins with the *toledot* formula: "These are the generations [*toledot*] of Jacob" (37:2). As always the *toledot* story focuses on the next generation, in this case Joseph and his brothers.[495] We have previously been introduced to Reuben, Simeon, and Levi as significant characters in the story, but from here onward all

---
[494] This version of the chiasm is taken from Mathews, *Genesis 11:27–50:26*, 680.
[495] On the *toledot* formula cf. comment on 2:4–7. We tend to focus on the central role of Joseph in the chapters that follow, but God is at work in the whole family; cf. Mathews, *Genesis 11:27–50:26*, 666.

twelve of the brothers will take center stage. This is the tenth and final use of the formula, demonstrating conclusively that the formula begins an episode rather than closing one. The story from here to the end of Genesis is part of a single narrative arc that concludes the story begun in Genesis 1:1 while at the same time preparing for the events that follow in the book of Exodus.

The first brother to be introduced is Joseph (37:2). A character's first appearance on the biblical stage can be quite revealing, and Joseph seems rather self-absorbed.[496] As a seventeen-year-old assisting his brothers Dan, Naphtali, Gad, and Asher—the sons of the maidservants, Bilhah and Zilpah—out in the fields, his role would normally be quite minor. In Hebrew the text says, "He was a boy with the sons of Bilhah and Zilpah" (v. 2),[497] which is as much a job description as it is a reference to his age.[498] He is sent along with his brothers to do all the menial and unimportant jobs. Yet Joseph brings a bad report to his father (v. 2), which certainly would not endear his brothers to him.

In English a "bad report" may be true or false; in Hebrew, however, this particular phrase (*dibbatam ra'ah*) has the connotations of a false or malicious report.[499] During the wilderness wanderings the ten spies bring the same kind of "bad report" back to the people of Israel concerning the land of Canaan, telling them it is not worth fighting for (Num. 13:32). In Proverbs 10:18 the word *dibbah* is translated "slander." This suggests that Joseph's report to his father is a fabricated, or at least exaggerated, account of their misdeeds. Whether the bad report is justified or unjustified—whether Joseph is a righteous whistleblower or a self-righteous pharisee—it inevitably strains relations between them, with Joseph elevating himself into a position of authority over them (as *merely* the sons of maidservants?).

37:3–4 Joseph's bad report to his father against his brothers is compounded by his father's favoritism: Jacob loves him "more than any other of his sons" (Gen. 37:3). Joseph is not the only "son of his old age" (v. 3); Benjamin was actually born after him. However, Joseph is also the firstborn son of Jacob's favored wife, Rachel. By calling Joseph "the son of his old age" (Hb. *lizqunav*) the narrator links Joseph with Isaac, the child that Sarah bore to Abraham in his old age; the same word is used of Isaac in Genesis 21:2. It was when Joseph was born that Jacob's thoughts turned to the journey back to the Promised Land (30:25), and, when it seemed that Esau and his men might threaten the safety of the whole family, Jacob had carefully placed Rachel and Joseph at the rear of the caravan, where their prospects of escape would have been the greatest (33:2).

---

[496] Alter, *Five Books of Moses*, 206.
[497] Referring to them as "the sons of Bilhah and Zilpah" rather than by name already highlights the family divisions.
[498] Speiser, *Genesis*, 289. When my grandfather began work as a farm servant in Aberdeenshire in the early twentieth century, his title was "Orra Loon" ("Other Boy").
[499] Hamilton, *Genesis 18–50*, 406. Currid suggests that the Hebrew can be translated to suggest that Joseph brought his father a bad report that the brothers had made about him (*Genesis 25:19–50:26*, 185; cf. KJV), but this seems less likely. After all, if the brothers had already made the bad report about him, there would have been no need for Joseph to bring it to his father's attention.

It is striking that the text says that "*Israel* loved Joseph more than any other of his sons" (37:3). The alternation between Jacob and Israel is not a random choice or the result of the use of different sources; rather it often reflects Jacob's self-awareness. When he is at his best, he is Israel; when he is regressing, he is Jacob.[500] Here it seems that the name Israel acts as a clue to Jacob's thinking: his favoritism toward Joseph is not merely a personal preference for the child who is most amenable or most like him, as was Isaac's preference for Esau (27:4). Rather, Jacob's preference for Joseph is rooted in his assumption that Joseph must be the child of the promise, the one who will carry on the line of the Messiah, the promised seed of the woman of Genesis 3:15. Surely God will not choose a child from unloved Leah, still less from one of the maidservants, to bear this blessing? This is perhaps why it is as *Israel* that he loves Joseph the best. But of course Jacob is mistaken: the God who chose him, the younger brother, as bearer of the blessing is quite capable of choosing one of the children of unloved Leah for that privilege.

That favoritism for Joseph is embodied in the richly ornamented coat (37:3; *ketonet*) that his father bestows upon him. It is not necessarily a "robe of many colors," a rendering based on the LXX; the exact meaning of the Hebrew is uncertain. However, in the only other place where this phrase occurs in the Bible it refers to a royal garment worn by a princess, David's daughter Tamar (2 Sam. 13:18). There the English translations, once again following the LXX, render it as a "long robe with sleeves." Since the Hebrew *pas* can mean the palms of the hand or the soles of the feet, it seems that the most plausible rendering is as a "robe that reaches to the extremities of the arms and legs."[501]

Whatever precise kind of robe it is, it is certainly not the kind of clothing that a person would wear to engage in manual labor. It striking that this robe is mentioned after Joseph brings the bad report to his father about his brothers (Gen. 37:2). There seems to be a sequence of events here: Joseph goes to serve and work under his brothers while they are shepherding; he brings home a bad report about them; his father rewards him with a splendid coat. The next time the brothers go out shepherding, later in the chapter, Joseph is no longer with them. Instead he is relaxing at home in his fancy coat, while his brothers do the dirty work of shepherding. In light of this it is not surprising that Joseph's clothing will have an important role to play throughout the narrative.[502]

Joseph's brothers hate him because of his father's preferential treatment toward him (v. 4). The Hebrew text says "They could not say shalom to him"—that is, they cannot even give him the most basic greeting (*shalom leka*; v. 4).[503] If this reflects their attitude toward Joseph before he receives his dreams, it is not surprising that after they hear his dreams they hate him all the more (v. 8). In fact, the text notes their rising hatred for Joseph three times (vv. 4, 5, 8). This is ominous, particularly given the bloodthirsty history of Simeon and Levi.

---

500 Wenham, *Genesis 16–50*, 351.
501 Cf. Mathews, *Genesis 11:27–50:26*, 689.
502 V. Matthews, "The Anthropology of Clothing in the Joseph Narrative," *JSOT* 65 (1995): 25–36.
503 Westermann, *Genesis: A Practical Commentary*, 263.

37:5–11 Joseph's place in the divine plan appears cemented when he receives two dreams that seem to affirm his status as God's favorite as well as Jacob's. Doubling is a feature of the Joseph narrative: alongside his two dreams, the two dreams of the Egyptian officials (40:5), and the two dreams of Pharaoh (41:1–8), Joseph experiences two confinements, in a pit and in an Egyptian prison (37:24; 39:20); the brothers make two journeys down to Egypt (42:3; 43:15); and so on.[504] In the ancient world doubled dreams had the reputation of being certain to come true (41:32). The prominence of dreams also marks a shift from the earlier patriarchal narratives; in those accounts God's presence was more immediate and direct, through appearances and explicit actions, while in the Joseph account God is still present and active but less overt in his actions.[505]

Joseph's first dream involved an agricultural setting: "In the field."[506] There, while Joseph and his brothers are binding sheaves as part of the harvesting process, Joseph's sheaf stands upright and the sheaves of his brothers gather round and bow down to his sheaf (37:7).[507] Even though Jacob and his family are primarily pastoralists, they would be involved in planting and harvesting as well (cf. 26:12);[508] the dream also foreshadows Pharaoh's second dream and Joseph's control over the granaries of Egypt (cf. 41:22–23). Some divinely inspired dreams have a complexity that requires expert interpretation, as in the dreams given to Pharaoh and his officials, but this dream is sufficiently transparent that the brothers instantly recognize its import: it is a claim of Joseph's supremacy over all his brothers (37:8). The brothers resent this claim to reign and rule over them, as well as the way in which he presents it to them; it is not merely for the dreams that the brothers hate him but for "his words" as well (v. 8).[509]

If it is unwise for Joseph to report his first dream to his brothers in this manner, the second dream underscores the point. Joseph is not responsible for receiving the dream, to be sure, but he chooses to report it in a similar fashion, punctuated with two more "Beholds" (*hinneh*) for emphasis (v. 9). This dream is even more affirmative of Joseph—Alter describes it as "teetering on the brink of blasphemy."[510] Now it is not merely sheaves of wheat that are bowing down to Joseph but the sun, the moon, and eleven stars (v. 9). In context these heavenly bodies represent Jacob's parents and his brothers,[511] but in the ancient world, where the stars were

---

[504] Greidanus, *Preaching Christ from Genesis*, 337.
[505] W. L. Humphreys, *The Character of God in the Book of Genesis: A Narrative Appraisal* (Louisville: Westminster John Knox, 2001), 205–216.
[506] Many things happen "in the field" in Genesis, good and bad, but in the context of Joseph's recounting his dreams to his brothers it seems ominous that Cain's murder of Abel also took place "in the field" (Gen. 4:8).
[507] As the particle that introduces unexpected events, it is not surprising to find *hinneh* in dream accounts, but the threefold *hinneh* ("Behold") seems to be an excessive exclamation point for Joseph to add; cf. Alter, *Five Books of Moses*, 207.
[508] Sarna, *Genesis*, 256.
[509] The infinitive absolutes in the brothers' reply, rendered as "indeed" twice in 37:8, suggest their incredulity at this potential outcome; cf. Ross, *Creation and Blessing*, 600.
[510] Alter, *Five Books of Moses*, 208. Of course, as heir of God's promise in Genesis 3:15 of the seed of the woman, Joseph typologically points forward to the one greater than himself, Jesus Christ, before whom all creation must truly bow.
[511] Joseph's mother, Rachel, has died already by this point (Gen. 35:18), so it is plausible that the moon represents Leah, Jacob's remaining wife. She is not literally Joseph's mother but could still be given that title as Jacob's wife. Alternatively, it may refer to Rachel's maidservant, Bilhah, who may have been intimately involved in raising Joseph (cf. Genesis Rabbah 84.11). Bilhah and Zilpah are referred to as Jacob's "wives" in

regarded as semidivine, the dream would be loaded with extra freight. In the same way that in Hebrew parallelism the second phrase does not merely repeat the first but often carries a force of "and what is more," so too here the second dream repeats and heightens the first one. Even Jacob rebukes Joseph for this dream, though, unlike Joseph's brothers, who are merely jealous, Jacob "kept the saying in mind" (v. 11). It likely further seals Jacob's conviction that Joseph is indeed the son of promise, chosen by God.

In giving Joseph these dreams God himself is bringing this family conflict to a head, in some ways contributing to the evil events that follow—which of course he intends for good (50:20). God is not to blame for the sinful reaction of Joseph's brothers, but he sovereignly directs all Joseph's steps through a difficult pathway to accomplish his designs in Joseph's heart, as well as in the hearts of his brothers. In the days that lie ahead Joseph will have a mixed evaluation of these dreams. On the one hand they are the occasioning incident of so much of his suffering, but on the other hand his faith in the promises of God that they represent keeps his hope alive in the most difficult of circumstances.

Response

Upon first introduction Joseph's character seems somewhat overconfident and arrogant. In the typical fashion of Hebrew narrative the text makes no explicit moral evaluation, but, just as we were not surprised that Esau wanted to kill Jacob, it is similarly unsurprising that Joseph provokes his brothers to jealousy. Of course, that jealousy would likely be present in any event, however Joseph might conduct himself, since divine election tends to provoke human anger, as it has ever since Cain and Abel. But Joseph's actions seem to exacerbate it in this case. If so, the pathway God has prepared for Joseph will humble and mature Joseph, forcing him to live by faith in circumstances in which it seems impossible that God's promises could ever find fruition.

The sovereign purposes of God are on full display in this chapter, in which every event is necessary in order for Joseph to end up as a slave in Egypt. The worst human sins do not prevent God's salvation from triumphing; on the contrary, God uses human sin—and deeply dysfunctional families—to accomplish his good purposes in the lives of his people and the world at large. This should encourage us when we are frustrated by the sins and brokenness we see around us in the church, in our families of origin, and even in our own hearts and lives. God is not finished with us yet, nor is he finished with those around us; he will use even the worst sins to accomplish his sanctifying goals in us.

As noted earlier, the dreams in this chapter are too big to be about Joseph alone. To be sure, to some extent they foreshadow later events, as Joseph's brothers will come down to Egypt and bow down to him. Yet, when Jacob blesses his sons in Genesis 49, he tells Judah, not Joseph, that his father's sons will bow down before

---

37:2. However, both of these explanations may be too literalistic, and the image may simply represent Joseph's whole family as bowing before him.

him. It is from the tribe of Judah that the one will ultimately come of whom the promise in Genesis 3:15 speaks and who is the true fulfillment of Joseph's dreams. Joseph's life foreshadows Christ's life in profound ways, but he is not the Christ himself. The promised Christ will be the son of Judah's line, yet he will be far greater even than Judah—he is God himself, the one before whom the sun, the moon, and the stars themselves truly bow.

GENESIS 37:12–36

¹² Now his brothers went to pasture their father's flock near Shechem. ¹³ And Israel said to Joseph, "Are not your brothers pasturing the flock at Shechem? Come, I will send you to them." And he said to him, "Here I am." ¹⁴ So he said to him, "Go now, see if it is well with your brothers and with the flock, and bring me word." So he sent him from the Valley of Hebron, and he came to Shechem. ¹⁵ And a man found him wandering in the fields. And the man asked him, "What are you seeking?" ¹⁶ "I am seeking my brothers," he said. "Tell me, please, where they are pasturing the flock." ¹⁷ And the man said, "They have gone away, for I heard them say, 'Let us go to Dothan.'" So Joseph went after his brothers and found them at Dothan.

¹⁸ They saw him from afar, and before he came near to them they conspired against him to kill him. ¹⁹ They said to one another, "Here comes this dreamer. ²⁰ Come now, let us kill him and throw him into one of the pits.[1] Then we will say that a fierce animal has devoured him, and we will see what will become of his dreams." ²¹ But when Reuben heard it, he rescued him out of their hands, saying, "Let us not take his life." ²² And Reuben said to them, "Shed no blood; throw him into this pit here in the wilderness, but do not lay a hand on him"—that he might rescue him out of their hand to restore him to his father. ²³ So when Joseph came to his brothers, they stripped him of his robe, the robe of many colors that he wore. ²⁴ And they took him and threw him into a pit. The pit was empty; there was no water in it.

²⁵ Then they sat down to eat. And looking up they saw a caravan of Ishmaelites coming from Gilead, with their camels bearing gum, balm, and myrrh, on their way to carry it down to Egypt. ²⁶ Then Judah said to his brothers, "What profit is it if we kill our brother and conceal his blood? ²⁷ Come, let us sell him to the Ishmaelites, and let not our hand be upon him, for he is our brother, our own flesh." And his brothers listened to him. ²⁸ Then Midianite traders passed by. And they drew Joseph up and lifted him out of the pit, and sold him to the Ishmaelites for twenty shekels[2] of silver. They took Joseph to Egypt.

²⁹ When Reuben returned to the pit and saw that Joseph was not in the pit, he tore his clothes ³⁰ and returned to his brothers and said, "The boy is gone, and I, where shall I go?" ³¹ Then they took Joseph's robe and slaughtered a goat and dipped the robe in the blood. ³² And they sent the robe of

many colors and brought it to their father and said, "This we have found; please identify whether it is your son's robe or not." **33** And he identified it and said, "It is my son's robe. A fierce animal has devoured him. Joseph is without doubt torn to pieces." **34** Then Jacob tore his garments and put sackcloth on his loins and mourned for his son many days. **35** All his sons and all his daughters rose up to comfort him, but he refused to be comforted and said, "No, I shall go down to Sheol to my son, mourning." Thus his father wept for him. **36** Meanwhile the Midianites had sold him in Egypt to Potiphar, an officer of Pharaoh, the captain of the guard.

¹ Or *cisterns*; also verses 22, 24 ² A *shekel* was about 2/5 ounce or 11 grams

Section Overview

Given the backstory already recounted in this chapter, it is certainly surprising that Jacob sends Joseph to inquire after his brothers—in his fancy coat (37:23)!—while they are out in the field, watching the flocks. This presents them with the perfect opportunity to do away with the dreamer who has so provoked their jealousy. Their initial plan is to kill Joseph, but later they decide simply to sell him into slavery and be done with him forever, bringing an end to him and his disturbing dreams while making a profit at the same time (vv. 18–28). As a result, Joseph is trafficked down to Egypt, and Jacob is cleverly deceived into thinking that his beloved son has died at the hands of wild animals (vv. 32–36). Jacob's deep despair is accounted for by his assumption that with the death of Joseph, whom Jacob imagined to be the child of promise, God's promise had also failed. God's purposes are not so easily derailed, however, and God will use the brothers' heinous sins to advance his perfect plan for humanity, as well as for the survival of Jacob's family and the ultimate reconciliation of the brothers.

Section Outline

XI. The Family History of Jacob (37:1–50:26) . . .
    B. The Brothers Sell Joseph (37:12–36)

Comment

37:12–17 Joseph's brothers go to pasture the flock near their former home of Shechem, some 50 miles (80 km) from Hebron, where Jacob is staying at this time (vv. 12–14). The family still owns property in the region (33:19), which may give them added incentive to travel to the area. After the earlier incident in which Joseph brought a bad report about his brothers (37:2), he is no longer working with them. Apparently he is exempt from the arduous task of shepherding, remaining comfortably at home in his fashionable robe, which would further inflame the other brothers' jealousy.

The location of the brothers at Shechem, near the site of their earlier slaughter of its inhabitants, might have given Jacob pause, but he seems to be oblivious to any potential danger. Instead he sends Joseph after them to inquire into their *shalom* ("See if it is well with your brothers"; v. 14), even though the brothers had been unwilling to give Joseph a *shalom* while they were at home (v. 4). As a dutiful son, Joseph readily agrees to his father's request ("Here I am"; v. 13) and journeys alone to find them.

When Joseph arrives in Shechem, however, the brothers are nowhere to be found (v. 15). This could easily be the end of Joseph's journey, forcing him to return home with no news. Coincidentally (providentially!), however, Joseph just happens to meet a man while wandering around in the fields, and that man just happens to know where the brothers have gone—to Dothan (v. 17), 13 miles (21 km) farther from home and from anyone who might know Jacob.[512] Significantly (and again providentially) Dothan is on a major caravan route to Egypt, unlike Shechem—another crucial step in the unfolding of God's plan. Dothan later becomes known as the place where God opens the eyes of Elisha's servant to see the invisible chariots and horsemen protecting Israel from the surrounding enemy army (2 Kings 6:13–17). God is no less present with Joseph at Dothan to protect him from danger, even though his eyes are never opened to see that reality.[513]

37:18–24 Joseph may find his brothers in Dothan (Gen. 37:17), but it is his brothers who see him coming from afar off and, recognizing him, cold-bloodedly decide to do away with him (v. 18). This is no crime of passion but premeditated murder. Their mocking comment could be rendered "Behold, here comes this master of dreams [*ba'al hakhalomot*]" (v. 19); if they kill him, they believe they will prevent his dreams of leadership over the family from coming to pass. The brothers' initial plan is to kill Joseph and dispose of the body by throwing it into one of the pits used for water storage, with which the area is dotted (v. 20). A person traveling through the open country on his own might easily encounter and be killed by a wild animal, though, and if his remains are never found, there would be little need for the brothers to account for his disappearance. In this way the brothers seek to forestall Joseph's dreams by disposing of their subject (v. 20): If Joseph is dead, how could they be forced to prostrate themselves before him?

Joseph's silence after he meets his brothers is unexpected.[514] In the earlier part of the chapter Joseph was full of words: he brought a report to his father (v. 2), he recounted his dreams (vv. 5–10), he responded "Here I am" when his father sent him to his brothers (v. 13), and he explained his mission to the man in the field at Shechem (v. 16). But at the crucial point when his brothers seize him this man of many words falls silent in a manner that foreshadows another servant who will suffer: "Like a sheep that before its shearers is silent, so he opened not his mouth" (Isa. 53:7).

At this point Reuben, the oldest brother, intervenes, seeking to rescue Joseph (Gen. 37:21). His motivation is clear, as it is repeated in the text—he desires to

---

[512] Perhaps assuming that Joseph is looking for lost animals, the stranger asks him, "What [*mah*] are you seeking?" rather than "Whom [*mi*] are you seeking?"
[513] Kidner, *Genesis*, 181.
[514] Greidanus, *Preaching Christ from Genesis*, 338.

rescue Joseph and restore him to his father (vv. 21–22)—but his reason for that desire is not given. Since he has been out of his father's favor since sleeping with his father's concubine Bilhah (35:22), it may be that he thinks to ingratiate himself with Jacob by preserving the life of his favorite son. He does not try to dissuade his brothers from disposing of Joseph at this point; he merely seeks to keep them from killing Joseph directly. That would constitute "shedding of blood" (37:22), which might leave them liable to judgment, whether by God (cf. 9:5–6) or by some form of cosmic justice. Instead they should simply cast Joseph into a pit alive, where they could let thirst and hunger do their dirty work for them.

Since these pits are used as cisterns to hold water, Joseph could potentially drown, but the particular pit the brothers choose is dry (37:24). We are not told whether they take any effort to check that fact ahead of time; Reuben might have, considering his plan to rescue Joseph later, or it may be a time of year when such pits are typically dry; the narrator simply records it as a bare fact. Joseph has been wearing his fancy coat with long sleeves (v. 23; cf. v. 3), and the brothers take him and strip off his garment before throwing him in a pit (vv. 23–24).[515] If his father's investiture of Joseph with the robe marked him out as the heir of the promise and the family favorite, then his robe's removal by his brothers marks the destruction of such hopes and his lowering of status to that of a common slave.

37:25–28 Having disposed of Joseph, at least temporarily, the brothers sit down to their lunch, as if it were a normal day like any other (v. 25). Meanwhile, a caravan of traders comes along, taking spices down from Gilead to sell in Egypt. These traders are variously described as "Midianites" or "Ishmaelites" at different points in the story (Ishmaelites: 37:25, 27, 28; 39:1; Midianites: 37:28, 36). The terms seem to be interchangeable, with "Ishmaelite" perhaps serving as a functional description of camel-riding spice traders, while "Midianite" serves more as an ethnic description.[516] It is certainly ironic that all those involved in selling Joseph into slavery in Egypt are part of the Abrahamic family—his brothers and cousins.[517]

The Ishmaelites' cargo is described as "[aromatic] gum, balm, and myrrh" (v. 25). These are precisely the kinds of cargo one would expect such traders to carry; however, they also find an ironic echo in the list of gifts that the brothers will later take down to Egypt to appease the unrecognized Joseph in 43:11, with "gum" and "myrrh" occurring in only these two places in the OT.[518] The Ishmaelites are not slave-traders by occupation, but they are apparently not averse to diversifying their merchandise on request.

Having earlier listened to Reuben's argument for keeping Joseph alive, the brothers now follow the lead of Judah in a signal of the impending power shift

---

515 The verb "stripped off" (Gen. 37:23; a form of of *pashat*) is also used of skinning animals, for example in Leviticus 1:6; cf. Wenham, *Genesis 16–50*, 354.
516 Much as "Canaanite" is both an ethnic designation and a term for a trader (s.v. כְּנַעֲנִי, HALOT, 2.485). On Ishmaelites and Midianites cf. Wenham, *Genesis 16–50*, 355. Cf. also Judges 8:22–24 for a similar linkage of Ishmaelites and Midianites. On camels cf. comment on 12:10–20.
517 Sarna, *Genesis*, 260.
518 Currid, *Genesis 25:19–50:26*, 199.

from firstborn brother to the ultimate leader of the family. However, at this point Judah's leadership is far from sanctified; he suggests selling Joseph rather than killing him, though he does recognize that "he is our brother, our own flesh" (37:27).[519] It is profit rather than compassion that motivates the brothers to change their mind; they sell Joseph to the Ishmaelites for twenty shekels of silver, the average price of a young male slave in antiquity.[520] Most slaves in Egypt would have been prisoners of war, but the commercial trading of people from the Near East to Egypt is well attested in this era.

37:29–36 The implication of the story is that, in order to enjoy their lunch in peace, the brothers have moved a little distance from the pit into which Joseph was unceremoniously dumped. After going back to the pit to extricate Joseph and sell him to the Ishmaelites, they then return to their encampment, leaving Reuben—who has been away on some unspecified errand—to discover Joseph's absence from the pit. Distraught, and perhaps imagining that the brothers have killed Joseph in his absence, Reuben tears his clothing as a sign of grief (v. 29).

Meanwhile the brothers take Joseph's special coat and dip it in the blood of a young goat, using it to deceive their father (v. 32). The irony is profound: since Jacob used a young goat and his brother's clothing to deceive his own father (cf. 27:9, 15, 16), the same deception is perpetrated upon him. However, whereas Jacob told his father an outright lie (27:19), his sons merely produce the garment and let him draw his own conclusions, saying, "This we have found; please identify whether it is your son's robe or not" (37:32). They do not speak Joseph's name nor call him their "brother"; he is "your son," reflecting the family favoritism as clearly as in chapter 27, where Esau was Isaac's son (27:1, 5, 18, 20, 21, 24, 26, 27) and Jacob was Rebekah's (27:6, 8, 17, 43). But, whereas Isaac was unable to identify Jacob (27:23), Jacob has no difficulty identifying Joseph's robe (37:33). The layers of irony continue to unfold later, when Joseph recognizes his brothers but they fail to recognize him (42:7–8).

Jacob's response to Joseph's presumed death is dramatic and enduring. He not only tears his clothing, as Reuben had earlier (37:34; cf. v. 29), but he also puts on sackcloth—the first recorded use of that mourning habit in the Bible. He mourns for "many days," in contrast to the more limited time of mourning over Jacob's own death at a good old age (50:3, 10), and refuses the comfort offered by his children (37:35).[521] On the contrary, he declares, "I shall go down to Sheol to my son, mourning" (v. 35). The righteous are never said to go to Sheol in the OT; it is the home of the unrighteous dead and of the souls of those who are not at rest (cf. Ezekiel 31–32).[522] Jacob's assumption that Joseph is in Sheol may be connected with

---

519 As noted earlier, the word "brother" (Hb. *'akh*) occurs no fewer than twenty-one times in this chapter, and the cluster of uses around this verse heightens the irony of the brothers' unbrotherly action.
520 Sarna (*Genesis*, 261) cites Leviticus 27:5 and Code of Hammurabi §116, 214, 252.
521 Reference to his "daughters" may include daughters-in-law or additional daughters beside Dinah, the only daughter mentioned in the biblical account.
522 On Sheol cf. Philip S. Johnston, *Shades of Sheol: Death and the Afterlife in the Old Testament* (Downers Grove, IL: InterVarsity Press, 2002).

his supposed violent death, and his death means the loss not only of an earthly future for Jacob but of his own future in the afterlife as well. It is not just Joseph's dreams that have been shattered by the events that have transpired; Jacob's dreams are destroyed as well.

Why though, is Jacob's world so completely overturned, so that he mourns for Joseph as though he were his only son? One answer is the fact that Joseph was his favorite son, the "son of his old age" (Gen. 37:3). This connection with Abraham's love for Isaac as the son of his old age (21:2, 7) suggests a deeper reason, however. Jacob saw Joseph as the child through whom the Lord's promise of a messianic seed would be fulfilled. With Joseph's apparent death, how would that promise be fulfilled? The dream that Jacob has stored up in his heart—Joseph's dream of the sun, moon, and stars' coming and bowing down to him (37:9–11), an image far too big simply to point to leadership in a small nomadic family—is a dream that now cannot be fulfilled. Jacob interprets the death of Joseph as the end not merely of his own hope but of all hope for the world.

Yet the narrator strikingly juxtaposes Jacob's intense grief with the announcement of Joseph's safe arrival in Egypt, where he is sold into Potiphar's house (v. 36). Joseph's story is not yet over; he was not in Sheol but merely down in Egypt, which is precisely where God's providential plan has brought him. God will continue to be with Joseph there, and in due season Jacob will see his son again.

Potiphar is described in Hebrew as a *saris* (v. 36), a word that can denote either a eunuch or a member of the royal bureaucracy (many of whose members would have been eunuchs, either so they could work around the women of the royal family or to prevent the danger of their leading any kind of coup). Eunuchs were often married in antiquity, so Potiphar's married status does not argue against his being one.[523] If he is a eunuch, that might add an additional dimension to the events of Genesis 39, though it should be noted that Pharaoh's chief cupbearer and baker are also termed *sarisim* in 40:2. The title given to Potiphar, "captain of the guard" (v. 36), means "chief of the slaughterers" (*sar hattabbakhim*); it may indicate some kind of military policeman, such as the position held by Nebuzaradan in 2 Kings 25:8 or Arioch in Daniel 2:14. On the other hand, it is possible that the "slaughtering" refers to killing animals for food and that therefore Potiphar is more of a chief cook or butler.[524]

Response

God is sovereign over all things that take place in this world. That includes the seemingly meaningless "coincidences" that happen to us. If Joseph had not met the man in the field, or if the man had not overheard the brothers, or if the brothers had not moved on to a place frequented by camel caravans, or if there had not happened to be a caravan at just the right time, then Joseph would not have ended

---

523 Cf. G. E. Kadish, "Eunuchs in Ancient Egypt," in *Studies in Honor of John A. Wilson*, ed. G. E. Kadish (Chicago: University of Chicago Press, 1969), 59.
524 The LXX calls him an *archimageiros* ("chief butler"); cf. Mathews, *Genesis 11:27–50:26*, 702.

up in Egypt. If he had been purchased by someone other than Potiphar, his story might have worked out differently. This story contains so many "chance" coincidences, but all of them work together to accomplish God's plan for his own glory and the good of his people.

Yet God's sovereignty in the Joseph story does not merely cover coincidences; it also explicitly covers the sinful acts of human beings. The brothers meant to kill Joseph, and then chose to profit instead through human trafficking. Yet those decisions too were part of God's will to accomplish his holy purposes; what they meant for evil, God meant for good (Gen. 50:20). This is a universal principle, as Paul records in Romans 8:28, but it is comforting to be reminded that even the worst sins perpetrated against us (or even by us!) cannot remove us from God's good plan for our lives. What others mean against us for evil, and what we mean for evil against others, God intends for our good and his glory.

At the same time we must not minimize the pain or suffering that such "coincidences" and sins may cause God's people. It may take years to see how God means good out of this evil—if we ever do—and in the meantime Christians may shed many tears over the bitterness of what has been lost. Certainly, God's plan for his people often involves deep hurts in the present, even if by faith we confess that such suffering is not worth comparing to the glory awaiting us in Christ (Rom. 8:18). At such times we must come alongside and weep with those who weep rather than offering mere platitudes (Rom. 12:15).

Our hope in the midst of this sad world lies in the gospel, which is prefigured in striking ways in this chapter. God the Father sent his own beloved Son into this world to seek our *shalom*, our welfare, knowing ahead of time exactly how we would receive him (cf. Matt. 21:33–41). Neither the Father nor the Son was surprised by the cross. God surrendered his Son into the hands of wicked men who stripped him not of a royal robe but of a simple peasant's garment and then brutally beat and executed him.

Jesus exercised his sovereignty even over his own death at the hands of wicked men. They had no power to commit such a sin against him except the power that he himself had given them. Every breath with which they mocked him came from him. The strength in the arm that drove each nail into his flesh was strength that God himself had supplied.[525] As Acts 2:23 puts it, Jesus was "crucified and killed by the hands of lawless men," but that very sinful act took place "according to the definite plan and foreknowledge of God."

Yet this Father's response to his Son's death was different from Jacob's. Jacob believed that the forces of darkness and chaos had won, but the divine Father knew that his Son's death was proof that divine love had triumphed. The bloodstained cross that declared the story of Jesus' death would be the gateway to new life for millions upon untold millions of sinful men and women who would be redeemed and given new hope by it. This gift of forgiveness comes to us freely as we simply

---

[525] Cf. Steven Estes and Joni Eareckson Tada, *When God Weeps: Why Our Sufferings Matter to the Almighty* (Grand Rapids, MI: Zondervan, 2000), 53–54.

trust in what Jesus has done for us. Instead of trying to stand before God dressed in our own righteousness, seeking to be justified by our own best efforts to do what is good and right, we put on the bloodstained robe of another and ask God to recognize his Son's robe. This is our only claim to righteousness and the pathway through which hope of new creation comes to this lost and hopeless world.

GENESIS 38

38 It happened at that time that Judah went down from his brothers and turned aside to a certain Adullamite, whose name was Hirah. ² There Judah saw the daughter of a certain Canaanite whose name was Shua. He took her and went in to her, ³ and she conceived and bore a son, and he called his name Er. ⁴ She conceived again and bore a son, and she called his name Onan. ⁵ Yet again she bore a son, and she called his name Shelah. Judah¹ was in Chezib when she bore him.

⁶ And Judah took a wife for Er his firstborn, and her name was Tamar. ⁷ But Er, Judah's firstborn, was wicked in the sight of the LORD, and the LORD put him to death. ⁸ Then Judah said to Onan, "Go in to your brother's wife and perform the duty of a brother-in-law to her, and raise up offspring for your brother." ⁹ But Onan knew that the offspring would not be his. So whenever he went in to his brother's wife he would waste the semen on the ground, so as not to give offspring to his brother. ¹⁰ And what he did was wicked in the sight of the LORD, and he put him to death also. ¹¹ Then Judah said to Tamar his daughter-in-law, "Remain a widow in your father's house, till Shelah my son grows up"—for he feared that he would die, like his brothers. So Tamar went and remained in her father's house.

¹² In the course of time the wife of Judah, Shua's daughter, died. When Judah was comforted, he went up to Timnah to his sheepshearers, he and his friend Hirah the Adullamite. ¹³ And when Tamar was told, "Your father-in-law is going up to Timnah to shear his sheep," ¹⁴ she took off her widow's garments and covered herself with a veil, wrapping herself up, and sat at the entrance to Enaim, which is on the road to Timnah. For she saw that Shelah was grown up, and she had not been given to him in marriage. ¹⁵ When Judah saw her, he thought she was a prostitute, for she had covered her face. ¹⁶ He turned to her at the roadside and said, "Come, let me come in to you," for he did not know that she was his daughter-in-law. She said, "What will you give me, that you may come in to me?" ¹⁷ He answered, "I will send you a young goat from the flock." And she said, "If you give me a pledge, until you send it—" ¹⁸ He said, "What pledge shall I give you?" She replied, "Your signet and your cord and your staff that is in your hand." So he gave them to her and went in to her, and she conceived by him. ¹⁹ Then she arose and went away, and taking off her veil she put on the garments of her widowhood.

²⁰ When Judah sent the young goat by his friend the Adullamite to take back the pledge from the woman's hand, he did not find her. ²¹ And

he asked the men of the place, "Where is the cult prostitute[2] who was at Enaim at the roadside?" And they said, "No cult prostitute has been here." 22 So he returned to Judah and said, "I have not found her. Also, the men of the place said, 'No cult prostitute has been here.'" 23 And Judah replied, "Let her keep the things as her own, or we shall be laughed at. You see, I sent this young goat, and you did not find her."

24 About three months later Judah was told, "Tamar your daughter-in-law has been immoral.[3] Moreover, she is pregnant by immorality."[4] And Judah said, "Bring her out, and let her be burned." 25 As she was being brought out, she sent word to her father-in-law, "By the man to whom these belong, I am pregnant." And she said, "Please identify whose these are, the signet and the cord and the staff." 26 Then Judah identified them and said, "She is more righteous than I, since I did not give her to my son Shelah." And he did not know her again.

27 When the time of her labor came, there were twins in her womb. 28 And when she was in labor, one put out a hand, and the midwife took and tied a scarlet thread on his hand, saying, "This one came out first." 29 But as he drew back his hand, behold, his brother came out. And she said, "What a breach you have made for yourself!" Therefore his name was called Perez.[5] 30 Afterward his brother came out with the scarlet thread on his hand, and his name was called Zerah.

[1] Hebrew *He* [2] Hebrew *sacred woman*; a woman who served a pagan deity by prostitution; also verse 22
[3] Or *has committed prostitution* [4] Or *by prostitution* [5] *Perez* means *a breach*

Section Overview

God promised Jacob that he would become a "company of nations" (Hb. *qahal goyim*; 35:11), but at this point the chosen family is coming apart at the seams. Reuben, Simeon, and Levi have all disqualified themselves from leadership in a variety of ways, while Joseph has been sold into Egypt as a slave; no one expects to see him again (37:36). Now Judah, the fourth son in line after Reuben, Simeon, and Levi, abandons his dysfunctional family to go and live among the Canaanites (38:1). He marries a Canaanite wife, and, though he produces three sons, it appears that his line will come to a halt in the next generation due to the wickedness of two of those sons and his unwillingness to risk the life of the youngest (38:7–11). Yet through his daughter-in-law's bold (and morally dubious) decision to dress up as a prostitute and sleep with Judah, his line is preserved. Not only so, but the line of promise will ultimately descend through the fruit of this sexual encounter, resulting in Tamar's becoming one of four women of questionable origins or character referenced in the genealogy of Jesus, alongside Ruth, Bathsheba ("the wife of Uriah"), and Mary (Matt. 1:1–17). The one who comes to save his people from their sins is himself descended from a long line of sinners (male and female).[526]

Genesis 38 is often treated as an intrusive element in the larger storyline of Joseph, but in fact it is a masterpiece of literary artistry far more tightly connected to the surrounding narrative than often recognized. The opening verse explicitly

---

526 M. G. Kline, *Genesis: A New Commentary* (Peabody, MA: Hendrickson, 2016), 122.

links it to the larger narrative as occurring "at that time" (Gen. 38:1), and the delay in continuing Joseph's story heightens suspense. Moreover, the story of Judah's sexual immorality (along with his sons') enhances our appreciation for Joseph's religiously motivated chastity under far greater temptation in chapter 39. Most importantly, however, Genesis 38 is absolutely necessary to the wider storyline in providing the explanation for the profound change in Judah's character, from the man willing to sell his brother for the price of a slave (37:26–27) and sleep with a prostitute (38:15–18) to the man willing to offer himself as a slave in his brother's place (44:18–34). Without it the wider narrative would be incoherent. The events of chapter 38 cover almost exactly the same time period as Genesis 37–44, and Judah's experience of sin and grace in this chapter leave a profound impact on his heart, accounting for his dramatically different persona later in the story.

Section Outline

XI. The Family History of Jacob (37:1–50:26) . . .
   C. Judah and Tamar (38:1–30)

Comment

38:1–2 The narrator directly links this episode with the events of the preceding chapter via the phrase "At that time" (Hb. *ba'et khahi*'; v. 1) rather than the more general "After these things" (cf. Gen. 15:1; 22:1). That is, Judah's decision to abandon the family of promise and join the Canaanites is linked directly to the brothers' selling of Joseph into slavery and deceiving their father (37:19–36). Judah played a central role in those actions (37:26–27), but now he wants nothing more to do with his brothers, a motive underlined by the fact that his leaving is described explicitly as going down from his brothers (38:1), rather than from Hebron or from his father. Like Joseph, who went down to Egypt, Judah also goes down, only in his case the departure from the family is voluntary rather than involuntary. Physical geography can be a marker of spiritual geography in the Bible, and Judah's journey is downhill in both aspects.[527]

It is not obvious that Judah has a particular destination in view when he leaves home, which reinforces his desperation to leave his family—anywhere would be better than remaining at home. However, he "turns aside" (or perhaps "pitches his tent") to see an Adullamite by the name of Hirah. The verb "turn aside" (*natah*) is not often used of visiting someone, so it may reflect spiritual as well as physical geography, a departure from the proper path (cf. 1 Sam. 8:3).[528] While he is there Judah sees a Canaanite woman (Gen. 38:2). There is no mention of Judah's loving her (cf. 24:67; 29:18) or even of her name; she is identified only as "the daughter of a certain Canaanite whose name was Shua."[529] The narrator simply tells us that

---

[527] Compare the similar movements of Samson in Judges 14 and Jonah in Jonah 1. Leaving the Israelite heartland always involves a physical descent, but sometimes more is at play than merely altitude.
[528] Currid, *Genesis 25:19–50:26*, 207.
[529] Perhaps that is her name, along the lines of "Bath-sheba" (2 Sam. 11:3; cf. 1 Chron. 2:3), but here and in Genesis 38:12 she is simply introduced as the (nameless) daughter of a man named Shua.

"he saw ... he took," phraseology that echoes Eve's original sin (3:6; cf. also the desire of the sons of God for the daughters of men in 6:2, and Pharaoh for Sarai in 12:15). Not only has Judah abandoned the Abrahamic family; he has now married a Canaanite woman (despite the prohibitions in 24:3; 28:1), seemingly confirming his definitive exit from the line of promise.

38:3–5 "He took her and went in to her, and she conceived and bore a son" (38:2–3)—the rapid succession of Hebrew verbs suggests a similarly rapid sequence of events. Judah names his son Er, which means something like "watchful," though no explanations are given in the text for the names of Judah's sons. Second and third sons rapidly follow, Onan and Shelah; there is no struggle with barrenness for Judah in his pathway away from the Abrahamic blessing. Only Er is named by Judah; Onan and Shelah are apparently named by his (unnamed) wife, while Judah may even be living in an entirely different town when Shelah is born, the town of Chezib, whose name can be translated "Deceit" (v. 5).[530] Deceit has been a consistent feature of Jacob's family, and it will be the same in Judah's subsequent dealings with Tamar.

38:6–11 Judah then takes a wife, Tamar ("palm tree"), from the local populace for his oldest son, Er. However, we are told that Er—whose firstborn status is reiterated—is evil in the sight of the Lord, and so the Lord puts him to death (v. 7).[531] The nature of his wickedness is not specified, though the language is used often of idolatry (cf. Deut. 4:25). This is a remarkable statement, given that the events of chapter 34 and 37 have elicited no direct response from the Lord, and Judah and his brothers remain unscathed; the word "evil" (Hb. *ra'*) and its deadly consequences link the sin of Er (and subsequently Onan) to the events leading to the flood (cf. Gen. 6:5; 8:21). Judah's decision to live among the Canaanites has had a fatal impact on his family.

If Er's sin is left unspecified, Onan's sin is clearly described (Gen. 38:9). Onan is instructed to follow the pattern of Levirate marriage and have sexual intercourse with his dead brother's widow in order to raise up offspring who will be counted as belonging to his brother rather than to himself (cf. Deut. 25:5–10). This practice was widely attested throughout the ancient Near East and provided a compassionate means of providing for widows within the family into which they had married, as well as of preserving the name of the deceased.[532]

However, although Onan is willing to join himself to Tamar and enjoy himself sexually, he makes sure there is little risk of any procreation, thus undermining the purpose of the institution (Gen. 38:9). The form of the Hebrew indicates that this is Onan's regular practice, not merely a one-time act.[533] His motivation may be financial. After Er's death, Onan stands to inherit the double share due to the

---

[530] Sarna, *Genesis*, 265. The MT places Judah in Chezib at the time, though the LXX suggests that his wife was the one who was located there.
[531] The Hebrew word for evil (*ra'*) is essentially Er's name backward (*'er*).
[532] Sarna, *Genesis*, 266.
[533] Wenham, *Genesis 16–50*, 367.

firstborn—provided there is no heir. If Onan fathers a son by Tamar, that son will be reckoned as Er's and thus inherit the firstborn's double portion. This abuse of both Tamar and the institution of Levirate marriage makes him "wicked in the sight of the LORD," just as his brother Er had been,[534] and he meets a similar fate: the Lord puts him to death as well (v. 10). Strikingly, there is no mention of Judah's mourning the death of either of his sons, unlike Jacob's intense mourning for Joseph (37:34–35).

Judah is now left with a dilemma: faced with the death of two of his sons, he should in due course give his third son, Shelah, to Tamar, in order to raise up seed for his brothers (38:11). Yet he is convinced that Tamar is under a curse—despite the obvious fact that the problem lies far more with the wickedness of his sons. In any event Tamar ends up not only childless and abused but socially shamed as well, sent back to her father's house in disgrace to await the summons in due course to marry Shelah.

38:12–19 Meanwhile, time passes,[535] and it becomes evident to Tamar that Judah has no intention of marrying her to Shelah, who by now is old enough for marriage (v. 14). Judah too, like Onan, is illegitimately withholding offspring from her, though for his own distinct reasons. Meanwhile, Judah's wife, the daughter of Shua, also dies, but once again Judah seems to be fairly rapidly comforted (v. 12).[536] Certainly there is a contrast here with Tamar, who maintains her mourning attire a much longer time (v. 14). Before long Judah is on his way to the annual sheepshearing festivities at Timnah along with his friend, Hirah the Adullamite (Gen. 38:12; cf. v. 1). Sheepshearing in the ancient world was a time of intensely hard work followed by equally intense celebration,[537] an important fact in the events that follow. In the Canaanite context cultic prostitution was a means of celebrating the blessing of fertility and acknowledging the role of Baal and Asherah in providing increase for the flocks, though it is not clear that Judah's interest in Tamar has any particular religious connotations (cf. comment on 38:20–23).

When the news of Judah's plans to attend the sheepshearing is relayed to Tamar, she puts into motion a plan of her own. She takes off her mourning attire and puts on a veil, which is necessary to conceal her identity from her father-in-law. The exact significance of being veiled in that cultural context is debated by commentators. Middle Assyrian laws forbade any common prostitute or an unmarried temple prostitute from wearing a veil, which leads Mathews to conclude,

---

[534] The similarity in the description of their sinful character and its consequences led the rabbis to speculate that their sin was also similar and that Er also practiced *coitus interruptus*. In his case the rabbis imagined his motivation to have been a selfish desire to avoid the challenges of parenting or to preserve Tamar's beauty for himself (cf. Sarna, *Genesis*, 266).

[535] In Hb. "The days grew many"; this can cover any time period from about one to twenty years. Narrative time slows down at this point, with the events of the rest of the chapter covering about a year, compared to something more like twenty years for the chapter to this point; cf. Steven D. Mathewson, *The Art of Preaching Old Testament Narrative* (Grand Rapids, MI: Baker, 2002), 54–55.

[536] The Hebrew is merely a sequence of *vav*-consecutives, which often convey immediately consequent actions, with little time lapse in between. Hence the KJV: "The daughter of Shua Judah's wife died and Judah was comforted and went up . . ."

[537] Steven D. Mathewson, "Exegetical Study of Genesis 38," *BSac* 146 (1989): 378.

"A woman's veil was the garment not of a harlot but of a betrothed woman,"[538] while Currid draws the opposite implication, that in donning a veil Tamar is dressing herself as a (married) cult prostitute.[539] The evidence of Song of Solomon 1:7 suggests that a veiled woman certainly ran the risk of being seen as a person of loose character,[540] while the text itself suggests that Tamar's covered face communicates to Judah that she is an ordinary prostitute (Hb. *zonah*; Gen. 38:15).

Tamar's location alongside the road likely adds to that impression. She stations herself along Judah's route to Timnah at the entrance of the town of Enaim ("twin springs"; v. 14). The place name is loaded with irony: not only will Judah "scatter his springs abroad" here (cf. Prov. 5:16 for this image of sexual activity), resulting in the birth of twins (Gen. 38:28–30), but the phrase "entrance to Enaim" (*petakh 'enayim*) could also mean "opening of the eyes." And the result of this encounter would certainly be eye-opening for Judah (cf. vv. 24–26).

Whether because of her veil, her location, or her clothing, Judah takes Tamar to be a prostitute (v. 15), though it is made clear in the text that her concern is simply the legitimate desire to have offspring, which Judah is blocking by withholding Shelah (v. 14). Not knowing the identity of the woman with whom he is about to sleep (cf. 29:23), Judah propositions her, and they negotiate a price. He will give her a "young goat from the flock" (38:17). This is the same kind of animal with which Isaac was deceived by Jacob in 27:9, 16, as well as with which Jacob was deceived by his sons in 37:31. Since Judah is obviously not traveling with such an animal in his possession, a pledge is required (38:17). Tamar's plan requires an identifiable object, and Judah's seal and his staff fit the bill perfectly (v. 18). The seal, perhaps cylindrical and in ancient times often carried on a cord around the person's neck or arm rather than on a ring,[541] was used to sign documents and mark objects as belonging to an individual. Meanwhile, the staff was often intricately carved and served as a symbol of a patriarch's authority as clan chieftain (cf. Numbers 17). This is thus the ancient equivalent of asking for Judah's driver's license and credit cards.[542]

The price is no sooner agreed than the deed is committed. Unlike in her earlier unfruitful relationships with Judah's sons, Tamar immediately conceives (Gen. 38:18). As a symbol of her return to her former position, Tamar takes off her prostitute's clothing and changes back into her widow's clothes, as if nothing has happened (v. 19). But fundamentally everything has now changed—both for Tamar and, ultimately, for Judah.

38:20–23 Although Judah's sexual morality leaves much to be desired, he is a man of his word; indeed, he goes to far greater lengths to fulfill what he has promised

---

[538] Mathews, *Genesis 11:27–50:26*, 718.
[539] Currid, *Genesis 25:19–50:26*, 211. Both positions seem to assume that the Middle Assyrian laws were invariably kept, but the opposite may actually be the case, that the laws were needed precisely because it was common for prostitutes to use veils to disguise their identity.
[540] Cf. Michael V. Fox, *The Song of Songs and the Ancient Egyptian Love Songs* (Madison: University of Wisconsin Press, 1985), 103.
[541] W. W. Hallo, "'As the Seal upon Thy Heart': Glyptic Roles in the Biblical World," BR 1 (1985): 22.
[542] Alter, *Art of Biblical Narrative*, 9.

this "prostitute" than what he had promised his own daughter-in-law. He sends his friend, Hirah, to Enaim with the young goat he has promised, hoping to retrieve his important personal possessions from the prostitute (v. 20). However, once there, not only can Hirah not find the woman, but no one seems to know who she is. Hirah refers to her in his conversations with the locals as a "cult prostitute" (Hb. *qedeshah*) rather than using the narrator's term, "prostitute" (*zonah*). These terms may be interchangeable, as some commentators believe,[543] but it is striking that it is only Hiram who calls her a "cult prostitute," suggesting that he is attempting to provide a cover of social acceptability for his friend.[544] Certainly, nothing about their original encounter smacked of any religious dimension. Visiting a cult functionary was probably viewed as more acceptable than engaging a roadside prostitute, however.

Hirah's failure to find any trace of Tamar, or anyone who has seen her, contrasts starkly with Joseph's immediate success in chapter 37 in finding someone who knew where his brothers had gone (37:15–16). Hirah is left with no choice but to return home empty handed and acknowledge his failure to Judah (38:22). Judah, for his part, seems unperturbed. He has fulfilled his part of the deal, and he feels that his hands are clean in the matter.

38:24–26 Three months later Tamar's condition becomes clear to all, and she is charged with acting like a prostitute (Hb. *zanetah*; v. 24). Judah does not seem to wait for the two or three witnesses required under the law (Deut. 17:6), nor does he carry out any sort of formal trial. Perhaps her condition is considered sufficient proof in the absence of a husband, but, considering his own recent dalliance with a prostitute, Judah's immediate pronouncement of the sentence to burn her reeks of inordinate haste (Gen. 38:24; Hb. "Bring her out and let her be burned" is only two words).[545] Even though Tamar is living in her own father's house at this point, Judah still has legal power over her as his daughter-in-law. Moreover, in the interests of his own family line he has his own reasons for wanting to get rid of her: once she is gone, Judah will be free to marry Shelah to someone else, someone not affected by Tamar's curse, by whom Judah's family line might continue. The irony is that, had he succeeded in his plan, it would have been his own offspring he would have been putting to death along with Tamar.

At the crucial moment Tamar is able to produce the evidence of Judah's hypocrisy and his paternity of her child: Judah's seal and staff (v. 25). Just as Judah and his brothers asked Jacob to identify Joseph's robe (37:32), so now she asks Judah to identify his possessions. He is forced to confess that she is righteous and not he (38:26).[546] Tamar is not "right" in the sense of being completely without moral guilt but is right in this situation, in which Judah's behavior with Shelah has driven her

---

[543] Mathews, *Genesis 11:27–50:26*, 719.
[544] Alter, *Art of Biblical Narrative*, 9.
[545] Burning was an extreme punishment, reserved for cases of exceptional depravity (cf. Lev. 20:14; 21:9), and Judah's sentence here is out of proportion with the punishments that would be normal for adultery or prostitution; cf. Sarna, *Genesis*, 269.
[546] For the translation "She is righteous, not I" rather than "She is more righteous than I" cf. Waltke (*Genesis*, 513), who calls it a comparison of exclusion.

to take drastic measures. Judah's eyes are opened, in contrast to their being shut tight at Enaim. He does not sleep with her again, however (v. 26); to do so would be to take advantage of her vulnerable position and would be unnecessary, since she already has the offspring that she sought.

38:27–30 There is still room for one more twist in the narrative. As with Rebekah before her, there are twins in Tamar's womb, and there is another conflict involving the color red and a younger child's supplanting the older (v. 27; cf. 25:22–26). In this case the first child to put out a hand, marked by the midwife with a scarlet thread, is actually the second child to be born (38:30). He is given the name Zerah but is upstaged by his brother, Perez, who overtakes him and manages to be born first. It is Perez ("breakthrough") whose line will ultimately become the more significant of the two, though his story extends far beyond the pages of the book of Genesis. His name recurs as the ancestor of Boaz—and thus of David—in Ruth 4:18–22, another story with themes reminiscent of levirate marriage. The "breakthrough" that gives Perez his name represents a breakthrough for Judah, for it is at this point in the story that Judah's thoughts must turn homeward to his own family; the next time we encounter Judah he is back within the fold (cf. Gen. 43:3). In the long run Perez's birth also represents a breakthrough for God's people; it is significant that in the book of Ruth there are ten generations from Perez to David, and Perez's name begins the genealogy, not Judah's, as we might have expected (Ruth 4:18).[547]

Response

In many ways Tamar was an innocent victim of the sins of Judah and his family. The trap she laid for Judah was about her getting justice and righting a wrong. Yet at the same time her trap was risky, not to mention highly questionable ethically, morally, and legally. She was intentionally engaging in prostitution to entrap Judah. Their relationship as father-in-law and daughter-in-law raised the issue of incest. As a result the text emphasizes strongly that Judah did not knowingly sleep with his daughter-in-law (Gen. 38:15) and that they did not have further sexual encounters after this incident (v. 26). Tamar set out to right a wrong, but she did so in a profoundly disturbing and wrong way.

This is a common reality. When we suffer at the hands of others, we often respond wrongly. We may lack Judah's position of authority to enforce oppression or Tamar's audacity to fight back. Yet we can still wage war against those who have hurt us in our minds, nursing bitterness, harboring resentment, and reveling in their sufferings and failings. Sometimes we turn the hurt inward in a cycle of self-loathing and self-harm. Others respond by retreating from relationships with others or with God, finding safety by seeking to control every aspect of one's existence. In our brokenness we continue the cycle of sin and counter-sin in ways that make sense within our own stories even though they do not give us the

---

[547] The formula "These are the *toledot* of Perez" (Ruth 4:18) represents another striking connection to the Genesis narrative.

safety and satisfaction we seek. But is there any way to break the cycle of sufferers-turned-sinners and victims-turned-perpetrators?

Judah was transformed by having his own sin exposed to public view, which led to his public confession and repentance. Tamar's words parallel exactly what Judah and his brothers said to Jacob when they brought him Joseph's bloodied coat (37:32; 38:25). If there was one thing that Judah gained from all the painful experiences and losses he suffered, it was a greater sympathy for his father. Judah now knew from personal experience what it was like to lose sons. Like Jacob, he too had tried desperately to protect his youngest, even at the cost of hurting others. He too had been duped by a mysterious veiled woman into a different relationship than the one he had expected. As Jacob had not recognized Leah (29:25), so Judah had failed to recognize Tamar. Judah's confrontation with the true depths of his own sin ultimately fostered reconciliation with his brothers, and especially with his father. Recognizing his own brokenness drove him back to reconnect with his broken family. His eyes were opened to his sin, and his heart was changed within him—a change whose impact resonates later in the story, when he volunteers to take Benjamin's place as Joseph's captive in Egypt (44:30–34).

What an incredible picture of the grace of God—the God who exalts the humble and brings down the proud! We are all profoundly broken people, just like Tamar and Judah. Yet that is precisely why Jesus came to this earth, to seek and to save that which is lost. Through Judah and Tamar Jesus was the son of a sinner and a prostitute. Indeed, Jesus spent much of his time on earth with sinners and prostitutes (cf. Matt. 21:31–32), telling them joyfully about the triumph of his grace over all our sin and failure. Jesus accomplished this by inverting what Judah did to Tamar. While Judah blamed Tamar for his sins to maintain his own innocence, planning to put her to death, Jesus himself took all our shame, enduring at the cross the death we deserved. He now covers us with his perfection, saying to us, "You are righteous," taking away our sins, and making us acceptable to his Father (2 Cor. 5:21). In that way he removes our curse forever and welcomes us safely into the family of God, where we can be loved and blessed by him, broken sinners though we still are.

GENESIS 39

39 Now Joseph had been brought down to Egypt, and Potiphar, an officer of Pharaoh, the captain of the guard, an Egyptian, had bought him from the Ishmaelites who had brought him down there. ² The LORD was with Joseph, and he became a successful man, and he was in the house of his Egyptian master. ³ His master saw that the LORD was with him and that the LORD caused all that he did to succeed in his hands.

⁴ So Joseph found favor in his sight and attended him, and he made him overseer of his house and put him in charge of all that he had. ⁵ From the time that he made him overseer in his house and over all that he had, the LORD blessed the Egyptian's house for Joseph's sake; the blessing of the LORD was on all that he had, in house and field. ⁶ So he left all that he had in Joseph's charge, and because of him he had no concern about anything but the food he ate.

Now Joseph was handsome in form and appearance. ⁷ And after a time his master's wife cast her eyes on Joseph and said, "Lie with me." ⁸ But he refused and said to his master's wife, "Behold, because of me my master has no concern about anything in the house, and he has put everything that he has in my charge. ⁹ He is not greater in this house than I am, nor has he kept back anything from me except you, because you are his wife. How then can I do this great wickedness and sin against God?" ¹⁰ And as she spoke to Joseph day after day, he would not listen to her, to lie beside her or to be with her.

¹¹ But one day, when he went into the house to do his work and none of the men of the house was there in the house, ¹² she caught him by his garment, saying, "Lie with me." But he left his garment in her hand and fled and got out of the house. ¹³ And as soon as she saw that he had left his garment in her hand and had fled out of the house, ¹⁴ she called to the men of her household and said to them, "See, he has brought among us a Hebrew to laugh at us. He came in to me to lie with me, and I cried out with a loud voice. ¹⁵ And as soon as he heard that I lifted up my voice and cried out, he left his garment beside me and fled and got out of the house." ¹⁶ Then she laid up his garment by her until his master came home, ¹⁷ and she told him the same story, saying, "The Hebrew servant, whom you have brought among us, came in to me to laugh at me. ¹⁸ But as soon as I lifted up my voice and cried, he left his garment beside me and fled out of the house."

¹⁹ As soon as his master heard the words that his wife spoke to him, "This is the way your servant treated me," his anger was kindled. ²⁰ And Joseph's master took him and put him into the prison, the place where the king's prisoners were confined, and he was there in prison. ²¹ But the LORD was with Joseph and showed him steadfast love and gave him favor in the sight of the keeper of the prison. ²² And the keeper of the prison put Joseph in charge of all the prisoners who were in the prison. Whatever was done there, he was the one who did it. ²³ The keeper of the prison paid no attention to anything that was in Joseph's charge, because the LORD was with him. And whatever he did, the LORD made it succeed.

Section Overview

After a chapter-long digression, following Judah's story downward away from the Abrahamic family and ending with the birth of the twins who will ultimately redirect Judah toward home, the narrator returns to the main storyline as it ended in chapter 37, with Joseph down in Egypt (39:1; cf. 37:36). There he has been sold as a slave to a man named Potiphar, an official (eunuch?)[548] at the Egyptian court.

---

548 Cf. comment on 37:29–36.

From that inauspicious starting point Joseph prospers, because the Lord is with him (39:2). Because of the Lord's presence with him, everything Joseph touches succeeds; in a virtuous cycle of blessing his master observes that the Lord is with him and so gives everything over into Joseph's control, which results in even more success and mutual blessing (vv. 3–5). Their relationship is a miniature embodiment of the Abrahamic blessing (12:1–3): as Potiphar submits control of his life to Joseph, he is in turn blessed by Joseph's God. The result is *shalom* for Potiphar, a life of ease in which he has nothing with which to concern himself except whatever is served for dinner (39:6).

Yet Potiphar's *shalom* does not last. Joseph is handsome and good-looking (v. 6), and Potiphar's wife notices him and seeks to seduce him (v. 7). Whether she is sexually frustrated with being married to a eunuch or merely a bored wealthy woman, she demands that Joseph sleep with her (vv. 8–12); when he refuses, she accuses him of attempted rape (vv. 13–16). Whether or not Potiphar is convinced by her accusations, Joseph finds himself once again at the bottom of the heap, this time as a prisoner in an Egyptian jail (v. 20).

Yet the Lord is still with Joseph, and so Joseph begins once again to find favor in the eyes of those around him and to be a blessing to them (v. 21). In language reminiscent of the earlier verses about the Lord's blessing on Potiphar the Lord's blessing now rests on the keeper of the prison, for Joseph's sake (v. 23). These events must have seemed very confusing to Joseph at the time. His "reward" for his faithfulness to his master and to the Lord was to be demoted and imprisoned? How could that happen if the Lord were really with him and showing him steadfast love (Hb. *khesed*; v. 21)? Yet the Lord's plan is exactly on track for Joseph, and every uncomfortable step is necessary not only to place him where he needs to be when Pharaoh dreams his dreams but also to form him into the kind of person the Lord wants him to be.

Section Outline

XI. The Family History of Jacob (37:1–50:26) ...
    D. Joseph and Potiphar (39:1–23)

Comment

39:1–6a Genesis 39:1 resumes where chapter 37 left off, recounting from the opposite perspective the transaction whereby Joseph ends up with Potiphar. In Genesis 37:36 Joseph was sold by the Midianites to Potiphar; here he is bought by Potiphar from the Ishmaelites.[549] This shift naturally focuses our attention on Potiphar, who, along with his wife, is the main character in this chapter. He is once again described as "an officer [*saris*] of Pharaoh, the captain of the guard" (39:1); we noted earlier the ambiguity of the first descriptor, which routinely (though not always) in the OT refers to eunuchs (cf. comment on 37:29–36). The Egyptian

---

[549] On the dual identification of the Midianites/Ishmaelites cf. comment on 37:25–28.

identity of Joseph's master is mentioned three times for emphasis (39:1, 2, 3): Joseph's God-given prosperity while in Egyptian captivity forms a paradigm for the later prosperity of the Israelites in their own Egyptian captivity (anticipated in the Lord's words to Abraham in 15:13).[550] It is also stressed (twice) that Joseph has been "brought down" (causative form of *yarad*) to Egypt, heightening the comparison and contrast with Judah, who "went down" (simple form of *yarad*) to live among the Canaanites of his own volition (38:1).

The divine name, Yahweh, is not used elsewhere in the Joseph narrative; however, it occurs no fewer than six times in this chapter, three at the beginning and three at the end (Gen. 39:2, 3, 5, 21, 23 [2x]).[551] Joseph's blessing comes not from some generic deity (*'elohim*) but from the personal presence of Israel's deity, which results in blessing for him and all those who trust in him. "The Lord was with Joseph," and so he prospers; these themes are underscored repeatedly in this chapter as cause and effect. Despite the difficulty of Joseph's situation, he advances rapidly in positions of responsibility and trust because the Lord gives him favor in the eyes of his owner (v. 4).

The first mark of this prosperity is Joseph's working in Potiphar's house with the higher class of slaves rather than out in the fields (v. 2). Of course, this location in the house will later put him in the pathway of Potiphar's wife, with significant consequences. In any case his master notices the success of everything placed under his care and promotes him first to be his personal assistant (ESV: "attended him") and then to be overseer over the whole house and estate (v. 4). The narrator chooses an unusual idiom in verse 6 to describe the transfer of power from Potiphar to Joseph; instead of the normal "he gave [*natan*] into the hand of Joseph" the narrative uses the verb *'azab* ("he left" [or "abandoned"]). This prepares for the next scene, in which Joseph in turn "abandons" his garment in the hand of Potiphar's wife (cf. vv. 12, 13, 15).[552] Potiphar's only concern is "the food he ate" (v. 6)—whether literally or as an idiom for needing to think only of his personal interests.

39:6b–10 Thus far the narrative might sound like a moralistic wisdom tale: those who serve God will prosper, along with everyone around them. However, this trajectory is rudely interrupted by Potiphar's wife. Joseph is "handsome in form and appearance" (v. 6), like his mother, Rachel, the only other person in Scripture to be given this double accolade. Potiphar's wife "cast her eyes on Joseph," an idiom of desire familiar from other ancient Near Eastern literature.[553] There is no seduction or romance in her approach to him. Rather, she issues him a simple command as his superior, as she might command him to move a piece of furniture: "Lie with me" (v. 7).

---

550 Wenham, *Genesis 16–50*, 373.
551 Sarna, *Genesis*, 271. Sarna points out that the divine name always occurs in the narrator's words and never in direct speech. In the one place we might expect it in direct speech, in Joseph's justification of his actions in verse 9, it makes sense for him to use the generic *'elohim* since he is addressing an outsider, Potiphar's wife.
552 Sarna, *Genesis*, 272.
553 Cf. Speiser, who cites the Gilgamesh epic (*Genesis*, 303).

It would have been easy for Joseph to justify submitting to her demands. Promiscuity was a given in most slave societies, and Joseph has seen so much taken from him. Why should he not take a little pleasure when it is offered? Ingratiating himself with his master's wife might lead to all sorts of little privileges, while turning her down might have unforeseen consequences. However, Joseph categorically refuses her. As the narrator has highlighted by repeatedly calling her "his master's wife," she does not belong to him—indeed, she is the only one of his master's belongings that he keeps for himself (v. 9). To sleep with her would be a sin against his master and, more importantly, a sin against God (v. 9). Indeed, it would be "great wickedness" (Hb. *hara'ah haggedolah*) to do such a thing; the word "wickedness" relates this temptation to the sins of Er and Onan in the previous chapter, which led to their deaths (38:7, 10), while also relating to the sins of the prefall generation in Genesis 6:5.

Potiphar's wife is far from deterred by Joseph's refusal, however. On the contrary, she continues to harass him on a daily basis "as she was speaking [*kedabberah*] with him" (39:10), which suggests a constant flow of speech. Meanwhile, his only recourse is to refuse to listen to her or to put himself in any kind of potentially compromising position (v. 10). To "lie beside her" or "to be with her" might not necessarily require Joseph to engage in sexual activity, but under the circumstances any close contact would be dangerous, and the latter phrase could be used as a euphemism for sex (cf. 2 Sam. 13:20). Joseph's steadfast refusal under constant temptation contrasts sharply with Judah's sexual sin with Tamar after simply seeing her sitting veiled beside the road on one occasion (Gen. 38:15–16).[554]

39:11–18 If this story were a morality tale, Joseph's steadfast faithfulness to God under temptation would be result in his being freed, or perhaps being given some high office. Instead, his faithfulness is precisely what brings him down. One day, when Joseph happens to be working in the house and none of the other servants are around, she confronts him again, taking hold of his outer garment (Hb. *beged*; 39:12).[555] He has no alternative but to leave his cloak in her hand and flee the house (v. 12).[556]

Not for the first time in his life Joseph finds his own clothing used against him. His brothers used his distinctive coat to convince his father he had been killed by a wild animal (37:31–33). Now his cloak is used by Potiphar's wife as the evidence that he has assaulted her (39:13–15). She marshals her case well, immediately summoning her other servants and claiming an atrocity has occurred, as evidenced by

---

[554] Calvin comments, "Holy Joseph ... must have been endowed with extraordinary power of the Spirit, seeing that he stood invincible to the last, against all the allurements of the impious woman" (*Genesis*, 2.297–298).
[555] Von Rad argues that it must have been an inner garment, since outer garments were not worn indoors, and that therefore Joseph fled in a state of undress (*Genesis*, 361). However, the Hebrew *beged* is a very general word for clothing, and we cannot be sure of its precise import here, which suggests that the state of Joseph's dress is not the main point of the narrator.
[556] Sarna (*Genesis*, 274) suggests that the combination of the two verbs, "he fled" and "he went out," suggests that Joseph ran hastily out of the room but slowed to a more normal pace as he went outside in order to avoid attracting attention.

the cloak. She calls Joseph a "Hebrew," identifying him as a dangerous foreigner,[557] and blames her husband for his presence in their midst ("He has brought among us a Hebrew"; v. 14). Meanwhile, she suggests that Joseph's presence is an intentional insult to all of them by her husband; she and the servants are together ("us") in being mocked by this alien.[558] Potiphar's wife claims that, when Joseph threatened her, she cried out with a loud voice (v. 15), an important demonstration of resistance to an attempted rape (Deut. 22:24, 27), though in fact in the earlier verses she called out only after Joseph had fled (Gen. 39:13–14).

When Potiphar returns home, she retells her story, with key differences. Potiphar is still assigned blame for bringing the Hebrew into their midst, but now Joseph's servant status is emphasized (v. 17). Joseph's intent was to mock (or sexually assault) her alone, rather than mocking both her and the other servants (v. 17). In both recountings she claims that Joseph left his cloak beside her, avoiding any mention of the more incriminating fact that it was actually left in her hand (v. 18; cf. v. 12).[559]

39:19–23 Potiphar is left with the unenviable choice of siding with a slave and exposing his wife as a liar or getting rid of Joseph. He chooses the latter course, though the fact that he merely has Joseph thrown in prison rather than executed suggests he does not entirely believe his wife's story. It seems that in many contexts in Egypt at this time the husband could decide whether or not to press for the death penalty in cases of adultery, but the normal punishment for such an offense would have been immediate execution.[560] There seems little reason for Potiphar to grant clemency if he really believes her story; however, if he has his doubts about her veracity, the decision makes perfect sense. While the text notes that Potiphar is furious, it refrains from identifying the target of his anger, supporting the possibility that at least part of that anger is directed toward his wife.[561]

Joseph thus finds himself at the bottom of the heap once again. After Joseph was sold into slavery by his brothers, the Lord's presence with him had permitted his meteoric rise to become the steward over all of Potiphar's possessions (vv. 3–6). Yet his downfall, through no fault of his own, does not mean that the Lord has now abandoned him. Joseph is now in the royal prison rather than in Potiphar's house (v. 20), but the Lord is still with him, with similar results. The Lord gives him favor in the eyes of the keeper of the prison (v. 21; cf. v. 4); everything Joseph does prospers (v. 23; cf. v. 3), so that he ends up in charge of the household, while his master lives a life entirely free from concern (vv. 22–23; cf. v. 6).

---

557 The term "Hebrew" is often used by outsiders to identify an Israelite, as well as by Israelites to identify themselves to outsiders (cf. Gen. 40:15; 41:12); cf. von Rad, *Genesis*, 362.
558 *Tsakhaq* ("to laugh at us") can also have connotations of sexual activity (compare English "fool around with"). In Genesis 26:8 it describes behavior that convinces Abimelech that Isaac and Rebekah are married.
559 Alter, *Art of Biblical Narrative*, 110.
560 Claus Westermann, *Genesis 37–50: A Continental Commentary*, trans. J. J. Scullion (Minneapolis: Fortress, 1986), 67.
561 Currid, *Genesis 25:26–50:26*, 230. Currid also notes that imprisonment was a distinctively Egyptian form of punishment, unknown in the rest of the ancient Near East—a detail that adds veracity to the story.

These close parallels between the beginning and the end of the chapter make the one unique statement in these verses stand out: "The LORD ... showed [Joseph] steadfast love" (Hb. *khesed*; 39:21). The casual observer would never conclude from Joseph's circumstances that he is the recipient of the *khesed* of his God, but appearances can be deceptive. In fact, it is the Lord's steadfast faithfulness to his promises to make the children of Israel into a community of nations and through them to bless the world that is being worked out through all this seemingly adverse providence. God has placed Joseph exactly where he needs to be for the next part of his storyline to unfold, and the Lord's blessing remains upon Joseph, even in the most difficult of circumstances.

Response

Preachers often turn to Genesis 39 as a model for how to resist temptation. That makes sense, since Joseph does indeed resist sexual temptation—in stark contrast to his brother Judah in Genesis 38—and there are lessons that may be legitimately drawn from his approach. Yet that is not really the point of Genesis 39, any more than the point of 1 Samuel 17 is to teach us how to take on the giants that threaten us in our own spiritual lives.

The main point of the chapter is that God is with Joseph, even in the most untoward of circumstances, and that his presence with Joseph not only enables him to succeed personally but also makes him a blessing to all those around him. In this way God is demonstrating his faithfulness to the Abrahamic blessing, of which Joseph acts as representative. God is also demonstrating the power of his providence in orchestrating all things, even horrendous situations of sin and abuse, to accomplish his holy purposes; Genesis 50:20 applies just as much to the actions of Potiphar's wife as it does to the actions of Joseph's brothers. Joseph must be in the royal prison at the end of Genesis 39 in order for the next part of God's plan to unfold.

Of course, the Lord may not have such dramatic plans for our lives as Christians, but we should learn not to equate success automatically with God's favor; the Lord may be with us on the slave auction block or in prison on a trumped-up charge just as much as he is with us in our best moments. His *khesed* will never leave us nor forsake us; it will pursue us all the days of our lives, wherever we find ourselves (Ps. 23:6).

The Lord was with Joseph, enabling him to be a blessing to Egyptians in the midst of his own undeserved pain, betrayal, suffering, and temptation, not simply so that he could become an example for us to imitate in temptation (though he is that) but so that he could be an exemplar pointing forward to Jesus. Jesus is the only one who has ever suffered entirely without fault of his own. In the wilderness he experienced far greater temptations than Joseph ever faced (Matthew 4). Joseph may have resisted temptation in this situation, but he was not sinless. There were doubtless times when Joseph lost hope and gave in to self-pity or anger. Yet in his moments of shining faithfulness Joseph points us beyond himself to Jesus.

Where was God on the day when Jesus suffered on the cross? What we—sinful humanity—meant for evil, God meant as part of his wonderful and holy plan of redemption. The Father allowed the Son to be falsely accused and falsely condemned, sinfully abused and murdered. In that terrible moment at the cross the Father was not with Jesus, so that he might be with us forever. As a result, the penalty was paid in full for all those times when we have joined Judah in plunging headlong into sin instead of siding with faithful Joseph. Instead of that penalty we have now been credited with the perfect righteousness of Christ, who withstood every temptation in our place. By his wounds we are healed. By his righteousness our filth is dealt with, fully and finally, so that the Lord's smile rests upon us forever for his sake.

This truth gives us assurance and hope as we face the darkest hours of God's plan for our own lives. We will all suffer in this life, and, as we do, we may be tempted to believe such suffering means that God is angry with us or has abandoned us. Nothing could be further from the truth. God has poured out all his anger against our sin on Jesus, which means that our present sufferings can only have a redemptive purpose, teaching us to die to sin and bringing others to see and know the God whom we have met in Jesus Christ. He is with us and will never leave us nor forsake us.

GENESIS 40

40 Some time after this, the cupbearer of the king of Egypt and his baker committed an offense against their lord the king of Egypt. ² And Pharaoh was angry with his two officers, the chief cupbearer and the chief baker, ³ and he put them in custody in the house of the captain of the guard, in the prison where Joseph was confined. ⁴ The captain of the guard appointed Joseph to be with them, and he attended them. They continued for some time in custody.

⁵ And one night they both dreamed—the cupbearer and the baker of the king of Egypt, who were confined in the prison—each his own dream, and each dream with its own interpretation. ⁶ When Joseph came to them in the morning, he saw that they were troubled. ⁷ So he asked Pharaoh's officers who were with him in custody in his master's house, "Why are your faces downcast today?" ⁸ They said to him, "We have had dreams, and there is no one to interpret them." And Joseph said to them, "Do not interpretations belong to God? Please tell them to me."

⁹ So the chief cupbearer told his dream to Joseph and said to him, "In my dream there was a vine before me, ¹⁰ and on the vine there were three branches. As soon as it budded, its blossoms shot forth, and the clusters ripened into grapes. ¹¹ Pharaoh's cup was in my hand, and I took the grapes and pressed them into Pharaoh's cup and placed the cup in

Pharaoh's hand." ¹²Then Joseph said to him, "This is its interpretation: the three branches are three days. ¹³In three days Pharaoh will lift up your head and restore you to your office, and you shall place Pharaoh's cup in his hand as formerly, when you were his cupbearer. ¹⁴Only remember me, when it is well with you, and please do me the kindness to mention me to Pharaoh, and so get me out of this house. ¹⁵For I was indeed stolen out of the land of the Hebrews, and here also I have done nothing that they should put me into the pit."

¹⁶When the chief baker saw that the interpretation was favorable, he said to Joseph, "I also had a dream: there were three cake baskets on my head, ¹⁷and in the uppermost basket there were all sorts of baked food for Pharaoh, but the birds were eating it out of the basket on my head." ¹⁸And Joseph answered and said, "This is its interpretation: the three baskets are three days. ¹⁹In three days Pharaoh will lift up your head—from you!—and hang you on a tree. And the birds will eat the flesh from you."

²⁰On the third day, which was Pharaoh's birthday, he made a feast for all his servants and lifted up the head of the chief cupbearer and the head of the chief baker among his servants. ²¹He restored the chief cupbearer to his position, and he placed the cup in Pharaoh's hand. ²²But he hanged the chief baker, as Joseph had interpreted to them. ²³Yet the chief cupbearer did not remember Joseph, but forgot him.

Section Overview

In Genesis 39 the Lord was with Joseph, who prospered in the house of Potiphar, bringing blessing to those around him—until his success came to a crashing halt when he was falsely accused by Potiphar's wife. The same trajectory began again at the end of that chapter: the Lord was with Joseph in the prison and gave him favor in the eyes of the keeper of the prison,[562] bringing blessing to those around him, albeit in more humble surroundings (39:21–23). The expectation is that this will once again lead to Joseph's promotion, and indeed it does—eventually. The means of that promotion is less predictable, however; Joseph's reputation as "master of dreams" had first brought him into this situation of bondage in Egypt, and it is his mastery of dreams that will eventually get him out of it (Genesis 40–41), though not before a significant and frustrating period of waiting. God's providence is once again the overarching theme of the narrative, a providence that is utterly sovereign but is in no hurry to accomplish its divine purposes.

Section Outline

XI. The Family History of Jacob (37:1–50:26) . . .
    E. The Cupbearer's and Baker's Dreams (40:1–23)

Comment

40:1–4 The gap between Genesis 39 and 40 is left undefined, described only with the vague phrase "Some time after this" (Hb. *'akhar haddebarim ha'eleh*; v. 1).

---

[562] The Hebrew calls it a "prison-*house*" (*bet-hassohar*) to underline the parallels.

Likely it is a period of several years, during which Joseph continues to serve his new master faithfully in the royal prison (the period from 37:2 to 41:46 covered a total of thirteen years). The prison is described as "the house of the captain of the guard" (40:3), the same title borne by Potiphar (cf. 39:1); although the text does not explicitly identify the two figures, it is possible that the site of Joseph's detention is literally at the doorstep of his previous success.

Two high-profile officials of Pharaoh are committed to the prison, and Joseph is assigned by the captain of the guard to serve them (40:4). These men are described as Pharaoh's "chief cupbearer" (*sar-hammashqim*; v. 2) and his "chief baker" (*sar-ha'ofim*; v. 2). These officials are far more important than their names might suggest to modern readers; they have personal access to the king daily and are perhaps trusted to sample the king's food before he eats it, to protect against poisoning. Since Pharaoh has absolute power, having his ear gives these men enormous influence (cf. Neh. 1:11).

The two have incurred Pharaoh's anger because they have "committed an offense" (*khate'u*, "sinned") against their master, the king of Egypt (Gen. 40:1). This highlights the contrast between their reason for imprisonment and Joseph's, who is there for refusing to sin (*khata'*) against his master, God (39:9).[563] The nature of their offense is left unspecified, but the king of Egypt is angry (*qatsaf*) with them, a term commonly used of God's anger against sinful humans. Since these two men are personal servants of Pharaoh and their fate has not been decided, it is not unreasonable that the prison governor would assign his most reliable man, Joseph, to watch over their needs.[564]

40:5–8 After they have been in custody for some time,[565] with Joseph attending to them daily, the two Egyptian officials have simultaneous dreams (40:5). Egyptians placed a high value on the significance of dreams in general and the fact that both have ominous dreams at the same time would heighten their sense of the importance of these revelations; as Joseph will later say, the doubling of dreams indicates the certainty that the depicted events will in fact occur (41:32).[566] The irony of these words' coming from a man whose own doubled dream in Genesis 37 seems very far from likely to come true at this point should not be missed. Joseph's faith in God's revelation through dreams has not been disturbed by his own experience.

The Egyptian officials are deeply disturbed by their dreams,[567] especially since there is no one available to interpret them (40:6). Since dreams typically pertain to

---

563 Waltke, *Genesis*, 524.
564 This service is thus hardly "as low as possible" or a contradiction to the earlier note about Joseph's significant role in the prison (*pace* von Rad, *Genesis*, 365). Rather, it is a position of extraordinary responsibility and delicacy.
565 The Hebrew *yammim* (Gen. 40:4) indicates an unspecified period of time, though it often seems to have in view about a year (cf. comment on 4:1–5).
566 In Genesis 37 and 41 the paired dreams are reinforcing, describing the same events in different imagery. Here, however, the paired events are discriminatory, anticipating different outcomes of the two men's incarceration. For that reason the dreams are given to two individuals here rather than both being given to the same man. The same reinforcing principle applies, however. On the phenomenon of duplicate dreams in the ancient Near East cf. Hamilton, *Genesis 18–50*, 487–488.
567 Since the Hebrew word *za'af* can describe a storm-tossed sea, the ESV's "troubled" fits well as a translation.

future events, understanding the meaning of the dream leaves open the possibility that adverse events could be forestalled, or at least borne with stoic endurance, while positive outcomes might be encouraged. An uninterpreted dream means unidentified dangers hanging over the dreamer's head, or potential triumphs that might slip through his fingers. It is not surprising, therefore, that the interpretation of dreams became an industry in Egypt, with many claiming the power to read and understand the symbology of such apparitions. As becomes clear in the next chapter, such professional dream interpreters were readily available at the royal court, but not in prison.

Joseph's concern for the welfare of the men he is serving is such that he notices their downcast faces and inquires after the cause (v. 7). When they share it with him, he boldly attributes the interpretation of dreams to God,[568] not professional dream interpreters, and invites them to share their dreams with him. He does not promise an interpretation, which lies in God's hands, but invites them to be open to the possibility that God might speak even through him. Since Joseph is aware of the Lord's presence with him, he may have a degree of confidence that the Lord will give him the required interpretation, just as Daniel does in Daniel 2:16–19.

40:9–19 The first to recount his dream is the cupbearer. The dream fits his calling, an element that would heighten his sense that the dream has a significant meaning concerning himself. It was common in Egyptian dream omens for the dreamer to be a central character in the dream and his actions within the dream to be significant.[569] In the cupbearer's dream he saw a vine with three branches, each of which budded, blossomed, and ripened immediately (Gen. 40:10). It was as though, under God's blessing, the normal agricultural cycle had been dramatically accelerated—an image that would instantly remind Moses' first audience of the budding and blossoming of Aaron's rod in Numbers 17. The cupbearer then took the grapes in the dream, crushed them into Pharaoh's cup, and gave the cup to his master (Gen. 40:11).

Joseph then gives his interpretation: the three branches represent three days,[570] after which Pharaoh will lift up the cupbearer's head and restore him to his former position (v. 13). To "lift up someone's head" is an idiom from the world of the ancient court. It was customary, whenever the king made a public appearance, for the people to prostrate themselves in his presence; however, those that the king favored might be invited to lift up their heads and approach him.[571] This expression can also be used to indicate a royal pardon, which would release a person from imprisonment (2 Kings 25:27).[572] So Joseph interprets the dream to mean that

---

568 More specifically Joseph refers to *'elohim* (God, or "the gods"), rather than explicitly naming Yahweh, since he is speaking to outsiders to the covenant.
569 On the Egyptian understanding of dreams cf. John Currid, *Ancient Egypt and the Old Testament* (Grand Rapids, MI: Baker, 1997), 224–228.
570 As Mathews (*Genesis 11:27–50:26*, 747) points out, the number three is underlined by the three aspects of the vine's flourishing (budding, blossoming, and ripening; Gen. 40:10) and the three actions of the cupbearer (taking the grapes, squeezing them, and placing the cup in Pharaoh's hand; 40:11).
571 Von Rad, *Genesis*, 367.
572 Waltke, *Genesis*, 526.

Pharaoh will summon the cupbearer from prison into his presence and restore him to his office within a very short space of time.

In lieu of payment for his interpretation, after Joseph predicts the cupbearer's release and restoration to power, he says to him, "Only remember me [*zakar* in the Qal], when it is well with you, and please do me the kindness [*khesed*] to mention me [*zakar* in the Hiphil] to Pharaoh, and so get me out of this house" (Gen. 40:14). In Genesis 39:21 we were told that the Lord had showed *khesed* to Joseph, a combination of love and loyalty that meant God had not forgotten him, even in prison. Now Joseph asks the cupbearer to remember him when he is released from prison and to take the appropriate action that goes with that memory; that is, he should use his access to Pharaoh to put in a good word and get Joseph released from the prison (40:14).

As further justification for his request, Joseph boldly proclaims the undeserved nature of his situation on two grounds: he had become a slave not through indebtedness or as a prisoner of war, which were generally regarded in the ancient world as legitimate grounds to enslave a person, but rather through manstealing, which was a capital offense in many ancient law codes (v. 15).[573] This highlights Joseph's brothers' crime against him and in turn makes it all the more striking that, when he later has the opportunity for vengeance against the brothers, he does not execute them. Moreover, Joseph has done nothing at all during his time in Egypt to deserve his imprisonment (v. 15)—indeed, quite the opposite, as chapter 39 makes clear. Joseph's life has gone from a literal pit (37:24) to a metaphorical pit (40:15) through no fault of his own. Unfortunately, it is necessary to God's plan that Joseph not yet be delivered from the pits, so the cupbearer does not remember Joseph for quite some time (v. 23).

Emboldened by the favorable interpretation that Joseph gives the royal cupbearer, the chief baker then recounts his own dream, carefully making it match the other dream as much as possible (v. 16). It also depicted his return to his old task, in his case bringing baked goods for Pharaoh to enjoy. Sarna points out that the Egyptians were justifiably renowned for their baking, with references found in hieroglyphic texts to fifty-seven varieties of bread and thirty-eight different types of cake.[574] However, in a scene evoking the classic film of Alfred Hitchcock, the baker dreamed that, as he walked along with three baskets of baked goods on his head,[575] he was assaulted by marauding birds (v. 17). Ominously, the baker was powerless to protect the baked goods against the birds, which ate from the uppermost basket, presumably because the baskets were stacked, protecting the lower two layers. The baker's failure to protect Pharaoh's food contrasts with Abraham's successful defense of the sacrifices against predatory birds in the night vision of Genesis 15:11.

---

[573] Exodus 21:16; Deuteronomy 24:7. On the term "Hebrews" cf. comment on 39:11–18.
[574] Sarna, *Genesis*, 279.
[575] The Hebrew word *khori* is of uncertain meaning. It could describe either the contents of the basket (NASB 1995: "white bread," which would be the finest kind of bread, in comparison to the dark bread that peasants would make from coarser grains) or the construction of the basket of wicker or other woven material (ESV "cake baskets"); cf. Hamilton, *Genesis 18–50*, 481.

Joseph's interpretation of the chief baker's dream begins exactly like that of the cupbearer: the three baskets represent three days, after which Pharaoh will lift up the baker's head (Gen. 40:19). Yet the baker must surely suspect that the final significance will be very different. Whereas the cupbearer will have his head "lifted up" in the sense that he will be restored to his previous position of power and influence, the baker's head will be "lifted up" in the sense of being hanged on a tree (v. 19). In an Egyptian context it is unlikely that being hanged means death by strangulation on the gallows. More probably this punishment means that his body will be impaled on a wooden spike and left to die or his corpse will be publicly displayed in this way after death by some other means.[576] Such a fate was a sign of being under an enduring curse throughout the ancient world (Deut. 21:22–23) but was perhaps a particular horror for Egyptians, for whom the proper care of dead bodies was a necessary prerequisite to a comfortable afterlife. It was thus an Egyptian's worst nightmare to have his body left after death to become food for the birds of the air—exactly what will happen to the chief baker in a gruesome real-life fulfillment of the birds' assault in the dream (Gen. 40:19).

40:20–23 Joseph's interpretation of the three branches and three baskets as three days may earlier have seemed arbitrary, or even simply a vague representation of a short period of time,[577] but it turns out to be an exact prediction of events. We are not told whether Joseph knew ahead of time that Pharaoh's birthday was three days away (v. 20),[578] but it turns out to be the decisive moment for both the cupbearer and the chief baker: both of their heads are "lifted up" among his servants (v. 20), with opposite outcomes, exactly as Joseph had predicted. The cupbearer is restored to his position, while the chief baker is impaled on a tree (vv. 21–22). However, the cupbearer does not show *khesed* to Joseph, as requested. On the contrary he forgets Joseph, leaving him languishing in the pit (v. 23). What must earlier have seemed to Joseph to be God's providential means of securing his release from prison ends with profound disappointment. Yet what really matters is not whether the cupbearer remembers Joseph but whether God remembers him.[579] Though it is not yet God's time for Joseph to be delivered, he has not forgotten Joseph.

Response

God's timing is perfect, as it always is. If the cupbearer remembered Joseph immediately after he was released from prison, he would have remembered him

---

[576] It is possible that the idiom of "lifting the head" can be used not merely of a favorite's being invited to lift up his face to behold the king's favor but also of a condemned man's being commanded to lift his face and hear the pronouncement of sentence; cf. E. A. Speiser, "Census and Ritual Expiation in Mari and Israel," *BASOR* 149 (1958): 21.
[577] There are passages in the OT in which "three days" seems simply to mean "a few days"; the events of Joshua 2, for example, which themselves stretch over several days, seem to fit within the "three days" of Joshua 1:11.
[578] Technically the form here of *yalad* means not "to be born" but "to be fathered," though the distinction is not very great, and in Ezekiel 16:4–5 it clearly refers to birth. However, James Hoffmeier has suggested that "the day of Pharaoh's being fathered" refers not to his birthday but rather to the celebration of his acknowledgment as the divine son of Ra; cf. Hoffmeier, *Israel in Egypt: The Evidence for the Authenticity of the Exodus Tradition* (Oxford: Oxford University Press, 1999), 89–91.
[579] Mathews, *Genesis 11:27–50:26*, 752.

too soon. Joseph might have been released from prison and lost from sight when God's moment for him came. God's purpose in all this—which at this stage is completely invisible and mysterious to Joseph—is to have him bear witness for him before kings and to deliver both Egypt and his own family from the impending famine. In order for that plan to progress Joseph must continue to experience yet more injustice and broken *khesed* at the hands of men. He must go on suffering undeserved pain in order ultimately to free others from death. Joseph endures two more years of his prison nightmare until God's time is finally ripe. Nonetheless, God will ultimately work for good everything that Joseph must endure as evil.

There are important lessons that we learn only in the furnace of suffering (cf. Rom. 5:3–5). God never forgets us amid our worst trials but promises to work all our painful experiences together for good (Rom. 8:28). The Lord's *khesed* never fails; it is new every morning because of his great faithfulness—even when our outward circumstances seem to declare the opposite (Lam. 3:22–23). To endure suffering is a call to wait patiently for the Lord, trusting that he will remember us and act to restore us at exactly the right time (Lam. 3:25–26).

We cannot do anything to merit such remembrance. We deserve to share the fate of the baker, not the cupbearer. We have truly sinned against our Master (Gen. 40:1), and the wages of such sin is death (Rom. 6:23). And yet, in the ultimate twist of providence, not merely was the one to whom we appeal for such remembrance himself sold, abused, and wrongly imprisoned; his body was hung upon a tree, under a curse, even though he had committed no crime. The one to whom we cry out, "Remember me!" is the very one we ourselves pierced (Zech. 12:10). Joseph's suffering is a pale shadow of the sufferings of Christ—yet Jesus promises not only to remember us and lift up our heads when he comes in his kingdom but also to be with us at every step of our earthly pilgrimage.

Not only do we ask Jesus to remember us; he also asks us to remember him. At the institution of the Lord's Supper Jesus said, "Do this in remembrance of me" (1 Cor. 11:24–25). It is as we remember Jesus' suffering and glory ("Proclaim the Lord's death until he comes"; 1 Cor. 11:26) that we find help to wait in hope while enduring our own present sufferings. Our losses, however deep and real they may be, are not worth comparing with what Jesus suffered in our place or with the glory to be revealed in us (Rom. 8:18). God ultimately enabled Joseph to recognize that the sins that other people committed against him were under God's sovereign control and would work for his good, as well as for God's divine purpose. May the Spirit instill the same confidence regarding God's sovereign love and gracious faithfulness in each of our hearts as well.

GENESIS 41

41 After two whole years, Pharaoh dreamed that he was standing by the Nile, ²and behold, there came up out of the Nile seven cows, attractive and plump, and they fed in the reed grass. ³And behold, seven other cows, ugly and thin, came up out of the Nile after them, and stood by the other cows on the bank of the Nile. ⁴And the ugly, thin cows ate up the seven attractive, plump cows. And Pharaoh awoke. ⁵And he fell asleep and dreamed a second time. And behold, seven ears of grain, plump and good, were growing on one stalk. ⁶And behold, after them sprouted seven ears, thin and blighted by the east wind. ⁷And the thin ears swallowed up the seven plump, full ears. And Pharaoh awoke, and behold, it was a dream. ⁸So in the morning his spirit was troubled, and he sent and called for all the magicians of Egypt and all its wise men. Pharaoh told them his dreams, but there was none who could interpret them to Pharaoh.

⁹Then the chief cupbearer said to Pharaoh, "I remember my offenses today. ¹⁰When Pharaoh was angry with his servants and put me and the chief baker in custody in the house of the captain of the guard, ¹¹we dreamed on the same night, he and I, each having a dream with its own interpretation. ¹²A young Hebrew was there with us, a servant of the captain of the guard. When we told him, he interpreted our dreams to us, giving an interpretation to each man according to his dream. ¹³And as he interpreted to us, so it came about. I was restored to my office, and the baker was hanged."

¹⁴Then Pharaoh sent and called Joseph, and they quickly brought him out of the pit. And when he had shaved himself and changed his clothes, he came in before Pharaoh. ¹⁵And Pharaoh said to Joseph, "I have had a dream, and there is no one who can interpret it. I have heard it said of you that when you hear a dream you can interpret it." ¹⁶Joseph answered Pharaoh, "It is not in me; God will give Pharaoh a favorable answer."[1]

¹⁷Then Pharaoh said to Joseph, "Behold, in my dream I was standing on the banks of the Nile. ¹⁸Seven cows, plump and attractive, came up out of the Nile and fed in the reed grass. ¹⁹Seven other cows came up after them, poor and very ugly and thin, such as I had never seen in all the land of Egypt. ²⁰And the thin, ugly cows ate up the first seven plump cows, ²¹but when they had eaten them no one would have known that they had eaten them, for they were still as ugly as at the beginning. Then I awoke. ²²I also saw in my dream seven ears growing on one stalk, full and good. ²³Seven ears, withered, thin, and blighted by the east wind, sprouted after them, ²⁴and the thin ears swallowed up the seven good ears. And I told it to the magicians, but there was no one who could explain it to me."

²⁵Then Joseph said to Pharaoh, "The dreams of Pharaoh are one; God has revealed to Pharaoh what he is about to do. ²⁶The seven good cows are seven years, and the seven good ears are seven years; the dreams are one. ²⁷The seven lean and ugly cows that came up after them are seven years, and the

seven empty ears blighted by the east wind are also seven years of famine. ²⁸ It is as I told Pharaoh; God has shown to Pharaoh what he is about to do. ²⁹ There will come seven years of great plenty throughout all the land of Egypt, ³⁰ but after them there will arise seven years of famine, and all the plenty will be forgotten in the land of Egypt. The famine will consume the land, ³¹ and the plenty will be unknown in the land by reason of the famine that will follow, for it will be very severe. ³² And the doubling of Pharaoh's dream means that the thing is fixed by God, and God will shortly bring it about. ³³ Now therefore let Pharaoh select a discerning and wise man, and set him over the land of Egypt. ³⁴ Let Pharaoh proceed to appoint overseers over the land and take one-fifth of the produce of the land² of Egypt during the seven plentiful years. ³⁵ And let them gather all the food of these good years that are coming and store up grain under the authority of Pharaoh for food in the cities, and let them keep it. ³⁶ That food shall be a reserve for the land against the seven years of famine that are to occur in the land of Egypt, so that the land may not perish through the famine."

³⁷ This proposal pleased Pharaoh and all his servants. ³⁸ And Pharaoh said to his servants, "Can we find a man like this, in whom is the Spirit of God?"³ ³⁹ Then Pharaoh said to Joseph, "Since God has shown you all this, there is none so discerning and wise as you are. ⁴⁰ You shall be over my house, and all my people shall order themselves as you command.⁴ Only as regards the throne will I be greater than you." ⁴¹ And Pharaoh said to Joseph, "See, I have set you over all the land of Egypt." ⁴² Then Pharaoh took his signet ring from his hand and put it on Joseph's hand, and clothed him in garments of fine linen and put a gold chain about his neck. ⁴³ And he made him ride in his second chariot. And they called out before him, "Bow the knee!"⁵ Thus he set him over all the land of Egypt. ⁴⁴ Moreover, Pharaoh said to Joseph, "I am Pharaoh, and without your consent no one shall lift up hand or foot in all the land of Egypt." ⁴⁵ And Pharaoh called Joseph's name Zaphenath-paneah. And he gave him in marriage Asenath, the daughter of Potiphera priest of On. So Joseph went out over the land of Egypt.

⁴⁶ Joseph was thirty years old when he entered the service of Pharaoh king of Egypt. And Joseph went out from the presence of Pharaoh and went through all the land of Egypt. ⁴⁷ During the seven plentiful years the earth produced abundantly, ⁴⁸ and he gathered up all the food of these seven years, which occurred in the land of Egypt, and put the food in the cities. He put in every city the food from the fields around it. ⁴⁹ And Joseph stored up grain in great abundance, like the sand of the sea, until he ceased to measure it, for it could not be measured.

⁵⁰ Before the year of famine came, two sons were born to Joseph. Asenath, the daughter of Potiphera priest of On, bore them to him. ⁵¹ Joseph called the name of the firstborn Manasseh. "For," he said, "God has made me forget all my hardship and all my father's house."⁶ ⁵² The name of the second he called Ephraim, "For God has made me fruitful in the land of my affliction."⁷

⁵³ The seven years of plenty that occurred in the land of Egypt came to an end, ⁵⁴ and the seven years of famine began to come, as Joseph had said. There was famine in all lands, but in all the land of Egypt there was bread. ⁵⁵ When all the land of Egypt was famished, the people cried to Pharaoh for bread. Pharaoh said to all the Egyptians, "Go to Joseph. What he says to you, do."

⁵⁶ So when the famine had spread over all the land, Joseph opened all the storehouses⁸ and sold to the Egyptians, for the famine was severe in the land of Egypt. ⁵⁷ Moreover, all the earth came to Egypt to Joseph to buy grain, because the famine was severe over all the earth.

¹ Or (compare Samaritan, Septuagint) *Without God it is not possible to give Pharaoh an answer about his welfare* ² Or *over the land and organize the land* ³ Or *of the gods* ⁴ Hebrew *and according to your command all my people shall kiss the ground* ⁵ *Abrek*, probably an Egyptian word, similar in sound to the Hebrew word meaning *to kneel* ⁶ *Manasseh* sounds like the Hebrew for *making to forget* ⁷ *Ephraim* sounds like the Hebrew for *making fruitful* ⁸ Hebrew *all that was in them*

Section Overview

At the end of Genesis 40 the cupbearer forgot Joseph (40:23). By the beginning of Genesis 41 Joseph would have just about forgotten the cupbearer. When the cupbearer was released, Joseph must have anticipated his freedom every time someone entered the jail; by two years later it would have seemed evident that his freedom would be unlikely to come from that source. Yet in the space of a single day Joseph goes from his humdrum life in prison to appearing before the throne of one of the world's most powerful men, Pharaoh himself. At the right time the cupbearer does remember him, and Joseph is summoned to interpret Pharaoh's dreams. His world is instantly turned upside down; he goes from being virtually powerless to being a governor of Egypt, from being incarcerated to being free, and from being penniless to being rich beyond belief.

Yet the import of Pharaoh's dreams is ominous, depicting a world turned upside down in a different way. Seven years of agricultural abundance will be followed by seven years of famine (41:29–31). It will take wise leadership to prepare for the approaching cataclysm—and Pharaoh is immediately convinced that Joseph is the man to provide leadership for the task (v. 38). The man who, under the Lord's blessing, had previously risen to manage Potiphar's household (39:5–6) and after his imprisonment had risen to manage the prison (39:22–23) is now tasked with governing the entire country of Egypt. The result is the preservation of many Egyptian lives when the famine arrives. The son of Abraham is bringing the Abrahamic blessing to the nation where God has sent him (cf. 12:1–3).

Yet the Lord's plan for Joseph is far bigger than simply making him a blessing to Egypt. The famine is far wider than Egypt, so that "all the earth" comes to Egypt to buy grain from Joseph (41:57). All nations find for themselves a blessing when they come and prostrate themselves before Joseph. But Joseph's dreams had specifically referred to his own family's prostrating themselves before him (37:5–11), and the famine will provide an opportunity for those dreams to be fulfilled, as well as for Joseph ultimately to be restored to fellowship with his brothers. They too will find themselves hungry because of the famine and forced to go down to Egypt to buy bread from the Egyptian ruler. Although they know nothing of this yet, their world is also in the process of being turned upside down.

Section Outline

XI. The Family History of Jacob (37:1–50:26) . . .
    F. A World Turned Upside Down (41:1–57)

Comment

41:1–8 Two complete years later (Hb. "after two years of days"),[580] Pharaoh has a dream (v. 1). The timing perhaps suggests that the dreams occur exactly two years later, on Pharaoh's birthday, which would add weight to their importance.[581] In his dream Pharaoh finds himself standing beside the Nile (v. 1), whose regular flow provides most of the water for Egyptian agriculture and whose annual floods enrich the soil. This is much more than a mere geographical referent; Pharaoh's own welfare and happiness, along with that of his people, rests on the health of the Nile and on the favor of the gods believed to control its flow.[582]

As with the cupbearer's and baker's dreams, Pharaoh is himself a participant in his dream, watching as various creatures emerge from the Nile (v. 2). As with Joseph's dream in Genesis 37, the surprising content of the dream is highlighted by the repeated use of *hinneh* ("Behold"; vv. 1 [Hb.], 2, 3, 5, 6, 7). Pharaoh's dreams also occur as a matched pair, with the pairing drawing parallels (as with Joseph's dreams) rather than contrasts (as with the cupbearer's and baker's dreams). The initial portent of the dream is positive, with seven "attractive"[583] and fat cows emerging from the Nile and feeding on the grassy margins of the river.[584] Seven is the number of completeness, and pictures of seven cows are prominent in Egyptian art.[585] It is a happy pastoral scene to warm Pharaoh's heart (v. 2). It does not take long for the dream to take an ominous turn, however. Seven ugly and thin cows (Hb. "evil of flesh and thin of appearance") emerge from the Nile shortly after the fat cows, and before long the ugly, thin cows consume the beautiful, fat cows (v. 4). Cannibalistic cows must surely be a negative omen, especially since the thin cows triumph by consuming the fat cows. On that discordant note Pharaoh awakes from sleep (v. 4).

A single bad dream might be dismissed as an aberration, but two similar dreams, especially on Pharaoh's birthday, cannot be ignored. After Pharaoh falls asleep, he dreams again. The second dream is similar to the first; initially it seems promising, with seven plump ears of grain growing from a single stalk, which would normally produce only a single ear (v. 5). However, these productive ears are followed by seven thin ears; these have been exposed to the hot, dry, east wind from the desert, which has stunted their growth (v. 6). Yet the thin ears swallow up the fat ears of grain, leaving nothing behind (v. 7). The unity of the dreams is underlined by the use of a single Hebrew verb (*'alah*) to describe the cows' coming

---

[580] Hamilton, *Genesis 18–50*, 484.
[581] Wenham, *Genesis 16–50*, 390.
[582] Brueggemann, *Genesis*, 327.
[583] In Hebrew they are "beautiful of form" (*yefot-mar'eh*), like Joseph in Genesis 39:6.
[584] The Hebrew word translated "reed grass" (*'akhu*; 41:2) is an Egyptian loanword that referred originally to the inundated areas around the Nile; cf. Hamilton, *Genesis 18–50*, 484.
[585] One important Egyptian goddesses, Hathor, was often depicted as a cow (Steinmann, *Genesis*, 379).

up out of the Nile and the stalks of grain's emergence from the ground, as well as by the reference to both apparitions with the singular noun "dream" (vv. 7, 8). Between the two subdreams both the pastoral and the agricultural sectors of the Egyptian economy are threatened.[586]

In the morning Pharaoh summons all his professional dream interpreters, his "magicians" and "wise men" (v. 8). "Magicians" (*khartumim*) were specialists in the manipulation of the spiritual world through the use of occult books and spells to ward off danger and acquire blessing for their clients. Such practices were forbidden in Israel because God did not need to be cajoled and could not be manipulated (Lev. 19:26; Deut. 18:10–11); his blessing rested upon his people freely by grace (Num. 6:22–27), and his judgments could not be thwarted, even by professional diviners (cf. Numbers 22–24). "Wise men" (*khakamim*) is often a more general term for people with knowledge or experience who can provide guidance and counsel, though here the term likely has in view expert interpreters who claim understanding into the world of dreams and visions.

It is notable that, unlike the cupbearer's and the butler's experiences in prison, there is no shortage of potential interpreters at Pharaoh's beck and call, but none of them is able to interpret Pharaoh's dreams (Gen. 41:8). This does not necessarily mean that they do not attempt to do so; however, Pharaoh apparently finds their interpretations unconvincing. The fact that the magicians refer to the dreams (plural) while Pharaoh refers to the dream (singular) suggests one possible source of disagreement, with the magicians interpreting the dreams as having different referents while Pharaoh recognizes the one dream's unity.[587] The failure of Pharaoh's magicians to comprehend and control Israel's God foreshadows the outcome of a similar contest in Exodus 7–9.[588]

41:9–13 Finally it is time for the cupbearer to remember Joseph. For those who have read chapter 40, Genesis 41:9–13 is a recap that serves to slow down the narrative and build to the inevitable climax when Joseph interprets the dreams. That does not make these verses irrelevant, however; the manner in which characters choose to remember events is always significant. For example, the cupbearer tells Pharaoh that he "remembered [his] offenses"; Pharaoh likely understands this as a reference to his sins against Pharaoh himself, for which the cupbearer was imprisoned (v. 9). The use of the verb "remember" (Hb. *zakar*) suggests that the cupbearer realizes he has not shown Joseph *khesed* by remembering him sooner to Pharaoh (40:14), but he makes no mention of his failure in this regard. Nor does he mention Joseph's claim that the interpretation of dreams belongs to God (40:8). Instead of explicitly calling Joseph a prisoner, he represents him as the "servant of the captain of the guard" who happened to be there with them (41:12). The cupbearer thus makes it sound as though this young Hebrew is a gifted dream interpreter in his

---

[586] Lindsay Wilson, *Joseph Wise and Otherwise: The Intersection of Wisdom and Covenant in Genesis 37–50* (Carlisle, UK: Paternoster, 2004), 124.
[587] Sternberg, *Poetics of Biblical Narrative*, 394–400. Westermann (*Genesis 37–50*, 88) suggests a possible unwillingness on the part of these court functionaries to be the bearers of such bad news, but that seems less likely.
[588] Sarna, *Genesis*, 282.

own right, able to give the meaning of any dream he hears (vv. 12–13).[589] The cupbearer does not specifically request Pharaoh to summon Joseph—such decisions must come from Pharaoh himself, not least in case Joseph proves unable to deliver an interpretation—but he set events rolling firmly in that direction.

41:14–24 Pharaoh responds as expected and summons Joseph from the (metaphorical) "pit" (Hb. *habbor*; v. 14), a word that harks back to Joseph's request to the cupbearer to remember him and deliver him from prison in Genesis 40:14, as well as to the literal pit into which his brothers threw him in Genesis 37. Joseph has waited a long time for this day to arrive, but when it does the change in his circumstances is breathtakingly fast.[590] Pharaoh's officials bring him "quickly" from the prison, and, after a brief pause to "shave"[591] and change clothing, he is presented before Pharaoh himself (41:14). Joseph's clothing has marked his status throughout this narrative: his position as favored son was marked by the gift of the ornamental robe (37:3), which was stripped from him when he was sold into slavery (37:23). His accusation by Potiphar's wife was accompanied by the supporting evidence of the robe left in her hand (39:12). Now his new clothes mark the beginning of Joseph's meteoric rise to power over all Egypt.

Pharaoh's initial words to Joseph highlight his need and the reason for Joseph's presence: he has had a dream that none can interpret, and he has heard that Joseph has the power to interpret any dream (41:15). This is exactly what the cupbearer told Pharaoh, but Joseph is eager to point attention away from himself to God as the true dream interpreter (v. 16): "It is not in me" is shorter and more of an exclamation in Hebrew ("Not me!").[592] Joseph says this not because of any lack of confidence that he can interpret Pharaoh's dream. On the contrary, he is sure that God will give Pharaoh an interpretation—but he seeks to make clear that the credit is entirely due to God and not to his own powers. Moreover, even before he hears Pharaoh's dream, he affirms that the answer will be favorable (Hb. "peace"; *shalom*; v. 16) to Pharaoh. The *shalom* that his brothers would not give him when he was still at home (37:4) and that he sought for his brothers when visiting them (37:14) will now come to Pharaoh through the God-given interpretation of the dream. In other words, God has given Pharaoh this dream not merely as a portent of doom, as with the chief baker's dream, but as a sign to help him prepare for the difficult days ahead, whose events lie in the sovereign hands of God.

Pharaoh then recounts his dream to Joseph (41:17–24). The reader has already heard the dream described in 41:1–7, but its repetition adds a certain intensity, not least by putting it in first-person perspective. The healthy cows are still "plump and attractive," but there is now an added emphasis on the unhealthy cows, which are

---
[589] Hamilton, *Genesis 18–50*, 490.
[590] As so often in Hebrew a sequence of *vav*-consecutive verbs indicates a rapid sequence of actions; cf. Donald B. Redford, *A Study of the Biblical Story of Joseph (Genesis 37–50)* (Leiden: Brill, 1970), 76. The Egyptians literally "run" (Hb. *ruts*) Joseph from the prison to Pharaoh.
[591] The Hebrew verb *galakh* likely implies shaving of the head as well as the beard in order to make Joseph presentable before Pharaoh (cf. Num. 6:9, 18); cf. Alter, *Five Books of Moses*, 232.
[592] Currid, *Genesis 25:19–50:26*, 257.

described as "poor and very ugly and thin" rather than as simply "ugly and thin" (vv. 3, 19); they are unlike any that Pharaoh has ever seen before (v. 19). Now it is made explicit that, after consuming the fat cows, the thin cows are as emaciated as ever (v. 21). The second dream, which concerns the ears of grain, is reported in similar terms to the original narrative, though with the addition of the word "withered" (Hb. *tsenumot*) to underline the supremacy of the ruined ears over the healthy ones (v. 23).[593] There is one other omission: Pharaoh does not introduce his second dream with the words "I dreamed a second time" (cf. v. 5), since he apparently already recognizes the unity of the dreams.[594]

41:25–36 The conclusion of Pharaoh's speech, "There was no one who could explain it to me" (v. 24), prepares the way for Joseph, with God's help, to fill the void. Without any hesitation Joseph confirms that the two dreams of Pharaoh are one in their meaning, as were his own dreams in Genesis 37. The fact that the dreams were doubled is due to the fact that the events they describe are certain and imminent ("Fixed by God, and God will shortly bring it about"; 41:32), a remarkable assertion in the context of Joseph's own as-yet-unfulfilled dreams. The interpretation is relatively straightforward once it is revealed. The number seven represents seven years; the fat cows/ears of grain are years of plenty, to be followed (and consumed by) the thin cows/ears of grain, which are years of famine. The effects of the famine will be so devastating to the land that the prosperity of the good years will be entirely forgotten (v. 31)—a point underlined by Joseph's devoting five sentences to the years of famine in comparison to one for the years of plenty.[595] These dreams have been given to Pharaoh on behalf of his people.

God's sovereignty is the necessary prerequisite for such predictive dreams; a God who cannot control the future is in no place to announce it with certainty ahead of time (cf. Isa. 44:6–8). Yet God's sovereignty is not fatalism; the Lord speaks to people ahead of time in order for them to repent and respond appropriately in a way that may forestall coming judgment, a belief expressed in classic form by the king of Nineveh in Jonah 3:9 ("Who knows? God may turn and relent and turn from his fierce anger, so that we may not perish"). It is not coincidental that Joseph uses the language of divinely inspired visions with reference to the dream; God has made Pharaoh see (Hiphil of *ra'ah*; Gen. 41:28) what is to happen.[596] In Egypt's case there is no call for repentance, since the coming famine is not connected explicitly to sin; Pharaoh is simply being given time to make wise preparation for the coming storm.

Joseph is bold in his prescriptions for what wisdom looks like in such a situation:[597] Pharaoh should appoint a discerning and wise man to oversee a period of intense preparation, with regional overseers under him (vv. 33–34). During the

---

[593] Cf. Sailhamer, *Pentateuch as Narrative*, 214.
[594] He also refers to it as "my dream" (singular) in 41:15, 22; cf. Waltke, *Genesis*, 532.
[595] Hamilton, *Genesis 18–50*, 497.
[596] Kidner, *Genesis*, 195.
[597] In speech "And now" (Hb. *ve'atah*; Gen. 41:33) often introduces the conclusion to the preceding argument (e.g., Gen. 4:11; Ex. 3:9).

seven years of plenty Pharaoh should impose a 20 percent tax in order to create a strategic grain reserve to provide resources to deal with the seven years of famine (vv. 34–36). Such a move will undoubtedly be painful and unpopular, but it will save the land from perishing during the difficult years. All this should be done "under the authority of Pharaoh" (v. 35).

41:37–45 It is unlikely that Joseph is proposing himself as a candidate for the position whose creation he recommends. He has neither the experience nor the court connections that would normally have been a prerequisite for such an exalted office—after all, until that very morning he had been residing in one of Pharaoh's prisons! Yet, like Potiphar and the prison warden earlier, Pharaoh recognizes the presence of God with Joseph, asking, "Can we find a man like this, in whom is the Spirit of God?" (v. 38).[598] Although Pharaoh and all his servants approve of Joseph's proposal, it is notable that the actual decisions are made by Pharaoh alone. He recognizes that, because of God's power displayed through Joseph, no one else meets Joseph's twin criteria of being "discerning and wise" (v. 39; cf. v. 33) as well as Joseph himself does.

Just as Joseph rose to the highest position in Potiphar's house and then in the house of the prison warden, so also he rises to the highest position in Egypt, second only to Pharaoh himself (v. 40; cf. 39:6, 23). Everyone in Egypt will be required to pay homage before him (41:40),[599] a status underlined by the repetition of the words "[Pharaoh] set him over all the land of Egypt" (vv. 41, 43). There was a history of foreigners' rising to positions of power and influence in Egypt,[600] although few others could have experienced as meteoric a rise as Joseph. It is doubly ironic that the person whose interpretation of his own God-given dreams had been met with flat incredulity by his family is believed and honored by Egyptians, even though he is a convicted felon.

This position of power and authority is marked by the accoutrements of office: Pharaoh's own ring (Hb. *taba'at*; v. 42),[601] symbolizing his power to rule; garments of fine linen (*shesh*), that is, linen produced in Egypt, the home of the best quality fabric, enabling him to be properly dressed to appear before Pharaoh in court on a regular basis; and a gold chain (or "collar")[602] of authority around his neck (v. 42). Unlike ordinary people, who walked everywhere, Joseph is granted Pharoah's

---

[598] Given the fact that this speech is in the mouth of an Egyptian, it is tempting to translate "In whom is the spirit of the gods?" (cf. ESV mg.; Dan. 5:14). However, in the following verse Pharaoh uses a singular verb with *'elohim* ("Since God has shown you all this"; Gen. 41:39), suggesting that the singular is appropriate. We need not assume that Pharaoh has converted to monotheism; he may simply be reflecting Joseph's own depiction of who has revealed the information to him, since Joseph has repeatedly used *'elohim* with a singular verb in this passage (vv. 16, 25, 28, 32).
[599] ESV's "All my people shall order themselves as you command" emends a difficult text, which reads "upon your mouth shall all my people kiss." The text becomes clearer when it is recognized that "Upon your mouth" is to be understood not as the location of the kiss but rather as a literary expression for "At your word"; the action of kissing (often a hand or a ring) is a common way of paying homage to a superior. Hence the NASB (1995) is most likely correct with its translation: "According to your command all my people shall do homage." Cf. Kenneth A. Kitchen, "The Term *Nšq* in Genesis xli.40," *ExpTim* 69 (1957): 30.
[600] Hoffmeier, *Israel in Egypt*, 93–95.
[601] This Hebrew word specifically denotes a ring, which may or may not include a seal to sign documents, in contrast to a *khotam*, a seal that may or may not be in the form of a ring (cf. Gen. 38:18). The ESV, along with most English versions, translates it as "signet ring," probably correctly in this context (cf. Est. 3:10, 12).
[602] Cf. Alter, *Five Books of Moses*, 235.

second chariot, with envoys proceeding ahead of him and crying out, *abrek* (v. 43), an obscure Egyptian word that means something like "Make way" (CEV) or "Bow the knee" (ESV; KJV).[603] The public humiliation that led to Joseph's imprisonment is now replaced by public adulation on all sides.

The similarity of Pharaoh's declaration of self-identity, "I am Pharaoh" (v. 44), to the Lord's declaration, "I am Yahweh" (seven times in Exodus 6–7 alone), is not coincidental. Pharaoh is laying claim to divine status and authority that empower him to make binding decrees on the inhabitants of his land—in this case, the decree that Joseph will have absolute authority of his own under him over all the inhabitants of Egypt (Gen. 41:44). No one can lift up a hand or foot—or, as we might say, no one can lift a finger—without his permission. Joseph gets to work right away, going out over the land of Egypt, presumably to start making preparations (v. 45).

Moreover, Pharaoh gives Joseph a new Egyptian name, Zaphenath-paneah, which means "God speaks and he lives,"[604] along with an Egyptian wife, Asenath, the daughter of a noble family of priests from On (v. 45).[605] In many ways Joseph's life has been transformed utterly in the course of a single day. In other ways, though, Joseph is tied more firmly than before to his Egyptian home and identity, and his own dreams from Genesis 37 seem as far away from fulfillment as ever. The Egyptians might prostrate themselves in front of Joseph, but the possibility that his own family will do the same remains unlikely. Nor is Joseph now free to return to the land of Canaan and set things right with his own family; any such plans will have to wait.

41:46–52 Thirteen years have now passed since Joseph's arrival in Egypt (v. 46; cf. 37:2). He faithfully carries out his task of storing grain during the good years so that there will be a reserve for the coming bad years (41:47–48). As master of the grain of all Egypt, his original dream, in which eleven sheaves bowed down to him, seems to be coming true in ironic fashion (37:7).

Another link to the earlier narrative in Genesis is the description of the abundance of the grain in Egypt as being "like the sand of the sea" (41:49), the same metaphor applied to the promise of patriarchal offspring (22:17; 32:12). It is not coincidental that the text then addresses Joseph's own fruitfulness during these seven years of plenty in the shape of two sons, Manasseh and Ephraim (41:51–52). The names given to them are significant, as was the case for Joseph and his brothers earlier in the story (cf. Genesis 29–30). Joseph calls his firstborn Manasseh because "God has made me forget all my hardship and all my father's house" (41:51), and he names the second Ephraim, "For God has made me fruitful in the land of my

---

603 This is probably an Egyptian loanword with no linguistic connection to the similar sounding Hebrew verb *berek*, which means "to kneel." It means to prostrate oneself in the presence of authority; cf. Hamilton, *Genesis 18–50*, 506–507.
604 Redford, *Biblical Story of Joseph*, 230.
605 Her father's name, Potiphera, is the same as that of Joseph's previous master, Potiphar, but it was a common name in Egypt, meaning "He whom Re gives." Since On (Heliopolis) was the center for worship of the sun god, Re, the name is hardly surprising.

affliction" (v. 52). Both names affirm Joseph's recognition that God has been at work through all his difficult circumstances: God has made him forget, and God has made him fruitful. Joseph's two children are no more accidental than Pharaoh's two dreams or Joseph's additional two years in prison; they are the means by which God is doing something significant in his life.

There is a certain irony in Joseph's calling Manasseh "forgetful," since names are inevitably a constant reminder. There is a sense in which Joseph can never forget the injustices he has suffered or his family of origin, of which Manasseh's name is a permanent witness. Indeed, the subsequent narrative depends on such remembering by Joseph! Yet from now on Joseph will remember those tragic events and losses in the context of God's larger work for good, which gives them a deeper meaning and a new significance in his thinking. The marks of the wounds remain in his life and can never be forgotten, but those scars have been beautifully incorporated into the intricate pattern of God's grace in his life, and Joseph is determined not to forget that.

Ephraim's name also represents a profound reflection on Joseph's experiences. God has not delivered Joseph *out of* the land of his affliction, as he has presumably prayed repeatedly. Instead, God has made him fruitful *in* the land of his affliction (v. 52), making him a blessing to all those around him throughout all he has suffered. Ephraim's name also serves as a reminder to Joseph that Egypt is not home; despite his elevation to power and his acquisition of an Egyptian wife and two half-Egyptian sons, Egypt is still "the land of his affliction" for Joseph, as it will later prove to be for his descendants (cf. 15:13; Ex. 3:7).[606] Canaan is still the location where God has promised long-term blessing for his people, even if he is more than able to provide abundantly for them outside the Land of Promise when necessary.

41:53–57 The seven years of plenty swiftly come to an end, to be replaced by the famine that Pharaoh's dreams have anticipated (Gen. 41:53–54). Because of Joseph's careful planning, there is food in Egypt, unlike in the rest of the ancient world. At Pharaoh's decree Joseph becomes the administrator of the sale of grain, just as he oversaw its collection (v. 55). To hoard away stored grain in a time of famine was regarded as reprehensible (Prov. 11:26). Indeed, not only does all Egypt come to Joseph to receive food, but "all the earth" likewise comes to Joseph to buy grain (Gen. 41:57), for the famine stretches far beyond Egypt's borders (a detail not included in Joseph's interpretation of the original dreams). Without Joseph's wisdom it is not only the Egyptians who will die. The descendant of Abraham is fulfilling his calling to be a blessing to all nations (cf. 12:3) as they come and bow down before him, even if his trajectory to this point has been unexpected. At the same time, the shift in focus to the wider picture of a world outside Egypt prepares the way for the narrative to shift its attention to Joseph's father and brothers back in Canaan.

---

[606] Kidner (*Genesis*, 209) points out that these are distinctively Hebrew and not Egyptian names, unlike later names at the time of the exodus, such as Moses and Phinehas.

Response

God's providence takes its own time. God is not slow in remembering Joseph, though it must have seemed that way to him, waiting two full years for the cupbearer to remember his promise. God's timing is perfect, and it results in Joseph's elevation to a position of unthinkable power and authority in Egypt. The Lord makes him fruitful in the land of his affliction and enables him to forget (or at least put in perspective) his many sufferings at the hands of his family of origin (41:50–52). Nor is this prosperity for Joseph's sake alone; by this means Joseph is enabled to be a blessing to the entire world, as his preparations during the seven years of famine lead to a sufficient abundance of stored grain to meet the needs not merely of Egypt but of surrounding peoples as well.

Yet Joseph is not merely an example to us of the working of God's providence. Throughout his life Joseph is a shadow and forerunner of a greater deliverer to come. Before Joseph can even begin to fulfill his calling as a shadow savior he must endure repeated and long-lasting suffering that will leave permanent scars. But after that painful preparation God uses him to be a blessing to the nations. Jesus follows the same pattern of suffering and then exaltation and public acclamation. Jesus is not merely second in line behind an Egyptian pharaoh; he is the King of kings and Lord of lords, before whom every knee will bow and every tongue confess that he is Lord (Phil. 2:9–11).

Yet this one before whom all nations will bow also learns obedience through what he suffers and becomes fruitful through his afflictions. Jesus' resurrected and glorified body still bears the scars of his suffering: there are still nail prints in his hands and a wound in his side (John 20:27) as perpetual reminders of the cross and his profound sufferings at the hands of his brothers. But Jesus will never forget the fruit borne of that suffering: a new family of men and women from every tribe and nation, who receive new life from his hands.

Just as Joseph's exaltation is not merely for himself, so too Jesus' exaltation leads to blessing for all nations, if they will come and bow the knee before him. Jesus is the true bread of heaven, the one whose broken body is the source of all life. He invites all those who are hungry to come to him and eat and all those who are thirsty to come to him and drink (Isa. 55:1–3). This feast is given to us freely, without cost, offered to helpless refugees seeking sustenance. We come with empty hands and nothing to give, asking Jesus to give us the perfect righteousness we need in order to stand before a holy God. All who come to Jesus on those terms will be welcomed into the final wedding feast of the Lamb, which will mark the coming of his kingdom in fullness (Rev. 19:9). This world is, and will continue to be, the land of our afflictions, but there is another land prepared for us where our citizenship truly belongs, where our God will wipe away all our tears (Rev. 21:4).

GENESIS 42

42 When Jacob learned that there was grain for sale in Egypt, he said to his sons, "Why do you look at one another?" **2** And he said, "Behold, I have heard that there is grain for sale in Egypt. Go down and buy grain for us there, that we may live and not die." **3** So ten of Joseph's brothers went down to buy grain in Egypt. **4** But Jacob did not send Benjamin, Joseph's brother, with his brothers, for he feared that harm might happen to him. **5** Thus the sons of Israel came to buy among the others who came, for the famine was in the land of Canaan.

6 Now Joseph was governor over the land. He was the one who sold to all the people of the land. And Joseph's brothers came and bowed themselves before him with their faces to the ground. **7** Joseph saw his brothers and recognized them, but he treated them like strangers and spoke roughly to them. "Where do you come from?" he said. They said, "From the land of Canaan, to buy food." **8** And Joseph recognized his brothers, but they did not recognize him. **9** And Joseph remembered the dreams that he had dreamed of them. And he said to them, "You are spies; you have come to see the nakedness of the land." **10** They said to him, "No, my lord, your servants have come to buy food. **11** We are all sons of one man. We are honest men. Your servants have never been spies."

12 He said to them, "No, it is the nakedness of the land that you have come to see." **13** And they said, "We, your servants, are twelve brothers, the sons of one man in the land of Canaan, and behold, the youngest is this day with our father, and one is no more." **14** But Joseph said to them, "It is as I said to you. You are spies. **15** By this you shall be tested: by the life of Pharaoh, you shall not go from this place unless your youngest brother comes here. **16** Send one of you, and let him bring your brother, while you remain confined, that your words may be tested, whether there is truth in you. Or else, by the life of Pharaoh, surely you are spies." **17** And he put them all together in custody for three days.

18 On the third day Joseph said to them, "Do this and you will live, for I fear God: **19** if you are honest men, let one of your brothers remain confined where you are in custody, and let the rest go and carry grain for the famine of your households, **20** and bring your youngest brother to me. So your words will be verified, and you shall not die." And they did so. **21** Then they said to one another, "In truth we are guilty concerning our brother, in that we saw the distress of his soul, when he begged us and we did not listen. That is why this distress has come upon us." **22** And Reuben answered them, "Did I not tell you not to sin against the boy? But you did not listen. So now there comes a reckoning for his blood." **23** They did not know that Joseph understood them, for there was an interpreter between them. **24** Then he turned away from them and wept. And he returned to them and spoke to them. And he took Simeon from them and bound him before their eyes. **25** And Joseph gave orders to fill their bags with grain, and to replace every man's money in his sack, and to give them provisions for the journey. This was done for them.

²⁶ Then they loaded their donkeys with their grain and departed. ²⁷ And as one of them opened his sack to give his donkey fodder at the lodging place, he saw his money in the mouth of his sack. ²⁸ He said to his brothers, "My money has been put back; here it is in the mouth of my sack!" At this their hearts failed them, and they turned trembling to one another, saying, "What is this that God has done to us?"

²⁹ When they came to Jacob their father in the land of Canaan, they told him all that had happened to them, saying, ³⁰ "The man, the lord of the land, spoke roughly to us and took us to be spies of the land. ³¹ But we said to him, 'We are honest men; we have never been spies. ³² We are twelve brothers, sons of our father. One is no more, and the youngest is this day with our father in the land of Canaan.' ³³ Then the man, the lord of the land, said to us, 'By this I shall know that you are honest men: leave one of your brothers with me, and take grain for the famine of your households, and go your way. ³⁴ Bring your youngest brother to me. Then I shall know that you are not spies but honest men, and I will deliver your brother to you, and you shall trade in the land.'"

³⁵ As they emptied their sacks, behold, every man's bundle of money was in his sack. And when they and their father saw their bundles of money, they were afraid. ³⁶ And Jacob their father said to them, "You have bereaved me of my children: Joseph is no more, and Simeon is no more, and now you would take Benjamin. All this has come against me." ³⁷ Then Reuben said to his father, "Kill my two sons if I do not bring him back to you. Put him in my hands, and I will bring him back to you." ³⁸ But he said, "My son shall not go down with you, for his brother is dead, and he is the only one left. If harm should happen to him on the journey that you are to make, you would bring down my gray hairs with sorrow to Sheol."

Section Overview

Chapters 39–41 focused on Joseph's fortunes down in Egypt; twenty years passed, during which Joseph endured many trials, after which he was elevated to the highest position in the land, second only to Pharaoh himself (Gen. 41:40). Yet at the end of chapter 41 the camera pans out to bring into focus the rest of the world, now linked to Egypt through the common experience of famine (41:57). It is time to see how Joseph's family is doing in the land of Canaan. It soon becomes apparent that, like everyone else, they have no food and must go down to Egypt to acquire sustenance (42:2).

On arrival in Egypt Joseph's brothers meet him, seeking to buy food (v. 6). He immediately recognizes them — presumably he has anticipated the possibility of their arrival at some point — but they remain in the dark about his identity (v. 8). Joseph could immediately identify himself to them and either execute them for their crimes or else pursue reconciliation with them. Instead Joseph chooses a complex strategy designed to determine whether his brothers have changed at all over the intervening twenty years or are the same hardened, unfeeling men as before. If they are unchanged, Joseph has little interest in renewing their acquaintance — in a profound sense, God has already made him forget his father's household (41:51). Yet, if the brothers have changed with the passage of time, then perhaps their relationship can be restored.

Section Outline
XI. The Family History of Jacob (37:1–50:26) . . .
    G. Joseph's Brothers Seek Grain (42:1–38)

Comment

42:1–5 Like everyone else around them, Jacob and his sons have been affected by the severe famine gripping the entire world (41:57). When the news arrives that there is still grain for purchase in Egypt, Jacob immediately sends his sons there to purchase food, so that they might live and not die (42:2). The very survival of the family is at stake and, along with it, the survival of God's promise, yet the inactivity of the sons—"looking at each other" instead of acting (v. 1)—contrasts sharply with Joseph's wise preparations for the famine. "Life" and "death" are key motifs in this episode (cf. v. 18, 20; 43:8). On the one hand this emphasis reinforces the message that the future of the family is at stake, while on the other it subtly hints at the theme of divine judgment for sin, as well as the possibility of forgiveness for those who repent (cf. Ezek. 18:28).[607]

Jacob sends ten of his remaining eleven sons on the perilous journey to Egypt, which would take about a week to complete. He keeps Benjamin safely at home to ensure that he does not undergo an "accident" like that which befell Joseph (Gen. 42:4; cf. 37:33). It is not clear whether Jacob fears that Benjamin will be harmed by his brothers or fears that he will suffer a natural accident on the journey; either way, he is taking no chances with Joseph's one remaining brother (42:4). Jacob's toxic favoritism toward the sons of his favorite wife, Rachel, is still on full display, since he shows no equal concern over the harm that might befall his other sons on this dangerous expedition. In chapter 37 Jacob sent Joseph to seek the *shalom* of his ten brothers (37:14); now he unwittingly sends the ten brothers to Joseph, so that the *shalom* of the family may be fully restored. Here they are called the "sons of Israel" (42:5) rather than of Jacob to focus our attention on their role as bearers of God's promises.

42:6–17 Joseph's role as "governor" (Hb. *shallit*; "vizier") leads to his taking an active role in the sale of grain (v. 6). It is hard to imagine that this hands-on approach is unconnected to Joseph's expectation that sooner or later his brothers will need to come to Egypt to buy supplies. Joseph's brothers prostrate themselves before him when they come in, just as Joseph's dream had anticipated (vv. 6, 9; cf. 37:7). Joseph immediately "recognizes" his brothers (form of *nakar*), but he "acts like a stranger" toward them (a different form of *nakar*), and they do not recognize him;

---

[607] As Daniel Block comments with regard to Ezekiel 18:28, "God's mercy and grace move him to plead with men and women to accept that way, to repent of their sin and find life in him"; Block, *Ezekiel 1–24*, NICOT (Grand Rapids, MI: Eerdmans, 1997), 590.

the same verb was used in 37:32–33 when Jacob "recognized" Joseph's cloak. Joseph addresses the brothers harshly (42:7), questioning them about their origins and identity and accusing them of being spies (v. 9). Specifically, Joseph accuses the brothers of having come "to see the nakedness of the land" (v. 9)—a metaphorical use of an image that elsewhere implies sexual sin (cf. Leviticus 18). The major threat to Egypt during much of its history was across the land bridge from Asia, so this is not an implausible accusation.[608] The language of "By the life of Pharaoh" (or "as Pharaoh lives"; Gen. 42:15, 16) parallels the form of an oath taken in the name of a deity (cf. "as the LORD lives"; e.g., Ruth 3:13).

The brothers' response is a strong denial, couched in carefully deferential terms ("my lord"; "your servants"; Gen. 42:10). Far from being spies representing a military force, they are part of a single family, come down to Egypt to buy food like everyone else (v. 10). They are honest men, they claim—although Joseph knows them rather better than they imagine. Joseph's aggressive tone forces the brothers to say more than they had expected as they cast around for means of defense against his accusations.[609] They are part of a larger family of twelve brothers from the land of Canaan, they say, though one brother remains home with their father and the other is no more (v. 13). Such a single-family unit could hardly pose a threat to Pharaoh's Egypt. Little do they know that the "other brother" of whom they speak is standing right in front of them!

42:18–22 This admission gives Joseph the opportunity he seeks to put the brothers to the test: they are required to leave one brother behind as a hostage and to go home with the food they have purchased (v. 19); then they are to return with their younger brother, Benjamin, as proof that they have been telling the truth (v. 20). Only then will the brother who remains as a hostage be released. In this way Joseph seeks to discover how determined the brothers are to keep intact what is left of the family, as well as to see how Benjamin is doing and ensure that they have not already disposed of him. These men had plotted Joseph's death in cold blood and then changed their minds, not out of any remorse but simply in order to profit financially (cf. 37:26). Joseph therefore seeks to determine whether there is now any remorse or sorrow in their hearts over their sin. By not choosing which brother must remain behind, Joseph leaves the brothers to make the difficult choice of who the hostage will be.

What Joseph puts his brothers through is mild compared to his own sufferings. He speaks harshly to them and imprisons them for three days in the guardhouse (42:17); fittingly, this is the same location where Joseph was earlier held (40:4). Whereas earlier he had threatened to imprison all of them and send a single brother back to fetch Benjamin (42:16), now he allows nine of the brothers to return home, leaving a single hostage (v. 19). Joseph explains his kindness by saying "I fear God" (v. 18), a fear of God that the brothers had signally failed to display

---

[608] Currid, *Genesis 25:19–50:26*, 282.
[609] The three brief disconnected sentences in 42:11 have a defensive tone to them (cf. Alter, *Five Books of Moses*, 241).

in their earlier mistreatment of Joseph himself. The fear of God is not exclusive to the family of promise—Abimelech had earlier evidenced it, despite Abraham's doubt (20:11)—but it provides reassurance to the brothers that they can expect the Egyptian authorities to behave responsibly toward them. The charge "Do this and you will live" prefigures the similar declaration by the Lord in Leviticus 18:5, reinforcing the message that Joseph's demands are not capricious. The brothers eagerly agree to Joseph's conditions (Gen. 42:20), though in reality they have little alternative.

This inexplicable situation, in which the ruler of all Egypt has chosen to single them out for negative treatment, immediately begins to work on the consciences of Joseph's brothers. They interpret this situation to be the result of karma (or, perhaps more fittingly in an Egyptian context, *ma'at*), as their earlier sins against Joseph are now coming home to roost. They saw his "distress" (*tsarah*) and did nothing to alleviate it; now a corresponding "distress" (*tsarah*) has come on them (v. 21). They acknowledge to one another their guilt in not listening to Joseph's cries for help.[610] These cries were not mentioned earlier, being held back by the narrator in order to increase their force as an expression of the vividness of the brothers' conviction of sin.

It is Reuben, the firstborn as well as the one brother who had intended to free Joseph from the pit, who speaks first—although not to propose a solution but to attempt to clear himself from the corporate blame they share.[611] "Did I not tell you not to sin against the boy?[612] But you did not listen" (v. 22). He had indeed persuaded the brothers not to kill Joseph at once (37:21–22), but he was hardly completely innocent in the wider narrative. He had encouraged them to throw Joseph into a pit and had gone along with their later plan to deceive their father (37:32–33). All the brothers were equally implicated in the reckoning now coming due for the blood of Joseph.

42:23–28 Joseph has been listening to this entire exchange, though of course the brothers do not realize that this "Egyptian" understands Hebrew, a ruse preserved by Joseph's use of an interpreter (42:23). The impact of these expressions of guilt and remorse from the brothers moves Joseph to tears, though he is careful that these tears remain unobserved (v. 24). Remorse and feelings of guilt are not enough by themselves, however; the brothers must exhibit evidence of genuine change. As a result, Joseph takes and binds Simeon as a hostage in front of the brothers (v. 24). We are not told why Simeon is singled out for this role; it may have seemed more logical to choose Reuben, as firstborn. However, Simeon is second in line after Reuben, and Reuben's recounting of his role in trying to rescue Joseph may have saved him from being chosen for imprisonment.[613]

---

610 The Hebrew idiom is "each to his brother," which underlines the theme word *'akh* ("brother").
611 Reuben's intervention here is ultimately ineffectual, as it was in chapter 37. It thus provides a negative foil for Judah's later intervention, where he offers to take Benjamin's place in Egyptian bondage (Gen. 44:18–34). Reuben makes no similar offer to become the hostage left behind in Egypt: that fate befalls Simeon (42:24).
612 Calling Joseph a *yeled* (at seventeen years old!) highlights his helplessness during these events.
613 Steinmann, *Genesis*, 399.

Meanwhile the grain is loaded into the sacks of the remaining brothers, while the money they have paid is returned to them, hidden in the grain. They are also gifted provisions necessary for the journey (v. 25). This is a deliberate attempt on Joseph's part to mystify his brothers: if *ma'at* could explain the negative part of their experience as punishment for their treatment of Joseph, what could explain this unexpected graciousness on the part of the Egyptians? The silver would serve as yet another reminder of the brothers' guilt, recalling the silver they received for selling Joseph to Egypt in the first place (37:28).

In this effort Joseph is successful. When the brothers stop overnight and go to feed their animals, one brother finds his money in his sack (Gen. 42:27). This astonishing outcome leaves them dumbfounded. It requires a larger explanation than *ma'at*, which dealt only in punishments fitting the crime and appropriate rewards for good behavior. Undeserved kindness could be attributed only to God, who is now referenced by Joseph's brothers for the first time in the narrative (v. 28). Yet such an unexpected turn of events leaves the brothers terrified rather than overjoyed (v. 28), for they know God to be a God of justice in addition to his grace. What could this strange providence mean? Perhaps they will now be accused of being thieves as well as spies on their return to Egypt.[614] This unexpected turn of events also jeopardizes their claim to be "honest men" (v. 11).

42:29–35 Upon the brothers' return to Jacob they tell him "all that had happened to them" (v. 29), although, as is usually the case in such circumstances, they omit certain key details. They do not mention their collective three-day imprisonment or that Simeon was bound in front of their very eyes, nor that their money had been mysteriously returned to their packs. They begin by mentioning the hostility and power of their interrogator and their own protestations of innocence, and only afterward do they explain the conditions he had imposed upon them (vv. 30–34). Nahum Sarna plausibly argues that the brothers must have found all the money in their sacks during the week-long journey home—as they tell Joseph in 43:21—and so the scene in which the brothers "discover" their money returned to them in 42:35 must be a careful staging for their father's benefit.[615] Awkward details casting doubt on the safety of a return trip to Egypt are suppressed, however, in hopes of persuading their father to allow Benjamin to accompany them, which is their only hope of retrieving Simeon and securing food supplies for the future.

42:36–38 The brothers' efforts to present the news as positively as possible are fruitless; the impact of seeing their money returned in their sacks provokes fear not simply in their hearts but, more importantly, in their father's heart as well (v. 35). If Jacob would not allow Benjamin to go to Egypt with his brothers in the first place, he is now even more committed not to let him go, even though it means giving up any hope of Simeon's return. Perhaps he suspects that their story about Simeon's fate is not entirely truthful and that, if he allows Benjamin to go

---

614 Westermann, *Genesis 37–50*, 112.
615 Sarna, *Genesis*, 296.

with them, his youngest son will have another of those "accidents" that had earlier caused Joseph's disappearance (37:33).

Yet, for all his concern for Benjamin, Jacob's primary concern is for himself. His reaction to the loss of Simeon and the potential loss of Benjamin is to say, "You have bereaved me of my children.... All this has come against me." (42:36). Despite all the experiences in which God has repeatedly demonstrated his ability to provide for Jacob's needs, Jacob remains a proud, self-centered old man. God's message of powerful grace despite—and even through—Jacob's weakness has not yet really taken hold on Jacob's heart.

Once again, as firstborn, Reuben takes the lead in attempting to intervene (v. 37), though his intervention is as fruitless as his earlier efforts at leadership had been (37:22; 42:22). This is the last time he acts as leader of the group. Reuben offers his own two children as surety for Benjamin's safe return (v. 37), seemingly unaware of the fact that it would hardly be comforting for Jacob to put to death two of his own grandsons in vengeance for the death of one (or perhaps more) of his sons! The effect of Reuben's words is to confirm Jacob in the unchangeableness of his grief: Benjamin cannot go down to Egypt because his brother Joseph is dead and there is no one else left (v. 38). None of the other brothers forms part of Jacob's equation,[616] for he has pinned the entirety of his hope in the Abrahamic blessing on the sons of Rachel; to lose both of them would mean the end of the Lord's promise, an outcome that would bring Jacob's gray hairs down to Sheol,[617] the home of the cursed dead, in sorrow. The remainder of his life would be marked by deep sadness and mourning.

Response

Many people who suffer as much as Joseph have no desire for reconciliation with those who have caused their pain. Such a response is thoroughly understandable. Not all human relationships can be restored this side of heaven. Yet in Genesis 42 God is the primary driver of reconciliation between Joseph and his brothers, having caused the worldwide famine that brings the brothers to Egypt. Joseph does not directly initiate the reconciliation, but neither is he opposed to it. He could easily seek vengeance on his brothers as soon as they arrive, but instead he sets in motion a plan to discover whether there is any real repentance in their hearts. It is a costly plan for Joseph, one that will leave him in tears on at least three occasions (42:24; 43:30; 45:2), but he is willing to pay the price necessary for the family to be fully restored.

Joseph's strategy involves orchestrating the brothers' circumstances in such a way that they will perceive the work of a higher hand in their lives. This "invisible hand" is not merely the imparter of judgment for their past sins but also the bringer of undeserved grace into their lives, for, as the apostle Paul reminds the Roman Christians, it is the kindness of God that brings us to the first steps on the road to repentance (Rom. 2:4).

---

616 They are not referred to as "my son," as Benjamin is (Gen. 42:38).
617 On Sheol cf. comment on 37:29–36.

Yet the gospel brings us a far greater reconciliation than that depicted in the Joseph narrative. In the gospel we hear of a Father willing to send his only begotten Son into mortal danger, knowing that we would beat and wound him and then crucify him on a cross (John 3:16). We hear of a brother willing to take the initiative in seeking after lost sinners, not merely so they might extend their earthly lives but so they might receive the gift of eternal life (Matt. 1:21). When Jesus calls us to faith in himself, he invites us to recognize him as our brother, like us in every way except sin, and as our Lord, who rules over us for our protection, our good, and our joy. Through Christ we have reconciliation and peace with our heavenly Father (Rom. 5:1)—a peace that no one or nothing in this world can take away from us.

What is more, we are called to extend that reconciliation to others, especially those within the church, the family of God. We are invited to forgive others as we ourselves have been forgiven and to seek their good as Christ has sought our good. We are required to love even our enemies; how much more, then, should we love the fellow members of the body of Christ, for whom he died. This is not an easy calling; sometimes it will cost us many tears, as was the case for Joseph. But it is a faithful response to the profound reconciliation that Christ has accomplished between ourselves and our God.

GENESIS 43

43 Now the famine was severe in the land. ² And when they had eaten the grain that they had brought from Egypt, their father said to them, "Go again, buy us a little food." ³ But Judah said to him, "The man solemnly warned us, saying, 'You shall not see my face unless your brother is with you.' ⁴ If you will send our brother with us, we will go down and buy you food. ⁵ But if you will not send him, we will not go down, for the man said to us, 'You shall not see my face, unless your brother is with you.'" ⁶ Israel said, "Why did you treat me so badly as to tell the man that you had another brother?" ⁷ They replied, "The man questioned us carefully about ourselves and our kindred, saying, 'Is your father still alive? Do you have another brother?' What we told him was in answer to these questions. Could we in any way know that he would say, 'Bring your brother down'?" ⁸ And Judah said to Israel his father, "Send the boy with me, and we will arise and go, that we may live and not die, both we and you and also our little ones. ⁹ I will be a pledge of his safety. From my hand you shall require him. If I do not bring him back to you and set him before you, then let me bear the blame forever. ¹⁰ If we had not delayed, we would now have returned twice."

¹¹ Then their father Israel said to them, "If it must be so, then do this: take some of the choice fruits of the land in your bags, and carry a present

down to the man, a little balm and a little honey, gum, myrrh, pistachio nuts, and almonds. **12** Take double the money with you. Carry back with you the money that was returned in the mouth of your sacks. Perhaps it was an oversight. **13** Take also your brother, and arise, go again to the man. **14** May God Almighty[1] grant you mercy before the man, and may he send back your other brother and Benjamin. And as for me, if I am bereaved of my children, I am bereaved."

15 So the men took this present, and they took double the money with them, and Benjamin. They arose and went down to Egypt and stood before Joseph.

16 When Joseph saw Benjamin with them, he said to the steward of his house, "Bring the men into the house, and slaughter an animal and make ready, for the men are to dine with me at noon." **17** The man did as Joseph told him and brought the men to Joseph's house. **18** And the men were afraid because they were brought to Joseph's house, and they said, "It is because of the money, which was replaced in our sacks the first time, that we are brought in, so that he may assault us and fall upon us to make us servants and seize our donkeys." **19** So they went up to the steward of Joseph's house and spoke with him at the door of the house, **20** and said, "Oh, my lord, we came down the first time to buy food. **21** And when we came to the lodging place we opened our sacks, and there was each man's money in the mouth of his sack, our money in full weight. So we have brought it again with us, **22** and we have brought other money down with us to buy food. We do not know who put our money in our sacks." **23** He replied, "Peace to you, do not be afraid. Your God and the God of your father has put treasure in your sacks for you. I received your money." Then he brought Simeon out to them. **24** And when the man had brought the men into Joseph's house and given them water, and they had washed their feet, and when he had given their donkeys fodder, **25** they prepared the present for Joseph's coming at noon, for they heard that they should eat bread there.

26 When Joseph came home, they brought into the house to him the present that they had with them and bowed down to him to the ground. **27** And he inquired about their welfare and said, "Is your father well, the old man of whom you spoke? Is he still alive?" **28** They said, "Your servant our father is well; he is still alive." And they bowed their heads and prostrated themselves. **29** And he lifted up his eyes and saw his brother Benjamin, his mother's son, and said, "Is this your youngest brother, of whom you spoke to me? God be gracious to you, my son!" **30** Then Joseph hurried out, for his compassion grew warm for his brother, and he sought a place to weep. And he entered his chamber and wept there. **31** Then he washed his face and came out. And controlling himself he said, "Serve the food." **32** They served him by himself, and them by themselves, and the Egyptians who ate with him by themselves, because the Egyptians could not eat with the Hebrews, for that is an abomination to the Egyptians. **33** And they sat before him, the firstborn according to his birthright and the youngest according to his youth. And the men looked at one another in amazement. **34** Portions were taken to them from Joseph's table, but Benjamin's portion was five times as much as any of theirs. And they drank and were merry[2] with him.

---

[1] Hebrew *El Shaddai* [2] Hebrew *and became intoxicated*

Section Overview

Shalom is an important word in the OT, in the Joseph narrative, and in this chapter. More than simply "peace," *shalom* suggests wholeness in relationships with God, creation, and the other humans around us. Joseph had been sent to seek his brothers' *shalom* in Genesis 37:14—the same brothers who would not give him a *shalom* in greeting at home; the answer to Pharaoh's dreams through Joseph was intended to bring him *shalom* (41:16); and now, as the narrative of Joseph and his brothers heads toward a resolution, the word *shalom* occurs no fewer than four times in Genesis 43 (vv. 23, 27 [2x], 28). The Lord is at work behind the scenes and through Joseph to restore the chosen family's fractured *shalom*, a necessary step if they are ever to become the united worshiping "assembly of nations" they have been called out of the world to become (cf. 28:3; 35:11). Although Joseph would perhaps be glad to put his father's house and the experiences suffered there behind him (cf. the naming of Manasseh in 41:51), God has better plans for him, plans for a restoration of their relationship. Moreover, in this unlikely story of reconciled sinners there is a profound anticipation of the goal of creation, in which men and women from all the different warring tribes of earth come together in worship of the living God (cf. Revelation 4–5).

Genesis 43 is the first part of a three-chapter narrative that provides the resolution of the brothers' broken relationship.[618] The length of the narrative indicates the complexity of the task. Joseph cannot simply welcome in his brothers and forgive them without evidence of heart change. It would have been a simple matter for Joseph to recognize them and condemn them, but restoration of relationship is a far more challenging goal.

Section Outline

XI. The Family History of Jacob (37:1–50:26) . . .
    H. Restoring Shalom (43:1–34)

Comment

43:1–10 At the end of the previous chapter Jacob ruled out any possibility of sending Benjamin to Egypt, which was the precondition for Simeon's release—effectively condemning Simeon to permanent enslavement in Egypt. Nothing that the brothers could say would change his mind, since Jacob saw them as the cause of the problem ("You have bereaved me of my children"; 42:36). But circumstances make inevitable the outcome that Jacob has resisted: "Now the famine was severe in the land" (43:1). The same situation that drove Abraham down to Egypt in 12:10 now leaves Jacob with few other choices. The food that the brothers brought back from Egypt was not going to last forever, and the day comes when Jacob tells his sons that the journey to Egypt is once again necessary. A hint of acknowledgment of the difficulty of this task is found in Jacob's words: "Buy us a little food" (43:2). This is more modest than his earlier request for them to "go down [to Egypt] and buy grain" (42:2).

---

[618] Wenham, *Genesis 16–50*, 419.

However, Judah immediately points out the problem. Unless they bring Benjamin with them to Egypt, they stand no chance of buying grain or even of being received into the presence of the mysterious man who controls the sale of grain. He had insisted that they must bring their younger brother with them (43:3–4).[619] Jacob's response is revealingly self-centered ("Why did you treat me so badly?"; v. 6), but the reality is that at this point he has no choice but to release Benjamin to go with his brothers. Whatever risks that course of action entails, the alternative is a slow death via starvation for the whole family.

Judah's leadership of his brothers emerges as the passage unfolds. Whereas the other brothers merely reiterate the problem to their father in verse 7, Judah provides the solution in verse 8. Reuben had made a rather clumsy personal commitment of Benjamin's safety at the end of the previous chapter, offering the death of his two sons (Jacob's grandsons!) if he did not bring Benjamin home successfully. Judah, however, offers his own person rather than his two sons. If Benjamin does not come back, Judah will bear the blame forever. He declares that he will have sinned against his father forever (v. 9). He himself will be the pledge; his father can demand payment from him.

The mention of a pledge connects this story with Genesis 38:18 and the pledge (Hb. *'erabon*, the noun derived from the same Hebrew verb) that Judah offered Tamar in exchange for their brief sexual encounter. These similarities invite us to see the differences as well. In Genesis 37 and 38 Judah's plan to sell Joseph and his offer of a pledge to Tamar were strategies designed to serve himself and advance his own interests by using others, while he seeks to serve others and bring them life, at whatever cost to himself. God is at work to change Judah even before he makes the trip back to Egypt. It is not yet a complete change, of course; there is no confession here by Judah of the ways in which he and his brothers have already "sinned against his father forever" in the matter of Joseph, for instance. But substantive change is rarely an immediate transformation. It usually happens in small steps.

From here onward Judah will be the prime spokesman for the brothers. He confidently asserts that there will be a positive outcome to their journey. Instead of the further bereavement that Jacob fears, "we [will] live and not die" (43:8), and by bringing home food they will secure the future not just of Jacob and his sons but also of "our little ones," the children depending on them to provide food (v. 8). Indeed, Judah rebukes his father's lack of faith in not sending them back to Egypt earlier; had they returned to Egypt immediately, they could have already returned (with Simeon in tow; v. 10). This is not mere self-confidence on the part of Judah but a growing faith in God's power and protection.

43:11–14 Reluctantly Jacob sends the brothers off on their journey along with a selection of gifts for the mysterious man who is running Egypt. These gifts ironically mirror the cargo that the Midianites had carried down to Egypt along with

---

[619] The cognate phrase *ha'ed he'id* is used of solemn warnings, often of life-and-death matters (Ex. 19:21, 23; 1 Sam. 8:9; 1 Kings 2:42); cf. Hamilton, *Genesis 18–50*, 538.

Joseph: gum, balm, and myrrh (v. 11; cf. 37:25), along with honey,[620] pistachio nuts, and almonds. There is no discrepancy between the existence of small quantities of these precious foods and the reality of a more general famine; they would have been preserved as ready currency for precisely such a situation as this. These gifts are described as a *minkhah* ("present"; 43:11), which could also be rendered "tribute"—these are the offerings required for entrance into the presence of an important figure (cf. 1 Kings 10:25).

Since the brothers had discovered that their money had been returned in their sacks on their previous journey, Jacob instructs them to take twice the money with them this time, in case there had been some mistake or their lack of proper payment had been observed (Gen. 43:12; cf. 42:35). Along with the money they may take Benjamin—though Jacob is not able to speak his name here, instead calling him "your brother" (43:13). Without Benjamin there is no prospect of being able to see the man who had made that demand of them. Finally, Jacob gives the brothers his blessing in the name of *'El-Shaddai* ("God Almighty"; v. 14), a poetic title emphasizing God's power, as the English translation suggests.[621] The request for God to grant someone mercy before a great ruler is a common motif later in the OT (1 Kings 8:50; Neh. 1:11; Jer. 42:12); it presupposes that the hearts of rulers are in the hands of the Lord to direct wherever he wills (Prov. 21:1). Jacob's favoritism is still evident from the fact that in the blessing Benjamin is now named, while Simeon is simply called "your other brother" (Gen. 43:14).

Jacob's blessing ends in a self-pitying cry: "If I am bereaved of my children, I am bereaved" (v. 14). This hardly has the heroic ring of an Esther, risking her own death before the potentially hostile King Ahasuerus with the words "If I perish, I perish" (Est. 4:16). On the contrary, Jacob's sole concern is himself. It is clear that the term "my children" extends only to the offspring of Rachel—Joseph, whom he thinks already dead, and Benjamin, whom he fears losing above all else. After all, he has been apparently untroubled about being bereaved of Simeon and makes no effort to rescue him from Egypt. Meanwhile, if Jacob were to be bereaved of his children, that would mean that the brothers themselves would be dead, which is surely a much worse fate. To Jacob, life without Joseph and Benjamin would become a living Sheol: a gray, hopeless, shadowy existence, without meaning or purpose (cf. Gen. 42:38). Yet in reality the Lord's purpose is not to bereave him but to unbereave him—to restore to him the sons he has lost, not to take more sons from him.

In the meantime God takes away all Jacob's sons, leaving him completely alone, so that he will once again be forced to trust in God alone to fulfill the Abrahamic promise that he will have descendants like the sand of the sea (32:12). God puts Jacob in a situation in which he will have to walk by faith in the promise of God over the many weeks that have to pass before he will see his sons again. He is old,

---

620 It is possible that *debash* has in view date syrup rather than bee's honey, since apiculture was not practiced during this period of history. However, wild honey was a known and valued commodity from earliest times (Deut. 32:13; Judg. 14:8; 1 Sam. 14:25).
621 On *'El-Shaddai* cf. comment on 17:1–8.

and their journey is long and perilous. He is left with nothing to comfort him in this situation except his faith in the bare word of God's promise.

43:15–25 Verse 15 is transitional, bridging the gap between Egypt and Canaan. It records the fact that the brothers take the present, double the money, and Benjamin—as though Benjamin were simply one more object to carry with them—and that they arrive safely in Egypt and present themselves before Joseph. The lengthy journey is covered briefly, but the subsequent events will be played out almost in slow motion in order to build suspense.[622]

From verse 15 onward the brothers are referred to simply as "the men" rather than "Joseph's brothers" (cf. 42:6–8), since their relationship to Joseph going forward is precisely the question. The relationship will be confirmed in Genesis 45:1–3, after they pass the test that Joseph devises for them. Seeing that they have indeed brought Benjamin with them, as instructed, Joseph commands his steward to bring the brothers into his house and leave them cooling their heels while they await the noon meal, which they will eat together with Joseph (43:16). In Genesis 37 the brothers and Joseph met in the open field, and he was in their power; now they meet indoors, where they are in his power.

This unusual invitation to dine with the mysterious ruler of Egypt causes the brothers considerable concern (v. 18). The fact that high Egyptian officials were known to have dungeons in their houses probably adds to their alarm. They immediately remember the strange occurrence on the first trip, when they found their money returned to them in their sacks (v. 18; cf. 42:26–28). They conjecture that perhaps Joseph wants to appropriate their donkeys, a rather quaint idea considering he has all the power and riches of Egypt at his disposal. If he were merely interested in their animals, he could be considerably more direct about it. The same is true if Joseph is concerned simply with enslaving him—the brothers are entirely in his power. Their fears reflect the fact that they earlier dispossessed Joseph and sold him into slavery: if the Egyptian does the same to them, it would be no more than they deserve.

The brothers' guilty consciences force them to go to Joseph's steward and confess that their money had been returned to them on the previous visit by person or persons unknown (Gen. 43:20–22). The steward,[623] presumably following a script given to him ahead of time by Joseph, explains it as an act of God—and not just any god but specifically "the God of your father" (v. 23),[624] a remarkably Israelite turn of phrase for an Egyptian. The steward seeks to calm their fears by claiming that he had received their money.[625] Their God could apparently multiply silver, even in faraway Egypt! The steward also brings out Simeon to them and provides

---

[622] Von Rad, *Genesis*, 38.
[623] It is a rich irony that Joseph, who once rose to be over Potiphar's house (Gen. 39:4–5), now has a servant over his own house.
[624] The phrase translated by most English versions as "Your God and the God of your father" could be rendered "Your God, that is, the God of your father," taking the *vav* as epexegetical (cf. *IBHS*, 39.2.4). On the formula "God of your father" cf. comment on 31:36–55.
[625] The steward uses a legal formula known from other ancient Near Eastern sources for payment received in full; cf. J. Muffs, "Two Comparative Lexical Studies," *JANES* 5 (1973): 287–294.

the brothers with water with which to wash their feet and straw for their donkeys (v. 24), as though deliberately rebuking their concern that Joseph's secret goal is to enslave them and steal their donkeys. He then leaves them to await Joseph's arrival at noon.

43:26–34 When the meal is finally served, the brothers bring their gifts and bow before Joseph, once again fulfilling the dream of Genesis 37 (43:26; cf. 37:7–8; 42:6). Joseph inquires after the brothers' *shalom*—the same *shalom* they had been unwilling to give him at home (37:4) and that he had been sent to seek after in 37:14—as well as the *shalom* of their elderly father (43:27). Restoring the family *shalom* is the key focus of this narrative unit. It is surely considerable comfort to Joseph to find out that Jacob is still alive and in good health (*shalom*), just as it is to see his brother Benjamin unharmed. He feigns ignorance of Benjamin's identity, asking, "Is this your youngest brother?" but he surely knows who he is. The sight of Benjamin is too much for his composure, so after a brief blessing ("God be gracious to you, my son!"; v. 29) Joseph withdraws to find a place to weep (v. 30).[626] In verse 14 Jacob had prayed for the Egyptian ruler to have compassion on the brothers; now his prayer has been answered. At the same time, if the fire of jealousy is still powerfully present in the brothers' hearts, Joseph's special attention to Benjamin is calculated to stoke it further.

When the meal is served, Joseph eats separately from the brothers, according to Egyptian custom that regarded the presence of foreigners as defiling (v. 32), a custom also reported by Herodotus.[627] Joseph heightens the effect of mysterious divine forces at work by arranging the brothers in exact order of age in the seating plan for the meal, a feat that the brothers find to be astonishing and unnerving (v. 33). Meanwhile, Joseph ensures that, even though his guests all have plenty of food, Benjamin is visibly favored with the best of the best: five times the portions of the other brothers (v. 34). It is plain for all to see which of the brothers is the favorite, not merely of the mysterious man but of the God who is apparently pulling all the strings of this encounter. Once again, if there is still jealousy and enmity at work among the brothers, this behavior would surely stir it up. Then on the next day Joseph will provide the brothers with a perfect opportunity to dispose of this unloved favorite, in circumstances for which they need not be held liable. The brothers would be able to return to Canaan with the food they need, without the brother they hate, and with an unimpeachable excuse.

To lend maximum credibility to the story about a stolen cup that the brothers will be told the next day, Joseph arranges for them to "drink and make merry"—to get drunk (*vayyishkeru*; Gen. 43:34), as this word combination signifies elsewhere (e.g., Jer. 25:27).[628] Joseph wants the brothers to have only hazy memories of the

---

626 "His compassion grew warm" could be rendered "His compassion boiled over"; cf. Hamilton, *Genesis 18–50*, 552. The plural *rakhamim* ("compassion") is likely a plural of intensification.
627 Alter, *Five Books of Moses*, 251.
628 See Alter's translation in *Five Books of Moses*, 252.

previous night's celebration in order to make them believe it is entirely possible that Benjamin has stolen the cup while under the influence of alcohol.

Joseph's motive throughout this chapter is for his brothers' *shalom*: anything less would not require such a costly interplay with them on Joseph's part; he could simply have condemned them from a distance. What is more, the abundant feast provides a picture of what restored *shalom* looks like.[629] Yet the *shalom* has not yet been completely restored; the brothers and Joseph still consume their feasts separately. The fullness of *shalom* requires that gap also to be bridged.

Response

Joseph's costly pursuit of his brother's consciences provides an insight into the costliness of all *shalom*-making. It is not only the guilty party who has to pay the price of reconciliation. The person who has been sinned against also has to be willing to bear the cost. There will be many tears on both sides before true *shalom* can be accomplished. Sometimes it may seem much easier simply to forget the whole endeavor and go back to living unreconciled lives; at other times we will face the temptation to gloss over the sin and rush to reconciliation before real change has taken place. True reconciliation is never accomplished lightly.

The same is true on a still grander scale with the reconciliation that God has provided for us in Christ. Far from clinging to his beloved Son fearfully, as Jacob did with Benjamin, the Father sent him into this broken and pain-filled world to restore our broken *shalom*. The Father knew what that reconciliation would cost Jesus and what the cost would be to himself. The Father knew that his own chosen people would reject Jesus and scorn him, preferring the darkness in which they lived to the light that he came to bring. He knew that Jesus' earthly brothers would take him and sell him for silver before torturing him and killing him. What must it have cost a Father's heart to watch his beloved Son undergo such terrible agony?

Yet that painful journey through a world of suffering and brokenness was necessary in order for Jesus to heal our shattered *shalom*, reconciling us to God at the cost of his own blood. God himself has paid the full cost of our reconciliation to him. All we have to do is humble ourselves before him and ask him to restore us to his favor. God himself pays the incalculable debt that we owe in order that we may receive the glorious inheritance that Christ has earned.

This *shalom* with God that is now ours summons us to seek the same *shalom* with our brothers and sisters in Christ (Eph. 2:16). That process will be painful and costly, as was our own reconciliation. We cannot simply ignore the sins that separate us. That journey may take all the wisdom with which Joseph sought *shalom* with his brothers, and it will likely bring into our lives tears we would rather have avoided. But in light of the reconciliation we have received how can we refuse to seek peace with our brothers and sisters? The one who has the power to raise

---

[629] Wilson, *Joseph Wise and Otherwise*, 161.

Christ from the dead also has the power to restore dead relationships to new life in him and make them a testimony to his grace.

However, not all our relationships will be restored here and now. We might have brothers and sisters in Christ who are still unwilling to speak *shalom* to us. Yet the *shalom* God accomplished at the cross enables us to live at peace with that reality as well. We are called to seek peace with others, but we are also called to be at peace when we cannot achieve reconciliation (Rom. 12:18; 2 Cor. 13:11). If God is for us, then all our failures are atoned for; if we are reconciled with God through Christ, then we may have peace in the midst of troubled earthly relationships that remain unresolvable. One day even those breaches will finally be healed, when we are all finally made fully new in Christ.

GENESIS 44:1–45:15

44 Then he commanded the steward of his house, "Fill the men's sacks with food, as much as they can carry, and put each man's money in the mouth of his sack, ² and put my cup, the silver cup, in the mouth of the sack of the youngest, with his money for the grain." And he did as Joseph told him.

³ As soon as the morning was light, the men were sent away with their donkeys. ⁴ They had gone only a short distance from the city. Now Joseph said to his steward, "Up, follow after the men, and when you overtake them, say to them, 'Why have you repaid evil for good?¹ ⁵ Is it not from this that my lord drinks, and by this that he practices divination? You have done evil in doing this.'"

⁶ When he overtook them, he spoke to them these words. ⁷ They said to him, "Why does my lord speak such words as these? Far be it from your servants to do such a thing! ⁸ Behold, the money that we found in the mouths of our sacks we brought back to you from the land of Canaan. How then could we steal silver or gold from your lord's house? ⁹ Whichever of your servants is found with it shall die, and we also will be my lord's servants." ¹⁰ He said, "Let it be as you say: he who is found with it shall be my servant, and the rest of you shall be innocent." ¹¹ Then each man quickly lowered his sack to the ground, and each man opened his sack. ¹² And he searched, beginning with the eldest and ending with the youngest. And the cup was found in Benjamin's sack. ¹³ Then they tore their clothes, and every man loaded his donkey, and they returned to the city.

¹⁴ When Judah and his brothers came to Joseph's house, he was still there. They fell before him to the ground. ¹⁵ Joseph said to them, "What deed is this that you have done? Do you not know that a man like me can indeed practice divination?" ¹⁶ And Judah said, "What shall we say to my lord? What shall we speak? Or how can we clear ourselves? God has found out the guilt of your servants; behold, we are my lord's servants, both we and he also in whose hand the cup has been found." ¹⁷ But he said, "Far be

it from me that I should do so! Only the man in whose hand the cup was found shall be my servant. But as for you, go up in peace to your father."

¹⁸ Then Judah went up to him and said, "Oh, my lord, please let your servant speak a word in my lord's ears, and let not your anger burn against your servant, for you are like Pharaoh himself. ¹⁹ My lord asked his servants, saying, 'Have you a father, or a brother?' ²⁰ And we said to my lord, 'We have a father, an old man, and a young brother, the child of his old age. His brother is dead, and he alone is left of his mother's children, and his father loves him.' ²¹ Then you said to your servants, 'Bring him down to me, that I may set my eyes on him.' ²² We said to my lord, 'The boy cannot leave his father, for if he should leave his father, his father would die.' ²³ Then you said to your servants, 'Unless your youngest brother comes down with you, you shall not see my face again.'

²⁴ "When we went back to your servant my father, we told him the words of my lord. ²⁵ And when our father said, 'Go again, buy us a little food,' ²⁶ we said, 'We cannot go down. If our youngest brother goes with us, then we will go down. For we cannot see the man's face unless our youngest brother is with us.' ²⁷ Then your servant my father said to us, 'You know that my wife bore me two sons. ²⁸ One left me, and I said, "Surely he has been torn to pieces," and I have never seen him since. ²⁹ If you take this one also from me, and harm happens to him, you will bring down my gray hairs in evil to Sheol.'

³⁰ "Now therefore, as soon as I come to your servant my father, and the boy is not with us, then, as his life is bound up in the boy's life, ³¹ as soon as he sees that the boy is not with us, he will die, and your servants will bring down the gray hairs of your servant our father with sorrow to Sheol. ³² For your servant became a pledge of safety for the boy to my father, saying, 'If I do not bring him back to you, then I shall bear the blame before my father all my life.' ³³ Now therefore, please let your servant remain instead of the boy as a servant to my lord, and let the boy go back with his brothers. ³⁴ For how can I go back to my father if the boy is not with me? I fear to see the evil that would find my father."

45 Then Joseph could not control himself before all those who stood by him. He cried, "Make everyone go out from me." So no one stayed with him when Joseph made himself known to his brothers. ² And he wept aloud, so that the Egyptians heard it, and the household of Pharaoh heard it. ³ And Joseph said to his brothers, "I am Joseph! Is my father still alive?" But his brothers could not answer him, for they were dismayed at his presence.

⁴ So Joseph said to his brothers, "Come near to me, please." And they came near. And he said, "I am your brother, Joseph, whom you sold into Egypt. ⁵ And now do not be distressed or angry with yourselves because you sold me here, for God sent me before you to preserve life. ⁶ For the famine has been in the land these two years, and there are yet five years in which there will be neither plowing nor harvest. ⁷ And God sent me before you to preserve for you a remnant on earth, and to keep alive for you many survivors. ⁸ So it was not you who sent me here, but God. He has made me a father to Pharaoh, and lord of all his house and ruler over all the land of Egypt. ⁹ Hurry and go up to my father and say to him, 'Thus says your son Joseph, God has made me lord of all Egypt. Come down to me; do not tarry. ¹⁰ You shall dwell in the land of Goshen, and you shall be near me, you and your children and your children's children, and your

flocks, your herds, and all that you have. ¹¹ There I will provide for you, for there are yet five years of famine to come, so that you and your household, and all that you have, do not come to poverty.' ¹² And now your eyes see, and the eyes of my brother Benjamin see, that it is my mouth that speaks to you. ¹³ You must tell my father of all my honor in Egypt, and of all that you have seen. Hurry and bring my father down here." ¹⁴ Then he fell upon his brother Benjamin's neck and wept, and Benjamin wept upon his neck. ¹⁵ And he kissed all his brothers and wept upon them. After that his brothers talked with him.

¹ Septuagint (compare Vulgate) adds *Why have you stolen my silver cup?*

Section Overview

Genesis 44 forms the middle of the three-chapter unit that documents the reconciliation between Joseph and his brothers. As such it focuses on the test that Joseph sets for his brothers (44:1–13), which leads to Judah's crucial intervention (vv. 14–34). It is Judah's willingness to sacrifice himself on behalf of Benjamin, out of deep concern for his father, that enables Joseph to see the change that has taken place in his brothers. This paves the way for Joseph to reveal his identity to his brothers and for the reconciliation to reach completion (45:1–15). Afterward the focus of the narrative shifts to Jacob's journey to Egypt (45:16–46:27) and to Jacob and Joseph's reunion (46:28–34). The good that God is working to bring about will finally become visible to the humans through whom and in whom he is working (cf. 45:5).

Section Outline

XI. The Family History of Jacob (37:1–50:26) . . .
    I. Joseph Reconciles with His Brothers (44:1–45:15)

Comment

44:1–2 At the end of chapter 43 the brothers were enjoying Joseph's hospitality to the full, even to the point of excess (43:34). They had successfully retrieved Simeon from his Egyptian captivity and thought they would be heading home the next day laden with grain they had purchased. It seemed that a trip with so many potential ways to go wrong was turning out far better than they had dared hope.

Yet Joseph was simply setting the brothers up for the ultimate test, as becomes clear when he gives his instructions to his steward the following morning. Not only is the steward to fill the brothers' sacks to the brim ("as much as they can carry," 44:1); he is once again to return the brothers' money in their sacks. No reason is given for this action, and it is not referenced later in the narrative, but it will likely heighten the brothers' sense of divine activity when they discover it, especially since the steward had deliberately attributed the earlier return of their money to "the God of [their] father" (43:23). It will also confirm to them that Benjamin is innocent of the charges against him.

The steward is further instructed to place Joseph's silver cup in the sack of the youngest brother, Benjamin, making it appear that he has violated his host's generous hospitality by stealing a prized possession (44:1–2). The word for "cup" here (Hb. *gabia'*) usually has in view a container for liquid larger than a normal drinking vessel, generally something used for sacred purposes such as libations.[630] Later the claim is made that Joseph uses this vessel for divination (vv. 5, 15), perhaps through studying oil trails in water or similar phenomena. The claim is probably designed as part of Joseph's Egyptian disguise, as well as to provide an explanation for how he could discern hidden things such as Benjamin's alleged theft, rather than being a statement to be taken at face value. Divination is later forbidden to Israel (Deut. 18:10).

44:3–13 The brothers leave with their grain sacks and donkeys at first light, probably still nursing hangovers from the night before (Gen. 43:34), but it is not long before Joseph sends the steward after them with a scripted accusation of having broken the sacred trust of ancient Near Eastern hospitality and doing undeserved evil against Joseph (44:4–6). Specifically, they are to be accused of theft—and not just of the common or garden variety but of stealing Joseph's own silver cup,[631] which he uses for sacred purposes (v. 5). The initial irony, of course, lies in the fact that they have indeed done undeserved evil against Joseph, selling him for silver, the same material as that of which the cup is made. They are thus truly guilty men, even though they are completely innocent of this particular charge.[632] The deeper irony may be seen in the fact that God's purpose in all of this is to do them undeserved good, even though their intentions have been truly evil (50:20).

Sure enough, the steward rapidly overtakes the heavily laden brothers, making his rehearsed speech (44:6). The brothers' response is full of aggrieved innocence (vv. 8–9). The insistence on death for the person who has stolen a precious object is reminiscent of Laban's search for his household gods, when Jacob made a similar commitment—not knowing that Rachel had indeed stolen them (31:32). The brothers "quickly" lower their sacks to be examined, confident that the search will prove fruitless (44:11).

Unimpressed by the brothers' loud protestations of innocence (not least because he himself earlier planted the allegedly stolen cup in Benjamin's sack), Joseph's steward begins to open their sacks, one by one. As with the seating of the brothers at the banquet, he starts with the oldest, Reuben, and works his way down to Benjamin, with the suspense building as he goes (v. 12). As he begins to open the sacks and the brothers see their money once again, they must have a sinking feeling. Perhaps they begin to feel like Lady Macbeth, doomed to be haunted forever by the silver they received in exchange for their brother.[633]

---

630 Wenham, *Genesis 16–50*, 424.
631 The Hebrew text does not explicitly mention the cup, only "this from which my lord drinks and practices divination," which assumes that at this point the steward will have already uncovered the cup in the brothers' sacks. The LXX adds "Why did you steal my silver cup?"
632 Hamilton, *Genesis 18–50*, 566.
633 Cf. Alter, *Five Books of Moses*, 253.

This sinking feeling must turn to profound panic when the searchers reach Benjamin's sack and find the stolen goblet (v. 12). The brothers likely suspect that it has been planted there, just like their money was. However, their chances of convincing Joseph of this fact are slim, especially since he (or someone in his household) seems to have planned their downfall. Yet, in light of recent events, in which one inexplicable circumstance has been piled on top of another, they may suspect a higher hand at work in all this. The steward has been promoting this connection from the beginning with his assertion that their God had returned their money on the previous trip (43:23). The logical conclusion is that this time their God not only has returned their money but also has miraculously planted the cup in Benjamin's sack to repay them for their former misdeeds. Their distress is evident as they tear their garments,[634] reload their donkeys, and return with heavy hearts to the city. It is striking that by this means the brothers *all* demonstrate their sorrow, even though the steward has already informed them that only Benjamin will suffer for his "crime" (44:10).

44:14–17 When the brothers return to Joseph's house, he is waiting to meet them (v. 14). Rather than leaving this task for a subordinate to carry out, he puts his business to one side in order to deal with them himself. The brothers once again prostrate themselves before him in fulfillment of his dream (v. 14; cf. 37:7); the addition of the phrase "to the ground" emphasizes their helplessness before him. Joseph does not need to reiterate the charge: his words are rhetorical, aimed at heightening the brothers' sense of participation in a divine drama. If Joseph is able to divine the identity of the thief, it must be because God has given him the insight (cf. 41:16). This explains Judah's reply: "God has found out the guilt of your servants" (44:16). He cannot be referring to the stolen cup, since the brothers are not guilty of that crime. This must be an acknowledgement of divine judgment upon the brothers for the sin of selling Joseph into slavery. The punishment fits the guilt of their earlier crime: since they sold Joseph to slavery in Egypt, they will now become slaves in Egypt.

It is significant that at this point Judah steps forward as the undisputed leader of the brothers to make the longest speech in the book of Genesis.[635] Previously, as firstborn, Reuben made the initial proposals, though in each case Judah's voice ultimately prevailed (37:22–28; 42:37–43:9); now, however, Judah's voice alone is heard in a lengthy speech on behalf of them all. The initial focus of his speech is the brothers' solidarity with Benjamin (44:16). The steward had suggested that, as the guilty individual, Benjamin alone would be enslaved; the other brothers would be free to return home with their grain (v. 10). This offer is calculated to appeal to the brothers' jealousy of Benjamin, which Joseph has fanned by showing special favoritism to the younger brother in speech (43:29) and action (43:34). Joseph reiterates the offer himself: only the guilty party will be enslaved, while

---

[634] This action mirrors Jacob's reaction to the death of Joseph (Gen. 37:34); as the chapter unfolds, the brothers previous callous disregard for their father's distress morphs into far greater compassion for his feelings.
[635] Mathews, *Genesis 11:27–50:26*, 803. Cf. Calvin, *Genesis*, 2.370.

the other brothers can go up "in peace" (Hb. *beshalom*; 44:17) to their father. Here is a golden opportunity for the brothers to be rid of their rival once for all, with no personal blame attaching to them in the least. It would be easy for the brothers to rationalize this choice, arguing that, if they all remain in Egypt, there will be no one to carry the grain home to their families in Canaan, who will then inevitably perish.

44:18–34 Judah's second speech is triggered by Joseph's words "Go up in peace [*beshalom*] to your father" (v. 17). There will be no *shalom* engendered by the brothers' returning to their father without Benjamin. This, of course, requires Judah to give a lengthy explanation to Joseph of the family situation. His language is extremely deferential, as befits conversation with a man of such power ("like Pharaoh himself"; v. 18), especially under such circumstances. Judah is aware that even speaking before Joseph is a privilege and not a right. Of course, the positive side of Joseph's undisputed power is his ability to determine appropriate punishment and grant clemency in this situation; there is no other man to whom he is accountable in his administration of justice.

Judah's appeal is ultimately on behalf of his father, not his own interests or even those of Benjamin; in this speech he uses the word "father" no fewer than fourteen times.[636] His recounting of their history is a loose paraphrase of events, focusing on why they had no choice but to bring Benjamin with them on this return visit to Egypt, as well as on Benjamin's special relationship with his father. The former is the result of Joseph's own unrelenting demand, while the latter is due to Benjamin's being the child of Jacob's old age and to the earlier death of Benjamin's brother (though, of course, Judah is at that moment unwittingly speaking to the "dead" brother, Joseph!). The unusual extensive use of second-level reporting—quoting earlier direct speech verbatim—lends Judah's words additional directness and pathos. The conclusion Judah hammers home is that if the brothers return home without Benjamin, it will kill their father (vv. 30–34). The father's life is bound up in the boy's, and Judah has personally pledged to bring Benjamin home safely or bear the guilt forever. Jacob's favoritism of Benjamin is no longer the reason for fraternal jealousy but now becomes a reason for Joseph to show compassion on the boy.

In conclusion Judah proposes a solution that honors both justice and peace: let Judah take Benjamin's place as the one condemned to slavery in Egypt, and let Benjamin return home to his father with the other brothers (v. 33). Judah will stand "in the place of" (*takhat*) Benjamin, as surely as the ram stood "in place of" (*takhat*) Isaac on Mount Moriah (v. 33; cf. 22:13).[637] This is fitting since it was originally Judah who had proposed selling Joseph into slavery (37:26–27), and now Judah cannot face the devastating impact that the alternative scenario would have on his father (44:34). With this conclusion the change in the brothers, as represented by

---

636 Greidanus, *Preaching Christ from Genesis*, 427.
637 Mathews, *Genesis 11:27–50:26*, 806. It is not coincidental that Isaac was also a "child of his old age" (Gen. 21:2, 7; 44:20), deeply beloved of his father.

Judah, is clear. Earlier they had no concern for the "evil" that would overtake their father when he was shown Joseph's bloody robe and concluded that his beloved son was dead (37:31–35); now Judah is willing to sacrifice himself in order to avoid any repetition of that scene.

45:1–15 At this moment the dramatic tension reaches the climax to which it has been building for several chapters. The future not only of Jacob, Benjamin, and the brothers lies in the balance, but indeed that of the Abrahamic promise itself. How could it be fulfilled unless the brothers are able to return home successfully with the grain? The resolution is swift and successful, as Joseph is overcome once again with emotion (45:1). He sends out his Egyptian entourage so that the moment of reconciliation with his brothers will be for them alone—although so great is the emotional outpouring that the sound of their weeping is heard more broadly, not just among Joseph's attendants but as far as the household of Pharaoh (v. 2). The division in the family engendered by jealousy in chapter 37 is finally resolved into harmony through repentance, grace, and forgiveness, demonstrated by the fact that Joseph summons the brothers to draw near to him (45:4) and that the brothers who had earlier been unwilling even to speak to Joseph (37:4) now finally talk with him (45:15).

Joseph's first words to his brothers, after confirming his identity, concern his father: "Is my father still alive?" (v. 3). He had already asked the brothers that question in 43:27, and indeed Judah's lengthy speech made little sense if Jacob were not still alive, but Joseph wants to hear the news once more for reassurance. His brothers are understandably stunned and dismayed at Joseph's self-revelation: if they had feared that the mysterious ruler of Egypt held a grudge against them before, now they have proof that he had abundant reason to do so. But, far from Joseph's being determined to destroy them, he has pursued this entire complex plan in order to facilitate their reconciliation.

Joseph's forgiveness of his brothers is remarkable. He identifies himself not as their lord and master but as their brother (v. 4).[638] Not only does he not hold their sin against them, but he urges them not to hold it against themselves (v. 5). This magnanimity on Joseph's part flows from an understanding of what God has been doing in and through their sin: "You sold me here," but "God sent me before you to preserve life," both the life of the Egyptian people and, especially, the lives of his chosen family (v. 5). As he looks back over his long and painful journey, Joseph can recognize that, ultimately, it was not the brothers who sent him into slavery in Egypt but God (v. 8).[639] While the brothers were truly guilty of their sin, God's sovereignty extended over Joseph's enslavement, even to the point of his deliverance from slavery and meteoric rise to become ruler over all Egypt, second only to Pharaoh (v. 8). It was not fate or circumstances that had made Joseph lord of all Egypt, but God (vv. 8–9).

---

638 Wilson, *Joseph Wise and Otherwise*, 174.
639 Cf. Calvin, *Genesis*, 2.377.

The famine is only just beginning at this point; they are a mere two years into the seven-year cycle of drought (v. 6). As a result, the best way for Jacob and all his family to survive the coming hardship is for them to come to Egypt with all their possessions and to settle in the fertile land of Goshen, in the Nile Delta, near Joseph (vv. 9–10). There Joseph will be able to provide for them, so that they will remain alive and avoid poverty (v. 11). The brothers now have to go back to their father and report the news of Joseph's place in Egypt—an awkward conversation, if ever there was one—and bring him down to join Joseph in Egypt (v. 13). Joseph then embraces all his brothers, beginning with Benjamin (v. 15); he earlier wept separately, but now in the culmination of their reconciliation they weep together.

Response

Joseph recognizes that it is not only his circumstances that are subject to God's overriding providence but even the worst sins of his brothers; God has good purposes in Joseph's life, even when he is brutally sinned against. That is easier to acknowledge in the abstract than in times when we are faced with the specifics of our own lives, where those closest to us—family and friends—have sinned against us in ways that seem to have destroyed our hopes and robbed us of years of happiness, but it is nonetheless true (v. 5). As the text makes clear, we should not in any way minimize sin, as though it does not really matter since God plans it for good. True repentance is a necessary prerequisite for reconciliation, and some relationships may be too broken to be restored this side of heaven. This is especially true when those who have sinned against us are unwilling or unable to recognize and admit their sin. The life to which God calls us and sovereignly ordains for us is often a difficult and challenging one.

We should not miss the fact that God's wonderful plan to feed his people by bringing them to Egypt also includes the next period in their history: their oppressive bondage under a pharaoh who forgets Joseph (Exodus 1), from which the Lord will subsequently liberate them through the exodus (Exodus 3–14). How ironic that the slavery in Egypt that Joseph does not impose on the brothers comes upon a subsequent generation, which in turn becomes the means for them to see the power of God at work in a new and incredible way in their own day! Far from bypassing suffering and victimization God's wonderful plan for our lives often takes us through the middle of searing pain and loss. Affliction is, after all, the soil in which the fruit of patience, endurance, perseverance, and hope most richly grow (James 1:2–4).

As Christians, we are called to forgive others as we ourselves have been forgiven (Matt. 18:1–34). This is a difficult calling, to be sure. Yet we serve a God who has himself experienced the difficulty of the task to which he calls us. Before the foundation of the world God developed a far more complicated and costly plan than Joseph's that would both satisfy the claims of justice *and* allow us to receive the mercy and grace we need in order to be reconciled to him. In the fullness of time God sent his only Son, Jesus, into this world of affliction and pain to effect this reconciliation with him.

Jesus' love for us is far greater than Judah's love for his father. Jesus not only had to be willing to bear the undeserved punishment of another's sin but also had to carry that willingness through to the bitter end. Judah may have offered to become Joseph's slave, but Judah's greater son went much further than that, bearing upon his back the blame we truly deserved. He came to bear a lifetime of limitation, sickness, rejection, and undeserved abuse, taking the form of a servant, in order to free us from our bondage to sin, death, and hell (Phil. 2:5–11). He obeyed faithfully all the way to the cross, where he bore the weight of divine rejection and torment that our sins deserved. In that way, through immense human sin and great suffering, God accomplished his purpose of redeeming a people for himself. We sinned, but God purposed it for good (Acts 2:23–24).

GENESIS 45:16–46:34

16 When the report was heard in Pharaoh's house, "Joseph's brothers have come," it pleased Pharaoh and his servants. 17 And Pharaoh said to Joseph, "Say to your brothers, 'Do this: load your beasts and go back to the land of Canaan, 18 and take your father and your households, and come to me, and I will give you the best of the land of Egypt, and you shall eat the fat of the land.' 19 And you, Joseph, are commanded to say, 'Do this: take wagons from the land of Egypt for your little ones and for your wives, and bring your father, and come. 20 Have no concern for[1] your goods, for the best of all the land of Egypt is yours.'"

21 The sons of Israel did so: and Joseph gave them wagons, according to the command of Pharaoh, and gave them provisions for the journey. 22 To each and all of them he gave a change of clothes, but to Benjamin he gave three hundred shekels[2] of silver and five changes of clothes. 23 To his father he sent as follows: ten donkeys loaded with the good things of Egypt, and ten female donkeys loaded with grain, bread, and provision for his father on the journey. 24 Then he sent his brothers away, and as they departed, he said to them, "Do not quarrel on the way."

25 So they went up out of Egypt and came to the land of Canaan to their father Jacob. 26 And they told him, "Joseph is still alive, and he is ruler over all the land of Egypt." And his heart became numb, for he did not believe them. 27 But when they told him all the words of Joseph, which he had said to them, and when he saw the wagons that Joseph had sent to carry him, the spirit of their father Jacob revived. 28 And Israel said, "It is enough; Joseph my son is still alive. I will go and see him before I die."

46 So Israel took his journey with all that he had and came to Beersheba, and offered sacrifices to the God of his father Isaac. 2 And God spoke to Israel in visions of the night and said, "Jacob, Jacob."

And he said, "Here I am." ³ Then he said, "I am God, the God of your father. Do not be afraid to go down to Egypt, for there I will make you into a great nation. ⁴ I myself will go down with you to Egypt, and I will also bring you up again, and Joseph's hand shall close your eyes."

⁵ Then Jacob set out from Beersheba. The sons of Israel carried Jacob their father, their little ones, and their wives, in the wagons that Pharaoh had sent to carry him. ⁶ They also took their livestock and their goods, which they had gained in the land of Canaan, and came into Egypt, Jacob and all his offspring with him, ⁷ his sons, and his sons' sons with him, his daughters, and his sons' daughters. All his offspring he brought with him into Egypt.

⁸ Now these are the names of the descendants of Israel, who came into Egypt, Jacob and his sons. Reuben, Jacob's firstborn, ⁹ and the sons of Reuben: Hanoch, Pallu, Hezron, and Carmi. ¹⁰ The sons of Simeon: Jemuel, Jamin, Ohad, Jachin, Zohar, and Shaul, the son of a Canaanite woman. ¹¹ The sons of Levi: Gershon, Kohath, and Merari. ¹² The sons of Judah: Er, Onan, Shelah, Perez, and Zerah (but Er and Onan died in the land of Canaan); and the sons of Perez were Hezron and Hamul. ¹³ The sons of Issachar: Tola, Puvah, Yob, and Shimron. ¹⁴ The sons of Zebulun: Sered, Elon, and Jahleel. ¹⁵ These are the sons of Leah, whom she bore to Jacob in Paddan-aram, together with his daughter Dinah; altogether his sons and his daughters numbered thirty-three.

¹⁶ The sons of Gad: Ziphion, Haggi, Shuni, Ezbon, Eri, Arodi, and Areli. ¹⁷ The sons of Asher: Imnah, Ishvah, Ishvi, Beriah, with Serah their sister. And the sons of Beriah: Heber and Malchiel. ¹⁸ These are the sons of Zilpah, whom Laban gave to Leah his daughter; and these she bore to Jacob—sixteen persons.

¹⁹ The sons of Rachel, Jacob's wife: Joseph and Benjamin. ²⁰ And to Joseph in the land of Egypt were born Manasseh and Ephraim, whom Asenath, the daughter of Potiphera the priest of On, bore to him. ²¹ And the sons of Benjamin: Bela, Becher, Ashbel, Gera, Naaman, Ehi, Rosh, Muppim, Huppim, and Ard. ²² These are the sons of Rachel, who were born to Jacob—fourteen persons in all.

²³ The son[3] of Dan: Hushim. ²⁴ The sons of Naphtali: Jahzeel, Guni, Jezer, and Shillem. ²⁵ These are the sons of Bilhah, whom Laban gave to Rachel his daughter, and these she bore to Jacob—seven persons in all.

²⁶ All the persons belonging to Jacob who came into Egypt, who were his own descendants, not including Jacob's sons' wives, were sixty-six persons in all. ²⁷ And the sons of Joseph, who were born to him in Egypt, were two. All the persons of the house of Jacob who came into Egypt were seventy.

²⁸ He had sent Judah ahead of him to Joseph to show the way before him in Goshen, and they came into the land of Goshen. ²⁹ Then Joseph prepared his chariot and went up to meet Israel his father in Goshen. He presented himself to him and fell on his neck and wept on his neck a good while. ³⁰ Israel said to Joseph, "Now let me die, since I have seen your face and know that you are still alive." ³¹ Joseph said to his brothers and to his father's household, "I will go up and tell Pharaoh and will say to him, 'My brothers and my father's household, who were in the land of Canaan, have come to me. ³² And the men are shepherds, for they have been keepers of livestock, and they have brought their flocks and their herds and all that they have.' ³³ When Pharaoh calls you and says, 'What

is your occupation?' ³⁴ you shall say, 'Your servants have been keepers of livestock from our youth even until now, both we and our fathers,' in order that you may dwell in the land of Goshen, for every shepherd is an abomination to the Egyptians."

[1] Hebrew *Let your eye not pity* [2] A *shekel* was about 2/5 ounce or 11 grams [3] Hebrew *sons*

Section Overview

For most of the previous chapters the narrative has focused on a significant threat to the fulfillment of the Abrahamic promise: internal conflict within the family, which led to some of the brothers' being ejected or voluntarily leaving. This threat has now been satisfactorily resolved, and family harmony has been restored. Yet in the background another, longer lasting threat has reemerged: famine. It would not help the family to have its internal *shalom* restored if it then perished from hunger. In this passage that threat is removed as Joseph—at Pharaoh's suggestion (45:17)—invites his father and brothers to come down to Egypt to live close to him. In this way they will not have to make the perilous journey from Canaan to Egypt repeatedly over the next five years in order to resupply themselves with food. Instead they will be given some of the best land of Egypt, so that they and their flocks may be sustained (47:6).

Yet journeying to Egypt to avoid a famine is not self-evidently a good option in Genesis. Abraham follows that route in 12:10, with near catastrophic consequences. Moreover, a generation later the Lord specifically instructs Isaac not to go to Egypt under similar circumstances (26:1–4). So it is fitting that Jacob should first consult the Lord at Beersheba about the journey (46:1). In response the Lord tells him to go down to Egypt without fear; the Lord will go with them, and in due time he will bring them back home to the Land of Promise as a multiplied nation (vv. 3–4). At this point the patriarchal narrative is beginning to connect clearly with the stories of the first hearers of the book, in the wilderness on their way back to the "home" none of them had ever seen.

Section Outline

XI. The Family History of Jacob (37:1–50:26) . . .
    J. The Lord's Blessing in Egypt (45:16–46:34)

Comment

45:16–20 Earlier the sound of the brothers' weeping reached Pharaoh's household (v. 2); the explanation for this unexpected outpouring of emotion also reaches the highest levels, with Pharaoh not merely being apprised of the fact that Joseph's brothers have come but approving of their arrival (v. 16). As a result, the invitation for Jacob and for Joseph's brothers to relocate to Egypt comes not merely from Joseph but from Pharaoh himself, assuring them of a warm welcome. This is no grudging toleration of their presence but an invitation to come and experience the very best that Egypt has to offer, eating the "fat of the land" (v. 18)—no small privilege in a time of universal famine. Of course, Pharaoh's approval reflects the fact that without Joseph to interpret his dreams there would be no "fat of the land" left in Egypt. They would be struck as severely as everyone else. Joseph's presence in their midst has been a blessing to Egypt, just as the Abrahamic blessing anticipated (12:1–3).

Even the transportation needs for Jacob and his family are to be provided for in the shape of wagons to ease the journey for the wives and children, so that they might arrive not as refugees but as dignitaries. These wagons may not sound especially significant to modern readers, but they are impressive enough to merit being mentioned no fewer than four times in the narrative (45:19, 21, 27; 46:5). Jacob's family does not even need to bring more of its possessions than absolutely necessary, for it will receive better replacements upon arrival in Egypt (45:20). In this way the journey can be expedited and the family can arrive safely in Egypt sooner. This repeated invitation for the sons of Israel to experience royal largesse on such a grand scale upon their arrival in Egypt provides a sharp contrast to the difficulties of two years of intense famine for the brothers, but it would also strike a painfully ironic note for those of Moses' hearers who have experienced the worst of the Egyptian oppression prior to their departure from there.

45:21–24 Joseph provides abundantly for his brothers, just as Pharaoh has commanded, giving them provisions for the journey as well (v. 21). These would presumably be considerably less than the sacks of grain they had originally packed, since they need sustenance only for their travels. Joseph also gives each of the brothers a new set of clothing, indicating their now elevated status in Egyptian society (v. 22), as well as replacing the garments they tore as an indication of their sorrow over the discovery of Joseph's cup (44:13). Again the irony is profound, considering that they previously stripped Joseph of his ornate clothing before sending him to Egypt, representing his significantly lowered status as an ordinary slave (37:23; cf. his reclothing before his appearance in front of Pharaoh in 41:14).

Joseph once again singles out Benjamin for special attention, giving him five changes of clothes to match the fivefold portion of food given him at the feast (Gen. 45:22; cf. 43:34); Joseph also gives him three hundred shekels (roughly 7.5 pounds [3.4 kg]) of silver, an enormous amount of money considering that the price for Joseph as a slave was a mere twenty shekels (37:28). Now that the brothers have demonstrated their changed hearts, there is no danger in showing such favoritism to one brother over the others. These gifts are evidence not only of Joseph's goodwill toward his brothers but also of his abundant ability to supply all their needs.

For this reason Joseph sends an even more abundant gift to his father, Jacob: twenty donkeys laden with staples and delicacies, more than enough to provide for Jacob's needs on the journey to Egypt (45:23). This gift is undoubtedly intended in part to reinforce the remarkable story that the brothers will have to tell Jacob, which might seem incredible to him. The twenty donkeys are tangible proof of the unlikely tale. Earlier the brothers had worried that Joseph was scheming to take their donkeys (43:18), yet in the end they arrive home with far more beasts of burden than they owned previously. Joseph's thoughtfulness is evident also in his final command to his brothers as they are about to depart on their journey: "Do not quarrel on the way" (45:24). It would be easy for dissension and mutual recrimination to be sparked among them on the journey home as they seek to work out how to break the news to their father, and especially how to apportion the inevitable blame among themselves. Now that Joseph has forgiven them, however, the brothers need to forgive one another as well.

45:25–28 When he last saw his sons, Jacob had been despairingly concerned that he would be bereaved of Benjamin as well as Joseph (43:14); now his sons return instead with the news that Joseph is still alive and, not only that, has become ruler over all Egypt (45:26), thus more than fulfilling Joseph's dream of ruling over his family (37:8). Perhaps unsurprisingly, having readily believed the evidence of Joseph's bloody cloak, Jacob finds their words hard to swallow: "His heart became numb [or "grew cold"], for he did not believe them" (45:26). The narrator passes over in silence the exact form of words that the brothers use, leaving us wondering about the completeness of their confession of their own complicity in Joseph's fate. Sooner or later, however, the truth must come out. But, as the brothers recount Joseph's words—and, perhaps more decisively, when Jacob sees the Egyptian wagons with his own eyes—his spirit is revived (v. 27).

Just as Abraham had to give up Isaac in Genesis 22 only to receive him back, as it were, from the dead, so too has Jacob's son been restored to him against all expectations ("my son"; 45:28). It is significant that in this moment when Jacob makes the decision to go down to Egypt to see Joseph he is called not Jacob but Israel (v. 28). Jacob's new name acquired at Penuel in Genesis 32 does not characterize him constantly but is used at particular moments of decisive significance as head of the new covenant community. This is one of those moments. It is as the head of the nascent nation of Israel that he makes the journey down to Egypt (cf. 46:1).[640] His interest in going there is not primarily to seek respite from the famine or to enjoy the good things Egypt has to offer; it is sufficient that he may see Joseph again.

46:1–4 Before he turns his back on the Promised Land at Pharaoh's invitation, Jacob makes sure to submit his decision to the Lord's approval. Significantly, he is once again named Israel here, since this decision will have profound ramifications for the nation that will come from him (vv. 1–2; though when the Lord addresses him by name he calls him Jacob). He travels to Beersheba, presumably to the tamarisk tree where his grandfather Abraham had called upon the Lord (21:33), and there Jacob offers sacrifices (Hb. *zebakhim*) to the God of his father, Isaac (46:1)—the same God who had told Isaac not to go down to Egypt during a famine (26:1–4).

---

640 Hamilton, *Genesis 18–50*, 587.

There at Beersheba the Lord appears to him, calling him by name (46:2). The doubling of his name ("Jacob, Jacob") gives the Lord's address added intensity, as when Abraham was about to sacrifice Isaac (22:11) and when God calls Moses from the burning bush (Ex. 3:4), while the use of the plural form of the word for "vision" (*mar'ot*; Gen. 46:2) emphasizes its significance: "An important vision."[641] There God identifies himself as "the God of his father,"[642] underlining his covenant commitment to Abraham and his family, and he reiterates his promises: Jacob will become a great nation (cf. 12:2), and God will bring this nation back up from Egypt, so Jacob need not be afraid to go there (46:3). In fact, God will go to Egypt with him (v. 4). The Lord is not merely a localized god in Canaan but the sovereign God over all nations (as he will later prove by powerfully bringing Israel out of Egypt at the exodus; cf. also 31:13, where God is with Jacob throughout his time in Paddan-aram).

Yet the Lord's words to Jacob are personal as well as national. The "you" is singular in these verses: God will be with Jacob personally, not merely with the nation that will come from him, and he will bring him back to the land in person, not just in the form of his offspring. His death will be a good one, faithfully attended by Joseph, who will personally "close [his] eyes," the final duty of a faithful son (46:4). Jacob had feared that he would die while still in mourning over Joseph (37:35), but in fact the reverse will be the case. Nor will Jacob have to await the exodus in order to return to the Promised Land; he will make that journey ahead of the others in order to be buried in the family tomb (cf. 50:4–13).

46:5–7 Encouraged by his encounter with God, Jacob sets out from Beersheba to go down to Egypt, along with his sons and their wives and the little ones—the very people who had been in danger of starving to death just a short while earlier (46:5; cf. 43:8). The all-inclusiveness of the language is underlined by reference to Jacob's daughters and granddaughters, who are often unmentioned (46:7). They are conveyed in style by the wagons Pharaoh has provided, accompanied by the livestock and goods accumulated in the land of Canaan (v. 6). They are to make a clean break with the Land of Promise, leaving no one and nothing behind, though retaining the Lord's promise that one day they will return there, this time not as a large family but as a nation (v. 3). God's promise of a land of their own has not been abandoned; it is merely put on hold until the right time—when the sins of the Amorites is complete (15:16).

46:8–25 The genealogy that follows (46:8–25) may seem intrusive to modern readers, but it is an integral part of the narrative. It shifts the focus of the journey from Jacob to the multiple generations that travel to Egypt with him. The genealogy forces us to slow down and reflect on the progress already made toward the promise that God would make Abraham into a great nation (12:2). In chapter 28, when Jacob left home, besides his father there was still only one person in

---

641 Sarna, *Genesis*, 312.
642 On the formula "God of your father" cf. comment on 31:36–55.

the line of the promised family, Jacob himself. Now the family has expanded to become seventy persons. These include not only sons but grandsons, and these seventy will form the nucleus of the expansion that follows once they arrive in Egypt, so that by the time they leave they have become a significant people.[643] Seventy is itself a number of completeness, as with the table of seventy nations in chapter 10.[644]

The genealogy is arranged in order of birth mother rather than the birth order of the children: the first six names are the sons of Leah (46:8–15), followed by the two from her maid, Zilpah (vv. 16–18), then Rachel's two children (vv. 19–22),[645] and finally those of Rachel's maidservant, Bilhah (vv. 23–25). In most cases the genealogy goes only to the second generation from Jacob, but the line of Judah through Perez is given special prominence by inclusion of the third generation (v. 12). This is despite the fact that Perez is very young when Jacob's family travels to Egypt, so his sons could not yet be born; nonetheless, his is the family through whom the messianic line will ultimately descend (cf. Ruth 4:18).[646] Perez's sons, Hezron and Hamul, may also serve as a kind of replacement for the two sons of Judah already killed by the Lord before the journey to Egypt, Er and Onan.

46:26–27 The genealogy lists seventy offspring of Jacob through his four wives (33 + 16 + 14 + 7). However, it is said that sixty-six persons of his offspring go down to Egypt, making a total of seventy (v. 27). It is clear that two of the difference of four are Joseph's two sons, already in Egypt, but the identity of the other two is not so clear. It might be Joseph and Jacob, but of them only Joseph was included in the earlier count of seventy, leaving a discrepancy between the two accounts.[647] Alternatively, the other two omitted persons might be Er and Onan, who are already dead before the journey, but that leaves unexplained why Joseph is included both in the sixty-six and in the four additional persons (Jacob, Joseph, and his two sons) who make up the seventy. Kidner solves this question by adding Dinah into the sixty-six rather than Joseph,[648] but he does not explain why she is included now after being omitted from the earlier numbering scheme. Perhaps the number seventy may simply be a round number and is not to be pressed too hard. The original hearers of this account in the days of Moses would have marveled still more that this relatively small family had multiplied in Egypt into a nation

---

643 Cf. D. J. A. Clines, *The Theme of the Pentateuch*, JSOTSup 10, 2nd ed. (Sheffield: Sheffield Academic Press, 1997), 48–49. The opening words of Genesis 46:8 ("These are the names of the descendants of Israel, who came into Egypt") are repeated verbatim in Exodus 1:1 (Westermann, *Genesis 37–50*, 159).
644 The numbers listed in the genealogy are not a simple totaling of the names. The count of thirty-three for Jacob's offspring by Leah (Gen. 46:15) excludes his daughter, Dinah, even though she is listed among the "sons and daughters"; Asher's daughter, Serah, is similarly listed but not counted among the total of Zilpah's sixteen descendants (vv. 17–18). It also includes Perez's two children, as well as Er and Onan, even though none of them personally makes the journey to Egypt.
645 Only Rachel is explicitly named as Jacob's wife.
646 Sarna, *Genesis*, 314. The sons of Asher are also listed to the third generation, however, for no obvious reason.
647 The LXX further complicates matters by adding more sons to reach a total of seventy-five. Acts 7:14 mentions seventy-five, though it is possible that this number includes Jacob's daughters-in-law, who are not counted in Genesis (so Currid, *Genesis 25:19–50:26*, 340). For a fuller discussion cf. Hamilton, *Genesis 18–50*, 597–599.
648 Kidner, *Genesis*, 220.

of more than a million (Ex. 12:37) despite Pharaoh's oppression. God has been faithfully fulfilling his promises.

46:28–34 Judah's undisputed leadership among the brothers is demonstrated by the fact that Jacob sends him ahead to prepare the way for arrival in the land of Goshen, one of the most fertile regions of Egypt, in the Nile delta (Gen. 46:28). However, the most poignant reunion is between Joseph and his father, who is here once again named Israel in recognition of his role as patriarch of the promised family (vv. 29–30).[649] Joseph "fell on his [father's] neck and wept," just as he earlier fell on Benjamin's neck and wept (v. 29; cf. 45:14). The special nature of this gesture is underlined by the fact that in comparison Joseph merely "kissed all his brothers and wept upon them" (45:15). Father and son are completely overcome with emotion, and Jacob, who earlier expressed repeatedly the likelihood that his sorrow at losing Joseph would accompany him to an unquiet grave in Sheol (37:35; cf. 42:38; 44:29), now expresses his readiness to die in peace since Joseph is still alive (46:30).

As noted earlier, the only explanation for the magnitude of this transformation in Jacob's perspective lies in his (mistaken) belief that the future of the messianic promise lies in the person of Joseph or, failing him, Benjamin, the offspring of his beloved Rachel. To receive Joseph back from the grave, as it were, means a resurrection of his faith in God's promises.[650] The similarity to the words of the aged Simeon on seeing the infant Jesus should not be overlooked:

Lord, now you are letting your servant depart in peace,
    according to your word;
for my eyes have seen your salvation
    that you have prepared in the presence of all peoples,
a light for revelation to the Gentiles,
    and for glory to your people Israel. (Luke 2:29–32)

Joseph has hoped and planned for this day for some time and has also thought through the future of Israel in Egypt. Rather than assimilation into the Egyptian community, which might seem advantageous given Joseph's exalted status, he wants to ensure that the Israelites remain a separate and distinct community. In pursuit of that goal he seeks to take advantage of the Israelites' occupation as pastoralists, since he knows that this occupation is an abomination to the Egyptians (Gen. 46:34). The low status of animal herders was common in many ancient societies, especially in comparison to urban elites.[651] Shepherding is hard work, out in the open air, and leaves little time or energy for cultural pursuits.

It might seem counterintuitive for the brothers to introduce themselves to their new neighbors by the one thing they know the Egyptians will find most offensive about them, but this is precisely what Joseph coaches them to do in order to preserve their distinctiveness. This itself is a step of faith that God will one day

---

649 Mathews, *Genesis 11:27–50:26*, 842.
650 Cf. comment on 37:29–36.
651 Cf. Currid, *Genesis 25:19–50:26*, 345, who cites Herodotus, among others.

bring his people back out of Egypt to the land of Canaan, just as he has promised (cf. 15:16). Nothing must be allowed to get in the way of that goal, no matter how much easier it would make life for Israel in the meantime if the people would assimilate. Indeed, it is noticeable that in the Exodus account of the departure from Egypt the livestock will play an important role (cf. Ex. 10:26). The location in Goshen, in northeast Egypt, keeps Israel close to the Egyptian border, whence it will be easier to leave when the time comes to return home.

Response

If the previous chapters might have tempted us to think of the Joseph narrative as essentially a story of timeless truths about God's providence and the power of forgiveness, this passage firmly grounds Joseph's experience within the unfolding narrative of the Pentateuch. Despite the human weakness and wickedness on full display in the midst of the chosen family, their numbers are growing and the Lord has brought them safely to Egypt, where they will grow further and remain a distinct people as they await the time when the sin of the Amorites will be full and the Lord will bring them back to the land of Canaan (Gen. 15:16). Despite Jacob's preference for Joseph and Benjamin, the offspring of his beloved Rachel, the Lord has chosen Judah, the third child of unloved Leah, as the leader of the family through whose offspring the promise will descend. Providence is not merely at work to protect the lives of God's chosen people from individual dangers but is shaping the course of economics and politics at the global level, as God sends a widespread drought and famine and positions Joseph to rise to power in Egypt. As with all nations, Egypt will find blessing only in bowing down to Abraham's offspring (cf. 12:2–3). These are aspects of the Joseph narrative often overlooked by Christian readers.

The passage also addresses contemporary readers in the post-Christian West who are finding their place at the central table of society barred to them. Joseph could have brought his brothers and father into the center of Egyptian society, where their opportunities for personal comfort, advancement, and profit would have been far greater. Instead, he sends them to a backwater location in Egypt, where they will continue their poorly regarded but honest work as shepherds. As a result they maintain a reputation distinct from that of the wider culture around them. This paradigm of being strangers and aliens in a land not their own shapes much of Israel's history, to the point that even in the land of Canaan they are to camp out every year at the time of the autumn Feast of Booths to remind themselves that the Promised Land itself is not their true home. Like their father, Abraham, they are not *of* this world, even while living *in* it (cf. Deut. 26:5).[652] The same perspective ought to be ours as Christians as well (Heb. 11:13–16).

Even the genealogy in this passage has much to teach us. The similarity in number between the seventy family members who go down to Egypt and the

---

[652] Brueggemann, *Genesis*, 355.

seventy nations in Genesis 10 reminds us that the nascent Israel is a microcosm of the larger people of God of all times and places who will gather in heaven before the throne of the Lamb (cf. Revelation 4–5).[653] The genealogy includes some whose names are well known even among those who have never read the Bible, as well as others whose identities are virtually unknown even to those who read the Bible annually. In the same way, relatively unknown saints are every bit as much members of God's church as those saints are who happen to be household names. The list of God's people includes notorious sinners such as Judah (Genesis 38), Reuben (35:22), and Simeon and Levi (cf. Genesis 34), as well as faithful servants such as Joseph, which reminds us that all may find a welcome in this "company of nations" (35:11), no matter one's background. The patriarchs of old were saved by grace alone through faith in Christ alone every bit as much as we are.

Finally, Jacob's joy over the "resurrection," as it were, of Joseph invites us to think of the Father's joy at the resurrection of Jesus on the third day. Sometimes Christians are so focused on Christ crucified that we forget that the same Christ was also raised from the dead and exalted to his Father's right hand! There, all three members of the Trinity share in "the joy . . . set before him" (Heb. 12:2), which is not merely the resurrection of Christ himself but the resurrection of countless Christians united to him forever in glory. How great is the joy of our reconciliation to our heavenly Father!

GENESIS 47

47 So Joseph went in and told Pharaoh, "My father and my brothers, with their flocks and herds and all that they possess, have come from the land of Canaan. They are now in the land of Goshen." ² And from among his brothers he took five men and presented them to Pharaoh. ³ Pharaoh said to his brothers, "What is your occupation?" And they said to Pharaoh, "Your servants are shepherds, as our fathers were." ⁴ They said to Pharaoh, "We have come to sojourn in the land, for there is no pasture for your servants' flocks, for the famine is severe in the land of Canaan. And now, please let your servants dwell in the land of Goshen." ⁵ Then Pharaoh said to Joseph, "Your father and your brothers have come to you. ⁶ The land of Egypt is before you. Settle your father and your brothers in the best of the land. Let them settle in the land of Goshen, and if you know any able men among them, put them in charge of my livestock."

⁷ Then Joseph brought in Jacob his father and stood him before Pharaoh, and Jacob blessed Pharaoh. ⁸ And Pharaoh said to Jacob, "How many are the days of the years of your life?" ⁹ And Jacob said to Pharaoh, "The days

---

[653] John Sailhamer comments, "The writer has gone to great lengths to portray the new nation of Israel as a new humanity and Abraham as a second Adam. The blessing that is to come through Abraham and his offspring is a restoration of the original blessing of Adam, a blessing that was lost in the fall" (*Genesis*, 261).

of the years of my sojourning are 130 years. Few and evil have been the days of the years of my life, and they have not attained to the days of the years of the life of my fathers in the days of their sojourning." ¹⁰ And Jacob blessed Pharaoh and went out from the presence of Pharaoh. ¹¹ Then Joseph settled his father and his brothers and gave them a possession in the land of Egypt, in the best of the land, in the land of Rameses, as Pharaoh had commanded. ¹² And Joseph provided his father, his brothers, and all his father's household with food, according to the number of their dependents.

¹³ Now there was no food in all the land, for the famine was very severe, so that the land of Egypt and the land of Canaan languished by reason of the famine. ¹⁴ And Joseph gathered up all the money that was found in the land of Egypt and in the land of Canaan, in exchange for the grain that they bought. And Joseph brought the money into Pharaoh's house. ¹⁵ And when the money was all spent in the land of Egypt and in the land of Canaan, all the Egyptians came to Joseph and said, "Give us food. Why should we die before your eyes? For our money is gone." ¹⁶ And Joseph answered, "Give your livestock, and I will give you food in exchange for your livestock, if your money is gone." ¹⁷ So they brought their livestock to Joseph, and Joseph gave them food in exchange for the horses, the flocks, the herds, and the donkeys. He supplied them with food in exchange for all their livestock that year. ¹⁸ And when that year was ended, they came to him the following year and said to him, "We will not hide from my lord that our money is all spent. The herds of livestock are my lord's. There is nothing left in the sight of my lord but our bodies and our land. ¹⁹ Why should we die before your eyes, both we and our land? Buy us and our land for food, and we with our land will be servants to Pharaoh. And give us seed that we may live and not die, and that the land may not be desolate."

²⁰ So Joseph bought all the land of Egypt for Pharaoh, for all the Egyptians sold their fields, because the famine was severe on them. The land became Pharaoh's. ²¹ As for the people, he made servants of them[1] from one end of Egypt to the other. ²² Only the land of the priests he did not buy, for the priests had a fixed allowance from Pharaoh and lived on the allowance that Pharaoh gave them; therefore they did not sell their land.

²³ Then Joseph said to the people, "Behold, I have this day bought you and your land for Pharaoh. Now here is seed for you, and you shall sow the land. ²⁴ And at the harvests you shall give a fifth to Pharaoh, and four fifths shall be your own, as seed for the field and as food for yourselves and your households, and as food for your little ones." ²⁵ And they said, "You have saved our lives; may it please my lord, we will be servants to Pharaoh." ²⁶ So Joseph made it a statute concerning the land of Egypt, and it stands to this day, that Pharaoh should have the fifth; the land of the priests alone did not become Pharaoh's.

²⁷ Thus Israel settled in the land of Egypt, in the land of Goshen. And they gained possessions in it, and were fruitful and multiplied greatly. ²⁸ And Jacob lived in the land of Egypt seventeen years. So the days of Jacob, the years of his life, were 147 years.

²⁹ And when the time drew near that Israel must die, he called his son Joseph and said to him, "If now I have found favor in your sight, put your hand under my thigh and promise to deal kindly and truly with me. Do not bury me in Egypt, ³⁰ but let me lie with my fathers. Carry me out of

Egypt and bury me in their burying place." He answered, "I will do as you have said." **31** And he said, "Swear to me"; and he swore to him. Then Israel bowed himself upon the head of his bed.[2]

[1] Samaritan, Septuagint, Vulgate; Hebrew *he removed them to the cities* [2] Hebrew; Septuagint *staff*

Section Overview

At the end of Genesis 46 Jacob traveled to Egypt and was reunited with his beloved Joseph (46:29–30). The brothers were reconciled to each other, and the threat of famine was removed, as Joseph proposed settling them in the land of Goshen (46:28). Much of the narrative tension that has been driving the story from chapter 37 onward has been successfully defused. In one sense the remainder of Genesis is an extended conclusion to the story and could easily be seen as anticlimactic. Yet the conclusion of the book of Genesis is important because the Genesis narrative is not a freestanding story but is part of a larger Pentateuchal (and indeed biblical) narrative, to which these chapters have great relevance. As a protected and respected minority, Israel's initial experience of life in Egypt is quite different than its final years there. What is more, Pharaoh himself is blessed by Jacob (47:10), and, as the book of Hebrews reminds us, the lesser is always blessed by the greater (Heb. 7:7). Jacob's blessings upon his children and grandchildren (Genesis 48–49) and Jacob's and Joseph's burials (Genesis 50) also have important messages to communicate, both to the first readers of the book and to us as well.

Section Outline

XI. The Family History of Jacob (37:1–50:26) . . .
    K. Israel in Egypt (47:1–31)

Comment

47:1–6 Thus far Joseph has been in charge of the arrangements for his brothers' arrival and lodgings in Egypt. Pharaoh has promised to give them the best of the land of Egypt (45:18) and has left the specifics for Joseph to organize, but now the arrangements have to be ratified by Pharaoh himself. This requires a representative sample ("five men") of the brothers and their father to appear before Pharaoh; all twelve might have felt like too imposing of a presence (47:2). It is not clear whether these are the most impressive brothers or merely a random assortment.[654] The brothers have been coached carefully by Joseph to reply to Pharaoh's question about their occupation by saying they are shepherds, as in fact they are (v. 3; cf. 46:34).[655] This answer has a twofold function, first to assure Pharaoh that they are not politically ambitious and second to affirm that they are no threat to Egyptian society.

---

[654] In favor of selectivity cf. von Rad, *Genesis*, 350; in favor of randomness cf. Sarna, *Genesis*, 319.
[655] Some commentators have sought to distinguish between "shepherds" (Hb. *ro'eh tson*; Gen. 47:3) and "keepers of livestock" (*'anshe-miqneh*; 46:34), but the two terms seem virtually interchangeable in Genesis 46:32. The former may describe the care of sheep and goats while the latter deals with cattle, but it seems unlikely that Pharaoh would see much of a distinction between the two terms, and Jacob's family takes care of both species.

All they want is to be allowed to raise their animals peacefully—preferably in the land of Goshen, as Joseph has planned (cf. comment on 46:28–34). Their presence in Egypt is not intended to be a permanent relocation; rather, they have come to "sojourn" (Hb. *ger*, a verb indicating a temporary stay) in the land for the duration of the famine (47:4; cf. 15:13).[656]

Pharaoh agreeably gives them exactly what they seek: royal permission to occupy the best of the land, including, if they so choose, Goshen. What is more, he offers them royal patronage, inviting Joseph to put the most skillful of the brothers to work in caring for the royal flocks and herds (47:6). Although this offer would no doubt be an attractive one for anyone set on advancement in Egyptian society, we hear no more about this opportunity subsequently, since Joseph's purpose for his brothers is exactly the opposite: to keep them distinct and separate from Egyptian society in the somewhat isolated region of Goshen. In this way they will be near the road leading back to the land of Canaan, ready to return home when the call finally comes.

47:7–12 Having first presented his brothers to Pharaoh, Joseph now brings in his aged father, Jacob, to meet one of the most powerful men of the ancient world. Far from being intimidated by the occasion, Jacob blesses Pharaoh (v. 7). The scene may have looked incongruous to Pharaoh's servants: an elderly nomadic figure solemnly pronounces his benediction on the semidivine ruler of all Egypt, as though he has something to impart to Pharaoh, as opposed to being the impoverished recipient of Pharaoh's generosity in recognition of his son's achievements. Yet Jacob is deliberately invoking Genesis 12:2–3, the Abrahamic blessing that promises good for all who bless Abraham's offspring.[657] Since Pharaoh has dealt kindly with Jacob and his family, he deserves to receive a blessing in the name of Israel's God, the God of all creation. As Abraham's heir, Jacob is authorized to deliver such a blessing, which he does both upon entering and upon leaving Pharaoh's presence (47:7, 10).

If Jacob's blessing of Pharaoh is an act of faith in Israel's God, the substance of his conversation with Pharaoh is less doxological. Pharaoh asks a politely conversational question, "How many are the days of the years of your life?" (v. 8), just as he earlier asked Joseph's brothers about their occupation (v. 3). This question provides Jacob with the opportunity not merely to give a number in reply but to reflect on the nature of those "days of the years of [his] life" (v. 8), which he does. Yet, instead of giving clear testimony to the Lord's faithfulness to him over his long and challenging life (as he does when meeting Esau in 33:5–11), his response to Pharaoh is largely bitter and negative: "The days of the years of my sojourning are 130 years. Few and evil have been the days of the years of my life, and they have not attained to the days of the years of the life of my fathers in the days of their sojourning" (47:9).

---

656 Hamilton, *Genesis 18–50*, 607.
657 Sailhamer, *Genesis*, 264.

In reality, Jacob is not yet about to die. To be sure, his impending death has been on Jacob's mind for some time. When he saw Joseph's bloodstained robe many years earlier, he was sure he was about to go down to Sheol in sorrow (37:35). When the brothers wanted to take Benjamin down to Egypt on the second trip, Jacob's concern was that, should anything happen to his son on the journey, it would kill him (42:38). When Jacob heard that Joseph was still alive, he declared that he would go to see him before he died (45:28). Even when he finally saw Joseph, Jacob said, "Now let me die, since I have seen your face and know that you are still alive" (46:30). Yet Jacob has another seventeen years to live in Joseph's company (47:28), the same length of time he spent with Joseph during the first years of his life. It is too soon for him to summarize the length of his days. He will reach 147 years, an age that, while short of Abraham's 175 years (25:7) and Isaac's 180 (35:28), is longer than nearly anyone will live after him. In comparison Joseph lives to be 110 years old (50:22) and Moses to 120 (Deut. 34:7). In Egypt 110 years was considered the ideal life span.[658]

It is interesting to speculate whether Jacob's response to Pharaoh would have been different had he been asked it at the end of those seventeen peaceful years in Egypt; his blessings in Genesis 48–49 have a more positive tone to them. Yet Pharaoh's question invites a positive reflection on the way in which the Lord has transformed his mourning over the son he thought he had lost into great joy, while providing abundantly for all his needs in the famine. God has been with Jacob from the day he left his father's house with nothing other than the staff in his hand until the point upon which he has become a family of more than seventy persons, with abundant livestock and material goods (cf. Gen. 32:10). Now that Jacob has arrived in Egypt, Joseph has given his father and brothers an inheritable "possession" (Hb. *'akhuzzah*; 47:11) in the best of the land, the land of Goshen,[659] and supplied them with sufficient food to see them through the remaining five years of famine (v. 12).

One aspect of Jacob's response to Pharaoh is a clear word of testimony. He makes it clear to Pharaoh that this world is not his home. There is a crucial difference between Pharaoh's question to Jacob and Jacob's answer. Pharaoh asks, "How many are the days of the years of *your life*?" But Jacob responds, "The days of the years of *my sojourning* are 130 years" (vv. 8–9). Jacob knows that his time here on earth is merely a sojourn, a temporary stay and not a permanent residence.[660] His grandfather Abraham had left Ur to sojourn in the land of Canaan, and now Jacob is sojourning in the land of Egypt. Even though Egypt probably provides the best living situation that Jacob has ever experienced, it will never be home. The Lord

---
658 Wenham, *Genesis 16–50*, 490.
659 The land of Goshen is here (probably anachronistically) called the "land of Rameses" in order to make a connection between this story of the arrival in Egypt and the exodus narrative (cf. Ex. 1:11; 12:37). Most believe that it does not acquire that name until the thirteenth century BC, when Ramesses II rebuilds the city of Tanis and makes it his capital. Similar scribal updating of place names occurs also at Genesis 14:14 and its mention of the city of Dan, which does not exist by that name until the time of the Judges. However, some scholars argue that the region already bore the name Rameses from a much earlier date.
660 Von Rad, *Genesis*, 407–408.

who promised to go down to Egypt with him had also promised to bring him back up to Canaan (46:4); that land is his true and everlasting "possession" (*'akhuzzah*; 17:8; cf. 47:11; 48:4). The departure of Jacob and his family from the Promised Land is only temporary, a faith commitment evidenced in Jacob's making Joseph swear that after his death he will not bury him in Egypt but will take his body back to the family burial plot at Machpelah (47:29–31).

47:13–26 There is a sharp contrast between the fortunes of Joseph's family, which is protected and provided for at every turn, and the rest of the Egyptian people (as well as those remaining in the land of Canaan), whose fortunes gradually get worse and worse. The pairing of "the land of Egypt" with "the land of Canaan," which occurs three times in verses 13–15, is very unusual and evokes the standard calls by critical scholars to emend the text. But there were strong ties between Egypt and the Canaanite city-states during at least some of this general period, as witnessed by the Amarna letters, which may account for the connection historically. From a literary perspective the point is much simpler: the populations of *both* Egypt and Canaan are suffering at this point, despite their rainfall's being dependent on different factors.

It must have seemed strange to Moses' audience to recall a time in which *they* were the favored class in Egypt while the Egyptians were suffering and oppressed. Jacob and Joseph's brothers seem to have plenty of food to eat without having to come to Joseph repeatedly and beg for provisions; they are even given their own portion of Goshen as their "possession" (Hb. *'akhuzzah*; v. 11). Meanwhile the native-born Egyptians become progressively poorer. First they lose their financial resources, as Joseph gathers into the royal coffers all the money in Egypt in exchange for grain (v. 14). Next, after the money is gone, Joseph takes ownership of all their livestock in exchange for food (vv. 16–17). As the most valuable animals, horses head the list of livestock.[661] Finally, Joseph purchases all the land of Egypt for Pharoah and reduces its inhabitants to slavery in return for food (vv. 16–21). Apart from Israel, only the priests are excepted from the general ruination of the land, since they receive an allowance of food directly from Pharaoh (v. 22); everyone else becomes Pharaoh's slaves. The irony is rich when the Egyptians, to whom Joseph was once sold as a slave, come to him and ask him to buy them and their land (v. 19).

As a result of this purchase of land and people by Pharaoh, the Egyptians are now indebted as sharecroppers to their overlord; 20 percent of the produce of their fields is to be remitted to Pharaoh, while the remaining 80 percent is theirs.[662] Yet the Egyptian people are grateful to their master, saying, "You have saved our lives; may it please my lord, we will be servants to Pharaoh" (v. 25). The implications ought not to have been lost on Moses' hearers: they and their children had also

---

[661] In an Israelite setting horses were used predominantly in military contexts. As Egypt was a major producer of horses, their ownership seems to have been more widespread there (cf. Deut. 17:16).

[662] This is a relatively modest demand by ancient Near Eastern standards, where the average amount claimed by the crown was around a third (cf. Waltke, *Genesis*, 591). *First Maccabees* 10:30 notes a tax of one third of grain and one half of fruit.

been delivered from death in Egypt and promised a possession (*'akhuzzah*) in the land of Canaan, where the Lord required a mere tithe (10 percent) of their agricultural produce, whether vegetable or animal, as a mark of his overlordship.[663] How much more should they come to their Overlord with gratitude and say, "You have saved our lives; may it please my lord, we will be servants to the Lord" (cf. Josh. 24:14–24)? Out of that tithe the Lord will provide for his priests and Levites, just as Pharaoh provides for the Egyptian priests (cf. Num. 18:21). These laws continue to be valid down to the time of the writer (Gen. 47:26), an assertion that presupposes familiarity with the extant Egyptian tax code—a familiarity that makes perfect sense for someone like Moses but seems less likely of a hypothetical Israelite author writing at a much later time.

There is extensive discussion in the commentaries as to whether these actions on the part of Joseph ought to be viewed as repressive against the Egyptian people, as a demonstration of Joseph's wisdom and a model of good governance, or merely as an explanation of ancient taxation practices.[664] These discussions tend to miss the point that the original readers would have discerned from the account. Joseph is undoubtedly a wise ruler over Egypt, whose measures save the lives of the Egyptians at a time when they would otherwise perish. The Egyptian people are depicted as grateful rather than grumbling in response to Joseph's provision of a means for them to purchase food under such circumstances, even at the cost of their personal freedom.[665] Yet the lesson for the Israelites is found in the contrasting fate of nascent Israel, provided with abundant food in Rameses by Joseph at no cost and gaining ownership of land at a time when everyone else in Egypt is losing theirs.[666] How much more grateful should they be to the God who thus provides for all their needs—and who later, when they have lost their own freedom and are themselves slaves in Egypt, delivers them from there and promises them a land of their own in return for the light yoke of tithing their agricultural produce?

47:27–31 The final verses of Genesis 47 also deal with life and death and with Egypt and Canaan. In contrast to the desperate struggles of the Egyptians throughout the famine the Israelites prosper, gaining property (the Hb. verb *'akhaz* in the Niphal is related to the noun *'akhuzzah* in v. 11) in the land of Goshen and demonstrating that the Lord's blessing is upon them by being fruitful and multiplying greatly, just as God promised Jacob (v. 27; cf. 1:28; 9:1; 17:6; 28:3; 35:11). Of course, that very fruitfulness will later become an issue, as a later pharaoh will feel threatened by the fertility and number of the Israelites (cf. Exodus 1).

Up to this point in Genesis the name Israel has referred primarily to Jacob. Even as recently as 46:1–2 Israel was construed with singular pronouns; when Israel went

---

663 On tithing in the Bible and in contemporary application cf. Duguid, *Should Christians Tithe? Excelling in the Grace of Giving* (Glenside, PA: St. Colme's Press, 2018).
664 See the extensive discussion in Wilson, *Joseph Wise and Otherwise*, 191–194.
665 Debt slavery in the ancient world was a voluntary provision that established a means for those who had fallen on hard times to preserve their lives by submitting themselves to the service of others. It was often temporary and generally better than the alternative of slow starvation, and it was quite distinct from chattel slavery.
666 Mathews uses the language of a "foil" (*Genesis 11:27–50:26*, 853).

down to Egypt, it was *his* journey with all that *he* had. Now, as the death of Jacob approaches, Israel has become a collective noun: "Israel settled in the land of Egypt, ... and *they* gained possession in it" (Gen. 47:27). As for Jacob, he lives for another seventeen years in Egypt, enjoying the same length of time in Joseph's company as he did at the beginning of Joseph's life (v. 28; cf. 37:2). The number of the years of his life, which he earlier characterized to Pharaoh as "few and evil" (47:9), stretches to 147 years, with a peaceful ending surrounded by his reconciled children.

Before Jacob dies he needs to pronounce a final set of benedictions on his children and grandchildren, blessings that will shape their destinies, for better or worse, into the distant future. Because of the significance of his words, he is now once again titled Israel (v. 29). Jacob's final request of Joseph is so important that he makes Joseph swear an oath by putting his hand on Jacob's thigh (v. 29; cf. 24:2–3, where Abraham charges his servant with a similarly weighty responsibility). This is a matter of steadfast love and faithfulness (47:29; *khesed va'emet*, "deal kindly and truly"), language used of a firm covenant commitment to another person and used even to describe the nature of the Lord himself (24:49; Ex. 34:6).

What Jacob asks of Joseph is no small matter: he wants Joseph to pledge to take his body back to the land of Canaan after his death, to be buried with his fathers in the family grave at Machpelah (Gen. 47:29–30). Where a person was buried was a matter of great significance in the ancient world, which is why, when Ruth pledges her loyalty to Naomi, the highest level of commitment for Ruth is not merely to take Naomi's God as her own but also to be buried alongside Naomi (Ruth 1:16–17). To make such a decision is to be bonded to a person and his or her God not merely in life but for all eternity. So too Jacob's desire to be buried in the family grave is not mere nostalgia or sentimentalism; it is a fundamental declaration of faith in the promises of God, an assertion that in death, as in life, the land of Canaan is his promised home—and ultimately that the Lord will take him to be with himself forever.[667] As Kidner points out, Jacob expects to sleep with his fathers prior to Joseph's carrying his corpse to join them physically in his last resting place in earth.[668]

The final sentence of the chapter is not entirely clear. Jacob bows himself either on the top of his bed (*hammittah*), as the text is vocalized in the MT, or on the top of his staff (*hammatteh*), as read by the LXX, which is in turn followed by Hebrews 11:21. Jacob's bed makes another appearance in Genesis 48:2, while Jacob's staff would connect this scene back to his earliest days, when his staff was his sole possession (though the Hebrew word used in 32:10 is different, *maqqel*). In favor of the latter reading, "head" (*ro'sh*) is more commonly used of vertical extremities (of stones, mountains, buildings, etc.). There are also different understandings of Jacob's bowing: Is he prostrating himself before Joseph or before the Lord, or is he

---

667 Modern scholars are usually skittish about the idea that ancient believers had faith in an afterlife, but, while it is not often explicitly described in the detail we find in the NT, the belief in a personal future beyond death is the presupposition without which many actions of OT saints make any sense at all. If God's promises to Abraham, Isaac, and Jacob have any meaning at all, they require something more than the blessings that the patriarchs obtain in this world.
668 Kidner, *Genesis*, 223.

simply fatigued? Since the staff is a sign of a person's authority, bowing at its head most likely means that Jacob is submitting himself to the Lord in thanksgiving, in response to Joseph's willingness to carry his corpse back to Canaan.[669]

Response

Christians should always be ready to give an answer to those who ask us about the hope that is within us (1 Pet. 3:15). Jacob has a prime opportunity to share his faith with Pharaoh, yet he responds to Pharaoh's question about his life by saying, in effect, that it has been solitary, poor, nasty, brutish, and short. Jacob has certainly suffered much, though many of his wounds have been at least partially self-inflicted. But, like so many of us, he is unprepared when the opportunity arises to recount God's faithfulness and abundant mercy to him. Nevertheless, he does bless Pharaoh (Gen. 47:7, 10), an audacious act in a world in which the greater blesses the lesser and not vice versa. He knows that as the heir of Abraham he has a blessing that is not merely for his own descendants but for the wider world as well, because he serves the God of all creation and the Lord of all history.

God demonstrates his power over creation and history in the widespread famine for which he has sent Joseph to Egypt to enable them to prepare ahead of time. Like the ark of Noah's day, Egypt becomes a refuge for God's people from the surrounding devastation, a place where they can be fruitful and multiply, even while the Egyptians are reduced to impoverished servitude. Later Israelites will also testify to how the Lord distinguishes between them and the Egyptians when bringing multiple plagues on the land (cf. Exodus 7–12).

The Lord's purpose is to bring his people back in due time to the land of Canaan, which he has promised to give them. Jacob's faith in that promise is evidenced by the vow he makes Joseph swear to carry his bones back to his ancestral burial place. Yet even Canaan is not Jacob's true home. The Promised Land is itself emblematic of the true city with foundations for which the patriarchs longed. Here on earth, they would always be sojourners, as all Christians are as well. But God has prepared a place for them ahead of time, to be entered by faith, not works. That heavenly *'akhuzzah*, or possession, will not be given to them as the gift of Pharaoh, or even Joseph, but is found in the true Son of Israel, Jesus Christ. He endures a life that is much more solitary, poor, nasty, brutish, and short than Jacob's. He is a man of sorrows, acquainted with sickness and many griefs (Isa. 53:4), culminating in a shameful death on the cross (Phil. 2:5–11). But that death and subsequent resurrection enable Christ to be the first of many brothers (Rom. 8:29), pioneering the way to our true heavenly home (Heb. 12:1–2), which we now receive from him as our inheritance (1 Pet. 1:3–5). Just as God is faithful to his promise to be with Jacob and his sons in Egypt, bringing them at last to the Promised Land, so also is he faithful to be with us wherever our earthly sojourning leads us until it is time to take us to our eternal home.

---

[669] Cf. Currid, *Genesis 25:19–50:26*, 362.

GENESIS 48

48 After this, Joseph was told, "Behold, your father is ill." So he took with him his two sons, Manasseh and Ephraim. ²And it was told to Jacob, "Your son Joseph has come to you." Then Israel summoned his strength and sat up in bed. ³And Jacob said to Joseph, "God Almighty[1] appeared to me at Luz in the land of Canaan and blessed me, ⁴and said to me, 'Behold, I will make you fruitful and multiply you, and I will make of you a company of peoples and will give this land to your offspring after you for an everlasting possession.' ⁵And now your two sons, who were born to you in the land of Egypt before I came to you in Egypt, are mine; Ephraim and Manasseh shall be mine, as Reuben and Simeon are. ⁶And the children that you fathered after them shall be yours. They shall be called by the name of their brothers in their inheritance. ⁷As for me, when I came from Paddan, to my sorrow Rachel died in the land of Canaan on the way, when there was still some distance[2] to go to Ephrath, and I buried her there on the way to Ephrath (that is, Bethlehem)."

⁸When Israel saw Joseph's sons, he said, "Who are these?" ⁹Joseph said to his father, "They are my sons, whom God has given me here." And he said, "Bring them to me, please, that I may bless them." ¹⁰Now the eyes of Israel were dim with age, so that he could not see. So Joseph brought them near him, and he kissed them and embraced them. ¹¹And Israel said to Joseph, "I never expected to see your face; and behold, God has let me see your offspring also." ¹²Then Joseph removed them from his knees, and he bowed himself with his face to the earth. ¹³And Joseph took them both, Ephraim in his right hand toward Israel's left hand, and Manasseh in his left hand toward Israel's right hand, and brought them near him. ¹⁴And Israel stretched out his right hand and laid it on the head of Ephraim, who was the younger, and his left hand on the head of Manasseh, crossing his hands (for Manasseh was the firstborn). ¹⁵And he blessed Joseph and said,

> "The God before whom my fathers Abraham and Isaac walked,
>   the God who has been my shepherd all my life long to this day,
> ¹⁶ the angel who has redeemed me from all evil, bless the boys;
>   and in them let my name be carried on, and the name of my fathers Abraham and Isaac;
>   and let them grow into a multitude[3] in the midst of the earth."

¹⁷When Joseph saw that his father laid his right hand on the head of Ephraim, it displeased him, and he took his father's hand to move it from Ephraim's head to Manasseh's head. ¹⁸And Joseph said to his father, "Not this way, my father; since this one is the firstborn, put your right hand on his head." ¹⁹But his father refused and said, "I know, my son, I know. He also shall become a people, and he also shall be great. Nevertheless, his

younger brother shall be greater than he, and his offspring shall become a multitude[4] of nations." ²⁰ So he blessed them that day, saying,

> "By you Israel will pronounce blessings, saying,
> 'God make you as Ephraim and as Manasseh.'"

Thus he put Ephraim before Manasseh. ²¹ Then Israel said to Joseph, "Behold, I am about to die, but God will be with you and will bring you again to the land of your fathers. ²² Moreover, I have given to you rather than to your brothers one mountain slope[5] that I took from the hand of the Amorites with my sword and with my bow."

[1] Hebrew *El Shaddai* [2] Or *about two hours' distance* [3] Or *let them be like fish for multitude* [4] Hebrew *fullness* [5] Or *one portion of the land*; Hebrew *shekem*, which sounds like the town and district called *Shechem*

Section Overview

The final words of famous persons are often recorded, on the grounds that, when everything else loses its importance as death approaches, we are more likely to say profound things. This is not always the case; many famous people have uttered the most banal trivialities on their deathbeds, but Jacob's final pronouncements in Genesis 48–49 are full of significance and faith.[670] Through divine insight Jacob understands the nature of his various offspring and speaks profoundly about their future—and particularly that of their progeny—in the plan and purpose of God. Unsurprisingly, given Jacob's own history, those blessings center around Joseph and his two sons, who are singled out for the double blessing that would normally be reserved for the firstborn son. This prominence flows from Jacob's expectation that the Abrahamic promise will surely flow through the children borne him by his beloved Rachel, whose place in his heart is memorialized in Genesis 48:7.

Yet the subsequent history of Israel eventually makes clear that the line of promise will descend through the tribe of Judah, who is also singled out for special mention in chapter 49. The Lord's purposes are clearly laid out for those with eyes to see, even if Jacob himself cannot discern the Lord's purposes. All twelve of his offspring will have an important part to play in the future of Israel, the Lord's chosen people, but some tribes will be more significant than others.

Section Outline

XI. The Family History of Jacob (37:1–50:26) . . .
    L. Jacob Blesses Ephraim and Manasseh (48:1–22)

Comment

48:1–7 The end of chapter 47 may have seemed like a deathbed scene (cf. 47:29), but there is still an "after this" (48:1) before Jacob's final illness. Yet clearly the news that his father is ill concerns Joseph profoundly, and the decision to take his two

---

[670] The writer to the Hebrews identifies this moment in Jacob's life as one of the great moments of faith in the OT (Heb. 11:21); Cf. Kidner, *Genesis*, 224.

sons with him to visit his ailing father anticipates the prospect of a final blessing (v. 1). Unlike Jacob's own attempt to steal a blessing from his aging father in Genesis 27, there is no deception in this visit; though Jacob's eyesight is failing, as Isaac's had been (48:10), his mind is clear, and he gathers his strength and sits up in bed to pronounce the blessing (v. 2).

First, Jacob takes the time to remind Joseph of the source and nature of the blessing. He is not merely passing on his own hopes and dreams, a sentimental wish for good for his descendants. Rather, he is passing on the blessing he himself received from God Almighty (*'El Shaddai*)[671] at Bethel (here described by its Canaanite name, Luz; v. 3; cf. 28:13–15). This point is underlined in the text by the shift in his own name from Jacob in the first half of verse 2 to Israel in the second.[672] In fact the blessing Jacob pronounces is larger than that found in Genesis 28; it also includes the expanded blessing that Jacob received on his return to Bethel, now bearing his new name, Israel (cf. 35:10–12). There God promised Jacob fruitfulness and that his offspring would become a "company" (Hb. *qahal*, "assembly")[673] of peoples who would receive the land of Canaan as a permanent possession (*'akhuzzah*; 48:4; cf. 17:8), in contrast to the temporary *'akhuzzah* that Joseph has given them in the land of Egypt (cf. 47:11). In light of the Lord's promise of fruitfulness it cannot escape Jacob's attention that one of his grandchildren standing before him bears the name "Fruitful" (Ephraim; cf. 41:52). The reference here foreshadows the elevation of the younger son, Ephraim, over the older, Manasseh, which is the theme of the later part of the chapter.

In light of this it is fitting that Jacob then effectively adopts Joseph's two sons, Ephraim and Manasseh, as his own, granting them equal inheritance rights with their uncles and thus effectively granting Joseph a double share of the inheritance, such as would normally be given to the firstborn (48:5). The normal entitlement to the firstborn's birthright had earlier been forfeited by Reuben because of his sin (35:22; 1 Chron. 5:1–2). Any subsequent children born to Joseph in Egypt will be counted as Joseph's own; indeed, they will receive their inheritance through their brothers and not in their own right (Gen. 48:6).[674] This special status of Joseph's two sons reflects Jacob's unique love for Rachel, Joseph's mother, and his great sadness when she died on the way to Ephrath (or Bethlehem) and had to be buried there rather than in the family burial plot at the cave of Machpelah (v. 7; cf. Genesis 23; 25:9).[675] Yet she is still buried in the Land of Promise, as Jacob himself longs to be. The two events Jacob mentions—his meeting with God at Luz/Bethel and the death of Rachel—bracketed his time outside the Promised Land, during all of which time the Lord had been with him.

---

[671] On the divine title *'El Shaddai* cf. comment on 17:1–8.
[672] Cf. Delitzsch, *Genesis*, 2.357.
[673] Cf. comment on 27:41–28:5.
[674] Passages such as this imply that biblical genealogies, like other similar ancient Near Eastern documents, are rarely simply records of the "facts" of natural family relationships. Other factors may complicate issues. For example, though it is a matter of principle that Jacob/Israel has twelve sons, the ability to substitute Ephraim and Manasseh for Joseph maintains the "twelve tribe" structure even when the tribe of Levi is separated out (e.g., in the wilderness camp in Numbers 2, or in the division of the land in Joshua 13–21).
[675] "To my sorrow" (Gen. 48:7) reflects the Hebrew "by me" (*'alay*), capturing accurately the mood of Jacob's reflection. See the similar construction in Psalm 42:6.

48:8–14 When Jacob's grandchildren are brought to him by Joseph, his first response is "Who are these?" (48:8). Jacob's apparent failure to recognize his grandchildren, whom he has now known for the past seventeen years, has puzzled commentators. Yet several factors could account for this, including Jacob's dimmed eyesight (v. 10). More significantly, if this episode represents an adoption ceremony, as Nahum Sarna argues, then the formal identification of the parties would be an important legal step.[676] It also serves as an important connection between this blessing scene and Genesis 27, where a similarly sight-challenged Isaac asks the same question of Jacob (27:18). These similarities serve to highlight the profound differences between the stories. In this case there is no deception or trickery involved—even though once again the younger son receives the greater blessing (48:17–19). Yet there will be a blessing for both Ephraim and Manasseh, and indeed for all Israel's other sons, who will share in the promise of becoming a multitude of nations.

When Joseph brings his two sons to his father, Jacob kisses and embraces them both, overwhelmed by the unexpected work of God in his own life. He had given up hope of ever seeing Joseph's face again after that fateful journey to visit his brothers, yet now he has seen not only Joseph but Joseph's children as well (v. 11). In the OT, given the relatively high mortality rate, to see one's children's children was a blessing, not an expectation (cf. Ps. 128:6); here even more is at stake, since Jacob identifies Joseph's sons as his "seed" (Hb. *zeraʻ*), alluding once more to the promises to his ancestors.[677] Out of deep respect for his father Joseph prostrates himself before him and then formally presents the two boys before Jacob so that they might receive his blessing, carefully positioning the older son, Manasseh, by Jacob's right hand and the younger, Ephraim, by his left hand, so that the older might be blessed first by his grandfather (Gen. 48:13). Israel, however—called by this name here in recognition of the long-term impact of the actions that will follow—switches his hands so that the primary blessing is given to Ephraim, the younger son, and not to Manasseh.

48:15–16 Despite Jacob's favoring of Ephraim over Manasseh—a final time in the book of Genesis that a younger son is raised over the older—the blessing that Jacob pronounces is for both boys (v. 16). Ephraim will be *primus inter pares* ("first among equals") over Manasseh rather than a blessed brother over against a cursed one, as was the case for Isaac and Ishmael and for Jacob and Esau.

The blessing begins by identifying the God who will provide it, the God of Jacob's father, Isaac, and his grandfather, Abraham (v. 15). Just as Abraham and Isaac had "walked before God" (cf. 17:1; 24:40), so too this God has been Jacob's shepherd throughout his life (48:15). This is the first use of what will become a favorite appellation for Israel's God as the biblical narrative unfolds (49:24; Pss.

---

676 Sarna, *Genesis*, 326. It should also be noted that, if Joseph spent the bulk of his time at Pharaoh's court, then his family may have grown up at a distance from Jacob and Joseph's brothers, who lived in Goshen, so Jacob may not necessarily have seen his grandchildren frequently.
677 Mathews, *Genesis 11:27–50:26*, 877.

23:1; 28:9; 80:1; Eccles. 12:11; Isa. 40:11; etc.). The metaphor of shepherd encompasses both strength and protection, along with tender care for the flock, and thus is a natural image to describe the Lord's care for his people.

Jacob also calls the Lord "the angel who has redeemed me from all evil" (Gen. 48:16). Calling God an "angel" is unusual and likely represents the same idea as "angel of the LORD," who seems to represent God on earth in unique ways, so that, when the angel speaks, God speaks (cf. Ex. 3:2–4). The angel of the Lord has not been explicitly mentioned in the Jacob narrative, though his role as a redemptive figure was clear in Genesis 16; 22, where he came to rescue Hagar and then Isaac, and angels have figured significantly in Jacob's life, most notably in Genesis 33 at Penuel.[678] The divine nature of the angel in Genesis 48:16 is clear both from the parallelism with the previous clauses and by the fact that Jacob seeks a blessing from him; nowhere else in the Bible does an angel possess the authority to bless anyone (except perhaps 32:27–30, where the figure is clearly a manifestation of God himself).

The content of the blessing includes God's protection and redeeming presence with the boys, as alluded to in the titles ascribed to the God from whom the blessing comes. This is the first use in the Bible of the Hebrew verb *ga'al* ("redeem"; 48:16), which, together with the noun form, *go'el* ("kinsman-redeemer"), will become a key descriptor of God's work on behalf of his people (Ex. 6:6; 15:13; Isa. 44:6; etc.). Jacob also asks that through these boys the family names—Abraham, Isaac, and Jacob (cf. Ex. 33:1; Deut. 9:27; 2 Kings 13:23; Jer. 33:26; Matt. 8:11; Acts 7:32)—might continue to be remembered. This family name that will be pronounced upon them is encapsulated in the form "Israel," given to Jacob at Penuel (Genesis 33). This perpetual remembering contrasts with the name Manasseh, which means "forgetting" (41:51): Joseph can never truly forget his father's household.

Finally, Jacob prays that God's blessing upon the boys would result in their "growing into a multitude in the midst of the earth" (48:16). This would represent a fulfillment of the divine blessing to "be fruitful and multiply" (cf. v. 4). The word translated "grow" (*dagah*) is elsewhere unattested; some have seen a connection to a similar root meaning "fish," suggesting that their fruitfulness is being compared to the teeming hordes of the sea (1:21–22; cf. 48:16 ESV mg.). The connection between the verbal roots is uncertain, though the abundance of the tribes of Ephraim and Manasseh is already apparent during the time of the exodus and the conquest.[679] Given the focus elsewhere in Jacob's blessing on the land of Canaan, the word *'erets* ("earth") could be rendered "land" here; what is in view is not global domination but fruitfulness in the Land of Promise.[680]

---

[678] There is also a striking similarity between this blessing and Daniel 3. There, after one "like a son of the gods" appears alongside Shadrach, Meshach, and Abednego in the fiery furnace (Dan. 3:25), Nebuchadnezzar says, "Blessed be the God of Shadrach, Meshach, and Abednego, who has sent his angel and delivered his servants" (Dan. 3:28).
[679] Cf. Sarna, *Genesis*, 328.
[680] One might compare Jesus' beatitude in Matthew 5:5, which almost all English translations render as "The meek shall inherit the earth" even though Jesus is almost certainly citing Psalm 37:11, where the same

48:17–22 Jacob earlier crossed over his hands in order to bestow the primary blessing on the younger son, Ephraim, rather than the older son, Manasseh (v. 14). In response Joseph is displeased and, assuming at first that this is the result of confusion on the part of his elderly father, seeks to switch his father's hands back so that Manasseh, the firstborn, might receive the primary blessing (v. 17). Yet Jacob insists on giving Ephraim the primary blessing. Manasseh too will become a great people, to be sure, but the younger brother will be even more blessed and his offspring even more abundant (v. 19). Indeed, in later years, after the northern kingdom secedes from the tribal alliance, the north is known interchangeably as Israel and Ephraim (e.g., Isaiah 7). Both of their names will be used as a blessing, but Ephraim's will come before Manasseh's (Gen. 48:20).

Jacob's concluding words in this scene are for Joseph, granting him a special blessing distinct from his brothers. He promises that God will be with Joseph, just as he had earlier been with Jacob, and will bring him back to the land of Canaan, a promise fulfilled long after Joseph's death, when his descendants bring his bones from Egypt to bury them in the Promised Land (50:25; Ex. 13:19)—a privilege that does not seem to be afforded to any of his brothers. Jacob also grants Joseph a special personal bequest, a particular piece of property that he took by conquest from the Amorites (Gen. 48:22). The exact nature and location of this property is uncertain and much debated, but the primary point is clear and has been central to this whole chapter. Jacob's favoritism of Joseph remains intact until the end; he is determined that Joseph receive a double blessing, both directly and through his children. What is more, the gift is a further act of faith on the part of Jacob, for the bequest will be of no value to Joseph as long as he and his descendants remain in Egypt. It will be appropriated only if God brings his people back to the land of Canaan and grants it to them as their lasting inheritance.

Response

Faith is central in this chapter (cf. Heb. 11:21). The name of God is frequently on the lips of Jacob and Joseph, both as the one who has made their reunion possible (Gen. 48:9–11) and as the one who has been and will be with the family in the days ahead. During his own lifetime Jacob does not see anything close to fulfillment of the great promises he inherits from Abraham. He first receives the promise at Luz (Bethel) while leaving the land, running for his life (Genesis 28); when he returns to Canaan, that return is marked not by triumphal entry into his promised inheritance but by the deepest pain and loss possible, the death of his beloved spouse (35:16). But the God who has been with Jacob throughout his life is able to be with his people and bless them in Egypt, just as he has in the land of Canaan, even though Egypt is not their home. We too can trust that this same God will be with us and bless us as we sojourn in this difficult world, looking onward toward our heavenly home.

---

translations render the clause "The meek shall inherit the land." "Land" focuses our attention on the spiritual nature of the inheritance of the meek as the true heirs of Abraham, Isaac, and Jacob.

It is important, too, to recognize that the faith in view here is not an abstract sense of optimism about the future, that things will eventually turn out well. Even though Jacob's story does have a happy ending, much of his earthly journey is hard and bitter (47:9), and, like his fathers, he dies without seeing the fullness of the rich promises received from God—promises that each man in turn passes on to the next generation. Biblical faith is not the power by which we receive the answers to all our prayers and acquire the object of all our desires. Rather, it is a God-given ability to cling to him throughout the storms of life, trusting that the God who made us for himself has prepared for us a glorious future with him in heaven. Jacob's faith in God's promises of land and offspring pulsates throughout these chapters; he believes firmly that God will bring his offspring into the land he has promised and that ultimately from his seed will come the seed of the woman, promised to bruise the head of the serpent once for all (3:15).

The corresponding truth to our faith is God's faithfulness, which also undergirds these chapters. Without God's faithfulness our faith would be utterly in vain. Our God is a faithful Shepherd and Redeemer of his people, a God who deals with families and not merely disconnected individuals. Without the promise of his Spirit for us and for our children (Acts 2:39), we would have little solid hope for the salvation of our children, but, armed with that promise, we can confidently call them to faith in Christ.

When Jacob calls the Lord "the God . . . who has redeemed me from all evil," what does he mean? The Hebrew word *ra'* covers both situational and moral evil, but it is clear that the Lord has not protected Jacob from every difficult life circumstance. From the pain of losing a beloved spouse to spending years thinking that his son Joseph was dead, the Lord hardly spares Jacob from life's most difficult challenges. What Jacob is affirming is that his God has *redeemed* all that evil. It is not that bad things have never happened to him but rather that these bad things have been planned and worked by God into something good. Instead of destroying Jacob, these traumatic experiences have been so ordained by God that now good flows from them instead of evil. None of Jacob's pain has been wasted. None of his sorrow has been fruitless wandering in the wilderness. Throughout all the days of Jacob's life the good Shepherd has been leading him along the right pathways, whether to green pastures or through the valley of deep shadow, providing good for him and redeeming his evil, bringing blessing and hope out of the darkest and most desperate of life's situations (cf. Psalm 23).

But Jacob's deepest need is for redemption from his own inner evil, the twistedness that has dogged his life at every turn, as it does all of us. As the spiritual descendants of Jacob and members of the "Israel of God" (Gal. 6:16), we who are Christians can see and testify even more fully than Jacob that the Lord is our faithful Shepherd who redeems our evil. We can see more clearly what it truly cost God to become our Redeemer.

In order to become the kinsman who redeems us, God's own Son had to leave the eternal smile of his Father's blessing and enter this world of suffering and evil. Jesus Christ had to expose himself to the hatred and enmity that this world has for whatever is good and holy and to learn through harsh experience how to trust his Father in the dark times as well as the good ones. Jesus received a body that could experience evil in its most vicious forms. He had a back that could be scourged and beaten until it was bloody and raw, hands and feet of living flesh that could be pierced by cruel nails, a side that could be stabbed with a spear, and a heart that could be broken by hypocrisy, treachery, ingratitude, faithlessness, and abandonment. The one who was himself the Good Shepherd took the place of his errant sheep in order to rescue us from the dangers of the valley of death's deep shadow. The faithful Son was abandoned by his own Father in order to buy us back from our bondage and return to us the inheritance we had squandered through our own sin and evil. He redeemed us from *all* evil by taking upon himself the punishment that our sin has deserved and covering us with his perfect holiness and purity. This is the power proclaimed by the cross: that the Son of God who was slain for us now clothes us with his perfect righteousness, thereby accomplishing God's eternal purpose for a holy people who will belong to him forever.

GENESIS 49:1–27

49 Then Jacob called his sons and said, "Gather yourselves together, that I may tell you what shall happen to you in days to come.

2 "Assemble and listen, O sons of Jacob,
 listen to Israel your father.

3 "Reuben, you are my firstborn,
 my might, and the firstfruits of my strength,
 preeminent in dignity and preeminent in power.
4 Unstable as water, you shall not have preeminence,
 because you went up to your father's bed;
 then you defiled it—he went up to my couch!

5 "Simeon and Levi are brothers;
 weapons of violence are their swords.
6 Let my soul come not into their council;
 O my glory, be not joined to their company.
 For in their anger they killed men,
 and in their willfulness they hamstrung oxen.
7 Cursed be their anger, for it is fierce,
 and their wrath, for it is cruel!
 I will divide them in Jacob
 and scatter them in Israel.

8 "Judah, your brothers shall praise you;
   your hand shall be on the neck of your enemies;
   your father's sons shall bow down before you.
9 Judah is a lion's cub;
   from the prey, my son, you have gone up.
  He stooped down; he crouched as a lion
   and as a lioness; who dares rouse him?
10 The scepter shall not depart from Judah,
    nor the ruler's staff from between his feet,
   until tribute comes to him;[1]
    and to him shall be the obedience of the peoples.
11 Binding his foal to the vine
    and his donkey's colt to the choice vine,
   he has washed his garments in wine
    and his vesture in the blood of grapes.
12 His eyes are darker than wine,
    and his teeth whiter than milk.

13 "Zebulun shall dwell at the shore of the sea;
    he shall become a haven for ships,
    and his border shall be at Sidon.

14 "Issachar is a strong donkey,
    crouching between the sheepfolds.[2]
15 He saw that a resting place was good,
    and that the land was pleasant,
   so he bowed his shoulder to bear,
    and became a servant at forced labor.

16 "Dan shall judge his people
    as one of the tribes of Israel.
17 Dan shall be a serpent in the way,
    a viper by the path,
   that bites the horse's heels
    so that his rider falls backward.
18 I wait for your salvation, O LORD.

19 "Raiders shall raid Gad,[3]
    but he shall raid at their heels.

20 "Asher's food shall be rich,
    and he shall yield royal delicacies.

21 "Naphtali is a doe let loose
    that bears beautiful fawns.[4]

22 "Joseph is a fruitful bough,
    a fruitful bough by a spring;
    his branches run over the wall.[5]
23 The archers bitterly attacked him,
    shot at him, and harassed him severely,
24 yet his bow remained unmoved;
    his arms[6] were made agile

> by the hands of the Mighty One of Jacob
> (from there is the Shepherd,[7] the Stone of Israel),
> 25 by the God of your father who will help you,
> by the Almighty[8] who will bless you
> with blessings of heaven above,
> blessings of the deep that crouches beneath,
> blessings of the breasts and of the womb.
> 26 The blessings of your father
> are mighty beyond the blessings of my parents,
> up to the bounties of the everlasting hills.[9]
> May they be on the head of Joseph,
> and on the brow of him who was set apart from his brothers.
>
> 27 "Benjamin is a ravenous wolf,
> in the morning devouring the prey
> and at evening dividing the spoil."

[1] By a slight revocalization; a slight emendation yields (compare Septuagint, Syriac, Targum) *until he comes to whom it belongs*; Hebrew *until Shiloh comes*, or *until he comes to Shiloh* [2] Or *between its saddlebags* [3] *Gad* sounds like the Hebrew for *raiders* and *raid* [4] Or *he gives beautiful words*, or *that bears fawns of the fold* [5] Or *Joseph is a wild donkey, a wild donkey beside a spring, his wild colts beside the wall* [6] Hebrew *the arms of his hands* [7] Or *by the name of the Shepherd* [8] Hebrew *Shaddai* [9] A slight emendation yields (compare Septuagint) *the blessings of the eternal mountains, the bounties of the everlasting hills*

Section Overview

In Genesis 48, as Jacob perceived his approaching death, he gave a special blessing to Joseph and his two sons. Now in Genesis 49 he gathers all twelve of his sons to give each of them a final blessing (including Joseph). In previous generations the Abrahamic blessing was passed on to a single son, but now that Jacob has become Israel, the father of a "company of nations" (35:11), the blessing must be passed on to all twelve of his sons. Yet each son does not receive the exact same blessing, as though they were products rolling off an assembly line. Each receives a "blessing suitable to him" (49:28). As a result of the blessings' being matched to the individual, some blessings sound more like curses (e.g., v. 7). Indeed, the form of Jacob's words sounds more like the style of the prophets than a conventional blessing. Perhaps the closest parallel is the oracles of Balaam, which are likewise styled as "blessings" but also contain prophetic elements (cf. Numbers 23–24).

Jacob's blessings for his sons reflect the impact on subsequent generations of the sins of the fathers (cf. Ex. 34:7). Yet, though the effects of those sins are real, we should not miss the grace that is also present in the fact that all twelve sons receive Jacob's blessing and are included in God's larger plans to make them a great nation, give them a land, and use them as a blessing for the nations. Sin pays very real and very costly wages, as Jacob's descendants will attest, but God's grace can triumph over even the greatest human sin by redeeming us from our evil (cf. Gen. 48:16). Indeed, that is the fundamental message of the book of Genesis: God's blessing will triumph over human evil. The storyline is necessarily incomplete—as we near the conclusion of the book, that blessing has been restored only very partially. However, the forward-looking nature of the final chapters would remind the original hearers (and us) that God's great work of redemption and blessing is unfolding and will surely reach its final goal.

Section Outline

XI. The Family History of Jacob (37:1–50:26) . . .

M. Mixed Blessings (49:1–27)

Comment

49:1–2 The prophetic style is strongly evident in Jacob's opening words, as he gathers his sons to tell them what will happen "in days to come" (Hb. *be'akharit hayyamim*; v. 1). This phrase often refers to climactic events in history (cf. Isa. 2:2; Ezek. 38:16; etc.) but can also be used for more indeterminate periods in the future, especially in the Pentateuch (Num. 24:14; Deut. 31:29). The summons to Israel's sons to "assemble and listen" also appears in the prophets, gathering the people to hear the Lord's word (Isa. 45:20; 48:14). This introduction gives a solemn tone to what follows, marking it out not merely as Jacob's words but as the Lord's words through him. It is also fitting given the specificity of many of the blessings assigned to the forefathers of the tribes, whose later experiences will demonstrate the accuracy of Jacob's words.

49:3–4 The blessings are arranged in order of birth mother rather than in strict sequence of age,[681] beginning with Leah's six children (Reuben–Issachar), followed by the four children of the maidservants, Bilhah and Zilpah (Dan–Naphtali),[682] and concluding with Rachel's two children (Joseph and Benjamin).

As firstborn, Reuben was born into a position of privilege and primacy; he is described as Jacob's might and the firstfruits of his strength, preeminent in dignity and power (49:3). Normally in the ancient Near East the firstborn might have expected to receive a double share of the inheritance to match his position of dignity and honor. In this case, however, Reuben's father has no words of blessing for him. Reuben's volatility—evidenced by his sleeping with his father's concubine, Bilhah (35:22)—leads to his losing his position of leadership among the sons. He is as reliable to lean on as a pillar of water (49:4). This instability was already noticeable in the earlier account. When the brothers plotted against Joseph, Reuben planned to help his brother escape, but he was absent at the crucial moment when the other brothers sold Joseph into slavery and so was unable to effect a rescue (37:29–30). Later Reuben pledged the life of his two sons as surety that Benjamin would return safely from the proposed trip to Egypt, but his offer was rejected by his father (42:37–38). Circumstances and his own character (or lack thereof) constantly conspire against Reuben's attempts to provide leadership for the family.

---

[681] Kline, *Genesis*, 139.
[682] These are also presented out of (birth) order, with Bilhah's two children bracketing Zilpah's.

Moreover, this trait of unreliability is passed on to the tribe that comes from him. In the days of the Judges, when Ephraim, Benjamin, Zebulun, Issachar, and Naphtali come and fight alongside Deborah, the tribe of Reuben apparently remains at home: "Among the clans of Reuben there were great searchings of heart. Why did you sit still among the sheepfolds, to hear the whistling for the flocks? Among the clans of Reuben there were great searchings of heart" (Judg. 5:15–16). While the other tribes are out fighting for their lives, the Reubenites are at home thinking about it. They are as unreliable as their forefather.

49:5–7 Simeon and Levi, next in line, receive a similarly negative assessment. In their case they face the consequences of the violence and ruthlessness with which, after the rape of Dinah, they tricked the men of Shechem into being circumcised in order to massacre them (Gen. 49:5–6; cf. ch. 34). At the time Jacob took no action beyond a mild word of reproof that focused more on the impact of their actions on Jacob's reputation than on the outrage of their behavior (34:30). Now, however, Jacob declares that, as a lasting result of their sin, their descendants will be scattered throughout Israel. As Simeon and Levi were joined together in their iniquity, so the tribes that come from them will together be scattered in their judgment. The nature of this pronouncement as a divine oracle is clear from the first-person-singular language ("I will divide them in Jacob and scatter them in Israel"; 49:7), where it is clear that the "I" cannot refer to Jacob but must be the Lord's own personal commitment.

These words work their way out in the future of Israel. Simeon is one of the smaller tribes from the outset, becoming largely absorbed into Judah. Meanwhile, the ferocious anger of Levi is harnessed in the Lord's service after the incident of the golden calf (Ex. 32:26–29). As a result, their curse is transformed into a blessing. They are still scattered among the tribes of Israel, but that status enables them to serve the whole nation as the priestly tribe, teaching Torah throughout Israel and serving at the sanctuary.

49:8–12 Judah's blessing is not the longest—that privilege is unsurprisingly reserved for Joseph—but is the most remarkable. Jacob begins by affirming (twice) Joseph's childhood dream that his brothers would praise him (Gen. 49:8; cf. 37:5–8). There is a play on words here, as Judah's own name means "praise" (cf. 29:35). Jacob describes Judah in distinctly royal terms. Triumphing over all his enemies,[683] he is majestic and lionlike; none will dare rouse him to anger (49:9). It is therefore no surprise to hear that, in addition to preeminence over his brothers, Judah will possess the scepter and the ruler's staff (v. 10). This blessing is also prophetic, foreshadowing the future history of Israel, in which the family of Judah will become the royal tribe through the line of David. This blessing also affirms by faith God's earlier promise that kings would come from Abraham's line (17:6).

---

[683] To place one's hand on another's neck is a sign of authority over that person, much like a policeman might grab a criminal by the shoulder or neck.

Yet Jacob's prophecy anticipates something even greater than the substantial blessings experienced by Judah in the time of David and Solomon, who rule over all Israel at the time of its greatest prosperity. After the scepter first arrives in Judah in the time of David, the scepter will remain with Judah until the arrival of a still greater future figure. The Hebrew text of verse 10 is complex, with the MT reading "until Shiloh comes" (cf. ESV mg.; KJV).[684] The ESV, like some other versions, has chosen to revocalize the text slightly to render it "Until tribute comes to him," which fits well with the following line, "And to him shall be the obedience of the peoples."[685] However, most ancient and modern translations have understood this verse to be a messianic prophecy, rendering it "Until he comes to whom it [the scepter] belongs" (cf. ESV mg.).[686] This messianic interpretation is already clear in later biblical passages that allude to this verse. Ezekiel 19 and 21:27 pick up on the imagery of lions and scepters to denigrate the Davidic kings of the immediate preexilic period. Zechariah 9:9–10 anticipates a messianic figure who will come riding on "a colt, the foal of a donkey" (Hb. *'al 'ayir ben 'atonot*; both terms come from Gen. 49:11); meanwhile, in Revelation 5:5 "the Lion of the tribe of Judah" is Jesus.

This enigmatic "one to come," to whom rulership properly belongs, will not reign only over the nation of Israel (i.e., over Judah's brothers). His reign will extend more widely, receiving the obedience of the peoples (Gen. 49:10; cf. Psalm 72). He will be unmatched in his beauty, with "eyes are darker than wine, and his teeth whiter than milk" (Gen. 49:12), and his arrival will usher in an age of unparalleled prosperity. This abundant prosperity is the significance of his tethering his young donkey to a choice vine (v. 11): since the donkey would immediately begin to eat the vine and any grapes it has borne—as especially a young and vigorous donkey would do—the image might be compared to someone in our culture using one-hundred-dollar bills to light a fire. Such a person's wealth is so vast that normal cautions may be cast to the wind.[687] In the same way, washing garments in wine is another emblem of extraordinary abundance. Yet the image of this figure's washing his robes in wine also has a negative aspect: the picture of a person whose clothing is stained red with the blood (!) of grapes is evocative of outright warfare (cf. Pss. 58:10; 68:23). These images (harvest and judgment, winepress and blood) are merged in Revelation 14:20 ("The winepress was trodden outside the city, and blood flowed from the winepress, as high as a horse's bridle, for 1,600 stadia"), while the figure riding to war on a white horse in Revelation 19:13 is described as wearing a garment "dipped in blood."

It is not difficult to see this figure reflected in the person of Jesus. In Jesus' first miracle he replaces water with wine at Cana on a vast scale, filling jars meant for washing with abundant wine (John 2:6, 9). In Matthew's account of the trium-

---

684 Some also see this as a reference to a location, Shiloh ("Until he comes to Shiloh").
685 So Sarna, *Genesis*, 336.
686 There is support for this reading in some manuscripts of the MT tradition; cf. Mathews, *Genesis 11:27–50:26*, 894.
687 Alter, *Five Books of Moses*, 286.

phal entry Jesus is also depicted as the humble king, riding into Jerusalem on a colt, the foal of a donkey (Matt. 21:1–8). Jesus is the one of unmatched beauty, to whom the obedience of the nations properly belongs. His saints now wash their garments and make them clean, not in blood-red wine nor in the blood of God's enemies but in what the wine of the Lord's Supper symbolizes: the "blood of the Lamb" himself (Rev. 7:14).

49:13–15 Compared to the glorious heights of the blessing pronounced upon Judah, the blessings assigned to Zebulun and Issachar are decidedly mixed.[688] On the one hand they speak of prosperity and comfort ("a haven for ships"; "a resting place was good"; "the land was pleasant"; Gen. 49:13–15). On the other hand, however, Zebulun will be dangerously dependent upon the Phoenicians for its prosperity (cf. below), and Issachar will end up in subjugation and forced labor. The statement that Zebulun will dwell beside the seashore does not reflect his tribe's subsequent location during the conquest of the land (cf. Josh. 19:10–16); its maritime trade is always carried out through its Phoenician neighbors, for whom Sidon stands as a representative.[689] Though Zebulun is not itself a coastal people, it benefits significantly from the fact that some of the main roads for coastal trade pass through its territory.

Issachar is blessed with strength, like a donkey (Gen. 49:14), though the compliment is double-edged, since donkeys are not exactly known for initiative or leadership. He would rather lie down among the saddlebags than use his strength for productive work (v. 14).[690] The tribe of Issachar is not even mentioned in Judges 1, which lists the successes and setbacks of the Israelite tribes in the conquest, suggesting that it has little role to play in such events. It seems that comfort and ease are more important to the tribe than freedom, and so it gradually settles into a role of servitude rather than leadership. A "resting place" (Hb. *menukhah*) in a pleasant land ought to be a great blessing (v. 15), but for Issachar that blessing will become a curse because of the price at which it purchases its peace, submitting itself to the imposition of forced labor.

49:16–18 As with Judah's name, Dan's name speaks of his high calling; it means "he judges," and Jacob's blessing upon him declares that he will indeed "judge his people" (v. 16). This sounds positive by itself, but the following verse throws doubt on that positive perspective. The "serpent" here is likely a horned viper that conceals itself in the sand along caravan routes in pursuit of its prey—small rodents that might be attracted by food particles left behind. If threatened by a passing horse or camel, it would strike, causing the animal to shy away and

---

[688] We would expect Issachar to be blessed before Zebulun, as the older of the last pair of sons of Leah. It is possible that the reversal in order is due to the theme of the younger's having precedence over the older (similarly in Deut. 33:18).

[689] Hamilton, *Genesis 18–50*, 664. This is a clear indication that the text is ancient, predating the settlement of the land. No later author would be likely to have described Zebulun's location in these terms.

[690] The ESV translates *mishpetayim* as "sheepfolds," but it is dual in form, so "saddlebags" seems more fitting (so ESV mg.). It only occurs here and in Judges 5:16, also in the context of Issachar; in that context "sheepfolds" seems to fit better than "saddlebags."

potentially dismount its rider (v. 17).⁶⁹¹ The question is whether Dan will really provide justice for the whole of Israel, or will he prove instead to be a snake in the grass? This aspect of Dan's legacy finds apt expression in the person of Samson, called by God from before his birth to be set apart for holy service (Judges 13) but in practice committed mostly to serving his own interests rather than judging the Lord's people (Judges 14–16).

Of Jacob's first seven children, six have had little to commend them. Apart from the high point of Judah and the prospect of the future messiah, the remainder of his blessings have been something of an anticlimax. Perhaps this is why Jacob cries out at this point: "I wait for your salvation, O LORD" (Gen. 49:18). Jacob's hopes rest not in the prospect of vindication by an earthly judge, expressed in the name Dan, nor in the fleeting wealth and comfort of this world, pursued by Issachar and Zebulun. As he is about to die, at the end of a short and painful life, surrounded by offspring who seem largely unable to fulfill their potential, Jacob looks up to the Lord and expresses his attitude of patient waiting until the Lord provides salvation. It is clear that his request is not for an extended earthly existence; he knows he is about to die (v. 29), but his hope extends beyond the grave. Jacob's faith is in a heavenly inheritance, a salvation from the Lord that no one and nothing can take from him.

49:19–21 Gad, Asher, and Naphtali are dealt with quickly. Gad's location in the Transjordan after the conquest of the land gives him property ideal for cattle (Num. 32:1) but also leaves him exposed to constant raids, especially from the Ammonites and the Moabites (cf. Judges 11). Gad's blessing too contains a play on his name: Gad will be raided by raiders (Hb. *gad gedud yegudenu*; Gen. 49:19), but he will raid (*yagud*) at their heels. In other words, though he will suffer at the hands of marauders, from them he will learn how to fight (cf. 1 Chron. 12:8–14).

Asher's blessing alludes to the provision of rich food, both for itself and for the royal court (Gen. 49:20). Certainly its tribal portion in western Galilee is well watered and fertile (cf. Deut. 33:24), but again its location in Galilee leaves it dangerously exposed to invasions at various points in history. Moreover, Judges 1:31 notes how the Asherites failed to drive out the Canaanites living in the land, settling among them instead. They may have fed royal courts, but many of those kings were not Israelites.

The blessing on Naphtali is the most enigmatic of all Jacob's blessings. It is not immediately apparent why this tribe should be compared to a doe that bears beautiful fawns (Gen. 49:21).⁶⁹² A female deer is sometimes used as a metaphor of feminine beauty (Prov. 5:19) or of speed and surefootedness on the mountains (2 Sam. 22:34; Hab. 3:19). Perhaps this is as simple as an image of unrestrained joy and freedom, suitable to the mountainous nature of Naphtali's subsequent home.

---

691 Sarna, *Genesis*, 340. At this point in history horses were used primarily to pull chariots rather than for riding, so this may have charioteers in view rather than equestrians.
692 The phrase *'imrei shafer* could also be translated "beautiful words" (cf. ESV mg.; NASB 1995), in which case the animal metaphor would end with the first half-line. However, the use of the participle seems to link the two halves together; if they were distinct, a finite verb would be more usual.

49:22–26 God's ability to bring good out of evil and to redeem painful circumstances is prominent in the longest of Jacob's blessings, unsurprisingly bestowed on his favorite son, Joseph. Joseph is compared to a fruitful plant,[693] located beside the abundant water of a spring, whose branches (Hb. "daughters") transcend even the protection of its walled vineyard (Gen. 49:22). The metaphor of a well-watered plant as an image of flourishing is common throughout the OT (Ps. 1:3; Ezek. 17:5). Yet that abundant prosperity comes in the context of bitter affliction and assault: Joseph is attacked by the archers (Gen. 49:23), a reference to all the slanders and injustices he has had to endure throughout his lifetime. Arrows are often used figuratively in the OT for verbal assaults (Ps. 57:4; Prov. 25:18; Jer. 9:3). Despite their ferocity these assaults have been ineffective; Joseph's own bow remains unmoved, ready to destroy his enemies (Gen. 49:24).

Yet the central word in Jacob's blessing upon Joseph is not Joseph's native fruitfulness, nor his bitter affliction, nor even his ability to withstand the assault; rather it is the affirmation of God's purposes in Joseph's life. Joseph's blessing flows from the Mighty One of Jacob, whose own arms strengthen Joseph's (v. 24). The title "Mighty One of Jacob" (Hb. *'abir ya'aqob*) occurs elsewhere only in Psalm 132 and in Isaiah and echoes the similar epithet applied to the God of Jacob's father, "the Fear of Isaac" (Gen. 31:42, 53).

The clause "From there[694] is the Shepherd, the Stone of Israel" (49:24) is less clear. Jacob earlier called the Lord his shepherd in 48:15; this is a natural image of protection and provision (cf. Psalm 23). However, the "Stone of Israel" (*'eben yisra'el*) is nowhere else used as a title for God. Elsewhere he is called the "Rock of Israel" (*tsur yisra'el*), but that is a quite different Hebrew word. "Rock" (*tsur*) generally refers to a natural outcrop, whereas stones (*'eben*) are much smaller. The memorials raised by God's people to remind them of his faithfulness, such as the one near Mizpah called Ebenezer ("stone of help"; 1 Sam. 7:12) or the stone pillar Jacob raised at Bethel to symbolize God's promise to bless him, are often called "stones" (Gen. 28:18). The latter incident may be in view, with Bethel being the "from there" mentioned in the verse. The Lord has been Jacob's shepherd and protector, the Mighty One of Jacob ever since Bethel, and he will similarly support and defend Joseph in all his struggles and difficulties, enabling him to bear fruit in abundance. God has set Joseph apart from his brothers and has maintained his faith in the face of every bitter assault.

This is why, even though Joseph has already achieved heights of greatness in Egypt, second only to Pharaoh and possessing wealth, status, and power in abundance, Jacob still blesses him. The blessings that Joseph needs do not consist in things that Egypt can give him. Rather they are the same blessings promised to Joseph's grandfather Isaac and his great-grandfather Abraham by *'El Shaddai* (49:25; cf. 17:1). Jacob blesses Joseph with the blessing of the heights and depths

---

693 ESV "fruitful bough"; the Hebrew is *ben porat*, "son of a fruitful one"—that is, "son of" in the sense of "sharing the quality of." An allusion to the name of Joseph's son Ephraim is likely.
694 Many commentators want to revocalize "from there" (Hb. *mishsham*) as "by the name of" (*mishshem*), but that form invariably uses the preposition *beth*, not *min*; cf. Sarna, *Genesis*, 343.

("heaven above, blessings of the deep that crouches beneath"), a merism that includes everything between these ultimate boundaries (cf. Genesis 1).[695] Since the Lord rules over all creation, all its bounty is his to grant. More specifically, Jacob asks for Joseph the blessings of "breasts"[696] and womb, representing fruitfulness in offspring, which is not only a key ingredient for prosperity generally in the ancient world but also a central part of the Abrahamic blessing (cf. 12:2–3). Another part of that Abrahamic blessing is found in the "bounties of the everlasting hills" (49:26), namely, the blessing of land. Jacob's blessing on Joseph reiterates his blessing on Ephraim and Manasseh, that they would become great in the Land of Promise, receiving the fullness of what God promised to Abraham (48:16).

In light of everything that has gone before, Jacob's declaration that Joseph is "set apart from his brothers" (49:26) can only mean that Jacob still regards Joseph's line as the one through whom the promised seed will be born. In this Jacob is mistaken—but, after all he has gone through, his faith that there will be a promised seed is nonetheless commendable. His belief in God's promise is firm, even though his expectation of how that future will unfold is misguided.

49:27 The last blessing is reserved for Benjamin, Jacob's youngest child, a blessing that is once again brief and largely negative. Benjamin is a ravenous wolf, an image that is never a positive picture in Scripture (v. 27; cf. John 10:12). At morning and evening he carves up the spoil collected from those weaker than himself. This is hardly the picture one would imagine from Benjamin's own story, but it proves fitting enough for the tribe that descends from Joseph's younger brother. Benjamin is the home of one of the early judges who saves Israel, Ehud (Judg. 3:15), and of the first king, Saul, who also delivers his people through military victory (1 Samuel 11). Less positively, the Benjaminites fight against the remainder of Israel in a civil war at the end of Judges (Judges 19–21).

Response

Jacob's blessings reflect the individual nature of his children and prophetically anticipate the future for each of the tribes that come from them (Gen. 49:28). As such they reflect the ongoing impact that parental sin has on the next (and subsequent) generations. Many of the tribes receive negative consequences because of their ancestors' sins (cf. Ex. 34:7). This reminds us of the profound significance of our sin, due to its impact not merely on ourselves but also on subsequent generations. None of us is independent or free in his actions. Yet alongside the suffered consequences of a parent's sin we also see illustrations of the transforming power of God's grace. For every Simeon, whose tribe is scattered in Israel and ultimately largely absorbed into Judah, there is a Levi, whose scattering is turned from a curse to a blessing. One tribe is defined by its ancestor's failure, while for the other the consequences of its father's curse become the context in

---

695 Currid, *Genesis 25:19–50:26*, 384.
696 There is a play on words between the Almighty (*'El Shaddai*) and "breasts" (*shadayim*).

which it becomes a blessing to others. Where sin abounds, grace abounds all the more (Rom. 5:20).

Most important, we should notice that all these sinners, along with their sin-damaged offspring, are nonetheless incorporated into the line of promise. Israel is built not simply on the foundation of righteous Joseph, or even transformed Judah, but on the foundation of all twelve patriarchs. Unstable Reuben, violent Simeon and Levi, comfort-loving Issachar, and dangerous Benjamin are all included as part of God's saving purpose for a holy people for himself. Our redeeming God does not go searching through the world for the best and most faithful people to save; rather, he comes seeking and saving lost sinners (Matt. 1:21). God pursues and rescues those whose lifestyles make them the object of the world's scorn, as well as those whose sin the world admires and lauds. From the start our salvation has been entirely by God's grace and not by our works. There is no room in this list of our spiritual ancestors for any boasting or pride in human accomplishment. The work of our salvation is God's from start to finish.

It is not clear how much of his prophetic blessings Jacob understands. The one to come, to whom authority belongs, will not be merely a future human king. If we are to be saved, then the Lord himself must be our redeemer. In Isaiah 63 the Lord is depicted as coming from the east, from Bozrah in Edom, with his garments stained red with blood, like a trampler of grapes. The Lord promises himself to bring salvation to his people and judgment upon their enemies, to redeem all those who belong to him and to establish true righteousness and lasting peace (Isa. 63:1–7).

The Lord did not need to enter our world and share our humanity to condemn us. That could have been done from a safe distance, as the Almighty. However, in order to redeem us Jesus had to be made like us, subject to far more ferocious attacks from his brothers than Joseph ever experienced, yet upheld by his Father through them all. In order to rescue us from our lostness, God himself had to take on flesh and stain his garments with his own precious blood at the cross. He took up our affliction so that we can now wash our sin-stained garments, not in blood-red wine but in the "blood of the Lamb" himself (Rev. 7:14). As we wash our garments in his cleansing blood, they come out dazzlingly clean and white, as pure and spotless as though we had never sinned.

Like Jacob, we are still awaiting the fullness of our salvation (Gen. 49:18). There is a day coming when the Lord will return in triumph and every knee will bow before him (Phil. 2:10). On that day the Lord will wipe away all our tears and sorrows and finally eliminate our remaining sin (Rev. 21:4). On that day all his promises will be fulfilled and we will be gathered to "our people," those from every tribe and nation gathered to worship the Lamb (Rev. 5:9). In the meantime we are called to wait with patient endurance and hope, looking forward to the day of his return.

GENESIS 49:28–50:26

²⁸ All these are the twelve tribes of Israel. This is what their father said to them as he blessed them, blessing each with the blessing suitable to him. ²⁹ Then he commanded them and said to them, "I am to be gathered to my people; bury me with my fathers in the cave that is in the field of Ephron the Hittite, ³⁰ in the cave that is in the field at Machpelah, to the east of Mamre, in the land of Canaan, which Abraham bought with the field from Ephron the Hittite to possess as a burying place. ³¹ There they buried Abraham and Sarah his wife. There they buried Isaac and Rebekah his wife, and there I buried Leah— ³² the field and the cave that is in it were bought from the Hittites." ³³ When Jacob finished commanding his sons, he drew up his feet into the bed and breathed his last and was gathered to his people.

50 Then Joseph fell on his father's face and wept over him and kissed him. ² And Joseph commanded his servants the physicians to embalm his father. So the physicians embalmed Israel. ³ Forty days were required for it, for that is how many are required for embalming. And the Egyptians wept for him seventy days.

⁴ And when the days of weeping for him were past, Joseph spoke to the household of Pharaoh, saying, "If now I have found favor in your eyes, please speak in the ears of Pharaoh, saying, ⁵ 'My father made me swear, saying, "I am about to die: in my tomb that I hewed out for myself in the land of Canaan, there shall you bury me." Now therefore, let me please go up and bury my father. Then I will return.'" ⁶ And Pharaoh answered, "Go up, and bury your father, as he made you swear." ⁷ So Joseph went up to bury his father. With him went up all the servants of Pharaoh, the elders of his household, and all the elders of the land of Egypt, ⁸ as well as all the household of Joseph, his brothers, and his father's household. Only their children, their flocks, and their herds were left in the land of Goshen. ⁹ And there went up with him both chariots and horsemen. It was a very great company. ¹⁰ When they came to the threshing floor of Atad, which is beyond the Jordan, they lamented there with a very great and grievous lamentation, and he made a mourning for his father seven days. ¹¹ When the inhabitants of the land, the Canaanites, saw the mourning on the threshing floor of Atad, they said, "This is a grievous mourning by the Egyptians." Therefore the place was named Abel-mizraim;¹ it is beyond the Jordan. ¹² Thus his sons did for him as he had commanded them, ¹³ for his sons carried him to the land of Canaan and buried him in the cave of the field at Machpelah, to the east of Mamre, which Abraham bought with the field from Ephron the Hittite to possess as a burying place. ¹⁴ After he had buried his father, Joseph returned to Egypt with his brothers and all who had gone up with him to bury his father.

¹⁵ When Joseph's brothers saw that their father was dead, they said, "It may be that Joseph will hate us and pay us back for all the evil that we did to him." ¹⁶ So they sent a message to Joseph, saying, "Your father gave this com-

mand before he died: **17** 'Say to Joseph, "Please forgive the transgression of your brothers and their sin, because they did evil to you."' And now, please forgive the transgression of the servants of the God of your father." Joseph wept when they spoke to him. **18** His brothers also came and fell down before him and said, "Behold, we are your servants." **19** But Joseph said to them, "Do not fear, for am I in the place of God? **20** As for you, you meant evil against me, but God meant it for good, to bring it about that many people[2] should be kept alive, as they are today. **21** So do not fear; I will provide for you and your little ones." Thus he comforted them and spoke kindly to them.

22 So Joseph remained in Egypt, he and his father's house. Joseph lived 110 years. **23** And Joseph saw Ephraim's children of the third generation. The children also of Machir the son of Manasseh were counted as Joseph's own.[3] **24** And Joseph said to his brothers, "I am about to die, but God will visit you and bring you up out of this land to the land that he swore to Abraham, to Isaac, and to Jacob." **25** Then Joseph made the sons of Israel swear, saying, "God will surely visit you, and you shall carry up my bones from here." **26** So Joseph died, being 110 years old. They embalmed him, and he was put in a coffin in Egypt.

[1] *Abel-mizraim* means *mourning* (or *meadow*) *of Egypt* [2] Or *a numerous people* [3] Hebrew *were born on Joseph's knees*

Section Overview

The closing section of Genesis details two good deaths, those of Jacob and Joseph. Having shown us the introduction of death into the world through the fall (cf. Genesis 3), Moses wants us to see that in Adam all must indeed die (1 Cor. 15:22). Yet this story is not simply about death; it is more precisely about death and burial. There is more to death than dying. Jacob and Joseph do not die well merely in the sense that they die comfortably at a good old age, surrounded by loving caregivers. They die well in the sense of dying in faith, knowing that their death is not the end of the real story of their lives. For Jacob and Joseph the end of life on earth is merely the closing page of one volume that leads into a new and better sequel. It is this that makes their burials so significant: each in his own way professes his confidence in God's promise of exodus from Egypt and a return to the Promised Land. That faith would be a great encouragement to the first generation of hearers in the wilderness as they sought to accomplish the goals in which Jacob and Joseph so passionately believed.

Section Outline

XI. The Family History of Jacob (37:1–50:26) . . .
    N. Death Is Not the End (49:28–50:26)

Comment

49:28–33 With Jacob's blessings on his children concluded,[697] he reiterates his request to be buried in the land of Canaan, at the ancestral tomb in the cave

---

697 Jacob's children are referred to as the "tribes of Israel" (Gen. 49:28), reflecting a later perspective from the time of Moses and acknowledging the forward-looking nature of his words. The blessings are intended

of Machpelah (vv. 29–30; cf. 23:17–19). In that cave are the mortal remains of Abraham and Sarah, along with Isaac and Rebekah (49:31). Moreover, in the ultimate irony, there too lie the remains of Leah, Jacob's "unloved" wife (49:31; cf. 29:31). Rachel had to be buried elsewhere, as Jacob recalls with sadness in 48:7, but in death Jacob is reunited with his first wife. In this sense Jacob will be "gathered to [his] people" (49:29). Yet Jacob's motivation is not a sentimental attachment to the people buried there; it is an act of faith in the promise of God that the land of Canaan will ultimately belong to his descendants. After his death he will foreshadow the journey that he fervently believes his descendants will make when their time in Egypt is complete and they return to the land. Indeed, Jacob's wish to be "gathered to his people" is recorded as being complete in the last verse of the chapter, well before his body is transferred to the family tomb. His final words are thus a powerful testimony to his faith in the Lord and the promise that transcends the very best this world has to offer.

50:1–6 Although Jacob made it clear that he would rather be buried simply in Canaan than with all state honors in Egypt, his funeral is nothing less than a state occasion as a mark of the honor in which Pharaoh holds Joseph and his aged father. The experts are summoned to preserve Jacob's corpse (50:2), not out of respect for the Egyptian beliefs about death and the afterlife but to ease the transportation of his body to its final resting place.[698] The process takes forty days and is doubtless very expensive. Meanwhile, the formal period of mourning for Jacob goes on for a total of seventy days (v. 3), only two fewer than the length of time prescribed for the death of a Pharaoh.[699]

Despite his elevated position Joseph must still defer to Pharaoh on matters of importance, such as his request to take his father's body to the land of Canaan and bury it there. His approach is suitably deferential, made through the members of Pharaoh's household rather than directly,[700] and he omits his father's negative requests not to be buried in Egypt (47:29–30), framing the issue positively as a desire to be buried in his own personal tomb (50:5).[701] He also adds a necessary commitment that he will return to his responsibilities in Egypt after the journey to bury his father is complete (v. 5). A key element of Joseph's case is the fact that his father forced him to swear an oath to that effect prior to his death (v. 5; cf. 47:29–31). Joseph therefore asks Pharaoh to let him go up (*'alah*) from Egypt to Canaan, introducing one of the key verbs in this chapter, a verb that will later be used for Israel's own exodus from Egypt. Pharaoh responds using the same verb: "Go up, and bury your father" (50:6).

---

not merely for their immediate recipients but for many generations to come. From this point onward the "twelve tribes of Israel" are a fundamental biblical unit.
698 The Hebrew text calls them "physicians" (*harofe'im*) rather than "embalmers" (*khanetim*; Gen. 50:2). Some commentators have argued that, since these are distinct professions, Joseph deliberately chose to avoid the magical rites of professional embalmers (e.g., Kidner, *Genesis*, 233), but this may be an oversubtle distinction.
699 Von Rad, *Genesis*, 430.
700 His recent contact with his father's corpse would also make it inappropriate for him to present himself directly to Pharaoh; cf. Hamilton, *Genesis 18–50*, 693.
701 Greidanus, *Preaching Christ from Genesis*, 466. The fact that he is said to have "cut" his own tomb probably refers simply to a separate chamber within the cave itself.

50:7–14 Joseph's journey to bury his father is recorded in considerable detail, highlighting the importance of the event. As well as by Joseph, his household, and his brothers, the body is accompanied by a very large party of prominent Egyptians (vv. 7–8).[702] However, the Israelites' children, flocks, and herds are left behind in the land of Goshen, ensuring that Joseph and his family will have to return to Egypt (v. 8).[703] The natural route to follow from Goshen to Canaan would be along the coastal road, but in verse 10 we are told that the party is lamenting at the threshing floor of Atad, near the Jordan River. No reason is given in the text for the apparent decision to go around the eastern side of the Dead Sea and then cross the Jordan in order to enter the Promised Land. Commentators have speculated about various plausible political and historical reasons that might have favored that eastern route over the more direct one. However, it would hardly have escaped the notice of Moses' original audience that this was exactly the same route they were following from Egypt to the Promised Land. Jacob's corpse is prefiguring what would happen to his descendants some four hundred years later.[704]

This prefiguring of the exodus also explains the rather curious reference to the Egyptian chariots and horsemen among the procession (v. 9). They seem rather unnecessary at a funeral, but they will have a key part to play in the later exodus, albeit on that occasion in pursuit of the Israelites. Indeed, in the first four books of the Bible this is the only reference to chariots and horsemen apart from those in the later exodus account (Exodus 14–15). Even the Canaanites notice the dramatic lamentation of the Egyptians, memorializing it as a place name. However, the central point is the fact that Jacob's sons do exactly as he instructed them, laying him to rest in the family tomb, alongside his father and grandfather (Gen. 50:12–13). This is the initial fulfillment of God's promise to Jacob in Genesis 46:3–4: "I am God, the God of your father. Do not be afraid to go down to Egypt, for there I will make you into a great nation. I myself will go down with you to Egypt, and I will also bring you up (*'alah*) again." Jacob's exodus is what the NT would call the "firstfruits" of the promise of Israel's exodus out of Egypt (cf. 1 Cor. 15:20).

50:15–21 Upon the brothers' return to Egypt they are immediately concerned for their own future. They are worried that Joseph has merely been delaying his revenge out of concern for his father but, now that Jacob had died, will now destroy them (as Esau had planned to do with Jacob; cf. Gen. 27:41). It is to their credit that they acknowledge that they committed evil against Joseph (50:15). However, their strategy in response to their fears is less than ideal. They send Joseph a message that purportedly came from Jacob prior to his death: "Your father gave this command before he died: 'Say to Joseph: "Please forgive the transgression of your

---

[702] "The largeness of the procession is reinforced by the threefold use of *kol* in vv. 7 and 8" (Hamilton, *Genesis 18–50*, 696).
[703] Later, in Exodus, Pharaoh will suggest that the Israelite men go out into the wilderness to worship the Lord but that their wives, children, and livestock remain behind (Ex. 10:9–11, 24).
[704] Wenham (*Genesis 16–50*, 488) comments, "His burial procession from Egypt to Canaan is doubtless seen as a pledge or acted prophecy of the nation's future move (cf. 50:24–25 with Exod 13:19)"; so also Sailhamer, *Genesis*, 382.

brothers and their sin, because they did evil to you."' And now, please forgive the transgression of the servants of the God of your father" (v. 17). This message is likely a fabrication, since, if he had intended to communicate anything like this to Joseph, he would have had plenty of opportunity to do so personally prior to his death.[705]

Joseph's response to his brothers' fear is to weep afresh, just as he had done when they were finally reconciled (v. 17; cf. 45:2). Their doubts about his intentions reopen old wounds. Even then the brothers are still fearful, prostrating themselves before him and offering themselves as his slaves, fulfilling Joseph's boyhood dreams one final time (50:18). Yet Joseph has no desire for vengeance, for the same reason that he had no desire to sin with Potiphar's wife: his faith in God takes priority over personal desires (v. 19; cf. 39:9). He acknowledges the reality of a divine judge, which frees him from needing to pursue vengeance for himself (Lev. 19:18; Rom. 12:19, quoting Deut. 32:35). As a result, because he is not God, he can say to his brothers what God often says to his people: "Do not fear" (Hb. *'al-tira'u*; Gen. 50:19).

Not only does Joseph not need to exact vengeance from his brothers; he has learned to recognize the good hand of God in his sufferings and losses. He too does not minimize his brothers' sin; they genuinely meant to do evil against him, and they carried that evil plan through. However, God's plan has triumphed over theirs, bringing good out of their evil (v. 20).[706] God's purpose in permitting the brothers to do evil was to save lives—the lives of the brothers, as well as many innocent men, women and children, both within the family of promise and outside it (v. 20). This plan has now successfully been carried out, so who is Joseph to hold a grudge against his brothers?

Joseph's response goes much further than a refusal to exact vengeance against his brothers. On the contrary, he himself (the "I" is emphatic in Hebrew) will continue to provide for them and for their little ones, repaying evil with good (v. 21; cf. Luke 6:27–31).[707] The famine has been over for many years at this point, but Joseph's position of power means he can still help his family in many ways. The contrast would be sharp for the original readers of Genesis, who had grown up under an oppressive Egyptian regime that had forgotten Joseph and his many contributions to its welfare (Ex. 1:8). The result had been oppression and bondage for Israel, precisely the judgment that Joseph has chosen not to execute on his brothers.

50:22–26 The book of Genesis closes with another good death, bracketing the reiterated forgiveness of Joseph's brothers. In this case it is the death of Joseph at 110 years old, the ideal lifetime in Egyptian thinking (vv. 22). Joseph not only

---

[705] Cf. Philip E. Satterthwaite, "Narrative Criticism: The Theological Implications of Narrative Techniques," in *A Guide to Old Testament Theology and Exegesis*, ed. Willem A. VanGemeren (Grand Rapids, MI: Zondervan, 1999), 126.
[706] God's unique power to discriminate between good and evil, as well as his power to bring good out of repeated human evil, has been a consistent theme throughout Genesis. Cf. Mathews, *Genesis 11:27–50:26*, 927.
[707] Kidner, *Genesis*, 234.

sees his children's children—a great blessing in a context of generally short life expectancy—but the third generation as well (v. 23).[708] The children of Machir, Manasseh's son, are (Hb.) "born on Joseph's knees," (v. 23; cf. ESV mg.). In context this may mean no more than that the children are placed in Joseph's lap when they are born, so that he might see them (cf. NIV), or it may have a more formal sense of adoption into special rights of inheritance (ESV: "counted as Joseph's own"; cf. 30:3; 48:12). Given Jacob's favoring of the younger son, Ephraim, over Manasseh (48:18–19), it would be striking for Joseph to single out one of Manasseh's grandsons for special treatment.

Joseph's final words are delivered to "his brothers" (50:24), which here likely has the sense of his kinsmen of the next generation, since Joseph's actual brothers are mostly older than him and he lives an unusually long life. They are the same group as the "sons of Israel" mentioned in verse 25. To the next generation Joseph passes on his own assurance of faith that God will continue to be with them in Egypt after his death (v. 24). For God to "visit" his people (Hb. *paqad*; vv. 24, 25) means a significant intervention in their lives for blessing or judgment.[709] In context this suggests either that their situation in Egypt has already worsened[710] or that Joseph anticipates that their future situation will not be as favorable after his death as it once had been, necessitating divine deliverance. God has already told Abraham that his offspring would be servants in another land for four hundred years (15:13), so Joseph's words may simply reflect that oracle. Either way, Joseph has faith that God will not abandon Israel but will at the right time bring them back to the Land of Promise.

Jacob had expressed his faith in the promise by insisting that his sons swear that his corpse will be repatriated to the land of Canaan upon his death and buried there (47:29–31). Joseph exhibits his faith in a different way, making his descendants swear to bury him in a portable coffin so that, when the Israelites make their journey to the Promised Land, they might bring his bones with them (50:25; cf. Heb. 11:22).[711] In some respects this is an act of even greater faith than Jacob's, since he is quite literally staking his permanent resting place on the realization of the Lord's promise. If Israel remains in Egypt forever, then Joseph's bones will do likewise.

So Joseph dies at a good old age surrounded by his family, as Jacob had done (Gen. 50:26). He too is embalmed, as Jacob had been, not out of Egyptian superstition but in order to prepare his body for its final journey, when God fulfills his word to his people. Genesis thus ends on a slightly anticlimactic note; the end of

---

708 Ephraim's children of the third generation are probably Ephraim's grandchildren, to match the grandchildren of Manasseh in the second half of the verse; the same unusual blessing is granted to Job in Job 42:16.
709 Ross (*Creation and Blessing*, 716) comments, "The verb *paqad*, 'visit,' signifies divine intervention for the sake of blessing or cursing—both, in the case of the exodus, in which Israel was delivered at the expense of the Egyptians. The word usually carries the connotation that destinies would be changed by the visitation from on high."
710 So Sarna (*Genesis*, 351), who also notes the absence of any extended national mourning period recorded after the death of Joseph.
711 Coffins—or, to be more precise, sarcophagi—were characteristic of Egyptian burial practices and are nowhere else mentioned in the Bible; cf. Hamilton, *Genesis 19–50*, 712.

this book is simply the introduction to the next chapter in the story, which will relate Israel's exodus out of Egypt and the journey of Joseph's bones to their homeland. Exodus begins by listing those who make the journey to Egypt with Jacob and Joseph's death (Ex. 1:1–6). It recounts God's affirmation that he has "observed" (*paqad*) his people (Ex. 3:16). And it notes the presence of Joseph's bones alongside Moses and the people on their journey out of the land of Egypt (Ex. 13:19). The book of Genesis is a book of beginnings, but its end is very far from the end of the story of God's work among his people.

Response

Death is not the end. Both Jacob and Joseph in their own ways use their deaths and burials as opportunities to proclaim their faith in God's promises of the land and thus, ultimately, what the land promise has always pointed to: an eternal heavenly inheritance. Christians too die, and we inter our bones in the ground in the sure hope of the resurrection of the dead. Death remains the final enemy, but in Christ that enemy has been defeated; its sting is gone, because our sins have been forgiven. Christ himself has gone through death and been raised as the firstfruits from the dead, assuring us of our own resurrection if we are in him (cf. 1 Corinthians 15). We may therefore face death without fear, confident that in due time God will visit our perishable bodies and raise them imperishable in a glorified state.

Genesis 50 also addresses the challenge of living, especially as those who are sinners and are sinned against, as people who must forgive others and need their forgiveness in turn. Joseph shows us that forgiveness does not mean denying the existence of evil or sin; if there is no sin, there is nothing to forgive. We do not merely make mistakes or mess up our lives; we commit acts of evil against one another—sometimes premeditated and deliberate acts. Forgiveness means acknowledging the reality of that evil and the genuine pain we have suffered, while at the same time refusing to hold that pain against the other person. Forgiveness acknowledges that evil fully deserves judgment, and forgiveness leaves room for God to judge, while also removing ourselves from that judicial role. Forgiveness is thus freeing for the forgiver as well as for the person forgiven, acknowledging that God has planned good out of that evil.

The brothers, meanwhile, demonstrate by their response how hard it can be to receive forgiveness and genuinely believe that we have been forgiven. This is true not merely on a human level but as sinners before a holy God. Our failure to believe that we are forgiven leaves us fearful and evasive, seeking constantly to find assurance of God's favor. We live our lives perpetually convinced that God is out to get us, interpreting every providential setback as further proof that God is our enemy.

The declaration "You meant evil against me, but God meant it for good" (Gen. 50:20) holds a climactic position in the book of Genesis, inviting readers to regard the whole book through this lens. Adam and Eve's sin, which brought death and destruction into the world, was genuinely sinful and continues to have horrific effects on their descendants after them. Evil is real, and the world is deeply scarred as a result. Yet God planned even their sin and is working to bring his good out of all things that transpire in this world, good and evil alike.

The supreme example of the plans of wicked men being part of God's good plan for his people comes at the cross, the ultimate visitation of God for blessing and judgment, as Peter told his hearers on the day of Pentecost: "This Jesus, delivered up according to the definite plan and foreknowledge of God, you crucified and killed by the hands of lawless men. God raised him up, loosing the pangs of death, because it was not possible for him to be held by it" (Acts 2:23–24). At the cross we see evil judged in the person of Jesus, the only completely innocent person who ever lived. All of God's outrage at the horrific damage that our sin causes in this world, from Adam onward, was laid upon him. He was cut off from the loving gaze of his Father and enveloped in the coldness and darkness of hell's utter abandonment. But at the cross we also see the most profound evil being turned around for the most profound good, as through that terrible death we are set free from the wrath of God and enveloped in the eternal smile of the Father's favor and blessing. The one who sits in God's place as our judge says to us, "I do not condemn you; now go, and sin no more." Not only does God not judge us, but in Christ he blesses us with every spiritual blessing in the heavenly realm (Eph. 1:3–14).

It is in Christ that we see the fulfillment of the promises set in motion in Genesis. He is the seed of the woman who came to bruise the serpent's head (Gen. 3:15). In him the land and seed blessings given to Abraham become blessing to the whole world, as the Gentiles too become spiritual children of Abraham through faith in Christ (Rom. 4:16–17). Through Christ we gain access to the tree of life in the new Jerusalem, a blessing that no sin will ever jeopardize. The God who created all things for himself and his own glory in Genesis 1 will bring that perfect plan to fruition in the new creation in Revelation 22, and the key to that fulfillment is Jesus Christ.

EXODUS

Jay Sklar

INTRODUCTION TO

EXODUS

Overview

As Exodus begins the Israelites are enslaved in Egypt and in danger of being wiped out by Pharaoh and the Egyptians (ch. 1). As Exodus ends the Israelites are free and safely encamped at Mount Sinai, where the Lord has entered into a covenant relationship with them and has come down in glory to dwell in their midst (ch. 40). Exodus tells the story of how this change in fortunes happens. It emphasizes the Lord's faithfulness to his covenant promises, his power to keep those promises, his desire to dwell among his covenant people, and his call for them to be a holy nation that embodies his character for all the world to see.[1]

The story may be thought of in six movements. The Lord delivers his people from slavery (1:1–15:21), leads them to Mount Sinai (15:22–17:16), and enters into a covenant relationship with them (18:1–24:11). Desiring to be near his covenant people, he gives Moses instructions for building his royal residence, the tabernacle, in their midst (24:12–31:18). While this is taking place the people commit full-scale rebellion against the Lord, making and worshiping a golden calf. The covenant is broken, and the story now describes the consequences that come as well as how the Lord graciously restores the covenant (32:1–34:35). With the covenant renewed the Lord's royal tabernacle is built, and then the Lord comes down in glory to dwell in the midst of his covenant people (35:1–40:38).

Considering each of these movements in more detail will help to sharpen our understanding of the story's shape and emphases.

THE ISRAELITES' NEED OF DELIVERANCE AND HOW

THE LORD BRINGS IT ABOUT (1:1–15:21)

Exodus begins with the Israelites in desperate need of deliverance and the Lord powerfully at work to provide it. By rescuing Israel the Lord shows his faithfulness

---

[1] Exodus often addresses issues that arise also in the books of Leviticus and Numbers, making those latter books especially helpful in illuminating Exodus. Throughout this commentary I will weave in observations from commentaries I have written on Leviticus and Numbers but will usually footnote those observations if the quotation is particularly lengthy. Those commentaries are Jay Sklar, *Leviticus: An Introduction and Commentary*, TOTC (Downers Grove, IL: InterVarsity Press, 2014); Jay Sklar, *Leviticus: A Discourse Analysis of the Hebrew Bible*, ZECOT (Grand Rapids, MI: Zondervan Academic, 2023); Jay Sklar, *Numbers*, The Story of God Bible Commentary (Grand Rapids, MI: Zondervan Academic, 2023).

to his covenant promises and also his sovereign strength over all earthly and heavenly powers.

As the book opens the Israelites are suffering under brutal Egyptian slavery and are under threat of being annihilated by Pharaoh and the Egyptians (ch. 1). A deliverer is clearly needed. Chapter 2 then introduces Moses, whom the Lord will use to lead his people out of Egypt, but by the chapter's end Moses is forced to flee Egypt and live in Midian, far away from the people he is to deliver. How can the Israelites be saved?

To this point Exodus has made little mention of the Lord. That now changes, and chapter 2 ends by noting how the Lord has heard the Israelites' cries for help and has decided to act in keeping with his covenant promises (2:23–25). Salvation will come, because God will bring it about! From this point onward the Lord and his appointed deliverer, Moses, are the story's central characters.

In chapters 3–4 the Lord reveals himself to Moses as the great I Am and equips him for the task of delivering Israel. The deliverance itself takes place over many chapters (5:1–15:21), with a strong emphasis on the ways in which the Lord shows that he, not Pharaoh, is the true king of power and that he, not Egypt's gods, is the true heavenly king. This theme is well captured by the song that concludes chapter 15, especially its last line: "The LORD will reign forever and ever!" (15:18).

THE LORD LEADS HIS PEOPLE TO MOUNT SINAI (15:22–17:16)

These chapters describe the Israelites' travel from Egypt to Mount Sinai. Testing is a theme here: the Lord faithfully tests the people for their good, and the people faithlessly test the Lord in their doubt (15:22–17:7). The stories thus introduce us to the Israelites' fickle faith and the Lord's patience and grace with his slow-to-believe people. He is truly "merciful and gracious, slow to anger, and abounding in steadfast love and faithfulness" (34:6). The testing stories are followed by another instance of the Lord's delivering his people from an enemy nation (17:8–16), underscoring that he is a God of power who protects and watches over his people.

THE LORD ENTERS INTO A COVENANT RELATIONSHIP WITH HIS PEOPLE (18:1–24:11)

Having brought the Israelites to Mount Sinai, the Lord prepares them to enter into a covenant relationship with him (18:1–19:25), and then he enters into that covenant with them (20:1–24:11). He does not want simply to rescue them; he wants to be in relationship with them.

As chapter 18 begins, someone from the nations (Jethro) recognizes that "the LORD is greater than all gods" (18:11), which reemphasizes the theme of the Lord's sovereign might—and reminds us that God's desire to bless the nations through Israel is not forgotten (Gen. 12:3). Chapter 18 finishes by describing Israel's judicial system (Ex. 18:13–27), which prepares us for the giving of the law that is about to come. In the meantime the Israelites must prepare themselves for the Lord's appearing by keeping themselves ritually pure (19:1–15), a signal that the Lord who will appear to them is holy. When the Lord then comes down in glory on the mountain, the sight is so awesome that it leaves the Israelites trembling with fear (19:16–25). This is no accident. The Lord is encouraging them to the type of godly fear that leads to faithful obedience (20:20). His people must keep the covenant if the world is to have any chance of learning who the Lord is.

In this awe-inspiring context the Lord delivers his covenant laws (20:1–23:33). In keeping with ancient Near Eastern convention the covenant is expressed as a "suzerain-vassal" (or "king-servant") covenant, in which the Lord is covenant king and the Israelites are his covenant people. The laws he gives them help them to know how to live as his "kingdom of priests and a holy nation" (19:6), since they show the Israelites how to embody his character of goodness, mercy, justice, and love. This in turn will enable them to make known to the world the glory of who the Lord is and the glory of being in relationship with him.

THE LORD GIVES MOSES INSTRUCTIONS FOR BUILDING HIS TABERNACLE IN ISRAEL'S MIDST (24:12–31:18)

In Israel's day a king could enter into a covenant with distant nations among whom he never lived. For example, Ahaz, king of Judah, became covenant servant of Tiglath-Pileser, king of Assyria (2 Kings 16:7), who never lived in Judah. This was common in the ancient Near East. But the Lord is a covenant king who wants to dwell in the very midst of his covenant people. He therefore commands a tabernacle to be built.

The Lord's instructions make clear the tabernacle is a palace-tent: it has rich fabrics, ornate furniture, uniformed palace servants (the priests), and a throne room in which the Lord sits enthroned over the ark. The ark is in the tabernacle's innermost room (the Most Holy Place) and contains the covenant tablets. Their placement here, in the tabernacle's very heart, testifies to the covenant's central importance in Israel's relationship with the Lord and to the fact that he sits enthroned over those tablets as a divine witness to what they say. Moreover, his presence in the tabernacle testifies to his desire to be with his people, which is a main reason that he redeemed them: "They shall know that I am the LORD their God, who brought them out of the land of Egypt *that I might dwell among them*" (Ex. 29:46). He is a God who longs to be with us, near us, and among us.

THE PEOPLE REBEL AGAINST THE LORD; MOSES INTERCEDES; THE LORD GRACIOUSLY RENEWS THE COVENANT (32:1–34:35)

The story now plunges into a valley of tragedy before rising again to the heights of glory, a rise that can occur only because of the intercession of a faithful servant and the forgiving mercy of a compassionate God.

At the same time the Lord is giving instructions that will enable him to draw near to his people, his people abandon the very covenant they have just entered with him. Fearing that Moses will never return, they build a golden calf to go before them and worship it with wild excitement (32:1–18). When Moses learns of their faithlessness, he shatters the covenant tablets to symbolize graphically what they have done (32:18–20). He spends the rest of chapters 32–34 bringing judgment to bear for their infidelity (32:21–29) but also interceding on their behalf, asking the Lord not to abandon them but to show his grace and mercy by renewing the covenant (32:30–34:35). Moses is a shepherd who cares deeply for his sheep. The Lord hears Moses' prayers and, in so doing, provides one of the fullest descriptions of his own character to this point in the Bible, a description that emphasizes above all his strong mercy, forgiveness, and steadfast love (34:6–7a). Yes, he is a God who brings judgment and discipline for sin (34:7b), but his deepest longing is that we might know his merciful love, a merciful love that makes it possible for him to have relationship with sinful people.

THE TABERNACLE IS BUILT, AND THE LORD COMES TO DWELL IN THE MIDST OF HIS PEOPLE (35:1–40:38)

The story comes to a glorious climax: the Israelites are renewed in their faith, and the Lord comes down to dwell amid his covenant people.

With the covenant reestablished, the tabernacle may now be built (35:1–40:33). The Israelites demonstrate their renewed faith by contributing with great generosity to the tabernacle's needs (35:20–36:7) and carrying out the Lord's commands exactly as he has given them (38:22; 39:1, 5, 7, 42). The tabernacle is built both beautifully and faithfully.

The moment the tent is complete, the Lord comes down in glory to dwell within it (40:34–38). "It's as if God could not wait to be where he had wanted to be all along—in the midst of his people."[2] He has redeemed them so that he might have relationship with them.

Exodus thus finishes by sounding a theme central to the biblical story. In Eden God comes to *walk* in the garden with Adam and Eve (Gen. 3:8); in the tabernacle he comes down so he might *walk* among the Israelites in their midst (Lev. 26:12). In the tabernacle he comes to *dwell* among them (Ex. 29:45); in Jesus he comes to *dwell* in our midst (John 1:14), and through his Spirit he makes his *dwelling* among the people of his church and *walks* among us (2 Cor. 6:16). At the end of time, when the heavenly city comes down to earth, a loud voice will declare, "Behold, *the dwelling place* of God is with man. He will *dwell* with them, and they will be his people, and God himself will be with them as their God. He will wipe away every tear from their eyes" (Rev. 21:3–4a). This is the God we see in Exodus. This is the God we see in Jesus. This is the God who invites us into relationship with him today through Christ.

Title

The Hebrew title of this book is "Names." This is because the Hebrew names of Pentateuchal books are taken from the first few words of each book's opening sentence. In this case, "These are the *names* of the sons of Israel" (Ex. 1:1). The LXX and Vulgate use the title "Exodus," which has been followed in the Christian tradition and means "going out, departure." This name highlights the central role in the book of the Lord's leading his people out of slavery and toward the Promised Land.

---

[2] Christopher J. H. Wright, *Exodus* (Grand Rapids, MI: Zondervan, 2021), 610.

Author and Date

Since the date of the material is connected directly to questions of authorship, we may begin with the latter. Three questions will guide our discussion. First, who was the source of the material found in Exodus? Second, does Exodus fit historically within the time period the Bible assigns to it? Third, who put the material in its final form?

WHO WAS THE SOURCE OF THE MATERIAL FOUND IN EXODUS?

Although the Lord is the ultimate source of Scripture, he also inspired humans to record it (2 Tim. 3:16). From this perspective, who was the human source of the material found in Exodus? Close attention to the book suggests the answer to be Moses.

First, Moses is identified explicitly as writing down certain portions of Exodus: the beginning of chapter 17 (cf. 17:14), most of chapters 20–23 (cf. 24:4, 7), and 34:11–26 (cf. 34:27–28).

Second, the content of Exodus 20–23, which Moses is commanded to write down, is revelation he received for the Israelites while on Mount Sinai (24:4, 7). But the text is also clear that Moses received chapters 25–31 for the Israelites while on Mount Sinai (cf. 31:18), and a natural assumption is that he wrote down these words as well. Stated differently, it is natural to assume that chapters 20–23 set a pattern Moses followed elsewhere, namely, to record revelation given by the Lord for the Israelites so they would know what the Lord wanted them to do.

Third, Exodus 17:14 and Numbers 33:2 both give clear examples of Moses' writing down various experiences of Israel in the wilderness. In other words he recorded not only revelation but also historical events to which he was witness. Once more a natural assumption is that he followed this pattern elsewhere, making it plausible that Moses would be the one responsible for recording his early flight from Egypt (Ex. 2:11–25), the Lord's deliverance of the Israelites in the book's beginning (chs. 3–19), and the story of their building the tabernacle at the book's end (chs. 35–40).[3] The plausibility of this understanding is strengthened by the fact that Moses not only was an eyewitness to the events of these chapters but also received revelation from the Lord during them (which, as argued above, he was likely to record). These chapters repeatedly refer either to the Lord's speaking to Moses (3:4, 15; 6:1, 10; 7:1, 8, 14; 8:5; 10:1; 40:1; etc.) or to Moses as the one passing on the Lord's words (35:1, 4, 30).

Finally, since Moses is the central dialogue partner with the Lord in Exodus 32–34, he is the most natural source of that material.

The above suggests that Moses was the primary source of most of the material found in Exodus. In light of on the biblical data, it seems he would have recorded this material sometime in the fifteenth to thirteenth centuries BC, depending on the date of the exodus (cf. Interpretive Challenges: The Date of the Exodus). This leads to our next question.

---

[3] As for the story of Moses' birth, hiding, and adoption (2:1–10), it is not a stretch to think that Moses learned of them from his family, nor a stretch to think that Moses learned of Israel's experience in Exodus 1 from his family or other Israelites.

DOES EXODUS FIT HISTORICALLY WITHIN THE TIME PERIOD THE BIBLE ASSIGNS TO IT?

From the end of the nineteenth century through much of the twentieth a majority of historical-critical scholars embraced Wellhausen's articulation of the documentary hypothesis, which argued that the Pentateuch consists of sources that came long after the biblical time of Moses.[4] In this schema Exodus consists mostly of the J source (c. 840 BC), E source (c. 700 BC), and P source (c. 500–450 BC). Scholars in this camp thus tend to view Exodus as historically unreliable since they understand it to have come long after the events it describes.[5] Rather than being a historical account dating to the second half of the second millennium BC, the material is understood to reflect political or religious interests of much later writers.

Beginning in the second half of the twentieth century and continuing to the present day, however, historical-critical scholars have begun to reflect a wider diversity of views on the origins of the Pentateuch. While North American and Israeli scholars still tend to accept some version of Wellhausen's formulation of the documentary hypothesis, European scholars do not, even to the point of questioning the existence of the J and E sources (though typically not questioning that the Pentateuchal material is late).[6] On the one hand this shows that historical-critical scholars have not reached a consensus regarding the Pentateuch's formation. On the other hand, as far as the historicity of the Pentateuch's contents is concerned, a general historical skepticism remains.

Is such a skepticism warranted? The biblical authors certainly did not think so. They constantly refer to God's acts in Exodus as historical events that reveal his character and thus have ongoing implications for us today (cf. Relationship to the Rest of the Bible and to Christ).

But is there warrant for such belief? More specifically, is there warrant for thinking that Exodus overlaps enough with the historical and cultural realities of the second half of the second millennium that its material could date to that time and could therefore accurately represent actual historical events?

Many have answered this question in the negative by pointing out a lack of direct evidence in certain key areas. But, as the archaeological proverb states, "Absence of evidence is not evidence of absence." Hawkins expands on this point:

> Historian David Hackett Fischer calls this approach the myth of "negative proof," which he describes as "an attempt to sustain a factual proposition

---

[4] For a helpful survey and critique of this approach cf. T. D. Alexander, *From Paradise to the Promised Land: An Introduction to the Pentateuch*, 4th ed. (Grand Rapids, MI: Baker, 2022), 229–301.
[5] A related issue is that many historical-critical scholars approach the text from naturalistic presuppositions. "Since the eighteenth century historical research has been dominated by certain important presuppositions: (1) the central role of human reason in the quest for truth, and (2) the rejection of divine revelation. Under the influence of 'modern naturalism' it is no longer fashionable to consider divine interventions as occurring. Consequently, it is assumed that miraculous events never occur, and God himself does not appear or speak"; T. Desmond Alexander, *Exodus*, ApOTC 2 (Downers Grove, IL: InterVarsity Press, 2017), 16. Such presuppositions would mean large swaths of Exodus do not—indeed, cannot—correspond to historical reality. As Alexander goes on to note, however, "These presuppositions regarding the centrality of human reason and a closed universe are articles of faith and, therefore, are open to scrutiny and rejection" (17).
[6] See overview in Thomas B. Dozeman, Konrad Schmid, and Baruch J. Schwartz, eds., *The Pentateuch: International Perspectives on Current Research*, FAT 78 (Tübingen: Mohr Siebeck, 2011), xi–xii.

merely by negative evidence." He argues that evidence must always be positive, and that "Negative evidence is a contradiction in terms—it is not evidence at all."[7]

The above is especially important to remember with regard to four specific areas in Exodus regarding which there is a lack of confirmatory evidence. Table 2.1 summarizes Hawkins' discussion.[8]

TABLE 2.1: Responding to Skepticism about Exodus's Historicity

Area Where Evidence Is Lacking	Response
No mention of "Hebrews" or "Israelites" in official Egyptian records of the time.	Egyptians called their West Semitic slaves "Asiatics," with no further distinctions; one therefore does not expect to read of "Hebrews" or "Israelites" in particular.
No inscriptional evidence on Egyptian monuments of the events in Exodus.	"Public stelae were designed to laud the pharaoh and his achievements, not highlight his gaffes. A pharaoh would not have commissioned a stele that acknowledged a failure on his part."[9]
No non-inscriptional evidence (such as on papyrus) of the Israelites in the Egyptian Delta.	"There are almost no papyri from dynastic times, and none at all have been found in the eastern Nile Delta where the Hebrews dwelled. It is not that there are no papyri from the eastern Nile Delta that relate to the events in the book of Exodus; there are no papyri from the eastern Nile Delta at all."[10]
No archaeological evidence of Israelite campsites.	"While it is true that sedentary people in settled areas usually leave a lot of archaeological evidence, in desert areas the opposite is true. The archaeological evidence produced by nomadic societies is negligible, such that they are often archaeologically invisible."[11]

But this still leaves the question of whether Exodus fits well within the historical and cultural realities of the second half of the second millennium. If this question can be answered affirmatively, it would not prove that Exodus was written at this time but would leave open the possibility that it was and thus also the possibility that it does correspond to actual historical events.

Since the end of the twentieth century, several specialists have answered the question positively by comparing what we find in Exodus to what we know of

---

[7] Ralph K. Hawkins, *Discovering Exodus: Content, Interpretation, Reception* (Grand Rapids, MI: Eerdmans, 2021), 23–24; the citations are from David Hackett Fischer, *Historians' Fallacies: Toward a Logic of Historical Thought* (New York: Harper & Row, 1970), 47, 62.
[8] Hawkins, *Discovering Exodus*, 22–23, 31–34.
[9] Hawkins, *Discovering Exodus*, 23.
[10] Hawkins, *Discovering Exodus*.
[11] Hawkins, *Discovering Exodus*, 32. See the similar conclusion in Thomas W. Davis, "The Elusive Signature of Nomads in Sinai," in *Did I Not Bring Israel out of Egypt? Biblical, Archaeological, and Egyptological Perspectives on the Exodus Narratives*, ed. James K. Hoffmeier, Alan R. Millard, and Gary A. Rendsburg, BBRSup 13 (Winona Lake, IN: Eisenbrauns, 2016), 226: "Finding direct evidence of a single-use campsite of a nomadic group that can be dated in isolation in the Sinai is a totally unrealistic expectation." This is due to several factors: pottery is one of the main archaeological artifacts to look for, but its use was rare among nomads (who preferred skins, since they were lightweight and traveled more easily); desert wind can erode sites, collapsing one site into another, making it extremely difficult to isolate one site from another; and nomads use tents, which "by their nature leave very little in the archaeological record"; Davis, "Elusive Signature," 225–226. The last citation is from Michael Homan, *To Your Tents O Israel: The Terminology, Function, Form and Symbolism of Tents in the Hebrew Bible and the Ancient Near East* (Leiden: Brill, 2002), 55. See also the summary in James K. Hoffmeier, *Ancient Israel in Sinai: The Evidence for the Authenticity of the Wilderness Tradition* (New York: Oxford University Press, 2005), 150–153.

historical and cultural realities in Egypt and the ancient Near East during the second half of the second millennium.[12] They have identified not only many indications that Exodus fits *well* in this time period but also some that indicate it fits *best* in this time period (and not a later one). The following is a noncomprehensive list of some of these finds.

Indications That Exodus Fits Well in the Second Half of the Second Millennium BC

(1) The description of brickmaking in Exodus aligns with realities dating back to the second millennium, including oversight by taskmasters who used corporal punishment, the difficulty of meeting brick quotas, and the importance of straw for the work.[13]

(2) "Tents were widely used in the ancient Near East during the second millennium as the dwelling for nomadic and traveling folk ... and ... as a shrine."[14] This fits with the Exodus account of the Israelites' use of tents for their dwellings (16:16) and the Lord's use of a tent for his (40:34).

(3) The layout of the tabernacle complex, with the Lord in his tent as king surrounded by a rectangular courtyard (27:9–19), parallels the plans of the camp of Ramesses II (mid-13th century BC), in which his tent is similarly surrounded by a rectangular courtyard. Moreover, in both cases the length-to-width ratio of the complex and camp is two to one, while the length-to-width ratio of each tent is three to one.[15]

(4) The materials used in the tabernacle—from the acacia wood to the gold overlay to the fine linen—all fit well in an Egyptian context of the second half of the second millennium.[16]

(5) The ark was a box associated with the deity (the Lord), covered in gold, with winged heavenly beings, and carried by priests on poles. All these features parallel boxes used as portable shrines in Egypt in the second half of the second millennium.[17]

Indications That Exodus Fits Best in the Second Half of the Second Millennium BC

(1) The form of the covenant between the Lord and Israel introduced in Exodus and concluded in Leviticus parallels Hittite treaties known from the second half of the second millennium and is closer in form to them than to first-millennium treaties.[18]

(2) In a study of the forty-two names mentioned in the exodus generation Hess notes that many of their verbal roots occur in West Semitic or Egyptian sources in the second millennium (where the Bible places the exodus) and the first millen-

---

[12] Cf. esp. James K. Hoffmeier, *Israel in Egypt: The Evidence for the Authenticity of the Exodus Tradition* (New York: Oxford University Press, 1997); Hoffmeier, *Ancient Israel in Sinai*; K. A. Kitchen, *On the Reliability of the Old Testament* (Grand Rapids, MI: Eerdmans, 2006); Hoffmeier, Millard, and Rendsburg, *Did I Not Bring Israel out of Egypt?*
[13] Hoffmeier, *Israel in Egypt*, 115; K. A. Kitchen, "From the Brickfields of Egypt," *TynBul* 27 (1976): 137–147.
[14] Hoffmeier, *Ancient Israel in Sinai*, 198; cf. fuller discussion on 196–198.
[15] Hoffmeier, *Ancient Israel in Sinai*, 205–208.
[16] Hoffmeier, *Ancient Israel in Sinai*, 209–212.
[17] Hoffmeier, *Ancient Israel in Sinai*, 213–214.
[18] Hoffmeier, *Ancient Israel in Sinai*, 183–192.

nium (long after the biblical date of the exodus). But he also notes that *none* of their roots is currently attested only in the first millennium (the time when historical-critical scholars date the book), and two or three of them occur *only* in the second millennium. "It remains to be explained how roots that have no clear attestation in West Semitic personal names of the first millennium BC would have been used to invent early Israelite person names."[19] This suggests that the names in Exodus are "authentic personal names from the Late Bronze Age [i.e., 1550–1200 BC] of the West Semitic world."[20]

In short, while the above evidence does not prove that the material in Exodus dates to the second half of the second millennium BC, it does show that it is plausible (and in some cases likely) that Exodus was written during this time. This also means it is plausible that a man named Moses who lived during this time was the primary human source of the book's material (as the book itself suggests), and this commentary will proceed on that assumption. This also leads to a final question.

WHO PUT THE MATERIAL IN ITS FINAL FORM?

By and large, conservative scholars have understood Moses to be not only the human source of Exodus but also the human source and author of a substantial amount of the Pentateuch. I use the word "substantial" for the simple reason that most conservative scholars agree that Moses did not write his own death notice (Deut. 34:5–12) and that other Pentateuchal passages provide descriptions that seem to come from after Moses' time, such as the mention of Dan (Gen. 14:14) and the reference to Israel's having already conquered the land (Deut. 2:12b).[21] To this we could add two verses that occur back-to-back in Exodus:

> "The people of Israel ate the manna forty years, till they came to a habitable land. They ate the manna till they came to the border of the land of Canaan." (Ex. 16:35)

> "(An omer is the tenth part of an ephah.)" (Ex. 16:36)

The first of these describes an event from after Moses' death (cf. Josh. 5:12), while the second suggests a period of time when the omer measurement was no longer in use.[22]

There is no question, therefore, that some editorial work took place on the Pentateuch—including Exodus—after the death of Moses. But how much of such editorial work exists, and why was it done?

---

19 Richard S. Hess, "Onomastics of the Exodus Generation in the Book of Exodus," in in *Did I Not Bring Israel out of Egypt? Biblical, Archaeological, and Egyptological Perspectives on the Exodus Narratives*, ed. James K. Hoffmeier, Alan R. Millard, and Gary A. Rendsburg, *BBRSup* 13 (Winona Lake, IN: Eisenbrauns, 2016), 48.
20 Hess, "Onomastics of the Exodus Generation," 48.
21 While affirming the presence of editorial work sometimes makes conservative scholars nervous, it need not. The Lord can inspire those who edit material just as he does those who first write it, as the Gospel of Luke so well attests (Luke 1:1–4). Cf. M. A. Grisanti, "Inspiration, Inerrancy, and the OT Canon: The Place of Textual Updating in an Inerrant View of Scripture," *JETS* 44/4 (2001): 577–598.
22 At the same time, "The reference to an omer and the need to explain it argue for the story's antiquity" (i.e., that the material comes from an early time); Peter Enns, *Exodus*, NIVAC (Grand Rapids, MI: Zondervan, 2000), 328.

Did such editorial work include simply the isolated examples above, which tend to update place names, explain customs no longer known to later readers, and note when an event came to completion, or was there a much more thorough revision of the materials?

Further, was the purpose of such potential work simply to update the text with historic and linguistic facts so that a later generation could better understand it, or was the goal to shape the material more fully to address specific issues a later generation was facing?

While scholars will undoubtedly continue to debate the answers to these questions, it may be noted that Exodus invites us to read it as a work that came to the Israelites as they fled Egypt and headed toward the Promised Land. As such, we are invited to step into that world while reading, meaning our first question of the text should always be to ask what the text would have meant to the first and second generation of Israelites coming out of Egypt. Only then will we be ready to ask what the text means for the Lord's followers today.[23]

Genre and Literary Features

Above all else, the book of Exodus tells a story: a story of a people in hardship and of a God who delivers them and comes to dwell in their midst. The most commonly used genre in the book is narrative, the perfect vehicle for communicating the various elements of a story from initial conflict, to plot turns and twists, and to final resolution. Indeed, Exodus's overarching story consists of several smaller stories, each with its own crisis and resolution, such as Pharaoh's attempting to decimate the Israelites and the Lord's preserving them (Exodus 1); the possible death of Moses as a baby and his rescue and adoption by Pharaoh's daughter (ch. 2); Pharaoh's refusal to release the Israelites and his driving the people out of his land (chs. 5–12); the Israelites' being trapped between the sea and the Egyptian army, facing certain death, and the Egyptian army's being the ones who die in the sea (ch. 14); the Israelites' lacking food and water in the wilderness and the Lord's miraculously providing it (chs. 16–17); and the Israelites' breaking the covenant and deserving to be wiped out and the Lord's restoring the covenant, taking them back as his people, and coming to dwell in their midst (chs. 32–34; 40). If Exodus is compared to a mountain range, each of these smaller stories is a mountain forming that range.

But narrative is not the only genre found within the book, since different aspects of its story require different tools to tell them well. Major events in a nation's life may be remembered by means of annual celebrations or regular customs, which gives rise in Exodus to instructions for the Passover, the Feast of

---

[23] Those who believe much more thorough revision and/or shaping of the text was done in order to have the material address specific issues facing a later generation will also want to ask an intermediary question: "What would this have meant to the later generation for whom the shaping of the text was done?" At this point in our knowledge, however, it is not clear that we can confidently identify who such an audience might have been. See especially the helpful reminders in Benjamin D. Sommer, "Dating Pentateuchal Texts and the Perils of Pseudo-Historicism," in *The Pentateuch: International Perspectives on Current Research*, ed. Thomas B. Dozeman, Konrad Schmid, and Baruch J. Schwartz, FAT 78 (Tübingen: Mohr Siebeck, 2011), 85–108.

Unleavened Bread, and the consecration of the firstborn (chs. 12–13). A nation's major events are also often celebrated in song, which is what we find in the musical poetry of Exodus 15 as the Israelites celebrate the Lord's defeat of Egypt's army in the sea. The covenant the Lord enters into with Israel takes the form of an ancient Near Eastern treaty between a sovereign king and a nation, which includes a preamble, a historical prologue, stipulations, and blessings and curses, all of which can be found in Exodus 20–23.[24] And building a tabernacle requires something comparable to a construction manual, the focus of Exodus 25–31.

All the genres described above have been woven together into the beautiful tapestry that is Exodus. The job of the interpreter is to recognize these different genres as they occur and to adopt the reading strategy appropriate for each. At appropriate points in the commentary I have sought to identify such strategies, especially when approaching genres that might be more unfamiliar to many readers.[25] Keeping such strategies in mind is one of the most helpful ways to appreciate what the text is saying and thus both the meaning and the beauty of Exodus's story.

A further aid in understanding the book is to appreciate its different literary features. Wright has provided a helpful listing, of which the following is a summary:[26]

- *Change of pace.* Exodus 2 covers a period of more than forty years, while Exodus 3–4 slows down to capture a single conversation, highlighting the importance of the conversation that takes place there.
- *Dialogue.* Dialogue is very "effective . . . in sustaining interest, illuminating conflicts, creating emotional and theological tension, and stretching out the resolution of issues. The dialogues between Moses and God are particularly rich, especially in the call narrative (chs. 3–4), and they carry the whole theological freight of those breathtaking chapters 32–34."[27]
- *Suspense.* Suspense is a common feature of storytelling, since it maintains our interest as we wait to find out what will happen. Chapter 14 begins with the Lord's telling the Israelites to turn back and camp by the sea, an event he says he will use to defeat Pharaoh (vv. 1–4). Just *how* he will do so is not revealed and, indeed, seems increasingly unlikely as the story continues and Israel is trapped between the Egyptian army and the sea. This only deepens the suspense—and keeps us reading! Such use of suspense occurs repeatedly in the book.
- *Patterning and threading.* "The account of the plagues on Egypt displays a subtle patterning—a triple series of threes, with certain repeating structural features. . . . Through the whole sequence are threaded some

---

[24] Cf. comments on 20:1–21; Section Overview of 23:20–33.
[25] Cf. discussion on Hebrew poetry in comment on 15:1–19 or on Hebrew law in the Section Overview of 20:1–21.
[26] Cf. Wright, *Exodus*, 6–8.
[27] Wright, *Exodus*, 7.

significant themes through the repetition of key words and phrases."[28] Recognizing such patterning and threading helps to make clear the text's narrative flow and emphases.

- *Repetition.* One of the features of Exodus that can puzzle modern readers is the large amount of repetition between Exodus 25–31 (which describes how to make the tabernacle) and Exodus 35–40 (which describes the Israelites' construction of it). From an efficiency perspective one could simply replace Exodus 35–40 with a summary statement, "The Israelites made the tabernacle just as the Lord had commanded." But doing so would miss an important point: by repeating so many of the details from Exodus 25–31 chapters 35–40 make clear the Israelites are obeying the Lord *exactly*, a central theme in this section.[29]

Further literary features—such as hyperbole, foreshadowing, and the like—will be pointed out in the commentary as we come across them. But the above summary of Exodus's genres and literary features is enough to show that its story is wonderfully rich and requires careful attention to understand and appreciate it in all its beauty.

Purpose and Theology of Exodus

The purpose of Exodus is to reveal God's character and his will for his people, Israel. Stated differently, its goal is to make clear who God is and who he wants his people to be. It achieves this purpose by focusing on various theological themes. We may begin with the themes describing God's character. The first five focus on the Lord as Israel's King, and the last two on the Lord as Israel's Father.[30]

YAHWEH, THE KING

In Exodus, kingship is one of the main means used to describe the Lord. This can be seen explicitly in the song of redemption, which concludes, "The LORD *will reign* forever and ever" (15:18). It can be seen implicitly in two of the book's main features: covenant and tabernacle. The covenant into which the Lord enters with Israel is a suzerain-vassal (or king-servant) covenant in which he is the sovereign king and Israel is his servant.[31] The tabernacle is his royal palace-tent in which he sits enthroned over the ark as covenant king (cf. comment on 25:17–22). Yahweh is thus the reigning covenant king.

But kingship by itself is not a virtue. History is full of kings who are devoted to their people's well-being but also of those who reign as cruel tyrants. Exodus therefore makes clear what type of king the Lord is—and the picture it paints is one of breathtaking awe and beauty.

---

28 Wright, *Exodus*, 8; cf. Overview of 7:8–11:10.
29 Cf. Overview of 35:1–40:38.
30 The following section is an expansion of introductory notes in Jay Sklar, "Exodus," The Gospel Coalition Commentary, https://www.thegospelcoalition.org/commentary/exodus.
31 Cf. comments on 20:1–21.

YAHWEH, THE KING OF COVENANT FAITHFULNESS

As Exodus begins we are told the Lord will deliver the Israelites from their trials because he has "remembered his covenant with Abraham, with Isaac, and with Jacob" (2:24). When he makes a promise, he keeps it. The rest of Exodus makes this clear by showing how the Lord begins to fulfill the promises he has made to Abraham, Isaac, and Jacob (cf. table 2.2). Yahweh is a king who is faithful to his covenant promises, and that faithfulness should encourage his people to obey him with bold trust.

TABLE 2.2: The Lord's Promises and Faithfulness in Genesis and Exodus

The Lord's Covenant Promises in Genesis	The Lord's Covenant Faithfulness in Exodus
To become a great nation (Gen. 12:2; 15:5; 17:5–6; 26:4; 28:14; 35:11; 46:3).	"The people of Israel were fruitful and increased greatly; they multiplied and grew exceedingly strong, so that the land was filled with them" (Ex. 1:7).
To give them a land (Gen. 12:1; 15:18–20; 26:3–4; 28:13; 35:12).	The Lord delivers Israel in order to bring them to the Promised Land (Ex. 3:8, 17; 6:8), and he provides his angel to lead them there (Ex. 23:20–23).
To curse the one who dishonors them (Gen. 12:3).	The Lord brings devastating strikes on Pharaoh and the Egyptians (chs. 7–12) and defeats them fully and finally in the sea (ch. 14).
To be their covenant God (Gen. 17:7–8; 28:15).	The Lord promises to redeem them in order to take them as his people (Ex. 6:6–7) and proceeds to do so, redeeming them (chs. 7–14) and then entering into covenant relationship with them (chs. 20–24).

YAHWEH, THE KING OF POWER

One reason the Lord can be faithful to his covenant promises is his sovereign power. No one can oppose his plans, for he is the true and sole King of heaven and earth. The strikes he brings on Egypt show that he is the true and sole King *of heaven* as the Egyptians' so-called "gods" are powerless before him (cf. comments on Ex. 7:8–13; 7:14–19; 10:21; 12:3–13 [at v. 12]; 15:1–19). Jethro, after hearing of the Lord's mighty redemption of Israel, states it succinctly: "Now I know that the LORD is greater than all gods" (18:11). But the Lord's defeat of Pharaoh and all his forces—the most powerful on the planet—shows that he is also the true and sole King *of earth*, the one before whom all other kings must bow in reverence (7:1–5; 9:13–30). Indeed, the text repeatedly notes that the Lord is sovereign over the decisions of Pharaoh's very heart (cf. comment on 4:21–23). The Lord is the true and sole King of heaven and earth, who reigns in sovereign majesty and might. All peoples are to obey him fully, and those who know him as their covenant God can rely on his strong protection and care.

YAHWEH, THE KING OF PRESENCE

As noted above (Cf. Overview), a king could enter into covenant with distant nations and never dwell among them. But the Lord is a king who seeks to live in the very midst of his people. Dwelling among them is in fact one of the very reasons that he redeems Israel: "I will dwell among the people of Israel and will be their God. And they shall know that I am the LORD their God, *who brought them out of the land of Egypt that I might dwell among them*. I am the LORD their God" (29:45–46). For the Lord redemption is always for the sake of relationship.

YAHWEH, THE KING OF FAITHFUL LOVE

The Lord's description of his character to Moses contains some of the most beautiful and hopeful words in Scripture: "The LORD, the LORD, a God merciful and gracious, slow to anger, and abounding in steadfast love and faithfulness, keeping steadfast love for thousands, forgiving iniquity and transgression and sin" (34:6–7a). Yes, he also brings discipline to bear on sin—as any loving parent does (34:7b). But the focus of his description is on his mercy and grace. His heart's first impulse toward his people is not judgment but faithful, kind, forgiving love (cf. comment on 34:1–8 [at vv. 5–7]). This in fact explains his desire to be with his people: we long to be near those we love.

YAHWEH, THE ADOPTING FATHER-KING

Pastor Tim Keller once tweeted that the only person who dares wake up a king at 3:00 a.m. for a glass of water is the king's child. His point was that God's people know him not simply as King but also as Father—which means they receive his special attention and care. Exodus affirms this reality for the Israelites when it records how the Lord refers to them as his firstborn son (4:22–23). As the comments on that passage will show, being a firstborn son in ancient Israel meant enjoying a special place of worth in the family, which in turn meant the Lord cared for Israel with a special love. He is a king who adopts those he rescues. They are his children, and he will protect, love, and care for them as his very own.

YAHWEH, THE REDEEMING FATHER-KING

Redemption connects naturally to the Lord's role as Father-King. The concept of redemption finds its roots in the social sphere, where it refers to one relative's rescuing another relative from servitude (Lev. 25:47–55). As applied to the Israelites' situation, the Lord is rescuing his son from cruel slavery in Egypt into the glorious freedom found in serving him. As Alexander aptly summarizes, "Since God has already spoken of Israel as his son (4:22), the liberation of the Israelites may be viewed . . . as a family affair."[32]

The book of Leviticus returns to the Lord's role as redeemer in the exodus. One of the reasons the Lord establishes the laws of jubilee is to create an ongoing institution of exodus-like redemption among his people (Lev. 25:54–55). As Hubbard notes,

> Put simply, redemption [in Lev. 25:54–55] amounts to an institutional Exodus in Israel. . . . It perpetuates the first liberation—that from Egyptian

---

32 Alexander, *Exodus*, ApOTC, 126.

slavery—within later, settled Israel. *It frees her from unending servitude to later Pharaohs within her own ranks.* . . . In short, through this institution, Yahweh provides . . . a "safety net" for vulnerable Israelites. In so doing, he shows himself to be the Great Kinsman, the powerful protector of the weak. Through redemption, he saves hopelessly poor citizens from an endless cycle of poverty. *He prevents a reversal of the Exodus—a relapse into the cruel hands of Israelite Pharaohs.*[33]

Through and through, the Lord is Israel's redeeming Father-King.

Having seen the themes of Exodus regarding the Lord, we may now turn to those regarding Israel. Three may be identified, each of which relates directly to the themes above regarding the Lord. This is no surprise. Exodus tells the story of the Lord's entering into relationship with Israel, and Israel is thus described in terms of the way she is to relate to him.

ISRAEL AS SERVANT

"Let my people go, that they may serve me" (Ex. 8:1; cf. 7:16; 8:20; 9:1, 13; 10:3). This text is programmatic for the book. Exodus describes how the Lord liberates his people from enslavement to a wicked ruler in order to serve him, the gracious King.

As noted at 3:12, the word "serve" (*'abad*) refers commonly to worship and its rites (cf. 5:1, 3 with 7:16; 10:7, 8; 10:24–26; cf. also Deut. 4:19; 5:8–9). But such worship was to be only one expression of whole-life obedience (Deut. 10:12–13; 11:13). In other words the Israelites were to serve the Lord in all of life, with worship being one aspect of this service. From daily work to tabernacle worship the Israelites were his servants.

Understanding Israel's role as a servant sheds light on the severity of various sins in Exodus. On the one hand it shows that Pharaoh's sin of refusing to let the people go to serve the Lord is all the more severe because he is holding back the true King's servants from performing their duty. At the same time it shows that Israel's apostasy with the golden calf is all the more severe because by it she is rebelling against her faithful king.

But understanding Israel's role as servant also sheds light on the book's entire flow, which can be thought of as follows: the Lord redeems his people to serve him (Exodus 1–19); he describes how to serve him in all aspects of life through obedience to his law (chs. 20–24); he gives them instructions for building a tabernacle so that he can dwell in their midst and they can serve him in worship (chs. 25–31); he renews the covenant with them after their rebellion so that they can reenter the freedom of serving him as their king (chs. 32–34); and he comes down and dwells in the tabernacle they have built so that they can come before him to serve him in worship (chs. 35–40). The Lord is the redeeming king who gives the Israelites the tremendous privilege of serving him in all of life.

---

[33] Robert L. Hubbard, Jr., "The Go'el in Ancient Israel: Theological Reflections on an Israelite Institution," *BBR* 1 (1991): 11, 13; emphasis added.

ISRAEL AS SON

As noted above, however, the Lord is not simply the Israelites' king, and they are not simply his servants; he is also their father, and they his children. In particular the Lord calls Israel "my firstborn son" (4:22). The implications are twofold.

First, being the Lord's firstborn means the Israelites know the Lord has a special love for them and will protect and care for them as his very own (cf. above: Yahweh, the Adopting Father-King). No wonder he also calls them a "treasured possession" (19:5); that is how parents feel about their children. They are the apples of their parents' eyes.

Second, being the firstborn means having a special role. As noted at 4:21–23, firstborn sons were to be "preeminent in dignity and preeminent in power" (Gen. 49:3), since they were responsible to maintain the household's well-being and honor.[34] This means they had to learn the father's business and would "serve" him during his life: "Let my son go that he may serve me" (Ex. 4:23). The Israelites are thus no longer to "serve" Pharaoh as slaves but are to "serve" Yahweh as sons,[35] obeying the Lord in all of life and maintaining his honor in the world. And this leads naturally to their role as a kingdom of priests and a holy nation.

ISRAEL AS KINGDOM OF PRIESTS AND HOLY NATION

The Lord states Israel's mission succinctly in 19:6: "You shall be to me a kingdom of priests and a holy nation." We may begin with the latter. The call to be a holy nation is a call to obedient living, which the Lord emphasizes in different ways throughout the book, from calls to obedience (19:5; 20:20; 23:21a) and commending examples of obedience (38:22; 39:1, 5, 7, 42; 40:16) to warnings against disobedience (23:21b; 34:7b) and the discipline and judgment that come for disobeying (32:25–29, 35). Clearly, the Lord wants his people to be faithful, and this is true not only in terms of general obedience to his covenant commands but specifically in terms of being faithful to serve and worship him alone. The Ten Commandments thus begin with two that require Israel to worship the Lord alone (20:3–6), and this command is reinforced multiple times throughout the book (20:22–23; 23:23–25, 32–33; 32:7–10, 25–29; 34:11–17). He is the King, and Israel is to be his faithful servant. He is the Father, and Israel is to be his obedient son. He is the husband, and Israel is to be his faithful wife. Israel's call to be a holy nation through faithful obedience is thus a major theme explaining who the Lord wants his people to be.

Importantly, Israel's obedience is to have a missional thrust. They are to be not simply a "holy nation" but a "kingdom of priests." These two go together. As noted in the comment on 19:3–6:

> The language of priesthood and holy nation . . . points to Israel's role in the Lord's world. Within Israel the Lord's priests are to live holy lives, teaching the Israelites his ways and helping them to know how to live in relationship

---

[34] Cf. Victor. H. Matthews, "Family Relationships," in *Dictionary of the Old Testament: Pentateuch*, ed. T. Desmond Alexander and David W. Baker (Downers Grove, IL: IVP Academic, 2003), 293.
[35] Based on an observation by my students Christina Hannah and Nelson and Nicole Hall.

with him (Lev. 10:10–11; 21:1–23). Israel is to do the same within the world. This will take place especially by embodying the Lord's holy character in the people's own lives, thereby showing others the beauty and glory of who he is (Lev. 19:2; 20:26). Put differently, Israel is not simply to be the Lord's treasured servant; she is to help the world understand why the Lord is to be treasured. Peter makes this very point to early Christians when referring to this passage: "You are a chosen race, a royal priesthood, a holy nation, a people for his own possession, *that you may proclaim the excellencies of him who called you out of darkness into his marvelous light*" (1 Pet. 2:9). To enter into the Lord's care is to receive his commission to help his world know, worship, obey, and love him.

SUMMARY

Exodus thus presents a picture of the Lord as the one who is the true and sole King of heaven and earth, full of majesty and might, yet overflowing with mercy, forgiveness, kindness, and love. This king longs to be with his people and calls them as his servants and sons and priests to embody his very character in their lives—for his glory, their good, and the world's blessing. This should all sound very familiar to the believer today, since Jesus is this same type of king and gives us this same type of calling (cf. comments on 15:1–19; 15:20–21; 25:8–9; 29:43–46; 32:25–29; 34:29–35; 40:34–38). In him we are freed from our slavery to sin into the glorious freedom of serving the true and living God. In him we are adopted as God's own children. In him we are a kingdom of priests and holy nation, "that [we] may proclaim the excellencies of him who called [us] out of darkness into his marvelous light" (1 Pet. 2:9).

Relationship to the Rest of the Bible and to Christ

Biblical authors in the OT and NT return frequently to Exodus. They do so in different ways, from picking up on general themes and alluding to specific events to using direct quotes. They also return to Exodus for different reasons, from applying its teaching anew for the people of God to showing how it prepares us to understand the person and work of Jesus. While the commentary goes into greater detail at relevant points, we may summarize the way other biblical authors use Exodus under four headings.

THE LORD'S MATCHLESS CHARACTER

In response to Moses' pleas for the Lord to forgive Israel for the golden calf, the Lord offers one of the most moving descriptions of his character in all the Pentateuch (Ex. 34:6–7). The description makes clear he disciplines for sin but emphasizes that he is a God of mercy, grace, love, and forgiveness. Many later biblical books return to this description and do so for different reasons:

- to appeal for forgiveness for Israel's sin (Num. 14:18–19; Neh. 9:17);
- to appeal for the Lord's help when facing the enemy (Ps. 86:15);
- as one of many reasons for praising him (Ps. 103:8; 145:8);

- to exhort sinners to repent before him (Joel 2:13);
- to complain (!) that the Lord shows mercy and forgiveness to foreigners (Jonah 4:2).

Whether in prayer, praise, command, or even complaint, God's people recognize that the Lord's character is unchanging and that the reality of who he is has implications for their lives today.

THE LORD'S FAITHFULNESS AND DEEDS IN EXODUS

The Bible refers regularly to the events of Israel's exodus from Egypt. A small sampling of these texts follows, arranged according to the reason(s) the exodus events are cited:

- to make known to following generations the Lord's mighty deeds, thus encouraging faithfulness to him (Ps. 78:1–8, 12–16, 44–51);
- to remind Israel that such deeds show that his steadfast love endures forever (Psalm 136; cf. esp. vv. 10–15);
- to urge those listening to praise the Lord for the way such deeds show his glory and his faithfulness to his promises and to follow this faithful and powerful God with their whole lives (Pss. 105 [esp. vv. 1–4, 24–45]; 135:8–9);
- to remember the Lord's faithful past deeds in order to give hope to present sufferers that the Lord will deliver them (Psalm 77);
- to provide a picture of how the Lord will protect the Israelites in the future (Isa. 4:5–6);
- to provide a picture of how the Lord will deliver the Israelites from exile (Isa. 11:16; 51:10–11; Jer. 23:7–8).

The frequent appeal to such a central event is unsurprising. Deeds are a demonstration of character, and the Lord's deeds in the exodus events give his people every reason to praise him as a God of faithful power and love who is worthy of praise, trust, and allegiance.

ISRAEL'S FAITHLESSNESS IN EXODUS

The Lord's faithfulness in Exodus stands in contrast to Israel's lack of it. The Bible uses such faithlessness in different ways:

- as a warning to later Israelites generations as how not to behave (Deut. 6:16; Ps. 95:7–11), a warning picked up and applied by the NT to followers of Jesus (Heb. 3:7–11; cf. 1 Cor. 10:1–13);
- to contrast with the Lord's faithfulness and care, the latter of which are reasons the current generation should follow him faithfully so that they, too, may experience the same (Ps. 81:6–10, 13–16);
- to confess similar faithlessness (Ps. 106:6–12, 19–23) yet also to remember how the Lord showed his faithfulness even to his sinful people, and to pray that he would do so again now (106:44–47; cf. Nehemiah 9).

As the story of the Bible continues, the ultimate sign of the Lord's faithfulness is seen in the coming of Jesus Christ, which leads to a further way in which the Bible uses Exodus.

EXODUS AND JESUS

Later biblical writers saw Exodus as preparing us to understand different aspects of Jesus' life and ministry:

- Just as the Lord declares himself to be the great "I AM" (Ex. 3:14), so Jesus declares himself to be the same (John 8:58).
- Just as the Passover lamb is sacrificed to deliver the Israelites from destruction, so Jesus is sacrificed at Passover (Matt. 26:2) as the perfect Lamb to deliver us (cf. Ex. 12:46; John 19:36; cf. also 1 Cor. 5:7).
- Just as the Israelites celebrate the Lord's protective deliverance during the Passover, Christians do the same during Communion, which Jesus institutes during the Passover (Luke 22:1–23), to celebrate his protective deliverance.
- Just as the Lord provides bread from heaven to satisfy the Israelites' physical hunger (Ex. 16:4), so he provides Jesus as the true bread from heaven to satisfy our spiritual hunger (John 6:31–35).
- Just as the Sinai covenant is inaugurated with the sacrificial blood of animals (Ex. 24:8), so the new covenant is inaugurated with the sacrificial blood of Jesus (cf. Luke 22:20; Heb. 9:15–28).
- Just as in the old covenant the Israelites' responsibilities include being "a kingdom of priests and a holy nation" (Ex. 19:6), so in the new covenant Jesus has rescued us to be the same (1 Pet. 2:9).
- Just as the Lord dwells in Israel's midst in the tabernacle and manifests his glory there (Ex. 40:34–35), so has he dwelt in our midst in the person of Jesus and manifested his glory there (John 1:14).
- Just as Moses' face beams with God's glory after being in God's presence on the mountain (Ex. 34:29–32), so Jesus' face beams with God's glory after being in his presence on the mountain (Matt. 17:2). But, whereas Moses veils the glory on his face (Ex. 34:33, 35), in Jesus God's glory is unveiled (2 Cor. 4:6), so that those who turn to him in faith are "being transformed into the same image from one degree of glory to another" (2 Cor. 3:18).
- Just as in an earthly tabernacle priests make atonement for God's people, so in the heavenly tabernacle Jesus, the Great High Priest, makes perfect atonement for us (cf. Ex. 25:40 and Leviticus 16 with Heb. 8:1–7; 9:1–14).

Once more, the above list is not exhaustive. But it is enough to show that what God has done for his people in Exodus he has done again for his people today in Jesus—though with a strength and glory that outshines Exodus as the sun outshines a birthday candle. "What once had glory has come to have no glory at all, because of the glory that surpasses it," seen in Jesus (2 Cor. 3:10)!

Preaching from Exodus

SCOPE OF COVERAGE

For those preaching or teaching through the whole book I have divided the commentary into thirty-six units. Each unit ends with a Response section showing how that unit relates to a life of faith today. Response sections are typically divided into three or four parts, each concentrating on a main point to develop in preaching or teaching. Each part also begins with a question (instead of a statement) to aid those wanting to approach their preaching or teaching inductively.[36]

Many will choose to cover Exodus in far less than thirty-five sessions. I have therefore compiled suggestions for possible sermon series and put these freely online.[37]

APOLOGETIC ISSUES

Different aspects of the Bible may seem to be not only confusing but also wrong or unjust. Aside from the natural rebellion that exists in our sinful hearts, there are at least two main reasons for these feelings. On the one hand every culture has values and assumptions that conflict with the Lord's values as laid out in the Bible. And because cultural values and assumptions are often felt deeply, if even at the subconscious level, the Bible will feel confusing, wrong, or unjust when it embodies conflicting values. In such cases preachers or teachers may need to spend appropriate time naming their culture's values and assumptions, explore where these values and assumptions do well but also where they leave us wanting, and turn to consider how the Lord's values and assumptions provide a better story of the world and our place within it.[38]

On the other hand some aspects of the Bible will seem confusing, wrong, or unjust because God seems to go against his own values. For example, God gives people equal value as his image bearers, yet he issues laws regulating slavery of one person to another (Ex. 21:2–11). In such cases the preacher or teacher will need to be honest with the tensions we feel while also doing the necessary work to show how such tensions can be resolved.

In the commentary I have sought to provide help at various points for apologetic issues that stood out to me as I read Exodus (for an example with slavery, cf. comment on 21:2–6). But commentators can never anticipate the apologetic issues of all readers, since those issues vary widely across cultures. Where I have missed an issue relevant to one's culture, my humble hope is that the commentary's approach to other apologetic issues models an approach anyone might be able to adapt for one's own context.

---

36 For homiletical suggestions on how to present narratives in teaching or preaching cf. Jay Sklar, *Additional Notes on Exodus* (St. Louis, MO: Gleanings Press, 2023), Appendix 1. I have made this available online; an internet search for the book's author and title should find it quickly.
37 Cf. note 36 above. The sermon series may be found in Appendix 2 of that work.
38 Cf. Joshua D. Chatraw, *Telling a Better Story: How to Talk about God in a Skeptical Age* (Grand Rapids, MI: Zondervan Reflective, 2020); Timothy Keller, *The Reason for God: Belief in an Age of Skepticism* (New York: Dutton, 2008); Keller, *Making Sense of God: An Invitation to the Skeptical* (New York: Viking, 2016).

PRINCIPLES OF APPLICATION TO KEEP IN MIND

Narrative and law are two of the most common genres in Exodus.[39] In making application from these genres preachers and teachers must keep important principles in mind.

With narrative, preachers and teachers must remember the importance of avoiding moralism and of staying centered on the gospel. Consider narrative examples of negative behavior. Moralism results if we only say, "The Israelites sinned here. Do not be like them! Be obedient." That is telling people, "Pull yourself up by your own moral bootstraps." Instead, we must always point our hearers to the Lord's provision for their lives of faith. The author of Hebrews certainly warns his audience not to be like the sinful Israelites, even quoting Psalm 95:7–11 (cf. Heb. 3:7–11). But he prefaces that warning with an exhortation to "consider Jesus" (Heb. 3:1), follows it by declaring that the Israelites' sin was to "fall away from the living God" (Heb. 3:12), and concludes the larger section to which Hebrews 3 belongs by pointing people to the reality of Jesus as our "great high priest" as the reason we should "hold fast our confession" (Heb. 4:14). In other words, instead of simply saying, "Do not be like them," the author says, "The reason for their disobedience was rooted in forgetting who God is; do not do the same! Remember him, especially what he has done in and through Jesus, so you might walk in paths of obedience." The author thus uses disobedience as both negative example and positive exhortation to refocus one's faith on the Lord as the only source of hope. In this way hearers are not left to pull themselves up by their own moral bootstraps but may look to the Lord for strength to follow him obediently.[40]

Similarly, with a positive narrative example, moralism results when we simply say, "Look at Moses' faith here. You should have the same faith!" Far better to say, "Look at Moses' faith here. How can he have such faith? Because of the reality of who God is. He is so worthy of our faithful trust. Let us put our faith in him!" In this way we use Moses' positive example to point beyond him to the Lord as the one who gives us reason to have Moses-like faith.

As for applying law, preachers and teachers must bear several factors in mind.[41] From the perspective of redemptive history the laws in Exodus are part of the Sinai covenant. Because Jesus inaugurated a new covenant (Luke 22:20; Heb. 8:6–13), we cannot simply assume OT laws are in force in the same way today.

At the same time they remain incredibly relevant to Christian living. Laws express the lawgiver's values. Most societies value life and the right to personal property and therefore prohibit murder and theft. Their laws express their values. Similarly, the Lord's laws in Exodus express his values.

Moreover, since his values flow from his character, which is perfect and constant (Mal. 3:6; Heb. 13:8; James 1:17), we should expect the values behind his laws to

---

[39] Narrative: most of chapters 1–11; 14; 16–19; 24; 32–34; 35–40. Law: most of chapters 20–23.
[40] The same approach can be seen in Psalm 95. The psalm ends with the Israelites' disobedience as negative example (95:7–11), but it begins with exhortations to sing for joy to the Lord and to acknowledge the greatness of who he is (95:1–6). Heeding the psalm's first part—with its focus on looking to God—is what enables one to avoid the negative example of the psalm's second half.
[41] The following is a slightly revised version of comments found in Sklar, *Numbers*, 27–28.

have some application today. Because these laws give us a window into the Lord's heart, those seeking to reflect his image have much to learn from them.

In preaching or teaching from a section of law we should therefore begin by identifying the value(s) being communicated to the original audience. If obeyed, what would that law have taught the Israelites about God's character and the values he wanted his people to embody? Once these questions are answered, it is a short step to ask how the Lord demonstrates these same values in the NT, especially in his Son, Jesus. And then we can consider how the NT commands us as Christians to live out these values in the world today.[42]

Finally, we must remind ourselves and our hearers that law was never given to save us. Law does not *establish* our relationship with the Lord; it *regulates* and *guides* it. The Lord did not say to Israel, "Keep these laws and then I will redeem you." He redeemed them first (Exodus 1–19) and then gave laws teaching them how to live in relationship with him (chs. 20–23). To obey the Lord's laws is to respond to the redeeming King with appropriate worship, reverence, and love (cf. 20:2 with 20:3–17).

Old Testament or New, God's laws are not a to-do list to earn relationship with him; they are loving directions from a heavenly Father that show us how to live in fellowship with him and reflect his character into the world. And, while we must repent of failing to obey them and of not reflecting his character well, we should preach and teach on law in such a way that our hearers can join the Israelites in praying Psalm 119, rejoicing that God has loved us so much that he has given us good laws to guide us in walking in paths that keep us close to him.[43]

Interpretive Challenges

THE DATE OF THE EXODUS

Debate surrounds the date of the events in Exodus. The Merneptah Stela (1207 BC) lists Israel as an inhabitant of Canaan, meaning the exodus happened before that date. Traditionally the exodus has been placed at 1446 BC, since 1 Kings 6:1 states that Solomon's temple-building began in the fourth year of his reign (966 BC), 480 years after the exodus. For others the store city "Raamses" in Exodus 1:11 is named after Ramesses II, a thirteenth-century pharaoh, placing the exodus at that time. (If so, the 480 years mentioned in 1 Kings 6:1 would be symbolic.) Conservative scholars have tended to favor the earlier date, though some go with the later one.[44]

In discussing this question Wright wisely observes, "There are many further questions and difficulties that scholars address—biblical scholars, archaeologists, Egyptologists, etc.—and we ought to recognize that there is as yet no conclusive or agreed certainty around the question."[45] What can be said, however, is that those fol-

---

[42] For a more detailed discussion of how OT laws apply today cf. Christopher J. H. Wright, *Old Testament Ethics for the People of God* (Downers Grove, IL: InterVarsity Press, 2004), 314–324, esp. 321–324 (his discussion complements the above; cf. also 403–408 for questions related to Israel as a theocratic nation). Cf. also Sklar, *Leviticus*, ZECOT, 33–39. For a helpful summary of various approaches to this question cf. Derek Tidball, *The Message of Leviticus: Free to Be Holy*, BST (Downers Grove, IL: InterVarsity Press, 2005), 28–31.
[43] For other general principles on reading law cf. comments on 20:1–21; Response section on 20:1–21, "How Should the Ten Commandments Be Read?"; Overview of 21:1–23:19.
[44] For a full discussion cf. J. H. Walton, "Exodus, Date of," *DOTP*, 258–272.
[45] Wright, *Exodus*, 14.

lowing the biblical data agree that the exodus took place sometime in the fifteenth to thirteenth century BC—and with that we might have to be content for now.

LARGE NUMBERS IN THE BOOK OF EXODUS[46]

Exodus 12:37 states that "about six hundred thousand men on foot, besides women and children," departed Egypt in the exodus. This number corresponds to Exodus 38:26 and Numbers 1:46, which list the adult Israelite males as 603,550 (Levites not included; Num. 1:47). How such large numbers should be understood is widely debated. Four main approaches may be identified.[47]

(1) *The numbers should be taken at face value.* While the most traditional approach is to take the numbers at face value, this creates tensions with biblical and archaeological data.[48] For example, Israel is called "the fewest of all peoples" (Deut. 7:7), and its small numbers are the reason the Lord will drive out the land's inhabitants slowly over time (Ex. 23:30; Deut. 7:22). Yet simply adding a wife and three children per family leads to a total population of at least three million Israelites if we take the numbers at face value. If we add older men and the Levites not counted in the census, the number goes as high as four million. Such a population dwarfs the 140,000 people estimated to have lived in Canaan between 2000 and 1500 BC, the period just before Israel entered the land. Even if we multiply the estimation of 140,000 by ten—and it should be noted that the estimation is based on significant amounts of archaeological work and regional surveys—Israel's population is still twice that of Canaan's, conflicting with the biblical texts cited above. This suggests that a different approach is warranted.

(2) *The numbers are symbolic.* In the first of two approaches, the symbolism is explained using gematria, a code in which numbers correspond to letters of the alphabet, spelling out different words. In the second, the numbers relate to astronomical phenomena. For example, Benjamin's total of 35,400 (Num. 1:37) divided by 100 is the same as the days in a short lunar year, 354. Few have adopted these approaches since they either fail to explain all the data or can explain it only by complex (and many would say arbitrary) calculations.

(3) *The word 'elef has been misunderstood.* The Hebrew word *'elef* used in Exodus 12 and Numbers 1 usually means "a thousand" but can also mean "family" or "clan," and a word built on the same root can mean "tribal leader." Some suggest the text originally referred to one of these other meanings. So, for example, Reuben's 46,500 (Num. 1:21) could represent 46 *families* totaling 500 people. The problem is that such approaches often assume a significant number of scribal errors. Given the lack of textual evidence for such errors, this approach is highly conjectural.

(4) *The numbers involve deliberate hyperbole.* The final approach, which has the fewest problems, understands the numbers to be inflated intentionally. Some suggest an inflation factor of ten, though others say the amount is no longer

---

[46] This is a slightly adapted version of what is found in Sklar, *Numbers*, 30–32.
[47] For fuller discussion cf. Aaron J. Goldstein, "Large Census Numbers in Numbers: An Evaluation of Current Proposals," *Presbyterion* 38/2 (2012): 99–108.
[48] The following summarizes Hoffmeier, *Ancient Israel in Sinai*, 153–156.

discernible.[49] Although many modern people believe numbers are misleading if they are not reported with scientific accuracy, in the ancient Near East numbers were often inflated, particularly in military contexts (as demonstrated by Ugaritic and Assyrian texts of the same general time period).[50] Doing so was neither unusual nor extraordinary. Given this convention, the Pentateuch's first audience would have immediately recognized the numbers to be inflated and would have grasped the true communicative intent of the numbers: rather than seeing this as deceptive, they may have seen it as simply a way of emphasizing the Lord had been faithful to his covenant promise to make Abraham into a numerous people (Gen. 12:2; 15:5).

In sum the first approach to the large numbers in Exodus 12, 38, and Numbers 1 is historically the most common, though the last appears most likely. In either case, however, the numbers' large size underscores that the Lord is a promise keeper: what he had sworn to Abraham has come to pass. And, since he has been faithful to that covenant promise, he can be trusted to fulfill his covenant promise to give his people a land. Israel could march into Canaan with full confidence in its covenant King.

Outline

As a quick comparison of commentaries will show, Exodus can be outlined in different ways. In the commentary outline I have sought to keep in front of the reader the geographical location of the Israelites, which is central to Exodus's story, as well as the central themes of the relevant sections. This leads to eight main sections:

I. Israel in Egypt: the Lord promises deliverance (1:1–11:10)
II. Israel leaves Egypt: the Lord provides deliverance (12:1–15:21)
III. Israel travels through the wilderness to Sinai: the Lord tests his people and provides for their needs (15:22–17:16)
IV. Israel arrives at Sinai: the Lord prepares his people to receive his covenant and its laws (18:1–19:25)
V. Israel at Sinai: the Lord gives his covenant to Israel (20:1–23:33); the covenant is ratified (24:1–11)
VI. Israel at Sinai: the Lord gives instructions for the building of his palace-tent among them (24:12–31:18)
VII. Israel at Sinai: the people break the covenant; the Lord renews the covenant (32:1–34:35)
VIII. Israel at Sinai: the Lord's palace-tent is built and he comes to dwell among his covenant people (35:1–40:38)

---

49 For the number of 603,550 (Ex. 38:26; Num. 1:46), another explanation of the inflation presents itself. In Exodus 38:25–26 the amount of silver used in the tabernacle corresponds *exactly* to the census count of 603,550 men. If the census count is not taken at face value (due to the factors named above in approach 4), and if the silver's weight is taken at face value—which is the universal approach with other tabernacle measurements—then the simplest solution is that the silver's weight represents the accurate needs of the tabernacle, and the census numbers were calculated based on that weight (hence the exact correspondence between the two). In reality the actual census numbers would be lower, meaning that additional silver would be required in addition to that collected in the census and could have come from the additional contributions of silver mentioned in 35:24.
50 Cf. Goldstein, "Large Census Numbers," 106.

If we pay less attention to Israel's geographical location and seek to form groups at a higher level, we could reduce the eight sections to six:

I. The Lord delivers Israel (1:1–15:21)
II. The Lord tests Israel (15:22–17:16)
III. The Lord enters into covenant with Israel (18:1–24:11)
IV. The Lord gives instructions for building his palace-tent in Israel's midst (24:12–31:18)
V. The Lord renews the covenant Israel has broken (32:1–34:35)
VI. The Lord has his palace-tent built and comes to dwell in Israel's midst (35:1–40:38)

If we think more broadly still and try to group the above under one-word titles, we could reduce the six sections to four:[51]

I. Deliverance (1:1–15:21)
II. Testing (15:22–17:16)
III. Covenant (18:1–24:11)
IV. Presence (24:12–40:38)[52]

Each of the above approaches has strengths and weaknesses. Generally speaking, with an outline that includes more main sections, one can capture finer emphases or nuances of the text but might not grasp the big picture. The opposite is true with fewer main sections. Deciding which approach to take will depend in large part on the interpreter's audience and goals.

What follows below is the commentary outline of eight main sections and the next level of outlining for each section, thus giving the reader the big picture and some idea of how each section is developed. In the commentary itself the Section Outline at the beginning of each unit often goes into more detail to bring even greater clarity to that unit's flow of thought.[53]

I. Israel in Egypt: the Lord promises deliverance (1:1–11:10)
   A. Israel's suffering in Egypt and need of a deliverer (1:1–2:22)
   B. The Lord calls and commissions the deliverer: Moses (2:23–4:17)
   C. Moses returns to Egypt (4:18–31)
   D. An initial attempt at deliverance (5:1–6:9)
   E. Preparation for the deliverance to come (6:10–7:7)
   F. The Lord's coming deliverance of Israel by great signs and wonders, showing his sovereignty over Pharaoh and Egypt's gods (7:8–11:10)

---

[51] The following is a modification of Wright (*Exodus*, 11), who combines 1:1–15:21 and 15:22–17:16 into one group with the title "Redemption."
[52] The theme of the Lord's presence with Israel is central to both the tabernacle narratives (chs. 25–31; 35–40) and the dialogue between Moses and the Lord after the golden calf (chs. 32–34; cf. esp. 33:1–7, 12–17).
[53] The higher levels of outlining in this section are heavily indebted to Douglas K. Stuart, *Exodus*, NAC 2 (Nashville: B&H, 2006), 183–184.

II. Israel leaves Egypt: the Lord provides deliverance (12:1–15:21)
   A. The institution of the Passover, the Feast of Unleavened Bread, and the consecration of the firstborn; the Lord's deliverance of Israel through the last strike and Israel's exodus from Egypt (12:1–13:16)
   B. The Lord's leading of his people out of Egypt and his final defeat of Pharaoh (13:17–15:21)
III. Israel travels through the wilderness to Sinai: the Lord tests his people and provides for their needs (15:22–17:16)
   A. Three stories of testing and provision in the wilderness (15:22–17:7)
   B. Israel defeats Amalek with the Lord's help (17:8–16)
IV. Israel arrives at Sinai: the Lord prepares his people to receive his covenant and its laws (18:1–19:25)
   A. Jethro's visit, his expression of faith and advice to Moses, his departure (18:1–27)
   B. The Lord's invitation of special covenant relationship; his arrival in glory (19:1–25)
V. Israel at Sinai: the Lord gives his covenant to Israel; the covenant is ratified (20:1–24:11)
   A. Fundamental stipulations of the covenant: the Ten Commandments, spoken by the Lord to the people (20:1–17)
   B. The people's fearful response to the Lord's special appearance (20:18–21)
   C. The Lord's further commands regarding false gods and proper worship, spoken to Moses for the people (20:22–26)
   D. Further stipulations of the covenant, spoken to Moses for the people (21:1–23:19)
   E. Warnings against disobedience, and the blessings of obedience, on the way to the Promised Land and once within it, spoken to Moses for the people (23:20–33)
   F. The covenant is ratified (24:1–11)
VI. Israel at Sinai: the Lord gives instructions for the building of his palace-tent among them (24:12–31:18)
   A. Moses goes up the mountain to receive the stone tablets from the Lord (24:12–18)
   B. Tabernacle contributions (25:1–9)
   C. Tabernacle building instructions (25:10–27:21)
   D. The priests' garments (28:1–43)
   E. The ordination ceremony for the priests (29:1–35)
   F. The altar of burnt offering and its offerings (29:36–42)
   G. The tent's purpose (29:43–46)
   H. Further instructions for items used in connection with the tabernacle (30:1–38)

  I. The artisans who will make the tabernacle, its furniture and related items (31:1–11)
  J. Keeping the Sabbath as the sign of the covenant (31:12–17)
  K. The Lord gives the stone tablets of the covenant to Moses (31:18)
VII. Israel at Sinai: the people break the covenant; the Lord renews the covenant (32:1–34:35)
  A. The people's idolatry, the Lord's anger, Moses' first act of intercession for Israel (that the Lord would not wipe out the people) (32:1–14)
  B. Moses' anger at the people's idolatry, his confrontation of Aaron, and his execution of justice (32:15–29)
  C. Moses' second act of intercession for Israel (that the Lord would forgive the people) (32:30–33:6)
  D. Moses' third act of intercession for Israel (that the Lord would go in Israel's midst) (33:7–17)
  E. Moses asks to see the Lord's glory (33:18–23)
  F. The Lord reveals his glory (34:1–8)
  G. Moses' fourth act of intercession for Israel (that the Lord would renew the covenant) (34:9–28)
  H. The shining face of Moses (34:29–35)
VIII. Israel at Sinai: the Lord's palace-tent is built and he comes to dwell among his covenant people (35:1–40:38)
  A. Introduction (35:1)
  B. Command to keep the Sabbath (35:2–3)
  C. Gathering the materials for the tabernacle and related components (35:4–36:7)
  D. Making the tabernacle and related components (36:8–39:43)
  E. The setting up of the tabernacle (40:1–33)
  F. The glory of the Lord fills the tabernacle (40:34–38)

OVERVIEW OF
EXODUS 1–11

This opening section of Exodus tells the story of Israel's need for deliverance and how the Lord will bring it about. It focuses on the character of the Lord, who shows himself to be the God who cares attentively for his people, who faithfully keeps his covenant promises, and who is fully sovereign over all earthly and heavenly powers.

  The story consists of six sections. The first introduces us to Israel's need for deliverance and to the Lord's deliverer, Moses (1:1–2:22). The second describes

Moses' call to be Israel's deliverer and focuses especially on the faithful and powerful character of the Lord who calls him (2:23–4:17). The third section narrates briefly Moses' return to Egypt and reunion with Aaron and highlights again the Lord's sovereign power and covenant care for his people (4:18–31). The fourth describes the failure of Moses' initial attempt at deliverance but reemphasizes that the Lord cares for his people and will powerfully deliver them (5:1–6:9). The fifth section is a transition that provides further background on Israel's main leaders (Moses and Aaron) and offers a preview of how the Lord will display his sovereign power over Egypt when he delivers his people (6:10–7:7). This leads to the final section, in which the Lord sends a series of miraculous judgments against the Egyptians but not against the Israelites to make clear he is the divine ruler and cares deeply for his people (7:8–11:10). Taken together, the sections certainly offer insight into human characters (Moses, Pharaoh, the Israelites), but their overall focus is on the Lord, the one who sees his people's suffering, who is committed to care for them and keep his covenant promises, and who can do so because he is the sovereign king.

EXODUS 1

1 These are the names of the sons of Israel who came to Egypt with Jacob, each with his household: ² Reuben, Simeon, Levi, and Judah, ³ Issachar, Zebulun, and Benjamin, ⁴ Dan and Naphtali, Gad and Asher. ⁵ All the descendants of Jacob were seventy persons; Joseph was already in Egypt. ⁶ Then Joseph died, and all his brothers and all that generation. ⁷ But the people of Israel were fruitful and increased greatly; they multiplied and grew exceedingly strong, so that the land was filled with them.

⁸ Now there arose a new king over Egypt, who did not know Joseph. ⁹ And he said to his people, "Behold, the people of Israel are too many and too mighty for us. ¹⁰ Come, let us deal shrewdly with them, lest they multiply, and, if war breaks out, they join our enemies and fight against us and escape from the land." ¹¹ Therefore they set taskmasters over them to afflict them with heavy burdens. They built for Pharaoh store cities, Pithom and Raamses. ¹² But the more they were oppressed, the more they multiplied and the more they spread abroad. And the Egyptians were in dread of the people of Israel. ¹³ So they ruthlessly made the people of Israel work as slaves ¹⁴ and made their lives bitter with hard service, in mortar and brick, and in all kinds of work in the field. In all their work they ruthlessly made them work as slaves.

¹⁵ Then the king of Egypt said to the Hebrew midwives, one of whom was named Shiphrah and the other Puah, ¹⁶ "When you serve as midwife to the Hebrew women and see them on the birthstool, if it is a son, you shall kill him, but if it is a daughter, she shall live." ¹⁷ But the midwives feared God and did not do as the king of Egypt commanded them, but let the male children live. ¹⁸ So the king of Egypt called the midwives and said

to them, "Why have you done this, and let the male children live?" ¹⁹ The midwives said to Pharaoh, "Because the Hebrew women are not like the Egyptian women, for they are vigorous and give birth before the midwife comes to them." ²⁰ So God dealt well with the midwives. And the people multiplied and grew very strong. ²¹ And because the midwives feared God, he gave them families. ²² Then Pharaoh commanded all his people, "Every son that is born to the Hebrews[1] you shall cast into the Nile, but you shall let every daughter live."

[1] Samaritan, Septuagint, Targum; Hebrew lacks *to the Hebrews*

Section Overview

In Genesis, the Lord promises to make the Israelites into a great nation (e.g., Gen. 22:17) and to give them the land of Canaan (e.g., 17:8). By the end of Genesis the first promise is fulfilled (47:27) but the second is not: the Israelites are in Egypt, not Canaan, so Genesis ends with an assurance that the promise of land will one day be fulfilled (50:24–25). It is a hopeful note, and Exodus begins similarly, making clear the Lord has indeed turned his people into a great nation, as he said (Ex. 1:1–7). But the mood immediately changes. Instead of receiving a land, Israel is cruelly enslaved (vv. 8–14), and its very existence is threatened when Pharaoh commands the death of every newborn male (vv. 15–22). The Israelites are in desperate need of deliverance—preparing us for Moses' introduction in chapter 2.

Section Outline

I. Israel in Egypt: the Lord promises deliverance (1:1–11:10)
   A. Israel's suffering in Egypt and need of a deliverer (1:1–2:22)
      1. Pharaoh's attempts to wipe out fruitful Israel (1:1–22)
         a. Israel fills all the earth/land of Egypt (1:1–7)
         b. Pharaoh's attempts at controlling the Israelite population (1:8–14)
         c. Pharaoh's attempts at wiping out the Israelite population (1:15–22)

Comment

1:1–5 These verses are a hinge between Genesis and Exodus.[54] Genesis ends with Joseph's dying words to his brothers, who, along with Jacob, have joined him in Egypt. Confident that God will keep his land promise made to Abraham, Isaac, and Jacob (e.g., Gen. 12:2; 22:17), Joseph makes his brothers swear to carry his bones up from Egypt when the promise is fulfilled (Gen. 50:24–25). These words give the reader hope that God will act soon as we come into Exodus.

Exodus indeed begins hopefully. It recaps the list of Jacob's sons who went down to Egypt, grouping them by the mother who bore them (Ex. 1:1–4): Leah

---

[54] Exodus begins with a conjunction (untranslated in ESV): "And these are the names." Also, the Hebrew of Exodus 1:1 begins in the same way as Genesis 46:8, further tying the books together.

(Reuben through Zebulun), Rachel (Benjamin), Bilhah (Dan and Naphtali), and Zilpah (Gad and Asher). Once the households were included, the total came to seventy people (v. 5a), including Jacob and also Joseph, the latter of whom was already in Egypt (v. 5b).[55] Like the number seven, the number seventy connotes fullness and plenty.[56] This is the beginning hint that God is fulfilling his promise to make Israel into a great nation (Gen. 12:2).

1:6–7 This fulfillment is immediately confirmed. After Joseph's generation died (Ex. 1:6), its descendants, the Israelites, "were *fruitful* and increased greatly; they *multiplied* and grew exceedingly strong, so that the *land* [or "earth"][57] was *filled* with them" (1:7; cf. Gen. 47:27). This language comes from the Lord's original command to humanity: "*Be fruitful* and *multiply* and *fill the earth*" (Gen. 1:28). The Lord also used this language in his promises to Israel's forefathers (Gen. 35:11; 48:4). Why? Because he is working out his intent for mankind by blessing his people. His actions toward them show what he longs to do for his world.

1:8–14 With the fruitfulness promise fulfilled we might now expect to hear that God fulfills the land promise, but the story's mood changes. At some point after Joseph's death "there arose a new king over Egypt" (Ex. 1:8). Exodus does not name any pharaohs, perhaps because the story is often telescoped, collapsing the similar experiences of many generations (and the similar actions of many pharaohs) together.[58] Whatever the reason for not naming the pharaohs, we are left with the impression that what is said of one of them would be true of all the rest in terms of how they treat Israel.

The important point here is that this pharaoh "did not know Joseph" (v. 8) and so looks unfavorably on his descendants. He is worried their vast numbers will continue increasing, presenting a double threat: joining forces with anyone who attacks Egypt, and then leaving (vv. 9–10). The latter concern suggests they are already serving the Egyptian economy in some way. Financial concerns often drive oppressive activity.

Pharaoh's first solution—which he describes as "dealing shrewdly [or "wisely"]"[59] with the Israelites (v. 10)—is to "afflict" them with heavy burdens (v. 11; cf. Gen. 15:13). This includes building projects, such as the store cities of Pithom and Raamses (Ex. 1:11).[60] Such projects would be backbreaking work, meant to weaken the Israelites and stifle their growth. "Hard labor always resulted in the death of many laborers."[61] But oppression of the Lord's people leads God to new levels of

---

[55] Cf. Genesis 46:8–27. Acts 7:14 has "seventy-five." Howard notes, "The figure of seventy-five persons is based on the LXX of Genesis 46:27 and Exodus 1:5, while the Hebrew text has 70. The larger total is arrived at by omitting Jacob and Joseph and including the remaining seven of Joseph's nine sons. In both cases the number is the total of Jacob's descendants who went down into Egypt or were born there." I. Howard Marshall, *Acts: An Introduction and Commentary*, TNTC 5 (Downers Grove, IL: Intervarsity Press, 1980), 146.
[56] For seventy cf. Genesis 50:3; Exodus 24:1. For seven cf. Exodus 22:30; 29:35; Leviticus 4:6; 26:18.
[57] The Hebrew word *'erets* can be translated as "earth" (Gen. 1:28) or "land" (Ex. 1:7); I include both to make the Genesis 1:28 allusion clear.
[58] Exodus 1–2 takes place over many generations (Ex. 12:40; cf. Gen. 15:13) but reads as though only one or two have passed. By telescoping events the author can focus on major themes.
[59] The Hebrew root usually refers to wisdom but can be translated as "shrewd, crafty" in some contexts.
[60] For discussion of these sites cf. Sklar, *Additional Notes on Exodus*, at 1:11. For the function of store cities cf. 2 Chronicles 32:28.
[61] W.H. Gispen, *Exodus*, trans. Ed van der Maas, BSC (Grand Rapids, MI: Zondervan, 1982), 34.

faithfulness by multiplying them further (v. 12), and Pharaoh's "wisdom" is shown for the folly it truly is. Opposing God's plans is ultimately disastrous. Nonetheless, gripped with fear, the Egyptians continue their wickedness, ruthlessly afflicting the Israelites with hard labor (vv. 13–14). "The reader is expected to identify with the unfairness of this. 'The recalling of oppression is to lead to an identification with those who suffer.'"[62]

1:15–21 Seeing that his "wise" attempts at population control have failed, Pharaoh takes a more diabolical approach: genocide. He gives an order to Shiphrah and Puah, "the midwives of the Hebrews" (v. 15 AT). Whether they are Egyptian midwives *for* the Hebrews or Israelite midwives *from* the Hebrews is unclear, though, given the Israelites' numbers, it seems likely they represent all such midwives.[63] Regardless, the irony is rich: the world's most powerful man is nameless, while the names of these ordinary women are known to this day. "In the biblical scale of values these lowly champions of morality assume far greater historic importance than do the all-powerful tyrants who ruled Egypt."[64]

Pharaoh's order makes his wickedness clear: the midwives are to kill any newborn Israelite sons (v. 16). In a day when descent is traced through the male, this would wipe out the Israelite nation, as any girls would be absorbed into Egyptian society through intermarriage.[65]

"But the midwives feared God" far more than Pharaoh, knowing that God is the one to whom they will ultimately give account, and so "did not do as the king of Egypt commanded them," choosing to honor the holy king of heaven instead of this wicked earthly tyrant (v. 17). When questioned by Pharaoh, their excuse to him is laughable (v. 19).[66] That Pharaoh believes it shows he is not only wicked but also a fool.

"So God dealt well with the midwives," perhaps by giving them favor in Pharaoh's eyes so they can continue in their role,[67] "and the people multiplied and grew very strong," a fact now mentioned a third time for emphasis (v. 20).[68] God's will for his people cannot be thwarted. The story returns briefly to the midwives, naming a further blessing appropriate to their obedience: for sparing the Israelites' families the Lord blesses them with families of their own (v. 21).

1:22 Sadly, Pharaoh has not learned the futility of fighting against God's people and now outdoes himself in evil by commanding all his people to cast newborn Israelite sons into the Nile (v. 22). Ironically, the next chapter tells the story of an

---

62 Stuart, *Exodus*, 71, 71n60, citing Terence E. Fretheim, *Exodus*, Interpretation (Louisville: John Knox Press, 1991), 30.
63 In 1:19 they speak of "the midwives" as including women other than themselves.
64 Nahum M. Sarna, *Exodus*, JPSTC (Philadelphia: Jewish Publication Society, 1991), 7.
65 John D. Currid, *A Study Commentary on Exodus*, vol. 1 (Auburn, MA: Evangelical Press, 2000), 52.
66 While truth is owed to others in normal life circumstances, one may legitimately ask, "Is truth owed here, where someone is attempting to slaughter the innocent?" The story provides no explicit answer, but the narrator's comment (Ex. 1:17) and God's response (vv. 20–21) paint these women in the most positive light, suggesting we should as well.
67 Cornelis Houtman, *Exodus*, vol. 1, trans. Johan Rebel and Sierd Woudstra, HCOT (Leuven: Peeters, 1993), 259. This makes good sense of the following clause.
68 U. Cassuto, *A Commentary on the Book of Exodus*, trans. Israel Abrahams (Jerusalem: Magnes Press, 1967), 15.

Israelite baby saved from the Nile, whom the Lord will use to defeat Pharaoh. Such ironies make clear God will return evil on its own head.

Response

HOW DOES THE STORY BEGIN?

As Exodus begins, the Lord's promise to make Israel a great nation is fulfilled as Jacob's descendants grow in keeping with God's design in Genesis 1, becoming "fruitful" and "multiplying" and "filling" the land of Egypt (Ex. 1:7; cf. Gen. 1:28). Exodus begins hopefully. It also begins missionally. By linking Israel's growth to the Lord's goal for humanity in creation, it signals that the Lord is making Israel his "starting point for realizing the divine intentions for all."[69] The blessing he gives them shows his commitment to make this world a place of fruitfulness and flourishing and to use his people as the ones through whom "all the families of the earth shall be blessed" (Gen. 12:3). Old Testament or New, the Lord blesses his people and intends for them to be his conduit of blessing (Ex. 19:5–6; 1 Pet. 2:9).

HOW DOES THE STORY GO HORRIBLY WRONG?

Instead of seeing the Israelites' fruitfulness as a blessing that should lead to praise of their God, Egypt's new king sees it as a threat to his power. He responds with severe oppression, first through heavy labor (Ex. 1:11), then through ruthlessly hard labor (vv. 13–14), and finally through attempts at genocide (vv. 15–22).

Even so, the Lord reigns. The Bible teaches that suffering is a reality and yet that God is still in control *and at work*. The Israelites are oppressed (vv. 9–11), "but the more they were oppressed, the more they multiplied" (v. 12; cf. also vv. 15–19 with v. 20). Even while his people are suffering, God is in control and at work.

This does not mean enduring suffering is easy. Jesus' suffering on the cross was incalculable: "My God, my God, why have you forsaken me?" (Matt. 27:46; cf. Ps. 22:1). And yet his final words express an underlying trust: "Father, into your hands I commit my spirit" (Luke 23:46; cf. Ps. 31:5). In the darkest moment of human history Jesus trusted the Father because he knew he was in control *and at work*. Jesus expresses his pain and hurt but, like the psalmist, fences it within the reality of God's sovereign goodness (cf. Ps. 13:1–4 with 13:5–6), in this way setting a model for his disciples (1 Pet. 2:21–23).

WHAT IS OUR PART IN THE STORY?

God's sovereignty does not mean we simply sit back and watch life unfold. Exodus begins with two lowly women disobeying the most powerful ruler in the world. Why? They "feared God" (Ex. 1:17), that is, they understand that there is a greater king to whom they must give account, causing them to resist evil and live righteously (cf. Deut. 6:2; 10:12; 13:4). They do so shrewdly (Ex. 1:19) but courageously. Living in light of God's kingship leads not to passivity but to fighting evil actively.

---

69 Fretheim, *Exodus*, 25.

For those who know that "every knee [will] bow . . . and every tongue confess that Jesus Christ is Lord" in the future (Phil. 2:10–11), resisting evil becomes a way for them to kneel before him in the present and to say with the disciples, "We must obey God rather than men" (Acts 5:29). What might this look like in one's own context as an employee or citizen? Wisdom again is called for (Matt. 10:16), but we can obey Jesus confidently, knowing that he is in control *and at work*.

EXODUS 2:1–22

2 Now a man from the house of Levi went and took as his wife a Levite woman. ² The woman conceived and bore a son, and when she saw that he was a fine child, she hid him three months. ³ When she could hide him no longer, she took for him a basket made of bulrushes[1] and daubed it with bitumen and pitch. She put the child in it and placed it among the reeds by the river bank. ⁴ And his sister stood at a distance to know what would be done to him. ⁵ Now the daughter of Pharaoh came down to bathe at the river, while her young women walked beside the river. She saw the basket among the reeds and sent her servant woman, and she took it. ⁶ When she opened it, she saw the child, and behold, the baby was crying. She took pity on him and said, "This is one of the Hebrews' children." ⁷ Then his sister said to Pharaoh's daughter, "Shall I go and call you a nurse from the Hebrew women to nurse the child for you?" ⁸ And Pharaoh's daughter said to her, "Go." So the girl went and called the child's mother. ⁹ And Pharaoh's daughter said to her, "Take this child away and nurse him for me, and I will give you your wages." So the woman took the child and nursed him. ¹⁰ When the child grew older, she brought him to Pharaoh's daughter, and he became her son. She named him Moses, "Because," she said, "I drew him out of the water."[2]

¹¹ One day, when Moses had grown up, he went out to his people and looked on their burdens, and he saw an Egyptian beating a Hebrew, one of his people.[3] ¹² He looked this way and that, and seeing no one, he struck down the Egyptian and hid him in the sand. ¹³ When he went out the next day, behold, two Hebrews were struggling together. And he said to the man in the wrong, "Why do you strike your companion?" ¹⁴ He answered, "Who made you a prince and a judge over us? Do you mean to kill me as you killed the Egyptian?" Then Moses was afraid, and thought, "Surely the thing is known." ¹⁵ When Pharaoh heard of it, he sought to kill Moses. But Moses fled from Pharaoh and stayed in the land of Midian. And he sat down by a well.

¹⁶ Now the priest of Midian had seven daughters, and they came and drew water and filled the troughs to water their father's flock. ¹⁷ The shepherds came and drove them away, but Moses stood up and saved them, and watered their flock. ¹⁸ When they came home to their father Reuel, he said, "How is it that you have come home so soon today?" ¹⁹ They said, "An Egyptian delivered us out of the hand of the shepherds and even drew

water for us and watered the flock." ²⁰ He said to his daughters, "Then where is he? Why have you left the man? Call him, that he may eat bread." ²¹ And Moses was content to dwell with the man, and he gave Moses his daughter Zipporah. ²² She gave birth to a son, and he called his name Gershom, for he said, "I have been a sojourner[4] in a foreign land."

[1] Hebrew *papyrus reeds* [2] *Moses* sounds like the Hebrew for *draw out* [3] Hebrew *brothers* [4] *Gershom* sounds like the Hebrew for *sojourner*

Section Overview

Exodus 1 makes clear that Israel needs a deliverer. Exodus 2 introduces us to him. The chapter's opening describes his birth and rescue from imminent death (2:1–10). Women are again central, especially in rescuing the child. The story then jumps years ahead, describing why Moses flees Egypt (vv. 11–15) and where he settles down (vv. 16–22), setting the stage for his eventual return to deliver his people. The chapter emphasizes Moses' role as deliverer by describing his birth with language reminiscent of Noah, an earlier deliverer, and recounting three instances in which Moses delivers the oppressed. In the midst of his people's suffering the Lord is faithful to raise up a deliverer.

Section Outline

I. Israel in Egypt: the Lord promises deliverance (1:1–11:10)
   A. Israel's suffering in Egypt and need of a deliverer (1:1–2:22) . . .
      2. The introduction of Israel's deliverer (2:1–22)
         a. The birth and deliverance of the deliverer (2:1–10)
         b. Moses' escape to Midian and life there (2:11–22)

Comment

2:1–4 Exodus 1 ends with Israel's desperate need of deliverance as Pharaoh commands his people to throw any Israelite newborn sons into the Nile (1:22). Exodus 2 begins with the birth of an Israelite son. Is this the deliverer? How will he escape Pharaoh's genocidal plan? Tensions of hope and fear are high and are sustained by the delayed mention of the child's name until the section's concluding verse (2:10).

The son is born to a couple from Levi's tribe (v. 1). Their names are given later (6:20), since the story's focus is the child, but their tribal affiliation would undoubtedly cause many Israelites to wonder, "Could their newborn be Moses or Aaron, who were from this tribe?" The suspense has just been magnified.

In the ancient world infant mortality was high, and it might quickly be evident that a baby would not live. But this is a "fine child" (2:2) or, in today's language, a "healthy, beautiful baby."[70] Seeing he would live, his mother hides him three months, presumably by keeping him at home and not publicizing his birth. Her

---

[70] The Hebrew word translated "fine" (*tob*) can describe a healthy, robust living being (BDB 373.3; cf. Gen. 18:7).

need to do so implies that other babies are being killed. The text does not mention such barbarism. Some acts are too evil to name.

A predictable problem arises. In dense populations hiding a newborn indefinitely is impossible, so an alternate plan is needed. Moses' mother waterproofs a bulrush basket, lays him in it, and places it among the Nile's "reeds" (2:3). Her thinking behind this action is not given; possible insight will come shortly. What is clear is that outside of Exodus 2 the word basket (Hb. *tebah*) occurs only in Genesis 6–9 to describe Noah's ark, also covered in pitch (Gen. 6:14). The similarity hints that this child, like Noah, will be a covenant representative who will save others (Gen. 6:18), in this case by bringing the Israelites "relief from [their] work and from the painful toil of [their] hands" (Gen. 5:29). (For a comparison to Noah at the end of the book, cf. comment on 40:16–33.)

As the little ark bobs among the reeds, the baby's sister—also unnamed—watches to see what will happen (2:4), her youth enabling her to do so with less suspicion than could a woman of childbearing age.

2:5–9 No sooner does she start watching than Pharaoh's daughter comes to bathe in the Nile. Perhaps this is a regular event, known to the child's mother, who has taken a calculated risk that Pharaoh's daughter will respond with compassion and offer her newborn son the best possible protection. Whatever the case, when the daughter opens the lid and sees the child crying, her compassion is aroused. She notes that it is a Hebrew child, opening the door for Moses' sister to intervene, offering to find a Hebrew woman to nurse it (v. 7). Pharaoh's daughter agrees, and the girl calls the child's own mother to fulfill this role (v. 8)! The beautiful irony continues: Pharaoh's daughter tells her to nurse the child on her behalf (in the days before baby formula, wet nurses were needed for women unable to nurse their own children) and also assures the mother of payment (v. 9).

2:10 "When the child grew older," presumably at least to the point of weaning (cf. Gen. 21:8),[71] his mother brings him to Pharaoh's daughter, who adopts him. Finally the child is named—and it is none other than Moses himself![72] For the Israelite audience the puzzle pieces come together immediately: this child, presented in Noah-type language, will indeed become their covenant representative and save them from their toil and labor. Moreover, in God's providence he is not only spared but taken into Pharaoh's house, the exact preparation needed for his later interactions with Pharaoh as his people's deliverer.[73] But Moses' role as

---

[71] Children in traditional societies nurse three to four years; cf. Katherine A. Dettwyler, "A Time to Wean: The Hominid Blueprint for the Natural Age of Weaning in Modern Human Populations," in *Breastfeeding: Biocultural Perspectives*, ed. Patricia Stuart-Macadam and Katherine A. Dettwyler (New York: Aldine de Grutyer, 1995), 43.

[72] As pointed out in the ESV mg., "Moses" sounds like the Hebrew word "draw out." Some have held that the name also relates to an Egyptian word, though this view is not without difficulties. See brief overview in Hess, "Onomastics of the Exodus Generation," 39.

[73] "That Moses was raised in Pharaoh's court (Ex. 2:10) resonates with the Egyptian royal educational institution known as the . . . royal nursery, where royal children were reared and educated. Egyptian textual evidence shows that for the first time, during the New Kingdom [16th–11th centuries BC] foreign princes were trained in the [royal nursery] and took the title . . . 'child of the nursery'" (Hoffmeier, *Ancient Israel in Sinai*, 180; cf. Acts 7:22).

deliverer will not occur until he is eighty (Ex. 7:7), so the story turns quickly to what happens in between.

2:11–15 Many years pass, and Moses becomes an adult. Although he grows up in an Egyptian home, he does not forget his Hebrew roots, which verse 11 emphasizes by speaking twice of "his people" ("his brothers"; cf. ESV mg.). The Israelites are his true family.

Going into their midst, he sees the "burdens" Pharaoh has inflicted on them (cf. 1:11), as well as an Egyptian's "beating/striking down [*nakah*] one of his brothers" (2:11). Moses responds in turn, "striking down" (*nakah*) the Egyptian and secretly burying the body (v. 12). In context this act is motivated by his solidarity with the Israelites.[74] But it does not endear him to his people. The very next day he comes across two fighting Israelites and rebukes the one who is wrongly "striking" (again *nakah*) the other (v. 13). The use of the same word for "striking" makes the rebuke's implication clear: "Egyptians do this (v. 11), not Israelites!" The offender responds with his own rebuke, saying in effect: "Who made you judge? And what are you going to do about it? Kill me like you killed that Egyptian?" (v. 14). Realizing the secret is out, Moses fears and for good reason: when Pharaoh learns of it, he tries to have Moses killed (v. 15a). Moses is forced to flee to Midian, an area "probably located in northwestern Arabia, just to the east of the Gulf of Elat (Aqaba),"[75] where he sits "down by a well" (v. 15b).

2:16–22 No sooner does he sit down than seven daughters of Midian's priest show up to water their father's flocks (v. 16). (The religion for which Jethro was a priest is never identified, though he does come to be a Yahweh worshiper [18:10–12].) They draw water and fill the troughs, but other shepherds arrive and chase them away, taking advantage of their hard work (2:17a). For the third time Moses' sense of justice is provoked (cf. v. 11, 13),[76] and he steps in, "saving" them from the other shepherds (v. 17b)—a foretaste of how the Lord will use him to save his people.

The daughters return home sooner than normal (v. 18) and explain to their father, Reuel—known also as Jethro (cf. comment on 3:1–3)—how Moses not only rescued them but even watered the flocks (2:19). They also describe him as Egyptian, perhaps because of his language or his clothing and haircut or both. Reuel tells them to bring Moses over for a meal, leading to Moses' living with Reuel's family and marrying his daughter Zipporah (vv. 20–21). She gives birth to his first son, Gershom, the first half of whose name sounds like the Hebrew word for "sojourner" (*ger*), a fitting testimony to Moses' status in this new land (v. 22; cf. comment on 18:2–5).[77]

---

[74] Cf. Ex. 2:11. Also, given how the two acts are similarly described, the narrator may be highlighting that Moses "struck down" someone who was wrongly "striking down" another. In modern language, he used lethal force on someone who was committing murder.
[75] Bruce Wells, *Exodus*, ZIBBC (Grand Rapids, MI: Zondervan Academic, 2016), 172.
[76] Fretheim, *Exodus*, 45.
[77] "Gershom" could come from Hebrew *garash* ("to drive away") or from West Semitic *geresh*, meaning "yield, produce." For other options cf. William H. C. Propp, *Exodus 1–18: A New Translation with Introduction and Commentary*, AB 2 (New York: Doubleday, 1999), 174. The link to Hebrew *ger* ("sojourner") is a play on words; cf. note 72 within comment on 2:10.

Response

HOW DOES THE LORD FIGHT AGAINST PHARAOH?

Exodus 1 and 2 share a common theme: the Lord delights to use the weak to shame the strong. In these chapters he uses the faithful actions of "unimportant" people to thwart the plans of earth's most powerful man (cf. Heb. 11:23). Note the central role of women in particular, be it the midwives refusing to kill Israelite babies because they fear God (Ex. 1:17–21), Moses' mother hiding him when he is born (2:2), or his sister—a young girl!—bravely stepping in to speak to Pharaoh's daughter (2:7–8). Fretheim summarizes nicely:

> "In the refusal of women to cooperate with oppression, the liberation of Israel from Egyptian bondage has its beginnings." . . . It can rightfully be said that women are here given such a crucial role that Israel's future is made dependent upon their wisdom, courage, and vision.[78]

Especially if we are weak in the world's eyes, we must remember that the Lord delights to use simple faithfulness for his purposes and glory (cf. 1 Cor. 1:27–29).

WHAT DOES THE LORD PROVIDE IN THE MIDST OF SUFFERING?

Such faithfulness is needed because of severe suffering—in this instance the unspeakable crime of genocide. Into this horror a baby is born who is presented as a second Noah, a person who will come to save (cf. comment on 2:1–4). In the midst of his people's suffering the Lord provides a deliverer to rescue them.

For the early disciples this was a picture of the Lord's provision of Jesus. Matthew 2 therefore draws parallels to this chapter. In each place an infant is saved from a tyrant intent on wiping out Israelite male babies. In each the infant saved will become his people's savior. The Lord's purpose for Moses to save the Israelite nation is a miniature picture of the Lord's purpose for Jesus to save the entire world, rescuing us not from Pharaoh but from the tyranny of sin that enslaves us and rewards us only with death (Rom. 6:16–23). The Lord has not overlooked the suffering our sin causes us. In Jesus he has provided a deliverer.

WHAT DO DELIVERERS DO?

Returning to Exodus 2, we note how the narrator highlights three different times that Moses rescues the suffering, whether his people (Ex. 2:11–12, 13) or strangers (v. 17). And, while some question the moral legitimacy of the first of these (though cf. note 74 within comment on 2:11–15), the good impulse underlying each is the same. Deliverers rescue those who are suffering, even if it is personally costly.[79]

---

78 Fretheim, *Exodus*, 33, quoting J. Cheryl Exum, "You Shall Let Every Daughter Live: A Study of Exodus 1:8–2:10," *The Bible and Feminist Hermeneutics* (1983): 63.
79 Cf. Hebrews 11:24–26. On 11:26 Cockerill writes, "The 'reproach' Moses suffered was 'the reproach of the coming Messiah with whom he was united by faith' (Hughes, 497). See John 5:46." Gareth Lee Cockerill, *The Epistle to the Hebrews*, NICNT (Grand Rapids, MI: Eerdmans, 2012), 572n35, citing Philip E. Hughes, *A Commentary on the Epistle to the Hebrews* (Grand Rapids, MI: Eerdmans, 1977).

Moses and Jesus help sufferers in an ultimate way, Moses by delivering Israel from Egypt and Jesus by delivering us from sin and death. Such ultimate acts of deliverance are unique. No one else in his generation is like Moses, and no one else in history is like Jesus. But Moses and Jesus also model helping sufferers in particular ways. In Luke 4:18–19 Jesus describes his ministry using the words of Isaiah 61:1–2:

> The Spirit of the Lord God is upon me,
>   because the Lord has anointed me
> to bring good news to the poor;
>   he has sent me to bind up the brokenhearted,
> to proclaim liberty to the captives,
>   and the opening of the prison to those who are bound;
> to proclaim the year of the Lord's favor,
>   and the day of vengeance of our God;
>   to comfort all who mourn.

He came to help those who were suffering. And, while Jesus' help again finds fulfillment in an ultimate and unique way in his rescuing us from sin and evil spiritual forces, it finds fulfillment also in a particular way in his emphasis on helping those suffering materially and physically: "When you give a feast, invite the poor, the crippled, the lame, the blind" (Luke 14:13; cf. James 2:1–13). Because Jesus came to help sufferers, his followers should want to do the same. What might it look like for us in practical terms to help those who suffer materially or physically? In answering we do well to remember: the Lord uses simple faithfulness for his purposes and glory.

EXODUS 2:23–4:17

²³ During those many days the king of Egypt died, and the people of Israel groaned because of their slavery and cried out for help. Their cry for rescue from slavery came up to God. ²⁴ And God heard their groaning, and God remembered his covenant with Abraham, with Isaac, and with Jacob. ²⁵ God saw the people of Israel—and God knew.

3 Now Moses was keeping the flock of his father-in-law, Jethro, the priest of Midian, and he led his flock to the west side of the wilderness and came to Horeb, the mountain of God. ² And the angel of the Lord appeared to him in a flame of fire out of the midst of a bush. He looked, and behold, the bush was burning, yet it was not consumed. ³ And Moses said, "I will turn aside to see this great sight, why the bush is not burned." ⁴ When the Lord saw that he turned aside to see, God called to him out of the bush, "Moses, Moses!" And he said, "Here I am." ⁵ Then he said, "Do not come near; take your sandals off your feet, for the place on which you are standing is holy ground." ⁶ And he said, "I am the God of your father,

the God of Abraham, the God of Isaac, and the God of Jacob." And Moses hid his face, for he was afraid to look at God.

⁷Then the Lord said, "I have surely seen the affliction of my people who are in Egypt and have heard their cry because of their taskmasters. I know their sufferings, ⁸and I have come down to deliver them out of the hand of the Egyptians and to bring them up out of that land to a good and broad land, a land flowing with milk and honey, to the place of the Canaanites, the Hittites, the Amorites, the Perizzites, the Hivites, and the Jebusites. ⁹And now, behold, the cry of the people of Israel has come to me, and I have also seen the oppression with which the Egyptians oppress them. ¹⁰Come, I will send you to Pharaoh that you may bring my people, the children of Israel, out of Egypt." ¹¹But Moses said to God, "Who am I that I should go to Pharaoh and bring the children of Israel out of Egypt?" ¹²He said, "But I will be with you, and this shall be the sign for you, that I have sent you: when you have brought the people out of Egypt, you shall serve God on this mountain."

¹³Then Moses said to God, "If I come to the people of Israel and say to them, 'The God of your fathers has sent me to you,' and they ask me, 'What is his name?' what shall I say to them?" ¹⁴God said to Moses, "I AM WHO I AM."[1] And he said, "Say this to the people of Israel: 'I AM has sent me to you.'" ¹⁵God also said to Moses, "Say this to the people of Israel: 'The Lord,[2] the God of your fathers, the God of Abraham, the God of Isaac, and the God of Jacob, has sent me to you.' This is my name forever, and thus I am to be remembered throughout all generations. ¹⁶Go and gather the elders of Israel together and say to them, 'The Lord, the God of your fathers, the God of Abraham, of Isaac, and of Jacob, has appeared to me, saying, "I have observed you and what has been done to you in Egypt, ¹⁷and I promise that I will bring you up out of the affliction of Egypt to the land of the Canaanites, the Hittites, the Amorites, the Perizzites, the Hivites, and the Jebusites, a land flowing with milk and honey."' ¹⁸And they will listen to your voice, and you and the elders of Israel shall go to the king of Egypt and say to him, 'The Lord, the God of the Hebrews, has met with us; and now, please let us go a three days' journey into the wilderness, that we may sacrifice to the Lord our God.' ¹⁹But I know that the king of Egypt will not let you go unless compelled by a mighty hand.[3] ²⁰So I will stretch out my hand and strike Egypt with all the wonders that I will do in it; after that he will let you go. ²¹And I will give this people favor in the sight of the Egyptians; and when you go, you shall not go empty, ²²but each woman shall ask of her neighbor, and any woman who lives in her house, for silver and gold jewelry, and for clothing. You shall put them on your sons and on your daughters. So you shall plunder the Egyptians."

4 Then Moses answered, "But behold, they will not believe me or listen to my voice, for they will say, 'The Lord did not appear to you.'" ²The Lord said to him, "What is that in your hand?" He said, "A staff." ³And he said, "Throw it on the ground." So he threw it on the ground, and it became a serpent, and Moses ran from it. ⁴But the Lord said to Moses, "Put out your hand and catch it by the tail"—so he put out his hand and caught it, and it became a staff in his hand— ⁵"that they may believe that the Lord, the God of their fathers, the God of Abraham, the God of Isaac, and the God of Jacob, has appeared to you." ⁶Again, the Lord said to him, "Put your hand inside your cloak."[4] And he put his hand inside his cloak, and when he took it out, behold, his hand was leprous[5] like snow. ⁷Then

God said, "Put your hand back inside your cloak." So he put his hand back inside his cloak, and when he took it out, behold, it was restored like the rest of his flesh. ⁸"If they will not believe you," God said, "or listen to the first sign, they may believe the latter sign. ⁹If they will not believe even these two signs or listen to your voice, you shall take some water from the Nile and pour it on the dry ground, and the water that you shall take from the Nile will become blood on the dry ground."

¹⁰But Moses said to the Lord, "Oh, my Lord, I am not eloquent, either in the past or since you have spoken to your servant, but I am slow of speech and of tongue." ¹¹Then the Lord said to him, "Who has made man's mouth? Who makes him mute, or deaf, or seeing, or blind? Is it not I, the Lord? ¹²Now therefore go, and I will be with your mouth and teach you what you shall speak." ¹³But he said, "Oh, my Lord, please send someone else." ¹⁴Then the anger of the Lord was kindled against Moses and he said, "Is there not Aaron, your brother, the Levite? I know that he can speak well. Behold, he is coming out to meet you, and when he sees you, he will be glad in his heart. ¹⁵You shall speak to him and put the words in his mouth, and I will be with your mouth and with his mouth and will teach you both what to do. ¹⁶He shall speak for you to the people, and he shall be your mouth, and you shall be as God to him. ¹⁷And take in your hand this staff, with which you shall do the signs."

¹ Or *I AM WHAT I AM*, or *I WILL BE WHAT I WILL BE*   ² The word Lord, when spelled with capital letters, stands for the divine name, YHWH, which is here connected with the verb *hayah*, "to be" in verse 14
³ Septuagint, Vulgate; Hebrew *go, not by a mighty hand*   ⁴ Hebrew *into your bosom*; also verse 7   ⁵ *Leprosy* was a term for several skin diseases; see Leviticus 13

Section Overview

Chapter 2 has introduced us to the Lord's deliverer, Moses; this section describes his call. It begins with a transition emphasizing Israel's suffering, the Lord's awareness of it, and his commitment to deliver Israel from it because of his faithfulness to his covenant promises (2:23–25). The call and commission that follow (3:1–4:17) are thus rooted in the Lord's faithful covenant love.

Whereas chapter 2 covered Moses' birth to his adulthood, 3:1–4:17 takes place in one day. By slowing the narrative pace the author highlights the importance of what happens here. In fact these chapters provide an interpretive framework through which to understand the story that follows. Their themes center on the Lord and include his holiness (3:1–5), his role as the God of the Israelites' forefathers (vv. 6, 13–16), his awareness of the Israelites' suffering (vv. 7, 9, 16), his sovereign power and might (vv. 14–15, 19–20; 4:11), the deliverance he will accomplish (3:8, 10, 17, 21–22), his presence with Moses in accomplishing it (v. 12; 4:1–9, 12, 15), and the good land he will give Israel (3:8, 17). We may be reading about Moses' call, but the focus is really on the caller (in the Hebrew, the Lord's words are more than five times as many as Moses'). Israel's ultimate hope is the Lord, not Moses.

The encounter between Moses and the Lord is similar in form to other OT (and ancient Near Eastern) theophanies, that is, appearances of a deity.[80] One of the com-

---

[80] Cf. Jeffrey J. Niehaus, *God at Sinai: Covenant and Theophany in the Bible and Ancient Near East* (Grand Rapids, MI: Zondervan, 1995), 31–32.

mon elements in such theophanies is a divine message that is met with some form of protest. In chapters 3–4 Moses responds with some sort of protest or refusal to the Lord five different times (3:11, 13; 4:1, 10, 13). As noted below, these responses spring from fear and lack of faith more than from humility. That the Lord does not rebuke Moses until the fifth time (4:14–17) underscores the Lord's merciful patience with his weak and fearful people. That he does rebuke Moses shows that there is an end to his patience. There comes a point when obedience must be done.

Section Outline

I. Israel in Egypt: the Lord promises deliverance (1:1–11:10) . . .
   B. The Lord calls and commissions the deliverer: Moses (2:23–4:17)
      1. God heeds Israel's suffering and remembers his covenant (2:23–25)
      2. The Lord calls and commissions Moses (3:1–4:17)
         a. The Lord's appearance to Moses (3:1–3)
         b. The Lord's introduction to Moses (3:4–6)
         c. The Lord's commission of Moses (3:7–10)
         d. Moses resists the Lord's command; the Lord's response (3:11–12)
         e. Moses resists a second time; the Lord's response (3:13–22)
         f. Moses resists a third time; the Lord's response (4:1–9)
         g. Moses resists a fourth time; the Lord's response (4:10–12)
         h. Moses resists a fifth time; the Lord's response (4:13–17)

Comment

2:23–25 "During those many days," in which Moses was living in Midian, "the king of Egypt died" (v. 23). But the new king continued the Israelites' affliction, as the language here graphically portrays (vv. 23–24). The verb "groaned" (Hb. *'anakh*) can communicate the pain of a broken heart (Ezek. 21:6) or of a woman in labor (Jer. 22:23), while the noun "groaning" (*ne'aqah*) can communicate a wounded man's suffering (Ezek. 30:24). "Crying out" (*za'aq*) is done elsewhere by those needing deliverance from oppression (Judg. 3:9, 15), a "cry for rescue" (*shaw'ah*) by those thinking they will die (2 Sam. 22:7; Ps. 40:1–2), while the Israelites' "slavery" (*'abodah*) is mentioned twice to identify their agony's source (Ex. 2:23). They are suffering profoundly and profoundly, in need of help.

But help is coming! Their cry "came up to God" (v. 23), entering his courts and becoming his attention's focus, implying that he will act. His activity is in fact highlighted. "By repeating 'God' as the subject of all four verbs in verses 24–25"—instead of replacing "God" with "he"—"the narrator emphasizes God's importance."[81] He hears, remembers, sees, and knows—and that means he loves the Israelites and will deliver them (cf. Response section).

---

81 Alexander, *Exodus*, ApOTC, 71.

3:1–3 The story shifts back to Moses (v. 1). The Lord will use him as the deliverer. Moses has become a shepherd for his father-in-law, Reuel, known also as Jethro. (Many biblical characters have two or more names, e.g., Jacob/Israel, Esau/Edom, Hoshea/Joshua. Reuel means "friend of God," and Jethro means "his excellency.") Searching for good pasture, Moses eventually leads the flock "to the mountain of God, to Horeb" (NET), that is, to the mountain of God within the Horeb region,[82] most commonly named Mount Sinai. The name "mountain of God" (v. 1; 4:27; 18:5; 24:13) presumably derives from the Lord's appearances there to Moses and later to all Israel. Use of that name here prepares the audience for what is next: "The angel of the LORD appeared to him" (3:2). Earlier stories recount this angel's speaking on the Lord's behalf (Gen. 16:7–12; 22:11–12). The word for "angel" may in fact be translated "messenger," which is his function here, speaking and acting on the Lord's behalf, like a king's messenger (cf. 2 Kings 18:19–25). This also explains why the text can switch back to the Lord as subject (Ex. 3:4): though the angel is in the bush, he represents the Lord.[83]

The angel appears as a "flame of fire" (v. 1). This is a common way for the Lord to appear (13:21; 19:18; 24:17), perhaps because fire expresses his glory's brilliance (cf. 24:17) and his impurity-destroying character (cf. Lev. 10:1–2; Num. 11:1–3). This also foreshadows the Lord's later appearance in a fiery cloud on Mount Sinai before all the people (Ex. 19:17–18).[84] The fire is clearly miraculous, since it does not burn up the bush, drawing an amazed Moses to investigate (3:3).

3:4–6 The Lord now calls to him from the bush's midst. Moses responds with a simple (but perhaps startled) "Here I am" (v. 4; cf. Gen. 22:11).

The Lord commands Moses to come no closer, for this is "holy ground" (Ex. 3:5). The Lord's strong holiness spreads like a beam of sunshine to whatever it touches, sanctifying the area around the bush as long as he is there (cf. Josh. 5:15). Moses must therefore remove his sandals, as priests will do in the holy tabernacle (Ex. 30:18–21), presumably because sandals regularly contact non-holy ground and are inappropriate to place on holy property. In modern language, to walk across someone's white carpet with muddy boots is severe disrespect.

The Lord identifies himself as the God of Israel's forefathers (and thus the God of the covenant with them; 3:6; cf. 2:24). Moses immediately hides his face, fearing to gaze upon God.[85] Israelites assumed one could not look at God's glory directly (cf. Gen. 32:30; Judg. 6:22; 13:22; Isa. 6:5), perhaps because the proper response before a king was not to look but to bow to the ground, awaiting his favorable response (cf. 1 Sam. 24:8; 2 Sam. 14:33; for the connection to the Lord's

---

82 It has been suggested that Horeb is a larger region in which Mount Sinai (and the Sinai Wilderness) is found (Sarna, *Exodus*, 14; Alexander, *Exodus*, ApOTC, 81–82). Alexander's discussion is the most robust. Mount Sinai's exact location is disputed; for thorough discussion and analysis cf. Hoffmeier, *Ancient Israel in Sinai*, 115–148.
83 Cf. Genesis 22:11 with 22:12; cf. also Exodus 23:21–22, esp. 23:22, where the Lord says of his angel, "If you carefully obey *his voice* and do all that *I say*."
84 Austin Surls, *Making Sense of the Divine Name in Exodus: From Etymology to Literary Onomastics*, BBRSup 17 (Winona Lake, IN: Eisenbrauns, 2017), 43.
85 Surrounding verses use the more common word *ra'ah* for "see" (3:2–4, 7). Here the word for "look" is *nabat*, which may indicate "to look intently, gaze" (Gen. 15:5; Ex. 33:8).

kingship cf. Isa. 6:5). At the least this would have made gazing upon the Lord a sign of severe disrespect. Whatever the reason for the Israelites' understanding, the Lord later confirms their instincts (cf. comment on 19:20–25), making Moses' reaction entirely appropriate.

3:7–10 The Lord's next words expand on his concern expressed in 2:24–25 and ring with hope: "I have surely seen[86] the affliction of my people . . . and have heard their cry because of their taskmasters. I know their sufferings"[87] (3:7). He will therefore remember and act on his covenant promises to "deliver them out of the hand of the Egyptians and . . . bring them . . . to a good and broad land, a land flowing with milk and honey," a poetic way of describing a land that will abundantly meet all their physical needs (cf. Deut. 8:7–10). It is a land inhabited by many peoples, but one he has promised on oath to them (Ex. 3:7–8). (For lists of peoples living in Canaan cf. Gen. 15:19–21; Ex. 3:17; 13:5; Num. 13:29; Deut. 7:1; etc. Those listed here are some of the most commonly mentioned.) In short, "I know your suffering and will act in keeping with my promises." The Lord emphasizes this by repeating the same idea in the verses to follow (cf. table 2.3). He also makes clear he will use Moses to deliver Israel.

TABLE 2.3: The Lord's Awareness and Action in Exodus 3

Awareness	Action
I have seen, heard, and know (3:7).	I will rescue them and give them a land (3:8).
Their cry has come to me and I have seen (3:9).	I will send you to deliver them (3:10).

3:11–12 But for the first of five times Moses resists the Lord (v. 11; cf. v. 13; 4:1, 10, 13). Some understand him to be expressing humility ("Who am I? This honor is too great!"). But the unfolding story makes clear that his words flow from fear and insecurity. Knowing this, the Lord focuses not on Moses' ability but on his presence with Moses (3:12a). In effect, "What matters is not who you are but the presence of the great 'I am' with you."[88]

Along with his presence the Lord promises a sign (3:12b). Its identification is debated. As translated by most versions the sign will be the Israelites' serving God in worship[89] on this mountain when they leave Egypt. That is the most natural reading of the Hebrew but is so far in the future that it does not address Moses' current need for encouragement (cf. Judg. 6:14–24). Another possible translation is, "And this [the burning bush] is[90] the sign for you, that I have sent you," a miracle to

---

[86] The Hebrew phrase emphasizes the activity.
[87] The sense is "to take note of and have concern about" (cf. Gen. 3:7; 39:6; Pss. 31:7; 144:3).
[88] Cf. Genesis 26:24; 31:3; Deuteronomy 31:23 (noted by Sarna, *Exodus*, 240n35); cf. also Psalm 23:4; Matthew 28:20.
[89] The word "serve" (Hb. *'abad*) commonly refers to worship and its rites (cf. Ex. 5:1, 3 with 7:16; 10:7, 8; 10:24–26; cf. also Deut. 4:19; 5:8–9), though such worship is to be accompanied by a life of obedience (Deut. 10:12–13; 11:13).
[90] Instead of "will be." In Hebrew the verb "to be" is omitted here (as it often is); it has to be supplied, and its tense must be determined from context.

assure him of his call (cf. Ex. 4:1–9), giving Moses confidence that "when you have brought the people out of Egypt, you shall serve God on this mountain." In either case the Lord promises clearly his presence and that Moses will deliver the people.

3:13–15 But Moses resists a second time. "If I come to the people of Israel and say to them, 'The God of your fathers has sent me to you,' and they ask me, 'What is his name?' what shall I say to them?" (v. 13). The answer will be important for establishing Moses' credibility. If he claims to speak on behalf of the God of the Israelites' forefathers, he needs to be able to identify him by name.[91]

The name itself is given in verse 15, though its pronunciation is debated. Its four consonants are *yhwh*, and the majority position understands the pronunciation to be "yahweh."[92] But the Hebrew text was originally written without vowels. For reasons lost to history, Jews at some point stopped pronouncing the name and instead said the Hebrew word for "my Lord" (*'adonay*) whenever they came across the divine name (leaving us unsure as to how it was really pronounced). The Greek translation followed suit, using the Greek word for "Lord" (*kyrios*) in place of the divine name. Most English translations follow this tradition, putting the word "Lord" in small capital letters to let the reader know that the divine name is being translated.

But what meaning, if any, should be given to this name? The debate is extensive.[93] There is agreement that the statement "I AM WHO I AM" (v. 14), which uses the verb "to be" (root *hyh*), is related to the divine name Yahweh (*yhwh*) (v. 15). A majority in fact holds that the name Yahweh is built on an older form of the verb "to be" (root *hwh*),[94] though the minority position may be correct that Yahweh simply sounds like the verb "to be."[95] In either case the "I am/I will be" statement is in some way related to the meaning of the divine name. But how?

We may consider this question by looking at three different approaches to the words "I AM WHO I AM." The first adjusts the vowels of "I am/I will be," leading to "I will cause to be what I will cause to be," that is, Yahweh is the Creator, who brings things into existence.[96] This description of Yahweh is theologically sound, but there is no textual evidence to support changing the vowels in verse 14, nor are there any instances in the OT of the verb "to be" being used causatively.

A second approach is well represented by Austin Surls in his *Making Sense of the Divine Name in Exodus*.[97] He notes that "I will be what I will be" is an *idem per idem* ("the same thing") statement, in which the same verb form appears twice, usually on either side of a relative particle. One use of *idem* statements is to describe the

---

[91] If the name Yahweh was not known previously, it would have done no good for Moses to find out his name in Exodus 3, since the Israelites "would not likely accept a completely new name for the god of their forefathers" (Surls, *Making Sense*, 49n30).
[92] See summary in Henry O. Thompson, "Yahweh," *ABD* 6.1011; for more detail cf. David N. Freedman and M. P. O'Connor, "יהוה YHWH," *TDOT* 5:501–512. For a contrasting opinion cf. Surls, *Making Sense*, 63–79.
[93] See the concise summary in Surls, *Making Sense*, 1–6.
[94] Cf. Freedman and O'Connor, "יהוה YHWH," 511–512; Roland de Vaux, "The Revelation of the Divine Name YHWH," in *Proclamation and Presence: Old Testament Essays in Honour of Gwynne Henton Davies*, ed. John I. Durham and J. R. Porter (Richmond, VA: John Knox, 1970), esp. 59–63.
[95] Surls, *Making Sense*, 63–67. For similar examples cf. Genesis 4:1; 5:29; 29:34. In each case the name sounds like the verb that explains it but is not necessarily built on that verb's root.
[96] Cf. Freedman and O'Connor, "יהוה YHWH," 500–521.
[97] Surls, *Making Sense*, 50–58.

widest range of activity. For instance 1 Samuel 23:13 could be woodenly rendered, "They went wherever they went," but is well translated, "They went wherever they could go." If we apply this to Exodus 3:14, the translation would be, "I will be whoever I will be," which Surls understands to be a way for the Lord to say that he "*would make sense of his name in the future*,"[98] that is, the Lord will reveal his character in what is to come in the rest of Exodus.

If we momentarily grant this translation of the name, we may still ask, "Is the Lord's intent to communicate by this phrase that he will make sense of his name in the future?" While this is not impossible, it may be noted that in describing a wide range of activity *idem* constructions can communicate a person's free will to do activity X without limits. "Bake what you will bake and boil what you will boil" (Ex. 16:23) is a way to say the person may bake or boil as much as he pleases, and the Lord's statement "I will speak the word that I will speak" (Ezek. 12:25) is his way of saying he will say whatever, and as much as, he wants to say. Taken in this way, "I will be whoever I will be" would be Yahweh's claim that no one can limit him in any way whatsoever; he is completely sovereign.[99] As noted further below, this claim of sovereignty fits very well with the upcoming narrative, since Yahweh's sovereignty over the so-called gods of Egypt is exactly what the text goes on to emphasize.

But it may also be questioned whether this translation of the phrase is correct. While the Lord certainly will show his character in what is to come, and this translation captures one possible understanding of the *idem* usage, such constructions can have another function as well (cf. below). Moreover, this translation leads to a possible tension in the verse's second half, where the name's explanation is shortened: "Tell the Israelites, 'I will be has sent me to you.'" The shortened "I will be" reads more as an affirmation of future existence, which is different in feel from "I will be whoever I will be" as an affirmation that the Lord will reveal his character.

This leads to the third approach, which translates either "I AM WHO I AM" or "I WILL BE WHO I WILL BE."[100] Either way, the focus is on the fact of the Lord's existence. Indeed, while an *idem* statement may describe a wide range of activity (cf. above), in some instances it expresses emphasis: "So *I fell down* before the LORD forty days and nights, which *I fell down*" (Deut. 9:25 AT), that is, "I fell *flat* on the ground for forty days and nights" (NET; cf. Deut. 1:46). As applied to Exodus 3:14, the idea would be, "I am—I really am!"[101]

---

98 Surls, *Making Sense*, 57, emphasis original.
99 Surls (*Making Sense*, 39–41) examines all fifty-two naming wordplays in the Pentateuch, placing them in one of three groups: description, commemoration, or anticipation. He notes that, "as a general rule," proper names explained by nouns belong in the description category, while proper names explained by verbs belong in the commemoration or anticipation category (56). He thus concludes that Exodus 3:14, which explains a proper name with a future-tense verb, belongs in the anticipation category, as describing a future event. But "general rule" is different than "absolute rule," and Surls himself identifies at least two examples in which a proper name in the description category is explained by a verb (Gen. 16:13–14; Num. 11:34b; cf. *Making Sense*, 39, 41). The same is equally possible here.
100 So most modern translations. Either translation is possible, thought most go with the present translation. The Hebrew verb form (*yiqtol*) is translated most often as an English future but can be translated as a present (cf. Joüon §113a, c, d).
101 For the significance of what the Lord is communicating by such emphasis, see further below, pp. 482–483.

This third approach explains why the Lord can shorten the name simply to "I am" in 3:14b, since both clauses now focus on the same point: the Lord's existence. But still, what does such a focus on existence communicate? In a word, the Lord is sovereignly unique, in terms both of his divinity (there is no god like him) and of his existence (there is no god but him). He *is* in a way that other gods are not, and *he* is while other gods are not. This understanding may be seen by paying close attention to the immediately following chapters (Exodus 5–12), which provide a narrative description of the significance of Yahweh's name, and by a later text that looks back on these narratives (Deut. 4:34–35). In Exodus 5 Pharaoh defiantly asks, "*Who is the* LORD, *that I should obey his voice and let Israel go?*" Yahweh then proceeds to forcefully answer that question! Primarily, he gives powerful signs that show his sovereignty over Pharaoh (Ex. 9:16), the gods of Egypt (12:12), and the entire earth (9:29; cf. 8:22). In the midst of these displays he draws specific attention to his name, proclaiming, "I am Yahweh" (7:17; 8:22; 10:2; 12:12; etc.), and also highlights that he is utterly unique: "This time I will send all my plagues on you yourself . . . so that you may know that *there is none like me* in all the earth" (9:14; cf. 8:10). He stresses the incomparable uniqueness of his divinity; no other god is like him (cf. 1 Kings 8:23; Ps. 86:8). He *is* in a way that other gods are not.

But to this must immediately be added that his divinity is so unique that it cancels out the thought that anything else exists that can even be called a god. When Deuteronomy looks back on all the signs the Lord performed in Exodus, it concludes with these words: "To you it was shown, that you might know that Yahweh is God; *there is no other besides him*" (Deut. 4:35 AT). In other words, *he* is, and other gods are not.

Indeed, the Bible holds together the ideas that the Lord is unique in terms of his divinity (no god is like him) and his existence (no god exists but him). The same verse can alternate between the two: "How great you are, Sovereign Yahweh! There is *no one like you*, and there is *no God but you*" (2 Sam. 7:22 AT; cf. 1 Sam. 2:2). This also explains why the plague narratives can focus on the fact that there is no god *like* him (Ex. 8:10; 9:14) even while Deuteronomy can look back on these narratives and focus on the fact that there is no god *but* him (Deut. 4:35). Biblically speaking, these are two sides of the same coin, and both sides of that coin are on display in Exodus.

In short, whether the second or the third translation above is correct, either may be understood to emphasize Yahweh's sovereign uniqueness: there is no god like him and no god but him—and the Israelites are to take deep comfort in such truth.

In the midst of the debate what must not be missed is that God has a name. If he had autographed the tablets with the Ten Commandments, he would have signed "Yahweh." He is not some nameless power. He is a divine person who acts sovereignly on his people's behalf, in this case by sending his appointed deliverer (the text emphasizes three times the Lord sent Moses; Ex. 3:13–15). Furthermore, he is the same God as that of the Israelites' forefathers, known to them by this name (v. 15a) and to be remembered by this name for the coming generations (v. 15b).

And because he is this same God he will fulfill the promises he made to Israel's forefathers—as he now goes on to make clear.

3:16–22 Moses is to gather the people's representatives (the elders) and let them know that their forefathers' God has appeared to him and taken favorable note of them and their suffering, and he will deliver them and lead them to a good land (vv. 16–17; cf. vv. 7–8).[102] The Lord then summarizes how the deliverance will occur, providing an overview of the coming chapters:

- The elders will believe him (v. 18; cf. 4:31).
- They will all ask Pharaoh's permission to go and worship the Lord; Pharaoh will refuse (3:18–19; cf. 5:1–4).[103]
- The Lord will strike Egypt with his wonders; Pharaoh will eventually agree to the people's leaving (3:20; cf. 7:1–12:32).
- When the people leave, the Lord will give them such favor before the Egyptians that they will be able to plunder their jewelry and clothing—appropriate compensation for years of bitterly hard service![104]—simply by asking for material goods, placing these things on the very children whom the Egyptians had tried to destroy (3:21–22; cf. 12:33–36 and Gen. 15:14).

In short, the Lord will deliver and richly supply them; their salvation and gifts come completely from him.

4:1–9 But Moses continues to resist (v. 1), and his claim that "they will not . . . listen to my voice" (v. 1) goes directly against the Lord's promise only a few verses earlier that "they will listen to your voice" (3:18). This paints Moses negatively. But the Lord, who is "slow to anger" (34:6), responds patiently, providing Moses with three signs to confirm Moses' status as the Lord's spokesman (4:2–9; cf. 1 Kings 17:22–24).[105]

The first sign involves Moses' staff, an item commonly carried by shepherds[106] but also by leaders (Num. 17:2), perhaps foreshadowing Moses' coming role. The Lord's question ("What is that in your hand?") draws his attention to the staff and its ordinary nature. When Moses throws it down and it turns into a snake, he is as surprised as anyone and runs away in fear (Ex. 4:3)!

The Lord's next command is to grasp it by the tail. Debate exists whether this approach is more dangerous (since the head is free to bite), therefore requiring more faith, or the safer approach (taken by some today working with larger

---

[102] The word "observed" (3:16) can refer to observing with favor or showing favorable care (cf. this word's use for "visit" [with favor] in Gen. 21:1 and "care for him" in Ps. 8:4).
[103] The elders are not mentioned in Exodus 5:1–4, perhaps because the narrator focuses on Moses and Aaron as the group's spokesmen. For "mighty hand" (3:19) cf. 6:1, "strong hand."
[104] Sarna, *Exodus*, 19, citing earlier commentators to this end.
[105] Confirming Moses' status is the signs' primary role. Suggestions have been made about secondary messages the signs may be communicating by means of symbolism, but the text does not give enough information to raise any of these suggestions above the level of guesswork.
[106] Though using a different Hebrew word; cf. Leviticus 27:32; Psalm 23:4; Micah 7:14.

snakes)¹⁰⁷ and therefore a more logical command. Either way, Moses is not a snake handler! Reaching out to grasp a snake is presumably an unnatural act requiring faith. When Moses obeys, the snake turns back into a staff (v. 4), and the Lord affirms that this sign will lead the Israelites to believe he has appeared to Moses (v. 5).

But, if not, there is a second sign. The Lord commands Moses to put his hand inside his cloak or, more woodenly, on his "chest/bosom" (v. 6 ESV mg.). When he pulls it out, it is ravaged by disease, leaving it covered in dead or blistered skin that flakes off like snow.¹⁰⁸ The Lord then commands him to put his diseased hand back inside his cloak onto his healthy body—another unnatural act requiring faith! When he does, the hand is perfectly restored (v. 7), and the Lord affirms that the second sign will serve as further proof if the Israelites do not believe the first (v. 8).

In case they do not believe the first two signs, the Lord gives Moses a third.¹⁰⁹ In this case he is to take Nile water and pour it on the ground, and it will turn into blood (v. 9). Unlike the first two signs, he cannot perform this one now (he is nowhere near the Nile), but in light of the first two he has every reason to believe that the third is possible and that the Lord is with him.

4:10–12 And yet Moses resists a fourth time, appealing to his inability to speak well (v. 10). To be "slow of speech and of tongue" may refer to a speech impediment or may refer simply to a lack of persuasive eloquence. The context supports the latter, since the Lord promises to teach Moses "what you shall speak" (not "how to speak," v. 12; cf. comment on 6:10–12). Either way, the Lord is asking him to do something he feels unqualified to do.

The Lord meets Moses' weakness with his own strength and presence. In terms of strength he is the sovereign King; he has made people's mouths so they can speak, and he can make people deaf or mute, seeing or blind (v. 11). How much more can he do something as simple as enabling Moses to speak well! In terms of presence he promises, "I will be with your mouth"—the word "I" is emphasized in Hebrew—"and teach you what you shall speak" (v. 12). What he requires of his servants he equips them to do. Indeed, Moses' two uses of "I" in verse 10 are met with the Lord's two uses of "I" in verses 11–12. "Moses feels his 'I' is inadequate for the task; Yahweh responds by saying that it is his 'I' that is to be reckoned with."¹¹⁰

4:13–17 Yet Moses does not embrace his call but resists a fifth and final time. Unlike with the first four instances, he now provides no excuse. He simply asks the Lord to send someone else—anyone but him. His refusal of the Lord's call is now clear (v. 13).

---

107 A search for "Steve Irwin Africa's Deadliest Snakes" should result in videos showing this approach—though his actions should not be imitated by nonprofessionals!
108 The word translated "leprous" refers to various skin diseases (cf. ESV mg.). Whether leprosy was among them is debated, but the Hebrew term is clearly very broad; cf. Sklar, *Leviticus*, TOTC, 183–184.
109 This should serve as final confirmation, since in ancient Israel to do or say something three times was to emphasize it (1 Sam. 20:41; Isa. 6:3); cf. Richard S. Hess, "Leviticus," in *Genesis–Leviticus*, ed. Tremper Longman III and David E. Garland, rev. ed., EBC 1 (Grand Rapids, MI: Zondervan, 2008), 703.
110 Enns, *Exodus*, 111.

Whereas the Lord previously responded patiently, this time his anger is aroused (v. 14). The Lord is abundantly merciful with our weaknesses and lack of faith, but there comes a point when he says, "Enough! You must take me at my word!"

Even here, however, he accommodates Moses' fear by providing a support in the person of his brother, Aaron, three years his elder (7:7) and able to speak well (4:14). The mention of Aaron's being a Levite perhaps prepares us for his priestly role,[111] or it may be a play on words anticipating Aaron's joining with Moses.[112] The mention of Aaron's being glad when he comes assures Moses that Aaron still loves him after all these years and will be happy to work with him (v. 14).[113] But even here the Lord reemphasizes his own empowering and guiding presence: "I will be with your mouth and with his mouth and will teach you both what to do" (v. 15b; cf. v. 12). The Lord's help remains his people's ultimate need.

The Lord also clarifies Moses and Aaron's respective roles, telling Moses, "You shall ... put the words in his mouth" (v. 15a), that is, the words the Lord will speak to Moses. The Lord reiterates this when he says, "He [Aaron] shall speak for you [Moses] to the people, and he shall be your mouth, and you shall be as God to him" (v. 16)—that is, he will receive the divine message from you (which you will receive from me) and will pass it along to the people on your behalf (cf. 7:1–2).

The Lord gives a final command: "Take in your hand this staff, with which you shall do the signs" (4:17). But would Moses not naturally take his staff with him? And why mention "signs," since the staff is involved with only one of the three just given? As will become clear, this staff will be central to many of the signs the Lord will perform through Moses (9:23; 10:13; 14:16), and the Lord's focus on it here foreshadows the significant role it will play.

Response

WHO IS THE LORD?

At the burning bush the hot glow of the Lord's holiness spreads like heat from a furnace, sanctifying the very ground around it (cf. comment on 3:4–6). To be holy is to be set apart as unique,[114] and the Lord's self-description—"I AM WHO I AM"—emphasizes how unique he is. There is no god like him and no god but him (cf. comment on 3:13–15). The opening chapters especially emphasize how unique the Lord is in his love and power.

First, the Lord shows his love through his awareness of the Israelites' suffering and his commitment to rescue them (2:24–25; 3:7–10, 16–17). Exodus 2:24–25 uses the word "God" four times to emphasize his activity and then describe it with richly significant terms. We might paraphrase, "God gave heed[115] to Israel's

---

[111] The phrase could also be translated "your brother Levite," thus emphasizing Moses and Aaron's Levite heritage (Sarna, *Exodus*, 22, 241n11, citing Deut. 15:12).
[112] The Hebrew for "Levite" sounds like the Hebrew for "to join" (cf. Num. 18:2; Cassuto, *Commentary on the Book of Exodus*, 50).
[113] "He is coming out" (Ex. 4:14) can be translated "he will be coming out"; cf. Houtman (*Exodus*, vol. 1, 181) notes that a participle after "behold" can refer to an imminent event; cf. 4:23; 7:17). This approach to 4:14 fits well with 4:27.
[114] Cf. Leviticus 20:26; cf. also Sklar, *Leviticus*, ZECOT, Introduction, §3b.
[115] For "hear" (*shama'*) with this sense cf. Genesis 16:11; Exodus 3:7.

groaning, and God determined to act according to his covenant promises.[116] Indeed, God looked compassionately on his people [cf. Gen. 29:32; Ex. 3:7; 4:31] and with concern took notice of their sufferings [cf. Gen. 39:6; 3:7; Pss. 31:7; 144:3]." He loves them and will deliver them.

This leads to his power. As Exodus 3 ends, the Lord previews that his deliverance will be seen by displaying his "mighty hand" through "wonders" (Ex. 3:19–20). These wonders will go off like nuclear bomb blasts, so powerful that Pharaoh and all Egypt will know that "there is none like [the Lord] in all the earth" (9:14; cf. 8:10). Power is praiseworthy only when directed to good ends, but that is exactly the case here: his power is guided by his love, which leads him to deliver his people from evil.

The greatest demonstration of such power and love is seen in Jesus. The Lord's statement, "I AM WHO I AM" (3:14), reminds us of the day Jesus told religious leaders, "Before Abraham was, I am" (John 8:58). He was equating himself to Yahweh, and the leaders did not miss it, wanting to execute him on the spot for blasphemy—and sadly missing that the God of love and power had shown up in Jesus to deliver them, not from political power but from slavery to sin's power (Rom. 8:38–39; Col. 1:13; Rev. 1:5). Only God can rescue us from the mess we have gotten ourselves into with our sin, and he has done so, with power and love, through Jesus, the ultimate deliverer.

WHO IS MOSES?

The topic of deliverance brings us back to Moses. Chapter 2 introduced us to him as the one the Lord would use to deliver Israel. Chapters 3–4 describe his call and commission as deliverer. But they also show it to be a call and commission he does not want.

As soon as the Lord tells Moses he will be Israel's deliverer, Moses questions his ability to play that role (3:10–11). This is the first of five times Moses will resist the Lord's call, and, while it may appear he is being humble, by the end it is clear he is driven by fear, finally asking the Lord to send anyone but him (4:13).

Why highlight Moses' five responses? Doing so shows on the one hand that his rise to leadership is not fueled by a desire for power or glory (cf. Num. 11:29; 12:1–9). He ultimately takes this role out of obedience, not longing. At the same time his responses show his weakness and frailty. The Lord does not choose a courageous man with deep faith. He chooses a man whose courage and faith are small, then teaches him over the years how to find courage and strength in his God. As Paul notes, "God chose what is weak in the world to shame the strong ... so that no human being might boast in the presence of God" (1 Cor. 1:27, 29). The portrayal of Moses encourages us that God can still use us in our weakness. It also humbles

---

[116] "In a context like this, 'remember' means to act in faithfulness to His word of promise"; Allan Harman, *Exodus* (Glasgow, UK: Christian Focus, 2017), 63–64, citing Gen. 8:1; cf. also Gen. 9:15, 16; Ex. 6:5; Lev. 26:45. Ortlund summarizes: "*Remember* . . . is covenant language. It is relational. This is remembering not as the alternative to forgetting but as the alternative to *forsaking*"; Dane Ortlund, *Gentle and Lowly: The Heart of Christ for Sinners and Sufferers* (Wheaton, IL: Crossway, 2020), 165, emphasis original.

us, reminding us that, when God does use us, we have a chance to give him honor and glory for using weak things to accomplish his purposes.

Still, for Moses to resist the call of God himself is no small matter, leading to a final question.

HOW DOES THE LORD RESPOND TO MOSES?

The Lord's first response is not indignation or anger. He has just shown up to Moses in a miraculous way, clearly showing himself to be God—and Moses still resists him. The Lord would be just to say immediately, "Do you not know who you are talking to? Do you not see my miraculous power before your very eyes? Now do as I command!"

But the Lord is "merciful and gracious, slow to anger, and abounding in steadfast love and faithfulness" (Ex. 34:6), and so he responds with patient grace the first four times, reassuring and providing for legitimate needs. To Moses' sense of inadequacy (3:11) he reassures with his presence (v. 12). In effect, "What matters is not who you are but the powerful presence of the great 'I am' with you" (cf. Ps. 23:4; Matt. 28:20; Acts 18:9–10). To Moses' question about God's name (Ex. 3:13) he not only identifies it but describes the bountiful protection and care he will show his people (vv. 14–22). To Moses' concern about the people not believing him (4:1) he reassures with powerful signs that will affirm his call (vv. 2–9). To Moses' lack of gifting he speaks of his own power and promises his equipping presence for the task (vv. 11–12). In each case the Lord shows patient grace. He knows we are but dust, and he is much more patient with us than we are with ourselves.

But his patience finally comes to an end. After Moses' fifth response, in which he asks the Lord to send anyone but him (v. 13), the "anger of the LORD was kindled against Moses" (v. 14). Even in our weakness the Lord expects obedience, not because we have the strength within ourselves but because he promises to give the strength we need. By faith we look to him for strength, and by faith we receive strength from him, so that by faith we might live a life pleasing to him.

Even in his anger, however, the Lord continues to show Moses tremendous grace. He begins by providing human help in Aaron, a man well gifted for the task (v. 14). But more importantly he reemphasizes his empowering and guiding presence: "I will be with your mouth and with his mouth and will teach you both what to do" (v. 15; cf. v. 12). The Lord's help remains his people's ultimate need. And he provides it freely to those who look to him in faith.

EXODUS 4:18–31

¹⁸ Moses went back to Jethro his father-in-law and said to him, "Please let me go back to my brothers in Egypt to see whether they are still alive." And Jethro said to Moses, "Go in peace." ¹⁹ And the Lord said to Moses in Midian, "Go back to Egypt, for all the men who were seeking your life are dead." ²⁰ So Moses took his wife and his sons and had them ride on a donkey, and went back to the land of Egypt. And Moses took the staff of God in his hand.

²¹ And the Lord said to Moses, "When you go back to Egypt, see that you do before Pharaoh all the miracles that I have put in your power. But I will harden his heart, so that he will not let the people go. ²² Then you shall say to Pharaoh, 'Thus says the Lord, Israel is my firstborn son, ²³ and I say to you, "Let my son go that he may serve me." If you refuse to let him go, behold, I will kill your firstborn son.'"

²⁴ At a lodging place on the way the Lord met him and sought to put him to death. ²⁵ Then Zipporah took a flint and cut off her son's foreskin and touched Moses'[1] feet with it and said, "Surely you are a bridegroom of blood to me!" ²⁶ So he let him alone. It was then that she said, "A bridegroom of blood," because of the circumcision.

²⁷ The Lord said to Aaron, "Go into the wilderness to meet Moses." So he went and met him at the mountain of God and kissed him. ²⁸ And Moses told Aaron all the words of the Lord with which he had sent him to speak, and all the signs that he had commanded him to do. ²⁹ Then Moses and Aaron went and gathered together all the elders of the people of Israel. ³⁰ Aaron spoke all the words that the Lord had spoken to Moses and did the signs in the sight of the people. ³¹ And the people believed; and when they heard that the Lord had visited the people of Israel and that he had seen their affliction, they bowed their heads and worshiped.

[1] Hebrew *his*

Section Overview

With his call and commission now complete (Ex. 2:23–4:17) Moses returns to Egypt (vv. 18–20). Sometime before or during the journey the Lord again previews how he will deliver the Israelites (vv. 21–23; cf. 3:16–22), emphasizing his sovereignty over Pharaoh and Israel's status as his firstborn son—a status implying Israel both is loved by the Lord and has obligations to serve him (cf. comment on 4:21–23).

The journey is interrupted by the bridegroom of blood episode (vv. 24–26), which seems to underscore, at the least, that all Israelites (leaders not excepted) must raise their children as covenant members. The story resumes with Aaron and

Moses' joyful reunion (vv. 27–28) and return to Egypt, where they inform their fellow Israelites that the Lord has taken favorable note of them and will deliver them (vv. 29–31). The Israelites believe their words and worship the Lord (v. 31), leaving us with a sense of unity and faith among the Lord's people—a unity and faith that soon will be sorely tested.

Section Outline

I. Israel in Egypt: the Lord promises deliverance (1:1–11:10) . . .
   C. Moses returns to Egypt (4:18–31)
      1. Moses departs for Egypt (4:18–20)
      2. The Lord previews what will happen (4:21–23)
      3. The "bridegroom of blood" episode (4:24–26)
      4. The reunion of Aaron and Moses (4:27–28)
      5. Their return to Egypt and the people's worshipful response to the Lord's message (4:29–31)

Comment

4:18–20 Moses returns from the mountain to his father-in-law, Jethro, seeking permission to return to Egypt (v. 18). For Moses to take his wife and children (Jethro's daughter and grandchildren) and leave without asking would seriously breach family protocol (cf. Gen. 31:17–28).

Moses does not tell Jethro the full story at this point (though we are not told why). Rather, he mentions his natural desire to see whether his "brothers" are still living—likely a reference either to his relatives (the same word is translated "kinsmen" in Gen. 13:8) or to fellow Israelites in general.[117] Jethro agrees to the request, and after an unspecified amount of time the Lord commands Moses to return to Egypt, assuring him that those seeking his life have died (Ex. 4:19; cf. 2:15). So Moses puts his wife (Zipporah) and his sons (Gershom and Eliezer) onto a donkey and begins the journey (4:20a). The narrator highlights that Moses takes his "staff" with him (v. 20b), signaling again that it will be central to the coming drama (cf. comment on 4:13–17). Indeed, it is called the "staff of God" (cf. 17:9), presumably because God will work miracles by it. In any case to have a "staff of God" is to have a divine weapon and to be equipped to do mighty things.

4:21–23 Either before or during the journey the Lord again gives Moses a preview of what will take place in Egypt (vv. 21–23; cf. 3:16–22). He focuses especially on his sovereignty over Pharaoh and on Israel's status as his firstborn son.

In terms of sovereignty the Lord commands Moses to perform the signs before Pharaoh and then states, "But I"—the Hebrew emphasizes the pronoun—"will harden his heart, so that he will not let the people go" (4:21). References to Pharaoh's heart's being "hard" occur throughout these chapters (7:3, 13, 14, 22; 8:15, 19, 32; 9:7, 12, 34, 35; 10:1, 20, 27; 11:10; 14:4, 8; cf. 14:17). Although it is

---

117 Exodus 2:11 (Cassuto, *Commentary on the Book of Exodus*, 53).

hard to see in English translations, three different Hebrew roots are used (*hazaq, qashah, kaved*). These appear to be used interchangeably, however, so that a consistent English translation such as "to harden/be hard" or "to make stubborn/be stubborn" is justifiable.[118] It may also be noted how the words are used with three different subjects: (1) the Lord, who hardens Pharaoh's heart (4:21; 7:3; etc.); (2) Pharaoh, who hardens his own heart (8:15, 32; 9:34); and (3) Pharaoh's heart, which is said to be hard/hardened (7:13, 14; 8:19; etc.).

In Exodus to have a "hard heart" is not to lack compassion (which is what English speakers often mean by such language). Rather, the phrase refers to a heart that is rebelliously stubborn in its refusal to change. Once the signs of chapters 7–14 start a discernible pattern is evident. *Before* the sign Pharaoh stubbornly refuses to obey the Lord's command. This is named first in 5:1–2 and stays consistent throughout the chapters. *After* the sign Pharaoh continues his stubborn refusal to obey the Lord's command (7:14, 22; 8:15, 19, 32; 9:7, 12, 34, 35; 10:20, 27–28; 14:4, 8). In between these two responses his heart is said to be hard or to be hardened by himself or the Lord (7:13, 14, 22; 8:15, 19, 32; 9:7, 12, 34, 35; 10:1, 20, 27; 11:10; 14:4, 8; cf. 14:17). In short the effect of his heart's being hard or hardened is that Pharaoh continues in his sinful path, impervious to change and even strengthened in his rebellious stubbornness.

To return to our passage, when the Lord says, "I will harden his heart" (4:21), he is not speaking of taking a good heart and making it bad. Pharaoh has long ago decided to treat the Israelites as slaves and oppress them brutally.[119] Rather, the Lord is saying he will take a heart hardened in rebellion and make it harder still, strengthening it in its deepest convictions,[120] "seconding, as it were," Pharaoh's own earlier decision to harden it.[121] In a sobering punishment that fits the crime the Lord sometimes judges us by giving us over to our heart's evil desires and then bringing his justice to bear against us for the evil we commit (cf. esp. 9:34 with 10:1; cf. also Ps. 81:11–12 and esp. Rom. 1:28–32). This is a severe warning about the danger of sin, which coats our hearts like quick-drying cement, making repentance increasingly difficult and judgment increasingly certain.

In sum the sense of "hardening" with each of the different subjects is as follows: (1) the Lord "hardens" Pharaoh's stubborn heart, that is, makes it harder still (4:21; 7:3; 9:12; 10:20, 27; 11:10; 14:4, 8, 17 [Egypt's heart]); (2) Pharaoh "hardens" his stubborn heart, that is, makes it harder still (8:11, 28; 9:34 [joined by his servants]);

---

118 Cf. Exodus 7:13 (Hb. *hazaq*) with 7:14 (*kaved*) and 7:3–4a (*qashah*).
119 Cf. Exodus 4:7–8. Pharaoh's actions in 5:2–9 only further his brutal oppression of the Israelites.
120 Alexander, *Exodus*, ApOTC, 187.
121 Walter C. Kaiser, *Exodus*, in *Genesis–Leviticus*, 359. Paul anticipates the philosophical objection this raises: "You will say to me then, 'Why does [God] still find fault? For who can resist his will?'" (Rom. 9:19). Paul's own answer is twofold: (1) Humans are in no place to question God's sovereign will (Rom. 9:20–21; cf. 11:33–36), and (2) God's judgment for sin makes his mercy for sinners stand out all the more (Rom. 9:22–29). Ultimately, Paul is not attempting to resolve the philosophical tension between God's complete sovereignty and humans' moral responsibility. Such tensions exist elsewhere in the Bible, for example, in the Trinity (How can each member be fully God and yet there be only one God?) or the nature of Christ (How can he be fully God and fully man?). The presence of such tensions is no surprise. Full understanding of the infinite God is beyond our finite capacities. In Exodus these chapters emphasize both the Lord's sovereign power over Pharaoh by hardening his heart and Pharaoh's culpability for his rebellion.

and (3) Pharaoh's stubborn "heart is hard/hardened," that is, continues in its stubborn rebellion and becomes harder still (7:13, 14, 22; 8:15; 9:7, 35).

Along with his sovereignty over Pharaoh the Lord also highlights Israel's status as his "firstborn son" (4:22–23). This status has at least two implications. First, it assumes the Lord's special love for his people.[122] In ancient Israel firstborn sons held a special place in the family. Men were heads of households, and their firstborn sons were known as the "firstfruits" of the father's "strength," an image in which the man's offspring are like a bountiful field and the firstborn the firstfruits of that field's harvest (Gen. 49:3; Pss. 78:51; 105:36). And, since the firstfruits were especially valuable (Num. 18:12), to describe firstborn sons with such language speaks to their special worth (cf. Mic. 6:7; Zech. 12:10).

Second, being the firstborn meant having a special role. Firstborns were to be "preeminent in dignity and preeminent in power" (Gen. 49:3), since they were responsible to maintain the well-being of the household and its honor.[123] This explains why they received a double inheritance, known as the "right of the firstborn" (Deut. 21:17), since resources were needed in order to carry out this role. It also meant they had to learn the father's business and would "serve" him during his life, which is the focus here: "Let my son go that he may serve me" (Ex. 4:23). They are no longer to "serve" Pharaoh as slaves but to "serve" Yahweh as sons.[124] How so?

On the one hand the word "serve" in this context describes worship (cf. comment on 3:11–12). Moses' later requests to Pharaoh can substitute the word "serve" with "hold a [religious] feast to" the Lord (5:1; cf. 10:9, 24–26) or "[make] sacrifice to the LORD" (5:3). At the same time, when used in combination with Israel's description as "firstborn son," the word "serve" evokes the larger social background just named: Israel is to obey the Lord in all of life, maintaining the Lord's honor in this world.

The above also means that to harm Israel, or even to prevent him from serving his heavenly Father, is beyond serious. (We might consider how wrong it would seem to us if someone came and took away and enslaved our child.) The threat is therefore most serious as well: the death of Egypt's firstborn sons. As the story unfolds the fulfillment of this threat is delayed. The Lord warns Egypt repeatedly about its wickedness, sending nine different plagues, like warning shots across the bow, but to no avail. This leads finally to the last plague, a shot now aimed at the ship's very heart: those who have refused to release Israel, the Lord's firstborn son, will lose their own—through death (4:23).[125]

But this punishment raises serious ethical questions for some. Is it not unjust to single out the firstborn for death? Why not just kill Pharaoh himself? Any answers

---

[122] Cf. Jeremiah 31:9, 20; Hosea 11:1; C. F. Keil, *Biblical Commentary on the Old Testament: Exodus*, vol. 1, *The Pentateuch*, trans. James Martin (1864; repr. Grand Rapids, MI: Eerdmans, 1988), 458.
[123] Cf. Matthews, "Family Relationships," 293.
[124] Based on an observation by my students Christina Hannah and Nelson and Nicole Hall.
[125] In Exodus 4:23 the Lord is addressing Pharaoh directly and therefore mentions only Pharaoh's firstborn, but the sign's fulfillment will apply to all Egyptian firstborn (11:5). We might note as well that translating 4:23b as conditional ("if") is possible (ESV), but the usual translation would be nonconditional (so most versions and commentators).

to these questions must begin by acknowledging the difficulty most feel regarding them. This passage is hard, even painful, for many. Personally, I have wrestled with this passage over the years more than almost any other in the Bible. How do we square this story with the biblical teaching that God is good?

In surveying the various approaches taken, I have found it helpful to begin with two steps.[126] The first is to remember that the term "firstborn" in general refers to birth order, not age, meaning it would refer to refer to any firstborn, including grown sons who were mature adults. The second is then to discuss separately the firstborn old enough to be morally culpable and the firstborn too young to be morally culpable. I begin with the firstborn old enough to be morally culpable and make four observations.

First, guilt for this situation cannot be isolated to Pharaoh.

> It would seem reasonable to suggest that . . . Pharaoh was hardly the only guilty party in the oppression of the Israelites. His order had to be carried out throughout the entire land, and this required the willing cooperation of his own court officials, regional administrators, military general officers and lesser officers, and civilians of all ranks and types.[127]

Pharaoh might have been most guilty, but the nation helped (just as Hitler might have been most guilty, but the nation helped). This was a guilt problem for Egypt as a whole, including mature firstborn sons.

But why make them the focus of the judgment? This leads to the next three observations: targeting the firstborn was a display of God's sovereignty, a punishment corresponding to the crime, and an act of judgment tempered by mercy. In terms of God's sovereignty firstborn sons were known as the firstfruits of someone's strength (Gen. 49:3; Pss. 78:51; 105:36), representing the household's vitality and, as the future head of the household, its very heart. To kill the firstborn of a nation is thus to proclaim God's sovereignty over its very existence. By this plague the Lord thus displays his sovereign power over the heart of Egypt's own strength (its firstborn) and his sovereign ability to deliver his own firstborn, the nation of Israel (Ex. 12:12; 13:14–16; Pss. 78:51; 105:36; 135:8; 136:10).

In terms of this being a punishment corresponding to the crime, because Israel was the Lord's own firstborn son, the punishment comes upon Egypt's firstborn sons. This would bring home to Egyptians, in the most personal of ways, the nature and severity of their wrong.

And yet, while the Egyptians would have experienced this as incredibly painful, it was judgment tempered by mercy. Whereas the Egyptians were trying to wipe out all Israelite males (Ex. 1:22), the Lord focused on the Egyptian firstborn, a much smaller number. The loss was still incredibly severe, but the judgment was targeted, not indiscriminate like the Egyptians' attempts.

---

126 Some of the ideas of the following paragraphs have been helped over the years by thoughts drawn from papers by my students. Two group papers were particularly helpful: that of Cole Lescher, Jeremy McNeill, and Joshua Hammans and of Jeremy King, Victor Mallin, and Zach Schwartzbeck.
127 Stuart, *Exodus*, 265; cf. Exodus 1:22; 2:11; 5:10–14.

This leaves the more difficult issue of the firstborn not old enough to be morally culpable for the wrongs done to Israel. I have found it helpful here to distinguish between temporal judgment and eternal destiny. The death of the firstborn was clearly the former; they died as a sign of God's judgment on the sin of Pharaoh and Egyptian society, even if they did not participate in the community's wrongs. The same happens elsewhere in punishments brought on a community: when the Lord punished Israel with defeat in war and exile for the sin of its society, many Israelite children would have died that were innocent of the wrongs that led to the punishment. The death of these covenant children in the community's temporal judgment did not mean they would suffer eternal judgment. Rather, their death only brought them sooner into the joys of heaven itself. In short an important distinction exists between temporal judgment and eternal destiny. In Exodus the former is the focus, not the latter. And, while the Bible nowhere addresses the eternal destiny of children who die outside of the covenant community, I find myself at this point remembering the question of Abraham: "Shall not the Judge of all the earth do what is just?" (Gen. 18:25). And I rest in that.

4:24–26 At first glance the next episode is one of the most curious in Exodus (and, some would say, the entire OT). The text leaves much unsaid, leading to a wide range of opinions concerning its meaning.[128] Most agree that the Lord seeks to kill Moses (Ex. 4:24) and that Zipporah's actions save him (vv. 25–26). But what is the connection between the two? And why does the Lord seek Moses' death in the first place?

Circumcision is central to this story (v. 25). Earlier, the Lord had commanded Abraham to circumcise his sons as the covenant sign, a sign that was to be applied throughout the generations (Gen. 17:10–13). All those who were not circumcised were considered covenant breakers and were to be cut off from the Lord's people (Gen. 17:14). That Moses' son—presumably his firstborn (cf. Ex. 4:25 with 2:21–22)—is not circumcised puts Moses in the same position as Pharaoh: just as Pharaoh is withholding firstborn son Israel from the Lord by not releasing him (4:22–23), Moses is withholding his firstborn son from the Lord by not applying to him the covenant sign. That the Lord seeks Moses' death underscores the wrong's severity (and is a warning to all Israelites to be sure to raise their children in the Lord's covenant). It also explains why Zipporah's action saves Moses, since she immediately resolves the problem by applying the covenant sign to their son.

While not all agree with the approach just named, the diversity of opinion increases tenfold when we ask, "But why does Zipporah touch the foreskin to Moses' feet[129] and describe him as a 'bridegroom of blood' (vv. 25–26)?" Here one is on much shakier ground, as it seems that answering these questions with any

---

[128] For an overview of approaches cf. Houtman, *Exodus*, vol. 1, 439–447; more succinctly, Wright, *Exodus*, 151–155 (his conclusions overlap with those above); Stuart, *Exodus*, 152n112.

[129] Most understand Moses as the referent of "his" and "him" throughout, and such an approach causes the fewest difficulties (e.g., whoever is touched appears to be the same person called a "bridegroom," which must apply to Moses). Another question is whether "feet" is here a euphemism for the genitals (for such a use of "feet" compare ESV with NIV and NET on Isa. 7:20).

degree of certainty requires background knowledge the text assumes but does not state. To the second question one may note that verse 26 implies this saying to be well-known among Israelites. Its meaning, however, remains mysterious, as does the action accompanying it, and the preacher or teacher would do well to avoid building any points of application on proposed answers to these two specific questions.

4:27–28 While Moses is headed from Midian to Egypt, the Lord commands Aaron to meet him in the wilderness (v. 27a). They meet at the mountain of God—Mount Sinai (cf. comment on 3:1–3)—and Aaron gives him a typical family greeting (4:27b; cf. Gen. 29:13; Ex. 18:7). Since Aaron is to be Moses' spokesman (4:15–16), Moses conveys to him the Lord's words and also the signs he is to perform to certify the Lord has sent him (v. 28; for the latter, cf. 4:1–9).

4:29–31 Returning together to Egypt, Moses and Aaron gather the Israelite elders (cf. 3:16), who represent the people, and Aaron declares the Lord's words to them and performs the signs (4:29–30), the latter perhaps at Moses' command (cf. 7:9–10, 19; 8:5–6). The people see and believe and are able to hear that the Lord has taken favorable note of them (cf. note 102 within comment on 3:16–22 for this sense of "visit") and understands their affliction (4:31a; cf. 3:7–9, 16). Appropriately, they bow in homage and worship the Lord (4:31b). As noted in the Section Overview, this leaves the reader with a sense of unity and faith among God's people—a unity and faith soon to be sorely tested.

Response

WHAT IS THE SIGNIFICANCE OF BEING A FIRSTBORN SON?

As previously noted (4:21–23), the Israelites' status as the Lord's firstborn son has two implications. First, they are the object of God's special fatherly love, an image the Bible returns to frequently: "In the wilderness ... you have seen how the LORD your God carried you, as a man carries his son" (Deut. 1:31); "When Israel was a child, I loved him, and out of Egypt I called my son" (Hos. 11:1).[130] In light of this image we do well to ask whether we view God the Father as having that kind of tender love and care for us. Do we take comfort from the love of Christ (Phil. 2:1)? If such love and care are real, how should that impact how we feel in the midst of worry? How should we face trials or the future?

The second implication of Israel's firstborn status is its responsibility to "serve" the Lord. This word refers to worshiping the Lord but also evokes Israel's social context, in which firstborn sons are to serve their father faithfully and so maintain his honor (cf. comment on 4:21–23). Israel will do so by obeying the Lord wholeheartedly. Since his laws are wise and good, following them will show the world the glories of belonging to this household and the glories of the Lord to whom it belongs (Deut. 4:5–8). As Jesus will later say, "Let your light shine before oth-

---

[130] Cf. Isaiah 46:3; Matthew 7:11; Romans 8:15; 2 Corinthians 6:18; Revelation 21:7. For other images expressing the same tender love cf. Deuteronomy 32:11; Isaiah 40:11.

ers, so that they may see your good works and give glory to your Father who is in heaven" (Matt. 5:16). Like a good father, the Lord gives us his commands in love. To follow them is to honor him with obedience and to show the world the glories of following a God so good and loving—and hopefully to make others long to become members of his household.

Pharaoh, however, has no such longing, repeatedly oppressing the Lord's people because of his hardened heart. This leads to a second question.

WHAT DOES IT MEAN TO HAVE A HARDENED HEART?

To have a hardened heart does not mean to lack compassion, and to harden a heart does not mean to take a good heart and make it bad. To harden a heart means to take a heart already hardened in rebellion and to make it harder still (cf. comment on 4:21–23). Pharaoh does this to himself in rebellion (8:11, 28; 9:34), and the Lord does this to him in judgment (4:21; 7:3; etc.).

This last point is especially sobering. The Lord's judgment sometimes involves giving us over to our heart's evil desires. As noted above, this is a stark warning about the danger of sin, which coats our hearts like quick-drying cement, making repentance increasingly difficult and judgment increasingly certain. It is no wonder, then, that Jesus warns us to gouge out our eye or cut off our hand if it leads us to sin, explaining, "It is better that you lose one of your members than that your whole body be thrown into hell" (Matt. 5:29, 30). He knows sin's power to harden our hearts and to cause us to reject the Lord of life. Given this reality, do we view sin as a mortal enemy? Do we see it as a life-or-death matter? How would such attitudes show themselves practically in our lives?

Pharaoh shows no such concern about avoiding sin, and the results are tragic, for him and the nation. This leads to a third question.

WHY PUNISH THE FIRSTBORN SONS OF EGYPT?

See full discussion at Exodus 4:21–23.

As the story continues and Moses travels down to Egypt, one of the most curious stories in the OT occurs. This leads to a final question.

WHAT IS GOING ON IN THE BRIDEGROOM OF BLOOD ACCOUNT?

Despite all the remaining questions with this account, it seems clear that a main point is the importance of Israelites' applying the covenant sign (circumcision) to their sons, thus showing that they will raise him as a covenant member (cf. comment on 4:24–26). As a general principle, parents must raise their children in covenant faith.

This principle is seen throughout the OT and NT, which exhorts parents to teach their children the Lord's ways. Sometimes this takes place through rituals, where the teaching happens through physical illustrations (Ex. 12:24–27; 13:3–10, 11–16; cf. 1 Cor. 11:23–26). Often this takes place in the context of everyday life: "You shall teach them diligently to your children, and shall talk of them when you sit in your house, and when you walk by the way, and when you lie down, and when you rise" (Deut. 6:7). In either case such instruction is to be done with tender love: "Fathers, do not provoke your children to anger, but bring them up in the discipline and instruction of the Lord" (Eph. 6:4; cf. Col. 3:21). When truth is given without love, many children will assume it to be a lie. Just as the Lord who gives us his truth also shows us his tender love, so parents are to give their children truth and show them tender love—and in this way be the best physical illustration possible of who the Lord is.

EXODUS 5:1–6:9

5 Afterward Moses and Aaron went and said to Pharaoh, "Thus says the LORD, the God of Israel, 'Let my people go, that they may hold a feast to me in the wilderness.'" ² But Pharaoh said, "Who is the LORD, that I should obey his voice and let Israel go? I do not know the LORD, and moreover, I will not let Israel go." ³ Then they said, "The God of the Hebrews has met with us. Please let us go a three days' journey into the wilderness that we may sacrifice to the LORD our God, lest he fall upon us with pestilence or with the sword." ⁴ But the king of Egypt said to them, "Moses and Aaron, why do you take the people away from their work? Get back to your burdens." ⁵ And Pharaoh said, "Behold, the people of the land are now many,¹ and you make them rest from their burdens!" ⁶ The same day Pharaoh commanded the taskmasters of the people and their foremen, ⁷ "You shall no longer give the people straw to make bricks, as in the past; let them go and gather straw for themselves. ⁸ But the number of bricks that they made in the past you shall impose on them, you shall by no means reduce it, for they are idle. Therefore they cry, 'Let us go and offer sacrifice to our God.' ⁹ Let heavier work be laid on the men that they may labor at it and pay no regard to lying words."

¹⁰ So the taskmasters and the foremen of the people went out and said to the people, "Thus says Pharaoh, 'I will not give you straw. ¹¹ Go and get your straw yourselves wherever you can find it, but your work will not be reduced in the least.'" ¹² So the people were scattered throughout all the land of Egypt to gather stubble for straw. ¹³ The taskmasters were urgent, saying, "Complete your work, your daily task each day, as when there was straw." ¹⁴ And the foremen of the people of Israel, whom Pharaoh's taskmasters had set over them, were beaten and were asked, "Why have you not done all your task of making bricks today and yesterday, as in the past?"

¹⁵ Then the foremen of the people of Israel came and cried to Pharaoh, "Why do you treat your servants like this? ¹⁶ No straw is given to your servants, yet they say to us, 'Make bricks!' And behold, your servants are beaten; but the fault is in your own people." ¹⁷ But he said, "You are idle, you are idle; that is why you say, 'Let us go and sacrifice to the LORD.' ¹⁸ Go now and work. No straw will be given you, but you must still deliver the same number of bricks." ¹⁹ The foremen of the people of Israel saw that they were in trouble when they said, "You shall by no means reduce your

number of bricks, your daily task each day." ²⁰ They met Moses and Aaron, who were waiting for them, as they came out from Pharaoh; ²¹ and they said to them, "The LORD look on you and judge, because you have made us stink in the sight of Pharaoh and his servants, and have put a sword in their hand to kill us."

²² Then Moses turned to the LORD and said, "O Lord, why have you done evil to this people? Why did you ever send me? ²³ For since I came to Pharaoh to speak in your name, he has done evil to this people, and you have not delivered your people at all."

6 But the LORD said to Moses, "Now you shall see what I will do to Pharaoh; for with a strong hand he will send them out, and with a strong hand he will drive them out of his land."

² God spoke to Moses and said to him, "I am the LORD. ³ I appeared to Abraham, to Isaac, and to Jacob, as God Almighty,² but by my name the LORD I did not make myself known to them. ⁴ I also established my covenant with them to give them the land of Canaan, the land in which they lived as sojourners. ⁵ Moreover, I have heard the groaning of the people of Israel whom the Egyptians hold as slaves, and I have remembered my covenant. ⁶ Say therefore to the people of Israel, 'I am the LORD, and I will bring you out from under the burdens of the Egyptians, and I will deliver you from slavery to them, and I will redeem you with an outstretched arm and with great acts of judgment. ⁷ I will take you to be my people, and I will be your God, and you shall know that I am the LORD your God, who has brought you out from under the burdens of the Egyptians. ⁸ I will bring you into the land that I swore to give to Abraham, to Isaac, and to Jacob. I will give it to you for a possession. I am the LORD.'" ⁹ Moses spoke thus to the people of Israel, but they did not listen to Moses, because of their broken spirit and harsh slavery.

¹ Samaritan *they are now more numerous than the people of the land* ² Hebrew *El Shaddai*

Section Overview

The previous section ended with the Israelites united in hope and worshipful, believing Moses' and Aaron's words (4:29–31). This section ends with them despondent and angry, blaming Moses and Aaron for their renewed suffering (5:20–21; 6:9). The difference is due to Pharaoh, who responds with sarcastic mockery to the Lord's command to release the people (5:1–2) and then shows his cruelty and cunning by making the Israelites' lives increasingly difficult in order to turn them against Moses and Aaron (vv. 3–18). His plan succeeds, and the Israelites ask the Lord himself to judge Moses and Aaron for the harm they have caused (vv. 19–21).

Moses prays to the Lord, lamenting the current situation and implicitly pleading for help (vv. 22–23). The Lord reassures him that he will deliver his people from Pharaoh by means of his strong hand (6:1). He then responds to Pharaoh's sarcastic "Who is Yahweh?" (5:2) with a speech threaded with the declaration "I am Yahweh!" (6:2, 6, 8), a statement explained by a description of his awareness of his people's sufferings, his faithfulness to his promises, the mighty salvation he will accomplish for his people, and the land with which he will bless them (6:3–8a). *This* is who Yahweh is.

But the suffering people refuse to listen to Moses (6:9). Moses and Aaron's mission, which had seemed so hopeful (4:29–31), now seems a lost cause, and we are left to wonder how the situation can possibly be made better.

Section Outline

I. Israel in Egypt: the Lord promises deliverance (1:1–11:10) . . .
    D. An initial attempt at deliverance (5:1–6:9)
        1. Pharaoh's rejection of the Lord's command and his own command to increase the people's burden (5:1–9)
        2. Pharaoh's command carried out (5:10–14)
        3. The Israelite foremen's plea for mercy and Pharaoh's merciless response (5:15–18)
        4. The foremen confront Moses and Aaron in anger (5:19–21)
        5. Moses' plea to the Lord (5:22–23)
        6. The Lord's reassurance of deliverance (6:1–8)
        7. The people's inability to hear Moses' words (6:9)

Comment

5:1–9 Approaching Pharaoh for the first time, Moses and Aaron issue the Lord's command to let the Israelites go so that they may hold a communal feast in the Lord's honor (5:1; cf. 10:9; 32:5–6). That it is to be in the wilderness, outside Egypt (cf. comment on 8:25–27), perhaps signals to Pharaoh that the end goal is much more permanent.[131] In any case, by giving Pharaoh a command, the Lord makes clear he is king, not Pharaoh.[132] And by calling Israel his people he makes clear they belong to him, not Pharaoh.

Pharaoh's reply is laced with sarcasm: "Who is the Lord, that I should obey his voice and let Israel go?" (5:2). This is akin to other questions, such as David's "Who is this uncircumcised Philistine, that he should defy the armies of the living God?" (1 Sam. 17:26).[133] In these cases the questioner looks down on the person in question. We might paraphrase, "The Lord? Ha! He is in no way worthy of my obedience!" The following statement—"I do not know the Lord"—emphasizes this thinking, since "to know" someone can refer to acknowledging that person's authority (cf. 1 Sam. 2:12; Prov. 3:6). Pharaoh refuses to do so and therefore refuses the Lord's command—not realizing that the Lord will answer his sarcastic question with frightening clarity in the coming chapters!

Moses and Aaron try again, noting that disobedience could have disastrous consequences for them, be it through human attack or deadly disease (Ex. 5:3). But Pharaoh remains unmoved, commanding the people to return to their "burdens"

---

[131] "In the style of Near Eastern requesting favors, the initial request was purposefully stated in a modest way, although what was really being sought was much more: full permanent departure" (Stuart, *Exodus*, 161, referencing Gen. 23:1–16). Compare today's question "Have you got a second?," which is a request for more time than an actual second (Stuart, *Exodus*, 125).
[132] Cf. Dorian Coover Cox, "The Hardening of Pharaoh's Heart in Its Literary and Cultural Contexts," *BSac* 163/651 (2006): 302.
[133] *IBHS* §18.2g. Cf. Judges 9:28; 1 Samuel 25:10; noted by Cox, "Hardening of Pharaoh's Heart," 296.

(an implicit acknowledgment of the work's severity; v. 4). He thinks it especially bad if they are not working, either because it means much work remains undone or because it gives them time to unite in rebellion—or both (v. 5).[134] He in fact increases their workload. One of the Israelites' main slave-tasks is to make bricks, central to which is straw, which serves as an adhesive and helps the bricks maintain their shape.[135] Pharaoh commands the Israelites' overseers to stop providing straw and yet requires the same daily quota of bricks, greatly increasing their workload (v. 8a). He claims this is necessary to teach them not to be lazy by requesting time off to worship (v. 8b). He also does this so they will "pay no regard to lying words" (v. 9), that is, Moses and Aaron's. He wants to turn the people against them— a strategy that eventually works (cf. v. 21).

5:10–14 The taskmasters and foremen relay Pharaoh's command (vv. 10–11), and the people face an impossible task. Not only do they have to spend time traveling to get straw, but the only straw they can find is scraps of stubble from harvested fields, which is painstakingly slow to gather (v. 12). But their Egyptian taskmasters are undeterred, urgently demanding that the same quota of bricks be made (v. 13), beating the Israelite foremen when the impossible task is not achieved (v. 14a),[136] and, ridiculously, asking why the Israelites have slowed down on the job (v. 14b).

5:15–18 The question's injustice is profound and the humiliation and anger it causes undoubtedly strong. The foremen's cry to Pharaoh is humble (name themselves his servants) and honest (they make the injustice clear) (vv. 15–16). But Pharaoh continues in his obstinate cruelty, underscoring his accusation of laziness by repeating it (v. 17) and doubling down on his unjust demand (v. 18).

5:19–21 The foremen see that their situation is disastrous and, as Pharaoh hoped, blame Moses and Aaron (vv. 19–21; cf. v. 9). They even ask the Lord himself to bring his justice to bear against Moses and Aaron for putting the Israelites in such a dire situation.[137]

5:22–23 Moses "turned to the LORD," perhaps a way of saying he leaves the foremen's presence and seeks a place to pray.[138] He questions why the Lord has harmed the Israelites[139] and why he ever sent Moses (v. 22), that is, why he has harmed them by sending Moses to them. What is more, the Lord has not delivered his people *at all* (v. 23). In noting such things he is asking the Lord's help to resolve them.

---

134 Cf. George Bush, *Commentary on Exodus* (1843; repr., Grand Rapids, MI: Kregel, 1993), 75. For the second option cf. 1:9–14; so Stuart, *Exodus*, 163.
135 Sarna, *Exodus*, 28.
136 For the foremen's being Israelite cf. Exodus 5:15–21. To have Israelite foremen is practical: they know the people better and can organize them most efficiently. It may also be tactical, an effort to split the people's anger between the Egyptians and their own foremen.
137 "In the sight of" (Ex. 5:21) translates the Hebrew "in the eyes of," which can mean "in the opinion of" (cf. Josh. 22:33). This explains why the eyes are mentioned instead of the nose (Houtman, *Exodus*, vol. 1, 482).
138 Stuart, *Exodus*, 168; cf. Ex. 32:31.
139 The Hebrew word (*ra'a*) can mean "to do evil" but can also describe doing harm in general (compare the ESV's translation of the same verb in Gen. 31:7; 43:6).

6:1–8 The Lord answers, beginning with an overarching promise: he will send forth his strong hand,[140] displaying his power and might by great acts of judgment (cf. 6:6; 7:4–5), leading Pharaoh not simply to release the people reluctantly but to drive them out urgently (6:1; cf. 12:39).[141]

With great reassurance the Lord then offers the reasons for his deliverance: he was known to Israel's forefathers, had covenanted to give them the land of Canaan, and now, deeply aware of their suffering—the word "I" is emphasized in the clause "I have heard" (6:5)[142]—is going to show his faithfulness to his covenant promise (vv. 2–5; cf. note 116 within Response Section on 2:23–4:17). In short, awareness of his people's suffering and faithfulness to his covenant promises are the driving force behind his coming actions.

It must also be noted that a question arises regarding 6:3, which most versions translate similarly to the ESV: "I appeared to Abraham, to Isaac, and to Jacob, as God Almighty [*'el shadday*], but by my name the LORD [*yhwh*] I did not make myself known to them." In short, the forefathers knew him by the name El-Shaddai,[143] not Yahweh. This is in tension with the fact that the name Yahweh is used throughout Genesis, not simply by the narrator (Gen. 12:1; 13:10; etc.) but also in the Lord's own self-description (15:7; 26:24; 28:13) and by the forefathers themselves (14:22; 26:22; 27:20). It is also in tension with the fact that Exodus 3:13–15 seems to presume the Israelites already know this name as the one their forefathers used (cf. comment on 3:13–15 and note 91).

Commentators have proposed at least three solutions to solve these two tensions.[144] The first two assume the above translation.

(1) The author of Genesis uses the name "Yahweh" anachronistically so that the Israelites would know that the God who later revealed his name as Yahweh was the same God their forefathers worshiped.[145] This explanation is theoretically possible for most of Genesis but might not work well in Genesis 22:14, where the name Yahweh is central to a well-known phrase that apparently pre-dated Exodus's audience. Moreover, it does not address Exodus 3:13–15, which seems to assume Israel's forefathers knew Yahweh's name. Finally, with the traditional translation, the transition to 6:4 feels disjointed in its use of "also": "I appeared to [them] as God Almighty, but by name the LORD I did not make myself known to them. ⁴I also established my covenant with them . . ."

---

140 "With a strong hand" is best understood as referring to the Lord's strong hand (note the preceding words: "What *I* will do to Pharaoh"). Compare Ex. 3:19, where the ESV renders the same words as "The king of Egypt will not let you go unless *compelled by a mighty hand*," namely, the Lord's (cf. 3:20; 7:4–5; 13:9).
141 During this period of history the language of having a strong arm is often applied to pharaohs, raising the possibility that the language is polemic: Yahweh has the strong arm, not Pharaoh! Cf. James K Hoffmeier, "The Arm of God versus the Arm of Pharaoh in the Exodus Narratives," *Biblica* 67/3 (1986): 378–387.
142 Keil, *Exodus*, vol. 1, 468.
143 "El" means "God"; the meaning of "Shaddai" is uncertain, since "its etymology remains elusive"; Kenneth Mathews, *Genesis 11:27–50:26*, NAC (Nashville: B&H, 2005), 64. The rendering "Almighty" derives from the LXX.
144 A fourth approach—taken by many source-critical scholars—sees the tensions resulting from contradicting sources. As argued above, a good approach exists that solves the tensions without resorting to source-critical theories.
145 G. J. Wenham, "The Religion of the Patriarchs," in *Essays on the Patriarchal Narratives*, ed. A. R. Millard and D. J. Wiseman (Leicester, UK: InterVarsity Press), 157–188, cited by Alexander, *Exodus*, ApOTC, 115.

(2) The Lord's words in verse 3 mean the patriarchs did not know the Lord by his name's full implications.[146] In various verses—including the upcoming verse 7—knowing Yahweh is connected to miraculous signs that show his character's nature (Ex. 7:5; 14:4; 1 Kings 20:13; Isa. 52:6; etc.). Further, this approach works with Exodus 3:13–15, since it does not deny that the forefathers knew the name. However, Exodus 3 and 6 both underscore that Yahweh was God to Israel's forefathers (3:13, 15; 6:8), thus emphasizing similarity, while this understanding emphasizes difference.[147] Another possible weakness is that the bumpy transition to verse 4 remains.

(3) The third solution proposes a different translation: "I appeared to Abraham, to Isaac, and to Jacob, as God Almighty, and by my name the LORD, did I not make myself known to them? I also established my covenant with them . . ."[148] While Hebrew often marks questions with an interrogative particle, at times it leaves them unmarked, allowing the context to indicate that a question is being asked.[149] Similar examples with negative questions include "Will they not stone us?" (8:26); "Would I not tell you?" (1 Sam. 20:9); "Should not I pity Nineveh . . . ?" (Jonah 4:11). Translating similarly in Exodus 6:3 immediately resolves the two tensions named above. Further, it leads to a smoother connection with verse 4: not only did I reveal my name to them, but I also entered into covenant with them.

The third solution appears to solve the problem most simply and cleanly, though the second may not be ruled out. Either way, the Lord's awareness of his people's suffering and his faithfulness to his covenant promises are clearly driving his actions (Ex. 6:4–5). He knows, he cares, and he acts.

Having laid this foundation, God reinforces and builds upon it, focusing on the deliverance he will grant his people (vv. 6–8). The declaration "I am Yahweh" frames the speech (vv. 6a, 8b), as though to make clear that delivering his people is the ultimate answer to Pharaoh's sarcastic "Who is Yahweh?" (5:2). The "I am Yahweh" frame also makes the Lord's character the source of the many promises he now gives his people. They are true and trustworthy because they are *Yahweh's* promises. The promises focus on his deliverance (6:6), his entering into relationship with them (v. 7), and the promise of land (v. 8).[150] We might paraphrase:

> I am Yahweh, and therefore[151] in view of my faithfulness and care and might:
> I will bring you out from under the very burdens Pharaoh just told you to return to (5:4).

---

146 Cassuto, *Commentary on the Book of Exodus*, 77–79 ; Sarna, *Exodus*, 31.
147 Cf. Alexander, *Exodus*, ApOTC, 116.
148 Stuart, *Exodus*, 169n164; Alexander, *Exodus*, ApOTC, 116–117 (cf. further references there).
149 Cf. *GKC* §150a; Joüon §161a.
150 Cassuto, *Commentary on the Book of Exodus*, 80.
151 Cf. Joüon §119e for the consequential sense of "and" in this context.

I will deliver you from slavery, the very thing I have just been accused of not doing at all (5:23).

I will redeem you, rescuing you from slavery—as a kinsmen does his relative[152]—by means of my arm outstretched in power and strength,[153] fighting against your enemies with terrifying displays of miraculous power (cf. Deut. 4:34; 7:19; 26:8), rendering judgment on them for their evil (cf. 2 Chron. 24:24; Ezek. 5:9–10; 28:22–23).

I will take you to be my people, like a father's adopting an orphan son, or a husband's marrying his wife, entering into a close relationship of love and care, and I will be your God,[154] watching over you so you may know by personal experience that I am your redeeming God.

I will bring you into the land I swore to your forefathers as a covenant promise, and I will give it to you for a possession, like an inheritance, since you are their descendants and my children (cf. Gen. 15:7–8, 18–21; Lev. 20:24).

Yes, all this I can and will do because I am Yahweh, who is faithful to his covenant, cares for you, and is mighty to save!

6:9 Moses seeks to reassure the people with these promises, but they pay no attention (v. 9). As Pharaoh intended (cf. 5:9), they have given up hope in Moses' words because of their frustration and anger at their hardship.[155] Without faith our hearts are overwhelmed and embittered by trials, making God's promises impossible to believe.

Response

WHAT KIND OF KING IS PHARAOH?

A king can wreak havoc on his servants. Pharaoh illustrates this starkly. He keeps the Israelites enslaved under heavy labor and then makes it heavier still, fails to deliver them from unjust beatings, and then sadistically accuses them of laziness (5:6–18). Their pain is his pleasure, and he does all he can to increase their misery and divide their leadership (5:9, 19–21; 6:9).

His cruelty is no surprise. His question, "Who is the LORD, that I should obey his voice?" (5:2), derides the Lord as unworthy of obedience (cf. comment on 5:1–9). He has no fear of God and therefore rules without boundaries. This does not mean

---

152 In the social sphere "redeem" can refer to one relative's rescuing another relative from servitude (Lev. 25:47–55). The mention of slavery here recalls that social context. Alexander (*Exodus*, 126) adds, "Since God has already spoken of Israel as his son (4:22), the liberation of the Israelites may be viewed ... as a family affair." Cf. Introduction: Purpose and Theology of Exodus: Yahweh, the Redeeming Father-King.
153 "Outstretched arm" elsewhere parallels "mighty hand" (Deut. 4:34; 5:15) and "great power" (Deut. 9:29; 2 Kings 17:36). The image may be that of an arm stretched out holding a sword or other weapon (cf. 1 Chron. 21:16; Ezek. 30:21–25). As in our passage it often occurs when the Lord judges by means of miraculous displays of power (Isa. 14:26; Jer. 21:5–6; Ezek. 20:33–34).
154 The language "to be to *person x* for *role y*" is highly relational and similar to that describing adoption (cf. Ex. 2:10; 2 Sam. 7:14; Jer. 31:9) and marriage (cf. Gen. 20:12; 24:67a; Num. 36:11). It thus refers to a very close relationship.
155 "Broken spirit" is in the Hebrew "short of spirit"; phrases using the same roots elsewhere describe a "hasty temper" (Prov. 14:29) or "impatience" (Job 21:4). Numbers 21:4 uses a related phrase for the Israelites' impatience at hardships, which leads to complaints against God and Moses.

that only God-fearing leaders can lead well. God's common grace and his fashioning us in his image enable even those who do not follow him to strive for justice and human flourishing. But with Pharaoh, as with leaders throughout history, denying God leads quickly to a rule centered on self-interest at the expense of others. We rightly shrink from such leadership—and ask God's help not to reflect it in our own lives.

WHAT KIND OF KING IS THE LORD?

The Lord's kingship is the polar opposite of Pharaoh's. To Pharaoh's question, "Who is the LORD?," the Lord will respond in word (6:1–9) and then in deed (7:3–5; 7:14–13:16).[156] The former is the focus here, and his promises to Israel make clear that

- he enters into close relationship with his people, like that of a parent and child or husband and wife (6:4, 7a);
- he is not distant and aloof but close and concerned about his people's suffering (v. 5);
- he uses his power not to oppress but to deliver from evil (vv. 6, 7b);
- and he keeps his covenant promises and gives good gifts to his people (vv. 5b, 8).

As a result, he will deliver his people from cruel service to a wicked king into the freedom of blessed service to a good king.

This last point is important: the Lord's deliverance is never about freedom alone but *freedom to serve the right king*. Jesus invites "all who labor and are heavy laden" to come to him for rest but also makes clear that such rest is found when we take his yoke upon us, learning from him (Matt. 11:28–30). True rest comes from being yoked to the right master.

HOW DOES THE LORD'S TYPE OF KINGSHIP ENABLE OUR LAMENTS?

While the above is completely true, it does not mean that life is free from suffering. Moses knew this full well as he experienced hardships while waiting for the Lord to fulfill his promise of deliverance. So he pours out his heart to the Lord, expressing his pain while raising his questioning eyes to heaven (Ex. 5:22–23).

Moses' words are like the prayers of lament in the Psalms, in which the psalmist is open with the Lord about his pain and suffering, reminds the Lord of his covenant promises, and looks to him for help and deliverance (cf. Psalms 3–7; 13; 22; 31; 44). Moses can pray this way is that he knows the type of king to whom he is praying. He brings his pain and questions to the Lord because he knows the Lord cares and can help. Such lament is different than complaint. In lament the sufferer is honest about his pain and suffering but also looks to God for help and deliverance. In lament we still look to our King for help. In complaint we deny his kingship.

That lament is a proper response to suffering is shown in the example of Jesus:

---

156 For the latter cf. Response section on 6:10–7:7, "What Is the Relationship between the End of This Story and God's Character?"

Jesus himself lamented in the midst of the most severe trial imaginable: his death on behalf of humanity. At one point on the cross, he cries out, "My God! My God! Why have you forsaken me?" (Matt. 27:46). Jesus is quoting Ps. 22:1, which comes from a lament psalm written by an Israelite believer in severe trial. The words are brutally honest but are still a prayer. And that is the point: the psalmist still looks to God in his suffering, and Jesus does the same. Indeed, lament psalms typically include honest expressions of grief together with deep expressions of trust and hope. Significantly, Jesus' final words on the cross—"Into your hands I commit my spirit" (Luke 23:46)—also come from a lament psalm (Ps. 31:5) and are rooted in his knowing that no matter what trial we go through, God is there in the midst of it, is good, and will listen to our prayers. What does it look like for us to do this in the midst of our trials? And how does the fact Jesus has already done this encourage us to look to him for strength to do the same?[157]

EXODUS 6:10–7:7

[10] So the LORD said to Moses, [11] "Go in, tell Pharaoh king of Egypt to let the people of Israel go out of his land." [12] But Moses said to the LORD, "Behold, the people of Israel have not listened to me. How then shall Pharaoh listen to me, for I am of uncircumcised lips?" [13] But the LORD spoke to Moses and Aaron and gave them a charge about the people of Israel and about Pharaoh king of Egypt: to bring the people of Israel out of the land of Egypt.

[14] These are the heads of their fathers' houses: the sons of Reuben, the firstborn of Israel: Hanoch, Pallu, Hezron, and Carmi; these are the clans of Reuben. [15] The sons of Simeon: Jemuel, Jamin, Ohad, Jachin, Zohar, and Shaul, the son of a Canaanite woman; these are the clans of Simeon. [16] These are the names of the sons of Levi according to their generations: Gershon, Kohath, and Merari, the years of the life of Levi being 137 years. [17] The sons of Gershon: Libni and Shimei, by their clans. [18] The sons of Kohath: Amram, Izhar, Hebron, and Uzziel, the years of the life of Kohath being 133 years. [19] The sons of Merari: Mahli and Mushi. These are the clans of the Levites according to their generations. [20] Amram took as his wife Jochebed his father's sister, and she bore him Aaron and Moses, the years of the life of Amram being 137 years. [21] The sons of Izhar: Korah, Nepheg, and Zichri. [22] The sons of Uzziel: Mishael, Elzaphan, and Sithri. [23] Aaron took as his wife Elisheba, the daughter of Amminadab and the sister of Nahshon, and she bore him Nadab, Abihu, Eleazar, and Ithamar.

---

[157] Sklar, *Numbers*, 182.

24 The sons of Korah: Assir, Elkanah, and Abiasaph; these are the clans of the Korahites. 25 Eleazar, Aaron's son, took as his wife one of the daughters of Putiel, and she bore him Phinehas. These are the heads of the fathers' houses of the Levites by their clans.

26 These are the Aaron and Moses to whom the LORD said: "Bring out the people of Israel from the land of Egypt by their hosts." 27 It was they who spoke to Pharaoh king of Egypt about bringing out the people of Israel from Egypt, this Moses and this Aaron.

28 On the day when the LORD spoke to Moses in the land of Egypt, 29 the LORD said to Moses, "I am the LORD; tell Pharaoh king of Egypt all that I say to you." 30 But Moses said to the LORD, "Behold, I am of uncircumcised lips. How will Pharaoh listen to me?"

7 And the LORD said to Moses, "See, I have made you like God to Pharaoh, and your brother Aaron shall be your prophet. 2 You shall speak all that I command you, and your brother Aaron shall tell Pharaoh to let the people of Israel go out of his land. 3 But I will harden Pharaoh's heart, and though I multiply my signs and wonders in the land of Egypt, 4 Pharaoh will not listen to you. Then I will lay my hand on Egypt and bring my hosts, my people the children of Israel, out of the land of Egypt by great acts of judgment. 5 The Egyptians shall know that I am the LORD, when I stretch out my hand against Egypt and bring out the people of Israel from among them." 6 Moses and Aaron did so; they did just as the LORD commanded them. 7 Now Moses was eighty years old, and Aaron eighty-three years old, when they spoke to Pharaoh.

Section Overview

This section transitions between the failed attempt at deliverance that led to the people's discouragement (5:1–6:9) and the coming display of the Lord's mighty hand that will lead to the people's departure (7:8–11:10). It comprises three parts. In the first the Lord reissues his charge to Moses to go to Pharaoh, and Moses expresses his inability to do so (6:10–12). In the second the story is interrupted to provide Moses and Aaron's genealogy (vv. 13–27). This is significant information for the original audience (cf. discussion below) and appropriately placed for the central role Moses and Aaron are about to play. The third part resumes the story and gives an overview of the coming chapters, underscoring the Lord's coming deliverance of Israel (6:28–7:7). This should give the audience hope as the narrative turns to describe Moses and Aaron's confrontations with Pharaoh (7:8–11:10).

Section Outline

I. Israel in Egypt: the Lord promises deliverance (1:1–11:10) . . .
   E. Preparation for the deliverance to come (6:10–7:7)
      1. The preparation begins: the Lord reissues his command for Moses and Aaron to confront Pharaoh (6:10–12)
      2. The genealogy of Moses and Aaron (6:13–27)
      3. The preparation resumed and an overview of what is to come (6:28–7:7)

Comment

6:10–12 The Lord commands Moses to go again to Pharaoh and demand the people's release (v. 11; cf. 4:22–23; 5:1), and Moses again questions his ability to do so, describing himself as being "of uncircumcised lips" (6:12; cf. 4:10; 6:30). This is a metaphor that means his lips cannot do what they are supposed to do (just as an "uncircumcised heart" or "uncircumcised ears" do not do what they are supposed to do; Lev. 26:41; Jer. 6:10). The context suggests this is not because of a speech impediment but because he lacks eloquence (he focuses on his inability to come across believably to the Israelites; cf. comment on 4:10–12). In either case his point is clear: Since the Israelites, his own people, have not listened to him, why should Pharaoh?

6:13–27 These verses are carefully arranged. A matching outer frame notes that Moses and Aaron have been charged to bring the Israelites out of Egypt (vv. 13, 26–27) and an inner core provides Moses and Aaron's genealogy (vv. 14–25; cf. Section Outline).

Why interrupt the story with a genealogy? Tribal societies are structured along relational lines that inform marriage decisions and business dealings, give people a general sense of belonging, and in certain cases (such as with the Levites) reveal a person's societal role. Knowing someone's genealogical heritage therefore helps another to know how to relate to that person and how he should relate to others.

This genealogy focuses on Levi's tribe and provides four important pieces of information: (1) the genealogical heritage of Moses and Aaron, who are about to lead the Israelites out of Egypt (cf. vv. 26–27);[158] (2) the genealogy of the priestly line (Levi → Kohath → Amram → Aaron → Eleazar → Phinehas); (3) the genealogical structure of the main Levite clans (Gershonites, Kohathites, Merarites), which rises to importance in Numbers (cf. Numbers 3–4); and (4) the genealogical heritage of key characters in the comings narratives.[159] In this way a relational context is given so that the Israelite listeners might have a sense of how to relate to these characters and how these characters should relate to them.

The genealogy begins with a brief mention of Reuben and Simeon (vv. 14b–15), the first two sons borne to Jacob by Leah, and then focuses on their third son, Levi (vv. 16–25).[160] It names Levi's three sons—who will form the three main Levite branches (cf. Numbers 3–4)—and their respective sons (Ex. 6:16–19). It then expands on the middle son, Kohath, from whom have descended Moses, Aaron,

---

[158] Their sister Miriam is not mentioned (cf. Num. 26:59) because the family line typically descended through males, leading Hebrew genealogies to focus on sons.

[159] (1) Korah (Ex. 6:21), who rebels against Moses and Aaron (cf. Num. 16:1–33); (2) Mishael and Elzaphan (Ex. 6:22), who carry the bodies of Nadab and Abihu away from the tabernacle (Lev. 10:4; Elzaphan [= Elizaphan] also leads the Kohathite clan [Num. 3:30]); (3) Aaron's priestly sons (Ex. 6:23): Nadab and Abihu (who die for improper tabernacle activity [Lev. 10:1–3]), Eleazar (who becomes high priest [Num. 20:28] and is the Levites' chief leader [Num. 3:32] and oversees the Kohathites in particular [Num. 4:16]), and Ithamar (who oversees the Gershonites and Merarites [Num. 4:28, 33]); (4) Phinehas (Ex. 6:25), famous for his godly zeal in the Baal of Peor incident (Num. 25:6–13).

[160] Cf. Genesis 29:31–34. The "heads of their fathers' houses" (Ex. 6:14) may refer to Reuben, Simeon, and Levi, that is, to tribes (cf. Num. 17:2–3), and the word "clans" to divisions within those tribes (cf. Num. 26:2 with 26:5), though at other times "heads of the fathers' houses" can refer to a division smaller than a tribe that then consists of "clans" (as in Ex. 6:25; cf. Num. 3:21–24). In either case "clan" is the smaller of the two groupings. As for the high ages listed here, cf. note 121 within comment on 4:21–23.

and the priestly line, going as far as Aaron's grandson, Phinehas (vv. 20–25).[161] As noted above, in addition to Moses and Aaron several of the people mentioned along the way play key roles in the larger coming story.

This section's last two verses (vv. 26–27) parallel its opening verse (v. 13). Arranged as a chiasm, they mirror one another in reverse order, emphasizing in the central section the key theme of Exodus' opening half: Israel's deliverance from Egypt.

6:28–7:7 This passage resumes the narrative begun in 6:10–12 by summarizing briefly those verses (vv. 28–30),[162] and the Lord now replies to Moses' fear by stating, "See, I have made you like God to Pharaoh" (7:1a), that is, you will be the source of my words to him (7:2a), "and your brother Aaron shall be your prophet" (7:1b), that is, you will tell him these words, and he will proclaim them to Pharaoh (7:2b; cf. 4:14–16). Moses' fear is therefore addressed, and the command to address Pharaoh is repeated. Moreover, the Lord makes clear it is his words, not Moses', that will confront Pharaoh.

The Lord then overviews the coming events (7:3–5). He begins by affirming his sovereignty over Pharaoh: "I will harden Pharaoh's heart" (v. 3a), that is, he will take Pharaoh's heart, which is already hardened in rebellion, and make it harder still (cf. comment on 4:21–23). This will lead to several results:

(1) The Lord will multiply in Egypt his signs and wonders, which continually witness to Pharaoh and the Egyptians that he is the Lord and should be heeded (7:3b).
(2) Despite the signs, Pharaoh will repeatedly refuse to heed the Lord's words (7:4a).
(3) Nonetheless, the Lord will put his hand on Egypt and bring his people out with great judgments on Egypt's evil (7:4b; cf. 2 Chron. 24:24; Ezek. 5:9–10; 28:22–23).
(4) Therefore, the Egyptians will know that he is the Lord (Ex. 7:5).

In short: "Moses and Aaron, your faithfulness will seem to have no effect, and for a time my mighty acts will seem to have no effect, but my purposes and power will prevail, so that I will lead Israel—my people!—out of Egypt, showing all Egypt that I am Yahweh, sovereign God and King!"

Just as verses 3–5 overviewed what the Lord would do in the coming days, verse 6 overviews what Moses and Aaron will do, namely, obey the Lord's commands. Verse 7 provides one final detail, letting us know Moses and Aaron's ages as they embark on their mission. "It is a common feature of Biblical narratives for the age of their heroes to be stated at the time when some momentous event befalls them."[163]

---

[161] Aaron's wife, Elisheba, comes from a leading family of Judah's tribe (Ex. 6:23; cf. Num. 1:7; 2:3), thus forming a link between the priests and David's line (cf. Ex. 6:23; Ruth 4:19–22).
[162] For a similar resumption compare Genesis 37:36 with 39:1; M. Kalisch, *Exodus* (London: Longman, Brown, Green and Longmans, 1855), 105.
[163] Cassuto, *Commentary on the Book of Exodus*, 90–91, citing Genesis 16:16; 17:24–25; 25:26; 41:46.

Response

WHAT IS THE RELATIONSHIP BETWEEN THE BEGINNING OF OUR STORY AND OUR USEFULNESS?

In Israel's world a person's genealogy had possible implications for his social standing. This was true in terms of family of origin, with wealthier families often having more social sway. But it was true also (for males) in terms of birth order, with firstborn sons being regarded as the "firstfruits" of a father's strength (Gen. 49:3) and entrusted with extra family responsibilities (cf. comment on 4:21–23).

In this genealogy, however, many key characters neither are the firstborn nor do they descend from the firstborn. The Levites play a crucial role at the all-important tabernacle but descend from Jacob's third son (6:14–16). The priestly family is the most important among the Levites but come from Levi's second son (6:16, 18, 20, 23, 25). And second-born Moses, not firstborn Aaron, is Israel's key leader. The same occurs elsewhere. The Lord chooses second-born Jacob over firstborn Esau (Gen. 25:23). He likewise chooses David, who is *eighth*-born and the youngest of his brothers (1 Sam. 16:6–12).

Such decisions make clear the Lord does not abide by society's rules when choosing those he will use. No matter our social status, family of origin, or place in our family, the Lord can use us as much as anyone else. If anything, the weaker we are in the world's eyes, the more God delights to use us, so that the world might see that someone far greater than us has chosen to work through us (cf. 1 Cor. 1:26–29). This leads to a second question.

WHAT STANDS BEHIND OUR USEFULNESS?

While the Lord sends Moses and Aaron to deliver Israel, he will clearly be the one at work through them. He repeats the word "I" like hammer blows when describing Israel's deliverance (Ex. 7:3–5). Moses and Aaron are his servants, but he is Israel's ultimate deliverer.

Moses and Aaron need to hear this. By themselves, they cannot convince the world's most powerful ruler to turn from his cruelty and give up a source of free labor. But it is just at this point that the Lord emphasizes that *he himself* will do this impossible task—because only he can do it. And Moses and Aaron respond in faith, relying not on their own strength but on the strength of Yahweh, the great I Am (7:6). We find strength to obey, even to try the impossible, not because of what we find within ourselves but because of the one we look to in faith to use us for his glory.

WHAT IS THE RELATIONSHIP BETWEEN THE END OF THIS STORY AND GOD'S CHARACTER?[164]

To Pharaoh's sarcastic "Who is the Lord?" (5:2) the Lord has already answered in word (6:1–9)[165] and now describes how he will answer in deed (7:3–5). These deeds

---

[164] This section's comments are especially informed by Fretheim, *Exodus*, 94–95.
[165] Cf. discussion in the Response section on 5:1–6:9, "What Kind of King Is the Lord?"

will show all Egypt, and ultimately "all the earth" (9:16), who he is. His deeds will include both judgment and deliverance.

In terms of judgment, Fretheim's comments are worth citing at length:

> *Public* acts of judgment are in view. What Pharaoh and the Egyptians have done to God's work of life and blessing in the world will not be overlooked. God will not be indifferent to evil. Acts of cruelty and ruthlessness, which bring people to the brink of despair, must be brought to justice and publicly exposed for what they are, so that the world will know that such anticreation deeds will not be tolerated. Indeed, unless there is judgment, the creation that God intends will be turned into chaos. . . . The reference to other nations hearing of God's deeds (15:15–16; cf. 18:1, 8–12) focuses at just this point—they may well be next on God's agenda for wiping out the evils of the world.[166]

In terms of deliverance, by bringing his people out of Egypt the Lord makes clear to Egypt and the world that he is Israel's powerful God as well as their redeeming God. He not only fights against evil; he also fights to restore good. In Israel's case he will lead her to "a land flowing with milk and honey" (3:8), a second Eden where his people can flourish under his loving care and provision. This pictures his intent for his creation and looks forward, together with his public judgments, to the day when in and through Jesus he will bring full and final justice to bear for all wrongs, dwell in the midst of his people as their God, wipe every tear from their eyes, and restore the world to the place of goodness, justice, mercy and love he intends it to be (Rev. 21:1–8). And that means that, as these stories unfold, they serve both as warnings to repent of evil and as encouragements to look to God for deliverance in the midst of it, fixing our eyes with hope on the return of Jesus, when all will be made right and new.

EXODUS 7:8–11:10

⁸ Then the LORD said to Moses and Aaron, ⁹ "When Pharaoh says to you, 'Prove yourselves by working a miracle,' then you shall say to Aaron, 'Take your staff and cast it down before Pharaoh, that it may become a serpent.'" ¹⁰ So Moses and Aaron went to Pharaoh and did just as the LORD commanded. Aaron cast down his staff before Pharaoh and his servants, and it became a serpent. ¹¹ Then Pharaoh summoned the wise men and the sorcerers, and they, the magicians of Egypt, also did the same by their secret arts. ¹² For each man cast down his staff, and they became serpents.

---

[166] Fretheim, *Exodus*, 95.

But Aaron's staff swallowed up their staffs. ¹³ Still Pharaoh's heart was hardened, and he would not listen to them, as the Lord had said.

¹⁴ Then the Lord said to Moses, "Pharaoh's heart is hardened; he refuses to let the people go. ¹⁵ Go to Pharaoh in the morning, as he is going out to the water, and stand on the bank of the Nile to meet him. Take in your hand the staff that turned into a serpent. ¹⁶ And you shall say to him, 'The Lord, the God of the Hebrews, sent me to you, saying, "Let my people go, that they may serve me in the wilderness." But so far, you have not obeyed. ¹⁷ Thus says the Lord, "By this you shall know that I am the Lord: behold, with the staff that is in my hand I will strike the water that is in the Nile, and it shall turn into blood. ¹⁸ The fish in the Nile shall die, and the Nile will stink, and the Egyptians will grow weary of drinking water from the Nile."'" ¹⁹ And the Lord said to Moses, "Say to Aaron, 'Take your staff and stretch out your hand over the waters of Egypt, over their rivers, their canals, and their ponds, and all their pools of water, so that they may become blood, and there shall be blood throughout all the land of Egypt, even in vessels of wood and in vessels of stone.'"

²⁰ Moses and Aaron did as the Lord commanded. In the sight of Pharaoh and in the sight of his servants he lifted up the staff and struck the water in the Nile, and all the water in the Nile turned into blood. ²¹ And the fish in the Nile died, and the Nile stank, so that the Egyptians could not drink water from the Nile. There was blood throughout all the land of Egypt. ²² But the magicians of Egypt did the same by their secret arts. So Pharaoh's heart remained hardened, and he would not listen to them, as the Lord had said. ²³ Pharaoh turned and went into his house, and he did not take even this to heart. ²⁴ And all the Egyptians dug along the Nile for water to drink, for they could not drink the water of the Nile.

²⁵ Seven full days passed after the Lord had struck the Nile.

8 ¹ Then the Lord said to Moses, "Go in to Pharaoh and say to him, 'Thus says the Lord, "Let my people go, that they may serve me. ² But if you refuse to let them go, behold, I will plague all your country with frogs. ³ The Nile shall swarm with frogs that shall come up into your house and into your bedroom and on your bed and into the houses of your servants and your people,² and into your ovens and your kneading bowls. ⁴ The frogs shall come up on you and on your people and on all your servants."'" ⁵ ³ And the Lord said to Moses, "Say to Aaron, 'Stretch out your hand with your staff over the rivers, over the canals and over the pools, and make frogs come up on the land of Egypt!'" ⁶ So Aaron stretched out his hand over the waters of Egypt, and the frogs came up and covered the land of Egypt. ⁷ But the magicians did the same by their secret arts and made frogs come up on the land of Egypt.

⁸ Then Pharaoh called Moses and Aaron and said, "Plead with the Lord to take away the frogs from me and from my people, and I will let the people go to sacrifice to the Lord." ⁹ Moses said to Pharaoh, "Be pleased to command me when I am to plead for you and for your servants and for your people, that the frogs be cut off from you and your houses and be left only in the Nile." ¹⁰ And he said, "Tomorrow." Moses said, "Be it as you say, so that you may know that there is no one like the Lord our God. ¹¹ The frogs shall go away from you and your houses and your servants and your people. They shall be left only in the Nile." ¹² So Moses and Aaron went out from Pharaoh, and Moses cried to the Lord about the frogs, as he had agreed with Pharaoh.⁴ ¹³ And the Lord did according to the word

of Moses. The frogs died out in the houses, the courtyards, and the fields. ¹⁴ And they gathered them together in heaps, and the land stank. ¹⁵ But when Pharaoh saw that there was a respite, he hardened his heart and would not listen to them, as the Lord had said.

¹⁶ Then the Lord said to Moses, "Say to Aaron, 'Stretch out your staff and strike the dust of the earth, so that it may become gnats in all the land of Egypt.'" ¹⁷ And they did so. Aaron stretched out his hand with his staff and struck the dust of the earth, and there were gnats on man and beast. All the dust of the earth became gnats in all the land of Egypt. ¹⁸ The magicians tried by their secret arts to produce gnats, but they could not. So there were gnats on man and beast. ¹⁹ Then the magicians said to Pharaoh, "This is the finger of God." But Pharaoh's heart was hardened, and he would not listen to them, as the Lord had said.

²⁰ Then the Lord said to Moses, "Rise up early in the morning and present yourself to Pharaoh, as he goes out to the water, and say to him, 'Thus says the Lord, "Let my people go, that they may serve me. ²¹ Or else, if you will not let my people go, behold, I will send swarms of flies on you and your servants and your people, and into your houses. And the houses of the Egyptians shall be filled with swarms of flies, and also the ground on which they stand. ²² But on that day I will set apart the land of Goshen, where my people dwell, so that no swarms of flies shall be there, that you may know that I am the Lord in the midst of the earth.⁵ ²³ Thus I will put a division⁶ between my people and your people. Tomorrow this sign shall happen."'" ²⁴ And the Lord did so. There came great swarms of flies into the house of Pharaoh and into his servants' houses. Throughout all the land of Egypt the land was ruined by the swarms of flies.

²⁵ Then Pharaoh called Moses and Aaron and said, "Go, sacrifice to your God within the land." ²⁶ But Moses said, "It would not be right to do so, for the offerings we shall sacrifice to the Lord our God are an abomination to the Egyptians. If we sacrifice offerings abominable to the Egyptians before their eyes, will they not stone us? ²⁷ We must go three days' journey into the wilderness and sacrifice to the Lord our God as he tells us." ²⁸ So Pharaoh said, "I will let you go to sacrifice to the Lord your God in the wilderness; only you must not go very far away. Plead for me." ²⁹ Then Moses said, "Behold, I am going out from you and I will plead with the Lord that the swarms of flies may depart from Pharaoh, from his servants, and from his people, tomorrow. Only let not Pharaoh cheat again by not letting the people go to sacrifice to the Lord." ³⁰ So Moses went out from Pharaoh and prayed to the Lord. ³¹ And the Lord did as Moses asked, and removed the swarms of flies from Pharaoh, from his servants, and from his people; not one remained. ³² But Pharaoh hardened his heart this time also, and did not let the people go.

9 Then the Lord said to Moses, "Go in to Pharaoh and say to him, 'Thus says the Lord, the God of the Hebrews, "Let my people go, that they may serve me. ² For if you refuse to let them go and still hold them, ³ behold, the hand of the Lord will fall with a very severe plague upon your livestock that are in the field, the horses, the donkeys, the camels, the herds, and the flocks. ⁴ But the Lord will make a distinction between the livestock of Israel and the livestock of Egypt, so that nothing of all that belongs to the people of Israel shall die."'" ⁵ And the Lord set a time, saying, "Tomorrow the Lord will do this thing in the land." ⁶ And the next day the Lord did this thing. All the livestock of the Egyptians died, but

not one of the livestock of the people of Israel died. ⁷ And Pharaoh sent, and behold, not one of the livestock of Israel was dead. But the heart of Pharaoh was hardened, and he did not let the people go.

⁸ And the Lord said to Moses and Aaron, "Take handfuls of soot from the kiln, and let Moses throw them in the air in the sight of Pharaoh. ⁹ It shall become fine dust over all the land of Egypt, and become boils breaking out in sores on man and beast throughout all the land of Egypt." ¹⁰ So they took soot from the kiln and stood before Pharaoh. And Moses threw it in the air, and it became boils breaking out in sores on man and beast. ¹¹ And the magicians could not stand before Moses because of the boils, for the boils came upon the magicians and upon all the Egyptians. ¹² But the Lord hardened the heart of Pharaoh, and he did not listen to them, as the Lord had spoken to Moses.

¹³ Then the Lord said to Moses, "Rise up early in the morning and present yourself before Pharaoh and say to him, 'Thus says the Lord, the God of the Hebrews, "Let my people go, that they may serve me. ¹⁴ For this time I will send all my plagues on you yourself,⁷ and on your servants and your people, so that you may know that there is none like me in all the earth. ¹⁵ For by now I could have put out my hand and struck you and your people with pestilence, and you would have been cut off from the earth. ¹⁶ But for this purpose I have raised you up, to show you my power, so that my name may be proclaimed in all the earth. ¹⁷ You are still exalting yourself against my people and will not let them go. ¹⁸ Behold, about this time tomorrow I will cause very heavy hail to fall, such as never has been in Egypt from the day it was founded until now. ¹⁹ Now therefore send, get your livestock and all that you have in the field into safe shelter, for every man and beast that is in the field and is not brought home will die when the hail falls on them."'" ²⁰ Then whoever feared the word of the Lord among the servants of Pharaoh hurried his slaves and his livestock into the houses, ²¹ but whoever did not pay attention to the word of the Lord left his slaves and his livestock in the field.

²² Then the Lord said to Moses, "Stretch out your hand toward heaven, so that there may be hail in all the land of Egypt, on man and beast and every plant of the field, in the land of Egypt." ²³ Then Moses stretched out his staff toward heaven, and the Lord sent thunder and hail, and fire ran down to the earth. And the Lord rained hail upon the land of Egypt. ²⁴ There was hail and fire flashing continually in the midst of the hail, very heavy hail, such as had never been in all the land of Egypt since it became a nation. ²⁵ The hail struck down everything that was in the field in all the land of Egypt, both man and beast. And the hail struck down every plant of the field and broke every tree of the field. ²⁶ Only in the land of Goshen, where the people of Israel were, was there no hail.

²⁷ Then Pharaoh sent and called Moses and Aaron and said to them, "This time I have sinned; the Lord is in the right, and I and my people are in the wrong. ²⁸ Plead with the Lord, for there has been enough of God's thunder and hail. I will let you go, and you shall stay no longer." ²⁹ Moses said to him, "As soon as I have gone out of the city, I will stretch out my hands to the Lord. The thunder will cease, and there will be no more hail, so that you may know that the earth is the Lord's. ³⁰ But as for you and your servants, I know that you do not yet fear the Lord God." ³¹ (The flax and the barley were struck down, for the barley was in the ear and the flax was in bud. ³² But the wheat and the emmer⁸ were not struck

down, for they are late in coming up.) ³³ So Moses went out of the city from Pharaoh and stretched out his hands to the Lord, and the thunder and the hail ceased, and the rain no longer poured upon the earth. ³⁴ But when Pharaoh saw that the rain and the hail and the thunder had ceased, he sinned yet again and hardened his heart, he and his servants. ³⁵ So the heart of Pharaoh was hardened, and he did not let the people of Israel go, just as the Lord had spoken through Moses.

10 Then the Lord said to Moses, "Go in to Pharaoh, for I have hardened his heart and the heart of his servants, that I may show these signs of mine among them, ² and that you may tell in the hearing of your son and of your grandson how I have dealt harshly with the Egyptians and what signs I have done among them, that you may know that I am the Lord."

³ So Moses and Aaron went in to Pharaoh and said to him, "Thus says the Lord, the God of the Hebrews, 'How long will you refuse to humble yourself before me? Let my people go, that they may serve me. ⁴ For if you refuse to let my people go, behold, tomorrow I will bring locusts into your country, ⁵ and they shall cover the face of the land, so that no one can see the land. And they shall eat what is left to you after the hail, and they shall eat every tree of yours that grows in the field, ⁶ and they shall fill your houses and the houses of all your servants and of all the Egyptians, as neither your fathers nor your grandfathers have seen, from the day they came on earth to this day.'" Then he turned and went out from Pharaoh.

⁷ Then Pharaoh's servants said to him, "How long shall this man be a snare to us? Let the men go, that they may serve the Lord their God. Do you not yet understand that Egypt is ruined?" ⁸ So Moses and Aaron were brought back to Pharaoh. And he said to them, "Go, serve the Lord your God. But which ones are to go?" ⁹ Moses said, "We will go with our young and our old. We will go with our sons and daughters and with our flocks and herds, for we must hold a feast to the Lord." ¹⁰ But he said to them, "The Lord be with you, if ever I let you and your little ones go! Look, you have some evil purpose in mind.⁹ ¹¹ No! Go, the men among you, and serve the Lord, for that is what you are asking." And they were driven out from Pharaoh's presence.

¹² Then the Lord said to Moses, "Stretch out your hand over the land of Egypt for the locusts, so that they may come upon the land of Egypt and eat every plant in the land, all that the hail has left." ¹³ So Moses stretched out his staff over the land of Egypt, and the Lord brought an east wind upon the land all that day and all that night. When it was morning, the east wind had brought the locusts. ¹⁴ The locusts came up over all the land of Egypt and settled on the whole country of Egypt, such a dense swarm of locusts as had never been before, nor ever will be again. ¹⁵ They covered the face of the whole land, so that the land was darkened, and they ate all the plants in the land and all the fruit of the trees that the hail had left. Not a green thing remained, neither tree nor plant of the field, through all the land of Egypt. ¹⁶ Then Pharaoh hastily called Moses and Aaron and said, "I have sinned against the Lord your God, and against you. ¹⁷ Now therefore, forgive my sin, please, only this once, and plead with the Lord your God only to remove this death from me." ¹⁸ So he went out from Pharaoh and pleaded with the Lord. ¹⁹ And the Lord turned the wind into a very strong west wind, which lifted the locusts and drove them into the Red Sea. Not a single locust was left in all the

country of Egypt. ²⁰ But the Lord hardened Pharaoh's heart, and he did not let the people of Israel go.

²¹ Then the Lord said to Moses, "Stretch out your hand toward heaven, that there may be darkness over the land of Egypt, a darkness to be felt." ²² So Moses stretched out his hand toward heaven, and there was pitch darkness in all the land of Egypt three days. ²³ They did not see one another, nor did anyone rise from his place for three days, but all the people of Israel had light where they lived. ²⁴ Then Pharaoh called Moses and said, "Go, serve the Lord; your little ones also may go with you; only let your flocks and your herds remain behind." ²⁵ But Moses said, "You must also let us have sacrifices and burnt offerings, that we may sacrifice to the Lord our God. ²⁶ Our livestock also must go with us; not a hoof shall be left behind, for we must take of them to serve the Lord our God, and we do not know with what we must serve the Lord until we arrive there." ²⁷ But the Lord hardened Pharaoh's heart, and he would not let them go. ²⁸ Then Pharaoh said to him, "Get away from me; take care never to see my face again, for on the day you see my face you shall die." ²⁹ Moses said, "As you say! I will not see your face again."

11 The Lord said to Moses, "Yet one plague more I will bring upon Pharaoh and upon Egypt. Afterward he will let you go from here. When he lets you go, he will drive you away completely. ² Speak now in the hearing of the people, that they ask, every man of his neighbor and every woman of her neighbor, for silver and gold jewelry." ³ And the Lord gave the people favor in the sight of the Egyptians. Moreover, the man Moses was very great in the land of Egypt, in the sight of Pharaoh's servants and in the sight of the people.

⁴ So Moses said, "Thus says the Lord: 'About midnight I will go out in the midst of Egypt, ⁵ and every firstborn in the land of Egypt shall die, from the firstborn of Pharaoh who sits on his throne, even to the firstborn of the slave girl who is behind the handmill, and all the firstborn of the cattle. ⁶ There shall be a great cry throughout all the land of Egypt, such as there has never been, nor ever will be again. ⁷ But not a dog shall growl against any of the people of Israel, either man or beast, that you may know that the Lord makes a distinction between Egypt and Israel.' ⁸ And all these your servants shall come down to me and bow down to me, saying, 'Get out, you and all the people who follow you.' And after that I will go out." And he went out from Pharaoh in hot anger. ⁹ Then the Lord said to Moses, "Pharaoh will not listen to you, that my wonders may be multiplied in the land of Egypt."

¹⁰ Moses and Aaron did all these wonders before Pharaoh, and the Lord hardened Pharaoh's heart, and he did not let the people of Israel go out of his land.

[1] Ch 7:26 in Hebrew [2] Or *among your people* [3] Ch 8:1 in Hebrew [4] Or *which he had brought upon Pharaoh* [5] Or *that I the Lord am in the land* [6] Septuagint, Vulgate; Hebrew *set redemption* [7] Hebrew *on your heart* [8] A type of wheat [9] Hebrew *before your face*

Section Overview

This textual unit consists of eleven sections describing eleven miraculous signs that show the Lord's sovereignty over Pharaoh, Egypt, and her gods (cf. comment on 7:14–11:10). Uniquely, the first is performed only before Pharaoh and his servants and harms neither them nor the land (7:8–13). But the next ten are set apart in being much more public and harming the Egyptians or their property (7:14–11:10). They are traditionally known as the "ten plagues," though "ten signs and wonders" perhaps describes them better (cf. comment on 7:14–11:10).[167]

Of these ten, the first nine occur in cycles of three, as shown by parallels between the cycles (cf. table 2.4).[168] From a literary perspective this structure sets apart the final (and most dramatic) sign yet to come: the death of the firstborn. From a theological perspective, since threefold repetition emphasizes the repeated element, the three cycles underscore Pharaoh's obstinate rebellion.

TABLE 2.4: Parallels between First Nine Strikes

	Sign	Forewarning	Time of Warning	Instruction Formula
First Series	Blood	Yes	"In the morning"	"Go to Pharaoh; stand"
	Frogs	Yes	None	"Go in to Pharaoh"
	Gnats	No	None	None
Second Series	Flies	Yes	"In the morning"	"Present yourself to Pharaoh"
	Livestock	Yes	None	"Go in to Pharaoh"
	Boils	No	None	None
Third Series	Hail	Yes	"In the morning"	"Present yourself before Pharaoh"
	Locusts	Yes	None	"Go in to Pharaoh"
	Darkness	No	None	None

As for the final sign, it is clearly the climax and results in one of the signs' main goals: the Israelites' release. Chapter 11 describes this sign in terrifying detail and prepares the audience for the next literary unit, in which the sign and its impact are fully described (12:1–13:16).

The above leads to the following broad outline of this section:

I. Introductory sign (7:8–13)
II. Three cycles of three signs (7:14–10:29)
III. The final sign (11:1–10)

Section Outline

I. Israel in Egypt: the Lord promises deliverance (1:1–11:10) . . .
   F. The Lord's coming deliverance of Israel by great signs and wonders, showing his sovereignty over Pharaoh and Egypt's gods (7:8–11:10)[169]
      1. First sign: Aaron's rod swallows up the Egyptians' rods (7:8–13)
      2. Second sign, first strike: water turns to blood (7:14–25)[170]

---

167 This paragraph is especially informed by Stuart, *Exodus*, 184–185.
168 The following chart is adapted very slightly from Enns, *Exodus*, 208.
169 The higher levels of outlining in this section are indebted heavily to Stuart, *Exodus*, 183–184.
170 As noted earlier, 7:8–13 is the first "sign" but, unlike the next ten, not a "strike" that harms Egypt (cf. Section Overview of 7:8–11:10). This explains the language above of "second sign, first strike."

3. Third sign, second strike: a frog infestation (8:1–15)
4. Fourth sign, third strike: a gnat infestation (8:16–19)
5. Fifth sign, fourth strike: a fly infestation (8:20–32)
6. Sixth sign, fifth strike: Egyptian livestock die (9:1–7)
7. Seventh sign, sixth strike: boils (9:8–12)
8. Eighth sign, seventh strike: hail (9:13–35)
9. Ninth sign, eighth strike: a locust infestation (10:1–20)
10. Tenth sign, ninth strike: darkness (10:21–29)
11. Announcement of eleventh sign, tenth strike: death of all Egyptian firstborn (11:1–10)

Comment

7:8–13 The previous section let us know a showdown was coming between Pharaoh and the Lord (Ex. 7:1–7). In this section the showdown begins. When Moses and Aaron provide a sign (vv. 8–10), Pharaoh's servants seem to match it (vv. 11–12a), only to have their sign undone by that of Moses and Aaron (v. 12b), which makes clear where the real power lies. Pharaoh, however, remains unmoved from his rebellion (v. 13).

The Lord tells Moses and Aaron that Pharaoh will ask them for a miracle that proves that a god has sent them. Moses is therefore to command Aaron to throw down his staff, which will become a serpent (7:9; cf. 4:1–5). Moses and Aaron obey and the miracle occurs, but Pharaoh's servants immediately imitate it (7:10–12). These servants are "wise men" and "sorcerers," described generally as "magicians." The latter word could also be translated "sorcerer-priest,"[171] as the Hebrew term "appears related to an Egyptian word often used to refer to theological specialists in ancient Egypt, who studied their culture's sacred literature and knew an array of secret charms, spell, and rituals."[172]

But how do they perform the sign? Aaron's act is truly miraculous.[173] As for how the sorcerer-priests imitate it, commentators propose that their imitation is performed either by means of illicit supernatural powers or by some sleight of hand or snake-charming methods that make serpents stiff like rods and then enliven them by throwing them on the ground.[174] However their imitation is actually accomplished, the sorcerer-priests present themselves as using their "secret arts" to access the power of Egyptian gods. This makes it even more significant that "Aaron's staff swallowed up their staffs" (v. 12). Because staffs represent power and authority, this act shows the Lord's superiority over the sorcerer-priests—and any Egyptian gods thought to empower them.

Nonetheless, Pharaoh's heart continues in its stubborn rebellion, and he will not listen to Moses and Aaron, just as the Lord has warned (7:13; cf. 4:21).

---
171 Alexander, *Exodus*, ApOTC, 160.
172 Wells, *Exodus*, 188 (cf. references there). This understanding fits with the mention of "secret arts" (Ex. 7:11).
173 Moses' surprise in Exodus 4:3 shows that the transformation happens supernaturally, not through sleight of hand or snake charming.
174 Cf. overview in John D. Currid, *Ancient Egypt and the Old Testament* (Grand Rapids, MI: Baker, 1997), 94–95.

7:14–11:10 Alexander notes that "this section of Exodus is usually called the 'ten plagues' in Christian tradition [and] the 'ten strikes' (Hb. *'eser hammakkot*) in Jewish tradition,"[175] though the Bible uses neither phrase. Because some of the ten "plagues" are not plagues in the word's modern sense, "ten strikes" is more appropriate, especially since many of the terms describing them relate to Hebrew words referring to "strikes" or "blows" or "wounds."[176]

As Alexander also notes, however, later biblical books refer to them frequently by the phrase found in 7:3, "signs and wonders" (Deut. 4:34; 6:22; 7:19; Neh. 9:10; Ps. 105:27; etc.)[177]—they are miraculous displays of the Lord's sovereign power. In light of these facts I will usually refer to these events as "strikes" or "signs and wonders" rather than as "plagues."

We may ask two questions to guide our discussion of this section. First, were the strikes natural or supernatural events? Second, what were the purposes of the strikes?

First, were these strikes natural or supernatural? While the strikes have traditionally been understood to be miracles of the Lord, more recent arguments claim that they resulted from completely natural processes.[178] Generally speaking, the first six strikes are said to follow a natural ecological sequence: (1) flagellates or dirt inundate the Nile, making it look red and killing the fish; (2) frogs are forced from the Nile and killed by anthrax that breeds in the rotting fish or by dehydration; (3) mosquitoes and (4) flies breed in water left by the flooding Nile and pass disease (such as anthrax) to (5) animals and (6) humans. The next three strikes are natural events: though rare, (7) hailstorms do occur in Egypt, (8) locust plagues are well known, and (9) desert sandstorms can occur in Egypt that obscure the light. The last strike (death of the firstborn) is variously explained, such as being related to high infant mortality rates or being an actual event (the death of Pharaoh's firstborn) that is applied to the whole people.

In evaluating the above it may be noted that the original question—Were these strikes natural or supernatural events?—introduces a false disjunction (one often assumed in these conversations). While many of the Bible's miracles cannot be explained naturally (such as the turning of water into wine), the Lord performs other miracles by supernaturally directing natural means to his ends, such as causing a "strong east wind" to blow all night and divide the sea (14:21). A natural explanation for an event does not prove that the Lord was uninvolved in it.

Several other problems with a purely naturalistic explanation may be noted. Stuart provides a substantial list, from which four may be highlighted: (1) "The biblical account describes the plagues as the result of commands given by Moses

---

175 Alexander, *Exodus*, ApOTC, 146.
176 These include the Hebrew verb *nakah*, which refers to "striking" (Ex. 7:17, 20, 25; 8:16; 12:12; etc.), the verb *nagaf* (8:2) and the related nouns *maggefah* (9:14) and *negef* (12:13), which all relate to a root meaning "to strike," and the noun *nega'* (11:1; cf. note 230 within the Response section on Exodus 11, "Who Is the Lord?").
177 Alexander, *Exodus*, ApOTC, 147.
178 For an early exposition of this approach cf. Greta Hort, "The Plagues of Egypt," *ZAW* 69/1–4 (1957): 84–103. For more recent approaches cf. references in Alexander (*Exodus*, 155). The following summary relies heavily on Stuart (*Exodus*, 192) and Wells (*Exodus*, 192), both of whom describe the naturalistic approach but also critique it.

and Aaron," beginning and ending precisely in keeping with their word (not from "natural" timing). (2) "The magicians saw the third, irreproducible plague as 'the finger of God' (8:19), rather than as something that normally happens in Egypt." (3) "The plagues differentially affected the Egyptians but left the Israelites unscathed." (4) "The final plague, that of the death of the firstborn, has no natural explanation at all. It was a special judgment of God (how could any natural disease strike only firstborn children and not harm others?)."[179] In short, Exodus presents the Lord as bringing these strikes on Egypt in his sovereign power.

This leads naturally to the second question: What were the purposes of these strikes? At least four may be identified. First, to punish disobedience (7:16–18; 8:2–4, 21–22; etc.). Pharaoh may be ruler of Egypt, but Yahweh is ruler of the universe, and rebelling against him brings punishment, as expected for those rebelling against a king.

The second purpose is related: to force Pharaoh to do what is right. These strikes punish Pharaoh but are also to lead to righteous behavior: releasing the people from their cruel slavery into the service of King Yahweh (3:19–20; 6:1; 11:1, 4–8; esp. 12:29–33).

A third purpose is to authenticate the messenger (4:1–9, 30–31; 7:8–9; 14:31). It is one thing to claim to speak on a deity's behalf; it is another to back up such claims with miraculous signs.

But above all by these signs the Lord demonstrates his character and purposes. At several points he states that these signs are so that people will "know" or "acknowledge"—the Hebrew word can mean either (cf. comment on 5:1–9)—that he is Yahweh, which means to "know/acknowledge" something that is true about his character and purposes. Pharaoh and the Egyptians are to know/acknowledge that Yahweh has set apart Israel as his beloved people (8:21–23; 9:4, 26; 11:7), has sovereign power throughout the earth (7:17; 8:10, 19, 22), and is mightier than Pharaoh or any of the "gods" the Egyptians worship (8:10; 12:12). This last point is a special focus and will be returned to below (cf. Response section on 7:8–11:10, "Who Is the Lord?").

As for the Israelites, they are to know/acknowledge all the above and especially to learn that Yahweh is their redeeming God who is faithful to his covenant promises (6:6–8; 10:2). He will keep his word not only because he is powerful enough but also because he overflows with faithful love (cf. Response section on 7:8–11:10, "What Does It Mean to Know the Lord?").

In sum the signs make clear that Israel—and the entire world (9:14–16)—is to obey Yahweh reverently because of his power, confidently because of his faithfulness, and joyfully because of his love.

7:14–25 Whereas the last sign did not harm Pharaoh or Egypt (Ex. 7:8–13), the next ten will (7:14–11:10). In each the Lord strikes Egypt with a punishing miracle that makes clear that he is the sovereign God. In this case the Nile and its waters

---

[179] Stuart, Exodus, 193.

are turned to blood (7:14–25), causing hardship for the Egyptians (vv. 21, 24) but also showing Yahweh's sovereignty over Egypt and her gods (cf. comment on 7:14–19 [at v. 17]).

The passage begins and ends by emphasizing the stubbornness of Pharaoh's heart (vv. 14, 22–23), drawing our attention to the root of his rebellion. When Pharaoh's sorcerer-priests imitate the sign carried out by Moses and Aaron (vv. 20–22a)—which ironically only add to Egypt's woes!—their imitation confirms Pharaoh's stubborn rebellion (vv. 22b–23), and the passage ends with his people's suffering the price for a full seven days (vv. 24–25).

7:14–19 Pharaoh's hardened heart and refusal to obey the Lord (v. 14; cf. vv. 22–23) is a theme running throughout these chapters (8:15, 19, 32; 9:7; etc.), making clear that these chapters narrate a battle between Pharaoh, the most powerful of earthly kings, and Yahweh, the king of the universe. Yahweh is clearly the superior, bringing his punishing strikes on Pharaoh and his land at will. That Pharaoh never learns his lesson underscores the depth of his rebellion and pride.

In this case the Lord commands Moses to meet Pharaoh as the latter goes out to the Nile, perhaps to bathe (cf. 2:5). The setting is fitting, since the Nile will be the object of the Lord's action. Moses must bring the "staff that turned into a serpent" (7:15), also known as the "staff of God," by which he (or Aaron on his behalf) will perform signs (cf. 4:17, 20). Clearly, another sign is about to come.

Moses is to remind Pharaoh of the king's disobedience and to warn him of the coming sign of judgment: the Lord will turn the Nile's water to blood, its fish (a primary Egyptian food source) will die, and the Egyptians will be unable to drink its water (7:17–18).[180] The very water in which the Egyptians were told to kill Israelite baby boys (1:22) now becomes water upon which the Egyptians can no longer depend to sustain life. All this will be a sign so that Pharaoh—who earlier boasted he did not know Yahweh (5:2)—will know clearly that Yahweh, the Hebrews' God, is Lord of heaven and earth (7:17). Moreover, since the Egyptians personify the yearly inundation of the Nile as the god Hapi[181] and also associate it "with the resurrection of [the god] Osiris,"[182] it is easy to imagine how this sign shows Yahweh's sovereign power over Egypt's gods.

The Lord then tells Moses and Aaron how to bring the sign about and notes that the affected waters will go far beyond the Nile to include all surface waters in the land (7:19). He also focuses the judgment on the Egyptians (note the use of "their" throughout v. 19).[183]

The question of whether the waters turn to actual blood is debated. Several argue that this is phenomenological language—that is, it describes what happens

---

[180] "[They] will grow weary of drinking water from the Nile" is in Hebrew "[They] will grow weary to drink water from the Nile," that is, "grow weary *from trying* to drink water from the Nile" due to the extreme water collection efforts they will have to follow (cf. 7:24; for a similar use of "to grow weary" cf. Gen. 19:11).
[181] Enns, *Exodus*, 200n16, citing D. P. Silverman, "Divinity and Deities in Ancient Egypt," in *Religion in Ancient Egypt: Gods, Myths, and Personal Practice*, ed. B. W. Shafer et al. (Ithaca, NY: Cornell University Press, 1991), 34.
[182] Hoffmeier, *Israel in Egypt*, 150.
[183] Enns, *Exodus*, 202.

with reference to how something looks to the naked eye, not how it actually is. (Compare the familiar "the sun rises," which is how a sunrise appears even though the sun does not actually rise in the air). In support many cite Joel's statement in a judgment context that "the sun shall be turned to darkness, and the moon to blood" (Joel 2:31). There "blood" refers not to actual blood but to the moon's bloodlike red color. The same could be true in Exodus 7, with suggestions for what turns the water red ranging from red soil to algae (or both).[184] But whether or not the water turns to actual blood, use of the term "blood" is a foreboding way to describe the water, especially given blood's association with judgment and death (Deut. 32:42; Ps. 58:10; Isa. 49:26; etc.). What is more, the endpoint is the same either way: the water will be undrinkable, and this will be Yahweh's doing.

7:20–23 Moses and Aaron obey, and the sign occurs (7:20–21). As they did before (vv. 11–12a) and will do again (8:7), Pharaoh's sorcerer-priests imitate the sign (7:22a; presumably using water sourced as outlined in v. 24). But "ironically, all that the magicians can do is make matters worse: more snakes, more bloody water, more frogs!"[185] As Houtman notes, "They cannot reverse the catastrophes, but only increase them, thus contributing to YHWH's fight against Pharaoh."[186] Pharaoh misses the irony. His heart remains hardened, using the sorcerer-priests' deed as an excuse (v. 22). Indeed, "he did not take even this to heart" (v. 23), meaning he does not apply his heart to learn what he should.[187] Clearly Pharaoh has a heart problem.

7:24–25 Since all surface water has been turned to blood (v. 19), the Egyptians are forced to dig for fresh water, or perhaps for water that has been filtered through the earth and drained of whatever has made it red (v. 24). In either case it is exhausting work that lasts at least seven days (v. 25).[188] But no word from Pharaoh comes, so the Lord prepares to strike Egypt again.

8:1–15 In the second strike frogs infest the land. The sign is first described (vv. 1–5), then carried out (v. 6), then repeated by Pharaoh's servants (v. 7), who thus make the plague worse—and can do nothing about it! This forces Pharaoh to know/acknowledge Yahweh's sovereign power (v. 8), and the Lord's deliverance is supposed to have the very same effect (v. 10). Sadly, once that deliverance comes (vv. 12–13), Pharaoh doubles down on his rebellious disobedience (v. 15). He has acknowledged the Lord in word but not in deed.

8:1–5 The Lord commands Moses both to repeat to Pharaoh the demand to let the Israelites go and worship the Lord (v. 1; cf. 5:1, 3; 7:16) and also to warn Pharaoh

---

[184] Cf. summary in Kaiser, *Exodus*, in *Genesis–Leviticus*, 350.
[185] Fretheim, *Exodus*, 113.
[186] Houtman, *Exodus*, vol. 1, 534.
[187] The same Hebrew phrase occurs in Proverbs 22:17 ("apply our heart"); 24:32 ("I considered"); 27:23 ("give attention to").
[188] Commentators debate whether to connect 7:25 to what precedes or to what follows. If the simple passing of time is the point, we might expect "And it came to pass after seven days" and connect it with what follows (cf. Gen. 22:1; 39:7; 40:1). I take Exodus 7:25 with what precedes to indicate the sign's length: "And seven days were completed after the Lord's striking of the Nile"; that is, the sign finished after seven days (cf. Gen. 25:24; 29:21).

of the consequences for refusing: a pestilence of frogs (8:2). The frogs will show no respect of rank, making themselves at home in Pharaoh's very bed! Everyone else will be similarly plagued, with frogs infesting the very implements used to make daily bread (v. 3). Pharaoh apparently refuses, and Moses tells Aaron to raise the staff of God over Egypt's waters once more (v. 5; cf. 7:19).

8:6 Aaron obeys, and the frogs cover the land like a swarming green slime. The infestation afflicts the Egyptians but may also have symbolic value. In Israel frogs will be ritually unclean (cf. Lev. 11:10–12), as will their carcasses (Lev. 11:24–25), so Israelites may view the punishment as going beyond hardship to include ritual defilement (cf. Ex. 9:10–11). By the end of the sign the Egyptians and their homes are entirely defiled.[189]

8:7–11 Pharaoh's sorcerer-priests imitate the sign—ironically causing more frogs to infest the land! What is worse, they cannot make the frogs leave. With his own bed full of frogs, Pharaoh promises to release the people if Moses and Aaron will plead to Yahweh—he uses the Lord's proper name[190]—to remove the frogs (8:8). Pharaoh is beginning to "know/acknowledge" that only Yahweh can fix this problem (cf. comment on 5:1–9); Egypt's king and gods are powerless before him.

Moses invites Pharaoh to name when he would like the frogs to leave (8:9).[191] Pharaoh's response of "Tomorrow" (v. 10a) could be understood as "By tomorrow,"[192] the sense being, "Pray this is resolved by tomorrow!" Moses agrees but also makes clear that when this occurs—the resolution of a national infestation within twenty-four hours—it will be a sign so that Pharaoh may know there is no one like Yahweh; he alone is God (v. 10b).[193] Pharaoh's boast of not knowing Yahweh (5:2) is being answered in the most public and painful of ways (cf. 7:17).

8:12–14 Moses and Aaron leave Pharaoh's presence, and Moses "cried to the LORD," indicating earnest prayer (8:12; cf. 14:10; 17:4). He does not take the Lord's help for granted but pleads earnestly for it, asking the Lord to reveal his power and strength by taking away "the frogs, which he had brought upon Pharaoh" (8:12; cf. ESV mg.). The Lord answers, and the frogs die throughout the land (v. 13). The Egyptians gather them into heaps and heaps—the Hebrew repeats the word "heaps" to convey how many frogs there are—and the land soon reeks of death, just as the Nile had because of the dead fish (v. 14; cf. 7:21). The stench is a lingering

---

189 The Israelites are presumably unaffected. Sometimes the Lord foretells that he will strike the Egyptians but not the Israelites (Ex. 8:22–23; 9:4; 11:7); at other times, however, the distinction is reported after the fact (9:26; 10:23). In this case it is presumed, as suggested by how the narrator focuses on the Egyptians as the target (8:3–4).
190 "LORD" in small caps represents the name Yahweh; cf. comment on 3:13–15.
191 "Be pleased to command me" is in Hebrew "Honor yourself/boast over me," often understood as a way of giving Pharaoh the honor of naming when the frogs should leave (so ESV and most versions). Alternately, Moses is challenging him, with the sense of 8:9–10 being, "Give yourself a reason to boast by telling me to fix this problem by an impossible time—but it will not work, since the Lord will do it and make his sovereignty crystal clear"; cf. Brevard S. Childs, *The Book of Exodus: A Critical, Theological Commentary* (Louisville: Westminster John Knox, 1974), 156.
192 The word "tomorrow" is preceded by a preposition that can mean "by" when used with reference to time. Compare the phrase "by morning" in Exodus 34:2.
193 Cf. Exodus 9:14; 15:11; Deuteronomy 4:35, 39; 1 Kings 18:36–37 (the latter noted by Kaiser, *Exodus*, in *Genesis–Leviticus*, 352).

reminder of Pharaoh's stubborn rebellion and the ultimate end of those who rebel against the Lord.

8:15 With the frogs gone Pharaoh hardens his heart and refuses to honor his promise. For many, promises made to God in desperation are quickly broken when relief comes. How much more so when the promiser has a proud and stubborn heart: "If favor is shown to the wicked, he does not learn righteousness" (Isa. 26:10).[194]

8:16–19 In the third strike gnats come on both humans and animals. The initial verses quickly introduce the gnat plague's coming upon the land (vv. 16–17). For the first time the sorcerer-priests are unable to replicate the sign (v. 18). They also speak for the first time, warning Pharaoh that divine handiwork is involved in this sign! But Pharaoh's hardened heart will not be moved (v. 19b).

As noted above (cf. Section Overview of 7:8–11:10), the first nine strikes occur in cycles of three, and the third strike in each cycle comes without explicit warning. Perhaps a warning did occur (Pharaoh and his servants know the strike is the Lord's doing; 8:18–19), but by not mentioning one the narrator makes an important point: if someone resists the Lord, judgment may come unannounced.

Aaron again stretches out the staff of God to bring about a strike (8:16; cf. 7:19; 8:5), in this case literally striking the ground and turning the dust into some form of insect, often translated as "gnats" (though certainty is difficult). The fact that they are on "man and beast" suggests a biting insect, with guesses ranging from lice to mosquitos. Whatever the case, there is no escaping them: "*All* the dust of the earth became gnats in *all* the land of Egypt."

For the first time Pharaoh's sorcerer-priests fail to imitate the sign (v. 18). They warn Pharaoh, "This is the finger of God" (v. 19), which is to say, "This is divine handiwork" (cf. Ps. 8:3). Moreover, by referring to a single "finger" they acknowledge that the hand's owner is so powerful that he needs only one finger to accomplish such miracles.

It may be noted that the phrase "finger of God" could be translated "finger of a god." In other words the sorcerer-priests avoid the question of which god is at work. We are not told why. (Are they worried about angering Pharaoh by naming Moses and Aaron's God?) Whatever the reason, their words do acknowledge that a divine power is at work, one greater than any power to which they have access, with the context making clear that it is Israel's God, Yahweh, who is doing these things. Moreover, the sorcerer-priests say this as Egypt's theological experts (cf. comment on 7:8–13), so Pharaoh now has testimony about Yahweh's power from his own trusted advisors.

But Pharaoh's remains hardened. He will not give up his rebellious obstinacy (8:19).

8:20–32 With the fourth strike flies invade the land. As the passage begins, the Lord's warning returns (cf. comment on 8:16–19). It is apparently unheeded, and

---
[194] Bush, *Commentary on Exodus*, 103.

the strike occurs, with emphasis placed on the fact that it impacts all Egyptians but no Israelites (vv. 20–24). Seeking relief, Pharaoh agrees at first to a partial concession and then to a full one if Moses will pray to the Lord on his behalf (vv. 25–29). Moses does so, and the Lord relents (vv. 30–31), but Pharaoh once more hardens his heart and again breaks his promise (v. 32; cf. v. 8, 15).

8:20–23 The second cycle of strikes begins (on the cycles cf. Overview at 7:8–11:10). Moses is once more to confront Pharaoh as he goes to the Nile, perhaps to bathe (8:20a; cf. 2:5; 7:15). The warning Moses gives to Pharaoh about not letting the people go could be woodenly rendered, "If you are not *sending* my people, behold, I am *sending* swarms of flies" (8:21). In other words, if Pharaoh refuses to send the people out, the Lord will send swarms of flies in! And while the translation "flies" (Hb. *'arob*) is uncertain,[195] they will clearly fill the homes of all the Egyptians (vv. 21, 24), causing significant distress and a desperate desire for relief (v. 28).

The land of Goshen, in which the Israelites live, however, will be spared (vv. 21b–22).[196] Such a distinction will be mentioned explicitly in four more of the ten strikes (9:4, 6; 9:26; 10:23; 11:7), though it is presumably made in the others as well (cf. note 189 within comment on 8:6). In this instance the Lord states that the distinction is so Pharaoh might "know/acknowledge [cf. comment on 5:1–9] that I am Yahweh in the midst of the earth" (8:22), that is, he is the king dwelling in it and sovereign over all that happens there (cf. 19:5; Deut. 23:14; Ps. 74:12). The Lord then underscores that the distinction will be between "my people," who will be dwelling in safety and peace, and "your [Pharaoh's] people," who will be oppressed and afflicted and not delivered by their king or their gods (Ex. 8:23). The impotence of Pharaoh's kingship before that of Yahweh will be on public display. Moses is to finish the warning by letting Pharaoh know that the strike will occur by the next day (v. 23). For reasons not explained significant events in Exodus often take place the following day.[197] In this case announcing the timing makes clear that the event starts at the Lord's bidding, and it also gives Pharaoh time to repent.

8:24 Pharaoh apparently refuses to repent, and the sign is fulfilled. The narrator focuses on the widespread nature of the affliction; all the Egyptians are affected.

8:25–27 Pharoah begins with a qualified concession: the Israelites may go and sacrifice to the Lord, but, instead of going a three days' journey into the wilderness (5:1, 3), they must remain within the land, that is, among the Egyptian population (8:25). Moses repeats the original demand, arguing that, were they to sacrifice in the Egyptian's presence, they would be stoned since the Egyptians would view their sacrifices as a detestable act (vv. 26–27).[198] No reason is given for the Egyptian

---

[195] Psalm 78:45 could suggest a biting insect here, unless it is using the language of "devour" as a poetic way of describing a draining affliction (cf. Gen. 31:40).
[196] Goshen is thought to be in the eastern Nile Delta and was especially good for grazing livestock (Gen. 46:34).
[197] Cf. Exodus 8:29; 9:5, 18; 10:4; 32:5; Numbers 16:5; cf. Cornelis Houtman, *Exodus*, vol. 2, trans. Johan Rebel and Sierd Woudstra, *HCOT* (Leuven: Peeters, 1996), 49–50.
[198] Since Moses knew the Lord could protect the Israelites, it seems plausible that he is responding to Pharaoh's cunning in Exodus 8:25 with his own shrewdness: "You know that we cannot sacrifice in this land

view (just as it is not explained why Egyptians thought it was detestable to eat with Israelites, Gen. 43:32, or to be a shepherd, Gen. 46:34). Usual guesses are that the Israelites would not sacrifice according to Egyptian religious regulations or would sacrifice animals considered sacred by the Egyptians (or both), though it may also be noted that some cultural views are simply inherited, with new generations simply assuming, "That is just the way it is." Whatever the reason for the Egyptians' perspective, Moses' argument works (cf. note 198).

8:28–29 While Pharaoh agrees to the demand, he warns that the people may not go far. From his perspective, this is to be a temporary situation. He then asks Moses to pray on his behalf, which Moses agrees to do, though not without his own warning: Pharaoh must not break his promise again (cf. v. 15).

8:30–32 As before, the Lord hears Moses' prayer, and the flies are removed (cf. v. 13). But Pharaoh again hardens his heart, doubling down on his stubborn rebellion and refusing to let the people go (cf. v. 15).

9:1–7 The fifth strike decimates Egyptian livestock with a plague. As previously, the Lord warns Pharaoh that he will distinguish between his people and the Egyptians in this judgment (Ex. 9:1–4; cf. 8:21–23). When the strike happens, this distinction is maintained, a fact that Pharaoh himself corroborates (9:6–7a). Nonetheless, his hardened heart is impervious to change (v. 7b).

9:1–5 Once more Moses is to demand that Pharaoh release the Israelites so that they may go and worship the Lord (v. 1; cf. note 89 within comment on 3:11–12). If he refuses, a very severe plague will devastate Egyptian livestock, impacting military endeavors (cf. 14:23) and depriving many Egyptians of food and income.[199] The plague will occur because "the hand of the LORD will fall" on the livestock (9:3),[200] making clear that Israel's God, the Lord, is sovereign king in the land (cf. 7:4–5). This will be evident not only from the plague's severity but also from that the fact that it will not affect the Israelites (9:4). As before, Moses is to announce that the strike will happen tomorrow (v. 5; cf. comment on 8:20–23).

9:6–7 The next day the strike occurs, and "all the livestock of the Egyptians died" (v. 6). The word "all" is hyperbolic, since livestock are mentioned just a few verses later (vv. 9, 19; cf. also v. 25 with 10:15), but the point of the hyperbole must not be missed: this blow is widespread and devastating. The Israelites, however, are protected (9:6), which Pharaoh himself confirms (v. 7)!

---

because of *your* people's customs, and that doing so could be fatal." In saying this Moses could be: (1) allowing Pharaoh to save face in not enforcing his demand, (2) appealing to Pharaoh's desire to avoid chaos in the land, (3) appealing to Pharaoh's desire not to lose his workforce (through death), or (4) a combination of the above (cf. Enns, *Exodus*, 214; cf. also Stuart, *Exodus*, 217, 217n77).

199 Abel Ndjerareou, *Exodus*, in *Africa Bible Commentary: A One-Volume Commentary Written by 70 African Scholars*, ed. Tokunboh Adeyemo (Grand Rapids, MI: Zondervan, 2006), 98. Some see the mention of camels as an anachronism, but cf. J. D. Currid ("Travel and Transportation," *DOTP*, 871–872) for evidence of camel domestication in the Levant by the beginning of the second millennium BC.

200 This is one of many passages illustrating that consequences for our sin can affect not only us but those connected to us (cf. Num. 14:33). For how human sin can impact creation and animals in particular cf. Jeremiah 7:20; 12:4; Hosea 4:1–3.

Sadly, even after confirming the sign himself, his heart doubles down in its stubborn rebellion (v. 7). Hardened hearts do not seek truth, only self-confirmation.

9:8–12 Debilitating sores now break out on people and animals. As with the third strike, no warning is mentioned. (For patterns within the strikes cf. Section Overview of 7:8–11:10.) When the strike occurs, the text emphasizes its impact on the (clearly powerless) magicians (9:11). In a punishment corresponding to the crime the Lord himself then hardens Pharaoh's already hardened heart, giving him over to his willfully proud rebellion (v. 12).

9:8–9 To this point Aaron has been performing the actions leading to judgment. From this point onward Moses will be in the lead role, which suggests that his earlier fears have been addressed (cf. comment on 3:11–12). In this case he and Aaron are to take soot from a furnace, presumably placing it in a container,[201] and then Moses is to throw it in the air before Pharaoh (9:8). The soot will become a dust afflicting people and animals with "boils breaking out in sores" (v. 9). While the exact meaning of "sores" is unclear, the term for "boils" clearly refers to a painful skin condition (cf. v. 11; Deut. 28:35; Job 2:7–8) that can be fatal (2 Kings 20:1–7).

9:10–11 Moses and Aaron obey, and the "boils breaking out in sores" afflict people and animals, presumably Egyptians in particular (cf. v. 11b). If the laws of Leviticus 13:18–22 reflect understandings already present among Israelites regarding defilement, the people would have viewed this strike not only as a physical punishment but also as a judgment rendering the Egyptians ritually impure (cf. comment on 8:6). And, while everyone was afflicted, the text highlights the impact on Pharaoh's magicians. Although they had imitated earlier signs, they are so afflicted by this one they cannot even stand in Moses' presence—and will not be heard from again. They and the gods they represent have been utterly defeated before Yahweh.

9:12 To this point either Pharaoh has hardened his own heart (8:15, 32) or the text has described his heart as hardened (7:13–14, 22; 8:19; 9:7). But now the Lord brings his judgment to bear by taking this heart hardened in rebellion and making it harder still, "seconding, as it were," Pharaoh's own earlier decision to harden it.[202] As noted above (cf. comment on 4:21–23), the Lord sometimes judges us by giving us over to our heart's evil desires. This is a severe warning about the danger of sin, which coats our hearts like quick-drying cement, making repentance increasingly difficult and judgment increasingly certain (cf. comment on 4:21–23 and note 121).

9:13–35 In the seventh strike a hailstorm of apocalyptic proportions decimates the land. As seen elsewhere, the text includes a warning about the consequences of disobedience (vv. 13–19). But the narrative especially emphasizes how the Lord will show himself unique among the gods by this strike (v. 14) and how the Lord has established Pharaoh's throne so that he may use Pharaoh's disobedience as an

---

201 Cassuto, *Commentary on the Book of Exodus*, 113.
202 Kaiser, *Exodus*, in *Genesis–Leviticus*, 359.

opportunity to show the nations his own glorious character (vv. 15–16). Through this strike Yahweh's kingship will become crystal clear.

This passage is also unique in describing for the first time how Pharaoh's servants respond to the warnings, distinguishing between those who fear the Lord's word and those who do not (vv. 20–21). When the strike occurs, the narrator emphasizes the destruction's widespread nature in Egypt (vv. 23–25) and contrasts this with the peace and safety enjoyed by the Lord's people (v. 26). For the first time Pharaoh acknowledges his and his people's wrong (vv. 27–28), though Moses' response leads us to doubt that Pharaoh or his servants have learned the lesson (vv. 29–30). Sure enough, when the Lord ends the hailstorm, Pharaoh again hardens his heart, as do his servants, and he refuses to let the people go (vv. 33–35). The heart is in fact a focus throughout: the Lord sent this strike "to Pharaoh's heart" that he might finally acknowledge the Lord (cf. comment on 9:13–14), Pharaoh's servants who do not fear the Lord's word "did not take it to heart" (cf. comment on 9:20–21), and Pharaoh and his servants "hardened their hearts" in continued rebellion against the Lord (v. 34). As goes the heart, so goes the person.

9:13–14 Once more Moses is to meet Pharaoh early in the morning, demand he release the Lord's people to go and worship him (v. 13; cf. note 89 within comment on 3:11–12), and warn him of disobedience's consequences (vv. 14–19). The warning is particularly long. When the Lord says, "For this time I will send all my plagues" (v. 14),[203] he means either that this strike will involve a combination of judgments (lethal hail, deafening thunder, blinding lightning, torrential rain) or that this time—that is, in this third cycle of strikes and the final strike following it—he will send his remaining judgments on the land.[204] Either way, terrifying judgments will occur. Significantly, the Hebrew of verse 14 reads, "I will send all my plagues to your heart," which refers to Pharaoh himself (cf. ESV mg.) but is more specific, naming the very place causing his rebellion, as though to say, "Your proud heart should be humbled by what you see so that you [singular] finally know/acknowledge"—the word can be translated either way (cf. comment on 5:1–9) —"that there is no god like me in all the earth!"[205]

9:15–16 To further humble him the Lord states that he could have already wiped Pharaoh and his people from the face of the earth. "Instead," he says to Pharaoh, "I have established you as king"—Pharaoh's very throne is dependent on Yahweh!—"so that I could use your reign, with all its stubborn rebellion, as an opportunity to show forth my mighty power, so all nations might hear and know who I am!"[206] Even the Lord's judgment has salvation ultimately in view, and that

---

[203] The word "plagues" could also be translated "(lethal) strikes." Cf. 2 Samuel 17:9 ("slaughter") and the use of the verb built on the same root in Exodus 21:22; Leviticus 26:17.
[204] Among others cf. Kalisch (*Exodus*, 153) for the former and Cassuto (*Commentary on the Book of Exodus*, 115) for the latter. For "all" with the sense "all that remain" cf. "rest of the blood" (Hb. "all of the blood") in Exodus 29:12 ESV mg. (Kaiser, *Exodus*, in *Genesis–Leviticus*, 361).
[205] Cf. Exodus 15:11 and discussion of the third approach in comment on 3:13–15. Fretheim (*Exodus*, 124) describes 9:14b as a "statement of God's incomparability extended to universal proportions."
[206] To "proclaim the name" is to tell of the praiseworthy deeds done by the one bearing that name (cf. Pss. 22:22; 102:21). Note Paul's citation of this passage in Romans 9:17 to illustrate God's sovereignty.

on a worldwide scale. He is God of all the earth (cf. 9:14; Ps. 24:1) and wants all the earth to know him.

9:17–19 The specific consequence is now named: unprecedented hail that will come the next day (vv. 17–18; for "tomorrow" cf. comment on 8:20–23). The Lord then warns Pharaoh to get all his remaining animals (cf. comment on 9:6–7) and all his people that are out in the fields to shelter lest they die when the hail comes (v. 19). The warning is both a mercy and a test: Will Pharaoh submit his kingship to Yahweh's by listening?

9:20–21 Pharaoh's servants also hear the warning and respond in two ways. Some "feared the word of the LORD," that is, obeyed it reverently (cf. Prov. 13:13). But others did not. The Hebrew of Exodus 9:21 begins, "Whoever did not *set his heart* to the word of the LORD." To "set one's heart" is an idiom that refers to "paying attention" to something or "taking it to heart" (cf. 2 Sam. 13:33; 19:20; Isa. 41:22 [ESV "consider"]). In this context it emphasizes that their problem, like Pharaoh's, lies in the heart, leading them to leave their servants and livestock fatally exposed.

9:22–25 The Lord now commands Moses to stretch toward the heavens his hand, which is holding the staff of God (v. 22; cf. v. 23). This action will be an enacted prayer (cf. comment on 9:29–30), which the Lord will answer by sending hail on everything exposed in Egypt's fields: people, animals, and plants. When Moses obeys, the Lord responds and the narrator slows down, taking three verses to describe the storm's terrifying nature and consequences (vv. 23–25). Relentless hail (the word is mentioned six times) falls, accompanied by constant lightning strikes and explosions of thunder. The results are apocalyptic:[207] people and animals are killed, crops wiped out, and trees splintered into bits. This is loss of life and financial disaster rolled into one, since losing one's servants, livestock, crops, and trees (esp. those bearing fruit; cf. 10:15) would lead to economic ruin. Egypt is utterly devastated.

9:26 Against the backdrop of Egypt's ruin stands the peaceful tranquility of Goshen, where the Israelites dwells. Once more the Lord sets his people apart, protecting them with his fatherly love and care and making clear that it is their God, Yahweh, who is doing these things (cf. 8:22–23; 9:4, 6; 10:23; 11:7; cf. note 189 within comment on 8:6).

9:27–28 For the first time Pharaoh acknowledges his wrong: "This time I have sinned" (v. 27). Commentators debate whether he means "This time (but not the previous times) I have sinned," "This time I (acknowledge that I have) sinned," or "This (one last) time I have sinned (but will not do so again)." In favor of the third understanding is his use of the near identical words in 10:17, where "this one last

---

[207] Indeed, Revelation will also speak of hail strikes that come in judgment (Rev. 8:7; 16:21).

time" fits the context very well.[208] In any case what is clear is that he acknowledges "The LORD is in the right" in demanding his people's release, "and I and my people are in the wrong" for not doing so.[209] He then pleads with Moses to pray for deliverance, and he promises release (9:28).

9:29–30 Moses responds that he will "stretch out [his] hands to the LORD"— an action that often accompanied prayer (1 Kings 8:22; Ps. 143:6; Isa. 1:15)[210]—and promises that the thunder and hail will cease so that Pharaoh (the "you" is singular) "may know that the earth is the LORD's" (9:29)—that is, that Yahweh is sovereign king over the world and controls all that occurs within it (cf. Ps. 24:1). He is the Lord; Pharaoh and his gods are not.

Moses then notes that Pharaoh and his servants "do not yet fear the LORD God" (Ex. 9:30). In contrast to some servants who did have an appropriate fear (v. 20) Pharaoh and his remaining servants do not. Often to "fear the Lord" means to show him obedience and love (Deut. 5:29; 6:2; 10:12), the emphasis being more on revering him than on actual terror. But the form of the phrase used here occurs in contexts in which the emphasis appears to be on the emotion of fear itself, perhaps because of the direct presence of the source of that fear (cf. esp. Deut. 2:4; 5:5; 7:18; 20:1; Ps. 3:6). Here the sense would be, "You are not afraid of the Lord's judgment despite his clear presence in these miracles." It may also be noted that at first glance this reads as an accusation, a way for Moses to affirm he is not fooled by Pharaoh's words. Possibly, however, Moses means this more as a challenge, a way to ask, "Do you really mean it?"—just as Joshua challenges the Israelites after their promise of obedience (cf. Josh. 24:14–20). If so, it is to give Pharaoh a chance to reaffirm ("I do really mean it!"), a response that in this case is notably missing (cf. Josh. 24:21). Either way, Pharaoh and his officials are painted negatively. Despite the clear work of God's hand in their midst, they still have not learned to fear his judgment (cf. Isa. 9:13; Jer. 2:30; Hag. 2:17).

9:31–32 The narrator interrupts the story to explain that this strike takes place while "the barley was in the ear and the flax was in bud" (Ex. 9:31), that is, sometime "in February or early March."[211] This orients the audience to the time of year and informs them of which crops are destroyed. The mention that "the wheat and the emmer were not struck down, for they are late in coming up" (v. 32) underscores the time of year and perhaps also helps the audience figure out which crops are destroyed in the next strike (cf. 10:5, 12, 15).[212]

---

[208] Cf. Genesis 18:32; Judges 6:39. The idea in Exodus 9:27 would be, "I have learned my lesson and will not do this again!" If so, 9:34 identifies the lie for what it is: as opposed to this being the last time, "he sinned yet again" and did not let the people go.
[209] Cassuto, *Commentary on the Book of Exodus*, 120. See the use of similar phrases to describe the innocent and guilty in legal cases (Deut. 25:1; 1 Kings 8:31–32).
[210] The reason he does so "outside the city" is not clear, though Moses regularly leaves Pharaoh's presence to pray (Ex. 8:12, 30; 10:18); cf. 5:22, which may suggest he seeks particular places to pray (cf. note 140 within comment on 6:1–8).
[211] Propp (*Exodus 1–18*, 335) notes that in Israel barley is harvested in March or April, but in Egypt "crops ripen earlier than in Canaan."
[212] The wheat harvest appears to have been seven weeks later than the barley; cf. Leviticus 23:10 (which refers to barley) with 23:15–16 (which refers to wheat).

9:33–35 As before, Moses prays and the Lord answers, ending the storm (v. 33; cf. 8:12–13, 30–31). And, as before, Pharaoh sins: he hardens his heart (cf. 8:15, 32)—this time joined by his servants—and refuses to let the people go (9:34–35; cf. note 208 within comment on 9:27–28).

10:1–20 In the eighth strike locusts invade the land. As the passage begins, the Lord encourages Moses by telling him that he is sovereignly overseeing Pharaoh's rebellion and using it to his own glorious ends (vv. 1–2). God's graphic warning of the coming strike (vv. 3–6) leads Pharaoh's own servants to urge him to let at least some Israelites go (v. 7). When Moses makes clear the Lord wants all to be released, Pharaoh again rebels (vv. 8–11), and the locusts decimate the land (vv. 12–15). For only the second time Pharaoh admits his wrong, then asks for forgiveness and deliverance (vv. 16–17). When Moses prays on his behalf, the Lord answers and then reasserts his sovereignty over Pharaoh once more by taking his already hardened heart and making it harder still (vv. 18–20). The Lord's hardening of Pharaoh's heart frames the passage (cf. vv. 1–2) and encourages God's people to recognize that it is Yahweh, not Pharaoh, who reigns as the true king and is working all things to his glory.

10:1–2 In the previous passage Pharaoh and his servants hardened their hearts (9:34–35); in this passage the Lord states he has also done so to their hearts (10:1a). As noted earlier, he sometimes judges people by giving them over to their hearts' evil desires (cf. comments on 4:21–23 [esp. note 121]; 9:12). That he does so here is meant to encourage Moses: despite Pharaoh's rebellion the Lord is in full control.

Returning to themes found in 9:14–16, the Lord explains he is using the rebellion of Pharaoh and his servants to accomplish far greater purposes, namely, displaying his miraculous judgment signs in their midst (10:1). The Israelites will then be able to tell future generations how the Lord used these signs in his dealings with the Egyptians (v. 2). Indeed, the term "dealt harshly" can "mean 'abuse' or 'mistreat' but in the sense of 'humiliate,'"[213] as someone might humiliate an enemy king. As the Egyptians and their king have humiliated the Israelites, now the true King will deliver the Israelites and humiliate their abusers. As a result, future generations (the "you" is plural) will know that Yahweh is the sovereign king (v. 2b). We help our children to know him when we recount to them his work in our own lives.[214]

10:3–6 Moses and Aaron deliver the Lord's message to Pharaoh. Their opening question reveals Pharaoh's central problem: a refusal to humble himself and acknowledge the Lord as sovereign king (v. 3). The command to let the people go and worship the Lord is then repeated (v. 3b; cf. note 89 within comment on 3:11–12), followed by a long warning about disobedience's consequences (10:4–6; for "tomorrow" cf. comment on 8:20–23). The Lord will bring so many locusts that

---

213 Stuart, *Exodus*, 244, citing Numbers 22:29; 1 Samuel 31:4; Jeremiah 38:19; etc.
214 Cf. Psalm 78:1–8. To see how this was done in song cf. Psalms 77:11–20; 78:43–53; 105:26–38; 106:7–12; 114:1–3; 135:8–9; 136:10–15 (Kaiser, *Exodus*, in *Genesis–Leviticus*, 365).

they will cover the land like a living, swarming blanket, devouring any crops left by the hail (cf. 9:32), destroying any recovering trees, and filling every home with insects.[215] This will not be the first locust plague in Egypt's history, but it will be a thousand times worse than any before it.

Having issued the warning, Moses and Aaron leave (10:6). The next move belongs to Pharaoh.

10:7 Pharaoh's servants appeal to him. They describe Moses as a "snare," that is, an instrument that captures something so it can be killed. The only way to escape the snare is to agree to Moses' request, so they tell Pharaoh, "Let the men go, that they may serve the LORD their God." Why specify "men" when the Lord had said "people" (cf. v. 3)? Perhaps to ensure the Israelites return, knowing the men will not leave permanently without their families. Whatever the reason, this is half-hearted obedience. Nonetheless, the servants still have the sense to name what Pharaoh is ignoring: the Lord has utterly ruined the land. Something must be done.

10:8–11 Moses and Aaron are brought back, and Pharaoh tells them to go and serve the Lord. This seems promising until Pharaoh asks who is to go (v. 8). "Everyone," Moses says, including the animals, for the people will hold a "feast" to the Lord (cf. 3:18)—that is, a community festival with sacrifices to the deity being honored (10:9; 32:5–6). Pharaoh is furious, perhaps understanding this to be an understated request for the whole nation to leave permanently (cf. note 131 within comment on 5:1–9). He begins sarcastically, as if to say, "May the Lord be with you if I ever send you off. But that is not going to happen!" (10:10). Little does he know how ironic his sarcasm is, as it will not be long before he does send them off, asking Moses to bless him when he does (12:32)! He then turns to accusation: "You are plotting evil!" before finishing by deceptively mischaracterizing the request: "So take only the men and go, for that is all you really want!" 10:10–11 AT). The king has spoken, and Moses and Aaron are driven out from his presence with their request denied. Pharaoh has made a fatal move.

10:12–15 The Lord commands Moses to lift the staff—the action again serving as an enacted prayer (cf. comment on 9:22–25)—so that locusts might come and devour anything left by the hail (10:12). In response to Moses' prayer the Lord directs an east wind to bring the locusts by the next morning (v. 13). As with the hail, the locusts come in unprecedented and apocalyptic proportions (vv. 14–15; cf. Rev. 9:1–12; cf. comment 9:22–25, esp. note 207). They so cover the land that it is "darkened." At the least this language refers to a physical phenomenon, such as thick clouds of locusts' obscuring the sunlight or spreading like a dark blanket across the earth's surface, or both. But darkness is also associated regularly with judgment (Isa. 5:30; Ezek. 32:8; Joel 2:10)—as it will be in full force in the

---

[215] For a poetic description of a locust plague as an invading army (or perhaps of an invading army as a locust plague) cf. Joel 2:1–11. Locust plagues continue today. The Food and Agriculture Organization of the United Nations notes that a swarm of just 0.4 square miles (1 km^2) can eat enough food in one day to feed 35,000 people; cf. "Desert Locust," accessed May 15, 2024, https://www.fao.org/locusts/en/.

next strike (Ex. 10:21–29)—and the Hebrew phrase used in verse 15 suggests an ominous reading here.[216] The judgment plays out in utter decimation, the text emphasizing that the locusts eat *all* the land and tree crops so that *not a green thing* of tree crops remains.[217] The devastation is total.

10:16–17 This time Pharaoh "hastily" summons Moses and Aaron (v. 16). There is no time to lose! For the second time he confesses his wrong, this time acknowledging he has sinned against both the Lord and his representatives (cf. 9:27). He asks to be forgiven "only this once" (10:17), which may mean "this one last time—I will not do it again!"[218] He then pleads that the Lord end the strike, calling it "this death" in light of its horrific consequences on the land (v. 17). Though unstated, the implication is that he will let the people go once the strike is ended.

10:18–19 Leaving Pharaoh's presence, Moses prays and the Lord answers, bringing a very strong western wind to drive the locusts into the Red Sea. The concluding statement—"Not a single locust was left"—seems to anticipate what happens when the Lord drowns Pharaoh's army in the Red Sea, such that "not one of them was left" (14:28 AT).[219]

10:20 For the second time we read that the Lord hardens Pharaoh's heart, that is, takes his already hardened heart and makes it harder still (v. 20; cf. comment on 9:12). Pharaoh then rebelliously refuses to let the Israelites go, setting up himself and his people for even further judgment.

10:21–29 In the ninth strike darkness covers the land so deeply for three days that the Egyptians might as well be blind (vv. 21–23). This is a foreboding sign of judgment, and the only ones to escape it are the Israelites, who are once again set apart as the Lord's people (v. 23). When Pharaoh again gives Moses qualified permission to leave (v. 24), Moses again insists the entire nation must go (vv. 25–26). Once more the Lord further hardens the already hardened heart of Pharaoh (v. 27), who refuses to let the people go and threatens Moses with death if he ever again appears before him (v. 28). Moses affirms he never will see him again (v. 29), giving a sense of finality to his encounters with Pharaoh. Matters will come to a head very soon.

10:21 As is common for the third strike in each series (cf. 8:16; 9:8–9), the judgment is announced immediately: "Stretch out your hand toward heaven, that there may be darkness over the land of Egypt, a darkness to be felt" (10:21).[220] As noted above, the Bible often associates darkness with judgment (cf. comment

---

[216] The Hebrew reads "They covered the eye of the whole land and the land was darkened." While "the eye of the whole land" refers idiomatically to the land's surface (Num. 22:5, 11), its use with "being darkened" suggests the judgment of blindness (cf. Ps. 69:23).
[217] Cf. Psalm 105:34–35. Fretheim (*Exodus*, 127) notes that the word "all" occurs eleven times in the Hebrew of Exodus 10:12–15.
[218] Cf. comment on 9:27–28, esp. note 208. The second use of "only" in this verse may have the same sense: "Only [this one and final time] to remove this death from me" (Cassuto, *Commentary on the Book of Exodus*, 128).
[219] The Hebrew verb is the same as in 10:19. Cf. note 282 within comment on 14:23–28.
[220] Or "a darkness causing [one] to grope around," as though blind (so also Stuart, *Exodus*, 256–257). This is the only time the verb occurs in this conjugation, which is typically causative; cf. the verb in a different conjugation in Deuteronomy 28:29; Job 12:25.

on 10:12–15), a judgment particularly pointed in Egypt's case since "the sun was worshiped as a manifestation of various deities, such as Atum, Re, Amun, and Amun-Re."[221] In obliterating the sun's light this judgment obliterates any deities it represents.

10:22–23 The darkness that comes is so thick that the Egyptians "did not see one another." As we might say, they could not see their hand in front of their face. Many commentators suggest the darkness is due to a type of sandstorm known as the *khamsin*. This is not impossible (the Lord elsewhere uses natural phenomena in a supernatural way; v. 13; 14:21), but the text does not say, focusing instead on the darkness's effect. The hardship is physical, making it virtually impossible to move around, but undoubtedly emotionally terrifying as well, as the darkness continues unabated for three days, leaving people unsure whether it is day or night and in little doubt that divine judgment is at work. The Israelites, however, experience none of this. Their God, Yahweh, continues to shine his light on their place of dwelling (10:23).

10:24 Presumably after the darkness has abated, Pharaoh summons Moses. Pharaoh's obstinacy is underscored when for the third time he puts limits on who can leave Egypt (cf. 8:25–28; 10:8–11). The situation would be comical were it not so tragic. Having been struck by the Lord nine different times, Pharaoh is in no position to haggle, but pride blinds him to his true situation, and he tells Moses that he and the people can go and worship the Lord (cf. note 89 within comment on 3:11–12) but must leave their animals behind. This is a hostage-taking maneuver. Pharaoh knows the people will not ultimately leave without their animals, which are so central to economic well-being.

10:25–29 Moses begins either by stating that Pharaoh himself must provide them with sacrifices (ESV) or by rhetorically asking whether he will do so (NET).[222] Either way, he insists that all their animals must go with them so they can make proper sacrifices when they worship the Lord (v. 26). They surely would not be asked to kill every last animal, but it makes good sense to understand that Moses is again following an approach to negotiation in which the full goal is not stated explicitly but implied, namely, the nation and all their belongings are leaving the land for good (cf. note 131 within comment on 5:1–9). In such negotiations it is wise to present an argument with even minimal plausibility if it can communicate the full goal. Pharaoh's angry response makes clear he gets the message.

While the earlier strikes noted that Pharaoh hardened his heart or that his heart continued in a hardened state, the later strikes have emphasized the Lord's involvement in hardening Pharaoh's heart. This functions as a sobering punishment corresponding to the crime: If one harden his heart against the Lord, he

---
[221] Wells, *Exodus*, 200.
[222] The ESV represents the majority approach among English translations, though it may be noted the NET ("Will you also provide us with sacrifices and offerings?") fits very well with Exodus 10:26, the general idea being: "Will *you* put sacrifices into our hand? No! So *we* need to bring sacrificial animals."

may bring his justice to bear by making the heart harder still and then judging the person for his hardness (cf. comments on 4:21–23 [esp. note 121]; 9:12). He does so here for the third time (cf. 9:12; 10:1), and Pharaoh again refuses to let the people go (v. 27). A sense of finality is introduced as Pharaoh warns Moses never to return to see Pharoah's face, on pain of death (v. 28). Moses responds that Pharaoh will never see his face again (v. 29), leaving the reader to conclude that things are about to come to a head and that Moses will indeed be leading the people out of Egypt, never to see Pharaoh again.[223] Pharaoh has become an unwitting prophet of his own defeat.[224]

11:1–10 This passage announces the tenth strike. It begins with a narrative aside that jumps ahead and describes the strike's final outcome: the people's release and experience of favor (vv. 1–3). It then returns to where chapter 10 left off, and Moses describes the final plague in terrifying detail and emphasizes how the Lord will care for his people in the midst of it (vv. 4–8). Moses then departs in fierce anger over Pharaoh's stubborn disobedience (v. 8), and the passage concludes by returning to earlier themes of Pharaoh's rebellion and the Lord's sovereignty over it (vv. 9–10). In short, this passage is a transition.[225] Looking forward, it announces the coming final strike (vv. 1–8), setting the stage for the description of Passover preparations and the final strike itself (ch. 12). Looking backward, it revisits themes that explain how the narrative has arrived at this point, underscoring the Lord's sovereignty over the events leading to this final act of judgment (11:9–10).

11:1–3 As many commentators argue, the narrator provides verses 1–3 as an aside that previews what is to come.[226] The effect is to draw in the audience, making it wonder, "How did the story turn out like that?" One might compare how some movies begin with a climactic scene from the story's end and then go back to the story's beginning after showing a subtitle that reads "Two days earlier" or something similar. In this case the audience is told clearly that Israel will finally be released—and will go out with extreme favor.

The aside begins with the Lord's words, which focus on the effects the last strike will have on Pharaoh and Egypt (vv. 1–2).[227] The timing of his speaking these words is not stated, but their meaning is clear. He begins with a promise. Because of the last strike, Pharaoh will not simply let the people go but will most certainly drive them out due to the strike's severity (the Hb. of v. 1 is extremely emphatic).[228] The

---

223 At least, not in the capacity of a visit Moses initiates, which has been the primary way in which Moses and Aaron have come before Pharaoh to this point (Ex. 7:15; 8:1, 20; 9:1, 13; 10:1). After the last strike Pharaoh is the one who summons Moses and Aaron and asks them to leave (12:31). Cf. Stuart (*Exodus* 260, note 192), who notes that 10:29b could be translated, "I will not keep seeing your face," that is, in the way that I have been.
224 Stuart, *Exodus*, 260.
225 Childs, *Book of Exodus*, 160–161.
226 This approach explains how Moses can say he will no longer see Pharaoh's face (Ex. 10:29) and yet not leave his presence until 11:8. Simply stated, he has not yet left; 11:1–3 is an aside, and the story resumes in verses 4–8. So also Keil, *Exodus*, vol. 1, 499; Cassuto, *Commentary on the Book of Exodus*, 131; Sarna, *Exodus*, 52.
227 The word translated "plague" (Hb. *nega'*; 11:1) can refer to sickness (Gen. 12:17) but also to a wounding "strike" (Deut. 17:8; 21:5). The latter sense is preferable here, since Exodus 11:1 assumes the previous nine signs could also be labeled with this word, and not all of them are "plagues" in the word's modern sense (which focuses on infestation or disease), though all of them are "strikes."
228 Cf. Carol Meyers, *Exodus* (Cambridge: Cambridge University Press, 2005), 92.

Lord then gives a command. The Israelites must ask their Egyptian neighbors for gold and silver items so that they do not leave empty handed (v. 2; cf. comment on 3:21–22). The narrator tells us the request will be met because the Lord will grant his people favor in the Egyptians' eyes. We also learn that Moses has similar favor, being considered a great man by Pharaoh's servants and all the people (11:3). In short Israel will be delivered and experience tremendous favor. So how does this come about?

11:4–8a The narrator now picks up where the story left off in 10:29, and Moses declares to Pharaoh a final announcement of judgment. In the middle of the night the Lord will go out in the midst of Egypt,[229] and all the firstborn will die (cf. comment on 4:21–23 for discussion of the death of the firstborn). This will happen at all levels of Egyptian society—from Pharaoh's firstborn to the slave's firstborn—and to livestock as well as people (11:5). All Egypt will experience this judgment in one way or another, and a cry of unprecedented suffering will rise throughout the land (v. 6). The word for "cry" is in fact "the very term used to give expression to Israel's misery under Egyptian enslavement [Ex. 3:7, 9]. The anguished cry of the oppressed yields to the cry of their oppressors and tormentors."[230] The only ones excepted will be the Israelites, who will face no hardship (the apparent meaning of "not a dog shall growl against" them). The result will be that Pharaoh and his servants (the "you" is plural) will know that the Israelites are Yahweh's people and thus experience his protection and love (11:7). Indeed, Pharaoh's own servants will come and bow before Moses instead of Pharaoh and plead with him to leave, an act that humbly recognizes that the God whom Moses represents is the true king (v. 8a).

11:8b Moses then goes "out from Pharaoh in hot anger." No reason is given, but the context suggests it is because of Pharaoh's stubborn and rebellious refusal to let the people go (v. 8a). As elsewhere, rebellion against the Lord angers Moses (cf. 32:19).

11:9–10 The last two verses summarize Pharaoh's disobedience and the Lord's sovereignty over it. In verse 9 the Lord again alerts Moses that Pharaoh will continue to refuse to listen and then explains how he will use Pharaoh's disobedience as an opportunity to display his miraculous signs of power.[231] In verse 10 the narrator notes that Moses and Aaron have performed these signs before Pharaoh but that Pharaoh has not obeyed because the Lord further hardens his already hardened heart. In short the Lord is sovereign over Pharaoh's disobedience and uses it to make his power and glory known in the earth. Israel need not fear Pharaoh but has every reason instead to worship the Lord.

---

229 Not that night, as preparations for the Passover will take place over several days (cf. 12:3 with 12:6), but at some upcoming night (Keil, *Exodus*, vol. 1, 500).
230 Sarna, *Exodus*, 53.
231 Alternately, Exodus 11:9 could refer summarily to the Lord's past statements: "The LORD had said to Moses" (cf. 7:3–4; cf. 7:13, 22; 8:15, 19; 9:12). This would not change the overall point above.

Response

WHO IS THE LORD?

These chapters, and the signs and wonders they narrate, are like a display window, allowing us to see who God is and what he is like. They focus on his power, his faithfulness, and his love.

First, the signs and wonders show the Lord's power over Egypt's gods. Turning the Nile into blood has plausibly been suggested as an attack against Hapi or Osiris (cf. comment on 7:14–19), while the darkening of the sun would be an attack against one of the gods associated with it (cf. comment on 10:21); further, the death of the firstborn is explicitly named as judgment on "all the gods of Egypt" (12:12), all of whom are powerless before this crushing blow.[232]

But the plagues also show the Lord's power over Pharaoh. Pharaoh asks, "Who is the LORD, that I should obey his voice?" (5:2), and the Lord answers him with power, using his strong hand to force Pharaoh to let Israel go (3:19; 6:1). These strikes target Pharaoh as much as they target Egypt's gods. Indeed, at this point in Egypt's history Pharaoh was seen as the earthly representative and image of an Egyptian god (or gods) and was responsible in the land to maintain cosmic order (known in Egypt as *ma'at*). In particular, maintaining order meant the Nile was to inundate regularly so that crops could grow and the land could be bountiful.[233] But maintaining such order was the very thing Pharaoh is powerless to do when confronted by the Lord, who turns the Nile to blood and decimates the land's crops. "What the plagues of Exodus show is the inability of the obstinate king to maintain [*ma'at*]. Rather, it is Yahweh and his agents, Moses and Aaron, who overcome in the cosmic struggle, demonstrating who really controls the forces of nature."[234] The Lord is sovereign; Pharaoh and any gods he represents are powerless before him.

It is worth pausing here. God is not impressed by a person's power or pedigree, by his rank or resources. No matter what signs of worldly authority or power we have—and Pharaoh had all the worldly authority and power possible—they are nothing in comparison to the Lord's. If his power is like the blazing sun that lights up the entire earth, then ours is less than a smoldering candle that cannot even light up a small room. We are usually comfortable with such power of the Lord if he uses it to help our life go as smoothly as possible, but we often want such help without any implications for how we are to live our lives before him. The Bible, however, emphasizes that, because God is big enough to help us out of our worst problems, he is also worthy of our absolute worship and loyalty. He is the king, we are the servants, and he does not hesitate to direct his power against us when we rebel against him. We must avoid the temptation to tame God. "The LORD your God is a consuming fire," Moses will write later (Deut. 4:24), and the signs and wonders in these chapters testify to that fact repeatedly, like nuclear explosions of

---

[232] Cf. comments on 7:8–13; 7:14–19; 8:7–11; 8:20–23; 9:10–11; 9:13–14; 9:29–30; 10:21. The point is not that each strike was aimed at a specific deity (cf. 12:12!) but that the Lord clearly showed through these signs that he was the sovereign God before whom Egyptian "deities" were powerless.
[233] Hoffmeier, *Israel in Egypt*, 151–153.
[234] Hoffmeier, *Israel in Egypt*, 153.

power that witness to all that the Lord is as a God of unrivalled might. If we resist him like Pharaoh does, he may crush us and show us to be the mere mortals we are.

But this is not his heart's desire! He has created us not for judgment but for life—life found in relationship with him. As noted above (cf. comment on 9:15–16), the Lord's words to Pharaoh in verse 16 might be paraphrased, "I have established you as king so that I could use your reign, with all its stubborn rebellion, as an opportunity to show forth my own mighty power, *so all the nations might hear and know who I am!*" Even the Lord's judgment has salvation ultimately in view, and that on a worldwide scale. He is God of all the earth (cf. 9:14; Ps. 24:1) and desires all those in the earth to know him.

As these chapters also make clear, people are to know about far more than the greatness of his power. By itself, power can quickly become tyranny. Not so with the Lord. If his power is like a huge and powerful train, then the tracks on which this train runs are faithfulness and love. In Exodus opening chapters the Lord makes clear repeatedly that he has seen, knows, and understands his people's suffering, that he has not forgotten them or the promises he made to their forefathers, and that he will be faithful to those promises and deliver them from suffering (Ex. 2:23–25; 3:7–10, 16–17; 4:31; 6:5–8). His displays of power in these chapters are in service of bringing those promises about and making clear to Israel, Egypt, and the entire world that the Israelites are like a beloved firstborn to him (cf. comment on 4:21–23). His faithfulness and love propel him to deliver his people from Pharaoh's cruel tyranny and slavery into the glorious freedom of serving him, their redeeming God and heavenly Father. This is who God is, and he wants us to know him as such. This leads to a second question.

WHAT DOES IT MEAN TO KNOW THE LORD?

As noted above, throughout these chapters God explains that these signs are so that people will "know" or "acknowledge"—the Hebrew word can mean either—that he is Yahweh. As also noted above, close attention to these texts shows that to "know/acknowledge" that he is Yahweh means to "know/acknowledge" something that is true about his character and purposes, namely, that he is a God of power, faithfulness, and love.

Throughout these chapters Pharaoh shows us what it means to refuse to know the Lord. The Lord's question in 10:3 reveals the heart of the issue: "How long will you refuse to humble yourself before me?" At times Pharaoh admits his mistakes (9:27; 10:16), but this is only when he feels the Lord's discipline most keenly. Once the discipline ends, his obedience evaporates. In this regard he is like a bow: the Lord's discipline is like pulling the bow's string, momentarily changing the bow's shape, but once the discipline is removed and the tension released Pharaoh springs back to his former self and continues in his proud rebellion.[235]

To put it differently, the heart of the issue is the issue of the heart. Repeatedly Pharaoh hardens his heart throughout these chapters (8:15, 32; 9:34; for details cf.

---

[235] Bush, *Commentary on Exodus*, 111.

comments on 4:21–23; 9:12). As noted at 9:14, in the Hebrew of that verse the Lord says, "I will send all my plagues to your heart," naming the very place causing his proud rebellion, as though to say, "Your proud heart should be humbled by what you are about to see so that you (singular) finally know/acknowledge that there is no god like me in all the earth!"[236] Indeed, some of his servants imitate his hardheartedness. As noted at 9:21, the Hebrew describes those who disobey the Lord's commands as those who "do not *set their heart* to the word of the LORD," emphasizing that their problem, like Pharaoh's, lies in the heart—with fatal results for those they are supposed to care for (9:21, 25). Tragically, a hard heart leads ultimately to destruction, not only for the rebels but also for those connected to them (cf. 10:7).

In contrast to Pharaoh and his hard-hearted servants are some of his servants who "feared the word of the LORD" (9:20), that is, who obey it reverently instead of proudly despising it (cf. Prov. 13:13). They bring their own servants and livestock in to shelter before the seventh strike promised by the Lord comes to pass (lethal hail). In doing so they save many lives (cf. Ex. 9:21, 25). These servants acknowledge through obedience their belief in what God has said and in so doing give us a picture of what it means to know the Lord—and of the practical benefits that spill over to those connected to those who do know him.

In short to know or acknowledge the Lord is to show through our obedience to his commands that we believe him to be a God of absolute power, faithfulness, and love. At this point in redemptive history this means obedience to the Father and the Son. In speaking of Jesus, the apostle John writes, "By this we know that we have come to know him, if we keep his commandments" (1 John 2:3). The type of wholehearted obedience we owe to the Father is the same type of obedience we owe to the Son, because Jesus is one with the Father, and the Father has "highly exalted him and bestowed on him the name that is above every name, so that at the name of Jesus every knee should bow, in heaven and on earth and under the earth, and every tongue confess that Jesus Christ is Lord, to the glory of God the Father" (Phil. 2:9–11).

In light of this we do well to ask questions such as these: How might obedience show my belief in Jesus' *power*? Are there commands of his I consider too hard to obey or steps of faith I am too afraid to take? What might obedience look like instead? And how might obedience show my belief in Jesus' *faithfulness* and *love*? How can his faithfulness encourage me to obey boldly and to quiet my heart's fears? How can his love serve as a bedrock of assurance out of which I am free to live with wild abandon to him, knowing he will never let me go? To know the Lord is the most grounding and freeing way to live, because we have been created to do these very things. As Augustine prayed, "You have made us for yourself, and our hearts are restless until they find their rest in you."[237]

---

[236] Fretheim (*Exodus*, 124) describes Exodus 9:14 as "a statement of God's incomparability extended to universal proportions"; cf. 15:11.
[237] Augustine, *Confessions*, 1.1.1.

OVERVIEW OF

EXODUS 12:1–15:21

Just as mountain ranges can have major peaks and minor peaks, so too can stories. These chapters are one of Exodus's main peaks, as Israel's long-awaited deliverance from Egypt finally arrives.

The chapters comprise two main sections. In the first (12:1–13:16) we read of the Lord's actions that finally release his people (12:29–42) and of the instructions he gives the Israelites to commemorate how he has saved them (12:1–28; 12:43–13:16).

In the second section (13:17–15:21) we read of the Israelites' initial departure route (13:17–22), the Lord's demonstration of his power in defeating Pharaoh and his army (14:1–31), and the Israelites' jubilant songs of praise in response (15:1–22). The Lord is a warrior who fights for his people, delivering them from their enemies and exalting his name as worthy of praise.

EXODUS 12:1–13:16

12 The LORD said to Moses and Aaron in the land of Egypt, **2** "This month shall be for you the beginning of months. It shall be the first month of the year for you. **3** Tell all the congregation of Israel that on the tenth day of this month every man shall take a lamb according to their fathers' houses, a lamb for a household. **4** And if the household is too small for a lamb, then he and his nearest neighbor shall take according to the number of persons; according to what each can eat you shall make your count for the lamb. **5** Your lamb shall be without blemish, a male a year old. You may take it from the sheep or from the goats, **6** and you shall keep it until the fourteenth day of this month, when the whole assembly of the congregation of Israel shall kill their lambs at twilight.¹

7 "Then they shall take some of the blood and put it on the two doorposts and the lintel of the houses in which they eat it. **8** They shall eat the flesh that night, roasted on the fire; with unleavened bread and bitter herbs they shall eat it. **9** Do not eat any of it raw or boiled in water, but roasted, its head with its legs and its inner parts. **10** And you shall let none of it remain until the morning; anything that remains until the morning you shall burn. ¹¹ In this manner you shall eat it: with your belt fastened, your sandals on your feet, and your staff in your hand. And you shall eat it in haste. It is the Lord's Passover. ¹² For I will pass through the land of Egypt that night, and I will strike all the firstborn in the land of Egypt, both man and beast; and on all the gods of Egypt I will execute judgments: I am the Lord. ¹³ The blood shall be a sign for you, on the houses where you are. And when I see the blood, I will pass over you, and no plague will befall you to destroy you, when I strike the land of Egypt.

¹⁴ "This day shall be for you a memorial day, and you shall keep it as a feast to the Lord; throughout your generations, as a statute forever, you shall keep it as a feast. ¹⁵ Seven days you shall eat unleavened bread. On the first day you shall remove leaven out of your houses, for if anyone eats what is leavened, from the first day until the seventh day, that person shall be cut off from Israel. ¹⁶ On the first day you shall hold a holy assembly, and on the seventh day a holy assembly. No work shall be done on those days. But what everyone needs to eat, that alone may be prepared by you. ¹⁷ And you shall observe the Feast of Unleavened Bread, for on this very day I brought your hosts out of the land of Egypt. Therefore you shall observe this day, throughout your generations, as a statute forever. ¹⁸ In the first month, from the fourteenth day of the month at evening, you shall eat unleavened bread until the twenty-first day of the month at evening. ¹⁹ For seven days no leaven is to be found in your houses. If anyone eats what is leavened, that person will be cut off from the congregation of Israel, whether he is a sojourner or a native of the land. ²⁰ You shall eat nothing leavened; in all your dwelling places you shall eat unleavened bread."

²¹ Then Moses called all the elders of Israel and said to them, "Go and select lambs for yourselves according to your clans, and kill the Passover lamb. ²² Take a bunch of hyssop and dip it in the blood that is in the basin, and touch the lintel and the two doorposts with the blood that is in the basin. None of you shall go out of the door of his house until the morning. ²³ For the Lord will pass through to strike the Egyptians, and when he sees the blood on the lintel and on the two doorposts, the Lord will pass over the door and will not allow the destroyer to enter your houses to strike you. ²⁴ You shall observe this rite as a statute for you and for your sons forever. ²⁵ And when you come to the land that the Lord will give you, as he has promised, you shall keep this service. ²⁶ And when your children say to you, 'What do you mean by this service?' ²⁷ you shall say, 'It is the sacrifice of the Lord's Passover, for he passed over the houses of the people of Israel in Egypt, when he struck the Egyptians but spared our houses.'" And the people bowed their heads and worshiped.

²⁸ Then the people of Israel went and did so; as the Lord had commanded Moses and Aaron, so they did.

²⁹ At midnight the Lord struck down all the firstborn in the land of Egypt, from the firstborn of Pharaoh who sat on his throne to the firstborn of the captive who was in the dungeon, and all the firstborn of the livestock. ³⁰ And Pharaoh rose up in the night, he and all his servants and all the Egyptians. And there was a great cry in Egypt, for there was not a house where someone was not dead. ³¹ Then he summoned Moses and Aaron by night and said, "Up, go out from among my people, both you and the people of Israel; and go, serve the Lord, as you have said.

⁣³² Take your flocks and your herds, as you have said, and be gone, and bless me also!" ³³ The Egyptians were urgent with the people to send them out of the land in haste. For they said, "We shall all be dead." ³⁴ So the people took their dough before it was leavened, their kneading bowls being bound up in their cloaks on their shoulders. ³⁵ The people of Israel had also done as Moses told them, for they had asked the Egyptians for silver and gold jewelry and for clothing. ³⁶ And the Lord had given the people favor in the sight of the Egyptians, so that they let them have what they asked. Thus they plundered the Egyptians.

³⁷ And the people of Israel journeyed from Rameses to Succoth, about six hundred thousand men on foot, besides women and children. ³⁸ A mixed multitude also went up with them, and very much livestock, both flocks and herds. ³⁹ And they baked unleavened cakes of the dough that they had brought out of Egypt, for it was not leavened, because they were thrust out of Egypt and could not wait, nor had they prepared any provisions for themselves.

⁴⁰ The time that the people of Israel lived in Egypt was 430 years. ⁴¹ At the end of 430 years, on that very day, all the hosts of the Lord went out from the land of Egypt. ⁴² It was a night of watching by the Lord, to bring them out of the land of Egypt; so this same night is a night of watching kept to the Lord by all the people of Israel throughout their generations.

⁴³ And the Lord said to Moses and Aaron, "This is the statute of the Passover: no foreigner shall eat of it, ⁴⁴ but every slave[2] that is bought for money may eat of it after you have circumcised him. ⁴⁵ No foreigner or hired worker may eat of it. ⁴⁶ It shall be eaten in one house; you shall not take any of the flesh outside the house, and you shall not break any of its bones. ⁴⁷ All the congregation of Israel shall keep it. ⁴⁸ If a stranger shall sojourn with you and would keep the Passover to the Lord, let all his males be circumcised. Then he may come near and keep it; he shall be as a native of the land. But no uncircumcised person shall eat of it. ⁴⁹ There shall be one law for the native and for the stranger who sojourns among you."

⁵⁰ All the people of Israel did just as the Lord commanded Moses and Aaron. ⁵¹ And on that very day the Lord brought the people of Israel out of the land of Egypt by their hosts.

13 The Lord said to Moses, ² "Consecrate to me all the firstborn. Whatever is the first to open the womb among the people of Israel, both of man and of beast, is mine."

³ Then Moses said to the people, "Remember this day in which you came out from Egypt, out of the house of slavery, for by a strong hand the Lord brought you out from this place. No leavened bread shall be eaten. ⁴ Today, in the month of Abib, you are going out. ⁵ And when the Lord brings you into the land of the Canaanites, the Hittites, the Amorites, the Hivites, and the Jebusites, which he swore to your fathers to give you, a land flowing with milk and honey, you shall keep this service in this month. ⁶ Seven days you shall eat unleavened bread, and on the seventh day there shall be a feast to the Lord. ⁷ Unleavened bread shall be eaten for seven days; no leavened bread shall be seen with you, and no leaven shall be seen with you in all your territory. ⁸ You shall tell your son on that day, 'It is because of what the Lord did for me when I came out of Egypt.'

⁹And it shall be to you as a sign on your hand and as a memorial between your eyes, that the law of the Lord may be in your mouth. For with a strong hand the Lord has brought you out of Egypt. ¹⁰You shall therefore keep this statute at its appointed time from year to year.

¹¹"When the Lord brings you into the land of the Canaanites, as he swore to you and your fathers, and shall give it to you, ¹²you shall set apart to the Lord all that first opens the womb. All the firstborn of your animals that are males shall be the Lord's. ¹³Every firstborn of a donkey you shall redeem with a lamb, or if you will not redeem it you shall break its neck. Every firstborn of man among your sons you shall redeem. ¹⁴And when in time to come your son asks you, 'What does this mean?' you shall say to him, 'By a strong hand the Lord brought us out of Egypt, from the house of slavery. ¹⁵For when Pharaoh stubbornly refused to let us go, the Lord killed all the firstborn in the land of Egypt, both the firstborn of man and the firstborn of animals. Therefore I sacrifice to the Lord all the males that first open the womb, but all the firstborn of my sons I redeem.' ¹⁶It shall be as a mark on your hand or frontlets between your eyes, for by a strong hand the Lord brought us out of Egypt."

¹ Hebrew *between the two evenings* ² Or *servant*; the Hebrew term *'ebed* designates a range of social and economic roles (see Preface)

Section Overview

This section centers on the Lord's final strike against Egypt and his leading his people out of bondage (12:29–42). On either side of that center are instructions regarding the main rites the people are to perform throughout their generations in order to remember the Lord's deliverance: they are to celebrate Passover, celebrate the Feast of Unleavened Bread, and consecrate their firstborn sons and animals to the Lord (vv. 1–28; 12:43–13:16). The Lord's deliverance and the importance of remembering it are thus clearly the focus (for the latter cf. esp. 12:24–27a; 13:8–10, 14–16). Complementary themes include the centrality of the Passover lamb's blood for deliverance (12:21–23), the Lord's faithfulness to his covenant promises (cf. comments on 12:37–42; 13:3–10), and his desire for the nations to be among his people (12:38, 48–49). This is a God who faithfully saves his people—and longs for the nations of the world to be counted among them.

Section Outline

    II. Israel leaves Egypt: the Lord provides deliverance (12:1–15:21)
        A. The institution of the Passover, the Feast of Unleavened Bread, and the consecration of the firstborn; the Lord's deliverance of Israel through the last strike and Israel's exodus from Egypt (12:1–13:16)
            1. The Lord's instructions regarding the Passover (12:1–13)
            2. The Lord's instructions regarding the Feast of Unleavened Bread (12:14–20)

3. Moses passes on Passover instructions to the Israelites (12:21–27a)
4. The people's response of worship and obedience (12:27b–28)
5. The final strike and Israel's exodus from Egypt (12:29–42)
6. Further instructions regarding the Passover (12:43–50)
7. Further instructions regarding the Feast of Unleavened Bread and instructions regarding the consecration of the firstborn (12:51–13:16)

Comment

12:1–2 The Lord's Passover instructions begin by identifying that the current month, in which the Israelites will leave Egypt, will become the start of their year (v. 2). Their calendar will thus begin with a reminder of the Lord's redemption.

The month is called Abib (13:4) and later Nisan (Est. 3:7). (The former name is Canaanite in origin; the latter, Babylonian.) It falls sometime in our March or April.

12:3–13 On the tenth of the month[238] each household is to take a lamb from among its sheep or goats (Ex. 12:3). If that provides too much meat for the household, neighbors are to share a lamb (v. 4). The lamb cannot have physical blemishes, which would make it less valuable and improper to use as one of the Lord's sacrifices (cf. Mal. 1:8), and it must be male, perhaps because it is given in place of a firstborn son.[239] It also must be a year old, which seems to be ideal for sacrificial animals.[240] The lamb is not to be slaughtered until the fourteenth day of the month (Ex. 12:6a). No reason is given for the four-day wait, and there is no scholarly consensus around the various guesses proposed.[241]

The lamb is to be slaughtered at twilight (v. 6b), perhaps since that is the beginning of night, the time when the Lord will pass through the land and therefore when the lamb's blood will play its role. The blood is to be smeared with hyssop branches on each house's doorposts and lintel (vv. 7, 22), signifying to the Lord that he should not enter that door to kill the firstborn since the lamb's lifeblood stands in its place. The Lord will therefore "pass over" that home in peace (cf. vv. 13, 23).

As for the meat, it is to be eaten roasted, not raw or boiled (vv. 8a, 9a). The prohibition against consuming blood (Gen. 9:4) explains why the meat cannot be raw; the reason it cannot be boiled—which is allowed for in other sacrifices (Lev. 6:28; 1 Sam. 2:13; 2 Chron. 35:13)—is less clear.[242] In any case the entire lamb is to be eaten, accompanied by unleavened bread and bitter herbs (Ex. 12:8b, 9b).

---

[238] The tenth day of the month may have held special significance in Israel. The Day of Atonement took place on the tenth day of the seventh month (Lev. 16:29).
[239] C. F. Keil, *Biblical Commentary on the Old Testament: Exodus*, vol. 2: The Pentateuch, trans. James Martin (1864; repr., Grand Rapids, MI: Eerdmans, 1988), 11; cf. Exodus 13:13b–15.
[240] "Keeping an animal for one year gets it to the point of reaching maximum meat weight with minimum investment"; Oded Borowski, *Every Living Thing* (Walnut Creek: AltaMira, 1998), 57.
[241] Cf. overview in Houtman, *Exodus*, vol. 2, 169–170; 173–174.
[242] The two most common guesses are the following: (1) roasting helps to remove the animal's fat, which will soon be prohibited (Ex. 29:13; Lev. 3:16–17); and (2) if Exodus 12:9 implies the animal has to be kept whole, then roasting on a spit is the only way to do so (cf. v. 46). The latter leads to the question of why the animal must be kept whole. No consensus exists among commentators.

(Some societies are not used to eating the entire animal, but in many societies this is more common.) The unleavened bread commemorates the haste with which the Israelites leave Egypt (cf. vv. 34, 39). The word for "bitter herbs" is related to the verb describing how the Egyptians had made the Israelites lives "bitter" with hard labor (1:14), suggesting these herbs are to remind the Israelites that the Lord is delivering them from a bitter existence.

All the meat is to be eaten that night and any leftovers burned (12:10). Once more, no reason is given, but the same requirement applies to peace offerings of thanksgiving (Lev. 7:15), and the context suggests the meat is considered holy and is to be burned to lessen the chance of its becoming defiled. While eating, the Israelites are to be ready to leave at a moment's notice (Ex. 12:11a), dressing as though ready for a journey (cf. 2 Kings 4:29) and eating the food quickly, as though in anxious haste.

The text then gives the sacrifice's name, which in Hebrew is *pesakh* (Ex. 12:11) and is translated "Passover" for reasons the Lord explains momentarily. But first he repeats his earlier description, stating he will strike dead the firstborn among both man and beast (v. 12; cf. 11:4–5). He adds that this will be an act of judgment "on all the gods of Egypt" (12:12).[243] The Egyptians believed in many gods. While previous strikes may have highlighted that certain ones of their gods were powerless before Yahweh (cf. comments on 7:8–13; 7:14–19; 8:7–11; 8:20–23; 9:10–11; 9:13–14; 9:29–30; 10:21), the crushing devastation of this strike will make clear they are *all* powerless before him, so that all might know that Israel's God, Yahweh, is the true God. None can deliver from his hand. Yahweh is God; the other gods are not (Deut. 4:35).

The Lord immediately notes, however, that when he sees the blood on the Israelites' homes he will not strike down their firstborn. Instead, he promises to "pass over" them (Ex. 12:13), using the Hebrew verb *pasakh*, which explains why the sacrifice is called *pesakh* (= Passover).[244] Indeed, this is "the LORD's Passover" (v. 11), that is, the Passover to be celebrated unto him, with him as the focus (cf. 13:5; Lev. 23:34, 41). Every time the Israelites celebrate this sacrifice, or simply mention its name, they have an opportunity to remember the Lord's merciful salvation.

12:14–20 When the Passover is celebrated in the future, it is to be followed immediately by the seven-day Feast (or Festival) of Unleavened Bread. This feast's purpose is to remember "this day" (Ex. 12:14), that is, the coming day on which the Lord will lead Israel out of Egypt (v. 17). The Lord's salvation is the foundation of his people's existence and must be kept in the forefront of their thoughts (vv. 14, 17b).

The festival is to take place over seven days, and any bread eaten during that time must be unleavened (v. 15). As later verses explain, this commemorates the

---

[243] The Hebrew has a plural ("judgments"), but plurals can be used to indicate intensity or to describe abstract actions, in which case an English singular is usually best (cf. Joüon §136f, i); cf. 2 Chronicles 24:24, where the same phrase ("execute judgments") is brought across with the singular ("executed judgment").

[244] The Hebrew verb *pasakh* is rare; in at least one context it parallels verbs that mean "to protect, deliver" (Isa. 31:5), which meaning would also fit here, though the endpoint is the same; whether the Lord "passes over" them or "protects" them, the Israelites suffer no harm.

fact that the Israelites depart so quickly when the Lord delivers them that they must take unleavened dough with them (vv. 34, 39; cf. Deut. 16:3). Those who refuse to follow these instructions are effectively saying that the event they are commemorating—the Lord's redemption—is of no importance. They are to be "cut off" from their people (Ex. 12:15), a penalty that could range from exile to death.[245] This is a punishment corresponding to the crime: having spurned the Lord's redemption of Israel, these people are removed from Israel's midst.

The festival is to begin and end with a "holy assembly" (v. 16), implying a communal celebration (cf. Lev. 23:8), and because it is holy no work is to be done, allowing people to focus on celebrating before the Lord. The only exception is the food-preparation work necessary for the festival (Ex. 12:16).

The Lord then repeats most of what he has just said in order to underscore it. This festival is to be observed throughout the coming generations to celebrate the Lord's deliverance (v. 17). It will be seven days long, with the start and end times specified,[246] and no leavened bread will be eaten during this time—whether by native Israelite or resident alien[247]—upon penalty of exile. Only unleavened bread can be eaten (vv. 18–20).

12:21–27a Moses now passes the instructions to Israel's elders (v. 21), who will in turn inform the people. Since Moses would need to say more than what is here in order for the Israelites to keep the Passover properly, the narrator presumably summarizes, focusing on two key themes.

The first is the importance of the blood to deliver the Israelites from the last strike (vv. 21–23). Using hyssop, the Israelites are to apply the blood to the doorframe and keep everyone safe within the home until morning. The Lord is passing through Egypt that night and will not allow "the destroyer" to enter such homes to kill. If the translation "the destroyer" is correct, it could refer to an angel who works alongside the Lord and does the actual killing (cf. 2 Sam. 24:15–16). Alternately, it is possible to translate that the Lord will not allow "destruction" to enter such homes (cf. the use of the same term in Ex. 12:13). In either case the lamb's lifeblood stands in place of the firstborn's to protect it.

The second theme is the importance of observing this rite in the coming generations (vv. 24–27a). Doing so is an opportunity to teach future generations about the Lord's deliverance "so that they should set their hope in God and not forget the works of God, but keep his commandments" (Ps. 78:7). Properly understood, rituals are to be not dry and dusty but rich with story, celebrating who the Lord is and what he does for his people as they look to him in faith. In these ways they help our children to see that God is worthy of love and obedience.

---

245 Cf. discussion in Sklar, *Leviticus*, TOTC, 64, 136.
246 How does Exodus 12:18 relate to Leviticus 23:5–8 and Numbers 28:16–25, which specify that the festival begins on the fifteenth day? Perhaps the simplest solution is that Exodus 12:18 is stating that unleavened bread will be eaten starting with the Passover on the evening of the fourteenth (in keeping with 12:8), while Leviticus and Numbers focus on the day the opening "holy gathering" is held (the morning after the Passover, on the 15th).
247 It is not clear whether this applies to all resident aliens or only to those who have been circumcised, so that they can partake of the Passover (Ex. 12:48–49). For "resident alien" cf. note 254 within comment on 12:43–50.

12:27b–28 As the Israelites did when Moses first came and told them the Lord was aware of their suffering, they now "bowed their heads and worshiped" (Ex. 12:27b; cf. 4:31). In short, they believe the Lord is about to deliver them, praise him for it, and then make the appropriate preparations (12:28).

12:29–33 On the fourteenth the Lord goes through the land at night, killing all Egyptian firstborn, along with the firstborn animals (v. 29; for apologetic issues related to the death of the firstborn cf. comment on 4:21–23). Egyptians at all levels of society cry out in great anguish (cf. comment on 11:4–8a); no one is exempt (12:30).

Pharaoh immediately summons Moses and Aaron and commands them to leave: "Go, serve the LORD, as you have said. Take your flocks and your herds, as you have said, and be gone" (12:31b–32a).[248] The repetition of "as you have said" underscores that he is finally yielding to the Lord's commands through Moses and Aaron. For the moment his hard heart has been broken. His further request— "And bless me also!" (v. 32b)—implicitly acknowledges that Yahweh, whom Moses and Aaron serve, is the one with power to curse and to bless. Pharaoh knows he needs Yahweh's help.

Similar to Pharaoh, the Egyptian people also urge the Israelites to leave and to do so quickly, "For they said, 'We shall all be dead'" (v. 33). They need the Israelites to leave, lest these punishments from Yahweh continue to befall them, another acknowledgment that Israel's God is sovereign over the events taking place.

12:34–36 The Israelites depart in such haste that "the people took their dough before it was leavened" (v. 34), meaning either before they have added leaven to it or before the dough has had a chance to rise. The fact that the dough is referred to later as unleavened (v. 39), even after it presumably would have had time to rise, supports the former understanding. In either case the detail underscores how hastily the Israelites leave and also explains why eating unleavened bread will commemorate their departure. The additional note about their carrying their kneading bowls on their shoulders in their cloaks (as though in a backpack) shows the importance of equipment for daily bread-baking in that day and age (v. 34).

In keeping with the Lord's command (3:22; 11:1) the people have asked the Egyptians for gold and silver jewelry and clothing (12:35). The Lord grants the Israelites favor in the Egyptians' eyes, who by this point are awestruck by the strength of Israel's God (cf. 8:19; 9:20; 10:7) and therefore give the Israelites "what they asked. Thus they plundered the Egyptians" (12:36). As noted earlier, this is appropriate compensation for years of bitterly hard service (cf. 3:16–22). What is more, such plundering—equivalent to stripping valuables off dead soldiers —normally occurs only after bloody battle (cf. 1 Sam. 31:8; 2 Sam. 23:10). In this case, however, the Israelites do not even have to raise a finger to fight. The Lord has fought the battle on their behalf.

---

[248] For how this relates to 10:28–29 cf. note 226 within comment on 11:1–3.

12:37–42 The Israelites "journeyed from Rameses [toward] Succoth, about six hundred thousand men on foot, besides women and children" (v. 37). (The Israelites' travels toward the Promised Land are described in summary form in Num. 21:10–20; 33:3–49; Deuteronomy 1–3.) The word translated "on foot" (Hb. *ragli*) is used elsewhere to refer to foot soldiers (1 Sam. 4:10; 2 Sam. 8:4; etc.), giving the announcement a military feel. As noted in the Introduction, the number 600,000 may be deliberately inflated, as common in ancient Near Eastern military contexts (and thus expected by an Israelite audience).[249] Inflated or not, however, the point is clear: in keeping with his earlier promises to their forefathers the Lord has indeed caused the people to be fruitful and increase greatly (Ex. 1:7; cf. comments there).

Along with the Israelites and their animals—which would provide food and wool and could be used in sacrifice—is a "mixed multitude" of people (12:38), that is, people from different nationalities. This observation undoubtedly explains to the original audience the presence of such people in their midst (cf. Num. 11:4).[250] It also reads as a continued affirmation of the Lord's covenant promises: not only has he made Israel a great nation, but he is also bringing blessing to other nations through them (Gen. 12:3).

The narrator returns to the Israelites' unleavened dough (Ex. 12:39; cf. 12:34), explaining they make it into "unleavened cakes" because they are driven out in such haste that they cannot delay, nor have they prepared the type of provisions one might gather ahead of a journey (cf. Josh. 1:11). The Israelites have known their departure was coming but are apparently surprised at just how quickly and forcefully the Egyptians demand that they leave. This, too, makes clear how devastating the final strike is to the Egyptian nation.

The section's closing verses emphasize that the Israelites' leave Egypt 430 years after entering there (Ex. 12:40–41). This is in keeping with the round number the Lord used earlier when telling Abram that his descendants would be afflicted in a foreign land for four hundred years but then would be delivered by the Lord and depart with "great possessions" (Gen. 15:13–14). Commentators are divided whether "on that very day" refers to the end of the 430 years (i.e., "430 years to the day, all the hosts") or to the day of deliverance already mentioned (i.e., "after 430 years, on that very day of deliverance, all the hosts"). The use of the same phrase at Exodus 12:17, 51 with regard to the day of deliverance supports the latter. What is clear is that the Lord has delivered them. Indeed, just as he has kept vigil that night for the Israelites to lead them out of Egypt, so they are to keep vigil on this same night in the generations to come to honor him for what he has done (v. 42). This leads back to a discussion of how that night is to be kept (vv. 43–51).

12:43–50 Previous Passover instructions focused on properly choosing a lamb, killing it, applying its blood to the home, and eating it (vv. 3–13, 21–27). The instructions of verses 43–50 focus on who may join in the Passover celebration

---

[249] Cf. Introduction: Interpretive Challenges: Large Numbers in the Book of Exodus.
[250] In Numbers 11:4 the word that many versions translate as "rabble" occurs only in that verse and is built on a root meaning "to gather." It may simply refer to a mixed gathering (as in Ex. 12:38) and not a "rabble" per se.

and are especially important considering that a "mixed multitude" leaves Egypt with Israel (v. 38).

The instructions first describe who can eat the meal. Since the Passover celebrates the Lord's deliverance of his covenant people (Israel), only members of the covenant community can partake. This naturally includes Israelites and any of their household servants,[251] who have been grafted into the household and received the covenant sign, circumcision (v. 44; cf. Gen. 17:12–13, 23).[252] This also explains why non-Israelites and hired workers (who are not a part of the household) cannot partake (Ex. 12:43, 45): they have not received the covenant sign.

The text digresses briefly to discuss three laws related to the Passover lamb: it must be eaten in one house, none of it can be taken outside, and none of its bones may be broken (v. 46). The requirement to keep it in one house and not take it outside may be to assure it is eaten only by those qualified to do so, then disposed of properly (cf. vv. 3–4, 10). As for why the bones cannot be broken, there is no consensus. One of the only other biblical passages that mentions breaking animal bones does so in the context of preparing the meat for boiling (Mic. 3:3), so the prohibition here against breaking bones may be to underscore the commands of Exodus 12:8–9.[253] Whatever the case, the apostle John cannot help but notice that Jesus, who is crucified at the time of the Passover, does not have his bones broken, a detail John includes to help us see that Jesus is the far greater Passover lamb (John 19:14, 33–36).

The text then returns to who may partake in the Passover, emphasizing that all Israelites must do so but also making clear that non-Israelites may if their males are circumcised (Ex. 12:47–48).[254] Just as baptism today indicates a person has been joined to the church as a follower of Jesus, so circumcision indicates a person has joined Israel as a follower of Yahweh. When non-Israelites do so, they are therefore declaring their allegiance to Yahweh (and, in the case of their circumcised infants, their commitment to raise them as Yahweh's followers). Once this occurs, they are to be considered as native Israelites as far as the Passover is concerned and treated as such when it comes to celebrating it (12:48–49; cf. Num. 9:14). Such a law, right at the start of the Israelites' history as a nation, underscores that the Israelites are to be welcoming non-Israelites into their midst as Yahweh's followers so that "all the families of the earth shall be blessed" (Gen. 12:3).

12:51–13:2, 11–16 After mentioning again the day of the Lord's deliverance of the Israelites (v. 51), the text turns to other events meant to commemorate it: the

---

[251] "Servant" is to be preferred to "slave"; cf. ESV mg. and further discussion in Sklar, *Leviticus*, TOTC, 307–308.
[252] Women are not circumcised but are certainly able to participate. The father is the head of the family and thus the family representative. If he receives the sign of the covenant, then all who are members of the family—including all females—are considered covenant members as well (cf. Gen. 6:18).
[253] So Propp (*Exodus 1–18*, 418), who also lists a broad survey of suggested explanations for the prohibition against bone breaking.
[254] "Stranger" (Ex. 12:48) is the same word rendered "sojourner" in verse 19 and is comparable to our phrase "resident alien," that is, a nonnative living in the land who is given most of the same rights, protections, and responsibilities under the law as full citizens (Ex. 23:9; Lev. 19:33–34; Deut. 1:16). This included observing laws that might today be classified as religious (cf. Ex. 20:10; Lev. 17:10; 24:16; Num. 19:10), though there were some religious laws that applied only to the resident aliens who chose to partake in certain activities, such as eating the Passover (Ex. 12:48–49).

consecration of the firstborn and the Feast of Unleavened Bread. The events are arranged as a chiasm.

(A) Consecration of the firstborn (13:1–2)
   (B) The Feast of Unleavened Bread (13:3–10)
(A') Consecration of the firstborn (13:11–16)

The chiasm is held together by a focus on using these events to teach the next generation (cf. 13:8–10 with 13:14–16).

We may begin with the outer frames. The Lord commands that all firstborns, whether human or animal, be "consecrated" to him (v. 2), that is, "set apart" to him (v. 12). The word translated "set apart" elsewhere describes the transfer of property from one person to another (Num. 27:7, 8). In this context it means to give the child or animal to the Lord as his special property. For ritually clean animals this would be done by sacrificing them (cf. Ex. 13:15; 22:30). But ritually unclean animals (such as a donkey) could not be sacrificed, nor could children, since the Lord abhors human sacrifice (Deut. 12:31). Instead they are to be "redeemed" (Ex. 13:13), that is, a payment is to be given to the Lord so that ownership may be transferred back to the Israelites. For animals the payment is a lamb, which is ritually clean and presumably sacrificed.[255] If no payment is given, the animal's neck is broken, which has the practical effect of making sure God's property is not put to profane use and is perhaps a nonsacrificial way of returning the animal's life to God. For sons later texts explain that the Israelites are to offer a five-shekel payment to support the Lord's work at the tabernacle (Num. 3:47–48; 18:16).

As with the Passover and the Feast of Unleavened Bread, this event is to be used to teach the next generation about the Lord's powerful deliverance (Ex. 13:14–15; cf. 12:26–27; 13:7–8). Parents can explain to their children, "Pharaoh would not release us from slavery, so the Lord, in his great power, struck down all the Egyptian firstborn but spared all our firstborn because they were protected by the Passover lambs' blood. By giving this protection, the Lord set apart our firstborn as belonging to him in a special way. Those rescued by the Lord belong to him.[256] We acknowledge his ownership by giving our firstborn animals to him through sacrifice and by redeeming our firstborn sons from him by payment. But this helps us remember that it is not only our firstborn that belong to him. The Lord has described all of us as his 'firstborn son' (Ex. 4:23), so every time we perform the rite of the firstborn we remember that we, too, belong to him in a special way. For he has rescued all of us, and we owe him our wholehearted worship and love."[257]

13:3–10 Between the commands about consecrating the firstborn the Lord issues further commands regarding the celebration of the Feast of Unleavened Bread (vv. 3–10; cf. the earlier commands of 12:14–20). He begins (13:3–4) with a sum-

---

[255] It is not entirely clear whether the law of Leviticus 27:27 is meant to replace the laws of Exodus 13:13; 34:20 or is meant simply to supplement them.
[256] Fretheim, *Exodus*, 147.
[257] For 13:16 cf. comment on 13:3–10 (at v. 9).

mary highlighting the reason for celebrating the feast (to remember the Lord's powerful deliverance), the feast's main feature (eating unleavened bread), and the month in which it is to be held (Abib; cf. comment on 12:1–2). He then turns to more specific instructions (13:5–9).

The instructions look forward to the time when the Israelites will be in the Promised Land (v. 5),[258] a notice that reminds us that what the Lord promises, he will do. The instructions then summarize earlier commands: unleavened bread is to be eaten seven days, with a feast to the Lord on the last day (vv. 6–7; cf. 12:15–16, 19–20). The instructions then add something new, focusing on how the feast is meant to strengthen and engender faith. Parents are to use this feast to tell their children about how the Lord has rescued his people and how they personally experienced it (13:8; cf. comment on 12:21–27a). In this way the feast is to serve "as a sign on your hand and as a memorial between your eyes"—like "tying a string around a finger," we might say—so that "the law of the LORD may be in your mouth" (13:9), that is, so that the Israelites, by retelling the Lord's amazing salvation, will in turn remember all that this redeeming God has commanded them, speak it to one another, and strive together to obey it (cf. Deut. 6:6–9). They owe such allegiance to him for a simple reason: "With a strong hand the LORD has brought you out of Egypt" (Ex. 13:9). He is their redeeming King and utterly worthy of their loyalty.

Response

FROM WHAT AND TO WHAT DOES THE LORD DELIVER ISRAEL?

At the end of Exodus 2 we learn that God has heard his people's cry for deliverance (2:23–25). At the beginning of Exodus 3 we see God's calling Moses to go and be the agent of this deliverance (3:7–10). Now, at long last, deliverance happens (12:29–42). Simply put, the Lord is the God who delivers his people from distress.

But this deliverance is both *from* something bad and *to* something good. The verses surrounding this deliverance speak of Israel's being delivered "out of the house of *slavery*" (13:3, 14), and Pharaoh's command for the Israelites to leave includes the words "Go, *serve* the LORD" (12:31). The terms translated "slavery" and "serve" are built on the same Hebrew root and help to show that salvation is not simply freedom from a cruel taskmaster but includes freedom to serve the right master. Stated differently, the Lord not only delivers us from evil but also calls us into his service (cf. 1 Pet. 2:16). And, because we have been created by him and for him, serving him gives us true freedom.

Jesus once said, "Come to me, all who labor and are heavy laden, and I will give you rest. Take my yoke upon you, and learn from me, for I am gentle and lowly in heart, and you will find rest for your souls. For my yoke is easy, and my burden is light" (Matt. 11:28–30). We might ask, How can we find rest by taking a yoke upon our shoulders? But that is the wrong question, because everyone bears a yoke.

---

[258] For details on this verse cf. comment on 3:7–10. For the original land promise cf. Genesis 12:7; 26:3; 28:13.

The real question is, What yoke are we bearing? If we do not serve God, we will serve somebody or something else, whether ourselves, other people, the things of this world, or manmade gods. But we are not designed to serve such things as our primary loyalty. Doing so is like being yoked to a field plow and trying to break up a parking lot. Field plows are not designed for that, and those bearing such a yoke will find it difficult and heavy. But through Jesus we can enter the service of God, knowing him, walking with him. Doing so is like being yoked to a field plow and breaking up a field. This is what the plow is designed for, and, compared to the parking lot, it now slices through the earth like a hot knife through butter. Jesus' yoke is in this way easy and his burden light because he frees us to live in accord with our design: serving God wholeheartedly.

Old Testament or New, the Lord is the God who delivers us from cruel taskmasters into the glorious freedom of serving him, the good and glorious King. This leads naturally to a second question.

WHAT ASPECTS OF GOD'S DELIVERANCE ARE
THE ISRAELITES TO REMEMBER?

On either side of the story of God's deliverance is a series of commands about celebrating the Passover and the Feast of Unleavened Bread and about giving firstborn children and animals to the Lord (Ex. 12:1–28; 12:43–13:16). Each one of these elements serves as a reminder of different aspects of the Lord's deliverance.

The Passover is a reminder that God's deliverance protects from judgment (cf. 12:26–27). Although in many contexts today it is not comfortable to speak of judgment, the Bible is clear that a day is coming when the Lord will bring his justice to bear against evil. All those who have committed evil are subject to that judgment unless they are protected by the lifeblood of another. In Israel's case the Lord allows the lifeblood of a spotless lamb to offer that protection. In our case he has sent his own son, Jesus, who has given his own lifeblood as "our Passover lamb" (1 Cor. 5:7) to deliver us from God's wrath (1 Thess. 1:10). And just as the Israelites celebrated the Lord's protective deliverance during the Passover, Christians do the same during the communion meal, instituted by Jesus at the Passover feast (Luke 22:1–23), where they remember and proclaim, "Jesus, you are the mighty Savior, the sacrificial lamb of God who takes away the sin of the world!"[259]

The Passover was immediately followed by the Feast of Unleavened Bread, which is a reminder that God's deliverance is powerful. Twice the text explains that the Israelites eat unleavened bread because they are told to leave the land so quickly that they so not have time to prepare adequate provisions (Ex. 12:33–34, 39). The reason for such haste is that the Lord deals such a mighty blow to Egypt that it shows his absolute and supreme power over all the Egyptian "gods" (12:12), and all the Egyptians are terrified (12:33). While the Bible speaks often of God's salvation in terms of delivering people from sin's slavery, it also speaks of it in terms of powerfully defeating the spiritual forces of evil. During his earthly ministry

---

[259] Cf. Isaiah 53:5–12; John 1:29; 19:33–36.

Jesus regularly commanded demons to leave people (Matt. 9:32–33; 12:22; Mark 5:1–13) and spoke several times of the devil's defeat and judgment (Luke 10:18; John 12:31; 16:11). At the end of his earthly ministry he died so "that through death he might destroy the one who has the power of death, that is, the devil" (Heb. 2:14). In his resurrection he has been exalted as Lord "far above all rule and authority and power and dominion, and above every name that is named, not only in this age but also in the one to come" (Eph. 1:21) and will, at the end of days, "[deliver] the kingdom to God the Father after destroying every rule and every authority and power" (1 Cor. 15:24). In short, if the Passover reminds us that Jesus is a vicarious substitute, then the Feast of Unleavened Bread reminds us that he is a victorious warrior.

Finally, consecrating the firstborn to God is a reminder that God sets apart those he has delivered as his own. Put simply: when he rescues someone, that person belong to him. This is certainly true of the firstborn on the night of the Passover but is equally true of Israel as a whole, whom the Lord himself calls his "firstborn son" (Ex. 4:23). Indeed, in the song celebrating the Lord's deliverance in Exodus 15 the Israelites describe themselves as "the people ... whom [the LORD has] purchased" (15:16), like those ransomed by a good and gracious master from cruel slavery. The NT continues this line of thinking, urging followers of Jesus to live holy lives, "knowing that you were ransomed from the futile ways inherited from your forefathers, not with perishable things such as silver or gold, but with the precious blood of Christ, like that of a lamb without blemish or spot" (1 Pet. 1:18–19). Those ransomed by Jesus owe their all to him and should live lives of joyful reverence and wholehearted worship, not to gain his love but because of his love. He is a good and gracious Lord!

The good news of the Lord's deliverance is not to end with the first generation of Israelites. This leads to a final question.

HOW DO THEY KEEP THIS MEMORY ALIVE?

One of the main purposes of celebrating these feasts and consecrating the firstborn is to have an opportunity to remember and pass on to the next generation the story of God's deliverance (Ex. 12:26–27; 13:7–9, 14–16). On the one hand this means Israelite parents must know and understand God's act of salvation well enough to describe it to their children. In today's context this means understanding God's ultimate act of salvation in Jesus and being able to describe it to our children.

At the same time the first recipients of this command are being exhorted to pass on *their own experience of the Lord's salvation*. Moses is speaking to people who will personally experience being delivered from Egypt. In telling their children what happens they will be explaining not simply historical facts but also how they personally experience the reality of God's salvation. We do well to ask what it looks like to tell our children (or anyone else) not only what God has done by sending Jesus but also the difference that has made *and continues to make* in our lives. How does knowing Jesus continue to change us, day after day, week after week, month after month? Do our children and others who know us see that we have a *living* relationship with God, one in which we continue to experience his loving care and the joys of growing in relationship with him? If not, what would it take for that to become a reality?

I remember hearing a Christian businessman describe how he was in a foreign country and was asked to share his testimony. In his past experience to share one's testimony meant describing the moment in the past when one became a Christian, and he dutifully recounted that story. His audience listened politely, but, when he had finished, they said, "That is all well and good, but, when we share our testimonies, we speak of what God is doing in our lives today. Please tell us, what is he doing in your life today?" Great question! How would we respond?

EXODUS 13:17–15:21

¹⁷ When Pharaoh let the people go, God did not lead them by way of the land of the Philistines, although that was near. For God said, "Lest the people change their minds when they see war and return to Egypt." ¹⁸ But God led the people around by the way of the wilderness toward the Red Sea. And the people of Israel went up out of the land of Egypt equipped for battle. ¹⁹ Moses took the bones of Joseph with him, for Joseph¹ had made the sons of Israel solemnly swear, saying, "God will surely visit you, and you shall carry up my bones with you from here." ²⁰ And they moved on from Succoth and encamped at Etham, on the edge of the wilderness. ²¹ And the Lord went before them by day in a pillar of cloud to lead them along the way, and by night in a pillar of fire to give them light, that they might travel by day and by night. ²² The pillar of cloud by day and the pillar of fire by night did not depart from before the people.

14 Then the Lord said to Moses, ² "Tell the people of Israel to turn back and encamp in front of Pi-hahiroth, between Migdol and the sea, in front of Baal-zephon; you shall encamp facing it, by the sea. ³ For Pharaoh will say of the people of Israel, 'They are wandering in the land; the wilderness has shut them in.' ⁴ And I will harden Pharaoh's heart, and he will pursue them, and I will get glory over Pharaoh and all his host, and the Egyptians shall know that I am the Lord." And they did so.

⁵ When the king of Egypt was told that the people had fled, the mind of Pharaoh and his servants was changed toward the people, and they said, "What is this we have done, that we have let Israel go from serving us?" ⁶ So he made ready his chariot and took his army with him, ⁷ and took six hundred chosen chariots and all the other chariots of Egypt with officers over all of them. ⁸ And the Lord hardened the heart of Pharaoh king of Egypt, and he pursued the people of Israel while the people of Israel were going out defiantly. ⁹ The Egyptians pursued them, all Pharaoh's horses and chariots and his horsemen and his army,

and overtook them encamped at the sea, by Pi-hahiroth, in front of Baal-zephon.

¹⁰ When Pharaoh drew near, the people of Israel lifted up their eyes, and behold, the Egyptians were marching after them, and they feared greatly. And the people of Israel cried out to the Lord. ¹¹ They said to Moses, "Is it because there are no graves in Egypt that you have taken us away to die in the wilderness? What have you done to us in bringing us out of Egypt? ¹² Is not this what we said to you in Egypt: 'Leave us alone that we may serve the Egyptians'? For it would have been better for us to serve the Egyptians than to die in the wilderness." ¹³ And Moses said to the people, "Fear not, stand firm, and see the salvation of the Lord, which he will work for you today. For the Egyptians whom you see today, you shall never see again. ¹⁴ The Lord will fight for you, and you have only to be silent."

¹⁵ The Lord said to Moses, "Why do you cry to me? Tell the people of Israel to go forward. ¹⁶ Lift up your staff, and stretch out your hand over the sea and divide it, that the people of Israel may go through the sea on dry ground. ¹⁷ And I will harden the hearts of the Egyptians so that they shall go in after them, and I will get glory over Pharaoh and all his host, his chariots, and his horsemen. ¹⁸ And the Egyptians shall know that I am the Lord, when I have gotten glory over Pharaoh, his chariots, and his horsemen."

¹⁹ Then the angel of God who was going before the host of Israel moved and went behind them, and the pillar of cloud moved from before them and stood behind them, ²⁰ coming between the host of Egypt and the host of Israel. And there was the cloud and the darkness. And it lit up the night² without one coming near the other all night.

²¹ Then Moses stretched out his hand over the sea, and the Lord drove the sea back by a strong east wind all night and made the sea dry land, and the waters were divided. ²² And the people of Israel went into the midst of the sea on dry ground, the waters being a wall to them on their right hand and on their left. ²³ The Egyptians pursued and went in after them into the midst of the sea, all Pharaoh's horses, his chariots, and his horsemen. ²⁴ And in the morning watch the Lord in the pillar of fire and of cloud looked down on the Egyptian forces and threw the Egyptian forces into a panic, ²⁵ clogging³ their chariot wheels so that they drove heavily. And the Egyptians said, "Let us flee from before Israel, for the Lord fights for them against the Egyptians."

²⁶ Then the Lord said to Moses, "Stretch out your hand over the sea, that the water may come back upon the Egyptians, upon their chariots, and upon their horsemen." ²⁷ So Moses stretched out his hand over the sea, and the sea returned to its normal course when the morning appeared. And as the Egyptians fled into it, the Lord threw⁴ the Egyptians into the midst of the sea. ²⁸ The waters returned and covered the chariots and the horsemen; of all the host of Pharaoh that had followed them into the sea, not one of them remained. ²⁹ But the people of Israel walked on dry ground through the sea, the waters being a wall to them on their right hand and on their left.

³⁰ Thus the Lord saved Israel that day from the hand of the Egyptians, and Israel saw the Egyptians dead on the seashore. ³¹ Israel saw the great power that the Lord used against the Egyptians, so the people feared the Lord, and they believed in the Lord and in his servant Moses.

15 Then Moses and the people of Israel sang this song to the Lord, saying,

"I will sing to the Lord, for he has triumphed gloriously;
  the horse and his rider[5] he has thrown into the sea.
2 The Lord is my strength and my song,
  and he has become my salvation;
 this is my God, and I will praise him,
  my father's God, and I will exalt him.
3 The Lord is a man of war;
  the Lord is his name.

4 "Pharaoh's chariots and his host he cast into the sea,
  and his chosen officers were sunk in the Red Sea.
5 The floods covered them;
  they went down into the depths like a stone.
6 Your right hand, O Lord, glorious in power,
  your right hand, O Lord, shatters the enemy.
7 In the greatness of your majesty you overthrow your adversaries;
  you send out your fury; it consumes them like stubble.
8 At the blast of your nostrils the waters piled up;
  the floods stood up in a heap;
  the deeps congealed in the heart of the sea.
9 The enemy said, 'I will pursue, I will overtake,
  I will divide the spoil, my desire shall have its fill of them.
  I will draw my sword; my hand shall destroy them.'
10 You blew with your wind; the sea covered them;
  they sank like lead in the mighty waters.

11 "Who is like you, O Lord, among the gods?
  Who is like you, majestic in holiness,
  awesome in glorious deeds, doing wonders?
12 You stretched out your right hand;
  the earth swallowed them.

13 "You have led in your steadfast love the people whom you have redeemed;
  you have guided them by your strength to your holy abode.
14 The peoples have heard; they tremble;
  pangs have seized the inhabitants of Philistia.
15 Now are the chiefs of Edom dismayed;
  trembling seizes the leaders of Moab;
  all the inhabitants of Canaan have melted away.
16 Terror and dread fall upon them;
  because of the greatness of your arm, they are still as a stone,
 till your people, O Lord, pass by,
  till the people pass by whom you have purchased.
17 You will bring them in and plant them on your own mountain,
  the place, O Lord, which you have made for your abode,
  the sanctuary, O Lord, which your hands have established.
18 The Lord will reign forever and ever."

19 For when the horses of Pharaoh with his chariots and his horsemen went into the sea, the Lord brought back the waters of the sea upon

them, but the people of Israel walked on dry ground in the midst of the sea. ²⁰ Then Miriam the prophetess, the sister of Aaron, took a tambourine in her hand, and all the women went out after her with tambourines and dancing. ²¹ And Miriam sang to them:

> "Sing to the Lord, for he has triumphed gloriously;
> the horse and his rider he has thrown into the sea."

¹ Samaritan, Septuagint; Hebrew *he* ² Septuagint *and the night passed* ³ Or *binding* (compare Samaritan, Septuagint, Syriac); Hebrew *removing* ⁴ Hebrew *shook off* ⁵ Or *its chariot*; also verse 21

Section Overview

At the end of chapter 13 the story is headed in a very hopeful direction: at long last the Israelites have left Egypt with the Lord in their midst, and he leads them by means of a pillar of cloud and fire (vv. 17–22). But the Lord is not finished bringing his justice to bear on Pharaoh and his forces, and he makes Pharaoh's hardened heart harder still, leading him to pursue after the Israelites—right into a trap of divine making. This results in Pharaoh and his forces' being fully defeated as the Lord makes his power and glory miraculously known (14:1–28). The Israelites respond with appropriate fear and reverence (14:29–31) and break out in jubilant songs of praise, giving glory to God for his powerful deliverance and loving redemption (15:1–21).

Themes in this section include the Israelites' propensity to fear and disbelief (14:10–12), Moses' strong faith in the Lord's word and promises (vv. 13–14), the Lord's continual presence with his people (13:21–22), his judgment of sin and his making his character known (vv. 1–4, 17–18), and especially his power and love in rescuing his people and defeating their enemies (vv. 13–14, 21–29; 15:1–21). This is a divine king who uses his awesome power to deliver his people.

Section Outline

II. Israel leaves Egypt: the Lord provides deliverance (12:1–15:21) . . .
   B. The Lord's leading of his people out of Egypt and his final defeat of Pharaoh (13:17–15:21)
      1. The Lord leads Israel out of Egypt (13:17–22)
      2. The Lord's final defeat of Pharaoh (14:1–31)
      3. The Israelites celebrate the Lord's victory in song (15:1–21)

Comment

13:17–22 Having provided a brief overview of Israel's exodus from Egypt in 12:31–42, the text now returns to offer further details. First we read the initial route that the Lord leads Israel to follow (13:17–18). The route is greatly debated by scholars.[260] The most direct path to Canaan would have been the by the "way of the land of the Philistines,"[261] but this would have involved immediate battles, either because the

---

[260] Cf. James K. Hoffmeier, "The Exodus and Wilderness Narratives," in *Ancient Israel's History: An Introduction to Issues and Sources*, ed. Bill T. Arnold and Richard S. Hess (Grand Rapids, MI: Baker Academic, 2014), 59–80.
[261] For the possible anachronism of "Philistines" cf. Sklar, *Additional Notes on Exodus*, at 13:17.

way itself was fortified²⁶² or because it would have led Israel very quickly to Canaan, where the nation would have been forced to fight immediately.²⁶³ Either way, the Lord knows his people are not prepared for this (cf. their response in 14:10–12), so he leads them instead "by the way of the wilderness toward the Red Sea²⁶⁴ ... equipped for battle" (13:18). Since it is odd to note the Israelites are "equipped for battle" (v. 18) just after noting they are too fearful to engage in it (v. 17), some suggest that this rare term refers more generally to a large group of people moving in an ordered way²⁶⁵ or that it is related to the Hebrew root for "five" and refers to the people's leaving in groups of fifty.²⁶⁶ What is clear is that they leave and that the Lord guides their journey.

Briefly the text notes that Moses fulfills the oath that Joseph made his sons swear, namely, to take his bones out of Egypt and to the Promised Land (v. 19; cf. Gen. 50:25). This notice ties up a loose end from Genesis and underscores that God has indeed "visited" his people, that is, shown them his special care.²⁶⁷ It is also noted that after Succoth, where the Israelites initially stop after leaving Egypt (Ex. 12:37), they go on to Elam, on the wilderness' edge (13:20). They will soon turn back from here, giving Pharaoh the false impression that the wilderness has trapped them (cf. comment on 14:1–4).

Finally, this section tells us how the Lord guides his people: "By day in a pillar of cloud to lead them along the way, and by night in a pillar of fire to give them light, that they might travel by day and by night" (13:21). These are not two different pillars but one, with the Lord lighting up the cloud at night with fire (cf. 14:24; 40:38; cf. Num. 9:15; 14:14), making it a giant "night light" to guide them. By day or night this cloud will assure them of the Lord's presence all the way to the Promised Land (Ex. 13:22; cf. 40:38).

14:1–4 At this point the narrative takes an unexpected twist. The Lord has just led the people away from the way of the Philistines lest they see war and "return" (Hb. *shub*) to Egypt (13:17). Now he uses the very same term when he tells them to "turn back" (*shub*; 14:2), that is, turn back from the wilderness (13:20) toward Egypt (or areas controlled by it).²⁶⁸ Why?

He immediately explains: "For Pharaoh will say of the people of Israel, 'They are wandering in the land; the wilderness has shut them in'" (14:3), that is, Pharaoh

---

262 Egyptian sources from the fourteenth and thirteenth centuries BC make clear "that several Egyptian forts" lay along this route; Nahum M. Sarna, *Exploring Exodus: The Origins of Biblical Israel* (New York: Shocken, 1986), 105. Cf. Hoffmeier ("Exodus and Wilderness Narratives," 65–69) for the relevant archaeological discoveries confirming the presence of fortresses in this general period.
263 Cassuto, *Commentary on the Book of Exodus*, 156.
264 "Red Sea" is in the Hebrew "Sea of Reeds," which some suggest refers in certain passages (such as this one) to marshy lakes north of what is today known as the Red Sea—e.g., Hoffmeier, "The Exodus and Wilderness Narratives" (78–80) and more fully, *Israel in Egypt* (199–222), where he notes (206) that in other passages it can refer to the Gulf of Suez (Num. 33:10, 11) or the Gulf of Aqaba (Ex. 23:31; Deut. 1:40), which are extensions of the Red Sea.
265 Cassuto, *Commentary on the Book of Exodus*, 156–157.
266 Stuart, *Exodus*, 324; the LXX translates "in the fifth generation," but this is less likely (cf. Gen. 15:16).
267 Cf. note 102 within comment on 3:16–22. The Israelites later bury these bones in an area of the Promised Land allotted to Joseph's tribe (Josh. 24:32).
268 The location described in 14:2 is again uncertain, but the details describing it suggest the ancient audience would have been able to identify the spot (cf. Hoffmeier, "Exodus and Wilderness Narratives," 72–80, and more briefly Alexander, *Exodus*, ApOTC, 273–274). Significantly it is "by the sea," the importance of which becomes clear as the story unfolds.

might think they got to the wilderness, thought it was impossible to journey through, turned back, and are now wandering around, distressed[269] and trapped!

In reality, however, "it is his armies that were marching into a trap of divine making."[270] The Lord explains, "I will harden Pharaoh's heart," that is, take Pharaoh's already hardened heart and make it harder still, confirming him in his rebellion and once more displaying God's sovereign power over him.[271] As a result, Pharaoh will "pursue" the Israelites, either to destroy or re-enslave them, but "I will get glory over Pharaoh and all his host" by a miracle of divine judgment[272] so that "the Egyptians shall know that I am the LORD," the God of sovereign might who is worthy of their honor (14:4a; for "know the LORD" cf. Response section on 7:8–11:10, "What Does It Mean to Know the Lord?"). We are not yet told what this miraculous judgment will be, but the Israelites obey and turn back (14:4b).

14:5–8 Meanwhile, the reality of the Israelites' departure is sinking in on Pharaoh and his servants, who regret losing their slave labor (v. 5). Preparing his chariot, Pharaoh leads his army after them, including six hundred choice chariots and myriads of others, all commanded by leading officers (vv. 6–7; cf. 15:4). Since chariots were the ancient equivalent of tanks, this is a formidable force. Verse 8 then summarizes: the Lord has hardened Pharaoh's heart, and Pharaoh has pursued after the Israelites, who are leaving Egypt "with an uplifted hand" (Hb.), that is, a hand lifted either in "defiance" or in "triumph," or both.[273] Clearly their departure is humiliating to Pharaoh, and he cannot leave it unaddressed.

14:9–14 The story resumes, and Pharaoh and his vast army overtake Israel (v. 9), that is, draw within sight of the Israelites (v. 10).[274] The Israelites are trapped, with an advancing wall of soldiers before them and an impassable wall of water behind them. Annihilation looks certain, and it is no surprise that they cry out to the Lord in great fear. The Lord certainly welcomes fearful cries as much as parents do when their little ones cry out during a storm. The problem here is that the Israelites are crying out with fear but no faith (vv. 11–12). Children who cry out during a storm believe their parents can defend them. The Israelites lack such childlike faith. Repeatedly they respond to difficulties with temper tantrums of unbelief (15:24; 16:1–3; 17:1–3; Num. 11:1; 14:1–3; etc.). This is especially ironic here. "God has just stressed the importance of passing on memories [of his deliverance] (ch. 13), but already the people have completely forgotten his spectacular actions on their behalf."[275]

But Moses has not forgotten, and his response is filled with faith (14:13–14). He does not know how the Lord will deliver them, but he knows he will (cf. v. 4).

---

269 The verb translated "wander" occurs two other times, each in a context of agitation or distress (Est. 3:15; Joel 1:18); a related noun refers to distressed confusion (Isa. 22:5; Mic. 7:4).
270 Hoffmeier, "Exodus and Wilderness Narratives," 74.
271 Cf. comments on 4:21–23; 11:9–10.
272 See the use of the verb translated in 14:4 as "get glory" in Exodus 14:17–18; Leviticus 10:3; Ezekiel 28:22.
273 "With an uplifted hand" and related phrases refer elsewhere to rebellion against the Lord or a king (Num. 15:30; 33:3; 1 Kings 11:26) and to victory in battle (Deut. 32:27).
274 Cassuto, *Commentary on the Book of Exodus*, 162–163.
275 Ndjerareou, *Exodus*, in *Africa Bible Commentary*, 105.

His faith is sure of what his eyes cannot see. He assures the Israelites they will not need to fight. The Lord will fight on their behalf, as he did while they were in Egypt. They could remain "silent"—a word that can refer to silence with the sense of inaction (Gen. 24:21; Judg. 16:2; Est. 4:14)—and "see" the Lord's salvation. The word "see" is used three times for emphasis,[276] as though to say, "As you trust in the Lord, what you will see is his salvation, and what you will never ever see again are your enemies!"[277]

14:15–18 The Lord now explains in broad terms how his deliverance will occur. His opening question—"Why do you cry to me?" (Ex. 14:15)—is best understood as being spoken to Moses in his role as the people's representative, the sense being, "Why is Israel crying out to me in fear with no faith? Do they not trust I can deliver them?"[278] The solution is for Moses to speak to the people, explaining what the Lord will do so they can move forward. The Lord's plan is twofold.

First, Moses is to lift his staff—the same "staff of God" that has already produced so many signs (4:17, 20; 7:19; 8:5, 16; 9:23; 10:13)—so that the sea will divide and the Israelites can march through on dry land (14:16). In short the Lord will create a miraculous escape route, though we are not told how.

Second, he will harden the Egyptians' hearts so they will chase the Israelites and then come to "know [he is] the LORD" when he has "gotten glory over Pharaoh, his chariots, and his horsemen" (v. 18). The implication is that he will judge Pharaoh and the Egyptians in a miraculous way that will show his sovereign power and make clear he is worthy of honor and praise (cf. v. 4). Again, the Lord does not explain how he will do so. The general plan is clear, but suspense is created in terms of the details.

14:19–22 For this plan to work time will be needed, so the angel of God who has been leading the Israelites moves from the camp's front to its rear, between the Israelites and the Egyptians. This is the first mention of an angel since 3:2, where it was noted that angels can speak and act on the Lord's behalf, like a king's messenger. In this case the text seems to assume that, just as this angel appeared on the Lord's behalf in the burning bush (3:2), he has been appearing on the Lord's behalf in the pillar of cloud (cf. 14:19 with 13:21 and 14:24), which now moves with the angel and forms a protective barrier between the camps.[279]

With this barrier in place Moses carries out the Lord's command and stretches out his hand, lifting his rod over the sea. As before, this is like an enacted prayer (cf. comment on 9:22–25), which the Lord answers by sending an east wind to drive the sea back, dividing it in two and making the seafloor dry (14:21). This allows

---
276 Cassuto, *Commentary on the Book of Exodus*, 164.
277 Unless dead (Ex. 14:30)! In the Hebrew the end of 14:13 reads, "You will no longer see them unto eternity," that is, never ever again.
278 Note that the verb "cry out" in 14:15 is the same used to describe the people's action in verse 10. Houtman (*Exodus*, vol. 2, 266) also observes that Moses has just been presented as full of faith (vv. 13–14); he is not crying out inappropriately.
279 As the ESV mg. shows, the translation of "And it lit up the night" is debated. As the Hebrew text stands, the most common understanding has been that the Egyptians are in darkness and the Israelites have light (cf. Houtman, *Exodus*, vol. 2, 267–269, and more briefly, Stuart, *Exodus*, 341).

the Israelites to walk right through the sea during the night (cf. v. 24), the water standing like a wall on either side (v. 22).[280]

14:23–28 With the Israelites safely through, the angel and cloud apparently move out of the way, allowing the massive Egyptian army to pursue, rushing right into the heart of the sea (v. 23). It is a death trap. The time is the morning watch (v. 24), just as day is breaking (cf. v. 27), meaning the final victory will be seen by all. The Lord—that is, the angel acting on his behalf (cf. comment on 14:19–22; compare 3:4 with 3:2)—looks down from the pillar of fire and cloud and throws the "Egyptian forces into a panic" (14:24). This is something the Lord often does on his people's behalf when fighting for them (23:27; Josh. 10:10; 1 Sam. 7:10). He does so here by crippling their chariots in some way "so that they drove heavily," that is, with difficulty (Ex. 14:25). This is a punishment corresponding to the crime: the word for "heavily" is built on the same root as one of the words that describes the Egyptians' hardened hearts (v. 4), so that those with heavy/difficult hearts are now having heaviness/difficulty driving their chariots.[281] They have been stripped of their most powerful weapon and quickly realize Israel's God is involved: "Let us flee from before Israel, for the LORD fights for them against the Egyptians!" (v. 25). As the Lord said, they have come to understand just how powerful he is (cf. v. 4).

But it is too late. The Lord instructs Moses to stretch out his hand once more over the sea, and its waters return to their normal state (vv. 26–27). For the Egyptians there is no escape. The Lord picks up their chariots with his waves and throws them into the heart of the sea, where they sink like a stone (v. 27; cf. Neh. 9:11). The army's devastation is total; all who have pursued after Israel are drowned. As with the army of locusts that the Lord drove into the sea (Ex. 10:19), so too with Egypt's army: "Not one of them remained" (14:28).[282]

14:29–31 The chapter concludes with a summary. As Moses had promised (vv. 13–14), the Lord has saved Israel from the Egyptians, whom the Israelites now see dead, washed up on the shore (vv. 29–30). The Lord's display of power is undeniable. The beginning of verse 31 could be woodenly translated, "When Israel saw the *powerful hand* with which the Lord acted in Egypt." As God had promised, he had delivered them from "the hand of the Egyptians" (v. 30) by means of his own much more powerful hand (v. 31; cf. 3:8, 19). As a result, the Israelites "feared the LORD" (14:31), an expression often accompanied by phrases emphasizing obedience, loyalty, and love for God and his commands (Deut. 5:29; 6:2; 10:12; 13:4; etc.). In these contexts the word could also be translated as "revere," with a focus on worshipful love and obedience flowing from reverence and awe. Seeing the Lord's signs, the Israelites understand that reverential obedience and love are the proper response toward him. The signs also made clear they can trust the Lord

---

[280] The term for "wall" refers most commonly to city walls, leading Stuart (*Exodus*, 342) to conclude the Israelites walked through a deep channel of water, "not a shallow path through mud or ankle-deep brine."
[281] Cf. NET text note on Exodus 14:4.
[282] Ndjerareou, *Exodus*, in *Africa Bible Commentary*, 105, citing 10:19, where "not a single locust *was left*" uses the same verb as here: "Not one of them *remained*."

and his promises (cf. Gen. 15:1–6) and trust that he has appointed Moses as his spokesman (Ex. 14:31; for the latter cf. 4:1–5, 30–31; 19:9).

Israel's nightmare of slavery in Egypt is now over. The Egyptians have been well and fully defeated and the Israelites well and fully freed. Their response of joyful song therefore comes as no surprise (15:1–21).

15:1–19 At various points in the biblical story God's people break out in spontaneous songs of praise to the Lord when he saves them (cf. Num. 21:16–18; 2 Sam. 22:1; cf. also Judges 4 with Judges 5). This is appropriate. The Lord's salvation is so marvelous that everyday speech can feel inadequate to describe it. We need songs, which are open fields of space for our hearts to run free, giving voice to the breadth and depth of our emotions.

So Moses and the Israelites sing, exchanging prose and simple speech for poetry and joyful song. The song focuses on *the Lord's* rescue of Israel. It does not even mention Moses, focusing instead on how the Lord himself and the Lord alone has accomplished salvation for his people.[283]

Great debate surrounds the song's structure,[284] which is unsurprising, since poetry does not always evince a crisp logical flow. Compared to prose, poetry is far more likely to make its points by repeated and overlapping waves of expression. In this case those waves focus on the Lord's defeat of Pharaoh and his forces, describing this from a first- and third-person perspective (Ex. 15:1–5) and then from a second-person one (vv. 6–12). Remaining in the second person,[285] the song then shifts and focuses on the Lord's leading of his people safely to the place where he himself will dwell (vv. 13–17). It then concludes with a third-person burst of praise affirming the Lord's enduring kingship (v. 18). The song could be paraphrased as follows:[286]

> I will sing to the Lord, who has abundantly shown his majesty and strength by defeating Egypt's forces, picking up each horse and rider as easily as an archer does an arrow and then shooting them into the heart of the sea (v. 1b). The Lord has exercised his saving strength on my behalf, and because of him I can sing with joy, rejoicing in the salvation he has accomplished for me (v. 2a). I give allegiance to him as my God and will describe the beauty of who he is; indeed, my ancestors gave their allegiance to him, and I will lift his name on high as the one worthy of praise (v. 2b). By defeating the Egyptians in war, he has made known that he, Yahweh, is the sovereign God of power in the earth (v. 3). He hurled Pharaoh's chariots and army into the sea where they sank, they and the very best of Egypt's officers (v. 4). The watery depths covered them like a blanket, and they sank like a stone into the heart of the sea (v. 5).

---

[283] Cf. Sarna, *Exodus*, 75. Cf. discussion in Response section.
[284] For an overview of at least six different approaches cf. Houtman, *Exodus*, vol. 2, 246.
[285] I understand 15:14–16a to function like 15:16b, that is, they are said out loud to the Lord (and thus still in second person).
[286] For notes explaining the decisions made in the paraphrase cf. Sklar, *Additional Notes on Exodus*, at 15:1–18.

O Lord, your strong right hand towers in majestic strength and shatters the enemy in defeat (v. 6). In the greatness of your majesty and strength you tear down those who rise up against you; you release your burning wrath on them, and it consumes them like stubble in the fire (v. 7). Your nostrils flared with anger, and at their blast the waters were heaped up like grain, forming into tall piles, becoming like two solid walls (v. 8). After we left Egypt and were escaping through the channel you made in the sea the enemy said, "I will pursue and overtake them! I will plunder their goods! I will feast myself full on them! I will empty my sword out of its sheath and will drive them away with no land to dwell in!" (v. 9). But you, O Lord, blew the waters back into place and covered them so that they sank like lead in the mighty waters (v. 10). Who is like you among the gods, O Lord? No one! What god is there whose utter uniqueness is so majestic, who is so worthy of reverential awe when being praised, who is able to do such miraculous wonders? None (v. 11)! You stretched out your right hand like a warrior in battle and caused the earth to swallow up the enemy in the sea (v. 12).

As for your people, Israel, you not only rescued them from difficulty; you are leading them in your gracious steadfast love, protecting them like a strong shepherd as you bring them like sheep to your holy pasture land in Canaan (v. 13). The other nations who hear of all you have done will quake with dread (v. 14a), including four of Israel's archenemies: Philistia's inhabitants will writhe in anguish like a woman in childbirth (v. 14b), Edom's chiefs will be paralyzed with terror (v. 15a), Moab's leaders will tremble with fear (v. 15b), and Canaan's inhabitants will melt away in dread (v. 15c). Yes, terror and dread will fall on them! When they see how great and powerful your miraculous acts of redemption prove you to be, they will be petrified, as still as stone, letting your people, whom you have redeemed and acquired as your servant, pass by unharmed (v. 16). You will then bring your people and plant them like a vine so they can take root and flourish in your land, which is like a majestic mountain, one that you are preparing, O Lord, to be the very place in which you dwell, a holy place, O Lord, that your own hands will establish (v. 17).

The Lord, he is the one who will reign as eternal King (v. 18)!

After the song a summary of its main theme is provided: this is the story of the Lord's defeating Pharaoh's forces in the sea and leading Israel safely through it (v. 19; cf. 14:28–29).

15:20–21 Miriam now enters the picture. We are told she is a prophetess and Aaron's sister (v. 20). Since Moses and Aaron are brothers (6:20), it is not clear why she is described simply as Aaron's sister (cf. Num. 26:59). This perhaps reflects an emphasis on the authority associated with the oldest male child.[287] Whatever the

---
[287] Sarna, *Exodus*, 83, 248n77, citing Genesis 4:22; 28:9; 36:22.

reason, by calling her a prophetess the text identifies her role within Israel and suggests that the song she is about to sing is divinely inspired.

Holding a tambourine, Miriam leads the women of Israel in singing and dancing (15:20b), a response we see from women elsewhere in the Bible who celebrate an Israelite victory (Judg. 11:34; 1 Sam. 18:6). The text notes she sings "to them" (Ex. 15:21). Since the word "them" is masculine here, many plausibly suggest that some form of antiphonal singing is going on, with the women singing the shorter chorus and the rest of Israel singing the larger song.[288] Whatever the case may be, Miriam's song focuses on the larger song's main theme, exhorting the Israelites to give praise to God for his victory and deliverance (15:21b; cf. comment on 15:1–19 [at v. 1]). In this way this section closes with a scene of utter jubilation: the women are playing music and dancing, and all Israel is raising its voices in a joyful song of praise and thanksgiving to the Lord.

Response

In this section the Israelites go from seeming deliverance (13:17–22) to seeming defeat (14:1–10), then from astounding rescue (14:13–29) to awestruck worship (14:30–15:21). Along the way they experience nearly every human emotion, from feelings of relief and triumph as they finally leave Egypt (14:8) and terror and fear as Pharaoh's army looks certain to overtake them (14:10–12) to reverential awe as they see the Lord's powerful deliverance (14:31) and profound joy and thanksgiving as they express worship to him (15:1–21). We may elaborate on how this story relates to us today by asking three questions.

WHAT IS THE HOPE?

Jesus once said, "Each tree is known by its own fruit" (Luke 6:44), meaning that our actions reveal our character. In this section of Scripture the Lord's actions reveal much about his character. Primarily they demonstrate that he is a God of love who desires relationship with his people and therefore delivers them with great power from their enemies. The Lord's love is celebrated in Exodus 15:13: "You have led in your steadfast love the people whom you have redeemed; you have guided them by your strength to your holy abode." As noted at 34:6–7, when describing the Lord the word for "steadfast love" (Hb. *khesed*) refers to a demonstration of love through favorable action. In this case the Lord's love leads him not only to deliver his people from evil ("the people whom you have redeemed") but also to lead them into relationship with himself ("guided them by your strength to your holy abode"). The Lord's salvation always has relationship in view.

Significantly, this salvation takes place by means of the Lord's demonstration of his supreme power, which is a constant theme of the narrator: "The LORD will fight for you" (14:14); "the LORD drove the sea back" (v. 21); "the LORD ... threw

---

[288] Bush (*Commentary on Exodus*, 194) suggests the shorter chorus was sung after each verse of the longer song in the same way that "his love endures forever" occurs at the end of each verse in Psalm 136. Certainty on this point is not possible.

the Egyptian forces into a panic" (v. 24); "the LORD fights for [Israel] against the Egyptians" (v. 25); "the LORD saved Israel that day from the hand of the Egyptians . . . [and] Israel saw the great power that the LORD used against the Egyptians" (vv. 30–31); "I will sing to the LORD, for he has triumphed gloriously; the horse and his rider he has thrown into the sea" (15:1).[289] By the end of this account the Lord is clearly a God of ultimate and sovereign power.

But perhaps most important to note is that the way in which the Lord brings about salvation from Egypt is a picture of how he brings about his far greater act of salvation from sin at the cross of Jesus. The verses just mentioned make clear that the Lord, and the Lord alone, is the one who saves his people. They cannot save themselves, and the song celebrating their deliverance in chapter 15 does not once mention anything they or Moses have done to contribute to their salvation. "The LORD is a man of war" who does battle for them.[290] Indeed, Moses exhorts them to be still and to watch as the Lord fights on their behalf to save them (cf. comment on 14:9–14). And that is the point. Salvation is not something humans achieve but something they receive as God's gracious gift. Only he can do it. We cannot save ourselves. He is the deliverer; we are the delivered. With great love and power Jesus has now defeated sin and death on our behalf so that we might be forgiven, cleansed, and adopted as the Father's own. He has fought the battle on our behalf and won (for Jesus as divine warrior cf. 1 Cor. 15:24–28; Heb. 2:14–15). This provides a sure and steady hope to those who believe, trusting not in themselves but in the God who delights to save those who cannot save themselves.

As glorious as the Lord's salvation is, there is another side to the coin. Whereas the Israelites march safely through the sea, experiencing the Lord's salvation, the Egyptians are drowned in it, experiencing the Lord's judgment. This leads to a second question.

WHAT IS THE WARNING?

It has long been suggested that the drowning of the Egyptian army in the sea is a punishment corresponding to the crime: just as the Egyptians had sought to kill Israelite male babies in the Nile (Ex. 1:22), now they themselves are drowned in the sea.[291] But there is far more to say. Just as the Israelites' deliverance serves as a picture of the Lord's ultimate act of salvation, the Egyptians' punishment serves as a picture of the Lord's ultimate act of judgment.

For many the idea of judgment goes against their modern sensibilities. We want to think of God as an elected official, someone who gains our support as long as he does what we want or gives us the help we need. But the Bible's perspective is that God is a king. Kingship is not a part of most people's lives today. The closest parallel in most societies will be that of parents and children. In the

---

[289] Cf. 15:1–21 as a whole, which drips with this theme. Later biblical writers look back continually to the exodus as a demonstration of God's power and love on his people's behalf (Josh. 24:7; Neh. 9:9–11; Pss. 66:6; 74:13; 78:13; 106:8–11; 136:13–14; Isa. 51:10; 63:11–14).
[290] For the theme of God as a warrior cf. the overview in Tremper Longman III, *Confronting Old Testament Controversies* (Grand Rapids, MI: Baker, 2019), 123–206, esp. 123–144.
[291] Cf. Houtman, *Exodus*, vol. 2, 274; he cites very early writers noting the same.

family children quickly learn that their parents are not elected officials, and the family is not a democracy! Their parents—their creators—are in authority. Yes, the parents are to love and care for their children, but they are also to be obeyed and honored. Kingship works the same, only much more so. Like a parent, a king is to love and care for his subjects but also to be obeyed and honored. And yet the stakes are greater. When children rebel against parents, they are being disobedient and can cause harm to a family, but, when subjects rebel against the king, they are being treasonous and can cause harm to a kingdom. By undermining the king's authority rebels threaten the stability of the entire nation. This explains why treason throughout history is normally met with incredibly high and severe penalties.

In this case the problem is not simply that the Egyptians have done great evil to the Israelites but especially that they will not yield to the Lord's kingship. Twice in this story the Lord says he is bringing his justice to bear against the Egyptians so they "shall know that I am the LORD" (14:4, 18). In context this means he is going to perform a miracle of divine judgment that will make clear to them that he is the sovereign King who is worthy to be honored and obeyed (cf. comment on 14:1–4; 14:15–18). This is what the Egyptians have refused to do. One cannot be neutral toward God. If someone is not yielding to God, he is rebelling against God because he is saying God is not really King.

The drowning of the Egyptians in the sea thus becomes a preview—and warning!—of the final judgment to come. Normally, the Lord displays his common grace to us, making "his sun rise on the evil and on the good, and send[ing] rain on the just and on the unjust" (Matt. 5:45). But at the end of time common grace ends and a final judgment takes place, in which the Lord divides between those who have yielded to him and those who have not (Matt. 25:31–33; Luke 3:17; Rev. 20:15). In passages such as ours this end-time judgment breaks into time and space, serving as the possible strongest warning to those who behold it: repent and bow the knee to the King who is the Creator.[292] This leads to a final question.

HOW DO WE RESPOND?

Biblical stories often serve as warnings to avoid imitating certain characters and as invitations to follow others. In this case the warning is clear: we must not be like the Egyptians by having a hard heart and refusing to acknowledge the Lord as King. But the invitation is equally clear. By the end of the story the Israelites look on the great power and love that God has displayed in rescuing them, and they "feared the LORD" (Ex. 14:31). As noted above, this does not mean they were terrified of him. Rather, it means they revered him with awe, bowing the knee to him as their King of power and Lord of love. Have we done this with Jesus? It is impossible to be neutral toward him. If we are not yielding to him, we are saying

---

[292] The ideas of the above paragraph are indebted especially to Meredith Kline, "The Intrusion and the Decalogue," *WTJ* 16 (1953): 1–22, esp. 15–16; Tremper Longman III, "Spiritual Continuity," in *Show Them No Mercy: Four Views on God and Canaanite Genocide*, ed. Stanley N. Gundry (Grand Rapids, MI: Zondervan, 2003), 159–187; Longman, *Confronting Old Testament Controversies*, 123–206, esp. 195–205. Another instance of such judgment is the flood, which Jesus explicitly points to as a warning to prepare for God's end-time judgment (Matt. 24:37–41).

he is not really King. But, if we do yield to him, we receive all the benefits of his victory over sin and death on our behalf and, most of all, experience the profound joy that comes from knowing him, the King of power and the Lord of love.

OVERVIEW OF

EXODUS 15:22–17:16

This section begins with three narratives that share similar themes. In all three the Israelites face a crisis and grumble or quarrel with their leaders, and the Lord miraculously provides for their needs (cf. table 2.5). The texts are further linked by the theme of testing: in the first two the Lord tests his people (15:25–26; 16:4–5), while in the last the people test the Lord (17:2, 7).

TABLE 2.5: Thematic Parallels in Exodus 15–17

15:22–27	16:1–36	17:1–7
No water to drink (15:23)	No food to eat (16:3)	No water to drink (17:1)
People grumble against Moses (15:24)	People grumble against Moses and Aaron (16:2)	People quarrel with Moses (17:2)
The Lord graciously provides water (15:25, 27)	The Lord graciously provides food (16:13–15)	The Lord graciously provides water (17:5–6)

The ways in which these themes work together becomes clearer when the nature of testing is remembered. Biblically speaking, when the Lord tests his people he gives them an opportunity to show faithfulness to him in difficult situations, where faith may be hard, and obedience harder still. In turn these situations allow them to see the Lord at work in their lives and are thus viewed as doing good for them in the end (Deut. 8:16; cf. Response section on 17:1–7, "Why Does God Test His People?"). When people test the Lord, however, it is always viewed negatively, since such testing expresses unbelief in his presence and care (cf. comment on 17:1–7).

In these accounts the Israelites consistently respond to difficult situations of testing with a lack of faith instead of obedient trust. And, while they do obey in some instances (16:17–18, 30), their overall posture is unbelieving complaint (cf. table 2.5), culminating in the incredibly faithless act of testing the Lord (17:2, 7). That their failure is seen in three narratives in a row only underscores it, because to repeat an action two additional times is to emphasize it (cf. note 109 within comment on 4:1–9).

This also means, however, that the Lord's graciousness is also emphasized, since in all three texts he does not punish his people; instead he provides for their needs. Later he will discipline them for their complaints (Num. 11:1–3, 33–34), but at this point he responds with gracious provision (cf. Response section on 17:1–7, "How Does the Lord Respond to the Israelites").

He does so again in this section's last narrative, as he helps the Israelites defeat Amalek (Ex. 17:8–16). Up to this point in Exodus the Israelites have not had to lift a finger against their adversaries; the Lord has defeated them directly on Israel's behalf. In this case, however, the Israelites must engage directly in battle. Even so, the text emphasizes that Israel's victory comes about only through the Lord's help (vv. 11–13), an important lesson (and encouragement) for them as they anticipate the coming battles in the Promised Land.

Viewed as a whole, this section emphasizes how the Israelites are slow to believe and quick to complain. This in turn makes the Lord's character shine all the brighter as he patiently, graciously, and bountifully provides and cares for his people. He is truly "merciful and gracious, slow to anger, and abounding in steadfast love and faithfulness" (34:6).

EXODUS 15:22–27

²² Then Moses made Israel set out from the Red Sea, and they went into the wilderness of Shur. They went three days in the wilderness and found no water. ²³ When they came to Marah, they could not drink the water of Marah because it was bitter; therefore it was named Marah.[1] ²⁴ And the people grumbled against Moses, saying, "What shall we drink?" ²⁵ And he cried to the Lord, and the Lord showed him a log,[2] and he threw it into the water, and the water became sweet.

There the Lord[3] made for them a statute and a rule, and there he tested them, ²⁶ saying, "If you will diligently listen to the voice of the Lord your God, and do that which is right in his eyes, and give ear to his commandments and keep all his statutes, I will put none of the diseases on you that I put on the Egyptians, for I am the Lord, your healer."

²⁷ Then they came to Elim, where there were twelve springs of water and seventy palm trees, and they encamped there by the water.

[1] *Marah* means *bitterness* [2] Or *tree* [3] Hebrew *he*

Section Overview

As noted above, this is the first of three testing narratives in this section. The situation causing the test is a lack of water (vv. 22–23), the Israelites' response is one of grumbling (v. 24), and the Lord's response is to provide for his people's needs

(vv. 24–25a). At this point we are also introduced to the theme of testing that links the first three narratives (vv. 25b–26). The Lord emphasizes the covenantal nature of testing, namely, that being tested is an opportunity for the Israelites to demonstrate covenant faithfulness to the Lord, their covenant God. This theme runs throughout the Pentateuch. The Lord has saved the Israelites not simply from slavery but also into covenant relationship with him, a relationship in which he obligates himself to show them faithful care and in which they obligate themselves to show him faithful obedience. The passage ends with a fitting testimony of how lavishly the Lord cares for his people (v. 27).

Section Outline

III. Israel travels through the wilderness to Sinai: the Lord tests his people and provides for their needs (15:22–17:16)
  A. Three stories of testing and provision in the wilderness (15:22–17:7)
    1. The Lord first tests the Israelites and provides for their needs (15:22–27)

Comment

15:22–26 With Pharaoh's forces defeated (14:26–29) Moses now leads the Israelites away from the Red Sea (cf. note 264 within comment on 13:17–22). They travel to the Wilderness of Shur (15:22), which is east of Egypt and known also as the "wilderness of Etham" (Num. 33:8). After a three-day journey, they have not found water. Traveling farther, they find water, but it is too bitter to drink, leading them to name the place Marah (Ex. 15:23; in Hebrew "Marah" means "bitter"; cf. Ruth 1:20).

This is a crisis. When water supplies run out in the wilderness, death soon follows. The Israelites could call out in faith, asking the Lord to deliver them from this crisis as he has just delivered them from another (cf. Ex. 14:13–31), but instead they respond again with unbelief (15:24; cf. 14:10–12). The word "grumbling" refers to a strong expression of discontent with the Lord or his leaders (cf. 16:2–3, 7; 17:3; Num. 14:2, 27, 29; 16:41). Faced with their response, Moses cries out to the Lord for help, and the Lord provides a solution: he shows Moses a log to throw into the waters that will make them drinkable (Ex. 15:25).

While some have explained this by noting that certain types of wood have natural properties that make bitter waters drinkable,[293] no such wood has been identified in the Sinai region, nor is it clear that a single log with such properties could purify the large amount of water needed for the people. It is far more likely that this is a miracle—the Lord himself has again rescued Israel. In doing so he provides an object lesson: just as the Lord is the one who has "healed" the water (v. 25), he is the one who "heals" Israel (v. 26; cf. Deut. 32:39).[294] Indeed, while he

---

[293] Fretheim, *Exodus*, 177.
[294] The verb in 15:25 is "to make sweet," but making waters sweet could be viewed as "healing" them (cf. 2 Kings 2:21). This points the way to the above understanding of the text's symbolism.

mentions his discipline ("I will put none of the diseases on you that I put on the Egyptians"), he focuses on his love for his people ("for I am the LORD, your healer"). He leans toward them with care, not judgment.

But this does not mean the Israelites can live any way they like. The Lord provides "a statute and rule" by which he will "test" them (Ex. 15:25). In the singular the language of "statute and rule" often refers to a binding custom or law (Num. 9:14; 27:11; 1 Sam. 30:25). In this case the "statute and rule" is that, if Israel is faithful to the Lord, then he will protect them from harm and bless them with good (Ex. 15:26). This is a "test" insofar as it establishes a standard of behavior by which Israel will be measured, namely, obedience to their covenant king (cf. also the use of "test" in Ex. 16:4; Deut. 8:2; 13:3; Judg. 2:22; 3:4).

It may be noted that the Pentateuch frequently emphasizes the importance of Israel's continued faithfulness to the covenant in order to experience the Lord's covenant blessings (Lev. 26:3–12; Deut. 4:1; 5:31–33; 26:16–19; 30:16). Deuteronomy 7:11–16 even appears to look back to Exodus 15:26 when it states that one sign of the Lord's blessing for Israel's faithfulness is his healing of diseases that the Israelites knew in Egypt (Deut. 7:15). But it would be wrong to think their obedience somehow earns his love. As I wrote elsewhere on a related verse (Lev. 18:5), the Israelites were not

> in some way earning the LORD's *salvific* favor. As the larger context demonstrates, redemption (Ex. 1–19) comes *before* law (Ex. 20–23). Or, to put it the other way, "The law was given to the covenant people *after* their redemption from Egypt (Lev. 18:3), not as a moral hurdle they had to clear if they wished to be saved."
>
> What, then, is the relationship between [obedience] and [blessing]? God's law may be thought of as marking the borders of his kingdom or the borders of the fields in which he walks. Those who stay within the borders stay close to the King, maintaining fellowship with him and experiencing the blessings he loves to give to his faithful children. As Jesus said to his disciples, "If you keep my commandments, you will remain in my love, just as I have kept my Father's commandments and remain in his love" (John 15:10; see also John 14:21). Obedience is not about earning God's love but about remaining in his love and experiencing its rich rewards. Put differently, the Lord is a King who rescues out of sheer love and who delights to shower that love in blessings and rewards on his faithful children.[295]

In short this is a king who saves his servants in sheer love and then loves to reward their faithful service with good things.

15:27 As though to underscore how the Lord shows his care, the text mentions the Israelites' arrival at Elim, "where there were twelve springs of water," enough

---

[295] Sklar, *Leviticus*, ZECOT, 479; the quote is from Gordon J. Wenham, *The Book of Leviticus*, NICOT 3 (Grand Rapids, MI: Eerdmans, 1979), 261, emphasis mine.

to provide one spring for each tribe, "and seventy palm trees," with the number seventy having connotations of fullness and plenty (cf. note 56 within comment on 1:1–5). Even in the wilderness the Israelites can obey the Lord with full trust, knowing that he can provide abundantly for their needs.

Response

See Response section on 17:1–7.

EXODUS 16

16 They set out from Elim, and all the congregation of the people of Israel came to the wilderness of Sin, which is between Elim and Sinai, on the fifteenth day of the second month after they had departed from the land of Egypt. ²And the whole congregation of the people of Israel grumbled against Moses and Aaron in the wilderness, ³and the people of Israel said to them, "Would that we had died by the hand of the Lord in the land of Egypt, when we sat by the meat pots and ate bread to the full, for you have brought us out into this wilderness to kill this whole assembly with hunger."

⁴Then the Lord said to Moses, "Behold, I am about to rain bread from heaven for you, and the people shall go out and gather a day's portion every day, that I may test them, whether they will walk in my law or not. ⁵On the sixth day, when they prepare what they bring in, it will be twice as much as they gather daily." ⁶So Moses and Aaron said to all the people of Israel, "At evening you shall know that it was the Lord who brought you out of the land of Egypt, ⁷and in the morning you shall see the glory of the Lord, because he has heard your grumbling against the Lord. For what are we, that you grumble against us?" ⁸And Moses said, "When the Lord gives you in the evening meat to eat and in the morning bread to the full, because the Lord has heard your grumbling that you grumble against him—what are we? Your grumbling is not against us but against the Lord."

⁹Then Moses said to Aaron, "Say to the whole congregation of the people of Israel, 'Come near before the Lord, for he has heard your grumbling.'" ¹⁰And as soon as Aaron spoke to the whole congregation of the people of Israel, they looked toward the wilderness, and behold, the glory of the Lord appeared in the cloud. ¹¹And the Lord said to Moses, ¹²"I have heard the grumbling of the people of Israel. Say to them, 'At twilight you shall eat meat, and in the morning you shall be filled with bread. Then you shall know that I am the Lord your God.'"

¹³In the evening quail came up and covered the camp, and in the morning dew lay around the camp. ¹⁴And when the dew had gone up, there was on the face of the wilderness a fine, flake-like thing, fine as frost on the ground. ¹⁵When the people of Israel saw it, they said to one another, "What is it?"[1] For they did not know what it was. And Moses said to them, "It is the bread that the Lord has given you to eat. ¹⁶This is what the

Lord has commanded: 'Gather of it, each one of you, as much as he can eat. You shall each take an omer,[2] according to the number of the persons that each of you has in his tent.'" [17] And the people of Israel did so. They gathered, some more, some less. [18] But when they measured it with an omer, whoever gathered much had nothing left over, and whoever gathered little had no lack. Each of them gathered as much as he could eat. [19] And Moses said to them, "Let no one leave any of it over till the morning." [20] But they did not listen to Moses. Some left part of it till the morning, and it bred worms and stank. And Moses was angry with them. [21] Morning by morning they gathered it, each as much as he could eat; but when the sun grew hot, it melted.

[22] On the sixth day they gathered twice as much bread, two omers each. And when all the leaders of the congregation came and told Moses, [23] he said to them, "This is what the Lord has commanded: 'Tomorrow is a day of solemn rest, a holy Sabbath to the Lord; bake what you will bake and boil what you will boil, and all that is left over lay aside to be kept till the morning.'" [24] So they laid it aside till the morning, as Moses commanded them, and it did not stink, and there were no worms in it. [25] Moses said, "Eat it today, for today is a Sabbath to the Lord; today you will not find it in the field. [26] Six days you shall gather it, but on the seventh day, which is a Sabbath, there will be none."

[27] On the seventh day some of the people went out to gather, but they found none. [28] And the Lord said to Moses, "How long will you refuse to keep my commandments and my laws? [29] See! The Lord has given you the Sabbath; therefore on the sixth day he gives you bread for two days. Remain each of you in his place; let no one go out of his place on the seventh day." [30] So the people rested on the seventh day.

[31] Now the house of Israel called its name manna. It was like coriander seed, white, and the taste of it was like wafers made with honey. [32] Moses said, "This is what the Lord has commanded: 'Let an omer of it be kept throughout your generations, so that they may see the bread with which I fed you in the wilderness, when I brought you out of the land of Egypt.'" [33] And Moses said to Aaron, "Take a jar, and put an omer of manna in it, and place it before the Lord to be kept throughout your generations." [34] As the Lord commanded Moses, so Aaron placed it before the testimony to be kept. [35] The people of Israel ate the manna forty years, till they came to a habitable land. They ate the manna till they came to the border of the land of Canaan. [36] (An omer is the tenth part of an ephah.)[3]

[1] Or *"It is manna"*; Hebrew *man hu* [2] An *omer* was about 2 quarts or 2 liters [3] An *ephah* was about 3/5 bushel or 22 liters

Section Overview

As noted above (cf. Overview of 15:22–17:16), this is the second of three testing narratives in this section. In the previous narrative the Israelites lacked water to drink; in this one they lack food to eat. The narrative's overall outline is similar to the last's: the Israelites grumble (16:2–3), and the Lord miraculously and graciously provides for their needs (vv. 13–15). This account, like the last, also identifies a test the Lord makes of the Israelites (vv. 4, 16–21), one that some initially fail (vv. 19–21, 25–30). But this account also notes how Moses and Aaron rebuke the people for their grumbling, making clear such grumbling is ultimately against the Lord (vv. 7–8) and implicitly warning them not to repeat such wicked behavior. This narrative also provides the Israelites instructions for commemorating the Lord's faithful provision (vv. 31–36), just as they were to do by commemorating his faithful deliverance from Egypt (13:1–16). These requirements are no surprise: remembering the Lord's faithfulness in the past is one of the greatest means to encourage his people's obedient trust in the present.

Section Outline

III. Israel travels through the wilderness to Sinai: the Lord tests his people and provides for their needs (15:22–17:16)
    A. Three stories of testing and provision in the wilderness (15:22–17:7) . . .
        2. The Lord again tests the Israelites and provides for their needs (16:1–36)

Comment

16:1 Departing Elim, the Israelites travel toward Sinai and arrive at the Wilderness of Sin (v. 1). (The word "Sin" is simply a transcription of the place's Hebrew name; it is not connected to the English word "sin" in any way.) Since they departed Egypt on the evening of the fourteenth of the first month (12:2–6), their arrival here on the fifteenth of the second month means they have been traveling for one month. It also means the memories of the Lord's deliverance (12:29–36; 14:13–31) and provision (15:22–27) should be very fresh.

16:2–3 Nonetheless, a new trial leads to renewed grumbling (vv. 2–3). This is done by "the whole congregation," which aims complaints like missiles at Moses and Aaron, in effect saying, "It would have been better if the Lord had killed us with the Egyptians during the plagues! At least in Egypt we had plentiful food. Instead, you have brought us into the wilderness to kill us with famine!" The language may be hyperbolic, but the hyperbole underscores the Israelites' depth of emotion—and severe lack of faith. Fear and anxiety have many causes, but they are often rooted in a lack of trust in the Lord.

16:4–5 The Lord responds graciously. Instead of raining hail on them in judgment as he did to Egypt (9:18), he will rain a day's worth of bread from heaven for them to gather each day (16:4a). In doing so he will also test them to see whether they will obey him as covenant king (v. 4b; this recalls the theme of covenant obedience introduced at 15:25–26). We are not told what the test will be until later (16:22–26), but a clue is given: on the sixth day the Israelites will be able to gather two days' worth of food (v. 5).

16:6–8 When Moses and Aaron pass along the Lord's message, they begin by correcting the Israelites' narrative, saying in effect, "This evening, the Lord will do such a miracle that it will again become clear that he led you miraculously out of Egypt, not us! He will underscore this in the morning with another miracle that will make clear how worthy of glory he is!"[296] It is him you're grumbling against; we are nothing!" (vv. 6–7). Moses then underscores the same, this time explicitly naming the miracles that will provide exactly for the Israelites' needs (v. 8).

16:9–12 That Moses knows about meat and not just bread indicates that verses 4–5 is a summary of what the Lord says to Moses. The story now flashes back and gives the fuller picture (vv. 9–12). Moses had instructed Aaron to assemble the Israelites to receive a message from the Lord (v. 9). "As soon as Aaron spoke to the whole congregation … they looked toward the wilderness," where the pillar of cloud was, leading the camp,[297] "and behold, the glory of the LORD appeared in the cloud" (v. 10). If other appearances of the Lord's glory are any indication, the Israelites would have seen the cloud light up with flashes of lightning and divine fire so that it was abundantly clear the King of glory was now in their midst (cf. note 296 within comment on 16:6–8; cf. also 19:16–18; 20:18; 24:17). Moses presumably approaches the cloud, and the Lord states that he will provide meat and bread in such a way that the Israelites will "know that I am the LORD your God" (16:12), that is, they will come to know and acknowledge the Lord's character, and especially his power and might, in response to the miracle (cf. 6:7; 7:5, 17; 8:22; 10:1–2; 14:4, 18). In this case the Israelites will especially see how he uses his power on their behalf; he is not simply the Lord but the Lord *their* God. They should have already been convinced of this fact (cf. 6:7; 10:1–2), but "their grumbling indicates that they do not truly know him."[298] Like the Egyptians, they are slow to believe (cf. 7:5, 17; 8:22; 14:4, 18).

16:13–15 That evening the Lord provides meat by sending quail (v. 13). Just as he had judged Egypt by causing countless frogs and locusts to "come up" and "cover" the land (8:2; 10:14–15), he now blesses Israel by having countless quail "come up" and "cover" the camp (16:13). The next morning he provides bread by sending manna (vv. 13b–15). When the daily dew evaporates, "there was on the face of the wilderness a fine, flake-like thing, fine as frost on the ground" (v. 14). The Israelites have never seen it before ("They did not know what it was"), so Moses has to explain it is the Lord's provision of bread (v. 15). Various naturalistic attempts have been made to explain the manna, but none can account for the amounts produced (enough daily for the entire nation), the fact that it does not appear on the Sabbath (vv. 26–27), or the fact that it ceases on the day that Israel first eats of the Promised Land's produce (Josh. 5:12). God's miraculous intervention is thus clear. We later learn it is "like coriander seed," which is the light-colored seed of the

---

[296] The "glory of the LORD" can refer particularly to the Lord's spectacular display of his presence in the cloud (Ex. 16:10; 24:16–17; 40:34–35). This is called "the glory of the LORD" because the proper response to such an awesome display is to give him glory for his strength and majesty: "O most powerful LORD, worthy are you to receive all glory and honor and praise!" In this context "the glory of the LORD" refers to the miracle the Lord will perform that shows he is worthy of glory and praise; cf. Numbers 14:22, where "glory" and "signs" help explain one another; cf. John 11:40–44 (Bush, *Commentary on Exodus*, 204–205).
[297] Cassuto, *Commentary on the Book of Exodus*, 193–194.
[298] Alexander, *Exodus*, ApOTC, 323.

cilantro plant, like a peppercorn in size, "white, and the taste of it was like wafers made with honey" (Ex. 16:31; cf. Num. 11:7) and thus flavorful and sweet.[299] The Israelites learn various ways to prepare it for eating (Ex. 16:23; Num. 11:8). Its name in Hebrew is *man* (no relation to the English word "man"), which appears to be a variant of the Hebrew for "what" and is linked to their original response to seeing it: "What is it?" (*man hu*; Ex. 16:15; cf. v. 31).[300]

16:16–21 The Lord then provides two sets of instructions for collecting the manna. As indicated earlier, these instructions will be a means to test whether Israel will trust and obey the Lord (v. 4). The first set of instructions concerns the daily gathering of manna (vv. 16–21). Every day the Israelites are to gather enough for the daily eating needs of everyone in their household,[301] estimated roughly at one omer per person (v. 16).[302]

"And the people of Israel did so" (v. 17), that is, they followed these instructions to the letter. Some gather more (if they have larger households) and others less (if they have smaller households), but they both gather exactly what they need (vv. 17–18).[303]

But the obedience of some is short lived. Moses commands not to save any manna for the next day (v. 19). Not doing so is part of the test, because it will require the Israelites to trust the Lord to provide their daily bread. "Some," however, "left part of it till the morning, and it bred worms and stank" (v. 20). This spoilage shows in dramatic fashion the futility of not trusting the Lord or obeying his word. Indeed, the manna's stinking replicates what happened to the Nile in the first strike (7:18, 21) and to the land in the second (8:14). It is as though Israel has invited the Lord's judgment into their midst, and Moses is understandably angered by their disobedience (cf. Ex. 32:19; Num. 31:14–16). The paragraph's concluding verse adds a detail ("When the sun grew hot, [the manna] melted")[304] but otherwise suggests that the Israelites learn their lesson and go back to gathering a day's worth each morning obediently (Ex. 16:21).

16:22–26 While the first set of instructions concerns gathering manna daily (vv. 16–21), the second set concerns collecting manna on the sixth day. Earlier the

---

[299] Cf. Numbers 11:7–8, where it is compared to the flavorful taste of cakes made with oil, which, as a fat, adds a sweet creaminess.
[300] English "manna" is built on the root *man* and perhaps comes via the LXX, which sometimes renders Hebrew *man* as *manna* (Wells, *Exodus*, 220).
[301] "As much as he can eat" in the Hebrew is more woodenly "according to the proportion of his eating," that is, as much as a person typically eats in a day (not as much as a person can possibly eat in a day).
[302] Estimates of modern equivalents for the omer range from 1–3.5 quarts (1.2–3.9 l); cf. E. M. Cook, "Weights and Measures," *ISBE* 4:1051, with Jacob Milgrom, *Leviticus 1–16*, AYB (New Haven, CT: Yale University Press, 1998), 895. An ephah is a tenth of a homer (Ezek. 45:11) and the omer a tenth of an ephah (Ex. 16:36) and thus a hundredth of a homer (Cook, "Weights and Measures," *ISBE* 4:1051).
[303] The English of Exodus 16:17–18 could read as though some gathered *too* much or little, with the amounts then miraculously evening out. The obedience formula at the beginning of verse 17, however, points in the direction above (so also Cassuto, *Commentary on the Book of Exodus*, 197; Stuart, *Exodus*, 379). In this regard verse 18 could read, "And they measured with an omer so that the one gathering much did not exceed and the one gathering little did not lack; each person gathered according to the proportion of his eating." Paul later cites verse 18 when encouraging generosity (2 Cor. 8:15), his point being that, when God's people see their brothers and sisters in need, they do not hoard their resources but share so that there is provision for all (cf. Alexander, *Exodus*, ApOTC, 330).
[304] This detail may be to explain why it is gathered in the morning (Keil, *Exodus*, vol. 2, 68) or to make clear the manna is provided fresh each day (Houtman, *Exodus*, vol. 2, 345).

Lord commanded the Israelites to collect twice as much manna on the sixth day, but no rationale was given (v. 5). Here the Israelites obey the command, the leaders report this to Moses (v. 22), and he gives the rationale (v. 23). The seventh day is a day of "rest" (Hb. *shabbaton*), a holy "Sabbath" (*shabbat*) to the Lord. Both words are built on the same root, which refers to "rest," pointing to the fact that rest is at the Sabbath's heart; no work is to be done on it. Consequently the Israelites must prepare two days' worth of food on the sixth day and, unlike on the other days, leave a portion for the next day (the Sabbath). This will provide them with food to eat that day without having to work to prepare it.

The word "Sabbath" occurs here for the first time in the Bible. And since Moses is just now explaining how it relates to the command to gather two days' worth of food on the sixth day, it seems the Israelites are learning of the Sabbath for the first time. As such, this passage anticipates the fuller giving of the Sabbath law in 20:8–11, which explains more fully that the Israelites are to rest on the Sabbath in imitation and honor of the Lord, the one who rested on the seventh day of creation (cf. comment on 20:8–11). Even here, however, the phrase "holy Sabbath *to the Lord*" communicates that the Israelites are to keep this day holy to honor and recognize him as their covenant God (cf. Lev. 23:3, 5, 6, 34, 41; 25:2).

The Israelites obey (Ex. 16:24). Unlike what occurred when they saved food disobediently (v. 20), this food keeps perfectly. Moses then underscores that the seventh day is a Sabbath to the Lord and therefore on it no manna will be found (vv. 25–26). There is no point in trying to gather on this day; resting in honor of the Lord is what they must do.

16:27–30 Once again, however, some Israelites disobey, going out to collect on the seventh day but finding none (v. 27). Earlier the Lord rebuked Pharaoh for his disobedience by asking, "*How long will you refuse* to humble yourself before me?" (10:3). This time he rebukes his people with the same language: "*How long will you refuse*[305] to keep my commandments and my laws?" (16:28). This is an ominous warning: the Israelites are treading the same rebellious ground as Pharaoh. The Lord's commands are a test to see whether they will honor him as the God worthy of their obedience (v. 4), and this is the second time some of them have failed the test (cf. v. 20). This is not a promising start.

The Lord goes on to explain that he himself has given them the Sabbath to observe, implying that obedience is required, not optional. But he also notes how he graciously provides so they might rest on the Sabbath instead of going out to gather (v. 29).[306] Thankfully, the people take the Lord's words to heart (v. 30).

16:31–36 As verses 34–35 suggests, the narrator now jumps forward in time, continuing the focus on manna by describing what the Lord later commands the Israelites to do to preserve their memory of it (for other places where the narrator

---

305 The verb is plural; the rebuke is spoken to Moses as the Israelites' leader but is meant for the Israelites.
306 The context makes clear the Lord is not prohibiting them from leaving their homes on the Sabbath but prohibiting them from leaving their homes *to gather manna* (Bush, *Commentary on Exodus*, 212).

jumps forward in time cf. Deut. 3:14; Josh. 4:9; 8:28; 13:13). The passage begins with a brief description of its name, appearance, and taste (Ex. 16:31; cf. comment on 16:13–15), then Moses commands the Israelites and Aaron to preserve some for posterity. They are to take an omer of manna—the exact amount the Lord has provided each day for every Israelite—and keep it so that future generations can see the bread with which the Lord blessed them when he rescued them from Egypt (v. 32). The Lord wants his people to remember not only his mighty acts of rescuing them but also his daily acts of providing for their needs.

In terms of keeping the manna Moses instructs Aaron to put it in a jar and "place it before the LORD" (v. 33), which implies placing it in the tabernacle (cf. the use of "before the LORD" in 27:21; 28:29, 30, 35; etc.). This is confirmed when we read that "Aaron placed it before the testimony" (16:34), that is, in front of the ark of the covenant, which rested in the Most Holy Place and contained the covenant law, which was known also as "the testimony" (25:16, 21; 31:18).[307] Given that the Israelites are to "see" it (16:32), it must have been brought out on occasion (perhaps when the tabernacle was taken down and moved) and used as a visual aid when the story of the Lord's provision of manna was retold and embedded in the nation's memory.

We learn that the Israelites will eat the manna until they come to the promised "land of Canaan" (v. 35), here identified as a "habitable land," or an "inhabited land," another possible translation. In either case the land stands in stark contrast to the wilderness, and arriving there marks the end of the Israelites' wanderings, which last forty years (cf. Num. 14:33–34). During this time the Lord will provide bountifully for their daily needs (cf. Deut. 2:7). Once in Canaan, a land flowing with milk and honey, he will provide from its produce to feed them (Ex. 16:35; cf. Josh. 5:12). The chapter closes with a notation about the size of the omer in comparison to the ephah (Ex. 16:36; cf. note 302 within comment on 16:16–21), perhaps added for later readers familiar with the latter measurement but not the former (for further discussion cf. Introduction: Author and Date: Who Put the Material in Its Final Form?).

Response

See Response section on 17:1–7.

---

[307] At a later point in history it seems the jar of manna is put in the ark, as is Aaron's rod (cf. Num. 17:10; Heb. 9:4). "Later reference to the tablets bearing the Ten Commandments as the only contents of the ark may have suggested that something else had once also been located therein" (Cockerill, *Epistle to the Hebrews*, 377–378, citing 1 Kings 8:9 [// 2 Chron. 5:10]).

EXODUS 17:1–7

17 All the congregation of the people of Israel moved on from the wilderness of Sin by stages, according to the commandment of the Lord, and camped at Rephidim, but there was no water for the people to drink. ² Therefore the people quarreled with Moses and said, "Give us water to drink." And Moses said to them, "Why do you quarrel with me? Why do you test the Lord?" ³ But the people thirsted there for water, and the people grumbled against Moses and said, "Why did you bring us up out of Egypt, to kill us and our children and our livestock with thirst?" ⁴ So Moses cried to the Lord, "What shall I do with this people? They are almost ready to stone me." ⁵ And the Lord said to Moses, "Pass on before the people, taking with you some of the elders of Israel, and take in your hand the staff with which you struck the Nile, and go. ⁶ Behold, I will stand before you there on the rock at Horeb, and you shall strike the rock, and water shall come out of it, and the people will drink." And Moses did so, in the sight of the elders of Israel. ⁷ And he called the name of the place Massah[1] and Meribah,[2] because of the quarreling of the people of Israel, and because they tested the Lord by saying, "Is the Lord among us or not?"

[1] *Massah* means *testing* [2] *Meribah* means *quarreling*

Section Overview

This is the third of three testing narratives in this section (cf. Overview of 15:22–17:16). Similarly to the previous two, the people have a need, doubt the Lord's goodness, and then see him miraculously and graciously provide. Unlike in the previous two, in which the Lord tested his people, this time the people test the Lord—an act universally condemned in the Bible as a sign of unbelief (cf. 17:2). Indeed, whereas the last passage ended by commemorating the Lord's faithfulness (16:31–36), this passage ends by commemorating the people's faithlessness (17:7), a tragic reminder of what rebellious unbelief looks like in action. The Lord is to be trusted, not tested.

Section Outline

    III. Israel travels through the wilderness to Sinai: the Lord tests his people and provides for their needs (15:22–17:16)
        A. Three stories of testing and provision in the wilderness (15:22–17:7) . . .
            3. The Israelites test the Lord and he provides for their needs (17:1–7)

Comment

17:1–7 The Israelites continue their travels, eventually arriving at Rephidim (v. 1; cf. Num. 33:12–14 for the different stages of their travel). Once more they cannot find water to drink (17:1; cf. 15:22–23), but, since they have come here "according to the commandment of the LORD," they should not fear. Considering how the Lord has so recently provided for their needs of both water (15:25–27) and food (16:1–36), they have every reason to pray expectantly and hopefully for his help.

Instead they "quarreled with Moses" about the lack of water (17:2a), that is, they argue heatedly with him over it (cf. the use of the same verb in Gen. 26:20–22; 31:36 ["berated"]; Ex. 21:18). Just as they had accused him of bringing them out of Egypt to kill them with hunger (cf. comment on 16:2–3), they now accuse him of doing so to kill them with thirst (17:3). And just as Moses had told them their real complaint was against the Lord (16:7–8), he now tells them the same is true here (17:2). Indeed, whereas the Lord was the one "testing" Israel in the previous two scenes to see whether they would trust him obediently (15:25–26; 16:4), now the Israelites are "testing" him to see whether he is faithful. Biblically speaking, God's testing of his people is ultimately for their good and is thus seen positively (Deut. 8:16; cf. Response section below, "Why Does God Test His People?"); the people's testing of God expresses unbelief in his presence and care (cf. Ex. 17:7) and is thus seen negatively (Num. 14:22–23; Pss. 78:41; 95:9; 106:14; etc.). Moses will in fact refer to this very incident when he later commands Israel never to test the Lord (Deut. 6:16), a verse Jesus himself quotes when rebuking the devil (Matt. 4:7).

The people's grumbling and anger are so severe that Moses feels his life is at risk, and so he again cries out to the Lord, asking what he (Moses) could do to address their concerns (Ex. 17:4; cf. 15:25).[308] His question is really a plea for help: "What can I do for this people? Nothing! I cannot give them water! I need your help, O Lord!" The Lord tells him to pass on ahead of the people and take some of the elders, who on the people's behalf will witness what is about to occur (17:5–6). He also stresses that Moses is to bring the staff with which he struck the Nile (v. 5; cf. 7:20), that is, the staff of God through which the Lord performed miraculous signs (cf. comment on 4:18–20). This time, instead of striking the Nile and turning its waters putrid, Moses is to strike a rock so that fresh waters will flow from it (17:6). This will take place at a rock in the Horeb region (cf. comment on 3:1–3 and note 82), presumably ahead of the camp, where the Lord will "stand,"[309] manifesting his presence in a spectacular way at the rock so that it is clear that he is the one causing water to flow from it like a river.[310]

---

[308] "What shall I do *with* this people?" could also be translated "What shall I do *for* this people?" (Cf. Gen. 30:31; 42:25; Ex. 14:13; 18:14.)

[309] The phrase "to stand before" can describe one person's having an audience with a more prominent person, whether human (Gen. 43:15) or divine (Gen. 18:22), but also can have "the sense 'to be in the service of,' e.g. of a king (1 Sam. 16:22 . . .) and of God (1 Kings 17:1 . . .)" (Houtman, *Exodus*, vol. 2, 364). Here it could have the second sense (the Lord is indicating he will help Moses) or it may simply be the most natural way to describe that, physically speaking, the Lord's presence has moved on ahead of Moses and will be standing before him when Moses arrives.

[310] While naturalistic explanations of this passage are sometimes offered (e.g., Sarna, *Exodus*, 94), and the Lord does use natural means elsewhere (cf. comment on 7:14–11:10), the text makes no comment one way

Moses obeys the Lord's command in front of Israel's elders, who will be able to report to Israel the miraculous deed (17:6).[311] The miracle could have led to the place's being called "Glory" or "The Lord Provides" but instead it is called "Massah" (i.e., "Testing") and "Meribah" (i.e., "Quarreling"), etching the Israelites' sinful behavior into the nation's collective memory (v. 7). In light of all the Lord has done for them, to ask "Is the LORD among us or not?" is the height of faithless unbelief, and the location's name stands as a sad warning not to follow this example (cf. Deut. 6:16; Ps. 95:8; Heb. 3:8).

Response

WHY DOES GOD TEST HIS PEOPLE?

It is one thing to profess faith and love for God but quite another to trust and love him in real life. Tests of faith help to show whether our profession matches our behavior (Deut. 8:2; 13:3; Judg. 2:21–22; 3:1–4). As in our passage, the test often consists of a difficult situation requiring obedient faith (Gen. 22:1–2; Deut. 8:2, 16). True faithfulness is shown not when obedience is easy but when it is hard. Will we follow God not only when the sun shines but also when dark clouds gather? True faith shows itself most clearly when we march on during the storm, "looking to Jesus, the founder and perfecter of our faith, who for the joy that was set before him endured the cross" (Heb. 12:2).

But testing not only gives us an opportunity to show faithfulness; it also helps us to become more faithful. Moses later explains that the Israelites were tested in order to humble them, putting them into situations where their self-reliance was shown to be bankrupt (Deut. 8:2–3, 16). Such humbling is never easy. It involves dying to self and can make it feel like our bones are being broken. But God does not break his people's bones to cause pain; he does so to straighten their crooked limbs. This is why testing is described as doing Israel "good in the end" (Deut. 8:16). The humbling is meant to help them to stop living as though they are their own saviors and to start living with the Lord as their Savior (Deut. 8:3). Indeed, as the testing narratives in Exodus 15–17 make clear, the Lord is present during the test all along, ready to help, strengthen, and deliver. In short, tests are meant to rescue us from foolish self-reliance and to bring us to reliance on the God who faithfully walks with us in our trials. This is the lesson Paul would learn. During a trial that made his weakness clear, he came to rejoice because the trial also helped him to experience the grace and strength of Christ to make him strong (2 Cor. 12:7–10; cf. Heb. 12:4–11; James 1:2–4).

All this should lead us to ask, How am I responding to the trials in my life right now? Can I see ways the Lord might be humbling me through this and wanting me to learn to rely on him instead of myself? These are the questions the Israelites should have been asking themselves, but sadly they did not.

---

or the other as to whether he does so here. What it does do, by highlighting the staff and the Lord's standing on the rock, is to stress that this is his miraculous provision.

311 Not stated is whether the waters flow back to the people or the people advance and catch up to Moses and the elders. In either case the point is that the elders witness the miraculous origin of the provision of water.

HOW DO THE ISRAELITES RESPOND TO THESE TESTS?

In each of the three scenes the Israelites respond to the test by grumbling or quarreling (Ex. 15:24; 16:2; 17:2). While they aim their complaints at Moses, he makes clear that they are actually complaining about the Lord (16:7–8; 17:2). It was the Lord who had led them out of Egypt, and it was his pillar of cloud and fire that is leading them through the wilderness. This, too, is a reminder: if God really is the sovereign King, grumbling or complaining is something we ultimately do against him.

The Israelites' complaints are especially tragic considering what has recently occurred. The Lord heard their cries for help in Egypt and delivered them through miraculous and unheard-of strikes against the land. He then came down in a pillar of cloud and fire and led them out of that land and remained among them as a faithful guide. He divided the sea in two so that they could walk safely through, and then he destroyed the most powerful army on earth in order to protect them. And, even after he provides for their thirst and hunger in the first two narratives, they are still complaining in the third.

In fact, it is worse, for now they put God to the test, asking, "Is the LORD among us or not?" (17:7). Their question differs from those in lament psalms. There the psalmists ask similar questions but from a posture of belief; they seek to understand as they remember the goodness of God's character and deeds. Not surprisingly, their prayers typically end with affirmations that God is good and can be trusted (Psalm 13 is a classic example, though cf. Psalms 3–7; 9–10; 22; 25; 27–28; etc.). In this text the Israelites' posture is rebellious unbelief, as they choose to ignore or forget what they have learned about God's good character and deeds. As a result, they look at their difficulty and conclude God cannot be good and therefore cannot be trusted—unless he meets their demands to show them otherwise. This is the wrong posture for the creation to take before its Creator, and numerous passages use this and similar passages to warn that testing God is something his people must never do (Num. 14:22–23; Deut. 6:16; Pss. 78:17–20, 40–41, 56; 95:7–11; 106:13–15; Matt. 4:7; Heb. 3:7–12).

Sadly, the Israelites' complaining is accompanied by disobedience, especially in the second narrative, in which the Lord issues very specific commands about not leaving any manna for the next day (Ex. 16:16, 19) and not collecting any manna on the seventh (vv. 5, 23, 25–26). Following these commands takes obedient trust, since the natural instinct in the wilderness would be to gather as much food as possible while it is available and to ration what one gathers. This is in fact what some of the Israelites do (vv. 20, 27–29). When choosing between trusting God's commands versus following their natural intuitions, their intuitions win out.

This is not simply an ancient problem.

> The same sort of challenge exists today. If people think God demands a behavior that runs against their intuitive sense of what is right, or pleasurable, or reasonable, or just "not so bad" (sex out of marriage, e.g.), it is

easy for them not to take a commandment seriously, which (although few realize it) is the same as not taking God seriously.[312]

Are there ways in which we might be following the footsteps of the Israelites? In every culture certain parts of the Bible will feel unnatural, even counterintuitive. How is this the case in our culture? The life of faith is one that evaluates culture in light of biblical standards, not the Bible in light of cultural standards. The Israelites struggle with this, which leads to a final question.

HOW DOES THE LORD RESPOND TO THE ISRAELITES?

Fortunately, the Lord responds to his slow-to-believe people with tremendous grace. This can be seen in two ways. First, he withholds punishment for their complaints and disobedience. In later passages the Lord will respond to complaints and disobedience with strong discipline (Num. 11:1–3, 33–34; 14:20–23, 26–37; etc.). In these three accounts, however, he does not. This is similar to Exodus 3–4, in which the Lord responds very patiently with Moses' reluctance to obey—up to a point (cf. 3:1–4:13 with 4:14–17). Like a good parent, the Lord eventually meets disobedience with discipline but begins with patience and grace as the child is learning to obey. Here the Israelites are in their infancy in their relationship with the Lord, and he responds patiently to their childlike complaining and disobedience.

But the Lord also provides bountifully for their physical needs, turning bitter waters sweet (15:25, 27), raining meat and bread into the camp (16:13–15), giving them a day of rest (16:23), and causing water to pour out of the rock (17:5–6). Not surprisingly, later OT writers look back on these events and break out in praise and thanksgiving for how lavishly the Lord provides for his people's material needs (Neh. 9:15; Pss. 78:15–16, 20, 23–25; 105:40–41; 114:8; Isa. 48:21).

In the NT at least two passages look back on some of the same events and see them as early signs of how the Lord will lavishly provide for our spiritual needs in Jesus. The first is very brief and found in 1 Corinthians 10:4, where "Paul alludes to this passage, implying that when the Israelites physically drank and ate in the wilderness, they shared spiritually with those who centuries later would feast on Christ."[313] In short the provision of manna points to the provision of life in Jesus. The second passage, which is more extended, does the same. As John 6 begins, Jesus miraculously provides bread for a large crowd (John 6:1–13). The next day the crowd asks him to do the same and refers to the manna provided in the wilderness (John 6:30–31). Jesus responds, "I am the bread of life; whoever comes to me shall not hunger, and whoever believes in me shall never thirst" (John 6:35). Once more the manna points ahead to Jesus. There is a hunger of the soul that can be satisfied only in him. Just as our stomachs need the nourishment that only food provides, so our souls need the nourishment that only Jesus provides. Our temptation is to attempt to satisfy that hunger with earthly things, which Jesus

---

312 Stuart, *Exodus*, 375.
313 Alexander, *Exodus*, ApOTC, 336.

warns against in this passage: "Do not work for the food that perishes, but for the food that endures to eternal life, which the Son of Man will give to you" (John 6:27; cf. 6:49–51).

That God provides such sustenance for us in Jesus testifies again to his lavish provision for our needs, which brings us full circle to the issue of testing. If God has provided for our deepest needs so richly in Jesus, is he not worthy of our trust in the face of current trials? As Paul asks,

> He who did not spare his own Son but gave him up for us all, how will he not also with him graciously give us all things? . . . Who shall separate us from the love of Christ? Shall tribulation, or distress, or persecution, or famine, or nakedness, or danger, or sword? . . . No, in all these things we are more than conquerors through him who loved us. For I am sure that neither death nor life, nor angels nor rulers, nor things present nor things to come, nor powers, nor height nor depth, nor anything else in all creation, will be able to separate us from the love of God in Christ Jesus our Lord. (Rom. 8:32, 35, 37–39)

No matter what trial may come, we know that the love the Father has shown us in Christ has not left us and never will. And that is why we can continue to trust and obey.

EXODUS 17:8–16

⁸ Then Amalek came and fought with Israel at Rephidim. ⁹ So Moses said to Joshua, "Choose for us men, and go out and fight with Amalek. Tomorrow I will stand on the top of the hill with the staff of God in my hand." ¹⁰ So Joshua did as Moses told him, and fought with Amalek, while Moses, Aaron, and Hur went up to the top of the hill. ¹¹ Whenever Moses held up his hand, Israel prevailed, and whenever he lowered his hand, Amalek prevailed. ¹² But Moses' hands grew weary, so they took a stone and put it under him, and he sat on it, while Aaron and Hur held up his hands, one on one side, and the other on the other side. So his hands were steady until the going down of the sun. ¹³ And Joshua overwhelmed Amalek and his people with the sword.

¹⁴ Then the Lord said to Moses, "Write this as a memorial in a book and recite it in the ears of Joshua, that I will utterly blot out the memory of Amalek from under heaven." ¹⁵ And Moses built an altar and called the name of it, The Lord Is My Banner, ¹⁶ saying, "A hand upon the throne¹ of the Lord! The Lord will have war with Amalek from generation to generation."

¹ A slight change would yield *upon the banner*

Section Overview

In the previous three narratives the Israelites had to trust that the Lord would provide for material needs (Ex. 15:22–17:7). In this narrative they must trust that he will help them defeat an enemy. The account is told very efficiently. The Amalekites come to attack (17:8), and Moses gives Joshua battle commands while also indicating that the Lord will help (v. 9). The battle is engaged (v. 10a), and the text then slows down, drawing special attention to Moses' actions with the staff of God (vv. 10b–12). The Lord's help in winning the battle is thus highlighted. With the battle won (v. 13) the text again slows down to focus on the importance of commemorating the Lord as the Israelite's help (v. 15) and especially on his ongoing hostility to Amalek (vv. 14, 16).

Section Outline

   III. Israel travels through the wilderness to Sinai: the Lord tests his people and provides for their needs (15:22–17:16)...
      B. Israel defeats Amalek with the Lord's help (17:8–16)
         1. Amalek comes to war against Israel (17:8)
         2. Moses gives Joshua battle commands (17:9)
         3. The battle takes place and the Lord gives Israel victory (17:10–13)
         4. The event's commemoration (17:14–16)

Comment

17:8 As the Israelites are camping at Rephidim, the Amalekites come to wage war against them (v. 8). Geographically, the Amalekites are associated with the Negeb (in Canaan's south; Num. 13:29) and Edom (just east of the Negeb; Gen. 36:16); both locations are east of Israel's current encampment. Relationally, the Amalekites come from Esau's descendants (Gen. 36:12), making them the Israelites' distant cousins, which might suggest they should interact as family. Instead the Amalekites come to make war, and this will be the first time since leaving Egypt that the Israelites will have to engage in battle. The stakes are high. Whatever happens here might foreshadow, positively or negatively, what will happen when the Israelites have to fight in the Promised Land.

17:9 Moses commands Joshua to choose men who can engage Amalek in battle the next day. This is the first mention of Joshua; later texts will let us know that as a young man he became Moses' helper (Num. 11:28), that he is young in this passage (cf. Ex. 33:11), and that he is evidently courageous (Num. 13:16), as we also see here. While Joshua leads the troops to battle, Moses will go to a hill overlooking the battle and take with him the staff with which he has performed miracles on the Lord's behalf (cf. comment on 4:18–20). Joshua and the Israelites are to fight, but the Lord will in some way also fight for them.

17:10–13 On the next day Joshua leads the Israelite army into battle while Moses goes to the hilltop with Aaron and Hur (v. 10). This is also the first mention of Hur;

later texts make clear that he is one of Israel's top leaders (24:14) and belongs to Judah's tribe (31:2; 1 Chron. 2:3–5, 18–19). Alongside Aaron's his role is likewise crucial. Whenever Moses lifts his hands with the staff, Israel prevails, but whenever he grows tired and lowers his hands, Amalek prevails (Ex. 17:11). Aaron and Hur therefore place Moses on a stone so that they can stand on either side and keep his hands and the staff lifted all day long. As a result, Joshua and the Israelites soundly defeat Amalek (vv. 12–13).

Such a path to victory might strike some moderns as primitive magic, but this would be to miss the event's symbolism. Outstretched hands are a common sign of prayer (1 Kings 8:22; Ps. 143:6; Isa. 1:15), and the "staff of God," as its name implies, represents the Lord's power and presence among his people (cf. comment on 4:18–20). The events on the hill will make clear to the Israelites that they must depend continually on the Lord's power and presence in their midst; without him they should expect nothing but defeat (cf. the similar event in Josh. 8:18–26). Indeed, the text's entire focus is not on Israel's fighting but on what is taking place with the staff of God on the hill.[314] He is the one fighting this battle through them.

17:14–16 With the victory won the Lord commands Moses to record it in a book (i.e., a scroll) so that it can be remembered (Ex. 17:14). He especially wants to make sure that Joshua is aware that in response to the Amalekites' actions the Lord plans to wipe them off the face of the map[315] (and thus Joshua should not attempt to engage in peaceful relations with them, v. 14; cf. Response section).

After the victory Moses builds an altar (v. 15). The Israelites' forefathers did this often, usually in response to the Lord's making his presence known in a special way or answering a prayer (Gen. 12:7, 8; 13:4, 18; 26:24–25; 33:18–20; 35:1, 3, 7; cf. Ex. 24:4–5). The altar serves to commemorate the event and also to provide Israel a place to offer sacrificial worship, which Moses presumably does here. He names the altar "The LORD Is My Banner" (17:15). In the ancient Near East a "banner" (or "standard" or "signal") was a rallying sign to which members of a people or fighting force could flee, finding safety in the company of those gathering to it and marching forward under it (Isa. 31:9; Jer. 4:21). To say "the LORD is my banner" is to say that he is his people's leader, the one they rally around, and that he will go before his people as they face the foe.

Debate surrounds the beginning of Exodus 17:16, since the Hebrew is somewhat unclear. Some versions understand it to refer to the taking of an oath; the verse's second half would then be the content of the oath.[316] Others understand it to refer to opposition (from Amalek) against the Lord, which then explains the penalty in the verse's second half.[317] Whatever the case may be, the verse ends clearly, stating that "the LORD will have war with Amalek from generation to generation"

---

[314] Enns, *Exodus*, 348.
[315] "Utterly blot out" well translates the emphasis of the Hebrew.
[316] So NASB, NET; ESV preserves the ambiguity.
[317] NIV, NLT. Still others amend the text from "throne" (Hb. *kes*) to "banner" (*nes*) (NRSV, NJB; cf. esp. Childs, *Book of Exodus*, 311–312; cf. ESV mg.), suggesting that the Lord's banner should be seized in the hand as one goes out to battle Amalek.

(v. 16), that is, they will face his opposition in the coming generations. This is to encourage the Lord's people that he himself will wage war against their enemies. He is their banner; let them follow him in faith.

Response

HOW IS THIS STORY A WARNING?

The closing verses of this text make crystal clear that the Lord intends to bring the Amalekite nation to an end (vv. 14–16). Why such a severe response?

Moses helps answer this question in Deuteronomy: "Remember what Amalek did to you on the way as you came out of Egypt, how he attacked you on the way when you were faint and weary, and cut off your tail, those who were lagging behind you, and he did not fear God" (Deut. 25:17–18; our passage presumably picks up on events the next day, after this cowardly attack). As Christopher Wright observes,

> Those lagging behind would have been the elderly and the very young, the sick, pregnant women, etc. To attack such defenseless people is a sign of extreme human callousness, which in turn is evidence of no fear of God. [Note] that noncovenant nations are still assumed to be morally accountable to God for fundamental norms of human behavior. The Amalekites are to be judged, then, not just because they had been *anti-Israel*, but because they had been *anti-human* by disregarding basic human obligations instilled by the creator God.[318]

Wright's observations are in keeping with other verses that speak of the ways in which "the law is written on [our] hearts" (Rom. 2:15)—that is, God has wired us to know fundamental norms of right and wrong and will hold us accountable for disregarding them (cf. 2:16 and also 1:19–32). The Amalekites experienced such judgment in severe measure, which strongly warns of what to expect if we disregard the moral fabric that God has woven into his world. He has created this to be a world of goodness, justice, mercy, and love—a world that reflects his own glory and is for humanity's blessing. His commitment to such a world means that those who destroy it can expect his judgment, whether in this life or the next.

But the Amalekites are not simply a warning. Defeating the Amalekites was also meant to be a strong encouragement to the Israelites.

HOW IS THIS STORY AN ENCOURAGEMENT?

At this point in their history the Israelites are on their way to the Promised Land. They know the land is already inhabited (Ex. 3:8; 13:5) and can anticipate that they will have to engage in battles there (cf. 23:22–30). How will those go? How can the Israelites, who have been enslaved with no experience in battle, ever hope to defeat nations far more experienced in warfare?

This passage anticipates those questions and provides a reassuring answer. The army's leader is Joshua, which is significant since he will later lead the Israelites

---

[318] Christopher J. H. Wright, *Deuteronomy*, NIBC 4 (Peabody, MA: Hendrickson, 1996), 267–268, emphasis original. Cf. 1 Samuel 15 for the next time that the Lord returns to the judgment decreed here.

in their initial battles in the Promised Land. Whatever happens here is what the Israelites can expect to happen there. While Joshua and chosen Israelites go into battle, Moses, Aaron, and Hur climb a hill overlooking the battlefield. As noted above, the text focuses on their activity and especially on how the Israelites are successful in battle whenever Moses lifts his hands (a posture of prayer) and holds the "staff of God" (signifying the Lord's help and power; cf. comments on 17:9; 17:10–13). The message is clear: Joshua and his men may fight, but they succeed only with the Lord's help.

The text thus refutes the mistake of those who say that everything is up to God and therefore human activity and agency are unimportant. On the contrary Joshua and his men must take up arms! But the text also refutes the mistake of those who say that everything is up to us. Joshua and his men are successful only when the Lord fights through them.

The lesson for us is twofold: our agency really does matter, and we are to look to the Lord for his help and strength in the tasks of our hands. Paul understands this twofold lesson very well. He describes in a profound way his labors of helping people mature in their faith: "For this *I toil*, struggling with all *his energy* that *he powerfully works within me*" (Col. 1:29). Paul is toiling and struggling but doing so in Jesus' strength (cf. Phil. 4:13).

We do well to ask ourselves, Am I more likely to think that my agency does not matter, or I am more likely to think that everything is up to me? If I think my agency does not matter, what does it look like to take my agency and God's call to contribute to his world seriously—to toil on his behalf? If I think everything is up to me, what does it look like to depend more on Jesus—to toil in his strength? We might not have a military battle to fight, but, whatever our calling, God gives us the privilege of representing him in this world and the courage to do so because he makes his strength and help available to us.

OVERVIEW OF

EXODUS 18–19

Chapters 18–19 transition the narrative from the Lord's deliverance (chs. 1–17) to his giving of the law (chs. 20–23). Chapter 18 highlights the Lord's deliverance (vv. 1–12) before explaining how the coming covenant law will be administered (vv. 13–27). Chapter 19 then describes the Israelites' accepting the Lord's invitation to covenant relationship (vv. 1–8) and how he appears in order to give his covenant law to them through his servant Moses (vv. 9–25). The stage is now set for the covenant law to be given (chs. 20–23).

EXODUS 18

18 Jethro, the priest of Midian, Moses' father-in-law, heard of all that God had done for Moses and for Israel his people, how the Lord had brought Israel out of Egypt. ² Now Jethro, Moses' father-in-law, had taken Zipporah, Moses' wife, after he had sent her home, ³ along with her two sons. The name of the one was Gershom (for he said, "I have been a sojourner[1] in a foreign land"), ⁴ and the name of the other, Eliezer[2] (for he said, "The God of my father was my help, and delivered me from the sword of Pharaoh"). ⁵ Jethro, Moses' father-in-law, came with his sons and his wife to Moses in the wilderness where he was encamped at the mountain of God. ⁶ And when he sent word to Moses, "I,[3] your father-in-law Jethro, am coming to you with your wife and her two sons with her," ⁷ Moses went out to meet his father-in-law and bowed down and kissed him. And they asked each other of their welfare and went into the tent. ⁸ Then Moses told his father-in-law all that the Lord had done to Pharaoh and to the Egyptians for Israel's sake, all the hardship that had come upon them in the way, and how the Lord had delivered them. ⁹ And Jethro rejoiced for all the good that the Lord had done to Israel, in that he had delivered them out of the hand of the Egyptians.

¹⁰ Jethro said, "Blessed be the Lord, who has delivered you out of the hand of the Egyptians and out of the hand of Pharaoh and has delivered the people from under the hand of the Egyptians. ¹¹ Now I know that the Lord is greater than all gods, because in this affair they dealt arrogantly with the people."[4] ¹² And Jethro, Moses' father-in-law, brought a burnt offering and sacrifices to God; and Aaron came with all the elders of Israel to eat bread with Moses' father-in-law before God.

¹³ The next day Moses sat to judge the people, and the people stood around Moses from morning till evening. ¹⁴ When Moses' father-in-law saw all that he was doing for the people, he said, "What is this that you are doing for the people? Why do you sit alone, and all the people stand around you from morning till evening?" ¹⁵ And Moses said to his father-in-law, "Because the people come to me to inquire of God; ¹⁶ when they have a dispute, they come to me and I decide between one person and another, and I make them know the statutes of God and his laws." ¹⁷ Moses' father-in-law said to him, "What you are doing is not good. ¹⁸ You and the people with you will certainly wear yourselves out, for the thing is too heavy for you. You are not able to do it alone. ¹⁹ Now obey my voice; I will give you advice, and God be with you! You shall represent the people before God and bring their cases to God, ²⁰ and you shall warn them about the statutes and the laws, and make them know the way in which they must walk and what they must do. ²¹ Moreover, look for able men from all the people, men who fear God, who are trustworthy and hate a bribe, and place such men over the people as chiefs of thousands, of hundreds, of fifties, and of tens. ²² And let them judge the people at all times. Every great

matter they shall bring to you, but any small matter they shall decide themselves. So it will be easier for you, and they will bear the burden with you. ²³ If you do this, God will direct you, you will be able to endure, and all this people also will go to their place in peace."

²⁴ So Moses listened to the voice of his father-in-law and did all that he had said. ²⁵ Moses chose able men out of all Israel and made them heads over the people, chiefs of thousands, of hundreds, of fifties, and of tens. ²⁶ And they judged the people at all times. Any hard case they brought to Moses, but any small matter they decided themselves. ²⁷ Then Moses let his father-in-law depart, and he went away to his own country.

¹ *Gershom* sounds like the Hebrew for *sojourner* ² *Eliezer* means *My God is help* ³ Hebrew; Samaritan, Septuagint, Syriac *behold* ⁴ Hebrew *with them*

Section Overview

Chapter 18 serves as a hinge.[319] The chapter's first half focuses on the Lord as his people's deliverer (vv. 1–12), in keeping with the first part of Exodus (chs. 1–17). Jethro's family connection to Moses is another theme (eight times he is called Moses' father-in-law: 18:1, 2, 5–8 [4x], 12 [2x]), as is the Lord's deliverance of Israel (mentioned four times in vv. 8–10). The chapter's second half focuses on the proper administration of the law (vv. 13–27), anticipating the announcement of the law to come in the second part of Exodus (chs. 19–40). Other themes include Moses' unique role as the intermediary between the people and the Lord (18:15–16), the importance of shared leadership (vv. 17–23), and the necessity of upstanding character among the Lord's leaders, especially those deciding between right and wrong (v. 21). Holding both halves of the chapter together is the character of Jethro, who draws special attention to the Lord's character (vv. 10–11).

Section Outline

IV. Israel arrives at Sinai: the Lord prepares his people to receive his covenant and its laws (18:1–19:25)
   A. Jethro's visit, his expression of faith and advice to Moses, his departure (18:1–27)
      1. Jethro's visit and his praise of the Lord as the greatest of all gods (18:1–12)
      2. Jethro's advice to Moses about the administration of justice (18:13–27)

Comment

18:1 When Moses originally fled Egypt, he settled in Midian and became son-in-law to a priest named Jethro (also known as Reuel; 2:15–22).[320] Before Moses returned to Egypt he first sought and received Jethro's blessing to do so (4:18–20). Since Jethro has not been mentioned since then, the narrator reminds us of who

---

319 The thoughts of this paragraph draw from Meyers, *Exodus*, 136, and Alexander, *Exodus*, ApOTC, 345.
320 Exodus 2:15–22; for the names Jethro and Reuel cf. comment on 3:1–3.

he is as he reenters the story (18:1).³²¹ Somehow, Jethro has heard that the Lord has delivered the Israelites, and he goes to meet them.³²²

18:2–5 The narrative pauses to provide further background information (vv. 2–4). When Moses left Midian to return to Egypt, he took with him his wife, Zipporah, and their two sons, Gershom and Eliezer (4:20). In Hebrew the beginning of Gershom (*gershom*) sounds like the word for "sojourner" (*ger*), a reminder of Moses' status when he came to Midian (cf. comment on 2:16–22 and note 77), while the name Eliezer (*eliezer*) means "God of [*eli*] help [*ezer*],"³²³ a testimony to how the Lord delivered Moses from Pharaoh (18:3–4; cf. 2:15). At some point after leaving Midian Moses sent his wife and sons back there. When and why he did so are nowhere stated. Perhaps he sent them back soon after leaving Midian and before coming to Egypt (perhaps for reasons of safety), or perhaps he sent them back once Israel had left Egypt and was getting close to Midian (so Zipporah and the boys could visit their family).³²⁴ In either case Jethro had naturally received them and is now bringing them back to Moses, who by this point has arrived with the Israelites "at the mountain of God" (18:5), that is, Mount Sinai (cf. comment on 3:1–3).³²⁵

18:6–7 Jethro has sent word ahead that he is coming (v. 6), and Moses goes out to greet him, presumably leaving the camp to meet Jethro before he arrives (v. 7; cf. Gen. 29:13; 32:3–6). Moses' bowing down shows appropriate respect to his elder father-in-law, and a kiss of greeting, even between men, is typical (cf. Ex. 4:27), as is asking of each other's welfare (cf. Gen. 43:27). Returning to the camp, they go into Moses' tent to catch up more properly.

18:8 Moses tells Jethro how the Lord fought for Israel while they were in Egypt and then how he has continued to help them during hardships they have faced since leaving there. He is a God who delivers his people from evil.

18:9–12 The text now underscores the theme of God's deliverance. Jethro's response to all that Moses shared is to rejoice over the good the Lord has shown Israel and particularly how he has delivered them from the Egyptians (Ex. 18:9). His rejoicing breaks out into words of blessing and praise,³²⁶ giving glory to the

---

321 Cassuto, *Commentary on the Book of Exodus*, 213.
322 The news could have come from caravans, since 2:19 implies Egyptians came Jethro's way often enough that they were recognizable to his family (Stuart, *Exodus*, 403–4). Depending on when Zipporah was sent back, she also could have brought some of the information (cf. comment on 18:2–5).
323 Cf. Stuart, *Exodus*, 404n220. Others suggest "My God is help." The end point is the same.
324 The word translated "sent her" (Ex. 18:2) is based on a root that can refer elsewhere to divorce, but nothing in the context suggests anything other than a simple sending. Indeed, the last time we read of Zipporah, she underscored their marital relationship (4:25), and Sarna (*Exodus*, 98) notes that Jethro refers to Zipporah as Moses' wife (18:6).
325 The account of the Israelites' arrival there does not come until the next chapter (Ex. 19:1–2), but the narrator jumps ahead and places the events of chapter 18 here to provide a smooth bridge from the exodus narrative to the Sinai narrative (cf. Section Overview). The narrator can then focus the following chapters on the Lord's entering into covenant relationship with the Israelites (chs. 19–24). As for when Jethro's visit occurs, Deuteronomy 1:9–19 might suggest it is toward the end of Israel's time at Sinai (cf. fuller discussion in Sarna, *Exodus*, 97), though "at that time" in Deuteronomy 1:9 could simply mean "when we were at Mount Sinai" (as opposed to its meaning "at that exact moment, just before we left Sinai").
326 When God blesses people, he shines his favor on them in some tangible way (cf. Deut. 28:1–14). When people say "Blessed be the LORD," they are saying that his name should be praised (cf. Ps. 103:1–2 with 103:3–14).

Lord for delivering his people both in battle and from slavery (v. 10). The Lord had repeatedly said that his miraculous signs of deliverance would result in people's "knowing" or "acknowledging"—the Hebrew can mean either—his true nature (7:17; 8:10, 22; 10:2; etc.). Jethro does just that, using the Lord's personal name to do so: Yahweh is greater than all gods (18:11).[327] Whether Jethro is coming to believe in Yahweh for the first time or coming to a higher view of Yahweh is not clear. What is clear is the exalted position Yahweh now has in his view of the world.

Jethro follows his words of praise with sacrificial worship (v. 12). The burnt offering would be entirely burned up on the altar (Lev. 1:1–9). It has an atoning function (Lev. 1:4) and can also serve as a costly expression of praise that underscores how worthy the Lord is of one's very best (Ps. 66:15–20).[328] "Sacrifices" refer to peace offerings,[329] parts of which would be burned on the altar (Lev. 3:1–5) and parts of which would be consumed by the offerer and others invited to the sacrificial meal (Lev. 7:15–18, 28–34)—in this context, Aaron and Israel's elders (along with Moses, who is assumed). They comes to eat "bread" (i.e., "food"[330]) with Jethro, the centerpiece of which would be the sacrificial meat. Sharing a meal is especially significant since the peace offering has overtones of a covenantal meal (cf. comments on 24:3–8 [at v. 5]; 24:9–11), signifying the close bond now existing between Jethro and Israel and between all of them and Israel's covenant God, Yahweh, before whom they eat. In Abraham's offspring the nations are indeed being blessed (Gen. 12:3).

18:13–23 A second narrative is now related that focuses on Jethro's advising Moses about administering justice. When Moses spends the entire day hearing people's legal cases and rendering judgment (Ex. 18:13), the older and wiser Jethro immediately sees how problematic this is. He asks Moses why he is taking this approach, focusing especially on the fact that he is doing it alone and all day long (v. 14). Moses responds that, since he is God's spokesman, the Israelites bring their cases to him so that he can render a decision and instruct them in God's statutes and laws (vv. 15–16). From Moses' perspective he has no choice, but Jethro knows otherwise.

He first points out that Moses' approach is neither sustainable nor efficient (vv. 17–18). Because the task is too great for Moses to do alone, it will "certainly wear [him] out,"[331] a verb normally used to describe a withered leaf (Ps. 1:3; Isa. 34:4; Ezek. 47:12). The same weariness will be true for the people, many of whom will have to wait for countless hours (perhaps days?) for the simplest case to be heard.

---

[327] The word for "deal arrogantly" (Hb. *zid*; Ex. 18:11) and other words built on its root (*zed, zadon*) often refer to wicked behavior that flows from an arrogant or presumptuous attitude toward others (Ex. 21:14; Deut. 1:43; 17:12–13; Neh. 9:10, 16). In this context the "they" most likely refers to Pharaoh and the Egyptians (as opposed to their gods; cf. Neh. 9:10). The sense is that, by delivering the Israelites, Yahweh showed his power over the gods of those who plotted harm against them.
[328] Cf. Sklar, *Leviticus*, TOTC, 94–95.
[329] When mentioned with burnt offerings, peace offerings are sometimes simply referred to as "sacrifices" (Num. 15:3; cf. Lev. 23:37; Josh. 22:26).
[330] The Hebrew word for "bread" often refers generally to food (Judg. 13:16; 1 Sam. 14:24; Ps. 136:25; cf. BDB 536.2).
[331] "Certainly" captures the fact that the verb "wear yourself out" is emphasized in the Hebrew.

Jethro's solution is as simple as it is wise. He recognizes that Moses has a unique leadership role to play and should continue in it, namely, in representing the people to God, bringing their cases to him, and revealing his statutes and laws so the people know how to act (Ex. 18:19–20). But Jethro also recognizes that, when a burden is too heavy, others are needed to help carry it. He therefore identifies ways in which Moses can delegate responsibilities (vv. 21–22). Moses is to find men of skill ("able men") and especially of character,[332] in particular those who have deep reverence of God and obey his ways ("men who fear God"; cf. Gen. 22:12; Deut. 10:12; 13:4), who are fully reliable ("trustworthy"),[333] and who cannot be persuaded to pervert the course of justice ("hate a bribe"; cf. Deut. 16:19; 1 Sam. 8:3). As always in the Bible, good character is the necessary foundation for leadership (cf. 1 Tim. 3:1–13). Moses is then to arrange the people in groups of varying sizes and place over them the chosen men, to whom the people will first go when they have legal cases to resolve. The appointed judges will address the simpler cases in keeping with the laws Moses has already revealed and will leave the more complicated cases for Moses (who can seek God's guidance when need be; cf. Lev. 24:10–23; Num. 9:6–14; 15:32–36; 27:1–11; 36:1–9). This will drastically reduce Moses' burden, protecting him from burnout and also enabling the people to resolve their cases much more quickly, undoubtedly lowering their frustrations ("go to their place in peace," Ex. 18:23).[334] In short, sharing leadership responsibilities is good for both the leader and those being led.

18:24–26 Moses listens to Jethro's wise counsel. All truth is God's truth and all wisdom God's wisdom, whether or not it comes from someone who has been walking with the Lord a long time. In terms of how Moses selects the judges, Deuteronomy 1:9–18 informs us that Moses consults the people since they know who will meet the qualifications.

18:27 We next read of Jethro's departure. Whether this takes place immediately or some time later is not stated, since it does not matter. The focus of this chapter has been on Jethro's bringing back Moses' wife and children, acknowledging Yahweh's superiority to all other gods, and giving wise advice to Moses about administering the law. This latter element is an especially helpful transition to the chapters that follow, in which the law is given to Moses on Mount Sinai.

Response

While Jethro is the thread that holds the two narrative of this chapter together, each half has its unique emphasis. This may be seen by asking two questions.

---

[332] Alternately, "able" could refer to having a character of moral strength, which the verse would now be detailing (Keil, *Exodus*, vol. 2, 87, citing the use of the same phrase in 1 Kings 1:52).
[333] Also translated as "faithful(ness)"; cf. Genesis 24:27; 32:10; 47:29 ("truly"); Exodus 34:6.
[334] The translation "God will direct you" involves a unique understanding of the relevant verb (Hb. *tsiwwah*). Many translate "And [if] God so commands you" (NASB, NIV, NET, etc.). The sense would then be that Jethro is saying that his advice is subject ultimately to God's approval.

WHAT DO WE LEARN ABOUT SHARING OUR FAITH?

In 9:16 the Lord said to Pharaoh, "For this purpose I have raised you up, to show you my power, so that my name may be proclaimed [*sapper*] in all the earth." Now in 18:8 we read, "Moses told/proclaimed (*sapper*) [to] his father-in-law all that the LORD had done to Pharaoh and to the Egyptians for Israel's sake, all the hardship that had come upon them in the way, and how the LORD had delivered them." Tying the two verses together, Fretheim observes, "Moses is the first of God's witnesses to another individual and another people. His witness serves to establish the exodus faith for the first time in a non-Israelite community.... What Moses has done, Israel and all of God's people are also called upon to do (cf. Pss. 18:49; 57:9; 96:3–4, 10; 113:3; cf. also 40:9–10; 67:4)."[335] In short, Moses is modeling what the Lord expects of his people: sharing of their faith with others.

What may be particularly noted is that Moses shares his faith not abstractly but by describing concretely what he had seen the Lord do in protecting and delivering his people (Ex. 18:8). What does it look like for us to share our faith in a similar way? How do we share with people not only that Jesus has died on the cross for us and risen again to defeat death on our behalf but also that he has delivered us in very personal ways, rescuing us from our own sins and struggles, transforming our lives to be more like his, strengthening us in our trials and comforting us in our sorrows? To be a Christian is not simply to believe about an act of deliverance Jesus did in the past but to experience that deliverance in an ongoing and transforming way in the present. Sharing our faith involves both aspects of that deliverance.

What Jethro receives from Moses in this first narrative is a tremendous gift. In the second account Jethro gives Moses a tremendous gift, leading to our second question.

WHAT DO WE LEARN ABOUT LEADERSHIP?

Jethro teaches Moses two very important lessons about leadership. First, the sharing of leadership responsibilities is important for the good of leaders and those being led. The weight of Moses' responsibilities is going to "wear [him] out" (18:18). As we might say today, he is going to suffer burnout. Moreover, because he cannot get to everything in a timely way, the people themselves are getting worn down with frustration (cf. comment on 18:13–23). The simple solution is for Moses to share the load. Just as Aaron and Hur came and held up Moses' hand when they grew too "heavy" for him (17:12)—the Hebrew of 17:12 could be woodenly translated "But Moses' hands grew heavy"—he now needs leaders to come alongside him to help bear this burden that has also grown too "heavy" (18:18).

Asking for help takes great humility on the part of leaders, but it is essential to the long-term well-being of themselves and those they lead.[336] Self-aware leaders recognize their own limits and seek help in places that their gifts are not strong or when they are simply overburdened. A leader's asking for help communicates,

---
335 Fretheim, *Exodus*, 197.
336 Cf. Bob Burns, Tasha D. Chapman, and Donald Guthrie, *Resilient Ministry: What Pastors Told Us about Surviving and Thriving* (Downers Grove, IL: InterVarsity Press, 2013), esp. chs. 5–6.

"This ministry/job/project is not about me. I am not the Christ. I cannot do it all. What is more, others have important gifts and abilities that need to be put to use." Moses is sometimes slow to learn this lesson. At a later point during the people's complaining he cries out, "I am not able to carry all this people alone; the burden is too heavy for me" (Num. 11:14). The Lord graciously responds by specially appointing and gifting seventy elders to help (Num. 11:16–25). It is an act of wisdom, however, to share leadership responsibilities before one gets to the breaking point.

The sharing of leadership responsibilities leads to the second lesson: such responsibilities must be shared with people who have character sufficient for the task. When Jethro describes the type of leaders needed, he focuses on their character (Ex. 18:21; cf. comment there). Skill is of course also required, but from a biblical perspective putting people into positions of leadership with skill but no character is as dangerous as building a house on a foundation of shifting sand. This is certainly true of leadership roles in the church, such as elders or deacons (1 Tim. 3:1–13; Titus 1:5–9), but the Bible also speaks of the importance of character for those in more public roles, such as the king (Prov. 30:1–9) or, as here, those deciding cases of justice. This means that, while it is true that those outside the church are not called to be our spiritual leaders, it is still important that they have good character, especially the higher in leadership one goes.[337] It is not only ministries that have collapsed due to the weak moral character of their leaders but businesses and governments as well—often to the great harm of those being led.

This means that, if we are choosing leaders, we must do so wisely, putting due focus on the person's character. And if we are in positions of leadership it means we should pay even more attention to cultivating our relationship with Jesus so that he can increasingly conform us to his image. This we can do confidently, knowing that he delights to help us to become like him.

EXODUS 19

19 On the third new moon after the people of Israel had gone out of the land of Egypt, on that day they came into the wilderness of Sinai. ² They set out from Rephidim and came into the wilderness of Sinai, and they encamped in the wilderness. There Israel encamped before the mountain, ³ while Moses went up to God. The Lord called to him out of the mountain, saying, "Thus you shall say to the house of Jacob, and tell the people of Israel: ⁴ 'You yourselves have seen what I did to the Egyptians, and how I bore you on eagles' wings and brought you

---

[337] Christians should therefore not excuse the poor character of political leaders by saying, "I'm not electing this person to be my pastor." The Bible emphasizes the importance of a leader's character in and outside the church.

to myself. ⁵ Now therefore, if you will indeed obey my voice and keep my covenant, you shall be my treasured possession among all peoples, for all the earth is mine; ⁶ and you shall be to me a kingdom of priests and a holy nation.' These are the words that you shall speak to the people of Israel."

⁷ So Moses came and called the elders of the people and set before them all these words that the Lord had commanded him. ⁸ All the people answered together and said, "All that the Lord has spoken we will do." And Moses reported the words of the people to the Lord. ⁹ And the Lord said to Moses, "Behold, I am coming to you in a thick cloud, that the people may hear when I speak with you, and may also believe you forever."

When Moses told the words of the people to the Lord, ¹⁰ the Lord said to Moses, "Go to the people and consecrate them today and tomorrow, and let them wash their garments ¹¹ and be ready for the third day. For on the third day the Lord will come down on Mount Sinai in the sight of all the people. ¹² And you shall set limits for the people all around, saying, 'Take care not to go up into the mountain or touch the edge of it. Whoever touches the mountain shall be put to death. ¹³ No hand shall touch him, but he shall be stoned or shot;¹ whether beast or man, he shall not live.' When the trumpet sounds a long blast, they shall come up to the mountain." ¹⁴ So Moses went down from the mountain to the people and consecrated the people; and they washed their garments. ¹⁵ And he said to the people, "Be ready for the third day; do not go near a woman."

¹⁶ On the morning of the third day there were thunders and lightnings and a thick cloud on the mountain and a very loud trumpet blast, so that all the people in the camp trembled. ¹⁷ Then Moses brought the people out of the camp to meet God, and they took their stand at the foot of the mountain. ¹⁸ Now Mount Sinai was wrapped in smoke because the Lord had descended on it in fire. The smoke of it went up like the smoke of a kiln, and the whole mountain trembled greatly. ¹⁹ And as the sound of the trumpet grew louder and louder, Moses spoke, and God answered him in thunder. ²⁰ The Lord came down on Mount Sinai, to the top of the mountain. And the Lord called Moses to the top of the mountain, and Moses went up.

²¹ And the Lord said to Moses, "Go down and warn the people, lest they break through to the Lord to look and many of them perish. ²² Also let the priests who come near to the Lord consecrate themselves, lest the Lord break out against them." ²³ And Moses said to the Lord, "The people cannot come up to Mount Sinai, for you yourself warned us, saying, 'Set limits around the mountain and consecrate it.'" ²⁴ And the Lord said to him, "Go down, and come up bringing Aaron with you. But do not let the priests and the people break through to come up to the Lord, lest he break out against them." ²⁵ So Moses went down to the people and told them.

¹ That is, shot with an arrow

Section Overview

The Israelites arrive at Mount Sinai and will remain here until Numbers 10, a period of time just under one year but narrated over fifty-nine chapters. "This level of interest in such a short period of time is unique in the Old Testament" and shows how important the events of Mount Sinai are.[338] A house can stand well only on a strong foundation, and the same is true for a nation; the Lord builds just such a foundation during this time.

Exodus 19 begins building this foundation by focusing on the Lord's invitation to the Israelites to enter into a special covenant relationship with him (vv. 1–6), an invitation they wholeheartedly accept (vv. 7–8). The rest of the chapter focuses on the Lord's special arrival at Mount Sinai (vv. 9–25). It begins by making clear the importance of ritual cleansing in preparation for the arrival of a holy God and the need to respect his holiness by not transgressing boundaries around his holy mountain (vv. 9–15). It then describes the Lord's arrival in terrifying detail and makes clear that Moses is the Lord's appointed spokesman (vv. 16–19). It ends by repeating the necessity of not transgressing the mountain's boundaries, with the exception of Moses and Aaron, in this way underscoring the Israelites' need to respect the Lord's holiness and to recognize those who have been set apart to have a special role within the nation (vv. 20–25).

Section Outline

IV. Israel arrives at Sinai: the Lord prepares his people to receive his covenant and its laws (18:1–19:25) . . .
    B. The Lord's invitation of special covenant relationship; his arrival in glory (19:1–25)
        1. The Israelites' arrival at Sinai (19:1–2)
        2. The Lord's invitation of special covenant relationship (19:3–6)
        3. The people accept the Lord's invitation (19:7–8a)
        4. Preparations for the Lord's arrival (19:8b–15)
        5. The Lord's special arrival takes place (19:16–19)
        6. The Lord reinforces his commands about who may and may not go up the mountain (19:20–25)

Comment

19:1–2 The opening verses appear to be a flashback (cf. note 325 within comment on 18:2–5 for possible reasons why ch. 18 is not in chronological sequence). Previously, the Israelites had been camped at Rephidim (ch. 17). They moved from there to the wilderness of Sinai and camped in front of Mount Sinai itself. Exodus 18 describes Jethro's coming to meet them there (18:5), and chapter 19 now returns to describe when the Israelites arrived there from Rephidim, namely, in the third month of the year (19:1–2).[339]

---

338 Alexander, *Exodus*, ApOTC, 355.
339 "Exod 19:1 could be woodenly translated, 'In the third new moon/month with regard to the children of Israel's going out from the land of Egypt'—that is, not three new moons/months after leaving but the third new moon/month of their departure year—'on that very day, they came into the wilderness of Sinai.' Since they came out on the evening of month one day fourteen, they arrive here roughly one and a half months later if 'that very day' refers to month three day one, and two months later if 'that very day' refers to the day

19:3–6 While they camp before Sinai, Moses goes up to receive a message from God, who calls to him "out of the mountain" (v. 3) or "from the mountain," perhaps with the mountain's top particularly in mind (cf. v. 20).[340] In the message the Lord underscores Israel's experience of his deliverance ("You *yourselves* have seen what I did to the Egyptians") and metaphorically describes his bringing the Israelites to himself as though they were flying through the wilderness on eagles' wings—that is, they have come swiftly and safely to his presence at Sinai as though to a secure mountain nest (v. 4; cf. 2 Sam. 1:23; Jer. 49:16; Obad. 4).[341]

Having recounted how he rescued them, God now invites them into a covenant relationship, describing their obligations and his (Ex. 19:5–6). True, they are already in relationship with the Lord because of the Abrahamic covenant (2:24; 6:4–5), which means the covenant of Sinai does not replace the Abrahamic covenant as much as show how it applies to the Israelites as a nation. As Alexander notes, "The [Sinai] covenant establishes a new phase in an already existing relationship, a phase linked to the creation of Israel as 'a kingdom of priests and a holy nation'. With the making of this covenant, God comes to dwell among the Israelites, an outcome that marks a major new development in the divine plan of salvation."[342] At the same time there is a fresh invitation here for Israel to choose to embrace covenant relationship with the Lord and all it entails. (For more on the nature of a covenant cf. Response section.)

At first glance the Lord's invitation in 19:5 reads as though the Israelites must earn relationship with him, but such a reading would miss what has just been said: he has already redeemed them (v. 4), and that completely apart from their own merit. Rather, the Lord's invitation is comparable to what transpires when a king rescues a helpless people from evil and then invites them to become his loyal subjects with all the responsibilities and benefits that entails. There are responsibilities, yes: they need to listen to the King ("You will indeed obey my voice and keep my covenant"; v. 5a). But there are benefits as well, since the King himself guarantees his ongoing care of them ("You shall be my treasured possession among all peoples"; v. 5b). Indeed, in this case the King of the universe, to whom all people belong ("All the earth is mine"), offers the Israelites a covenant relationship that sets them apart in a special way. The language of "treasured possession" refers elsewhere to a king's treasure (1 Chron. 29:3; Eccles. 2:8), something to be safeguarded and valued to the utmost.[343] To change the metaphor, this is akin to a marriage proposal to Israel: "If you enter into faithful marriage with me, you will experience a husband who will guard you, watch over you, and view you as

---

of the third month parallel to their departure day (day fourteen). Arguments in favor of either position are evenly balanced" (Sklar, *Numbers*, 51n7).
340 Kalisch, *Exodus*, 328.
341 Possibly Exodus 19:4 should be understood to mean that the Lord is the eagle carrying Israel on his own wings in keeping with Deuteronomy 32:11, though that verse uses a different word ("pinions," not "wings"), and the verse's meaning is debated; cf. Hendrik G. L. Peels, "On the Wings of the Eagle (Deut. 32:11)–An Old Misunderstanding," *ZAW* 106 (1994): 300–303. At the least our passage is saying that the Lord has brought Israel to this point and done so swiftly and safely (cf. comments above).
342 *Exodus*, 374–375.
343 Related words occur in other ancient Near Eastern contexts to refer to servants—be it of gods or kings—that were especially valued. Cf. Sarna, *Exodus*, 104.

his treasured possession."[344] That is not a promise to earn love; it is a promise to experience love.

The Lord extends the idea of his special care when he says the Israelites will "be to me a kingdom of priests and a holy nation" (Ex. 19:6). Priests had an honored role in the biblical world (Gen. 14:18–20; 47:22, 26), and to be holy can refer to being set apart as belonging to the Lord in a special way (Lev. 20:26). In short these are two more ways of describing what it means to be a treasured possession. This explains why Deuteronomy 26:18–19, when referring to our passage, describes Israel as a treasured possession that will be set "in praise and in fame and in honor high above all nations that [the Lord] has made, and . . . [Israel] shall be a people holy to the LORD [its] God."

Along with underscoring Israel's special status, the language of priesthood and holy nation also points to Israel's role in the Lord's world. Within Israel the Lord's priests are to live holy lives, teaching the Israelites his ways and helping them to know how to live in relationship with him (Lev. 10:10–11; 21:1–23). Israel is to do the same within the world. This will take place especially by embodying the Lord's holy character in the people's own lives, thereby showing others the beauty and glory of who he is (Lev. 19:2; 20:26). Put differently, Israel is not simply to be the Lord's treasured servant; she is to help the world understand why the Lord is to be treasured. Peter makes this very point to early Christians when referring to this passage: "You are a chosen race, a royal priesthood, a holy nation, a people for his own possession, *that you may proclaim the excellencies of him who called you out of darkness into his marvelous light*" (1 Pet. 2:9). To enter into the Lord's care is to receive his commission to help his world know, worship, obey, and love him.

19:7–8a Having come down the mountain, Moses reports the Lord's words to the elders to pass on to the people (Ex. 19:7). Their response is unified and wholehearted: "*All* the people answered *together* and said: '*All* that the LORD has spoken we will do'" (v. 8a).

19:8b–13 Like a messenger returning to a king, Moses goes back up the mountain and reports the people's response to the Lord (v. 8b). Now that they have accepted his invitation into covenant relationship, the Lord explains they must prepare for a special manifestation of his presence (vv. 9–13). They have agreed to enter into relationship with the King of kings, and he is now going to show up in full—and terrifying!—royal splendor.

The Lord describes in general how he will appear, namely, in a thick cloud (v. 9a), to protect Moses and the people from the consequences of seeing his glory directly (cf. comment on 19:20–25). The Lord also identifies Moses as the main recipient of his appearing ("you" in v. 9 is singular) and states that his visible representation and audible speech to Moses will confirm to the people that Moses really is God's prophet (v. 9b; cf. 4:5; 14:31).

---

344 So also Alexander (*Exodus*, 375), who notes that according to this analogy the wedding (the confirmation of the covenant relationship) occurs in Exodus 24:3–11. To carry this further, Exodus 40 would then be the groom's "moving in" to live with his new bride.

The Lord next states that the people must prepare themselves for his special appearance by cleansing themselves of ritual impurity (19:10–11). In ancient Israel, as in other ancient Near Eastern societies, the concept of ritual states was part of the cultural landscape.[345] God's law describes three basic states: impurity, purity, and holiness. Most importantly, ritual impurity is never to come into contact with ritual holiness. Since the Lord is the ultimate expression of holiness, those coming before him must cleanse themselves of ritual impurity. (To use a modern analogy, a doctor does not walk into an operating room unless he has disinfected himself. Nor does a subject wear dirty clothes when appearing before a king.) Moses is therefore to consecrate the people by having them go through typical activities for cleansing and for avoiding ritual impurity (vv. 14–15): letting time pass ("today ... tomorrow ... and be ready for the third day"), washing garments (a natural symbol of cleansing), and avoiding sexual contact (since sexual relations would result in ritual impurity). It should not be difficult for the Israelites to realize that, if the Lord requires their ritual purity, how much more does he likewise require their moral purity.[346]

Moses is also to warn them not to touch the mountain, on pain of death (vv. 12–13a). The implication is that the Lord's presence makes the mountain so holy that even ritually pure Israelites may not touch it. (Stated differently, his presence makes the mountain like a sanctuary; cf. comment on 24:1–2.) As Numbers makes clear, only those the Lord has set apart as ritually holy can come in contact with objects that are ritually holy (Num. 3:38; 4:15). To do otherwise is to disrespect the object's holiness and the one who makes the object holy, the Lord. Indeed, those who touch the mountain are to be killed by stones or arrows so that they will not be touched. Not stated is whether this is because they now share in some of the mountain's holiness (and, like it, cannot be touched) or because the crime is so heinous that touching the guilty is thought to be defiling. Either way, the warning is clear: the Lord's holy space must be respected.

The Lord concludes by stating, "When the trumpet sounds a long blast, they shall come up to the mountain" (Ex. 19:13). This could mean a certain trumpet blast signals the Israelites to come to the foot of the mountain but not to touch it (cf. vv. 16–17). Alternately, it could mean that the trumpet blast signals that the Lord's special presence has left the mountain and that the people may again go up on it. (In favor of the latter, the phrase "come up to the mountain" [v. 13] uses the same Hebrew words as the phrase "go up into the mountain" [v. 12], where the sense is climbing the mountain.) Either way, there are clearly times at which the people must not touch the mountain at all.

19:14–19 Moses now comes back down the mountain and prepares the people for the Lord's special appearance (vv. 14–15).[347] Three days later it occurs, with

---

[345] For details on ritual states cf. Sklar, *Leviticus*, TOTC, 44–49; for the concept among Israelites before Exodus 19 cf. Genesis 35:2.
[346] Bush, *Commentary on Exodus*, 241; cf. further discussion in Sklar, *Leviticus*, TOTC, 48–49.
[347] "Do not go near a woman" (Ex. 19:15) refers to having sexual relations, which were ritually defiling (Lev. 15:18).

a pyrotechnic display of the Lord's power and might. Visually, the Israelites see Sinai wrapped in a dense cloud lit up with lightning. Audibly, they hear thunder crashing down from the heavens and the mighty blast of a trumpet. They are so scared that they literally tremble (v. 16). Moses leads them out of the camp toward the foot of the mountain (v. 17), and what they experience only deepens their fear: smoke appears to be billowing out of the mountain as out of a furnace, covering all of it, because the Lord has descended with a fire of nuclear strength, causing the massive mountain to tremble as much as the Israelites now standing at its base (v. 18). As the trumpet blast intensifies, Moses begins speaking to God, and the Lord answers him with a thunderous voice (v. 19).[348] There can be no doubt among the people that the Lord is present here and has direct dialogue with Moses his servant (cf. v. 9; cf. 20:18–19).

19:20–25 While the dialogue begins at the mountain's base in front of the people so that they can witness it, it will continue further up the mountain. The narrator restates that the Lord has descended on Sinai, specifying he has come down at its very top, in order to introduce this as the place to which the Lord now summons Moses (v. 20). The Lord reemphasizes to Moses the importance of the people's not going beyond the boundaries at the mountain's base, which some might seek to do in order to get past the smoke and attempt to see the Lord (v. 21). This would be a fatal mistake. To gaze on a king uninvited is a severe sign of disrespect (cf. comment on 3:4–6). What is more, to gaze on the magnitude of this king's glory might be fatally overwhelming. The idea might be that, if merely earthly circumstances can so overwhelm a person's senses that he loses consciousness, then the sight of the heavenly Lord's glory might so overwhelm a person's senses that he loses life itself. It would be like a power surge of glory that fatally overwhelms and short-circuits a person's mortal capacities.

The Lord adds a command for the priests (19:22). While the Lord does not set aside Aaron's family as official priests until 28:1, presumably the Israelites, like other ancient Near Easterners, have people that function as priests (cf. Gen. 14:18; Ex. 2:16). What exactly their role looks like at this point is not certain, though the language of "drawing near" occurs elsewhere to describe those approaching the Lord in prayer (Gen. 18:23) or performing ritual duties (Lev. 21:21). What is clear is that they cannot rest on their priestly credentials when performing such deeds; like the rest of the people, they have to consecrate themselves lest they face the Lord's wrath (cf. Ex. 19:10, 14–15).

Moses repeats back to the Lord his earlier commands that boundaries be set around the mountain (v. 23; cf. v. 12). Perhaps Moses thinks that giving the warning again is unnecessary—an opinion the Lord corrects (v. 24). Whatever the reason behind Moses' words, the narrator accomplishes two goals by recording Moses' repetition of the earlier commands. First, the repetition underscores the impor-

---

[348] Translations are divided on whether to translate Exodus 19:19 as "God answered him in thunder" or "God answered him with a voice." In favor of the latter is that the relevant Hebrew word (*qol*) is singular; when this word refers to thunder elsewhere in Exodus it is always plural (as in 19:16; cf. 9:23, 28–29, 33–34; 20:18).

tance of the Israelites' showing due respect and reverence to the Lord's holiness. This will be especially important for the people to remember as Moses will soon be spending extended time at the mountain's top, and the temptation to follow him up could grow with each passing day. Second, the repetition sets the stage for two clarifications the Lord now provides. First, Aaron will be allowed to come up the mountain with Moses. Second, even after the priests have consecrated themselves, they, like the people, may not come on the mountain at all, despite their priestly credentials (v. 24). In short Moses and Aaron are the only two exceptions at this point, a message Moses dutifully reports to the people (v. 25).

Response

As Abraham's descendants, the Israelites are already members of the Abrahamic covenant. In this chapter, however, the Lord invites them afresh to embrace a covenant relationship with him. We may explore what this means by asking four questions.

WHAT IS A COVENANT RELATIONSHIP?

In the ancient Near East to enter into a covenant was to enter into a relationship with another party. Israel's covenant relationship with the Lord was the type of relationship that was to be much more personal than a contract and much more permanent than an ordinary relationship.[349] Stated differently, this was not a business relationship but a personal one, like a marriage. And it was to be not a short-lived relationship but a permanent one, as also a marriage is supposed to be: "Till death us do part."

WHERE DOES RELATIONSHIP WITH THE LORD BEGIN?

Significantly, this relationship is rooted in the Lord's redeeming love. He begins his invitation in this way: "You yourselves have seen what I did to the Egyptians, and how I bore you on eagles' wings and brought you to myself" (v. 4). Israel is to accept the Lord's invitation not in order to earn his love but as the proper response to the overwhelming love he has already shown.

Such an understanding is at odds with how God's love is thought of today, sometimes even in Christian circles. Too often his love is presented as meager food for which one must labor all day long in the hopes of getting a scrap. But in the Bible God's love is like a lavish banquet on which he invites us to feast all day long in order to fuel our life. Or, again, we think of his love as something we must climb to heaven to secure by means of our good works, when in reality he has already come down from heaven to rescue us and embrace us with his love. Biblically speaking, God always takes the initiative. He is the pursuer; we are the

---

[349] The above description is adapted from Timothy J. Keller, *Preaching: Communicating Faith in an Age of Skepticism* (New York: Viking, 2015), 104; cf. Michael D. Williams, *Far as the Curse Is Found: The Covenant Story of Redemption* (Phillipsburg, NJ: P&R, 2005), 139–147, esp. 144–147. For a much more detailed discussion and definition of covenant cf. Gordon P. Hugenberger, *Marriage as a Covenant: A Study of Biblical Law and Ethics Governing Marriage, Developed from the Perspective of Malachi* (Leiden: Brill, 1994), 168–184.

pursued. He is the rescuer; we are the rescued. He is the lover: we are the loved. As Paul puts it, "God shows his love for us in that *while we were still sinners*, Christ died for us" (Rom. 5:8).

WHAT DOES RELATIONSHIP WITH THE LORD ENTAIL?

In most meaningful relationships both parties have obligations, especially the obligation of faithfulness. Whether in a relationship between friends, best friends, or spouses, a certain level of faithfulness is assumed. The same is true in the Lord's covenant relationship with Israel: each party is expected to be faithful to the other.

That faithfulness may be described in terms of the type of covenant in view. As discussed in more detail below (cf. comments on 20:1–21), the Sinai covenant resembles other ancient Near Eastern treaties between a greater king (a suzerain) and a lesser king (a vassal, i.e., a servant). In such treaties the greater king is obligated to offer military protection while the lesser king is obligated to offer absolute loyalty.[350]

For his part the Lord shows his faithfulness by rescuing the Israelites from slavery and will show his ongoing faithfulness by treating them as his "treasured possession" (19:5). The word translated "treasured possession" refers elsewhere to a king's treasure (1 Chron. 29:3; Eccles. 2:8), something to be highly safeguarded and valued (cf. comment on 19:3–6). That is what the Lord will do with Israel. As Moses will later say, "[The Lord] kept [Israel] as the apple of his eye" (Deut. 32:10; cf. Zech. 2:8).

For Israel's part they are to be faithful to the Lord's covenant law ("Obey my voice and keep my covenant"; Ex. 19:5). It is how they show their loyalty. What is more, by doing so they will live out the special calling the Lord has given them: to be a kingdom of priests and a holy nation. Just as priests within Israel are to help the Israelites know, love, and worship God, so Israel as a nation is to help the rest of the world do the same. Indeed, as a holy nation they are to embody God's own character on earth so that the nations may come to understand who their Creator is and what it means to live in his world. In short the Lord has called Israel into unique relationship, not because he wants to save them and not the world but so that through them the world might be saved (cf. Gen. 12:3). "All the earth is mine" (Ex. 19:5), says the Lord, and I have called Israel to spread my kingdom throughout all of it. As noted above, the Lord extends the exact same call to believers today (1 Pet. 2:9; cf. comment on 19:3–6). He not only calls us in love; he gives us the privilege of embodying his love in this world and calling others to feast upon it.

WHO IS THIS LORD WHO INVITES US INTO RELATIONSHIP?

I have focused thus far on the Lord's lavish love shown for his people and how it calls forth a response of obedient love from them. But this chapter also emphasizes the Lord's incomparable holiness and what that means for his people.

---

[350] Cf. Sandra L. Richter, *The Epic of Eden: A Christian Entry into the Old Testament* (Downers Grove, IL: InterVarsity Press, 2008), 73–75.

To be holy is to be set apart as distinct or unique.[351] Here the Lord shows his utter uniqueness in terms of his power and purity. In terms of his power he comes down from heaven to earth with a display of such terrifying might that both the people and the mountain itself are left trembling. Here is a King before whom all must fall on their faces. In terms of his purity he emphasizes the importance of the Israelites' cleansing themselves to prepare for his coming and the fact that even then they may not approach too close without suffering death. His moral purity makes him like the sun, and our sin makes us like snowmen; to enter unshielded into his presence is to melt.

What this means for his people, among other things, is that they approach him with great reverence. To many this may feel like an irreconcilable tension. If someone is loved, is not the proper response love instead of reverence? But this is a false choice. Biblically speaking, loving and revering the Lord who loves us is as natural as loving and revering a loving parent.

What is more, the Bible is clear that this reverence is due not simply to God the Father but also to God the Son, since the Son shares equally in his holiness. When the apostle John catches glimpses of Jesus in a vision, he beholds someone of unspeakable power and blazing purity (Rev. 1:12–18; 19:11–16). Similarly, the author of Hebrews describes him as "the radiance of the glory of God and the exact imprint of his nature . . . [who] upholds the universe by the word of his power" (Heb. 1:3). And Paul is clear that "God has highly exalted [Jesus] and bestowed on him the name that is above every name, so that at the name of Jesus every knee should bow" (Phil. 2:9–10).

What might this look like in the life of the believer today? What does it mean practically to rejoice and bask in God's love for us in Christ and also to bow our knees in reverence before the Father and the Son? Does one of these come more naturally to us than the other? If so, why? And what might growth in the other area look like? Whatever the answers to these questions may be, we can take comfort in hearing the Father's invitation, now made even louder in Christ, to become his treasured possession, the apple of his eye, the one he will watch over both now and forever.

---

351 Cf. discussion in Sklar, *Leviticus*, TOTC, 39–40.

OVERVIEW OF

EXODUS 20:1–24:11

In chapter 19 the Lord invited Israel to enter a new covenant with him, an invitation the people willingly accepted (vv. 5–8). In chapters 20–24 the Lord gives the covenant to the Israelites (chs. 20–23) and both parties ratify it (ch. 24). Covenant is clearly this section's theme.

As noted below, the covenant's form is most comparable to ancient Near Eastern treaties in which a king (in this case the Lord) enters a covenant relationship with a nation (in this case Israel) who will serve him (cf. comments on 20:1–21). Reading this section well therefore requires doing so through the lens of a king's entering a covenant with a people who will serve him. The king is both Creator and Redeemer, who rescues his people in sovereign power, faithfulness, and love. The people are those rescued from cruel servitude to Pharaoh into glorious servitude to the Lord. The service with which he privileges them is to worship him and show his kingdom of goodness, justice, mercy, and love to his world. Covenant with the Lord is always relational, relationship with him is always for the good and blessing of his people, and his people are always to mediate that good and blessing to his world.

EXODUS 20:1–21

20 And God spoke all these words, saying, ² "I am the Lord your God, who brought you out of the land of Egypt, out of the house of slavery.

³ "You shall have no other gods before[1] me.

⁴ "You shall not make for yourself a carved image, or any likeness of anything that is in heaven above, or that is in the earth beneath, or that is in the water under the earth. ⁵ You shall not bow down to them or serve them, for I the Lord your God am a jealous God, visiting the iniquity of the fathers on the children to the third and fourth generation of those who hate me, ⁶ but showing steadfast love to thousands[2] of those who love me and keep my commandments.

⁷ "You shall not take the name of the Lord your God in vain, for the Lord will not hold him guiltless who takes his name in vain.

⁸"Remember the Sabbath day, to keep it holy. ⁹ Six days you shall labor, and do all your work, ¹⁰ but the seventh day is a Sabbath to the LORD your God. On it you shall not do any work, you, or your son, or your daughter, your male servant, or your female servant, or your livestock, or the sojourner who is within your gates. ¹¹ For in six days the LORD made the heavens and the earth, the sea, and all that is in them, and rested on the seventh day. Therefore the LORD blessed the Sabbath day and made it holy.

¹²"Honor your father and your mother, that your days may be long in the land that the LORD your God is giving you.

¹³"You shall not murder.³

¹⁴"You shall not commit adultery.

¹⁵"You shall not steal.

¹⁶"You shall not bear false witness against your neighbor.

¹⁷"You shall not covet your neighbor's house; you shall not covet your neighbor's wife, or his male servant, or his female servant, or his ox, or his donkey, or anything that is your neighbor's."

¹⁸ Now when all the people saw the thunder and the flashes of lightning and the sound of the trumpet and the mountain smoking, the people were afraid⁴ and trembled, and they stood far off ¹⁹ and said to Moses, "You speak to us, and we will listen; but do not let God speak to us, lest we die." ²⁰ Moses said to the people, "Do not fear, for God has come to test you, that the fear of him may be before you, that you may not sin." ²¹ The people stood far off, while Moses drew near to the thick darkness where God was.

¹ Or *besides* ² Or *to the thousandth generation* ³ The Hebrew word also covers causing human death through carelessness or negligence ⁴ Samaritan, Septuagint, Syriac, Vulgate; Masoretic Text *the people saw*

Section Overview

In chapter 19 the Lord summoned his people to the base of Mount Sinai, on which he descended in an awe-inspiring demonstration of power (19:16–19). He now begins to give them the commands and stipulations they are to obey in order to live as his holy nation, beginning with the Ten Commandments (20:1–17). In keeping with ancient Near Eastern treaties these commandments open with a preamble and historical prologue that describe the Lord's status and his recent history with Israel (vv. 1–2; cf. comment below). The commandments themselves then begin with four that explain to Israel how to love God properly (vv. 3–11), followed by six explaining how to love one another properly (vv. 12–17).[352] The concluding verses record how the Israelites are terrified by hearing the Lord's voice come from the fiery thundercloud and how they ask that all future communication be given to Moses on their behalf (vv. 18–21). These verses explain why the stipulations that follow in chapters 21–23 are spoken only to Moses. They also affirm that the people will view those stipulations as having the same God-breathed authority as the Ten Commandments they have just heard themselves.

---

352 Our love for neighbor is ultimately an expression of our love for God; the two loves are inseparably linked. Nonetheless, Jesus lists the commands to love God and love neighbor individually and states that all the Law and the Prophets hang on both commands (Matt. 22:37–40). Paul also lists several of the last six commandments and states that they are "summed up in this word: 'You shall love your neighbor as yourself'" (Rom. 13:9).

Section Outline

V. Israel at Sinai: the Lord gives his covenant to Israel; the covenant is ratified (20:1–24:11)
   A. Fundamental stipulations of the covenant: the Ten Commandments, spoken by the Lord to the people (20:1–17)
      1. Preamble (20:1–2a)
      2. Historical prologue (20:2b)
      3. First commandment: Do not have other gods (20:3)
      4. Second commandment: Do not make or worship idols (20:4–6)
      5. Third commandment: Do not use the Lord's name in false oaths (20:7)
      6. Fourth commandment: Observe the Sabbath (20:8–11)
      7. Fifth commandment: Honor parents (20:12)
      8. Sixth commandment: Do not murder (20:13)
      9. Seventh commandment: Do not commit adultery (20:14)
      10. Eighth commandment: Do not steal (20:15)
      11. Ninth commandment: Do not bear false witness (20:16)
      12. Tenth commandment: Do not covet (20:17)
   B. The people's fearful response to the Lord's special appearance (20:18–21)
      1. The people's experience of the Lord's special appearance (20:18a)
      2. The people's fearful response (20:18b–19)
      3. Moses' response of reassurance and instruction (20:20)
      4. The people stay at a distance while Moses approaches God (20:21)

Comment

Two beginning observations may be helpful. First, the discovery and study in the last century of ancient Near Eastern treaties has greatly enhanced our understanding of Exodus 19–24. In particular the covenant at Sinai has significant parallels to a type of treaty found in Hittite and Assyrian sources known as a suzerain treaty (sometimes called a vassal treaty), that is, a treaty between a suzerain (a more powerful king) and a vassal (a less powerful king). Wells is worth citing at length:

> While both Hittite and Assyrian texts offer parallels to the biblical idea of covenant, the Hittite treaties have often been the focal point of comparison.[353]
>
> A comprehensive analysis of these texts shows that they tend to contain a regular sequence of elements: (1) a preamble, with the name and titles of the suzerain, in this case the Hittite king; (2) a historical introduction

---

[353] The Hittite texts are from the mid-second millennium BC; the Assyrian from early to mid-first millennium BC. Note added by author.

that describes any previous relations between the Hittites and the vassal state and points out historical reasons why the latter should be loyal to the Hittite king; (3) provisions and stipulations that impose duties on the vassal; (4) a list of those deities who are to witness the agreement and can enforce punishments if necessary; (5) a collection of curses and blessings, either of which could ensue depending on whether or not the vassal state fulfills its obligations and duties.

The description of the covenant in Exodus does not present a tidy sequence of elements in exactly the same manner as the Hittite treaties, but several of the same elements occur. The statement "I am the LORD your God" in 20:2 serves well as a preamble. References to Yahweh's deliverance of the Israelites from Egypt (19:4; 20:2) constitute an appropriate historical introduction. The laws in Exodus 20–23 form a list of stipulations—and a rather lengthy one at that. Element 4 would have served little purpose for monotheistic Israelites, and a specific counterpart to element 5 in Hittite treaties also seems to be missing from Exodus, though other biblical texts (Leviticus 26; Deuteronomy 28) contain blessings and curses related to the Sinai covenant.[354]

In short we do well to keep in mind the image of the Lord as king and Israel as servant as we read this section of Scripture. The commentary below will return frequently to this reality and its significance for the text.

The second observation is that, whereas the Lord speaks the laws of chapters 21–23 to Moses alone after Moses has gone back up the mountain, he speaks the Ten Commandments to all the Israelites gathered at the mountain's base; the whole assembly hears him speak these words (Ex. 20:19; cf. Deut. 4:12–13; 5:4–24, esp. vv. 22–24). This underscores the Ten Commandments' central role in the Israelites' lives. These laws alone are the ones he speaks to them directly. Indeed, they are the foundation on which the following laws are built and are crucial in forming Israel into the holy nation the Lord has called it to be. As Wright observes,

> Liberation from Egyptian bondage would be no advantage in itself unless it were consolidated into social structures and moral principles that would sustain the covenant community both vertically in relation to God and horizontally in relation to one another. The Decalogue is the foundation block of such social consolidation, upon which the rest of the laws and institutions of the Torah build their constitution-shaping edifice.[355]

20:1–2 Similar to what he does in 19:4–6, the Lord in chapter 20 precedes his commands with a reminder of his deliverance. He is worthy of Israel's worship because he is Creator, but as Creator *and* Redeemer he is especially worthy. This

---

[354] Wells, *Exodus*, 226–227. For element 5, however, cf. Section Overview of 23:20–33. For the possible ancient Near Eastern significance of there being two tablets on which the Ten Commandments were written cf. comment on 31:18.
[355] Wright, *Exodus*, 357.

opening statement is also a reminder that redemption by the Lord always precedes relationship with him. Indeed, Exodus itself has "nineteen chapters of salvation before any chapters of law."[356] The law is meant not to save but to guide those who have been saved in living a life pleasing to their Savior. It answers the question, How do we live out our calling as God's kingdom of priests and holy nation? In this way it describes the "lifestyle of the redeemed."[357]

20:3 The Lord's opening commands are later identified as the Ten Commandments and equated with the heart of the covenant (cf. esp. 34:28; Deut. 4:13). In what follows I explain each command and, where known, its penalty. (The Ten Commandments do not list specific penalties; these are identified in other passages for all but the tenth, for which cf. comment on 20:17.)

As noted above (cf. Section Overview), the first four commands direct Israel in how to show love to God. Not surprisingly, the first command is for the Israelites to have no other gods. Since the Lord has made us for himself, the most important thing we can do is to give ourselves to him and him only. As a fish is made for water, we are made for the Lord. To worship anyone or anything else would be like a fish's leaving the life-giving ocean to suffocate on dry land.

Understanding the command's nuance depends on how one understands the Hebrew phrase translated "before me." (*'al panaya*). Its sense could be (1) "You shall have no other gods *physically* before me in the tabernacle" (no idols allowed!), (2) "You shall not *prefer another god in place of me*," or (3) "You shall have no other gods besides me" (cf. ESV mg.)—that is, in addition to me.[358] Since the following commandment covers idols specifically (vv. 4–5a), the second or third nuance seems more likely, but the main point remains the same: we must worship the Lord exclusively. To return to the suzerain-vassal treaty concept, just as the vassal must be absolutely faithful to the suzerain,[359] so the Israelites (the vassal) must be absolutely faithful to the Lord (the suzerain). "Just as a nation would never bind itself to more than one suzerain (unless they liked to live dangerously), Israel was not to bind herself to more than one deity."[360] This also explains why the penalty for violating both this command and the next one is death. To worship other gods is an act of high treason, a capital crime in various societies to this day. In the biblical worldview to rebel against the King of creation is to forfeit one's right to live in that creation.

20:4–6 The second command prohibits making or worshiping idols. Israel must have no other gods (v. 3) and so must avoid the practice by which other gods are worshiped: idolatry (vv. 4–6). This prohibition forbids making idols to represent the Lord (cf. Deut. 4:12, 15) but is stated broadly enough to forbid idols of any kind.

---

[356] Wright, *Exodus*, 356–357.
[357] J. A. Motyer, *Look to the Rock: An Old Testament Background to Our Understanding of Christ* (Leicester, UK: Inter-Varsity Press, 1996), 41; cited in Alexander, *Exodus*, ApOTC, 428–429.
[358] For these different uses of the phrase translated here as "before me" cf. Exodus 33:19 ("before you"); Deuteronomy 21:16 ("in preference to"); Job 16:14 ("upon," i.e., "in addition to"); cf. also BDB 815.7a.(a)-(c).
[359] For this element in ancient Near Eastern treaties cf. F. Charles Fensham, "Clauses of Protection in Hittite Vassal-Treaties and the Old Testament," *VT* 13/2 (1963): 135–138.
[360] Richter, *Epic of Eden*, 86. This commandment does not affirm that other gods exist; it simply addresses the reality that people worship other gods and prohibits the Israelites from doing so.

Making and worshiping idols was as prevalent in ancient Near Eastern cultures as materialism is today in Western cultures (cf. Response section on 32:1–34:35, "Why Was Idolatry Such a Temptation?"). Archaeological discoveries have uncovered gods worshiped in all sorts of forms, from birds (the "likeness of anything that is in heaven above") and various land creatures (anything "that is in the earth beneath") to aquatic creatures (anything "that is in the water under the earth").[361] These three categories correspond to the creatures the Lord made on days five and six of creation (Gen. 1:20–35), and they are just that: creatures, not the Creator. To worship or serve them in place of him is as useless as it is foolish.

The Lord next gives the reason for the prohibitions (Ex. 20:5b–6). He begins by describing himself as a "jealous God," which raises immediate questions, since we often use the words "jealous" and "jealousy" with negative connotations. But there are cases in which

> jealousy, and even jealous anger, is not petty but proper. A husband or wife is right to feel jealous anger if his or her spouse is unfaithful. This explains how the same root can refer to the Lord's jealousy when his people have committed spiritual adultery against him by worshiping other gods (Ex. 20:5; Deut. 4:24; 5:9) and why it can parallel his anger (Deut. 32:16).[362]

In short just as we should not look negatively at a spouse's anger over his or her partner's physical adultery, we should not look negatively at the Lord's anger over his people's spiritual adultery. His jealousy actually testifies to his love for his people:

> The covenant relationship between God and God's people really means something only if God is totally committed to it, so much so that he rejects and resists anything that draws us away from the blessing and security it provides. A God who was not jealous in his commitment to us (that is, a God who did not particularly care whether or not we love him in return or just wander off with other gods) would be as contemptible as a husband or wife who did not care whether or not their spouse was faithful to them or was just playing around with others.[363]

The Lord says he that will show his anger by "visiting the iniquity[364] of the fathers on the children to the third and the fourth generation of those who hate me." As Stuart notes,[365] this cannot mean God targets children for sins they did not commit, which goes against his statement in Deuteronomy 24:16: "Fathers shall not be put to death because of their children, nor shall children be put to death because of their fathers. Each one shall be put to death for his own sin." As for what the phrase does mean, two explanations are most likely, each with biblical warrant.

---

361 Cf. esp. *ANEP*, images 568 and 573. Compare the listing in Deuteronomy 4:16–18. Describing the water as "under the earth" is a way to say that bodies of water are "lower than the solid ground" (Keil, *Exodus*, vol. 2, 115; cf. Deut. 4:18).
362 Sklar, *Numbers*, 318.
363 Wright, *Exodus*, 363.
364 That is, bringing sin's judgment to bear on the sinner (cf. Ex. 32:34–35; 34:7).
365 Stuart, *Exodus*, 454.

Boda identifies the first: "Yahweh is committed to disciplining those who rebel against him, and this sort of discipline extends through the family unit, which was typically comprised of four generations, until the death of the offender."[366] Numbers 14:33 is a key text here. In Numbers 14 the Lord has just told the Israelites who refuse to enter the Promised Land that he will punish them by causing them to wander in the wilderness for forty years. He then says, "And your children shall be shepherds in the wilderness forty years *and shall suffer for your faithlessness*, until the last of your dead bodies lies in the wilderness" (Num. 14:33). In short, the Lord is not angry with the "third and fourth generations"; rather, the family is cohesive, like a body of water, and, when the Lord brings his supernatural discipline to bear on the sinner, the impact can ripple throughout the family.

Alexander identifies the second explanation:

> Although God's patience may extend for several generations, in the end his judgment will fall justly upon those who remain intransigent. In such instances, when they have walked in their fathers' footsteps, the accumulated guilt of a family will fall on later generations. An important example of this comes in the book of Kings, where the sins of Manasseh are included with those of his descendants when God punishes the people of Judah at the time of the Babylonian exile (cf. 2 Kings 23:26; 24:3).[367]

In other words the Lord in his mercy may not punish immediately, but he will surely bring punishment to bear when sin is ongoing, even if not until the third or fourth generation.[368]

The fact that the first approach is clearly illustrated in the Pentateuch weighs in its favor as the most likely explanation of this Pentateuchal passage.[369] Having said that, we can recognize how the Lord states things generally enough that his words would allow for the second approach as well. Importantly, both approaches make clear that sin must be avoided at all costs because the Lord will surely bring his justice to bear against it.

The Lord follows this severe warning with the gracious promise that he shows "steadfast love to thousands of those who love me and keep my commandments" (Ex. 20:6). As noted earlier, the word translated "steadfast love" (Hb. *khesed*), especially when used of the Lord, could also be referred to as *gracious* steadfast love

---

[366] Mark J. Boda, *A Severe Mercy: Sin and Its Remedy in the Old Testament*, Siphrut 1 (Winona Lake, IN: Eisenbrauns, 2009), 45.

[367] Alexander, *Exodus*, ApOTC, 406–407. In the first explanation the words "those who hate me" in Exodus 20:5 would refer to the fathers, not to the three or four subsequent generations. In the second explanation it would refer to the fathers *and* the succeeding generations. Commentators are divided between these options. Further, the words "love" and "hate" in this passage refer primarily not to an emotion but to whether or not one is faithful to the Lord (to be faithful to him is to love him, while to be unfaithful to him is to hate him; cf. Deut. 7:9–10; cf. also Stuart, *Exodus*, 441n8).

[368] This understanding would explain why the Lord follows his statement of mercy in Exodus 34:6 with his assurance that he will "by no means clear the guilty" (34:7), namely, he is emphasizing that, while he is so merciful he might not punish sin in the sinner's lifetime, his punishment for ongoing sin will come at some point. This understanding would also explain why later Israelites repent not only of their sin but also of their forefathers': they understand the Lord has finally brought due punishment to bear for the sin of many generations, and thus the sin of those generations must be repented of (Lev. 26:40; Ezra 9:7; Neh. 9:2; Jer. 14:20; Dan. 9:16; cf. Isa. 65:6–7; Jer. 16:11–12).

[369] In addition to Numbers 14:33, cf. comment on 34:1–8 (at v. 7).

since it refers to his demonstrating love through favorable action toward someone, giving that person something good (cf. comment on 34:1–8 [at vv. 6–7]). In our context such gracious steadfast love is shown to those who are not apostates (20:5) but faithful covenant members (20:6), not because they are earning his love but because they are walking with him in his life-giving ways and remaining within the sphere of his blessing (cf. comment on 15:22–26, esp. toward the end of the comments there). That the Lord shows such steadfast love to "thousands," as compared to showing punishment to the "third and the fourth generation," shows us something of the Lord's heart: "By the greatest numerical contrast in the Bible (three/four to thousands), God identified eloquently his real desire: to have his people remain loyal forever so that he might in turn show them the rich blessings of his resulting loyalty to them."[370]

20:7 The third commandment prohibits using the Lord's name improperly in speech, such as by false oath or blasphemy.[371] As such, to "take the name of the LORD ... in vain" is not primarily a reference merely to using it as a profanity (though such a use is naturally prohibited by the respect for his name that this command assumes); rather, it refers to misusing (or abusing) his name in any way in speech.

Various ancient Near Eastern texts show concern about misusing a deity's name in false oaths or blasphemy.[372] The same concerns existed in ancient Israel. For example, Israelites commonly took oaths in the Lord's name to affirm a promise or the truth of one's words.[373] Invoking his name meant calling him as divine witness. Given human nature, however, false oaths in the Lord's name were made, as several texts show (Lev. 6:3, 5 [cf. 19:12]; Jer. 5:2; 7:9; Isa. 48:1; Zech. 5:4). This serious offense denies the Lord's sovereign ability to hold humans accountable and treats his holiness with contempt by using his name and reputation for evil purposes. Blasphemy is equally serious to taking false oaths, because it abuses the Lord's name and therefore his person, expressing severe contempt for him (cf. Lev. 24:10–16).

That the misuse of the Lord's name in speech is in view here finds support in various lines of evidence. (1) The phrase "take ... in vain" is found also in Psalm 24:4, where it is parallel to "swearing deceitfully,"[374] clearly showing the phrase can refer to misusing the Lord's name in speech. This is no surprise, because (2) the word translated "take" (Hb. *nasa'*) is used in many contexts to refer to an act of

---

370 Stuart, *Exodus*, 454.
371 The majority opinion understands this command to refer to misuse of the Lord's name in speech, though the question of which type(s) of speech might be in view is debated. For a survey of these variations and other approaches cf. Carmen Imes, *Bearing Yhwh's Name at Sinai: A Reexamination of the Name Command of the Decalogue*, BBRSup 19 (University Park, PA: Eisenbrauns, 2018), 7–45.
372 Cf. overview in David L. Baker, *The Decalogue: Living as the People of God* (Downers Grove, IL: IVP Academic, 2017), 62–63.
373 Cf. Exodus 22:11; Leviticus 19:12; Deuteronomy 6:13; 10:20; etc. For taking oaths in a deity's name elsewhere in the ancient Near East cf. Imes, *Bearing Yhwh's Name*, 13–15.
374 The parallelism in Hebrew is especially strong; the last two clauses both begin with a negative particle + verb + preposition *le* + noun. A wooden rendering would read: "*has not lifted up vainly/falsely* my soul, and *has not sworn deceitfully*" (italics represent grammatical parallels). In this case "my soul" refers to the Lord; especially in poetry "soul" can be used for the person to whom it belongs (cf. BDB 659.4; several MSS and versions read "his soul" in place of "my soul," which is the easier reading and thus less likely). The JPS captures the sense well: "Who hath not taken My name in vain, and hath not sworn deceitfully."

speech, especially of a "formal and solemn utterance."³⁷⁵ In two of these contexts *nasa'* occurs in a fuller phrase involving the lips or mouth; for example, "To the wicked God says: 'What right have you to recite my statutes or take my covenant on your lips?'" (Ps. 50:16).³⁷⁶ In the majority of contexts, however, the word *nasa'* occurs in a shortened phrase, the reference to the lips or mouth being understood: "Raise/take up a lamentation on the bare heights" (Jer. 7:29)—that is, take it up in your mouth and speak it.³⁷⁷ (3) That *misuse* of the Lord's name in speech is in view here is evident from the word translated "in vain," which consists of a preposition (*le*) plus a noun that can be translated "vanity" or "falsehood" (*shabe'*). Aside from its use in Deuteronomy 5:11, which repeats this command, the noun occurs only twice elsewhere in the Pentateuch, both in contexts of words or speech that cannot be trusted (Ex. 23:1; Deut. 5:20). This usage is common outside the Pentateuch (Pss. 12:2; 41:6; 139:20; 144:8, 11; Prov. 30:8; Isa. 59:4; Ezek. 13:8) and is again in line with misusing the Lord's name in speech.³⁷⁸ (4) Finally, this understanding explains why the Lord follows the command with a warning that he will be aware of the wrong (and, by implication, bring punishment for it), the idea being, "If you do swear falsely by my name, or blaspheme my name, *though no one else may know, I certainly will* and will not hold him guiltless who takes my name in vain."³⁷⁹ The penalty is not stated but does not need to be: opening oneself up to divine judgment should be threat enough to deter such activity.³⁸⁰

20:8–11 The fourth commandment requires Israelites to "remember the Sabbath day." "This is not merely a cognitive exercise, any more than remembering your wedding anniversary means simply recalling it. . . . Biblical remembrance requires action. . . . [When] God remembers Israel in their slavery . . . [it] means delivering them from Egypt."³⁸¹ As applied to the Sabbath, Israel is to keep the day's obligations (cf. Deut. 5:12), setting it apart as unique and thus treating it as "holy," like a "sanctuary of time" (Ex. 20:8).³⁸² The obligation is straightforward: do no work

---

375 BDB 669.1.b(6).
376 The last three words could also be translated "in your mouth"; cf. also Psalm 16:4.
377 Cf. Exodus 23:1; Numbers 23:7; Job 27:1; Jeremiah 9:10; Amos 5:1; Micah 2:4; Habakkuk 2:6; etc. Cf. BDB 669.1.b(6)-(7). Cf. esp. the end of 2 Kings 9:25, which in Hebrew reads, "The LORD took up this pronouncement against him," and which English versions typically translate, "The LORD made/spoke/uttered this pronouncement against him" (ESV, NIV, NET, NRSV, etc.).
378 Especially noteworthy is the fact that Exodus 23:1, coming only a few chapters later, uses two of the main words from 20:7—"take" and "falsehood"—to refer to someone's "*taking up* a report of *falsehood*," that is, committing an evil act of speech by "spreading a false report" (cf. note 377 above). In both cases evil speech is in view.
379 A minority approach is to translate, "You shall not bear the name of the LORD your God in vain," the idea being that, just as the high priest "bears the name" of the Israelites before the Lord as their representative (Ex. 28:12), the Israelites "bear the name" of the Lord before the world as his. As such, their calling is to represent him faithfully to the world in everything they do; they must not bear his name (i.e., represent him) in vain. For a full defense of this position cf. Imes, *Bearing Yhwh's Name*. While this approach is grammatically possible, and Imes identifies various points that weigh in its favor, it is not clear to me that these points are weightier than those above. Also, its final understanding makes this command exceedingly broad: do not misrepresent the Lord in any way. (For its broad nature cf. Imes, *Bearing Yhwh's Name*, 180–181.) This gives it a categorically different feel than the other nine commandments, all of which target specific behaviors. This does not make the position wrong but does mean it bears the burden of proof to show why it is more likely than the above, which is also grammatically possible, also has various points that weigh in its favor, and has the added weight that it keeps the command parallel to the other nine in prohibiting a specific type of behavior.
380 For what confession and atonement looks like in cases of false oaths cf. Leviticus 6:1–7.
381 Enns, *Exodus*, 418; cf. Exodus 2:24; 6:5.
382 Fretheim, *Exodus*, 229, citing Dale Patrick, *Old Testament Law* (Atlanta: John Knox, 1985), 50.

so that everyone may rest (vv. 9–10). Work is to be done for six days but ceases on the seventh, which is a Sabbath—the word itself is built on a root meaning "cease, desist"—"to the Lord" (v. 10). The phrase "to the Lord" occurs with other special days and times (Lev. 23:5, 6, 34, 41; 25:2) and emphasizes that such events are centered on the Lord, serving as time for the Israelites to celebrate him and remember that he is their covenant God. Not surprisingly, the Sabbath will become the sign of Israel's covenant relationship with him—like a wedding ring that identifies a covenant partner. This also explains why breaking the Sabbath is a capital crime: to break it is to break the covenant and commit treason against the Lord.[383]

It is important to note that the emphasis is on ceasing work so that everyone can rest. The Sabbath is certainly a day to remember covenant relationship with the Lord and thus gather for corporate worship; Leviticus 23:3 assumes as much by calling the Sabbath a "holy convocation," that is, a holy gathering (cf. Heb. 10:24–25). But the text emphasizes rest. This applies to everyone, and the text is careful to identify all possible working members of the Israelite household (adults, children, servants, even animals), as well as other workers ("the sojourner who is within your gates").[384] None is to do typical weekday labors, whether the "gathering of food (Ex. 16:29–30), plowing and reaping (Ex. 34:21), kindling fire (Ex. 35:3), [or] gathering wood (Num. 15:32–36)."[385] They are instead to rest and "be refreshed" (Ex. 23:12). As Jesus will later say, "The Sabbath was made for man" (Mark 2:27).

The Lord concludes the command by referring to his own activity in creating all things, noting that he made the world in six days and rested on the seventh, in this way blessing it and setting it apart as unique, thus making it holy (Ex. 20:11; cf. Gen. 2:2–3). His world is to honor its Maker by following his lead and resting on this day. "God's resting [on day seven] is a divine act that builds into the very created order of things a working/resting rhythm. Only when that rhythm is honored by all is the creation what God intended it to be."[386]

In summary, the Sabbath has a theological and social function. Theologically, by focusing one day in seven on the Lord, it functions "as a brake on the temptation to idolatry . . . [by] *protect[ing] the uniqueness of Yahweh* as creator and redeemer."[387] Socially, by giving everyone a day of rest—including servants and temporary workers—it functions "as a brake on [the temptation to] economic exploitation and oppression . . . [thus] preserv[ing] the social liberation that *reflect[s] the character of Yahweh*."[388] In these ways the Sabbath is a benevolent gift meant to bless those who honor the Lord by keeping it (Ex. 23:12; Deut. 5:14–15; Mark 2:27). With his typical grace the Lord commands the Israelites to proclaim their loyalty to

---

383 For treason as a capital crime cf. 21:15. For further thoughts on explaining such judgment in a modern age cf. Response sections on 13:17–15:21: "What Is the Warning?"; "How Do We Respond?"
384 "Sojourner" refers to a "resident alien; cf. note 254 within comment on 12:43–50. "In your gates" is a way to refer to someone living within the town (cf. Deut. 12:17; 14:21, 27 [ESV "within your towns"]).
385 Jacob Milgrom, *Leviticus 23–27*, AYB (New Haven, CT: Yale University Press, 2001), 1960.
386 Fretheim, *Exodus*, 230.
387 Wright, *Exodus*, 369, emphasis original.
388 Wright, *Exodus*, 369.

him (observing the Sabbath) in a way that brings them blessing (needed rest and refreshment; cf. Mark 2:27).[389]

20:12 The commandments now turn from describing how to love God properly (commandments 1–4) to describing how to love fellow humans properly (commandments 5–10; cf. Section Overview).[390] The fifth commandment centers on the foundational context for human relationship: the family (cf. note 400 within comment on 20:14). Indeed, the family is the basic building block of a stable society, so it is little wonder that the Lord includes this command, which protects that foundational social unit. The commandment in fact encompasses both a command and a promise.

The command is to honor one's parents. To honor someone is to treat that person as worthy of respect and esteem (1 Sam. 15:30; Mal. 1:6; cf. those described as honored in Gen. 34:19; Num. 22:15). In the context of the parent-child relationship Israelites are to obey and serve their parents:

> They were to obey especially in terms of their parents' covenant instruction [see Gen. 18:19; Ex. 12:26–27; 13:14; Deut. 6:1–2, 6–7]; to fail to do so was to reject the covenant itself. They were to serve especially in terms of caring for aging parents,[391] the very application Jesus later makes of the fifth commandment in Mark 7:10–13: To honor one's parents includes supporting and caring for them as they become less able to do so themselves. By such obedience and care, the family—the bedrock of covenant instruction and care—would be protected, and faithful covenant living could continue.[392]

This command therefore includes childhood obedience (cf. Eph. 6:1–3) but also speaks to the honor and care we are to show our parents long after we become adults.[393] It does not root such honor and care in our parents' being perfect (which is not even possible) or even easy to get along with; it roots such honor in the simple fact that they are our parents. Three friends of mine with difficult parents come immediately to mind. None of them was relationally close to his parents, yet each persisted in being respectful and caring for them as they aged, doing deeds of honor and love to honor the Lord. In Israel dishonoring one's parents was so serious that it not only would result in being under a curse (Deut. 27:16) but,

---

389 For whether the Sabbath should be observed today cf. Christopher J. Donato, ed., *Perspectives on the Sabbath: Four Views* (Nashville: B&H, 2011). Because the Sabbath command is rooted in creation (cf. Ex. 20:8–11), I understand it to have ongoing relevance today.
390 In addition, obedience to the fourth commandment ("Remember the Sabbath") was also to benefit our fellow humans (20:10), making it an excellent transition to commandments five through ten (Wright, *Deuteronomy*, 75). Cf. also note 352 within Section Overview on 20:1–21.
391 This understanding is supported by the positive examples in other biblical texts of those who care for their aging parents (Joseph in Gen. 45:9–11; 47:12) and negative examples of those who abandon such care (Prov. 19:26; 23:22). For evidence that adult children were expected to care for aging parents in other ancient Near Eastern societies cf. David L. Baker, "The Fifth Commandment in Context," in *On Stone and Scroll: Essays in Honor of Graham Ivor Davies*, ed. James K. Aitken, Katharine J. Dell, and Brian A. Mastin (Berlin: de Gruyter, 2011), 257–258. As Meyers (*Exodus*, 192) notes, "Caring for the few parents who lived into old age was the only way for the senior members of a family, no longer physically able to provide for themselves, to survive."
392 Sklar, *Leviticus*, ZECOT, 525–526. Cf. 1 Timothy 5:3–4, 8, 16.
393 Wright, *Exodus*, 369.

depending on the nature of dishonor shown, could be punishable by death (Ex. 21:15, 17; Lev. 20:9; Deut. 21:18–22).[394]

The promise is "that your days may be long in the land that the LORD your God is giving you," that is, that you may have a long life, as the expanded parallel in Deuteronomy 5:16 suggests: "Honor your father and your mother, as the LORD your God commanded you, that your days may be long [i.e., that you may live a long life], and that it may go well with you in the land that the LORD your God is giving you." This promise certainly contains a natural element: the type of honor and care intended here leads to a stable society and also models for the next generation how to care for the current generation when it is older, all of which would lead to longer lives. But, since the threats in Exodus 20:5–6 and 20:7 have the supernatural element of curse, it seems likely that a supernatural element of blessing is meant here. This blessing is a fit reward to those who keep this command faithfully: having cared for their parents into old age, they themselves will experience old age and peace.[395]

20:13 While the fifth commandment focused on parents, commandments six through ten focus on human relationships more broadly. Positively stated, they explain various ways in which we must love our neighbors as ourselves (Rom. 13:9).

The sixth commandment has sometimes been translated "Thou shall not kill" (AV, RSV), but, since capital punishment is prescribed for certain crimes—including this one (Ex. 21:12; Lev. 24:17)—and lethal warfare is at times commanded (Num. 21:31–35; 31:1–12; Deut. 20:1–18; etc.), a specific type of killing must be in view here, which most modern versions capture well: "You shall not murder."

Genesis 9:6–7 provides the rationale for this command: "Whoever sheds the blood of man, by man shall his blood be shed, for God made man in his own image. And you, be fruitful and multiply, increase greatly on the earth and multiply in it." Because God made humans in his image, they are to be respected, valued, and cared for so that they may flourish. As God's image bearers, humans have supreme worth and are to be treated as such (cf. James 3:9); this value must

---

394 Cf. Exodus 21:15, 17. The Lord's commands and laws typically assume the usual situation, which in this case would be parents who provide for their children and raise them with typical—but far from perfect!—parental care. How this command applies to those who have suffered serious abuse requires great pastoral wisdom. At the least, children experiencing abuse ought to be removed immediately from such environments wherever possible. What happens when they are adults? Certainly, believers must forgive others' wrongs, even as they themselves have been forgiven (Mark 11:25; Eph. 4:32). At the same time, while forgiveness means we no longer hold the wrong against the one who has wronged us, it does not mean we must immediately reenter into relationship. In some cases this is neither wise nor safe, meaning that care for aging parents might not be possible in all cases. But this would be the exception, not the rule, and best discerned with the counsel of mature and wise pastors or elders and also with mature siblings and trusted family members who best know the relational dynamics involved.

395 The covenant blessings and curses must not be read as mechanistic laws that apply always and immediately to every individual, so that righteous people always prosper and wicked people always suffer. This misguided thinking is demonstrated by Job's friends—whom the Lord rebukes (cf. Job 4:7; 8:4, 20; 11:13–20; 22:4–11 with 42:7). Indeed, the Psalms make clear that the righteous often suffer and the wicked often prosper (Pss. 10:1–11; 17:1–15; 34:19; 73:1–14). At the same time these promises are real, and Israelites may well expect that, generally speaking, the Lord will indeed shine his favor on his obedient people by blessing them—a point Paul appears to assume for the believer today (Eph. 6:1–3). As for the promise of long life in particular, which does not always happen for faithful believers, Calvin notes that long life is simply an expression of divine favor. The early death of a believer, who now enters the Lord's presence directly, is the greatest favor the Lord can show. Rather than proof the Lord has broken a promise, it is comparable to the Lord's promising one acre and giving one hundred instead (*Institutes of the Christian Religion*, 2.8.37).

guide all our personal relationships and ethical reasoning.[396] In fact, it explains what appears at first glance to be an irony: requiring the death penalty for murderers (Ex. 21:12; Lev. 24:17). In reality such a penalty emphasizes the tremendous worth of human beings. Human life is, in fact, so valuable that anyone ending it is to face ultimate justice. No one can take the life of another without forfeiting his or her own.[397]

20:14 The seventh commandment prohibits adultery, that is, a married person's engaging in sexual activity with someone other than one's spouse (cf. Lev. 20:10).[398] This command is repeated elsewhere in both OT and NT (Lev. 18:20; 1 Cor. 6:9; Heb. 13:4). Like murder, adultery is so serious a wrong that the capital penalty is required (Lev. 20:10). It is considered an act of treachery against one's spouse (Jer. 3:20; Mal. 2:14), as well as a sin against God (Gen. 20:6; 39:9), who created marriage between man and woman as the cornerstone of a stable human society (Gen. 2:18–24) and who designed sex as the physical expression of the marriage covenant.[399] To engage in adultery is thus to betray our covenant partner and to rebel against our Creator by undermining his vision for human flourishing.[400]

20:15 The eighth commandment prohibits stealing, that is, taking others' property, typically by stealth (Gen. 31:19; 44:8; Ex. 22:7; etc.). Doing so damages their well-being for the sake of our own, putting our desires ahead of theirs—the very opposite of loving our neighbors as ourselves. Stealing is also a crime against society, whose flourishing is undermined when a person's property is wrongly taken from him since property is connected to financial security and the ability to survive and prosper.[401]

The penalties for theft are financial (Ex. 22:1; Lev. 6:1–5). This contrasts with certain ancient Near Eastern laws that stipulate that theft is punishable by death (Code of Hammurabi §§9–10, 22, 25). Not so in Israel; a human life is too valuable

---

[396] The latter noted esp. by Wright, *Deuteronomy*, 78.
[397] For a survey of approaches to the question of capital punishment today cf. Erik C. Owens, John D. Carlson, and Eric P. Elshtain, eds., *Religion and the Death Penalty: A Call for Reckoning* (Grand Rapids, MI: Eerdmans, 2004).
[398] Many hold that adultery in the OT could be committed only when a married woman slept with someone other than her husband, that is, that adultery did not apply to a married man who lay with an unmarried woman. Hugenberger makes a strong case that this is largely an argument from silence and, in fact, that "a number of texts, including Job 31:1; Hos. 4:14; and particularly Prov. 5:15–23, make clear that, whether or not there was any *legal* obligation, there definitely was a *moral* obligation for exclusive sexual fidelity on the part of husbands"; Gordon Hugenberger, *Marriage as a Covenant: A Study of Biblical Law and Ethics Governing Marriage, Developed from the Perspective of Malachi*, VTSup 52 (Leiden: Brill, 1994), 338. For his full discussion, including interaction with opposing views, cf. 313–338. Not surprisingly, then, Jesus speaks of a man's committing adultery against his wife (Mark 10:11; cf. Hugenberger, *Marriage as a Covenant*, 318n153).
[399] Sexual union is the physical expression of "leave and cleave and become one flesh" (Gen. 2:24; cf. Hugenberger, *Marriage as a Covenant*, 158–165, 248–278, esp. 266). The underlying principle is that in God's design sexual relations are to be carried out only in the context of heterosexual marriage (cf. Heb. 13:4). This explains why other texts prohibit homosexual sexual activity (Lev. 18:22; 1 Cor. 6:9; 1 Tim. 1:10) and sexual immorality in general, which is broader than adultery (note the mention of both in 1 Cor. 6:9; Heb. 13:4). On the principle above sexual immorality would include (but not necessarily be limited to) all nonmarital sexual activity.
[400] Cf. Sklar, *Numbers*, 107, at "How Does This Law Relate to Our Sexual Practices Today?" As noted there, modern studies have repeatedly shown the personal and social benefits of strong families; cf. Linda J. Waite and Maggie Gallagher, *The Case for Marriage: Why Married People Are Happier, Healthier, and Better Off Financially* (New York: Doubleday, 2000). Insofar as adultery undermines the marital bond, it undermines society. As Fretheim notes, "This commandment insists that *issues of sexuality are not a casual matter* for the good order of God's world" (*Exodus*, 235; emphasis original).
[401] Kalisch, *Exodus*, 372.

to be ended for such a crime. As Wright notes, "The priority of the sixth commandment ["You shall not murder"] over the eighth, then, was more than just numerical. It reflects a scale of values in which human life is of immeasurably higher value than property."[402]

20:16 The ninth commandment forbids false testimony in court against a "neighbor," a term that can refer to someone living near you (Ex. 11:2) but can also refer more broadly to a fellow citizen (cf. Lev. 19:18a with 19:18b).[403] The latter understanding fits better with the all-encompassing role the Ten Commandments appear to have for Israelite society. This commandment differs from the third in that the third is concerned with the misuse of the Lord's name, whether by false oaths, which could be made in a wide variety of contexts, or by blasphemy (cf. comment on 20:7). This commandment is concerned with false testimony in court, which could occur apart from any oath in that culture and would thus not automatically be covered by the third commandment.

While witnesses are a fundamental part of judicial systems today, they were especially important in ancient times, when forensic science did not exist. Due to human nature, however, false testimony was a problem then as now and was offered "for a variety of reasons and pressures. These can include: fraud and greed (Lev. 19:11–13), slander and hatred (vv. 16–18), crowd pressure or conspiracy (Ex. 23:1–2), misplaced favoritism or pity (Ex. 23:3, Lev. 19:15), and even family loyalties (Deut. 13:6–11)."[404] Such testimony leads to general injustice and to particular harm to anyone falsely accused, who may suffer loss of reputation, standing or property, physical harm (in the case of corporal or capital punishment; cf. 1 Kings 21:1–13; Matt. 26:59), or a combination of these. The temptation to harm may have been especially great in local courts, where a witness would likely know the accused: "In the intimate atmosphere of a local trial it would be particularly easy for neighbors to let their feuds and personal animosities distort the proceedings."[405] Not surprisingly, later texts seek to mitigate false testimony by requiring two or three witnesses to establish a charge (Deut. 19:15). The Lord is a God of justice; his people must testify truthfully so that justice may be done.

The penalty for false testimony corresponds to the crime: whatever harm the false witness would have caused to the accused is to be brought to bear against the false witness so that everyone may "hear and fear, and shall never again commit any such evil among you" (Deut. 19:20; cf. Deut. 19:18–21 as a whole).

20:17 The tenth commandment forbids coveting what belongs to others (for "neighbor" cf. comment on 20:16) and is the only command that repeats its prohibition: *"You shall not covet your neighbor's* house; *you shall not covet your neighbor's*

---
402 Kalisch, *Exodus*, 376.
403 That this commandment also applies to noncitizens can be deduced from the mention of the resident alien in Exodus 20:10, from the way in which the command to "love your neighbor as yourself" in Leviticus 19:18 is specifically applied to the resident alien in Leviticus 19:34, and from the insistence that Israelite law be applied equally to resident aliens (Lev. 24:22).
404 Wright, *Exodus*, 378.
405 Wenham, *Leviticus*, 268.

wife, or his male servant."[406] The relationship between the prohibitions could be understood in one of two ways. If the word "house" refers to the physical structure (cf. Gen. 33:17), then the second prohibition *lists things in addition to the house* that may not be coveted (although, if this were the sense, we might expect to see all the items listed together instead of their being separated by a repetition of the command not to covet). But if the word "house" refers more broadly to the household and household property (cf. Gen. 39:4–9), then the second prohibition *explains what the first means by "house"* (which perhaps makes more sense of the repetition of the command not to covet). Either way, the result is the same, as the end of the command makes clear: "You shall not covet . . . anything that is your neighbor's."

The English word "covet" can be defined as "to desire (what belongs to another) inordinately or culpably."[407] This is close to the way in which the Bible uses the relevant Hebrew term (*khamad*) but is not quite strong enough, since the Hebrew term typically denotes desire of something coupled with an attempt to obtain it; they are two sides of the same coin. The sense is perhaps best captured by our phrase "to set the heart on something," meaning to desire something and to take the necessary steps to get it. At seminary, when I set my heart on winning the affections of a fellow student named Ski, I not only desired to do so but took the necessary steps to seek her affections. (Thankfully, I was successful!) Similarly, the Hebrew term translated "covet" refers to a desire one chooses to engage with action. This is true of its use outside the Pentateuch[408] but also within it, as in Deuteronomy 7:25: "The carved images of their gods you shall burn with fire. You shall not *covet* [i.e., set your heart on] the silver or the gold that is on them [and[409]] *take* it for yourselves." While it could be argued that this verse refers to two distinct actions, it seems better to understand these as two sides of the same coin. Indeed, the connection between desiring and taking is so strong that Exodus 34:24, which assures Israelites that they can visit the Lord's central sanctuary without fear of invasion, simply states, "I will cast out nations before you and enlarge your borders; no one shall *covet* your land, when you go up to appear before the LORD your God three times in the year." This is not a promise that no one will desire their land; it is a promise no one will set their heart on it and attempt to take it, and the Hebrew term communicates both ideas strongly enough that the word for "take" is unnecessary.[410] In short the tenth commandment could be rendered, "You shall

---

406 The list does not name every item of value (thus the concluding words: "or anything that is your neighbor's"). It also does not assume everything has the same value, such that the wife is somehow parallel to the ox. On the contrary, especially if the word "house" refers to "household and household property" (cf. above), the list appears to begin with the most valuable (the wife) and go in descending order from there (cf. Deut. 5:21, where this becomes even more explicit). For the fact that wives were not considered the property of their husbands cf. Christopher J. H. Wright, *God's People in God's Land: Family, Land, and Property in the Old Testament* (Grand Rapids, MI: Eerdmans, 1990), 182–221.
407 *Merriam-Webster*, s.v. "covet," accessed January 9, 2024, https://www.merriam-webster.com/dictionary/covet.
408 The connection between desiring and taking is so strong that the word can refer to "choosing something because one delights in it," either positively (Ps. 68:16, where "desired" [*khamad*] refers to "chose") or negatively (Prov. 1:22; Isa. 1:29; in both places "delight in/desired" [*khamad*] refers to something the people choose to do or pursue).
409 While this could be translated "or" (so ESV), it is the regular Hebrew conjunction, which most commonly has the sense of "and."
410 For ancient Near Eastern examples of desire and action as two sides of the same coin cf. Baker, *The Decalogue*, 144–145.

not set your heart on your neighbor's house, wife, etc.," implying one must not attempt to take these things for oneself.

This understanding helps answer two questions often raised about this commandment. The first question assumes that "covet" simply means "desire" and therefore asks, "How can a commandment prohibit a desire, which often arise involuntarily?" The short answer is that this commandment is not simply about desire; it is about desire that we choose to engage, desire that we allow to govern our actions. This is where the rendering "You shall not *set your heart on* your neighbor's house" is so helpful. Many sinful desires—hatred, lust, envy, greed—can be indulged or turned from, nursed or repented of (and, if my own struggle reflects that of the typical believer, one may need to repent of the same sinful desire a hundred times in the same day). Saints of previous generations described this war against sinful desires as "mortifying the flesh," that is, putting to death the desires of our sinful nature through continually repenting and turning away from them. They recognized that the battle against sin begins in the heart and that repentance must start there as well. This commandment points the way, forbidding us from indulging sinful desires by setting our hearts on that which belongs to another.

This also helps answer the second question often raised: How does this commandment differ from the eighth ("You shall not steal")? Simply stated, this commandment is broader, since setting our hearts on what belongs to others can lead to a multitude of sins. If we covet property, this could certainly lead to stealing (8th commandment) but also false swearing, false testimony, or murder (3rd, 9th and 6th commandments; cf. 1 Kings 21:1–13); if we covet another's spouse, this could lead to adultery (7th commandment). This commandment gets at the heart of many sins we commit. Indeed, if the Ten Commandments begin by making sure that we have the right foundation in place by worshiping God alone, then they end by teaching us that the battle to be faithful to him is waged in our hearts, which we must guard with all diligence.[411]

No punishment is listed here or elsewhere for breaking this commandment, perhaps because coveting often expresses itself in ways covered by other laws (e.g., stealing or adultery or murder).

20:18–21 We now return to the people and what they are experiencing. To imagine it is to appreciate their response. As they hear the Lord's majestic, powerful voice boom out each of the Ten Commandments directly to them,[412] four other things are happening repeatedly:[413] thunder is rumbling, lightning flashing, the earth-shaking trumpet sounding, and the furnace-like smoke billowing (Ex. 20:18). Understandably terrified, they "tremble," a word used elsewhere of swaying trees (Judg. 9:9, 11) and staggering drunkards (Ps. 107:27), meaning the Israelites are literally tottering with fear, barely able to stand. While they have respected the

---
411 Cf. Bush, *Commentary on Exodus*, 285, 286.
412 Cf. Deuteronomy 5:4–24, esp. 5:22–24; for the power of the Lord's voice cf. Psalm 29:3–9.
413 The word translated "saw" is a participle in the Hebrew, in this case indicating repeated or ongoing action in the past (cf. Joüon §121f).

boundaries the Lord had set around the mountain by staying at its foot (Ex. 19:17), they now draw further back and plead with Moses, "You speak to us, and we will listen; but do not let God speak to us, lest we die" (20:19).[414] By stating that they will listen, they make clear they are not drawing back in rebellion. Rather, they are drawing back in terror; they have seen the Lord's nuclear power and fear it will melt them.

At first, Moses' response seems contradictory. Using the same Hebrew root, he tells them not to "fear" while also saying the Lord has come so that his "fear" might be before them (v. 20). The contradiction disappears once his words are put in context, the thought being, "Do not fear that you will die, as you just said (v. 19), for God has come not to kill you but to test you to see whether you will be obedient to his commands.[415] He has also come so that[416] the fear of him may be before you,[417] meaning you must keep before your eyes the reality of his power and ability to bring his justice to bear against evil and therefore must have the appropriate fear of experiencing it, with the result that you not sin."[418] Ideally, children obey their parents from a heart of love, but, because a child's love is often overrun by sinful desires, parents must use discipline to instill a fear of doing wrong as another motivation toward obedience. So it is with God and his people. Like a good father, he shows his children tender care and love while also disciplining them in such a way that they fear doing wrong. They are to delight to obey him because of their great love toward him, while also feeling literal fear of disobeying him, because his discipline is so sure. And, as with all good discipline, the end goal is the good of the one disciplined: "Oh that they had such a heart as this always, to fear me and to keep all my commandments, that it might go well with them and with their descendants forever!" (Deut. 5:29).[419]

We might summarize Moses' words in this way: "Do not live in constant dread of him, since his goal is not at all your harm. But, if you consider rebelling against him, then you should be very much afraid!" That the Lord makes the point so strongly shows he is well aware how weak the Israelites' love and faith are at this point.

Exodus 20:21 then marks an important transition indicating that God has granted the people's request and will speak directly to Moses instead (cf. Deut. 5:22–33, which also shows he does not view their request negatively). The clause "the people stood far off" is repeated from the end of Exodus 20:18 to indicate

---

414 Or perhaps simply, "May God not speak with us"; the form of the verb (jussive) indicates the speaker's wish and is not necessarily a command to Moses.
415 The Lord's "tests" center around whether his people will obey him (cf. Ex. 16:4; comment on 15:22–26 [at v. 25]). In view here could be the commands he is giving in chapters 20–23 or the commands he has already given about not coming up the mountain (cf. 19:21–24)—or both.
416 The Hebrew could be woodenly rendered, "Moses said to the people, 'Do not fear, for God has come *in order to* test you, *and so that* his fear would be before you, so you do not sin.'" The "testing" and the "fearing" are two separate reasons he has come.
417 The phrase could be woodenly translated "before your face" and is the same used in the first command (Ex. 20:3). Tying the two together, the idea would be, "You shall have no other gods *before my face*; instead, the fear of me shall be *before your face*!"
418 Cf. how an absence of fearing God leads to sin (Gen. 20:11; Ps. 36:1) while fearing him leads to avoiding it (Neh. 5:15; Prov. 16:6).
419 Noted by Wright, *Exodus*, 349.

they do not return close to the mountain to hear God's voice. (Deut. 5:30 fills out the picture, letting us know the Lord instructs them to return to their tents.) The text then notes, "Moses drew near to the thick darkness where God was," that is, to the ominous storm cloud on the mountain (Ex. 19:16; Deut. 5:22), to receive further revelation to pass on to the people. It is now clear to them that they should treat any future revelation to Moses—such as that which is about to come in the following chapters—as bearing the same authority as the Ten Commandments they have just heard the Lord himself speak to them.[420]

Response

HOW DO THE TEN COMMANDMENTS BEGIN?

As noted above (cf. Comment section above), a treaty between a king and a people in the ancient Near East often began with the king's reminding the people of who he was and of his recent history with them. In this case the Lord focuses on the fact that he is already in relationship with Israel ("I am the LORD your God") and has redeemed them ("who brought you out of the land of Egypt, out of the house of slavery"; 20:2). This leads to two observations.

First, by speaking of his redemption *before* giving the Israelites his commandments, the Lord makes clear that his laws are meant not for them to earn relationship with him but to guide them in the relationship that already exists. Second, while it is true that he is speaking to them as a king and therefore is to be obeyed, he is especially worthy of their obedience because he is a *redeeming* king, a *rescuing* king, a *good* king who has delivered them from cruel slavery into his joyful service. Obedience to his commands is to be not drudgery but delight fueled by gratitude and wonder at his unspeakably kind salvation. Paul pulls these ideas together in his epistle to the Romans. Having spent three chapters recounting God's glorious salvation in Christ (Romans 9–11), he writes, "Therefore," in light of all these "mercies of God" in Christ, "present your bodies as a living sacrifice" (Rom. 12:1), not to gain relationship with God but in joyful gratitude for the glorious relationship he has secured with you in and through Jesus. We obey not simply because he is the king but because he is a king who is unspeakably worthy of obedience.

HOW SHOULD THE TEN COMMANDMENTS BE READ?

At least three principles should guide our reading of the Ten Commandments. First, as noted above (cf. Overview), the first four commands focus on how to love God and the last six on how to love others (cf. esp. note 352 within Section Overview). That is, they address the vertical aspect of our lives (relationship with God) and the horizontal aspect of our lives (relationship with one another). Or again, they help explain the two greatest commandments: how to love God with all our heart, soul, and mind (1–4) and how to love our neighbors as ourselves (5–10).

Second, these commandments are given in a corporate context; they are to guide the Israelites as a people to live holy lives. When reading them, we should

---

[420] Cf. Houtman, *Exodus*, vol. 3, 73; cf. 19:9.

not think simply of private morality but should expect these commands to have significant implications for community life and the way we as individuals contribute (or not) to a community's flourishing.

Third, following these commands at a surface level is not the same as living a righteous life. One can follow them all and still be morally corrupt and wicked. For example, just because someone has not committed adultery does not mean he has been a good husband.

helpfully explains this point,[421] noting that laws often function to identify a minimum standard of behavior, an "ethical floor" beneath which one should not sink. But behind the laws are ethical and theological principles and values that explain not only why a particular negative behavior should be avoided but also why others should also be avoided and why various positive behaviors should be embodied—the "ethical ceiling" to which the underlying values point. For example, "Do not murder" is the floor, the very minimum of behavior one must not do. But the command flows out of the worth humans have as God's image bearers and his desire that they flourish (cf. Gen. 9:1–7). These values point toward other negative behaviors one should likewise avoid (such as undue anger toward others, the very point Jesus makes in Matt. 5:22) as well as to a higher ethic—the ceiling—one is to aim for, namely, the types of behaviors that lead to human flourishing because they embody the Lord's own values.

In the comments that follow I begin by assuming the explanation of the commandment given in the commentary above. I then identify the commandment's underlying ethic and further negative behaviors each commandment would forbid as well as positive behaviors (the ceiling) each commandment implies.[422] For those teaching or preaching through these commandments, enough material is here to take them one sermon/lesson at a time. Such sermons/lessons can easily become moralistic, simply exhorting people to do better in their own strength to please God. To avoid this, make sure to keep the context of God's grace always in view (cf. above, "How Do the Ten Commandments Begin?") and to point to Jesus as the one who not only commands the same obedience and models it for us but also keeps the commandments for us, so that his righteousness is reckoned to us as though it were our own and strengthens us to follow after him in his holy ways (Eph. 6:10–11; Phil. 4:13).[423]

(1) *You shall have no other gods before me*; that is, you shall not worship other gods.

Underlying ethic: The Lord is worthy of our exclusive loyalty.

Other behaviors prohibited: In general any activity in which we put our trust for ultimate salvation or meaning in anyone or anything besides the Lord. In particular syncretism, by which we mix elements of biblical faith with other

---

[421] Cf. Gordon J. Wenham, "The Gap between Law and Ethics in the Bible," *JJS* 48 (1997): 17–29.
[422] The identification of these negative and positive behaviors follows the model of historic catechisms such as the WLC (questions 102–148) and the HC (questions 94–113). Each paragraph below was written before consultation with these catechisms and then occasionally filled out with observations made by the catechisms.
[423] For a helpful exposition of the Ten Commandments that pays special attention to apologetic issues cf. John Dickson, *A Doubter's Guide to the Ten Commandments* (Grand Rapids, MI: Zondervan, 2016).

religions or cultic practices (Lev. 19:31; Ezek. 8:3–11); materialism, by which we make possessions and wealth the measure and source of meaning and worth (Luke 12:16–21; Col. 3:5); secularism, by which we deny the Lord the worship he is due and live unto ourselves (Pss. 10:4; 14:1); pluralism, by which we claim that there are many ways to God, thus denying the unique revelation given by the Lord to his people (cf. John 14:6; Acts 17:16–31; for further comments on idolatry cf. Response section on 32:1–34:35).

Other behaviors commanded: In general loving the Lord with all our heart, soul, and might (Deut. 6:5). In particular regular participation in worship and prayer, both public and private, by which we honor the Lord as our God (Pss. 84:10; 122:1; Matt. 6:6; Acts 2:42; Heb. 10:24–25); the ordering of our lives according to God's values and priorities, thereby showing him to be our God (Matt. 6:33); fleeing from sin and temptation and any other thing that would draw us away from obedience to God and instead pursuing after the Lord (1 Tim. 6:11; 2 Tim. 2:22); and cultivating habits and disciplines that keep our lives focused on the Lord (Matt. 6:19–21; 1 Tim. 4:7–8).

(2) *You shall not make idols*, whether of the Lord or any other god.

Underlying ethic: The Lord is worthy of our exclusive loyalty.

Other behaviors prohibited: In general any activity in which we put our trust for ultimate salvation or meaning in anyone or anything besides the Lord or misrepresent his nature in any way. In particular the making of any images of the Godhead for worship (Ex. 32:4–5; Deut. 4:15–18); the making of any images at all for worship (Lev. 19:4; 26:1); teaching false doctrines, by which we distort or deny God's character (Matt. 15:8–9); and storing up for ourselves treasures on earth, by which we make earthly things our focus and give to them our hearts (Matt. 6:19–21; for further comments on idolatry cf. Response section on 32:1–34:35).

Other behaviors commanded: In general loving the Lord with all our heart, soul, and might (Deut. 6:5). In particular keeping our worship free from any images of the Godhead or any other person or object that might lead people to worship them (Ex. 32:4–5); regular teaching in worship on the true nature and character of God (1 Tim. 4:13, 16) and meditation on the same in private (Josh. 1:8; Ps. 1:2); defending the faith from false doctrine or from attacks that seek to undermine or destroy it (Acts 17:16–31; 1 Tim. 1:3); and storing up for ourselves treasures in heaven, knowing that "where your treasure is, there your heart will be also" (Matt. 6:19–21).

(3) *You shall not take the name of the Lord your God in vain*; that is, you shall not misuse his name as one might do in false oaths or blasphemy.

Underlying ethic: The Lord's name, which represents his character and person, is not to be misused in any way.

Other behaviors prohibited: In general, any activity in which our behavior does not align with the character of the Lord, thereby bringing dishonor to his name (Prov. 30:9; Amos 2:6–7). In particular being untruthful in our speech and promises, especially those made in his name (Lev. 19:12); lifting up his name in worship while living in unrepentant sin before God or others (Isa. 1:15–17; Matt. 5:23–24); false acts of piety done in his name (Acts 5:1–11); avoiding obedience to his commands by means of unbiblical religious traditions or practices done in his name (Matt. 5:3–10); and using his name as a profanity, thereby treating it as unworthy of respect.

Other behaviors commanded: In general to live a life consistent with his character, in this way bringing honor to his name (Matt. 5:17). In particular being truthful in all our speech and promises (Matt. 5:37; Eph. 4:25) and keeping any vows made in his name (Deut. 23:21; Ps. 76:11; Acts 18:18); repenting quickly of sin before God and others so that our worship of his name may be pure and undefiled (Isa. 1:15–17; Matt. 5:23–24); singing praises to his name and speaking of his glorious deeds and character (Pss. 7:17; 66:1–4; 71:15); praying that his named would be hallowed, that is, that ourselves and others would treat the Lord with the full respect and worship due his person and character (Matt. 6:9); and confessing Jesus' name as the one above all others and submitting to him (Phil. 2:9–11).

(4) *Remember the Sabbath day* by not working on it so that you and others can rest and celebrate the Lord as your covenant God.

Underlying ethic: The Lord has set a pattern of rest in creation that is to be followed in recognition and honor of him.

Other behaviors prohibited: In general any activities by which we nullify the day of rest or make it a day devoid of any remembrance and worship of the Lord. In particular denying others rest on this day (Ex. 23:12; Deut. 5:14); resting our bodies from work but setting our minds on it or focusing our conversations on it; and filling the day with leisure activities and leaving no room for the praise and worship of God (cf. comment on 20:8–11).

Other behaviors commanded: In general any activities that encourage rest and the worship of God. In particular the worship of God in public and private, by which we honor him (cf. comment on 20:8–11); engaging in activities that bring rest to our bodies (Ex. 23:12; Deut. 5:14); and encouraging the saints through public worship and deeds of mercy (1 Cor. 16:2; Heb. 10:24–25).

(5) *Honor your father and your mother* by showing them respect all your days and caring for them into their old age.

Underlying ethic: The Lord has ordained the family such that children are to honor their parents.

Other behaviors prohibited: In general any activity by which we show dishonor to our parents or others in authority over us. In particular disobeying their covenant instruction in the Lord (cf. Deut. 6:1–2, 6–7); disobeying them in general (Deut. 21:18–20; Col. 3:20); cursing them (Ex. 21:17) or otherwise disrespecting them in our speech; and failing to care for them as they age (Prov. 19:26; 23:22; Mark 7:10–13; 1 Tim. 5:8).

Other behaviors commanded: In general any activity by which we show honor and care to our parents and others in authority over us. In particular heeding their covenant instruction in the Lord (Gen. 18:19; Ex. 12:26–27; 13:14; Deut. 6:1–2, 6–7); obeying them in general (Lev. 19:3; Prov. 1:8; 6:20; Col. 3:20); respecting them with our speech (cf. Ex. 21:17; Prov. 20:20); and caring for their needs as they age (Gen. 45:9–11; 47:12; 1 Tim. 5:3–4, 16).

(6) *You shall not murder.*

Underlying ethic: Human beings bear God's image and are therefore to be respected, valued, and cared for so that human life may flourish (Gen. 9:6–7).

Other behaviors prohibited: In general any activity that destroys human life or diminishes its flourishing. In particular deeds by which we oppress and afflict others, leading to their financial or physical harm (Lev. 19:13; Jer. 22:13); gossip or slanderous words, by which we destroy others' reputation or endanger them in the courts (Ex. 23:1; Lev. 19:16; Ps. 101:5; Prov. 16:28); nursing hatred toward others in our hearts, which leads to harmful actions and attitudes toward them (Lev. 19:17; 1 John 3:15); showing unjust anger to others or abusing them with our speech (Matt. 5:21–22); and failing to take safety precautions for the physical safety of others (Ex. 21:29).

Other behaviors commanded: In general any activity that promotes human flourishing. In particular deeds by which we help to supply the needs of others so that they may flourish materially (Ex. 23:11; Deut. 24:19–20; Prov. 14:21, 31; 28:8); defending and protecting others from unjust oppression (Ps. 72:4; Isa. 1:17); promoting love and good deeds (Heb. 10:24); being kind and gentle with one another (Eph. 4:32; 1 Pet. 3:8); blessing others with our words and building them up with encouragement (Prov. 15:23; Eph. 4:29); dealing with anger quickly so that it does not take root (Lev. 19:17; Eph. 4:26–27); being quick to forgive, even our enemies (Matt. 5:38–45; Eph. 4:32); and taking appropriate safety precautions for the physical safety of others (Deut. 22:8).[424]

(7) *You shall not commit adultery.*

Underlying ethic: As modeled in creation, sexual activity is to be expressed only in the context of heterosexual marriage (Gen. 2:21–25; cf. esp. note 399 within comment on 20:14).

Other behaviors prohibited: In general any activity by which we engage in sexual activity outside our marriage or that leads us toward marital infidelity. In particular giving our hearts over to lustful thoughts or using pornography, by which we encourage adulterous thoughts (Matt. 5:27–28); putting ourselves in situations in which compromise is more likely (Proverbs 7); failing to repent quickly of sin in our marriage, by which we introduce distance and increase the chances of infidelity; emotional affairs, by which someone looks for relational intimacy in members of the opposite sex aside from one's spouse, often leading

---

[424] The last two points are recognized in the WLC, question 135.

to sexual affairs;[425] and withholding sex from one's spouse, thereby increasing temptation to infidelity (1 Cor. 7:3–5).

Other behaviors commanded: In general any activity that strengthens and safeguards the marriage bond and fidelity to it. In particular the fostering of the marital relationship through submission and self-sacrificial love (Eph. 5:22–33); regularly enjoying sexual relations with one's spouse (1 Cor. 7:3–5); fleeing from lustful thoughts and from situations that could lead to compromise (Job 31:1; Prov. 5:8; 7:1–27; Matt. 5:27–30); and focusing one's sexual and emotional thought life on one's spouse (Prov. 5:18–19).

(8) *You shall not steal.*

Underlying ethic: The property rights of others are to be respected.

Other behaviors prohibited: In general any activity by which we defraud others of what is theirs or otherwise lead to their financial harm. In particular using deceptive business practices to gain extra money (Lev. 19:35–36; Deut. 25:13–15; Prov. 11:1); oppressing others, for example by excessive interest, leading to their financial hardship (Prov. 28:8; Ezek. 22:12); taking advantage of the financial need of others, even if by legal means, to our prospering and their harm (Neh. 5:1–12); being slow to pay workers their wages (Lev. 19:13); a lack of generosity toward the poor (Lev. 19:9–10; Deut. 14:28–29; Job 31:16–23); cheating on our taxes (Rom. 13:7); and relying on others to provide for our needs when we might otherwise be able to work (2 Thess. 3:10–11).[426]

Other behaviors commanded: In general any activity by which we help safeguard the property of others and otherwise contribute to their financial stability. In particular conducting our business dealings with others fairly (Prov. 11:1; 16:11); being generous toward the poor and those in need (Lev. 19:9–10; Deut. 14:28–29; Isa. 58:5–10), especially those among the people of God (Rom. 12:13; 2 Cor. 8:1–5, 13–15; Gal. 6:10); being generous in general toward others instead of hoarding our goods (Prov. 11:26); safeguarding the poor and less powerful from oppression (Prov. 22:22–23); granting justice to the poor in lawsuits (Ex. 23:6); paying workers their wages promptly (Deut. 24:14–15); and working with our own hands so that we might be able to share with others (Eph. 4:28).[427]

(9) *You shall not bear false witness against your neighbor* by means of false testimony in court.

Underlying ethic: We must seek justice, and not commit injustice, in the courts.

Other behaviors prohibited: In general any activity by which we deny or pervert justice in the courts. In particular failing to provide relevant testimony so that justice is denied or perverted (Lev. 5:1); the paying of bribes to deny or pervert

---

[425] This happens often enough that psychologists have identified it as one of three or four classic affair scenarios. For outlines of these scenarios cf. Frank S. Pittman, *Private Lies: Infidelity and the Betrayal of Intimacy* (New York: Norton, 1990), 132–134; David Carder and Duncan Jaenicke, *Torn Asunder: Recovering from an Extramarital Affair*, 3rd ed. (Chicago: Moody, 2008), 52–60. A summary may be found in Sklar, *Numbers*, 109–110.
[426] The last two points are observed in the WLC, questions 141–142.
[427] The last point is observed in the WLC, question 141.

justice (Deut. 27:25); and showing partiality in judgments, whether to the rich or to the poor (Lev. 19:15; Deut. 16:19).

Other behaviors commanded: In general any activity by which justice is properly upheld. In particular providing relevant testimony to legal proceedings (Lev. 5:1); refusing to take bribes (Ex. 23:8; Deut. 16:19); rendering judgments without partiality or intimidation (Lev. 19:15; Deut. 1:17); and defending those who might be unjustly taken advantage of in the courts (Prov. 31:8–9).[428]

(10) *You shall not covet*, setting your heart on what belongs to another and taking the necessary steps to acquire it.

Underlying ethic: We must not wrongly set our hearts on what belongs to others, leading to all manner of wrong in taking it.

Other behaviors prohibited: In general any wrongful setting of our heart on what belongs to others such that we wrongly take it. In particular setting our hearts on that which belongs to our neighbors such that we break any of commandments six through nine in order to get it, be it through murder, adultery, theft, or false witness, or any of the negative activities such commandments prohibit (cf. relevant discussions above).

Other behaviors commanded: In general any activity by which we arrive at contentment for what we have and a rejoicing in the blessings of others. In particular keeping our lives free from the love of money and being content with what we have, knowing we have God's own presence with us as our greatest good (Heb. 13:5); keeping a pure heart and putting to death covetous desires (Ps. 51:10; Col. 3:5);[429] storing up for ourselves treasures in heaven, not on earth, knowing that the treasures in which we invest our energies will capture our hearts (Matt. 6:19–21); valuing godliness and likeness to Christ above material comforts (1 Tim. 6:6–8; James 1:2–4); looking to Jesus for strength in whatever situation we are in so that we might be content (Phil. 4:11–13); valuing the knowledge and beauty of the Lord above all other things (Pss. 27:4; 65:4; 84:10); giving thanks to him for the gifts he has provided us and being content with them, be they physical or spiritual (Prov. 30:7–9; Matt. 15:36; 1 Cor. 12:4–26); and rejoicing in the good favor shown to others, knowing that our heavenly Father has equal love for us (Rom. 12:15; 1 Cor. 12:25–27).[430]

WHAT IS THE FEAR OF THE LORD?

As noted above (cf. comment on 20:18–21), the Israelites are shaken to the core by the powerful splendor of the Lord's appearance and think they are going to die. While Moses exhorts them not to fear instant death, which is not the Lord's intent for them, he affirms that God's "shock and awe" appearance is meant to give them a healthy fear of rebelling against the Lord. Stated simply, if we are considering doing wrong, we should be terrified at what the Lord might do by way of discipline or judgment. He is not a God to be trifled with.

---

[428] The last point is observed in the WLC, question 144.
[429] WLC, question 148.
[430] The last point is observed in the WLC, question 147.

This is not to say we should live in terror of God. He is a loving Father, a tender Savior, and, just as a child comes to an earthly loving father with joy and the assumption of loving acceptance, so we should come to our heavenly Father. But we miss out on an important aspect of biblical teaching when we reduce the "fear of the Lord" to "deep respect for the Lord." Deep respect is certainly involved, but there is more. What does it mean to *fear* him?

Briefly stated, we show our fear of the Lord through obedience to his commands. This is why so many passages can put fearing him alongside serving and obeying him (Deut. 5:29; 6:2, 24; 8:6; 10:20; 13:4; etc.). This obedience can come from two different sources. Ideally, it comes from a heart of joyful reverence and love to the God who leaves us in awe—not just respectful but in awe—of both his power and his loving rescue. In this regard we can note how some passages put fearing him alongside loving him (Deut. 10:12; 13:3–4). But our love is often weak and fickle, meaning there are times when our obedience will need to come from a literal fear—a bone-shaking terror—of what this God of incomparable power and authority may do to us if we rebel against him.

This understanding of the fear of the Lord is not limited to the OT. In Acts 5 two professing believers, Ananias and Saphira, lie to the Lord about a financial gift they have given. When the sin is exposed, he judges them with immediate death, "and great fear came upon the whole church and upon all who heard of these things" (Acts 5:11). The same understanding of the fear of the Lord is found in Hebrews 12:18–29, which actually refers to Exodus 20. In this passage the writer contrasts what happens here at Mount Sinai with what God has done in and through Jesus to make a way to heaven, which he describes metaphorically as Mount Zion, the heavenly Jerusalem. His point is a warning: if God's appearance at Mount Sinai is terrifying, and if those who refuse to follow what he says to them on earth can be sure of judgment, how much more severe and terrifying judgment can we expect if we refuse to follow what he has said to us from heaven in and through Jesus? His concluding words drive the point home: "For our God is a consuming fire" (Heb. 12:29).

But again, such fear is meant to help us only if the temptation to sin overwhelms our love of God. This same passage in Hebrews identifies our normal response to the glories of what God has done in Jesus: "Therefore let us be grateful for receiving a kingdom that cannot be shaken, and thus let us offer to God acceptable worship, with reverence and awe" (12:28). Grateful, awe-struck, obedient reverence is always the proper response to God's amazing salvation in and through Christ.

EXODUS 20:22-26

²² And the LORD said to Moses, "Thus you shall say to the people of Israel: 'You have seen for yourselves that I have talked with you from heaven. ²³ You shall not make gods of silver to be with me, nor shall you make for yourselves gods of gold. ²⁴ An altar of earth you shall make for me and sacrifice on it your burnt offerings and your peace offerings, your sheep and your oxen. In every place where I cause my name to be remembered I will come to you and bless you. ²⁵ If you make me an altar of stone, you shall not build it of hewn stones, for if you wield your tool on it you profane it. ²⁶ And you shall not go up by steps to my altar, that your nakedness be not exposed on it.'"

Section Overview

Moses has now returned from the people to the mountain in order to receive word from the Lord (v. 21). The Lord begins with a series of commands centered on proper worship. These serve as a transition between the Ten Commandments just given—which begin with a focus on proper worship—and the more detailed laws in 21:1–23:19. The commands prohibit the making of idols (20:22–23) and instruct Israel on the proper making and use of altars (vv. 24–26). These latter commands anticipate the covenant's ratification in the very next section, in which an altar is built and sacrifices made (24:1–8; cf. 20:24).[431]

Section Outline

V. Israel at Sinai: the Lord gives his covenant to Israel; the covenant is ratified (20:1–24:11) . . .
   C. The Lord's further commands regarding false gods and proper worship, spoken to Moses for the people (20:22–26)
      1. The prohibition against making idols (20:22–23)
      2. Commands about the making and use of altars (20:24–26)

Comment

20:22–26 The Lord's opening commands reinforce the first two of the Ten Commandments. Since the Israelites have heard his voice speaking to them from *heaven*, they must be sure not to make *earthly* gods of silver or gold (vv. 22–23). These can never represent the true God. If there is any difference

---
[431] Alexander, *Exodus*, ApOTC, 442.

between the two halves of verse 23, it may be, "Do not make gods of silver to accompany me, and do not make gods of gold to worship as me (or, in place of me)."

The Lord then turns to items central to worship—sacrificial altars—and issues three commands. First, altars must be made of earth (v. 24). No rationale is given for this, though verse 25 may suggest that the goal is to avoid using materials—such as metal or hewn stone—that could have the appearance of an idol. Along with this command is a promise: the Lord will "cause my name to be remembered" (Hb. *hizkir*) in various places, that is, he will establish places of worship where people can acknowledge him in worship (cf. Deut. 12:5; 16:6; 26:2).[432] When Israelites present sacrificial worship to him at such places, he promises to draw near to them and bless them. This confirms he does not want them to live in terror of him (Ex. 20:20); his real desire is to be with them and to care for them. The promise perhaps also comes at this point in order to assure them that an earthen altar would suffice.

However, if the Israelites do want to build an altar of stones, the second command states that they must use unhewn stones, since formed stones would "profane" the altar, that is, disqualify it for use in a "holy" worship ceremony (v. 25). Why? Of the proposed rationales, the simplest argues that, because figured stones are items of worship at this time (cf. Lev. 26:1), the goal of this verse is to prohibit idolatry, in keeping with the immediate context.

The third command assumes that altars could be built high enough that stairs or a ramp would be needed for access (Ex. 20:26). For example, the altar of burnt offering is roughly 4.5 feet (1.4 m) high (cf. comment on 27:1–8), making it difficult to arrange all the wood and sacrificial pieces while standing on the ground (cf. also Lev. 9:22; 1 Sam. 2:28). This verse prohibits the use of stairs because these could cause the person climbing them to lift his leg high enough to expose his nakedness, a real possibility when undergarments were not the norm and tunics could be loose fitting.[433] The reason for the prohibition of nakedness is not stated. Some suggest this is to ensure that no sexual rites are introduced into the Lord's worship,[434] though this would be a very indirect way of achieving that goal. A simpler suggestion is that exposing oneself in worship, even accidentally, is tremendously inappropriate, a disrespectful insult to the Lord.[435]

Response

WHY WAS IDOLATRY SUCH A TEMPTATION?

See Response section on 32:1–34:35.

---

[432] For *hizkir* with the sense "acknowledge in worship" cf. Exodus 23:13: "*Make no mention* of the names of other gods," that is, do not acknowledge them as your own and therefore worthy of worship (cf. Josh. 23:7). Cf. Psalm 20:7: "We *trust* in the name of the LORD our God."
[433] Priests are told specifically to wear undergarments when in the sanctuary (Ex. 28:42–43).
[434] Sarna, *Exodus*, 117.
[435] Cf. Stuart, *Exodus*, 473. Other texts associate public nakedness with shame or disgrace (Isa. 47:3; Jer. 13:26; Nah. 3:5).

HOW DOES GOD RESPOND TO PROPER WORSHIP?

"In every place where I cause my name to be remembered I will come to you and bless you" (Ex. 20:24). As noted above, the places where the Lord causes his name to be remembered are worship sites. When the Israelites go to these places and present proper worship, they are not simply to go through a religious ceremony. Their worship is to be a physical expression of their covenant commitment to the Lord and their love for him. "Burnt offerings" would be completely consumed on the altar, the costliest gift that could be given. These serve different goals, including acknowledging a worshiper's deep need of forgiveness from the Lord (Lev. 1:4), underscoring his complete dependence on God for help (1 Sam. 7:9; 13:8–12; Ps. 20:1–5), and emphasizing that God is worthy of one's highest praise (Ps. 66:13, 15). "Peace offerings" are the only ones from which offerers eat, doing so as an expression and celebration of their covenant commitment to the Lord and one another (cf. comments on 24:3–8; 24:9–11). In short, when done properly, these offerings are to be physical expressions of sincere covenant faith in the Lord and love for him. This is what worship is to be. It is not simply the singing of a song; it is the presenting of one's entire self to the Lord in faith and love (Rom. 12:1).

The Lord responds to such faith and love with blessing (Ex. 20:24).[436] This is his basic posture toward his people. His face is quick to break into a smile, as it were, and he loves to shine his beaming countenance on his people and to bless them. He is lavish with his favor and blessing, not stubborn or frugal.

But what does it mean to be "blessed"? The following comments on Leviticus 26 list the types of blessings the Lord promises his faithful people (Lev. 26:4–12).

Ross provides a helpful definition of a "blessing" and the different types found in these verses:

> A blessing is some gift, some enrichment of life, or some enablement for prosperity that comes from God. By usage it most often represents a physical benefit, such as wealth, prosperity, children, success, or peace; but the blessing may also be spiritual, such as grace and peace from God (Num. 6:22–27) or communion with God (Ps. 144:15). Both physical and spiritual blessings are found in Lev. 26.[437]

The fact that both physical and spiritual blessings are found here should help us avoid two mistakes. The first is to so emphasize the spiritual that we deny that the Lord, who has made us physical beings and wants to care for our bodies. "Jesus teaches us to pray for our physical needs ('Give us today our daily bread') and promises our heavenly Father will provide for them (Matt. 6:11, 25–34; cf. Phil. 4:19)."[438]

---

[436] For the relationship between obedient faith and blessing—and especially the fact that the relationship is not meritorious—cf. comment on 15:22–26 (esp. v. 26).
[437] Allen P. Ross, *Holiness to the Lord: A Guide to the Exposition of the Book of Leviticus* (Grand Rapids, MI: Baker Academic, 2002), 467.
[438] Sklar, *Leviticus*, TOTC, 315.

As one commentator notes, "He that is so gracious in blessing the soul is not sparing in his kindness to the body."[439]

The second mistake is that of the "prosperity Gospel," which "errs by making material blessings life's ultimate goal and claiming they will come automatically and abundantly as long as we have enough faith."[440] In fact, these verses save the spiritual blessings as the climax, the most precious gifts the LORD can give (Lev. 26:11–12). He has created us for himself, and our greatest good is found in knowing him and walking with him (cf. Matt. 6:25–33).[441]

The thrust of this passage is thus to flee from false gods that cannot satisfy to the one true God, who can bless us with what we need in both body and soul. This happens today in Jesus, through whom the Lord will provide for physical needs (Phil. 4:19) but also in whom the Lord "has blessed us ... with every spiritual blessing" (Eph. 1:3), so that we might find rest for our souls (Matt. 11:28–30). Our responsibility is to come to him in faith, worshiping him with our entire lives—and being assured that his smile of blessing beams down us with a warmth and love we cannot even imagine (Eph. 3:18–19).

OVERVIEW OF
EXODUS 21:1–23:19

Excursus: Covenant Stipulations of 21:1–23:19

Exodus 20:22–23:33 is a long section of speech from the Lord to Moses. In the speech's center is a list of stipulations—as is typical for ancient Near Eastern covenants (cf. Comment section on 20:1–21)—for the Israelites to follow (21:1–23:19). The list is framed by exhortations focusing on proper worship (20:22–26) and on obeying the stipulations and worshiping the Lord alone (23:20–33). This frame therefore emphasizes that covenant obedience begins and ends with acknowledging who the Lord is and worshiping him rightly.

Regarding the covenant stipulations the Israelites are to obey (21:1–23:19), two general observations may be made. First, some of these either repeat the Ten Commandments (e.g., 20:23; 23:10–12) or flesh them out with specific applications (e.g., 21:12–14, 17; 22:1, 3–4, 20; 23:1–3, 7), though many others come alongside

---

439 Bonar, *Leviticus*, 471.
440 Sklar, *Leviticus*, TOTC, 315. A good critique of the prosperity gospel may be found in Femi Adeleye, *Preachers of a Different Gospel: A Pilgrim's Reflections on Contemporary Trends in Christianity* (1999; repr., Grand Rapids, MI: Hippo Books, 2011).
441 Sklar, *Leviticus*, ZECOT, 724.

the Ten Commandments to fill out the picture of what it means for Israel to live as the Lord's "kingdom of priests and a holy nation" (19:6). Second, the stipulations themselves are often referred to as the Covenant Code, since they are understood to make up the "Book of the Covenant" mentioned in 24:7. But, as suggested at 24:3–11, it is perhaps better to understand 24:7 as referring to most or all of 20:1–23:33. Either way, 21:1–23:19 is clearly a distinct section in which the Lord now speaks directly to Moses and not to all the Israelites, as he did in 20:1–17.

In addition to these general observations it may be noted that there is some debate regarding how the stipulations in 21:1–23:19 are to function in Israel's everyday life and, in particular, whether they are to guide courts of law. These stipulations are similar in form (and in some cases content) to other collections of ancient Near Eastern laws.[442] These other collections have traditionally been referred to as "law codes," but this designation is commonly called into question today since we currently use the term "law code" to refer to systematically arranged legislation, often comprehensive in nature, that law courts consult. By way of contrast ancient Near Eastern law collections are not systematic in today's sense of the word, nor comprehensive, nor is there strong evidence that the courts consulted them regularly. Consequently, many have argued that these collections are primarily "the work of scribes in their attempt to construct what can be called scientific or academic treatises."[443] And, while some conclude that such treatises were descriptive of actual legal practice, others argue that these treatises were theoretical in nature and not representative of, nor intended for, actual legal practice.[444]

This perspective regarding ancient Near Eastern law has impacted the discussion surrounding biblical law. For example there is an increased preference to use the term "law collection" in place of "law code" to refer to material such as Exodus 21:1–23:19. This is a positive development insofar as it helps us not to read modern conceptions of law codes—such as their systematic or comprehensive nature—onto ancient law collections.[445] But there is also an increased tendency to distance what is found in biblical laws from Israel's actual legal practice. For some, biblical law is primarily theoretical, with no real relationship to Israelite courts. For others, biblical law describes the reality of Israel's legal practice even if it was not consulted as binding legislation in the same way a court might consult a body of law today. Still others disconnect biblical law from legal practice and connect it to the life of wisdom, viewing its goal as directing moral or religious behavior and not life in the courts.[446]

---

442 For a brief description of the main ancient Near Eastern collections that have been found cf. Cassuto, *Commentary on the Book of Exodus*, 258–259.
443 Bruce Wells, "What Is Biblical Law?: A Look at Pentateuchal Rules and Near Eastern Practice," *CBQ* 70/2 (2008): 228. Wells is simply describing this view, not endorsing it.
444 Cf. overview in Wells, "What Is Biblical Law?," 228–231.
445 With regard to the comprehensiveness of Exodus 21–23 Sarna (*Exodus*, 117) notes that this section "is silent on important areas of legal practice, such as inheritance, the transfer of property, commerce, and marriage." Moreover, as noted below, at various points the Israelites need to ask for further guidance from the Lord in order to guide their courts in making decisions.
446 For these and other perspectives cf. overview in Wells, "What Is Biblical Law?," 228–229, 230–31.

In deciding between these options at least two conclusions may be drawn in light of the immediate and larger contexts of Exodus 21–23. First, the stipulations found in Exodus 21:1–23:19 were indeed to guide the Israelites' moral and religious lives. This is evident from the simple fact that their immediate context is one of covenant (cf. Comment section on 20:1–21); as such, these stipulations are to guide the Israelites' behavior before the Lord, their covenant King. To put it differently, in his covenant with the Israelites the Lord has called them to be "a kingdom of priests and a holy nation" (19:6); these stipulations describe what that looks like. Thus it is little wonder that the Israelites are commanded to "teach them diligently to your children, and . . . talk of them when you sit in your house, and . . . write them on the doorposts of your house and on your gates" (Deut. 6:7–9).[447] These are central to faithful covenant living.

But second, the larger Pentateuchal context makes it most natural to conclude that these stipulations are to guide local courts. Whether or not other ancient Near Eastern societies looked to their law collections to inform legal practice,[448] at least two narratives indicate the Israelites are supposed to and in fact do so. In Numbers the daughters of Zelophehad bring a question regarding inheritance rights (Num. 27:3–4), which local courts would be expected to adjudicate. But since this is a new situation Moses brings their case before the Lord, who responds by issuing a ruling to guide this case and then a series of case laws to guide further decisions regarding inheritance (Num. 27:5–11). As a later passage makes clear, the Lord's original ruling and the subsequent case laws are both considered binding (cf. Num. 36:1–9). Similarly, in Leviticus 24 the Israelites are unsure about what to do in a matter that requires formal judgment. Moses again seeks direction from the Lord, who responds by naming the penalty to carry out (Lev. 24:14)—which the Israelites do (Lev. 24:23)—and then by naming the underlying legal stipulations informing what to do in similar situations in the future (Lev. 24:15–16). In short, when the Lord provides stipulations through Moses in Numbers 27 and Leviticus 24, they are to guide Israelite courts going forward, making it most natural to assume this to be the case with the stipulations in Exodus 21:1–23:19 as well, which the Lord also provides through Moses. This conclusion also fits beautifully in light of the immediate context, which has just described a series of judges that Moses is to appoint and then teach the Lord's laws (Ex. 18:13–26), making it natural to conclude that the stipulations Moses receives in chapters 21–23 are to be passed on to guide their decisions.

Three important principles must be kept in mind when reading and applying laws. First, laws reflect the lawgiver's values. One reason that most societies prohibit murder and theft is because they value life and the right to private property. As applied to biblical law, the stipulations found in 21:1–23:19 provide us an opportu-

---

447 Cf. Wright, *Exodus*, 426n28.
448 Bruce Wells notes that while there are discrepancies between the ancient Near Eastern law collections and the practice of law in the courts, there are also points of overlap, leading him to conclude that the evidence at this point is "indecisive" with respect to the extent to which the collections do or do not reflect actual legal practice. Cf. Wells, "What Is Biblical Law?," 230–231.

nity to learn what the Lord values, both for individuals and society, and we do well to identify those underlying values where we can. Second, as discussed earlier, laws often indicate a minimum standard of behavior, an "ethical floor" below which one must not sink. The underlying values, however, often point to a higher ideal, an "ethical ceiling" for which we are to strive in order to embody the Lord's character (cf. esp. Response section on 20:1–21, "How Should the Ten Commandments Be Read?"). Finally, these stipulations are best read as legal paradigms, models that could be applied to related issues even when not specifically mentioned by the stipulation. Exodus 21:23–25, for example, states that, when one person injures another, the punishment must be "life for life, eye for eye, tooth for tooth, hand for hand, foot for foot, burn for burn, wound for wound, stripe for stripe." But this list is not exhaustive (no mention is made of the ear or the nose, e.g.) but it does not need to be; as a model, this law teaches the principle that punishments must be appropriate to the crime, and Israelite courts are expected to apply this principle to physical injuries of any sort even if not listed here. In reading any law the sensitive interpreter will therefore ask, How might the values and principles underlying this law relate to other situations even if they are not explicitly named?[449]

EXODUS 21:1–11

21 "Now these are the rules that you shall set before them. ² When you buy a Hebrew slave,[1] he shall serve six years, and in the seventh he shall go out free, for nothing. ³ If he comes in single, he shall go out single; if he comes in married, then his wife shall go out with him. ⁴ If his master gives him a wife and she bears him sons or daughters, the wife and her children shall be her master's, and he shall go out alone. ⁵ But if the slave plainly says, 'I love my master, my wife, and my children; I will not go out free,' ⁶ then his master shall bring him to God, and he shall bring him to the door or the doorpost. And his master shall bore his ear through with an awl, and he shall be his slave forever.

⁷ "When a man sells his daughter as a slave, she shall not go out as the male slaves do. ⁸ If she does not please her master, who has designated her[2] for himself, then he shall let her be redeemed. He shall have no right to sell her to a foreign people, since he has broken faith with her. ⁹ If he designates her for his son, he shall deal with her as with a daughter. ¹⁰ If he takes another wife to himself, he shall not diminish her food, her clothing, or her marital rights. ¹¹ And if he does not do these three things for her, she shall go out for nothing, without payment of money."

[1] Or *servant*; the Hebrew term *'ebed* designates a range of social and economic roles; also verses 5, 6, 7, 20, 21, 26, 27, 32 (see Preface)   [2] Or *so that he has not designated her*

---

[449] This commentary does so for many of the laws of chapters 21–23 in the relevant Response sections (cf. the approach taken above to the Ten Commandments in the Response section on 20:1–21); cf. also Stuart's commentary on 21:1–23:19, in which he consistently identifies the range of issues to which each law would apply.

Section Overview

Verse 1 briefly introduces the stipulations found in 21:2–23:19. These stipulations then open by addressing servanthood (21:2–11). This is no surprise. The Israelites have suffered cruel bondage; these opening stipulations teach them not to inflict the same on others. Instead, just as the Lord is a gracious master to the Israelites as his servants, the Israelites are to be gracious masters to their servants.

Two series of laws are listed here. The first addresses the length of service for male servants, as well as questions relating to a wife or children such servants might have (vv. 2–6). The second series addresses the rights of women sold as servants for the eventual purpose of marriage (vv. 7–11).

Section Outline

    V. Israel at Sinai: the Lord gives his covenant to Israel; the covenant is ratified (20:1–24:11) . . .
        D. Further stipulations of the covenant, spoken to Moses for the people (21:1–23:19)
           1. Introduction to 21:1–23:19 (21:1)
           2. Stipulations regarding servants (21:2–11)
               a. Male servants (21:2–6)
               b. Female servants (21:7–11)

Comment

21:1 The Lord refers to the covenant stipulations that follow as "rules," a word that refers elsewhere to binding regulations (v. 31; Lev. 18:4–5, 26; 24:22). These are not optional for Israelite behavior. By following them the Israelites will avoid behavior displeasing to their covenant King. What is more, the stipulations reflect principles and values that point to a positive ethic for the Israelites to embody, displaying their King's character in the world.[450]

21:2–6 Many of the initial stipulations are formulated as case laws. A case law begins by identifying a situation (or "case") with an "if" or "when" clause. This is known as the protasis. It is followed by a clause, known as the apodosis, that describes what to do in that situation.[451] Exodus 21:28 illustrates this form:

Protasis: "When an ox gores a man or woman to death"
Apodosis: "the ox shall be stoned"

The opening case laws deal with a Hebrew slave/servant,[452] which ESV translates as "slave" but also notes "servant" as a possibility, since the Hebrew term

---

[450] Cf. esp. Response section on 20:1–21, "How should the Ten Commandments be read?," third paragraph.
[451] In a series of case laws Hebrew often uses *ki* to introduce the main case (as in 21:2, 7) and *'im* to introduce subcases (as in 21:3–6, 8–11). "The sequence runs something like this: 'In the case of . . .' (main situation); 'if, however . . .' (additional or qualifying circumstances)" (Wright, *Exodus*, 397n13).
[452] The term "Hebrew" is sometimes understood in this and other passages to refer not to an ethnic group (the Israelites) but to a low social class. But the term is applied first to Abraham without any such connotation (Gen. 14:13) and is naturally understood as a reference to his descendants (cf. esp. Gen. 43:32, where "Hebrews"

'ebed designates a range of social and economic roles. For some modern readers the term "slave" might call to mind the slave trade of past centuries in which slaves were often kidnapped and sold and thus viewed as chattel—property that masters could treat as they wished. Verse 16, however, forbids both the kidnapping and the selling of a kidnapped person (and makes either action a capital offense); following this law alone would have decimated most historical slave trading. In contrast,

> servants had legal rights in Israel. Israelite law stipulated they went free if their masters abused them (Ex. 21:26–27), and they had the right to rest on the Sabbath (Ex. 20:10).[453] In addition, Israelite masters were commanded to treat their servants with compassion (Deut. 15:12–15; 16:11–12). Indeed, servants who escaped from cruel masters were not to be returned (Deut. 23:15–16).[454]

In short, servants in Israel were seen not as chattel but as humans, made in God's image and to be respected as such (Deut. 15:12–15 illustrates this perspective beautifully).

One of the most common causes of servitude was debt, causing the debtor to sell into servitude either himself (cf. Lev. 25:39–43, 47–55) or his children (cf. 2 Kings 4:1; Neh. 5:4–5). While such debt is never good, the protective nature of such servitude should be noted:

> Servitude, if performed under the humane conditions required by law, "could be said to be little different *experientially* from many kinds of paid employment in a cash economy" (Wright, 2004: 333). In both cases, one person submits to the control of another and provides labor in exchange for certain benefits, whether money (in many of today's economies) or food and shelter (in ancient Israel). Indeed, the potential benefits were great enough that some people sought to become permanent servants (Deut. 15:16–17; cf. Ex. 21:5–6). These benefits included protection from poverty, provision of regular food and shelter, and a place in a stable family. For those in poverty or facing it, this type of servitude was literally a lifesaver.[455]

Because this was a commercial arrangement, language is used that is normally reserved for speaking of property, such as "buys" (Ex. 21:2). At first glance such language gives the impression that servants were dehumanized and thought of as mere property. But such a conclusion would ignore what has been noted above

---

contrasts with "Egyptians," the latter reference clearly to an ethnic group). Leviticus 25:39–46 does make a distinction between Israelite servants and those from other nations (in other words, it makes a distinction based on ethnicity). See discussion on those verses, and especially Ex. 25:44–46, in Sklar, *Leviticus* ZECOT, 700–701.
453 Cf. Wright, *Old Testament Ethics for the People of God*, 334–335.
454 Sklar, *Leviticus*, ZECOT, 697.
455 Sklar, *Leviticus*, TOTC, 698; the quote is from Wright (*Old Testament Ethics for the People of God*, 333). Stuart (*Exodus*, 480) also uses the analogy of military service, which includes many of the same benefits as above (plus pay) and which people sign up for either for limited amounts of time or, through repeated enlistments, for an entire career.

about a servant's humanity and would also miss the fact that we use the same type of language in similar situations today.

> In English, we regularly use commercial language to describe people when the context is commercial, for example, "trading" a player to another team (as one might "trade" a stock), or "transferring" an employee to another location (as one might "transfer" money). We do not use this language because we view the people involved as less than human; we use it because it accurately describes their circumstances in a given commercial context.[456]

The use of such language here is not to put servants on the level of furniture, any more than to say that "trading" sports stars puts them on the level of a stock.[457]

As with many of the laws in chapters 21–22, this passage contains a series of case laws. Each case answers questions related to the commercial or financial aspects of servitude or marriage. The first questions are straightforward: What is the maximum length of a Hebrew servant's term, and what might he owe at the term's end? The answers are that the maximum term length is six years and that he owes nothing at the term's end (21:2).[458] The next question is also straightforward: What if he comes in single and does not marry? The answer is simple: he goes out single (v. 3). But now the questions become more complex. Stated most broadly, What if he is already married or gets married during his servanthood? The cases of verses 3–6 answer these questions. To understand these answers it must be remembered that marriage in ancient Israel was often preceded by a betrothal in which a gift would be given to the bride's family.[459] Such a gift enabled the legal transfer of the wife from her father's household to her groom's. It also entailed financial implications to betrothal and marriage, and those implications give rise to at least three specific questions that verses 3–6 answers.

First, if a man who becomes a servant is already married when he enters into servitude, what happens to his wife when his servitude is over? She goes with him, since he has already given any necessary betrothal gift (v. 3).

---

456 Sklar, *Leviticus*, TOTC, 308–309.
457 The law also makes clear the servant's term is only six years, meaning the servant is not "bought" outright, like a piece of property. The situation is more like acquiring the right to the servant's services, much like a sports team "acquires" a player (Stuart, *Exodus*, 474; indeed, the Hebrew verb may be translated "acquire" instead of "buy"; BDB 888).
458 Debate surrounds how Exodus 21:2 and its parallel in Deuteronomy 15:12 relate to Leviticus 25:41, which states that Israelite servants are not set free until the Jubilee, which occurred every fiftieth year (cf. Lev. 25:8–10). Cf. Gregory Chirichigno, *Debt-Slavery in Israel and the Ancient Near East*, JSOTSup 141 (Sheffield, UK: JSOT Press, 1993), 334–336. Chirichigno argues that Leviticus 25 is addressing a case in which the head of a household is so impoverished that he must sell himself and his entire household into servitude, while Exodus 21:2 and Deuteronomy 15:12 address a situation in which an Israelite landowner with far less debt sells a dependent into servitude. For similar arguments cf. Wright, *God's People in God's Land*, 253–257. This understanding of Leviticus 25:41 finds strong support in the text (cf. Sklar, *Leviticus*, TOTC, 303). This understanding is also plausible for Exodus 21:2 and Deuteronomy 15:12, since (1) it would explain why the term of service is only six years (i.e., the debt is smaller) and (2) the very next law in Exodus 21 clearly involves a father's selling a daughter into servitude (vv. 7ff.).
459 Genesis 34:12; Exodus 22:16–17; 1 Samuel 18:25; 2 Samuel 3:14; Hosea 12:12. Cf. Hugenberger, *Marriage as a Covenant*, 246–247. Cf. comment on 22:16–17.

Second, what if he is given a wife from the master's household and she has children? Since his being sold into servitude implied he had no financial means, he could not give a betrothal gift, meaning the woman (and any offspring she bore) was still legally part of the master's household. Consequently, the man may not simply leave with them when his servitude is over (v. 4). Importantly, the law is not assuming that this is what the man will do (as v. 5 goes on to make clear); it simply focuses on the narrow question: In light of betrothal practice, to whose household do the wife and her children legally belong?

Third, is there anything the servant can do to keep his family together? Certainly! "If the slave plainly says, 'I love my master, my wife, and my children,'" then he can become a permanent servant, in which case his service will make him part of the same household (vv. 5–6).[460] The parallel passage in Deuteronomy makes clear the servant's love for his master is due to the beneficial treatment the servant has received from him (Deut. 15:16), while the claim to love a wife and children is what Israelites would expect to be the reality. The thought of leaving without them (Ex. 21:4) is out of the question. In other words verse 4 makes clear to whose household the wife and children legally belong, but it is not sanctioning the husband's leaving without them; verses 5–6 describe the action the husband is expected to take. Moreover, because this law is publicly known, it means that servants who accepted a wife from the master went into the situation with their eyes wide open (and had the freedom not to do so if they knew the master to be unkind). Indeed, given the servant's financial situation, this may have been one of the only hopes he had of marrying and starting a family and thus may have been something he was eager to do (cf. note 460).

By way of summary, moderns are tempted to read this law as condoning chattel slavery, condoning a man's abandonment of his wife and children, and forcing a slave into lifelong servitude if he wanted to keep his family. Set in its historical context, however, this law describes indentured servitude in order to clear a debt, assumes that the man would in fact stay with his wife and children out of his love for them, and assumes he willingly entered the marriage and the servitude that went with it in order to have a chance at having a family.

Two final comments may be made on some of the details in verses 2, 6. First, verse 2 sets an upper limit of six years on the period of service (for Lev. 25:41 cf. note 458). This is a helpful safeguard for the person in debt who could otherwise be forced to accept unreasonable conditions from the person holding the debt (cf. Jer. 34:8–22, where the Lord condemns Israelites for disregarding this very law and forcing permanent servitude upon fellow Israelites). At the end of the six years the debtor goes out "free" (i.e., as a free person, no longer a servant; see the use of the term in Deut. 15:12–13, 18) and the debt is discharged (he owes "nothing"). Second, regarding Exodus 21:6, debate exists whether to translate "His master

---

[460] Compare Jacob's serving fourteen years for Leah and Rachel (Gen. 29:15–30). The situation there differs in that permanent servitude is not required, perhaps because he is family or because he does not start out in a position of debt.

shall bring him to God" or "His master shall bring him to the judges." If the former ("to God"), the idea may be that the entire rite is carried out at a worship site, with God as divine witness,[461] or that the matter is at least confirmed at a worship site, after which they return home and pierce the servant's ear there. If the latter ("to the judges"), the idea may be that the rite takes place at an official place (such as the city gate), where the leaders of the community would gather or, again, that it is confirmed there and the ear-piercing then done at home. Of the two translations ("to God" and "to the judges"), normal usage favors the former since the relevant word usually refers to God (or in a pagan context to gods).[462] Moreover, though in some passages the word possibly refers to judges or leaders (Ex. 22:8–9; Judg. 5:8; 1 Sam. 2:25; cf. BDB 43.1a), the data is not clear, leading many standard translations to maintain "God" (or "gods," depending on the context) in some or all those passages.[463] In either case, however, the goal of the rite is to make official the servant's decision to enter into permanent servitude.

21:7–11 Having answered questions related to male Hebrew servants, the text now answers questions related to female Hebrew servants (that these servants are also Hebrew is implied in Ex. 21:8). To understand the text an important aspect of the social context must be kept in mind, namely, marriages in Israel were often arranged—that is, brides and grooms were chosen for each other by their families (or by servants acting on the family's behalf; cf. Gen. 24:2–4). This is foreign today to most from the West, where marriage is thought of in terms primarily of romance, where an individual's choices reign supreme, and where building a self-sustaining career as a single person is a readily available option for many. But the situation in Israel was entirely different.

To begin, prioritizing romance as the reason for marriage is a very modern way of thinking. In biblical times (and throughout much of history) the "various factors in a marriage to be weighed in the negotiations involved social parity, economic advantage and expansion of the kinship network."[464] This does not preclude romance, but it was not the leading factor.

Second, in contrast to modern individualism, Israelites thought corporately, bearing in mind the ways that their choice of marriage partner impacted their clan and tribe. Finally, building a self-sustaining career as a single person was both foreign to the Israelites' family-centered way of thinking and, for most women in an ancient Near Eastern context, not a practical option (note how often "widows" are grouped alongside the poor and oppressed: Deut. 10:18; 14:29; 16:11; etc.). From this perspective ensuring one's daughter had a home with her own family was not cruel but incredibly loving, especially for the poor, for whom the type of

---

[461] For an ancient Near Eastern parallel of an important event being carried out in the gate of the temple of a god cf. F. Charles Fensham, "New Light on Ex 21:6 and 22:7 from the Laws of Eshnunna," *JBL* 78/2 (1959): 160–161.
[462] For "gods" cf. Genesis 31:30; Exodus 18:11; etc. The singular, however, is by far the most common use of the term (Gen. 5:22; 6:9; Ex. 1:17; 3:6; Num. 22:10; Deut. 4:35; etc.).
[463] Cf. ESV; JPS; NRSV. Indeed, in no one passage do the standard translations agree that *'elohim* should be translated as "judges."
[464] Matthews, "Family Relationships," 294.

arranged marriage described here might be the only way to provide their daughter with a better life.[465]

With that background in mind, we turn to the case laws in Exodus 21:7–11 and the questions they answer. Verse 7 describes the main case: a father has sold his daughter as a servant. The first question is simply, Does she, too, go out free in year seven (cf. v. 2)? The answer is no. Why not? Presumably, while a motivating factor for the father's action was poverty (cf. Neh. 5:5), the overarching goal was an arranged marriage, as shown by the focus on marriage and marital rights in the laws that immediately follow (this distinguishes it from Deut. 15:12, where servitude more generally is addressed). In light of this, while she began as a maidservant, the end goal was always that she experience care and stability by becoming a permanent part of the household as a wife.

This understanding also sheds light on the questions answered by the laws in Exodus 21:8–11. First, what if she was to be the master's wife (he had "designated her for himself") but she was displeasing to him and he no longer wished to marry her?[466] His canceling of the arranged marriage was considered an act of broken faith against her. (The Hb. for "break faith" is strongly negative, with connotations of treachery and deceit; cf. Pss. 59:5; 78:57; Prov. 11:3; Isa. 24:16. For a marriage context cf. Jer. 3:8, 11, 20; Mal. 2:14–16.) He could not sell her to a foreign people but had to let her be redeemed, that is, had to allow payment be given to release her (Ex. 21:8). Presumably this was done by her father or, if he was unable, by one of her relatives (cf. Lev. 25:47–49).

Second, what if the arranged marriage was between her and the master's son? Then the master "shall deal with her as with a daughter" (Ex. 21:9), which could imply many things: he will make sure she has adequate food and clothing; he will not have sexual relations with her; he will treat her as a full family member, not a second-class one. In short, whether the marriage occurs immediately or is a few years away, he shall treat her as his own flesh and blood.

Third, what if he marries another wife? The word for "another" (*'akher*) can mean "another in addition to" (Gen. 8:10; 29:27), in which case he has already married the woman sold as a servant. However, the word can also mean "another instead of," that is, a "different" one (Gen. 29:19; Num. 14:24; Deut. 24:2), in which case he has not married the servant woman.[467] In favor of the second approach the final verse mentions release but no divorce (Ex. 21:11), suggesting no marriage has taken place. So what happens if he marries another woman instead of the servant? If her family is unable to redeem her and she stays (v. 8), the master must not reduce any of the physical provision he would have given her before the marriage (v. 10). This includes food, clothing, and "marital rights/habitation." Debate surrounds

---
465 Cf. NET note on Exodus 21:7.
466 That the marriage has not taken place is suggested by the fact that divorce is not mentioned in 21:8. Note also that the ESV follows the marginal reading of the Hebrew text (also followed by the LXX and Vulgate). The alternate reading of the Hebrew is found in the ESV mg.: "If she does not please her master, so that he has not designated her [e.g., for a son], then he shall . . ." The difference in Hebrew is whether one reads the relevant word as *lo* or *lo'*. In either case the arranged marriage is called off.
467 Hugenberger, *Marriage as a Covenant*, 322.

the last of these. The Hebrew word (*'onah*) occurs only here in the OT, and the underlying root has several different meanings, leading to a variety of views as to its meaning. One use of the root refers to sexual relations, leading some to understand the term to refer to "marital (i.e. conjugal) rights." Against this approach it may be noted that the use of the root is found in negative contexts as opposed to normal marital contexts (Gen. 34:2; Deut. 22:24, 29; Judg. 19:24; etc.), and, again, the law seems to presuppose marriage has not taken place. Another use of the root is related to "dwelling" (cf. Deut. 33:27), meaning the term in question would refer to shelter.[468] In favor of this approach "shelter" naturally complements food and clothing and does not need to assume that marriage has taken place.

But a final question remains. What if the master is unwilling to continue to provide such food, clothing, and shelter? She is released from her servitude (Ex. 21:11); no redemption payment is needed, since he has been unfaithful in his responsibilities.

In short these laws provide tremendous protection for the woman who is sold as a servant for the eventual purpose of marriage. At every turn her rights are guarded and the master's ability to wrong her (even through neglect) is restricted.[469]

Response

Perhaps more so than any other passage in Exodus 21:1–23:19 these verses raise significant apologetic and pastoral questions for the modern reader. I begin by naming three of those questions below and pointing to the places where I have sought to answer them in the commentary. I then consider two broader questions of application.

IS THE BIBLE CONDONING SLAVERY?

See the opening discussion in comment on 21:2–6.

DO VERSES 1–6 CONDONE A MAN'S LEAVING HIS WIFE AND
CHILDREN AND FORCING HIM INTO LIFELONG SLAVERY?

See the remaining opening discussion in comment on 21:2–6 and the three questions and answers that immediately follow them.

DO VERSES 7–11 CONDONE TREATING A DAUGHTER
AS MERE PROPERTY TO BUY AND SELL?

See comment on 21:7–11, which focuses on the different aspects of the passage that lead to this question.

WHAT DO THESE LAWS DO FOR MASTERS?

These verses make clear that servants are expected to fulfill their contractual obligations to their masters. For example male servants are expected to serve out

---

[468] Hugenberger, *Marriage as a Covenant*, 321.
[469] I am grateful to my students Chris Jameson, Ryan Northfield, and Charles Stover for the use of "restriction" language to describe these laws' effect on the master.

their six-year term and to understand that there are financial implications if they choose to receive a wife from the master. In short masters have a right to see that financial obligations made toward them are kept, and servants are to be faithful in their responsibilities toward the master.

In today's context the closest parallel to the servant-master relationship would be that of employee to employer. In that context the underlying question to ask would be, What does it mean for employees to be faithful to their contractual obligations to their employer? Christians in particular are exhorted to serve those over them in authority with such faithfulness and good character that it makes the gospel attractive (1 Tim. 6:1; Titus 2:9–10). A related question would be, What does faithfulness look like regarding any contractual obligation we have undertaken, whether in a work context or elsewhere? Christians are expected to be people of their word (cf. Ps. 15:4; Matt. 5:37) and in this way testify that they follow a God of truth.

WHAT DO THESE LAWS DO FOR SERVANTS?

While these laws provide safeguards for masters, they also provide significant protections for servants. Servanthood itself provides a way for those in debt to clear it while being part of a stable household. The six-year limit for male servants protects the person in debt from having to accept unreasonable conditions from his creditor. And female servants are protected from being sold like a piece of property, are in fact to be treated like a daughter, and are given rights of release if the master is unfaithful in his contractual responsibilities. All of this should make good sense to an Israelite. Since humans bear God's image, they are worthy of being treated with justice, respect, and fairness. To take advantage of them in their weakness would be to disregard their nature as God's image bearers.

As applied to the employee-employer relationship, the underlying question to ask would include, What does it look like for employers to treat their employees with justice, respect, and fairness as God's image bearers? More specific questions might include, What accountability measures are in place if employers are not faithful in their contractual responsibilities? Are there currently accepted labor practices by which employers can take unfair advantage of vulnerabilities among employees—and which Christian employers should therefore reject? Christian employers especially are to remember that they are servants of the Lord, their heavenly master, and are to imitate him in the way they treat those under their authority (Eph. 6:9; Col. 4:1). Just as the Lord showed himself to be a kind and gracious master in redeeming the Israelites from slavery, so he has shown himself to be a kind and gracious master by redeeming us in Jesus. Those under our authority should experience the same kindness and grace from us.

EXODUS 21:12–17

¹² "Whoever strikes a man so that he dies shall be put to death. ¹³ But if he did not lie in wait for him, but God let him fall into his hand, then I will appoint for you a place to which he may flee. ¹⁴ But if a man willfully attacks another to kill him by cunning, you shall take him from my altar, that he may die.

¹⁵ "Whoever strikes his father or his mother shall be put to death.

¹⁶ "Whoever steals a man and sells him, and anyone found in possession of him, shall be put to death.

¹⁷ "Whoever curses[1] his father or his mother shall be put to death."

[1] Or *dishonors*; Septuagint *reviles*

Section Overview

These offenses strike at "fundamental moral values that were to underpin Israelite society,"[470] such as the value of human life and of the family. Due to the offenses' severity, the penalty for each is capital. The offenses include murder (with a distinction made between murder and manslaughter; vv. 12–14), mistreatment of parents (vv. 15, 17), and kidnapping and human trafficking (v. 16).

Section Outline

V.D. Further stipulations of the covenant, spoken to Moses for the people (21:1–23:19) . . .
  3. Stipulations related to capital offenses (21:12–17)
     a. Murder versus manslaughter (21:12–14)
     b. Striking a parent (21:15)
     c. Kidnapping and human trafficking (21:16)
     d. Cursing a parent (21:17)

Comment

21:12–14 The first three stipulations address killing. The first gives the general rule: whoever kills another person has committed a capital offense (v. 12). Because human beings bear God's image, they are of immeasurable value. To destroy a life of such worth is to forfeit one's right to one's own (Gen. 9:6). But the community may not apply this penalty lightly, and other laws make clear that at least two witnesses are necessary in murder cases (Num. 35:30; for the capital penalty today cf. note 397 within comment on 20:13).

---

[470] Alexander, *Exodus*, ApOTC, 479.

The second and third stipulations address related subcases. In the second the killer "did not lie in wait, ... but God let [the victim] fall into his hand" (Ex. 21:13). What does this mean? If the focus is on premeditation (the killer did not plan the killing in advance), this leaves room for a crime of passion, what would be classified today as second-degree murder. If the focus is on intention (the killer did not mean to kill), this leaves room only for accidental death, what we know today as manslaughter. The fullest law that treats the same subject elsewhere appears to assume the second, manslaughter (Num. 35:16–25). This is perhaps also the best way to understand the words "but God let [the victim] fall into [the killer's] hand," that is, it was "an act of God," for which there is no human liability.[471] In such cases the killer is able to flee to a place of refuge, which at this point in time is perhaps a sanctuary (cf. Ex. 21:14). Once Israel enters the land, the Lord will establish cities of refuge to which an unintentional killer could flee (Num. 35:9–29; Deut. 4:41–43; 19:1–13; Joshua 20). This arrangement would protect the killer from any relatives seeking blood vengeance and also protect the land from being defiled by the slain person's blood (Num. 35:31–34). The unintentional killer would remain there "until the death of the high priest" (Num. 35:25), at which point he would be allowed to go free. As many commentators observe, the high priest's death appears to function as an atoning sacrifice, his blood being taken as a substitute for that of the unintentional killer and cleansing the land of innocent blood.[472]

The third stipulation returns to a case in which "a man willfully attacks another to kill him by cunning" (Ex. 21:14). In contrast to verse 13, the killing in this verse is intentional, and the phrase "by cunning" suggests some form of premeditation, what would be classified today as first-degree murder. This does not necessarily mean crimes of passion are not included. The point of describing it as premeditated may be simply to emphasize that it is not an accident, in support of which is the fact that the fullest treatment of such cases elsewhere (Num. 35:16–25) seems to distinguish only in terms of whether or not the death is accidental.[473] In such nonaccidental cases of murder the killer is to be executed. As Exodus 21:14 goes on to explain, this applies even to one who goes and clings to the altar, an act that would normally guarantee someone's safety, perhaps because it was thought that contact with God's property gave the person God's protection (cf. 1 Kings 1:50–53). In the case of guilty murderers, however, such protective measures do not apply (cf. 1 Kings 2:28–34).

21:15 Biblically speaking, God has established a structure within the family in which parents are in the position of authority. As such, he commands that they be honored and revered (Ex. 20:12; Lev. 19:3), meaning their instruction is to be heeded and they are to be shown respect and care, especially as they age and are less able to care for themselves (cf. comment on 20:12). Such respect and care are

---

[471] E.g., Deuteronomy 19:4–5 (Bush, *Commentary on Exodus*, 313).
[472] Cf. Sklar, *Numbers*, 415 ("How Does the Death of the High Priest ... ?).
[473] Cf. Sklar, *Numbers*, 411–412.

also in keeping with God's vision for a flourishing society, central to which are healthy families (cf. Response section).

The very opposite of such respect and care is to strike one's parents, causing them physical harm and expressing utmost contempt for their authority. This is not only an act of treachery against those who have cared and provided for a child (cf. 1 Tim. 5:4); it is also an act of treason against the Lord, since it is a rejection of his express covenant command (Ex. 20:12) and an attack on the type of society that his command is to help establish. Just as treason is a capital offense in many countries to this day, so also here, with adult children particularly in view (cf. comment on 21:17). If this strikes us as overly severe, it may be worth asking if part of the reason is because we live in a society with too low a view of the family, of parental authority, and of the elderly.[474]

21:16 "Kidnapping, presumably with the intention of selling the victim into slavery, was apparently tantamount to taking a life [cf. 21:12] and is punished similarly."[475] As noted above, had earlier generations paid attention to such a verse, the slave trade of most of human history would have been decimated.

This verse's translation is debated. The ESV assumes more than one guilty person could be described here: the kidnapper and the purchaser (although they could be the same person). Most translations and commentators assume the kidnapper is described both times, e.g., "He who kidnaps a man, whether he sells him or he is found in his possession, shall surely be put to death" (NASB 1995).[476] In either case both kidnapping and human trafficking are considered capital offenses.

21:17 The honor and care due to parents have been discussed at verse 15.[477] That verse addresses the opposite of such respect and care from a physical perspective: striking them. This verse addresses the opposite of such respect and care from a verbal perspective: cursing them.

> The word "to curse" (*qillel*) can refer to abusive or dishonoring speech in general [2 Samuel 16:6–7] or to uttering a formal "curse" in particular [Deuteronomy 23:4; 1 Sam. 17:43]. Though the option in view here is unclear, either way, the point is the same: to curse someone is to treat him as an enemy and wish great harm on him [see Josh. 24:9; 2 Sam. 16:13; 2 Kings 2:24].... While this law applies directly to verbal curses, it would apply equally to actions that communicate the same. In short, it describes those who have shown by word or deed that they wished their parents were dead. Note this verse does not have in mind young children and their typical disobedience. In light of ... other commands to honor and revere

---

[474] In other instances, however, some will struggle to have a high view of the family and parental authority because of serious mistreatment by the parents; cf. note 394 within comment on 20:12.
[475] Meyers, *Exodus*, 192.
[476] Cf. Kalisch, *Exodus*, 399; note also Joüon §175b.
[477] Why does Exodus 21:17 not follow verse 15? Perhaps to arrange verses 15–17 as a chiasm (cf. vv. 12–14; Stuart, *Exodus*, 487) or because verses 15–17 are in descending order of severity (Alexander, *Exodus*, ApOTC, 479).

parents (which apply especially to adult children who are to care for their aging parents),[478] this verse has adult sons or daughters in view, those who are old enough to bear the responsibility of caring for aging parents but have scorned their parents' words and their parents' needs.[479]

For further discussion on the penalty cf. comment on 21:15.

Response

As noted above (cf. Section Overview), the penalty for these offenses is capital because the offenses themselves are incredibly severe, striking at values fundamental to a biblical worldview. The first of these is the value of human life.

WHY IS HUMAN LIFE SO VALUABLE?

In the biblical story it is not simply human life that is of value. In Genesis 6–9 God ensures that animals also make it safely into the ark and names them as members of the covenant he makes with Noah (Gen. 6:18–20; 8:1; 9:9–10). In the Pentateuch various laws encourage compassion toward animals (Ex. 22:30; 23:5, 11–12a; Deut. 22:6–7), and Proverbs describes the righteous as those who care for their beasts (Prov. 12:10). Clearly, animal life matters.

But the Bible also makes clear that human life matters uniquely since humans alone bear God's image (Gen. 1:26–27). On the one hand this gives them value because they are God's representatives. They have been appointed by God to represent him and his rule (Gen. 1:28), and this role gives them a special dignity and honor (Ps. 8:3–8). At the same time they have value because they are the special objects of his affection and care. Just as parents believe their children, who are in their own image and likeness (cf. Gen. 5:3), are priceless, God views mankind, which is in his own image and likeness, as priceless. God's first words to humanity are words of blessing (Gen. 1:28). No parent is surprised by this. We cannot help but love those who bear our image.

Moral implications flow from this. To disrespect, harm, or destroy God's representatives is to show utter disregard for God himself. How can we say we love God while we show hate to those made in his image (cf. James 3:8–9)? The way someone treats a king's representative says much about what that person thinks of the king. Further, just as parents view it as the greatest wrong when someone harms their children, who bear their image, so also does God view it as great harm when we harm someone who bears his image. For these reasons to kill someone in his image (Ex. 21:12, 14) or to kidnap and sell someone like a piece of property (v. 16) is an offense of the greatest nature and met with a penalty that is equally severe.[480] For further implications on the types of behavior expected toward humans in light of their value as God's image bearers see Response section on 20:1–21, "You shall not murder."

---

478 Cf. comment on 20:12.
479 Sklar, *Leviticus*, ZECOT, 560.
480 For further thoughts on biblical penalties cf. Sklar, *Leviticus*, TOTC, 62–63, 65–67.

But this passage does not only speak of the value of human life. It also emphasizes a second value: the family.

WHY SUCH A FOCUS ON PARENTAL AUTHORITY?

As noted at 21:15, the emphasis on respecting and caring for parents is in keeping with the biblical view that healthy families are foundational to a flourishing society. The book of Proverbs, which casts a vision for how to live properly in God's world, is full of admonitions to listen to one's parents (Prov. 1:8–9; 6:20; 23:22), describes in the most negative light those who do not care for them (Prov. 19:26; 28:24; 30:11, 17), and makes extensive exhortations to be faithful in marriage (Prov. 5:1–23; 6:20–35; 7:1–27). Clearly, the family is foundational to society in a biblical worldview. As Sarna notes in comments on the penalty in Exodus 21:15 and 17, "[In] biblical religion . . . the integrity of the family is the indispensable prerequisite for a wholesome society. There is also here the unassailable conviction that the dissolution of the family unit must inevitably rend to shreds the entire social fabric."[481]

The above is not meant to heap guilt on those whose marriages have split apart nor shame on those who come from broken or single-parent homes. The purpose of the above is to seek to make clear that the Bible sees strong families, and therefore respect toward parents and care for them, as foundational to God's ordering of the world for humanity's good and blessing.[482] He therefore weaves respect and care for parents into his law so that this value might in turn be woven into Israelite society (21:15, 17).

In light of this Christians will want to ask about what types of behavior they should practice in order to honor and care for their parents in particular (cf. Response section on 20:1–21,"Honor your father and your mother"). To do so is to follow in Jesus' own steps, who was obedient to his parents (Luke 2:51) and, even while hanging on the cross, made sure his mother would be cared for (John 19:26–27). Christians will also want to ask in what ways they might help strengthen families in their church and in society in general. In many cases this will mean coming alongside not only existing two-parent families but especially other family arrangements, where special support may be needed, or coming alongside those who do not have their own family, be it the orphan, the widow (Deut. 14:28–29; 1 Tim. 5:3–16; James 1:27), or, increasingly in the modern world, the single person. God has adopted us into his family in love and asks us to show that same love to those around us.

---

[481] Sarna, *Exodus*, 122. Cf. note 394 within comment on 20:12.
[482] For a summary of studies showing the personal and societal benefits of strong families cf. Waite and Gallagher, *Case for Marriage*.

EXODUS 21:18–32

¹⁸ "When men quarrel and one strikes the other with a stone or with his fist and the man does not die but takes to his bed, ¹⁹ then if the man rises again and walks outdoors with his staff, he who struck him shall be clear; only he shall pay for the loss of his time, and shall have him thoroughly healed.

²⁰ "When a man strikes his slave, male or female, with a rod and the slave dies under his hand, he shall be avenged. ²¹ But if the slave survives a day or two, he is not to be avenged, for the slave is his money.

²² "When men strive together and hit a pregnant woman, so that her children come out, but there is no harm, the one who hit her shall surely be fined, as the woman's husband shall impose on him, and he shall pay as the judges determine. ²³ But if there is harm,[1] then you shall pay life for life, ²⁴ eye for eye, tooth for tooth, hand for hand, foot for foot, ²⁵ burn for burn, wound for wound, stripe for stripe.

²⁶ "When a man strikes the eye of his slave, male or female, and destroys it, he shall let the slave go free because of his eye. ²⁷ If he knocks out the tooth of his slave, male or female, he shall let the slave go free because of his tooth.

²⁸ "When an ox gores a man or a woman to death, the ox shall be stoned, and its flesh shall not be eaten, but the owner of the ox shall not be liable. ²⁹ But if the ox has been accustomed to gore in the past, and its owner has been warned but has not kept it in, and it kills a man or a woman, the ox shall be stoned, and its owner also shall be put to death. ³⁰ If a ransom is imposed on him, then he shall give for the redemption of his life whatever is imposed on him. ³¹ If it gores a man's son or daughter, he shall be dealt with according to this same rule. ³² If the ox gores a slave, male or female, the owner shall give to their master thirty shekels[2] of silver, and the ox shall be stoned."

[1] Or *so that her children come out and it is clear who was to blame, he shall be fined as the woman's husband shall impose on him, and he alone shall pay.* ²³*If it is unclear who was to blame* [2] A *shekel* was about 2/5 ounce or 11 grams

Section Overview

The stipulations of Exodus 21:18–32 direct Israel's response in cases of physical injury or negligent death. They again assume the high value of human life, requiring that those harming others must give appropriate compensation (vv. 18–27) and warning that those responsible for negligent death may also be subject to death (vv. 23, 29).

The passage begins by considering four cases in which one person injures another (vv. 18–27) and then turns to three variations of a case in which an animal kills a person (vv. 28–32).

Section Outline

V.D. Further stipulations of the covenant, spoken to Moses for the people (21:1–23:19) . . .
   4. Stipulations related to one person causing another person physical harm (21:18–27)
   5. Stipulations related to an animal causing a person to die (21:28–32)

Comment

21:18–19 In the first case a quarrel leads to physical aggression, and one person is incapacitated (v. 18). If that person can recover (even if this involves time using a crutch), then the injuring party must pay the injured party for any missed work and make sure to give any necessary support until full healing takes place (v. 19). This implies that, if the injury is permanent, the guilty party must give ongoing support to whatever extent necessary to sustain the injured party.

21:20–21 Whereas verses 18–19 concern one citizen's striking of another, verses 20–21 concern a master's striking of his servant. Two cases are described. In the first the servant apparently dies during, or in very close proximity to, the master's striking (v. 20).[483] The master, however, does not have the right to kill his servant intentionally, and the servant is therefore to be "avenged" (v. 20), a term referring to hostile action taken against a wrongdoer on behalf of oneself or someone else (cf. Num. 31:2; Deut. 32:43). In most Pentateuchal uses of the term death is in view (Gen. 4:15, 24; Lev. 26:25; Num. 31:2; Deut. 32:43),[484] and this seems likely here as well.[485] The master is thus held to full account, presumably by one of the servant's relatives, who would act as the "avenger of blood" and execute the guilty party (Num. 35:19).[486]

But this applies only if the master clearly intended to kill the servant. If the servant survived for a day or two and then died, no vengeance is allowed, since the master did not intend death (Ex. 21:21). It was manslaughter, not murder. As difficult as the thought may be for many today, the passage assumes that corporal punishment is within the rights of masters to administer.[487] The historical context must be remembered. Day workers had intrinsic motivation to work hard and do a good job; otherwise they would not be rehired. Not so with servants, who were

---

[483] The phrase "under his hand" could refer simply to the servant's being under the master's authority (cf. use of the phrase in Gen. 41:35; Ex. 18:10), though this seems redundant considering the servant language just used. Alternately, the phrase "under his hand" underscores that the servant died "under his hand" on the spot, that is, he was beaten to death.
[484] Leviticus 19:18 is the only possible exception.
[485] Linguistically the penalty is emphasized: he shall *certainly* be avenged. This language is the language not of the courts but of a person (or God himself) who is exacting justice, which in the case of a death in ancient Israel was the "avenger of blood" who executed the guilty (cf. above). Theologically in Israel's world all humanity is created in God's image (Gen. 1:26–27), meaning the capital penalty is appropriate in cases of murder (Gen. 9:6), even of a servant. Cf. also Wright, *Exodus*, 414–416.
[486] The Hebrew term for "avenger" in Numbers 35:19 is different than the term found in Exodus 21:20, but the underlying idea is the same. What if there was no relative? Presumably the community would step in.
[487] Cf. Proverbs 26:3; esp. 29:19; William H. C. Propp, *Exodus 19–40: A New Translation with Introduction and Commentary*, AB 2A (New York: Doubleday, 2006), 218.

often working off a debt in the master's household for a fixed period of time that did not change no matter how hard they worked. This meant there was not the same intrinsic motivation as day laborers to work hard, since masters were more or less stuck with them. Physical discipline was therefore a needed motivation at times for lazy servants. In this regard describing the servant as the master's "money" is not to dehumanize the servant but to point to the fact that this is a commercial arrangement in which masters have the ability to administer corporal punishment.

It should immediately be noted, however, that, just because cases of manslaughter could occur, this did not mean that masters had the right to beat servants severely. As noted below (vv. 26–28), servants suffering permanent injury went free, thus discouraging masters from even heading in that direction. In short while verse 21 addresses cases of manslaughter that could occur, the surrounding laws put strong safeguards around servants by making clear that murdering a servant is a capital crime (v. 20) and that severely injuring them means they are to go free (vv. 26–27).

21:22–25 Two men are in the midst of a physical fight and one of them ends up hitting a pregnant woman. As a result, she either gives birth prematurely or miscarries (the word translated "come out" occurs in contexts of both live birth [Gen. 25:25; 38:29] and still birth [Num. 12:12]). The text does not specify which, though Sprinkle notes that premature births before modern medicine were often fatal and that the other ancient Near Eastern laws closest to this one appear to presume miscarriage (Ex. 21:22a).[488]

The text goes on to consider two different scenarios, one in verse 22 and the other in verses 23–25. Understanding them is complicated by two rare and disputed words. The term translated "harm" (Hb. *'ason*) in verses 22–23 occurs in only three other verses, each time referring to the harm Jacob feared would happen to Benjamin (Gen. 42:4, 38; 44:29). The harm in view there is obviously serious and possibly fatal, though it is uncertain whether the term itself refers necessarily to lethal harm. Indeed, Exodus 21:23–25 assumes the harm could be fatal ("life for life") or not ("eye for eye").[489] The term translated "judges" (*palil*) at the end of verse 22 is also relatively rare and also disputed, with possible translations of the relevant clause including "And he shall pay as the judges determine" (ESV), "The payment [is] to be based on reckoning" (JPS), or "[He] shall pay ... in accordance with an assessment."[490] Since it seems unlikely a husband would be allowed to demand whatever he wanted, it would make good sense if this phrase were in some way indicating a standard or a supervising third party that ensured the demand was reasonable.[491]

---

[488] Joe M. Sprinkle, *The Book of the Covenant: A Literary Approach*, JSOTSup 174 (Sheffield, UK: JSOT Press, 1994), 93, cited in Enns, *Exodus*, 447. On a different note the Hebrew text of verse 22 indeed has a plural ("Her children come out"), though a slight emendation leads to "And her child comes out." In either case the blow triggers a birth.
[489] Propp, *Exodus 19–40*, 222.
[490] Childs, *Book of Exodus*, 443.
[491] Cassuto, *Commentary on the Book of Exodus*, 275.

TABLE 2.6: Three Approaches to Exodus 21:22–25

	Scenario 1 (v. 22)	Scenario 2 (vv. 23–25)
Approach One	The woman suffers no serious or fatal harm; the man who caused the premature birth or miscarriage must pay a fine for the child's harm or death.	The woman herself suffers serious or fatal harm; the man who caused the harm is prosecuted according to the law of talion ("life for life, eye for eye").
Approach Two	The child suffers no serious or fatal harm; the man who caused the premature birth must pay a fine for hitting the wife hard enough to cause premature labor.	The child suffers serious or fatal harm; the man who caused the harm is prosecuted according to the law of talion.
Approach Three	Neither the woman nor the child suffers serious or fatal harm; the man who caused the premature birth must pay a fine for hitting the wife hard enough to cause premature labor.	The child or the woman suffers serious or fatal harm; the man who caused the harm is prosecuted according to the law of talion.

In light of the above the two scenarios could be approached in three different ways (cf. table 2.6). Deciding between these approaches is complex. Some ancient Near Eastern laws concerning a stricken pregnant woman discuss harm to the child and harm to the mother;[492] this favors the first or third approach. Other ancient Near Eastern laws, however, appear to focus only on the harm to the child;[493] this favors the second approach. Further, in most ancient Near Eastern laws the man who causes an early miscarriage is subject only to a fine, favoring the first approach, but in at least one instance he is subject to death,[494] favoring the second or third. As noted above, however, it is also true that the relevant ancient Near Eastern laws seem to presume that a woman who gives birth prematurely typically miscarries (cf. above). If this was indeed the historical reality, it speaks against the second and third approaches (since scenario 1 in those approaches is now unlikely) and in favor of the first.

If the first approach is correct, then the payment of only a fine in verse 22 need not imply "that the fetus did not have the status of a viable human."[495] From a broader biblical perspective the way in which other texts describe the Lord's personal involvement in the formation of children in the womb presumes that they are as much in the image of God as those fully born (Job 31:15; Ps. 139:13–15; Jer. 1:5). These are not simply "embryos"; they are little image bearers. But even if we stay in the present context we see only a few verses later that fines are allowed in the case of a goring ox in which fully grown humans are killed (Ex. 21:30–32). In other words the presence of a fine does not mean we are dealing with nonviable humans. Indeed, what verse 22 and verses 30–32 share in common is that in both instances the death is indirect: the woman is struck, not the child; the ox does the killing, not the person. This indirectness may explain why the guilty party is able

---

[492] Cf. Code of Hammurabi §209–14 (*ANET*, 175); Middle Assyrian Laws (tablet A) §50 (*ANET*, 184). Cf. note 488 within comment on 21:22–25.
[493] Cf. *ANET*, 525, §1–2; HL §17–18 (*ANET*, 190).
[494] Middle Assyrian Laws (tablet A) §50 (*ANET*, 184).
[495] So Meyers, *Exodus*, 192–193.

to pay a fine instead of having to flee to a city of refuge (as in 21:13; the indirectness would also make this situation very different than abortion, which is direct and intentional). Striking the woman, however, is direct, and thus the law of talion is invoked in verses 23–25 to make clear the man will be subject to death if the woman dies ("life for life") and to lesser penalties if she is injured ("eye for eye").[496]

This leads to the law of talion itself: "You shall pay life for life, eye for eye, tooth for tooth," (vv. 23–24). This appears to be a stereotyped formula that is repeated in full here even if not all the wounds apply in this specific situation (such as a "burn").[497] As I wrote elsewhere on the similar penalty described in Leviticus 24:19–20:

> This law came to be known as the *lex talionis*, a Latin phrase that translates roughly as the "law of compensation in kind."[498] Similar expressions are found elsewhere in Old Testament [Exod. 21:23–25; Deut. 19:16–21] and ancient Near Eastern law.[499] Interpreted literally, it would require that the same injury be done to the offender as the offender has committed. Such an approach seems to have been taken in ancient Israel with regard to murder: the killer was to die [cf. Lev. 24:19–20 with 24:21c–d]. In non-lethal cases, however, the law seems to have been taken "as a guiding principle, 'a handy way of saying that the punishment must fit the crime.'"[500]

When physical injuries are treated in Exodus 21:18–19 and 21:26–27, in neither situation is there a literalistic application of the lex talionis. Indeed, such an approach would be of no real help to the injured party. What is found in both cases is proper justice: an injured person must be supported until becoming self-sufficient again (vv. 18–19); a servant is released from the tyranny of a cruel master (vv. 26–27).

> In short, the law of compensation in kind was not some literalistic, primitive form of vengeance. In Israel, it functioned as a guiding principle to ensure judges gave penalties appropriate to the crimes—the very principle that is "the basis for all civilized legal systems" today.[501] In this way, the law actually served to limit vengeance, which often demands a penalty far exceeding the bounds of justice.[502] It emphasized instead that justice be fair and equitable.[503]

---

[496] Might the judges have freedom to determine whether the blow to the woman was unintentional and thus not a capital crime? Or does the very fact the men were already engaged in violent behavior somehow void any appeal to unintentionality? A firm answer to these questions is elusive.
[497] Cassuto, *Commentary on the Book of Exodus*, 276.
[498] In Latin, *lex* is law and *talionis* is the genitive of *talio*, meaning "compensation in kind, recompense."
[499] Cf. Code of Hammurabi §§196–97, 200. Important differences, however, existed in terms of application. In the Code of Hammurabi, if you were responsible for the death of another's child, your child should be killed (§§209–210, 229–30), an approach the Bible expressly forbids (Deut. 24:16).
[500] Sklar, *Leviticus*, ZECOT, 660; the quote is from Wright, *Old Testament Ethics for the People of God*, 310. So also Wenham, *Leviticus*, 312; Sarna, *Exodus*, 126–127.
[501] John W. Kleinig, *Leviticus*, Concordia Commentary (St. Louis: Concordia, 2003), 529. Note original.
[502] Kleinig, *Leviticus*, 529; cf. Genesis 4:23–24. Note original.
[503] Sklar, *Leviticus*, ZECOT, 660–661. How does this relate to Matthew 5:38–42? Many have suggested Jesus is critiquing not this law but those who are taking it out of the realm of the courts (where it belongs) and using

Practically speaking, this meant that, if the woman died, the man who struck her would also be put to death: "life for life" goes into effect (and thus the mention of the law of talion instead of simply a notice of a fine). But if the woman was injured, he would need to give financial compensation in keeping with the nature of the injury.[504]

21:26–27 As noted directly above, these verses show that the "eye for eye" principle is to be applied not in a literalistic way but as a means of assuring that the penalty is appropriate to the crime. Blinding the eye of the master or knocking out his tooth would do the servant little good. Instead, the servant is freed from the master's tyrannical rule, which also means any outstanding debts are cancelled. Clearly, Israelite masters are not to treat their servants as chattels but to respect them as image bearers of the divine King.[505]

21:28–32 Five different cases are considered. In the first an ox for the first time gores a man or woman to death (v. 28). Because of the incomparable value that humans have as God's image bearers, the ox must be killed (cf. Gen. 9:5). In addition its meat may not be eaten. Is this because it is considered to be defiled with bloodguilt? Or because having a barbecue at the cost of someone's life would be grotesque? Or both? The text does not say. It makes clear, however, that the ox's owner is not liable, since this is new behavior.

In the second case the owner has been warned about his ox's dangerous behavior but has not restrained it properly (Ex. 21:29). This is culpable negligence, and he is now liable for any death that occurs; not only is the ox killed but the owner as well.

The third case identifies a possible way the owner may escape death: "If a ransom is imposed on him, then he shall give for the redemption of his life whatever is imposed on him" (v. 30). The text says not, "If he decides to pay a ransom," but, "If a ransom is imposed on him." The option of paying ransom is not up to him but is determined by a third party, presumably the family of the slain person.[506] Should they allow the ox's guilty owner to pay a ransom to rescue his life, it would be an act of sheer grace on their part. They may hold him fully liable due to his negligence (v. 29), but they may also view him as being guilty of a type of manslaughter (instead of murder) and allow him to ransom himself from death.[507]

The fourth case specifies that, even if the victim is not fully grown ("a man's son or daughter"), the situation is the same as the death of an adult, and the ox's

---

it to justify personal revenge in everyday relationships. He is teaching that in personal relationships love, not retaliation, is the mark of the righteous person. (For details cf. Sklar, *Leviticus*, TOTC, 295).
504 Other ancient Near Eastern laws identify specific fines for various injuries—for example, "a mina of silver for the blinding of an eye . . . or a third of a mina for the loss of the tooth" (Cassuto, *Commentary on the Book of Exodus*, 276, citing Code of Hammurabi §§198, 200). Presumably Israel had similar fines.
505 Sarna (*Exodus*, 127) notes, "This biblical law . . . is without parallel in other ancient Near Eastern legislation; the latter simply does not concern itself with the well-being of the slave."
506 Cf. Exodus 21:22 (Sarna, *Exodus*, 128).
507 I say "a type of manslaughter" because this case differs from Exodus 21:13, where the guilty party must flee to a city of refuge. The difference appears to be that in verse 13 the person causes the death with his own hands whereas in this case the death is caused by a third party (the ox), whose execution perhaps accounts for the blood defilement of the land that the city of refuge is meant to address (cf. v. 13).

owner will be dealt with "according to this same rule" (v. 31). Whether the "rule" in question is that of verse 30 in particular or verses 28–30 as a whole is debatable, although, since verse 30 presumes verses 28–29, the endpoint is the same either way.

The fifth case answers the question, "If the person killed is a servant, what type of financial compensation goes to the servant's master?" The answer is thirty shekels (v. 32), that is, roughly 12 oz (340 grams; for details cf. comment on 30:11–16). The case does not answer the question, To what extent do the stipulations of 21:29–31 also apply? That verse 32 mentions the ox must be stoned could be taken to mean, "You pay the thirty shekels and stone the ox and nothing else." But the fact that the stoning requirement repeats statements from the preceding laws (cf. vv. 28, 29) could also be taken to mean that those stipulations are assumed to apply in addition to the thirty-shekel fine. I lean toward the latter of these options on the basis of the treatment of the one killing a servant in verse 20 and also because a servant could be from a local Israelite family (v. 2), and it is hard to imagine that stepping into that role somehow nullifies the family's right to seek justice according to the stipulations of verses 29–31.

Response

WHO BEARS GOD'S IMAGE?

At the end of the previous section it was noted that human life is of special value because humans alone bear God's image (cf. Response section on 21:12–17, "Why Is Human Life So Valuable?"). As a result, taking a human life was met with serious consequence. The same is true in this section. An animal that kills a human being must be put to death (v. 28). A person who is culpably negligent in causing a death is subject potentially to the death penalty (v. 29). If the family of the slain allows him to live, a penalty must still be paid (v. 30). One cannot take the life of one made in God's image without consequence.

But this section makes especially clear that all people bear God's image. The murder of a servant or a woman bystander is a capital offense (vv. 20, 23), and sons or daughters who are not fully grown have the same worth as adults (v. 31). In short all people have value, since all people are made in God's image (Gen. 1:26–27; 9:6).

This simple fact is to be a great equalizer in how we relate to others. A natural human tendency is to treat the beautiful, the gifted, the rich, or the powerful as though they have more value than others. The Bible repeatedly speaks against this. Old Testament or New, the Lord commands his people to make sure they defend, care for, and support the lowly (Ex. 22:21–24; Deut. 14:28–29; 24:19; Isa. 1:17; Jer. 22:3; James 1:27; 2:1–9). Jesus himself repeatedly embodies such love and compassion to those on the lowest rungs of the social ladder. He in fact goes out of his way to show them special care. How does he respond to the unclean and untouchable leper who pleads for help? "Moved with pity, he stretched out his hand and touched him," healing him of his disease (Mark 1:40–42). To the blind men who want to see? "And Jesus in pity touched their eyes, and immediately they recovered their sight and followed him" (Matt. 20:34). To the everyday people who were "harassed and helpless, like sheep without a shepherd"? "He had compassion for them" (Matt. 9:36). Jesus sees people not as rich or poor, beautiful or ugly, popular or misfits. He sees them as those who bear God's image and are therefore worthy of respect, love, and care. We do well to ask if our posture toward others is the same.

WHAT IS OUR RESPONSIBILITY TO THOSE WE HAVE HARMED?

Given that all people have dignity and worth, harming them is not something we can view lightly. Where possible, we must account properly for any harm done to others.

This passage focuses especially on physical harm and various forms of compensation owed to the person harmed. This can be monetary, as when one citizen who harms another pays damages for various injuries (cf. 21:24–25) or compensates him for time lost at work, supporting him until he becomes self-sufficient again (v. 19). The harm does not even have to be intentional; culpable negligence results in compensation owed (cf. vv. 24–25). But compensation can also mean releasing others from various obligations if it means freeing them from the possibility of further harm, such as the servant who is permanently injured by the master (vv. 26–27). There is likely a financial element to this in many cases, since any debt the servant may be working off would thus be forgiven, but there is also a protective and preventative element, insofar as the servant is protected from an abusive master and masters are incentivized not to mistreat their servants in the first place.

While this passage focuses on accounting properly for the ways we may have harmed others physically, the basic principle applies also when we have harmed people in other ways, as when we slander them and harm their reputation. Accounting for such harm may involve financial remuneration (if they or their business lose income as a result) but may also involve publicly correcting our error in order to undo the damage we have done. Most generally speaking, any way in which we harm others is to be acknowledged, repented of (if due to sin), and corrected and compensated so far as possible. By doing so we show that we view others as Jesus does: as God's image bearers and therefore worthy of honor and care.

EXODUS 21:33–22:15

³³ "When a man opens a pit, or when a man digs a pit and does not cover it, and an ox or a donkey falls into it, ³⁴ the owner of the pit shall make restoration. He shall give money to its owner, and the dead beast shall be his.

³⁵ "When one man's ox butts another's, so that it dies, then they shall sell the live ox and share its price, and the dead beast also they shall share.

36 Or if it is known that the ox has been accustomed to gore in the past, and its owner has not kept it in, he shall repay ox for ox, and the dead beast shall be his.

22 ¹ "If a man steals an ox or a sheep, and kills it or sells it, he shall repay five oxen for an ox, and four sheep for a sheep. ² ² If a thief is found breaking in and is struck so that he dies, there shall be no bloodguilt for him, ³ but if the sun has risen on him, there shall be bloodguilt for him. He³ shall surely pay. If he has nothing, then he shall be sold for his theft. ⁴ If the stolen beast is found alive in his possession, whether it is an ox or a donkey or a sheep, he shall pay double.

⁵ "If a man causes a field or vineyard to be grazed over, or lets his beast loose and it feeds in another man's field, he shall make restitution from the best in his own field and in his own vineyard.

⁶ "If fire breaks out and catches in thorns so that the stacked grain or the standing grain or the field is consumed, he who started the fire shall make full restitution.

⁷ "If a man gives to his neighbor money or goods to keep safe, and it is stolen from the man's house, then, if the thief is found, he shall pay double. ⁸ If the thief is not found, the owner of the house shall come near to God to show whether or not he has put his hand to his neighbor's property. ⁹ For every breach of trust, whether it is for an ox, for a donkey, for a sheep, for a cloak, or for any kind of lost thing, of which one says, 'This is it,' the case of both parties shall come before God. The one whom God condemns shall pay double to his neighbor.

¹⁰ "If a man gives to his neighbor a donkey or an ox or a sheep or any beast to keep safe, and it dies or is injured or is driven away, without anyone seeing it, ¹¹ an oath by the LORD shall be between them both to see whether or not he has put his hand to his neighbor's property. The owner shall accept the oath, and he shall not make restitution. ¹² But if it is stolen from him, he shall make restitution to its owner. ¹³ If it is torn by beasts, let him bring it as evidence. He shall not make restitution for what has been torn.

¹⁴ "If a man borrows anything of his neighbor, and it is injured or dies, the owner not being with it, he shall make full restitution. ¹⁵ If the owner was with it, he shall not make restitution; if it was hired, it came for its hiring fee."⁴

¹ Ch 21:37 in Hebrew ² Ch 22:1 in Hebrew ³ That is, the thief ⁴ Or *it is reckoned in* (Hebrew *comes into*) *its hiring fee*

Section Overview

The text now turns from harming humans (21:1–32) to harming or stealing property (21:33–22:15), emphasizing that others' property must be respected. When our actions damage others' property, even through negligence, full repayment must be made (21:33–34, 36; 22:5–6, 12). Theft of others' property is even more serious, requiring full repayment plus a penalty (22:1, 4, 7, 9). But the stipulations also recognize that damage or harm can come for reasons beyond our control (21:35; 22:10–11, 13), in which case no repayment is required. In these ways protections are given to property owners and to those entrusted with caring for property.

The stipulations cover a range of property matters common at this point in history: dead livestock (21:33–36), stolen livestock (22:1–4), destruction of crops (vv. 5–6), and theft or damage to property that one person entrusts to another (vv. 7–15).

Section Outline

> V.D. Further stipulations of the covenant, spoken to Moses for the people (21:1–23:19) . . .
> 6. Stipulations related to livestock dying (21:33–36)
> 7. Stipulations related to theft of livestock (22:1–4)
> 8. Stipulations related to the destruction of crops (22:5–6)
> 9. Stipulations related to theft or damage to property entrusted or lent to another (22:7–15)

Comment

21:33–34 In biblical lands water was often in short supply, and so pits known as cisterns were dug to trap water (Lev. 11:36). Because an open pit is a safety hazard, the pit's owner is expected to cover it, perhaps with planks or large sticks bound together. In this case someone has taken the cover off and failed to replace it, or has dug the pit and never covered it, and an ox or donkey (or by implication any other animal) falls into it and dies (Ex. 21:33).[508] The negligent party must repay the owner for the animal's loss; the dead animal then belongs to the negligent party, who can presumably make use of its meat and hide (v. 34; cf. v. 28). The underlying principle is that we are financially responsible for negligent behavior that causes others financial harm. The same is true for the following two verses.

21:35–36 Two cases are considered. In the first a person's ox is violent for the first time and kills another person's ox. There is no negligence involved, and therefore no fault is assigned to the first person, and the financial loss is borne equally by both parties: they divide any proceeds from the first ox's sale (or one of them by implication could buy out the other) and divide the dead ox's meat (v. 35). But if the first person knows his ox is violent and does not restrain it properly, this negligence leads to full financial responsibility for any harm done (cf. comment above). In a nonagrarian context we might say that, if a pet has shown itself to be dangerous (biting, scratching), its owner bears responsibility for any future harm it causes.

22:1–4 Five cases addressing theft are considered. In the first someone steals an ox or a flock animal[509] and either butchers it (to eat) or sells it; in either case the animal is gone (v. 1). Because intentional theft is far more serious than negligence (cf. 21:33–36), the thief must not simply pay for the stolen animal but must pay additional penalties as well (note that Zacchaeus acknowledges the same and may

---

[508] Stuart (*Exodus*, 495) helpfully notes that, because farm animals were such a common part of Israelite life, laws dealing with accidents to or by them are as natural as laws today regarding vehicle accidents.
[509] The word translated "sheep" here refers to an animal from the sheep or goat flocks.

have this verse in mind when mentioning the fourfold repayment he will give to anyone he has defrauded; Luke 19:8). These penalties scale to the animal's worth. The more costly the animal, the greater the offense and the greater the penalty (cf. in modern law how the penalty for car theft is typically greater than that for bicycle theft). The thief must therefore pay four times a flock animal's worth but five times the worth of the more costly ox. Thieves are not, however, to be put to death, as they are in Hammurabi's law code (§21). "The biblical scale gives priority to the protection of life—even the life of the burglar—over the protection of property."[510]

In the second and third cases a homeowner kills the thief while he is breaking in (Ex. 22:2–3a). In darkness the exact danger posed is unclear, and the homeowner is not guilty of bloodshed for taking extreme measures to protect family and property (v. 2). Daylight, however, affords a clearer evaluation of the situation and easier access to nonlethal actions, so killing the thief in daytime makes the homeowner guilty of bloodshed and thus is a capital crime (v. 3a; for the capital penalty today cf. note 397 within comment on 20:13). Taking human life must never be a starting point but always a last resort, even with burglars, since they too bear God's image.

The fourth case returns abruptly to the thief (some translations insert "the thief" in place of "he" to make this clearer, cf. ESV mg.; v. 3b). It emphasizes that a thief without the means to repay will be sold into servitude—which could be for a period of up to six years (21:2)—in order to cover the debt (naturally, all the laws protecting servants would apply; cf. comment on 21:2–6). This penalty emphasizes how important it is to compensate others for financial harm done to them.

The fifth case identifies what to do if the stolen property is found with the thief (22:4). Unlike the command in verse 1, here the original animals are returned, meaning the owner has not lost any work that had been put into training them, which might explain why the penalty is less and the thief pays double the animal's worth instead of four or five times its worth. Still, the penalty is steep and emphasizes again that others' property must be completely respected.[511]

22:5–6 These stipulations cover damage to crops through carelessness. In each case full restitution must be made; carelessness does not excuse responsibility.

As it currently stands, verse 5 addresses one person's animal's grazing in another person's field or vineyard. The animal's owner must not simply replace what the animal ate but replace it with the best produce possible. This assures the second person in no way suffers loss and, because of the cost involved, encourages the animal's owner to be more careful in the future. The LXX, the SP, and at least one Qumran manuscript,[512] however, insert an additional clause in the midst of the verse that alters its sense slightly: If the animal destroys only a portion of the field or vineyard, the animal's owner simply repays from his own field. But, if it destroys the entire field or vineyard, then restitution must be with the best of the

---

510 Sarna, *Exodus*, 130.
511 In 22:4 the thief has been caught with the property. A later law will specify that confessing to the crime and returning the lost item voluntarily results in a 120 percent penalty rather than 200 percent (Lev. 6:1–5), in this way encouraging confession and repentance before one is caught.
512 Cf. Propp, *Exodus 19–40*, 124.

owner's crops. The presence of the clause in three ancient versions is strong support for its originality,[513] and the point would then seem to be that for incidental damages simple repayment suffices but for significant damages the responsible party bears more guilt and must make sure repayment is not only full but robust.

In verse 6 someone starts a fire that gets out of control and destroys harvested or unharvested crops. Again, the guilty party must make full restitution, presumably along the lines of verse 5.

22:7–15 These stipulations all deal with theft or damage to property entrusted or loaned by one person to another. The basic principles for trustees are that they must repay any damage or loss only when they can reasonably be held responsible (vv. 12, 14), not when such damage or loss is due to natural circumstances (vv. 10–11, 13), and that they must pay double if they have lied about such damage or loss (v. 9). At the same time those lending objects are taught that they must not make false accusations of theft (v. 9) and that they must not hold trustees responsible for matters beyond their control (vv. 10–11, 13).

22:7–9 In this scenario one person entrusts an object to another for safekeeping, and the latter at some point reports it as stolen (v. 7a). If the thief is caught with the property, he pays double (v. 7b; cf. v. 4). Verses 8–9 lay out what to do if the thief is not caught, but their exact meaning and how they relate to the verses that follow are debated. To my thinking the solution that accounts most simply for all the data understands verses 8–9 to describe two different scenarios.

In the first the money or property is gone and the person guarding it is brought "near to God"[514] to take an oath to see "whether or not he has put his hand to his neighbor's property" (v. 8). Although an oath is not mentioned in verse 8, it ends in the same way as verse 11, meaning the front half of each verse may also describe the same thing (which in v. 11 is clearly an oath; cf. table 2.7). In other words the house owner would swear, "As the LORD lives, I did not take this property" (cf. the oath formula in Judg. 8:19; 1 Sam. 14:39; etc.; cf. also 1 Kings 8:31–32). Though this is not stated, it would then be expected that he would have to repay for what was stolen since he had agreed to guard it (cf. Ex. 22:12).[515]

TABLE 2.7: Parallelism in Exodus 22:8 and 22:11

"The owner of the house shall come near to God . . .	. . . to show whether or not he has put his hand to his neighbor's property" (22:8)
"An oath by the LORD shall be between them both . . .	. . . to see whether or not he has put his hand to his neighbor's property" (22:11)

---

513 For how the clause may have dropped out cf. Propp, *Exodus 19–40*, 124.
514 Here and in Exodus 22:9 some versions translate "judges" in place of "God." The Hebrew word is *'elohim*, which normally refers to "God" and only possibly in a few passages refers to "judges," though this is far from certain. Cf. last paragraph within comment on 21:2–6.
515 Compare also Code of Hammurabi §125. It could be argued that, because Exodus 22:12 mentions repayment and verse 8 does not, no repayment is expected in verse 8. But it could also be argued that, because verses 11 and 13 mention nonrepayment and verse 8 does not, nonrepayment is not an option in verse 8. In other words the mention of nonmention of repayment is not decisive. I assume repayment here simply because verse 8 is very similar to verse 12 in terms of the situation being addressed.

In the second scenario the house owner claims the property has been stolen, but the property owner claims to be able to identify it among the trustee's goods: "Look! That is my garment, not his! This is a breach of trust!" (v. 9). In this case both parties come before the Lord, and "the one whom God condemns shall pay double to his neighbor," whether it is the house owner who lied or the property owner who made a false accusation.[516] How God would identify the person is not stated. It may be that the guilty party refuses to take an oath, which would prove guilt, or it may be that the priest somehow seeks a decision by the Lord directly (cf. Num. 27:21) or performs a thorough investigation himself (cf. Deut. 19:16–21).

22:10–13 In these verses one person has asked another to watch over an animal, and something then happens to it. It must be remembered that animals were not only kept safe in pens but also allowed to roam to find pasture. This helps explain the three scenarios considered here.

In the first the trustee claims the animal either died, was injured, or was driven away, but no one saw; that is, any of these three things happened while the animal was out grazing, it never returned, and no one has any idea where it is (Ex. 22:10). In this case the trustee swears an oath before the Lord that he did not take the animal, the animal's owner must believe the trustee's word, and no restitution is paid since this is a natural hazard of letting animals graze (v. 11).

In the second scenario the animal is stolen, that is, it has not simply wandered off or been taken when it was out to pasture but was taken in such a way that could have been prevented by more care; for example, it was stolen from a pen that should have been guarded (v. 12). In this case the trustee is responsible and must repay with another animal.

In the third scenario the animal was attacked by another animal and died. This, too, is a hazard of raising animals, so the trustee needs simply to return the carcass to the owner and not make further restitution (v. 13).

22:14–15 Just as farmers today might borrow or rent a tractor from one another to plow a field, Israelites might do the same with an ox. Three scenarios are considered. In the first a borrowed animal is injured or dies and the owner is not there, that is, the one borrowing it was the one working it and therefore fully responsible for any harm. Any damages must therefore be paid by the borrower (v. 14). In the second the owner was there, that is, the owner was working the animal or overseeing its use and therefore responsible for any damages (v. 15a). In the third the animal's owner rented it out, and "the rental fee was expected to include 'insurance' on the animal,"[517] meaning the owner bore the loss (v. 15b).

Response

WHAT DO THESE LAWS DO FOR PROPERTY OWNERS?

When our property is harmed or stolen, we bear loss and cost: loss from the damage or theft and cost to fix or replace it. These laws take such loss and cost seriously

---

516 For the latter cf. Deuteronomy 19:16–21 (Wells, *Exodus*, 242).
517 Stuart, *Exodus*, 508.

by requiring that appropriate compensation be made from the party responsible for the harm or theft. Such compensation is required even in cases of negligence (21:33–34, 36; 22:5–6, 12). This is as it should be. If I accidentally back my car into my neighbor's, it is only fair I pay for any damage. In addition thieves unable to make compensation from their own resources had to work off the debt (v. 3). This especially underscores the high view we are to have of others' property and the importance of compensating them fairly for any harm we have done to it. At the end of the day, property is an extension of its owner; to harm it is in some way to harm him. Proper compensation is therefore not only fair but also a way to acknowledge that the owner is God's image bearer and therefore worthy of honor and respect. And, while these laws focus on harm done to physical property, the principle of appropriate compensation would also apply to harm in other areas, such as damaging someone's reputation (cf. Response section on 21:18–32, "What Is Our Responsibility to Those We Have Harmed?").

While these laws focus on protecting the rights of property owners, they also provide protections for those entrusted with property.

WHAT DO THESE LAWS DO FOR THOSE ENTRUSTED WITH PROPERTY?

As noted in the Section Overview, damage or harm can come to property for reasons beyond our control. Animals can fight and injure one another (21:35, but note the important qualification of v. 36; 22:13), die a natural death, or get lost and fail to return (v. 10). Property owners therefore do not have an automatic right of compensation, which gets at the worth of human beings from a different angle: we respect others as God's image bearers by not placing unjust expectations on them. In other words we love our neighbors as ourselves when we do not ask of them what we would feel it unjust for them to ask of us.

There is a related principle at work, namely, that the compensation expected of responsible parties is equivalent to, not greater than, the damage done (21:33–34, 36; 22:5–6, 12). It is true that in cases of theft extra damages need to be paid to the person wronged (22:1, 4, 7, 9), to which we will return in a moment. But in normal situations, when the damage comes through mistake or negligence, the compensation paid should equal the damages done, which is both fair and prevents vengeful or angry property owners from demanding excessive compensation from those causing the damage. Even parties in the wrong must be treated with complete fairness, something we can struggle to do in situations in which we have suffered financial loss. These laws remind us that "tooth for tooth" is the principle, not "head for tooth" (cf. discussion of the law of talion within comment on 21:22–25). This reminder also leads to a final question.

WHAT PRINCIPLES STAND BEHIND CRIMINAL PENALTIES IN BIBLICAL LAW?

While biblical law is sometimes viewed as primitive and simplistic, the reality is that it is informed by some of the same principles informing many modern laws today. In the above cases, in which financial loss caused by someone's mistake or negligence results in compensation equivalent to the loss, but financial loss due to theft results in equivalent compensation plus additional penalties (22:1, 4, 7, 9), at least three different principles may be seen to be at work.

The first is the respect due not simply to people's property but also to people themselves. Financial loss that comes from a mistake or negligence is not aimed at the property owner; stealing someone else's property is entirely different because it is intentionally causing the property owner harm. Paying damages acknowledges that harm by publicly affirming to the victim that the wrong was not simply against his property but against him personally. In this way the importance of respecting individuals is underscored. Indeed, the fact that thieves pay financial penalties instead of being subject to the death penalty gets at the same point from a different angle: human life is of far more value than material goods (cf. comment on 22:1–4).

The second principle is that greater crime requires greater penalty. Stealing and selling a flock animal requires fourfold repayment, but stealing and selling the more valuable ox requires fivefold repayment (v. 1). As noted above, it makes intuitive sense that the penalty for stealing a car should normally be greater than that of stealing a bicycle because of the greater worth of the car and the increased financial damage to its owner. Not all crimes are equal; those causing more damage call for a greater punishment.

A final principle is that penalties can act as a deterrent. This is named explicitly in Deuteronomy 19:16–19, which commands that a false witness should be punished with the same punishment that would have befallen the person falsely accused. One of the results will be that "the rest shall hear and fear, and shall never again commit any such evil among you" (Deut. 19:20). It is not hard to imagine the same effect here. To see a thief having to pay heavy penalties, or even becoming a servant until the debt from their theft is cleared, would doubtless cause others to think twice before committing a similar deed.[518]

In short, intentional harm to others results in compensation plus additional penalties, penalties should be greater or lesser according to the crime's severity, and deterrence is one of the goals of such penalties. These principles inform many modern justice systems, and for good reason: they acknowledge the respect we should show others and encourage a society in which harming others is seen as wrong and as something to be avoided.

As a final comment, it may be remembered that, while laws often identify a minimum standard of behavior one should not sink below, they also have underlying values that point to an ideal of behavior for which one should aim (cf. esp. Response section on 20:1–21, "How Should the Ten Commandments Be Read?"). For how this plays out in terms of theft in particular cf. Response section on 20:1–21, "You shall not steal." Jesus' teaching in the Sermon on the Mount is that the righteous person is the one who embodies the ideals to which these laws point (cf. Matt. 5:20 with 5:21–30). In this way we show the world that we follow a God who is not simply free from evil but abounding in love and mercy toward those made in his image.

---

[518] For further thoughts on biblical penalties and their aims cf. Sklar, *Leviticus*, TOTC, 62–63.

EXODUS 22:16–17

16 "If a man seduces a virgin[1] who is not betrothed and lies with her, he shall give the bride-price[2] for her and make her his wife. **17** If her father utterly refuses to give her to him, he shall pay money equal to the bride-price for virgins."

[1] Or *a girl of marriageable age*; also verse 17 [2] Or *engagement present*; also verse 17

Section Overview

These laws stipulate what to do when a man seduces an unbetrothed virgin. The laws provide important protections for the woman and emphasize that sex is meant for marriage. The first law requires a betrothal gift and marriage (v. 16); the second explains what to do when the marriage is disallowed (v. 17).

Section Outline

V.D. Further stipulations of the covenant, spoken to Moses for the people (21:1–23:19) ...
    7. Stipulations related to a man seducing a virgin who is not betrothed (22:16–17)

Comment

22:16–17 Three aspects of historical and theological context shed light on what these stipulations are protecting against. First, in the ancient Near East issues of continuing the family line and passing property on to legitimate heirs were central to the purpose of marriage. As a result, "traditions favoring premarital virginity as well as legislation requiring marital fidelity [were] common,"[519] since both help assure that any offspring would be legitimate heirs. Second, it was also common for a man who wanted to marry a woman to give an "engagement present" (cf. ESV mg.), which would "often be returned to the woman as part of her dowry or inheritance, thus providing for her financial well-being."[520] Third, from a theological perspective the Bible understands sexual activity to be a physical way for a husband

---

519 Matthews, "Family Relationships," 296.
520 Jay Sklar, *Additional Notes on Leviticus* (St. Louis, MO: Gleanings Press, 2023), at 19:20. For details cf. Hugenberger, *Marriage as a Covenant*, 243–244, note 126; Sarna, *Exodus*, 135. For examples of such gifts cf. Genesis 34:12; 1 Samuel 18:25; 2 Samuel 3:14; Hosea 12:12. On a related note there is no need to conclude that, since many of the immediately preceding stipulations concern property, Exodus 22:16–17 is thinking of the woman as property. If verses 16–17 share a similarity with the preceding stipulations, it may simply be in the fact that a fine is required (Cassuto, *Commentary on the Book of Exodus*, 288) or that financial loss is involved, in this case the potential loss of the betrothal gift for virgins (Alexander, *Exodus*, ApOTC, 499).

and wife to act out and confirm the covenant commitment they have made to one another in marriage; as they have promised to cleave in covenant loyalty to one another for all of life, sexual activity becomes the physical way they confirm, reaffirm, and strengthen this commitment throughout marriage. This is why sex must be marital: it relates to a covenant commitment two people have already made.[521]

This context in turn helps to clarify the purpose of these stipulations. They concern a case in which "a man seduces"[522] and then "lies with" a "virgin[523] who is not betrothed," meaning she has not been pledged in marriage (cf. note 459 within comment on 21:2–6 and attendant discussion). This is an important detail. In Israel betrothal was somewhere between modern engagement and marriage. Like engagement it was a promise to wed. Like marriage it required sexual fidelity, such that sexual relations with another person during betrothal was considered adultery (leading to adultery's penalty for the guilty parties; Deut. 22:23–24). But in this case she is not betrothed, so no such punishment applies. Instead the man is now to give the betrothal present and take her to be his wife (Ex. 22:16). This protects the woman socially. Since she is no longer a virgin, her chances of marriage may be harmed, and the man is therefore prevented from leaving her in a potentially vulnerable state. "A man cannot 'love her and leave her': by sleeping with her he has assumed the obligation to marry her."[524] (By way of comparison, we might think of the expectation—fading in many modern contexts but very strong only a generation or two ago—that a man should marry a woman if she becomes pregnant by him.) Moreover, as already noted, it appears that the betrothal present the man must give will provide "indirectly for the financial wellbeing of the bride (as the marriage present . . . was customarily returned to brides in the dowry)."[525] Finally, requiring marriage reinforced God's purpose for sexual relations by underscoring the bond between sexual activity and marriage. Indeed, the man has led the woman to commit the covenantal act of marriage without entering a covenant with her. By preventing him from misusing sex and the woman in this way the law points to the true nature of what sexual activity is to be: an expression of marital commitment.

But the law is not naive and does not give the man the automatic right to marriage. The woman's father is able to deny the union (v. 17). This may have been

---

521 For helpful discussion cf. Timothy Keller with Kathy Keller, *The Meaning of Marriage: Facing the Complexities of Commitment with the Wisdom of God* (New York: Dutton, 2011), 219–236; Hugenberger, *Marriage as a Covenant*, 158–165. Cf. note 399 within comment on 20:14.
522 The word for "seduces" often refers to some form of persuasion, which can be positive (Prov. 25:15; Hos. 2:14) but is usually negative, with one person tricking another in some way (Deut. 11:16; Judg. 14:15; 16:5; 2 Sam. 3:25; 1 Kings 22:20–22). In either case the man is the responsible party; he has somehow convinced the woman to sleep with him.
523 The Hebrew word translated "virgin" is *betulah*. It "refers to a female who was not necessarily a virgin (otherwise Gen. 24:16 is redundant) but was expected to be (Deut. 22:14–19), was not married (Ex. 22:16–17; Lev. 21:3), was young (see Deut. 32:25, where the term is parallel to a term for 'young man'), and was under her father's care (Gen. 24:16–51; Ex. 22:17; Deut. 22:16). The term thus seems closest to the English terms 'maid' or 'maiden'; that is, 'an unmarried girl or woman esp. when young' ('Maid,' Merriam-Webster, http://www.merriam-webster.com/dictionary/maid; cf. John H. Walton, 'בְּתוּלָה,' *NIDOTTE* 1:782–83)"; Sklar, *Leviticus*, ZECOT, 586n10.
524 T. Frymer-Kensky, "Virginity in the Bible," in *Gender and Law in the Hebrew Bible and the Ancient Near East*, ed. B. M. Levinson, T. Frymer-Kensky, and V. H. Matthews, JSOTSup 262 (Sheffield, UK: JSOT, 2009), 91, cited in Alexander, *Exodus*, ApOTC, 499.
525 Hugenberger, *Marriage as a Covenant*, 254.

an expected right in a culture where the head of the household was responsible for all major decisions within it, but a protective function also accompanies this right. Various lines of evidence suggest females "generally married soon after puberty,"[526] meaning the normal case of seduction would involve a woman who was quite young and whose decision-making capabilities were not fully developed. The father's right to deny the marriage gives the daughter an important protection, whether from the lack of wisdom that comes with youth or from a man of ill repute who has taken advantage of her in some way. That the man still has to pay the equivalent of the betrothal gift punishes him for his wrong and discourages men from engaging in premarital sex, emphasizing again that God has created sexual union for the context of marriage.

Response

In many modern contexts these laws are strange at best and offensive at worst. Are they teaching that wives are something men can buy? And why do fathers have such a say in who their daughters marry? Any attempt to answer such questions must begin with a clear understanding of the cultural and theological context surrounding these laws.

WHAT ASPECTS OF CULTURAL AND THEOLOGICAL CONTEXT NEED TO BE KEPT IN MIND?

See the opening paragraph in the Comment section for three important cultural and theological factors informing these laws.

IN WHAT WAYS DO THESE LAWS ACTUALLY PROTECT WOMEN?

Requiring the man to marry the woman protects her both socially and financially. See the second paragraph in the Comment section. Giving the father the right to disallow the marriage protects the seduced woman from a potentially unwise youthful decision or from marriage to an unsavory character.

WHAT DO THESE LAWS TEACH US ABOUT GOD'S VIEW OF THE PROPER CONTEXT FOR SEXUAL ACTIVITY?

These laws emphasize that God has created sexual activity for the context of marriage. First, they require the man who has seduced a young woman and slept with her to marry her (22:16). If physical activity is the cart, marriage is the horse. The couple may have put the cart before the horse in this instance, but horse and cart go together. Sexual activity is marital.[527] Second, if the marriage is disallowed, the man still has to pay the equivalent of the betrothal gift (v. 17). This not only

---

[526] Cf. Hugenberger, *Marriage as a Covenant*, 315. Cf. note 523 within comment on 22:16–17.
[527] Does this mean that those who fornicate today must also get married? Not necessarily. On the one hand the passage itself notes that disallowing marriage in such an instance is possible, perhaps especially when factors such as youth or deceptive motive are involved (cf. comment above, third paragraph). Moreover, in many cultures today a nonvirgin woman is not at the same risk of being unable to find a husband, meaning she might not need the same social protections named above (cf. comment above, second paragraph). At the same time this should not lead us to deemphasize what the Bible makes clear: God intends sexual activity for the context of marriage. To engage in it outside of that context is to rebel against him.

penalizes him for his wrong but also had a deterrent effect, discouraging others from engaging in fornication. It also again makes clear that sexual union and marriage go together. Honoring God's design therefore means not only saving sexual activity for marriage but also avoiding adultery and other forms of non-marital sexual activity. See discussion in the Response section on 20:1–21, "You shall not commit adultery."

In a world of sexual brokenness, it is also vital to remember that, when we have failed in any of the above ways, we need not only to repent of the wrong but also to embrace God's promise that "if we confess our sins, he is faithful and just to forgive us our sins and to cleanse us from all unrighteousness" (1 John 1:9). Sexual sin is not beyond God's forgiveness. In Jesus cleansing from any sin is always full and complete.

EXODUS 22:18–20

¹⁸ "You shall not permit a sorceress to live.
¹⁹ "Whoever lies with an animal shall be put to death.
²⁰ "Whoever sacrifices to any god, other than the LORD alone, shall be devoted to destruction.¹

¹ That is, set apart (devoted) as an offering to the Lord (for destruction)

Section Overview

Earlier stipulations required the capital penalty for various crimes committed directly against other people (21:12, 14–17). These three laws require the capital penalty for various crimes—sorcery (22:18), bestiality (v. 19), and apostasy (v. 20)—that rise to the level of treason against the Lord and/or his purposes in creation.

Section Outline

V.D. Further stipulations of the covenant, spoken to Moses for the people (21:1–23:19) . . .
    8. Further stipulations related to capital offenses (22:18–20)
       a. Sorcery (22:18)
       b. Bestiality (22:19)
       c. Apostasy (22:20)

Comment

22:18 In several passages the Bible lists various people who in some way seek to access divine power or knowledge by illicit means, such as magicians, diviners, mediums, or spiritualists. Sorcerers fall in the midst of such lists (Deut. 18:10; 2 Chron. 33:6) as those who attempt to access divine power by means of incantations or spells.[528] As such, they are either appealing to gods other than the Lord or presuming they can manipulate the Lord's own power. Either way, sorcery is a treasonous rejection of the Lord as sovereign King, so the penalty for treason applies. (The specification of "sorceress" suggests that women were more likely to practice sorcery; the law would naturally apply to men doing the same.)

22:19 The Hittite laws suggest that certain forms of bestiality were considered permissible among at least some of Israel's neighbors. "In the Hittite laws, bestiality is permitted with a horse or mule (HL §200A), but is interdicted . . . with an ox (§187), a sheep (§188), or a dog (§199)."[529] This verse prohibits it absolutely, a prohibition repeated in Leviticus 18:23. In comments on that verse I note:

> [Leviticus 18:23] emphasizes the negative nature of bestiality by describing it as a "perverse act" (*tevel*), a word likely built on a root that refers to "mixing, confusing" (cf. Gen. 11:7, 9; Lev. 2:4). The noun appears only here (in reference to bestiality) and [Lev] 20:12 (in reference to a man having sexual relations with his daughter-in-law). The sense is obviously negative, referring to an illicit "mixing" in terms of sexual relationship, that is, a "perverse act." In this law, the point is that human sexuality is just that: *human* sexuality. As the creation narrative attests, no suitable partner for humanity exists among the animals (Gen. 2:20). The person who breaks this law thus goes directly against the Creator's design for sex—and so denies the Creator.[530]

Denial through such twisted behavior puts the guilty party among the treasonous and subject to treason's penalty.

22:20 The Ten Commandments begin by prohibiting the worship of others gods (Ex. 20:3–4). This verse describes the penalty for those who ignore the prohibition: they shall be "devoted to destruction." This Hebrew term refers to giving something to the Lord or his tabernacle in a permanent way (cf. Lev. 27:28), which in judgment contexts takes place through death (cf. Num. 21:2; Deut. 13:13–16). In this case the punishment corresponds to the crime: having sacrificed to other gods instead of the Lord, the guilty are handed over to the Lord through death for judgment.

Response

HOW DO THESE LAWS FUNCTION AS MODELS, AND WHAT ARE THE "FLOOR" AND THE "CEILING" OF EACH OF THEM?

In earlier comments it was noted that biblical laws often function as models that can be applied to related issues. It was further noted that laws often require a

---

528 They are parallel to those who use "enchantments" (Isa. 47:9, 12). The Hebrew root is *kashaf*; an Akkadian verb built on the same root (*kašāpu*) is used to refer to casting an evil spell (cf. CAD, *kašāpu*).
529 Jacob Milgrom, *Leviticus 17–22*, AYB (New Haven, CT: Yale University Press, 2000), 1570.
530 Sklar, *Leviticus*, ZECOT, 502–503.

minimum standard of behavior (the floor) but also have an underlying value that points to a higher ethical ideal (the ceiling; cf. Response section on 20:1–21, "How Should the Ten Commandments Be Read?"). How do these principles apply to the three laws considered above?

The first law would prohibit not only sorcery but any biblically illicit activity by which someone tries to access or manipulate divine knowledge or power, such as magic, divination, or being a medium, spiritualist, fortune teller, or omen interpreter (Lev. 19:26; Deut. 18:10; 2 Chron. 33:6; in a modern context, things such as reading palms, writing horoscopes, or using Ouija boards, tarot cards, or crystal balls would also be included). Instead we are expected to look to the Lord alone as the source of divine knowledge and power. In terms of divine knowledge the Bible's view of the primary way to gain it is clear: study, learn, and pass on God's Word (Deut. 6:1–9; Pss. 1:1–6; 19:7–14; 119:1–176; 2 Tim. 3:16–17). In terms of divine power, instead of our trying to wield it in our own hands (as sorcerers do), the Bible exhorts us to pray, looking to the Lord for deliverance from our trials and enemies as well as a more general experience of blessing and favor from him (Psalms 3–7; Phil. 4:6–7).

For the law prohibiting bestiality see the Response section on 20:1–21, "You shall not commit adultery." For the law prohibiting sacrificing to other gods see the Response section on 20:1–21, "You shall have no other gods before me."

WHY ARE THESE CRIMES SO SERIOUS?

What unites these crimes is that they are all serious acts of treason against the Lord and/or his purposes in creation. Sorcerers look to gods other than the Lord or attempt to manipulate the Lord's own power (cf. 22:18). Bestiality explicitly rejects divisions that God established in creation, twisting and denying his purposes for sexual intimacy and thereby denying him as well (cf. v. 19). Worshiping other gods is a direct rejection of the Lord as sovereign King and God (v. 20). As serious acts of treason, they result in treason's penalty: death. The Bible does not hesitate to say that the God who has the right to judge us when we die has the right to exercise such judgment while we live. For further thoughts on explaining such judgment in a modern age see the Response section on 13:17–15:21, "What Is the Warning?" and "How Do We Respond?"

EXODUS 22:21–27

²¹ "You shall not wrong a sojourner or oppress him, for you were sojourners in the land of Egypt. ²² You shall not mistreat any widow or fatherless child. ²³ If you do mistreat them, and they cry out to me, I will surely hear their cry, ²⁴ and my wrath will burn, and I will kill you with the sword, and your wives shall become widows and your children fatherless.

²⁵ "If you lend money to any of my people with you who is poor, you shall not be like a moneylender to him, and you shall not exact interest from him. ²⁶ If ever you take your neighbor's cloak in pledge, you shall return it to him before the sun goes down, ²⁷ for that is his only covering, and it is his cloak for his body; in what else shall he sleep? And if he cries to me, I will hear, for I am compassionate."

Section Overview

Proper treatment of the weak and disadvantaged unites the stipulations of Exodus 22:21–27. Since every person bears God's image, every person deserves honor, respect, and care.

The opening verses prohibit mistreatment of the socially weak, whether the resident alien (v. 21) or the widow and fatherless (vv. 22–24). The concluding verses encourage compassionate treatment to those in financial difficulty, whether in lending practices (v. 25) or the ways in which financial obligations are enforced (vv. 26–27).

Section Outline

> V.D. Further stipulations of the covenant, spoken to Moses for the people (21:1–23:19) . . .
> 9. Stipulations related to the proper treatment of resident aliens, widows and the fatherless (22:21–24)
> 10. Stipulations related to lending and to holding garments in pledge (22:25–27)

Comment

22:21–24 These stipulations prohibit oppressing or taking advantage of the socially vulnerable. The word "sojourner" may also be translated "resident alien," that is, someone living in a foreign land (Gen. 15:13; Ex. 2:22). Resident aliens did not own land and thus had to make their living by hiring out their labor (Ex.

23:12; Lev. 25:39–40; Deut. 5:14; 29:11) or perhaps from trade. Their lack of land ownership, combined with their possibly starting from scratch in a foreign land among its unfamiliar language, customs, and prices, made sojourners vulnerable to financial difficulty and exploitation (cf. note 254 within comment on 12:43–50). In a modern context this category might include resident aliens, refugees, or migrant workers.[531] The Israelites are forbidden from "wronging" them (Ex. 22:21), a word that "usually connotes economic exploitation, the deprivation of property, or denial of legal rights."[532] Neither could they "oppress" them, a word used earlier in Exodus to describe Pharaoh's cruel mistreatment of the Israelites (3:9). Not only did the Lord abhor such wronging and oppression (Isa. 3:14; 10:1–2; Amos 5:11–12; etc.), but the Israelites personally experienced these horrors when they "were sojourners in the land of Egypt" (Ex. 22:21; cf. 23:9). Loving their neighbors as themselves meant not putting sojourners through the same type of treatment (cf. Lev. 19:33–34) and in fact extending to them compassion and care (Lev. 19:9–10; Deut. 10:18–19).

"Widows" and the "fatherless" were also socially vulnerable if not taken into a larger household to enjoy economic security. Not surprisingly, they are often listed with "resident aliens" as those who are especially susceptible to oppression and poverty (Deut. 10:18; 24:17, 19; etc.). The Israelites must in no way "mistreat" them (Ex. 22:22), a word used also to describe the ways in which the Israelites were "afflicted" and "oppressed" in Egypt (1:11–12; the Hb. verb is the same in each instance). If the Israelites do so, the Lord will be sure to hear the resulting cries for help, and his "wrath will burn" at such cruelty and injustice. He himself will "surely hear their cry" and take up their cause, fatally punishing their oppressors, with the result that their own wives will become widows and their own children fatherless (22:23–24).[533]

22:25–27 These stipulations encourage generosity and kindness to those in financial difficulty. Two situations are considered. In the first a fellow Israelite has become poor.[534] Those who lend money to them should not act as a normal money lender and charge interest (v. 25). These Israelite poor are fellow members of God's people, and therefore family rules apply: just as someone would not charge interest to a brother or sister in financial difficulty, neither should one with a fellow Israelite.[535] But this is a loan, not a gift. In Israel's context the loan could be used to plant crops and produce a harvest, enabling the loan's repayment and the borrower's escape from poverty. There is always some risk involved, however,

---

[531] The second is noted by Ndjerareou, *Exodus*, in *Africa Bible Commentary*, 116, and the third by T. Desmond Alexander, *Exodus*, TTC (Grand Rapids, MI: Baker, 2016), 129.
[532] Levine, *Leviticus*, 134; cf. Leviticus 25:14; Jeremiah 22:3; etc.
[533] Childs (*Book of Exodus*, 478) observes, "The style [in vv. 23–24] shifts to the first person as God places himself directly in the role of special protector."
[534] Cf. Leviticus 25:35–38. Given the focus on the poverty of the borrower, these prohibitions might not apply to commercial loans (cf. Wright, *Deuteronomy*, 251), although the principles stated here and elsewhere would prohibit predatory or otherwise exploitative lending.
[535] Family rules do not always apply elsewhere, so it is no surprise that non-Israelites may be charged interest (Deut. 23:20); the latter was a business relationship, not a family one. Sarna (*Exodus*, 139) also suggests that reciprocity was a contributing factor in cases such as the one described in Deuteronomy 23:20, since Israelites would undoubtedly need to pay interest if borrowing from non-Israelites.

so lending is viewed as an act of generosity, is praised elsewhere as a mark of the righteous (Pss. 15:1–5; 37:26; cf. esp. Luke 6:34),[536] and is said to be rewarded by the Lord himself (Prov. 19:17).

In the second situation the lender asks the borrower to give a "pledge," that is, an item of worth that will cover the loan if the borrower defaults (Ex. 22:26–27). The Bible recognizes that many cannot afford to risk loans that default and also affirms that those who borrow should repay, so asking for collateral is only fair. The pledge in this instance is a garment. Garment making in the ancient Near East was very labor intensive, since all the materials and the garment itself had to be made by hand. This in turn made them very valuable and possible pledge items. The context suggests that the "cloak" was an outer garment worn over other clothes (no one would have given his only garment in pledge, since public nakedness was forbidden). Apparently it decently covered the body and could serve as a type of blanket in the cold desert evenings (Deut. 24:12–13). Given the function of this garment, the lender had to return a neighbor's cloak by sunset so that the neighbor could avoid undue hardship. If not, the Lord would again hear and show his compassion by judging the lender and helping the borrower. The Israelites were to avoid this judgment by showing such compassion themselves, the principle being that loving a neighbor well sometimes means temporarily suspending one's own financial rights. (For related laws cf. Deut. 15:7–11; 24:6, 10–13, 17.)

Response

WHAT DO THESE LAWS PROHIBIT?

As noted above, resident aliens, widows, and the fatherless were socially vulnerable for various reasons (cf. comment on 22:21–24). The opening laws prohibit taking advantage of them in any way and provide at least two reasons. First, the Israelites themselves were shown the Lord's special care when socially vulnerable and were to embody that same care toward others. The passage's prohibitions against mistreating the socially vulnerable use the very same words used to describe how Pharaoh and the Egyptians mistreated the Israelites (cf. vv. 21–22). In other words, "Israel, in your weakness you experienced cruel mistreatment. Do not do the same to the weak among you. Instead, love your neighbor as yourself by embodying the same love you received from the Lord."

The second reason that the Israelites may not mistreat the weak is that the Lord himself is their protector. This is in keeping with the fact that they bear his image. To mistreat them is to provoke the one whose image they bear—with serious consequences (vv. 23–24). Rather than suffering such a fate, the Israelites should show compassion and care to the socially vulnerable and in this way embody the Lord's own character, who is a father to the fatherless and a defender of widows (Ps. 68:6; cf. Deut. 10:18; Pss. 10:18; 146:9). The Lord's people must show to others the

---

[536] Houtman, *Exodus*, vol. 3, 218.

same compassion and care they themselves have received from the Lord (cf. Matt. 18:21–35; Eph. 4:32). This leads to a second question.

WHAT DO THESE LAWS COMMAND?

The Israelites were not simply to avoid mistreating the weak; they were also to show them generosity and kindness. This is seen especially in the laws concerning loans and pledges (Ex. 22:25–27). We may first consider loans. As noted at verse 25, extending personal loans in ancient Israel was viewed as an act of generosity because there was always some risk involved for the lender. In this case the generosity is further enhanced by the fact that no interest is to be charged (for how this relates to commercial loans cf. note 534 within comment on 22:25–27). An underlying principle is that we use our resources not to take advantage of the poor but to help them get back on their feet. The Lord's followers are to embody compassion.

The same is true regarding pledges, which in Israel's day were a means of securing the loan, as someone might do by giving over a valuable outer garment (cf. comment on 22:25–27). Technically, a lender should be able to retain such a garment until the loan is repaid, but the Israelites are prohibited from doing so, since, as noted above, a poor person without his outer garment would suffer in the cold desert evenings (Deut. 24:12–13). Returning it to the borrower was therefore an act of compassion in which one's own rights were temporarily suspended in order to imitate the Lord's own compassion (Ex. 22:27).

In short God showed his compassion to Israel in their physical poverty; they are to show the same compassion to those in poverty around them. The same posture is true for the believer today. Paul notes that in the person of Jesus God entered the world and became materially poor to deliver us from our spiritual poverty and make us spiritually rich (2 Cor. 8:9). Paul makes that observation in the context of appealing to a group of early Christians in Corinth to give generously to support poor believers in Jerusalem (cf. 2 Cor. 8:1–15; 9:1–15; cf. Rom. 15:25–28). The idea is clear: the grace and compassion we have received from Jesus should lead us to show grace and compassion to others and to do so in all areas of life, including through the meeting of material needs.[537]

---

[537] For discussion of how such care might be shown today cf. Wright (*Old Testament Ethics for the People of God*, 207n16), who recommends John D. Mason, "Biblical Teaching and Assisting the Poor," *Transformation* 4/2 (1987): 1–14.

EXODUS 22:28–31

28 "You shall not revile God, nor curse a ruler of your people.
29 "You shall not delay to offer from the fullness of your harvest and from the outflow of your presses. The firstborn of your sons you shall give to me. 30 You shall do the same with your oxen and with your sheep: seven days it shall be with its mother; on the eighth day you shall give it to me.
31 "You shall be consecrated to me. Therefore you shall not eat any flesh that is torn by beasts in the field; you shall throw it to the dogs."

Section Overview

These verses are unified in their exhortation to honor and respect certain authorities, both human and divine. They begin by prohibiting cursing God or earthly rulers (Ex. 22:28), then command honor of God by giving to him from the material blessings he has bestowed (vv. 29–30) and by avoiding a specific behavior not in keeping with being his holy people (v. 31).

Section Outline

V.D. Further stipulations of the covenant, spoken to Moses for the people (21:1–23:19) . . .
    11. Stipulations related to cursing God and earthly authorities (22:28)
    12. Stipulations related to offerings given to God (22:29–30)
    13. Stipulations related to dietary marks of holiness (22:31)

Comment

22:28 The word translated "revile" is the same used in 21:17 and translated "curse": "Whoever curses his father or his mother shall be put to death." As noted there, the word refers to speech that abuses or dishonors someone and can refer to a formal curse. In either situation the act entails hostility toward someone by speaking or wishing evil against him. To do so with God is to reject him as King over his world and, not surprisingly, to forfeit one's right to live within it (Lev. 24:15–16). The Bible assumes that the God who has the right to judge us when we die also has the right to do so while we live.[538]

Cursing earthly rulers is also prohibited. The word for "curse" here refers more regularly to a formal curse in which one person calls down some type of misfortune on another (Gen. 3:14; 4:11; 9:25). The endpoint, however, is the same: someone

---
[538] For further thoughts on explaining such judgment in a modern age cf. Response sections on 13:17–15:21: "What Is the Warning?"; "How Do We Respond?"

utterly opposes the one he curses and wishes him harm. Doing so is forbidden, since the Lord has established civil authorities for the community's good, and they are to be honored as such (cf. Rom. 13:1–7; 1 Pet. 2:17).[539] See further in the Response section.

22:29–30 The underlying principle of these commands is that the Lord is to be honored as King and provider by returning to him from the material blessings he has given to his people. This applies in three contexts: harvests (v. 29a), children (v. 29b) and animals (v. 30).

In terms of harvest the Israelites are elsewhere commanded to present their firstfruits as well as a tenth of their harvests to the Lord (v. 19; Lev. 23:9–14; 27:30–31). Given the focus on the firstborn in Exodus 22:29b–30, the focus in verse 29a may be on firstfruits in particular,[540] though the command would also apply to the tithe (cf. 23:16).

Because the firstfruits are the harvest's best (Num. 18:12), to give them to the Lord is a way for Israel to recognize that he is worthy of his people's greatest honor and praise. It is also a way to celebrate his faithfulness to his covenant promises in giving them such a fruitful land (cf. Deut. 26:1–10). Giving back to him acknowledges him as the good giver of gifts. As for the tithe, it was common practice in the ancient Near East to give a tithe to kings, gods, or priests.[541] And, since the Lord is Israel's God and heavenly King (cf. 1 Sam. 8:7), tithing is a natural way to honor him as such. What is more, the firstfruits and tithe are a way to provide for the priests and Levites, enabling them to focus on Israel's spiritual needs, and are also a way to provide for the poor (Num. 18:12–13, 21–29; Deut. 14:28–29).[542] For the command not to delay in giving these things see the Response section.

The Israelites are also to present their firstborn sons and animals to the Lord (Ex. 22:29b–30; for explanation cf. comment on 12:51–13:2, 11–16). Exodus 22:30 adds that firstborn animals from the herd and flock are to remain with their mother a full week before being sacrificed to the Lord on the eighth day. The same command is repeated in Leviticus 22:27, where the context suggests compassion as a motivating factor:

> Various laws in the Pentateuch appear to be motivated by concern for the animal's well-being (see Ex. 23:5, 11–12a; Deut. 22:6–7; cf. also Prov. 12:10), and this motivation also fits well here.
>
> This is perhaps clearest for [Lev.] 22:28: "But an ox or a flock animal—it and its young you must not slaughter on the same day" (22:28); that is,

---

539 The same is true of parents (Ex. 20:12; 21:17; Prov. 20:20; Eph. 6:2) and church leaders (1 Thess. 5:12; 1 Tim. 5:17; Heb. 13:17).
540 Keil, *Exodus*, vol. 2, 143.
541 For an overview cf. Richard E. Averbeck, "מַעֲשֵׂר," *NIDOTTE* 2:1035–1036.
542 For further details cf. Sklar, *Leviticus*, TOTC, 333. For how the various tithing laws in Leviticus–Deuteronomy relate cf. Sklar, *Additional Notes on* Leviticus, at 27:30–33, which follows Averbeck in understanding that all three books refer to one annual tithe, with Deuteronomy specifying its distribution at the sanctuary in years 1–2, 4–5 (Deut. 14:22–27) and in local towns in years 3 and 6 (Deut. 14:28–29; 26:12–15). Cf. Averbeck, "מַעֲשֵׂר," *NIDOTTE* 2:1041–1050, esp. 1041, 1046–1049.

slaughter for sacrifice. This calls to mind Deut. 22:6–7, which appears to view it as unjust to kill an entire family of animals on the same day.

A rationale of compassion also fits well with [Lev.] 22:27: a newborn herd or flock animal "must remain seven days with its mother" before it may be sacrificed, giving them at least "seven days" together, which in Leviticus was considered a thorough amount of time.[543] The LORD shows compassion to his creation (Ps. 104:14a; 147:9; Matt. 6:26); his followers must do the same.[544]

22:31 To be "consecrated" (or "holy") is to be set apart; to be "consecrated to the Lord" is to show in some way that someone belongs especially to him (cf. note 114 within Response section on 2:23–4:17). Just as this is to be true of the firstborn (vv. 29–30), so is it to be true of Israel as a whole, in this case by not eating the meat of animals killed by wild beasts.[545] Other texts make clear that eating such meat makes one ritually impure (Lev. 17:15), though the reason that this is the case is nowhere explained. Whatever the reason, by not eating such meat the Israelites signal to the nations that purity matters to them because it matters to their God.

Response

As noted above (cf. Section Overview), these verses are unified in their exhortation to honor and respect certain authorities, both human and divine. We may unpack this by asking two questions.

HOW ARE WE TO RESPOND TO OUR CIVIL LEADERS?

As noted at Exodus 22:28, the Lord has established civil authorities for the community's good, and they are to be honored as such (cf. Rom. 13:1–7; 1 Pet. 2:17). Indeed, the word for "rulers" refers not simply to the main leader but to rulers more generally (cf. Ex. 16:22; 34:31; cf. also Acts 23:5). True, they can rule tyrannically instead of reflecting God's good and just rule, but the appropriate response is not cursing (cf. Acts 23:1–5). Instead, a believer's first response is to pray, knowing that the Lord, who is King of all kings, can move in rulers' hearts to do good (Ezra 6:22; 7:27; Neh. 2:1–8; Prov. 21:1; 1 Tim. 2:1–2). In modern democracies the Lord has also granted believers the privilege of using their vote and various forms of advocacy to seek to install leaders that will rule justly. But this, too, is done under the umbrella of trust in God's sovereignty and a commitment to pray, not to curse, when votes do not go our way. Especially at times when we disagree with our leaders should Christians be noted for doing so with respect.

WHAT ARE PRACTICAL WAYS TO HONOR THE LORD?

Generally speaking, Exodus 22:29–31 identifies two practical ways for the Israelites to honor the Lord. The first is to return to him from the material bless-

---

543 Cf. note 56 within comment on 1:1–5.
544 Sklar, *Leviticus*, ZECOT, 610.
545 For how this compares with Leviticus 17:15–16 cf. Sklar, *Leviticus*, TOTC, 222–223.

ings he has given them. But not just any gift will do. As noted at verse 29, the firstfruits were the harvest's best, meaning that the Israelites are taught that the Lord is not simply worthy of praise but worthy of the best praise they can give. Some farmers' fields will undoubtedly produce better firstfruits than others', but this does not matter. The question is not whether one person's gift is better than another's; the question is whether each person is giving his best.

Related to this, the text commands Israelites not to delay (or fail entirely) in bringing their gifts (v. 29). A person in charge of receiving charitable gifts at our seminary once said that one of his team's operating principles was to "Thank before you bank," that is, write a note of thanks before depositing the check to ensure that appropriate thanks are given. So too here: giving to the Lord is to be done not last, with the remnants, but first, with the very best. This is how to honor a king, especially one as generous as the Lord.

The second way for the Israelites to honor the Lord is through costly obedience. Verse 31 commands them not to eat ritually defiling meat, for they belong to a holy God. As noted there, by not eating such meat the Israelites signal to the nations that purity matters to them because it matters to their God. Indeed, at a time when eating meat would be rare, throwing otherwise good meat to the dogs would require sacrificial obedience from the Israelites, both in terms of denying themselves and in terms of being willing to look strange before others. (That this command even exists suggests that eating such meat was common elsewhere.) But this is the point: the Lord is worthy of our obedience, no matter the cost personally or socially.

In all the above, such costly gifts and obedience are given not to earn God's favor but simply because he is worthy. He is worthy by his very nature as divine King; that is reason enough. But he is especially worthy because he is a divine King who leans toward us with the utmost compassion and love, not only in providing daily bread, and often far beyond our daily needs, but in sending Jesus to rescue us from our sin, defeat the powers of evil, and make a way for us to be adopted in God's own family. That is worthy of costly praise indeed. As Paul writes, "I appeal to you therefore, brothers, *by the mercies of God*, to present your bodies as a living sacrifice, holy and acceptable to God, which is your spiritual worship" (Rom. 12:1).

EXODUS 23:1–9

23 "You shall not spread a false report. You shall not join hands with a wicked man to be a malicious witness. ² You shall not fall in with the many to do evil, nor shall you bear witness in a lawsuit, siding with the many, so as to pervert justice, ³ nor shall you be partial to a poor man in his lawsuit.

⁴ "If you meet your enemy's ox or his donkey going astray, you shall bring it back to him. ⁵ If you see the donkey of one who hates you lying down under its burden, you shall refrain from leaving him with it; you shall rescue it with him.

⁶ "You shall not pervert the justice due to your poor in his lawsuit. ⁷ Keep far from a false charge, and do not kill the innocent and righteous, for I will not acquit the wicked. ⁸ And you shall take no bribe, for a bribe blinds the clear-sighted and subverts the cause of those who are in the right.

⁹ "You shall not oppress a sojourner. You know the heart of a sojourner, for you were sojourners in the land of Egypt."

Section Overview

These verses are arranged as a chiasm, with the outer sections detailing commands concerning justice (vv. 1–3, 6–9) and the center section outlining case laws addressing love of enemy (vv. 4–5).[546] The overall effect is to emphasize that the Israelites must show justice and love to all.

Section Outline

   V.D. Further stipulations of the covenant, spoken to Moses for the people (21:1–23:19) . . .

   14. Stipulations related to justice in legal proceedings (23:1–3)
   15. Stipulations related to loving one's enemy as oneself (23:4–5)
   16. Further stipulations related to justice in legal proceedings (23:6–9)

Comment

23:1–3 These stipulations command that justice be done in legal proceedings. Five commands are given, the first four of which overlap in various ways. We might paraphrase, "You shall not spread a false report" (v. 1a), whether by means of slander in general or by means of testifying falsely in particular so that justice is perverted or denied (cf. comment on 20:16). Nor shall you "join hands with a

---
[546] So also Stuart, *Exodus*, 523.

wicked man to be a malicious witness" (23:1b), plotting together with others to give false testimony in a legal proceeding to the harm of the accused (cf. 1 Kings 21:13; cf. also Deut. 19:15–21). Indeed, even if you must stand alone, "you shall not fall in with the many to do evil" (Ex. 23:2a) in any of the ways that justice can be perverted,[547] making sure you do not testify falsely by "siding with the many, so as to pervert justice" (v. 2b). God's people must embody God's justice.

But it is also possible to commit injustice by siding with the weaker party, especially when compassion tempts one to rule in favor of the disadvantaged. The fifth command therefore states the Israelites may not "be partial to a poor man in his lawsuit" (v. 3; cf. Lev. 19:15 and Ex. 23:6). Justice is to be fair and impartial.

23:4–5 These two stipulations focus on loving our enemies as ourselves. In the first an Israelite comes across an ox or donkey that has wandered away from its owner's field (v. 4a), likely a common occurrence in a day and age when labor and material costs made it impractical to build long fences or walls for cattle. The animal's owner is an "enemy," which in this context refers not to someone from an enemy nation but to a nearby Israelite, most likely a neighbor, with whom the first Israelite is at odds (cf. Num. 35:23). The reason for the enmity is not stated because it does not matter: just as someone would want his lost valuable possession returned to him, whether by friend or foe, so he must do the same (Ex. 23:4b). The same applies when an enemy's animal lies down under its load and help is needed getting it up (or, in a modern context, when an enemy's tractor breaks down and help is needed to fix it). In short, just as one would want help in difficult situations, whatever they might be, that person must extend the same help to another, even if he is an enemy (v. 5). (Though perhaps not the focus of v. 5, this command also encourages compassion to animals; cf. comment on 22:29–30.) See further in the Response section. For related laws see Deuteronomy 22:1–4.

23:6–9 As in verses 1–3, these verses include five commands requiring that justice be done in legal proceedings. Again we might paraphrase, "Though the poor are often powerless, you shall not pervert the justice due to them in court, whether from spite or by siding with the rich or powerful; justice must be applied equally to all (v. 6; cf. Lev. 19:15; Prov. 22:22–23). Do not have anything to do with a false charge (Ex. 23:7a); indeed, do not kill or in any way wrong the innocent with your judgments, for I, the Lord, am watching and will hold you to account (v. 7b)! Make sure to take no bribes, since they blind you to what is just so that the words and causes[548] of those in the right are overthrown (v. 8; cf. comment on 18:13–23 [at v. 21]). All of this applies to resident aliens as well,[549] whom you must not oppress, since you know from your time in Egypt exactly what it is like to be wrongly mistreated as an alien (23:9; cf. comment on 22:21–24)." The justice and deliverance

---

547 The word for "evil" is plural.
548 The word translated "cause" (Hb. *debarim*) is plural and could also be rendered "causes" or even "words."
549 Cf. Deuteronomy 1:16 (Kalisch, *Exodus*, 447); 24:17; 27:19 (Keil, *Exodus*, vol. 2, 145). For "sojourner" as "resident alien" cf. note 254 within comment on 12:43–50.

the Lord did for the Israelites in their weakness is the same they must do for the weak in their midst.

Response

WHAT ARE THE KEYS TO PROPER JUSTICE?

Exodus 23:1–9 identifies three principles central to the proper execution of justice in the courts. First, witnesses and judges must hold an unwavering commitment to truth. Verses 1–3 emphasize that witnesses must not lie or mislead in any way. Verses 6–9 emphasize that judges must not listen to false charges or take bribes and so pervert justice.[550] The temptation to compromise truth could come from the desire for gain or revenge or, as emphasized in verses 1–3, from the pressure of others. Especially in ancient Israel, where communities were small and the witnesses in a local court were likely to be one's friends or families, going along with the majority would have been a very strong temptation.[551] But fear of God and a commitment to his truth must trump fear of others, leading one to "swim against the tide, if it flows toward evil."[552]

Second, special concern must be shown to the weak and powerless. Verses 6 and 9 focus on the poor and the resident alien, both of whom were socially vulnerable. As noted further above, a natural human tendency is to treat the beautiful, the gifted, the rich, or the powerful as though they have more value than others. The Bible repeatedly speaks against this. Old Testament or New, the Lord commands his people to make sure they defend, care for, and support the lowly (22:21–24; Deut. 14:28–29; 24:19; Isa. 1:17; Jer. 22:3; James 1:27; 2:1–9; cf. Response section on 21:18–32, "Who Bears God's Image?").

Third, while special concern must be shown to the weak and powerless, we must also make sure that compassion does not lead us to pervert justice in their favor (Ex. 23:3). Justice is the foundation of moral order in society and must be applied fairly and impartially. In many societies today justice is personified as a woman who holds scales by which the evidence is to be weighed, who bears a sword that represents authority to make and enforce legal decisions, and who wears a blindfold to indicate that justice is fair and impartial.[553] God is no respecter of persons; his people must not be so either.

While the above principles are meant to guide behavior in the courts, they apply to many other contexts as well. This includes "organizations, businesses, and schools where individuals or committees are responsible to investigate charges against members, employees, or students."[554] In today's social media age it applies also to the court of public opinion, where people's actions are quickly evaluated and judged on any number of media platforms and where the temptation to follow

---

550 In ancient Israel judgment could be rendered by an individual (Ex. 18:24–26) or by a group of elders (Deut. 22:15–19), the latter loosely comparable today to a jury.
551 Stuart, *Exodus*, 524. Cf. comment on 20:16 for further discussion of what might tempt one to false testimony.
552 Cassuto, *Commentary on the Book of Exodus*, 296.
553 Alexander, *Exodus*, TTC, 134.
554 Stuart, *Exodus*, 527. Churches would be included as one such organization.

the majority is strong. What does it look like in these contexts for God's people to have an unwavering commitment to truth, to show special care for the weak and powerless, and to make sure that the judgments we make or encourage are fair and impartial? How might our businesses or social media feeds look different as a result? How *should* they look different as a result?

WHAT SHOULD BE OUR POSTURE TOWARD OUR ENEMIES?

Amid these commands regarding proper justice we find two commands about loving our enemies as ourselves (23:4–5). This is no surprise. Our enemies are the ones we might be most tempted to wrong in matters of justice. These verses steer us away from such behavior by commanding us to show compassion to our enemies. In particular, just as we would want help in difficult situations, so must we extend the same help to others, even an enemy. In short we must love our enemies as ourselves.

The original command to "love your neighbor as yourself" is spoken in the context of how to interact with someone who has wronged another (cf. Lev. 19:18b with 19:18a). Stated differently, the "neighbor" in view in Leviticus 19:18 is not first and foremost the person whom someone likes and gets along with but the one with whom another has conflict. In comments elsewhere on that verse I note,

> Jesus ... [addresses] those who sought to limit this command to friends (Matt. 5:43), emphasizing that it also applies to enemies. He teaches us even to pray for them and explains that only when we show love to all people can we become living examples of God's generous care and love for the entire world (Matt. 5:44–45). Similarly, when asked to explain what loving our neighbor as ourselves entails, Jesus tells the parable of a good Samaritan who showed practical love and care for a man who would normally be considered his enemy (Luke 10:29–37). He concludes the parable by saying "Go and *do* likewise" (10:37), making clear that loving our neighbor means showing God's love and care to all those we encounter, whether friend or foe, and doing so in very practical ways.[555]

WHAT MOTIVATES OUR OBEDIENCE?

In all the above, obedience is motivated by two different factors. First, God himself is watching. "Keep far from a false charge, and do not kill the innocent and righteous, *for I will not acquit the wicked*" (Ex. 23:7). God will hold us to account for wrongs we have done, even when others are powerless to do so (cf. 22:23–24, 27). "Be sure your sin will find you out" (Num. 32:23) is one of the Bible's most sobering warnings.

But the Israelites should not even need this warning, in light of the second factor: the tremendous justice and mercy they have already received from the Lord. "You shall not oppress a sojourner. You know the heart of a sojourner, for you were sojourners in the land of Egypt" (Ex. 23:9). By appealing to the Israelites' own experience of suffering and misery the Lord also recalls how he has exercised

---

555 Sklar, *Leviticus*, ZECOT, 534.

justice and mercy on their behalf. The Israelites are in turn to be a conduit of this same justice and mercy toward others.

Throughout the Bible God's behavior toward his people is to be the model of how they treat others. Jesus tells his disciples, "A new commandment I give to you, that you love one another: just as I have loved you, you also are to love one another" (John 13:34). Other verses also speak of the love we have received from the Father and the Son as the model and motivation for the love we are to show others (Eph. 5:2; 1 John 4:11; from a warning perspective, cf. Matt. 18:21–35). Whether in the courts of criminal or civil justice or in the courts of public opinion, whether in our interactions with our friends or in those with our enemies, Christians have the privilege of embodying to others the love of Jesus. And that is the strongest testimony we can ever give.

EXODUS 23:10–19

¹⁰ "For six years you shall sow your land and gather in its yield, ¹¹ but the seventh year you shall let it rest and lie fallow, that the poor of your people may eat; and what they leave the beasts of the field may eat. You shall do likewise with your vineyard, and with your olive orchard.

¹² "Six days you shall do your work, but on the seventh day you shall rest; that your ox and your donkey may have rest, and the son of your servant woman, and the alien, may be refreshed.

¹³ "Pay attention to all that I have said to you, and make no mention of the names of other gods, nor let it be heard on your lips.

¹⁴ "Three times in the year you shall keep a feast to me. ¹⁵ You shall keep the Feast of Unleavened Bread. As I commanded you, you shall eat unleavened bread for seven days at the appointed time in the month of Abib, for in it you came out of Egypt. None shall appear before me empty-handed. ¹⁶ You shall keep the Feast of Harvest, of the firstfruits of your labor, of what you sow in the field. You shall keep the Feast of Ingathering at the end of the year, when you gather in from the field the fruit of your labor. ¹⁷ Three times in the year shall all your males appear before the Lord God.

¹⁸ "You shall not offer the blood of my sacrifice with anything leavened, or let the fat of my feast remain until the morning.

¹⁹ "The best of the firstfruits of your ground you shall bring into the house of the Lord your God.

"You shall not boil a young goat in its mother's milk."

Section Overview

This section focuses on special seasons and days the Israelites are to celebrate as the Lord's people. The opening commands focus on how celebrating the Sabbath year and the Sabbath day is a way to show the Lord's comprehensive care to humanity and his creation (vv. 10–12). The latter commands focus on three festivals that will remind the Israelites of the Lord's redemption and material blessing and allow them to express appropriate worship and praise (vv. 14–19). Acting as a hinge between these two groups of commands, the middle command underscores that the Israelites must worship the Lord alone (v. 13).

Section Outline

V.D. Further stipulations of the covenant, spoken to Moses for the people (21:1–23:19) . . .
    17. Stipulations related to the Sabbath year and day (23:10–12)
    18. Stipulations related to proper worship of the Lord (23:13–19)

Comment

23:10–11 To show that they are the Lord's people, the Israelites are to rest not only one day in seven but also one year in seven. The Sabbath year of rest applies especially to the full scope of agricultural work, from beginning to end (sowing to gathering), whether in the fields, vineyards, or olive orchards (vv. 10, 11c). The Israelites' food will come from the previous year's harvest and from what grows naturally in the fields (Lev. 25:6–7).

There are three reasons behind the command: so that the land may rest,[556] the poor may eat freely from the land's fruit,[557] and the animals may eat whatever the poor leave. The Lord has compassion for all people and all things, including the land and the animals (cf. Gen. 6:18–20; 8:1; 9:8–10; Lev. 25:4–5; Ps. 104:10–18; Matt. 10:29). So great is his concern that he institutionalizes this care in the rituals his people are to follow, both here and in Exodus 23:12, providing them with a constant reminder to show his compassion to his world. This focus, here and in verse 12, also connects these verses naturally to the preceding. For a more detailed expression of this law see Leviticus 25:1–7, 18–22.

23:12 The command to rest every seventh day is now repeated (cf. comment on 20:8–11). Picking up on the rationale of the preceding verses, 23:12 focuses on compassion for animals, who are the objects of God's own care, and compassion for all people, who are made in his image, whether the lowliest member of a household ("the son of your servant woman") or those from a different people ("the alien"; for "alien" cf. note 254 within comment on 12:43–50). None of these are to be treated as lifeless tools but are to be shown compassion as living beings in need of rest and refreshment.

23:13 A more wooden rendering of this verse might begin, "In everything I have said to you, keep yourselves!"—that is, they are to stay exactly within the commands he has given them. This especially means showing exclusive loyalty to the

---

[556] This is implied in the language of Exodus 23:11, which could be rendered literalistically, "But in the seventh year you must release it [i.e., the land] and leave it." Leviticus 25:4–5 makes the point more explicitly.
[557] This would be in addition to other regular ways in which the poor are to be supported; cf. comment on 22:29–30.

Lord by not even mentioning the names of other gods, whether by praising them, praying to them, or taking oaths in their name (v. 13b; cf. note 432 within comment on 20:22–26). In short the rejection of other gods is to be absolute. "Idols shall not only be banished from the hearts, but also from the lips."[558] The Lord alone is to be the Israelites' God.

23:14–17 In light of verse 13 one way in which the Israelites will show their exclusive devotion to the Lord is when Israelite males, as family representatives, travel to the sanctuary three times during the year to hold various feasts in honor of the Lord.[559] The passage begins and ends with this command in order to emphasize it (vv. 14, 17). Other community rituals and offerings are also to be held (cf. table 2.8), but this passage focuses on the only three that will require Israelites to travel to the sanctuary.

The first feast is the "Feast of Unleavened Bread" (Ex. 23:15), which is celebrated together with the Passover (cf. comments on 12:14–20 and 12:3–13, respectively; for "Abib" cf. comment on 12:1–2).[561] The focus here, as in chapter 12, is the way in which this feast commemorates the Lord's deliverance of the Israelites. Their year thus begins with a celebration of his redemption. And since they are coming before him as their redeeming King, it is appropriate for them to bring tribute to him in the form of offerings and not come empty-handed.[562] The same will apply to the following feasts.[563]

The next sanctuary feast is the Feast of Harvest, which goes by other names as well (cf. how today we use "Communion," "the Lord's Supper," and "the Eucharist" to refer to the same meal). One of these is "Feast of Weeks" (Ex. 34:22), as it comes seven weeks after the offering of the firstfruits of the barley harvest,[564] and another is "Pentecost," used in NT times (Acts 2:1) and deriving from the Greek word for "fiftieth" (*pentēkos*) since it occurs on the fiftieth day after the offering of the firstfruits (cf. Lev. 23:16). This feast celebrates the Lord as provider of the harvest (for further details cf. table 2.8 and Lev. 23:15–22).

The final sanctuary feast is known as the "Feast of Ingathering" since it takes place "at the end of the year," with the final harvest (Ex. 23:16b),[565] and is a time

---

558 Kalisch, *Exodus*, 452.
559 At least one text suggests, however, that entire families typically traveled to the sanctuary during the Festival of Weeks (Deut. 16:11), and other texts mention entire households' going to the sanctuary to worship and partake of sacrificial meals (Deut. 12:10–12, 18). How often this actually occurred is impossible to know, but, when it did, it seems to have been viewed as a natural occurrence. As Alexander notes, "Women are not prohibited from attending, but mandatory attendance would prove exceptionally difficult for those who might be pregnant or have small children" (*Exodus*, TTC, 137).
561 Passover and Unleavened Bread are sometimes treated together (cf. Deut. 16:16 with 16:1–8), so the text can speak of "three" times Israelites are to appear before the Lord (Ex. 23:14).
562 Cf. the offerings described Numbers 28:19–24, no doubt collected from the whole people, since very few individuals could afford such lavish gifts; cf. also note 563.
563 Deuteronomy 16 makes clear that contributions are to be brought to each of the three feasts (Deut. 16:16) and that "every man shall give as he is able, according to the blessing of the Lord your God that he has given you" (Deut. 16:17; Keil, *Exodus*, vol. 2, 147).
564 Cf. Leviticus 23:10–11 with Leviticus 23:15. Wheat comes later than barley, so the "firstfruits" in Exodus 23:16 is a reference to the firstfruits of the wheat harvest (cf. 34:22), with its final harvest coming several weeks later, during ingathering (23:16b).
565 Since the new calendar year begins in our March or April, and this feast occurs in our September or October (cf. table 2.8), "end of the year" may refer here to the agricultural year rather than to the calendrical year.

TABLE 2.8: The Lord's Holy Times[560]

Reference	Event	Month	Day	Season/Modern Calendar	Work Prohibition	Males Required to Go to Sanctuary?	Purpose
Lev. 23:3	Weekly Sabbath	Every	Every 7th	—	Total	No	Sign of the covenant; an opportunity for rest.
First Half of Year							
Lev. 23:5	Passover	1	14	Spring/March-April	None stated	Yes	To celebrate how the Lord rescued them in the midst of his judgment of Egypt and led them from the land of slavery.
Lev. 23:6–8	Festival of Unleavened Bread	1	15–21	Spring/March-April	Partial on days 1, 7	Yes	As immediately above.
Lev. 23:9–14	Offering of the firstfruits	—	Day after first Sabbath of harvest	Spring/April	None stated	No	Honor the Lord as provider by returning to him from firstfruits of the harvest; likely pray for his continued blessing on the harvest.
Lev. 23:15–22	Festival of Weeks/Festival of Harvest/Pentecost	—	50th day after the offering of the first-fruits	Spring-Summer/May-June	Partial	Yes	As immediately above.
Second Half of Year							
Lev. 23:23–25	Day of trumpet blasts	7	1	Fall/September-October	Partial	No	To acknowledge the Lord as their God and to ask him to show them his favor and to be faithful to his covenant promises to them.
Lev. 23:26–32	Day of Atonement	7	10	Fall/September-October	Total	No	The making of atonement for their sins and impurities.
Lev. 23:33–36, 39–43	Festival of Booths/Succoth/Festival of Ingathering	7	15–21	Fall/September-October	Partial on day 1	Yes	Celebrate the Lord's provision in the harvest; teach future generations of the Lord's deliverance of Israel from Egypt
Lev. 23:36	Festival of Booths closing assembly	7	22	Fall/September-October	Partial	Yes	As immediately above; also, closes out the festival.

[560] Sklar, *Leviticus*, ZECOT, 624–625.

to praise the Lord again for his provision. It is also known as the "Feast of Booths" (Lev. 23:34) since the Israelites are to construct "booths"—known in Hebrew as *sukkot*, the name often used for the festival in Jewish circles—to remember and teach about the Lord's deliverance of Israel from Egypt (cf. table 2.8 and Lev. 23:33–43, and further in the Response section).

23:18–19 As do the preceding verses, these also focus on matters related to the Lord's proper worship and, in particular, matters relevant to the feasts just mentioned. While verse 18 could be read as a general comment on sacrifices, the approach that makes best sense of all the data understands it to refer to the Passover in particular (celebrated together with the Festival of Unleavened Bread). This is certainly true of the phrase "my feast" in the verse's second half, since the parallel verse in 34:25 substitutes "Feast of the Passover" in its place. It also makes good sense of the first half of 23:18, as it focuses on keeping anything leavened from accompanying the sacrifice, which is the main focus of Passover. In this light the terms "my sacrifice" and "my feast" are parallel, with the verse emphasizing earlier commands related to the Passover: any bread eaten with the meal must be unleavened, and none of it may be left until morning.[566] (Cf. comment on 12:3–13 for further explanation.)

Exodus 23:19a continues the theme of worshiping the Lord properly by commanding the Israelites to bring "the best of the firstfruits" of their harvest to him (which they will do in part during the Festival of Weeks; Lev. 23:17). He is worthy of their highest honor and praise (cf. comment on 22:29–30). Exodus 23:19b also relates to the Lord's proper worship. Boiling appears to have been a common way to prepare sacrificial meat (Lev. 6:28–29; 1 Sam. 2:13; Zech. 14:21), which would have been done during the three festivals above. Why such meat should not be boiled in its mother's milk is not explained. Many have suggested this is prohibiting the Israelites from imitating a pagan rite, though there is no clear evidence that such a rite was practiced by other nations.[567] Since other verses imply that a level of respect and compassion should be shown with regard to the relationship between an animal and its offspring (cf. comment on 22:29–30), it should not surprise us if the same principle is at work here, the thought being that using a mother's life-giving milk to prepare her dead offspring for consumption is uncaring at best and grotesque at worst. At our current state of knowledge this understanding is perhaps the most plausible, though it cannot be affirmed with certainty.

Response

WHY DOES THE LORD GIVE THE SABBATH?

The Lord gives his people the Sabbath for different though complementary reasons. Some texts emphasize that it serves as a sign of the Israelites' covenant

---

[566] Exodus 23:18b might mention "fat" in particular since this is the one part Israelites are not to eat (Lev. 3:17) and therefore the part most likely to be set aside while they focus on the meat they can eat. Exodus 34:25 makes clear the command applies to any of the animal's meat (cf. 12:10).
[567] Appeal has been made to a possible Ugaritic parallel (Cassuto, *Commentary on the Book of Exodus*, 305), but the meaning of the Ugaritic text cited in support is disputed (cf. extensive references in Alexander, *Exodus*, ApOTC, 525).

relationship with the Lord, much like a wedding ring is a sign of a marriage relationship (Ex. 31:13–17). Keeping the Sabbath year and the Sabbath day are thus physical proclamations of faith, a way for Israelites to say with their bodies that they follow the Lord, the one who created all things in six days and then rested on the seventh.

But these verses emphasize other reasons for the Sabbath, namely, rest and provision, especially for those who might not be able to rest otherwise or who struggle to provide for themselves. Among people the Lord zeroes in on the poor and lowly (23:11–12), reminding Israelites that all are in God's image and therefore to be shown compassion and care, both in allowing them to provide for their needs and in giving them needed rest and refreshment. But the Lord also makes note of the land and the animals (vv. 11–12), which are equally to be given the opportunity to rest and, in the animals' case, to provide for themselves. This is no surprise. This is God's creation, and he cares for it as his own. We do well to ask: What does it look like for believers today, especially those who employ others, to provide rest and refreshment for others, including the poor and lowly? And what does it look like for believers today to have the Lord's posture toward the earth and the creatures within it? This is our Father's world; we should care for it as such.

WHY DOES THE LORD INSTITUTE VARIOUS FEASTS?

The Sabbath and the Sabbath year are not the only special times in Israel's calendar. Others include the offering of the firstfruits, the day of trumpet blasts, the Day of Atonement, and three festivals at the sanctuary: Passover and Unleavened Bread (celebrated together), Weeks, and Booths (cf. table 2.8). This passage focuses on these latter three (for details on each of the feasts cf. comments on 23:10–19).

By keeping these feasts the Israelites begin their year with a reminder of the Lord's redemption (Passover and Unleavened Bread), which would be like our beginning the calendar with Easter. As the year went on, the countrywide harvest is punctuated near its beginning (Weeks) and end (Booths) with reminders of the Lord's provision and an opportunity to pass on again the story of his redemption. The calendar is both a catechism, teaching the Israelites who the Lord is, and a worship service, providing them opportunity to respond in thanksgiving and praise. How might we structure the life of our churches in similar ways? Aside from Sunday worship, what types of regular events could remind people of God's goodness in providing salvation through Christ and in providing material blessing? And how can we structure these events to give God's people a chance to respond with appropriate celebration and praise?

EXODUS 23:20–33

²⁰ "Behold, I send an angel before you to guard you on the way and to bring you to the place that I have prepared. ²¹ Pay careful attention to him and obey his voice; do not rebel against him, for he will not pardon your transgression, for my name is in him.

²² "But if you carefully obey his voice and do all that I say, then I will be an enemy to your enemies and an adversary to your adversaries.

²³ "When my angel goes before you and brings you to the Amorites and the Hittites and the Perizzites and the Canaanites, the Hivites and the Jebusites, and I blot them out, ²⁴ you shall not bow down to their gods nor serve them, nor do as they do, but you shall utterly overthrow them and break their pillars in pieces. ²⁵ You shall serve the Lord your God, and he[1] will bless your bread and your water, and I will take sickness away from among you. ²⁶ None shall miscarry or be barren in your land; I will fulfill the number of your days. ²⁷ I will send my terror before you and will throw into confusion all the people against whom you shall come, and I will make all your enemies turn their backs to you. ²⁸ And I will send hornets[2] before you, which shall drive out the Hivites, the Canaanites, and the Hittites from before you. ²⁹ I will not drive them out from before you in one year, lest the land become desolate and the wild beasts multiply against you. ³⁰ Little by little I will drive them out from before you, until you have increased and possess the land. ³¹ And I will set your border from the Red Sea to the Sea of the Philistines, and from the wilderness to the Euphrates,[3] for I will give the inhabitants of the land into your hand, and you shall drive them out before you. ³² You shall make no covenant with them and their gods. ³³ They shall not dwell in your land, lest they make you sin against me; for if you serve their gods, it will surely be a snare to you."

[1] Septuagint, Vulgate *I* [2] Or *the hornet* [3] Hebrew *the River*

Section Overview

Having given Moses specific stipulations for the Israelites (21:1–23:19), the Lord now warns them against disobedience and describes the blessings of obedience, both on the way to the Promised Land and within it. On the way to the Promised Land the Israelites must obey the guidance the Lord gives them through his angel (23:20–22). Failure to do so will result in judgment, but obedience will result in the Lord's fighting on their behalf. Once they arrive in the Promised Land they must be sure to destroy any false worship objects they find and not make any covenants of peace with the land's inhabitants, lest the objects or inhabitants lead them astray (vv. 23–24, 32–33). Instead they must serve the Lord alone, who will pour abundant blessings on his faithful servants (vv. 25–31).

To find such warnings and blessings here is no surprise. Ancient Near Eastern treaty documents from the second millennium often ended in similar ways. Like this passage, they also list blessings for the obedient. Unlike our passage, they list formal curses for the disobedient, though the warning of judgment for disobedience in verse 21 ought to have a similar effect. In short, while later biblical passages hold more exact parallels to the blessings and curses of second-millennium treaties (cf. Lev. 26:3–39; Deut. 27:9–28:68), this passage is a close cousin and a natural conclusion to the preceding covenant stipulations.

Section Outline

V. Israel at Sinai: the Lord gives his covenant to Israel; the covenant is ratified (20:1–24:11) . . .
  E. Warnings against disobedience, and the blessings of obedience, on the way to the Promised Land and once within it, spoken to Moses for the people (23:20–33)
    1. Warnings against disobedience, and the blessings of obedience, on the way to the Promised Land (23:20–22)
    2. Warnings against disobedience, and the blessings of obedience, once in the Promised Land (23:23–33)
      a. Command not to worship the nations' gods (23:23–24)
      b. The blessings the Lord will give his faithful servants (23:25–31)
      c. Command not to let the nations remain and tempt Israel to worship their gods (23:32–33)

Comment

23:20–22 This is the third time we read of an angel of the Lord (cf. 3:2; 14:19). The word for "angel" also means "messenger," and, like a king's messenger, angels can both speak and act on the Lord's behalf (cf. comment on 3:1–3). Chapter 3 emphasizes the angel's speaking role. Chapter 14 emphasizes the way he acts to protect the Israelites as they leave Egypt. Chapter 23 emphasizes the angel's role as both protector and speaker. As protector, the angel will go before the Israelites to bring them safely into the Promised Land (v. 20). But in doing so he will also communicate to them on the Lord's behalf: "If you carefully obey *his voice* and do all that *I say*" (v. 22). Just what this communication looks like is nowhere explained. In chapter 14 the angel's presence is especially associated with the movement of the pillar of cloud that leads the Israelites (cf. v. 19 with 13:21 and 14:24), so following his lead via the cloud into battle and the Promised Land may be especially in view in chapter 23. What is clear is that the angel will lead the Israelites into that land and that the Lord has already prepared it for their arrival; their job is simply to follow the angel into it.

Two motivations for obeying the angel are given. First, failure to obey him will have serious consequences (v. 21). When the Lord declares that "My name is in him," he conveys that the angel speaks on his behalf (cf. the prophet in Deut.

18:19). For this reason disobeying the angel will result in judgment: "He will not pardon your transgression." The idea is not that forgiveness is impossible for the repentant (Ex. 34:6–7a) but that judgment will be sure to come for the rebellious (v. 7b; cf. Josh. 24:19 with 24:20; cf. Response section).

Second, and more positively, the Lord will protect and deliver those who obey his direction through the angel (Ex. 23:22)—not because obedience somehow earns blessing but because those who align themselves with a king have the king himself to fight for them (cf. comment on 15:22–26; Response section below). The Lord goes before the Israelites; they need simply to follow in his wake.

23:23–24 The Lord now commands the Israelites regarding their actions after entering the land. He warns them to remain faithful to him in it and describes the blessings he will bestow on them there. He begins with the warning. The Israelites will come to a land inhabited by many different peoples (cf. comment on 3:7–10) with many different gods. When the Lord blots out these nations, the Israelites must not worship their gods by making use of any idols or cultic objects left behind, such as sacred pillars (23:23–24)[568] or altars or Asherim (cf. comment on 34:11–16). Instead they must utterly destroy such objects. One of the surest ways to resist sin is to remove whatever might lead to it (cf. Matt. 5:29–30).

23:25–31 Rather than serving the nations' gods, the Israelites must "serve the LORD" alone (Ex. 23:25a). As noted earlier, the word "serve" (Hb. *'abad*) refers commonly to worship,[569] though such service is also to include a life of worshipful obedience (Deut. 10:12; 11:13). The Lord delivers the Israelites from cruel service to Pharaoh not so they might serve false gods but so that they might know the freedom of serving him, the one true God.

The Lord now makes clear that those who enter his service enter a realm of blessing (Ex. 23:25b–31). The blessings focus on practical matters necessary for physical survival and well-being. This is no surprise. The Lord has made us as physical creatures with physical needs; he describes here how he will meet those needs in abundant ways. We might paraphrase, "I will provide you bountifully with food ("bless your bread and your water"), keep you physically healthy ("take sickness away from among you"), grant you fruitfulness of womb ("none shall miscarry or be barren"), give you long life ("fulfill the number of your days"), cause your enemies to flee in defeat before you ("send my terror before you [cf. Josh. 2:9–11] . . . make all your enemies turn their backs to you . . . send hornets before you, which shall drive out [the nations] before you"), yet drive them out gradually ("not . . . in one year"), so that other dangers do not become a problem ("lest the land become desolate and the wild beasts multiply against you")[570] and so that you

---

[568] A pillar is apparently a single stone (cf. Ex. 23:24; 34:13) set up to function in the worship of false gods (cf. Deut. 7:5; 12:3), though its exact use is less clear. Pillars can, however, also serve in other more noble ways; cf. comment on 24:3–8.
[569] Cf. note 89 within comment on 3:11–12. Cf. 5:1, 3 with 7:16; 10:7, 8; 10:24–26; cf. also Deuteronomy 4:19; 5:8–9.
[570] See the same in Deuteronomy 7:22. Many modern people, especially urban dwellers, might have difficulty appreciating this danger, but for ancient agrarians the threat was very real (cf. Lev. 26:22) and made all the

have time to multiply and take over the land responsibly ("until you have increased and possess the land"), with the end result being that I will give you an abundant area of land in which to dwell ("from the Red Sea to the Sea of the Philistines . . . from the wilderness to the Euphrates").[571] In short, in the context of worshiping and following the Lord the Israelites will experience abundant peace, security, and provision in a fruitful land. This is nothing less than a return to Eden on a large scale (cf. also Lev. 26:3–13; Deut. 7:12–15; 28:1–14).

23:32–33 The Lord now turns from blessings back to warnings (cf. Ex. 23:23–24). Having earlier commanded the Israelites to destroy any objects related to false worship (v. 24), he now commands them not to enter into a covenant of peace with the land's inhabitants or their gods and not to let the inhabitants continue living in the land, lest they lead the Israelites away from the Lord (vv. 32–33).[572] Expanding on this warning later, the Lord describes how the land's inhabitants will invite the Israelites to the sacrifices of their foreign gods and that the Israelites will also be tempted to intermarriage, again leading to foreign worship practices (34:12–16). As later passages will show, this is not a theoretical concern (cf. Num. 25:1–9; cf. also Ps. 106:34–39). The Lord knows that ongoing temptation to unfaithfulness, especially in a relational context, is a deathtrap that ensnares many.

Response

WHAT ARE THE TWO ASPECTS OF OBEDIENCE?

Obedience is a two-sided coin: *following after* on the one side and *running away from* on the other. First and foremost, obedience means following after the Lord, walking with him in his ways. To "carefully obey" and "do all" he says (Ex. 23:22) means that his word is our command; where he leads, we will follow. Jesus does not tell us simply to believe theoretical truths about him; he tells us, "*Follow* me" (Matt. 4:19; 8:22; 9:9; 16:24).

But following after the Lord also means running away from sin and temptation—not walking away but running away. As Paul's stresses, "*Flee* from sexual immorality. . . . *Flee* from idolatry. . . . *Flee* youthful passions!" (1 Cor. 6:18; 10:14; 2 Tim. 2:22). Sin and temptation are not harmless rubber snakes; they are living, coiled vipers ready to strike and destroy those who get too close. We are to avoid them at all costs. The Lord emphasizes the same in our passage. Israel is not simply to put false gods into storage; she is to "utterly overthrow them" (Ex. 23:24), leaving no trace behind. As noted above, one of the surest ways to resist sin is to remove whatever

---

worse by a lack of modern weaponry. A friend of mine was camping, completely unarmed, and awakened in the night by a bear outside his tent. Verses like this took on a whole new meaning to him.
571 This is a list of "four 'terminal points': 'from the Red Sea [south(east)], to the Sea of the Philistines [= Mediterranean; northwest], and from the desert [southwest] to the River [= Euphrates; northeast]"; Carl G. Rasmussen, *Zondervan Atlas of the Bible*, rev. ed. (Grand Rapids, MI: Zondervan, 2010), 254, use of square brackets are his. It would not be until the time of Solomon that something close to such an extensive area was controlled (1 Kings 4:21). For the possible anachronism with "Philistines" cf. Sklar, *Additional Notes on Exodus*, at 13:17.
572 Note that 23:33 could be translated more strongly, "They shall not dwell in your land, lest they make you sin against me, *for you will serve their gods, for this will be a snare to you*" (cf. BDB 474.3d). Other texts go into more detail on the Israelites' role in defeating the land's inhabitants. For some of the apologetic questions this raises cf. Response section on 13:17–15:21, "What Is the Warning?", esp. the resources in note 292.

might lead to it. Jesus teaches, "If your right eye causes you to sin, tear it out and throw it away.... And if your right hand causes you to sin, cut it off and throw it away. For it is better that you lose one of your members than that your whole body go into hell" (Matt. 5:29–30). The language is clearly hyperbole; a one-handed person can still commit sin with his remaining hand. But hyperbole is used to emphasize a point, which in this case is clear: sin has the power to drag us into hell. And Jesus loves us too much for that. His warning is that of a parent who drills into his child the need to avoid running into the street. Jesus knows that sin wants to turn us into roadkill.

This leads naturally to a second question.

WHAT ARE THE RESULTS OF DISOBEDIENCE?

Sin leads naturally to judgment—supernatural judgment. It is true that sin has natural negative consequences. For example, if we are known for lying, people stop believing us. If we are known for gossip, people stop sharing with us. But this passage emphasizes the supernatural element of judgment that comes to those who rebel against the Lord. The warning that the angel "will not pardon your transgression" means not that forgiveness is impossible for the penitent but that judgment is sure for the rebellious (cf. comment on Ex. 23:20–22).

The context matters. The Lord is speaking to Israelites, those who claim to be his followers. The Bible certainly speaks of final judgment for anyone who rejects the Lord, even if that person never claimed to be his follower, but it also speaks of the ways in which the Lord brings judgments into the lives of those who claim to be his followers. Leviticus 26 is instructive here. It lists a long series of curses—such as defeat in war, famine, or sickness—that will come on the Israelites if they are faithless to the Lord (Lev. 26:14–39). But throughout the passage the Lord emphasizes these judgments are to "discipline" his people so they might "listen" to the Lord and "turn" back to him (Lev. 26:18, 23, 27–28). It is not their destruction he desires but their salvation. As with a good father, his discipline, even if painful, is meant as a warning that brings his people back to the path of obedience, where they might flourish.

Such disciplining judgments are not simply an OT phenomenon. Paul speaks of those in the Corinthian church who have become sick and even died for partaking of the Lord's Supper in an unworthy manner (1 Cor. 11:27, 30). And he explains this in the same kinds of terms as those used in Leviticus 26: "When we are *judged* by the Lord, we are *disciplined* so that we may not be condemned along with the world" (1 Cor. 11:32). As the Father's children, Christians should expect discipline to come if they wander from his ways. He wants something far better for them. And this leads to the final question.

WHAT ARE THE RESULTS OF OBEDIENCE?

The strongest focus of this passage is that those who follow and serve the Lord enter a realm of blessing (Ex. 23:2b–31). It cannot be otherwise. Just as good parents seek to bless their children with love and protection, so does the Lord with his own children. Just as a good king seeks to bless his servants with love and protection, so does the

Lord with his own servants. The Israelites must choose whether to enter such service; if they do, they can be assured their King will surround them with his love and care. (Cf. comment on 15:22–26 for the relationship between obedience and blessing.)

In the Bible blessings take on many forms. Leviticus 26 is again instructive. It begins with a list of physical and material blessings for the faithful that overlap with those in our passage (Lev. 26:3–10). The list then reaches an apex by describing the blessing of intimate relationship with the Lord (Lev. 26:11–12). That it saves what might be called spiritual blessings for last—as the highest and best of the blessings!—rescues us from the error and theological poverty of the prosperity gospel, which teaches that the ultimate goal in life is to be rich and healthy. The Bible disagrees. As the psalmist prays, "You are my Lord; *I have no good apart from you*" (Ps. 16:2). It is only in the yoke of Jesus that our weary souls find rest (Matt. 11:28–30; cf. note 440 within the Response section on 20:22–26, "How Does God Respond to Proper Worship?").

At the same time, Leviticus 26, similarly to our passage, also lists physical and material blessings necessary for physical flourishing (cf. Ex. 23:25–31). This rescues us from overspiritualizing life and downplaying the reality of living as a physical creature in God's physical world. This is something the Bible does not do. The Israelites were to gather regularly to feast and celebrate the harvest (Lev. 23:39–41). The psalmist rejoices in the Lord's good gifts of food, drink, and provision for both people and beasts (Pss. 104:14–15; 145:15–16). Jesus healed the sick, fed the hungry, taught us to pray for our physical needs, and promised that our heavenly Father would provide for his disciples (Matt. 6:11, 25–34; cf. Phil. 4:19). And Paul condemns those who "require abstinence from foods that God created to be received with thanksgiving. . . . For everything created by God is good" (1 Tim. 4:3–4).

How should these truths impact our lives? First, we should rejoice in the Lord's good gifts of material blessings. In avoiding the tragic error of the prosperity gospel we must make sure not to make the opposite error of disregarding the goodness of God's material blessings. Second, we are to have confidence that the Lord will meet our material needs (Matt. 6:11, 25–34; Phil. 4:19). Third, if the Lord has blessed us materially or physically, we should seek to imitate him by sharing such blessings with those in need. The Lord delights to meet our needs and to give us the privilege of being his agents in meeting the needs of others (cf. 2 Cor. 8:8–15).

EXODUS 24:1–11

24 Then he said to Moses, "Come up to the Lord, you and Aaron, Nadab, and Abihu, and seventy of the elders of Israel, and worship from afar. ² Moses alone shall come near to the Lord, but the others shall not come near, and the people shall not come up with him."

³ Moses came and told the people all the words of the LORD and all the rules.¹ And all the people answered with one voice and said, "All the words that the LORD has spoken we will do." ⁴ And Moses wrote down all the words of the LORD. He rose early in the morning and built an altar at the foot of the mountain, and twelve pillars, according to the twelve tribes of Israel. ⁵ And he sent young men of the people of Israel, who offered burnt offerings and sacrificed peace offerings of oxen to the LORD. ⁶ And Moses took half of the blood and put it in basins, and half of the blood he threw against the altar. ⁷ Then he took the Book of the Covenant and read it in the hearing of the people. And they said, "All that the LORD has spoken we will do, and we will be obedient." ⁸ And Moses took the blood and threw it on the people and said, "Behold the blood of the covenant that the LORD has made with you in accordance with all these words."

⁹ Then Moses and Aaron, Nadab, and Abihu, and seventy of the elders of Israel went up, ¹⁰ and they saw the God of Israel. There was under his feet as it were a pavement of sapphire stone, like the very heaven for clearness. ¹¹ And he did not lay his hand on the chief men of the people of Israel; they beheld God, and ate and drank.

¹ Or *all the just decrees*

Section Overview

In Exodus 19 the Lord invited Israel to enter covenant relationship with him, an invitation they willingly accepted: "All that the LORD has spoken we will do!" (19:8). In chapters 20–23 the Lord appeared in glory and proclaims the covenant stipulations. Now in 24:1–11 the covenant is confirmed after the Israelites reaffirm their willingness to enter into it by repeating their earlier statement: "All the words that the LORD has spoken we will do!" (24:3; cf. v. 7). This repetition ties chapters 19–24 together.⁵⁷³ The covenant invitation has been accepted and ratified.

As for the covenant ratification itself, this will require identifying an Israelite delegation (24:1–2), an affirmation from the people of their agreement to the covenant (vv. 3–8), and a meal sealing the relationship between the covenant parties (vv. 9–11). Emphases include the Israelites' affirmation of obedience (vv. 3, 7), the Israelite delegation's seeing God (vv. 10, 11), and the centrality of blood to this particular covenant (vv. 6–8).

As noted earlier, the Israelites are already in covenant relationship with the Lord by means of the Abrahamic covenant (cf. comment on 19:3–6 and esp. note 342). The Sinai covenant does not replace it as much as show how it applies to Israel as a nation. Yet the Sinai covenant is also a very real invitation for the Israelites to embrace their calling, as heirs of Abraham, to be a conduit of blessing to the nations, especially by being a kingdom of priests and a holy nation that embody and spread God's kingdom on earth (19:4–6). The stipulations of the Sinai covenant explain what such a kingdom looks like; by ratifying it the Israelites commit to being such a kingdom.

---

573 Alexander, *Exodus*, ApOTC, 547, citing Childs, *Book of Exodus*, 502–503.

Section Outline

V. Israel at Sinai: the Lord gives his covenant to Israel; the covenant is ratified (20:1–24:11)...
   F. The covenant is ratified (24:1–11)
      1. The Israelite delegation party and three zones of proximity to the Lord (24:1–2)
      2. The Israelites confirm their allegiance to their covenant Lord (24:3–8)
      3. The delegation party ratifies the covenant before the Lord (24:9–11)

Comment

24:1–2 Continuing to speak to Moses, the Lord identifies the delegation that will represent the Israelites: Moses, Aaron, Aaron's two eldest sons (Nadab and Abihu; 6:23), and seventy of Israel's elders (24:1a).[574] The sense of verse 1 is thus, "Then the LORD gave a particular instruction to Moses himself: 'After you go down and give these stipulations to the Israelites, then come up, you and Aaron and the others.'"[575]

The Lord next describes three different zones of physical proximity to himself and the identity of those who may enter each one (vv. 1b–2). These may be explained by thinking of a palace. While the public may have access to the edge of palace grounds, only a select few may enter the palace itself, and fewer still may go freely into the throne room. In this case the Lord's presence makes the mountain to be like a palace-sanctuary, and, as with the palace-sanctuary to come in chapter 40 (the tabernacle), three zones can be identified (cf. table 2.9).[576]

TABLE 2.9: Comparison of a Palace, Mount Sinai, and the Tabernacle: Three Zones and Who May Enter Them

A Palace	Throne room: a king's select servants	Palace itself (aside from throne room): other servants of the king	Border of palace grounds: the people
Mount Sinai	Near to God on the mountain: Moses	On the mountain: Israelite delegation	Border of mountain's base: Israelites
Tabernacle	Most Holy Place: high priest only	Holy Place: priests	Courtyard: Israelites

As table 2.9 shows, the only person authorized to draw very near to the Lord at the mountain's top is his special servant, Moses (cf. 19:20), not the delegation ("the others") nor the people (who may not even "come up with" Moses; cf. 19:12). As for the members of the delegation, while they are allowed to come on the mountain,

---

574 The number seven is associated with completeness in the Pentateuch (cf. note 56 within comment on 1:1–5), suggesting that seventy elders would be a good and thorough representation on Israel's behalf.
575 Cf. 19:24–25 (Kalisch, *Exodus*, 470).
576 Cf. Sarna, *Exodus*, 105.

they are to "worship from afar" (24:1). The word rendered "worship" can also mean "bow down in reverence," as one does before a person of eminence (Gen. 18:2; 19:1) or a king (1 Sam. 24:8). Since the Lord is the King of supreme eminence, Israelites commonly bow before him when they worship (Gen. 24:26; Ex. 4:31; 12:27). As applied to this context, the delegation is to go partially up the mountain and approach the Lord on the Israelites' behalf but is to bow low in reverence and worship without drawing too close. It must be remembered that a certain protocol existed in ancient Israel for entering a king's throne room, one that showed respect for the king's person and authority. Disregarding it demonstrated little regard for the king. To barge into the throne room was therefore a treasonous act of disrespect that could be met with the penalty given traitors: death.[577] Instead, by bowing low in worship from a distance, the delegation declares its tremendous respect and honor for the Lord as supreme covenant King.

24:3–8 Having come down the mountain, Moses recounts to the Israelites "all the words of the LORD and all the rules" (v. 3). The "rules" are those given in 21:1–23:19 (cf. 21:1). The "words" are either (1) the Ten Commandments (20:1–17; cf. 20:1), (2) the words the Lord spoke to Moses in addition to the rules (20:22–25; 23:20–33), or (3) both. I lean toward option 2, since the word for "told" appears most frequently in contexts in which new information is being given (Gen. 24:66; Ex. 18:8; etc.), and the Israelites have already heard the Ten Commandments. Nevertheless, given the centrality of the Ten Commandments in chapters 19–23 as a whole, it seems hard to imagine that they would not also be assumed when the Israelites proceed to say, "All the words that the LORD has spoken we will do" (24:3), nor should it surprise us if they were included when Moses "wrote down all the words of the LORD" (v. 4).

Hearing the people's initial agreement to the covenant stipulations, Moses takes steps to formalize it. The discovery of numerous ancient Near Eastern covenants shows that it was common at that time to write down a covenant made between a king and a people, and this is what Moses proceeds to do (v. 4). He then puts various objects in place for the ceremony in which the Israelites will officially confirm their agreement to the covenant terms. This takes place "at the foot of the mountain," where the people may gather (cf. 19:12). Sacrifices will be needed, so an altar is built, and twelve pillars are erected (24:4). While pillars can be erected as part of illicit worship (Deut. 7:5; 12:3), they can also be erected as a witness to a covenant ceremony (Gen. 31:41–52).[578] This fits the context here perfectly. Moreover, given that these pillars are explicitly said to represent Israel's tribes (Ex. 24:4) and that this covenant is between them and the Lord, it makes good sense to see the altar

---

[577] Though from a later period, cf. 1 Kings 1:16, 23; outside of Israel (and also later) cf. Esther 4:11. More closely, we can consider the fate of Nadab and Abihu, who "died before the LORD" for attempting to barge into the Most Holy Place (Lev. 10:1–2; cf. Lev. 16:1 with 16:2; cf. Sklar, *Leviticus*, TOTC, 156–157).

[578] Although the word "pillar" is not used, the stone that Joshua erects has a similar function in a covenant context. Sarna (*Exodus*, 151) draws special attention to Joshua 24:27: "Behold, this stone shall be a witness against us, for it has heard all the words of the LORD that he spoke to us. Therefore it shall be a witness against you, lest you deal falsely with your God."

as representing the Lord.⁵⁷⁹ In this way all thirteen objects stand together in unity as witness to the covenant relationship now being enacted.

Next come the sacrifices (v. 5), which are an important part of properly approaching the Lord and will also function here as central to the covenant.⁵⁸⁰ The reason that Moses sends "young men" to offer these is not explained, though their presence does seem to be a contrast to the "elders," and it may be reasonably suggested that the handling of oxen required special strength.⁵⁸¹ "Burnt offerings" and "peace offerings" were a common pair of sacrifices (20:24; 32:6). As noted at 18:9–12, burnt offerings were totally burned on the altar and were a way to make atonement and offer costly praise. Peace offerings were partially burned on the altar and partially consumed by the offerer, making this like a shared meal between the Lord and his people. In short, as atonement has been made (burnt offering), the way is opened for fellowship (peace offering). The occurrence of the peace offering is especially significant in a covenant context, since sharing a meal together was one way to confirm a covenant, and it should not surprise us if the elders partook of this meat in their feast before the Lord (cf. comment on 24:9–11).

Central to sacrifices is the proper use of sacrificial blood. We first read that Moses takes half the sacrificial blood and sets it aside in basins (v. 6a). This is unusual, but Moses' rationale will shortly become clear. He then takes the remaining half and throws it on the altar (v. 6b), a much more expected action—in fact, a necessary one—for burnt and peace offerings (Lev. 1:5; 3:2). Doing so appears to have been a way of presenting the animal's lifeblood to the Lord to atone for the offerer.⁵⁸²

With the sacrifices complete, Moses now takes the Book of the Covenant, which contains most (or all) of the words the Lord has spoken in Exodus 20–23 (cf. 24:3), and reads it before the people (v. 7). Earlier Moses had told them the Lord's words, and they had agreed to them (v. 3), but this public reading and response appear to formalize the people's commitment.⁵⁸³ And the commitment is wholehearted: "*All* that the LORD has spoken *we will do*, and *we will be obedient*."

Attention now shifts to the remaining sacrificial blood, which Moses describes as the "blood of the covenant" (v. 8). Moses describes the covenant in two further ways. First, it is the "covenant that the LORD has made with you." The Lord initiates the covenant with Israel, as he did earlier with Abraham (Gen. 15:18) and Noah (Gen. 9:11). We do not initiate relationship with him; in his grace and love he initiates relationship with us. Israel's responsibility (and ours) is to respond to his initiation and redemption with obedient worship and love.⁵⁸⁴ Second, the

---

579 This is a common view among commentators; e.g., Cassuto, *Commentary on the Book of Exodus*, 311; Sarna, *Exodus*, 151; Alexander, *Exodus*, ApOTC, 544.
580 Cf. Psalm 50:5 (Houtman, *Exodus*, vol. 3, 290).
581 So also Houtman, *Exodus*, vol. 3, 290; Stuart, *Exodus*, 554.
582 Cf. Leviticus 17:11; Sklar, *Leviticus*, TOTC, 91, 102, 220–222.
583 "Interestingly, some Hittite treaty texts require periodic public recital of the terms of the pact before the vassal and his people" (Sarna, *Exodus*, 152, citing *ANET*, 205); cf. Deuteronomy 31:11; Joshua 8:34–35 (Stuart, *Exodus*, 553n295).
584 The Sinai covenant "is not an enforced submission, such as a conquering empire imposes on a vassal state, but a willing acceptance of the authority and will of the God who had demonstrated his faithfulness, love,

Lord has made this covenant "in accordance with all these words" (Ex. 24:8), that is, in accordance with all the covenant stipulations the Lord has just spoken. His commands define the covenant.

As for the blood, just as Moses threw it on the altar, he now throws it on the people. The intent of doing so is not explained. If the altar does represent the Lord (cf. v. 4), then the blood may symbolically tie the Lord and people together in covenant relationship. Moreover, later in Exodus Moses will place sacrificial blood on Aaron and his sons as part of a consecrating rite (Ex. 29:19–21), so there may be an element here of cleansing and consecrating the Israelites for their covenantal role as a kingdom of priests and holy nation. At the least, placing the "blood *of the covenant*" on the people after their public agreement to it would seem to be a way of confirming them as covenant members. They are literally wearing the covenant sign.

24:9–11 Now that the people have confirmed their allegiance to the covenant, the Israelite delegation goes up the mountain to ratify the covenant before the Lord (v. 9). When the Lord first came down on the mountain, the Israelites "saw the thunder and the flashes of lightning . . . and the mountain smoking" (20:18). This delegation, however, "saw the God of Israel" (24:10). This cannot mean they see God's glory in an unfiltered way, since he himself will later tell Moses, "You cannot see my face, for man shall not see me and live" (33:20; cf. also John 1:18; 1 Tim. 6:16). But there is a directness in their seeing that is new; the storm cloud is removed and they see something of his essence or glory that is normally concealed from human view.[585]

It is tempting at this point to fill in the picture with the fuller one given in Ezekiel 1:26–28, or Isaiah 6:1–3, or Revelation 4:1–11, but that would be to ignore the direction of this passage. No description of God himself can be given, only of what lies beneath his feet. Is this because what lies above his feet is shrouded in cloud or fire? Or because it is important not to give the Israelites, who are prone to idolatry, any descriptions that they might attempt to make into an image (cf. Deut. 4:15–18)? Or both? The text does not say. It simply describes the appearance of "a pavement of sapphire stone" under his feet. Debate exists whether to translate "sapphire stone" or "lapis lazuli," though both types of stones occur in a brilliant blue, which seems to be the point here, as the further comparison to the "very heaven for clearness" suggests. In short, this pavement is like a clear blue sky, which contrasts with the earlier picture of storm clouds and, given the pavement's apparent material, also speaks to the Lord's magnificent splendor as the one whose rules stretches higher than the heavens.

The idea of the Lord's kingship also relates to the delegation's ability to see God. The Lord had earlier warned that Israelites who bypassed the limits at the

---

and saving power on [the Israelites'] behalf" (Wright, *Exodus*, 457). Cf. Response section on 19:1–25, "Where Does Relationship with the Lord Begin?"
585 Cf. Exodus 23:22. Compare Ezekiel 1:26–28a, which describes a vision of God (cf. v. 1), with verse 28b, which describes this vision as "the *appearance* of the *likeness* of the glory of the LORD" (but not the Lord himself).

mountain's base to look at the Lord in his glory would perish, in part because it was a sign of severe disrespect to gaze on a king without his permission (cf. comment on 3:4–6). But this delegation has been especially invited to enjoy an audience with him. As a result, "he did not lay his hand on the chief men of the people of Israel"; instead, "they beheld[586] God" (24:11)—here repeated for emphasis (cf. v. 10)—implying he has favorably accepted them into his presence.[587] Such favorable acceptance also explains the notice that the delegation "ate and drank." While curious to many moderns, this notice perfectly fits the covenantal context. As several texts illustrate, one way to ratify a covenant in the ancient Near East was for the two parties to partake of a meal together (Gen. 26:28–30; 31:44–46, 53–54). The text does mention the meal's contents or source, but, given the covenantal associations with the peace offering, it would be no surprise if the delegation ate meat that came from the very sacrifices the Israelites had just made: the Lord's share had been given to him on the altar, and the delegation now eats Israel's share in his presence. Whatever the case, the covenant is now ratified, and this meal before the Lord serves as a perfect picture of the covenant fellowship Israel is now to enjoy with him.

Response

WHAT IS A COVENANT, AND WHAT ARE ITS IMPLICATIONS?

See the Response section on 19:1–25, which goes into significant detail about the nature of the covenant and its implications. In keeping with those comments we can note especially the overlap here between the Lord's status as covenant initiator (cf. comment on 24:3–8 [at v. 8]) and the importance of Israelite obedience (emphasized by the Israelites' repeated promise of faithfulness in v. 3 and v. 7; for a further area of overlap see the last question below). What is new in this context is the centrality of the sacrificial blood to the Sinai covenant. This leads to a second question.

WHAT IS THE SIGNIFICANCE OF BLOOD?

As noted above, sacrificial blood has different functions in Israel. The sprinkling of the altar is associated with making atonement (cf. comment on 24:3–8 [at v. 6]), a deep need whenever sinful people come before a holy God. When placed on people, blood can also have a cleansing function (cf. v. 8), so there may be an element of cleansing and consecrating the Israelites for their covenantal role as a kingdom of priests and holy nation. What is most clear is that the blood is called the "blood *of the covenant*," meaning it serves here as the covenant's sign. Those marked with it are members of that covenant. For many of the Israelites this mark will remain on their clothing for years to come, a constant reminder of their covenant relationship with the Lord and all it entails.[588]

The NT uses the picture of the blood of the Sinai covenant to explain what Jesus has accomplished by giving his lifeblood on the cross. Just as the Sinai covenant

---

[586] This verb commonly refers to "seeing/beholding" a vision in general or one of God in particular (Num. 24:4, 16; Isa. 1:1; 2:1; 13:1; Ezek. 12:27).
[587] With a human king cf. Genesis 43:3; Exodus 10:28; 2 Samuel 14:24.
[588] Stuart, *Exodus*, 555.

was inaugurated with the sacrificial blood of animals, the new covenant has been inaugurated with the sacrificial blood of Jesus (cf. Luke 22:20; Heb. 9:15–28). Just as the shedding of that blood was followed by a covenantal meal, so Christians remember the shedding of Jesus' blood by partaking of the covenantal meal of Communion.[589] And just as the Israelites' covenant responsibilities included being "a kingdom of priests and a holy nation," so has Jesus in the new covenant rescued us to be the same (1 Pet. 2:9). In the Bible redemption is always a springboard to mission. God saves us that we may know him—and make him known.

As this passage draws to a close, there is a final curiosity: we are told two different times that the Israelite delegation sees God (Ex. 24:10, 11). This leads to the last question.

WHY DOES THE TEXT EMPHASIZE THAT THE
ISRAELITE DELEGATION SEES GOD?

In a covenant between a greater king and a lesser king the primary obligation of the greater king was military protection (cf. note 350 in the Response section on 19:1–25, "What Does Relationship with the Lord Entail?"). In the Israelites' case this becomes incredibly personal. Not only has the Lord already delivered them from the greatest military power of the day (Exodus 1–15), and not only will he continue to protect them when they enter the Promised Land (23:22–23, 27–30), but he will view them as a "treasured possession" (19:5), which refers elsewhere to a king's treasure (1 Chron. 29:3; Eccles. 2:8), something to be safeguarded and valued to the utmost (cf. note 343 within comment on 19:3–6).

This passage gets at the same idea by way of emphasizing that the Israelite delegation was able to see God in his glory and partake of a meal before him. Ancient Near Eastern royal protocol helps to explain. As noted at Exodus 24:9–11, the delegation's ability to see God's glory without harm meant that he, as divine King, had welcomed them into his royal presence. As also noted there, by eating and drinking before him the delegation not only seals the covenant but does so in a way that pictures the covenant fellowship they now enjoy with the Lord. Certainly, they must be his faithful servants, but, if they can eat at the King's table, they can know that the King himself has accepted them and will provide for their needs and protect them (cf. 2 Samuel 9).

This takes on special significance for the Christian, who, through Jesus, is able to come freely before the Lord as King. Indeed, because of Jesus we can "*with confidence* draw near to *the throne of grace*, that we may receive mercy and find grace to help in time of need" (Heb. 4:16; cf. Heb. 10:19–22). Mercy and grace in time of need flow from the throne of the heavenly King with whom we have covenant fellowship. What fears does this promise still? What anxieties does it calm? Because of Jesus, such things are freely ours. *Lavishly* ours. The King is with us! Let us no longer fear.

---

[589] Note the language of 1 Corinthians 11:25: "In the same way also [Jesus] took the cup, after supper, saying, 'This cup is the *new covenant* in my blood. Do this, as often as you drink it, in remembrance of me.'" Cf. Sklar, *Leviticus*, ZECOT, 638.

OVERVIEW OF

EXODUS 24:12–31:18

The next major section in Exodus introduces the tabernacle. It begins in 24:12 with the Lord's stating his intent to give Moses the law on stone tablets and ends in 31:18 with his doing so.[590] The flow of the entire section is very straightforward. The Lord summons Moses into his presence on Mount Sinai (24:12–18) and then makes a long speech describing the design of the tabernacle complex and related items (such as the uniforms the priests must wear when ministering; 25:1–30:38). The Lord then identifies two men, Bezalel and Oholiab, who will oversee the making of everything necessary for the sanctuary complex (31:1–11) and emphasizes the importance of keeping the Sabbath, which he identifies as the sign of the covenant between him and the Israelites (vv. 12–17). With this the speech ends and he gives the covenant tablets to Moses (v. 18).

The covenant is in fact an important thread that ties together this section of Exodus with its final two sections (chs. 32–34; 35–40).

(1) 24:12–31:18: In response to the covenant's confirmation (24:1–11) the Lord commands the building of his palace-tent in Israel's midst, where he will sit enthroned as covenant King over the ark containing the covenant tablets (25:16; 31:18). As just noted, this section ends with a command to keep the Sabbath, explicitly identified as the sign of the covenant (31:13, 16–17).

(2) 32:1–34:35: By building a golden calf Israel breaks the covenant, which Moses graphically portrays by shattering the covenant tablets (32:15–19). The rest of the section describes how the covenant is renewed through Moses' intercession on the Israelites' behalf and by the Lord's graciously showing them his mercy and forgiveness (cf. esp. 34:1–28).

(3) 35:1–40:38: With the covenant reestablished this section begins with a renewed call for the Israelites to keep the covenant's sign, the Sabbath (35:1–3; cf. 31:12–17). The rest of the section then describes the Israelites' building and setting up the dwelling of their covenant King and finishes with the Lord's descent in glory to his palace-tent in Israel's midst (40:34–38). In this way the book concludes with the Israelites' faithfully doing what their covenant King commands and the King's coming himself to dwell in the midst of his covenant people.

---

590 Houtman, *Exodus*, vol. 3, 298.

As a result, one cannot think of the tabernacle without thinking of covenant. The tabernacle is a constant witness to the Israelites that their covenant King dwells among them, which should assure them that he will be faithful to his covenant promises to them and also remind them of their covenant obligations to him.

The tabernacle itself will be described in detail in the coming chapters, but a brief overview may be helpful here.[591] Most broadly speaking it consists of a frame with four coverings and measures 45 feet (13.7 m) in length and 15 feet (4.6 m) in width and height. In terms of size this is not like a camping tent but more like a tent used today at festivals or outdoor receptions. More specifically speaking its frame is made of gold-covered acacia frames fastened together into a roofless rectangular box oriented lengthwise on an east-west axis. On the east of the rectangle is a screened entrance. The screen is made of blue, purple, and scarlet wool as well as fine linen—colors and materials fit for a king (cf. comment on 25:3–7). Inside the rectangle are two rooms. From the east the first room is known as the Holy Place and measures 30 feet (9.1 m) in length and 15 feet (4.6 m) in height and width. It contains an incense altar, a lamp, and a table, all made of gold or covered with gold, just as one might expect in a king's palace. At the far end of the room is a veil made of the same materials as the screen, with cherubim woven into it, speaking to the heavenly nature of the dwelling and symbolically guarding the way into the second room behind it. That room is known as the Most Holy Place, measuring 15 feet (4.6 m) square and serving as the Lord's throne room. It contains the ark of the covenant, a rectangular box overlaid with gold and with a solid golden lid. Four different coverings then go over the frame. The first is a series of curtains joined together that are likely to cover the top, back, and most of the sides of the frame. They are made similarly to the veil so that those standing in the tabernacle will see cherubim seemingly floating above them, an appropriate setting for the heavenly Lord's dwelling. The second covering is a series of curtains joined together and made of woven goat's hair, while the third and fourth coverings are made of animal skins, all of which will protect the tent from the elements. Outside the tent's entrance is a basin and the altar of burnt offering, which stand in a courtyard marked out by joined curtains forming a rectangular wall measuring 150 feet (46 m) in length, 75 feet (23 m) in width, and 7.5 feet (2.3 m) in height. Like the tent, its entrance is to the east and covered by a screen made of the same royal materials (blue, purple, and scarlet wool and fine linen). In short, from the courtyard's entrance to the very interior room of the tent royal and heavenly symbolism is very strong. This is the palace-tent of the King of heaven.

It may be noted briefly that many have questioned the historical plausibility of the construction of such a tent in the Mosaic period. Wellhausen argued that the tabernacle was invented at a far later period and based on the Jerusalem temple.[592] This and similar approaches have not been uncommon in biblical

---

591 For very helpful illustrations of what the tabernacle and its furniture may have looked like cf. *ESV Study Bible* (Wheaton, IL: Crossway, 2008), 184–188, 190–191, 194, or search online for "ESV pictures of the tabernacle," "ESV pictures of the altar of incense," and the like.
592 See summary of his position in Averbeck, "Tabernacle," *DOTP,* 818.

studies.⁵⁹³ As modern understanding of the ancient Near East has grown, however, it has become clear that such a tent is completely in keeping with Egyptian construction techniques from even before the time of Moses.⁵⁹⁴ Indeed, based on his wide-ranging study of tents in the ancient Near East "Homan concludes that 'the many [ancient Near Eastern] parallels to the Tabernacle in form and function support its historicity.'"⁵⁹⁵ This is not the same as proving the tabernacle's historicity, but it does show that the biblical account of the tabernacle, including its time period, is completely plausible.

With regard to this section's major themes four in particular may be noted. First, the Lord guides his people, be it through calling Moses once again up the mountain to give him instruction (24:12) or naming the tent of meeting as the future place where he will continue to give Moses revelation for the people (25:22). Second, the Lord desires to be near his people and have relationship with them, which are explicitly named as the goals of both redemption (29:46) and the building of the tent (25:8).⁵⁹⁶ Third, he will dwell in their midst as covenant King, as evidenced by the tent's many royal associations as well as the larger context of the suzerain-vassal covenant he has just made with Israel.⁵⁹⁷ Finally, the Lord is holy, which the tabernacle itself communicates in numerous ways.⁵⁹⁸ Taken together, these themes underscore the Lord's transcendence (he is a king who is holy) and his immanence (he desires to be among his people and guide them). He is unspeakably other and unbelievably personal. He moves his throne room from heaven to earth to be near those he has redeemed—those he cares for and protects as the very "apple of his eye" (Deut. 32:10).

As a final comment, it may be noted that this section presents certain challenges to the translator and interpreter—to the translator because many technical terms are used that are fairly rare and to the interpreter because a certain amount of knowledge is presumed of the reader. Both challenges are in fact expected amid technical instructions. For example, recipes often use technical language uncommon to everyday speech. Some cooks might know what "barding" is, but most people would need to be told that it means covering meat with slices of bacon. Moreover, recipes assume important pieces of knowledge, such as when they say to add two eggs without telling the cook to crack them and dispose of their shells! As it relates to these chapters, there will be times when we are left with some questions or uncertainty regarding various particulars of the tabernacle or the priests' clothing. Fortunately, however, enough is clear to give a very helpful general understanding of what these items would have looked like and, as already suggested, an even clearer understanding of what they are meant to represent.

---

593 For a broad overview cf. Averbeck, "Tabernacle," *DOTP*, 818.
594 Cf. esp. K. A. Kitchen, *On the Reliability of the Old Testament* (Grand Rapids, MI: Eerdmans, 2006), 276–280.
595 Alexander, *Exodus*, ApOTC, 558, citing Michael M. Homan, *To Your Tents, O Israel!* (Leiden: Brill, 2002), 184.
596 Cf. Wright, *Exodus*, 494–495.
597 For the latter cf. comments on 20:1–21.
598 For themes two through four cf. esp. Response section on 24:12–25:9, "What Does the Tabernacle Teach Us about the Kind of God He Is?"

EXODUS 24:12–25:9

 ¹² The Lord said to Moses, "Come up to me on the mountain and wait there, that I may give you the tablets of stone, with the law and the commandment, which I have written for their instruction." ¹³ So Moses rose with his assistant Joshua, and Moses went up into the mountain of God. ¹⁴ And he said to the elders, "Wait here for us until we return to you. And behold, Aaron and Hur are with you. Whoever has a dispute, let him go to them."

¹⁵ Then Moses went up on the mountain, and the cloud covered the mountain. ¹⁶ The glory of the Lord dwelt on Mount Sinai, and the cloud covered it six days. And on the seventh day he called to Moses out of the midst of the cloud. ¹⁷ Now the appearance of the glory of the Lord was like a devouring fire on the top of the mountain in the sight of the people of Israel. ¹⁸ Moses entered the cloud and went up on the mountain. And Moses was on the mountain forty days and forty nights.

25 The Lord said to Moses, ² "Speak to the people of Israel, that they take for me a contribution. From every man whose heart moves him you shall receive the contribution for me. ³ And this is the contribution that you shall receive from them: gold, silver, and bronze, ⁴ blue and purple and scarlet yarns and fine twined linen, goats' hair, ⁵ tanned rams' skins, goatskins,¹ acacia wood, ⁶ oil for the lamps, spices for the anointing oil and for the fragrant incense, ⁷ onyx stones, and stones for setting, for the ephod and for the breastpiece. ⁸ And let them make me a sanctuary, that I may dwell in their midst. ⁹ Exactly as I show you concerning the pattern of the tabernacle, and of all its furniture, so you shall make it."

¹ Uncertain; possibly *dolphin skins*, or *dugong skins*; compare 26:14

Section Overview

In this section's opening verses the Lord summons Moses to ascend the mountain in order to receive the covenant law written on tablets of stone (vv. 12–18). The focus here is on the covenant's centrality to the nation (as witnessed by the Lord's inscribing a copy of the covenant's foundational commandments himself) as well as on Moses' special status as the one who can stand in the Lord's presence and bring communication back to the people from him. A brief comment is also made about Joshua (v. 13), preparing us for his mention later, when Moses descends the mountain (32:17).

The instructions that immediately follow in 25:1–9 about contributions for the Lord's tabernacle come as a special surprise: this is a God who not only offers covenant relationship but desires to dwell in his people's very midst (v. 8). Emphasis is placed on the voluntary nature of the contributions (v. 2), their costly nature

(vv. 3–7), and the need to build them into a tabernacle exactly as the Lord says (vv. 8–9). In short this will be a tabernacle the Israelites are to build in worshipful love and to make in a manner worthy of their most holy covenant King.

Section Outline

VI. Israel at Sinai: the Lord gives instructions for the building of his palace-tent among them (24:12–31:18)
   A. Moses goes up the mountain to receive the stone tablets from the Lord (24:12–18)
      1. The Lord commands Moses to come up the mountain to meet him (24:12)
      2. Moses goes up with his assistant, Joshua (24:13)
      3. The instructions Moses gave the elders before going up (24:14)
      4. An overview of what Moses experienced on the mountain (24:15–18)
   B. Tabernacle contributions (25:1–9)
      1. What the Israelites are to gather: contributions (25:1–2a)
      2. From whom to gather them: those whose heart moves them (25:2b)
      3. What they are to consist of (25:3–7)
      4. What they will be used for: a holy dwelling place for God in Israel's midst (25:8)
      5. What the dwelling place will be modeled after: the pattern God reveals (25:9)

Comment

24:12–14 With the covenant ratification ceremony complete (vv. 9–11) the delegation returns to the people (cf. v. 14). From here the Lord again summons Moses to ascend the mountain, offering the following reason: "That I may give you the tablets of stone, with the law and the commandment, which I have written for their instruction" (v. 12). Later passages make clear that the stone tablets contain the Ten Commandments (34:28; Deut. 10:4), meaning the sense here is "the tablets of stone, with the law and the commandment [written on them, namely, the Ten Commandments], which I have written for their instruction." The word for "law" is built on the same root as the word rendered "for their instruction" and points to the teaching nature of the Ten Commandments, while the word "commandment" makes clear that the teaching is not optional. Positively stated, the Lord has called his people to be a kingdom of priests and a holy nation and graciously gives them the instructions they must follow in order to carry out this calling.[599] While the Lord has already given many other covenant stipulations that Moses has written down (Ex. 24:4), the Ten Commandments are fundamental, as indicated by their

---

[599] Wright, *Exodus*, 462–463.

placement at the head of the stipulations (20:1–17) and by the fact that they are spoken directly to Israel by the Lord (cf. comment on 20:18–21). They can therefore represent all the stipulations. Stated differently, as a wedding ring serves as a symbol of a marriage covenant, the Ten Commandments serve as a symbol of the Sinai covenant.[600]

Moses goes up as the Lord commands, taking with him Joshua (24:13), whom we met earlier (17:9). He becomes Moses' servant while still a young man (Num. 11:28), though it is important to note that the word for servant here (Hb. *mesharet*) differs from that used in places such as Exodus 21:2 (*'ebed*). The latter often refers to a debt servant or permanent servant, while the word in this passage refers simply to someone who works as an attendant to another (Num. 8:26; 2 Sam. 13:17; 2 Kings 4:43). In short, Joshua is Moses' right-hand man; where Moses goes, Joshua follows. Having been mentioned, he now recedes into the background. He will reappear in Exodus 32:17, but until then the text focuses simply on the Lord and Moses.

Briefly the narrative backtracks to describe what Moses tells the elders before ascending Sinai (24:14). This is clearer in the Hebrew, which avoids normal word order at the beginning of verse 14 and could be rendered, "Now to the elders Moses *had said*."[601] Moses names Aaron and Hur, two of the nation's top leaders (cf. comment on 17:10–13), as judges over any disputes that arise, that is, any disputes too difficult for the people's regular judges (cf. 18:24–26). Moses' action also implies the entire delegation has returned to the Israelites' midst; since the people are not allowed on the mountain (19:12), Aaron and Hur must be among them in order to hear their cases (24:14).

24:15–18 Moses leaves the nation in what he thinks are capable hands (cf. 32:1–6!) and goes up the mountain with Joshua (24:15). An overview is given of what he experiences there.

First, for six days the Lord's cloud covers the mountain (vv. 15–16), presumably the top in particular, since Moses is on the mountain but does not enter the cloud until day seven (v. 18; cf. 19:20 and 24:17). Within the cloud appears "the glory of the LORD,"[602] that is, a spectacular display of the Lord's presence that in this case is "like a devouring fire on the top of the mountain," visible for the entire nation to see (v. 17). See further comments in the Response section.

Second, the Lord summons Moses into the cloud on the seventh day (v. 16b).[603] On the one hand it is noteworthy that Moses does not enter the cloud until summoned. As noted above (vv. 1–2), one dare not barge into the presence of a king. But the reason that the Lord waits until day seven to summon Moses is not explained. Possibly the mention of "six days . . . seventh day" is meant to recall

---

[600] For the possible ancient Near Eastern significance of there being two tablets on which the Ten Commandments are written cf. comment on 31:18.
[601] So also Propp, *Exodus 19–40*, 299; cf. NRSV.
[602] Cf. 16:10; 40:34–35. It is said to "dwell" on the mountain, the Hebrew for which is *shakan*, leading to the word Shekinah, used in later Jewish sources to describe "the majestic presence or manifestation of God which has descended to 'dwell' among men"; "Shekinah," *The Jewish Encyclopedia*, vol. 11 (1906), 258.
[603] The Hebrew phrase can mean "called to" or "summoned" (for the latter cf. Ex. 10:24; Lev. 10:4). "Summoned" makes good sense here since Moses' response is to enter the cloud (Ex. 24:18).

the creation account. If so, this would mean at the least that the God of Sinai is the God of creation—a point underscored at the end of the tabernacle instructions (31:17).[604] But it is also true that many significant events, with no evident tie to creation, either take place on the seventh day after a six-day wait or take seven days to accomplish: Noah waits six days in the ark until the flood comes on day seven (Gen. 7:7–10); Joseph mourns his father seven days (Gen. 50:10); the Feast of Unleavened Bread is to last seven days, with a special feast on day seven (Ex. 13:6); Aaron and his sons will be ordained over seven days (Ex. 29:35); and purification from a major ritual impurity takes seven days (Lev. 15:13). In short seven days appear to represent a complete and full amount of time (cf. comment on 1:1–5), though unfortunately that still leaves unanswered why such a wait is necessary here and why it was not required earlier (Ex. 19:2–3, 20).[605] What is clear, however, is that Moses enjoys a particularly close relationship with the Lord. He alone is able to draw this close to the Lord's glory (cf. 24:2), and his degree of access should assure the Israelites that the words he brings back to them really are from the Lord (cf. 19:9).

Third, Moses enters the cloud and goes up the mountain (24:18a), that is, to the very top, where the Lord's glory has settled in the cloud (v. 17). Moses remains there forty days and forty nights (v. 18), a period of time that similarly might be associated with thoroughness and completeness (Gen. 7:4; Num. 13:25).[606] It is certainly long enough to make the Israelites wonder whether he is coming back (Ex. 32:1). The reason such time is required is again not stated, though it surely speaks again to Moses' special status as the Lord's servant. Others could not even go in the cloud; he is allowed to stay there no fewer than forty days!

25:1–2 Having summoned Moses into his presence (24:15–18), the Lord begins giving him instructions for building a tabernacle where the Lord will dwell in the Israelites' midst as their covenant King. For this reason the tabernacle is best thought of as a palace-tent. Thus its fabrics will contain royal colors (blue and scarlet), its furniture will be made with or covered with precious metals (gold and silver and bronze), and its royal attendants (the priests) will wear special uniforms. (Cf. Response section, "What Does the Tabernacle Teach Us about the Kind of God He Is?")

"Contributions" will be necessary to build the tent (v. 2). This word appears often in the Pentateuch and "designates that which is separated from a larger

---

[604] Wright, *Exodus*, 463–464. Wright also suggests that the creation allusion is meant to underscore Yahweh as Creator-King, the one who entered the resting place of his cosmic temple on day seven of creation and now, as King, calls Moses on day seven into his royal presence to give him instructions for his people. This is not impossible but depends on understanding Genesis 1 as describing the building of a cosmic temple, which some scholars have argued for but is not a majority opinion.

[605] Some suggest this is a period of spiritual preparation (Cassuto, *Commentary on the Book of Exodus*, 316; Houtman, *Exodus*, vol. 3, 303); although this did occur earlier (Ex. 19:11), then it took three days, not six. The suggestion that the Lord is taking six days to make a model of the tabernacle (cf. references in Propp, *Exodus 19–40*, 299) is sheer speculation. Sometimes we are simply not able to identify a solution that is either certain or even a more likely possibility among others.

[606] In some contexts "forty" is possibly used idiomatically to mean "a good many," the way that English uses the word "dozens," as in, "I've told you dozens of times" (cf. Stuart, *Exodus*, 561). A possible example is the use of "forty years" in Judges 3:11; 5:31; 8:28; 13:1. (It seems curious that it would be exactly forty years each time.)

quantity for a sacred purpose,"⁶⁰⁷ for example, building materials for the tabernacle (Ex. 25:2–3; 35:5, 21, 24; 36:3, 6), specific portions of a sacrifice (Ex. 29:27–28; Lev. 7:32, 34; 10:14–15; Num. 6:20), or different "holy gifts" (most often food items; Lev. 22:12; Num. 5:9; 18:18–19, 21–24, 26–29). The Lord does not receive these contributions via taxation. He invites those "whose heart moves" them to contribute (Ex. 25:2), that is, those compelled by inner desire and longing to give gifts to their gracious redeemer and King (cf. 35:5, 21–22; 1 Chron. 29:9). As Paul will later write, "Each one must give as he has decided in his heart, not reluctantly or under compulsion, *for God loves a cheerful giver*" (2 Cor. 9:7). And no wonder—gifts given voluntarily are the clearest sign of love.

25:3–7 As noted above, the goal of the contributions is to build a palace-tent for the Lord, including all its furniture and the uniforms for his palace attendants (the priests). As a result, many precious materials are listed (Ex. 24:3–7). If an earthly king's palace is identifiable by its beauty and grandeur, how much more that of the heavenly King. No other tent in Israel will be like this in beauty or size.

The contributions may be placed into seven groupings:⁶⁰⁸

(1) Precious metals: gold, silver, and bronze (v. 3). These will be for covering or making pieces of furniture (such as the ark and the altars; vv. 10–11; 27:1–2; 30:1–3) and for certain accessories and structural elements (such as curtain clasps and pillar sockets; 26:11, 37).

(2) Yarns and textiles (25:4). The yarns are to be "blue and purple and scarlet," which are colors associated elsewhere with royalty (2 Sam. 1:24; Est. 1:6; Ezek. 23:6)⁶⁰⁹ and are appropriate for the Lord's palace. They will be used in the high priest's uniform (Ex. 28:1–5) and in various curtains, including those used as a first covering over the tabernacle's frame (26:1). "Fine twined linen" also occurs in royal contexts (Gen. 41:42) and is listed as parallel to other fine materials (Prov. 31:22; Ezek. 16:10, 13; 27:7), again making it appropriate for the Lord's palace.⁶¹⁰ Generally speaking, it will be used in the same way as the yarns (Ex. 26:1, 31, 36; 28:1–5). "Goats' hair" could be spun (35:26) and will be used to make curtains to form a second covering over the tabernacle (26:7).

(3) Skins (25:5a). "Tanned rams' skins" are used to make a third covering over the tabernacle, and "goatskins"⁶¹¹ make the final covering (26:14). Together these will provide strong protection from the elements. The

---

607 Childs, *Book of Exodus*, 523.
608 The text does not number the groupings, and alternate arrangements are possible (e.g., 25:4–5a could be taken together under the category of materials for clothing, curtains, and coverings).
609 In the ancient world the dyes required to make such materials were especially costly, explaining their association with royalty: only the wealthy could afford them in large quantities.
610 Linen is made from flax; cf. James K. Hoffmeier, "פֵּשֶׁת," *NIDOTTE* 3:711, who cites Proverbs 31:13 and Hosea 2:5, 9 and also describes how it is made.
611 The meaning of the Hebrew term (*takhash*) is debated. Cf. Benjamin J. Noonan, "Hide or Hue? Defining Hebrew *taḥaš*," *Biblica* 93/4 (2012): 580–589, esp. 586–589, where he concludes that the word may well refer to a type of leather.

word "tanned" could be rendered "dyed red," which, as noted above, is a royal color and would be in keeping with the tent's royal nature. Later texts inform us that Israelites have some of these materials on hand and contribute them (35:23) and also make more (36:7). For example, women spin yarn and fine linen by hand (35:25–26)—a labor of love for their King.

(4) "Acacia wood" (25:5b). This will be used for the tent's structural elements (such as various boards and bars; 26:15, 26) and for various pieces of furniture (such as the ark and the table; 25:10, 13). The acacia tree is "a thorny tree, growing up to 10 m [32.8 feet] high, prob. *Acacia seyal*, Red acacia, prized for its timber."[612]

(5) "Oil" (25:6a), that is, olive oil (27:20). It will be used for lamps, namely, the seven lamps held by the golden lampstand (25:37), and will also serve as the base of the anointing oil (30:22–25).

(6) "Spices" (25:6b). These are for the holy anointing oil and the sacred incense, described in further detail in 30:22–24, 34–35.

(7) Precious "stones" (25:7). The names of the twelve tribes will be inscribed on two onyx stones,[613] six tribes per stone, and the stones mounted on the high priest's ephod as "stones of remembrance" before the Lord (28:9–12). The high priest will also wear a breastpiece set with twelve precious stones ("stones for setting"), each inscribed with the name of an Israelite tribe (28:17–21).

As noted in 36:3–7, the Israelites give generously. One might ask where recently enslaved Israelites get some of these materials, especially the more costly ones. The answer was given in 12:35–36: "The people of Israel had also done as Moses told them, for they had asked the Egyptians for silver and gold jewelry and for clothing. And the LORD had given the people favor in the sight of the Egyptians, so that they let them have what they asked. Thus they plundered the Egyptians." Made with these materials, the tabernacle will become a visible reminder of the Lord's salvation.

25:8–9 Finally the Lord names the purpose of the contributions: "And let them make me a sanctuary, *that I may dwell in their midst*" (v. 8). Relationship and fellowship with his creation is always the Lord's goal. When the covenant ceremony was finished in Exodus 24, the Lord could have sent the Israelites on to the Promised Land. But he wanted more than a formal agreement; he wanted to be with them, in their midst (cf. 29:45–46). We always want to be near those we love. And so the Lord pauses and takes the next six chapters to describe the home the Israelites are to build for him in their midst.

The Lord's dwelling goes by three main names in Exodus, each referring to a different aspect of the physical structure and emphasizing a different aspect

---

612 *DCH*, 332.
613 Or possibly red carnelian stones (so *HALOT*).

of the Lord's character.[614] The Hebrew word for "sanctuary" (25:8) refers often to the sanctuary complex as a whole, from the tent to the courtyard (cf. 25:8 with 25:9–27:21). The term is built on the root for "holiness" and points to the holy nature of both the dwelling and the one who lives within it. (The English word "sanctuary" is similar, tracing back to a Latin word meaning "holy," *sanctus*.)

The Hebrew word for "tabernacle" (25:9) refers especially to the interior frame and the first covering stretched over it (cf. 26:1–6, 15–30 with 26:7–14). The term is built on the root for "dwelling, living"; its verbal form can describe someone's dwelling in a tent (Gen. 9:27). (Note that the word "tabernacle" is again similar, being an old English word for a dwelling that traces back to a Latin word for "tent," *tabernaculum*.) In other words the Israelites live in their tents, and the Lord will live in their midst in his. He wants to be near them (Ex. 29:45–46; 40:34–38).

Finally, the term "tent of meeting" refers to the entire tent structure, that is, the tabernacle and its covering as well as the other coverings stretched over it as a tent (26:7; 40:29). The term highlights that here is where the Lord will "meet" with the Israelites and receive their worship (29:42–46) and also "meet" with Moses, giving him laws for the people (25:22; in Hebrew the verb for "meet" in these verses is built on the same root as the noun "meeting" in the term "tent of meeting"). The Lord does not simply want to be in the Israelites' midst; he wants them to come before him in repentance and worship so that they might experience his forgiveness and mercy and have their hearts filled with the joy and love that stream from him like beams of light from the sun.

The Lord's dwelling and its furniture are to be built exactly as he shows Moses on the mountain (v. 9). Whether the word "pattern" here refers to a physical model (Josh. 22:28), a visual likeness (Ezek. 10:8), or a blueprint (1 Chron. 28:11–12) is unclear. As a result, commentators debate whether the Lord shows Moses an actual tabernacle in heaven to replicate, gives him a vision of a heavenly tabernacle, or gives him a vision or plan of how the earthly tabernacle is to look (with no necessary correspondence to a heavenly tabernacle).[615] Whatever the case, the tabernacle's plan comes from the Lord and must be built exactly as he says.[616] This becomes especially important when we remember his dwelling will be the place of worship. Biblically speaking, worshiping God properly is not something we can invent, for to worship him properly is to worship him as he is. Only God can reveal that to us. To put this differently biblical worship is something that originates not with us but with God. He is real, he desires us to know him, and in his grace and love he reveals to us who he is and how to relate to him properly. The tabernacle is a part of that revelation and is meant to help Israel know and

---

614 A fourth name, "tent of the testimony," occurs in Numbers (9:15; 17:7, 8; 18:2) and 2 Chronicles (24:6). "Testimony" refers to the covenant tablets housed in the ark of the covenant (cf. Ex. 25:16 and 31:18), making the tent a constant reminder of the Lord's covenant promises and Israel's covenant obligations.

615 Hebrews 8:5 supports one of the first two options. "As 'pattern and shadow' 'the tabernacle was a rough reminiscence intended to suggest the idea of the original and to train the people of God to appreciate the heavenly reality itself'"; Cockerill, *Epistle to the Hebrews*, 361, citing William L. Lane, *Hebrews*, WBC (Dallas: Word, 1991), 1:206.

616 The word "pattern" is actually repeated in the Hebrew: "Exactly as I show you concerning the pattern of the tabernacle, and the pattern of all its furniture, so you shall make it."

worship him correctly. For this reason alone it must be built exactly as he says. As a coming chapter will show, to worship him according to our invention is to worship him not at all (Exodus 32).

Response

WHAT IS THE GLORY OF THE LORD?

At various points in Exodus the Lord manifests his presence in visible ways. His appearance is so awesome it makes our grandest firework displays look like mere birthday candles. Mountains shake (19:18). Lightning strikes repeatedly (19:16; 20:18). Deafening thunder pounds (19:16, 19; 20:18). Fire blazes (19:18). Smoke billows (19:18; 20:18). In this passage the mountain's rocky top appears to be engulfed in a continual devouring flame (24:17).

So why is this called the "glory of the LORD"? To use an analogy, when I am listening to a beautiful piece of music, sometimes I cannot help but say to those around me, "Did you hear that? That was amazing!" Or, when I see a masterful sports play, I cannot help but say, "Did you see that? That was incredible!" What I witness causes me to give glory to the person responsible for my amazement. This helps explain the phrase "glory of the LORD." It describes an appearance of the Lord so awesome in power and might that the only proper response is to give him glory. Put differently, the Lord is so glorious that it should cause the beholder to recognize and acknowledge his glory. (Cf. Ps. 19:1: "The heavens declare the glory of God," that is, they testify to the power, strength, and wonder of their Maker and bid the one observing them to give God glory.)

Such an awesome display of the Lord's glory also reminds us of his majesty. He is not our "buddy." Reverence must always be present in our relationship with him. He is the King, and we are the servants. Yes, he is a loving and a merciful king, but a king nonetheless, and reverence is due him. He is the Father, and we are the children. Yes, he is a loving and a merciful father, but a father nonetheless, and reverence is due him. Even when Jesus calls us friends, he does so in the context of saying we must do what he commands (John 15:14). Reverence is due him. In short we are to be secure in God's love for us in Christ and yet always revere him. The writer of Hebrews assures us, "We have *confidence* to enter the holy places by the blood of Jesus" (Heb. 10:19), and also exhorts us, "Let us offer to God acceptable worship, *with reverence and awe,* for our God is a consuming fire" (Heb. 12:28–29).

But this passage teaches more than the fact that God is worthy of our reverence. The tabernacle instructions in particular reveal several other aspects of God's character.

WHAT DOES THE TABERNACLE TEACH US ABOUT THE KIND OF GOD HE IS?

Many Bible readers may be tempted to skip six chapters of detail about tabernacle construction. But careful attention to these chapters rewards us with a rich theology of who God is. At least three aspects of God's character are displayed here.

First, he is the Israelites' King, as evidenced by the tabernacle's function as a palace-tent in their midst. Exodus and Leviticus together give several indications that the tent functions in this way:

(1) The Israelites bring their tribute here (Ex. 25:1–9), just as a people would bring tribute to a king's palace.
(2) They comes here to "stand before" the LORD (Lev. 9:5), just as one "stands before" a ruler or person in authority (1 Kings 1:28; 3:16; Est. 8:4).
(3) Its ornate furniture and tapestries are unlike those of any other tent in Israel (Ex. 25:10–26:37; 30:1–10; cf. also at 25:4). This is clearly a tent fit for a king.
(4) Just as a king's servants wears special uniforms and minister before him in the palace (1 Kings 10:5), so the Lord's servants (the priests) wear special uniforms (Exodus 28) and minister before him here (28:43).
(5) It has a throne room—the Most Holy Place—where the Lord's glory sits enthroned over the ark among the cherubim (1 Sam. 4:4; Ps. 99:1), who serve as the attendants at his royal throne (cf. the seraphim in Isa. 6:1–2).
(6) The curtain before the Most Holy Place is woven with cherubim (Ex. 26:31–33), who not only symbolically guard the entrance into this throne room (cf. Gen. 3:24) but are heavenly beings, thus making clear it is the throne room of the heavenly King.[617]

Second, this king is holy. Generally speaking the tabernacle complex is called the Lord's "sanctuary," the Hebrew of which is built on the root for "holiness," pointing to the holiness of the place and the one who dwells within it (Ex. 25:8). More specifically the tabernacle complex has different grades or zones of holiness, and the holiest is reserved for the Lord. These grades of holiness are seen in three different ways:

(1) *The titles of the different rooms.* The first room a priest enters when going into the tent is known as the "Holy Place"; the second, where the Lord manifests his presence, is the "Most Holy Place" (26:33; cf. 25:21–22). The Lord's supreme holiness requires the holiest of places for his dwelling.
(2) *The materials used to construct it.* In the outer court the altar is covered with bronze (27:1–2), but, the closer one gets to the Most Holy Place, the more precious and costly the materials become, so that within the Most Holy Place one finds only silver and gold (25:10–11; 26:6, 15–30). This gradation in materials reflects the gradation in holiness that occurs as one draws near to the Lord's presence.

---
617 Adapted slightly from Sklar, *Leviticus*, ZECOT, 11.

(3) *The personnel.* Laymen and priests are allowed into the courtyard (Lev. 1:3; 12:6).[618] Priests—who, unlike laymen, are ritually holy (Lev. 8:30)—are allowed into the Holy Place (Ex. 28:43). But only the high priest—the holiest of the priests (Lev. 8:12)[619]—is allowed into the Most Holy Place, and then only once a year (Lev. 16:2, 32–34). The gradation in holiness with regard to access underscores the Lord's supreme holiness.[620]

Finally, the tabernacle texts show the Lord is not only a king who is holy but also a king who desires to be with his people. This is the very reason he gives for the building of the tabernacle: "Let them make me a sanctuary, *that I may dwell in their midst*" (Ex. 25:8). As noted at verse 8, we want to be near the ones we love. The Israelites are in their tents; the Lord will be in their midst in his (cf. v. 8). His is not a "tent of seclusion" but a "tent of meeting," where the Israelites can come before him in repentance and praise to experience his forgiveness, mercy, glory, and love (cf. v. 9). This has been God's desire from the beginning. In the account of creation the Bible uses a relatively rare form of a verb to describe the Lord's "*walking* in the garden" of Eden (Gen. 3:8).[621] The same verb is used again in Leviticus, when the Lord promises the Israelites, "I will make my dwelling among you . . . and *I will walk* among you" (Lev. 26:11–12). Eden is revisited in the tabernacle. God again comes to walk with his people.[622]

This finds its ultimate expression in Jesus. Speaking of him as the Word of God, John writes, "The Word became flesh and dwelt among us" (John 1:14). The Greek words for "dwelt" and "tabernacle" are built on the same root,[623] making John's point clear: in Jesus God has again come to dwell in our midst. To ensure we do not miss it John adds, "And we have seen his glory" (1:14). Just as the glory of the Lord came to the tabernacle after it was built (Ex. 40:34–35), so it came in Jesus' life and ministry. God had drawn nearer than ever before. He brushed shoulders with us, shared a cup with us, touched us to heal us, placed his hands upon us to bless us. All of this points to where the world's story is headed for those who have faith in Jesus:

> I heard a loud voice from the throne saying, "Behold, the dwelling place[624] of God is with man. He will dwell with them, and they will be his people, and God himself will be with them as their God. He will wipe away every tear from their eyes, and death shall be no more, neither shall there be

---

618 "The entrance of the tent of meeting" refers to a space within the courtyard of the tabernacle complex. Cf. Leviticus 1:5, which places the altar of burnt offering, which is clearly in the tabernacle courtyard, "at the entrance of the tent of meeting."
619 Only Aaron has the holy anointing oil placed on his head; cf. Leviticus 8:12 with 8:30.
620 For further discussion cf. Philip P. Jenson, *Graded Holiness: A Key to the Priestly Conception of the World*, JSOTSup 106 (Sheffield, UK: JSOT Press, 1992), 89–209.
621 The Hebrew verb is *hithallek*; it occurs only eleven times in the Pentateuch and only four times in the phrase "to walk in/among," the phrase found in Genesis 3:8 and Leviticus 26:12. Cf. further above.
622 For further parallels between Eden and the tabernacle cf. Gordon J. Wenham, "Sanctuary Symbolism in the Garden of Eden Story," in *Proceedings from the Ninth Congress of Jewish Studies, Division A: The Period of the Bible* (Jerusalem: World Union of Jewish Studies, 1986), 19–25, esp. 20–22.
623 The Greek verb is *skēnoō*; the LXX regularly translates the Hebrew word "tabernacle" with *skēnēs*.
624 The Greek for "dwelling place" is the same word used in the LXX for the tabernacle; cf. note 623.

mourning, nor crying, nor pain anymore, for the former things have passed away." (Rev. 21:3–4)

WHAT IS THE PROPER RESPONSE?

How are we to respond to a God like this? One thing is clear: we must not try to earn his love. To do so would be to deny the story's direction. God always comes down to us, whether in the garden, on the mountain, in the tabernacle, or in Jesus. Christianity is not about working one's way to heaven to earn his love; it is about the Maker of heaven's coming to earth in his amazing love for us. His love is received, not earned. But along with receiving his love we must bow before his power and holiness. God remains a consuming fire (Heb. 12:29). So a proper response to him involves rejoicing in his love and bowing before him in reverent worship. How do these work together?

The answer is already hinted at in this passage. The tabernacle's building materials have two characteristics: they are costly (Ex. 25:3–7) and must be given voluntarily (v. 2). Their costliness acknowledges the Lord's greatness. He is the holy and powerful King of kings, worthy of costly sacrifice. To give less than our entire selves is to say he is not worthy of our worship. But their voluntary nature points to the spirit with which such sacrifices are made: one not of duty but of love, not to earn his mercy and love but in response to the greatness of his mercy and love. Paul makes this same connection in Romans. After taking three chapters to describe the mercy and love God has shown us in Jesus (Romans 9–11), he concludes, "I appeal to you therefore, brothers, *by the mercies of God*, to present your bodies as a living sacrifice, holy and acceptable to God, which is your spiritual worship" (Rom. 12:1). We give ourselves to him not to earn his mercy but because he has already shown such rich mercy to us in Jesus.

In light of the above we do well to ask, In what practical ways can I present myself as a living sacrifice to the Lord? And do I consider such sacrifices as religious duty to a strict, austere God? Or do I think of such sacrifices as heartfelt worship to a holy, loving God who has shown me unspeakably great mercy in Christ?

EXODUS 25:10–27:21

[10] "They shall make an ark of acacia wood. Two cubits[1] and a half shall be its length, a cubit and a half its breadth, and a cubit and a half its height. [11] You shall overlay it with pure gold, inside and outside shall you overlay it, and you shall make on it a molding of gold around it. [12] You shall cast four rings of gold for it and put them on its four feet, two rings on the one side of it, and two rings on the other side of it. [13] You shall make poles of acacia wood and overlay them with gold. [14] And you shall put the poles

into the rings on the sides of the ark to carry the ark by them. ¹⁵ The poles shall remain in the rings of the ark; they shall not be taken from it. ¹⁶ And you shall put into the ark the testimony that I shall give you.

¹⁷ "You shall make a mercy seat² of pure gold. Two cubits and a half shall be its length, and a cubit and a half its breadth. ¹⁸ And you shall make two cherubim of gold; of hammered work shall you make them, on the two ends of the mercy seat. ¹⁹ Make one cherub on the one end, and one cherub on the other end. Of one piece with the mercy seat shall you make the cherubim on its two ends. ²⁰ The cherubim shall spread out their wings above, overshadowing the mercy seat with their wings, their faces one to another; toward the mercy seat shall the faces of the cherubim be. ²¹ And you shall put the mercy seat on the top of the ark, and in the ark you shall put the testimony that I shall give you. ²² There I will meet with you, and from above the mercy seat, from between the two cherubim that are on the ark of the testimony, I will speak with you about all that I will give you in commandment for the people of Israel.

²³ "You shall make a table of acacia wood. Two cubits shall be its length, a cubit its breadth, and a cubit and a half its height. ²⁴ You shall overlay it with pure gold and make a molding of gold around it. ²⁵ And you shall make a rim around it a handbreadth³ wide, and a molding of gold around the rim. ²⁶ And you shall make for it four rings of gold, and fasten the rings to the four corners at its four legs. ²⁷ Close to the frame the rings shall lie, as holders for the poles to carry the table. ²⁸ You shall make the poles of acacia wood, and overlay them with gold, and the table shall be carried with these. ²⁹ And you shall make its plates and dishes for incense, and its flagons and bowls with which to pour drink offerings; you shall make them of pure gold. ³⁰ And you shall set the bread of the Presence on the table before me regularly.

³¹ "You shall make a lampstand of pure gold. The lampstand shall be made of hammered work: its base, its stem, its cups, its calyxes, and its flowers shall be of one piece with it. ³² And there shall be six branches going out of its sides, three branches of the lampstand out of one side of it and three branches of the lampstand out of the other side of it; ³³ three cups made like almond blossoms, each with calyx and flower, on one branch, and three cups made like almond blossoms, each with calyx and flower, on the other branch—so for the six branches going out of the lampstand. ³⁴ And on the lampstand itself there shall be four cups made like almond blossoms, with their calyxes and flowers, ³⁵ and a calyx of one piece with it under each pair of the six branches going out from the lampstand. ³⁶ Their calyxes and their branches shall be of one piece with it, the whole of it a single piece of hammered work of pure gold. ³⁷ You shall make seven lamps for it. And the lamps shall be set up so as to give light on the space in front of it. ³⁸ Its tongs and their trays shall be of pure gold. ³⁹ It shall be made, with all these utensils, out of a talent⁴ of pure gold. ⁴⁰ And see that you make them after the pattern for them, which is being shown you on the mountain.

26 "Moreover, you shall make the tabernacle with ten curtains of fine twined linen and blue and purple and scarlet yarns; you shall make them with cherubim skillfully worked into them. ² The length of each curtain shall be twenty-eight cubits,⁵ and the breadth of each curtain four cubits; all the curtains shall be the same size. ³ Five curtains shall be coupled to one another, and the other five curtains shall be coupled to one

another. ⁴ And you shall make loops of blue on the edge of the outermost curtain in the first set. Likewise you shall make loops on the edge of the outermost curtain in the second set. ⁵ Fifty loops you shall make on the one curtain, and fifty loops you shall make on the edge of the curtain that is in the second set; the loops shall be opposite one another. ⁶ And you shall make fifty clasps of gold, and couple the curtains one to the other with the clasps, so that the tabernacle may be a single whole.

⁷ "You shall also make curtains of goats' hair for a tent over the tabernacle; eleven curtains shall you make. ⁸ The length of each curtain shall be thirty cubits, and the breadth of each curtain four cubits. The eleven curtains shall be the same size. ⁹ You shall couple five curtains by themselves, and six curtains by themselves, and the sixth curtain you shall double over at the front of the tent. ¹⁰ You shall make fifty loops on the edge of the curtain that is outermost in one set, and fifty loops on the edge of the curtain that is outermost in the second set.

¹¹ "You shall make fifty clasps of bronze, and put the clasps into the loops, and couple the tent together that it may be a single whole. ¹² And the part that remains of the curtains of the tent, the half curtain that remains, shall hang over the back of the tabernacle. ¹³ And the extra that remains in the length of the curtains, the cubit on the one side, and the cubit on the other side, shall hang over the sides of the tabernacle, on this side and that side, to cover it. ¹⁴ And you shall make for the tent a covering of tanned rams' skins⁶ and a covering of goatskins on top.

¹⁵ "You shall make upright frames for the tabernacle of acacia wood. ¹⁶ Ten cubits shall be the length of a frame, and a cubit and a half the breadth of each frame. ¹⁷ There shall be two tenons in each frame, for fitting together. So shall you do for all the frames of the tabernacle. ¹⁸ You shall make the frames for the tabernacle: twenty frames for the south side; ¹⁹ and forty bases of silver you shall make under the twenty frames, two bases under one frame for its two tenons, and two bases under the next frame for its two tenons; ²⁰ and for the second side of the tabernacle, on the north side twenty frames, ²¹ and their forty bases of silver, two bases under one frame, and two bases under the next frame. ²² And for the rear of the tabernacle westward you shall make six frames. ²³ And you shall make two frames for corners of the tabernacle in the rear; ²⁴ they shall be separate beneath, but joined at the top, at the first ring. Thus shall it be with both of them; they shall form the two corners. ²⁵ And there shall be eight frames, with their bases of silver, sixteen bases; two bases under one frame, and two bases under another frame.

²⁶ "You shall make bars of acacia wood, five for the frames of the one side of the tabernacle, ²⁷ and five bars for the frames of the other side of the tabernacle, and five bars for the frames of the side of the tabernacle at the rear westward. ²⁸ The middle bar, halfway up the frames, shall run from end to end. ²⁹ You shall overlay the frames with gold and shall make their rings of gold for holders for the bars, and you shall overlay the bars with gold. ³⁰ Then you shall erect the tabernacle according to the plan for it that you were shown on the mountain.

³¹ "And you shall make a veil of blue and purple and scarlet yarns and fine twined linen. It shall be made with cherubim skillfully worked into it. ³² And you shall hang it on four pillars of acacia overlaid with gold, with hooks of gold, on four bases of silver. ³³ And you shall hang the veil from the clasps, and bring the ark of the testimony in there within the veil. And

the veil shall separate for you the Holy Place from the Most Holy. ³⁴ You shall put the mercy seat on the ark of the testimony in the Most Holy Place. ³⁵ And you shall set the table outside the veil, and the lampstand on the south side of the tabernacle opposite the table, and you shall put the table on the north side.

³⁶ "You shall make a screen for the entrance of the tent, of blue and purple and scarlet yarns and fine twined linen, embroidered with needlework. ³⁷ And you shall make for the screen five pillars of acacia, and overlay them with gold. Their hooks shall be of gold, and you shall cast five bases of bronze for them.

27 "You shall make the altar of acacia wood, five cubits⁷ long and five cubits broad. The altar shall be square, and its height shall be three cubits. ² And you shall make horns for it on its four corners; its horns shall be of one piece with it, and you shall overlay it with bronze. ³ You shall make pots for it to receive its ashes, and shovels and basins and forks and fire pans. You shall make all its utensils of bronze. ⁴ You shall also make for it a grating, a network of bronze, and on the net you shall make four bronze rings at its four corners. ⁵ And you shall set it under the ledge of the altar so that the net extends halfway down the altar. ⁶ And you shall make poles for the altar, poles of acacia wood, and overlay them with bronze. ⁷ And the poles shall be put through the rings, so that the poles are on the two sides of the altar when it is carried. ⁸ You shall make it hollow, with boards. As it has been shown you on the mountain, so shall it be made.

⁹ "You shall make the court of the tabernacle. On the south side the court shall have hangings of fine twined linen a hundred cubits long for one side. ¹⁰ Its twenty pillars and their twenty bases shall be of bronze, but the hooks of the pillars and their fillets shall be of silver. ¹¹ And likewise for its length on the north side there shall be hangings a hundred cubits long, its pillars twenty and their bases twenty, of bronze, but the hooks of the pillars and their fillets shall be of silver. ¹² And for the breadth of the court on the west side there shall be hangings for fifty cubits, with ten pillars and ten bases. ¹³ The breadth of the court on the front to the east shall be fifty cubits. ¹⁴ The hangings for the one side of the gate shall be fifteen cubits, with their three pillars and three bases. ¹⁵ On the other side the hangings shall be fifteen cubits, with their three pillars and three bases. ¹⁶ For the gate of the court there shall be a screen twenty cubits long, of blue and purple and scarlet yarns and fine twined linen, embroidered with needlework. It shall have four pillars and with them four bases. ¹⁷ All the pillars around the court shall be filleted with silver. Their hooks shall be of silver, and their bases of bronze. ¹⁸ The length of the court shall be a hundred cubits, the breadth fifty, and the height five cubits, with hangings of fine twined linen and bases of bronze. ¹⁹ All the utensils of the tabernacle for every use, and all its pegs and all the pegs of the court, shall be of bronze.

²⁰ "You shall command the people of Israel that they bring to you pure beaten olive oil for the light, that a lamp may regularly be set up to burn. ²¹ In the tent of meeting, outside the veil that is before the testimony, Aaron and his sons shall tend it from evening to morning before the LORD. It shall be a statute forever to be observed throughout their generations by the people of Israel."

---

¹ A *cubit* was about 18 inches or 45 centimeters ² Or *cover* ³ A *handbreadth* was about 3 inches or 7.5 centimeters ⁴ A *talent* was about 75 pounds or 34 kilograms ⁵ A *cubit* was about 18 inches or 45 centimeters ⁶ Or *of rams' skins dyed red* ⁷ A *cubit* was about 18 inches or 45 centimeters

Section Overview

Having just stated, "Let [the Israelites] make me a sanctuary" (25:8), the Lord now begins describing its design. (For a summary cf. Overview of 24:12–31:18.) Generally speaking he begins with the heart of the tabernacle and works outward. He begins with three pieces of sanctuary furniture (25:10–40), the most important being the golden ark of the covenant (vv. 10–22) in the tabernacle's inner room, the Most Holy Place. He then moves to the tabernacle's outer room, the Holy Place, and describes the golden table (vv. 23–30) and the golden lampstand there (vv. 31–40). (For the golden incense altar cf. comment on 30:1–10.) Emphasis is placed throughout on the use of gold, especially pure gold, in construction (25:11, 17, 24, 31). This furniture is for the home of the King of kings. He is worthy of the best his people can offer.

Having described various pieces of furniture within the tabernacle, the Lord next describes the tabernacle itself, including its four coverings (26:1–14), frame (vv. 15–30), inner veil, and curtained doorway (vv. 31–37). This leads to a discussion of the altar in front of the tabernacle (27:1–8) and the curtained walls forming the courtyard (vv. 9–19). Chapter 27 finishes with a description of the oil for lighting in the tabernacle (vv. 20–21), which, as the priests' responsibility, serves as a good transition to a description of their clothing in chapter 28.

The closer one gets to the Lord's throne room, the more beautiful and costly the materials become, a visual reminder of the majesty of the one who sits on the throne and the glory due his name.

Section Outline

VI. Israel at Sinai: the Lord gives instructions for the building of his palace-tent among them (24:12–31:18) . . .
   C. Tabernacle building instructions (25:10–27:21)
      1. The golden ark of the covenant (25:10–22)
      2. The golden table (25:23–30)
      3. The golden lampstand (25:31–40)
      4. The tabernacle's covering of curtains (26:1–6)
      5. The tabernacle's goat hair tent (26:7–13)
      6. The tent's two further coverings (26:14)
      7. The tabernacle's inner structure (26:15–30)
      8. The tabernacle's veil and screen (26:31–37)
      9. The altar of burnt offering (27:1–8)
      10. The walls of the tabernacle's courtyard (27:9–19)
      11. The oil for the golden lampstand (27:20–21)

Comment

25:10–16 The first item described is the most important: the ark of the covenant. Not only are the stone tablets placed inside as a witness to the covenant between the Lord and Israel (v. 16), but the ark itself serves as the place where the Lord will manifest his presence as covenant King and will instruct his people through Moses (v. 22).

The Hebrew word for "ark" (*'aron*) is used elsewhere to refer to boxes in which objects could be placed, such as a money chest (2 Kings 12:9) or a coffin (Gen. 50:26). The tabernacle's ark is made to contain the covenant tablets (cf. below). Made of acacia wood, it is the size of a travel trunk, measuring 3.75 feet (1.1 m) in length and 2.25 feet (0.7 m) in width and height (25:10)[625] and overlaid with pure gold inside and out (Ex. 25:11).[626] The word "pure" suggests gold of the highest value, as does the fact that such gold is reserved for the tabernacle's main pieces of furniture (the ark, the table and its dishes, the lampstand and its utensils, and the incense altar; cf. 25:24, 29, 31, 33 [cf. 39:25], 36, 38–39; 30:3) and for various pieces of the high priest's clothing.[627]

Around the ark is some form of golden molding (25:11), though its design (plain or ornamented?) and position (high, middle, or low?) are not given. (These are some of the many unnamed details in the tabernacle instructions that Moses may have been able to provide based on his viewing of the pattern the Lord had shown him; v. 9.) The ark has four feet, which will keep it off the ground when at rest,[628] and four golden rings attached to the feet (v. 12). The rings are for holding gold-covered acacia poles. When the tabernacle is on the move, the Levites will use the poles to carry the ark on their shoulders (Num. 4:5–6; 7:9; 1 Chron. 15:15), which is perhaps an extra sign of reverence (a later passage speaks of a king who is carried by his servants; Song 3:7).[629] The poles are treated as one piece with the ark and left in place even when it is not being carried (Ex. 25:15).[630] Finally, Moses is to put "into the ark the testimony" (v. 16), that is, the covenant tablets.[631] At least one other ancient Near Eastern example from this time describes the placement of a written copy of a covenant in a deity's temple, and several list deities as witnesses to covenants. These observations suggest the covenant tablets here are kept under the place the Lord will manifest his

---

[625] A cubit is usually assumed to be based "the distance from an average man's elbow to his fingertips" (Propp, *Exodus 19–40*, 380), that is, roughly 18 inches (45 cm). For details on acacia wood cf. at Exodus 25:5.
[626] "In Egypt, wooden furniture was covered with gold either by nailing on hammered plates or by gluing on foil" (Propp, *Exodus 19–40*, 380).
[627] Cf. Exodus 28:14, 22, 36. Since chemical refining techniques were likely not developed at this time, pure gold likely "refers to the highest grade of naturally occurring gold—that is, ores with the fewest traces of other metals. It can also include awareness of the 'washing' technique necessary to separate alluvial gold, the most common source of gold in the ancient Near East, from its matrix"; Meyers, *Exodus*, 227, citing Carol L. Meyers, *The Tabernacle Menorah: A Synthetic Study of a Symbol from the Biblical Cult*, 2nd ed. (Piscataway, NJ: Gorgias Press, 2003), 41–43; cf. passages that speak of certain gold as being of special value (Gen. 2:12; Job 28:16).
[628] Stuart, *Exodus*, 568.
[629] While many of the tabernacle's curtains and structural items are carried in carts (cf. Num. 4:21–33 with 7:7–9), all the furniture and vessels from inside the tabernacle, which are used more directly in worship, are hand carried, as is the important altar of burnt offering and its utensils (Num. 4:5–14).
[630] This seems to conflict with the traditional translation of Numbers 4:6, which notes that the Levites will "put in [the ark's] poles" when they get ready to transport it. "One possible explanation is that the poles would be temporarily removed when the ark was wrapped for transport but then immediately reinserted. Alternatively, and perhaps more persuasively, Eichler (Raanan Eichler, *The Ark and the Cherubim* [Tübingen: Mohr Siebeck, 2021], 112–113) has made a good case that there were four poles—two at each end—that were retractable, noting the exact same construction in a 14th century BC chest from Tutankhamen's tomb. The poles would be pushed under the ark when at rest (hiding them) and pulled out to be 'put [in place]' for carrying when the ark was being moved (Num. 4:6). (For translating the relevant verb [Hb. *sim*] as 'put in place,' see its use in ESV of Ex. 40:28 and see also *DCH*, 135, range of meaning 2.)" (Sklar, *Numbers*, 81n27).
[631] Cf. Exodus 31:18 and esp. Deuteronomy 10:1–5 (Wright, *Exodus*, 480).

presence to make clear he will serve as divine witness to the covenant (cf. comment on 31:18).

25:17–22 The ark's lid is described next. Made of pure gold, it is the same length and breadth as the ark (3.75 ft by 2.25 ft [1.1 m by 0.7 m]; v. 17). The Hebrew word for the lid (*kapporet*) is variously translated as "mercy seat" (ESV, NRSV), "atonement lid" (NET), or "atonement cover" (NIV). I will use "atonement lid" to highlight that the word is built on the same root as the verb "to make atonement" (*kipper*) and is explicitly linked with that verb in Leviticus 16:14–16, where Aaron "makes atonement" (*kipper*) on the Day of Atonement in part by sprinkling sacrificial blood on and before the "atonement lid" (*kapporet*). (The word used in the LXX for this lid—*hilastērion*—is the word Paul uses to describe Jesus and the work he accomplishes with his sacrificial death: "Whom God put forward as a *propitiation* by his blood"; Rom. 3:25.) Making atonement at this very place—where the Lord manifests his presence (cf. below)—may communicate that sins are nothing less than rebellion against him and that he is the one who graciously grants cleansing and forgiveness to those who repent.

On top of the lid are two cherubim, celestial figures made of hammered gold and of one piece with the lid (Ex. 25:18–19).[632] In terms of function cherubim serve as guardians (Gen. 3:24), a metaphorical chariot on which the Lord rides (1 Chron. 28:18; Ps. 18:10), or divine attendants at his throne (2 Sam. 6:2; Pss. 80:1; 99:1; cf. the heavenly attendants around the throne in 1 Kings 22:19; Isa. 6:1–2).[633] The latter fits the context here well since the tabernacle functions as the Lord's palace-tent, making it natural to see the Most Holy Place as the Lord's throne room, where he sits enthroned over the ark and surrounded by his heavenly attendants. In terms of form we learn from Exodus that the cherubim are winged creatures with faces, presumably standing on each end of the lid as they stretch their wings over it (Ex. 25:20). Ezekiel goes into greater detail describing cherubim (Ezek. 1:5–11; 10:20–22), but whether all cherubim look exactly the same is unclear, making it difficult to know how much of Ezekiel's description to read back into Exodus. (In fact the cherubim in Ezekiel have four faces [1:5–6], whereas those here apparently have only one.) Whatever their exact form here, they are to be stationed at each end of the ark, facing one another with heads toward the mercy seat, either bowed in reverence[634] or looking on as guards,[635] or both (Ex. 25:18–20). Moreover, just as the cloud on Sinai prevents direct sight of the Lord (24:16–17), the cherubim's wings spread forward over the atonement lid, screening the place where the Lord will manifest his presence (25:20, 22).

---

632 The word translated "hammered" is rare and its meaning disputed, though it is different from the word used for "casting" metal (Ex. 25:12). It describes the lampstand also (vv. 31, 36), which, like the cherubim, is a complex object.
633 While many versions translate the relevant Hebrew in these verses as "the Lord who sits enthroned *on* the cherubim," the word "on" is not in the Hebrew, which could also be translated "the Lord who sits/dwells/ is enthroned among the cherubim," that is, surrounded by his heavenly attendants (cf. *IBHS* 9.5.2f). The sense of "enthroned" is favored in light of Psalm 99:1, where it is parallel to "reign (as king)."
634 Cf. how Moses "hid his face" before God's presence (Ex. 3:6), as do the angelic beings attending the Lord in Isaiah's vision (Isa. 6:2); Cassuto, *Commentary on the Book of Exodus*, 335.
635 Houtman, *Exodus*, vol. 3, 388.

After highlighting again that the ark will contain the covenant tablets (v. 21), the Lord explains that there, above the atonement lid, he will "meet" with Moses,[636] manifesting his presence and continuing to give him commandments to pass on to the Israelites (v. 22). Mention of the "testimony" in two consecutive verses (vv. 21–22) underscores the covenant's centrality to the Israelites' relationship with the Lord and the importance of their following his covenant instruction, especially since he manifests his presence above the ark as divine witness to the covenant's stipulations (cf. comment on 25:10–16 [at v. 16]). The fact that the Lord will continue to give such instruction means the Israelites need not fear he will be absent or silent once they leave Mount Sinai. The tabernacle will function as a portable Mount Sinai in their midst, a constant assurance of the Lord's presence and guidance (for further connections between the tabernacle and Mount Sinai cf. 40:34–38).

25:23–30 Two items from the Holy Place are described next: a table that stands on the room's north side and a lampstand on the south (26:35). The table is described first. Made of acacia wood, it is covered in pure gold and looks more like a long side table than a dining table at 3 feet (0.9 m) in width, 1.5 feet (0.5 m) in depth, and 2.25 feet (0.7 m) in height (25:23). It is the same height as the ark though slightly smaller in length and width. Like the ark, it is overlaid with pure gold, has a gold molding all around it, and will be carried on gold-covered poles inserted into four rings (vv. 24–28). Unlike the ark, it has a rim around it, with an additional molding around the rim. The two perhaps function together to add beauty to the table and stability to its structure (v. 25). In keeping with its table design it has legs instead of feet, and the rings are fastened to the legs near the table's rim (vv. 26–27).[637] It holds plates for food (and perhaps the bread of the Presence in particular), dishes possibly for incense for the incense altar (cf. 30:1–9) or frankincense for the bread (cf. Lev. 24:7)[638] or both,[639] and flagons and bowls that can be used for daily drink offerings in the Holy Place (Ex. 25:29).[640] Like the table, all these are of pure gold (v. 29). Finally, the "bread of the Presence" is to be placed on the table (v. 30). Further details are found in Leviticus 24:5–9, which states the bread consists of twelve flat loaves placed in two stacks and replaced weekly. The loaves represent the twelve tribes of Israel, and the emphasis in Leviticus 24 (and Exodus 25) is that they are to be continually before the Lord. Indeed, the phrase "bread of the Presence" (v. 30) may be more woodenly translated as "bread of the face," that is, the bread constantly before the Lord's face (cf. the end of v. 30: "before me regularly"; cf. Response section for significance).[641]

---

636 In Hebrew the verb "meet" is built on the same root as the noun "meet" in the phrase "tent of meeting"; cf. comment on 25:8–9.
637 In Hebrew the word translated "frame" in 25:27 is the same word translated "rim" in verse 25.
638 Kalisch, *Exodus*, 481.
639 These are interpretive suggestions. The word translated "dishes for incense" is indeed used elsewhere for a dish that holds incense (Num. 7:14), though it is possible such dishes could be used for other things.
640 Cf. Numbers 28:3–8. A drink offering is often offered along with a sacrifice and grain offering and, in this way, completes the "meal": meat (the sheep), "bread" (even if uncooked), and drink, a robust expression of praise offered to the Lord. For sacrifice as a meal cf. Sklar, *Leviticus*, ZECOT, 122–124, 645 (esp. comments on 24:5–9).
641 Cassuto, *Commentary on the Book of Exodus*, 340; Propp, *Exodus 19–40*, 397.

25:31–40 The second item from the Holy Place to be described is the lampstand. (The third item, the altar of incense, is described in 30:1–10.) Like the atonement lid, it is to be a hammered work of pure gold, with all its different parts of one piece with it (25:31, 36; cf. note 632 within comment on 25:17–22). Generally speaking it is to resemble a miniature flowering almond tree—native to the Middle East—with a main trunk ("stem"), three branches coming off each side for a total of six, and twenty-two flowering almond buds,[642] three on each of the branches and four on the trunk (vv. 32–35).[643] The lamps for the lampstand number seven, a full and complete number (cf. note 56 within comment on 1:1–5). Presumably there is one for each of the six branches and one for the trunk, placed to cast light toward the golden table (25:37).[644] The stunning result is a miniature golden tree with golden blossoms, shining with golden light.[645]

Various implements are required to tend the lamps—tongs for moving hot lamps or coals (cf. Isa. 6:6), or perhaps hot wicks, and trays (or "censers") for holding hot lamps or any coals used for lighting them—and these too are to be made of pure gold (Ex. 25:38). About 75 pounds (34 kg) of pure gold ("a talent") is needed to make everything (v. 39; for the talent's weight cf. note 819 in table 2.10). The passage concludes by stating that these items must be made exactly according to the pattern shown Moses on the mountain (v. 40), which repeats what was said just before the first tabernacle item of furniture was described (v. 9), thus tying together the section.

Other texts inform us that the lampstand's lamps are to be kept burning continually through the night (27:20–21; Lev. 24:1–4; for significance cf. Response section).

26:1–6 The tabernacle consists of a frame measuring roughly 45 feet (13.7 m) in length on an east-west axis and roughly 15 feet (4.6 m) in height and width (cf. Ex. 25:15–25; for the use of "roughly" cf. note 647). As noted above, this is not the size of a modern-day camping tent; it is more the size of a festival or outdoor reception tent. Over the frame hangs ten huge bolts of cloth joined together as a tapestry.[646] The word for the individual bolts is usually rendered "curtains." The curtains are long and relatively narrow, measuring about 42 feet (12.8 m) long by 6 feet (1.8 m) wide (v. 2; for the cubit cf. note 625 within comment on 25:10–16).

---

642 Described as cups with a calyx and flower. "Calyx" refers to the leaves, usually green, that surround and protect the budding flower.
643 I understand 25:35 as an explanation of 25:34, but it is also possible that 25:35 describes three additional calyx formations. On a different note commentators debate whether the almond blossoms are meant to symbolize anything and what that symbolism might be. At the least they beautify the lampstand, which in itself reminds us God values aesthetics—as any close attention to his creation also makes clear!
644 Perhaps the wick is at one side of the lamp, not the center, and placed toward the front (Keil, *Exodus*, vol. 2, 174). The word translated "set up" could also be translated "made to burn" (cf. Lev. 24:2).
645 While definite parallels exist between the tabernacle and the garden of Eden (cf. Response section on Ex. 35:1–40:38, "What Does the Tabernacle Have to Do with Eden?"), it is difficult to affirm, despite several commentators' claims (Stuart, *Exodus*, 577; Wells, *Exodus*, 249, 251), that the lampstand is to be viewed as a symbolic tree of life. Such a view would be more likely if there were explicit verbal links to the language describing the tree of life in Genesis 2–3.
646 This is the majority view. A minority view suggests the final tapestry is hung by hooks to the interior of the frame so the frame's boards and planks so not conceal it from view (Kalisch, *Exodus*, 477–478), though this only creates a new problem in that the golden boards would be completely obscured (Cassuto, *Commentary on the Book of Exodus*, 350–351).

Five are joined together along their lengths, presumably by some sort of stitching, to make one large curtain measuring 42 feet (12.8 m) long by 30 feet (9.1 m) wide (26:3). Fifty blue loops are added to its long edge. The same process is performed with the other five, and the two large curtains are then joined at the loops by golden clasps (vv. 4–6).

Taking this approach probably makes things easier to handle and assemble; as anyone who has dealt with a large amount of material knows, it can become very heavy. In this case the final product, when joined together, is a huge tapestry measuring 60 feet by 42 feet (18.3 m by 12.8 m)—one third longer than the tabernacle and roughly three times as wide. This would allow it to cover the tabernacle's top and most of its sides. When placed over the frame, the tapestry would come within 1.5 feet (45 cm) of the ground on the long northern and southern sides and, since a separate screen hangs on the eastern side (vv. 36–37), is likely placed to cover most of the western end (the back of the Most Holy Place), leaving little to nothing on the eastern front.[647]

The curtains are a combination of fine twined linen and colorful yarns (v. 1), materials elsewhere associated with royalty (cf. 25:4). Cherubim, the Lord's heavenly attendants (cf. 25:18), are woven into them (26:1). When the curtains are joined and spread over the frame, the view from inside would be remarkable. Any priest entering the Holy Place would be bathed in golden light as the lampstand's seven lamps reflected off the golden table, the golden altar, and the golden frames along the northern and southern walls. Looking up, the priest would see the ornate tapestry, with cherubim "floating" above him. Similarly, as he looked forward, he would see cherubim floating before him on the veil in front of the Most Holy Place (v. 31). Clearly this is the palace-tent of the King of heaven.

The cherubim are said to be "skillfully worked," a word that might also be rendered "the work of a skilled worker." The underlying Hebrew term refers elsewhere to someone especially gifted to make beautiful designs (31:4). Significantly, this ability is linked to Spirit-filled wisdom and "knowledge" (31:3), which challenges us to realize that the arts are within the sphere of God's direct involvement and that wisdom and knowledge extend to creating beauty (cf. comment on 31:1–11).

26:7–13 A second series of slightly larger curtains is then made, this time of goat's hair, to serve as a "tent" over the tabernacle (v. 7). The first set of curtains seems to

---

[647] For the tabernacle's dimensions cf. comment on 26:15–30. From the south it measures roughly 15 feet (4.6 m) up, across, and down, that is, roughly 45 feet (13.7 m). (I say "roughly" because it is not clear how much height the silver bases add to the tabernacle's frames, though any such additions would be relatively minor; Homan, *To Your Tents*, 178n148, estimates no more than half an inch to an inch [1–2 cm] based on their weight, which is 75 pounds [34 kg] each; cf. comment on 26:15–30 [at v. 19].) This dimension is 3 feet (90 cm) more than the tapestry, leaving a shortage of 1.5 feet (45 cm) on each side. The next covering makes up for this shortage (v. 13). From the west the tabernacle measures roughly 15 feet (4.6 m) up, 45 feet (13.7 m) long, and 15 feet (4.6 m) down, that is, 75 feet (22.9 m), which is 15 feet (4.6 m) more than the tapestry. (I say "roughly" because of the issue of the bases and also because it is not clear how much height and width the corner frames add, though again any such additions would be relatively minor.) If it was not hung to cover the front, which had its own screen, the 60-foot (18.3 m) tapestry would cover the back end and top, leaving the front open. As Keil (*Exodus*, vol. 2, 176–177) notes, this would also mean that the fifty loops and golden clasps—which are at the halfway point of the 60 feet (18.3 m)—would be right over the division between the Most Holy Place (which is 15 feet [4.6 m] square) and the Holy Place (cf. also v. 33).

be simply draped over the frame; the second set then covers the first, with room to spare, and is staked into the ground (cf. 27:19).

In this case there are eleven curtains (vv. 7–8), each measuring 45 feet (13.7 m) by 6 feet (1.8 m). Five are joined into one larger curtain and six into another, each again having fifty loops (vv. 8–11). When the two are joined together—this time with bronze clasps[648]—the tent would measure 66 feet (20 m) by 45 feet (14 m), making it 3 feet (0.9 m) longer than the tapestry on one side and 6 feet (1.8 m) longer on the other, and thus able to cover it fully. If it is placed evenly over the tapestry, it would overhang it by 1.5 feet (45 cm) on each of the long northern and southern sides (v. 13), thus hanging to the ground, and by 3 feet (0.9 m) on each of the eastern and western sides. On the eastern side, at the front, the 3 feet (0.9 m) would hang down from the top and would be doubled up (v. 9); no rationale is given. On the western side, at the back, the 3 feet (0.9 m)—equivalent to the width of half a curtain (v. 12)—is not doubled up but allowed to hang freely off the rear of the tabernacle to the ground.

26:14 Two additional coverings are then made, presumably for added protection, one of tanned rams' skins and one of goatskins. For the materials cf. comment on 25:3–7.

26:15–30 The tabernacle structure is now described. Acacia wood "frames" form walls on the two longer sides (north and south) and the far end (west). The east is left open for the entryway. The frames are overlaid with gold and measure 15 feet (4.6 m) in height and 2.25 feet (0.7 m) in width (vv. 15–16, 29). (Many homes today have ceilings 8–9 feet high [2.4–2.7 m], meaning the tabernacle is just over one and a half times higher.) These frames are traditionally understood to be planks, though a good case has been made that they are instead ladderlike.[649] If so, each frame's sides would be connected with rungs, with the sides themselves functioning like "tenons" inserted into a silver base in which the frame stands upright (v. 19). (In 38:27 we learn each base weighs one talent, that is, about 75 pounds [34 kg]. For the talent's weight cf. note 819 within table 2.10). In short the frames stand next to one another in the bases, forming a three-sided structure made of ladderlike golden walls.

The longer northern and southern sides of the tabernacle each have twenty frames and forty silver bases for a total length of 45 feet (13.7 m) per side (26:18–21). The back has six regular frames and two corner frames (vv. 22–25). The shape of the corner frames is debated due to a lack of detail in the text and questions surrounding the translation of verse 24, but it seems reasonable to conclude they function to reinforce the tabernacle structure. Their effect on the tent's overall width and length is also debated, since their shape is unknown and it is unclear

---

648 Gold (cf. Ex. 26:6) is unnecessary since these will not be visible from within the tabernacle, where only the finest materials may be used—as is fitting for a king.
649 Cf. Propp, *Exodus 19–40*, 411–412. With some adjustments he is following A. R. S. Kenney, "Tabernacle," in *A Dictionary of the Bible*, ed. J. Hastings (Edinburgh: Clark, 1898), 660. If they are frames, that would reduce the size of tree required to make them, since they could consist of many different pieces of wood as opposed to a single plank (cf. the construction of wooden ladders today).

how they are joined to the back and side walls, though many plausibly suggest they would be arranged to maintain either an internal or external symmetry of 15 feet (4.6 m) square for the Most Holy Place and a doubled length of 30 feet (9.1 m) for the Holy Place (cf. note 647 within comment on 26:1–6).

To reinforce the walls acacia wood bars, again covered in gold, are inserted through rings attached to the frames (vv. 26–29), five bars per wall. The reason the middle bar alone is specified as running from end to end is unclear (v. 28). Some suggest the others are attached to rings on the frames while the middle bar is inserted into holes bored through the frames, though such holes would weaken the frames' structural integrity. Possibly the middle bar is simply the longest, running from end to end, with the others shorter but placed to maximize reinforcement (perhaps overlapping in some way), or maybe the middle bar is on the inside of the walls and the others are outside.[650] Whatever the case, the tabernacle's materials and coverings have now been described, and the Lord makes clear they are to be assembled according to what he has revealed to Moses at Mount Sinai (v. 30). This is the Lord's house, and its various parts are to be built (vv. 9, 40) and assembled (v. 30) exactly according to his directions.

26:31–35 On the inside the tabernacle is divided into two rooms. The first is the Holy Place, about 30 feet (9.1 m) long. In this room are the golden table on the right (the north), the golden lampstand on the left (the south), and the golden incense altar between them toward the back of the room (v. 35; 30:6; for the incense altar cf. comment on 30:1–10). At the end of the room is a floor-to-ceiling curtain known as the "veil." Like the tabernacle's first covering, it is made of royal materials and colors, with cherubim woven into it (26:31; cf. v. 1). It hangs on golden hooks on four gold-covered acacia wood pillars positioned under the clasps joining the two large sections of the first covering (vv. 32–33; cf. v. 6).[651] On the other side of the veil is the Most Holy Place, approximately 15 feet (4.6 m) square. It contains the ark of the testimony with its atonement lid (vv. 33b–34) and serves as the Lord's throne room within his royal palace-tent (cf. comment on 25:17–22). The veil thus separates the rooms, its cherubim symbolically standing guard to prevent illicit entry.

26:36–37 At the tent's entrance is a screen. Like the veil, it is made of the same royal colors and materials and hangs from gold-covered acacia wood pillars. But there are also differences. No mention is made of cherubim (Is this to keep the Israelites from seeing figures they might worship?). Instead the screen is to be "embroidered with needlework," perhaps suggesting a rich mosaic of colors. There are also five pillars instead of four. This could be to provide extra support, since the screen forms the exterior front wall of the tent and would be exposed to the wind in a way the interior veil is not. It could also be to ensure that none of the holy furniture could be removed from the tabernacle once it is erected.[652] Or perhaps

---

650 Homan, *To Your Tents*, 150–151, noting Exodus 26:28 might be rendered "And the middle bar *inside* the frames," that is, on the inside of the structure (not the outside).
651 ESV "From the clasps" (26:33) can be translated more woodenly as "under the clasps."
652 For the latter cf. Cassuto, *Commentary on the Book of Exodus*, 361.

it is simply a design feature. There is no way to be certain. As a final note, the pillars' bases are to be bronze instead of silver, likely because they are further from the Lord's throne room. The closer one gets to the place of the Lord's presence, the more costly the materials become, a visual way to signal that one is approaching the person worthy of supreme honor.

27:1–8 Altars link earth to heaven. They are the interface between the Israelites and the Lord, translating their physical offerings into prayers of forgiveness, petition, and worship. As such, they are of fundamental importance. A tabernacle with no functioning altar would be like a body with no heart.

This passage describes the main altar. It stands in the courtyard and goes by two names: the "altar of burnt offering" (30:28; 38:1), likely because the daily burnt offerings would be made there (29:38–42), and the "bronze altar," due to its bronze overlay (38:30; 39:39). Animal offerings could be made only on this altar (the incense altar is for incense only, as its name implies; 30:9). This makes it the centerpiece of Israelite worship, and appropriately it is placed somewhere in front of the tabernacle's entrance (40:6) so Israelites could present their offerings before the Lord.

The altar is a hollow wooden box, overlaid with bronze, measuring 7.5 feet (2.3 m) square and 4.5 feet (1.4 m) high (27:1). Priests likely access it by a ramp so they can more easily build fires and place sacrificial portions on its top (cf. 20:26; Lev. 9:22; 1 Sam. 2:28). On each of its top corners is a projection known as a "horn" (Ex. 27:2). In some sacrificial rites these horns represent the altar; when the priest places the blood on them, he is cleansing the entire altar (Lev. 8:15), as rites done to one part of a person or object can be considered to apply to the entire object or person (cf. Lev. 8:12, 23–24). Exemplars of horned altars have been found at sites such as Dan and Beersheba;[653] the "horns" in such cases are like small, pointed pillars on each of the corners (more like the pointed horns of a baby goat than the long curved horns of a mature goat).

The making of sacrifices calls for various implements (Ex. 27:3). Clearing the altar's ashes requires shovels and pots so they can be scooped up and carried away (cf. Lev. 6:10–11). Sacrificial blood is collected in basins for use in various rites (cf. Ex. 29:20; Lev. 1:5). Forks aid in moving sacrificial meat (cf. 1 Sam. 2:13–14). Fire pans hold live coals for starting fires and can be used as censers to present incense offerings (Lev. 10:1; 16:12). Like the altar, these implements are to be of bronze.

The altar also has a bronze "network" (or "net"). The same word describes nets to catch people or animals (Hos. 7:12), suggesting a crisscross pattern. It has a ring on each of its four corners to hold poles for carrying the altar (Ex. 27:4–7). (The fact that the altar is a hollow box would make carrying it easier; cf. v. 7b with v. 8a.) The network is to be placed under a ledge that goes around the altar, though commentators debate various questions: Where exactly is the altar's ledge? (At the top? Partway down from the top?) Is the network seated horizontally inside the altar, or is it more like a panel around the outside? If outside, does it cover the altar's

---

[653] Sarna, *Exodus*, 172; cf. citations noted there.

bottom half or top half? What function does it serve? (Ornamental? Allowing air flow?[654]) None of this is a mystery to the Israelites, since Moses sees the altar's design on the mountain (v. 8b), and the text emphasizes again the Israelites must follow that design exactly (cf. 25:9, 40; 26:30). Given the altar's centrality to worship, this is no surprise: we must approach God on his terms, not ours.

27:9–19 The tabernacle is surrounded by a series of four walls made of curtains. The walls measure 150 feet (45.7 m) in length on the north and south and 75 feet (22.9 m) in width on the east and west and stand 7.5 feet (2.3 m) high (v. 18), forming a courtyard a quarter of an acre (0.1 hectares) in size. About five courtyards could fit on an American football field and seven on an international soccer field. Since the walls are half the tabernacle's height (cf. 26:16), the tabernacle's top would be visible throughout the camp. The walls' main function is to create a courtyard around the tabernacle and clearly distinguish it from the camp. To enter the courtyard is to enter a space set aside in a special way for drawing near to the Lord for service, worship, and fellowship.

Centered on the eastern wall of curtains is the entrance ("gate"), 30 feet (9.1 m) wide, consisting of the same royal colors and materials as the tabernacle's screen (27:16; cf. 26:36). The remaining walls on the east and on the other three sides are made of fine-twined linen curtains. These hang on pillars of acacia wood, spaced every 7.5 feet (2.3 m), the same measurement as the height of the curtains, which suggests the walls are not a single continuous curtain but a series of square curtains hanging between pillars. The pillars have bronze bases but silver hooks, capitals, and fillets (27:10–17; 38:17), the latter term perhaps describing a type of band that goes around the pillar, either for decoration or to secure the curtains, or both.[655] Unlike the tabernacle's pillars, which are covered in gold and have golden hooks (26:29, 32), only the tops of the courtyard's pillars seem to be covered in metal, this time silver, with silver hooks and fillets (27:10).[656] The contrast underscores again: the closer to the Lord's presence one is, the more costly and precious are the construction materials, a visual way of communicating the honor due this King.

The tabernacle's utensils and pegs are to be of bronze (v. 19). Since the various utensils used within the tabernacle are gold (25:39), those mentioned here are perhaps tools or implements used to set up the tabernacle, while the pegs would be used to secure the tabernacle and the curtained walls to the ground by means of ropes or cords (cf. 35:18; 39:40; Num. 3:37).

The positioning of the tabernacle within the court is nowhere stated. It would make sense if it were further toward the back of the courtyard on the west, providing more room in front to perform the various offerings and sacrifices.[657] Many suggest its entrance would be at the halfway point of the court and that it would be centered between the courtyard's northern and southern walls, in which

---

654 Cf. fuller list in Houtman, *Exodus*, vol. 3, 445–446.
655 Cassuto, *Commentary on the Book of Exodus*, 365.
656 Exodus 27:10 could be more woodenly rendered, "And its twenty pillars, and their twenty bases of bronze"—that is, the bases are of bronze, not the pillars; so also verse 11.
657 Bush, *Commentary on Exodus*, 436.

case the Most Holy Place, and the ark within it, would be perfectly centered in the courtyard's second half.[658] Given the careful symmetry of the sanctuary complex, this suggestion is not unreasonable.

27:20–21 Having mentioned the tools used in setting up the tabernacle (Ex. 27:19), the text now mentions another item necessary once it is up and running: oil for the golden lampstand, which stands in the Holy Place in front of the veil that screens off the ark of the covenant (or "testimony"; cf. 16:34). The oil is to be "pure," that is, either not mixed with other spices (cf. 30:22–25)[659] or free of impurities, or both. It is also to be "beaten," a word used elsewhere to describe oil given by one king to another (1 Kings 5:11) and therefore suggesting a high quality. This is no surprise: this oil is meant for the lamp in the palace of the King of kings. It "was either included among the supplies carried out of Egypt or was acquired in the wilderness from caravanners."[660]

The priests—Aaron and his sons—are responsible for making sure the lamp burns continually throughout the night. Its light represents the Lord's presence within the tent (cf. Response section, "What Do We Learn of the Lord's Desire for Relationship with His People?"); by keeping the lamp burning continually the priests acknowledge the Lord's constant presence and show their continual willingness to serve him.

A final clause notes this is to be a "statute forever,"[661] that is, throughout the Israelite generations (cf. Ex. 12:14; Lev. 17:7). In some contexts "forever"—sometimes translated "everlasting"—can mean "always, as long as time endures" (Gen. 21:33), while in other contexts it means "always, as long as certain conditions endure" (1 Sam. 2:30). In the context of the Mosaic covenant it means this rite is to be practiced as long as that covenant endures. Once the new covenant comes and replaces the Mosaic covenant (Heb. 8:6–13), such rites are no longer required.

Response

As the comments above have shown, the tabernacle and its furniture are not simply functional. They have much to teach about the Lord's character and his ways with his people. Five questions will help identify some of the key lessons taught by this furniture; a sixth question will show how these lessons relate to Jesus.[662]

WHAT DO WE LEARN OF THE LORD'S DESIRE FOR
RELATIONSHIP WITH HIS PEOPLE?

These chapters make clear the Lord's desire for relationship with his people. The King of heaven establishes in the Most Holy Place a throne room on earth, right in his people's midst, that he might live among them in his tent as they live around

---

658 E.g., Sarna, *Exodus*, 174.
659 Cf. also 30:34, where "pure frankincense" is frankincense unmixed with other spices.
660 Sarna, *Exodus*, 175.
661 The clause could also be rendered, "It [i.e., the oil] shall be a perpetual due throughout their generations from the people of Israel."
662 Teachers and preachers might want to cover questions one and two in one session and questions three through five in a second session. The relevant parts of the sixth question would be spread across both sessions.

him in theirs (cf. Ex. 25:18–19; 26:31–35). At this tent they can come "before the LORD" (Lev. 1:3; 3:1; 4:4; etc.), whether to pray for help, ask for forgiveness, or praise him for his goodness and his answers to prayer. Whatever the case, the Lord desires that his people know him and enjoy fellowship with him—so much so that he bridges the distance from heaven to earth to be with them.

The same is seen again in the tabernacle's equipment and furniture. As noted above (Ex. 27:1–8), altars allow Israelites to present their sacrifices and offerings as physical prayers, and, while they cannot enter the tent (cf. below), the altar standing in front is an open invitation from the Lord to draw near to him in worship and prayer. When Israelites do so, they are literally only steps away from his holy throne and are able to come that close because of his invitation. He desires that they know him and have fellowship with him.

These chapters and others also emphasize the continual or regular nature of the rites done with or on the various pieces of furniture. The table is to be laden with food continually (25:30), the lampstand is to burn through the night continually (27:20–21), and the incense on the altar (described in 30:1–10) is to be burned regularly (cf. 30:7–8). As with the ark, this communicates that the Lord is continually present among his people. As Averbeck notes,

> The combination of the daily lighting of the lampstand and associated burning of incense (Lev. 24:3 with Ex. 30:7–8), plus the bread constantly on the table, impresses one with the fact that the Lord had truly taken up residence in the tabernacle. If there is a lamp burning, incense burning, and bread on the table, then someone is "home."[663]

The analogy must not be pressed too far, such as by assuming the Israelites do this in order to feed the Lord or that he is somehow physically present there (or spiritually absent elsewhere). No biblical text indicates that the Israelites view the Lord as needing actual food (cf. Ps. 50:13). It is just the opposite. "That its purpose was display, not consumption, is . . . indicated by the fact that it is replaced weekly, not daily as elsewhere in the ancient Near East."[664] At the same time, the analogy does make clear that this is a God who is near. In fact, he is the King next door![665] He is a King who seeks to have relationship with his people.

WHAT DO WE LEARN OF THE LORD'S ONGOING HELP?

Central to his relationship with his people is the Lord's giving them the help they need. Fellowship with him means receiving care from him. The bread and the lampstand together communicate the Israelites' need of such help and assure them the Lord will provide it. For example, the lampstand is positioned so that it casts its light forward onto the golden table with the bread of the Presence (Num. 8:2–3). The twelve loaves of that bread represent the twelve tribes and their covenant

---

663 Richard E. Averbeck, "Tabernacle," *DOTP*, 815.
664 Jeffrey Tigay, "Exodus," in *The Jewish Study Bible: Jewish Publication Society, Tanakh Translation*, ed. Adele F. Berlin, Marc Z. Brettler, and Michael A. Fishbane (New York: Oxford University Press, 2004), 167.
665 A phrase I first heard from my student Anna Ochoa.

relationship with the Lord (Lev. 24:5–8) and also serve as a request for the Lord to remember his favor toward them (Lev. 24:7). So, not only do the lampstand and the bread speak of the Lord's presence among his people who serve him continually, but they also work together to show how the light of his presence shines on them to assure them of his love and favor. The Hebrew word for "light up" in Numbers 8:2 and Exodus 25:37 is "exactly the same Hebrew word that the priestly blessing used of God's face shining upon his people (6:25)."[666] As a result,

> What we see in Numbers 8:1–4 is a visual metaphor. What the priests declared in the words of their benediction [The Lord make his face shine on you, Num. 6:25] the lampstand of the tabernacle proclaimed as a daily reality: the light of the Lord's blessing rested upon all of the tribes of his people. . . . God's love and acceptance of those who were his was depicted at the very heart of the tabernacle.[667]

WHAT DO WE LEARN OF THE LORD'S COMMANDS?

While this King desires fellowship with his people and promises them his care, he is also a King who commands and guides them (Ex. 25:22). He is the gracious, redeeming King; they are to be his loyal, faithful servants. He is the Father who promises them his care; they are the children who are to be obedient to their Father.

The ark reminds his people that following the Lord's commands is central to their relationship with him. Not only does it contain the covenant tablets (25:16), which he sits over as divine witness (cf. comment on 25:10–16), but it rests in the heart of the Lord's tent (40:2–3; Lev. 16:2). As vows are central to a marriage, the covenant's commands are central to the Israelites' relationship with the Lord. In both OT and NT obedience is not optional for the Lord's followers; it is how they proclaim their faith in him and love for him (John 14:15, 21, 23; James 2:14–26).

The rites done with the furniture in the Holy Place are not occasional or haphazard but regular and continual, showing that the Israelites are to be the Lord's continual servants. This is seen especially in the significance of the bread of the Presence. In Leviticus 24:8 it is called a "covenant," that is, a sign of the covenant between the Lord and Israel (cf. Gen. 17:10–11). Calling the bread of the Presence a "covenant" thus indicates that, just as the Israelites demonstrate their covenant faithfulness by circumcising their sons (Gen. 17:10–11), so they are to do the same by continually placing the bread of the Presence before the Lord. Indeed, since bread is so common at meals, it is an especially appropriate covenant sign, because covenants in the ancient Near East were often sealed by eating a meal. In this case the priests eat the bread on the people's behalf (cf. Ex. 24:9–11), confirming the covenant with the Lord every time they do so. In short the Israelites are the Lord's perpetual and permanent servants who are to fulfill faithfully their covenant obligations to their King.

---

666 Duguid, *Numbers*, 109.
667 Duguid, *Numbers*, 109.

At the same time the covenant commands are not hurdles to jump over or hoops to jump through but loving, wise guidance, as from a father to his children, helping the Israelites to know best how to live. Stated differently, his laws are meant to guide the Israelites in his paths, and his paths are paths of goodness, justice, love, and peace. Following them is meant to be not a burden but a blessing. The psalmist does not miss it: "Your word is a lamp to my feet and a light to my path" (Ps. 119:105).

WHAT DO WE LEARN OF THE LORD'S FORGIVENESS?

But the Lord also knows his people will fail, leading to the fourth aspect of his character on display here: merciful, forgiving love. The atonement lid especially testifies to such love (Ex. 25:17–22). As we learn from Leviticus 16, it features centrally in the Day of Atonement, that one day in Israel's year that assures the people all their sins are cleansed and forgiven. In that day's opening ritual the Israelites' sins are pictured as a defiling substance clinging to the throne of the Lord, against whom they have rebelled. The high priest therefore takes sacrificial blood, the most powerful purifying agent in ancient Israel, and sprinkles it on and before the atonement lid, cleansing away all sin and impurity (vv. 11–16). Yes, sin is rebellion against the Lord, but he is a King who in his love makes a way to deal with our wrongs so that we might be made right with him.

WHAT DO WE LEARN OF THE LORD'S HOLINESS (AND OUR SIN)?

While the Lord provides a way of dealing with his people's sins, which allows them to continue in relationship with him and him to continue to dwell in their midst, something is still missing. In Eden the Lord walked with Adam and Eve in the garden (Gen. 3:8–9). But now a level of separation remains between the Lord and his people. The Israelites can enter the courtyard in front of the tabernacle but not the tabernacle itself. Only ritually holy priests can do that (cf. Num. 18:1–7). But they too face restrictions. Within the tabernacle a curtain separates the first room, the Holy Place, from the second, the Most Holy Place (Ex. 26:31–35), which serves as the Lord's throne room. Only the high priest—the most ritually holy—can go in, and then only once a year (Lev. 16:2, 34).

On the one hand these distinctions underscore for Israelites that the Lord is set apart from them in terms of his moral purity, which shines like the sun in its strength, destroying impurity as light destroys darkness. This is why they may not simply walk into his throne room: as humans, their sin and impurity are so entwined in their lives that the radiance of his holy purity would obliterate them. In this regard the curtain separating the Holy Place from the Most Holy Place reminds us that sin and impurity separate us from God.

On the other hand this separation shows that mankind cannot enjoy fully the type of fellowship for which it has been created. The Lord will need to provide deeper, fuller, stronger way of atonement that can deal with sin and impurity once and for all. This will require a far greater priest or a far greater sacrifice—or both.

HOW DO THESE QUESTIONS RELATE TO JESUS?

Having considered the above five questions in the context of the tabernacle, we can now consider them in the context of who Jesus is and what he came to do. First, in the incarnation God wondrously—shockingly!—bridges the gap between heaven and earth by taking on the flesh of his creation, dwelling among us not in a tent but as the God-man (John 1:14), no longer cordoned off behind a curtain in the Most Holy Place but taking children in his arms to bless them (Mark 10:13–16), placing his hands on the eyes of the blind to give them sight (Matt. 9:27–30), and touching the untouchable lepers to make them whole (Matt. 8:1–3). God's desire to be near us and have relationship with us is so great that he has taken on our flesh to do it.

Second, even though he has returned to the glories of heaven, Jesus promises us his ongoing help and care. In his final words in Matthew's Gospel Jesus not only commands his disciples to bring the glorious good news of his kingdom to all nations but also assures them that they can do so boldly because of his ongoing presence with them: "And behold, I am with you always, to the end of the age" (Matt. 28:20). Having come down to earth to dwell among his people, Jesus does not leave them as orphans after his return to heaven. Through his Holy Spirit his presence remains with his people (John 14:16, 26; 16:7).

Third, Jesus also gives us commands that guide us in the Lord's good and life-giving paths. Just as the Lord is giving instruction from the mountain in these chapters, Matthew's Gospel records how Jesus begins his teaching ministry by going up "on the mountain" (Matt. 5:1) and giving his followers commands that teach them how to embody God's character so that others will "see your good works and give glory to your Father who is in heaven" (Matt. 5:16).

Fourth, in Jesus atonement is made for those who put their trust in him. As noted above (cf. comment on 25:17–22), the word used in the LXX for the atonement lid (*hilastērion*) is the very word Paul uses to describe Jesus and the work he accomplishes with his sacrificial death: "Whom God put forward as a *propitiation* by his blood" (Rom. 3:25). And John beautifully notes the cleansing power of Jesus' blood: "The blood of Jesus . . . cleanses us from all sin. . . . If we confess our sins, he is faithful and just to forgive us our sins and to cleanse us from all unrighteousness" (1 John 1:7, 9).

Finally, in Jesus atonement is full and complete because he is a far greater priest offering a far greater sacrifice. Unlike the sinful Israelite priests, who are continually replaced because they die, Jesus is a high priest without sin who lives forever to make intercession on behalf of those who trust in him (Heb. 5:1–3; 7:23–27). And unlike the Israelites' sacrifices, which have to be offered again and again to make fresh atonement, Jesus' sacrifice of himself is so powerful that no other sacrifice is needed (Heb. 9:24–26). Indeed, when Jesus dies, the curtain separating the Holy Place from the Most Holy Place—the curtain representing our ongoing separation from God because of our sin and impurity—is torn in two (Matt. 27:50–51), a visual symbol that Jesus' sacrifice is so strong and cleanses us so deeply that no separation remains. As a result, we can now have "confidence to enter the holy places by the blood of Jesus, by the new and living way that he opened for us through the curtain" (Heb. 10:19–20).

In short whether through the tabernacle and its furniture or even more fully through Christ, the character that the Lord displays is magnificent. He is eager to be near us and have relationship with us. He continues to watch over and care for us daily. He gives us commands we must obey for our good and his glory. He moves toward us in merciful love and compassion when we fail and joyfully provides a way to be restored to him. Is this how we think of the Lord? In the crush of life we can lose sight of these aspects of who he is. We do well to ask, How should such a view of God and Christ inform how we pray, how we think of his Word and our obedience to it, how we relate to those around us (esp. when they sin against us or him), or how we face our fears and concerns? In Christ God is with us, guides us, forgives us, watches over us. Let us live in the glorious light of those realities.

EXODUS 28–29

28 "Then bring near to you Aaron your brother, and his sons with him, from among the people of Israel, to serve me as priests— Aaron and Aaron's sons, Nadab and Abihu, Eleazar and Ithamar. ² And you shall make holy garments for Aaron your brother, for glory and for beauty. ³ You shall speak to all the skillful, whom I have filled with a spirit of skill, that they make Aaron's garments to consecrate him for my priesthood. ⁴ These are the garments that they shall make: a breastpiece, an ephod, a robe, a coat of checker work, a turban, and a sash. They shall make holy garments for Aaron your brother and his sons to serve me as priests. ⁵ They shall receive gold, blue and purple and scarlet yarns, and fine twined linen.

⁶ "And they shall make the ephod of gold, of blue and purple and scarlet yarns, and of fine twined linen, skillfully worked. ⁷ It shall have two shoulder pieces attached to its two edges, so that it may be joined together. ⁸ And the skillfully woven band on it shall be made like it and be of one piece with it, of gold, blue and purple and scarlet yarns, and fine twined linen. ⁹ You shall take two onyx stones, and engrave on them the names of the sons of Israel, ¹⁰ six of their names on the one stone, and the names of the remaining six on the other stone, in the order of their birth. ¹¹ As a jeweler engraves signets, so shall you engrave the two stones with the names of the sons of Israel. You shall enclose them in settings of gold filigree. ¹² And you shall set the two stones on the shoulder pieces of the ephod, as stones of remembrance for the sons of Israel. And Aaron shall bear their names before the Lord on his two shoulders for remembrance. ¹³ You shall make settings of gold filigree, ¹⁴ and two chains of pure gold, twisted like cords; and you shall attach the corded chains to the settings.

¹⁵ "You shall make a breastpiece of judgment, in skilled work. In the style of the ephod you shall make it—of gold, blue and purple and scarlet

yarns, and fine twined linen shall you make it. ¹⁶ It shall be square and doubled, a span¹ its length and a span its breadth. ¹⁷ You shall set in it four rows of stones. A row of sardius,² topaz, and carbuncle shall be the first row; ¹⁸ and the second row an emerald, a sapphire, and a diamond; ¹⁹ and the third row a jacinth, an agate, and an amethyst; ²⁰ and the fourth row a beryl, an onyx, and a jasper. They shall be set in gold filigree. ²¹ There shall be twelve stones with their names according to the names of the sons of Israel. They shall be like signets, each engraved with its name, for the twelve tribes. ²² You shall make for the breastpiece twisted chains like cords, of pure gold. ²³ And you shall make for the breastpiece two rings of gold, and put the two rings on the two edges of the breastpiece. ²⁴ And you shall put the two cords of gold in the two rings at the edges of the breastpiece. ²⁵ The two ends of the two cords you shall attach to the two settings of filigree, and so attach it in front to the shoulder pieces of the ephod. ²⁶ You shall make two rings of gold, and put them at the two ends of the breastpiece, on its inside edge next to the ephod. ²⁷ And you shall make two rings of gold, and attach them in front to the lower part of the two shoulder pieces of the ephod, at its seam above the skillfully woven band of the ephod. ²⁸ And they shall bind the breastpiece by its rings to the rings of the ephod with a lace of blue, so that it may lie on the skillfully woven band of the ephod, so that the breastpiece shall not come loose from the ephod. ²⁹ So Aaron shall bear the names of the sons of Israel in the breastpiece of judgment on his heart, when he goes into the Holy Place, to bring them to regular remembrance before the LORD. ³⁰ And in the breastpiece of judgment you shall put the Urim and the Thummim, and they shall be on Aaron's heart, when he goes in before the LORD. Thus Aaron shall bear the judgment of the people of Israel on his heart before the LORD regularly.

³¹ "You shall make the robe of the ephod all of blue. ³² It shall have an opening for the head in the middle of it, with a woven binding around the opening, like the opening in a garment,³ so that it may not tear. ³³ On its hem you shall make pomegranates of blue and purple and scarlet yarns, around its hem, with bells of gold between them, ³⁴ a golden bell and a pomegranate, a golden bell and a pomegranate, around the hem of the robe. ³⁵ And it shall be on Aaron when he ministers, and its sound shall be heard when he goes into the Holy Place before the LORD, and when he comes out, so that he does not die.

³⁶ "You shall make a plate of pure gold and engrave on it, like the engraving of a signet, 'Holy to the LORD.' ³⁷ And you shall fasten it on the turban by a cord of blue. It shall be on the front of the turban. ³⁸ It shall be on Aaron's forehead, and Aaron shall bear any guilt from the holy things that the people of Israel consecrate as their holy gifts. It shall regularly be on his forehead, that they may be accepted before the LORD.

³⁹ "You shall weave the coat in checker work of fine linen, and you shall make a turban of fine linen, and you shall make a sash embroidered with needlework.

⁴⁰ "For Aaron's sons you shall make coats and sashes and caps. You shall make them for glory and beauty. ⁴¹ And you shall put them on Aaron your brother, and on his sons with him, and shall anoint them and ordain them and consecrate them, that they may serve me as priests. ⁴² You shall make for them linen undergarments to cover their naked flesh. They shall reach from the hips to the thighs; ⁴³ and they shall be on Aaron and on his sons when they go into the tent of meeting or when they come near the altar

to minister in the Holy Place, lest they bear guilt and die. This shall be a statute forever for him and for his offspring after him.

29 "Now this is what you shall do to them to consecrate them, that they may serve me as priests. Take one bull of the herd and two rams without blemish, ² and unleavened bread, unleavened cakes mixed with oil, and unleavened wafers smeared with oil. You shall make them of fine wheat flour. ³ You shall put them in one basket and bring them in the basket, and bring the bull and the two rams. ⁴ You shall bring Aaron and his sons to the entrance of the tent of meeting and wash them with water. ⁵ Then you shall take the garments, and put on Aaron the coat and the robe of the ephod, and the ephod, and the breastpiece, and gird him with the skillfully woven band of the ephod. ⁶ And you shall set the turban on his head and put the holy crown on the turban. ⁷ You shall take the anointing oil and pour it on his head and anoint him. ⁸ Then you shall bring his sons and put coats on them, ⁹ and you shall gird Aaron and his sons with sashes and bind caps on them. And the priesthood shall be theirs by a statute forever. Thus you shall ordain Aaron and his sons.

¹⁰ "Then you shall bring the bull before the tent of meeting. Aaron and his sons shall lay their hands on the head of the bull. ¹¹ Then you shall kill the bull before the Lord at the entrance of the tent of meeting, ¹² and shall take part of the blood of the bull and put it on the horns of the altar with your finger, and the rest of⁴ the blood you shall pour out at the base of the altar. ¹³ And you shall take all the fat that covers the entrails, and the long lobe of the liver, and the two kidneys with the fat that is on them, and burn them on the altar. ¹⁴ But the flesh of the bull and its skin and its dung you shall burn with fire outside the camp; it is a sin offering.

¹⁵ "Then you shall take one of the rams, and Aaron and his sons shall lay their hands on the head of the ram, ¹⁶ and you shall kill the ram and shall take its blood and throw it against the sides of the altar. ¹⁷ Then you shall cut the ram into pieces, and wash its entrails and its legs, and put them with its pieces and its head, ¹⁸ and burn the whole ram on the altar. It is a burnt offering to the Lord. It is a pleasing aroma, a food offering⁵ to the Lord.

¹⁹ "You shall take the other ram, and Aaron and his sons shall lay their hands on the head of the ram, ²⁰ and you shall kill the ram and take part of its blood and put it on the tip of the right ear of Aaron and on the tips of the right ears of his sons, and on the thumbs of their right hands and on the great toes of their right feet, and throw the rest of the blood against the sides of the altar. ²¹ Then you shall take part of the blood that is on the altar, and of the anointing oil, and sprinkle it on Aaron and his garments, and on his sons and his sons' garments with him. He and his garments shall be holy, and his sons and his sons' garments with him.

²² "You shall also take the fat from the ram and the fat tail and the fat that covers the entrails, and the long lobe of the liver and the two kidneys with the fat that is on them, and the right thigh (for it is a ram of ordination), ²³ and one loaf of bread and one cake of bread made with oil, and one wafer out of the basket of unleavened bread that is before the Lord. ²⁴ You shall put all these on the palms of Aaron and on the palms of his sons, and wave them for a wave offering before the Lord. ²⁵ Then you shall take them from their hands and burn them on the altar on top of the burnt offering, as a pleasing aroma before the Lord. It is a food offering to the Lord.

26 "You shall take the breast of the ram of Aaron's ordination and wave it for a wave offering before the Lord, and it shall be your portion. 27 And you shall consecrate the breast of the wave offering that is waved and the thigh of the priests' portion that is contributed from the ram of ordination, from what was Aaron's and his sons'. 28 It shall be for Aaron and his sons as a perpetual due from the people of Israel, for it is a contribution. It shall be a contribution from the people of Israel from their peace offerings, their contribution to the Lord.

29 "The holy garments of Aaron shall be for his sons after him; they shall be anointed in them and ordained in them. 30 The son who succeeds him as priest, who comes into the tent of meeting to minister in the Holy Place, shall wear them seven days.

31 "You shall take the ram of ordination and boil its flesh in a holy place. 32 And Aaron and his sons shall eat the flesh of the ram and the bread that is in the basket in the entrance of the tent of meeting. 33 They shall eat those things with which atonement was made at their ordination and consecration, but an outsider shall not eat of them, because they are holy. 34 And if any of the flesh for the ordination or of the bread remain until the morning, then you shall burn the remainder with fire. It shall not be eaten, because it is holy.

35 "Thus you shall do to Aaron and to his sons, according to all that I have commanded you. Through seven days shall you ordain them, 36 and every day you shall offer a bull as a sin offering for atonement. Also you shall purify the altar, when you make atonement for it, and shall anoint it to consecrate it. 37 Seven days you shall make atonement for the altar and consecrate it, and the altar shall be most holy. Whatever touches the altar shall become holy.

38 "Now this is what you shall offer on the altar: two lambs a year old day by day regularly. 39 One lamb you shall offer in the morning, and the other lamb you shall offer at twilight. 40 And with the first lamb a tenth measure[6] of fine flour mingled with a fourth of a hin[7] of beaten oil, and a fourth of a hin of wine for a drink offering. 41 The other lamb you shall offer at twilight, and shall offer with it a grain offering and its drink offering, as in the morning, for a pleasing aroma, a food offering to the Lord. 42 It shall be a regular burnt offering throughout your generations at the entrance of the tent of meeting before the Lord, where I will meet with you, to speak to you there. 43 There I will meet with the people of Israel, and it shall be sanctified by my glory. 44 I will consecrate the tent of meeting and the altar. Aaron also and his sons I will consecrate to serve me as priests. 45 I will dwell among the people of Israel and will be their God. 46 And they shall know that I am the Lord their God, who brought them out of the land of Egypt that I might dwell among them. I am the Lord their God.

[1] A *span* was about 9 inches or 22 centimeters [2] The identity of some of these stones is uncertain [3] The meaning of the Hebrew word is uncertain; possibly *coat of mail* [4] Hebrew *all* [5] Or *an offering by fire*; also verses 25, 41 [6] Possibly an ephah (about 3/5 bushel or 22 liters) [7] A *hin* was about 4 quarts or 3.5 liters

Section Overview

The last three chapters have described the tabernacle (25:10–27:21); the next two describe what is necessary for priests to work there (28:1–29:42) and remind us of its purpose (29:43–46).

First, chapter 28 identifies the priestly family who will serve in the tabernacle and describes their special uniforms (vv. 1–43). The chapter focuses on the high priest's uniform, which consists of eight articles, many costly and ornate (vv. 5–39). Briefer attention is paid to the regular priests' uniforms (v. 40), which comprise only four articles and are less elaborate. These differences testify to the differences in function and authority between the high priest and regular priests.

Chapter 29 begins by describing the ordination rites necessary to make the family of priests ritually holy so they can work in the tabernacle (vv. 1–35). It describes an elaborate ceremony and includes materials to be gathered (vv. 1–3), clothing to be worn (vv. 4–9), and sacrifices to be offered (vv. 10–35). The altar of burnt offering is also made holy and prepared for the priests' daily service (vv. 36–42).

The chapter finishes by reminding readers why all this is necessary: the holy, redeeming God wants to come and live in the midst of the people he has rescued (vv. 43–46). The Lord always redeems for the sake of relationship.

Section Outline

VI. Israel at Sinai: the Lord gives instructions for the building of his palace-tent among them (24:12–31:18) . . .
    D. The priests' garments (28:1–43)
        1. The priestly family, their priestly garments, and the garments' makers (28:1–4)
        2. The high priest's uniform (28:5–39)
        3. The regular priests' uniforms: coats and sashes and caps (28:40)
        4. The function of the priestly uniforms (28:41)
        5. The linen undergarments (28:42–43)
    E. The ordination ceremony for the priests (29:1–35)
        1. Title (29:1a)
        2. Gathering the necessary materials (29:1b–3)
        3. The ordination ceremony (29:4–35)
    F. The altar of burnt offering and its offerings (29:36–42)
        1. The altar's purification and consecration (29:36–37)
        2. The altar's daily burnt offerings (29:38–42)
    G. The tent's purpose (29:43–46)
        1. The Lord will meet with Israel (29:43a)
        2. The Lord will sanctify the tent and everything connected to it (29:43b–44)
        3. The Lord will dwell in their midst and be their God (29:45)
        4. Israel will know the Lord redeemed them for relationship with him (29:46)

Comment

28:1–4 Although all the Israelites are to be the Lord's servants, he sets aside one family to serve him as priests at his tabernacle: Aaron and his four sons (v. 1).

Others from the tribe of Levi can help transport and guard the tabernacle (Num. 3:5–4:49), but only Aaron's family may serve as priests, a point the text emphasizes three times (Ex. 28:1, 3, 4).

This chapter describes the special uniforms that distinguish the priests. The introductory verses make five general points. First, the garments are ritually holy (28:2, 4). Just as a surgeon needs sterilized clothing in order to work in a sterile operating room, the priests need ritually holy clothing in order to work in the ritually holy tabernacle. The clothing must be appropriate for the space.

Second, just as putting on a wedding ring helps moves a groom into the married state, donning the appropriate clothing helps move a priest into a ritually holy state: these are "garments *to consecrate him* for my priesthood" (v. 3).

Third, the garments will be for "glory and for beauty" (28:2, 40). These two words are in many cases translated "honor" since the type of glory or beauty in mind marks its bearer as worthy of honor and respect.[668] The idea is that the garments will help set apart Aaron and the priests as the Lord's special servants, who are thus to be shown honor and dignity by the Israelites. As the chapter goes on to explain, the priests' uniforms will be made of the same sorts of material as the tabernacle itself, and the high priest's uniform in particular will match the tabernacle's design. Just as the Israelites are to respect the Lord's tabernacle, so too should they respect his servants who are dressed like his tabernacle and serve in his courts.

Fourth, just as the tabernacle's ornate features require special skill to make (31:1–11), so will the priests' garments, which will be made by those whom the Lord has "filled with a spirit of skill" (28:3; cf. 35:10).

Finally, the high priest's garments will consist of several distinct pieces: "A breastpiece, an ephod, a robe, a coat of checker work, a turban, and a sash" (28:4). (Undergarments are not mentioned here but assumed, cf. vv. 42–43; the golden crown is also assumed as belonging with the turban, cf. vv. 36–37.) Most of the chapter will focus on describing each piece in detail.

28:5–14 Artists' renditions of the priests' garments are easily found online. Comparing them shows that, just as various aspects of the tabernacle are debated, so also are the priests' garments. (The text sometimes lacks clarifying detail unnecessary for the original audience, who understood its technical language and had Moses to guide them if questions remained.) Areas of debate will be noted in the comments that follow.

The priests' garments will be made with the same materials already gathered and used in the tabernacle: "Gold, blue and purple and scarlet yarns, and fine twined linen" (v. 5; cf. 25:3–4, 11; 26:1). As such, the priests' garments match the holiness of the tabernacle. As chapter 29 makes clear, the pieces of his uniform are to be put on in the following order: undergarments, coat, sash, robe, ephod, breastpiece, turban, golden crown (vv. 5–6). In this chapter, however, the list begins with the ephod and the breastpiece, testifying to their importance. As discussed

---

[668] For "glory" (Hb. *kabod*) cf. Genesis 45:13; Numbers 24:11; 1 Samuel 2:8. For "beauty" (*tiferet*) cf. Deuteronomy 26:19; Judges 4:9; Isaiah 4:2.

below, the Lord gives the breastpiece for making his will clear to the Israelites. And, since the breastpiece is attached to the ephod, the ephod is described first.

The ephod is an ornate vest made of the same royal materials as the tabernacle's first covering and curtains: a combination of fine twined linen and colorful yarns (28:6; cf. at 25:4 and 26:1, 31, 36; for "skillfully worked" cf. comment on 26:1–6). Gold threads woven into it (39:3) further enhance its beauty and value. A later passage notes how the gold threads are woven throughout, perhaps giving the garment a golden sheen (39:3).[669] Its shape is debated. While some commentators believe it to cover the torso,[670] many see it more as an apron covering the waist.[671] They also debate how the shoulder pieces join it together and to which part of the ephod they are attached.[672] It seems clear that it ties around the body with a band of cloth attached to the ephod and made of the same material (28:8).

Each shoulder piece bears an onyx stone enclosed in "settings of gold filigree"—that is, artistic gold settings—and engraved with the names of the Israelite tribes in their birth order (vv. 9–11), six on one stone (Reuben, Simeon, Levi, Judah, Dan, Naphtali) and six on the other (Gad, Asher, Issachar, Zebulun, Joseph, Benjamin). Aaron will bear these stones on his shoulders when he goes in before the Lord for the sake of "remembrance," a word repeated to underscore the stones' purpose (v. 12).

The language of "remembrance" does not mean the Lord might forget his people—an impossible act for him (cf. Isa. 49:15–16)! Rather, such language refers to the Lord's showing his people that they are in the forefront of his thoughts, which he does by granting them favor (Gen. 8:1; 19:29) and by being faithful to his covenant promises (Gen. 9:15, 16; Ex. 2:24). As Palmer beautifully summarizes, "To evoke Yahweh's remembrance is to call upon his blessing, provision, and care."[673] The high priest evokes such remembrance every time he wears his uniform into the tabernacle. He is a visual, walking prayer, bringing the Israelites by name before the Lord and asking him to bless them, provide for them, and care for them. Moreover, by bearing their names on his shoulders, he shows he does his priestly work as their representative. "It is as if all Israel is brought before the presence of Yahweh to participate in ritual service through the sacral apparel of the man who embodies their worship."[674] In short the stones are a request that the Lord show his favor on his faithful worshipers.[675]

The ephod's description concludes by noting that two chains of pure gold, ropelike in appearance, are attached to the stones' settings (28:13–14). These will be connected to the breastpiece, which is now described.

---

669 Christine Palmer, "Israelite High Priestly Apparel: Embodying an Identity between Human and Divine," in *Fashioned Selves: Dress and Identity in Antiquity*, ed. Megan Cifarelli (Havertown, PA: Oxbow Books, 2019), 122. Woodenly translated 39:3 might read, "And they hammered out gold leaf, and he cut it into threads to work into the midst of the blue and into the midst of the purple and into the midst of the scarlet yarns, and into the midst of the fine twined linen, in skilled design." The repetition of "into the midst of" makes clear the golden threads are everywhere throughout the fabric.
670 Stuart, *Exodus*, 606; Alexander, *Exodus*, TTC, 160.
671 E.g., Cassuto, *Commentary on the Book of Exodus*, 373; Houtman, *Exodus*, vol. 3, 485–487; Milgrom, *Leviticus 1–16*, 506; Wells, *Exodus*, 253.
672 Cf. Propp, *Exodus 19–40*, 435–436.
673 Palmer, "Israelite High Priestly Apparel," 122.
674 Palmer, "Israelite High Priestly Apparel," 122.
675 Cf. Numbers 10:10; 2 Kings 20:3; Nehemiah 13:14.

28:15–30 The breastpiece is a square pouch when doubled and made of the same material as the ephod (v. 15; cf. v. 6). Its length and breadth is a "span" (v. 16), a measurement nowhere specified. One text makes clear it is less than a cubit (cf. 1 Sam. 17:4), and another compares it to a measurement made with the hand (Isa. 40:12); most commentators therefore assume it to be about half a cubit, that is, 9 inches (23 cm; cf. note 625 within comment on 25:10–16 for the cubit). The breastpiece features twelve stones, set in four rows of three, each bearing the name of an Israelite tribe (Ex. 28:17–21).[676] Commentators debate the identity of many of the stones but agree they are precious, which again speaks to the ornate and royal character of the high priest's uniform.[677]

The breastpiece attaches firmly to the ephod by golden chains and blue cords (vv. 22–28). While debate surrounds the details, the breastpiece features four golden rings. Two attach to the golden settings of the shoulder pieces via the rope-like chains of gold mentioned in verse 14, and two attach via blue cords to two other golden rings on the ephod somewhere below the golden shoulder settings. As a result, the breastpiece will "not come loose from the ephod" (v. 28), which is important given its twofold function.

First, like the stones of remembrance on the shoulder pieces, the breastpiece stones are to "bring [the Israelites] to regular remembrance before the LORD" (v. 29), asking him to bless and care for his people (cf. v. 12). The stones are compared to "signets" (v. 21), that is, the stamp signet seals used in the ancient Near East to represent the owner when sealing important documents with wax or clay.[678] Thus the inscribed stones communicate that the high priest is representing Israel in all he does. He seeks favor and blessing for Israel's tribes as he performs his duties and brings their names for "remembrance" before the Lord.

Second, this remembrance is linked in its function as a "breastpiece of judgment" (vv. 29–30) by which the high priest can ask the Lord on Israel's behalf to make his judgment or decision about a certain matter clear. ("Breastpiece of decision" is in fact another possible translation of the phrase; cf. note 679) The "Urim and Thummim" used for this are apparently a system of lots by which the Lord's guidance on various matters may be sought; for example, "Is it time to break camp and move on?" (cf. Num. 27:21), or "Is this person guilty of a certain wrong that has been done?" (cf. 1 Sam. 14:41–42).[679]

Together the breastpiece's two functions serve as a way for the high priest wearing it to pray during his priestly duties: "Just as the Israelites are on my heart and in my thoughts, O Lord, may they be on your heart and in your thoughts![680] May

---

676 If the birth order in Exodus 28:10 is in mind (cf. there for details), the stones may be listed in accordance with that order, so that "Reuben" is inscribed on the sardius stone, "Simeon" on the topaz stone, and so on.
677 Cf. Ezekiel 28:11–13, which describes a king whose covering consists of nine stones listed here and describes them as "precious." Given the stones' precious and royal nature, it is no surprise that at least eight are listed in Revelation 21:19–20 as foundation stones in the walls of the heavenly city.
678 For details cf. Christine Palmer, "High Priestly Dress in Ancient Israel" (PhD diss., Hebrew Union College–Jewish Institute of Religion, 2016), 142–146.
679 Cf. Proverbs 16:33: "The lot is cast into the lap, but its every decision is from the LORD." The word translated "decision" here is the same word translated "judgment" in Exodus 28:29–30.
680 See the use of the phrase "on the heart" in Isaiah 46:8; 65:17; Jeremiah 3:16 (often translated "to mind" or "into mind").

you bless them, provide for them, care for them, and would you do this especially as they seek your guidance and will!"

28:31–35 The ephod is to be worn over a robe of woven blue material with a woven binding around the neck so it cannot be torn (Ex. 28:31–32). In Israel tearing one's garment is a visible sign of mourning (Gen. 37:34; 2 Sam. 1:11), comparable to wearing black in many societies today. The high priest is forbidden from performing such mourning rituals (Lev. 21:10). In Israel mourning rites and ritual impurity go together (Lev. 21:1, 3, 4), perhaps because such rites are done near corpses, which are ritually defiling. Moreover, the Lord has set the high priest apart into the most holy of states through anointing (cf. Ex. 29:7). That anointing marks him as belonging to the Lord in the same way a wedding ring marks one person as belonging to another. For him to defile his ritually holy status would be comparable to the disrespect one would show by stomping one's wedding ring into the ground.

The robe's hem is decorated with alternating pomegranates and golden bells (28:33–34). The pomegranates are made of the same blue, purple and scarlet yarns as the ephod, underscoring the costly and royal nature of the high priest's uniform and increasing its beauty. As for the golden bells, their sound is perhaps a respectful way for Aaron to "clock in" and "clock out" of his priestly duties (v. 35). To change the metaphor, just as we show respect by knocking before entering a home and saying "goodbye" when we leave, the golden bells sound as Aaron enters and leaves the Lord's home.[681] Of course, the Lord is fully aware of when Aaron comes and goes, but the bells remind Aaron himself to show the necessary respect to the Lord—and thus avoid the lethal consequences of failing to do so (v. 35).

28:36–38 On his head the high priest wears a fine linen "turban" (vv. 37, 39), a term built on a root suggesting it to be a headwrap of some sort (the root is *tsanaf*, which means to wind, roll, or "whirl" in Isa. 22:18). In one text it is parallel to a standard word for "crown" (Ezek. 21:26), suggesting it has royal overtones. Attached to the front of the turban by a blue cord is a "plate of pure gold" (Ex. 28:36), also referred to as a "crown" (29:6; 39:30), another word with royal overtones (2 Sam. 1:10; 2 Kings 11:12). Clearly the high priest is the most exalted of the Lord's royal servants.

The plate is inscribed with the words "Holy to the LORD." This phrase refers elsewhere to a person, property, day, or festival set apart as belonging to the Lord in a special way (Ex. 12:14; 13:12; 31:15; Lev. 27:14, 21). In this case the high priest is stamped, as it were, as the Lord's special property. And because he wears this plate as Israel's representative Israel as a whole is identified as belonging to the Lord in a special way. Indeed, the plate's phrase—"holy *to the Lord*"—recalls Exodus 19:5, where the Lord says of Israel, "You shall be *to me* a treasured possession among all peoples" (AT).

At the same time our text focuses on a different function of the plate. By wearing it "Aaron shall bear any guilt from the holy things that the people of Israel

---

[681] Similarly Bush, *Commentary on Exodus*, 463; Cassuto, *Commentary on the Book of Exodus*, 383; Stuart, *Exodus*, 614.

consecrate as their holy gifts ... that they[682] may be accepted before the LORD" (28:38). Several of these words and phrases require comment. The word translated "accepted" could also be translated "favorably accepted." It refers to the Lord's being well pleased with the offerer and offering, as made clear from passages that compare these words to the Lord's pleasure or that contrast them with his displeasure (cf. Pss. 30:5; 51:16–17; Jer. 14:10–12; Hos. 8:13). In sacrificial contexts offerers can be assured of the Lord's favor if they present their offerings properly and with a sincere heart of faith. The "holy things" include various sacrifices and food offerings the Israelites might present to the Lord (Num. 18:8–19).

But what if the sacrificial animal has some blemish unknown to the offerer, or another unknown problem occurs with the offering? Normally it would be disqualified and the favorable acceptance the offerer desired would be denied, much as an expired ticket denies entry into an event (cf. Lev. 22:18–20). To avoid this the "holy to the LORD" plate allows the priest to "bear any guilt from the holy things," that is, to bear it away and make it null and void (cf. Lev. 16:21–22).[683] Exactly how the plate achieved this is not explained. Is its phrase a way to say that the Israelites intended to present holy gifts and that therefore they should be treated as such? Or is the high priest's holiness a substitute for any lack of holiness in the gifts? We do not know. What is clear is that the sacrifice or offering will still count so that the Israelites will receive the Lord's favorable acceptance. This will take place because of the high priest's intercessory role.

28:39 One of the first garments the high priest puts on is a fine linen checkered[684] coat (or "tunic"). This garment would cover the body sufficiently (cf. Gen. 3:21; the regular priests wear similar coats as their main clothing, Ex. 28:40). A linen sash is tied around it at the waist (cf. Lev. 8:7). It is beautifully embroidered with the costly blue, purple, and scarlet yarns used for other pieces of the high priest's uniform and the tabernacle fabrics (Ex. 39:29). For the turban cf. comment on 28:36–38.

28:40 The text now turns to the regular priests' uniforms. Like the high priest, they also wear linen coats and sashes and some form of headdress ("caps"; cf. Lev. 8:13), and, like the high priest, their garments are "for glory and beauty" (or "glory and honor"), setting them apart as the Lord's special servants and therefore to be shown honor and dignity by the Israelites (cf. comment on 28:1–4). But, unlike the high priest, they have no ephod, breastpiece, or robe, and their headdress (a "cap" instead of a "turban") has no golden plate. Their simpler uniforms still identify them as priests while also marking their lower rank, much as a regular soldier's simpler uniform makes clear he holds a lower rank than the more elaborately dressed general.

28:41 A marriage ceremony usually involves rituals that, when taken together, transition a person from one state (singleness) to another (marriage). Similarly,

---

[682] That is, the Israelites. But even if this refers to the gifts, the endpoint is the same, since Israel's acceptance depends on their offerings' being acceptable (Lev. 22:18–20).
[683] Cf. fuller discussion in Jay Sklar, *Sin, Impurity, Sacrifice, Atonement: The Priestly Conceptions* (Sheffield, UK: Sheffield Phoenix Press, 2005), 88–99, esp. 98–99.
[684] The word's meaning is debated. If "checkered" is the sense, it might refer to the type of weave as opposed to a variation of color (cf. 39:27).

Aaron and his sons will go through an ordination ceremony with rituals that, when taken together, will transfer them from one state (lay Israelites) to another (ritually holy priests). The ceremony is described in the next chapter and carried out in Leviticus 8, but the main sequence is summarized here: they are first clothed in priestly garb (as bride and groom are clothed in wedding attire), then anointed with holy oil, and then ordained over a seven-day period, at the end of which they are ritually holy and may serve as priests (cf. ch. 29 for details). The point made here is that their clothing is a foundational part of this process.

28:42–43 The clothing put on first—the undergarments—are saved for last, perhaps because they are hidden and are not "for glory and for beauty," as the other garments are (cf. v. 40).[685] Still, the undergarments are important for covering the priests' nakedness and thus protecting them from fatally exposing themselves before the Lord. (Cf. comment on 20:22–26, where it is suggested that exposing oneself in worship, even accidentally, is an insult to the Lord.[686])

29:1–3 Having described the ordination clothing of Aaron and his sons, the text now describes the ordination ceremony.[687] It begins with its purpose: to set Aaron and his sons into a ritually holy state so that they might serve the Lord as priests (v. 1a). It then identifies the appropriate materials to gather: a bull and two rams for sacrifices and various unleavened breads to be offered on the altar as well as eaten (vv. 1b–3).[688] These will be taken to the "entrance of the tent of meeting" (v. 4), that is, to the area in front of the tent's entryway (cf. note 618 within the Response section on 24:12–25:9). This ensures the ceremony will take place before the Lord.

29:4–9 Attention now turns to Aaron and his sons, who are also to be at the tent's entrance. The ceremony's purpose is to move Aaron and his sons into the highest state of ritual purity: holiness. Therefore the first step will be for them to go through a rite frequently associated with ritual purification: washing with water (29:4; cf. 30:18–21; Lev. 14:9; 15:5–8, etc.).

Next they are to be dressed in their priestly uniforms. In the ancient Near East special clothing indicated that a person had entered into a specific state (such as mourning; 2 Sam. 14:2) or had a specific role (such as a ruler; Gen. 41:42). The same is true today, as with a soldier's uniform, a bride's wedding dress, or a mourner's black clothing. The priests' special clothing therefore identifies them as being set apart by the Lord into a specific state (ritual holiness) in order to carry out a specific role (to approach his holy altar and minister in his holy tabernacle; Ex. 28:3, 40–43; 39:41). As noted above, it also signals to the Israelites the dignity and honor due to those who bear such a weighty responsibility (Ex. 28:2; cf. 1 Tim. 5:17).

---

685 Keil, *Exodus*, vol. 2, 205.
686 Cf. Stuart, *Exodus*, 473; other texts also associate public nakedness with shame or disgrace (Isa. 47:3; Jer. 13:26; Nah. 3:5).
687 Exodus 29 describes the ordination ceremony that is to take place for Aaron and his sons. Leviticus 8 narrates the actual ceremony. Since Leviticus 8 repeats much of what is stated here, and I have written on that chapter elsewhere (Sklar, *Leviticus*, TOTC, 141–149), the following comments are an edited version of my earlier ones.
688 For reasons nowhere explained leavened breads cannot be offered on the altar (Lev. 2:11). For further discussion cf. Sklar, *Leviticus*, TOTC, 99.

The high priest is to be dressed first (Ex. 29:5–6; cf. 28:5–39 for description of the clothing). He will then be anointed on the head with "anointing oil" (29:7), which consists of olive oil and spices (30:23–25). It is made for tabernacle use and thus especially holy; whatever it touches becomes consecrated (set apart as ritually holy; 30:25–30). By pouring it on Aaron's head Moses will both consecrate him for the ordination ceremony and set him apart as the priests' leader (Lev. 21:10; cf. 1 Sam. 10:1).

The text then briefly describes how the regular priests are to be dressed (Ex. 29:8–9)[689] and highlights again the clothing's function: to set apart Aaron and his family as the Lord's priests (v. 9). Everything will now be in place to offer the ordination ceremony's three main sacrifices: the purification offering (vv. 10–14), the burnt offering (vv. 15–18), and the ordination offering (vv. 19–28; as noted below, this is a type of peace offering).

29:10–14 The first offering to be presented is the sin offering, called by many commentators the "purification offering," a term I will use here.[690] This offering normally precedes burnt or peace offerings (cf. Lev. 8:14 and 8:18; Lev. 9:8 and 9:12; etc.). The order is logical, since cleansing sin and impurity (purification offering) naturally precedes expressions of general worship or atonement (burnt offering) or expressions of covenant fellowship (peace offering/ordination offering).

The sacrificial procedure here generally follows the description of the high priestly purification offering in Leviticus 4:3–12. First, Aaron and his sons are to "lay their hands on the head of the bull" (Ex. 29:10), indicating that it is being sacrificed on their behalf (cf. Lev. 1:4). Priests are as sinful and impure as other Israelites and equally in need of atonement (cf. Heb. 5:1–3). After slaughtering the bull Moses will perform a special blood rite (Ex. 29:11–12). Sin and impurity defile the Lord's dwelling place (cf. Lev. 16:16, 19). As Ndjerareou notes, "People's sins pollute their surroundings, and so it was not just the people who needed this annual rite of atonement, but also any objects connected with them."[691] Moses will therefore take the sacrificial blood, the most powerful cleansing agent available (cf. Lev. 16:19), and go to the burnt-offering altar (which perhaps represents the tabernacle as a whole). He will place some of the blood on the altar's horns, thus purifying it (cf. Lev. 4:5–7) and perhaps the entire tabernacle as well. He will pour out the rest at the altar's base, perhaps as a means of proper disposal. Next, all the animal's fat portions are to be burned on the altar (Ex. 29:13). While many moderns look negatively at fat, it represents the best portion and is therefore to be given totally to the Lord, the one worthy of our highest honor and praise (Lev. 3:16–17).[692] The remaining portions are to be burned outside the camp (Ex. 29:14). While priests would normally eat portions of the people's purification offerings

---

[689] The phrase "And bind caps on them" (Ex. 29:9) refers to the regular priests; Aaron and his sons all wear sashes, but Aaron wears a "turban" (28:39) while his sons wear "caps" (28:40).
[690] Cf. Sklar, *Leviticus*, TOTC, 111.
[691] Ndjerareou, *Exodus*, in *Africa Bible Commentary*, 124. Similarly, Alexander (*Exodus*, ApOTC, 599) notes that "humans, due to their sinfulness, are a source of defilement."
[692] Cf. 1 Samuel 2:15; Israelites used the word "fat" to describe the very best of something, such as the "finest [Hb. fat] of the wheat" (Ps. 147:14; cf. Gen. 45:18).

(Lev. 6:24–30), they are forbidden from eating their own, perhaps because it is inappropriate for them to benefit from their own sin.

29:15–18 Moses will next present a burnt offering for Aaron and his sons. A burnt offering is the only offering entirely burned on the altar and thus the most costly. It can atone for the offerers' general sinfulness (Lev. 1:4) and serve as a way for them to acknowledge the Lord as the one worthy of all praise (Ps. 66:13–20). It may functioned in both ways here, and its overall goal is clear: to be a "pleasing aroma . . . to the LORD," that is, for the Lord to be pleased with the offerer and favorably accept the smoke as representing a legitimate sacrifice presented with heartfelt worship (cf. Gen. 8:21; Ezek. 20:41; for further details on the burnt offering cf. Lev. 1:3–9).[693]

29:19–28 The ordination offering is a type of peace offering, as suggested by their many similarities: the blood is thrown "against the sides of the altar" (Ex. 29:20; cf. Lev. 3:2); the fat is burned on the altar (Ex. 29:25; cf. Lev. 3:3–5); most of the meat is split between the officiant (Moses) and the offerers, the priests (Ex. 29:26–28, 31–33; cf. Lev. 7:15–21, 29–34); and any meat not consumed within a certain time must be burned up (Ex. 29:34; cf. Lev. 7:15–18).

To offer a type of peace offering is appropriate, for peace offerings serve as meals that confirm a covenant (cf. comments on 24:3–8; 24:9–11), and the priesthood is a covenantal promise to Aaron and his sons (Num. 18:19; 25:13; cf. Jer. 33:21; Mal. 2:4). In short, after making atonement for their sin and impurity (purification offering, burnt offering) and acknowledging the Lord as the one worthy of all praise (burnt offering) the priests will now confirm the covenant of priesthood that the Lord is bestowing on them (ordination offering/peace offering).

29:19–21 After the hand-laying rite and bull slaughtering, Moses will again perform a special blood rite. Just as blood is placed on the extremities of the altar to make it holy (Ex. 29:12), it will also be placed on the extremities of Aaron and his sons—from top to bottom—to make the whole of their bodies holy (v. 20; cf. comment on 29:10–14). The blood will be placed on their extremities on the right, the favored side (cf. Gen. 48:13–20; 1 Sam. 11:2).

After throwing the rest of the blood against the altar, Moses will take some of it and the anointing oil for another ritual.[694] These liquids are used also for cleansing and consecration (cf. Ex. 29:7, 12). Up to this point the oil will have been put on Aaron (v. 7) and the blood on Aaron and his sons (v. 20). Now Moses will take both liquids and sprinkle Aaron, his sons, and their garments, making them all holy (v. 21). In context this means not making them holy for the first time (cf. vv. 7, 20) but deepening their holiness, much like a second coat of paint deepens the color of the first.

---

693 "Food offering" could also be translated "offering by fire" (ESV mg.; details in Sklar, *Leviticus*, ZECOT, 94). Even if "food offering" is retained, Psalm 50:13 shows that this term should be understood as a metaphor, since the Lord is a spirit and has no need of actual food.
694 The sequence in Leviticus 8 differs here. Exodus 29 may be arranged topically (keeping all the anointing actions together) and Leviticus 8 temporally.

29:22–25 Next Moses will perform a wave offering. Waving an item before the Lord appears to be a way of dedicating it to him (cf. Num. 8:15–16). Moses will do this on the priests' behalf, using some of the animal's best portions: the fat (cf. Ex. 29:13) and the right thigh (cf. 1 Sam. 9:24).[695] He will also present various unleavened breads made of the finest flour (cf. Ex. 29:2). In this way the priests will be dedicating the very best to the Lord and thereby acknowledging his greatness. For verse 25 cf. comment on 29:15–18.

29:26–28 Moses will receive the breast of the offering, perhaps because he is part of the priestly family (cf. Lev. 7:31) or because a portion normally goes to the supervising priest (his role here; cf. Lev. 7:32). Either way, he will present it as a wave offering according to the Lord's command (Ex. 29:26; cf. Lev. 7:29–30). By setting apart as holy the right thigh and the breast in this ordination offering (which, as noted above, is a type of peace offering; cf. comment on 29:19–28) a model has now been set for Israelites to bring a peace offering: the right thigh and the breast will be set apart as holy to the Lord, who will in turn assign it to his priests, his holy servants (vv. 27–28; cf. Lev. 7:28–36, esp. vv. 34–36).

29:29–30 A brief aside now explains that the high priesthood is to pass to Aaron's descendants. Presumably it will pass to the eldest surviving son (cf. Num. 20:26–28), who will don the high priestly uniform, be anointed with oil on the head, and then go through a seven-day ordination ceremony.

29:31–34 The text now turns to the ram of the ordination offering. Its meat is to be prepared in a holy place and then eaten, along with any remaining breads, by Aaron and his sons at the entrance to the tent of meeting, that is, the area of the courtyard in front of the tent (Ex. 29:31–32). The idea is straightforward: holy meat must be eaten by holy people in a holy place. This also explains why an "outsider"—that is, a layman, outside the priestly family (cf. Num. 16:40)—may not eat it, since lay Israelites are not ritually holy (Ex. 29:33; cf. Lev. 22:10). The food's holiness might also explain why any that is left over must be burned, which would reduce the risk of its being somehow defiled (Ex. 29:34; cf. 12:10).

29:35 A summary verse makes clear that the above procedures—presumably the sacrifices in particular—are to be repeated every day for seven days (cf. v. 36; Lev. 8:31–35). Seven days represents a full amount of time (cf. comment on 1:1–5), meaning that the consecration is thorough and complete.

29:36–42 The ordination ceremony will bring not only Aaron's family into a holy state but the altar of burnt offering as well (v. 36).[696] For seven days the purification offering will cleanse the altar of sin and impurity, and the anointing oil will

---

[695] Priests normally receive the right thigh of fellowship offerings (Lev. 7:32–33), along with one each of the various breads (Lev. 6:14–16). Aaron and his sons do not receive them in this rite because here they are treated as offerers, not priests.

[696] In the Hebrew the normal verbal sequence is interrupted at Exodus 29:36, leading most commentators to understand this verse as beginning a new section concerning the altar.

set it apart as holy—indeed, as "most holy" (v. 37).[697] Little wonder that Aaron and his sons must be consecrated: only holy people can interact with an object so holy (cf. 30:26–29).

A functioning altar is of primary importance. As noted earlier (cf. comment on 27:1–8), altars link earth to heaven. They serve as the interface between the Israelites and the Lord, translating their physical offerings into prayers of forgiveness, petition, and worship. A tabernacle with no functioning altar would be like a body with no heart.

Having mentioned the tabernacle's main altar, the text now describes the daily offering made there (29:38–42). It may be described as follows:

> First commanded in Exodus 29:38–42 (cf. Lev. 6:8–13), the Israelites were to present a continual burnt offering of two lambs each day, one in the morning and the other in the evening. The finest ingredients are called for, whether for the animals (year-old lambs without blemish) or for the grain and drink offerings accompanying them (the finest flour,[698] oil from [beaten] olives,[699] and [wine]). This was an offering fit for the King. . . .
>
> Burnt offerings had many purposes, including atonement (Lev. 1:4) and to "serve as an exclamation point to an offeror's prayers," whether prayers of praise and thanksgiving (Lev. 22:18–20; Num. 6:13–20; Ps. 66:13–16) or prayers "asking the LORD for help in grave situations, such as war (1 Sam. 7:9; 13:8–12) or suffering (Ps. 20:1–5 [2–6])." The Israelites' day was thus bordered, morning and evening, with a collective prayer: "You, O LORD our King, dwell in our midst and are worthy of our most costly praise! Look on us with favor! Forgive our sin! Receive our praises and give ear to our cries for help!"[700]

29:43–46 Verse 42 ends with the Lord's noting that this offering must be made before the tent, "where I will meet with you, to speak to you there." This leads him to stress the tent's overall purpose: to be a place where he can dwell among his people.

He begins by giving a preview of what is to come in the events described in chapter 40, in which his presence will come down on the tent in a cloud of glory in front of all the Israelites, clearly setting it apart as his holy dwelling (29:43; cf. 40:34–35). He then underscores that he will set apart as holy the tent, its altar, and Aaron and his sons to serve as priests (29:44) and that he will do so with one overarching goal in mind: "I will dwell among the people of Israel and will be their God" (v. 45). The last part of that sentence could be rendered woodenly, "And I will be to them for a God." As noted earlier (cf. note 154 within comment on 6:1–8), the language "to be to *person x* for *role y*" is highly relational and similar to descriptions

---

[697] For the translation of Exodus 29:37b cf. note 730 within comment on 30:22–33.
[698] In the Hebrew no measurement for the flour is given, though many versions insert "ephah" on the basis of Numbers 28:5.
[699] Cf. comment on 27:20–21.
[700] Sklar, *Numbers*, 348. The quotes are from Sklar, *Leviticus*, ZECOT, 99, 191.

of adoption (cf. Ex. 2:10; 2 Sam. 7:14; Jer. 31:9) and marriage (cf. Gen. 20:12; 24:67; Num. 36:11), thus referring to a very close relationship. The Lord does not simply want to live in Israel's midst; his goal has always been relationship (cf. Ex. 6:7; 19:5; Deut. 4:20; 7:6; 26:18; 2 Sam. 7:23–24). And to make that clear he emphasizes it one last time, noting that his presence among them will demonstrate the fact that he has redeemed them with this goal in mind: to dwell in their midst (Ex. 29:46). As noted above, the Lord always redeems for the sake of relationship.

Response

Exodus 28–29 focuses on Israel's priests. To understand these chapters' relevance today we may ask five questions. The first three address parallels between Israel's priests and today's church leaders. The fourth addresses parallels and contrasts between Israel's priests and Jesus. The fifth addresses why Exodus gives so much space to the priesthood and tabernacle.

WHAT DO PRIESTS DO? (PART 1)

While priests in Israel have many different functions, these chapters highlight their intercessory role, that is, their seeking the Lord's favor on the Israelites' behalf. Twice in chapter 28 we read that by wearing his uniform the high priest will "bear [the Israelites'] names before the LORD . . . for remembrance" (28:12; cf. v. 29). As discussed above, "To evoke Yahweh's remembrance is to call upon his blessing, provision, and care,"[701] meaning the high priest does this every time he wears his uniform into the tabernacle. He is a visual, walking prayer, bringing the Israelites by name before the Lord and asking him to bless them, provide for them, and care for them. (Cf. further at 28:5–14 and esp. vv. 15–30.)

This same intercessory role applies to church leaders today, especially elders. For example, one goal of instituting the office of deacon in Acts 6 to help meet the physical needs of poor Christians is to free elders to devote themselves "*to prayer and to the ministry of the word*" (Acts 6:4). Paul begins many of his letters with words similar to 1 Thessalonians 1:2: "We give thanks to God always for all of you, *constantly mentioning you in our prayers*" (cf. Eph. 1:16; Phil. 1:3–5; Col. 1:3–4, 9). Simply put, shepherds are to pray for their sheep. What does making this a priority mean for those of us serving as spiritual leaders?

WHAT ARE PRIESTS' QUALIFICATIONS?

What does it take to serve as a priest? Aside from belonging to the priestly family, one fundamental need is highlighted: priests must be ritually holy (Ex. 28:3; 29:1, 44). Because they work in a ritually holy space (the tabernacle), their own ritual state must be one of holiness. Surgeons do not enter an operating room covered in filth; they enter in the highest possible state of physical cleanliness and wear a sterilized gown. Similarly, priests cannot enter the tabernacle stained with ritual impurity; they must enter in a state of ritual holiness and wear a ritually holy uniform.

---

701 Palmer, "Israelite High Priestly Apparel," 122.

At first glance, this seems far removed from a day and age in which the Lord has set aside the categories of ritual states (cf. Mark 7:19). But even in Israel's time lessons surrounding ritual states were meant to serve as lessons regarding moral states (cf. comment on Ex. 19:8b–13 and also note 346). Yes, priests must be ritually holy, but they are also expected to be morally holy (cf. 1 Sam. 2:13–17, 22, 27–36). And moral holiness is the primary qualification for serving as a spiritual leader today. For example, when Paul lists the qualifications for serving as elder or deacon, he focuses on issues of character and stresses the need for spiritual maturity above all else (cf. 1 Tim. 3:1–13). This is a call to self-examination for spiritual leaders and a reminder to those choosing them to focus on character ahead of his gifting or success.

HOW ARE ISRAELITES TO INTERACT WITH PRIESTS?

While the Bible expects much from the leaders of God's people, it also expects much from God's people as they interact with their leaders and, in fact, commands them to show their leaders honor and respect. Exodus 28 twice mentions that the priests' garments will be "for glory and for beauty" (28:2, 40). As noted above, the sense of the phrase is "for glory and for honor" (cf. v. 2), that is, the garments set Aaron and the priests apart as the Lord's special servants, and therefore the Israelites are to treat them with honor and dignity (cf. comment on 28:1–4).

The NT emphasizes the same regarding church leaders:

> We ask you, brothers, to respect those who labor among you and are over you in the Lord. (1 Thess. 5:12)

> Let the elders who rule well be considered worthy of double honor, especially those who labor in preaching and teaching. (1 Tim. 5:17)

> Obey your leaders and submit to them, for they are keeping watch over your souls, as those who will have to give an account. Let them do this with joy and not with groaning, for that would be of no advantage to you. (Heb. 13:17)

Our leaders are not perfect. Indeed, many are keenly aware of their deficiencies—often because we do such a good job of highlighting them! How can we instead offer encouragement more than critique and prayers more than complaints? Do we act in such a way that our leaders really can do their work "with joy and not with groaning"?

WHAT DO PRIESTS DO? (PART 2)

While Israelite priests are similar to church leaders today in many ways, we also see important differences. One is that Israel's priests perform atonement rites on the Israelites' behalf. As noted above, priests offer the burnt offering every morning as a way not only to ask for the Lord's favor on the Israelites but also to make atonement for them and ask the Lord's forgiveness (cf. comment on 29:36–42). And the high priest, by means of the "Holy to the LORD" plate, is able somehow to bear away any guilt that attaches to the Israelites' offering (cf. comment on 28:36–38). In short the priests are not simply intercessors; they are atoning mediators whom God gives in his love to help remove his people's sin so they can have fellowship with him.

Today, however, only Jesus fulfills this role of atoning mediator. Paul boldly states, "There is one mediator between God and men, the man Christ Jesus" (1 Tim. 2:5), and the book of Hebrews identifies Jesus as both the "mediator of a new covenant" (Heb. 12:24) and the final high priest who takes away sin (Heb. 2:17; 3:1; 7:23–8:2; 9:11–12, 25–28). Hebrews also describes Jesus as the final sacrifice by whose blood his people are "sanctified" (10:10, 14; 13:12). What the high priest in Israel does with the Israelites' offerings—making them "holy to the Lord"—Jesus does with his followers! And only Jesus can do this.

This means leaders should remind themselves and their people often, "I am not the Christ!" (John 1:20). We are not our people's saviors and should in no way think or pretend we can be. Moreover, leaders must point people to Jesus as the only one who can deal fully and finally with sin. Exalting Jesus as Savior and Lord must be the motivating principle of all we do.

WHY HAVE PRIESTS AND A TABERNACLE ANYWAY?

In the midst of the above discussion we must not forget the Lord has taken five full chapters to discuss—often in more detail than some may desire!—how to build his tabernacle and clothe and ordain his priestly servants. Why such a focus?

He provides the answer in Exodus 29:45–46: "I will dwell among the people of Israel and will be their God. And they shall know that I am the LORD their God, who brought them out of the land of Egypt that I might dwell among them. I am the LORD their God." Simply put, he desires to be with his people and to be known by them.

Do we think of God like this? As wanting to be with us? As wanting to be known by us? As noted (cf. Introduction: Overview), this is, in fact, the story of the Bible from one end to the other. In Eden God comes to *walk* in the garden with Adam and Eve (Gen. 3:8); in the tabernacle he comes down so he might *walk* among the Israelites in their midst (Lev. 26:12).[702] In the tabernacle he comes to *dwell* among them (Ex. 29:45); in Jesus he comes to *dwell* in our midst (John 1:14),[703] and through his Spirit he makes his *dwelling* among the people of his church and *walks* among us (2 Cor. 6:16).[704] At the end of time, when the heavenly city comes down to earth, a loud voice will declare, "Behold, *the dwelling place* of God is with man. He will *dwell* with them, and they will be his people, and God himself will be with them as their God. He will wipe away every tear from their eyes" (Rev.

---

702 Both passages use a relatively rare form of the verb "walk" (Hb. *hithallek*); cf. note 838 within Response section on 35:1–40:38, "What Does the Tabernacle Have to Do with Eden?"
703 The verb for "dwell" (*skēnoō*) in John 1:14 is built on the same root as the LXX word for "tabernacle" (*skēnēs*). In Jesus God "tabernacled" among us.
704 This passage cites Exodus 29:45 and Leviticus 26:12. In other words God's collective people have become the tabernacle!

21:3–4).[705] Think of it: Jesus will be so near to us that he will reach out his hand to brush away every tear of pain from our eyes. Do we think of God like this? In Jesus we see this is exactly the type of God that he is. If we have not come to know him in this way, what is stopping us? And, if we have, what does it mean for the ways in which we face our fears and sorrows? He loves us, wants to be with us, and wants us to know him. Jesus came in our flesh to prove that it is so. This is who God is.

EXODUS 30

30 "You shall make an altar on which to burn incense; you shall make it of acacia wood. ² A cubit¹ shall be its length, and a cubit its breadth. It shall be square, and two cubits shall be its height. Its horns shall be of one piece with it. ³ You shall overlay it with pure gold, its top and around its sides and its horns. And you shall make a molding of gold around it. ⁴ And you shall make two golden rings for it. Under its molding on two opposite sides of it you shall make them, and they shall be holders for poles with which to carry it. ⁵ You shall make the poles of acacia wood and overlay them with gold. ⁶ And you shall put it in front of the veil that is above the ark of the testimony, in front of the mercy seat that is above the testimony, where I will meet with you. ⁷ And Aaron shall burn fragrant incense on it. Every morning when he dresses the lamps he shall burn it, ⁸ and when Aaron sets up the lamps at twilight, he shall burn it, a regular incense offering before the Lord throughout your generations. ⁹ You shall not offer unauthorized incense on it, or a burnt offering, or a grain offering, and you shall not pour a drink offering on it. ¹⁰ Aaron shall make atonement on its horns once a year. With the blood of the sin offering of atonement he shall make atonement for it once in the year throughout your generations. It is most holy to the Lord."

¹¹ The Lord said to Moses, ¹² "When you take the census of the people of Israel, then each shall give a ransom for his life to the Lord when you number them, that there be no plague among them when you number them. ¹³ Each one who is numbered in the census shall give this: half a shekel² according to the shekel of the sanctuary (the shekel is twenty gerahs),³ half a shekel as an offering to the Lord. ¹⁴ Everyone who is numbered in the census, from twenty years old and upward, shall give the Lord's offering. ¹⁵ The rich shall not give more, and the poor shall not give less, than the half shekel, when you give the Lord's offering to make atonement for your lives. ¹⁶ You shall take the atonement money from the people of Israel and shall give it for the service of the tent of meeting, that it may bring the people of Israel to remembrance before the Lord, so as to make atonement for your lives."

---

705 The term for "dwelling place" in Revelation 21:3 is the same term used in the LXX for "tabernacle" (*skēnēs*). In other word, an obvious link exists between God's dwelling in his tabernacle in Exodus, his dwelling among us in Jesus (John 1:14), and his dwelling again on the earth in the final days (Rev. 21:3). He is driven to be with us.

¹⁷ The Lord said to Moses, ¹⁸ "You shall also make a basin of bronze, with its stand of bronze, for washing. You shall put it between the tent of meeting and the altar, and you shall put water in it, ¹⁹ with which Aaron and his sons shall wash their hands and their feet. ²⁰ When they go into the tent of meeting, or when they come near the altar to minister, to burn a food offering⁴ to the Lord, they shall wash with water, so that they may not die. ²¹ They shall wash their hands and their feet, so that they may not die. It shall be a statute forever to them, even to him and to his offspring throughout their generations."

²² The Lord said to Moses, ²³ "Take the finest spices: of liquid myrrh 500 shekels, and of sweet-smelling cinnamon half as much, that is, 250, and 250 of aromatic cane, ²⁴ and 500 of cassia, according to the shekel of the sanctuary, and a hin⁵ of olive oil. ²⁵ And you shall make of these a sacred anointing oil blended as by the perfumer; it shall be a holy anointing oil. ²⁶ With it you shall anoint the tent of meeting and the ark of the testimony, ²⁷ and the table and all its utensils, and the lampstand and its utensils, and the altar of incense, ²⁸ and the altar of burnt offering with all its utensils and the basin and its stand. ²⁹ You shall consecrate them, that they may be most holy. Whatever touches them will become holy. ³⁰ You shall anoint Aaron and his sons, and consecrate them, that they may serve me as priests. ³¹ And you shall say to the people of Israel, 'This shall be my holy anointing oil throughout your generations. ³² It shall not be poured on the body of an ordinary person, and you shall make no other like it in composition. It is holy, and it shall be holy to you. ³³ Whoever compounds any like it or whoever puts any of it on an outsider shall be cut off from his people.'"

³⁴ The Lord said to Moses, "Take sweet spices, stacte, and onycha, and galbanum, sweet spices with pure frankincense (of each shall there be an equal part), ³⁵ and make an incense blended as by the perfumer, seasoned with salt, pure and holy. ³⁶ You shall beat some of it very small, and put part of it before the testimony in the tent of meeting where I shall meet with you. It shall be most holy for you. ³⁷ And the incense that you shall make according to its composition, you shall not make for yourselves. It shall be for you holy to the Lord. ³⁸ Whoever makes any like it to use as perfume shall be cut off from his people."

¹ A *cubit* was about 18 inches or 45 centimeters ² A *shekel* was about 2/5 ounce or 11 grams ³ A *gerah* was about 1/50 ounce or 0.6 gram ⁴ Or *an offering by fire* ⁵ A *hin* was about 4 quarts or 3.5 liters

Section Overview

This chapter provides final instructions for items used in connection with the tabernacle. It begins with the incense altar, describing both its form (vv. 1–5) and its function (vv. 6–10) and emphasizing that it is a most holy altar used to present regular incense offerings on the Israelites' behalf. This makes it comparable to the burnt offering altar and its regular offerings just described (29:38–42), which may partly explain why it is described here and not earlier with the other furniture of the Holy Place (cf. comment on 30:1–10).

The text then transitions to the census tax, which is linked to the preceding passage by the idea of atonement (cf. v. 10 with v. 16) and to the larger context by explaining how the tax will be used for building the tabernacle (v. 16). These verses emphasize the atoning role the tax serves (vv. 12, 15–16) as well as the way its presentation will be used as a visual reminder in the tabernacle to "bring the people of Israel to remembrance before the LORD" (v. 16).

The last piece of tabernacle furniture is then described: a bronze basin for holding water. Through repetition emphasis is placed on its function of enabling priests to wash before performing certain duties. By doing so they will remove ritual impurity and so protect themselves from the Lord's judgment (vv. 17–21).

Chapter 30 concludes by describing the holy anointing oil (vv. 22–33) and the holy incense (vv. 34–38). The Hebrew root for "holy/holiness/making holy" occurs fifteen times in this section, underscoring the holiness of these objects—and, in the case of the anointing oil, its role in making other objects or people holy. Both passages also warn against making these items for use outside the sanctuary, on pain of being "cut off from [their] people" (vv. 33, 38)—thus underscoring they are the Lord's holy property and to be respected as such.

Section Outline

VI. Israel at Sinai: the Lord gives instructions for the building of his palace-tent among them (24:12–31:18)...

    H. Further instructions for items used in connection with the tabernacle (30:1–38)

        1. The golden altar of incense (30:1–10)
        2. The half-shekel census tax (30:11–16)
        3. The bronze basin (30:17–21)
        4. The holy anointing oil (30:22–33)
        5. The holy incense (30:34–38)

Comment

30:1–10 The tabernacle's first room is the Holy Place. It contains three pieces of furniture: the golden lampstand, the golden table, and the golden incense altar. The first two were described in chapter 25, but the altar was not. This was perhaps because of the many parallels between the altar of burnt offering at the end of chapter 29 and the golden incense altar at the beginning of chapter 30: blood is put on the altars' horns, and atonement is made for them (29:36–37 [cf. v. 12]; 30:10); the altars are used for a "regular" daily offering each morning and evening (29:38–42; 30:8); and the Lord speaks in each passage of the altars' being in front of a place in the tent "where I will meet with you" (29:42; 30:6). These parallels naturally suggest that the incense altar is described here in order to keep like with like. Indeed, doing so helps to highlight the importance of maintaining the altars' ritual state so they may be used in the regular offerings, which are central to Israel's relationship with the Lord who meets with them at the tent.[706]

---

[706] Cf. Cassuto, *Commentary on the Book of Exodus*, 390; Sarna, *Exodus*, 193; Wright, *Exodus*, 535n2. For a survey of other approaches to this question cf. Alexander, *Exodus*, 559.

30:1–5 The incense altar is a rectangular box measuring 1.5 feet (45 cm) in length and width and 3 feet (90 cm) in height. Made of acacia wood, it is covered in pure gold and has "horns" on its top corners and some form of molding around it (vv. 1–3; for further description of altar horns cf. 27:1–8 [at v. 2]). Under the molding on two sides are golden rings to hold gold covered wooden poles for carrying it (30:4–5).

30:6–10 Having described its design, the Lord now turns to the altar's placement and function, which are closely related. The altar is to stand toward the back of the Holy Place, in front of the curtain screening off the Most Holy Place (v. 6). On the curtain's other side stands the ark (v. 6),[707] above which the Lord will manifest his presence in a special way to meet with Moses (the "you" in singular). See comment on 25:17–22 [at vv. 21–22]. This means the incense altar, which stands before the curtain in front of this special place of the Lord's presence, is perfectly situated for presenting incense offerings to the Lord.

The text nowhere explains an incense offering's function, probably because the original audience understood it. We can note, however, that animal offerings are frequently described as a "pleasing aroma to the LORD" (Ex. 29:18, 25, 41; Lev. 1:9; 3:5; 4:31; etc.), that is, an offering by which one seeks the Lord's favorable acceptance (cf. comment on 29:15–18). It seems likely that incense offerings function in the same way since, by their very nature, they produce a pleasing aroma. Indeed, the continual incense offering here parallels the continual burnt offering just described: both are offered every morning and every evening (29:38–42; 30:7–8). As the daily burnt offering is a way to seek the Lord's favor (cf. comment on 29:36–42), so is the daily incense offering. Not surprisingly, later Israelites will compare their prayers for the Lord's help to an incense offering (Ps. 141:1–2).[708]

Aaron[709] is to burn "fragrant incense" on the altar. Whether he burns it directly on the top or in a bowl or censer placed on the top is unclear.[710] Presumably he uses the incense described in Exodus 30:34–38, which, like the incense altar, is to be "before the testimony" (v. 36; cf. v. 6).[711] This special incense may not be used for everyday purposes; it is "holy to the LORD" and to be used only for him (v. 37). Using any other incense on the incense altar is thus "unauthorized" and strictly forbidden (v. 9a),[712] as is any other type of offering in general, whether animal, grain, or drink offering (v. 9b). This altar is to be used only for incense offerings.

---

[707] Hebrews 9:4, which describes the Most Holy Place as "having the golden altar of incense," is best understood as meaning the incense altar "belongs to" the Most Holy Place in a special way; that is, its function is closely related to it—which our text in fact emphasizes; cf. Roy Gane, *Cult and Character: Purification Offerings, Day of Atonement, and Theodicy* (Winona Lake, IN: Eisenbrauns, 2005), 27n7; and more fully Cockerill, *Hebrews*, 376–377. Gane cites 1 Kings 6:22 as having the same sense, and Cockerill notes the difference between the table and lamp as being "in" the Holy Place (Heb. 9:2) and the Most Holy Place as "having" the incense altar (Heb. 9:4).
[708] For the NT cf. Revelation 5:8; 8:3–4 (Stuart, *Exodus*, 633).
[709] And presumably his sons; cf. Ex. 27:21 with 30:7–8, which show that references to Aaron sometimes use his name as a way of referring to priestly action in general (Sarna, *Exodus*, 194).
[710] Propp, *Exodus 19–40*, 474, citing Leviticus 10:1; 16:12; Numbers 16:6–7, 17–18, 38–39; 2 Chronicles 26:19 (cf. 2 Chron. 26:16); Ezekiel 8:11.
[711] The word translated "fragrant" in Exodus 30:7 is the same word rendered as "sweet spices" twice in verse 34.
[712] The situation in Leviticus 10:1–2 differs in that Nadab and Abihu are presenting not unauthorized incense but unauthorized fire, that is, they are presenting an incense offering in the Holy Place that has not

A final note refers to an annual rite of atonement the high priest will make by applying the blood of a purification offering[713] to the altar's horns (v. 10a). A similar rite takes place with the burnt offering altar during the priest's ordination ceremony to cleanse it of sin and defilement (cf. comment on 29:10–14). This same rite will take place every year on the Day of Atonement for the incense altar.[714] As a result, it will maintain its most holy status and therefore continue as a place where incense offerings may be made on Israel's behalf (30:10b).

30:11–16 These verses describe a census tax, which at first glance seems to have little to do with the tabernacle. As the passage concludes, however, it becomes clear this tax will serve an important role for the functioning of the tabernacle (cf. below).

For reasons nowhere explicitly explained in Scripture, taking a census is considered dangerous at this point in Israel's history. Among the many guesses of commentators some suggest that counting lives is considered something only God should do; others suggest that counting lives is somehow a sign of sinful ambition.[715] Whether either of these is correct is impossible to know. What is clear, however, is that those counted in the census endanger their lives and therefore must give a "ransom" (v. 12). While this word is often used in English to refer to a payment made on behalf of an innocent party (a kidnapped person) to a guilty party (the kidnapper), it is just the opposite in the Pentateuch, where it refers to a payment made to rescue a guilty party from a deserved penalty (cf. Ex. 21:28–32; Num. 35:30–34).[716] In this case it will rescue Israelites from a "plague," that is, an unnamed but lethal form of judgment from the Lord (cf. Ex. 12:13; Num. 16:46–49).

The payment to be given is "half a shekel according to the shekel of the sanctuary" (Ex. 30:13). The mention of a "shekel of the sanctuary" suggests there may have been different standards for weights and measures in Israel (cf. 2 Sam. 14:26); the text thus makes clear which standard to use and even identifies it more precisely as equaling twenty "gerahs." (Based on archaeological evidence, a shekel is understood to weigh about 0.4 ounces [11–12 g].[717] It is "not a coin" at this point in history "but a measure of weight."[718]) The half-shekel is to be paid by all those counted who are at least twenty years of age (Ex. 30:14); later texts note the purpose is to count Israelite males for military service (cf. 38:25–26 with Num. 1:3, 46).[719]

---

been authorized (and are apparently trying to barge into the Most Holy Place as well; cf. Lev. 16:1–2). Cf. Sklar, *Leviticus*, TOTC, 156–157.

713 Or "sin offering"; cf. comment on 29:10–14.

714 Cf. Leviticus 16:16, which assumes Aaron performs atoning rites in the outer room to atone for it just as he does for the inner room. Leviticus 16:18–19 is describing the altar of burnt offering. Cf. Sklar, *Leviticus*, TOTC, 210–212. (Note that in Lev. 16:16 "Holy Place" refers to the "Most Holy Place"; cf. Lev. 16:2; Sklar, *Leviticus*, ZECOT, 143n26.)

715 For these and other suggestions cf. Song-Mi Suzie Park, "Census and Censure: Sacred Threshing Floors and Counting Taboos in 2 Samuel 24," *HBT* 35 (2013): 21–41, esp. 22–28.

716 Cf. fuller discussion in Sklar, *Sin, Impurity, Sacrifice, Atonement*, 44–79, esp. 48–61.

717 Cook, "Weights and Measures," *ISBE* 4:1054.

718 Propp, *Exodus 19–40*, 478.

719 Numbers 1 records the census but does not mention the tax. It may be that the tax is provisionally collected at this point in Exodus so that the tabernacle can be built, with Numbers 1 describing the actual enrollment of names (a much longer process) carried out after the tabernacle's construction (Cassuto, *Commentary on*

The fact that poor and rich paid the same amount underscores that every life has the same value before the Lord (Ex. 30:15).[720]

The ransom payment is described in verse 16 as "atonement money," since the idea of ransom is central to the biblical concept of atonement.[721] Verse 16 also explains that the atonement money will both rescue the Israelites' lives and be used for the service of the tabernacle. As such, it will bring them "to remembrance before the LORD"; that is, it will serve as a request for the Lord to show them his favor and care (cf. comment on 28:5–14). As 38:25–28 goes on to explain, the silver will be used to make parts of the tabernacle's structure and accessories. Thus the items made with the ransom money will be a constant "reminder" of the Israelites' acknowledged need for atonement and their desire to worship the Lord faithfully and experience his loving care and protection.

30:17–21 Rather than describing the bronze basin earlier with the other courtyard items, the Lord describes it here, following his discussion of the priests' ordination in chapter 29, likely because it is key to their maintenance of ritual purity.

Ritually holy priests are the only people who can enter the tent of meeting or present offerings at the altar. But they still live in a world full of ritual impurity, which they are most likely to contact physically, with their feet or hands. Since water is a cleansing agent for ritual impurity (Lev. 15:5–8), priests must wash their feet and hands before entering very sacred space (the tent) or touching very sacred items (sacrifices and the altar) in order to remove any trace of impurity (Ex. 30:19–20). (Compare how surgeons scrub their hands before operating to remove any trace of bacteria.) By doing so the priests show respect to the Lord's holy property and therefore to the Lord himself. Failing to do so would show treasonous disrespect and merit the judgment typically due the treasonous: death (vv. 20–21). Indeed, the text repeats how they are to "wash . . . so that they may not die," emphasizing the text's focus: priests must show due reverence to the Lord.

The water is to come from a basin on a stand in the courtyard, somewhere between the altar of burnt offering and the tent (v. 18). Like the altar, it is to be made of bronze, since the courtyard holds a lower level of holiness than the tent and therefore requires less costly materials than the tent's golden furniture.[722] We later learn that the bronze comes "from the mirrors of the ministering women who ministered in the entrance of the tent of meeting," (38:8).[723] Little is known of these women. They are mentioned again in 1 Samuel 2:22, and the same "ministering" language that describes them also describes the male Levites who perform

---

the Book of Exodus, 471). For how to understand the census numbers cf. Introduction: Interpretive Challenges: Large Numbers in the Book of Exodus (esp. note 49).
720 When the offering is potentially very expensive (such as an animal), options given take into account a person's financial ability so as not to burden those with fewer means (cf. Lev. 1:1–17; 5:7–13; 12:8).
721 Cf. Sklar, *Leviticus*, TOTC, 50–54, esp. p. 50.
722 Cf. Response section on Exodus 24:12–25:9, "What Does the Tabernacle Teach Us about the Kind of God He Is?"
723 Since the tabernacle has not yet been built, this verse may be describing these women from the perspective of the role they will later play. Alternately, it may be describing women who are currently serving at the entrance to the tent mentioned in Exodus 33:7 and will later transfer this service to the tabernacle (cf. 1 Sam. 2:22).

various nonpriestly tasks important for the proper functioning of the tent and its worship (cf. Num. 4:23; 8:24, where the Hb. word translated "doing duty" is the same word translated "ministering/ed" in our verse). For the women this may include "utensil cleanup, general courtyard cleanup, water resupply, ancillary food preparation, guiding and assisting other women worshipers, [or] washing priests' clothes."[724] These tasks may seem mundane—but are no more so than the Levites' work! Indeed, these are important acts of service: without them the Lord's palace cannot function as a place of worship. Whatever acts of service these women do, they contribute directly to the Lord's people's ability to worship. And they do so in a costly way. "Handheld mirrors . . . were greatly valued. When monarchs exchanged gifts, mirrors were often included. They were made of highly polished metal, often bronze, copper, silver, gold, and electrum."[725] These women band together and give out of devotion and love what might be their most costly possession, as a special gift for the work of the Lord's home. How pleasing to the Lord this must be. After all, costly love is the truest type.

30:22–33 The chapter concludes with two final items to be made for the tabernacle and its worship: anointing oil (Ex. 30:22–33) and incense (vv. 34–38). Both make use of costly spices, both are holy, and both may be used only in connection with the tabernacle.[726] These could have been described earlier with other tabernacle components (cf. their placement in 37:29), but, since the description of the incense altar was delayed until 30:1–6 (cf. explanation above), it makes sense that description of the incense burned upon it would likewise be delayed, together with the anointing oil.

Five ingredients constitute the anointing oil. The first four are 12.5 pounds (5.7 kg) of liquid myrrh, 6.25 pounds (2.8 kg) of sweet-smelling cinnamon, the same of aromatic cane, and 12.5 pounds (5.7 kg) of cassia (assuming 0.4 oz [11 g] per shekel).[727] These are to be mixed with a "hin of olive oil" (vv. 22–25),[728] usually understood to be between 0.95 and 1.7 gallons (3.6–6.5 l).[729] The first four ingredients are not simply "spices" but "finest spices," as appropriate for use in the king's service. Indeed, spices were often quite valuable in the ancient world and could even be included in gifts for a king (1 Kings 10:2, 10). Here they are to be made into a "holy anointing oil" used to anoint the tabernacle and its objects and to move them into a state of ritual holiness (Ex. 30:25–29).[730] Likewise the oil

---

724 Stuart, *Exodus* 767.
725 Philip J. King and Lawrence E. Stager, *Life in Biblical Israel* (Louisville: Westminster John Knox Press, 2001), 283–284.
726 Cf. Meyers, *Exodus*, 251–252.
727 Of these four, identification of the last is least certain. Commentators also debate whether the myrrh is liquid.
728 Noting that the weight of the spices is far greater than that of the oil, Propp (*Exodus 19–40*, 483) writes, "Job 41:23 implies that the 'compounder's work' involves boiling. . . . The Talmud preserves one method for imparting scent to oil, corroborated by Egyptian, Mesopotamian and classical sources. . . . The herbs were soaked in water and oil, and then either the water was boiled away or the oil skimmed off. . . . Thus savor was transferred from the spices to the water to the oil." It is for this reason a person skilled in making perfume is required (Ex. 30:25).
729 Cook, "Weights and Measures," *ISBE* 4:1051. Most authorities lean toward the lower end of this scale.
730 Commentators debate whether to translate Exodus 30:29 as "Whatever touches them will become holy" or "Whoever touches them must be holy." Either option is possible, although a clear flow of thought results

is to be put on Aaron and his sons—on Aaron's head and clothes (29:7, 21) and his sons' bodies and clothes (29:21)—to move them into a state of ritual holiness in order to work in the tabernacle and handle its holy objects (30:30). The result? Holy servants in a holy palace serving a holy king.

The Lord then emphasizes that the Israelites are to respect this oil as being especially holy by never copying its formula for use in other purposes (vv. 31–33). It can be used only in the sanctuary and placed on it and on priests the Lord approves. Anyone who makes it and puts it on someone outside the priestly family—which is the sense of the word "outsider" here (cf. 29:33; Num. 16:40)—either treats the Lord's holy oil as an everyday object or rejects his priesthood by trying to start his own. Not surprisingly, such a person will be "cut off from his people," a penalty that ranges from exile to premature death by means of judgment (Ex. 31:14; cf. note 245 within comment on 12:14–20). It is a fearful thing to dismiss God's holiness and reject his authority.

30:34–38 Five ingredients also constitute the holy incense: equal parts of sweet spices (stacte, onycha, galbanum) and pure frankincense,[731] along with an unspecified amount of salt (vv. 34–35). Commentators debate the identity of the first two sweet spices, though there is more agreement that the third is galbanum (a "resin from *Ferula galbaniflua Boisser et Buhse* and related species originally indigenous to Persia and Afghanistan"[732]) and that frankincense is "a gum resin of a species of the *Boswellia* species . . . indigenous to southern Arabia, Ethiopia, Somalia, and India."[733] Frankincense is a costly spice: "Pure, genuine frankincense was imported (from Sheba: Jer. 6:20; Isa. 60:6) and therefore both valuable and expensive (cf. Isa. 43:23)."[734] Given the value of spices in general (cf. comment on 30:22–33), the sweet spices are likely also costly. This incense is fit for a king and will be offered to the Lord, the heavenly King, every morning and evening (vv. 7–8). The salt might serve a practical purpose,[735] but other texts also inform us that salt is to be a part of all offerings since—for reasons nowhere explained—it serves as a reminder of the Lord's eternal covenant with Israel (Lev. 2:13; Num. 18:19).

The incense is described as "pure and holy" and "most holy" (Ex. 30:35, 36); this makes it suitable for tabernacle use. It is kept in the tabernacle (v. 36), presumably near the incense altar (cf. v. 6), ready for use in the daily incense offering (cf. vv. 7–8). Grinding it "very small" may make it burn evenly.

Anyone who makes this incense for everyday use will face the same penalty as those who make the holy anointing oil for everyday use: he will be cut off from the people (vv. 37–38; cf. vv. 31–33). These are holy items to be used only in

---

from the latter: because the altar is "most holy" and because those who touch it "must be holy" (v. 29), Aaron and his sons must be made holy to minister at it (v. 30).
731 It may be that the sweet spices are mixed and considered together, meaning one part of the sweet-spice mixture and one part frankincense.
732 Propp, *Exodus 19–40*, 485.
733 Houtman, *Exodus*, vol. 1, 170.
734 D. Kellermann, "לְבֹנָה," *TDOT* 7:443.
735 Sarna states that salt can "enhance the rate of burning and smoking" (*Exodus*, 199). I have not been able to confirm whether this is correct.

service of the holy King. To do otherwise would be to disregard the holy King to whom they belong.

Response

Atonement and holiness are two of the main themes in chapter 30. Each may be considered in turn.

WHAT IS ATONEMENT, AND WHY DO WE NEED IT?

Our sin and impurity have different effects. On the one hand they defile us. Most of us know how doing something wrong can make someone feel dirty afterward. We sense a deep need to be cleansed. On the other hand our sin and impurity endanger us. Most of us know how doing something wrong also makes someone feel like he deserves punishment. We sense a deep need to be rescued. In both cases atonement is the answer, since it refers to cleansing and ransom.[736] In fact this chapter displays both ideas—atonement as cleansing and atonement as ransom.

The cleansing side of atonement is seen in 30:10. The incense altar has become defiled with sin and impurity; Aaron performs an atonement rite by placing blood on it to remove the defilement and make it holy (cf. comments on 29:10–14; 30:6–10). Atonement results in profound cleansing.

The very next paragraph highlights the ransom idea of atonement in the census tax requirement (vv. 11–16). As noted above, when the Bible speaks of ransom it refers to a payment that rescues a guilty party from a deserved penalty. The reason a census is dangerous is unclear (cf. discussion above), but the Israelites are in danger, and the "atonement money" rescues their lives from certain death. Atonement results in profound rescue.

And this leads us directly to Jesus, whose death on our behalf leads to both cleansing and rescue. In terms of cleansing the apostle John promises, "If we confess our sins, [God] is faithful and just to forgive us our sins and to cleanse us from all unrighteousness" (1 John 1:9). Just as the sacrificial blood cleanses the altar of sin and impurity in Exodus 30:10, Jesus' blood cleanses us of our sin and impurity—and does so profoundly and completely. The writer of Hebrews notes how the blood of Jesus "purif[ies] our conscience" (Heb. 9:14) and gives us "hearts sprinkled clean from an evil conscience" (Heb. 10:22). Freedom from the guilt and shame of past sin is found in the cleansing blood of Jesus.

In terms of rescue Jesus says that he comes not "to be served but to serve, and to give his life as a ransom for many" (Mark 10:45; cf. 1 Pet. 1:18–19). He is the ransom payment on our behalf. His lifeblood for ours. Freedom from the fear of future judgment is found in the ransoming blood of Jesus.

What this means is that Jesus is the one who allows us to live in the present not only with a clear conscience but also with confidence that God leans toward us with love and acceptance, not judgment. But it does not stop there. Jesus "gave himself for us to redeem us from all lawlessness and to purify for himself a people

---

[736] For further discussion cf. Sklar, *Leviticus*, TOTC, 50–54.

for his own possession *who are zealous for good works*" (Titus 2:14). In other words those he rescues and cleanses are those he calls to live as his holy people in this world. This leads to a second question.

WHAT IS CONSECRATION, AND WHY DO WE NEED IT?

The word "consecrate" (Ex. 30:30)—which can also be translated "sanctify"—refers to holiness. In this chapter it refers to setting someone or something apart as the Lord's. Sprinkling the priests and the tabernacle with the Lord's holy anointing oil marks them as the Lord's special property (vv. 26–30). And, once a person or an object is set apart as the Lord's special property, he or it is considered holy. Just as an earthly king's property is considered royal property since it belongs to someone royal, the Lord's property is considered holy property since it belongs to someone holy.

Once something or someone belongs to the Lord, important implications follow. Holy objects are to be shown respect and not treated lightly. In this instance the Lord's holy anointing oil and holy incense are to be respected by using them only in his tabernacle (vv. 31–33, 37–38). These are not everyday types of oil and incense. An NT parallel would be the Lord's Supper. This is not an everyday meal but one set apart by Jesus to remember and celebrate what he has done. As such it is to be respected and not taken in an unworthy manner—a point Paul emphasizes, noting that some who take it in an unworthy manner have experienced the Lord's disciplinary judgment (1 Cor. 11:17–30).

The most important implication for holy people—all those who belong to Jesus—is that they are to live in keeping with that holy status. This means repenting when we commit sin. Exodus 30:17–21 helps illustrate this. The priests are set apart as ritually holy yet become ritually polluted throughout the week. Washing their hands and feet at the basin removes this ritual impurity so they can come newly cleansed before the Lord. Similarly, sin and impurity defile us throughout the week. Coming to Jesus in repentance to have his blood again wash away our defilement leaves us newly cleansed before the Lord.

But we also live in keeping with our holy status by living holy lives. Now that we are God's children, we are to live in a way that pleases our heavenly Father. Just as the Lord needed a holy tabernacle for his dwelling in Exodus, believers are to be a holy tabernacle for his dwelling now. Paul picks up on both themes, saying God has appointed his children to be his holy temple so that he can walk among us and be a father to us (2 Cor. 6:16–18). He concludes, "Since we have these promises, beloved, let us cleanse ourselves from every defilement of body and spirit, bringing holiness to completion in the fear of God" (2 Cor. 7:1). The Christian does not say, "I have been forgiven; I can live however I want." The Christian says, "O Lord, through Jesus you have pulled me out of the muck and mire of my sin and shame, washed me clean, given me your name, and called me to reflect your holy love into the world. Help me to do so with love and reverence before you. And in seeing me may others glimpse you—and run to you for cleansing and rescue."

EXODUS 31

31 The Lord said to Moses, ² "See, I have called by name Bezalel the son of Uri, son of Hur, of the tribe of Judah, ³ and I have filled him with the Spirit of God, with ability and intelligence, with knowledge and all craftsmanship, ⁴ to devise artistic designs, to work in gold, silver, and bronze, ⁵ in cutting stones for setting, and in carving wood, to work in every craft. ⁶ And behold, I have appointed with him Oholiab, the son of Ahisamach, of the tribe of Dan. And I have given to all able men ability, that they may make all that I have commanded you: ⁷ the tent of meeting, and the ark of the testimony, and the mercy seat that is on it, and all the furnishings of the tent, ⁸ the table and its utensils, and the pure lampstand with all its utensils, and the altar of incense, ⁹ and the altar of burnt offering with all its utensils, and the basin and its stand, ¹⁰ and the finely worked garments,¹ the holy garments for Aaron the priest and the garments of his sons, for their service as priests, ¹¹ and the anointing oil and the fragrant incense for the Holy Place. According to all that I have commanded you, they shall do."

¹² And the Lord said to Moses, ¹³ "You are to speak to the people of Israel and say, 'Above all you shall keep my Sabbaths, for this is a sign between me and you throughout your generations, that you may know that I, the Lord, sanctify you. ¹⁴ You shall keep the Sabbath, because it is holy for you. Everyone who profanes it shall be put to death. Whoever does any work on it, that soul shall be cut off from among his people. ¹⁵ Six days shall work be done, but the seventh day is a Sabbath of solemn rest, holy to the Lord. Whoever does any work on the Sabbath day shall be put to death. ¹⁶ Therefore the people of Israel shall keep the Sabbath, observing the Sabbath throughout their generations, as a covenant forever. ¹⁷ It is a sign forever between me and the people of Israel that in six days the Lord made the heavens and the earth, and on the seventh day he rested and was refreshed.'"

¹⁸ And he gave to Moses, when he had finished speaking with him on Mount Sinai, the two tablets of the testimony, tablets of stone, written with the finger of God.

¹ Or *garments for worship*

Section Overview

This chapter concludes the section that began in 24:12, which has focused on the building of the tabernacle. Coming on the heels of chapter 30, which concluded the description of the tabernacle and its contents, this chapter begins by describing those who will make them (31:1–11). The master artisans will be Bezalel (vv. 1–5) and Oholiab (v. 6), though others will help them (v. 6). Focus is placed on the Lord as the one who divinely gifts them to do this work (vv. 3, 6), showing that creative arts are within the sphere of his activity and concern. Focus is also placed on the wisdom, intelligence, and knowledge required for such work (vv. 3, 6), showing that wisdom includes skillful work of the hands and not only intellectual ability of the mind. The passage concludes by emphasizing a theme found throughout chapters 25–31: the importance of making everything in the tabernacle exactly as the Lord has commanded (31:6–11).

The second half of chapter 31 (vv. 12–17) shifts the discussion from sacred space (the tabernacle) to sacred time (the Sabbath). It emphasizes the importance of keeping the Sabbath, offering two reasons: the Sabbath serves as the sign of Israel's covenant relationship with the Lord, and he has set it aside as holy. It also names severe consequences for breaking the Sabbath: anyone who does so will be cut off from the covenant community by death. The Israelites must keep the Sabbath, resting one day in seven—as did their covenant King in creation.

The chapter's final verse then states how the Lord inscribes the covenant commands on two stone tablets and gives them to Moses (v. 18). Moses will now go down the mountain and see what Israel has been doing in his absence. It will be a tragic scene.

Section Outline

VI. Israel at Sinai: the Lord gives instructions for the building of his palace-tent among them (24:12–31:18) . . .
  I. The artisans who will make the tabernacle, its furniture and related items (31:1–11)
    1. The divinely gifted artisans (31:1–6b)
    2. (A) The importance of following the Lord's commands in making these things (31:6c)
    3. (B) The items to be made (31:7–11a)
    4. (A') The importance of following the Lord's commands in making these things (31:11b)
  J. Keeping the Sabbath as the sign of the covenant (31:12–17)
    1. (A) The command to keep the Sabbath and first rationale (31:12–13)
    2. (B) The command to keep the Sabbath, the second rationale, and the punishment for breaking it (31:14–15)
    3. (A') The command to keep the Sabbath and first rationale (31:16–17)
  K. The Lord gives the stone tablets of the covenant to Moses (31:18)

Comment

31:1–11 The Lord now turns from describing the tabernacle to identifying the artisans who will make it. Bezalel is described first, here and in other passages (35:30–34; 38:21–23), suggesting he is the chief. He is the grandson of Hur (31:2;

1 Chron. 2:20), presumably the same Hur who is one of Israel's top leaders (Ex. 24:14; cf. comment on 17:10–13).

The Lord "called [Bezalel] by name" (31:2), that is, he commissions him for this task (cf. Isa. 45:1–3; 49:1–3). But he does not call him without preparing him for the task: "I have filled him with the Spirit of God" (Ex. 31:3).[737] This does not refer to salvation (though we should presume Bezalel is a man of faith and a true covenant member). The Spirit of God elsewhere equips people for certain tasks who do not seem to be true believers (Num. 24:2; cf. Josh. 13:22; 2 Pet. 2:15). In other words the filling refers here to a divine gifting, in this case "with ability and intelligence, with knowledge and all craftsmanship" (Ex. 31:3), that is, with the wisdom, skill, and know-how for a wide variety of artistic endeavors (vv. 4–5). The fact that God gives such gifts means that creation of beauty is within the sphere of his direct involvement. The fact that creating beauty takes wisdom and knowledge means that wisdom and knowledge extend beyond merely intellectual pursuits to include hands-on labors. See further comments in the Response section.

The Lord also provides helpers to Bezalel. His main colaborer is Oholiab (v. 6), who is later identified as being gifted as "an engraver and designer and embroiderer in blue and purple and scarlet yarns and fine twined linen" (38:23). Complementing this, Bezalel is identified as being gifted "to devise artistic designs, to work in gold, silver, and bronze, in cutting stones for setting, and in carving wood, to work in every craft" (31:4–5). Some overlap between these lists may exist, but taken together they indicate that Bezalel and Oholiab can do and oversee all the work necessary for making the tabernacle's components.

Other helpers are also named, and the second half of verse 6 could be woodenly rendered, "And into the heart of all who are wise of heart I have put wisdom so they might make all that I have commanded you." Again such gifting is associated with wisdom from God (cf. v. 3). He gifts wisdom to men (such as Bezalel and Oholiab) and women (35:25–26),[738] all of whom are involved in making the tabernacle and its contents, which are now listed (31:7–11; fuller lists are provided in 35:10–19; 39:32–41). To have artistic gifts does not mean there is no room for growth in using them. We later read of how Bezalel and Oholiab are "inspired . . . to teach" (35:34), that is, to serve as master artisans who apprentice others. Developing a skill takes long, exhausting, mind-numbing, hard work. Any artisan knows this. Nonetheless, God grants to all the artisans the gifting to do the work in the first place. He is its source. And the artisans are to use these gifts by being careful to make everything in keeping with the Lord's commands (31:11), a theme found throughout chapters 25–31 (25:9, 40; 27:8; 31:6; etc.). The tabernacle is his home and must be made according to his desires.

---

[737] This could also be rendered "I have filled him with a spirit from God" (cf. LXX: "divine spirit"), but this would not affect the overall point above, since it still means that the wisdom described is ultimately a divine gift.
[738] The word translated as "skillful" and "skill" (Hb. *hokhmah*) in Exodus 35:25–26 is the same word translated in our passage as "ability" (31:6), a word often rendered as "wisdom."

31:12–17 As many commentators have noted, from the beginning of the tabernacle instructions in 25:1 this is the seventh section introduced by the clause "The Lord said to Moses" (31:12; cf. 25:1; 30:11, 17, 22, 34; 31:1). This makes it especially appropriate that it centers on the Sabbath. The passage focuses on reasons for keeping the Sabbath and makes clear the penalty for desecrating it.

Two complementary reasons are given for keeping the Sabbath. First, the Lord explains that it "is a sign between me and you throughout your generations" (v. 13). The word for "sign" occurs elsewhere to describe a visible symbol of a covenant, such as the rainbow in the covenant with Noah (Gen. 9:12, 13, 17) or circumcision in the covenant with Abraham (Gen. 17:11). Here keeping the Sabbath as a day of solemn rest is a sign of the covenant the Lord is entering into with Israel at Sinai (Ex. 31:16–17).[739] (The reasons for choosing the Sabbath as the covenant sign are discussed below in the Response section.)

Second, the Sabbath is "holy to the Lord" (v. 15; cf. 31:14). As explained earlier, by resting on this day "the Lord blessed the Sabbath day and made it holy" (20:11), that is, set it apart as unique and to be recognized as his special day (cf. comment on 20:8–11). As the tent is to be a holy tabernacle in space, the Sabbath is to be a holy tabernacle in time.[740]

These reasons show why breaking the Sabbath is so serious. It is like ripping off a wedding ring and stomping it into the ground, only more so. To break the Sabbath is to reject and deny the Creator and desecrate what he has declared holy. Put differently, if keeping the Sabbath is how Israel declares her faith in this covenant God, then breaking it is to abandon faith in him, reject his covenant, and spit on his holy property (cf. Ezek. 20:12–13, 20–21). Thus the punishment fits the crime (Ex. 31:14–15). Those who reject the covenant sign are cut off from the covenant community. Those who desecrate that which is holy are judged by the Holy One. Those who reject the covenant King experience the punishment given for treason: death itself. Having rejected the earth's Creator, the guilty have rejected their right to live in his creation.

By ending his tabernacle instructions with a discussion of the Sabbath, the Lord makes clear the Israelites must not work on the Sabbath in making the tabernacle.[741] Moreover, since Israel is to keep the Sabbath perpetually as a covenant sign, the Lord also underscores that covenant faithfulness extends beyond building the tabernacle (or doing any other "religious" activities for that matter). It involves faithfulness to all his covenant commands, summarized beautifully in the Ten Commandments, where the command to keep the Sabbath occurs in the midst of nine others that emphasize the importance of loving the Lord with all one's heart and loving one's neighbor as oneself (20:1–17). That is the covenant faithfulness the Lord requires of his people (cf. Matt. 22:37–40).

---

739 The phrase "Sabbath of solemn rest" usually refers to a day on which no work at all may be done (Lev. 16:31; 23:3, 32), in comparison to other special days, on which limited work can be done (cf. Lev. 23:3 with 23:7–8).
740 Propp, *Exodus 19–40*, 494, citing B. Jacob, *The Second Book of the Bible: Exodus*, trans. W. Jacob (Hoboken, NJ: KTAV, 1992), 853–854.
741 Keil, *Exodus*, vol. 2, 218.

31:18 Having finished this portion of covenant instruction, the Lord gives Moses the "two [stone] tablets of the testimony ... written with the finger of God," that is, inscribed by the Lord himself with covenant laws (for "testimony" as covenant law cf. comment on 16:31–36). Later passages state that the laws are written on both sides (32:15) and consist of the Ten Commandments in particular (34:28; Deut. 10:4), which serve as a summary of the entire covenant (cf. comment on 24:12–14). Their size is nowhere stated, though they must be small enough to fit inside the ark and to be carried by Moses down the mountain (25:16; 32:15).[742]

Why two tablets? Many assume the commandments are spread over both, with the four that regulate our behavior to God on the first tablet and the remaining six, which regulate our behavior toward others, on the second. This is possible, though no evidence supports it.

Another answer suggests itself. As noted earlier, significant parallels exist between the Sinai covenant and ancient Near Eastern treaties (cf. comments on 20:1–21; Section Overview of 23:20–33). These parallels might explain not only why there are two tablets but also why they are placed in the tabernacle. "A treaty between the Hittite King Shuppiluliumas (ca. 1375–1335 B.C.) and King Mattiwaza of Mittani in Upper Mesopotamia noted that each of the contracting parties deposited a copy in his respective temple before the shrine of the deity,"[743] and this and other treaties list the gods as divine witnesses to and enforcers of the treaty.[744] This suggests that each of the two stone tablets contains a full copy of the Ten Commandments (31:18), one tablet being Israel's and the other the Lord's. Since the tabernacle is the shared holy space of Israel and the Lord, both copies are placed there, in the ark, over which the Lord sits enthroned as divine witness. Such an understanding cannot be proved, but it enjoys the advantage of aligning with the cultural realities of the time.

In any case Moses can now go down the mountain and show the Israelites the covenant documents the Lord himself has written. The reader might expect this to be a joyful reunion, with the Israelites breaking out in praise that the Lord would offer such relationship to them. Tragically, however, a much different situation is about to unfold.

Response

This chapter is united by the twin themes of work and rest: work in creating the tabernacle in all its beauty (vv. 1–11) and rest as a sign every seventh day that Israel is in relationship with the Lord (vv. 12–17). We may consider these themes by asking two questions.

WHAT DOES BEAUTY HAVE TO DO WITH WISDOM AND WITH GOD?

The work this chapter has in view is the building of the tabernacle, work that will be headed up by a man named Bezalel. Bezalel is introduced to us as someone

---
742 Keil, *Exodus*, vol. 2, 219–220.
743 Sarna, *Exodus*, 108; cf. *ANET*, 205 (Mattiwaza was also known as Kurtiwaza; Sarna uses the former, *ANET* the latter); cf. also *COS* 2.106 (§27).
744 Cf. *ANET*, 200–201, 205–206.

whom the Lord "fills with the Spirit of God [cf. note 737 within comment on 31:1–11], with ability and intelligence, with knowledge and all craftsmanship" to create the tabernacle and its items (vv. 3–5). This leads to three observations.

First, the word for "ability" can also be translated "skill" (35:26) and is the same word usually translated "wisdom" (Hb. *hokhmah*). It is used here with the term "intelligence" and "knowledge." While we sometimes consider intelligence to be only the thinking we do with our heads, the Lord extends it to the work we do with our hands. In this passage in particular the Lord uses the words *wisdom*, *intelligence*, and *knowledge* in describing those gifted to make aesthetically pleasing items, whether for the eyes (the tabernacle, its furniture, the priestly clothing) or for the nose (the perfumed anointing oil and fragrant incense). From a biblical perspective creating beauty takes nothing less than wisdom, intelligence, and knowledge—which should encourage us to value those with wisdom and intelligence in the arts as much as we do those with wisdom and intelligence in the sciences.

Second, the Lord is both the ultimate source of beauty and a lover of it. God gifts Bezalel with the wisdom and intelligence to create the tabernacle and its rich fabrics, gleaming furniture, delightful smells, and resplendent uniforms. God enables a way for everything to be soaked in beauty, for he delights in it. He does not simply give his law; he encases it in beauty.[745] He does not simply give priests; he robes them in beauty. He does not simply make a tent; he establishes a palace of beauty. None of this is surprising. God introduces himself to us as the master Creator (Genesis 1), the maker of all things beautiful. Where beauty exists, it points to him.

This does not mean that all who create beauty know God. God, in his common grace, does not reserve these gifts for believers only. He showers them over his creation so that the beauty he loves can fill his world and point to him even in places where his gospel has not yet been heard. If God so values beauty, what are the implications for believers today? What does it mean for our churches and worship services to be places where beauty matters—as it did in the tabernacle? How can we encourage those divinely gifted with wisdom and knowledge in the arts to use their gifts to create beauty—whether inside or outside the church? That God gifts people to create beauty shows us how much he values it. May we value it as he does.

Finally, if God grants people "ability and intelligence, with knowledge" in creative pursuits, surely he grants people these things in other pursuits. And this has important implications. It calls us to acknowledge that all our gifts are given by God. He is the one who grants us our skills and abilities. It also calls us to think of intelligence and skill in all its forms as something God cares about. He gifts the pastor, teacher, clerk, homemaker, businessman, construction worker, and janitor alike. Whatever one's gifts, they are given by God, and, if he has given them, they are valuable. To put this differently: someone is not a second-class Christian whose gifts are in areas outside church ministry. Gifts are valuable and purposeful because

---

[745] This thought and the two that follow come from my friend Dan Myers.

God has given them, and that brings dignity to work, whatever one's God-glorifying field. A believer does not have to become a minister to serve God and bring him glory. A believer can do so as he uses his gifts in the context of a life of obedience to him. Famed nineteenth-century pastor Charles Spurgeon captures this reality beautifully:

> You housemaids, you cooks, you nurses, you plowmen, you housewives, you traders, you sailors—your labor is holy if you serve the Lord Christ in it, if by living unto Him as you ought to live! The sacred has absorbed the secular! The overarching temple of the Lord covers all your houses and your fields! My brothers and sisters, this ennobles life! . . . This ensures us a reward for all we do![746]

WHY MAKE THE SABBATH THE SIGN OF THE COVENANT?

If the first half of the chapter relates to work, the second relates to rest, and in particular Sabbath rest. For general discussion of the Sabbath command cf. comments on 20:8–11; 31:12–17. As a complement I will focus here on the question, Why make the Sabbath the sign of the covenant? At least two answers may be given.

First, it shows that Israel follows the Lord because by keeping it she is imitating his activity. In other words, if asked why he rests every seventh day, an Israelite could respond, "Because I follow the Lord, the one who made the heavens and the earth in six days and then on the seventh day rested and was refreshed."[747] In this way the Sabbath reminds Israel—for an entire day once a week!—that the Lord has "sanctified" them (31:13), that is, set them apart to be his very own and therefore to walk with him in his ways. Keeping the Sabbath is Israel's declaration that they are his (one author calls this "definitional holiness") and will follow him (what the same author calls "ethical holiness").[748] It entails relationship with the Lord and faithfulness to him. As a wedding ring serves as both a sign of the covenant relationship between husband and wife and a call to be faithful to that covenant, the Sabbath serves as the sign of the covenant relationship between the Lord and Israel and a call to be faithful to that covenant. In this way it is a sign with present implications in terms of Israel's resting every seventh day and being faithful to the covenant commands throughout the week.[749]

Second, from a larger biblical perspective it points to the final salvific rest the Lord will bring about for those in covenant relationship with him. In Hebrews 4

---

[746] Charles H. Spurgeon, "All for Jesus! Sermon #1205," *Metropolitan Tabernacle Pulpit*, vol. 20; cited in Wright, *Exodus*, 544.
[747] The Bible often describes the Lord in human terms so that we can get a sense of who he is or what he has done, but the language must not be pressed too far. The Lord is a warrior on our behalf (Jer. 20:11), meaning he defeats our enemies—but not because he literally holds a weapon in his hand. Here we read that the Lord "rested and was refreshed." Since the Lord has no physical body and never grows tired or weary (Isa. 40:28), the sense here is that he ceased from his work of creating the world (rested) to enjoy the labor of his hands, the satisfaction that comes from a job well done (was refreshed). When used of humans, however, the word "refreshed" focuses more on recharging one's strength (Ex. 23:12; 2 Sam. 16:14). Even so, the point is not lost: if the Lord, who never grows weary, "rests" and is "refreshed" one day in every seven, how much more should his easily tired creatures do the same!
[748] Daniel C. Timmer, *Creation, Tabernacle, and Sabbath: The Sabbath Frame of Exodus 31:12–17; 35:1–3 in Exegetical and Theological Perspective* (Göttingen: Vandenhoeck & Ruprecht, 2009), 176–177.
[749] For the question on whether Christians should keep the Sabbath today cf. note 389 within comment on 20:8–11 and also following paragraph above.

the author describes the full and final experience of the Lord's salvation as a "Sabbath rest for the people of God" (Heb. 4:9). What does the Lord have in store for those who know him through Jesus? Not thorns and thistles but the life-giving rest that comes to those who have been delivered from all evil and ushered into full fellowship with God, enjoying him and all his good gifts. It is a profound, bone-strengthening, soul-nourishing, heart-refreshing, eternally overflowing rest. It is the same rest Jesus speaks of when describing why he came: to relieve us of heavy burdens and provide *rest* for our souls (Matt. 11:28–29). This means that to keep the Sabbath—to cease from work in order to experience a small measure of this rest and enjoyment of the Lord and the good gifts of his creation—is to get a foretaste of that rest to come in the new heavens and earth.

If such a foretaste does not appeal to us, we do well to ask, What has so shaped my tastes and desires that I do not long for that which God promises as my greatest good? In some cultures productivity has become its own god, worshiped so strongly that it makes resting feel heretical. But in the Bible enjoying the Sabbath is one of the truest signs of orthodoxy, for in doing so we imitate our Creator and anticipate the full and final rest promised in Jesus.

OVERVIEW OF
EXODUS 32–34

Over the last twelve chapters the covenant has been made and the Lord has given instructions to build a tabernacle so that he can dwell in his people's midst (chs. 20–31). Next what we would hope to see would be the Israelites' building the tabernacle.[750] Instead we read that they build a golden calf and worship wildly before it. This covenant-shattering act of treachery leads to the main question this section will answer: Can the relationship between the Israelites and the Lord be restored so that he will indeed come to live in his people's midst?

In answering, several themes are highlighted that occur frequently in the Pentateuch, such as the Israelites' tendency to rebel, Moses' role as intercessor and mediator, and the Lord's dual response of justice and mercy.[751] These will be developed in some detail below.

---

[750] The events of Exodus 32–34 are recounted in Deuteronomy 9–10, which telescope them in order to highlight specific themes. Thus Deuteronomy does not focus on chronological precision as much as making the themes clear. Stated differently, chronology is put in the service of the themes. Cf. J. G. McConville, *Deuteronomy* (Downers Grove, IL: IVP Academic, 2002), 178–181; more briefly Wright, *Deuteronomy*, 135–136.

[751] For a fuller exploration cf. Jay Sklar, "Sin and Atonement: Lessons from the Pentateuch," BBR 22/4 (2012): 467–491.

But several other themes are also present. First, at the Lord's command the Levites execute justice on a portion of the idolaters, highlighting the special role they will come to play in Numbers (cf. Numbers 3–4), as well as the dangers of idolatry (cf. Numbers 25). God clearly demands undivided allegiance and does not look lightly on acts of spiritual adultery. He is a faithful husband and expects faithfulness in return.

Second, Exodus 32 paints an unflattering picture of Aaron (vv. 2–5, 21–25), showing us how the Bible does not hesitate to point out the weaknesses and failings of even major characters. Later narratives will do so for Aaron again (Numbers 12; 20:2–13), Miriam (ch. 12), and Moses himself (20:2–13). This is both a warning to those in leadership and an encouragement: the Lord uses sinners to lead his people and accomplish his purposes, which gives us hope, emphasizes his grace, and points to him as ultimate deliverer. Salvation comes despite us and because of him!

Third, what matters most is God's presence in his people's midst. Earlier God said he had redeemed his people so that he could live with them (Ex. 29:46). This is his deepest desire; he has made us for himself and longs for us not simply to know him but to be near him. Stated from our perspective, we find our fullest joy when he is near, for we have been made for his presence. Thus when the Lord says in these chapters that he will not come to dwell among his people (32:34; 33:3, 5), it is a national tragedy (33:4), and Moses becomes laser-focused on pleading for the Lord to reconsider (33:12–13, 15–16; 34:9). This underscores that our purpose as humans is to know God not in theory but in practice, experiencing his presence in the midst of all we do. The Bible begins with an earthly paradise where the Lord walks with Adam and Eve (Gen. 3:8) and ends with a heaven-on-earth paradise where the Lord walks with his people (Rev. 21:3–4). These bookends show us how the story is to play out in between: God will walk in his people's midst, and his people will walk with him.

EXODUS 32–34

32 When the people saw that Moses delayed to come down from the mountain, the people gathered themselves together to Aaron and said to him, "Up, make us gods who shall go before us. As for this Moses, the man who brought us up out of the land of Egypt, we do not know what has become of him." ² So Aaron said to them, "Take off the rings of gold that are in the ears of your wives, your sons, and your daughters, and bring them to me." ³ So all the people took off the rings of gold that were in their ears and brought them to Aaron. ⁴ And he received the gold from their hand and fashioned it with a graving tool and made a golden¹ calf.

And they said, "These are your gods, O Israel, who brought you up out of the land of Egypt!" ⁵ When Aaron saw this, he built an altar before it. And Aaron made a proclamation and said, "Tomorrow shall be a feast to the LORD." ⁶ And they rose up early the next day and offered burnt offerings and brought peace offerings. And the people sat down to eat and drink and rose up to play.

⁷ And the LORD said to Moses, "Go down, for your people, whom you brought up out of the land of Egypt, have corrupted themselves. ⁸ They have turned aside quickly out of the way that I commanded them. They have made for themselves a golden calf and have worshiped it and sacrificed to it and said, 'These are your gods, O Israel, who brought you up out of the land of Egypt!'" ⁹ And the LORD said to Moses, "I have seen this people, and behold, it is a stiff-necked people. ¹⁰ Now therefore let me alone, that my wrath may burn hot against them and I may consume them, in order that I may make a great nation of you."

¹¹ But Moses implored the LORD his God and said, "O LORD, why does your wrath burn hot against your people, whom you have brought out of the land of Egypt with great power and with a mighty hand? ¹² Why should the Egyptians say, 'With evil intent did he bring them out, to kill them in the mountains and to consume them from the face of the earth'? Turn from your burning anger and relent from this disaster against your people. ¹³ Remember Abraham, Isaac, and Israel, your servants, to whom you swore by your own self, and said to them, 'I will multiply your offspring as the stars of heaven, and all this land that I have promised I will give to your offspring, and they shall inherit it forever.'" ¹⁴ And the LORD relented from the disaster that he had spoken of bringing on his people.

¹⁵ Then Moses turned and went down from the mountain with the two tablets of the testimony in his hand, tablets that were written on both sides; on the front and on the back they were written. ¹⁶ The tablets were the work of God, and the writing was the writing of God, engraved on the tablets. ¹⁷ When Joshua heard the noise of the people as they shouted, he said to Moses, "There is a noise of war in the camp." ¹⁸ But he said, "It is not the sound of shouting for victory, or the sound of the cry of defeat, but the sound of singing that I hear." ¹⁹ And as soon as he came near the camp and saw the calf and the dancing, Moses' anger burned hot, and he threw the tablets out of his hands and broke them at the foot of the mountain. ²⁰ He took the calf that they had made and burned it with fire and ground it to powder and scattered it on the water and made the people of Israel drink it.

²¹ And Moses said to Aaron, "What did this people do to you that you have brought such a great sin upon them?" ²² And Aaron said, "Let not the anger of my lord burn hot. You know the people, that they are set on evil. ²³ For they said to me, 'Make us gods who shall go before us. As for this Moses, the man who brought us up out of the land of Egypt, we do not know what has become of him.' ²⁴ So I said to them, 'Let any who have gold take it off.' So they gave it to me, and I threw it into the fire, and out came this calf."

²⁵ And when Moses saw that the people had broken loose (for Aaron had let them break loose, to the derision of their enemies), ²⁶ then Moses stood in the gate of the camp and said, "Who is on the LORD's side? Come to me." And all the sons of Levi gathered around him. ²⁷ And he said to them, "Thus says the LORD God of Israel, 'Put your sword on your side each of you, and go to and fro from gate to gate throughout the camp, and each of you kill his brother and his companion and his neighbor.'" ²⁸ And the

sons of Levi did according to the word of Moses. And that day about three thousand men of the people fell. ²⁹ And Moses said, "Today you have been ordained for the service of the LORD, each one at the cost of his son and of his brother, so that he might bestow a blessing upon you this day."

³⁰ The next day Moses said to the people, "You have sinned a great sin. And now I will go up to the LORD; perhaps I can make atonement for your sin." ³¹ So Moses returned to the LORD and said, "Alas, this people has sinned a great sin. They have made for themselves gods of gold. ³² But now, if you will forgive their sin—but if not, please blot me out of your book that you have written." ³³ But the LORD said to Moses, "Whoever has sinned against me, I will blot out of my book. ³⁴ But now go, lead the people to the place about which I have spoken to you; behold, my angel shall go before you. Nevertheless, in the day when I visit, I will visit their sin upon them."

³⁵ Then the LORD sent a plague on the people, because they made the calf, the one that Aaron made.

33 The LORD said to Moses, "Depart; go up from here, you and the people whom you have brought up out of the land of Egypt, to the land of which I swore to Abraham, Isaac, and Jacob, saying, 'To your offspring I will give it.' ² I will send an angel before you, and I will drive out the Canaanites, the Amorites, the Hittites, the Perizzites, the Hivites, and the Jebusites. ³ Go up to a land flowing with milk and honey; but I will not go up among you, lest I consume you on the way, for you are a stiff-necked people."

⁴ When the people heard this disastrous word, they mourned, and no one put on his ornaments. ⁵ For the LORD had said to Moses, "Say to the people of Israel, 'You are a stiff-necked people; if for a single moment I should go up among you, I would consume you. So now take off your ornaments, that I may know what to do with you.'" ⁶ Therefore the people of Israel stripped themselves of their ornaments, from Mount Horeb onward.

⁷ Now Moses used to take the tent and pitch it outside the camp, far off from the camp, and he called it the tent of meeting. And everyone who sought the LORD would go out to the tent of meeting, which was outside the camp. ⁸ Whenever Moses went out to the tent, all the people would rise up, and each would stand at his tent door, and watch Moses until he had gone into the tent. ⁹ When Moses entered the tent, the pillar of cloud would descend and stand at the entrance of the tent, and the LORD² would speak with Moses. ¹⁰ And when all the people saw the pillar of cloud standing at the entrance of the tent, all the people would rise up and worship, each at his tent door. ¹¹ Thus the LORD used to speak to Moses face to face, as a man speaks to his friend. When Moses turned again into the camp, his assistant Joshua the son of Nun, a young man, would not depart from the tent.

¹² Moses said to the LORD, "See, you say to me, 'Bring up this people,' but you have not let me know whom you will send with me. Yet you have said, 'I know you by name, and you have also found favor in my sight.' ¹³ Now therefore, if I have found favor in your sight, please show me now your ways, that I may know you in order to find favor in your sight. Consider too that this nation is your people." ¹⁴ And he said, "My presence will go with you, and I will give you rest." ¹⁵ And he said to him, "If your presence will not go with me, do not bring us up from here. ¹⁶ For how shall it be known that I have found favor in your sight, I and your people? Is it not in

your going with us, so that we are distinct, I and your people, from every other people on the face of the earth?"

¹⁷ And the LORD said to Moses, "This very thing that you have spoken I will do, for you have found favor in my sight, and I know you by name." ¹⁸ Moses said, "Please show me your glory." ¹⁹ And he said, "I will make all my goodness pass before you and will proclaim before you my name 'The LORD.' And I will be gracious to whom I will be gracious, and will show mercy on whom I will show mercy. ²⁰ But," he said, "you cannot see my face, for man shall not see me and live." ²¹ And the LORD said, "Behold, there is a place by me where you shall stand on the rock, ²² and while my glory passes by I will put you in a cleft of the rock, and I will cover you with my hand until I have passed by. ²³ Then I will take away my hand, and you shall see my back, but my face shall not be seen."

34 The LORD said to Moses, "Cut for yourself two tablets of stone like the first, and I will write on the tablets the words that were on the first tablets, which you broke. ² Be ready by the morning, and come up in the morning to Mount Sinai, and present yourself there to me on the top of the mountain. ³ No one shall come up with you, and let no one be seen throughout all the mountain. Let no flocks or herds graze opposite that mountain." ⁴ So Moses cut two tablets of stone like the first. And he rose early in the morning and went up on Mount Sinai, as the LORD had commanded him, and took in his hand two tablets of stone. ⁵ The LORD descended in the cloud and stood with him there, and proclaimed the name of the LORD. ⁶ The LORD passed before him and proclaimed, "The LORD, the LORD, a God merciful and gracious, slow to anger, and abounding in steadfast love and faithfulness, ⁷ keeping steadfast love for thousands,³ forgiving iniquity and transgression and sin, but who will by no means clear the guilty, visiting the iniquity of the fathers on the children and the children's children, to the third and the fourth generation." ⁸ And Moses quickly bowed his head toward the earth and worshiped. ⁹ And he said, "If now I have found favor in your sight, O Lord, please let the Lord go in the midst of us, for it is a stiff-necked people, and pardon our iniquity and our sin, and take us for your inheritance."

¹⁰ And he said, "Behold, I am making a covenant. Before all your people I will do marvels, such as have not been created in all the earth or in any nation. And all the people among whom you are shall see the work of the LORD, for it is an awesome thing that I will do with you.

¹¹ "Observe what I command you this day. Behold, I will drive out before you the Amorites, the Canaanites, the Hittites, the Perizzites, the Hivites, and the Jebusites. ¹² Take care, lest you make a covenant with the inhabitants of the land to which you go, lest it become a snare in your midst. ¹³ You shall tear down their altars and break their pillars and cut down their Asherim ¹⁴ (for you shall worship no other god, for the LORD, whose name is Jealous, is a jealous God), ¹⁵ lest you make a covenant with the inhabitants of the land, and when they whore after their gods and sacrifice to their gods and you are invited, you eat of his sacrifice, ¹⁶ and you take of their daughters for your sons, and their daughters whore after their gods and make your sons whore after their gods.

¹⁷ "You shall not make for yourself any gods of cast metal.

¹⁸ "You shall keep the Feast of Unleavened Bread. Seven days you shall eat unleavened bread, as I commanded you, at the time appointed in the month Abib, for in the month Abib you came out from Egypt. ¹⁹ All that

open the womb are mine, all your male[4] livestock, the firstborn of cow and sheep. [20] The firstborn of a donkey you shall redeem with a lamb, or if you will not redeem it you shall break its neck. All the firstborn of your sons you shall redeem. And none shall appear before me empty-handed.

[21] "Six days you shall work, but on the seventh day you shall rest. In plowing time and in harvest you shall rest. [22] You shall observe the Feast of Weeks, the firstfruits of wheat harvest, and the Feast of Ingathering at the year's end. [23] Three times in the year shall all your males appear before the Lord GOD, the God of Israel. [24] For I will cast out nations before you and enlarge your borders; no one shall covet your land, when you go up to appear before the LORD your God three times in the year.

[25] "You shall not offer the blood of my sacrifice with anything leavened, or let the sacrifice of the Feast of the Passover remain until the morning. [26] The best of the firstfruits of your ground you shall bring to the house of the LORD your God. You shall not boil a young goat in its mother's milk."

[27] And the LORD said to Moses, "Write these words, for in accordance with these words I have made a covenant with you and with Israel." [28] So he was there with the LORD forty days and forty nights. He neither ate bread nor drank water. And he wrote on the tablets the words of the covenant, the Ten Commandments.[5]

[29] When Moses came down from Mount Sinai, with the two tablets of the testimony in his hand as he came down from the mountain, Moses did not know that the skin of his face shone because he had been talking with God.[6] [30] Aaron and all the people of Israel saw Moses, and behold, the skin of his face shone, and they were afraid to come near him. [31] But Moses called to them, and Aaron and all the leaders of the congregation returned to him, and Moses talked with them. [32] Afterward all the people of Israel came near, and he commanded them all that the LORD had spoken with him on Mount Sinai. [33] And when Moses had finished speaking with them, he put a veil over his face.

[34] Whenever Moses went in before the LORD to speak with him, he would remove the veil, until he came out. And when he came out and told the people of Israel what he was commanded, [35] the people of Israel would see the face of Moses, that the skin of Moses' face was shining. And Moses would put the veil over his face again, until he went in to speak with him.

[1] Hebrew *cast metal*; also verse 8 [2] Hebrew *he* [3] Or *to the thousandth generation* [4] Septuagint, Theodotion, Vulgate, Targum; the meaning of the Hebrew is uncertain [5] Hebrew *the ten words* [6] Hebrew *him*

Section Overview

"Make us gods who shall go before us" (32:1)—this single request plunges the Israelites' story into the realm of treachery and coming judgment, leaving the reader to wonder whether the Israelites will even come out alive, let alone in a continued relationship with the Lord.

The opening verses introduce the tragic event that derails the narrative: while Moses is up the mountain receiving the covenant tablets from the Lord, the Israelites make a golden calf, proclaim it as their savior, and worship with wild revelry before it (vv. 1–6). Seeing their treachery, the Lord commands Moses to descend. He threatens to wipe them out and begin the patriarchal promises anew through Moses (vv. 7–10). The Israelites have broken the covenant, shattering their relationship with the Lord. Moses must try and piece it back together, which he does through four acts of intercession that spread over chapters 32–34.

In the first he pleads for the Lord not to wipe out the people as they deserve (32:11–13). In the second he asks the Lord to forgive them (vv. 31–32). In the third he beseeches the Lord to go in the people's midst (33:12–13, 15–16). And in the fourth he begs that the Lord would renew the covenant (34:9). It is a slow process, and no wonder—severe relationship breaches are seldom healed instantly. In this case especially, the offending party needs time to own the wrong and show genuine repentance for it.

The Lord agrees to each of Moses' requests and in several instances implicitly encourages him to intercede in the first place (cf. comments on 32:7–10; 33:1–6; 34:9). This is a God who seeks to forgive and continue in covenant relationship with his sinful people. For the people's part we see various acts of faithfulness (32:26–28), repentance (33:4–6), and worship (34:10) along the way. By the end of chapter 34 the restoration is complete, and Moses comes down the mountain with new covenant tablets (34:29–35).[752]

In the midst of the four acts of intercession Moses makes one request of his own: to see the Lord's glory (33:18). This is partly for Israel's sake: if the Lord reveals himself fully to Moses, it guarantees that Moses has found favor in his eyes and that God will answer Moses' prayers on Israel's behalf. But Moses also seems to ask because he desires to know God more deeply and fully. The Lord's answer leads to the most complete and beautiful description of God to this point in the Bible (34:6–7). It corresponds to the very things we see in these chapters. On the one hand he is a God who brings justice to bear against sin (34:7b), which he does at two different points in chapter 32 (32:27, 35). But he is also a God who overflows with forgiving mercy and faithful love (34:6–7a), which he shows each time that he responds to Moses' prayers on the people's behalf. The end result warns us against the dangers of sin while encouraging us that, no matter how great our sin, his merciful love is greater still—if only we turn to him with repentant hearts. He has not created his people for judgment; he has created us for relationship with him and leans toward us with the mercy and love we need for this relationship to work.

Section Outline

VII. Israel at Sinai: the people break the covenant; the Lord renews the covenant (32:1–34:35)

    A. The people's idolatry, the Lord's anger, Moses' first act of intercession for Israel (that the Lord would not wipe out the people) (32:1–14)

---

[752] Exodus 34 has many parallels to chapters 19–24: Israel and/or Moses are to "be ready" for a special appearance of the Lord's glory (19:11; 34:2), the Israelites and their animals must stay off the mountain (19:12–23; 34:3), the Lord comes down to the top of the mountain (19:20; 34:2, 5), and the Lord gives Moses the Ten Commandments over a period of forty days and nights (20:1–17; 24:18; 34:10–28). The effect is to let us know that the covenant has been renewed: the golden calf incident is a thing of the past, and the Lord will pick up with his people where he left off in chapter 31. Cf. comments on 35:1–3.

1. The people worship the golden calf (32:1–6)
2. The Lord's angry response (32:7–10)
3. Moses' intercession and the Lord's merciful response (32:11–14)

B. Moses' anger at the people's idolatry, his confrontation of Aaron, and his execution of justice (32:15–29)
   1. Moses' anger at the people's idolatry (32:15–20)
   2. Moses confronts Aaron (32:21–24)
   3. Moses has judgment executed (32:25–29)

C. Moses' second act of intercession for Israel (that the Lord would forgive the people) (32:30–33:6)
   1. Moses tells the people his plan (32:30)
   2. Moses' request: please forgive the people (32:31–32)
   3. The Lord's response (32:33–34)
   4. Flash forward: the Lord's judgment on the people (32:35)
   5. Flashback: the Lord's response (33:1–3)
   6. The people's response (33:4–6)

D. Moses' third act of intercession for Israel (that the Lord would go in Israel's midst) (33:7–17)
   1. The place of intercession: the first tent of meeting (33:7–11)
   2. Moses' request: please be present in our midst (33:12–17)

E. Moses asks to see the Lord's glory (33:18–23)
   1. Moses asks to see the Lord's glory (33:18)
   2. The Lord's response (33:19–23)

F. The Lord reveals his glory (34:1–8)
   1. The Lord's commands of preparation (34:1–3)
   2. Moses obeys and goes up the mountain (34:4)
   3. The Lord comes down in the cloud and proclaims his name (34:5–7)
   4. Moses' response of worship (34:8)

G. Moses' fourth act of intercession for Israel (that the Lord would renew the covenant) (34:9–28)
   1. Moses' request (34:9)
   2. The Lord's response: the covenant is renewed (34:10–28)

H. The shining face of Moses (34:29–35)
   1. Moses' face shines (34:29)
   2. The people's response of fear (34:30)
   3. Moses passes on the Lord's commands (34:31–32)
   4. Moses' use of a veil (34:33–35)

Comment

32:1–6 Moses spends forty days and nights on the mountain (24:18). At some point the people give up on his ever returning and take matters into their own hands

(32:1). Moses has been not only their leader but also their connection to God and his protective help and power. In Moses' absence they need a new way to connect to the divine, and they resort to the most common approach of the day: physical idols. Israel has been taken out of Egypt, but much of Egypt remains in Israel (cf. Acts 7:39). Sin's muscle memory can be very strong.

To start they "gathered themselves together to Aaron" (Ex. 32:1), which might also be translated "gathered themselves together *against* Aaron." The phrase occurs three other times in the Pentateuch, always with a threatening connotation (Num. 16:3, 42; 20:2). One senses that emotions are running high.

Next they demand he make them a god "who shall go before us" (Ex. 32:1)[753]—to protect and provide for them as they move from that place. Moses had indeed brought them up from Egypt, but, they claim, "we do not know what has become of him," and they seek to ensure access to divine aid. They believe an idol to be the most certain way of doing so.

Aaron immediately gives in, asking them for the golden earrings of their wives and children (v. 2).[754] This is perhaps the same jewelry the Lord gave them as plunder from the Egyptians (3:22) and was to be used to make the tabernacle as a sign that their redeeming God wanted to live in their midst. Instead, Aaron turns the gold into a calf (32:4),[755] that is, a young version of a bull. Bulls were commonly worshiped as idols in the ancient Near East.[756] Seeing it, the people blasphemously describe it as their true deliverer.[757]

In light of their response Aaron builds an altar in front of the calf and proclaims, "Tomorrow shall be a feast to the LORD" (v. 5). He may be attempting to salvage the situation by suggesting the calf represents the Lord. But even this would be a treacherous disregard of the Lord's earlier commands (20:4–5, 23). Not surprisingly, we later learn the Lord is so angry with Aaron "that he was ready to destroy him" (Deut. 9:20). The people, in any case, appear to miss Aaron's possible nuance and seem to view the calf itself as the god who has delivered them (Ex. 32:4; cf. also 32:8; comment on 32:25–29). They have broken the second commandment (20:4–5) as well as the first (20:3).[758]

The next day the Israelites feast on the meat of the peace offerings they have made before the idol (32:6). This is especially tragic, as peace offerings function as a shared covenant meal (cf. comments on 24:3–8; 24:9–11), meaning the Israelites are proclaiming their fidelity to the golden calf—and doing so with great enthusiasm! The word translated "to play" is used elsewhere for laughing

---

[753] The Hebrew of verse 1 could be rendered either "Make us a god" or "Make us gods," and the Hebrew of verses 4 and 8 either "This is your god" or "These are your gods." English versions are divided. In favor of the former translations is the fact that there was just one golden calf. For grammatical justification cf. *GKC* §145h.
[754] The word translated "take off" is used elsewhere with a violent sense of "tearing off" (Zech. 11:16) or "stripping off" (Ezek. 19:12). Aaron is perhaps matching the crowd's emotion and exhorting it to do this with haste.
[755] For the calf's construction cf. comment on 32:15–20 (at v. 20).
[756] "Among the Egyptians the bull represented [the god] Apis in the pantheon while among the Canaanites he symbolized Baal" (Childs, *Book of Exodus*, 565). That the word "calf" can refer to a young bull finds support in Genesis 15:9, which uses the feminine form of this word to refer to a three-year-old animal (Alexander, *Exodus*, 622).
[757] For "These are your gods" cf. note 753 within comment on 32:1–6.
[758] Ndjerareou, *Exodus*, in *Africa Bible Commentary*, 125.

(Gen. 17:17) or entertaining (Judg. 16:25) and can have sexual overtones (Gen. 39:17). It refers here to festive singing and dancing (Ex. 32:18–19), perhaps with lewd behavior implied (cf. v. 25), and is undoubtedly fueled by the drinking just mentioned (v. 6). The resulting behavior is so rowdy that Joshua mistakes its sound for the sound of war (v. 17). This is a raucous and drunken party in honor of their newfound god.

32:7–10 Meanwhile, on the mountain the Lord has just finished inscribing and giving the covenant tablets to Moses. Seeing what is happening below, he is understandably furious. The people just confirmed their relationship with him only forty days before (24:1–11). Their treacherous worship of another god so soon is like "adultery on one's wedding night."[759] And just as adultery jeopardizes a marriage, so the Israelites' idolatry has jeopardized their relationship with the Lord.

The Lord commands Moses to go down to "your people" (32:7). This is an ominous description. Throughout Exodus the Lord has repeatedly referred to Israel as "my people" (3:7, 10; 5:1; 6:7; 7:4, 16; etc.). Now he distances himself from them. Or perhaps more accurately he names the distance they have created: "They [have] exchanged the glory of God for the image of an ox that eats grass" (Ps. 106:20). To this point in history the exodus has been the most significant act of salvation the Lord has accomplished for a people, and the Israelites have now attributed it to a piece of calf-shaped metal. This is akin to someone's telling his mother that a woman he just met gave him birth, and he will act as her child from now on.

The Lord describes what he will do. To this point in Exodus, when he "sees" his people, he is paying attention to them because their suffering is so great (2:25; 3:7, 9; 4:31). Now what he "sees" most is that they are "stiff-necked," that is, stubbornly sinful, unwilling to yield to discipline or correction (Deut. 31:27; Neh. 9:16–17). As a result, he will consume them in his wrath and make Moses into a great nation in their place (Ex. 32:9–10). It is as though he says, "Moses, I will make you like a second Abraham, to whom I made the same promise four hundred years ago (cf. Gen. 12:2). I will not abandon faithfulness to that promise, but I need to start all over again." Significantly, however, the Lord prefaces his statement of judgment with the command "Now therefore let me alone" (Ex. 32:10). If the Lord's decision to abandon Israel were absolute and final, such a statement would be unnecessary. Thus the Lord's statement hints at the fact that, if Moses intercedes, a way of mercy may yet be found. In other words this is more an invitation to pray than a command not to—an invitation Moses immediately accepts.[760]

32:11–14 Moses does not simply pray; he "implored the LORD his God," a term commonly used to refer to seeking someone's favor (of seeking God's favor: 1 Sam. 13:12; 1 Kings 13:6; etc.; of seeking man's favor: Job 11:19; Prov. 19:6). Moses'

---

[759] R. W. L. Moberly, "How May We Speak of God? A Reconsideration of the Nature of Biblical Theology," *TynBul* 53 (2002): 198; cited in Wright, *Exodus*, 551.
[760] Stuart (*Exodus*, 670) compares this to the statement "Yet forty days, and Nineveh will be overthrown" (Jonah 3:4), which is actually an invitation to repent so that the destruction does not occur—an invitation the Ninevites happily accept, allowing them to escape destruction.

words could be paraphrased, "O Lord, please do not let your anger burn against Israel.[761] They are not simply my people (Ex. 32:7) but *your* people (v. 11)! You are the one who brought them out of Egypt (v. 11b)! You are the one who showed your great power before Egypt, the mightiest nation on earth. Do not give Egypt the opportunity to speak ill of you (v. 12a)![762] Have I mentioned these are *your* people? Please do not carry out your judgment (v. 12b)! After all, you made promises to our fathers. You swore promises by your own self (Gen. 22:16) — the greatest name by which one can swear[763] — and these promises are for the Israelites! Do not start over with me; continue with them (Ex. 32:13)!"

This is the first of Moses' four acts of intercession on Israel's behalf in chapters 32–34 (cf. Section Overview). The Lord listens to his prayer and relents of the disaster he had threatened (32:14). This speaks to his merciful nature. He wants not to judge his people but to show them patient forgiveness and steadfast love—which he will soon emphasize to Moses (34:6–7). At the same time, what he relents of is his threat to wipe out the people completely (32:10); he still may execute some form of judgment or discipline. Just because a parent forgives a child of great wrong does not mean there will not be consequences, even very severe ones—as Israel soon learns.

32:15–20 In the meantime Moses heads down the mountain (v. 15a). The text pauses to describe the stone tablets he carries: they are covenant tablets ("testimony" refers to a covenant; cf. comment on 16:31–36) written on both sides and are God's work; that is, God has made the tablets and engraved the covenant on them (32:15b–16; cf. comment on 31:18). The reason they are mentioned becomes clear momentarily.

We learned earlier that Moses' assistant, Joshua, had gone with him up the mountain (cf. 24:13; whether he went all the way up with Moses or only partway up is nowhere stated). Joshua now reenters the story as he and Moses draw nearer to the Israelite camp at the mountain's base. He hears such a loud commotion that he assumes the people are shouting as they either celebrate victory or lament loss in war (32:17). Moses replies that it is neither; they are simply singing loudly (v. 18). In other words a riotous party is taking place.

As Moses draws near enough to see the golden calf and the people worshiping before it with singing and dancing, his "anger burned hot" (v. 19). The same phrase was just used to describe the Lord's anger (v. 10)—the very anger Moses asked the Lord to avert (v. 11). Now seeing its cause, Moses has the same response; the people's treachery against their faithful Lord is rightly infuriating. Moses throws the God-made, God-engraved tablets to the ground, shattering the covenant into a thousand pieces at the foot of the mountain—the very place where the people had first pledged covenant faithfulness (cf. 24:4–8).[764] Shattering the tablets here

---

[761] For a question as a request cf. Joüon §161h.
[762] Cf. Numbers 14:15–16; Deuteronomy 9:28; 32:26–27 (Sarna, *Exodus*, 261n26).
[763] Bush, *Commentary on Exodus*, 514. Cf. Hebrews 6:13.
[764] Houtman, *Exodus*, vol. 3, 658.

is a visual picture of what the people have just done with their idolatrous worship (32:19).

Moses then turns his attention to the golden calf. Sarna suggests it is a "wooden model... overlaid with gold."[765] This might explain how Moses could burn it and then ground the charcoal remains and the melted gold overlay into fine pieces (v. 20; cf. Deut. 9:21), though it is also possible the language of this verse is simply "a conventional way to describe demolition and is not a literal description of how a statue might be destroyed."[766] Either way, the point remains: he demolishes it completely. Casting the idolatrous mixture on the water flowing down the mountain, he makes the people drink it (Ex. 32:20; cf. Deut. 9:21). Some have suggested this is similar to the ritual in Numbers 5:11–28 and that some visual mark appears on those guilty of idolatry, identifying them for the Levites. The idolatrous, however, number far more than merely three thousand people (Ex. 32:3, 7–10, 35).[767] Perhaps this is simply a punishment corresponding to the crime, a way of saying, "You long this much for an idol? Then I will make sure to fill your bellies with it!" Either way, the calf is shown to be what it really is: not a god but merely a completely ordinary statue.

32:21–24 Moses now confronts Aaron (v. 21). He had left Aaron in charge when he went up the mountain (24:14), and now he demands to know what the people could possibly have done to make Aaron lead them into such great sin. Moses' question is instructive. He is experienced enough in leadership to know the people may have pressured Aaron, and yet he views leadership highly enough to know Aaron still bears responsibility.

Aaron's answer begins honestly enough. He notes the people's tendency to evil—a tendency Moses himself has experienced (14:11; 15:24; 16:2, 20; etc.)—and accurately and fully describes their reason for desiring an idol (32:23; cf. v. 1).[768] But he abbreviates his role in the events and finishes laughably, at best: "I threw [the gold] into the fire, and out came this calf" (v. 24). In reality Aaron himself had "fashioned [the gold] with a graving tool and made a golden calf" (v. 4). Many of us can identify with Aaron's evasiveness and selective recounting. It is far easier to describe other's sin in detail than even to admit our own.

32:25–29 The situation has now gotten out of control. The people have "broken loose" (v. 25), language used elsewhere to describe unkempt hair allowed to hang loose and do whatever it wants (Lev. 10:6; 21:10). The picture here is of the people's having cast off even the basics of orderly society as they worship the idol in drunken and riotous rebellion. Aaron's responsibility is again emphasized, since he is the one who "had let them break loose to the derision of their enemies." No enemy is currently watching Israel, so this phrase must describe how the enemies

---

[765] Sarna, *Exodus*, 203, citing Isaiah 30:22; 40:19; Hosea 8:6; so also Cassuto, *Commentary on the Book of Exodus*, 412.
[766] Meyers, *Exodus*, 260; cf. 2 Kings 23:15.
[767] Houtman, *Exodus*, vol. 3, 659.
[768] On the question of whether to translate "god" or "gods" in Exodus 32:23 cf. note 753 within comment on 32:1–6.

will react once Israel's behavior becomes known to them. And while there is some question about whether to translate this as "derision" or "gloating" of their enemies, the endpoint is not much different: in either case their enemies will look on Israel not as a righteous people to emulate but as a drunken laughingstock.

Moses takes decisive action. He stands at the camp's "gate" (Ex. 32:26), that is, the place considered the camp's entrance, and summons any whose first allegiance is to the Lord. The only tribe to respond is that of Levi. Moses conveys the Lord's command for them to take up a sword and go throughout the camp to execute the Lord's judgment on the treasonous—even family and friends (v. 27).[769] The Levites obey immediately, executing three thousand people (v. 28). Since this is only a fraction of the non-Levites in the camp, clearly not every guilty person is punished. This suggests the Levites kill the ringleaders or the most serious offenders. In doing so they set themselves apart for the Lord's service and blessing (v. 29), a fact later celebrated in song (Deut. 33:8–9). But this comes at great personal cost, since deciding for the kingdom of God often means deciding against family and friends ("each one at the cost of his son and of his brother"; Ex. 32:29; cf. Matt. 10:37; Luke 14:26).

32:30–35 The next day is very somber. While the Lord has agreed not to wipe out the entire nation (Ex. 32:14), the Israelites have broken the covenant and been given no assurance they will receive its promises. Moses knows the people are therefore still in great danger, and so he tells them he will attempt to make atonement on their behalf (v. 30). But there is no guarantee, so he chooses his words carefully: "*Perhaps* I can make atonement for your sin." If we compare this to a marriage, we could say that the Lord has biblical grounds for divorce, and Moses does not know what the Lord will do.

Moses goes back up the mountain to make his second act of intercession in chapters 32–34 (cf. Section Overview). He acknowledges the people's great sin and pleads for the Lord's forgiveness (32:31–32a). He underscores the request by asking for God, if forgiveness is not given, to "blot me out of your book that you have written" (v. 32b). In other words, "You write history as one writes a book,[770] and I would rather be blotted out of the story at this point if Israel is not forgiven." He is not offering himself as a sacrifice (kill me *instead of* the people); he is simply saying that, if they are not forgiven, he would rather not live (cf. Num. 11:10–15).[771] In doing so he shows his deep commitment to the people and his deep desire for their well-being. Moses is a true shepherd.

---

[769] For treason as a capital crime cf. comment on 21:15. For further thoughts on explaining such judgment in a modern age cf. Response section on 13:17–15:21, "What Is the Warning?"; "How Do We Respond?" The fact that family members are killed suggests that "all" in 32:26 is hyperbole to indicate that the vast majority of the tribe draws near.

[770] Cf. Psalm 139:16.

[771] So also Houtman, *Exodus*, vol. 3, 673; Stuart, *Exodus*, 685n72; Wright, *Exodus*, 559. I once spoke with a man who used Exodus 32:32–33 as proof that Jesus could not have been substituted on our behalf because God in this verse rejects the idea of substitutionary atonement. But Moses is not actually offering himself as a self-substitute. As for the idea of substitutionary atonement, other Scriptures are clear that this occurs not only with animals on people's behalf (Lev. 4:27–31; 16:6, 11; 17:11; etc.) but also with the Lord's servant on people's behalf (Isa. 53:1–12)—and that this was Jesus' own self-understanding (Mark 10:45; 14:24).

The Lord begins by stating that he will not wipe Moses out with the guilty; he will judge those who have sinned (Ex. 32:33). But he follows this with words of assurance and warning. The assurance is that Moses may "lead the people to the place" the Lord has promised them. Israel will still inherit the Promised Land, and the Lord's angel will continue to go before them (v. 34a). Clearly some level of forgiveness has happened. The warning is that punishment for sin will still come (v. 34b). As noted above, forgiveness does not mean the absence of discipline (as any parent knows).

That discipline is now named: "The LORD *sent a plague*" (v. 35a). The same word is used in 12:23, 27 to refer to a fatal blow, and the noun built on the same root occurs elsewhere in the Pentateuch to refer to fatal consequences (Num. 14:37; 16:48–49; 25:8–9). The implication is that many more of the people die as a result of their sin. The verse ends by making clear that, while Aaron made the calf, he did so because the people desired it be made, the sense being, "*The Israelites are the ones who had this calf made*, the one Aaron made."

33:1–6 Verses 1–2 resume the thought of 32:34a. This suggests that verse 35 describes a judgment that occurs later—showing the threat of verse 34b is carried out—and that 33:1 returns to the present, as the Lord continues his speech to Moses.[772]

Moses earlier reminded the Lord of his promise to the patriarchs to give the Promised Land to their descendants (32:13), and the Lord affirms he will keep that promise and carry it out by means of a conquering angel who will go before the Israelites (33:1–2). This sounds similar to the Lord's promise in 23:20–23 to send an angel before them, but there is a key difference. The Lord followed his earlier promise by commanding Israel to collect materials for a sanctuary so that he could dwell in Israel's midst (25:1–8). Here he follows his promise by stating, "I will not go up among you, lest I consume you on the way, for you are a stiff-necked people" (33:3). To be stiff-necked is to adopt a posture of proud rebellion (cf. comment on 32:7–10), and those in such a posture are most at risk of the Lord's judgment. He therefore will not dwell among them; it is far too dangerous for them. So all the tabernacle instructions in chapters 25–31 have been for nothing; a tabernacle is no longer needed. Indeed, the whole point of the exodus ("I am the LORD their God, who brought them out of the land of Egypt *that I might dwell among them*"; 29:46) seems to have been nullified. This is a tragedy of epic proportions.

In response the people mourn and do not put on their ornaments (33:4). This is in keeping with the Lord's command: "Take off your ornaments, that I may know what to do with you" (v. 5). The people's taking off ornaments is an appropriate sign of mourning over their sin and its consequences—not only because mourners do not dress in their finest (Gen. 37:34; 2 Sam. 14:2) but also because ornaments include earrings (Hos. 2:13), the very things the Israelites had used to make the

---

[772] So also Cassuto, *Commentary on the Book of Exodus*, 424; he sees a similar approach when comparing Numbers 14:26–35 and 14:36–38 with 14:39.

golden calf (Ex. 32:2–3). But all is not lost. The statement "That I may know what to do with you" (33:5) is both sobering and hopeful. It is sobering because it indicates the possibility of further punishment; it is hopeful because it leaves open the door that Lord may respond positively to their repentance.

The people obey, stripping themselves of their jewelry and mourning in repentance for their sin. This also sets up an opportunity for Moses to intercede again on their behalf.

33:7–11 The text now pauses to let us know where the intercession takes place. Instead of going up the mountain every time he needs to speak with God, Moses speaks with him at a tent he sets up "*outside* the camp, *far off* from the camp" (v. 7). It is not stated how long he has been doing so, whether it has been since their arrival at Sinai or prior to that, nor, if the former, whether it was in response to the Lord's rebuke in chapter 32 or beforehand. Whatever the answer, the emphasis on its placement outside the camp is a sad reminder that God will not dwell in the Israelites' midst due to their sin.

Moses names it "the tent of meeting" since he may meet with the Lord there (vv. 7–8), as may others seeking the Lord (presumably when Moses is there to mediate[773]). The tabernacle is likewise called "the tent of meeting" since it is to have the same function (29:42–43), though it will not be built until chapters 35–40, and it is not clear at this point in the narrative whether it will ever be built. All that to say, these verses concern a different tent, far less glorious than the coming tabernacle and pitched far away from the camp instead of in its midst (cf. Num. 2:2).

Those who seek the Lord include those needing guidance in legal disputes (Ex. 18:15–16) or life events (Gen. 25:22; 2 Sam. 21:1) and those desiring to pursue the Lord in repentance or worship (Deut. 4:29; Ps. 40:16). Whenever Moses goes out to the tent, the Israelites watch intently (cf. note 85 within comment on 3:4–6). And no wonder—every time he goes inside, the Lord's cloud of glory descends to the tent's entrance, leading the people to worship the Lord from a distance, each at one's own tent (Ex. 33:8–10). This too is a positive sign: repentance for sin is now matched with worship of Israel's Redeemer.

Verse 11 finishes with two notices. First, "the LORD used to speak to Moses face to face." This does not contradict the Lord's comment to Moses in a few verses ("You cannot see my face, for man shall not see me and live"; v. 20). It is a figurative expression that refers to personal and intimate communication, as the next phrase makes clear: "As a man speaks to his friend."[774] The Lord speaks with other prophets in visions or dreams or riddles; with Moses he speaks directly (cf. Num. 12:6–8). The point is that Moses has a uniquely direct and personal relationship with the Lord (cf. Deut. 34:10), which helps explain the direct and personal conversations that ensue.[775]

---

773 Stuart, *Exodus*, 696.
774 Cf. also Deuteronomy 5:4 (Alexander, *Exodus*, 635).
775 Sarna, *Exodus*, 211.

Second, whenever Moses returns to the camp, his assistant Joshua stays at the tent. No reason is given for this practice, though the tent's association with the Lord's presence and as the place for people to seek the Lord paints Joshua in a positive light and further establishes his credibility as Moses' successor (cf. Ex. 17:9–13).

33:12–17 We now return to Moses' third intercession in these chapters (cf. Section Overview). The Lord has said he will not go up in his people's midst (33:3, 5). Moses now asks him to reconsider, repeatedly using the verb "to know" and the phrase "to find favor in your sight" (vv. 12–13). His prayer could be paraphrased, "You have said, 'Lead this people up,' but you have not *made me know* who will go with me in your place. Yet you have said *you have known me* very personally (by name!) and that I have *found favor in your sight*. If I have *found favor in your sight*, then *make me know* your ways in our very midst—it is your presence for which I am truly asking!—*that I may know you* even more deeply, so *that I may indeed find favor in your eyes* (in keeping with what you have said). And do this not only for my sake. Consider also that this nation is your people,[776] which is one more reason that you should go up among us. Not just for my sake; also for theirs!"

The Lord responds positively: "My presence will go with you, and I will give you rest" (v. 14); that is, I myself will lead you into the land and give you rest from your enemies (cf. Deut. 12:10; 25:19).[777]

In biblical times it was not uncommon to ask someone to confirm that he meant what he had just agreed to do, somewhat akin to when a parent says, "I will take you to the zoo," and the child responds, "Do you promise?"[778] Moses does something similar here, stating that, if the Lord does not go to the Promised Land with them—and he mentions "*I and your people*" twice to emphasize that the Lord's promise applies to all Israel—it is better that they not go. Why? Only the Lord's presence shows the nations that Moses and Israel have found favor in the Lord's sight and that Israel is his treasured possession (Ex. 33:15–16; cf. 19:5; Num. 14:14). Only then can Israel carry out its role as a "kingdom of priests and a holy nation" (Ex. 19:6), so that "every other people on the face of the earth" can know the reality and nature of the Lord.

The Lord reassures Moses that he will indeed go with Israel, emphasizing that Moses has found favor in his sight—the fifth time this expression is used!—and that he knows him by name (33:17; cf. v. 12). Moses is thus assured of the Lord's presence with Israel and the Lord's special favor toward him in particular. His prayers have made the difference.

33:18–23 Moses now makes one further request: "Please show me your glory" (v. 18). The "glory of the LORD" has already appeared elsewhere in the book, where it refers to the Lord's display of his presence in a spectacular but veiled way (16:10;

---

[776] In the Hebrew Moses puts "your people" first for emphasis: *Your people* is this nation!
[777] Woodenly translated Exodus 33:14 might read, "My presence/face is going, and I will give you rest." The "you" is singular, but the Lord uses the singular elsewhere in the immediate context when he is speaking to Moses and yet addressing all Israel (so also in 33:3, 5; 34:10–12; etc.).
[778] For a biblical example cf. Joshua 24:14–22.

24:16–17; for details cf. note 296 within comment on 16:6–8; cf. also comment on 16:9–12). Based on the Lord's response (33:20), Moses seems to be asking to see the Lord's presence directly, with no cloud acting as a veil. He wants to see God as he is in all his fullness. This would put it beyond a shadow of a doubt that Moses has found favor in the Lord's eyes and that the Lord will answer his prayer to go with Israel. It also shows us that Moses is a man who wants to know God deeply. He has seen more of God's power and has more direct communication with him than has any human to this point in history. But, like those who take a first bite of the most delicious meal they have ever tasted, he wants to keep eating. He is hungry for more.

The Lord will answer his prayer—in part. We might paraphrase, "Everything about me is goodness (Pss. 31:19; 145:7), and I will allow you *to see* more physical manifestation of it than others and *to hear* me describe my character ("name"). And what you will hear me describe is that I am characterized above all by mercy and grace, which I am free to show without limit!"[779]

But God cannot answer Moses' prayer in full. Again to paraphrase: "But you cannot see my face, for to see me unveiled, shining in all my brilliance and splendor and glory, would be fatal" (Ex. 33:20). Why? As noted earlier (19:20–25), the idea might be that if merely earthly circumstances can so overwhelm a person's senses that he loses consciousness, then the sight of the heavenly Lord's full glory can so overwhelm a person's senses that he loses life itself. It is like a power surge of glory that fatally overwhelms and short-circuits our mortal capacities.

The Lord tells Moses of a place on "the rock"—which here refers to the mountain's peak (34:2; cf. Num. 23:9)—where Moses is to stand (Ex. 33:21). Then as now standing was a sign of respect and the posture of those attending a king (1 Sam. 22:6) or awaiting a response from a deity (Num. 23:6). While the Lord passes by, he will put Moses in a cleft and obscure his view with his hand but at some point remove it, allowing Moses to see his "back" but not his "face" (Ex. 33:22–23). The Lord describes himself here in human terms, not because he has a body (John 4:24) but so we may understand his point: just as we get an idea of a person by seeing his back but learn more upon seeing his face, so Moses will get to see more of God's glory than the average person but will not be able to see God's glory in all its fullness.

34:1–8 Earlier Moses had shattered the covenant tablets to portray physically what Israel had done by making and worshiping the golden calf (Ex. 32:19). Now, in

---

779 "I will be gracious to whom I will be gracious, and will show mercy on whom I will show mercy" (33:19) is an *idem per idem* construction (cf. comment on 3:13–15). In some contexts these phrases describe a person's freedom to do activity X without limits. When the Lord says, "I will speak the word that I will speak" (Ezek. 12:25), he is declaring he will say whatever he wants. No one can limit him. As applied to Exodus 33:19, the *idem* construction means on the one hand that his sovereign choice determines who receives his grace and mercy (cf. Rom. 9:15–16). They are not earned and must not be presumed upon. At the same time the immediate context emphasizes that the Lord delights to show grace and mercy *to thousands* (Ex. 34:6–7; these verses resume the thought of 33:19 by repeating some of its language: "proclaim," "grace," "mercy"). Stated differently, he uses his sovereign freedom to be *generous* with grace and mercy, not stingy. To put it more colloquially: the Lord can show grace and mercy to whomever he darn well pleases—and he is darn well pleased to show it to many! This is the core of who he is.

words full of hope, the Lord commands Moses to make two new tablets so he can write on them the same covenant words as before (34:1). This will occur the next day, after Moses goes up to the mountain top and presents himself before the Lord (34:2). Aaron, who went up with Moses the first time (19:24), is not mentioned, perhaps because of his part in the golden calf incident. Whatever the case, the mountain will be especially consecrated by God's presence and thus off limits to everyone except Moses (34:3; cf. 19:12–13).

Moses obeys and early the next morning takes the stone tablets and ascends the mountain (34:4). The Lord then comes down in the cloud of glory (v. 5a). The phrase "And stood with him there" could mean that the Lord stood with Moses or that Moses stood with the Lord. In favor of the latter is verse 2, where "present yourself" uses a similar sounding root to describe what Moses is to do—but the endpoint is the same. The Lord then "proclaim[s] the name of the LORD" (v. 5b; cf. 33:19), which, as the context shows, refers to his describing his own essential nature and character (34:6b–7).[780] In keeping with what he said earlier (33:19) the Lord does this as he "passes before" Moses (34:6), who is presumably hidden in the rock as described in 33:21–23.

The words that follow are the most detailed self-description the Lord has given to this point in the Bible (34:6–7). Not surprisingly, biblical characters and writers return to this text continually when thinking of the glories of who the Lord is and why these perfections matter for the lives of God's people.[781] They did not get to see what Moses saw, but these verses allow them to hear what he heard so that they (and we!) get a clear window into God's very heart.

The terms fall into four natural pairings: (1) merciful and gracious, (2) slow to anger and abounding in steadfast love and faithfulness, (3) keeping steadfast love and forgiving sin, and (4) not clearing the guilty but visiting the father's iniquity upon the children. As will be seen, the progression is natural from one pairing to the next. Perhaps most noteworthy, however, is that mercy, patience, and love (the first three pairings) all come before judgment for sin (the fourth) and are all elaborated in much greater detail than judgment for sin is (three pairings versus one). He stresses that he a God of mercy and love who desires us to know him as such.

Mercy and grace are the first aspects of God's character. That these come first tell us something about his heart's instinctive reflex toward his people. "Merciful" (Hb. *rakhum*) is built on a root that often refers to the compassion God shows to those suffering punishment for sin or those worthy of punishment for sin (Deut. 30:3; Isa. 49:13; 54:8, 10; 55:7; Jer. 31:20; Hab. 3:2). "Gracious" (*khanun*) is built on a root that often refers to his showing undeserved favor to someone (Gen. 33:5, 11; Num. 6:25), even someone experiencing punishment for sin (2 Sam. 12:22; Pss.

---

[780] Compare the English phrase "to drag someone's name through the mud," that is, to speak negatively of his or her person and character. Thus in both Hebrew and English "name" can be shorthand for someone's "character."

[781] Numbers 14:18; Nehemiah 9:17; Psalms 86:15; 103:8; 145:8; Joel 2:13; Jonah 4:2. Cf. further discussion in Introduction: Relationship to the Rest of the Bible and to Christ: The Lord's Matchless Character.

31:9–10; 41:4; 51:1; Amos 5:15). In both cases he withholds or stops due punishment because he leans toward his people with mercy and grace.

Not surprisingly, God is therefore "slow to anger" when confronted with his people's sin. This is not a God who is spring-loaded with judgment, ready to pounce at his people's slightest misstep. He is awash with merciful and gracious patience. And not only patience, as though gritting his teeth while trying to remain calm; his patience is paired with his "steadfast love and faithfulness." If his patience causes him to withhold or stop due punishment, then his steadfast love and faithfulness propel him to show kindness and love. When used of the Lord, the word translated "steadfast love" (*khesed*) refers to a love characterized by graciousness and faithfulness, that is, to "gracious steadfast love" or "gracious loyal love." The gracious aspect of *khesed* is seen in that it often refers to the Lord's love demonstrated through favorable action toward someone, giving him something good, be it a spouse (Gen. 24:12, 14), material prosperity (Gen. 32:10–11), favor in the eyes of a superior (Gen. 39:21), or forgiveness and general loving kindness instead of punishment and wrath (Ex. 20:6; 34:6–7; Num. 14:18–19). The faithful aspect of this love is seen in that showing *khesed* can be paralleled to keeping the covenant, since both acts demonstrate the faithfulness expected from one covenant member to another (Deut. 7:9, 12; cf. the use of *khesed* in the context of oaths in Gen. 47:29; Josh. 2:12, 14). For this reason *khesed* is often paired with the word "faithfulness" (*'emet*), the terms together referring to the faithful expression of covenant loyalty and love (Gen. 24:27, 49; 32:10; Ex. 34:6). And the Lord does not simply *have* steadfast love and faithfulness; he is *abounding* in them. They pour from him, cascading down on his people like a waterfall of faithful love and grace.

This leads naturally to the third pairing. Because he overflows with faithful steadfast love, he faithfully maintains such love toward his people ("keeping steadfast love")—not just to a few generations but to *thousands* (cf. ESV mg.), stretching forward as far as the eye can see. And this is despite the fact that his people are still sinful! Indeed, what enables him to maintain such love toward a sinful people is that he forgives so lavishly ("forgiving iniquity"). As in relationships between people, if there is no forgiveness for wrongs, there will be no more relationship. The Lord's forgiveness clears the way for his relationship with his people to continue. He continues to show his people steadfast love because he continues to forgive their sin—and not just sin but their "iniquity and transgression and sin" (v. 7). The terms for sin are multiplied to show that, no matter how great the sin, the forgiving mercy of God is greater still. His people cannot out-sin it. He is spring-loaded to forgive. It is his natural reflex. He delights to forgive us.

But this does not mean sin should be taken lightly (cf. Rom. 6:1). This leads to the final pairing. The Lord "by no means clears the guilty." This cannot mean he does not forgive (as has just been emphasized). It means he will hold sinners to account and will do so by "visiting the iniquity of the fathers on the children and the children's children, to the third and the fourth generation" (Ex. 34:7). This last phrase occurs in 20:5 in a context contrasting those who were persisting in sin ("those who hate me") with those who were persisting in righteousness ("those who love me and keep my commandments"; 20:6). Here the contrast is missing; the preceding statement is simply that he "by no means clears the guilty," which could also be rendered, "he does not remit all punishment."[782] In other words, "Yes, I abound in forgiveness for sinners, but do not think forgiveness means absence of discipline. Good parents can forgive wrongs and discipline their children for them at the same time. They do this for their good because they love them. Shall I, your heavenly father, who loves his people infinitely more, not do the same (Heb. 12:5–11)? So take sin very seriously! Remember discipline can impact not only you but also the three to four generations of your family who live with you and are connected to you!"[783] The idea is not that discipline happens every single time we sin but that God can and does bring his discipline to bear, especially the more serious or persistent the sin.

Yet his deepest desire is not that we know his discipline; it is that we know his forgiving love. As noted at Exodus 20:4–6, the fact that steadfast love is shown to "thousands," as compared to punishment shown to the "third and the fourth generation," shows us something of the Lord's heart: "By the greatest numerical contrast in the Bible (three/four to thousands), God identified eloquently his real desire: to have his people remain loyal forever so that he might in turn show them the rich blessings of his resulting loyalty to them."[784] As noted above (cf. Section Overview), he has not created his people for judgment; he has created us for relationship with him, and he overflows with the mercy, grace, patience, love, and forgiveness we need in order to make this relationship a reality.

Moses responds to the Lord's display of glory and proclamation of his name by casting himself face down on the ground in reverent worship, paying him homage as the King of kings (34:8; cf. 1 Kings 1:16; cf. also Job 42:1–6).

34:9 While the Lord's appearance is profoundly sobering to Moses, it also encourages him that the Lord views him with favor. Added to this, the Lord has already told him to come up the mountain with two new stone tablets so he can write on them the words of the covenant (Ex. 34:1). With this dual encouragement Moses intercedes for the fourth and final time on Israel's behalf in these chapters (cf. Section Overview), praying for full and final restoration of the covenant relationship. "O Lord, my ruler and king,[785] if I have found favor in your sight as you have said (and as your special appearing to me in glory confirms), then please go in our midst in the tabernacle, as you have also said, even though[786] this is a stiff-necked people (as you have noted, 32:9). But I am bold to pray for this because, as you have just said (34:7), you overflow

---

[782] NJPS; so also Bush, *Commentary on Exodus*, 545; Childs, *Book of Exodus*, 602. Cf. Jeremiah 30:11 and 46:28, where the same verb is translated in ESV with "I will by no means leave you unpunished" and is parallel to "I will discipline you in just measure."
[783] For a narrative example cf. Numbers 14: Moses quotes Exodus 34:6–7 (Num 14:18), asks for forgiveness (v. 19), is assured of his people's pardon by the Lord (v. 20) but is also told there will be punishment (vv. 21–23, 28–30, 32)—and that this punishment will impact the Israelites' children (v. 33)!
[784] Stuart, *Exodus*, 454.
[785] Moses uses not the divine name here but the title "Lord," that is, a ruler. Cf. comment on 34:9.
[786] The word translated "for" can also be translated as "although" (cf. Ex. 13:17), which well fits the context here.

with steadfast love that you keep for thousands by forgiving their transgression and sin. So please forgive the transgression and sin of this people and take us as your inheritance, your chosen lot, your treasured possession."[787] If the Lord answers this prayer, it would will renewing the covenant the people have broken.

34:10 And that is exactly what he does. "Behold, I am making a covenant" (v. 10), that is, "I am remaking the covenant with the Israelites that they have broken. And they will know this because I will do unheard of marvels in their sight that will show not only Israel, but the surrounding nations, that the Lord is in covenant relationship with this people." The marvels are not named here, but the fact that the Lord speaks of their happening in view of the nations and that he tells Israel, "It is an awesome thing I will do *with you*," suggests the marvels relate to the coming conquest.[788] Not surprisingly, the next occurrence of the word "marvels" is found at Joshua 3:5 to describe the Lord's stopping the waters of the Jordan so Israel can cross into the Promised Land. This is followed by a series of events to which the same term could also apply, though it is not explicitly used: the collapse of the walls of Jericho (Josh. 6:20) and the sun's standing still at Gibeon (Josh. 10:12–13). Indeed, the conquest as a whole is described as "the work that the LORD did for Israel" (Josh. 24:31; cf. "the work of the LORD" in Ex. 34:10).

34:11–16 A covenant, however, requires faithfulness, so the Lord immediately exhorts the Israelites to obedience, giving a general command to obey (v. 11a) followed by specific examples (vv. 11b–26). The commands repeat or echo Exodus 23:12–33, that is, the very end of the first covenant commands. Indeed, the fact that the Lord will rewrite the Ten Commandments (34:1), which occur at the beginning of the original covenant, and here repeats the commands from the end of that covenant makes clear that he is renewing all of it.[789] The specific commands he cites focus on the twin themes of not worshiping false gods (vv. 11b–17) and worshiping the Lord correctly (vv. 18–26). In other words, Israel must turn from false worship and practice true worship. The focus on such commands is no surprise, given the golden calf tragedy two chapters prior. Of all the things Israel needs at this point in time, proper worship is at the top of the list.

The Lord therefore begins with commands to turn from false worship (vv. 11b–17). He will drive out the idolatrous nations in the Promised Land (v. 11b), but not all at once (23:27–30). So he warns the Israelites not to enter into a covenant relationship with them, lest they be led into worshiping their gods (34:12–16). Instead they are to destroy anything related to such worship, whether altars, sacred pillars (cf. note 568 within comment on 23:23–24), or Asherim,[790] and must avoid

---

[787] For "take us for your inheritance" cf. also Deuteronomy 4:20 (cf. Deut. 7:6; 14:2); Psalm 33:12.
[788] I understand "all the people" to refer to the nations mentioned in Exodus 34:11 (cf. 23:27) and "with you" as a reference to Israel (cf. the use of "you" in v. 11).
[789] Stuart, *Exodus*, 722.
[790] These were wooden objects set up in a sacred place, such as beside an altar (cf. Deut. 16:21; Judg. 6:25; 1 Kings 14:23). "It is unlikely that the 'poles' referred to in this verse are images of the goddess [Asherah]; rather, they are probably religious objects used in rituals associated with Asherah worship or perhaps with non-Yahwistic fertility rites in general" (Wells, *Exodus*, 262).

intermarriage, lest false worship enter Israel through the family.[791] This is rooted in the fact that "the LORD, whose name is Jealous, is a jealous God" (34:14) and will therefore view spiritual adultery with the same anger and hatred as a spouse would view physical adultery.[792] In other words, this jealousy is that not of petty envy but of betrayed love (cf. comment on 20:4–6).

34:17 To drive the point home, the Lord also forbids the Israelites from making "any gods of cast metal." The term here for "cast metal" is the same term used to describe the golden calf in 32:4, 8. What happened there must never happen again.

34:18–26 Having commanded the Israelites to avoid false worship, the Lord now commands them to practice true worship. When practiced according to the Lord's commands, worship is not only a vehicle for giving glory to God; it is also a classroom, teaching us who God is and forming our thoughts and affections after his own. To keep the Feast of Unleavened Bread and to give or redeem the firstborn are reminders of the Lord's deliverance and in particular the way in which he spared the Israelites' firstborn (vv. 18–20). This is a redeeming God. The Sabbath is a reminder of the covenant relationship with the Lord as well as the fact that he is the one who provides for our needs such that we actually can rest (v. 21). Celebrating the three feasts is a way to remember the Lord's deliverance from evil as well as his bountiful provision (vv. 22–24). In every way he is a provider. The remaining commands emphasize such themes as respecting the Lord by celebrating his redemption according to his ordinances (v. 25), honoring him as worthy of the very best one has (v. 26a), and imitating his compassion toward his creation (v. 26b). Taken together, these practices are a curriculum that teaches Israel who their God is and how to honor him. The takeaway is clear: if we want to know God well, we must cultivate the habit of regular worship into our lives.

Since this section's commands more or less repeat earlier ones, the commentary will refer the reader to the appropriate place in the previous comments and will add new comment only on notable new features.

34:18 Cf. comment on 23:14–17.

34:19–20 Cf. comment on 12:51–13:2, 11–16.

34:21 Cf. comments on 20:8–11; 23:12; 31:12–17. The mention of plowing and harvest is unique here but underscores that even the busiest times of life do not take precedence over the Sabbath.

34:22–23 Cf. comment on 23:14–17. As observed there (note 564), "firstfruits of the wheat harvest" describes the Feast of Weeks. The three feasts are thus Unleavened

---

[791] Cf. comments on 23:23–24; 23:32–33. Stuart notes that the focus of 34:16 on false worship that comes through women is due to the fact that women left their homes and moved in with the man's family, meaning false worship would enter the nation primarily through foreign women who brought it with them (Stuart, *Exodus*, 726).
[792] Cf. Deuteronomy 32:21–22 with Proverbs 6:32–35 (Bush, *Commentary on Exodus*, 549).

Bread, Weeks (also known as the Feast of Harvest or Pentecost), and Ingathering (also known as the Feast of Booths).

34:24 This verse answers a practical question raised by the previous two: Who will protect the land if they leave it three times a year to go to the Lord's place of worship? The answer is that the Lord will give them such success in battle and make them so great that no one will set his heart on the land and try to take it (cf. comment on 20:17 for this understanding of "covet").

34:25 Cf. comment on 23:18.

34:26 Cf. comment on 23:19.

34:27–28 The covenant commands are now written down. In 34:27 the Lord commands Moses to write down "these words," a reference to verses 11–26 at the least, though it should not surprise us if all the covenant commands from chapters 20–23 are to be rewritten, since that entire covenant is now being renewed (cf. 24:4). And, since the Lord said at the beginning of chapter 34 that he himself would rewrite the Ten Commandments on the tablets (34:1), it makes sense that the Lord is the "he" mentioned in the last half of verse 28: "And he [the LORD] wrote on the tablets the words of the covenant, the Ten Commandments," that is, those originally given in 20:2–17.[793]

The process takes forty days and nights, during which Moses abstains from both bread and water (34:28). While managing forty days without food is possible for some people, no one can survive forty days without water. We may be reading of a miracle, though neither this text nor those describing parallel situations note the Lord's special involvement (cf. Deut. 9:9, 18). Another possibility is that the text is using idiom or hyperbole; perhaps "forty days and nights" is a way to say "a good many days and nights" (cf. note 606 within comment on 24:15–18) or "neither ate bread nor drank water" could mean "a lot of fasting." Whatever the case, we know that fasting accompanies earnest seeking of the Lord (Judg. 20:26; 2 Sam. 12:16; Ezra 8:23) and therefore underscores the seriousness with which Moses undertakes his intercession for Israel and his role as covenant mediator. (Jesus' forty-day-and-night fast in the wilderness [Matt. 4:2] points to him as a second Moses who gives God's law, though he is infinitely greater than Moses himself [Heb. 3:1–6].)

34:29–35 As he did in 32:15, Moses comes down from the mountain with the two covenant tablets in his hand, but this time is different: "The skin of his face shone because he had been talking with God" (34:29).[794] Given that Moses had talked

---

[793] Cf. Deuteronomy 10:4, which makes this connection clear between the Ten Commandments and Exodus 20:2–17. Depending on how they are counted, the commands given in 34:11–26 also come to ten. This should not surprise us: since the original list of ten was meant to represent the entire covenant (cf. comment on 24:12–14), it is natural to have another list of ten here that does the same, a list that focuses this time on the most pressing pastoral need, namely, the need to avoid false worship and practice true worship. As 34:1 makes clear, however, the list the Lord rewrites on the stones in 34:28 is the original list.

[794] The Hebrew root translated "shone" can also refer to a "horn," perhaps because "rays" of light project out like horns (cf. "rays" in Hab. 3:4, also built on this root). The Vulgate, however, translates "[Moses'] face

with God the first time he received the Ten Commandments, why does his face shine now when it did not then? The most natural answer focuses on an important difference between the previous reception of the commandments and this one: Moses receives an even greater glimpse of God's glory than he ever had before (33:18–34:7), and this exposure leaves a beaming residue of glory on his face.

Having never seen anything like it, Aaron and the Israelites are initially too frightened to come near Moses (34:30). Eventually he is able to persuade Aaron and the leaders to return so that he can speak with them (v. 31). The rest of the people soon follow, and Moses "commanded them all that the LORD had spoken with him on Mount Sinai" (v. 32). During this time his face continues to shine with the Lord's glory, which surely confirms his authority as the one with whom God has spoken directly and who speaks on God's behalf. After passing on God's commands he veils his face (v. 33) and leaves it veiled until he returns to speak with the Lord (vv. 34–35). In short, when speaking with God or communicating God's word to the people, he is unveiled, meaning the Israelites will know he is communicating words received directly in God's glorious presence.[795] The rest of the time he is veiled. No reason is given here—though, in light of Israel's initial response of fear, constant exposure to this sight of God's glory may simply be too much for them (and cf. below on 2 Corinthians 3).

The account of Jesus' transfiguration in Matthew 17:1–8 bears several parallels to this passage: Jesus is high up a mountain (Matt. 17:1), his face shines "like the sun" (v. 2), Moses appears with him (as does Elijah, another great OT prophet; v. 3), a cloud of glory appears (v. 5), and the disciples with Jesus fall on their faces in fear (v. 6; cf. Moses in Ex. 34:8). By tying this event to Exodus 34 Matthew emphasizes that God's glory now beams from Jesus' face. Moreover, when the cloud appears, the Lord's voice declares, "This is my beloved Son, with whom I am well pleased; listen to him" (Matt. 17:5). Jesus is not simply a prophet, as Moses is, but the very Son of God. His face shines God's glory because "he is the radiance of the glory of God and the exact imprint of his nature" (Heb. 1:3).

A second NT passage making use of the account of Moses' shining face is 2 Corinthians 3, where Paul contrasts the old covenant with the new. The old was written on tablets of stone, resulted ultimately in condemnation and death for the Israelites, and was coming to an end due to its temporary nature.[796] The new is written with the Spirit on human hearts, results in righteousness and life, and will continue forever due to its eternal nature (2 Cor. 3:3–11). In making the contrast Paul points out that, if the former covenant came with glory, how much greater is the glory that comes with an infinitely better covenant (2 Cor. 3:7–11)! What is

---

was horned" in Exodus 34:29, leading some artists in previous centuries to produce paintings or sculptures of Moses with horns coming from his head.

795 Cf. 19:9 (Fretheim, *Exodus*, 311).

796 The clause translated "Which was being brought to an end" (ESV) is sometimes translated "which was fading," but the key Greek term (*katargeō*) "means to nullify or abolish or bring to naught"; Dane Ortlund, *2 Corinthians*, in *Romans–Galatians*, ESVEC (Wheaton, IL: Crossway, 2020), 442. The old covenant and its glory are now replaced by the new covenant and its far greater glory. As Wright (*Exodus*, 594) explains, "The old glory was not so much a flashlight that faded out as it was a flashlight that gets switched off when the sun shines."

more, unlike the veiling of God's glory on Moses' face, God's glory is unveiled in Jesus (cf. 2 Cor. 4:6) so that those who turn to him in faith are "being transformed into the same image from one degree of glory to another" (2 Cor. 3:18). In other words the Christian life is one in which, through the indwelling Holy Spirit, we come to know Jesus better and better and, as a result, become more and more like him, reflecting his glory—God's glory—increasingly in our lives for all the world to see.

Response

These chapters recount the history of a people whose sin runs deep, of a leader who stands in the gap and intercedes on his people's behalf, and of a God whose love and mercy more than meets the need of the moment. We can follow this text by asking three questions.

WHY WAS IDOLATRY SUCH A TEMPTATION?

There is a reason the Ten Commandments begin with two that forbid the worship of other gods (Ex. 20:3–6). Even a cursory reading of Israel's history will show that idolatry was one of her greatest temptations.[797] Various reasons have been summarized by Stuart,[798] including the following:

(1) Idols provide an assured, tangible point of access to the divine. Humans have a natural aversion to uncertainty; idols are a way of saying, "You can know you have access to the god."

(2) In Israel's day idolatry was normal (cf. materialism in many Western cultures today). It would be easy to think, "How could something so normal for most people be wrong?"

(3) The worship of more than one god was also normal. In ancient Mesopotamia people could have a great god and also a personal god, who was often a lesser deity among many.[799] The Israelites might naturally assume they could be faithful to the Lord, the great god of Israel, and to lesser gods as well.

(4) Finally, whether the Israelites were eyeing the Canaanites' good crops or the general success of neighboring superpowers (Egypt, Assyria), they might link a nation's success to its idols. It was a large step of faith for Israelites to pursue success by worshiping the Lord alone and not using idols to do so.[800]

In other words two of idolatry's driving forces are the temptation to conform to surrounding culture and the desire for security and control. Both are displayed here. Creating an image of an animal to represent the deity was commonplace in

---

[797] Exodus 32:1–6; Numbers 25:1–3; Judges 2:10–13; 2 Kings 17:7–16; etc. Cf. the warnings in Exodus 20:3–6, 23; Deuteronomy 6:14; 8:19; etc.
[798] Stuart, *Exodus*, 450–454.
[799] Cf. Daniel C. Snell, *Religions of the Ancient Near East* (Cambridge, UK: CUP, 2011), 27–28.
[800] Sklar, *Leviticus*, ZECOT, 722.

Egypt, where the Israelites had been living for four hundred years; this was the way it was done. In addition security came from possessing a physical representation of a god, so the Israelites naturally wanted an idol as a guarantee they would be safe.

Sadly, the Israelites' failure is not just an ancient problem. Cultural conformity and the desire for security create new idols for us to worship today. When a culture does not make loving the Lord wholeheartedly its highest priority, it will prioritize and normalize other things as ultimate loves. In some cases this could be actual pagan gods other than the Lord. In others it can be material success and fortune, power, human relationships, or physical pleasures such as sexual intimacy, food, or drink. Not all of these latter things are wrong in and of themselves, and many of them are in fact quite good. After all the Bible teaches we have been created for human relationship (Gen. 2:18; Eccles. 4:9–12), counsels us to save for material needs (Prov. 27:23–27), speaks positively of sexual relations within marriage (Proverbs 5; 1 Cor. 7:3–5), and praises God as the one who blesses his creation with food and drink (Ps. 104:10–15; 1 Tim. 4:3–4). The problem is that often we take these good things and turn them into ultimate things, sometimes out of greed or out of a desire for security and control. "Our hearts deify [these things] as the center of our lives, because, we think, they can give us significance and security, safety and fulfillment, if we attain them."[801] In short the temptation to conform and the desire for security and control come together, resulting in any number of things—aside from the Lord—that might control our lives by determining our values and habits and leading us further and further away from the only source of true security and significance. We turn away from a clear, flowing stream to broken pots that cannot hold a drop of water (Jer. 2:13).

Thus the Lord's commands to avoid idolatry are one of the greatest kindnesses he could give us. Like a loving parent, he leads us to a good and rich path for our best. Only his love can satisfy our hearts' deepest longings, for he has made us for himself. In knowing him we find true rest for our souls, since we can eat and drink ourselves full from the storehouses of his love. In light of this we do well to ask, Who or what occupies the throne in my heart? To what extent might I be making secondary things, even good things, central in my life? How do my habits, values, and priorities shed light on the answers to these questions? What does repentance look like, in practical terms, if I have been putting other things ahead of the Lord?

For the Israelites it is an actual, golden idol they worship, leading to God's judgment. They need someone to step into the gap and intercede for them. This leads to our second question.

IF GOD IS SOVEREIGN, WHY PRAY?

God's sovereignty is clear in these chapters. No Israelite who saw the Lord's descent in a fiery pillar of cloud would have questioned it. Moses at one point addresses the Lord with the word *adonai* (Ex. 34:9), Hebrew for "sovereign, master" (Gen. 40:1;

---

[801] Timothy Keller, *Counterfeit Gods: The Empty Promises of Money, Sex, and Power, and the Only Hope That Matters* (New York: Dutton, 2009), xiv.

Ex. 21:4). So, if God is sovereign, why pray? Some answer by noting that prayer changes us. This is true enough. Simply talking to God often reminds us of what is true and helps to form our thoughts and affections after his. But these chapters give a different answer. They show how prayer changes not only us but *history*.

In Exodus 33:17 the Lord responds to Moses' prayer by stating, "This very thing that you have spoken I will do, for you have found favor in my sight, and I know you by name." Indeed, four times throughout these chapters Moses prays for the Lord's mercy, and four times the Lord answers his prayers (cf. Section Overview). Moses' prayers make a difference. The psalmist sees it clearly:

> He said he would destroy them—
>   had not Moses, his chosen one,
>   stood in the breach before him,
>   to turn away his wrath from destroying them. (Ps. 106:23)

The NT says something similar of Elijah: "He prayed fervently that it might not rain, and for three years and six months it did not rain on the earth" (James 5:17). Like Moses', his prayers made a difference.

So the Bible teaches that God is sovereign and that prayer changes things. There is an element of mystery here, but in his sovereignty God has chosen to make our prayers effective in carrying out his will.[802] And because of that he commands us to pray. Moses' prayers make a difference. Elijah's prayers make a difference. *Our* prayers make a difference.

One might respond, "I am not a prophet like Moses or Elijah." True enough, but, as James points out, "*Elijah was a man with a nature like ours*, and he prayed fervently that it might not rain, and for three years and six months it did not rain on the earth" (James 5:17). In other words one need not be a prophet for one's prayers to make a difference; we simply have to be *people who pray*.

The questions therefore are simple: Do we believe that prayer matters? Do we pray as though our prayers can make a difference? As though they *do* make a difference? We can pray as though prayer changes things—because it does! And this brings us to the one to whom we pray. Moses prays with confidence because of the nature of the one to whom he prays, which leads to our last question.

WHO IS GOD?

As noted in the commentary, Exodus 34:6–7 contains the most detailed self-description that the Lord has given to this point in the Bible. If he had a business card, these words would be on it. If he had a website, they would be on the "About Me" page.[803] Later biblical characters and writers return to them repeatedly (cf. note 781 within comment on 34:1–8). They do not simply describe a God of

---

[802] A similar question could be asked regarding evangelism. If God has already chosen the elect, why evangelize? The answer is that because in his sovereignty he has ordained the preaching of the gospel as the way in which people are saved; cf. J. I. Packer, *Evangelism and the Sovereignty of God* (Chicago: InterVarsity, 1961), esp. 96–98.
[803] I borrow the idea from Ortlund, *Gentle and Lowly*, 21.

unsurpassed glory; they give us a window into the depths of his unspeakably good, kind, and just heart.

The comments above explain these verses. Here we can highlight how the apostle John ties together this description and its context with Jesus. His main point is that in Jesus God has come more fully and wonderfully nearer than on Sinai (John 1:14–18). John's words could be paraphrased, "In Exodus God dwelled in his people's midst in the tabernacle; in Jesus God dwelled in our midst in human flesh (v. 14a). In Exodus God's people saw his glory in the cloud and heard of his glory as the one who would be gracious to whom he would be gracious and who was faithful and true. In Jesus we have seen this same glory in a person full of God's grace and truth (v. 14b). In fact through him we have received and known firsthand this grace and truth, a grace that has come in a new, greater, stronger way (v. 16)![804] Indeed, in Exodus God showed tremendous grace in giving his people a law that revealed his character to them in words and taught them his truth. But in Jesus the same grace and truth have come in the flesh (v. 17). To this day none of us has seen God in all his fullness. But Jesus has and knows him as intimately as anyone can be known and has made him known to us in stunning detail (v. 18)." As Jesus later says, "Whoever has seen me has seen the Father" (John 14:9). In Jesus God has shown up *face to face* (cf. 2 Cor. 4:6). Thus Moses' prayer "Show me your glory" (Ex. 33:18) has been answered for us in the most unimaginable way.

What does this mean for our lives? If Moses "quickly bowed his head toward the earth and worshiped" in response to God's self-description in Exodus (34:8), how much more should we bow our heads toward the earth and worship in response to God's self-revelation in Jesus? If this is who Jesus is, the only proper response is reverent and humble adoration and worship. This does not necessarily mean formally worshiping or actually bowing all day long every day. But those who know us best should be able to say about us, "This person's life is oriented by the thought, 'How might I bring glory to Jesus?' This person cares most about making Jesus known because he or she believes Jesus is the most wonderful person who can be known and that knowing him is the only way to know God." Would those who know us best say this? If so, may God continue refreshing our souls with the river of delights found in Jesus and use us as channels of Jesus' grace to others! If not, what actions, priorities, or values might need to change so that our lives point to the grace and truth of God found in Jesus?

---

[804] Commentators debate whether the phrase "grace upon grace" should be understood as "grace in Jesus is a fresh wave coming after the grace of the law" or "grace in Jesus now replaces the grace of the law." The second approach more strongly emphasizes the redemptive-historical change of times; cf. D. A. Carson, *The Gospel according to John*, PNTC (Grand Rapids, MI: Eerdmans, 1991), 131–134. In either case both Jesus and the law are characterized by grace. The contrast in this passage is not that the law is bad and Jesus is good; it is that the law is good but Jesus is far better!

OVERVIEW OF
EXODUS 35–40

In Exodus 25–31 the Lord describes in detail how the Israelites are to make the tabernacle components. Chapters 35–39 now repeats much of that material to describe the Israelites' construction of those components (and chapter 40 describes the tabernacle's final assembly). The following verses offer a typical example of this dynamic:

> You shall make bars of acacia wood, five for the frames of the one side of the tabernacle. (26:26)

> He made bars of acacia wood, five for the frames of the one side of the tabernacle. (36:31)

Indeed, chapters 35–39 repeat most of chapters 25–31 verbatim,[805] which some modern readers may find tedious. But there are two reasons that such repetition is not surprising. First, similar examples can be found in other ancient Near Eastern and biblical texts. The classic ancient Near Eastern example is the Ugaritic myth known as the Keret epic, in which "The god El commands King Keret in a dream to do a considerable number of things." And, when he does so, "The text repeats more than ninety lines of instruction almost but not entirely verbatim. . . . This is precisely the phenomenon that occurs in Exodus 25–31 and 35–40."[806] As for biblical texts, examples include (1) the initial recounting of the events involving Abraham's servant in Genesis 24:12–27 and his repeating of those events in verses 34–48[807] and (2) the twelve identical lists of tabernacle gifts in Numbers 7 that differ only according to the name of the Israelite tribal leader who gives them. Clearly the literature of that time was comfortable with a high level of repetition.

Second—and more to the point—such repetition draws our attention to something important. In Genesis 24, for example, the repetition makes clear that the Lord has sovereignly directed Abraham's servant and granted him favor in fulfilling his task; the repeated lists in Numbers 7 emphasize that all tribes contribute equally in bringing gifts to the Lord. As for Exodus 25–31 and 35–39, the repetition shows that the Israelites have followed the Lord's commands exactly,

---

[805] The variations that exist are relatively minor, such as the natural change of "You shall make" in earlier chapters to "And he made" in later chapters, or the omission of statements from earlier chapters about an item's purpose (Ex. 25:22) or about arranging furniture (26:33–35) in later chapters (36:35–38; 37:1–9), which focus more narrowly on the items being made.
[806] Stuart, *Exodus*, 743; cf. Cassuto, *Commentary on the Book of Exodus*, 453.
[807] Stuart, *Exodus*, 743n252, citing Duane Garrett, *Rethinking Genesis: The Sources and Authorship of the First Book of the Pentateuch* (Fearn, UK: Christian Focus/Mentor, 2000), 22–23.

a central theme in this section of Exodus. For further discussion cf. Overview, as well as the Response section, "What Should Obedience Look Like?"

EXODUS 35–40

35 Moses assembled all the congregation of the people of Israel and said to them, "These are the things that the LORD has commanded you to do. ² Six days work shall be done, but on the seventh day you shall have a Sabbath of solemn rest, holy to the LORD. Whoever does any work on it shall be put to death. ³ You shall kindle no fire in all your dwelling places on the Sabbath day."

⁴ Moses said to all the congregation of the people of Israel, "This is the thing that the LORD has commanded. ⁵ Take from among you a contribution to the LORD. Whoever is of a generous heart, let him bring the LORD's contribution: gold, silver, and bronze; ⁶ blue and purple and scarlet yarns and fine twined linen; goats' hair; ⁷ tanned rams' skins, and goatskins;[1] acacia wood, ⁸ oil for the light, spices for the anointing oil and for the fragrant incense, ⁹ and onyx stones and stones for setting, for the ephod and for the breastpiece.

¹⁰ "Let every skillful craftsman among you come and make all that the LORD has commanded: ¹¹ the tabernacle, its tent and its covering, its hooks and its frames, its bars, its pillars, and its bases; ¹² the ark with its poles, the mercy seat, and the veil of the screen; ¹³ the table with its poles and all its utensils, and the bread of the Presence; ¹⁴ the lampstand also for the light, with its utensils and its lamps, and the oil for the light; ¹⁵ and the altar of incense, with its poles, and the anointing oil and the fragrant incense, and the screen for the door, at the door of the tabernacle; ¹⁶ the altar of burnt offering, with its grating of bronze, its poles, and all its utensils, the basin and its stand; ¹⁷ the hangings of the court, its pillars and its bases, and the screen for the gate of the court; ¹⁸ the pegs of the tabernacle and the pegs of the court, and their cords; ¹⁹ the finely worked garments for ministering[2] in the Holy Place, the holy garments for Aaron the priest, and the garments of his sons, for their service as priests."

²⁰ Then all the congregation of the people of Israel departed from the presence of Moses. ²¹ And they came, everyone whose heart stirred him, and everyone whose spirit moved him, and brought the LORD's contribution to be used for the tent of meeting, and for all its service, and for the holy garments. ²² So they came, both men and women. All who were of a willing heart brought brooches and earrings and signet rings and armlets, all sorts of gold objects, every man dedicating an offering of gold to the LORD. ²³ And every one who possessed blue or purple or scarlet yarns or fine linen or goats' hair or tanned rams' skins or goatskins brought them. ²⁴ Everyone who could make a contribution of silver or bronze brought it as the LORD's contribution. And every one who possessed acacia wood of any use in the work brought it. ²⁵ And every skillful woman spun with her hands, and they all brought what they had spun in blue and purple and

scarlet yarns and fine twined linen. ²⁶ All the women whose hearts stirred them to use their skill spun the goats' hair. ²⁷ And the leaders brought onyx stones and stones to be set, for the ephod and for the breastpiece, ²⁸ and spices and oil for the light, and for the anointing oil, and for the fragrant incense. ²⁹ All the men and women, the people of Israel, whose heart moved them to bring anything for the work that the Lord had commanded by Moses to be done brought it as a freewill offering to the Lord.

³⁰ Then Moses said to the people of Israel, "See, the Lord has called by name Bezalel the son of Uri, son of Hur, of the tribe of Judah; ³¹ and he has filled him with the Spirit of God, with skill, with intelligence, with knowledge, and with all craftsmanship, ³² to devise artistic designs, to work in gold and silver and bronze, ³³ in cutting stones for setting, and in carving wood, for work in every skilled craft. ³⁴ And he has inspired him to teach, both him and Oholiab the son of Ahisamach of the tribe of Dan. ³⁵ He has filled them with skill to do every sort of work done by an engraver or by a designer or by an embroiderer in blue and purple and scarlet yarns and fine twined linen, or by a weaver—by any sort of workman or skilled designer.

36

"Bezalel and Oholiab and every craftsman in whom the Lord has put skill and intelligence to know how to do any work in the construction of the sanctuary shall work in accordance with all that the Lord has commanded."

² And Moses called Bezalel and Oholiab and every craftsman in whose mind the Lord had put skill, everyone whose heart stirred him up to come to do the work. ³ And they received from Moses all the contribution that the people of Israel had brought for doing the work on the sanctuary. They still kept bringing him freewill offerings every morning, ⁴ so that all the craftsmen who were doing every sort of task on the sanctuary came, each from the task that he was doing, ⁵ and said to Moses, "The people bring much more than enough for doing the work that the Lord has commanded us to do." ⁶ So Moses gave command, and word was proclaimed throughout the camp, "Let no man or woman do anything more for the contribution for the sanctuary." So the people were restrained from bringing, ⁷ for the material they had was sufficient to do all the work, and more.

⁸ And all the craftsmen among the workmen made the tabernacle with ten curtains. They were made of fine twined linen and blue and purple and scarlet yarns, with cherubim skillfully worked. ⁹ The length of each curtain was twenty-eight cubits,³ and the breadth of each curtain four cubits. All the curtains were the same size.

¹⁰ He⁴ coupled five curtains to one another, and the other five curtains he coupled to one another. ¹¹ He made loops of blue on the edge of the outermost curtain of the first set. Likewise he made them on the edge of the outermost curtain of the second set. ¹² He made fifty loops on the one curtain, and he made fifty loops on the edge of the curtain that was in the second set. The loops were opposite one another. ¹³ And he made fifty clasps of gold, and coupled the curtains one to the other with clasps. So the tabernacle was a single whole.

¹⁴ He also made curtains of goats' hair for a tent over the tabernacle. He made eleven curtains. ¹⁵ The length of each curtain was thirty cubits, and the breadth of each curtain four cubits. The eleven curtains were the same size. ¹⁶ He coupled five curtains by themselves, and six curtains by themselves. ¹⁷ And he made fifty loops on the edge of the outermost curtain of the one set, and fifty loops on the edge of the other connecting curtain.

¹⁸ And he made fifty clasps of bronze to couple the tent together that it might be a single whole. ¹⁹ And he made for the tent a covering of tanned rams' skins and goatskins.

²⁰ Then he made the upright frames for the tabernacle of acacia wood. ²¹ Ten cubits was the length of a frame, and a cubit and a half the breadth of each frame. ²² Each frame had two tenons for fitting together. He did this for all the frames of the tabernacle. ²³ The frames for the tabernacle he made thus: twenty frames for the south side. ²⁴ And he made forty bases of silver under the twenty frames, two bases under one frame for its two tenons, and two bases under the next frame for its two tenons. ²⁵ For the second side of the tabernacle, on the north side, he made twenty frames ²⁶ and their forty bases of silver, two bases under one frame and two bases under the next frame. ²⁷ For the rear of the tabernacle westward he made six frames. ²⁸ He made two frames for corners of the tabernacle in the rear. ²⁹ And they were separate beneath but joined at the top, at the first ring. He made two of them this way for the two corners. ³⁰ There were eight frames with their bases of silver: sixteen bases, under every frame two bases.

³¹ He made bars of acacia wood, five for the frames of the one side of the tabernacle, ³² and five bars for the frames of the other side of the tabernacle, and five bars for the frames of the tabernacle at the rear westward. ³³ And he made the middle bar to run from end to end halfway up the frames. ³⁴ And he overlaid the frames with gold, and made their rings of gold for holders for the bars, and overlaid the bars with gold.

³⁵ He made the veil of blue and purple and scarlet yarns and fine twined linen; with cherubim skillfully worked into it he made it. ³⁶ And for it he made four pillars of acacia and overlaid them with gold. Their hooks were of gold, and he cast for them four bases of silver. ³⁷ He also made a screen for the entrance of the tent, of blue and purple and scarlet yarns and fine twined linen, embroidered with needlework, ³⁸ and its five pillars with their hooks. He overlaid their capitals, and their fillets were of gold, but their five bases were of bronze.

37 Bezalel made the ark of acacia wood. Two cubits[5] and a half was its length, a cubit and a half its breadth, and a cubit and a half its height. ² And he overlaid it with pure gold inside and outside, and made a molding of gold around it. ³ And he cast for it four rings of gold for its four feet, two rings on its one side and two rings on its other side. ⁴ And he made poles of acacia wood and overlaid them with gold ⁵ and put the poles into the rings on the sides of the ark to carry the ark. ⁶ And he made a mercy seat of pure gold. Two cubits and a half was its length, and a cubit and a half its breadth. ⁷ And he made two cherubim of gold. He made them of hammered work on the two ends of the mercy seat, ⁸ one cherub on the one end, and one cherub on the other end. Of one piece with the mercy seat he made the cherubim on its two ends. ⁹ The cherubim spread out their wings above, overshadowing the mercy seat with their wings, with their faces one to another; toward the mercy seat were the faces of the cherubim.

¹⁰ He also made the table of acacia wood. Two cubits was its length, a cubit its breadth, and a cubit and a half its height. ¹¹ And he overlaid it with pure gold, and made a molding of gold around it. ¹² And he made a rim around it a handbreadth[6] wide, and made a molding of gold around the rim. ¹³ He cast for it four rings of gold and fastened the rings to the four corners at its four legs. ¹⁴ Close to the frame were the rings, as holders

for the poles to carry the table. ¹⁵ He made the poles of acacia wood to carry the table, and overlaid them with gold. ¹⁶ And he made the vessels of pure gold that were to be on the table, its plates and dishes for incense, and its bowls and flagons with which to pour drink offerings.

¹⁷ He also made the lampstand of pure gold. He made the lampstand of hammered work. Its base, its stem, its cups, its calyxes, and its flowers were of one piece with it. ¹⁸ And there were six branches going out of its sides, three branches of the lampstand out of one side of it and three branches of the lampstand out of the other side of it; ¹⁹ three cups made like almond blossoms, each with calyx and flower, on one branch, and three cups made like almond blossoms, each with calyx and flower, on the other branch—so for the six branches going out of the lampstand. ²⁰ And on the lampstand itself were four cups made like almond blossoms, with their calyxes and flowers, ²¹ and a calyx of one piece with it under each pair of the six branches going out of it. ²² Their calyxes and their branches were of one piece with it. The whole of it was a single piece of hammered work of pure gold. ²³ And he made its seven lamps and its tongs and its trays of pure gold. ²⁴ He made it and all its utensils out of a talent[7] of pure gold.

²⁵ He made the altar of incense of acacia wood. Its length was a cubit, and its breadth was a cubit. It was square, and two cubits was its height. Its horns were of one piece with it. ²⁶ He overlaid it with pure gold, its top and around its sides and its horns. And he made a molding of gold around it, ²⁷ and made two rings of gold on it under its molding, on two opposite sides of it, as holders for the poles with which to carry it. ²⁸ And he made the poles of acacia wood and overlaid them with gold.

²⁹ He made the holy anointing oil also, and the pure fragrant incense, blended as by the perfumer.

38

He made the altar of burnt offering of acacia wood. Five cubits[8] was its length, and five cubits its breadth. It was square, and three cubits was its height. ² He made horns for it on its four corners. Its horns were of one piece with it, and he overlaid it with bronze. ³ And he made all the utensils of the altar, the pots, the shovels, the basins, the forks, and the fire pans. He made all its utensils of bronze. ⁴ And he made for the altar a grating, a network of bronze, under its ledge, extending halfway down. ⁵ He cast four rings on the four corners of the bronze grating as holders for the poles. ⁶ He made the poles of acacia wood and overlaid them with bronze. ⁷ And he put the poles through the rings on the sides of the altar to carry it with them. He made it hollow, with boards.

⁸ He made the basin of bronze and its stand of bronze, from the mirrors of the ministering women who ministered in the entrance of the tent of meeting.

⁹ And he made the court. For the south side the hangings of the court were of fine twined linen, a hundred cubits; ¹⁰ their twenty pillars and their twenty bases were of bronze, but the hooks of the pillars and their fillets were of silver. ¹¹ And for the north side there were hangings of a hundred cubits; their twenty pillars and their twenty bases were of bronze, but the hooks of the pillars and their fillets were of silver. ¹² And for the west side were hangings of fifty cubits, their ten pillars, and their ten bases; the hooks of the pillars and their fillets were of silver. ¹³ And for the front to the east, fifty cubits. ¹⁴ The hangings for one side of the gate were fifteen cubits, with their three pillars and three bases. ¹⁵ And so for the other side. On both sides of the gate of the court were hangings of

fifteen cubits, with their three pillars and their three bases. ¹⁶ All the hangings around the court were of fine twined linen. ¹⁷ And the bases for the pillars were of bronze, but the hooks of the pillars and their fillets were of silver. The overlaying of their capitals was also of silver, and all the pillars of the court were filleted with silver. ¹⁸ And the screen for the gate of the court was embroidered with needlework in blue and purple and scarlet yarns and fine twined linen. It was twenty cubits long and five cubits high in its breadth, corresponding to the hangings of the court. ¹⁹ And their pillars were four in number. Their four bases were of bronze, their hooks of silver, and the overlaying of their capitals and their fillets of silver. ²⁰ And all the pegs for the tabernacle and for the court all around were of bronze.

²¹ These are the records of the tabernacle, the tabernacle of the testimony, as they were recorded at the commandment of Moses, the responsibility of the Levites under the direction of Ithamar the son of Aaron the priest. ²² Bezalel the son of Uri, son of Hur, of the tribe of Judah, made all that the LORD commanded Moses; ²³ and with him was Oholiab the son of Ahisamach, of the tribe of Dan, an engraver and designer and embroiderer in blue and purple and scarlet yarns and fine twined linen.

²⁴ All the gold that was used for the work, in all the construction of the sanctuary, the gold from the offering, was twenty-nine talents and 730 shekels,⁹ by the shekel of the sanctuary. ²⁵ The silver from those of the congregation who were recorded was a hundred talents and 1,775 shekels, by the shekel of the sanctuary: ²⁶ a beka¹⁰ a head (that is, half a shekel, by the shekel of the sanctuary), for everyone who was listed in the records, from twenty years old and upward, for 603,550 men. ²⁷ The hundred talents of silver were for casting the bases of the sanctuary and the bases of the veil; a hundred bases for the hundred talents, a talent a base. ²⁸ And of the 1,775 shekels he made hooks for the pillars and overlaid their capitals and made fillets for them. ²⁹ The bronze that was offered was seventy talents and 2,400 shekels; ³⁰ with it he made the bases for the entrance of the tent of meeting, the bronze altar and the bronze grating for it and all the utensils of the altar, ³¹ the bases around the court, and the bases of the gate of the court, all the pegs of the tabernacle, and all the pegs around the court.

39 From the blue and purple and scarlet yarns they made finely woven garments,¹¹ for ministering in the Holy Place. They made the holy garments for Aaron, as the LORD had commanded Moses.

² He made the ephod of gold, blue and purple and scarlet yarns, and fine twined linen. ³ And they hammered out gold leaf, and he cut it into threads to work into the blue and purple and the scarlet yarns, and into the fine twined linen, in skilled design. ⁴ They made for the ephod attaching shoulder pieces, joined to it at its two edges. ⁵ And the skillfully woven band on it was of one piece with it and made like it, of gold, blue and purple and scarlet yarns, and fine twined linen, as the LORD had commanded Moses.

⁶ They made the onyx stones, enclosed in settings of gold filigree, and engraved like the engravings of a signet, according to the names of the sons of Israel. ⁷ And he set them on the shoulder pieces of the ephod to be stones of remembrance for the sons of Israel, as the LORD had commanded Moses.

⁸ He made the breastpiece, in skilled work, in the style of the ephod, of gold, blue and purple and scarlet yarns, and fine twined linen. ⁹ It was square. They made the breastpiece doubled, a span¹² its length and a span its breadth when doubled. ¹⁰ And they set in it four rows of stones. A row of sardius, topaz, and carbuncle was the first row; ¹¹ and the second row,

an emerald, a sapphire, and a diamond; ¹² and the third row, a jacinth, an agate, and an amethyst; ¹³ and the fourth row, a beryl, an onyx, and a jasper. They were enclosed in settings of gold filigree. ¹⁴ There were twelve stones with their names according to the names of the sons of Israel. They were like signets, each engraved with its name, for the twelve tribes. ¹⁵ And they made on the breastpiece twisted chains like cords, of pure gold. ¹⁶ And they made two settings of gold filigree and two gold rings, and put the two rings on the two edges of the breastpiece. ¹⁷ And they put the two cords of gold in the two rings at the edges of the breastpiece. ¹⁸ They attached the two ends of the two cords to the two settings of filigree. Thus they attached it in front to the shoulder pieces of the ephod. ¹⁹ Then they made two rings of gold, and put them at the two ends of the breastpiece, on its inside edge next to the ephod. ²⁰ And they made two rings of gold, and attached them in front to the lower part of the two shoulder pieces of the ephod, at its seam above the skillfully woven band of the ephod. ²¹ And they bound the breastpiece by its rings to the rings of the ephod with a lace of blue, so that it should lie on the skillfully woven band of the ephod, and that the breastpiece should not come loose from the ephod, as the Lord had commanded Moses.

²² He also made the robe of the ephod woven all of blue, ²³ and the opening of the robe in it was like the opening in a garment, with a binding around the opening, so that it might not tear. ²⁴ On the hem of the robe they made pomegranates of blue and purple and scarlet yarns and fine twined linen. ²⁵ They also made bells of pure gold, and put the bells between the pomegranates all around the hem of the robe, between the pomegranates— ²⁶ a bell and a pomegranate, a bell and a pomegranate around the hem of the robe for ministering, as the Lord had commanded Moses.

²⁷ They also made the coats, woven of fine linen, for Aaron and his sons, ²⁸ and the turban of fine linen, and the caps of fine linen, and the linen undergarments of fine twined linen, ²⁹ and the sash of fine twined linen and of blue and purple and scarlet yarns, embroidered with needlework, as the Lord had commanded Moses.

³⁰ They made the plate of the holy crown of pure gold, and wrote on it an inscription, like the engraving of a signet, "Holy to the Lord." ³¹ And they tied to it a cord of blue to fasten it on the turban above, as the Lord had commanded Moses.

³² Thus all the work of the tabernacle of the tent of meeting was finished, and the people of Israel did according to all that the Lord had commanded Moses; so they did. ³³ Then they brought the tabernacle to Moses, the tent and all its utensils, its hooks, its frames, its bars, its pillars, and its bases; ³⁴ the covering of tanned rams' skins and goatskins, and the veil of the screen; ³⁵ the ark of the testimony with its poles and the mercy seat; ³⁶ the table with all its utensils, and the bread of the Presence; ³⁷ the lampstand of pure gold and its lamps with the lamps set and all its utensils, and the oil for the light; ³⁸ the golden altar, the anointing oil and the fragrant incense, and the screen for the entrance of the tent; ³⁹ the bronze altar, and its grating of bronze, its poles, and all its utensils; the basin and its stand; ⁴⁰ the hangings of the court, its pillars, and its bases, and the screen for the gate of the court, its cords, and its pegs; and all the utensils for the service of the tabernacle, for the tent of meeting; ⁴¹ the finely worked garments for ministering in the Holy Place, the holy garments for Aaron the priest, and the garments of his sons for their service as priests. ⁴² According to all that

the Lord had commanded Moses, so the people of Israel had done all the work. ⁴³ And Moses saw all the work, and behold, they had done it; as the Lord had commanded, so had they done it. Then Moses blessed them.

40 The Lord spoke to Moses, saying, ² "On the first day of the first month you shall erect the tabernacle of the tent of meeting. ³ And you shall put in it the ark of the testimony, and you shall screen the ark with the veil. ⁴ And you shall bring in the table and arrange it, and you shall bring in the lampstand and set up its lamps. ⁵ And you shall put the golden altar for incense before the ark of the testimony, and set up the screen for the door of the tabernacle. ⁶ You shall set the altar of burnt offering before the door of the tabernacle of the tent of meeting, ⁷ and place the basin between the tent of meeting and the altar, and put water in it. ⁸ And you shall set up the court all around, and hang up the screen for the gate of the court.

⁹ "Then you shall take the anointing oil and anoint the tabernacle and all that is in it, and consecrate it and all its furniture, so that it may become holy. ¹⁰ You shall also anoint the altar of burnt offering and all its utensils, and consecrate the altar, so that the altar may become most holy. ¹¹ You shall also anoint the basin and its stand, and consecrate it. ¹² Then you shall bring Aaron and his sons to the entrance of the tent of meeting and shall wash them with water ¹³ and put on Aaron the holy garments. And you shall anoint him and consecrate him, that he may serve me as priest. ¹⁴ You shall bring his sons also and put coats on them, ¹⁵ and anoint them, as you anointed their father, that they may serve me as priests. And their anointing shall admit them to a perpetual priesthood throughout their generations."

¹⁶ This Moses did; according to all that the Lord commanded him, so he did. ¹⁷ In the first month in the second year, on the first day of the month, the tabernacle was erected. ¹⁸ Moses erected the tabernacle. He laid its bases, and set up its frames, and put in its poles, and raised up its pillars. ¹⁹ And he spread the tent over the tabernacle and put the covering of the tent over it, as the Lord had commanded Moses. ²⁰ He took the testimony and put it into the ark, and put the poles on the ark and set the mercy seat above on the ark. ²¹ And he brought the ark into the tabernacle and set up the veil of the screen, and screened the ark of the testimony, as the Lord had commanded Moses. ²² He put the table in the tent of meeting, on the north side of the tabernacle, outside the veil, ²³ and arranged the bread on it before the Lord, as the Lord had commanded Moses. ²⁴ He put the lampstand in the tent of meeting, opposite the table on the south side of the tabernacle, ²⁵ and set up the lamps before the Lord, as the Lord had commanded Moses. ²⁶ He put the golden altar in the tent of meeting before the veil, ²⁷ and burned fragrant incense on it, as the Lord had commanded Moses. ²⁸ He put in place the screen for the door of the tabernacle. ²⁹ And he set the altar of burnt offering at the entrance of the tabernacle of the tent of meeting, and offered on it the burnt offering and the grain offering, as the Lord had commanded Moses. ³⁰ He set the basin between the tent of meeting and the altar, and put water in it for washing, ³¹ with which Moses and Aaron and his sons washed their hands and their feet. ³² When they went into the tent of meeting, and when they approached the altar, they washed, as the Lord commanded Moses. ³³ And he erected the court around the tabernacle and the altar, and set up the screen of the gate of the court. So Moses finished the work.

³⁴ Then the cloud covered the tent of meeting, and the glory of the Lord filled the tabernacle. ³⁵ And Moses was not able to enter the tent of

meeting because the cloud settled on it, and the glory of the Lord filled the tabernacle. ³⁶ Throughout all their journeys, whenever the cloud was taken up from over the tabernacle, the people of Israel would set out. ³⁷ But if the cloud was not taken up, then they did not set out till the day that it was taken up. ³⁸ For the cloud of the Lord was on the tabernacle by day, and fire was in it by night, in the sight of all the house of Israel throughout all their journeys.

¹ The meaning of the Hebrew word is uncertain; also verse 23; compare 25:5 ² Or *garments for worship*; see 31:10 ³ A *cubit* was about 18 inches or 45 centimeters ⁴ Probably Bezalel (compare 35:30; 37:1) ⁵ A *cubit* was about 18 inches or 45 centimeters ⁶ A *handbreadth* was about 3 inches or 7.5 centimeters ⁷ A *talent* was about 75 pounds or 34 kilograms ⁸ A *cubit* was about 18 inches or 45 centimeters ⁹ A *talent* was about 75 pounds or 34 kilograms; a *shekel* was about 2/5 ounce or 11 grams ¹⁰ A *beka* was about 1/5 ounce or 5.5 grams ¹¹ Or *garments for worship* ¹² A *span* was about 9 inches or 22 centimeters

Section Overview

Finally we come to the building of the tabernacle. It is a highlight of the story. "The building of the tabernacle at the end [of Exodus] is not an appendix but a climax. Exodus moves from 'service' (slavery) to Pharaoh in Egypt to the 'service' (worship) of Yahweh at Sinai."⁸⁰⁸ The Lord now condescends into the Israelites' midst in the tabernacle so that this service and worship may continue throughout their journeys. God's goal in redemption is always to be near his people and in relationship with them. That goal is realized powerfully in this last section of the book.

The section's opening verses (35:1–3) begin by recapping the Sabbath commands given in 31:12–17. Since the Sabbath is the covenant sign, these verses highlight a main theme of the section: the importance of covenant obedience. And, since they recap the verses immediately preceding the golden calf incident in chapter 32, they allow us to pick up on the other side of that account and resume the narrative as it was supposed to be: Israel is moving forward in obedience to the Lord.

The text then turns to the tabernacle contributions and the gifted artisans who will use them to craft the tabernacle and its furniture (35:4–36:7). We read of a river of joyful givers from across the community whose generosity exceeds the artisans' needs. As for the artisans, emphasis is again placed on their divine gifting from the Lord, whose wisdom extends even to how one practices one's trade or craft. Covenant obedience is again highlighted; the clause "the Lord has/had commanded" occurs no fewer than five times (35:4, 10, 29; 36:1, 5).

With the materials now in place the text describes the Israelites' crafting of the tabernacle and related items (36:8–39:43), such as the priestly clothing. Chapter 39 especially emphasizes how they are careful to do everything "as the Lord had commanded Moses," with some variation of that clause occurring ten times (39:1, 5, 7, 21, 26, 29, 31, 32, 42, 43).

That emphasis continues into the final chapter (40:1–33), which describes the setting up of the tabernacle and mentions Moses' obedience to the Lord's commands seven different times (40:16, 19, 21, 23, 25, 27, 29), as well as the priests'

---

808 B. G. Webb, "Heaven on Earth: The Significance of the Tabernacle in Its Literary and Theological Context," in *Exploring Exodus: Literary, Theological, and Contemporary Approaches*, ed. B. S. Rosner and P. R. Williamson (Nottingham, UK: Inter-Varsity, 2008), 155; cited in Alexander, *Exodus*, 554.

obedience in their future ministry (40:32). This emphasis on obedience throughout Exodus 35–40 underscores that we are reading no longer of the disobedient calf-worshiping Israelites but of the Israelites as they are meant to be obeying their Lord and King cheerfully, faithfully, and wholeheartedly.

This prepares us for the closing verses, in which the Lord comes down in glory to dwell in the tabernacle in the midst of his faithful people (40:34–38). This achieves one of the Lord's major goals of the exodus, as he had previously stated it: "I am the LORD their God, who brought them out of the land of Egypt *that I might dwell among them*" (29:46). What is more, that he comes down to dwell with his people so soon after the golden calf tragedy (chs. 32–34) is especially significant. It is "not that the events of those chapters would ever be *forgotten*. But the arrival of God's glory and the resumption of the journey demonstrated that they had been *forgiven*."[809] This makes clear he truly is a God "merciful and gracious, slow to anger, and abounding in steadfast love and faithfulness, keeping steadfast love for thousands, forgiving iniquity and transgressions and sin" (34:6–7). Hallelujah!

Section Outline

VIII. Israel at Sinai: the Lord's palace-tent is built and he comes to dwell among his covenant people (35:1–40:38)
  A. Introduction (35:1)
  B. Command to keep the Sabbath (35:2–3)
    1. The command (35:2a)
    2. The punishment for breaking it (35:2b)
    3. A specific application of the command (35:3)
  C. Gathering the materials for the tabernacle and related components (35:4–36:7)
    1. The call for tabernacle contributions (35:4–9)
    2. The items to be made for the tabernacle (35:10–19)
    3. The bringing of the tabernacle contributions (35:20–29)
    4. The divinely gifted tabernacle artisans (35:30–36:1)
    5. The command to stop bringing tabernacle contributions (36:2–7)
  D. Making the tabernacle and related components (36:8–39:43)
    1. The tabernacle's covering of curtains (36:8–13)
    2. The tabernacle's goat hair tent (36:14–18)
    3. The tent's two further coverings (36:19)
    4. The tabernacle's inner structure (36:20–34)
    5. The tabernacle's veil (36:35–36)
    6. The tabernacle's screen (36:37–38)
    7. The ark of the covenant (37:1–9)
    8. The golden table (37:10–16)
    9. The golden lampstand (37:17–24)

---

[809] Wright, *Exodus*, 607.

10. The golden altar of incense (37:25–28)
11. The holy anointing oil and holy incense (37:29)
12. The altar of burnt offering (38:1–7)
13. The bronze basin (38:8)
14. The walls of the tabernacle's courtyard (38:9–20)
15. The record of the tabernacle donations (38:21–31)
16. The priestly garments (39:1–31)
17. The tabernacle items are brought to Moses (39:32–43)

E. The setting up of the tabernacle (40:1–33)
   1. The Lord commands the tabernacle to be set up (40:1–8)
   2. The Lord commands for the tabernacle and its priests to be made holy (40:9–15)
   3. The tabernacle is set up according to the Lord's commands (40:16–33)

F. The glory of the Lord fills the tabernacle (40:34–38)

Comment

35:1 Moses now assembles the people in order to pass along the Lord's commands. What 34:32 mentioned in overview the following chapters now describe in detail.

35:2–3 Commands to keep the Sabbath occur just prior to the golden calf incident (31:12–17) and just after the Israelites have been fully forgiven (35:2–3). This helps to bracket out the Israelites' unfaithfulness as a thing of the past; they can now move beyond it. It is as though the Lord is saying, "I will now pick up where I left off before you built that calf. I was speaking about keeping the Sabbath, which is what I want to emphasize before you begin building my tabernacle." At the same time, repetition of the commands regarding the Sabbath—the covenant sign—emphasizes the importance of covenant faithfulness. The Lord most desires not a fancy tent but his people's faithful love. Even the noble work of building the tabernacle, which the Lord will now describe, must not override faithfulness to his commands.

For comments on Sabbath keeping cf. comment on 31:12–17. Exodus 35:3 expands the earlier commands by providing an example of breaking the Sabbath, namely, kindling fires in one's dwelling.[810] This may seem to us like a small thing, but kindling fire was part of the day's normal work activities, necessary for such things as baking bread, which was especially labor intensive when it required one to grind one's own flour. And, since women or servants were more likely to undertake this work, the command of verse 3 makes especially clear that they too must be relieved of work on this day.[811]

35:4–9 Cf. comments on 25:1–2; 25:3–7.

---

[810] This helps explain why the man collecting sticks on the Sabbath is considered to have broken it: it is the first stage of kindling a fire. Cf. Numbers 15:32–36.
[811] In keeping with this Exodus 16:23 suggests that any food needed for the Sabbath should be prepared the preceding day so the Sabbath can be a full day of rest.

35:10–19 The tabernacle is to be made by "every skillful craftsman" (v. 10), which could be rendered more woodenly "all those wise of heart." Earlier texts have explained how the Lord has gifted certain people with skill/wisdom in using their hands (28:3; 31:6); they are now called to use those gifts (cf. comment on 31:1–11).

The text then identifies that which they are to use their skills to make: the tabernacle and its related components (35:11–19). These items fall into six groupings:

(1) the tent of meeting (35:11), consisting of the tabernacle (the inner ornate curtains, cf. comment on 26:1–6), the tent of goat hair that covers these curtains (cf. comment on 26:7–13), and the additional coverings on top (cf. comment on 26:14)[812]

(2) the items related to the Most Holy Place (35:12), that is, the ark (cf. comment on 25:10–16), the atonement lid (cf. comment on 25:17–22), and the veil (cf. comment on 26:31–35)

(3) the items related to the Holy Place (35:13–15), that is, the table and bread (cf. comment on 25:23–30), the lampstand and its oil (cf. comments on 25:31–40; 27:20–21), the altar of incense (cf. comment on 30:1–10), the anointing oil and incense (cf. comment on 30:22–33; 30:34–38), and the screen for the tent (cf. comment on 26:36–37)

(4) the items related to the courtyard (35:16–17), namely, the altar of burnt offering (cf. comment on 27:1–8), the basin (cf. comment on 30:17–21), the court walls, and the court's gateway screen (cf. comment on 27:9–19)

(5) the pegs and ropes for the tabernacle and courtyard (35:18; cf. comment on 27:9–19)

(6) the priestly garments (35:19; cf. comments on 28:1–43)

35:20–29 Having heard which items need to be made (vv. 10–19), the people now depart to collect the necessary materials (v. 20). The text has emphasized that the contribution is to be voluntary (25:2; 35:5), and it returns to that emphasis here: the list of items brought (vv. 22–28) is bracketed by notices that they are a freewill offering given by those with willing hearts (vv. 21, 29)—an idea also threaded throughout the list itself (vv. 22, 26; cf. 25:1–2). The tabernacle is built not through oppressive taxation or guilt-infused pressure tactics but through gifts given in joyful love.

The gifts are listed in natural groupings: gold items (v. 22),[813] yarns, textiles and skins (v. 23), silver and bronze (v. 24a), acacia wood (v. 24b), freshly spun yarns and textiles (vv. 25–26), precious stones (v. 27), and spices and oil (v. 28). (For details cf. comment on 25:3–7.) The first items mentioned are gold, including earrings, the very things Israelites brought to make the golden calf (35:22; cf. 32:2). This highlights the fact that they are now using their goods for proper worship. They truly have repented and turned back to the Lord.

---

[812] Exodus 26:14 makes clear that there are two coverings, one of ram skin and one of goat, though these are considered to work together and can thus be described as a singular covering (as here; so also 36:19; 39:34; 40:19).

[813] The words "Every man dedicating an offering of gold to the LORD" could be rendered "thus did every man presenting a wave offering of gold to the Lord." For "wave offering" cf. comment on 29:22–25.

Two observations may be made about the giving. First, the entire community participates. The text highlights how both men and women donate (35:22, 29), and the list shows that this includes those able to give expensive gifts (vv. 27–28), as well as those giving a single earring (v. 22). It is a picture of widespread giving from all sectors of society because of widespread desire to worship God in this way. Indeed, the people are eventually told to stop because they have already brought more than enough (36:3–7)! These truly are cheerful givers (2 Cor. 9:7). Second, while some give from their treasures, others give from their talents and time by using their skills to make the needed goods (Ex. 35:25–26; cf. 31:1–11). One need not be wealthy to give; the poorest person could use his gifts to contribute to the Lord's tabernacle in joyful love.

35:30–36:1 Now that the materials are gathered, who will transform them into the tabernacle? Moses answers this question by introducing the lead artisans the Lord has equipped: Bezalel and Oholiab. He notes how God has gifted them to apprentice others, identifies their wide-ranging abilities that will enable them to do and oversee the work, and emphasizes that they and their team must work in accordance with the Lord's commands (a key theme regarding the tabernacle; cf. 31:11). For further detail cf. comment on 31:1–11.

36:2–7 Moses now summons the artisans and passes along the people's contributions (vv. 2–3a). But so much keeps coming every morning that all the artisans from every aspect of the work tell Moses that they have "much more than enough" (v. 5), a fact emphasized again in verse 7. This is a river of generosity at flood stage! Moses therefore commands the people to stop—surely one of the rare instances in the history of God's people that generosity is so great that it must be restrained (vv. 6–7).

36:8–39:43 The tabernacle work now begins in earnest. From 36:4 we know that various pieces are being worked on simultaneously, though the text naturally describes them one at a time. The reasons for such extensive repetition between this section and the earlier sections describing the pieces are discussed above in (cf. Overview of Exodus 35:1–40:38). Due to the repetition, in what follows the comments typically point the reader to the earlier discussion and provide additional comment only in the few instances of new material.

36:8–13 Cf. comment on 26:1–6. For 36:8 cf. comment on 31:1–11 (esp. v. 6).[814]

36:14–19 Cf. comments on 26:7–13; 27:14.

36:20–34 Cf. comments on 26:15–30.

36:35–36 Cf. comment on 26:31–35.

---

[814] Exodus 25–31 begins with the tabernacle's furniture (25:10–39) and then describes the tabernacle itself (26:1–37), whereas Exodus 35–39 begins with the tabernacle itself (36:8–38) and then describes its furniture (37:1–28). As such, Exodus 25–31 describes the tabernacle from most holy to least holy, thus making distinctions especially important for Israel to understand (cf. esp. Num. 4:1–20), while Exodus 35–39 describes the tabernacle in terms of the order in which it is erected (cf. 40:18–27), which is very practical now that the items have been made.

36:37–38 Cf. comment on 26:36–37.[815]

37:1–9 Cf. comment on 25:10–16; 25:17–22. The ark is the most important piece of tabernacle furniture. Not surprisingly, the text specifies that Bezalel himself, the chief artisan, makes it.[816]

37:10–16 Cf. comment on 25:23–30.

37:17–24 Cf. comment on 25:31–40.

37:25–28 Cf. comment on 30:1–5.

37:29 Cf. comment on 30:22–33; 30:34–38.

38:1–7 Cf. comment on 27:1–8.

38:8 Cf. comment on 30:17–21.

38:9–20 Cf. comment on 27:9–19.

38:21–31 We learn that Moses has commanded a record to be made of the materials used for the tabernacle components (v. 21; for "testimony" cf. 16:34). (Though not stated here, one reason for such a record may be to make sure all donations are accounted for properly; cf. 2 Kings 12:9–15.) The tabernacle is called the "tabernacle of the testimony," that is, the tabernacle in which the covenant law is found (cf. comment on Ex. 16:31–36). The phrase is relatively rare.[817] Its use here draws attention to the covenant, which stands at the heart of Israel's relationship with God.

It appears that the phrase "the responsibility of the Levites" (38:21b) refers to the fact that they will do the counting of the tabernacle donations. The Levites comprise three major divisions: Kohathites, Gershonites, and Merarites (Num. 3:14–20). The latter two are in view here, since they will be the ones to come under the oversight of Aaron's son, Ithamar (4:28, 33). That they should do the counting makes sense, for the majority of the precious metals recorded will be used for the tabernacle's structural elements, the very elements these divisions are responsible for transporting (3:36–37; 4:28, 33). The text also naturally highlights the chief artisans, Bezalel and Oholiab, who oversee the use of the materials to make the tabernacle components. Cf. comment on 31:1–11.

The record of the materials come next. "The inventory described here is in accord with Egyptian practice. Egyptian art depicting scenes of metalworking regularly features the master weigher weighing the metals on balances and the scribes recording the results in their ledgers before issuing the materials to the artisans."[818]

---

815 Exodus 36:38 could be rendered "He overlaid their capitals and their fillets with gold." The mention of the capitals' gold overlay is perhaps made to distinguish the capitals clearly from the courtyard capitals, which are overlaid with silver (38:10). It does not mean the rest of the pillar is *not* also overlaid with gold (cf. 26:37).
816 Keil, *Exodus*, vol. 2, 249. Sarna (*Exodus*, 227) notes that, just as "the house that King Solomon built" (1 Kings 6:2) means "King Solomon was responsible for having this house built," Moses' statement "I made an ark" (Deut. 10:3) means "I was responsible for having this ark made."
817 It occurs only three other times (Num. 1:50, 53; 10:11); "tent of the testimony" occurs five times (Num. 9:15; 17:7, 8; 18:2; 2 Chron. 24:6).
818 Sarna, *Exodus*, 231; as one example he cites *ANEP*, no. 133.

TABLE 2.10: The Making of the Tabernacle Components

Material	Biblical Amount	Modern Equivalent[819]	Source	Use
Gold	29 talents and 730 shekels	2,193 pounds (995 kg)	Wave offering from the people (38:24)[820]	Sanctuary items
Silver	100 talents and 1,775 shekels	7,544 pounds (3,422 kg)	Census tax (cf. 30:11–16)	Bases for the sanctuary and veil, hooks, overlay for capitals, fillets[821]
Bronze	70 talents and 2,400 shekels	5,310 pounds (2,409 kg)	Voluntary contributions from the people (35:24)	Bases for entrance to tent of meeting, bronze altar and grating, utensils of burnt offering altar, bases for court walls, bases for gate of the courts, all pegs[822]

The precious metals alone—which presumably come from long-held belongings as well as ones recently acquired through the despoiling of the Egyptians (12:35–36)—weigh close to 15,000 pounds (6,800 kgs) and are described here as completely sufficient to make all that is needed (cf. comment on 36:2–7). (It may be noted that the Levites responsible to transport the heaviest items are given carts and oxen to help; Num. 7:3–9.)

For the mention of "those of the congregation who were recorded" (Ex. 38:25) cf. comment on 30:11–16. For the census number in 38:26 cf. Introduction: Interpretive Challenges: Large Numbers in the Book of Exodus (esp. note 49).

39:1–31 Having described the making of the tabernacle components (36:8–38:31), the text now describes the making of the garments for the priests who will serve at the tabernacle. The people do so "as the Lord had commanded Moses," a clause that occurs seven times in order to make clear that their obedience is full and complete.[823]

39:1–7 Cf. comment on 28:5–14.

39:8–21 Cf. comment on 28:15–30.

39:22–26 Cf. comment on 28:31–35.

39:27–29 Cf. comments on 28:39; 28:40; 28:42–43.

39:30–31 Cf. comment on 28:36–38.

---

[819] This assumes a value of 75 pounds (34 kg) for the talent and 0.4 ounces (11.3 g) for the shekel (Cook, "Weights and Measures," *ISBE* 4:1054). The number of shekels per talent can be calculated from 38:25–26. If 603,550 people give a half-shekel each, the total is 301,775 shekels. If we remove the overage of 1,775 shekels, then 300,000 are left. Dividing this by the 100 talents results in a ratio of 3,000 shekels per talent. Multiplying this by 0.4 ounces (11.3 g) leads to the value of 75 pounds (34 kg) per talent. For "shekel of the sanctuary" cf. comment on 30:11–16 (at v. 13).
[820] Cf. 35:22 and note 813 within comment on 35:20–29.
[821] For "fillets" cf. comment on 27:9–19.
[822] The absence of the basin is no surprise here, since we have already learned that its material comes from a different source (Ex. 38:8).
[823] Cf. comment on 1:1–5 and also the use of this same phrase seven times in 40:17–33.

39:32–43 The text now lists all the tabernacle items that the people make (vv. 33–41; cf. comment on 35:10–19 for details). The list begins and ends by noting three separate times that the people make all these things in exact keeping with the Lord's commands (39:32, 42–43). The emphasis must not be missed: Israel has followed the Lord's commands to the very letter, a model that succeeding generations are to follow. Moses responds by blessing them (v. 43), that is, by saying a prayer over them in which he asks the Lord to show them his special favor (cf. Num. 6:23–27). This, too, is not to be missed: the Lord delights to bless his obedient children. That is a good father's natural response—and the Lord is the very best father there is.

40:1–15 With everything ready the Lord now commands that the tabernacle be set up and the priests consecrated.

40:1–8 The tabernacle setup is to take place "on the first day of the first month ... in the second year" (vv. 2, 17), that is, the second year after the Israelites' deliverance from Egypt and some ten months after their arrival at Sinai (cf. note 339 within comment on 19:1–2). This timing is especially meaningful. When the Lord led Israel out of Egypt so that he could eventually dwell in their midst (29:46), he declared the month of their redemption to be the new beginning of their year (cf. comment on 12:1–2). Now, almost one year later, Israel is to set up the tabernacle on the first day of that same month, a moving reminder that God's purpose in redemption has been accomplished.

Everything is set up in logical order: the tent is set up first (40:2b), the furniture is then moved in (vv. 3–5), and finally the surrounding courtyard and its items are put in place (vv. 6–8). The process is described in more detail in verses 16–33.

40:9–15 Once the tabernacle is set up, it must be made ritually holy, as do its priests. This is due to the Lord's own holiness: a holy king requires a holy dwelling place and holy servants to work within it.

First, the Lord commands that the tabernacle and everything within it, as well as the altar and basin in the court, be anointed (vv. 9–11). For further details cf. comment on 30:22–33 (at vv. 26–29).[824]

The Lord then commands the priests' consecration, which involves a ceremonial washing, dressing with the priestly garments, and anointing (40:12–15).[825] Cf. comments on Exodus 29:1–46, especially verses 1–9, where the process is described more fully.

---

[824] While only the altar of burnt offering is identified as "most holy" (Ex. 40:10), 30:29 makes clear that all tabernacle items are "most holy." The altar's holiness is perhaps emphasized because it is in the court, not the tent, and thus most at risk of being inappropriately touched by worshipers who are bringing sacrifices (Keil, *Exodus*, vol. 2, 255). The emphasis on its holiness thus serves as a reminder that only the ritually holy priests may touch it; cf. note 730 within comment on 30:22–33.

[825] In Leviticus 8 the tent's anointing comes after Aaron is clothed, not before as here (cf. Lev. 8:7–9 with 8:10–12). "It may be that the account in Exodus is thematically arranged, thus keeping all the actions related to the Tabernacle together (40:1–11) before turning to the actions regarding the priests (40:12–15), whereas Leviticus 8 is providing the actual temporal sequence: Aaron is prepared for anointing (8:7–9) and then the anointing of the Tabernacle and of Aaron occurs (8:10–12; this actually makes good practical sense, as the anointing may now all be done at once)"; Sklar, *Additional Notes on Leviticus*, at 8:10–13; cf. also note 694 within comment on 29:19–21.

40:16–33 Once again exact obedience is emphasized: "This Moses did; according to all that the LORD command him, so he did" (v. 16). The wording is virtually identical to Genesis 6:22, which describes Noah's exact obedience. Just as the beginning of Exodus describes Moses with Noah-like language to emphasize his role as a deliverer (cf. 2:1–4), the end of the book describes him with Noah-like language to emphasize his role as an obedient man of God.

The text now describes that obedience with regard to setting up the tabernacle (40:17–33). (Moses' obedience with regard to making the priests holy will be told in Leviticus 8; cf. comment on 40:34–38.) Moses is described as carrying out all the actions, not because he personally does all the work (it is far too great for one person) but because he ensures that it is done correctly.[826] At the same time, Moses does perform certain priestly actions—such as burning the incense (v. 27) or making the offerings (v. 29)—since he alone has a state of ritual purity great enough to perform them (the priests are not yet consecrated).

The description of setting up the tabernacle is broken into eight sections. The first seven end with the refrain "As the LORD had commanded Moses." Just as this phrase occurred seven times in 39:1–31 to emphasize the thoroughness of the people's obedience, it occurs here seven times to emphasize the thoroughness of Moses' obedience.[827] The eighth section ends with the statement "So Moses finished the work" (40:33), which echoes Genesis 2:2 and encourages us to see a link between the tabernacle and Eden (cf. Response section, "What Does the Tabernacle Have to Do with Eden?"). The setting up proceeds as follows:

(1) The tabernacle proper is erected, from its frame to its coverings (40:18–19). For 40:18 cf. comments on 26:15–30; 26:31–35; for 40:19 cf. comments 26:1–14.

(2) The ark is prepared,[828] placed in the Most Holy Place, and screened (40:20–21). Cf. comments on 25:10–16; 25:17–22; 26:31–35.

(3) The golden table is placed in the Holy Place and the bread of the Presence arranged on it (40:22–23). Cf. comments on 25:23–30; 26:31–35.

(4) The golden lampstand is placed in the Holy Place and its lamps are set up (40:24–25).[829] Cf. comments on 25:31–40; 26:31–35.

(5) The golden altar is placed in the Holy Place and incense burned on it (40:26–27). Cf. comments on 26:31–35; 30:1–5; 30:6–10; 30:34–38.

(6) The screen is placed at the tabernacle's entrance, the altar of burnt offering is placed before the tabernacle, and a burnt offering and grain offering are made (40:28–29). Cf. comments on 26:36–37; 29:36–42.[830]

---

[826] Cf. 1 Kings 6:2, which describes the temple as the "house that King Solomon built," not because he built it by himself but because he was responsible for its being built (cf. note 816 within comment on 37:1–9).
[827] Wright, *Exodus*, 609. For "seven" as a mark of thoroughness cf. comment on 1:1–5.
[828] The full process is named here even though some of this preparation—such as the placing of the poles—has already occurred (cf. 40:20 with 37:5).
[829] The word translated "set up" could also be rendered "lighted" (NASB) or "lit up" (JPS); cf. Leviticus 24:2, where the word is translated "may be kept burning."
[830] Because Exodus 40 is more like a summary, the text mentions only the grain offering (v. 29); the drink offering is understood (cf. 29:40).

(7) The basin is placed somewhere between the altar of burnt offering and the tent of meeting and is filled with water (40:30); its use is then described (40:31–32). (While Moses might have used it immediately, the text appears to focus on its future use for Moses and the priests.) Cf. comment on 30:17–21.

(8) The courtyard walls and the screen for its entryway are set up (40:33). Cf. comment on 27:9–19.

40:34–38 After the tabernacle is set up it is to be anointed and the priests consecrated (vv. 9–15). But this does not occur here; we must wait until Leviticus 8—and for good reason. The priests' consecration will require numerous sacrifices, several of which are described in Leviticus 1–7, which outlines the Israelite sacrificial system. Moreover, because the ordination will take seven days (Lev. 8:33), placing Leviticus 1–7 before the ceremony helps to give the sense of the passage of time between the erecting of the tabernacle (Exodus 40) and its anointing at the priests' consecration (Leviticus 8).

But the Lord does not wait for the priests' consecration to be complete! As soon as the tabernacle is set up, he comes down in his cloud of glory (Ex. 40:34).[831] "It's as if God could not wait to be where he had wanted to be all along—in the midst of his people."[832] This is, in fact, one of the main reasons he has redeemed them: "They shall know that I am the LORD their God, who brought them out of the land of Egypt *that I might dwell among them*" (29:46). Simply put, this is a God who longs to be with us, near us, among us.

As for the cloud of glory, it may be described as a two-part reality: the cloud and the glory within it. The "cloud" would look like those in the skies, while the "glory"—which is not always present (cf. 16:10)—refers to the Lord's lighting up the cloud with such an awesome display of his presence that the only proper response is to give him glory (cf. comment on 24:15–18 and at Response section on 24:12–25:9, "What Is the Glory of the Lord?"). Practically speaking, however, when the glory is present, it so transforms the cloud's appearance that the two fuse into a single glory-cloud.

Due to the cloud's presence over and filling the tent, Moses cannot go in (40:35). The use of the word "filled" might suggest that the Lord's glory is so palpable and thick that there is no room for Moses to enter. But a comparison with chapter 24 suggests a different possibility. When the Lord's glory appeared within the cloud on Mount Sinai (vv. 15–18), Moses entered the cloud, but not until summoned (v. 16); one dare not barge into the presence of a king uninvited (cf. vv. 1–2). The same is true here: the Lord's glory has again lit up the cloud covering and filling the tent, making clear that he is present within. Moses is therefore "not able to enter" (40:35). As a sign of reverence and respect, he waits until being summoned (cf. Lev. 1:1).[833]

The text concludes by describing two important functions of the cloud. First, the Lord will guide the Israelites by it. When he takes up the cloud from the

---

[831] The cloud itself would immediately consecrate the tabernacle and its contents (Ex. 29:43). The later anointing in Leviticus 8 will underscore and confirm this consecration.
[832] Wright, *Exodus*, 610.
[833] Presumably, the Lord would have withdrawn his presence into the Most Holy Place by the time we reach the events of Leviticus 1:1 (cf. Ex. 25:22; Num. 7:89).

tabernacle and moves on, they will take down the tabernacle and follow him (Ex. 40:36–38). He is their ultimate leader during their journey to the Promised Land (cf. comment on 13:17–22; cf. also Num. 9:15–23). Second, the cloud shows that the Lord is present in their midst. It is a visible reminder—day and night, throughout all their journeys—that he is with them (Ex. 40:38).

To come at this second point from another angle: clear parallels exist between the Lord's coming down on Mount Sinai and his coming down on the tabernacle (cf. table 2.11; the words in italics are the same in Hebrew).[834] The parallels are a way to say, "Israelites, when you leave Mount Sinai, where you have seen the Lord's presence in your midst so clearly, do not worry about whether he is still with you. He has given you this tabernacle as a 'portable Mount Sinai,' a continual guarantee of his presence with you." He never forsakes those he rescues—and he will lead them safely to his Promised Land of rest.

TABLE 2.11: Parallels between the Lord's Coming Down on Sinai and the Tabernacle

Exodus 24:15b–16a, 17, 18a; 25:1–2a	Exodus 40:34–35; Leviticus 1:1–2
"The (1) *cloud covered* the mountain, and (2) *the glory of the* LORD settled (3) *on Mount Sinai* . . . and (4) *he called to Moses* on the seventh day *from* within the cloud. . . . And the appearance of the Lord's glory was like a consuming fire on the top of the mountain in the sight of the Israelites. Then (5) *Moses entered the midst of the cloud* and went up into the mountain. . . . And (6) *the Lord spoke to Moses, saying, 'Speak to the Israelites.'*"	"Then the (1) *cloud covered* the tent of meeting, and the (2) *glory of the* LORD filled (3) *the tabernacle*. And (5) *Moses was not able to enter the tent of meeting* because the cloud had settled upon it, and the glory of the LORD filled the tabernacle. Then (4) *the* LORD *called to Moses* and the (6) Lord *spoke to him from* the tent of meeting, *saying, 'Speak to the Israelites.'*"

Response

We may consider some of this section's main lessons by asking four questions that center around the tabernacle. The first is about giving, the next two are about obedience, and the last is about God's purposes in creation.

WHY DO WE GIVE GIFTS TO GOD?

By the time we reach the end of Exodus we might lose sight of how it began: with the Lord's rescue of his people from cruel bondage in Egypt (Exodus 1–15). That rescue connects directly to what is taking place at the book's end, especially when we remember one of the main reasons the Lord gives for rescuing Israel: "They shall know that I am the LORD their God, who brought them out of the land of Egypt *that I might dwell among them*" (29:46). Redemption by the Lord is always for the sake of relationship with him. In Israel's case this means he will come and physically dwell in its midst in his tabernacle.

But the Israelites must build the tabernacle and provide its materials. In other words this is one of the first capital campaigns God's people ever undertake. And

---

[834] Averbeck, "Tabernacle," *DOTP,* 823–824, citing E. Blum, *Studien zur Komposition des Pentateuch*, BZAW 189 (Berlin: de Gruyter, 1990), 312–313.

how do they respond? With a tsunami of generosity. When the Lord first calls for contributions he emphasizes that they are to be voluntary (25:2). But the Israelites' contributions are not only voluntary; they are community wide (35:20–22, 27). They consist not only of material gifts (35:20–29) but also of acts of service (35:25–26; 36:2). And they are so abundantly given that the artisans soon have more than they can use (36:5–7). This is one problem most pastors would be happy to have!

But why does this happen? Surely because the people remember that this is a God who not only redeemed them to begin with (chs. 1–15) but also has forgiven them and taken them back after they have messed up so badly (chs. 32–34). The proper response to God's initial grace in redemption and his ongoing grace in forgiveness is not only obedience in general but joyful, cheerful, sacrificial giving in particular. The Israelites do not give in order to be rescued or forgiven. They have already experienced both! And this is the point: generous and cheerful giving is a proper response to the God who has been so gracious to us. Such giving might come in the form of material gifts (35:20–29) or acts of service (35:25–26; 36:2), *but true thankfulness always seeks an outlet of expression* (cf. Response section on 24:12–25:9, "What Is the Proper Response?").

When the Israelites give, they do so in keeping with what the Lord commands them to give (35:4; 36:5). This leads to a section question.

WHAT SHOULD OBEDIENCE LOOK LIKE?

A major theme of this last section of Exodus is the Israelites' obedience to the Lord. This is highlighted not only by the text's numerous statements that they do "as the Lord commanded" (cf. Overview of 35:1–40:38) but also in its extensive repetition between the Lord's commands in chapters 25–31 and the Israelites' obedience to them in chapters 35–39. Such repetition is intended to make clear that the Israelites have followed the Lord's commands exactly. This is especially important in the context of Exodus. Only a few chapters earlier they had rebelled against the Lord's commands regarding proper worship by making a golden calf (ch. 32). Now a chastened and repentant people are following his commandments precisely in building the place where they will worship him. When understood this way, the repetition is meant to inspire us to an obedience that follows God's commands *to the letter*. To put it as a question, If someone were to describe God's commands and then describe our obedience to them, would there be the same level of repetition as we find between chapters 25–31 and 35–39?

We can note further that the obedience highlighted in this section centers around the place of God's worship. This leads to the next question.

WHY DOES PROPER WORSHIP MATTER?

"Worship is absolutely basic to a proper relationship to God."[835] This is because worship involves acknowledging who God is and responding appropriately with obedience, thanksgiving, and praise. But we can respond appropriately only when

---

835 Stuart, *Exodus*, 779.

we are responding to who God actually is—which is why our worship must be in direct keeping with what he has revealed about himself in his Word.

The final chapters of Exodus are a case in point. When the Israelites make and worship a golden calf, the Lord's responds with judgment and even considers wiping out his people (ch. 32). When the Israelites make and set up the tabernacle exactly in keeping with God's commands, he comes down to dwell in their midst (chs. 35–40). These contrasting responses make a crucial point: not all ways of worship lead to the same place. There are wrong ways, which God condemns, and a correct way, which he blesses and reveals to us in his Word.

This has important implications for us today. Jesus says, "I am the way, and the truth, and the life. No one comes to the Father except through me" (John 14:6). He is in effect saying, "Every other way to God that does not go through me is like a golden calf, and those taking such paths can expect the Lord to respond in the way he did with Israel. But the one who comes to God through me can know him truly, and 'we will come to him and make our home with him'" (John 14:23). We need to know Jesus because only in him can we come to know God and have fellowship with him—which is the very reason we have been created. This leads to a final question.

WHAT DOES THE TABERNACLE HAVE TO DO WITH EDEN?

Commentators frequently note the parallels between the tabernacle account in Exodus 39–40 and the creation account in Genesis 1–2 (cf. table 2.12; the words in italic are the same Hebrew words). These parallels are in keeping with other passages that encourage us to see a link between the tabernacle and creation, and in particular with the garden of Eden. For example, as noted earlier,[836] the Bible uses a relatively rare form of a verb to describe the Lord's "*walking* in the garden" of Eden (Gen. 3:8) and then uses that same verb when recounting the Lord's promise to the Israelites, "I will make my dwelling/tabernacle[837] among you ... and *I will walk among you*" (Lev. 26:11–12).[838] Such passages encourage us to see that the tabernacle realizes a main purpose of Eden: God is again "walking" among his people.[839]

TABLE 2.12: Parallels between Tabernacle Account and Creation Account

"Thus all the work of the tabernacle of the tent of meeting was *finished*, and the people of Israel *did* according to all that the LORD had commanded Moses; so they *did*. ... So Moses *finished* the work" (Ex. 39:32; 40:33b)	"Thus the heavens and the earth were *finished* ... and on the seventh day God finished his *work* that he had *done*" (Gen. 2:1a, 2a)
"And Moses *saw* all the work, *and behold*, they had *done* it. ... Then Moses *blessed* them" (Ex. 39:43)	"And God *saw* everything that he had *made, and behold*, it was very good. ... So God *blessed* the seventh day" (Gen. 1:31; 2:3a)

---

836 Cf. comments on 24:12–25:9; Response section, "What Does the Tabernacle Teach Us about the Kind of God He Is?"
837 The Hebrew word for "dwelling" is the same word used for the Lord's "tabernacle."
838 The Hebrew verb is *hithallek*; it occurs only eleven times in the Pentateuch and only four times in the construction "to walk in/among," the one found in Genesis 3:8; Leviticus 26:12.
839 For further links between the tabernacle and Eden cf. G. K. Beale, "The Final Vision of the Apocalypse and Its Implications for a Biblical Theology of the Temple," in *Heaven on Earth. The Temple in Biblical Theology*, ed. S. Gathercole and T. D. Alexander (Carlisle, UK: Paternoster, 2004), 197–199.

We must not miss the fact that God's desire to be with his creation is not restricted to these passages. It is the heartbeat that drives the biblical story forward from beginning to end. To return to earlier comments,[840] in Eden God comes to *walk* in the garden with Adam and Eve (Gen. 3:8); in the tabernacle he comes down so he might *walk* among the Israelites in their midst (Lev. 26:12).[841] In the tabernacle he comes to *dwell* among them (Ex. 29:45); in Jesus he comes to *dwell* in our midst (John 1:14),[842] and through his Spirit he makes his *dwelling* among the people of his church and *walks* among us (2 Cor. 6:16).[843] At the end of Revelation, when the heavenly city comes down to earth, John hears a loud voice declare, "Behold, *the dwelling place* of God is with man. He will *dwell* with them, and they will be his people, and God himself will be with them as their God. He will wipe away every tear from their eyes" (Rev. 21:3–4).[844] God will be so near to us that it will be as though he reaches out his hand to brush away every tear of pain from our eyes. Do we think of God like this? In Jesus we see that this is exactly the type of God he is. If we have not come to know him in this way, what is stopping us? And if we have, what does it mean for how we face our fears and sorrows? He loves us, seeks to be with us, and desires us to know him. Jesus came in our flesh to prove that it is so. This is who God is.

---

840 Cf. Response section on Exodus 28–29, "Why Have Priests and a Tabernacle Anyway?"
841 As noted above, both passages use a relatively rare form of the verb "walk"; cf. note 838 within Response section on 35:1–40:38, "What Does the Tabernacle Have to Do with Eden?"
842 The verb for "dwell" (*skēnoō*) in John 1:14 is built on the same root as the LXX's word for "tabernacle" (*skēnēs*). In Jesus God "tabernacled" among us.
843 This passage cites Exodus 29:45 and Leviticus 26:12. In other words God's collective people have become the tabernacle!
844 The term for "dwelling place" in Revelation 21:3 is the same term used in the LXX for "tabernacle" (*skēnēs*). Also, in both John 1:14 and Revelation 21:3 the verb for "dwell" (*skēnoō*) is built on the same Greek root as that for "dwelling place." In other words an obvious link exists between God's dwelling in his tabernacle in Exodus, his dwelling among us in Jesus (John 1:14), and his dwelling again on the earth in the final days (Rev. 21:3).

LEVITICUS

Christine Palmer

INTRODUCTION TO
LEVITICUS

Overview

Leviticus is the central book of the Pentateuch and the midpoint of a single narrative that spans from the creation of the world (Gen. 1:1) to the threshold of the Promised Land (Num. 36:13). Leviticus addresses the ruptured divine-human relationship in Genesis by forging the way back into God's presence through sacrifice. It realizes the mission of God's redeemed people to be a holy nation (Ex. 19:6) by ordaining a priesthood and inaugurating worship at the tabernacle. It further looks beyond Sinai to the other side of the wilderness journeys recounted in Numbers to describe holy living in the land of Canaan that anticipates the covenant focus of Deuteronomy. At the heart of the Pentateuch's redemptive narrative, Leviticus celebrates the gift of God's presence in worship, where he is said to walk among his people once again, as he had with Adam in the garden sanctuary: "I will walk among you and will be your God, and you shall be my people" (Lev. 26:12). God's people are instructed in a life of holiness wherein they, together with the Lord, re-create another Eden in which to dwell in fellowship together.

Leviticus develops along five thematic movements. The first is an *invitation to worship through sacrificial offerings* (chs. 1–7). The Lord calls Israel into his presence by way of the sacrificial altar, instructing his people on offerings that they may bring in order to express wholehearted dedication, covenant loyalty, and thanksgiving, as well as expiatory offerings that are required for attaining forgiveness and cleansing from sin. Sacrifice is the way to relationship with God in all its facets, whether in penitence or praise, seeking his forgiveness or favor.

The second is the *ordination and ministry of the priesthood* (chs. 8–10). The tabernacle was designed as a re-created heaven on earth, adorned with gold and precious stones that were plentiful in Eden, a lampstand crafted as a stylized tree that recalled the tree of life, and cherubim woven into the embroidered veil that barred the way into the divine throne room (Gen. 2:9, 12; 3:24). In this setting the priesthood is consecrated to mediate the nation's worship before the presence of a holy God.

The next thematic movement involves *ritual purity and access to God* (Leviticus 11–15). In order for the Lord to dwell among his people they will be required to "distinguish between the holy and the common, and between the unclean and the clean" (10:10). An Israelite could become unclean through contact with animal carcasses, blood loss from childbirth, defiling skin disease, or bodily discharges. A state of ritual impurity is incompatible with God's holiness and could defile the sanctuary (15:31). Worshipers must discern sources of impurity and cleanse themselves in order to approach the Lord.

The cleansing of all impurity—along with all sin—culminates on the *Day of Atonement* (ch. 16), the fourth movement. Only on this day does the high priest enter behind the veil into the divine throne room to cleanse the sanctuary from defilement and atone for sin through the sprinkling of sacrificial blood. The nation's sins are placed on the head of an animal substitute that is driven away from God's presence into the wilderness. Sacred space is renewed and relationship with a holy God restored. The Day of Atonement is the centerpiece of Leviticus, bringing to conclusion laws on sacrifice and ritual purity (chs. 1–15) and charting the course toward a life of holiness made possible by the Lord's abiding presence (chs. 17–27).

Moral purity and holy community (chs. 17–27) highlight the final movement, in which the call to holiness extends outward from the courts of the tabernacle to the people as a whole. The land is viewed as a sanctuary and the covenant people as priests with agency to guard their inheritance from defilement and to nurture holiness in community. Holy living takes the shape of conforming to the Lord's holiness through obedience to the covenant's ethical demands of faithfulness, justice, and love. The final chapter on redeeming dedicated gifts brings the book full circle back to the tent of meeting, where the Lord dwells among his people to receive their worship.

Title

In keeping with the ancient tradition of naming a literary work after its first word the book's title in Hebrew is *wayyiqra'* ("And [the LORD] called"). The Lord calls Moses to instruct the Israelites in worship in seamless continuity with the tabernacle's construction in Exodus.[1] The English title is inherited from the Latin Vulgate's translation of the LXX title, *Leuitikon* ("relating to the Levites"), which understands the book as a manual for the Levitical priests. Similarly, later Hebrew tradition calls it the *torat kohanim* ("instructions for or by the priests"; Mishnah, Megillah 3:5). Most of the book, however, is addressed to the people of Israel, instructing them on how to approach the Lord in worship and live a life of purity and holiness that keeps them covenantally bound to his sanctifying presence.[2]

Author and Date

While all Scripture is God's divinely inspired Word, no other book makes as strong of a claim to be the Lord's direct speech as Leviticus does. About 85 percent of the book is introduced as divine speech, with the clause "The LORD said" at the head of almost every chapter. The Lord's words are recorded as spoken to Moses, once to

---

[1] The Hebrew verbal form of the book's opening word is used in narrative texts to signal continuity. From a grammatical point of view these speeches are of a single narrative flow with Exodus.
[2] The sections explicitly addressed to priests are 6:8–7:10; 21:1–22:16.

Aaron alone (10:8), and several times to both Moses and Aaron (11:1; 13:1; 14:33; 15:1). The Pentateuch identifies Moses as its author,[3] a tradition that becomes well established by the time of the NT.[4]

Since the emergence of higher critical scholarship in the nineteenth century, authorship of the Pentateuch has been attributed to different sources or literary strands (JEDP), each reflecting a particular theological focus.[5] Most germane to the study of Leviticus are the purported priestly source (P) and holiness code (H) that separate the book into two parts: chapters 1–16 (P) and chapters 17–27 (H). Proponents argue that the ritual material in 1–16 is authored by a different hand than the laws in 17–27 concerned with ethical holiness, a claim that a close reading of the book will reveal to be overstated. Ethical constraints can be seen to govern ritual practice, as, for example, in making provision for the poor to be equally cleansed and forgiven with an offering proportionate to their means (5:7, 11; 12:8) or in the humanitarian concern for a worshiper to select an animal that is not offered on the same day as its mother (22:27–28; Mal. 1:8). By the same token, ritual is interspersed throughout the ethical material that contains an entire chapter on the festival calendar (Leviticus 23) and regulations on sacrificial meat consumption next to caring for the poor (19:5–10). The commentary will address how holiness in worship (chs. 1–16) logically and theologically extends to the entire community (chs. 17–27).

Dating Leviticus cannot be done without reference to the exodus, since the tent of meeting from which the Lord speaks to his people is set up the year after Israel's deliverance from Egypt (Ex. 40:17). Arriving at a date for the exodus is a complex question rife with presuppositions, leading to greatly divergent dates from as early as 1446 BC to the fifth century BC, with some even doubting the exodus as historical at all.[6] Although the discussion is complex, two markers help establish limits to the chronology, one biblical and the other extrabiblical. First Kings 6:1 records that Solomon began construction on the temple "in the four hundred and eightieth year after the people of Israel came out of the land of Egypt." Taken literally, this situates the exodus at 1446 BC. Archaeology supplies the second marker: a monumental inscription known as the Merneptah Stele (1207 BC) that mentions Israel as an unsettled people group in the land of Canaan. Allowing for forty years in the wilderness and the initial stages of conquest, a date range of 1446–1250 BC honors the biblical and material evidence. Leviticus seems most at home in this chronological milieu, as reflected by its frequent mention of a wilderness setting and by rituals that bear similarity with ancient Near Eastern counterparts of that time period.

Occasion

Leviticus finds Israel encamped at the foot of Mount Sinai, rescued from Egypt and brought into covenant as Yahweh's own people and treasured possession out

---

[3] Exodus 17:14; 24:4, 7; 34:27; Deuteronomy 28:58; 30:10; et al.
[4] Mark 7:10 on Leviticus 20:9; Luke 5:14 on Leviticus 14; John 8:5 on Leviticus 20:10; Romans 10:5 on Leviticus 18:5.
[5] J = (J)Yahweh; E = Elohim; D = Deuteronomy; P = priestly source. Cf. John E. Hartley, *Leviticus*, WBC 4 (Dallas, TX: Word, 1992), xxxv–xliii.
[6] For a more in-depth look at the evidence cf. Jay Sklar, *Exodus*, in this volume.

of all the earth.[7] The great exodus redemption ends with the construction of the tabernacle "in the *first month* in the second year" (Ex. 40:17). The narrative picks up again "in the second year, in the *second month*," with the tabernacle dismantled and the people departing for the land of Canaan (Num. 10:11). In the intervening month the Lord who had descended from the summit of Sinai to inhabit the sacred tent speaks to his people in thirty-seven speeches that constitute Leviticus. The blueprint for the Lord's divine dwelling was given from the mountaintop. Now at the foot of the mountain Israel receives the blueprint for life with her Sovereign. Leviticus is a stop in the journey and a pause in the plot wherein Israel receives the Word of God that shapes her identity as a worshiping people.

Genre and Literary Features

The majority of the book is divine instruction, with a relatively small portion of narrative (Lev. 8:1–10:20; 24:10–23). Viewed within the broader canonical landscape, the divine instruction of Leviticus inhabits the Sinai narrative (Exodus 19–Numbers 10). Following a dramatic rescue from Egypt, Israel is brought to Mount Sinai to be wed in covenant to the Lord and instructed on life together with him.

The Lord's instruction is presented as legal material: "These are the statutes and rules and laws that the Lord made between himself and the people of Israel through Moses on Mount Sinai" (Lev. 26:46). Ten occurrences of the word *torah* ("instruction, law") are divided evenly between laws for offerings (6:9, 14, 25; 7:1, 11) and laws on purity (11:47; 12:7; 13:59; 14:2, 32, 54–57; 15:32). Ethical imperatives are found as both apodictic commands ("*You shall not . . .*") and case laws that establish legal precedent ("*If . . . then*"). Compared to law collections of the ancient Near East, Israel's statutes are undergirded by motive clauses that encourage obedience by teaching hearers "to understand how ethical practice is the outworking of underlying theological and covenantal commitments."[8] Intentional obedience is both invited and commanded.

Theology of Leviticus

Leviticus is a deeply theological book. Its theology, however, is not formulated as doctrinal statements. It is instead embedded in prescribed rituals and rhythms of daily living that are bodily enacted by the worshiping congregation.

HOLINESS

The theme of holiness pervades every aspect of the book. It resounds in the Lord's declaration of his own holiness (11:44–45; 19:2; 20:7, 26; 21:8), the call for Israel in turn to be holy (19:2; 20:7, 26; 21:6, 8), and in the ritual enactments and covenant living predicated upon the Lord's sanctifying presence among his people.

---

[7] The Sinai setting is invoked throughout Leviticus, in 1:1; 7:38; 25:1; 26:46; 27:34.
[8] Philip Peter Jenson, *Leviticus: The Priestly Vision of Holiness*, T&T Clark Study Guides to the Old Testament (London: T&T Clark, 2021), 68.

Holiness is a divine quality. The Lord alone is inherently holy: holiness is the essence of his person in all his purity, excellence, and moral perfection. He is the source and measure of all holiness. The Lord chooses to magnify his holiness by sharing it with those whom he brings into special relationship with him. Holiness for God's people, therefore, is personal, relational, and anchored in the Lord's divine nature. It always begins with God's work. The only way for Israel to be made holy is through covenantal union and communion with Yahweh: "I am the LORD who sanctifies you" (20:8).

Holiness for Israel is learned through lived experience of it. A worshiper appearing at the sanctuary would encounter God's holiness in the built environment through increasing degrees of sanctity in space, objects, and priestly servants as the worshiper drew closer to the Lord's presence. A lay Israelite may enter only the outer court to have his gift offered on the bronze altar of sacrifice. He is not permitted into the Lord's dwelling of wool and linen textiles of vibrant purple, blue, and scarlet. Only priests had access to the Holy Place inside the sanctuary that housed furnishings of gold—a table and altar overlaid with pure gold and a lampstand of hammered gold. The Most Holy Place is the Lord's throne room and hidden from the sight of all. Restricted access impresses upon Israelites the Lord's transcendence and otherness. Ritual objects crafted of increasingly precious material in proximity to God's presence teach them of the Lord's kingship and worth.

The Israelites' experience at the tabernacle should also remind the Israelites that they are the Lord's holy possession, redeemed from the world, brought near as his precious treasure, and called to be holy in all aspects of life. Worshipers who offer their unblemished sacrifices by the hands of unblemished priests see for themselves that those who stand in God's presence are made whole. Again, holiness always begins with the work of God, who not only cleanses his people from their sin and pollution so he can remain among them (chs. 4; 16) but also provides for them the means necessary to live holy lives. For example his righteous commands form his character within them so they can remain planted in the land (18:30). Moreover, Israel is invited into holy time to appear before the Lord and offer him worship in the weekly and monthly rhythms of Sabbaths and appointed festivals (23:3–4; Ex. 31:13). Holiness for Israel is the consecrated life. The Lord provides the holy institutions that will keep Israel abiding in him and him with Israel. The command to be holy is meant to be not an impossibility for the people to attain but an invitation into his presence and ways so that he can form them increasingly into his image—for his glory, their good, and the world's blessing.

SACRIFICIAL WORSHIP

Israel is called to the priestly vocation of worshiping the Lord as the firstfruits of the praise of the whole earth (Pss. 22:27; 86:9–10). Worship is addressed in every single chapter in Leviticus.[9] It is Israel's orienting center.

---

[9] Commands that forbid ritually impure persons from eating holy foods (Lev. 7:20; 22:3–4) indicate that worship is implicit even in purity laws (chs. 11–15). Chapters known for their ethical focus do not fail to contain injunctions against idolatry and instructions regarding proper worship (18:21; 19:4–8, 30–31; 20:2–5, 27).

The Lord invites his people to commune with him through sacrifice and be restored to his presence. Sacrifice is the means to restoring relationship ruptured by the fall. Israelites approach as individuals to express exclusive devotion and covenant loyalty and to fulfill vows that culminate in a joyful fellowship meal. They seek the Lord's forgiveness and cleansing from sin and make offerings that repair relationship with God and neighbor. Sacrificial gifts are offered in an act of dedication that represents the surrender of oneself and anticipates the surrendered life of the beloved Son. God's people gather as a worshiping community in feasts that celebrate their historic exodus deliverance, trust the Lord for the forgiveness of sin, and demonstrate dependence on him to sustain life in the land of Canaan. Their encounter of the Lord in worship reveals his character as a merciful savior, faithful provider, and forgiver of sin.

The altar is the centerpiece of worship, the place where the Lord appeared visibly in theophany and is tacitly present in every subsequent act of worship to receive offerings and grant favorable acceptance to the offerer (Lev. 1:4; 9:24). Priests are called and consecrated to serve at the altar on the worshiper's behalf by arranging the sacrificial animal and applying its blood. They alone are qualified to handle the blood that has power to cleanse the sinner, purify the sanctuary, and accomplish atonement. They pronounce forgiveness and blessing issuing from the Lord as divine gifts of grace. The tabernacle's service is centered around substitutionary sacrifice and the ministry of the anointed high priest, who bridges the worlds of heaven and earth in a ministry of reconciliation. These point to the coming of a greater High Priest, who will serve at the altar with his own blood and reconcile us to God (Rom. 5:10; 2 Cor. 5:18).

PRIESTLY PEOPLE IN HOLY COMMUNITY

Since the Lord dwells among his people, all of life is to be lived with reference to his sanctifying presence. The ethical vision of Leviticus has unfairly been separated from sacrificial worship, but in reality the one cannot exist apart from the other. The worship of God is the first ordering principle of life together. To worship rightly is to live rightly.

Holiness begins in the sanctuary and its objects, offerings, and officiants and from there extends into society to encompass all Israel in what may be envisioned as mapping the sanctuary onto the land and lending it its holiness. The people are the priesthood of the land-sanctuary. They were sprinkled with blood when set apart to the Lord by covenant (Ex. 24:8; Lev. 8:23–24). They wear a tassel of priestly blue on the edges of their garments to prompt obedience to the Lord's commands (Ex. 28:33; Num. 15:38). They groom their hair and keep their bodies whole like priests (Lev. 19:27–28; 21:5). They each bear the divine name—as their high priestly representative does—to be marked as Yahweh's very own (Num. 6:27; Ex. 28:36). They are invited to consecrate themselves by observing boundaries between holy/common and clean/unclean as these touch upon their daily lives (Lev. 10:10–11). They are tasked with guarding the land from defilement as the Levites guard the sanctuary (22:31–33). Their priest-likeness is lived out in obedience in everyday life that takes the shape of separation from impurity and of conformity to the ethical demands of the covenant (chs. 17–26). Ritual and ethical holiness are inseparable, as both body and soul are trained toward godliness.

Israel is invited to share in God's holiness and be transformed into a holy people who reflect his image in the world. Holiness is to be attained not through lonely asceticism but only as a community in life together. Abiding by his laws, God's people will build a holy community in which marriage and the family are protected (chs. 18; 20), the stranger is welcomed as a brother (ch. 19), debtors are forgiven as the people themselves have been forgiven (ch. 25), and every person loves his neighbor as himself, a command Jesus himself quotes as one of the greatest (Matt. 22:37–40).

Relationship to the Rest of the Bible and to Christ

Leviticus shapes Israel's worldview in an all-encompassing manner. There is hardly a portion of Scripture that remains untouched by its theological vision. Prophetic voices seize on Leviticus's teaching to indict Israel for failure to worship the Lord (Mal. 2:1–9). They condemn God's people for not living up to the Lord's call for justice and love for neighbor. They are especially trenchant against the priestly leaders, in whose power it is to guard the sanctity of worship and uphold righteousness: "Her priests have done violence to my law and have profaned my holy things. They have made no distinction between the holy and the common, neither have they taught the difference between the unclean and the clean, and they have disregarded my Sabbaths, so that I am profaned among them" (Ezek. 22:26). The punishment of exile is ultimately attributed to a corruption of worship and failure of the land to keep the Sabbath (2 Chron. 36:21).

If Leviticus provides the legal grounds for banishing the nation into exile, it also provides the road map for restoration. The prophetic ministry inspires hope by reprising the nation's call to holiness (Isa. 61:6–7). God's spokesmen envision a time of cleansing from all defilement that will be accomplished representatively through the person of the high priest (Zech. 3:1–7). They prophesy of a restoration phrased in the familiar idiom of purity but with a promised renewal and inner transformation that will never be undone (Ezek. 36:22–32; 43:7). The Lord will dwell among his people once more and make all things holy (Ezek. 48:35; Zech. 14:20–21). Upon Israel's return from exile the programmatic vision for rebuilding the community looks to Leviticus to recover an identity as a priestly people. The book of Chronicles constructs a narrative of hope by placing the temple at the heart of the nation's life and the Levites as guardians of Israel's holy call to worship (1–2 Chronicles).

The NT authors live in continuity with the world shaped by the theology of Leviticus. Their cultural and religious practice revolve around theological categories that guide all human life to be experienced in the presence of a holy God—sacrifice and worship, atonement and forgiveness, observance of boundaries between holy and profane, and bodily states of clean and unclean. They record the historic events that fully realize Leviticus's vision of worship in the person and work of Jesus Christ.

GOD'S HOLY PEOPLE IN PRIESTLY SERVICE

By the first century a large body of rabbinic commentary known as the oral law had been added to the biblical teaching of Leviticus. Various sects of Judaism gave increased attention to the politics of ritual purity by adopting priestly requirements for themselves in their ordinary lives. Among them were the Pharisees, whom Jesus critiques for missing the heart of what ritual purity was indicating: the far deeper need for moral purity. Jesus moves quickly from a discussion of ritual impurity to locate the ultimate source of moral defilement within the human heart: "What comes out of a person is what defiles him. For from within, out of the heart of man, come evil thoughts, sexual immorality, theft, murder, adultery, coveting, wickedness, deceit, sensuality, envy, slander, pride, foolishness" (Mark 7:20–22). In other words cleansing oneself from ritual impurity is to be a reminder of the call to cleanse oneself from moral impurity and live in keeping with the Lord's call to be his holy people (Leviticus 18; 19). To focus on the former (ritual purity) and not the latter (moral purity) is to miss the point. Indeed, contrary to much of the teaching in Jesus' day, dealing properly with ritual impurity was not meant as an end in itself. It was rather for the sake of entering the Lord's presence in transformative worship, where there was holy potential to be restored to God's image and re-created after his likeness (Lev. 19:2). In keeping with this NT believers are exhorted, "Be imitators of God. . . . Walk in love, as Christ loved us and gave himself up for us, a fragrant offering and sacrifice to God" (Eph. 5:1–2). When all is said and done, holiness is anchored in a person—to be holy is to be Christlike.

The NT authors continue to draw on the rich theology of Levitical worship to articulate Christian identity. In continuity with Israel's call and vocation Paul frequently addresses believers in Christ as "saints" ("holy ones"). They have inherited Israel's vocation as "a royal priesthood, a holy nation, a people for his own possession" (1 Pet. 2:9). The NT is not merely applying the same terminology to the new covenant community but invoking a sustained biblical image of those who are called into God's presence. Priestly ministry shares a close affinity with our call to discipleship. Their daily service revolved around sacrifice at the altar as we are called to live a cruciform life defined by the altar (Gal. 2:20).

Paul articulates his own missionary labor among the Gentiles as priestly service to God. After nearly twenty-five years of preaching and teaching Paul embarks for Jerusalem with a freewill offering accompanied by seven men who represent the fruit of his mission (Acts 20:3–5). He acts with thoughtful intentionality to embody the unity of the new covenant community and to enact the eschatological pilgrimage of the nations (Isa. 2:1–4; 60:1–5). Out of a worldview shaped by Leviticus he describes the meaning of his actions as priestly service. He understands himself as a "*minister* [*leitourgos*, "priestly officiant"] of Christ Jesus to the Gentiles in the *priestly service* of the gospel of God, so that the *offering* of the Gentiles may be *acceptable, sanctified* by the Holy Spirit" (Rom. 15:16). He sees his life poured out for Christ like a drink offering was poured on the primary sacrifice in temple worship (Phil. 2:17; 2 Tim. 4:6; cf. Ex. 29:40).

JESUS CHRIST: HIGH PRIEST AND SACRIFICE

The most sustained treatment of Christ's priesthood and sacrificial self-offering is found in the letter to the Hebrews. The same God who in the past had spoken from the tent of meeting now "has spoken to us by his Son" (Heb. 1:2). Priestly ministry foreshadowed the work of Christ until his service as both high priest and atoning sacrifice brought it to climactic fulfillment. Christ's saving work is depicted as analogous to the high priest's ministry on the Day of Atonement. Hebrews assumes familiarity with the sacred space, sacrificial service, and holy convocations of Leviticus but distinguishes Christ's priesthood from that of the Levitical priests as unique in location, kind, and eternal consequence. Jesus was not of Levitical lineage and consequently did not serve in an earthly temple but instead officiated in heaven, the original and eternal divine dwelling after which the temple was patterned. As the high priest would enter God's throne room to sprinkle blood on the mercy seat, Christ enters "the greater and more perfect tent (not made with hands, that is, not of this creation)... once for all into the holy places, not by means of the blood of goats and calves but by means of his own blood, thus securing an eternal redemption" (Heb. 9:11–12). His offering is superior because the atoning blood he offers is his own—a sinless life that accomplishes perfect purification and secures eternal forgiveness. His priesthood is eternal because it is based not on human descent but on a holy and indestructible life (Heb. 7:16). Finally, his work is eternally efficacious. After entering the Most Holy Place "he sat down at the right hand of the Majesty on high" (Heb. 1:3; cf. 8:1; 10:12). Christ is enthroned as God, taking his place upon heaven's mercy seat to live and make intercession for his own (Heb. 7:24–25). He does what no priest of the old covenant could do by rending the veil and opening the way for believers to approach the throne of grace with boldness (Heb. 4:16; 10:19–22).

Christ's sacrificial offering empowers his people to live out of the same self-giving that characterized Christ's earthly life (Phil. 2:5–8). Paul makes an appeal in light of God's great and merciful salvation that believers would offer their lives back to God as a sacrificial act: "Present your bodies as a living sacrifice, holy and acceptable to God, which is your spiritual worship" (Rom. 12:1). The surrender of oneself to the service of God is our proper worship, since we have been bought at a price and no longer belong to ourselves. We are not destined to be consumed on a physical altar, but our bodily lives *are* to be spent in dedicated service to the Lord (Heb. 10:5). Whereas the rest of the world experiences corruption and progressive degradation because of its failure to worship (Rom. 1:24–32), God's people are re-created in Christ to recover the human vocation of priestly service to the Lord.

THE CONSUMMATION OF ALL THINGS

The final book of the Bible depicts the consummation of redemptive history in language and imagery drawn directly from the divine service inaugurated in Leviticus. Whereas the voice of God once called from the tent, it now calls as the voice of Jesus Christ from within the heavenly sanctuary (Rev. 1:10–11). Jesus appears as a priest standing among golden lampstands that locate him in the Holy Place. He is next seen seated on the throne of God, having entered the Most Holy Place to be acclaimed as worthy of worship on account of his sacrificial self-offering (Rev. 5:6).

Revelation is presented as a dynamic scene of congregational worship in response to the Lord's saving actions. At the center the Lamb of God receives the adoration of all creation for his atoning sacrifice: "By your blood you ransomed people for God from every tribe and language and people and nation, and you have made them a kingdom and priests to our God" (Rev. 5:9–10). As Leviticus teaches, the life is in the blood (Lev. 17:11). Christ's shed blood on the heavenly altar of God pays the ransom for our sin. His followers will themselves be martyred, and their blood, according to sacrificial practice, will be poured out at the base of the altar, from whence it will cry out to God (Rev. 6:9). In the end they will share in Christ's victory over evil "by the blood of the Lamb and by the word of their testimony" (Rev. 12:11).

The holy city, new Jerusalem, is akin to Eden, using language that recalls the covenant promise of God's dwelling with his people (Rev. 21:3; cf. Lev. 26:11–12). The city of God descends from heaven adorned with precious stones that fuse together images of Eden and the sanctuary. Its shape is in the dimensions of the Most Holy Place—multiplied by one thousand—and speaks to the dissolution of boundaries and barriers that separated man from God's presence (Rev. 21:16; cf. 1 Kings 6:20). There is no separate sanctuary here, for the entire city *is* the sanctuary, and all has been made holy for the dwelling of God: "Nothing unclean will ever enter it, nor anyone who does what is detestable or false, but only those who are written in the Lamb's book of life" (Rev. 21:27). The river of life flows out from God's throne room to renew the earth in perpetual cleansing as anticipated by Leviticus's purity laws and atonement rites (Rev. 22:1; cf. Ezek. 47:1–12). The identity of God's people is fully realized—a re-created and redeemed humanity that, as a kingdom of priests, bears the Lord's name and worships him face to face forever (Rev. 22:4).

Preaching from Leviticus

Preach with God at the center. God is at the center of Leviticus, his voice ringing out from the wilderness tent pitched in the middle of the camp. Faithful preaching will draw the listener to see and hear the Lord. In the same way that the Lord gave laws that revealed his character and re-created a people after his image, the preaching moment must provide an opportunity for a transformational encounter with the Lord. Leviticus reveals the Lord in his holiness—a Savior offering forgiveness through substitutionary sacrifice, a Redeemer restoring a fallen world for all to flourish. It is inconceivable that the Lord's presence among his people would leave them unchanged. Making the Lord both the subject and the object of one's preaching shapes the covenant community to reflect his character in the world.

Preach the person and work of Christ. Charles Spurgeon famously taught developing preachers, "From every text of Scripture there is a road to Christ. And my dear brother, your business is, when you get to a text, to say, now, what is the road to Christ?"[10] There are a number of different roads through the biblical text to arrive to Christ. Sidney Greidanus offers helpful advice in charting a course.[11] Most relevant for preaching Leviticus involve typology, analogy, NT Scripture references, and redemptive-historical approaches.

- Typology considers how OT types prefigure Christ. It is an effective way to preach the various sacrifices, the role of the high priest, as well as the festivals. Jesus brings the sacrificial system to its intended goal in himself: his is the perfect and sinless life that paid for our sins and pleased the Father for our acceptance. In Christ we have a perfect high priest consecrated for the unique ministry of reconciliation between a holy God and humanity through his service at the altar. His work on the cross is compared meaningfully with the Day of Atonement, on which sin is banished from God's presence and the world is created anew. Christ inaugurates his ministry by alluding to the Year of Jubilee and proclaiming that release from spiritual bondage and restoration to our heavenly inheritance would be fulfilled in him (Luke 4:18–21). The fulfillment of these types in Christ augments, or magnifies, the original symbol.
- Analogies make careful comparisons between two situations understood to be similar and develop the capacity to apply insights from one domain to another. Analogical reasoning is found in Scripture as an important first-century hermeneutical principle known as the *qal wakhomer* (Hb. "the light and the heavy"). If the first proposition (*qal*, "light") is true, then "how much more" is the second (*khomer*, "heavy") certainly true. This method models an assurance of the consistency of God's person, character, and redemptive purposes. An example of a clear *qal wakhomer* comes from the author of Hebrews: "*If* the blood of goats and bulls . . . *how much more* will the blood of Christ . . . purify our conscience from dead works to serve the living God" (Heb. 9:13–14). If a preacher can help his congregation to see the work of God in Leviticus, how much more clearly will the people behold it in the person and work of Christ!
- Another way to preach Leviticus is to make explicit reference to the many direct NT quotations of and allusions to the book. There are 283 OT quotations in the NT, including 19 that come from Leviticus. Jesus quotes Leviticus 19:18, "You shall love your neighbor as yourself," as

---
10 Charles Spurgeon, *Lectures to My Students* (Grand Rapids, MI: Baker, 1975), 49.
11 Sidney Greidanus, *Preaching Christ from Leviticus: Foundations for Expository Sermons* (Grand Rapids, MI: Eerdmans, 2021), 25–26.

one of two passages that summarize the law of God (Matt. 22:39). The apostles frequently cite Leviticus to describe the life of faith characterized by love (Rom. 13:9; Gal. 5:14; James 2:8). Peter admonishes all who have received God's grace in Christ, "Be holy in all your conduct, since it is written, 'You shall be holy, for I am holy'" (1 Pet. 1:14–16, quoting Lev. 11:44). Added to these are various allusions to the book (many of which will be picked up on in the commentary).

- A redemptive-historical reading traces the unfolding plan of God through Scripture to locate the climax of redemptive activity in the life, death, and resurrection of Jesus Christ. Along the way there may be elements of discontinuity within the larger continuity of purpose and ultimate end goal. For example, when early church leadership met to resolve issues related to the inclusion of the Gentiles (Acts 15:19–20), it applied Leviticus's prohibition against blood, idolatry, and sexual immorality (Leviticus 17–20), but also recognized that purity laws were now obsolete, having served their purpose in keeping Israel set apart until Christ's coming. A new age of redemptive history had dawned, in which Jew and Gentile shared equal status in the body of Christ.

Allow Leviticus to provide a biblical vision of hope. Leviticus supplies a theological concreteness to the shape of redemptive hope. Those who came to worship at the sacred tent entered a world in which Yahweh was sovereign, sin was being defeated by the shed blood of sacrifice, and worshipers were cleansed and made whole. The world of Leviticus is one wherein to be human is to be restored to God's presence. Preachers need to represent faithfully this world that reclaims the imagination and suffuses it with heavenly hope. They must resist always resorting to a biblical metanarrative of failure. Scripture is transparently honest about human failure (ch. 10), yet that is not its only message. Eschatological hope has broken into the present age to work its way into all aspects of human living until the Lord has reclaimed and redeemed all things. Portions of the book call us to embrace radical self-giving. Others call us to work toward a vision of justice in all things, while still others inspire transformative worship that looks forward to the worship of an eternal heavenly kingdom: "Worthy are you . . . for you were slain, and by your blood you ransomed people for God from every tribe and language and people and nation, and you have made them a kingdom and priests to our God" (Rev. 5:9–10).

Interpretive Challenges

MISPERCEPTION OF THE NATURE OF THE BOOK

The first interpretive challenge of Leviticus is the widespread misperception of the nature and content of the book. Many Christian readers view the book as a set of obscure laws no longer applicable to the life of discipleship. But Leviticus must be read instead within the relational context of covenant, not as an impersonal legal code. The Lord who dwells in visible holiness among his redeemed people reveals his personal will to shape their lives. His speech is written down and transmitted as the text of Scripture, which is "breathed out by God and profitable for teaching, for reproof, for correction, and for training in righteousness, that the man of God may be complete, equipped for every good work" (2 Tim. 3:16–17). Embracing this portion of Scripture as the beautiful center of the Pentateuch that guides us toward worship puts us in a posture of hearing Leviticus as the sanctifying Word of God with relevance for our own lives.

RITUAL-THEOLOGICAL WORLDVIEW

Another great challenge is the specialized vocabulary and ritual concepts that are difficult to translate into the experience of modern readers. Leviticus calls upon a rich vocabulary of worship in order to relate all aspects of life, even the most personal, to the Lord's sanctifying presence in Israel's midst. It is important to understand such language because it creates the theological categories with which the Lord relates to his people. Concepts such as sin, sacrifice, atonement, holiness, defilement, clean and unclean, all inform the work of Christ and the world of the NT.

Leviticus's theological categories divide the world along lines of that which has been brought into the Lord's use versus whatever remains as part of the ordinary world (holy/common), as well as in terms of fitness to appear before him at the sanctuary (clean/unclean). The starting point of persons and objects in their natural state is common and clean. From that position they can be defiled and become ritually unclean or be acted upon by God to be made holy. While a status or condition can be degraded unintentionally, an elevation of status always requires ritual action.

Holy/Common (Status)

Objects and persons that have been withdrawn from common use and brought into the Lord's sphere in close proximity to him are holy. In addition space (sanctuary) and time (Sabbath, holy convocations, Year of Jubilee) may be designated as holy because they serve as vehicles through which the Lord meets with his people. Gifts dedicated to the sanctuary become the Lord's holy possession and may not go back into common use. Priests are holy because they have been consecrated to the Lord's service. They are able to move between the worlds of holy and common to share in them both, connecting them and mediating the relationship between the two. To treat something holy as though it were common is to profane (desecrate) it. The high priest is not permitted to come near a dead body lest he profane his consecration and the sanctuary itself (21:11–12). God's people are warned not to profane the Lord's holy name by bringing their impurities into contact with the sanctuary (15:31) or by engaging in immoral practices, such as idolatry (20:3).

Clean/Unclean (Condition)

A person can be either clean (pure) or unclean (impure). Purity has to do with how the body relates to the sanctuary and other holy objects (such as a sacrificial meal).

Impurity (uncleanness) is contracted through natural and unavoidable processes such as childbirth and bodily discharges, skin disease, and contact with corpses or animal carcasses (chs. 11–15). It is first and foremost not a moral category but a ritual one, making a person ritually unfit for God's presence. Those who are unclean must normally separate themselves from appearing at the sanctuary (unless coming there as part of a purification ceremony; cf. ch. 12) and from partaking of holy foods. Impurity is impermanent, allowing for the worshiper to be restored to the worshiping community through the ritual process of purification, which at its simplest involves washing and the passage of time or, at its most complex, washing, laundering, and the offering of sacrifice.

Ritual/Moral Impurity

The sins of idolatry, sexual immorality, and murder result in moral impurity (chs. 18–20). Whereas ritual impurity is an impermanent bodily condition, moral impurity is a serious moral condition that cannot be washed away. It pollutes the sinner (20:3), the sanctuary, and the land itself (18:24–25). No individual sacrifices are prescribed for these acts. Instead those who commit them are typically "cut off" (exiled or executed), thus ridding the community and land of their defiling influence, though it may be noted that we see instances in which a mediator can achieve atonement on behalf of God's people for such sins (Exodus 32–34; Numbers 25).[12] This anticipates the atonement that Jesus will make available as our final mediator, whose sacrifice is great enough to cleanse even our deepest moral impurities.

Reading Ritual Texts for Meaning

For an exposition on the general topic of relating the law to the Christian the reader is referred to other works.[13] The interest of this section is to provide some reflection on reading ritual (ceremonial law) in the book of Leviticus.

The laws on sacrifice were given to a people already familiar with making offerings (Genesis 22). Every man had already acted as the priest of his household by slaughtering the Passover lamb that paved the way for Israel's redemption from Egypt. For this reason not every detail about the actual sacrificial procedure needed to be explained. Reading chapters 1–7 is like reading a theater script that notes the most essential stage instructions, an experience that is not nearly as satisfying—or understandable—as watching the performance. Faith is meant to be enacted, and the drama of worship is meant to be experienced. If aspects of ritual performance are beyond our understanding, it is because we are separated in time and culture from practices familiar in the ancient world.

As outsiders, we tend to characterize ritual as a thoughtless performance of obligatory acts. It would be more accurate to think of it as enacting belief. Ritual has been defined as a "way of construing, actualizing, realizing, and bringing into

---

[12] Cf. fuller discussion in Jay Sklar, "Sin and Atonement: Lessons from the Pentateuch," *BBR* 22/4 (2012): 485–490.
[13] Richard E. Averbeck, *The Old Testament Law for the Life of the Church* (Downers Grove, IL: IVP, 2022), and Jay Sklar, *Leviticus*, ZECOT (Grand Rapids, MI: Zondervan, 2023), 33–39.

being a world of meaning and ordered existence. Ritual is, thus, seen as a means of enacting one's theology."[14] Its efficacy depends not on the performance of the act itself but on the Lord who commands it. Gane makes the point that the physical act of slaughtering a goat on the Day of Atonement and applying its blood in the sanctuary does not achieve cleansing. Instead it produces a mess of "bloodstains, smoke, and ashes." Cleansing of the sanctuary from impurity and sin is accomplished by the Lord who prescribes the ceremony. Gane writes, "While the activities themselves do not produce this goal through physical cause and effect, as they would be expected to in ordinary life, they serve as a vehicle for transformation that takes place on the level of symbolic meaning."[15]

Finally, ritual is polyvalent, that is, it communicates a surplus of meaning. It may be likened to the celebration of communion in the worshiping life of Christian community. The Lord's Supper is invested with a surplus of meaning: it is an act of faithful remembrance, participation in the covenant community, a proclamation of Christ's death and coming again, and an invitation to deeper faith. Participating in the Lord's Supper is enacted theology that preaches the gospel of Christ's sacrificial offering and puts on display the redeemed people of God. As a ritual act, its regular celebration becomes more meaningful over time and forms the worshiper as well as the worshiping community. The best way to approach ritual in Leviticus is to understand it as practical theology.

Outline

I. Sacrificial Worship (1:1–7:38)
    A. Burnt Offering (1:1–17)
        1. Invitation to Worship (1:1–2)
        2. The Burnt Offering (1:3–17)
            a. From the Herd (1:3–9)
            b. From the Flock (1:10–13)
            c. From the Birds (1:14–17)
    B. Grain Offering (2:1–16)
        1. Offering the Sacrifice of Uncooked Grain (2:1–3)
        2. Offering the Sacrifice of Cooked Grain (2:4–10)
        3. Further Rules Regarding Leavening and Salt (2:11–13)
        4. Offering the Firstfruits (2:14–16)
    C. Peace Offering (3:1–17)
        1. Sacrificing a Peace Offering from the Herd (3:1–5)
        2. Sacrificing a Peace Offering from the Flock (3:6–16)
            a. Sheep (3:6–11)
            b. Goat (3:12–16)
        3. Giving to the Lord What Is His Alone (3:17)

---

14 Frank H. Gorman, Jr., *The Ideology of Ritual: Space, Time, and Status in the Priestly Theology*, LHBOTS (London: T&T Clark, 1990), 19.
15 Roy Gane, *Cult and Character: Purification Offerings, Day of Atonement, and Theodicy* (Winona Lake, IN: Eisenbrauns, 2005), 17.

D. Sin Offering (4:1–5:13)
  1. Introduction to Unintentional Sin (4:1–2)
  2. The High Priest's Sin Offering (4:3–12)
  3. The Congregation's Sin Offering (4:13–21)
  4. A Tribal Leader's Sin Offering (4:22–26)
  5. An Individual's Sin Offering (4:27–35)
  6. Sins of Omission Requiring a Sin Offering (5:1–4)
     a. Failure to Testify (5:1)
     b. Prolonged Impurity from an Animal Source (5:2)
     c. Prolonged Impurity from a Human Source (5:3)
     d. Failure to Fulfill an Oath (5:4)
  7. Sacrificial Procedure (5:5–13)
     a. Confession and Offering (5:5–6)
     b. Alternate Offerings (5:7–13)
E. Guilt Offering (5:14–6:7)
  1. Introduction to the Guilt Offering (5:14)
  2. Case of Sacrilege (5:15–16)
  3. Case of Suspected Sacrilege (5:17–19)
  4. Case of Sacrilege in Swearing Falsely (6:1–7)
F. Instructions for Priests (6:8–7:38)
  1. Law of the Daily Burnt Offering (6:8–13)
  2. Law of the Daily Grain Offering (6:14–23)
     a. Congregational Grain Offering (6:14–18)
     b. High Priestly Grain Offering (6:19–23)
  3. Law of the Sin Offering (6:24–30)
  4. Law of the Guilt Offering (7:1–7)
  5. Summary of Priestly Portions (7:8–10)
  6. Law of the Peace Offering (7:11–36)
     a. Peace Offering (7:11–21)
     b. Sacrificial Portions (7:22–36)
  7. Concluding Summary (7:37–38)
II. Inauguration of Public Worship (8:1–10:20)
  A. Ordination of the Priesthood (8:1–36)
     1. Preparation for Ordination Ceremony (8:1–5)
     2. Consecration of Tabernacle and Priesthood (8:6–13)
     3. Sacrificial Service of Ordination (8:14–30)
     4. Completing the Ordination (8:31–36)
  B. The First Worship Service (9:1–24)
     1. The Call to Worship (9:1–5)
     2. Inaugural Worship at the Altar (9:6–22)
        a. Introduction (9:6–7)
        b. Sacrifices for the Priests (9:8–14)

       c. Sacrifices for the People (9:15–21)
       d. Priestly Blessing (9:22)
    3. The Appearance of the Lord (9:23–24)
  C. The Priesthood's Costly Lesson on Holiness (10:1–20)
    1. The Unholy Death of Nadab and Abihu (10:1–7)
    2. The Lord's Direct Address to Aaron on Making Distinctions (10:8–11)
    3. Ministry That Respects God's Holiness (10:12–20)
III. Ritual Impurity (11:1–15:33)
  A. Clean and Unclean Animals (11:1–47)
    1. Introduction (11:1–2a)
    2. Clean and Unclean Animals (11:2b–23)
       a. Land Animals (11:2b–8)
       b. Aquatic Animals (11:9–12)
       c. Flying Animals (11:13–19)
       d. Flying Insects (11:20–23)
    3. Carcass Impurity (11:24–40)
    4. Swarming Creatures (11:41–45)
    5. Summary (11:46–47)
  B. Purification after Childbirth (12:1–8)
    1. Introduction (12:1–2a)
    2. Time Required for Purification If the Child Is Male (12:2b–4)
    3. Time Required for Purification If the Child Is Female (12:5)
    4. Sacrifice Required for Purification (12:6–7)
    5. Provision for a Woman of Lower Economic Status (12:8)
  C. Diagnosing Skin Disease (13:1–59)
    1. Introduction (13:1)
    2. Diagnosis of Diseased Persons (13:2–44)
    3. Consequence: Removal from the Camp (13:45–46)
    4. Diagnosis of Diseased Garments (13:47–51)
    5. Consequence: Burning, Washing (13:52–58)
    6. Concluding Summary (13:59)
  D. Purification from Skin Disease (14:1–14:57)
    1. Introduction to the Purification Rite (14:1–3)
    2. First Stage: Restoration to the Camp (14:4–8)
    3. Second Stage: Restoration to the Sanctuary (14:9)
    4. Third Stage: Restoration to the Worshiping Community (14:10–20)
    5. Provision for the Poor (14:21–32)
    6. Purification of Houses (14:33–53)
    7. Concluding Summary (14:54–57)

- E. Bodily Impurities (15:1–33)
    1. Introduction (15:1–2)
    2. Abnormal Male Discharge (15:3–15)
    3. Normal Male Discharge (15:16–17)
    4. Marital Intercourse (15:18)
    5. Normal Female Discharge (15:19–24)
    6. Abnormal Female Discharge (15:25–30)
    7. Reason for These Laws (15:31–33)
- IV. Day of Atonement (16:1–34)
    - A. Introduction (16:1–2)
    - B. Ritual Preparation for the Rites of Atonement (16:3–10)
    - C. Day of Atonement Rites (16:11–28)
        1. Purification of the Sanctuary (16:11–19)
        2. Atonement for the People (16:20–22)
        3. Worship Restored (16:23–28)
    - D. The People's Participation (16:29–31)
    - E. Conclusion (16:32–34)
- V. Life Is in the Blood (17:1–16)
    - A. Introduction (17:1–2)
    - B. Slaughter of Domestic Animals (17:3–7)
    - C. Slaughter of Sacrificial Animals (17:8–9)
    - D. Eating Blood Is Forbidden (17:10–12)
    - E. Disposal of Blood from Game (17:13–14)
    - F. Purification Contingencies (17:15–16)
- VI. Moral Holiness (18:1–20:27)
    - A. Sexual Ethics for a Holy People (18:1–30)
        1. Exhortation: Holy Living Leads to Life (18:1–5)
        2. Laws of Incest (18:6–18)
        3. Forbidden Sexual Practices and Worship (18:19–23)
        4. Unholy Living Leads to Death (18:24–30)
    - B. A Community of Holy Love (19:1–37)
        1. Call to Holiness (19:1–2)
        2. Holiness in Worship (19:3–8)
        3. Holiness in Community (19:9–18)
        4. Holiness in All of Life (19:19–36a)
        5. Final Charge (19:36b–37)
    - C. Penalties for Sexual Offenses (20:1–27)
        1. Introduction (20:1–2a)
        2. Idolatry and Divination (20:2b–6)
        3. Exhortation to Holiness (20:7–8)
        4. Dishonoring Parents, Sexual Sins (20:9–21)
        5. Exhortation to Holiness (20:22–26)
        6. Divination (20:27)

VII. Holy Institutions (21:1–27:34)
   A. Priesthood (21:1–24)
      1. Holiness in Mourning and Marriage: Regular Priests (21:1–9)
      2. Holiness in Mourning and Marriage: High Priest (21:10–15)
      3. Blemishes That Disqualify Service at the Altar (21:16–23)
      4. Moses' Obedience to Relay the Instructions (21:24)
   B. Sacrifices (22:1–33)
      1. Introduction (22:1–2)
      2. Eating in Holiness (22:3–9)
      3. Rights to Priestly Portions (22:10–16)
      4. Disqualifying Animal Blemishes (22:17–25)
      5. Additional Sacrificial Laws (22:26–30)
      6. Exhortation to Holiness (22:31–33)
   C. Calendar (23:1–44)
      1. Introduction to Holy Times (23:1–2)
      2. Sabbath (23:3)
      3. Feast of Passover and Unleavened Bread (23:4–8)
      4. Feast of Firstfruits (23:9–14)
      5. Feast of Weeks (23:15–22)
      6. Feast of Trumpets (23:23–25)
      7. Day of Atonement (23:26–32)
      8. Feast of Booths (23:33–43)
      9. Conclusion (23:44)
   D. Tent of Meeting (24:1–23)
      1. Kindling the Lamps of the Lampstand (24:1–4)
      2. Setting Out the Bread of the Presence (24:5–9)
      3. The Crime of Blaspheming the Name (24:10–23)
   E. Covenanted Land (25:1–55)
      1. Sabbatical Year (25:1–7)
      2. Jubilee Year (25:8–17)
      3. The Lord's Promise to Sustain (25:18–22)
      4. Jubilee Redemption Laws (25:23–55)
         a. Theology of Land (25:23–24)
         b. Sale of Landholdings (25:25–34)
         c. Provision of Interest-Free Loans (25:35–38)
         d. Entering Indentured Servitude (25:39–55)
   F. Covenant Blessings and Curses (26:1–46)
      1. Worship as the Basis of the Covenant (26:1–2)
      2. Blessings of the Covenant (26:3–13)
         a. Introduction (26:3)
         b. First Blessing: Rains in Season (26:4–5)
         c. Second Blessing: Peace (26:6)
         d. Third Blessing: Victory over Enemies (26:7–8)

        e. Fourth Blessing: Prosperity (26:9–10)
        f. Fifth Blessing: Yahweh's Personal Presence (26:11–12)
        g. Conclusion (26:13)
     3. Curses of the Covenant (26:14–39)
        a. Introduction (26:14–15)
        b. First Discipline: Panic (26:16–17)
        c. Second Discipline: Drought (26:18–20)
        d. Third Discipline: Wild Beasts (26:21–22)
        e. Fourth Discipline: War (26:23–26)
        f. Fifth Discipline: Military Defeat (26:27–39)
     4. Yahweh Is Faithful to Restore His Wayward People (26:40–45)
     5. Conclusion (26:46)
  G. Dedicated Gifts (27:1–34)
     1. Introduction (27:1–2a)
     2. Voluntary Votive Offerings (27:2b–25)
        a. Pledges of Persons (27:2b–8)
        b. Animal Pledges (27:9–13)
        c. Property and Land Pledges (27:14–25)
     3. Nonredeemable Offerings (27:26–33)
        a. Firstborn (27:26–27)
        b. Devoted Things (27:28–29)
        c. Tithes (27:30–33)
     4. Conclusion (27:34)

LEVITICUS 1

1 The LORD called Moses and spoke to him from the tent of meeting, saying, ² "Speak to the people of Israel and say to them, When any one of you brings an offering to the LORD, you shall bring your offering of livestock from the herd or from the flock.

³ "If his offering is a burnt offering from the herd, he shall offer a male without blemish. He shall bring it to the entrance of the tent of meeting, that he may be accepted before the LORD. ⁴ He shall lay his hand on the head of the burnt offering, and it shall be accepted for him to make atonement for him. ⁵ Then he shall kill the bull before the LORD, and Aaron's sons the priests shall bring the blood and throw the blood against the sides of the altar that is at the entrance of the tent of meeting. ⁶ Then he shall flay the burnt offering and cut it into pieces, ⁷ and the sons of Aaron the priest shall put fire on the altar and arrange wood on the fire. ⁸ And Aaron's sons the priests shall arrange the pieces, the head, and the fat, on the wood that is on the fire on the altar; ⁹ but its entrails and its legs he

shall wash with water. And the priest shall burn all of it on the altar, as a burnt offering, a food offering[1] with a pleasing aroma to the LORD.

¹⁰ "If his gift for a burnt offering is from the flock, from the sheep or goats, he shall bring a male without blemish, ¹¹ and he shall kill it on the north side of the altar before the LORD, and Aaron's sons the priests shall throw its blood against the sides of the altar. ¹² And he shall cut it into pieces, with its head and its fat, and the priest shall arrange them on the wood that is on the fire on the altar, ¹³ but the entrails and the legs he shall wash with water. And the priest shall offer all of it and burn it on the altar; it is a burnt offering, a food offering with a pleasing aroma to the LORD.

¹⁴ "If his offering to the LORD is a burnt offering of birds, then he shall bring his offering of turtledoves or pigeons. ¹⁵ And the priest shall bring it to the altar and wring off its head and burn it on the altar. Its blood shall be drained out on the side of the altar. ¹⁶ He shall remove its crop with its contents[2] and cast it beside the altar on the east side, in the place for ashes. ¹⁷ He shall tear it open by its wings, but shall not sever it completely. And the priest shall burn it on the altar, on the wood that is on the fire. It is a burnt offering, a food offering with a pleasing aroma to the LORD."

[1] Or *an offering by fire*; so throughout Leviticus [2] Or *feathers*

Section Overview

The arc of the redemptive drama begun in Exodus continues to unfold in Leviticus. Abraham's descendants, delivered from Egypt and brought into covenant as God's own people, have stopped at Mount Sinai, where they have built the Lord's tabernacle and are now further instructed on the shape of life as a "kingdom of priests and a holy nation" (Ex. 19:6).[16]

Leviticus begins with the Lord's speaking out of his divine dwelling. His voice rings out through the chapters of the book in thirty-seven speeches that invite his people to draw near to him in worship and that instruct them in the way of holy living. To deliver this invitation the introduction to the book (Lev. 1:1–2) uses three distinct verbs of speaking (5x) coupled with the verb "to bring near" (4x). The opening lines of this call to worship therefore reveal "that the book of Leviticus will be about connections, both spoken and acted, between God and people, between the divine and human worlds."[17]

The Lord's invitation to covenant fellowship begins by addressing the sacrificial offerings (1:3–7:38). That the laws on sacrifice canonically follow the filling of the tabernacle with divine glory (Ex. 40:35) makes the theological statement that the right response to God's presence is worship. Leviticus 1–3 provides ritual instruction for the burnt, grain, and fellowship offerings, which Israelites can

---

[16] Exodus ends on the climactic note of the construction of the Lord's dwelling "in the *first month* in the second year, on the first day of the month" (Ex. 40:17). Numbers picks up the narrative "on the first day of the *second month*, in the second year after they had come out of the land of Egypt" (Num. 1:1). Leviticus relates the divine instruction of the Lord in that intervening month.
[17] Bryan D. Bibb, *Ritual Words and Narrative Worlds in the Book of Leviticus* (London: T&T Clark, 2009), 78.

bring voluntarily (Lev. 22:18, 21) but which are in some instances mandatory (cf. 14:19–20), while 4:1–6:7 describes the sin and guilt offerings, which are always mandatory (12:6; 14:12, 19).[18] Finally, Leviticus 6–7 provides additional instructions, primarily for the priests who perform these rituals, though at times also for the lay Israelites who bring the offerings.

In reading through the opening chapters we see that Israel's sacrificial system is robust and runs the gamut of the expression of worship and human emotion. Coming to the Lord with an offering is analogous to today's going to church, lifting up prayers, offering thanksgiving for answered prayer, confessing one's sins, making peace with one's neighbor, expressing wholehearted devotion, and participating in the Lord's Supper. In short, sacrifice expresses relationship with God in all its facets.

Section Outline

I. Sacrificial Worship (1:1–7:38)
   A. Burnt Offering (1:1–17)
      1. Invitation to Worship (1:1–2)
      2. The Burnt Offering (1:3–17)
         a. From the Herd (1:3–9)
         b. From the Flock (1:10–13)
         c. From the Birds (1:14–17)

Comment

1:1–2a The Lord calls to Moses as he has done throughout the exodus from Egypt. Only now, instead of calling "out of the mountain" (Ex. 19:3) or "out of the midst of the cloud" (Ex. 24:16), he speaks from behind the veil of the tent of meeting, where he has taken up residence. It is appropriate that in Leviticus the Lord's dwelling is almost exclusively referred to as the "tent of meeting," emphasizing the relational goal of the Lord's abiding presence.[19] Yahweh descends from Sinai to inhabit his earthly sanctuary and call his people to meet with him. They will meet through the ordained sacrifices at the altar.

The Lord's instructions are for the "people of Israel," inviting every covenant son and daughter into the fellowship of worship. This is in contrast with practices of the ancient world, where typically only the priestly class held the knowledge of ritual performance. In Israel all are invited to approach the Lord in recognition of their priestly call as a nation (Ex. 19:5–6).

1:2b The opening line of the sacrificial laws is simple in its phrasing but generous in its inclusion: "When *any one* of you . . ." The Hebrew behind this translation is *'adam*, referring to a human person. The invitation to worship the Lord through the offering of sacrifice is extended to men and women alike with language that

---

18 Sklar, *Leviticus*, ZECOT, 81.
19 "Tabernacle" is used only four times in the book (Lev. 8:10; 15:31; 17:4; 26:11), which prefers instead to use "tent of meeting," in this way emphasizing the Lord's relational goals with his people.

echoes humanity's creation (Gen. 1:27).[20] Indeed, the tent of meeting creates sacred space that evokes the setting of Eden (cf. Introduction) and becomes the place where the Lord will once again meet with humanity in fellowship, healing the rift created by sin through substitutionary sacrifice.

The language of sacrifice communicates volumes about its theology. The offering a worshiper must bring (Hb. *qorban*) derives from the verb "to draw near" (*qarab*), variations of which appear four times in this verse. A worshiper draws near to the Lord through that which he brings near, an idiom that may best be captured in English as "[to] present a present."[21] Fellowship with God is accomplished through a gift of domesticated livestock, whether from the herd, the flock, or the birds, listed in descending order of economic value. What the worshiper brings from his own household represents more than his resources, as it personally represents and stands in for him.

1:3 The burnt offering takes pride of place to introduce the sacrifices and serves as a template for the ritual procedure to be followed for all the offerings. In other words it is paradigmatic. In English translations the emphasis falls on the *burning* of the sacrifice on the altar: the animal is consumed in flames as it is dedicated in its entirety to the Lord. The LXX adds to this the notion of completeness: the *whole* animal is burned on the altar, rendered in the LXX as *holokautōma* ("whole burnt offering"). But this is only part of the picture. In Hebrew *'olah* most literally means the "ascending" offering, a term that captures its dynamic movement upward as it rises in smoke to the Lord. The focus, therefore, is not on the animal's being incinerated by fire but its being conveyed upward through fire and smoke.

The burnt offering may be one of the oldest and most foundational sacrifices, brought by the faithful even before the covenant at Sinai (Gen. 8:20). This is the offering of wholehearted devotion required of Abraham: "Take your son, your only son Isaac, whom you love, and go to the land of Moriah, and offer him there as a burnt offering" (Gen. 22:2). The burnt offering is at the heart of Israel's worship, offered daily on the altar at dawn and at twilight (Ex. 29:38–42; Num. 28:3–8). It is the most common offering on public celebrations such as covenant making (Ex. 24:5), priestly ordination (Leviticus 8), and the annual festivals (Numbers 28–29). As a personal offering, it is a fitting expression of worship for a broad range of occasions—fulfilling a vow or offering thanksgiving (Lev. 22:18), making petitions (1 Sam. 13:12), and seeking atonement (Lev. 14:19–20).

Coming to the Lord with an offering begins before the actual moment of sacrifice. Each household takes care to breed and cull the flock and herd for animals that are whole and without defect. The worshiper then selects an animal according to that which is fitting for his petition (chs. 1–5) and according to his means (1:3, 10, 14). He physically examines the animal from head to tail to ensure that it is free of blemish or injury (22:22–24). For a burnt offering he must bring a male

---

20 Access to the Lord in the OT is on the basis not of gender but of ritual purity (chs. 12–15). Women are excluded not from making offerings but from serving as priests (as are all Israelites of non-Aaronic descent).
21 James W. Watts, *Leviticus 1–10*, HCOT (Peeters, 2013), 181.

without blemish. Male animals are generally preferred for daily and public sacrifices in Israel's worship, and female for private offerings, though in this instance private burnt offerings had to be male.[22] No reason is given. What is clear is that selecting an offering pleasing to the Lord and presenting it according to his laws means that the worshiper and his household will be accepted through its acceptance and find favor with God.

1:4 The offering is brought to the entrance of the tent of meeting, where the worshiper presses his hand on the animal's head in an act of presentation and dedication. This gesture—a firm leaning rather than simply resting of the hand—signifies that the item that has been in his grasp, in his sphere of ownership, is now surrendered to the Lord. In this act of presentation the offerer also identifies with his offering as he leans his weight on the animal that will represent him, as though saying, "This creature stands in for me." The Levites are dedicated with a similar gesture when the people of Israel lay their hands on them to dedicate them to the Lord's service on their behalf (Num. 8:10, 16).

The animal is "accepted for him" as a gift that secures atonement. The theological concept of atonement, literally at-one-ment, expresses the reconciliation and restoration of relationship between two estranged parties. This is achieved in two main ways: one avenue is through purification from sin (Leviticus 16), and the other is through the payment of a ransom. Since there is no particular sin or offense in view here, atonement must be in the sense of appearing before a holy God through sacrifice that serves as a ransom, that is, the offering is accepted in place of the offerer, such as the ram that Abraham offered "instead of his son" (Gen. 22:13).

The aim of the offering is to be accepted by the Lord with favor for blessing (Ex. 28:38; Isa. 56:7).[23] The language in these verses alternates between the Lord's accepting the offering (Lev. 1:3) and accepting the offerer (v. 4), blurring the boundary to bring to the fore that the offering stands in for the offerer.[24]

1:5 The worshiper slaughters the bull by passing a sharp knife over its throat (cf. Gen. 22:10), while the priests handle the blood that makes atonement (cf. Lev. 17:11). The animal is the worshiper's to offer, but the blood that represents its life is the Lord's and so is returned to him by those consecrated to handle the life-liquid. The act of sacred killing is passed over quickly; death is not the goal of sacrifice but is only the beginning of the ritual of drawing near to the Lord. What receives more attention is the handling of blood, which throughout all the instructions

---

[22] Male animals are required for the daily sacrifice (Ex. 29:38–42), Passover (Ex. 12:5), Tabernacles (Num. 29:12–34), and Day of Atonement (Lev. 16:3–11). They are also required as a sin offering for a leader or the congregation as a whole (4:3, 14, 22–23), whereas a layman may bring a female (4:28). A female animal may also be brought for a peace offering that furnishes the meat for the offerer and his extended family (3:1, 6). The reason that male animals are required for the burnt offering goes unstated but may be related to animal husbandry practices: more females than males were required for breeding, meaning that males were often culled. Cf. Roland Boer, *The Sacred Economy of Ancient Israel* (Louisville: Westminster John Knox, 2015), 62.

[23] Here again Abraham's burnt offering is instructive. Because Abraham was willing to surrender his son to death, God's favor is articulated in blessing: "Because you have done this and have not withheld your son ... I will surely bless you" (Gen. 22:16–17).

[24] This is true throughout—the offering is accepted (Lev. 19:7; 22:21) that the offerer may be accepted (7:18; 19:5; 22:29).

for sacrifice is drained, splashed, poured, sprinkled, and smeared in the variety of its applications. Priests catch the animal's blood in bronze bowls (Ex. 27:3) to toss upon the sides of the altar or pour at its base (Lev. 4:7).[25] Some of the freely flowing blood might make contact with the offerer, spattering him as it is splashed on the altar, reinforcing the blood bond that binds every Israelite in covenant to the Lord: "Moses took half of the blood and put it in basins, and half of the blood he threw against the altar. . . . [Then he] took the blood and threw it on the people and said, 'Behold the blood of the covenant that the LORD has made with you in accordance with all these words'" (Ex. 24:6, 8).

1:6–7 The worshiper continues to prepare his offering by stripping the carcass of its hide and butchering it into cuts of meat, likely on tables in the area of the courtyard (cf. Ezek. 40:39). He is, however, prohibited from setting the offering on the altar. The priests are the ones to arrange the wood and kindle the altar's fire, having been consecrated to serve and invested with a holiness akin to that of the altar (Leviticus 8). Instructions for the handling of the sacrificial animal alternate perspectives between worshiper and priest, as they work in concert to present an offering to the Lord.

1:8–9a The offerer washes the entrails and lower part of the legs to remove any soiling. He then relinquishes his offering to the priest, who arranges the animal's pieces on the altar according to the ritually prescribed order: the quartered cuts, the head, suet, and finally the innermost parts. Some see a deeper significance to this order, suggesting that, as the animal's innermost parts are laid bare before the eyes of the Lord for examination, so is the worshiper whom the animal on the altar represents (Jer. 11:20; 17:10).

1:9b The animal in its entirety is placed on the altar and given to the Lord, with nothing held back but its hide for the officiating priest (Lev. 7:8). The Hebrew word translated "burn" (*hiqtir*) could also be rendered "turned to smoke," the focus being on the offering's now rising from the earthly sphere to the heavenly. The "ascending" offering passes from the offerer's hand to the hands of the priest and on to the altar's consuming fire, where it is transformed into a pillar of smoke reaching toward the Lord.

It reaches him as a "pleasing aroma,"[26] a sensory metaphor for divine favor. The sense of smell as a means of experiencing and interpreting the world was finely developed in Israel, as with many cultures around the world today. Distinctive odors, foul or favorable, lend discernment to interpret that which is not visible. For example Isaac must rely on smell to discern the person who speaks to him in Jacob's voice yet smells like his firstborn, Esau (Gen. 27:27). Smell naturally serves as a way of expressing social relationships: an odious stench in the nostrils signals

---

25 Such a bowl dating to the eighth century BC has been discovered in a ritual context at Tel Dan in northern Israel. The shallow bowl (16 cm [6 in]wide x 4.5 cm [2 in] high) was unearthed at the base of a small altar together with three incense shovels and a pot of animal bones.
26 Lev. 1:9, 13, 17; 2:2, 9, 12; 3:5, 16; 4:31; 6:15, 21; 8:21, 28; 17:6; 23:13, 18.

fractured bonds and adversarial relationships (Gen. 34:30; Ex. 5:21; 1 Sam. 13:4; 27:12; 2 Sam. 10:6; 16:21). When the Lord refuses to smell the smoky aroma of sacrifice (Lev. 26:31), he is rejecting the offering and ultimately the offerer (Gen. 4:5–7; Mal. 2:13). To accept the fragrance of an animal consumed on the altar, however, is to accept the worshiper who has surrendered it: "As a pleasing aroma I will accept you" (Ezek. 20:41; cf. Phil. 4:18).

This is the worshiper's gift offered as "food."[27] The Hebrew uses a technical term that can refer to sacrificial meat (Ex. 29:18; Lev. 3:5), grain (2:2), baked bread (24:9), or wine (Num. 15:10). This should be understood in the sense not of providing sustenance but of giving a valued gift. The offerer surrenders to the Lord that which is *his* food and livelihood: domesticated animals, agricultural produce, and the fruit of the vine. But unlike with Israel's neighbors, who bring food offerings and place them before the images of their gods, Israel's worship celebrates that their God is self-sufficient and Sustainer of all (Pss. 50:10–15; 145:15–16).

1:10–11 A worshiper who brings an offering from the flock, a sheep or goat, follows the same protocol laid out above, though we learn additional details from other texts. As the worshiper enters the east-facing entrance to the tent of meeting to present his animal to the priest (Ex. 27:13), he is in a direct line with the sanctuary where the Lord is enthroned. Facing toward the tent, he is simultaneously presenting himself to the Lord. He then moves to the north side of the altar, where the animal is slain (Lev. 1:11) and the priests catch the blood that is tossed around the four sides of the altar.

1:12–13 The ritual continues with the priest's handwashing in the laver to the west (Ex. 40:30), going up a ramp beside the 4.5 foot (1.8 m) altar to arrange the animal's portions (cf. Ex. 20:26; Lev. 9:22), and finally discarding the remains in an ash heap to the altar's east (1:16). The ritual at the altar is clearly the focal point, underscoring the Lord's grace in providing the sacrificial system so that his people can draw near to him in worship and fellowship.

1:14 The final instruction is regarding an offering of birds (dove or pigeon). The provision of an offering for the poor ensures that all Israelites may participate in worship and in the giving of themselves to the Lord. Remarkable equality is found in the declaration that this is no less a "pleasing aroma" and acceptable offering to the Lord. Though the worshiper may bring as he is able, he must nevertheless bring the best that he is able.

1:15–17 The smaller size requires different sacrificial handling to be performed by the hand of the priest: the bird's head is pinched off, its blood drained by the side of the altar, its crop discarded, and its body cavity laid open on the altar. Just as the larger animals are arranged with their innards for the Lord's inspection, birds likewise are laid fully bare before the eyes of the Lord (cf. Heb. 4:13).

---

[27] This word could also be translated as "fire offerings." More explicit references to gifts in the form of "food" include Leviticus 3:11, 16; 21:6, 8, 17, 21, 22; 22:25.

Response

The burnt offering is unique among the offerings in its complete surrender to the Lord. It is not difficult to see how this gift communicates a wholehearted dedication that makes it a most fitting expression of covenant loyalty.

This is the gift Abraham is called to bring—out of his household he selects the offering pleasing to the Lord (Gen. 22:2) and makes Moriah's ascent to "worship" (Gen. 22:5). It is there that the Lord reveals his will to provide a substitute, having found Abraham faithful because he has "not withheld your son, your only son" (Gen. 22:12). On this same mountain (2 Chron. 3:1) Israel's covenant worship will rise from the altar in burnt offerings, day in and day out, anticipating the time when the Lord himself will turn to his household to select a pure and spotless Lamb to offer on the altar (Rom. 8:32; 1 Pet. 1:18–19). The beloved Son unreservedly holds nothing back, pouring out his life to the Father as a ransom for many (Mark 10:45; 1 Pet. 3:18). His is the perfect offering, worthy of the Father's pleasure (Mark 1:11), a pleasing aroma and "fragrant offering and sacrifice to God" (Eph. 5:2).

The language of sacrifice, far from having become obsolete, characterizes our own discipleship as followers of Christ. We are called to conform our lives after Jesus' own self-abandonment, who held nothing back but emptied himself completely to death on a cross in sacrificial obedience (Phil. 2:5–8). In the same way we offer back to the Lord our very lives that he has redeemed, serving him with a radical self-giving that embraces all of life: "Present your bodies as a living sacrifice, holy and acceptable to God, which is your spiritual worship" (Rom. 12:1). We are sacrifices that are living, brought to life by faith in Christ, so that we can offer ourselves back to him in lives lived for his purposes in the world.

LEVITICUS 2

2 "When anyone brings a grain offering as an offering to the LORD, his offering shall be of fine flour. He shall pour oil on it and put frankincense on it ²and bring it to Aaron's sons the priests. And he shall take from it a handful of the fine flour and oil, with all of its frankincense, and the priest shall burn this as its memorial portion on the altar, a food offering with a pleasing aroma to the LORD. ³But the rest of the grain offering shall be for Aaron and his sons; it is a most holy part of the LORD's food offerings.

⁴"When you bring a grain offering baked in the oven as an offering, it shall be unleavened loaves of fine flour mixed with oil or unleavened wafers smeared with oil. ⁵And if your offering is a grain offering baked on a griddle, it shall be of fine flour unleavened, mixed with oil. ⁶You shall break it in pieces and pour oil on it; it is a grain offering. ⁷And if your

offering is a grain offering cooked in a pan, it shall be made of fine flour with oil. ⁸ And you shall bring the grain offering that is made of these things to the Lord, and when it is presented to the priest, he shall bring it to the altar. ⁹ And the priest shall take from the grain offering its memorial portion and burn this on the altar, a food offering with a pleasing aroma to the Lord. ¹⁰ But the rest of the grain offering shall be for Aaron and his sons; it is a most holy part of the Lord's food offerings.

¹¹ "No grain offering that you bring to the Lord shall be made with leaven, for you shall burn no leaven nor any honey as a food offering to the Lord. ¹² As an offering of firstfruits you may bring them to the Lord, but they shall not be offered on the altar for a pleasing aroma. ¹³ You shall season all your grain offerings with salt. You shall not let the salt of the covenant with your God be missing from your grain offering; with all your offerings you shall offer salt.

¹⁴ "If you offer a grain offering of firstfruits to the Lord, you shall offer for the grain offering of your firstfruits fresh ears, roasted with fire, crushed new grain. ¹⁵ And you shall put oil on it and lay frankincense on it; it is a grain offering. ¹⁶ And the priest shall burn as its memorial portion some of the crushed grain and some of the oil with all of its frankincense; it is a food offering to the Lord."

Section Overview

This chapter describes offering the yield of cultivated land, meaning it is anticipating that Israel will be settled in the land promised to her forefathers (Gen. 12:7; 26:2–3). This land was promised to Israel while she was still in Egypt (Ex. 3:8; 6:6–8). Israel's redemption looks beyond flight from the land of her oppressors to finding a home in this world, "a good land ... a land of wheat and barley" (Deut. 8:7–8), a physical place in which to live as God's people. Life lived in covenant faithfulness will bring the Lord's provision through bountiful yield (Lev. 26:1–4). No longer will it be miraculous, as with the heavenly manna. Instead, through Israel's faithful cooperation to steward this divine gift the Lord's provision will extend to all, sustaining the landowner, the poor, and the resident alien (19:9–10; 25:6–7).

Grain is the backbone of the Israelite diet,[28] so much so that the word for bread (Hb. *lehem*) can mean "food" in general (cf. 21:6). Although the grain offering is not a blood sacrifice, its value should not be underestimated. Israelites were farmers who kept small livestock; both agricultural and pastoral gifts represented the offerer's livelihood and were offered as an act of worship to honor the Lord. Grain farming began in November-December, after the first rains softened the heat-parched land and farmers could break it up with the plow and sow seed (Deut. 11:13–14). When it was time to harvest (barley in April and wheat in May), reapers gathered in the fields—men and women and servants of the extended household (Ruth 2:23). Stalks were harvested with sickles or pulled out by hand to keep the grain intact and then bound into sheaves for transport to the threshing floor beyond the

---

[28] The staples of the ancient Israel diet were grain, wine, and oil (Deut. 7:13; Jer. 31:12). All three are found in the sanctuary (Ex. 29:40; Lev. 23:13).

village (Ruth 3:2). Grain was beaten with a stick by hand (Ruth 2:17) or threshed with a sledge dragged by animals. Men were responsible for winnowing by tossing the grain into the air with a pitchfork to separate the grain from the chaff, while women further separated edible and inedible parts with sieves.[29] To bring a gift from one's daily bread involved the labor of the entire household and made for a fitting offering to the Lord in whose land Israel dwelled.

Section Outline
   I. Sacrificial Worship (1:1–7:38) . . .
      B. Grain Offering (2:1–16)
         1. Offering the Sacrifice of Uncooked Grain (2:1–3)
         2. Offering the Sacrifice of Cooked Grain (2:4–10)
         3. Further Rules regarding Leavening and Salt (2:11–13)
         4. Offering the Firstfruits (2:14–16)

Comment

2:1 The word used to refer to the offerer is "living being" (Hb. *nefesh*). Like the use of *'adam* in 1:2, this phrasing is inclusive of men and women who are invited to worship through the grain offering.[30] Grinding grain and baking bread was a woman's daily work (26:26). Grain was ground on grinding slabs or small hand-mills by the women of the household and cooked in ovens or over firepits located in the home's open courtyard. It took an estimated five hours a day to produce enough bread for a household.[31]

The grain offering is called the *minkhah,* which in secular contexts designates tribute offered by a vassal to his sovereign (Judg. 3:15–17; 2 Sam. 8:6; 1 Kings 4:21). In a religious context it comes to designate the grain offering. This suggests that the sacrifice is best understood as covenant tribute, a gift to the Lord who has given the land and its life-sustaining produce. In the service the grain offering appears to have followed the burnt offering (Lev. 14:20; 2 Kings 16:13, 15; 1 Chron. 21:23).

Just as Israelites are commanded to bring the best from the flock, they are to bring the best of the produce of the land. "Fine flour" is semolina, or the inner kernel of durum wheat grown in the Middle East. It is mixed with olive oil (1 Kings 17:12–13), making it burn more easily on the altar's fire, and offered up with frankincense that makes it fit for the table of the King (1 Kings 10:2, 10; Matt. 2:11). Images of kings from the ancient world picture them with censers before their royal throne.[32]

---

29 Oded Borowski, *Agriculture in Iron Age Israel* (Boston: American Schools of Oriental Research, 2002), esp. 47–69.
30 Most laws are formulated using the Hebrew word *nefesh*, as in this verse (cf. Lev. 4:2; 5:1; 7:27). The Lord breathes the breath of life into Adam, who becomes a "living being," connecting *'adam* and *nefesh* in reference to humanity (Gen. 2:7).
31 Jenni R. Ebeling, *Women's Lives in Biblical Times* (London: T&T Clark, 2010), 48.
32 An example is an image carved in stone of a royal audience hall where two censers stand before the enthroned Darius II and his successor, crown prince Xerxes (biblical Ahasuerus; cf. Est. 1:1). For incense in a royal context cf. Psalm 45:8; Esther 2:12.

2:2 Like the burnt offering surrendered to the priest, who handles its blood, the grain offering changes hands from offerer to priest. A portion or "handful" of the flour is mixed with oil and burned on the altar while the remainder is the Lord's provision for the priests. The flour offered on the altar is the "memorial portion." This representative portion stands for the entire grain offering, which will not be directly consumed on the altar. The fistful calls to mind the whole, which in turn brings to remembrance the worshiper who gives it.[33] To be remembered by the Lord is to be remembered for covenant blessing (Lev. 26:45).

Frankincense is added for a "pleasing aroma," metaphorically meaning it makes for an acceptable sacrifice to the Lord. Practically speaking, since uncooked flour does not produce a savory aroma, as cooked grain does, frankincense may be offered with raw flour for the sake of emitting a pleasing odor.[34] Meat offerings whose fat sizzles on the altar are a pleasing aroma (1:9; 3:5; 4:31), and cooked bread likewise is a pleasing aroma (2:9).

2:3 Aaron and his sons consume the remainder of the offering as their portion, designated as "most holy," meaning it must be eaten in the ritually holy place of the courtyard and only by ritually holy people (6:16–18; 7:6).

The priests are privileged to serve the Lord on holy ground and are allotted no inheritance in the land: "To the tribe of Levi Moses gave no inheritance; the LORD God of Israel is their inheritance, just as he said to them" (Josh. 13:33).[35] They are instead to live in dependence on the Lord, who will feed them through Israel's tithes and offerings (Num. 8:18–19; Deut. 18:1–5, Josh. 13:14). Without this offering the servants of God do not eat, and the ministry falters (cf. Neh. 13:10–13). To this day God's people are called to share their bread with those who serve the church by giving to the Lord to feed the ministers of his Word (1 Cor. 9:14; Gal. 6:6).

2:4–7 Israel's tribute could be brought prepared in a variety of ways, as commonly would be found on the table. When not offered raw, the grain may be baked as round loaves or as flatbread in an oven (Lev. 2:4), griddle (vv. 5–6), or pan (v. 7). Grain in ancient Israel could be prepared in other ways as well. It was often soaked in water and boiled to make a porridge or gruel, but that does not feature among the acceptable offerings fit for the King's table. The Lord's offerings are all made by fire.

Bread was baked in clay ovens (v. 4) in the shape of a beehive and heated by fire at the bottom. The dough would be pressed against the hot interior wall to bake. The soft flatbread was eaten torn into pieces by hand and drizzled with olive oil. An offering could also be cooked on a flat, iron griddle (vv. 5–6) over an open

---

33 In the case of the wife suspected of adultery it is explicitly forbidden that frankincense accompany the grain offering (Num. 5:15). It is an offering of remembrance with the negative sense of exposing sin and calling forth the Lord's judgment.
34 Jonathan Grossman, "The Significance of Frankincense in Grain Offerings," *JBL* 138/2 (2019): 285–296. However, frankincense is also added to the firstfruit ears of grain, which would have emitted savory odors in roasting (Lev. 2:14–15).
35 The Levites receive no tribal inheritance and no land in a strict sense. They are, however, given forty-eight cities and their surrounding pasturelands in which to dwell (Num. 35:2–5).

fire (Ezek. 4:3). These breads would be thinner and less soft and thus crumbled before oil was added. Bread cooked in a deeper pan with a lid may have been fried with oil (Lev. 2:7).

2:8–10 These verses refer to the grain offering cooked as bread. Once more the worshiper gives the entirety "to the LORD," as it belongs to him as tribute and as food for his table. The Lord in turn shares the bread of his table with his servants. After the officiating priest presents the gifts at the altar and burns a memorial portion the priests again receive the remainder from the Lord (cf. v. 3), not the offerer. Both lay Israelite and priest look to the Lord for his daily bread: "The eyes of all look to you, and you give them their food in due season. You open your hand; you satisfy the desire of every living thing" (Ps. 145:15–16).

2:11–12 Leaven and honey are two substances prohibited in the preparation of the grain offering. Bread was made by mixing flour with water and salt and was typically leavened with a fermented starter from a previous batch (sourdough). "Honey" could refer to bee honey but more likely should be identified as date syrup, since Leviticus 2:12 classifies it as "firstfruits" that could be offered to the Lord.[36] Leavened bread and date syrup could be presented to the Lord as firstfruits (i.e., first-processed agricultural products), which the priests could eat (Lev. 23:20; Num. 18:12–13), but these could not be consumed by fire on the altar (2 Chron. 31:5).

The reason for forbidding baking with a leavening agent and flavoring with date syrup is not explained. It is sometimes suggested that fermentation was viewed as decay and that any hint of death would be incompatible with the sanctuary, meaning that leaven (which experiences fermentation) and date syrup (which was possibly susceptible to fermentation) were prohibited on the altar.[37] Another suggestion is that leavened cakes sweetened with raisins and dates might have too closely resembled offerings to the Canaanite fertility goddess Asherah (Jer. 7:18; Hos. 3:1). Again, the lack of explanation in the text itself makes it difficult to be certain.

2:13 All grain offerings must be seasoned with the "salt of the covenant."[38] Salt was the foremost preservative in the ancient world, preventing decay associated with death. On the altar's fire salt does not burn or change but is permanent and unalterable. Because of these properties it is used in covenant-making ceremonies to communicate the binding and enduring nature of the agreement.[39] This language is picked up when referring to the Lord's promised provision of regular portions for the priesthood (Num. 18:19). Sharing salt creates a bond among partakers and an obligation that must be honored (cf. Ezra 4:14). Salting the sacrifices reminds

---

[36] In Deut. 8:8 honey is listed among cultivated agriculture such as vines, fig trees, and olive trees, reinforcing that this refers to dates.
[37] Roy Gane, *Leviticus, Numbers*, NIVAC (Grand Rapids, MI: Zondervan Academic, 2004), 80.
[38] The verse begins with addressing the grain offering but ends with including all offerings. Ezekiel reflects the practice of offering salt with the meat of burnt offerings (Ezek. 43:24).
[39] Cf. Jacob Milgrom, *Leviticus 1–16*, AYB (New Haven, CT: Yale University Press, 1998), 191.

the Israelites with every offering that they are covenant allies with the Lord, who requires their allegiance and tribute. The enduring nature of the Lord's covenant with Israel is evoked by the phrase "everlasting covenant" (Gen. 17:7; Isa. 24:5, 61:8; Jer. 32:40; Ezek. 37:26).

2:14–16 The closing verses likely refer to the other grain in the Israelite diet, barley. The word translated as "firstfruits" may be understood as "first ripe." Barley is harvested before wheat as the first ripe grain (Ruth 2:23). The grain is roasted over fire and rubbed to release its kernels. A memorial portion of crushed grain is offered with oil and frankincense as with the uncooked wheat (Lev. 2:2).

Response

Israel's grain tribute affirms the Lord as Ruler of the world who renews humanity's call to be stewards over his creation (Gen. 1:28–29). He entrusts to Israel a land pregnant with potential for abundance (Deut. 8:7–10). He invites them to co-labor with him toward another Eden—to push back the effects of the curse, cultivate the earth to its fullest life-giving potential, and bring the best it has to offer to the praise of God. The Lord is honored as Israel's Sovereign when he is offered a gift of the fruit of the land. Yet it is *he* who first graciously gives the land, brings the rains, and showers his people with blessing (Deut. 11:10–12; Ps. 65:9–11). A theology of giving in proper perspective reveals it is the Lord who gives and to the Lord that it all belongs, as David recognizes in his prayer: "All that is in the heavens and in the earth is yours.... But who am I, and what is my people, that we should be able thus to offer willingly? For all things come from you, and of your own have we given you" (1 Chron. 29:11, 14).

It is humbling to acknowledge that anything we could ever offer the Lord has been given us first from him: our innate talents, cultivated skills, spiritual gifts, everything in our possession, and even the fruit of our labors (1 Cor. 4:7). He invites us to partner with his Spirit in a redemptive vision of work that transforms all we have been given into a pleasing aroma offered back to him. Giving is first and foremost an act of worship acknowledging the lordship of Jesus Christ. Here also we encounter the profound giving of the Lord, perfectly embodied in Christ, who as the true Bread of Life (John 6:35) gave himself up to the Father to set a table with his broken body that would satisfy his people into eternity: "I am the living bread that came down from heaven. If anyone eats of this bread, he will live forever. And the bread that I will give for the life of the world is my flesh" (John 6:51).

LEVITICUS 3

3 "If his offering is a sacrifice of peace offering, if he offers an animal from the herd, male or female, he shall offer it without blemish before the Lord. ²And he shall lay his hand on the head of his offering and kill it at the entrance of the tent of meeting, and Aaron's sons the priests shall throw the blood against the sides of the altar. ³And from the sacrifice of the peace offering, as a food offering to the Lord, he shall offer the fat covering the entrails and all the fat that is on the entrails, ⁴and the two kidneys with the fat that is on them at the loins, and the long lobe of the liver that he shall remove with the kidneys. ⁵Then Aaron's sons shall burn it on the altar on top of the burnt offering, which is on the wood on the fire; it is a food offering with a pleasing aroma to the Lord.

⁶"If his offering for a sacrifice of peace offering to the Lord is an animal from the flock, male or female, he shall offer it without blemish. ⁷If he offers a lamb for his offering, then he shall offer it before the Lord, ⁸lay his hand on the head of his offering, and kill it in front of the tent of meeting; and Aaron's sons shall throw its blood against the sides of the altar. ⁹Then from the sacrifice of the peace offering he shall offer as a food offering to the Lord its fat; he shall remove the whole fat tail, cut off close to the backbone, and the fat that covers the entrails and all the fat that is on the entrails ¹⁰and the two kidneys with the fat that is on them at the loins and the long lobe of the liver that he shall remove with the kidneys. ¹¹And the priest shall burn it on the altar as a food offering to the Lord.

¹²"If his offering is a goat, then he shall offer it before the Lord ¹³and lay his hand on its head and kill it in front of the tent of meeting, and the sons of Aaron shall throw its blood against the sides of the altar. ¹⁴Then he shall offer from it, as his offering for a food offering to the Lord, the fat covering the entrails and all the fat that is on the entrails ¹⁵and the two kidneys with the fat that is on them at the loins and the long lobe of the liver that he shall remove with the kidneys. ¹⁶And the priest shall burn them on the altar as a food offering with a pleasing aroma. All fat is the Lord's. ¹⁷It shall be a statute forever throughout your generations, in all your dwelling places, that you eat neither fat nor blood."

Section Overview

The third and final voluntary offering is an invitation to the Lord's table. If the burnt offering expresses a worshiper's total dedication and the grain offering a response to Yahweh's covenant lordship, then the peace offering best expresses joy in covenant fellowship. The first three sacrifices in Leviticus are listed in order of increasing spheres of consumption: the burnt offering is consumed whole by the Lord on the altar; the grain offering is shared with his servants, the priests;

and the peace offering is shared among the Lord, the priests, and the worshipers, who enjoy the largest portion. The ritual is given in concise instructions, but what must be envisioned is the fullness of the Lord's hospitality this offering extends. Feasting is an act of worship and an experience of real communion with the Lord.

Israel first tasted of the Lord's hospitality when she entered into covenant with him at Sinai. Moses, Aaron, and the seventy elders enjoyed a meal in the Lord's presence and, as Israel's representatives, feasted on peace offerings (Ex. 24:5, 9–11) since it was customary for table fellowship to conclude treaties (Gen. 31:54). This way of concluding treaties is no surprise; since eating is an activity shared with family, a covenant meal enacts a kinship identity, bringing covenant allies into a new relationship with obligations similar to those of natural kin. Moreover, while priestly families regularly shared meals from God's table as Israel's representatives (cf. Leviticus 6–7), the peace offering gave every Israelite access to the table. They were hosted by the Lord, invited to eat in his courts and to live out their identity as a covenanted kingdom of priests (Ex. 19:6).

It is in the context of communion with the Lord that this offering provides meat for the worshiper's household. And for most worshipers the eating of meat was not common. The typical Israelite diet consisted of bread, wine, and olive oil (Deut. 11:14), modestly and seasonally supplemented with fruit, vegetables, legumes, and dairy products. Feasting on meat marked a peace offering as a special event to savor joyously the Lord's benefaction: "Oh, taste and see that the LORD is good!" (Ps. 34:8; cf. Deut. 12:11–12).[40] Celebration over a shared meal nurtures spiritual and emotional bonds, fosters community, and instills in all partakers a shared identity as God's people.

Section Outline

I. Sacrificial Worship (1:1–7:38) . . .
    C. Peace Offering (3:1–17)
        1. Sacrificing a Peace Offering from the Herd (3:1–5)
        2. Sacrificing a Peace Offering from the Flock (3:6–16)
           a. Sheep (3:6–11)
           b. Goat (3:12–16)
        3. Giving to the Lord What Is His Alone (3:17)

Comment

3:1 English versions bring across the meaning of this offering through a variety of translations: "peace offering" (ESV) and "sacrifice of well-being" (NRSV) are based on etymology deriving from *shalom* ("wholeness, peace")[41] whereas "fellowship offering" (NIV) is descriptive of its function. The range of *shalom* is broad,

---

40 Scripture forges a strong connection between sacrificial feasting and joy. Gary A. Anderson notes that almost all expressions of joy found in the biblical text are in the context of sacrificial feasting: *A Time to Mourn, A Time to Dance: the Expression of Grief and Joy in Israelite Religion* (State College, PA: Pennsylvania State University Press, 1991, 19–26).
41 The Hebrew name of the sacrifice is *shelamim*, which is based on the same root as the word *shalom*.

conveying well-being that speaks to both the motivation and the spiritual effect of the sacrifice. *Shalom* involves wholeness brought about by satisfaction or repayment, evident in the fulfillment of a vow. Most importantly, *shalom* has covenant overtones as the blessed state of being in right relationship with God (Lev. 26:6; Num. 6:24–26; Rom. 5:1). Wholeness brought about through the peace offering extends beyond the individual to the entire household that participates in table fellowship (Lev. 7:11–18, 28–36). It is a communal offering expressive of the covenant relationship.

Reading together with chapter 7, we see that a worshiper may bring a peace offering as an expression of thanksgiving, in fulfillment of a vow, or as a freewill offering (7:12, 16). Thanksgiving is enacted by offering a spontaneous sacrifice in gratitude to the Lord for his blessings (a bountiful harvest, a baby's safe delivery, physical protection, etc.) and is accompanied by praise: "Let them offer sacrifices of thanksgiving, and tell of his deeds in songs of joy!" (Ps. 107:22; cf. Ps. 116:17–18). A worshiper may vow an offering to the Lord, as with Hannah in her prayer for a son (1 Sam. 1:10–11, 24–28), or in prayers for deliverance and protection (Gen. 28:20; Pss. 56:12; 66:13–15; Jonah 2:9). Freewill offerings are a voluntary gift beyond the required tithe or firstfruits and can be offered at any time.[42]

All these occasions are a source of joy for the giver: "You shall sacrifice peace offerings and shall eat there, and you shall rejoice before the LORD your God" (Deut. 27:7). Indeed, Israel's worship shows that sacrificial offerings are accompanied by public praise: "I will tell of your name to my brothers; in the midst of the congregation I will praise you. . . . My vows I will perform before those who fear him" (Ps. 22:22, 25).[43] A worshiper's offering provides the occasion for giving testimony of the Lord's faithfulness before all family and friends who join the table. Feasts have the power to catechize.

3:2 The sacrificial procedure follows the same order as that for the burnt offering: the offerer lays his hand on his offering in an act of presentation before the Lord. It is slaughtered in the area of the courtyard, and the priests collect the blood to spatter against the side of the altar. In the peace offering, however, the worshiper may bring either a male or female animal, bull or cow, provided it is unblemished (Lev. 3:1, 6).[44] Keeping with the joyous spirit of the offering's freewill and spontaneous nature, the worshiper is given freedom of choice over the sacrifice he will offer.

3:3–4 The animal's preparation continues in the careful removal of the fat covering the internal organs and kidneys (along with the kidneys and long lobe of the liver,

---

42 Freewill offerings could also include other material contributions such as precious metals, gemstones, and fabrics for the construction of the tent of meeting (Ex. 25:2; 35:21, 29) and temple (Ezra 1:6).

43 The author of Hebrews places these words in Jesus' mouth. Having endured suffering unto death (Ps. 22:1–21), Jesus now rejoices in God's deliverance through death's defeat and his bodily resurrection (Ps. 22:22–31). In the assembly of the redeemed, who have become his brothers and sisters, Christ pays his vows by testifying to the Father's covenant faithfulness in words echoing the fulfillment of vows of praise (Heb. 2:12). These words also include the fellowship meal: "My vows I will perform before those who fear him. The afflicted shall *eat and be satisfied*" (Ps. 22:25–26).

44 Leviticus 22:23 allows for an exception in the case of the freewill offering only: "You may present a bull or a lamb that has a part too long or too short for a freewill offering, but for a vow offering it cannot be accepted."

which appear to be considered as part of the fat). This is not the fat stored in the animal's muscle tissue but the protective layer around the vital organs. There is no need to separate out portions in the burnt offering, since the animal is dedicated in its entirety to the Lord and burned whole on the altar. The sacrificial meat of the peace offering, however, is shared with priests and worshipers, so the Lord's portion is separated. In Israel's subsistence economy, wherein meat is consumed sparingly, fat is highly regarded as the animal's richest portion and thus given to the Lord to show him the honor he is due. In many cultures fat still speaks to high value: the higher the degree of marbling in beef, the higher the quality grade and more expensive the cut. Because fat is associated with nourishment and abundance, it is used metaphorically to refer to the choicest land and its produce (Gen. 45:18; Ps. 147:14 [ESV "finest"]). Prophetic images of restoration anticipate a time when quality wine and meat with all its fat will satisfy every Israelite in "a feast of rich food, a feast of well-aged wine, of rich food full of marrow, of aged wine well refined" (Isa. 25:6).

3:5 The peace offering is set on top of the burnt offering, implying that, in the daily sacrificial service at the tent of meeting, freewill offerings follow the regular burnt offering (Lev. 6:12). When the worshiper's offering (fat, kidneys, and liver lobe) is added to the smoldering remains of the communal offering (lamb and grain), an individual household's expression of praise joins with that of the entire covenant community.

3:6–8 A peace offering taken from the flock may be either male or female, provided it is unblemished (cf. 22:18–25). The offerer presents the sheep (ram or ewe) before the Lord by laying his hand on the offering, and he ritually slaughters it before the tent of meeting, the nearest a worshiper may draw before the divine presence.

3:9–10 Israelites domesticated a breed of broad-tailed sheep indigenous to the Middle East known as the awassi (*Ovis laticaudata*). Its characteristic tail has a large accumulation of stored fat used for nourishment in the autumn and early winter, when food is scarce. A ram's tail is close to 12 inches (30 cm) long and can reportedly weigh up to 15 pounds (6.8 kg).[45] The fat tail is removed in its entirety to be offered to the Lord together with the fat, kidneys, and long lobe of the liver.

3:11 These are all offered on the altar as a "food offering," or the Lord's portion.[46] The image of a shared meal is the vehicle for expressing communion with God, since meals are the quintessential occasions for celebrating the bonds of family and friendship. The fellowship meal that will sustain offerer and priest reserves the choicest of portions for the Lord. The breast and right thigh are given to the officiating priest (7:30–34), while the largest part is retained by the worshiper.

---

[45] Oded Borowski, *Every Living Thing: Daily Use of Animals in Ancient Israel* (Walnut Creek, CA: Altamira, 1998), 66.
[46] The word *lekhem*, "bread, food," appears here for the first time and also in Lev. 7:13; 21:6, 8, 17, 21, 22; 22:25.

3:12–16 An offering from the flock of a goat or nanny requires different preparation. Although similar to a sheep in its ritual presentation and slaughtering, it lacks a fatty tail.

3:17 The conclusion to the peace offering marks the boundary in what the worshiper is allowed to consume: the fat and blood of a sacrificial animal are reserved exclusively for the Lord, drawing a sharp distinction between the worshiper and his God (7:25–26). The Lord is both host of the banquet and most honored guest and thus given the best portion (the fat; cf. comment on 3:3–4). As for why he is given the blood, 17:11–12 explains: "The life of the flesh is in the blood, and I have given it for you on the altar to make atonement for your souls, for it is the blood that makes atonement by the life. Therefore I have said to the people of Israel, No person among you shall eat blood, neither shall any stranger who sojourns among you eat blood." That which representatively constitutes the best part of an animal (fat) and the very essence of its life (blood) belongs to the Lord.

While the peace offering is consumed before the Lord's presence, this law applies to all Israel's "dwelling places," referring to individual households (13:46; 23:3, 17; 25:29). All meat eaten in the home must be drained of its blood (17:13–14). The law of the sanctuary extends into every Israelite home, linking the altar to the table of every household.

Response

A whole animal shared between Lord, his priestly servants, and the offerer's extended household is the physical symbol that brings them all together. Feasting on the peace offering's sacrificial meat is the means through which worshipers commune with God and with one another. It is a table fellowship that casts its shadow forward to the meal of a sacrificial offering that would be our peace and conclude a covenant whose bonds are everlasting (Eph. 2:14–16; Col. 1:19–20). The feast as an act of worship and communion with God reaches its fullest and truest expression at the Last Supper. Here the altar and the table become one: "And he took bread, and when he had given thanks, he broke it and gave it to them, saying, 'This is my body, which is given for you.... This cup that is poured out for you is the new covenant in my blood'" (Luke 22:19–20).

Gathering around this shared fellowship meal is the central and defining enactment of the early Christian church. The preached Word and the celebration of communion (also called the Eucharist, from Gk. *eucharistia*, "thanksgiving") defines the gathered believers as followers of Christ (Acts 2:42). Feasting on the body and blood of the Lord unites the corporate body of Christ through the shared bonds of covenant loyalty: "Because there is one bread, we who are many are one body, for we all partake of the one bread" (1 Cor. 10:17). As with the peace offering, there is an element of public proclamation in the Lord's Supper, that of Christ's atoning death that ratifies a new covenant (1 Cor. 11:26). This regular remembrance and symbolic enactment in the life of the church is eschatological, looking forward to the time when the Lord as the Host of the banquet will serve up the ultimate feast, the marriage supper of the Lamb, at the consummation of human history (Rev. 19:9). Gratitude and joy surround the table of the Lord, who calls us into communion with him and brings peace into all relationships. Celebration of the Lord's Supper roots our identity as people who belong to God's household as his children and to one another as brothers and sisters. We receive the gift of belonging from our heavenly Father and join the feast with thanksgiving and praise!

LEVITICUS 4

4 And the Lord spoke to Moses, saying, **2** "Speak to the people of Israel, saying, If anyone sins unintentionally[1] in any of the Lord's commandments about things not to be done, and does any one of them, **3** if it is the anointed priest who sins, thus bringing guilt on the people, then he shall offer for the sin that he has committed a bull from the herd without blemish to the Lord for a sin offering. **4** He shall bring the bull to the entrance of the tent of meeting before the Lord and lay his hand on the head of the bull and kill the bull before the Lord. **5** And the anointed priest shall take some of the blood of the bull and bring it into the tent of meeting, **6** and the priest shall dip his finger in the blood and sprinkle part of the blood seven times before the Lord in front of the veil of the sanctuary. **7** And the priest shall put some of the blood on the horns of the altar of fragrant incense before the Lord that is in the tent of meeting, and all the rest of the blood of the bull he shall pour out at the base of the altar of burnt offering that is at the entrance of the tent of meeting. **8** And all the fat of the bull of the sin offering he shall remove from it, the fat that covers the entrails and all the fat that is on the entrails **9** and the two kidneys with the fat that is on them at the loins and the long lobe of the liver that he shall remove with the kidneys **10** (just as these are taken from the ox of the sacrifice of the peace offerings); and the priest shall burn them on the altar of burnt offering. **11** But the skin of the bull and all its flesh, with its head, its legs, its entrails, and its dung— **12** all the rest of the bull—he shall carry outside the camp to a clean place, to the ash heap, and shall burn it up on a fire of wood. On the ash heap it shall be burned up.

13 "If the whole congregation of Israel sins unintentionally[2] and the thing is hidden from the eyes of the assembly, and they do any one of the things that by the Lord's commandments ought not to be done, and they realize their guilt,[3] **14** when the sin which they have committed becomes known, the assembly shall offer a bull from the herd for a sin offering and bring it in front of the tent of meeting. **15** And the elders of the congregation shall lay their hands on the head of the bull before the Lord, and the bull shall be killed before the Lord. **16** Then the anointed priest shall bring some of the blood of the bull into the tent of meeting, **17** and the priest shall dip his finger in the blood and sprinkle it seven times before the Lord in front of the veil. **18** And he shall put some of the blood on the horns of the altar that is in the tent of meeting before the Lord, and the rest of the blood he shall pour out at the base of the altar of burnt offering that is at the entrance of the tent of meeting. ¹⁹ And all its fat he shall take from it and burn on the altar. ²⁰ Thus shall he do with the bull. As he did with the bull of the sin offering, so shall he do with this. And the priest shall make atonement for them, and they shall be forgiven. ²¹ And he shall carry the bull outside the camp and burn it up as he burned the first bull; it is the sin offering for the assembly.

²² "When a leader sins, doing unintentionally any one of all the things that by the commandments of the Lord his God ought not to be done, and realizes his guilt, ²³ or the sin which he has committed is made known to him, he shall bring as his offering a goat, a male without blemish, ²⁴ and shall lay his hand on the head of the goat and kill it in the place where they kill the burnt offering before the Lord; it is a sin offering. ²⁵ Then the priest shall take some of the blood of the sin offering with his finger and put it on the horns of the altar of burnt offering and pour out the rest of its blood at the base of the altar of burnt offering. ²⁶ And all its fat he shall burn on the altar, like the fat of the sacrifice of peace offerings. So the priest shall make atonement for him for his sin, and he shall be forgiven.

²⁷ "If anyone of the common people sins unintentionally in doing any one of the things that by the Lord's commandments ought not to be done, and realizes his guilt, ²⁸ or the sin which he has committed is made known to him, he shall bring for his offering a goat, a female without blemish, for his sin which he has committed. ²⁹ And he shall lay his hand on the head of the sin offering and kill the sin offering in the place of burnt offering. ³⁰ And the priest shall take some of its blood with his finger and put it on the horns of the altar of burnt offering and pour out all the rest of its blood at the base of the altar. ³¹ And all its fat he shall remove, as the fat is removed from the peace offerings, and the priest shall burn it on the altar for a pleasing aroma to the Lord. And the priest shall make atonement for him, and he shall be forgiven.

³² "If he brings a lamb as his offering for a sin offering, he shall bring a female without blemish ³³ and lay his hand on the head of the sin offering and kill it for a sin offering in the place where they kill the burnt offering. ³⁴ Then the priest shall take some of the blood of the sin offering with his finger and put it on the horns of the altar of burnt offering and pour out all the rest of its blood at the base of the altar. ³⁵ And all its fat he shall remove as the fat of the lamb is removed from the sacrifice of peace offerings, and the priest shall burn it on the altar, on top of the Lord's food offerings. And the priest shall make atonement for him for the sin which he has committed, and he shall be forgiven."

[1] Or *by mistake*; so throughout Leviticus [2] Or *makes a mistake* [3] Or *suffer for their guilt*, or *are guilty*; also verses 22, 27, and chapter 5

Section Overview

As noted above (cf. Section Overview of Leviticus 1), Leviticus 1–3 provides ritual instruction for the burnt, grain, and fellowship offerings, which Israelites could bring voluntarily (22:18, 21) but were in some instances mandatory (cf. 14:19–20). Leviticus 4:1–6:7 provides ritual instruction for the sin and guilt offerings, which were always mandatory (12:6; 14:12, 19). In broad terms the "sin offering" cleanses the offerer and the sanctuary, where sin's impurity leaves its stain. The "guilt offering" repairs relationship with the Lord through restitution. In making amends for transgression Israel's expiatory offerings guard God's holiness by bringing sin's effect to light and making provision for its remedy. The invitation into the Lord's presence continues in these offerings so that those who are polluted by sin or impurity may find cleansing and forgiveness.

Two important points serve to clarify the role of the sin offering. The first is that its name (Hb. *khatta't*) is a word that is used both for *sin* (4:3, 14, 23, 28, 35) and for the *offering* that removes sin's effects (4:3, 8, 20, 21, 24, 25, 29, 32, 33, 34, 35). In essence the offering de-sins, that is, decontaminates from sin's pollution.[47] Second, in addition to cleansing impurity generated by sin, it also cleanses from ritual impurity, where there is clearly no sin (such as childbirth or consecration to service). Therefore many commentators prefer to call this the "purification offering,"[48] a name that highlights its cleansing character. Whether it is defilement from sin or ritual impurity incompatible with God's holiness, the sin offering cleanses the worshiper and restores relationship with the Lord.

The four main occasions for making a sin offering are the following:

(1) inadvertent sin against the Lord's commands (4:1–5:13);
(2) purification from ritual impurity, such as childbirth (12:6–8), leprosy (14:19, 31), bodily emissions (15:14–15, 29–30), or contact with death (Num. 6:11; 19:13);
(3) consecration of priests and Levites into the Lord's service as an extension of purification (Lev. 8:14–17; Num. 8:8, 12);
(4) and purification of the sanctuary on the Day of Atonement (Lev. 16:11–19).

This chapter addresses purification from inadvertent sin. It is arranged as four cases in descending order from the nation's spiritual head to the individual worshiper. The offerer's social standing determines the offering animal and the distinctive handling of sacrificial blood. The logic of the sin offering is as follows: transgression of the Lord's commands generates impurity that clings to the sinner and contaminates God's holy dwelling. Sin's impact is mapped in the sanctuary, where it leaves its mark on holy ground. The ritual space where purification is performed is reflective of the access each member of society has to the Lord's presence: sacrificial blood to cleanse from the sin of individuals and leaders is applied in the outer courts, where they worship, whereas that of the high priest must be applied deeper in the tent of meeting, where he appears before the Lord.

---

47 From a grammatical perspective the name of the offering derives not from a simple form of the verb that means "to sin" but from the form of the verb that means to "de-sin, to decontaminate or cleanse from the effects of wrong-doing."

48 Milgrom, *Leviticus 1–16*, 253–254; Hartley, *Leviticus*, 55; Gordon J. Wenham, *Leviticus*, NICOT (Grand Rapids, MI: Eerdmans, 1979), 88–89; Sklar, *Leviticus*, TOTC, 107–108; Gane, *Leviticus, Numbers*, 96. Since this chapter deals with the consequences of inadvertent sin rather than cleansing from ritual impurity, retaining the name of "sin offering" is adequate to the task.

Sin and its effects are put on display vividly in the tabernacle. Sin not only defiles the sinner but reaches in to pollute the sanctuary, clinging to the altar that is the very symbol of the covenant relationship. Since the tabernacle is designed to reflect an image of the world, it is an inescapable conclusion that our sin defiles the earth itself.

Section Outline

I. Sacrificial Worship (1:1–7:38) . . .
  D. Sin Offering (4:1–5:13)
    1. Introduction to Unintentional Sin (4:1–2)
    2. The High Priest's Sin Offering (4:3–12)
    3. The Congregation's Sin Offering (4:13–21)
    4. A Tribal Leader's Sin Offering (4:22–26)
    5. An Individual's Sin Offering (4:27–35)

Comment

4:1–2 The sin offering law is stated quite generally, with only a few specific offenses listed at the end of the legislation (5:1–4). The lack of specificity may be intentional to cover the broadest possible range of transgression for which the offering could atone.

The offering is stipulated for "unintentional" sin, that is, an inadvertent or unpremeditated offense. Its basic meaning is to stray—as wandering sheep go astray (Ezek. 34:6)—aptly illustrating how anyone may veer off course into error.[49] "With my whole heart I seek you; let me not wander from your commandments!" (Ps. 119:10). In contrast sin at the other end of the spectrum is said to be perpetrated with a "high hand" (Num. 15:30). A high-handed sin is intentional, brazen, and in open rebellion against the Lord's authority. There is no sacrifice for the one who has sinned defiantly because he "has despised the word of the LORD and has broken his commandment, that person shall be utterly cut off; his iniquity shall be on him" (Num. 15:31; cf. Heb. 10:26–27). The contrast between the two postures is at the heart of defining unintentional sin, that is, straying into error as opposed to rebelling against God.[50]

Even if committed in error, sin endangers relationship with the Lord. It brings guilt on the offender and causes pollution to accumulate in the sanctuary. The Lord himself provides the solution for those defiled by sin to find cleansing and forgiveness through accepting an offering for sin. "Sacrificial [atonement] is a privilege granted by YHWH, not an inalienable right."[51]

4:3–4 The first case deals with the spiritual head of the nation, who is called here the "anointed priest," an uncommon title highlighting his consecration (Lev. 4:3, 5, 16).[52] The wording recalls his installation to office via anointing with holy oil

---

[49] R. Knierim, "šgg to err," *TLOT*, 1302–1304.
[50] For more detail cf. Jay Sklar ("Sin and Atonement," 467–491), who also discusses sins that fall in between the two categories above in that they are intentional and yet atonable by means of sacrifice (as in Lev. 6:1–7).
[51] Gane, *Cult and Character*, 204.
[52] The Hebrew for "anointed one" is *mashiakh*, from which we get our word *messiah*. This is the only place in the Pentateuch where this word appears.

that consecrates him, the sanctuary, and the altar over a period of seven days (Ex. 29:35–37; Lev. 8:10–12).

When the anointed priest sins, it has consequences for the entire nation. The passage refers to the priest's acting in his official capacity and not as an individual.[53] Since he represents the worshiping community before the Lord, his inadvertent sin results in the community's straying into error. Whether he has failed to guard the holiness of the sanctuary, perform worship according to the divine commands, or teach the people the Lord's requirements, he has brought guilt upon those on whose behalf he ministers when in fact his charge is to "bear any guilt from the holy things that the people of Israel consecrate" (Ex. 28:38). As guilt has been incurred by priest and congregation alike, it must be redressed by both fully (cf. Lev. 4:13–21).

The high priest is to bring a bull, an offering to the scale of his status within the community. The value of his offering is equivalent to that of the congregation, since he represents them (v. 14; cf. table 3.1).

TABLE 3.1: Offenders and Offerings

Offender	Offering	Blood Rite	Sacrificial Portions
high priest	bull	veil and incense altar	none: carcass burned
congregation	bull	veil and incense altar	none: carcass burned
tribal leader	male goat	sacrificial altar	officiating priest
ordinary citizen	female goat	sacrificial altar	officiating priest

Israel's lived experience is reflected in the animals required for sacrifice. God's people are given a land suited ideally for pasturing flocks. Cattle are less common since they require an amount of water and grass that is scarce. Israelites keep flocks that are two-thirds sheep and one-third goats, with a few head of cattle for labor in cultivating the land.[54] The representative symbolism of the sin offering is based on an analogy: as with Israel's flocks, so with the Lord's flock (Pss. 95:7; 100:1–5). Thus the structure of Israelite society is reflected in the animals that cleanse their sin. The high priest who represents the congregation must bring a bull (head of the herd). A tribal leader must bring a male goat (head of the flock), whereas an ordinary citizen brings of the more plentiful females that constitute the greater part of the flock. The offering represents the offerer and underscores that the animal is a substitute for the offerer.[55]

4:5–6 Unlike with other sacrifices, the blood of the sin offering is brought inside the sanctuary. The high priest carries the sacrificial blood into the ritual space

---

[53] Personal sin is acknowledged in the sacrifices offered on the Day of Atonement when the high priest brings a sin offering for himself and his household before making atonement for the nation; Leviticus 16:6.
[54] Sites throughout Israel have yielded a high number of bones from sheep and goats, with only 15 percent identified as cattle bones. Estimates are that a village of a hundred people would be supported by three hundred sheep and goats and only about a dozen cattle, used primarily for labor (Boer, *Sacred Economy*, 64).
[55] Cf. comments on 1:2b; 1:4; Section Overview of Leviticus 11.

where he ministers and sprinkles it seven times in front of the veil separating the Holy Place from the Most Holy Place. The veil marks the closest he is permitted to approach as he burns incense daily on the golden altar. The blood is sprinkled "before the LORD," locating the ritual action both directionally and theologically. The Lord is the one toward whom the ritual is directed and the one who is approached for forgiveness. Performing the sprinkling seven times emphasizes the completeness of the cleansing.[56]

4:7 The high priest then applies blood to the horns of the incense altar "before the LORD" in the Holy Place. The remaining blood is poured out in the courtyard at the base of the altar of burnt offering, so called because of the burnt offering made on it twice daily. These two altars serve as focal points in the performance of the sin offering: the incense altar for the high priest and congregation and the altar of sacrifice for the leader and ordinary citizen.

The blood is applied not to the altar in general (as with other sacrifices, 1:5; 3:2; 7:2) but to its horns. Applying blood to the altar's extremities cleanses the impurity and sin that has obstructed fellowship and reconsecrates the altar for continued intercession (cf. 8:15). Sacrifice is not an end in itself but the means to reconciliation with God for ongoing worship.

4:8–10 The priest separates out the Lord's portions—the fat and kidneys and lobe of the liver—and offers them on the altar, as is ritual procedure (cf. 3:3–5). The Lord is honored and acknowledged as covenant Sovereign with the animal's richest portions.

4:11–12 Rather than being offered on the altar the bull's carcass is carried to the ash heap outside Israel's camp, where it is burned along with its hide and entrails. Its incineration on a wood fire is expressed in a different way (Hb. *saraf*) than is an offering that smolders on the altar (*qatar*), making it clear that this is not a sacrificial act but a ritual disposal. The "clean place" is also where the ashes and unusable parts of the burnt offering are discarded (1:16; 6:11).[57] Since the offering is payment for transgression (4:20–21), to eat of it would be to rescind payment in some way. The offering has been made holy by its presentation to the Lord, so it must be treated as holy by not allowing its use for any other purpose; therefore, it is eliminated by burning. When a sin offering is made for a leader or ordinary citizen, the meaty portions go to the officiating priest as compensation for his service, but an offering for the high priest or congregation is never to be consumed (6:30).

4:13–14 The second case involves the inadvertent sin of the congregation. Although its sin is initially hidden from its eyes, the congregation later realizes its guilt, or, as Sklar clarifies, it "suffers guilt's consequences,"[58] meaning the people

---

[56] For "seven" having the sense of completeness or thoroughness cf. Leviticus 26:18; cleansing from major impurities requires a wait of seven days (12:2; 15:13), that is, a thorough wait (Sklar, *Leviticus*, ZECOT, 143).
[57] The "pure place" is contrasted with an "impure place," where those things contaminated with spreading disease are disposed (Lev. 14:40, 41, 45).
[58] Sklar, *Leviticus*, TOTC (Downers Grove, IL: IVP Academic, 2014), 113.

experience the Lord's disfavor in some way, alerting them to possible sin. The sin itself is vague and without specifics. The same language of hiddenness and realization is used in 5:2–4 to refer to a person who has come in contact with impurity but has not handled it properly. Perhaps this is also the situation envisioned here.

4:15 The offering for the congregation—a bull—is the same as that for the high priest, which is no surprise given that the high priest represents the congregation in worship. The elders who represent the people legally are the ones to bring and dedicate the animal by placing their hands on its head. Again the ritual of presentation and slaughter take place "before the LORD."

The elders represent the congregation at Sinai, ratifying the covenant and feasting in God's presence on behalf of the nation (Ex. 19:7–8; 24:9–11). Their leadership as heads of the families of tribes is exercised in civic (Num. 11:16–25; Deut. 21:18–21) as well as ritual matters (Ex. 12:21; Ps. 107:32; Joel 1:14). Significantly, they have authority to stand on the people's behalf in rituals that cleanse guilt, as in this passage and in the case of bloodguilt from an unsolved murder (Deut. 21:6–7).[59]

4:16–18 As with the high priest's offering, the blood is brought inside the Holy Place and sprinkled before the veil seven times, symbolizing completeness. The high priest then dips his finger and applies the blood to the altar of incense in front of the veil. The rest he carries outside to the courtyard and pours out at the base of the bronze altar of sacrifice.

The blood that achieves cleansing for the congregation is brought all the way into the Holy Place even though no Israelite may ever enter the tent. The blood rite suggests that the congregation is in fact regarded as having entered this space by virtue of its need for cleansing. How so? As the high priest dons his ceremonial garments daily, he representatively brings all Israel before the Lord's presence: "Aaron shall bear the names of the sons of Israel in the breastpiece of judgment on his heart, when he goes into the Holy Place, to bring them to regular remembrance before the LORD" (Ex. 28:29). It is as though all the people have appeared before the Lord when their names are carried into the sanctuary by their priestly mediator.

4:19 In the same sacrificial procedure as for the high priest's offering, the fat portions are placed on the altar. Although the instructions do not mention them explicitly, these portions would include the kidneys and long lobe of the liver, which are considered part of the fat (cf. 4:8–9).

4:20 The priest makes atonement for the congregation, and as a result they are forgiven. Atonement is a richly textured term with a dual value in the sin offering. In the context of sin it ransoms the sinner by providing a substitute in exchange.

---

[59] In the case of an unsolved murder elders from the town nearest the discovered corpse take an unworked heifer to a water source, slaughter it, and, declaring their innocence, wash their hands in order to make atonement and purge guilt from among them. Expiation comes through the heifer's blood and cleansing by water.

The animal reflective of the offerer's status in the community "pays" for the sinner. In the context of the Lord's holy dwelling the blood of sacrifice cleanses the impurity and contamination that has spoiled relationship with God and by extension the guilt from the offender.

Transgression incurs guilt even if unintentional. Yet the persistent refrain throughout the sin and guilt offerings is that "they shall be forgiven" (vv. 20, 26, 31, 35; 5:10, 13). The Lord who provides the substitute also provides assurance of his forgiveness through the word of his mediator. The priest is given authority to declare what only the Lord can do: forgive. (It is for this reason that the high priest's rite lacks the statement that he will be forgiven. Since he is officiating on his own behalf, he cannot pronounce forgiveness on himself, though he would certainly know the Lord has forgiven him because of the atoning sacrifice.)

4:21 As with the offering for the high priest, the bull's carcass is carried to the clean ash heap outside Israel's camp and burned in its entirety.

4:22–23 Tribal leaders are addressed next: "Chiefs of their ancestral tribes, the heads of the clans of Israel" (Num. 1:16). A tribal chief is a secular leader who represents the tribe (cf. Num. 7:1–88). His required offering is an unblemished male goat. Goats constitute a third of Israel's flocks, with males being less common than females, therefore making this offering consonant with the leader's position in tribal society.

4:24 The goat is slaughtered north of the altar, where the smaller animals are ritually slain (Lev. 1:11). The bull, as a larger animal, is slain in the more spacious area in front of the altar, by the entrance to the tent of meeting (4:4, 14–15; cf. 1:3). The statement "It is a sin offering" could reflect what the offerer says as he presents his animal to distinguish it from the burnt offering.

4:25–26 This time the blood is not brought into the Holy Place but applied to the horns of the altar in the outer court, where lay Israelites appear before the Lord. The sacrificial altar is "most holy," sanctified by holy oil and divine glory, and the place where the Lord meets with his people to receive their worship (Ex. 29:37, 42–43). It symbolizes the promise of enduring relationship, like the blood rite that sealed the covenant between Israel and their God (Ex. 24:6–8). A worshiper may swear an oath before the altar (1 Kings 8:31) or plead asylum (1 Kings 1:50) as though standing before the Lord himself. The application of blood cleanses the altar from sin's impurity, achieves forgiveness for the sinner, and reestablishes communion between the Lord and the worshiper.

Unlike with the offering for the high priest or for the congregation, there is no mention that the carcass is burned. Instead, later the Lord allocates the meat portions for the officiating priest and the male priests of his household (Lev. 6:26, 29). As a most holy portion, it must be eaten within the area of the sanctuary's courtyard. The person on whose behalf the offering has been made, however, cannot partake of it.

4:27–28 While the tribal leader who sins is required to bring a male goat, an individual brings a female. Females were more prevalent among the flocks, as they were needed for reproduction and for their milk. It is a fitting analogy for a member of the community.

4:29–31 Standing north of the altar, the offerer lays his hand on the head of the goat that is his substitute and slaughters it. The officiating priest applies its blood to the horns of the altar in the outer court. The individual's offering remains in the area where the individual Israelite is granted access to the Lord—its blood on the altar's horns and its flesh consumed by priests in the altar's vicinity (6:26).

4:32–35 Alternately, an Israelite citizen who has strayed into error may bring a lamb. In the graded scale of offerings from rarest to most common, female lambs are most plentiful among Israel's flocks. The procedure is the same as that of offering a female goat, with care given to removing the fat portion that belongs to the Lord.

Response

The sin offering teaches Israel that sin, even if committed in ignorance or error, is first and foremost an offense against the Lord (Ps. 51:4). Far from private, its effects are a pollution that defiles not only the individual but also the sanctuary where the Lord dwells. This contamination requires cleansing through blood, because "everything is purified with blood, and without the shedding of blood there is no forgiveness of sins" (Heb. 9:22). The offering of sacrifice atones for the guilty, achieves forgiveness, and restores relationship with the Lord, whose "eyes" are "purer ... than to see evil" (Hab. 1:13). The scaled offerings, from those for the high priest to those for an individual, make clear that "All we like sheep have gone astray" and are in need of one to bear the "iniquity of us all" (Isa. 53:6). Offerings specific to one's status underscore that they represent the sinner and reveal the mercy of God to provide a substitute. At this moment in redemptive history, though inadequate in itself, the blood of animals will serve to communicate that a life atones for a life and that the blood of the blameless ransoms the guilty.

For the NT believer the sin offering has shaped how the church understands and articulates the atoning work of Christ. He comes as the *offerer*, presenting an offering on behalf of fallen humanity, just as Israel's representatives were legally authorized to bring an offering on behalf of the nation (Lev. 4:15). He serves as the anointed *high priest*, making atonement and declaring forgiveness (v. 20) but having no need to bring an offering of his own because he is sinless (Heb. 4:15; 7:26–28). He is the *sacrifice*, shedding his blood on the altar of God as the unblemished substitute who takes the place of the sinner (1 Pet. 1:18–19). He gave his life in place of ours, slain to atone for our sins and cleanse us from all impurity (2 Cor. 5:21). His blood has been sprinkled in the true heavenly dwelling, beyond the veil in the Father's presence, to restore fellowship with him (Heb. 9:11–12). The sin offering, whose instructions are so carefully scripted, was fulfilled in the historic death of the Messiah, the anointed High Priest who was crucified outside the holy city of Jerusalem, just as the offering's carcass was discarded outside the camp (Lev. 4:12; John 19:20). "So Jesus also suffered outside the gate in order to sanctify the people through his own blood" (Heb. 13:12).

The shed blood of Jesus Christ has the power to bring us into communion with a holy God and to redeem all creation, even as the sin offering purifies both the sinner and the sanctuary representing the world (Rom. 8:18–22). The Lord is at work reconciling the world to himself through Christ (2 Cor. 5:19; cf. John 1:29). Atonement is the work of God, his divine initiative and activity on our behalf, yet as a redeemed people we have the priestly privilege of proclaiming the gospel that relationship with God may be restored through faith in Jesus and his substitutionary sacrifice on our behalf: "For our sake he made him to be sin who knew no sin, so that in him we might become the righteousness of God" (2 Cor. 5:21).

LEVITICUS 5:1–13

5 "If anyone sins in that he hears a public adjuration to testify, and though he is a witness, whether he has seen or come to know the matter, yet does not speak, he shall bear his iniquity; ² or if anyone touches an unclean thing, whether a carcass of an unclean wild animal or a carcass of unclean livestock or a carcass of unclean swarming things, and it is hidden from him and he has become unclean, and he realizes his guilt; ³ or if he touches human uncleanness, of whatever sort the uncleanness may be with which one becomes unclean, and it is hidden from him, when he comes to know it, and realizes his guilt; ⁴ or if anyone utters with his lips a rash oath to do evil or to do good, any sort of rash oath that people swear, and it is hidden from him, when he comes to know it, and he realizes his guilt in any of these; ⁵ when he realizes his guilt in any of these and confesses the sin he has committed, ⁶ he shall bring to the LORD as his compensation¹ for the sin that he has committed, a female from the flock, a lamb or a goat, for a sin offering. And the priest shall make atonement for him for his sin.

⁷ "But if he cannot afford a lamb, then he shall bring to the LORD as his compensation for the sin that he has committed two turtledoves or two pigeons,² one for a sin offering and the other for a burnt offering. ⁸ He shall bring them to the priest, who shall offer first the one for the sin offering. He shall wring its head from its neck but shall not sever it completely, ⁹ and he shall sprinkle some of the blood of the sin offering on the side of the altar, while the rest of the blood shall be drained out at the base of the altar; it is a sin offering. ¹⁰ Then he shall offer the second for a burnt offering according to the rule. And the priest shall make atonement for him for the sin that he has committed, and he shall be forgiven.

11 "But if he cannot afford two turtledoves or two pigeons, then he shall bring as his offering for the sin that he has committed a tenth of an ephah[3] of fine flour for a sin offering. He shall put no oil on it and shall put no frankincense on it, for it is a sin offering. **12** And he shall bring it to the priest, and the priest shall take a handful of it as its memorial portion and burn this on the altar, on the LORD's food offerings; it is a sin offering. **13** Thus the priest shall make atonement for him for the sin which he has committed in any one of these things, and he shall be forgiven. And the remainder[4] shall be for the priest, as in the grain offering."

[1] Hebrew *his guilt penalty*; so throughout Leviticus [2] Septuagint *two young pigeons*; also verse 11 [3] An *ephah* was about 3/5 bushel or 22 liters [4] Septuagint; Hebrew *it*

Section Overview

In order to present new material in continuity with the previous chapter this section begins with the same clause that introduced the sin offering there ("If anyone sins," v. 1; cf. 4:2). These instructions are added as an appendix to the sin offering and outline borderline cases that do not conform fully with the regular offering.[60] While the regular offering is for general inadvertent transgressions, the instructions here name specific sins of omission. Taking the two chapters together, we see that sin is understood to include both an active straying into error (commission) and a passive neglect (omission). Both require sacrifice for forgiveness. In the appendix specific sins are mentioned, and it lists different offering possibilities for those with more limited means.

The cases are balanced in a chiasm, with the first and last dealing with neglect in the legal sphere and the middle two dealing with neglect in matters of ritual. The structure conveys the sin offering's dual purpose to achieve cleansing from impurity as well as forgiveness of sin (cf. ch. 4).

(A) failure to respond to an oath
    (B) prolonged animal impurity
    (B') prolonged human impurity
(A') failure to fulfill an oath

Section Outline

I.D. Sin Offering (4:1–5:13) . . .
    6. Sins of Omission Requiring a Sin Offering (5:1–4)
        a. Failure to Testify (5:1)
        b. Prolonged Impurity from an Animal Source (5:2)
        c. Prolonged Impurity from a Human Source (5:3)
        d. Failure to Fulfill an Oath (5:4)
    7. Sacrificial Procedure (5:5–13)
        a. Confession and Offering (5:5–6)
        b. Alternate Offerings (5:7–13)

---

60 Milgrom, *Leviticus 1–16*, 309–310.

Comment

5:1 The first case treats the failure to come forward and testify when there is a public call for witnesses. Such proclamations usually involved an oath with an attached curse for not coming forward with information (cf. Judg. 17:2; Prov. 29:24). A witness may be afraid for himself or reluctant to incriminate close relatives. Regardless, he is held accountable for withholding evidence that obstructs justice. As long as he remains silent, he "bears his iniquity." This biblical idiom means the offender is heavily laden with guilt and liable to suffer its punishment (in this instance the curse uttered before the Lord).[61]

Sin is expressed in vivid language that draws from known images and experiences of everyday life to lend concreteness and make the intangible quality of sin tangible. The previous chapter portrayed sin as a pollution that needed to be cleansed from the sinner and sanctuary. Here sin is expressed as a weight. The guilty carries the crushing weight of his own sin without relief, bearing its consequences.[62] The Lord provides the means of relief and unburdening through confession and sacrifice (Lev. 5:5–6).

5:2 The second case involves contracting impurity by contact with the carcass of an unclean animal. Normally this type of impurity does not require a sacrifice but is resolved by washing one's clothes and waiting until evening (11:24–25). The offender in this instance, however, has neglected to handle it properly since it was "hidden from him," that is, he forgot about it (cf. the use of the same phrase in 5:4). He therefore remains in his impurity and is held liable for not carrying out the Lord's commands.

5:3 A mirror case deals with impurity from contact with human uncleanness, such as a bodily discharge or an object that has touched an unclean person (cf. chs. 12; 15). Again this is normally resolved by laundering clothes, washing the body, and waiting until evening. But because they slipped the person's mind these procedures were not done. This is not only an offense; it also had the potential to defile the Lord's dwelling: "Thus you shall keep the people of Israel separate from their uncleanness, lest they die in their uncleanness by defiling my tabernacle that is in their midst" (15:31).

At some point the offender "realizes his guilt" (cf. comments on 4:13–14; 5:17). God's people are held accountable for knowing the law that brings awareness of transgression: "I have stored up your word in my heart, that I might not sin against you" (Ps. 119:11; cf. Rom. 3:20). Yet there are others, such as the priests and the broader community, who also have a role in bringing sin to light for the good of the sinner and the entire congregation (cf. Gal. 6:1–2; James 5:19–20; 1 John 1:7–8).

---

61 The range of punishments elsewhere for those "bearing sin" range from childlessness (Lev. 20:20) to being cut off from the community (19:8) and death itself (22:9; 24:14–15).
62 Our conceptualization of sin affects our understanding of its remedy. The same language describing sin is also a rich metaphor for forgiveness. Sin is borne by either the sinner or a substitute. When borne by the sinner, the expression speaks to suffering sin's punishment; when carried by a substitute, it speaks to receiving forgiveness. Forgiveness is the *bearing away* of sin, taken up by another so that the guilty is set free (Lev. 16:22; Isa. 53:12).

5:4 The final case involves a person who utters an oath carelessly without taking stock fully of its implications. An oath is a solemn promise to keep one's word faithfully. Oaths are taken in the name of the Lord with the addition of a curse should a person fail to keep his promise, typically expressed as "May God do so to me and more also . . ." (2 Kings 6:31). Having called on the Lord to vouch for one's word, the swearer sins by failing to fulfill it (Num. 30:2). In this case the oath was "rash," being quickly and thoughtlessly spoken and then quickly forgotten ("hidden from him"); it thus remained unfulfilled.

5:5–6 When the offender realizes his guilt in any of the above situations, he must first confess his sin and then bring a sacrifice. His offering is that of a female lamb or goat, the same as that which is required of an individual for the regular offering (4:27–28, 32). (Coming verses will identify less costly offerings for those unable to afford a flock animal.)

Next the worshiper must make things right, first with respect toward those he has wronged and then to the Lord. These instructions are given from the perspective of the sanctuary and naturally focus on repairing relationship with the Lord through sacrifice, but this does not limit the scope of what needs to be set aright. The offender must first come forward and testify, cleanse himself from impurity, and fulfill the sworn oath. At that point sacrifice can then be given (cf. 6:5–7).

The Hebrew expression for confession conveys great richness that reveals the Lord's purposes in the sacrificial system. The word "to confess" (*yada*) is a secondary form of the verb that primarily means to declare praise. This makes clear two things: sin must be acknowledged aloud,[63] and confession is a vital aspect of the worship of God. Confession grounds critical moments in the worshiping life of the congregation, found at the beginning (5:5), middle (16:21), and end (26:40) of Leviticus. An individual worshiper is restored to the Lord by declaring publicly that he has violated the Lord's moral-ritual order. "I acknowledged my sin to you, and I did not cover my iniquity; I said, 'I will confess my transgressions to the LORD,' and you forgave the iniquity of my sin" (Ps. 32:5). In his admission he separates himself from his sin and trusts in the Lord's provision of forgiveness (Lev. 4:20, 26, 31, 35; 5:10, 13, 16, 18; 6:7). Without confession he is bound to bear his iniquity (5:1). Public confession mediated by the high priest takes center stage on the Day of Atonement (16:21). It is the act of confession on behalf of the nation that places Israel's sins on the head of the scapegoat. Without confession, though the goat be driven out into wilderness, the people's sins are not on his head for him to bear away (cf. 1 John 1:10). Finally, corporate confession closes the book with a look to the future. The Lord holds out hope to his estranged people that he will

---

[63] The declaration may have been brief, taking responsibility for sin and acknowledging the Lord as righteous Judge, such as, "I have sinned; the LORD is in the right, and I [am] . . . in the wrong" (Ex. 9:27; cf. 2 Sam. 12:13), or simply, "I have sinned" (Num. 22:34; 1 Sam. 15:30). Sin against another may have been voiced as "I have sinned against the LORD . . . and against you" (Ex. 10:16). Corporately there was naming and taking responsibility for the transgression: "We have sinned against you, because we have forsaken our God and have served the Baals" (Judg. 10:10; cf. 1 Kings 8:47; Psalm 106).

be prompted to overturn punishment and turn toward them again with blessing when in humility they confess their waywardness (Lev. 26:40–42).

Israel's history bears testimony to the Lord's purposes through confession. The returning exiles at the time of Nehemiah petition the Lord in communal repentance and mourning for a quarter of the day (Neh. 9:1–3). As the law is interpreted by the priests and the people's sin is brought to light (Neh. 8:5–8), the Word of God fuels their confession as well as their resolve to recommit to the covenant (Neh. 10:28–39). Recorded prayers alternate between acknowledgment of sin and God's faithfulness to forgive, recalling the wording of Leviticus 4–5. Confession and praise of God's saving acts go hand in hand, turning the humble admission of failure into a recital of the Lord's mercy and faithfulness.[64]

5:7 Since it is critical for continued relationship that sin be atoned for through the mandatory offerings, the Lord makes concessions for the poor, "for there is no one who does not sin" (1 Kings 8:46). Instead of a lamb God will accept either two pigeons or two turtledoves.[65] It is apparent that the two birds are meant to be offered together since they are brought as a pair, the two constituting one whole offering. One is sacrificed in the manner of a sin offering, whose blood is applied to the altar and its meat given to the priest; the other as a burnt offering to provide the portion that goes to the Lord.

5:8–10 As with the regular sin offering, attention continues to focus on the sacrificial blood through which atonement is made. The blood from a small bird is likely not enough to apply to the altar's four horns, so it is sprinkled on the side instead.

5:11 In the case of deep poverty the worshiper may bring grain instead of animals from the flock. The prescribed amount, a tenth of an ephah, is equivalent to a day's ration (Ruth 2:17).[66] The Lord's gracious accommodation to accept a lesser offering is balanced by sin's costliness. Sin's cost is calculated not with the Lord in mind but with the sinner. The offering must be costly to each person, proportionate to his economic situation. As David emphatically insists, "I will not offer burnt offerings to the LORD my God that cost me nothing" (2 Sam. 24:24). The law shapes a vision of sacrifice that foreshadows sin's great cost to the Father, who gives his only begotten Son for our forgiveness.

5:12–13 The sacrificial procedure resembles the grain offering—a memorial portion is offered on the altar and the rest given to the priest—but it notably does not create a "pleasing aroma" (cf. Lev. 2:2). It is not offered with the oil and frankincense that produce a soothing scent pleasing to the Lord, since sin is quite the opposite.

---

[64] In the NT confession is both an acknowledgment of sin and an acknowledgment of Christ's lordship (Rom. 10:9–10).
[65] These are the same offerings required for ritual purification from bodily uncleanness (Lev. 15:14–15, 29–30).
[66] Milgrom, *Leviticus 1–16*, 306.

Response

Recently a Christian university in the midwestern United States experienced a special move of God. It began when a few students lingered after chapel to seek the Lord, praying and confessing their sins to one another. Their prayer was answered by an outpouring of the Spirit that drew into worship the rest of the campus and thousands from across the nation. Consonant with what we see in the Scripture, their worship came in an alternating ebb and flow of the proclamation of God's Word, confession of sin, praise, and giving testimony.[67] Historical outpourings of the Spirit in the worldwide church have begun with a heightened consciousness to sin that leads to confession, dramatic witness to the works of God, and ultimately an abiding commitment to walk with him in greater personal holiness.

Confession reaches deeper than an admission of guilt; it owns responsibility for sin, acknowledges the Lord's righteousness, and yields to his sovereign rule to order our lives. Implicit in this act is our desire to direct our will toward change. Grateful for his forgiveness and renewing presence, we earnestly seek the Lord's empowerment to uproot sin from our lives and embrace sanctifying fellowship with him.

This portion of Leviticus teaches us that confession is also a vital part of worship. Although it is natural to think of repentance as something that happens when we come to faith, it has continual relevance for a believer's walk with Christ. A posture that seeks not to grieve the Holy Spirit but grieves over sin, a desire to remain in close communion with the Lord, and a mindful turning back to him are the marks of intentional discipleship. Seasons of individual and corporate repentance in our worship allow us to be restored to the Lord and to one another (James 5:16). We bear witness that "if we confess our sins, he is faithful and just to forgive us our sins and to cleanse us from all unrighteousness" (1 John 1:9). It is to the praise of God that the worship of the gathered church lives out our identity as a people forgiven by the Lamb of God, who takes away the sins of the world (John 1:29).

LEVITICUS 5:14–6:7

14 The LORD spoke to Moses, saying, 15 "If anyone commits a breach of faith and sins unintentionally in any of the holy things of the LORD, he shall bring to the LORD as his compensation, a ram without blemish out of the flock, valued[1] in silver shekels,[2] according to the shekel of the sanctuary, for a guilt offering. 16 He shall also make restitution for what he has done amiss in the holy thing and shall add a fifth to it and give it to the

---

[67] Nehemiah 9; Acts 2; 4; 8; 10.

priest. And the priest shall make atonement for him with the ram of the guilt offering, and he shall be forgiven.

¹⁷ "If anyone sins, doing any of the things that by the LORD's commandments ought not to be done, though he did not know it, then realizes his guilt, he shall bear his iniquity. ¹⁸ He shall bring to the priest a ram without blemish out of the flock, or its equivalent, for a guilt offering, and the priest shall make atonement for him for the mistake that he made unintentionally, and he shall be forgiven. ¹⁹ It is a guilt offering; he has indeed incurred guilt before³ the LORD."

6 ⁴ The LORD spoke to Moses, saying, ² "If anyone sins and commits a breach of faith against the LORD by deceiving his neighbor in a matter of deposit or security, or through robbery, or if he has oppressed his neighbor ³ or has found something lost and lied about it, swearing falsely—in any of all the things that people do and sin thereby— ⁴ if he has sinned and has realized his guilt and will restore what he took by robbery or what he got by oppression or the deposit that was committed to him or the lost thing that he found ⁵ or anything about which he has sworn falsely, he shall restore it in full and shall add a fifth to it, and give it to him to whom it belongs on the day he realizes his guilt. ⁶ And he shall bring to the priest as his compensation to the LORD a ram without blemish out of the flock, or its equivalent, for a guilt offering. ⁷ And the priest shall make atonement for him before the LORD, and he shall be forgiven for any of the things that one may do and thereby become guilty."

¹ Or *flock, or its equivalent* ² A *shekel* was about 2/5 ounce or 11 grams ³ Or *he has paid full compensation to* ⁴ Ch 5:20 in Hebrew

Section Overview

While the language of atonement and forgiveness binds the sin and guilt offerings together (Lev. 5:16, 18; 6:7), these offerings are distinct. Whereas the sin offering cleanses the offerer and the sanctuary from sin's impurity, the guilt offering atones for sacrilege and repairs the relationship broken through sin. Moreover, unlike the sin offering, the guilt offering is not scaled according to status or economic ability but requires the costly sacrifice of a ram in every situation.

Translations traditionally have rendered this as the "guilt offering." The Hebrew *asham* refers to the guilt incurred by a sinner as well as to the offering that atones for it. It captures the experience of guilt and its consequences (5:17; 6:4), as well as the penalty for wrongdoing (5:6, 15), which in the case of sacrilege is an unblemished ram. In light of the latter some modern commentators suggest it be called a "reparation offering."[68]

The guilt offering is mandated for sin directly against the Lord—his sacred gifts and holy name. Since it is sin committed against the Lord, it is sacrilege. This idea is expressed by the Hebrew *ma'al*, which fundamentally means a breach of covenant loyalty. A parallel passage on violations and restitution includes in its discussion the case of the wife suspected of infidelity, driving home the point that disloyalty is personal (Num. 5:6–31). Sacrilege violates not only God's holy

---

[68] Gane, *Leviticus, Numbers*, 132; Hartley, *Leviticus*, 72; Sklar, *Leviticus*, TOTC, 121.

property but his person. It removes what is the Lord's from the status of holy to treat it as common and makes light of his awesome holiness.

The cases are laid out in a clear progression, beginning with known inadvertent violation (vv. 15–16), unknown inadvertent violation (vv. 17–19), and intentional violation (6:1–7). The final violation of another's property is included in the laws of sacrilege because a false oath taken in the Lord's name is an offense that steals something of his honor. The sacrificial procedure for guilt offerings is not rehearsed but taken up in subsequent instructions to the priests (7:1–7). The focus is rather on what the offender must do to repair relationship, namely, make restitution and offer an unblemished ram.

The occasions for making a guilt offering are the following:

(1) inadvertent violation of the Lord's holy property (5:15–19),
(2) violation of the Lord's holy name to defraud another of their property (6:1–7),
(3) reintroduction of a leper into holy community (14:12, 21),
(4) profaning a betrothed slave girl (19:20–21), and
(5) desecration of holy Nazirite status (Num. 6:7–12).

Section Outline

    I. Sacrificial Worship (1:1–7:38) . . .
        E. Guilt Offering (5:14–6:7)
            1. Introduction to the Guilt Offering (5:14)
            2. Case of Sacrilege (5:15–16)
            3. Case of Suspected Sacrilege (5:17–19)
            4. Case of Sacrilege in Swearing Falsely (6:1–7)

Comment

5:14 The introduction marks what follows as divine speech. The guilt offering is commanded by the Lord as the only one who sees hidden sin and can prescribe its remedy.

5:15 The first case of a "breach of faith" (Hb. *ma'al*) is trespass against the gifts dedicated to the Lord that have passed from the worldly, common sphere to become the Lord's holy possession. Sacrilege is so serious a sin that theft of sanctuary property or sacred goods is often punishable by death (Laban's gods, Gen. 31:32; Joseph's divination cup, Gen. 44:9; Belshazzar's feast that profanes the temple vessels, Dan. 5:23, 30). Sacrilege is grasping for one's own use that which belongs to God, illustrated vividly by Achan's theft of devoted things of "silver and gold, and the vessels of bronze and of iron . . . put into the treasury of the house of the LORD" (Josh. 6:24). Achan's sacrilege (*ma'al*) exposed the entire community to divine wrath.

The guilt offering is the Lord's provision for the unintentional violation of holy things, such as when someone inadvertently eats a portion of the firstfruits of his harvest or fails to redeem the firstborn of his male animals that rightly belong to the Lord (Num. 18:12–18). Or when someone other than a priest, such as a guest or daughter married outside of the priestly clan, partakes of the most holy sacrificial portions reserved for those who minister at the altar (Lev. 2:3; 6:25, 29; 7:1, 6; cf. 22:10–16). In these situations the Lord is owed compensation for misappropriated and desacralized holy things. The offender must bring a ram, a choice offering as head of the flock. The ram is "valued in silver shekels," suggesting the offerer has the option to purchase the sacrificial ram at the sanctuary (cf. 2 Kings 12:16).

The shekel in this passage is not currency but more accurately a measure of weight, about 0.4 troy ounces (11.2 g).[69] Before coins were in use payment was made in fragments of precious metal, small ingots, or coiled bracelets weighed out on a balance against stone weights. Payment in the shekel of the sanctuary implies there may have been different weights in use at the temple and marketplace (2 Sam. 14:26). In NT times temple offerings were made only in Tyrian shekels, which were prized for their purity, being over 90 percent silver and weighing 0.45 troy ounces (14 g) (Mishnah, Bekhorot 8:7; cf. Matt. 21:12).[70] Temple offerings would include vows (Leviticus 27), tithes (Deut. 14:24–26), and the redemption of firstborn (Num. 18:15–16), as well as the half shekel atonement money for every male Israelite twenty years and older counted in a census (Ex. 30:11–16). The sanctuary shekel standardizes payment so that rich and poor alike make equal restitution to the Lord whose holiness they have offended.

5:16 As the Lord's instructions continue, it becomes clear that the offering alone is not enough. There must be restitution. Restitution assumes responsibility for the wrong that has ruptured relationship and takes ownership for setting it right by repaying at full cost plus an additional one-fifth of the value. (For a similar 20 percent penalty surrounding holy things cf. comment on 27:11–13).

The offender brings his payment to the priest, servant of the Lord's estate, who makes atonement for the sinner. The divine and human dimensions of forgiveness are both at play. The Lord graciously provides the means to atonement through accepting a ram as a guilt offering, but the sinner must respond to the Lord's initiative in obedience and faith.

5:17 This case is different from the previous one in that the offerer suspects he has violated the Lord's holy things but does not know exactly how. At some point he "realizes his guilt," that is, he suffers the effects of his guilt, which prompts him to bring an offering. "He does not know [what he has done], but he suffers guilt's consequences and bears his punishment."[71] Abimelech suffered the effects of his guilt when the Lord prevented conception in his household before making his sin known in a dream (Gen. 20:17–18).

---

69 David Hendin, *Guide to Biblical Coins*, 6th ed. (New York: American Numismatic Society, 2021), 54. Biblical texts value the sanctuary shekel at 20 gerahs (lit., "grain"), the smallest and most basic unit of measurement (Ex. 30:13; Num. 3:47; Ezek. 45:12). Numerous small limestone scale weights have been found in Israel inscribed with symbols that mark them as shekel weights.
70 Hendin, *Guide to Biblical Coins*, 442. The single coin in the fish's mouth that paid the half shekel tax for both Jesus and Peter was a Tyrian shekel (Matt. 17:24).
71 Sklar, *Leviticus*, TOTC, 122.

Prayers from the ancient world voice the suffering of worshipers who know their affliction is divine but do not know the sin that has caused it.[72] The Bible likewise attributes disease, agricultural disasters, and military defeat to the Lord's divine discipline, all the while affirming that his attention-getting chastisement is to produce repentance and restoration (Lev. 26:14–39).[73] Guilt—its physical effects and emotional experience—gives room for the inward working of the law to shape a conscience that responds to the Lord.

5:18 The offender is liable and will bear the consequences of his wrongdoing despite not being fully aware of his sin. The priest makes atonement for him at the altar, and, if his suffering has been caused by unintentional sin, he will be forgiven and find relief. There is no mention of additional restitution, since the offerer continues to lack knowledge of the specifics. Fear of offending the Lord's holiness is deep rooted and often borne out of piety, as with Job, who makes offerings on behalf of his children to atone for any unknown unintentional sin (Job 1:5).

5:19 A summary statement as with other offerings may have been spoken by the priest in the guilt offering's presentation (Lev. 2:6; 4:24). Instead of rehearsing that the worshiper has "incurred guilt," the second part of the sentence may alternatively be read as "he has paid full compensation to the LORD" (cf. ESV mg.), resounding with the assurance of forgiveness and the clearing of the offerer's conscience.

6:1–3 The third case that requires a guilt offering is one in which the sin has been intentional, as opposed to the first two cases, in which it has been inadvertent. The range of sinful deeds in these verses are all situations in which someone has sworn falsely about something deposited, pledged, robbed, withheld, or lost. These examples are all related to the abuse of power through seizing a pledge given as security against a loan (Deut. 24:6, 10–13), forcibly taking another's property (Mic. 2:1–2), withholding a worker's wages (Lev. 19:13; Deut. 24:14–15), or failing to restore lost property (Deut. 22:1–3). What makes these a breach of faith (Hb. *ma'al*) against the Lord is that the offender has lied under oath.

When it cannot be proven that someone has committed a wrong, an appeal is made to a higher justice. The offender swears by taking an oath in the Lord's name, calling on him to confirm the truthfulness of his testimony (Ex. 22:7–8, 11). God's name is synonymous with God himself. His name represents him and expresses his revealed character (Ex. 3:13–15). In swearing by the Lord's name to cover up sin the offender makes the Lord an accomplice to the crime, dishonoring him and

---

[72] In the popular Mesopotamian composition known as the *Poem of the Righteous Sufferer* the worshiper endures physical illness and mental anguish that make him question how he has sinned, but his fault is never revealed: "Whoever could learn the reasoning of a god, the innermost core of heaven? A (goddess's) intentions, the unknowable depths of the earth, who could fathom them? Where might mere human beings have learned the ways of the gods?"; Righteous Sufferer (Ludlul bēl nēmeqi), II.36–38, https://doi.org/10.5282/ebl/l/2/2.
[73] By no means is personal sin the cause of all suffering, as Job's friends (Job 34:11; 36:6) and Jesus' disciples (John 9:2) come to learn. Yet it is a premise of the covenant that the Lord blesses obedience and punishes disobedience. While in the end God exercises sovereign freedom, cultivating a sensitivity to sin's very real consequences keeps the conscience alive before God.

injuring his reputation. The offender distorts the character of God, who is "exalted in justice" and the "Holy God [who] shows himself holy in righteousness" (Isa. 5:16; cf. Deut. 32:4; Pss. 9:7; 33:5). He misrepresents the Lord, who is the defender of the needy, helper of the weak, and advocate of the vulnerable (Ex. 22:25–27; Ps. 68:5). Swearing falsely profanes the name of the Lord and tarnishes its holiness, when it was every Israelite's privilege to sanctify it instead (Lev. 22:32; Ps. 41:13).

6:4–5 A person who has intentionally sinned but comes to an awareness of his guilt must repay the item in full and add 20 percent to its total. In other laws someone who does not voluntarily confess but is caught with the stolen object in his possession must pay double its value (Ex. 22:4). If he has taken the next step to sell or slaughter the stolen animal, he must pay four to five times its value (Ex. 22:1). But here the person has come forward to confess, and thus the penalty is less.

The offender confesses his sin, as suggested by the parallel passage in Numbers 5:7 and implied by the return of the stolen property.[74] The fruit of genuine repentance is to make restitution to the victim (Matt. 3:8). This acknowledges that all are accountable to the Lord and enacts justice among the covenant community, a theme whose full force will be developed in the second half of the book but which is enduringly present in the sacrificial system.

6:6–7 The Lord is also owed damages, as his name has been misused, and the "LORD will not hold him guiltless who takes his name in vain" (Ex. 20:7; cf. Zech. 5:2–4; 8:16–17). After restitution to the victim a ram is presented at the sanctuary. This order is prioritized also by Jesus: "First be reconciled to your brother, and then come and offer your gift" (Matt. 5:23–24). The offender is reconciled to the person he has wronged and to the Lord on the same day, as was the chief tax collector Zacchaeus, who vowed a fourfold restitution to those he defrauded and dined with the Lord on the same day (Luke 19:8–10).

Response

In soul-searching theological reflection after the exile Israel's story is poignantly retold as one of brazen sacrilege (Hb. *ma'al*). The people persist in idolatry and their kings in rejecting God's law (2 Chron. 12:2; 26:16; 28:19, 22–25) until they progressively become profaned and are no longer recognizable as God's holy nation. It is covenant disloyalty (*ma'al*) that leads to their fall—Israel to Assyria (1 Chron. 5:25–26) and Judah to Babylon (1 Chron. 9:1; 2 Chron. 36:14–16).

Indeed, the story of the world is one of breaking faith with the Lord. Failing to trust that God had given them all they could ever need, Adam and Eve rebelled and violated divinely set boundaries to commit sacrilege against forbidden holy

---

[74] Ritual texts leave much implied. Although confession is not mentioned explicitly, neither is the sacrificial procedure. Milgrom (*Leviticus 1–16*, 301–302) argues that confession changes the status of the offense from "deliberate sins into inadvertences, thereby qualifying them for sacrificial expiation." Viewed more personally, a change of heart in genuine repentance changes the Lord's response toward the sinner. The Lord makes allowance for his intentional (though not "high-handed") sin to be treated as inadvertent and remedied by sacrifice, allowing for the maximal extension of grace.

things. They seized what was not theirs to take and incurred a debt of sin they could never repay. They were expelled from holy ground, their glory desecrated (Rom. 3:23). Yet the Lord, rich in his mercy, forged a way to forgiveness when he sent his own son as a guilt offering (*asham*) to satisfy our debt and heal the chasm of sin's separation (Isa. 53:10). The justice of God demanded satisfaction, and the mercy of God provided its means. Redemption could never be bought with rams in the thousands (Mic. 6:7), but it was purchased by the precious blood of Christ (1 Pet. 1:18–19).

Our debt has been assumed and satisfied by Christ. We are a blood-bought, forgiven people whose only remaining debt is the debt of gratitude for the mercy we have received. We love and forgive one another (Matt. 18:23–35; Rom. 13:8), righting our wrongs and repairing relationship with our brothers and sisters whom we see in the flesh to demonstrate our love for the Lord, whom we cannot see (1 John 4:20–21). He who has forgiven our debts calls us to do the same (Matt. 6:12), displaying to all the world that sin has been defeated, God's redeemed are being sanctified by his indwelling Spirit, and the current of all redemptive history is moving toward holiness.

LEVITICUS 6:8–30

8 1 The LORD spoke to Moses, saying, 9 "Command Aaron and his sons, saying, This is the law of the burnt offering. The burnt offering shall be on the hearth on the altar all night until the morning, and the fire of the altar shall be kept burning on it. 10 And the priest shall put on his linen garment and put his linen undergarment on his body, and he shall take up the ashes to which the fire has reduced the burnt offering on the altar and put them beside the altar. 11 Then he shall take off his garments and put on other garments and carry the ashes outside the camp to a clean place. 12 The fire on the altar shall be kept burning on it; it shall not go out. The priest shall burn wood on it every morning, and he shall arrange the burnt offering on it and shall burn on it the fat of the peace offerings. 13 Fire shall be kept burning on the altar continually; it shall not go out.

14 "And this is the law of the grain offering. The sons of Aaron shall offer it before the LORD in front of the altar. 15 And one shall take from it a handful of the fine flour of the grain offering and its oil and all the frankincense that is on the grain offering and burn this as its memorial portion on the altar, a pleasing aroma to the LORD. 16 And the rest of it Aaron and his sons shall eat. It shall be eaten unleavened in a holy place. In the court of the tent of meeting they shall eat it. 17 It shall not be baked with leaven. I have given it as their portion of my food offerings. It is a thing most holy, like the sin offering and the guilt offering. 18 Every male among the children of Aaron may eat of it, as decreed forever throughout

your generations, from the LORD's food offerings. Whatever touches them shall become holy."

19 The LORD spoke to Moses, saying, 20 "This is the offering that Aaron and his sons shall offer to the LORD on the day when he is anointed: a tenth of an ephah[2] of fine flour as a regular grain offering, half of it in the morning and half in the evening. 21 It shall be made with oil on a griddle. You shall bring it well mixed, in baked[3] pieces like a grain offering, and offer it for a pleasing aroma to the LORD. 22 The priest from among Aaron's sons, who is anointed to succeed him, shall offer it to the LORD as decreed forever. The whole of it shall be burned. 23 Every grain offering of a priest shall be wholly burned. It shall not be eaten."

24 The LORD spoke to Moses, saying, 25 "Speak to Aaron and his sons, saying, This is the law of the sin offering. In the place where the burnt offering is killed shall the sin offering be killed before the LORD; it is most holy. 26 The priest who offers it for sin shall eat it. In a holy place it shall be eaten, in the court of the tent of meeting. 27 Whatever touches its flesh shall be holy, and when any of its blood is splashed on a garment, you shall wash that on which it was splashed in a holy place. 28 And the earthenware vessel in which it is boiled shall be broken. But if it is boiled in a bronze vessel, that shall be scoured and rinsed in water. 29 Every male among the priests may eat of it; it is most holy. 30 But no sin offering shall be eaten from which any blood is brought into the tent of meeting to make atonement in the Holy Place; it shall be burned up with fire."

[1] Ch 6:1 in Hebrew [2] An *ephah* was about 3/5 bushel or 22 liters [3] The meaning of the Hebrew is uncertain

Section Overview

At first glance Leviticus 6–7 appears to repeat the offerings already outlined in the previous five chapters. A closer look, however, reveals that, while the opening words on sacrifice were for the "people of Israel" (1:2), these commands are addressed to both the "people of Israel" (7:23, 29) and the priests who minister at the altar (6:9, 25).

The offerings in this section are arranged in a slightly different order. Israel's call to worship began with first treating the sacrifices that could be voluntary or mandatory (burnt, grain, and peace offerings) and then treating the sacrifices that are always mandatory (sin and guilt offerings). The offerings in this section are presented from the perspective of the priests, who are entrusted with mediating the encounter of a holy God with his covenant people. The concern is for correct ritual performance: distinguishing holy from most holy, properly distributing the sacrificial portions, and overseeing the disposal of sacrificial remains. The offerings are therefore ordered according to their degree of holiness, which is communicated by way of those who partake of their portions. Leading the list is the burnt offering, which is wholly consumed by the Lord, followed by the similarly "most holy" grain, sin, and guilt offerings, portions of which are eaten by the priests, and finally the "holy" peace offering, the greatest portion of which is enjoyed by the offerer. Appropriately, the verb "to eat" holds the laws together, as it appears twenty-nine times throughout these chapters.[75] Equally important is the disposal of the sacrificial remains: the ashes of the burnt offering are removed to a clean place outside the camp, the grain, sin, and guilt offerings are eaten by priests, and the peace offering is burned up if it is not consumed by the conclusion of the allotted ritual time.

TABLE 3.2: Offering, Portions, and Remains

Offering	Sacrificial Portions	Disposal of Remains
Burnt Offering *most holy*[76]	God: whole animal except the skin Officiating priest: animal hide	fatty ashes brought to clean place outside the camp
Grain Offering (Daily) *most holy*	God: handful "memorial" portion mixed with oil, frankincense; unleavened and unfermented Priesthood: the rest; also leavened loaves	eaten by the priesthood
Grain Offering (Priestly)	God: entire grain offering	burned on the altar
Sin Offering *most holy*	God: fat, kidneys, lobe of the liver Officiating priest: meat from the animal; none if offered for the high priest or community	eaten by officiating priest, priests on duty; if high priest / community offering, remains burned outside camp
Guilt Offering *most holy*	God: fat, kidneys, lobe of the liver Officiating priest: meat from the animal	eaten by officiating priest, priests on duty
Peace Offering *holy*	God: fat, kidneys, lobe of the liver Officiating priest: right hindlimb of sacrificial animal; loaves of bread, leavened and unleavened Priesthood & families: breast Worshiper: the rest (most) of animal's meat	eaten by worshiper; if time limit exceeded, then remains are burnt

Food makes a theological statement: "If food is treated as a code, the messages it encodes will be found in the pattern of social relations being expressed. The message is about different degrees of hierarchy, inclusion and exclusion, boundaries and transactions across the boundaries."[77] Grades of holiness in the tent of meeting separate people, places, and food portions, and these distinctions give expression to the Lord's holiness. The priests' role is to safeguard the divine presence by safeguarding these distinctions so that Israelites may continue to meet with the holy God among them, who share his table. Through proper ritual performance and administration of holy things the priests maintain the Lord's presence—the divine fire—in the midst of Israel without themselves being consumed (cf. Ex. 3:2).

Section Outline

I. Sacrificial Worship (1:1–7:38)...
    F. Instructions for Priests (6:8–7:38)

---

[75] John W. Kleinig, *Leviticus*, ConC (St. Louis, MO: Concordia, 2003), 139.
[76] Though not explicit, this is inferred by the fact that all of it is consumed by the Lord.
[77] Mary Douglas, "Deciphering a Meal," *Daedalus* 101 (1972): 61.

1. Law of the Daily Burnt Offering (6:8–13)
2. Law of the Daily Grain Offering (6:14–23)
   a. Congregational Grain Offering (6:14–18)
   b. High Priestly Grain Offering (6:19–23)
3. Law of the Sin Offering (6:24–30)

Comment

6:8–9 The Lord's speech to Moses addresses the priests who serve at the altar. This is the *torah*, ("law" or "divine ritual instruction") given to the priests for carrying out their duties in handling holy things.[78] Priests who have been instructed in the law are responsible for embodying it and teaching it to Israel—how to distinguish between clean and unclean, divide the holy from common, and live within the boundaries set by the Lord (10:10–11). A priest's duty is to safeguard the Lord's holy worship (Ezek. 22:26; Mal. 2:6–7).

Each day at the tent of meeting the burnt offering is sacrificed as the first and last act of worship (Ex. 29:38–42). Since the procedure for making an offering has already been articulated for the worshiper (Lev. 1:1–17), the ritual instruction to the priests covers how to dispose of its remains, giving special attention to the tending of the altar's fire. The whole burnt offering must be left on the altar to be consumed fully by the fire that never goes out (cf. 6:12–13). It is always burning and always ascending as a pleasing aroma before the Lord.

6:10–11 The priest who handles the remains of the daily offering is attired in a white linen tunic and undergarments for propriety as he ascends the altar to remove the ashes and set them by its east side (Ex. 28:42–43). The linen garments are laid aside when the priest steps outside holy ground and exits the camp to dispose of the ashes. His ceremonial dress has been consecrated for service, sprinkled with the blood of the ordination sacrifice and holy oil (Ex. 29:8–9, 21). It is holy and must remain in a holy space (Ex. 28:2; Ezek. 44:19).

Dress is instrumental in ritual performance. The graded spheres of holiness in Israel's sacred tent are signaled by fabric, color, and weave, as cloth demarcates ritual boundaries and defines spheres of service. In keeping with this the priesthood is clothed in fabrics reflective of its sphere of ministry. Priests who serve in the outer court are dressed in tunics and caps of twined linen corresponding to the linen outer hangings that set apart holy ground from the camp surrounding it (Ex. 27:9). The high priest's layered dress corresponds to the linen of the outer court as well as the sanctuary's elaborate fabrics of blue, purple, and scarlet yarns interwoven with gold; he is invested with divine authority to minister within all the holy spaces of the Lord's dwelling place (Exodus 28). The Lord's servants cross the boundaries of holy and common. It is because of their ability to do so that they can represent Israel before the Lord and the Lord to his covenant people.

---

[78] *Torah*, a Hebrew noun deriving from the verb "to teach," is used to refer to the stipulations of the covenant as well any type of instruction.

6:12–13 Live coals that have been left smoldering overnight are stoked into a holy fire in the morning (Lev. 6:9, 12, 13; Ps. 134:1). The altar's fire is never to go out but burns perpetually, aided by the addition of the fat of the peace offerings throughout the day. The command to keep the fire burning is repeated, drawing attention to the fire's importance in sacrificial ministry. While there is no explicit reason given in these preliminary instructions to worship, we see that the fire is lit by the Lord himself at the inauguration of public worship. In the first theophany since Sinai the Lord descends as fire to consume the offerings on the altar and validate visibly the priestly ministry at the tabernacle (Lev. 9:24).

The fire burns "continually" as one of the ongoing rites of tabernacle worship that are performed regularly and uninterruptedly. These include the morning and evening burnt offering accompanied by a grain offering (Ex. 29:38–42), the lighting of the golden lampstand in the Holy Place (Lev. 24:1–4), the burning of fragrant incense (Ex. 30:7–9), the setting out of the showbread on the golden table (Ex. 25:30), and the continual grain offering of the priests (Lev. 6:20; Num. 4:16). To these may be added the high priest's ministry of bringing Israel to remembrance before the Lord at the appointed times of worship through his ceremonial dress (Ex. 28:29–30, 38). These are the daily rituals and physical signs that testify of the Lord's abiding and committed covenant presence among his people. The ongoing regular rites reflect the worship that is his in heaven as it has come to earth. Indeed, with the exception of the showbread set out weekly on the Sabbath, these rites are performed twice daily, creating a continuous flow of offerings on the altar, light in the tent, and incense wafting heavenward throughout the day. This is worship without ceasing.

6:14–15 The grain offering is addressed next since it is offered on the altar as part of the daily offering at the tent of meeting. The instructions rehearse Leviticus 2:2–3 in scripting how the priests must offer a memorial portion of a handful of grain mixed with oil, along with frankincense. The instructions detail where the grain must be eaten, all the while emphasizing its holiness. Priestly consumption is part of the ritual process.[79]

6:16–18 After the token handful of grain is offered on the altar the Lord assigns the remainder to the priests as their daily portion (2:3, 10). The use of "portion" is telling, as it is the typical way of referring to the land allotments given to the rest of the tribes of Israel. Although Levi has no share in the land, it receives its daily bread from God's table, as he assures the Levites in his own words: "I am your portion and your inheritance among the people of Israel" (Num. 18:20).

The grain is "most holy," meaning two things: (1) it cannot be taken out of the sacred precincts but must be eaten in the area of the courtyard beside the altar (Lev. 10:12–13), and (2) it must be eaten only by the priests who minister there. The priestly instructions include as an aside that this holds true for the

---

[79] Baruch A. Levine, *Leviticus*, JPSTC (Philadelphia, PA: Jewish Publication Society, 1989), 37.

sin and guilt offerings as well; they are in the category of most holy. That which is most holy is consumed in the Lord's presence, therefore priests may not share it with their households as the peace offering (7:34–35). Later, special rooms in the temple complex are reserved for the priests' consumption of the most holy offerings (Ezek. 42:13).

The explanation that "whatever touches them [the offerings] shall become holy" allows for different readings. Grammatically, it can be interpreted in one of two ways: anyone who touches this flesh will *become* holy (i.e., contract holiness from the holy meat) or *must be* holy (i.e., be in the appropriate ritual state in order to consume holy food). Since the context of these laws relates to the priestly portions of sacrificial offerings, it is best to understand these instructions as underscoring that only those who are holy can consume the sacrificial food portions. This is closely related to another set of instructions directed to the priesthood: no priest who has come in contact with uncleanness "may eat of the holy things until he is clean" (Lev. 22:4) nor "eat of the holy things unless he has bathed his body in water" (22:6). Israel's sacred tent features graded levels of holiness in space, persons, and offerings, and it is the priesthood's role to ensure boundaries are not breached when consuming the sacrificial portions.

6:19–21 On the day the high priest is ordained to serve at the altar and every day thereafter he is to offer a tenth of an ephah of flour, approximately a day's ration of about 1 dry gallon (2.2 l), on behalf of himself and his sons. The flour is soaked in oil, cooked on a griddle, and broken into pieces. Half of it he offers in the morning and half in the evening to accompany the daily burnt offering (Ex. 29:40–41).

6:22–23 It is the privilege of every high priest who will succeed Aaron to offer the priestly grain portion as an expression of homage to the Lord who provides for the priestly family its daily bread (Lev. 2:3; 24:9). It is a daily tribute (Hb. *minkhah*) of loyalty.[80] The crumbled grain is wholly consumed on the altar. No one may eat of it. This daily offering allows the priests to join their worship to that of the nation's in tangible symbols of devotion.

6:24–26 The sin offering is to be slaughtered in the same place as the burnt offering, that is, on the north side of the altar (1:11). The officiating priest is given the meaty portions after the fat is separated for burning on the altar and the entrails and legs for burning outside the camp (4:11–12). Since the meat is "most holy," he must eat it in the courtyard's holy area and so stay within the appropriate ritual boundaries for the food's most holy status (cf. 10:12).

The expression "the priest who offers it for sin" is unique in Leviticus, focusing attention on the priest who serves at the altar on behalf of the worshiper. Instructions given to the Israelites on bringing a sin offering likewise highlight the priest's role as the one who makes atonement for the sinner and pronounces

---

[80] Roy E. Gane, "Ritual and Religious Practices," in *The Oxford Handbook of Ritual and Worship in the Hebrew Bible*, ed. Samuel E. Balentine (Oxford: Oxford University Press, 2020), 229.

the Lord's forgiveness (cf. 4:20, 26, 31, 35). Therefore, the command in 6:25, that the officiating priest must consume the sin offering, must serve a purpose. Derek Kidner proposes the reason for this may be that, as the priest eats the sacrifice, he representatively enacts the Lord's acceptance of it.[81]

6:27–28 In the course of presenting the sin offering the blood applied to the horns of the altar and poured at its base may spatter the priest's garments (cf. 4:25). He is to wash his garments "in a holy place." The concern that comes through is to keep that which is holy in the holy sphere, taking care in how holy meat and its blood are handled. It is reiterated that whatever, or *whoever*, touches the offering must be holy.

The vessels in which sacrificial meat is cooked must be cleansed thoroughly after being used for a meal that was "most holy." Ceramic pots, which are porous with permeable boundaries, are broken and put out of use. Bronze vessels, whose boundaries are nonpermeable, are scoured, polished clean, and rinsed in water. To wash garments and pots ensures that whatever is most holy will not be brought into contact with the common.[82]

6:29–30 The meat of an individual's sin offering may be eaten by the male priests who have been consecrated to serve at the altar and are at a level of holiness in keeping with the offering. The exception is with a sin offering made on behalf of the high priest or the congregation, whose blood has been brought into the Holy Place (4:11–12, 21). It may not be eaten.

Response

One of the most monumental boundary crossings in history has been humanity's crossing into outer space. The first people to ever set foot on the moon, Buzz Aldrin and Neil Armstrong, deposited a plaque on the moon's surface to commemorate their journey into unexplored realms: "Here men from the planet Earth first set foot upon the moon July 1969, A.D. We came in peace for all mankind."

A lesser-known aspect of their visit was the performance of a symbolic act of even greater significance. Searching for a way to express the gratitude and magnitude of the moment, Buzz Aldrin had brought among his personal effects elements of the Lord's table—a piece of broken bread from a loaf that he had shared in communion with his church in Houston and a small vial of wine. He recalls partaking of holy food in unity with the body of Christ on earth: "I poured the wine into the chalice our church had given me. In the one-sixth gravity of the moon the wine curled slowly and gracefully up the side of the cup. It was interesting to think that the very first liquid ever poured on the moon, and the first food eaten there, were communion elements."[83]

---

81 Quoted in Hartley, *Leviticus*, 98.
82 Sklar, *Leviticus*, TOTC, 131.
83 "Guideposts Classics: When Buzz Aldrin Took Communion on the Moon," Finding Life Purpose, Guideposts, accessed May 24, 2024, https://guideposts.org/positive-living/health-and-wellness/life-advice/finding-life-purpose/guideposts-classics-when-buzz-aldrin-took-communion-on-the-moon.

Whatever we make of Aldrin's actions, it is clear that food makes a theological statement. The Lord who extends his presence and redemptive activity to reclaim a fallen world does so "through human agents, ritual symbols, and material objects, to the farthest reaches of the cosmos."[84] And he does so as an act of love that invites belief and looks forward to the day when all those who trust in him will feast at the marriage supper of the Lamb (Rev. 19:9).

LEVITICUS 7

7 "This is the law of the guilt offering. It is most holy. ²In the place where they kill the burnt offering they shall kill the guilt offering, and its blood shall be thrown against the sides of the altar. ³And all its fat shall be offered, the fat tail, the fat that covers the entrails, ⁴the two kidneys with the fat that is on them at the loins, and the long lobe of the liver that he shall remove with the kidneys. ⁵The priest shall burn them on the altar as a food offering to the Lord; it is a guilt offering. ⁶Every male among the priests may eat of it. It shall be eaten in a holy place. It is most holy. ⁷The guilt offering is just like the sin offering; there is one law for them. The priest who makes atonement with it shall have it. ⁸And the priest who offers any man's burnt offering shall have for himself the skin of the burnt offering that he has offered. ⁹And every grain offering baked in the oven and all that is prepared on a pan or a griddle shall belong to the priest who offers it. ¹⁰And every grain offering, mixed with oil or dry, shall be shared equally among all the sons of Aaron.

¹¹"And this is the law of the sacrifice of peace offerings that one may offer to the Lord. ¹²If he offers it for a thanksgiving, then he shall offer with the thanksgiving sacrifice unleavened loaves mixed with oil, unleavened wafers smeared with oil, and loaves of fine flour well mixed with oil. ¹³With the sacrifice of his peace offerings for thanksgiving he shall bring his offering with loaves of leavened bread. ¹⁴And from it he shall offer one loaf from each offering, as a gift to the Lord. It shall belong to the priest who throws the blood of the peace offerings. ¹⁵And the flesh of the sacrifice of his peace offerings for thanksgiving shall be eaten on the day of his offering. He shall not leave any of it until the morning. ¹⁶But if the sacrifice of his offering is a vow offering or a freewill offering, it shall be eaten on the day that he offers his sacrifice, and on the next day what remains of it shall be eaten. ¹⁷But what remains of the flesh of the sacrifice on the third day shall be burned up with fire. ¹⁸If any of the flesh of the sacrifice of his peace offering is eaten on the third day, he who offers it shall not be accepted, neither shall it be credited to him. It is tainted, and he who eats of it shall bear his iniquity.

¹⁹"Flesh that touches any unclean thing shall not be eaten. It shall be burned up with fire. All who are clean may eat flesh, ²⁰but the person

---

84 Samuel E. Balentine, *Leviticus*, Interpretation (Louisville: Westminster John Knox, 2011), 67.

who eats of the flesh of the sacrifice of the Lord's peace offerings while an uncleanness is on him, that person shall be cut off from his people. ²¹ And if anyone touches an unclean thing, whether human uncleanness or an unclean beast or any unclean detestable creature, and then eats some flesh from the sacrifice of the Lord's peace offerings, that person shall be cut off from his people."

²² The Lord spoke to Moses, saying, ²³ "Speak to the people of Israel, saying, You shall eat no fat, of ox or sheep or goat. ²⁴ The fat of an animal that dies of itself and the fat of one that is torn by beasts may be put to any other use, but on no account shall you eat it. ²⁵ For every person who eats of the fat of an animal of which a food offering may be made to the Lord shall be cut off from his people. ²⁶ Moreover, you shall eat no blood whatever, whether of fowl or of animal, in any of your dwelling places. ²⁷ Whoever eats any blood, that person shall be cut off from his people."

²⁸ The Lord spoke to Moses, saying, ²⁹ "Speak to the people of Israel, saying, Whoever offers the sacrifice of his peace offerings to the Lord shall bring his offering to the Lord from the sacrifice of his peace offerings. ³⁰ His own hands shall bring the Lord's food offerings. He shall bring the fat with the breast, that the breast may be waved as a wave offering before the Lord. ³¹ The priest shall burn the fat on the altar, but the breast shall be for Aaron and his sons. ³² And the right thigh you shall give to the priest as a contribution from the sacrifice of your peace offerings. ³³ Whoever among the sons of Aaron offers the blood of the peace offerings and the fat shall have the right thigh for a portion. ³⁴ For the breast that is waved and the thigh that is contributed I have taken from the people of Israel, out of the sacrifices of their peace offerings, and have given them to Aaron the priest and to his sons, as a perpetual due from the people of Israel. ³⁵ This is the portion of Aaron and of his sons from the Lord's food offerings, from the day they were presented to serve as priests of the Lord. ³⁶ The Lord commanded this to be given them by the people of Israel, from the day that he anointed them. It is a perpetual due throughout their generations."

³⁷ This is the law of the burnt offering, of the grain offering, of the sin offering, of the guilt offering, of the ordination offering, and of the peace offering, ³⁸ which the Lord commanded Moses on Mount Sinai, on the day that he commanded the people of Israel to bring their offerings to the Lord, in the wilderness of Sinai.

Section Overview

The offering laws continue, with directives on priestly portions and the disposal of sacrificial remains (cf. table 3.2 in Section Overview of 6:8–30). The Lord instructs his people as divine householder of all creation. All belongs to him (Ps. 50:10–15), and he apportions it according to his will, giving each his or her due (Ps. 145:14–15). These laws put on display the Lord's kingship; as host of the great banquet feast, he invites his people to eat from his table. Priests who have been consecrated to serve on holy ground dine daily in his presence. Lay Israelites who come bringing offerings of praise also enjoy the hospitality of the royal table. As a king feeds his courtiers, so the Lord feeds his royal household (cf. 2 Sam. 9:7; Est. 2:9; Jer. 52:33–34; Dan. 1:5). The protocol of the sacrificial table orients every Israelite's life-sustaining activity of eating toward the kingship claims of Yahweh.

Section Outline

I.F. Instructions for Priests (6:8–7:38) . . .
    4. Law of the Guilt Offering (7:1–7)
    5. Summary of Priestly Portions (7:8–10)
    6. Law of the Peace Offering (7:11–36)
        a. Peace Offering (7:11–21)
        b. Sacrificial Portions (7:22–36)
            i. Blood and Fat Prohibitions (7:22–27)
            ii. Priestly Portions (7:28–36)
    7. Concluding Summary (7:37–38)

Comment

7:1–2 Instructions regarding Israel's gifts continue with the guilt offering, whose holiness is underscored at the beginning and end of the instructions (vv. 1, 6). The sacrificial procedure is similar to that for the sin offering—slaughtered on the north side of the altar, the fat turned to smoke, and its meat portions eaten by the priests in the vicinity of the altar. The difference between the two is in how the blood is handled: the blood of the guilt offering is dashed against the sides of the altar, whereas that of the sin offering is sprinkled inside the tent and smeared on the altar's horns (cf. ch. 4).

7:3–5 Table protocol calls for honoring the Lord by separating out his portion first (cf. 1 Sam. 2:15–17). The sacrificial animal's choicest portion is offered, consisting of the fat around its vital organs together with the liver lobe and kidneys.

7:6–7 The officiating priest then receives the meat he is to share with his male family members, that is, those serving in the tabernacle, as well as with other priests on duty. Since the guilt offering is "most holy," its flesh must remain in the sacred precincts and be eaten in the outer court by the priests who have been ordained to approach the "most holy" altar. The offering's holiness is guarded by keeping it near the anointed altar (Ex. 30:26–29), to be consumed by the anointed priesthood (Ex. 30:30). The image is that of the Lord's priestly household gathered around his table.

7:8 Having detailed the priestly portions for the guilt and sin offerings, the instructions look back to the burnt and grain offerings. The officiating priest who presents a worshiper's burnt offering is entitled to its hide.[85] Animal skins were valued for

---

[85] This law refers to the individual's gift ("any man's burnt offering"). The hides of the public burnt offering may have likewise gone to the officiating priest or may have even been used for writing. It was a priestly responsibility to oversee the copying of the law for the king (Deut. 17:18) and to read it to the congregation every seven years (Deut. 31:9–13).

the leather goods that could be produced from them, such as sandals, belts, water flasks, and tent coverings.

7:9–10 As for the cooked grain offerings (Lev. 2:4–7), they are apportioned to the priest who presents them, while the raw grain offerings (2:3) belong to the entire priesthood. Raw grain could be stored and shared with all priests who came to serve at the tabernacle (priestly rotations are later systematized for temple service; cf. 1 Chronicles 24; Luke 1:8–9).

7:11 The peace offering is celebrated as a communal meal shared among the Lord, his priests, and the worshiper. It is a voluntary offering brought to express thanksgiving for answered prayer or praise at the fulfillment of a vow, or as a spontaneous gift of gratitude. Instructions on the various sacrificial portions address each of these three occasions to supplement the teaching of Leviticus 3.

7:12–14 In addition to a male or female animal of the offerer's choosing a thanksgiving offering must be accompanied by bread to round out the meal.[86] Unleavened loaves and wafers were made by mixing flour and water with oil to soften the dough, to which a pinch of salt was added. Leavened loaves were the same recipe, with added sourdough from a previous batch. These are offered to the Lord but go to the officiating priest as his share for performing the sacrificial ministry. They are a "gift to the LORD," or contribution (Hb. *terumah*), set apart to maintain those who minister at the altar. "One loaf from each offering," leavened and unleavened, goes to the priest and his family, while the rest are eaten by the worshiper and his household as part of the fellowship meal.

7:15 The worshiper retains the largest portion of the meat to eat in the Lord's presence, which could be the courtyard area[87] but could also presumably be at home if the home is ritually pure.[88] In either case that which is usually a priestly privilege is extended to the covenant family, as lay Israelites are welcomed to the table of the Lord to feast as his guests.

The sacrificial meat of the thanksgiving offering must be wholly consumed on the day it is slaughtered. No reason is given, but the outcome would be to help prevent the meat from becoming profaned (cf. 22:29–30) and to encourage a spirit of generosity in inviting the greater community to share in the feast. A single household could not consume the entire animal in a single day, so the extended family, neighbors, and friends—including the poor, widow, and the orphan among them—are folded into the celebration (Deut. 12:10–12; Luke 14:12–14).

---

86 Filling out the image of the meal, Numbers 15:2–5 prescribes that wine should also be offered.
87 Milgrom, *Leviticus 1–16*, 458. At the site of biblical Dan (Tel Dan) cooking pots, bones, and feasting remains were found in the open-air courtyard beside the altar, supporting the interpretation that worshipers feasted there; Jonathan S. Greer, *Dinner at Dan* (Leiden: Brill, 2013). In NT times the entire city of Jerusalem was regarded as having the holiness of the altar area, allowing worshipers to eat the Passover meal in homes within the city (Mishnah, Zevahim 5:6–8).
88 Cf. Leviticus 10:14. Later verses explain what is to be done with leftover portions on days two and three (7:16–17). It seems most likely these are leftover portions at the offerer's home, not leftover portions that remain in the tabernacle courtyard overnight.

An occasion of great joy for the worshiper is not contained within his household alone but overflows into the life of the congregation. As part of the celebration the worshiper gives public testimony of the Lord's faithfulness before all who join the table (Pss. 56:12–13; 107:19–22). The praise of God's goodness and exaltation of his character is no less a "sacrifice of thanksgiving" than the slaughtered animal (Pss. 50:14; 116:17).

7:16–18 The worshiper who brings an offering in fulfillment of a vow or as a freewill offering can eat its meat until the second day, but not on the third. Since the animal has been offered to the Lord, its meat is part of a holy meal that the worshiper receives back from the Lord's table and so must be treated properly; otherwise the gift is rejected and, rather than making the offerer acceptable before the Lord (Lev. 1:3), counts against him.[89] Any leftovers must be burned. Israelites are encouraged to eat the meat fresh and not keep it (cf. the commands about the manna in the wilderness; Ex. 16:19–20). This posture of daily dependence cultivates not only trust in the Lord for daily bread but also generosity toward others.

7:19–21 Great concern must be shown in guarding the holiness of the Lord's table, especially as the peace offering invites lay Israelites to feast on meat dedicated to the Lord. Instructions dealing with ritual purity highlight this is no ordinary meal but one consumed *in God's presence*. Therefore only those who are in a state of ritual purity may feast on sacrificial meat, because in partaking of this meal they are coming before the Lord. Those who are ritually impure[90] or have been in contact with anything unclean[91] are disqualified from the meal (Lev. 22:3; Hag. 2:13). Every participant examines himself, acting as a priest tasked with discriminating between clean and unclean (Lev. 10:10) and discerning whether he is fit to appear before the Lord.

A breach of table protocol carries the penalty of being "cut off." A person can be cut off from his people,[92] from Israel,[93] from the midst of the assembly,[94] or from the Lord's presence.[95] Cutting off spans a wide arc to encompass the potential extinction of one's family line, ostracism from the covenant community, exclusion from the sanctuary, or ultimately, estrangement from the Lord in life or in death (for the latter cf. comment on 20:4–5). The expression may be related to the solemn ceremony of "cutting covenant" (Hb. *karat berit*), in which parties pass through the pieces of animals cut in half (Gen. 15:9–10), symbolically taking curses upon themselves should they fail to keep the covenant: "The men who transgressed my

---

89 In this case third-day meat is considered "tainted," a term that refers elsewhere not to spoiled meat but to meat considered ritually offensive; cf. Isa. 65:4; Ezek. 4:14. "Lev 19:7–8 uses it to describe sacrificial meat that has been 'profaned,' that is, treated as common instead of as holy—a terrible ritual offense" (Sklar, *Leviticus*, ZECOT, 231).
90 Ritual impurity could result from childbirth (Lev. 12:2, 5), genital discharges in general (15:2), or "leprous" eruptions on the body, clothing, or home (13:3, 55; 14:44).
91 Examples include coming in contact with the carcass of an unclean animal (Lev. 11:24–26), human corpse (Num. 19:11), or someone with a discharge (Lev. 15:4, 20).
92 Exodus 30:33, 38; 31:14; Leviticus 7:20, 21, 25, 27; 17:4, 9; 18:29; 19:8; 20:18; 23:29; Numbers 9:13; 15:30.
93 Exodus 12:15, 19; Numbers 19:13.
94 Numbers 19:20.
95 Leviticus 22:3.

covenant and did not keep the terms of the covenant that they made before me, I will make them like the calf that they cut in two and passed between its parts" (Jer. 34:18). The severest of penalties is to be cut off from the covenanted people and even from life itself.

Offenses carrying the penalty of being cut off are primarily against the Lord and his holy worship.[96] Notably, a considerable number relate to food: failing to fast on the Day of Atonement (Lev. 23:29), appropriating the Lord's portion (3:17; 7:25–27; 17:10, 14), consuming yeast during the Feast of Unleavened Bread (Ex. 12:15, 19), or eating in fellowship with the Lord in the incompatible state of ritual impurity (Lev. 7:20–21; 19:8; 22:3). The laws of the Lord's table are taken seriously (cf. the cutting off of Eli's house for dishonoring the sacrificial meal in 1 Sam. 2:29–34).

7:22–36 The law of the peace offering continues with specifying the sacrificial portions for the Lord (Lev. 7:22–27) and his servants, the priests (vv. 28–36).

7:22–25 The fat of all sacrificial animals belongs to the Lord; anyone who consumes the Lord's portion will be cut off. This applies to all sacrifices. As for fat that cannot be offered on the altar, such as that from a carcass or mauled animal, it may be put to other use—as lamp oil, hand salve, soap, or hair oil.

7:26–27 Equally prohibited is the consumption of blood (in the meat) of any animal, sacrificial or not.[97] The command to refrain from eating blood "in any of your dwelling places" that ends the peace offering is repeated for emphasis (3:17).

7:28–30 Since the meat of the peace offering belongs primarily to the worshiper, there is a different protocol for offering its reserved portions: a worshiper is to present the fat and breast with "his own hands." The fat is surrendered to the priest for burning on the altar as usual, but the breast is elevated before the Lord in imitation of the upward ascent of offerings on the altar as they rise heavenward in smoke (cf. 1:9). It appears the priests are the ones who lift the designated portions to dedicate them to the Lord's use (9:21; 14:12; cf. esp. 23:12 with 23:11). The initial contact with the worshiper's hands, however, makes clear the identity of the offerer.

The translation of "wave offering" (Hb. *tenufah*) suggests a back-and-forth movement, variously interpreted as either a side-to-side or a raising-and-lowering motion. Evidence of ritual practice in paintings and reliefs from the ancient Near East suggests that dedication was performed as an upward lifting toward the deity, favoring the motion of elevation, which is why this is sometimes called an "elevation offering."[98] The meaning of the ritual gesture, however, is beyond

---

96 Examples include the desecration of the Sabbath (Ex. 31:14), practicing divination and idolatry (Lev. 20:3, 5, 6), failing to celebrate the Lord's deliverance in the Passover sacrifice (Num. 9:13), and misappropriating the holy anointing oil and incense for personal use (Ex. 30:33, 38).
97 Birds, which were not offered as fellowship offerings, are mentioned here, suggesting that this verse is prohibiting consuming blood in the meat of any animal.
98 Milgrom, *Leviticus 1–16*, 469–473; Hartley, *Leviticus*, 91.

dispute: by being "waved [or "elevated"] ... before the LORD"[99] the sacred gift is transferred from the worshiper's possession into the Lord's and from the common sphere to sacred use.

7:31 The breast is the portion assigned "for Aaron and his sons," meaning all the priests and their families. The breast (brisket) is a choice cut, meaty enough to provide for the priestly servants ministering at the tabernacle. It is generous but not extravagant (priests are entitled to the sheep and goats of the sin and guilt offerings but only a share of the beef). Notably, in the case of priests who do not present the particular offering, no family among them receives a preferential portion; they all receive from the specified share.[100] There is equality around the Lord's table.

7:32–33 The right thigh is given to the priest who presents the peace offering. The animal's right hindlimb is set apart as a "contribution" (Hb. *terumah*), a consecrated gift, to the Lord reserved for the officiating priest and his family (Num. 18:19).[101] The hindlimb must have been considered a special portion; when Saul was anointed king, he was made an honored guest at a banquet, given a position at the head of the table, and served the reserved thigh portion (1 Sam. 9:22–24).

7:34–36 The brisket and right shank are the Lord's gift to the priesthood, encapsulated in a wordplay through the unusual word for "portion" (Hb. *mishkhah*) that sounds like the word "anoint" (*mashakh*). From the day the priests are anointed and ordained to ministry (Lev. 8:30) they are entitled to the "anointed" share for their service. The portion matches the person in holiness. While this rightly may be thought of as their payment for serving at the altar, it is not spoken of as such. Rather it is viewed as the Lord's apportioning their due. Priestly portions are allotted to the tribe of Levi in the same way that territorial portions have been allotted to the rest of Israel (Ezek. 44:28–30). For all other Israelites their sustenance will come from working the land, but the priests will "feast on the abundance of [God's] house" (Ps. 36:8).

7:37–38 These verses summarize Leviticus 6:8–7:36 as laws for the ritual performance of Israel's major offerings. Included among them is the ordination offering, a type of peace offering that anticipates the priesthood's installation into office in the following chapter. This section concludes the sacrificial laws and prepares the way for the priesthood's ordination (ch. 8) and its ministry in the tent of meeting (ch. 9).

---

99 Examples of such offerings include sacrificial portions from the priesthood's ordination ceremony (Lev. 8:25–27), grain sheaves and baked loaves (23:11, 17), and precious materials for the tabernacle's construction (Ex. 35:22).
100 Temple records from Egypt and Mesopotamia show that different classes of priests received prebends according to their rank. In the Mesopotamian temple of Eanna, for example, the chief priest was allotted the heart, a kidney, and a choice shoulder cut, whereas the singers received the head and the butcher the hide. (Cf. also Hannah's favored portion in 1 Sam. 1:5.)
101 Feasting activities at the idolatrous temple at Tel Dan show that priests ate in side rooms to the west of the courtyard, where bone remains of priestly portions (right-sided hindlimbs and animal hides) have been found.

Response

In the Lord's kingdom economy he chooses sacrificial giving as the path to meeting the needs of his people. While he could have given the priests land and the ability to provide for themselves and their families, he chooses not to. This is so that priest and worshiper can serve one another—the priests by mediating at the altar and worshipers by sharing a portion of their sustenance. They each give out of obedience and trust *in the Lord*—the priests live in faith that he will provide for their needs and the worshipers bring their offerings in faith that he will find them pleasing and acceptable. The Lord cultivates an ethic of mutual dependence and selfless giving among the people who make him known in the world (Phil. 2:4).

This is still the Lord's will for us today, as Paul reasons: "Do you not know that those who are employed in the temple service get their food from the temple, and those who serve at the altar share in the sacrificial offerings? In the same way, the Lord commanded that those who proclaim the gospel should get their living by the gospel" (1 Cor. 9:13–14; cf. Gal. 6:6). In practical advice on living out the faith we are called to set aside a "priestly portion" to sustain those who have dedicated their lives to ministry. Pastors, missionaries, and servants of the gospel who have consecrated their lives to the Lord's service are worthy of being supported for their honorable work in God's kingdom (1 Tim. 5:18).

As the community of faith is shaped by selfless giving, it reflects the Lord's divine self-giving. Israelite worshipers feasted *in anticipation* of the sacrificial meal the Lord was preparing for his people since the foundation of the world. Indeed, Jesus is our portion, and he invites us to the table to give us his body as nourishment for our souls (Luke 22:19–20). As worshipers in the old covenant had to examine themselves lest they come with ritual impurity, so we are called to examine ourselves and guard the holiness of the Lord's table. The Lord's Supper requires the respect of a sacrificial meal: it must be eaten in purity, after we have confessed our sins and reconciled with our covenant family. To come to the table unworthily or without regard for our brothers and sisters who eat with us brings judgment (1 Cor. 11:27–32). No doubt Paul had Leviticus 6–7 in mind when he said that many in Corinth were ill and had died, recalling that those who ate in contempt of the Lord would be cut off (Lev. 7:20–21). The meal celebrated in community that nurtures our fellowship in the faith cannot be one that we come to with flagrant sin, unrepentant hearts, or divisions. We cannot come dissatisfied with our portion, seeking more than is given us at the expense of others (1 Cor. 11:20–21). Eating in fellowship with the Lord and with one another requires unity of spirit and the purity and righteousness that come from being in communion with the Holy One. We feast together in remembrance but also *in anticipation*. As we await the marriage banquet of the Lamb, may we display faithfully the generous and self-giving character of our King.

LEVITICUS 8

8 The LORD spoke to Moses, saying, 2 "Take Aaron and his sons with him, and the garments and the anointing oil and the bull of the sin offering and the two rams and the basket of unleavened bread. 3 And assemble all the congregation at the entrance of the tent of meeting." 4 And Moses did as the LORD commanded him, and the congregation was assembled at the entrance of the tent of meeting.

5 And Moses said to the congregation, "This is the thing that the LORD has commanded to be done." 6 And Moses brought Aaron and his sons and washed them with water. 7 And he put the coat on him and tied the sash around his waist and clothed him with the robe and put the ephod on him and tied the skillfully woven band of the ephod around him, binding it to him with the band.¹ 8 And he placed the breastpiece on him, and in the breastpiece he put the Urim and the Thummim. 9 And he set the turban on his head, and on the turban, in front, he set the golden plate, the holy crown, as the LORD commanded Moses.

10 Then Moses took the anointing oil and anointed the tabernacle and all that was in it, and consecrated them. 11 And he sprinkled some of it on the altar seven times, and anointed the altar and all its utensils and the basin and its stand, to consecrate them. 12 And he poured some of the anointing oil on Aaron's head and anointed him to consecrate him. 13 And Moses brought Aaron's sons and clothed them with coats and tied sashes around their waists and bound caps on them, as the LORD commanded Moses.

14 Then he brought the bull of the sin offering, and Aaron and his sons laid their hands on the head of the bull of the sin offering. 15 And he² killed it, and Moses took the blood, and with his finger put it on the horns of the altar around it and purified the altar and poured out the blood at the base of the altar and consecrated it to make atonement for it. 16 And he took all the fat that was on the entrails and the long lobe of the liver and the two kidneys with their fat, and Moses burned them on the altar. 17 But the bull and its skin and its flesh and its dung he burned up with fire outside the camp, as the LORD commanded Moses.

18 Then he presented the ram of the burnt offering, and Aaron and his sons laid their hands on the head of the ram. 19 And he killed it, and Moses threw the blood against the sides of the altar. 20 He cut the ram into pieces, and Moses burned the head and the pieces and the fat. 21 He washed the entrails and the legs with water, and Moses burned the whole ram on the altar. It was a burnt offering with a pleasing aroma, a food offering for the LORD, as the LORD commanded Moses.

22 Then he presented the other ram, the ram of ordination, and Aaron and his sons laid their hands on the head of the ram. 23 And he killed it, and Moses took some of its blood and put it on the lobe of Aaron's right ear and on the thumb of his right hand and on the big toe of his right foot. 24 Then he presented Aaron's sons, and Moses put some of the blood

on the lobes of their right ears and on the thumbs of their right hands and on the big toes of their right feet. And Moses threw the blood against the sides of the altar. ²⁵ Then he took the fat and the fat tail and all the fat that was on the entrails and the long lobe of the liver and the two kidneys with their fat and the right thigh, ²⁶ and out of the basket of unleavened bread that was before the Lord he took one unleavened loaf and one loaf of bread with oil and one wafer and placed them on the pieces of fat and on the right thigh. ²⁷ And he put all these in the hands of Aaron and in the hands of his sons and waved them as a wave offering before the Lord. ²⁸ Then Moses took them from their hands and burned them on the altar with the burnt offering. This was an ordination offering with a pleasing aroma, a food offering to the Lord. ²⁹ And Moses took the breast and waved it for a wave offering before the Lord. It was Moses' portion of the ram of ordination, as the Lord commanded Moses.

³⁰ Then Moses took some of the anointing oil and of the blood that was on the altar and sprinkled it on Aaron and his garments, and also on his sons and his sons' garments. So he consecrated Aaron and his garments, and his sons and his sons' garments with him.

³¹ And Moses said to Aaron and his sons, "Boil the flesh at the entrance of the tent of meeting, and there eat it and the bread that is in the basket of ordination offerings, as I commanded, saying, 'Aaron and his sons shall eat it.' ³² And what remains of the flesh and the bread you shall burn up with fire. ³³ And you shall not go outside the entrance of the tent of meeting for seven days, until the days of your ordination are completed, for it will take seven days to ordain you. ³⁴ As has been done today, the Lord has commanded to be done to make atonement for you. ³⁵ At the entrance of the tent of meeting you shall remain day and night for seven days, performing what the Lord has charged, so that you do not die, for so I have been commanded." ³⁶ And Aaron and his sons did all the things that the Lord commanded by Moses.

¹ Hebrew *with it* ² Probably Aaron or his representative; possibly Moses; also verses 16–23

Section Overview

This chapter takes place at the foot of Mount Sinai, a year after the exodus from Egypt. The Lord has given specific instructions to Moses about the construction of his dwelling place (Exodus 25–31), and the people have carried them out according to his word (Exodus 35–39). What remains is for the tabernacle to be consecrated as holy ground and for servants to be set apart to minister in its courts. Leviticus 8 picks up the narrative with the final preparations before formal worship at the tabernacle begins (cf. Ex. 40:12–16).

Arrayed in holy garments, the priests undergo a weeklong consecration rite to become fit for divine service. Aaron and his sons are passive recipients of the rites performed upon them—washing, ceremonial robing, anointing with oil, and sprinkling with blood. Moreover, they do not offer their own sacrifices; Moses does so on their behalf. They are ever aware of being acted upon as they are transformed from common men into holy priests. The congregation witnessing the ceremony is ever aware of the weightiness of approaching the Lord. The ordination ceremony sanctifies space and servants to make communion with God possible: "I will consecrate the tent of meeting and the altar. Aaron also and his sons I will consecrate to serve me as priests. I will dwell among the people of Israel and will be their God" (Ex. 29:44–45). The message of this moment in redemptive history brings to light that it is the Lord himself who sanctifies his people: "I am the LORD who sanctifies you" (Lev. 20:8; cf. Lev. 21:8, 15; 22:9, 32). The installation is a visible means by which Aaron and his sons are transformed into a divinely ordained priesthood (Leviticus 8) so that God may fulfill his promises to dwell among his people (Leviticus 9).

Section Outline
   II. Inauguration of Public Worship (8:1–10:20)
        A. Ordination of the Priesthood (8:1–36)
           1. Preparation for Ordination Ceremony (8:1–5)
           2. Consecration of Tabernacle and Priesthood (8:6–13)
           3. Sacrificial Service of Ordination (8:14–30)
           4. Completing the Ordination (8:31–36)

Comment

8:1–5 The Lord's first command is for Moses to call Aaron and his sons, making it clear that they are called and appointed by God (v. 2). The priesthood is given to the house of Aaron as a gift for its zeal in guarding the holiness of the Lord in the face of false worship (Ex. 32:26–29; Num. 25:11–13; Deut. 33:8–11). Aaron's divine election is evident in his serving in a priestly role prior to the grant of the priesthood, as in Exodus 7:1–2, where he stands as mediator, speaks the words of the Lord, and demands the freedom to worship the one true God.

The Lord also commands Moses to gather the ritual objects for the ceremony (Lev. 8:2) and to summon the congregation (v. 3). The ceremony is especially significant for the worshiping community. The community assembles at the entrance to the tent of meeting, that is, in the courtyard in front of the altar. The people participate as witnesses to the installation and affirm the priesthood's role to mediate on their behalf. Once sacrificial worship is instituted, the people will return to this designated place to bring their offerings to the Lord, and the priests will present them on their behalf (cf. Lev. 3:2; 12:6; 14:11; 17:8–9).

8:6 The requirements of ordination begin with washing, an act of purification the congregation also performed in order to stand before the presence of the Lord at Sinai (Ex. 19:10). Washing is a public sign that the priest who enters God's service must present himself in a state of purity. From this point forward whenever a priest enters the tent of meeting or approaches the altar to minister, he will repeat this act by the ritual washing of his hands and feet at the basin (Ex. 30:17–21). This demonstrates in a tangible way that those who approach the Lord must be holy (cf. Ps. 24:3–4).

8:7–9 Next Aaron is clothed with the distinctive apparel of the priesthood in the sight of the congregation. Aaron does not dress himself; he is invested ceremoniously by Moses. While the priestly garments are described in rich detail when instructions are given for their fashioning (Exodus 28), the interest of this passage is to highlight how the garments function in the ritual of ordination. The sacral garments transform a man into a priest by moving him from the domain of the common into the domain of the holy. In other words putting on these garments is the act of investiture that confers the office of priesthood. At the death of Aaron Eleazar will succeed him to become high priest by being dressed in the priestly garments and anointed with holy oil: "The holy garments of Aaron shall be for his sons after him; they shall be anointed in them and ordained in them" (Ex. 29:29; cf. Num. 20:25–26). When Eleazar wears the priestly garments, he is not simply *perceived* to be acting as high priest but has in fact succeeded his father to *become* the next high priest.

The high priest's garments are eight in number: four that all priests wear and four unique to his position. The four articles of clothing that all priests wear are linen undergarments, a linen tunic, a sash, and a linen turban. Among the wealth of detail relating to priestly dress there is no mention of footwear. It seems likely that priests minister barefoot on holy ground (cf. Ex. 3:5; Josh. 5:15). In this passage Aaron and his sons are understood to be clad in the linen undergarments, a requisite covering for all priests from the loins to the thigh so that their nakedness not be exposed at the altar (cf. Ex. 28:42).

In terms of the clothing unique to the high priest the first to be mentioned is the robe (Lev. 8:7). Aaron is dressed in a stately robe of a single piece of cloth (cf. Ex. 28:31–35). It has a blue-purple color achieved by a costly dye deriving from a marine snail found in the Mediterranean. This was the most famous dye of antiquity, highly esteemed for its beauty and colorfast properties. The robe's hem is embellished with hanging, tassel-like pomegranates of blue-purple, red-purple, and crimson yarns that alternate with golden bells. As Aaron ministers in the tabernacle, the bells ring to announce his presence in the courts of the Lord as one would be announced in the presence of a king.

He is robed next with the ephod, an apron-like article of clothing held up by broad shoulder straps and fastened around the waist with a decorated belt. It is open in the front for attaching the breastpiece (cf. Ex. 28:6–14). The ephod is crafted of dyed yarns of blue-purple, red-purple, and crimson, interwoven with gold wire thread (Ex. 39:3). Mounted on the shoulder straps are two onyx stones inscribed with the names of the tribes of Israel, six on each stone, that the high priest may bear the tribes for remembrance in God's presence.

The breastpiece (Lev. 8:8), attached to the ephod by rings of gold and blue cords, is a fabric pouch that serves as a receptacle for the Urim and Thummim and also as a canvas for mounting the twelve engraved gemstones representing the tribes of Israel (cf. Ex. 28:15–30). Although the exact nature of the Urim and Thummim remains enigmatic, they are some type of sacred lots for the revelation of God's will to his people. These have been entrusted to the tribe of Levi in response to covenant faithfulness (cf. Deut. 33:8). They are carried on the person of the high priest, who alone is authorized to read and interpret them. Twelve gemstones are mounted on the breastpiece in four rows of three stones each, engraved according to the birth order of Jacob's sons. The stones are identifying emblems of the tribes that communicate the high priest's role in representing all Israel in worship. Carried before the Lord's covenant presence on the breastpiece of the high priest, all Israel can participate in worship.

The last distinctive item of apparel is a gold frontlet (Lev. 8:9) inscribed with the epithet "Holy to the LORD" and affixed over the high priest's linen turban (Ex. 28:36). To be holy to the Lord speaks of dedication (Lev. 27:14, 21, 30). It is a mark of ownership on the priest's forehead, designating that he has come into God's possession. The priests are regarded as holy because they are in special relationship with the Lord, chosen from among the tribes to serve him and given the right to participate in the sphere of the holy. The inscription on the priestly frontlet speaks to the consecration of the priest in his ritual role, as well as the consecration of all Israel, whom he represents (Ex. 19:6).

8:10–12 Following Aaron's investiture, attention turns to the sanctuary. The high priest and the space in which he will serve are consecrated together. Moses anoints the tabernacle, its furnishings, and Aaron with the oil reserved exclusively for the sanctuary and those who minister in its courts. The oil is the work of a perfumer, infused with fragrant spices of two parts finest myrrh, two parts cassia, and one part each of sweet-smelling cinnamon and aromatic cane (Ex. 30:23–24). The anointing oil is holy; its use on any other article or person outside of the holy sphere is strictly forbidden (Ex. 30:32).

Special attention is given to the altar, as it is sprinkled "seven times" (Lev. 8:11). The number seven in Leviticus communicates completeness. Sanctification is a process that will take the fullness of time for both the ritual objects and the priests who will minister before the Lord. By means of anointing, the altar is brought into the highest state of ritual purity: "The altar shall be most holy" (Ex. 29:37). This is where the sacrifices of the worshiping community will be offered and where the Lord will meet with his people. The altar functions as a meeting point between heaven and earth.

Aaron is not merely sprinkled but has the oil of anointing poured upon his head (Lev. 8:12).[102] Anointing is the supreme ritual act that sets the high priest apart from the rest of the priesthood, conferring upon him the titles of "anointed priest" (Lev. 4:3; 16:32) and "priest who is chief among his brothers" (21:10). It is worth noting that the high priest is the first person in Scripture to be anointed, followed by kings (1 Sam. 10:1; 16:13; 1 Kings 1:39). Anointing sets a person apart as divinely elected and consecrated to the Lord's service and is indicative of the Spirit's empowerment for office (Isa. 61:1).

---

[102] This becomes an image of the Lord's blessing in the poetic rendering of Psalm 133:2: "It is like the precious oil on the head, running down on the beard, on the beard of Aaron, running down on the collar of his robes!"

8:13 Moses now turns to dress Aaron's sons ceremoniously in accordance with the Lord's instructions. The garments of the ordinary priesthood are of a simpler nature and made of fine linen, a ritually clean fabric (Ezek. 44:18). White linen communicates purity and holiness, imagery the psalmist picks up on: "Let your priests be clothed with righteousness" (Ps. 132:9). Aaron's sons are clothed in a linen tunic, with a sash bound around them. The sash is a piece of cloth that could be wrapped around the waist to secure a garment or worn as an official mark of status. It is found almost exclusively with priestly dress. Lastly the priest's heads are covered with a rounded headdress. Though not as elaborate as Aaron's, these garments also carry the sanctity and authority of the priestly office.

8:14–17 A large part of this chapter is concerned with the offerings that consecrate sacred space and its servants. No less than three sacrifices are required to ordain the priesthood. This communicates the significance of the sacrificial system in providing a way to approach a holy God. Because the priesthood has not yet been ordained Moses serves at the altar in a priestly role. Over the course of the seven-day ceremony the status of Aaron and his sons will be changed from lay Israelites to functioning priests.

The first sacrifice ever offered on the altar of the sanctuary is a sin offering to make atonement for the priests who will officiate over worship at the tent. Moses brings a bull as prescribed for the anointed priest (cf. Lev. 4:3–12). Neither Aaron nor his sons eats any of the sacrificed meat, underscoring that it has been offered on their behalf to make atonement. At the very outset of their ordination the priests are confronted with the barrier that stands between every person and a holy God. (In the future, when they preside over the holiest day of the year, the Day of Atonement, they will begin the ceremony by offering a bull for their own sin as a reminder that they are in need of forgiveness and that they approach the altar by grace; cf. 16:6). In addition to making atonement for the priests this sacrifice purifies and consecrates the altar for every subsequent sacrifice that will be offered on it (8:15).

8:18–21 The second sacrifice of the ordination service is a burnt offering in which the animal is wholly turned to smoke and sent up to the Lord in worship (cf. Lev. 1:2–17). In the worshiping life of Israel the burnt offering is the cornerstone of the sacrificial system, offered on the altar every morning and evening (Ex. 29:38–42) and on festival days of the year (Numbers 28–29). This sacrifice covers the range of human emotions in life lived before the Lord. It could be offered for such diverse reasons as making atonement (Lev. 1:4), or fulfilling a vow and expressing thanksgiving (Lev. 22:17–19). It is a gift on the altar yielded utterly to the Lord; the worshiper holds back nothing for himself. It is no surprise that it would be foundational in the ordination rite to atone fully for the life of the priests. The ram is offered on their behalf and serves as their substitute, perhaps in part also illustrating that the lives of Aaron and his sons will be given fully to the Lord's service. This moment is likewise an occasion for thanksgiving as the priesthood enters into the service of the Lord and is granted the privilege of drawing near to him on behalf of the people.

8:22–28 The ceremony culminates in a sacrifice unique to the priesthood's installation—the ram of ordination—that resembles a peace offering fellowship meal (cf. 3:1–17). Moses offers the ram and places in the hands of Aaron and his sons its right thigh, the fat of the offering, and three loaves. This represents the portion allotted to the priesthood from the Lord's table (cf. 7:31–36). The priests in turn offer this up as a wave offering, raising it to heaven in a symbolic gesture of complete dedication. The thigh, fat, and loaves are then placed upon the altar, as the priests surrender their portion to the Lord. The significance of this act comes across in the idiom for ordination, expressed in the Hebrew as "to fill the hand." Filling the hand means to install to priestly office (Ex. 29:9; Lev. 21:10; 1 Kings 13:33). The installation ceremony quite literally fills the hands of the priests with portions of the "ram of filling." Aaron and his sons begin their ministry by taking the gifts that have filled their hands and offering them back to the Lord in worship.

The most striking aspect of this sacrifice involves the ram's blood. In the eyes of the gathered congregation Moses has taken the blood of the previous two offerings and applied it to the altar. The expectation is that he will do the same for the third sacrifice, but instead he applies it to Aaron and his sons, daubing it on their right ear lobe, right thumb, and right toe (Lev. 8:23–24). The remainder of the blood is dashed against the altar. An identification is intended between the priests and the altar at which they will serve. In the same manner that the altar's extremities are ritually applied with blood, so are the priests' extremities.

The blood daubing ritual poignantly recalls the covenant at Sinai, the only other occasion when the blood of sacrifice is halved to sprinkle both offerer and altar (cf. Ex. 24:6–11). There Moses built an altar, commanded the offering of sacrifices, and after reading from the book of the covenant took half of the sacrificial blood to sprinkle the gathered Israelites while he dashed the remainder against the altar. Afterward he and seventy elders were granted access into the Lord's presence to eat and drink before him. This ceremony represented the ratification of the covenant between the Lord and his people. The ordination ceremony closely follows the same pattern of sacrifice, blood ritual, and meal, suggesting its role is to bring the priests into the covenant service of the Lord. From this time forward they will have access to his presence, serve at the place of his feet, and eat from his table. The Lord's presence on Mount Sinai will find a new dwelling in the tabernacle, and all Israel's future encounters with their God will be through her priestly mediators.

8:29 Moses receives as his portion the breast of the ordination ram, which is the portion given to the priestly family (Lev. 7:31; note that Moses and Aaron are brothers, Ex. 6:20). He is not entitled to the right thigh, which is the designated portion of the officiating priest (Lev. 8:26; cf. 7:32–33), because he is not an ordained priest. Rather he is acting in a priestly capacity to install the priesthood and institute worship at the tabernacle. Moses is given the authority to anoint those called by

God and to make them priests in the same way that prophets anoint those called by God to make them kings.

8:30 In a final act of consecration Moses mixes some of the sacred anointing oil with the sacrificial blood from the altar and sprinkles the priestly garments. From this point forward the priesthood's blood-spattered dress bears the symbol of the covenant that committed it to the Lord's service. This becomes the third application of a purifying substance on the high priest's person to consecrate him to the Lord's service (cf. vv. 12, 23, 30). Aaron has been elevated to a holier status than that of his sons, who have only their garments sprinkled.

8:31–35 Aaron and his sons are commanded to remain in the courts of the tabernacle at the entrance to the tent of meeting for a full seven-day cycle (vv. 33, 35). The sacrificial service is to be repeated each day of the ordination period "as has been done today" (v. 34). During that time Moses will make offerings on the altar and Aaron and his sons will feast in the Lord's presence. Since meals often conclude covenants, an ordination banquet is a fitting way to celebrate the installation of the priesthood.

The seven-day period is a symbolic time frame in ancient Israelite thought. Rituals that bring about a change of status or acts of dedication typically follow a seven-day pattern. Seven days of a wedding celebration mark the change from singleness to entering the covenant of marriage (Gen. 29:27). In the practice of circumcision a child lives a full seven-day cycle before taking on the mark of the covenant on the eighth day to be dedicated as a member of the covenant community. A sacrificial animal remains with its mother for a full seven-day cycle before becoming eligible to be dedicated to the Lord in sacrifice (Ex. 22:30; Lev. 22:27). Likewise the seven-day cycle accomplishes the priests' consecration so that on the eighth day they serve as dedicated, full-fledged ministers of the covenant (cf. 9:1).

8:36 Moses is faithful to relay the Lord's command (v. 35), and Aaron and his sons are faithful to perform it. The chapter concludes as it has begun, with the obedience of Moses and Aaron to the Lord's commands. The congregation can be assured of the favor of the Lord and acceptance of its worship since all has been done according to his will.[103] The ceremony concludes with a fully functioning sanctuary and attendants to serve within its sacred space for the proper worship of the Lord.

Response

This unique moment in redemptive history ordains a priesthood to serve the living God. If Solomon will later wonder how the Lord could dwell in a temple built

---

[103] This is an important idea in the chapter, which repeats seven times that Moses executes everything according to the Lord's command (Lev. 8:4, 9, 13, 17, 21, 29, 36). The sevenfold repetition presents the ordination as seven acts of obedience to the Lord. Also, the structuring of the account into seven sections strongly echoes the seven-day creation account of Genesis. Creation themes are woven throughout the description of the tabernacle to signal that this tent will be the Lord's dwelling place on earth. The creation of sacred space is in part a return to Eden, though with the need for priests to serve as mediators, whereas there was no need for intermediaries before the fall.

by human hands, one wonders how any man could be made worthy to serve him with human hands. Through a solemn ordination ("filling of the hand") ceremony Aaron and his sons are consecrated for service. Consecration is to set apart for the exclusive use of the Lord and to make at home in the realm of the Holy One. The installation of the priesthood transfers its citizenship from the realm of the common to the realm of the holy. Its ordination is not just a series of ceremonial rites but the divinely ordained way through which Aaron and his sons are made holy to approach the Lord and to offer up worship for all Israel.

The call into God's service is humbling. It reveals the true condition of man before a holy God. The first sacrifice ever offered upon the altar of the sanctuary is a sacrifice of atonement for the sins of Aaron and his sons. Those who are called by the Lord into ministry are confronted by their sinfulness and utter inadequacy (Ex. 3:6; Isa. 6:5; Luke 5:8). In the words of the apostle Paul, "Who is sufficient for these things?" (2 Cor. 2:16). Yet the Lord does not leave those he calls in their inadequacy. He sanctifies them. He invites Aaron and his sons to draw near to him, gives them access to the altar, and seats them at his table. They are made holy so that they can serve him in worship.

The priesthood's installation anticipates the coming of Christ, called and appointed by God the Father to serve as the "High Priest of our confession" (Heb. 3:1). Though sinless, he is washed in baptism and anointed by the Holy Spirit (Matt. 3:13–17). Jesus the Messiah is the ultimate and final Anointed One. He dedicates himself to the Father's will, that through his sacrificial death he may sanctify a people in the service of God (John 17:19). Christ's consecration is to offer up his life as an atonement for sin and to inaugurate a new covenant by the blood of his priestly sacrifice (Heb. 10:29).

The new covenant holds out a vision of a new priesthood instituted by a perfect, sinless High Priest who enters a "more perfect tent (not made with hands, that is, not of this creation)" (Heb. 9:11; cf. Heb. 2:10–11). Christ stands before the throne of God to present a priestly people who have been washed by his Word (John 13:8; Heb. 10:22) and whose consciences have been sprinkled and purified to serve the living God (Heb. 9:14). His followers are anointed with the Spirit, who not only fills their hands but indwells them, filling their lives. They are clothed in the blood-spattered garments that speak of an enduring covenant (Rev. 7:14). Indeed, they are even clothed with Christ as their lives take on the shape of his consecration, renewed in the image of his holiness (Rom. 13:14; Eph. 4:24; Col. 3:10). By grace they have been granted access to the Lord, and their citizenship has been recorded in heaven (Phil. 3:20). Their consecration makes them a priestly people who worship the Lord with their lives.

LEVITICUS 9

9 On the eighth day Moses called Aaron and his sons and the elders of Israel, ²and he said to Aaron, "Take for yourself a bull calf for a sin offering and a ram for a burnt offering, both without blemish, and offer them before the Lord. ³And say to the people of Israel, 'Take a male goat for a sin offering, and a calf and a lamb, both a year old without blemish, for a burnt offering, ⁴and an ox and a ram for peace offerings, to sacrifice before the Lord, and a grain offering mixed with oil, for today the Lord will appear to you.'" ⁵And they brought what Moses commanded in front of the tent of meeting, and all the congregation drew near and stood before the Lord. ⁶And Moses said, "This is the thing that the Lord commanded you to do, that the glory of the Lord may appear to you." ⁷Then Moses said to Aaron, "Draw near to the altar and offer your sin offering and your burnt offering and make atonement for yourself and for the people, and bring the offering of the people and make atonement for them, as the Lord has commanded."

⁸So Aaron drew near to the altar and killed the calf of the sin offering, which was for himself. ⁹And the sons of Aaron presented the blood to him, and he dipped his finger in the blood and put it on the horns of the altar and poured out the blood at the base of the altar. ¹⁰But the fat and the kidneys and the long lobe of the liver from the sin offering he burned on the altar, as the Lord commanded Moses. ¹¹The flesh and the skin he burned up with fire outside the camp.

¹²Then he killed the burnt offering, and Aaron's sons handed him the blood, and he threw it against the sides of the altar. ¹³And they handed the burnt offering to him, piece by piece, and the head, and he burned them on the altar. ¹⁴And he washed the entrails and the legs and burned them with the burnt offering on the altar.

¹⁵Then he presented the people's offering and took the goat of the sin offering that was for the people and killed it and offered it as a sin offering, like the first one. ¹⁶And he presented the burnt offering and offered it according to the rule. ¹⁷And he presented the grain offering, took a handful of it, and burned it on the altar, besides the burnt offering of the morning.

¹⁸Then he killed the ox and the ram, the sacrifice of peace offerings for the people. And Aaron's sons handed him the blood, and he threw it against the sides of the altar. ¹⁹But the fat pieces of the ox and of the ram, the fat tail and that which covers the entrails and the kidneys and the long lobe of the liver— ²⁰they put the fat pieces on the breasts, and he burned the fat pieces on the altar, ²¹but the breasts and the right thigh Aaron waved for a wave offering before the Lord, as Moses commanded.

²²Then Aaron lifted up his hands toward the people and blessed them, and he came down from offering the sin offering and the burnt offering and the peace offerings. ²³And Moses and Aaron went into the tent of meeting, and when they came out they blessed the people, and the glory

of the LORD appeared to all the people. ²⁴ And fire came out from before the LORD and consumed the burnt offering and the pieces of fat on the altar, and when all the people saw it, they shouted and fell on their faces.

Section Overview

The tabernacle was constructed in all its details according to the Lord's commands: "And Moses saw all the work, and behold, they had done it; as the LORD had commanded, so had they done it. Then Moses blessed them" (Ex. 39:43). The priesthood has also been ordained according to the Lord's commands (Lev. 8:36). It is now time to inaugurate covenant worship according to the Lord's commands (9:7, 10, 21). This is a new beginning for God's people, in which the Lord will make his covenant-dwelling among them and receive their worship. The new beginning is signaled by patterns and language recalling the Genesis creation account, most obvious of which is the pattern of command and fulfillment: Israel responds in obedience and fulfills the Lord's commands, just as did all of creation at the beginning of time (Gen. 1:3, 7, 9, 11, 15, 24). Indeed, at the institution of covenant worship the Lord blesses his people (Lev. 9:22, 23), just as he did all creation in the beginning (Gen. 1:22, 28; 2:3).

Priests and altar take center stage in the drama of worship as this chapter gives us a close and personal view of the ritual performance that takes place at the tent of meeting. First, the Lord calls the people to assemble. Standing in his presence, they are aware that they need to be cleansed from impurity and to rely on the sacrifices made through their priestly mediators in order to atone for their sins and express their worship through both meat and grain offerings. The action then focuses on the altar and the person of the high priest in a retelling that invites us to *see* his sacrificial service executed in a faithful obedience that wins the Lord's approval. The blood of sacrifice especially is painted in vivid detail: smeared on the horns of the altar, dashed against its every side, and poured at its base, where it is soaked up by the earth. The gathered congregation that has receded into the background is brought into view again at the climactic moment when the offerings are consumed by fire that comes out from the presence of the Lord, and the people fall down to pay him homage. Worship culminates in fellowship with the Lord through a shared meal, words of blessing, and the real experience of his personal presence.

Section Outline

II. Inauguration of Public Worship (8:1–10:20) . . .
    B. The First Worship Service (9:1–24)
        1. The Call to Worship (9:1–5)
        2. Inaugural Worship at the Altar (9:6–22)
            a. Introduction (9:6–7)
            b. Sacrifices for the Priests (9:8–14)
            c. Sacrifices for the People (9:15–21)
            d. Priestly Blessing (9:22)
        3. The Appearance of the Lord (9:23–24)

Comment

9:1 The book of Leviticus begins with the Lord's *calling* from the tent of meeting to give the laws of sacrifice to his people in a series of speeches (1:1). The very next instance of calling involves Moses, who summons the priests and the elders to put into practice the way of worship through sacrifice.

It is the eighth day after the ordination of the priesthood, a time recognized for new beginnings (cf. comment 8:31–35). Significantly, God's activity in creation lasted seven days, and the eighth day marked a new beginning of human stewardship. The priestly ordination lasts seven days, with the eighth day marking a new era in the life of God's people. The Lord will dwell and be worshiped in the tabernacle that was set up on the first day of the new year (Ex. 40:17) and has now become a fully functional *tent of meeting*.

9:2–4 Preparation for worship begins with carefully selecting the offerings to be brought to the Lord, first for the priest and then for the congregation. This pattern of describing sacrifices before worship has already been established by the book's structure, which begins with the enumeration of sacrifices (Leviticus 1–7) before arriving to the practice of covenant worship (Leviticus 9). Requirements for the priests include a bull calf as a sin offering (vv. 8–11) and a ram as a burnt offering (vv. 12–14).[104] Requirements for the people include a male goat as a sin offering (v. 15), a calf and lamb as a burnt offering (v. 16), a grain offering (v. 17), and finally an ox and ram as a peace offering (vv. 18–21). Aaron is the one to instruct the people, as the priesthood will continue to do in the course of its ministry. Every sacrifice the Lord has thus far required of his people will be offered at the inaugural service with the exception of the guilt offering, since that is the offering of an individual and not fitting for public worship (5:14–6:7). In all there are seven animal offerings in addition to the grain offering, bringing the total to eight sacrifices on the eighth day.[105]

9:5 Having brought their offerings, the priests, elders, and all the congregation expectantly assemble to stand before the Lord. To stand in the presence of a ruler speaks to the privilege of access and audience with him, as attendants in a royal court (1 Kings 10:8; Dan. 1:5) or as servants before their master (Deut. 1:38). On this day Israel is privileged to stand in these ways before her Lord and Sovereign.

9:6 The goal of covenant worship is fellowship with the Lord. The offerings will thus be made so "that the glory of the LORD may appear to you" (cf. Lev. 9:4, 23). Fellowship for *all* Israel will be possible because of the priesthood's ministry at the altar. The daily worship service at the tent of meeting testifies to a God who is present among his people and who promises to meet with them through sacrifice.

---

104 Typically a bull is required for the priestly sin offering (Lev. 4:3). It could be that a younger animal is chosen due to the prior ordination sacrifices that cleansed and consecrated the priesthood. It could also be that the calf is considered more valuable and fitting in light of the anticipated appearance of the Lord (Sklar, *Leviticus*, TOTC, 151–152).

105 Gane, *Leviticus, Numbers*, 178.

9:7 Aaron is called up to the altar to begin his ministry formally as high priest. He is officially commissioned and installed through the performance of the sacrificial service. The emphasis is on atonement, underscored for both priestly ministers and congregation.

9:8–11 Aaron approaches the altar to slaughter the sin offering for himself and his household. The deliberate repetition of his drawing near to the altar together with the rehearsal of sacrificial procedure highlights that the ritual has been executed according to the Lord's command. The sin offering is described in shorthand; the fuller procedure is assumed (4:3–12), though the description features only how it intersects with the altar.[106]

Repetition also slows down the action so that we are able to visualize Aaron's approach and the choreography of sacrificial service. The very personal nature of his identification with the sin offering comes across in the way the blood is handled: Aaron dips his finger in the life-liquid that purifies him. He smears the blood on the horns of the altar and then pours out the rest at its base, returning the animal's life back to its Giver.[107] Aaron's sons assist him in handling the blood of sacrifice (also 9:12, 18), presenting it to him in ritual vessels that are part of the altar's assemblage (cf. Num. 4:14; 1 Kings 7:40). The physicality of this ritual enactment powerfully communicates blood's potency to cleanse, atone, and secure covenant relationship.

9:12–14 The burnt offering for the priests follows the ritual script of Leviticus 1:10–13. Aaron's sons hand him the sacrificial portions piece by piece in a vivid image of the dismembered animal's arrangement on the altar. This detail of the priestly family serving together is found nowhere else in the biblical text.

9:15–21 Aaron now presents offerings on behalf of the congregation as its mediator. The sequence of offerings evinces a ritual logic: the sin offering (v. 15) is for purification and removal of sin, the burnt offering (v. 16) is for atonement and worship, the grain offering (v. 17) is a gift of tribute to Israel's Sovereign, and finally the peace offering (vv. 18–21) enacts covenant fellowship through a shared meal between the Lord and his people. The fullness of the sacrificial system is on display at the inaugural service. While atonement is emphasized, it is part of a larger picture of worship that culminates in fellowship and blessing.

9:22 The service concludes as the creation account concludes, with God's blessing over his people. Blessing has been woven into the Lord's relationship with humanity since creation (Gen. 1:28) and is perpetuated in the world through covenant worship (Deut. 28:1–14). From the altar the high priest raises his hands to pronounce the benediction (cf. Deut. 10:8; 2 Chron. 30:27). Lifted hands are a common

---

[106] Milgrom, *Leviticus 1–16*, 579.
[107] In the future the blood of the sin offering will be brought inside the tent to be sprinkled in front of the veil and smeared on the incense altar (Lev. 4:5–7), but, since no priests have yet entered the tent, the blood is applied to the altar in the courtyard.

gesture of prayer (Pss. 28:2; 63:4; 1 Tim. 2:8), but here Aaron raises his hands *toward* the congregation. Elevated at the altar,[108] his physical body bridging heaven and earth, he visibly mediates between the Lord and his people. The hands that were dipped in the blood of sacrifice are now stretched toward Israel. Aaron's words are *performative*—not merely a wish but a pronouncement spoken with authority to actualize the blessings of the covenant resulting from the ministry of atonement.

The priestly blessing that Aaron may have used is preserved in Numbers 6:24–26:

> The LORD bless you and keep you;
> The LORD make his face to shine upon you and be gracious to you;
> The LORD lift up his countenance upon you and give you *peace*.

Aaron is to articulate the divine name three times in this blessing, invoking the protection, grace, and peace that come from relationship with the Lord. Priestly mediation brings the people into communion with their God and speaks over them his life-giving covenantal intention to bless. The significance of blessing for the worshiping community is not simply that of a parting ceremonious word but one that has the power to shape the life of every worshiper. Blessing rings out and ends on the resounding note of *peace*.

9:23 While Moses has already been in the tent (cf. Lev. 8:10), Aaron has not. Sacrificial ministry at the altar changes this forever. Aaron and the priests are now granted access into the Holy Place, paving the way for ministry in the Lord's house. Aaron and his sons will henceforth have access to the Lord in the tent as Moses had access on Sinai. Moses enters together with Aaron to confirm him in his role as priestly mediator.

After their audience with the Lord both Moses and Aaron emerge to pronounce blessing on the people again. As they had brought the people's gifts to the Lord through the altar, they now bring the Lord's gift to his people in blessing. The Lord stamps his presence on these spoken words by appearing in glory. Glory refers to a manifestation of the Lord's presence that can be *seen* (cf. Ex. 24:17). He appears in royal radiant splendor to all the people, manifesting his glory as fire wrapped in a cloud of smoke, with flashes of luminous lightning and a rainbow brilliance (cf. Isa. 6:4; Ezek. 1:26–28).

The Lord's glory validates the pronouncement of blessing and foreshadows that from now on he will appear through his anointed representative. When the high priest concludes the daily service with the benediction, the congregation will view a representative image of the Lord's glory through the priest—clothed in the luminous splendor of the golden ephod, gleaming stones of the breastpiece, and golden diadem on the forehead, he displays an image of God's glory and the shining face of his favor (Num. 6:25).

---

[108] The altar is 4.5 feet (1.4 m) high (Ex. 27:1). The detail that Aaron "came down" assumes a ramp to the altar (cf. Ex. 20:26).

9:24 At this moment fire comes out from before the Lord's presence (his throne room in the inner sanctuary), consuming the offerings. He thus validates the ministry of the newly ordained priesthood by showing he has accepted his people's offerings.[109] The fire is a sign of God's presence that is never to be let die but must continue to burn on the altar as he continues to accept his people's worship (Lev. 6:9, 12, 13). The inaugural service marks the only time in Leviticus that the glory of the Lord appears. In the future, when the people approach the Lord with their offerings, they will do so in faith that he is present to receive them, as promised: "It shall be a regular burnt offering throughout your generations at the entrance of the tent of meeting before the LORD, *where I will meet with you*, to speak to you there" (Ex. 29:42).

The people's response is to "shout," a word used elsewhere to refer to shouts of joy or even joyful singing. This is a far cry from when the Lord appeared to them wrapped in thick smoke on Sinai's summit and they stood far off in fear and trembling (Ex. 20:18). Their exultant praise at the Lord's coming is captured by the prophet Isaiah, who uses this same expression: "*Sing*, O heavens, for the LORD has done it; shout, O depths of the earth; *break forth into singing*. . . . For the LORD has redeemed Jacob, and will be glorified in Israel" (Isa. 44:23). The great King has arrived to receive their worship, and the people fall on their faces in homage before him. What is often brought across in English translations as "worship" is the physical act of bowing low with face to the ground (2 Chron. 20:1–3; 29:29). Worship is thus both planned and spontaneous: careful preparation and execution of God's revealed will finds spontaneous response at the advent of his presence.

Response

The tabernacle extends to Israel the invitation to commune with her God in a re-created heaven on earth.[110] Worship in the sacred tent is initiated by the Lord, who desires to meet with his redeemed people, inviting their participation through the offering of gifts and offering to them in return the gift of his presence (cf. Ex. 33:16). This rich theological vision scripts worship around substitutionary sacrifice and the ministry of the anointed high priest, who bridges the gap between God and man. The altar is the centerpiece of OT worship. It is here, in the daily sacrifice, that the Lord meets with his people. Our gaze has been so captivated by the divine glory resident in the Most Holy Place that in our teaching and preaching we tend to highlight the lack of access in Israel's worship. Rather, we should appreciate that at this time in redemptive history all eyes are turned to the *altar*, waiting expectantly through the ages for the appearance of the Lord.

Historically, the Lord fulfills his promise to meet his people at the altar. Christ comes as the high priest who is chosen, anointed, and invested with authority to

---

[109] The Lord's approval will come as divine fire at Solomon's dedication of the temple (2 Chron. 7:1) and Elijah's sacrifices on Mount Carmel (1 Kings 18:38).
[110] Cf. Gordon J. Wenham, "Sanctuary Symbolism in the Garden of Eden Story," in *I Studied Inscriptions from before the Flood*, ed. Richard S. Hess and David Toshio Tsumura (Winona Lake, IN: Eisenbrauns, 1994), 399–404.

draw near to the Lord as his divinely appointed mediator: "I am the way, and the truth, and the life. No one comes to the Father except through me" (John 14:6). Christ our High Priest mediates at the intersection of heaven and earth, serving at the altar of the cross that he drenches with his own blood. The enduring symbol of the altar is a testimony to the centrality of atonement that makes our access to God—and our worship—possible. Jesus reaches out his nail-scarred hands in blessing over his people (Luke 24:50–51) and imparts covenant peace that is lasting (John 14:27). His sacrificial ministry has the Father's wholehearted approval, which he demonstrates in sending fire from heaven that births the church (Acts 2:3). It is a fire that has not gone out; the Lord's redeemed encounter it anew in every generation and carry its witness throughout the world. At Pentecost the people of God began new life with a new identity. They started to gather for worship on the eighth day, the day of Christ's resurrection and the dawn of the new creation (Acts 20:7; Rev. 1:10). The Lamb of God has inaugurated a heavenly liturgy wherein all are now called to draw near to the Lord's unveiled presence, be received into his glory, and bow before him in eternal worship.

LEVITICUS 10

10 Now Nadab and Abihu, the sons of Aaron, each took his censer and put fire in it and laid incense on it and offered unauthorized[1] fire before the Lord, which he had not commanded them. 2 And fire came out from before the Lord and consumed them, and they died before the Lord. 3 Then Moses said to Aaron, "This is what the Lord has said: 'Among those who are near me I will be sanctified, and before all the people I will be glorified.'" And Aaron held his peace.

4 And Moses called Mishael and Elzaphan, the sons of Uzziel the uncle of Aaron, and said to them, "Come near; carry your brothers away from the front of the sanctuary and out of the camp." 5 So they came near and carried them in their coats out of the camp, as Moses had said. 6 And Moses said to Aaron and to Eleazar and Ithamar his sons, "Do not let the hair of your heads hang loose, and do not tear your clothes, lest you die, and wrath come upon all the congregation; but let your brothers, the whole house of Israel, bewail the burning that the Lord has kindled. 7 And do not go outside the entrance of the tent of meeting, lest you die, for the anointing oil of the Lord is upon you." And they did according to the word of Moses.

8 And the Lord spoke to Aaron, saying, 9 "Drink no wine or strong drink, you or your sons with you, when you go into the tent of meeting, lest you die. It shall be a statute forever throughout your generations. 10 You are to distinguish between the holy and the common, and between the unclean and the clean, 11 and you are to teach the people of Israel all the statutes that the Lord has spoken to them by Moses."

¹² Moses spoke to Aaron and to Eleazar and Ithamar, his surviving sons: "Take the grain offering that is left of the LORD's food offerings, and eat it unleavened beside the altar, for it is most holy. ¹³ You shall eat it in a holy place, because it is your due and your sons' due, from the LORD's food offerings, for so I am commanded. ¹⁴ But the breast that is waved and the thigh that is contributed you shall eat in a clean place, you and your sons and your daughters with you, for they are given as your due and your sons' due from the sacrifices of the peace offerings of the people of Israel. ¹⁵ The thigh that is contributed and the breast that is waved they shall bring with the food offerings of the fat pieces to wave for a wave offering before the LORD, and it shall be yours and your sons' with you as a due forever, as the LORD has commanded."

¹⁶ Now Moses diligently inquired about the goat of the sin offering, and behold, it was burned up! And he was angry with Eleazar and Ithamar, the surviving sons of Aaron, saying, ¹⁷ "Why have you not eaten the sin offering in the place of the sanctuary, since it is a thing most holy and has been given to you that you may bear the iniquity of the congregation, to make atonement for them before the LORD? ¹⁸ Behold, its blood was not brought into the inner part of the sanctuary. You certainly ought to have eaten it in the sanctuary, as I commanded." ¹⁹ And Aaron said to Moses, "Behold, today they have offered their sin offering and their burnt offering before the LORD, and yet such things as these have happened to me! If I had eaten the sin offering today, would the LORD have approved?" ²⁰ And when Moses heard that, he approved.

¹ Or *strange*

Section Overview

As one of the few narrative portions of the book of Leviticus, chapters 8–10 are meant to be read together.[111] This narrative continues the inauguration of priestly ministry on the eighth day after the priests' consecration. The climax of celebration is interrupted by tragedy—the Lord, who had descended on Mount Sinai as fire (Ex. 19:18) and further descended to fill the tabernacle with his presence (Ex. 40:38), now breaks out in fiery judgment. Whereas Moses and Aaron took pains to do everything "as the LORD commanded"[112] for the ordination of the priesthood and the inauguration of public worship, the young priests Nadab and Abihu strike out on their own to do that "which he had not commanded" (Lev. 10:1).

The tension that develops between chapters 8–9 and chapter 10 is concretized in the divine fire that can in one moment consume the people's offerings with pleasure (9:24) and the wayward priests in the next with displeasure (10:2). Theologically expressed, this judgment illustrates the tension that exists when a holy God dwells among a sinful people. This chapter provides an answer to that tension *in part*: the Lord will dwell among his people because he has instituted a priesthood to mediate his presence by the careful observance of making

---

[111] Warning notes that "fire" is the theme word that ties these chapters together, appearing seven times (8:17, 32; 9:11, 24; 10:1 [2x], 2); Wilfred Warning, *Literary Artistry in Leviticus* (Leiden: Brill, 1999), 75–76.
[112] Leviticus 8:4, 9, 13, 17, 21, 29; 9:7, 10.

distinctions between holy/common and clean/unclean and by teaching the people to do likewise. Nadab and Abihu's deaths, quickly recounted in two verses, serve as an object lesson that introduces this twofold commission to distinguish and teach, highlighted by the Lord's direct speech. The chapters that follow (chs. 11–15) expound on how the priesthood is to lead the people in separating clean from unclean. These instructions in turn lead to the Day of Atonement, on which the tension is resolved *in full* with the provision of atonement that allows Israel to continue as the Lord's set-apart, holy nation.

Although priestly ministry begins with tragedy and failure, it culminates with the Lord's commitment to entrust Aaron's house with making atonement for the nation. In its inaugural ministry the priesthood is shown to be as prone to sin as all the congregation is (Heb. 5:3). By chapter 16 we see that provision has been made to atone for the sins of the priesthood (Lev. 16:6, 11), as well as for all Israel (vv. 15–16), since "all have sinned and fall short of the glory of God" (Rom. 3:23). The shedding of the blood of sacrifice for the atonement of sin is how a holy God can dwell among his people and begin to sanctify them by his holy presence (Leviticus 17–26).

Section Outline

II. Inauguration of Public Worship (8:1–10:20) . . .

C. The Priesthood's Costly Lesson on Holiness (10:1–20)

1. The Unholy Death of Nadab and Abihu (10:1–7)
2. The Lord's Direct Address to Aaron on Making Distinctions (10:8–11)
3. Ministry That Respects God's Holiness (10:12–20)

Comment

10:1–2 Elsewhere Nadab and Abihu are prominently mentioned as Aaron's oldest sons (Ex. 6:23), in line to inherit the high priesthood. They, together with their father and seventy elders, had been invited to feast in the presence of the Lord, who received them and "did not lay his hand" on them (Ex. 24:11). They were permitted to approach halfway up the mountain but no further (Ex. 24:1–2). After the construction of the tabernacle and the beginning of public worship there is a standing invitation to approach (partway) into the Lord's presence and continue to eat at his covenant table.

In a rash move perhaps heightened by emotion at the appearance of the Lord in fire Nadab and Abihu fill their firepans to present "unauthorized" fire. This may also be translated as "foreign" or "strange" fire, meaning something alien to the holy environment of the tabernacle, suggesting they introduce something common into a space that is holy. As this incident is brought up again in the legislation for the Day of Atonement, looking to chapter 16 can help clarify what goes wrong. Aaron is instructed "not to come *at any time* into the Holy Place *inside the veil*" (Lev. 16:2), leaving us to infer that Nadab and Abihu try to enter the holiest part of the tent, which is off limits except for once a year to make atonement for the nation. On that day the high priest *alone* is to bring a firepan filled with coals and incense from the golden altar before the Most Holy Place (16:12–13). The coals are holy because they come from the sacrificial altar that the Lord ignited by the fire of his presence and never extinguished (6:13). The incense is holy because it is exclusive to the sanctuary, with aromas of the Lord's personal presence (Ex. 30:34–37). Any fire other than that lit by coals from the altar or burning anything other than sacred incense is foreign to the sanctuary. When once a year the high priest is given access to the Lord's most holy throne room, he must come with holy fire and incense as the one consecrated by holy oil (Ex. 29:7; Lev. 21:10) and dressed in holy garments (Ex. 28:2). Nadab and Abihu presumably attempt to intrude into the holiest realms of God's presence with "unauthorized incense" (Ex. 30:9), that is, a recipe other than the sanctuary's. In this way they demonstrate error in judgment by not respecting the Lord's most holy things and treating the holy as profane.

Fire comes out from the Most Holy Place and consumes the priests who trespass into his presence.[113] The Lord strikes them down with punishment that fits the crime: if one tries to present unauthorized fire, he will be consumed by fire itself. Before the eyes of all the people the commands on offering the right sacrifices (Leviticus 1–7) must now seem more relevant than ever.

10:3 Moses is given a message to pass on to Aaron that is sure to be passed down to all the priesthood with every retelling of this transgression. Its memorable quality is due to its delivery in poetic verse of two parallel lines. The first line refers to the priests. They are the ones "who draw near to me to minister to me" (Ezek. 43:19), chosen from all the tribes of Israel to approach the Lord. The very essence of priesthood consists of "access to the presence of God, particularly the presence of God associated with the altar, and above all the sanctuary."[114] Among the priests the Lord will show himself to be holy, as he has done on this day to defend his holiness.

The parallel line expands upon the first by broadening the audience to all Israel. To the people he will reveal himself in his weighty glory as he has just done to consume their offerings—"the glory of the LORD appeared to all the people" (Lev. 9:23)—and as he will do to consume anything that profanes his presence (22:9). The Lord will display his glory in both mercy and judgment (Ex. 33:18; 34:6–7), depending on priestly mediation. In this instance he does so in judgment, as though to say, "If you do not set me apart by your actions as the God worthy of reverence, I will use your death as an opportunity to remind all the people that I am indeed the God who is to be revered above all."[115] The first to be in need of atonement are those who have been called into God's service (cf. 1 Tim. 1:15–16).

---

[113] How they meet their death will be repeated with Korah and his followers, who attempt to usurp the priesthood and disregard those set apart to holiness. The Lord judges them by fire as they are offering incense (Num. 16:35).
[114] John A. Davies, *A Royal Priesthood: Literary and Intertextual Perspectives on an Image of Israel in Exodus 19.6*, JSOTSup 395 (London: T&T Clark, 2004), 162.
[115] Sklar, *Leviticus*, TOTC, 157–158.

Aaron's silence speaks volumes. He does not protest the Lord's chastisement but humbly receives his hand of discipline. By his actions Aaron acknowledges the Lord's just judgment in the transgression of his holiness. At the same time Aaron's silence is also a sign of mourning (Job 2:13).

10:4–5 The order of first importance is to remove the ritually defiling corpses from before the Most Holy Place. Moses calls Aaron's cousins Mishael and Elzaphan to take the bodies outside the camp for burial. For Eleazar and Ithamar to touch their brothers' corpses would be ritually defiling and render them unfit for service (Lev. 21:2), and Aaron is not permitted to tend to their bodies at all (21:11). The cousins carry them by their linen tunics so that they avoid even touching those who have fallen under the judgment of God (Num. 19:11).

10:6–7 After the shock of Nadab and Abihu's sudden death it would be natural for Aaron to begin mourning by raising his voice in lament, tearing his garments, removing his turban, and disheveling his hair (cf. Ezek. 24:17), as is the custom. But Moses tells Aaron and his remaining sons that this is not fitting for priests. Mourning at the time of their consecration would be defiling to their holy status (even though at a different time this would be permissible for the brothers; cf. Lev. 21:2). The consecrating oil of anointing has been poured out upon them, moving them out of the sphere of the common and into the Lord's domain as his very own set-apart servants (8:12, 30). They are therefore not to leave the sanctuary but to remain in its courts for the remainder of their consecration period (9:7), which includes the inaugural service (8:33). To leave and bury their dead would be to make Nadab and Abihu's mistake in reverse by bringing holy things (their bodies) into profane space. Instead, Aaron and his sons are called to make a distinction between their holy, set-apart status and the necessities of burying the dead, something that Jesus himself would call his followers to do (Luke 9:60). The rest of the nation will mourn, including perhaps their mother, sisters, wives, children, and "all . . . Israel," as later at Aaron's death (Num. 20:29).

10:8–11 For the only time in Leviticus the Lord speaks to Aaron directly, without an intermediary. He holds Aaron accountable for the conduct of his sons and entrusts to him their oversight. He commands them particularly not to indulge in wine or strong drink when they exercise their priestly duties. (Wine was present at the tabernacle and offered twice daily to the Lord as part of the daily offering; Ex. 29:40–41.) Though not always evident in English, there are three reasons given for the command.

The first is so the priests do not die (Lev. 10:9). Entering into holy space is potentially dangerous for the simple reason that missteps here could show severe disrespect to the Lord's holiness, with lethal consequences—as Nadab and Abihu have just made clear.[116] Second, priests must refrain from consuming alcohol while

---

[116] Though not explicitly stated, the fact that the command of Lev. 10:9 comes so soon after vv. 1–2 may imply that Nadab and Abihu had been lax in their diligence because they had been drinking.

they are serving at the tent precisely because it dulls discernment on matters of the holy and the profane (v. 10). The priesthood is especially called to observe distinctions between the ritual categories the Lord has ordained for holy living. The holy is that which has been dedicated to the Lord's use and brought into his sacred sphere of ownership; the common is that which is ordinary and nonholy. Something common could be either clean or unclean.[117] While the normal state of things is that they are clean, uncleanness must be dealt with through ritual purification to restore the item in question to a clean state. These binary categories define all Israel's decisions of obedience, and priests must be ready at all times while on duty to distinguish between them properly.

Third, an important aspect of priestly ministry is teaching Israel how to live life in light of God's holiness, keeping away from practices that pollute and embracing practices that sanctify (vv. 10–11; cf. Ezek. 22:26). Priestly instruction encompasses such specific things as proper offerings, celebrating holy days, clean and unclean foods, and diagnosing skin disease, all in obedience to the all-encompassing covenant they will read aloud every seven years in the people's hearing (Deut. 31:10–13). Drunken priests would falter in their holy charge to render judgments (Deut. 17:8–13) when instead the "lips of a priest should guard knowledge, and people should seek instruction from his mouth, for he is the messenger of the LORD of hosts" (Mal. 2:7).

10:12–15 The tabernacle's inaugural service concludes when the priests partake their portion of the offerings. After the events of the day eating could hardly seem appropriate (cf. Deut. 26:14). How could Eleazar and Ithamar feast when their brothers had perished? Yet eating at the Lord's table today is more important than ever because it declares unwavering covenant solidarity with him. Aaron and his sons are entitled to the most holy "grain offering" (Lev. 9:17) meant to be eaten in the holy precincts by the altar, while the breast and thigh (9:21) could be eaten in any ritually clean place, such as their homes and with their families. While these instructions might come across as a mundane concern, they underscore the distinctions between holy and most holy food, the people who would consume it, and the places where it could be consumed (10:10). The theme of clean and unclean distinctions in food consumption will continue into the next chapter.

10:16–18 Moses now inquires about the goat that had been sacrificed as a sin offering for the people (9:3, 15), only to find that Aaron and his sons burned it. Proper protocol called for them to eat its meat in the tabernacle's court (6:26). The only occasion for burning it would be when its blood had been brought into the Holy Place for atonement (6:30), as in the case of purification rites for the sin of the congregation (4:20; 16:15).

The handling of the sin offering is no trifling matter. When properly consumed, it contributes to the people's atonement by allowing for the priests to bear their

---

117 For more on these categories cf. Section Overview of Leviticus 10.

sin (10:17).[118] They act as substitutes, bearing the sin of the nation until it was placed on an animal substitute and driven away from the camp (Leviticus 16). They, however, are not touched by its consequence because of their holy status. When priests eat the sin offering, they embody "a profound theological statement: holiness has swallowed impurity; life can defeat death."[119]

10:19–20 It is fitting that Aaron responds on behalf of his sons after the Lord's direct charge to him in verses 9–10. His response assumes responsibility and also to some measure guilt for his family. How could they bear sin, atone for the people, if they themselves have fresh guilt with which to deal? Nadab and Abihu's sacrilege was committed *after* the sin offering had been offered for the priestly household (9:11), leaving Aaron to believe that another offering for atonement was needed on behalf of the priestly family. He may reasoned that the sin offering for the people atoned for the priests as well, in which case they should not have eaten its meat (4:3–12).

Moses is satisfied that Aaron's reasoning has been with attention to distinguishing between the holy and common and his actions have been in keeping with honoring the Lord and the spirit of the law. Moses' approval is as the Lord's approval.

Response

The consecration that the Lord requires of those he brings to himself in service is wholehearted, unwavering, and unapologetic. One of the most well-known English preachers, Charles Spurgeon, on taking the pulpit at a church aptly named the Tabernacle inaugured his ministry with a sermon of consecration:

> It appears that the one subject upon which men preached in the apostolic age was *Jesus Christ*. The tendency of man, if left alone, is continually to go further and further from God, and the Church of God itself is no exception to the general rule. . . . Gradually the Church departed from the central point, and began rather to preach ceremonials and church offices than the person of their Lord. . . . I would propose that the subject of the ministry of this house, as long as this platform shall stand, and as long as this house shall be frequented by worshipers, shall be the person of Jesus Christ.[120]

These words call to mind Paul, who determined to preach nothing but the crucified Christ, relying not on his human frailty or any rhetoric of persuasion but on the gospel's power to convict and convert (1 Cor. 2:1–5). For whatever reason Nadab and Abihu did not rely on God's real, visible, and tangible presence in their midst to validate their ministry. They produced a fire of their own, adding spectacle to ceremony, human effort to divine service, the profane to the holy.

---

[118] This is made most explicit for the high priest, who bears their iniquity on his head (Ex. 28:38) and at his death atones for the unintentional manslayer (Num. 35:25).
[119] Milgrom, *Leviticus 1–16*, 638.
[120] Charles Spurgeon, *Sermons*, vol. 7, no. 369; delivered March 25, 1861.

The privilege of leading God's people comes with great responsibility. It also comes with great pressure to perform in a way that appears to validate the leader in ministry. This passage challenges and exhorts Christian leaders to guard themselves against the temptation to bring an offering of their own making. It is easier than it seems to embellish a presentation of the gospel with a mixture of other things—a reliance on technology, a spirit of entertainment, an appeal to practical psychology; the list goes on. The temptation is ever-present to preach words that are not one's own under pressure to appear dynamic and charismatic, or to labor to appear spiritual in public while losing battles in private. The church of Jesus Christ needs holy leaders, not ones who appear successful. It needs leaders who know their greatest resource in ministry is the living presence and abiding fellowship of the Lord.

This passage calls all ministers to center their hope on Christ's atoning death, which offers deep cleansing to "purify our conscience from dead works to serve the living God" (Heb. 9:14). It calls them to consecrate themselves afresh, to embrace a proper and reverent fear of the Lord, rejecting a posture of overfamiliarity with a God who is a consuming fire and rightly deserving to be worshiped with reverence and awe (Heb. 12:28–29). It summons ministers to commit themselves anew to their calling and to find their purpose in this world in being set apart for God's use.

Jesus consecrated himself with a singularity of focus and purpose to offer himself as the sacrifice that atones for sin and restores humanity to the Father's presence. He required no sacrifice of his own (Heb. 7:26–27) but carried our sin to its final destruction, where it was "swallowed up in victory" (1 Cor. 15:54–56). In all holiness and perfection Jesus fulfilled all the requirements of the law and in perfect obedience did only what he saw his Father doing (John 5:19; 6:38). He is a High Priest who can be trusted in every way because he did not seek to please himself or aggrandize his ministry but came to please the Father (Matt. 12:18; John 8:29). In what has come to be known as his high priestly prayer (John 17:1–26) Jesus prays for his disciples to participate in the same consecration: "For their sake I consecrate myself, that they also may be sanctified in truth" (John 17:19). As his disciples, we draw confidence that he has left us not only with his example but with his empowering presence to live a life of obedience in which the fire of his holiness will sanctify us and not consume us.

LEVITICUS 11

11 And the Lord spoke to Moses and Aaron, saying to them, **2** "Speak to the people of Israel, saying, These are the living things that you may eat among all the animals that are on the earth. **3** Whatever parts the hoof and is cloven-footed and chews the cud, among the animals, you may eat. **4** Nevertheless, among those that chew the cud or part the hoof, you shall not eat these: The camel, because it chews the cud but does not part the hoof, is unclean to you. **5** And the rock badger, because it chews the cud but does not part the hoof, is unclean to you. **6** And the hare, because it chews the cud but does not part the hoof, is unclean to you. **7** And the pig, because it parts the hoof and is cloven-footed but does not chew the cud, is unclean to you. **8** You shall not eat any of their flesh, and you shall not touch their carcasses; they are unclean to you.

9 "These you may eat, of all that are in the waters. Everything in the waters that has fins and scales, whether in the seas or in the rivers, you may eat. **10** But anything in the seas or the rivers that does not have fins and scales, of the swarming creatures in the waters and of the living creatures that are in the waters, is detestable to you. **11** You shall regard them as detestable; you shall not eat any of their flesh, and you shall detest their carcasses. **12** Everything in the waters that does not have fins and scales is detestable to you.

13 "And these you shall detest among the birds;[1] they shall not be eaten; they are detestable: the eagle,[2] the bearded vulture, the black vulture, **14** the kite, the falcon of any kind, **15** every raven of any kind, **16** the ostrich, the nighthawk, the sea gull, the hawk of any kind, **17** the little owl, the cormorant, the short-eared owl, **18** the barn owl, the tawny owl, the carrion vulture, **19** the stork, the heron of any kind, the hoopoe, and the bat.

20 "All winged insects that go on all fours are detestable to you. **21** Yet among the winged insects that go on all fours you may eat those that have jointed legs above their feet, with which to hop on the ground. **22** Of them you may eat: the locust of any kind, the bald locust of any kind, the cricket of any kind, and the grasshopper of any kind. **23** But all other winged insects that have four feet are detestable to you.

24 "And by these you shall become unclean. Whoever touches their carcass shall be unclean until the evening, **25** and whoever carries any part of their carcass shall wash his clothes and be unclean until the evening. **26** Every animal that parts the hoof but is not cloven-footed or does not chew the cud is unclean to you. Everyone who touches them shall be unclean. **27** And all that walk on their paws, among the animals that go on all fours, are unclean to you. Whoever touches their carcass shall be unclean until the evening, **28** and he who carries their carcass shall wash his clothes and be unclean until the evening; they are unclean to you.

29 "And these are unclean to you among the swarming things that swarm on the ground: the mole rat, the mouse, the great lizard of any kind, **30** the gecko, the monitor lizard, the lizard, the sand lizard, and the chameleon. ³¹ These are unclean to you among all that swarm. Whoever touches them when they are dead shall be unclean until the evening. ³² And anything on which any of them falls when they are dead shall be unclean, whether it is an article of wood or a garment or a skin or a sack, any article that is used for any purpose. It must be put into water, and it shall be unclean until the evening; then it shall be clean. ³³ And if any of them falls into any earthenware vessel, all that is in it shall be unclean, and you shall break it. ³⁴ Any food in it that could be eaten, on which water comes, shall be unclean. And all drink that could be drunk from every such vessel shall be unclean. ³⁵ And everything on which any part of their carcass falls shall be unclean. Whether oven or stove, it shall be broken in pieces. They are unclean and shall remain unclean for you. ³⁶ Nevertheless, a spring or a cistern holding water shall be clean, but whoever touches a carcass in them shall be unclean. ³⁷ And if any part of their carcass falls upon any seed grain that is to be sown, it is clean, ³⁸ but if water is put on the seed and any part of their carcass falls on it, it is unclean to you.

³⁹ "And if any animal which you may eat dies, whoever touches its carcass shall be unclean until the evening, ⁴⁰ and whoever eats of its carcass shall wash his clothes and be unclean until the evening. And whoever carries the carcass shall wash his clothes and be unclean until the evening.

⁴¹ "Every swarming thing that swarms on the ground is detestable; it shall not be eaten. ⁴² Whatever goes on its belly, and whatever goes on all fours, or whatever has many feet, any swarming thing that swarms on the ground, you shall not eat, for they are detestable. ⁴³ You shall not make yourselves detestable with any swarming thing that swarms, and you shall not defile yourselves with them, and become unclean through them. ⁴⁴ For I am the LORD your God. Consecrate yourselves therefore, and be holy, for I am holy. You shall not defile yourselves with any swarming thing that crawls on the ground. ⁴⁵ For I am the LORD who brought you up out of the land of Egypt to be your God. You shall therefore be holy, for I am holy."

⁴⁶ This is the law about beast and bird and every living creature that moves through the waters and every creature that swarms on the ground, ⁴⁷ to make a distinction between the unclean and the clean and between the living creature that may be eaten and the living creature that may not be eaten.

¹ Or *things that fly*; compare Genesis 1:20 ² The identity of many of these birds is uncertain

Section Overview

The sacrilege of Aaron's sons culminates in a fearful display of God's judgment. Because the Lord dwells among his people, it is critical that they learn to guard against violating his holiness. The priesthood is entrusted with teaching Israel to make distinctions in their daily lives "between the holy and the common, and between the unclean and the clean" (10:10–11). The first topic of Israel's discipleship is how to eat in holiness by distinguishing between clean and unclean animals. At the conclusion of this teaching the charge is given to the people themselves: "Make a distinction between the unclean and the clean and between the living creature that may be eaten and the living creature that may not be eaten" (11:47).

Israelites are invited to participate in their sanctification and to pursue the Lord's intentions for covenant fellowship.

Eating receives a lot of attention in Leviticus. The book begins with the offerings that grace the Lord's table (chs. 1–5), moves to the holy portions allotted to priests and their families (chs. 6–7), and then continues with the meat fit for Israel's table (ch. 11). The second half of the book, on holy living, takes up the theme of covenant eating again: refraining from blood (ch. 17), circumstances in which priests must refrain from holy portions, and, finally, refraining from offering blemished sacrifices (ch. 22), coming back full circle to the table of the Lord. Eating expresses relationship with the Lord and shapes the identity of those who feast with him (cf. Rev. 3:20).

The chapter is shaped to reflect the creation account of Genesis 1:20–25. Animals are presented according to their habitats: land (Lev. 11:2–8, 29–30, 41–42), water (vv. 9–12), and sky (vv. 13–23). Since the Lord now indwells creation in the midst of his people, creatures in each of these realms are related to his holiness and deemed clean or unclean. The Lord's instructions thus reach beyond a mere patterning after creation to address the human vocation of stewarding creation. As Adam named the animals because he understood something essential about their nature (Gen. 2:19–20), Israel discerns whether those animals may be brought to table fellowship. The Lord's table is connected to his people's: offerings made at the altar put meat on the menu for Israelites (Lev. 17:8–9).[121] In light of God's revealed will the people must discern whether the flesh of a living being facilitates communion with the Lord or draws them apart. A meal eaten in fellowship with family and community strengthens spiritual bonds and identity as a people while at the same time serving to distinguish Israelites from those outside the covenant community.

The Lord draws upon metaphors from Israel's life experience to communicate his redemptive purposes. Membership in the household of God is illustrated through the metaphor of domesticated animals: "You are my sheep, human sheep of my pasture, and I am your God, declares the Lord GOD" (Ezek. 34:31; cf. Pss. 95:7; 100:1–5). This analogy is foundational for Israelites' understanding of themselves, their community, and the world around them. A domesticated, sacrifice-able animal corresponds to an individual, which is precisely what makes it "an apt gift and even a symbolic counterpart for the worshiper, who sacrifices a creature analogous to him/herself to God."[122] On the level of society, ranking within the community is reflected in the sacrifices of the sin offering brought according to the animal hierarchy of a mixed flock: the high priest offers a bull, a tribal leader a male goat, and an ordinary citizen a female goat or lamb (ch. 4). As Leviticus progressively develops a vision of holiness that subsumes all of life, another layer is added to

---

121 Once Israel settled in the land, domestic animals could be eaten away from the sanctuary so long as their blood was ritually disposed (Deut. 12:15–16).
122 Ronald Hendel, "Table and Altar: The Anthropology of Food in the Priestly Torah," in *To Break Every Yoke: Essays in Honor of Marvin L. Chaney*, ed. R. B. Coote and N. K. Gottwald (Sheffield, UK: Sheffield Phoenix Press, 2007), 136.

the analogy in this chapter relating to divisions in the world: Israel is as clean animals and the nations are as unclean.[123] The implication is that dietary laws serve as "a sign of Israel's identity and calling, a wall of separation between Israel and the nations. Israel had been chosen of God and cleansed, and so possessed, with his dwelling in their midst, fullness of life; the Gentiles were still exiled from the divine Presence, unclean and in the realm of death."[124]

A variety of approaches have sought to explain the dietary laws, many that can be traced back to antiquity. In brief the most common include the following:[125]

(1) *Hygienic*: unclean animals carry diseases that pose health concerns; for example, pigs could carry trichinosis or shellfish could be contaminated. This view reflects mainly modern health concerns and has not found strong support among interpreters who point out the ritual (not medical) interest of these laws. If hygiene was of primary concern, it is doubtful that Jesus would have abolished the distinctions of clean and unclean (Mark 7:19).

(2) *Creational order*: clean animals display characteristics compatible with their creational realms, whereas unclean animals do not fit the pattern; for example, aquatic animals that do not swim but instead scuttle along the bottom are unclean.[126] Much remains unaccounted for, such as why anomalous animals like the donkey are prized for labor but not for lunch.

(3) *Ethical*: by avoiding certain animals Israel learned the sanctity of life and how to restrain their appetite.[127] This reading notes a progression from humanity's original diet (Gen. 1:29) to the concession of meat (Gen. 9:3–4). The dietary laws restrict Israel's fare further to only clean animals. But if restraint is the goal, is this achieved simply by limiting Israel's choices of what it can eat (but putting no limits on how much it can eat)?

(4) *Arbitrary*: there is no discernible rationale to the division of clean and unclean, but these laws nevertheless teach the valuable lesson of obedience.[128] Without question obedience is at the heart of relationship with the Lord. Yet the dietary laws are in close conversation with God's work in creation and redemption, both thematically and by repeated phrases, thus suggesting intentional theological reflection in how they are conceived.

---

[123] Subsequent chapters continue to develop the theme by addressing how an animal's life may substitute for that of the worshiper (Lev. 17:11) and how an acceptable sacrifice must be pure and unblemished (22:19–25).
[124] L. Michael Morales, *Who Shall Ascend the Mountain of the Lord?*, NSBT (Downers Grove, IL: InterVarsity Press, 2015), 163.
[125] For a survey cf. Walter Houston, *Purity and Monotheism: Clean and Unclean Animals in Biblical Law*, JSOT Supp. 140 (Sheffield, UK: JSOT Press, 1993), 68–123.
[126] Mary Douglas, *Purity and Danger*, 55–57. A fruitful application of Douglas' categories may be found in Wenham, *Leviticus*, 164–185.
[127] Milgrom, *Leviticus 1–16*, 731–736; Balentine, *Leviticus*, 96–98; Houston, *Purity and Monotheism*, 257–258.
[128] Gane's approach emphasizes an actionable aspect of demonstrating faith even if the commands are no longer binding (*Leviticus, Numbers*, 208–209).

While we may not understand fully the rationale behind the dietary laws, staying close to the biblical text allows us to find their ultimate purpose. The theological reason for making distinctions between clean and unclean is for Israel to be holy as the Lord is holy so it may remain in life-giving fellowship with him (Lev. 11:44–45). Therefore it is best to approach these laws as the original hearers did, making redemptive-theological connections. The dietary laws are for Israel's discipleship and training in godliness. In their every meal Israelites consecrated themselves to the Lord and separated themselves from the nations (20:24–26). With each act of obedience they set themselves apart as the Lord's holy people, envisioning the world as a sanctuary with themselves as the new humanity within it.

Section Outline

III. Ritual Impurity (11:1–15:33)
    A. Clean and Unclean Animals (11:1–47)
        1. Introduction (11:1–2a)
        2. Clean and Unclean Animals (11:2b–23)
            a. Land Animals (11:2b–8)
            b. Aquatic Animals (11:9–12)
            c. Flying Animals (11:13–19)
            d. Flying Insects (11:20–23)
        3. Carcass Impurity (11:24–40)
        4. Swarming Creatures (11:41–45)
        5. Summary (11:46–47)

Comment

11:1–2a The Lord addresses Aaron in addition to Moses for the first time. The narrative of the priesthood's ordination, inaugural worship service, and Nadab and Abihu's ritual transgression ended on a question concerning holy eating. Moses reprimanded Aaron for not eating the sin offering. Aaron countered that, considering the day's tragedy, the Lord would not have approved, and Moses, hearing his reasoning, agreed (10:20). In this exchange we saw Aaron become an authority on matters of ritual eating. He and all the priestly servants will now teach the people to make distinctions as they select meat for their tables.

11:2b–3 As Israelites prepare to set their table, they must select clean animals and reject the unclean. Clean animals meet two criteria: they chew the cud and have divided hooves. This refers primarily to domesticated herds and flocks, with the inclusion of game such as deer and gazelle, roebuck, wild goat and ibex, antelope, and mountain sheep (Deut. 14:5). Cud-chewing animals are herbivores who do not feed on flesh.

A subtle word choice encourages the hearer to draw connections between the dietary laws and Israel's redemption. The expression "to bring up" the cud (*'alah*) readily resonates with God's work to "bring up" (*'alah*) Israel out of Egypt, a theological point that frames the laws in this chapter: "You shall not defile yourselves. ... For I am the LORD who *brought you up* out of the land of Egypt to be your God" (Lev. 11:44–45). This serves to make the point that, as Israelites separate clean from unclean creatures, they enact their own status as a redeemed people. Their eating secures their identity: they are a people who have been brought up out of Egypt by the Lord.

11:4–7 The discussion moves from that which is permitted to that which is prohibited to eat, exactly as the Lord commands in Genesis: "*You may surely eat* of every tree of the garden, but of the tree of the knowledge of good and evil *you shall not eat*" (Gen. 2:16–17). Unclean animals meet only one of the two criteria. The camel, rock badger, and hare appear to bring up the cud (though they are not technically ruminants) but do not have fully divided hooves. On the other hand the pig has a divided hoof but does not bring up the cud. Firmage notes that all unclean animals could have been prohibited by the single specification that they have divided hooves. The law's phrasing therefore explicitly singles out pork: "The pig has a special place, for it alone in the entire animal world known to Israel has cloven hooves but does not chew the cud."[129] Pork avoidance becomes the most enduring and defining dietary identity marker for the Jewish people, one that continues to this day.

Israel's neighbors, the Philistines, raised pigs for food. Pig bones are plentiful in the coastal cities where the Philistines settled, but in Israelite territory very few pig bones have been found.[130] By the Hellenistic Period (323–31 BC) pork consumption marked a hard ethnic boundary. The Seleucid emperor Antiochus Epiphanes infamously slaughtered a sow on the temple's altar, desecrated the scrolls of the law with it, and forced the high priest to eat its flesh.[131] In NT times pig raising continued to be associated with Gentile territory (Mark 5:1, 13).

11:8 The rejection of unclean animals is comprehensive. They are not suitable for Israel's table; moreover, their carcasses cannot even be touched, echoing the language of Genesis: "You shall not eat ... neither shall you touch it" (Gen. 3:3). The topic of carcass impurity is brought up as an aside and will be taken up again (Lev. 11:24–28, 39–40). Those later verses suggest that the point of verse 8 is that Israelites must realize they cannot touch these carcasses without contracting impurity. As for live unclean animals, they do not convey impurity. The patriarchs rode camels (Gen. 24:10, 19–20), and Israelite farmers used donkeys as pack animals for travel and labor (Gen. 42:26).

11:9 Fish with fins and scales are clean to eat. Fish were a small part of the Israelite diet, mainly tilapia and carp from the freshwater Sea of Galilee and Jordan River,

---

129 Edwin Firmage, "Zoology," *ABD*, 6:1125.
130 Borowski, *Every Living Thing*, 143. This point has been greatly nuanced by recent archaeology but still seems to hold true generally.
131 Moving accounts of Jewish martyrdom recount how women, the elderly, and the young were tortured for their refusal to be force-fed pork (*2 Macc.* 6:18–31). In response to this oppression the Maccabean Revolt succeeded in seizing and purifying the temple. Referred to in the NT as the Festival of Dedication (John 10:22), it is celebrated by Jews to this day as the Feast of Hanukkah.

with Nile perch and grouper coming from Egypt and the Mediterranean through trade (Neh. 13:16).[132]

11:10–12 Swarming creatures describe small creatures that move about in large numbers.[133] The wordplay in Hebrew—"swarming" creatures (*sheretz*) are "detestable" (*sheqetz*)—makes the phrase memorable, especially since the word "detestable" is used four times in these verses.[134] The strong language creates a heightened consciousness for the need of separation. The force of the term "detestable" is to reorient Israel's perception and align it with the divine will. That which the Lord deems abhorrent should not be perceived as a "delight to the eyes" (Gen. 3:6) but should be faithfully avoided.

11:13–19 Israelites are not given criteria by which to distinguish edible birds from inedible ones. Instead a list of twenty banned birds is given according to their "kind" (Lev. 11:14, 15, 16, 19), an obvious allusion to the creation account (Gen. 1:12, 21, 24, 25). Most of the forbidden birds feed on live prey or carrion, meaning they come in contact with carcasses and feed on blood, something Israelites are categorically forbidden from doing (Lev. 11:24, 31; cf. 7:26–27; 17:10).[135] Clean birds include doves and pigeons, geese and ducks, hens and quails, and sparrows.[136] In Hellenistic times doves and pigeons were raised in underground rock-carved niches known as columbaria. It is thought that some of the birds were used as sacrificial offerings in the temple.

11:20–23 Among flying insects (Hb. "winged swarmers") those that walk on all fours are forbidden. However, those with jointed legs that hop may be eaten: the locust, bald locust, cricket, and grasshopper. These are indeed eaten in many places in the world today, and John the Baptist famously ate "locusts and wild honey" (Matt. 3:4).

11:24–28 The Lord's instructions continue to expand on the pollution that unclean animals convey. Anyone who touches the carcass of an unclean animal contracts a minor impurity and must wait until evening. Anyone who carries a carcass, having more sustained contact to presumably remove and bury it, must wash his clothes and wait until evening.

11:29–30 Having already discussed swarmers among aquatic and flying creatures (Lev. 11:10–12, 20–23), the instructions pick up the topic of land swarmers that are unclean and not permitted to eat. Eight creatures are listed, among them rodents and reptiles.

11:31–36 Carcasses of unclean swarming creatures could easily contaminate a home; being small, they could drop into water jugs, food containers, or cooking

---

[132] Borowski, *Every Living Thing*, 170–175.
[133] James W. Watts, *Leviticus 11–20*, HCOT (Leuven: Peeters, 2023), 86.
[134] Eleven times total: Lev. 11:10, 11, 12 (2x), 13 (2x), 20, 23, 41, 42, 43.
[135] Milgrom, *Leviticus 1–16*, 661–664. For possible identifications cf. Peter Altmann, *Banned Birds: The Birds of Leviticus 11 and Deuteronomy 14* (Tübingen: Mohr Siebeck, 2019), 77–127. Altmann classifies *most* birds as carnivorous, with some exceptions, such as the ostrich.
[136] Kleinig, *Leviticus*, 245.

ovens. Wood, cloth, or leather on which a carcass has dropped must be submerged in water to be cleansed (cf. Num. 31:20). A ceramic vessel, on the other hand, must be smashed and everything in it discarded (cf. Lev. 15:12). Clay ovens in the courtyard of Israelite homes also had to be broken if contaminated by a swarming creature. Clay ovens in the shape of a beehive had an opening at the top for pressing dough to bake against the sides, through which a swarmer could easily fall.[137] As an exception, cisterns that collect rainwater do not contract impurity. They are a source of purity instead that cleanses those things that have become unclean.

11:37–38 Dry seed does not become contaminated by an animal carcass, but dampened seed does, likely because water is a medium that conducts impurity or because the water may have caused the seed casing to crack and germinate, exposing whatever is inside.

11:39–40 Carcasses are polluting, even those of clean animals that are permitted as food. Ritual slaughter does not, of course, pollute a person, and a clean animal that dies of natural causes may be eaten, though the handling of its flesh necessitates washing and waiting until evening to be clean (17:15).

11:41–45 The topic of swarming creatures is taken up in a highly structured unit interwoven with commands and motives urging obedience (cf. table 3.3).[138]

TABLE 3.3: Commands and Motives in Leviticus 11:41–45

(A) command: do not make yourselves detestable (v. 43)	(A') command: do not defile yourselves (v. 44b)
(B) motive: I am the Lord (v. 44a)	(B') motive: I am the Lord (v. 45a)
(C) command: be holy (v. 44a)	(C') command: be holy (v. 45b)
(D) motive: I am holy (v. 44a)	(D') motive: I am holy (v. 45b)

Why is there such an emphasis on avoiding creatures that walk close to the ground or crawl on their "belly" (v. 42)? Conspicuously, the single other mention of "belly" (Hb. *gakhon*) is in the curse on the serpent, that he slither on his belly all his days (Gen. 3:14). Israelites' obedience to reject swarming creatures from their table would enact the priestly task of banishing from their homes those creatures associated with the serpent who originally defiled humanity. If Israelites allow themselves to become defiled by detestable things, they likewise become detestable (Lev. 11:43), taking on a nature different from that which they are meant to have as God's people.

First appearing here, "I am the LORD your God" is a refrain that will echo throughout the rest of the book.[139] Israel's identity derives from the Lord, with

---

[137] Cynthia Shafer-Elliott, *Food in Ancient Judah: Domestic Cooking in the Time of the Hebrew Bible* (Milton Park, UK: Routledge, 2013), 120.
[138] Adapted from Sklar, *Leviticus*, TOTC, 171.
[139] Leviticus 18:2, 4, 30; 19:2, 3, 4, 10, 25, 31, 34, 36; 20:7, 24; 23:22, 43; 24:22; 25:17, 38, 55; 26:1, 13, 44.

whom it is bound in covenant. The privilege of sharing in his holiness comes with the obligation to separate from all defiling practices.

11:46 The passage ends with a summary of the law (Hb. *torah*, "instruction"). The Lord provides four categories for Israelites to discern between clean and unclean: clean land animals chew the cud and part the hoof; clean aquatic animals have fins and scales; twenty birds are forbidden; clean flying insects have jointed legs and hop. The fifth category is forbidden with no qualifications: swarmers are all unclean.

11:47 Israelites are to make distinctions (Hb. *badal*) as the Lord did when dividing light from darkness, the waters above the heavens from those below, and day from night (Gen. 1:4, 6–7, 14). Similarly, the Lord created a holy nation by setting it apart (*badal*) from the nations as a distinct people (Lev. 20:24). In imitation of its Sovereign, Israel must continue to enact divisions in its daily lives to keep itself set apart: "I am the LORD your God, who has separated you from the peoples. You shall therefore separate the clean beast from the unclean" (20:24–25).

By eating in obedience to the Lord's commands Israel is to live out its identity among the nations. Its meat comprises domesticated animals because Israel is the Lord's flock. Ruminants that bring up the cud perpetuate the memory that Israel had been brought up out of Egypt. Israelites avoided carnivorous scavengers as they themselves were commanded to avoid touching carcasses or ingesting blood. They kept separate from "whatever goes on its belly" in remembrance of the enduring enmity between themselves and the serpent's offspring (Gen. 3:14–15).

Response

The dietary laws given to Israel prepare us for the invitation to come to that table where we find our true identity in the consummate meal prepared by the Lord. We eat the bread and drink the wine to commemorate Christ's death and to enact bodily our belief that we have been redeemed by the broken body and shed blood of our Savior, Jesus Christ. Through a sacred covenant meal we proclaim his coming and the hope of eternal life in him (John 6:50–55).

Jesus uses meals, a deeply embedded symbol in Israel's cultural life, to draw people to himself. He feasts with those on the margins, eating with sinners and welcoming them into the kingdom of God by welcoming them first to the table (Mark 2:15–17). He uses the Passover meal to explain his sacrificial death to his disciples, showing them that it is soon coming to fulfillment in himself as he will inaugurate the new covenant (Matt. 26:26–29). Those who eat at table with him feast in fulfillment of prophetic anticipations of commensality with God (Isa. 25:6–9). After his resurrection Jesus chooses to reveal his identity through a meal: "When he was at table with them, he took the bread and blessed and broke it and gave it to them. And their eyes were opened, and they recognized him" (Luke 24:30–31). Meals define identity. As the banquet host, the Lord invites us to partake in the meal of his flesh and blood that defines our belonging to his body.

In the new covenant dietary regulations that once separated Israelites from the surrounding nations are no longer binding. The inclusion of the Gentiles is revealed to Peter in a vision that a faithful Jew living out of Leviticus would understand: a sheet descended at mealtime filled with all kinds of unclean animals for him to kill and eat (Acts 10:10–16).[140] Peter's objection testifies to how strong a covenant boundary-marker the dietary laws had become and how effectively they had separated Jews and Gentiles for generations. But through this vision Peter understands that the nations have *become clean* through faith in Christ: "God has shown me that I should not call any person common or unclean" (Acts 10:28). Gentiles have been granted "repentance that leads to life" (Acts 11:18), cleansed from all unrighteousness, and filled with the Holy Spirit, just as Jewish believers have been (Acts 15:8–9). Israel's election had always been for the sake of the nations, who are now invited to the table as full participants in the covenant community.

The church wrestled with the nature of this multicultural table fellowship, as chronicled in the book of Acts and Paul's letters. The Jerusalem Council agreed on four nonnegotiables to bring Jewish and Gentile believers to the same table, drawn in large measure from Leviticus's laws on holy living for the resident alien. Gentiles had to refrain from things polluted by idols (1 Cor. 8:1–13; 10:18–22), sexual immorality (Lev. 18:6–30), anything strangled (7:24; 17:15), and the ingesting of blood (7:26–27; 17:10–16). Covenant identity has always been meant to be enacted around a shared meal. The meal that is now of eternal significance is the one made up of the body and blood of Jesus, the meal that levels all boundaries to create a new redeemed people, called to "come from east and west and recline at table with Abraham, Isaac, and Jacob in the kingdom of heaven" (Matt. 8:11).

LEVITICUS 12

12 The LORD spoke to Moses, saying, ² "Speak to the people of Israel, saying, If a woman conceives and bears a male child, then she shall be unclean seven days. As at the time of her menstruation, she shall be unclean. ³ And on the eighth day the flesh of his foreskin shall be circumcised. ⁴ Then she shall continue for thirty-three days in the blood of her purifying. She shall not touch anything holy, nor come into the sanctuary, until the days of her purifying are completed. ⁵ But if she bears a female child, then she shall be unclean two weeks, as in her menstruation. And she shall continue in the blood of her purifying for sixty-six days.

⁶ "And when the days of her purifying are completed, whether for a son or for a daughter, she shall bring to the priest at the entrance of the tent of meeting a lamb a year old for a burnt offering, and a pigeon or a

---

140 The Greek *tetrapoda tēs gēs* ("animals"; Acts 10:12) literally translates "four-footed animals of the ground" and refers to the creatures that swarm on the ground of Leviticus 11:46.

turtledove for a sin offering, ⁷and he shall offer it before the Lord and make atonement for her. Then she shall be clean from the flow of her blood. This is the law for her who bears a child, either male or female. ⁸And if she cannot afford a lamb, then she shall take two turtledoves or two pigeons,¹ one for a burnt offering and the other for a sin offering. And the priest shall make atonement for her, and she shall be clean."

¹ Septuagint *two young pigeons*

Section Overview

The topic of childbirth introduces the section that deals with bodily impurities (chs. 12–15). These chapters define those who merit exclusion from the sanctuary and the means through which they may be integrated back into the worshiping community. The opening chapter addresses the uncleanness of a woman from the blood loss of childbirth, and the closing chapter addresses purification from genital discharges (male and female), ending on the topic of menstrual blood. The instructions thus come full circle, beginning and ending with a woman's loss of life fluids. Inside this envelope is the diagnosis (ch. 13) and purification of skin disease (ch. 14). The arrangement helps make the instructions memorable, something especially important for a culture that is predominantly aural.[141]

The concern of this passage is with how to restore a woman to a state of ritual purity after delivering a child. A period of separation followed by sacrifice provides the way for a mother to be reincorporated into the worshiping community, with access to the sanctuary. The Lord's instructions recognize the woman as a worshiper.

Glimpses of Israel's worshiping life reveal a vibrant female presence, especially as part of the larger household. Women are found at the sanctuary earnestly seeking the Lord (1 Sam. 1:10–16), fulfilling vows as individuals (Num. 30:3–15; 1 Sam. 1:21–24), and participating with their husbands in making sacrificial offerings (Judg. 13:15–23; 1 Sam. 1:24–25).[142] They feast in God's presence on meat that has been offered on the altar (1 Sam. 1:3–5).[143] They sing and lead worship, as Miriam with tambourine in hand to celebrate the Lord's deliverance (Ex. 15:20–21). They are free to set themselves apart to the Lord for a season by taking a Nazirite vow (Num. 6:2). They are found serving at the entrance to the tabernacle and tending to God's house (Ex. 38:8; 1 Sam. 2:22). They observe holy days and participate in celebrations of repentance and rejoicing (Lev. 16:29; Deut. 12:12). They are included, together with their children, in the public reading of God's Word and are charged with obeying it (Deut. 31:10–13; Neh. 8:1–3). The fact that children are welcome not only speaks to the concern for passing down the faith to the next generation but significantly allows for women, the primary caregivers of the young, to be present in public worship.

---

141 Sklar, *Leviticus*, TOTC, 174.
142 Women as worshipers in Leviticus is implied by the use of inclusive language in the instructions for sacrifice (cf. comment on 1:2b).
143 Both the sons and the daughters of Aaron gather around the table to eat the holy portions from the altar (Lev. 10:14).

Section Outline

III. Ritual Impurity (11:1–15:33) . . .

    B. Purification after Childbirth (12:1–8)

        1. Introduction (12:1–2a)

        2. Time Required for Purification If the Child Is Male (12:2b–4)

        3. Time Required for Purification If the Child Is Female (12:5)

        4. Sacrifice Required for Purification (12:6–7)

        5. Provision for a Woman of Lower Economic Status (12:8)

Comment

12:1–2a The Lord gives instructions to Moses, who in turn addresses the people regarding a woman who has given birth. One can imagine in the generations to come that these instructions would be repeated and faithfully passed down from mother to daughter. The legislation that follows may span just a few verses, but it touches on a very significant aspect of a woman's life experience. The Bible paints the picture that childbirth is a regular occasion for women to draw near to the Lord in faith.

Women seek the Lord, believing that conception is his work (Ruth 4:13; Ps. 139:13) and that it is ultimately in his hand to either open or close the womb (Gen. 29:31; 30:22; Ruth 4:13). They not only pray to conceive (1 Sam. 1:10–11) but continue to trust the Lord throughout their pregnancy as the one who knows the children in the womb (Gen. 25:22–23; Jer. 1:5). Childbirth, then as now, could be life threatening, and women often came to the threshold of death when bringing forth life (Gen. 35:17–19). The experience of pregnancy and childbirth could shape a mother's vision of her child's future, which is reflected in its naming (Gen. 4:1; 21:6–7; 25:24–26; 29:32–35; etc.) and nurtured in its upbringing (Gen. 16:11–12; Judg. 13:3–5). Childbirth in Scripture is oftentimes a struggle of faith (Gen. 18:11–15), sometimes even a struggle between life and death (cf. Matt. 2:16), but always the work of the Lord (Gen. 4:1).

12:2b Discussion of purification begins with the case of a woman who bears a male child. In giving birth a woman becomes unclean. Why should childbirth cause a woman to become unclean if God's mandate to humanity is to bring forth life—"be fruitful and multiply" (Gen. 1:28)—and if a woman's role as a mother is highly valued (Gen. 3:20)? Impurity after childbirth has to do with the bodily discharge of blood and is strictly the designation of a ritual state, not a moral state (cf. Lev. 15:19–26). There is nothing sinful, shameful, or undignified about a mother's postpartum condition.

A woman's postpartum blood flow is likened to her menstruation, meaning that for the first week after giving birth her impurity can be communicated to those who come in contact with her directly or with anything on which she has sat or lain (Lev. 15:19–20; cf. Gen. 31:34–35). It also means that her husband may have no sexual relations with her (Lev. 18:19). There is nothing particularly unusual about these restrictions, which the woman would have kept every month prior to her pregnancy. Their practical effect is to place the mother in the welcome position to receive care from her immediate household while her body heals from the trauma of childbirth.[144] She would be allowed to rest, begin lactation, and bond with her newborn in a pro-natal culture that values the lives of both mother and child. While the benefits to the mother are many, it is important to keep in mind that the primary reason for these laws is to remove the mother's impurity so that she may have access to the sanctuary and to the Lord, who is the source of all holiness for his people (Lev. 20:8). As a creature of the sixth day, her primary calling in life is to worship him and reflect his own holiness in the world.

12:3 The focus of attention momentarily shifts from the mother to the male child and the command that he be circumcised on the eighth day. The phrase "flesh of his foreskin" is identical to that of the Bible's first circumcision, recalling the sign of the covenant given to Abraham: "You shall be circumcised in the flesh of your foreskins, and it shall be a sign of the covenant between me and you" (Gen. 17:11).[145]

Circumcision is a family matter, performed in the home usually by the father (Gen. 17:12, 23; 21:4) and at a most urgent moment by the mother, though it is hard to know whether this was ever common practice (Ex. 4:25). Circumcision is a mark of Israel's identity and a physical sign of the covenant worn on the body.[146] A male child is ceremoniously welcomed into the worshiping community on the eighth day with the privilege and obligation to live according to the treaty of the great King (cf. Leviticus 26).

12:4 The mother's purification continues another thirty-three days for a total of forty days, a familiar number from Scripture marking transitionary periods.[147] In this secondary period of separation the mother is to "not touch anything holy, nor come into the sanctuary," clarifying that her impurity is defined with respect to the sanctuary and its holy things, such as the food of peace offerings (7:20–21). She is now in the "blood of her purifying," which is different from the initial blood "as at the time of her menstruation" (12:2), as she no longer communicates uncleanness to others and can therefore reenter normal societal relations without fear of passing on ritual impurity. This is also different from a woman with an abnormal issue of blood "beyond the time of her impurity" (15:25), which also continues to cause uncleanness.

---

144 A typical Israelite household included the extended family; Philip J. King and Lawrence E. Stager, *Life in Biblical Israel*, LAI (Louisville: Westminster John Knox, 2002), 40. Those who helped the new mother and came in contact with her would be ritually unclean until evening, which would not affect them greatly unless they were going to the sanctuary (Lev. 15:19). There is nothing to suggest that a husband avoided the mother of his newborn child.
145 This wording occurs only in this verse and in Genesis 17 (vv. 11, 14, 23, 24, 25), suggesting that the phrasing is intended to recall the sign of the covenant given to Abraham. The laws in Leviticus flow in continuity with the earliest inception of the nation.
146 Covenant ceremonies were attended by sacrifices and symbolic actions that put on display the consequences of disobedience. Covenant partners walked through the halved pieces of a sacrificed animal (cf. Gen. 15:9-10) to enact their taking on the curse of being cut off like the animal if they failed to keep the covenant (cf. Jer. 34:18). The promise of descendants to Abraham is marked by circumcision, the cutting of the flesh, as a sign of allegiance to Yahweh as covenant Sovereign.
147 Kleinig, *Leviticus*, 267.

The two-stage process marks a passage from one ritual state to another through separation, transition, and a return to society, classically known as a rite of passage.[148] The mother who has been separated from the community due to the impurity of childbirth begins a gradual reassimilation first into society at large (after seven days) and then into the household of God (after forty days). The passage of time allows for a transition between ritual states while she is moving closer to the sanctuary and the center of holiness, which is the Lord.

12:5 If the woman bears a female child, she is unclean twice as long: two weeks, as in her menstruation, and an additional sixty-six days in secondary purification, for a total of eighty days. In the absence of an explicit explanation in the text it is difficult to pinpoint the reason for this doubling. There are numerous suggestions as to why this might be.[149] Some interpreters take the view that this is because Israel's worship is greatly opposed to Canaanite fertility religions that viewed the childbearing woman as ritually potent. Biblical law, therefore, removes the new mother from the realm of the holy and her presence from the sanctuary. Others posit that a female child may have needed extra social and ritual protection than a male.

Another suggestion comes from closer attention to the chapter's arrangement, which noticeably interrupts the ritual legislation in the case of a male child to address circumcision (cf. comment on 12:3). This may be important. It is possible that allowance is made for a shorter purification period in the case of a male child so that the mother can participate in another important rite of passage, that of her son's circumcision.[150] Otherwise she would be unclean and unable to celebrate the rite that brings her son into the covenant community. Thus, rather than understanding the birth of the female child as prolonging ritual impurity, it could be that the birth of a male child curtails it.

In the absence of a clearly stated rationale it is possible that ancient Israelites themselves did not know the reason either but followed established cultural practices. It is the nature of ritual to focus on practice, not interpretation. Second, and most importantly, the very first chapter of the Bible makes clear that men and women equally bear God's image and thus have equal value before him (Gen. 1:27), meaning Israelites were not to view the differing lengths of time for impurity as a commentary on the value of male or female children.[151]

12:6–7 If there was any question whether a female child defiles more than a male, these verses quickly dispel it. The sacrifice required is the same for both male and

---

[148] A rite of passage entails (1) a period of separation from the state and status of an older identity, (2) entry into a liminal, or in-between, stage, and (3) a return to society having been transformed to a new state and status. Cf. Arnold Van Gennep, *The Rites of Passage*, trans. Monika B. Vizedom and Gabrielle L. Caffee (Chicago: University of Chicago Press, 1960). The installation of the priesthood in chapter 8 follows such a pattern. Aaron and his sons are separated from the rest of the people, they are in a liminal state for seven days, and on the eight day they function as priests at the altar. Their identity has been redefined with respect to the sanctuary, from common men to a holy priests.
[149] For a review of interpretations cf Milgrom, *Leviticus 1–16*, 750–751.
[150] In Jewish practice the sanctity of the Sabbath may be breached for circumcision on the eighth day, demonstrating that the sign of entrance into the covenant community takes precedence over other religious laws (Mishnah, Sukkah 18:3). This type of thinking may have applied in earlier times to the mother's ritual impurity.
[151] Gane, *Leviticus, Numbers*, 223.

female (stated twice in these verses for emphasis). The mother is to bring a burnt offering (a yearling lamb) and a sin offering (pigeon or turtledove) to complete her purification, and she will be clean from the blood loss of childbirth.[152] The need for a sin offering does not imply that she has sinned; rather, a sin offering is given for purification so that she may once again have access to worship at the sanctuary (cf. comment on 4:3–4). The call to all God's people is to be holy as he is holy (Lev. 11:44, 45; 19:2; 20:7, 26) and to bring his holy standards into every aspect of their lives (Lev. 10:10). The burnt offering is given as the "first act of worship after being restored to purity."[153] Ritual transition requires the passage of time and the shed blood of sacrifice.

The requirements after the new mother's period of purification are very clearly stated using the feminine form of the verb ("She shall bring"). This is what the woman herself must do, not what others will do on her behalf. She counts off the days of her purification, she is familiar with the requirements of the law, and she brings the offering to the tent of meeting. The mother is responsible and accountable for her relationship with the Lord. In all this, however, she does not act alone but would undoubtedly travel with her husband to the sanctuary and bring her nursing baby with her. This would make a child's first encounter with the Lord the result of a mother's obedience to come before the Lord in worship.

12:8 Concluding the legislation on impurity at childbirth is the provision for a woman of lower economic status to bring a turtledove instead of a lamb. As with all sacrifices, access to God is not limited to those of means; all Israel is enabled to obedience.

Response

Among every woman who fulfilled the requirements of this law in ancient Israel one stands out above the rest. The Gospel of Luke records Mary's appearing at the temple together with Joseph to make the purification sacrifice and to dedicate her firstborn son (Luke 2:24). Familiarity with the law of Leviticus illuminates this moment.

As an initial observation, the time given to a new mother before she is required to come before the Lord with an offering comes across as a great kindness. Allowing for at least a forty-day recovery shows the Lord's compassion for the vulnerability of a young mother and her infant child, a concern that surfaces throughout Scripture (Isa. 40:11; Matt. 19:13–15; 23:37).

The first time Jesus is found in his "Father's house" (Luke 2:49) is when he is brought by his mother in her obedience to appear before the Lord, an obedience his earthly parents would continue throughout their life as worshipers (Luke 2:41). But this first time is especially unique since Jesus is revealed publicly as the expected Messiah, Light to the Gentiles, and Savior of the world through the prophetic word

---

[152] These are the same offerings required at the ordination of the priesthood, which is also a rite of passage (Lev. 8:14, 18).
[153] Levine, *Leviticus*, 74; cf. also Gane, *Leviticus, Numbers*, 221.

at the temple (Luke 2:29–38). Mary and Joseph come with a "sacrifice according to what is said in the Law of the Lord, 'a pair of turtledoves, or two young pigeons'" (Luke 2:24). We recognize in this humble offering the Lord's allowance for the poor. While Mary and Joseph bring an offering out of their poverty, their baby boy is proclaimed by Simeon and Anna to be God's glorious riches for the world!

The coming of Christ into the world not as a fully grown man in his prime but as a vulnerable infant born to poor parents reaches deeply into human culture and promises to transform it. To begin, godless cultures are antilife; they exploit the vulnerable and persecute children (Ex. 1:15–16; Matt. 2:16–18). Biblical culture values life and protects it. It celebrates the role of a mother (Ps. 113:9) and regards children as a blessing from the Lord (Ps. 127:3–5). What is more, the legislation of Leviticus 12 encourages us to press even further into biblical culture to find our identity rooted in relationship with the Lord and our place of belonging in *his* house. This is a welcome refining of our vision. In our zeal to value life and Christian family rightly, there may be ways that we inadvertently set the expectation that the highest and most fulfilling expression of a woman's calling is in her role as a mother rather than her role as a worshiper. The anguish of barrenness is as real today as it was in ancient Israel (Gen. 30:1; 1 Sam. 1:10). Our actions may be adding stigma and isolation to a woman's hidden pain. The lens of Leviticus helps us to remember that a woman's core identity is in relationship to the Lord and her highest calling is to be a worshiper of Christ.

LEVITICUS 13

13 The LORD spoke to Moses and Aaron, saying, ² "When a person has on the skin of his body a swelling or an eruption or a spot, and it turns into a case of leprous[1] disease on the skin of his body, then he shall be brought to Aaron the priest or to one of his sons the priests, ³ and the priest shall examine the diseased area on the skin of his body. And if the hair in the diseased area has turned white and the disease appears to be deeper than the skin of his body, it is a case of leprous disease. When the priest has examined him, he shall pronounce him unclean. ⁴ But if the spot is white in the skin of his body and appears no deeper than the skin, and the hair in it has not turned white, the priest shall shut up the diseased person for seven days. ⁵ And the priest shall examine him on the seventh day, and if in his eyes the disease is checked and the disease has not spread in the skin, then the priest shall shut him up for another seven days. ⁶ And the priest shall examine him again on the seventh day, and if the diseased area has faded and the disease has not spread in the skin, then the priest shall pronounce him clean; it is only an eruption. And he shall wash his clothes and be clean. ⁷ But if the eruption spreads in the skin, after he has shown himself to the priest for his cleansing, he shall appear again before the priest. ⁸ And the priest shall look, and if the eruption has spread in the skin, then the priest shall pronounce him unclean; it is a leprous disease.

⁹ "When a man is afflicted with a leprous disease, he shall be brought to the priest, ¹⁰ and the priest shall look. And if there is a white swelling in the skin that has turned the hair white, and there is raw flesh in the swelling, ¹¹ it is a chronic leprous disease in the skin of his body, and the priest shall pronounce him unclean. He shall not shut him up, for he is unclean. ¹² And if the leprous disease breaks out in the skin, so that the leprous disease covers all the skin of the diseased person from head to foot, so far as the priest can see, ¹³ then the priest shall look, and if the leprous disease has covered all his body, he shall pronounce him clean of the disease; it has all turned white, and he is clean. ¹⁴ But when raw flesh appears on him, he shall be unclean. ¹⁵ And the priest shall examine the raw flesh and pronounce him unclean. Raw flesh is unclean, for it is a leprous disease. ¹⁶ But if the raw flesh recovers and turns white again, then he shall come to the priest, ¹⁷ and the priest shall examine him, and if the disease has turned white, then the priest shall pronounce the diseased person clean; he is clean.

¹⁸ "If there is in the skin of one's body a boil and it heals, ¹⁹ and in the place of the boil there comes a white swelling or a reddish-white spot, then it shall be shown to the priest. ²⁰ And the priest shall look, and if it appears deeper than the skin and its hair has turned white, then the priest shall pronounce him unclean. It is a case of leprous disease that has broken out in the boil. ²¹ But if the priest examines it and there is no white hair in it and it is not deeper than the skin, but has faded, then the priest shall shut him up seven days. ²² And if it spreads in the skin, then the priest shall pronounce him unclean; it is a disease. ²³ But if the spot remains in one place and does not spread, it is the scar of the boil, and the priest shall pronounce him clean.

²⁴ "Or, when the body has a burn on its skin and the raw flesh of the burn becomes a spot, reddish-white or white, ²⁵ the priest shall examine it, and if the hair in the spot has turned white and it appears deeper than the skin, then it is a leprous disease. It has broken out in the burn, and the priest shall pronounce him unclean; it is a case of leprous disease. ²⁶ But if the priest examines it and there is no white hair in the spot and it is no deeper than the skin, but has faded, the priest shall shut him up seven days, ²⁷ and the priest shall examine him the seventh day. If it is spreading in the skin, then the priest shall pronounce him unclean; it is a case of leprous disease. ²⁸ But if the spot remains in one place and does not spread in the skin, but has faded, it is a swelling from the burn, and the priest shall pronounce him clean, for it is the scar of the burn.

²⁹ "When a man or woman has a disease on the head or the beard, ³⁰ the priest shall examine the disease. And if it appears deeper than the skin, and the hair in it is yellow and thin, then the priest shall pronounce him unclean. It is an itch, a leprous disease of the head or the beard. ³¹ And if the priest examines the itching disease and it appears no deeper than the skin and there is no black hair in it, then the priest shall shut up the person with the itching disease for seven days, ³² and on the seventh day the priest shall examine the disease. If the itch has not spread, and there is in it no yellow hair, and the itch appears to be no deeper than the skin, ³³ then he shall shave himself, but the itch he shall not shave; and the

priest shall shut up the person with the itching disease for another seven days. ³⁴ And on the seventh day the priest shall examine the itch, and if the itch has not spread in the skin and it appears to be no deeper than the skin, then the priest shall pronounce him clean. And he shall wash his clothes and be clean. ³⁵ But if the itch spreads in the skin after his cleansing, ³⁶ then the priest shall examine him, and if the itch has spread in the skin, the priest need not seek for the yellow hair; he is unclean. ³⁷ But if in his eyes the itch is unchanged and black hair has grown in it, the itch is healed and he is clean, and the priest shall pronounce him clean.

³⁸ "When a man or a woman has spots on the skin of the body, white spots, ³⁹ the priest shall look, and if the spots on the skin of the body are of a dull white, it is leukoderma that has broken out in the skin; he is clean.

⁴⁰ "If a man's hair falls out from his head, he is bald; he is clean. ⁴¹ And if a man's hair falls out from his forehead, he has baldness of the forehead; he is clean. ⁴² But if there is on the bald head or the bald forehead a reddish-white diseased area, it is a leprous disease breaking out on his bald head or his bald forehead. ⁴³ Then the priest shall examine him, and if the diseased swelling is reddish-white on his bald head or on his bald forehead, like the appearance of leprous disease in the skin of the body, ⁴⁴ he is a leprous man, he is unclean. The priest must pronounce him unclean; his disease is on his head.

⁴⁵ "The leprous person who has the disease shall wear torn clothes and let the hair of his head hang loose, and he shall cover his upper lip² and cry out, 'Unclean, unclean.' ⁴⁶ He shall remain unclean as long as he has the disease. He is unclean. He shall live alone. His dwelling shall be outside the camp.

⁴⁷ "When there is a case of leprous disease in a garment, whether a woolen or a linen garment, ⁴⁸ in warp or woof of linen or wool, or in a skin or in anything made of skin, ⁴⁹ if the disease is greenish or reddish in the garment, or in the skin or in the warp or the woof or in any article made of skin, it is a case of leprous disease, and it shall be shown to the priest. ⁵⁰ And the priest shall examine the disease and shut up that which has the disease for seven days. ⁵¹ Then he shall examine the disease on the seventh day. If the disease has spread in the garment, in the warp or the woof, or in the skin, whatever be the use of the skin, the disease is a persistent leprous disease; it is unclean. ⁵² And he shall burn the garment, or the warp or the woof, the wool or the linen, or any article made of skin that is diseased, for it is a persistent leprous disease. It shall be burned in the fire.

⁵³ "And if the priest examines, and if the disease has not spread in the garment, in the warp or the woof or in any article made of skin, ⁵⁴ then the priest shall command that they wash the thing in which is the disease, and he shall shut it up for another seven days. ⁵⁵ And the priest shall examine the diseased thing after it has been washed. And if the appearance of the diseased area has not changed, though the disease has not spread, it is unclean. You shall burn it in the fire, whether the rot is on the back or on the front.

⁵⁶ "But if the priest examines, and if the diseased area has faded after it has been washed, he shall tear it out of the garment or the skin or the warp or the woof. ⁵⁷ Then if it appears again in the garment, in the warp or the woof, or in any article made of skin, it is spreading. You shall burn with fire whatever has the disease. ⁵⁸ But the garment, or the warp or the

woof, or any article made of skin from which the disease departs when you have washed it, shall then be washed a second time, and be clean."

⁵⁹ This is the law for a case of leprous disease in a garment of wool or linen, either in the warp or the woof, or in any article made of skin, to determine whether it is clean or unclean.

¹ *Leprosy* was a term for several skin diseases ² Or *mustache*

Section Overview

The laws on bodily impurity continue with the topic of ritually defiling skin disease: its diagnosis (ch. 13) and ritual restoration (ch. 14). These two chapters must be read theologically. As the Lord's presence among his people reorders their lives around his holiness, it shines a light on whatever is out of step with his redemptive purposes. The defiling presence of disease and decay is incompatible with God's holiness. Although contracting impurity is a normal part of life, it is not to be associated with the divine life. And although there is no mention of sin here, bodily disease is a result of sin and death in a fallen world. Read together as one, these chapters point to the abnormality of death and decay in God's presence and how they will ultimately be overcome by the Lord of life. The first chapter mandates the separation of impurity from the community, while the second shows the way back to the God who heals and restores to his presence.

The instructions on diagnosing impurity proceed as seven distinct yet closely related cases of "skin disease" (Hb. *tsara'at*). These specific cases are phrased as "if-then" conditional statements that describe a protocol for diagnosing diseased persons and objects as well as the outcome for each. Each case includes (1) observable symptoms, (2) ritual examination by the priest, (3) identification of symptoms, (4) confirmation (or not) of bodily disease, and (5) pronouncement of ritual status by the priest.[154] It is important to note that there is no prescription for treatment (as there is in 2 Kings 20:7). The priest pronounces the diseased person as ritually "unclean" to confirm the already-present disease and "clean" to confirm his healing. The priesthood's ministry establishes a person's ritual status with respect to the sanctuary.

The Hebrew *tsara'at* frequently translated as "leprous disease" requires some explanation.[155] The term "leprosy" today refers to Hansen's disease, but there is no evidence of this medical condition in the Mediterranean world before 200 BC. The LXX chose the word *lepra* for the Hebrew *tsara'at* because it applied to a variety of skin disorders. "Leprous disease" as described in this portion of Leviticus appears to resemble conditions such as psoriasis, vitiligo, eczema, and favus. Since it could also affect textiles, leather, and homes, it is best to think of it as a "ritually defiling skin disease/infestation."[156] An important characteristic is its spreading nature.[157]

---

154 Kleinig, *Leviticus*, 280.
155 Cf. ESV mg., which also points in this direction: "*Leprosy* was a term for several skin diseases."
156 Sklar, *Leviticus*, TOTC, 184, 189.
157 The Hebrew verb *pasah*, meaning "to spread," appears twenty-two times in chapters 13–14 but nowhere else in the Bible.

The disease manifests as a growing, visible spread of peeling, flaking skin that could expose raw flesh underneath. The flaking makes the sufferer look "as one dead, whose flesh is half eaten away when he comes out of his mother's womb" (Num. 12:12). As such, its appearance is a mark of physical death incompatible with God's holiness.[158] For fear of the contagion of ritual impurity those afflicted with skin disease were removed from the camp to live in isolation on its perimeter.

The amount of text dedicated to diagnosing skin disease and its ritual resolution is considerable, leading to the conclusion that it is best to understand this teaching as a paradigmatic case of the diseased body.[159] When compared with the consecrated and ritually fit body of the high priest, we see between the two a symbolic display of life versus death. The skin-diseased person (the most impure Israelite body) and the high priest (the holiest Israelite body) stand on two opposite ends of the holiness spectrum (cf. table 3.4). The high priest is the closest person to the divine presence and consecrated to share in the sanctuary's holiness through ceremonial investiture and anointing with sacral oil (Lev. 8:10–12). The skin-diseased person is the furthest from the divine presence and must announce his pollution by crying out "Unclean! Unclean!" The diseased body is the least ritually fit for sacred space and the consecrated body the most ritually fit. The nearer one draws to the Lord, the closer one comes to life itself. The further one is driven from God's presence, the closer one is to death and decay.

TABLE 3.4: The Skin-Diseased Person and the High Priest

Skin-Diseased Person	High Priest
Hair disheveled	Hair groomed and never disheveled
Garments rent	Garments never rent
	Body anointed with oil
Outside the camp, furthest from the divine presence	Before the sanctuary veil, nearest the divine presence
Represents death in his diseased and blemished body	Represents life in his whole and unblemished body

Section Outline

III. Ritual Impurity (11:1–15:33) . . .

    C. Diagnosing Skin Disease (13:1–59)

        1. Introduction (13:1)

        2. Diagnosis of Diseased Persons (13:2–44)

---

158 Milgrom, *Leviticus 1–16*, 819–820; Kleinig, *Leviticus*, 286; Gane, *Leviticus, Numbers*, 238.
159 Philip Peter Jenson, *Graded Holiness: A Key to the Priestly Conception of the World*, JSOTSup 106 (London: T&T Clark, 1992), 140. Eleven different conditions could qualify a skin condition as *tsara'at*: swelling (Lev. 13:2), rash (v. 2), discoloration ("spot"; vv. 2, 38), leprous disease (v. 2), boil (v. 18), itch (v. 30), leukoderma (v. 39), crown baldness (v. 40), forehead baldness (v. 41), eruption (vv. 42, 57), and malignant eruption (ESV "persistent leprous disease" v. 51); drawn from David Tabb Stewart, "Leviticus-Deuteronomy," in *The Bible and Disability: A Commentary*, ed. Sarah J. Melcher, Mikeal C. Parsons, and Amos Young (Waco, TX: Baylor University Press, 2017), 70. These signs of disease restrict a person's access to the sanctuary. Similarly, there are twelve conditions that disqualify priests and sacrificial animals from coming into contact with the altar (21:17–20; 22:22–24).

3. Consequence: Removal from the Camp (13:45–46)
4. Diagnosis of Diseased Garments (13:47–51)
5. Consequence: Burning or Washing (13:52–58)
6. Concluding Summary (13:59)

Comment

13:1 Instructions regarding the diagnosis of skin disease are addressed to Moses and Aaron but not to the "people of Israel" (unlike in 11:2; 12:2; 15:2) since it is a priestly responsibility both to diagnose skin disease as well as to preside over its ritual resolution (cf. Deut. 24:8).

13:2–8 The first case appears through three visible marks on the skin as "a swelling or an eruption or a spot" (Lev. 13:2). Three diagnostic terms describe the bodily affliction. The first term is best understood as a mark or discoloration that produces a visible blemish on the skin. The second term may indicate a scab or flaking skin. The third term indicates a spot that can be clearly seen. Bodily disease is diagnosed with terms that are rare and suggest technical terminology.[160]

The diseased person is brought to the priest, likely outside the camp (14:3). If the priest observes that the hair in the diseased area has turned white and the affected area is more than skin deep, the person is pronounced ritually unclean. The diseased person is required to quarantine outside the camp, far from the sanctuary, because of his impurity (13:45–46). However, if the priest does not observe these two signs, the person is placed in quarantine for seven days and then reexamined. If the disease has not spread, he is quarantined for an additional week. If the disease still has not spread, the priest pronounces the person ritually clean. After ritual washing he is reintegrated into the worshiping life of the community.

13:9–17 The second case presents a visible white swelling in a raw wound that has caused the hair to turn white. There is no need for a quarantine period to make a diagnosis since a long-standing disease is clearly apparent. The priest pronounces the sufferer ritually unclean, and isolation outside the camp must follow (vv. 45–46). If, however, the disease runs its course and the inflamed area turns white from the growth of new skin, the person is pronounced clean.[161] Any further lesions that appear as "raw flesh" (vv. 14–15) indicate that the skin disease has returned, and the diseased person must be isolated from the community.

13:18–23 The following cases are when *tsara'at* appears as a secondary complication. The third case concerns a boil that has healed but develops a secondary condition. Hezekiah and Job both suffered from such ulcerous lesions (2 Kings 20:7; Job 2:7). If the boil later presents a white swelling or a reddish-white spot that

---
160 James W. Watts, *Leviticus 11–20*, HCOT (Leuven: Peeters, 2023), 160.
161 Levine, *Leviticus*, 78; Sklar, *Leviticus*, TOTC, 185. Hartley (*Leviticus*, 191) interprets the white skin not as regrowth but as loss of pigmentation as occurs in leukoderma. The person is clean because there are no open sores and raw flesh.

appears deeper than the skin, and its hair has turned white, the priest pronounces the sufferer unclean. If the hair has not turned white and the mark on the skin's surface begins to fade, a seven-day quarantine follows (Lev. 13:21). If the disease does not spread after seven days, the spot is only a scar. The person is pronounced ritually clean and may participate fully in worship.

13:24–28 The next case concerns a visible burn on the body that later develops a reddish-white or white spot in its wound. The remaining details of this case follow closely the pattern established in verses 18–23.

13:29–37 The next case is one of suspected skin disease that has spread underneath the hair. The instructions relate to both men and women (as with previous cases), but here this is made explicit. If a person has a disease that is more than skin deep and the hair has yellowed and thinned out, then the priest pronounces him or her unclean. The condition translated as "itch" (only here and 14:54) derives from a verb meaning to tear or uproot. The translation supposes the sufferer is scratching his skin,[162] though it may also be understood as a disease of the hair follicle.[163] If the disease appears only skin deep but there is no healthy black hair typical of Israelites, then a seven-day quarantine is required. The person is required to shave the area surrounding the disease and wait another seven days. If the disease has spread, the person is unclean, but if it has not and instead healthy black hair has grown back, he or she is pronounced clean and reintegrated into the community after ritual washing.

13:38–39 The next case presents as white patches on the skin but with no accompanying raw flesh, wounds, or red spots that typically signal the presence of *tsara'at*. If the patches are dull white, it is not diseased, and the person is pronounced clean. The condition is what is translated as "leukoderma," a loss of pigmentation that causes discolored patches on the skin.

13:40–44 The next case addresses baldness. Hair loss on the top of the head, thinning hair at the temples, and a receding hairline indicate not disease but normal aging. If a reddish-white area appears, the priest examines the person; if the area matches the previously described cases, the person is pronounced ritually unclean.

13:45–46 Although impurity may be unavoidable, it is still incompatible with God's holiness, and the afflicted person is sent to live outside the camp (Num. 5:2–3; Deut. 24:8–9). The sufferer takes on the appearance of a mourner by tearing his clothes and letting his hair hang loose. Through ritual gestures that symbolically enact the body's dissolution he identifies with death. That skin disease is viewed as a symbolic death is further suggested by the fact that an afflicted person is likened to a corpse (Num. 12:12; cf. Job 18:13). Not surprisingly, the purification ritual that restores the healed to the covenant community recalls cleansing from

---

162 Hartley, *Leviticus*, 192.
163 Levine, *Leviticus*, 80.

corpse contamination (Lev. 14:4–7; cf. Num. 19:1–13). To be separated from God's presence is certain death (Gen. 2:17; 3:24).

In memorable passages the Lord strikes with skin disease those who trespass his holiness: Miriam, for challenging divinely appointed authority (Num. 12:14); Gehazi, for deceiving Naaman in the Lord's name (2 Kings 5:27); and Uzziah, for encroaching upon holy ground and priestly duties (2 Chron. 26:16–21). This is not to say that everyone who suffers from skin disorders is being punished by God; when the Lord *does* visit divine judgment, however, this particular affliction communicates his censure effectively by banishing the person from his presence.

During isolation the ritually impure person remains unclean "as long as he has the disease" (Lev. 13:46).[164] Healing can come only from the Lord; when it does, it is a testimony that "there is no God in all the earth but in Israel" (2 Kings 5:15). Scripture is filled with the prayers of those who seek the Lord for healing (Num. 12:13; 2 Kings 20:2–6; Ps. 6:1–5; Jer. 17:14). A sufferer longs for the courts of the Lord, to be restored to the covenant community and worship in God's presence: "A day in your courts is better than a thousand elsewhere" (Ps. 84:10).

13:47–51 The second section of divine instruction concerns the presence of disease in garments (textiles and leather), which in the ancient world were viewed as an extension of the self. The word "skin" for leather illustrates continuity between human skin and animal skin that could be infected with *tsara'at*, the same word applied to the observable signs of spreading decay in humans.[165] If the disease appears greenish or reddish in a wool or linen garment or on leather or anything made of leather, the priest examines it for immediate quarantine.

13:52–58 If after an initial quarantine of seven days the disease spreads, the garment has a ritually defiling infestation and must be burned with fire (Lev. 13:52). But if after seven days the disease has not spread, the garment must be washed and quarantined for an additional seven days. If the diseased area persists, the garment is burned; if it fades, that portion of the garment is torn out (v. 56). Should the disease appear again and continue to spread, the garment must be destroyed. When the disease is removed after an initial washing of textile or leather, the item must be washed a second time to be pronounced clean (v. 58).

13:59 The concluding summary restates this is the law for diagnosing whether garments and worked leather are clean or unclean.

Response

Death and disease are incompatible with God's presence. They exist in the world outside of Eden, a world the Lord is reclaiming and remaking for Abraham's

---

[164] Uzziah lived out the rest of his days contaminated and unclean in a house of isolation. At his death he was buried outside the city and not laid to rest in the royal cemetery with his forefathers (2 Chron. 26:23). As Jerusalem expanded in the first century, Uzziah's burial site had to be moved outside the new city limits. His bones were reburied and marked with a plaque that reads: "Here were brought the bones of Uzziah king of Judah—do not open!" Cf. "Epitaph of King Uzziah of Judah," The Israel Museum, accessed May 28, 2024, https://www.imj.org.il/en/collections/353190-0.

[165] The ESV remains consistent by using the term "leprous disease."

descendants until it extends throughout the whole earth. Sickness is a persistent reminder that the world is fallen and stands in need of restoration, repair, and renewal. The removal of those with defiling skin disease outside the camp is an important aspect of Israel's practical, concrete expression of holiness that is instructive to the entire community. The Lord who dwells in the glory of his perfect wholeness and holiness provides his people with a theological understanding of bodily decay and its ultimate reversal (Isa. 26:19; 65:17). These laws look forward to the day when impurity itself will be banished outside the camp (Lev. 16:22). Those who must be separated in their impurity from the life of the community and the worship of God earnestly long for restoration. We likewise embrace a biblical hope that looks forward to a bodily resurrection and life eternal that is no longer susceptible to disease, death, or decay.

This hope is realized in the incarnation, wherein Christ assumed a fully embodied human life. He met those afflicted with skin disease and had compassion (Mark 1:40–42). He reached out with divine authority in his public ministry to cleanse them as a sign that God's kingdom had come (Matt. 9:35–36; 11:5). Jesus revealed his messianic identity through healings that spoke to a restoration of all things: "The blind receive their sight, the lame walk, *lepers are cleansed*, and the deaf hear, the dead are raised up, the poor have good news preached to them" (Luke 7:22). Sickness and disease are borne and removed by him to fulfill the prophetic promise: "He took our illnesses and bore our diseases" (Matt. 8:17; cf. Isa. 53:4). As the feast of the Passover and Jesus' imminent self-offering were drawing near, he reclined at the table of Simon the leper while a woman anointed his body (Mark 14:3). A man healed of disease and death's decay eating at a table with the anointed High Priest preparing for his own death is a sign that the kingdom has arrived and the way to fellowship with God has been made open.

Jesus' atoning death and bodily resurrection triumph over sin, disease, and death. Humanity is designed for an embodied eternity that will be accomplished through a physical resurrection from the dead. Creation itself longs to be "set free from its bondage to corruption and obtain the freedom of the glory of the children of God" (Rom. 8:21). Not only creation but we ourselves eagerly await the "redemption of our bodies" (Rom. 8:23). The climax of biblical redemption takes place when the

> dwelling place of God is with man. He will dwell with them, and they will be his people, and God himself will be with them as their God. He will wipe away every tear from their eyes, and death shall be no more, neither shall there be mourning, nor crying, nor pain anymore, for the former things have passed away. (Rev. 21:3–4)

Disease and death will one day be overturned and will be no more.

LEVITICUS 14

14 The Lord spoke to Moses, saying, **2** "This shall be the law of the leprous person for the day of his cleansing. He shall be brought to the priest, **3** and the priest shall go out of the camp, and the priest shall look. Then, if the case of leprous disease is healed in the leprous person, **4** the priest shall command them to take for him who is to be cleansed two live[1] clean birds and cedarwood and scarlet yarn and hyssop. **5** And the priest shall command them to kill one of the birds in an earthenware vessel over fresh[2] water. **6** He shall take the live bird with the cedarwood and the scarlet yarn and the hyssop, and dip them and the live bird in the blood of the bird that was killed over the fresh water. **7** And he shall sprinkle it seven times on him who is to be cleansed of the leprous disease. Then he shall pronounce him clean and shall let the living bird go into the open field. **8** And he who is to be cleansed shall wash his clothes and shave off all his hair and bathe himself in water, and he shall be clean. And after that he may come into the camp, but live outside his tent seven days. **9** And on the seventh day he shall shave off all his hair from his head, his beard, and his eyebrows. He shall shave off all his hair, and then he shall wash his clothes and bathe his body in water, and he shall be clean.

10 "And on the eighth day he shall take two male lambs without blemish, and one ewe lamb a year old without blemish, and a grain offering of three tenths of an ephah[3] of fine flour mixed with oil, and one log[4] of oil. **11** And the priest who cleanses him shall set the man who is to be cleansed and these things before the Lord, at the entrance of the tent of meeting. **12** And the priest shall take one of the male lambs and offer it for a guilt offering, along with the log of oil, and wave them for a wave offering before the Lord. **13** And he shall kill the lamb in the place where they kill the sin offering and the burnt offering, in the place of the sanctuary. For the guilt offering, like the sin offering, belongs to the priest; it is most holy. **14** The priest shall take some of the blood of the guilt offering, and the priest shall put it on the lobe of the right ear of him who is to be cleansed and on the thumb of his right hand and on the big toe of his right foot. **15** Then the priest shall take some of the log of oil and pour it into the palm of his own left hand **16** and dip his right finger in the oil that is in his left hand and sprinkle some oil with his finger seven times before the Lord. **17** And some of the oil that remains in his hand the priest shall put on the lobe of the right ear of him who is to be cleansed and on the thumb of his right hand and on the big toe of his right foot, on top of the blood of the guilt offering. **18** And the rest of the oil that is in the priest's hand he shall put on the head of him who is to be cleansed. Then the priest shall make atonement for him before the Lord. **19** The priest shall offer the sin offering, to make atonement for him who is to be cleansed from his uncleanness. And afterward he shall kill the burnt offering. **20** And the priest shall offer the burnt offering and the grain offering on the altar. Thus the priest shall make atonement for him, and he shall be clean.

21 "But if he is poor and cannot afford so much, then he shall take one male lamb for a guilt offering to be waved, to make atonement for him, and a tenth of an ephah of fine flour mixed with oil for a grain offering, and a log of oil; 22 also two turtledoves or two pigeons, whichever he can afford. The one shall be a sin offering and the other a burnt offering. 23 And on the eighth day he shall bring them for his cleansing to the priest, to the entrance of the tent of meeting, before the Lord. 24 And the priest shall take the lamb of the guilt offering and the log of oil, and the priest shall wave them for a wave offering before the Lord. 25 And he shall kill the lamb of the guilt offering. And the priest shall take some of the blood of the guilt offering and put it on the lobe of the right ear of him who is to be cleansed, and on the thumb of his right hand and on the big toe of his right foot. 26 And the priest shall pour some of the oil into the palm of his own left hand, 27 and shall sprinkle with his right finger some of the oil that is in his left hand seven times before the Lord. 28 And the priest shall put some of the oil that is in his hand on the lobe of the right ear of him who is to be cleansed and on the thumb of his right hand and on the big toe of his right foot, in the place where the blood of the guilt offering was put. 29 And the rest of the oil that is in the priest's hand he shall put on the head of him who is to be cleansed, to make atonement for him before the Lord. 30 And he shall offer, of the turtledoves or pigeons, whichever he can afford, 31 one[5] for a sin offering and the other for a burnt offering, along with a grain offering. And the priest shall make atonement before the Lord for him who is being cleansed. 32 This is the law for him in whom is a case of leprous disease, who cannot afford the offerings for his cleansing."

33 The Lord spoke to Moses and Aaron, saying, 34 "When you come into the land of Canaan, which I give you for a possession, and I put a case of leprous disease in a house in the land of your possession, 35 then he who owns the house shall come and tell the priest, 'There seems to me to be some case of disease in my house.' 36 Then the priest shall command that they empty the house before the priest goes to examine the disease, lest all that is in the house be declared unclean. And afterward the priest shall go in to see the house. 37 And he shall examine the disease. And if the disease is in the walls of the house with greenish or reddish spots, and if it appears to be deeper than the surface, 38 then the priest shall go out of the house to the door of the house and shut up the house seven days. 39 And the priest shall come again on the seventh day, and look. If the disease has spread in the walls of the house, 40 then the priest shall command that they take out the stones in which is the disease and throw them into an unclean place outside the city. 41 And he shall have the inside of the house scraped all around, and the plaster that they scrape off they shall pour out in an unclean place outside the city. 42 Then they shall take other stones and put them in the place of those stones, and he shall take other plaster and plaster the house.

43 "If the disease breaks out again in the house, after he has taken out the stones and scraped the house and plastered it, 44 then the priest shall go and look. And if the disease has spread in the house, it is a persistent leprous disease in the house; it is unclean. 45 And he shall break down the house, its stones and timber and all the plaster of the house, and he shall

carry them out of the city to an unclean place. ⁴⁶ Moreover, whoever enters the house while it is shut up shall be unclean until the evening, ⁴⁷ and whoever sleeps in the house shall wash his clothes, and whoever eats in the house shall wash his clothes.

⁴⁸ "But if the priest comes and looks, and if the disease has not spread in the house after the house was plastered, then the priest shall pronounce the house clean, for the disease is healed. ⁴⁹ And for the cleansing of the house he shall take two small birds, with cedarwood and scarlet yarn and hyssop, ⁵⁰ and shall kill one of the birds in an earthenware vessel over fresh water ⁵¹ and shall take the cedarwood and the hyssop and the scarlet yarn, along with the live bird, and dip them in the blood of the bird that was killed and in the fresh water and sprinkle the house seven times. ⁵² Thus he shall cleanse the house with the blood of the bird and with the fresh water and with the live bird and with the cedarwood and hyssop and scarlet yarn. ⁵³ And he shall let the live bird go out of the city into the open country. So he shall make atonement for the house, and it shall be clean."

⁵⁴ This is the law for any case of leprous disease: for an itch, ⁵⁵ for leprous disease in a garment or in a house, ⁵⁶ and for a swelling or an eruption or a spot, ⁵⁷ to show when it is unclean and when it is clean. This is the law for leprous disease.

¹ Or *wild* ² Or *running*; Hebrew *living*; also verses 6, 50, 51, 52 ³ An *ephah* was about 3/5 bushel or 22 liters ⁴ A *log* was about 1/3 quart or 0.3 liter ⁵ Septuagint, Syriac; Hebrew *afford*, ³¹*such as he can afford, one*

Section Overview

Chapter 14 complements the previous chapter to describe how the person healed of skin disease is restored to the sanctuary and the covenant community. Whereas the previous laws detailed a diseased person's diagnosis and period of separation, these outline the purification rite for restoration. The Lord is revealed as the one who heals the sick, overcomes death with life, and restores the afflicted to his courts of praise. As prophetic hope will articulate, "After two days he will revive us; on the third day he will raise us up, that we may live before him" (Hos. 6:2). To be restored to the Lord is to have life.

The movement back is progressive, transitioning through stages in which the one healed is pronounced clean three times in steadily increasing degrees of purity (Lev. 14:7, 9, 20). The priest examines the person outside the camp to verify his healing and then performs the first rite of purification involving two birds, one that is slaughtered and the other released into the open country. The person being cleansed may then move inside the camp but may not yet enter his tent. The second stage is a seven-day liminal period with shaving and bathing on either side. The third stage concludes with his appearing before the Lord with offerings. The person healed from defiling skin disease offers all the atoning sacrifices (guilt, sin, and burnt offerings) and is reintegrated through a consecration rite involving the daubing of blood and oil on his bodily extremities. The body once touched by death has been brought back to life. He who was in exile outside the camp is now restored to his people. These ritual passages are mediated by the priests, who, as agents of the Lord's restoration, cross spatial and ritual boundaries to reconcile the outsider to the presence of the Lord.

Section Outline

III. Ritual Impurity (11:1–15:33) . . .
   D. Purification from Skin Disease (14:1–14:57)
      1. Introduction to the Purification Rite (14:1–3)
      2. First Stage: Restoration to the Camp (14:4–8)
      3. Second Stage: Restoration to the Sanctuary (14:9)
      4. Third Stage: Restoration to the Worshiping Community (14:10–20)
      5. Provision for the Poor (14:21–32)
      6. Purification of Houses (14:33–53)
      7. Concluding Summary (14:54–57)

Comment

14:1–2a The Lord gives instructions to Moses concerning the ritual restoration of the person who has been healed of defiling skin disease. The instructions describe the purification rites following his healing.

14:2b–3 The purification rite shows a steady and progressive movement through space (toward the sanctuary) and time (toward the eighth day) to signal newness of life. The rite begins outside the camp, where the person had been forced to live while he was afflicted (13:46). The priest goes out to inspect the person who has received healing from the Lord. Priests are enabled to move through the spheres of holy ground inside the tabernacle and common space outside the camp to facilitate the rites that move the unclean person into a clean ritual state.

14:4 Two wild birds are taken together with cedarwood, scarlet yarn, and hyssop outside the camp, where the rite will be performed. These same materials are found also in the rite of purification from corpse contamination (Num. 19:6), further supporting the view that the spreading skin disease is identified conceptually with death (Lev. 13:45; Num. 12:12). The skin-diseased person and the one who has touched a corpse are in the same category of having had a brush with death.

The two birds must be "living," a word that could also be rendered "wild." The use of a wild bird makes it more likely that it will fly away when released into the open.[166] The only other use of a "living"/"wild" animal is the goat for the purification rite on the Day of Atonement (Lev. 16:10, 20–21). It is possible that specifying these animals as wild signals that they are not sacrifices, since only domesticated animals are offered as sacrifices.[167] In addition identifying the birds

---
[166] Milgrom, *Leviticus 1–16*, 833.
[167] This is especially important on the Day of Atonement so that it is not perceived that an offering is made as the sin-carrying goat is sent out into the wilderness.

as "living"/"wild" touches on a number of other usages of this word: skin disease that makes a person unclean by exposing raw flesh (Hb. "living" flesh; 13:10, 14, 15, 16, 24) is purified by blood from "living" birds (14:4, 6, 7), mixed with "living" water (vv. 5, 6). The drumbeat of life courses through the chapter.

Cedarwood is fragrant and durable, resisting decay. Hyssop (wild marjoram) is a bushy shrub whose leaves absorb liquid. It was tied together in bunches and used to sprinkle blood on the doorposts of Israelite houses at the Passover (Ex. 12:22–23). Associated with the sprinkling of purification rites (Num. 19:18), it appears in the prayer of the penitent longing to be cleansed: "Purge me with hyssop, and I shall be clean; wash me, and I shall be whiter than snow" (Ps. 51:7). Cedarwood and scarlet yarn have a red hue that associates them with blood, the most powerful agent of purification,[168] perhaps to amplify its power.

14:5–7 The two birds play an important role in the person's movement from outside to inside the camp. One of the birds supplies the blood for the purification ceremony. Its neck is wrung over an earthen vessel and its blood mixed with "fresh water" (Hb. "living water"; Lev. 14:6, 50, 51, 52), that is, water that comes from a flowing source, such as a spring or a running stream. Living water is used for cleansing major impurities (15:13; Num. 19:17 [cf. ESV mg.]).

The performance of the rite suggests that the hyssop branch is tied to the cedarwood with the scarlet yarn, dipped into the blood of the slain bird, and used as a brush for sprinkling. The sevenfold sprinkling recalls the Day of Atonement purification rites (16:15, 19). However, this is the only rite wherein blood is sprinkled on a person for cleansing. Sprinkling with blood is found in two other solemn rites: the ordination that consecrates the priesthood for service on holy ground (8:24, 30) and the covenant ceremony in which the people are dashed with the blood of sacrifice (Ex. 24:8). Read together, these inform how the skin-diseased person who has been outside of the covenant community is readmitted into the congregation. The ordination rite enabled Aaron and his sons to cross the boundary from common into holy ground. The purification rite enabled an Israelite to cross the boundary from exile into the camp. The blood-bond of the covenant is worn upon his healed body through sprinkling as a renewal of his membership among the people of God.

The person healed of skin disease is declared ritually "clean," just as he had formerly been pronounced "unclean." The live bird is then dipped in the earthen vessel with the blood of the slain bird and released into the open field. The release of the live bird anticipates the rite on the Day of Atonement, wherein one goat is offered as a purification sacrifice and the other is released into the wilderness, where it removes the community's impurity (Lev. 16:8–10, 21–22). Here one bird is killed and the other released into the open country. Does the released bird carry away the person's impurity, like the scapegoat does for the nation?[169] Does

---

[168] Sklar, *Leviticus*, TOTC, 191. Purification from corpse contamination specifies a red heifer, perhaps for the same associations (Num. 19:2).
[169] Sklar, *Leviticus*, TOTC, 191; Hartley, *Leviticus*, 195; Gane, *Leviticus, Numbers*, 247.

dipping the live bird in the blood of the slain symbolize the sufferer's close brush with death and his freedom in newness of life?[170] Leviticus itself does not explain the symbolism. Those undergoing the rite do so in faith that it cleanses them (cf. 2 Kings 5:13–14). Although the text does not explain what the two birds symbolize, it is clear that purification is a process through which the healed person is passing from death (outside the camp) to life (inside the camp).

14:8 The person being purified bathes and launders his clothes, as in cleansing from a major impurity (Lev. 15:13). In addition he shaves off all his hair. Once within the camp the person being cleansed must wait a full seven days before appearing at the sanctuary, a period of time marking passage from one ritual state to another. The weeklong waiting period is shared in common with other major impurities (15:13, 24, 28). The difference in the case of skin disease is that the person may not enter his own tent during this time, suggesting that some residual impurity associated with death still clings to him. Death's impurity would contaminate every person and object inside a home (21:11; Num. 19:14).

14:9 The seven-day period is transitional, a liminal state at the ritual boundary in which the person is readmitted to the camp but not yet fully restored to the congregation. It recalls the ordination of the priests, who must remain at the entrance to the tent of meeting for seven days to complete their consecration (Lev. 8:33). On the seventh day the person being cleansed once again shaves all his hair, especially that of his head and face. Shaving embodies a new identity and ritual status, seen with the completion of a Nazirite vow, the consecration of Levites to service, and the assimilation of a captive woman into an Israelite household (Num. 6:18; 8:7; Deut. 21:12). The person then launders his clothes and bathes in preparation for meeting with the Lord. He must be restored to the Lord before being restored to his family and community.

14:10–11 On the eighth day the person being cleansed assembles a substantial collection of offerings: two male lambs, one ewe lamb a year old, and a tenth of an ephah of fine flour for each of the three lamb offerings. He also brings a measure of oil (about 1/3 quart [0.4 l]) that will be used to anoint him. Such a great amount of sacrificial offerings for an average worshiper speaks to the extreme impurity he has suffered. The purified person is stationed "before the LORD," a technical phrase signifying the closest a person may come into God's presence (Lev. 14:12, 16, 18, 24, 27, 29, 31).[171] In this act of presentation he is once more recognized as a worshiper.

14:12–18 The lamb of the guilt offering and the measure of oil are "waved" before the Lord in an act of dedication that consecrates the blood and oil to be applied

---

170 Tikva Frymer-Kensky, "Pollution, Purification, and Purgation in Biblical Israel," in *The Word Shall Go Forth*, ed. Carol L. Meyers and M. O'Connor (Winona Lake, IN: Eisenbrauns, 1983), 400; Kleinig, *Leviticus*, 297–298.
171 Michael B. Hundley, "Before YHWH at the Entrance of the Tent of Meeting: A Study of Spatial and Conceptual Geography in the Priestly Texts" *ZAW* 123 (2011): 15–26.

to the person's body for purification. A guilt offering is typically made in cases of sacrilege that violate the Lord's holy property (5:15), though there is no indication that the skin-diseased person has sinned.[172]

Throughout the multiple stages of the rite its focus is always purification. Could the offering be to atone for an unknown sacrilege that may have brought about the disease (cf. 5:17)?[173] Could the sanctuary's loss be that of tithes and offerings while the person was afflicted with skin disease?[174] Conceptually the offering may be likened to the guilt offering brought by the Nazirite, whose consecration is desecrated by contact with death (Num. 6:9–12). It could be that the diseased person himself is regarded as the Lord's "holy property" and his entanglement with death, even symbolically, as theft from the living God. The guilt offering is mandated for holy things that have been desacralized. This is precisely the situation of one of God's holy people (Ex. 19:6) who has been cut off from the sanctuary. The guilt offering is the logical choice for reparation to the Lord and repatriation into holy community.

Some of the blood of the guilt offering is reserved and applied to the physical extremities of the recovered person: the lobe of the right ear, the thumb of the right hand, and the big toe of his right foot, recalling the ordination of the priests, who were set apart for divine service by these same actions (Lev. 8:23–24). As the daubing of blood on the priestly bodies consecrated them to holy ground, so the blood application to the body of the one healed of skin disease reestablishes his relationship to the sanctuary.

Next the priest takes some of the oil, pours it in his palm, and sprinkles it with his finger toward the sanctuary ("before the LORD") seven times—perhaps to consecrate it—before applying it to the person. It is applied to the same bodily extremities as was the blood, and the rest is poured over the head, again recalling priestly anointing (8:12, 30). The act speaks to an elevation of status, especially as one emerges from mourning into the joyous fellowship of life with anointing "instead of ashes, the oil of gladness instead of mourning" (Isa. 61:3).

14:19–20 The remaining sacrifices emphasize atonement that leads to the restoration of covenant relationship with the Lord. The sin (purification) offering on its own is for cleansing the sanctuary from defilement (Lev. 16:14–19), but, when it also involves the ritual purification of a worshiper (which is the focus here), it is accompanied by other offerings (12:6–7; 15:15, 30; Num. 6:11), underscoring that purification is not an end in itself but the first step to restoring fellowship with God. The burnt offering together with its grain portion is made for atonement and to reestablish the worship of the exiled person, who has now come home. With sanctuary and worshiper fully cleansed the person restored from sickness and death is pronounced clean for the final time (Lev. 14:20).

---

172 Cf. comment on 13:45–46 for cases in which the Lord visits judgment through skin disease. If the intention was to clear a person of sin, we would expect him to make a confession over the bird that is released into the wild as in the parallel rite of atonement (Lev. 16:21).
173 Milgrom, *Leviticus 1–16*, 856–857.
174 Wenham, *Leviticus*, 210.

14:21–22 Throughout Scripture the Lord makes provision for the poor to participate in worship (5:7–13; 12:8). Those who are unable to afford the array of sacrifices may bring instead as their offering one male lamb for a guilt (reparation) offering, a tenth (in place of three tenths) of a measure of fine flour, and two turtledoves or pigeons (in place of flock animals) for the sin and burnt offerings. The lamb for the guilt offering and log of oil for anointing are nonnegotiable and remain the same, demonstrating their importance in the performance of purification.

14:23–32 The ritual performance for complete restoration is the same: sacrifice of the guilt offering and anointing with blood and oil, followed by the purification and burnt offerings. Even though a poor person's contribution is less, it may represent a greater sacrifice than that of those with means (Mark 12:42–44).

14:33–42 The final section on restoration from *tsara'at* disease addresses the diagnosis and purification of infected houses, just as the previous chapter addressed the diagnosis and purification of infected garments (Lev. 13:47–59). These laws also anticipate life in the land of Canaan where people will dwell in houses of stone (14:34, 40).

If a case of disease appears in a home, the owner must report it to the priest and empty the house of all possessions, lest these be shut up in quarantine or pronounced unclean (v. 36). The priest examines the house as he might examine a person. If signs of disease, decay, or death appear on the walls, presenting as a visible mold, mildew, or fungus with greenish or reddish spots, the home is quarantined for seven days (vv. 37–38). If after seven days the disease has spread, the affected stones and plaster are removed and cast into an unclean location beyond the city's boundary (v. 40). The inside of the house is scraped and the dismantled walls replaced with fresh stones and replastered.

14:43–47 If the contaminating disease continues to spread in the house, it is pronounced unclean (v. 44). It is torn down and its construction materials of stone, timber, and plaster discarded outside the city's boundary. Should anyone go inside the house while it is under quarantine, he will contract a secondary impurity (cf. 15:5–11, 16–18, 21–23). Anyone who eats or sleeps in it will contract impurity that requires laundering his clothes.

14:48–53 If the priest inspects the house and finds that the disease has not spread after being replastered, the house is declared clean and the disease "healed" (v. 48). The procedure for cleansing the house recalls the ritual for restoring impure persons. The priest performs the same rite with two birds, together with cedarwood and scarlet yarn and hyssop. One bird is killed, and the other is dipped into the mixture of blood and water. The home is sprinkled seven times, as a skin-diseased person might be, and pronounced clean. The other bird is released into the open country, removing defilement and purging the house from impurity (v. 53).

14:54–57 The concluding statement brings the two chapters together in its summary. Divine instruction given to the priests is for any case of afflicting disease, whether on persons, clothing, or houses, so that Israel might distinguish between unclean and clean.

Response

On his final journey to Jerusalem, where he will suffer and die, Jesus is met by ten lepers. Not surprisingly, they are on the outskirts of a village, standing "at a distance" (Luke 17:12), their physical distance a visual display of their outcast status. Lifting up their voices, they cry, "Jesus, Master, have mercy on us" (Luke 17:13). They want not just to be clean; they want to be whole. It will take a miracle that no ordinary priest has the authority to command, but Jesus is no ordinary priest. While ordinary priests can declare a healed person clean, Jesus is a priest that can miraculously bring about the healing—which is exactly what he decides to do. He instructs the lepers to follow the protocol laid out in Leviticus: "Go and show yourselves to the priests" (Luke 17:14), and, as they made their way, they were healed.

At this point nine of the lepers continue on to show themselves to the priests in Jerusalem. After all, in keeping with the steps of ritual purification laid out in Leviticus, restoration to the temple is critical for reintegration into society. But one leper, a Samaritan, returns. Instead of going to the temple he brings his worship to Christ, prostrating himself and offering his praises as a sacrifice of thanksgiving. Having been restored as a worshiper before the Lord Jesus, he can now return home. Jesus Christ is the priest, the temple, and the atoning sacrifice that makes the defiled clean and gives the outcast the right to stand in God's presence.

Bodily affliction will be overcome ultimately by bodily resurrection. Jesus, our great High Priest, is raised bodily after his sacrificial obedience unto death, recalling his words "I am the resurrection and the life. Whoever believes in me, though he die, yet shall he live" (John 11:25). Indeed, many of those deeply familiar with the priestly ministry recognize his work: "The word of God continued to increase, and the number of the disciples multiplied greatly in Jerusalem, and a great many of the priests became obedient to the faith" (Acts 6:7). Sinful, earthly, mortal priests worship Jesus, the sinless, heavenly, eternal priest who is "able to save to the uttermost those who draw near to God through him, since he always lives to make intercession for them" (Heb. 7:25).

LEVITICUS 15

15 The Lord spoke to Moses and Aaron, saying, ²"Speak to the people of Israel and say to them, When any man has a discharge from his body,¹ his discharge is unclean. ³And this is the law of his uncleanness for a discharge: whether his body runs with his discharge, or his body is blocked up by his discharge, it is his uncleanness. ⁴Every bed on which the one with the discharge lies shall be unclean, and everything on which he sits shall be unclean. ⁵And anyone who touches his bed shall wash his clothes and bathe himself in water and be unclean until the evening. ⁶And whoever sits on anything on which the one with the discharge has sat shall wash his clothes and bathe himself in water and be unclean until the evening. ⁷And whoever touches the body of the one with the discharge shall wash his clothes and bathe himself in water and be unclean until the evening. ⁸And if the one with the discharge spits on someone who is clean, then he shall wash his clothes and bathe himself in water and be unclean until the evening. ⁹And any saddle on which the one with the discharge rides shall be unclean. ¹⁰And whoever touches anything that was under him shall be unclean until the evening. And whoever carries such things shall wash his clothes and bathe himself in water and be unclean until the evening. ¹¹Anyone whom the one with the discharge touches without having rinsed his hands in water shall wash his clothes and bathe himself in water and be unclean until the evening. ¹²And an earthenware vessel that the one with the discharge touches shall be broken, and every vessel of wood shall be rinsed in water.

¹³"And when the one with a discharge is cleansed of his discharge, then he shall count for himself seven days for his cleansing, and wash his clothes. And he shall bathe his body in fresh water and shall be clean. ¹⁴And on the eighth day he shall take two turtledoves or two pigeons and come before the Lord to the entrance of the tent of meeting and give them to the priest. ¹⁵And the priest shall use them, one for a sin offering and the other for a burnt offering. And the priest shall make atonement for him before the Lord for his discharge.

¹⁶"If a man has an emission of semen, he shall bathe his whole body in water and be unclean until the evening. ¹⁷And every garment and every skin on which the semen comes shall be washed with water and be unclean until the evening. ¹⁸If a man lies with a woman and has an emission of semen, both of them shall bathe themselves in water and be unclean until the evening.

¹⁹"When a woman has a discharge, and the discharge in her body is blood, she shall be in her menstrual impurity for seven days, and whoever touches her shall be unclean until the evening. ²⁰And everything on which she lies during her menstrual impurity shall be unclean. Everything also on which she sits shall be unclean. ²¹And whoever touches her bed shall wash his clothes and bathe himself in water and be unclean until the

evening. ²² And whoever touches anything on which she sits shall wash his clothes and bathe himself in water and be unclean until the evening. ²³ Whether it is the bed or anything on which she sits, when he touches it he shall be unclean until the evening. ²⁴ And if any man lies with her and her menstrual impurity comes upon him, he shall be unclean seven days, and every bed on which he lies shall be unclean.

²⁵ "If a woman has a discharge of blood for many days, not at the time of her menstrual impurity, or if she has a discharge beyond the time of her impurity, all the days of the discharge she shall continue in uncleanness. As in the days of her impurity, she shall be unclean. ²⁶ Every bed on which she lies, all the days of her discharge, shall be to her as the bed of her impurity. And everything on which she sits shall be unclean, as in the uncleanness of her menstrual impurity. ²⁷ And whoever touches these things shall be unclean, and shall wash his clothes and bathe himself in water and be unclean until the evening. ²⁸ But if she is cleansed of her discharge, she shall count for herself seven days, and after that she shall be clean. ²⁹ And on the eighth day she shall take two turtledoves or two pigeons and bring them to the priest, to the entrance of the tent of meeting. ³⁰ And the priest shall use one for a sin offering and the other for a burnt offering. And the priest shall make atonement for her before the LORD for her unclean discharge.

³¹ "Thus you shall keep the people of Israel separate from their uncleanness, lest they die in their uncleanness by defiling my tabernacle that is in their midst."

³² This is the law for him who has a discharge and for him who has an emission of semen, becoming unclean thereby; ³³ also for her who is unwell with her menstrual impurity, that is, for anyone, male or female, who has a discharge, and for the man who lies with a woman who is unclean.

¹ Hebrew *flesh*; also verse 3

Section Overview

The chapter on bodily impurities is arranged as a balanced parallel of male and female discharges. Female discharges are listed after those of a male in the reverse order to create a chiasm, a literary feature that calls attention to its center. Sexual intercourse is at the midpoint of the laws, marking a pivot from male to female impurity and highlighting the one-flesh union of husband and wife. The parity in treatment of male and female discharges shows that all human bodies are touched by ritual impurity.[175] A ritually impure person's separation from the sanctuary makes the theological statement that the Lord alone is holy and pure.

(A) abnormal male discharge (vv. 3–15)
   (B) normal male discharge (vv. 16–17)
      (C) marital intercourse (v. 18)
   (B') normal female discharge (vv. 19–24)
(A') abnormal female discharge (vv. 25–30)

---

[175] Impurity contracted from unclean animals, scale disease, corpse contamination, and bodily emissions affects both sexes equally. This chapter likewise achieves balance between the sexes to show that ritual impurity is common to all humanity.

Every Israelite worshiper had to be conscious of his or her ritual fitness in presenting himself before a holy God. Ritual impurity was not sinful and was usually temporary. Certain bodily fluids—such as sweat, urine, tears, or blood from wounds—do not generate impurity; only genital emissions do, and these can be classified as abnormal (those due to disease or sickness) or normal (those involved with sex or menstruation). Abnormal discharges produce a major impurity that require a longer purification period and sacrifice, while normal discharges can be resolved with waiting and washing and do not require sacrifice.

Several key words repeat throughout this passage that would stand out to the original listeners to whom the Word of God came in spoken form: "unclean" (34x),[176] "touch" (10x),[177] "wash" (11x), and "bathe" (11x). The effect is to urge every Israelite to guard against uncleanness and to be ever mindful of his or her ritual fitness with respect to the sanctuary.

Section Outline

III. Ritual Impurity (11:1–15:33)...
    E. Bodily Impurities (15:1–33)
       1. Introduction (15:1–2)
       2. Abnormal Male Discharge (15:3–15)
       3. Normal Male Discharge (15:16–17)
       4. Marital Intercourse (15:18)
       5. Normal Female Discharge (15:19–24)
       6. Abnormal Female Discharge (15:25–30)
       7. Reason for These Laws (15:31–33)

Comment

15:1–2a The Lord's instruction is to both Moses and Aaron, as is found with other teaching on impurity (11:1; 13:1; 14:33). Priests are responsible for teaching the people as well as protecting the boundaries of the sanctuary from all uncleanness (15:31).

15:2b The first case is treated in the most extensive detail and informs the ones to follow. Israelites must be conscious of their bodily purity: any male with an unusual genital discharge is ritually unclean. Because bodily discharges are a private matter, every Israelite must learn to make distinctions between unclean and clean ritual states—to live by them and perform the required washings and sacrificial offerings outlined below.

15:3 More details now follow. A man with a genital discharge that is either flowing as clear liquid or creating blockage by pus is unclean. Commentators tend to associate these symptoms with gonorrhea, but it is not crucial to identify the precise medical disease; multiple urinary and genital infections causing long-term

---
[176] The word *tame'* appears as a verb (24x), adjective (4x), and noun (6x); Kleinig, *Leviticus*, 317.
[177] Touch is an important refrain in the purity laws, occurring seventy-four times in Leviticus 11–15.

discharge are included within this broad description. The burden of the passage is not to diagnose but rather to communicate the procedure for cleansing and protecting others in the community from secondary impurity.

For the individual a state of ritual impurity translates to not being permitted in the sanctuary nor being able to eat food sacrificed on the altar (7:20–21; 22:3–7). For the community it means taking care not to become polluted through objects the impure person has touched—but, if so, to take the necessary steps of cleansing (5:3).

15:4–6 An abnormal discharge classifies as a major impurity. As a result, an object the diseased person has touched can now communicate impurity to others. Thus anyone who comes into contact with the bedding or an object on which a man with a discharge has sat himself contracts impurity. That person, however, has only a minor impurity, which can be resolved by laundering clothes, bathing in water, and waiting until the evening.

15:7–8 Direct contact with the sufferer initiated by someone who is clean renders that person unclean. A person with an abnormal genital discharge can intentionally contaminate another person by spitting on him.

15:9–10 Because the man with the discharge has a major impurity, he is contagious and makes those objects directly under him unclean, such as a seat or saddle, so that anyone who comes into contact with such an object will also become unclean. The same is the case for menstrual blood (vv. 20–23). Impurity is communicated through touch (vv. 7, 10, 11, 12, 19, 21, 22, 23, 27), sitting (vv. 4, 6, 20, 22, 23), or lying (vv. 4, 20, 26). This means that a long-term discharge will impact daily living, since a man will be aware of what he touches or where he sits while at home or at work farming and tending livestock and will be conscious to maintain distance from others if he is not to convey his impurity.

15:11–12 The diseased man must be diligent to wash his hands lest he convey impurity to those he touches (cf. Mark 7:1–4). The vessels he handles can also be affected if he does not wash his hands: ceramic pots, which are porous, are broken and put out of use, but wood can be washed and reused (Lev. 11:32–33). Priests serving in the tent of meeting regularly follow these protocols to maintain the holiness required in the Lord's dwelling (Ex. 30:18–20; Lev. 6:27–28). In NT times tableware and storage vessels will be crafted out of stone so as not to be contaminated (John 2:6).

15:13–15 After the infection has healed and the man no longer has a discharge he must wait a full seven days, a period of time that marks passage from one ritual state to another. He then must wash the clothes that have touched his body and bathe in "fresh water." The expression in Hebrew is "living water," meaning it comes from a flowing spring or running river and is not stagnant (14:5–6).[178]

---

[178] The influence of Leviticus is encountered at every turn in excavations of the land of Israel, which have uncovered approximately one thousand ritual baths carved into bedrock. Immersion pools are built with

Flowing, living water has power to cleanse the abnormal flow without itself becoming contaminated.

On the eighth day that marks the beginning of a new status the man healed of the abnormal discharge offers a sacrifice of two birds, either turtledoves or pigeons. The two offerings work together—the sin (purification) offering cleanses from impurity and the burnt offering restores fellowship through sacrifice. With this act of worship he is once more welcomed into the holiness of God's presence through the priestly mediation of atonement.

15:16–17 A man who has a nocturnal emission not associated with sexual intercourse becomes ritually unclean, as does any clothing and bedding touched by his semen. He washes his clothes and his body and is clean by that evening. Although this is a normal condition, it is incompatible with sacred space and holy offerings.

15:18 Both husband and wife become ritually unclean after sexual intercourse and must bathe. It strikes us as unexpected that the couple becomes unclean through a union the Lord has blessed so that his image bearers may "be fruitful and multiply and fill the earth" (Gen. 1:28). Although sexual intimacy between a husband and wife is honored in Scripture, it produces a temporary restriction on access to the sanctuary. Sexuality is strictly distanced from the realm of the holy, perhaps to communicate that worship of Israel's God must not be equated to the fertility cults of Canaan. Sexuality and the sacred are incompatible in this way.

When all Israel was to meet with the Lord to ratify the Sinai covenant, it was instructed to wash its clothes and abstain from sexual relations (Ex. 19:10, 15). The congregation consecrated itself to prepare for an encounter with the Lord (while there was no physical structure, Sinai itself was a sanctuary).[179]

15:19 A woman's menstrual cycle puts her in a state of ritual impurity for seven days (even if her blood flow ends sooner). Israelite women would have had fewer menstrual cycles in their lifetime than is typical today since marrying at an early age, frequent pregnancies, and breastfeeding till the age of three affected the frequency.

Anyone who touches the menstruant contracts a minor impurity and is unclean for the rest of the day. As with the impurity of childbirth (12:2–5), this does not hinder others in the household from sharing daily life beside her but only makes them conscious that, should they touch her, they must stay away from holy things. For most Israelites only special occasions will bring them to the tabernacle (later, the temple), such as making an offering, fulfilling a vow, or celebrating the pilgrimage festivals (Deut. 16:1–17).

Bathing at the end of the seven-day period is not mentioned but is implied, since it is required for an equivalent state of impurity (Lev. 15:16–17). Other

---

channels that fill them with rainwater or are dug below the water table so that fresh water naturally seeps in, thereby fulfilling the command to bathe in "living water." The Pool of Siloam is the most famous ritual immersion pool, used by worshipers making pilgrimage to Jerusalem, who would first immerse before ascending to the temple to offer sacrifice.

[179] David and his men assured Ahimelech that they had not had relations with women in order to be given the holy bread (1 Sam. 21:2–7).

passages are suggestive. Bathsheba was "purifying herself from her uncleanness" (2 Sam. 11:4) when David saw her from his palace. Her bathing signaled the end of the purification period after her monthly cycle. The detail is supplied in the narrative to make clear that the child she conceived could only have been David's.

15:20–23 Anything on which the woman lies or sits has the potential to convey her impurity to others (cf. Gen. 31:34–35, where Rachel uses this excuse to conceal household idols in her saddle). Should someone come into contact with her bedding or seat, that person must wash his or her clothes and body and wait until evening to be clean. It is probably to be understood that household items she touches contract impurity (Lev. 15:11–12).

Ritual separation does not make for social isolation. There is no indication that a menstruating woman is isolated from her household (unlike the leper, who must dwell outside the camp); she is restricted only from appearing at the sanctuary or participating in a holy meal. No sacrifices are required at the end of her cycle.

15:24 If a husband and wife are sexually intimate and do not realize that the woman's period has begun, he becomes unclean like her for seven days and likewise conveys her impurity. Were he simply to *touch* his wife, it would make him unclean for only the day. Intercourse, however, causes him to share his wife's impurity because sexual intimacy enacts their one-flesh union (Gen. 2:24). Normally sexual intercourse makes them both unclean for a day (Lev. 15:18), the same duration as that for a normal seminal emission (v. 16). If his semen touches her, she becomes unclean like him; if her blood touches him, he becomes unclean like her. Deliberate intercourse while she is menstruating is prohibited (18:19).

15:25–27 A woman with irregular vaginal or prolonged bleeding beyond her regular period remains ritually unclean and unfit to approach the Lord at the sanctuary. The rules of impurity are the same as those for her regular menstrual flow. She will have to avoid the touch of others and be aware of the ways her impurity may impact others. She must be careful where she sits and where she lies. The lives of her family and community will have to adjust to her prolonged discharge.

15:28–30 When the woman is healed of her abnormal blood flow, she counts off seven days and follows the same purification rite as that of a male with abnormal emission (vv. 13–15). A long-term discharge requires sacrifice to be restored to purity, unlike the regular normal impurity of menstruation.

15:31–33 These laws are given to protect God's people so they do not approach him in their uncleanness and die. The call for Israel to be separate from its uncleanness points to its priestly vocation among the nations. This separation is phrased in a unique way based on the Hebrew word *nazir*, from which the word Nazirite is derived. A Nazirite takes a vow to consecrate himself to the Lord by separating *from* wine and separating *unto* the Lord (Num. 6:2–3). Israel's separation *from* ritual impurity enables its consecration *to* the Lord and conformity with his holy dwelling.

Because the Lord is among his people, he is pushing life in the direction of bodily purity and sanctification. Even though bodily impurity is part of the normal course of life, the Lord provides a way for bodies to be made compatible with the sanctuary and enabled to stand in his presence. Aligning the body according to the ritual purity of the sanctuary anticipates how one day all believers will become sanctified to be as the temple of the Holy Spirit (1 Cor. 6:19).

Response

In the days of his earthly ministry multitudes are drawn to Jesus, pressing in on all sides: "All the crowd sought to touch him, for power came out from him and healed them all" (Luke 6:19; cf. Mark 3:7–10). Indeed, in his compassion Jesus is moved to stretch out his hand and touch an unclean leper. The power that flows out of him is the power of his divine life that overturns disease and even death itself.

We see this again in the account of a hemorrhaging woman who has spent all her money on medical care, has been left destitute and depleted, and is resolved to touch Jesus (Luke 8:43–48). It is a desperate act, knowing that touching him will make him ritually unclean. At least, that is what would have normally happened. But at the moment she touches the hem of his garment her flow of blood ceases immediately. Not only does Jesus not contract her impurity, but his holiness issues forth to make her clean. We can imagine the fullness of life awaiting the woman—wholeness of body and emotion, social inclusion in the community, restored intimacy with her husband, and maybe even the conception of a child. The greatest restoration of all will be to the temple, as she will be able to enter its courts once more as a worshiper. For twelve years she has not been able to make her way to meet with the Lord, but *he* meets *her* in her infirmity and makes her whole.

LEVITICUS 16

16 The LORD spoke to Moses after the death of the two sons of Aaron, when they drew near before the LORD and died, ²and the LORD said to Moses, "Tell Aaron your brother not to come at any time into the Holy Place inside the veil, before the mercy seat that is on the ark, so that he may not die. For I will appear in the cloud over the mercy seat. ³But in this way Aaron shall come into the Holy Place: with a bull from the herd for a sin offering and a ram for a burnt offering. ⁴He shall put on the holy linen coat and shall have the linen undergarment on his body, and he shall tie the linen sash around his waist, and wear the linen turban; these are the holy garments. He shall bathe his body in water and then put them on. ⁵And he shall take from the congregation of the people of Israel two male goats for a sin offering, and one ram for a burnt offering.

⁶ "Aaron shall offer the bull as a sin offering for himself and shall make atonement for himself and for his house. ⁷ Then he shall take the two goats and set them before the LORD at the entrance of the tent of meeting. ⁸ And Aaron shall cast lots over the two goats, one lot for the LORD and the other lot for Azazel.¹ ⁹ And Aaron shall present the goat on which the lot fell for the LORD and use it as a sin offering, ¹⁰ but the goat on which the lot fell for Azazel shall be presented alive before the LORD to make atonement over it, that it may be sent away into the wilderness to Azazel.

¹¹ "Aaron shall present the bull as a sin offering for himself, and shall make atonement for himself and for his house. He shall kill the bull as a sin offering for himself. ¹² And he shall take a censer full of coals of fire from the altar before the LORD, and two handfuls of sweet incense beaten small, and he shall bring it inside the veil ¹³ and put the incense on the fire before the LORD, that the cloud of the incense may cover the mercy seat that is over the testimony, so that he does not die. ¹⁴ And he shall take some of the blood of the bull and sprinkle it with his finger on the front of the mercy seat on the east side, and in front of the mercy seat he shall sprinkle some of the blood with his finger seven times.

¹⁵ "Then he shall kill the goat of the sin offering that is for the people and bring its blood inside the veil and do with its blood as he did with the blood of the bull, sprinkling it over the mercy seat and in front of the mercy seat. ¹⁶ Thus he shall make atonement for the Holy Place, because of the uncleannesses of the people of Israel and because of their transgressions, all their sins. And so he shall do for the tent of meeting, which dwells with them in the midst of their uncleannesses. ¹⁷ No one may be in the tent of meeting from the time he enters to make atonement in the Holy Place until he comes out and has made atonement for himself and for his house and for all the assembly of Israel. ¹⁸ Then he shall go out to the altar that is before the LORD and make atonement for it, and shall take some of the blood of the bull and some of the blood of the goat, and put it on the horns of the altar all around. ¹⁹ And he shall sprinkle some of the blood on it with his finger seven times, and cleanse it and consecrate it from the uncleannesses of the people of Israel.

²⁰ "And when he has made an end of atoning for the Holy Place and the tent of meeting and the altar, he shall present the live goat. ²¹ And Aaron shall lay both his hands on the head of the live goat, and confess over it all the iniquities of the people of Israel, and all their transgressions, all their sins. And he shall put them on the head of the goat and send it away into the wilderness by the hand of a man who is in readiness. ²² The goat shall bear all their iniquities on itself to a remote area, and he shall let the goat go free in the wilderness.

²³ "Then Aaron shall come into the tent of meeting and shall take off the linen garments that he put on when he went into the Holy Place and shall leave them there. ²⁴ And he shall bathe his body in water in a holy place and put on his garments and come out and offer his burnt offering and the burnt offering of the people and make atonement for himself and for the people. ²⁵ And the fat of the sin offering he shall burn on the altar. ²⁶ And he who lets the goat go to Azazel shall wash his clothes and bathe his body in water, and afterward he may come into the camp. ²⁷ And the bull for the sin offering and the goat for the sin offering, whose blood was brought in to make atonement in the Holy Place, shall be carried outside the camp. Their skin and their flesh and their dung shall be burned up

with fire. ²⁸ And he who burns them shall wash his clothes and bathe his body in water, and afterward he may come into the camp.

²⁹ "And it shall be a statute to you forever that in the seventh month, on the tenth day of the month, you shall afflict yourselves² and shall do no work, either the native or the stranger who sojourns among you. ³⁰ For on this day shall atonement be made for you to cleanse you. You shall be clean before the LORD from all your sins. ³¹ It is a Sabbath of solemn rest to you, and you shall afflict yourselves; it is a statute forever. ³² And the priest who is anointed and consecrated as priest in his father's place shall make atonement, wearing the holy linen garments. ³³ He shall make atonement for the holy sanctuary, and he shall make atonement for the tent of meeting and for the altar, and he shall make atonement for the priests and for all the people of the assembly. ³⁴ And this shall be a statute forever for you, that atonement may be made for the people of Israel once in the year because of all their sins." And Aaron³ did as the LORD commanded Moses.

¹ The meaning of *Azazel* is uncertain; possibly the name of a place or a demon, traditionally a scapegoat; also verses 10, 26 ² Or *shall fast*; also verse 31 ³ Hebrew *he*

Section Overview

As the book of Leviticus unfolds in a series of the Lord's speeches to his covenant people, chapter 16 marks the central speech. The book itself anchors the center of the Pentateuch, thus making the Day of Atonement the literary and theological heart of the law.[180] The significance of its subject matter is further communicated through subtle literary artistry, with atonement referenced sixteen times[181] and the Holy Place and mercy seat each seven times.[182] Within the book this chapter serves as a hinge between two major sections, bringing to conclusion the sacrificial (chs. 1–7) and purity laws (chs. 11–15) and charting the path forward for a life of holiness made possible through the abiding presence of a holy God (chs. 17–27). As Hartley observes, "It may be said that the moral and spiritual energy for the people to fulfill the laws in chaps. 17–26 comes out of their finding complete expiation on the Day of Atonement."[183]

The opening verse unexpectedly takes us back to the death of Aaron's sons and the unresolved theological tension of how Israel can maintain ongoing covenant communion with the Lord in the face of her rebellion and uncleanness. The effects of sin, far from being private, are a virulent pollution that defiles the person, the land, and the sanctuary wherein God dwells. It clings to the horns of the sacrificial altar, accrues in the tabernacle, and spills out onto the land until it must be dealt with in judgment (18:28). The Lord's presence is a dangerous privilege: "You shall keep the people of Israel separate from their uncleanness, lest they die in their uncleanness by defiling my tabernacle that is in their midst" (15:31).

The tension is resolved through the rituals of this sacred day, which the Lord ordains for the purging of sin and cleansing of the sanctuary so that he may

---

[180] Warning, *Literary Artistry in Leviticus*, 40–46; Morales, *Who Shall Ascend*, 29.
[181] Leviticus 16:6, 10, 11, 16, 17 (2x), 18, 20, 24, 27, 30, 32, 33 (3x), 34.
[182] Holy Place (Lev. 16:2, 3, 16, 17, 20, 23, 27) and mercy seat (vv. 2 [2x], 13, 14 [2x], 15 [2x]).
[183] Hartley, *Leviticus*, 217.

continue to dwell among his people. It is a sacrificial provision without which Israel's uncleanness would accumulate like that of the nations whom the Lord will judge and expel from the land (Gen. 15:16; cf. Lev. 26:33). By God's grace Israel will not be expelled from his presence, but a substitute in her place will carry the people's sins into the inaccessible wilderness wasteland.

Section Outline

IV. Day of Atonement (16:1–34)
    A. Introduction (16:1–2)
    B. Ritual Preparation for the Rites of Atonement (16:3–10)
    C. Day of Atonement Rites (16:11–28)
        1. Purification of the Sanctuary (16:11–19)
        2. Atonement for the People (16:20–22)
        3. Worship Restored (16:23–28)
    D. The People's Participation (16:29–31)
    E. Conclusion (16:32–34)

Comment

16:1 The Day of Atonement is introduced with reference to the death of Aaron's sons, recalling the narrative of the inauguration of tabernacle worship (chs. 8–10). Israel's covenant worship enacts the fellowship between God and humanity that had been known previously in Eden (cf. Introduction; comment on 26:11–12). In this context Nadab and Abihu's sin followed by the Lord's swift judgment replays another fall of humanity. But it does more than that. Introducing the Day of Atonement in light of grave transgression brings into focus that which the sacrificial system is intended to achieve: the cleansing of all unrighteousness in order to restore relationship with the Lord.

16:2 The Lord prohibits approach into his presence "at any time" of Aaron's choosing. Rather, the time and manner of approach before the throne of God will be determined by him. The Holy Place is the Lord's audience hall and the Most Holy Place his throne room, concealed from visibility by a veil embroidered with figures of guardian cherubim. Behind the veil rests the holiest article of furniture, the ark of the covenant, crowned with a cover of pure gold from whose ends rise two cherubim of pure gold (Ex. 25:17–22). The cherubim are turned inward, facing each other, and their outstretched wings create a seat where the Lord is envisioned as enthroned (Ps. 99:1; Isa. 37:16). This cover, translated as "mercy seat" (ESV) or "atonement cover" (NASB), derives its name from the Day of Atonement ceremonies because it is the focal point of ritual activity on this day (Lev. 16:13–15).[184]

Verses 2–3 set before the readers of this text a contrast between the proper and improper ways of approaching the Lord, recalling the priesthood's charge to dis-

---

[184] The LXX translates as *hilastērion* ("instrument of propitiation"), highlighting its role as a place where sin is purged and God's wrath turned away.

tinguish between holy and common / clean and unclean (10:10) and setting a tone that guards from overfamiliarity with the God who makes his dwelling among his people. The Lord pledges his personal presence in the sanctuary—"I will appear in the cloud over the mercy seat" (Lev. 16:2; cf. Ex. 25:22)—a presence that both visits judgment on sin (Lev. 10:2) and secures forgiveness for the penitent (16:30).

16:3–5 The ritual first specifies the offerings: a bull for a sin offering and a ram for a burnt offering for Aaron's household (v. 3) and two male goats for a sin offering and a ram for a burnt offering on behalf of the people (v. 5). In addition to the offerings a change of clothing is specified. The change of dress is no mere outward formality but speaks to an inner disposition. The high priest must humble himself by laying aside his sumptuous garments in favor of plain linen robes (Exodus 28; Lev. 8:7–9). His role on this day is to represent the people before the Lord, so he dresses in a linen tunic of the common priesthood in identification with every Israelite. Aaron washes his body before dressing, thereby signaling a more thorough ritual cleansing and consecration not required on other days of his priestly ministry, likely because he will be drawing closer than ever to the presence of the Lord.

16:6 Verses 6–10 offer a preliminary description of the sacrificial ritual that will be enacted at the appointed time. This verse anticipates the sin offering for the priestly household that is fulfilled in verse 11.

16:7–8 The focus now shifts to the sin offering that will be made for the people at the appointed time (cf. v. 15). Aaron must present the two male goats to the Lord, and it is the Lord who will select by lot which one will be for purification and which will be sent into the wilderness (vv. 9–10). The use of lots is a sanctioned means of discerning God's will: "The lot is cast into the lap, but its every decision is from the LORD" (Prov. 16:33).

Azazel is mentioned only here in the Bible,[185] making it difficult to decipher its identity with any certainty. Several avenues of interpretation have been proposed, all which depend on etymology. Azazel could be taken either as a personal name, a geographical location, or a description of the goat's function. First, since it appears in parallel with the name of the Lord, Azazel may be a personal name containing the words *'ez* ("goat") and *'el* ("mighty"). Reading this chapter together with the following one, some interpreters suggest that Azazel is the name of a goat demon (cf. Lev. 17:7).[186] In this scenario the nation's sin is placed on the goat and dispatched to a realm believed to be associated with demons.

Another reading understands Azazel to derive from the Arabic *'azazu*, meaning "rough and rocky precipice," possibly referring to the type of terrain or location to

---

[185] Leviticus 16:8, 10 (2x), 26.
[186] Milgrom, *Leviticus 1–16*, 1020–1021; Gane, *Leviticus, Numbers*, 288. This interpretation presents the theological difficulty of the Lord's prescribing a ritual practice that appears to validate the existence of demonic beings and their appeasement through sacrifice. Those who make this argument note that Azazel appears in parallel with the name of the Lord. The parallelism, however, is one of designation and can apply grammatically to any of the suggested meanings, such as a goat "for the Lord" or a goat "for the cut-off land."

which the goat is banished (cf. 16:10, 22).[187] This proposal sees the nation's sin as being transferred onto a carrier destined to the precipice, which cuts it off from human habitation.

Related to its function, Azazel may represent a combination of the words '*ez* and '*azal* to mean "goat that departs." In distinction to the goat offering whose blood cleanses the sanctuary, Azazel's function is to remove sin from the congregation by carrying it outside of the boundaries of the Lord's domain. The traditional rendering of scapegoat ("*escape*-goat") derives from this explanation.[188] It is important to bear in mind that etymology alone can be interpreted in a variety of ways, yet the goat's ritual function is clear and best comports with this final meaning.[189]

16:9–10 The two goats, one slain and one released alive, will accomplish the twofold work of atonement. The first goat's sacrificial blood will cleanse from impurity and sin (purification), while the second goat will carry away all sin and its lethal burden.

16:11 The day's ceremonies begin with a sin offering for the high priest and his household, as did the inaugural service evoked in verse 1 (cf. 9:8).

16:12–13 Aaron fills his censer (fire pan) with live coals from the "altar before the LORD," that is, the golden altar in front of the veil drawn before the Most Holy Place. To the coals he adds two handfuls of holy incense, compounded of fragrant resins, spices, and herbs finely ground and mixed with salt for combustion (Ex. 30:34–35). This incense is "most holy" and exclusive to the sanctuary; any other use is forbidden and results in the user's being cut off from God's people (Ex. 30:36–38). Incense is burned daily on the golden altar (Ex. 30:7–8), producing a cloud that permeates boundaries that otherwise cannot be crossed as it drifts through the separating veil into the Most Holy Place. On this day Aaron brings his censer behind the curtain so that the incense cloud hovers over the mercy seat (cf. Lev. 16:2). The ark is referred to here as the ark of the testimony to emphasize the tablets of the covenant it contains and the covenant obligations that have been violated throughout the year (Ex. 31:18; 40:21).

To be granted access into the innermost chamber of God's throne room Aaron must create his own veil of separation, shielding himself behind the smoky, sweet-smelling cloud. This cloud will "cover the mercy seat," over which the Lord appears (Lev. 16:2), "so that [Aaron] does not die" (v. 13), for no one can see the Lord in all his glory and live (Ex. 33:20). Aaron is thus permitted entry, not as a stranger but as a welcome priest into the Lord's throne room to make atonement, an act that

---

[187] Hartley, *Leviticus*, 237.
[188] Levine, *Leviticus*, 102.
[189] Sklar, *Leviticus*, TOTC, 210. In support the LXX renders Azazel as *apopompaios* ("sending away"), which lacks any nuance of personality (as would be necessary for a goat demon). For an overview of the earliest interpretations cf. Lester L. Grabbe, "The Scapegoat Tradition: A Study in Early Jewish Interpretation" *JSJ* 18 (1987): 152–167. It is instructive to note that all interpretations above can be traced back to early Jewish and Christian exegesis, with Jewish traditions favoring the interpretation of a goat demon and Christian traditions seeing Christ prefigured in the scapegoat banished from God's presence.

looks forward to a far greater priest performing a far greater work of atonement in the throne room of heaven itself (cf. Heb. 9:23–24).

16:14 It is for the purpose of atonement that the high priest is granted access behind the cherubim-embroidered veil that replicates the separation between God and humanity that has existed since the guardian cherubim were first stationed at the entrance to Eden (Gen. 3:24). Israel's sins throughout the year have generated pollution that has accumulated in the sanctuary and infiltrated even into the Lord's throne room. Aaron takes the blood of his household's sin offering and sprinkles it on the cover of the mercy seat and in front of it seven times, a number signifying completion. God's throne and the ground on which it rests are thus cleansed when atonement is made.

16:15 Aaron then slaughters the goat chosen by lot as the people's sin offering (Lev. 16:9) and brings its blood inside the Most Holy Place to sprinkle as he did the bull's.

16:16 The blood of the sin offerings cleanses the innermost sanctuary and entire tent of meeting pitched amid a sinful people. This verse implies that the ritual performed in the Most Holy Place is also to be performed in the Holy Place, most likely by sprinkling the altar of incense seven times and applying blood on its horns (cf. vv. 18–19).

In the first movement of the ritual of atonement the Lord's dwelling is thoroughly cleansed of all sin, categorized as "uncleannesses" (chs. 11–15), willful "transgressions," and all other "sins" that have polluted the sanctuary (chs. 4–5). While "impurity" and "sin" have been the subject of Leviticus's laws, "transgression" appears for the first time, recognizing that people also sin willfully and defiantly. The Hebrew term (*pesha'*) carries the sense of rebellion, such as that of a vassal against his suzerain (1 Kings 12:19; 2 Kings 8:20). In Israel's covenant with the Lord willful and defiant sin is open rebellion against his rule over his people's lives. Yet on this day all sin—including defiant sin—is atoned for so that the Lord may continue to dwell among his people.

16:17 To underscore the gravity of the day's rites and uniqueness of the mediator the instructions clarify that no one but the high priest is permitted in the tent during the purification of the sanctuary, "from the time he enters . . . until he comes out." This is the work exclusively of the man who stands as mediator between the Lord and his people.[190]

16:18–19 The blood that was brought inside the veil (v. 15) is carried outward to cleanse the Holy Place (v. 16) and then the sacrificial altar in the courtyard (v. 18). The progressive movement from God's throne room to the courtyard where worshipers gather bears witness that it is the Lord who cleanses his people from their

---

[190] One cannot help but hear a faint note of Nadab and Abihu's transgression in this prohibition. Aaron's role as ritual mediator in the tabernacle is like Moses' role of covenant mediator on Sinai.

sins. The same movement is observed in Ezekiel's prophetic vision of restoration, where cleansing waters instead of blood flow from God's throne to bring to new life everything in their path (Ezekiel 47).

The high priest takes the bull's blood (priestly sin offering) and the goat's blood (people's sin offering) and mixes them together to apply to the horns of the altar and to sprinkle the altar itself. For the third time there is mention of a sevenfold sprinkling, drawing on language rich with symbolism to illustrate a complete cleansing.[191] The application of blood purifies the altar and reconsecrates it, removing defilement and making it ritually fit for God's people to utilize in meeting with him again through the sacrifices and gifts of covenant worship. The sprinkling recalls the altar's original consecration (Lev. 8:11, 15) and signals the new beginning that the Day of Atonement achieves.

16:20 Once the tent of meeting has been purified (vv. 11–19) the Day of Atonement continues with the second of the two goats.

16:21 As elsewhere in the Bible, sin is conceived of here as a physical burden carried about as "an encumbrance, an ever-present yoke, under whose strain [the sinner] may eventually be crushed."[192] When carried by the sinner, it inevitably leads to suffering sin's consequence and punishment (5:17; 22:9; Num. 18:22). When carried by a substitute, it is carried away for forgiveness as the sinner is freed from the burden of his iniquity (Ex. 34:7; Pss. 32:5; 85:2; Isa. 53:11; Mic. 7:18). This background helps make clear what is occurring in these verses.

To begin Aaron presents the live goat before the Lord, places both his hands on the goat's head, and confesses over it Israel's sins. As high priest, he thus representatively stands in for all sinners, since it is always the offerer who leans his hand on the sacrificial victim (Lev. 1:4) and the guilty who makes a confession of sin (5:5).[193] Aaron confesses the *iniquity* and *transgressions* of the Israelites—all their *sins*—thereby transferring them onto the goat's head.[194] This language expresses the totality of sins the substitute carries, repeating the very language of the totality of the Lord's forgiveness when he reveals himself a God rich in mercy, "forgiving *iniquity* and *transgression* and *sin*" (Ex. 34:7). Aaron then expels the goat and all Israel's sins with it by means of a man designated for the task.

---

191 Jacob Milgrom counts forty-nine (7 x 7) separate blood sprinklings to make a superlative atonement: 1x on the mercy seat with bull's blood and 1x with goat's blood; 7x in front of the mercy seat with bull's blood and 7x with goat's blood; 7x on the altar of incense with bull's blood and 7x with goat's blood; 4x on its horns with bull's blood and 4x with goat's blood; and finally 7x on the altar of sacrifice + 4x on its horns with combined bull-and-goat blood (*Leviticus 1–16*, 1038–1039).

192 Baruch J. Schwartz, "The Bearing of Sin in the Priestly Literature," in *Pomegranates and Golden Bells: Studies in Biblical, Jewish, and Near Eastern Ritual, Law, and Literature in Honor of Jacob Milgrom*, ed. David P. Wright, David Noel Freedman, and Avi Hurvitz (Winona Lake, IN: Eisenbrauns, 1995), 10.

193 The people are not summoned to the sanctuary as on the appointed feasts (Deut. 16:16) but rather observe the day in their dwellings in fasting and repentance.

194 Unlike in the separate purification offerings for the priesthood and the people, all sins are carried by the Azazel goat. Later Jewish sources record this prayer as having been prayed by the high priest: "O God, thy people, the House of Israel, have committed iniquity, transgressed, and sinned before thee. O God, forgive, I pray, the iniquities and transgressions and sins which thy people, the House of Israel, have committed and transgressed and sinned before thee; as it is written in the law of thy servant Moses, *For on this day shall atonement be made for you to cleanse you: from all your sins shall ye be clean before the Lord*" (Mishnah, Yoma 6:2; italics added).

16:22 The ritual landscape now extends to the limits of the known world when the goat on whose head Israel's sin has come to rest is driven out into the wilderness. In Israel's worldview the wilderness represents chaos, the opposite of the Lord's ordered and life-giving presence (cf. Matt. 4:1; 12:43). It is forsaken, unsown, and uncreated, a restless haunt for predators (Jer. 4:23–26). This solitary, cut-off land is the antithesis of the life of the redeemed community. As the animal is driven away in the opposite direction from God's presence and people, it illustrates what happens to those who bear their own sin apart from forgiveness (Lev. 7:27; 18:26–29; 20:2–5; Isa. 53:8).[195]

The handling of the Azazel goat dispels any thought it could be a sacrifice: it carries the nation's sin away into those realms unclaimed by the redemptive purposes of God. Sin is pushed back into the realm of chaos, and the realm of the Lord's holy dwelling (sanctuary, people, and land) becomes rid of its pollution.

16:23–25 After the purification and elimination rites Aaron removes the linen garments worn on this special day, washes in a holy place (cf. Lev. 6:27), and once again dons the distinctive high priestly dress to offer two rams—one on behalf of the priests and the other on behalf of the people—together with the sin offering's fat portions (cf. 4:8–10). His change of dress signals a change in ritual movement. The last time in the narrative that ram offerings were made was at the inaugural service (9:2, 4), linking the passages to imply a restart to the tabernacle's sacrificial ministry.[196] On the day that sin is banished from the community of the redeemed, worship of the Lord begins anew.

16:26 The designated man who leads the live goat into the wilderness must wash the clothes that have been in the presence of the nation's sin. After he washes his body outside the camp he is then able to rejoin the congregation.

16:27–28 Another man, one in charge of burning the remains of the sin offering's hide, flesh, and offal, also has to wash before returning to the camp (cf. 4:11–12; Num. 19:8). As the Israelites witness this process, sin's contagion would be hard to miss. The men remain nameless, emphasizing the importance of Aaron in his high priestly role.

From a literary perspective the instructions for the Day of Atonement begin and end with the sin offerings, creating a frame around the other rituals and interpreting all activities as cleansing the sanctuary and community from all sin (Lev. 16:11, 27).[197]

16:29–31 The high priest is the mediator of the nation's atonement, but the people are no afterthought. They are addressed for the first time in the text, although

---

[195] Rabbinic traditions record that in the Second Temple period the goat was pushed off a precipice to its death (Mishnah, Yoma 6:2). The purpose of the ritual, however, is not to put the goat to death but to drive it away, cutting it off so that it removes sin's pollution and suffers the punishment of the sinner, who deserves to be cut off (e.g., Lev. 7:27; 20:3, 5, 6, 17).
[196] All offerings on this day serve the purposes of atonement (Lev. 16:6, 10, 11, 16, 17, 18, 20, 24, 27, 30, 32, 33, 34).
[197] Gane, *Leviticus, Numbers*, 276.

they have been participants all along. On this day their act of worship is to "afflict themselves"[198] by fasting and offering prayers of repentance (cf. Ps. 35:13; Isa. 58:5). Anyone who does not humble himself in repentance before the Lord is to be cut off from his people (cf. Lev. 23:29). This is the only mandatory fast day in the law, and in calling the covenant community to *afflict* itself much more than fasting is in view. The people are to abase themselves as one does when mourning, weeping, and interceding in sackcloth and ashes (Est. 4:3; Joel 2:12–13). They are commanded to be in a posture of sorrow over their sin to teach that "godly grief produces a repentance that leads to salvation" (2 Cor. 7:10).[199] Fasting, furthermore, is of no benefit unless it is accompanied by works that testify to a changed heart, such as feeding the hungry, caring for the poor, and championing the cause of the oppressed (Isa. 58:6–8).

This solemn day is a "Sabbath of Sabbaths," on which work is strictly prohibited for the Israelite and the resident alien,[200] as both are held accountable under the same law (Lev. 24:22) for sin that pollutes the land.[201] If anyone does any work, he is to be cut off from his people (cf. 23:30). In the ancient world work was necessary for survival. To abstain from both work *and* food effectively disconnects a person from all that is life-sustaining. The rite of atonement takes center stage so that Israel learns it is only cleansing from sin that brings life.

Verses 29–31 are arranged in a chiasm, the bookends of which describe the Day of Atonement as a perpetual statute and a day of rest (vv. 29, 31). Highlighted in between is the declaration that Israel will be cleansed and made clean, repeated for emphasis (v. 30). There is a day written into Israel's calendar—the tenth day of the seventh month—on which sin is banished from God's presence and forgiveness is won for the penitent through the ministry of the high priest.

16:32–34a The ritual legislation ends on a note highlighting the high priestly office. It looks forward to Aaron's descendants who will succeed him, coming back full circle to the beginning of the chapter, which makes mention of the two sons who did not respect the Lord's holiness. Humble obedience to the Lord's commands assures the perpetuation of Aaron's priestly lineage and its performance of atonement for the sanctuary, priesthood, and the people of Israel.

16:34b The reckless tragedy of the opening line is reversed through obedience: Aaron is faithful to perform all that the Lord has commanded through Moses.

---

198 The language of affliction appears again in Psalm 35:13; Isaiah 58:3, 5 connected with fasting. That this was the means of the people's participation in the Day of Atonement is evident by how it later comes to be known as the "Great Fast Day" (Josephus, *Antiquities* 3.10.3; Mishnah, Yoma 74b).
199 Later Jewish sources underscore that the day does not atone unless the people repent (Mishnah, Yoma 8:8).
200 What is translated as "stranger" or in other places "sojourner" refers to a non-Israelite who has left his homeland and settled among the Israelites. In modern terms his status is best understood as a "resident alien." Like Israelites, resident aliens are required to cease from work on the Sabbath (Ex. 20:10; Deut. 5:14) and also on this Sabbath of sabbaths.
201 The holy living required of the resident alien is the same as that of the Israelite, including the prohibitions of eating blood (Lev. 17:10–13), transgressing social-familial boundaries in sexuality (18:6–23), and sacrificing children to false gods (20:2). These are the practices that brought the Lord's judgment upon the land's previous inhabitants (18:26–28).

Response

On the Day of Atonement time comes to a standstill, as all daily rhythms of toil and table are suspended. When it comes to the need for atonement, everyone is treated on an equal plane, whatever one's role (master or servant) or status (all are humbled). The experience of the day must have been one that reverberated with the sentiment that "all have sinned and fall short of the glory of God" (Rom. 3:23). All awaited the atonement mediated by the high priest before the throne of God. After the cleansing blood was applied, the sin-laden goat sent away, and sacrifices offered on the reconsecrated altar, time could restart, as though the whole world had begun anew through the gift of redemption and propitiation by blood (cf. Rom. 3:24–25).

The yearly rite enacting the removal of sin and the purification of the sanctuary ultimately prefigured the offering of a high priest who would secure a lasting atonement (Heb. 10:11–14). In the fullness of time, on a day written into redemptive history, Christ, having divested himself of his glory to come as a man (Phil. 2:6–8), entered into the divine throne room in heavenly places with his own blood (Heb. 9:11–12). He was received as the Father's very image (Col. 1:15), sent to "reconcile to himself all things, whether on earth or in heaven, making peace by the blood of his cross" (Col. 1:20). Having offered up himself as the perfect sacrifice, he did not turn to leave but remained and "sat down at the right hand of the Majesty on high" (Heb. 1:3). The separating veil was torn in two, showing that the way into the Father's presence stands wide open forever (Mark 15:38; Heb. 10:19–22). The human longing never to be separated from God's presence has been answered in Christ, who restores fellowship with the Father and continues to indwell his redeemed through the Spirit. In his sacrificial death and resurrection the world has indeed begun anew as he inaugurates a new creation.

LEVITICUS 17

17 And the Lord spoke to Moses, saying, ² "Speak to Aaron and his sons and to all the people of Israel and say to them, This is the thing that the Lord has commanded. ³ If any one of the house of Israel kills an ox or a lamb or a goat in the camp, or kills it outside the camp, ⁴ and does not bring it to the entrance of the tent of meeting to offer it as a gift to the Lord in front of the tabernacle of the Lord, bloodguilt shall be imputed to that man. He has shed blood, and that man shall be cut off from among his people. ⁵ This is to the end that the people of Israel may bring their sacrifices that they sacrifice in the open field, that they may bring them to the Lord, to the priest at the entrance of the tent of meeting, and sacrifice them as sacrifices of peace offerings to the Lord. ⁶ And the priest shall

throw the blood on the altar of the Lord at the entrance of the tent of meeting and burn the fat for a pleasing aroma to the Lord. ⁷ So they shall no more sacrifice their sacrifices to goat demons, after whom they whore. This shall be a statute forever for them throughout their generations.

⁸ "And you shall say to them, Any one of the house of Israel, or of the strangers who sojourn among them, who offers a burnt offering or sacrifice ⁹ and does not bring it to the entrance of the tent of meeting to offer it to the Lord, that man shall be cut off from his people.

¹⁰ "If any one of the house of Israel or of the strangers who sojourn among them eats any blood, I will set my face against that person who eats blood and will cut him off from among his people. ¹¹ For the life of the flesh is in the blood, and I have given it for you on the altar to make atonement for your souls, for it is the blood that makes atonement by the life. ¹² Therefore I have said to the people of Israel, No person among you shall eat blood, neither shall any stranger who sojourns among you eat blood.

¹³ "Any one also of the people of Israel, or of the strangers who sojourn among them, who takes in hunting any beast or bird that may be eaten shall pour out its blood and cover it with earth. ¹⁴ For the life of every creature¹ is its blood: its blood is its life.² Therefore I have said to the people of Israel, You shall not eat the blood of any creature, for the life of every creature is its blood. Whoever eats it shall be cut off. ¹⁵ And every person who eats what dies of itself or what is torn by beasts, whether he is a native or a sojourner, shall wash his clothes and bathe himself in water and be unclean until the evening; then he shall be clean. ¹⁶ But if he does not wash them or bathe his flesh, he shall bear his iniquity."

¹ Hebrew *all flesh* ² Hebrew *it is in its life*

Section Overview

After the high point of the Day of Atonement this chapter continues the focus on lifeblood by setting parameters around its usage. It also serves as a hinge to the second part of the book, which addresses holy living (chs. 17–27). The theological center of gravity has thus far revolved around the tent of meeting as it has addressed the maintaining of relationship with the Lord through sacrifices that atone for sin, offer worship, and cleanse from impurity. The center of gravity now moves outward to the societal implications of a life lived in holiness. As the first part of the book opened with the whole burnt offering that represents total dedication to the Lord, the second part bridges to holy living by addressing the blood of sacrifice that is wholly dedicated to the Lord.

From a canonical perspective the people of God have witnessed the ransoming power of sacrificial blood on the doorframes of their houses to protect them from the plague of the firstborn (Ex. 12:21–23). They have experienced the blood bond that brought them into covenant with the Lord at Sinai (Ex. 24:6–8). They have gathered around Aaron and his sons, who were ordained to service through blood that consecrated the altar and those who officiate before it (Lev. 8:15, 23–24, 30). They have seen the ritual handling of blood restore relationship with God as it was sprinkled before the curtain (4:6–7), splashed against the sides of the altar (1:5; 3:2; 7:2; 9:12), and poured at its base (4:7; 9:9). They have considered how the numerous blood applications of the Day of Atonement will cleanse the sanctuary from all impurity and sin (16:14–19). Now, as the call to holiness extends from the sanctuary and priesthood into the life of every Israelite, they themselves are instructed on the proper use of this atoning, purifying, life-giving substance.

The command to refrain from eating blood "in all your dwelling places" (3:17; 7:26–27) has been growing in force until it reaches its fullest exposition in this chapter. The chapter is structured around five proclamations regarding blood's proper and improper use, thematically held together by the thirteenfold appearance of the word "blood."[202] Woven throughout is the theological rationale for these laws, which bring to light the lifeblood's ritual significance (17:5–7, 11–12, 14). The surrounding nations all offer sacrifices to their gods, but none ascribe as much importance to the blood as Israel does. God's people are entrusted with a revelation that is unique in the ancient world.

Section Outline

V. Life Is in the Blood (17:1–16)
    A. Introduction (17:1–2)
    B. Slaughter of Domestic Animals (17:3–7)
    C. Slaughter of Sacrificial Animals (17:8–9)
    D. Eating Blood Is Forbidden (17:10–12)
    E. Disposal of Blood from Game (17:13–14)
    F. Purification Contingencies (17:15–16)

Comment

17:1–2 The Lord's words are addressed to priests and people alike, making them binding upon all Israelites. These commands go beyond ritual performance at the sanctuary to touch on practices of daily life for the community. This is emphasized throughout the chapter by underscoring how these laws are for "any one" (vv. 3, 8, 10, 13). The sojourner is included in four of the five commands, extending the requirements of holy living to all who are associated with the covenant community (vv. 8, 10, 12, 13, 15).

17:3–4 The first prohibition concerns the *place* of animal slaughter. A person who butchers a domestic animal, whether inside the camp (around the home) or outside the camp (herding livestock), without bringing it to the tent of meeting as an offering is regarded as guilty of bloodshed and thus worthy of being cut off (cf. 7:20). The punishment interprets the *nature* of animal slaughter: every act of animal slaughter is a sacrificial act.

The ox, lamb, and goat appear in lists together as domestic animals that may be offered as a peace offering, the only offering from which the offerer may eat

---

[202] Leviticus 17:4 (2x), 6, 10 (2x), 11 (2x), 12 (2x), 13, 14 (3x).

(7:23; 22:27).²⁰³ An Israelite who slaughters an animal for its meat must bring it as a gift to the Lord (17:5) and honor him with the fat portions, but the worshiper may feast on the rest. Most importantly, the blood must be handled in a sacral manner and applied to the altar (v. 6). If not, then the person is considered to have "shed blood," the biblical idiom for unjust killing. Killing an animal apart from the sanctuary is equated with murder, meaning that all non-sacrificial slaughter is banned. Slaughter is never secular, as the animal's blood must be disposed of in a way that returns life to its Maker. The pronouncement strikes an ethical note, a concern that will continue to unfold in subsequent chapters that deal with the ethics of a holy people (chs. 18–25).

Yet, practically speaking, occasions could arise wherein it would not be appropriate for an animal to be offered as a sacrifice, and ordinary slaughter would be more fitting. Animals that were blemished or sick could not be offered on the altar (22:20–25). Additionally, the herd or flock would be culled to breed for desirable traits (Gen. 30:37–43), to increase milk productivity, or to keep the flock at optimal size for the pasturage.²⁰⁴ Must every slaughter be a sacrifice?

It is important to bear in mind that the setting of these laws is the wilderness, and their aim is to orient the life of every Israelite around the presence of a holy God. Once Israel settles in the land, the law accommodates to the new lived reality. Within the land of their inheritance Israelites must still bring their sacrifices and tithes to the sanctuary, but, if they crave meat and live at a distance, "Then you may kill any of your herd or your flock, which the LORD has given you, as I have commanded you, and you may eat within your towns whenever you desire" (Deut. 12:21). If an animal is blemished, "You shall eat it within your towns. The unclean and the clean alike may eat it, as though it were a gazelle or a deer" (Deut. 15:22). However, under no circumstance are the people to eat its blood (cf. comment on 17:10).

17:5–6 The reason for mandating that all slaughter take place at the tabernacle is because the people are sacrificing in the open country. They should bring their gifts to the sanctuary, where the Lord has established his presence and priesthood, slaughter them there as peace offerings that honor him with the fat portions, and be free to feast on the rest. Most importantly, the blood must be ritually dashed against the "altar *of the* LORD," named and marked as his own. The name of the Lord rings out seven times in these laws to direct the worshipers' attention continually to their covenant Sovereign, who commands their exclusive worship.²⁰⁵ Any slaughter apart from the Lord's altar leads to idolatry (cf. 1 Kings 12:25–13:2).

The command articulated here will develop into one of the most enduring cornerstones of OT worship. A worshiper must approach the Lord only at the place where his covenant presence dwells: "You shall seek the place that the LORD your

---

203 It is instructive that the command to abstain from eating blood thus far has been in the context of the peace offering (Lev. 3:17; 7:26–27), supporting the understanding that any animal slaughtered for meat is offered as a peace offering.
204 Boer, *Sacred Economy*, 62.
205 Leviticus 17:4 (2x), 5 (2x), 6 (2x), 9.

God will choose out of all your tribes to put his name and make his habitation there. There you shall go, and there you shall bring your burnt offerings and your sacrifices, your tithes and the contribution that you present, your vow offerings, your freewill offerings, and the firstborn of your herd and of your flock" (Deut. 12:5–6; cf. Deut. 12:11–14). From the time Israel enters the land until the destruction of the temple in AD 70 all will stream to Jerusalem, the place of the Lord's habitation, to honor him with their gifts. There is only one legitimate place to seek the Lord, one place consecrated by his presence, and one altar that has been ignited by his fire.

17:7 It now becomes clear that the reason for the severity of the cutting-off penalty (Lev. 17:4) is the gravity of the offense. What is brought across as "goat demons" literally translates as "hairy ones, shaggy creatures," a common term for goats though in this context one that clearly refers to some form of supernatural being worshiped by some Israelites. Although this is distant from us in its specific details, we catch a glimpse of an idolatrous practice that will be repeated in Israel's history (cf. 2 Chron. 11:15). Such practices are absolutely forbidden. Whether inside the camp, where the Holy One dwells, or outside the camp, where impurity is banished (Lev. 16:21–22), the Lord reigns over all. Dominion is his alone.

Without validating belief in demonic spirits the law denounces their worship in a decisive blow—anyone who sacrifices to idols "whores" after false gods (cf. Ex. 34:14–17; Deut. 31:16). The Lord's covenant with Israel is a marriage, demanding exclusive faithfulness to him to whom they are bound in trust through blood (Jer. 2:2; Hos. 2:2). To worship other gods is tantamount to infidelity, rejecting the Lord's claims and abandoning the marriage for other lovers (Jer. 3:1–2, 6–10; Ezekiel 16; 23; Hos. 2:5; 5:4). Bringing sacrifices to the house of the Lord will be a statute forever, even after the wilderness period, when Israel is settled in the land. Although the social setting may change in the years to come, the Lord's requirements will remain the same (cf. Deut. 12:10–14).

17:8–9 The prohibition continues to unfold, focusing on sacrificial animals and extending to address resident aliens, who are likewise responsible for bringing offerings to the one designated place of worship. Offering worship to the Lord is not restricted to Israel but open to all who approach him by faith (Num. 15:14). Resident aliens can bring burnt offerings and peace offerings, provided they follow the proper sacrificial protocol outlined here: slaughtering the animal at the sanctuary, abstaining from the blood of sacrifice or game, and purifying themselves in the event of eating meat from animals that die naturally or from predation (Lev. 17:10, 12, 13, 15; cf. 22:18).[206]

17:10 The blood prohibition is the axis around which this chapter revolves, clarifying the laws on sacrificial animals that have come before and the laws on

---

[206] Foreigners who had witnessed the Lord's power in Egypt joined the Israelites in a "mixed multitude" (Ex. 12:38) and were granted the right to celebrate the Passover as long as they were circumcised (Ex. 12:48). Cf. comment on 16:29–31, notes 200 and 201.

non-sacrificial animals to follow. The peculiar phrase "to *eat* blood" refers to eating an animal's flesh with the blood still in it, meaning it has not been drained in slaughter (cf. Gen. 9:4; Deut. 12:16, 23). Discourse on the ritual handling of lifeblood expands from a negative decree to a positive one—blood may not be consumed because it is reserved for the specific and sacred purpose of expiation.

The Lord's voice breaks into the speech mediated through Moses to confront every hearer: "*I* will set my face against... and will cut off." The cutting-off penalty that earlier had been expressed passively (Lev. 17:4, 9) becomes active in the mouth of the Lord, who promises to carry it out himself against any who defies him. The ultimate break in relationship is when the Lord no longer shines his countenance in blessing upon the worshipers but sets his face against them in opposition.

17:11 The statement "The life of the flesh is in the blood" is key to understanding the theology and ritual logic behind the sacrificial system. This evocative image conveys that blood is that which makes a living being alive; blood and life are inextricably linked. In the case of a person blood has power and contains something of the life of the person that continues to have agency even after death. The blood of the innocent slain cries from the ground to be avenged, from the first murder to the martyrs before the altar at the end of time (Gen. 4:10–12; Deut. 21:7–9; Isa. 26:21; Rev. 6:9–10).

That the life is in the blood may be easily observed: as blood pours out of a mortal wound, so does the life of a living being. What cannot be observed but must be revealed by the Lord is that he will accept the blood as atonement for the life of the worshiper. The verse unfolds in associative logic: (1) Life is in the blood of all living beings. (2) Blood makes atonement for human life. And (3) the blood of sacrificial animals makes efficacious atonement because of the life in it. The Lord will graciously accept its life as a substitute for the life of the offerer.

Up until now the people have observed priests' placing (Hb. *natan*) the blood on the altar (Lev. 4:25; 8:15; 9:9; 16:18). This verse, however, contends that all along it has been the *Lord* who has placed it on the altar—"I have given [*natan*] it for you on the altar to make atonement for your souls." The wording reframes how Israel is to understand the sacrificial procedure, as though the Lord is saying, "It is not you who are placing the blood on the altar for me, for my benefit, but rather the opposite: it is I who have placed it there for you—for your benefit."[207] The blood serves as a ransom, as payment for the life of the worshiper because the Lord has ordained the principle of a life for a life (Ex. 21:23; Lev. 24:18; Deut. 19:21).

17:12 The Lord quotes himself, reaching back to what he has already commanded (3:17; 7:26–27) in order to repeat, restate, and emphasize the absolute certainty of this issue.

According to traditional herding practices Israel made use of the slaughtered animal in its entirety: the meat and its byproducts of milk and cheese for food,

---

[207] Baruch Schwartz, "Prohibitions Concerning the 'Eating' of Blood," in *Priesthood and Cult in Ancient Israel* (New York: Bloomsbury, 2009), 51.

wool and hides for clothing, bones for tools such as spindles and knife handles, and its horns for calling the congregation to assemble.[208] The cultural context thus marks the blood prohibition as striking, especially in light of cooking methods in the ancient world that made use of blood, as does modern global cuisine.[209] The Lord emphatically sets apart the animal's blood for *his* use, and in obedience the covenant people enact with every slaughter the reality that life belongs to the Lord.

17:13 Clean animals that are hunted, though not offered on the altar, must be treated according to the law that regulates blood disposal. Game could be hunted for meat, as requested by Isaac to bestow blessing on Esau: "Take your weapons, your quiver and your bow, and go out to the field and hunt game for me" (Gen. 27:3). Meat dishes of "deer, gazelles, roebucks, and fattened fowl" are said to have graced Solomon's kingly table (1 Kings 4:23). Game native to Israel (Deut. 14:5) and still abundant today includes the wild goat known as the ibex (*Capra ibex*) and the mountain gazelle (*Gazella gazella*). Once Israel settles in the land and relies on its cultivation, archaeological evidence shows that these become a very minor part of their diet.[210]

The blood of a hunted animal must be drained and covered with earth. The parallel passage in Deuteronomy directs that the blood be poured out "on the earth like water" but does not mention covering it (Deut. 12:24). The legislation of Leviticus focuses on a different factor: since improper slaughter is equated with bloodguilt (Lev. 17:4), the blood must be covered over as though it were a living entity that is receiving burial.

17:14 The repetition of the command to refrain from consuming blood takes the reader back to the origins of human history. After the flood waters recede and Noah and his family emerge onto a renewed earth with renewed blessing they are permitted to eat meat. Having stewarded the lives of living creatures within the confines of the ark, humanity is to steward them in the world and use some for food, always acknowledging the Lord, who gives them into their hand: "But you shall not eat flesh with its life, that is, its blood" (Gen. 9:4). The blood prohibition applies to all humanity, but it is for Israel to understand this divine revelation as it relates to its standing before God.

17:15–16 The chapter concludes with an allowance for a person who has eaten the meat of an animal that has died naturally or by predation (this allowance does not apply to priests; 22:8–9).[211] This is the only legal case that does not conclude with

---

208 Borowski, *Every Living Thing*, 52–71.
209 Surviving recipes from Mesopotamia show that blood was used for seasoning and as thickener for stews. A recipe for goat stew reads: Singe the head, legs, and tail. Prepare water; add fat, onion, leek and garlic; bind with blood; adapted from Jean Bottéro, *The Oldest Cuisine in the World* (Chicago: University of Chicago Press, 2004), 27. Examples are plentiful in modern cuisine, including dishes such as blood sausage, blood pudding, blood pancakes, and blood stews such as Korean *seonji-guk* and Philippine *dinuguan*.
210 Nathan MacDonald, *What Did the Ancient Israelites Eat? Diet in Biblical Times* (Grand Rapids, MI: Eerdmans, 2008), 34.
211 This law "would also assume previously stated laws, in particular, that Israelites may eat animals that die naturally (Lev. 11:39–40), but not those torn by wild animals (Exod. 22:31). As a result, the law addresses only three scenarios: a native-born Israelite eating an animal that had died naturally; a resident alien eating

one's being cut off; rather it offers a solution to address the impurity. An animal that has died by the hand of nature or by predation (1 Sam. 17:34–35) will bring impurity on the eater (perhaps because its blood has not been properly drained, and its carcass is unclean; Lev. 11:39–40). The remedy is for the person to wash his body and clothes. Should he not bathe to cleanse himself from impurity, then he is culpable and will be held responsible by the Lord for his disobedience.

Response

Israel is chosen and called to live as a holy nation out of all the peoples and to put on display the Lord's character and wisdom. To God's people is revealed the power of sacrificial blood to atone for the life of the offerer. Day after day, as they guard the handling of lifeblood, they enact that it is for the Lord's use alone. As the blood was poured, dashed, and smeared on the altar, the people become beneficiaries of forgiveness and restored relationship with God.

Jesus came to Jerusalem, the chosen "city of the great King" (Matt. 5:35), to bring to fulfillment this centuries-long practice. He came as God in the flesh with authority to lay down his life and shed his blood as a ransom for many (Mark 10:45; John 10:18). On a hill outside the city called the Skull (Matt. 27:33) he officiated as priest over his own self-sacrifice, pouring out his life as "great drops of blood falling down to the ground" (Luke 22:44) and as blood and water from his side (John 19:34). He had interpreted his death to his disciples the previous night over the Passover meal when he took the cup and, telling them to drink, explained, "This is my blood of the covenant, which is poured out for many for the forgiveness of sins" (Matt. 26:28). They struggled to reconcile his words with that which every devout Jew knew could not be done: the drinking of blood. And yet they drank, and in time, through revelation by the Spirit, they understood this heavenly wisdom (1 Cor. 1:21–24).

All who come to Christ must be awakened spiritually. The Lord's revelation is necessary in order for one to grasp the significance of Jesus' death for our forgiveness. His death is more than the death of an innocent man. His lifeblood upon the altar of God pays the ransom for our sin, and his life is accepted as a substitute for ours—a life for a life, his lifeblood for mine. His blood continues to speak to the Father, but it "speaks a better word than the blood of Abel" (Heb. 12:24). It does not cry to be avenged but cries, "Father, forgive them, for they know not what they do" (Luke 23:34). The blood that has power to ransom has power to forge eternal covenant bonds that bring us into communion with a holy God: "Whoever feeds on my flesh and drinks my blood abides in me, and I in him" (John 6:56). Its efficacy is certain because it is guaranteed by the Lord, who has given it on the altar for atonement (Heb. 9:11–12).

---

the same; a resident alien—but not an Israelite (Exod. 22:31)—eating an animal torn by wild beasts." Sklar, *Leviticus*, TOTC, 222–223.

LEVITICUS 18

18 And the Lord spoke to Moses, saying, **2** "Speak to the people of Israel and say to them, I am the Lord your God. **3** You shall not do as they do in the land of Egypt, where you lived, and you shall not do as they do in the land of Canaan, to which I am bringing you. You shall not walk in their statutes. **4** You shall follow my rules[1] and keep my statutes and walk in them. I am the Lord your God. **5** You shall therefore keep my statutes and my rules; if a person does them, he shall live by them: I am the Lord.

6 "None of you shall approach any one of his close relatives to uncover nakedness. I am the Lord. **7** You shall not uncover the nakedness of your father, which is the nakedness of your mother; she is your mother, you shall not uncover her nakedness. **8** You shall not uncover the nakedness of your father's wife; it is your father's nakedness. **9** You shall not uncover the nakedness of your sister, your father's daughter or your mother's daughter, whether brought up in the family or in another home. **10** You shall not uncover the nakedness of your son's daughter or of your daughter's daughter, for their nakedness is your own nakedness. **11** You shall not uncover the nakedness of your father's wife's daughter, brought up in your father's family, since she is your sister. **12** You shall not uncover the nakedness of your father's sister; she is your father's relative. **13** You shall not uncover the nakedness of your mother's sister, for she is your mother's relative. **14** You shall not uncover the nakedness of your father's brother, that is, you shall not approach his wife; she is your aunt. **15** You shall not uncover the nakedness of your daughter-in-law; she is your son's wife, you shall not uncover her nakedness. **16** You shall not uncover the nakedness of your brother's wife; it is your brother's nakedness. **17** You shall not uncover the nakedness of a woman and of her daughter, and you shall not take her son's daughter or her daughter's daughter to uncover her nakedness; they are relatives; it is depravity. **18** And you shall not take a woman as a rival wife to her sister, uncovering her nakedness while her sister is still alive.

19 "You shall not approach a woman to uncover her nakedness while she is in her menstrual uncleanness. **20** And you shall not lie sexually with your neighbor's wife and so make yourself unclean with her. **21** You shall not give any of your children to offer them[2] to Molech, and so profane the name of your God: I am the Lord. **22** You shall not lie with a male as with a woman; it is an abomination. **23** And you shall not lie with any animal and so make yourself unclean with it, neither shall any woman give herself to an animal to lie with it: it is perversion.

24 "Do not make yourselves unclean by any of these things, for by all these the nations I am driving out before you have become unclean, **25** and the land became unclean, so that I punished its iniquity, and the land vomited out its inhabitants. **26** But you shall keep my statutes and my rules and do none of these abominations, either the native or the stranger who sojourns among you ²⁷ (for the people of the land, who were before you, did all of these abominations, so that the land became unclean), ²⁸ lest the land vomit you out when you make it unclean, as it vomited out the nation that was before you. ²⁹ For everyone who does any of these abominations, the persons who do them shall be cut off from among their people. ³⁰ So keep my charge never to practice any of these abominable customs that were practiced before you, and never to make yourselves unclean by them: I am the LORD your God."

¹ Or *my just decrees*; also verse 5 ² Hebrew *to make them pass through* [the fire]

Section Overview

The next three chapters (18–20) form a single unit like a triptych—a work of art with three panels that each portrays different elements of a single narrative. The outer panels that frame the composition deal with sexual ethics, chapter 18 painting the prohibitions and chapter 20 the penalties. The central panel, highlighted and supported by those on either side, expands the vision of family to extend the ethics of holiness to the entire community, from brother to resident alien.

The first panel paints a picture of the Israelite family and defines a holy sexual ethic in a sexually disordered world. The laws progress from family (vv. 6–16) and clan (vv. 17–18) to the entire nation (vv. 19–23). The chapter itself is bookended by two exhortations, stated first in the positive (vv. 1–5) and then in the negative (vv. 24–30). The Lord as head of the household of faith orders the expression of sexuality according to his design. He draws boundaries to protect the integrity of the family and its vulnerable members because it is his will that they all enjoy safety and flourishing (Deut. 33:26–29; Isa. 11:6–9).

Life under God's rule is, in a theological sense, a return to Eden. Leviticus is in conversation with a vision of sexuality shaped by the Lord's work in creation. The first marriage in Scripture is ordained by God, who as Father arranges a marriage for his son. Adam's longing for a companion is met first by a series of unsuitable mates. Among all the Lord's created works "there was not found a helper fit for him" (Gen. 2:20) until the Lord fashioned Eve out of Adam's own "flesh" (Hb. *basar*). Eve is a soulmate built out of his side, not the soil of the earth. Adam's marriage vows celebrate her as "bone of my bones and flesh of my flesh." He names her after himself, calling her "Woman [*'ishah*] because she was taken out of Man [*'ish*]" (Gen. 2:23). Their marriage is exclusive. They must cling and "hold fast" to one another in unfailing covenant loyalty that should never be breeched, for to do so would threaten the unity of their mission to be fruitful and extend God's rule in the world. The Lord who arranged their marriage also indwells it; therefore it must be kept holy (cf. Heb. 13:4).

The incest prohibitions follow the Genesis pattern to articulate clearly a series of unsuitable sexual partners (Lev. 18:6–18). In so doing they tacitly define the only suitable union as a monogamous, heterosexual marriage. Kinship ties within the extended family are viewed as a part of oneself and appropriately called "close relatives" (v. 6). The Lord who indwells the family of Israel gives them his laws for a holy sexual ethic that protects the exclusive rights of marriage partners and the extended family.

The prohibitions are strongly worded in order to evoke emotions of disgust. Not only are sexually disordered behaviors identified as morally wrong, but emotions are also recruited to buttress legal boundaries with psychological ones. Prohibited unions are polluting, making one's own body and the very land "unclean" (*tame'*; vv. 19, 20, 23, 24, 25, 27, 28, 30). They are "depravity" (*zimma*; v. 17; 20:14), an "abomination" (*to'eba*; 18:22, 26, 27, 29, 30; 20:13), and "perversion" (*tebel*; 18:23; 20:12). Indeed, they are so repugnant that those who practice them will be vomited out by the land in disgust (18:25, 28).

Section Outline

VI. Moral Holiness (18:1–20:27)
    A. Sexual Ethics for a Holy People (18:1–30)
        1. Exhortation: Holy Living Leads to Life (18:1–5)
        2. Laws of Incest (18:6–18)
            a. Near Relatives (18:6–17)
            b. Bridging Law (18:18)
        3. Forbidden Sexual Practices and Worship (18:19–23)
        4. Unholy Living Leads to Death (18:24–30)

Comment

18:1–2 The incest laws are introduced with the very same words that introduce the covenant: "I am the LORD your God" (Ex. 20:2; Deut. 5:6).[212] The well-known statement links these laws to Israel's deliverance from Egypt, which made them God's very own people. It frames Israel's obedience as allegiance to their Sovereign, whose moral authority stands behind these prohibitions. Evoking the covenant of Sinai is especially fitting for laws that deal with the covenant of marriage.

18:3–4 The exhortation not to conform to the practices of the nations comes at both the beginning and the end of the chapter, forming an envelope around prohibited sexual practices (Lev. 8:2, 4, 5, 30). Having left Egypt behind and setting its sights toward Canaan, Israel is urged to neither look back nor embrace the customs of where it is going, but to look to the holy God who dwells in its midst and to conform to his character. His people are to live as a people set apart to him—in the world but not of it (20:26; John 17:15–16).

By associating disordered sexual behavior with Egyptians and Canaanites the law effectively defines sexual sins as "foreign" to the people of God.[213] Israel is called

---

[212] Stated a total of six times in this chapter (Lev. 18:2, 4, 5, 6, 21, 30). The Lord's self-identification is threaded through chapters 18–26 a total of fifty times, expanded as "*who sanctifies you*" (20:8; 21:15, 23; 22:9, 16, 32), "*brought you out of Egypt*" (19:36; 22:32–33; 25:38; 26:13), and "*separated you from the peoples*" (20:24, 26).
[213] Israel's neighbors are not known to have such a lengthy and detailed enumeration of forbidden relationships. In the ancient world Leviticus 18 is a comprehensive treatment that serves to differentiate Israel

to be a holy people who do "not walk in their statutes" (Lev. 18:3), for the Israelites have bound themselves by covenant to walk in the Lord's (v. 4). Although the world competes for their allegiance and affection, they must demonstrate their covenant commitment by pursuing God's righteousness with their bodies, in worship (chs. 1–16) and in ethical living (chs. 17–27).

18:5 These laws are ordained by God and lead to life. The reward for obedience is life; the consequence of disobedience is delayed until the end of the chapter (vv. 24–30). Life is built into the commands because they keep Israel in right relationship with the Lord who is Life himself. The Lord will uphold those who walk in obedience and cause them to flourish (26:9, 11–12). By walking in his ways they will enjoy life in the land and not be expelled, like the nations before them were (18:24–30; Deut. 5:33). Life will work its way into their families as they renounce practices that betray marriage's sacred trust, violate the vulnerable, and hinder life's potentiality through unions that are not fruit bearing.

18:6 This verse is an introduction to the incest laws, which prohibit sexual relations with "close relatives," which in biblical thought includes relatives by blood (Lev. 18:7, 9, 10, 12, 13) or marriage (vv. 8, 11, 14, 15–17). The Hebrew expression is two nearly identical words: *basar she'er* ("flesh of [his] flesh"). Becoming one flesh is the bond of a new family unit.[214] Flesh defines family.[215]

The laws are given from the perspective of the male head of family, whose household includes two to three generations of blood kin as well as family by marriage (vv. 8, 15–18). The "father's household" (*bet 'ab*) includes his wife, married sons and their wives, unmarried daughters, and unmarried female blood relatives, such as a widowed mother, aunts, and sisters. Young women who marry into the household become "flesh family" through marriage. Close kin is spoken of as sharing the same flesh and bone, as Laban declares to his nephew Jacob, "Surely you are my bone and my flesh!" (Gen. 29:14; cf. Gen. 37:27; 2 Sam. 5:1).

Every Israelite has formal responsibilities toward his flesh family: to protect and provide (Ruth 2:20; 4:1–6), redeem from debt slavery (Lev. 25:47–55), redeem ancestral inheritance (25:23–25; Jeremiah 32), provide an heir to continue lineage (Deut. 25:5–10), pass down knowledge of God's saving acts (Ps. 78:5–7), provide proper burial (2 Sam. 21:8–14), and even avenge murder (Num. 35:19).

It is also his responsibility not to engage in illicit sexual relations by uncovering or revealing a woman's nakedness (Lev. 18:7–16). Sexual intimacy is more commonly expressed as "to lie with"[216] or "to know"[217] someone. The phrase "to uncover one's nakedness" is used of prohibited sexual relations in which there

---

among the nations. Hammurabi's Law Code §154–158 prohibits only sexual relations with one's daughter, daughter-in-law, mother, or stepmother.
214 Gordon P. Hugenberger, *Marriage as Covenant: Biblical Law and Ethics as Developed from Malachi* (Eugene, OR: Wipf & Stock, 1994), 163.
215 The implications for the incarnation are immediately apparent. In order to work our redemption as our Kinsman Redeemer the Lord first became our kinsman by becoming part of the human family: "The Word became flesh and dwelt among us" (John 1:14; cf. Heb. 2:14).
216 Genesis 30:15; Leviticus 15:33; 19:20; 20:11, 12, 13, 18, 20.
217 Genesis 4:1; 24:16; Judges 11:39; 21:12; Hosea 2:10.

is sexual vulnerability, exposure, and shame.[218] This is in stark contrast with nudity in marriage, through which there is a mutual vulnerability with no shame (Gen. 2:25).

Whose nakedness is being exposed? Most of the time it is the woman's own (Lev. 18:9, 11, 15, 17, 18, 19), while at other times it is an offense against the man who is in a marriage covenant, with exclusive conjugal rights to his wife's sexuality (vv. 8, 16). The prohibitions are not worded as a husband's rights to his wife's body, as though she were property (to the contrary cf. v. 19), but rather they locate the proper union for sharing holy intimacy. By prohibiting a whole web of sexual relations the law protects the sexual union of a husband and wife, guarding the sanctity of marriage.[219]

18:7 Sexual transgressions against one's father and mother are strictly prohibited, something that is universal in all human culture. The prohibition is stated as protecting the right of a husband's access to his wife's sexuality, covenanted exclusively to him. A mother's nakedness is equated with a father's nakedness, since they belong to one another. A husband and wife are one flesh through the bonds of marriage, and thus to expose her is to expose him.

18:8 Sexual relations are forbidden with the wives of one's father, whether secondary wives or those married after a mother's death, because they violate the father's conjugal rights. Reuben, Jacob's firstborn, violated his father's rights by having sexual relations with Bilhah, his father's concubine (Gen. 35:22; 49:3–4). The act challenged his father's authority and leadership of the family (also 2 Sam. 16:21–22). Reuben forfeited his birthright as a result (1 Chron. 5:1). The penalty is prescribed in Leviticus 20:11.

18:9 Sisters and half-sisters (born to one's father or mother by another union) are protected from sexual advances. Whether raised in the same family household or another, sisters are off limits.[220] The law is binding even when they do not live in proximity. Instead an Israelite male bears responsibility to protect and provide for his unmarried or widowed sister (21:3), and custom demanded that he even avenge her honor, as do Jacob's sons for their sister, Dinah, (Genesis 34) and Absalom for Tamar (2 Sam. 13:20).[221] The penalty is prescribed in Leviticus 20:17.

18:10 A male head of the household may not approach his granddaughter sexually. The explanation that "their nakedness is your own nakedness" refers to shared blood ties. A granddaughter (and implicitly a daughter) is one's own flesh and

---

218 In addition to the occurrences in this chapter the expression is used by the prophets to evoke the feelings of shame (Isa. 47:3; Ezek. 16:36, 37; 22:10; 23:10, 18, 29).
219 "The law forbidding adultery in this chapter (18:20) implies the incest laws do not have in view relations with these women while they are married (otherwise, the adultery law would have sufficed). These laws are prohibiting relations with such women while they are unmarried or after a former marriage has ended (through death or divorce)." Sklar, *Leviticus*, ZECOT, 482.
220 Abraham, who married his half-sister Sarah (Gen. 20:2, 12–16), did so before the law was given to his descendants and may have reflected the customs of Mesopotamia.
221 It is difficult to know whether Tamar says she could be given in marriage to Amnon in order to protect herself from sexual violence or whether it was permissible to marry a half-brother born to another mother.

blood. It is a man's responsibility to bless, protect, and pass down the faith to his children and his "children's children" (Gen. 48:8–16; Deut. 4:9–10).

18:11 Sexual relations with one's half-sister born of another mother (concubine) are forbidden. The stepsister is to be treated as a natural-born sister, meaning she has entered the household to be provided for and protected. She is accorded full status as a sister.

18:12–13 Aunts from either side of the family are protected from sexual advances because they are a father's or mother's own flesh relations. The balanced prohibitions from both sides of the family respect the ties forged between the two households through marriage. A family's strength comes from the loyalty of its relationships. The penalty is prescribed in 20:19.

18:14 Adultery with a paternal uncle's wife offends an uncle's sexual rights by marriage covenant. His wife has become one's aunt through marriage. The penalty is prescribed in 20:20.

18:15 A daughter-in-law who has come into the household of her husband is protected from sexual advances of other men in the family even after his death (cf. 18:8). The law upholds a son's rights and sets limits for the family's patriarch. Heads of households do not have rights to the women of their extended family but rather are charged to care for and protect them (Ruth 2:9). Marriage creates kinship ties and alliances between families. The penalty is prescribed in Leviticus 20:12.

Judah's obligation toward Tamar, which he was lax in fulfilling, led to the breach of this prohibition (Gen. 38:13–26). Tamar is praised for her loyalty in protecting her deceased husband's rights to an heir by crossing boundaries to bear a son who would legitimately continue his lineage.

18:16 It would be dishonorable to both one's brother and his wife to make sexual advances toward a sister-in-law. It would not only degrade his wife but also confuse family inheritance. In the case of a brother's death his widowed wife is protected from abuse. She is not treated as property that passes among brothers. The penalty is prescribed in 20:21.

A different passage deals with one's responsibility toward a brother's widowed wife if she has no sons. A man whose brother has died with no heirs is to take his brother's place. He weds his sister-in-law to produce an heir so that his brother's lineage and share in the family estate are not lost (Deut. 25:5–10). To perpetuate his name and memory is to allow him to live on through his descendants. The arrangement provides security for the widow in a legitimate relationship (Ruth 1:9).

18:17 This law protects the rights of a wife by guarding the covenant union of marriage. It implicitly prohibits incest with one's daughter as legislated from the perspective of his wife. A woman's female descendants, her daughters and granddaughters, are never permitted as potential partners. The law protects not only the daughters but, importantly, also the bond between mother and child by not making a daughter equal in the relationship. God judges this as depravity (Hb. *zimmah*), a word used of such acts as forcing a daughter into prostitution or the rape of the Levite's concubine (Judg. 20:6). The penalty is prescribed in Leviticus 20:14.

18:18 This law may be taken as preventing the marriage of biological sisters or, taking the word "sister" more broadly, as outlawing polygamy.[222] It bridges the laws of forbidden sexual unions within the family (vv. 6–17) and those of other forbidden sexual practices (vv. 19–23). If the word "sister" is taken strictly, the law protects a wife's honor with respect to her own female blood relatives. If the word "sister" is understood more broadly, the law protects the bonds of loyalty and intimacy between a husband and wife that a rival would compromise. Biblical narratives of polygamy paint the anguish of women's vying for their husband's affection in competition for children (Gen. 16:5; 21:10; 30:1–24; 1 Samuel 1). The Lord's ordering of relationships restores peace to family dynamics threatened by the fall.

18:19 Even within God-ordained sexual unions there are boundaries to conjugal rights: a husband may not pursue sexual relations with his wife during her menstrual impurity (Lev. 12:2, 5). This law recognizes that, though husband and wife belong to each other, ultimate authority over a woman's body is the Lord's (1 Cor. 7:3–5). Mutuality and respect are understood by this ruling. The penalty is prescribed in Leviticus 20:18.

18:20 Marital fidelity is the foundation of the marriage covenant, guarded by the Decalogue (Ex. 20:14; Deut. 5:18). Adultery is defined as sexual relations with a woman who is married or betrothed (Deut. 22:22–24). Sexual relations are powerful, creating physical, emotional, and relational bonds. In the wrong context, however, such relations destroy already existing bonds to forge new ones that threaten marriage, family, and society. Children conceived from the union are on the margins (Deut. 23:2; Judg. 11:1–3). Disordered sexual practices are disordering and result in moral defilement.[223] Jesus gets to the heart of adultery by locating it not only in the physical act but also in its contemplation (Matt. 5:27–28). The penalty is prescribed in Leviticus 20:10.

18:21 Child sacrifice is included in these laws because children are the fruit of sexual union. This verse is linked to the previous one by the keyword "seed" (Hb. *zera'*), referring to semen or offspring. Those who participate in the pagan

---

[222] Polygamy was not common. An ordinary Israelite would have difficulty affording the bride price and support of multiple wives. The practice is seen among the patriarchs who build the nation (Gen. 16:1–16; 30:3–8) and kings who build their dynasty, although even they are restrained from amassing large harems (Deut. 17:17).

[223] Commenting on Leviticus 18:20, Sklar notes, "Until this point in Leviticus, the word [unclean] has referred to impurity that comes from events or circumstances that are not immoral, such as childbirth (12:2) or leprosy (13:14). This type of impurity is allowed, may be removed by ritual means (bathing, laundering, sacrifice) and does not lead to further penalty. It is commonly called 'ritual impurity'. In this verse, however, the word [unclean] refers to impurity that comes from moral wrongdoing. This type of impurity is forbidden, cannot be removed by ritual means and does lead to further penalty. It is commonly called 'moral impurity'. ... Actions that cause such impurity—and therefore rupture one's relationship with the Lord—are to be avoided at all costs." Sklar, *Leviticus*, TOTC, 236–237.

practice of giving their children to Molech profane the name of Yahweh (19:12; 20:3). To profane or make common is to tarnish the Lord's reputation and make him appear as the gods of the nations. The penalty is prescribed in 20:2.

18:22 Homosexuality is prohibited as a violation of God's creational design. Man (Hb. *'ish*) and woman (*'ishah*) belong together, as much as their names share a fundamental unity. The phrase to "lie . . . as with a woman" already implicitly communicates that a man belongs with a woman. Substituting a male for a female and sexually behaving as though a man were a woman is a union the Lord neither intended nor blessed at creation.

Homosexuality is called an "abomination" (*to'ebah*), as are all prohibited sexual practices in this chapter (vv. 26, 27, 29, 30). Yet this is the only one individually labeled as such. Hebrew *to'ebah* is used for that which is wholly incompatible with God's character and, as Crouch observes, refers particularly to the "delineation and protection of boundaries."[224] This is a nonnegotiable boundary for the Israelites, who are urged to avoid behaviors that must never define God's people. Israel must keep separate from the practices of the nations in order to remain united with the Lord.

The phrasing of this law continues the legal pattern of addressing the male head of household but would apply naturally to women as well. Lesbianism is explicitly condemned in the NT (Rom. 1:26). The penalty is prescribed in Leviticus 20:13.

18:23 Bestiality involves a different violation of creational boundaries. According to the Lord's design animals are to mate and reproduce after their own kind. Only a human being can ever be a suitable covenant partner and life companion for another human being (Gen. 1:24–31; 2:20). This prohibition speaks volumes to the nature of humanity. Although created on the sixth day alongside other living beings, a human is not a more sophisticated animal but a unique creation in the very image and likeness of God. Human sexual intimacy is a gift dignified and blessed by God and quite unlike the animalistic drive to mate. To engage sexually with an animal is "perversion" (Hb. *tebel*), an expression that points to a confusion of categories.[225] It is disordered sexuality. The verse begins by addressing men and then makes explicit that the law applies also to women. The penalty is prescribed in Leviticus 20:15–16.

18:24–25 The chapter ends with a threat of expulsion that recalls the expulsion from the garden (Gen. 3:23–24). As it makes ready to enter the land, Israel is reminded that the nations are being evicted because of their sexual immorality.

---

[224] C. L. Crouch, "What Makes a Thing Abominable? Observations on the Language of Boundaries and Identity Formation from a Social Scientific Perspective," VT 65 (2015): 517. What classifies as *to'ebah* is the worship of other gods (Deut. 13:1–15; 27:15), child sacrifice (Deut. 12:31), sorcery (Deut. 18:9–12), and cross-dressing (Deut. 22:5).

[225] The noun *tebel* is derived from the verb *balal* ("to mix"), used of the Lord's judgment on Babel (Gen. 11:7, 9). The confusion of languages was a fitting punishment for a people who confused the boundaries between God and mortal man.

The Lord is the divine householder entrusting the land into Israel's care as its share of the paternal estate. The land must be treated as holy because the Lord himself inhabits it among his covenant family and from this promised plot extends his reign throughout the earth (Ex. 15:17).

A rightly ordered sexual ethic is critical to preventing uncleanness that would cause the people to forfeit their inheritance.[226] Like a mirror, the land reflects Israel's standing with its heavenly Father. If God's people live by his commandments and conform to his character, they will remain secure in the land; if they neglect his commands and conform to the practices of the nations, they will be evicted.

18:26 The resident alien will be held accountable for practices that defile the land. Under godly covenant stewardship the land will sustain both native and resident alien. While resident aliens cannot permanently own the land deeded to Abraham's descendants,[227] their poor can glean from the land's yield to satisfy their hunger (19:10; 23:22).

18:27–30 As covenant witness, the land will testify against the moral impurity within it (Deut. 30:19; Isa. 24:4–5). The land is personified, taking on human qualities to express disgust at its defilement and pollution. The word for "land" is grammatically feminine in Hebrew, painting the striking image of a woman who is retching at the sexual sin perpetrated against her. In disgust she vomits out her violators until she can have rest from wrongdoing (Lev. 26:34–35).

Israel's election is an act of God's grace. He takes them as his people by covenant and invites them into a dynamic relationship wherein they participate in their sanctification. The privilege of election carries with it the obligation of obedience in order to avoid defiling ways. The Lord is not judging the nations because of their ethnicity but holding them accountable for their sin (Gen. 15:16). Should Israel stray from his life-giving laws, she will deserve the same.

Response

Whether we are single or married, the way in which we live out our sexuality is an important aspect of our holiness as God's people. The theological vision of Leviticus honors sexuality as a God-given gift with the potential to shape our human capacities for love, self-giving, and exclusive commitment. For this very reason it is protected. Sexuality that is unfaithful or outside its holy boundaries cripples our capacity for covenant love and corrupts the marital intimacy whereby we are known and unashamed, committed and constrained, self-giving and self-denying. As believers we are called to be unshaped by a worldly vision of sex as indiscriminate self-gratification, a commodity to be bought and sold, as objectification that

---

[226] In addition to sexual immorality sins that are said to pollute the land include bloodshed (Num. 35:33–34), illicit worship (Lev. 19:31; Jer. 16:18), exposing a corpse overnight (Deut. 21:23), and a twice-divorced woman remarrying her first husband (Deut. 24:4). Cf. also comment on 18:20, note 223.
[227] They can lease it from Israelites who have fallen on hard times and need to sell their harvests until they can redeem it, or until the jubilee (Lev. 25:47–55).

harms the vulnerable among us. Instead we must model transformed lives that embody a moral and ethical purity in the way we honor God-given boundaries. Paul writes to new believers:

> This is the will of God, your sanctification: that you abstain from sexual immorality; that each one of you know how to control his own body in holiness and honor, not in the passion of lust like the Gentiles who do not know God; that no one transgress and wrong his brother in this matter, because the Lord is an avenger in all these things, as we told you beforehand and solemnly warned you. For God has not called us for impurity, but in holiness. (1 Thess. 4:3–7)

The Lord's demand for sexual holiness in Leviticus 18 and the punishments described for unrepented sexual sin in Leviticus 20 appear in the narrative *after* the account of the sacrificial system (chs. 1–7) and the priestly ministry of atonement and forgiveness (chs. 16–17). The God revealed in Scripture forgives the repentant, restores the broken, and makes the unclean clean. The Lord reaches out with redeeming hope to heal our damaged emotions, sanctify our polluted imagination, wash us from shame, and restore our abused bodies (2 Cor. 5:17). The church must reclaim a truly biblical vision of sexuality, one that has never been repressive but is a reflection of the passionate love and enduring commitment of our Savior. Christian marriage especially has the potential to be attractive and missional, displaying the mystery of God's covenant participation as he indwells our marriages and suffuses them with his life-giving love and extravagant self-giving. The remedy for our sexual disorder is to immerse ourselves in a biblical and sanctifying vision of sexuality as the Lord's gift, to be enjoyed in safety and wholesome beauty, without shame or regret but in praise of his goodness.

LEVITICUS 19

19 And the Lord spoke to Moses, saying, ² "Speak to all the congregation of the people of Israel and say to them, You shall be holy, for I the Lord your God am holy. ³ Every one of you shall revere his mother and his father, and you shall keep my Sabbaths: I am the Lord your God. ⁴ Do not turn to idols or make for yourselves any gods of cast metal: I am the Lord your God.

⁵ "When you offer a sacrifice of peace offerings to the Lord, you shall offer it so that you may be accepted. ⁶ It shall be eaten the same day you offer it or on the day after, and anything left over until the third day shall be burned up with fire. ⁷ If it is eaten at all on the third day, it is tainted; it will not be accepted, ⁸ and everyone who eats it shall bear his iniquity,

because he has profaned what is holy to the Lord, and that person shall be cut off from his people.

9 "When you reap the harvest of your land, you shall not reap your field right up to its edge, neither shall you gather the gleanings after your harvest. 10 And you shall not strip your vineyard bare, neither shall you gather the fallen grapes of your vineyard. You shall leave them for the poor and for the sojourner: I am the Lord your God.

11 "You shall not steal; you shall not deal falsely; you shall not lie to one another. 12 You shall not swear by my name falsely, and so profane the name of your God: I am the Lord.

13 "You shall not oppress your neighbor or rob him. The wages of a hired worker shall not remain with you all night until the morning. 14 You shall not curse the deaf or put a stumbling block before the blind, but you shall fear your God: I am the Lord.

15 "You shall do no injustice in court. You shall not be partial to the poor or defer to the great, but in righteousness shall you judge your neighbor. 16 You shall not go around as a slanderer among your people, and you shall not stand up against the life[1] of your neighbor: I am the Lord.

17 "You shall not hate your brother in your heart, but you shall reason frankly with your neighbor, lest you incur sin because of him. 18 You shall not take vengeance or bear a grudge against the sons of your own people, but you shall love your neighbor as yourself: I am the Lord.

19 "You shall keep my statutes. You shall not let your cattle breed with a different kind. You shall not sow your field with two kinds of seed, nor shall you wear a garment of cloth made of two kinds of material.

20 "If a man lies sexually with a woman who is a slave, assigned to another man and not yet ransomed or given her freedom, a distinction shall be made. They shall not be put to death, because she was not free; 21 but he shall bring his compensation to the Lord, to the entrance of the tent of meeting, a ram for a guilt offering. 22 And the priest shall make atonement for him with the ram of the guilt offering before the Lord for his sin that he has committed, and he shall be forgiven for the sin that he has committed.

23 "When you come into the land and plant any kind of tree for food, then you shall regard its fruit as forbidden.[2] Three years it shall be forbidden to you; it must not be eaten. 24 And in the fourth year all its fruit shall be holy, an offering of praise to the Lord. 25 But in the fifth year you may eat of its fruit, to increase its yield for you: I am the Lord your God.

26 "You shall not eat any flesh with the blood in it. You shall not interpret omens or tell fortunes. 27 You shall not round off the hair on your temples or mar the edges of your beard. 28 You shall not make any cuts on your body for the dead or tattoo yourselves: I am the Lord.

29 "Do not profane your daughter by making her a prostitute, lest the land fall into prostitution and the land become full of depravity. 30 You shall keep my Sabbaths and reverence my sanctuary: I am the Lord.

31 "Do not turn to mediums or necromancers; do not seek them out, and so make yourselves unclean by them: I am the Lord your God.

32 "You shall stand up before the gray head and honor the face of an old man, and you shall fear your God: I am the Lord.

33 "When a stranger sojourns with you in your land, you shall not do him wrong. 34 You shall treat the stranger who sojourns with you as the native among you, and you shall love him as yourself, for you were strangers in the land of Egypt: I am the Lord your God.

³⁵ "You shall do no wrong in judgment, in measures of length or weight or quantity. ³⁶ You shall have just balances, just weights, a just ephah, and a just hin:³ I am the LORD your God, who brought you out of the land of Egypt. ³⁷ And you shall observe all my statutes and all my rules, and do them: I am the LORD."

¹ Hebrew *blood* ² Hebrew *as its uncircumcision* ³ An *ephah* was about 3/5 bushel or 22 liters; a *hin* was about 4 quarts or 3.5 liters

Section Overview

The chapters framing Leviticus 19 narrowly circumscribe family unions to construct the boundaries within which an expansive and compelling vision of holiness characterized by love may flourish in community. As the congregation heeds the Lord's sanctifying words, it is transformed by his holiness.

Perhaps nowhere else in Leviticus is the divine voice heard more directly than here. The declaration "I am the LORD your God" and the shorter "I am the LORD" ring out sixteen times throughout the chapter to tie these laws together.²²⁸ The human mouthpiece fades from awareness as attention is directed to the Lord, who stands behind these commands with every mention of his name.

The Decalogue is in conversation with this collection of laws to shape life lived in holy community. For a people with a priestly vocation worship and ethical living go hand in hand.²²⁹ It is no surprise to find reflexes of almost all the Ten Commandments in a book that preserves the "statutes and rules and laws that the LORD made between himself and the people of Israel through Moses on Mount Sinai" (26:46; cf. table 3.5).

TABLE 3.5: The Decalogue in Leviticus 19

Ten Commandments	Leviticus 19
No other gods	v. 4
No idols	v. 4
God's name in vain	v. 12
Keep the Sabbath	vv. 3, 30
Honor parents	v. 3
Do not murder	v. 16
Do not commit adultery	v. 29
Do not steal	vv. 11, 13, 35–36
No false witness	vv. 11, 16

---

228 Leviticus 19:2, 3, 4, 10, 12, 14, 16, 18, 25, 28, 30, 31, 32, 34, 36, 37. The formula rings out forty-eight times in the span of chapters 18–26 and twice in 11:44–45.
229 In NT times the Ten Commandments were recited as part of temple worship close to the time of the daily offering (Mishnah, Tamid 5:1). This tradition continued as part of early Christian worship (Pliny the Younger 10.96.9) and was revitalized by the Reformers. Calvin placed the recitation of the Ten Commandments after the confession of sin and words of pardon to emphasize that obedience is the right covenantal response for believers who have received forgiveness.

Section Outline

VI. Moral Holiness (18:1–20:27) . . .

    B. A Community of Holy Love (19:1–37)

        1. Call to Holiness (19:1–2)

        2. Holiness in Worship (19:3–8)

        3. Holiness in Community (19:9–18)

        4. Holiness in All of Life (19:19–36a)

        5. Final Charge (19:36b–37)

Comment

19:1–2 The call to holiness opens the Lord's address. Israel is to model a holiness of character linked to his, to live and to love in the ways that she herself has seen and experienced from her faithful kinsman-redeemer and covenant King. The Lord alone is holy and shares his holiness with Israel to display his perfection to the world. As Sklar observes, "Holiness is not accomplished by withdrawing from the world, but by engaging actively in it, living out the Lord's righteous character in every sphere of life."[230]

Israel is addressed as a "congregation," showing that holiness must be pursued within community and cannot be arrived at alone. It is within the community of the redeemed that every person is called to live out the ethic of love that characterizes the people of God.

19:3–4 The command to "revere" (Hb. *yare'*, "fear, honor") one's mother and father is expressed by a verb normally reserved for fearing the Lord (v. 14). The mother is listed before the father, in reverse order from the Ten Commandments (Ex. 20:12). Honoring one's parents is the Decalogue's pivot from covenant obligation toward the Lord to covenant obligation toward others. Leviticus reverses the order to begin with an emphasis on community: honoring parents (5th commandment), observing the Sabbath (4th commandment), and prohibiting idolatry (2nd commandment). This is fitting for an exposition on a community characterized by holy love.

The most regular act of worship for the Israelite family is Sabbath observance in imitation of the Lord who rested at the conclusion of his work (Ex. 20:11). His people join him in that rest, just like the family and its attached servants and animals rest at the householder's command (Ex. 20:10). Worship is lived out in the home. To disrespect parental authority is to break the living link between one's home and the household of God.

19:5–8 The peace offering is the most communal of the offerings. The worshiper's extended household gathers to feast on the offering's sacrificial meat. Leviticus 7 already introduced different reasons for bringing a peace offering, and these verses seem to have especially in mind those brought to fulfill a vow or as voluntary

---

[230] Sklar, *Leviticus*, TOTC, 243.

expressions of praise (cf. comment on 7:16–18). It is an occasion to testify of the Lord's faithfulness in prayer and deliverance in the context of the community of faith. The time restriction for consuming sacrificial meat encourages a spirit of generosity. It prompts Israelites to invite others to the table beyond their own household. A spirit of openness and generosity around the table contributes to a culture that is open to receiving the "other" among them.

19:9–10 The following verses are grouped as couplets that each conclude with the declaration "I am the LORD," motivating an obedience that will shape every person's life according to God's character and transform the people collectively into a holy nation.

Israelites are to harvest the land in a way that acknowledges the Lord's ownership of it (25:23). They are to welcome the poor and resident alien to glean in their fields with dignity and be sustained by the Lord's generosity (Ruth 2:2). Hospitality is extended beyond the kinship group to those in need. There can be no life together if there is no sharing of life-sustaining resources with those in need. God's ways value people over profit and challenge the hearer not to guard his margins but to give them away.

19:11–12 Acts of defrauding one's neighbor are typically covered up by deception and lies that involve taking the Lord's name in a false oath (cf. Lev. 6:2–3). Laws in Leviticus are especially concerned with guarding the divine name (18:21; 20:3; 21:6; 22:2, 32). As a priestly people, Israel is privileged to bless the Lord's name in her worship and call upon it in prayer (Pss. 105:1–3; 106:47; 113:1–3; 116:4). Yahweh is the saving God among Israel who sanctified her by his name (Lev. 21:6; 22:32). Treating the Lord's name with disrespect endangers not only the individual (24:11) but the entire congregation, which is made holy by his abiding presence.

19:13–14 Hired workers and day laborers depend on daily wages to feed their families. Withholding their pay exploits the most vulnerable and is equal to robbery. Elsewhere God's law instructs employers to return a garment taken in pledge so the laborer will not suffer cold (Deut. 24:12–13). When Israelites see their hired workers as people and show concern over whether they go hungry or cold, they begin to image the Lord, who is the defender of the needy, helper of the weak, and advocate for the vulnerable (Ex. 22:26–27).

In a similar vein the Lord warns against wielding power over the helpless cruelly, to ridicule or oppress them. As legislation protecting the disabled, this is unique in the ancient Near East. The Lord sees and hears on behalf of the blind and deaf to avenge them and reserves a day when they will be a sign of the restoration of his kingdom (Isa. 35:4–5; Matt. 11:5–6). The admonition not to curse the disabled but to fear the Lord links this verse to obligation to one's parents: to fear (Lev. 19:3) and not curse them (20:9). Holy living obliges us toward those who are in authority over us and those over whom we have authority.

19:15–16 The clarion call to justice is to conform to the Lord's judgments enshrined in his law.[231] Land-owning male citizens are involved in their local village law courts, whether as elders who judge cases at the city gate or as witnesses who can influence the outcome. They are warned not to be swayed by anyone's status and position in society but to pursue justice with impartiality. Slander is connected to the courts: an attack on a fellow kinsman's reputation judges him in advance and subverts true justice (James 4:11–12). Maligning and defaming one's neighbor is likened to standing over his life, that is, becoming a direct agent of harm who profits from another's victimization.

19:17–18 Conflict in the covenant community must be addressed without delay. Harboring hatred in one's heart is the concealed version of slander's public animosity. The Lord condemns them both. An open rebuke staves off resentment that might lead to taking revenge (cf. Eph. 4:15; Heb. 12:14–15). Love is commanded instead, countering a negative prohibition with a positive command.

Each of the previous verses refers to a fellow Israelite with varying degrees of relational closeness in expressions that tease the boundaries of kinship ties—fellow Israelite, close friend, kinsman, neighbor, brother.[232] The circle of kinship obligation extends from blood brother to fellow citizen and radiates out to include the resident alien (Lev. 19:34). The obligation to love encompasses every member of the community and most especially the vulnerable—the destitute gleaner, day laborer, disabled, and wrongly accused. Its generous inclusiveness calls for embracing the other as closest kin because all are of the household of God. The implications of this kind of love in holy community unfold further in chapter 25.

The command to love "as yourself" cannot mean that self-love is the measure for the love we are to show to others. This command is situated among laws that elevate the welfare of others above one's own. God's people are to love as *he* loves, emulating the loyalty, justice, and compassion they themselves have received from him who loved them first (1 John 4:19–21). It is a love that embraces the one with whom they have conflict as their own brother or sister. It is a love that can be commanded as a covenant obligation because it is not merely emotional attachment but action that seeks the welfare of the other (Rom. 13:8).

19:19 A holy people must maintain the boundaries the Lord drew at creation by keeping species distinct in animal breeding, crop cultivation, and weaving, specifically in ways that might produce a hybrid. Some suggest these prohibitions might serve as a metaphor to forbid mingling with the nations in intermarriage, a topic the Pentateuch speaks to clearly elsewhere (Deut. 7:1–3).[233]

---

231 The coming Messiah will be blind and deaf to any other means of judgment but the Lord's: "He shall not judge by what his eyes see, or decide disputes by what his ears hear, but with righteousness he shall judge the poor, and decide with equity for the meek of the earth" (Isa. 11:3–4). Cf. John 5:30; 6:38.
232 The variety of terms for a fellow Israelite crescendo in the fullest expression of kinship in the command to love everyone in the family of God: fellow citizen (*'amit*; Lev. 19:11–12); neighbor (*re'a*; vv. 13–14); fellow citizen + people (*'am*) + neighbor (vv. 15–16); brother (*'akh*) + fellow citizen + kinsman (*bene 'am*) + neighbor (vv. 17–18).
233 Wenham, *Leviticus*, 269–270.

Upon closer look, such mixtures are found only in the sanctuary. Should a farmer sow two different types of seed, his crop becomes sacrosanct and must be dedicated to the sanctuary (Deut. 22:9).[234] Blended fabrics of dyed wool interwoven with twined linen make up the sacral textiles of the tabernacle and priestly dress (Ex. 26:31; 28:6, 15). The Most Holy Place houses the throne of God, guarded by cherubim, creatures that elsewhere appear as part ox, eagle, and lion with a human face (Ezek. 1:5–11). Israel is prohibited from bringing sacred mixtures into secular life because they are relegated to holy space.

19:20–22 If a man sleeps with a female slave who has been assigned to marry another man, neither one is put to death because she has not yet been given her freedom (perhaps suggesting no betrothal has yet taken place). Had she been free, this same act would carry the death penalty (Deut. 22:23–24). The law is meant to protect a slave girl whose lower status creates an unequal power dynamic that makes it difficult to thwart unwanted advances from her master. It also condemns the act as morally wrong by requiring the man to bring a costly guilt offering for the sin he has committed.

19:23–25 Holy living reclaims the human vocation of care for God's creation in Israel's cultivation of the land. The people may not eat the fruit of newly planted fruit trees for the first three years because it is "forbidden" (lit., "uncircumcised"). The immature trees have not yet come of age in order for their harvest to be dedicated to the Lord. In the same way animals may be offered only after the eighth day, the same time frame as circumcision for Israelite boys (Gen. 17:12; Ex. 22:30). They must allow their orchards of olives, dates, figs, pomegranates, and almond trees to mature and become fully established. In the fourth year the Lord receives their praise (as firstfruits; Lev. 23:10–14), and only in the fifth year can their caretakers enjoy their yield. The circumcision imagery calls upon the Lord's blessing and covenant promise of fruitfulness in all areas of life (Gen. 1:22; 17:2, 6).

19:26 To remain in right standing with the Lord, under no circumstances may the covenant people eat meat with its blood, for to do so could lead to idolatry (Lev. 17:7, 10). In pagan rites the blood of a slain animal was manipulated to conjure spirits of the underworld. Israelites are forbidden from engaging in the occult and seeking omens, as is customarily done among their neighbors through reading the stars, inspecting an animal's internal organs, observing the movement of birds, and the like (2 Kings 17:17; 21:6). The Lord expressly forbids ascribing power to false gods and impersonal forces that feign to foretell things to come. He alone knows the end from the beginning because he directs all human history to accomplish his will (Isa. 45:20–22).

---

[234] The ESV translation of Deuteronomy 22:9 that the yield is "forfeited" indicates it is removed from common use and forfeited to the sanctuary. Cf. ESV mg. ("become holy"), which highlights how the Hebrew verb *qadash* regularly means "be/become holy" (*HALOT*, 1073). (Cf. LXX, which renders as *hagiazō* ["sanctified"].)

19:27–28 Shaving the head and gashing the body are mourning rites that degraded the body (cf. Deut. 14:1). God's people are holy, a theological identity worn on their bodies through wholeness and ritual purity. They are to leave the edges (Hb. *pe'ah*) of their beards untrimmed, just as they leave the edges (*pe'ah*) of their fields ungleaned (Lev. 19:9–10).

Tattooing is included with the mourning prohibitions because it disfigures the body. There is no evidence that tattooing was practiced as part of mourning rites in the ancient Near East. Rather, it was identified with slave markings. Slaves in Mesopotamia were branded or tattooed on the forehead and hand; captives in Egypt were marked as belonging to the priesthood or state. The Lord has redeemed his people from slavery in Egypt to make them walk with their heads held high (26:13). He alone reserves the right to mark them, which he does with his name as a sign of his holy ownership (Num. 6:27).

19:29–30 A woman's sexuality is intended only for her future husband. It is furthermore to be guarded by her family (cf. Leviticus 18; Song 8:8–9). A father must not give his daughter into prostitution or exploit her for economic gain. She is a person under his care, not property. Prostitution is frequently connected with idolatrous shrines. A woman known as a *qedeshah*, "holy one," sold her body (Deut. 23:17; Hos. 4:14), as Judah mistakenly assumed of Tamar (Gen. 38:21). In condemning such prostitution the Bible's strong message is that sexual relations are holy only in the context of marriage. Prostitution instead "profanes" a woman and defiles the land. That which sanctifies Israel is the Sabbath, on which Israel meets with the Lord in holy time, and the sanctuary (lit., "holy place"), where he receives his people's worship (Lev. 26:2).

19:31 The Lord condemns mediums who summon ancestral spirits, asking, "Should they inquire of the dead on behalf of the living?" (Isa. 8:19). Saul resorts to necromancy because the Lord no longer reveals his will through the priestly Urim and Thummim, dreams, or the prophetic word (1 Sam. 28:6). It is futile to conjure spirits of the dead for help and knowledge of the future. They are not omniscient or holy but instead pollute and defile. The Israelites have the living God among them, guiding their lives with his life-giving words (Lev. 18:5; Deut. 4:7–8).

19:32 Respect for elders recalls the command to revere one's parents (Lev. 19:3) and extends it out into the larger community. God's people are to show deference to the elders, who uphold the rights of the community through their judicial decisions (Ruth 4:1–2). By way of contrast to summoning the spirits of deceased ancestors (Lev. 19:31) the people are enjoined to respect their elders' wisdom and life experience and seek out their blessing (Job 12:12).

19:33–34 The resident alien is a non-Canaanite foreigner living within the boundaries of Israel's inheritance. At the time of the giving of these laws the foreigner may be among the "mixed multitude" (Ex. 12:38) that has come out of Egypt. After Israel's settlement in the land resident aliens come as laborers, craftsmen, merchants, and mercenaries. They are to be protected and, although not part of the family of God, invited into the community of faith through circumcision (Ex. 12:19, 48–49). They can seek sanctuary in a city of refuge since they have taken refuge with the Lord (Num. 35:15).

The command to love reaches beyond the kinship of ethnic Israel to bridge the gap with the foreigner, anticipating that a community fully formed in the image of God will mature into a people through whom "all the families of the earth shall be blessed" (Gen. 12:3). To see the other as one's self is the transformative power of love. The command comes with an appeal for sympathy based on Israel's own experience as foreigners in the land of Egypt.

19:35–36a Honest weights and balances ensure a just society. The word "just" appears four times, driving home the point that they are to be a people just and righteous. Picking up the theme of business dealings for self gain (Lev. 19:11, 13), these laws are included near the ones governing the resident alien perhaps because they are most vulnerable to exploitation.

19:36b–37 The weighty words that began the Lord's speech to the congregation ("I am the LORD"; v. 3) now find their resolution ("who brought you out of the land of Egypt"; v. 36; cf. Ex. 20:2). The resounding conclusion on how Israel will live as a holy community is found in the teaching between these two phrases. Israel's path to holiness is to live individually and collectively in imitation of the God of Sinai, who rescued his people from Egypt to shape their character according to his.

Response

"And who is my neighbor?" a man trained in biblical law asked Jesus (Luke 10:29). The former had just recited the two greatest commandments in summary of the law. He knew them by rote, familiar with every word for kinsman, companion, neighbor, and friend. But what was his covenant obligation in light of the law? Jesus answered him with a parable about a good Samaritan, the Jews' geographical neighbors and sworn enemies for at least the last four hundred years. Jesus' parable confronts the heart's hidden hatred (Lev. 19:17). The priest and Levite who maintain their separate distance in order not to contract impurity betray an essential misunderstanding of the nature of holiness. To love God is to "love your neighbor as yourself" (19:18; Matt. 22:37–40). It is to recognize the other as a brother within the bonds of familial kinship and move toward him with mercy (Luke 10:37). In the Sermon on the Mount Jesus extends the boundaries of kinship to include even the ultimate outsider, an avowed enemy (Matt. 5:43–45). Jesus' followers live in imitation of their heavenly Father in striving toward a holiness that is expressed in love for their neighbor, honored throughout the NT by its frequent mention.[235]

---

235 Matthew 5:43; 19:19; 22:39 (parallels in Mark 12:31, 33; Luke 10:27); Rom. 13:9; Gal. 5:14; James 2:8.

LEVITICUS 20

20 The Lord spoke to Moses, saying, ² "Say to the people of Israel, Any one of the people of Israel or of the strangers who sojourn in Israel who gives any of his children to Molech shall surely be put to death. The people of the land shall stone him with stones. ³ I myself will set my face against that man and will cut him off from among his people, because he has given one of his children to Molech, to make my sanctuary unclean and to profane my holy name. ⁴ And if the people of the land do at all close their eyes to that man when he gives one of his children to Molech, and do not put him to death, ⁵ then I will set my face against that man and against his clan and will cut them off from among their people, him and all who follow him in whoring after Molech.

⁶ "If a person turns to mediums and necromancers, whoring after them, I will set my face against that person and will cut him off from among his people. ⁷ Consecrate yourselves, therefore, and be holy, for I am the Lord your God. ⁸ Keep my statutes and do them; I am the Lord who sanctifies you. ⁹ For anyone who curses his father or his mother shall surely be put to death; he has cursed his father or his mother; his blood is upon him.

¹⁰ "If a man commits adultery with the wife of¹ his neighbor, both the adulterer and the adulteress shall surely be put to death. ¹¹ If a man lies with his father's wife, he has uncovered his father's nakedness; both of them shall surely be put to death; their blood is upon them. ¹² If a man lies with his daughter-in-law, both of them shall surely be put to death; they have committed perversion; their blood is upon them. ¹³ If a man lies with a male as with a woman, both of them have committed an abomination; they shall surely be put to death; their blood is upon them. ¹⁴ If a man takes a woman and her mother also, it is depravity; he and they shall be burned with fire, that there may be no depravity among you. ¹⁵ If a man lies with an animal, he shall surely be put to death, and you shall kill the animal. ¹⁶ If a woman approaches any animal and lies with it, you shall kill the woman and the animal; they shall surely be put to death; their blood is upon them.

¹⁷ "If a man takes his sister, a daughter of his father or a daughter of his mother, and sees her nakedness, and she sees his nakedness, it is a disgrace, and they shall be cut off in the sight of the children of their people. He has uncovered his sister's nakedness, and he shall bear his iniquity. ¹⁸ If a man lies with a woman during her menstrual period and uncovers her nakedness, he has made naked her fountain, and she has uncovered the fountain of her blood. Both of them shall be cut off from among their people. ¹⁹ You shall not uncover the nakedness of your mother's sister or of your father's sister, for that is to make naked one's relative; they shall bear their iniquity. ²⁰ If a man lies with his uncle's wife, he has uncovered his uncle's nakedness; they shall bear their sin; they shall die childless. ²¹ If a man takes his brother's wife, it is impurity.² He has uncovered his brother's nakedness; they shall be childless.

²² "You shall therefore keep all my statutes and all my rules and do them, that the land where I am bringing you to live may not vomit you out. ²³ And you shall not walk in the customs of the nation that I am driving out before you, for they did all these things, and therefore I detested them. ²⁴ But I have said to you, 'You shall inherit their land, and I will give it to you to possess, a land flowing with milk and honey.' I am the LORD your God, who has separated you from the peoples. ²⁵ You shall therefore separate the clean beast from the unclean, and the unclean bird from the clean. You shall not make yourselves detestable by beast or by bird or by anything with which the ground crawls, which I have set apart for you to hold unclean. ²⁶ You shall be holy to me, for I the LORD am holy and have separated you from the peoples, that you should be mine.

²⁷ "A man or a woman who is a medium or a necromancer shall surely be put to death. They shall be stoned with stones; their blood shall be upon them."

¹ Hebrew repeats *if a man commits adultery with the wife of* ² Hebrew *menstrual impurity*

Section Overview

The discussion in chapter 18 on sexual ethics is written as apodictic law, that is, absolute decrees addressed to every Israelite ("You shall not . . ."). Chapter 20 presents the corresponding penalties as case laws that establish legal precedent for the community to adjudicate when the commands are violated ("If . . . then"). The parallel chapters work together, the one urging obedience and the other detailing the consequences for disobedience. The case laws unfold inside bookends of exhortation that call Israel to participate in the holiness that defines her as God's people (vv. 7–8, 26). They are to guard their holiness, which, if tainted, could lead to their expulsion from the land.

The punishment of sexual sin demonstrates the Lord's commitment to recreating a holy people among whom he will dwell after Eden's pattern. The covenant people in turn are responsible for cooperating with the Lord's righteous judgments to create a just society. McClenney-Sadler writes,

> A neighborly love (chap. 19) cannot exist without holy sexual relations between humans on one side (chap. 18), and consequences for failure to maintain those relationships in a holy manner on the other (chap. 20).²³⁶

We see here a sanctioned interplay between the Lord and the holy community to eradicate sin that threatens the covenant relationship. While the community is most often identified as the ones to carry out the penalty (20:2, 9–18), the Lord himself is also involved (vv. 3–5, 6), and the very fact he is giving these laws makes clear that, even when the community acts, it does so on the Lord's behalf.

The penalties must be contextualized within Israel's legal system. A juridical process establishes guilt and punishment in local courts comprising elders (1 Kings 21:8–11) or, later, in the royal court presided over by the king (2 Sam. 15:2–6;

---

236 Madeline McClenney-Sadler, "Leviticus," in *The Africana Bible* (Minneapolis: Fortress, 2010), 92.

1 Kings 3:28). Legal proceedings called on eyewitnesses to testify and require two or three witnesses for capital punishment (Deut. 17:6–7). Capital punishment is not carried out as a blood vendetta but involves the community, which joins in judging the crime as being outside the will of God. The people collectively reject sin as transgressing the covenant. Were they to not judge it, they would become its silent accomplices.

Technical legal terms are threaded throughout the chapter. The language of "Their blood is upon them" is analogous to the guilty verdict (Lev. 20:9, 11, 12, 13, 16). It means that the offender deserves the punishment he has brought upon himself and that those who execute him are not held liable for his blood. Similarly, "They shall bear their iniquity" means there is no atonement for the wrongdoing; the guilty will bear the consequence of his sin. "They shall surely be put to death" (vv. 2, 10, 11, 12, 13, 15, 16, 27) is a technical term for the death penalty, handed down by a court and carried out by the community.

After the introduction (vv. 1–2a) the chapter alternates punishments for sin (vv. 2b–6, 9–21, 27) with calls to holiness (vv. 7–8, 22–26). Israel is to heed the latter, not only to avoid the former but also to fulfill its privileged mission as the Lord's holy people.

Section Outline

VI. Moral Holiness (18:1–20:27) . . .
    C. Penalties for Sexual Offenses (20:1–27)
        1. Introduction (20:1–2a)
        2. Idolatry and Divination (20:2b–6)
        3. Exhortation to Holiness (20:7–8)
        4. Dishonoring Parents, Sexual Sins (20:9–21)
        5. Exhortation to Holiness (20:22–26)
        6. Divination (20:27)

Comment

20:1–2a While Leviticus is pervasively marked as the Lord's speech, it is especially important to remember this here. The Lord is still speaking from Sinai with the same authority that spoke the blessings and curses of the covenant. These laws are given to the "people of Israel," who will be responsible as a community for judging sin.

20:2b–3 The penalty begins most emphatically to include every single Israelite and resident alien.[237] Idolatry is the first order of concern in the Sinai covenant (Ex. 20:3). The offense of turning to other gods is only magnified by the way in which devotion is shown to Molech in offering one's children. The Lord had judged the genocidal king of Egypt and claimed all Israelite children through the redemption

---

[237] This literally reads "man, man" in Hebrew, with a distributive meaning of "each and every person." Not surprisingly the phrase is thus found in contexts that apply to both Israel and the nations (Lev. 17:3, 8, 10, 13; 18:6; 20:9; 22:18; 24:15), and in 15:2 it refers to both men and women.

of the firstborn (Ex. 13:11–15). To give them up willingly to false gods is a betrayal of the Lord's saving work among his people. It profanes the holy name of Yahweh by making him appear as the depraved gods of the nations.

Child sacrifice was practiced among Israel's neighbors, and in their darkest apostasy by Israelites themselves (2 Kings 23:10; Jer. 32:35). Ancient literary sources and archaeological remains attest to how children were offered as sacrifice by passing through fire. Cemeteries in North Africa, Sicily, Sardinia, and Cyprus preserve the cremated remains of infants in ceramic urns with dedicatory inscriptions.

The community is to execute the violator and purge evil from among the nation. Stoning is prescribed as the method of execution for idolatry and the practice of the occult (Lev. 20:2, 27), rebellion against parental authority (v. 9), and adultery (v. 10). Elsewhere it is prescribed for blasphemy (24:16) and the desecration of the Sabbath (Num. 15:32–36).

20:4–5 If the community is lax in enforcing the death penalty, the Lord himself will arise as a kinsman, avenging wrong by judging the sinner with the extinction of his family line and judgment beyond the grave. He will judge the clan that should have restrained the sinner but instead chose to close its eyes (cf. Josh. 7:25).

In Leviticus 20:3, 5 the Lord threatens to "set [his] face against that man" in a reversal of the blessing for the Lord to shine his face upon his people with favorable acceptance (Num. 6:24–26). Instead of granting favor and peace God will oppose the idolater who profanes his divine name.

20:6 Spiritism involves seeking knowledge from other gods and from a different realm, often by possession (cf. 19:31).

20:7–8 The Lord sanctifies Israel (v. 8), but she must also consecrate herself (v. 7). The people participate in their sanctification through obedience to the Lord's commands. Holiness allows for relationship: God's people draw near to him in worship and live under his blessing. It is their priestly task to guard themselves from sin, as the Levites were zealous to guard the Lord's holiness (Exodus 26–29; Deut. 33:8–9).

20:9 The laws begin with those whose penalty is death (vv. 9–16), followed by those whose penalty is not (vv. 17–21). The death penalty for cursing one's parents conveys the gravity of the offense. This law is directed toward adult children, who have a solemn obligation to care for their parents in their old age (and even beyond, as in Gen. 50:5, 12–13). Dishonoring one's parents undermines the kinship bonds of loyalty and authority that exist in the parent-child relationship (and that ultimately mirror the same bonds that exist in one's relationship with the Lord). Furthermore, cursing invokes a supernatural power. If blessing is thought to have the spiritual power to shape the course of one's life, so is cursing. Jacob was desperate for his father's blessing but fearful of his curse (Gen. 27:11–13). The Lord condemns anyone who would wish destruction on his parents, through whom he has received protection, blessing, life instruction, and knowledge of the Lord. Both parents are to bring their son to the town's elders, who call witnesses and judge the case (Deut. 21:18–21). No one in the extended family or village community can excuse the crime or cover up this sinful behavior.

20:10–21 The following penalties appear to be addressing consensual forbidden unions, since they specify that both parties are to be put to death, to be cut off, to bear their guilt, or to die childless.

20:10 Adultery is a weighty transgression against the Lord and the covenant of marriage (Ex. 20:14). Among Israel's neighbors adultery was referred to as the "great sin" and was punishable by death. In Israel both adulterer and adulteress are executed by stoning in a public place (Deut. 22:24). In complementary biblical laws provision is made to protect a woman who may have been sexually assaulted. If she cried out for help, the sexual encounter is deemed nonconsensual. She is spared, and her rapist is put to death for violating her (Deut. 22:25–27). Falsely accusing a woman of adultery during the betrothal period results in flogging and a staggering fine of 100 shekels (Deut. 22:18–19).[238]

Adultery is difficult to prove in a court that requires eyewitnesses to the act. A husband therefore has recourse to a divine court at the tabernacle (Num. 5:11–31), where he appeals to the Lord to uncover and punish sin. It may be up to the wronged husband's discretion whether he pursues a trial or divorce (cf. Matt. 1:19).[239] Through the prophetic word it is up to the Lord to model that which is outside the purview of the legal genre to convey—forgiveness and reconciliation (Hosea 2; John 8:3–11). See Leviticus 18:20.

20:11–12 A sexual liaison between a man and his father's wife or a man and his daughter-in-law is incest and a capital offense. It dishonors the relationship between father and son and disorders family dynamics involving household leadership and inheritance. Judah unknowingly violated this law with Tamar but later exonerated her as more righteous than he when he recognized his complicity in driving her to that desperate act (Gen. 38:26). See Leviticus 18:8, 15.

20:13 Capital punishment is prescribed for same-sex intercourse. Homosexuality is embedded within other penalties for sexual sin that, though apparently consensual, defy the Lord's commands and pollute the community's holiness. The severe punishment strikes at eradicating personal sin that endangers the entire nation of coming under God's wrath (vv. 22–24).

In the same way that child sacrifice (v. 2), incest (vv. 11–12), and bestiality (vv. 15–16) have ongoing relevance so does the prohibition against homosexuality, as clearly reflected in the NT (Rom. 1:24–27; Rev. 22:15). In fact Paul coins a word

---

[238] According to the estimated wage of a shekel per month, this fine represents eight years of labor, making it roughly equivalent to the bride price paid by Jacob.
[239] In Deuteronomy 24:1 the translation of "indecency" as grounds for divorce is literally "the nakedness of a matter." Although this can be interpreted as any kind of marital impropriety, "nakedness" is used most often idiomatically for sexual intercourse (cf. Leviticus 18). Understood this way, it would imply that adultery could end in divorce instead of death even in OT times.

for those who practice homosexuality that is drawn directly from the LXX of this verse: *arsenokoitai* combines the word for male (*arseno*) and bed (*koitē*) to refer to men who take other men to bed (1 Cor. 6:9; 1 Tim. 1:10). For Paul this is not just an aberrant sexual practice but one that the authority of Scripture clearly condemns. In the old covenant as in the new the Lord holds out hope for the penitent, preferring "that the wicked [person should] turn from his way and live" (Ezek. 33:11, 14–16). Turning away from a sinful lifestyle to walk in forgiveness and newness of life is possible because of the power of God made available "in the name of the Lord Jesus Christ and by the Spirit of our God" (1 Cor. 6:11). See Leviticus 18:22.

20:14 The law and its penalty are given from the perspective of the wife. The prohibition in 18:17 is stated from the mother's perspective ("woman and . . . her daughter"), while here it is stated from the daughter's perspective ("woman and her mother"). The focus is the relationship between the two women. Such a marriage is a betrayal of the natural bond between mother and child that was protected even among Israel's livestock (22:28). It is perversion (Hb. *zimmah*). As noted above, the unions appear to have been consensual, since the husband and both of his wives are held liable and punished by burning, a form of execution seen not usually with men but with women who have engaged in illicit sexual behavior (21:9; Gen. 38:24). Burning communicates a decisive eradication of sin and purification of the community. The Lord himself punishes by fire when he judges sexual sin (Gen. 19:24), transgression of holy boundaries (Lev. 10:2), and evil in general (Rev. 20:10).

20:15–16 The sin of bestiality can be committed by either men or women. Livestock is overnighted in stables on either side of a home's central courtyard, where daily cooking activities take place. Inclusion of bestiality in the family laws shows that animals are part of the Israelite household. They rest on the Sabbath, just as the householder and his servants do (Ex. 23:12); they feed on the land, just as the poor do (Lev. 25:6–7); they are held liable for shedding a person's blood, just as human murderers are (Gen. 9:5; Ex. 21:28–32). Since both animal and human have transgressed the Lord's boundaries, both are to be put to death. See Leviticus 18:23.

20:17 A man who has sexual intercourse with his sister or half-sister is guilty. While both are held liable to punishment, a brother's culpability is singled out ("He shall bear his iniquity") because he is responsible for protecting his sister and guarding her honor but instead has betrayed and shamefully debased her. As Tamar objected to Amnon, "Such a thing is not done in Israel" (2 Sam. 13:12). That which is to separate Israel from the nations is love and care for the other within holy boundaries (Leviticus 19).

For the "cutting off" penalty cf. 7:19–21. Given that the penalty in 20:9–16 is clearly stated as being put to death, the switch to the "cutting off" penalty here suggests that excommunication, not death, is in view.[240] For the parallel laws cf. 18:9.

---

[240] Sklar, *Leviticus*, TOTC, 258.

20:18 The man and woman who pursue sexual relations during the woman's menstrual cycle are likewise punished by being cut off from the community. This is a different situation from that of 15:24, in which the couple was intimate without realizing menstruation had begun. Deliberate intercourse during menstruation is a moral issue because it is a flagrant violation of the Lord's commands—his exposing "her fountain" and her "uncovering the fountain of her blood." See 18:19.

20:19–20 Sexual relations with aunts from either the mother's or the father's side of the family bring guilt upon the offenders that will be punished by the Lord. A man who seduces his uncle's wife (presumably after his death) will be punished with childlessness (cf. sexual sin and lack of conception in Gen. 20:17–18). The Lord will bring justice to an immoral union by ending that family line. The expression that they will "bear their sin/iniquity" instills the fear of God in situations that are difficult to expose. The Lord takes it upon himself to visit punishment in the absence of human agency. See Leviticus 18:12–14.

20:21 The case of a man's taking his brother's wife is equated with having relations with a menstruating woman. The Hebrew for "impurity" (Hb. *niddah*), which refers elsewhere to menstruation (12:2, 5; 15:19–33; 18:19), is used rhetorically to communicate the uncleanness and disgust of a polluting sexual union in violation of God's commands. John the Baptist confronted Herod Antipas precisely on this prohibition, as he had unlawfully divorced his wife and married Herodias, his brother Philip's wife (Mark 6:17–18). Cf. Leviticus 18:16.

20:22–24 The way in which Israel lives in the land will determine her destiny. The choice is clear: will God's people live by the Lord's statutes and inherit the land, or will they live like the nations, which were vomited out? They will soon be acting as an instrument of God's judgment on the Canaanites. How can they possibly fight wars of conquest or take possession of the land if they have not rooted out the evil from among them? If the Lord detests these practices, his covenant partners should also (Ps. 139:21–22; Rom. 12:9).

20:25–26 Israel participates in her sanctification by obedience in daily living. Drawing distinctions between clean and unclean separates Israel *from* the nations and *to* the Lord. Consuming unclean food would make the people "detestable" (Hb. *shaqats*; 11:11, 13, 43), a word intended to elicit disgust. The Lord who made a distinction between his people and the Egyptians (Ex. 8:23) urges them to maintain their distinctiveness in the land. The distinctiveness they are to have at the ritual level in relation to food is a constant reminder of the distinctiveness they are to have at the moral level in relation to sexuality and worship practices.

20:27 The final case law comes full circle to the beginning of the chapter: idolatry and divination will not go unpunished. The public and dramatic execution will be a stern warning to all.

Response

The character of God and our Christian witness are at stake as we approach this passage. It is crucial, now more than ever, that the church recover a holy fear of the Lord's hatred of sin. To some extent we are all accountable for the alarming rates of adultery, pornography, and sexual abuse within the church. Were we too embarrassed to confront our brother? Were we worried about offending our sister? Have we been too polite in the face of sexual sin, which does tremendous violence to the lives of its victims and whose consequences are felt over generations? Have we unknowingly perpetuated cultural norms in the name of Christian love?

The burden of this chapter is to convince us that there is no place for deliberate sin in the holy Christian community. For the believer who has found refuge in Christ's shed blood, it should cause us great heartache to think that we would willingly crucify him all over again. The Lord has revealed the profound mystery of his character as being both merciful and just (Ex. 34:6–7). It is God's royal prerogative to show mercy to his subjects. But we are never to forget the cost. Were the punishment not so steep, the mercy would not be so unfathomable. Mercy does not make sin less abhorrent. Christ has borne the righteous wrath of a holy God and the death penalty for all so that we would live holy lives that testify to his power to save sinners. As a kingdom of priests, we are called to mediate a knowledge of the Lord to those around us. Without holiness we become indistinguishable from the world and are of little use in God's redemptive mission. As Jesus declares, salt that has lost its taste is "no longer good for anything" (Matt. 5:13).

LEVITICUS 21

21 And the Lord said to Moses, "Speak to the priests, the sons of Aaron, and say to them, No one shall make himself unclean for the dead among his people, ² except for his closest relatives, his mother, his father, his son, his daughter, his brother, ³ or his virgin sister (who is near to him because she has had no husband; for her he may make himself unclean). ⁴ He shall not make himself unclean as a husband among his people and so profane himself. ⁵ They shall not make bald patches on their heads, nor shave off the edges of their beards, nor make any cuts on their body. ⁶ They shall be holy to their God and not profane the name of their God. For they offer the Lord's food offerings, the bread of their God; therefore they shall be holy. ⁷ They shall not marry a prostitute or a woman who has been defiled, neither shall they marry a woman divorced from her husband, for the priest is holy to his God. ⁸ You shall sanctify him, for he offers the bread of your God. He shall be holy to you, for I, the LORD, who sanctify you, am holy. ⁹And the daughter of any priest, if she profanes herself by whoring, profanes her father; she shall be burned with fire.

¹⁰ "The priest who is chief among his brothers, on whose head the anointing oil is poured and who has been consecrated to wear the garments, shall not let the hair of his head hang loose nor tear his clothes. ¹¹ He shall not go in to any dead bodies nor make himself unclean, even for his father or for his mother. ¹²He shall not go out of the sanctuary, lest he profane the sanctuary of his God, for the consecration of the anointing oil of his God is on him: I am the LORD. ¹³And he shall take a wife in her virginity.¹ ¹⁴A widow, or a divorced woman, or a woman who has been defiled, or a prostitute, these he shall not marry. But he shall take as his wife a virgin² of his own people, ¹⁵ that he may not profane his offspring among his people, for I am the LORD who sanctifies him."

¹⁶And the LORD spoke to Moses, saying, ¹⁷ "Speak to Aaron, saying, None of your offspring throughout their generations who has a blemish may approach to offer the bread of his God. ¹⁸For no one who has a blemish shall draw near, a man blind or lame, or one who has a mutilated face or a limb too long, ¹⁹or a man who has an injured foot or an injured hand, ²⁰or a hunchback or a dwarf or a man with a defect in his sight or an itching disease or scabs or crushed testicles. ²¹ No man of the offspring of Aaron the priest who has a blemish shall come near to offer the LORD's food offerings; since he has a blemish, he shall not come near to offer the bread of his God. ²² He may eat the bread of his God, both of the most holy and of the holy things, ²³but he shall not go through the veil or approach the altar, because he has a blemish, that he may not profane my sanctuaries,³ for I am the LORD who sanctifies them." ²⁴ So Moses spoke to Aaron and to his sons and to all the people of Israel.

¹ Or *a young wife* ² Hebrew *young woman* ³ Or *my holy precincts*

Section Overview

Whereas chapters 18–20 shape the vision for Israel to embrace living in the Lord's holiness, chapters 21–22 script a course for Israel's priesthood. Priests are to live out an embodied sanctification in their primary relationships and in the physical wholeness of their bodies. The concept of *drawing near* (Hb. *qarab*)[241] is a key to understanding the theme of these laws: flesh and blood relationships that priests may draw near to at home (21:1–15), followed by requirements of flesh and blood in drawing near to God at the sanctuary (vv. 16–23).

A society's marriage and mourning practices bring to the fore family relationships and obligations. The priestly purity laws tighten the circle of family obligation to only the nearest of kin and further define who may enter that circle to become kin through marriage. Regular priests may become unclean for the sake of their closest blood relatives because in addition to being the Lord's servants they are also sons, brothers, and fathers who must perform rites for the dead. In the case of the high priest, however, he must not be touched by death at all, for he is

---

[241] Leviticus 21:6, 8, 17 (2x), 18, 21 (2x).

dedicated exclusively to the Lord, holy to him, and set apart in a way transcending natural family relations.

After restrictions on familial duties relating to the body itself (vv. 1–15) the second half of the chapter addresses restrictions on priestly duties as they relate to bodily wholeness (vv. 16–23). Since holiness is nonnegotiable for access into God's presence, priests have to live according to stricter standards than those of laymen. They live, wed, and minister in physical and unblemished wholeness because they represent something beyond themselves—a picture of life lived in God's presence.

Section Outline

VII. Holy Institutions (21:1–27:34)
    A. Priesthood (21:1–24)
        1. Holiness in Mourning and Marriage: Regular Priests (21:1–9)
        2. Holiness in Mourning and Marriage: High Priest (21:10–15)
        3. Blemishes That Disqualify Service at the Altar (21:16–23)
        4. Moses' Obedience to Relay the Instructions (21:24)

Comment

21:1 These instructions are given to the sons of Aaron, the regular priests. They describe the limits of contracting impurity in mourning the dead. Mourning in ancient Israel is fully embodied and encompassed more than emotion. It is expressed by such physical acts as the rending of garments (Gen. 37:34; Job 1:20), dressing in coarse sackcloth (2 Sam. 3:31), heaping ashes on the head (Josh. 7:6; Jer. 6:26), fasting (2 Sam. 1:12), and lamenting with loud weeping and wailing (Gen. 37:34–35; 2 Sam. 1:11–12; Job 2:12).

The body's burial is so important that to remain unburied is regarded as being accursed (Deut. 28:26). Nevertheless, death leads to a major impurity that comes about through physical contact with the dead (e.g., when preparing the body for burial) or even through being in a home with the dead body (Num. 19:11, 14). Death's defilement is ritual (not moral) and temporary, lasting for seven days (Num. 19:11). A common Israelite could intentionally become unclean to bury the dead, so long as he cleansed himself with water for cleansing on the third day (after the burial) and again on the seventh day (at the end of the period of uncleanness; Num. 19:12). During his uncleanness he is not permitted to approach the sanctuary.

21:2 Mourning the loss of a loved one not only is validated in Scripture but comes with the promise that God himself will comfort the mourner (cf. 2 Cor. 1:3–4). The Lord makes provision for a priest to mourn his closest family but limits this provision to kin who are "closest" (Hb. root *qarab*), that is, blood relatives. The biological family includes those toward whom he has formal responsibilities and who also happen to be those with whom he lives in the paternal household—father, mother, brother, children, and unmarried sisters.[242] They are therefore "close" in blood lineage and also in literal proximity.

The family household is the building block of ancient Israelite society and the source of all identity and relationships. In the words of one biblical archaeologist, "The family and household provide the central symbol about which the ancient Israelites created ... the world in which members of that society expressed their relationships to each other, to their leaders ... and to the deity."[243] These are the very relationships dealt with in this chapter.

21:3 An unmarried sister is still part of the paternal household and a "near" relative. The obligation to care for her falls to the males in her family (2 Sam. 13:20) until she marries and becomes part of her husband's household (Gen. 24:58).

21:4 The phrasing of this verse may be elliptical, that is, not fully expressing what is meant by the priest "as a husband" among his people or tribe. Does it mean that he may not mourn his wife or not mourn family relations through marriage? Although a wife is not strictly blood lineage, the Bible assumes husband and wife to share the closest of kinship bonds, expressed as "bone of my bones and flesh of my flesh" (Gen. 2:23). Sharing flesh and bone is kinship language (cf. Gen. 29:13–14).[244] It may be tacitly understood that a priest's wife is included in the blood relatives for which he may defile himself; otherwise we would expect a clearer negative prohibition. Practically speaking, defilement would be very difficult to avoid; a priest is not immune from becoming defiled by the sudden death of his wife, with whom he shares a home (Num. 19:14).

It requires reading this verse within the broader context of Scripture to understand the exact prohibition. When the Lord commands Ezekiel not to mourn his wife, it surprisingly departs from common practice, therefore making for an attention-getting prophetic parable (Ezek. 24:15–24). The expression "as a husband" among his people or tribe thus likely prohibits the priest from mourning related to family relations through marriage, such as his in-laws.

21:5–6 The allowance to mourn the nearest of kin comes with the restriction of altering the body: a priest may become defiled but not disfigured. At this point in Israel's history shaving the head and gashing the body appears to be practiced among Israel's pagan neighbors (cf. Deut. 14:1). Not only are the Israelites to live distinctly from these neighbors when it comes to these practices, but the priests are to take the lead in doing so because they have been set apart to the Lord to offer (Hb. root *qarab*, "bring near") sacrifices at his altar. In the same manner a priest is profaned by identifying with a household other than his own kin (Lev.

---

[242] The paternal home typically comprises three generations living together under the leadership of the patriarch. The household is such a strongly defined unit that families remain together beyond death, often buried together in a family tomb, as seen with Jacob, who wishes his remains to be brought to the family burial site in Canaan and laid to rest with his forefathers (Gen. 49:29–33). Consequently, one of the most familiar ways of expressing death in the Bible is by the phrase "gathered to his people [kin]" (Gen. 25:8; 35:29).
[243] King and Stager, *Life in Biblical Israel*, 5.
[244] The expression is used for the blood bond of biological family, or the covenant bond that brings people into the same relationship as a biological family (2 Sam. 5:1; 19:12–13).

21:4), the Lord is profaned if the priest identifies with practices that do not belong in the household of God. A priest's body represents the Lord and belongs to the Lord's household.

21:7 Since marriage is a covenant union of "one flesh," the status of a priest's wife is of critical importance. Union with a woman who has already had sexual relations with another man—promiscuous, defiled, or divorced—is out of bounds. This may reflect the high concern that any children born to the union must be the priest's own so that they can properly serve as priests (and thus properly enable worship to continue).

21:8 The voice shifts to addressing the congregation directly with the exhortation to guard priestly holiness. Priests are holy because they have been dedicated to the Lord's service. They are able to move between the worlds of holy and common, sharing in them both and mediating the relationship between the two, but they are always to be regarded as set apart. The congregation is to help the priests maintain their holy status carefully, thus allowing them to continue to serve as intermediaries between the people and the Lord who sanctifies them.

21:9 In the same way a priest must not join his flesh to a prostitute, his daughter, an extension of his flesh and blood, must not become a prostitute. A priest's family shares in his holiness by virtue of blood kinship and through the holy priestly portions from the Lord's table (10:14).[245] A daughter who profanes her body does more than merely damage her father's reputation; she profanes him, compromising his own embodied sanctity and showing utter disregard for the Holy One he represents. The only way to cleanse such profaning of the holy is through the same punishment meted out to Nadab and Abihu, that of burning (10:2).

21:10–12 Different holiness requirements between regular priests and the high priest reflect the different spheres of ministry to which they each have access within the tabernacle. Since the high priest ministers closest to God's throne and personal presence, he must embody a higher standard of holiness. A priest's body is holy; the high priest's body is holier still.

The high priest must not dishevel his hair nor tear the garments that ordained him to service, even for father or mother (cf. Lev. 10:6; cf. Matt. 12:48). He must not defile himself with mourning, since the oil of anointing has been lavishly poured upon his head to consecrate him—"precious oil on the head, running down on the beard, on the beard of Aaron, running down on the collar of his robes" (Ps. 133:2; cf. Lev. 4:3). He shares in the sanctuary's holiness through anointing with oil and blood (Lev. 8:10–12, 23–24). He is dressed in layered garments that replicate the holy fabrics of the tent's coverings so that his body appears as a scaled-down tent.[246] He is naturally allowed to leave the tent for many reasons, not least of

---

245 Gane, *Leviticus, Numbers*, 373.
246 Christine Palmer, "Israelite High Priestly Apparel: Embodying an Identity between Human and Divine," in *Fashioned Selves: Dress and Identity in Antiquity*, ed. Megan Cifarelli (Oxford, UK: Oxbow, 2019), 117–127.

which would be carrying on regular family life at home. But in the case of death his holy status means he is not allowed to leave the tent of the Lord (21:12) to go into a tent to mourn the dead of his paternal household (v. 11); if he does so, he profanes the sanctuary he represents. To remain in the Lord's tent after the death of a close relative is an act that embodies a statement of allegiance declaring that *the Lord* is his nearest kin and that the tabernacle is his Father's household (cf. Luke 2:49).[247]

21:13–15 Instructions regulating the marriage of the high priest are stated in both the negative and the positive. Negatively, he is prohibited from marrying the women unsuitable for regular priests, with the addition of the widow. Positively, the only suitable wife is a virgin from a priestly family. Since the two will become one flesh, she must present a bodily wholeness comparable to his. What was inferred above (Lev. 21:7) is made explicit now: priestly lineage and the hereditary priestly office must be kept holy.

21:16–23 These instructions are addressed to Aaron as head of his family and chief minister in God's house. He is responsible to ensure that those with physical blemishes do not "draw near, approach" (Hb. *qarab*) the altar (vv. 17, 18, 21).

A "blemish" may be understood as a physical abnormality caused by a congenital birth defect (i.e., blindness), disease (i.e., boils), or an external agent (i.e., a broken arm). The following list of twelve blemishes that disqualify a priest from service are virtually identical with those that disqualify animals from being offered as sacrifices on the altar (22:22–25). (A possible implication is that, if the body of a priest is as the body of a sacrificial offering, then priestly service must be envisioned as a *living* sacrifice.)

The reason priests with physical blemishes are prohibited from ministering at the altar is because doing so would "profane" the Lord's holy precincts (v. 23), that is, treat them as an ordinary thing instead of as sacred space. But why would such profanation be the end result? While the text does not say, the underlying rationale may be that wholeness is a symbolic sign of the nature of holy space and the Holy One who indwells it. The inner sanctuary behind the veil is the place of his enthronement (Ex. 40:38), and the altar in the courtyard is the place where his fiery presence alighted (Lev. 9:24). Both are regarded as "most holy" (Ex. 26:33; 29:37) because they are places where heaven touches earth. The place of the Lord's presence is must not lack wholeness in any way. Thus a priest with a bodily defect is prohibited from ministering in the places most directly identified with the Lord's manifest presence.

While these verses might read to many today as being prejudiced against the physically disabled, the Lord includes instructions here to make sure that these priests are still treated with great honor and respect, especially by emphasizing

---

[247] Israelite society was structured as ever-increasing, nested households: the paternal household, the clan, the tribe, the king's household, and, over all, the God of Israel as Father over the household of his covenanted kindred (King and Stager, *Life in Biblical Israel*, 4–5).

that disabled priests are prohibited only from presenting sacrificial offerings; they are otherwise welcomed to the Lord's table in order to feast with him and the rest of their kin from the most holy and holy offerings of the sanctuary.[248]

21:24 The chapter closes with Moses' obedience to relay the instructions to Aaron and his household as well as to the household of Israel. While the instructions concern the priesthood, they are delivered before all the people. In the Lord's kindness the responsibility for priestly purity is shared alike by priests, their families, and all Israel, which will be affected by the priesthood's consecration in marriage, mourning, and all matters of life.

Response

Priestly purity requirements may seem strange on the surface, yet they create categories and shape expectations that find fulfillment ultimately in Christ. The blood bond of the paternal household through which social obligations were expressed becomes redefined around the person of Jesus Christ. It is the bond of *his* shed blood that brings us into his Father's covenant household (John 14:1–4). Christ's call for an exclusive allegiance that denies a son to bury his father (Luke 9:59–60) would meet our ears as an impossible saying were it not for the high priest's example of devotion. The teaching that our bodies are not our own but belong to the Lord who sanctifies them and charges us to honor *him* with them (1 Cor. 6:19–20) would be merely an abstract notion were it not lived out by the old covenant priesthood. In the tabernacle's courts those who draw near, whether offering or priest, must be perfect and whole because they put on display what it means to be *restored to God's presence*. Death and physical blemishes have no place in the sanctuary not because God's holiness is threatened by them but because the tabernacle is a prophetic image of the coming renewed creation, wherein death and sin have been overturned, defeated, and exchanged for life and wholeness through the atoning work of Christ. Before all Israel the priesthood embodies the reality and future hope that those who are called to draw near to the Lord will be cleansed and made whole.

In the new covenant it is Christ who *draws near*, moving outward from the Father's presence and bringing redemptive renewal in his wake (Mal. 4:2). He moved with pity toward the disabled and the dead, raising a woman from her crippling deformity and a ruler's twelve-year-old daughter and widow's son from the dead (Mark 5:41–42; Luke 7:14). He laid his hands on the "blemished" blind, deaf, and mutilated and restored them to wholeness (Matt. 9:29, 20:34; Mark 7:32–33; Luke 22:51; John 5). For those who had eyes to see he was God's presence in their midst, moving out toward humanity to redeem from sin and restore to wholeness (Matt. 11:5). The incarnate Jesus Christ was holy ground on the move, his body the

---

[248] Most holy food includes portions from the grain offering, the sin offering, and the guilt offering, as well as the weekly bread of the presence, eaten in the sacred precincts of the tabernacle (Lev. 2:3, 10; 6:17, 25, 29; 7:1, 6; 24:9). Holy food includes the breast and right thigh from peace offerings, shares from firstfruit offerings, and tithes, which may be brought back to the disabled priest's household to be enjoyed with his family (Lev. 7:31–34; Num. 18:12–19, 26).

place where heaven had touched down on earth. The crowds who saw what was enacted among them knew the kingdom of God had drawn near to them in Christ.

As a priestly people who put on display the kingdom of God among us, we are called to live in moral purity without spot or blemish before the world (Eph. 5:27; Phil. 2:15; 2 Pet. 3:14). We are called to live as Christ, not preserving our bodies but giving them up for the sake of the world. He who took on flesh to enter the world he would redeem as a fully embodied human, free of the blemish of sin, consecrated himself to his Father's will: "When Christ came into the world, he said, 'Sacrifices and offerings you have not desired, but a body have you prepared for me. . . . Behold, I have come to do your will'" (Heb. 10:5–7). He worked our salvation by offering up his body—physically suffering and dying on a cross—and bodily rising from the dead on the third day. He now calls us to imitate him in offering up our bodies to draw near to a hurting world and spend our lives for the sake of the gospel, denying ourselves to reach the unreached, serving the poor, ministering to the sick, caring for the orphan, and even embracing persecution to stand with Christ. We offer our bodies to be broken and our lives to be poured out because he did so first. In the words of Charles Spurgeon, "It is our duty and our privilege to exhaust our lives for Jesus. We are not to be living specimens of men in fine preservation, but living *sacrifices*, whose lot is to be consumed; we are to spend and to be spent."[249]

LEVITICUS 22

22 And the LORD spoke to Moses, saying, ² "Speak to Aaron and his sons so that they abstain from the holy things of the people of Israel, which they dedicate to me, so that they do not profane my holy name: I am the LORD. ³ Say to them, 'If any one of all your offspring throughout your generations approaches the holy things that the people of Israel dedicate to the LORD, while he has an uncleanness, that person shall be cut off from my presence: I am the LORD. ⁴ None of the offspring of Aaron who has a leprous disease or a discharge may eat of the holy things until he is clean. Whoever touches anything that is unclean through contact with the dead or a man who has had an emission of semen, ⁵ and whoever touches a swarming thing by which he may be made unclean or a person from whom he may take uncleanness, whatever his uncleanness may be— ⁶ the person who touches such a thing shall be unclean until the evening and shall not eat of the holy things unless he has bathed his body in water. ⁷ When the sun goes down he shall be clean, and afterward he may eat of the holy things, because they are his food.

---

[249] Charles H. Spurgeon, "The Minister's Fainting Fits," in *Lectures to My Students* (Grand Rapids, MI: Baker, 1995), 170.

⁸He shall not eat what dies of itself or is torn by beasts, and so make himself unclean by it: I am the Lord.' ⁹They shall therefore keep my charge, lest they bear sin for it and die thereby when they profane it: I am the Lord who sanctifies them.

¹⁰ "A lay person shall not eat of a holy thing; no foreign guest of the priest or hired worker shall eat of a holy thing, ¹¹ but if a priest buys a slave¹ as his property for money, the slave² may eat of it, and anyone born in his house may eat of his food. ¹² If a priest's daughter marries a layman, she shall not eat of the contribution of the holy things. ¹³ But if a priest's daughter is widowed or divorced and has no child and returns to her father's house, as in her youth, she may eat of her father's food; yet no lay person shall eat of it. ¹⁴ And if anyone eats of a holy thing unintentionally, he shall add the fifth of its value to it and give the holy thing to the priest. ¹⁵ They shall not profane the holy things of the people of Israel, which they contribute to the Lord, ¹⁶ and so cause them to bear iniquity and guilt, by eating their holy things: for I am the Lord who sanctifies them."

¹⁷ And the Lord spoke to Moses, saying, ¹⁸ "Speak to Aaron and his sons and all the people of Israel and say to them, When any one of the house of Israel or of the sojourners in Israel presents a burnt offering as his offering, for any of their vows or freewill offerings that they offer to the Lord, ¹⁹ if it is to be accepted for you it shall be a male without blemish, of the bulls or the sheep or the goats. ²⁰ You shall not offer anything that has a blemish, for it will not be acceptable for you. ²¹ And when anyone offers a sacrifice of peace offerings to the Lord to fulfill a vow or as a freewill offering from the herd or from the flock, to be accepted it must be perfect; there shall be no blemish in it. ²² Animals blind or disabled or mutilated or having a discharge or an itch or scabs you shall not offer to the Lord or give them to the Lord as a food offering on the altar. ²³ You may present a bull or a lamb that has a part too long or too short for a freewill offering, but for a vow offering it cannot be accepted. ²⁴ Any animal that has its testicles bruised or crushed or torn or cut you shall not offer to the Lord; you shall not do it within your land, ²⁵ neither shall you offer as the bread of your God any such animals gotten from a foreigner. Since there is a blemish in them, because of their mutilation, they will not be accepted for you."

²⁶ And the Lord spoke to Moses, saying, ²⁷ "When an ox or sheep or goat is born, it shall remain seven days with its mother, and from the eighth day on it shall be acceptable as a food offering to the Lord. ²⁸ But you shall not kill an ox or a sheep and her young in one day. ²⁹ And when you sacrifice a sacrifice of thanksgiving to the Lord, you shall sacrifice it so that you may be accepted. ³⁰ It shall be eaten on the same day; you shall leave none of it until morning: I am the Lord.

³¹ "So you shall keep my commandments and do them: I am the Lord. ³² And you shall not profane my holy name, that I may be sanctified among the people of Israel. I am the Lord who sanctifies you, ³³ who brought you out of the land of Egypt to be your God: I am the Lord."

¹ Or *servant*; twice in this verse ² Hebrew *he*

Section Overview

Chapter 22 continues the teaching on the priesthood's embodied consecration. In the previous chapter priests were instructed in how to live and minister in physical and unblemished wholeness in order to maintain the holiness of God's presence. They guard themselves against pollution by marrying and mourning in holiness (21:1–15). They guard the tabernacle's holiness from a blemished priestly servant's ministering at the altar or sanctuary veil and thus profaning them (21:16–23).

Attention now turns to guarding the sanctity of Israel's sacrificial offerings in their consumption (22:1–16, 29–30) and selection (22:17–28). The first responsibility of spiritual leaders is to model a right reverence and respect for the holy things the Lord has placed into their hands. Those who minister at the altar must handle their dedicated portions with as much respect in their homes as they do in the Lord's courts. Moreover, along with the priestly servants who offer them, sacrificial offerings dedicated by worshipers must also be free of physical blemish. Above all, the Lord's worship must be holy because through it he makes his people holy.

Section Outline

VII. Holy Institutions (21:1–27:34) . . .
   B. Sacrifices (22:1–33)
      1. Introduction (22:1–2)
      2. Eating in Holiness (22:3–9)
      3. Rights to Priestly Portions (22:10–16)
      4. Disqualifying Animal Blemishes (22:17–25)
      5. Additional Sacrificial Laws (22:26–30)
      6. Exhortation to Holiness (22:31–33)

Comment

22:1–2 The Lord continues his instructions to the priesthood, charging it to guard the holiness of priestly portions and sacrificial offerings. God's holiness that sanctifies his covenant people requires that he be respected in the treatment of the sacred gifts to prevent the desecration of his holy name (21:6, 12; 22:32).

22:3–7 Priests who are ritually unclean in any manner by which any Israelite may become unclean must abstain from their regular priestly portions. Offerings dedicated to the Lord are holy, and no one who is ritually unclean may eat them. Physically impaired priests, though unable to perform the sacrificial ministry at the altar, are still entitled to the dedicated food portions, which are their livelihood (21:22). A priest with ritual impurity, however, is sternly admonished from eating the food portions and profaning that which is holy.

Anyone with either major impurities (22:4a) or minor impurities (vv. 4b–7) must go through the necessary purification rites in order to be able to come in contact with holy things. This holds true for laymen as well as for priests (7:20–21).

22:8 The restrictions here are stricter than they are for laymen and resident aliens (cf. comments on 17:15), which is in keeping with the higher ritual standards for priests elsewhere (cf. 21:1–4, 7). Priests must be especially diligent to maintain holiness.

22:9 The privilege of serving the Lord in his courts must be tempered by respect. Priests must guard against an overfamiliarity with the things of God and the temptation to think that the laws of the sanctuary do not apply to them. Those who treat the holy food portions as common will die, a consequence not too far from their experience or imagination (10:2).

22:10–11 Priestly families are fed by designated portions from the Lord's table. Any member of the priestly household can eat of the holy offerings. A guest from a nonpriestly family or a hired worker who is temporarily in the priest's home does not qualify. A non-Israelite slave who has been brought into the household may eat of the food because he has become part of the priestly family (25:44–46).

22:12–13 A priest's daughter is entitled to portions from fellowship and votive offerings and any firstfruits that are brought home, but not to the holiest food (meat from the sin and guilt offerings or bread of the presence), which must be eaten in the sacred precincts of the tabernacle (Num. 18:11–19). If she marries a man outside the priestly clan, her husband's land will sustain them. If she becomes widowed or divorced with no children who can inherit their father's land and support her, however, she returns to her father's household for sustenance.

22:14–16 If someone not of the priest's immediate household accidentally eats from the dedicated offerings, his mistake can be rectified by paying back the monetary value (or in kind) of the priestly portion and adding a fifth. He will also need to offer a ram for misappropriating the Lord's holy things according to the law of the guilt offering (Lev. 5:14–16). Priests are responsible for what occurs in their home and are admonished to respect the holiness of the sacred gifts even when outside the boundaries of the sanctuary. Their table is an extension of the Lord's table and should be guarded appropriately. Failure to do so will result in guilt for laymen in "eating their holy things" (22:16), that is, eating the holy things they had brought as sacrificial offerings to the Lord.

22:17–20 This section begins with a reminder to the priesthood and all worshipers that burnt offering sacrifices must be without defect to be acceptable, even if they are voluntary and not expiatory offerings. Up until this point sacrificial instructions have specified that animals must be *tamim*: whole, perfect, and "without blemish" (1:3; 3:1; 4:3; 5:15, et al.). The Lord adds to these instructions by enumerating blemishes that disqualify sacrificial animals. Offerings must conform to all the Lord's requirements to be accepted, so that in turn the worshiper may be accepted by the Lord (1:4; 19:5; 23:11). The theme of favorable acceptance strongly resonates throughout the remaining sacrificial laws (22:19, 20, 21, 23, 25, 27, 29).

Resident aliens are invited to offer sacrifices to Israel's God (17:8–9). It is the hope, as they live among God's people and experience the Lord's kindness through the covenant community (19:10, 33–34; Deut. 16:13–15), that they will be drawn to worship (1 Kings 8:41–43).

22:21–23 The instructions now turn from burnt offerings to peace offerings. The list of blemishes that disqualify a sacrificial animal from being offered on the altar corresponds directly to priestly blemishes that disqualify them from service (Lev. 21:18–20). The altar is holy and may be approached only by those who are whole. That both priest and sacrifice should be required to approach the Lord in perfection is not surprising. What is unexpected, however, is that the twelve blemishes forge an explicit association between priests and sacrificial animals through parallel blemishes.

The description proceeds in the order by which a priest might inspect an animal for ritual fitness: head, limbs, hide, and, finally, genitals. Both lists begin with blindness and end with genital damage, with a greater number of eye defects listed for priests and more testicular injuries for animals:[250]

TABLE 3.6: Priestly and Animal Blemishes

Priestly Blemishes	Animal Blemishes
blind, eye defect	blind
injured arm or leg, lame, mutilated	injured, maimed, mutilated
hunchback or dwarf	
itch, scab	discharge, itch, scab
extended limb	extended or contracted limb
crushed genitals	crushed, bruised, torn genitals

Certain exceptions can be made: an animal with a contracted or extended limb can be offered as a freewill peace offering, but not as a votive (dedicated) peace offering. Freewill offerings are a voluntary gift beyond the required tithe or firstfruits. A dedicatory vow, on the other hand, is the promise to devote something or someone to the Lord in answer to prayer (ch. 27). In keeping with the joyous spirit of the freewill offering's spontaneous nature a worshiper can sacrifice either a male or female animal and even one that is lame. A worshiper who has vowed to dedicate an animal to the Lord, however, has the time to select a healthy one to make good on his promise (cf. Mal. 1:7–8, 14).

22:24–25 The prohibition of offering an animal whose testicles are damaged may be related to Deuteronomy 23:1: "No one whose testicles are crushed or whose male organ is cut off shall enter the assembly of the LORD." Since the sign of the covenant is worn on the male organ, the organ must be whole (Gen. 17:10–11).[251]

Israelites are not to offer a blemished sacrificial animal purchased from a foreigner. This does not ban the purchase of whole and unblemished sacrifices, as

---

[250] The defects have been chiastically arranged: animal blemishes are in groupings of six, two, and four and priestly ones in groupings of four, two, and six (Hartley, *Leviticus*, 360).
[251] Prophetic hope holds out mercy for the eunuch who has put his faith in the Lord. He will be remembered in covenant faithfulness with a memorial *within* the temple ("in my house and within my walls"), making his name endure beyond a natural, physical genealogy (Isa. 56:4–5).

we may assume is the case with David, who purchases animals from Ornan the Jebusite to make an acceptable offering to the Lord (1 Chron. 21:21–27).

22:26–28 A newborn animal is to remain with its mother for seven days before it can be offered in sacrifice. On the eighth day it is an animal in its own right, independent of its mother and beginning life on its own, much like a male child, who is received into the covenant community through circumcision on the eighth day (12:3; Ex. 22:30).[252] Even after a newborn reaches maturity, it is not to be slaughtered on the same day as its mother. Israelites caring for their herds and flocks must be closely aware of family relationships to follow such a law. These commands have been taken as reflecting humanitarian concerns (cf. Ex. 23:5, 10–12; Deut. 22:6–7; Prov. 12:10).

22:29–30 A sacrifice made in thanksgiving must be consumed on the same day it is offered. Since the concern of these laws is to guard the holiness of offerings, it is possible that the time restriction will encourage worshipers to feast on holy ground in the vicinity of the tabernacle. This will prevent the meat from being brought into the common context of the household and becoming profaned. A holy meal is not to be confused with a common one.[253]

22:31–33 The concluding exhortation reminds Israelites that they have been redeemed from Egypt in order to find life in covenant relationship with the Lord. In this way he has set them apart as his own and given them a holy status and calling ("I am the LORD who sanctifies you"). They live out that calling as they obey his charge to "keep" (Hb. *shamar*) the Lord's commands, a charge that ties chapters 18–22 together (18:1–5, 24–30; 19:37; 20:7–8, 22–26). To "keep" (*shamar*) was Adam's priestly task in guarding the holiness of the garden sanctuary (Gen. 2:15). Israel is to guard the holy things of God brought to the tabernacle sanctuary by not treating them as common. In guarding them the Israelites set the Lord apart as the Holy One of Israel, the one worthy of holy worship by his holy and redeemed people.

Response

The sublime identification of the priestly body with that of a sacrificial offering foreshadows that in the fullness of time the priest will *become* the offering. In daily enactment at the altar Israel's sacrifices declare that redemption will come through a perfect sacrifice, a "lamb without blemish or spot" (1 Pet. 1:19), presided over by the perfect priest. Jesus comes to offer himself "without blemish to God" (Heb. 9:14)—through a perfect life, without sin—and to fulfill all that is anticipated in the old covenant. The love of God revealed in Christ sanctifies a people that he presents in worship as holy and without blemish: "Christ loved the church and

---

[252] The lives of their animals in ways mirror their own: the firstborn of the flock and herd is dedicated to the Lord, just as firstborn male children are (Ex. 13:2; 22:29–30).
[253] Allen P. Ross, *Holiness to the Lord: A Guide to the Exposition of the Book of Leviticus* (Grand Rapids, MI: Baker Academic, 2006), 394.

gave himself up for her, that he might sanctify her, having cleansed her by the washing of water with the word, so that he might present the church to himself in splendor, without spot or wrinkle or any such thing, that she might be holy and without blemish" (Eph. 5:25–27). The covenant relationship between the Lord and his people is held together by a holy and blameless sacrifice, one that is not desecrated but sanctified by both the Lord and his redeemed people.

Guarding the holiness of our corporate worship that shapes us into Christlikeness is still of the utmost importance, as demonstrated in the ministry of John Calvin. When he began pastoral ministry in Geneva at the age of twenty-seven, sexual infidelity was a tolerated sin in the church. Calvin stood firm to deny communion to a prominent church member who was overt about his mistress. The man appealed the decision to the city council and the following Sunday defiantly asserted his right to eat from the Lord's table. Calvin descended from the pulpit, flung his arms around the vessels to protect them from sacrilege, and cried out with a loud voice: "These hands you may crush, these arms you may lop off, my life you may take, my blood is yours, you may shed it; but you shall never force me to give holy things to the profaned, and dishonor the table of my God." "After this," attest eyewitnesses, "the sacred ordinance was celebrated with a profound silence, and under solemn awe in all present, as if the Deity Himself had been visible among them."[254] May the Lord give us a similar love and zeal to protect the honor of his worship!

LEVITICUS 23

23 The LORD spoke to Moses, saying, ² "Speak to the people of Israel and say to them, These are the appointed feasts of the LORD that you shall proclaim as holy convocations; they are my appointed feasts.

³ "Six days shall work be done, but on the seventh day is a Sabbath of solemn rest, a holy convocation. You shall do no work. It is a Sabbath to the LORD in all your dwelling places.

⁴ "These are the appointed feasts of the LORD, the holy convocations, which you shall proclaim at the time appointed for them. ⁵ In the first month, on the fourteenth day of the month at twilight,¹ is the LORD's Passover. ⁶ And on the fifteenth day of the same month is the Feast of Unleavened Bread to the LORD; for seven days you shall eat unleavened bread. ⁷ On the first day you shall have a holy convocation; you shall not do any ordinary work. ⁸ But you shall present a food offering to the LORD for seven days. On the seventh day is a holy convocation; you shall not do any ordinary work."

⁹ And the LORD spoke to Moses, saying, ¹⁰ "Speak to the people of Israel and say to them, When you come into the land that I give you and reap its

---

[254] Henry Henderson, *Calvin in His Letters* (Eugene, OR: Wipf & Stock, 1996), 78.

harvest, you shall bring the sheaf of the firstfruits of your harvest to the priest, ¹¹ and he shall wave the sheaf before the Lord, so that you may be accepted. On the day after the Sabbath the priest shall wave it. ¹² And on the day when you wave the sheaf, you shall offer a male lamb a year old without blemish as a burnt offering to the Lord. ¹³ And the grain offering with it shall be two tenths of an ephah[2] of fine flour mixed with oil, a food offering to the Lord with a pleasing aroma, and the drink offering with it shall be of wine, a fourth of a hin.[3] ¹⁴ And you shall eat neither bread nor grain parched or fresh until this same day, until you have brought the offering of your God: it is a statute forever throughout your generations in all your dwellings.

¹⁵ "You shall count seven full weeks from the day after the Sabbath, from the day that you brought the sheaf of the wave offering. ¹⁶ You shall count fifty days to the day after the seventh Sabbath. Then you shall present a grain offering of new grain to the Lord. ¹⁷ You shall bring from your dwelling places two loaves of bread to be waved, made of two tenths of an ephah. They shall be of fine flour, and they shall be baked with leaven, as firstfruits to the Lord. ¹⁸ And you shall present with the bread seven lambs a year old without blemish, and one bull from the herd and two rams. They shall be a burnt offering to the Lord, with their grain offering and their drink offerings, a food offering with a pleasing aroma to the Lord. ¹⁹ And you shall offer one male goat for a sin offering, and two male lambs a year old as a sacrifice of peace offerings. ²⁰ And the priest shall wave them with the bread of the firstfruits as a wave offering before the Lord, with the two lambs. They shall be holy to the Lord for the priest. ²¹ And you shall make a proclamation on the same day. You shall hold a holy convocation. You shall not do any ordinary work. It is a statute forever in all your dwelling places throughout your generations.

²² "And when you reap the harvest of your land, you shall not reap your field right up to its edge, nor shall you gather the gleanings after your harvest. You shall leave them for the poor and for the sojourner: I am the Lord your God."

²³ And the Lord spoke to Moses, saying, ²⁴ "Speak to the people of Israel, saying, In the seventh month, on the first day of the month, you shall observe a day of solemn rest, a memorial proclaimed with blast of trumpets, a holy convocation. ²⁵ You shall not do any ordinary work, and you shall present a food offering to the Lord."

²⁶ And the Lord spoke to Moses, saying, ²⁷ "Now on the tenth day of this seventh month is the Day of Atonement. It shall be for you a time of holy convocation, and you shall afflict yourselves[4] and present a food offering to the Lord. ²⁸ And you shall not do any work on that very day, for it is a Day of Atonement, to make atonement for you before the Lord your God. ²⁹ For whoever is not afflicted[5] on that very day shall be cut off from his people. ³⁰ And whoever does any work on that very day, that person I will destroy from among his people. ³¹ You shall not do any work. It is a statute forever throughout your generations in all your dwelling places. ³² It shall be to you a Sabbath of solemn rest, and you shall afflict yourselves. On the ninth day of the month beginning at evening, from evening to evening shall you keep your Sabbath."

³³ And the Lord spoke to Moses, saying, ³⁴ "Speak to the people of Israel, saying, On the fifteenth day of this seventh month and for seven days is the Feast of Booths[6] to the Lord. ³⁵ On the first day shall be a holy con-

vocation; you shall not do any ordinary work. ³⁶ For seven days you shall present food offerings to the Lord. On the eighth day you shall hold a holy convocation and present a food offering to the Lord. It is a solemn assembly; you shall not do any ordinary work.

³⁷ "These are the appointed feasts of the Lord, which you shall proclaim as times of holy convocation, for presenting to the Lord food offerings, burnt offerings and grain offerings, sacrifices and drink offerings, each on its proper day, ³⁸ besides the Lord's Sabbaths and besides your gifts and besides all your vow offerings and besides all your freewill offerings, which you give to the Lord.

³⁹ "On the fifteenth day of the seventh month, when you have gathered in the produce of the land, you shall celebrate the feast of the Lord seven days. On the first day shall be a solemn rest, and on the eighth day shall be a solemn rest. ⁴⁰ And you shall take on the first day the fruit of splendid trees, branches of palm trees and boughs of leafy trees and willows of the brook, and you shall rejoice before the Lord your God seven days. ⁴¹ You shall celebrate it as a feast to the Lord for seven days in the year. It is a statute forever throughout your generations; you shall celebrate it in the seventh month. ⁴² You shall dwell in booths for seven days. All native Israelites shall dwell in booths, ⁴³ that your generations may know that I made the people of Israel dwell in booths when I brought them out of the land of Egypt: I am the Lord your God."

⁴⁴ Thus Moses declared to the people of Israel the appointed feasts of the Lord.

¹ Hebrew *between the two evenings* ² An *ephah* was about 3/5 bushel or 22 liters ³ A *hin* was about 4 quarts or 3.5 liters ⁴ Or *shall fast*; also verse 32 ⁵ Or *is not fasting* ⁶ Or *Tabernacles*

Section Overview

Israel's calendar for holy living revolves around the saving acts of God and the right response to his mercy.[255] The Lord ordains a rhythm of sacred time that shapes Israel's identity and makes her into a holy people. The calendar is set with "appointed times" (Hb. *mo'ed*), language that picks up the idiom of creation. God fashioned the heavenly lights to serve "for signs and for seasons [*mo'ed*; i.e., appointed times], and for days and years" (Gen. 1:14). Creation itself is put to the service of marking out special times for the worship of the Creator. Seasonal feasts orient the nation toward the Lord and synchronize every Israelite to celebrate in community as well as in continuity with his forefathers. Israel's present is lived out in light of God's faithfulness in the past and his promises for the future.

The chapter's arrangement shows that the year is divided into two halves. In the spring the first-month holy days include Passover, Unleavened Bread, and Firstfruits. In the fall the seventh-month holy days include Trumpets, Day of Atonement, and Booths. The two cycles of spring and fall festivals conclude with the declaration "I am the Lord your God" (Lev. 23:22, 43), structuring

---

[255] In the Pentateuch are several other iterations of the calendar, each with a certain focus depending on its context. Exodus 23:14–17 and 34:18–26 emphasize the pilgrimage festivals, Numbers 28–29 enumerates the offerings for each festival, while Deuteronomy 16:1–17 considers celebrations from the perspective of the community and highlights the centrality of the sanctuary. Leviticus 23 treats Israel's celebrations from the perspective of holy time.

the chapter and signaling that sacred time is a revelation of the Lord. A closer look at the calendar reveals a subtle progression of redemptive themes: God as Creator (vv. 1–3), God as Deliverer (vv. 4–8), God as Sustainer (vv. 9–22), God as Remember-er (vv. 23–25), God as Forgiver (vv. 26–32), and God as Ingatherer (vv. 33–43). The festivals are an appointment to meet with the Lord and to know him in covenant relationship.

Section Outline

VII. Holy Institutions (21:1–27:34) . . .

    C. Calendar (23:1–44)

        1. Introduction to Appointed Times (23:1–2)

        2. Sabbath (23:3)

        3. Feast of Passover and Unleavened Bread (23:4–8)

        4. Feast of Firstfruits (23:9–14)

        5. Feast of Weeks (23:15–22)

        6. Feast of Trumpets (23:23–25)

        7. Day of Atonement (23:26–32)

        8. Feast of Booths (23:33–43)

        9. Conclusion (23:44)

Comment

23:1–2 Israel's festival calendar is the Lord's invitation to meet together at regular times. Moses is to make known the times the Lord has ordained as holy, and in turn the people are to join in proclaiming them as holy. In this way Israel's calendar sets seasonal appointments with the Lord as a continuing call to worship. Appointed meeting times (Hb. *moʿed*) echo the language of the tent of meeting (*moʿed*). As the tabernacle marks out sacred space, so the calendar marks out sacred time that the Lord will inhabit with his people as a "sanctuary in time."[256]

23:3 The calendar of holy days begins with sacred time ordained at creation: "God blessed the seventh day and *made it* holy" (Gen. 2:3). The Lord sanctifies the Sabbath and commands his covenant people "to *keep it* holy" (Ex. 20:8). Israel is invited to enter into God's rest by observing a total cessation from its labors. In doing so Israel images its Sovereign, who ceased from his work at the beginning of time. Israel celebrates "in all your dwelling places," that is, in homes gathered with families. Holy time is lived out in every Israelite household as a weekly reorientation to the Lord's sovereignty and as a reminder of the covenant that makes Israel his holy people (Ex. 31:13).

The Lord establishes sacred times and Israel responds to observe them so that both God and his people participate in setting apart those times as "holy." The Sabbath models a meeting together in time that will serve as a pattern for the

---

[256] My paraphrase of Abraham Joshua Heschel's designation of the Sabbath as a "palace in time." *The Sabbath: Its Meaning for Modern Man* (New York: Farrar, Straus & Giroux, 2005).

rest of the appointed feasts throughout the year. The Sabbath pattern leaves its imprint on all other holy days that are observed with either a complete (as here) or a partial day of rest (cf. comment on 23:6–8). As holy time celebrated on the seventh day, the Sabbath begins the cycle of seven appointed feasts. The number seven features prominently in each half of the calendar in celebrations of a seven-day festival (Unleavened Bread in the spring and Feast of Booths in the fall). Seven weeks are counted off from the elevation of the firstfruits to the celebration of the Feast of Weeks. This intentional patterning ties all Israel's appointed feasts back to creation. Israel's sacred calendar envisions created time as a dimension in which to meet with God.

23:4 An introduction to the appointed feasts the Sabbath has heralded opens the treatment of the calendar.

23:5 The Lord's deliverance of his people inaugurates the cycle of Israel's appointed feasts. This is the first month of the ritual calendar, signaling that Israel was given new life as a redeemed people (Ex. 12:2).[257] The Passover and Unleavened Bread are two distinct feasts that nevertheless commemorate the same historic saving act. These festivals bring forward into the present Yahweh's deliverance so that it continues to shape Israel's covenant identity.

The Passover begins at "twilight," the very time when on that momentous night in Egypt all Israel slaughtered its lambs as the prelude to freedom (Ex. 12:6). Israelites reenact the sacrifice that delivered them and through the ceremonial Passover meal pass down the story of their redemption to the next generation (Ex. 12:24–27). It is celebrated for one day and is the first of the three pilgrimage feasts, which also include the Feast of Weeks (Pentecost) and the Feast of Booths.

23:6–8 The following day begins the Feast of Unleavened Bread, which is observed for seven days, including holy convocations at its beginning and its conclusion, when all work is forbidden except for the preparation of food (cf. Ex. 12:16).[258] During this time Israelites eat unleavened bread to commemorate their hasty passage out of Egypt, when they packed their dough before it had been leavened (Ex. 12:39). Memory of the exodus that is marked first by eating the Passover meal continues for seven days by eating bread with no leaven.

23:9–11 In this ceremony of "firsts" the first yield of the land is offered on the first day of the week, on the Sunday following the beginning of the barley harvest.[259] The feast anticipates dwelling in the land promised to the patriarchs by commanding the offering of its yield to the Lord as an act of worship. The offerer brings a sheaf from his harvest to the sanctuary for the priest to lift heavenward in

---

[257] Later known as the month of Nisan, it begins in March or April.
[258] This suggests that the phrase "ordinary work" (Lev. 23:7) refers to the regular work one does to make a living (such as farming).
[259] "On the day after the Sabbath" could possibly be interpreted as referencing the Sabbath following the Feast of Unleavened Bread. Since Leviticus 23:9 begins a new speech, however, it is best taken as not being tied to the previous feast. The barley harvest in the land of Canaan comes in the early spring, around April, the time of the celebration of Passover and Unleavened Bread.

a gesture of presentation,²⁶⁰ while the worshiper makes the following declaration of the Lord's faithfulness:

> The LORD brought us out of Egypt with a mighty hand and an outstretched arm, with great deeds of terror, with signs and wonders. And he brought us into this place and gave us this land, a land flowing with milk and honey. And behold, now I bring the first of the fruit of the ground, which you, O LORD, have given me. (Deut. 26:8–10)

The worshiper's confession brings the Lord's past saving acts into the present as he lives out the fulfillment of God's promises to his forefathers.

23:12–13 The worshiping community brings a male yearling lamb together with grain and drink offerings to accompany the presentation of firstfruits. The offering closely resembles the daily offering at the sanctuary, with the addition of an extra portion of grain (*two* tenth measures of fine flour; cf. Ex. 29:40). The amount of grain is double that of the daily offering, likely in celebration of the harvest.

23:14 This is an important ceremony and joyous occasion for Israelites, who may eat of the land's yield only after it has first been offered to the Lord. Before anyone may benefit from its sustenance the first portion of the new crop is offered to God in recognition that it is *he* who feeds his people from the fruit of the earth (cf. Gen. 1:29; Ps. 145:15–16). The first yield of the first harvest acknowledges symbolically all that the worshipers have and all that they are belong to the Lord. To honor him by giving him priority invites the blessing of abundance intended for humanity (cf. Gen. 1:28; Prov. 3:9–10). Only then may Israel eat "in all your dwellings"—worship in God's presence affects life at home.

23:15–16a The Feast of Weeks follows "seven full weeks" after the beginning of the barley harvest to celebrate the firstfruits of the wheat harvest (which would occur in May or June). Although it remains unnamed here, the feast is known from other portions of Scripture as the Feast of the Harvest (Ex. 23:16) or the Feast of Weeks (Ex. 34:22; Deut. 16:10). The feast may be more familiar by its designation as Pentecost, deriving from the Greek *pentēkostos*, meaning "fifty" (Acts 2:1), because of counting off fifty days from when the first sheaf is presented to the Lord.²⁶¹ It lasts for one day and always falls on a Sunday ("the day after the seventh Sabbath"), the first day of the week.

23:16b–17 Israelites present to the Lord an elevation offering of two loaves of leavened bread baked of flour from the wheat harvest. While it is a single sheaf

---

260 For "wave" (Lev. 23:11) cf. comment on 7:28–30. As noted there, the action represented here is best understood as an upward motion of elevating the worshiper's gift to heaven rather than a right-to-left waving motion. This gesture symbolizes a complete dedication to the realm of the holy; the raising up to heaven "indicates the transfer of the offering from the profane to the sacred, from the offerer's domain to God's." Jacob Milgrom, *Studies in Cultic Theology and Terminology*, SJLA, vol. 36, ed. Jacob Neusner (Leiden: Brill, 1983), 158.
261 Seven weeks from the day following the first day of the festival equals forty-nine days. So why is Pentecost celebrated as day 50? If the first Sunday is counted as day 1, then the seventh Sunday would be day 50 in inclusive reckoning. Cf. Sklar, *Leviticus*, TOTC, 283n7.

that is elevated at the beginning of the grain harvest, loaves of bread are elevated at its end. Israel's worship is a concrete image that whatever the Lord provides to grow out of the ground the people offer back to him, joining their work to his in creation.

23:18–21 A burnt offering again accompanies the wave offering, this one of seven lambs (perhaps one for each week), two rams, and one bull. To this is added a sin offering to make atonement and a peace offering to celebrate restored fellowship.

23:22 Festivals around the grain harvest naturally give rise to the commandment to cultivate the land and harvest its crops in a manner that will sustain all who dwell in it, from the land owner to the poor among God's people. A segment of one's fields must remain unreaped and their harvested portions ungleaned in order to provide for the poor and sojourner. Gratitude for the harvest is lived out in imitation of the Lord, who provides for his people from the yield of the land.

23:23–25 This feast is commemorated with blasts of the trumpet to signal the beginning of the cycle of holy days in the seventh month (which would fall in September or October). During her wilderness sojourns trumpet blasts summoned Israel to assemble before the Lord or to break camp for setting out in her divisions to follow his lead (Num. 10:3–8). The Feast of Trumpets is both an announcement and a summons. It announces the arrival of the seventh month, the holiest month of the year, and summons Israel to prepare to meet with the Lord by participating in sacred time.

The feast is a *memorial*. According to Numbers 10:10 blasts of the ram's horn serve as a reminder of Israel before her God on every feast day. Reminders are significant in the covenant relationship between the Lord and his people, and both covenant partners are given reminders of their obligations to the other. Festivals, holy convocations, and tassels on garments assure a remembrance that is not merely cognitive for Israel but leads to obedience: "Remember all the commandments of the LORD, *to do them*" (Num. 15:39). When the Lord in turn remembers his covenant, he does so for blessing: "For their sake he remembered his covenant, and relented according to the abundance of his steadfast love" (Ps. 106:45; cf. Lev. 26:42–45; Ps. 105:8). Within the context of Israel's worship remembrance is a sign of continued relationship: "God's memory is not a re-creating of the past, but a continuation of the self-same purpose."[262]

23:26–28 The Day of Atonement ceremonies are described in full in chapter 16. The interest of the festival calendar is to bring into focus the people's responsibility to observe a time of fasting and ceasing from their work in the seventh month, on the tenth day. On this day, Israelites are to "afflict themselves," that is, to fast and humble themselves in sorrow over their sin as they petition the Lord in complete dependence (cf. comment on 16:29–31).

---

[262] Brevard S. Childs, *Memory and Tradition in Israel* (Naperville, IL: Allenson, 1962), 42.

23:29–30 The gravity of this day is reflected by the severity of punishment for not observing it as the Lord commands. Anyone who does not humble himself in fasting and repentance before the Lord will be cut off from his people, and anyone who does any work will be destroyed by the Lord.[263] Stated otherwise, these commands teach that repentance is necessary for forgiveness and that atonement is the work not of man but of God. He who does not humble himself will not receive cleansing from sin and has in effect already cut himself off from the Lord.

23:31–32 The Day of Atonement is observed for only one day, yet this day is one of the most important in the calendar and designated a Sabbath of complete rest.

23:33–36 The Feast of Booths marks the high point of celebrations. It is inaugurated on the fifteenth day of the seventh month by a holy convocation around which no work is done. Sacrificial offerings are made on each of its seven days, and it concludes with another holy convocation on day eight. It is also called the Feast of Ingathering, as implied by verse 39, which refers to gathering the land's produce (Ex. 23:16; 34:22).

23:37–38 For a moment the passage takes its eyes off the Feast of Booths to speak of the importance of bringing all the offerings of these festivals "each on its proper day" (Lev. 23:37) and to make clear that these are in addition to other regular offerings that are made (v. 38).

23:39–41 The passage now returns to the Feast of Booths. Native Israelites whose forefathers came out of Egypt are commanded to construct huts of leafy boughs as temporary dwellings to commemorate their time journeying to the Promised Land. Appointed feasts are an opportunity for each Israelite to relive in his or her own generation the historic saving acts of God. Remembering the past by enacting it in the present teaches Israel that she is a sojourning people, a worshiping community whose journey with Yahweh continues even after having received the land of its inheritance.

Rejoicing is commanded as part of the celebration in the same way that constructing booths is: "You shall rejoice before the Lord your God seven days." It is remarkable that only five days after humbling herself in fasting and repentance Israel is commanded to rejoice. Can joy indeed be mandated? It seems so (cf. Neh. 8:9–12). In the Scriptures rejoicing is more than an emotional state or attitude of the heart. To rejoice is an embodied act of obedience expressed in approaching the Lord with offerings at the sanctuary (Deut. 12:12; 14:26; cf. 2 Cor. 9:6–7).[264] The heart is trained to rejoice in the Lord through the offering of worship.

23:42–43 Israel's calendar of appointed feasts concludes with exceedingly great joy. Celebration is catechism, given so that "your generations may know." Living out

---

[263] To be "cut off" is to experience exile or premature death (cf. comment on 7:19–21).
[264] Gary A. Anderson, *A Time to Mourn, A Time to Dance: The Expression of Grief and Joy in Israelite Religion* (State College, PA: Pennsylvania State University Press, 1991), 20.

the Lord's commands leads to knowing him. All Israel is brought together in God's appointed times to embed in his people the redemptive story that shapes their covenant identity. It is during the Feast of Booths that the Law is read every seven years (Deut. 31:10–13; cf. Neh. 8:1). In postexilic times the Feast of Ingathering acquires an eschatological flavor, undergirding the expectation that time, though cyclical, is also moving toward an ultimate end or goal that includes the ingathering of the nations in the spirit of joyful worship (Zech. 14:16–21).

23:44 Moses has faithfully relayed the festivals of Israel's calendar as the Lord has commanded him.

Response

Israel's life is ordered around a day of rest and a succession of festivals at appointed times that cultivate the expectation of meeting with the Lord. The Lord ordains the seasons, and the Israelites' response of glad obedience brings Israel and the Lord together in sacred time. Israel's worship requires faith, whether it is rest from one's labor, offering the cultivated fruit of the land, actively humbling oneself, or constructing and dwelling in booths. In all this the people enact the redemptive narrative that the Lord has written into the history of the world. They meet him in the feasts as Creator (Sabbath), Deliverer (Passover/Unleavened Bread), Sustainer (Firstfruits/Weeks), Forgiver of sins (Day of Atonement), and Ingatherer (Booths). Israel lives out her covenant identity in light of her worship, acknowledging her dependence and gratitude to the Lord and holding him as her highest joy. Worship is formative: through meeting with the Lord in these holy times Israel is formed into a holy people.

The regular cycle of festivals celebrated week after week and year after year builds anticipation that the Lord will appear to meet with his people at the appointed time. This rhythm of life finds ultimate fulfillment in Christ: "When the fullness of time had come, God sent forth his Son" (Gal. 4:4). The incarnate Son of God enters into time to reveal himself through Israel's feasts as the one to whom they pointed and that he comes to fulfill. Jesus is revealed as Lord of the Sabbath, healing and restoring his creation on the seventh day (Matt. 12:8–13). He is the Passover Lamb, who inaugurates a new covenant in his blood (Luke 22:14–20; 1 Cor. 5:6–8) and offers his life as a ransom for many (Mark 10:45). His sacrificial death on a cross at the Passover reveals him to be God's appointed Redeemer and Forgiver. Christ is the firstfruits of the resurrection (1 Cor. 15:20), elevated before the Father on Sunday, the first day of the week, in order to inaugurate the new creation. He is the Sustainer who feeds his people with the bread of life, which is his own body (John 6). He is the Lord of the harvest who commissions his church on Pentecost. Christ will come again as the Ingatherer to bring God's kingdom to fulfillment and time itself to its ultimate goal of God's rest (Matt. 11:28; Heb. 4:9–10).

Time is not an abstract measurement in the biblical worldview. It is created as a dimension through which to know the Lord (Gen. 1:14). Time must never be thought of as our own possession to save or give according to our own discretion. It belongs to God and is ordered by him to serve the purpose of our covenant relationship. As Christians, we take our own journey through seasons of appointed time to meet with the Lord, offer him our worship, and remember who we are as the church. Regular gatherings on Sunday, weekly or monthly celebrations of being hosted at the Lord's table, and rhythms throughout the year can tell the story of redemption and prepare our hearts to encounter the God of our salvation. Holy rhythms of life are formative in building our identity in Christ. As the church commemorates the saving acts of our Lord Jesus, it is fitting to approach these appointed times with genuine anticipation of being met by him. Our weekly worship most significantly testifies that we have entered a new time, the first day of the week, signaling the new creation in Christ. Our gathering as a church around the globe testifies that all time is destined for consummation in the worship of God and that we are a people whose ultimate destiny is to be participants in the eternal liturgy of the heavenly kingdom.

LEVITICUS 24

24 The Lord spoke to Moses, saying, 2 "Command the people of Israel to bring you pure oil from beaten olives for the lamp, that a light may be kept burning regularly. 3 Outside the veil of the testimony, in the tent of meeting, Aaron shall arrange it from evening to morning before the Lord regularly. It shall be a statute forever throughout your generations. 4 He shall arrange the lamps on the lampstand of pure gold¹ before the Lord regularly.

5 "You shall take fine flour and bake twelve loaves from it; two tenths of an ephah² shall be in each loaf. 6 And you shall set them in two piles, six in a pile, on the table of pure gold³ before the Lord. 7 And you shall put pure frankincense on each pile, that it may go with the bread as a memorial portion as a food offering to the Lord. 8 Every Sabbath day Aaron shall arrange it before the Lord regularly; it is from the people of Israel as a covenant forever. 9 And it shall be for Aaron and his sons, and they shall eat it in a holy place, since it is for him a most holy portion out of the Lord's food offerings, a perpetual due."

10 Now an Israelite woman's son, whose father was an Egyptian, went out among the people of Israel. And the Israelite woman's son and a man of Israel fought in the camp, 11 and the Israelite woman's son blasphemed the Name, and cursed. Then they brought him to Moses. His mother's name was Shelomith, the daughter of Dibri, of the tribe of Dan. 12 And they put him in custody, till the will of the Lord should be clear to them.

13 Then the Lord spoke to Moses, saying, 14 "Bring out of the camp the one who cursed, and let all who heard him lay their hands on his head, and let all the congregation stone him. 15 And speak to the people of Israel,

saying, Whoever curses his God shall bear his sin. ¹⁶ Whoever blasphemes the name of the LORD shall surely be put to death. All the congregation shall stone him. The sojourner as well as the native, when he blasphemes the Name, shall be put to death.

¹⁷ "Whoever takes a human life shall surely be put to death. ¹⁸ Whoever takes an animal's life shall make it good, life for life. ¹⁹ If anyone injures his neighbor, as he has done it shall be done to him, ²⁰ fracture for fracture, eye for eye, tooth for tooth; whatever injury he has given a person shall be given to him. ²¹ Whoever kills an animal shall make it good, and whoever kills a person shall be put to death. ²² You shall have the same rule for the sojourner and for the native, for I am the LORD your God." ²³ So Moses spoke to the people of Israel, and they brought out of the camp the one who had cursed and stoned him with stones. Thus the people of Israel did as the LORD commanded Moses.

¹ Hebrew *the pure lampstand* ² An *ephah* was about 3/5 bushel or 22 liters ³ Hebrew *the pure table*

Section Overview

After setting the rhythm for meeting with the Lord in regular appointed times throughout the year Moses now turns to the daily and weekly rituals through which Yahweh makes himself known. The subject of this chapter is the manifest presence of God in the midst of his people. It is divided into two parts: ritual prescriptions concerning God's dwelling place (vv. 1–9) and a narrative concerning judgment on a blasphemer (vv. 10–23). The theme of sacred time subtly continues in the regular lighting of the lampstand and arrangement of the bread of the Presence. As the chapter unfolds, the case of the blasphemer may initially appear to be out of place. Yet there is a thematic inner logic in contrasting human activity that invites God's indwelling presence with that which endangers it. The narrative introduces tension over the real danger of losing Yahweh's abiding presence and then resolves it through the actions of the community.

As part of the book that deals with holiness, the scope of vision in these chapters moves from the outside in with ever-increasing proximity to the source of all holiness in God. There is a steady progression of holiness that begins with the covenant people (chs. 19–20), moves in to the priestly circle (21:1–22:16), touches on the sacrifices offered in the outer court (22:17–33) and the appointed times that occasion them (ch. 23), extends to the oil and bread inside the tent (24:1–9), and finally reaches the name of the Lord, whose presence fills the Most Holy Place (24:10–23).[265]

Section Outline

VII. Holy Institutions (21:1–27:34) . . .
    D. Tent of Meeting (24:1–23)
        1. Kindling the Lamps of the Lampstand (24:1–4)
        2. Setting Out the Bread of the Presence (24:5–9)
        3. The Crime of Blaspheming the Name (24:10–23)

---

[265] Kleinig, *Leviticus*, 514.

Comment

24:1–4 The Lord speaks to Moses, and Moses in turn speaks to God's people regarding the regular offerings for the sanctuary. The people are tasked with providing "pure oil"[266] for the lampstand and "fine flour" for the bread on the table (v. 5). Of all Israel's prescribed offerings (chs. 1–7) the oil and flour are unique in that they are brought into the Holy Place, nearest to God's presence. The lampstand's light is to burn "regularly" (Hb. *tamid*), in daily repetition from evening to morning.[267] Every morning the attending priest is to fill the lamps with fresh oil, and every evening he is to light them (cf. 1 Sam. 3:3). The ritual is performed in the inner sanctuary at the same time as the burning of incense on the golden altar before the veil (Ex. 30:7).

The lampstand is set on the southern wall, before the veil that separates the throne room of God (Ex. 40:24), and is solid gold, crafted as a "single piece of hammered work of pure gold" (Ex. 25:36).[268] It is designed as a single shaft, with three branches on either side decorated with almond blossoms, calyxes, and flowers (Ex. 25:31–40). Seven lamps are placed atop the lampstand, "set up so as to give light on the space in front of it" (Ex. 25:37). The lampstand visually resembles a stylized tree.[269] When the lampstand is lit, it is a tree ablaze in reflective gold. Taken on its own it recalls the manifest presence of God, who appears to Moses from within the burning bush (Ex. 3:4). Viewed in its setting in sacred space the lampstand is aglow in a room filled with a smoky cloud of incense that partly veils its fire and light, re-creating the pillar of cloud and fire that attended Israel on her journeys. Laymen would not have seen the lampstand in the Holy Place. Instead, as they gazed at the tabernacle in the evenings, they would have seen the diffusing of soft light and smoke from the edges of the layered tent, replicating the fire and cloud on Sinai and communicating that Yahweh is among his people. It may have been the Lord's intention for the lampstand to reproduce a "little theophany, the nightly theophany that corresponded to his daily theophany in fire at the altar (Lev. 9:23–24)."[270]

24:5–6 The fine flour is an offering from the community for baking twelve loaves, two tenths of an ephah each.[271] The loaves are most commonly referred to as the "bread of the Presence" (Ex. 25:30; 35:13; 39:36) since they are placed "before the LORD" (i.e., in his immediate presence).[272] The bread is set in two "piles" (or

---

[266] The finest quality oil was obtained from olives beaten in a vat by hand. The pulp was then placed in baskets that were stacked on top of stone slabs with grooves around the edges and pressed by weighted beams, expelling the oil into storage jars. The sanctuary's sacred oil was skimmed from the first beating before being crushed in the olive press. Cf. Lawrence E. Stager and Samuel R. Wolff, "Production and Commerce in Temple Courtyards: An Olive Press in the Sacred Precinct at Tel Dan," *BASOR* 243 (1981): 96.

[267] Some versions translate *tamid* as "continually," but its sense is regular, repeated ritual acts rather than a rite that goes on perpetually; Menahem Haran, *Temples and Temple-Service: An Inquiry into the Character of Cult Phenomena and the Historical Setting of the Priestly School* (Oxford: Oxford University Press, 1979), 207.

[268] The other furniture in the Holy Place (altar of incense and table of showbread) are crafted of acacia wood and overlaid with gold. The lampstand is fashioned of solid gold.

[269] Carol Meyers, "Lampstand," *ABD*, 4:141–143.

[270] Kleinig, *Leviticus*, 517.

[271] The loaves are generous, made of two tenths of an ephah, which amounts to sixteen cups of flour per loaf. It is likely they are baked without leaven, like the grain offerings brought to the sacrificial altar (Lev. 2:11).

[272] Elsewhere their mention is found as the "regular showbread" (Num. 4:7) because they are set out at a fixed time, once a week. "Rows of showbread" is another designation (Neh. 10:33), no doubt because of its arrangement on the golden table.

"arrangements") on the table of acacia wood overlaid with pure gold. The table stands opposite the lampstand, on the northern wall of the Holy Place. Though not explicitly stated, it is understood that the twelve loaves represent the twelve tribes.

24:7 Each pile of six loaves is topped with pure frankincense as a "memorial portion." The frankincense marks this as a special type of grain offering to the Lord that nonetheless is shared with his consecrated priests. The incense is likely burned on the small golden altar of the inner sanctuary as a token portion (cf. Lev. 2:2).

24:8–9 Fresh loaves are laid out on the Sabbath, the day on which the people cease from their labors to enjoy the hospitality of the Lord. While the people rest, the Lord lays out a table for the week ahead, ensuring his presence and provision (cf. Ps. 23:5). The priests eat the old loaves on behalf of all Israel in a holy place. The pattern for representatively eating a meal in God's presence was set when the Lord brought Israel into covenant relationship with himself at Sinai. A select group—Moses, Aaron and his sons, and seventy elders—was invited to approach halfway up the mountain and there enjoy Yahweh's hospitality. They were granted access to the place of his feet and feasted on a covenant meal in his presence (Ex. 24:9–11). Once God's presence descends to fill the tent patterned as an enduring Sinai, the priesthood representatively sits at the table with the Lord to eat the bread of the covenant on behalf of the people. In this way arranging the loaves for sharing a meal before the Lord points to the covenant-making ceremony at Sinai. It is perpetuated in the tabernacle as a tangible sign of Yahweh's covenant presence, memorializing and enacting "a covenant forever." It is not lost on us that the sign of the covenant is the offering brought by the "people of Israel," the human agency in the divine-human relationship.

24:10–11 The subject now turns to an incident involving a man from a mixed marriage.[273] In contrast with the Israelite mother, whose name and lineage are given, her son remains unnamed. In a narrative whose subject is the "Name" that sanctifies all Israel this may be an important detail foreshadowing that the blasphemer will be cut off from the community and his name blotted out from under heaven (cf. Ex. 32:33).

The quarrel between the half-Israelite and the Israelite in the camp is not given much explanation, but we are not left with the impression that the Lord's name was uttered in a heated moment.[274] Rather it was deliberate contempt for the God of Israel. In Israel's experience the name of Yahweh is a revelation of his identity (Ex. 34:6–7). It is entrusted to his people in covenant relationship (Ex. 3:14–15) and is the means by which he displays to the nations his power to save (Ex. 7:5; 9:16). The divine name defines Israel as a people set apart to the Lord for blessing:

---

[273] In biblical times descent was traced through the father as reflected in the genealogies of the Bible. In modern times Jewish descent is traced through the maternal line.
[274] Two verbs are brought together to represent a single action, thereby intensifying their meaning: "He pronounced by cursing blasphemously" (Levine, *Leviticus*, 166). Later Jewish tradition forbids the very use of the divine name in an effort to protect its sanctity and to avoid inadvertently making light of the Holy One of Israel.

"So shall they put my name upon the people of Israel, and I will bless them" (Num. 6:27). Israel's identity as a people is tied to his. To misuse Yahweh's name is not to utter a forbidden word but to malign the very person of God, who is represented by his name. It is "to treat his gift lightly, to underestimate his power, to scorn his Presence, and to misrepresent to the family of humankind his very nature as 'The One Who Always Is.'"[275]

24:12 In the case of an Israelite the law forbids cursing the Lord (Ex. 22:28) and spells out judgment in the Ten Commandments: "The LORD will not hold him guiltless who takes his name in vain" (Ex. 20:7).[276] Treating his name without regard for its sanctity is a violation of the covenant and a capital crime. But what about the nations? Will they be held accountable? Moses thus seeks the Lord's wisdom for the unprecedented case of how to judge the one who has cursed the divine name if he is not a full-fledged Israelite. (The ruling given in Lev. 24:16, 22, with its mention of the "sojourner," clarifies that this is the nature of the legal problem.)[277]

24:13–16 All who are witnesses to the sacrilege are called to place their hands on the offender's head so that he will "bear his sin" (cf. 5:1). This gesture conveys the antithesis of the sacrificial system, which provides the means for sin to be borne by an animal substitute to atone for the sinner (cf. discussion in chapter 16). Instead of the sin's being placed on a substitute, he who has defiantly sinned against Yahweh must bear his own guilt. In such a case "his iniquity shall be on him" (Num. 15:31), and he must be punished accordingly. The laying of hands on the blasphemer's head acknowledges that he bears his guilt upon his own head and that the witnesses are absolved of the blood guilt in executing him.[278] As expressed in Deuteronomy, "The hand of the witnesses shall be first against him to put him to death, and afterward the hand of all the people. So you shall purge the evil from your midst" (Deut. 17:7).[279] "All the congregation" participates in executing the blasphemer and takes action together to remove evil from its midst.

24:17–22 The case of blasphemy occasions the introduction of the laws found in the following verses. Legal material in the Bible is always set within the context of narrative, underscoring that Israel's laws are not abstract principles but a national charter given in the context of *covenant relationship* (cf. Deut. 4:7–8). All law proceeds from the Lord, who elected Israel as his very own people and gave them his statutes for holy living. It is personal. The laws (including Lev. 24:16b) are arranged as a chiasm:[280]

---

275 Durham, *Exodus*, 288.
276 To take the Lord's name "in vain" is idiomatic for equating the name of Yahweh with vanity, that which is trivial and fleeting. This is the opposite of God's glory, which is expressed in terms of weight and value. Yahweh's fame and reputation in the world is at stake in how his people treat his name. To treat Israel's sovereign without deference and respect is tantamount to treason.
277 For another case in which Moses seeks the Lord due to lack of precedent cf. Numbers 15:32–36.
278 A similar gesture is found in Deuteronomy 21:6–9; in that instance, since the perpetrator remains unknown, the elders symbolically wash their hands of the blood guilt of the slain.
279 Cf. the martyrdom of Stephen, who is executed for blasphemy by stoning outside the city (Acts 7:54–60).
280 Hartley, *Leviticus*, 405–406; Wenham, *Leviticus*, 312.

    (A) one law for sojourner and native (v. 16b)
        (B) death for taking a man's life (v. 17)
            (C) restitution for taking an animal's life (v. 18)
                (D) lex talionis ("eye for an eye"; vv. 19–20)
            (C') restitution for taking an animal's life (v. 21a)
        (B') death for taking a man's life (v. 21b)
    (A') one law for sojourner and native (v. 22)

The pronouncement of one law for the sojourner and the native frames the relevant legislation. The effect of a chiastic arrangement is to highlight the central idea as the most important one (vv. 19–20).

As Sklar notes, given that the frame emphasizes that justice must be applied equally to all (vv. 16, 22), it makes sense to read the verses in between as "also stating principles of justice," namely, that "crimes against humans are far more serious than crimes against property (v. 21)" and that "penalties must be appropriate to the crimes (vv. 19–20)."[281]

24:17 This verse addresses murder, not manslaughter (for the latter cf. Ex. 21:12–14; Num. 35:11, 15). Because human beings alone bear God's image (Gen. 1:26–27), they are of incomparable worth, meaning the penalty for killing them is the highest possible: death itself.

24:18 By way of contrast animals are not made in God's image, so the penalty for killing them is not capital but financial, restoring to the animal's owner an animal of equal worth ("life for life"), though presumably the fair market value of the animal could also be given to its owner (cf. the more detailed law in Ex. 21:33–34).

24:19–21 The formulation of the legal principle for punishment is known as lex talionis, or the law of retribution. The heart of the law aims at having the punishment fit the crime, that is, that it be proportionate in its scope and severity and not outweigh it. Although this legal formulation is familiar from elsewhere in Scripture (Ex. 21:23–25; Deut. 19:21), it is phrased differently in Leviticus. This passage introduces the category of injury with a unique theological perspective, using the term *mum*, which in the preceding chapters is translated as "blemish" (Lev. 21:17–18, 23; 22:20–21, 25). Blemishes disqualify animals from being offered on the altar and priests from offering the bread of the presence. Injury is conceived as a disfigurement of man made in the image of God and a marring of his wholeness (cf. ch. 21).

24:22 Both the sojourner and the native are held to the same standard of holiness. Although the nonnative is not bound by covenant to worship Yahweh, he lives in the land and is capable of polluting it, thereby alienating the divine presence.[282] The Lord's dwelling among his people has implications for how life is lived within

---
281 Sklar, *Leviticus*, TOTC, 293.
282 Jacob Milgrom, *Leviticus 23–27*, AB (New Haven, CT: Yale University Press, 2001), 2132.

24:23 The narrative concludes with the people's carrying out the Lord's judgment on the blasphemer in a public execution by stoning. The man who treated the divine name with contempt is put to death, and defilement is eradicated from the camp. Thus all Israel has exercised its priestly vocation by eliminating impurity and guarding the holiness of God.

Response

The Lord gives Israel tangible signs of his covenant presence: the light of the lampstand, the bread of the presence, and his holy "Name" (24:11). Daily worship at the tabernacle testifies to a God who is present with his people. The closest Israel ever came to beholding the physical manifestation of the divine presence was at the inauguration of the tabernacle, when Yahweh sent out fire from his presence to consume the sacrifices on the altar (9:24). At all other times that the people approached the Lord with their offerings they did so in *faith* that he was present to receive them: "Whoever would draw near to God must believe that he exists and that he rewards those who seek him" (Heb. 11:6). The daily ordering of his house, the preparation of his table, and priests to serve in the divine household are signs and symbols of his presence. Although these activities may appear to be the seemingly mundane tasks of daily life, they nevertheless profoundly testify to a God who is with his people. It is in the daily living that the Lord meets with his people and invites his worship to pervade their lives.

To lack this level of concreteness in Christian worship can sometimes leave us looking for the Lord in a worship *experience* rather than in the familiar symbols of our faith. The gift of God's presence in the life of a new covenant believer is nearer than ever (cf. Deut. 30:11–14). As we gather in communal worship, Christ is present in the preached Word. He is present in fellowship at the table. He assures us of his abiding presence by his unfailing word of promise: "I am with you always, to the end of the age" (Matt. 28:20b). Nearer still, he has endowed us with his Spirit, who, manifesting like fire, was sent to fill the church as he once filled the tabernacle (Acts 2:1–4). Every believer is now indwelt by the Spirit, who leads us into all truth so that we may image the Lord rightly in the world (John 14:18; 16:13). His presence pervades our daily lives and even our very being: "He dwells with you and will be *in you*" (John 14:17).

It is no less the case in the new covenant that it is a grievous insult to treat lightly the God of our salvation and the Spirit with whom we have been "sealed for the day of redemption" (Eph. 4:30). Anyone who blasphemes the Spirit, who unites us in fellowship to the life of the Trinity, will be held accountable (Mark 3:28–30).[283] We are chastened not to disfigure the image of God that is being rec-

---

[283] The "eternal sin" of blasphemy in Mark 3:22–30 has to do with those who saw the coming of the kingdom in its power and ascribed it to the powers of darkness in direct rejection of God's power to save.

reated in us and through which the world comes to see Christ. We are charged to be worthy bearers of the name. Jesus has perfectly revealed the Father by embodying his name among his followers: "I made known to them your name, and I will continue to make it known, that the love with which you have loved me may be in them, and I in them" (John 17:26). As Christians, we zealously guard Christ's reputation in the world by living in obedience to his will and extending his fame to the ends of the earth. Paul's prayer for the Thessalonians is a timely encouragement to the church today: "To this end we always pray for you, that our God may make you worthy of his calling . . . so that the name of our Lord Jesus may be glorified in you, and you in him, according to the grace of our God and the Lord Jesus Christ" (2 Thess. 1:11–12).

LEVITICUS 25

25 The Lord spoke to Moses on Mount Sinai, saying, **2** "Speak to the people of Israel and say to them, When you come into the land that I give you, the land shall keep a Sabbath to the Lord. **3** For six years you shall sow your field, and for six years you shall prune your vineyard and gather in its fruits, **4** but in the seventh year there shall be a Sabbath of solemn rest for the land, a Sabbath to the Lord. You shall not sow your field or prune your vineyard. **5** You shall not reap what grows of itself in your harvest, or gather the grapes of your undressed vine. It shall be a year of solemn rest for the land. **6** The Sabbath of the land¹ shall provide food for you, for yourself and for your male and female slaves² and for your hired worker and the sojourner who lives with you, **7** and for your cattle and for the wild animals that are in your land: all its yield shall be for food.

8 "You shall count seven weeks³ of years, seven times seven years, so that the time of the seven weeks of years shall give you forty-nine years. **9** Then you shall sound the loud trumpet on the tenth day of the seventh month. On the Day of Atonement you shall sound the trumpet throughout all your land. **10** And you shall consecrate the fiftieth year, and proclaim liberty throughout the land to all its inhabitants. It shall be a jubilee for you, when each of you shall return to his property and each of you shall return to his clan. **11** That fiftieth year shall be a jubilee for you; in it you shall neither sow nor reap what grows of itself nor gather the grapes from the undressed vines. **12** For it is a jubilee. It shall be holy to you. You may eat the produce of the field.⁴

13 "In this year of jubilee each of you shall return to his property. **14** And if you make a sale to your neighbor or buy from your neighbor, you shall not wrong one another. **15** You shall pay your neighbor according to the number of years after the jubilee, and he shall sell to you according to the number of years for crops. **16** If the years are many, you shall increase the price, and if the years are few, you shall reduce the price, for it is the number of the crops that he is selling to you. ⁷¹⁷ You shall not wrong one another, but you shall fear your God, for I am the Lord your God.

¹⁸ "Therefore you shall do my statutes and keep my rules and perform them, and then you will dwell in the land securely. ¹⁹ The land will yield its fruit, and you will eat your fill and dwell in it securely. ²⁰ And if you say, 'What shall we eat in the seventh year, if we may not sow or gather in our crop?' ²¹ I will command my blessing on you in the sixth year, so that it will produce a crop sufficient for three years. ²² When you sow in the eighth year, you will be eating some of the old crop; you shall eat the old until the ninth year, when its crop arrives.

²³ "The land shall not be sold in perpetuity, for the land is mine. For you are strangers and sojourners with me. ²⁴ And in all the country you possess, you shall allow a redemption of the land.

²⁵ "If your brother becomes poor and sells part of his property, then his nearest redeemer shall come and redeem what his brother has sold. ²⁶ If a man has no one to redeem it and then himself becomes prosperous and finds sufficient means to redeem it, ²⁷ let him calculate the years since he sold it and pay back the balance to the man to whom he sold it, and then return to his property. ²⁸ But if he does not have sufficient means to recover it, then what he sold shall remain in the hand of the buyer until the year of jubilee. In the jubilee it shall be released, and he shall return to his property.

²⁹ "If a man sells a dwelling house in a walled city, he may redeem it within a year of its sale. For a full year he shall have the right of redemption. ³⁰ If it is not redeemed within a full year, then the house in the walled city shall belong in perpetuity to the buyer, throughout his generations; it shall not be released in the jubilee. ³¹ But the houses of the villages that have no wall around them shall be classified with the fields of the land. They may be redeemed, and they shall be released in the jubilee. ³² As for the cities of the Levites, the Levites may redeem at any time the houses in the cities they possess. ³³ And if one of the Levites exercises his right of redemption, then the house that was sold in a city they possess shall be released in the jubilee. For the houses in the cities of the Levites are their possession among the people of Israel. ³⁴ But the fields of pastureland belonging to their cities may not be sold, for that is their possession forever.

³⁵ "If your brother becomes poor and cannot maintain himself with you, you shall support him as though he were a stranger and a sojourner, and he shall live with you. ³⁶ Take no interest from him or profit, but fear your God, that your brother may live beside you. ³⁷ You shall not lend him your money at interest, nor give him your food for profit. ³⁸ I am the Lord your God, who brought you out of the land of Egypt to give you the land of Canaan, and to be your God.

³⁹ "If your brother becomes poor beside you and sells himself to you, you shall not make him serve as a slave: ⁴⁰ he shall be with you as a hired worker and as a sojourner. He shall serve with you until the year of the jubilee. ⁴¹ Then he shall go out from you, he and his children with him, and go back to his own clan and return to the possession of his fathers. ⁴² For they are my servants,⁵ whom I brought out of the land of Egypt; they shall not be sold as slaves. ⁴³ You shall not rule over him ruthlessly but shall fear your God. ⁴⁴ As for your male and female slaves whom you may have: you may buy male and female slaves from among the nations that are around you. ⁴⁵ You may also buy from among the strangers who

sojourn with you and their clans that are with you, who have been born in your land, and they may be your property. ⁴⁶ You may bequeath them to your sons after you to inherit as a possession forever. You may make slaves of them, but over your brothers the people of Israel you shall not rule, one over another ruthlessly.

⁴⁷ "If a stranger or sojourner with you becomes rich, and your brother beside him becomes poor and sells himself to the stranger or sojourner with you or to a member of the stranger's clan, ⁴⁸ then after he is sold he may be redeemed. One of his brothers may redeem him, ⁴⁹ or his uncle or his cousin may redeem him, or a close relative from his clan may redeem him. Or if he grows rich he may redeem himself. ⁵⁰ He shall calculate with his buyer from the year when he sold himself to him until the year of jubilee, and the price of his sale shall vary with the number of years. The time he was with his owner shall be rated as the time of a hired worker. ⁵¹ If there are still many years left, he shall pay proportionately for his redemption some of his sale price. ⁵² If there remain but a few years until the year of jubilee, he shall calculate and pay for his redemption in proportion to his years of service. ⁵³ He shall treat him as a worker hired year by year. He shall not rule ruthlessly over him in your sight. ⁵⁴ And if he is not redeemed by these means, then he and his children with him shall be released in the year of jubilee. ⁵⁵ For it is to me that the people of Israel are servants.⁶ They are my servants whom I brought out of the land of Egypt: I am the LORD your God."

¹ That is, the Sabbath produce of the land ² Or *servants* ³ Or *Sabbaths* ⁴ Or *countryside* ⁵ Hebrew *slaves* ⁶ Or *slaves*

Section Overview

Chapters 25–27 anticipate life in the land of Israel's inheritance. This new section is marked as commandments given on Mount Sinai (25:1–26:46). Chapter 27, which adds to the jubilee laws, has the same setting (27:34). Most of the Lord's words to his people have been spoken from the tent of meeting (1:1), so the note that these words were spoken from Sinai is rare and gives rhetorical emphasis.

Entering into covenant with the Lord at Sinai was never meant to remain a mountaintop experience but was to be lived out in the plains and valleys, in the hill country and fortified cities of the Land of Promise. Israel must live according to the covenant in its own land. The people will cross the Jordan into a place of nourishment and flourishing, freedom and worship. They will go from being redeemed slaves to being children receiving their inheritance. The land is given to make possible a life lived in imitation of the holiness of the Father who gives it. The Lord, who promises the land on oath and gives it by covenant, describes the shape that obedience will take. Israel must take careful, patient care to cultivate the soil under the Lord's divine decrees, providing for the poor, observing cessation of labor for man and beast, and living righteously in the land to create a space where humanity and the Lord can dwell together (26:11–12).

This chapter outlines the economics of the kingdom at the intersection of creation and redemption. The sabbatical pattern leaves its mark in ever-expanding concentric circles: the seventh day mandates rest from one's labor, the seventh year enjoins rest for the land's labor, and the year after the seventh cycle of seven years ushers in release from debt and rest from displacement. It is rest for both covenant people and covenant land.

Section Outline

VII. Holy Institutions (21:1–27:34) . . .

    E. Covenanted Land (25:1–55)

        1. Sabbatical Year (25:1–7)

        2. Jubilee Year (25:8–17)

        3. The Lord's Promise to Sustain (25:18–22)

        4. Jubilee Redemption Laws (25:23–55)

            a. Theology of Land (25:23–24)

            b. Sale of Landholdings (25:25–34)

            c. Provision of Interest-Free Loans (25:35–38)

            d. Entering Indentured Servitude (25:39–55)

Comment

25:1 The Lord speaks from Sinai, from the geographical setting of covenant making, to instruct Israel regarding rest and redemption. The Sabbath is a template for holy time established from creation that casts its ever-increasing sphere of influence over life in the land. Israel's obedient response to the Lord's invitation to rest under his sovereign rule will result in the sanctification of time, land, and people.

25:2 Until now the people have been instructed on the importance of observing the Sabbath as a sign of the covenant: "Above all you shall keep my Sabbaths, for this is a sign between me and you throughout your generations, that you may know that I, the LORD, sanctify you" (Ex. 31:13; cf. Ex. 31:14–17). In a surprising turn the Lord's royal decree from Sinai mandates that the *land* observe a Sabbath rest.

25:3–4 After Israel takes possession of her inheritance the land is to have a season of rest from its labor, that is, its work of producing crops to sustain humanity. In every seventh year the Israelites must neither sow nor reap, plant nor harvest, but allow the land to lie fallow in complete rest as it reverts to its natural, unworked, and unmanaged state (Gen. 2:5–6). This charge envisions the Lord as the divine householder of all creation. Because he owns the land (Lev. 25:23), all within his household will enjoy Sabbath rest, including his children, servants, animals, and even the personified land (Ex. 20:8–11). Should Israel not cooperate with the Lord's commands but instead subject the land to ceaseless production, she will be evicted and sent into exile so that the land may enjoy its Sabbaths (Lev. 26:34–35).

25:5–7 At first blush these verses appear to contradict the sabbatical vision by stating that "all its yield shall be for food" (v. 7). Although the land may not be cultivated, it will still produce "aftergrowth," natural growth from seeds that fell to the ground during the previous year's harvest. This aftergrowth is not just for the field's owners but also for the landless poor, as the parallel passage in Exodus makes explicit: "The seventh year you shall let it rest and lie fallow, that the poor of your people may eat; and what they leave the beasts of the field may eat. You shall do likewise with your vineyard, and with your olive orchard" (Ex. 23:11).[284] The law thus envisions that in the sabbatical year everyone will gather as the landless do. Every seventh year the divine Landlord will supply his people's needs as they glean from his land. Everyone will be equally dependent on the Lord's provision, and everyone will be equally at rest from one's labors, from owner to hired worker. Jubilee legislation envisions equality among the covenant community.

The aim of the sabbatical year is not to promote greater productivity or yield from the land as a result of letting it lie fallow but rather to grant it a rest from its labors in a "public affirmation of the land's freedom under Yahweh's sovereign rule."[285] That the land is redeemed (Lev. 25:23), as are Abraham's descendants (v. 42), entwines the destinies of both within the covenant context. A Sabbath for the land suggests it is in covenant relationship with the Lord and that there is a purpose to its redemption that will continue on to the new creation (Rom. 8:19–21).

25:8–9 The jubilee crowns the seventh cycle of seven years, culminating in the fiftieth year.[286] The cycle of sevens draws attention to the pattern of time established at creation and ultimately the design of creation itself. As the seventh day heralds the goal of creation—the Lord's enthronement in worship—the seventh seven both recapitulates creation's original state and foreshadows its ultimate goal. The jubilee is a portrait of both beginning and end. In language that looks back to Eden the land is reordered along the lines of covenant relations, in which all are family and all is the Lord's. In a prophetic look forward the jubilee anticipates the re-creation of the world itself.

The jubilee is announced with a trumpet[287] in the fall, the beginning of Israel's agricultural calendar (the ritual calendar begins in the spring, with Passover; see 23:5).[288] The name "jubilee" is taken from the ram's horn (*yobel*) that is trumpeted to sound the advent of its celebration. A trumpet blast in the context of Sinai (v. 1) is associated with the Lord's appearance and the sound of his unmediated voice (Ex. 19:16, 19; 20:18). Trumpet blasts also announce the coronation of kings as

---

[284] When Israelites brought in the harvest, they were not to reap their fields in their entirety, nor strip their olive groves and vines of all fruit, but to leave some behind for the poor in the land to glean (Lev. 19:9–10; Deut. 24:19–22). This was to be every landholder's practice every year until the seventh year, when he himself would glean from the land—not as owner but as an Israelite at rest.

[285] Richard H. Lowery, *Sabbath and Jubilee* (St. Louis, MO: Chalice Press, 2000), 61. As a point of note, for the land to lie fallow one year out of seven is hardly enough. It is more common to practice crop rotation and let the land lie fallow one year out of three. Therefore it becomes even clearer that this legislation is for religious rather than practical reasons and to shape a people through theological versus agricultural concerns.

[286] The relationship between the seventh sabbatical year and the jubilee has occasioned several proposals, the most convincing of which is that it was celebrated on the fiftieth year, which also counted as the first year of the new cycle. For a careful and cogent accounting of jubilee chronology cf. Gane, *Leviticus, Numbers*, 432–435.

[287] The shofar is a ram's horn.

[288] The sabbatical pattern signaling new beginnings is observed in the new ritual status of the priesthood following the seven-day ordination, purification after seven days (Lev. 14:23; 15:14, 29), and circumcision on the eighth day (Gen. 17:12). According to this analogy (cycle of 7 +1) the jubilee (7 x 7 + 1) signals a new beginning.

they take up their throne (2 Sam. 15:10; 1 Kings 1:39; 2 Kings 9:13). In the people's experience this would have suggested the Lord's advent as king in their midst.

The celebration is announced on the Day of Atonement. On the day that the sanctuary is cleansed from all sin and defilement the land reverts to its original state and debtors are released from their debts. The pattern of 7 x 7 that purifies the sanctuary through blood extends now to the land,[289] which is consecrated by a pattern of 7 x 7 cycles in time (Lev. 25:10).

25:10–13 Legislation for the jubilee comes with special vocabulary shared with Israel's neighbors. The "liberty" (Hb. *deror*) proclaimed throughout the land is reflected in a similar Mesopotamian institution known as *anduraru*, an edict of release issued by kings to prevent economic collapse and uprisings in their realm. The sense means "to move about freely," as those bound in indentured labor are released from their debt servitude.[290] Israel's practice differs in that, instead of an unpredictable edict of debt forgiveness when society is on the brink of collapse, the jubilee guarantees release and return once in every generation. Israel's Sovereign, whose proclamation goes forth and is set in motion by this very passage, decrees liberty in every generation. The King whose throne is founded on righteousness and justice brings freedom in his train (Ps. 89:14).

The heart of the jubilee is the release from debts that brings about the return of each debtor to his family and the return of all land to its original tribal allotments. This practice is firmly grounded in Israel's history. Yahweh redeemed his firstborn son, Israel, from Pharaoh's oppression and slavery (Ex. 4:22). As Father, he bequeathed to them an inalienable family inheritance as tribal allotments in the land of Canaan (Num. 26:52–56). Israel's inheritance is a gift not given apart from relationship; it is evidence of sonship and a place to commune with him as they dwell *together* in the land. Each generation that recovers ancestral property and returns to the land relives the redemptive narrative of God's people. This is the land where the Lord chose to plant his people: "You will bring them in and plant them on your own mountain, the place, O LORD, which you have made for your abode, the sanctuary, O Lord, which your hands have established" (Ex. 15:17). It is the holy ground of relationship with God, in which every covenant son and daughter finds rootedness and belonging that shape the identity of the covenant people.

25:14–17 Fair and just economic dealings are predicated upon the fact that all land is owned by the Lord, who will reapportion the tribal allotments in every generation. Land sale, therefore, is not the right to ownership but rather the right to the land's produce. The buyer purchases its use and the right to its harvests. The land's purchase value is calculated according to the number of years until the coming redemption. The closer to the jubilee year of release, the less the land is worth because of its anticipated reclamation by its original owner.

---

289 Cf. comment on 16:18–19, note 191.
290 Levine, *Leviticus*, 171.

The admonition not to wrong one another forms an envelope around these verses (Lev. 25:14, 17), speaking directly to the temptation to take advantage of the one who sold his land out of need. Wronging one's neighbor is decried by the prophets, who address the wealthy who seize lands to add to their own estates:

> They covet fields and seize them,
>   and houses, and take them away;
> they oppress a man and his house,
>   a man and his inheritance. (Mic. 2:2)

25:18–22 The text takes up the sabbatical year again, anticipating how fear could stand in the way of keeping the commandment and in so doing voicing concerns that would arise also in the seventh round of seventh years. If the land is left uncultivated in the forty-ninth year and remains unworked in the fiftieth year also, the people will not reap a harvest until the third year. Is it possible that in God's economy they could escape starvation? The Lord answers with the promise of a bumper crop in the sixth year that will last through the fallow seventh year and to the planting of the eighth (jubilee) year. Crops planted in the fall of the eighth year would yield a harvest in the spring of the ninth year, making Israel rely on the Lord's promise to sustain her.[291]

Israel is about to embark on a forty-year journey through the wilderness, in which the Lord will prove his ability to provide for his people every day. He will embed within their experience the testimony of an increased yield of manna every sixth day that will sustain them into the seventh (Ex. 16:5). The manna will prove miraculous in both its provision and its preservation not to spoil (Ex. 16:24). This weekly rhythm of being fed by the Lord will train the people to exercise faith once settled in the land and to put their trust not in the works of their hands but in the Lord's unfailing provision. The Lord promises not only survival if Israel obeys but a flourishing such as was known in the beginning of God's creation.

25:23–24 The theological vision of land finds its source with God as owner and the status of his people as analogous to resident aliens and immigrants, with no claims to property. When Israel recites its humble origins in gratitude at the harvest, the people are reminded that their ethics stem from their own experience as sojourners in Egypt: "A wandering Aramean was my father. And he went down into Egypt and sojourned there" (Deut. 26:5). Many a time the community of faith will rehearse this spiritual truth in worship (1 Chron. 29:15; 1 Pet. 2:11). The land is entrusted to Israel for cultivation, a portion of which will be brought back to the Lord in thanksgiving and worship, and the majority of which will sustain and satisfy his people's needs. This ultimately stages a different power dynamic among the community of Israel, in which God as landowner has the power to host or to evict his people. It is not for an Israelite to lord it over another with an accumulation of fields or houses (Isa. 5:8).

---

[291] Gane, *Leviticus, Numbers*, 434.

25:25–28 Three successive stages of descent into increasing debt are treated in the jubilee laws: loss of a portion of land, loss of all of land, and loss of freedom. Each of these situations begins with the conditional clause "If your brother becomes poor," situating the commands in the framework of kinship relations that are sure to evoke sympathy and counter the tendency to dismiss personal responsibility. In fact the laws address those who have the power to act and make "care for the poor *the litmus test of covenant obedience*."[292] They refer to a fellow Israelite as a "brother,"[293] a term first introduced in parallel with "neighbor": "You shall not hate your brother in your heart. . . . You shall love your neighbor as yourself" (Lev. 19:17–18). The jubilee is in conversation with the passage on brotherly love to spell out in practical detail what the Israelites have already learned from their stories of origin: they are their brother's keeper (Gen. 4:9).

The first situation concerns an Israelite who is forced by his circumstances to sell some of his land. The reasons could be multiple, from failed crops to mismanagement, but the fact that none are mentioned means that his situation is not judged. He is entitled to recover his ancestral estate because the Lord gives it, not because he deserves it. The extended family serves as a safety net, calling for the "nearest redeemer" to acquire the property so that it does not leave the family's holdings (cf. Jer. 32:7). In the event that the seller's economic situation improves and he acquires the means he may buy back his land, but, if not, he must wait for the jubilee year for his land to revert to his family's holdings.

The concern that ancestral land not be lost is brought to life vividly in the book of Ruth, wherein Boaz acts as redeemer to buy back the property of his clan member Elimelech.[294] In the process he goes beyond that which the law envisions in order to restore Naomi and Ruth to the family property through marriage and producing a living descendant. The narrative brings to the fore that which is behind the jubilee, namely, the bond between land and identity.

25:29–31 Real estate is an exception to the law of redemption. Should someone sell a house in a walled city, he is given a year's time to buy it back; otherwise it will permanently remain in the possession of the buyer. Houses are not like fields, which provide the means for the life sustenance of a family. Village homes, however, are accounted as one with their land parcel and fall under the same laws of land redemption; they can be recovered at the jubilee.

25:32–34 Special provision is made for the Levites, who have no tribal inheritance (Josh. 13:33). They are allotted no land to farm but instead given forty-eight cities and their surrounding lands for pasturing their flocks (Num. 35:7; Josh. 21:1–42). If a Levite sells a house in a city, the house will revert to him in the jubilee, since that is his only possession. Land for grazing and gardening held in common, however, must not be sold at all.

---

292 Wright, *Old Testament Ethics*, 174, emphasis original.
293 In Hebrew at Leviticus 25:14, 25 (2x), 35, 36, 39, 46 (2x), 47, 48.
294 Boaz declares to the elders his intentions to redeem the land parcel of "our relative Elimelech," which could be rendered woodenly as "our brother Elimelech," echoing the phrasing of the jubilee laws.

If land sale is not an option, then what kind of safety valve do Levites have in economic crisis? The Lord intends for the Levites to be supported by the tithes and offerings brought to the sanctuary (Num. 18:24; Deut. 18:1–2; Josh. 13:14). The Levites are found grouped together with the vulnerable fatherless and widow as the Lord urges charity, mercy, and beneficence toward them (Deut. 14:27–29).

25:35 After the clauses of exceptions the laws of redemption pick back up with the situation of an Israelite who, having been forced to sell some of his landholdings, now faces complete insolvency and must be supported as though a resident alien or sojourner, that is, as being in the same social class as the landless. The loss of farmland exposes a family to the very real possibility of starvation. In the kin-based society of ancient Israel poverty strikes at the heart of a person's very identity, unrooting him from a place tied to identity. In his vulnerability he must be treated as a brother, with the same dignity and compassion with which the Lord treats his people, all of whom are accounted as "strangers and sojourners" (Lev. 25:23). Even for those without land and power the Lord affirms equality of personhood.

25:36–37 In a measure that protects the poor from exploitation Israelites are forbidden from charging interest on a loan made to a brother Israelite in need (cf. Ex. 22:25). Exacting no interest brings loans under the economy of the household, as family lending to family. Profiting from a brother's misfortune and driving him deeper into debt destroys not only him but also the bonds of community.[295]

Gracious dealings with one's brothers are motivated by the fear of God, a holy reverence for the Father in whose patrimony all have a right to live. This is Nehemiah's appeal amid the mounting debt crisis of those who have returned to an impoverished homeland. Farmers have mortgaged their land and indentured their children with no hope of recovery, while the upper class prosper through charging interest on loans. Invoking the fear of the Lord (Neh. 5:9, 15), Nehemiah shames those taking advantage of their covenant brothers and makes them return the fields seized as collateral and the interest made on loans. Brothers protect and do not profit.

25:38 The section appropriately ends with a strong charge to imitate the Lord, who released his people from servitude and gave them the land as a possession.

25:39–41 The final scenario is one in which persistent and unalleviated financial distress presses an Israelite to enter another's household as a servant. In this situation he must be treated as a bond servant, not a chattel slave. The difference between the two is teased out carefully in the following verses. Debt slavery is an institution known in the ancient world that, though not abolished here, sees

---

[295] The parallel law in Deuteronomy makes explicit that for those outside the covenant family the normal business practice of charging interest may take place (Deut. 23:19–20), which would be in keeping with the fact it was a business relationship, not a family one (though Wright also suggests that the reference to interest-bearing loans to foreigners has commercial loans in mind; cf. Wright, *Old Testament Ethics*, 165).

limits and boundaries set for what the Lord will permit at this time. Above all is the exhortation to uphold human dignity in all one's dealings.

An Israelite is never to be less than a hired resident worker, whose wages go toward paying off his loans. At the jubilee he is released to return to his land, as he and his children are restored once again to their ancestral inheritance. The children are mentioned here since the release looks forward to their future. The jubilee assures that families will not be trapped in an endless cycle of poverty with no hope or a future but that each generation will see the possibility of a clean slate and a new start.

25:42–43 The exhortation to treat a fellow Israelite as a hired laborer and not oppress him is rhetorically stirring and theologically compelling. No Israelite can ever be reduced to a slave, for the Lord released all of them from Pharaoh's service to enter his own.[296] It would challenge his ownership were they to become objects of human slavery. This claim continues with redemptive-historical power, as Paul argues for the release of Onesimus based on the Lord's claim on him and his master (Philem. 16–21). In his opening greetings of his letters Paul calls himself a bondservant of Christ (Rom. 1:1; Gal. 1:10; Phil. 1:1; Titus 1:1). To put every Israelite on the same level is to acknowledge that all are debtors before God.

25:44–46 An exception can be made with respect to slaves from among foreigners and resident aliens. The only ones in servitude in Israel should be foreigners, acquired as captives of war (Deut. 21:10–14) or purchase (Gen. 37:28). Their slavery is permanent, with no change of status. Slaves become a part of the household (Gen. 17:12–14) and are entitled to certain rights as rest on the Sabbath and can even celebrate the Passover (Ex. 12:44).[297]

25:47–54 Finally, if an Israelite must enter into the service of a household outside his clan (or even outside the covenant community), the obligation rests with the clan to redeem him, from nearest to most distant extended family member. In this situation the redeemed Israelite will work for his kinsman rather than a foreigner. As with land, all calculations for his redemption are made in light of the upcoming jubilee. In all transactions of redemption, whether of land parcel or person, all value is accorded with respect to the ultimate proclamation of release. In this way the debtor is released when his land is released so that he has a place in this world to which to return.

25:55 The chapter closes with the Lord's statement of ownership that undergirds the laws on indentured servants and all jubilee practices. It is a statement of identity and hope. Israelites may not be enslaved, for they are the Lord's servants. Since they belong to him by right of redemption from Egypt, they live in the promise that he will continue to redeem them and repatriate them, as he has in the past (Isa. 43:5–7; 49:8–12).

---

296 The Hebrew word *'ebed* means both "servant" and "slave," as does the Greek *doulos*.
297 For more on these verses and some of the apologetic issues they raise cf. Sklar, *Leviticus*, ZECOT, 696–703.

Response

The laws given to Israel on Mount Sinai shape the identity of the covenant community. They chart a path of hope for the future and inspire one's imagination to cast a vision for life lived in the presence of the Lord as it ought to be. It is not utopian or idealized but rather eschatological, painting a picture of how the world can flourish in freedom under human stewardship that itself is aligned with the kingship of God. The Sabbath is only one day out of seven, the Year of Jubilee only one out of fifty, yet the pattern of seven established at creation and woven into the rhythms of covenanted life points forward to a time when we will live in the perpetual 7 + 1 day, the eternal fiftieth year. Debts will be canceled, slaves released, and the world with those who inherit it will enter God's rest (Rom. 8:19–21).

The significance of the jubilee only increases in the course of Israel's history. Exile and expulsion from the land give rise to a yearning for a restoration to the land that is promised by covenant and for a redemption on the scale of a jubilee. The prophet Isaiah voices this hope throughout his prophecies, presenting an image of the Lord as a redeemer who will appoint a servant to bring about the jubilee (Isa. 49:8–9). The hope for a jubilee is pinned on a person, one anointed by the Spirit to proclaim release to the prisoners as the sign of the Lord's coming reign (Isa. 61:1–3).

This daring vision of justice and restoration that is nothing short of the reordering of the world is the message Jesus preaches to initiate and interpret his ministry. He picks up the scroll of Isaiah and placed himself in the role of the anointed messenger, heralding salvation from sin to the poor and liberty to the captives, ushering in the jubilee (Isa. 61:1–2).[298] Jesus defines his ministry in terms of a jubilee liberator, a Savior who will restore people to their inheritance (cf. Acts 1:6). The Lord who saved his people out of bondage from Egypt steps into redemptive history to enact a second exodus, this time from sin, and to bring to fulfillment the jubilee vision.

---

[298] The quotation in Luke merges the text of Isaiah 61:1, which clearly evokes the release of the jubilee, and Isaiah 58:6, which makes reference to the Day of Atonement. This is not accidental, since the jubilee was proclaimed on the Day of Atonement, making explicit a connection between the release from bondage and cleansing from all sin. The passages that follow Jesus' message in Luke center on outsiders receiving the message/prophet of God (cf. 1 Kings 17:1–16; 2 Kings 5:1–14). Interpretation continues to follow on the theme of jubilee, namely, that the kingdom would be redistributed from those who have held it in their power to all those who will by repentance and faith become equal heirs (Jews and Gentiles) in the year of rest.

LEVITICUS 26

26 "You shall not make idols for yourselves or erect an image or pillar, and you shall not set up a figured stone in your land to bow down to it, for I am the Lord your God. ² You shall keep my Sabbaths and reverence my sanctuary: I am the Lord.

³ "If you walk in my statutes and observe my commandments and do them, ⁴ then I will give you your rains in their season, and the land shall yield its increase, and the trees of the field shall yield their fruit. ⁵ Your threshing shall last to the time of the grape harvest, and the grape harvest shall last to the time for sowing. And you shall eat your bread to the full and dwell in your land securely. ⁶ I will give peace in the land, and you shall lie down, and none shall make you afraid. And I will remove harmful beasts from the land, and the sword shall not go through your land. ⁷ You shall chase your enemies, and they shall fall before you by the sword. ⁸ Five of you shall chase a hundred, and a hundred of you shall chase ten thousand, and your enemies shall fall before you by the sword. ⁹ I will turn to you and make you fruitful and multiply you and will confirm my covenant with you. ¹⁰ You shall eat old store long kept, and you shall clear out the old to make way for the new. ¹¹ I will make my dwelling[1] among you, and my soul shall not abhor you. ¹² And I will walk among you and will be your God, and you shall be my people. ¹³ I am the Lord your God, who brought you out of the land of Egypt, that you should not be their slaves. And I have broken the bars of your yoke and made you walk erect.

¹⁴ "But if you will not listen to me and will not do all these commandments, ¹⁵ if you spurn my statutes, and if your soul abhors my rules, so that you will not do all my commandments, but break my covenant, ¹⁶ then I will do this to you: I will visit you with panic, with wasting disease and fever that consume the eyes and make the heart ache. And you shall sow your seed in vain, for your enemies shall eat it. ¹⁷ I will set my face against you, and you shall be struck down before your enemies. Those who hate you shall rule over you, and you shall flee when none pursues you. ¹⁸ And if in spite of this you will not listen to me, then I will discipline you again sevenfold for your sins, ¹⁹ and I will break the pride of your power, and I will make your heavens like iron and your earth like bronze. ²⁰ And your strength shall be spent in vain, for your land shall not yield its increase, and the trees of the land shall not yield their fruit.

²¹ "Then if you walk contrary to me and will not listen to me, I will continue striking you, sevenfold for your sins. ²² And I will let loose the wild beasts against you, which shall bereave you of your children and destroy your livestock and make you few in number, so that your roads shall be deserted.

²³ "And if by this discipline you are not turned to me but walk contrary to me, ²⁴ then I also will walk contrary to you, and I myself will strike you sevenfold for your sins. ²⁵ And I will bring a sword upon you, that shall execute vengeance for the covenant. And if you gather within your cities,

I will send pestilence among you, and you shall be delivered into the hand of the enemy. 26 When I break your supply[2] of bread, ten women shall bake your bread in a single oven and shall dole out your bread again by weight, and you shall eat and not be satisfied.

27 "But if in spite of this you will not listen to me, but walk contrary to me, 28 then I will walk contrary to you in fury, and I myself will discipline you sevenfold for your sins. 29 You shall eat the flesh of your sons, and you shall eat the flesh of your daughters. 30 And I will destroy your high places and cut down your incense altars and cast your dead bodies upon the dead bodies of your idols, and my soul will abhor you. 31 And I will lay your cities waste and will make your sanctuaries desolate, and I will not smell your pleasing aromas. 32 And I myself will devastate the land, so that your enemies who settle in it shall be appalled at it. 33 And I will scatter you among the nations, and I will unsheathe the sword after you, and your land shall be a desolation, and your cities shall be a waste.

34 "Then the land shall enjoy[3] its Sabbaths as long as it lies desolate, while you are in your enemies' land; then the land shall rest, and enjoy its Sabbaths. 35 As long as it lies desolate it shall have rest, the rest that it did not have on your Sabbaths when you were dwelling in it. 36 And as for those of you who are left, I will send faintness into their hearts in the lands of their enemies. The sound of a driven leaf shall put them to flight, and they shall flee as one flees from the sword, and they shall fall when none pursues. 37 They shall stumble over one another, as if to escape a sword, though none pursues. And you shall have no power to stand before your enemies. 38 And you shall perish among the nations, and the land of your enemies shall eat you up. 39 And those of you who are left shall rot away in your enemies' lands because of their iniquity, and also because of the iniquities of their fathers they shall rot away like them.

40 "But if they confess their iniquity and the iniquity of their fathers in their treachery that they committed against me, and also in walking contrary to me, 41 so that I walked contrary to them and brought them into the land of their enemies—if then their uncircumcised heart is humbled and they make amends for their iniquity, 42 then I will remember my covenant with Jacob, and I will remember my covenant with Isaac and my covenant with Abraham, and I will remember the land. 43 But the land shall be abandoned by them and enjoy its Sabbaths while it lies desolate without them, and they shall make amends for their iniquity, because they spurned my rules and their soul abhorred my statutes. 44 Yet for all that, when they are in the land of their enemies, I will not spurn them, neither will I abhor them so as to destroy them utterly and break my covenant with them, for I am the LORD their God. 45 But I will for their sake remember the covenant with their forefathers, whom I brought out of the land of Egypt in the sight of the nations, that I might be their God: I am the LORD."

46 These are the statutes and rules and laws that the LORD made between himself and the people of Israel through Moses on Mount Sinai.

[1] Hebrew *tabernacle* [2] Hebrew *staff* [3] Or *pay for*; twice in this verse; also verse 43

Section Overview

The Lord's speech begun in 25:1 continues and now concludes with the rewards of obedience and the consequences for disobedience. The language of this chapter is common to ancient political treaties that were part of Israel's world and with which they would have been familiar. Treaties legally brought into diplomatic relationship a regional superpower who would agree to protect and come to the aid of its vassal state in exchange for allegiance and tribute. Just like legal documents today follow a specific format, treaties between nations were shaped in a recognizable way. Treaties between a great king (suzerain) and a lesser king (vassal) typically included the following elements:

(1) introduction of the speaker (the suzerain's right to proclaim the treaty)
(2) historical prologue (the relationship between the parties, defined in terms of the suzerain's kindness to the vassal)
(3) stipulations (core of the treaty laying out the benefits of the suzerain's protection and the obligations for the vassal's obedience)
(4) witnesses (typically gods of both parties)[299]
(5) blessings and curses (actions of the gods if the treaty is violated)[300]

The chapter follows this pattern loosely. The introduction of the speaker and historical prologue are found in the preceding verse: "It is to me that the people of Israel are servants. They are my servants whom I brought out of the land of Egypt: I am the LORD your God" (Lev. 25:55). Yahweh has a right to dictate the obligations of the covenant relationship (stipulations) because he has delivered Israel from bondage. The stipulations are brief but all-encompassing as they relate to Israel's obligation toward its Suzerain (vv. 1–2). The essence of a vassal's obedience is allegiance, and for Israel that means offering Yahweh its exclusive worship. The greater part of the speech is structured as five blessings and five curses, with the curses expounded at a greater length, as typical in ancient covenants (cf. Deuteronomy 28). As blessings and curses would conclude treaties by spelling out the consequences of abiding by the covenant or breaking it, so this chapter comes near the end of Leviticus in a manner suggesting that all of it should be read in light of Israel's covenant obligations. Ancient Israelites would have understood that they were vassals under a great King to whom they were indebted and rightly owed their undivided allegiance. They also would have understood the legally binding nature of the covenant and Yahweh's justice to enforce the consequences for disobedience.

Canonically, the first time we encounter blessing and curse is at creation. The Lord creates humanity for blessing, personally pronouncing his purpose to cause mankind to flourish (Gen. 1:28). It is only when sin enters the world that the Lord responds with curses—not on humanity directly but over its labor and unique creative contribution to the world (Gen. 3:16–17). Pain, sorrow, unfulfilled potential, resistance in work, fractured relationships, and most significantly the loss of the intimate presence of God are all the results of disobedience in the garden, echoed

---

[299] In the biblical context there were no other gods to serve as witnesses; in some cases, however, creation itself could be called on to testify (cf. Deut. 4:26; 31:26–28).
[300] John Walton, *Ancient Israelite Literature in its Cultural Context: A Survey of Parallels between Biblical and Ancient Near Eastern Tests* (Grand Rapids, MI: Zondervan, 1989), 95–107.

anew in the curses of the covenant. As long as the Israelites embrace obedience, the covenant restores them to God's presence, to walk with him in fellowship as humanity once did in the garden.

Section Outline

VII. Holy Institutions (21:1–27:34) . . .
    F. Covenant Blessings and Curses (26:1–46)
        1. Worship as the Basis of the Covenant (26:1–2)
        2. Blessings of the Covenant (26:3–13)
            a. Introduction (26:3)
            b. First Blessing: Rains in Season (26:4–5)
            c. Second Blessing: Peace (26:6)
            d. Third Blessing: Victory over Enemies (26:7–8)
            e. Fourth Blessing: Prosperity (26:9–10)
            f. Fifth Blessing: Yahweh's Personal Presence (26:11–12)
            g. Conclusion (26:13)
        3. Curses of the Covenant (26:14–39)
            a. Introduction (26:14–15)
            b. First Discipline: Panic (26:16–17)
            c. Second Discipline: Drought (26:18–20)
            d. Third Discipline: Wild Beasts (26:21–22)
            e. Fourth Discipline: War (26:23–26)
            f. Fifth Discipline: Military Defeat (26:27–39)
        4. Yahweh Is Faithful to Restore His Wayward People (26:40–45)
        5. Conclusion (26:46)

Comment

26:1–2 Yahweh's speech continues with an admonition to remain true to the heart of relationship with him. Israel's covenant obligation at its most foundational is worship: "Let my son go so he may worship me" (Ex. 4:23 AT).[301] Yahweh redeems Israel to create a worshiping people among whom he will dwell and sanctify by his presence and through whom make himself known to the nations (Ex. 4:23; 19:5–6). They are a people distinct among the nations because they are the Lord's (Ex. 33:15–16).

Their eyes are now drawn to the commandments against idolatry and to keeping the Sabbath because those exemplify what it means to be a holy people.[302] Bowing down before idols and giving allegiance to false gods breaks the covenant relationship. The importance of the Sabbath cannot be overstated. It is both a sanctuary

---

[301] Or "so he may serve me" (ESV), as the word for "serve" is often used to refer to service in worship in particular (cf. Ex. 7:16 with 5:1, 3).
[302] The subject matter of Leviticus 26 corresponds to Deuteronomy 28. The literary form of Deuteronomy is recognized as being cast in the ancient international treaty pattern, whereas Leviticus is not a treaty but rather deals with requirements for worship and holy living. It therefore suits the purpose of Leviticus to abbreviate the covenant terms (stipulations) to the most salient obligations with respect to worship and attach them to culturally recognizable consequences for disobedience (vv. 13–39).

in time, blessed for meeting with the Lord (Gen. 2:3), and a sign of the covenant (Ex. 31:13). This verse links the sanctuary (place) to the Sabbath (time), bringing together the intersection of human existence where the Lord makes his dwelling (Lev. 26:11). The treaty of the great King can be summed up as faithful worship.

26:3 The literary arrangement of this section reflects the theology that blessing is dependent on obedience to the covenant. It begins with the conditional clause "If you walk in my statutes" (v. 3) and ends with "I will walk among you" (v. 12). The frame around the covenant blessings is cast as Eden regained: the Lord who first walked in fellowship with Adam and Eve once again will walk with his people (Gen. 3:8). Since creation, blessing has been woven into God's relationship with mankind for fruitfulness and flourishing to fill the earth. Blessing is his intention for his elect people so that through them blessing may once again be realized in a fallen world (Gen. 12:1–3). Wright insightfully clarifies: "Blessing is the prior reality of God's grace. . . . Obedience, therefore, like faith, is the means of *appropriating* God's grace and blessing, not the means of *deserving* it."[303]

26:4–5 The gift of land is the all-important setting in which life is lived in relationship with the Lord (cf. ch. 25). If Israel obeys, the Lord will actively respond to her obedience by causing the land to respond in abundant fruitfulness that will amply satisfy all his people's needs (cf. Hos. 2:21–22). Unlike Egypt, which is irrigated by the Nile, Canaan is dependent on the early and latter rains for agriculture.[304] To this day prayers for rain are lifted up in Israel during the rainy season, and historic Jewish texts view God's provision of rain as a tremendous blessing: "The day when rain falls is as great as the day on which heaven and earth were created" (Ta'anit 8b). Such will be the abundance that the barley harvest (March) will overtake the wheat harvest (May), which will overtake the grape harvest (July). Israel will eat and be satisfied, providing yet another conceptual link with Eden.

26:6 Peace will pervade the land so that Israel will lie down unafraid, pictured as the Lord's flock protected from wild animals, who are their enemies. This promise is astonishing. Israel's complex geopolitical setting made it improbable that it could know peace apart from Yahweh's protection and care. Located between the powerful civilizations of Egypt and Mesopotamia, the land of Israel is a bridge in the middle of the world and also of its conflict (cf. Ezek. 5:5).

26:7–8 Under the Lord's blessing Israel's history will take a decisive turn. The people who were chased out of Egypt will now chase their enemies, and, though

---

[303] Christopher Wright, *Deuteronomy*, NIBC, ed. Robert L. Hubbard, Jr., and Robert K. Johnston (Peabody, MA: Hendrickson, 1996), 280–281.

[304] Life in the land will be successful not by human effort but by the personal and providential care of the Lord: "The land that you are entering to take possession of it is not like the land of Egypt, . . . where you sowed your seed and irrigated it, like a garden of vegetables. But the land that you are going over to possess is a land of hills and valleys, which drinks water by the rain from heaven, a land that the Lord your God cares for. The eyes of the Lord your God are always upon it, from the beginning of the year to the end of the year. And if you will indeed obey my commandments that I command you today, to love the Lord your God, and to serve him with all your heart and with all your soul, he will give the rain for your land in its season, the early rain and the later rain" (Deut. 11:10–14).

the Israelites are not as numerous (Deut. 7:7), they will pursue and overtake those enemies (cf. Ex. 15:9). The expression is memorable, cast in poetic parallelism found also in Deuteronomy: "How could one have chased a thousand, and two have put ten thousand to flight?" (Deut. 32:30).

26:9–10 The favor of the Lord is embodied in his turning toward his people in relationship. Bound together with Yahweh in covenant, they will know a life overflowing with creative abundance in recovery of the human vocation (Gen. 1:28; 9:1) and in fulfillment of the promises laid in store for Abraham's descendants (Gen. 17:1–6; 35:11–12). Yahweh will "maintain" the covenant by acting as the Suzerain who makes good on his promises.

26:11–12 The blessings crescendo with Yahweh's promise to make his "dwelling" among his people, literally "place my tabernacle." The height of the Lord's nearness is found in the sanctuary, which he fills with his presence and wherein he receives his people's worship and provides the means for atonement so that his soul will not "abhor" them. This rare word depicts a feeling of deep aversion and even disgust as a response to filth, a fitting way for Leviticus to express the sinful condition.[305] This will be the reaction when Israel walks in disobedience (vv. 15, 30, 43, 44).

Yahweh's promise to walk among his people recalls nothing less than the fellowship the first man and woman shared with the Lord when "walking in the garden in the cool of the day" (Gen. 3:8).[306] Restoration of relationship is the ultimate goal of the covenant. The covenant relationship is deeply personal and expressed here in what resembles the solemn vow of marriage or adoption in the ancient world: "I will be your God, and you shall be my people." This promise reverberates throughout the Scriptures (cf. Gen. 17:7–8; Ex. 6:7; Deut. 29:13; 2 Sam. 7:24; Jer. 24:7; 31:1; Ezek. 11:20; 34:30; 37:23, 27; Hos. 2:23; Zech. 8:8; Rev. 21:3, 7).

26:13 The epilogue to the blessings echoes the introduction of the covenant Suzerain in Leviticus 25:55: "It is to me that the people of Israel are servants. They are my servants whom I brought out of the land of Egypt: I am the LORD your God." Yahweh identifies himself as the one who is able to fulfill his stated rewards for obedience because of his actions in the past. Belonging to Yahweh brings freedom, a point that is not abstract for Israel but historically grounded in her deliverance from Egypt and from Pharaoh's oppression. Not only does the Lord redeem his people in a one-time historical event, but he continues to do so throughout their history together (cf. John 8:36).

26:14–15 The subject now turns to curses that will unfold with increasing severity should Israel break its treaty with the great King. Israel's idolatry shows abhorrence for the Lord (Lev. 26:15, 43), which he will answer with abhorrence of Israel (v. 30). Careful attention to the language makes it clear that this is deserved punishment

---

[305] Levine, *Leviticus*, 184.
[306] The verbal form for "walk among" in Leviticus 26:12 is the same as that found in Gen. 3:8 ("walking"), which intentionally connects covenant blessings to the garden.

and heavenly discipline for a wayward nation. The consequences for disobedience are stated conditionally: "If . . . then I will do this to you" (vv. 14, 16). Punishment is ascribed directly to the Lord. It is critical that Israel understands how these are not natural misfortunes but the chastisement of the Lord. At the same time the conditional language also entertains the possibility that the nation may turn away from its unfaithfulness and return to the Lord.

The curses spell out disasters familiar to the ancient world that aptly foreshadow the devastation Israel will come to face in its own history, so much so that certain scholars want to read this portion of Scripture as having been authored at the time of exile, after Israel's experience of it. The Lord's speech, however, is historically anchored at Sinai, as recorded no fewer than three times in this section (25:1; 26:46; 27:34). Yahweh makes known "the end from the beginning and from ancient times things not yet done" (Isa. 46:10), also sending his prophets so that his people can interpret the times and know he is the sovereign Lord of history.

26:16–17 The curses of the covenant are expressed as a reversal of the Lord's blessing.[307] Instead of turning his face favorably toward Israel as the recipient of his attention and blessing, the Lord turns his personal presence away from the broken relationship. Instead of the great King's ruling over Israel, she will be dominated by her enemies. Instead of enjoying the fruit of one's labor as under Yahweh's rule (Lev. 26:5), God's people will see their crops consumed by their conquerors. In fear they will retreat instead of putting their enemies to flight (vv. 7–8). An emotional state of alienation from the Lord will prevail. Israel will be broken and hopeless, led to despair, depression, and anxiety.

26:18 If still Israel will not heed the Lord, she will merit a "sevenfold" measure of his discipline, a figurative expression indicating increasing severity (cf. Gen. 4:24).[308] This verse makes clear that curses are divine "discipline" visited upon Israel for the purpose of turning her away from disobedience.

26:19–20 In particular the Lord will wage war against the pride that comes from Israel's sense of self-sufficiency. The verse unfolds to suggest the people's misplaced source of strength is their own land. Therefore, instead of yielding its crops, the land will now resist stubborn Israel to become as unyielding as iron and bronze (a reversal of vv. 4–5). The language of "heavens of iron and . . . earth of bronze" is common to ancient Near Eastern treaties and implies injurious drought. This curse traces its roots all the way back to Eden: the land will not cooperate with the efforts of man to cultivate it (Gen. 3:17–19).

26:21–22 Israel's continued hostility will be met with a greater escalation of the Lord's hostility. Wild beasts will prey upon the vulnerable and unprotected children and livestock in a reversal of the covenant blessing: "Be fruitful and multiply and fill the earth. The fear of you and the dread of you shall be upon every beast of the

---

307 This same pattern can be observed with the first curses in the garden (Gen. 3:16–19).
308 Hartley, *Leviticus*, 465.

earth" (Gen. 9:1–2). Cities will be depopulated, and well-traveled thoroughfares will lie deserted. Such is the fate of the northern kingdom when it is exiled by the Assyrians and wild beasts invade the land (2 Kings 17:25–27; cf. Lam. 5:18). As with a suzerain king, when Yahweh removes his personal protection, Israel is left unprotected, its dominion diminished.

26:23–26 The litany of Yahweh's opposition continues in direct proportion to the people's sin: "Walk contrary to me, then I also will walk contrary to you" (Lev. 26:23–24). The Lord will bring war as punishment from which there is no retreat; it will follow after them in their cities with pestilence and famine. In an image of the pitiable lack of food and struggle for survival ten women crowd around one oven.[309] War is the sword that will "execute vengeance for the covenant," an experience Israel comes to know well in its history, more so than the blessed promise of peace (v. 6).

26:27–29 Ever-escalating apostasy brings punishment to a shrill intensity. As the result of siege, famine, and military defeat, the people will be brought to the point of eating the flesh of their own children. Tragically, Jerusalem does suffer the horror of such desperation (Lam. 2:20; 4:10). The dissolution of the covenant whose dominant note is progeny and land (Gen. 12:1–3) is illustrated in heart-wrenching detail.

26:30–35 The reason for the Lord's judgment is given in the following verses, coming full circle to the heart of covenant relationship that opens this chapter: "You shall not make idols for yourselves.... You shall keep my Sabbaths" (Lev. 26:1–2). Yahweh will avenge himself by tearing down idolatrous sanctuaries and incense offered to other gods. He will dispossess Israel of its land and scatter the people among the nations. Their decaying corpses will be heaped upon the idols of the land in measure-for-measure judgment. Because they worshiped lifeless idols, they will become lifeless. Because the people did not observe the Sabbath, sabbatical rest will be enforced. The God of covenant who made a way not to abhor but to grant his people his personal presence (v. 11) will now abhor them.

26:36–39 The surviving remnant will fare no better but be overcome by fear with no power to stand, though these people could have held their heads high (vv. 6, 13). They will waste away in exile in a reversal of the flourishing that could have been theirs. The words are strong, meant to intimidate and strike fear in the heart of the hearer. Yet the Lord interprets fear for his people as beneficial to deterring sin (Ex. 20:20).

26:40–43 "But if" marks a turning point in Israel's relentless dissolution. Confession, humility, and deeds flowing out of repentance are what the Lord requires to restore the wayward nation. This should come as no surprise, given

---

[309] The triad of sword, pestilence, and famine is the choice David is given as discipline from the Lord (1 Chron. 21:11–13). David models a posture of repentance. Receiving the correction of the Lord restores relationship and his presence among his people (1 Chron. 22:1).

the message of Leviticus. The purpose of the sacrificial system is to provide the means to reconciliation, and, as the Day of Atonement has shown, that comes only by humility and repentance (cf. Leviticus 16).

26:44–45 In one of the most hope-filled phrases of Scripture ("Yet for all that") the tide of the Lord's opposition turns. There is hope even in exile, for Yahweh will remain steadfast to his purposes to make Israel a blessing to the world despite her not remaining steadfast to him (cf. Deut. 30:3–4).[310] The section ends with the declaration "I am the LORD," appearing here for the forty-ninth and final time in Leviticus.[311] The number is significant, sounding a note that picks up on the themes of restoration and forgiveness. At the conclusion of forty-nine years the Year of Jubilee is inaugurated (Lev. 25:8), and after forty-nine sprinklings of blood on the Day of Atonement the sanctuary is purified (16:14–19). Despite the sevenfold discipline of God (26:18, 21, 24, 28) the final word is that Yahweh's commitment to his own purposes stands.

26:46 The final verse of the chapter looks back to all the instruction the Lord has given to his people through Moses at Sinai. The inclusive phrase "statutes and rules and laws" encompasses all the covenant stipulations found in chapters 1–25 and thus concludes the chapter with an admonition cast in the language of blessings and curses, as would be expected in treaties of the ancient world. The familiar language signals to Israel that she is a covenanted people whose treaty with the great King is based on exclusive allegiance and worship of him.

Response

The Lord draws on Israel's shared cultural heritage with the ancient world to present himself as her great King and to communicate the consequences of abiding by his laws or rejecting them. The legal nature of the covenant makes clear that the relationship is based not on cheap grace but on a mutual agreement that the God who delivers deserves Israel's sole allegiance. Blessings and curses are expressed in a way that is appropriate to their ancient context but at their heart are tied to the personal presence of God. In his presence there is fullness of life; apart from him there is loss, death, and devastation.

The curses may be the most difficult aspect of the covenant with which to identify. At least two observations are in order. First, the Lord makes known from the beginning the consequences for disobedience. Israel has been forewarned. Second, the calamities brought upon Israel are in response to the people's apostasy and are intended to call them back into faithful relationship. Ultimately punishment is visited on God's people to produce repentance.

Contrary to popular teaching in parts of the world today, blessing is not an impersonal principle set in motion as a result of human effort that indiscriminately unfolds to return prosperity. The blessings of the covenant cannot be obtained

---

[310] "If we are faithless, he remains faithful—for he cannot deny himself" (2 Tim. 2:13).
[311] Gane, *Leviticus, Numbers*, 455.

apart from a relationship with the Lord. Furthermore, blessing is not for personal, individual success. The promise of blessing is given to the nation as it relates to its mission in the world. Yahweh's blessing upon his people is for the sake of actualizing redemption and restoration in the world. As in the garden, God's blessing has a wider scope in view to include all creation.

We stand at the crossroads of time to appreciate fully the fulfillment of this portion of Scripture. Written in a balanced five blessing plus five curse structure, the final section (vv. 44–45) stands outs and stands alone. Even when the people do not fulfill their obligation to the covenant, and even though the Lord would be justified in rejecting them entirely, he will remain committed. How this will be achieved is left unsaid, but hope rings out over the curse and leads us to the cross, where "Christ redeemed us from the curse of the law by becoming a curse for us" (Gal. 3:13). Through Christ we stand in right relationship with the great King, and his soul does not abhor us. Instead he lavishes upon us the blessings of Abraham (Gal. 3:14). We have peace with God that nothing can destroy (John 14:27; Phil. 4:7), the spiritual resources for life and godliness (2 Pet. 1:3–4), his unyielding commitment to be for us and not against us (Rom. 8:31–32), his unfailing covenant love (Eph. 3:17–19), and most importantly his eternal, abiding presence (Rev. 21:3). This is not for our benefit alone, as through us God brings blessing to the world around us and calls forth the hope of a world restored to God: "No longer will there be anything accursed, but the throne of God and of the Lamb will be in it, and his servants will worship him" (Rev. 22:3).

LEVITICUS 27

27 The LORD spoke to Moses, saying, ² "Speak to the people of Israel and say to them, If anyone makes a special vow to the LORD involving the valuation of persons, ³ then the valuation of a male from twenty years old up to sixty years old shall be fifty shekels¹ of silver, according to the shekel of the sanctuary. ⁴ If the person is a female, the valuation shall be thirty shekels. ⁵ If the person is from five years old up to twenty years old, the valuation shall be for a male twenty shekels, and for a female ten shekels. ⁶ If the person is from a month old up to five years old, the valuation shall be for a male five shekels of silver, and for a female the valuation shall be three shekels of silver. ⁷ And if the person is sixty years old or over, then the valuation for a male shall be fifteen shekels, and for a female ten shekels. ⁸ And if someone is too poor to pay the valuation, then he shall be made to stand before the priest, and the priest shall value him; the priest shall value him according to what the vower can afford.

⁹ "If the vow² is an animal that may be offered as an offering to the LORD, all of it that he gives to the LORD is holy. ¹⁰ He shall not exchange

it or make a substitute for it, good for bad, or bad for good; and if he does in fact substitute one animal for another, then both it and the substitute shall be holy. ¹¹ And if it is any unclean animal that may not be offered as an offering to the Lord, then he shall stand the animal before the priest, ¹² and the priest shall value it as either good or bad; as the priest values it, so it shall be. ¹³ But if he wishes to redeem it, he shall add a fifth to the valuation.

¹⁴ "When a man dedicates his house as a holy gift to the Lord, the priest shall value it as either good or bad; as the priest values it, so it shall stand. ¹⁵ And if the donor wishes to redeem his house, he shall add a fifth to the valuation price, and it shall be his.

¹⁶ "If a man dedicates to the Lord part of the land that is his possession, then the valuation shall be in proportion to its seed. A homer[3] of barley seed shall be valued at fifty shekels of silver. ¹⁷ If he dedicates his field from the year of jubilee, the valuation shall stand, ¹⁸ but if he dedicates his field after the jubilee, then the priest shall calculate the price according to the years that remain until the year of jubilee, and a deduction shall be made from the valuation. ¹⁹ And if he who dedicates the field wishes to redeem it, then he shall add a fifth to its valuation price, and it shall remain his. ²⁰ But if he does not wish to redeem the field, or if he has sold the field to another man, it shall not be redeemed anymore. ²¹ But the field, when it is released in the jubilee, shall be a holy gift to the Lord, like a field that has been devoted. The priest shall be in possession of it. ²² If he dedicates to the Lord a field that he has bought, which is not a part of his possession, ²³ then the priest shall calculate the amount of the valuation for it up to the year of jubilee, and the man shall give the valuation on that day as a holy gift to the Lord. ²⁴ In the year of jubilee the field shall return to him from whom it was bought, to whom the land belongs as a possession. ²⁵ Every valuation shall be according to the shekel of the sanctuary: twenty gerahs[4] shall make a shekel.

²⁶ "But a firstborn of animals, which as a firstborn belongs to the Lord, no man may dedicate; whether ox or sheep, it is the Lord's. ²⁷ And if it is an unclean animal, then he shall buy it back at the valuation, and add a fifth to it; or, if it is not redeemed, it shall be sold at the valuation.

²⁸ "But no devoted thing that a man devotes to the Lord, of anything that he has, whether man or beast, or of his inherited field, shall be sold or redeemed; every devoted thing is most holy to the Lord. ²⁹ No one devoted, who is to be devoted for destruction[5] from mankind, shall be ransomed; he shall surely be put to death.

³⁰ "Every tithe of the land, whether of the seed of the land or of the fruit of the trees, is the Lord's; it is holy to the Lord. ³¹ If a man wishes to redeem some of his tithe, he shall add a fifth to it. ³² And every tithe of herds and flocks, every tenth animal of all that pass under the herdsman's staff, shall be holy to the Lord. ³³ One shall not differentiate between good or bad, neither shall he make a substitute for it; and if he does substitute for it, then both it and the substitute shall be holy; it shall not be redeemed."

³⁴ These are the commandments that the Lord commanded Moses for the people of Israel on Mount Sinai.

---

[1] A *shekel* was about 2/5 ounce or 11 grams [2] Hebrew *it* [3] A *homer* was about 6 bushels or 220 liters [4] A *gerah* was about 1/50 ounce or 0.6 gram [5] That is, set apart (devoted) as an offering to the Lord (for destruction)

Section Overview

Leviticus closes with words from Sinai that look to the future of life in the land, a theme linking this section (chs. 25–27). This chapter mirrors chapter 25 in its treatment of people, land, and that which is consecrated to the Lord. The jubilee laws speak of faithfulness in person-to-person debts in light of coming redemption; laws on dedicated offerings address both faithfulness in satisfying debts to the Lord and also his allowance for redemption.

The chapter has two main halves. It begins by describing voluntary votive offerings (27:2b–25). A votive offering may be understood as a debt voluntarily entered into in times of distress or blessing. A vow is a conditional promise to be fulfilled if the Lord answers the worshiper's prayer. This ancient custom and very human experience is addressed from the perspective of the sanctuary, regulating the times that an offerer can redeem a votive offering (27:2b–25). The chapter's second half then describes various nonvotive offerings that can never be redeemed (vv. 26–33).

Leviticus thus ends having brought the worshiper back to the sanctuary. Leviticus has revealed the tent of meeting as the seat of the Lord's kingship and its sacrificial ministry as the center of Israel's holiness. It has shaped the practice of personal wholeness and holiness through ritual and moral purity. It now connects the day-to-day life of God's people with worship through voluntary contributions as well as nonredeemable contributions. Personal faith and economic commitment go hand in hand. The Lord whose voice went forth from the tent of meeting (1:1) gives final instructions on how his people should continue its operation through their gifts in order to sustain the vision of the world that Leviticus has shaped.

Section Outline

VII. Holy Institutions (21:1–27:34) . . .
    G. Dedicated Gifts (27:1–34)
        1. Introduction (27:1–2a)
        2. Voluntary Votive Offerings (27:2b–25)
            a. Pledges of Persons (27:2b–8)
            b. Animal Pledges (27:9–13)
            c. Property and Land Pledges (27:14–25)
        3. Nonredeemable Offerings (27:26–33)
            a. Firstborn (27:26–27)
            b. Devoted Things (27:28–29)
            c. Tithes (27:30–33)
        4. Conclusion (27:34)

Comment

27:1–2a This is the last speech of the Lord recorded in Leviticus. The final verse will note that these words are spoken from Sinai.

27:2b–25 In each of the cases in this section special gifts are vowed to the Lord. A vow may be taken in situations of life and death (Jonah 2:9), urgent need of the Lord's help (Num. 21:1–3; Judg. 11:30–31), or longed-for answer to prayer, usually for children (Prov. 31:2). Elkanah is no stranger to vows (1 Sam. 1:21) but it is Hannah's that is best remembered: "She vowed a vow and said, 'O Lord of hosts, if you will indeed . . . give to your servant a son, then I will give him to the Lord all the days of his life'" (1 Sam. 1:11). Anyone could make a vow as an act of devotion. A woman who makes a vow, however, may be released from its obligation if it is objected to by her father if she is unmarried, or her husband if she is married (Num. 30:3–8; cf. Jer. 44:15–19). A vow is a sacred obligation to which a person binds himself; once spoken, it must be fulfilled and cannot be dissolved (Num. 30:2; Josh. 9:19–21). The importance of vows in Israel's worship can be seen in how frequently the Psalms articulate vows, especially for the Lord's deliverance (e.g., Pss. 22:25; 50:14–15; 56:12–13; 66:13–14; 116:14).[312]

27:2b–7 Voluntary offerings are introduced with the personal vow of dedication.[313] This is called a "special vow," a phrase found only one other time, there regarding the Nazirite, a person who has dedicated himself to the Lord for a season by voluntarily taking on the purity requirements of the priesthood and living out his consecration by abstaining from wine and all fruit of the vine, not coming near a corpse, and, most conspicuously, leaving his hair untrimmed (Num. 6:2–8). It is a special vow because it exceeds normal expressions of devotion by making explicit what in the sacrificial system is implicit—the giving of one's self to the Lord (cf. Leviticus 1). While both describe a similar dedication of oneself, the Nazirite lives his out while the vower may fulfill his through money paid to the sanctuary.

People could be pledged to serve the Lord as temple servants (cf. 1 Chron. 9:2; Ezra 2:43), and in certain cases a child might be dedicated to Nazirite status from the womb (Judg. 13:4–5; 1 Sam. 1:22–28). While the custom of vowing a child to the temple was known in the ancient world,[314] it appears this is less common in Israel, in which a priestly tribe is elected to serve. Every firstborn is to be dedicated to the Lord's service because he was redeemed at the exodus. In practical terms, however, the Levites take the place of the firstborn and are consecrated to serve on holy ground instead (Num. 3:12–13; 8:16–19). The firstborn male is redeemed, or bought back, at a redemption price of five shekels (Ex. 13:13; 34:19–20; Num. 18:15–16).

The redemption prices registered here (cf. table 3.7) are in the same tradition as the firstborn—the vow of one's intended service is calculated in terms of its

---

312 Votive offerings continue to be an important part of Jewish worship in the NT period, technically referred to as *korban* (cf. Mark 7:11), and the temple treasury that contained them as *korbanas* (Matt. 27:6; Josephus, *Jewish War* 2.175).
313 Josephus mentions the practice of dedicating oneself (*korban*) and explains it as a "gift," *doron* in Greek, which is a LXX word for sacrifice (*Antiquities* 4.73).
314 In Mesopotamia there was a special class of consecrated servants who had been dedicated to the temple known as the *shirku* (CAD 3:110). They were not temple personnel responsible for the performance of ritual but worked the temple lands and pastured the flocks. Those who had been dedicated for life were permanently marked with a star.

equivalence in silver. The differing prices, which are embedded within the context of legislation that deals with economic transactions related to sanctuary pledges, reflect labor capacity or potential. Valuations represent the equivalent of a person's labor dedicated to the sanctuary and are given in the standard sanctuary shekel (Lev. 27:25). They are not a statement of personal worth nor the relative value of men and women in Israelite society. In fact the inestimable value of human life is communicated in laws on homicide that emphatically reject monetary compensation for the loss of life (Num. 35:31–34).

TABLE 3.7: Redemption Prices

Age	Male	Female
1 month – 5 years of age	5 shekels	3 shekels
5–20 years of age	20 shekels	10 shekels
20–60 years of age	50 shekels	30 shekels
over 60 years of age	15 shekels	10 shekels

A person's labor potential varies by age. The youngest age group (one month to five years)[315] represents the lowest valuation, given that children are too young to contribute but instead require a significant investment. The second lowest valuations are found in persons over the age of sixty, when age decreases capability for manual labor. Yet this valuation represents only a modest decrease from ages five to twenty for males while remaining the same for females and speaks to the great respect accorded to the elderly for their contribution in wisdom and life experience. As expected, labor in the prime of life between twenty and sixty years is valued most highly.

One of the more noticeable aspects of redemption prices is the lower valuation of female to male. The greatest disparity is found in five to twenty age range, with women's value half that of men. This coincides with a young woman's childbearing years, which begin soon after marriage at puberty and curtail her labor potential. It bears repeating that these numbers do not reflect the inherent worth of a person.

27:8 Redemption prices are not insignificant. Based on such passages as the yearly wage of ten pieces of silver for priestly duties (Judg. 17:10), it is estimated that the average wage was a shekel a month.[316] If a laborer in his prime saved all his earnings, it would take him a little over four years to pay his redemption price. If a person is unable to redeem his pledge, he presents himself to the priest for a fair assessment according to his means, recalling the extenuating provisions for the poor that are worked into the sacrificial laws (Lev. 5:7; 12:8; 14:21–22). Anyone can petition the Lord as an expression of worship, not least of all the poor.

---

315 The valuations begin at a month because this is when they are first eligible to be redeemed (Num. 18:16).
316 Gane, *Leviticus, Numbers*, 469.

27:9–10 The most common pledge is an animal offered as a sacrifice (7:16; 22:18–19, 21; 23:37–38). Vowed to the Lord, it acquires the status of "holy," meaning it is incorporated into the sanctuary as the Lord's property. Once the animal is pledged, a substitute will not be accepted, either of greater or lesser value or even of a different species. In fact if a person seeks to exchange his pledge for another, then both animals will be holy—the one vowed and the one intended to replace it. This shows that the vow was considered binding when it was spoken: "You shall be careful to do what has passed your lips, for you have voluntarily vowed to the LORD your God what you have promised with your mouth" (Deut. 23:23; cf. Num. 30:3–5).

But why would someone make a substitution? It could be out of dishonesty; Malachi chastises worshipers who own better animals that they choose to make the subject of their vow, offering the lesser valued instead (Mal. 1:12–14). Or it could be that the vow was open ended, with the person pledging to dedicate the next born from the flock or herd for a sacrificial feast only to find that the animal born was undesirable for the feast (Lev. 7:16; Deut. 12:17, 26; 14:23).[317] Either way, a person cannot replace what he has vowed. It has become holy to the Lord.

27:11–13 If the pledge is an unclean animal that cannot be offered on the altar, then the vower must present it to the priest to be assessed. Instead of a fixed valuation, as with persons, the amount is determined by the priest according to the particular situation. If the vower wishes to buy back his pledged animal, he must pay a fifth more than the assessment price. This amount is familiar from the reparation offering but differs in its application (cf. Lev. 5:16). There is no sin involved, but there is a breach of intention. The additional fifth may especially relate to the fact that the animal is moved out of the Lord's domain and into the owner's possession (cf. 22:14).[318] It also may serve as a deterrent from entering unadvisedly into rash vows: "It is a snare to say rashly, 'It is holy,' and to reflect only after making vows" (Prov. 20:25).

27:14–15 A person may also wish to dedicate his house to the Lord. There is debate whether this is being thought of in this passage as a spontaneous vow (cf. Prov. 20:25) or as a simple declaration of dedication (perhaps Judg. 17:3), though in either case the house has become consecrated, that is, committed to the holy domain of the Lord. And, whereas some vows might take some time to fulfill (since the object becomes dedicated only after a prayer is answered), the consecration in view here becomes effective as it is declared.

When a person consecrates his house as a "holy gift," the priest appraises it and gives a valuation. If the donor wishes to redeem it, it can be bought back for its original appraisal plus an additional fifth of its value.

27:16–19 Arable land can also be dedicated to the Lord. The priest arrives at an appraisal by determining the amount of barley seed required to sow the parcel.

---

[317] Richard E. Averbeck, "מעשר," *NIDOTTE*, 1042.
[318] Compare Gane, *Leviticus, Numbers*, 465.

The measure of a homer, deriving from a word for "donkey," is the load of seed that a donkey could carry, roughly 29–53 gallons (135–240 l).[319] It is estimated a homer would sow 3.75 acres.[320] The field's valuation is then calculated at fifty shekels per homer if consecrated on a jubilee year or, if otherwise, prorated to adjust for the years remaining till the jubilee (Lev. 25:15–16). If the donor wishes to redeem the field, he must add a fifth to its valuation to withdraw it from the sacred domain.

Land may exchange hands, but it is not considered permanently given over to the sanctuary; only its agricultural yield belongs to the sanctuary, and that for a specified period of time—until redemption by its donor or the jubilee (25:10, 28). At the jubilee all land reverts to the original allotments in order to restore each family's access to the means of production and to God's provision of covenant blessing. The law does not inordinately favor the priesthood over common Israelites, in stark contrast to the economies of neighboring Mesopotamia and Egypt, where palaces and temples controlled vast estates.

There is debate on who works the consecrated field. Some commentators believe it to be the priests (cf. 27:21). (While the tribe of Levi may not have been allotted an inheritance, this did not preclude it from holding land.) Alternately, if the consecrated parcel was part of a larger estate, the owner may have continued to work it on behalf of the priests, bringing its yield to the sanctuary. Deciding between these is difficult, as the precise arrangement is not spelled out, and the interest of these laws is the redemption of consecrated property. What we do know is that it took many hands to work the land (Ruth 2).

27:20–21 This next case is difficult but seems to suggest the following: a person sells his field to a buyer and then subsequently consecrates it to the Lord.[321] The jubilee laws suppose the only reason anyone would part with his inheritance is because he can no longer afford to work the land (Lev. 25:25). If this is read within the context of the circumstances envisioned in chapter 25, we see that a person who has fallen on hard times may sell his land to pay off his debts. Should he not seek to redeem his field but desires to consecrate it to the Lord instead, it is with the understanding that he intends to relinquish his ancestral inheritance permanently. When the field is released from the buyer in the jubilee year, rather than reverting to the owner it passes into the landholdings of the sanctuary and can never be bought back; it is a permanent consecration likened to a nonredeemable devoted object (cf. comment on 27:28–29). The land comes into the possession of the priest, meaning the priesthood will work or manage it. Although the tribe of Levi is allotted no land, property could pass into its control if permanently devoted to the sanctuary. The case of the nonredeemable land begins to cast a look forward to the second part of the chapter.

---

319 Wenham, *Leviticus*, 339n6.
320 Hartley, *Leviticus*, 483.
321 With Milgrom, *Leviticus 23–27*, 2385. The difficulty is evidenced by the variety of interpretations. Some read this as though the person first dedicates the field to the Lord and then subsequently leases it to another buyer. The loss of land is thus the penalty for this illegal sale.

27:22–24 In a different scenario a person who has purchased a field that is not his ancestral inheritance may still consecrate it to the sanctuary. The priest appraises it as outlined above (vv. 16–18), and the donor pays the full amount on the day of its appraisal. In this way the owner of the field may redeem and reclaim his land at any time from the lessee, with no competing claims from the sanctuary. There is no mention of the additional added fifth, possibly because it is not his land.

27:25 The standard for assessing the redemption prices is the sanctuary shekel, weighing under half an ounce (up to 12 grams) and valued at 20 gerahs (Ex. 30:13; Num. 3:47; Ezek. 45:12; cf. comment on 5:15). The sanctuary ensures just weights and measures for all transactions in the land.

27:26–27 The transition to offerings that may not be redeemed opens with firstborn animals, which by virtue of the Lord's historic saving acts already belong to him and cannot be rededicated through a separate vow. When God strikes down the firstborn of Egypt, he claims all the firstborn of Israel—whether children or animals—as his own, and every subsequent act of a firstborn's dedication is a celebration and reminder of the Lord's saving power (Ex. 13:2, 11–15). Therefore a firstborn animal may not be pledged to the Lord, for it already is his own. (Firstborn sons were redeemed; Ex. 13:13; Num. 18:15–16.)

In contrast an unclean firstborn animal that cannot be offered on the altar may be bought back by the vower, providing he pays its valuation price and an additional fifth. If he chooses not to redeem it, the priests may make use of the animal (such as a donkey on a farm) or sell it at the cost of its set value.

27:28–29 Another category of property and persons that belong unequivocally to the Lord are those that have been devoted as *kherem*, withdrawn from secular use and consecrated exclusively to the Lord for his purposes. The concept in its most general sense covers that which is forbidden from common use. This is encountered in two ways in the Bible: in the context of peace as an especially sacred offering (Lev. 27:28) and in the context of warfare as an offering of total destruction (v. 29).[322] (Since Israel's battles were fought as holy war, these are not unrelated.) In this law's usage *kherem* is a binding dedication similar to an oath, whereby the vow is irrevocable and its substance unrecoverable.

Devoted property declared *kherem* has become "most holy" and incorporated into the Lord's sphere of possessions; it cannot be bought back (as v. 21). The inclusion of persons devoted to destruction (v. 29) could anticipate Israel's wars of conquest (Num. 21:2), and even extend to the idolater within the community

---

[322] An example is Joshua's putting the city of Jericho under *kherem*, translated as "devoted to the Lord for destruction" (Josh. 6:17). The spoils of war are dedicated to the Lord: the city and all its inhabitants are destroyed by fire, but its silver, gold, and vessels of bronze are accounted as holy and deposited into the treasury (Josh. 6:19, 24). Achan's theft places the devoted plunder within the camp and makes all Israel fall under *kherem* until sin is purged from among her and God's justice is satisfied against the transgressor (Josh. 7:11–12). Jericho was dedicated by destruction as "most holy," and therefore anyone who attempted to rebuild it transgressed the Lord's holy property (Josh. 6:26; cf. 1 Kings 16:34).

(Ex. 22:19; Deut. 13:13–15). This law seeks to prevent a misstep such as that by Saul, who allows the king of the Amalekites and the best of the flock to live even though they had been "devoted to destruction" (1 Sam. 15:9).

27:30–33 The tithe is the Lord's by virtue of his kingship over Israel. He is honored with a tenth of the produce of the land and increase of the flock in the manner that kings in the ancient world were paid taxes and tribute (1 Sam. 8:15–17; 2 Kings 3:4). A tithe to the Lord is first vowed by Jacob as he leaves his father's house: "Then Jacob made a vow, saying, '*If* God will be with me and will keep me in this way that I go . . . *then the* LORD *shall be my God*, and this stone, which I have set up for a pillar, shall be God's house. And of all that you give me I will give a full tenth to you" (Gen. 28:20–22). Jacob promises covenant allegiance that will be demonstrated by building the Lord a place of worship and supplying it with his tithe. Tithes of grain, wine, oil, and animals of the flock and herd supply the house of the Lord for its sacrificial ministry and provide for his servants (Num. 18:21–24; Neh. 13:10–12).

If it becomes necessary for a person to retain a portion, "*some* of his tithe," likely by reason of need, the Lord will allow for the agricultural produce of crops and orchards to be bought back at their valuation plus a fifth. Tithe animals, however, are not subject to this accommodation (Num. 18:17). The Lord himself selects every tenth newborn of the flock and herd as it passes under the shepherd's staff to be counted, whether "good or bad" (Jer. 33:13; Ezek. 20:37). Should anyone attempt to replace it with a substitute, both will be regarded as holy and forfeited to the sanctuary (cf. comment on 27:9–10).

27:34 The concluding words of the book echo the closing statement of 26:46.[323]

Response

In 1505 a young law student caught in a terrifying thunderstorm vowed, were he to be saved, "I will become a monk!" He did indeed survive the storm and made good on his pledge, entering the monastery and trading the study of law for theology. His life of consecration and commitment to the vow he made in distress was honored by the Lord, and his life came to have far-reaching impact. That man was Martin Luther. Vows and binding promises are a serious matter. The Lord does not require them, but, if compelled by faith and love a person makes them, God insists they be fulfilled.

God's generous grace leads to generous giving back to him. Even when vows were not involved, the early NT believers were compelled by love to sell their possessions and use the proceeds to serve the needs of their brothers and sisters. They went beyond the tithe and firstlings of animals and produce prescribed in the laws

---

[323] Later scribes known as the Masoretes (AD 500–1000) added a notation to aid in their sacred task of copying God's Word and to guard its accurate transmission. It can be found in editions of the Hebrew text at the end of the book and reads, "The sum of the verses of the book: 859; its middle: 'And whoever touches the body' [15:7], and its divisions 25." The Lord's words from Sinai have been preserved through the ages with meticulous care.

of Leviticus to sell their land holdings as an extraordinary gift commensurate to the extraordinary grace they had each received in Christ (Acts 4:36–37).

Voluntary offerings in addition to tithes continue to support the ministry of the church. The worshiping life of the body of Christ needs to be nurtured and supported through the gifts of God's people. Indeed, the book's final words look forward to the ongoing ministry of the tent of meeting as God's people respond to his generous care with generous giving and are formed into a holy nation through relationship with him. They in turn invite us to bring our use of money in line with kingdom priorities, to see our finances in light of our covenant commitments, and to be shaped by a call to holiness characterized by relentless generosity.

NUMBERS

Ronald Bergey

INTRODUCTION TO
NUMBERS

Overview

Numbers recounts the history of God's direction, discipline, and deliverance of his people, the Israelites, throughout their wilderness sojourn. His instructions prepare the exodus generation for its journey from Sinai. He guides them to Kadesh on the border of Canaan, where they tragically refuse to enter the Promised Land. Due to their disobedience, all those of at least twenty years of age die in the wilderness. God guides the generation that will enter Canaan to the plains of Moab across the Jordan from Jericho. His instructions prepare them for life in the land. Despite their waywardness, the Lord remains faithful to his people and the promises made to their fathers.

Title

The title "Numbers" stems from the Latin Vulgate (*Numeri*), whose title for the book is drawn in turn from the LXX (*Arithmoi*). These names reflect censuses of the exodus generation (ch. 1) and the succeeding generation (ch. 26). The title also reflects other censuses (chs. 3; 4), as well as quantified lists of offerings (chs. 7; 28–29) and the tallied spoils of war (ch. 31).

The Hebrew title "In the wilderness of [Sinai]" (*bemidbar* [*sinay*]; 1:1) covers the first ten chapters, spanning the final nineteen days the Israelites spend at Sinai. But the name serves the entire book well. To arrive at Sinai from Egypt Israel first traverses the "wilderness of Etham" (33:8), then the "wilderness of Sin" (33:11). Numbers covers Israel's thirty-eight-year sojourn in the "wilderness of Paran" (e.g., 10:12) and the "wilderness of Zin" (e.g., 13:21). "Wilderness" also describes portions of the Transjordan (21:23; 24:1).

Author

Whereas the expression "The Lord spoke to Moses" occurs over forty times in Numbers, only once is it said that "Moses wrote down . . . by command of the Lord" (33:2). What he transcribed was the travel log of forty stations between the Israelites' departure from Egypt and their arrival at the plains of Moab. That Moses did write more of Numbers is deduced from Deuteronomy, which is explicitly attributed to his authorship (Deut. 31:9, 22, 24). His Deuteronomy discourses depend upon Numbers. The Israelites' wilderness journey is clearly recalled (Deut. 1:1–3:29; 8:2–3), as are characters such as Dathan and Abiram (Deut. 11:6; Num. 16:1–33), Sihon and Og (Deut. 29:7; Num. 21:21–35), and Balaam (Deut. 23:4–5; Numbers 22–24). Moses mentions crucial moments such as the Kadesh revolt (Deut. 9:23; Num. 13:25–14:4), the Baal of Peor debacle (Deut. 4:3; Num. 25:1–3), his own forfeiture of entrance into Canaan (Deut. 1:37; 4:21; Num. 20:8–13), and Joshua's appointment to succeed him (Deut. 3:28; 34:9; Num. 27:15–23). Laws from Numbers are expounded in Deuteronomy, such as those regarding the cities of refuge (Deut. 19:1–13; Num. 35:9–34). If these things were written down by Moses in Deuteronomy, it is likely he wrote their source (in Numbers) too.

To argue that someone else wrote Numbers many say that Moses would never have written, "Now the man Moses was very meek, more than all people who were on the face of the earth" (Num. 12:3). Mosaic authorship of Numbers does not necessarily require that every word be attributable to him. (Just as he did not write his own obituary in Deut. 34:5–8.) He did not record all of the details of the Transjordan tribal settlement (Num. 32:34–39), which took place under Joshua (Num. 32:28–29; cf. Joshua 13). He unlikely would have known that Zelophehad's daughters married sons of their father's brothers (Num. 36:11), nor that their "inheritance remained in the tribe of their father's clan" (v. 12). Minor supplemental redactions such as these were made under the same superintendence of God's Spirit as that guiding the principal author.

The testimony of Deuteronomy supports Mosaic authorship of Numbers. This was the conclusion of nearly all interpreters until the literary-criticism movement nurtured by rationalistic historicism. The canonical division—"the Law of Moses and the Prophets and the Psalms" (Luke 24:44; cf. 16:16, 29, 31)—long predates its mention in the NT (cf. *Sir.* 1:1). "The Law of Moses" designates the Pentateuch, which includes Numbers. If nowhere explicitly stated, Mosaic authorship of Numbers is nonetheless scripturally implied.

Date and Occasion

Numbers contains an internal chronology. The book spans thirty-eight years. It opens on the first day of the second month of the second year after the exodus (1:1). Numbers 7:1–10:10 reverts to the first month (cf. 7:1; 9:1, 15). The departure from Sinai resumes the second-month chronology on the twentieth day (10:11). The chronology ends in the months between Aaron's death in the fifth month of the fortieth year (33:38) and Moses' discourses on the plains of Moab in the eleventh month of that year (Deut. 1:3). In light of the chronological statement at 1 Kings 6:1, it is possible to date the exodus to early in the second half of the fifteenth century BC, that is, 480 years before the construction of the temple, which began in the fourth year of Solomon's reign. As such, Numbers would cover most of the latter half of that century.

Various elements in Numbers reflect a period prior to Israel's national existence. For example, the form of the tabernacle, with the sacred tent representing God's presence in Israel's midst, mirrors the Egyptian military camp surrounding the tent of Rameses II. The shared custodial tabernacle responsibilities of priests and Levites is found also in Hittite sanctuary practice. The boundaries of Canaan as presented in Numbers are similar to those described in Egyptian sources from the fifteenth to the thirteenth century BC.[1]

The book includes two static settings at which Moses addresses the people. The first involves the instructions given at Sinai to the exodus generation shortly before its departure from there (chs. 1–10). The other comprises instructions given on the plains of Moab to the generation that will soon enter Canaan (chs. 26–36). While the intervening chapters 11–25 have no one specific setting—various episodes occur at different locations—it is noteworthy that the wilderness wanderings are virtually passed over in silence. Their different settings can be chiefly linked to or near Kadesh at the beginning and end of that period (13:26; 20:1, 22).

Genre and Literary Features

A striking literary feature of Numbers is the book's plethora of genres (narrative, law, story, discourse, song, administrative lists, cultic calendars, travelogue, etc.) and its sundry subjects (people's camps, bodily discharges, embezzlement, marital jealousy, Nazirite vow, offerings, seven lamps, silver trumpets, battles, tassels, the red heifer, vows and oaths, spoils of war and captive women, borders, inheritance, cities of refuge, etc.).

Another literary feature is the book's alternance of narrative (N, including discourse) and law (L, including instructions and lists): 1:1–10:10 (L); 10:11–14:45 (N); ch. 15 (L); chs. 16–17 (N); chs. 18–19 (L); chs. 20–25 (N); 26:1–27:11 (L); 27:12–23 (N); chs. 28–30 (L); 31:1–33:49 (N); 33:50–36:13 (L). This alternance in not arbitrary but mutually reinforcing. Narrative can respond to law—for example, instructions regarding the departure (1:1–10:10) are executed in narrative form (10:11–14:45). And law can respond to narrative—for example, after the rebellion of the preceding narrative (10:11–14:45), laws (ch. 15) affirm God's commitment to bring the Israelites' children into the land. Placement of these diverse materials is far from arbitrary.

Theology of Numbers

Various theological themes, such as land and blessing, are addressed in the Section Overview and Comment sections (e.g., Section Overview of Numbers 13; 22; 34). Levitical ministry is nowhere more extensive developed than in Numbers. This too is developed in the comments, especially on chapters 3–4 and 18. Although they could rightly be treated here, the motifs of holiness and purity are treated in Interpretive Challenges as part of the discussion of the literary unity of Numbers.

---

[1] Jacob Milgrom, *Numbers*, JPSTC (Philadelphia: Jewish Publication Society, 1990), xxxii–xxxv.

The focus here is on examples of OT allusions to Numbers, taken as the cue to the book's theological emphases. This summary dovetails with the following section of the Introduction (Relationship to the Rest of the Bible and to Christ).

The Welsh minister Matthew Henry (1662–1714) remarked in his commentary, "An abstract of much of this book we have in a few words [in] Ps. 95:10, 'For forty years I was grieved with this generation,' and an application of it to ourselves [in] Heb. 4:1, 'let us fear lest we seem to come short.'"[2] Henry implicitly points to the typological relationship of the nation of Israel to the church and of the Promised Land and life in it to the promise of eternal life in Christ and life in him indwelt by the Holy Spirit.

In the fourth book of the Psalter Psalm 106 echoes the tragic story of the exodus generation, as recounted in this fourth book of the Pentateuch:

> Then they despised the pleasant land,
> > having no faith in his promise.
> They murmured in their tents,
> > and did not obey the voice of the LORD.
> Therefore he raised his hand and swore to them
> > that he would make them fall in the wilderness. (Ps. 106:24–26; cf. Num. 13:27–14:4, 32–35)

The same psalm also speaks of the earth's opening and swallowing up of Dathan, Abiram, and their followers at Korah's rebellion (Ps. 106:17–18; cf. Num. 16:27–35). It recalls the licentious Baal of Peor idolatry of the next generation and Phinehas's making atonement to save them from God's wrath (Ps. 106:28–31; cf. Num. 25:1–13).

If Numbers stresses God's judgment on sin, it also accentuates his mercy. Immediately after he pronounces judgment barring the exodus generation from the Promised Land, God shows his mercy to its children and his faithfulness to his covenant promise: "I will bring [your children] in" (14:31). He assures them by giving them laws applicable to that situation: "When you come into the land . . ." (15:2). He repeatedly reminds them that his commands are a "statute forever throughout your generations" (15:15, 23; 18:23; 35:29). He guides the new generation, as he had its parents, to the doorstep of Canaan at Kadesh, this time "beyond the Jordan at Jericho" (Num. 22:1; 26:3; 36:13).

For God's people a millennium later Numbers is a reminder for Nehemiah and the remnant that his mercy triumphs over judgment: "Nevertheless, in your great mercies you did not make an end of them or forsake them, for you are a gracious and merciful God" (Neh. 9:31). After seventy years of wilderness exile, Nehemiah's generation returns to the Promised Land.

These OT examples support the conclusion that in Numbers God's grace is projected against the somber background of his people's sinful faithlessness.

---

2 Cited by George Bush, *Notes, Critical and Practical, on the Book of Numbers* (1858; repr., Minneapolis: Klock & Klock, 1981), iv.

The Relationship to the Rest of the Bible and to Christ

The importance of Numbers for God's people under the old covenant can be garnered from citations of and allusions to it in Deuteronomy (Deut. 1:1–3:29; 4:3, 45–49; 8:2–3, 15–16; 9:22–24; 11:6; 23:3–5, 21–23; 24:9; 29:7; 31:2; 32:49–52; 34:9), the Prophets (former prophets, Josh. 1:12–15; 2 Kings 18:4; latter prophets, Ezek. 20:13–24; 46:4, 13, 15; Hos. 9:10; Mic. 6:5; 7:14–15; Amos 2:10, 12; 5:25; Zech. 12:13), the Psalms (Pss. 78:14–41; 80:1–2; 95:7–11; 99:8; 102:4–8; 106:24–33; 121:4–8; 135:11; 136:20) and other books within the Writings (2 Chron. 30:2; Neh. 9:31; 13:2).

Such passages throughout the OT canon, combined with citations of and allusions to Numbers in the NT, underscore the book's relevance for God's people throughout the ages. Luke reports, "Beginning with Moses and all the Prophets, [the risen Christ] interpreted to them in all the Scriptures the things concerning himself" (Luke 24:27). Numbers contains key anticipations that Christ and NT authors interpret as realized in his person and work.

Jesus speaks of himself as the manna from heaven that sustained the Israelites in the wilderness, typifying the true Bread of Eternal Life (John 6:48–50; cf. Num. 11:7–9). Paul declares that Christ was the spiritual Rock that followed the Israelites in the wilderness, providing saving spiritual drink (1 Cor. 10:4; cf. Num. 20:8–11). Jesus remarks that the bronze serpent hung on a pole by which anyone mortally bitten was delivered by obeying the command to look upon it pointed to his death on the cross for the eternal life of those who look to him in faith (John 3:14–16; cf. Num. 21:9).

Through the NT Scriptures Numbers continues to exhort and warn the church. God's dealings with his people recorded in Numbers were, says Paul, "written down for our instruction" (1 Cor. 10:11). The exodus generation's failure to attain the promised rest in Canaan due to unbelief in God's promises served as a warning to the next generation, which arrived across the Jordan from Jericho. This principle is applied to the Hebrews—fearful judgment also awaits all who refuse to take hold of the promises of salvation rest in Christ (Hebrews 3–4; cf. Num. 14:34–35; Ps. 95:8–11). The Israelites' rebellions in the wilderness serve, says Paul, "as examples for us, that we might not desire evil as they did" (1 Cor. 10:6), referring to the immorality at Baal-peor (1 Cor. 10:7–8; cf. Num. 25:1–9). Paul advises the church not to "put Christ to the test, as some of them did and were destroyed by serpents" (1 Cor. 10:9; cf. Num. 21:4–9). He exhorts Gentile Christians, "Note then the kindness and the severity of God: severity toward those who have fallen, but God's kindness to you, provided you continue in his kindness. Otherwise you too will be cut off" (Rom. 11:22). Peter warns of self-indulgent teachers in the church, likening them to those who "followed the way of Balaam" (2 Pet. 2:15; cf. Numbers 22–24; Rev. 2:14). Jude warns his readers, "I want to remind you . . . that Jesus, who saved a people out of the land of Egypt, afterward destroyed those who did not believe" (Jude 5; cf. Num. 26:64–65). Jude likens false teachers who beset the church to Korah (Jude 11; cf. Numbers 16). Referring to the Baal-peor incident, Christ warns the church in Pergamum, "You have some there who hold the teaching of Balaam, who taught Balak to put a stumbling block before the sons of Israel, so that they might eat food sacrificed to idols and practice sexual immorality" (Rev. 2:14).

Understanding how God dealt with his people in the wilderness increases Christians' awareness of God's holiness and his just judgment of sin. This realization drives them to lay hold of his goodness and grace by faith in Christ Jesus alone for salvation from sin and judgment. Such goodness and grace provide the incentive and strength to live in a way pleasing to him.

Preaching from Numbers

Often considered theologically insignificant and literarily obscure, Numbers may be one of the least preached books of all Scripture. The early-third-century church father Origen acknowledged this and sought to remedy the problem via a series of sermons on Numbers.[3]

The temptation exists to preach moralizing sermons from Numbers. The book certainly does not lack examples to make the point that living contrary to God's Word brings undesired results (the exodus generation died in the wilderness!). To emphasize that reality alone, however, misses the main point. Numbers reveals something far deeper.

The failure of God's people to live in a way that brings divine blessing is deeply rooted in the covenant relationship between the Lord and his people. If tension in the relationship did not exist, there would be no need for a covenant. The Sinai covenant was made with a sinful people. It governed and adjudicated the relationship of corrupt people with a holy God. But it is God who chose his people in his goodness and initiated the covenant to restore a relationship lost in the fall and to sustain it with his blessing. It was predicated on redeeming grace: "I am the LORD your God, who brought you out of the land of Egypt, out of the house of slavery" (Ex. 20:2). This fulfilled a promise made to Abraham also sealed in a covenant (Gen. 15:13–14). Keeping covenant with him by heeding his warnings, believing his promises, and obeying his commands was and is God's will and desire. Doing so results in life and blessing, for God will always keep his covenant. Sadly, the human heart tends to fixate on desires contrary to the way of life blessed by God. As underscored in Numbers, this results in unhappiness, complaining, and turning away from the Lord. This in turn leads to his chastisement.

Moses' intercessory prayers point to the way to confront the head-on collision in the relationship between sinful people and a holy God (Num. 14:13–19). As covenant mediator, he stands in the gap by seizing on God's promises and character, especially his goodness and mercy as revealed in his covenant. Any need or

---

[3] Dennis T. Olson, *Numbers*, Interpretation (Louisville: John Knox, 1996), 1. Other helpful sermonic commentaries include Raymond Brown, *The Message of Numbers*, BST (Downers Grove, IL: InterVarsity, 2002); Iain M. Duguid, *Numbers: God's Presence in the Wilderness*, PTW (Wheaton, IL: Crossway, 2006).

crisis was matched by God's faithfulness and covenant-keeping character. Certainly the Lord disciplines his wayward people—that too had been promised!—but he does so to draw them back into a relationship with him so they might live a life of blessing.

As demonstrated in Numbers, grace remains the key ingredient in the struggle against ungodly desires and living (Titus 2:11–12). Laying hold of God's promises yields the fruit of godliness and provides the off-ramp from bad desires (2 Pet. 1:4). God does not require what he by his grace has not first provided. His greatest gift was in sending his Son, the mediator of the new covenant, who as the Great High Priest lives to make intercession based on his accomplished work of redemption (Heb. 4:14; 7:25).

If cues are taken from the overall theological thrust of Numbers and the way in which the book relates to the rest of Scripture and Christ, the preacher will find the book a rich mine to ply with his exegetical pickaxe. Preaching Numbers will unveil its precious treasure. God's people will be warned of his judgment and strengthened in his grace.

Interpretive Challenges

Questions concerning large census numbers will be treated in the Comment section on Numbers 1. Those related to the way of the wilderness journey and the location of Mount Sinai are addressed in the Section Overview and Comment sections on chapter 33.

Two challenges are broached here: the unity of the book of Numbers and literary approaches to Numbers. Is there an overall structure of the book and a common thread binding the diverse genres and subjects together? And can the book be rightly understood by reading the present text as a whole?

UNIFYING STRUCTURE OF NUMBERS

Remarks on unifying ties between individual chapters are made in the corresponding Section Overview and Comment sections. The focus here is on the overall internal structure of Numbers as the backbone of the book's cohesion. Despite the ongoing debate as to whether the book's diverse genres and seemingly unrelated subjects fit together, commentators do concur that Numbers contains a tripartite geographical structure based on Israel's presence (1) in the wilderness of Sinai, (2) at and around Kadesh in the wilderness of Paran, and (3) in the Transjordan highlands and the plains of Moab. Travel narratives bridge these major movements.[4]

These geographical indices are generally used to outline the book. But the demarcations in verses, even chapters, often varies, particularly between the second

---

[4] In light of the "three important geographical references which help both to shape the structure of the book, and also serve to move Israel from Sinai to the borders of Canaan ... [the] work is on the whole well ordered." Philip J. Budd, *Numbers*, WBC 5 (Waco, TX: Word, 1984), xvii. The overly negative opinion of M. Noth is often cited: Numbers "lacks unity, and it is difficult to see any pattern in its construction." Martin Noth, *Numbers*, OTL (London: SCM, 1968), 1.

and third parts. For example, the outline in the hallmark commentary of G. B. Gray is the following:

I. 1:1–10:10
II. 10:11–*21:9*
III. *21:10*–36:13[5]

The highly regarded commentary of J. de Vaulx presents another:

I. 1:1–10:10
II. 10:11–*22:1*
III. *22:2*–36:13[6]

Comparing these and other outlines reveals that the differences (such as those italicized) involve the bridging travel narratives—chiefly, as here, that of the journey from Kadesh to the plains of Moab (20:22–22:1). Gray divides it at the narrative point at which, after leaving the Sinai Peninsula, the Israelites travel across the Arabah, south of the Dead Sea en route to Transjordan (21:9; cf. v. 10). De Vaulx includes the entire travel narrative, all the way to the encampment in the plains of Moab (22:1), in the second part of his outline.

Given the multiple interpretations of the literary contours of the topographical data, some commentators have opted for a binary division of Numbers: chapters 1–25; chapters 26–36. In support of this division literary and thematic echoes are pointed out; in particular both "halves" open with a census: the first of the "old" exodus generation (ch. 1) and the second of the "new" generation (ch. 26).[7] Notwithstanding this and other pertinent parallels, several factors should be borne in mind regarding this generational and literary division.

First, a literary division of the book based on the two genealogies does not really reflect a thematic "old" and "new" generational divide, which is fundamental to this binary division. When those twenty years old and upward of the "old" exodus generation are condemned to perish in the wilderness (14:29), those under twenty years are already present and part of the "new" generation that will enter the Promised Land (14:31). Thus, from the beginning to the end of Numbers the new generation is present. The new generation increases during the thirty-eight-year sojourn while the old generation decreases and ultimately ceases.

Second, locating the divide between the old and new generations—based on the census of the latter in chapter 26—sidesteps the internal chronology of Numbers. Aaron's death corresponds to the end of the traditional forty years (33:38) of the wilderness sojourn. His death is reported in chapter 20. Thus the old generation has passed away before the Israelites leave Kadesh (20:22) or reach the

---

[5] George Buchanan Gray, *Numbers*, ICC (Edinburgh: T&T Clark, 1903), xxvi–xxix.
[6] J. de Vaulx, *Les Nombres*, Sources Bibliques (Paris: Gabalda, 1972), 427–429. The same outline is proposed by Eryl W. Davies, *Numbers*, NCBC (Grand Rapids, MI: Eerdmans, 1995), liii.
[7] Largely inspired by Dennis T. Olson, *The Death of the Old and the Birth of the New: The Framework of the Book of Numbers and the Pentateuch*, BJS 71 (Chico, CA: Scholars Press, 1985), 83–124. In forty-six commentaries from the preceding one hundred years Olson found eighteen different outlines based on the geography of Israel's journeys (35). Cf. Davies's critique of Olson's approach (*Numbers*, lii–liii).

Transjordan (ch. 21; Deut. 2:14). Viewed as such, the twenty-four thousand who die in a plague for engaging in licentious idolatry at Peor (Num. 25:1–5, 9) are not the last remaining of the old generation. The death of the exodus generation reported in Numbers 26:64–65 antedates chapters 21–25.

Third, the old and new generation binary division smooths the edges of the sharp break within chapters 1–25, viewed as the first half of the book. Geographically, in chapter 10 Israel leaves Sinai for Kadesh (v. 11–12; cf. 13:26). Chronologically, chapters 1–10 involve a period of nineteen days, whereas chapters 11–25 cover the entire wilderness period. Thematically, the prompt obedience characterizing the leaders and the people in chapters 1–10 contrasts with their rife disobedience narrated in chapters 11–25, resulting in the forfeiture of their inheritance in Canaan.[8] Also, viewed as the second half of Numbers, chapters 26–36 cover but a few months, which seems disproportional chronologically, not to mention literarily, compared to the other half (chs. 1–25). Moreover, the picture-perfect obedience often attributed to the "new" generation in those last eleven chapters is undermined by Moses' own descriptions of them (e.g., "You have risen in your fathers' place, a brood of sinful men"; 32:14) and other Scripture (cf. Section Overview of Numbers 26). It is difficult to see how their obedience could be measured by instructions pertaining mainly to their future life in the land.

The tripartite outline proposed here draws upon literary features that dovetail with the geographical format.

The suggested structure contains outer frames: chapters 1–10 and chapters 26–36. Each is headed by a census, one of the exodus generation at Sinai and the other of the following generation in the plains of Moab. Each contains instructions, the former for the wilderness journey and the latter for life in the Promised Land. The twice occurring "In the midst of which I dwell" describes, in the first frame, the Lord's presence in the midst of the wilderness camp that must not be defiled (5:3) and, in the second frame, his future presence in the midst of the land the new generation must not defile (35:34). The first frame covers a few weeks and the second several months.

This framing is reinforced by bracketing chapters. Within the chapter 1–10 side frame, after the census (ch. 1) chapters 2 and 10 form brackets. Chapter 2 contains instructions regarding the arrangement of the tribal camps and how they "shall set out" (2:9, 16, 17, 24, 31). Chapter 10 narrates the execution of these instructions as they "set out" (10:12, 13, 14, 17, 18, 21, 22, 25, 28, 33, 34, 35) from Sinai. Within the Numbers 26–36 side frame, headed by a census (ch. 26), the bracketing chapters 27 and 36 contain rulings concerning the land inheritance of the "daughters of Zelophehad."

The framed center of Numbers (chs. 11–25) is also bracketed. Chapter 11 depicts the complaining, revolting exodus generation—the object of the Lord's "anger"

---

[8] Commentators who do adopt the binary division do, of course, recognize the break between chapters 10 and 11, or precisely between 10:10 and 10:11. Olson (*Numbers*, 9, 60) divides chapters 1–25 between "Obedient Beginnings..." (chs. 1–10) and "An Abrupt Slide into Rebellion..." (chs. 11–25).

(vv. 1, 10, 33) and a "plague" (v. 33). It contains a supplement on Joshua (1st mention), whom Moses asks, "Are you jealous for my sake?" (v. 29). Chapter 25 describes the licentious idolatry of the new generation—also an object of the Lord's "anger" (vv. 3, 4) and a "plague" (vv. 8, 9, 18). The chapter contains a supplement on Phinehas (his 1st mention), who was, Moses reports, "jealous for his God" (v. 13).

The side frames and the framed center are definable as compositional units. The book of Numbers is thus a structured whole.

UNIFYING SUBJECTS OF HOLINESS AND PURITY

In addition to the unifying structure of Numbers, the ritual realm is inherently related to the unity of the book. This realm encompasses four states, or spheres, presented in Leviticus 10:10 (cf. Ezek. 44:23) as paired opposites: holy (sacred) and common (ordinary/profane); unclean (impure) and clean (pure).[9] The suggestion made here is that holiness and purity and their opposites bind together the diverse contents of Numbers.

These matters did not concern only the clergy; they were part of everyone's daily life. In the compass of the whole book the chief concern in Numbers is for the Israelites not to defile (1) the camp in the wilderness and (2) the land of Canaan once they settle it. The reason for these concerns is one and the same: they occur at places "in the midst of which I [the holy God] dwell" (Num. 5:3; 35:34). Uncleansed impurity is dangerous, even potentially lethal, because it profanes the holy: God's name. Safeguard against desecration of the holy and defilement of the pure is crucial not only for survival in the wilderness; dwelling in the land will depend on it. Everyone—priests, Levites, and laity—has a critical role to play. Otherwise they will suffer God's wrath. The wilderness experience is the occasion for training in purity and holiness, which can then be applied to life in the Land of Promise.

To protect the people from God's wrath, spaces are delimited to safeguard the holy from desecrating encroachment. The tabernacle has the tent of meeting, consisting of the Most Holy Place and the Holy Place and their sacred furnishings, the court and the holy altar, all surrounded by a high curtain. Outside the curtain, on the four compass points of the tabernacle, was a cordon made by the camps of the priests and Levites (1:53; 3:23, 29, 35, 38). Around that was a second cordon of the people's military camps (1:52; 2:1–34; 10:1–36). The space beyond that was "outside the camp," which also had a vital role in preventing the defilement of the sanctuary (e.g., 5:3–4; 15:35; 19:9; 31:13, 19).

In addition, clerics were assigned to protect the holy. From inside the tabernacle the priests safeguarded the tent of meeting, its sacred furnishings, and the altar from desecration. They prevented unqualified priests or Levites from intruding the sacred space. From outside the tabernacle, and from between the altar and the tabernacle entry, the Levites prevented encroachment by the people. Any intruder was to be put to death. By their mutual service the priests and Levites saved them-

---

9 Cf. Gordon J. Wenham, *The Book of Leviticus*, NICOT (Grand Rapids, MI: Eerdmans, 1979), 18–23; Jay Sklar, *Leviticus*, TOTC (Downers Grove, IL: InterVarsity Press, 2014), 44–49.

selves (3:10; 4:19–20; 18:3, 7) and the people from the wrath of a holy God (1:51, 53; 8:19; 18:5). The people also played a vital role by keeping their camp pure by applying instructions given them to cleanse impurities (5:4; 19:12; 31:24).

Desecration of the holy was strictly forbidden and harshly punished (cf. below on legitimate desacralization). It involved encroachment, intentional sins, and uncleansed impurities. The following examples are, for the most part, limited to Numbers.

Encroachment involved unauthorized people or objects' entering into the holy space and also ritual misdeeds performed there. Encroachment was not merely an accidentally incurred impurity and therefore could not be cleansed. The death of the intruder was the only answer. For their transgressions in the ritual realm Aaron's sons, the priests Nadab and Abihu, and thousands of Korahite Levites and their followers perished (3:4; 16:32–35). Even the ritually purified Levites were forbidden to touch or look upon the most holy furnishings (4:15, 19–20).

Intentional sins desecrated the sanctuary, and so the guilty were cut off (15:30–31). As with encroachment, there was no ritual remedy for intentional sin. Examples include the Sabbath breaker (15:32–36), anyone who did not keep the Passover (9:13), the entire exodus generation for rebellion (14:32, 35), and anyone guilty of murder (35:30–34).

Anyone with certain impurities had to leave the camp to maintain its purity; they were quarantined "outside the camp" (5:2–3), especially those who contracted the highly contagious corpse impurity (19:13, 22; 31:19). Impurity outside the camp did not desecrate the holy if the proper cleansing procedure was followed. Once cleansed from their impurity, the person could reenter the camp (19:19; 31:24). But anyone not purified by the prescribed rituals in the given time frame while outside the camp would be cut off for having polluted the holy place (19:13, 20).

Desecration provoked God's wrath (1:53; 16:46; 18:5; 25:11; cf. also 11:10, 33; 12:9; 25:3–4; 32:14), which was manifested in various ways. It could break out in a plague (8:19; 11:33; 14:37; 16:46; 25:8–9, 18; 26:1; 31:16) or fire (11:1; 16:35; 26:10). In some cases the offender was to be executed by the hand of man, either by the sword of priests or Levites ("He shall be put to death," Hb. *yumat*; Ex. 32:27; Num. 1:51; 3:10, 38; 18:7) or by civil execution (15:35; 35:17). In other cases the punishment came directly from the hand of God ("They shall die," *yamut*; 14:35; 17:13; 20:26; 26:65), sometimes by cutting off (*karat*) the offending party and/or his lineage (4:18; 9:13; 19:13, 20). The misdeeds of one or a few sometimes resulted in many deaths in the community at large (17:12–13; 18:5; 25:9; 31:16). The death of the entire exodus generation in the wilderness was due to the bad report of ten men (14:32, 35; 26:65).

A legitimate form of desacralization occurred in the redemption of the holy firstborn by the Levites (3:13), which returned the redeemed firstborn from a holy to the common state (3:40–41). Terminating a Nazirite vow necessitated the return from a holy state comparable to that of the high priest to the common state by a complex ritual process (cf. comment on 6:13–21). After a portion ("a contribution") of holy first dough was offered, the rest could be used in an ordinary way (15:20–21). Once the contributions from the holy offerings were lifted, the remainder could be eaten by the priest's family (18:11). After the Levites tithed ("a contribution") the holy tithe from the people (18:26–28), the remaining nine-tenths was at their disposal (18:30–31). Priests who worked while performing Sabbath rituals also legitimately profaned the Sabbath (28:9–10; Matt. 12:5; John 7:23).

Contact with impurity defiled anyone or anything pure. Like infectious diseases, some physical impurities were contagious. Some of these impurities disappeared after a brief lapse of time and by washing. More severe ones required quarantine outside the camp (Num. 5:2–3) and offerings (cf. Lev. 13:46; 14:12; 15:2, 14–15, 29–30; cf. the special case of the Nazirite; Num. 6:9–12). Outside the camp had a pure place where the ashes from the red heifer were kept to make water for (i.e., to cleanse) impurity (19:9). The most defiling impurity, contact with a dead body, necessitated all the above antidotes in addition to the double aspersion with the water for impurity (9:10; 19:11–13; 31:19). Metallic objects made impure by contact with corpses could be purified by passing them through fire and sprinkling them with water for impurity; things that could not withstand fire were passed through the water (31:22–23). Once purified, people and objects were allowed back into the camp (31:24).

Impurities also resulted from unintentional sins (6:9–11). These were cleansed ceremonially. Their seriousness varied according to the level of responsibility in the hierarchy of religious or civil authority of anyone who caused the impurities, ranging from a high priest to a commoner (Lev. 4:3, 13, 15, 22, 27). The gravity was also signaled by the holy furnishing contaminated by the impurity and the means required to remove the impurity.

The common denominator in making purification was the "[de-]sin offering" (or "purification offering," *hatta't*), mentioned nearly forty times in Numbers (e.g., 15:25). To make purification the blood of a substitute animal was applied to the tabernacle furnishing that had been made impure (Ex. 29:36). If the impurity was caused by a high priest or another religious leader, it was purged by the blood of a bull applied to the incense altar in the Holy Place (Lev. 4:7, 14, 18). If the impurity was caused by a civil leader or commoner, it was purged by the blood of a goat at the altar in the court (Lev. 4:25, 30; Ezek. 43:20). Impurity could even penetrate the Most Holy Place and defile the most sacred atonement cover (*kapporet*, "mercy seat"; cf. comment on Num. 7:89) of the ark of the covenant, which represented the Lord's throne. Purging it with blood was done on the annual Day of Atonement by the high priest (Lev. 16:15). On other days blood was sprinkled seven times in front of the veil hiding the ark from view (Lev. 4:6). The sin offering is called the "sin offering of atonement" (Num. 29:11). Purging by substitutional blood was a means of making atonement (from *kpr*; Ex. 29:36; Lev. 14:19; Num. 6:11; 8:12, 19, 21; 15:25, 28; 28:22, 30; 29:5), which led to forgiveness (15:25, 26, 28). It necessitated the life (blood) of an animal as a vicarious payment for anyone who caused the impurity.

As stated in the NT, "Under the law almost everything is purified with blood, and without the shedding of blood there is no forgiveness of sins" (Heb. 9:22).

UNIFYING THEME OF LIFE AND DEATH

Keeping the spheres or states of the ritual realm separate—particularly the holy from the impure—saved life. But mixing or confusing them led to death. Warnings include "You shall not profane the holy things . . . lest you die" (Num. 18:32) and "If the man who is unclean does not cleanse himself, that person shall be cut off from the midst of the assembly, since he has defiled the sanctuary of the LORD" (19:20; cf. v. 13). In ritual contexts life and death are juxtaposed as binary opposites (e.g., "That they [the ritually pure Kohathite Levites] may live and not die when they come near to the most holy things"; 4:19).[10] The priest, Phinehas, as mediator "stood between the dead and the living" (16:48). Indeed, the life and death motif undergirds all the ritual states surveyed above and unifies the diverse contents in Numbers.

Although this was generally expressed in negative terms (death), saving life was the implicit goal. As with any law, a prohibition makes unnecessary the stating of all that is permitted. Obviously, avoiding what causes death by observing the commandments on holiness and purity preserves life.

In relation to the tabernacle everything is organized in Numbers to preserve life. The people in the camps (militia and their families) are kept from encroaching the tabernacle by the Levites (1:50) "so that there may be no wrath on the congregation of the people of Israel" (v. 53; 18:5). God's wrath spells death (e.g., 25:11). The Levites are kept from encroaching the sanctuary and the altar by the priests, "lest they die" (4:15). Thereby the priests protect themselves and the Levites, "lest they, and you, die" (18:3). "If any outsider comes near, he shall be put to death" (3:10; 18:7).

The death motif is recurrent in the laws and instructions. The law on impurity (5:1–4) addresses "contact with the dead" (5:2). The law on the Nazirite vow (6:1–12), requires that a Nazirite "shall not go near a dead body" (6:6) and specifies what must be done "if any man dies . . . beside him" (6:9). The instructions on the seven lamps (8:1–4) is vital, since the lamps illuminate the dark Holy Place. When leaving an encampment to set out on a journey, the priests are instructed to wrap the most holy furnishings carefully so that the Levites who carry them do not touch or even see them, "lest they die" (4:15, 20). In the second Passover law (9:6–14) "touching a dead body" (9:10) exempts anyone made impure from the first-month Passover. The law on tassels on garments (15:37–41) aims at preventing death by reminding Israel not to go "whor[ing] after" foreign gods (15:39; cf. Ex. 34:15–16; Deut. 31:16; Hos. 6:10). Conversely, touching tassels could restore life (Matt. 9:20; 14:36). Laws on the duties of priests and Levites (Numbers 18) reiterate their role of preventing encroachment, "lest they [the Levites], and you

---

10 The verb "die" (Hb. *mot*) in its various forms has a high frequency in Numbers—88 times, twice as many as in Leviticus. It occurs 60 times in Exodus and 55 times in Deuteronomy. The verb "to live" (*hayah*) occurs only 8 times in Numbers (4:19; 14:38; 21:8, 9; 22:33; 24:23; 31:15, 18). But this notion is more often expressed in negative terms, such as "That the manslayer may not die" (35:12; cf. 4:19; 26:11) or "They must not . . . lest they die" (4:15; cf. v. 20; 17:10; 18:3, 22, 32).

[the priests], die" (18:3; cf. v. 32) and "lest they [the people] . . . die" (18:22). The law on the red heifer and water for impurity made from its ashes (19:2, 11–22) concerns "whoever touches a dead person" (19:13).

The second census (ch. 26) contains obituary notices of well-known figures from the past (e.g., "Er and Onan died in the land of Canaan"; 26:19; cf. vv. 10, 61) and the contemporaneous comment "But the sons of Korah did not die" (26:11). It also reports the judgment pronounced on the exodus generation, "'They shall die in the wilderness.' Not one of them was left" (26:65). The legal appeal involving Zelophehad's daughters (chs. 27; 36) depends on their father's "[dying] for his own sin" (27:3), that is, not dying for being among those who rebelled. In the laws on the cities of refuge pertaining to manslaughter (35:16–34), a murderer is "guilty of death" and thus "shall be put to death" (35:30–31). Unpremeditated bloodshed remains unpurged until the "death of the high priest" (35:25, 28).

The Numbers narratives report a record number of deaths, posing a constant danger of corpse contamination. Hundreds of thousands of "dead bodies" (14:32) would fall in the wilderness; "there they shall die" (14:35). Notable individuals who "died" include Nadab and Abihu (3:4; 26:61), Miriam (20:1), Aaron (v. 28; 33:38), and Balaam (31:8). Korah, Dathan, Abiram, and their families "went down alive into Sheol" (16:33). Aaron's staff that budded was put into the ark as a sign to the grumbling people, "lest they die" (17:10); the grumblers stated their fear—"Everyone . . . who comes near to the tabernacle of the LORD, shall die" (17:13). From poisonous snakes "many people of Israel died," but by looking at the bronze serpent anyone "shall live" (21:6, 8). This motif is related to another: "I have set before you life and death, blessing and curse. Therefore choose life, that you and your offspring may live" (Deut. 30:19). Blessing and curse is the main motif in the Balaam story and discourses (Numbers 22–24; cf. Section Overviews). Recognizing God's blessing upon Jacob, Balaam exclaims, "Let me die the death of the upright" (23:10).

War is a constant threat, along with its own prospect of death. The censuses were designed to assign to companies those "able to go to war" (1:3; 26:2). In the law of the silver trumpets (10:1–10) one of their uses is to signal "when you go to war" (10:9). The people refuse to enter Canaan for fear they will "fall by the sword" (14:3). The law concerning the water for impurity prescribes its use on anyone who has touched someone "killed with a sword" (19:16). Military conflicts are waged in the wilderness with Amalekites (14:39–45), Canaanites (21:1–3), and Amorites (21:21–35). After the vengeance on the Midianites (31:1–8), purification is made for "whoever of you has killed any person and whoever has touched any slain" (31:19). Astonishingly, among Israel's soldiers, "there [was] not a man missing" (31:49). There will be deaths in future battles in Canaan (cf. 10:9; 33:50–56).

Laws and narratives contain the "breaking faith" (*ma'al*) offense, a term applied to high-handed or flagrant violations resulting in the perpetrator's being "cut off" (15:30–31). In chapter 5 the civil case (vv. 5–7) and the moral case (vv. 12–30) each involve "breaking faith" (vv. 6, 12, 27). Each case contains mitigating circumstances averting the death penalty (cf. comments on 5:5–10; 5:11–31). The plague at Peor that kills twenty-four thousand strikes those who acted "treacherously" (*ma'al*; 31:16), referring to licentious idolatry. Even Moses will die outside the Promised Land for "breaking faith" (Deut. 32:51) at Meribah for not treating God as holy (Num. 20:11–13; he rebelled against God, 27:14). There are those who can or will be "put to death" (1:51; 3:10, 38; 15:35; 18:7; 35:16, 17, 18, 21, 30, 31) or "shall die" (14:35; 17:13; 20:26; 26:65) for various offenses.

Behind all impurity representing decay and death is the underlying opposite principle of purity as representing well-being and life. Menstruation causes impurity of an otherwise pure person (Lev. 15:19), as does emission of semen (Lev. 15:16). The grouping of abnormal discharges from sexual organs with leprosy and corpse contact in Numbers 5:2–3 is revealing. Being struck with the impurity of leprosy (5:2) results in being "as one dead" (12:12). Even menstruation or ejaculation, both sources of life, apparently represent death.[11]

The prescribed antidote to death is "You shall therefore keep my statutes and my rules," which is followed by the promise "If a person does them, he shall live by them: I am the LORD" (Lev. 18:5).[12] But this promise applies to those who neither spurn God's grace nor tempt his wrath. This is seen clearly in Numbers. Anyone who would—in obedience of faith in the promise of deliverance—look at the bronze serpent "shall live" (Num. 21:8).

Putting into practice God's law preserves life. It involves a life of growing in holiness and purity, hallmarks of godly living. The Christian is exhorted, "Let us cleanse ourselves from every defilement of body and spirit, bringing holiness to completion in the fear of God" (2 Cor. 7:1), "for God has not called us for impurity, but in holiness" (1 Thess. 4:7).

DIACHRONIC AND HOLISTIC LITERARY APPROACHES

Commentaries on Numbers from the nineteenth century to the present can be divided into two basic types: (1) diachronic or historical-critical, which interprets the text after dissection by source, tradition, or redaction criticism; and (2) synchronic or holistic, which interprets the text as is.

Concerning the former type, in the introduction to his recent two-volume Numbers commentary B. Levine defends the "proposition that in order to understand a Torah book we are required to disassemble and reassemble its sources in chronological sequence." Such an approach, he argues, "holds forth the promise of identifying significantly different perceptions of the wilderness experience, perceptions that might be lost to us were we to study only the final product of the biblical process at the expense of the phases reflected in its literary development."[13] Levine's principal guide is G. B. Gray's 1903 commentary, which became the

---

[11] "Life" and "blood" can be synonyms (Gen. 9:4). Blood is lifeblood (Lev. 17:11). Milgrom (*Numbers*, 346) writes, "Blood and semen represent the forces of life; their loss, therefore, signifies death." For Sklar, this rationale behind certain impurities is a "*possible*" solution but lacks proof that it is "*probable*" (*Leviticus*, 47–48, emphasis his).
[12] Leviticus 18:5 is also cited by Milgrom, *Numbers*, 346.
[13] Baruch A. Levine, *Numbers 1–20: A New Translation with Introduction and Commentary*, AYB 4 (New York: Doubleday, 1993; New Haven, CT: Yale University Press, 2008), 49.

twentieth-century standard for a source-critical reading of Numbers. Gray's work represented a counterreaction to C. F. Keil's conservative (holistic) commentary published thirty-five years earlier. Gray considered Keil's commentary "untenable" given the advance of critical scholarship.[14] Ninety years later, Levine lauds Gray's work, saying he knows of no other modern critical commentary on Numbers "as instructive as his."[15] Levine's commentary also illustrates that, since Gray, for those who still adhere to the classical source-critical theory, literary boundaries have not appreciably moved concerning what is commonly labeled "priestly" (P) postexilic redaction (lists, laws, etc.), forming over three quarters of Numbers.

A prime example of the holistic type is the Numbers commentary of J. Milgrom. Concerning the holistic method Milgrom says, "It refuses to dissect the whole into parts and then consider these parts as having meaning apart from the whole. Rather, it studies a literary piece as a whole by demonstrating the interaction of its parts." He concludes, "Actually, this approach is not new at all."[16] Indeed, the goal of centuries of traditional or conservative interpretation has been to ascertain the intended meaning of the present text as is.

Admittedly, juxtaposing these two types of commentaries runs the risk of oversimplifying the question, since diachronic and synchronic approaches are often used concurrently. Classification of those commentaries depends on which method has the upper hand.[17]

One final point. Since "priestly" material (labeled P) constitutes the bulk of Numbers, it should be noted that the postexilic date generally assigned to it has been challenged on all fronts by scholars who themselves hold to some form of literary criticism. They have shown on linguistic and other grounds that priestly materials are at least preexilic if not at home in the second millennium BC.[18]

Outline

I. Instructions for the Exodus Generation Preparing to Leave Sinai for Canaan (1:1–10:36)
    A. The First Census of Men for Military Service (1:1–54)
        1. Census Preparation and Execution (1:1–19)
        2. Census Totals (1:20–46)
        3. Levites Exempted (1:47–54)

---

14 Gray, *Numbers*, vii. C. F. Keil, *The Book of Numbers* (Edinburgh: T&T Clark, 1869).
15 Levine, *Numbers 1–20*, 88. In addition to Gray and Levine, other Numbers commentators who emphasize historical-critical issues include M. Noth (1968), J. de Vaulx (1972), J. Sturdy (1976), P. J. Budd (1984), E. W. Davies (1995), and R. P. Knierim and G. W. Coats (2005). Since the end of the twentieth century, traditional source-criticism has largely been abandoned in Europe, particularly in France, Germany, and Switzerland, though the diachronic impulse persists.
16 Milgrom, *Numbers*, xii. Other commentators employing a holistic approach include G. Bush (1858), A. Noordtzij (1941; English translation 1983), G. J. Wenham (1981), R. B. Allen (1990), R. K. Harrison (1990), T. R. Ashley (1993), and R. D. Cole (2000).
17 The commentaries of M. Douglas (1993), K. D. Sakenfeld (1995), and D. T. Olson (1996) are characteristically holistic but do reach some literary-critical conclusions.
18 Cf. A. Hurvitz, "The Evidence of Language in Dating the Priestly Code," *RB* 81 (1974): 24–56; Hurvitz, *A Linguistic Study of the Relationship between the Priestly Source and the Book of Ezekiel* (Paris: Gabalda, 1982). On cultic institutions cf. Menahem Haran, *Temples and Temple-Service in Ancient Israel* (Winona Lake, IN: Eisenbrauns, 1985).

B. The Camp Arrangement and Order of March (2:1–34)
    1. General Instructions (2:1–2)
    2. The Judah Camp (2:3–9)
    3. The Reuben Camp (2:10–16)
    4. The Levites (2:17)
    5. The Ephraim Camp (2:18–24)
    6. The Dan Camp (2:25–31)
    7. Summary (2:32–34)
C. The First Census of the Tribe of Levi, the Levites' Roles and Arrangement around the Tabernacle (3:1–51)
    1. Priests Distinguished from the Levites (3:1–4)
    2. Levites Assigned Their Duties and Positions around the Tabernacle (3:5–39)
    3. Levites Redeem the Firstborn (3:40–51)
D. Levite Responsibilities and Totals (4:1–49)
    1. Kohathite Responsibilities and Totals (4:1–20, 34–37)
    2. Gershonite Responsibilities and Totals (4:21–28, 38–41)
    3. Merarite Responsibilities and Totals (4:29–33, 42–45)
    4. Summary (4:46–49)
E. Laws on Purity of the Camp (5:1–31)
    1. Physical Impurities (5:1–4)
    2. Fraud (5:5–10)
    3. Suspicion of Adultery (5:11–31)
F. The Nazirite Consecration (6:1–27)
    1. Requirements of the Nazirite Vow (6:1–12)
    2. Completion of the Nazirite Vow (6:13–21)
    3. Divine Blessing (6:22–27)
G. Offerings at the Tabernacle's Consecration (7:1–89)
    1. Gifts for the Transportation of the Tabernacle (7:1–9)
    2. Gifts for the Dedication of the Altar (7:10–88)
    3. The Voice Speaking to Moses (7:89)
H. Preparing for Service in the Tabernacle (8:1–26)
    1. The Lampstand (8:1–4)
    2. The Cleansing and Separation of the Levites (8:5–22)
    3. The Senior Levites Redeployed (8:23–26)
I. The Passover and the Cloud (9:1–23)
    1. Keeping the Passover (9:1–14)
    2. The Cloud Covering the Tabernacle (9:15–23)
J. On the Way from Sinai to Canaan (10:1–36)
    1. Silver Trumpet Signals (10:1–10)
    2. The Orderly March (10:11–28)
    3. Moses Requests Hobab's Services (10:29–32)
    4. Guidance by Ark and Cloud (10:33–36)

II. Trials in the Wilderness of Paran, the Transjordan Highlands, and the Plains of Moab (11:1–25:18)
  A. Incidences at Taberah and Kibroth-hattaavah (11:1–35)
    1. Complaining at Taberah, Divine Judgment, Moses' Prayer (11:1–3)
    2. Weeping over the Manna (11:4–10)
    3. Moses' Plea (11:11–15)
    4. Elders Appointed to Share Moses' Burden (11:16–30)
    5. Quail and a Plague at Kibroth-hattaavah (11:31–35)
  B. Miriam's and Aaron's Contention with Moses (12:1–16)
    1. The Complaint (12:1–3)
    2. The Lord's Reply and Remonstrance (12:4–10)
    3. Aaron's Confession, Moses' Plea, and Travel Resumed (12:11–16)
  C. Scouting the Land of Canaan (Num. 13:1–33)
    1. Commissioning the Scouts (13:1–20)
    2. Sending the Scouts (13:21–24)
    3. Return and Report of the Scouts (13:25–33)
  D. The Aftermath of the Scouts' Report (14:1–45)
    1. Immediate Reaction to the Scouts' Report (14:1–10)
    2. The Lord's Initial Response and Moses' Intercession (14:11–19)
    3. The Lord's Answer to Moses' Prayer (14:20–25)
    4. His Sentence Pronounced (14:26–38)
    5. Aborted Attempt to Enter the Promised Land (14:39–45)
  E. Regulations for Life in the Land (15:1–41)
    1. Laws on Offerings (15:1–21)
    2. Laws on Inadvertent and Willful Sins (15:22–31)
    3. Sentence of a Sabbath Breaker (15:32–36)
    4. Garment Tassel-Reminders (15:37–41)
  F. The Rebellion over the Priesthood and Leadership (16:1–50)
    1. Korah, Dathan, and Abiram Rebel (16:1–19)
    2. Judgment (16:20–35)
    3. Atonement (16:36–50)
  G. Test of Twelve Staffs (Num. 17:1–13)
    1. Twelve Tribes' Staffs Put before the Lord (17:1–7)
    2. Aaron's Staff Bears Almonds (17:8–13)
  H. Service and Revenues of Priests and Levites (18:1–32)
    1. Responsibilities and Rights of Priests and Levites (18:1–7)
    2. Priests' Revenues from the Offerings (18:8–19)
    3. Levites' Revenues from Tithes (18:20–32)
  I. Red Heifer Ashes and Water for Impurity (19:1–22)
    1. Preparation of Water for Impurity (19:1–10)
    2. Application of Water for Impurity (19:11–22)

- J. Final Incidents around Kadesh (20:1–29)
    1. Miriam's Death (20:1)
    2. The Waters of Meribah (20:2–13)
    3. Edom Refuses Passage (20:14–21)
    4. Aaron's Death (20:22–29)
- K. Journey from the Negeb to Transjordan (21:1–35)
    1. Arad Destroyed (21:1–3)
    2. Bronze Serpent (21:4–11)
    3. In Moab (21:12–20)
    4. Amorite Kings Sihon and Og Defeated (21:21–35)
- L. Balaam's Mission (22:1–41)
    1. His Summons (22:1–21)
    2. His Journey (22:22–41)
- M. Balaam's First Two Discourses (23:1–30)
    1. Discourse One (23:1–12)
    2. Discourse Two (23:13–30)
- N. Balaam's Final Two Discourses (24:1–25)
    1. Discourse Three (24:1–14)
    2. Discourse Four (24:15–25)
- O. Baal Worship at Peor (25:1–18)
    1. Israel's Infidelity (25:1–9)
    2. Phinehas's Zeal (25:10–15)
    3. Consequences for Midian (25:16–18)

III. Instructions beyond the Jordan at Jericho for the Generation Soon to Enter Canaan (26:1–36:13)
- A. Census of the New Generation (26:1–65)
    1. Census Ordered and Taken (26:1–51)
    2. Census and Land Inheritance (26:52–62)
    3. Reminder of the Reason for the Second Census (26:63–65)
- B. Succession to Property and Leadership (27:1–23)
    1. Succession to Property by Zelophehad's Daughters (27:1–11)
    2. Succession to Leadership by Joshua (27:12–23)
- C. Regular Offerings (28:1–31)
    1. Daily Offerings (28:1–8)
    2. Sabbath Offerings (28:9–10)
    3. Monthly Offerings (28:11–15)
    4. Passover and Feast of Unleavened Bread Offerings (28:16–25)
    5. Feast of Weeks Offerings (28:26–31)
- D. Offerings on the Seventh Month (29:1–40)
    1. Offerings for the Feast of Trumpets (29:1–6)
    2. Offerings for the Day of Atonement (29:7–11)
    3. Offerings for the Feast of Booths (29:12–38)
    4. Conclusion (29:39–40)

E. Vows and Oaths (30:1–16)
   1. Vows and Oaths of Men (30:1–2)
   2. Vows and Oaths of Women (30:3–16)
F. Vengeance on Midian (31:1–54)
   1. War against Midian (31:1–11)
   2. Return from War (31:12–18)
   3. Purification (31:19–24)
   4. Division of Plunder (31:25–47)
   5. Commanders' Offering (31:48–54)
G. Transjordan Inheritance of Reuben, Gad, and Manasseh (32:1–42)
   1. The Tribes' Request and Moses' Remonstrance (32:1–15)
   2. The Tribes' Proposition and Moses' Consent (32:16–32)
   3. The Tribes' Transjordan Inheritance (32:33–42)
H. The Forty-Year Itinerary and Land Inheritance Instructions (33:1–56)
   1. From Egypt to Sinai (33:1–15)
   2. From Sinai to [Kadesh] (33:16–18a)
   3. From [Kadesh] to Kadesh (33:18b–36)
   4. From Kadesh to the Jordan at Jericho (33:37–49)
   5. Instructions on Taking Possession of Canaan (33:50–56)
I. Inheriting the Land of Canaan (34:1–29)
   1. Boundaries of the Land to Be Inherited (34:1–15)
   2. Leaders Appointed to Oversee the Inheritance (34:16–29)
J. Cities for Levites and Cities of Refuge (35:1–34)
   1. Cities for Levites (35:1–8)
   2. Cities of Refuge (35:9–34)
K. Marriage of Daughter-Heirs (36:1–13)
   1. The Problem (36:1–4)
   2. The Solution (36:5–13)

OVERVIEW OF

NUMBERS 1–10

Numbers 1–10 contains instructions to prepare the Israelites for their departure from the wilderness of Sinai for the land of Canaan. Chapter 1 opens the book's "second year" supplement (1:1–10:10) to the Sinai pericope (Ex. 19:1–Lev. 27:34), which closes with Israel's departure from Sinai nineteen days later (Num. 10:11). The Numbers 1–10 frame opens with a census (ch. 1) and then is literarily bracketed by chapter 2, containing instructions on the camps' order of march, and by chapter 10, narrating those instructions' execution. The same compositional pattern is found in the Numbers 26–36 frame (cf. Introduction: Interpretive Challenges: Unifying Structure of Numbers).

NUMBERS 1

1 The Lord spoke to Moses in the wilderness of Sinai, in the tent of meeting, on the first day of the second month, in the second year after they had come out of the land of Egypt, saying, 2 "Take a census of all the congregation of the people of Israel, by clans, by fathers' houses, according to the number of names, every male, head by head. 3 From twenty years old and upward, all in Israel who are able to go to war, you and Aaron shall list them, company by company. 4 And there shall be with you a man from each tribe, each man being the head of the house of his fathers. 5 And these are the names of the men who shall assist you. From Reuben, Elizur the son of Shedeur; 6 from Simeon, Shelumiel the son of Zurishaddai; 7 from Judah, Nahshon the son of Amminadab; 8 from Issachar, Nethanel the son of Zuar; 9 from Zebulun, Eliab the son of Helon; 10 from the sons of Joseph, from Ephraim, Elishama the son of Ammihud, and from Manasseh, Gamaliel the son of Pedahzur; 11 from Benjamin, Abidan the son of Gideoni; 12 from Dan, Ahiezer the son of Ammishaddai; 13 from Asher, Pagiel the son of Ochran; 14 from Gad, Eliasaph the son of Deuel; 15 from Naphtali, Ahira the son of Enan." 16 These were the ones chosen from the congregation, the chiefs of their ancestral tribes, the heads of the clans of Israel.

17 Moses and Aaron took these men who had been named, 18 and on the first day of the second month, they assembled the whole congregation together, who registered themselves by clans, by fathers' houses, according to the number of names from twenty years old and upward, head by head, 19 as the Lord commanded Moses. So he listed them in the wilderness of Sinai.

20 The people of Reuben, Israel's firstborn, their generations, by their clans, by their fathers' houses, according to the number of names, head by head, every male from twenty years old and upward, all who were able to go to war: 21 those listed of the tribe of Reuben were 46,500.

22 Of the people of Simeon, their generations, by their clans, by their fathers' houses, those of them who were listed, according to the number of names, head by head, every male from twenty years old and upward, all who were able to go to war: 23 those listed of the tribe of Simeon were 59,300.

24 Of the people of Gad, their generations, by their clans, by their fathers' houses, according to the number of the names, from twenty years old and upward, all who were able to go to war: 25 those listed of the tribe of Gad were 45,650.

26 Of the people of Judah, their generations, by their clans, by their fathers' houses, according to the number of names, from twenty years old and upward, every man able to go to war: 27 those listed of the tribe of Judah were 74,600.

28 Of the people of Issachar, their generations, by their clans, by their fathers' houses, according to the number of names, from twenty years old and upward, every man able to go to war: 29 those listed of the tribe of Issachar were 54,400.

30 Of the people of Zebulun, their generations, by their clans, by their fathers' houses, according to the number of names, from twenty years old and upward, every man able to go to war: 31 those listed of the tribe of Zebulun were 57,400.

32 Of the people of Joseph, namely, of the people of Ephraim, their generations, by their clans, by their fathers' houses, according to the number of names, from twenty years old and upward, every man able to go to war: 33 those listed of the tribe of Ephraim were 40,500.

34 Of the people of Manasseh, their generations, by their clans, by their fathers' houses, according to the number of names, from twenty years old and upward, every man able to go to war: 35 those listed of the tribe of Manasseh were 32,200.

36 Of the people of Benjamin, their generations, by their clans, by their fathers' houses, according to the number of names, from twenty years old and upward, every man able to go to war: 37 those listed of the tribe of Benjamin were 35,400.

38 Of the people of Dan, their generations, by their clans, by their fathers' houses, according to the number of names, from twenty years old and upward, every man able to go to war: 39 those listed of the tribe of Dan were 62,700.

40 Of the people of Asher, their generations, by their clans, by their fathers' houses, according to the number of names, from twenty years old and upward, every man able to go to war: 41 those listed of the tribe of Asher were 41,500.

42 Of the people of Naphtali, their generations, by their clans, by their fathers' houses, according to the number of names, from twenty years old and upward, every man able to go to war: 43 those listed of the tribe of Naphtali were 53,400.

44 These are those who were listed, whom Moses and Aaron listed with the help of the chiefs of Israel, twelve men, each representing his fathers' house. 45 So all those listed of the people of Israel, by their fathers' houses, from twenty years old and upward, every man able to go to war in Israel— 46 all those listed were 603,550.

47 But the Levites were not listed along with them by their ancestral tribe. 48 For the LORD spoke to Moses, saying, 49 "Only the tribe of Levi you shall not list, and you shall not take a census of them among the people of Israel. 50 But appoint the Levites over the tabernacle of the testimony, and over all its furnishings, and over all that belongs to it. They are to carry the tabernacle and all its furnishings, and they shall take care of it and shall camp around the tabernacle. 51 When the tabernacle is to set out, the Levites shall take it down, and when the tabernacle is to be pitched, the Levites shall set it up. And if any outsider comes near, he shall be put to death. 52 The people of Israel shall pitch their tents by their companies, each man in his own camp and each man by his own

standard. ⁵³ But the Levites shall camp around the tabernacle of the testimony, so that there may be no wrath on the congregation of the people of Israel. And the Levites shall keep guard over the tabernacle of the testimony." ⁵⁴ Thus did the people of Israel; they did according to all that the LORD commanded Moses.

Section Overview

The opening verses of Numbers join the book canonically, historically, and theologically to Genesis, Exodus, and Leviticus. Were Numbers to be read with no knowledge of the earlier books, everything mentioned in 1:1–3 would be incomprehensible. Who is "the LORD"? Who are "Moses" and the "people of Israel"? Why are they in the "wilderness of Sinai"? What is the "tent of meeting"? How did they "come out of the land of Egypt"? Why did the Lord command Moses to "take a census" of men who "are able to go to war"? All of this presupposes—as does the answer to the question not raised here, "Where are they going?"—the understanding that the Lord has delivered his chosen people from slavery, as promised to Abraham, so that they might honor, serve, and enjoy life in covenant relationship with him in the land he covenanted to the fathers and their descendants. The census is a critical step in that direction.

Chapter 1 begins with a command given by the Lord to Moses and ends with a compliance summary, "They did according to all that the LORD commanded Moses" (v. 54). An obedient response also punctuates the chapter (v. 19), as is repeatedly the case in the first part of the book.

Section Outline

I. Instructions for the Exodus Generation Preparing to Leave Sinai for Canaan (1:1–10:36)
   A. The First Census of Men for Military Service (1:1–54)
      1. Census Preparation and Execution (1:1–19)
      2. Census Totals (1:20–46)
      3. Levites Exempted (1:47–54)

Comment

1:1–19 "The LORD spoke to Moses" (v. 1) occurs over forty times in Numbers. This expression confirms Moses' role as spokesman and intermediary for the Lord before the people and for the people before the Lord. "The Lord [who] spoke" defines the God of Israel as the God who reveals himself in words and thereby sets himself apart from the gods of other nations, who cannot speak (e.g., Ps. 115:5). In addition to his word (special revelation) the Lord manifests himself also through his works of creation and providence (general revelation). Redemption from bondage in Egypt and the law given at Sinai were primordial demonstrations of these revelatory modes through Moses. The Lord demonstrated his mighty power as King by delivering his people and crushing their enemy (cf. Ex. 15:2–12; Isa. 43:14–15; 44:6). By Moses he gave his law to Israel, which is now a nation, and renewed his covenant bond he had established with their fathers. He will now lead them to their inheritance in the Promised Land (Ex. 15:13–18).

"The wilderness of Sinai" (Num. 1:1) occurs ten times in Numbers, whereas Mount Sinai is mentioned only as the locus of the institution of the Aaronic priesthood (3:1) and the ordinance of the burnt offering (28:6). These latter elements are part of the Sinai covenant, while the census instructions are not. The wilderness of Sinai and Mount Sinai are geographically indissociable (Ex. 19:2; Lev. 7:38; Acts 7:30). The location of one depends on the other (cf. Section Overview of Numbers 33; comment on 33:1–15 [at v. 15]). The wilderness of Sinai is only part of what is today called the Sinai Peninsula.

The Sinai Peninsula is shaped like an upside-down triangle, with its base in the north and its apex in the south. The base merges into the semiarid Negeb (meaning "dry"; 13:17) along the southern border of Canaan. The northern half of the peninsula is sandwiched between Egypt on the western side and the Arabah to the east—the geological rift between the Dead Sea and the head of the Gulf of Aqaba/Elath. The southern half is flanked by the two branches of the Red Sea, the Gulf of Suez to the west (33:10–11) and the Gulf of Aqaba to the east (21:4). Despite low levels of precipitation that decrease from the northern parts of the peninsula to the southern regions, large areas in the northern half are suitable for pasturage and, in pockets, crops. The Israelites have large flocks and herds to tend during their year in the wilderness of Sinai (Ex. 12:38; 34:3; Num. 3:41, 45; 7:87–88). "Wilderness" (Hb. *midbar*) often refers to "pasture" (e.g., Gen. 36:24; 1 Chron. 6:78; Ps. 65:12; Jer. 9:10).

The locus of revelation to Moses is no longer Mount Sinai (Lev. 26:46) but now "in the tent of meeting" (*'ohel mo'ed*; Num. 1:1), designated over fifty-five times in Numbers. This generally defines the tent containing the Holy Place and the Most Holy Place (Ex. 40:22–26; Lev. 4:5–6; 24:3; Num. 7:89). The Lord had promised he would meet with Moses there (Ex. 30:36). As mediator between the Lord and his people, Moses no longer ascends the mountain but goes to the tent to hear the Lord speaking to him from above the mercy seat and between the cherubim (Num. 7:89; cf. Ex. 25:22; 30:6, 36). As prophet-mediator, Moses delivers to the people the word he receives (e.g., Num. 1:54; 2:34). To prevent the people from approaching the mountain, limits had been set around it. The mountain where the Lord manifested his presence could neither be looked upon nor touched, under the pain of death (Ex. 19:12, 21). Now the tent of meeting is where the presence of the Lord is manifested. Even the Levites who encamp around the tabernacle can neither touch nor look upon the sacred furnishings in the tent of meeting, lest they die (Num. 4:15, 20).

When the word "tent" appears alone, it refers to the goat hair covering of the sacred objects, that covering itself being enclosed with ram skins and goatskins (Ex. 36:14, 19; 40:19; Num. 3:25). *Mo'ed* alone can signify, as here, a sacred appointed "meeting" place or, as elsewhere, a sacred appointed "meeting" time, such as Passover (9:2). The Sinai revelatory trajectory of *mo'ed* is significant. In Exodus sacred festivals (*mo'adim*) were to be held around the tent of meeting (*'ohel mo'ed*), where the Lord would meet (*y'd*) with his gathered people. Exodus ended with the cloud covering the tent of meeting and the glory filling the tabernacle. But Moses was not able to enter the tent of meeting (Ex. 40:35)—now that God's holy presence was manifested there, it could not yet be a meeting place between God and his people. Still to be provided were the Levitical laws on approaching the tent of meeting through priest-mediated offerings (Leviticus 1–10), laws on maintaining its purity (chs. 11–15), laws on its purification on the Day of Atonement (ch. 16), laws on maintaining its holiness (chs. 17–22), and laws on sacred festivals in the sacred calendar, when God would meet with his people (chs. 23–25)—with blessings and curses related to all the regulations (ch. 26). These laws will be supplemented in Numbers, and others added. Also, worship at the tent of meeting awaits the offerings of the chiefs of Israel for the consecration of the tabernacle and the dedication of the altar (Num. 7:2–88), which is linked chronologically to the setting up of the tabernacle (vv. 1, 89). Instructions are needed to safeguard the holiness of the tent of meeting, which requires priestly and Levitical service and the purity of the peoples' camp (chs. 1–6; 18–19).

The exodus—on the day after the first-year, first-month Passover (Ex. 12:29, 51)—is a chronological benchmark in Israel's history, 430 years after the descent to Egypt (cf. Gen. 15:13; Ex. 12:40–41) and 480 years before the construction of Solomon's temple (1 Kings 6:1; cf. Introduction: Date and Occasion). The tabernacle was erected on the "first day of the first month" in the second year (Ex. 40:2; cf. Num. 7:1). Between the first and second months Aaron and his sons were consecrated (Exodus 29), the chiefs' offerings were presented for the tabernacle's consecration (Numbers 7), and the second Passover was celebrated (9:1–5). Israel left Sinai on the twentieth day of the second month (10:11). Numbers 1:1–10:10 therefore spans nineteen days. Two other second-year, second-month events are recorded in revelation history: the cloud's lifting from over the tabernacle—signaling Israel's departure from the wilderness of Sinai (10:11)—and the commencement of temple reconstruction upon the people's return from exile (Ezra 3:8).

The first words spoken by the Lord to Moses are commands and instructions. "Take a census" (Num. 1:2; lit., "Lift the head") does not mean they were physically to count the heads of the people one by one. The same expression is used for inventorying plunder, which involved no heads (31:26)! The parallel expression "Taking the number of . . . names" (3:40; lit., "Lift the number of names") shows that the census is based on lists of names (cf. comment on 1:20–46 [at v. 20]). "Head by head" means "each one" (Ex. 16:16).

Those counted are designated from general to specific. "All" (Hb. *kol*) in this context narrowly delimits the "congregation of the people of Israel" according to gender ("every male"; Num. 1:2) and age ("from twenty years old and upward"; v. 3). "Congregation" (*'edah*; v. 2) views Israel's civil identity, in its broadest sense, as the sum of its individuals (a body) or, in a narrow sense, as its representatives (cf. comments on v. 18; 16:1–19 [at v. 13]). *'Edah* is translated "swarm" if referring to bees (Judg. 14:8) and "herd" if cattle (Ps. 68:30). "The people of Israel," literally "the sons of Israel," is an ethnological expression designating a people (cf. Deut. 2:19) who are descendants of one of Jacob's/Israel's sons, the twelve tribal ancestors.

Socially, the Israelites are organized by tribes, clans, and fathers' houses (Num. 1:2; cf. Josh. 7:14, 16–18; Judg. 6:15). Synchronically, members of fathers' houses are members of clans (cf. Josh. 2:12–13, 18; 6:23, 25), just as members of clans are also members of tribes (Num. 1:4; cf. comment on 3:5–39 [at v. 20]). Diachronically, fathers' houses are nuclear families, each with three or four generations of one lineage living at the same time.[19] This household unit may be behind the recurrent expression "Third and fourth generations" (Ex. 20:5; 34:7; Num. 14:18; Deut. 5:9; cf. Job 42:16). Apparently, the oldest living man is the household head, and upon his death the title passes to his junior.

"Number" (*mispar*; Num. 1:2) refers to a sum (3:22), not a count. The census is done via names on lists. This factor and the fact that the census is undertaken for all the tribes simultaneously explains how it is accomplished in under twenty days (cf. 1:4; 10:11).

"From twenty years old and upward" (1:3) implies that the lists of names are birth records (cf. comments on v. 18; 1:20–46 [at v. 20]). In addition to fifteen occurrences in chapter 1, this expression occurs four times elsewhere in Numbers, twice referring to the exodus generation, which dies in the wilderness (14:29; 32:11), and twice to the new generation (26:2, 4). According to Josephus the upper age limit was fifty (*Antiquities*, 3.12.4). Fifty years of age is the upper limit of the Levites' census for tabernacle work (Num. 4:3), at which age they assume less strenuous duties (cf. comment on 8:23–26 [at v. 25]).

"Who are able to go to war" (*yotse' tsaba'*; 1:3) further defines those counted. The same expression rendered in 2 Chronicles 25:5 as "fit for war" is qualified as "those . . . able to handle spear and shield." Some are unable to do so, such as those with a physical handicap. "To war" (*tsaba'*) may be rendered "military service." "War" is normally expressed as *milkhamah* (cf. Num. 10:9; 21:14, 33; 31:6, 14, 21, 27, 28, 49). *Tsaba'* also refers to the Levites' tabernacle duty (4:3).

The reason to take the "census" in Numbers 1 differs from that given in Exodus 30:11–16. There the census determined the number for whom a ransom—atonement money—was to be paid (Ex. 30:16; cf. Num. 31:50). A half shekel was paid for "everyone . . . listed in the records, from twenty years old and upward, for 603,550 men" (Ex. 38:26). This figure is precisely the one given in Numbers 1:46. The literary position of the census in Exodus 30 indicates it was taken to raise

---

19 Including his own, Joseph's "father's house" includes four generations (Gen. 50:22–23), as does Achan's "household" (Josh. 7:18).

funds for the construction of the tabernacle, the contributions in silver used for the bases (Ex. 38:25–27). The tabernacle was completed on the first day of the first month, in the second year after the exodus (Ex. 40:2, 16; cf. Num. 7:1). The Numbers 1 census instructions are given on the first day of the second month (1:1). The Numbers census apparently employs the conscription registration of those already numbered in Exodus 30 (cf. discussion Num 1:18).[20] As will be suggested, the "census" in Numbers has to do more with appointment to a sphere of service than with counting.

Both from the tribe of Levi, Moses' closest collaborator is his brother, Aaron, who is three years his senior (Ex. 7:7). Their names appear together in over fifty verses in Numbers. Aaron was progenitor of the priesthood (Ex. 40:12–15). Moses is the archetypical prophet (Num. 12:8; Deut. 34:10). The brothers' respective roles are complementary: ministers of the Word and sacraments (cf. Deut. 33:8, 10). Moses' Torah teaching reveals God's justice and holiness, the righteousness and purity required to live in his presence, and the blessings for obedience and curses for disobedience. Aaron's officiating at the altar allows the people to draw near to God, seek his forgiveness through atonement, and give thanks for his grace. Both men require help to carry out their tasks. Moses is aided by elders and Joshua (Num. 11:14–17, 25, 28), Aaron and his sons by the Levites (3:9; 18:6; for tribal leaders who helped both cf. discussion on 1:4–16).

Moses and Aaron are instructed to "list them, company by company" (1:3). The immediate goal is to organize the men into military companies (cf. v. 52). In this context the verb translated "list" (Hb. *paqad*) may be rendered "appoint" (cf. v. 50; 3:10, 36).[21] The complement "company by company" is literally "to their companies" (*letsib'otam*). Numbering, listing, or registering is part of a process that culminates in appointment to military (1:3) or Levitical units (cf. v. 50; "appoint").

On a larger scale the twelve secular tribes are organized into four "camps," each consisting of three "companies" (cf. ch. 2). On a smaller scale each company comprises blood relatives living together as extended families. This organization facilitates the mustering of troops in time of war. Bivouacking together with kin provides an additional incentive for them to fight to defend the family (cf. Ezra 8:15–23). Similarly, families would provide supplies for their sons in time of war (1 Sam. 17:17).

Numbers 1:4–16 contains the names of one man from each tribe who assists Moses and Aaron in the census. None of their composite theophoric names has the abridged form of Yahweh (*yah*). The short form of Elohim (*'el*) is either

---

[20] So C. F. Keil, "The Fourth Book of Moses" in *The Pentateuch*, Commentary on the Old Testament 1 (Grand Rapids, MI: Eerdmans, 1973), 4.
[21] *Paqad* has been variously translated here: "list" (ESV), "number" (RSV, NASB), "count" (NIV), and "register" (CSB, NLT). Cf. *CDCH*, 363. "Count/number" is problematic since, as suggested, the counting had already been done (cf. comment on 1:1–19 [at v. 3]). Moreover, other verbs mean "count/number," e.g., Num. 23:10: "Who can count [*manah*; cf. Gen. 13:16; Ps. 90:12] the dust of Jacob or number [*sapar*; cf. Gen. 15:3; 2 Chron. 2:16] the fourth part of Israel?" Solomon said Israel was "too many to be numbered [*manah*] or counted [*sapar*] for multitude" (1 Kings 3:8). The range of proposed translations reflects a challenge that surfaces in passages such as "number [*paqad*] the people, that I may know the number [*mispar* from *sapar*] of the people" (2 Sam. 24:2).

prefixed (e.g., "Elizur"; v. 5) or suffixed (e.g., "Shelumiel"; v. 6). The epithet Shaddai (*shaddai*, translated "Almighty"; cf. comment on 24:1–14 [at v. 4]) also appears (e.g., "Ammishaddai"; 1:12). Other names reflect kinship ties: "people" (*'am*; e.g., "Amminadab," v. 7 [the father of Aaron's wife, Ex. 6:23; ancestor of Christ, Luke 3:33]), "father" (*'ab*; e.g., "Eliab," Num. 1:9), and "brother" (*'ah*; e.g., "Ahiezer," v. 12). Each is the "head of the house of his fathers" (v. 4). They are also the "chiefs of their ancestral tribes, the heads of the clans of Israel" (v. 16; cf. Ex. 6:14, 25; Num. 7:2). Their titles bring together three social levels of Israelites: tribe (*matteh/shebet*), clan (*'elep/mishpakhah*), and father's house (*bet 'ab*).

The verb and its complement "assist you" (1:5) may be translated "stand with you" (*ya'amdu 'itkem*). An inferior who stands with a superior is at his service. They are the "ones chosen from the congregation" (v. 16). "Chosen" is grammatically bound to the following word and read together may be translated "ones called/ convened from the congregation" (the verb is *qara'*, "call/convoke," not *bahar*, "choose"; cf. 17:5). Those whom the Lord tells Moses will assist him are already recognized leaders upon whom the Lord indicates his approval by naming them individually.

Numbers 1:17–19 present the response to the census instructions. Moses and Aaron carry them out "on the first day of the second month" (v. 18), the very day they are given. Delayed obedience generally ends in disobedience. They are assisted by the men who "had been named" (*niqqbu beshemot*; v. 17), an expression used for officials serving in national civil and ceremonial capacities (e.g., 1 Chron. 12:32; Ezra 8:20). The verb (*naqab*) suggests their names are inscribed (cf. "engravings"; Ezek. 28:13).

The subjects of the verb "they assembled" (Num. 1:18) are Moses and Aaron, no doubt assisted by the twelve named men (v. 17). This is the first occurrence in Numbers of "assemble" (*qahal*; cf. comments on 10:1–10 [at v. 7]; 16:1–19 [at v. 3]). As in 1:2, "the whole congregation" (v. 18) refers to those twenty years old or older eligible for military service. Elsewhere the whole congregation refers, in a broad sense, to the Israelites (20:1) and, in a restricted sense, to their representatives (Lev. 4:13 [cf. "elders," v. 15]; Num. 27:22).

The grammatical voice of "who registered themselves" (from *yalad*, "be born/ give birth"; v. 18) is not a regular reflexive (in which the subject and object are the same, both performing and receiving the action of the verb) but rather an indirect reflexive (in which the subject is the beneficiary but not the performer of the action)—thus "who got themselves registered" (cf. comment on 8:5–22 [at v. 21]). The verb indicates being registered by genealogy (cf. comment on 1:20–46 [at v. 20; "generations"]).[22]

"According to the number of names" (v. 18; cf. v. 2)—specified for each tribe (e.g., vv. 20, 22)—is how the whole congregation of those "twenty years old and upward, head by head" is assembled. It is done based on written records, not physical presence. "So he listed them" (*paqad*; v. 19) states the compliance to the

---

22 On Numbers 1:18 cf. CHALOT, s.v. ילד: "Have oneself entered in a family register."

instructions (v. 3) and prefaces what is said for each tribe, "those listed of the tribe of" (e.g., v. 21).[23] "Listed" may be rendered "assigned," here to military companies (e.g., 2:4; cf. comment on 1:3).

1:20–46 The census totals are given by tribal ancestors: Reuben, Simeon, Gad, Judah, Issachar, Zebulun, Joseph (Ephraim and Manasseh), Benjamin, Dan, Asher, and Naphtali (vv. 20–43). Except for Gad, these names are in the same order as in verses 5–15. Once again, the two "sons/people of Joseph" (vv. 10, 32), Ephraim and Manasseh, are mentioned, bringing the total to twelve tribes, with Levi not included. Since we have not yet been told the reason, Levi's absence is surprising and hints at what will follow. The sons of Levi will have a special role that sets them apart from the other tribes (vv. 47–54).

In connection with the lists of their names, the birth order of the tribal ancestors is significant. Reuben, Simeon, Levi, and Judah were sons born to Leah, Jacob's first wife (Gen. 29:31–35). Then Dan and Naphtali were born to Rachel's servant, Bilhah (Gen. 30:4–8), after which Gad and Asher were born to Zilpah, Leah's servant (Gen. 30:10–13). Then Leah bore Issachar and Zebulun (Gen. 30:17–20). Finally, Joseph and Benjamin were born to Rachel (Gen. 30:23–24; 35:16–18).

In Numbers 1 the order is presented differently than their birth order. Leah's honor and rights are, in a sense, posthumously restored as she is implicitly highlighted. Two of Leah's rights had been violated. As the first wife of Jacob, she should have been the matriarch, not Rachel. Leah's son Reuben, Jacob's firstborn, should have been heir, not Joseph, who through his sons Ephraim and Manasseh received a double portion. What Jacob did to Leah and her firstborn was later forbidden (Deut. 21:15–17). The sons she bore are mentioned first: Reuben, Simeon, and Judah, as well as the two she bore later, Issachar and Zebulun. These two were born after the four sons born to her servant and Rachel's. In addition, Levi, not yet mentioned, will hold a special position. Judah too will have preeminence, signaled by his tribe's position in the camp and the marching order (Num. 2:3, 9). Moreover, that Leah's son Reuben was "Israel's firstborn" is recalled in 1:20. This notice may be a harbinger of the Reubenite challenge raised in chapter 16.

Genealogical records are necessary to establish new registration lists of those of draft age. For each tribe, records by "their generations" (Hb. *toledot*, from *yalad*; e.g., v. 20; NIV "records") are available from fathers' houses.[24] These involve birth registers (cf. Gen. 25:12–15; Ps. 87:6). The totals are given of each of the twelve tribes (e.g., Num. 1:21, 23), then their sum (v. 46). Each total for the tribes is preceded by "those listed" (e.g., vv. 21, 23), and then their sum is preceded by "all those listed" (*kol happequdim*; v. 46). "All" (*kol*) means "the total," as in "the total of those assigned."[25] They were to be assigned "company by company."

---

23 The Mari royal archives show how armies were mustered. Based on quotas set by the king, military scribes entered tribal camps and made lists of men to be levied. Forces were mustered from different locations. Cf. G. E. Mendenhall, "The Census of Numbers 1 and 26," *JBL* 77 (1958): 64.
24 R. K. Harrison calls them "records of ancestry," which were indispensable for tribal membership and inheritance. Cf. Harrison, *Numbers*, WEC (Chicago: Moody, 1990), 41.
25 Rolf P. Knierim and George W. Coats, *Numbers*, FOTL 4 (Grand Rapids, MI: Eerdmans, 2005), 50.

A summary (vv. 44–46) concludes the census list, forming an inclusio with the introduction (cf. 2–5a), juxtaposed in table 4.1. The repetition of "able to go to war," used fourteen times in chapter 1, emphasizes the goal and its realization.

TABLE 4.1: Inclusio in Numbers 1:1–46

"Take a census . . . of the people of Israel" (v. 2)	"all those listed of the people of Israel" (v. 45; cf. v. 46)
"you . . . shall list them" (v. 3)	"These are those who were listed" (v. 44)
"you and Aaron" (v. 3)	"Moses and Aaron" (v. 44)
"a man from each tribe, . . . head of the house of his fathers" (v. 4)	"twelve men, each representing his fathers' house" (v. 44)
"twenty years old and upward" (v. 3)	"twenty years old and upward" (v. 45)
"all in Israel who are able to go to war" (v. 3)	"every man able to go to war in Israel" (v. 45)

The summary is concluded by the grand census total of those enlisted: 603,550 (v. 46; 2:32; cf. Ex. 38:26). This figure remains an object of debate.[26]

To grasp the significance of this total it must first be understood that neither the grand total here nor that of the second census (Num. 26:51) gives the size of Israel's standing army. It is instead the number of men "able to go to war" (e.g., 1:3, 45; 26:2), those eligible to be called up to active duty.[27] Israel never had a standing army of over 600,000. For example, against Midian there were "out of the thousands of Israel, a thousand from each tribe, twelve thousand armed for war" (31:5). In their first two military engagements in Canaan the armies at Jericho and at Ai numbered 40,000 and 30,000, respectively (Josh. 4:13; 8:3).[28] These figures of fighting men are comparable to army sizes known from ancient Near Eastern texts.[29]

Second, the numbers of those engaging in actual combat were far less than the size of the fielded army. Alongside those who did bear arms were some who guarded the supplies; these formed as many as one-third of David's forces (1 Sam. 25:13; cf. 23:13; also 17:22; 30:24). In a protracted battle, some would rest while others fought (1 Sam. 30:9–10). Some would remain to protect the families the warriors left behind. This may explain why no upper age limit is given for the conscription of those "twenty years old and upward." Those who were older would no longer do battle (2 Sam. 21:17), but they could still stand guard. As with the Levites, there is no stated age limit for those who do guard duty (Num. 3:5–7, 15), but there is for porterage (4:3).

---

26 For discussions of problems related to census figures in Numbers cf. Ronald B. Allen, *Numbers*, in *Numbers–Ruth*, EBC 2 (Grand Rapids, MI: Zondervan, 1990), 680–691. Also cf. Gordon J. Wenham, *Numbers*, TOTC (Downers Grove, IL: InterVarsity Press, 2008), 60–66; Milgrom, *Numbers*, 336–339; Timothy R. Ashley, *The Book of Numbers*, NICOT (Grand Rapids, MI: Eerdmans, 1993), 60–66; R. Dennis Cole, *Numbers*, NAC (Nashville: B&H, 2000), 78–82.
27 Confusing the conscription census figures with actual army sizes has sometimes led to undue observations that the figures are inconsistent with army sizes in other texts.
28 Even if 40,000 refers not to all Israel but only to soldiers from Reuben, Gad, and the half-tribe of Manasseh (Josh. 4:12), their conscription total of 124,350 still supports the point made.
29 *ANET*, 278–279. In the first half of the second millennium BC a major military operation could call a force of 60,000; F. Malbran-Labat, "Military Organization in Mesopotamia," *ABD* 4.827.

If the figure 603,550 is taken literally, the estimated population of Israel would be as large as 2,500,000. Given this vast population, it is hard to understand why it is said the nations in Canaan are "more numerous and mightier" (Deut. 7:1) than the "fewest of all peoples" (Deut. 7:7), or why these are nations the Lord would clear away "little by little" as the Israelite population increased (Deut. 7:22; cf. Ex. 23:29–30). When the conquest dust settled—whether viewed from the perspective of the "whole land" taken or of the "land that yet remains" to be taken (Josh. 10:40; 13:2)—the Israelites possessed, in addition to the Negeb, a region comparable to the West Bank today. The Israelite population of that area, apart from the indigenous Canaanite population, would have been as dense as today's population.[30] This consideration does not, however, address the question of how two and a half million people could sojourn in the wilderness, and that in relative proximity.[31] The main answer given in Numbers and Deuteronomy is the miraculous provision of food and water.

Another difficulty surfaces when the 603,550 male adults are juxtaposed with the 22,273 firstborn males a month old and upward (3:43). The number of males under twenty cannot be determined, nor can the number of adult firstborn among the 603,550 twenty years old and upward. But if only that number were divided by the number of those one month and upward, there would have been twenty-seven males per family.[32] This calculation would mean each mother bore about fifty children, assuming the number of girls was close to that of males. The juxtaposition of these two tallies gives pause.

Some have suggested that *'elep* in the census means military "unit" or "clan" rather than "thousand." Thus a tribe such as that of Reuben, listed at 46,500, would have contained 46 units (or clans) of 500 people. This means the given sum derived from the addition of the figures for all the tribes, 603,550, would have to come from an originally unintended and erroneous redaction. More promising is the idea that these military census figures are intentionally high. Rhetorical or hyperbolic war language is found in Numbers and elsewhere in the Pentateuch:

> Our sister, may you become
> > thousands of ten thousands,
> and may your offspring possess
> > the gate of those who hate him! (Gen. 24:60)

Whenever the ark set out, Moses said, "Arise, O Lord, and let your enemies be scattered, and let those who hate you flee before you." And when it rested, he said, "Return, O Lord, to the ten thousand thousands of Israel [i.e., thousands of tens of millions]." (Num. 10:35–36)[33]

---

30 The Arab population of the West Bank in 2017 was 2.3 million, with a total population over 3.2 million.
31 The current population of the entire peninsula, including the Negeb, is approximately 1.4 million.
32 Or a 27:1 ratio of adult to firstborn males; cf. Wenham, *Numbers*, 61. To address this disproportion Keil posited that only the firstborn in the thirteen months between the exodus and adult census were numbered ("Fourth Book of Moses," 9–12). The firstborn census instructions do not mention that timeframe, nor do those for the military census. If the census demographic applied to the Levites ("every firstborn who opens the womb"; 3:12) also applied to the other Israelite firstborn (v. 43), they would be the firstborn of both husband and wife, bearing in mind a man could have more than one wife.
33 The word translated "ten thousand" (Hb. *rebabah*) refers to an incalculable sum, as does the LXX "myriads."

Five of you shall chase a hundred, and a hundred of you shall chase ten thousand, and your enemies shall fall before you by the sword. (Lev. 26:8; cf. Deut. 32:30; 33:17; 1 Sam. 18:7; Ps. 91:7)

Declaring massive numbers of forces was apparently part of military strategy in the ancient Near East. The notable example is the three million mustered in the Ugaritic legend of King Keret.[34] A possible rhetorical role for the number ten is suggested by the fact that all the census figures in Numbers are rounded to the hundred (Gad to fifty; Num. 1:25), thus being divisible by ten.[35] Some suggest that the military census numbers are magnified by a factor of ten. If so, the grand total would be 60,355 (cf. 2:32).[36] Moreover, dividing these 60,000 male adults by 22,000 firstborn (3:39) yields a 3:1 ratio, which is consistent with family sizes around the time of the exodus.[37] This can apply elsewhere without creating a conflict with other numbers (e.g., 31:32–35) and is applicable to both army census figures (2 Sam. 24:9) and army sizes (e.g., Judg. 20:2). Viewing census figures as rhetorical or hyperbolic in their cultural context does not imply that they are erroneous, unlike other methods of reducing the numbers down to "realistic" levels.

Finally, commentators in general agree that large census numbers make an important theological point: the Lord has kept the promises made to the fathers and has blessed his people.[38] Israel's military might has truly increased exponentially, since "the LORD is a man of war" (Ex. 15:3). By relying on the Lord's strength Israel will be victorious over the mightiest of foes (Num. 10:35–36). Even before entrance into the Promised Land this is demonstrated in the great victories over the Transjordan Amorite kings, Sihon and Og (21:21–35). Balaam prophesies that Israel, a blessed people, will defeat her foes and rule over them (23:20, 24; 24:8–9, 17–25). The totals serve to underscore the Lord's presence to grant victory: "One man of you puts to flight a thousand, since it is the LORD your God who fights for you, just as he promised you" (Josh. 23:10; cf. Isa. 30:17).

1:47–54 With no previous introduction "the Levites" are mentioned. Before Numbers, the Levites are virtually unknown. Genesis mentions "the sons of Levi" once (46:11), as does Exodus several times (6:16; 32:26, 28; cf. 6:19, 25), but only once as "Levites" in connection with tabernacle responsibilities (38:21; cf. 4:14). Notwithstanding its title, Leviticus refers to "Levites" only twice, concerning redemption rights (25:32–33), and never pertaining to tabernacle service. Reference to Levi, Levites, or the tribe/sons of Levi is made nearly eighty times in Numbers. A major distinction is yet to be drawn between "priests," who are themselves sons of

---

34 M. Hoegger, "L'interprétation des grands nombres dans l'Ancien Testament," *Hokhma* 25 (1984): 9. Hoegger also draws attention to a force of 360,000 under the king of Kuthra, which he labels the closest parallel to 600,000 in Numbers (10). Cf. D. Fouts, "A Defense of the Hyperbolic Interpretation of Large Numbers in the Old Testament," *JETS* 40 (1997): 377–387.
35 This is also the case in the Mari royal archives, listing forces mustered from different locations: 1,000 from one, 600 from another, until 6,000 was reached. The king added 10,000 and the city of Eshnunah 6,000. An army of 20,000 was a strong army (Mendenhall, "Census of Numbers 1 and 26," 64).
36 Allen, *Numbers*, 688–691; 709–711.
37 R. I. Vasholz, "Military Census in Numbers," *Presbyterion* 18 (1992): 122–125.
38 Cf. Bush, *Book of Numbers*, 24; Allen, *Numbers*, 710–711; Olson, *Numbers*, 15.

Levi, and the nonpriestly "Levites" (cf. ch. 3). The same is true of the three Levitical branches (ch. 4). However, some of the details in the following verses already presume these differentiations (cf. discussion on 1:50, 51).

The tribe of Levi did not figure in the tribal appointments made to military companies (Num. 1:47). The Lord had commanded Moses, "You shall not list, ... not take a census of them" (v. 49). It is not that they are not adept for military service. Levi and his descendants were renowned for their weaponry prowess. Levi slew the Shechemites with the sword (Gen. 34:25; 49:5). By the sword sons of Levi executed God's wrath at the golden calf incident (Ex. 32:25–29) and by a spear the Levitical priest Phinehas stayed his wrath at Peor (Num. 25:7–8; Deut. 4:3). But their service is described with the same term (*tsaba'*; cf. Num. 4:3, "come on duty") as soldiers ("go to war"; 1:3). Moses must "appoint the Levites over the tabernacle" (v. 50). Their compatriots were appointed to military companies (v. 3); the Levites are appointed to tabernacle service. Their calling is to slay any who encroach on the sacred space (cf. discussion on v. 51).

The tabernacle is qualified as being "of the testimony" (*ha'edut*; v. 50; 10:11), because the tabernacle is the tent that houses the ark and, more specifically, the two tablets of the testimony in it (Ex. 31:18; 32:15; 34:29; esp. Ex. 40:20). "Tabernacle" transliterates *tabernaculum* (Vulgate), which renders the Hebrew *mishkan*, "dwelling place" (from the verb *shakan*, "to dwell"). "Tabernacle" used alone generally refers to the tent housing the Holy Place and the Most Holy Place (Ex. 35:15; 40:2, 6), but occasionally it can be applied to the entire complex (e.g., Num. 1:50b–51). It was where God manifests his promised presence: "I will dwell [*shakan*] among [them]" (Ex. 29:45). In the wilderness he dwells in the midst of Israel's camp by means of the tabernacle (Num. 5:3). He will ultimately dwell in Israel's midst in the Promised Land (35:34) by means of the place he will choose for his sanctuary (Deut. 12:11).

The Levites have service responsibilities whether the tabernacle is static or in transit. They "carry" (or "transport") it and its furnishings, they "take care" (*shrt*) of it, and they "camp around" it (Num. 1:50) in order to "keep guard" (*shamar*).[39] *Shrt* is often used for service rendered to a superior (cf. comment on 8:23–26 [at v. 26]). The Levites are supervised by Aaron's sons (3:32; 4:28). When the tabernacle is "to set out," they "take it down," and when it is "to be pitched" (lit., "when encamping"), they "set it up" (1:51). Carrying the furnishings will be confined to the Kohathites (4:15; 10:21a), and taking the tabernacle down, transporting it on wagons, and setting it up to the Gershonites and the Merarites (4:24–26, 31–33; 7:7–8; 10:17, 21b).

The verb translated "set out" (*nasa'*) can mean "travel/journey," describing the movement between two locations (e.g., 10:25). Since *nasa'* is employed as the opposite of "camp" (*khanah*, nearly seventy times in Numbers; e.g., 2:17), the distinction drawn is between being mobile (traveling) and being static (encamped). Whether

---

[39] For Milgrom *shamar* is subsumed under *shrt*, pointing to 3:6b, 7a; 18:2a, 3a (*Numbers*, 10; ESV renders *shrt* as "minister"). *Shamar mishmeret*, especially in connection with divine wrath for intrusion (cf. 1:53), suggests guard duty. Cf. Milgrom, *Numbers*, 11.

when stationary or when traveling, the Levites must prevent intrusion by any outsider. Any unauthorized person must be "put to death" (1:51).

"The people of Israel" (v. 52) introduces a distinction between them and the Levites. The phrase containing both the noun "camp" (*makhaneh*) and the denominative "to camp" (*khanah*; "pitch") reads literally "The sons of Israel shall camp ... each man in his own camp." They will bivouac in military camps. "Companies" (*tsaba'*) is also a military term. In chapter 2 the tribes are organized in four camps, each consisting of three companies. On "standard" (1:52) cf. comment on 2:1–2.

The Levites shall "camp around the tabernacle of the testimony" and "keep guard over the tabernacle of the testimony" (1:53). By camping around the tabernacle they create a barrier and a buffer zone around it. The repetition of "testimony" emphasizes that their encampment and keeping guard will prevent encroachment and the resulting desecration of the sanctuary furnishings, especially the ark. Their compliance will ensure there will be "no wrath on the congregation" (v. 53). Whatever form it takes—fire, plague, or sword—God's "wrath" (*qetseph*) destroys the offender (e.g., 16:21).

Numbers 1:54 contains a compliance response to the entire chapter. Translated woodenly, "They did ['*asah*], the people of Israel, according to all that the Lord commanded Moses; thus they did ['*asah*]." In fact, nothing is said in chapter 1 about the people's doing anything. What the Lord commanded Moses is actually carried out by Israel's leaders, working in concert with the people. What their leaders-representatives have done is reckoned by the Lord as the people's doing too, whether good or bad! This underlines the prevalent principle of corporate solidarity.

Response

God makes provisions to shield the Israelites from his wrath (Num. 1:53; 18:5). Wrath strikes anyone who flaunts sinful behavior in God's holy face (16:46; 25:11). Given Paul's use of examples drawn from Numbers of God's dealings with the Israelites in the wilderness to exhort and warn the church (cf. Introduction: Theology of Numbers), he perhaps has Numbers in mind when he assures the Christians in Rome, "Since, therefore, we have now been justified by his blood, much more shall we be saved by him from the wrath of God" (Rom. 5:9).

Paul also warns those in the church, "Let no one deceive you with empty words, for because of these things the wrath of God comes upon the sons of disobedience" (Eph. 5:6). John states, "Whoever believes in the Son has eternal life; whoever does not obey the Son shall not see life, but the wrath of God remains on him" (John 3:36). Believing and obeying are two sides of the same coin. The commands the Lord gives in Numbers 1 draw the obedient response of the Israelites. Obedience expresses their faith. Walking by faith with the Lord in their midst, they can experience a safe wilderness journey and anticipate a new life in Canaan. So too for the Christian: faith and obedience constitute the experiential tandem giving evidence of new life in Christ. With them comes the assurance expressed by Paul: "God has not destined us for wrath, but to obtain salvation through our Lord Jesus Christ" (1 Thess. 5:9).

NUMBERS 2

2 The Lord spoke to Moses and Aaron, saying, ²"The people of Israel shall camp each by his own standard, with the banners of their fathers' houses. They shall camp facing the tent of meeting on every side. ³Those to camp on the east side toward the sunrise shall be of the standard of the camp of Judah by their companies, the chief of the people of Judah being Nahshon the son of Amminadab, ⁴his company as listed being 74,600. ⁵Those to camp next to him shall be the tribe of Issachar, the chief of the people of Issachar being Nethanel the son of Zuar, ⁶his company as listed being 54,400. ⁷Then the tribe of Zebulun, the chief of the people of Zebulun being Eliab the son of Helon, ⁸his company as listed being 57,400. ⁹All those listed of the camp of Judah, by their companies, were 186,400. They shall set out first on the march.

¹⁰"On the south side shall be the standard of the camp of Reuben by their companies, the chief of the people of Reuben being Elizur the son of Shedeur, ¹¹his company as listed being 46,500. ¹²And those to camp next to him shall be the tribe of Simeon, the chief of the people of Simeon being Shelumiel the son of Zurishaddai, ¹³his company as listed being 59,300. ¹⁴Then the tribe of Gad, the chief of the people of Gad being Eliasaph the son of Reuel, ¹⁵his company as listed being 45,650. ¹⁶All those listed of the camp of Reuben, by their companies, were 151,450. They shall set out second.

¹⁷"Then the tent of meeting shall set out, with the camp of the Levites in the midst of the camps; as they camp, so shall they set out, each in position, standard by standard.

¹⁸"On the west side shall be the standard of the camp of Ephraim by their companies, the chief of the people of Ephraim being Elishama the son of Ammihud, ¹⁹his company as listed being 40,500. ²⁰And next to him shall be the tribe of Manasseh, the chief of the people of Manasseh being Gamaliel the son of Pedahzur, ²¹his company as listed being 32,200. ²²Then the tribe of Benjamin, the chief of the people of Benjamin being Abidan the son of Gideoni, ²³his company as listed being 35,400. ²⁴All those listed of the camp of Ephraim, by their companies, were 108,100. They shall set out third on the march.

²⁵"On the north side shall be the standard of the camp of Dan by their companies, the chief of the people of Dan being Ahiezer the son of Ammishaddai, ²⁶his company as listed being 62,700. ²⁷And those to camp next to him shall be the tribe of Asher, the chief of the people of Asher being Pagiel the son of Ochran, ²⁸his company as listed being 41,500. ²⁹Then the tribe of Naphtali, the chief of the people of Naphtali being Ahira the son of Enan, ³⁰his company as listed being 53,400. ³¹All those listed of the camp of Dan were 157,600. They shall set out last, standard by standard."

³²These are the people of Israel as listed by their fathers' houses. All those listed in the camps by their companies were 603,550. ³³But the

Levites were not listed among the people of Israel, as the LORD commanded Moses.

³⁴ Thus did the people of Israel. According to all that the LORD commanded Moses, so they camped by their standards, and so they set out, each one in his clan, according to his fathers' house.

Section Overview

After the census of men from the twelve secular tribes eligible for military service (Num. 1:2–46) and the general instruction concerning their camp companies (v. 52), the next step in chapter 2 involves the composition of their camps in companies around the tabernacle and their order of march. The orderly departure in chapter 10 executes the instructions given here. (On the literary bracketing role of chapters 2 and 10 cf. Introduction: Interpretive Challenges: Unifying Structure of Numbers.)

The twelve tribes are arranged around the tabernacle in four camps. Each camp comprises three companies of tribes, with one of the three as the head. The first of two general organizing principles is the encampment position, one camp "on every side" (2:2) of the tabernacle, "east," "south," "west," and "north" (vv. 3, 10, 18, 25). The second is how they will "set out" on the march by camps: "first," "second," "third," and "last" (2:9, 16, 24, 31, 34).

The Israelites will "set out" from the wilderness of Sinai in the hope of settling in the land God had promised the patriarchs and their descendants (e.g., 13:2; 15:2; cf. Gen. 12:7; Ex. 6:4–8; Lev. 25:38). These instructions are thus an encouragement for the Israelites to reach that goal. The individual tribes' census figures and the grand total are repeated from Numbers 1 (2:32; cf. 1:46), emphasizing God's blessing upon them. His blessing will remain upon them as they travel (6:23–27; 24:9). The summary statement (2:32–33a) and the compliance statement (vv. 33b–34) cover chapters 1 and 2 both.

Section Outline

I. Instructions for the Exodus Generation Preparing to Leave Sinai for Canaan (1:1–10:36) . . .
   B. The Camp Arrangement and Order of March (2:1–34)
      1. General Instructions (2:1–2)
      2. The Judah Camp (2:3–9)
      3. The Reuben Camp (2:10–16)
      4. The Levites (2:17)
      5. The Ephraim Camp (2:18–24)
      6. The Dan Camp (2:25–31)
      7. Summary (2:32–34)

Comment

2:1–2 "The people of Israel" (vv. 2, 34) refers principally to the conscripted males. They are organized in four camps, each comprising three tribal companies.

According to his tribal affiliation, each man is in a "camp" (Hb. *makhaneh*)—e.g., "the camp of Judah" (v. 3)—and a "company" (*tsaba*'; cf. 1:52)—e.g., the company of Judah, the company of Issachar, and the company of Zebulun (2:4, 6, 8). "Each by his own standard" (v. 2) refers to the standard of his camp (e.g., Judah), since a "standard" (*degel*) is associated only with the four camps (vv. 3, 10, 18, 25). "Banners" (pl. *'oth*) identifies the "fathers' houses" of the soldiers and their extended families (vv. 2, 34; cf. comment on 1:1–19 [at v. 2]).

The overall arrangement is by tribe. For example, Judah is the head tribe of the camp comprising the companies of Judah, Issachar, and Zebulun (2:3–9). For each tribe, a "chief of the people" is named (e.g., representing Judah is "Nahshon the son of Amminadab"; v. 3). These chiefs are the same men who assisted Moses in taking the census (1:5–15).

The tribes camp "facing the tent of meeting" (2:2) "on every side [of]" (*sabib*, v. 2; lit., "around," here rectangularly) the tent of meeting.[40] The four groups of three tribes camp on the four compass points of the tabernacle (cf. Section Overview). The distance from the tent of meeting is not indicated. Rabbinic interpretation based on Joshua 3:4 puts the distance at 2,000 cubits (1,000 yards or 900 meters; cf. comment on 35:1–8 [at vv. 4–5]). The area occupied by the camps may have been about 3 square miles (8 sq km; cf. comment on 33:37–49 [at v. 49]).[41]

2:3–9 In addition to being first in the list, the preeminence of the tribe of Judah is seen from three other vantage points. First, "Judah" (v. 3) heads the camp comprising two additional Leah tribes, Issachar and Zebulun (vv. 5, 7). Second, his "camp" is assigned to the prominent "east" (Hb. *qedem*: "forward," v. 3; cf. Gen. 13:11) position, also qualified as being "toward the sunrise." The priests' camp, including Moses, is also on the east side of the tabernacle. Orientation in the OT is always eastward. Third, when breaking camp, Judah leads not only his camp of three companies but all the Israelite tribes. The order of march anticipates what is to come: the departure of the cloud and the trumpet signal given by the priests to set out (Num. 10:5–6, 11–13).

These are steps toward the ultimate unveiling of the messianic fulfillment of the prophetic blessing bestowed upon Judah by his father. Jacob's benediction forecast his son's preeminence:

> The scepter [*shebet*] shall not depart from Judah,
>   nor the ruler's staff from between his feet,
> until tribute comes to him;
>   and to him shall be the obedience of the peoples. (Gen. 49:10)

In Jacob's blessings, Zebulun and Issachar come directly after Judah (Gen. 49:13–15). The three tribes' being grouped into one camp in Numbers 2 recalls these ancient blessings.

---

40 The rectangular form of the encampments (e.g., 3:26) enveloping the ark is like that employed in Egyptian military campaigns surrounding the pharaoh (cf. Ashley, *Book of Numbers*, 73).
41 C. J. Ellicott, "Numbers," in *Ellicott's Bible Commentary* (Grand Rapids, MI: Zondervan, 1972), 150.

2:10–16 The "south side" (from *yamin*; Num. 2:10, "right") is on the right side of the tabernacle from the perspective of an eastward orientation. Reuben's camp includes "Simeon" and "Gad." Reuben was Leah's first son, thus Jacob's firstborn. Simeon was her second son, and Gad was the first son born to her servant Zilpah. Levi's position as Leah's third son was filled by Gad (cf. 1:24).

Among Jacob's blessings were reproaches addressed to Reuben and to Simeon and Levi:

> Unstable as water, you [Reuben] shall not have preeminence,
> > because you went up to your father's bed;
> > > then you defiled it—he went up to my couch! (Gen. 49:4)

As concerns Reuben's birthright, Jacob declared him forfeit for having had relations with Rachel's servant Bilhah (Gen. 35:22–23), by whom Jacob had fathered Dan and Naphtali.

> Cursed be their [Simeon's and Levi's] anger, for it is fierce,
> > and their wrath, for it is cruel!
> I will divide them in Jacob
> > and scatter them in Israel. (Gen. 49:7; cf. vv. 5–6)

This was the consequence of these brothers' disproportionate vengeance on the inhabitants of Shechem after their sister, Dinah, was raped (Genesis 34).

"All those listed of [or assigned to] the camp of Reuben" are those from his tribe and from Simeon's and Gad's tribes. They form the second camp comprising three companies. When time comes to march, the Reuben camp "shall set out second."

In Numbers considerable emphasis is placed on the Leah tribes, which increases as the book unfolds. This begins in Numbers 1 (cf. comment on 1:1–19 [at vv. 5–15]); as were the first six tribes in that chapter, here the first *seven* are Leah tribes. In chapter 1 Reuben was first in the census order as the "firstborn" (1:20). In chapter 2 Judah is preeminent. His tribe is encamped on the prominent east side and will march in the lead of all the others when they set out. The tribe of Levi has a special place in Numbers. Not only is Levi the ancestor of Miriam, Moses, and Aaron; his name is memorialized in "the Levites" (2:17), who will profoundly mark the spiritual history of Israel and the church.

2:17 "The tent of the meeting shall set out" (v. 17) after the Reubenite camp and before the Ephraimite camp (vv. 16, 24). The Kohathite Levites carry its sacred furnishings (4:15; 10:21). The "Levites" who set out "in the midst [*betok*] of the camps" (2:17) are the Kohathites, who set out between (*betok*) the Reuben and Ephraim camps (10:18, 21–22; cf. comments on 2:18–24; 10:11–28 [at v. 21]). Implicitly, a distinction is drawn between the Kohathites and the two other Levitical families, the Gershonites and the Merarites.

"As they camp, so shall they set out" (2:17) refers to the three Levitical families and apparently the secular camps also (cf. "standard by standard"). The Gershonites and the Merarites set out between the Judah and Reuben camps (10:17), ahead of the Kohathites. In that way the tent could be erected and ready to be furnished by the time the Kohathites arrive (10:21).

"Standard by standard" (*lediglehem*; 2:17) means "according to/by their standards," as the identical Hebrew term is translated in verse 34 ("by their standards"). Verse 17 may refer to the Judah and Reuben camps, and verse 34 to the Ephraim and Dan camps. All together the four military camps have four "standards" (vv. 3, 10, 18, 25). Nowhere is there reference to any "standard of the tribe of Levi," which would have been over the three Levitical camps.

2:18–24 The sons of Joseph—Rachel's firstborn (Gen. 30:22–24)—Ephraim (Num. 2:18) and his brother, Manasseh (2:20), received their grandfather Jacob's blessing. Thereby Joseph received a double portion, like a firstborn (cf. Deut. 21:17). Joseph's sons became heirs of that which would have been Reuben's and Simeon's (Gen. 48:5). The tribe of Joseph's younger brother, Benjamin (Num 2:22), also belonged to the "camp of Ephraim" (v. 18).

The three Rachel tribes were "on the west side" of the tabernacle (v. 18; lit., "seaward," Hb. *yamah*, with the "sea" being the Mediterranean; e.g., Deut. 11:24). From an eastward orientation, west is also "behind the tabernacle" (*'ahar*; Num. 3:23). After the Judah and Reuben camps, the camp of Ephraim "shall set out third on the march" (2:24). Psalm 80:1–2 seems to allude to this passage, declaring that the shepherd-king of Israel, enthroned upon the cherubim, goes before Ephraim, Benjamin, and Manasseh to save them by his might.

2:25–31 "On the north [*tsaphon*] side" is the camp of Dan (2:25), which includes, in addition to his own company, those of Asher (v. 27) and Naphtali (v. 29). Dan was the firstborn of Rachel's servant Bilhah and therefore the firstborn of the sons Jacob fathered through his wives' servants. Bilhah also gave birth to Naphtali (Gen. 30:3–8). Asher was the second son born to Leah's servant Zilpah (Gen. 30:12–13). "They shall set out last" (Num. 2:31): the Israelites journey in a linear fashion, with Judah in the lead and Dan bringing up the rear, "acting as the rear guard of all the camps" (10:25).

FIGURE 4.1: "Standard" (Hb. *degel*) Positions around the Tabernacle (T) Compass Points

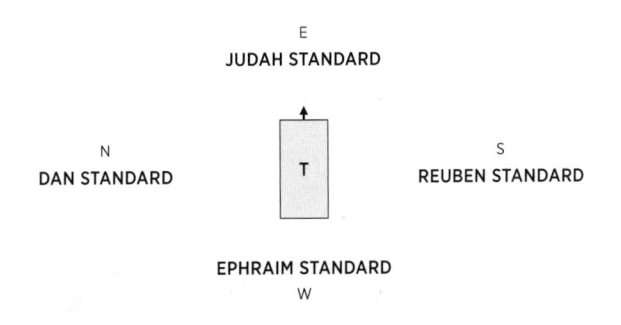

```
                        E
                  JUDAH STANDARD
                        ↑
      N                ┌─┐              S
  DAN STANDARD         │T│         REUBEN STANDARD
                       └─┘

                 EPHRAIM STANDARD
                        W
```

2:32–34 The summary (2:32–33a) and the compliance formula (vv. 33b–34) recall the three main activities up to this point: how the conscripted were assigned to military companies and camps, how they "camped," and how they "set out." It also notes that "the Levites were not listed" (v. 33); that is, they were not assigned to a military company and camp (cf. 1:47–50). The compliance formula ("As the Lord commanded Moses.... According to all that the Lord commanded Moses"; 2:33–34) links and closes chapters 1–2, emphasizing the people's complete obedience to the Lord's commands.

Response

"Nahshon the son of Amminadab" (2:3), a descendant of Judah, is an important figure in the genealogy of Christ. His son, Salmon, who married Rahab, was the ancestor of Boaz, who married Ruth the Moabite. Their son, Obed, was a grandfather of David (Ruth 4:16–22; Matt. 1:3–5).

In light of the emphasis on the Leah tribes in the lists, one cannot help but think that Leah herself may be in view in Paul's statement, "We know that for those who love God all things work together for good, for those who are called according to his purpose" (Rom. 8:28). Although she worshiped the Lord (Gen. 29:35), she was unloved (lit., "hated," Hb. *sane'*; vv. 31, 33) by Jacob. Being hated meant her husband failed to respect her rights by marriage, a covenant, or those of her sons. But their rightful due was ultimately restored. Through the godly Leah and her sons Levi and Judah came the greatest blessings the world has ever known.

Under Moses, descendant of Levi, the royal priesthood was established in the Sinai covenant. As mediator and administrator of this old or first covenant, Moses is called a house servant (Heb. 3:5). Through Jesus, the descendant par excellence of Judah, an eternal spiritual kingdom and an eternal priestly order are established under the new and better covenant of which he is mediator. Because of his greater glory, Christ is over God's house as a son; "And we are his house, if indeed we hold fast our confidence and our boasting in our hope" (Heb. 3:6). Being assured of their part in Christ's house, which has a distinguished history and a glorious future, boosts Christians' confidence in this life and nourishes their hope for the life to come, to which they are exhorted to hold fast.

NUMBERS 3

3 These are the generations of Aaron and Moses at the time when the LORD spoke with Moses on Mount Sinai. ² These are the names of the sons of Aaron: Nadab the firstborn, and Abihu, Eleazar, and Ithamar. ³ These are the names of the sons of Aaron, the anointed priests, whom he ordained to serve as priests. ⁴ But Nadab and Abihu died before the LORD when they offered unauthorized fire before the LORD in the wilderness of Sinai, and they had no children. So Eleazar and Ithamar served as priests in the lifetime of Aaron their father.

⁵ And the LORD spoke to Moses, saying, ⁶ "Bring the tribe of Levi near, and set them before Aaron the priest, that they may minister to him. ⁷ They shall keep guard over him and over the whole congregation before the tent of meeting, as they minister at the tabernacle. ⁸ They shall guard all the furnishings of the tent of meeting, and keep guard over the people of Israel as they minister at the tabernacle. ⁹ And you shall give the Levites to Aaron and his sons; they are wholly given to him from among the people of Israel. ¹⁰ And you shall appoint Aaron and his sons, and they shall guard their priesthood. But if any outsider comes near, he shall be put to death."

¹¹ And the LORD spoke to Moses, saying, ¹² "Behold, I have taken the Levites from among the people of Israel instead of every firstborn who opens the womb among the people of Israel. The Levites shall be mine, ¹³ for all the firstborn are mine. On the day that I struck down all the firstborn in the land of Egypt, I consecrated for my own all the firstborn in Israel, both of man and of beast. They shall be mine: I am the LORD."

¹⁴ And the LORD spoke to Moses in the wilderness of Sinai, saying, ¹⁵ "List the sons of Levi, by fathers' houses and by clans; every male from a month old and upward you shall list." ¹⁶ So Moses listed them according to the word of the LORD, as he was commanded. ¹⁷ And these were the sons of Levi by their names: Gershon and Kohath and Merari. ¹⁸ And these are the names of the sons of Gershon by their clans: Libni and Shimei. ¹⁹ And the sons of Kohath by their clans: Amram, Izhar, Hebron, and Uzziel. ²⁰ And the sons of Merari by their clans: Mahli and Mushi. These are the clans of the Levites, by their fathers' houses.

²¹ To Gershon belonged the clan of the Libnites and the clan of the Shimeites; these were the clans of the Gershonites. ²² Their listing according to the number of all the males from a month old and upward was[1] 7,500. ²³ The clans of the Gershonites were to camp behind the tabernacle on the west, ²⁴ with Eliasaph, the son of Lael as chief of the fathers' house of the Gershonites. ²⁵ And the guard duty of the sons of Gershon in the tent of meeting involved the tabernacle, the tent with its covering, the screen for the entrance of the tent of meeting, ²⁶ the hangings of the court, the screen for the door of the court that is around the tabernacle and the altar, and its cords—all the service connected with these.

⁲⁷ To Kohath belonged the clan of the Amramites and the clan of the Izharites and the clan of the Hebronites and the clan of the Uzzielites; these are the clans of the Kohathites. ²⁸ According to the number of all the males, from a month old and upward, there were 8,600, keeping guard over the sanctuary. ²⁹ The clans of the sons of Kohath were to camp on the south side of the tabernacle, ³⁰ with Elizaphan the son of Uzziel as chief of the fathers' house of the clans of the Kohathites. ³¹ And their guard duty involved the ark, the table, the lampstand, the altars, the vessels of the sanctuary with which the priests minister, and the screen; all the service connected with these. ³² And Eleazar the son of Aaron the priest was to be chief over the chiefs of the Levites, and to have oversight of those who kept guard over the sanctuary.

³³ To Merari belonged the clan of the Mahlites and the clan of the Mushites: these are the clans of Merari. ³⁴ Their listing according to the number of all the males from a month old and upward was 6,200. ³⁵ And the chief of the fathers' house of the clans of Merari was Zuriel the son of Abihail. They were to camp on the north side of the tabernacle. ³⁶ And the appointed guard duty of the sons of Merari involved the frames of the tabernacle, the bars, the pillars, the bases, and all their accessories; all the service connected with these; ³⁷ also the pillars around the court, with their bases and pegs and cords.

³⁸ Those who were to camp before the tabernacle on the east, before the tent of meeting toward the sunrise, were Moses and Aaron and his sons, guarding the sanctuary itself, to protect[2] the people of Israel. And any outsider who came near was to be put to death. ³⁹ All those listed among the Levites, whom Moses and Aaron listed at the commandment of the Lord, by clans, all the males from a month old and upward, were 22,000.

⁴⁰ And the Lord said to Moses, "List all the firstborn males of the people of Israel, from a month old and upward, taking the number of their names. ⁴¹ And you shall take the Levites for me—I am the Lord—instead of all the firstborn among the people of Israel, and the cattle of the Levites instead of all the firstborn among the cattle of the people of Israel." ⁴² So Moses listed all the firstborn among the people of Israel, as the Lord commanded him. ⁴³ And all the firstborn males, according to the number of names, from a month old and upward as listed were 22,273.

⁴⁴ And the Lord spoke to Moses, saying, ⁴⁵ "Take the Levites instead of all the firstborn among the people of Israel, and the cattle of the Levites instead of their cattle. The Levites shall be mine: I am the Lord. ⁴⁶ And as the redemption price for the 273 of the firstborn of the people of Israel, over and above the number of the male Levites, ⁴⁷ you shall take five shekels[3] per head; you shall take them according to the shekel of the sanctuary (the shekel of twenty gerahs[4]), ⁴⁸ and give the money to Aaron and his sons as the redemption price for those who are over." ⁴⁹ So Moses took the redemption money from those who were over and above those redeemed by the Levites. ⁵⁰ From the firstborn of the people of Israel he took the money, 1,365 shekels, by the shekel of the sanctuary. ⁵¹ And Moses gave the redemption money to Aaron and his sons, according to the word of the Lord, as the Lord commanded Moses.

---

[1] Hebrew *their listing was* [2] Hebrew *guard* [3] A *shekel* was about 2/5 ounce or 11 grams [4] A *gerah* was about 1/50 ounce or 0.6 gram

Section Overview

Chapters 3–4 augment the brief instructions concerning the Levites given in 1:47–53; 2:17, 33 and disclose how they are to be implemented. Chapter 3 defines the Levites' spheres of responsibility and camp positions around the tabernacle. Chapter 4 prescribes their duties in transporting it.

The secular tribes were assigned their camp positions on the four compass points of the tabernacle (ch. 2). Now the Levitical families—Gershonites, Kohathites, and Merarites, together with Moses, Aaron, and Aaron's sons—are assigned camp positions around it (3:23, 29, 35, 38). Their presence as a cordon between the tabernacle and the other tribes' camps is to safeguard the tabernacle from encroachment and thereby protect the congregation from God's wrath (3:7; cf. 1:53). The key word for "guard duty" occurs ten times (Hb. *mishmeret*; 3:7 [2x], 8, 25, 28, 31, 32, 36, 38 [2x]; with the related verb *shamar*; vv. 7, 8, 38).

Being exempt from military service, the Levites were not included in the previous census (1:47, 49). They are, however, part of two other censuses. The first one involves "every male from a month old and upward" (3:15), juxtaposed with a census of the "firstborn males of the people of Israel, from a month old and upward" (v. 40). The combined results reveal the number of Levites available for tabernacle service as substitutes for firstborn Israelite males (vv. 41–51). The second Levitical census comes in chapter 4.

Each part of chapter 3 contributes to the execution of the commands given earlier and is introduced by "The LORD spoke/said to Moses" (3:5, 11, 14, 40, 44). The major sections close with compliance summaries (vv. 39, 51).

Section Outline

I. Instructions for the Exodus Generation Preparing to Leave Sinai for Canaan (1:1–10:36) . . .
  C. The First Census of the Tribe of Levi, the Levites' Roles and Arrangement around the Tabernacle (3:1–51)
    1. Priests Distinguished from the Levites (3:1–4)
    2. Levites Assigned Their Duties and Positions around the Tabernacle (3:5–39)
    3. Levites Redeem the Firstborn (3:40–51)

Comment

3:1–4 This genealogy of Aaron seems unrelated to the subject of chapter 3 (the duties and camp arrangements of the tribe of Levi). But before these can be prescribed, a question must be answered: In what sense are Levites and priests different? They are all "sons of Levi" (Gen. 46:11; Ex. 6:16). Yet, although all priests are Levites by descent, not all Levites are priests. Only Aaron and his sons are.

"[Now] these are the generations of Aaron and Moses" (Num. 3:1): the "generations" (Hb. *toledot*) formula occurs twelve times in the OT, including ten times in Genesis; the only other Pentateuchal occurrence is here.⁴² Seven times, including here, "the generations of" begins with the demonstrative "these" with a prefixed conjunction (*ve-*; Gen. 10:1; 11:27; 25:12, 19; 36:1, 9; Num. 3:1; without the conjunction: Gen. 2:4; 6:9; 11:10; 37:2). In all these uses of this formula with the prefixed conjunction (often rendered "now") a distinction is drawn between the descendants mentioned before and those mentioned after. Genesis 25 offers two examples (the ESV does not translate the conjunction): "[Now] these are the generations of Ishmael.... [Now] these are the generations of Isaac" (Gen. 25:12, 19). The former draws a distinction between Ishmael and other sons of Abraham born to his concubines, while the latter distinguishes between Isaac's and Ishmael's descendants.

In a similar way, the conjunction used in Numbers 3:1 (suitably rendered "now") points to another distinction. Up until now "the Levites" were mentioned (1:47–53; 2:17, 33), but nothing was said about priests. Leviticus already prescribed in detail the sacred service of Aaron and his sons, but the Levites appear only in two verses related to property redemption (25:32, 33). Numbers now specifies the tabernacle responsibilities of the Levites according to their families (3:17–37). "Now[—there is a distinction!—]these are the generations of Aaron..." (3:1). After this follows the names of Aaron's sons, about whom is it said that they are "the anointed priests, whom [Moses] ordained to serve as priests" (vv. 2–3).

As sons of Amram, Aaron appears before Moses in genealogical lists since he is the older brother (Num. 26:59; cf. Ex. 6:20; 7:7; 1 Chron. 6:3; 23:13). This listing is not a typical linear genealogy. The emphasis is on the hereditary priesthood. Aaron's four sons are introduced: "Nadab the firstborn, and Abihu, Eleazar, and Ithamar" (Num. 3:2). Being "anointed" (*mashakh*) with holy oil (35:25), a high priest and his successor eldest son held a high, most sacred office, like those of prophets and kings (cf. 1 Kings 19:16; Pss. 89:20; 105:15). Although Moses had exercised priestly functions in anointing and consecrating Aaron and his sons (Ex. 28:41; 29:21; Lev. 8:30), none of Moses' sons are mentioned in the genealogy. They are named among the Levites (1 Chron. 23:14). Not even Moses has a claim to Aaron's priestly ministry.

"Mount Sinai" (Num. 3:1) is mentioned only twice in Numbers (cf. 28:6; on the question of identification cf. Section Overview of Numbers 33; comment on 33:1–15 [at v. 15]). Here it harks back to the law given there (Ex. 28:1). The locus of revelation is now no longer the mountain but the tent of meeting.

"Ordained" (Num. 3:3) translates "to fill the hands of." If taken in a concrete sense, anyone whose hands are full is entirely occupied with what is in them. In the ordination service the hands were filled with sacrificial bread and meat (Lev. 8:26–27), representing the offerings with which they would officiate. This ordination had been promised to the sons of Levi as a blessing for their having slain about three thousand men involved in the golden calf incident (Ex. 32:29).

---

42 The formula occurs also in Ruth 4:18.

The death of "Nadab and Abihu" (Num. 3:4), recorded in Leviticus 10:1–2, punished their misuse of censers and incense, "which [the Lord] had not commanded them" (Lev. 10:1). They offered "unauthorized fire before the LORD" (Num. 3:4; cf. Ex. 30:9, "unauthorized incense"), likely pointing to some misuse of the incense altar in the Holy Place,[43] though the precise nature of their offense remains a mystery. "Unauthorized" (*zar*) renders the same term translated "outsider" (1:51). In the ritual realm this term describes encroachment by unlawful presence or misdeed. Was something wrong with the incense (cf. Num. 4:16)? Did they attend the incense altar at a time other than at morning and twilight (Ex. 30:7–8)? Was only one of them supposed to burn incense (cf. Lev. 4:7; Num. 4:16; 1 Sam. 2:28)? Was there to have been but one censer (cf. Num. 16:46)? Did they err under the influence of alcohol (cf. Lev. 10:9)? Certainty is not possible, but the punishment is severe: "They had no children" (Num. 3:4). Eli's line was similarly wiped out later because he and his sons, Hophni and Phinehas, abused the Lord's offerings (1 Sam. 2:34; 3:13; 4:11).

Aaron's other sons, Eleazar and Ithamar, served as priests during their father's lifetime (Num. 3:4). Eleazar and Ithamar had oversight of the Levites (v. 32; 4:28, 33; 7:8); Eleazar succeeded his father after his death (20:28), and his son, Phinehas, followed him (25:7, 11; 31:6).

3:5–39 The duties of the "tribe of Levi" (v. 6) involve interrelated ministry spheres: the priesthood (representing the whole congregation), the tabernacle, and the people themselves (vv. 6–10). Added to this is the notice that the Levites will be substitutes for the firstborn (vv. 11–13).

Two imperatives describe what Moses must do with the tribe of Levi: "bring [them] near" and "set them before Aaron the priest" (v. 6). To "bring near" is ritual language, as with a sacrifice that must be brought near to the Lord (5:9; 15:4). That is, it is presented to the priest in the sanctuary, who then takes it and makes the offering on behalf of the offerer. By being brought near to Aaron, the Levites are brought near to the Lord himself (16:9). To "set them before" (lit., "make it [the tribe] stand before") is also priestly language. The priest stands before the Lord (Deut. 17:12; Ezek. 44:15). The one being served by the priest is also brought or set before the Lord (Lev. 14:11; Num. 5:16). The Levites, being brought before Aaron and his sons, are presented as an offering to the Lord (8:13). Thereupon, the Levites stand before the priests to serve them (cf. 18:2), and in so doing also stand before the people to serve them (cf. 16:9), just as the seven Greek men were "set before" (lit., "caused to stand before") the apostles to serve the people (Acts 6:6).

Executing these commands leads to three results, each rendered "that they may."[44]

---

[43] For Levine "unauthorized fire" means the same as "unauthorized incense." If so, what Aaron's sons did was not prescribed ritual practice (*Numbers 1–20*, 156).
[44] The syntax clearly marks the intended result or consequence of executing a command, as at 13:17–18: "go up [command] ... "and [so] see" (consequence, *vav* perfect). Cf. *IBHS* 529 (32.2.2, 1b).

The first result is "that they may minister to him" (Num. 3:6). To minister, as here to the priest, is also to minister to the congregation (Hb. *shrt*; 16:9) and to the Lord (*shrt*; cf. 1 Sam. 2:11). That which the Levites' ministry entails will be described in what follows.

The second result is "[that they may] keep guard over him" (*shamar* + *mishmeret*; Num. 3:7), that is, over Aaron the priest, and over the whole congregation, that is, their representatives. "Before the tent of meeting" (3:7) is in the holy space between the altar and the tent, which is guarded by preventing intrusion of an unqualified priest or lay leader (cf. 18:2–3) while the tabernacle was in service. They also "ministered at the tabernacle" (lit., "by doing the service of the tabernacle"; cf. v. 8; 4:30; 7:5; 8:11, 19; 16:9; 18:6), that is, doing physical labor.[45]

The third result is "[that they may] guard" (3:8) all the furnishings of the tent of meeting. The Levites (Kohathites) are responsible for the porterage of these sacred "furnishings" (*keley*; 1:50; cf. Ex. 31:7–9) when the tabernacle is in transit (Num. 10:21; cf. 3:31). They are to "keep guard over the people of Israel" by preventing encroachment during these times of especial risk. When the Israelites travel, the Levites (Gershonites and Merarites) must take down, transport, and set up the tabernacle (10:21b; cf. 1:51; 3:25–26, 36–37).

While priests minister daily within the court at the altar, between it and the tent, and in the Holy Place, the Levites serve both outside the court and also within it. For ceremonial purposes the people come to the entrance of the tabernacle, then inside the court between the entry and altar (cf. comment on 18:8–19 [at v. 10]; cf. also note there). The Levites' guard duty prevents encroachment by lay people beyond the altar. They thereby protect the priests, leaders, and the people from the wrath of God.

"You shall give [*natan*] the Levites to Aaron and his sons" (3:9): the commands and the results up to this point have described in a general way in what sense and for what reason the Levites "are wholly given" (v. 9; 8:16 renders the emphatic double cognate *netunim netunim*; cf. *netimim*, "temple servants"; 1 Chron. 9:2; Ezra 8:20).

Numbers 3:10 shifts from the Levites to the priests. The change is syntactically signaled. The double object "And . . . Aaron and his sons" precedes the verb "appoint" (*paqad*, used as an imperative; cf. NIV). It is followed by the intended result ("[that they may] guard," NASB), with the object "their priesthood"—that is, all their sacerdotal prerogatives distinguishing them from the Levites. "Any outsider . . . shall be put to death": the priests are required to prevent unqualified priests from serving at the altar (Lev. 21:17; Ezra 10:18; Neh. 7:64; 13:29) and the Levites from contact with the most holy furnishings. Levites who transport these items can neither touch nor see them; the furnishings must be

---

[45] Milgrom draws this distinction between *shamar mishmeret* and *'abodah* (*Numbers*, 16–17). He is followed, among others, by Wenham, *Numbers*, 70; Ashley, *Book of Numbers*, 78. E. W. Davies (*Numbers*, 28) doubts that the term rendered "guard duty" has such a precise meaning and argues that it refers more generally to various tabernacle functions such as helping the congregation with its offerings (e.g., 2 Chron. 29:34). For Levine *shamar mishmeret* for Levites means "to fulfill assigned tasks," and *'abad 'abodah* refers to their "maintenance functions" (*Numbers 1–20*, 156).

covered by the priests (Num. 4:15, 20). "Comes near" (from *qarab*; 3:10) forms an inclusio with "bring ... near" (v. 6); the opening verb refers to being brought into sacred service by divine appointment, and the closing verb to encroaching the sacred space.

Verses 11–13 introduce the reason "the Levites shall be mine" (vv. 12, 13): they are "taken" by the Lord "instead of every" Israelite "firstborn" (v. 12). "Opens the womb" (v. 12) indicates a woman's firstborn. The firstborn (male) has a special "consecrated" (*hiqdish*) status (v. 13). As a people, Israel is God's firstborn (Ex. 4:22). A redemptive-historical reason lies behind this requisition. After the exodus, the Lord commanded Moses to consecrate all the firstborn (Ex. 13:1–2). They represented the Israelites. The Israelites were delivered from slavery after the last plague, which resulted in the death of the Egyptian male firstborn, man and beast (Ex. 13:11–13). But Israelite firstborn were spared by the blood of the Passover lamb (12:12–13). For this reason the firstborn clean animals are sacrificed and the firstborn sons are redeemed (Num. 3:12–15), as are unclean animals (Lev. 27:26; Num. 18:15). Since they are redeemed by a blood price, firstborn do not belong to themselves; they are consecrated to the Lord for sacred service. Now the Levites will serve as their substitutes. The Levites redeem the firstborn Israelites by their own persons (3:41, 45) and the substitutional blood sacrifices made for them (8:11–12).

So that every firstborn male might find a Levite counterpart, censuses are taken of the Levites (3:14–16) and of all the firstborn in Israel (vv. 40–51). The census of the sons of Levi is taken "by fathers' houses and by clans," consisting of "every male from a month old and upward" (v. 15). As in the military census, their being "listed" (*paqad*; v. 16), that is "appointed" (cf. comment on 1:1–19 [at v. 3]) as substitutes, is done "by their names" (3:17), those of the three ancestral sons of Levi ("Gershon and Kohath and Merari") and those of their descendants "by their clans" (of Gershonites: Libnites and Shimeites [vv. 17, 21]; of Kohathites: Amramites, Izharites, Hebronites, Uzzielites [vv. 19, 27]; of Merarites: Mahlites, Mushites [vv. 20, 33]). Moses, Aaron, and Miriam are Amramite Kohathites (26:59). Failure to maintain a proper distinction between the Amramites and the Izharites leads to Korah's rebellion (cf. ch. 16).

"These are the clans of the Levites, by their fathers' houses" (3:20) forms an inverted inclusio (cf. v. 15, "sons of Levi, by fathers' houses and by clans"). The terms "fathers' houses" and "clans" can have different referents. Here "fathers' houses" refers to the three "sons of Levi" (v. 17), as in "fathers' house of the Gershonites" (v. 24). "Clans" here are descendants of these three fathers' houses (vv. 18, 19, 20, 21, 27, 33). In 17:2–3 "fathers' houses" are the "tribes" of Israel, including Levi. In 26:57 the sons of Levi—the Gershonites, Kohathites, and the Merarites—are "clans," as are their descendants—Libnites, Hebronites, Mahlites, and Mushites (26:58). Thus the meaning of "clan" and "father's house" can vary, as does the order in which they are mentioned (4:2, 22, 29; cf. Gen. 24:38, 40).

The census is taken (Num. 3:22, 28, 34, 39). The three Levitical ancestral fathers' houses structure this section containing their chiefs, census figures, assigned positions around the tabernacle, and responsibilities (cf. table 4.2).

TABLE 4.2: Gershon, Kohath, and Merari in Numbers 3:21–37

	Gershon	Kohath	Merari
Chiefs	Eliasaph (v. 24)	Elizaphan (v. 30)	Zuriel (v. 35)
Census Figures ("Number of all the males from one month old and upward")	7,500 (v. 22)	8,600 (v. 28)	6,200 (v. 34)
Assigned Portions (in relation to the tabernacle)	"on the west" (v. 23)	"on the south side" (v. 29)	"on the north side" (v. 35)
Responsibilities	the suspended items (tent coverings, screens, hangings, cords; vv. 25–26)	the furnishings (ark, table, lampstand, altars, vessels; v. 31)	the structuring parts (frames, bars, pillars, bases, pegs, cords, accessories; vv. 36–37)

The "tent of meeting" (3:25) is here specified as the "tabernacle," that is, its inner ten-curtain structure of fine linen (Ex. 26:1–6), the Holy Place and the Most Holy Place, and "tent with its covering" (Num. 3:25) of eleven goat's hair covers (Ex. 26:7–10), all being covered with rams and goats' skins (Ex. 26:14; 36:14, 19; 40:19). These coverings insulate the tent (hair) and make it impermeable (skins).

Their "guard duty" (Hb. *mishmeret*; Num. 3:25, 28, 31, 36) pertains to the section of the sanctuary that each Levitical branch protects from intruders and "all the service" (*'abodah*; vv. 26, 31, 36), that is, the "work" of dismantling, transporting, and reassembling it. When static, their service includes maintenance of the various pieces. The ark is generally transported by the Kohathites (v. 31; 4:15; Deut. 31:25), but it is carried by the priests (Deut. 31:9) when going into battle (e.g., Josh. 6:6).

The screen (*masak*; Num. 3:31) hiding the Most Holy Place is also called the *paroket hammasak* ("veil of the screen"). It is used by the priests to cover the ark for setting out (4:5). The Gershonites handle the other two screens, the "screen for the entrance of the tent" to enter the Holy Place and the "screen for the door of the court" (3:25, 26). "Vessels of the sanctuary" (*keley haqqodesh*; 3:31; 18:3; 31:6) could be rendered "holy vessels" (as in 1 Kings 8:4; cf. *shemen haqqodesh*, "holy oil"; Num. 35:25). They are called the "furnishings of the tent" (*keley ha'ohel*) and include the ark, table, lampstand, incense altar, and bronze altar and their respective utensils (Ex. 31:7–9).

Eleazar, Aaron's son, is the "chief over the chiefs of the Levites" (Num. 3:32). He has "oversight" (*pequddah*; v. 32; 4:16) over all "who kept guard" (*shomre mishmeret*), or "who guard what is to be guarded."

The area of the camp "toward the sunrise," "on the east," is reserved for Moses and Aaron and his sons (Num. 3:38–39). The east is the principal side, since the tabernacle court entrance is there. Mankind was banished from Eden to the east (Gen. 3:23–24). Like the sword-wielding cherubim at the east of Eden, Moses and the priests (cf. Ps. 99:6) on the east of the tabernacle are "guarding [*shamar*] the sanctuary . . . to protect" (*mishmeret*; lit., "for the protection of") the Israelites. The tabernacle is here termed "the sanctuary" (*hammiqdash*); it is described in this way elsewhere only at Numbers 10:21; 18:1. Any outsider who comes near, that is, any unauthorized person who encroaches, will forfeit his life. The three principal terms "tabernacle," "tent of meeting," and "sanctuary" appear here (3:38), which also underlines the exclusive and all-encompassing responsibilities of Moses, Aaron, and his sons.

The number of males one month old and upward "listed among the Levites . . . by clans" totals 22,000 (v. 39). But adding the figures for the three Levitical branches yields 22,300. Instead of 8,600 for the Kohathites (v. 28), the Greek (Lucianic recension) reads 8,300, which would bring the total to 22,000. Some suggest (cf. BHS) that the Hebrew number 6 (*shsh*) in 600 (8,600) originally read 3 (*shlsh*; thus 8,300), with the middle letter (*l*) later dropping out. Given the broad base of textual families that support the MT reading (SP, LXX), however, it is preferable to take 22,000 as a round figure.

3:40–51 According to their number, the firstborn of Israel and their cattle will be redeemed by the males and the cattle of the Levites, respectively (vv. 40–43, 45). Redemption is necessary given the sanctity of the firstborn, for which reason they belong to the Lord (Ex. 13:2; 34:19). As in the military census (Numbers 1), the number of firstborn is determined by "taking the number of their names" (3:40; cf. 1:2, 18). The names likely come from birth records. As in the census of the Levites, this census also involves males "a month old and upward" (3:40). The same age group in both cases is directly linked to the principle of substitution: "Take the Levites for me . . . instead of all the firstborn among the people of Israel" (v. 41; cf. vv. 12–13). Moses must "list" (Hb. *paqad*; v. 40; also v. 42) them, that is, "appoint" those to be redeemed.

The number of the Israelite firstborn, 22,273 (v. 43; cf. comment on 1:20–46 [at v. 46] for this total in relation to 603,550), exceeds the number of Levites who can redeem them. The shortfall is met by a monetary payment for the 273 Israelite males who outnumber the Levite redeemers (3:44–51). The "redemption price" (from *padah*; vv. 46, 48) here involves a substitutionary payment, in which no Levite's life of service could be substituted for the Israelite firstborn. "Five shekels per head" (v. 47) is not an onerous sum. The redemption price of a firstborn boy or a male unclean animal is five shekels (18:16), the same as the vow valuation, fixed on the person's age, for a male from one month to five years of age (Lev. 27:6). The "redemption money" (Num. 3:49, 51) comes to "1,365 shekels" (v. 50), a perquisite given "to Aaron and his sons" (v. 51).

The chapter ends with a unique double compliance statement: "According to the word of the LORD, as the LORD commanded Moses" (v. 51).

Response

The redemption of firstborn is a work of grace. Although grace is freely given, it comes at great cost. Levites perform their redeeming work as living substitutional sacrifices, at the cost of their own lives should they fail their responsibility of preventing God's wrath from destroying the people. Redemption is never without payment. This prefigures the work of Christ, who "redeemed us from the curse of the law by becoming a curse for us" (Gal. 3:13). The call "You shall be holy, for I am holy" (1 Pet. 1:16, cited from Lev. 11:44) is motivated by "knowing that you were ransomed from the futile ways inherited from your forefathers, not with perishable things such as silver or gold, but with the precious blood of Christ, like that of a lamb without blemish or spot" (1 Pet. 1:18–19). This ultimate grace and Christian response is concisely expressed: "You were bought with a price. So glorify God in your body" (1 Cor. 6:20).

NUMBERS 4

4 The LORD spoke to Moses and Aaron, saying, ²"Take a census of the sons of Kohath from among the sons of Levi, by their clans and their fathers' houses, ³from thirty years old up to fifty years old, all who can come on duty, to do the work in the tent of meeting. ⁴This is the service of the sons of Kohath in the tent of meeting: the most holy things. ⁵When the camp is to set out, Aaron and his sons shall go in and take down the veil of the screen and cover the ark of the testimony with it. ⁶Then they shall put on it a covering of goatskin[1] and spread on top of that a cloth all of blue, and shall put in its poles. ⁷And over the table of the bread of the Presence they shall spread a cloth of blue and put on it the plates, the dishes for incense, the bowls, and the flagons for the drink offering; the regular showbread also shall be on it. ⁸Then they shall spread over them a cloth of scarlet and cover the same with a covering of goatskin, and shall put in its poles. ⁹And they shall take a cloth of blue and cover the lampstand for the light, with its lamps, its tongs, its trays, and all the vessels for oil with which it is supplied. ¹⁰And they shall put it with all its utensils in a covering of goatskin and put it on the carrying frame. ¹¹And over the golden altar they shall spread a cloth of blue and cover it with a covering of goatskin, and shall put in its poles. ¹²And they shall take all the vessels of the service that are used in the sanctuary and put them in a cloth of blue and cover them with a covering of goatskin and put them on the carrying frame. ¹³And they shall take away the ashes from the altar and spread a purple cloth over it. ¹⁴And they shall put on it all the utensils of the altar, which are used for the service there, the fire pans, the forks, the shovels, and the basins, all the utensils of the altar; and they shall spread on it a covering of goatskin, and shall put in its poles. ¹⁵And when Aaron and his sons have finished covering the sanctuary and all the furnishings

of the sanctuary, as the camp sets out, after that the sons of Kohath shall come to carry these, but they must not touch the holy things, lest they die. These are the things of the tent of meeting that the sons of Kohath are to carry.

¹⁶ "And Eleazar the son of Aaron the priest shall have charge of the oil for the light, the fragrant incense, the regular grain offering, and the anointing oil, with the oversight of the whole tabernacle and all that is in it, of the sanctuary and its vessels."

¹⁷ The LORD spoke to Moses and Aaron, saying, ¹⁸ "Let not the tribe of the clans of the Kohathites be destroyed from among the Levites, ¹⁹ but deal thus with them, that they may live and not die when they come near to the most holy things: Aaron and his sons shall go in and appoint them each to his task and to his burden, ²⁰ but they shall not go in to look on the holy things even for a moment, lest they die."

²¹ The LORD spoke to Moses, saying, ²² "Take a census of the sons of Gershon also, by their fathers' houses and by their clans. ²³ From thirty years old up to fifty years old, you shall list them, all who can come to do duty, to do service in the tent of meeting. ²⁴ This is the service of the clans of the Gershonites, in serving and bearing burdens: ²⁵ they shall carry the curtains of the tabernacle and the tent of meeting with its covering and the covering of goatskin that is on top of it and the screen for the entrance of the tent of meeting ²⁶ and the hangings of the court and the screen for the entrance of the gate of the court that is around the tabernacle and the altar, and their cords and all the equipment for their service. And they shall do all that needs to be done with regard to them. ²⁷ All the service of the sons of the Gershonites shall be at the command of Aaron and his sons, in all that they are to carry and in all that they have to do. And you shall assign to their charge all that they are to carry. ²⁸ This is the service of the clans of the sons of the Gershonites in the tent of meeting, and their guard duty is to be under the direction of Ithamar the son of Aaron the priest.

²⁹ "As for the sons of Merari, you shall list them by their clans and their fathers' houses. ³⁰ From thirty years old up to fifty years old, you shall list them, everyone who can come on duty, to do the service of the tent of meeting. ³¹ And this is what they are charged to carry, as the whole of their service in the tent of meeting: the frames of the tabernacle, with its bars, pillars, and bases, ³² and the pillars around the court with their bases, pegs, and cords, with all their equipment and all their accessories. And you shall list by name the objects that they are required to carry. ³³ This is the service of the clans of the sons of Merari, the whole of their service in the tent of meeting, under the direction of Ithamar the son of Aaron the priest."

³⁴ And Moses and Aaron and the chiefs of the congregation listed the sons of the Kohathites, by their clans and their fathers' houses, ³⁵ from thirty years old up to fifty years old, everyone who could come on duty, for service in the tent of meeting; ³⁶ and those listed by clans were 2,750. ³⁷ This was the list of the clans of the Kohathites, all who served in the tent of meeting, whom Moses and Aaron listed according to the commandment of the LORD by Moses.

³⁸ Those listed of the sons of Gershon, by their clans and their fathers' houses, ³⁹ from thirty years old up to fifty years old, everyone who could come on duty for service in the tent of meeting— ⁴⁰ those listed by their clans and their fathers' houses were 2,630. ⁴¹ This was the list of the clans

of the sons of Gershon, all who served in the tent of meeting, whom Moses and Aaron listed according to the commandment of the Lord.

⁴² Those listed of the clans of the sons of Merari, by their clans and their fathers' houses, ⁴³ from thirty years old up to fifty years old, everyone who could come on duty, for service in the tent of meeting— ⁴⁴ those listed by clans were 3,200. ⁴⁵ This was the list of the clans of the sons of Merari, whom Moses and Aaron listed according to the commandment of the Lord by Moses.

⁴⁶ All those who were listed of the Levites, whom Moses and Aaron and the chiefs of Israel listed, by their clans and their fathers' houses, ⁴⁷ from thirty years old up to fifty years old, everyone who could come to do the service of ministry and the service of bearing burdens in the tent of meeting, ⁴⁸ those listed were 8,580. ⁴⁹ According to the commandment of the Lord through Moses they were listed, each one with his task of serving or carrying. Thus they were listed by him, as the Lord commanded Moses.

¹ The meaning of the Hebrew word is uncertain; compare Exodus 25:5

Section Overview

Numbers 4 develops the subject of Levitical organization and tabernacle duties addressed in chapter 3. It expands the Levites' responsibilities, especially regarding the transportation of the tabernacle. These instructions heighten the anticipation of the journey to the Promised Land. Supplementing the census of the Levites in chapter 3, the census in chapter 4 discloses the number available for tabernacle duty.

Chapter 4, like chapter 3, centers around three Levitical families: Kohathites, Gershonites, and Merarites. This distinction is functional, as each group has its own responsibilities and camp position around the tabernacle. The order in which the three are presented—Kohath, Gershon, Merari (4:2, 22, 29)—is not genealogical, since Gershon was the firstborn (cf. 3:17). Nor is it in the order in which they will set out, since the Gershonites and Merarites leave before the Kohathites (10:17, 21). The Kohathites are mentioned first since they are responsible for the most holy appurtenances. Aaron's sons supervise the Levites, with Eleazar over the Kohathites and Ithamar over the Gershonites and the Merarites (4:16, 28, 33).

Three principal words pairs—verb and cognate noun—describe the Levites' tabernacle duties: (1) carrying/transportation (*nasa'/massa'*); (2) physical labor of serving/service (*'abad/'abodah*), including dismantling, packing, loading, reassembling, and maintenance; and (3) guarding/guard duty (*shamar/mishmeret*) to prevent encroachment. The latter two sometimes summarize the Levites' responsibilities. Given the focus of chapter 3 on their camp positions around the tabernacle, the sevenfold accent there was on keeping guard/guard duty (*mishmeret*). With the emphasis on transporting the tabernacle in chapter 4, two terms—"burden" (*massa'*) and "service" (*'abodah*)—are used together seven times and are equally applied to all three Levitical families (vv. 19, 24, 27, 31, 32, 47, 49). A fourth term previously used describes the Levites' duty to "take care of" (*shrt*) the tabernacle.

Characteristically, the chapter begins with a command given by the Lord to Moses and ends with a compliance summary ("as the LORD commanded Moses"), a subtype of which punctuates the chapter (vv. 37, 41, 45).

Section Outline

I. Instructions for the Exodus Generation Preparing to Leave Sinai for Canaan (1:1–10:36)...

    D. Levite Responsibilities and Totals (4:1–49)

        1. Kohathite Responsibilities and Totals (4:1–20, 34–37)
        2. Gershonite Responsibilities and Totals (4:21–28, 38–41)
        3. Merarite Responsibilities and Totals (4:29–33, 42–45)
        4. Summary (4:46–49)

Comment

4:1–20, 34–37 Moses and Aaron are commanded to "take a census of the sons of Kohath" (v. 2; cf. comment on 1:1–19 [at v. 2]). The Kohathites are "sons of Levi" (v. 2), together with the Gershonites and Merarites. "From thirty years old up to fifty" (v. 3; cf. vv. 23, 30, 35, 39, 43, 47) is the age group of service for all three Levitical families. "From thirty" they will be thoroughly trained and "up to fifty" have the necessary vigor to dismantle, pack, transport, and reassemble the tabernacle, the focus of their work "when the camp is to set out" (4:5, 15). The Kohathites will carry the sacred furnishings on their shoulders (7:9).

"All who can come on duty [*tsaba'*]" (4:3, 23, 30, 35, 39, 43) is like the formula for military conscription ("All who can go to war [*tsaba'*]"; 1:3). Levites combat intruders to the holy to prevent desecration. The LXX reads "comes in to minister" (*leitourgeō*), the same term that describes the Jerusalem church's "worshiping" when it receives instructions to set apart the Levite Barnabas and Saul for service (Acts 13:2).

The Kohathites are responsible for "the most holy things" (*qodesh haqqodashim*; Num. 4:4, 15, 19), literally, "the holy of holies," sometimes referring to the Most Holy Place (Ex. 26:33; 1 Kings 8:6). "Things," added in the translation, refers to the furnishings in the Most Holy and the Holy Place and to the altar in the court (Num. 3:31). Two terms describe the Kohathites' responsibility: "work" (*mela'kah*; 4:3)—the only occurrence referring to Levitical duty—and "service" (*'abodah*; v. 4). The latter also defines the responsibilities of the Gershonites and the Merarites (vv. 23, 30).

Both terms were used in concluding statements on the tabernacle: "Thus all the work ['*abodah*] of the tabernacle of the tent of meeting was finished" (Ex. 39:32); "So Moses finished the work [*mela'kah*]" (Ex. 40:33). The latter term echoes the finished work of creation: "And on the seventh day God finished his work [*mela'kah*] that he had done, and he rested on the seventh day from all his work [*mela'kah*] that he had done" (Gen. 2:2). In Numbers 28–29 both words are combined in a fixed expression rendered "ordinary work" (*mela'keth 'abodah*), forbidden during the sacred feasts (cf. comment on 28:16–25 [at v. 18]). Paul uses the same two words as rendered in the LXX (4:3, *leitourgia*; v. 4, *ergon*) to describe Epaphroditus's labor: "He nearly died for the work [*ergon*] of Christ, risking his life to complete what was lacking in your service [*leitourgia*] to me" (Phil. 2:30). Paul often employs priestly language to describe sacred service in the church.

Numbers 4:5–15 describe the work Aaron and his sons do before the tabernacle can be transported. Because the Kohathites must not "touch" or "look" on the sacred furnishings (vv. 15, 20), the priests must cover the furniture and make ready the means of transportation. Since the inner sanctuary is pitch black (1 Kings 8:12; cf. Ps. 18:9), the instructions given on the seven lamps in the Holy Place (Num. 8:1–4) are essential to execute this responsibility.

TABLE 4.3: Covers and Transportation for the Sacred Furnishings

Furniture	Cover	Transportation
Ark of the testimony	veil, goatskin, blue cloth	poles
Table of bread of Presence	blue cloth, scarlet cloth, goatskin	poles
Lampstand	blue cloth, goatskin	carrying frame
Golden altar (incense)	blue cloth, goatskin	poles
Vessels	blue cloth, goatskin	carrying frame
Altar (burnt offerings)	purple cloth, goatskin	poles

The order of the furnishings, along with the number and color of their covers, reflects varying degrees of sacredness, which is also shown by the movement from the Most Holy Place to the Holy Place, then outward to the court.

Aaron and his sons will "take down the veil of the screen" (4:5), which curtains access to the Most Holy Place. Cherubim are embroidered in it (Ex. 26:31), like those placed at the eastern entrance to the garden of Eden to guard the way to the tree of life (Gen. 3:24). The veil is now used to "cover the ark of the testimony." The veil includes all of the majestic royal colors: blue, purple, and scarlet (Ex. 26:31–33). On top of this is a "covering of goatskin" (*takhash*; Num. 4:6; the meaning is uncertain, cf. Ex. 25:5 ESV mg.).[46] This skin covers all the furniture. Being impermeable, it protects from the elements. A "cloth all of blue" (*tekelet*, bluish purple or violet material) is put over the skin. The carrying poles must be removed to cover the ark, after which the priest must "put in its poles." Otherwise, they are never removed (Ex. 25:15).

The "table of the bread of the Presence" (Num. 4:7) is literally "table of the Presence" (cf. Ex. 25:30; 35:13; 39:36). "Regular" (*tamid*; Num. 4:7) also means "continual," since the "showbread" (*lehem*), consisting of twelve loaves arranged in two rows and representing the twelve tribes, is always on the table and replaced

---

[46] A similar word in Arabic for "dolphin" (*tuhas*) yields the translation "porpoise-hide" (and also seal-hide, dugong-hide, sea cowhide). Egyptian "leather" (*tkhs*) gives the rendering "goatskin" (also fine leather, durable leather; cf. Ezek. 16:10).

each Sabbath (Lev. 24:5–9; cf. 1 Sam. 21:6; 1 Chron. 9:32). The table is first covered with a "cloth of blue." Then the "plates ... dishes ... bowls ... and flagons" used in the sanctuary are put on the table. These are made of gold (Ex. 25:29; 37:16). The table and everything on it are covered with a "cloth of scarlet" (*tola'at*), then "goatskin" (Num. 4:8). The coverings show the table is second in sacredness only to the ark.

A "cloth of blue" first covers the lampstand (v. 9; cf. 8:1–4), which is made of gold and has six branches (Ex. 25:32) and seven lamps (Ex. 25:37; 37:23; Num. 8:2; Zech. 4:2). Then it, its lamps, and all its utensils are covered with goatskin and put on a "carrying frame" (*mot*; Num. 4:10). Elsewhere *mot* describes the pole used by two men to carry a grape cluster (13:23) and the poles used to shoulder the ark (7:9; cf. Ex. 25:14; 37:5). The translation "carrying frame" reflects a surface sufficiently wide and flat to place and transport the aforementioned items (cf. Num. 4:12). Either a carrying pole (the word is sg.) is attached to a frame or the pole itself is a flat-surfaced beam. The "golden altar" (v. 11), the altar of incense (Ex. 31:8), is covered in the same manner as the lampstand. "All the vessels of the service that are used in the sanctuary" (Num. 4:12; cf. 3:31)—other than those on the table of the bread of the Presence—are covered with cloth of blue and with goatskin, then put on the carrying frame (4:12).

After the ashes are removed and carried outside the camp to a clean place (Lev. 6:11; cf. Num. 19:9), the bronze altar (4:13) in the court is covered with a purple cloth. In the rank portrayed by the three colors, purple is lowest. As third ruler in the kingdom, Daniel is clothed in purple (Dan. 5:29). The soldiers place a purple robe on Jesus, then a crown of thorns, to mock him as king (John 19:2–3). Then, on top of the altar, the "fire pans, the forks, the shovels, and the basins, all the [bronze] utensils of the altar" are covered with goatskin (Num. 4:14; cf. Ex. 27:3).

Numbers 4:16 lists that over which "Eleazar ... shall have charge" (v. 16). The "oil for the light" is beaten olive oil (Lev. 24:2; cf. comment on Num. 28:1–8 [at v. 4]) for the golden lampstand (cf. 4:9). The "fragrant incense" (v. 16) is for the golden altar. Both the oil and the incense are burned in the Holy Place morning and evening (Ex. 30:7–8). The "regular grain offering" (Num. 4:16) is made with the regular burnt offering (cf. chs. 28–29); it is most holy (Lev. 10:12; Num. 18:9), made from fine flour, olive oil, and frankincense. The "anointing oil" (4:16), which is holy (Ex. 30:31; Num. 35:25), is used to consecrate Aaron and his sons (Ex. 29:21), as well as the tent and its furnishings, making them ceremonially most holy (Ex. 30:25–29; cf. Num. 18:9–10). Eleazar's "oversight of the whole tabernacle" (Num. 4:16) involves specifically "all that is in it," that is, "of the sanctuary and its vessels." "Vessels" (*kelim*) involve the furnishings in the Most Holy and Holy Places (cf. 1:50; 18:3; also Ex. 31:7; 1 Kings 7:48). "Charge" (Num. 4:16) renders the same Hebrew word (*pequddah*) translated "oversight" (v. 16). In the LXX this is translated by the words (*episkope/episkopos*) that in the NT describe the church office of "overseer" (1 Tim. 3:1) and Christ as the "Shepherd and Overseer of your souls" (1 Pet. 2:25).

"The LORD spoke to Moses and Aaron" (Num. 4:17; cf. v. 1) introduces additional instructions, including a warning. The plural imperative "Let not . . . be destroyed" (v. 18) is addressed to both. To "be destroyed" (*karat*; lit., "be cut off") describes the consequence of a grave violation (cf. v. 19), here encroachment by ritual misdeed. Any negligence on the part of the Kohathites, who bear responsibility for the most holy things, is extremely dangerous and will be charged to Moses and Aaron. Priestly inattention to ceremonial detail will incur divine wrath.

Moses and Aaron, and now also Eleazar, must ensure that the Kohathites "may live and not die" (v. 19). When called to "come near" (v. 19), that is, to approach holy things, Aaron and his sons must cover those items so that the Kohathites will "not touch" (v. 15; cf. Uzzah, 2 Sam. 6:6–7) or even "look on the holy things even for a moment, lest they die" (Num. 4:20; cf. the men of Beth-shemesh, 1 Sam. 6:19). The Hebrew rendered "for a moment" literally means "like swallowing" (*keballa'*; cf. Num. 16:32), a figure for about one second of time.[47]

4:21–28, 38–41 Given the similarities, the responsibilities of the Gershonites (vv. 21–28, 38–41) and the Merarites (vv. 29–33, 42–45) are commented on together here. What primarily distinguishes the two families is that which they transport. Otherwise, what is said of one could be said of the other.

"Take a census" (v. 22; cf. comment on 1:1–19 [at v. 2]) is said concerning the Gershonites only, but a Merarite census is obviously taken too (cf. 4:44). To "do duty" means to "do service in the tent of meeting" (vv. 23, 30), literally, "to work [*'abad*] the work of [*'abodah*]" the physical labor involved before, during, and after transporting the tabernacle.

The Gershonites shall carry (*nasa'*) the "curtains of the tabernacle and the tent of meeting with its [goat's hair] covering and the covering of goatskin . . . the screen for the entrance of the tent of meeting . . . the hangings of the court and the screen for the entrance of the gate of the court . . . their cords . . . the equipment" (4:25–26; cf. comment on 3:5–39 [at v. 26]). These are the fabric parts of the tabernacle. The Gershonites receive two wagons and four oxen to transport these elements (7:7). The Kohathites receive none, since they are to carry the sacred objects on their shoulders (7:9). In the summary statements the Gershonites' "service" (*'abodah*, physical labor) and "guard duty" (*mishmeret*; 4:28) and the Merarites' "service" (v. 31) are placed "under the direction of Ithamar the son of Aaron the priest" (v. 28, 33). Although it is not repeated in the summary, the Merarites have guard duty (cf. 3:36).

4:29–33, 42–45 The Merarites are "charged to carry" (v. 31) and "required to carry" (v. 32), both rendering the same expression (*mishmeret massa'am*; lit., "the guarding of their porterage").[48] The need for guarding against intrusion does not cease during the packing and transporting of the tabernacle. In fact, at those

---

47 "*As a swallowing* = for an instant"; BDB 118a.
48 Milgrom, *Numbers*, 31.

critical moments fatal errors of inadvertent encroachment could, and will, occur (cf. 2 Sam. 6:6–7). The transporting of the tabernacle involves the structural parts and hardware ("frames ... bars, pillars, and bases.... pegs, and cords, with all their equipment and all their accessories"; Num. 4:31–32). Given their heavy load, the Merarites receive four wagons and eight oxen (7:8; cf. Ex. 38:24–31). By the choice of words common to all three Levitical families, considerable effort is made to rule out any idea of favoritism or superiority among them, especially between the Kohathites and their brethren. Although tasks vary and spheres of ministry differ, the responsibilities of each clan involve doing "service in the tent of meeting" (Num. 4:4, 23, 30).

Verses 34–37, 38–41, 42–45 give the census totals for the three Levitical clans. Being an administrative list, they are presented in a repetitive manner. The Kohathite clan will illustrate this. The concentric literary pattern is similar for the two other clans.

> (A) Moses and Aaron ... listed the sons of the Kohathites, by their clans
> ... from thirty years old up to fifty years old (vv. 34–35a)
> > (B) [All] who could come on duty, for service in the tent of meeting (v. 35)
> > > (C) Those listed by clans were 2,750. This was a list of the clans of Kohathites (vv. 36–37a)
> > (B') All who served in the tent of meeting (v. 37a)
> (A') Whom Moses and Aaron listed according to the commandment of the LORD by Moses (v. 37b)

In addition to the shared vocabulary, the same literary structure for the census results of the three Levitical clans also underscores their equality, notwithstanding their varying service. The census figures in themselves suggest no Kohathite superiority, as they number 2,750 (v. 36) and the Gershonites 2,630 (v. 40). The Merarites have the greatest number 3,200 (v. 44); their load is the heaviest.

4:46–49 The concluding summary is characteristic of administrative census lists (e.g., 1:44–46; 2:32–34; 3:39). Restated are (1) the listed ("Levites"), (2) the listers ("Moses and Aaron and the chiefs"), (3) the categories of listing ("clans ... fathers' houses"; 4:46), (4) the age group ("from thirty years old up to fifty"), (5) the purpose ("the service of ministry and the service of bearing burdens in the tent of meeting"; v. 47), and (6) the total (8,580; v. 48).

Like the literary structure of the census summaries of each family, here the final verse (v. 49) is concentric:

> (A) According to the commandment of the LORD
> > (B) Through Moses they were listed
> > > (C) Each one with his task of serving or carrying.
> > (B') Thus they were listed by him,
> (A') As the LORD commanded Moses.

Rather than their numbers, their ministries are highlighted in the center of the structure. Although they are divided by clans and different spheres of ministry, all the Levites, down to "each one," have a common goal: their service to the Lord, his ministers the priests, and his people.

Response

The Levites' coming on "duty" (*tsaba'*; cf. comment on 4:1–20, 34–37 [at v. 3]) is described with the same word for soldiers' going to "war" (cf. comment on 1:1–19 [at v. 3]). The Levites do not have military duty. But they must wage war against all that would desecrate the holiness of the tabernacle. This may be behind NT expressions such as "take up the whole armor of God" (Eph. 6:13), "wage the good warfare" (1 Tim. 1:18), "a good soldier of Christ Jesus" (2 Tim. 2:3), and "no soldier gets entangled in civilian pursuits" (2 Tim. 2:4). Spiritual warfare involves three intermingled spheres: sin, Satan, and the world. By relying on the Holy Spirit, Christians do not persist in sinful behavior (Gal. 5:16; 1 John 3:6, 8, 9; 5:18). They submit to God and resist the Devil (James 4:7). They overcome the world by faith in Christ (1 John 5:5).

NUMBERS 5

5 The Lord spoke to Moses, saying, ² "Command the people of Israel that they put out of the camp everyone who is leprous¹ or has a discharge and everyone who is unclean through contact with the dead. ³ You shall put out both male and female, putting them outside the camp, that they may not defile their camp, in the midst of which I dwell." ⁴ And the people of Israel did so, and put them outside the camp; as the Lord said to Moses, so the people of Israel did.

⁵ And the Lord spoke to Moses, saying, ⁶ "Speak to the people of Israel, When a man or woman commits any of the sins that people commit by breaking faith with the Lord, and that person realizes his guilt, ⁷ he shall confess his sin that he has committed.² And he shall make full restitution for his wrong, adding a fifth to it and giving it to him to whom he did the wrong. ⁸ But if the man has no next of kin to whom restitution may be made for the wrong, the restitution for wrong shall go to the Lord for the priest, in addition to the ram of atonement with which atonement is made for him. ⁹ And every contribution, all the holy donations of the people of Israel, which they bring to the priest, shall be his. ¹⁰ Each one shall keep his holy donations: whatever anyone gives to the priest shall be his."

¹¹ And the Lord spoke to Moses, saying, ¹² "Speak to the people of Israel, If any man's wife goes astray and breaks faith with him, ¹³ if a man lies with her sexually, and it is hidden from the eyes of her husband, and

she is undetected though she has defiled herself, and there is no witness against her, since she was not taken in the act, ¹⁴ and if the spirit of jealousy comes over him and he is jealous of his wife who has defiled herself, or if the spirit of jealousy comes over him and he is jealous of his wife, though she has not defiled herself, ¹⁵ then the man shall bring his wife to the priest and bring the offering required of her, a tenth of an ephah³ of barley flour. He shall pour no oil on it and put no frankincense on it, for it is a grain offering of jealousy, a grain offering of remembrance, bringing iniquity to remembrance.

¹⁶ "And the priest shall bring her near and set her before the Lord. ¹⁷ And the priest shall take holy water in an earthenware vessel and take some of the dust that is on the floor of the tabernacle and put it into the water. ¹⁸ And the priest shall set the woman before the Lord and unbind the hair of the woman's head and place in her hands the grain offering of remembrance, which is the grain offering of jealousy. And in his hand the priest shall have the water of bitterness that brings the curse. ¹⁹ Then the priest shall make her take an oath, saying, 'If no man has lain with you, and if you have not turned aside to uncleanness while you were under your husband's authority, be free from this water of bitterness that brings the curse. ²⁰ But if you have gone astray, though you are under your husband's authority, and if you have defiled yourself, and some man other than your husband has lain with you, ²¹ then' (let the priest make the woman take the oath of the curse, and say to the woman) 'the Lord make you a curse and an oath among your people, when the Lord makes your thigh fall away and your body swell. ²² May this water that brings the curse pass into your bowels and make your womb swell and your thigh fall away.' And the woman shall say, 'Amen, Amen.'

²³ "Then the priest shall write these curses in a book and wash them off into the water of bitterness. ²⁴ And he shall make the woman drink the water of bitterness that brings the curse, and the water that brings the curse shall enter into her and cause bitter pain. ²⁵ And the priest shall take the grain offering of jealousy out of the woman's hand and shall wave the grain offering before the Lord and bring it to the altar. ²⁶ And the priest shall take a handful of the grain offering, as its memorial portion, and burn it on the altar, and afterward shall make the woman drink the water. ²⁷ And when he has made her drink the water, then, if she has defiled herself and has broken faith with her husband, the water that brings the curse shall enter into her and cause bitter pain, and her womb shall swell, and her thigh shall fall away, and the woman shall become a curse among her people. ²⁸ But if the woman has not defiled herself and is clean, then she shall be free and shall conceive children.

²⁹ "This is the law in cases of jealousy, when a wife, though under her husband's authority, goes astray and defiles herself, ³⁰ or when the spirit of jealousy comes over a man and he is jealous of his wife. Then he shall set the woman before the Lord, and the priest shall carry out for her all this law. ³¹ The man shall be free from iniquity, but the woman shall bear her iniquity."

¹ *Leprosy* was a term for several skin diseases; see Leviticus 13 ² Hebrew *they shall confess their sin that they have committed* ³ An *ephah* was about 3/5 bushel or 22 liters

Section Overview

After the civil and clerical instructions to organize the journey from Sinai to the Promised Land (Num. 1:1–4:49) come laws dealing with the purity of the lay camp, three in chapter 5 and one in chapter 6. All four concern both men and women (5:3, 6, 12; 6:2). Impurities could involve physical disorders, civil offenses, moral indecencies, or especially contact with a human corpse. Given the importance of the latter, it is addressed in chapters 5; 6; 19; 31.

Although diverse, these laws share a common concern: the Israelite camp must remain pure so as not to defile the sanctuary and thereby draw God's wrath. He dwells in their midst (5:3) by his symbolic presence in the sanctuary. This pedagogical wilderness period is a critical training ground for the future: the land in which the Israelites will live must not be defiled, since the Lord will dwell there in their midst (35:34).

The four laws are introduced by "The LORD spoke to Moses, saying," after which a law is given that he must transmit "to the people" (5:1–2, 5–6, 11–12; 6:1–2).

The priestly benediction (6:22–27) following the fourth law (6:1–21) is another encouragement to maintain the camp's purity.

Section Outline

I. Instructions for the Exodus Generation Preparing to Leave Sinai for Canaan (1:1–10:36) . . .
  E. Laws on Purity of the Camp (5:1–31)
    1. Physical Impurities (5:1–4)
    2. Fraud (5:5–10)
    3. Suspicion of Adultery (5:11–31)

Comment

5:1–4 The three general classes of physical impurities addressed in chapter 5 are a "leprous" condition, abnormal bodily "discharge," and "contact with the dead" (v. 2). Anyone who contracts any of these impurities is "put out of the camp." The summary fashion with which these cases are treated here presumes fuller exposition elsewhere. The first two are treated at length in Leviticus 13–15. Corpse contamination receives less attention in that book, as it deals only with priests' contact with the deceased (Lev. 21:1–4). Special instructions regarding corpse contamination are given in Numbers 6; 19.

The "leprous" (form of Hb. *tsaraʿ*; Num. 5:2) condition likely includes several skin diseases (Lev. 13:1–44).[49] While still in quarantine and after receiving a clean bill of health from the priest, who functions as a public health inspector, the affected person undergoes a complex process of purification ("atonement"; Lev. 14:19–20, 21–32).

---

49 Such as psoriasis, acute acne, or vitiligo; cf. Katharine Doob Sakenfeld, *Numbers: Journeying with God*, ITC (Grand Rapids, MI: Eerdmans, 1995), 33.

A "discharge" (*zav*; Num. 5:2) from a sexual organ could be normal or abnormal. Normal discharges involve emission of semen and menstruation. Ejaculation causes uncleanness until evening, menstruation for seven days (Lev. 15:16, 19). These require neither quarantine nor sacrifices. Abnormal masculine urethral discharge and vaginal bleeding do. After the discharge ceases, it requires a seven-day period of cleansing and sacrifices on the eighth day (cf. Lev. 15:2, 13–15, 25, 28–29).

Contamination by "contact with the dead" (Num. 5:2; cf. comment on 6:1–12 [at v. 6]), whether accidental or of necessity, results in the greatest danger. Among other rites, if not sprinkled twice with water for impurity made from the ashes of the red heifer, the contaminated person is to be cut off from Israel (19:11–22; cf. 9:6, 10). Impurities affect both genders in parallel, though not identical, fashion (5:3). "Outside the camp" (vv. 2, 4) is outside the double cordon of the camps of the Levites and the tribes—thus at the greatest distance from the tabernacle. Confinement there affords time for purification by the prescribed rites and physical restoration when needed. But, if purification is not made, the sanctuary will be defiled and the responsible person cut off (19:13, 20).

Although there is concern about hygiene and contagion, the only stated reason behind these stipulations is "Thus you shall keep the people of Israel separate from their uncleanness, lest they die in their uncleanness by defiling my tabernacle that is in their midst" (Lev. 15:31). "They may not defile their camp, in the midst of which I dwell" (*shakan*; Num. 5:3) is the only stated reason for the unclean to go outside the camp.

The title "tabernacle/dwelling place" (*mishkan*; e.g., v. 17) is cognate to "dwell" (*shakan*). The Lord's dwelling presence (the "Shekinah" of rabbinic tradition, based on the Targums) is of paramount importance. At this stage of the history of revelation this is the *summum* of the tripartite covenant promise "I will make my dwelling among you, and my soul shall not abhor you. And I will walk among you and will be your God, and you shall be my people," expressed fully for the first time in Leviticus (Lev. 26:11–12), proclaimed by the prophets especially in the context of the new covenant (e.g., Jer. 31:1, 33; Ezek. 36:28), and then realized ultimately in the NT (e.g., 2 Cor. 6:16). Both Leviticus and its citation in Corinthians state, "And I will walk [Hb. *vehithalakti*] among you," which echoes the Lord God's "walking in the garden" (Gen. 3:8; same verb form). The requirement to maintain purity is extended to the Promised Land, where the Lord will dwell in the midst of his people (cf. comment on Num. 35:9–34 [at v. 34]). The promise of his presence and its manifestation in the tabernacle anticipates "the Word [who] became flesh and dwelt [lit., "tabernacled"] among us" (John 1:14). Jesus' physical contact with lepers, the woman with an abnormal discharge of blood, and the dead all point to Jesus' fulfillment and transcendence of ceremonial laws (Matt. 8:1–4; Mark 5:25–34, 41). In his compassion he cleanses them from their defiling impurities.

5:5–10 This law regarding fraud presents a civil case adjudicated in the ritual domain. It is closely related to Leviticus 6:1–7 (Lev. 5:20–26 MT; cf. Ex. 22:7–9, 10–13), as table 4.4 shows.

TABLE 4.4: Connections between Numbers 5:5–10 and Leviticus 6:1–7

Sin of "breaking faith" (*ma'al*)	Num. 5:6	Lev. 6:2
Consequence "guilt" (*'asham*)	Num. 5:6	Lev. 6:4, 5, 6 [*'asham*; "guilt offering"]
Required "restitution" (*'asham*)	Num. 5:7	Lev. 6:4, 5
Reparation "adding a fifth"	Num. 5:7	Lev. 6:5
Offering "a ram"	Num. 5:8	Lev. 6:6
For "atonement"	Num. 5:8	Lev. 6:7
"Man or woman"	Num. 5:6 (cf. 5:3; 6:2)	

"Any of the sins that people commit" (Num. 5:6) renders the Hebrew "any sin of man/humanity," which could mean any sin *by* man or any sin *against* man. Here it is the latter: "To whom he did the wrong" (v. 7). The Leviticus parallel provides as case in point:

> If anyone sins and commits a breach of faith against the LORD by deceiving his neighbor in a matter of deposit or security, or through robbery, or if he has oppressed his neighbor or has found something lost and lied about it, swearing falsely—in any of all the things that people do and sin thereby. (Lev. 6:2–3)

The "sin" involves misappropriation, the wrongful keeping of something entrusted by its owner. Stealing profanes God's name (Prov. 30:9). Here it is aggravated by the embezzler's "breaking faith" (Hb. *ma'al*; Num. 5:6) by taking an oath in God's name to hide the fraud. A false oath is sacrilegious perjury. Swearing falsely profanes God's name (Lev. 19:12). Scripture provides notable examples of those who break faith in other ways. Achan steals sacrosanct spoil under the *kherem* ban (Josh. 6:19; 7:21). The charge is brought by God himself: "Israel has sinned; they have transgressed my covenant that I commanded them; they have taken some of the devoted things; they have stolen and lied and put them among their own belongings" (Josh. 7:11). Usurping priestly prerogative, Saul offers a sacrifice (1 Sam. 13:12; 15:22–23). Moses and Aaron fail to treat the Lord as holy. They all "break faith" (Deut. 32:51; Josh. 7:1; 22:20; 1 Chron. 2:7; 10:13), profane God's holy name, and therefore die. For profaning God's holy name (Ezek. 36:20) by their iniquity, the people of Israel go into captivity because they break faith with God ("Dealt so treacherously"; Ezek. 39:23). Whatever its form, breaking faith desecrates the Lord.

"Realizes his guilt" (*'asham*; Num. 5:6) suggests that strong guilt feelings drive the embezzler to turn himself in to make amends. This law provides the way.

"Confess his sin" (*yadah*; v. 7; cf. Lev. 5:5; cf. also Ps. 32:5; Prov. 28:13) means to acknowledge it to God and make it known in the presence of a priest and the victim. Sincerity is evidenced by the offender's burden of guilt and doing what is required of his own accord. David's guilt feelings and remorse drive him to confess his sins (Ps. 32:3–5). Confession is the only way he will not be chastened by God in his wrath (Ps. 38:1, 18). The principle is simple: "Godly grief produces a repentance that leads to salvation without regret, whereas worldly grief produces death" (2 Cor. 7:10).

In addition to openly admitting his willful wrongdoing, the embezzler must "make full restitution" (*'asham*) to the victim of what he has misappropriated and make reparation by "adding a fifth to it" (Num. 5:7). A thief who is apprehended must restore the stolen goods and make reparation anywhere from two to five times their value (Ex. 22:1–4). Here reparation is 20 percent of the value of the extorted item (Num. 5:7; cf. Lev. 6:4–5), since the offender voluntarily surrenders (cf. Ex. 22:1, 4; 2 Sam. 12:6). The action of doing wrong (*'asham*) results in guilt (*'asham*) and requires restitution (*'asham*) and, as mentioned in Leviticus, a guilt offering (*'asham*; Num. 6:6 [5:25 MT]). If the victim is deceased and there is "no next of kin," the priest receives the restitution payment (6:8).

Alongside confession, restitution, and reparation, a sacrifice is required (a "ram of atonement"), with which atonement is "made for him" (5:8). This involves a "guilt offering" (Lev. 6:6). The "atonement" (from *kpr*) made here for an intentional sin provides an exception to the fundamental principle that atonement can normally be made only for unintentional sins (Num. 15:27–29; Heb. 9:7). Intentional, or high-handed, sins are punished by the perpetrator's being cut off (*karat*; Num. 15:30–31). Once again, it seems the element of confession provides a mitigating factor.

Although forgiveness is not mentioned here, for the guilty party it is the goal of atonement (Lev. 6:7 [5:26 MT]). Forgiveness requires this purification sacrifice. Confession makes this possible even for high-handed sins (Ps. 51:3–4; cf. Ps. 32:5; Ezra 10:10–11). The blood of a sin or guilt offering (a substitute victim) dabbed, sprinkled, or splashed on the contaminated sacred object is the agent that purifies *it* (Lev. 8:15; 16:18–19; 17:11; Ps. 51:7; Ezek. 43:20). The guilty party is forgiven for having polluted it and for the act causing the pollution. Pardon for sin is probably pronounced by the priest, but it is granted by God alone.

In the NT Zacchaeus is guilty of defrauding. In Jesus' presence he confesses his sin and promises to make restitution. Jesus remarks in response, "Today salvation has come to this house, since he also is a son of Abraham. For the Son of Man came to seek and to save the lost" (Luke 19:9–10).

A "contribution" (*terumah*; Num. 5:9) is the priest's share of an offering. In Numbers it involves the first of the dough (15:20–21); the portion removed from the grain, sin, and guilt offerings, which are most holy (18:8–10, 18); and the Levites' tithe (v. 28). Numbers 5:8–10 illustrates how certain laws are added as supplements where they fit. Here the supplements center on priests' stipends (e.g., 6:21; 9:9–14).

5:11–31 This case involves a domestic matter: a wife suspected of adultery by her husband. As is the preceding civil case, it is adjudicated in the ritual domain. The sanctity of marriage is underscored by the prescribed imprecatory oath-ordeal; God himself will vindicate or judge the suspect.

The law covers two possibilities. In the first "she has defiled herself" (v. 13; cf. vv. 20, 29), whereas in the second "she has not defiled herself" (5:14; cf. v. 28). "Defiled" (Hb. *tame'*) defines immorality in ritual terms. Use of the term supposes a sacred counterpoint: the marriage bed (Gen. 49:4; Heb. 13:4). Two verbs describe the act of defiling oneself. First, "go astray" (*satah*; Num. 5:12, 19, 20, 29) appears in warnings to a son not to go astray by turning to prostitutes (Prov. 4:15; 7:25). Second, "breaks faith" (*ma'al*; Num. 5:12; cf. v. 27) links the law with the preceding one (cf. comment on 5:5–10 [at v. 6]). There it involved swearing in God's name that a falsehood was true. The action of the second verb (lying under oath) confirms the first (she went astray). The charge of adultery is thereby aggravated by sacrilegious perjury.

The noun cognate with "break faith" describes idolatry (Lev. 26:40, "treachery"; Num. 31:16, "act treacherously"). Turning to other gods is likened to adultery committed by Israel, the Lord's wife (e.g., Jer. 3:9; 31:32; Ezek. 16:32; Hos. 1:2; 2:2; cf. Ex. 34:15–16; Ps. 106:36–39; Jer. 13:26–27). Like the relationship with the Lord, marriage is a covenant bond (Mal. 2:14; cf. Prov. 2:17; Ezek. 16:8). In either case, breaking faith destroys trust and breaches the covenant bond (Josh. 7:11). Both adultery and idolatry call for capital punishment (Ex. 22:20; Lev. 20:3, 10).

In the present case if the wife is guilty there is no prescribed sentence to be executed by man's hand. The woman is protected before submitting to the oath-ordeal by mitigating circumstances: "It is hidden from the eyes of her husband, and she is undetected though she has defiled herself, and there is no witness against her, since she was not taken in the act" (Num. 5:13). First, if there is "no witness," the death sentence is precluded (Deut. 22:22), since it requires at least two witnesses (Deut. 17:6). Second, the term "adultery" (*na'aph*; e.g., Ex. 20:14; Lev. 20:10) is not used. Instead an expression describes it but applies only to the man involved.[50] A man other than her husband "lies with her sexually" (*shakab ... shikbat-zera'*; lit., "lies ... lying-seed"; Num. 5:13; cf. Lev. 15:16, 17, 18, 32 ["emission of semen"]) or has "lain" with her (*shakab*, Num. 5:19; *shekobet*, v. 20; cf. Lev. 18:20). The man's act described here is his consummated intercourse with the wife of another man. Numbers 5:20 does not mince words, which translated word for word reads, "A man put in you his lying instead of your man." Clearly, adultery is described without ever using the inculpatory word. Hidden sin and guilt, however, will ultimately meet God's judgment. This is the reason for the oath-ordeal if the wife is guilty.

That which has aroused the husband's "spirit of jealousy" (Num. 5:14, 30; Prov. 6:32–35; cf. Prov. 27:4; Song 8:6) is not stated. He "is jealous of his wife," that is, "because of" her. Perhaps she is pregnant, and he suspects he be not the father. The outcome of the oath-ordeal if undefiled—"she ... shall conceive children"

---

50 Milgrom, *Numbers*, 350.

(Num. 5:28)—may suggest this.[51] If she were pregnant and innocent, she would bear her husband's child. Jealousy as the basis of such a serious charge raises the second possibility: "She has not defiled herself" (v. 14). In this case the husband's suspicions are unfounded. Either way, jealousy has led him to undertake the prescribed measures.

In the absence of tangible evidence, how could the case be adjudicated? A ritual is employed. It is not a trial by ordeal, in which, presumed guilty, the wife would be proved innocent by her surviving a typically fatal act, such as being thrown into a river. In trials by ordeal, fire to burn and water to drown the accused are used to coerce confessions. Nothing but a miracle could save the innocent. Here, fire burns the sacrifice brought on behalf of the wife, and water is that which she consents to drink. The ritual itself is neutral as concerns her guilt or innocence. Before she drinks the water she pronounces a curse (cf. Jer. 49:12–13) upon herself, supported by an oath. This autoimprecation will prove her guilt or innocence by either materializing or not doing so. If she be guilty, only God can execute judgment by fulfilling the curse she has called upon herself.

The "offering required of her, a tenth of an ephah of barley" (Num. 5:15), is not the normal grain offering of fine wheat flour (cf. 4:16). Barley cost half as much as wheat (2 Kings 7:1, 16, 18; cf. Rev. 6:6); it was fed to horses (1 Kings 4:28 [5:8 MT]). "No oil" or "frankincense" (Num. 5:15) are to be used here, as they are with grain offerings (Lev. 6:15); frankincense would create a pleasing aroma to the Lord (Lev. 6:15; cf. Num. 15:10). The reason for this prohibition is that "it is a grain offering of jealousy, a grain offering of remembrance, bringing iniquity to remembrance" (Num. 5:15). The husband's "jealousy" has occasioned the ritual. "Remembrance" (*zikron*) is more than bringing something to mind. The word can refer to an official document containing vital affairs and juridical decisions (Est. 6:1). Because of the serious charges and, if she be guilty, the severe consequences, the sworn curse uttered by the woman is recorded (Num. 5:23). The accusation involves "iniquity" (*'avon*; vv. 15, 31), an intentional sin, breaking faith (vv. 12, 27), which cannot be atoned (15:30–31).

The priest is to "bring [the woman] near and set her before the LORD" (5:16; cf. vv. 18, 30). The two verbs "bring near" (form of *qarab*) and "set before" (form of *'amad*, lit., "make stand") are used together for the Levites brought near and stood before Aaron, the priest (3:6). To be brought near and stood "before the Lord" means the woman is brought before the priest officiating the altar. Her presence there suggests she is presumed innocent, undefiled. The priest must put "holy water in an earthenware vessel" (5:17) and "unbind the hair of the woman's head" (v. 18). Both an earthenware vessel and the unbinding of hair are part of the purification for leprous conditions (Lev. 14:5, 50; 13:45). The Hebrew verb translated "unbind" (*para'*) also describes the Israelites as "out of control" at the golden calf incident (Ex. 32:25; cf. 2 Chron. 28:19: "made [to] act sinfully"). The term "holy water" appears only here. It is perhaps taken from the bronze basin in the court. "Dust" from the

---

51 Levine, *Numbers 1–20*, 181, 193.

"floor of the tabernacle," mixed with the holy water (Num. 5:17), constitutes the "water of bitterness that brings the curse" (vv. 18, 24). The cursed serpent had to eat dust (Gen. 3:14; cf. Mic. 7:17). Moses made the Israelites involved in the golden calf incident drink water mixed with the powder of the burnt idol (Ex. 32:20).

The priest next puts the grain offering "in her hands," whereas "in his hand" he holds the water of bitterness (Num. 5:18). He makes her take "an oath" (*shebu'ah*; v. 19), an imprecation to the effect that "If I am guilty, let the Lord bring the words of this curse upon me." If so, the Lord will make her "a curse and an oath" among her people (vv. 20–21). This "curse" (*'alah*) is the effect of her own spoken words: her "body" or "womb" will "swell" and her "thigh" will "fall away." The Mishnah holds that the parts of her body with which she has sinned will be affected (Sotah 1:7). In that sense, "thigh" refers to genitals (cf. Gen. 46:26: "Who were his own descendants"; lit., "Who came out of his thigh"). If so, she will bear the curse in her body (cf. 1 Cor. 6:18). "Fall away" (*naphal*; Num. 5:27) is related to the Hebrew word for a spontaneous abortion (*nephel*; Ps. 58:8, "stillborn child"), which perhaps is the consequence. If she is already pregnant, or later becomes so, she will miscarry. If innocent, her vindication is her ability to "conceive children" (Num. 5:28). To this "oath of the curse" she adds "Amen, Amen" (v. 21, 22; cf. John 3:5, where "Truly, truly" renders Gk. *amen amen*). The priest must then "write these curses in a book and wash them off into the water of bitterness," which he shall "make the woman drink" (Num. 5:23–24). The water of bitterness (*marim*), conveying agent of the curse, enters her body (cf. Ps. 109:18) and, if she be guilty, will "cause bitter pain" (Num. 5:24), or bitterness (*marim*), the effect of the curse.

The priest must do five things with the "grain offering of jealousy": "take [it] out of [her] hand and shall wave [it] before the LORD and bring it to the altar," and there "take a handful ... and burn it" (vv. 25–26). The cadence of the five gestures of the priest with the grain offering gives the woman time to ponder her situation. (For "wave" cf. comment on 18:8–19 [at v. 11].) Then he makes the woman drink the water (5:27). She has sworn an oath upon the curse she pronounced on herself; she drinks the water of bitterness fully aware of potential consequences. Evidence of the woman's guilt or innocence is the outcome of the ritual oath-ordeal. The Lord is either her judge or her vindicator. His holiness will be vindicated through a mediator employing ritual means, in the same way his justice is established in a court of law. The outcome of a guilty verdict is already stated in terms of her womb and thigh. This condition has social ramifications, as it will make her a "curse among her people" (v. 27); her shame will be public. "But if the woman has not defiled herself and is clean, then she shall be free and shall conceive children" (v. 28). Her moral innocence is described in ritual terms: "not defiled" and "clean." Conceiving, a divine blessing, will publicly vindicate her.

The closing verses (vv. 29–31) summarize only the last of the three laws of chapter 5 (vv. 11–28), and only the cases in which the woman is guilty of adultery, whereas the case law also treats her innocence ("She has not defiled herself"; vv. 14, 28). These verses reiterate the circumstances requiring the law in the cases of jealousy: "When a wife . . . goes astray and defiles herself, or when the spirit of jealousy comes over a man" (vv. 29–30).

Two additional points are made in these verses. To say "the man shall be free from iniquity" (v. 31) is surprising.[52] "Free" (*nqh*) means "innocent, not guilty," the same word used for the innocent woman (v. 28). Is he free from iniquity only if his jealousy is well founded (v. 30)? Or even if his suspicions are unfounded?[53] Or will be free from iniquity for causing her punishment?[54] Perhaps the exculpation means he is free from *her* iniquity. The law underscores three times that she is "under her husband['s authority]" (*takhat 'ishha*; v. 29; cf. vv. 19, 20). The law on vows may shed light on this suggestion. Given his authority over her, a husband who learns of his wife's vow and remains silent the day he hears of it when he could legitimately nullify it, but then does so later, "shall bear her iniquity" (30:15)—that is, the iniquity she would have borne had she herself broken the vow. Given his suspicion of his wife's infidelity, the husband had two choices, either remain silent or evoke the law of jealousy (5:30). By doing the latter, the husband was "free from iniquity" (v. 31) in two ways. If she were guilty, he would be free from complicity and from obstruction of divine justice.

Nevertheless, "the woman shall bear her iniquity" (v. 31). Bearing one's iniquity means God will judge that person; no human court could condemn her in the absence of witnesses.

Response

The case of a wife suspected of adultery (Num. 5:11–31) is rooted in the creational mandate of "one flesh" (Gen. 2:24), the faithful marriage union of one man and one woman. There is a difference between what is tolerated under the law and the creational principles intended to govern a couple's relationship. In ancient Near Eastern cultures—as reflected in the OT—a man could take more than one wife and have concubines. Adultery consisted in having sexual relations with another man's wife, which even non-Israelites treated as a criminal offense (Gen. 12:17–20; 20:2–9; 26:10–11). But a man was not executed for having relations with a non-betrothed woman, a slave, or a war prisoner (e.g., Ex. 22:16; Lev. 19:20–21; Num. 31:17; Deut. 20:10–14; 22:28).

The OT mirrors the creational mandate in different ways. First, the Mosaic law condemns idolatry as marital infidelity by portraying the Lord, like the husband in Numbers 5, as a jealous husband (Ex. 20:5; 34:14; Num. 25:11). Implicitly, the Lord is the husband of one wife (and is faithful to her!), and his wife is to be faithful to him (e.g., Isa. 54:5–6; Hos. 2:2, 16). Second, marital infidelity is portrayed as ritual defilement in Numbers 5 and elsewhere (e.g., Ezek. 33:26). Marriage involves a covenant bond (Prov. 2:17; Ezek. 16:8; Mal. 2:4), in nature the same kind

---

[52] The word rendered "iniquity" (*'avon*) can mean "guilt" from iniquity or "punishment" for iniquity; cf. *CDCH*, 315; Milgrom renders as "free from punishment" (*Numbers*, 43).
[53] Budd, *Numbers*, 65. E. W. Davies, *Numbers*, 57. Cole, *Numbers*, 118.
[54] Rashi's view, even though it meant her death; cf. *Pentateuch with Rashi's Commentary*, vol. 4, *Numbers* (Jerusalem: Silberman Family, 1933), 27.

of bond undergirding the Lord's relationship to his people and their union with him. Defilement breaks the covenant (Isa. 24:5). Third, the narrative discreetly condemns violations of the creational principle. Abraham's relations with Hagar, which inflict great pains upon his marriage, are subtly condemned by their portrayal in terms of Adam's first sin. The narrative thus points back to the creational ideal.[55] Thus in various ways the "one flesh" principle is upheld throughout the OT, notwithstanding laws that tolerate the less-than-ideal.

The permanent faithful union of one man and one woman is reiterated in the NT. Jesus himself quotes the Genesis "one flesh" mandate (Matt. 19:4–6; cf. Mark 10:8). If the law tolerates divorce (Deut. 24:1–4), it is a concession: "Because of your hardness of heart Moses allowed you to divorce your wives, but from the beginning it was not so" (Matt. 19:8). "One flesh" is the norm for the church (Eph. 5:31; cf. 1 Cor. 6:16); reformulated as being "the husband of one wife," it is applied to elders and deacons (1 Tim. 3:2, 12; Titus 1:6). Warnings are given to all in ritual terms from the OT: "Let the marriage bed be undefiled, for God will judge the sexually immoral and adulterous" (Heb. 13:4). Exhortations have the same tone: "This is the will of God, your sanctification: that you abstain from sexual immorality; . . . For God has not called us for impurity, but in holiness" (1 Thess. 4:3, 7). The highest standard is "Husbands, love your wives, as Christ loved the church and gave himself up for her. . . . In the same way husbands should love their wives as their own bodies. He who loves his wife loves himself" (Eph. 5:25, 28). No man who loves his wife in this way would be unfaithful to her.

NUMBERS 6

6 And the LORD spoke to Moses, saying, [2] "Speak to the people of Israel and say to them, When either a man or a woman makes a special vow, the vow of a Nazirite,[1] to separate himself to the LORD, [3] he shall separate himself from wine and strong drink. He shall drink no vinegar made from wine or strong drink and shall not drink any juice of grapes or eat grapes, fresh or dried. [4] All the days of his separation[2] he shall eat nothing that is produced by the grapevine, not even the seeds or the skins.

[5] "All the days of his vow of separation, no razor shall touch his head. Until the time is completed for which he separates himself to the LORD, he shall be holy. He shall let the locks of hair of his head grow long.

[6] "All the days that he separates himself to the LORD he shall not go near a dead body. [7] Not even for his father or for his mother, for brother or sister, if they die, shall he make himself unclean, because his separation to God is on his head. [8] All the days of his separation he is holy to the LORD.

---

55 Ron Bergey, "The Torah of Eden and the Conception of Ishmael: Genesis 3:6 and 16:3–4," *Unio cum Christo* 5/1 (2019): 77–86.

⁹ "And if any man dies very suddenly beside him and he defiles his consecrated head, then he shall shave his head on the day of his cleansing; on the seventh day he shall shave it. ¹⁰ On the eighth day he shall bring two turtledoves or two pigeons to the priest to the entrance of the tent of meeting, ¹¹ and the priest shall offer one for a sin offering and the other for a burnt offering, and make atonement for him, because he sinned by reason of the dead body. And he shall consecrate his head that same day ¹² and separate himself to the Lord for the days of his separation and bring a male lamb a year old for a guilt offering. But the previous period shall be void, because his separation was defiled.

¹³ "And this is the law for the Nazirite, when the time of his separation has been completed: he shall be brought to the entrance of the tent of meeting, ¹⁴ and he shall bring his gift to the Lord, one male lamb a year old without blemish for a burnt offering, and one ewe lamb a year old without blemish as a sin offering, and one ram without blemish as a peace offering, ¹⁵ and a basket of unleavened bread, loaves of fine flour mixed with oil, and unleavened wafers smeared with oil, and their grain offering and their drink offerings. ¹⁶ And the priest shall bring them before the Lord and offer his sin offering and his burnt offering, ¹⁷ and he shall offer the ram as a sacrifice of peace offering to the Lord, with the basket of unleavened bread. The priest shall offer also its grain offering and its drink offering. ¹⁸ And the Nazirite shall shave his consecrated head at the entrance of the tent of meeting and shall take the hair from his consecrated head and put it on the fire that is under the sacrifice of the peace offering. ¹⁹ And the priest shall take the shoulder of the ram, when it is boiled, and one unleavened loaf out of the basket and one unleavened wafer, and shall put them on the hands of the Nazirite, after he has shaved the hair of his consecration, ²⁰ and the priest shall wave them for a wave offering before the Lord. They are a holy portion for the priest, together with the breast that is waved and the thigh that is contributed. And after that the Nazirite may drink wine.

²¹ "This is the law of the Nazirite. But if he vows an offering to the Lord above his Nazirite vow, as he can afford, in exact accordance with the vow that he takes, then he shall do in addition to the law of the Nazirite."

²² The Lord spoke to Moses, saying, ²³ "Speak to Aaron and his sons, saying, Thus you shall bless the people of Israel: you shall say to them,

24 The Lord bless you and keep you;
25 the Lord make his face to shine upon you and be gracious to you;
26 the Lord lift up his countenance[3] upon you and give you peace.

²⁷ "So shall they put my name upon the people of Israel, and I will bless them."

[1] *Nazirite* means *one separated*, or *one consecrated* [2] Or *Naziriteship* [3] Or *face*

Section Overview

Laws on maintaining the purity of the people's camp (Numbers 5–6) follow the instructions on their organization while encamped and voyaging (chs. 2–4). The camp must be pure in order not to desecrate the sanctuary, the Lord's abode in their midst (5:3). The case in chapter 6 involves anyone under a Nazirite vow who has contact with a corpse, a source of impurity already mentioned in 5:2. Corpse contamination is the most serious of impurities. At the close of this case Aaron is summoned to pronounce the Lord's blessing (6:22–27) on the "people of Israel" (v. 23), to whom this and the preceding laws were addressed (v. 2; cf. 5:2, 6, 12). Maintaining the purity of the camp and the tabernacle concerns everyone; everyone can enjoy God's blessing for his or her obedience.

The "vow of a Nazirite" (6:2) involves abstinence from certain things for a self-imposed period (vv. 3–7). The vow requires a high degree of ritual holiness (v. 8). Should the Nazirite be defiled by a dead body, the vow is voided. After a complex ritual purification, the vow is to be begun anew (vv. 9–12). Once the vow is completed, the Nazirite returns from his consecration to a common state. This desacralization involves a long ceremonial procedure (vv. 13–21).

Added to the overall purity theme are linguistic links connecting chapter 6 to the three cases in chapter 5. A Nazirite vow concerns a "man or a woman" (6:1), as do the laws on impurities (5:3, 6). The defilement (Hb. *tame'*) of a Nazirite is the major concern of this law (6:6–8, 9–12), as it was for the camp at large (5:2–3). "Atonement" must be made for the Nazirite (6:11) involving a "guilt offering" (*'asham*; v. 12), as with someone who embezzles and lies under oath (cf. comment on 5:5–10 [at v. 8]). The vow of a defiled Nazirite "shall be void" (*naphal*, "fall"; 6:12), while the adulterous woman's thigh "shall fall away" (*naphal*; 5:27).

Section Outline

I. Instructions for the Exodus Generation Preparing to Leave Sinai for Canaan (1:1–10:36) . . .
   F. The Nazirite Consecration (6:1–27)
      1. Requirements of the Nazirite Vow (6:1–12)
      2. Completion of the Nazirite Vow (6:13–21)
      3. Divine Blessing (6:22–27)

Comment

6:1–12 The gender parity of "a man or a woman" (v. 1) is noteworthy, since the high degree of ritual holiness for the Nazirite vow is on par with that for the high priest. The Mosaic law evinces great concern for females, especially those in precarious situations, such as widows, servants, and girls (e.g., Ex. 21:3–5, 7–11; 22:22). The previous law made provisions for a wife to be exonerated from guilt and shame due to the unfounded suspicions of a jealous husband (Num. 5:15, 28). Numbers legislates the right for daughters to succeed to their fathers' lands and transmit them to their children (chs. 27; 36). Whereas they may seem archaic today, these laws in their cultural context protect women from certain discriminatory practices and abuses.

"Makes a special vow, the vow of a Nazirite" (6:2; cf. Lev. 27:22) could read "Does something special by vowing [*nadar*] the vow of [*neder*] a Nazirite." The same form of *pala'* is translated "[do something] too hard" (Gen. 18:14), "bring on [something] extraordinary" (Deut. 28:59), and "do wonderful things" (Isa. 29:14). In this sense, what is "special" is that the vow is "the vow of the Nazirite." But the verb is perhaps more likely a biform of *palah*, meaning here "he set (himself) apart"[56] by vowing the Nazirite vow.

Deuteronomy 23:23 defines a vow as "What you have promised with your mouth" (cf. Ps. 66:14). Vows are voiced obligations to do or not to do something with a stated purpose, such as having a prayer answered (e.g., 1 Sam. 1:11). Nothing is said here about the content or purpose of the vow. The proper noun "Nazirite" (*nazir*; Num. 6:2, 13, 18, 19, 20, 21) is semantically and morphologically related to the verb rendered "separate" (from *nazar*; vv. 2, 3, 5, 6, 12) and the noun generally translated "separation" or occasionally "consecration" (from *nezer*; vv. 3, 4, 5, 7, 8, 9, 12 [2x], 13, 18 [2x], 19, 21 [2x]). The Nazirite must first "separate himself to the LORD" (v. 2) then "separate himself from" (v. 3) certain things. "All the days of his separation"[57] (v. 4; cf. vv. 5, 6, 8)—the number is determined by the Nazirite—he must abstain from three otherwise legitimate things and activities. He could consume "nothing ... produced by the grapevine" (v. 4); "no razor shall touch his head" (v. 5). He could not "go near a dead body. Not even for his father or for his mother" (vv. 6–7). All these temporary injunctions have a connection with the priesthood (cf. discussion on v. 11). Their reason is straightforward: "All the days of his separation [*nezer*] he is holy to the LORD" (v. 8).

These three prohibitions perhaps symbolize the deprivation of covenant blessing, even as someone under a curse, which may explain the pronouncement of benediction at the end of the chapter. The vine and its products are symbols of God's blessing (Lev. 26:5; Deut. 7:13; Isa. 65:8). Not enjoying the fruit of the vine is among the covenant curses (Deut. 28:30; cf. Isa. 24:7). Also, any product from an unpruned vine (called *nazir*; Lev. 25:5) is impure, since to prune a vine is to cleanse it (Gk. *kathairō*; John 15:2). Captives are exiled with shaved heads as a covenant curse (Jer. 48:37; Amos 1:15; cf. Isa. 15:2; Jer. 2:16; Ezek. 5:1–4; 27:31; 29:18). The shaving of hair is a sign of mourning for the dead (Jer. 16:6). A covenant curse for defiling the land leaves it filled with unburied corpses (Lev. 26:30; Deut. 28:26).

Numbers 6:9–12 prescribes what must occur "if any man dies very suddenly beside him and he defiles his consecrated [*nezer*] head" (v. 9). "Suddenly" implies either the Nazirite unintentionally makes physical contact with a corpse or his defilement is unavoidable. Purification requires a series of rites. Seven days (v. 9) is the standard lapse of time required for purification (e.g., Lev. 15:13). A leper's head is shaved on the seventh day (Lev. 14:8–9), and anyone contaminated by a corpse is sprinkled with water for impurity on the third and seventh days (Num. 19:12). But the Nazirite's purification is more complex. The next stage of purification, "on

---

56 Levine, *Numbers 1–20*, 216, 218; *CDCH*, 357, 358. The last consonants of the two verbs are interchangeable (cf. Ps. *palah*, 17:7; *pl'*, 31:22 [31:21 MT]), and in general the verb *pala'* (meaning "to do something wonderful or hard") only has the Lord as its subject.

57 "Vow of separation" (6:5); *neder* ("vow") and *nezer* ("separation") may be related morphologically (cf. Hebrew *zhb*; Aramaic *dhb*, "gold"). Levine suggests *nadar* and *nazar* are phonetic variants of the same root (*Numbers 1–20*, 218–219).

the eighth day," involves offering "two turtledoves or two pigeons" (6:10), one for a "sin offering" and the other for a "burnt offering" (v. 11). Cleansed lepers who are poor sacrifice turtledoves or pigeons for these same two offerings (Lev. 14:22). The higher degree of corpse contamination contracted by a Nazirite is underscored by the absence of water for impurity required in other cases (Num. 19:9).

Ritual infractions are sin, in this case the infraction of becoming impure. Two types of "atonement" (*kpr*) should be distinguished, one requiring blood and the other not requiring it (for the latter cf. comment on 16:36–50 [at v. 46]). Blood is always required in the ritual domain. Such blood always involves the death of a substitute, a life as payment. To make atonement the blood of an animal is sprinkled on the altar, smeared on its horns, or poured at its base. The blood cleanses or purifies the altar from defilement that has resulted from sin. Thereupon the guilty party is pardoned for having contaminated the altar and for the act that made it impure. Ritually, this is expressed as "his cleansing" (6:9). Drawing upon this ceremonial aspect of atonement, the shedding of Christ's blood is linked to purification and pardon in the NT (Heb. 9:22; cf. 1 John 1:7).

"He shall consecrate his head that same day" (Num. 6:11), the "same day" being the "eighth day," when atonement for him is made. "Consecrate" (from *qadash*) literally means to "make holy." "Consecrating his head" is the first step toward renewal of the voided Nazirite vow. This means "no razor shall touch his head. . . . He shall let the locks of hair of his head grow long" (v. 5). Letting hair grow is a sign of holiness. The head of a priest receives special attention. As high priest, Aaron's head is anointed with holy oil (Ex. 29:7). He wears a holy crown (*nezer haqqodesh*; Ex. 29:6) with a golden plate on which is written "Holy to the LORD" (Ex. 28:36–38; 39:30). The degree of Nazirite separation involves a ritual consecration second only to that of a high priest (Lev. 21:10–12). The hair of the high priest is the *summum* of holiness; it is not to be cut (Lev. 21:10; cf. Ezek. 5:1). The high priest can never let his hair "hang loose" (*paraʿ*; Lev. 21:10; cf. the hair of the woman that is unbound [*paraʿ*] by the priest; Num. 5:18). Like the Nazirite, the high priest "shall not go in to any dead bodies nor make himself unclean, even for his father or for his mother" (Lev. 21:11). On him is the "consecration of [*nezer*] the anointing oil" (Lev. 21:12).

The Nazirite must "separate himself [from *nazar*] to the LORD for the days of his separation" (*nezer*; Num. 6:12), that is, recommence his aborted vow (v. 5) for the initially pledged period. In addition to the sin and the burnt offerings, "a male lamb a year old for a guilt offering" (*ʾasham*; v. 12) is required. The law for cleansing a leper also requires a male lamb (Lev. 14:12). "The previous period shall be void" (Num. 6:12; lit., "the days shall fall")—that is, the period the Nazir voluntarily fixed for his vow is aborted (cf. 5:27), "because his separation [*nezer*] was defiled" (6:12).

6:13–21 This law stipulates how the Nazirite's ritual holiness is divested so that he can return to a normal life. Unlike those made lifelong Nazirites from birth—Samuel, Samson, and John the Baptist—the law here encompasses a self-imposed time limit. Two interrelated steps are taken to close the vowed period: sacrifices and shaving of the head. To do so, first "he shall be brought to the entrance of the tent of meeting" (v. 13; cf. v. 18). The verb, although in the active voice (*yabi'*; cf. v. 10: "he shall bring," *yabi'*), seemingly has no explicit subject and is rendered as a passive (cf. Lev. 14:2 the passive *yuba'*). However, the verb is in the active voice because it has an object, "him/it" (*'otho*, untranslated by ESV). The literal reading is "he/one shall bring him/it." "It" could render collectively the offerings that "he," the Nazirite, must bring.[58] Or, "one," possibly a Levite, must bring "him," the Nazirite, to the entrance after verifying the Nazirite has fulfilled his vow. This kind of guard duty could be done by Levites over fifty years old who no longer perform hard physical labor in tabernacle service (8:25–26). If it were a woman Nazirite, she could be accompanied by one of the women ministering at the tabernacle (Ex. 38:8). Such activities find echoes in the ministry of the church diaconate.

The first step to end the vow involves various offerings. "He shall bring his gift to the LORD" (Num. 6:14) requires mediation: "The priest shall bring [the offerings] before the LORD" (v. 16). "Gift" (*qorban*) is cognate with "shall bring" (form of *qarab*). The law stipulates that no one shall appear before the Lord empty-handed (Ex. 23:15; 34:20; Deut. 16:16). The gifts include a "male lamb," a "ewe lamb," and a "ram," each "without blemish," for, respectively, a "burnt offering," a "sin offering," and a "peace offering" (Num. 6:14). In addition, he is to bring a "basket of unleavened bread, loaves of fine flour mixed with oil, and unleavened wafers smeared with oil, and their grain offering and their drink offerings" (v. 15; cf. v. 17). Concerning the order of the burnt and sin offerings, as in verse 14, the Leviticus administrative order is for the burnt offering to come first (ch. 1), followed by the sin offering (ch. 4). But when actually made, the order is inverted.[59] The Nazirite offers the "sin offering" and then the "burnt offering" (Num. 6:16; cf. Lev. 9:7; 14:19–20). The sin offering "de-sins" or removes the stain of impurity, generally from the main altar, with blood that, like soap, washes it away. Only after purification is made by the sin offering could the burnt offering, which produces a pleasing aroma to the Lord, be made. Thereafter comes the "peace offering" (Num. 6:17).

The second step taken to terminate the vow involves shaving the head (vv. 18–20; cf. Acts 21:24). Since hair is a sign of the sacredness of its wearer (cf. comment on Num. 6:1–11 [at v. 9]), it is removed as part of the process of divesting ritual holiness. Hair shaving is also part of the leper's cleansing (Lev. 14:8–9). Shaving the "hair of his consecration" (Num. 6:19) reduces the Nazirite's state from holy to common. The shaved hair must be burned "under the sacrifice of the peace offering" (v. 18). The hair disappears, as does the holiness it represents (cf. Ezek. 5:1–2).

The unburnt parts of the peace offering—boiled "shoulder of the ram," "unleavened loaf," and "unleavened wafer"—are put in the hand of the Nazirite, who gives them back to the priest who had made them a "wave offering before the

---

58 Cole, *Numbers*, 125n39.
59 A. F. Rainey, "The Order of Sacrifices in Old Testament Ritual Texts," *Biblica* 51 (1970): 487–489 (on administrative order), 494–498 (on procedural order). Maimonides (1135–1204) had already made this observation.

LORD" (Num. 6:19–20). They are the priest's "holy portion," as are the "breast that is waved and the thigh that is contributed" (v. 20; cf. comment on 15:1–21 [at v. 20, regarding "contribution"]). Of the three types of peace offerings (freewill, thanksgiving, and votive), it is the last that is made in 6:15, 17, 19. "And after that the Nazirite may drink wine" (v. 20), resuming a normal life. The "law of the Nazirite" (v. 21) has been observed and the "vow of a Nazirite" (v. 2) fulfilled.

Verse 21 contains a supplement to the Nazirite vow "if he vows an offering to the LORD above his Nazirite vow." Two conditions are imposed: "as he can afford" and "in exact accordance with the vow that he takes." Other laws pertain to sacrifices offered to fulfill vows as freewill offerings (Lev. 22:21; Num. 15:3, 8; 29:39; Deut. 12:6, 11, 17). Behind these conditions is an implicit warning not to make a rash or hasty vow that, being difficult, someone may be tempted not to keep (Deut. 23:21–23; cf. Lev. 27:10; Num. 30:2; Judg. 11:35; Prov. 20:25).

6:22–27 This blessing is formulated by the Lord himself and communicated to Moses, who shall transmit it to Aaron and his sons, who in turn are to invoke it on the people (vv. 22–23). The literary pattern of the three-verse blessing in three double-clause lines is cumulative in Hebrew: three words (v. 24), five words (v. 25), seven words (v. 26). "The LORD" appears once in each line. The addressee is "you" (sg.) twice in each verse (e.g., "bless you . . . keep you"; v. 24), identified in the conclusion as "the people of Israel . . . them" (v. 27).

"Speak to Aaron and his sons" (v. 23) occurs only here in Numbers (elsewhere Lev. 6:18; 17:2; 22:2, 18). "Thus" (Hb. *koh*) introduces the manner in which the blessing is bestowed: "You shall bless [2nd person pl.] . . . say to them." God blesses through the mediacy of priests' speaking *his word* of blessing, "The LORD bless you" (v. 24). Pronouncing a blessing in the ritual domain, like officiating at the altar, is the exclusive domain of the priesthood. Aaron's blessing of the people is mentioned in Leviticus 9:22.

As may be seen from the Genesis blessing (1:28) and curse (3:17–19), as well as and the covenant blessings as compared with corresponding curses (Leviticus 26; Deuteronomy 28), divine blessing vivifies and promotes life, whereas a curse stifles life, which leads ultimately to death. The stark contrast is succinctly stated: "I have set before you life and death, blessing and curse" (Deut. 30:19). Both blessing and curse are providential (e.g., rain, Heb. 6:7; withered fig tree, Mark 11:20–21). The law promises life for obedience (Lev. 18:5) but is powerless at any time to deliver it to sinful people (Rom. 7:10; Gal. 3:12; cf. Luke 10:28). The supreme blessing is eternal life (Ps. 133:3), granted and restored since the fall by grace alone. It is promised in the Word (1 John 2:25; cf. John 12:49–50) and pictured in the sacraments, grace always anticipating Christ's accomplished redemptive work and the gospel-promise fulfillment (cf. Gal. 3:14; Eph. 1:3). The ultimate curse is the second death. The Lord's blessing and its benefic results are the antidote to the curse and its malefic effects (cf. Num. 5:27–28; Deut. 23:5). This is clearly illustrated in the Balaam narrative (Numbers 22–24).

The blessing here is for the "people of Israel" (6:23). What is reported in chapters 5–6 could leave "the people of Israel" (5:2, 6, 12; 6:2) with the question of whether anyone could receive God's favor, since no one is exempt from impurity; the high degree of holiness required by the Nazirite vow, while ritually attainable, is but temporary and must be relinquished. The blessing in this context reassures the Israelites that it is their God who, recognizing their fallen and frail human condition, blesses them by pure grace—not only because he is able but because he desires to do so.[60] This passage also anticipates Balak's scheme to have Balaam curse the people; in light of it, it is not surprising that Balaam cannot. God's blessing is his people's protection; he turns the curse scheme of their enemies into a blessing (24:9) because he loves his people (Deut. 23:5; cf. Josh. 24:10).

The Lord's keeping ("keep you"; *shamar*, "guard") in the immediate context points to his appointing priests and Levites to avert divine wrath by preventing the people's impurities from polluting the tabernacle (Num. 1:53; 18:5).

In a broader sense his keeping sustains life during the wilderness period. This is celebrated in Psalm 121:4–8 (translation of *shamar* italicized):

> Behold, he who *keeps* Israel
>   will neither slumber nor sleep.
> The LORD is your *keeper*;
>   the LORD is your shade on your right hand.
> The sun shall not strike you by day,
>   nor the moon by night.
> The LORD will *keep* you from all evil;
>   he will *keep* your life.
> The LORD will *keep*
>   your going out and your coming in
>   from this time forth and forevermore.

Concerning the Lord's "face" and "countenance" (both translate the same form of *paneh*), two actions in Numbers 6:25–26 ("make shine" and "lift") describe his acceptance, beneficence, and ultimately the salvation of those so blessed (cf. Pss. 4:6; 44:3; 80:3, 7, 19; 89:15). Seeing the face of the king is an honor enjoyed only by those highest in office (Est. 1:14). Being in the light of his face is life; the opposite is his wrath and death (Prov. 16:14–15). In recognition of Esau's mercy Jacob exclaims: "I have seen your face, which is like seeing the face of God, and you have accepted me" (Gen. 33:10; cf. Ps. 27:8). A fallen or turned face (Gen. 4:5; cf. 1 Kings 21:4) and a darkened or hidden countenance (Deut. 31:18; Job 23:17; Ps. 143:7) communicate strong displeasure and anger (cf. 2 Sam. 14:24; Ps. 27:9; Isa. 57:17; 59:2), even a covenant curse (Ezek. 39:23–24). The Lord spoke to his people through his spokesman mediator, Moses, "face to face" (Ex. 33:11; Deut. 5:4; cf. Num. 12:8: "mouth to mouth"). The Lord had said, "I will be gracious to

---

60 Ron Bergey, *Découvrir Dieu à travers le Pentateuque* (Romanel-sur-Lausanne: Maison de la Bible, 2016), 439.

whom I will be gracious.... But... [Moses] cannot see my face, for man shall not see me and live" (Ex. 33:19–20). He saw only God's back (Ex. 33:23; cf. Jer. 18:17). Seeing God's face in a theophany is not permissible, but seeing its manifestation in beneficent words and deeds is (cf. Jer. 18:17). His blessing permits faith to comprehend his attendant grace, expressed in physical terms.

His shining and lifted face leads to two benefits: he will "be gracious to you" and "give you peace." His being "gracious" (*khanan*), like his mercy, is consonant with his goodness (Ex. 33:19; cf. Isa. 30:18–19). In Exodus 33 his being gracious is predicated upon his pardon granted to the sinful people after Moses' intercession. Only then can God's "peace" (*shalom*) be experienced, the peace of reconciliation and the absolved guilt. In turn, the Israelites bless each other in personal greetings (Ruth 2:4; Ps. 129:8), a practice also attested in apostolic "grace and peace" salutations (e.g., 1 Cor. 1:3; Gal. 1:3; Eph. 1:2; Rev. 1:4).

The result of the blessing is described thus: "So shall they [the priests] put my name upon the people of Israel" (Num. 6:27). Only here it is said that the Lord's name is put upon the people. This implies that the people belong to him. A woman's being called by a man's name points to the one on whom she depends and to whom she belongs (Isa. 4:1). This name is "the LORD" (*yhwh*, from *hayah*, "to be," Ex. 33:19). When spoken of, his name is "He is" (*yhwh*; Ex. 6:2). When speaking of himself, his name is "I AM" (*'ehyeh*; Ex. 3:14).[61] He reveals his name at the second-greatest moment in redemption history (Ex. 3:14). The greatest revelation comes in the person of Jesus Christ, the "I am" (John 8:58), who accomplishes the eternal plan of redemption. His name is put on those who call upon him (Acts 15:17; Rev. 14:1; 22:4).

In the introduction, "You shall bless the people" (Num. 6:23) emphasizes the means of this grace, since the priesthood mediates the blessing (1 Chron. 23:13); in the conclusion, however, "I will bless them" (Num. 6:27) reminds the people that the Lord is the source.

Response

The priests who had temple night-watch blessed the Lord and invoked his blessing on his people (Ps. 134:1–3). Isaac Watts's "Joy to the World" brings the extent of God's beneficence to light. In his advent "He comes to make his blessings flow / Far as the curse is found." Because Christ has redeemed his people from the curse of the law, God's blessing upon Abraham reaches the Gentiles (Gal. 3:14). God's blessing entails Christ's imputed righteousness received apart from the works of the law (Rom. 4:6). In Christ Christians are blessed with every spiritual blessing in the heavenlies (Eph. 1:3). As a "royal priesthood" (1 Pet. 2:9), followers of Christ are exhorted by him to "bless those who curse you, pray for those who abuse you" (Luke 6:28). Paul likewise exhorts Christians, "Bless those who persecute you; bless and do not curse them" (Rom. 12:14).

---

61 The prefixed form of the stative verb *hayah* does not mean here "I/he will be." Having no present tense form in biblical Hebrew, the prefixed form is used, as is often the case of stative verbs (e.g., Ruth 2:13).

NUMBERS 7

7 On the day when Moses had finished setting up the tabernacle and had anointed and consecrated it with all its furnishings and had anointed and consecrated the altar with all its utensils, ²the chiefs of Israel, heads of their fathers' houses, who were the chiefs of the tribes, who were over those who were listed, approached ³and brought their offerings before the Lord, six wagons and twelve oxen, a wagon for every two of the chiefs, and for each one an ox. They brought them before the tabernacle. ⁴Then the Lord said to Moses, ⁵"Accept these from them, that they may be used in the service of the tent of meeting, and give them to the Levites, to each man according to his service." ⁶So Moses took the wagons and the oxen and gave them to the Levites. ⁷Two wagons and four oxen he gave to the sons of Gershon, according to their service. ⁸And four wagons and eight oxen he gave to the sons of Merari, according to their service, under the direction of Ithamar the son of Aaron the priest. ⁹But to the sons of Kohath he gave none, because they were charged with the service of the holy things that had to be carried on the shoulder. ¹⁰And the chiefs offered offerings for the dedication of the altar on the day it was anointed; and the chiefs offered their offering before the altar. ¹¹And the Lord said to Moses, "They shall offer their offerings, one chief each day, for the dedication of the altar."

¹²He who offered his offering the first day was Nahshon the son of Amminadab, of the tribe of Judah. ¹³And his offering was one silver plate whose weight was 130 shekels,¹ one silver basin of 70 shekels, according to the shekel of the sanctuary, both of them full of fine flour mixed with oil for a grain offering; ¹⁴one golden dish of 10 shekels, full of incense; ¹⁵one bull from the herd, one ram, one male lamb a year old, for a burnt offering; ¹⁶one male goat for a sin offering; ¹⁷and for the sacrifice of peace offerings, two oxen, five rams, five male goats, and five male lambs a year old. This was the offering of Nahshon the son of Amminadab.

¹⁸On the second day Nethanel the son of Zuar, the chief of Issachar, made an offering. ¹⁹He offered for his offering one silver plate whose weight was 130 shekels, one silver basin of 70 shekels, according to the shekel of the sanctuary, both of them full of fine flour mixed with oil for a grain offering; ²⁰one golden dish of 10 shekels, full of incense; ²¹one bull from the herd, one ram, one male lamb a year old, for a burnt offering; ²²one male goat for a sin offering; ²³and for the sacrifice of peace offerings, two oxen, five rams, five male goats, and five male lambs a year old. This was the offering of Nethanel the son of Zuar.

²⁴On the third day Eliab the son of Helon, the chief of the people of Zebulun: ²⁵his offering was one silver plate whose weight was 130 shekels, one silver basin of 70 shekels, according to the shekel of the sanctuary, both of them full of fine flour mixed with oil for a grain offering; ²⁶one

golden dish of 10 shekels, full of incense; ²⁷ one bull from the herd, one ram, one male lamb a year old, for a burnt offering; ²⁸ one male goat for a sin offering; ²⁹ and for the sacrifice of peace offerings, two oxen, five rams, five male goats, and five male lambs a year old. This was the offering of Eliab the son of Helon.

³⁰ On the fourth day Elizur the son of Shedeur, the chief of the people of Reuben: ³¹ his offering was one silver plate whose weight was 130 shekels, one silver basin of 70 shekels, according to the shekel of the sanctuary, both of them full of fine flour mixed with oil for a grain offering; ³² one golden dish of 10 shekels, full of incense; ³³ one bull from the herd, one ram, one male lamb a year old, for a burnt offering; ³⁴ one male goat for a sin offering; ³⁵ and for the sacrifice of peace offerings, two oxen, five rams, five male goats, and five male lambs a year old. This was the offering of Elizur the son of Shedeur.

³⁶ On the fifth day Shelumiel the son of Zurishaddai, the chief of the people of Simeon: ³⁷ his offering was one silver plate whose weight was 130 shekels, one silver basin of 70 shekels, according to the shekel of the sanctuary, both of them full of fine flour mixed with oil for a grain offering; ³⁸ one golden dish of 10 shekels, full of incense; ³⁹ one bull from the herd, one ram, one male lamb a year old, for a burnt offering; ⁴⁰ one male goat for a sin offering; ⁴¹ and for the sacrifice of peace offerings, two oxen, five rams, five male goats, and five male lambs a year old. This was the offering of Shelumiel the son of Zurishaddai.

⁴² On the sixth day Eliasaph the son of Deuel, the chief of the people of Gad: ⁴³ his offering was one silver plate whose weight was 130 shekels, one silver basin of 70 shekels, according to the shekel of the sanctuary, both of them full of fine flour mixed with oil for a grain offering; ⁴⁴ one golden dish of 10 shekels, full of incense; ⁴⁵ one bull from the herd, one ram, one male lamb a year old, for a burnt offering; ⁴⁶ one male goat for a sin offering; ⁴⁷ and for the sacrifice of peace offerings, two oxen, five rams, five male goats, and five male lambs a year old. This was the offering of Eliasaph the son of Deuel.

⁴⁸ On the seventh day Elishama the son of Ammihud, the chief of the people of Ephraim: ⁴⁹ his offering was one silver plate whose weight was 130 shekels, one silver basin of 70 shekels, according to the shekel of the sanctuary, both of them full of fine flour mixed with oil for a grain offering; ⁵⁰ one golden dish of 10 shekels, full of incense; ⁵¹ one bull from the herd, one ram, one male lamb a year old, for a burnt offering; ⁵² one male goat for a sin offering; ⁵³ and for the sacrifice of peace offerings, two oxen, five rams, five male goats, and five male lambs a year old. This was the offering of Elishama the son of Ammihud.

⁵⁴ On the eighth day Gamaliel the son of Pedahzur, the chief of the people of Manasseh: ⁵⁵ his offering was one silver plate whose weight was 130 shekels, one silver basin of 70 shekels, according to the shekel of the sanctuary, both of them full of fine flour mixed with oil for a grain offering; ⁵⁶ one golden dish of 10 shekels, full of incense; ⁵⁷ one bull from the herd, one ram, one male lamb a year old, for a burnt offering; ⁵⁸ one male goat for a sin offering; ⁵⁹ and for the sacrifice of peace offerings, two oxen, five rams, five male goats, and five male lambs a year old. This was the offering of Gamaliel the son of Pedahzur.

⁶⁰ On the ninth day Abidan the son of Gideoni, the chief of the people of Benjamin: ⁶¹ his offering was one silver plate whose weight was 130 shek-

els, one silver basin of 70 shekels, according to the shekel of the sanctuary, both of them full of fine flour mixed with oil for a grain offering; ⁶²one golden dish of 10 shekels, full of incense; ⁶³one bull from the herd, one ram, one male lamb a year old, for a burnt offering; ⁶⁴one male goat for a sin offering; ⁶⁵and for the sacrifice of peace offerings, two oxen, five rams, five male goats, and five male lambs a year old. This was the offering of Abidan the son of Gideoni.

⁶⁶On the tenth day Ahiezer the son of Ammishaddai, the chief of the people of Dan: ⁶⁷his offering was one silver plate whose weight was 130 shekels, one silver basin of 70 shekels, according to the shekel of the sanctuary, both of them full of fine flour mixed with oil for a grain offering; ⁶⁸one golden dish of 10 shekels, full of incense; ⁶⁹one bull from the herd, one ram, one male lamb a year old, for a burnt offering; ⁷⁰one male goat for a sin offering; ⁷¹and for the sacrifice of peace offerings, two oxen, five rams, five male goats, and five male lambs a year old. This was the offering of Ahiezer the son of Ammishaddai.

⁷²On the eleventh day Pagiel the son of Ochran, the chief of the people of Asher: ⁷³his offering was one silver plate whose weight was 130 shekels, one silver basin of 70 shekels, according to the shekel of the sanctuary, both of them full of fine flour mixed with oil for a grain offering; ⁷⁴one golden dish of 10 shekels, full of incense; ⁷⁵one bull from the herd, one ram, one male lamb a year old, for a burnt offering; ⁷⁶one male goat for a sin offering; ⁷⁷and for the sacrifice of peace offerings, two oxen, five rams, five male goats, and five male lambs a year old. This was the offering of Pagiel the son of Ochran.

⁷⁸On the twelfth day Ahira the son of Enan, the chief of the people of Naphtali: ⁷⁹his offering was one silver plate whose weight was 130 shekels, one silver basin of 70 shekels, according to the shekel of the sanctuary, both of them full of fine flour mixed with oil for a grain offering; ⁸⁰one golden dish of 10 shekels, full of incense; ⁸¹one bull from the herd, one ram, one male lamb a year old, for a burnt offering; ⁸²one male goat for a sin offering; ⁸³and for the sacrifice of peace offerings, two oxen, five rams, five male goats, and five male lambs a year old. This was the offering of Ahira the son of Enan.

⁸⁴This was the dedication offering for the altar on the day when it was anointed, from the chiefs of Israel: twelve silver plates, twelve silver basins, twelve golden dishes, ⁸⁵each silver plate weighing 130 shekels and each basin 70, all the silver of the vessels 2,400 shekels according to the shekel of the sanctuary, ⁸⁶the twelve golden dishes, full of incense, weighing 10 shekels apiece according to the shekel of the sanctuary, all the gold of the dishes being 120 shekels; ⁸⁷all the cattle for the burnt offering twelve bulls, twelve rams, twelve male lambs a year old, with their grain offering; and twelve male goats for a sin offering; ⁸⁸and all the cattle for the sacrifice of peace offerings twenty-four bulls, the rams sixty, the male goats sixty, the male lambs a year old sixty. This was the dedication offering for the altar after it was anointed.

⁸⁹And when Moses went into the tent of meeting to speak with the LORD, he heard the voice speaking to him from above the mercy seat that was on the ark of the testimony, from between the two cherubim; and it spoke to him.

---

¹ A *shekel* was about 2/5 ounce or 11 grams

Section Overview

Numbers 7:1–10:36 contains critical measures to prepare for the Israelites' departure from Sinai and travel to the wilderness of Paran. This section chronologically precedes chapters 1–6 (cf. comment on 7:1–9 [at v. 1]); literarily, it logically follows them. After the military census of the tribes, their assigned encampments around the tabernacle and marching order, the tabernacle duties and the arrangement of the camps of the Levites and priests (chs. 1–4), and the rules for maintaining the camp's purity (chs. 5–6), the tabernacle is prepared for worship and travel via the tribes' gifts (chs. 7:1–8:4). The Levites are cleansed to assist the priests as they minister there (8:5–26). Passover is celebrated (9:1–14). With the cloud to guide them and the trumpets to signal their departure (9:15–10:10), the Israelites will leave Sinai and begin their journey to the Promised Land (10:11–36).

Chapter 7 narrates the tribes' contributions of wagons and oxen for transporting the tabernacle and its furnishings (vv. 1–9) and their offerings for the dedication of the altar (vv. 10–88). The altar is dedicated a month earlier than the events contained in the first six chapters. Twelve identical offerings are presented over a twelve-day period, one each day. The only variation in the description is the names of the tribes and their chiefs presenting them. The redundancy is pedagogical. Although their population sizes and camp positions differ, each tribe has an equal stake in the tabernacle, not only in assisting its transportation by the gift of ox-drawn wagons but also in worship there before the altar. No one tribe contributes more or less than another. If the priests and Levites have special ministries, the people of Israel equally support the tabernacle service and thereby share in its ministry.

Section Outline

I. Instructions for the Exodus Generation Preparing to Leave Sinai for Canaan (1:1–10:36) . . .
    G. Offerings at the Tabernacle's Consecration (7:1–89)
        1. Gifts for the Transportation of the Tabernacle (7:1–9)
        2. Gifts for the Dedication of the Altar (7:10–88)
        3. The Voice Speaking to Moses (7:89)

Comment

7:1–9 "On the day when Moses had finished setting up the tabernacle" (v. 1) is the first day of the first month of the second year (Ex. 40:17). Chapters 1–6 took place "on the first day of the second month, in the second year" (Num. 1:1), a chronology extending to 10:10 (cf. 9:1: "in the first month of the second year"; 9:5: "Passover in the first month, on the fourteenth day"; 9:15: "on the day that the tabernacle was set up"). Numbers 10:11 returns the timeline to "the second month, on the twentieth day."

That Moses "had anointed and consecrated it" (7:1) could mean that he "had anointed, *that is* [*vav* explicative], made it holy" (piel of Hb. *qadash*). Anointing with holy oil (Ex. 30:25, 31) would consecrate the tabernacle, its furnishings, and the altar (Ex. 40:9–10).

Those who bring the offerings are the "chiefs of Israel, heads of their fathers' house[holds] ... chiefs of the tribes ... over those who were listed" (7:2)—these are the twelve men who had assisted Moses in the census (1:5–16, 44). The combination of these qualifications underlines the care taken to uphold the principle of parity in tribal representation. The two stages of presenting offerings are to "approach" and "bring" them (7:2–3). The offerings are brought to the altar ("before the LORD"; v. 3), and the wagons and oxen are brought to the entrance of the court ("before the tabernacle"; v. 3). Each tribe brings the same contribution: "six wagons[62] and twelve oxen, a wagon for every two of the chiefs, and for each one an ox" (v. 3).

The wagons given to assist the Levites in transporting the tabernacle with these gifts to the Promised Land reappear in Isaiah 66:19–21, which foresees the Israelite remnant, sent to the nations, returning to the holy mountain of Jerusalem with an offering. This return consists of brothers from all the nations riding on horses, mules, and dromedaries and using chariots and "litters" (*tsab*; Isa. 66:20; the only other occurrence). Among the remnant are those who will be appointed Levites and priests (Isa. 66:21). This Isaiah passage anticipates the apostolic gospel ministry to the diaspora, which yields a rich harvest, particularly among Gentiles (cf. Isa. 60:3–4; 66:19–21; Rom. 15:8–12). It also anticipates the universal priesthood of Christians, which has its roots in the Levitical-Aaronic sacred service (cf. Deut. 33:8–11; Isa. 66:21).

The "oxen" (*baqar*; Num. 7:3, 6, 7, 8) that draw the heavily laden wagons are large adults, not the young sacrificial animals (*ben-baqar*; 15:8). Such ox-drawn wagons could operate successfully only on level terrain, which is one of several reasons that argue against locating Mount Sinai in the craggy, mountainous southern part of the Sinai peninsula.

Moses must "accept" (*laqakh*; 7:5) these offerings he takes (*laqakh*, "took"; v. 6) from the chiefs. He obviously cannot take them into his hand, so his acceptance probably refers to a gesture. Moses receives them rather than Aaron and his sons because the offerings are not destined for the altar. Moreover, they are received at the same time as the consecration of the priests, on the first day of the first month (Ex. 40:15, 17). The priests would not be able to preside until the eighth day of that month (Lev. 9:1, 22).

Moses gives "two wagons and four oxen" to the "sons of Gershon" and "four wagons and eight oxen" to the "sons of Merari," in both cases "according to their service"

---

[62] The Hebrew rendered "wagons" (*'eglot tsab*; 7:3, 6, 7, 8) is translated "covered wagons" in some versions, both ancient (LXX, Vulgate) and modern (KJV, RSV; "covered carts," NASB, NIV). "Covered" may be supported by terms related to the first Hebrew word (*'agalah* from, *'gl*) which refers to round objects, such as "earrings" (*'agil*, 31:50), the "round" (*'agol*) rim of the cast metal sea (1 Kings 7:31), and the "round" top of a throne (10:19). The second term (*tsab*) also suggests roundness, e.g., the "swelling" (from *tsabah*) of the abdomen (Num. 5:21, 22, 27). Either term could signify a form like a covered wagon. Although some of what was carried on the wagons was protected by waterproof goatskin (Num. 4:25–26), covered wagons would provide protection from the penetrating, windblown desert dust and sand.

(Num. 7:7–8). The gifts correspond to the load each Levitical family will transport. The Gershonites transport the lighter load of curtains and screens, whereas the Merarites transport the heavier hardware: bases, structuring frames, and poles (4:24–27, 31–32). Ithamar (7:8) supervises the Gershonites and Merarites (4:28, 33).

"But to the sons of Kohath he gave none" (7:9); they transport the "holy things . . . carried on the shoulder" (v. 9). This is the first time "shoulder" is mentioned as the means of transportation of the furnishings (cf. 4:4, 15; 10:21). Inserted poles allow the weight of the ark, the table of the bread of the Presence, the lampstand, the golden incense altar, the bronze altar, and all the accompanying vessels to be distributed evenly on the porters (4:5–6, 7–8, 11, 14; 1 Chron. 15:15). The golden lampstand weighs no less than 75 pounds (34 kg; cf. ESV mg. on Ex. 25:39). The silver plates and basins and golden dishes presented at the altar's dedication will only increase the overall weight (cf. comment on Num. 7:10–88 [at v. 86]).

7:10–88 After the contribution of wagons and oxen for transporting the tabernacle, gifts are presented on the occasion of the dedication of the altar. These gifts precede the consecration of the altar and its utensils (reported in Lev. 8:11). "The day [the altar] was anointed" (Num. 7:10, 84) is also the first day of the first month (Ex. 40:10, 17). Its consecration makes it "most holy" (Ex. 40:10).

"The dedication of the altar" (Hb. *khanukkat hammizbeah*; Num. 7:10, 11, 84, 88; 2 Chron. 7:9; cf. *khanukkat habbayit*; Psalm 30 title, "dedication of the temple") is the direct object of the main verb, reading literally "the chiefs offered the dedication of the altar" (Num. 7:10). "Offerings for" is added in translation. The "dedication of the altar" is made possible by the gifts. The offerings are identical except that they are introduced and concluded by the name of the chief from each tribe presenting them, for example, "Nahshon . . . of the tribe of Judah" (vv. 12, 17). The repetitive style is likely due to the text's use as an administrative list.[63]

The order in which the gifts are given begins with Judah (v. 12). The order followed in the offering list is not the same as that in the census record in chapter 1. Here it follows the presentation of the camp arrangements around the tabernacle, given in chapter 4. The offerings are presented first by the east group (Judah, Issachar, Zebulun), then by the south (Reuben, Simeon, Gad), followed by the west (Ephraim, Manasseh, Benjamin) and then the north (Dan, Asher, Naphtali). This is particularly striking because the consecration of chapter 7 chronologically precedes the assignment of camp positions around the tabernacle (ch. 2; cf. comment on 7:1–9 [at v. 1]). It may be that this list forms the basis of the tribes' camp arrangements. Collectively, the nonpriestly tribes will henceforth be collaborators in the sanctuary service. It is fitting that this sacred service begins with an act of community worship—the service of giving unto the Lord.

Since the twelve offerings are identical, only the details of Judah's are commented on here (vv. 11–17). Each consists of three utensils: a silver bowl, a silver

---

[63] Levine says 7:10–88 "is composed in the form of an ancient Near Eastern temple account" (*Numbers 1–20*, 247).

basin, and a gold dish. The silver bowls are filled with a wheat grain offering made of fine flour mixed with olive oil. The gold dish contains incense. The use of silver and gold, that is, metals of lesser and greater value, respectively, is due to their different contents and place of use. The incense presented in the golden dish will be burnt on the golden altar in the Holy Place, while the grain offering presented in silver utensils will accompany a burnt offering (cf. v. 87) made on the bronze altar in the court.

Each of the animals presented is given for one of three offerings: "one bull . . . one ram, one male lamb a year old, for a burnt offering" (v. 15); "one male goat for a sin offering" (v. 16); and "for the sacrifice of peace offerings, two oxen, five rams, five male goats, and five male lambs a year old" (v. 17). The burnt offering, a fragrant aroma sacrifice, is mentioned first in descriptive lists, but, when it is offered with a sin offering, the latter is made first, since it "de-sins" or purges with blood any impurities from the altar. Thus purification atonement is made first. Peace offerings when specified involve freewill, votive, or thanksgiving offerings (Lev. 7:15–16).

The totals for the altar gifts are given in Numbers 7:64–88. The combined weight of silver plates and basins—each of the twelve weighing 130 shekels and 70 shekels, respectively—is 2,400 shekels (v. 85). The combined weight of the twelve golden dishes, each weighing 10 shekels, is 120 shekels (v. 86). The silver and gold vessels together thus weigh about 62 pounds (28 kg). These vessels for the altar dedication will be carried with the altar by the Kohathites (cf. 4:13–14).

The animals offered as burnt offerings are twelve of each of the following: bulls, rams, male lambs, and twelve male goats for the sin offering (7:87). Those offered in peace offerings are twenty-four bulls and sixty of each of the following: rams, male goats, male lambs (v. 88). Two hundred fifty-two animals are offered in total. Many Israelites were herdsmen and shepherds in Egypt (Gen. 47:1–6; Ex. 9:6; 10:9). They left Egypt with very many cattle (Ex. 12:38) and continued to herd animals during the entire wilderness period (Num. 11:22; 20:4, 8; 32:1).

"This was the dedication offering for the altar after it was anointed" (7:88) forms a framing summary and inclusio, echoing the initial command (v. 11).

7:89 The statement that Moses "went into the tent of meeting to speak with the LORD" (v. 89) is surprising. There is no report of what Moses says. What the voice says to Moses is reported in chapter 8. Elsewhere in Numbers the Lord initiates communication. This statement does, however, recall Moses' going "in before the LORD to speak with him" in Exodus 34:34, 35. There the tent of meeting was the one Moses made and placed outside the camp prior to the construction of the tabernacle (Ex. 33:7–11). The golden calf incident (Exodus 32) had, apparently, created some doubt as to whether the tabernacle would be set up. However, here the tent is pitched and furnished. There are two occurrences in which Moses says that "the LORD listened to me," recalling the Lord's response to his intercessory prayer (Deut. 9:19; 10:10; cf. 2 Kings 13:4). Perhaps Moses enters the tent of meeting to pray for the people. Not all of his prayers are recorded (e.g., Num. 11:2; 21:7).

That Moses "heard the voice [*qol*]" is reminiscent of Adam and Eve in the garden of Eden when they "heard the sound [or "voice," *qol*]" (Gen. 3:8) of the Lord God. They and the Israelites were fearful of "the voice" they heard, respectively, in Eden and from a cloud on Mount Sinai. The Israelites implored Moses to intervene (Deut. 5:23, 25, 26; 18:16). Now "the voice," once heard in the garden and from the mountain, is heard again in the tent of meeting speaking to a mediator. God's voice is also later heard from a cloud on a high mountain, saying of another (in Moses' presence), "This is my beloved Son; listen to him" (Mark 9:7).

From this position above the ark, "speaking to him from above the mercy seat ... from between the two cherubim" (Num. 7:89; as promised in Ex. 25:21–22), the Lord speaks as King, for he sits enthroned on the cherubim (1 Sam. 4:4; 2 Sam. 6:2; cf. Jer. 48:15). Viewed from his throne in heaven, the ark is his footstool (Ps. 132:7–8; 1 Chron. 28:2), as is the land (Isa. 66:1). The "mercy seat"[64] is the golden lid or cover of the ark on which stand the cherubim.[65] Occurring only here in Numbers, "mercy seat" (*kapporet*) is cognate with the verb "to make atonement" (*kipper*). The two ideas converge, since the blood sprinkled over and on the front of the lid on the annual Day of Atonement purges it, thereby cleansing impurities caused by the people's sins (Lev. 16:14–16, 33–34). Once blood atonement is made, forgiveness can be granted for the pollution and the sin causing it. The merciful Lord can therefore spare his people from judgment and remain in their midst.

The entire tabernacle portrays Christ, the incarnate Word who "dwelt" (Gk. *skanoō*; "tabernacled") among his people (John 1:14). As the tent of meeting is given by God to his people in the wilderness, Christ comes in flesh to his own. The ark more than any other furnishing of the tabernacle portrays his person and work. A few examples will suffice. The ark is made of acacia wood and covered with gold. Acacia wood is impermeable and resistant to insects and disease, a fitting picture of his sinless humanity. But wood can be destroyed, as Christ's body, the temple, is (John 2:19, 21). Gold is imperishable, suggesting Christ's eternal deity (e.g., John 1:1; 8:58; Heb. 1:8; 13:8). Inside the ark are the stone tablets inscribed with God's law and covenant that have already been broken by the people. Christ comes to fulfill all righteousness required by the law by his active and passive obedience. On the Day of Atonement the high priest enters the Most Holy Place to put the blood of a bull and a goat on the mercy seat to purge the accumulated impurities caused by the people's sins. This cleansing is the basis for divine pardon. Christ is both the offering and the Great High Priest. By his person and work he makes atonement once for all (Heb. 9:1–10:18). He enters not into a place made by human hands but into the very presence of God (Heb. 9:24). His blood cleanses his people from all sin, by which they are assured full forgiveness (1 John 1:7, 9).

---

64 The English "mercy seat," from the sixteenth-century Tyndale Bible, stems from Luther, who employed "mercy [grace] seat" (*Gnadenstuhl*) to translate the words from both the Hebrew and the Greek (*hilasterion*; Num. 7:89 LXX; Heb. 9:5).

65 Taking refuge "under his wings" (e.g., Ruth 2:12; Ps. 61:4 [61:5 MT]; Heb. 9:5) may refer to the wings of cherubim "overshadowing the mercy seat" (Ex. 25:20).

Response

In the ancient Near East sacred objects from the temples of defeated foes were transferred to victors' temples (1 Sam. 5:2; 2 Sam. 5:21; Ezra 5:14; Dan. 1:2; 11:8; Joel 3:5). The act demonstrated that the victor's god had defeated and exiled the enemy's god (Ex. 12:12; 2 Sam. 7:23; Jer. 43:12; 49:3; Dan. 11:8).

Precious objects of gold, silver, and bronze and other materials from the despoiled Egyptians (Ex. 12:36) are employed to make furnishings for the tabernacle (Ex. 25:3; 35:5; cf. Josh. 6:19, 24). David amasses war spoils used in the construction of Solomon's temple (2 Sam. 8:10–11; 1 Kings 7:51; 1 Chron. 18:8, 10–11; 26:26–27). In like manner Paul, drawing on Psalm 68:18, portrays the church as edified by the plunder of despoiled spiritual forces distributed as spiritual gifts to the church, that is, spiritually endowed believers (Eph. 4:7–12; cf. 1 Cor. 3:16; Col. 2:15). Like the tribal chiefs representing each tribe and everyone in them presenting their gifts for tabernacle worship, every Christian has a gift to employ for the mutual edification of the body of Christ (Rom. 12:3–8; 1 Cor. 12:1–29; Eph. 4:11–16; 1 Pet. 4:9–11), which "grows into a holy temple in the Lord" (Eph. 2:21).

By their generosity at the tabernacle's consecration the secular tribes support community worship and the ministries of those whose lives are devoted to sacred service. The earthly ministry of Jesus and his disciples is supported by those who desire to share in it (Luke 8:1–3). So too Paul's apostolic ministry (e.g., Rom. 16:1–2; 2 Cor. 11:8–9; Phil. 4:16–17). By their gifts, they all share in promulgating God's Word and the resulting worship of him. These examples of generosity are given in Scripture to encourage God's people to emulate them: "Having gifts that differ according to the grace given to us, let us use them . . . the one who contributes, in generosity" (Rom. 12:6–8).

NUMBERS 8

8 Now the Lord spoke to Moses, saying, ² "Speak to Aaron and say to him, When you set up the lamps, the seven lamps shall give light in front of the lampstand." ³ And Aaron did so: he set up its lamps in front of the lampstand, as the Lord commanded Moses. ⁴ And this was the workmanship of the lampstand, hammered work of gold. From its base to its flowers, it was hammered work; according to the pattern that the Lord had shown Moses, so he made the lampstand.

⁵ And the Lord spoke to Moses, saying, ⁶ "Take the Levites from among the people of Israel and cleanse them. ⁷ Thus you shall do to them to cleanse them: sprinkle the water of purification upon them, and let them go with a razor over all their body, and wash their clothes and cleanse

themselves. ⁸ Then let them take a bull from the herd and its grain offering of fine flour mixed with oil, and you shall take another bull from the herd for a sin offering. ⁹ And you shall bring the Levites before the tent of meeting and assemble the whole congregation of the people of Israel. ¹⁰ When you bring the Levites before the Lord, the people of Israel shall lay their hands on the Levites, ¹¹ and Aaron shall offer the Levites before the Lord as a wave offering from the people of Israel, that they may do the service of the Lord. ¹² Then the Levites shall lay their hands on the heads of the bulls, and you shall offer the one for a sin offering and the other for a burnt offering to the Lord to make atonement for the Levites. ¹³ And you shall set the Levites before Aaron and his sons, and shall offer them as a wave offering to the Lord.

¹⁴ "Thus you shall separate the Levites from among the people of Israel, and the Levites shall be mine. ¹⁵ And after that the Levites shall go in to serve at the tent of meeting, when you have cleansed them and offered them as a wave offering. ¹⁶ For they are wholly given to me from among the people of Israel. Instead of all who open the womb, the firstborn of all the people of Israel, I have taken them for myself. ¹⁷ For all the firstborn among the people of Israel are mine, both of man and of beast. On the day that I struck down all the firstborn in the land of Egypt I consecrated them for myself, ¹⁸ and I have taken the Levites instead of all the firstborn among the people of Israel. ¹⁹ And I have given the Levites as a gift to Aaron and his sons from among the people of Israel, to do the service for the people of Israel at the tent of meeting and to make atonement for the people of Israel, that there may be no plague among the people of Israel when the people of Israel come near the sanctuary."

²⁰ Thus did Moses and Aaron and all the congregation of the people of Israel to the Levites. According to all that the Lord commanded Moses concerning the Levites, the people of Israel did to them. ²¹ And the Levites purified themselves from sin and washed their clothes, and Aaron offered them as a wave offering before the Lord, and Aaron made atonement for them to cleanse them. ²² And after that the Levites went in to do their service in the tent of meeting before Aaron and his sons; as the Lord had commanded Moses concerning the Levites, so they did to them.

²³ And the Lord spoke to Moses, saying, ²⁴ "This applies to the Levites: from twenty-five years old and upward they[1] shall come to do duty in the service of the tent of meeting. ²⁵ And from the age of fifty years they shall withdraw from the duty of the service and serve no more. ²⁶ They minister[2] to their brothers in the tent of meeting by keeping guard, but they shall do no service. Thus shall you do to the Levites in assigning their duties."

[1] Hebrew *he*; also verses 25, 26 [2] Hebrew *He ministers*

Section Overview

Following the report on the offerings for the transportation of the tabernacle and the altar service (Numbers 7) come instructions on the illumination from the golden lampstand (8:1–4; cf. 3:31; 4:9). In addition to ministering daily at the altar, the priests will also need to enter the Holy Place, where the lamp stands. Also, the Levites must be ritually cleansed for their service of assisting the priests (8:5–26). This purification probably takes place when Aaron and his sons are consecrated on the first day of the first month (Ex. 40:2, 13–15, 17).[66] The lampstand is part of the tabernacle, which is completed on the first day of the first month. Like chapter 7, chapter 8 is also antecedent to chapters 1–6 (cf. Section Overview of Numbers 7; comment on 7:1–9 [at v. 1]).

Section Outline

I. Instructions for the Exodus Generation Preparing to Leave Sinai for Canaan (1:1–10:36) . . .
   H. Preparing for Service in the Tabernacle (8:1–26)
      1. The Lampstand (8:1–4)
      2. The Cleansing and Separation of the Levites (8:5–22)
      3. The Senior Levites Redeployed (8:23–26)

Comment

8:1–4 Moses is to "speak to Aaron" (8:2; seven other occurrences: Lev. 6:25; 16:2; 17:2; 21:17; 22:2, 18; Num. 6:23) what he heard in the tent of meeting (7:89). Seven lamps illuminate the Holy Place (8:2; cf. Ex. 25:37; Num. 8:3). Before the Kohathites can transport the sacred furnishings, Aaron and his sons must enter the Most Holy Place and the Holy Place to wrap the furnishings carefully so that the Levites neither see nor touch them (Num. 4:15, 20). In addition, Aaron is to enter the Holy Place morning and evening to keep the lampstand lamps lit (Lev. 24:2–4) and to burn incense on the golden altar (Ex. 30:7–8). Every Sabbath he is to arrange the bread of the Presence on the golden table (Ex. 25:30; Lev. 24:8).

"In front of the lampstand" (Num. 8:2, 3) provides the directions indicated in Exodus 40:22, 24, which states that the table is on the north side of the Holy Place and the lampstand on the south side. The entrance to the tent is on the east side. The lampstand is "hammered work of gold" (Num. 8:4). The other furnishings in the Holy Place are overlaid with gold. The lampstand is to be made "according to the pattern that the LORD had shown Moses" (v. 4; cf. Ex. 25:31–40). "Pattern" generally renders a different Hebrew word (*tabnit*), but here "appearance" (*mar'eh*) is used, along with the denominative "had shown" (form of *ra'ah*). These terms are combined in the conclusion of the orders on the lampstand and its utensils: "See that you make them after the pattern [*tabnit*] for them, which is being shown [from *ra'ah*] you on the mountain" (Ex. 25:40). "Pattern" also refers to that of the entire tabernacle (Ex. 25:9; Acts 7:44; Heb. 8:5).

8:5–22 Before doing any tabernacle service, the Levites are cleansed or made ritually pure (8:5–13). The priests are consecrated or made ritually holy (Ex. 29:1; Lev. 8:12). Only priests can officiate sacred rites. The Levites are separated from their fellow Israelites, for whom they do tabernacle service as substitutes for the firstborn (Num. 8:14–22). Their role is to help the priests (3:6).

---

[66] The consecration of Aaron and his sons takes seven days (Lev. 8:35). Adding the twelve days of tribal offerings would mean they overlap Passover, held on the fourteenth day (cf. Milgrom, *Numbers*, 362–364).

The Levites' cleansing involves three steps, the first of which involves the "water of purification" (*me hatta't*, 8:7; lit., "sin water" to de-sin). This water is perhaps taken from the main basin in the court used by the priests (Lev. 8:6), as opposed to being taken from the water for impurity (*me niddah*) made from the ashes of the red heifer (Num. 19:2–10), used primarily for cleansing corpse contamination. In "cleanse themselves" (8:7; form of *tahar*) the voice is not fully reflexive, with the subject and object being the same (i.e., the Levites doing and receiving the action of the verb "cleanse themselves"), but is partially indirect reflexive (i.e., with the subject "the Levites" as beneficiaries but not the sole performers of the action). Although the Levities wash their clothes and shave their bodies, Moses sprinkles the purification water "upon them" (v. 7).

Given their rank and responsibilities, the Levites must offer two bulls, one for a sin offering (v. 8) and the other for a burnt offering (vv. 8, 12). These same two animals were required for these two offerings made for sins of the high priest (Lev. 4:3, 7) and for the whole congregation (Lev. 4:13–14). "Its grain offering" (Num. 8:8) indicates that the first bull is a burnt offering, as specified in verse 12. The grain offering is presented as pan-baked "fine flour mixed with oil" (v. 8); it also accompanies peace offerings (6:17). After being cleansed, the Levites are offered, step by step, as a living sacrifice (8:9–13; cf. Rom. 12:1–2), having as their goal atonement on behalf of themselves (Num. 8:12) and the people (v. 19).

The people of Israel are to "lay their hands on the Levites" (v. 10), portraying an identification of "the people"—that is, their representatives—with the Levites. The closest parallel involves the elders' laying their hands on the bull to be sacrificed for their (the whole congregation's) sin (Lev. 4:13, 15). Aaron is then to offer the Levites "as a wave offering" (Num. 8:11, *tenuphah*; cf. discussion on v. 15), the cognate noun from the verb *nuph* (to "offer"). The Septuagint translates this as "set apart" (Gk. *aphorizō*), the same verb used to describe the setting apart of Barnabas (a Levite) and Saul from the Antioch church by the Holy Spirit for missionary service (Acts 13:2; notice the laying on of hands by the representatives of the community in Acts 13:3). The Levites are an offering "before the LORD" (Num. 8:11, 21; cf. v. 13, "to the LORD") "from the people of Israel" (v. 11) and are offered in their place to "do the service of the LORD" (v. 11). That is, as substitutes for the firstborn, they serve the Lord at the tabernacle instead of, and on behalf of, the people. The Levites then lay their hands on the heads of the bulls (v. 12), connecting the sins of the people with the sacrificial animals as their substitutional representatives. The priests offer the bulls, one for a "sin offering" the other for a "burnt offering," "to make atonement for the Levites" (v. 12)—that is, atonement on their behalf and for the people they represent.

When atonement is made with a burnt offering (Lev. 1:4; 14:20; 16:24; Num. 8:12), the blood of the animal, from the herd or the flock, is thrown against the sides of the altar in the court (regardless of the offeror's rank; Lev. 1:5, 11). The blood of the sin offering is manipulated more intricately. If it is a bull (for a high priest or the civil authorities representing the whole congregation), its blood is sprinkled seven times in front of the veil of the Most Holy Place, applied to the horns of the incense altar in the Holy Place, and poured out at the base of the altar of burnt offering in the court (Lev. 4:6–7). If it is a female goat/lamb (from a common person), its blood is put on the horns of the incense altar and poured out at the base of the altar of burnt offering (Lev. 4:25, 30, 34). Making atonement for the offeror involves purging with blood the furnishing that has been made impure by his or her sin. Blood sprinkled before the veil implies that the mercy seat on the ark has been polluted. But the high priest enters inside the veil only on the Day of Atonement to sprinkle the blood of a bull for his sin offering and a goat for the people's sin offering in front of the mercy seat (Lev. 16:14–16). Some of that same blood is applied to the horns of the incense altar and sprinkled on it (Lev. 16:18–19).[67]

Their purification and being offered as a living sacrifice "separated the Levites from among the people" (Num. 8:14; cf. v. 6). To "separate" (form of *badal*; v. 14) is an action undertaken to separate mixed things, as with the primordial elements in the sacred cosmos, such as light from darkness (Gen. 1:4). The priests must keep separate the holy and profane and the impure and pure (Lev. 10:10; cf. Ezek. 22:26). Mixing them defiles the pure and desecrates the holy. Even outside the ritual domain it is forbidden to mix two kinds of seeds, two kinds of animals when breeding or plowing, or two fabrics used for a garment (Lev. 19:19; Deut. 22:9–11). Blurring God-ordained distinctions is dangerous. God separates (*badal*) Israel from the other peoples (Lev. 20:24). Although the people must keep themselves from impurity and be holy in their conduct, they are never ceremonially consecrated as are the priests nor cleansed as are the Levites.

The Levites are "wholly given" to the priests to "do the service for the people at the tent of meeting" (Num. 8:16–19). The "service," or work (*'abodah*), they do as substitutes for the people involves cleaning, taking down, transporting, and setting up the tent and its furnishings. They are also to carry wood and water and slaughter daily and festival sacrifices. Finally, the Levites, as a living sacrifice, are given to "make atonement for the people of Israel" (v. 19), that is, on behalf of the people. Blood atonement to purify is made for them by sacrifices (cf. 5:25). This atonement made by Levitical service falls into the category of bloodless atonement to appease the anger of an offended party (cf. 31:50). The purpose is so "that there may be no plague ... when the people of Israel come near the sanctuary" (8:19). The form of the verb "come near" (*nagash*) is not the same form of this verb used for coming near with a sacrifice (Ex. 32:6; Lev. 2:8; also cf. *qarab*; Lev. 1:2; Num. 6:14). In this grammatical form *nagash* involves direct physical contact (Ex. 19:15). A plague manifests God's wrath for encroachment (Num. 16:46). As substitutes in proximity to the sacred, the Levites continually propitiate God and avert divine

---

[67] J. Milgrom argues that the blood of the sin and the guilt offerings make atonement (purification) more narrowly than the burnt offering—only for sins polluting sacred objects and the sanctuary—while the burnt offering may atone more broadly, for human sin, "such as the neglect of the performative commandments." Cf. "Sacrifices and Offerings, OT," *IDBSup*, 769.

wrath on the people.[68] The section closes with a major compliance statement (8:20), followed by a summary (vv. 21–22a) and a reiterating compliance statement (v. 22b). After the aforementioned ceremonies the Levites begin their tasks in and around the tabernacle (v. 22).

8:23–26 Based on age, a distinction is drawn between the younger Levites, who do heavy labor (Hb. *'abodah*), and their older relatives, who perform the lighter task of keeping guard (*mishmeret*) over the tabernacle. The Levites begin working here at "twenty-five years old and upward" (v. 24), while in chapter 4 the age at which the Levites begin to "do duty" is thirty. This difference perhaps reflects a period of five years' apprenticeship, beginning at twenty-five. Given the skill required to carry out their tasks, the Levites would need a period of training.[69]

The verb translated "to do" (*tsaba'*; 8:24) is the same rendered "warred" (e.g., 31:7), and the cognate object "duty" (*tsaba'*; cf. 4:3, 23) is elsewhere translated "war" (e.g., 31:3; 32:27); the terms thus describe the Levites' service as spiritual warfare. They bear arms (Ex. 32:26–27) to execute encroachers. Like soldiers, the Levites' duty is conscripted and regimented in turns of active service—8,580 Levites (Num. 4:48) could not all serve simultaneously. Nothing is said here about their divisions or rotation of duties (cf. 1 Chron. 23:6). "Service" (*'abodah*; Num. 8:24) is physical labor, involving maintaining the tabernacle and transporting it. The latter would include dismantling, packing, loading onto wagons or carrying parts on shoulders, and then setting up the tabernacle upon arrival at the next station.

At the age of fifty the Levites "withdraw from the duty of the service" (v. 25). There will be no more active hard-labor duty after this age. This is emphasized: "Serve no more" (v. 25); "do no [more] service" (v. 26). Instead "they minister to their brothers," in particular to the priests (3:7) but also to the people (3:8), "by keeping guard," which involves preventing intrusion by keeping station around the tabernacle during encampment and march (1:53; 2:17; 10:17, 21).

"Minister" (*sharat*; 8:26) in Numbers refers to the sacred task of the Levites: they "take care of" (same verb) the tabernacle and "minister" to Aaron and his sons, the priests (3:6; 18:2), and to the congregation (16:9). Ministering is done under someone else's authority. The verb describes Joseph's ministering to Potiphar (Gen. 39:4; "attended"), Joshua's ministering to Moses (Num. 11:28; "assistant"), and Samuel's ministering to the Lord as a boy under Eli the priest (1 Sam. 2:11). The Levites minister under the priests—the Kohathites under Eleazar (Num. 3:32; 4:16) and the Gershonites and Merarites under Ithamar (4:28, 33). No details are repeated here concerning this ministry of keeping guard, since the purpose of this law is to establish the age at which senior Levites are exempt from hard physical labor, which has already been prescribed in detail (3:5–4:49). At a later period the Levites' temple service under the priests will be multifaceted (e.g., as gatekeepers,

---

[68] Milgrom states that 8:19 implies the "Levites are a ransom for Israel, a lightning rod to attract the wrath of God upon themselves whenever an Israelite has encroached upon the sancta" (*Numbers*, 371).
[69] Levine, *Numbers 1–20*, 158.

musicians, praise leaders).[70] As teachers, the older Levites would be well versed in the Scripture (Neh. 8:7, 9).

Response

The priests are responsible for the Word and sacraments (Deut. 33:10). The non-priest Levites handle the material aspects of the sacred ministry. Their distinct roles anticipate pastoral and diaconal ministries in the church. The Levites' sacrificial service as substitutes for the Israelite firstborn provides a concrete example for Christian service in general.

The Levites are a living sacrifice chosen by the Lord to serve him by serving their brothers (the priests) and the people. Paul probably has their example in mind when exhorting Christians as living sacrifices to employ their God-given gifts in service to one another.

> I appeal to you therefore, brothers, by the mercies of God, to present your bodies as *a living sacrifice*, holy and acceptable to God, which is your spiritual worship.... For as in one body we have many members, and the members do not all have the same function, so we, though many, are one body in Christ, and individually members one of another. Having gifts that differ according to the grace given to us, let us use them ... if service, in our serving [*diakonia*]. (Rom. 12:1, 4–7)

NUMBERS 9

9 And the LORD spoke to Moses in the wilderness of Sinai, in the first month of the second year after they had come out of the land of Egypt, saying, ²"Let the people of Israel keep the Passover at its appointed time. ³On the fourteenth day of this month, at twilight, you shall keep it at its appointed time; according to all its statutes and all its rules you shall keep it." ⁴So Moses told the people of Israel that they should keep the Passover. ⁵And they kept the Passover in the first month, on the fourteenth day of the month, at twilight, in the wilderness of Sinai; according to all that the LORD commanded Moses, so the people of Israel did. ⁶And there were certain men who were unclean through touching a dead body, so that they could not keep the Passover on that day, and they came before Moses and Aaron on that day. ⁷And those men said to him, "We are unclean through touching a dead body. Why are we kept from bringing

---

[70] During the First and Second Temple periods the Levites' duties were many and varied as worship leaders (2 Chron. 8:14), musicians (2 Chron. 8:14; 23:18), armed guards (2 Chron. 23:7), priests' helpers to flay offerings (2 Chron. 29:34), scribes, officials, and gatekeepers (2 Chron. 34:13), and treasurers (1 Chron. 9:26; 26:20; 2 Chron. 34:9); cf. 1 Chron. 9:17–33; 23:2–32; 2 Chron. 30:16; 31:12; 35:12–13; Neh. 12:24–25.

the Lord's offering at its appointed time among the people of Israel?" ⁸ And Moses said to them, "Wait, that I may hear what the Lord will command concerning you."

⁹ The Lord spoke to Moses, saying, ¹⁰ "Speak to the people of Israel, saying, If any one of you or of your descendants is unclean through touching a dead body, or is on a long journey, he shall still keep the Passover to the Lord. ¹¹ In the second month on the fourteenth day at twilight they shall keep it. They shall eat it with unleavened bread and bitter herbs. ¹² They shall leave none of it until the morning, nor break any of its bones; according to all the statute for the Passover they shall keep it. ¹³ But if anyone who is clean and is not on a journey fails to keep the Passover, that person shall be cut off from his people because he did not bring the Lord's offering at its appointed time; that man shall bear his sin. ¹⁴ And if a stranger sojourns among you and would keep the Passover to the Lord, according to the statute of the Passover and according to its rule, so shall he do. You shall have one statute, both for the sojourner and for the native."

¹⁵ On the day that the tabernacle was set up, the cloud covered the tabernacle, the tent of the testimony. And at evening it was over the tabernacle like the appearance of fire until morning. ¹⁶ So it was always: the cloud covered it by day[1] and the appearance of fire by night. ¹⁷ And whenever the cloud lifted from over the tent, after that the people of Israel set out, and in the place where the cloud settled down, there the people of Israel camped. ¹⁸ At the command of the Lord the people of Israel set out, and at the command of the Lord they camped. As long as the cloud rested over the tabernacle, they remained in camp. ¹⁹ Even when the cloud continued over the tabernacle many days, the people of Israel kept the charge of the Lord and did not set out. ²⁰ Sometimes the cloud was a few days over the tabernacle, and according to the command of the Lord they remained in camp; then according to the command of the Lord they set out. ²¹ And sometimes the cloud remained from evening until morning. And when the cloud lifted in the morning, they set out, or if it continued for a day and a night, when the cloud lifted they set out. ²² Whether it was two days, or a month, or a longer time, that the cloud continued over the tabernacle, abiding there, the people of Israel remained in camp and did not set out, but when it lifted they set out. ²³ At the command of the Lord they camped, and at the command of the Lord they set out. They kept the charge of the Lord, at the command of the Lord by Moses.

[1] Septuagint, Syriac, Vulgate; Hebrew lacks *by day*

Section Overview

As instructed, Israel keeps Passover in the first month (Num. 9:1–5). However, a second month Passover could be observed under certain conditions (vv. 9–14). The section on the cloud covering the tabernacle (vv. 15–23) supplements the Exodus narrative (Ex. 40:34–38) from "the day that the tabernacle was set up" (Num. 9:15) and condenses the cloud's guidance throughout the wilderness sojourn: "So it was always" (v. 16). Like the two preceding chapters, chapter 9 falls into the first-month, second-year chronology, a month earlier than chapters 1–6. The celebration of the

Passover and the guiding cloud summary are literarily positioned close to Israel's departure from Sinai (10:11).

Section Outline
   I. Instructions for the Exodus Generation Preparing to Leave Sinai for Canaan (1:1–10:36) . . .
      I. The Passover and the Cloud (9:1–23)
         1. Keeping the Passover (9:1–14)
         2. The Cloud Covering the Tabernacle (9:15–23)

Comment

9:1–14 This section contains two parts. First, the Israelites heed the reminder that the Passover is to be celebrated at the appointed time (vv. 1–5). Second, those hindered by uncleanness or distance from keeping the Passover must keep it in the second month, on the fourteenth day (vv. 6–14).

The Lord's instructions come "in the first month [Abib (March/April)] of the second year" (v. 1) after the exodus (cf. Ex. 13:4; Deut. 16:1). Two temporal markers guide the keeping of "the Passover at its appointed time" (Num. 9:2): (1) the "fourteenth day" (v. 3), which was "that very day" (Ex. 12:41) of the exodus; (2) "at twilight" (Num. 9:3, 5, 11), when the Passover lamb was slaughtered (Ex. 12:6; cf. Deut. 16:6). In Second Temple practice "twilight" was the period between the highest and lowest position of the sun in the sky, during which daylight would begin to fade and darkness would start to overtake it. It framed the time when the second regular burnt offering could be slaughtered, from the sixth to the ninth hour (roughly 12:00–3:00 p.m.). If the eve of Passover fell on an eve of Sabbath, the burnt offering was slaughtered at half past the sixth hour and offered an hour later, followed by the Passover lamb (Mishnah, Pesahim 5:1). As the Passover Lamb of God (John 1:29, 36) Jesus' crucifixion was marked by darkness between the sixth and ninth hour, the latter being the hour he gave up his spirit (Matt. 27:45–46, 50).[71]

"Appointed time" (Num. 9:2, 3) translates the same term (*mo'ed*) used for an appointed place in the expression "tent of meeting" (*'ohel mo'ed*) and "appointed feasts" (e.g., 10:10). The time, place, and occasion of God's convocations are neither spontaneous nor arbitrary.

"All its statues and all its rules" (9:3) refers to the Passover instructions already given (Ex. 12:2–27, 43–51; Lev. 23:4–8; cf. Num. 9:11–12; 28:16–25; Deut. 16:1–8). Passover preparation begins on the tenth day of the first month with the selection a lamb, which is then slaughtered on the fourteenth day (Ex. 12:3, 6). This first section ends with a compliance statement: "They kept the Passover . . . so the people of Israel did" (Num. 9:5), a declaration reminiscent of their submitting to

---

[71] The "day of Preparation," mentioned in the Synoptic Gospels as the day of Jesus' death, was always the Friday before Sabbath (e.g., Mark 15:42), called the "day of Preparation of the Passover" (John 19:14). John not only links the Sabbath and the Passover. He also indicates that Pilate handed Jesus over for crucifixion at "about the sixth hour" (John 19:14), which opened the time frame for the slaughter of the Passover lamb.

the rules given at the first Passover (Ex. 12:28). With one previous exception (Num. 5:4), compliance statements have referred to Israel's leaders (e.g., 8:22). Here the people follow in their footsteps.

The second part of 9:1–14 contains a question about those hindered from celebrating the Passover at the appointed time (vv. 6–8) and the response (vv. 9–14). Becoming "unclean through touching a dead body" (v. 6) involves quarantine outside the camp (5:2–3) for seven days (19:11; 31:19), including ablutions with water for impurity (19:11–13). The Passover is a holy convocation (Lev. 23:4; Num. 28:18). Thus anyone partaking of it must be ritually pure. Anyone uncleansed from corpse contamination may not partake of it, lest they defile the sanctuary (19:13, 20).

"Certain men" (9:6) in this predicament desire to keep the Passover at the appointed time but are "kept" (*gara'*; v. 7) from it. A strict application of the law would deny them their legitimate part "among the people of Israel" in the Passover, which would mean having their inheritance "taken away" (*gara'*; cf. 27:7; 36:3, 4). Having no precedent, Moses inquires to "hear what the LORD will command" (9:8; cf. 15:33–35). The response (9:9–13) not only addresses anyone "unclean" but also applies to anyone "on a long journey" (v. 10). They must keep the feast "in the second month on the fourteenth day" (v. 11). Once the festivals become centralized pilgrimages, organizing a second Passover will be difficult. However, the Numbers 9 ruling provides the precedent for one such occasion in Hezekiah's day (2 Chron. 30:1–3).

The same rules apply to the second-month Passover: "They shall eat it.... [And] leave none of it until the morning" (Num. 9:11–12). The paschal lamb is roasted whole over fire; any leftovers are burnt (Ex. 12:8, 10). The regulation "nor [shall they] break any of its bones" (Num. 9:12; cf. Ex. 12:46) is cited as being fulfilled in Christ (John 19:36).

A warning is given against making this second-month Passover ruling an easy option for anyone who simply did not want to keep it in the first month. "But if anyone who is clean and is not on a journey fails to keep the Passover, that person shall be cut off [*karat*] from his people... that man shall bear his sin" (Num. 9:13). *Karat* is the statutory sentence for a high-handed sin (Num. 15:30–31), as in the stoning of the Sabbath breaker (15:32–36) or the blasphemer (Lev. 24:10–16). It applies to anyone who "profaned what is holy to the LORD" by, for example, eating peace offering meat on the third day (Lev. 19:8) or not being purified from corpse contamination, thereby defiling the sanctuary (Num. 19:13, 20). This punishment is generally meted out by God's own hand (e.g., 1 Sam. 2:25; 4:11; Acts 5:5, 10; 1 Cor. 5:5; 11:30; cf. comments on Num. 1:47–54 [at v. 51]; 17:8–13 [at v. 13]). It can also entail the extirpation of posterity (Ps. 37:28; Isa. 14:22) or exile (1 Kings 9:7; Ps. 37:22).

Passover is the only sacred festival punished by *karat* for nonobservance. Placed at the head of annual festivals, it commemorates Israel's deliverance from slavery, linked to the making of the Sinai covenant. Its antitype is the Lord's Supper and the institution of the new covenant. A warning against abuse of the Lord's Supper includes a similar penalty for its profanation (1 Cor. 11:27–30).

A "stranger" (*ger*; Num. 9:14) is a resident alien who can lawfully join Israelite festivals. Abraham described himself as a "sojourner and foreigner" (Gen. 23:4). No foreigner (*toshab*) is allowed to eat the Passover (Ex. 12:45). To keep the Passover, males must be circumcised (Ex. 12:48) as a sign of their belonging the covenant Lord and their engagement to keep the covenant. The fact that the stranger desires to keep the Passover of the Lord (Num. 9:14) demonstrates his heartfelt desire to worship the true God. Two implicit concurrent concerns are present. First, despite his restrictive civil status, the stranger has no fewer privileges or obligations regarding this religious observance. Second, the native must show no ceremonial discrimination regarding the covenant-keeping sojourner. The "statute of the Passover" and "its rule" applies alike to the "sojourner" (*ger*) and the "native" (v. 14; cf. Ex. 12:48–49).[72] This Passover is perhaps the last one observed in the wilderness. After forty years, the new generation is circumcised at Gilgal, also neglected all that time. Thereupon they hold the Passover (Josh. 5:5, 10).

9:15–23 The last verses of Exodus (Ex. 40:34–38), which tells us that the people "throughout all their journeys" (Ex. 40:38) set out if the cloud lifted and stayed if it remained, are taken up and supplemented in Numbers 9:15–23. "The day that the tabernacle was set up," when "the cloud covered the tabernacle, the tent of the testimony" (v. 15), is the first day of the first month of the second year (Ex. 40:2, 17), the same day the cloud filled the tabernacle with the glory of the Lord (40:34). The cloud covers the tabernacle as it had covered the mountain when Moses ascended (Num. 9:16; cf. Ex. 24:15; Deut. 4:11). The verb includes making the covered object invisible (e.g., Ex. 15:5; Ps. 32:1). In Psalm 105:39 this cloud is described as a curtain (*masak*, "cover"), like that which is spread over the entrance of the tabernacle courtyard and the inner tent ("screen"; Num. 3:26, 31), which hides from view that which is behind. The "cloud ['*anan*] ... by day" has the "appearance of fire by night" (9:16, 21; cf. Ex. 40:38). Its form is a "pillar" ('*amud*) when the Lord summons someone to the tent of meeting (Num. 12:5; Deut. 31:15). The pillar, whether cloud or fire, leads the Israelites when they journey (Num. 14:14; cf. Ex. 13:21; Neh. 9:12).

Although God himself is invisible, the cloud is a manifestation of his presence to protect and guide his people. Moreover, in a desert the darkness, like the cold at night, is penetrating. At night the fiery cloud provides both heat and light. In the day the cloud "over them" (Num. 10:34) shades the people from the burning sun and heat. Light and shade permit travel by day or night (Ex. 13:21; cf. Ps. 19:6; Isa. 4:5). The camp remains stationary "as long as the cloud rested over the tabernacle" (Num. 9:18). "Kept the charge" (v. 19) means that Israel followed the cloud signals (cf. 18:8). The length of time could range from "two days" to "a month," or even "a longer time" (lit., "days"; 9:22), which in context has been interpreted as "a year" (e.g., KJV, NIV), completing the day-month sequence.

Reference to the cloud's remaining in a fixed position for various lengths of time takes into account the entire wilderness experience: "So it was always" (v. 16;

---

[72] On "*ger*" cf. Milgrom, *Numbers*, 398–402.

cf. Ex. 40:36, 38: "throughout all their journeys"), a rare glimpse of the thirty-eight years of wanderings otherwise virtually passed over in silence. Notwithstanding his chastising them, the Lord remains present to protect his people and provide for their needs (Deut. 2:7; 8:4; 29:5). The temporal reckoning of the stations, like the list of forty encampments (Numbers 33), is a reminder that the days making up the decreed judgment are numbered (cf. 14:34; 32:13).

In the compliance summary (e.g., 1:54; 2:34) setting up camp and breaking camp are done "at the command of the LORD," repeated three times in 9:23 (cf. vv. 18, 20). The people "kept the charge of [*shamar mishmeret*] the LORD" by maintaining the purity of the camp while decamping, traveling, and encamping, much like the Levites, who prevent encroachment by keeping guard (*shamar mishmeret*; 1:53). The Lord's "command" is visual—the cloud's lifting and settling down. Moses' "command" is given to the priests, who blow trumpets to signal the move (10:5–6).

Response

The cloud's covering the tabernacle is portrayed poetically by John Newton in the third stanza of his "Glorious Things of Thee Are Spoken."

> Round each habitation hov'ring, / see the cloud and fire appear
> For a glory and a cov'ring, / showing that the Lord is near;
> Thus deriving from their banner / light by night and shade by day,
> Safe they feed upon the manna, / which he gives them when they pray.

This abiding and guiding divine presence is a call in the fourth stanza to reflect on God's grace and its attendant blessings:

> Savior, if of Zion's city / I, through grace, a member am,
> Let the world deride or pity; / I will glory in thy name.
> Fading is the worldling's pleasures, / all his boasted pomp and show;
> Solid joys and lasting treasure / none but Zion's children know.

NUMBERS 10

10 The LORD spoke to Moses, saying, ²"Make two silver trumpets. Of hammered work you shall make them, and you shall use them for summoning the congregation and for breaking camp. ³And when both are blown, all the congregation shall gather themselves to you at the entrance of the tent of meeting. ⁴But if they blow only one, then the chiefs, the heads of the tribes of Israel, shall gather themselves to you. ⁵When you blow an alarm, the camps that are on the east side shall set out. ⁶And when you blow an alarm the second time, the camps that are on the south side shall set out. An alarm is to be blown whenever they are to set out. ⁷ But when the assembly is to be gathered together, you shall blow a long blast, but you shall not sound an alarm. ⁸ And the sons of Aaron, the priests, shall blow the trumpets. The trumpets shall be to you for a perpetual statute throughout your generations. ⁹ And when you go to war in your land against the adversary who oppresses you, then you shall sound an alarm with the trumpets, that you may be remembered before the Lord your God, and you shall be saved from your enemies. ¹⁰ On the day of your gladness also, and at your appointed feasts and at the beginnings of your months, you shall blow the trumpets over your burnt offerings and over the sacrifices of your peace offerings. They shall be a reminder of you before your God: I am the Lord your God."

¹¹ In the second year, in the second month, on the twentieth day of the month, the cloud lifted from over the tabernacle of the testimony, ¹² and the people of Israel set out by stages from the wilderness of Sinai. And the cloud settled down in the wilderness of Paran. ¹³ They set out for the first time at the command of the Lord by Moses. ¹⁴ The standard of the camp of the people of Judah set out first by their companies, and over their company was Nahshon the son of Amminadab. ¹⁵ And over the company of the tribe of the people of Issachar was Nethanel the son of Zuar. ¹⁶ And over the company of the tribe of the people of Zebulun was Eliab the son of Helon.

¹⁷ And when the tabernacle was taken down, the sons of Gershon and the sons of Merari, who carried the tabernacle, set out. ¹⁸ And the standard of the camp of Reuben set out by their companies, and over their company was Elizur the son of Shedeur. ¹⁹ And over the company of the tribe of the people of Simeon was Shelumiel the son of Zurishaddai. ²⁰ And over the company of the tribe of the people of Gad was Eliasaph the son of Deuel.

²¹ Then the Kohathites set out, carrying the holy things, and the tabernacle was set up before their arrival. ²² And the standard of the camp of the people of Ephraim set out by their companies, and over their company was Elishama the son of Ammihud. ²³ And over the company of the tribe of the people of Manasseh was Gamaliel the son of Pedahzur. ²⁴ And over the company of the tribe of the people of Benjamin was Abidan the son of Gideoni.

²⁵ Then the standard of the camp of the people of Dan, acting as the rear guard of all the camps, set out by their companies, and over their company was Ahiezer the son of Ammishaddai. ²⁶ And over the company of the tribe of the people of Asher was Pagiel the son of Ochran. ²⁷ And over the company of the tribe of the people of Naphtali was Ahira the son of Enan. ²⁸ This was the order of march of the people of Israel by their companies, when they set out.

²⁹ And Moses said to Hobab the son of Reuel the Midianite, Moses' father-in-law, "We are setting out for the place of which the Lord said, 'I will give it to you.' Come with us, and we will do good to you, for the Lord has promised good to Israel." ³⁰ But he said to him, "I will not go. I will depart to my own land and to my kindred." ³¹ And he said, "Please do not leave us, for you know where we should camp in the wilderness, and you will serve as eyes for us. ³² And if you do go with us, whatever good the Lord will do to us, the same will we do to you."

³³ So they set out from the mount of the Lord three days' journey. And the ark of the covenant of the Lord went before them three days' journey,

to seek out a resting place for them. ³⁴ And the cloud of the LORD was over them by day, whenever they set out from the camp.

³⁵ And whenever the ark set out, Moses said, "Arise, O LORD, and let your enemies be scattered, and let those who hate you flee before you." ³⁶ And when it rested, he said, "Return, O LORD, to the ten thousand thousands of Israel."

Section Overview

In their literary position the silver trumpets' instructions (Num. 10:1–10) close the entire Sinai pericope (Ex. 20:1–Num. 10:10). Their coded blasts coordinate the Israelites' breaking camp. The departure is nineteen days after the census (10:11; cf. 1:1), which ends the "first month" pericope (7:1–10:10; cf. Section Overview of Numbers 7); the "second month" chronology of chapters 1–6 resumes. The tribes' order of setting out and march (10:13–28) executes the instructions given earlier (2:1–3:38). The general destination is the wilderness of Paran (10:12).

Moses requests the assistance of his wife's relative Hobab for the wilderness trek (vv. 29–32). With the ark of the covenant in the lead and the cloud to guide, Moses invokes the Lord to scatter his enemies and be with his people (vv. 33–36). The Israelites will soon be on the doorstep of Canaan.

As suggested in the Introduction (cf. Interpretive Challenges: Unifying Structure of Numbers), following the census (ch. 1) the literarily parallel chapter 2 instructions "They shall set out" and chapter 10 execution "They set out" bracket the opening frame (chs. 1–10) of the tripartite structure of Numbers. The same pattern is found in the end frame (chs. 26–36).

Section Outline

I. Instructions for the Exodus Generation Preparing to Leave Sinai for Canaan (1:1–10:36) . . .
   J. On the Way from Sinai to Canaan (10:1–36)
      1. Silver Trumpet Signals (10:1–10)
      2. The Orderly March (10:11–28)
      3. Moses Requests Hobab's Services (10:29–32)
      4. Guidance by Ark and Cloud (10:33–36)

Comment

10:1–10 Signals and directions during the desert march from Sinai to the wilderness of Paran are not only visual (the cloud) but also audible (silver trumpets). The cloud gives the signal to set out, and in response the trumpets give the order in which the camps depart. This is the first time "trumpets" (Hb. *hatsotserah*; Num. 10:2) are explicitly mentioned, although they were implied in Leviticus 23:24 ("blast"; with "of trumpets" rightly added, as in Num. 29:1). They are fabricated by "hammered work" (10:2), like the cherubim and lampstand (cf. Ex. 25:18, 31;

Num. 8:4). Josephus describes them as less than a cubit long,[73] thus unlike the long ones depicted on the Arch of Titus.

These trumpets have at least four uses. The first is in "summoning the congregation" (10:2). The noun translated "summoning" (*miqra'*) is generally found only in the expression "holy convocation" (*miqra' qodesh*) that qualifies the sacred gatherings, including the Sabbath (e.g., Num. 28:18, 25, 26; 29:1, 7, 12; exceptions include Isa. 1:13; 4:5). "Holy" does not qualify the summons, since it has a civil rather than a ceremonial purpose. If both trumpets are blown, the summons is for "all the congregation . . . at the entrance of the tent of meeting" (Num. 10:3). "Congregation" refers specifically to its representatives (cf. comment on 1:1–19 [at v. 2]), such as the seventy elders and the officers (11:16). If only one trumpet is blown, "the chiefs, the heads of the tribes of Israel" are summoned (10:4). Twelve chiefs head the national census (ch. 1), lead the tribal military companies making up the camps (e.g., 2:3–4, 10–11), and present the twelve-tribe offerings at the tabernacle dedication (7:2).

The second use of silver trumpets is for "breaking camp" (*massa'*; 10:2; cf. the verb *nasa'*; for both, Ex. 40:36). This use is the immediate concern, as the following section makes clear (Num. 10:11–28). The trumpets are blown in various ways (vv. 5–7). To signal breaking camp "an alarm" (*teru'ah*, v. 5; certainly a loud sound, cf. Josh. 6:5; 1 Sam. 4:5: "shout") is blown, first for the "east side" camps to move out (Num. 10:5; cf. 2:3–9), then a second time for the "south side" camps (10:6; cf. 2:10–16). The remaining order is not stated in the Hebrew text but completed in the LXX, following chapter 2: following the east and south side camps, the "west side" (2:18–24), and the "north side" camps are signaled (2:25–31). The "assembly [*qahal*] . . . to be gathered together [*qahal*]" (10:7) is a religious body. It is summoned by a "long blast . . . not . . . an alarm" (v. 7). There is little agreement on the nature of the sound (steady, staccato, quavering, etc.) or its length, however. An old rabbinic practice for the New Year shofar blasts consists of "three blasts," one sustained, one quavering, and another sustained (Mishnah, Rosh Hashanah 4:9).

The third use of these trumpets is to "sound an alarm" (*rw'*) when going "to war in your land" (Num. 10:9). Although it is "your land," it will not be taken without fierce resistance. At Jericho, signals are given by "trumpets [*shopharot*] of rams' horns" (Josh. 6:4). The city walls collapse at the blowing of the "rams' horns" (*qeren hayyovel*), the sound of the "trumpet" (*shophar*), and the people's "shout" (*teru'ah*; Josh. 6:5; the same term translated "alarm" in Num. 10:5, both from *rw'*). In Gideon's battle the Midianites are terrorized by the sound of smashing jars and blowing trumpets (*shophar*; e.g., Judg. 7:20; cf. 2 Sam. 2:28; 18:16; Ezek. 33:3). Apart from Numbers 10, in war contexts the use of *hatsotseroth* (translated "trumpets") is rare (2 Chron. 13:12, 14; cf. Hos. 5:8 parallel with *shophar*). It is more commonly named among the musical instruments used by Levites in temple worship (e.g., 2 Chron. 5:12). In times of war the blowing of these trumpets is so that "you may be remembered [*zakar*] before the LORD your God, and you shall be saved from

---

[73] Josephus, *Antiquities* 3.12.6.

your enemies" (Num. 10:9) and to "be a reminder [*zikkaron*] of you before your God" (v. 10). Priests' blowing the battle trumpets is like crying out to the Lord in prayer (2 Chron. 13:12, 14). When he heard the groaning of his people in servitude, God remembered his salvific covenant promises (Ex. 2:24; cf. Gen. 15:14, 18). He remembers the needs of his own and delivers them (Gen. 8:1; 19:29; 30:22; 1 Sam. 1:19; Pss. 98:3; 105:42; 106:45; 115:12).

The fourth use of these silver trumpets is to signal "appointed feasts" (pl. *moʿed*; Num. 10:10). "On the day of your gladness" refers to public sacred festivals, when "burnt offerings" and "peace offerings" are made for all the people (cf. Lev. 23:4–38; Num. 28:1–29:40; Deut. 16:1–17).

10:11–28 Dating the departure from Sinai marks this event's importance: "In the second year, in the second month, on the twentieth day of the month" (10:11) is nearly fourteen months after the exodus (Ex. 12:17, 51; 19:1), over eleven months after Israel's arrival at the mountain (Ex. 16:1), fifty days after the erection of the tabernacle (Ex. 40:17), and nineteen days after the census (Num. 1:1).

The main action sequence is that "the cloud lifted," the Israelites "set out," and "the cloud settled down." (10:11–12). "Set out" (*nasaʿ*), the key word, occurs sixteen times (e.g., vv. 12, 13, 34, 35). "Arrival" is mentioned only once (v. 21), when the Kohathites arrive with the sacred furnishings after the tabernacle has been set up. "By stages" (v. 12) reads literally "in *their* stages/settings out," which describes the camps' sequential departures (east camp, south camp, etc.; vv. 5–6, 14, 18) from their encampments before arriving in the wilderness of Paran, at Kibroth-hattaavah (11:34) and Hazeroth (12:16).

The "wilderness of Sinai" (10:12) is one of a handful of named wildernesses included in the Israelites' wilderness trek in the Sinai Peninsula (cf. Introduction: Title; comment on 1:1–19 [at v. 1]). Its position in the peninsula remains in doubt, since the identification of Mount Sinai is debated. If Mount Sinai is in the southern part of the Sinai Peninsula,[74] the Israelites would head north through the mountainous eastern part of the peninsula to travel to the wilderness of Paran. If Mount Sinai is in the west-central part of the peninsula—as held in this commentary (cf. Section Overview of Numbers 33; comment on 33:1–15 [at v. 15])—they would travel in an east-northeasterly direction. The general contours of the "wilderness of Paran" (10:12) can be determined. From there the Israelite scouts "go up into the Negeb" (13:17) to reconnoiter Canaan (32:8). The northern border of Paran merges into the Negeb and the wilderness of Zin south of Judah to the Negeb highlands (34:3). On the east is the Arabah, with the Gulf of Elath on the southeast fringe (cf. Gen. 14:6 reading El[ath]-paran). The wilderness of Shur and Egypt lay to its west (Gen. 20:1; 21:21). This data suffices to locate the wilderness of Paran in the limestone tableland covering a large swath in the center of the Sinai Peninsula, today called et-Tih ("Wanderings Wilderness"). To the south are the mountains of the

---

[74] Cf. G. I. Davies, *The Way of the Wilderness. A Geographical Study of the Wilderness Itineraries in the Old Testament*, SOTSMS 5 (Cambridge: Cambridge University Press, 1979), 63–69, 84–87.

southern peninsula. From antiquity a major route crossing the Paran wilderness connected Midian and Egypt (1 Kings 11:17–18), later known as the Darb al-Hajj, the Pilgrim Road, used by Muslims to go from Egypt to Mecca.[75]

"They set out for the first time at the command of the LORD by Moses" (Num. 10:13). Israel has "set out" earlier from several points before arriving at Mount Sinai (Ex. 15:22; 16:1; 19:2). This is the first time they set out from Sinai, and the first time organized and marching in military camps and companies. It is also the first step from Sinai toward the Promised Land. The Lord's command is audible (the silver trumpets; Num. 10:5–6) and visual (the cloud; vv. 11–12). Both signs attend the Lord's word delivered to the people "by Moses."

The order of march of the tribal camps (vv. 13–28) follows that laid out in chapter 2. The twelve tribes are organized in four camps, each camp consisting of three tribal military companies, with a standard of the camp of the lead tribe. The tribal camps' rectangular stationary positions on each side of the tabernacle become linear once they are on the move. The eastern group "set out first," led by "the standard of the camp . . . of Judah" (10:14). "Their companies" refers to their own [Judah's] company, the "company" of Issachar, and the "company" of Zebulun (vv. 15–16). They are followed by the Gershonite and Merarite Levites, who have "taken down" the tabernacle and "carried" it (v. 17), that is, have transported it on wagons (cf. 7:7–8). Then the southern Reuben camp sets out, consisting of its own company together with Simeon's and Gad's companies (10:18–20).

They are followed by the Kohathite Levites (v. 21), responsible for "carrying the holy things" (cf. 4:15) on their shoulders (cf. 7:9). The order of march allows the Gershonites and Merarites to arrive ahead of the Kohathites so that "the tabernacle was set up before [the Kohathites'] arrival" (10:21). The sacred furnishings can thus be put in place by Aaron and his sons. This order of march appears to differ from that in chapter 2, where the "tent of meeting" and the "Levites" set out (v. 17) between the Reuben and Ephraim companies (vv. 10–16, 18–24). However, the Levites there, as suggested, are Kohathites who here set out between these two companies.

After them the western Ephraim camp sets out with its company and those of Manasseh and Benjamin (vv. 22–24). Finally, the northern camp sets out with the Dan company, joined by the companies of Asher and Naphtali (vv. 25–27). The Dan camp is the "rear guard of all the camps" (v. 25; cf. comment on 2:17; cf. Josh. 6:9; Isa. 52:12; 58:8). The Danites are renowned for their fighting prowess (Gen. 49:16–17; Judg. 18:27). They guard all the companies from a rear attack (cf. Deut. 25:17–18).

The summary statement ("This was the order of march of the people of Israel by their companies, when they set out"; Num. 10:28) covers the early stages of travel in Numbers 10:29–12:16, culminating in the Israelites' making camp in the wilderness of Paran on the southern doorstep of the land of Canaan, at Kadesh.

---

75 Menashe Har-El, *Sinai Journeys: The Route of the Exodus* (San Diego, CA: Ridgefield, 1983), 322–324. Noordtzij identifies the wilderness of Paran with et-Tih covering the northern half of the peninsula, with the wilderness of Zin in its northernmost part; A. Noordtzij, *Numbers*, trans. Ed van der Maas, BSC (Grand Rapids, MI: Zondervan, 1983), 91.

10:29–32 Moses understands that God's guidance by the cloud (v. 12) and the ark (v. 33) does not preclude human agency for specific matters. Moses requests Hobab to remain with the people, "For you know where we should camp in the wilderness, and you will serve as eyes for us" (v. 31). The flocks and herds need pasture and water, neither being readily available nor easily accessible in the wilderness, especially since the Israelites have much livestock (Ex. 12:38; 17:3; Num. 11:22; 14:33; 20:8). With time already being well into the "second month" (10:11; April–May), grass on the highlands will soon become scarce. Moses' in-law is no stranger to desert herdsmanship (Ex. 3:1).

If "father-in-law" (Hb. *khoten*; Num. 10:29) refers to Reuel rather than Hobab, Hobab would be Moses' brother-in-law.[76] Judges 4:11 would be understood in the same sense (NIV: "brother-in-law; ESV: "father-in-law"). This harmonizes with Exodus 2, where "Reuel," who has "seven daughters" (Ex. 2:16; "their father," Ex. 2:18), gives "his daughter Zipporah" as wife to Moses (Ex. 2:21). Reuel is "the priest of Midian" (Ex. 2:16, 18). But elsewhere "Jethro, the priest of Midian" is called Moses' "father-in-law" (Ex. 3:1; 18:1). Does he perhaps have two names: Jethro and Reuel? Others certainly do, such as Jacob/Israel (Gen. 32:28; Num. 24:17; Hos. 12:12), Gideon/Jerubbaal (Judg. 6:32; 8:35), and Solomon/Jedidiah (2 Sam. 12:24–25). It is worth noting that in each case the second is a theophoric name (-*'el*, -*baal*, -*yah*), like Reu*el*, "Friend of God."

It is more likely that "Jethro" is a priestly title—or, more precisely, "Jether" (Hb. *yether* appears at Ex. 4:18, although it is conflated with "Jethro" in translation). A noun of the form *yether* would become "Jethro" whenever a third-person masculine singular suffix was attached.[77] "Jethro" would mean "his excellence/eminence" (Gen. 49:3, "preeminence," from *yatar*).[78] Jethro blesses the Lord and offers sacrifices (Ex. 18:10, 12), two principal priestly ministries (cf. 1 Chron. 23:13). So Reuel and Jethro could be one and the same person, Moses' father-in-law (Reuel) and priest (Jethro), with Hobab being Moses' brother-in-law.

Reuel is a "Midianite" (Num. 10:29) and Hobab a "Kenite" (Judg. 1:16; 4:11). Rather than being a gentilic (like "Kenite"), "Midianite" may refer to someone from Midian (Ex. 2:15; Num. 10:30, "my land," i.e., Midian; cf. "Jethro, the priest of Midian," Ex. 3:1; 18:1). The designation "Kenite" first appears in connection with Hobab after the settlement in Canaan, which suits the suggestion that Hobab is Moses' brother-in-law.

By acquiescing to Moses' request Hobab will share in the "good" (Num. 10:29) the Lord has promised Israel; that is, he will be a beneficiary of covenant favor

---

76 The syntax is ambiguous. *Khoten* could equally refer to Hobab (cf. Judg. 4:11). Rashi viewed Reuel as the grandfather of Moses' wife (*Pentateuch with Rashi's Commentary*, 4:50–51). Most modern evangelical commentators identify Reuel with Jethro (cf. Bush, *Book of Numbers*, 140; Wenham, *Numbers*, 105; Ashley, *Book of Numbers*, 196; Cole, *Numbers*, 176). The derived verb (form of *khatan*) means "be related by marriage" (e.g., Deut. 7:3). In addition to *khoten*, according to context, *khatan* means "bridegroom" (Ex. 4:25), "sons-in-law" (Gen. 19:14; cf. 1 Sam. 18:18), or "male related by marriage" (2 Kings 8:27). Cf. *CDCH*, 137.

77 Cf. *degel* ("standard") becomes *diglo* ("his own standard"; Num. 2:2); *nezer* ["separation"] becomes *nizro* ("his separation"; 6:5).

78 Noordtzij also concludes that Jethro is a priestly title meaning something like "eminence." He understands the "*o*" to be an ancient nominative case (*Numbers*, 92).

and hold an inheritance in the Promised Land (vv. 29, 32). Hobab initially declines Moses' invitation (v. 30), but he ultimately accepts it; he is among the Israelites at Jericho and the Kenites who settle in the Negeb of the tribe of Judah (Judg. 1:16; 1 Sam. 27:10).

The proximity of Midian and Mount Sinai can be deduced from this passage and others. Moses fled from Egypt to the land of Midian (Ex. 2:15), which was near Horeb, the mountain of God (Ex. 3:1, 12; 4:27)—both terms designating Mount Sinai (e.g., Ex. 24:13, 15; Deut. 1:6, 19; Acts 7:30). Moses went back to Egypt from Midian, taking his wife and children (Ex. 4:19). Moses returned to Midian, where Aaron, leaving Egypt, came to him (Ex. 4:27). Moses' father-in-law brought Moses' wife and children to him when the Israelites arrived at Sinai (Ex. 18:5). Then he returned to "his own country" (Ex. 18:27), namely, Midian. Midian lay on the route traversing Paran on the way to Egypt (1 Kings 11:18). The implied proximity and relative ease of travel further support a location of Mount Sinai in the western peninsula rather than in the rugged southern mountains.

10:33–36 The travel narrative that began with Israel's departure from Egypt halted in Exodus 19:1, when the people arrived at "the mountain" (Ex. 19:3). Now it resumes, as already indicated (Num. 10:11). Elsewhere "the mount of the LORD" (Hb. *har yhwh*) refers to the place in the land of Moriah where the Lord tested Abraham by ordering him to sacrifice Isaac (Gen. 22:1, 14). Solomon built the temple in Jerusalem on Mount Moriah (2 Chron. 3:1). Although the two places are geographically distinct, the common denominator between "the mount of the LORD" (i.e., Sinai) and "the mountain of the LORD" (also *har yhwh*; e.g., Isa. 30:29; i.e., Zion) is that both are linked to receiving and being instructed in the law of the Lord. They differ in that his law is given on the former to Israel, while from the latter it will go forth to instruct all peoples (Isa. 2:3; Mic. 4:2; Zech. 8:3). After his resurrection, Jesus returns to the Mount of Transfiguration in Galilee to meet his eleven disciples (Matt. 17:1–13; 28:16). There he announces the Great Commission to "make disciples of all nations, baptizing them" and "teaching them to observe all that I have commanded you" (Matt. 28:18–20).

"The ark of the covenant of the LORD" (Num. 10:33), the first of two occurrences of this title (cf. 14:44), is so named because the covenant law is placed within it (cf. "ark of the testimony" 4:5; 7:89; cf. comment on 1:47–54 [at v. 50], "testimony"). The ark "went before them" (10:33), which may imply that its being carried ahead of the people by Aaron and his sons on this first leg of the journey. In battle the priests carry the ark before the army (e.g., Josh. 6:12), though the Levites generally transport it in the midst of the marching camps (Num. 4:15; but cf. Deut. 31:9, 25; 2 Sam. 15:24). At the crossing of the Jordan the Israelites are to keep about 2,000 cubits (1,000 yards/900 meters) between themselves and the ark (Josh. 3:4). The three days refer to the journey to Kibroth-hattaavah, the first encampment before they arrive in the wilderness of Paran (Num. 11:34). Deuteronomy 1:2 speaks of an eleven-day journey between Horeb (Mount Sinai) and Kadesh-barnea (cf. Num. 13:26).

The ark goes "to seek out a resting place" (10:33; lit., "to scout out [*tur*] rest [*menuhah*] for them"). Before they left Sinai the Lord had promised, "My presence will go with you, and I will give you rest" (*nuakh*; Ex. 33:14). At the end of their journey on the plains of Moab Moses reminds the people that God "went before you in the way to seek you out a place to pitch your tents, in fire by night and in the cloud by day" (Deut. 1:33). Both the ark and the cloud are also reminders of God's faithfulness to his promise.

The cloud, which provides shade by day and fire by night, is their guide (Num. 9:16–17; 14:14). It is a manifestation of the angel of the Lord, who leads the people (Ex. 14:19; 23:20–23; cf. 33:14; Judg. 2:1). When the Israelites are traveling, the cloud is "over them by day" (Num. 10:34; 14:14). When stationary, it remains over the tent (Num. 9:15, 17). "Whenever the ark set out," so did Israel (10:35); "when it rested," so did they (v. 36).

Moses' invocation "Arise, O LORD" (v. 35) depicts a warrior stirred to battle: "Let your enemies be scattered [cf. Ps. 89:10], and let those who hate you flee before you" (Num. 10:35; cf. Deut. 28:7). David cites Moses' invocation, applying it to his enemies (Ps. 68:1; cf. 2 Chron. 6:41; Ps. 132:8). Moses' call "Return, O LORD" (Num. 10:36) anticipates a victorious return "to the ten thousand [pl. *rebabah*] thousands [pl. *'elep*] of Israel" (v. 36; cf. 1 Sam. 18:7, 8). This could be rendered "the multitude [pl. *rebabah*] of the clans/families [pl. *'elep*] of Israel" (cf. Num. 1:16; 10:4; Josh. 22:21, 30). Elsewhere the terms "ten thousand" and "thousand" refer to warriors (Lev. 26:8; Deut. 32:30; 1 Sam. 18:7; Pss. 68:17; 91:7; cf. Rev. 9:16). *'Elep* may be a term for a military unit, as in some other cases (e.g., 1 Sam. 17:18; NIV: "unit").[79] The Israelites are now organized into military units with marching orders. As their God and Great King (Ps. 95:3; Matt. 5:35), the Lord is in the midst of his forces, enthroned on the cherubim (cf. Num. 7:89). Notwithstanding the great size of Israel's forces, they cannot depend on their own strength.

Response

The ark goes "to seek out a *resting* place" (Num. 10:33). The Lord had promised, "My presence will go with you, and I will give you rest" (Ex. 33:14). The ark's seeking a resting place in the wilderness anticipates, step by step, the fulfillment of the Lord's promise to give his people rest in the Promised Land (Deut. 12:9; Josh. 1:13; Ps. 95:11). Jesus invites, "Come to me, all who labor and are heavy laden, and I will give you rest" (Matt. 11:28). The rest in the Promised Land foreshadows the rest promise of Jesus, the rest of salvation in God's Son entered by faith in his person and finished work (Heb. 3:18; 4:1–11).

---

[79] "Unit of a thousand men" (*CDCH*, s.v. אלף II.2, citing 1 Sam. 17:18); cf. *CHALOT*, s.v. אֶלֶף III: "'thousand,' military unit."

The ark goes "to seek out a resting *place*" (Num. 10:33). By his angel who went before the people to guard and guide them, the Lord promised "to bring you to the place I have prepared" (Ex. 23:20–23). The same angel who led them out of Egypt (Ex. 14:19) leads them to the Promised Land (Judg. 2:1). Christ's words to his disciples echo these: "If I go and prepare a place for you, I will come again and will take you to myself, that where I am you may be also" (John 14:3).

The messianic Psalm 68:1 cites Numbers 10:35, "Arise, O LORD, and let your enemies be scattered, and let those who hate you flee before you." The Psalm celebrates the Lord's victory over his enemies and his reign over them. Verse 18 is cited in the NT in reference to Christ's resurrection and ascension (Eph. 4:8; cf. Acts 1:9). After he fulfilled the law by his life and death, Christ in his resurrection dealt a mortal blow to sin, death, and Satan (Acts 26:18; Rom. 6:9; 8:11). His ascension inaugurated his reign over his former enemies (Rom. 5:10), now his people from all the nations of the earth (Matt. 28:19; Rom. 15:9–12, citing the Law, Prophets, and Psalms; 1 Tim. 3:16; Rev. 12:5).

Risen with Christ and seated with him in the heavenly places (Eph. 2:6), by faith Christians share in that reign in this life. And when faith will be sight, they will reign with Christ (2 Tim. 2:12) in the new heavens and the new earth (Rev. 20:6).

OVERVIEW OF

NUMBERS 11–25

The first section of Numbers, chapters 1–10, emphasized the Israelites' prompt execution of God's instructions (e.g., 1:54; 2:34; 9:23) preparing for their departure from Sinai for Canaan. The next major section, chapters 11–25, stands in stark contrast. It narrates the people's disaffection with their lot, leaders, and Lord. The exodus generation will die in the wilderness for refusing to enter Canaan. Will the new generation also fail to enter the Promised Land due to their disobedience?

Like the preceding and following sections, this section is literarily demarked by bracketing chapters, 11 and 25 (cf. Introduction: Interpretive Challenges: Unifying Structure of Numbers).

NUMBERS 11

11 And the people complained in the hearing of the Lord about their misfortunes, and when the Lord heard it, his anger was kindled, and the fire of the Lord burned among them and consumed some outlying parts of the camp. ² Then the people cried out to Moses, and Moses prayed to the Lord, and the fire died down. ³ So the name of that place was called Taberah,¹ because the fire of the Lord burned among them.

⁴ Now the rabble that was among them had a strong craving. And the people of Israel also wept again and said, "Oh that we had meat to eat! ⁵ We remember the fish we ate in Egypt that cost nothing, the cucumbers, the melons, the leeks, the onions, and the garlic. ⁶ But now our strength is dried up, and there is nothing at all but this manna to look at."

⁷ Now the manna was like coriander seed, and its appearance like that of bdellium. ⁸ The people went about and gathered it and ground it in handmills or beat it in mortars and boiled it in pots and made cakes of it. And the taste of it was like the taste of cakes baked with oil. ⁹ When the dew fell upon the camp in the night, the manna fell with it.

¹⁰ Moses heard the people weeping throughout their clans, everyone at the door of his tent. And the anger of the Lord blazed hotly, and Moses was displeased. ¹¹ Moses said to the Lord, "Why have you dealt ill with your servant? And why have I not found favor in your sight, that you lay the burden of all this people on me? ¹² Did I conceive all this people? Did I give them birth, that you should say to me, 'Carry them in your bosom, as a nurse carries a nursing child,' to the land that you swore to give their fathers? ¹³ Where am I to get meat to give to all this people? For they weep before me and say, 'Give us meat, that we may eat.' ¹⁴ I am not able to carry all this people alone; the burden is too heavy for me. ¹⁵ If you will treat me like this, kill me at once, if I find favor in your sight, that I may not see my wretchedness."

¹⁶ Then the Lord said to Moses, "Gather for me seventy men of the elders of Israel, whom you know to be the elders of the people and officers over them, and bring them to the tent of meeting, and let them take their stand there with you. ¹⁷ And I will come down and talk with you there. And I will take some of the Spirit that is on you and put it on them, and they shall bear the burden of the people with you, so that you may not bear it yourself alone. ¹⁸ And say to the people, 'Consecrate yourselves for tomorrow, and you shall eat meat, for you have wept in the hearing of the Lord, saying, "Who will give us meat to eat? For it was better for us in Egypt." Therefore the Lord will give you meat, and you shall eat. ¹⁹ You shall not eat just one day, or two days, or five days, or ten days, or twenty days, ²⁰ but a whole month, until it comes out at your nostrils and becomes loathsome to you, because you have rejected the Lord who is among you and have wept before him, saying, "Why did we come out of Egypt?"'" ²¹ But Moses said, "The people among whom I am number six

hundred thousand on foot, and you have said, 'I will give them meat, that they may eat a whole month!' ²² Shall flocks and herds be slaughtered for them, and be enough for them? Or shall all the fish of the sea be gathered together for them, and be enough for them?" ²³ And the LORD said to Moses, "Is the LORD's hand shortened? Now you shall see whether my word will come true for you or not."

²⁴ So Moses went out and told the people the words of the LORD. And he gathered seventy men of the elders of the people and placed them around the tent. ²⁵ Then the LORD came down in the cloud and spoke to him, and took some of the Spirit that was on him and put it on the seventy elders. And as soon as the Spirit rested on them, they prophesied. But they did not continue doing it.

²⁶ Now two men remained in the camp, one named Eldad, and the other named Medad, and the Spirit rested on them. They were among those registered, but they had not gone out to the tent, and so they prophesied in the camp. ²⁷ And a young man ran and told Moses, "Eldad and Medad are prophesying in the camp." ²⁸ And Joshua the son of Nun, the assistant of Moses from his youth, said, "My lord Moses, stop them." ²⁹ But Moses said to him, "Are you jealous for my sake? Would that all the LORD's people were prophets, that the LORD would put his Spirit on them!" ³⁰ And Moses and the elders of Israel returned to the camp.

³¹ Then a wind from the LORD sprang up, and it brought quail from the sea and let them fall beside the camp, about a day's journey on this side and a day's journey on the other side, around the camp, and about two cubits² above the ground. ³² And the people rose all that day and all night and all the next day, and gathered the quail. Those who gathered least gathered ten homers.³ And they spread them out for themselves all around the camp. ³³ While the meat was yet between their teeth, before it was consumed, the anger of the LORD was kindled against the people, and the LORD struck down the people with a very great plague. ³⁴ Therefore the name of that place was called Kibroth-hattaavah,⁴ because there they buried the people who had the craving. ³⁵ From Kibroth-hattaavah the people journeyed to Hazeroth, and they remained at Hazeroth.

¹ *Taberah* means *burning* ² A *cubit* was about 18 inches or 45 centimeters ³ A *homer* was about 6 bushels or 220 liters ⁴ *Kibroth-hattaavah* means *graves of craving*

Section Overview

This chapter narrates the first in a cyclical series of complaints of the exodus generation regarding their circumstances (Num. 11:1–3, 4–15, 31–33; cf. 14:1–4; 16:41–50 [17:6–15 MT]; 20:2–5; 21:4–9). The severe divine judgment these complaints provoke is due largely to the people's underlying sinful belief that life in Egypt as slaves was better than their current state (11:5, 18, 20; cf. 14:2–4; 20:4–5). Viewed from the overall perspective of Numbers—preparations for and journey to the Promised Land—reverting to Egypt in attitude is tacitly to turn in the opposite direction. Not only is it turning against God's ordained leader, Moses; it is turning against God himself.

Soon after the departure from the wilderness of Sinai, manna becomes the source of discontent (11:4–6). The miraculous provision of manna, which began after the Israelites crossed the sea after leaving Egypt, continues after they leave Sinai (Num. 11:9; cf. Ex. 16:14–18) and throughout the entire wilderness sojourn (Josh. 5:12).

Three toponyms are mentioned in Numbers 11: Taberah (v. 3), Kibroth-hattaavah (v. 34), and Hazeroth (v. 35). Their locations are unidentified. Halts there precede the Israelites' arrival at the wilderness of Paran, at Kadesh (cf. 10:12; 12:16; 13:26; 32:8).

Section Outline

II. Trials in the Wilderness of Paran, the Transjordan Highlands, and the Plains of Moab (11:1–25:18)
  A. Incidents at Taberah and Kibroth-hattaavah (11:1–35)
    1. Complaining at Taberah, Divine Judgment, Moses' Prayer (11:1–3)
    2. Weeping over the Manna (11:4–10)
    3. Moses' Plea (11:11–15)
    4. Elders Appointed to Share Moses' Burden (11:16–30)
    5. Quail and a Plague at Kibroth-hattaavah (11:31–35)

Comment

11:1–3 Following the Masoretic punctuation, verse 1 may be translated "When the people complained, [it was] evil in the hearing of the LORD . . ." (lit., "in the ears of the LORD," an expression found only here; more commonly "Evil in the *sight* [or "eyes"] of the LORD," e.g., Num. 32:13). The people's complaining recalls the Marah experience (Ex. 15:22–24), which, like here, followed a three-day march (v. 22; cf. Num. 10:33). The reason they complain is not stated. Many Israelites of the exodus generation worshiped idols in Egypt (Ezek. 20:7–8) and remain apostate in the wilderness. They are ungrateful for their deliverance from servitude and freely complain about their physical circumstances.

A closely related verb, "grumbled" (Hb. *lun*), appears almost exclusively in two major wilderness narratives, the first reporting the people's testing the Lord in the Marah and the Massah and Meribah incidents (Ex. 15:22–17:7), and the second reporting the Kadesh rebellion and Korah's revolt (Num. 14:1–17:13; 14:1–17:28 MT). The Hebrew verbs rendered "complained" (*'anan*) in Numbers 11:1 and "grumbled" (*lun*) in the above narratives are both translated by the same Greek term (*gongyzō*). Jewish authorities and even some disciples grumbled (*gongyzō*) in disbelief at Jesus' claim to be manna from heaven, which, if eaten, would give eternal life (John 6:41, 61–66).

"Burned" (*ba'ar*; Num. 11:1, 3) spawns the place-name "Taberah" (11:3). It is the manifestation of the Lord's anger. The "fire of the LORD" (vv. 1, 3) also destroyed Sodom and Gomorrah (Gen. 19:24), Aaron's two sons (Lev. 10:2; cf. Num. 3:4; 26:61), and those involved in Korah's rebellion (16:35). The fire "consumes" (*'akal*, "eat, devour"; 11:1), corresponding to the rabble's craving "to eat" (*'akal*; v. 4) meat.

The "outlying parts of the camp" (*qetseh hammakheneh*; v. 1) are a location as far as possible from the tabernacle, to which these people had withdrawn in the camp.

"The people cried out" (*tsaʿaq*; v. 2), reminiscent of the starving Egyptians' begging Pharaoh for food during the famine (Gen. 41:55). Since they are described as those in the "outlying parts of the camp" (Num. 11:1) and the "rabble that was among them" (v. 4), these people may be non-Israelite (cf. comment on 11:4–10 [at v. 4]). The sons of Israel had cried out earlier and were delivered (e.g., Ex. 14:10; Judg. 3:9); in Numbers 11:4 "the rabble" are distinguished from "the people of Israel."

Moses' prayer in verse 2 is not recorded here, nor is his intercession in Numbers 21:7. Elsewhere his prayers are (Ex. 33:12–16; Num. 12:13; 14:13–19; 16:20–22). Prayer is an essential tool of a prophet (Gen. 20:7; 1 Sam. 12:23; 2 Kings 4:33; Jer. 37:3; 42:2–4, 9). Proclaiming the word of the Lord to his people is inextricably bound to intercessory prayer for them (Isa. 37:4, 6). When praying, a prophet stands before God on behalf of the people. When proclaiming the word, he stands before the people on behalf of God.

"The fire died down" (*shaqaʿ*), like water draining away (Amos 9:5) or a stone sinking in water (Jer. 51:64; cf. Jer. 51:63). The expression suggests the fire is not a metaphor here for a plague or other natural disaster. No actual casualties are reported. Taberah is not mentioned in the itinerary (Num. 33:16), nor do we find the characteristic narrative formula (they set out from X and camped in Y; e.g., 12:16).

11:4–10 The word "rabble" (*haʾsapsup*; v. 4) occurs only here. The LXX uses the same word (*epimiktos*) to translate the Hebrew rendered "rabble," "mixed multitude" (Hb. *ʿereb rab*; Ex. 12:38), and "of foreign descent" (*ʿereb*; Neh. 13:3). Non-Israelites join in the exodus: the blasphemer in Leviticus 24:10 is the son of an Israelite mother and an Egyptian father, while Moses requests his Midianite in-law to join the Israelites.

Behind this incident is the riffraff's "strong craving" (Num. 11:4; *taʾavah*). The same noun describes Eve's reaction upon seeing the tree in the middle of Eden ("a delight [*taʾavah*] to the eyes"; Gen. 3:6). Deuteronomy 12:20 employs similar forms of both the verb and noun: "When the Lord your God enlarges your territory, as he has promised you, and you say, 'I will eat meat,' because you crave [*ʾavah*] meat, you may eat meat whenever you desire [n. *ʾavvah*]." Such "craving" or "desiring" is not necessarily wrong (cf. Deut. 14:26; 2 Sam. 3:21; 1 Kings 11:37; Prov. 13:12, 19). However, in this case the craving is preceded by complaining (Num. 11:1) and followed by weeping (v. 4). After the Kadesh revolt, both reactions, one verbal and the other emotional, are manifested simultaneously (14:1–2). Ingratitude for their long-term gain from their redemption and promised inheritance leads these people to grumble, complain, and weep over temporary circumstances, which in turn leads to rebellion, that is, a failure to believe and obey God (Deut. 9:23–24).

Not acting upon God's promises is unbelief (cf. Heb. 3:12, 15–19; 4:1–2). Behind unbelief is ingratitude toward God (Rom. 1:21), which naturally feeds complaining. What proceeds from the mouth not only reveals the state of the heart; it also "defiles a person" (Matt. 15:18–19; cf. Titus 1:15). The food and water incidents that resulted in grumbling before the giving of the Sinai law covenant did not incur divine judgment (Ex. 15:22–26; 16:1–18; 17:1–7). Increased revelation, however, brings increased responsibility (Rom. 4:15). After the law is given, sin becomes exceedingly sinful (Rom. 7:13). The presence of a holy God is incompatible with a people defiled of speech (cf. Isaiah 6).

The people then weep again (Num. 11:4): They previously wept when the burning from the Lord killed Aaron's sons (Lev. 10:6). They will weep at Aaron's and Moses' deaths (Num. 20:29; Deut. 34:8). Now they weep in frustration over their unsatiated craving. "Oh that" (*mi*; Num. 11:4) renders as an exclamation the interrogative "who," which is the subject of the following verb, "eat." The sentence literally reads, "Who will feed us meat to eat?" This defiant challenge is directed at Moses, but it is ultimately aimed at God as well. As the Psalter remarks, "They ... put God to the test in the desert" (Ps. 106:14). They could in fact have eaten meat from their own flocks and herds (Ex. 34:3; Num. 20:4).

They also lament the absence of the fish they ate in Egypt (11:5). Had they been traveling in the southern peninsula, the traditional location of the wilderness of Sinai, they could probably have had abundant fish from the Gulf of Suez or the Gulf of Elath.[80] Viewing life "in Egypt" as better than their current state—"but now" (v. 6)—was behind their charge leveled against Moses at the Red Sea (Ex. 14:12). They now claim the fish they ate in Egypt cost them nothing (Num. 11:5), presumably since these and the five vegetables (all *hapax legomena*) were part of the slave wages intended to sustain them sufficiently for work. "This manna" (v. 6) is deprecatory. They pine for their past rations for which they paid with sweat, and they despise God's gracious provision, which is genuinely "free."

Verses 7–9 describe "manna" (*man*): how it is prepared, its taste, and when and where it falls. This is their dietary staple until the next generation reaches Canaan (Ex. 16:35; Josh. 5:12). As "bread from heaven" (Ps. 105:40; cf. Ps. 78:25; John 6:31), manna is emblematic of God's care for his people. The daily gathering of manna on six days is to remind the people to attend to their daily spiritual need of God's word (Deut. 8:3; Matt. 4:4) and to respect the Sabbath rest (Ex. 16:26). Jesus speaks of himself as the true manna from heaven; those who eat of him will live forever (John 6:41–58). Manna, being "white," sweet like "honey" (Ex. 16:31), having the appearance of "bdellium" (a transparent aromatic tree resin), and falling with "the "dew," has led some to the conclusion that it is a natural phenomenon involving the tamarisk tree and insect excretion.[81] However, that so-called manna is found only two months a year and would not be accessible only six days a week. The variety of ways manna could be prepared—baked, boiled, or fried—and its different tastes—"like wafers made with honey" (Ex. 16:31) or "cakes baked with oil"—undermine the people's "nothing at all but" (Num. 11:6) complaint.

---

80 Cf. Har-El, *Sinai Journeys*, 373.
81 F. S. Bodenheimer, "The Manna of Sinai." *BA* 10 (1947): 2–6. Also John Sturdy, *Numbers*, CBC (Cambridge: Cambridge University Press, 1976), 84.

The Hebrew expression rendered "The anger of the LORD blazed" (v. 10) is literally "The Lord's nose got *very* hot" (cf. "The Lord's nose got hot"; e.g., vv. 1, 33). The exodus generation is the expressed object of the Lord's anger in four verses (11:33; 12:9; 32:10, 13), as will be the new generation in three (25:3, 4; 32:14). Just as the people's complaining was evil in the Lord's ears (11:1) so here in verse 10 the people's weeping is evil in Moses' eyes.

11:11–15 Moses' plea (vv. 11–15) is framed as a chiasm:

> "Dealt ill [*ra'*] . . . not found favor in your sight" (v. 11)
> "If I find favor in your sight . . . my wretchedness" (*ra'*; v. 15)

Moses' prayer emphasizes the "burden" (*massa'*) he must "carry" (the cognate verb, *nasa'*):

> "You lay the *burden* of all this people on me" (v. 11)
> "*Carry* them in your bosom, as a nurse *carries* a nursing child" (v. 12)
> "I am not able to *carry* all this people alone" (v. 14)
> "The *burden* [lit., "it"] is too heavy for me" (v. 14)

Did Moses "conceive" and "give birth" to the people, that God should expect him to carry them like a "nursing child" to the land he swore to give their fathers? (v. 12). God has already called Israel "my son" (Ex. 4:23). Implicitly, the son's mother is God (cf. Deut. 32:18; Isa. 42:14; 49:15; 66:13): Israel is his "firstborn." How could he, Moses, like a mother, provide enough sustenance for all people (Num. 11:13)? Paul also uses maternal language to describe his care for the church (Gal. 4:19; 1 Thess. 2:7).

"The land" (*ha'adamah*; Num. 11:12) is the first explicit reference in Numbers to the Promised Land. The Lord swore a covenant to give the land to Abram's offspring (Gen. 15:18; Num. 14:16, 23; 32:4), yet now Moses feels as if the burden of bringing them to Canaan is falling only on him. Moses pleads, "Kill me at once," if he be so treated by God (Num. 11:15). Jonah and Elijah make similar pleas (1 Kings 19:4; Jonah 4:8). Moses directs his complaint to God, not to the people. It is not unfounded, given the people's bitter reaction.

11:16–30 God has put Moses to the test. Now he responded to his servant's prayer. Seventy elders "shall bear [*nasa'*] the burden [*massa'*] of the people with you, so that you may not bear [*nasa'*] it yourself alone" (Num. 11:17; cf. vv. 11–15). Elders were part of Israel's socio-religious life in Egypt (e.g., Ex. 3:16). Seventy elders together with Moses, Aaron, and his sons witnessed the Sinai theophany and partook of the covenant meal (Ex. 24:9–11). "The whole congregation" often refers in practice to the elders (Lev. 4:13, 15). The seventy elders [LXX *presbyteroi*] of Israel are called in Exodus 24:9 LXX "the council [*gerousia*] of Israel"; *gerousia* refers to the seventy council members in Acts 5:21, the Sanhedrin. The apostles appoint "elders . . . (*presbyteroi*) in every church" (Acts 14:23; Titus 1:5).

The elders are also called "officers" (Num. 11:16, *shoterim*), the same term used for the "foremen" under the Egyptian taskmasters accountable for the Israelites' daily quota of bricks (Ex. 5:6–19). The LXX renders it "scribes" (*grammateus*), which also describes the "town clerk" of Ephesus (Acts 19:35). As record keepers (cf. Num. 11:26), these officers were probably among those who helped in the conscription census and subsequent military registers (cf. Deut. 20:5; 2 Chron. 26:11). Levites were among the *shoterim* (1 Chron. 23:4; 2 Chron. 19:11; 34:13).

The elders are to be gathered and taken (*laqakh*) to the tent of meeting (Num. 11:16), which refers to the tent outside the camp (cf. Ex. 33:7–11; 34:34–35). These elders are endowed with the Spirit. God's gifting them involves taking Moses' portion of the Spirit and distributing it among them (Num. 11:17; cf. Neh. 9:20). Moses is not left with less of the Spirit, nor do the elders receive fractions of what is taken from Moses. A candle flame used to light other candles does not diminish, nor are their flames lesser for having been so lit. Like Moses, none will lack spiritual endowment in proportion to his responsibilities. God's salvation is attested "by gifts of the Holy Spirit distributed according to his will" (Heb. 2:4). To Joshua's consternation, two men do "not [go] out to the tent" but nonetheless receive the Spirit (Num. 11:26). Afterward, Moses and the elders "returned to the camp" (v. 30).

The people are told to consecrate themselves (v. 18), involving purifying themselves by washing themselves and their clothes (cf. Gen. 35:2; Lev. 17:15). This is ominous (cf. Josh. 7:13), since the people have been rebellious in God's presence. Their words are turned into formal charges against them: they are rejecting (*ma'as*; Num. 11:20) the Lord, a word that occurs one more time in Numbers—for the land they reject (14:31).

Instead of the people's responding, Moses resumes his defense in 11:21. Since the Lord has assured the people they will eat meat, Moses responds by saying they outnumber his ability to provide; "six hundred thousand on foot" (*ragli*) refers to "foot soldiers" (11:21; cf. 1 Sam. 4:10; 1 Kings 20:29). In Exodus 12:37 *ragli*, distinguished from women and children, are "equipped for battle" (13:18). But, as they will soon see, the Lord is more than able to provide (Num. 11:23).

When the Spirit descends on the seventy elders, they prophesy (v. 25). Here and elsewhere prophesying is linked inextricably to God's Spirit (v. 26; 1 Sam. 10:6; 1 Kings 22:24; Mic. 3:8; Zech. 7:12; Acts 28:25; 2 Pet. 1:21; Rev. 19:10). However, this gift of prophecy is temporary (1 Sam. 10:10–13; 1 Cor. 13:8); "they did not continue doing it" (Num. 11:25; lit., "never again" or "no more," *velo' yosiphu*; e.g., Deut. 19:20; Judg. 8:28). The nature of their prophesying is unknown,[82] but they do not hold the office of prophet, as Moses does, along with the later canonical prophets.

It is not stated why "two men remained in the camp . . . Eldad . . . Medad" (Num. 11:26). "Registered" (v. 26) renders the same Hebrew word (*kethubim*; lit., "written") used for the Ten Commandments' being "written" on stone tablets (Ex.

---

[82] Keil believes it to be "speaking in an ecstatic and elevated state of mind . . . just like the 'speaking in tongues,' which frequently followed the gift of the Holy Ghost in the days of the apostles" ("Fourth Book of Moses," 70).

31:18; Deut. 9:10) and for the acts of kings' being formally "written" in the Book of the Chronicles of the Kings of Israel (e.g., 1 Kings 14:19). The use of this term for official records suggests that the Eldad and Medad hold high standing either as "men of the elders" from whom the seventy are appointed (Num. 11:24; cf. Ex. 24:9) or even as part of the seventy. "Seventy" may represent a quorum, like the Sanhedrin (cf. discussion above on Num. 11:16), with the two men as designated replacements, which may explain why "they had not gone they out to the tent" (v. 26) when the elders were summoned. Joshua's naming them to Moses proves them to be recognized figures (v. 28). They are perhaps considered part of the seventy, since the Spirit also rests upon them, and they prophesy.

"Joshua" (v. 28) appeared first in a military capacity (Ex. 17:9–10). He was Moses' "assistant" (from *sharat*; Ex. 24:13; 33:11; Josh. 1:1). The same Hebrew word refers to Elisha as Elijah's "assistant" (1 Kings 19:21) and to Elisha's "servant" (2 Kings 6:15). The Levites are similarly to "minister" (*sharat*) to the priests (Num. 3:6). Although no specific responsibilities are mentioned, the term connotes assisting a superior to accomplish a mission. Joshua has filled this role "from his youth" (11:28). He is also referred to as a "young man" (*na'ar*) in Exodus 33:11, where the term may have a vocational sense, "an apprentice." Jeremiah's pleading that he is but "a youth" (Jer. 1:6–7), may mean he is still an apprentice priest. Joshua is well suited to become Moses' successor (Num. 27:18–23).

11:31–35 "Wind" (v. 31) renders the Hebrew *ruakh*, which also signifies "Spirit" (v. 25). "Sprang up" (v. 31) is a rare sense (cf. Ps. 78:26) of the verb common in Numbers that is often translated "set out" or "journeyed" (*nasa'*; Num. 11:35; 20:22). In the exodus-Sinai pericope "the sea" is the Gulf of Suez, on the western side of the peninsula (cf. Ex. 14:2). After Sinai, "the sea" becomes the Gulf of Aqaba, on the eastern side of the peninsula, to the east of the Israelite camps. It was a southeasterly wind (Ps. 78:26) "from the LORD" that "brought quail" (cf. Ex. 16:13; Ps. 105:40) flying northward in the spring from the interior of Africa.[83]

The quail fall all around the camp (Num. 11:31, 32): "around" occurs regularly for the space outside the four sides of the tabernacle (e.g., 1:50). "On this side ... on the other side" translates *koh ... koh*; literally, "here ... there"). "About a day's journey" is a vague measure but could easily be 6–10 miles [10–16 km], perhaps more. Even if wind-driven quail flying over the peninsula at low altitude—"two cubits" (about 3 feet [90 cm])—is a natural seasonal phenomenon, the precise timing, their flight trajectory, and concentrated vast quantities are supernatural. The protracted time the people gather quail—"all that day and all night and all the next day" (v. 32)—and the quantity gathered reveal their craving for meat (cf. comment on 11:4–10 [at v. 4]). "Those who gathered least gathered ten homers" (about 60 bushels [2,015 L]) of quail, which suggests that those who gather do so on behalf of households consisting of three or four generations. "They spread them out" to cure the meat by the effects of the bright sun and dry air circulation.

---
83 Keil, "Second Book of Moses," in *Pentateuch*, 67; "Fourth Book of Moses," 72.

Two circumstantial clauses are juxtaposed: "While the meat was yet between their teeth" and "Before it was consumed" (v. 33). "Consumed" (from *karat*)—the same verb meaning "to be cut off" from one's people (e.g., 9:13) or "to cut down" a vine (13:23)—here means to "cut" the meat by chewing, which anticipates the consequence. The Lord's anger erupts after they bite ("between their teeth") the meat and before it is thoroughly chewed ("consumed"). The sentence was already pronounced in 11:20: "It comes out at your nostrils and becomes loathsome [or "nauseating," *zara*'] to you." The language evokes violent vomiting. Although the Lord has shown forbearance "a whole month" (v. 20), the sentence is now executed: "And the LORD struck down the people with a very great plague" (v. 33; cf. Ps. 106:15). The words "struck down" (*nakah*) and "plague" (*makkah*, from *nakah*) are also used for the plagues with which the Lord's struck Egypt (e.g., Ex. 3:20; 12:13). "Kibroth-hattaavah" fittingly means "the graves of craving," so named "because there they buried the people who had the craving" (Num. 11:34). As with Tombstone, Arizona, a toponym is coined.

Response

Satan is portrayed as a roaring lion seeking someone to devour (1 Pet. 5:8). In hunt a lion isolates its prey or goes after what is separated from the herd, often the weak or young. Those who complain in the Taberah incident (Num. 11:1–3) isolate themselves from God's people in the camp and distance themselves from the means of grace afforded by the tabernacle. This incidence serves as a reminder of the importance of fellowship and worship as principal means to escape the Devil's onslaught.

In his comment on Numbers 11:33 Augustine writes, "To some, indeed, who lack patience, the Lord God in his wrath grants them what they ask, just as in his mercy, on the other hand, he refused it to the apostle. We read what and how the Israelites asked and received, but when their lust had been satisfied, their lack of patience was severely punished."[84]

NUMBERS 12

12 Miriam and Aaron spoke against Moses because of the Cushite woman whom he had married, for he had married a Cushite woman. ² And they said, "Has the LORD indeed spoken only through Moses? Has he not spoken through us also?" And the LORD heard it. ³ Now the man Moses was very meek, more than all people who were on the face

---

84 Joseph T. Lienhard, ed., *Exodus, Leviticus, Numbers, Deuteronomy*, ACCS Old Testament 2, (Downers Grove, IL: InterVarsity Press, 2001), 219.

of the earth. ⁴And suddenly the Lord said to Moses and to Aaron and Miriam, "Come out, you three, to the tent of meeting." And the three of them came out. ⁵And the Lord came down in a pillar of cloud and stood at the entrance of the tent and called Aaron and Miriam, and they both came forward. ⁶And he said, "Hear my words: If there is a prophet among you, I the Lord make myself known to him in a vision; I speak with him in a dream. ⁷Not so with my servant Moses. He is faithful in all my house. ⁸With him I speak mouth to mouth, clearly, and not in riddles, and he beholds the form of the Lord. Why then were you not afraid to speak against my servant Moses?" ⁹And the anger of the Lord was kindled against them, and he departed.

¹⁰When the cloud removed from over the tent, behold, Miriam was leprous,¹ like snow. And Aaron turned toward Miriam, and behold, she was leprous. ¹¹And Aaron said to Moses, "Oh, my lord, do not punish us² because we have done foolishly and have sinned. ¹²Let her not be as one dead, whose flesh is half eaten away when he comes out of his mother's womb." ¹³And Moses cried to the Lord, "O God, please heal her—please." ¹⁴But the Lord said to Moses, "If her father had but spit in her face, should she not be shamed seven days? Let her be shut outside the camp seven days, and after that she may be brought in again." ¹⁵So Miriam was shut outside the camp seven days, and the people did not set out on the march till Miriam was brought in again. ¹⁶After that the people set out from Hazeroth, and camped in the wilderness of Paran.

¹ *Leprosy* was a term for several skin diseases; see Leviticus 13 ² Hebrew *do not lay sin upon us*

Section Overview

The people's contention with Moses (Numbers 11) is followed by that of his siblings (ch. 12). Miriam and Aaron contest Moses' primacy as the Lord's spokesman. Their remonstrance has far-reaching implications. Is Moses' mediatory role unique, not only as prophet but also as founder and head of the theocratic kingdom of Israel under the old covenant? As instigator of the crises, Miriam perhaps confuses her prophetic gift with Moses' office of prophet.

Section Outline

II. Trials in the Wilderness of Paran, the Transjordan Highlands, and the Plains of Moab (11:1–25:18) . . .
   B. Miriam's and Aaron's Contention with Moses (12:1–16)
      1. The Complaint (12:1–3)
      2. The Lord's Reply and Remonstrance (12:4–10)
      3. Aaron's Confession, Moses' Plea, and Travel Resumed (12:11–16)

Comment

12:1–3 "Miriam and Aaron spoke against Moses" (Num. 12:1; lit., "Miriam spoke [fem. sg. vb.] and Aaron." Miriam apparently persuaded her brother to join her. This is not the first time Aaron has been swayed to challenge his brother (cf. Ex.

32:22–23). Moses "had married" a "Cushite woman" (Num. 12:1). Traditionally "Cushite" is understood as Ethiopian (LXX, Vulg.), thus someone with dark skin (cf. Jer. 13:23).[85] "Cushite" may, however, refer to Zipporah, from a Midianite tribe (Ex. 2:21) of Cushan (cf. Hab. 3:7), a tribe also known from Egyptian and Assyrian texts, living south of Canaan.[86] It is unlikely that Moses has divorced Zipporah and remarried.[87] True, Moses "had sent her" (Ex. 18:2, ESV adds "home"), and "to send" is the technical term for divorce (Deut. 24:1–4), but this was only for the time he was in Egypt confronting Pharaoh, after which time she rejoined him (Ex. 18:6).

The reason for the complaint against Moses' wife's ethnicity is unstated. It is perhaps connected to the foreign contingent's involvement in the Taberah and Kibroth-hattaavah incidents (cf. comment on 11:4–10). Moreover, the connection between Miriam's and Aaron's contention concerning Moses' wife and what follows is not clear. But for older siblings, especially a sister, to challenge their younger brother's choice in marriage is certainly a way of getting his attention.

Miriam and Aaron challenge Moses' prophetic prerogative, and thus his unique mediatory role as God's spokesman (12:2). After all, Miriam is a worship leader and a prophetess (Ex. 15:20), and Aaron is high priest. As a spokesman for Moses, he too is called a prophet (Ex. 7:1). "And the LORD heard it" is literally "and the LORD heard" (Num. 12:2). The expression as an independent clause without a complement occurs only here and at 11:1. Elsewhere the verb always has an object (e.g., "And the LORD heeded [heard] the voice"; 21:3). His having "heard" is ominous. Speaking against Moses in the Lord's hearing has dire consequences, as seen in chapter 11.

The text declares, "Now the man Moses was very meek" (12:3). His being "very meek" ('*anav*; or "humble") is the hallmark of his leadership. Moses never sought his high position (Ex. 3:10–12; 4:1, 10). His status is not the fulfillment of personal ambition. He has already proven his willingness to seek the advice and help of others (Num. 10:31) and to share leadership responsibilities (11:14, 16), and even the right to prophesy (11:29). In the face of this new challenge, he does not assert his authority. If he says anything, it is not recorded. As in the face of Korah's challenge, he knows the rebellion is ultimately against the Lord, and he leaves the Lord to intervene (16:11, 28–30). He practices what he preaches concerning personal vengeance (Deut. 32:35, 41; cf. Rom. 12:19; Heb. 10:30).

In the LXX the word here translated "meek" is the same used in the Beatitudes: "Blessed are the meek [*praus*], for they shall inherit the earth" (Matt. 5:5, echoing Ps. 37:11: "the meek ['*anav*; LXX *praus*] shall inherit the land"). Although Moses does not receive an inheritance in Canaan, he has an eternal one (Ps. 37:18; cf. Ps. 37:9, 22, 29). Paul speaks of his own humility (Acts 20:19), which is a Christian fruit (Eph. 4:2; Phil. 2:3; cf. Gal. 5:22–23). Peter reminds his readers that "God opposes the proud but gives grace to the humble" (*tapenos*; 1 Pet. 5:5), citing

---

85 So Noth, *Numbers*, 94; cf. Gray, *Numbers*, 121.
86 De Vaulx, *Les Nombres*, 159.
87 Whether the Cushite wife was Zipporah or another woman remains much debated. Cf. Bush, *Book of Numbers*, 170–171; Ashley, *Book of Numbers*, 223–224. Levine, *Numbers 1–20*, 328.

Proverbs 3:34, where "humble" (*'anav*; LXX *tapenos*) renders the same Hebrew word used in Numbers 12:3.

12:4–10 "Suddenly" (*pith'om*; v. 4) occurs elsewhere in the Pentateuch at 6:9. "Come out ... to the tent of meeting" (12:4) suggests a location outside the camp. The order anticipates Miriam's becoming leprous, requiring quarantine in order not to defile the tabernacle (5:2–3; cf. 2 Chron. 26:19–20). That "the LORD came down" (Num. 12:5)—here "in a pillar of cloud" and before "in the cloud" (11:25; Ex. 34:5)—is an expression of his condescension and accommodation (cf. Gen. 11:5; Ex. 19:20).

The syntax of part of Numbers 12:6 is difficult: "If there is a prophet among you, I the LORD ..." reads literally "If there is your prophet the Lord in a vision to him I will make myself known." The reading "your prophet" (MT)[88] may refer to some prophet envisaged by Miriam and Aaron, or by the people, in contrast to "my servant Moses" (v. 7). The Lord has never said there is no other prophet. Miriam herself is a "prophetess" (Ex. 15:20), and the seventy elders prophesy (Num. 11:25). But a distinction is drawn between revelatory modes. With another prophet, the Lord reveals himself to him "in a vision ... in a dream" (Num. 12:6) or "in riddles" (v. 8). "Not so" (v. 7) with Moses, to whom he speaks "mouth to mouth" (v. 8) and whom he knows "face to face" (Deut. 34:10).

Hence the prophet Moses is not like other prophets, in that the revelatory mode to him is objective speech and audible communication, not subject to the interpretation of visions or dreams known only to the prophets themselves. If a dream were prophetic of the future and accompanied by a sign, its authenticity and veracity would have to be tested and proven (Deut. 13:1–2; 18:22). There is necessarily a more subjective element in that kind of revelatory mode. In addition, prophetic visions and dreams are generally given for special circumstances and times. In the history of revelation the Torah of Moses is the foundation upon which all subsequent writing prophets build (Mal. 4:4).[89]

In addition, Moses' mediatorial ministry is unique: "He is faithful in all my house" (Num. 12:7), or "In all my house he (alone/only) is authorized/established [*ne'eman*]," as Samuel is "established" as the Lord's prophet (1 Sam. 3:20) and David's throne is "established" (Ps. 89:35–37). As mediator, Moses represents the people before God and God before the people. Hence Moses is not only the chief among prophets; he surpasses them as the founder of the theocracy and the mediator of the Sinai covenant.

Given the unique way the Lord speaks to Moses and Moses' preeminence as covenant mediator in the Israelite economy, "Why then were you not afraid to speak against my servant Moses?" (Num. 12:8; cf. Heb. 3:5). This interrogation is a charge against Miriam and Aaron for their error. "My servant" (Num. 12:7, 8) is a title also ascribed to Abraham (Gen. 26:24), Caleb (Num. 14:24), David (e.g.,

---

[88] The LXX renders "Your [pl] prophet" (*nebi'akem*) as "a prophet of you"; the Vulgate reads "a prophet among you" (both reflecting a reading *nabi' bakem*). In this they are followed by many modern versions (e.g., ESV).
[89] R. Bergey, "Le cantique de Moïse: son reflet dans le prisme du canon des Ecritures," *RRef* 54/3 (2003): 76–98; Bergey, "The Song of Moses (Dt 32.1–43) and Isaianic Prophecies: A Case of Early Intertextuality," *JSOT* 28/1 (2003): 33–54.

2 Sam. 3:18), and his coming descendant (Isa. 42:1; 53:11), that is, Christ (Matt. 12:18, citing Isa. 42:1).

"The anger of the LORD was kindled" (Num. 12:9). Serious offenders kindle it, as those weeping over the manna (cf. 11:10), the rebellious exodus generation at Kadesh (32:10, 12), the lascivious idolaters at Baal-peor (25:3), and even Moses himself for resisting God's call to go to Pharaoh (Ex. 4:14). Now it is kindled against Miriam and Aaron. Before his anger manifests itself, the Lord departs (Num. 12:9) and the cloud is "removed" (v. 10) because Miriam becomes "leprous" (v. 10), an uncleanness incompatible with the Lord's holy manifested presence (5:3; 35:34). His departure spares Miriam and Aaron far worse consequences. Ultimately it is their sin that drives him away.

12:11–16 Upon seeing Miriam's condition Aaron immediately confesses, "We have done foolishly and have sinned" (v. 11). As brother and high priest he appeals to Moses, "let . . . not" (or "please [*na'*; cf. v. 13] do not let") Miriam's condition run its debilitating course (v. 12). Moses immediately "cries out" (*tsa'aq*; v. 13; cf. Gen. 27:34; Num. 11:2) to God. Aaron tacitly recognizes Moses unique mediatorial role, and he immediately exercises it. By his reply the Lord implicitly assures Moses that Miriam will be healed but must be "outside the camp seven days" (12:14), the quarantine duration for her condition (Lev. 13:4; cf. Num. 5:2). To spit in someone's face (Num. 12:14) is a sign of disgrace (Deut. 25:9; Job 17:6; Isa. 50:6; Matt. 27:30), which she must endure for seven days. However, she is not left behind: "The people did not set out on the march till Miriam was brought in again" (Num. 12:15). The Israelites are here at Hazeroth at least seven days (v. 14) before moving on to the Wilderness of Paran (v. 16). The next step will be scouting out the Promised Land (13:17), for which the wilderness of Paran, with the base at Kadesh, becomes mission control (13:26; 20:1; 32:8). There is abundant pastureland and water for flocks there (1 Sam. 25:1–2).

Response

"Moses was very meek" (Num. 12:3). Meekness is not weakness but a sign of strength. It takes courage to admit insufficiencies, inabilities, and need of help. Should meekness be considered weakness, an apt response would be that Christ's "power is made perfect in weakness" (2 Cor. 12:9).

Moses is "faithful in all my house" (Num. 12:7). The book of Hebrews refers to this verse ("Just as Moses also was faithful in all God's house"; Heb. 3:2) to contrast God's people living under Moses' Sinai covenant headship with life under Christ's new covenant headship ("But Christ is faithful over God's house as a son. And we are his house"; Heb. 3:6). Paul speaks of the "household of God, which is the church of the living God" (1 Tim. 3:15). The "living God" is an expression applied to the God who is unique since he speaks to a people who are unique because they hear his voice (Deut. 5:26). Paul's mention of the living God is bracketed by an exhortation toward "how one ought to behave" in the church and a declaration that the church is a "pillar and buttress of the truth" (1 Tim. 3:15). As under the Sinai covenant, the house under the new covenant is only as strong as its supporting pillar and buttress, both objectively in doctrine and subjectively in purity of life.

NUMBERS 13

13 The Lord spoke to Moses, saying, ² "Send men to spy out the land of Canaan, which I am giving to the people of Israel. From each tribe of their fathers you shall send a man, every one a chief among them." ³ So Moses sent them from the wilderness of Paran, according to the command of the Lord, all of them men who were heads of the people of Israel. ⁴ And these were their names: From the tribe of Reuben, Shammua the son of Zaccur; ⁵ from the tribe of Simeon, Shaphat the son of Hori; ⁶ from the tribe of Judah, Caleb the son of Jephunneh; ⁷ from the tribe of Issachar, Igal the son of Joseph; ⁸ from the tribe of Ephraim, Hoshea the son of Nun; ⁹ from the tribe of Benjamin, Palti the son of Raphu; ¹⁰ from the tribe of Zebulun, Gaddiel the son of Sodi; ¹¹ from the tribe of Joseph (that is, from the tribe of Manasseh), Gaddi the son of Susi; ¹² from the tribe of Dan, Ammiel the son of Gemalli; ¹³ from the tribe of Asher, Sethur the son of Michael; ¹⁴ from the tribe of Naphtali, Nahbi the son of Vophsi; ¹⁵ from the tribe of Gad, Geuel the son of Machi. ¹⁶ These were the names of the men whom Moses sent to spy out the land. And Moses called Hoshea the son of Nun, Joshua.

¹⁷ Moses sent them to spy out the land of Canaan and said to them, "Go up into the Negeb and go up into the hill country, ¹⁸ and see what the land is, and whether the people who dwell in it are strong or weak, whether they are few or many, ¹⁹ and whether the land that they dwell in is good or bad, and whether the cities that they dwell in are camps or strongholds, ²⁰ and whether the land is rich or poor, and whether there are trees in it or not. Be of good courage and bring some of the fruit of the land." Now the time was the season of the first ripe grapes.

²¹ So they went up and spied out the land from the wilderness of Zin to Rehob, near Lebo-hamath. ²² They went up into the Negeb and came to Hebron. Ahiman, Sheshai, and Talmai, the descendants of Anak, were there. (Hebron was built seven years before Zoan in Egypt.) ²³ And they came to the Valley of Eshcol and cut down from there a branch with a single cluster of grapes, and they carried it on a pole between two of them; they also brought some pomegranates and figs. ²⁴ That place was called the Valley of Eshcol,¹ because of the cluster that the people of Israel cut down from there.

²⁵ At the end of forty days they returned from spying out the land. ²⁶ And they came to Moses and Aaron and to all the congregation of the people of Israel in the wilderness of Paran, at Kadesh. They brought back word to them and to all the congregation, and showed them the fruit of the land. ²⁷ And they told him, "We came to the land to which you sent us. It

flows with milk and honey, and this is its fruit. ²⁸ However, the people who dwell in the land are strong, and the cities are fortified and very large. And besides, we saw the descendants of Anak there. ²⁹ The Amalekites dwell in the land of the Negeb. The Hittites, the Jebusites, and the Amorites dwell in the hill country. And the Canaanites dwell by the sea, and along the Jordan."

³⁰ But Caleb quieted the people before Moses and said, "Let us go up at once and occupy it, for we are well able to overcome it." ³¹ Then the men who had gone up with him said, "We are not able to go up against the people, for they are stronger than we are." ³² So they brought to the people of Israel a bad report of the land that they had spied out, saying, "The land, through which we have gone to spy it out, is a land that devours its inhabitants, and all the people that we saw in it are of great height. ³³ And there we saw the Nephilim (the sons of Anak, who come from the Nephilim), and we seemed to ourselves like grasshoppers, and so we seemed to them."

¹ *Eshcol* means *cluster*

Section Overview

Of the over eighty references to the Land of Promise in Numbers, all but two (10:9; 11:12) occur in 13:1–36:13.[90] Many are concentrated in chapters 13–14, dealing with the reconnaissance of Canaan and its aftermath.

Moses sends scouts to reconnoiter the land of Canaan (13:2). They are given a list of things to learn about the land (vv. 18–20). Upon their return they give their report. Unanimously they declare the land to be good, but for a majority its occupants and their defenses are too strong to overcome (vv. 27–29, 31–33). Caleb and Joshua dissent passionately (v. 30).

Section Outline

II. Trials in the Wilderness of Paran, the Transjordan Highlands, and the Plains of Moab (11:1–25:18) . . .

　　C. Scouting the Land of Canaan (Num. 13:1–33)

　　　　1. Commissioning the Scouts (13:1–20)

　　　　2. Sending the Scouts (13:21–24)

　　　　3. Return and Report of the Scouts (13:25–33)

Comment

13:1–20 The Lord gives Moses the order: "Send men" (v. 2). According to Deuteronomy, after Moses orders the people to go and take possession of the land, the people request him to send scouts to explore it (Deut. 1:21–23). The Lord apparently accommodates this demand. As with the quail incident, he grants their request, but in fulfilling their desire the people meet disaster (Num. 11:18–20, 33; Ps. 106:15). Those sent are "a man" from "each tribe," each a "chief" (Num. 13:2)

---

[90] Cf. David J. A. Clines, *The Theme of the Pentateuch*, JSOTSup 10 (Sheffield: JSOT Press, 1978), 39–40; cf. also his comments on the land-promise theme in Numbers (53–57).

and all "heads" of the people (v. 3). The latter is specified in Moses' blessing: "Thus the LORD became king in Jeshurun, when the *heads* of the people were gathered, all the tribes of Israel together" (Deut. 33:5). Divine lordship is exercised by these heads but under Moses as "ruler and redeemer" (Acts 7:35). These chiefs will lead the tribes into divine judgment.

The Lord's command specifies the purpose: "to spy out" (*tur*; cf. Num. 13:16, 17, 21, 25, 32), that is, "to scout/reconnoiter," as it is not done clandestinely (cf. 10:33; *tur*, "seek out"). In Hebrew "to spy out" (cf. the spies sent to Jericho) is a different verb (a form of *ragal*; Josh. 6:22). Another verb (*hapar*) describes the actions both here in Canaan ("explore"; Deut. 1:22) and later at Jericho ("search out"; Josh. 2:2; cf. Judg. 18:2, *ragal* ["to spy"] and *haqar* ["to explore"]). "The land of Canaan" occurs twelve times in Numbers. The earlier promise ("I will give"; Num. 10:29) is now in the present tense ("Which I am giving to the people of Israel"; 13:2; cf. 11:12). The land belongs to the Lord (Lev. 25:23), but he grants Israel usufruct rights, privileges, and responsibilities.

Moses sends the spies "from the wilderness of Paran" (Num. 13:3), more precisely from Kadesh-barnea (32:8; Deut. 1:2). The "names" of the men, one from each tribe (Num. 13:4–16), include none of those in preceding lists (1:5–15; 7:12–83). Two of them stand out, "from the tribe of Judah, Caleb" (13:6) and "from the tribe of Ephraim, Hoshea the son of Nun" (v. 8). The text notes that "Moses called Hoshea the son of Nun, Joshua" (v. 16), a change from "he saves" (*hoshe'a*) to "Yahweh saves" (*yehoshu'a*). Jesus (from *yeshu'a*) is an abridged form of the same name.

The spies are to "go up into the Negeb" (v. 17). Stretching some 60 miles (100 km) northward from Kadesh, the Negeb (meaning "dry") is a geographically well-defined semiarid region, here situated between the wilderness of Paran and the southern Judean "hill country" (v. 17; Josh. 11:21). The Negeb has always had a dimorph culture, with both agricultural and pastoral production, as illustrated by Isaac, who was both herdsman and husbandman in the northern Negeb (Gen. 26:12, 20) and today by the combination of fellahin (farmers) and shepherds.[91] It supported a sizable population in biblical times (Josh. 15:21–32). The Israelites were in and around the Negeb during much of the wilderness sojourn.

Numbers 13:18–20 defines the mission. Its scope is tactical and demographical (to learn whether the people are "strong or weak ... few or many"), martial (to determine whether the cities are "camps or strongholds," that is, unwalled or walled), and agricultural (to see if the land is "good or bad ... rich or poor" with "trees ... or not"). They should return with "some of the fruit of the land."

The reconnaissance begins in the "season of the first ripe grapes" (v. 20), around mid- to late-July or early August. Returning "forty days" later (v. 25) enables the twelve to return with a weighty cluster of grapes, figs, and pomegranates (v. 23) harvested toward the end of summer. This timeframe fits other chronological

---

[91] N. Glueck, *Rivers in the Desert: A History of the Negeb* (New York: Norton Library, 1959), 55, 181, 213. In the poorer areas of the Paran and Zin wildernesses are remains of ancient agriculture in the valleys (Har-El, *Sinai Journeys*, 337).

indices. Israel leaves Sinai on the twentieth day of the second month (10:11). The people spend at least a month at Kibroth-hattaavah (11:20), followed by seven days at Hazeroth (12:15–16). The travel time between those two sites and between Hazeroth and Kadesh is unknown.[92] But the earliest Israel could have arrived at Kadesh is in the fourth month (June–July). The forty-day reconnaissance would end sometime in the sixth month (August–September), the end of the summer harvest.

13:21–24 The narrative apparently combines the reconnaissance of two scouting groups. Verses 21–22 present two departure points, each with a specific destination in two widely separated regions, one extending to the northern extremity of Canaan and the other in the south. Leaving "from the wilderness of Paran" (v. 3), one group "went up into the Negeb and came to Hebron" (v. 22). Hebron is about 75 miles (120 km) north-northeast of Kadesh. The second group "went up ... from the wilderness of Zin to Rehob, near Lebo-hamath" (v. 21). The "wilderness of Zin" (v. 21) forms Canaan's southeastern border, contiguous with Edomite territory west of the Arabah (Num. 34:3; Josh. 15:1). It includes the Negeb highlands north of Nahal Zin. In Numbers Kadesh is in the wilderness of Paran (Num. 13:26) and the wilderness of Zin (20:1; 27:14; 33:36). Either Kadesh lay on the border of the Zin and Paran wildernesses, or else Zin formed the northern part of the greater Paran wilderness.[93] Israel's arrival at Kadesh from Sinai is linked to the Paran wilderness. The heading from Kadesh in a northerly direction is linked, as here, to the Zin wilderness (also cf. 20:1, 22; 21:1). "Rehob" is probably Beth-rehob (Judg. 18:28) in Dan rather than Rehob in Asher (Judg. 1:31).[94] About 200 miles (320 km) to the north of Kadesh, Lebo-hamath is the northern limit of Canaan (Judg. 3:3; 1 Kings 8:65; Amos 6:14). Leaving from the Zin wilderness, the scouts probably go northward via the Jordan Valley.

Anak's forefather Arba founded the city of Kiriath-arba (or Hebron; Josh. 21:11), and the three Anakite clans (of Ahiman, Sheshai, and Talmai) settled there before Caleb drove them out (Josh. 14:15; Judg. 1:20). The patronym "Anak" also refers to their impressive stature (Num. 13:33; Deut. 9:2). The Anakites lived mainly in the southern hill country but some settled on the coastal plain (Josh. 11:21–22). Hebron had a lengthy history even then, being built "seven years before Zoan" (Num. 13:22). Abraham bought a burial place for Sarah at Hebron, his only foothold in the Promised Land, in the days when it was known as Kiriath-arba (Gen. 23:2, 19–20). "Zoan" was one of the locations where God worked wonders in Egypt (Ps. 78:12, 43), so this historical note is perhaps a way of reminding the people that

---

[92] Travel distances measured in days—here the eleven-day journey between Horeb and Kadesh (Deut. 1:2)—refer to military or merchant-travel times. The Israelites' travel is slow, given their flocks and herds, their young and aged, and their heavily laden ox-drawn wagons. At least twenty travel days are needed to cover 120 miles (200 km) between Sin Bisher (on this identification with Mount Sinai in the western peninsula cf. Section Overview of Numbers 33; comment on 33:1–15 [at v. 15]) and Kadesh. This estimate is based on the rate of Bedouins moving camp with families and animals of 6 miles (10 km) per day (cf. Har-El, *Sinai Journeys*, 424).
[93] Denis Baly, *The Geography of the Bible: A Study in Historical Geography*, rev. ed. (New York: Harper & Row, 1974), 247, 250–251.
[94] Gray, *Numbers*, 140. Rehob in Asher was probably on the coastal plain of Acco; Yohanan Aharoni, *The Land of the Bible: A Historical Geography*, trans. A. F. Rainey, rev. ed. (Philadelphia: Westminster, 1979), 235, 281n135.

God has not forgotten his promise to Abraham and his descendants concerning the land to which they are now coming.

The "valley of Eshcol" (13:23) is perhaps Nahal Hebron, which joins Nahal Beersheba in the Negeb. Apart from the Jordan River, the land contains only wadis (seasonal streams). Irrigation is difficult (though possible by constructing dams in wadi beds), and so Canaan's fruitfulness depends almost entirely on seasonal precipitation (Deut. 11:10–11, 14; Joel 2:23). The fruit samples the scouts pick—grapes, pomegranates, and figs—are tangible proofs of its fertileness. The "pole" (*mot*) for carrying the grape cluster is the same word for the "carrying frame" used for transporting various tabernacle objects (Num. 4:10, 12). The place is given the name "Valley of Eshcol" because of the cluster ('*eshkol*) the spies bring back (13:24).

13:25–33 Mention of the "end of forty days" (v. 25) is a harbinger of the scouts' bad report (v. 32; cf. 14:34). Forty days is sufficient time to reconnoiter the land and to return to the base at Kadesh (13:26), a round trip of roughly 400 miles (650 km) on a straight line from Lebo-hamath to Kadesh. Kadesh occurs ten times in Numbers (13:26; 20:1, 14, 16, 22; 27:14; 33:36, 37; including Kadesh-barnea, 32:8; 34:4; on both identifications cf. comment on 33:18b–36 [at v. 36]).

The scouts go in two groups to Canaan, each with a designated itinerary. Their demographic report also reflects this dual objective. The scouts who go to Hebron report on the peoples of the Negeb and the hill country. Those who go to Rehob report on the inhabitants of the Jordan Valley and the coastal plain. If they went north by way of the Jordan Valley, they may have returned by the coastal plain. Moreover, each group reports on the peoples they have encountered, who characteristically live either in the Negeb and the hill country or in the plains and valleys (cf. Deut. 1:7; Josh. 5:1; 9:1; 11:3). The scouts' report is well founded. They give proof that the land agriculturally "flows with milk and honey" (Num. 13:27). This expression may summarize two principal economic forms, "milk"—dairy products from flocks and herds—and "honey" (Hb. *debash*)—fruit confiture (Arabic *dipsh*) from trees and vines. They also report on the military situation ("the people . . . are strong, and their cities are fortified and very large . . . the descendants of Anak"; v. 28), introduced with an expression to counter the testimony of the bountiful land ("however"; '*epes-ki*). The "Hittites" (v. 29) associated with the Amorites are probably not Anatolians (who occupy the region of modern Turkey) but more likely Hethites, descendants of Canaan (Gen. 10:15). Esau's Hittite wives were Canaanites (Gen. 36:2; cf. 26:34; 28:8). Linguistically the descendants of "Heth" (*heth*) were called "Hittites" (*hitti*). Ethnically, they were Hethite Canaanites (cf. Ezek. 16:3).

Caleb offers a minority report arguing in favor of military action (Num. 13:30), countering the majority viewpoint. "Go up" ('*alah*) in a military context means "mount an attack" (e.g., Josh. 6:5; 2 Sam. 5:19). He knows that delayed obedience is rebellion's foothold. "Occupy it" (*yarash*) is to be understood as first "dispossessing" the land's inhabitants (Num. 33:55), then taking possession of it (33:53). The other scouts repeat their initial claim: "We are not able to go up against the people, for they are stronger than we are" (13:31). Their comparison "we ... they" shows them to be depending on their own strength rather than God's. Their lack of faith distorts their view. Before it was a bountiful land. Now it is a "land that devours its inhabitants" (v. 32; cf. v. 27), as by drought or locusts (2 Chron. 7:13), ending in famine and pestilence (Ezek. 7:15).

The absence of faith falsely magnifies the strength of its inhabitants: "All the people that we saw in it are of great height.... We saw the Nephilim (the sons of Anak, who come from the Nephilim), and we seemed to ourselves like grasshoppers, and so we seemed to them" (Num. 13:32–33). The "Nephilim" were like the antediluvians who through their power and influence encouraged social decadence (Gen. 6:4–5). Rather than viewing the land and its inhabitants in the light of God's promises, as did Caleb, the other spies' eyes are blinded by a heart of unbelief.

Response

Instead of exercising faith, the scouts' unbelief prevents them from seeing the land as theirs. Faith sees what the eye does not nor cannot (2 Cor. 5:7; cf. 4:18). This sight is gained by the optics of the promises of God. Bishop Joseph Hall (1574–1656) remarked, "What needed they doubt of obtaining that which God promised to give? When we will send our senses to be our scouts in matters of faith, and rather dare trust men than God, we are worthy to be deceived." He added, "When we measure our spiritual success by our own power, we are vanquished before we fight. He that would overcome must neither look upon his own arm, nor the arm of his enemy, but to the mouth and hand of him that hath promised and can perform."[95]

NUMBERS 14

14 Then all the congregation raised a loud cry, and the people wept that night. ² And all the people of Israel grumbled against Moses and Aaron. The whole congregation said to them, "Would that we had died in the land of Egypt! Or would that we had died in this wilderness! ³ Why is the Lord bringing us into this land, to fall by the sword? Our wives and our little ones will become a prey. Would it not be better for us to go back to Egypt?" ⁴ And they said to one another, "Let us choose a leader and go back to Egypt."

⁵ Then Moses and Aaron fell on their faces before all the assembly of the congregation of the people of Israel. ⁶ And Joshua the son of Nun and Caleb the son of Jephunneh, who were among those who had spied out the land, tore their clothes ⁷ and said to all the congregation of the people of Israel, "The land, which we passed through to spy it out, is an exceed-

---

[95] Cited by Bush, *Book of Numbers*, 181, 193.

ingly good land. ⁸ If the Lord delights in us, he will bring us into this land and give it to us, a land that flows with milk and honey. ⁹ Only do not rebel against the Lord. And do not fear the people of the land, for they are bread for us. Their protection is removed from them, and the Lord is with us; do not fear them." ¹⁰ Then all the congregation said to stone them with stones. But the glory of the Lord appeared at the tent of meeting to all the people of Israel.

¹¹ And the Lord said to Moses, "How long will this people despise me? And how long will they not believe in me, in spite of all the signs that I have done among them? ¹² I will strike them with the pestilence and disinherit them, and I will make of you a nation greater and mightier than they."

¹³ But Moses said to the Lord, "Then the Egyptians will hear of it, for you brought up this people in your might from among them, ¹⁴ and they will tell the inhabitants of this land. They have heard that you, O Lord, are in the midst of this people. For you, O Lord, are seen face to face, and your cloud stands over them and you go before them, in a pillar of cloud by day and in a pillar of fire by night. ¹⁵ Now if you kill this people as one man, then the nations who have heard your fame will say, ¹⁶ 'It is because the Lord was not able to bring this people into the land that he swore to give to them that he has killed them in the wilderness.' ¹⁷ And now, please let the power of the Lord be great as you have promised, saying, ¹⁸ 'The Lord is slow to anger and abounding in steadfast love, forgiving iniquity and transgression, but he will by no means clear the guilty, visiting the iniquity of the fathers on the children, to the third and the fourth generation.' ¹⁹ Please pardon the iniquity of this people, according to the greatness of your steadfast love, just as you have forgiven this people, from Egypt until now."

²⁰ Then the Lord said, "I have pardoned, according to your word. ²¹ But truly, as I live, and as all the earth shall be filled with the glory of the Lord, ²² none of the men who have seen my glory and my signs that I did in Egypt and in the wilderness, and yet have put me to the test these ten times and have not obeyed my voice, ²³ shall see the land that I swore to give to their fathers. And none of those who despised me shall see it. ²⁴ But my servant Caleb, because he has a different spirit and has followed me fully, I will bring into the land into which he went, and his descendants shall possess it. ²⁵ Now, since the Amalekites and the Canaanites dwell in the valleys, turn tomorrow and set out for the wilderness by the way to the Red Sea."

²⁶ And the Lord spoke to Moses and to Aaron, saying, ²⁷ "How long shall this wicked congregation grumble against me? I have heard the grumblings of the people of Israel, which they grumble against me. ²⁸ Say to them, 'As I live, declares the Lord, what you have said in my hearing I will do to you: ²⁹ your dead bodies shall fall in this wilderness, and of all your number, listed in the census from twenty years old and upward, who have grumbled against me, ³⁰ not one shall come into the land where I swore that I would make you dwell, except Caleb the son of Jephunneh and Joshua the son of Nun. ³¹ But your little ones, who you said would become a prey, I will bring in, and they shall know the land that you have rejected. ³² But as for you, your dead bodies shall fall in this wilderness. ³³ And your children shall be shepherds in the wilderness forty years and shall suffer for your faithlessness, until the last of your dead bodies lies in the wilderness. ³⁴ According to the number of the days in which you spied out the land, forty days, a year for each day, you shall bear your iniquity forty years, and

you shall know my displeasure.' ³⁵ I, the Lord, have spoken. Surely this will I do to all this wicked congregation who are gathered together against me: in this wilderness they shall come to a full end, and there they shall die."

³⁶ And the men whom Moses sent to spy out the land, who returned and made all the congregation grumble against him by bringing up a bad report about the land— ³⁷ the men who brought up a bad report of the land—died by plague before the Lord. ³⁸ Of those men who went to spy out the land, only Joshua the son of Nun and Caleb the son of Jephunneh remained alive.

³⁹ When Moses told these words to all the people of Israel, the people mourned greatly. ⁴⁰ And they rose early in the morning and went up to the heights of the hill country, saying, "Here we are. We will go up to the place that the Lord has promised, for we have sinned." ⁴¹ But Moses said, "Why now are you transgressing the command of the Lord, when that will not succeed? ⁴² Do not go up, for the Lord is not among you, lest you be struck down before your enemies. ⁴³ For there the Amalekites and the Canaanites are facing you, and you shall fall by the sword. Because you have turned back from following the Lord, the Lord will not be with you." ⁴⁴ But they presumed to go up to the heights of the hill country, although neither the ark of the covenant of the Lord nor Moses departed out of the camp. ⁴⁵ Then the Amalekites and the Canaanites who lived in that hill country came down and defeated them and pursued them, even to Hormah.

Section Overview

Upon hearing the scouts' negative reconnaissance report regarding Canaan (Numbers 13), the people revolt (14:1–10). The Lord threatens to destroy them, but Moses' intercessory prayer staves off his immediate judgment (vv. 11–19). The people are forgiven, but the exodus generation, twenty years old and upward, is condemned to die in the wilderness (vv. 20–38). The ensuing presumptuous attempt to enter Canaan is thwarted by an Amalekite and Canaanite coalition (vv. 39–45).

Section Outline

II. Trials in the Wilderness of Paran, the Transjordan Highlands, and the Plains of Moab (11:1–25:18)...
   D. The Aftermath of the Scouts' Report (14:1–45)
      1. Immediate Reaction to the Scouts' Report (14:1–10)
      2. The Lord's Initial Response and Moses' Intercession (14:11–19)
      3. The Lord's Answer to Moses' Prayer (14:20–25)
      4. His Sentence Pronounced (14:26–38)
      5. Aborted Attempt to Enter the Promised Land (14:39–45)

Comment

14:1–10 The syntax of verse 1 is peculiar. It literally reads, "And all the congregation raised [no object!] and they gave their voice, and the people wept that night." In contexts of lament the normal expression is "lift up/raise one's voice and weep" (cf. Gen. 21:16; 27:38). "A loud cry" renders the Hebrew "they gave their voice," making it the object of "the congregation raised." The verb "raised" with no object could instead be like Habakkuk 1:3, rendered literally as "There is strife and contention; one lifts up." In this same sense "the congregation raised" could mean they rose up in dissension, which suits the context.

"Gave ... voice" followed by weeping is found also in Genesis 45:2 (lit., "Joseph gave his voice weeping"). Generally, "give" with the complement "voice" describes nonhuman sounds, such as a lion's roar (Amos 3:4), raging waters (Hab. 3:10), or a peal of thunder, particularly in a theophany (2 Sam. 22:14).[96] This suggests the "loud cry" is menacing, a tumultuous sound like that of an enemy breaching the walls of a city (Lam. 2:7). The next verse brings this out: Israel's grumbling is not merely complaining but is the voicing of rebellion (Num. 14:9). Grumbling against the leaders is grumbling against God (14:27, 29; 16:11; cf. Ex. 16:2, 8). The people had grumbled about water and food after leaving Egypt (Ex. 15:23–24; 16:2; 17:3; Num. 11:1–6). They had even rebelled at the Red Sea (Ps. 106:7)!

"Would that we had died in the land of Egypt! Or would that we had died in this wilderness!" (Num. 14:2) and "Would it not be better for us to go back to Egypt?" (v. 3) each recalls the people's reaction voiced earlier: "It would have been better for us to serve the Egyptians than to die in the wilderness" (Ex. 14:12); "Would that we had died by the hand of the LORD in the land of Egypt, when we sat by the meat pots and ate bread to the full, for you have brought us out into this wilderness to kill this whole assembly with hunger" (Ex. 16:3); "Why did you bring us up out of Egypt, to kill us and our children and our livestock with thirst?" (Ex. 17:3). Some among the generation that will enter Canaan also repeat the rebellious charge of the exodus generation: "Why have you brought us up out of Egypt to die in the wilderness? For there is no food and no water, and we loathe this worthless food" (Num. 21:5; cf. 20:29; 33:38). Their grumbling is fanned by the many obstacles they perceive in taking possession of Canaan. According to Nehemiah, "They ... appointed a leader to return to their slavery in Egypt" (9:17; cf. Num. 14:4). The Land of Promise is portrayed pejoratively as "this land."

In response Moses and Aaron "fell on their faces" (v. 5), while Joshua and Caleb "tore their clothes" (v. 6). Both are gestures of great distress (cf. 16:22; 20:6; Josh. 7:6). Joshua and Caleb remind the people that it is a good land and that God will give it to them (Num. 14:8). They exhort the people, "Only do not rebel" (*marad*; v. 9), as had the vassal kings against their Mesopotamian suzerain (Gen. 14:4). Israel's enemies are "bread for us" (Num. 14:9; cf. Ps. 14:4): defeated adversaries are often viewed as having been devoured (*'akal*; Num. 23:24; Deut. 32:42; Ps. 79:7).

The Hebrew word rendered "said" (*'amar*; Num. 14:10) here means "intend to," often with a view to harming someone (e.g., Ex. 2:14; 1 Sam. 30:6; 2 Chron. 28:10).[97] Stoning a superior is a sign of insurrection (1 Sam. 30:6; 1 Kings 12:18).

---

96 Cf. BDB 679b.
97 Cf. *CDCH*, s.v. אמר: "with [*le-*] + inf. of other verb, 'think, propose, threaten' to do something," citing Deuteronomy 9:25; 1 Kings 5:5 [5:19 MT]. Cf. also Gen. 4:8; Josh. 22:33; 2 Sam. 21:16; 2 Chron. 28:13; 32:1.

But before they can carry out their action, the glory of Yahweh appears (Num. 14:10). This first manifestation of his glory in Numbers, as elsewhere (16:19, 42; 20:6), is ominous as concerns the people. But it saves Moses and Aaron, and probably Joshua and Caleb too. The eternal Son is described as the "radiance of the glory of God" (Heb. 1:3).

14:11–19 Grumbling against the Lord's appointed leaders is rebellion (cf. comment on 14:1–10 [at v. 2]) that also despises the Lord, who appointed them (v. 11; cf. v. 23). To despise him is to despise his Word (cf. Isa. 1:4; 5:24). The people's unbelief is disobedience (Heb. 3:18–19). "Signs" (Num. 14:11) give evidence of God's power but in themselves do not produce faith (Luke 16:31; John 12:37; Rom. 10:17).

When God tells Moses that he will make of him "a nation greater and mightier than they" (Num. 14:12), this implies an adjustment of the promise that "Abraham shall surely become a great and mighty nation" (Gen. 18:18). The promise-lineage would then be traced through descendants of Levi rather than of Judah (Gen. 49:8–10; cf. comment on Num. 2:3–9 [at v. 3]; 10:11–28 [at v. 14]). This rouses Moses to take his stand in intercessory prayer, similar to his response to the golden calf incident. At that time, the Lord threatened to destroy Israel and make Moses into a great nation (Ex. 32:10), which drew Moses' intercession.

In his intercessory prayer (Num. 14:13–19) Moses first confronts the situation at hand with a threefold argument. First, God's honor is at stake. The "Egyptians" (v. 13), the "inhabitants of this land" (v. 14), and the "nations" (v. 15) will hear and say, "It is because the LORD was not able to bring this people into the land that he swore to give to them that he has killed them in the wilderness" (v. 16). Second, God should not violate his word: "As you have promised" (v. 17) in the very covenant made with Israel at Sinai and by the bestowal of blessing (cf. discussion on v. 12). Third, there is a way out: mercy would contradict neither his word nor his character, for "the LORD is slow to anger and abounding in steadfast love, forgiving iniquity and transgression" (v. 18). Appealing to the law covenant and to God's "abounding in steadfast love" in the same breath is saying, in Pauline terms, "The law came in to increase the trespass, but where sin increased, grace abounded all the more" (Rom. 5:20). Ultimately, grace or "steadfast love" (Hb. *hesed*) is salvific and freely shown, since a response to an appeal for *hesed* depends entirely on the Lord's ability and willingness to bestow it (cf. Pss. 6:4; 17:7; 40:10; 119:41; Isa. 54:10).[98] By praying that God "will by no means clear the guilty" (Num. 14:18b) after confessing his steadfast love (as is Ex. 34:7), Moses inverts the order in the Sinai covenant preamble, where this warning to the guilty precedes the promise of grace (Ex. 20:5).

Based on his argument Moses then makes his plea: "Please pardon the iniquity of this people" (Num. 14:19). "Please pardon" (*selah-na*'; cf. Amos 7:2) is the only viable appeal, since this iniquity (*'avon*), being high-handed, is unatonable and thus unpardonable. Statutorily, it is a capital offense (Num. 15:31; Jer. 31:30). Yet "by

---

[98] On *hesed* cf. K. D. Sakenfeld, "Love (OT)," *ABD* 4.335–381 (377–380); Sakenfeld, *Numbers*, 90–92.

steadfast love and faithfulness [*hesed ve'emeth*] iniquity is atoned for" (Prov. 16:6; cf. the Gk. equivalent *karis kai aletheia*, which come to us in Christ alone; John 1:14, 17). "This people" is generally deprecatory (e.g., Num. 14:11)—Moses does not downplay their unworthiness of divine favor. But from start to finish he rests his case on God's abounding grace ("According to the greatness of your steadfast love"; v. 19). Moses reminds God of the precedent: "Just as you have forgiven this people, from Egypt until now." "Forgiven" (*nasa'*), here with the indirect object "[*le*]people," may mean "spare" (Gen. 18:24, 26) but with a word for sin as complement (with *le-*) normally means "forgive" (Ex. 23:21; Josh. 24:19). Forgiveness here involves sparing the people, for, in so doing, the Lord does not immediately destroy them (cf. Isa. 48:9). His following response, however, shows that God does not expunge the consequences of their rebellion.

14:20–25 The Lord grants Moses' request since his "word" (v. 20) is in harmony with God's promises and attributes. Psalm 106:23 says that Moses "stood in the breach" (cf. Ezek. 22:30).

"But truly" (*ve'ulam*; Num. 14:21) nuances "I have pardoned" (v. 20) and could be rendered "however" (cf. Gen. 48:19, "nevertheless"; cf. comment on Num. 14:26–38 [at v. 28]). Although the oath formula "as I live" (v. 14:21) occasionally precedes a promise, as in Isaiah 49:18, it generally heralds judgment, as here. "As all the earth shall be filled with the glory of the LORD" (Num. 14:21) is not doxological; rather, the manifestation of the Lord's glory, especially its filling the whole land (*kol ha'arets*), signals disaster. In Isaiah 6, upon hearing the seraphim cry "Holy, holy, holy is the LORD of hosts; the whole earth [*kol ha'arets*] is full of his glory," Isaiah immediately exclaims, "Woe is me," recognizing that his own and the people's uncleanness have defiled the land. The manifestation of the glory of the holy God amid an unclean, rebellious people is a harbinger of impending judgment (cf. Num. 14:10; 16:19, 42; 20:6).[99]

God's glory and signs (14:22) are displays of his power to judge and to save "in Egypt and in the wilderness." Seeing these manifestations of God hardened many, like those who "have tasted the goodness of the word of God and the powers of the age to come" (Heb. 6:5) but nevertheless fell away (Heb. 6:6). In "[They] put me to the test these ten times" (Num. 14:22), "ten times" may mean "once too often" (cf. Gen. 31:7; Job 19:3).[100] Disobedience, whatever the form, is rebellion (cf. 1 Sam. 15:22–23). This generation loses the blessing of entering the Promised Land due to unbelief. Hebrews uses this incident to show that the obedience of faith in God's promise always was and is required in order to enter the rest of salvation (Heb. 4:1–3). In contrast, Caleb and his descendants will possess it (Num. 14:24;

---

[99] Ron Bergey, *Découvrir Dieu à travers Esaïe* (Romanel-sur-Lausanne: Maison de la Bible, 2018), 41.
[100] Though the LXX seems to take it literally, reading "this tenth time," in the Talmudic tradition (Arakhin 15a) the ten tests were twice at the Red Sea (before crossing it Ex. 14:11–12; when leaving it (Ex. 14:30), understood by Rashi to mean the people feared the Egyptians may have crossed another part of the sea (cf. Ps. 106:7); twice concerning manna (Ex. 16:20, 27); twice concerning quail (Ex. 16:3; Num. 11:4); twice lacking water (at Marah Ex. 15:24; at Rephidim 17:1); the golden calf (Ex. 32:1); the scouts' evil report (Num. 13:26). Rashi, *Pentateuch with Rashi's Commentary*, 4:68; cf. Appendix, 195. It is not clear why the manna test in Numbers is not included (11:6).

cf. Josh. 14:14), a testimony to the spiritual promise of the Lord's being the God of the fathers and their children (e.g., Deut. 30:6–7; Isa. 59:21; Acts 2:39).

The "Amalekites," descendants of Esau (Gen. 36:12), live in the Negeb basin (Gen. 14:7), while the "Canaanites" are generally associated with the plains (Num. 13:29; Josh. 17:16). These areas are grouped together as "valleys" (Num. 14:25; sg. *'emeq*),[101] in geographical opposition to "hills" (sg. *har*; 14:45; Josh. 17:16; Judg. 1:19; 1 Kings 20:28). These Amalekites and Canaanites referred to here may be those who live in the central Negeb lowlands as far west as Shur (cf. Num. 13:29; 1 Sam. 15:7). The Amalekites and Canaanites also live in the "hill country" (*har*; Num. 14:45) referring to the Negeb highlands (cf. comment on 21:1–3). A chain of fortified Canaanite cities, including Arad and Hormah (cf. 21:1, 3; 14:45; 33:40), lies across the entire Negeb.

The Israelites are ordered to "turn tomorrow and set out" (respectively *panah* and *nasa'*, imperatives elsewhere only for their leaving Horeb; Deut. 1:7), this time "for the wilderness by the way to the Red Sea" (Num. 14:25). Some have suggested that the Lord is telling them to do what they said they intended to do (v. 4) and to return to Egypt.[102] In fact, however, it seems they are to head in the direction of the Gulf of Aqaba—the other branch of the Red Sea (cf. comment on 21:4–11). This is confirmed by Deuteronomy, which details the Israelites' journeying "into the wilderness in the direction of the Red Sea" (Deut. 1:40) to a location where for "many days" they travel around "Mount Seir" (Deut. 2:1), that is, Edomite territory west of the Arabah, located on the southern border of Canaan, on the central eastern fringe of the Sinai peninsula.

14:26–38 The sentence pronounced by the Lord fulfills the people's own request ("Would that we had died in this wilderness!"; v. 2): "What you have said in my hearing I will do to you; your dead bodies shall fall in this wilderness" (vv. 28–29; cf. vv. 32, 35). "Dead bodies" recalls the curses for violating the Sinai covenant (Lev. 26:30; Deut. 28:26). The charge that calls down this sentence is that "They grumbled against me" (Num. 14:29). Their mouths confessed the rebellion in their hearts (cf. Matt. 12:34; Rom. 10:10). By their tongue they convicted themselves (Matt. 15:18; cf. Titus 1:15).

The punishment falls on those "twenty years old and upward ... listed in the census" (Num. 14:29; cf. 1:3), an age-span generationally framed in the warning "but he will by no means clear the guilty, visiting the iniquity of the fathers on the children, to the third and the fourth generation" (14:18). Three generations would encompass grandparents, parents, and adults led out of Egypt and guided by God to Mount Sinai, then to the entry of the Promised Land at Kadesh.

"I swore" (Num. 14:30) renders "I raised my hand," a gesture made when taking an oath. Before only Caleb was named as an exception (v. 24), but Joshua is added, as well as "your little ones" (v. 31), that is, those too young to have been

---

[101] *CDCH*, 333: "'lowland, plain,' rather than 'valley' Nm 14:25; 1 S 6:13"; cf. G. A. Smith, *The Historical Geography of the Holy Land* (London: Collins, 1966), 437–438.
[102] So Noordtzij, *Numbers*, 127.

numbered. Those under twenty will enter the Promised Land, but only after forty years of shepherding in the wilderness, until the last of the older generation's "dead bodies lies in the wilderness" (v. 33). Shepherding is a difficult task made even harder by confinement in the wilderness (cf. Gen. 31:40). The Hebrew rendered "faithlessness" (*zenuth*) is the same term translated "whoredom" (Jer. 3:2), which recalls the image of idolatrous Israel as God's unfaithful wife (Ezek. 16:15; Hos. 6:10). Whoredom defiles Israel (Hos. 6:10), pollutes the land (Jer. 3:2, 9), and results in their exile. The exodus generation children will forgo the blessing of life in the land for many years but will finally experience it after first witnessing God's sobering judgment upon their parents.

"Forty days, a year for each day, . . . forty years" (Num. 14:34) is an application of lex talionis, whereby the punishment fits the crime. From the exodus, forty years elapse by the time of Aaron's death (20:28; 33:38). The wilderness sojourn, bracketed by Israel's arrival and departure from Kadesh (13:26; 20:22), covers thirty-eight years (Deut. 2:14). "I, the LORD, have spoken" (Num. 14:35) is the only Pentateuchal occurrence of this phrase, used eleven times in Ezekiel to underline judgment (e.g., 5:15; 24:14) and occasionally an eschatological promise (34:24; 36:36; 37:14). "Surely" (*'im-lo'*; Num. 14:35) is here the emphatic affirmative of an oath; "In this wilderness" (Num. 14:35) is the Paran wilderness, where the Israelites will spend thirty-eight years, apparently in the Kadesh area. "There they shall die" (v. 35); as Jude reminds his readers, "Jesus, who saved a people out of the land of Egypt, afterward destroyed those who did not believe" (Jude 5).

14:39–45 "The people mourned greatly" (v. 39), not for the ten men who die in the plague (v. 37) but for being deprived of the blessing of life in the Promised Land. Like Esau, they seek to regain the forfeited blessing by their tears (Gen. 27:38; Heb. 12:17). "We have sinned" (Num. 14:40) is not a confession from godly grief producing true repentance (2 Cor. 7:9–10). Their resolve to "go up to the place that the LORD has promised" (Num. 14:40) is labeled by Moses for what it is: "Transgressing the command of the LORD" (v. 41). The "command" was that "you shall bear your iniquity forty years" (v. 34) in the wilderness. Their attempt to enter the land will not succeed because it is disobedience, the fruit of unbelief. Like Adam and Eve, who were barred from reentry into Eden to access the tree of life by the sword of the cherubim (Gen. 3:24), the sword of "the Amalekites and the Canaanites" will prevent Israel from entering the Promised Land. That "the LORD will not be with you" explains why they cannot be victorious. The vacuum created by his withdrawn presence is filled by that of the enemy.

Nonetheless, Israel presumes (*'pl*) to go up (14:44). Although the Hebrew word is different, David prays, "Keep back your servant also from presumptuous [*zed*] sins" (Ps. 19:13). Neither the ark nor Moses goes with the Israelites on this futile foray (Num. 14:44), suggesting that they disregard the value of Moses' mediatorial intercession and the Lord's sacramental presence by means of the ark required at such a time (cf. Num. 10:35; Ps. 60:10).

In fact, the Israelites do not have to "go up" (Num. 14:40, 44), since the enemy "came down" (v. 45) from the hill country, the Negeb highlands. Israel is "defeated" (*nkh*; v. 45), and the Amalekites pursue (*ktt*) Israel. Hormah may be the northern limit of the Canaanites' victory over the Israelites, stretching from Seir/Edom west of the Arabah (Deut. 1:44). "Hormah" as a general term is related to "devote" (*kharam*) to sacred use or destruction, like the city Zephath (Judg. 1:17). The identification of Hormah remains uncertain.[103] Its association with Arad (Num. 21:1; Josh. 12:14; Judg. 1:16) suggests it was situated near a major crossroads heading west to Beersheba, then Gaza, east leading to the Arabah, north joining the road from Beersheba into the Judean hill country, and south to Kadesh. By controlling these interior routes the Canaanites would have access to the route to Shur and Egypt and to the King's Highway and Transjordan (cf. comment on Num. 20:14–21). They thus control the southern flank of Canaan.

After this Hormah debacle, Deuteronomy 1 says Israel "remained at Kadesh many days" (Deut. 1:46; cf. Num. 20:1; Deut. 1:41–44). Biblical data suggests that Israel stays in the Kadesh region most of the wilderness period. At the end of the wilderness period, Numbers 20 takes up this thread: "They journeyed from Kadesh" (Num. 20:22; cf. 33:37) in the direction of Transjordan.

Response

Moses often intercedes for the people (e.g., Num. 14:13–19; cf. 11:2; 21:7). The Lord incites Moses to intercede, provocatively calling into question his own promises and very character (14:12). Moses makes appeal to them. The Lord does not merely acquiesce but responds in kind, "according to your word" (v. 20). Moses' word is God's very own. Prayer is designed to be instrumental, the key the Lord provides to open the door to his response according to his will (Matt. 6:10; James 5:15–16).

The Israelites put God to the test "ten times" (Num. 14:22). They fail God's testing of them (Ex. 16:4; 20:20). His testing of them is not to make them fall but to allow them to rise to the occasion by the obedience of faith. Jesus is led into the wilderness by the Spirit to be tempted (Luke 4:1; cf. Heb. 2:18; 4:15). As their representative and by his obedience Christ, God's "beloved Son" (Matt. 3:17) accomplished what the Israelites ("my son"; Ex. 4:23) and Adam ("the son of God"; Luke 3:38) by disobedience failed to do.

Those who hear the gospel are exhorted, "Do not harden your hearts as in the rebellion, on the day of testing in the wilderness, where your fathers put me to the test and saw my works for forty years" (Heb. 3:8–9).

Speaking of those heading toward opposite eternal destinies, C. S. Lewis writes, "There are only two kinds of people—those who say to God 'Your will be done,' and those to whom God says in the end, 'Your will be done.'"[104]

---

[103] Possibly T. Masos, 8 miles (13 km) east southeast of Beersheba, or T. Halif, 9.5 miles (15.5 km) northeast of Beersheba; Carl G. Rasmussen, *Zondervan Atlas of the Bible*, rev. ed. (Grand Rapids, MI: Zondervan, 2010), 239.
[104] C. S. Lewis, *The Great Divorce: A Dream* (San Francisco, CA: HarperCollins, 2009), 75.

NUMBERS 15

15 The Lord spoke to Moses, saying, ² "Speak to the people of Israel and say to them, When you come into the land you are to inhabit, which I am giving you, ³ and you offer to the Lord from the herd or from the flock a food offering¹ or a burnt offering or a sacrifice, to fulfill a vow or as a freewill offering or at your appointed feasts, to make a pleasing aroma to the Lord, ⁴ then he who brings his offering shall offer to the Lord a grain offering of a tenth of an ephah² of fine flour, mixed with a quarter of a hin³ of oil; ⁵ and you shall offer with the burnt offering, or for the sacrifice, a quarter of a hin of wine for the drink offering for each lamb. ⁶ Or for a ram, you shall offer for a grain offering two tenths of an ephah of fine flour mixed with a third of a hin of oil. ⁷ And for the drink offering you shall offer a third of a hin of wine, a pleasing aroma to the Lord. ⁸ And when you offer a bull as a burnt offering or sacrifice, to fulfill a vow or for peace offerings to the Lord, ⁹ then one shall offer with the bull a grain offering of three tenths of an ephah of fine flour, mixed with half a hin of oil. ¹⁰ And you shall offer for the drink offering half a hin of wine, as a food offering, a pleasing aroma to the Lord.

¹¹ "Thus it shall be done for each bull or ram, or for each lamb or young goat. ¹² As many as you offer, so shall you do with each one, as many as there are. ¹³ Every native Israelite shall do these things in this way, in offering a food offering, with a pleasing aroma to the Lord. ¹⁴ And if a stranger is sojourning with you, or anyone is living permanently among you, and he wishes to offer a food offering, with a pleasing aroma to the Lord, he shall do as you do. ¹⁵ For the assembly, there shall be one statute for you and for the stranger who sojourns with you, a statute forever throughout your generations. You and the sojourner shall be alike before the Lord. ¹⁶ One law and one rule shall be for you and for the stranger who sojourns with you."

¹⁷ The Lord spoke to Moses, saying, ¹⁸ "Speak to the people of Israel and say to them, When you come into the land to which I bring you ¹⁹ and when you eat of the bread of the land, you shall present a contribution to the Lord. ²⁰ Of the first of your dough you shall present a loaf as a contribution; like a contribution from the threshing floor, so shall you present it. ²¹ Some of the first of your dough you shall give to the Lord as a contribution throughout your generations.

²² "But if you sin unintentionally,⁴ and do not observe all these commandments that the Lord has spoken to Moses, ²³ all that the Lord has commanded you by Moses, from the day that the Lord gave commandment, and onward throughout your generations, ²⁴ then if it was done unintentionally without the knowledge of the congregation, all the congregation shall offer one bull from the herd for a burnt offering, a pleasing aroma to the Lord, with its grain offering and its drink offering, according to the rule, and one male goat for a sin offering. ²⁵ And

the priest shall make atonement for all the congregation of the people of Israel, and they shall be forgiven, because it was a mistake, and they have brought their offering, a food offering to the Lord, and their sin offering before the Lord for their mistake. ²⁶ And all the congregation of the people of Israel shall be forgiven, and the stranger who sojourns among them, because the whole population was involved in the mistake.

²⁷ "If one person sins unintentionally, he shall offer a female goat a year old for a sin offering. ²⁸ And the priest shall make atonement before the Lord for the person who makes a mistake, when he sins unintentionally, to make atonement for him, and he shall be forgiven. ²⁹ You shall have one law for him who does anything unintentionally, for him who is native among the people of Israel and for the stranger who sojourns among them. ³⁰ But the person who does anything with a high hand, whether he is native or a sojourner, reviles the Lord, and that person shall be cut off from among his people. ³¹ Because he has despised the word of the Lord and has broken his commandment, that person shall be utterly cut off; his iniquity shall be on him."

³² While the people of Israel were in the wilderness, they found a man gathering sticks on the Sabbath day. ³³ And those who found him gathering sticks brought him to Moses and Aaron and to all the congregation. ³⁴ They put him in custody, because it had not been made clear what should be done to him. ³⁵ And the Lord said to Moses, "The man shall be put to death; all the congregation shall stone him with stones outside the camp." ³⁶ And all the congregation brought him outside the camp and stoned him to death with stones, as the Lord commanded Moses.

³⁷ The Lord said to Moses, ³⁸ "Speak to the people of Israel, and tell them to make tassels on the corners of their garments throughout their generations, and to put a cord of blue on the tassel of each corner. ³⁹ And it shall be a tassel for you to look at and remember all the commandments of the Lord, to do them, not to follow⁵ after your own heart and your own eyes, which you are inclined to whore after. ⁴⁰ So you shall remember and do all my commandments, and be holy to your God. ⁴¹ I am the Lord your God, who brought you out of the land of Egypt to be your God: I am the Lord your God."

¹ Or *an offering by fire*; so throughout Numbers ² An *ephah* was about 3/5 bushel or 22 liters ³ A *hin* was about 4 quarts or 3.5 liters ⁴ Or *by mistake*; also verses 24, 27, 28, 29 ⁵ Hebrew *to spy out*

Section Overview

Following a wave of uprisings (Numbers 11–12) that crests in the Kadesh revolt (ch. 13–14), God renews his gracious promise to the children and grandchildren of the generation condemned to die in the wilderness: "When you come into the land you are to inhabit, which I am giving you" (15:2). All will suffer the consequences of sin to one degree or another, but the Lord remains "abounding in steadfast love" (14:18), a God who "pardons" (v. 20).

Accompanying the renewed promise are prescriptions for offerings "from the herd or from the flock," each accompanied by a "grain offering" (15:3–4). These point to bountiful pastoral and agricultural activities of a people settled in the land who will worship the Lord there. The laws apply "throughout your generations" (vv. 15,

21, 23, 38). That their children will enter Canaan is a consolation for the godly remnant among those twenty years of age and upward who will fall in the wilderness due to their leaders' rebellion. It is an encouragement to persevere in the faith for those under twenty, who will one day receive an inheritance in the Promised Land.

Section Outline

    II. Trials in the Wilderness of Paran, the Transjordan Highlands, and the Plains of Moab (11:1–25:18) . . .

        E. Regulations for Life in the Land (15:1–41)

            1. Laws on Offerings (15:1–21)

            2. Laws on Inadvertent and Willful Sins (15:22–31)

            3. Sentence of a Sabbath Breaker (15:32–36)

            4. Garment Tassel-Reminders (15:37–41)

Comment

15:1–21 This section contains instructions regarding the grain and drink offerings accompanying animal sacrifices (vv. 3–16) and the first-dough contribution (vv. 19–21). Each part opens with "When you come into the land" (vv. 2, 18). The new generation is reminded that the Lord will keep his covenant promise (Gen. 12:7; 15:18) despite the parents' failure at Kadesh to keep their oath made at Sinai ("All that the Lord has spoken we will do, and we will be obedient"; Ex. 24:7; cf. Ex. 19:8; 24:3). "You" (Num. 15:2) are those under twenty years of age at the rebellion (cf. 14:29) and those born to them (cf. 14:31). This is one of two occurrences in Numbers depicting their settlement in the Promised Land (cf. 35:29). "Which I am giving you" (15:2) reformulates the land promise made to the fathers in the present tense (cf. 10:29; 11:12; 14:16, 23).

The laws in 15:3–5 remind the people that the land is flowing with "milk and honey" (cf. comment on Num. 13:25–33 [at v. 37]). The offerings presuppose abundance in both major socioeconomic sectors: transhumant herding ("herd . . . flock"; 15:3) and sedentary husbandry ("grain . . . oil . . . wine"; vv. 4–5). This abundance is proof of God's blessing and goodness (10:29; Deut. 7:13; Jer. 31:12).

Animals from the flock (Num. 15:3) include the "lamb" (v. 5), "ram" (v. 6), and "young goat" (v. 11). "Lamb" (Hb. *she*) can refer to young sheep or goats (Ex. 12:5). From the "herd" (Num. 15:3) here means a "bull" (v. 8). "Bull or ram" (v. 11) are paired, perhaps since rams would be separated from the flock and placed with the herd until breeding time. A "food offering" (*'ishshah*; v. 3) is made by fire (*'esh*), as the name suggests (Lev. 3:5). All offerings on the altar are food offerings, since the altar is "the Lord's table" (Mal. 1:7), an anthropomorphic image, as if the Lord ate sacrifices and drank their blood (Ps. 50:12–13). This portrays his communing at table with his people (Ps. 23:5; Rev. 3:20; 19:9), mirroring the practice of eating a covenant meal (Gen. 26:30; Ex. 24:11; 34:15; Matt. 26:28; 1 Cor. 11:20–22). ESV adds "or" before "a burnt offering"; a closer rendering is "And you make a food offering to the Lord, whether a burnt offering or a votive or freewill offering."

The "burnt offering" (*'olah*, lit., "ascending"; 15:3, 8) goes up in smoke and is totally consumed by fire (cf. LXX *holocaust*). As here, it is first in lists of sacrifices (Lev. 1:3). Its sprinkled blood is used in making atonement. The body is skinned and dismembered, with the legs and entrails washed and the pieces, including the head and fat, arranged on the wood (Lev. 1:5–9). The word "sacrifice" (*zebakh*; Num. 15:3) simply implies a slaughtered animal (cf. Isa. 34:6; *zebakh*, "sacrifice"// *tebakh*, "slaughter"). Here it is an abbreviation for "peace offerings" (*zebakh shelamim*; Lev. 22:21; *shelamim*; Num. 15:8).[105] These are often presented with burnt offerings (Lev. 6:12; Num. 15:8; 29:39; 2 Sam. 6:18). The fat, kidneys, and liver are burnt (Lev. 3:3–4). Two of the three kinds of peace offerings are mentioned in Numbers 15:3, "to fulfill a vow" and "freewill offering." The third ("thanksgiving sacrifice"; Lev. 7:11–12) is unspecified, since grain and drink accompaniments are not required.[106] The priest and his family receive the breast and right thigh, which are first ritually waved and contributed (Lev. 9:18, 21; 10:14). The remainder is eaten by the offeror (Lev. 7:15–16). "Appointed feasts" (*mo'ed*; Num. 15:3) are festive occasions on which community offerings will be made once Israel is in the land (vv. 2, 18).

"He who brings his offering shall offer" (v. 4) renders a unique three-word Hebrew phrase turning on the *qrb* stem; literally, "The one drawing near (*maqrib*) shall draw near (*hiqrib*) to the Lord, by means of his drawer-near (*qorban*)." The major concern of these regulations—that which is unique to Numbers (cf. Ex. 29:38–42; Lev. 2:1–16; 7:11–14)—is the detailed quantity of food accompaniment according to the offering and the animal offered (cf. Ezek. 46:11–15): "fine flour," in fractions of the "ephah" dry measure, and of olive "oil" and "wine," in fractions of the "hin" liquid measure (Num. 15:4–5, 8–10, 11). The underlying principle is that the greater the value (and size) of the animal is—lamb/goat, ram, bull—the greater the measured quantity must be—tenth, two-tenths, three-tenths of an ephah of flour and a quarter, third, half of a hin of wine and oil. Meat offerings are accompanied by bread, a "grain offering" (v. 4), flour mixed with oil, and "wine ... a drink offering" (*nesek*; v. 5) poured out either at the foot of the altar or on the offering.[107] Describing all these offerings as "a pleasing aroma to the LORD" (v. 10; cf. vv. 3, 7, 14, 24) portrays the Lord convivially at table in covenant communion with the offeror. The grain and drink offerings are not joined to sin or guilt offerings, nor does the pleasing aroma expression apply to them.[108]

The section ends by reiterating the general application, first concerning each offering. The stipulated dry and liquid measures, whether with a bull, ram, lamb, or goat, apply as follows: "As many as you offer, so shall you do with each one" (vv. 11–12). There is no distinction of person according to the animal offered or the quantity of grain and oil accompaniments. A second application concerns anyone presenting an offering, whether "native Israelite" (*'ezrah*), sojourning "stranger" (*ger*,

---

[105] Milgrom, *Numbers*, 119.
[106] Ibid., 118.
[107] The former is mentioned in *Sirach* 50:15; Josephus, *Antiquities* 3.9.4; cf. Milgrom, *Numbers*, 120.
[108] Milgrom also observes the Leviticus 4:31 exception of "pleasing aroma" from the sin offering, which may be explained by the fat being removed and burnt like that of the peace offering (*Numbers*, 118, 312n9).

a temporary resident), or anyone "living permanently" (perhaps a foreigner; cf. Gen. 23:4, *neker/nokri*), for all of whom there is "one law and one rule" (Num. 15:13–16), though with some restrictions for a foreigner (Ex. 12:43). Anyone in the land who desires, if qualified, can make an offering. These social distinctions anticipate life in the land, the very thing the previous generation doubted in unbelief.

The second part of the laws on sacrifices begins much like the first, "When you come into the land to which I bring you" (Num. 15:18; cf. v. 2). As do the former laws, this one anticipates agricultural abundance in the Promised Land. The reminders "When you eat of the bread of the land" (v. 19)—rather than manna—and "Throughout your generations" (v. 21)—beyond the generation that will die in the wilderness—reassure the people that for those who love and obey him, the Lord will keep covenant and steadfast love to a thousand generations (Ex. 20:6; Num. 14:18; Deut. 7:9).

The law introduced in Numbers 15:18 is unique (vv. 19–21; cf. Lev. 23:17). The bread in view is the "first of your dough" (Num. 15:20), a portion of which is to be presented (*rum*) to the Lord. The verb describes the action of presenting to the Lord that which is removed from the whole, that is, the portion contributed to the priest.[109] This does not necessarily imply that the contribution is held up or "heaved" (the language of the "heave offering" comes from the KJV, via the rabbis; cf. Mishnah, Menahot 5:6) any more than "raising an offering" means lifting it up. Such would be impossible given the weight of the gold, silver, and bronze contributions for the tabernacle (called a *terumah* in Ex. 35:5), a land contribution for the temple (Ezek. 45:1, "portion"), and large amounts of plunder (Num. 31:29, 41, 52). The contribution here, a "loaf," is part of a lump of "dough" made from some of the grain on the "threshing floor" (15:20). "First" here could refer to the first dough made at the time of the earliest grain harvest, or perhaps each time a new lump is made.[110]

15:22–31 This initial section on unintentional sins of the congregation parallels the more elaborate Leviticus 4:13–21 law, with some differences. For example, Leviticus 4 includes four case categories—high priest, congregation, leader, and individual—whereas the present law includes only two—congregation and individual. Leviticus 4 treats violations "not to be done" (e.g., Lev. 4:2) or prohibitive (do not do) commandments, whereas Numbers 15 deals with "all" commandments (Num. 15:22, 23), both prohibitive and prescriptive (to do).[111] Whether unintentional ritual or ethical infractions, in both passages they require atonement.

The plural verb in "if you [pl.] sin unintentionally [*shagah*]" (v. 22) refers to the unintentional sin of the congregation (cf. Lev. 4:13, pl. verb + "whole congregation"), that is, its representatives ("elders of the congregation," Lev. 4:15; but distinct from a leader, v. 22). The law on "one person" begins in Numbers 15:27 (cf. Lev. 4:27; "anyone of the common people"). *Shagah* describes sheep that wander (Ezek. 34:6)

---

109 The hiphil verb *rum* in a ritual context, rather than "raise, lift," means "contribute/present" a gift (cf. *CDCH*, s.v. רום; Milgrom states, "*herim* means 'dedicate' or 'set aside' and the noun *terumah* means 'gift' "; *Leviticus 1–16*, AYB (New Haven, CT: Yale University Press, 1998), 474–475.
110 Cf. Ashley, *Book of Numbers*, 282–283.
111 For a full treatment cf. Gray, *Numbers*, 178–182; Milgrom, *Numbers*, 402–405.

and people who stray from the commandments (Ps. 119:21; cf. Ps. 119:118, "go astray"). Sheep do so unawares. Implied in the verb is the notion "unintentionally," translating the cognate *shegagah* (Num. 15:24; v. 25, "mistake"; cf. v. 27, "sins unintentionally," *hata'* + *shegagah*). The act itself may be intentional, but not the awareness that it is sinful or occasions impurity.[112] An example would be someone who becomes impure by walking on an unmarked grave and later becomes aware of it (cf. 19:16). This law apparently includes inadvertent violations of the preceding ritual regulations.

Whether unintentional or not, sin is not limited to doing wrong (Lev. 4:13; "ought not to be done"); it includes, as here, not doing what is required (Num. 15:22). Guilt is incurred even if the violation is unintentional. Like the laws on future offerings in the land, this exhortation extends "onward throughout your generations" (v. 23). The fact that it is "without the knowledge of the congregation [i.e., the representatives]" (v. 24) reiterates the point that awareness of the error incriminating the entire community comes after the fact (cf. Lev. 4:13, *'asham*; "they realize their guilt"; Lev. 4:14, "sin . . . becomes known"). In Joshua 7 Israel suffers the consequences of the act of one man: from God's standpoint "Israel has sinned" (Josh. 7:11) although only "I [Achan] sinned" (Josh. 7:20).

The requisite "bull . . . for a burnt offering" (Num. 15:24) is for representatives of the congregation (elders). The "male goat for a sin offering" (Num. 15:24) is for a leader (*nasi'*; Lev. 4:23). A "female goat" (Num. 15:27) is for an ordinary member of the community (Lev. 4:28). The burnt offering is mentioned here before the sin offering (also in Num. 6:14–15; 7:15–16), indicating what is offered. The order in which they are offered is reversed. This ritual sequence shows that purification and forgiveness of sin, by the atoning sin (blood purification) offering, is required first before making a burnt offering, which exudes a fragrant aroma. Numbers 15:25 summarizes, "And the priest shall make atonement for all the congregation of the people of Israel, and they shall be forgiven, because it was a mistake, and they have brought their offering, a food offering to the LORD, and their sin offering before the LORD for their mistake." Even unintentional mistakes require atonement.

The priest intermediary makes ceremonial blood "atonement" (*kipper*) by smearing, sprinkling, or pouring/throwing the blood, by which impurity is symbolically removed from holy objects (altar of burnt offerings, incense altar, mercy seat). The blood from a "sin offering," applied to the altar, makes atonement for *it* (Ex. 29:36; 30:10; Lev. 8:15; 16:18–19; Ezek. 43:20; 45:18–20). This is done "for [on behalf of] all the congregation of the people of Israel" (cf. 8:19; 2 Chron. 29:24). The animal sacrificed is a substitute for those who have caused the defilement. After blood purges the impurity, "they shall be forgiven" for defiling the sacred and for "their mistake" causing the contamination. Although the priest probably announces the pardon, the Lord alone can forgive.

After the laws about unintentional sins (Num. 15:22–29) comes a ruling on intentional sin (vv. 30–31). Behind the sin qualified "anything with a high hand"

---

112 Cf. Ashley, *Book of Numbers*, 286.

(v. 30) is a defiant gesture, like that made at the exodus by the Israelites in the face of the Egyptians (Ex. 14:8, "defiantly"; Num. 33:3, "triumphantly"). Such a sin usually involves a willful violation of one of the Ten Commandments, as illustrated in the next section with the Sabbath (Num. 15:32–36).[113] To "cut [someone] off" (*karat*; v. 31) is a severe form of covenant curse (Gen. 8:21; cf. Gen. 9:11; Jer. 44:8), involving punishment for offenses that are unatonable and thus unpardonable.[114] "His iniquity"—his punishment for it—"shall be on him"; that is, the consequences are to be borne by him.

In Numbers 5 another kind of intentional sin was addressed. Blood atonement was made there under certain conditions—notably, true repentance and confession.[115] In David's case these actions mitigate the judgment upon high-handed sins for which there is no sacrifice—adultery and murder (Ps. 51:1, 4, 16–17).

15:32–36 The case is then introduced of a man "gathering sticks on the Sabbath day" (Num. 15:32). The law forbids lighting a fire on the Sabbath (Ex. 35:3; cf. Jer. 17:27). Gathering sticks is not in itself the problem since, if it were considered work, there would be no need to inquire of the Lord (cf. Ex. 31:14; 35:2). The question seems to regard whether gathering sticks is evidence of intent to make fire, and, if so, whether it is punishable, and to what extent. According to a strict interpretation, since no fire is made, there might be no infraction since no human court could prove intent.

Those who observed the man "brought him . . . to all the congregation" (Num. 15:33), that is, to the representatives. He is held "in custody" (in the *mishmar*, "guardhouse"; v. 34), but only until the case is decided (cf. Lev. 24:12). Imprisonment as punishment is foreign to the Israelite penal system. The question remains: What should they do next (Num. 15:34)? Identical language is used in the case of the blasphemous son of an Israelite and an Egyptian father (Lev. 24:11). In both cases the verb "be/make clear" (*parash*) involves a legal decision[116] derived from the law (cf. Neh. 8:8).

The Lord decrees: "The man shall be put to death" (Num. 15:35; or "shall surely be put to death," *mot yamut*; e.g., Gen. 26:7; Num. 35:16). "All the congregation," that is, the designated representatives, "shall stone him" to death. Stoning is the sentence for divination (Lev. 20:27), blasphemy (Lev. 24:16), idolatry (Deut. 17:3, 5), and adultery (Deut. 22:21). Anyone guilty of certain perversions could be burned with fire (Lev. 20:14; 21:9). Execution is "outside the camp" (Num. 15:35, 36) so as not to defile it (31:19; cf. 5:3). Thereafter a lifeless body could be hung on a tree (25:4; Josh. 10:26; 2 Sam. 4:12). Being so hung is a curse (Deut. 21:22; Gal. 3:13).

15:37–41 "Tassels" (Hb. *tsitsith*; v. 38; cf. Deut. 22:12; LXX *kraspeda*, "fringes," also Matt. 9:20; 14:36; 23:5) were worn on hems of garments of religious notables

---

113 Rainey, "Sacrifice and Offerings," *ZPEB* 5:204.
114 Cf. Milgrom, *Numbers*, 405–408; for all nineteen Pentateuchal cases cf. ibid., 406.
115 Ron Bergey, "La confession des péchés dans les lois sur les sacrifices," *RRef* 63/1 (2012): 1–9.
116 *CHALOT*, 1. "Be explained, decided" (299, citing Num. 15:34).

in Near Eastern antiquity.[117] "Corners" (*kanap*) more precisely indicates "border/hem,"[118] not "corner" (*pinnah*; cf. 1 Sam. 15:27 "skirt of his robe"). A "cord of blue" (Num. 15:38) is the color of royalty, a reminder, with the tassels, that Israel is a kingdom of priests (Ex. 19:6).

Tassels provide a sign "to look at and remember," positively "all the commandments... to do them" and negatively "not to follow after your own heart and your own eyes, which you are inclined to whore after" (Num. 15:39). "Heart" here is the seat of bad desires, while "eyes" indicates the visual enflaming of improper passions. "To follow" (*tur*) is the same verb translated "to spy out" in 13:2, a subtle way of reminding the people that they must submit to God's commands and believe his promises in order not to repeat their sinful rebellion at Kadesh. To "whore after" (from *zanah*) refers to idolatry (e.g., Ex. 34:15–16), also a capital offense. It defiles the person (Hos. 6:10) and pollutes the land (Jer. 3:2, 9). The new generation will succumb to lascivious idolatry at Peor (Num. 25:1).

To "do all my commandments, and be holy to your God" (Num. 15:40) is predicated upon their being a priestly kingdom (Ex. 19:6). Leviticus 20:7 commands them to "consecrate yourselves" (or "be holy yourselves"), while Leviticus 20:8 reminds, "I am the LORD who sanctifies you" (or "makes you holy"). God gives what he requires (cf. "circumcise... your heart"; "The LORD your God will circumcise your heart"; Deut. 10:16; 30:6). Obedience to God's Word ("my commandments") yields the fruit of holiness, since Scripture is essential to sanctification (John 17:17; Eph. 5:26; 1 Tim. 4:5), empowered by the Holy Spirit (Rom. 15:16; 2 Thess. 2:13). Failing to obey God's Word is failure to uphold him as holy, a sin that costs Moses and Aaron dearly (Num. 27:14). The stimulus for obedience is always the grace of the redeeming Lord, "who brought you out of the land of Egypt to be your God" (15:41).

Response

As with the Israelites, who are warned "not to follow after your own heart and your own eyes" (v. 39), there remains for us "all that is in the world—the desires of the flesh and the desires of the eyes" (1 John 2:16; cf. 2 Pet. 1:4), "passions... which wage war against your soul" (1 Pet. 2:11; James 4:1). These oppose the Spirit, but the Spirit combats them (Gal. 5:16–17; James 4:5). Paul reminds the believer, "Put on the Lord Jesus Christ, and make no provision for the flesh, to gratify its desires" (Rom. 13:14); and Peter declares, "Since therefore Christ suffered in the flesh, arm yourselves with the same way of thinking, for whoever has suffered in the flesh has ceased from sin" (1 Pet. 4:1; cf. Heb. 2:18; 4:15). Grace is an essential weapon in the struggle: "The grace of God has appeared, bringing salvation for all people, training us to renounce ungodliness and worldly passions, and to live self-controlled, upright, and godly lives in the present age" (Titus 2:11–12).

---

117 Milgrom, *Numbers*, 410–414. Tassels appear in Egyptian and Mesopotamian paintings, sculptures, and reliefs; cf. Davies, *Numbers*, 161.
118 *CDCH*, 179: "Skirt, hem, edge of garment Ru 3:9."

Robert Robertson captures the source of victory in this battle for the heart in the last stanza of "Come, Thou Fount of Every Blessing."

O to grace how great a debtor Daily I'm constrained to be;
Let that grace now, like a fetter, Bind my wandering heart to thee.
Prone to wander, Lord, I feel it; Prone to leave the God I love;
Here's my heart, O take and seal it; Seal it for thy courts above.

NUMBERS 16

16 Now Korah the son of Izhar, son of Kohath, son of Levi, and Dathan and Abiram the sons of Eliab, and On the son of Peleth, sons of Reuben, took men. ² And they rose up before Moses, with a number of the people of Israel, 250 chiefs of the congregation, chosen from the assembly, well-known men. ³ They assembled themselves together against Moses and against Aaron and said to them, "You have gone too far! For all in the congregation are holy, every one of them, and the Lord is among them. Why then do you exalt yourselves above the assembly of the Lord?" ⁴ When Moses heard it, he fell on his face, ⁵ and he said to Korah and all his company, "In the morning the Lord will show who is his,¹ and who is holy, and will bring him near to him. The one whom he chooses he will bring near to him. ⁶ Do this: take censers, Korah and all his company; ⁷ put fire in them and put incense on them before the Lord tomorrow, and the man whom the Lord chooses shall be the holy one. You have gone too far, sons of Levi!" ⁸ And Moses said to Korah, "Hear now, you sons of Levi: ⁹ is it too small a thing for you that the God of Israel has separated you from the congregation of Israel, to bring you near to himself, to do service in the tabernacle of the Lord and to stand before the congregation to minister to them, ¹⁰ and that he has brought you near him, and all your brothers the sons of Levi with you? And would you seek the priesthood also? ¹¹ Therefore it is against the Lord that you and all your company have gathered together. What is Aaron that you grumble against him?"

¹² And Moses sent to call Dathan and Abiram the sons of Eliab, and they said, "We will not come up. ¹³ Is it a small thing that you have brought us up out of a land flowing with milk and honey, to kill us in the wilderness, that you must also make yourself a prince over us? ¹⁴ Moreover, you have not brought us into a land flowing with milk and honey, nor given us inheritance of fields and vineyards. Will you put out the eyes of these men? We will not come up." ¹⁵ And Moses was very angry and said to the Lord, "Do not respect their offering. I have not taken one donkey from them, and I have not harmed one of them."

¹⁶ And Moses said to Korah, "Be present, you and all your company, before the Lord, you and they, and Aaron, tomorrow. ¹⁷ And let every one of you take his censer and put incense on it, and every one of you bring

before the Lord his censer, 250 censers; you also, and Aaron, each his censer." ¹⁸ So every man took his censer and put fire in them and laid incense on them and stood at the entrance of the tent of meeting with Moses and Aaron. ¹⁹ Then Korah assembled all the congregation against them at the entrance of the tent of meeting. And the glory of the Lord appeared to all the congregation.

²⁰ And the Lord spoke to Moses and to Aaron, saying, ²¹ "Separate yourselves from among this congregation, that I may consume them in a moment." ²² And they fell on their faces and said, "O God, the God of the spirits of all flesh, shall one man sin, and will you be angry with all the congregation?" ²³ And the Lord spoke to Moses, saying, ²⁴ "Say to the congregation, Get away from the dwelling of Korah, Dathan, and Abiram."

²⁵ Then Moses rose and went to Dathan and Abiram, and the elders of Israel followed him. ²⁶ And he spoke to the congregation, saying, "Depart, please, from the tents of these wicked men, and touch nothing of theirs, lest you be swept away with all their sins." ²⁷ So they got away from the dwelling of Korah, Dathan, and Abiram. And Dathan and Abiram came out and stood at the door of their tents, together with their wives, their sons, and their little ones. ²⁸ And Moses said, "Hereby you shall know that the Lord has sent me to do all these works, and that it has not been of my own accord. ²⁹ If these men die as all men die, or if they are visited by the fate of all mankind, then the Lord has not sent me. ³⁰ But if the Lord creates something new, and the ground opens its mouth and swallows them up with all that belongs to them, and they go down alive into Sheol, then you shall know that these men have despised the Lord."

³¹ And as soon as he had finished speaking all these words, the ground under them split apart. ³² And the earth opened its mouth and swallowed them up, with their households and all the people who belonged to Korah and all their goods. ³³ So they and all that belonged to them went down alive into Sheol, and the earth closed over them, and they perished from the midst of the assembly. ³⁴ And all Israel who were around them fled at their cry, for they said, "Lest the earth swallow us up!" ³⁵ And fire came out from the Lord and consumed the 250 men offering the incense.

³⁶ ² Then the Lord spoke to Moses, saying, ³⁷ "Tell Eleazar the son of Aaron the priest to take up the censers out of the blaze. Then scatter the fire far and wide, for they have become holy. ³⁸ As for the censers of these men who have sinned at the cost of their lives, let them be made into hammered plates as a covering for the altar, for they offered them before the Lord, and they became holy. Thus they shall be a sign to the people of Israel." ³⁹ So Eleazar the priest took the bronze censers, which those who were burned had offered, and they were hammered out as a covering for the altar, ⁴⁰ to be a reminder to the people of Israel, so that no outsider, who is not of the descendants of Aaron, should draw near to burn incense before the Lord, lest he become like Korah and his company—as the Lord said to him through Moses.

⁴¹ But on the next day all the congregation of the people of Israel grumbled against Moses and against Aaron, saying, "You have killed the people of the Lord." ⁴² And when the congregation had assembled against Moses and against Aaron, they turned toward the tent of meeting. And behold, the cloud covered it, and the glory of the Lord appeared. ⁴³ And Moses and Aaron came to the front of the tent of meeting, ⁴⁴ and the Lord spoke to Moses, saying, ⁴⁵ "Get away from the midst

of this congregation, that I may consume them in a moment." And they fell on their faces. ⁴⁶ And Moses said to Aaron, "Take your censer, and put fire on it from off the altar and lay incense on it and carry it quickly to the congregation and make atonement for them, for wrath has gone out from the LORD; the plague has begun." ⁴⁷ So Aaron took it as Moses said and ran into the midst of the assembly. And behold, the plague had already begun among the people. And he put on the incense and made atonement for the people. ⁴⁸ And he stood between the dead and the living, and the plague was stopped. ⁴⁹ Now those who died in the plague were 14,700, besides those who died in the affair of Korah. ⁵⁰ And Aaron returned to Moses at the entrance of the tent of meeting, when the plague was stopped.

¹ Septuagint *The LORD knows those who are his* ² Ch 17:1 in Hebrew

Section Overview

Chapter 16 narrates the mutinous challenge to Moses' leadership and Aaron's priestly prerogatives. This follows Miriam and Aaron's opposition to Moses' office of prophet (ch. 12) and the tribal leaders' revolt against his leadership (chs. 13–14). As before, the consequences of this latest uprising are tragic.

The leaders of the rebellion, Korah (from the tribe of Levi) and the Reubenites Dathan and Abiram, are all descendants of Leah, Jacob's first wife. Nursing old fraternal rivalries and current jealousies (Ps. 106:16–17), they launch their uprising, aided and abetted by 250 tribal chiefs. The Lord's gracious promises renewed after the Kadesh revolt (cf. Num. 15:2) neither temper their judgment nor foster their piety.

Numbers 16:1–18:32 comprises the traditional weekly Torah reading (*parashah*) titled "Korah." It underscores the primacy of the Aaronic priesthood that Korah challenges. These chapters, with chapter 19, contain a well-rounded theology of the priesthood, with its divine origin, sacred character, ritual responsibilities and revenues, relation to sin, and particularly its atoning role. Chapters 16–17 narrate the few known events from the thirty-eight years of wilderness wanderings.

Section Outline

II. Trials in the Wilderness of Paran, the Transjordan Highlands, and the Plains of Moab (11:1–25:18) . . .
    F. The Rebellion over the Priesthood and Leadership (16:1–50)
        1. Korah, Dathan, and Abiram Rebel (16:1–19)
        2. Judgment (16:20–35)
        3. Atonement (16:36–50)

Comment

16:1–19 In Hebrew the chapter begins "And Korah took [*vayyiqqakh*, from *laqakh*]," with no object; ESV has supplied the object "men." If the root is *yaqakh* (albeit unattested in biblical Hebrew), the meaning could be "Korah acted brazenly."[119] The instigator, Korah, is a Kohathite, the Levitical clan responsible for transporting the tabernacle's sacred furnishings. Moses, Aaron, and Miriam are also descendants of Kohath through his firstborn, Amram, whereas Korah is a descendant of Kohath's second son, Izhar (Ex. 6:18–21; Num. 3:19; 16:1).

Korah has Dathan and Abiram as co-conspirators. A third, On, is otherwise unknown. They are "sons of Reuben," Leah's firstborn. In deference to Rachel, Jacob had nullified Leah's matriarchal rights. Moreover, Reuben lost his primogeniture for his sin (Gen. 49:4). The descendants of Leah's third son, Levi, will receive no land inheritance. The Levitical Kohathites and the Reubenites are both camped on the south side of the tabernacle, which facilitates their conspiracy. The Reubenites perhaps also nurse grudges against the tribe of Judah, a younger son of Leah yet the preeminent tribe, assigned the head encampment on the east side of the tabernacle, contiguous with that of Moses, Aaron, and his sons. The Korahites challenge the exclusivity of the Aaronic priesthood (Num. 16:10–11). Dathan and Abiram begrudge Moses' supreme leadership (vv. 12–13; Ps. 106:16–17).

They have other accomplices: "250 chiefs" (Num. 16:2), apparently "elders" and "well-known men." "Chosen" could be rendered "called" (it comes from *qara'*, not *bahar*, which is used in v. 5: "chooses"); here they are called to an "assembly" (*mo'ed*). This gathering constitutes a representative civil "congregation" (*'edah*) or a religious "assembly" (*qahal*; v. 3). This is the only known reference to a representative assembly called a *mo'ed*.[120] The broad support of all these religious and civil leaders shows this is not a spontaneous revolt but a well-organized uprising.

"You [pl.] have gone too far!" (v. 3) is the opening salvo of a double offensive. First, Korah takes aim at the priesthood of Aaron and his sons, claiming, "All in the congregation are holy" (v. 3), which confuses sacerdotal ceremonial holiness with ethical holiness, the latter of which is required of every Israelite (cf. 15:40). Only priests are anointed and thus consecrated, or made ritually holy (Ex. 30:30). Levites are merely ritually purified with water (Num. 8:7, 21). Korah fails to distinguish between the universal priesthood of the Israelites (Ex. 19:6) and the particular divinely appointed mediatorial office of Aaron. Moses' response confirms Korah and his followers' intent: "Would you [pl.] seek the priesthood also?" (Num. 16:10). Their second accusation—"Why then do you exalt yourselves above the assembly [*qahal*] of the LORD?" (v. 3)—is aimed at the Aaronite representative position over the religious assembly.

Moses' response is twofold. First, he "fell on his face" (v. 4) to pray (cf. v. 22), although no words are recorded; his prostration acknowledges the Lord's consuming presence (cf. 22:31). Second, he replies to Korah (16:5): "In the morning the LORD will show [or "will make known"; from *yada'*] who is his, and who is holy."

---

[119] CDCH, s.v. *קיח*, "embolden," citing Job 15:12; Proverbs 6:25, 26, the former passage describing someone carried away with passion and the latter an adulteress enticing a man. BHS suggests reading either *vayyaqom*, "and he arose," or *vayyaqakh*, from *yqkh* = Arabic (*wqh*), "act imprudently." On this issue Milgrom presents at least ten distinct views (*Numbers*, 312–313).
[120] Levine, *Numbers 1–20*, 412.

That is, the Lord will determine publicly who holds the divinely appointed office of priesthood, emphasizing God's sovereign appointment of those who mediate at his altar.

A test involving incense censers will show Korah and all his company the one who "shall be the holy one" (v. 7). Priests are made ceremonially holy to minister in the holy sphere. No one else can do so, not even the Levites. "Censers" are bronze fire pans in which hot coals are placed from the altar ("fire"), followed by ground incense (Lev. 16:12). The test is extremely hazardous, as Aaron has already lost two sons, both priests, who died while manipulating incense censers (cf. Leviticus 10). That incident should have sufficed to warn the nonpriestly Levites, since, like Nadab and Abihu, they too must now take "censers" (Num. 16:6) with "fire" (i.e., coals; v. 37 [17:2 MT]) and "incense." Moses warns them, "You have gone too far" (16:7), their exact charge against Aaron and his sons (v. 3).

Moses appeals to the rebels by reminding them of the honor of their present ministry: "Is it too small a thing for you?" (v. 9). They are "separated" (from *badal*; cf. comment on 16:20–35 [at v. 21]) by God from the "congregation of Israel," that is, as Levites from the other secular tribes and as Kohathites from the other Levitical clans. Separation makes a clear distinction of that which must not be confused (*balal*; cf. comment on 8:5–22 [at v. 14]). This was done to "bring you near to himself," that is, to "cause you to approach" (*hiqrib*) the Lord in a sacred task, which is twofold: first, "to do service in the tabernacle" by assisting the priests and transporting the sanctuary and its most holy furnishings (cf. 3:6–9; 4:4, 15); second, "to stand before the congregation to minister to them [or for them]" in their stead. The Kohathites have the highest and most sacred calling among the Levites.

The test will settle whether Korah and the other "sons of Levi" (16:8), who already enjoy elite Levitical privileges (v. 9), could also claim a share in the "priesthood" (v. 10), hitherto the office of Aaron, the high priest, and his sons as his successors (Ex. 29:9; 40:15; Num. 25:13). Intrusion by a Levite into the priestly domain is punishable by death (Num. 3:10; 18:7). Moses reminds Korah and his allies that they have gathered (*ya'ad*; 16:11) against the Lord, as the rebels did against him at Kadesh (14:35); moreover, they are grumbling (*lun*) against Aaron as the people did against the Lord and Moses there (14:27, 36).

Moses then summons Dathan and Abiram (16:12), but they refuse to appear before him. The second rebellious salvo is promptly fired: "Must you [sg.] also make yourself a prince over us?" The Reubenites now challenge Moses' supremacy (cf. v. 3). They seem to stake their claim to authority on their ancestor's primogeniture as compared with Moses' and Aaron's descent. They accuse Moses of poor judgment for having led them out of Egypt, "a land flowing with milk and honey," and ineffectiveness for not leading them into "a land flowing with milk and honey" (vv. 13–14). Their blindness is willful. They attribute to the land of servitude the very essence of the land of liberty. They accuse Moses of trying to pull the wool over their eyes: "Will you put out the eyes of these men?" (v. 14). Everyone can see they are still in "the wilderness" (v. 13) and not in an "inheritance of fields and vineyards" (v. 14).

Moses' being "very angry" (v. 15) in response is justifiable. It is the Lord who has delivered them from Egypt and is guiding them in the wilderness. Moreover, it is the people who disobeyed the Lord by not entering the Promised Land. The identity of "their offering" (*minkhah*; v. 15) that Moses asks the Lord not to accept is unclear; God had not accepted Cain's *minkhah* (Gen. 4:3). Moses' assertion of honesty ("I have not taken one donkey ... not harmed"; Num. 16:15) is later echoed in Samuel's claim of just dealings (1 Sam. 12:3; cf. Deut. 16:19).

Moses then instructs Korah and his company to present themselves on the next day "before the LORD" (Num. 16:16), that is, between the altar and the entrance of the tent of meeting (v. 18). The day's delay will allow for purification from any light impurity Aaron might contract. It will also allow Korah and his company to consider what they are about to do. The test requires each to take "his censer" for "incense" and present it "before the LORD" (vv. 7, 17, 38), including 250 censers for all the chiefs, as well as censers for Korah and for Aaron (v. 17). Only a priest, however, can take an incense censer and enter the Holy Place to minister at the incense altar (v. 40; cf. Ex. 30:7–8; 1 Sam. 2:28; 2 Chron. 26:18). The rebels will pay dearly for their presumption. After taking their burning incense censers (Num. 16:18), "Korah assembled all the congregation" (v. 19; LXX "his congregation"), that is, those banded with him against Moses and Aaron. Then "the glory of the LORD appeared" (v. 19), an ominous portent of judgment (cf. 14:10).

16:20–35 The Lord orders Moses and Aaron, "Separate [*badal*, cf. comment on 16:1–19 (at v. 9)] yourselves from among this congregation" (v. 21). To no avail, Moses had reminded the Kohathites of their privilege of being separated from the Israelite congregation to serve the Lord and his people (v. 9). "Consume" (*'akal*; v. 21) is a frequent figure for annihilation (e.g., Ex. 32:10; Num. 16:45). In this case, "the earth opened its mouth and swallowed them up" (v. 32; cf. 2 Sam. 20:20). Moses and Aaron fall on their faces (Num. 16:22), a sign of consternation before the offenders (cf. 14:5; 16:4) and of submission to God, the Judge (20:6). He is called "the God of the spirits of all flesh" (16:22; cf. 27:16; Heb. 12:9; James 2:26), that is, the one who can destroy both body and soul in hell (Matt. 10:28; James 4:12). He has created heaven and earth and the spirit of man (Zech. 12:1). "Shall one man sin, and will you be angry with all the congregation?" (Num. 16:22) is a matter of principle: Because of "one," is it just to destroy "all"? Abraham's prayer was similar: In Sodom, should the righteous, though few, perish with the wicked (Gen. 18:23)?

The insurrectionists will be judged—Korah for encroaching the sacred sphere of the Aaronic priesthood and Dathan and Abiram for challenging Moses' invested authority. To be spared, the congregation must "get away" (*'alah*, "withdraw"; 2 Sam. 20:2; 23:9) from (*missabib*) the "dwelling" (*mishkan*) of the three rebel factions (Num. 16:24). The language recalls the proximity of the Kohathites and the Reubenites, who have their contiguous encampments on the south side of the tabernacle. The Simeonites and the Gadites also share the south side encampment with the Reubenites (2:10–14).

The elders of Israel (16:25) are on Moses' side, among whom are the "seventy" and the "officers" (cf. comment on 11:16–30). The "congregation" (16:26; cf. v. 24) is those dwelling adjacent to the leaders of the rebellion. They are instructed, "Depart... of these wicked men... touch nothing of theirs..." (v. 26; cf. vv. 2, 14). They and their possessions are defiled (cf. Lev. 11:8; Isa. 52:11), and anyone who covets them might be swept away (Num. 16:26; like Sodom, Gen. 19:15) with all their sins. This is not only because their defilement is contagious but also because of their impending judgment; those in near proximity could suffer the same fate. The actions of Dathan and Abiram together with their families—those who "came out and stood" (Num. 16:27)—signals their defiance, already witnessed by their refusal to heed Moses' summons (cf. v. 12).

To defend his divine appointment, which the two men have challenged (cf. v. 13), Moses calls upon God to confirm his words in an unheard-of way (vv. 28–30). "If they are visited" (*paqad*; v. 29) here means to "intervene with judgment" (cf. 14:18), not to "intervene with favor" (e.g., 1 Sam. 2:21); it never has that positive sense in Numbers. The same verb is rendered "list" in the opening genealogies (e.g., Num. 1:3; cf. comment on 1:1–19) and "appoint" (cf. 1:50; 3:10; 27:16).

The verb "creates" (*bara'*; 16:30) has a homonym, "cut down" (*bara'*: to "clear forestland," Josh. 17:15, 18; "cut down" with a sword, Ezek. 23:47). The object "something new" (*beriy'ah*) is generally taken as a cognate accusative of "create"; however, this noun may be related to the homonymic adjective "fat/healthy" (*beriy'ah*; e.g., Gen. 41:2, "plump" cows) and verb "fatten oneself" (form of *bara'*; 1 Sam. 2:29). If so, the expression would mean "But if the Lord cuts down someone healthy." This understanding fits with Moses' protasis challenge, "If these men die as all men die," answered in the apodosis as evidence of his mediatorial role, "then the LORD has not sent me" (Num. 16:29; cf. Jer. 27:15). It also answers to the conditional "If... they go down alive into Sheol," advanced as conclusive of their false claim, "then you shall know that these men have despised [*na'ats*] the LORD" (Num. 16:30; cf. comment on 14:20–25).

It appears that at this moment an enormous sinkhole providentially opens (16:31). The people may be in the vicinity of the Dead Sea, where cavernous dolines collapsing suddenly can leave a gaping hole several hundred yards (or meters) in diameter. "All the people who belonged to Korah" (v. 32) perish, but not his sons (26:10–11). Dathan and Abiram likewise perish (Deut. 11:6; Ps. 106:17). Descending to "Sheol" alive (Num. 16:33; cf. Ps. 55:15 [55:16 MT]) is a miracle second only to ascending from Sheol (1 Sam. 2:6; Hos. 13:14). "Fire... consumed the 250 men offering the incense" (Num. 16:35), an example of the lex talionis principle: they had "put fire" in their censers (v. 18), and now they are consumed by it.

16:36–50[121] "Eleazar the son of Aaron" (v. 37) is summoned since Aaron the high priest cannot have contact with a corpse. The "blaze" (Hb. *serephah*), fire from the Lord (v. 35), apparently cremates the men (so the LXX; cf. *serephah* of a funeral pyre,

---

121 In the Hebrew text this is 17:1–15.

2 Chron. 16:14). The term is related to "fiery serpent" (*saraph*; Num. 21:8; Isa. 30:6) and "seraphim" (Isa. 6:6). The "fire" (Num. 16:37) is the burning incense coals.

The flattened censers that Korah and his followers used are plated on the altar (v. 38) as a double reminder of the Aaronic priesthood's prerogative and the consequences of Korah's rebellion. The plates serve as a warning ("no outsider... should draw near"; v. 40) addressed particularly to the Levites ("Korah and his company"; v. 40; cf. 3:10) but also generally to anyone else (1:51). Even these censers of sinful men "became holy" (16:38) because they are "offered... before the LORD" (v. 38), that is, at the altar (cf. v. 40), which makes the offering sacred (Ex. 29:37; Matt. 23:19).

The people grumble against Moses and Aaron, claiming that they have killed the rebels (Num. 16:41). However, this is a false accusation. Previously, Moses was accused of being unable to lead them to the Promised Land. Now, he and Aaron are accused of exercising deadly supernatural powers. The people's grumbling is ultimately against the Lord (cf. vv. 8, 11; 17:5). It is therefore ominous when his glory appears (16:42) as an omen (cf. comments on 14:20–25; 16:1–19 [at v. 19]). The Lord is ready to consume the people in his wrath (v. 45), but Moses and Aaron fall on their faces, interceding for them (v. 45; cf. comment on 16:1–19 [at v. 4]).

Atonement within the ritual domain always requires blood to purge the sacred furnishings from impurity. A different kind of atonement is made without blood outside the sanctuary. Its purpose is to appease. Here Aaron makes "atonement" (*kipper*) with incense. Phinehas made it by thrusting a spear through the Moabite woman and the Israelite man (25:11, 13). At the golden calf incident, Moses made it by intercessory prayer (Ex. 32:30–32). In these three cases the mediatorial acts of these men turn away God's wrath from his people (cf. Ps. 78:38). In human relations, Jacob prepared gifts to "appease" (*kipper*) his brother, Esau (Gen. 32:20; cf. Prov. 16:14). Another kind of bloodless atonement involves a "ransom payment" (*koper*) to save someone's life.

God's wrath sends a plague (Num. 16:46). Such execution apparently involves destroying angels (cf. Ex. 12:23; Ps. 78:49–50; Heb. 11:28), as God removes his protection (cf. 2 Thess. 2:6–7). Aaron, however, stands between the dead and the living (Num. 16:48). In making atonement as mediator, he ministers on behalf of the people before God. His person and work literally stand between life and death. He mediates the benefits of atonement for "the living," defending those for whom the atonement is efficacious. The toll in human life is without parallel: "14,700, besides those who died in the affair of Korah" (Num. 16:49). Ironically, the main task of the Levites was to prevent a plague from smiting the people (8:19). No numbers are given for the plague that smote the people at Kibroth-hattaavah (11:34).

Response

Ezekiel warns those who will return from exile that, in the wilderness, the Lord will purge out the rebels, those who will not enter the land (Ezek. 20:34–35).

Moreover, Israel has already been idolatrous in Egypt (Josh. 24:14). It was only for his name's sake that the Lord did not destroy them there (Ezek. 20:8–9). The book of Hebrews also points to the wilderness judgments to warn those who persist in sin, refuse to acknowledge Christ's sacrificial death, and spurn his grace: "A fearful expectation of judgment, and a fury of fire . . . will consume the adversaries. . . . For our God is a consuming fire" (Heb. 10:27; 12:29). These repeated warnings come from the people's own history. The principle is timeless.

NUMBERS 17

17 ¹ The LORD spoke to Moses, saying, ² "Speak to the people of Israel, and get from them staffs, one for each fathers' house, from all their chiefs according to their fathers' houses, twelve staffs. Write each man's name on his staff, ³ and write Aaron's name on the staff of Levi. For there shall be one staff for the head of each fathers' house. ⁴ Then you shall deposit them in the tent of meeting before the testimony, where I meet with you. ⁵ And the staff of the man whom I choose shall sprout. Thus I will make to cease from me the grumblings of the people of Israel, which they grumble against you." ⁶ Moses spoke to the people of Israel. And all their chiefs gave him staffs, one for each chief, according to their fathers' houses, twelve staffs. And the staff of Aaron was among their staffs. ⁷ And Moses deposited the staffs before the LORD in the tent of the testimony.

⁸ On the next day Moses went into the tent of the testimony, and behold, the staff of Aaron for the house of Levi had sprouted and put forth buds and produced blossoms, and it bore ripe almonds. ⁹ Then Moses brought out all the staffs from before the LORD to all the people of Israel. And they looked, and each man took his staff. ¹⁰ And the LORD said to Moses, "Put back the staff of Aaron before the testimony, to be kept as a sign for the rebels, that you may make an end of their grumblings against me, lest they die." ¹¹ Thus did Moses; as the LORD commanded him, so he did.

¹² And the people of Israel said to Moses, "Behold, we perish, we are undone, we are all undone. ¹³ Everyone who comes near, who comes near to the tabernacle of the LORD, shall die. Are we all to perish?"

¹ Ch 17:16 in Hebrew

Section Overview

This passage details the sequel to Korah's rebellion. The focus is on the "people of Israel" (vv. 2, 5, 6, 9, 12), sympathizers who "grumbled against Moses and against Aaron," accusing them "You have killed the people of the LORD" (16:41; i.e., Korah and his followers). The Lord now declares to them he will put an end to the "grumblings of the people of Israel . . . against you [pl.]" (17:5). The challenges of the Israelite leaders to Moses' and Aaron's prerogatives have by now reached the grassroots of the people.

To show the legitimacy of the Aaronic priesthood—as descendant of the second son of Levi, Aaron is not the natural head but the divinely appointed one[122]—a test is made, with the staffs of the chiefs representing all the tribes of Israel. These staffs, each with the name of a tribe written on it, are placed before the testimony. The Lord will show his choice by the staff that sprouts. Aaron's staff not only buds and blossoms; it bears almonds. The Israelites now fear that anyone who comes near the tabernacle will perish (vv. 12–13). Chapter 18 describes how the Lord will allay their fears by reiterating the duties of the priests and Levites, which are designed to keep the people safe.

Section Outline

    II. Trials in the Wilderness of Paran, the Transjordan Highlands, and the Plains of Moab (11:1–25:18) . . .
        G. Test of Twelve Staffs (17:1–13)
            1. Twelve Tribes' Staffs Put before the Lord (17:1–7)
            2. Aaron's Staff Bears Almonds (17:8–13)

Comment

17:1–7[123] The people of Israel are represented by the "chiefs according to their fathers' houses" (v. 2). When assembled, the chiefs are "all the people of Israel" (cf. comment on 17:8–13). The staffs (Hb. *matteh*; vv. 3, 5) here are emblems of the tribes. Each staff is in the possession of the person in authority (cf. Ps. 110:2, "scepter"; Isa. 14:5). The same word also signifies "tribe" (e.g., Num. 18:2).

Moses is to "write Aaron's name on the staff of Levi" (17:3). The question is not concerning which of the twelve tribes the Lord has chosen for priestly service. Rather, which "man" (v. 5) has he chosen?[124] In other words, is the priesthood Aaronic? This may explain why "fathers' house" (vv. 2, 3, 6) is used here instead of "tribe," a term conspicuously absent in chapter 17. The question of whether all Kohathites are priests has been answered in the negative (ch. 16).

The staffs are to be deposited before "the testimony" (17:4), that is, the ark containing the law in the Most Holy Place (4:5; 7:89). If "before" the testimony refers to the curtain at the entry of the tent of meeting rather than the curtain separating the Most Holy Place from the Holy Place, then "Where I meet with *you* [pl.]" (v. 4; cf. v. 19 MT) must refer to meeting with the people (Ex. 29:42). The Lord met with Moses inside the tent (cf. Ex. 25:22). However, there is strong textual support for reading "meet with you [sg.]," in which case Moses alone is in view (Num. 17:9; SP, LXX, Vulg.). For a staff to sprout (*parah*; 17:5) would be miraculous, since it would be made of dead wood. The sign should be enough to

---

122 Ellicott, "Numbers," 159.
123 In the Hebrew text this is 17:16–22.
124 Levine, *Numbers 1–20*, 421.

bring Israel's grumblings to an end. To grumble against God's appointed servants is to grumble against him.

17:8–13[125] Not only does Aaron's rod sprout, but it "put forth buds and produced blossoms, and it bore ripe almonds" (v. 8). Centuries later, upon seeing an "almond [*shaqed*] branch" and hearing the Lord's response, "I am watching over [*shoqed*] my word to perform it" (Jer. 1:11, 12), Jeremiah, as prophet-priest, would no doubt have recalled Aaron's staff and its almonds (*sheqedim*). The people's twelve leaders now see incontrovertible proof of God's choice of Aaron and his family for the priesthood.

After Korah's rebellion, the hammered censers now plating the altar are a warning sign against grumbling (16:38; cf. 17:10). Grumbling expresses the heart's rebellion. The heart is the source of evil expressed by the mouth; such speech defiles (Matt. 15:11, 18). The people have already been warned that grumbling is a sin leading to death (Num. 14:29).

"Everyone who comes near . . . shall die" (17:13), except a priest from the Levitical family of Amram descended from Aaron (cf. comment on 16:1–19). "Are we all to perish?" renders a finite verb (*tamam*) and an infinitive (*gavaʿ*; cf. v. 12; 20:3, 29) that woodenly reads, "Shall we end up by perishing?" *Tamam* occurs three other times in Numbers for those doomed to die in the wilderness, referring to the "last of" (14:33) the bodies of those who would "come to a full end" (14:35) and were ultimately "gone" (32:13).

Response

Dissension over ecclesiology has remained a part of the history of God's people. The Reverend George Gillespie (1613–1648), a Scottish theologian, penned *Aaron's Rod Blossoming; or The Divine Ordinance of Church Government Vindicated* (1646). A strong defender of Presbyterian polity, Gillespie, by distinguishing between ecclesial and civil government, made the case for the exclusive spiritual jurisdiction in the church at a time in which the Church of Scotland was resisting strong English influence. Gillespie was a member of the Westminster Assembly of Divines and assisted in the preparation of its Confession of Faith. Aaron's rod is a reminder of distinctions that are, in principle, still valid. Although those in civil and ecclesiastical authority are servants of God, those serving in the kingdom "not of this world" (John 18:36) have qualifications of a higher standard (1 Tim. 3:1–13). Their spheres of authority and rule differ.

---

[125] In the Hebrew text this is 17:23–28.

NUMBERS 18

18 So the Lord said to Aaron, "You and your sons and your father's house with you shall bear iniquity connected with the sanctuary, and you and your sons with you shall bear iniquity connected with your priesthood. ² And with you bring your brothers also, the tribe of Levi, the tribe of your father, that they may join you and minister to you while you and your sons with you are before the tent of the testimony. ³ They shall keep guard over you and over the whole tent, but shall not come near to the vessels of the sanctuary or to the altar lest they, and you, die. ⁴ They shall join you and keep guard over the tent of meeting for all the service of the tent, and no outsider shall come near you. ⁵ And you shall keep guard over the sanctuary and over the altar, that there may never again be wrath on the people of Israel. ⁶ And behold, I have taken your brothers the Levites from among the people of Israel. They are a gift to you, given to the Lord, to do the service of the tent of meeting. ⁷ And you and your sons with you shall guard your priesthood for all that concerns the altar and that is within the veil; and you shall serve. I give your priesthood as a gift,¹ and any outsider who comes near shall be put to death."

⁸ Then the Lord spoke to Aaron, "Behold, I have given you charge of the contributions made to me, all the consecrated things of the people of Israel. I have given them to you as a portion and to your sons as a perpetual due. ⁹ This shall be yours of the most holy things, reserved from the fire: every offering of theirs, every grain offering of theirs and every sin offering of theirs and every guilt offering of theirs, which they render to me, shall be most holy to you and to your sons. ¹⁰ In a most holy place shall you eat it. Every male may eat it; it is holy to you. ¹¹ This also is yours: the contribution of their gift, all the wave offerings of the people of Israel. I have given them to you, and to your sons and daughters with you, as a perpetual due. Everyone who is clean in your house may eat it. ¹² All the best of the oil and all the best of the wine and of the grain, the firstfruits of what they give to the Lord, I give to you. ¹³ The first ripe fruits of all that is in their land, which they bring to the Lord, shall be yours. Everyone who is clean in your house may eat it. ¹⁴ Every devoted thing in Israel shall be yours. ¹⁵ Everything that opens the womb of all flesh, whether man or beast, which they offer to the Lord, shall be yours. Nevertheless, the firstborn of man you shall redeem, and the firstborn of unclean animals you shall redeem. ¹⁶ And their redemption price (at a month old you shall redeem them) you shall fix at five shekels² in silver, according to the shekel of the sanctuary, which is twenty gerahs. ¹⁷ But the firstborn of a cow, or the firstborn of a sheep, or the firstborn of a goat, you shall not redeem; they are holy. You shall sprinkle their blood on the altar and shall burn their fat as a food offering, with a pleasing aroma to the Lord. ¹⁸ But their flesh shall be yours, as the breast that is waved and as the right thigh are yours. ¹⁹ All the holy contributions that the people of Israel present to

the LORD I give to you, and to your sons and daughters with you, as a perpetual due. It is a covenant of salt forever before the LORD for you and for your offspring with you." ²⁰ And the LORD said to Aaron, "You shall have no inheritance in their land, neither shall you have any portion among them. I am your portion and your inheritance among the people of Israel.

²¹ "To the Levites I have given every tithe in Israel for an inheritance, in return for their service that they do, their service in the tent of meeting, ²² so that the people of Israel do not come near the tent of meeting, lest they bear sin and die. ²³ But the Levites shall do the service of the tent of meeting, and they shall bear their iniquity. It shall be a perpetual statute throughout your generations, and among the people of Israel they shall have no inheritance. ²⁴ For the tithe of the people of Israel, which they present as a contribution to the LORD, I have given to the Levites for an inheritance. Therefore I have said of them that they shall have no inheritance among the people of Israel."

²⁵ And the LORD spoke to Moses, saying, ²⁶ "Moreover, you shall speak and say to the Levites, 'When you take from the people of Israel the tithe that I have given you from them for your inheritance, then you shall present a contribution from it to the LORD, a tithe of the tithe. ²⁷ And your contribution shall be counted to you as though it were the grain of the threshing floor, and as the fullness of the winepress. ²⁸ So you shall also present a contribution to the LORD from all your tithes, which you receive from the people of Israel. And from it you shall give the LORD's contribution to Aaron the priest. ²⁹ Out of all the gifts to you, you shall present every contribution due to the LORD; from each its best part is to be dedicated.' ³⁰ Therefore you shall say to them, 'When you have offered from it the best of it, then the rest shall be counted to the Levites as produce of the threshing floor, and as produce of the winepress. ³¹ And you may eat it in any place, you and your households, for it is your reward in return for your service in the tent of meeting. ³² And you shall bear no sin by reason of it, when you have contributed the best of it. But you shall not profane the holy things of the people of Israel, lest you die.'"

¹ Hebrew *service of gift* ² A *shekel* was about 2/5 ounce or 11 grams

Section Overview

After the Kohathite challenge to the Aaronic priesthood (Numbers 16) and the subsequent test of the staffs proving Aaronic primacy (ch. 17), chapter 18 reformulates the distinct responsibilities of priests and Levites (vv. 1–7; cf. 1:50–53; 3:5–10; 4:4–33) and specifies their revenues (18:8–32). Korah's rebellion has neither nullified God's promises to the Kohathites nor revoked their responsibilities or privileges (3:29–31; 4:2–4, 15).

Because of the outbreak of God's wrath (cf. comment on 16:36–50)—a plague killing thousands (16:49)—the people are afraid to come near to the tabernacle (17:12–13). That dread is allayed in chapter 18 by the reiteration of the ministries of the priests and the Levites: "That there may never again be wrath on the people of Israel" (v. 5) and "So that the people of Israel do not come near the tent of meeting, lest they bear sin and die" (v. 22).

The priests' revenues listed in chapter 18 includes portions ("contributions"; cf. vv. 8, 19) of the grain, sin, and guilt offerings (vv. 8–10); best of produce; firstfruits; anything devoted; unburnt parts of sacrificed firstborn clean animals; and the redemption price of firstborn sons and unclean animals (vv. 11–18). The Levites receive tithes from the people and tithe those to the priests (vv. 21–32). Other sources of priestly revenues include restitution payments if there is no next of kin (5:8), a portion of plunder (also for Levites; 31:29–30), animal hides of burnt offerings (Lev. 7:8), and showbread (Lev. 24:9). Such revenues are their due for their tabernacle service and compensation for having no land inheritance (Num. 18:20–21). Failure to care for their needs forsakes the house of God (Neh. 13:10–11).

These foci of chapter 18 also demonstrate the faithfulness of God to his promises. The revenues derived from priestly service depends upon the people's settling in the Promised Land and enjoying its bounty.

Section Outline

II. Trials in the Wilderness of Paran, the Transjordan Highlands, and the Plains of Moab (11:1–25:18) . . .
    H. Service and Revenues of Priests and Levites (18:1–32)
        1. Responsibilities and Rights of Priests and Levites (18:1–7)
        2. Priests' Revenues from the Offerings (18:8–19)
        3. Levites' Revenues from Tithes (18:20–32)

Comment

18:1–7 By being directly addressed ("The LORD said to Aaron," vv. 1, 20; elsewhere only at Ex. 4:27; cf. "the Lord spoke to Aaron," Num. 18:8; elsewhere only Lev. 10:8), Aaron's sacerdotal prerogative is underscored. All three sections of chapter 18 (cf. Section Outline) are introduced by the Lord's addressing only Aaron. "Your sons" (18:1) are Aaron's, who are and will be priests (cf. 16:40; "descendants of Aaron"). Your "father's house with you" (18:1) is a reminder of the Kohath-Amramite ancestry of Aaron (Ex. 6:18, 20), as distinct from the Kohath-Izharite descendance of Korah (Num. 16:1), but also a reaffirmation of their common Kohathite ancestry. To "bear iniquity connected with the sanctuary" (18:1) is to bear the responsibility and the penalty for allowing any desecration of the sacred by intrusion of impurity or sin. Aaron and his sons are to ensure that the Kohathites do not die due to priestly negligence in the sanctuary (3:10; 4:14, 17–20). "The sanctuary" (18:1; Hb. *hammiqdash*, "the holy [place]") refers to the Most Holy Place and the Holy Place, along with their furnishings.

The priests bear the responsibility and the consequences of their personal infringements and ritual omission and commission violations (v. 1). Aaron's sons died for their violation (3:4), as could a high priest who wrongly goes inside the veil (Lev. 16:2). Priests must also prevent encroachment by an unqualified, maimed, or unclean fellow priest (Lev. 21:23; Neh. 7:64–65; cf. Ex. 28:43; Lev. 10:9). The priest also bears iniquity by eating certain of the sin/purification offerings of the people, with which the priest makes atonement (Lev. 10:17).[126] Given his mediatorial office, he performs the required blood ceremonies to make atonement (cf. comment on Num. 15:22–31 [at v. 25]).

"With you bring your brothers also" (Num. 18:2) emphasizes the mutual lineage of the priestly and nonpriestly Levites against the background of strained relations (ch. 16). "Tribe... tribe" renders synonyms, respectively *matteh* and *shebet*. The former is an echo of the "staff" (*matteh*) incident (17:2). "The tribe of Levi [*lvy'*] ... shall join [*lvh'*] you" (18:2) emphasizes paronomastically the joint ministry of the Levites and the priests. For "minister to you" (v. 2; *shrt*) cf. comments on 1:47–54 [at v. 50]; 8:23–26. The Levites are to keep guard over the priests and the whole tabernacle complex (18:3). By making a physical barrier around it, whether stationary or in transit, the Levites are to keep any unauthorized person or thing outside. However, they are not to come near to the vessels of the sanctuary or to the altar (v. 3). The priests protect the Levites from death from encroachment by covering the sanctuary furnishings and the altar (cf. 4:12, 14). The priests too will die if they fail to prevent Levite encroachment (18:3).

That "they shall keep guard" and that "no outsider shall come near you" (v. 4) reiterate the Levites' principal duty regarding the priests (1:51, 53; 3:10, 38). Encroachment will defile them (cf. Ezek. 44:19). The "service [*'abodah*] of the tent" is the physical labor involved in assisting the priests and transporting the tabernacle. The Levites must prevent the people with offerings from going beyond the altar in the court (Num. 18:22), although they themselves can, under certain conditions, assist the priests at the altar (cf. 2 Chron. 30:15, 17; 35:11).

To "keep guard over the sanctuary and over the altar" (Num. 18:5) refers to the duties of Aaron and his sons. Officiating in the sanctuary and at the altar is their exclusive prerogative. In addition they pack and cover the sanctuary furnishings, which the Kohathites can neither look upon nor directly touch as they transport them (4:15, 20). Eleazar supervises the Kohathites and all the chiefs of the Levitical clans (3:32). Ithamar supervises the Gershonites and the Merarites (4:28, 33).

The reason for this reiteration of the sacred service in response to the people's fear is so that there will "never again be wrath on the people" (18:5; cf. 17:12–13). "Wrath" has recently taken the form of devastating fire and deadly plagues (e.g., 16:35, 49; cf. comment on 16:36–50).

To call the Levites "your brothers" (Num. 18:2, 6; 2 Chron. 29:34) reminds Aaron, and all priests, of God's grace. Priests and Levites are "brothers" (Num. 8:26) not only physically but also in "service" (18:6; cf. Ps. 133:1). "They are a gift to you, given to the LORD" (Num. 18:6; cf. 3:9). The Levites belong to the Lord. Once purified, they are offered as a wave offering, substituted for Israelite firstborn, then given to Aaron and his sons (8:15–19, 21). This sovereign endowment is not nullified by Korah's rebellion.

---

126 On Leviticus 10:17 Milgrom (*Leviticus 1–16*, 622–625, 635–640) says if God is the subject of the verb, bearing iniquity means removing it (e.g., Num. 14:18). If a person is the subject, he himself bears the iniquity, that is, its punishment (e.g., Num. 18:1, 23). J. E. Hartley writes that "Bear the iniquity of the congregation" by a priest is grammatically explained: "To make atonement." *Leviticus 1–27*, WBC 4 (Dallas: Word, 1992), 136.

The four terms "Guard ... altar ... veil ... serve" (18:7) are shorthand for priestly duties and service spheres (cf. 3:31; 4:28). The verbs, "guard" (*shamar*) and "serve" (*'abad*), label the priests' primary responsibilities: preventing encroachment and performing ceremonial labor such as slaughtering, butchering, and flaying animal offerings. The "altar" in the court and the "veil" separating the Holy Place and the Most Holy Place delimit their ministry domains and the sacred furnishings involved. Priests enter the Holy Place morning and evening. The high priest enters the Most Holy Place once a year. If impurity breaches the court, the altar is defiled. Impurity also penetrates the Holy Place and pollutes the incense altar. It can penetrate the Most Holy Place and defile the mercy seat. "Any outsider" here is a Levite or a disqualified priest (cf. discussion on 18:1 above); one who comes near is to be "put to death" (cf. 3:10; 4:18–20) by man's hand (cf. comment on 17:8–13, "shall die").

18:8–19 The second section opens like the first and third, with the Lord addressing Aaron (v. 8; cf. vv. 1, 20). The "charge [*mishmeret*] of the contributions" (v. 8) now involves adhering to the regulations concerning sacred gifts, the measured "portion," the "perpetual due."

Priestly remuneration falls into two categories:

(1) "Contributions" (pl. *terumah*), some of which are "most holy," here specified as the parts "reserved from the fire," that is, removed from the rest of the sacrifice burned on the altar, of the "grain ... sin ... guilt offering[s]" that are partaken of by the officiating priest and his "sons" in a "most holy place" (Num. 18:8–10; cf. comment on 5:5–10 [at v. 9]).

(2) Less sacred "wave offerings" and "holy contributions," which could be shared with the priest's "sons and daughters" and "everyone who is clean" in his household (18:11, 19; cf. Lev. 22:4, 6–7). These offerings and contributions are listed in Numbers 18:12–19.[127]

In addition to these, in Numbers "contributions" includes holy donations in general (5:9), the thigh of the Nazirite's peace offering (6:20), the first dough (15:19–20), tithes (18:24–29), and plunder donated for the sanctuary (31:29, 41, 52). Apart from the offerings at the altar, the contributions are given directly to the priest (5:10). In addition, in Numbers "wave offerings" include the grain offering of the woman suspected of adultery (5:25), the ram's shoulder and bread of the Nazirite's peace offering (6:19–20), the breast and right thigh of the peace offering (6:20; 18:18), and the Levites themselves (8:11, 13, 15, 21). Wave offerings involve a ritual performed in the sanctuary before the offerings are given to priests.

The contributions are "made to me" from "the people of Israel" (18:8). The priest does not receive his revenue from the people; he receives a share of the people's gifts first given to the Lord. A "portion" (*moshkhah*) is a measured, quantifiable

---

127 On these offerings cf. Jacob Milgrom, *Leviticus 1–16*, AYB (New Haven, CT: Yale University Press, 1998), 461–473, 473–481; R. E. Averbeck, "*nuph*," NIDOTTE, 3:63–67; Averbeck, "*terumah*," NIDOTTE, 4:335–338.

allotment that could be, for example, the thigh contribution and the breast wave offering of the peace offering, each part of which could also be called a "portion" (*manah*; Lev. 7:33; 8:29).[128] "Perpetual due" (*hoq*) comprises these same parts (cf. Lev. 7:34), or in general all of the remunerations (cf. *hoq*, "fixed allowance" of Egyptian priests; Gen. 47:22). Their being "perpetual" ensures that they will continue for the priests in the land (2 Chron. 31:3–7; cf. Ezra 2:62–63).

The "most holy things" (Num. 18:9) in Hebrew is simply the "most holy" (*qodesh haqqodashim*), which elsewhere generally signifies "a most holy place" or "the Most Holy Place" (e.g., Ex. 26:34), its furnishings (Num. 4:4, 19), and food from sacrifices (2 Chron. 31:6; Ezra 2:63; Neh. 7:65). Here it qualifies priests' food, the designated portions of "every grain offering . . . every sin offering . . . and every guilt offering" (Num. 18:9; cf. Lev. 6:14–17; Ezek. 42:13). "Render to me" (*shub*) implies that these first belong to the Lord, who gives them to the offeror, who then returns them to the Lord by giving them to the priest.

Given the offerings' highest sacred status, they can be eaten only by a priest and his sons, "every male," in "a most holy place" (Num. 18:10; cf. Lev. 6:17–18, 25–26), that is, between the altar and the tent of meeting (Lev. 6:25–26; cf. Ezek. 42:13), whose status is perhaps elevated from holy to "most holy" by contact with these sacrifices (Ex. 29:37; Matt. 23:19).[129] In Ezekiel's vision, the priests eat these offerings in the north and south chambers (Ezek. 42:17–18).

Numbers 18:11–19 treats gifts of a lesser sacred status—"holy" (v. 19) but not most holy—that the priest and his entire household can enjoy. "Gifts" also refer to "every contribution" in verse 29. All "wave offerings" (*tenuphah*) are beforehand dedicated as a "contribution" (*terumah*) by the offeror.[130] This apparently explains why some offerings are both contributions and wave offerings (cf. Ex. 29:22–24, 27; 35:24; Lev. 9:18, 21; 10:14).

As stated above (cf. comment on Num. 15:1–21 [at v. 20]), the word "contribution" (*terumah*) is drawn from "lift up, raise" (*rum*), leading to the familiar translation "heave offering" (KJV), suggesting an up-and-down movement. But it would be impossible to lift some contributions (Ex. 35:24; cf. Ex. 38:25, 26; Num. 31:32–41, 52). A contribution is generally a portion lifted (removed) from a whole, like the tithe (18:24; cf. "lift an offering"), or bread made from a large lump of dough. For the peace offering, the right thigh contribution is removed and given to the priest (Lev. 7:32). The tithe and the tithed tithe are separated from the total that has been collected and is presented (*rum*) as a contribution (*terumah*; Num. 18:24, 26) to the Levites and priests, respectively. The cognate verb (*ramam*) also has this meaning (16:45, "get away"; i.e., "remove yourself," "separate"). Meanwhile, the denominative of "wave offering" (*tenuphah*; Num. 18:11) is "wave" (*nuph*; cf. comment on 8:5–22 [at v. 15]). If it involves a back-and-forth

---

[128] CDCH (249) links the noun *moshkhah* II ("'prescribed portion' of priests from sacrifices"; only Num. 18:8) to the verb *mshkh* III ("measure") found in a Qumran text.
[129] Haran argues that the area between the tabernacle entry and the altar has a minor degree of holiness. He calls the stricter holiness between the altar and the tent "contagious holiness" (*Temples and Temple-Service*, 184).
[130] Milgrom, *Leviticus 1–16*, 474–476; Milgrom, *Numbers*, 427.

gesture, "wave" may stem from the ritual practice of the priest, who, after receiving the offering, places it back in the hands of the offeror (cf. Num. 5:25; 6:19; cf. Ex. 29:24).[131] As a wave offering, the Levites (Num. 8:15) would be impossible to move physically.

The new "oil" (*yitshar*), new "wine" (*tirosh*),[132] and whole "grain" (*dagan*) are to be distinguished from the oil (*shemen*), wine (*yayin*), and ground grain (*soleth*) accompanying the regular burnt offerings (Lev. 23:12–13) and those offered at the Feast of Weeks (Num. 28:26–31). The former group of three is called *re'shith* ("firstfruits"; Num. 18:12; Deut. 18:4) and the latter group *bikkurim* ("first ripe fruits,"; cf. discussion on Num. 18:13 above).[133] The best of all of these belongs to the priests. "The firstfruits" (v. 12; *re'shitham*) involves the first processed produce of those three crops—oil (olives), wine (grapes), and grain (barley)—the latter coming from the threshing floor (v. 27) and thus being a hard grain separated from the head and chaff. These are a sign of God's blessing (Deut. 7:13; Jer. 31:12). Firstfruits (*re'shith*) include leaven, dough, wool (Lev. 2:12; Num. 15:20–21; Deut. 18:4), honey, and "all the produce of the field" (2 Chron. 31:5). Firstborn are also called firstfruits (Gen. 49:3; Ps. 105:36).

"The first ripe fruits" (*bikkurim*; Num. 18:13) are associated with the Feast of Weeks and the wheat harvest and are brought at the end of the agricultural year during the Feast of Booths (Ex. 34:22). As such, they are wave offerings (*tenuphah*), since the Israelites bring them "to the LORD" (Num. 18:13), that is, at the sanctuary (cf. Ex. 23:19; 34:26). The *re'shith*, as "contributions" (*terumah*), are given directly to the priest (Lev. 23:10–11). In Second Temple times *re'shit* and *bikkurim* were brought to the temple and stored in chambers for the priests and the Levites (Neh. 10:35, 37 [v. 36 MT], 38; 12:44). These gifts could be consumed by all the priest's family members (Num. 18:11) if they were ceremonially "clean" (v. 13), since they involved "holy contributions" (v. 19), not "most holy things" (v. 9).

"What they give to the LORD, I give to you" (Num. 18:12; cf. vv. 8, 11) is echoed in 2 Corinthians 8:5 concerning the Macedonian churches' offering: "They gave themselves first to the Lord and then by the will of God to us." Paul often describes service in the church in priestly language.

A "devoted thing" (*kherem*; Num. 18:14) is something voluntarily and irrevocably devoted to the Lord, in this case for the priests' revenue. It is transferred from the profane (common) to the sacred domain by the offeror and is most holy (Lev. 27:28), even though the devoting is not done in the sanctuary (cf. Acts 5:1–4). Several close connections can be seen between the Leviticus *kherem* law (27:28)

---

[131] Milgrom also adds Egyptian cultic evidence of an offering described formulaically like the wave offering and depicted in a relief placed in the hands of the offerer (*Leviticus 1–16*, 471).

[132] Cf. BDB: *yitshar*, "fresh oil, in unmanufactured state" (844a); *tirosh*, "fresh or new wine" (440b). If similar to current practice, new oil could be from the cold first pressing (which does not crush the seeds, as do heated further pressings), and the new wine from the first harvested grapes, quickly fermented—both are choice products still much appreciated in the Mediterranean region, where this commentator lives.

[133] Distinctions drawn between *re'shith* and *bikkurim* vary. According to Mishnaic interpretation *bikkurim* involve the produce in Deuteronomy 8:8 ("of wheat and barley, of vines and fig trees and pomegranates, . . . of olive trees and honey"; Bikkurim 1:3; cf. Berakhot 6:4). For Milgrom *re'shit* are first-processed produce and *bikkurim* first-ripe produce (*Numbers*, 427–428). Budd (*Numbers*, 205) and Ashley (*Book of Numbers*, 349) view the terms as used in Numbers 18 as synonymous.

and the Numbers law, including their contexts. The Leviticus law includes fields as *kherem* donations, which would no doubt include their produce for sanctuary use. In Numbers the *kherem* law comes immediately after the firstfruits gifts (18:12–13), which is followed by tithes, including those on those very products (vv. 27, 30). In Numbers the *kherem* law is immediately followed by the firstborn redemption laws (18:15–18), whereas in Leviticus they precede it (Lev. 27:26–27). As with the most holy devoted things in Leviticus (Lev. 27:28), Numbers delimits most holy offerings of grain, sin, and guilt offerings (Num. 18:9). These same three are summarized as priestly gifts in Ezekiel 44:29, to which is added "every devoted thing" (*kol kherem*).

"Everything that opens the womb" (Num. 18:15) refers to a mother's male firstborn of both "man or beast," which the people "offer to the LORD." Underlying the firstborn law here and elsewhere (Ex. 13:12–13; 22:29–30; 34:19–20; Lev. 27:26–27; Deut. 15:19–23) is a threefold division: clean male sacrificial animals, unclean male animals, and human males. The firstborn neither of man nor of unclean animals (Num. 18:16) could be offered on the altar. Therefore, "you shall redeem" (*padah*; vv. 15, 16) them. The "redemption price" (from *padah*; v. 16) belongs to the priests (cf. Lev. 27:27; Num. 3:41, 45, 47–51). This term for "redeem" (18:15, 16, 17; cf. 3:49) implies purchasing something not originally possessed by the owner—since it first belonged to the Lord (Lev. 27:26)—whereas another term also translated "redeem" (*ga'al*) refers to buying something back originally owned (e.g., Lev. 25:25).[134]

Being intrinsically clean animals and holy as firstborn, the "firstborn of a cow ... sheep ... or a goat" irrevocably belonged to the sacred domain and were to be sacrificed (Num. 18:17). "Cow" (*shur*) here refers to a female cow giving birth for the first time (cf. Lev. 22:28); the same distinction applies to sheep and goats. *Shur* generally refers to cattle collectively or to an ox when used individually. However, it also appears as "ox" when listed with the two other animals being offered as sacrifices (Lev. 17:3; 27:23), which may explain why *shur* is used here rather than the usual term for cow (*parah*; e.g., 1 Sam. 6:10; Job 21:10).

The terms "sprinkle [*zaraq*, or "throw"] their blood on the altar ... burn their fat ... pleasing aroma ... breast ... waved ... right thigh" (Num. 18:17–18) apply to the peace offering (Lev. 7:29–32, 34; 10:14; 17:6; Num. 6:18, 20), of which the thigh contribution and waved breast belong to the officiating priest (Lev. 7:34). Normally, the remaining flesh of the peace offering would be eaten by the offeror (Lev. 7:15–18). If it is a firstborn sacrifice, however, "their flesh shall be yours" (Num. 18:18), that is, the priest's.

Verse 19, forming an inclusio (cf. v. 11), summarizes all the holy contributions mentioned above, which are for "you," the priests, and "your sons and daughters." The "salt of the covenant" (*melakh [hab]berit*; Lev. 2:13) is added to unleavened grain offerings. Salt is also added to burnt offerings and sin offerings (Ezek. 43:24; cf. Ezra 6:9). In secular contexts, partaking of salt is synonymous with longstanding

---

134 N. H. Snaith, *Leviticus and Numbers*, Century Bible (London: Nelson, 1967), 268.

loyalty (Ezra 4:14),[135] a covenant requisite. Mention of this "covenant of salt" anticipates the covenant of peace made with Aaron's son, Phinehas, a covenant of perpetual priesthood (Num. 25:12). Divine covenants are corporate and transgenerational (e.g., Gen. 9:9; 17:7; Ps. 105:8–10), as are the promises they seal: "For you and for your offspring" (Num. 18:19; cf. Gen. 28:14; Acts 2:39; Gal. 3:14). Like the "everlasting [*'olam*] covenant" (Gen. 9:16; 17:19; 2 Sam. 23:5; Jer. 32:40), these holy gifts are a "perpetual [*'olam*] due" (Num. 18:19), that is, for as long as the law covenant is in effect.

18:20–32 Unlike the other tribes, the priests and Levites have no inheritance in the land (v. 20). Rather than a land inheritance, they have the Lord, with the gifts for priests for their sanctuary service and now tithes for the Levites and priests as their financial recompense (vv. 20, 23–24, 25–32; Deut. 18:2). "Portion" (*heleq*; v. 20) is not the same Hebrew word as in verse 8 (*moshkhah*). *Heleq* and "inheritance" (*nakhalah*) are often paired, referring to a heritage passed on to children (Gen. 31:14), Israel's inheritance of Canaan (1 Chron. 16:18; Ps. 105:11), the territory of a tribe (Josh. 17:14), and here the territory denied the tribe of Levi (cf. Deut. 10:9; 18:1). It can refer to land lots or fields (Josh. 18:5, 9; Mic. 2:4, "fields"). When land inheritance is the object, the cognate verb means "divide/allot" (*halaq*; Num. 26:53, 55, 56; Mic. 2:4).

The Levites' tithes (Num. 18:21) are treated first, since the priests' tithes depend on them. "Every tithe" (*ma'aser*) is a "one-tenth" unit (cf. *'eser*, "ten"). Livestock, grain, wine, and oil are tithed (Lev. 27:30, 32; Num. 18:30; Deut. 14:23; cf. 2 Chron. 31:5–6 for more tithed produce). In addition to vegetable and animal tithes, the Levites receive agricultural and pasturelands around their forty-eight cities (Num. 35:2–8; cf. Josh. 21:13–19; Ezek. 45:4). "In return" (Num. 18:21, *heleph*; only elsewhere in v. 31) is cognate with "to substitute" (*halaph*; Lev. 27:10). "Service" (*'abodah*; Num. 18:21) is physical labor, such as maintaining and transporting the tent of meeting (v. 21), measuring grain, wine and oil, and flaying animals for offerings (1 Chron. 23:29; 2 Chron. 35:11; Ezek. 44:11; cf. comment on Num. 8:23–26 and note on v. 26). The tithe is given by the people to the Lord (18:24), who in turn gives it to the Levites. This restates the principle concerning the priests' gifts (vv. 8, 11, 19).

"So that the people of Israel do not come near the tent of meeting" (v. 22) probably means they cannot go beyond the altar in the court (cf. Ex. 40:29; Lev. 1:5). The primary Levitical service is to prevent encroachment. By their encampments and their service ceremonially clean Levites make a hedge separating the sanctuary and the secular tribes' camps (Num. 1:50, 53), like the hangings around the tabernacle court and the wall around the temple (Ezek. 42:20). "Lest they bear sin and die" (Num. 18:22) restates the consequence of encroachment for the people (1:51, 53), which the Levite guards must prevent. If someone trespasses, the Levites "shall bear [the people's] iniquity [guilt consequences]" (18:23). Their lives, as a

---

[135] Milgrom cites a neo-Babylonian letter in which a tribe's allies are called those who have tasted its salt (*Numbers*, 154).

ransom substitute, "make atonement" (8:19). For encroachment the people bear sin (18:22), whereas priests and Levites bear iniquity (18:1, 23).[136] Although sin and iniquity are sometimes synonyms (e.g., Pss. 32:5; 51:2, 5), iniquity here may involve a greater offense, given the high office of those accountable. On the Day of Atonement blood atonement is made for the Holy Place because of the peoples' transgressions and sins (Lev. 16:16). But their iniquities are laid on the scapegoat, who bears them outside the camp (Lev. 16:21). Concerning the abased and exalted servant of the Lord, "the LORD laid on him the iniquities of us all"; regarding those he would make righteous, "he shall bear their iniquities" (Isa. 53:11; cf. Isa. 53:5, 6). He also deals with their transgressions and sins (Isa. 53:5, 12).[137]

The Lord now addresses Moses (Num. 18:25). Aaron is spared from telling his brothers how and what they should give to him and his sons (vv. 26–32). "You shall present [*rum*] a contribution [*terumah*]" (v. 26) involves presenting a part of a whole (cf. comment on 15:1–21 [at v. 20]), here a "tithe of the tithe," which delimits "contribution." The Levites' tithe for the priests is "as" (*ke-*) the people's firstfruits offering (18:27). Once the Levites tithe to the priests, they can use the rest just as the Israelites can, consuming or selling the remainder of their produce. "Fullness" (*mele'ah*) occurs only twice elsewhere (Ex. 22:29; Deut. 22:9). It may substitute for the expression "best of" (lit., "fat of") in connection with firstfruits (Num. 18:12). A related term (*melo'*) signifies what the earth produces (Deut. 33:16). The "winepress" (*yeqeb*) is used for wine and oil (cf. Joel 2:24, "vats"; cf. Isa. 5:2; 16:10). It has two cavities hewn in the rock and joined by a narrow channel, the higher cavity for pressing and the lower for collecting. This verse has in view the principal agricultural firstfruits: grain, wine, oil (Num. 18:12). The people tithe this produce for the Levites (Neh. 13:5, 12; cf. Deut. 12:17; 14:23). The Levites tithe it for the priests (Neh. 10:39).

The tithe is holy (Lev. 27:30; Deut. 26:13). The "contribution" (Num. 18:29) from it, "its best part" (v. 29; cf. comment on 18:8–19 [at v. 12]), is "dedicated" (*miqdesho*; v. 29), that is, the tenth of the tithe.[138] "The rest" (v. 30) involves the nine-tenths remaining after the one-tenth tithe contribution. The term "any place" (v. 31) assumes such a place is ritually clean, since the people's tithe they will "eat" is holy. The food supply is for everyone in the household ("you and your households"). "Reward" (*sakar*) could also be rendered "wage" (e.g., Gen. 30:28, 32). The Levites incur no punishment when they eat the remainder (Num. 18:32); however, they are not to "profane the holy things" (v. 32) by eating of the tithe before the one-tenth contribution is lifted or by eating the remainder in a state of uncleanness. Otherwise they will die like Nadab and Abihu (3:4) and like Korah and his followers (ch. 16).

---

136 On verse 23 and encroachment cf. Milgrom, *Numbers*, 155, 423–424.
137 Ron Bergey, "The Rhetorical Role of Reiteration in the Suffering Servant Poem, Isaiah 52:13—53:12," *JETS* 40 (1997): 177–188.
138 *CDCH* (240) has two entries for this word: *miqdash* ("'consecrated part' of an offering," citing Numbers 18:29) and **[miqdesh]* ("holiest part," for Numbers 18:29 alone). It cannot mean "most holy," since those gifts were restricted to the priests and their sons (v. 9), whereas the holy gifts, as this one, were for priests and their households (v. 31). The spelling anomaly *miqdesho* rather than *miqdasho* (e.g., Isa. 16:12) suggests the scribes deliberately avoided the superlative meaning.

Response

The Israelites support the priests' and Levites' service through their "tithes and offerings," which fittingly sums up Numbers 18. Malachi 3:9–10 will remind them that not to tithe is to rob God, which will lead to a curse (dearth), whereas tithing will bring blessing (abundance). On two occasions Paul cites "You shall not muzzle an ox when it is treading out the grain" (Deut. 25:4) to remind churches that they must provide generously for their ministers (1 Cor. 9:9; 1 Tim. 5:18). He exhorts them, saying, "In the same way, the Lord commanded that those who proclaim the gospel should get their living by the gospel" (1 Cor. 9:14; cf. Matt. 10:10, "the laborer deserves his food"). And again, "Let the elders who rule well be considered worthy of double honor [remuneration], especially those who labor in preaching and teaching. . . . The laborer deserves his wages" (1 Tim. 5:17–18).

Clearly, those called to minister should earn their living doing so. Generous salaries, housing allowances, expense accounts, medical insurance, and pension funds might entice some to enter ministry and to remain in it, but they ought not. Elders are warned not to fulfill their duties solely for financial gain (Titus 1:7), and certainly not for ill-gotten gain (1 Tim. 3:8; 1 Pet. 5:2), which can involve that which is derived from sinful motives. Yet the opposite is true too. Some do not enter ministry because there is little, insufficient, or sometimes no remuneration. Those who sacrificially minister labor knowing their eternal reward will be great (1 Pet. 5:4; cf. 1 Cor. 9:12). Yet that should be the exception, not the rule.

NUMBERS 19

19 Now the Lord spoke to Moses and to Aaron, saying, **2** "This is the statute of the law that the Lord has commanded: Tell the people of Israel to bring you a red heifer without defect, in which there is no blemish, and on which a yoke has never come. **3** And you shall give it to Eleazar the priest, and it shall be taken outside the camp and slaughtered before him. **4** And Eleazar the priest shall take some of its blood with his finger, and sprinkle some of its blood toward the front of the tent of meeting seven times. **5** And the heifer shall be burned in his sight. Its skin, its flesh, and its blood, with its dung, shall be burned. **6** And the priest shall take cedarwood and hyssop and scarlet yarn, and throw them into the fire burning the heifer. **7** Then the priest shall wash his clothes and bathe his body in water, and afterward he may come into the camp. But the priest shall be unclean until evening. **8** The one who burns the heifer shall wash his clothes in water and bathe his body in water and shall be unclean until evening. **9** And a man who is clean shall gather up the ashes of the heifer and deposit them outside the camp in a clean place. And they shall be kept for the water for impurity for the congregation of the people of Israel; it is a sin offering. ¹⁰ And the one who gathers the ashes of the heifer shall wash his clothes and be unclean until evening. And this shall be a perpetual statute for the people of Israel, and for the stranger who sojourns among them.

¹¹ "Whoever touches the dead body of any person shall be unclean seven days. ¹² He shall cleanse himself with the water on the third day and on the seventh day, and so be clean. But if he does not cleanse himself on the third day and on the seventh day, he will not become clean. ¹³ Whoever touches a dead person, the body of anyone who has died, and does not cleanse himself, defiles the tabernacle of the Lord, and that person shall be cut off from Israel; because the water for impurity was not thrown on him, he shall be unclean. His uncleanness is still on him.

¹⁴ "This is the law when someone dies in a tent: everyone who comes into the tent and everyone who is in the tent shall be unclean seven days. ¹⁵ And every open vessel that has no cover fastened on it is unclean. ¹⁶ Whoever in the open field touches someone who was killed with a sword or who died naturally, or touches a human bone or a grave, shall be unclean seven days. ¹⁷ For the unclean they shall take some ashes of the burnt sin offering, and fresh[1] water shall be added in a vessel. ¹⁸ Then a clean person shall take hyssop and dip it in the water and sprinkle it on the tent and on all the furnishings and on the persons who were there and on whoever touched the bone, or the slain or the dead or the grave. ¹⁹ And the clean person shall sprinkle it on the unclean on the third day and on the seventh day. Thus on the seventh day he shall cleanse him, and he shall wash his clothes and bathe himself in water, and at evening he shall be clean.

²⁰ "If the man who is unclean does not cleanse himself, that person shall be cut off from the midst of the assembly, since he has defiled the sanctuary of the Lord. Because the water for impurity has not been thrown on him, he is unclean. ²¹ And it shall be a statute forever for them. The one who sprinkles the water for impurity shall wash his clothes, and the one who touches the water for impurity shall be unclean until evening. ²² And whatever the unclean person touches shall be unclean, and anyone who touches it shall be unclean until evening."

[1] Hebrew *living*

Section Overview

In chapter 5 contact with a dead human body appeared with two other sources of impurity (v. 2). Chapter 6 described the ritual process for a Nazirite's cleansing from corpse defilement (vv. 9–12). Chapter 19 deals in depth with the cleansing of this impurity, whether involving direct or indirect contact with a cadaver, or even with a bone or grave. Unchecked, this impurity would defile the sacred sphere, and anyone uncleansed would be "cut off" (vv. 13, 20).

Given its contagion—death being the antithesis of life (cf. Introduction: Interpretive Challenges: Unifying Theme of Life and Death)—corpse contamination is treated differently than other impurities, such as those caused by bodily discharges. Those could require, among other rituals, a sin purification offering to make atonement. There is no sacrifice made on the altar for contact with the dead, nor any priest to make purification. The required cleansing by water for impurity is done outside the ritual domain, even outside the camp.

This chapter logically follows chapters 16–18. The revolt against Aaron and Moses resulted in the death of the instigators, their families, and thousands of others (ch. 16). The test of the staffs resulted in the people's fear of dying for approaching the sacred sphere (ch. 17). The service of priests and Levites would prevent their encroachment, lest they die (ch. 18). Chapter 19 also encompasses the untold number of deaths in the wilderness of the exodus generation decreed after the Kadesh revolt (chs. 13–14).

Section Outline

II. Trials in the Wilderness of Paran, the Transjordan Highlands, and the Plains of Moab (11:1–25:18) . . .
    I. Red Heifer Ashes and Water for Impurity (19:1–22)
        1. Preparation of Water for Impurity (19:1–10)
        2. Application of Water for Impurity (19:11–22)

Comment

19:1–10 "The statute of the law" (Hb. *huqqath hattorah*; v. 2) is addressed to Moses and Aaron. This formula here and at its only other occurrence (31:21) refers to ritual law. It is a "perpetual statute" (*lehuqqath 'olam*; also rendered "statute forever," 19:21), that is, until its ultimate foreshadowed fulfillment. Given the characteristic need for blood to purify (the purpose of this red heifer ritual), the red color is perhaps symbolically compensatory, since its flesh with the blood is burned (v. 5). Other burned red ingredients are among the ashes used to make the purification water (v. 6). A "heifer" (*parah*) is not necessarily a young cow (Gen. 41:2–4). In 1 Samuel 6:7 the same term signifies an adult that has calved.[139] "On which a yoke has never come" is also stipulated for the "heifer" (*'eglah*) slaughtered for an unsolved murder (Deut. 21:3). "Without defect, . . . no blemish" (Num. 19:2) applies to almost all sacrificial animals (Deut. 17:1).

"Eleazar the priest" (Num. 19:3, 4) supervises the preparation of the purification water. He also supervises the lamp oil and the incense (4:16). His new responsibility naturally follows his intervening ceremonially after the death of 250 followers of Korah (16:37–39). Eleazar's prominence in these chapters also anticipates his rise to the office of high priest upon Aaron's death (20:28). "Outside the camp" (occurring ten times: 19:3, 9; cf. 5:3, 4; 12:14, 15; 15:35, 36; 31:13, 19) is a sphere from which ceremonial impurities, if treated correctly, will not desecrate the holy (cf. Introduction: Interpretive Challenges: Unifying Subjects of Holiness and Purity). Outside the cordon of the camps of the various tribes, "outside the camp" is the remotest sphere from the holy space. Once "slaughtered" and "burned" (19:3, 5), the heifer's ashes are deposited there in a clean place (cf. discussion on v. 9 below).

---

[139] In English "heifer" can refer to a young cow that has not borne a calf. The debate recorded in the Mishnah indicates the red heifer could be anywhere from two to five years old (Parah 1:1).

Eleazar is to "sprinkle [*nazah*] . . . blood toward the front of the tent of meeting seven times" (v. 4), a ritual comparable to the sprinkling of blood of the bull sin offering for the high priest and the whole congregation (its representative leaders) seven times in front of the veil (Lev. 4:6, 17). On the Day of Atonement it is sprinkled in front of and on the mercy seat (Lev. 16:14, 19). Sprinkling seven times corresponds to the seven days needed to achieve purification (Num. 19:11, 12, 14, 16, 19). Hyssop is a leafy herb used to sprinkle blood (Lev. 14:51; Ps. 51:7; Heb. 9:19).

"Its skin, its flesh, and its blood, with its dung, shall be burned" (Num. 19:5), like the unsacrificed parts of the bull sin offering, except for its blood (Lev. 4:11). The blood of the red heifer is in the ashes used to make the purification water. The use of "cedarwood and hyssop and scarlet yarn" (Num. 19:6) probably stems from their relationship to blood: red color in the case of the cedar and yarn and means of sprinkling it in the case of hyssop.[140] All three are also used in cleansing lepers (Lev. 14:4).

The priest's uncleanness from sprinkling the blood and throwing the three elements into the fire requires cleansing by water and a lapse of time (one day; Num. 19:7). The same cleansing is required for the person "who burns the heifer" and the one "who gathers the ashes" (vv. 8, 10). The ash depository perhaps becomes "clean" (*tahor*, ritually "pure") from the ashes, like a pure sacrifice that becomes holy from contact with the altar (Ex. 29:37). The parts of the bull sin offering not offered on the altar are burned outside the camp in a clean place, on the ash heap (Lev. 4:12), where the ashes of the burnt offerings are deposited (Lev. 6:11).

The "water for impurity" (Num. 19:9) is made with ash dissolved in water to cleanse from impurity. "It is a sin offering" refers to the ash (masc. sg. '*epher*; v. 9). It is the dissolved ash—all that remains of the red heifer—that makes the water suitable. The ashes (dissolved in water) are for sin, that is, to de-sin or purify. The sin offering (cf. Leviticus 4) involves blood put on the altar to purify it and provide forgiveness for the one causing the defilement. Here water for impurity is applied to the person needing cleansing; no forgiveness is required. (On "perpetual statute", Num. 19:10, cf. comment on 19:11–21 [at v. 21]; cf. also 10:8; 15:15.) The same requirement for cleansing applies to all, whether Israelite or sojourner (v. 10).

19:11–22 The focus in verses 11–13 shifts from those who prepare the water for impurity (vv. 2–10) to its application to "whoever touches the dead body" (v. 11). Contamination is immediate. Many deaths are reported in Numbers (15:36; 16:32, 35, 49). More will come (20:1, 28; 21:6, 35; 25:9; 31:7)—ultimately, those of the whole exodus generation (14:29, 37). The duration of uncleanness is "seven days" (mentioned seven times: 19:11, 14, 16; cf. 12:14 [2x], 15; 31:19), assuming the regulations are scrupulously followed. This is the same period required for other types of physical impurities, followed on the eighth day by, among other ceremonies, the sin offering (*hatta't*) with a blood ceremony to make atonement (Lev. 12:2, 6–8; 14:9–13, 19; 15:13, 15).

---

140 R. Bergey, "Sang," *Dictionnaire de Théologie Biblique* (Cléon d'Andran: Excelsis, 2006), 932–935.

The grammatical voice of "he shall cleanse himself" (form of *hata'*; Num. 19:12; cf. 8:21) is not reflexive, with the subject and object being the same, but indirect reflexive, with the subject as the beneficiary but not the performer of the action—"he shall get himself cleansed"—since the water for impurity is "thrown on him" (cf. 19:13) by someone else. "With the water" (v. 12) follows the Targum and Vulgate, although the Hebrew reads "with it" (*bo'*, masc. sg.; *mayim*, "water," is pl.), likely referring to the ash (*'epher*, masc. sg., vv. 9, 10, 17) from the red heifer, which is dissolved into water.[141] The contamination remains on the body after the first washing, requiring a second application ("On the third day ... seventh day"; v. 12). Failure to do so on those two days means "he will not become clean" (v. 12).

Verse 13 concludes this section on direct contact with a corpse and warns of the consequences for "whoever ... does not cleanse himself" by having water "thrown [*zaraq*, "sprinkled"] on him." The one who applies the water is not specified. Since it is done outside the sanctuary and does not involve a sacrifice, it may be done by a Levite. This would explain the assumption that this person is ritually pure (vv. 10, 19, 21). He "defiles [*tm'*, "makes impure"] the tabernacle [*mishkan*]" since his contamination spreads like an infectious disease. Being cut off could involve the person's own death (Lev. 15:31), the extirpation of his lineage, and/or childlessness (Lev. 20:20–21; cf. Lev. 20:18–19).

The cases in Numbers 19:14–16 concern persons or objects in a tent in which someone has died (vv. 14–15) and anyone who inadvertently touches a corpse, bone, or grave (v. 16). This involves a seven-day uncleanness. The cleansing is treated together in verses 17–20. The "ashes of the burnt sin offering" (v. 17) refer to the ashes for purification, mixed with "fresh water" (*mayim hayyim*, "living/spring water"), not run-off water trapped in a cistern. A "clean person" (v. 18), perhaps a Levite, dips the hyssop into water and "sprinkles it" (from *nazah*) on all the indirectly contaminated persons and objects (v. 18). A person directly contaminated has water "thrown" (*zaraq*) on him (v. 13). The concluding verse 20 apparently uses "throw" and "sprinkle" synonymously. After two sprinklings (on the "third" and "seventh day") and the washing of his garments and body, "at evening" the unclean person is clean (v. 19).

Verse 20 concludes the section on indirect corpse contamination. Here the uncleansed person who has "defiled the sanctuary" (*miqdash*) "shall be cut off from the midst of the assembly" (*qahal*), which perhaps involves being banned from religious assemblies. But the parallel verse 13, with "defiles the tabernacle" and being "cut off from Israel," could point to synonymy with verse 20. On a "statute forever" (v. 21) cf. comment on 19:1–10 (at v. 9). This is a promise of grace in view of the decreed death of all those twenty years old and upward of the exodus generation (14:29) and the future confrontations with opposing nations in the Promised Land.

---

141 For Rashi the masculine suffix refers to *'epher* (*Pentateuch with Rashi's Commentary*, 4:92); cf. Milgrom, *Numbers*, 160. "Water" (*mayim*) is normally construed with pl. (e.g., adj. *mayim hayyim*, v. 17; it is normally the subject of a plural verb, 5:22, 24; 20:11; but sometimes with singular, 24:7).

Numbers 19:21–22 are summations having the underlying inverse notions that the water for impurity cleanses an impure person but makes impure a clean person. The person "who sprinkles the water" (v. 21) must wash his clothes, since the sprinkled water splashes them too; anyone who touches the water must wait in quarantine until evening. The "unclean person" (v. 22) refers to the one in verse 21. That person's uncleanness could be transmitted to anyone or anything he touches and it could in turn be transmitted to anyone who touches the contaminated object.

Response

Behind the pervasive defilement caused by death lies a sinister factor: "The wages of sin is death" (Rom. 6:23). Matthew Henry writes, "The preventing of sin is the preventing of wrath; and the mischief sin has done should be a warning to us for the future, to watch against it both in ourselves and others."[142]

Hebrews 9 contrasts the red heifer purification with that by Christ's blood:

> If the blood of goats and bulls, and the sprinkling of defiled persons with the ashes of a heifer, sanctify for the purification of the flesh, how much more will the blood of Christ, who through the eternal Spirit offered himself without blemish to God, purify our conscience from dead works to serve the living God. (Heb. 9:13–14)

Under the Sinai covenant the water for impurity's cleansing power—albeit only for "the flesh"—does not reside in it, nor in the ritual aspersion, but in the promise of cleansing wrought through faith by God's Spirit, who dwells among the people. Obeying the ceremonial commands, heeding the warnings, and believing the promises attached to them was living faith. But that could assuage the conscience only temporarily.

Christ blood purifies "our conscience." A purified conscience is also a tranquil conscience, since "the blood of Jesus [God's] Son cleanses us from all sin" (1 John 1:7). Based on this key point the apostle assures his readers: "By this we shall . . . reassure our heart before him; for whenever our heart condemns us, God is greater than our heart, and he knows everything. Beloved, if our heart does not condemn us, we have confidence before God" (1 John 3:19–21).

---

142 Cited by Bush, *Book of Numbers*, 258.

NUMBERS 20

20 And the people of Israel, the whole congregation, came into the wilderness of Zin in the first month, and the people stayed in Kadesh. And Miriam died there and was buried there.

2 Now there was no water for the congregation. And they assembled themselves together against Moses and against Aaron. 3 And the people quarreled with Moses and said, "Would that we had perished when our brothers perished before the Lord! 4 Why have you brought the assembly of the Lord into this wilderness, that we should die here, both we and our cattle? 5 And why have you made us come up out of Egypt to bring us to this evil place? It is no place for grain or figs or vines or pomegranates, and there is no water to drink." 6 Then Moses and Aaron went from the presence of the assembly to the entrance of the tent of meeting and fell on their faces. And the glory of the Lord appeared to them, 7 and the Lord spoke to Moses, saying, 8 "Take the staff, and assemble the congregation, you and Aaron your brother, and tell the rock before their eyes to yield its water. So you shall bring water out of the rock for them and give drink to the congregation and their cattle." 9 And Moses took the staff from before the Lord, as he commanded him.

10 Then Moses and Aaron gathered the assembly together before the rock, and he said to them, "Hear now, you rebels: shall we bring water for you out of this rock?" 11 And Moses lifted up his hand and struck the rock with his staff twice, and water came out abundantly, and the congregation drank, and their livestock. 12 And the Lord said to Moses and Aaron, "Because you did not believe in me, to uphold me as holy in the eyes of the people of Israel, therefore you shall not bring this assembly into the land that I have given them." 13 These are the waters of Meribah,[1] where the people of Israel quarreled with the Lord, and through them he showed himself holy.

14 Moses sent messengers from Kadesh to the king of Edom: "Thus says your brother Israel: You know all the hardship that we have met: 15 how our fathers went down to Egypt, and we lived in Egypt a long time. And the Egyptians dealt harshly with us and our fathers. 16 And when we cried to the Lord, he heard our voice and sent an angel and brought us out of Egypt. And here we are in Kadesh, a city on the edge of your territory. 17 Please let us pass through your land. We will not pass through field or vineyard, or drink water from a well. We will go along the King's Highway. We will not turn aside to the right hand or to the left until we have passed through your territory." 18 But Edom said to him, "You shall not pass through, lest I come out with the sword against you." 19 And the people of Israel said to him, "We will go up by the highway, and if we drink of your water, I and my livestock, then I will pay for it. Let me only pass through on foot, nothing more." 20 But he said, "You shall not pass through." And Edom came out against them with a large army and with a strong force.

21 Thus Edom refused to give Israel passage through his territory, so Israel turned away from him.

22 And they journeyed from Kadesh, and the people of Israel, the whole congregation, came to Mount Hor. 23 And the LORD said to Moses and Aaron at Mount Hor, on the border of the land of Edom, 24 "Let Aaron be gathered to his people, for he shall not enter the land that I have given to the people of Israel, because you rebelled against my command at the waters of Meribah. 25 Take Aaron and Eleazar his son and bring them up to Mount Hor. 26 And strip Aaron of his garments and put them on Eleazar his son. And Aaron shall be gathered to his people and shall die there." 27 Moses did as the LORD commanded. And they went up Mount Hor in the sight of all the congregation. 28 And Moses stripped Aaron of his garments and put them on Eleazar his son. And Aaron died there on the top of the mountain. Then Moses and Eleazar came down from the mountain. 29 And when all the congregation saw that Aaron had perished, all the house of Israel wept for Aaron thirty days.

[1] *Meribah* means *quarreling*

Section Overview

The people's grumbling at Meribah (Numbers 20) adds to the series of uprisings at Taberah, Kibroth-hattaavah (ch. 11), and Kadesh (chs. 13–14), including those by key leaders directed against Moses and Aaron (chs. 12; 16–18). The Meribah incident is so closely tied to Kadesh that it is called "Meribah of Kadesh" (27:14) and "Meribah-kadesh" (Deut. 32:51). It is likely that Numbers 15–19 have their setting there too (cf. 13:26).

The placename "Kadesh" (*qadesh*) and the attributive "holy" (*qadosh*) are key words in chapter 20. Kadesh is where Israel "stayed" (v. 1), "sent messengers from" (v. 14), "are in" (v. 16), and "journeyed from" (v. 22). Moses and Aaron are judged at Kadesh for not upholding the Lord as "holy" before the people (vv. 12, 13; cf. 27:14).

The deaths of Miriam and Aaron bracket chapter 20 (vv. 1–2, 22–29) and thereby frame the implicit announcement of Moses' death (v. 12). These deaths also bind the chapter thematically to chapter 19 on cleansing from corpse contamination. All three die outside the Promised Land. Aaron dies in the fortieth year after the exodus (33:38), the year that ends thirty-eight years of wilderness sojourn, during which time the exodus generation had perished. Those under twenty at the Kadesh rebellion and their offspring will leave Kadesh.

Section Outline

- II. Trials in the Wilderness of Paran, the Transjordan Highlands, and the Plains of Moab (11:1–25:18) . . .
    - J. Final Incidents around Kadesh (20:1–29)
        1. Miriam's Death (20:1)
        2. The Waters of Meribah (20:2–13)
        3. Edom Refuses Passage (20:14–21)
        4. Aaron's Death (20:22–29)

Comment

20:1 The wilderness of Zin (v. 1) is on the southern border of Canaan. Beyond it lies Edomite territory west of the Arabah (34:3; Josh. 15:1). "They stayed [*yashab*] in Kadesh" (Num. 20:1) is echoed in Deuteronomy, which states that Israel "remained [*yashab*] at Kadesh many days" (1:46). The wilderness sojourn in the Negeb highlands and the Mount Seir region not far from Kadesh also covers "many days" (Deut. 2:1; cf. Judg. 11:17). Kadesh is probably a central rallying point throughout the wilderness period.[143]

"In the first month" (Num. 20:1) is in the Passover month. The year is not given, but Israel's arrival at Kadesh from Sinai (12:16; 13:26; 32:8) and its departure from there bracket the wilderness period (20:22; 33:37). Viewed globally, "the time" (*hayyamim*, "the days") covers "thirty-eight years" (Deut. 2:14), ending forty years after the exodus.[144] Numbers 20 thus marks the end of the traditional forty wilderness years and the lifespan of the exodus generation (cf. Num. 14:34–35).[145]

"Miriam died there" (20:1) four months before Aaron dies (33:38) and about eleven months before Moses does (Ex. 7:7; Deut. 1:3; 29:5; 34:7–8; Josh. 1:1–2). Her character was forged as a young girl living during the Egyptian pogroms. She bravely watched over her baby brother, Moses (Ex. 2:4, 7–8). She encouraged the Lord's people by leading worship and pursuing her ministry as prophetess (Ex. 15:20–21; Mic. 6:4). She was unafraid to voice her opinion, at least once unduly so (Numbers 12). Her life and service would leave a void. Jesus' mother may have been named after her (LXX *Mariam* and Luke 1:27). Other OT prophetesses include Deborah, Huldah, Noadiah, and Isaiah's wife (Judg. 4:4; 2 Kings 22:14; Neh. 6:14; Isa. 8:3).

20:2–13 "There was no water" (v. 2): after crossing the Red Sea (Ex. 15:22), a similar crisis had confronted the exodus generation at Rephidim (Ex. 17:1; Num. 33:14). The Kadesh area has the richest water supply of the northern Sinai Peninsula and is its most important oasis (cf. "En["spring of"]-mishpat . . . Kadesh"; Gen. 14:7).[146] It is located about 50 miles (80 km) south-southwest of Beer("well of")sheba. During periods of drought, however, even the abundant springs in the Kadesh region are reduced to a trickle.[147] Due to drought, Abram had to leave there to seek refuge in Egypt (Gen. 12:9–10). The current crisis in the water supply may be the providential tool to pry the people from remaining at Kadesh. It may explain why the Israelites head to the Transjordan highlands. The family of Elimelech went to Moab to escape a drought-induced famine in the Judean hills (Ruth 1:1–2).

"They assembled themselves together against Moses and against Aaron" (Num. 20:2), exactly as did those in Korah's rebellion from the exodus generation (16:3).

---

[143] Noordtzij affirms that Kadesh remained the home base where the tabernacle stayed and annual feasts were held, while tribal and family units moved around independently in search of food for man and beast (*Numbers*, 8, 127–128). For Aharoni, Kadesh-barnea served as a central assembly point during the wilderness period (*Land of the Bible*, 200).
[144] Noordtzij puts the thirty-eight years between Numbers 10:11 and 20:1 (*Numbers*, 6).
[145] Cf. Gray, *Numbers*, 259–260; Levine, *Numbers 1–20*, 483.
[146] Aharoni, *Land of the Bible*, 70, 74.
[147] Har-El, *Sinai Journeys*, 335.

"The people quarreled" (20:3), as had the exodus generation at Rephidim (Ex. 17:2). "Quarreled" here implies a formal accusation, formulated in Numbers 20:4–5. "Would that we had perished when our brothers perished before the LORD" (v. 3) draws the parallel to those who perished suddenly (16:35, 49) or otherwise in the wilderness (14:32).

"Why? . . . And why?" (20:4, 5) introduces a double accusation against Moses and Aaron. First, they are charged with malfeasance against the "assembly of the LORD" (v. 4, cf. 16:3 recalling Korah's rebellion), that is, injury due to a breach of duty for having brought them into the wilderness "that we should die here, both we and our cattle" (20:4). Not only have the springs failed; drought has dried up the pastureland. Throughout the wilderness period the Israelites have maintained large livestock holdings ("cattle," be'irah, vv. 4, 8, 11; "livestock," miqneh, v. 19).

Second, Moses and Aaron are charged with misfeasance, that is, after leading the people out of Egypt, they have (allegedly) failed to bring them to the promised destination, instead leading them to "this evil place," with "no place for" crops and, worse, "no water to drink" (v. 5). Turning the deliverance "out of Egypt" into an accusation is recurrent in both the old and the new generations (Ex. 14:11; 17:3; Num. 11:20; 21:5).

The prophet Moses and the high priest Aaron (Deut. 18:15; Ps. 99:6; Hos. 12:13) both "fall on their faces" to intercede at the "entrance of the tent of meeting" (Num. 20:5). They stand in the gap between the assembly and the Lord. By his grace, "the glory of the LORD appeared to them" (v. 6)—only to Moses and Aaron—lest the others be consumed, as threatened when the glory appeared before (cf. Num. 14:10–12; 16:19–21, 42, 45 [17:7, 10 MT]).

The narrative of water from the rock (20:2–13) is similar to, yet also different from, the previous incident in which there was no water (Ex. 17:1–7). Resemblances include the name of the incidents ("Meribah," "quarrelling"; Ex. 17:7; Num. 20:3), the people's accusing Moses of leading them out of Egypt to the wilderness only to kill them there with thirst (Ex. 17:3; Num. 20:4), and the flow of water after Moses strikes the rock with a staff (Ex. 17:6; Num. 20:11). Differences clearly distinguish the two narratives, however. The former occurred in the three-month period after leaving Egypt, at Rephidim in the wilderness of Sin (Ex. 17:1; Num. 33:14); the latter occurs forty years later, in the wilderness of Zin (20:1). Only the former is branded "Massah" ("testing"; Ex. 17:7). Only the latter is labeled "Meribah-kadesh" (Deut. 32:51). In the former Moses is told to strike the rock with his staff (Ex. 17:6); in the latter he is to speak to it (Num. 20:8). The difference of greatest import, though, is Moses' and Aaron's conduct here, for which they forfeit entry into the Promised Land (v. 12; cf. Deut. 32:51).

Moses and Aaron are to "tell [pl.] the rock . . . to yield its water" (Num. 20:8), though that which they are to say is left unstated. Moses' question ("Shall we bring water for you out of this rock?"; v. 10) could be understood by the people as a claim that they have the power to give the people water. But it echoes God's instructions ("You shall bring water out . . . give drink," v. 8; both verbs are in the singular).

Several of their actions (vv. 10–11) differ from the Lord's instructions (v. 8). First, Moses addresses the people. "Hear now" (v. 10) introduces an accusation (12:6; 16:8; Isa. 7:13; Jer. 5:21); "you rebels" is a serious charge. Moses and Aaron are never told to speak to the people. Second, "Moses . . . struck the rock with his staff twice" (Num. 20:11). "His staff" is the one used to strike the Nile and bring other plagues on Egypt, the same staff used to strike the rock at Horeb/Meribah (Ex. 17:5; cf. Ex. 10:13). Moses is ordered to "take the staff" (Num. 20:8), the one "from before the LORD" (v. 9), perhaps "the staff of Aaron before the testimony" (17:10; synonymous with "before the LORD," Ex. 27:21; Num. 17:9). Moses and Aaron also fail to do what God orders them to do: speak to the rock. Moses thus does two things that are not commanded: he speaks to the people (Ps. 106:33 says he "spoke rashly") and strikes the rock—and that twice in anger, possibly using "his staff" of judgment on God's enemies, contrary to the order to take Aaron's staff, now a symbol of mediatorial grace for God's people.

The charge against Moses and Aaron is that "you did not believe in me" (v. 12). Believing is demonstrated by acting in accord with a command (Deut. 9:23; Rom. 1:5). God's holiness has been profaned by their disobedience; they were supposed to "uphold me as holy." And their sin has been overt ("in the eyes of the people of Israel"), which makes their guilt all the greater.

To the indictment is added, "because you rebelled [*marah*] against my command at the waters of Meribah" (Num. 20:24), which echoes Moses' accusation of the people as being "rebels" (form of *marah*; v. 10). Unbelief, disobedience, and rebellion go hand in hand (1 Sam. 15:22–23; Heb. 3:16, 18–19). "Therefore" (*laken*)—because of what Moses and Aaron did and did *not* do—"you shall not bring this assembly into the land" (Num. 20:12). They are the highest representatives of Israel before God and are God's representatives before the people. Their punishment for this one act is exceptionally severe. Deuteronomy 32:51 adds that Moses and Aaron "broke faith" (*ma'al*), which is tantamount to sacrilege. Breaking faith also results in the deaths of Achan and Saul (Josh. 7:1; 1 Chron. 2:7; 10:13) and in Judah's exile (1 Chron. 9:1). As leaders, Moses and Aaron will suffer both fates (death and exile). Together with the exodus generation they die outside the Promised Land.

A summary closes the "Meribah" incident (Num. 20:13), a name derived from the "quarrel" (*rib*; v. 3). "The people . . . quarreled with the LORD" by their "quarrel[ing] with Moses" (v. 3; cf. 16:11). "Through [*b-*] them he showed himself holy" (20:13), using the same verb (*qadash*) in form and syntax as the statement "Among [*b-*] those who are near me I will be sanctified" (Lev. 10:3). There the Lord was sanctified through the deaths of Nadab and Abihu. Here his holiness is shown by the sentence passed on Moses and Aaron.

20:14–21 From Kadesh Moses sends "messengers" (Hb. *mal'akim*; v. 14; same word for "angel," v. 16) to the king of Edom. On a kinship level they appeal to Edom as a "brother" (v. 14; Deut. 2:9). Jacob/Israel and Esau/Edom had the same parents. The message is sent from "Kadesh, a city on the edge [*qetsah*] of your territory [*gebul*, "border"]" (Num. 20:16). As G. A. Smith observes, "Edom's land stretched west as well as east of the Arabah."[148] Israelite contact with Edom in the wilderness period is west of the Arabah.

Moses makes two propositions. First, "Let us pass through your land. We will not pass through field or vineyard, or drink water from a well. We will go along the King's Highway" (*derek hammelek*; v. 17). Second, "We will go up by the highway ... drink of your water ... will pay for it" (v. 19). The two are similar: the request for passage by the "highway" (*messilah*; v. 19), a raised, leveled road for military and commercial use. The road here is probably the northernmost Sinai branch of the King's Highway joining Edom, through Kadesh, to western Sinai.[149] The Transjordan north-south trunk road descends from Damascus to the Gulf of Aqaba (21:22). The main difference between Moses' two proposals is remuneration. In the first he gives only verbal assurances that they will not take Edomite crops nor use their water. It is met with a threat to "come out with the sword against you" (20:18). In the second Moses promises to pay the highway toll and a fee for water consumption. This one is met with a "large army" against them (v. 20). Because Edom refuses passage, Israel turns away (*natah*; v. 21). Subsequently, they go toward Arad in a northeasterly direction around Edomite territory in the eastern Sinai (21:1).

20:22–29 As K. D. Sakenfeld observes, "The resumption of the march [from Kadesh] ... must be understood as the end of the traditional forty years in the wilderness."[150] Although the precise location of Mount Hor is uncertain, it is somewhere along the route joining Kadesh and Arad (21:1; 33:40).[151] It is "on the border of" (Hb. *gebul*; 20:23; cf. *qatseh*, "on edge of"; 33:37) Edom and thus probably near where the Nahal Zin valley separates the Negeb highlands from Mount Seir to the south. In the itinerary Mount Hor is the first station after Kadesh (33:37).

"Aaron [is] gathered to his people" (20:24, 26; Deut. 32:50), as is also said of Abraham, Ishmael, Isaac, and Jacob (Gen. 25:8, 17; 35:29; 49:33). The expression may suggest the grouping of the bones of a defunct family into an ossuary (2 Sam. 21:13; cf. Gen. 50:25; Ex. 13:19; Josh. 24:32; Jer. 8:1; Matt. 23:27; cf. the opposite, "scatter" bones, Ps. 53:5; Ezek. 6:5). Thirty days of mourning (Num. 20:29; also for Moses, Deut. 34:8) is sufficient time for bodily decomposition, permitting the gathering of Aaron's bones to his sister's. "He shall not enter ... you rebelled" (pl., Num. 20:24) reiterates the charge and sentence pronounced earlier, "You did not believe ... you shall not bring" (both pl. verbs; cf. v. 12).

"Strip Aaron of his garments and put them on Eleazar his son" (v. 26) signals Aaron's divestiture and Eleazar's investiture (cf. v. 28). The removal of the holy

---

148 Smith, *Historical Geography of the Holy Land*, 368.
149 Aharoni mentions two east-west branches of the King's Highway, the northern branch connecting the Zin wilderness, Kadesh, and Egypt by the way to Shur and the southern branch connecting the northern tips of both Red Seas, at Elath and Suez (*Land of the Bible*, 56; cf. 44, map 3). The northern branch would be the Darb es-Sultan and the southern the Darb el-Hagg, still used to make pilgrimages from Egypt to Mecca and Medina.
150 Sakenfeld, *Numbers*, 112.
151 Given its location somewhere on the Kadesh-Arad trajectory, Aharoni posits Imaret el-Khureisheh, about 8 miles (13 km) northeast of Kadesh (*Land of the Bible*, 202; cf. Rasmussen, *Zondervan Atlas*, 91). For other identifications in that area cf. de Vaulx, *Les Nombres*, 231; Cole, *Numbers*, 339.

apparel (Ex. 28:2) is not to humiliate Aaron. Had Aaron died wearing them, the holy garments would have been defiled. Moreover, as high priest Eleazar could have no contact with a dead family member (Lev. 21:11; cf. Num. 6:9–12). So "Moses stripped Aaron of his garments and put them on Eleazar. . . . Aaron died" (20:28). The order of these actions safeguards against ritual impurity. "Aaron . . . perished" (*gavaʿ*, v. 29; also in 17:13; 20:3); he dies at 123 years of age (33:39). He was more than eighty-three at the time of the exodus (Ex. 7:7).

Response

On the new generation that "assembled themselves together against Moses and against Aaron" (Num. 20:2) Bush comments, "The present was a new outbreak of that characteristic perversity, which though occasionally suppressed by severe judgments, seems never to have been effectively subdued. But while they thus proved themselves the children of their fathers, we should not forget that our waywardness proves equally that we are *their* children in moral relationship, and that the deed of our fathers we continue to do."[152]

The Lord once again displays his holiness through public judgment of leaders' sin (v. 12; cf. 3:4; 12:15). As the psalmist writes, "You were a forgiving God to them, but an avenger of their wrongdoings" (Ps. 99:8), referring to God's dealing with Moses and Aaron following the Meribah incident (Num. 20:10–13). Both are denied the blessing of entering Canaan, apparently for the manner in which Moses, abetted by his brother, speaks to the people (Ps. 106:33). Their punishment provides a solemn example of what Jesus warns, "Whoever causes one of these little ones who believe in me to sin, it would be better for him if a great millstone were hung around his neck and he were thrown into the sea" (Mark 9:42). Jesus' brother James adds, "Not many of you should become teachers, my brothers, for you know that we who teach will be judged with greater strictness" (James 3:1). And Paul instructs Timothy, "As for those [elders] who persist in sin, rebuke them in the presence of all, so that the rest may stand in fear" (1 Tim. 5:20). It is likely that the lapses in holy living of Miriam, Aaron, and Moses contribute to the waywardness of the new generation. Church leaders must not only watch over the conduct of congregants; they must carefully watch over their own and strive to set an example of godliness.

---

[152] Bush, *Book of Numbers*, 288–289.

NUMBERS 21

21 When the Canaanite, the king of Arad, who lived in the Negeb, heard that Israel was coming by the way of Atharim, he fought against Israel, and took some of them captive. **2** And Israel vowed a vow to the Lord and said, "If you will indeed give this people into my hand, then I will devote their cities to destruction."[1] **3** And the Lord heeded the voice of Israel and gave over the Canaanites, and they devoted them and their cities to destruction. So the name of the place was called Hormah.[2]

4 From Mount Hor they set out by the way to the Red Sea, to go around the land of Edom. And the people became impatient on the way. **5** And the people spoke against God and against Moses, "Why have you brought us up out of Egypt to die in the wilderness? For there is no food and no water, and we loathe this worthless food." **6** Then the Lord sent fiery serpents among the people, and they bit the people, so that many people of Israel died. **7** And the people came to Moses and said, "We have sinned, for we have spoken against the Lord and against you. Pray to the Lord, that he take away the serpents from us." So Moses prayed for the people. **8** And the Lord said to Moses, "Make a fiery serpent and set it on a pole, and everyone who is bitten, when he sees it, shall live." **9** So Moses made a bronze[3] serpent and set it on a pole. And if a serpent bit anyone, he would look at the bronze serpent and live.

10 And the people of Israel set out and camped in Oboth. **11** And they set out from Oboth and camped at Iye-abarim, in the wilderness that is opposite Moab, toward the sunrise. **12** From there they set out and camped in the Valley of Zered. **13** From there they set out and camped on the other side of the Arnon, which is in the wilderness that extends from the border of the Amorites, for the Arnon is the border of Moab, between Moab and the Amorites. **14** Therefore it is said in the Book of the Wars of the Lord,

"Waheb in Suphah, and the valleys of the Arnon,
15 and the slope of the valleys
   that extends to the seat of Ar,
   and leans to the border of Moab."

16 And from there they continued to Beer;[4] that is the well of which the Lord said to Moses, "Gather the people together, so that I may give them water." **17** Then Israel sang this song:

"Spring up, O well!—Sing to it!—
18 the well that the princes made,
   that the nobles of the people dug,
   with the scepter and with their staffs."

And from the wilderness they went on to Mattanah, ¹⁹ and from Mattanah to Nahaliel, and from Nahaliel to Bamoth, ²⁰ and from Bamoth to the valley lying in the region of Moab by the top of Pisgah that looks down on the desert.⁵

²¹ Then Israel sent messengers to Sihon king of the Amorites, saying, ²² "Let me pass through your land. We will not turn aside into field or vineyard. We will not drink the water of a well. We will go by the King's Highway until we have passed through your territory." ²³ But Sihon would not allow Israel to pass through his territory. He gathered all his people together and went out against Israel to the wilderness and came to Jahaz and fought against Israel. ²⁴ And Israel defeated him with the edge of the sword and took possession of his land from the Arnon to the Jabbok, as far as to the Ammonites, for the border of the Ammonites was strong. ²⁵ And Israel took all these cities, and Israel settled in all the cities of the Amorites, in Heshbon, and in all its villages. ²⁶ For Heshbon was the city of Sihon the king of the Amorites, who had fought against the former king of Moab and taken all his land out of his hand, as far as the Arnon. ²⁷ Therefore the ballad singers say,

> "Come to Heshbon, let it be built;
>   let the city of Sihon be established.
> ²⁸ For fire came out from Heshbon,
>   flame from the city of Sihon.
> It devoured Ar of Moab,
>   and swallowed⁶ the heights of the Arnon.
> ²⁹ Woe to you, O Moab!
>   You are undone, O people of Chemosh!
> He has made his sons fugitives,
>   and his daughters captives,
>   to an Amorite king, Sihon.
> ³⁰ So we overthrew them;
>   Heshbon, as far as Dibon, perished;
>   and we laid waste as far as Nophah;
>   fire spread as far as Medeba."⁷

³¹ Thus Israel lived in the land of the Amorites. ³² And Moses sent to spy out Jazer, and they captured its villages and dispossessed the Amorites who were there. ³³ Then they turned and went up by the way to Bashan. And Og the king of Bashan came out against them, he and all his people, to battle at Edrei. ³⁴ But the LORD said to Moses, "Do not fear him, for I have given him into your hand, and all his people, and his land. And you shall do to him as you did to Sihon king of the Amorites, who lived at Heshbon." ³⁵ So they defeated him and his sons and all his people, until he had no survivor left. And they possessed his land.

¹ That is, set apart (devote) as an offering to the Lord (for destruction); also verse 3 ² *Hormah* means *destruction* ³ Or *copper* ⁴ *Beer* means *well* ⁵ Or *Jeshimon* ⁶ Septuagint; Hebrew *the lords of* ⁷ Compare Samaritan and Septuagint; Hebrew *and we laid waste as far as Nophah, which is as far as Medeba*

Section Overview

Chapter 21 narrates the Israelites' journey from the northern Negeb to Transjordan's highlands. They leave Mount Hor in the direction of Arad, which draws Canaanite resistance. The victory over the Canaanites (vv. 1–3) is a sign of God's presence with the new generation. Thirty-eight years earlier the old generation had been defeated by the Canaanites and Amalekites (14:39–45). Notwithstanding their deliverance, the people speak against God and Moses, drawing a scourge of deadly venomous serpents. By the obedience of faith in the Lord's promise, any snakebitten person who looks at the bronze serpent is delivered (21:4–9). Ascending the great Zered Gorge, the Israelites penetrate Transjordan to the east of Moab (Judg. 11:18). Beyond the Arnon on Moab's northern border are the Amorites (Num. 21:10–20). The Lord gives the generation that will enter Canaan another great victory, this time over the Amorite kingdoms of Sihon and Og (vv. 21–35).

Numbers 20–21 presents the new generation against the backdrop of the exodus generation (cf. table 4.5). These parallels support an underlying theme of the old generation as an example for the new. God's dealings with both generations serve as examples for his people of all ages (cf. Introduction: Theology of Numbers).

TABLE 4.5: New Generation Compared to Exodus Generation

New Generation	Old Generation
At Kadesh after 38 wilderness years (20:1)	At Kadesh after Mount Sinai (chs. 13–14)
Zin wilderness Meribah incident (20:2–13)	Sin wilderness Meribah incident (Ex. 17:1–7)
Victory over Canaanites-Hormah (21:1–3)	Defeat by Amalekites and Canaanites-Hormah (14:44–45)
Complaint about deliverance from Egypt (21:5)	Complaints about deliverance from Egypt (14:2–4; cf. Ex. 14:11–12; 16:3; 17:3)
Confession "we have sinned" (21:7)	Confession "we have sinned" (14:40)
Moses prayed, no words mentioned (21:7)	Moses prayed, no words mentioned (11:2)
Serpent "pole" (*nes*) deliverance (21:8) from judgment	"Warning" (*nes*; 26:10) about Korah's judgment (ch. 16)
Victory "Book of the Wars" (21:14)	Victory "memorial in a book" (Ex. 17:14)

Section Outline

II. Trials in the Wilderness of Paran, the Transjordan Highlands, and the Plains of Moab (11:1–25:18)...

    K. Journey from the Negeb to Transjordan (21:1–35)

        1. Arad Destroyed (21:1–3)

        2. Bronze Serpent (21:4–11)

        3. In Moab (21:12–20)

        4. Amorite Kings Sihon and Og Defeated (21:21–35)

Comment

21:1–3 The "Canaanite" (v. 1; a gentilic having no number or gender) people (cf. v. 3, "Canaanites"; same word form) are associated with the Amalekites in the same region at Hormah (cf. comment on 14:20–25). "Arad" probably refers to a region, named after the chief city, since the territory of the "king of Arad ... in the Negeb" (21:1) includes "cities" (vv. 2, 3). Aharoni lists nine Canaanite cites in the Negeb and believes this chain is what forces Israel to turn eastward to Transjordan.[153] Canaanite Arad is generally distinguished from Tell Arad in the eastern Negeb, 17 miles (27 km) south of Hebron. Canaanite Arad is located 4 miles (6.5 km) away at Tell el-Malhata, 11 miles (18 km) east of Beersheba.[154] Both locations lie north of Kadesh, joined by the "way of Atharim" (v. 1).[155] Tell el-Malhata, in the center of the Arad basin, lies at the headway of the road to Kadesh and the road to the main descent into Nahal Zin, via the ascent of Akrabbim.[156] The Zin valley separates the wilderness of Zin from Edomite territory to its south (34:3; cf. 20:16; cf. Josh. 15:1; Judg. 1:36).

By taking "some of [the Israelites] captive" (Num. 21:1) the king perhaps thinks he can avert retaliatory aggression from an overwhelming Israelite force, hold the captives as hostages to be ransomed by his wealthy adversary, or sell them to slave traders. (Israel later takes Midianite women and children captive [31:9].) In response, the Israelites "vowed a vow" (21:2) to "devote [them] to destruction" (v. 2), which translates one word, a form of *kharam* (LXX *anathematizō*). *Kherem* encompasses three spheres: martial, social, and cultic.[157] First, in wartime, cities under *kherem* could be destroyed, as here; such examples during the conquest are rare (e.g., Josh. 6:24; 8:26; 11:13). The general rule is that, if attacked, cities of aggressors and their holdings are to be put under the *kherem* ban (Josh. 11:20; cf. cases of terms of peace Deut. 20:12; Josh. 11:19). Israel's policy in Canaan is not to destroy cities but to take them intact and inhabit them (Deut. 6:10; Josh. 24:13) after driving out their residents (Num. 33:52). Banishment is a form of *kherem* (2 Kings 19:11).

Second, any remaining inhabitants are put under a social *kherem*, cut off from the Israelites, who are forbidden to make covenants with them involving marriage or worship. Their places of worship are destroyed (Num. 33:52; Deut. 7:2–5; Judg. 2:2; 3:6; Neh. 13:23–27). Third, war plunder under *kherem* is devoted to the victor's sanctuary (Josh. 6:18–19; 8:26–27; 11:12, 14; "sacred gifts [*qodesh*]" 1 Kings 15:15; cf. Num. 18:14; 31:54).

"Hormah" (21:3; form of *kharam*) here refers to territory with "cities" defeated by the Israelites, not one specific site (cf. comment on 14:39–45). Hormah and Edomite Seir west of the Arabah are adjacent (Deut. 1:44). The Israelites are now in the territory that will be allotted to Judah (Josh. 15:30) and the Kenites, the family of Moses' wife (Judg. 1:16)—a foretaste of the Promised Land for the new generation.

21:4–11 "From Mount Hor" (v. 4) resumes the narrative from 20:22–29. Apparently, the Israelites remain encamped there while their armed forces make the assault on Arad. "By the way to the Red Sea" (Hb. *derek yam suph*; 21:4) may be "in the direc-

---

[153] Aharoni, *Land of the Bible*, 201.
[154] Ibid., 201, 215–216; Rasmussen, *Zondervan Atlas*, 226; Cole, *Numbers*, 344–345.
[155] Aharoni, *Land of the Bible*, 44 map 3; 58, 202, 203 map 14.
[156] Yehuda Karmon, *Israel: A Regional Geography* (London: Wiley-Interscience, 1971), 277.
[157] Ron Bergey, "Anathème, interdit," *Le Grand Dictionnaire de la Bible* (Charols: Excelsis, 2004), 59–63.

tion of the Red Sea." It is commonly held that this refers to either a southeasterly road linking Kadesh to Elath or a north-south route in the Arabah between the Dead Sea and Red Sea.[158] However, Israel's trajectory is northerly, from Kadesh to Arad. From Mount Hor the Israelites set out *in the direction of* the Red Sea "to go around [*sabab*] the land of Edom" (21:4; cf. comment on 20:1).[159] *Sabab* does not mean more here than that they skirt Edom's border (cf. 34:4). Nahal Zin forms the northern limit of Edomite Mount Seir (cf. 20:16).[160] The Israelites descend to the Arabah via Nahal Zin (cf. 34:4; "ascent of Akrabbim"),[161] which joins the Arabah about 20 miles (12 km) southwest of the Dead Sea near "Oboth" (cf. 33:43), the first encampment after Mount Hor.

Deuteronomy 2 also evokes Israel's sidestepping Edom/Mount Seir (Deut. 2:1, 4, 5; cf. Deut. 1:44). To do so, they are commanded to "turn northward" (Deut. 2:3), recalling Israel's leaving Kadesh in a northerly direction to Mount Hor and Arad (Num. 20:22; 21:1, 4). They are ordered to "pass through" (lit., "cross over"; Deut. 2:4) Edomite territory, literally "border" (*gebul*), no doubt referring to Nahal Zin. Israel's crossing the Arabah south of the Dead Sea to reach the Zered Valley (Num. 21:12; Deut. 2:13) may be recalled in their going "away from the Arabah road from Elath and Ezion-geber . . . in the direction of the wilderness of Moab" (Deut. 2:8). The Zered is the border between Moab and Edom. The verb translated "go over" (*'abar*, Num. 21:13; "crossed," v. 14) in context means they will "pass through" the Zered valley to reach Moab from the Arabah, just as Abram "passed through" (*'abar*) the land of Canaan, not from one side to another but from one end to the other (Gen. 12:9).

"The people became impatient" (Num. 21:4). "Impatient" describes the people's psychosomatic reaction (*qatsar nepesh*, "short of soul/breath"; cf. antonym "patient," *'erek nepesh*, "long of soul/breath"). Recent events probably contribute to this state: the lack of water at Meribah, then the death of Miriam and Aaron, followed by Edom's refusal of passage and the Canaanites' attack. As a result, the people's impatience overflows. Like the old generation that grumbled and murmured, the new generation (cf. Section Overview of Numbers 20; Numbers 21) accuses Moses, "Why have you brought us up out of Egypt to die in the wilderness?" (Num. 21:5; cf. Ex. 14:11–12; 15:24; 16:3; 17:2–3). The water supply, though miraculous, often depends on Israel's being led to springs or places where ground water could be dug (Num. 21:18), the water being readily found in wadi beds just below ground level (Gen. 21:25, 31; 26:15, 17–18). "We loathe" (*naphshenu qatsah*; Num. 21:5) renders an expression phonetically similar to "impatient" (v. 4; *qatsar nepesh*), suggesting that

---

[158] For the former cf. Har-El (*Sinai Journeys*, 75), Davies (*Way of the Wilderness*, 77) and Rasmussen (*Zondervan Atlas*, 92), who all posit the Gaza-Beersheba-Kadesh-Elath road. For the latter cf. Aharoni, *Land of the Bible*, 44 map 3.
[159] Many think 21:4 indicates Israel turns south to circumvent Transjordan Edom (e.g., Gray, *Numbers*, 264; Noordtzij, *Numbers*, 181; Ashley *Book of Numbers*, 402. Har-El (*Sinai Journeys*, 430) correctly states that Israel bypasses Edom by going north in the Negeb before reaching Moab via the Arabah and the Zered Valley. Cf. Wenham's maps (*Numbers*, 229), which trace the "Route of Israelites" from Kadesh to Moab by way of the Zered Valley.
[160] De Vaulx, *Les Nombres*, carte 2.
[161] Aharoni, *Land of the Bible*, 55.

their state of mind affects their taste. "This worthless [*qeloqel* is a *hapax legomenon*[162]] food" refers to the manna (Ex. 16:4; Ps. 105:40; cf. Ps. 78:24, "grain of heaven"; John 6:31, "bread from heaven"). The Israelites have manna every day until they cross the Jordan (Josh. 5:12). But they loathe God's good gift.

The "fiery" aspect of the serpents' name (*saraphim*; Num. 21:6; cf. "seraphim," Isa. 6:2) probably refers to inflammatory venomous bites rather than the snakes' physical appearance. There is also a play on words here: "Serpents [*nahash*] . . . bit [*nashak*]." Thus many died. The people's response, "We have sinned" (Num. 21:7), is an insincere confession, like the one made by the past generation (14:40). "Moses prayed" (21:7), but no words are recorded. "Moses prayed" similarly for the exodus generation at Taberah (11:2), also an unrecorded prayer.

In response to his intercessory prayer Moses is told to make a "fiery serpent" (*saraph*; 21:8; cf. v. 6). He constructs a "bronze serpent" (*nehash nehoshet*) that ultimately becomes a fetish (2 Kings 18:4, *nehushtan*). The eastern Arabah is a copper mining and smelting center (cf. comment on Num. 33:37–49, "Punon").[163] The connection between the venomous serpents and the bronze serpent is analogous to "sin water" as "water for purification" (Num. 8:7; cf. "water for impurity," 19:9) or a "sin offering" as being for purification (Ex. 29:36; Ezek. 43:22). The word translated "pole" (*nes*; Num. 21:8) occurs later as a homophone, "a warning" (26:10) of the judgment-example upon Korah's followers. Anyone who "sees" or "would look" at the suspended serpent will live (21:8, 9). Seeing and looking are responses of faith: salvation is found through the obedience of faith in God's promised deliverance.

"Oboth" (vv. 10, 11) apparently lies just south of the foot of Nahal Zin, in the western Arabah.[164] Oboth follows two encampments, Zalmonah and Punon, mentioned only in the itinerary (cf. 33:42). Iye ("ruins of")-abarim ("across"; 21:11) or "Iyim" (33:45) is across the northern side of the Zered Gorge in Moab.[165] Israel penetrates Transjordan "opposite Moab, toward the sunrise" (Num. 21:11; Deut. 2:8; Judg. 11:18), that is, heading eastward across the Arabah.

Excursus: Geographical Overview of Transjordan

The Transjordan is divided by four major wadi canyons. Two drain into the Jordan River: the Yarmouk, south of the Sea of Galilee, and the Jabbok, between the Yarmouk and the Dead Sea. Two more empty into the Dead Sea: the Arnon in the middle of the sea and the Zered at the southern end. Ammon lies between the Jabbok and the Arnon, Moab between the Arnon and the Zered, and Edom to the south of the Zered.

---

162 *CHALOT*, 319: "cogn. languages suggest a spec. (unappetizing) leguminous plant." *CDCH*, 396: "'cassia,' type of plant." Milgrom reports that in Ugaritic *qlql* appears to mean "horse fodder, i.e., menial food" (*Numbers*, 317n6).
163 A five-inch copper snake was found south of the Dead Sea at the Timnah copper mines dating between 1200 and 900 BC (Milgrom, *Numbers*, 175).
164 Baly notes two important springs near the foot of Nahal Zin in the Arabah: Oboth and Tamar. He identifies Oboth with Ain-Weiba (Yahab), about 15 miles (24 km) south of Nahal Zin (*Geography of the Bible*, 206).
165 Cf. Jan Jozef Simons, *The Geographical and Topographical Texts of the Old Testament* (Leiden: Brill, 1959), 55, 202. Simons locates Iye-abarim on the left bank (ascending) of upper Zered; cf. Aharoni, *Land of the Bible*, 55, 202.

The Transjordan also has four distinct regions: Bashan, Gilead, tableland (*mishor*), and wilderness (*midbar*).¹⁶⁶ The Bashan stretches from Mount Hermon to just south of the Yarmouk. Gilead begins there and straddles the Jabbok, divided into northern and southern halves by that wadi. Bashan and Gilead are geologically distinct, the former being basaltic with rich volcanic soils and the latter being limestone with chalky soil.¹⁶⁷ The plateau highlands (*mishor*) extend eastward from the mountain watershed between the Arnon and Jabbok. The wilderness lies to the east of Bashan, Gilead, and the tableland. The Amorite kingdoms of Sihon and Og stretch from the Arnon to Mount Hermon (Deut. 3:8).

The division of Transjordan between the tribes of Reuben and Gad and half the tribe of Manasseh is described in Numbers 32. Their inheritances are delimited by the topography. Manasseh inherits Bashan and the northern half of Gilead (Josh. 13:31). Gad inherits the southern half of Gilead (Deut. 3:12). Between the Jabbok and the Arnon, Gad's and Reuben's inheritances include the tableland. Gilead sometimes refers to the territory of these tribes, even to Transjordan in general (Josh. 22:9, 13, 15, 32). It is also a name of a descendant of Manasseh (Num. 27:1).

21:12–20 The "Valley [*nahal*, "wadi"] of Zered" (v. 12) is a massive gorge forming a natural boundary between Edom to the south and Moab to the north. Unlike most wadis, the Zered is perennial and has an oasis, perhaps providing a reason for the Israelites' taking this route from the Arabah.¹⁶⁸ From its head, waters descend almost 4,000 feet (1,200 m) into the southern end of the Dead Sea. Deep (1,700 feet [520 m]) and gaping at the top (2 miles [3.2 km]), the Arnon Gorge is the northern limit of Moab.¹⁶⁹ Its waters also enter the Dead Sea opposite Engedi. The Amorites, from Canaan across the Jordan, have pushed the Moabites south of the Arnon (v. 26) and the Ammonites to the east of Jabbok's sources. Sihon's territory is between these two wadi canyons (v. 24–25).

The "Book of the Wars of the LORD" (v. 14) is presumably an early source recording those events (cf. the writing of a "memorial in a book" of the war with Amalek; Ex. 17:14). The meaning of the transliterated "Waheb in Suphah" is unknown.¹⁷⁰ The expression may be explained epexegetically—"and [*vav*, "that is"], the valleys of the Arnon"—since about 15 miles (24 km) up the gorge from where its flow enters the Dead Sea the Arnon divides into northern and southern valleys, each splitting into two. The name "Suphah" may be preserved in the principal southern branch, called Saphiah.¹⁷¹ "Ar" (*'ar*; Num. 21:15, 28; SP *'r*) has not been identified. It appears in parallelism with Kir, Moab's capital (Isa. 15:1). If not a city, it may be synonymous with Moab (Deut. 2:9).

---

166 Transjordan *midbar* is semidesert steppeland merging into cultivated land (Baly, *Geography of the Bible*, 103).
167 Baly, *Geography of the Bible*, 31; Rasmussen, *Zondervan Atlas*, 29, 52. Bashan and Gilead seem to overlap in some texts. Havvoth ("towns/villages of")-jair, south of the Yarmouk, is found in Bashan (Josh. 13:30) and Gilead (1 Kings 4:13). These "sixty" (Josh. 13:30) towns or villages no doubt overlap both regions.
168 Wadi el-Hesa; cf. Simons, *Geographical and Topographical Texts*, 260; Baly, *Geography of the Bible*, 204, 233 ("Probably the 'Brook of the Willows' [Isa. 15:7]").
169 Smith, *Historical Geography of the Holy Land*, 377. He adds that the bed where the water flows is only 40 yards wide (37 m).
170 Cf. Ashley, *Book of Numbers*, 411–412; Cole, *Numbers*, 353.
171 Smith, *Historical Geography of the Holy Land*, 377–378; cf. "fords of the Arnon" (Isa. 16:2).

The people are led to "Beer" (Num. 21:16), meaning "well." As the people have been denied access to water first by Edom and then by Moab, the well is providential; when water is struck, "then Israel sang this song" (vv. 16–18). Digging for water in wadi beds is possible with "staffs" (v. 18), since the water table is close to the surface (Gen. 26:19). The synonymic parallel word "scepter" (*mekhoqeq*) has led to a range of old midrashic interpretations.[172] The places named in Numbers 21:19 have not been identified. "Bamoth" ("heights") reappears in compound names, "Bamoth-arnon" (v. 28; "heights of the Arnon"), "Bamoth-baal" (22:41), and "Beth-bamoth" (Moabite Stone, line 27; cf. comment on 32:33–42).

The "top of Pisgah" (Num. 21:20; 23:14) may define the highest point of Mount Nebo in the Abarim mountain chain (Deut. 3:27; 32:49; 34:1),[173] whereas the slopes of Pisgah (Deut. 3:17; 4:49) may describe the Moabite mountain range east of the Dead Sea.[174] "The desert" (Num. 21:20; 23:28) renders a determined noun (*hayeshimon*; anarthrous in Deut. 32:10; Ps. 107:4) that perhaps refers to the Jeshimon, overlooking the southern Jordan Valley and the northern Dead Sea from both the eastern (Num. 33:49; Beth-jeshimoth) and the western sides (1 Sam. 26:1, 3) of the Arabah. The "Jeshimon" would then be either the Judean wilderness or the wilderness east of the Jordan.[175]

21:21–35 "Israel sent messengers to Sihon king of the Amorites" (v. 21); the LXX and SP add "with words of peace" (cf. Deut. 2:26), meaning terms of surrender (cf. 1 Chron. 19:19), a stipulated military procedure against enemies outside the border of Canaan (Deut. 20:10). Both "Sihon" and "Og" are Amorites (Deut. 4:47). Cisjordan "Amorites" have expanded their territory to Transjordan (cf. Num. 13:29). Sihon refuses passage and makes war (21:23).

As with the Edomites, Israel is not permitted to disinherit its Moabite and Ammonite kinsmen (Deut. 2:5, 9, 19, 37). Moabite territory lies between the Zered and the Arnon (Num. 21:12–13, 24). The Ammonites hold the land between the Arnon and the Jabbok (Josh. 12:2; Judg. 11:13). The territories from the Arnon northward are now occupied, respectively, by Sihon and Og (Num. 21:24; Deut. 2:36; 3:8; Josh. 12:2–3; Judg. 11:22).

Sihon's "people" (*'am*; Num. 21:23) is his army (e.g., Ex. 14:6; in Judg. 8:5–6 "people" and "army" [*tsaba'*] are parallel; in Judges 9:43 "people" are divided into three companies; in 2 Sam. 24:2, 9 David's numbering the "people" involves those who draw the sword). The battle site, "Jahaz" (Num. 21:23), is not identified but according to ancient sources lies between Medeba and Dibon (cf. discussion on 21:30 below).[176] These latter two locations are on the mountain watershed branch of the King's Highway (21:22; cf. comment on 20:14–19 [at vv. 17, 19]). This road starts in the north at Rabbah (today Amman) and has a more easterly branch skirt-

---
172 Milgrom, *Numbers*, 461.
173 Bush, *Book of Numbers*, 336.
174 Simons, *Geographical and Topographical Texts*, 75. Baly (*Geography of the Bible*, 117) identifies the Pisgah as the edge of the Transjordan plateau (Num. 21:20; 23:14).
175 Smith, *Historical Geography of the Holy Land*, 381.
176 Jahaz's proximity to Dibon and Medeba is clear from Eusebius's *Onomasticon* and the Moabite inscription (Milgrom, *Numbers*, 180).

ing the eastern "wilderness" (21:23). Jahaz apparently lies on that route. Sihon seeks to block Israel from passing through his territory via this road.

The Arnon and Jabbok gorges (v. 24) form the natural borders of Sihon's territory. The Jabbok flows into the Jordan 15 miles (24 km) north of the Dead Sea. The Jabbok Gorge is the northern border of Ammonite territory (v. 24). The Amorites have pushed them east of the Jabbok's sources. Some suggest "strong" (*'az*) should read "Az" (NJPS), an unidentified toponym, or "Jazer" (LXX; cf. RSV, NASB), a city on the Ammonite border (v. 32). However, when a toponym is "on the border of" somewhere, it is signaled with the preposition *b-* (*bigebul*; e.g., 33:44; 1 Sam. 10:2), which is not the case here. This favors reading *'az* as an adjective.

Pride of mention among Sihon's cities is his capital, "Heshbon" (Num. 21:25, 26, 27, 28, 30). If it is modern Hesban, it is located 12 miles (19 km) southwest of Amman (OT Rabbah).[177] Ashtaroth is Og's capital (Josh. 9:10). Numbers 21:26 is a flashback: before Israel's arrival in Transjordan, Moab had lost possession of its territory north of the Arnon to the Amorites. Mention of the historical antecedent is necessary because Israel is forbidden to take Moab's land (cf. discussion on v. 21 above). The "ballad singers" (v. 27; cf. Judg. 5:11) may have first vaunted the Amorites' victory over the Moabites (Num. 21:26; cf. Jer. 48:45–46), a ditty later adapted by the Israelites ("we"; Num. 21:30) to boast their triumph over the Amorites. This would also serve to challenge any possible later claim by Moab that Israel has taken its land, as the Ammonites claim during the period of the judges. Jephthah counters this claim by noting that Israel took the land from the Amorites, who had defeated the Ammonites and the Moabites (Judg. 11:12–13, 21–28).

On "Ar" (Num. 21:28) cf. comment on 21:12–20 (at v. 15). The "heights" (*bamoth*; v. 28) may refer to cultic "high places" (33:52), since defeating a people involves destroying their gods and places of worship. The "people of Chemosh" (21:29; Jer. 48:46) are Moabite worshipers of their national deity (Judg. 11:24; 1 Kings 11:33). For Heshbon cf. discussion on Numbers 21:25 above. "Dibon," modern Dhiban, is 3.5 miles (5.5 km) north of the Arnon and 13 miles (21 km) east of the Dead Sea. "Fire" (v. 30) follows the SP and LXX, both reading *'esh* (cf. v. 28) rather than the MT's *'asher*, with the *-r* marked by scribes with special punctuation to indicate it is suspicious. "Medeba," modern Madaba, is 12.5 miles (20 km) east of the northern end of the Dead Sea and 20 miles (32 km) south of Ammonite Rabbah (modern Amman).[178] The King's Highway and the "tableland" (*mishor*; Deut. 3:10; Josh. 13:9), lying between the Arnon and the wadi Hesban—named after Heshbon—25 miles (40 km) south of the Jabbok, are controlled by these cities.

Although unidentified, "Jazer" (Num. 21:32) is located between wadi Hesban and the Jabbok.[179] Jazer is also the name of a rich pasture region (32:1; Josh. 13:25).

---

177 Smith, *Historical Geography of the Holy Land*, 375. Tell Hesban does not antedate the Iron Age. Nearby Jalul is a favored candidate, the only important Late Bronze Age site in the area (Rasmussen, *Zondervan Atlas*, 238; Milgrom, *Numbers*, 180).

178 On Dibon and Medeb cf. Rasmussen, *Zondervan Atlas*, 232, 244.

179 Perhaps Kh. Jazzir, 9.5 miles (15 km) west of Rabbah at the head of Wadi Su'eib, which flows into the Jordan. It corresponds linguistically and fits Eusebius's description (*Onomasticon* 12.1–4). Cf. J. L. Peterson, "Jazer," *ABD* 3:650–651.

It is apparently the northernmost city held by Sihon. To be "dispossessed" (*yarash*) involves losing lands and everything in them (Deut. 2:21). Another form of the verb means "to possess" (Num. 21:35). The Israelites head for Og's kingdom in Bashan (v. 33), which stretches from Gilead about 6 miles (10 km) south of the Yarmouk in the south to Mount Hermon in the north, including the Golan east of the Sea of Galilee.[180] "Edrei" (v. 33) is identified as modern Dera,[181] near the Yarmouk on the southeast border of Og's territory. Nothing is said of the Israelite forces' advances from the Jabbok through Gilead to Edrei.

"Do not fear him, for I have given him into your hand.... And you shall do to him as you did to Sihon" (v. 34). The Lord's command, linked to a promise and a reminder of their victory over Sihon, spurs the Israelites to victory over Og and possession of his territory (v. 35). After defeating the two Amorite kings, Israel claims their lands as its own since it has not taken them from the Moabites or the Ammonites (Judg. 11:19–27). Israel now controls the Transjordan. It also controls the entire Jordan Valley, since Sihon's territory there had extended from the Dead Sea to the Sea of Galilee (Josh. 12:2–3). Israel is therefore able to encamp securely "in the plains of Moab beyond the Jordan at Jericho" (Num. 22:1; 36:13) where it would remain until crossing the Jordan to enter the Promised Land.

The victory over the Arad Canaanites (21:1–3), followed by victory over Amorite kings and the possessing of their lands (vv. 24–25, 34–35), is proof of God's presence to fulfill his promise.

Response

Regarding the bronze serpent Charles Spurgeon remarks,

> This is a glorious gospel type. Jesus, numbered with the transgressors, hangs before us on the cross. A look at him will heal us of the serpent bite of sin.... The bronze serpent ... specifically aimed at those who were 'bitten.' Jesus died as a real Savior for real sinners. Whether the bite has made you a drunkard or a thief or an unfaithful or a profane person, a look at the great Savior will heal you of these diseases and make you live in holiness and communion with God. Look and live.[182]

Jesus applies the bronze serpent to his own mission: "As Moses lifted up the serpent in the wilderness, so must the Son of Man be lifted up, that whoever believes in him may have eternal life" (John 3:14–15). This is followed by the most well-known verse in the NT (John 3:16). The correlation of the serpent and the Son of Man is striking. The deadly serpent bite is a consequence of sin and God's judgment upon it, and the bronze serpent represents that curse. "In the likeness of sinful flesh" (Rom. 8:3) Christ is lifted up because he is made "to be sin who knew

---

180 Smith, *Historical Geography of the Holy Land*, 354; Rasmussen, *Zondervan Atlas*, 228.
181 Sixty miles (100 km) south of Damascus (Rasmussen, *Zondervan Atlas*, 232).
182 Spurgeon, *The Promises of God* (Wheaton IL: Crossway, 2019), April 10.

no sin, so that . . . we might become the righteousness of God" (2 Cor. 5:21). In so doing he becomes a curse for us (Gal. 3:13) so that we might receive the life-giving Spirit through faith (Gal. 3:14).

Sin is a sting resulting in death, like a venomous snake bite (1 Cor. 15:55–56). Sin is the irruption of evil in a world created good and blessed. The curse, death from sin, is its consequence. Death is an enemy (1 Cor. 15:26) especially because it is the ultimate expression of God's anger at sin (Ps. 30:5). No one is immune; nobody escapes the sentence. The only antidote to the venom is Christ's death on the cross, which through faith delivers from sin and divine judgment. By Christ's life and resurrection the blessing of eternal life is restored. "This is the will of my Father, that everyone who looks on the Son and believes in him should have eternal life, and I will raise him up on the last day" (John 6:40).

Represented as a serpent from Genesis (3:1) to Revelation (20:2), Satan epitomizes sin, malediction, and death. However, the woman's descendant crushes the head of the Serpent (Gen. 3:15; Ps. 91:13), the "ancient serpent, who is called the devil and Satan, the deceiver of the whole world" (Rev. 12:9; 20:2). "The reason the Son of God appeared was to destroy the works of the devil" (1 John 3:8). The Christian is assured, "The God of peace will soon crush Satan under your feet" (Rom. 16:20).

NUMBERS 22

22 Then the people of Israel set out and camped in the plains of Moab beyond the Jordan at Jericho. ² And Balak the son of Zippor saw all that Israel had done to the Amorites. ³ And Moab was in great dread of the people, because they were many. Moab was overcome with fear of the people of Israel. ⁴ And Moab said to the elders of Midian, "This horde will now lick up all that is around us, as the ox licks up the grass of the field." So Balak the son of Zippor, who was king of Moab at that time, ⁵ sent messengers to Balaam the son of Beor at Pethor, which is near the River[1] in the land of the people of Amaw,[2] to call him, saying, "Behold, a people has come out of Egypt. They cover the face of the earth, and they are dwelling opposite me. ⁶ Come now, curse this people for me, since they are too mighty for me. Perhaps I shall be able to defeat them and drive them from the land, for I know that he whom you bless is blessed, and he whom you curse is cursed."

⁷ So the elders of Moab and the elders of Midian departed with the fees for divination in their hand. And they came to Balaam and gave him Balak's message. ⁸ And he said to them, "Lodge here tonight, and I will bring back word to you, as the LORD speaks to me." So the princes of Moab stayed with Balaam. ⁹ And God came to Balaam and said, "Who are these men with you?" ¹⁰ And Balaam said to God, "Balak the son of Zippor,

king of Moab, has sent to me, saying, ¹¹ 'Behold, a people has come out of Egypt, and it covers the face of the earth. Now come, curse them for me. Perhaps I shall be able to fight against them and drive them out.'" ¹² God said to Balaam, "You shall not go with them. You shall not curse the people, for they are blessed." ¹³ So Balaam rose in the morning and said to the princes of Balak, "Go to your own land, for the LORD has refused to let me go with you." ¹⁴ So the princes of Moab rose and went to Balak and said, "Balaam refuses to come with us."

¹⁵ Once again Balak sent princes, more in number and more honorable than these. ¹⁶ And they came to Balaam and said to him, "Thus says Balak the son of Zippor: 'Let nothing hinder you from coming to me, ¹⁷ for I will surely do you great honor, and whatever you say to me I will do. Come, curse this people for me.'" ¹⁸ But Balaam answered and said to the servants of Balak, "Though Balak were to give me his house full of silver and gold, I could not go beyond the command of the LORD my God to do less or more. ¹⁹ So you, too, please stay here tonight, that I may know what more the LORD will say to me." ²⁰ And God came to Balaam at night and said to him, "If the men have come to call you, rise, go with them; but only do what I tell you." ²¹ So Balaam rose in the morning and saddled his donkey and went with the princes of Moab.

²² But God's anger was kindled because he went, and the angel of the LORD took his stand in the way as his adversary. Now he was riding on the donkey, and his two servants were with him. ²³ And the donkey saw the angel of the LORD standing in the road, with a drawn sword in his hand. And the donkey turned aside out of the road and went into the field. And Balaam struck the donkey, to turn her into the road. ²⁴ Then the angel of the LORD stood in a narrow path between the vineyards, with a wall on either side. ²⁵ And when the donkey saw the angel of the LORD, she pushed against the wall and pressed Balaam's foot against the wall. So he struck her again. ²⁶ Then the angel of the LORD went ahead and stood in a narrow place, where there was no way to turn either to the right or to the left. ²⁷ When the donkey saw the angel of the LORD, she lay down under Balaam. And Balaam's anger was kindled, and he struck the donkey with his staff. ²⁸ Then the LORD opened the mouth of the donkey, and she said to Balaam, "What have I done to you, that you have struck me these three times?" ²⁹ And Balaam said to the donkey, "Because you have made a fool of me. I wish I had a sword in my hand, for then I would kill you." ³⁰ And the donkey said to Balaam, "Am I not your donkey, on which you have ridden all your life long to this day? Is it my habit to treat you this way?" And he said, "No."

³¹ Then the LORD opened the eyes of Balaam, and he saw the angel of the LORD standing in the way, with his drawn sword in his hand. And he bowed down and fell on his face. ³² And the angel of the LORD said to him, "Why have you struck your donkey these three times? Behold, I have come out to oppose you because your way is perverse³ before me. ³³ The donkey saw me and turned aside before me these three times. If she had not turned aside from me, surely just now I would have killed you and let her live." ³⁴ Then Balaam said to the angel of the LORD, "I have sinned, for I did not know that you stood in the road against me. Now therefore, if it is evil in your sight, I will turn back." ³⁵ And the angel of the LORD said to Balaam, "Go with the men, but speak only the word that I tell you." So Balaam went on with the princes of Balak.

36 When Balak heard that Balaam had come, he went out to meet him at the city of Moab, on the border formed by the Arnon, at the extremity of the border. 37 And Balak said to Balaam, "Did I not send to you to call you? Why did you not come to me? Am I not able to honor you?" 38 Balaam said to Balak, "Behold, I have come to you! Have I now any power of my own to speak anything? The word that God puts in my mouth, that must I speak." 39 Then Balaam went with Balak, and they came to Kiriath-huzoth. 40 And Balak sacrificed oxen and sheep, and sent for Balaam and for the princes who were with him.

41 And in the morning Balak took Balaam and brought him up to Bamoth-baal, and from there he saw a fraction of the people.

[1] That is, the Euphrates [2] Or *the people of his kindred* [3] Or *reckless*

Section Overview

Numbers 22:1–24:25 contains the Balaam narrative. The scene shifts from the Israelites' Transjordan conquests to their encampment "in the plains of Moab beyond the Jordan at Jericho" (22:1). The Moabites, with the Midianites, fear the same demise as the two powerful Amorite kings, Sihon and Og. Balak, king of Moab, sends emissaries to summon Balaam, a diviner. His mission is to curse the Israelites so that Balak can drive them from his territory.

The Balaam account portrays the God who has blessed his people and so turns the curse of their adversaries on their own heads. Balaam cannot revoke God's blessing and curse the Israelites. Rather than invoking a curse on the Israelites, Balaam ends up pronouncing blessings, a theme accentuated in his discourses (chs. 23–24; cf. Section Overview of Numbers 23). The motif is introduced in chapter 22 (cf. table 4.6).

TABLE 4.6: Blessing Motif Introduced in Numbers 22

Action	Verse(s)
Balak's summons	"Come now, curse this people for me . . . to defeat them and drive them from the land, for I know that he whom you bless is blessed, and he whom you curse is cursed." (v. 6) "Come, curse this people for me." (v. 17)
God's order	"You shall not curse the people, for they are blessed." (v. 12)
Balaam reports Balak's summons to God	"Now come, curse them for me. . . . to fight against them and drive them out." (v. 11)

Linked to this motif is another: God's word by which he upholds his blessing on Israel. His giving Balaam permission to go to Moab is predicated upon two conditions: First, "Only do what I tell you" (vv. 20, 26). Second, "Speak only the word that I tell you" (v. 35). Upon his arrival Balaam tells Balak, "The word that God puts in my mouth, that must I speak" (v. 38). The Lord puts his word in Balaam's mouth in the form of prophetic discourses contained in chapters 23–24.

Given the underlying movement of Numbers—toward the land of Canaan (cf. Section Overview of Numbers 13)—the blessing motif is patently related. According to the Sinai covenant, if curse spells death in the land, defeat at the hand of the enemy, and ultimately exile, then blessing results in long life in peace and prosperity in the land (Lev. 26:4, 6, 17, 27–28, 31–33). Once in the land, the Balaam episode is recalled as part of the covenant renewal at Shechem: "Then Balak . . . invited Balaam the son of Beor to curse you, but I would not listen to Balaam. Indeed, he blessed you. So I delivered you out of his hand" (Josh. 24:9–10).

Section Outline

    II. Trials in the Wilderness of Paran, the Transjordan Highlands, and the Plains of Moab (11:1–25:18) . . .
        L. Balaam's Mission (22:1–41)
            1. His Summons (22:1–21)
            2. His Journey (22:22–41)

Comment

22:1–21 The people of Israel are "in the plains of [*'arabah*] Moab beyond the Jordan at Jericho" (v. 1; cf. comment on 26:1–51). On the other side of the Jordan the region is called the "plains of [*'arabah*] Jericho" (Josh. 4:13). In addition to the rift stretching from the Dead Sea to the Gulf of Aqaba, "Arabah" also designates the portion between the Dead Sea and the Sea of Galilee (Deut. 3:17). This southeastern end of the Jordan Valley is well watered and densely wooded in biblical times (Num. 24:2, 5–7; 2 Kings 6:4–5; Jer. 49:19; 50:44).[183] It is the physical setting of the remainder of Numbers and Deuteronomy, as well as the beginning of Joshua (cf. Num. 33:48; 36:13; Deut. 1:1; 34:1; Josh. 1:1; 3:1). Moses begins his discourses there on the first day of the eleventh month of the fortieth year (Deut. 1:3–5). The journey to Transjordan began after the thirty-day mourning period following Aaron's death in the fifth month of that year (Num. 20:29; 33:38).

"The Jordan" is the only perennial river in Canaan. From the Sea of Galilee it descends 65 miles (105 km) to the Dead Sea. Its meanderings more than double its length. The steep descent in elevation between these two seas (c. 650 feet [200 m]) conferred the name "Jordan" (*yarden*; from *yarad*, "descend").[184] The Israelites camp at Shittim (cf. comment on 25:1–9; cf. 33:49; Josh. 3:1). Across the river, Jericho, 9 miles (14 km) north-northwest of the Dead Sea, controls access to the hill country west of the plains (cf. comment on Num. 33:37–49 [at v. 48]). The Israelites will soon encounter Jericho (Josh. 2:1). Their presence in the plains of Moab has already caused Jericho's inhabitants to fear (Josh. 2:9). The Moabite king, Balak, has reason

---

[183] Baly, *Geography of the Bible*, 202; Aharoni, *Land of the Bible*, 34, 206.
[184] Physical characteristics are also determinate in the names of the Sea of Galilee, or "Sea of Chinnereth" (Num. 34:11), reflecting its "harp" shape, and the Dead Sea, or "Salt Sea" (34:3, 12), due to its 25–30 percent salinity, the highest of any sea or lake in the world.

for concern because he saw what had happened to the Amorites (Num. 22:2). Israel not only defeated the Amorites; they now control their territory from the Arnon to Mount Hermon. Moab is south of the Arnon.

Although Israel is not to war with them, nor to dispossess them (Deut. 2:9), the Moabites are nevertheless in "great dread [*gur*]" of Israel's vast numbers and "overcome with fear [*quts*]" of their presence (Num. 22:3). Their distress echoes the Lord's promise made to Israel just before their battles with the Amorites: "I will begin to put the dread [*pakhad*] and fear [*yir'ah*] of you on the peoples who are under the whole heaven, who shall hear the report of you and shall tremble and be in anguish because of you" (Deut. 2:25). The Moabites are descendants of Abraham's nephew, Lot (Gen. 19:36–37). The Midianites are Abraham's descendants by Keturah (25:2). Like the Amorites, the Midianites live both west and east of the Arabah (Num. 10:29). Midianite clans under elders live in Moab (cf. Gen. 36:35), ruled by a Moabite king.

The fear that Israel will "lick up" everything like an ox does "the grass of the field" (Num. 22:4) is not hyperbole, since the Israelites have vast flocks and herds. For herdsmen, controlling pasturelands and water sources was a regular source of conflict (Gen. 13:6–7; 26:20–21). For husbandmen, outlying marauding bands frequently penetrated cultivated lands after harvest time. There, they devoured readily available foods, and then made off with large quantities of harvested crops (Judg. 6:3, 11; 1 Chron. 11:13–14). Defending these resources required a militia. But Moab was vastly outnumbered by the Israelites.

If Balaam's name is derived from *bala'* (with a -*m* nominal ending),[185] there may be a play on words recalling the judgment of Korah and his company being "swallowed" (*bala'*; Num. 16:32; 26:10) by the earth. Balaam is a diviner (cf. discussion on 22:7 below; Josh. 13:22). He is never called a prophet (*nabi'*), nor a seer (*ro'eh* or *hozeh*; all three terms: 1 Chron. 29:29), nor viewed in a positive manner (Deut. 23:5; Josh. 13:22; 24:9–10; Mic. 6:5; 2 Pet. 2:15; Jude 11; Rev. 2:14). His most heinous deed leads to the death of twenty-four thousand Israelites (Num. 25:9; 31:16). His avarice and malice lead to his end (31:8).

Discovered east of the Jordan near the foot of the Jabbok, the Deir 'Alla inscription, in language dating to the eighth century BC, mentions a Balaam, son of Beor, in ways comparable to the biblical character. For example, he is said to be a diviner able to avert divine wrath by communicating with gods known as El and Shadday, the two appellations paired in Numbers in Balaam's discourses ("God [*'el*] . . . the Almighty [*shadday*]"; Num. 24:4, 16). Balaam is summoned at "Pethor, which is near the River" (22:5) "Pethor" is usually identified with Pitru in upper Mesopotamia, between Aleppo and Carchemish.[186] "The River" is the Euphrates (*hannahar*; e.g., Josh. 24:2 ESV mg.). Deuteronomy 23:4 says Balaam

---

[185] E.g., Hb. *melek* ("king"). Cf. Ammonite *milkom* ("[god] Milcom"; 1 Kings 11:5); Hb. *peh*, ("mouth"); Aramaic *pum* ("mouth"; Dan. 4:31).
[186] Near or at Tell el-Ahmar, 12 miles (20 km) south of Carchemish; cf. Rasmussen, *Zondervan Atlas*, 248; Gray, *Numbers*, 325. On the linguistic difficulties in reading Pethor as Pitru cf. Baruch A. Levine, *Numbers 21–36: A New Translation with Introduction and Commentary*, AYB 4 (New York: Doubleday, 2000), 147.

is from "Pethor of Mesopotamia," or "Pethor in Aram Naharaim" (NIV). Aram Naharaim, "the land of two rivers," refers to the region between the Euphrates to the west and the Habur River to the east.[187] Balaam says he was summoned from "Aram" (cf. comment on Num. 23:1–12 [at v. 7]). Each of the two round trips made between Moab and Pethor by Balaam's messengers to persuade Balaam to come would require months of travel (cf. Ezra 7:9).[188] During his mission Balaam resides in Moab. Afterward he returns to "his place" (Num. 24:25) somewhere in Moab, where he is killed by the Israelites (31:8) who have encamped at Shittim in the Jordan Valley.

The rendering "Amaw" (22:5) is based on ancient inscriptions that possibly mention a land of Amaw, but both the reading and its connection with Pitru are disputed.[189] The Hebrew reads "the sons of his people" (*bene-'ammo*), as does the LXX. The SP and Vulgate read "sons of Ammon" (cf. *'ammo* with a final *-n*).[190] The traditional reading is not difficult (although it never occurs elsewhere for a location), and the expression has parallels (e.g., "the sons of my people," Gen. 23:11; "the children of their people," Lev. 20:17). Moreover, Balaam speaks of his return to "my people" (Num. 24:14).

"Curse . . . cursed . . . bless . . . blessed" (22:6) are the key words around which the Balaam narrative and discourses turn (cf. Section Overview). Their twofold repetition in Balaam's first oracle ushers in a high frequency of occurrences of the terms throughout the narrative and the discourses. Balaam's third oracle ends with the terms in inverted order: "Blessed . . . bless . . . cursed . . . curse" (24:9). Forms of the word "curse" (*'arar*) occur seven times (22:6 [3x], 12; 23:7; 24:9 [2x]). Another term translated "curse" (*qabab*) occurs ten times (22:11, 17; 23:8 [2x], 11, 13, 25 [2x], 27; 24:10). The semantically related "denounce" (*za'am*) appears three times (23:7, 8 [2x]). Forms of "bless" (*barak*) occur fourteen times (22:6 [2x], 12; 23:11 [2x], 20 [2x], 25 [2x]; 24:1, 9 [2x], 10 [2x]).

Ultimately, God alone blesses (Num. 6:24; 24:1; cf. Gen. 1:22, 28) and curses (Num. 23:8; cf. Gen. 3:14, 17). His covenant blessing occasions strength, health, abundance, and victory (e.g., Lev. 26:4–9; Deut. 28:2–13). Covenant curses cause weakness, sickness, dearth, and defeat (e.g., Lev. 26:16–33; Deut. 28:15–68; cf. Mark 11:21). As polar opposites, blessing is life and good, whereas curse is death and evil (Deut. 30:15, 19). Blessing and curses are often expressed in terms of good/favor or evil/harm/disaster (Num. 10:29; Josh. 23:15; Job 2:10; Jer. 32:42; 39:16–18; 44:27; Zeph. 1:12). Intermediaries can invoke God to bless or curse (Num. 22:6, 12; Deut. 28:2, 15; Gal. 1:7–8) and, in some cases, directly invoke a blessing or curse (Num. 23:8; Deut. 33:1; 1 Cor. 5:5). Evil spirits enjoined by diviners can

---

[187] Much later (Polybius, 2nd century BC, and Strabo, 1st century AD) "Mesopotamia" described the land between the Tigris and the Euphrates (Rasmussen, *Zondervan Atlas*, 65, 226).
[188] It took Ezra at least four months to arrive at Jerusalem from Persia (Ezra 7:9; 8:31). Balaam traveled by donkey, an animal incompatible with a 400-mile (650 km) trip from upper Mesopotamia to Moab (cf. Milgrom, *Numbers*, 186; Gray, *Numbers*, 326). He may have traveled from northern Mesopotamia on camel and once in the mountainous Moabite region continued his voyage on donkey (cf. comment on 22:22–41 [at v. 25]).
[189] Milgrom, *Numbers*, 186; Levine, *Numbers 21–36*, 148.
[190] The reading adopted by Gray (*Numbers*, 326) and Levine (*Numbers 21–36*, 148).

inflict curses; but doing so is never outside divine purview (1 Kings 22:22–23; Job 1:12). Unless it is debilitated by curses, Israel will remain too powerful for Moab (Num. 22:6, 11).

"Fees for divination" renders one word (pl. *qesem*; lit., "divinations"; 22:7). If these are fees rather than instruments for divination,[191] they constitute a down payment; full receipt requires success (vv. 18, 37; 24:11). Balaam practices divination (*qasam*; Josh. 13:22) for hire. Ezekiel describes its practice in a military context: "The king of Babylon stands at the parting of the way, at the head of the two ways, to use divination. He shakes the arrows; he consults the teraphim; he looks at the liver" (Ezek. 21:21). Given all the sacrifices he orders, Balaam perhaps uses hepatoscopy (divination by studying the liver). Divination is forbidden to Israel (Lev. 19:31; Deut. 18:10, 14). It is a form of rebellion (1 Sam. 15:23) that involves mediums, the spirit world (1 Sam. 28:7–8), and, at times, child sacrifice (Deut. 18:10; 2 Kings 17:17). False prophets employ divination (e.g., Jer. 14:14). Balaam also uses "enchantments" and "omens" (both from *nahash*; Num. 23:23; 24:1, the term rendered "serpent[s]" in Num. 21:6, 7, 9).

"Lodge here tonight" (22:8) suggests that Balaam anticipates a nocturnal revelatory vision (cf. 24:4, 16). "As the LORD speaks" (v. 8) does not indicate Balaam is a true prophet any more than using the name "LORD" means he worships him. Like Balak, he has undoubtedly heard what the Lord has done to Egypt and the kingdoms of the Amorites. "God came to Balaam" (v. 9) as he had to Abimelech and Laban, both in a dream, warning them (Gen. 20:3; 31:24). God does not converse with Balaam by using his covenant name, though "the LORD" would put his word in the form of prophetic discourses in Balaam's mouth (Num. 23:5, 16). "And said" (22:9) suggests the revelation is auditory. God forbids Balaam to go with the messengers to "curse the people, for they are blessed" (v. 12; cf. v. 6). A curse could remove the hedge of blessing (cf. 5:19–28).

After Balaam declines the first summons (22:13–14), Balak sends a second delegation "more in number," with emissaries "more honorable" (*kabed*; v. 15), by whom he promises Balaam "great honor" (*kabed*; v. 17),[192] that is, greater wealth (*kabod*; Gen. 31:1), which Balaam knows to be "silver and gold" (Num. 22:18). As with the first summons, the goal of this second summons is to "curse this people" (v. 17; cf. v. 6). Although acknowledging that he cannot "go beyond the command of the LORD my God" (v. 18), Balaam entreats Balak's emissaries, "Please stay here tonight" (v. 19), as he had the first messengers (v. 8). God's "command" is already clear: "You shall not go" (v. 12). Nevertheless, he says he will "know what more the LORD will say to me" (v. 19). His feigned rejection of money is unmasked by his forestalling. Perhaps he hopes to up the ante.

God grants Balaam his desire to go for hire, but not the right to acquiesce to Balak's demand: "Only do what I tell you" (Num. 22:20). God gives Balaam over to his willfulness (Ps. 81:11–12; Acts 7:42). God sovereignly uses evil desires and

---
191 Cf. *CDCH*, 398.
192 *CHALOT*, 150: "reward richly," citing Numbers 22:17.

deeds to accomplish his purposes (Gen. 50:20; Judg. 14:1–4; Acts 2:23; Rom. 8:28) and then to punish those who indulge in them (Prov. 1:31; Jer. 21:14; Rom. 1:24, 26–27, 28). Balaam's avarice will be his demise by the hand of those he is commissioned to curse (Num. 31:8).

22:22–41 "God's anger was kindled" (v. 22; cf. 11:1; 32:13); "anger . . . kindled" is said also of Balaam's and Balak's anger (22:27; 24:10). The Lord's anger is kindled because Balaam went with the intention of enriching himself by cursing God's people (Deut. 23:5), not to do what God would tell him to do. Balaam's perversity (cf. Num. 22:32) draws God's anger.

The "angel of the LORD" (v. 22) appeared to Hagar, Abraham, and Moses (Gen. 16:7; 22:11; Ex. 3:2). There is no referential distinction between "angel of the LORD" and "angel of God" (cf. Ex. 14:19 and Judg. 2:1; Judg. 13:9 and Judg. 13:16). "Angel of the LORD" occurs ten times in the Balaam narrative. In a figurative sense, ten times means once too often (Gen. 31:7; Job 19:3). In Numbers 22:22 the tenth time leads to divine judgment. First, the angel of the Lord is Balaam's "adversary" (*satan*; v. 22; cf. v. 32, "oppose"; 1 Kings 5:4). In the second and seventh occurrences he appears with a "sword in his hand" (Num. 22:23, 31). The tenth time the angel of the Lord reiterates God's prior command, "Go with the men, but speak only the word that I tell you" (v. 35; cf. v. 20). Speaking as God himself, his command "Go" leads to Balaam's doom. If he had obeyed in the first place (v. 12), Balaam would not have suffered death (Num. 31:8), the ultimate expression of God's anger (Ps. 90:7–8) and judgment for his perverse advice that instigates the Baal-peor debacle.

A "narrow path between the vineyards" (Num. 22:24) describes stone-walled, terraced hillsides, perhaps already in Moab, reputed for wine production (Jer. 48:33). Such descriptions (cf. Num. 22:26) show that Balaam's encounter with the angel, rather than occurring on a route crossing the plains, comes in mountainous terrain, which fits well with where Balaam is received (cf. v. 36) and where he will preside over his rituals (v. 41; 23:3, 9, 14, 28). The donkey "lay down under Balaam" (22:27). The observation of animal behavior is part of divination. The Ugaritic Keret Legend includes a horse's lying down while drawing the chariot of a king or prince as an omen of failure in his mission (cf. 1 Sam. 6:8–9).[193]

"The LORD opened the mouth of the donkey" (Num. 22:28), anticipating the Lord's putting his word in Balaam's mouth (cf. v. 38). The donkey presents the opposite qualities of Balaam (vv. 23–30). It sees the angel, which Balaam does not. Balaam beats his donkey three times for actions which, as it turns out, save his life. The donkey has proven its selfless, faithful service to his master. Balaam proves himself self-serving and untrustworthy to God. "Then the LORD opened [*galah*] the eyes of Balaam" (v. 31): when having revelatory visions, Balaam claims his eyes have been "uncovered" (form of *galah*; 24:4, 16). Balaam confesses neither his greed nor his treachery but only that he erred by persisting to advance while

---

[193] De Vaulx, *Les Nombres*, 269. The legend dates to the Late Bronze Age (c. 1500–1200 BC).

the angel was blocking the path: "I did not know that you stood in the road." He proposes, "if it is evil in your sight," to "turn back" (22:34).

"Go... speak only the word that I tell you" (v. 35). Despite Balaam's intentions, God will use him to accomplish his purposes. There is no contradiction between the Lord's commands "You shall not go" (v. 12) and then "Go" (vv. 20, 35), since the former was linked to "You shall not curse the people" (v. 12) and the latter to "do" and "speak" (vv. 20, 35) only what God says to Balaam. In any event, God has already given Balaam over to his own willful desires in order to accomplish his sovereign will.

Balak greets Balaam "on the border formed by the Arnon," Moab's northern border (v. 36). The "extremity of the border" (v. 36) is apparently a western point from which the Israelites can be seen below (cf. discussion on v. 41 below). Irritated by Balaam's delay in coming, Balak angrily asks, "Am I not able to honor you?" (v. 37), that is, enrich Balaam (cf. comment on 22:1–21 [at v. 17]). Balaam's earlier stalling tactics—ostensibly waiting for revelation from God—have had their effect (vv. 8, 19). Balaam knows Balak will greatly reward him to get what he wants. He tells Barak he can only speak "the word that God puts in my mouth" (v. 38; cf. 23:5, 12, 16). Given his cupidity, Balaam thereby incites Balak to increase his offer. His subsequent actions of multiplying sacrifices (23:1, 14, 29) and using omens (24:1) all portray a complicit Balaam, "who loved gain from wrongdoing" (2 Pet. 2:15). He has indeed come to get rich by doing Balak's will.

"Bamoth-baal" (Num. 22:41, "Baal's high places"; cf. 21:19, Bamoth) here indicates a sacred site in a city, named as a city in Reuben's inheritance (Josh. 13:17). Balak calls on Baal, a pan-national deity, not the national god of Moab, Chemosh (Num. 21:29; 1 Kings 11:33). The reason Balaam seeks only a "fraction [*qatseh*, "extremity, edge"] of the people" is probably due to the distance and angle of vision from that vantage point, since the Israelites are encamped in the Jordan Valley around 4,250 feet below (1,300 m) and perhaps as distant as 25 miles (40 km; cf. Num. 22:36). From between the Zered and the Arnon, Moab overlooks the southern half of the Dead Sea. But the encamped Israelites can still be seen to the north of the sea. To be cursed the people have to be seen, if only some of them.

Response

A florilegium of Matthew Henry citations is worth considering.[194] Regarding God's command to Balaam ("Go with them"; v. 20), Henry writes, "As God sometimes denies the prayers of his people in love, so sometimes he grants the desires of the wicked in wrath."

Concerning Balaam's considering the angel to be his adversary (v. 22), he writes, "Those are really our best friends, and we are so to reckon them, that stop our progress in a sinful way."

---

[194] Cited by Bush, *Book of Numbers*, 351, 352, 359, 361.

Regarding Balaam's beating his donkey (v. 23), he writes, "Thus they who by willful sin are running headlong into perdition, are angry at those who would prevent their ruin."

On Balaam's seeing the angel (v. 31), Henry remarks, "When our eyes are opened we shall see what danger we are in in a sinful way, and how much it was for our advantage to be crossed in it, and what fools we were to quarrel with our crosses which helped to save our lives."

NUMBERS 23

23 And Balaam said to Balak, "Build for me here seven altars, and prepare for me here seven bulls and seven rams." ² Balak did as Balaam had said. And Balak and Balaam offered on each altar a bull and a ram. ³ And Balaam said to Balak, "Stand beside your burnt offering, and I will go. Perhaps the Lord will come to meet me, and whatever he shows me I will tell you." And he went to a bare height, ⁴ and God met Balaam. And Balaam said to him, "I have arranged the seven altars and I have offered on each altar a bull and a ram." ⁵ And the Lord put a word in Balaam's mouth and said, "Return to Balak, and thus you shall speak." ⁶ And he returned to him, and behold, he and all the princes of Moab were standing beside his burnt offering. ⁷ And Balaam took up his discourse and said,

> "From Aram Balak has brought me,
>   the king of Moab from the eastern mountains:
> 'Come, curse Jacob for me,
>   and come, denounce Israel!'
> ⁸ How can I curse whom God has not cursed?
>   How can I denounce whom the Lord has not denounced?
> ⁹ For from the top of the crags I see him,
>   from the hills I behold him;
> behold, a people dwelling alone,
>   and not counting itself among the nations!
> ¹⁰ Who can count the dust of Jacob
>   or number the fourth part¹ of Israel?
> Let me die the death of the upright,
>   and let my end be like his!"

¹¹ And Balak said to Balaam, "What have you done to me? I took you to curse my enemies, and behold, you have done nothing but bless them." ¹² And he answered and said, "Must I not take care to speak what the Lord puts in my mouth?"

¹³ And Balak said to him, "Please come with me to another place, from which you may see them. You shall see only a fraction of them and shall

not see them all. Then curse them for me from there." ¹⁴ And he took him to the field of Zophim, to the top of Pisgah, and built seven altars and offered a bull and a ram on each altar. ¹⁵ Balaam said to Balak, "Stand here beside your burnt offering, while I meet the LORD over there." ¹⁶ And the LORD met Balaam and put a word in his mouth and said, "Return to Balak, and thus shall you speak." ¹⁷ And he came to him, and behold, he was standing beside his burnt offering, and the princes of Moab with him. And Balak said to him, "What has the LORD spoken?" ¹⁸ And Balaam took up his discourse and said,

> "Rise, Balak, and hear;
>   give ear to me, O son of Zippor:
> ¹⁹ God is not man, that he should lie,
>   or a son of man, that he should change his mind.
> Has he said, and will he not do it?
>   Or has he spoken, and will he not fulfill it?
> ²⁰ Behold, I received a command to bless:
>   he has blessed, and I cannot revoke it.
> ²¹ He has not beheld misfortune in Jacob,
>   nor has he seen trouble in Israel.
> The LORD their God is with them,
>   and the shout of a king is among them.
> ²² God brings them out of Egypt
>   and is for them like the horns of the wild ox.
> ²³ For there is no enchantment against Jacob,
>   no divination against Israel;
> now it shall be said of Jacob and Israel,
>   'What has God wrought!'
> ²⁴ Behold, a people! As a lioness it rises up
>   and as a lion it lifts itself;
> it does not lie down until it has devoured the prey
>   and drunk the blood of the slain."

²⁵ And Balak said to Balaam, "Do not curse them at all, and do not bless them at all." ²⁶ But Balaam answered Balak, "Did I not tell you, 'All that the LORD says, that I must do'?" ²⁷ And Balak said to Balaam, "Come now, I will take you to another place. Perhaps it will please God that you may curse them for me from there." ²⁸ So Balak took Balaam to the top of Peor, which overlooks the desert.² ²⁹ And Balaam said to Balak, "Build for me here seven altars and prepare for me here seven bulls and seven rams." ³⁰ And Balak did as Balaam had said, and offered a bull and a ram on each altar.

¹ Or *dust clouds* ² Or *Jeshimon*

Section Overview

Numbers 23–24 contain Balaam's discourses. Their common features are highlighted here. "Discourse" (*mashal*; cf. comment on 23:1–2 [at v. 7]) is the sevenfold designation of Balaam's interventions (23:7, 18; 24:3, 15, 20, 21, 23). He delivers four major discourses (23:7–10, 18–24; 24:3–9, 15–19) and three minor ones

(24:20, 21–22, 23–24). The second two major discourses are also called "oracles" (*ne'um*; cf. comment on 24:1–14 [at v. 3]).

The first two discourses are words put into the mouth of Balaam by the Lord (23:5, 16). The third discourse comes after the Spirit of God has come upon him (24:4), a ministry that no doubt applies also to the fourth discourse. All the discourses are divinely revealed. They draw on the promises made to Abraham and his descendants. Israel will be immeasurably numerous (23:10; 24:7; cf. Gen. 13:16), delivered by their king (Num. 23:21; 24:7, 17, 19; cf. Gen. 17:6, 16; 35:11; cf. Gen. 36:31), and blessed (Num. 23:20; 24:9; cf. Gen. 12:2; 49:25). Moreover, the curse invoked by their enemies will boomerang upon them (e.g., Num. 24:9; cf. vv. 8, 17, 18; cf. Gen. 12:3; 27:29).

The discourse form appears in parallel synonymic doublets (e.g., "Come, curse Jacob for me, and come, denounce Israel!"; Num. 23:7), in antithetic doublets ("Blessed are those who bless you, and cursed are those who curse you"; 24:9), and in double doublets or quadruplets (e.g., "Like palm groves that stretch afar, like gardens beside a river, like aloes that the LORD has planted, like cedar trees beside the waters"; 24:6).

The theme here is Balak's scheme to curse Israel cannot supplant God's blessing (cf. Section Overview of Numbers 22; cf. table 4.7).

TABLE 4.7: Main Theme throughout Numbers 23–24

In Balaam's discourses	"How can I curse whom God has not cursed?" (23:8) "Behold, I received a command to bless: he has blessed, and I cannot revoke it." (23:20) "Blessed are those who bless you, and cursed are those who curse you." (24:9)
In Balak's responses	"I took you to curse my enemies, and behold, you have done nothing but bless them." (23:11) "Curse them for me from there." (23:13) "Perhaps it will please God that you may curse them." (23:27) "Do not curse them at all, and do not bless them at all." (23:25) "I called you to curse my enemies, and behold, you have blessed them these three times." (24:10)
In the narration	"Balaam saw that it pleased the LORD to bless Israel." (24:1)
In Scripture commentary	"But the LORD your God would not listen to Balaam; instead the LORD your God turned the curse into a blessing for you, because the LORD your God loved you." (Deut. 23:5) "And he sent and invited Balaam the son of Beor to curse you, but I would not listen to Balaam. Indeed, he blessed you. So I delivered you out of his hand." (Josh. 24:9–10) ". . . but hired Balaam against them to curse them—yet our God turned the curse into a blessing." (Neh. 13:2)

Instead of a cursed and conquered people, as Balak desired, Balaam's discourses foretell Israel as blessed, sovereign, and victorious over its enemies (Num. 23:7–11, 18–24; 24:3–9, 15–19, 20–24). On the heels of the defeat of Transjordan Amorites, the Israelites will be poised, with God's blessing, to take possession of the Promised Land.

Section Outline

II. Trials in the Wilderness of Paran, the Transjordan Highlands, and the Plains of Moab (11:1–25:18) . . .

    M. Balaam's First Two Discourses (23:1–30)
        1. Discourse One (23:1–12)
        2. Discourse Two (23:13–30)

Comment

23:1–12 The scene is set for the first two discourses with "seven altars . . . seven bulls . . . seven rams" (v. 1). Seven represents wholeness and perfection, intrinsic qualities of sacredness. Bulls and rams are the costliest of sacrifices. Each is a "burnt offering" (vv. 3, 6, 15, 17). By presiding over these rituals, Balaam colludes in Balak's scheme rather than dissuading him. However, when he states, "Whatever he shows me I will tell you" (v. 3), Balaam implicitly reiterates that he can do and say only what God orders (22:20, 35; cf. 23:5, 12, 26; 24:13). The Lord is the one who reveals his word to Balaam and opens his eyes to see visions (24:3, 15). The angel of the Lord had put his word in the donkey's mouth and opened Balaam's eyes to see the angel (22:28, 31). His order remains unchanged: "Thus you shall speak" (23:5), which serves as an introductory refrain to the first discourse (cf. discussion on v. 12 below).

"Discourse" (v. 7) renders a term also translated "proverb" (Hb. *mashal*; e.g., Prov. 1:1), belonging to the wisdom genre. Balaam's discourses are more like the instances of *mashal* found in the prophets (Isa. 14:4; Ezek. 12:22, 23; 16:44; 18:2, 3). Given the prophetic genre of Balaam's discourses, the term is well suited. Like the proverbs, these too are robed in poetical garb.

"Aram" (Num. 23:7) is north-northeast of Canaan. It extends from northern Transjordan to the upper Tigris-Euphrates valleys (cf. comment on 22:1–21 [at v. 5]).[195] "The eastern mountains" (*harrey-qedem*, 23:7; also rendered "ancient mountains," Deut. 33:15) may be those traversing northeastern Syria.

Balaam first restates Balak's wish: "Come, curse Jacob for me" (Num. 23:7). "Curse" (*'arar*) also describes the action directed at the Serpent and those who ill-treat Abraham's descendants (Gen. 3:14; 12:3). The parallel "denounce" (*za'am*; Num. 23:7, 8) is the rarer of the word pair. Balaam then reiterates God's restraining order: "How can I curse whom God has not cursed?" (v. 8), which employs a different verb (*qabab*). "A people dwelling alone, and not counting itself among the nations!" (v. 9) underscores the uniqueness of Israel, having the Lord as God and his law as their own (Deut. 4:7–8; 33:29; Ps. 147:19–20).

"Who can count the dust of Jacob?" (Num. 23:10) recalls God's promise to Abraham, "I will make your offspring as the dust of the earth, so that if one can count the dust of the earth, your offspring also can be counted" (Gen. 13:16; cf. Gen. 28:14). Since blessing brings increase, Balaam's rhetorical question is an implicit

---

[195] Rasmussen, *Zondervan Atlas*, 226. In 2 Chronicles 20:2 "Aram" appears in the context of the Moabites, the Ammonites, Engedi, and Mount Seir (2 Chron. 20:1, 10, 22). It is sometimes rendered "Edom" (e.g., RSV, ESV) following one Hebrew manuscript. Aram is in most Hebrew manuscripts and is also supported by the LXX and the Vulgate (cf. NASB). On "Assur" cf. comment on Num. 24:15–25 [at v. 22]; note 199.

blessing, just as Balak understands: "I took you to curse my enemies, and behold, you have done nothing but bless them" (Num. 23:11). "Must I not take care to speak what the LORD puts in my mouth?" (v. 12) forms an inclusio, an end frame of the first oracle (cf. discussion on v. 5 above; cf. vv. 16, 26).

23:13–30 The scene shifts "to another place" (v. 13), "to the field of Zophim ["Watchers"], to the top of Pisgah" (v. 14). As before, a total of fourteen burnt offerings are made on seven altars (v. 14; cf. v. 4). Pisgah, the summit of Mount Nebo, overlooks the southern Jordan Valley and the northern end of the Dead Sea from opposite Jericho (Deut. 3:17; 34:1). From there Moses will survey the Promised Land (Deut. 34:1–4), but Balaam can see only a "fraction" of the Israelites, albeit one sufficiently large to "curse them ... from there" (Num. 23:13).

"Thus shall you speak" (v. 16) introduces the discourse (cf. discussion on the inclusio below, v. 26). Balak's anticipatory query ("What has the LORD spoken?"; v. 17) is answered in two ways by Balaam. First, he affirms God's immutability: "God is not man, that he should lie, or ... change his mind" (v. 19). Consequently, "Has he said, and will he not do it? Or has he spoken, and will he not fulfill it?" (v. 19). Second, Balaam confirms, "Behold, I received a command to bless" (v. 20; lit., "I received to bless"), that is, a word of blessing from the Lord. Balaam can transmit only what he receives. God forbids Balaam to curse Israel, for *God* has blessed them (22:12). Consequently, "[God] has blessed, and I cannot revoke it" (23:20); "I cannot make it return" to the one who pronounced it. As the prophet later declares,

> So shall my word be that goes out from my mouth;
> > it shall not return to me empty,
> but it shall accomplish that which I purpose,
> > and shall succeed in the thing for which I sent it. (Isa. 55:11)

Balaam's powers are bridled. He can neither curse Israel nor revoke God's blessing. In fact, there is no trace of curse. On the contrary, "He has not beheld misfortune in Jacob, nor ... trouble in Israel" (Num. 23:21).

"Their God is with them" (v. 21) is a salvific promise, as are all "Immanuel" (*'immanu 'el*, "God with us") promises (e.g., 2 Chron. 13:12; Isa. 7:14; 8:8, 10; Matt. 1:21, 23). If "God [is] with us," there is victory.[196] Joshua and Caleb exhorted the people to enter the Promised Land and not to fear their adversaries, for "the LORD is with us" (*yhwh 'ittanu*; Num. 14:9). "Shout" (*teru'ah*) may refer to a war-trumpet alarm (Num. 31:6; Jer. 4:19) or a war cry (Josh. 6:5; Jer. 49:2). The king who is among them is "the LORD their God," who will swiftly triumph over the "king of Moab," Balak (Num. 22:4; cf. 21:1; 1 Chron. 1:43). This is the same God who "brings them out of Egypt," the greatest evidence of his ability to deliver Israel from an international power, one far greater than Moab (Num. 23:22). It irrefutably demonstrates his supremacy over all nations (Ex. 9:14, 16) and their gods (Ex. 12:12; Jer. 43:12–13).

---

[196] On the salvific import of the Immanuel promise cf. Ron Bergey, "La Prophétie d'Esaïe 7,14–16: accomplissement unique ou double?" *RRef* 46/1 (1995): 9–14.

In fulfillment of his covenant promise he purposed to bring Israel out of Egypt and lead the nation to the Promised Land (e.g., Gen. 15:13–14; Ex. 3:8; 32:13; Deut. 19:8; 31:7). This epitomizes his redemptive grace (*hesed*, "steadfast love"; e.g., Ex. 15:13; Ps. 136:11), which is incarnated ultimately in Christ (John 1:14, 17).

Here and in the third discourse the simile "Like the horns of the wild ox" is joined with "God brings them out of Egypt" (Num. 23:22; 24:8). He is "for them like the horns" (23:22). In ancient Near Eastern iconography gods are portrayed with horns. A "horn" is a royal image (Pss. 89:17–18; 132:17) symbolizing power (1 Kings 22:11; Dan. 8:6–7). This is tantamount to saying that if Egypt's magicians and diviners were no match for God, how could Balak expect Balaam to thwart him? No enchantment or divination is efficacious against God's power and blessing (Num. 23:23).

Another simile appears here and in the following discourse: "As a lioness . . . lion" (v. 24; 24:9 in inverted order). This applies not to God but to "a people" and recalls Jacob's blessing on Judah.

> Judah is a lion's cub;
> > from the prey, my son, you have gone up.
> He stooped down; he crouched as a lion
> > and as a lioness; who dares rouse him?
> The scepter shall not depart from Judah,
> > nor the ruler's staff from between his feet,
> until tribute comes to him;
> > and to him shall be the obedience of the peoples. (Gen. 49:9–10; cf.
> > > Deut. 33:20 in Moses' blessing, where Gad crouches like a lion)

"It does not lie down until it has devoured the prey and drunk the blood of the slain" (Num. 23:24) depicts the power of a people blessed by God their King, as well as the fate of anyone who curses them. The prophetic imagery is royal and messianic, ultimately delineated as "the Lion of the tribe of Judah, the Root of David, [who] has conquered" (Rev. 5:5).

Balak understands—temporarily at least—Balaam's impotence and asks, if Balaam cannot curse Israel, that he should at least not bless them even further (Num. 23:25). Balaam's discourse drives home the point that disaster awaits those who curse the people whom God has blessed. "All that the LORD says" (v. 26) forms an inclusio (cf. v. 16; cf. vv. 5, 12).

Balak's acquiescence, like Pharaoh's, is short lived. He again enjoins Balaam to come "to another place . . . that you may curse them for me from there" (v. 27; cf. v. 13). The location is portentous, "the top of Peor" (v. 28), anticipating the calamitous Baal of Peor incident (25:3). "Overlooks the desert" (*yeshimon*) refers here perhaps not to the Jeshimon in Judah west of the Dead Sea but to the Jeshimon east of the Jordan and north of the Dead Sea (cf. 21:20).[197] Balaam can now see all the Israelite encampments (24:2).

---

[197] Smith, *Historical Geography of the Holy Land*, 381n2.

Response

The redemptive grace of the Lord ("God brings them out of Egypt"; 23:22) is applicable to all who trust in the prefigured Pascal Lamb of God (John 1:29) who was slain (Rev. 5:12; 13:8) and now reigns (Rev. 22:1). "Jesus . . . saved a people out of the land of Egypt" (Jude 5) and led them in the wilderness (1 Cor. 10:4, 9). Many Israelites refused the spiritual redemptive grace displayed in the exodus experience and in God's care in the wilderness. They had no faith in God's promises and no hope of life in the land. In their unbelief, rather than entering Canaan they longed to return to Egypt. "Jesus . . . afterward destroyed those who did not believe" (Jude 5). He now leads a people who believe in him into the antitype of the Promised Land, the promised rest of salvation and all its benefits in this life and in the hope of eternal life (John 10:10; Titus 1:2; 3:7; Heb. 4:1–9).

NUMBERS 24

24 When Balaam saw that it pleased the LORD to bless Israel, he did not go, as at other times, to look for omens, but set his face toward the wilderness. ² And Balaam lifted up his eyes and saw Israel camping tribe by tribe. And the Spirit of God came upon him, ³ and he took up his discourse and said,

"The oracle of Balaam the son of Beor,
    the oracle of the man whose eye is opened,¹
⁴ the oracle of him who hears the words of God,
    who sees the vision of the Almighty,
    falling down with his eyes uncovered:
⁵ How lovely are your tents, O Jacob,
    your encampments, O Israel!
⁶ Like palm groves² that stretch afar,
    like gardens beside a river,
like aloes that the LORD has planted,
    like cedar trees beside the waters.
⁷ Water shall flow from his buckets,
    and his seed shall be in many waters;
his king shall be higher than Agag,
    and his kingdom shall be exalted.
⁸ God brings him out of Egypt
    and is for him like the horns of the wild ox;
he shall eat up the nations, his adversaries,
    and shall break their bones in pieces
    and pierce them through with his arrows.
⁹ He crouched, he lay down like a lion
    and like a lioness; who will rouse him up?
Blessed are those who bless you,
    and cursed are those who curse you."

10 And Balak's anger was kindled against Balaam, and he struck his hands together. And Balak said to Balaam, "I called you to curse my enemies, and behold, you have blessed them these three times. **11** Therefore now flee to your own place. I said, 'I will certainly honor you,' but the LORD has held you back from honor." **12** And Balaam said to Balak, "Did I not tell your messengers whom you sent to me, **13** 'If Balak should give me his house full of silver and gold, I would not be able to go beyond the word of the LORD, to do either good or bad of my own will. What the LORD speaks, that will I speak'? **14** And now, behold, I am going to my people. Come, I will let you know what this people will do to your people in the latter days."

15 And he took up his discourse and said,

"The oracle of Balaam the son of Beor,
    the oracle of the man whose eye is opened,[1]
16 the oracle of him who hears the words of God,
    and knows the knowledge of the Most High,
who sees the vision of the Almighty,
    falling down with his eyes uncovered:
17 I see him, but not now;
    I behold him, but not near:
a star shall come out of Jacob,
    and a scepter shall rise out of Israel;
it shall crush the forehead[3] of Moab
    and break down all the sons of Sheth.
18 Edom shall be dispossessed;
    Seir also, his enemies, shall be dispossessed.
    Israel is doing valiantly.
19 And one from Jacob shall exercise dominion
    and destroy the survivors of cities!"

20 Then he looked on Amalek and took up his discourse and said,

"Amalek was the first among the nations,
    but its end is utter destruction."

21 And he looked on the Kenite, and took up his discourse and said,

"Enduring is your dwelling place,
    and your nest is set in the rock.
22 Nevertheless, Kain shall be burned
    when Asshur takes you away captive."

23 And he took up his discourse and said,

"Alas, who shall live when God does this?
24   But ships shall come from Kittim
    and shall afflict Asshur and Eber;
    and he too shall come to utter destruction."

25 Then Balaam rose and went back to his place. And Balak also went his way.

---

[1] Or *closed*, or *perfect*; also verse 15 [2] Or *valleys* [3] Hebrew *corners* [of the head]

Section Overview

The final two discourses, with virtually identical preambles (Num. 24:3b–4a, 15b–16a), emphasize their source: the "words of God" and the "vision of the Almighty" (vv. 4, 16). As do the first two discourses, these last two continue the blessing-curse theme: "Blessed are those who bless you, and cursed are those who curse you" (v. 9; cf. Section Overview of Numbers 23; Numbers 24). The two discourses are also called "oracles" (24:3 [2x], 4, 15 [2x], 16). Following the last oracle are three short discourses in which Balaam predicts the demise of cursed nations (24:20–24). For shared characteristics of the four discourses cf. Section Overview of Numbers 23.

Section Outline

II. Trials in the Wilderness of Paran, the Transjordan Highlands, and the Plains of Moab (11:1–25:18) . . .
   N. Balaam's Final Two Discourses (24:1–25)
      1. Discourse Three (24:1–14)
      2. Discourse Four (24:15–25)

Comment

24:1–14 The opening verse highlights the theme of the Balaam account: "It pleased [or "it was good (Hb. *tob*) to"; cf. discussion on v. 5 below] the LORD to bless Israel" (v. 1). To "bless" is what is "good" to the Lord. Good and blessing are closely related (Gen. 26:29; Deut. 28:12; Prov. 16:20; 24:25). The Lord promises "good" (*tob*) to Israel (Num. 10:29, 32). His blessing makes mankind fruitful (Gen. 1:22) and Abraham and his descendants great (12:2), preserving them from their enemies (Num. 6:24). Balaam knows that God will curse any who dishonors those he has blessed (24:9; cf. Gen. 12:3). Balaam's awareness of these things draws two immediate reactions. This time he does not "look for omens" (cf. Num. 22:7), perhaps via animal entrails, even though sacrifices have been made (23:29–30). Second, he "set his face toward the wilderness" (24:1). "Wilderness" here describes the portion of the Arabah just north of the Dead Sea (Deut. 3:17), the plains of Moab (cf. comment on Num. 22:1–21). There he sees "Israel camping tribe by tribe" (Num. 24:2). "Camping" (*shakan*) appears in Numbers in anticipation of "dwelling" in the Promised Land (14:30; 35:34). Now his view is panoramic—before he only saw a fraction of the people (22:41; 23:13).

The Spirit of God comes upon Balaam (24:2). Elsewhere in the Pentateuch the Spirit of God is over the primeval waters covering the unformed and unfilled earth enshrouded in darkness (Gen. 1:2). Pharaoh recognizes the Spirit of God to be in Joseph (Gen. 41:38). The tabernacle craftsman, Bezalel, is endued by the Spirit of God (Ex. 31:3). Outside the Pentateuch the Spirit of God comes upon Saul and Saul's messengers who are sent to capture David; they all prophesy (1 Sam. 10:10; 19:20). The prophet Ezekiel is brought in a vision by the Spirit of God to the exiles in Babylonia (Ezek. 11:24). "The Spirit" occurs four times in Numbers, in connection with Moses, the seventy elders, and Eldad and Medad (Num. 11:17, 25, 26), all of whom prophesy. God's Spirit is the source of all true prophecy (e.g., 2 Sam. 23:2; Neh. 9:30; Zech. 7:12; Acts 28:25; Eph. 3:5; 2 Pet. 1:21). The Spirit directs the words, thus certifying their authenticity and veracity, even if the one prophesying lacks those qualities, such as Balaam and Caiaphas, whose prophecies are nonetheless true (John 11:50–51).

On "discourse" (*mashal*; Num. 24:3) cf. Section Overview of Numbers 23. This discourse is also called an "oracle" (*ne'um*; 24:3, 4, 15, 16). *Ne'um* occurs only twice elsewhere in the Pentateuch outside the Balaam narrative. In both cases the utterance is an oath made by the Lord: "As I live, declares [lit., "oracle of"] the LORD" (Num. 14:28; cf. Gen. 22:16). The word is used over three hundred times by the prophets for a prophetic declaration from the Lord (e.g., Isa. 1:24; Jer. 1:8). Prophetic visions are generally verbal and audible (Num. 24:4; cf. Isa. 2:1; Mic. 1:1). "Vision" here is not one of the more common terms (*mar'ah*, e.g., Num. 12:6; *hazon*, e.g., 1 Sam. 3:1) but a rarer one (*makhazeh*, elsewhere only Gen. 15:1; Num. 24:16; Ezek. 13:7).

"The Almighty" (*shadday*; Num. 24:4, 16; cf. Gen. 49:25), or "God Almighty" (*'el-shadday*; Gen. 17:1; 35:11; 43:14; 48:3), is associated with blessing in the patriarchal narratives (e.g., Gen. 48:3), particularly that of fruitfulness (Gen. 28:3; 35:11; 49:25; cf. 2 Cor. 6:18). This connection is perhaps evoked by a homophone, "breasts" (*shadayim*; Gen. 49:25). The Almighty who makes fruitful is ironically the one who makes Naomi bitter by depriving her of her husband and sons (Ruth 1:20–21; cf. Gen. 43:14). He can withdraw blessing, thereby unleashing covenant curses. Many of the thirty-one occurrences of this name in Job center on the Almighty's prerogative to bless, including by giving children (Job 29:5), and to deprive of blessing (Job 6:4; 21:20). "The Almighty" in Balaam's discourse is implicitly associated with blessing in the following verses.

Balaam exclaims, "How lovely [or "good" (vb. *tob*); cf. discussion on v. 1 above] are your tents, O Jacob, your encampments, O Israel!" (Num. 24:5). Ironically, the Israelites had found life "better" (*tob*) in Egypt (11:18; 14:3; cf. 20:5). The word "encampments" is the plural form of *mishkan* ("dwellings"; cf. discussion on v. 2 above); although Israel is poised for the conquest in military camps (*makhaneh*; e.g., 1:54), Balaam sees the nation as already settled in the land. Israel is portrayed as fertile and flourishing, like well-watered plants, gardens, and trees (Num. 24:6; cf. Ps. 104:16). Cedars are typically found on mountains, not by rivers. The employment of abnormal creation imagery seems rhetorical and suggests radical change (e.g., Isa. 41:18–20; 55:12; Ezek. 17:3–6; 19:10). It may anticipate the mountains' (where cedars grow) being turned into valleys (where water flows).

"Water" and "seed" (Num. 24:7) portray fertility and, metaphorically, fecundity. Increase in progeny is essential for Israel's "king" to establish "his kingdom" (v. 7; cf. 23:21) and to defeat "his adversaries" (24:8; cf. Gen. 22:17; 24:60; Ps. 127:5). "Agag" (Num. 24:7), known elsewhere as the Amalekite king slain by Samuel (1 Sam. 15:33), may be a common royal name, like Pharaoh (Gen. 12:15; Ex. 11:1) or Abimelech (Gen. 20:2; Psalm 34 title). On "wild ox" (Num. 24:8) cf. 23:22. On

"Lion ... lioness" (24:9) cf. 23:24. Numbers 24:9 returns to the themes of blessing and cursing that are central to these oracles.

In anger Balak reproaches Balaam: "I called you to curse my enemies, and behold, you have blessed them these three times" (v. 10). He "struck his hands" (v. 10), a sign of displeasure (cf. Job 34:37; Jer. 31:19; Lam. 2:15; Ezek. 21:14, 17; 22:13). "Your own place" (Num. 24:11) is not far away (cf. 22:5), since from there Balaam will instigate the Baal-peor incident (ch. 25; cf. 31:8). Balaam's response reiterates what he said at the outset concerning "his house full of silver and gold" (24:13; cf. 22:18). To do "either good or bad" (24:13) adds up to "not be[ing] able to go beyond" what the Lord has ordered (cf. 22:18, "to do less or more"; also Gen. 31:24, 29; Jer. 42:6; Rom. 9:11).

"The latter days" (*be'aharit hayyamim*; Num. 24:14) introduces blessings that contain eschatological messianic prophecies (Gen. 49:1–27; Num. 24:14–19; Deut. 31:29; 32:1–43; 33:2–29; cf. Response section on Numbers 24). The temporal "latter" (from *'ahar*) refers to the future. The same term can also be used spatially. Facing eastward, what is "behind" is unseen and unknown and therefore, timewise, "future." To be known, it must be revealed by prophetic utterance. The opposite and corresponding term (*qedem* and related forms), again spatially oriented eastward (from the Judean mountains), refers to the Salt (Dead) Sea as "before" or "on the east" (Num. 34:3). Temporally, what lies "before" is seen and known: the "days of old" (Ps. 44:1), "from of old" (Mic. 5:2).

24:15–25 Verses 15–16 repeat the opening of the preceding discourse (vv. 3–4) apart from the added "And knows the knowledge of the Most High" (*'elyon*; v. 16). In the Pentateuch the priest of God Most High, Melchizedek, invokes the Most High to bless Abram (Gen. 14:18–20). Abram calls the Most High the "Possessor of heaven and earth" (Gen. 14:22). With his Amorite allies Abram had just rescued Lot, his family, and other inhabitants of the cities near the Dead Sea from their powerful Mesopotamian adversaries. The Most High's sovereignty in the affairs of men is also underscored in Deuteronomy: "When the Most High gave to the nations their inheritance, when he divided mankind, he fixed the borders of the peoples according to the number of the sons of God" (Deut. 32:8).

Balaam foretells the reign of one from Israel, the focus of his fourth discourse: "A scepter shall rise out of Israel; . . . one from Jacob shall exercise dominion" (Num. 24:17, 19). The Most High's dominion will be exercised by a descendant of Judah (Gen. 49:10). Balaam also prophesies what "this people [Israel] will do to your people [Moab]" (Num. 24:14): the scepter "shall crush the forehead of Moab and break down the sons of Sheth" (v. 17). "Moab" and "Sheth" are probably synonymous.[198] The prophecy also concerns "Edom," synonymous with "Seir" (v. 18). The verbs used to refer to Moab/Sheth ("crush/break") show its fate to be worse than Edom/Seir, which shall be "dispossessed." Balak's desire to curse Israel draws a severer punishment. Since Edom/Seir lies both east and west of the Arabah

---

198 Cf. "Shutu," *ANET*, 329n4: "Probably Moab; cf. the 'sons of Sheth' in Num. 24:17."

(cf. Num. 21:4), Moab/Sheth may similarly refer to peoples on both sides of the Arabah.[199] "Sheth" is the same Hebrew name rendered elsewhere "Seth" (*sheth*; e.g., Gen. 4:25).

The demise of these peoples will come from "him," someone "not now . . . not near," described as "a star" and "a scepter" (Num. 24:17), The verb rendered "shall come out of" (*darak*; v. 17) in a military context means "tread, trample" (Deut. 33:29; Isa. 63:3). "Star . . . scepter" (Num. 24:17) portray royalty (cf. Ps. 45:6; Isa. 14:12; Matt. 2:2). Bar Kokbah, "son of the star," drew upon this prophecy to legitimize his uprising against the Romans in the early second century AD. The NT points to the realization of the "star" figure in Christ as the true descendant of David (Rev. 22:16; cf. Luke 1:32; Heb. 1:8). To "exercise dominion" (*radah*; Num. 24:19) describes mankind's dominion over creatures (Gen. 1:26, 28) and Solomon's dominion over all territory west of the Euphrates (1 Kings 4:24). *Radah* also means "tread," such as treading grapes with feet (Joel 3:13), portraying defeat and subjugation. Solomon describes enemy peoples as those whom the Lord puts "under the soles of [David's] feet" (1 Kings 5:3). David had subjugated Edom, Moab, and Ammon (2 Sam. 8:12).

Balaam's three minor discourses announce judgment on "Amalek" (Num. 24:20), "the Kenite/Kain" (vv. 21–22), and "Asshur and Eber" (vv. 23–24). "Amalek" (v. 20) was a grandson of Esau (Gen. 36:12). The Amalekites fiercely opposed the Israelites from the time they left Egypt (Ex. 17:8). "Amalek was the first [*re'shith*] among the nations, but its end [*'akharith*, "last"; cf. Num. 24:14, "latter days"] is utter destruction": Israel is to destroy Amalek (Deut. 25:19), which David does to those of his day (2 Sam. 8:11–12). The Amalekites here appear with Transjordanian peoples (cf. Judg. 6:3), but at different times they also control the entire Negeb (Gen. 14:7; cf. Num. 13:29; 1 Sam. 27:8; 30:1; 1 Chron. 4:42–43) and parts of Cisjordan hill country (Judg. 12:15; 1 Sam. 15:6).

"The Kenite" (*haqqini*; Num. 24:21) are a people whose ancestor is "Kain" (*qayin*; v. 22; cf. Tubal-*qayin*; Gen. 4:22); "nest" (*qen*; v. 21) sounds like Cain. Moses' father-in-law was a Kenite (Judg. 1:16). Some Kenites assimilated into the tribe of Judah (Judg. 1:16) and others into Asher or Naphtali (Judg. 4:11). They appear at times among the Negeb Amalekites (1 Sam. 15:6). The downfall of Cain is "Asshur" (Num. 24:22, 24); this might refer to the Assyrians (cf. discussion on v. 24 below), who deported all Galilee and beyond (2 Kings 15:29). "Takes you away captive" is perhaps a presage of the notorious Assyrian deportation policy (2 Kings 17:23–24).[200]

"Kittim" (Num. 24:24) as a people refers to the descendants of Javan (Gen. 10:4) and as a locality to the Mediterranean coastlands and islands, and perhaps specifically Cyprus (Isa. 23:1, 12; Jer. 2:10), known for its wood used for ships (cf. Ezek.

---

[199] As concerns Sheth, Milgrom thinks they are probably Sethites in Canaan, descendants of Abraham (*Numbers*, 208).
[200] De Vaulx believes that Assur, in the context of Kenites and Amalekites, refers to a northern Sinai tribe known from Genesis 25:3, 18 (*Les Nombres*, 295). In Psalm 83:8 "Asshur" is echoed by "children of Lot" in a context of Ammon, Moab, Edom, Hagirites, Ishmaelites, and Amalekites (Ps. 83:6–7). On "Aram" cf. comment on Num. 23:1–12 (at v. 7) and note 194.

27:6). Numbers 24:24 may predict the invasion of the Sea Peoples, known from Egyptian and Hittite sources, among whom were the Philistines (cf. Gen. 10:6, 14; 1 Chron. 1:12, descendants of Ham). Their incursions into Anatolia, bordering northern Mesopotamia, would bring them in conflict with "Asshur" and "Eber" (Num. 24:24). Eber is the name of the Hebrews' ancestor (Gen. 11:14), reflected in the LXX rendering *Ebraios* (translating the gentilic *'ibri*; e.g., Gen. 39:14, "Hebrew"). Shem's descendants include both Asshur and Aram (Gen. 10:21–22) and, through Aram, Eber (Num. 24:24). Asshur, linked to Elam (v. 22), may refer to eastern Mesopotamian Semites. Like Aram, Eber may refer to western Mesopotamian Semites.[201] "He too shall come to utter destruction" refers to Kittim, and thus ultimately to the fall of Rome (Dan. 11:30).

"Balaam ... went back to his place" (Num. 24:25). "Place" (*maqom*) may refer to a residence (Gen. 18:33) or a cultic center (Gen. 28:19; Acts 6:14). His instigation of Israelite involvement in Baal worship at Peor (Numbers 25) indicates he remains nearby; he is killed by Israelites encamped in the southern Jordan Valley (31:8).

Response

Balaam prophesies about "the latter days" (*ba'aharit hayyamim*; cf. Num. 24:14), an expression occurring in two other Pentateuchal texts introducing messianic prophecies. Genesis 49 contains Jacob's blessing, "The scepter shall not depart from Judah ... to him shall be the obedience of the peoples" (Gen. 49:10), echoed in Numbers 24: "a scepter shall rise out of Israel" (Num. 24:17). This royal image is applied to Christ in the NT: "Your throne, O God, is forever and ever, the scepter of uprightness is the scepter of your kingdom" (Heb. 1:8). So is the stellar image, "A star shall come out of Jacob" (Num. 24:17); "Jesus ... the bright morning star" (Rev. 22:16; cf. "his star" Matt. 2:2).

The other Pentateuchal messianic prophecy, the third introduced by "the latter days" (Deut. 31:29), is in the archetypical prophecy of the song of Moses (cf. Num. 12:6): "Rejoice, you Gentiles, with his people" (Deut. 32:43 LXX), cited in Romans 15:10 as referring to the Gentile ingrafting in Christ. Hebrews 1:2 says that "in these last days" God spoke by his Son, whom he appointed heir of all things. The NT Greek for "last days" (*eschatou ton hemeron*) is the same as the LXX rendering of the Hebrew *ba'aharit hayyamim* in the three Pentateuchal passages presented here. Those last days, also called the "end of the ages" (1 Cor. 10:11), was when the Son appeared to put away sin once for all by his self-sacrifice (Heb. 9:26).[202]

---

201 Cf. Keil, "Fourth Book of Moses," 199.
202 Ron Bergey, "Littérature et théologie dans le Pentateuque," *RRef* 50/4-5 (1999): 41–53.

NUMBERS 25

25 While Israel lived in Shittim, the people began to whore with the daughters of Moab. ² These invited the people to the sacrifices of their gods, and the people ate and bowed down to their gods. ³ So Israel yoked himself to Baal of Peor. And the anger of the LORD was kindled against Israel. ⁴ And the LORD said to Moses, "Take all the chiefs of the people and hang¹ them in the sun before the LORD, that the fierce anger of the LORD may turn away from Israel." ⁵ And Moses said to the judges of Israel, "Each of you kill those of his men who have yoked themselves to Baal of Peor."

⁶ And behold, one of the people of Israel came and brought a Midianite woman to his family, in the sight of Moses and in the sight of the whole congregation of the people of Israel, while they were weeping in the entrance of the tent of meeting. ⁷ When Phinehas the son of Eleazar, son of Aaron the priest, saw it, he rose and left the congregation and took a spear in his hand ⁸ and went after the man of Israel into the chamber and pierced both of them, the man of Israel and the woman through her belly. Thus the plague on the people of Israel was stopped. ⁹ Nevertheless, those who died by the plague were twenty-four thousand.

¹⁰ And the LORD said to Moses, ¹¹ "Phinehas the son of Eleazar, son of Aaron the priest, has turned back my wrath from the people of Israel, in that he was jealous with my jealousy among them, so that I did not consume the people of Israel in my jealousy. ¹² Therefore say, 'Behold, I give to him my covenant of peace, ¹³ and it shall be to him and to his descendants after him the covenant of a perpetual priesthood, because he was jealous for his God and made atonement for the people of Israel.'"

¹⁴ The name of the slain man of Israel, who was killed with the Midianite woman, was Zimri the son of Salu, chief of a father's house belonging to the Simeonites. ¹⁵ And the name of the Midianite woman who was killed was Cozbi the daughter of Zur, who was the tribal head of a father's house in Midian.

¹⁶ And the LORD spoke to Moses, saying, ¹⁷ "Harass the Midianites and strike them down, ¹⁸ for they have harassed you with their wiles, with which they beguiled you in the matter of Peor, and in the matter of Cozbi, the daughter of the chief of Midian, their sister, who was killed on the day of the plague on account of Peor."

¹ Or *impale*

Section Overview

Following their great victories over the two Amorites kings, Sihon and Og (Numbers 21), and Balaam's powerlessness to curse them at the behest of Balak, king of Moab (chs. 22–24), the Israelites fall into the insidious trap of licentious idolatry (ch. 25). The parallels between Baal worship at Peor and the golden calf incident at the foot of Mount Sinai are striking (Exodus 32). Both occur in great moments of Israelite history: receiving the law and the Land of Promise. Both involve profligate idolatry drawing God's wrath, executed by deadly plagues. Both plagues are halted by executions, the first carried out by the sons of Levi and the second by Phinehas, a priest and thus a son of Levi. Thereupon the Lord grants the Levites and Phinehas and their descendants perpetual covenanted sacred ministries.

The new generation—those from the exodus generation who were under twenty at the Kadesh rebellion and their children—suffers a great moral setback.[203] Will the new generation prove itself to be as fickle and faithless as the older generation, which fell in the desert? The grace of God is even more evident by his not condemning this generation too.

This closing chapter 25 in the middle section of Numbers (chs. 11–25) forms a literary bracket with the opening chapter 11 (cf. Introduction: Interpretive Challenges: Unifying Structure of Numbers).

Section Outline

II. Trials in the Wilderness of Paran, the Transjordan Highlands, and the Plains of Moab (11:1–25:18) . . .
    O. Baal Worship at Peor (25:1–18)
        1. Israel's Infidelity (25:1–9)
        2. Phinehas's Zeal (25:10–15)
        3. Consequences for Midian (25:16–18)

Comment

25:1–9 "Shittim" ("acacias") is located in the plains of Moab near the Jordan (cf. "Abel-shittim"; 33:49),[204] from whence scouts are sent to Jericho (Josh. 2:1) and Israel sets out to take possession of Canaan (Josh. 3:1). This is also likely where Moses renews the covenant with the people (Deut. 29:1). "Began to" (Num. 25:1) renders the consonantal verb *hll*, which, pointed slightly differently, means to "profane" (Lev. 21:9; cf. Lev. 19:29), as read in the LXX: "The people were profaned by whoring." "To whore" is not only a metaphor for idolatry (e.g., Hos. 4:15); mention of the "daughters of Moab" and the sequel indicate orgiastic relations. "The people" often refers to soldiers (cf. Num. 1:5; 26:2; Josh. 6:9–10; 10:21; Judg. 18:11, 22; 1 Kings 20:29). Some of the men involved with these women are soldiers who fought against the Amorites (cf. Num. 25:5, 9). On their mission they were to abstain from sexual relations (1 Sam. 21:5). No longer under this constraint, they

---

[203] For Olson, whose binary division of Numbers places chapter 25 at the end of the first half, "this last episode in the first half of Numbers brings the story of the generation of the exodus and Sinai to a tragic conclusion" (*Numbers*, 152; cf. 133). Consonant with the position held here (cf. Introduction: Interpretive Challenges: Unifying Structure of Numbers), Levine states that the Baal-peor incident reveals that the new generation was not immune to sinfulness (*Numbers 21–36*, 275).

[204] Probably T. el-Hammam, 8 miles (13 km) northeast of the Dead Sea, where Wadi Kefrein enters the Jordan Valley (Aharoni, *Land of the Bible*, 429; Rasmussen, *Zondervan Atlas*, 224, 251).

succumb to their impulses. Perhaps they minimize their actions by considering the Moabite women to be war captives (Num. 31:18; Deut. 21:11; Judg. 5:30).

Yielding to sexual temptation leads to idolatry. "The people ate" (Num. 25:2) describes an act of worship (cf. Ex. 32:6), since portions of sacrifices are eaten. Eating sacrifices also involves a covenant (Ex. 34:15; Judg. 2:2) by which "Israel yoked [*tsamad*] himself to Baal" (Num. 25:3). A related noun form (*tsemed*) describes yoked pairs of oxen (1 Kings 19:19). Paul's expression "unequally yoked with unbelievers" (2 Cor. 6:14) draws on the Peor incident. "Baal" (Num. 25:3) means "lord/master." Baal worship was widespread in the ancient Near East under various names, often coupled with localities (e.g., "of Peor" [v. 3; cf. 23:28] or "Baal-meon" [32:38; cf. comment on 22:22–41, "Bamoth-baal"]).

"The anger of the LORD was kindled against Israel" (25:3) occurs once elsewhere in Numbers and in the Pentateuch, the object being the exodus generation's sentence of forty years of wandering for rebelling at Kadesh (32:13). Once again on the threshold of Canaan, Israel—now the new generation—is again the object of the Lord's anger (cf. 11:10). That anger is directed first at the "chiefs of the people" (25:4). This precise expression occurs only once elsewhere (Neh. 10:14). It is unlikely that this office is the same as the exodus generation's chiefs of the twelve tribes (Num. 1:16; 7:2; 10:4; 13:3; cf. 30:1; 32:28; 36:1). If "the people" refers to soldiers (cf. 25:1), "the chiefs" would be their officers (cf. 31:48), who are held accountable to restrain those under them. Their sentence is representative: they are to be hanged. "Hang" (from *yqʻ*) suggests impalement, which could involve public exposure of the body after death (2 Sam. 21:6, 9; cf. Josh. 8:29; 10:26).

The "judges of Israel" (Num. 25:5; elsewhere 2 Sam. 7:7; 1 Chron. 17:6) are ordered to "kill those of his men." Whether tribal or military leaders, each is responsible to execute those from his own tribe. There is no record that they carry out the order, which is executed ultimately by "the plague" (Num. 25:9), unless the plague is a metaphor for destruction by their sword.[205] The verb "kill" (*harag*) is used for capital punishment (Lev. 20:16); the instrument could be the sword (Amos 9:4). The sword of the government is a means whereby God executes his wrath (Rom. 13:4–5).

The scene shifts from rampant Baal worship to an incident involving a couple presented as "one of the people of Israel" and "a Midianite woman" (Num. 25:6), or "the man of Israel" and "the woman" (v. 8). Their names and origins are disclosed later (vv. 14–15): Zimri, a Simeonite and son of Salu (a chief), and Cozbi, daughter of Zur (a Midianite tribal head). The Israelite "brought" her to his family (v. 6, lit., "to his brothers/kinsmen") in the Simeonite camp south of the tabernacle. Presenting her to them suggests his intention to marry her. The brazen act of Zimri occurs while Moses and the other leaders are weeping (v. 6) over the people's sinful behavior. The "entrance of the tent of meeting" (v. 6) is where ritual decisions are made (Ex. 38:8; Lev. 14:11; Num. 6:13) and legal matters handled (cf. Num. 27:2–3; Josh. 19:51).

The pedigree of Phinehas is mentioned twice as "son of Eleazar, son of Aaron the priest" (Num. 25:7, 11). At this point Eleazar is high priest, Aaron's successor

---

[205] So Bush, *Book of Numbers*, 410, 413.

(20:28). Phinehas "rose and left the congregation," that is, of the repentant leaders (25:7). He "pierced both of them" (v. 8). Phinehas' act cannot be performed by his father, for a high priest must avoid corpse contamination (cf. comment on 6:1–12 [at vv. 6–7]). When Aaron was high priest, Eleazar was commissioned to remove the censers of the 250 men consumed by fire from the Lord (16:37). "Her belly" (*qebah*, once elsewhere Deut. 18:3) sounds somewhat like "chamber" (*qubbah*, only occurrence), the latter perhaps the women's section of the family tent.[206] Consummating marriage generally took place in the mother's tent (Gen. 24:67; Song 3:4). Like idolatry, marriage with an unbeliever was forbidden (Deut. 7:3–4; Judg. 2:2; 3:6; cf. Ezra 9:2, 12; Neh. 13:25–27). Idolatry and marriages create covenant bonds (Ex. 34:15–16). Both are a breach of faith (*ma'al*), a sacrilege, for which, apart from special conditions, no blood purification can be made (cf. comments on Num. 5:5–10; 5:11–31 [at vv. 12, 27]; 25:10–15, "atonement"). Although the plague is halted by Phinehas' act, it nevertheless kills "twenty-four thousand" (25:9). The sharp census decrease of Simeonites is undoubtedly due to this (1:23; 26:14).

25:10–15 As the son of Eleazar, Phinehas no doubt succeeds his father as chief over the chiefs of the Levites who keep guard over the sanctuary (Num. 3:32). As priest, he is God's representative to the people and the people's representative before God. He is "jealous with my jealousy" (*qana'*; cf. Ps. 69:9 [69:10 MT]; John 2:17); the Lord's "wrath" and "jealousy" (Num. 25:11) are juxtaposed elsewhere (Deut. 29:20; Ezek. 16:42; 38:19; Zeph. 1:18; Zech. 8:2). Phinehas' act, rooted in righteous indignation, confines the impurity to the camp, halts its spread, and thereby prevents the profanation of the sanctuary. The Lord declares, "I did not consume [*kalah*, "bring to an end/finish"; Num. 7:1; 16:31] the people of Israel in my jealousy" (25:11)—as almost occurred in Korah's rebellion (16:21–24), here too all the people could have suffered the consequences. As mediator, Phinehas acts promptly on behalf of both God and the people. His deed saves many and vindicates God's justice. Yet it is God alone who spares the people, whose rebellion in some ways surpasses that of the generation that perished in the desert, given their firsthand awareness of the consequences of that rebellion.

Phinehas' spontaneous and unilateral act leaves him vulnerable to revenge sought by Zimri's kinsmen.[207] "My covenant of peace" (*beriti shalom*; 25:12; cf. Isa. 54:10; Ezek. 34:25; 37:26) promises protection for Phinehas. It is a "covenant of a perpetual priesthood" (Num. 25:13; cf. Jer. 33:21; Neh. 13:29). The priesthood promise has been made broadly to the tribe of Levi (Ex. 32:29; Deut. 33:8, 10; Mal. 2:4–8) and specifically to Aaron and his sons (Ex. 29:9; 40:15; Num. 3:10; 18:1; 1 Chron. 9:20). Psalm 106:31 recalls Phinehas' deed, which is "counted to him as righteousness [*tsedaqah*] from generation to generation forever." The generational promise is realized in his descendant Zadok (*tsadoq*; 1 Chron. 6:50–53), who serves as a priest during David's reign (2 Sam. 8:17) and is the father of the Zadokite priests (Ezek. 40:46; 44:15–16).

---

206 *CHALOT* defines *qubbah* as "women's quarters (in tent)" (311).
207 Cf. Milgrom, *Numbers*, 216. The slain parties' families are potential avengers.

The Lord has promised Israel that his "covenant of peace" (*berit shalom*) will endure (Isa. 54:10). By his covenant of peace with Israel, God will protect Israel (Isa. 54:10) like a shepherd over his sheep by means of his servant David (Ezek. 34:25; cf. Ezek. 34:23). This covenant of peace establishes David as prince forever, with God's sanctuary in the midst of his people (Ezek. 37:26; cf. Ezek. 34:25, 27–28). It is based on the triple promise, "My dwelling place shall be with them, and I will be their God, and they shall be my people" (Ezek. 37:27; cf. Lev. 26:11). This is the essence of the new covenant (Jer. 31:33; 2 Cor. 6:16; Heb. 8:10), foreshadowing eternal realties (Rev. 21:3). The covenant of peace thus combines priesthood and kingship. The prince of peace (Isa. 9:6), Christ in the order of Melchizedek, priest and king (Heb. 7:1–3; cf. Gen. 14:18), is established as king and priest forever (1 Tim. 1:17; Heb. 6:20; 7:11–28; Rev. 15:3).

When Phinehas makes atonement (*kapar*; Num. 25:13), it is not a sanctuary ceremony to make expiatory purification (cf. comment on 15:22–31; cf. Ezek. 43:20, 26). Atonement made without sacrificial blood outside the sacred sphere is propitiatory (cf. comment on Num. 16:36–50 [at v. 46]).

25:16–18 The command to "harass the Midianites" (v. 17) means to be adversarial (from *tsarar*; cf. n. *tsar*, "enemy," 10:9). Transjordanian Midianites live in Moab (cf. comment on 22:1–21 [at v. 4]; cf. 1 Chron. 1:46). Israel is to "strike them down" (*nakah*), meaning "take their life" (Deut. 19:6), because "they have harassed you" (from *tsarar*; Num. 25:18). Their sentence fits the crime. "The matter of Peor, and in the matter of Cozbi" (v. 18) are two separate instances (cf. comment on 25:1–9 [at v. 6]). However, as in this example, warnings against mixed marriages and idolatry are often juxtaposed (e.g., Ex. 34:15–16; Deut. 7:3–4; Josh. 23:12–13; 1 Kings 11:2). One leads to the other (Judg. 3:6). Both are subsumed under "Baal of Peor" (Deut. 4:3; Ps. 106:28). Numbers 31 records the vengeance on Midian, the execution of this order and one in which Balaam, who devised the devious scheme, is also killed (31:8).

Response

Great victory can give way to spiritual lassitude, leaving God's people vulnerable to temptation, as seen by the bronze serpent incident on the heels of the Israelite defeat of its enemies at Arad (21:1–9). After conquering the Amorites (21:21–35), the Israelites fall into lascivious Baal worship at Peor (25:1–2). After his baptism "to fulfill all righteousness" as Israel's representative, Jesus is led by the Spirit into the wilderness for forty days and forty nights, where he successfully relives the wilderness testing failed by the Israelites (Luke 4:1–13). After celebrating Passover with them, Jesus warns his disciples in Gethsemane, "Watch and pray that you may not enter into temptation. The spirit indeed is willing, but the flesh is weak" (Matt. 26:41). From their spiritual upper-room heights they will fall into the depths of defection. Facing the cross, Christ himself is tempted far greater than they (Matt. 26:39, 42, 45). Throughout his earthly life, in fact, he is "in every respect ... tempted as we are, yet without sin" (Heb. 4:15).

When tempted, the Christian must look to Christ and, like him, to God's promises. In 1 Corinthians 10 Paul combines the situation at Baal-peor with the case of the bronze serpent (1 Cor. 10:8–9) to warn the church, "Now these things happened to them as an example, but they were written down for our instruction, . . . Therefore let anyone who thinks that he stands take heed lest he fall" (1 Cor. 10:11–12). He closes with a promise, "No temptation has overtaken you that is not common to man. God is faithful, and he will not let you be tempted beyond your ability, but with the temptation he will also provide the way of escape, that you may be able to endure it" (1 Cor. 10:13). This promise assures the Christian that any temptation can be endured since it is not unique to him, nor is it greater than he is able to withstand; above all, God will provide the way out.

OVERVIEW OF NUMBERS 26–36

As suggested in the Introduction (cf. Introduction: Interpretive Challenges: Unifying Structure of Numbers), chapters 26–36 are framing chapters together with chapters 1–10. Each frame begins with a census chapter, after which the remaining unit is bracketed by parallel chapters, here those concerning the case of Zelophehad's daughters (chs. 27; 36). Many of the instructions for the generation that will enter Canaan concern its inheritance in the land (chs. 27; 32; 35; 36) and corporate worship there (chs. 28–29). Israel's journey from Egypt to the Jordan across from Jericho, as well as the boundaries of Canaan, are traced (chs. 33–34). The chapters in this final frame underline the Lord's faithfulness to his people and to the promises made to their fathers.

NUMBERS 26

26 After the plague, the LORD said to Moses and to Eleazar the son of Aaron, the priest, ² "Take a census of all the congregation of the people of Israel, from twenty years old and upward, by their fathers' houses, all in Israel who are able to go to war." ³ And Moses and Eleazar the priest spoke with them in the plains of Moab by the Jordan at Jericho, saying, ⁴ "Take a census of the people,¹ from twenty years old and upward," as the LORD commanded Moses. The people of Israel who came out of the land of Egypt were:

⁵ Reuben, the firstborn of Israel; the sons of Reuben: of Hanoch, the clan of the Hanochites; of Pallu, the clan of the Palluites; ⁶ of Hezron, the clan of the Hezronites; of Carmi, the clan of the Carmites. ⁷ These are the clans of the Reubenites, and those listed were 43,730. ⁸ And the sons of Pallu: Eliab. ⁹ The sons of Eliab: Nemuel, Dathan, and Abiram. These are the Dathan and Abiram, chosen from the congregation, who contended against Moses and Aaron in the company of Korah, when they contended against the LORD ¹⁰ and the earth opened its mouth and swallowed them up together with Korah, when that company died, when the fire devoured 250 men, and they became a warning. ¹¹ But the sons of Korah did not die.

¹² The sons of Simeon according to their clans: of Nemuel, the clan of the Nemuelites; of Jamin, the clan of the Jaminites; of Jachin, the clan of the Jachinites; ¹³ of Zerah, the clan of the Zerahites; of Shaul, the clan of the Shaulites. ¹⁴ These are the clans of the Simeonites, 22,200.

¹⁵ The sons of Gad according to their clans: of Zephon, the clan of the Zephonites; of Haggi, the clan of the Haggites; of Shuni, the clan of the Shunites; ¹⁶ of Ozni, the clan of the Oznites; of Eri, the clan of the Erites; ¹⁷ of Arod, the clan of the Arodites; of Areli, the clan of the Arelites. ¹⁸ These are the clans of the sons of Gad as they were listed, 40,500.

¹⁹ The sons of Judah were Er and Onan; and Er and Onan died in the land of Canaan. ²⁰ And the sons of Judah according to their clans were: of Shelah, the clan of the Shelanites; of Perez, the clan of the Perezites; of Zerah, the clan of the Zerahites. ²¹ And the sons of Perez were: of Hezron, the clan of the Hezronites; of Hamul, the clan of the Hamulites. ²² These are the clans of Judah as they were listed, 76,500.

²³ The sons of Issachar according to their clans: of Tola, the clan of the Tolaites; of Puvah, the clan of the Punites; ²⁴ of Jashub, the clan of the Jashubites; of Shimron, the clan of the Shimronites. ²⁵ These are the clans of Issachar as they were listed, 64,300.

²⁶ The sons of Zebulun, according to their clans: of Sered, the clan of the Seredites; of Elon, the clan of the Elonites; of Jahleel, the clan of the Jahleelites. ²⁷ These are the clans of the Zebulunites as they were listed, 60,500.

²⁸ The sons of Joseph according to their clans: Manasseh and Ephraim. ²⁹ The sons of Manasseh: of Machir, the clan of the Machirites; and Machir was the father of Gilead; of Gilead, the clan of the Gileadites. ³⁰ These are the sons of Gilead: of Iezer, the clan of the Iezerites; of Helek, the clan of the Helekites; ³¹ and of Asriel, the clan of the Asrielites; and of Shechem, the clan of the Shechemites; ³² and of Shemida, the clan of the Shemidaites; and of Hepher, the clan of the Hepherites. ³³ Now Zelophehad the son of Hepher had no sons, but daughters. And the names of the daughters of Zelophehad were Mahlah, Noah, Hoglah, Milcah, and Tirzah. ³⁴ These are the clans of Manasseh, and those listed were 52,700.

³⁵ These are the sons of Ephraim according to their clans: of Shuthelah, the clan of the Shuthelahites; of Becher, the clan of the Becherites; of Tahan, the clan of the Tahanites. ³⁶ And these are the sons of Shuthelah: of Eran, the clan of the Eranites. ³⁷ These are the clans of the sons of Ephraim as they were listed, 32,500. These are the sons of Joseph according to their clans.

³⁸ The sons of Benjamin according to their clans: of Bela, the clan of the Belaites; of Ashbel, the clan of the Ashbelites; of Ahiram, the clan of the

Ahiramites; ³⁹ of Shephupham, the clan of the Shuphamites; of Hupham, the clan of the Huphamites. ⁴⁰ And the sons of Bela were Ard and Naaman: of Ard, the clan of the Ardites; of Naaman, the clan of the Naamites. ⁴¹ These are the sons of Benjamin according to their clans, and those listed were 45,600.

⁴² These are the sons of Dan according to their clans: of Shuham, the clan of the Shuhamites. These are the clans of Dan according to their clans. ⁴³ All the clans of the Shuhamites, as they were listed, were 64,400.

⁴⁴ The sons of Asher according to their clans: of Imnah, the clan of the Imnites; of Ishvi, the clan of the Ishvites; of Beriah, the clan of the Beriites. ⁴⁵ Of the sons of Beriah: of Heber, the clan of the Heberites; of Malchiel, the clan of the Malchielites. ⁴⁶ And the name of the daughter of Asher was Serah. ⁴⁷ These are the clans of the sons of Asher as they were listed, 53,400.

⁴⁸ The sons of Naphtali according to their clans: of Jahzeel, the clan of the Jahzeelites; of Guni, the clan of the Gunites; ⁴⁹ of Jezer, the clan of the Jezerites; of Shillem, the clan of the Shillemites. ⁵⁰ These are the clans of Naphtali according to their clans, and those listed were 45,400.

⁵¹ This was the list of the people of Israel, 601,730.

⁵² The LORD spoke to Moses, saying, ⁵³ "Among these the land shall be divided for inheritance according to the number of names. ⁵⁴ To a large tribe you shall give a large inheritance, and to a small tribe you shall give a small inheritance; every tribe shall be given its inheritance in proportion to its list. ⁵⁵ But the land shall be divided by lot. According to the names of the tribes of their fathers they shall inherit. ⁵⁶ Their inheritance shall be divided according to lot between the larger and the smaller."

⁵⁷ This was the list of the Levites according to their clans: of Gershon, the clan of the Gershonites; of Kohath, the clan of the Kohathites; of Merari, the clan of the Merarites. ⁵⁸ These are the clans of Levi: the clan of the Libnites, the clan of the Hebronites, the clan of the Mahlites, the clan of the Mushites, the clan of the Korahites. And Kohath was the father of Amram. ⁵⁹ The name of Amram's wife was Jochebed the daughter of Levi, who was born to Levi in Egypt. And she bore to Amram Aaron and Moses and Miriam their sister. ⁶⁰ And to Aaron were born Nadab, Abihu, Eleazar, and Ithamar. ⁶¹ But Nadab and Abihu died when they offered unauthorized fire before the LORD. ⁶² And those listed were 23,000, every male from a month old and upward. For they were not listed among the people of Israel, because there was no inheritance given to them among the people of Israel.

⁶³ These were those listed by Moses and Eleazar the priest, who listed the people of Israel in the plains of Moab by the Jordan at Jericho. ⁶⁴ But among these there was not one of those listed by Moses and Aaron the priest, who had listed the people of Israel in the wilderness of Sinai. ⁶⁵ For the LORD had said of them, "They shall die in the wilderness." Not one of them was left, except Caleb the son of Jephunneh and Joshua the son of Nun.

¹ *Take a census of the people* is implied (compare verse 2)

Section Overview

The new generation is in the plains of Moab on the threshold of Canaan, where the Lord commands a new military census be taken (Num. 26:2–3). This will also be the basis of proportionate land allocation in the Promised Land (v. 53). The exodus generation has perished: "For the LORD had said of them, 'They shall die in the wilderness.' Not one of them was left, except Caleb the son of Jephunneh and Joshua the son of Nun" (v. 65). This occurs before the Israelites arrive in Transjordan: "The time from our leaving Kadesh-barnea until we crossed the brook Zered was thirty-eight years, until the entire generation, that is, the men of war, had perished from the camp, as the LORD had sworn to them" (Deut. 2:14; cf. Deut. 2:7–8, 16–18).

Will the new generation repeat the failure of the old? Shortly after it left Kadesh, it began to repeat the sins of the exodus generation (Num. 21:4–9). The people sinned grievously at Baal-peor (25:1–3). Moses remonstrates, "You have risen in your fathers' place, a brood of sinful men, to increase still more the fierce anger of the LORD against Israel!" (32:14). Before his death Moses warns them, "I know how rebellious and stubborn you are. Behold, even today while I am yet alive with you, you have been rebellious against the LORD. How much more after my death!" (Deut. 31:27; cf. Ezek. 20:18, 21).[208] The new generation faces faith challenges just as the old did.

Section Outline

III. Instructions beyond the Jordan at Jericho for the Generation Soon to Enter Canaan (26:1–36:13)
    A. Census of the New Generation (26:1–65)
        1. Census Ordered and Taken (26:1–51)
        2. Census and Land Inheritance (26:52–62)
        3. Reminder of the Reason for the Second Census (26:63–65)

Comment

26:1–51 Twenty-four thousand died (25:9) due to the idolatrous immorality of members of the new generation at Peor.[209] "The LORD said to Moses and to Eleazar" (26:1) replaces "The LORD said to Moses and Aaron" (20:12, 23), a reminder that Aaron too has died and a sign that the Lord is upholding his covenant promise made with Aaron and his sons (Ex. 40:15; Num. 25:13). "Take a census of all the congregation of the people of Israel" (26:2) repeats the first census command given in the wilderness of Sinai (1:2; 26:64). Men "twenty years old and upward . . . able to go to war" (v. 2) describes those to be numbered and the purpose, just as in the first census (1:3, 45). "Able to go to war" is mentioned only once here, as compared to fourteen times in chapter 1. A new reason for the current census is to divide the land proportionally (26:53–56).

The census will be taken "in the plains of Moab by [*'al*] the Jordan at Jericho" (v. 3), a location stated seven times in Numbers (v. 63; 31:12; 33:48, 50; 35:1; 36:13;

---

[208] These passages challenge the common view echoed by Sakenfeld that in chapters 26–36 the "new generation will be portrayed as perfectly obedient, even as the old generation has been portrayed as constantly rebellious" (*Numbers*, 143).
[209] Olson maintains that the Peor plague put to death the last of the first generation (*Numbers*, 160; cf Ashley, *Book of Numbers*, 531). However, that older generation had perished by the time the Israelites left the Kadesh region for Transjordan in Numbers 20.

cf. 22:1, "In the plains of Moab beyond [*me'eber*] the Jordan"). The first and second census reports begin with "Reuben, the firstborn of Israel" (26:5; cf. 1:20) and end with "Naphtali" (26:48; cf. 1:42). They follow the same order, except that Manasseh now precedes Ephraim (26:29, 35; cf. 1:32, 34), which increases the emphasis on this tribe through the Manassite daughters of Zelophehad in chapters 27; 36. The second census total (601,730; 26:51) is surprisingly close to the first (603,550; 1:46) in light of the four decades separating the two, the death of the old generation (26:64), and the recent death of twenty-four thousand of the new generation (25:9).

Concerning the totals of individual tribes, some increase, such as Judah's, Zebulun's, and Dan's, even sizably—Issachar's, Benjamin's, Asher's, and especially Manasseh's, from 32,200 (1:35) to 52,700 (26:34). Manasseh's increase is a blessing perhaps compensating his loss of rights of primogeniture to Ephraim (Gen. 48:14, 17; Jer. 31:9). Like a firstborn, the tribe of Manasseh receives a double land inheritance, one in Cisjordan and another in Transjordan (Num. 32:39–42). Other tribes decrease, such as Reuben, Gad, and especially Simeon, from 59,300 (1:23) to 22,200 (cf. 26:13). The Simeonites apparently suffer the brunt of the Peor plague, triggered by the brazen act of a Simeonite (cf. 25:9, 14). Ephraim and Naphtali each decrease by 8,000 (1:33, 43; 26:37, 50).

The collation of obituaries of those who died as a result of divine judgment also distinguishes this census report from the first: Dathan and Abiram, together with Korah and his company (26:10); Judah's sons, Er and Onan (v. 19; cf. Gen. 38:7, 10); and Nadab and Abihu (Num. 26:61). The fate of Korah serves as a "warning" (*nes*; v. 10)—like others mentioned—to incite obedience to the law as the rule for a blessed life in the land. "But the sons of Korah did not die" (v. 11; cf. comment on 26:52–62 [at v. 58]) is a reminder of God's grace in sustaining the Kohathite's ministry, "that there may never again be wrath on the people of Israel" (18:5).

A key feature of this report in contrast to the first census is the emphasis on the "clan/clans" (almost one-hundred occurrences in ch. 26) making up the tribes, e.g., "Reuben, . . . the clan [*mishpakhah*] of the Hanochites . . . These are the clans of the Reubenites" (vv. 5–7). In the former census only the tribe was named, e.g., "tribe of Reuben" (1:21). The new census will be used to allocate land inheritances proportionally. Clans are the basis of allocation (e.g., Josh. 13:15, 24, 29; 15:1). The emphasis on clans is the cue that God is about to fulfill his land-gift promise made to the fathers.

26:52–62 This section deals with both the secular tribes, which receive land (vv. 52–56), and the Levites, who do not (vv. 57–62). Inheriting land involves two criteria. The first is "according to the number of names" (v. 53) by "every tribe . . . its list" (v. 54). The "list" contains the names (cf. comment on 1:1–19 [at v. 2]). Thus, proportionally, "to a large tribe you shall give a large inheritance, and to a small tribe you shall give a small inheritance" (26:54, 56; 33:54). Second, land is apportioned "by lot" (26:55; 33:54). "According to lot" (26:56) is a unique expression. "According to" (Hb. *'al-pi*, lit., "by the mouth of") elsewhere in Numbers refers nearly always to God's spoken word or command (e.g., 3:16; 13:3). A decision by lot is considered God's decision (Josh. 7:14; Prov. 16:33; Acts 1:26; cf. "by lot," Judg. 20:9; "inquired of God ... the LORD said," Judg. 20:18). It is made before the Lord, at the sanctuary (Josh. 18:6, 8, 10; 19:51). Violation of decisions by lot will cause desecration. Any person who removes or moves landmarks of allotted land will face God's wrath (Hos. 5:10; cf. Deut. 19:14; Job 24:2).

The correlation of proportional distribution and allocation by lots is not apparent. It seems that assigning land inheritances involves at least two steps. First, the general location for each tribe is determined by lot. In Joshua 18:2–6 the land available for seven tribes is divided into seven parts, then lots are cast to determine which part each tribe will inherit (Josh. 18:11; 19:1, 10, 17, 24, 32, 40; cf. Num. 27:1, 4; 34:13). Second, the specific apportionment is made by clan (Num. 33:54; 36:8; cf. Josh. 18:11) and fathers' houses (Num. 34:14) according to their size. Intermediate steps are undoubtedly involved as well, such as measuring land area (Isa. 34:17, "lot"//"line" [*qav*]; Mic. 2:5, "cast the line [*hebel*] by lot"; cf. *naphal* + *hebel*: Josh. 17:5, "fell ... portions [of land]"; Ps. 16:6, "lines have fallen ... inheritance").

The Levites (Num. 26:57–62) are exempted from both general censuses of males twenty years old and upward since they neither serve in the army nor receive a tribal land inheritance (18:20; 26:62). A special Levite census had been made of males one month old and upward in view of their tabernacle service (3:27–39) and their redemption of firstborn (3:40–50). To the three principal Levitical clans—Gershonites, Kohathites, Merarites—are added five more, each related to one of the three main clans, among which are the "Korahites" (26:58). Descendants of the main clan of Kohath (16:1) through Izhar (16:1), Korah and his followers believed they too should have a stake in the priesthood and suffered God's judgment (26:10; cf. 16:32, 35). Despite their father's revolt, the "sons of Korah did not die" (26:11; cf. Ex. 6:24; 1 Chron. 6:22–26), a clear demonstration of God's grace. The Korahites become worship leaders in temple service (cf. Response section). Like Moses and Aaron, who were Kohathites and camped at the east side of the tabernacle (Num. 3:28), the Korahites will later occupy this place of honor as temple entrance gate-keepers (1 Chron. 9:19; 26:1, 19).

"Kohath was the father of Amram" (Num. 26:58); Moses, Aaron, and Miriam are Amramites (v. 59). The incident involving the death of "Nadab and Abihu," who offered "unauthorized fire" (3:4; 26:61; cf. Lev. 10:1), is recalled for the third time, a warning to priests that preserving the sanctity of the tabernacle requires their strict observance of ritual law. From the Levitical clans the males from a month old and upward increase from 22,200 to 23,000 (Num. 3:39; 26:62).

26:63–65 "These were those listed ... in the plains of Moab by the Jordan at Jericho" (v. 63) forms an inclusio (cf. vv. 2–3). Verses 64–65 recapitulate the latter census in contrast to the former: "But among these there was not one of those listed by Moses and Aaron ... in the wilderness of Sinai" (v. 64). Even Aaron had died (20:28), and Moses soon will too (27:13). Reference to this census is a reminder of divine judgment upon the exodus generation for its revolt at Kadesh (chs. 13–14): "They shall die in the wilderness" (26:65; cf. 14:29). The proof: "Not one of them was left, except Caleb . . . and Joshua" (26:65; cf. 14:30). These two had exhorted the Israelites to obey God, believe his promises, and enter the Promised Land (13:30; 14:6–9). Eleazar and Phinehas also enter the Promised Land (Josh. 14:1; 22:13). The tribe of Levi was not represented among the other tribes whose leaders reconnoitered the land and brought a bad report.

Response

"But the sons of Korah did not die" (Num. 26:11). Against the somber background of Korah's rebellion (ch. 16), God's grace is highlighted in chapter 18 and recalled here. The Lord does not exclude Korah's descendants from Levitical service because of their father's sin. The Korahites will have a vital ministry in the temple service as gatekeepers (1 Chron. 9:19), praise musicians (2 Chron. 20:19), and psalmists (cf. titles of Psalms 42; 44–49; 84; 85; 87; 88). Korahites are among David's mighty men (1 Chron. 12:6). In light of God's grace in Christ, Paul progressively sees himself as the "least of the apostles" (1 Cor. 15:9), the "very least of all the saints" (Eph. 3:8), and of "sinners . . . the foremost" (1 Tim. 1:15). These examples illustrate the fundamental principle in God's ultimate dealing with sinful creatures: "Where sin increased, grace abounded all the more" (Rom. 5:20; cf. Num. 14:19; Neh. 9:17, 19; James 2:13). Each generation should rejoice and give thanks for God's mercy in Christ.

NUMBERS 27

27 Then drew near the daughters of Zelophehad the son of Hepher, son of Gilead, son of Machir, son of Manasseh, from the clans of Manasseh the son of Joseph. The names of his daughters were: Mahlah, Noah, Hoglah, Milcah, and Tirzah. ²And they stood before Moses and before Eleazar the priest and before the chiefs and all the congregation, at the entrance of the tent of meeting, saying, ³"Our father died in the wilderness. He was not among the company of those who gathered themselves together against the Lord in the company of Korah, but died for his own sin. And he had no sons. ⁴Why should the name of our father be taken away from his clan because he had no son? Give to us a possession among our father's brothers."

⁵Moses brought their case before the Lord. ⁶And the Lord said to Moses, ⁷"The daughters of Zelophehad are right. You shall give them possession of an inheritance among their father's brothers and transfer the inheritance of their father to them. ⁸And you shall speak to the people of Israel, saying, 'If a man dies and has no son, then you shall transfer his

inheritance to his daughter. ⁹ And if he has no daughter, then you shall give his inheritance to his brothers. ¹⁰ And if he has no brothers, then you shall give his inheritance to his father's brothers. ¹¹ And if his father has no brothers, then you shall give his inheritance to the nearest kinsman of his clan, and he shall possess it. And it shall be for the people of Israel a statute and rule, as the LORD commanded Moses.'"

¹² The LORD said to Moses, "Go up into this mountain of Abarim and see the land that I have given to the people of Israel. ¹³ When you have seen it, you also shall be gathered to your people, as your brother Aaron was, ¹⁴ because you rebelled against my word in the wilderness of Zin when the congregation quarreled, failing to uphold me as holy at the waters before their eyes." (These are the waters of Meribah of Kadesh in the wilderness of Zin.) ¹⁵ Moses spoke to the LORD, saying, ¹⁶ "Let the LORD, the God of the spirits of all flesh, appoint a man over the congregation ¹⁷ who shall go out before them and come in before them, who shall lead them out and bring them in, that the congregation of the LORD may not be as sheep that have no shepherd." ¹⁸ So the LORD said to Moses, "Take Joshua the son of Nun, a man in whom is the Spirit, and lay your hand on him. ¹⁹ Make him stand before Eleazar the priest and all the congregation, and you shall commission him in their sight. ²⁰ You shall invest him with some of your authority, that all the congregation of the people of Israel may obey. ²¹ And he shall stand before Eleazar the priest, who shall inquire for him by the judgment of the Urim before the LORD. At his word they shall go out, and at his word they shall come in, both he and all the people of Israel with him, the whole congregation." ²² And Moses did as the LORD commanded him. He took Joshua and made him stand before Eleazar the priest and the whole congregation, ²³ and he laid his hands on him and commissioned him as the LORD directed through Moses.

Section Overview

The instructions on land allotment in Canaan, based on the recent census of the generation that will enter Canaan (Num. 26:52–56), raises the question of succession (1) to property by Zelophehad's daughters (27:1–11) and (2) to leadership by Joshua (vv. 12–23). Chapter 26 had mentioned both the daughters of Zelophehad (v. 33) and Joshua (v. 65).

The two narratives in chapter 27 are linguistically linked. The daughters "stood before" (27:2) Moses, Eleazar, and all the congregation; Moses makes Joshua "stand before" (v. 22; cf. v. 19) Eleazar and the whole congregation. They are also linked by homophony: "transfer" (from *'abar*; vv. 7, 8), describing property succession, and "Abarim" (from *'abar*; v. 12), where Moses learns Joshua will succeed him.

Section Outline

    III. Instructions beyond the Jordan at Jericho for the Generation Soon to Enter Canaan (26:1–36:13)...

        B. Succession to Property and Leadership (27:1–23)

            1. Succession to Property by Zelophehad's Daughters (27:1–11)

            2. Succession to Leadership by Joshua (27:12–23)

Comment

27:1–11 Repeating the family's genealogy ("Zelophehad the son of Hepher . . . Machir . . . from the clans of Manasseh"; v. 1; cf. 26:28–34) indicates the matter of succession to be urgent. The Machir clan belongs to the half-tribe of Manasseh that will settle in Transjordan, territory already conquered (21:31–35). As in chapter 26, the focus is on the inheritance of "clans." The same names as two of Zelophehad's daughters, "Noah" and "Hoglah," appear in the Samaria Ostraca (850–750 BC) as district names in the region of Samaria in Cisjordan Manasseh.[210] "Tirzah," another daughter, is also the name of one capital of the northern kingdom (1 Kings 16:23). These names suggest that prominent descendants of Zelophehad's daughters will settle in Cisjordan Manasseh.

The five daughters of Zelophehad "drew near" (Num. 27:1), that is, to a sacred place and "stood . . . at the entrance of the tent of meeting" (v. 2). The "entrance" (Hb. *petakh*) is akin to the city gate, where legal decisions about succession were made (Ruth 4:1, 10–11; cf. Num. 25:6). "And" (*ve-*) prefixed to "all the congregation" means "that is," with "Moses . . . Eleazar . . . [and] the chiefs" (27:2) thus as representatives. These chiefs probably number twelve (36:1; cf. 1:16; 7:2, 10, 84). The death of Zelophehad in the wilderness (27:3) makes the matter urgent; there are no apparent heirs. Zelophehad's death is not due to his being part of "the company of Korah," which involved Kohathite Levites, joined by some Reubenites and 250 chiefs of Israel (16:1–2). Implicitly, Zelophehad could have taken part in that rebellion, but "he died for his own sin" (27:3), unrelated to the rebellion. Making this point may imply that anyone executed for a civil or religious offense forfeits his property (cf. 1 Kings 21:1–16; Ezra 10:8). But Zelophehad dies like all those twenty years of age and over due to the Kadesh revolt. The problem is that "he had no sons" to succeed him.

This predicament surpasses their situation. Having no legitimate heir means Zelophehad's "name" could be "taken away from his clan" (Num. 27:4; cf. 2 Sam. 14:7). "Taken away" (*gara'*) is the opposite of "added to" (Num. 36:3). Land titles or deeds preserve the family name (cf. Ruth 4:5). The daughters desire to see their father's name perpetuated through them and their descendants by inherited land. "Clan" here is the extended family, as explained in "give to us a possession among our father's brothers" (Num. 27:4), that is, his blood relatives in Zelophehad's Hepherite clan. "Possession" (*'akhuzzah*) is personal property, implicitly an inheritance (*nakhalah*)—a term the daughters do not use, perhaps to allow the leaders to draw for themselves this inference from their stated case. "Their case" (*mishpat*; v. 5) requires legislation. A new law would not innovate a category of women landholders; such already exists. Job gives his three daughters an "inheritance among their [seven] brothers" (Job 42:15). Joshua gives his daughter land (Josh. 15:19). But there is no law providing daughters the right to succeed as heirs to property of fathers who have no sons.

---

[210] Levine, *Numbers 21–36*, 344.

The Lord's decision (Num. 27:6) grants them "possession [*'akhuzzah*] of an inheritance [*nakhalah*]," that is, land ownership based on the right of inheritance. The daughters get their request and more. They are granted the status of legitimate heirs. Their land possession is therefore inalienable and transmissible in their (father's) name, that is, their children will inherit from them. The "transfer" (*'abar*) of the inheritance (v. 7) involves not only the land possession but the inheritance rights of succession too, applicable to their children.

In verses 8–11 the new ruling regarding daughter-heirs (vv. 8–9a) becomes statutory law concerning a father with no son (vv. 9b–11; cf. Ruth 4:3–6). "Statute and rule" (*lekhuqqat mishpat*; Num. 27:11) describes a legal precedent, a formula occurring elsewhere only in 35:29 (also qualifying a precedent).

27:12–23 Moses looks out from "this mountain of Abarim" (v. 12), from the peak called Pisgah (Deut. 34:1; cf. Num. 21:20), part of Mount Nebo, across from Jericho (Deut. 32:49).[211] The Israelites camp in the Abarim before descending to the plains of Moab (Num. 33:47–48). For Moses to "go up" to the top of the mountain from the Jordan Valley means he ascended well over 2,600 feet (800 m) to "see the land that I have given to the people of Israel" (27:12). Although Moses will only see it, God reaffirms his promise first made to Abraham to "give" him and his descendants all the land he can "see" (Gen. 13:15). Centuries later, Moses stands directly across the Jordan Valley from where Abraham stood in Cisjordan, only 25 miles (40 km) away. Both view Canaan from afar, as neither will personally inherit (cf. Heb. 11:13). Moses will be gathered to his people, as his brother Aaron has been (Num. 27:13; cf. comment on 20:22–29 [at v. 24]). Both Moses and Aaron die on a mountain outside the Promised Land. Numbers reports Aaron's death (20:28–29; 33:38), but only Deuteronomy mentions his burial (10:6). Deuteronomy alone records Moses' death and burial (Deut. 34:5–6).

At the Meribah incident the Lord's charge against Moses was that he "did not believe" (Num. 20:12) and "broke faith" (Deut. 32:51). Now the Lord summarizes that it is "because you rebelled" (Hb. *marah*; Num. 27:14); not to believe is rebellion (Deut. 9:23; 1 John 3:23). Rebellion (Num. 20:24) and breaking faith (5:27; 31:16, "act treacherously") are capital offenses. "Failing to uphold me as holy [*qadash*]" (27:14) repeats the indictment handed down at Kadesh (from *qadash*). "The waters of Meribah" (v. 14; cf. 20:12) recalls the people's quarrel (*rib*; 20:3) that led to tragic consequences for Aaron and Moses (20:12; 27:13). On the "Wilderness of Zin" cf. comment on 13:21–24. "Moses spoke to the LORD" (Num. 27:15); this is the only occurrence of this expression that is otherwise always the other way around in the Pentateuch (over ninety times).

"The God of the spirits of all flesh" (Num. 27:16; cf. 1 Kings 8:39; Jer. 32:27) occurs only elsewhere in Moses and Aaron's intercession upon hearing God's threat to destroy the entire congregation because of Korah's rebellion (Num. 16:22). Moses

---

[211] "Abarim" (pl. *'abar*, "traversings") may refer to the mountain's western face, a geological transition from mountain to plain. Baly believes the Abarim are the eroded slopes below the Pisgah (*Geography of the Bible*, 117).

calls upon God to designate the person spiritually suited to lead the people (27:16), though the jussive form "Let the LORD ... appoint [*paqad*]" (Num. 27:16) tempers Moses' request. God had told Moses to appoint the Levites over the tabernacle (1:50) and Aaron and his sons over the priesthood (3:10). Moses' concern is not for himself but for his successor and the people his replacement will lead.

"Go out ... come in ... lead them out and bring them in" (27:17; cf. v. 21; Deut. 31:2; 1 Kings 3:7; 2 Chron. 1:10) describes the successor's leadership role in pastoral terms, so that the congregation may "not be as sheep that have no shepherd" (Num. 27:17; cf. 1 Kings 22:17; Matt. 9:36). The verb translated "appoint" (*paqad*; Num. 27:16) also describes the work of spiritual leaders as shepherds who should "attend" their flocks (Jer. 23:2). Jesus views the crowds harassed by blind spiritual leaders to be "as sheep that have no shepherd" (Matt. 9:36). The Good Shepherd is the door through which one enters to be "saved and [to] go in and out and find pasture" (John 10:9).

The Lord selects "Joshua the son of Nun" (Num. 27:18), a longtime, faithful associate of Moses (Ex. 17:9; Num. 11:28; 13:16). Moses' request to the "God of the spirits" for "a man" (27:16) is echoed in the Lord's response, "a man in whom is the Spirit" (v. 18), qualified as the "spirit of wisdom" (Deut. 34:9). Wisdom and spirit/Spirit are regularly paired (e.g., Isa. 11:2; Acts 6:3). "Spirits" (Num. 27:16) may refer to spiritual gifts (cf. 1 Cor. 14:12). "The Spirit" (Num. 27:18) empowers people for special tasks (e.g., Ex. 31:3; Judg. 3:10; Acts 13:9), particularly those who prophesy (e.g., Num. 11:17, 25–26; 24:2; Ezek. 3:24; Mic. 3:8). Like Joshua (*yeshuaʿ*), Jesus (Yeshua), upon crossing the Jordan, begins his ministry while led by the Spirit (Matt. 3:13, 16; 4:1; John 1:33; cf. Acts 10:38).

"Lay your hand on him" (Num. 27:18) portrays the transfer of invested leadership from Moses to Joshua. Eleazar the priest and all the congregation witness this at the tent of meeting (v. 19; Deut. 31:14). The Lord "commissions" Joshua (cf. Deut. 31:14) through Moses' acting as mediator and executing his orders (Deut. 31:22–23). "Authority" (Num. 27:20) translates *hod*, which occurs only here in the Pentateuch and elsewhere is usually translated "majesty" (e.g., 1 Chron. 29:25; Isa. 30:30) or "glory" (e.g., Ps. 8:1), as in ancient versions (Num. 27:20 LXX *doxa*; Vulg. *gloria*). Joshua is commissioned publicly, at which occasion the Lord's presence is manifested in the pillar of cloud at the tent (Deut. 31:15). The cloud and God's glory are inextricably related (Ex. 40:35; Num. 16:42).

The expression "By the judgment of the Urim" (Num. 27:21) is unique. It sheds light on the meaning of "some of" Moses' authority (v. 20) being given to Joshua. Moses has received the law, spoken to God face to face, and inquired directly from the Lord (v. 5). After Moses, "judgment" (*mishpat*) will come, in certain cases, through an instrument, "Urim," usually coupled with Thummim, pouched in the high priest's breastpiece (Ex. 28:30, "breastpiece of judgment"; Lev. 8:8). The Urim and Thummim are used to determine God's will in the absence of instruction (e.g., 1 Sam. 28:6). Used conjointly, they could show who was guilty or innocent (1 Sam. 14:41). Their meaning is uncertain, but they appear to have been used as lots (cf. 1 Sam. 14:42, "cast the lot"; Hb. simply "cast," one of several verbs for casting lots; cf. Jonah 1:7).

Response

Bishop Ellicott (1819–1905) once observed, "The law led men to 'see the promises afar off, and to embrace them' (Heb. 11:13), and it brought them to the borders of Canaan, but it could not bring them into it: that was reserved for Joshua, the type of Jesus."[212]

NUMBERS 28

28 The LORD spoke to Moses, saying, [2] "Command the people of Israel and say to them, 'My offering, my food for my food offerings, my pleasing aroma, you shall be careful to offer to me at its appointed time.' [3] And you shall say to them, This is the food offering that you shall offer to the LORD: two male lambs a year old without blemish, day by day, as a regular offering. [4] The one lamb you shall offer in the morning, and the other lamb you shall offer at twilight; [5] also a tenth of an ephah[1] of fine flour for a grain offering, mixed with a quarter of a hin[2] of beaten oil. [6] It is a regular burnt offering, which was ordained at Mount Sinai for a pleasing aroma, a food offering to the LORD. [7] Its drink offering shall be a quarter of a hin for each lamb. In the Holy Place you shall pour out a drink offering of strong drink to the LORD. [8] The other lamb you shall offer at twilight. Like the grain offering of the morning, and like its drink offering, you shall offer it as a food offering, with a pleasing aroma to the LORD.

[9] "On the Sabbath day, two male lambs a year old without blemish, and two tenths of an ephah of fine flour for a grain offering, mixed with oil, and its drink offering: [10] this is the burnt offering of every Sabbath, besides the regular burnt offering and its drink offering.

[11] "At the beginnings of your months, you shall offer a burnt offering to the LORD: two bulls from the herd, one ram, seven male lambs a year old without blemish; [12] also three tenths of an ephah of fine flour for a grain offering, mixed with oil, for each bull, and two tenths of fine flour for a grain offering, mixed with oil, for the one ram; [13] and a tenth of fine flour mixed with oil as a grain offering for every lamb; for a burnt offering with a pleasing aroma, a food offering to the LORD. [14] Their drink offerings shall be half a hin of wine for a bull, a third of a hin for a ram, and a quarter of a hin for a lamb. This is the burnt offering of each month throughout the months of the year. [15] Also one male goat for a sin offering to the LORD; it shall be offered besides the regular burnt offering and its drink offering.

---

212 "Numbers," 165.

ⁱ⁶ "On the fourteenth day of the first month is the Lᴏʀᴅ's Passover, ¹⁷ and on the fifteenth day of this month is a feast. Seven days shall unleavened bread be eaten. ¹⁸ On the first day there shall be a holy convocation. You shall not do any ordinary work, ¹⁹ but offer a food offering, a burnt offering to the Lᴏʀᴅ: two bulls from the herd, one ram, and seven male lambs a year old; see that they are without blemish; ²⁰ also their grain offering of fine flour mixed with oil; three tenths of an ephah shall you offer for a bull, and two tenths for a ram; ²¹ a tenth shall you offer for each of the seven lambs; ²² also one male goat for a sin offering, to make atonement for you. ²³ You shall offer these besides the burnt offering of the morning, which is for a regular burnt offering. ²⁴ In the same way you shall offer daily, for seven days, the food of a food offering, with a pleasing aroma to the Lᴏʀᴅ. It shall be offered besides the regular burnt offering and its drink offering. ²⁵ And on the seventh day you shall have a holy convocation. You shall not do any ordinary work.

²⁶ "On the day of the firstfruits, when you offer a grain offering of new grain to the Lᴏʀᴅ at your Feast of Weeks, you shall have a holy convocation. You shall not do any ordinary work, ²⁷ but offer a burnt offering, with a pleasing aroma to the Lᴏʀᴅ: two bulls from the herd, one ram, seven male lambs a year old; ²⁸ also their grain offering of fine flour mixed with oil, three tenths of an ephah for each bull, two tenths for one ram, ²⁹ a tenth for each of the seven lambs; ³⁰ with one male goat, to make atonement for you. ³¹ Besides the regular burnt offering and its grain offering, you shall offer them and their drink offering. See that they are without blemish."

¹ An *ephah* was about 3/5 bushel or 22 liters ² A *hin* was about 4 quarts or 3.5 liters

Section Overview

The questions raised in chapter 27 regarding succession of land inheritance and leadership succession have in view Israel's imminent arrival in the Promised Land. The ritual laws in chapters 15, 18–19 likewise have this outlook ("when you come into the land"; 15:2, 18; cf. Lev. 23:10; Deut. 26:1). Similarly, the laws on offerings in Numbers 28–29 presuppose a productive pastoral and agricultural life there.

The sacrifices here center on the burnt offering (e.g., Num. 28:6; 29:2) and the sin offering (e.g., 28:22; 29:5), with their accompanying grain and drink offerings given in precise measured amounts (cf. 15:1–16). The calendrical cycle of offerings starts with daily offerings, then Sabbath offerings, then new moon offerings (28:1–15), and finally those made annually at five feasts: Passover, Weeks, Trumpets, Day of Atonement, and Booths (28:16–29:40). Compared to other Pentateuchal lists of regulations on offerings linked to the festival calendar (Ex. 23:14–18; 29:38–42; 31:12–17; Leviticus 23), Numbers 28–29 is unparalleled for its completeness and orderly arrangement. The chapters point to the people's part in community worship as "a kingdom of priests and a holy nation" (Ex. 19:6).

The opening injunction addressed to Moses ("Command the people of Israel"; Num. 28:1) covers all the laws regarding offerings in chapters 28–29. The compliance formula ("Just as the Lᴏʀᴅ had commanded Moses") draws them to a close (29:40).

Section Outline

III. Instructions beyond the Jordan at Jericho for the Generation Soon to Enter Canaan (26:1–36:13) . . .
   C. Regular Offerings (28:1–31)
      1. Daily Offerings (28:1–8)
      2. Sabbath Offerings (28:9–10)
      3. Monthly Offerings (28:11–15)
      4. Passover and Feast of Unleavened Bread Offerings (28:16–25)
      5. Feast of Weeks Offerings (28:26–31)

Comment

28:1–8 Verse 2 is a superscription for chapters 28–29. For "my food offerings . . . pleasing aroma" cf. comment on 15:1–21 (at vv. 3, 10). For "appointed time" cf. comment on 15:1–21 (at v. 3, "appointed feasts"). The "food offering" in Numbers 28:3 is named as the "burnt offering" (v. 6), qualified here as "regular" (Hb. *tamid*, cf. Mishnah, Tamid 1:1–6:3) because it is offered "day by day," in the "morning" and at "twilight" (Num. 28:3–4; cf. comment on 9:1–14 [at v. 3]). In rabbinic tradition all the other offerings on special days are "additional" (*musaf*) since they are made "besides [*'al*] the regular burnt offering" (28:10). The burnt offering involves "two male lambs a year old without blemish" (v. 3), each lamb offered with a "grain offering" consisting of a "tenth of an ephah of fine flour," mixed with a "quarter of a hin of beaten oil," and a "drink offering" (vv. 5, 7, 8). "Beaten oil" (*katit*) is that from the olive press,[213] like the oil for the light in the Holy Place (Lev. 24:2). "Strong drink" (*shekar*; Num. 28:7; cf. 6:3), fermented from fruit or grain, is only once in these laws specified as "wine" (*yayin*; 28:14; cf. 15:5), the substance of the drink offering. A "drink offering" (*nesek*) is "pour[ed] out" (from *nasak*; 28:7; cf. 2 Tim. 4:6), not drunk.

"Mount Sinai" (Num. 28:6) is mentioned only once elsewhere in Numbers (3:1). "In the Holy Place" (28:7) is literally "in the holy"; the expression itself could refer to the holy vessel with which the drink offering is poured, since it is forbidden to pour drink offerings on the incense altar in the Holy Place (Ex. 30:9), where the vessels to pour them are kept (Ex. 25:29). But here "the Holy Place" probably describes the court (Lev. 6:16; cf. Num. 18:10), since drink offerings are apparently "pour[ed] out" (28:7) on the bronze altar there (cf. 2 Kings 16:13–14).

28:9–10 Sabbath burnt offerings are unique to Numbers. "On the Sabbath day" (v. 9) all ordinary work is forbidden (Ex. 31:15; 35:2; Num. 15:32) except by the priests, given their ritual duties (Matt. 12:5). "Two male lambs" are offered with their corresponding "two tenths" measure of flour for a "grain offering" and "drink offering" (Num. 28:9). Made "besides the regular burnt offering" (v. 10), the Sabbath offering is made after the morning burnt offering, which applies

---

[213] For "pressed in a mortar" cf. Milgrom, *Numbers*, 239; contrast *CHALOT*, 167: "(the first) oil (produced) from beaten (but not yet pressed) olives." *Katit* oil was pure (cf. Lev. 24:2: "pure oil"), whether extracted by pressing or by beating. If the whole olive with seeds is processed, the oil is cloudy.

to the other occasions, except at Passover, when the offering is made at twilight (Lev. 23:5).[214]

28:11–15 "At the beginnings of your months" (v. 11) is the first day of each month. "Two bulls from the herd, one ram, seven male lambs" (v. 11) are the same in species and quantity as that for the burnt offerings specified at Passover (v. 19) and the Feast of Weeks (v. 27). The proportions of the corresponding grain and drink offerings depend on the animal. "For each bull" the grain offering fine flour requirement is "three tenths of an ephah," but "two tenths . . . for the one ram" (v. 12). "For every lamb" the requirement remains the same as the daily offering, "one tenth" (v. 13; cf. v. 5). As for drink offerings, the quantities follow the same animal size and value principle: "Half a hin of wine for a bull, a third of a hin for a ram, and a quarter of a hin for a lamb" (v. 14).

In a list, the "sin offering" (vv. 15, 22, 30; 29:5, 11, 16, 19, 22, 25, 28, 31, 34, 38) follows the burnt offering. Given its goal "to make atonement" (28:30), the sin (atoning purification) offering is made first. Before the burnt offering can be "a pleasing aroma" (e.g., 28:2; 29:2), atonement must be made (cf. comments on 6:13–21 [at v. 16]; 15:22–31 [at v. 24]). It is not offered on the Sabbath, since purification is not made on that day. For "Besides the regular burnt offering" (28:15) cf. verses 6, 10.

28:16–25 The Passover calendar is reiterated as beginning on the evening of the "fourteenth day of the first month" (v. 16), when the Passover lamb is slaughtered and eaten in homes (Ex. 12:6; Josh. 5:10). The burnt offerings now specified show that Passover/Unleavened Bread observance has become community wide rather than a family commemoration (cf. Lev. 23:4–8). On the fifteenth day of this first month is the Feast of Unleavened Bread (Ex. 12:17; Num. 28:17). One of the three annual pilgrimage feasts (Deut. 16:16; 2 Chron. 8:13), this feast continues "seven days" (Num. 28:17) until the evening of the twenty-first day (Ex. 12:18; 13:6). A "feast" (Hb. *hag*) is more than a time of making food offerings and eating. "On the first day" (Num. 28:18) and "on the seventh day" (v. 25) there is "a holy convocation" (*miqra' qodesh*). This "convocation" is a mandatory assembly, "holy" because it is done at the sanctuary. Thus *hag* implies a pilgrimage.[215] It is a time of fellowship and joyful worship (2 Chron. 30:13, 21; Ezra 6:22). The "ordinary work" (*mela'ket 'abodah*; Num. 28:18) that is forbidden refers to routine occupational labor. Other activities are permitted during the feasts. Occupational "work" (*mela'kah*) is forbidden on the Sabbath (Ex. 20:10; Deut. 5:14) and on the Day of Atonement (Lev. 23:28; Num. 29:7).

"Food offering" (28:19) has been, until now, the only qualification concerning the community wide Passover offering (Lev. 23:8). It is "a burnt offering" and involves the same animals and their numbers as the new moon burnt offering, with their same measured "grain" and "drink" complements (Num. 28:19–20, 24; cf. vv. 11–13). Nor has the "goat for a sin offering" (v. 22; cf. comment on 28:11–15)

---

214 Levine, *Numbers 21–36*, 376.
215 Levine defines *miqra' qodesh* as "sanctuary convocation" and *hag* as "pilgrimage" (*Numbers 21–36*, 379–80).

been mentioned before in connection with the Passover. Blood from the sin offering is applied to the altar to cleanse the impurities, thus making "atonement" for it (cf. comment on 15:22–31 [at v. 25]; cf. Lev. 8:15), upon which basis the people are forgiven for having contaminated it and for that which has caused the impurity (cf. Lev. 4:30; 17:11; 2 Chron. 29:24). For "Besides the regular burnt offering" (Num. 28:24) cf. comments on 28:1–8; 28:9–10.

28:26–31 "The day of the firstfruits" (v. 26) does not specify a particular day or month. Here alone it is simply called "firstfruits" (*bikkurim*; cf. comment on 18:8–19 [at v. 12]) and abbreviated to "your weeks" (v. 26; ESV: "Your Feast of Weeks"); elsewhere with "feast" (*hag*) it is called the Feast of Harvest (Ex. 23:16) or the Feast of Weeks (*shabu'oth*; Ex. 34:22; Deut. 16:10, 16; 2 Chron. 8:13). "New grain" (Num. 28:26) refers to wheat (Ex. 34:22) harvested sometime in the third month (May/June). Barley harvest is in the first month (March/April). Since harvest times vary, the feast is set seven weeks after the beginning of the barley harvest (Deut. 16:9) or fifty days after the grain presentation (Lev. 23:15–16); for that reason it is called Pentecost (meaning "fiftieth"; Acts 2:1), a first day of the week (cf. Response section).

The "burnt offering" and the accompanying "grain" and "drink offering" (Num. 28:27, 28, 31) are the same as those for the monthly and Passover offerings. "One male goat" (v. 30) is for the unmentioned sin offering (vv. 15, 22). Although not indicated here, the peace offering is required in the Feast of Weeks (Lev. 23:19–20; cf. comment on 15:1–21 [at v. 3]).

Response

On the regularity of the daily offerings (28:3) Bush reflects, "In our private and domestic devotions, if we are remiss, inconsistent, and irregular, allowing trifling or inadequate occasions to break in upon the fixed routine of worship, we shall be very certain to forfeit and lose the tokens of the Lord's presence with us, and bring leanness into our souls." Regarding the Sabbath offerings over and above the daily offerings he adds (vv. 9–10), "This suggests to us the propriety of doubling our devotions on the Sabbath."[216] In the hymn "Safely through Another Week" John Newton refers to the Sabbath as the "Day of all the week the best, Emblem of eternal rest."

Certain language describing OT offerings is in the NT applied only to Christ; for example, "Christ, our Passover lamb, has been sacrificed" (1 Cor. 5:7). Some language refers to Christ and Christians; "firstfruits" (Num. 28:26) qualifies both Christ, the first resurrected (1 Cor. 15:20, 23), and his redeemed people, chosen "as the firstfruits to be saved" (2 Thess. 2:13; cf. James 1:18; Rev. 14:4), those who have the "firstfruits of the Spirit" (Rom. 8:23) and are eagerly awaiting their bodily redemption. Other language describes a single person such as Paul, who expects in martyrdom to be "poured out as a drink offering" (Phil. 2:17).

Christians in general are exhorted to "present your bodies as a living sacrifice, holy and acceptable to God, which is your spiritual worship" (Rom. 12:1). Paul

---

[216] Bush, *Book of Numbers*, 430, 431.

apparently has "a pleasing aroma to the Lord" (e.g., Num. 28:2; cf. 15:3; 29:2) in mind when writing, "We are the aroma of Christ to God among those who are being saved and among those who are perishing, to one a fragrance from death to death, to the other a fragrance from life to life" (2 Cor. 2:15–16). Just as the aroma of an offering was pleasing to the Lord, a scent detected by others, so too "we," as an "aroma of Christ" to God, are also a "fragrance" to those who hear the gospel.

Paul also describes the gift sent to him by the Philippians as a "fragrant offering" (Phil. 4:18). He uses "the first of your dough" (Num. 15:20) as an image of Israel: "If the dough offered as firstfruits is holy, so is the whole lump" (Rom. 11:16; cf. Num. 15:20). This expresses his hope that the inclusion of Gentiles will incite his fellow Jews to jealousy and lead to their salvation. As mentioned above, he views himself as being "poured out as a drink offering upon the sacrificial offering of your [Philippians'] faith" (Phil. 2:17; cf. Num. 15:5; 28:7; 29:6; 2 Tim. 4:6). The appropriate response to God's grace expressed in sacrificial terms is proffered in similar terms: "Through him then let us continually offer up a sacrifice of praise to God, that is, the fruit of lips that acknowledge his name" (Heb. 13:15).

NUMBERS 29

29 "On the first day of the seventh month you shall have a holy convocation. You shall not do any ordinary work. It is a day for you to blow the trumpets, ²and you shall offer a burnt offering, for a pleasing aroma to the LORD: one bull from the herd, one ram, seven male lambs a year old without blemish; ³also their grain offering of fine flour mixed with oil, three tenths of an ephah¹ for the bull, two tenths for the ram, ⁴and one tenth for each of the seven lambs; ⁵with one male goat for a sin offering, to make atonement for you; ⁶besides the burnt offering of the new moon, and its grain offering, and the regular burnt offering and its grain offering, and their drink offering, according to the rule for them, for a pleasing aroma, a food offering to the LORD.

⁷"On the tenth day of this seventh month you shall have a holy convocation and afflict yourselves.² You shall do no work, ⁸but you shall offer a burnt offering to the LORD, a pleasing aroma: one bull from the herd, one ram, seven male lambs a year old: see that they are without blemish. ⁹And their grain offering shall be of fine flour mixed with oil, three tenths of an ephah for the bull, two tenths for the one ram, ¹⁰a tenth for each of the seven lambs: ¹¹also one male goat for a sin offering, besides the sin offering of atonement, and the regular burnt offering and its grain offering, and their drink offerings.

¹²"On the fifteenth day of the seventh month you shall have a holy convocation. You shall not do any ordinary work, and you shall keep a feast to

the Lord seven days. ¹³ And you shall offer a burnt offering, a food offering, with a pleasing aroma to the Lord, thirteen bulls from the herd, two rams, fourteen male lambs a year old; they shall be without blemish; ¹⁴ and their grain offering of fine flour mixed with oil, three tenths of an ephah for each of the thirteen bulls, two tenths for each of the two rams, ¹⁵ and a tenth for each of the fourteen lambs; ¹⁶ also one male goat for a sin offering, besides the regular burnt offering, its grain offering and its drink offering.

¹⁷ "On the second day twelve bulls from the herd, two rams, fourteen male lambs a year old without blemish, ¹⁸ with the grain offering and the drink offerings for the bulls, for the rams, and for the lambs, in the prescribed quantities; ¹⁹ also one male goat for a sin offering, besides the regular burnt offering and its grain offering, and their drink offerings.

²⁰ "On the third day eleven bulls, two rams, fourteen male lambs a year old without blemish, ²¹ with the grain offering and the drink offerings for the bulls, for the rams, and for the lambs, in the prescribed quantities; ²² also one male goat for a sin offering, besides the regular burnt offering and its grain offering and its drink offering.

²³ "On the fourth day ten bulls, two rams, fourteen male lambs a year old without blemish, ²⁴ with the grain offering and the drink offerings for the bulls, for the rams, and for the lambs, in the prescribed quantities; ²⁵ also one male goat for a sin offering, besides the regular burnt offering, its grain offering and its drink offering.

²⁶ "On the fifth day nine bulls, two rams, fourteen male lambs a year old without blemish, ²⁷ with the grain offering and the drink offerings for the bulls, for the rams, and for the lambs, in the prescribed quantities; ²⁸ also one male goat for a sin offering; besides the regular burnt offering and its grain offering and its drink offering.

²⁹ "On the sixth day eight bulls, two rams, fourteen male lambs a year old without blemish, ³⁰ with the grain offering and the drink offerings for the bulls, for the rams, and for the lambs, in the prescribed quantities; ³¹ also one male goat for a sin offering; besides the regular burnt offering, its grain offering, and its drink offerings.

³² "On the seventh day seven bulls, two rams, fourteen male lambs a year old without blemish, ³³ with the grain offering and the drink offerings for the bulls, for the rams, and for the lambs, in the prescribed quantities; ³⁴ also one male goat for a sin offering; besides the regular burnt offering, its grain offering, and its drink offering.

³⁵ "On the eighth day you shall have a solemn assembly. You shall not do any ordinary work, ³⁶ but you shall offer a burnt offering, a food offering, with a pleasing aroma to the Lord: one bull, one ram, seven male lambs a year old without blemish, ³⁷ and the grain offering and the drink offerings for the bull, for the ram, and for the lambs, in the prescribed quantities; ³⁸ also one male goat for a sin offering; besides the regular burnt offering and its grain offering and its drink offering.

³⁹ "These you shall offer to the Lord at your appointed feasts, in addition to your vow offerings and your freewill offerings, for your burnt offerings, and for your grain offerings, and for your drink offerings, and for your peace offerings."

⁴⁰ ³ So Moses told the people of Israel everything just as the Lord had commanded Moses.

---

¹ An *ephah* was about 3/5 bushel or 22 liters ² Or *and fast* ³ Ch 30:1 in Hebrew

Section Overview

The Section Overview of Numbers 28 encompasses chapter 29 as well. Chapter 29 focuses on the three holy convocations held in the seventh month (29:1, 7, 12; September/October): on the first day the Feast of Trumpets (vv. 1–6), on the tenth day the Day of Atonement (vv. 7–11), and from the fifteenth through the twenty-second day the Feast of Booths (vv. 12–38). The repetitive style, especially that prescribing offerings during the eight-day Feast of Booths, would nurture the faith and hope of the Israelites in anticipation of their settlement and worship in a good land. The repetition emphasizes that true worship must be sustained by the means of grace afforded by sacred assemblies.

Section Outline

III. Instructions beyond the Jordan at Jericho for the Generation Soon to Enter Canaan (26:1–36:13) . . .
    D. Offerings on the Seventh Month (29:1–40)
        1. Offerings for the Feast of Trumpets (29:1–6)
        2. Offerings for the Day of Atonement (29:7–11)
        3. Offerings for the Feast of Booths (29:12–38)
        4. Conclusion (29:39–40)

Comment

29:1–6 The "first day of the seventh month" (v. 1) is the Feast of Trumpets. Although unnamed, it is designated "a day for you to blow the trumpets" (v. 1; cf. 10:10). Leviticus calls it a "memorial" (Hb. *zikron*, 23:24; cf. *zikkaron*, "remembrance," Num. 5:15, 18; "reminder," 10:10; 17:5; "memorial," 31:54). In the liturgical calendar the seventh month, Ethanim (1 Kings 8:2), is concomitant with the first month of the civil calendar, Tishri (September/October in the Gregorian calendar). From Tannaitic times the first of Ethanim was New Year's Day (Mishnah, Rosh Hashanah 1:1). The seventh month marks the end of the agricultural year (Ex. 23:16). The first day is to be observed as a holy convocation, which means no ordinary work may be undertaken (Num. 29:1; cf. 28:18).

The animal burnt offerings—bull, ram, lambs—with their grain and drink offering complements (29:2–4) are the same as those for the monthly offerings and those of the Passover and the Feast of Weeks except for the use of one bull (v. 2) rather than two, as in previous laws (28:11, 19, 27). One bull is offered on the Day of Atonement and one on the eighth day of the Feast of Booths (29:8, 36). The reason one bull rather than two is to be offered remains unanswered.

As in the preceding offerings, except on the Sabbath, a goat is sacrificed as "a sin offering, to make atonement" (v. 5; cf. 28:15). These offerings are in addition to the regular monthly offerings (29:6; cf. 28:11–15). "According to the rule for them" (*kemishpatam*; 29:6) is an abridged form of a longer expression occurring only in this chapter, rendered "in the prescribed quantities" (*bemisparam kamishpat*; vv. 18, 21, 24, 27, 30, 33, 37).

29:7–11 "On the tenth day of this seventh month" (v. 7) indicates the unnamed Day of Atonement (Lev. 23:27). To "afflict yourselves" (*'anah*; Num. 29:7) involves a deprivation of something normally done or permitted, particularly by fasting on this day (cf. Ps. 35:13; Isa. 58:3, 10). "The Fast" in Acts 27:9 is the Day of Atonement. Daniel's list of how he has humbled himself (Dan. 10:3; same verb, Dan. 10:12) is reproduced in the Mishnah, which adds sexual abstinence (Yoma 8:1). The latter can be deduced from the need for ritual purity on that day (Lev. 15:17; 16:16, 30). As on the Sabbath, no work is permitted (Num. 29:7; cf. 28:18); it is a "Sabbath of solemn rest" (Lev. 23:3, 32). The elaborate Day of Atonement rituals go unmentioned (cf. Leviticus 16) given the focus here, which is the quantity of required offerings (Num. 29:8–10).

Two goats for a sin offering are required, as in Leviticus 16:5. One is slain—here called the "sin offering of atonement" (Num. 29:11)—to purge the entire sanctuary (Lev. 16:15–19), while the other is sent away. One portrays the making of purification for sin of the people and the other the bearing and taking away of their sin from God's presence. The two depict the substitutionary work of Christ. He bears the sin of his people and removes it (e.g., John 1:29; 2 Cor. 5:21) and makes purification for it by his blood (Heb. 9:11–14).

29:12–38 Starting "on the fifteenth day" (Num. 29:12), a "feast" is to be held for "seven days" (v. 12). Although unnamed, this is the Feast of Booths (Lev. 23:34; Deut. 16:13), also called the Feast of Ingathering (Ex. 23:16; 34:22), the last of the three annual pilgrimages (Deut. 16:16). It is a pilgrim's model for a day of thanksgiving for a bountiful harvest. Although the daily number of rams (two), lambs (fourteen), and goats (one) remains constant, the number of bulls, starting on the first day with thirteen (Num. 29:13), is reduced by one each day so that on the seventh day seven bulls are offered (v. 32). The total number of bulls is seventy; lambs, ninety-eight. According to rabbinic tradition the bulls represent the seventy nations in Genesis 10, and the lambs the atonement for the ninety-eight curses in Deuteronomy 28.[217]

The eighth day is appended to the weeklong feast (Num. 29:35). "Solemn assembly" (*'atseret*; v. 35) designates a "holy convocation" (*miqra'*; e.g., vv. 1, 7; Isa. 1:13; Joel 1:14; 2:15) on the eighth day, following a seven-day cycle (Lev. 23:36; 2 Chron. 7:9; Neh. 8:18), or on the seventh day after a six-day cycle (Deut. 16:8). "Ordinary work" (Num. 29:35; cf. vv. 1, 12; cf. comment on 28:16–25 [at v. 18]) is precluded. Only one bull is required (29:36), as was the case during the two preceding seventh-month convocations (vv. 2, 8). On all eight days the grain and drink offerings are made in their ordinary "prescribed quantities" (v. 37; cf. comment on 29:1–6).

29:39–40 Verse 39 contains supplements to the laws on regular burnt offerings and peace offerings and their grain and drink offerings. The congregational "appointed feasts" also afford the opportunity to make individual vow offerings or freewill offerings, a familiar peace offering pair (Lev. 22:21; 23:38; Num. 15:3;

---

[217] Milgrom, *Numbers*, 247, 248.

Deut. 12:6, 17). Peace offerings of any kind—thanksgiving, vow, and freewill offerings—have not been mentioned before in Numbers 28–29 due to the emphasis on community wide offerings, not individual ones (cf. 6:17; 15:8), although for the congregation the peace offering is part of the Feast of Weeks (Lev. 23:19). Individuals make their peace offerings at the sanctuary at the appointed gatherings (cf. 1 Sam. 1:3, 11, 21–22). They are included among the burnt and sin offerings (cf. Num. 6:16–17). The mentioned peace offerings are accompanied by "grain" and "drink offerings." The unmentioned thanksgiving offering do not require them (Lev. 7:12).

Numbers 29:40 (30:1 MT) concludes chapters 28–29 with the words with which they opened. All the instructions given to Moses on the sacred calendar and public offerings are communicated to the Israelites (cf. 28:1; cf. Section Overview of Numbers 28). They are thereby encouraged and assured by the expounded law of Moses that they will enter the Promised Land and worship the Lord in a way pleasing to him by means of its bountiful harvests and large flocks and herds. The Lord does not require anything he does not provide. Mention of "vow offerings" at the end of chapters 28–29 provides a link to chapter 30, which is devoted to the subject of vows (cf. Num. 6:1–21). Vows are fulfilled or concluded by votive sacrifices (Num. 6:13–17; 1 Sam. 1:21).

Response

On repentance and the sin offering of atonement (Num. 29:11) Bush writes, "Even in our humiliation and repentance so many defects and infirmities mingle, that we have need of that virtue which was signified by the sin offering to make them acceptable." Thereupon he cites Matthew Henry: "Though we must not repent that we have repented, yet we must repent that we have not repented better."[218]

NUMBERS 30

30 Moses spoke to the heads of the tribes of the people of Israel, saying, "This is what the Lord has commanded. ² If a man vows a vow to the Lord, or swears an oath to bind himself by a pledge, he shall not break his word. He shall do according to all that proceeds out of his mouth.

³ "If a woman vows a vow to the Lord and binds herself by a pledge, while within her father's house in her youth, ⁴ and her father hears of her vow and of her pledge by which she has bound herself and says nothing to her, then all her vows shall stand, and every pledge by which she has bound herself shall stand. ⁵ But if her father opposes her on

---

[218] Bush, *Book of Numbers*, 435.

the day that he hears of it, no vow of hers, no pledge by which she has bound herself shall stand. And the LORD will forgive her, because her father opposed her.

⁶ "If she marries a husband, while under her vows or any thoughtless utterance of her lips by which she has bound herself, ⁷ and her husband hears of it and says nothing to her on the day that he hears, then her vows shall stand, and her pledges by which she has bound herself shall stand. ⁸ But if, on the day that her husband comes to hear of it, he opposes her, then he makes void her vow that was on her, and the thoughtless utterance of her lips by which she bound herself. And the LORD will forgive her. ⁹ (But any vow of a widow or of a divorced woman, anything by which she has bound herself, shall stand against her.) ¹⁰ And if she vowed in her husband's house or bound herself by a pledge with an oath, ¹¹ and her husband heard of it and said nothing to her and did not oppose her, then all her vows shall stand, and every pledge by which she bound herself shall stand. ¹² But if her husband makes them null and void on the day that he hears them, then whatever proceeds out of her lips concerning her vows or concerning her pledge of herself shall not stand. Her husband has made them void, and the LORD will forgive her. ¹³ Any vow and any binding oath to afflict herself,¹ her husband may establish,² or her husband may make void. ¹⁴ But if her husband says nothing to her from day to day, then he establishes all her vows or all her pledges that are upon her. He has established them, because he said nothing to her on the day that he heard of them. ¹⁵ But if he makes them null and void after he has heard of them, then he shall bear her iniquity."

¹⁶ These are the statutes that the LORD commanded Moses about a man and his wife and about a father and his daughter while she is in her youth within her father's house.

¹ Or *to fast* ² Or *may allow to stand*

Section Overview

The commands on vows and oaths logically follow offerings at appointed times (Numbers 28–29; cf. Leviticus 27). Votive offerings are made at those occasions at the sanctuary (cf. Num. 29:39). Like the holy feasts, vows and oaths are sacred (Lev. 27:9). They must be fulfilled (Num. 30:2; Deut. 23:21; Eccles. 5:4). Vows are made to the Lord (Num. 6:21; 30:2; cf. Gen. 28:20). Oaths are taken in God's name (Gen. 24:3; Josh. 9:18; Neh. 13:25; Zech. 5:4; 1 Thess. 5:27). Swearing falsely profanes his name (Lev. 19:12).

Given the binding force of vows, Numbers 30 addresses the circumstances under which vows can be nullified and, if so, the determination of the one who bears the responsibility for doing so. But an underlying basic concern is present: outside the ceremonial domain (under priestly authority) lies the domestic domain (under the authority of laymen). No one can offer an acceptable sacrifice without a priest. A girl living at home or a married woman who desires to fulfill a vow does so with the consent of her father or husband. Its being a domestic affair does not isolate it from the community. The violation of a sacred vow poses a threat to the community at large (cf. comment on 30:1–2).

NUMBERS 30

Section Outline

   III. Instructions beyond the Jordan at Jericho for the Generation Soon to Enter Canaan (26:1–36:13) ...

      E. Vows and Oaths (30:1–16)

         1. Vows and Oaths of Men (30:1–2)

         2. Vows and Oaths of Women (30:3–16)

Comment

30:1–2 Men's vows are treated first; the principles expressed here undergird the stipulations concerning women's vows as well. The expression "The heads of the tribes of the people of Israel" (v. 1) is unique to Numbers ("heads of the tribes of Israel," 10:4; cf. 1 Kings 8:1). These are "the chiefs of their ancestral tribes, the heads of the clans of Israel" (Num. 1:16; cf. 7:2), twelve in number. They deal with civil affairs, such as the military census. Although the vows in question are those made in a domestic context, they concern the entire community—due to the foundational principle of corporate solidarity—and thus these tribal heads. Saul breaks the vow made to the Gibeonites by Joshua, for which the Israelites suffer under David's reign (2 Sam. 21:1–2; cf. Josh. 9:3–17).

Although unspecified, given the preceding context (Numbers 28–29) the vows probably involve the ceremonial domain, such as donations vowed to the sanctuary (Leviticus 27), votive offerings (Num. 6:21), or a Nazirite vow (ch. 6). A vow is made "to the LORD" (30:2, 3), often in a time of trouble (Ps. 66:13–14) and as a conditional promise. For example, if God would protect him, Jacob vowed to worship him (Gen. 28:20–22); if God gave victory over the Canaanites, Israel vowed to devote them to destruction (Num. 21:2); if God granted him victory over the Ammonites, Jephthah vowed to offer whatever first came out of his house upon return (Judg. 11:31); if God gave her a son, Hannah vowed to give him to the Lord (1 Sam. 1:11). A vow could involve abstinence: for a Nazirite, from anything from the vine (Num. 6:3); for a woman, from conjugal relations (cf. comment on 30:3–16 [at v. 13]); for militia, from eating before the enemy was defeated (rashly in one instance; 1 Sam. 14:24). Thus vows involve self-imposed obligations to do or not do something.

"Swearing an oath" (Num. 30:2) invokes God's name (Lev. 19:12; Isa. 65:16; Jer. 4:2; Zech. 5:4; 1 Thess. 5:27), which calls on him as guarantor. This is not conditional, unlike a promissory vow. An oath is sworn concerning an action to be done (Josh. 2:12–17), concerning an action not to be done (Gen. 24:3–8), or that something has not been done (Ex. 22:11; Num. 5:19). It supports a promise (Matt. 14:7; Heb. 6:13–17). God swears by his own name to keep his covenant promise (Gen. 26:3; Deut. 7:8; Ps. 105:9; Ezek. 16:8; Heb. 6:17). A false oath involves breaking faith, a sacrilege (cf. comments on Num. 5:5–10; 5:11–31 [at v. 27]). Action contrary to what is sworn can draw a curse (Num. 5:19–22; 1 Sam. 14:24, 28; Zech. 5:3–4; cf. Mal. 1:14) and divine wrath (Josh. 9:20).

"To bind" (*'asar*, Num. 30:2; "binds," v. 3) in other contexts refers to physically binding someone (Gen. 42:24) or yoking cows (1 Sam. 6:7; cf. Jer. 46:4, "harness the horses"). "A pledge" (*'issar*; e.g., with the verb "bind," Num. 30:2, 3, or alone, e.g., v. 4) is a part of the oath that, combined in the expression "binding oath" (*shebu'at 'issar*, v. 13; v. 15 MT), is clearly prohibitive; a woman might pledge to "afflict herself," for example (cf. comment on 30:3–16 [at v. 13]).[219] The equivalent to *'issar* in Aramaic (*'esar*) refers to a prohibitive royal "injunction" (Dan. 6:8, 12, 16 [6:9, 13, 17 MT]).

A vow or an oath "proceeds out of his mouth" (Num. 30:2) or is an "utterance of her lips" (vv. 6, 8; cf. v. 12). The solemnity is underscored by two commands, one prohibitive ("He shall not break his word") and the other performative ("He shall do according to all that proceeds out of his mouth"; v. 2). "Break his word" is literally "profane [*khalal*] his word"[220] by not fulfilling a vow. A word, in the form of a sworn vow to the Lord, is holy (cf. Section Overview). False oaths necessarily defile those who take them (cf. Matt. 15:19) and profane God's holy name (Lev. 19:12). No extenuating circumstances permit the voiding of men's vows.

30:3–16 Four distinct cases concern a woman who makes a vow: (1) "while within her father's house in her youth," that is, "a daughter" (vv. 3–5, 16); (2) one who makes a vow before marriage but now "marries a husband" (vv. 6–8); (3) as a "widow" or divorcée (v. 9); (4) when "in her husband's house" (vv. 10–15). Cases 1 and 4 are the major ones, which are drawn together in the summary (v. 16). Case 2 has ties to both 1 and 4, whereas case 3 stands alone.

The general principle is that a girl's or woman's vow is as binding as a man's. Three concessions are offered. First, if she makes a vow while living in "her father's house" as a "youth" (*na'arah*, perhaps marriageable, even betrothed) and her father hears of the vow and opposes it, the vow does not stand (vv. 3–5). Second, if her vow was made and apparently consented to by (or unknown to?) her father before marriage, but "her husband hears of it" and opposes it, it is nullified (vv. 6–8). Third, if she makes a vow after marriage but her husband, upon hearing it, opposes it, it is void (v. 10–15). This last case includes her vow or oath "to afflict herself" (from *'anah*; v. 13), which involves some form of abstinence. Its omission in the section about oaths made in a father's house suggests the abstinence is from conjugal relations (cf. 29:7; cf. 1 Cor. 7:2, 4–5; cf. Mishnah, Nashim; Ketubbot 5:6–7). In all these cases a girl's or a woman's vow stands, whether made in her father's or husband's house, if on "the day that he hears/heard it" (Num. 30:5, 7, 12, 14) "he says/said nothing" (vv. 4, 7, 11, 14). By silence he consents.

As a rule, a woman's vow stands or falls on her father's or husband's assent or dissent. This is summarized in verse 16 "about a man and his wife" and "about a father and his daughter." In either case she is under a man's authority. Case 3

---

[219] Commentators often affirm that *neder* is positive or promissory, whereas *'issar* is negative or restrictive (Keil, "Fourth Book of Moses," 223; Noordtzij, *Numbers*, 266–267; Ashley, *Book of Numbers*, 577). For the view expressed above that both are positive and negative restrictive obligations cf. Milgrom, *Numbers*, 251, 488–490; Levine, *Numbers 1–20*, 215, 219; Levine, *Numbers 21–36*, 430.

[220] *CHALOT*, 105. "Break his word" and the definition "Make word invalid" (*CDCH*, 119) could downplay the idea that breaking a vow involves profanation. The notion is supported by the close connection between making a vow and devoting (*kharam*) someone to destruction (Num. 21:2–3) or something to the sanctuary (Lev. 27:2, 28). Whatever is devoted is most holy. Its violation is profanation, which incurs the death penalty (Lev. 27:29).

concerns vows of widows and divorcées. They have no male domestic authority. They alone bear responsibility should they violate a vow (v. 9).

The binding nature of a vow is underscored by the covenant language expressing it. A woman's vow "shall stand" (*qum*; vv. 4, 5, 7, 9, 11 [vv. 5, 6, 8, 11, 12 MT]), being "established" (same vb., vv. 13, 14 [vv. 14, 15 MT]) by her father or husband. *Qum* is used in Genesis 6:18 for "establish [my covenant]" (Gen. 17:7, 19, 21). The same verb for "making [a vow] null and void" (*parar*; Num. 30:8, 12, 13, 15 [vv. 9, 13, 15, 17 MT]) is rendered in Genesis 17:14 as "broken [my covenant]" and in Numbers 15:31 as "broken [his commandment]." "Oath" (30:2, 10, 13 [vv. 3, 11, 14 MT]) too is covenant language (Gen. 21:31–32; 26:3; Hos. 10:4). The relationship of the covenant to vows and oaths is stated clearly in Ezekiel 16:8, 59; 17:13, 18–19.

A final rule concerns the one who bears responsibility for a nullified vow, given the general principle that a vow is inviolable. First, as concerns a daughter or a wife, if her vow is nullified by her father or husband, "the LORD will forgive her" (Num. 30:5, 8, 12). "Forgive" (*salah*) is the opposite of "bear her iniquity" (cf. v. 15). A vow made by a woman before marriage in her youth but now nullified in marriage is called a "thoughtless utterance" (*mibta'*; vv. 6, 8, only occurrences).[221] Her rash vow failed to take into consideration her eventual marriage. Implicitly, a now-married daughter would be forgiven for having made her vow without the approbation of the one in authority over her.

Second, as concerns a husband, "he shall bear her iniquity" (v. 15). "Iniquity" points to either the act itself (breaking a vow) or the consequences (guilt) for breaking it. Does this mean that, by annulling his wife's vows, he bears the guilt of her not fulfilling them since he prevented her from doing so, even if he does so "on the day that he heard" (*beyom shom'o*; v. 14)? "After he has heard" (*'aharey shom'o*; v. 15) may mean "after [the day] he heard." In other words, "he shall bear her iniquity" if he voided her vow sometime "after" that fixed delay. The reading "his iniquity" (SP, LXX, Syr.) simplifies the traditional reading by emphasizing his liability, not hers. This case may be analogous to a vow unable to be fulfilled that requires a redemption payment (Leviticus 27). The terms "forgiven" (cf. Num. 30:5) and "bear iniquity" in a domestic context of vows and oaths underscore the concomitant nature of the sacred and domestic domains and the impact of domestic life on the entire community (cf. v. 1).[222]

Response

The fifth commandment ("Honor your father and your mother") undergirds Numbers 30, as it does the principle of submission to authority in general.[223] As concerns vows, a daughter's submission to the authority of her father in the home is an application of the commandment. Drawing from this principle, Paul exhorts

---

[221] "Rash vow" (*CHALOT*, 181); "impetuous utterance" (*CDCH*, 201). In the context of oaths the related verb (*bata'*) is rendered "speak rashly" (Lev. 5:4).
[222] Ron Bergey, "Parents as Covenant Mediators in Deuteronomy," in *Faithful Ministry: An Ecclesial Festschrift in Honor of the Rev. Dr. Robert S. Rayburn*, ed. Max Rogland (Eugene, OR: Wipf & Stock, 2019), 31–37.
[223] On the fifth commandment cf. WSC 64.

children to obey their parents in the Lord (Eph. 6:1; Col. 3:20). Wives are therefore instructed to submit to their husbands as the church must to its head, Christ (Eph. 5:22–24; Col. 3:18; 1 Pet. 3:5). Peter instructs young people to submit to their elders (1 Pet. 5:5). The church must submit to its leaders (Heb. 13:17). Submitting to one another in the church is done in reverence to Christ (Eph. 5:21). The reason given to submit to civil authorities is that God has instituted authority (Rom. 13:1). No one is exempt from submitting to God himself (James 4:7), nor therefore from his ordained authority in the home, the church, or society at large.

NUMBERS 31

31 The Lord spoke to Moses, saying, ² "Avenge the people of Israel on the Midianites. Afterward you shall be gathered to your people." ³ So Moses spoke to the people, saying, "Arm men from among you for the war, that they may go against Midian to execute the Lord's vengeance on Midian. ⁴ You shall send a thousand from each of the tribes of Israel to the war." ⁵ So there were provided, out of the thousands of Israel, a thousand from each tribe, twelve thousand armed for war. ⁶ And Moses sent them to the war, a thousand from each tribe, together with Phinehas the son of Eleazar the priest, with the vessels of the sanctuary and the trumpets for the alarm in his hand. ⁷ They warred against Midian, as the Lord commanded Moses, and killed every male. ⁸ They killed the kings of Midian with the rest of their slain, Evi, Rekem, Zur, Hur, and Reba, the five kings of Midian. And they also killed Balaam the son of Beor with the sword. ⁹ And the people of Israel took captive the women of Midian and their little ones, and they took as plunder all their cattle, their flocks, and all their goods. ¹⁰ All their cities in the places where they lived, and all their encampments, they burned with fire, ¹¹ and took all the spoil and all the plunder, both of man and of beast. ¹² Then they brought the captives and the plunder and the spoil to Moses, and to Eleazar the priest, and to the congregation of the people of Israel, at the camp on the plains of Moab by the Jordan at Jericho.

¹³ Moses and Eleazar the priest and all the chiefs of the congregation went to meet them outside the camp. ¹⁴ And Moses was angry with the officers of the army, the commanders of thousands and the commanders of hundreds, who had come from service in the war. ¹⁵ Moses said to them, "Have you let all the women live? ¹⁶ Behold, these, on Balaam's advice, caused the people of Israel to act treacherously against the Lord in the incident of Peor, and so the plague came among the congregation of the Lord. ¹⁷ Now therefore, kill every male among the little ones, and kill every woman who has known man by lying with him. ¹⁸ But all the young girls who have not known man by lying with him keep alive for yourselves. ¹⁹ Encamp outside the camp seven days. Whoever of you has killed any person and whoever has touched any slain, purify yourselves and your captives on the third day and on the seventh day. ²⁰ You shall purify every garment, every article of skin, all work of goats' hair, and every article of wood."

²¹ Then Eleazar the priest said to the men in the army who had gone to battle: "This is the statute of the law that the Lord has commanded Moses: ²² only the gold, the silver, the bronze, the iron, the tin, and the lead, ²³ everything that can stand the fire, you shall pass through the fire, and it shall be clean. Nevertheless, it shall also be purified with the water for impurity. And whatever cannot stand the fire, you shall pass through the water. ²⁴ You must wash your clothes on the seventh day, and you shall be clean. And afterward you may come into the camp."

²⁵ The Lord said to Moses, ²⁶ "Take the count of the plunder that was taken, both of man and of beast, you and Eleazar the priest and the heads of the fathers' houses of the congregation, ²⁷ and divide the plunder into two parts between the warriors who went out to battle and all the congregation. ²⁸ And levy for the Lord a tribute from the men of war who went out to battle, one out of five hundred, of the people and of the oxen and of the donkeys and of the flocks. ²⁹ Take it from their half and give it to Eleazar the priest as a contribution to the Lord. ³⁰ And from the people of Israel's half you shall take one drawn out of every fifty, of the people, of the oxen, of the donkeys, and of the flocks, of all the cattle, and give them to the Levites who keep guard over the tabernacle of the Lord." ³¹ And Moses and Eleazar the priest did as the Lord commanded Moses.

³² Now the plunder remaining of the spoil that the army took was 675,000 sheep, ³³ 72,000 cattle, ³⁴ 61,000 donkeys, ³⁵ and 32,000 persons in all, women who had not known man by lying with him. ³⁶ And the half, the portion of those who had gone out in the army, numbered 337,500 sheep, ³⁷ and the Lord's tribute of sheep was 675. ³⁸ The cattle were 36,000, of which the Lord's tribute was 72. ³⁹ The donkeys were 30,500, of which the Lord's tribute was 61. ⁴⁰ The persons were 16,000, of which the Lord's tribute was 32 persons. ⁴¹ And Moses gave the tribute, which was the contribution for the Lord, to Eleazar the priest, as the Lord commanded Moses.

⁴² From the people of Israel's half, which Moses separated from that of the men who had served in the army— ⁴³ now the congregation's half was 337,500 sheep, ⁴⁴ 36,000 cattle, ⁴⁵ and 30,500 donkeys, ⁴⁶ and 16,000 persons— ⁴⁷ from the people of Israel's half Moses took one of every 50, both of persons and of beasts, and gave them to the Levites who kept guard over the tabernacle of the Lord, as the Lord commanded Moses.

⁴⁸ Then the officers who were over the thousands of the army, the commanders of thousands and the commanders of hundreds, came near to Moses ⁴⁹ and said to Moses, "Your servants have counted the men of war who are under our command, and there is not a man missing from us. ⁵⁰ And we have brought the Lord's offering, what each man found, articles of gold, armlets and bracelets, signet rings, earrings, and beads, to make atonement for ourselves before the Lord." ⁵¹ And Moses and Eleazar the priest received from them the gold, all crafted articles. ⁵² And all the gold of the contribution that they presented to the Lord, from the commanders of thousands and the commanders of hundreds, was 16,750 shekels.[1] ⁵³ (The men in the army had each taken plunder for himself.) ⁵⁴ And Moses and Eleazar the priest received the gold from the commanders of thousands and of hundreds, and brought it into the tent of meeting, as a memorial for the people of Israel before the Lord.

---

[1] A *shekel* was about 2/5 ounce or 11 grams

Section Overview

The Israelites are ordered to take vengeance on Midian for the Baal-peor incident (Num. 31:1–11), a revenge already decreed (25:16–18). Upon return from battle, the soldiers and the spoil are purified (31:12–24) especially with "water for impurity" (v. 23) prepared from the ashes of the red heifer (ch. 19). Once cleansed, the spoil is distributed (31:25–47). Seeing their forces suffer no loss, the army commanders present an offering to the sanctuary (vv. 48–54).

Section Outline

III. Instructions beyond the Jordan at Jericho for the Generation Soon to Enter Canaan (26:1–36:13) . . .
    F. Vengeance on Midian (31:1–54)
        1. War against Midian (31:1–11)
        2. Return from War (31:12–18)
        3. Purification (31:19–24)
        4. Division of Plunder (31:25–47)
        5. Commanders' Offering (31:48–54)

Comment

31:1–11 The Midianites (cf. 10:29) living in Moab had followed Balaam's advice and induced Israel to licentious idolatry (31:16), resulting in a plague that had culminated in heavy loss of life (25:9). Avenging Israel "on" (Hb. *m-*; cf. 2 Kings 9:7) the Midianites is restitutive for this wrongful injury or loss; the Israelites will reap the spoils. The Lord's vengeance "on" (*b-*; cf. Jer. 50:15) Midian is also retributive; they will suffer defeat.[224] "Afterward you shall be gathered to your people" (Num. 31:2): already informed of his death in these very words (27:13; cf. Deut. 32:50), Moses now learns of his last mission.

"War" (*tsaba'*; Num. 31:3, 4, 5, and twelve other occurrences in ch. 31) waged by Israel is the instrument of the Lord's vengeance. The same Hebrew word is used for tabernacle "duty" (4:3; 8:25). In this context *tsaba'* suggests a holy war (cf. 31:14, "service [*tsaba'*] in the war [*milkhamah*]"; cf. comment on 32:16–32 [at v. 20]). War is sanctified (*qadash*; Jer. 6:4; 51:28, "prepare"; Joel 3:9 [4:9 MT], "consecrate"). The priest goes "to the war" with the soldiers (Num. 31:6), and the sacred ark is carried into battle (10:35–36; Josh. 6:4; 1 Sam. 4:5). Four hundred thousand foot soldiers who draw the sword constitute the "assembly of [*qahal*] the people of God" (Judg. 20:2); The *qahal* is a sacred body. Soldiers must be ritually pure and consecrated (Josh. 3:5; Isa. 13:3; Joel 3:9), which involves, among other things, abstention from sexual relations (1 Sam. 21:5; 2 Sam. 11:11). The bivouac must be holy because the Lord is in its midst (Deut. 23:14). Shields and perhaps other weapons are anointed with oil (cf. "shield . . . not anointed [*mashiakh*] with oil," 2 Sam. 1:21; "oil [*mashakh*] the shield," Isa. 21:5) to consecrate them (cf. discussion of Num.

---

224 On these syntactic-semantical nuances cf. Milgrom, *Numbers*, 255.

31:6, "vessels of the sanctuary"). Booty undergoes purification (vv. 23–24), and gold spoil goes to the sanctuary (vv. 52–54). Plunder is later "dedicated" (*qadash*) by David, and his commanders present "dedicated gifts" (*qodashim*) for the house of the Lord (1 Chron. 26:26). The sanctuary serves as an armory (1 Sam. 21:8–9; 2 Kings 11:10; 2 Chron. 23:9).

"A thousand from each tribe" or "twelve thousand armed for war" (Num. 31:5) constitute an Israelite army commensurate in size with other ancient armies.[225] The large census totals involved conscription numbers in excess of six hundred thousand (26:51), which was not reflective of those called up to active duty in a standing army (1 Kings 10:26) nor for an army mustered for battle (2 Sam. 7:1). Given the considerable differences of the conscription figures of each secular tribe, one thousand from each seems disproportionate. But, as with the identical offerings made by tribal leaders for the consecration of the tabernacle (Numbers 7), each tribe will share equally in the honor of victory over the Midianites and the recompense of the spoil.

The Hebrew verb *masar* (31:5)[226] occurs twice in biblical Hebrew, both times in this chapter, the second probably as a homonym (cf. comment on 31:12–18 [at v. 16]). Here it appears to mean, as in later Hebrew, "received, handed down."[227] In this sense the twelve thousand soldiers are those who have been "handed down" from the pool of over six hundred thousand eligible men.[228] Phinehas goes with the troops as a chaplain (v. 6) since Eleazar, as high priest, cannot become impure from contact with corpses (Lev. 21:11). To avoid such defilement Eleazar himself had earlier replaced Aaron the high priest in the aftermath of the incident with Korah (Num. 16:37).

The "vessels of the sanctuary" (*keley haqqodesh*; 31:6; cf. 3:31; 18:3), or "holy vessels" (cf. 1 Kings 8:4; cf. *shemen haqqodesh*, "holy oil," Num. 35:25), are perhaps weapons (cf. 1 Sam. 21:5 [21:6 MT], in which "vessels [*keley*] . . . holy" refer to weapons; so LXX, Vulg., NET, NAB). Alternatively, if the conjunction that begins Numbers 31:6 (*ve-*) is epexegetical, it would connect with the preceding words ("the holy vessels, *that is* [*ve-*] the trumpets"; cf. 10:9; cf. 2 Kings 12:13).[229] Since these vessels appear to be in the hand of Phinehas (Num. 31:6), and the priests blow battle trumpets (cf. comment on 10:1–10 [at v. 9]), the latter interpretation seems more likely.

"Slain" implies "pierced" (*khalal*), like Balaam, "with the sword" (31:8). "Zur" is Cozbi's father, a tribal head (25:15), here listed among the "five kings of Midian" (31:8). Within the confines of Moab, Midian is a confederation. Cozbi was the woman slain together with the Israelite by Phinehas (25:15). The Israelites "killed every male" (31:7) but "took captive the women . . . and their little ones" (v. 9), as

---

225 According to Harrison, "A military force of 10,000 was apparently common in the time of Hammurapi (c. 1790–1750 B.C.)" (*Numbers*, 47). The army size is also comparable to those in the Assyrian period; cf. *ANET* 278–279.
226 For Numbers 31:5 cf. *CDCH*, s.v. *מסר* I: "be counted, provided, conscripted"; s.v. *מסר* IV: "be selected."
227 *CDCH*, s.v. *מסר* II: "'hand down, transmit' commandments" (cf. CD 3:3); "'be handed over' to [le-] sword" (cf. CD 19:10). A related noun (*masoret*) refers to a military unit (1QM 3:3).
228 Levine translates "to separate, hand over, detach" (*Numbers 21–36*, 451).
229 Keil, "Fourth Book of Moses," 225; Davies, *Numbers*, 323.

stipulated in Deuteronomy 20:13–14. In contrast to "their cities" (Num. 31:10), the Midianite "encampments" (pl. *tirah*, not *makhaneh*) are nomadic tent encampments (Gen. 25:16; Ezek. 25:4).[230]

"Took as plunder" (*bazaz*; Num. 31:9; cf. comment on 31:25–47) refers to both animate and inanimate booty ("cattle . . . goods"). "Spoil" (*shalal*; vv. 11, 12) can also be both (e.g., Josh. 22:8; Judg. 5:30). "Plunder" (*malqoakh*; Num. 31:11, 12, 26, 27, 32) is probably only animate ("man" and "beast"; vv. 11, 26; Isa. 49:24, 25). Cf. comment on Num. 31:25–42.

31:12–18 The soldiers return to their camp on the plains of Moab, across the Jordan from Jericho (v. 12), where the Israelite families have encamped during the war. The Levites have kept guard over the tabernacle there (v. 47). The Midianite captives and plunder are brought to Moses, Eleazar, and the people "outside the camp" (v. 13), a sphere unaffected by someone or something ritually impure (cf. comment on 19:1–10 [at vv. 3, 9]). Eleazar has already returned to the camp. The soldiers drive the captured livestock and lead the captive women with their children at a slower pace.

That the female Midianites have been spared draws Moses' ire at the commanders (31:14–15). Normally, the Israelites could take captive women as wives (Deut. 20:14; 21:10–14), but in this case it is inconceivable. Even though they have acted "on Balaam's advice" (Num. 31:16; Rev. 2:14) "these" (Hb. *hen*, feminine) are held accountable for causing Israel to "act treacherously" (*limsor ma'al*; Num. 31:16). This verb (infinitive from *masar*)[231] is rendered as "by apostatizing" in the LXX (also an infinitive; cf. comment on 31:1–11 [at v. 5], *masar*). In Numbers 5:12, 27 the noun rendered "break faith" (*ma'al*) describes a wife's adultery, which, if corroborated by witnesses, draws the death sentence. In the "incident of Peor" (31:16) the immorality was blatant.

Another translation of *ma'al* ("faithlessness") describes intermarriage of Israelite returnees from exile—a "holy race" to a "holy place"—with the peoples of the land (Ezra 9:2, 4). They have "broken faith" (*ma'al*; Ezra 10:2, 10), or, as rendered elsewhere, "act[ed] treacherously" (Neh. 13:27). *Ma'al* impurity penetrates and desecrates the sacred realm, profaning God's name (Deut. 32:51). The generation to enter the land was warned about indigenous peoples who make the land unclean with their abominations (Lev. 18:27–28; Num. 33:52, 55). If the Israelites defile the holy land, God will drive them out just as he has those peoples (Lev. 20:22–23; Num. 33:56).

Israel is instructed to "kill every male among the little ones" (31:17). This harsh sentence is preemptive, so that there will be no Midianites in the vicinity to take revenge or make war on Israel. "Kill every woman who has known man by lying with him" (v. 17) is retaliatory, since the women had seduced the Israelite men (25:1, 8). Virgin women and now-orphaned girls remain; they might become domestic,

---

[230] Gray, *Numbers*, 421.
[231] Cf. *CDCH*, s.v. מסר III: "'offer,' i.e. commit, 'trespass against [*be*-]," citing Numbers 31:5.

civil, or cultic slaves (Lev. 25:44; Josh. 9:27). Midianites living elsewhere are unaffected (e.g., Judges 6–8).

31:19–24 Due to contact with corpses, the soldiers and their captives remain "outside the camp" (Num. 31:19; cf. comment on 31:12–18), beyond the perimeter of the tribes' encampments, quarantined seven days in order not to defile the camp. They must "purify" (Hb. *hata'*; cf. 19:12) themselves and their female captives "on the third" and "seventh day" (31:19), by the procedure prescribed for corpse contamination (19:11–12). This cleansing includes personal effects (31:20), "garment" (*beged*, "cloth, linen"; Gen. 41:42), "article of skin" (skins for water/milk/wine; Gen. 21:14; Judg. 4:19; 1 Sam. 1:24; skin garments, Lev. 13:48) and "of wood" (e.g., a vessel; Lev. 15:12), and "work of goats' hair" (e.g., curtains, tent; Ex. 26:7). "Eleazar the priest said" (Num. 31:21) is the only mention of Eleazar's transmitting Moses' instructions (cf. Josh. 22:31). "This is the statute of the law" (Num. 31:21; only elsewhere in 19:2) refers to ritual law (cf. comment on 35:9–34 [at v. 29]).

Metal objects, listed in order of value ("gold . . . bronze . . . lead"; 31:22) are purified by "fire" and "water for impurity" (*me niddah*, v. 23; cf. 19:9). "Whatever cannot stand the fire" is washed with "water" (31:23), then splashed with water for impurity. All "clothes" (v. 24; cf. v. 20, "garment") are washed on the seventh day. The Israelite soldiers and the Midianite virgins and little girls are now "clean" and can enter the "camp" (v. 24).

31:25–47 This section legislates the distribution of plunder and spoil. "Plunder" (Hb. *malqoakh*, v. 26; only elsewhere Isa. 49:24) is animate, "man" and "beast" (cf. comment on Num. 31:1–11 [at v. 11]). Half is distributed to the warriors and half to all the congregation (Num. 31:27; cf. 1 Sam. 30:25). Of the soldiers' share, "one out of five hundred" (0.2 percent) of the captive people and cattle is for the priest (Num. 31:28). Of the people's share, one out of every fifty (2 percent) is for the Levites (v. 30) who keep guard over the tabernacle of the Lord, a double reminder of their duty (vv. 30, 47; cf. 1:53). This probably serves to justify their receiving ten times more than the priests, although their superior number is reason enough. Their keeping guard is especially critical in times of epidemic corpse contamination due to war (cf. 31:54). The English "levy" (from *rum*, "lift"; v. 28) is borrowed from Old French *lever*, "to lift." "Tribute" (*mekes*, only in vv. 28, 37, 38, 39, 40, 41) is called a "contribution" (*terumah*, from *rum*; vv. 29, 41, 52; cf. 15:20), a tax levied for sanctuary service.

Numbers 31:32–41 provide the totals of the soldiers' half of persons and animals, from which is taken the "Lord's tribute" (vv. 37, 38, 39, 40), that is, the portion given "to Eleazar the priest" (vv. 29, 41). Verses 42–46 do the same in respect to Israel's half, from which comes the Levites' portion.

31:48–54 "Counted the men" (v. 49) renders the same Hebrew expression ("lift the heads") used for the inventory of plunder in verse 26 and earlier translated "take a census" (cf. 1:2; 4:2). That there is "not a man missing" (31:49) is why they bring "the LORD's offering" (v. 50; only elsewhere 9:7, 13). The military commanders offer "what each man found" (31:50), plunder consisting of "gold" jewelry (v. 50) and "crafted articles" (v. 51). The purpose is to "make atonement" (Hb. *kapar*; v. 50) for themselves—another case of bloodless atonement (cf. comments on 8:5–22 [at v. 12] and 16:36–50 [at v. 46]). The commanders perhaps fear a plague otherwise. David's later military census results in a pestilence that kills seventy thousand Israelites (2 Sam. 24:1, 15). The commanders' gift may be a ransom (*koper*), also a kind of bloodless atonement, to save lives (Ex. 21:30; Num. 35:31–32; cf. 1 Sam. 14:45 with the verb *padah*). To avert a plague, a ransom called "atonement money" (*kesep hakkippurim*) was levied for each person counted in the census (Ex. 30:12–16). To make atonement the army officers make an offering of gold plunder (Num. 31:50), which has been purified by passing it through fire (v. 23). The purification of Isaiah's lips by a burning coal from the altar is also called atonement (Isa. 6:6–7).

Although the word *kherem* is not employed, the offering is devoted. In the laws on redemption of vows it is stipulated, "No devoted thing [*kherem*] that a man devotes to the LORD, of anything that he has, whether man or beast, or of his inherited field, shall be sold or redeemed; every devoted thing [*kherem*] is most holy to the LORD" (Lev. 27:28). The "gold of the contribution [*terumah*; cf. Num. 15:20]" weighs "16,750 shekels" (31:52), or about 420 pounds (190 kg).

Devoted gifts go into the tent of meeting (v. 54; cf. Josh. 6:19; 2 Sam. 8:11–12; 1 Kings 7:51; 15:15; 1 Chron. 26:26). The gold's function as a "memorial" (*zikkaron*, "reminder") may be for the Lord to remember his people (Num. 10:10) or for the people to remember the Lord (16:40). The stored riches in the tent are another reason the Levites must keep guard (cf. 31:30, 47).

Response

To warn the Thessalonians Paul perhaps draws upon the vengeance of God on Midian for inciting Israel to morally corrupt themselves: "The Lord is an avenger in all these things" (1 Thess. 4:6). God's will is their sanctification, precisely that they abstain from sexual immorality (1 Thess. 4:3). God has called them not for impurity but in holiness. As in the wilderness, where uncleansed impurity defiled God's dwelling place and drew his wrath, so in the church impurity defiles the body in which the Holy Spirit dwells (1 Thess. 4:7–8). God's vengeance is an expression of his wrath against sin (Rom. 1:18; 12:19). Sexual immorality tops the list (Eph. 5:5–6; Col. 3:5–6). Paul reminds the Thessalonians, "God has not destined us for wrath, but to obtain salvation through our Lord Jesus Christ" (1 Thess. 5:9).

NUMBERS 32

32 Now the people of Reuben and the people of Gad had a very great number of livestock. And they saw the land of Jazer and the land of Gilead, and behold, the place was a place for livestock. ² So the people of Gad and the people of Reuben came and said to Moses and to Eleazar the priest and to the chiefs of the congregation, ³ "Ataroth, Dibon, Jazer, Nimrah, Heshbon, Elealeh, Sebam, Nebo, and Beon, ⁴ the land that the Lord struck down before the congregation of Israel, is a land for livestock, and your servants have livestock." ⁵ And they said, "If we have found favor in your sight, let this land be given to your servants for a possession. Do not take us across the Jordan."

⁶ But Moses said to the people of Gad and to the people of Reuben, "Shall your brothers go to the war while you sit here? ⁷ Why will you discourage the heart of the people of Israel from going over into the land that the Lord has given them? ⁸ Your fathers did this, when I sent them from Kadesh-barnea to see the land. ⁹ For when they went up to the Valley of Eshcol and saw the land, they discouraged the heart of the people of Israel from going into the land that the Lord had given them. ¹⁰ And the Lord's anger was kindled on that day, and he swore, saying, ¹¹ 'Surely none of the men who came up out of Egypt, from twenty years old and upward, shall see the land that I swore to give to Abraham, to Isaac, and to Jacob, because they have not wholly followed me, ¹² none except Caleb the son of Jephunneh the Kenizzite and Joshua the son of Nun, for they have wholly followed the Lord.' ¹³ And the Lord's anger was kindled against Israel, and he made them wander in the wilderness forty years, until all the generation that had done evil in the sight of the Lord was gone. ¹⁴ And behold, you have risen in your fathers' place, a brood of sinful men, to increase still more the fierce anger of the Lord against Israel! ¹⁵ For if you turn away from following him, he will again abandon them in the wilderness, and you will destroy all this people."

¹⁶ Then they came near to him and said, "We will build sheepfolds here for our livestock, and cities for our little ones, ¹⁷ but we will take up arms, ready to go before the people of Israel, until we have brought them to their place. And our little ones shall live in the fortified cities because of the inhabitants of the land. ¹⁸ We will not return to our homes until each of the people of Israel has gained his inheritance. ¹⁹ For we will not inherit with them on the other side of the Jordan and beyond, because our inheritance has come to us on this side of the Jordan to the east." ²⁰ So Moses said to them, "If you will do this, if you will take up arms to go before the Lord for the war, ²¹ and every armed man of you will pass over the Jordan before the Lord, until he has driven out his enemies from before him ²² and the land is subdued before the Lord; then after that you shall return and be free of obligation to the Lord and to Israel, and this land shall be your possession before the Lord. ²³ But if you will not do so,

behold, you have sinned against the LORD, and be sure your sin will find you out. ²⁴ Build cities for your little ones and folds for your sheep, and do what you have promised." ²⁵ And the people of Gad and the people of Reuben said to Moses, "Your servants will do as my lord commands. ²⁶ Our little ones, our wives, our livestock, and all our cattle shall remain there in the cities of Gilead, ²⁷ but your servants will pass over, every man who is armed for war, before the LORD to battle, as my lord orders."

²⁸ So Moses gave command concerning them to Eleazar the priest and to Joshua the son of Nun and to the heads of the fathers' houses of the tribes of the people of Israel. ²⁹ And Moses said to them, "If the people of Gad and the people of Reuben, every man who is armed to battle before the LORD, will pass with you over the Jordan and the land shall be subdued before you, then you shall give them the land of Gilead for a possession. ³⁰ However, if they will not pass over with you armed, they shall have possessions among you in the land of Canaan." ³¹ And the people of Gad and the people of Reuben answered, "What the LORD has said to your servants, we will do. ³² We will pass over armed before the LORD into the land of Canaan, and the possession of our inheritance shall remain with us beyond the Jordan."

³³ And Moses gave to them, to the people of Gad and to the people of Reuben and to the half-tribe of Manasseh the son of Joseph, the kingdom of Sihon king of the Amorites and the kingdom of Og king of Bashan, the land and its cities with their territories, the cities of the land throughout the country. ³⁴ And the people of Gad built Dibon, Ataroth, Aroer, ³⁵ Atroth-shophan, Jazer, Jogbehah, ³⁶ Beth-nimrah and Beth-haran, fortified cities, and folds for sheep. ³⁷ And the people of Reuben built Heshbon, Elealeh, Kiriathaim, ³⁸ Nebo, and Baal-meon (their names were changed), and Sibmah. And they gave other names to the cities that they built. ³⁹ And the sons of Machir the son of Manasseh went to Gilead and captured it, and dispossessed the Amorites who were in it. ⁴⁰ And Moses gave Gilead to Machir the son of Manasseh, and he settled in it. ⁴¹ And Jair the son of Manasseh went and captured their villages, and called them Havvoth-jair.[1] ⁴² And Nobah went and captured Kenath and its villages, and called it Nobah, after his own name.

[1] *Havvoth-jair* means *the villages of Jair*

Section Overview

The request of the tribes of Reuben and Gad to settle in Transjordan (Num. 32:1–5) follows the defeat of the Amorites (21:21–35) and the Midianites (ch. 31). The entire region from the Arnon to Mount Hermon is under Israelite control. Moses likens these tribes' request to settle outside Canaan to the revolt at Kadesh, in which the exodus generation refused to enter the Promised Land (32:6–15). Only after the Reubenites and the Gadites solemnly promise to cross the Jordan with the other tribes to fight with them and not to settle in Transjordan until the others have taken their possession (vv. 16–19, 31–32) does Moses consent (vv. 20–25, 28–30). Along with a grant of land and cities to Reuben and Gad (vv. 33–38), the half-tribe of Manasseh is also accorded a Transjordan inheritance (vv. 39–42). (Cf. Excursus before 21:12–20, "Geographical Overview of Transjordan".)

Section Outline

III. Instructions beyond the Jordan at Jericho for the Generation Soon to Enter Canaan (26:1–36:13) . . .
    G. Transjordan Inheritance of Reuben, Gad, and Manasseh (32:1–42)
        1. The Tribes' Request and Moses' Remonstrance (32:1–15)
        2. The Tribes' Proposition and Moses' Consent (32:16–32)
        3. The Tribes' Transjordan Inheritance (32:33–42)

Comment

32:1–15 The tribes of Reuben and Gad (v. 1) are encamped on the south side of the tabernacle (2:10, 14). Their "very great number of livestock" (32:1) is due in part to the Midianite plunder (31:32). However, the Israelites had left Egypt with much livestock (Ex. 12:38); they herded in the wilderness (Num. 11:22; 20:4, 8, 11, 19). In its broadest sense "livestock" (Hb. *miqneh*) can denote flocks and herds, including donkeys, mules, horses, and camels (Gen. 31:18; 32:13; Ex. 9:3). More narrowly, it defines herded, grazing ovine ("flocks"; Num. 31:9), distinguished from "cattle" (*behemah*; 31:9; 32:26), larger herded and nonherded animals, such as oxen and donkeys, respectively (Deut. 5:14; *behemah*, "livestock"). On "chiefs of the congregation" (Num. 32:2) cf. 4:34; 16:2; 31:13; Joshua 22:30.

The "land of Gilead" (Num. 32:1) in the broadest sense extends from the Arnon in the south to the Yarmouk in the north, divided by the Jabbok. In a more restricted sense it may refer to the northern half, whereas "the land of Jazer" may refer to the southern half, between the Jabbok and the Arnon.[232] Transjordan suits these tribes' needs and interests since it is recognized for its good grazing land for livestock (v. 1; cf. 2 Kings 3:4; Mic. 7:14).[233] Most of the nine cities mentioned in Numbers 32:3 and again in verses 34–38 have been identified.[234]

"Ataroth" (cf. v. 34) is 9 miles (15 km) northwest of "Dibon" (cf. 21:30), which is 13 miles (21 km) east of the Dead Sea and 3.5 miles (5.5 km) north of the Arnon. For "Jazer" cf. 21:32. "Nimrah" ("Beth-nimrah"; 32:36) is 18 miles (30 km) east of Amman (biblical Rabbah). "Heshbon" is almost centered between the Arnon and Jabbok.[235] "Elealeh" is northeast of Heshbon and 11 miles (18 km) southwest of Amman. "Sebam" (or "Sibmah," v. 38; SP *sbmh* and LXX *sebama*) is unidentified but was famous for its quality wines (Isa. 16:8–9; Jer. 48:32). "Nebo" (cf. Num. 23:13–14) is 9 miles (15 km) east of the north end of the Dead Sea. "Beon" ("Baal-meon," 32:38; "Beth Baal-meon," Josh. 13:17; "Beth-meon," Jer. 48:23) is 4.5 miles (7 km) southwest of Medaba, 10 miles (16 km) east of the Dead Sea, and 23 miles (37 km) southwest of Amman.

---

232 Cf. Davies, *Numbers*, 334. On the elasticity of the designation "Gilead" cf. Gray, *Numbers*, 427–428.
233 Smith notes that Ammon and Moab were wealthier (in water, pasturage, and agriculture) than Judah and Ephraim (*Historical Geography of the Holy Land*, 340).
234 Cf. Simons, "Appendix on Numbers 32," *Geographical and Topographical Texts*, 131–134; Aharoni, *Land of the Bible*, Site Identifications, 429–443.
235 Since no remains before the Iron Age have been found at Tell Hesban, 12 miles (19 km) southwest of Amman, it is generally held that the name was transferred from Jalul, the only Late Bronze site in the region (cf. Milgrom, *Numbers*, 180).

The "land that the LORD struck down" (Num. 32:4) is the land of Sihon and Og (v. 33). On "land for livestock" (v. 4) cf. verse 1. "Found favor" (*matsa' khen*; v. 5) is a common expression (e.g., 11:11, 15). Finding favor depends entirely on the kindly disposition of a superior (e.g., Gen. 6:8; 39:4; Num. 32:5; Ruth 2:10). "In your [sg.] sight" is addressed only to Moses, although the tribes have come to "Eleazar" and the "chiefs" (Num. 32:2).

Canaan's eastern border is the Jordan (34:2, 12). Had the Transjordan Amorite kings not attacked, no land east of the Jordan would have been taken by the Israelites. The Amorites who are part of the seven nations to be dispossessed are Cisjordan Amorites (e.g., Gen. 15:21; Josh. 5:1), descendants of Canaan (Gen. 10:15; 1 Chron. 1:13). Although the negative verb form attenuates their request not to be forced to cross the Jordan, Moses views it as a refusal to take part in the conquest and settlement "while you sit here" (Num. 32:6), that is, outside Canaan. Are these two new generation tribes about to repeat the failure of the old generation? Moses' remonstrance, "Will you discourage the heart of the people?" (v. 7), links their request to the Kadesh-barnea incident, when "your fathers . . . discouraged the heart of the people" (vv. 8–9). "Discourage" (*nu'*) is the same verb for preventing a vow from being fulfilled ("oppose"; 30:5, 8, 11).

Thirty-eight years earlier a bad report from ten scouts had demoralized the Israelites (14:36). "When I sent them from Kadesh-barnea" (32:8; cf. 33:4) is the first specific mention of the scouts' having been sent from this point (cf. Deut. 9:23; Josh. 14:7). Numbers 13 mentions their being sent from the wilderness of Paran (v. 3) and the people's encampment at Kadesh after reconnoitering the land (v. 26). Reference to "the land that the LORD has given them" (32:7, 9) recalls God's promise concerning Canaan (e.g., Ex. 12:25; Num. 11:12; 14:16, 23; 32:12).

After recounting God's judgment upon Israel for the Kadesh rebellion (vv. 8–13), Moses warns, "You have risen in your fathers' place, a brood of sinful men" (v. 14; "brood," *tarbut*, is a *hapax legomenon*). Moses sees in them the same sinful disposition as their fathers' and the potential to repeat their mistake. Having witnessed the anger of the Lord expressed in his judgment upon the exodus generation, they are even more accountable ("To increase still more the fierce anger of the LORD against Israel"; v. 14). "If you turn away from following him" (v. 15) implies they could refuse the grace of the one who has promised to go before them. The LXX renders the Hebrew expression translated "turn away" (*shub me'ahare*) with the same term used in the NT concerning those who have "turned away" (*apostrephō*) from the truth (2 Tim. 4:4; Titus 1:14).

Israel suffered collective judgment because of the leaders of ten tribes: "He will . . . abandon them in the wilderness, and you [tribes of Reuben and Gad] will destroy all this people" (Num. 32:15). Moses fears the same punishment because of two tribes. It takes only one man's disobedience to draw God's later wrath, resulting in Israel's defeat at Ai (Josh. 7:1, 12). "A little leaven leavens the whole lump" (1 Cor. 5:6).

32:16–32 There is no report of Moses' seeking God's directive in response to this extraordinary request, as he did earlier when he had no precedent upon which to draw (Num. 27:5; cf. 15:34–35).[236] Moses' anger is abated by the tribes' proposed compromise to settle only their families and livestock, then to send their armed men to join the other tribes to secure the Cisjordan, and only thereafter to return to Transjordan (32:16–19). "Ready to go" (v. 17) renders a verb meaning "hasten" (Hb. *khush*; e.g., Isa. 28:16). The LXX "vanguard" perhaps translates *khamushim*, a military term with the general sense "in battle-readiness" (e.g., Ex. 13:18, "equipped for battle").[237] Their proposal to go "before the people of Israel" (Num. 32:17) would not be literally possible if the Reuben camp, which includes the Gad and Simeon companies, set out to cross the Jordan as in the wilderness trek—in battle march second (2:16). "Before the LORD for the war" parallels "before the LORD to battle" (32:20, 27; cf. vv. 21, 22, "before the LORD"), underscoring the sacred nature of the conquest (cf. 31:3).

Moses repeats their proposal but with opposite conditions: "If you will take up arms . . . this land shall be your possession." But "if you will not do so," he warns them, "you have sinned against the LORD" (32:23), the same charge leveled against the exodus generation at the golden calf incident (Deut. 9:16; cf. Jer. 40:3; 44:23). Sin is personified as an active agent finding its author ("Be sure your sin will find you out," Num. 32:23; cf. Rom. 6:12). God warned Cain that sin desired to control him (Gen. 4:7). Sin is a pitiless master.

If these tribes keep their word, however, they will "be free of obligation" (*naqi*, "be free"; Num. 32:22; cf. 5:19, 28, 31), which indicates their promise is considered an oath (cf. Gen. 24:41 "free [*naqi*] from my oath"). To "be free" in Numbers 5 means not to experience effects of a curse for lying under oath (5:19, 28) and of the consequences of iniquity (5:31). The sworn obligation to be fulfilled is "to the LORD and to Israel" (32:22). "Do what you have promised" (or "do what proceeds from your mouths"; v. 24) expresses a vow or a sworn oath ("He shall do according to all that proceeds out of his mouth"; 30:2).[238] They affirm their commitment to their proposal (32:25–27). Moses then formulates it as an order to Eleazar, Joshua, and the leaders containing the conditions upon which the Transjordan inheritance rests (vv. 28–29). He adds, "If they will not pass over with you armed, they shall have possessions among you in the land of Canaan" (v. 30), a stipulation Joshua enforces (Josh. 1:12–15). Moses places no confidence in their promise. Only their actions will prove their intent.[239]

The tribes reaffirm their obligation (Num. 32:31–32). "We will do" (v. 31) is another oath formula (cf. Judg. 11:10; Neh. 5:12; Jer. 42:5). By repeating Moses' words (Num. 32:32) they reinforce their vow (cf. Josh. 2:12, 14, 17). To break a vow or oath is sacrilege (Num. 5:19; cf. 30:2). The inheritance they "have received" is one they "have taken" (*laqakh*; 34:14, 15; cf. Response section).

32:33–42 The territory and cities formerly belonging to the Amorites under Sihon and Og are given to Gad, Reuben, and half the tribe of Manasseh (v. 33). The cities

---

[236] Noordtzij calls this "a weak moment in Moses' life" (*Numbers*, 280).
[237] CDCH, 124.
[238] Cf. Levine, *Numbers 21–36*, 494.
[239] Olson views their response to Moses in the form of a compromise as positive, a contrast with the old generation, which rebelled (*Numbers*, 182). However, Moses is dubious (cf. Response section for Calvin's view).

Gad and Reuben rebuild are listed (vv. 34–38), supplemented by a summary of the territory and cities taken by Manasseh's descendants (vv. 39–42). A good number of the cities in the inheritances of Gad and Reuben are mentioned in the Moabite Stone (c. 830 BC).[240] King Mesha (cf. 2 Kings 3:4) claims to have rebuilt them, which indicates that the situation of the two tribes, especially Reuben's, is tenuous. Battles to control these rich lands are incessant (e.g., 1 Sam. 14:47; 1 Chron. 5:26).

"Fortified [*mibtsar*] cities" (Num. 32:36; cf. 13:19, "strongholds") is in opposition to "camps." "Folds for sheep" (32:36) are surrounded by stone walls. Only a portion of the conscripted men will cross the Jordan with the other tribes.[241] Others will stay behind to defend the women and children and care for the flocks.

Apart from a few exceptions, only those cities listed in 32:34–38, 41–42 not already mentioned in verse 3 are commented on here. "Ataroth" (v. 34; cf. v. 3) is mentioned in the Moabite Stone as a home of Gadites (line 10). For "Dibon . . . Jazer" (vv. 34, 35; Moabite Stone, line 20) cf. comments on 21:21–35 (at vv. 30, 32); 31:1–11 (at v. 3). "Aroer" (32:34; Moabite Stone, line 25) is about 14 miles (23 km) east of the Dead Sea, on the north bank of the Arnon gorge. "Atroth-shophan" (v. 35) is unidentified. "Jogbehah" is 7 miles (11 km) northwest of Amman (biblical Rabbah). In Gideon's day Midianites lived in that area (Judg. 8:11; cf. Num. 32:42). For "Beth-nimrah" (v. 36) cf. v. 3, Nimrah. "Beth-haran" ("Beth-haram"; Josh. 13:27) is 18 miles (30 km) west southwest of Amman.

For "Heshbon . . . Elealeh . . . Nebo . . . Baal-meon" cf. Num. 32:3, "Beon." The location of "Kiriathaim" (v. 37) is uncertain.[242] Although Nebo, Baal-meon, and Kiriathaim are mentioned in the Moabite Stone (lines 10, 14, 30), the Reubenites are not (cf. discussion on v. 34 above). "Their names were changed" (v. 38) because, like Baal, Nebo was a god (Isa. 46:1; cf. Ex. 23:13). The name Nebo reappears after the area reverts to the Moabites (Isa. 15:2; Jer. 48:1, 22). For "Sibmah" (Num. 32:38) cf. v. 3, Sebam.

The Manassite "Machir" (v. 39) clan settled in northern Gilead and Bashan ("Sons of Machir," v. 39; or "Machirites," 26:29). "Havvoth-jair" (32:41; "towns of Jair," Josh. 13:30; "villages of Jair," 1 Kings 4:13) are somewhere in northern Gilead, near the Yarmouk River. The Jair clan, descendants of Machir, has twenty-three cities in Gilead (1 Chron. 2:21–22). It settles in Bashan as far north as Mount Hermon (Deut. 3:14; 1 Kings 4:13), where it has sixty cities (Deut. 3:4; Josh. 13:30; 1 Kings 4:13). "Nobah" (Num. 32:42) captures "Kenath" and renames the city after himself, located 55 miles (90 km) east of the Sea of Galilee. In Gideon's day Midianites lived in the vicinity of Nobah (Judg. 8:11). With Zelophehad and others (Num. 27:1), Jair and Nobah are Machirite sons of Manasseh.

In summary, the inheritances of Reuben and Gad lie between the Arnon and Jabbok gorges, including for Gad the southern half of Gilead (Deut. 3:12, 16) and

---

240 ANET, 320–321.
241 Israel's first fielded army in Canaan was 40,000 men (Josh. 4:13), a fraction of the total conscription (601,730; Num. 26:51). Even if 40,000 refers to soldiers from Gad, Reuben, and half of Manasseh (Josh. 4:12), the figure would represent about a third of their combined conscription (26:7, 18, 34).
242 Possibly Qaryat el-Mekhaiyet, 9 miles (15 km) east of the Dead Sea (Rasmussen, *Zondervan Atlas*, 242). De Vaulx (*Les Nombres*, 366) notes that the cities of Reuben, located on a plateau, encircle Heshbon in a diameter of 15 miles (25 km).

the Arabah east of the Jordan. The Reubenites receive most of the territory stretching from the Arnon to Heshbon, the Moabite tableland, or *mishor*.[243] At some point the Gadite cities Dibon and Aroer (Num. 32:34) became Reubenite cities (Josh. 13:16–17). Conversely, some cities allotted to Reuben appear in Gad's territory, which suggests Reuben is ultimately integrated into Gad, much like Simeon's assimilation into Judah.[244] Gad's inheritance stretches from Heshbon in the south to Machanaim on the Jabbok and from east of Rabbah (Amman) to the Jordan, including the greater part of the eastern Jordan Valley (Josh. 13:25–27). Half the tribe of Manasseh inherits the land between the Jabbok and the Yarmouk, including the northern half of Gilead and Bashan (Deut. 3:13–16; Josh. 17:1). Bashan extends from the Yarmouk, ascending east of the Sea of Galilee to Mount Hermon in the north.

Response

The parallels with this chapter and the account of Lot are striking. Based on herding interests, Lot chose the Jordan Valley, east of the Jordan River, as it was well watered, with grass for livestock (Gen. 13:7, 10–11). Abram had proposed that Lot go to either the left or the right (Gen. 13:9), that is, when facing east, to go either north or south in the central mountain range in Canaan. Instead Lot "saw" (Gen. 13:10), as Reuben and Gad "saw" (Num. 32:1), that land to the east was good for livestock. Lot separated from Abram (Gen. 13:11) and settled outside of Canaan on the other side of the Jordan. Reuben and Gad (and half of Manasseh) also choose to settle outside Canaan on the other side of the Jordan. The short- and long-term results were disastrous for Lot's family and for the people of God, especially the outcome of his daughters' incest with him: the Moabites and the Ammonites (Gen. 19:36–38), the very people whose territories are now in Israelite possession. Similarly, the Transjordan tribes will pay dearly for their choice by the resurgence of the Midianites, Moabites, and Ammonites—as witnessed by both the former and the latter prophets (e.g., Josh. 24:9; Judg. 6:1; 11:27; 2 Kings 10:33; Isa. 11:14). Moreover, as Lot was taken captive by Mesopotamian kings (Gen. 14:12), these are the first tribes to suffer Assyrian deportation (1 Chron. 5:25; cf. 2 Kings 15:29).

Calvin labels the Gadite and Reubenite request to inherit in Transjordan a pursuit of self-interest to the injury of others. He believes they sin against the rule of love, which directs us not to seek our own interests (1 Cor. 10:24). By transgressing the limits of the Promised Land they "disunite themselves from the body of the Church, as if they desired to be emancipated from God. Hence ought we to be the more on our guard, lest we should go astray after our own lusts."[245] Bush cites an earlier commentator for whom "these two tribes were too much engaged in their affections to that portion of land, as Lot's mind was too much set upon the plains of Sodom."[246]

---

243 Smith, *Historical Geography of the Holy Land*, 354; Rasmussen, *Zondervan Atlas*, 55.
244 On this question cf. Noordtzij, *Numbers*, 283–284.
245 Calvin, *Commentaries on the Last Four Books of Moses*, trans. Charles William Bingham (Grand Rapids, MI: Baker, 1984), 4:280.
246 Bush, *Book of Numbers*, 452.

NUMBERS 33

33 These are the stages of the people of Israel, when they went out of the land of Egypt by their companies under the leadership of Moses and Aaron. ² Moses wrote down their starting places, stage by stage, by command of the Lord, and these are their stages according to their starting places. ³ They set out from Rameses in the first month, on the fifteenth day of the first month. On the day after the Passover, the people of Israel went out triumphantly in the sight of all the Egyptians, ⁴ while the Egyptians were burying all their firstborn, whom the Lord had struck down among them. On their gods also the Lord executed judgments.

⁵ So the people of Israel set out from Rameses and camped at Succoth. ⁶ And they set out from Succoth and camped at Etham, which is on the edge of the wilderness. ⁷ And they set out from Etham and turned back to Pi-hahiroth, which is east of Baal-zephon, and they camped before Migdol. ⁸ And they set out from before Hahiroth¹ and passed through the midst of the sea into the wilderness, and they went a three days' journey in the wilderness of Etham and camped at Marah. ⁹ And they set out from Marah and came to Elim; at Elim there were twelve springs of water and seventy palm trees, and they camped there. ¹⁰ And they set out from Elim and camped by the Red Sea. ¹¹ And they set out from the Red Sea and camped in the wilderness of Sin. ¹² And they set out from the wilderness of Sin and camped at Dophkah. ¹³ And they set out from Dophkah and camped at Alush. ¹⁴ And they set out from Alush and camped at Rephidim, where there was no water for the people to drink. ¹⁵ And they set out from Rephidim and camped in the wilderness of Sinai. ¹⁶ And they set out from the wilderness of Sinai and camped at Kibroth-hattaavah. ¹⁷ And they set out from Kibroth-hattaavah and camped at Hazeroth. ¹⁸ And they set out from Hazeroth and camped at Rithmah. ¹⁹ And they set out from Rithmah and camped at Rimmon-perez. ²⁰ And they set out from Rimmon-perez and camped at Libnah. ²¹ And they set out from Libnah and camped at Rissah. ²² And they set out from Rissah and camped at Kehelathah. ²³ And they set out from Kehelathah and camped at Mount Shepher. ²⁴ And they set out from Mount Shepher and camped at Haradah. ²⁵ And they set out from Haradah and camped at Makheloth. ²⁶ And they set out from Makheloth and camped at Tahath. ²⁷ And they set out from Tahath and camped at Terah. ²⁸ And they set out from Terah and camped at Mithkah. ²⁹ And they set out from Mithkah and camped at Hashmonah. ³⁰ And they set out from Hashmonah and camped at Moseroth. ³¹ And they set out from Moseroth and camped at Bene-jaakan. ³² And they set out from Bene-jaakan and camped at Hor-haggidgad. ³³ And they set out from Hor-haggidgad and camped at Jotbathah. ³⁴ And they set out from Jotbathah and camped at Abronah. ³⁵ And they set out from Abronah and camped at Ezion-geber. ³⁶ And they set out from Ezion-geber and camped in the

wilderness of Zin (that is, Kadesh). ³⁷ And they set out from Kadesh and camped at Mount Hor, on the edge of the land of Edom.

³⁸ And Aaron the priest went up Mount Hor at the command of the LORD and died there, in the fortieth year after the people of Israel had come out of the land of Egypt, on the first day of the fifth month. ³⁹ And Aaron was 123 years old when he died on Mount Hor.

⁴⁰ And the Canaanite, the king of Arad, who lived in the Negeb in the land of Canaan, heard of the coming of the people of Israel.

⁴¹ And they set out from Mount Hor and camped at Zalmonah. ⁴² And they set out from Zalmonah and camped at Punon. ⁴³ And they set out from Punon and camped at Oboth. ⁴⁴ And they set out from Oboth and camped at Iye-abarim, in the territory of Moab. ⁴⁵ And they set out from Iyim and camped at Dibon-gad. ⁴⁶ And they set out from Dibon-gad and camped at Almon-diblathaim. ⁴⁷ And they set out from Almon-diblathaim and camped in the mountains of Abarim, before Nebo. ⁴⁸ And they set out from the mountains of Abarim and camped in the plains of Moab by the Jordan at Jericho; ⁴⁹ they camped by the Jordan from Beth-jeshimoth as far as Abel-shittim in the plains of Moab.

⁵⁰ And the LORD spoke to Moses in the plains of Moab by the Jordan at Jericho, saying, ⁵¹ "Speak to the people of Israel and say to them, When you pass over the Jordan into the land of Canaan, ⁵² then you shall drive out all the inhabitants of the land from before you and destroy all their figured stones and destroy all their metal images and demolish all their high places. ⁵³ And you shall take possession of the land and settle in it, for I have given the land to you to possess it. ⁵⁴ You shall inherit the land by lot according to your clans. To a large tribe you shall give a large inheritance, and to a small tribe you shall give a small inheritance. Wherever the lot falls for anyone, that shall be his. According to the tribes of your fathers you shall inherit. ⁵⁵ But if you do not drive out the inhabitants of the land from before you, then those of them whom you let remain shall be as barbs in your eyes and thorns in your sides, and they shall trouble you in the land where you dwell. ⁵⁶ And I will do to you as I thought to do to them."

¹ Some manuscripts and versions *Pi-hahiroth*

Section Overview

Following an introduction and overview (Num. 33:1–2), the bulk of chapter 33 traces the Israelites' itinerary from Egypt to the Transjordan plains of Moab (vv. 3–49). In between are forty encampments and thus forty-two toponyms, including the points of departure and arrival. The remainder of the chapter contains instructions on taking possession of Canaan and its apportionment to the nine-and-a-half Cisjordan tribes (vv. 50–56). The other two-and-a-half tribes took Transjordan (ch. 32). Chapter 33 is a testimony to God's faithfulness, first to his people throughout their wilderness journeys and then to his covenant promises made to their fathers to bless and give them the land of Canaan. The order of the two parts of the chapter is significant. A look back on God's guidance over the past forty years will nourish the Israelites' faith; looking ahead to life in the Promised Land will foster hope.

The combined travel narratives (Ex. 12:33–19:2; Num. 10:11–12:16; 13:26; 20:1, 12–22:1) and the stage-by-stage itinerary (33:3–49) point in the general destination of Israel's travels en route to Canaan, first from Egypt to Sinai, then from Sinai to Kadesh, and finally from Kadesh to the Transjordan. The itinerary restates the first-year date of the departure from Egypt, "on the fifteenth of the first month" (v. 3: cf. Ex. 12:2; 13:4), just after Passover. It also dates Aaron's death to the "fortieth year ... on first day of the fifth month" (Num. 33:38; cf. 20:28), the year terminating the forty-year wilderness sojourn (32:13; cf. Ex. 16:35; Num. 14:33–35).

Not all the encampments mentioned in the narratives appear in the itinerary. And many encampments in the itinerary, especially those in 33:19–35, are not found in the narratives.[247] Fourteen wilderness encampments in verses 18b–30a are nowhere else mentioned in Scripture, nor are two among the Transjordan encampments in verses 41b–47a. Only two toponyms have been identified with a high degree of certainty: Kadesh and Ezion-geber. Other posited identifications are based on an assumed direction Israel took to arrive at Mount Sinai and from there at Kadesh.[248]

Since the location of Mount Sinai is debated, the overall orientation of the Israelites' itinerary is contested. After crossing the Red Sea, did the Israelites head toward the southern Sinai Peninsula, or did they go to a central western part? Then from Mount Sinai did they head northward toward Kadesh (from the southern peninsula) or eastward (from the western side)?

Located in the southern peninsula, Jebel Musa is the long-favored traditional Mount Sinai,[249] though there is no direct biblical data to support this identification.[250] Moreover, this identification squares poorly with biblical data. For example, according to the burning bush narrative Moses was shepherding on the "west side" (Ex. 3:1; *'aḥar*, "behind") of the wilderness of Sinai when he came "to Horeb, the mountain of God" (Mount Sinai). There Moses was shepherding for his Midianite father-in-law, a people associated with the Paran wilderness (1 Kings 11:18). From a Midianite perspective, "behind" was the Egyptian side.[251] The journey from the wilderness of Sinai to the wilderness of Paran (Num. 10:11), and thus to Kadesh (13:26), was made in the direction of Seir (Deut. 1:2).[252] The guiding theophany from Sinai is poetically portrayed as the dawn's light from Seir (and the parallel

---

[247] Cf. Frank Moore Cross, *Canaanite Myth and Hebrew Epic: Essays in the History of the Religion of Israel* (Cambridge, MA: Harvard University Press), 308–311, 314, 316. Cross observed that the twelve narratives of Israel's journeys correspond to the Numbers 33 itinerary stages—six from Egypt to Rephidim, the camp before Sinai (Ex. 12:37; 13:20; 14:1–2; 15:22; 17:1), and six from Sinai to the Plains of Moab (Ex. 19:2; Num. 10:12; 20:1; 20:22; 21:10–11; 22:1). The narratives do not name all the itinerary encampments, since they are subsumed under a general designation "wilderness X"; e.g., the wilderness of Paran (10:12), which incorporates the encampments from Kibroth-hattaavah to Kadesh in the itinerary (33:16–36). Cf. Milgrom's summary of Cross's observations (*Numbers*, 498).
[248] On the twenty-five stations between the Red Sea and Ezion-geber (33:8–35) Aharoni states, "It is impossible to identify even one with certainty, and the accepted identifications are made mainly on the basis of the hypothetical line of march" (*Land of the Bible*, 198).
[249] This is the favored location in Christian tradition since the fourth century. Eusebius' *Onomasticon* suggests the proximity of both Horeb and Rephidim (the location before Sinai) to Faran (the wilderness of Paran, after Sinai), which is considered compatible with a location in the southern peninsula. The specific identification with Jebel Musa comes from the later-fourth-century *Peregrinatio Egeriae*. Cf. Davies, *Way of the Wilderness*, 32–33.
[250] Affirmed by Simons, *Geographical and Topographical Texts*, 253.
[251] Cf. N. M. Sarna, *Exodus*, JPSTC (Philadelphia: JPS, 1991), 14.
[252] "By the way of Mount Seir" (Deut. 1:2) means "By the way to Mount Seir" (Aharoni, *Land of the Bible*, 45). The "way of the land of the Philistines" (Ex. 13:17) goes from Egypt to the coastal plain of Canaan.

Mount Paran, Deut. 33:2; cf. Hab. 3:3).[253] Seir was Edomite territory west of the Arabah, on the southern border of Canaan/Judah (Num. 34:3; cf. comment on 14:20–25 [at v. 25]; cf. Deut. 1:44; Josh. 15:1).[254] The guiding theophany-sunrise assumes an eastern orientation from Sinai. The first Israelite camp after Sinai was "on the east side toward the sunrise" (Num. 2:3, 9).

These factors, among others, suggest that Mount Sinai is in the central western peninsula opposite Seir in the central eastern peninsula. Jebel Sin Bisher in that region is considered a prime candidate for Mount Sinai, as has been long advocated by M. Har-El.[255] Jacob Milgrom agrees: "The identification of Sinai with Jebel Sin Bisher ... has much to commend it."[256]

According to the narratives, after leaving Mount Sinai Israel encamped at Hazeroth before arriving at Kadesh (Num. 11:35; 12:16; 13:26). Kadesh is not mentioned in the itinerary after Hazeroth (33:18a). Kadesh does appear in verse 36b after eighteen other encampments (vv. 18b–36a). However, Kadesh in verse 36 corresponds to Israel's presence there at the *end* of the wilderness wanderings (20:1; Deut. 2:14), not to its arrival there from Mount Sinai (Num. 13:26; 14:25; 32:28; Deut. 1:2, 19; 9:23; Josh. 14:7). The itinerary after Kadesh in Numbers 33:36b to the plains of Moab corresponds to the Transjordan narrative encampment stages, the last of the journey. Thus the preceding list of encampments in verses 18b–36a are those of the thirty-eight-year wilderness sojourn.[257]

The suggestion made here is that Kadesh's place in the itinerary between Hazeroth and Rithmah (v. 18) is tacitly understood, just as Mount Sinai is, although it too is unmentioned. In the Outline [Kadesh] refers to its presumed position in the itinerary after Hazeroth (v. 18).[258] The reasons for which Kadesh is not included there will be suggested in the comments.

Section Outline

III. Instructions beyond the Jordan at Jericho for the Generation Soon to Enter Canaan (26:1–36:13) ...

    H. The Forty-Year Itinerary and Land Inheritance Instructions (33:1–56)

        1. From Egypt to Sinai (33:1–15)

        2. From Sinai to [Kadesh] (33:16–18a)

---

253 Cf. Samuel R. Driver, *Deuteronomy*, 3rd ed., ICC (1901; Edinburgh: T&T Clark, 1973), 390. Driver rightly says this theophany describes the Lord's guidance on the journey from Sinai to Canaan. Some identify Mount Paran with Mount Mugrah (2,000 feet; 620 m) 30 miles (50 km) south of 'Ain Kadesh; others suggest the range on mountains on the eastern side of the peninsula dropping down to the western side of the Gulf of Elath.
254 Keil, "Fifth Book of Moses," in *Pentateuch*, 281. Baly, *Geography of the Bible*, 12. Har-El, *Sinai Journeys*, 337.
255 Har-El is Professor Emeritus of Historical Geography at Tel-Aviv University. For a summary of his research cf. "Sinai," *Encyclopaedia Miqra'ith*, vol. 5 (Jerusalem: Mosad Bialik, 1964–), cols. 1021–1022 [Hebrew]; Har-El, *Sinai Journeys*, 342–359, 415–431.
256 *Numbers*, 280. Others who support this identification include Wenham, *Numbers*, 224–227; Rasmussen, *Zondervan Atlas*, 90–91, 252; Cole, *Numbers*, 68–69, 523–524.
257 For Keil that Numbers 33:36 refers to Israel's second arrival at Kadesh, as in 20:1, is beyond doubt. He maintains that the encampments listed in verses 19 [from Rithmah]–36 are in the thirty-eight years of punishment in the wilderness ("Fourth Book of Moses," 242–244). Har-El places these encampments in the thirty-eight years of wandering, as does Wenham (*Numbers*, 228). On Israel's presence at Kadesh at the beginning and/or end of the wilderness period cf. Milgrom, *Numbers*, 164, 281.
258 Milgrom's list has "[Paran]" after Hazeroth (*Numbers*, 499).

3. From [Kadesh] to Kadesh (33:18b–36)
4. From Kadesh to the Jordan at Jericho (33:37–49)
5. Instructions on Taking Possession of Canaan (33:50–56)

Comment

33:1–15 Verses 1–2 introduce and summarize the itinerary. "Stages" (Hb. *massaʿ*; v. 1) can refer to treks from one encampment to another or to larger journeys involving several encampments, as from the wilderness of Sin to the wilderness of Sinai (Ex. 17:1; cf. Ex. 19:1–2) or from the wilderness of Sinai to the wilderness of Paran (Num. 10:12). "Their companies" (33:1) refers to military units (1:3). There were four camps, each comprising three tribal companies in marching formation, as described in chapter 2. Unless on mission, the soldiers lived and journeyed with their families. The order of march was described in 10:11–28.

On "Moses wrote down" (33:2) cf. Introduction: Author. He also "wrote down" all the words of the law (Ex. 24:4; Deut. 31:9). Other Pentateuchal passages mention Moses' authorship (Ex. 17:14; 34:28; Deut. 31:22, 24).

Each departure of Israel is stated as "They set out from" (*nasaʿ*; e.g., Num. 33:6) "by command [or "mouth"] of the LORD" (v. 2; cf. 9:18; 10:13; 13:3). The command was given by the cloud's lifting from the tabernacle (9:17–18, 20). The silver trumpets signaled the order in which they set out (10:5–6).

Numbers 33:3–4 recall the circumstantial setting of the itinerary within Egypt. Israel left Rameses in the first month on the fifteenth day, the day after the Passover. Moreover, they went out "triumphantly" (*beyad ramah*), or "defiantly," like ones shaking a fist, the same expression for "high handed" sins (15:30). This was "while the Egyptians were burying all their firstborn . . . [when] on their gods, also the LORD executed judgments." Against the God of Israel, Egypt's gods were utterly unable to defend the land or its inhabitants (cf. 2 Kings 17:26).

The ensuing itinerary (Num. 33:5–49) is punctuated by two verbs: "set out" and "camped." The itinerary pattern is well attested in ancient Near Eastern documents from the early second millennium and later (i.e., "They set out from A and camped at B; they set out from B and camped at C"[259]). Historical or geographical allusions are joined to some journeys or encampments (vv. 6, 7, 9, 14, 36, 37, 38–39, 40).

Among "Rameses . . . Succoth . . . Etham . . . Pi-hahiroth . . . Baal-zephon . . . Migdol" (vv. 5–7), only the (general) locations of the first two sites are known.[260] They all probably lay in a southeasterly direction toward Lake Timsah, then southward toward the Bitter Lakes, and finally to the Gulf of Suez (Red Sea).

The land of Rameses, or the land of Goshen, was where Jacob and his family had settled (Gen. 47:4, 11, 27). After assembling in Goshen (Ex. 8:22) as a rallying point, Israel's movement was toward "Etham" on the "edge of the wilderness" (Num. 33:6), that is, the western side of the "wilderness of Etham" (v. 8), also called

---

[259] G. I. Davies, "The Wilderness Itineraries," *TynBul* 25 (1974): 46–81; Milgrom, *Numbers*, 497–498.
[260] K. A. Kitchen, "Exodus, The," *ABD* 2:700–708 (esp. 703–704, 705–706). For Rameses and Succoth he posits the area of Khataʿana-Qantir-Tell-Dabʿa and Tell el-Maskhuta, respectively; cf. Davies, *Way of the Wilderness*, 75.

the "wilderness of Shur" (Ex. 15:22). Etham and Shur mean "wall" in Egyptian and Hebrew, respectively. "Etham/Shur" and "Migdol" (Num. 33:7 "fort/watchtower") were part of a line of defenses to deter migrant infiltration from the wilderness routes leading to Egypt's border.[261] From Kadesh the "way to Shur" went to Beersheba, then to Egypt (cf. Gen. 16:7, 14; 20:1; 1 Sam. 15:7). This wilderness road entered Egypt at Lake Timsah. This important juncture would have been fortified (at Etham?).

But from Etham the Israelites turned back (Num. 33:7) at the Lord's command (Ex. 14:1) to Pi [house of]-hahiroth, east of Baal-zephon, camping "before" Migdol (Num. 33:7).[262] This *volte face* was intended to make Pharaoh believe the Israelites were trapped (Ex. 14:3), not only by the wilderness but also by the sea. "From before" (Pi) Hahiroth they "passed through the midst of the sea" (Num. 33:8). The crossing of "the sea" (v. 10) is narrated and celebrated in Exodus 14:15–15:21. "Red" (Ex. 15:22) translates the LXX (*erythras*) rather than the Hebrew "reeds/rushes" (*suph*, cf. Ex. 2:3; but cf. discussion on Num. 33:10 below, "Camped by the Red Sea"). If no reeds grow in saltwater, this would rule out not only the Gulf of Suez as the crossing point but also the brackish lakes to the north. But *suph* also refers to seaweed kelp (Jonah 2:5). Some suggest the Israelites crossed at some point along the Bitter Lakes.[263] According to Isaiah they crossed the "tongue of the Sea of Egypt" (Isa. 11:15), which apparently describes a promontory of the Red Sea.[264]

After a three days' journey in the wilderness of Etham/Shur the Israelites reached Marah (Num. 33:8; cf. Ex. 15:22). The name was coined because the water was "bitter" (*marah*, "brackish"). Marah is possibly Bir el-Murrah ("the bitter well"), almost 25 miles (40 km) from the Bitter Lakes and 10 miles (16 km) east of Suez, in west-central Sinai.[265] The travel time fits the location, given the large number of people, including the aged and small children, livestock, and loaded wagons (cf. discussion on Num. 33:15; comment on 33:16–18a, "wilderness of Sinai"). There is no water source between the Bitter Lakes and Bir el-Murrah. They continued to "Elim," where there were "twelve springs" and "seventy palm trees" (Ex. 15:27; Num. 33:9). Twelve springs and a palm grove have been found at Ayin Musa ("Moses' spring"), 7.5 miles (12 km) south of Bir el-Murrah or 9 miles (14 km) southeast of Suez.[266]

Israel then "camped by the Red Sea" (Num. 33:10), that is, on the eastern side of the Gulf of Suez,[267] the western flank of the Sinai Peninsula. "Red Sea" (*yam suph*; cf. discussion on v. 8 above) also refers to the Gulf of Aqaba, the peninsula's eastern flank (Num. 14:25; 21:4; 1 Kings 9:26). *Suph* may be analogous to the Mishnaic

---

[261] Aharoni, *Land of the Bible*, 196. Rasmussen observes, "Etham and Migdol could be any one of a number of Egyptian forts located near the present-day Suez Canal" (*Zondervan Atlas*, 89).
[262] On these three locations cf. Davies, *Way of the Wilderness*, 81–82.
[263] Kitchen, "Exodus," 703: "part of the Bitter Lakes." Cf. S. R. Driver, *Exodus*, Cambridge Bible for Schools and Colleges (Cambridge: Cambridge University Press, 1911), 111. Driver suggested the possibility that there may have been a shallow extension of the Red Sea as far north as Lake Timsah. Reeds were found in areas where salt and freshwater mix.
[264] Cf. "tongue" (*lashon*) of the Dead Sea, referring to its extremities (Josh. 15:2; 18:19).
[265] Har-El, *Sinai Journeys*, 354–355 Rasmussen, *Zondervan Atlas*, 244.
[266] Har-El, *Sinai Journeys*, 355–356; Rasmussen, *Zondervan Atlas*, 233.
[267] Davies, *Way of the Wilderness*, 83.

Hebrew word for "shore" (*soph*; Yevamot 16:4) or to modern Hebrew "end/extremity" (*soph*), referring to the seas on the extremities of the southern peninsula.[268]

The "wilderness of Sin" (Num. 33:11) subsumes the following three encampments. "Dophkah" and "Alush" (vv. 12–14) are unmentioned in the narrative (Ex. 17:1). "Rephidim" (Num. 33:14–15) is associated with Horeb in Exodus 17, where the Massah-Meribah incident took place (vv. 1, 6–7; cf. Num. 20:2–13).[269] Exodus 16:1 reports the Israelites then came to "the wilderness of Sin, which is between Elim and Sinai, on the fifteenth day of the second month after they had departed from the land of Egypt," one month after the exodus. "After they had departed" is an infinitive (*letse'tam*) meaning "from their departing," that is from Rameses, the starting point. In other words, from Rameses their arrival in the wilderness of Sin took a month.

The "wilderness of Sinai" (Num. 33:15, 16) is the twelfth location and the eighth encampment in the itinerary (vv. 8–15). Mount Sinai is mentioned twice in Numbers (3:1; 28:6) but not in the itinerary. Naming the wilderness of Sinai as the arrival and departure point (Ex. 12:2; Num. 10:12) suggests the Israelites were spread out during that year, with the mountain and the tabernacle as rallying points.

If Mount Sinai is identified with Jebel Sin Bisher on the central western side of the peninsula, as suggested (cf. Section Overview and below), to approach this mountain the Israelites would have turned eastward to pass through the mountains at the Wadi Suder valley. The Suder pass leads to the most important crossroads in the peninsula.[270] Directly to the east, 185 miles (300 km) from the western Red Sea, lay Elath and Ezion-geber on the eastern Red Sea.

Added to the adduced factors in support of identifying Jebel Sin Bisher with Mount Sinai (cf. Section Overview) are the following considerations.[271] The proximity of Mount Sinai to Egypt is reflected in the comings and goings of Moses—and also his wife and children—and of Aaron (Ex. 4:20, 27, 29; 18:5–6; cf. Num. 10:30, "I will depart to my own land" on the proximity of Midian and Mount Sinai). Jebel Sin Bisher is 30 miles (50 km) from the northern tip of the Red Sea and 45 miles (75 km) from the southern end of the Bitter Lakes.[272] The implied proximity and relative ease of travel both point to a Mount Sinai location in the western peninsula rather than in the southern peninsula. Jebel Musa is about 155 miles (250 km) from the northern Red Sea.

The central Sinai route would also be ideal for their intermediary Kadesh destination near the southern border of Canaan. The route to Jebel Musa goes in the opposite direction from Canaan. The most direct northerly route from Egypt

---

268 G. I. Davies expresses a similar view (ibid., 74).
269 Dophkah, Alush, and Rephidim have not been identified (ibid., 84).
270 Har-El believes the ancient Darb el-Hajj (Pilgrims' Route from Egypt to Elath, then to Medina and Mecca) linking the northern extremities of the two arms of both Red Seas had its entry to the wilderness at the Suder valley (*Sinai Journeys*, 357 [map], 359, 418). This road follows the natural geographical division between the northern and southern peninsula. Together with the way to the land of the Philistines (Ex. 13:17) and the way to Shur (Gen. 16:7), this is the third main route in the Sinai Peninsula.
271 Wenham reiterates the difficulties of identifying Mount Sinai with Jebel Musa and counters the main objections to Sin Bisher (*Numbers*, 225–227); cf. Milgrom, *Numbers*, 280.
272 Har-El, *Sinai Journeys*, 420, 424.

to Canaan was avoided by the Israelites because of the military opposition they would have encountered there (Ex. 13:17). It is unlikely the Israelites would have gone as far from Canaan as possible and to a part of the peninsula in which copper and turquoise mines were heavily guarded by Egyptian forces.[273]

Jebel Sin Bisher accords with the three-day travel time between Egypt and Mount Sinai (Ex. 3:18; 5:3; 8:27), that is, the travel time for unburdened travelers on foot (such as Moses and Aaron, mentioned above), camel caravans (Isa. 30:6), or marching armies.[274] It obviously took longer for the Israelites, driving livestock, heavily laden beasts of burden, and donkey- and oxen-drawn wagons while assisting children and the aged. They would have averaged 6–8 miles (10–13 km) per day.[275] After crossing the sea, it took them three days to arrive at Marah (cf. Num. 33:8). They arrived in the Sin wilderness a month after the exodus (Ex. 16:1) and at Sinai by the third month (Ex. 19:1–2), or about forty days after the exodus. At 6 miles (10 km) per day it would have taken the Israelites forty consecutive days of travel to trek from Rameses to Jebel Musa. For Jebel Sin Bisher, it would have involved half that travel time, with as many days encamped.

At 125 miles (200 km) from Kadesh, Sin Bisher also fits into the eleven-day frame from Horeb (Deut. 1:2; cf. comment on Num. 13:1–20 [at v. 20]).[276] Given the Israelites' pace, Jebel Musa would not fit this timeframe to cover the 220 miles (350 km) from Kadesh.[277] What is more, the Suder Valley-Sin Bisher location suits the need for plentiful potable water and pasturage for the year the Israelites spent at Mount Sinai. When Moses heard God's calling from the burning bush, he was tending a flock at Horeb (Ex. 3:1) in the wilderness of Mount Sinai (Acts 7:30). The Israelites left Egypt with "flocks and herds" (Ex. 12:38), which they pastured at Mount Sinai (Ex. 34:3; cf. Num. 3:41, 45; 7:87–88). Suder Valley has abundant water sources and rich pastures.[278] At Horeb there was a brook (*nahal*; Deut. 9:21; cf. Ex. 17:6; Ps. 68:8–9). The overall region, the north-west plateau the of the et-Tih desert, affords plentiful pastureland in altitudes of 2,600 feet (800 m), including cultivable land on the slopes and valleys and ample water supply.[279] The mountainous apex of the Sinai Peninsula, with granite peaks and profound crags, lacks such lands or water for cattle-raisers and cultivators.

In addition, Scripture indicates that Mount Sinai could not have been too high nor too difficult to ascend. In a short period of time, the aged Moses ascended

---

[273] Ibid., 223; Wenham, "Numbers," OTG (Sheffield: Sheffield Academic, 1997), 48.
[274] Har-El considers 15 miles (25 km) per day the rate for pedestrians or armies (*Sinai Journeys*, 424). Cf. B. J. Beitzel, *The Moody Atlas of Bible Lands* (Chicago, IL: Moody, 1985), 91. Beitzel gives 20–23 miles (32–37 km) as the maximum caravan travel distance per day indicated in ancient itinerary texts.
[275] Har-El, *Sinai Journeys*, 195. The Israelites also had ox-drawn wagons (Num. 7:7–8), which could cover 9 miles (14 km) per day (as compared to a mule-drawn wagon, which could cover 19 miles [31 km], and a horse-drawn wagon, 32 miles [51 km] per day). Cf. Richard A. Gabriel, *Soldiers' Lives through History: The Ancient World* (Westport, CT: Greenwood, 2007), 102.
[276] Har-El, *Sinai Journeys*, 425. Nineteenth- and twentieth-century explorers, E. Robinson, J. Rowlands, and F. M. Abel, made the journey from Jebel Musa to Kadesh in eleven days; Moshe Weinfeld, *Deuteronomy 1—11*, AYB 5 (New York: Doubleday, 1991), 127. But, unlike the Israelites, these explorers traveled unimpeded.
[277] Har-El, *Sinai Journeys*, 196.
[278] Ibid., 361.
[279] The convergence of major routes in the Suder valley, the supply of water and pasturage, and the need to protect them explain the strong Midianite and Amalekite opposition to the Israelites (ibid., 358–359).

and descended four times (Ex. 19:3, 14, 20, 25; 32:15, 30–31; 34:4, 29), once with Aaron, his sons, and seventy elders (Ex. 24:9, 18). Moses and the people below heard the voice of God (Ex. 19:9, 17, 19; Deut. 4:12). Sin Bisher rises 1,000 feet (300 m) above its surroundings, a height which fits these climbs.[280] The altitude of Jebel Musa is 7,500 feet (2,300 m), however, which would seem to preclude such climbs.

Lastly, after the departure from Sinai, travel surfaces had to be level to transport the tabernacle on oxen-drawn wagons (Num. 7:3).[281] The gold, silver, and bronze used in the construction of the tabernacle and its accoutrements weighed about 15,000 pounds (6,800 kg), or 7.5 tons (6.8 metric tons; cf. Ex. 38:24–29). Added to this was the weight of all the other materials, such as wood, skins, and fabrics. To travel to Kadesh from the southern peninsula, with its jagged granite peaks, some reaching over 8,600 feet (2,600 m), and extremely deep craggy valleys not leading in one direction, stretches the imagination.[282] The Wadi Suder route leading from Sin Bisher would have afforded the travel conditions necessary for the Israelites.

In summary, biblical data and other factors support a central-western peninsula location for Mount Sinai and an eastern movement from Mount Sinai to Kadesh. Jebel Sin Bisher and its location correspond to the data. Conversely, there is no direct evidence that the Israelites traveled to the southern peninsula and from there northward to Kadesh. Several factors mentioned above would exclude such possibilities.

33:16–18a "By stages" includes the encampments on the way to Kadesh, "Kibroth-hattaavah . . . Hazeroth" (Num. 33:16–17; cf. 11:34–35). Both are unidentified. Those who posit a southern Mount Sinai generally identify Hazeroth with Ain/Wadi Hudeirat, about 40 miles (65 km) northeast of Jebel Musa in the mountains west of the Gulf of Aqaba.[283] According to the narratives, after Hazeroth the Israelites encamped in the wilderness of Paran (12:16). Neither the wilderness of Paran nor Kadesh, in the Paran wilderness (13:26), are mentioned in the itinerary where expected after Hazeroth (33:18).[284]

It may be that the Israelite's encampment at Kadesh was left blank in the itinerary to make a theological point. The great rebellion took place there

---

[280] Ibid., 26, 420–425. He adds that "Sin" preserves the name Sinai and "Bisher" the giving of the law (b-s-r, "promulgate, announce, proclaim"; 421). Cf. *bsr* in biblical Hebrew ("carry news," 2 Sam. 18:20; "good news," 1 Kings 1:42).
[281] Gabriel states that Philip of Macedon removed oxcarts from his army, given their slowness and inability to move over rough terrain (*Soldiers' Lives through History*, 102).
[282] Beitzel opines that from Mount Sinai in the southern peninsula the Israelites would have crossed the mountains on the eastern edge of the desert, descended into the Arabah, and headed north along the left bank of Gulf of Aqaba "with comparative ease" (*Moody Atlas*, 93). However, Har-El states the mountains along the western side of the Gulf of Aqaba descend so steeply that the coastal plain is cut off; in several places not even a pedestrian can continue (*Sinai Journeys*, 26, 35). He also states that steep gradient of the mountains that descend from the southern mountains prevent the passage of caravans along the coast of the gulf (14, 413); cf. Rasmussen, *Zondervan Atlas*, 60.
[283] Davies, *Way of the Wilderness*, 85. According to Simons there is no evidence of suitable localities or oases in the eastern part of et-Tih desert for Hazeroth (*Geographical and Topographical Texts*, 256).
[284] As noted, Milgrom puts "[Paran]" after Hazeroth (*Numbers*, 499). Cross considers that "wilderness of Paran" may have dropped out between Hazeroth and Rithmah by haplography (*Canaanite Myth and Hebrew Epic*, 315n4); cf. Num. 12:16: "And afterward the people journeyed from Hazeroth, and camped in the wilderness of Paran."

(Numbers 13–14). Similarly, Mount Sinai is not named, where the golden calf incident occurred (Exodus 32). These are the two darkest moments in the wilderness journey—indeed, in the revelation history of Israel. On each occasion God threatened the people's destruction.[285] The two are conspicuous by their absence. Omitting them appears intentional, suggesting that what occurred there, though not forgotten, was forgiven (Num. 14:19; cf. Ex. 32:32).

In some cases the use of figures in Numbers appears rhetorical. For example, "the land of Canaan" occurs twelve times (cf. comment on 34:1–15 [at v. 2]), as do repeatedly the names of the twelve tribes. The book contains seven lists of tribal chiefs (cf. Section Overview of Numbers 34). In chapters describing the Levites' responsibilities the key word for guard duty around the stationary tabernacle occurs ten times (cf. Section Overview of Numbers 3) and the combined terms describing their work burden seven times (cf. Section Overview of Numbers 4). The wilderness of Sinai is mentioned ten times (cf. comment on 1:1–19), as is the zone called "outside the camp" (cf. comment on 19:1–10 [at v. 3]). Mentioned seven times are the seven days required for cleansing from corpse contamination (cf. comment on 19:11–22; on the use of fourteen, ten, seven, and three in the Balaam story cf. comments on 22:1–21 [at v. 6]; 22:22–41).

As concerns Kadesh in Numbers, the figures ten and forty stand out. Kadesh is mentioned ten times (cf. comment on 13:25–33 [at v. 26]). The Lord said there that Israel had put him to the test ten times (14:22). Like the intentional limiting of the number of encampments in the itinerary to forty, forty concerning Kadesh is used rhetorically. In the narratives Kadesh is named only after the forty-day reconnaissance (13:26; cf. 14:34), even though scouts had been sent from there (32:8). Kadesh is where the forty-year judgment was decreed (14:33–34). After judgment came a season of grace. The departure from Kadesh (20:22), corresponding to the fortieth year (33:37), signaled a new beginning for the generation that would settle in Canaan. Then Kadesh appears in the itinerary (33:36).

33:18b–36 According to the Numbers narratives the Israelites were at Kadesh before the thirty-eight years of wilderness wanderings (13:26; 32:8; cf. Josh. 14:7) and left Kadesh at the end of that period in the direction of Transjordan (Num. 20:14, 22; cf. 33:36b; Deut. 2:14).

As mentioned in the Section Overview, the eighteen encampments in Numbers 33:18b–36a are those from the thirty-eight years of the wilderness sojourn. Apart from "Ezion-geber" (v. 36a), none has been identified with any degree of certainty.[286] They are probably located somewhere in the northern half of eastern Sinai and in the western Negeb highlands.[287] Those who believe they lie somewhere is the southeastern half between Jebel Musa and Ezion-geber fare no better in identifying them.[288]

---

[285] Nor is Massah, Meribah, or Taberah mentioned—all notorious places of uprisings.
[286] For a list of some suggested identifications cf. Davies, *Way of the Wilderness*, 88.
[287] Rasmussen, *Zondervan Atlas*, 91.
[288] Simons notes that the encampments in 33:16–36 "hardly lend themselves to even a tentative identification" (*Geographical and Topographical Texts*, 254).

"Rithmah" (v. 18) is the first encampment after the posited Kadesh.[289] "Hashmonah" (v. 29), if identified with Heshmon listed among the southernmost settlements of Judah (Josh. 15:27), is in the Negeb highlands.[290] "Bene-jaakan" (Num. 33:31) is also called "Beeroth ["wells of"] Bene[sons of]-jaakan" (Deut. 10:6). It was named after the Jaakan Seir/Horite clan, which points to an encampment near Seir west of the Arabah (1 Chron. 1:42; cf. Gen. 36:27–31).[291] "Jotbathah" (Num. 33:33) is qualified as "a land with brooks of water" (Deut. 10:7) which suited the needs of the Israelites during the wilderness sojourn, especially given their vast cattle holdings. "Ezion-geber" (Num. 33:35), a port associated with Elath (Deut. 2:8; 1 Kings 9:26), is located on or near the northern end of the oriental Red Sea.[292] The distance of several days march between Ezion-geber and Kadesh (Num. 33:36; 50 miles [80 km]) allows for unmentioned encampments between them (cf. v. 31).

The "wilderness of Zin (that is, Kadesh)" (v. 36) extends to the southern limit of Canaan and Judah, contiguous with Edom (cf. comment on 34:1–15 [at v. 3]). As in the Numbers narratives, the Zin wilderness is mentioned in the itinerary immediately before Israel's departure from Kadesh (33:37; cf. 20:1, 22) and its heading northward in the Negeb to Arad (33:40; cf. 21:1–3). Similarly, Israel's arrival at Kadesh from Sinai is associated with the "wilderness of Paran" (10:12; 12:16; 13:3, 26).

The location of Kadesh has been established, the only sure identification of all the encampments west of the Arabah. Ein Qadeis and Ein Qudeirat, 6 miles (10 km) to the north and northwest, are identified with Kadesh and Kadesh-barnea, respectively (32:8; cf. comment on 34:1–15 [at v. 4]).[293] The Kadesh region lies where the western Negeb highlands sink down to undulating terrain stretching to the Wadi El-Arish.

33:37–49 The remainder of the itinerary stages and the travel narratives are nearly parallel. Israel set out from Kadesh (33:37; cf. 21:22). It camped at Mount Hor, where "Aaron . . . died" (33:37–39; cf. 20:28). The people went north in the direction of Arad, where they met armed resistance in the Negeb, in the land of Canaan (33:40; cf. 21:1). They crossed the Arabah south of the Dead Sea (33:42–44; cf. 21:10–12), traversed Moab (33:44–47; cf. 21:13, 16, 18–20), and ultimately arrived in the plains of Moab, by the Jordan at Jericho (33:48–49; cf. 21:21–35).

---

289 Keil emphasizes the linguistic similarity with Abu Rithmat, a wadi not far to the south of Kadesh, citing the nineteenth-century Bible scholar and explorer E. Robinson, who described there "a wide plain with shrubs and *retem* [i.e., broom]" ("Fourth Book of Moses," 243).
290 Davies, *Way of the Wilderness*, 87. Simons identifies Hashmonah with Azmon (Num. 34:4, 5; Josh. 15:4) on Judah's southern border (*Geographical and Topographical*, 256).
291 Gray, *Numbers*, 447; Noordtzij, *Numbers*, 290.
292 Ezion-geber is traditionally located at Tell el-Kheleifeh. An alternative site is the modern Gezirat al-Fauran, 15 miles (24 km) south-southwest from Tell el-Kheleifeh (Cole, *Numbers*, 525). Davies believes both identifications fit biblical data "tolerably well" (*Way of the Wilderness*, 86). Encampment in the Arabah may be due to seasonal factors. Cf. G. A. Smith, *Deuteronomy*, Cambridge Bible for Schools and Colleges (Cambridge: Cambridge University Press, 1918), 31. Smith observed nomadic Arabs wintering there in the warmth.
293 About Kadesh and Ein Qadeis, Har-El writes, "It is interesting to note that this is the only place mentioned in connection with the wanderings of the Children of Israel where there is a correlation between the place-name, meaning, and geographical location" (*Sinai Journeys*, 334).

"Mount Hor" (33:37, 41) is probably located near the head of the Zin Valley (cf. 20:23). The Israelites left the Negeb highlands for the Arabah no doubt by descending the Nahal Zin (cf. 21:4).[294]

The chronological notice of Aaron's death—"in the fortieth year after the people of Israel had come out of the land of Egypt, on the first day of the fifth month" (33:38; cf. 20:29)—is a tribute to this first high priest. That same year marked the end of the forty-year judgment pronounced on the exodus generation (14:34; 32:13).

"Zalmonah" and "Oboth" (33:41, 43) are probably in the western Arabah near the foot of Nahal Zin (cf. 21:10, 11). "Punon" (33:42) is traditionally identified with Feinan, on the eastern border of the Arabah, 32 miles (50 km) south-southeast of the Dead Sea and north of Petra in Edom.[295] Given the copper mining and smelting near Feinan at Khirbet en-Nahas ("serpent"), the site is often linked to the bronze serpent incident (21:5–9). The narrative trajectory perhaps suggests the incident occurred in the Arabah (cf. 21:4, 10).[296] "Iye-abarim" (33:44; cf. comment on 21:4–11) is also called "Iyim" (33:45).

To access Transjordan the Israelites ascended the Zered Valley (cf. comment on 21:12–20; Deut. 2:13–14), the border between Edom and Moab.[297] Their going around Edom involved the Edomite territory west of the Arabah (cf. Num. 20:21). Three Transjordan encampments included in the narratives—Mattanah, Nahaliel, and Bamoth (21:19)—are not in the itinerary. "Dibon-gad" (33:45) is so named because it was rebuilt by Gad (32:34). Dibon (cf. 21:30) was originally allotted to Reuben (32:3). "Almon-diblathaim" (33:46) is possibly located 21 miles (34 km) southeast of Amman.[298] Nebo was among the Mountains of Abarim (v. 47; cf. 21:11; 27:12; cf. Deut. 32:49). "Abarim" ("across") may describe the imposing mountain range in Moab as viewed from Cisjordan.

"Jericho" (Num. 33:48), the "City of Palms" (Judg. 3:13), is located 6 miles (10 km) west of the Jordan and 10 miles (16 km) north-northwest of the Dead Sea.[299] "Beth-jeshimoth" (cf. Num. 21:20), part of the Reubenites' inheritance (Josh. 13:20), is north-northeast of "Abel-shittim" (Num. 33:49, "Meadow of Acacias"; cf. 25:1, "Shittim"), the latter being 8 miles (13 km) north-northeast of the Dead Sea.[300] The 11 miles (18 km) separating the two locations is an indication of the vast spread of the Israelite camps.

After completing this travelogue, the generation that would possess Canaan is poised to cross the Jordan.

---

[294] Aharoni supposes they descended Wadi Fuqrah (Nahal Zin; *Land of the Bible*, 55); cf. Davies, *Way of the Wilderness*, 90.
[295] Simons locates Oboth and Punon in the western and eastern Arabah south of the Dead Sea, the latter at Feinan, which preserves the name (*Geographical and Topographical Texts*, 259–260). Aharoni links Punon with Feinan (*Land of the Bible*, 202, 440).
[296] Aharoni, *Land of the Bible*, 204.
[297] Har-El affirms that Israel reached Moab via the Arabah, Punon, and the Zered Valley on Edom's northern border (*Sinai Journeys*, 430).
[298] Possibly, Khirbet Deleilat esh-Sherqiyeh. Cf. Aharoni, *Land of the Bible*, 430; Rasmussen, *Zondervan Atlas*, 225.
[299] Tel es-Sultan (Rasmussen, *Zondervan Atlas*, 240). Jericho dates to the eighth millennium BC (Aharoni, *Land of the Bible*, 5).
[300] Tel el-Azeimeh and Tel el-Hammam, respectively (Aharoni, *Land of the Bible*, 432, 429; Rasmussen, *Zondervan Atlas*, 229, 224).

33:50–56 From the plains of Moab (33:50) the Lord gives Moses instructions on how the Israelites should—after crossing the Jordan into the land of Canaan (v. 51)—deal with the inhabitants (vv. 52–53) and allot the land (v. 54). He warns them of what will happen if they fail to obey (vv. 55–56). Their crossing of the Jordan occurs in the spring, just before Passover (Josh. 5:10), when the water level is at its peak. Springtime is also the time kings typically make war (2 Sam. 11:1; 1 Kings 20:22; 2 Kings 13:20).

To take possession of their inheritance the Israelites must do two things. First, they should "drive out" (Hb. *yarash*; Num. 33:52, 55), or "dispossess" (as the verb is translated in 21:32; 32:39), the inhabitants.[301] The method of doing so is not stated. A typical way is to "expel/drive out" (*garash*; Ex. 23:28; Josh. 24:18; Judg. 2:3) the inhabitants. Many will flee in fear before the Israelite forces (Num. 10:35; Deut. 2:5), much as the Israelites will flee before the Philistines, abandoning to them their houses, possessions, and lands (1 Sam. 31:7). Second, the Israelites should "destroy" and "demolish" (both from *'abad*; Num. 33:52) the appurtenances of the inhabitants' idolatrous worship.[302] Leaving "images" and "high places" intact would tempt the Israelites to adapt their worship to them. To defeat an enemy, their gods must be overthrown (33:4; cf. 21:29). Thus the Israelites receive "great and good cities that you did not build, and houses full of all good things that you did not fill, and cisterns that you did not dig, and vineyards and olive trees that you did not plant" (Deut. 6:10–11).

Israel can then take "possession of the land" (*yarash*; Num. 33:53) thanks to the covenant promise reiterated here, "I have given the land to you," which the Lord swore to their fathers to fulfill (e.g., 11:12; 14:23; 32:11). This is the land of which he first said "I *will* give" (10:29), then "I *am* giving" (13:2; 15:2), and now "I *have* given" (33:53). "Settle in it" (*yashab*) also implies "remain in it." To "live long in the land" (Deut. 11:9; 30:18; Eph. 6:3) Israel must heed the Lord's covenant.

To "inherit the land" (*nahal*; Num. 33:54) is Israel's privilege as the Lord's firstborn (Ex. 4:22; Rom. 9:4). Land is attributed to the tribes "by lot." "Wherever the lot falls" (Num. 33:54; cf. 26:55) is considered the Lord's doing (Prov. 16:33). Thus they receive what the Lord has in store for them (cf. Ps. 16:6). Inheriting by lot neutralizes conflicting interests. Other factors are also at play. If a tribe is "large" or "small," the land inherited will be proportionate (Num. 33:54; cf. 26:54, 56). Land size based on census figures (26:51–53) also involves allocation "by lot according to your clans" (33:54; Josh. 15:1, 20). The manner in which these methods, and probably others, work together is unstated (cf. comment on Num. 26:52–62). Allotment is made in the presence of Eleazar the priest, Joshua, and one chief from each tribe (Num. 34:17; cf. 7:2; Josh. 14:1). If the Urim and Thummim were employed as lots, Eleazar had to be there (Num. 27:21). "Tribes of your fathers" (33:54) underscores the principle that ultimately inherited land belongs to the twelve ancestral tribes.

The imagery of inhabitants who will not be dispossessed, as "barbs in your eyes and thorns in your sides" (v. 55; cf. "a snare," Ex. 23:33; Deut. 7:16; Josh. 23:13), is

---

[301] *CDCH*, 166. A different form of the verb means "inherit" (Num. 33:54).
[302] Ron Bergey, "La conquête de Canaan: un génocide?," *RRef* 54/5 (2003): 61–79.

made concrete by "they shall trouble you" (*tsarar*; Num. 33:55). How so is suggested by three other occurrences of this word. Like an enemy "oppresses" (10:9), Israel will "harass" (25:17) the Midianites to death because they have "harassed" (25:18) Israel by means of seduction to idolatrous immorality. The warning is clear: "I will do to you as I thought to do to them" (33:56). Like the indigenous inhabitants, Israel could be banished.

Response

Like the banishment of Adam and Eve, then Cain, to the east of Eden (Gen. 3:24; 4:16), Israel's exile is to the east. Regarding the warning in Numbers 33:56 Matthew Henry reflects, "If we do not drive sin out, sin will drive us out; if we be not the death of our lusts, our lusts will be the death of our souls."[303] And as Spurgeon exhorts, "Our warfare involves putting the knife into sins of all sorts and sizes, whether of the body, the mind, or the spirit."[304] Paul writes, "Since we have these promises, beloved, let us cleanse ourselves from every defilement of body and spirit, bringing holiness to completion in the fear of God" (2 Cor. 7:1). Peter encourages, "Beloved, I urge you as sojourners and exiles to abstain from the passions of the flesh, which wage war against your soul" (1 Pet. 2:11).

NUMBERS 34

34 The LORD spoke to Moses, saying, ² "Command the people of Israel, and say to them, When you enter the land of Canaan (this is the land that shall fall to you for an inheritance, the land of Canaan as defined by its borders), ³ your south side shall be from the wilderness of Zin alongside Edom, and your southern border shall run from the end of the Salt Sea on the east. ⁴ And your border shall turn south of the ascent of Akrabbim, and cross to Zin, and its limit shall be south of Kadesh-barnea. Then it shall go on to Hazar-addar, and pass along to Azmon. ⁵ And the border shall turn from Azmon to the Brook of Egypt, and its limit shall be at the sea.

⁶ "For the western border, you shall have the Great Sea and its¹ coast. This shall be your western border.

⁷ "This shall be your northern border: from the Great Sea you shall draw a line to Mount Hor. ⁸ From Mount Hor you shall draw a line to Lebo-hamath, and the limit of the border shall be at Zedad. ⁹ Then the border shall extend to Ziphron, and its limit shall be at Hazar-enan. This shall be your northern border.

¹⁰ "You shall draw a line for your eastern border from Hazar-enan to Shepham. ¹¹ And the border shall go down from Shepham to Riblah on the east side of Ain. And the border shall go down and reach to the shoul-

---

303 Cited by Bush, *Book of Numbers*, 461.
304 Spurgeon, *Promises of God*, May 7.

der of the Sea of Chinnereth on the east. ¹²And the border shall go down to the Jordan, and its limit shall be at the Salt Sea. This shall be your land as defined by its borders all around."

¹³Moses commanded the people of Israel, saying, "This is the land that you shall inherit by lot, which the LORD has commanded to give to the nine tribes and to the half-tribe. ¹⁴For the tribe of the people of Reuben by fathers' houses and the tribe of the people of Gad by their fathers' houses have received their inheritance, and also the half-tribe of Manasseh. ¹⁵The two tribes and the half-tribe have received their inheritance beyond the Jordan east of Jericho, toward the sunrise."

¹⁶The LORD spoke to Moses, saying, ¹⁷"These are the names of the men who shall divide the land to you for inheritance: Eleazar the priest and Joshua the son of Nun. ¹⁸You shall take one chief from every tribe to divide the land for inheritance. ¹⁹These are the names of the men: Of the tribe of Judah, Caleb the son of Jephunneh. ²⁰Of the tribe of the people of Simeon, Shemuel the son of Ammihud. ²¹Of the tribe of Benjamin, Elidad the son of Chislon. ²²Of the tribe of the people of Dan a chief, Bukki the son of Jogli. ²³Of the people of Joseph: of the tribe of the people of Manasseh a chief, Hanniel the son of Ephod. ²⁴And of the tribe of the people of Ephraim a chief, Kemuel the son of Shiphtan. ²⁵Of the tribe of the people of Zebulun a chief, Elizaphan the son of Parnach. ²⁶Of the tribe of the people of Issachar a chief, Paltiel the son of Azzan. ²⁷And of the tribe of the people of Asher a chief, Ahihud the son of Shelomi. ²⁸Of the tribe of the people of Naphtali a chief, Pedahel the son of Ammihud." ²⁹These are the men whom the LORD commanded to divide the inheritance for the people of Israel in the land of Canaan.

¹ Syriac; Hebrew lacks *its*

Section Overview

Chapter 33 recalled how God had faithfully led his people "by stages" from Egypt, through the wilderness, to the doorstep of Canaan (33:1–49). There he gave them instructions on how they should take possession of the land promised to their fathers (33:50–56). Chapter 34 surveys the frontiers of Canaan (34:1–12; cf. "the territory of the Canaanites," Gen. 10:19), which "the LORD has commanded to give to the nine tribes and to the half-tribe" (Num. 34:13). Two tribes and a half-tribe have already "taken" Transjordan as their inheritance (cf. comment on 34:1–15 [at vv. 14–15]), as described in chapter 32. The list of leaders appointed to oversee the Cisjordan allotment (vv. 16–29) is the seventh list of tribal representatives (chs. 1; 2; 7; 10; 13; 26; 34). Among those named, Caleb alone is from the exodus generation (13:6; 34:19).

Section Outline

III. Instructions beyond the Jordan at Jericho for the Generation Soon to Enter Canaan (26:1–36:13) . . .
    I. Inheriting the Land of Canaan (34:1–29)
        1. Boundaries of the Land to Be Inherited (34:1–15)
        2. Leaders Appointed to Oversee the Inheritance (34:16–29)

Comment

34:1–15 "Command the people of Israel" (v. 1; cf. 5:2; 28:2; 33:2; 35:2) is echoed in the framing conclusion (34:29; cf. v. 13). The syntax of "when you enter" (Hb. *ki* + participle; v. 2; cf. 35:10, "when you cross") may be emphatic, thus yielding "for/now you are entering" (cf. Deut. 11:31; "For you are to cross"). The expression "land of Canaan" (Num. 34:2) occurs only twice in Exodus (Ex. 6:4; 16:35), three times in Leviticus (Lev. 14:34; 18:3; 25:38), and once in Deuteronomy (Deut. 32:49). The twelve occurrences in Numbers, mainly with the new generation in view (Num. 13:2, 17; 26:19; 32:30, 32; 33:40, 51; 34:2 [2x], 29; 35:10, 14), accentuate the land theme and accelerate the overall movement of the Israelites toward Canaan.

The language of "The land that shall fall ... inheritance" (34:2; Josh. 13:6; Ezek. 47:14) reflects either the distribution by lots, which, after cast, "fall" (*napal*, cf. Jonah 1:7), or an "inheritance" (*nakhalah*) that comes down like water in a wadi (*nakhal*). The extremities of the southern frontier of Canaan are, on the east, the "end of the Salt [Dead] Sea" (Num. 34:3) and, on the west, "the sea" (v. 5), that is, the "Great [Mediterranean] Sea" (v. 6). The latter forms the entire western border of Canaan, in fact. Between these perimeters lies the formidable "Brook of Egypt" (cf. v. 5).

On Canaan's "south side" (*pe'at negeb*, "southern edge"; v. 3) is the Negeb "wilderness of Zin alongside Edom" (34:3).[305] "Alongside" (*'al-yade*) indicates a stretch of border, not a point (cf. Judg. 11:26). Like Canaan's border, Judah's southeastern flank is also "to the boundary [*gebul*] of Edom" (Josh. 15:1), that is Edomite territory in the Sinai Peninsula. To reconnoiter Canaan the Israelite scouts went up through the Negeb (Num. 13:22) from Kadesh into the wilderness of Zin (13:21; 32:8; 33:36). The "southern border" (*gebul negeb*; 34:3) heads in a southwesterly direction from the "Salt Sea" (v. 3), which has 34 percent salinity, ten times greater than ocean water. "On the east" (*qedemah*, "forward"; v. 3) reflects an eastward orientation from southern Canaan, as does the "eastern [*qadmoni*, "before"] sea" (Ezek. 47:18), also designating the Dead Sea.

The "ascent of Akrabbim" (Num. 34:4; "Scorpions' Pass") is on the southeast corner of Canaan (v. 4) and Judah (Josh. 15:3; Judg. 1:36). It descends from the north side of Nahal Zin toward the Arabah about 20 miles (32 km) south of the Dead Sea. From Roman times Scorpions' Pass was identified with this ascent.[306] "Zin" (Num. 34:4) may refer to Nahal (wadi) Zin, like the Arnon and the Jabbok (21:24; neither qualified with "wadi") and the "Jordan" (34:12; not qualified with "river").[307] The Zin Valley, the most important and the largest connecting the Sinai to the Arabah, divides the Negeb highlands into northern and southern parts, forming a natural border of Canaan to the north and Edomite Sinai territory to the south.[308] The most important road connecting the Arabah and the Mediterranean coast, the Darb es-Sul-

---

305 Baly avers that Seir (Edom) as a regional name included the Negeb (*Geography of the Bible*, 12). For a description of this border cf. de Vaulx, *Les Nombres*, 385.
306 Cole, *Numbers*, 536. For this and other possibilities cf. de Vaulx, *Les Nombres*, map 5.
307 Simons suggests that Zin here is a specific place that has given its name to the wilderness (*Geographical and Topographical Texts*, 136).
308 Keil, "Fourth Book of Moses," 250–251.

tan, traverses the valley[309] and is no doubt taken by Israel to descend to the Arabah. "Its limit" (v. 4), that is, "its [the border's] going out/direction" (*yatsa'*), is westward.

"Kadesh-barnea" (v. 4; cf. comment on 33:18b–36 [at v. 36]) covers a region about 50 miles (80 km) south of Beersheba.[310] The two sites, moving westward from Kadesh, are often identified by following a series of springs, as are two others on Judah's southern border (Josh. 15:3). "Hazar-addar" (Num. 34:4; cf. Hezron and Addar, Josh. 15:3) is possibly Ein Qudeis/Qedeis or a nearby fort, 2 miles (3.2 km) west of Ein Qudeirat (Kadesh-barnea).[311] "Azmon" (or *'atsmonah*; LXX *asemona*; cf. comment and note on Num. 33:18b–36 [at v. 29], "Hashmonah") may be Ein Muweilih.[312]

The "Brook [*nakhal*] of Egypt" (34:5), the formidable Wadi el-Arish, separates Canaan and Egypt.[313] Originating in the upper reaches of the northern half of Sinai, its tributaries divide that half into eastern and western quarters. They funnel rainwaters into the main trunk, which, turning northwestward, drains into the Mediterranean about 40 miles (65 km) south of Gaza. "Western border" (*gebul yam*; v. 6) is literally "sea border." The "Great Sea" (vv. 6, 7) is also the "western" (*'aharon*, "behind" when oriented eastward) sea (Deut. 11:24); "to the sea" (*yammah*) also means westward (Gen. 13:14).

Like the southern border depicted geographically with the term *negeb* (cf. Num. 34:3), so perhaps the expression "northern border" (*gebul tsaphon*; Num. 34:7; cf. 2:25, "north side") may use as a geographical counterpoint *tsaphon*, namely, Mount Zaphon (Ps. 48:2 NIV; Isa. 14:13) overlooking the Mediterranean in northern Syria. This border connects five locations. On the northwestern corner of Canaan, "Mount Hor" (Num. 34:7, 8; not to be confused with Mount Hor in the Negeb, 33:37) is possibly Ras Shaqqah, 30 miles (50 km) north-northeast of Beirut on the Mediterranean.[314] Then the border reaches eastward to "Lebo-hamath" (34:8), the northern limit of Israel's exploration (cf. comment on 13:21–24). The equivalent transcription of "Lebo" in Egyptian and Assyrian sources indicates it to be a city near Riblah at the source of the Orontes River, south of Hamath, today's Lebweh.[315] The city of Hamath is midway on the route connecting Lebo, Riblah (cf. discussion on 34:11 below), Ebla, and Aleppo. Hamath marks the northern border in Ezekiel 47:17.

The "limit" (Num. 34:8, 9), or "going out/direction" (cf. v. 4), continues eastward to the next three northern points. The name "Zedad" (v. 8) is preserved in modern Sadad, 35 miles (55 km) northeast of Lehweh (Lebo), near the Damascus-Homs Road. Given its location on the desert border, the next two locations, "Ziphron" and "Hazar-enan" (v. 9), are identified with desert oases east of Zedad.[316]

---

309 Baly, *Geography of the Bible*, 35.
310 Glueck names eleven wells, among others, between Qadeis and Ain el-Qudeirat (Kadesh-barnea; *Rivers in the Desert*, 88). Aharoni says Kadesh-barnea (Ein Qudeirat) is the "richest and most centrally located of a group of springs on the southern edge of the Negeb" (*Land of the Bible*, 70). Har-El calls it "the largest oasis in northern Sinai" (*Sinai Journeys*, 335).
311 Baly, *Geography of the Bible*, 250; Aharoni, *Land of the Bible*, 72.
312 Aharoni, *Land of the Bible*, 72. De Vaulx posits Ain Queseima (*Les Nombres*, 385).
313 Aharoni, *Land of the Bible*, 64, 72.
314 Rasmussen, *Zondervan Atlas*, 238.
315 Aharoni, *Land of the Bible*, 72–73; Levine, *Numbers 21–36*, 534.
316 Aharoni, *Land of the Bible*, 73. Translating Lebo-hamath "entrée d'Hamath," de Vaulx says it designates the narrow passage between the mountains of south Lebanon and Hermon, which opens on the Beqaa Valley and the large plain of Hamath (*Les Nombres*, 386–387).

"Hazar-enan" (v. 10; cf. v. 9) marks the northeast corner of the "eastern border" (*qedemah*; v. 10; cf. discussion on v. 3 above), which descends "from Shepham to Riblah" (v. 11), both unidentified.[317] Riblah cannot be Riblah on the Orontes in the land of Hamath (2 Kings 23:33).[318] "Ain" (Num. 34:11) is identified as Khirbet ʿAyyun, 3 miles (5 km) east of the Sea of Galilee, north of the Yarmouk.[319] The border follows "the shoulder," perhaps the range of heights on the eastern side of the sea or the steep slope on the southeast side. The name "the Sea of Chinnereth" (v. 11) reflects the "harp" (*kinnur*) shape of the Sea of Galilee. The border then goes "down to the Jordan" (v. 12; cf. comment on 22:1–21; *yarden*, from *yarad*, "descend"), descending on its meandering course from 686 feet (209 m) below sea level at the Chinnereth to 1,284 feet (396 m) at the "Salt Sea" (34:12; cf. discussion on v. 3 above). In reference to Canaan, the Israelites are either "on the other side of the Jordan" or "on this side of the Jordan" (32:19). From Canaan, Transjordan is "beyond the Jordan" (34:15).

"The land of Canaan as defined by its borders" (v. 2) is now "your land as defined by its borders" (v. 12). "All around" (*sabib*) refers to the above boundary compass points, much like the Levites, who camp "around" the tabernacle compass points to safeguard it from defilement (1:53; cf. 3:23, 29, 35, 38). Like the tabernacle and the camp, the land must not be defiled (35:34; cf. 5:3; 19:13, 20).

Numbers 34:13–15 reiterate the distinction between the Cisjordan inheritance, which nine tribes and a half-tribe "shall inherit" (from *nahal*; v. 13), and the Transjordan inheritance, which two tribes and a half-tribe "by fathers' houses" (v. 14) "have received" (*laqakh*, "taken"; vv. 14, 15; cf. Section Overview; Josh. 13:8; 18:7). This sets the stage for next section.

34:16–29 "Eleazar the priest and Joshua" (v. 17) are given overall oversight of the land division. Under them, "one chief" (v. 18; cf. 7:2) is taken from each of the nine tribes and the half-tribe (34:19–28).

"Divide . . . for inheritance" (vv. 17, 18, 29) renders one Hebrew word, a verb (*nakhal*). In chapter 26 "divide for inheritance" was expressed with a different verb (*khalaq*) and a complement (*nakhalah*; 26:53, 56). The burden in chapter 34 is not so much dividing the inheritance as it is appointing chiefs who will oversee the actual inheritance transaction, who will "make inherit" (AT; causative form of *nakhal*) "the people of Israel" (34:29), the direct object.[320]

The order of names—Judah followed by Simeon (vv. 19–20, the only time in seven lists in Numbers)—supports this view, since it already assumes Simeon's inheritance within Judah's borders (Josh. 19:1). Moreover, the entire list moves from south to north and assumes the actual tribal allocations: Judah, Simeon, Benjamin, Dan (cf. Josh. 19:40–47), Manasseh, and Ephraim, all south of Jezreel;

---

317 Aharoni, *Land of the Bible*, 73.
318 Riblah in the MT reads *hariblah* (with *h*- determinative), SP *hrblh*, and LXX *Arbela*; cf. Sturdy, *Numbers*, 235; Ashley, *Book of Numbers*, 641; Cole, *Numbers*, 537–538.
319 Aharoni, *Land of the Bible*, 73.
320 The verb form here is understood as causative; cf. GKC (Oxford: Clarendon, 1974), §52g. It is followed by the accusative (*'et*).

Zebulun, Issachar, Asher, and Naphtali to the north. Viewed as such, the Lord's directives to Moses are prophetic. The lots to be cast (Num. 33:54; Joshua 15–19) will confirm his word. "The land of Canaan" (Num. 34:29) frames the chapter (cf. v. 2).

Response

The process of inheritance is done methodically and transparently. Although God determines the inheritance of each tribe, the people execute the multiple tasks involved in distributing it under the oversight of tribal chiefs, supervised by a religious and a civil leader, Eleazar and Joshua. In the NT, raising church support for material needs and sending it was done under apostles who appointed men to oversee the tasks, leaders of good repute inside and outside the church (Acts 6:1–3; 11:29–30; 12:25; 1 Cor. 16:1–3; 1 Tim. 3:6–7). Among God's people, such matters must be done transparently. Concerning the gift from the Corinthian church and the painstaking oversight in handling it, Paul says, "We take this course so that no one should blame us about this generous gift that is being administered by us, for we aim at what is honorable not only in the Lord's sight but also in the sight of man" (2 Cor. 8:20–21).

NUMBERS 35

35 The LORD spoke to Moses in the plains of Moab by the Jordan at Jericho, saying, ² "Command the people of Israel to give to the Levites some of the inheritance of their possession as cities for them to dwell in. And you shall give to the Levites pasturelands around the cities. ³ The cities shall be theirs to dwell in, and their pasturelands shall be for their cattle and for their livestock and for all their beasts. ⁴ The pasturelands of the cities, which you shall give to the Levites, shall reach from the wall of the city outward a thousand cubits¹ all around. ⁵ And you shall measure, outside the city, on the east side two thousand cubits, and on the south side two thousand cubits, and on the west side two thousand cubits, and on the north side two thousand cubits, the city being in the middle. This shall belong to them as pastureland for their cities.

⁶ "The cities that you give to the Levites shall be the six cities of refuge, where you shall permit the manslayer to flee, and in addition to them you shall give forty-two cities. ⁷ All the cities that you give to the Levites shall be forty-eight, with their pasturelands. ⁸ And as for the cities that you shall give from the possession of the people of Israel, from the larger tribes you shall take many, and from the smaller tribes you shall take few; each, in proportion to the inheritance that it inherits, shall give of its cities to the Levites."

⁹And the Lord spoke to Moses, saying, ¹⁰"Speak to the people of Israel and say to them, When you cross the Jordan into the land of Canaan, ¹¹then you shall select cities to be cities of refuge for you, that the manslayer who kills any person without intent may flee there. ¹²The cities shall be for you a refuge from the avenger, that the manslayer may not die until he stands before the congregation for judgment. ¹³And the cities that you give shall be your six cities of refuge. ¹⁴You shall give three cities beyond the Jordan, and three cities in the land of Canaan, to be cities of refuge. ¹⁵These six cities shall be for refuge for the people of Israel, and for the stranger and for the sojourner among them, that anyone who kills any person without intent may flee there.

¹⁶"But if he struck him down with an iron object, so that he died, he is a murderer. The murderer shall be put to death. ¹⁷And if he struck him down with a stone tool that could cause death, and he died, he is a murderer. The murderer shall be put to death. ¹⁸Or if he struck him down with a wooden tool that could cause death, and he died, he is a murderer. The murderer shall be put to death. ¹⁹The avenger of blood shall himself put the murderer to death; when he meets him, he shall put him to death. ²⁰And if he pushed him out of hatred or hurled something at him, lying in wait, so that he died, ²¹or in enmity struck him down with his hand, so that he died, then he who struck the blow shall be put to death. He is a murderer. The avenger of blood shall put the murderer to death when he meets him.

²²"But if he pushed him suddenly without enmity, or hurled anything on him without lying in wait ²³or used a stone that could cause death, and without seeing him dropped it on him, so that he died, though he was not his enemy and did not seek his harm, ²⁴then the congregation shall judge between the manslayer and the avenger of blood, in accordance with these rules. ²⁵And the congregation shall rescue the manslayer from the hand of the avenger of blood, and the congregation shall restore him to his city of refuge to which he had fled, and he shall live in it until the death of the high priest who was anointed with the holy oil. ²⁶But if the manslayer shall at any time go beyond the boundaries of his city of refuge to which he fled, ²⁷and the avenger of blood finds him outside the boundaries of his city of refuge, and the avenger of blood kills the manslayer, he shall not be guilty of blood. ²⁸For he must remain in his city of refuge until the death of the high priest, but after the death of the high priest the manslayer may return to the land of his possession. ²⁹And these things shall be for a statute and rule for you throughout your generations in all your dwelling places.

³⁰"If anyone kills a person, the murderer shall be put to death on the evidence of witnesses. But no person shall be put to death on the testimony of one witness. ³¹Moreover, you shall accept no ransom for the life of a murderer, who is guilty of death, but he shall be put to death. ³²And you shall accept no ransom for him who has fled to his city of refuge, that he may return to dwell in the land before the death of the high priest. ³³You shall not pollute the land in which you live, for blood pollutes the land, and no atonement can be made for the land for the blood that is shed in it, except by the blood of the one who shed it. ³⁴You shall not defile the land in which you live, in the midst of which I dwell, for I the Lord dwell in the midst of the people of Israel."

---

¹ A *cubit* was about 18 inches or 45 centimeters

Section Overview

The movement flows from instructions on allotting land to the secular tribes in Transjordan (Numbers 32) and within the borders of Canaan (ch. 34) to directives on apportioning forty-eight Levitical cities on both sides of the Jordan (ch. 35).

The Levites have their encampments "around" (Hb. *sabib*; 1:50, 53) the tabernacle on its cardinal compass sides (3:23, 29, 35, 38). The cardinal compass boundaries of the Promised Land (34:3, 6, 7, 10) "all around" (*sabib*; v. 12) are defined. The Levitical cities are distributed with their pasturelands "around" (*sabib*; 35:3, 4), that is, on cardinal compass sides of the cities (v. 5), including six cities of refuge, three on each side of the Jordan. The Levites primary task in the wilderness was to guard the sanctuary from desecration (1:53; 18:4). Their responsibility is now greatly increased. By their positions in the land, especially in the cities of refuge (35:9–33), they will guard the land from "blood" pollution and defilement (vv. 33–34). The camp "in the midst of which I [the LORD] dwell" (Num. 5:3) cannot be defiled; nor shall the land "in the midst of which I dwell" (35:34). In the First Temple period Levites serve as judges in civil and criminal cases, including those involving "bloodshed" (2 Chron. 19:8–10). They serve as military commanders and palace guards (2 Chron. 23:1–7) and temple gatekeepers to prevent any unclean person from entering (2 Chron. 23:9).

Section Outline

III. Instructions beyond the Jordan at Jericho for the Generation Soon to Enter Canaan (26:1–36:13) . . .
  J. Cities for Levites and Cities of Refuge (35:1–34)
    1. Cities for Levites (35:1–8)
    2. Cities of Refuge (35:9–34)

Comment

35:1–8 As sons of Levi, the priests and nonpriests do not receive a land inheritance (18:20; 26:62). Their heritage is sacred service to the Lord and his people (18:23–24). To carry out their ministry nationwide they will be scattered, as was prophesied (Gen. 49:7). In this way the curse pronounced on Levi by Jacob is turned into a blessing for them and God's people. Their disbursement is achieved by assigning them cities among the tribes (Num. 35:2). Joshua 20–21 narrates the execution of the command regarding the Levitical cities.

With the cities they receive the "pasturelands" (Hb. *migrash*; Num. 35:2, 3, 4, 7), a debated translation, since the term is thought to refer more generally to land around a city and under its jurisdiction, "suburbs" (Vulg. *suburbana*, also KJV) or "common land" (NEB; cf. 2 Chron. 11:14; 31:19).[321] Although the Hebrew word is related to "drive out" (*garash*), the semantic conflation "drive out (cattle) in pasturelands" is unlikely, since the verb is never used in connection with cattle. Usage in

---

[321] Cf. Davies, *Numbers*, 358.

the context of Levitical cities does, however, support the rendering "pasturelands." They are designated "for their cattle" (Num. 35:3; cf. Josh. 14:4; 21:2). Since the Levites receive cities but not dependent villages, the law provides lands because they are herdsmen (Num. 3:41; 31:30; 35:3), and their revenues include livestock (Lev. 27:32). In Leviticus 25:34 the Levites' "fields" are qualified as *migrash* ("pastureland"). The cities the other tribes inherit include their unwalled villages and their fields (Lev. 25:31; e.g., Josh. 15:32, 36).

The dimensions of these lands "reach from the wall of the city outward a thousand cubits all around ... outside the city, on the east ... south ... west ... north side two thousand cubits" (Num. 35:4–5). This enigma of two apparently conflicting measurements has long tantalized interpreters. The Mishnah queried, "How can we explain this?" One answer assumes the thousand cubits to be the outskirts (*migrash*) of the city and the two thousand cubits to be the (surrounding) fields and vineyards (Sotah 5:3). The LXX, or its source, may have harmonized verse 4 with verse 5, reading "two thousand cubits" both times. Josephus speaks only of two thousand cubits of land (*Antiquities* 4.4.3).[322]

Although these two measurements still appear irreconcilable to some,[323] there are reasonable explanations. For example, the cubits are measurements of frontage of land around the city with a depth of a thousand cubits (v. 4) and a width of two thousand (v. 5).[324] Another interpretation understands the measurements, being given symmetrically, as adaptable to varying city shapes and sizes.[325] Flexibility is necessary, since many of the Levitical cites are in mountainous regions, with contours depending on the terrain. In cases in which one side of the city has too little land, the corresponding number of cubits could be added to another side where there is sufficient footage.

Mention of "six cities of refuge" (v. 6) anticipates the following section (vv. 9–34). Their names and locations are given in Joshua 20. "Of refuge" (*miqlat*; Num. 35:6) qualifies only these cities. "Manslayer" (from *ratsakh*) here refers to anyone who intentionally or unintentionally kills someone. "To flee" from whom and why are not yet indicated (cf. v. 12). The cities of refuge are added to the forty-two cities (v. 6), making a total of forty-eight (v. 7) Levitical cities.

"In proportion to the inheritance" (v. 8) is the regulating principle for the number of Levitical cities within the tribes, based on a tribe's census being "larger" or "smaller" (26:54; 33:54).

---

[322] Medieval commentators differed. For Rashi of the two thousand cubits one thousand is open space (*migrash*). For Maimonides of three thousand cubits one thousand are suburbs and two thousand fields and vineyards; cf. Bush, *Book of Numbers*, 467; Snaith, *Leviticus and Numbers*, 342.
[323] E.g., Gray, *Numbers*, 468; Sturdy, *Numbers*, 238; Davies, *Numbers*, 358.
[324] Budd, *Numbers*, 376. For Bush the thousand cubits are measured outward at right angles to the city wall, whereas two thousand denotes the outside measurement parallel to the wall (*Book of Numbers*, 467). De Vaulx recognizes that the geometrical measurements, while not in themselves irreconcilable, cannot be applied strictly in a land with mountains and valleys such as Palestine's (*Les Nombres*, 392).
[325] Sotah 5:3 interprets the two thousand cubits as the permitted Sabbath travel distance from the city. Tannaitic sources specify the distance to be measured in every direction from the city walls regardless of the city's shape or size. M. Greenberg believes the same practicality is inherent in vv. 4–5. Cf. Moshe Greenberg, "Idealism and Practicality in Numbers 35:4–5 and Ezekiel 48," *JAOS* 88 (1968): 59–66. Wenham (*Numbers*, 235) shares Greenberg's view, and Milgrom (*Numbers*, 502–504) develops it. Keil ("Fourth Book of Moses," 259–260) posits a similar solution.

35:9–34 "When you cross [from *'abar*] the Jordan into the land of Canaan" (35:10) echoes word for word "When you pass over [from *'abar*] the Jordan into the land of Canaan" (33:51), or in other words, "When you enter the land of Canaan" (34:2). These clauses recall the words of promise addressed to those under twenty years of age of the exodus generation, "When you come into the land to which I bring you" (15:18), thus serving as a reminder of God's faithfulness. His promise will soon be realized. To "select" is to "make it happen" (form of *qarah*, 35:11; cf. Gen. 27:20 NASB, "cause it to happen"). "Cities of refuge" (cf. Deut. 19:1–13; Josh. 20:1–9) protect a manslayer from the avenger of blood. Refuge there includes, first, protection from the manslayer's arrival "until" his trial (Num. 35:12), and second, if he is exonerated, protection from premeditated murder from that time until the death of the high priest (v. 28). "Without intent" (*shegagah*; vv. 11, 15) is the same word rendered "mistake" (15:26, 28) and "unintentionally" (15:27, 29).

The "congregation" (35:12)—Levite adjudicator representatives (cf. Deut. 19:12 and Josh. 20:4, "elders"; 2 Chron. 19:8–10)—must render "judgment" (*mishpat*; cf. Num. 35:25), that is, weigh the evidence, determine whether or not the manslayer be guilty of first-degree murder, and pronounce the verdict. Although the plaintiff is the family of the avenger of blood (v. 24), to ensure impartiality the case is not judged by members of the deceased's family nor by those of the manslayer's.

The "avenger" (*go'el*, v. 12; cf. "avenger of blood," v. 19) is a close relative of the victim. The same word is also rendered "redeemer" or "kinsman." The *go'el* remedies premeditated murder by the lex talionis principle, "life for life" (Gen. 9:6; Ex. 21:24; Lev. 24:20; Deut. 19:21). In other cases the *go'el* redresses a situation *status quo ante* by fathering a child with the widow of a deceased brother who had no heir (Ruth 2:20; 4:4–6), by buying back an impoverished relative sold into slavery or his property (Lev. 25:25, 48), or by receiving restitution for a wrong done to a deceased relative (Num. 5:8).[326]

The Lord specifies "three cities beyond the Jordan, and three cities in the land of Canaan" (35:14) as cities of refuge. Transjordan is not part of Canaan (34:2, 12). Specifying three cities on each side of the river makes the distance the manslayer must flee not too great to take refuge before meeting the avenger (cf. Deut. 19:6). "Anyone" (Num. 35:15) may find refuge in a city of refuge; the sanctity of human life, regardless of ethnicity or civil status, stems from mankind's being created in the image of God (Gen. 1:27; 9:6). Beyond this is the concern of keeping the land from defilement (Num. 35:34; cf. Response section).

Verses 16–23 give instructions on how to determine intent in the case of homicide, which is difficult to prove. If a lethal object was used, whether made of iron, stone, or wood (vv. 16–18), or if there was no lethal object but there was malice aforethought, evinced by the manslayer's pushing someone in hatred, throwing something at him after lying in wait, or striking him with the hand in enmity (vv. 20–21), then the assailant is guilty of premeditated homicide. The avenger of

---

326 Noordtzij says that *go'el* means not "avenger" but "restorer" (*Numbers*, 297).

blood must "put him to death" (vv. 19, 21). "When he meets him" (vv. 19, 21) shows the manslayer has been removed from the city of refuge (cf. v. 25).

If premeditation is not proven, even if a stone has caused the death but was dropped unawares by the manslayer, who sought no harm (vv. 22–23; cf. Deut. 19:5), the accused is guilty of involuntary manslaughter. There is guilt but not enough to require his life. The congregation "shall rescue" (*natsal*) the manslayer from the avenger (Num. 35:25); this is the only occurrence in Numbers of this verb, which is used frequently elsewhere, often with the complement "from/into the hand of" (v. 25). God "delivered" (*natsal*) Abram's enemies into his hand (Gen. 14:20), Jacob from the hand of Esau (Gen. 32:12, 21), and his people from the hand of the Egyptians (Ex. 3:8; 18:9). Judging is based on rulings or judgments ("judge," *shaphat*; "rules," *mishpatim*; Num. 35:24)—a case is adjudicated on the basis of such laws or precedents.

The phrase "Shall restore [or "return"] him to his city of refuge" (Num. 35:25) is commonly taken to mean that the trial takes place elsewhere.[327] But Joshua 20:4 places it in the gates of the city of refuge.[328] "Restore him" may first view his provisional asylum upon his fleeing there, technically suspended during the trial but then definitively reinstated after a verdict of not guilty of premeditated homicide. If guilty of this, the manslayer is taken from the city of refuge to his own town in order to meet his fate (Deut. 19:12).

There the manslayer must fulfill two conditions to prevent the avenger from ever taking his life. First, he must remain in the city of refuge until the death of the high priest (Num. 35:25, 28), who among fellow priests is "anointed with the holy oil" (v. 25; cf. Ex. 30:30–32; Lev. 21:10; also the king cf. Ps. 89:20). His consecration depends on the anointing, not on his person. As such he can make atonement for himself, the entire nation, and the holy sanctuary (Ex. 29:26; Lev. 16:6, 16, 18, 33). Since in this case the one who has shed blood is not required to give his own life to purge the land polluted by blood (Num. 35:33), the high priest, as representative mediator, vicariously makes atonement by his death.[329] After his death the manslayer can return home. Justice and purification are accomplished by the death of the high priest. Second, the manslayer must stay within the "boundaries" of the city (v. 27), referring probably not to the walls but to the city's lands. If the manslayer leaves those confines, the avenger of blood can take his life with impunity (v. 27).

"Statute and rule" (*khukat mishpat*; v. 29) is civil law, as in 27:11, being distinct from "statute of the law" (*khukat hattorah*), or ritual law, as in 19:2; 31:21.[330] In the Levitical cities, including the cities of refuge, the priests and Levites are responsible for both.

---

327 Sturdy, *Numbers*, 242; Harrison, *Numbers*, 421; Ashley, *Book of Numbers*, 652; Milgrom, *Numbers*, 294.
328 Cole says that the manslayer appears at the city gate, but his being sent back suggests the trial takes place outside the walls to make it easier to turn him over eventually to the avenger (*Numbers*, 553–554).
329 The Mishnah (Makkot 2:6) and Talmud (Makkot 11b) consider the cities of refuge to be places of exile that punish but do not expiate bloodshed, which only the high priest's death can do. Cf. Keil, "Fourth Book of Moses," 265; Milgrom, *Numbers*, 294; Cole, *Numbers*, 554.
330 Milgrom, *Numbers*, 294.

Numbers 35:30–31 presents two legal restrictions to safeguard justice from being perverted. The first requires "evidence of witnesses" (v. 30; cf. Deut. 17:6, two or three) to execute the manslayer found guilty of premeditated homicide. This reduces the possibility of false testimony or mistaken identity. The second forbids "ransom" to deliver a manslayer from the death penalty or to release a manslayer from a city of refuge before the death of the high priest (Num. 35:31). Verses 33–34 explain why the law on Levitical cities is needed. The general principle is that "blood pollutes [*khanap*; the only Pentateuchal occurrence] the land" (v. 33)—that is, the shedding of "blood," whether involuntarily or voluntarily. The only way to purge the land is "by the blood of the one who shed it" (v. 33; cf. Gen. 9:6). In the case of premeditated murder the manslayer's own blood is required. In the case of involuntary manslaughter the death of the high priest is substitutionary.

"You shall not defile [*tame'*] the land in which you live" (Num. 35:34) by disregarding the "statute and rule" (v. 29) concerning bloodshed. The reason is that such bloodshed would occur in the land "in the midst of which I dwell, for I the LORD dwell in the midst of the people of Israel" (v. 34; cf. Section Overview). Defiling the land is tantamount to breaking God's eternal covenant, for which a curse would devour the land and the people would suffer their guilt (Isa. 24:5–6). They could be driven from their land into exile (Lev. 18:28; 20:22; 26:38).[331]

Response

The fundamental issue presented in the Numbers law on manslaughter is as follows: blood pollutes the land, which, in the case of premeditated murder, can be atoned (cleansed) only by the death of its author (Num. 35:33). Although this civil law on cities of refuge relates to national Israel in the land of Canaan and has thus been abrogated, the principle remains.

The prescription is a restatement of the Noahic law on homicide (Gen. 9:6), founded on man's being created "in the image of God" (Gen. 1:27). The wrongful taking of human life created in the image of God is an affront to God's holiness—it defiles and profanes his name. It is also an affront to his righteousness and justice, the foundations of his throne (Ps. 89:14, 35). God's intrinsic attributes are the ultimate principle behind capital punishment. These attributes are communicable: God's servant is the government whose sword expresses his wrath and executes his vengeance (cf. Rom. 13:4), which vindicates his throne and his holiness (Ezek. 36:23).

---

331 Ibid., 294, 331.

NUMBERS 36

36 The heads of the fathers' houses of the clan of the people of Gilead the son of Machir, son of Manasseh, from the clans of the people of Joseph, came near and spoke before Moses and before the chiefs, the heads of the fathers' houses of the people of Israel. ² They said, "The Lord commanded my lord to give the land for inheritance by lot to the people of Israel, and my lord was commanded by the Lord to give the inheritance of Zelophehad our brother to his daughters. ³ But if they are married to any of the sons of the other tribes of the people of Israel, then their inheritance will be taken from the inheritance of our fathers and added to the inheritance of the tribe into which they marry. So it will be taken away from the lot of our inheritance. ⁴ And when the jubilee of the people of Israel comes, then their inheritance will be added to the inheritance of the tribe into which they marry, and their inheritance will be taken from the inheritance of the tribe of our fathers."

⁵ And Moses commanded the people of Israel according to the word of the Lord, saying, "The tribe of the people of Joseph is right. ⁶ This is what the Lord commands concerning the daughters of Zelophehad: 'Let them marry whom they think best, only they shall marry within the clan of the tribe of their father. ⁷ The inheritance of the people of Israel shall not be transferred from one tribe to another, for every one of the people of Israel shall hold on to the inheritance of the tribe of his fathers. ⁸ And every daughter who possesses an inheritance in any tribe of the people of Israel shall be wife to one of the clan of the tribe of her father, so that every one of the people of Israel may possess the inheritance of his fathers. ⁹ So no inheritance shall be transferred from one tribe to another, for each of the tribes of the people of Israel shall hold on to its own inheritance.'"

¹⁰ The daughters of Zelophehad did as the Lord commanded Moses, ¹¹ for Mahlah, Tirzah, Hoglah, Milcah, and Noah, the daughters of Zelophehad, were married to sons of their father's brothers. ¹² They were married into the clans of the people of Manasseh the son of Joseph, and their inheritance remained in the tribe of their father's clan.

¹³ These are the commandments and the rules that the Lord commanded through Moses to the people of Israel in the plains of Moab by the Jordan at Jericho.

Section Overview

Chapter 36 supplements the law on daughter-heirs (Num. 26:33–34; 27:1–11).[332] The solution to the dilemma in chapter 27—Zelophehad has no sons, so his daughters will inherit—produced a conundrum: if his daughters married outside

---

[332] For Budd this supplement is an appendix to the entire book (*Numbers*, 390). So too Levine, *Numbers 21–36*, 575.

their Manassite tribe, their lands would become the possession of their husbands' tribes (36:1–3). But inherited land is inalienable (Lev. 25:10, 23). An amendment is adopted: daughter-heirs must marry within their tribe (Num. 36:5–9). Zelophehad's daughters comply (vv. 10–12).

As suggested (cf. Introduction: Interpretive Challenges: Unifying Structure of Numbers), the end-framing chapters 26–36 are, after the opening census (ch. 26), bracketed by the thematically related chapters 27 and 36. This follows the pattern of the initial-framing chapters 1–10, bracketed, after the census (ch. 1), by chapters 2 and 10.

Chapter 36 draws the book of Numbers to a fitting conclusion.

Section Outline

III. Instructions beyond the Jordan at Jericho for the Generation Soon to Enter Canaan (26:1–36:13) . . .
   K. Marriage of Daughter-Heirs (36:1–13)
      1. The Problem (36:1–4)
      2. The Solution (36:5–13)

Comment

36:1–4 For the third time the lineage of Zelophehad's daughters is evoked: Joseph, Manasseh, Machir, Gilead (v. 1), Hepher, and his son Zelophehad (26:28–33; 27:1; 36:2). Zelophehad's daughters will marry, bear children, and, by the land they inherit, carry on their father's name. The problem the Gileadite leaders raise addresses the possibility of these daughters' marrying outside the Manassite tribe, in which case their inheritance would pass to their husbands' tribe(s) (36:3). Their children would bear the fathers' names, as would land they inherit from their mothers. The inheritance would therefore be irretrievably lost to the tribe of Manasseh.

The reason for "the jubilee" (Hb. *hayyobel*; v. 4) to figure in the equation has drawn diverse suggestions. The jubilee law requires land that has been sold to return on the fiftieth year to the original owner (Lev. 25:10, 24–28). Here the question concerns land transferred to the "tribe into which they marry" (Num. 36:3). Are the leaders pointing out that the jubilee would not affect inherited land under the earlier ruling in Numbers 27?[333] Or are they indicating that the jubilee law is inapplicable here?[334] Indeed, how could land revert to its original owner if it were transferred by marriage to another tribe? Perhaps their appeal exposes a jubilee legal custom reflected only here. Perhaps land inherited by a daughter who marries someone from a different tribe could, in the event of her death, be redeemed by her family before the jubilee year. But "when the jubilee . . . comes," it will irrevocably become property of her husband's family.[335] If so, the

---
[333] Cf. Levine, *Numbers 21–36*, 578.
[334] So Noordtzij, *Numbers*, 303; Ashley, *Book of Numbers*, 659.
[335] Cf. de Vaulx, *Les Nombres*, 405.

Gileadite leaders' appeal has in view the likelihood that Zelophehad's daughters will outlive the jubilee.

36:5–13 The case presented, Moses makes a ruling concerning Zelophehad's daughters (vv. 5–6), a civil precedent for all daughter-heirs who marry (vv. 8–9). The daughters of Zelophehad can "marry whom they think best, only they shall marry within the clan of the tribe of their father" (v. 6). This ruling extends to "every daughter who possesses an inheritance in any tribe" (v. 8), which satisfies the inalienability principle: "So no inheritance shall be transferred from one tribe to another, for each of the tribes of the people of Israel shall hold on to its own inheritance" (v. 9; cf. v. 7). Zelophehad's daughters obey and marry as instructed, so that "their inheritance remained in the tribe of their father's clan" (v. 12; cf. 27:7).

Numbers 36:13, the last verse of the book, is a colophon covering "the commandments and the rules" given to the new generation camped "in the plains of Moab by the Jordan at Jericho" (cf. 26:3), which frames the instructions that begin with those on inheritance in chapter 27.[336]

Chapter 36 is a response to a major concern. Thirty-eight years earlier, the exodus generation was at the door of Canaan, but ten of their leaders refused to enter (Num. 13:25–14:38). Will leaders of the succeeding generation also fail to lay hold of God's promise and not enter the Promised Land? In particular, the request for an inheritance outside Canaan by the Transjordanian tribes—including Zelophehad's Manassite clan—has already been compared to the rebellion of the old generation at Kadesh (32:6–15). Zelophehad's daughters demonstrate their confidence in God's promise to give them an inheritance. The Manassite Gileadite leaders now also express their faith by requesting a ruling, applicable to all the tribes and to succeeding generations. As such, chapter 36, being more than a supplement or appendix, draws Numbers to a close on a note of faith and hope.

Response

Zelophehad's daughters live their faith by acting upon God's promises (cf. Response section on Numbers 27). As mothers and grandmothers, they influence generations of Israelites (cf. Response section on Numbers 2, concerning Leah). Their example still lives today and may have provided the thought behind the instructions Paul left for women in the church. As with Zelophehad's daughters, who could marry "whom they think best, only . . . within the clan" (36:6), Paul says that a woman (a widow) may be married "to whom she wishes, only in the Lord" (1 Cor. 7:39). Mothers and grandmothers have an important role in the spiritual well-being of the church. Older women are exhorted to train younger women "to love their husbands and children" (Titus 2:4). Paul reminds Timothy that his sincere faith dwelled first in his grandmother and mother (2 Tim. 1:5).

---

336 There is debate concerning the extent of legislation covered by the colophon. Some commentators believe it refers to chapters 27–36, or parts thereof, whereas others to the entire book. Cf. Davies, *Numbers*, 370.

Many in the church yesterday and today trace their faith to a godly mother's example, prayers, and teaching. Monica was the mother of Augustine of Hippo, one of the most influential Christian theologians of all history. In his *Confessions*, Augustine writes of her godly and prayerful life dedicated to his conversion and reformation. Another example is Susanna Wesley. Like Zelophehad's daughters, who would bequeath lands to their children, grandchildren, and generations to come, Susanna's sons John and Charles indelibly marked church history through their evangelistic ministries. Her grandson Samuel bequeathed to the church hymn lyrics such as "O for a Thousand Tongues to Sing" and melodies such as the one accompanying "The Church's One Foundation."

SCRIPTURE INDEX

Genesis
Book of 23–37
1 .... 34, 39, 40, 41, 42, 43, 47, 51, 52, 55, 57, 90, 99, 106, 138, 424, 433, 468, 705n604, 764
1–2 .... 56, 57, 59, 814
1–3 .... 23, 24
1–11 .... 23, 24, 28, 33, 76, 136n214
1:1 .... 41, 49, 323, 819
1:1–2:3 .... 38–49, 48, 50, 51, 81, 100
1:2 .... 41–42, 42, 46, 101, 105, 1258
1:3 901
1:3–4 43
1:3–5 42–44,
1:4 .... 922, 1145
1:5 44
1:6–7 922
1:6–8 .... 43, 44
1:6–9 101
1:7 901
1:8 44
1:9 .... 44, 108, 901
1:9–10 43
1:9–13 44–45
1:10 44
1:11 901
1:11–12 .... 46, 52n30
1:11–13 43
1:12 .... 44, 920
1:13 44
1:14 .... 45, 922, 1011, 1017
1:14–15 45
1:14–19 .... 43, 45
1:15 901
1:16 45
1:17–18 45
1:18 45
1:20 .... 45, 91
1:20–23 .... 43, 45–46
1:20–25 916
1:20–35 607
1:21 .... 45, 920
1:21–22 412
1:22 .... 46, 106, 137, 171, 901, 986, 1246, 1258
1:24 .... 52, 91, 901, 920
1:24–25 .... 43, 44
1:24–26 97
1:24–31 .... 46–47, 978
1:25 920
1:26 .... 30, 46, 127, 127n197, 1261
1:26–27 .... 43, 645, 648n485, 653, 1023
1:26–28 .... 27, 30, 40, 81
1:27 .... 43, 55, 841, 927, 1329, 1331
1:28 .... 47, 57, 74n81, 89, 111, 171, 241, 251, 272n395, 405, 466, 466n57, 468, 645, 901, 903, 925, 951, 1038, 1041, 1246, 1261
1:28–29 850
1:28–31 29
1:29 .... 97, 917, 1014
1:29–30 .... 46, 47, 111
1:31 .... 47, 814
2 .... 46, 48, 51, 52, 54n39, 55, 57
2–3 .... 29, 51, 136, 720n645
2:1 .... 41, 47
2:1–3 47–48
2:1–4 30
2:1a 814
2:2 .... 47, 810, 1109
2:2–3 .... 40, 611
2:2a 814
2:3 .... 312, 901, 1012, 1040
2:3a 814
2:4 .... 51, 1100
2:4–7 .... 26, 50, 51–52, 81, 94, 119, 131, 132, 318n487, 322n495
2:4–25 .... 40, 49–58
2:4–4:26 81
2:5 .... 52, 52n30
2:5–6 1028
2:6–7 52
2:7 .... 30, 51, 52, 89, 847n30
2:8 .... 51, 52, 114, 125, 125n188
2:8–9 57
2:8–17 .... 52–54, 205
2:9 .... 54, 62, 819
2:11 123
2:11–14 53
2:12 .... 717n627, 819
2:15 .... 51, 52, 69, 75, 114, 1008
2:16 .... 51, 54, 61
2:16–17 .... 30, 54, 56, 60, 919
2:17 .... 31, 57, 61, 68, 91, 936
2:18 .... 51, 54, 55, 57, 791
2:18–24 .... 30, 614
2:18–25 54–56
2:19 55
2:19–20 .... 42, 916
2:20 .... 54, 666, 972, 978
2:21 55
2:21–22 51
2:21–25 623
2:22 72
2:23 .... 55, 972, 999
2:24 .... 56, 87, 614n399, 952, 1123
2:24–25 56
2:25 65
3 .... 24, 34, 40, 51, 58–70, 72, 89, 90, 185, 427
3–4 .... 80, 107n145
3–6 91
3–11 24
3:1 .... 60, 61, 74n81, 113n153, 1241
3:1–5 60–62
3:1–6 .... 31, 72
3:3 .... 61, 919
3:4 .... 31, 61, 102, 188
3:4–5 62
3:5 .... 31, 62
3:6 .... 60, 61, 62, 67, 67n65, 87, 114, 146, 164, 304, 337, 920, 1165
3:6–7 .... 61, 62–63
3:7 .... 56, 63, 479n87, 486
3:7–13 62
3:8 .... 30, 63, 114, 440, 711, 711n621, 748, 767, 814, 814n838, 815, 1040, 1041, 1041n306, 1117, 1140
3:8–9 729
3:8–12 61
3:8–13 .... 63–65, 83
3:9 .... 63, 165, 179
3:10 64
3:11 .... 64, 165
3:12 64
3:12–13 75
3:13 .... 61, 64, 165
3:14 .... 60, 65, 672, 921, 1122, 1246, 1253
3:14–15 .... 61, 135, 922
3:14–19 .... 65–67, 74n80
3:15 .... 24, 25, 27, 31, 34, 53, 65, 66, 68, 69, 72, 77, 80, 84, 85, 86, 111, 116, 171, 198, 269, 324, 325n510, 327, 414, 433, 1241
3:16 .... 61, 66, 74, 74n80, 81, 132
3:16–17 1038
3:16–19 .... 1042n307
3:16–22 489
3:17 .... 75, 84, 135, 164, 1246
3:17–19 .... 61, 68, 1042
3:19 .... 73n79, 211, 313
3:20 .... 61, 63, 67, 72, 925
3:20–24 67–69
3:21 .... 68, 68n67, 107n145, 111, 114, 740

3:21–24	61	
3:22–24	68	
3:23	69, 73	
3:23–24	227, 978, 1105	
3:24	52, 69, 126, 127, 146, 710, 718, 819, 936, 959, 1110, 1187, 1320	
4	34, 66, 70–79, 88, 89, 233, 283	
4–11	73, 125	
4:1	72, 84, 480n95, 925, 974n217	
4:1–5	72–74	
4:2	72, 73	
4:3	73, 107, 1202	
4:3–4	73	
4:4	73, 107, 107n145, 111, 127	
4:4–5	73	
4:5	74, 1131	
4:5–7	844	
4:6–7	72, 74	
4:6–8	74–75	
4:6–15	136	
4:7	66, 66n62, 74, 1304	
4:8	74, 74n81, 114, 116, 325n506, 1183n97	
4:9	75, 1032	
4:9–16	75	
4:10	75	
4:10–12	968	
4:11	75, 135, 362n597, 672	
4:12	75	
4:13–14	75	
4:14	75	
4:15	75, 648	
4:16	75, 126, 146, 1320	
4:16–22	126	
4:17	75, 76, 89	
4:17–24	75–77	
4:19	87, 242, 264	
4:19–22	72	
4:19–24	80, 82, 90, 95	
4:20	76	
4:20–22	76	
4:21	76, 489	
4:21–23	489–493	
4:22	561n287, 1261	
4:23	76, 77, 199n296	
4:23–24	72, 651n502	
4:24	77, 648, 1042	
4:25	65, 72, 77, 84, 131, 1261	
4:25–26	77–78, 81, 165n254, 295n450	
4:26	72, 77, 81, 82, 90, 127	
5	24, 79–85, 86, 88, 88n108, 89, 95, 102, 110, 130, 131, 132n206, 133	
5:1	87	
5:1–2	81	
5:1–3	88	
5:1–5	81–82	
5:2	87	
5:3	88, 645	
5:3–5	82	
5:4	82	
5:5	82	
5:6–24	82–83, 95	
5:7	82	
5:8	82	
5:10	82	
5:11	82	
5:15	82	
5:18–22	76	
5:22	638n462	
5:22–24	131	
5:24	80, 82, 83, 95	
5:25–32	83–85	
5:29	80, 84, 105, 471, 480n95	
5:32	95, 114	
6	86, 88, 90, 95n118, 185, 304	
6–8	24, 31	
6–9	471, 645	
6:1	87, 89, 90n111, 125	
6:1–2	89	
6:1–4	86, 87–90	
6:1–5	95	
6:1–8	86–92	
6:2	87, 89, 146, 304, 337	
6:3	82, 89, 89n110	
6:4	89, 90, 90n111, 95, 116, 122, 137	
6:4–5	89, 1180	
6:5	86, 89, 90, 92, 95, 100, 107n148, 181, 337, 346	
6:5–8	90–91	
6:6	91	
6:7	86, 91	
6:8	91, 95, 1303	
6:9	83, 85, 86, 91, 95, 108, 116, 170, 638n462, 1100	
6:9–12	84, 94–96	
6:9–22	93–98	
6:10	114	
6:11	96	
6:11–12	95	
6:12	95, 100	
6:13	95, 165n254	
6:13–22	96–97, 112	
6:13–9:17	136	
6:14	471	
6:17	96	
6:18	96, 103, 112, 471, 547n252, 1292	
6:18–20	645, 681	
6:19	100	
6:20	97	
6:21	97	
6:22	97, 810	
7	98–103, 108	
7:1	100	
7:1–4	106	
7:1–5	99–100	
7:2	111	
7:2–3	100	
7:3	489	
7:4	100, 101, 106, 705	
7:5	100	
7:6	114	
7:6–10	100	
7:7–10	705	
7:7	188	
7:9	101n137	
7:10	100	
7:11	101, 105	
7:11–16	101–102	
7:13	114, 489	
7:14	489	
7:15	101	
7:16	102	
7:17–21	102	
7:17–24	102	
7:19–23	102	
7:22	102, 489	
7:23	102, 102n141, 106	
7:24	105	
8	103–108	
8:1	42, 104, 105, 189, 273, 486n116, 645, 681, 737, 1156	
8:1–2	104	
8:1–5	105–106	
8:2	105	
8:3	105	
8:4	105	
8:5	106	
8:6–13	106	
8:9	106	
8:10	106, 639	
8:11	106	
8:12	106	
8:13	106	
8:14	106	
8:14–19	106–107	
8:15	489	
8:15–17	106	
8:17	106, 171	
8:18–19	106	
8:19	489	
8:20	107, 111, 841	
8:20–22	107–108	
8:21	106, 107, 110, 113, 114, 116, 135, 185, 337, 743, 1195	
8:22	107	
8:32	489	
9	31, 109–117	
9:1	46, 111, 116, 123, 126, 171, 251, 405, 1041	
9:1–2	1043	
9:1–7	111–112, 620	
9:2	111	
9:3	111	
9:3–4	917	
9:4	111, 968, 969, 1071n11	
9:5	112, 652, 994	
9:5–6	330	
9:6	28, 47, 112, 116, 642, 648n485, 653, 1329, 1331	
9:6–7	613, 623	
9:7	46, 171, 489	
9:8–10	681	
9:8–17	112–113	
9:9	108, 1216	
9:9–10	645	
9:11	695, 1195	
9:12	489, 762	
9:12–17	113, 172	
9:13	116, 762	
9:15	113, 486n116, 737	
9:16	113, 486n116, 737, 1216	
9:17	762	
9:18	114	
9:18–29	113–116	
9:20	114	
9:21	110, 114, 190	
9:22–23	110	
9:23	114	
9:24	94n117, 119n165	
9:25	114, 115n157, 135, 138, 672	

9:25–27 110
9:26 115
9:26–27 130
9:27 . . . . 114, 115, 708
9:28 . . . . 110, 114
9:28–29 116
9:29 . . . . 80, 88
9:34 489
9:35 489
10 . . . . 24, 28, 49, 85, 113, 117–124, 130, 131, 132n206, 399, 1287
10:1 . . . . 119, 489, 1100
10:1–5 119–120
10:2 119
10:6 . . . . 120, 1262
10:6–20 . . . . 120–122, 239n346, 318n489
10:8 121
10:8–10 125
10:9 . . . . 121, 122
10:10 . . . . 122, 125n187
10:10–12 121
10:13–14 120
10:14 . . . . 120n172, 1262
10:15 . . . . 121, 1179, 1303
10:15–18 . . . . 161n247
10:15–19 121
10:17–18 121
10:19 . . . . 121, 1321
10:20 489
10:21 122
10:21–22 1262
10:21–32 122–123
10:22 123
10:23 . . . . 123n183
10:24 123
10:25 . . . . 123, 124
10:27 489
10:29 123
10:32 123
11 . . . . 24, 119, 125n187, 135, 255, 257
11:1 . . . . 125, 128
11:1–4 125–127
11:1–9 . . . . 24, 31, 122, 123, 124–129, 139, 146
11:2 . . . . 126, 128, 146, 151
11:3 . . . . 126, 128
11:3–4 127
11:4 . . . . 125, 126, 127, 128, 137, 255
11:5 . . . . 127, 128, 181
11:5–9 127–128
11:6 . . . . 127, 305n467
11:6–9 257
11:7 . . . . 127, 128, 666, 978n225
11:8 . . . . 125, 128
11:9 . . . . 125, 125n187, 128, 666, 978n225
11:10 . . . . 489, 1100
11:10–26 . . . . 130, 131,134
11:10–32 129–134
11:14 1262
11:18 123
11:26 . . . . 124, 131, 138
11:27 . . . . 132, 133, 210, 230, 1100
11:27–32 . . . . 130, 132–133, 136, 210
11:27–12:3 31
11:28–31 136
11:30 . . . . 131, 132, 138, 231, 238
11:31 133
11:32 . . . . 131, 136
12 . . . . 24, 99n131, 129, 133, 135, 140, 142, 150, 156, 193, 255
12–25 33
12–50 . . . . 23, 28
12:1 . . . . 136, 205, 205n303, 210, 218n322, 239, 449, 500
12:1–3 . . . . 23, 27, 46, 124, 129, 130, 131, 136–138, 136n214, 140, 180, 207, 228, 344, 358, 393, 1040, 1043
12:1–4 224
12:1–9 . . . . 24, 135–139
12:2 . . . . 76, 90, 136, 137, 138, 145, 171, 246, 395, 449, 460, 465, 775, 1252
12:2–3 . . . . 83, 154, 238, 243, 313, 398, 402, 424
12:3 . . . . 136, 137, 144, 146, 164, 192, 202, 239, 249, 256, 365, 449, 468, 546, 547, 589, 600, 988, 1252, 1253, 1258
12:4 . . . . 169, 221n329, 227
12:4–5 136
12:4–9 138–139
12:5 138
12:5–9 136
12:6 . . . . 136, 138
12:6–7 . . . . 139, 312
12:6–9 138
12:7 . . . . 65, 107, 147, 158, 210, 241, 549n258, 583, 846, 1092, 1191
12:7–8 . . . . 139, 205, 206
12:8 . . . . 107, 125n188, 142, 256, 583
12:9 . . . . 142, 1235
12:9–10 1226
12:10 . . . . 140, 141, 142, 150, 163, 238, 376, 392
12:10–20 . . . . 28, 137, 141–142, 218, 219n325, 279n416, 284n421, 330n516
12:10–13:4 140–143
12:11 . . . . 141, 264
12:11–20 . . . . 192, 259
12:14 193
12:15 . . . . 142, 337, 1259
12:16 . . . . 142, 163, 195, 240, 279
12:17 . . . . 533n227
12:17–20 . . . . 141, 1123
12:18–19 142
12:20 142
12:44 1034
13 . . . . 142, 152, 158, 186, 240
13–15 163
13–19 34
13:1 . . . . 142, 144
13:1–4 142
13:2 142
13:3 142
13:4 . . . . 142, 148, 583
13:5 145
13:5–7 144–145
13:5–18 143–148
13:6 . . . . 145, 156, 319
13:6–7 1245
13:7 . . . . 145, 161n247, 1306
13:8 . . . . 145, 489
13:8–9 145
13:8–13 145–147
13:9 . . . . 147, 232, 305, 1306
13:10 . . . . 28, 144, 146, 163, 190, 500, 1306
13:10–11 1306
13:11 . . . . 125n188, 126, 146, 146n227, 147, 232, 1306
13:12 147
13:13 . . . . 144, 146, 150, 153, 180, 185, 219
13:14 . . . . 147, 147n229, 232, 1323
13:14–16 147
13:14–18 147–148
13:15 1277
13:15–16 147
13:15–17 239
13:16 . . . . 158, 227, 256, 1083n21, 1252, 1253
13:16–17 157
13:17 147
13:18 . . . . 107, 147, 148, 152, 177, 205, 206, 583
14 . . . . 122, 149–155, 156
14:1–11 150
14:1–12 150–152
14:2 . . . . 146, 151
14:4 . . . . 151, 489, 1183
14:5–6 151
14:6 1156
14:7 . . . . 151, 152, 153, 1186, 1226
14:8 . . . . 146, 489
14:10 152
14:12 . . . . 147, 150, 152, 1306
14:12–14 152
14:13 . . . . 122, 152, 177, 634n452
14:13–16 152–153
14:14 . . . . 27, 152, 293, 403n659, 445
14:14–16 286
14:15 152
14:16 153
14:17 . . . . 153, 489
14:17–18 153
14:17–24 . . . . 153–154, 257n374
14:18 . . . . 249, 598, 1267
14:18–20 . . . . 150, 232, 1260
14:19–20 153
14:20 . . . . 153, 257n374, 1330
14:21 . . . . 150, 153, 154
14:21–23 305
14:22 . . . . 153, 154, 500, 1260
15 . . . . 27, 155–162, 169, 170n258, 172, 174, 192n286, 194, 228, 255
15:1 . . . . 156, 157, 179, 194, 336, 1259
15:1–5 156
15:1–6 . . . . 156–158, 192n286, 560
15:2 . . . . 138, 157, 164, 182, 218
15:2–3 157
15:3 . . . . 1083n21
15:4 . . . . 156, 157, 163

15:4–5 157	17:2 ....170, 227, 986	18:20............180
15:5 ....147n229, 165, 207, 227, 239, 449, 460, 478n85	17:3 170	18:20–21 186
	17:4 ....170, 171, 172, 227, 239	18:21............180, 181, 206
15:6 ....95, 100, 148, 158, 203, 316		18:21–22 185
	17:4–5 232	18:22............577n309
15:7 ....132, 133, 157, 500	17:5 ....137, 171, 226	18:22–33 181–182
15:7–8 502	17:5–6 ....173, 449	18:23............598, 1202
15:7–16..........158–160	17:6 ....171, 174n264, 405, 419, 986, 1252	18:23–33 ....34, 205
15:7–21..........156		18:24............1185
15:8 158	17:7 ....97, 112, 170, 171, 172, 288n436, 850, 1216, 1292	18:25............31, 181, 187, 189, 493
15:9 ....158, 774n756		
15:9–10..........887, 926n146		18:26............1185
15:10............158	17:7–8 ....449, 1041	18:27............181
15:11............353	17:8 ....172, 305, 404, 465	18:28............185n274
15:12............55, 157, 159, 160, 169	17:9 ....97, 170, 172, 489	18:32............177, 181, 185, 528n208
	17:9–14..........172–173	
15:13............25, 32, 159, 165n252, 172, 345, 365, 402, 431, 466, 466n58, 668, 1081	17:10............170, 306n469	18:33............182, 1262
	17:10–11 ....728, 1007	19................146, 147, 150, 177, 178, 181, 183–191, 254
	17:10–13 493	
	17:11............113, 762, 926, 926n145	
15:13–14 ....25, 546, 1062, 1255		19:1 ....147, 178, 186, 694
15:14............483, 1156	17:12............306n469, 926, 986, 1029n288	19:1–2 ....185, 186
15:14–16 159		19:1–3 186–187
15:15............159, 227	17:12–13 ....198, 547	19:2 ....179n267
15:16............116, 159, 161, 188, 219, 395, 398, 556n266, 956, 979	17:12–14 1034	19:2–3 178
	17:13............170, 173	19:3 ....186, 187
	17:14............169, 170, 493, 926n145, 1292	19:4 ....187, 188, 308n475
15:17............160		19:4–5 185
15:17–21 160–161	17:15............173	19:4–11 187–188
15:18............160, 695, 1156, 1167, 1191	17:15–22 173–174	19:5 187
	17:16............173, 313, 1252	19:7 ....186, 187
15:18–20 449	17:16–20 179	19:8 ....187, 190
15:18–21 502	17:17............173, 226, 227, 775	19:9 187
15:19–21 ....161, 479	17:18............174	19:10–11 187
15:21............1303	17:19............170, 174, 198, 1216, 1292	19:11............185, 519n180
16................77n88, 156, 162–167, 169, 172, 246, 269, 412		19:12............185
	17:19–20 175	19:12–14 ....100, 188
	17:19–21 203	19:13............188
16–21 232	17:20............174, 228	19:14............185, 186, 188, 1158n76
16:1 163	17:21............97, 170, 174, 179, 1292	
16:1–2 271		19:15............1203
16:1–6 ....163–165, 271n391	17:23............174, 547, 926, 926n145	19:15–22 181
16:1–16..........977n222		19:15–26 188–189
16:2 ....164, 199, 246	17:23–27 174	19:16............188
16:3 ....28, 67n65, 164	17:24............926n145	19:16–17 188
16:4 ....163, 164	17:24–25 ....507n163	19:17............188
16:5 ....165, 977	17:25............926n145	19:18............179n267
16:6 ....165, 199n296	17:26............174, 175	19:20............188
16:7 ....165, 1248, 1312, 1313n270	18................147n228, 176–183, 187, 194	19:20–21 189
		19:22–23 146
	18:1 177	19:23............186
16:7–12..........165–166, 478	18:1–8 177–179	19:24 .... 101, 189, 994, 1164
16:8 165	18:2 ....178, 694	
16:9 ....163, 165, 166	18:2–5 ....185, 186	19:26............185, 189, 217
16:10............163, 165, 228	18:3–5 178	19:27............189
16:10–12 228	18:6 178	19:27–29 189
16:11............166, 200, 485n115	18:6–8 187	19:28............189
16:11–12 925	18:7 ....178, 470n70	19:29............183, 186, 188, 737, 1156
16:12............166, 200n298, 226, 228	18:8 ....177, 179	
	18:9–15..........179–180	19:30............185, 190
16:13............165, 165n253, 166, 166n257, 206, 269	18:10............177, 179	19:30–38 ....34, 189–190
	18:11............179, 287	19:31–33 190
16:13–14 ....481n99	18:11–15 925	19:32............272
16:13–16 166–167	18:12–13 179	19:36–37 1245
16:14............166n257, 167, 223, 1312	18:13............179	19:36–38 1306
	18:13–14 179	19:37–38 ....144, 185, 190, 207n310
16:15............167	18:14............179, 1127	
16:16............507n163	18:15............179	20................191–195, 239n346
17................27, 43, 168–175, 179	18:16............180	20:1 ....193, 238, 1156, 1312
	18:16–21 180–181	
17:1 ....161, 170, 174, 250, 411, 423, 1259	18:17............93	20:1–2 193
	18:17–21 177	20:1–18..........137
17:1–6 1041	18:18............180, 256, 1184	20:2 ....192, 193, 975n220, 1259
17:1–8 ....169–172, 378n621, 410n671	18:19............180, 180n268, 182, 612, 623	
		20:2–9 1123

20:2–14 259
20:3 .... 193, 299, 1247
20:3–8 193–194
20:4 193
20:5 193
20:6 .... 194, 614
20:7 .... 156, 157n242, 192, 194, 232, 1165
20:8 194
20:8–11 240
20:9 194
20:9–18 194–195
20:11 .... 194, 202, 371, 618n418
20:12 .... 132, 502n154, 746
20:12–16 ...... 975n220
20:13 .... 192, 194
20:14 .... 195, 201
20:15 195
20:17–18 ...... 195, 873, 995
21 .... 24, 196–202, 204, 288
21:1 .... 198, 483n102
21:1–2 198
21:1–7 198
21:1–12 199
21:2 .... 323, 332, 387n637
21:3 .... 72, 198
21:4 .... 198, 206, 926
21:5 .... 199n296
21:6 .... 174, 197, 198
21:6–7 925
21:7 .... 198, 332, 387n637
21:8 471
21:8–9 197
21:8–21 198–200
21:9 .... 28, 199
21:9–13 166
21:10 .... 197, 199, 232, 977
21:10–11 227
21:11 199
21:12 .... 164, 197, 199, 219
21:12–13 199
21:12–14 ...... 226, 227
21:13 199
21:14 .... 199, 205, 1298
21:14–16 199
21:17 206
21:17–20 ...... 199n296
21:18 200
21:19 200
21:20 .... 199n295
21:21 .... 200, 217, 242, 1156
21:22 .... 200, 201, 241n351
21:22–24 241
21:22–34 ...... 197, 200–201, 238
21:23 .... 197, 200
21:25 .... 200, 1235
21:27 201
21:28–30 201
21:30–31 200
21:31 .... 242, 1235
21:31–32 1292
21:31–33 241
21:32 .... 120n172
21:33 .... 201, 394, 726
21:34 201
22 .... 25, 31, 32, 197, 208, 224, 226, 394, 412, 832
22:1 .... 203, 204, 206, 336, 520n188, 1159
22:1–2 204–205
22:1–16 206
22:1–19 202–209

22:2 .... 147n229, 175, 203, 204, 205, 205n303, 210, 226, 841, 845
22:3 205
22:3–8 205–206
22:4 .... 204, 205n306
22:5 .... 204, 205, 845
22:6 .... 204, 205, 208
22:7 .... 206, 248
22:8 .... 205, 206, 207
22:8–9 969
22:9 206
22:9–14 206–207
22:10 .... 206, 842
22:11 .... 199n297, 206, 395, 478n83, 1248
22:11–12 478
22:12 .... 175, 204, 206, 478n83, 590, 845
22:13 .... 175, 205n306, 207, 387, 842
22:14 .... 203, 207, 224, 500, 1159
22:15–19 207–208
22:16 .... 207, 776, 1259
22:16–17 ...... 842n23
22:16–18 207
22:17 .... 207, 223, 227, 293, 364, 465, 1259
22:18 .... 207, 211, 256
22:19 207
22:20–22 210
22:20–24 ...... 132n206, 210–211, 219, 220
22:20–23:20 .. 209–214
22:20–25:11 .. 210
22:21 211
23 .... 83, 145, 226, 299n456, 410
23–50 25
23:1 211
23:1–2 .... 210, 211, 226
23:1–16 .... 498n131
23:2 .... 211, 1178
23:3 211
23:3–20 .... 210, 211–213
23:4 .... 212, 213, 218, 1151, 1193
23:6 .... 179n267, 212, 271n393
23:8–9 212
23:9 212
23:11 .... 212, 213, 1246
23:13 213
23:15 213
23:16 213
23:17–19 428
23:19 213
23:19–20 1178
23:20 212
24 .... 142n222, 157, 200, 211, 214–225, 259, 261, 282, 794
24:1 .... 218, 222
24:1–7 217
24:1–9 218–219
24:2 .... 218, 219
24:2–3 406
24:2–4 638
24:3 .... 219, 250, 337, 1289
24:3–4 .... 218, 219
24:3–8 1290
24:4 136
24:5–8 218
24:6 .... 219, 250

24:6–9 219
24:10 .... 133, 219, 254, 259n376, 919
24:10–14 219–220
24:12 .... 219, 225, 784
24:12–21 218
24:12–27 794
24:14 .... 220, 784
24:15 220
24:15–28 220–221
24:16 .... 220, 220n327, 224, 261, 264, 663n523, 974n217
24:16–51 ...... 663n523
24:18–19 220
24:19–20 ...... 224, 919
24:20 220
24:21 .... 261, 558
24:22 221
24:22–25 221
24:23 220
24:24 220
24:26 694
24:27 .... 220, 590n333, 784
24:28 221
24:29–30 221
24:29–48 221–222
24:30 221
24:31 221
24:32 221
24:33 222
24:34–48 794
24:35 .... 222, 279
24:36 226
24:36–51 264
24:38 1103
24:40 .... 411, 1103
24:41 1304
24:43 .... 220n327
24:47 221
24:49 .... 222, 406, 784
24:49–61 222–223
24:50 .... 221, 222, 286, 286n429
24:50–51 261
24:51 222
24:52 222
24:53 .... 222, 222n330
24:54 222
24:54–59 222
24:54–61 286
24:55 223
24:58 .... 218, 223, 224, 999
24:59 223
24:60 .... 223, 1087, 1259
24:61 223
24:62 .... 167, 223
24:62–67 ...... 223–224, 265
24:63 223
24:63–64 223
24:65 .... 223, 225
24:66 .... 225, 694
24:67 .... 218, 221, 224, 336, 746, 1266
24:67a 502n154
25 .... 25, 171, 227, 235, 1100
25:1–6 226–227
25:1–18 .... 225–229, 230
25:2 1245
25:3 .... 1261n200
25:5 .... 226, 227
25:6 .... 226, 227
25:7 .... 226, 233, 239n346, 403

SCRIPTURE INDEX

25:7–8 226
25:7–11 227–228
25:8 .... 227, 315, 999n242, 1229
25:8–10 211
25:9 .... 213, 226, 410
25:9–10 228
25:11 .... 167, 226, 239
25:12 .... 28, 228, 231, 1100
25:12–15 1085
25:12–16 174
25:12–18 .... 33, 228, 317
25:13–15 228
25:17 .... 228, 315, 1229
25:18 .... 193, 226, 227, 228, 1261n200
25:19 .... 230, 1100
25:19–21 231–232
25:19–34 230–236
25:20 .... 123, 219n326, 226, 232, 242
25:21 .... 133, 226, 231, 232, 238, 270
25:22 .... 221n329, 232, 780
25:22–23 .... 232–233, 925
25:22–26 341
25:23 .... 231, 235, 246, 247, 255, 264, 291, 298, 508
25:24 .... 520n188
25:24–26 .... 233, 925
25:25 .... 234, 248, 649
25:26 .... 232, 233, 247, 507n163
25:27 .... 114, 234, 247, 260, 261
25:27–28 234
25:28 .... 234, 247
25:29 234
25:29–34 .... 234–235, 246
25:30 .... 233, 234
25:31 235
25:31–33 231
25:31–34 249
25:32 235
25:33 235
25:34 235
26 .... 231, 236–243, 288
26–36 33
26:1 .... 120n172, 193, 238, 239
26:1–4 .... 392, 394
26:1–6 238–239
26:2 239
26:2–3 846
26:2–5 238
26:3 .... 239, 549n258, 1290, 1292
26:3–4 449
26:3–5 227
26:5 239
26:6 239
26:7 .... 239, 1195
26:7–11 .... 239–240, 259
26:8 .... 239, 240, 347n558
26:9 240
26:10 240
26:10–11 1123
26:11 240
26:12 .... 240, 325, 1177
26:12–22 240–241
26:13 279
26:13–14 240
26:15 .... 240, 1235
26:17–18 1235
26:18 .... 242n352
26:18–21 240
26:18–35 238
26:19 1238
26:20 1177
26:20–21 1245
26:20–22 577
26:22 .... 240, 500
26:23–25 241
26:24 .... 241, 256, 288n436, 479n88, 500, 1173
26:24–25 583
26:25 241
26:26 .... 200n299
26:26–29 241
26:26–33 241–242
26:28 241
26:28–30 697
26:29 .... 241, 242, 1258
26:30 .... 242, 1191
26:32 242
26:33 .... 207n310, 242
26:34 .... 217, 218, 242, 247, 318, 1179
26:34–35 242
26:35 .... 242, 247
27 .... 227, 240, 246, 252, 284, 315n483, 410, 411
27:1 .... 247, 331
27:1–28:9 243–253
27:1–4 .... 246, 247
27:3 969
27:3–4 247
27:4 .... 247, 247n355, 324
27:5 .... 247, 331
27:5–10 247–248
27:5–17 246
27:6 .... 247, 331
27:6–10 246
27:7 247
27:8 .... 247, 331
27:9 .... 331, 339
27:9–10 247
27:11 .... 233, 246, 248, 254
27:11–13 992
27:11–17 248
27:13 .... 247, 248, 252
27:13–14 248
27:15 .... 233, 247, 331
27:15–16 248
27:16 .... 331, 339
27:17 .... 247, 248, 331
27:18 .... 248, 331, 411
27:18–29 .... 246, 248–249
27:19 .... 247n355, 248, 331
27:20 .... 247, 248, 331, 500, 1329
27:21 .... 247, 331
27:22 .... 248, 249
27:23 .... 292n439, 331
27:24 .... 247, 249n362, 331
27:25 .... 247n355, 248
27:26 .... 247, 299, 331
27:26–27 .... 249, 262
27:27 .... 247, 247n359, 249, 331, 843
27:28 .... 247n359, 249
27:28–29 .... 250, 255
27:29 .... 249, 298, 1252
27:30 .... 249, 292n439
27:30–40 249–250
27:31 .... 247n355, 249
27:32 .... 247, 249
27:33 249
27:34 1174
27:35 .... 306, 315
27:36 .... 249, 250
27:38 .... 1183, 1187
27:39 .... 250, 319
27:39–40 250
27:40 250
27:41 .... 250, 291, 297
27:41–46 246
27:41–28:5 .... 250–251, 410n673
27:42 247
27:43 .... 247, 250, 264, 285, 331
27:44 250
27:45 250
27:46 250
28 .... 257, 262, 267, 286, 292, 293, 301, 303, 310, 313, 315, 395, 413
28:1 .... 250, 337
28:1–5 246
28:3 .... 25, 32, 129, 251, 274, 276, 313, 376, 405, 1259
28:3–4 255
28:4 251
28:5 .... 123, 251
28:6–7 251
28:6–9 251
28:8 1179
28:9 .... 217, 251, 318, 318n488, 561n287
28:9–22 254
28:10 254
28:10–15 254–256
28:10–22 253–258
28:11 .... 254, 255, 316
28:12 .... 129, 254, 255, 256, 257
28:13 .... 255, 256, 257, 288n436, 449, 500, 549n258
28:13–15 .... 266, 276, 410
28:13–17 262
28:14 .... 256, 268, 274, 279, 1216, 1253
28:15 .... 256, 283, 300, 312, 449
28:16 256
28:16–19 256
28:17 .... 127, 256
28:18 .... 256, 313, 423
28:18–22 284
28:19 .... 256, 312, 313, 1262
28:19–22 .... 300, 311
28:20 .... 853, 1289
28:20–22 .... 256–257, 300, 312, 1053, 1290
28:21 .... 257, 300, 315
28:22 257
29 259
29–30 364
29:1 259
29:1–3 259–260
29:1–14 258–263
29:2 260
29:3 260
29:4–8 260
29:6 260
29:7–8 260
29:9 261
29:9–11 219
29:9–12 260–261
29:10 .... 260, 264

29:11..............260	30:31..............277, 577n308	31:55..............262, 288
29:12..............260n378	30:32..............275, 1217	32..................290–296, 394
29:13..............261, 262, 288, 299, 494, 588	30:33..............277, 284, 285	32:1................292
29:13–14........261–262, 999	30:35..............276, 278	32:1–2.............254, 291–292
29:14..............55n46, 262, 263, 974	30:35–43........278–279	32:2................292
	30:37–42........278, 283	32:3................292, 292n440, 319
29:15..............264, 277	30:37–43........276, 966	32:3–6.............292–293, 588
29:15–20........264–265	30:43..............279	32:4................276, 283, 292
29:15–30........263–267, 637n460	31....................280–289, 291	32:4–5.............292
29:17..............260, 261	31:1................276, 283, 1247	32:5................293
29:18..............262, 265, 336	31:1–2.............311	32:6................293, 298
29:18–28........217	31:1–3.............282–283	32:7................142n222
29:19..............639	31:2................282	32:7–8.............293
29:20..............265	31:3................283, 479n88	32:7–12...........293
29:21..............265, 520n188	31:4................283	32:9................293
29:21–30........265–266	31:4–16...........283–284	32:10..............254, 293, 403, 406, 590n333, 784
29:23..............265, 339	31:5................283, 283n419, 292, 312	
29:24..............266		32:10–11.........784
29:25..............265, 285, 315, 342	31:5–13..........277n407	32:11..............293
29:27..............266, 639, 898	31:7................280, 283, 499n139, 1185, 1248	32:12..............293, 364, 378, 1330
29:29..............266		32:13..............1302
29:30..............266	31:8–12...........278	32:13–21.........293
29:31..............133, 268, 269, 271, 273, 428, 925, 1096	31:11..............286	32:13–23.........293–294
	31:11–13.........311	32:15..............294n445
29:31–34........506n160	31:12..............284	32:18..............294
29:31–35........269–270, 1085	31:13..............284, 395	32:20..............294, 1204
29:31–30:24....267–274	31:14..............1216	32:21..............1330
29:31–30:34....273	31:14–16.........264, 284	32:21–23.........294
29:32..............269, 270n388, 486	31:15..............285	32:22..............285
29:32–35........925	31:16..............284	32:24..............294
29:32–30:24....72	31:17..............142n222	32:24–29.........298
29:33..............270, 1096	31:17–21.........284–285	32:24–31.........254
29:34..............270, 270n388, 480n95	31:17–28.........489	32:24–32.........294–296
	31:18..............1302	32:25..............294
29:35..............419, 1096	31:18–21.........211	32:26..............295
30....................164, 1083	31:19..............284, 285, 311, 614	32:27–30.........412
30:1................270, 271, 273, 314, 929	31:20..............284, 285	32:28..............271n393, 295, 313, 1158
	31:21..............285	
30:1–8............270–271	31:22..............286	32:30..............299, 316, 478
30:1–24..........977	31:22–35.........286–287	32:31..............254
30:2................269n387, 270	31:24..............286, 286n429, 299, 1247, 1260	32:32..............28, 296
30:3................164, 271, 431		33....................250, 291, 297–301, 412
30:3–8............977n222	31:25..............286	
30:4–13..........266	31:26..............285	33:1................298, 299
30:6................271	31:27..............223, 285	33:1–3.............298
30:8................271n393	31:28..............262	33:2................298, 323
30:9................271	31:29..............1260	33:3................298
30:9–21..........271–272	31:30..............285, 286, 638n462	33:4................299
30:10–13........1085	31:30–32.........289	33:4–11...........298–300
30:11..............271	31:32..............285, 287, 289, 314, 385, 872	33:5................299, 299n455, 783
30:12–13........1095		33:5–11...........402
30:13..............271	31:33..............287	33:7................298n452
30:14..............272, 273	31:34..............284, 287	33:8................299
30:14–16........270	31:34–35.........264, 925, 952	33:9................298, 299, 299n456, 300
30:15..............270n388, 272, 974n216	31:35..............179, 287	
	31:36..............577	33:10..............299, 299n455, 306, 1131
30:16..............272n398	31:36–42.........288n433	
30:17..............271, 272	31:36–55.........241n349, 287–288, 379n624, 395n642	33:11..............298, 299, 299n455, 783
30:17–20........1085		
30:18..............270n388, 272	31:38..............279	33:12..............300
30:20..............270n388, 272	31:38–40........261	33:12–14.........319
30:21..............272, 304	31:38–42........277	33:12–16.........298
30:22..............273, 925, 1156	31:39..............285, 287	33:12–17.........300
30:22–24........273	31:40..............523n195	33:14..............300
30:23..............273	31:41..............287	33:14–16.........300
30:23–24........1085	31:41–52.........694	33:15..............300
30:24..............273	31:42..............288, 301, 423	33:16–17.........300
30:25..............273, 275, 276, 323	31:43..............287	33:17..............616
30:25–28........276–277	31:44–46.........697	33:18..............138, 257, 300, 307
30:25–43........274–380	31:45–46.........287	33:18–20.........300–301, 583
30:27..............275, 277, 279, 283	31:46..............287, 288n433	33:19..............300, 313
30:28..............275, 277, 1217	31:49..............288n434	33:20..............300, 301, 311
30:29–34........277–278	31:53..............241n349, 288, 423	34....................272, 301, 302–309, 311, 314, 337, 399, 419, 975, 1094
30:30..............277, 279	31:53–54.........697	
	31:54..............852	

34:1 .... 303, 304, 308	36:1–5 318–319	37:22 .... 330, 373
34:1–7 304–305	36:1–8 319	37:22–28 386
34:2 .... 272, 303, 304, 640	36:2 .... 318n488, 318n490, 1179	37:23 .... 328, 330, 330n515, 361, 393
34:3 304	36:2–3 318	37:23–24 330
34:4 .... 303, 304, 305	36:4 319	37:24 .... 325, 330, 353
34:5 .... 303, 305, 308	36:4–5 318	37:25 .... 142n222, 330, 378
34:7 .... 305, 305n464	36:5 318	37:25–28 .... 25, 330–331, 344n549
34:8 305	36:6 319	37:26 370
34:8–12 305–306	36:6–8 319	37:26–27 .... 336, 387
34:10 .... 305, 307	36:7 319	37:27 .... 330, 331, 974
34:11–12 306	36:8 .... 318, 319	37:28 .... 330, 372, 393
34:12 .... 305, 636n459, 662n520	36:9 .... 319, 1100	37:29 331
34:13 .... 306, 315	36:9–19 319	37:29–30 418
34:13–19 306	36:9–43 319	37:29–36 .... 331–332, 344, 373n617, 397n650
34:15 .... 306n469	36:12 .... 582, 1186, 1261	37:30 .... 82n92
34:19 .... 307, 612	36:16 582	37:31 339
34:20 307	36:19 .... 318, 319	37:31–32 264
34:20–24 307	36:20 319	37:31–33 346
34:21 307	36:20–30 319	37:31–35 388
34:22 307	36:22 .... 561n287	37:32 .... 331, 340, 342
34:23 307	36:24 1080	37:32–33 .... 370, 371
34:24 .... 307n471	36:27–31 1317	37:32–36 328
34:25 .... 303, 307	36:31 320	37:33 .... 331, 369, 373
34:25–26 307	36:31–43 320	37:34 .... 331, 386n634, 739, 779, 998
34:25–31 307–308	36:35 1245	37:34–35 .... 273, 338, 998
34:27 307	36:43 .... 318, 320	37:35 .... 331, 395, 397, 403
34:27–29 307	37 .... 25, 273, 283, 286, 315n483, 337, 340, 343, 351, 351n566, 361, 364, 369, 371n611, 377, 379, 380, 388, 401	37:36 .... 330, 332, 335, 343, 344, 507n162
34:29 .... 307, 307n473		38 .... 316, 334–342, 348, 377, 399
34:30 .... 303, 308, 311, 312, 419, 844		38:1 .... 335, 336, 338, 345
34:31 .... 303, 308	37–44 336	38:1–2 336–337
35 309–316	37–50 33	38:1–30 322
35:1 .... 311, 583	37:1 322	38:2 .... 217, 336
35:1–8 311–313	37:1–2 322–323	38:2–3 337
35:2 .... 311, 597n345, 1168	37:1–11 321–327	38:3 72
35:2–4 289	37:2 .... 321, 322, 323, 324, 326n511, 329, 351, 364, 406, 1100	38:3–5 337
35:3 .... 312, 583		38:4–5 72
35:4 311		38:5 337
35:5 312	37:2–11 322	38:6–11 337–338
35:6 138	37:3 .... 323, 324, 330, 332, 361	38:7 .... 346, 1272
35:6–15 257		38:7–11 335
35:7 .... 257, 312, 583	37:3–4 .... 321, 323–324	38:9 337
35:8 .... 313, 316	37:3–50:26 51	38:10 .... 338, 346
35:9–13 .... 311, 313	37:4 .... 324, 329, 361, 380, 388	38:11 338
35:9–14 257		38:12 .... 336n529, 338
35:9–15 313	37:5 324	38:12–19 338–339
35:10–12 410	37:5–8 419	38:14 .... 338, 339
35:11 .... 251, 313, 320, 321, 335, 376, 399, 405, 417, 466, 1252, 1259	37:5–10 .... 321, 329	38:15 .... 339, 341
	37:5–11 .... 325–326, 358	38:15–16 346
	37:7 .... 325, 364, 369, 386	38:15–18 336
	37:7–8 380	38:17 339
35:11–12 1041	37:8 .... 324, 325, 325n509, 394	38:18 .... 339, 363n601, 377
35:12 449		38:19 339
35:14 313	37:9 325	38:20 340
35:15 313	37:9–11 332	38:20–23 ...... 338, 339–340
35:16 413	37:11 .... 270, 326	38:21 987
35:16–18 1085	37:12–17 328–329	38:22 340
35:16–20 314	37:12–36 ...... 322, 327–334	38:24 .... 340, 994
35:17 314	37:13 .... 204, 329	38:24–26 ...... 339, 340–341
35:17–19 925	37:14 .... 329, 361, 369, 376, 380	38:25 .... 340, 342
35:18 .... 314, 316, 325n511		38:25–27 1083
35:19 .... 289, 313	37:15 329	38:26 .... 340, 341, 993
35:20 314	37:15–16 340	38:27 341
35:21 314	37:16 329	38:27–30 341
35:21–29 314–315	37:17 329	38:28–30 339
35:22 .... 314, 316, 330, 399, 418, 975	37:18 329	38:29 649
	37:18–24 329–330	38:30 341
35:22–23 1094	37:18–28 328	39 .... 332, 336, 342–349, 350
35:23–26 ...... 314, 318	37:19 329	
35:27 .... 138, 314, 315, 322	37:20 329	
35:28 .... 315, 403	37:21 329	
35:29 .... 315, 316, 999n242, 1229	37:21–22 ...... 330, 371	39–41 368
36 .... 80, 171, 316–320		
36:1 .... 318, 319, 1100		

Reference	Pages
39:1	330, 343, 344, 345, 351,
39:1–6a	344–345
39:1–23	322
39:2	344, 345
39:3	345
39:3–5	344
39:3–6	347
39:4	345, 347, 1146, 1303
39:4–5	379n623
39:4–9	616
39:5	345
39:5–6	358
39:6	344, 345, 347, 359n583, 363, 479n87, 486
39:6b–10	345–346
39:7	272, 344, 345, 520n188
39:8–12	344
39:9	345n551, 346, 351, 430, 614
39:10	346
39:11–18	346–347, 353n573
39:12	345, 346, 347, 361
39:13	345
39:13–14	347
39:13–15	346
39:13–16	344
39:14	122, 152, 199, 240n348, 347
39:15	345, 347
39:17	347, 775
39:18	347
39:19–23	347–348
39:20	325, 344, 347
39:21	344, 345, 347, 348, 353, 784
39:21–23	350
39:22–23	347, 358
39:23	344, 345, 347, 363
40	286, 349–355, 360
40–41	350
40:1	350, 351, 355, 520n188, 791
40:1–4	350–351
40:1–41:57	322
40:2	332, 351, 1083
40:3	351
40:4	351, 351n565, 370
40:5	325, 351
40:5–8	351–352
40:6	351
40:7	352
40:8	360
40:9–19	352–354
40:10	352, 352n570
40:11	352, 352n570
40:12–15	1083
40:13	352
40:14	353, 360, 361
40:15	285, 347n557, 353
40:16	353
40:16–33	471
40:17	353
40:19	354
40:20	354
40:20–23	354
40:21–22	354
40:23	354, 358
41	25, 286, 351n566, 356–366, 368
41:1	359
41:1–7	361
41:1–8	325, 359–360
41:2	359, 359n584, 1203
41:2–4	1220
41:3	359, 362
41:4	359
41:5	359, 362
41:6	359
41:7	359, 360
41:8	360
41:9	360
41:9–13	360–361
41:12	347n557, 360
41:12–13	361
41:14	361, 393
41:14–24	361–362
41:15	361, 362n594
41:16	361, 363n598, 376, 386
41:17–24	361
41:19	362
41:21	362
41:22	362n594
41:22–23	325
41:23	362
41:24	362
41:25	363n598
41:25–36	362–363
41:28	362, 363n598
41:29–31	358
41:31	362
41:32	325, 351, 362, 363n598
41:33	362n597, 363
41:33–34	362
41:34–36	363
41:35	363, 648n483
41:37–45	363–364
41:38	358, 363, 1258
41:39	363, 363n598
41:40	363, 368
41:41	363
41:42	363, 741, 1298
41:43	363, 364
41:44	364
41:45	364
41:46	351, 364, 507n163
41:46–52	364–365
41:47–48	364
41:49	364
41:50–52	366
41:51	364, 369, 376, 412
41:51–52	364
41:52	365, 410
41:53–54	365
41:53–57	365
41:55	365, 1165
41:57	358, 365, 368, 369
42	367–374
42:1	369
42:1–5	369
42:1–43:34	322
42:2	368, 369, 376
42:3	325
42:4	369, 649
42:5	369
42:6	368, 369, 380
42:6–8	379
42:6–17	369–370
42:7	370
42:7–8	331
42:8	368
42:9	369, 370
42:10	370
42:11	370n609, 372
42:13	370
42:15	370
42:16	370
42:17	370
42:18	369, 370
42:18–22	370–371
42:19	370
42:20	369, 370, 371
42:21	371
42:22	371, 373
42:23	371
42:23–28	371–372
42:24	371, 371n611, 373, 1290
42:25	372, 577n308
42:26	919
42:26–28	379
42:27	372
42:28	372
42:29	372
42:29–35	372
42:30–34	372
42:35	372, 378
42:36	373, 376
42:36–38	372–373
42:37	373
42:37–38	418
42:37–43:9	386
42:38	373, 373n616, 378, 397, 403, 649
43	374–382
43–45	33
43:1	376
43:1–10	376–377
43:2	376
43:3	341, 697n587
43:3–4	377
43:6	377, 499n139
43:7	377
43:8	369, 377, 395
43:9	377
43:10	377
43:11	330, 378
43:11–14	377–379
43:12	378
43:14	378, 380, 394, 1259
43:15	325, 379, 577n309
43:15–25	379–380
43:16	379
43:18	379, 394
43:20–22	379
43:21	372
43:23	376, 379, 384, 386
43:26	380
43:26–34	380–381
43:27	376, 380, 388, 588
43:28	376
43:29	380, 386
43:30	373, 380
43:32	380, 524, 634n452
43:33	380
43:34	380, 384, 385, 386, 393
44	384
44–45	322
44:1	384
44:1–2	384–385
44:1–13	384
44:1–34	322
44:1–45:15	382–390
44:3–13	385–386
44:4–6	385
44:5	385
44:6	385
44:8	285, 614

44:8–9 385	46:15 .... 396n644	48:16 .... 411, 412, 417, 424
44:9 872	46:17–18 .... 396n644	48:17 .... 413, 1272
44:10 386	46:19–22 396	48:17–19 411
44:11 385	46:23–25 396	48:17–22 413
44:12 .... 385, 386	46:26 .... 219, 1122	48:18–19 431
44:13 393	46:26–27 396–397	48:19 .... 413, 1185
44:14 386	46:27 .... 118n162, 396, 466n55	48:20 .... 137, 413
44:14–17 386–387		48:22 413
44:14–34 384	46:28 401	49 .... 308, 314, 409, 417, 1262
44:15 .... 277n404, 385	46:28–34 .... 384, 397–398, 402	
44:16 386	46:28–47:12 322	49:1 418
44:17 387	46:29 397	49:1–2 418
44:18 387	46:29–30 .... 397, 401	49:1–27 .... 415–425, 1260
44:18–34 .... 336, 371n611, 387–388	46:30 397	49:3 .... 418, 452, 491, 492, 508, 1158, 1214
	46:32 .... 401n655	
44:20 .... 387n637	46:34 .... 397, 401, 401n655, 523n196, 524	49:3–4 .... 314, 418–419, 975
44:29 .... 397, 649		49:4 .... 418, 1094, 1120
44:30–34 .... 342, 387	47 399–407	49:5–6 .... 419, 1094
44:33 387	47:1–6 .... 401–402, 1139	49:5–7 .... 308, 309, 314, 419
44:34 387	47:2 401	49:7 .... 417, 419, 1094, 1327
45:1 388	47:3 .... 401, 401n655, 402	49:8 419
45:1–3 379	47:4 .... 402, 1311	49:8–10 1184
45:1–15 .... 384, 388–389	47:6 .... 392, 402	49:8–12 .... 34, 419–421
45:1–28 322	47:7 .... 402, 407	49:9 419
45:2 .... 373, 388, 392, 430, 1183	47:7–12 402–404	49:9–10 1255
	47:8 402	49:10 .... 316, 419, 420, 1260, 1262
45:3 388	47:8–9 403	
45:4 388	47:9 .... 402, 406, 414	49:11 420
45:5 .... 384, 388, 389	47:10 .... 401, 402, 407	49:12 420
45:6 389	47:11 .... 403, 404, 405, 410, 1311	49:13–15 .... 421, 1093
45:8 388		49:14 421
45:8–9 388	47:12 .... 403, 612n391, 623	49:15 421
45:9–10 389	47:13–15 404	49:16 421
45:9–11 .... 612n391, 623	47:13–26 404–405	49:16–17 1157
45:11 389	47:13–31 322	49:16–18 421–422
45:13 .... 389, 736n668	47:14 404	49:17 422
45:14 397	47:16–17 404	49:18 .... 422, 425
45:15 .... 388, 389, 397	47:16–21 404	49:19 422
45:16 392	47:19 404	49:19–21 422
45:16–20 392–393	47:22 .... 404, 1213	49:20 422
45:16–46:27 384	47:25 404	49:21 422
45:16–46:34 390–399	47:26 405	49:22 423
45:17 392	47:27 .... 405, 406, 465, 466, 1311	49:22–26 423–424
45:18 .... 393, 401, 742n692, 854		49:23 423
	47:27–31 405–407	49:24 .... 411, 423
45:19 393	47:28 .... 403, 406	49:25 .... 423, 1252, 1259
45:20 393	47:29 .... 219, 406, 409, 590n333, 784	49:26 424
45:21 393		49:27 424
45:21–24 393–394	47:29–30 .... 406, 428	49:28 .... 417, 424, 427n697
45:22 393	47:29–31 .... 404, 428, 431	49:28–33 427–428
45:23 393	48 .... 408–415, 417	49:28–50:26 426–433
45:24 394	48–49 .... 401, 403, 409	49:29 .... 83, 422, 428
45:25–28 394	48:1 .... 409, 410	49:29–30 428
45:26 394	48:1–7 409–410	49:29–32 213
45:27 .... 393, 394	48:1–49:28 322	49:29–33 .... 999n242
45:28 .... 394, 403	48:2 .... 406, 410	49:29–50:14 322
46 .... 25, 401	48:3 .... 410, 1259	49:31 .... 213, 315, 428
46:1 .... 392, 394	48:4 .... 25, 251, 404, 410, 412, 466	49:33 .... 315, 1229
46:1–2 .... 394, 405		50 401
46:1–4 .... 141, 394–395	48:5 410	50:1–6 428
46:1–27 322	48:6 410	50:1–13 25
46:2 395	48:7 .... 409, 410, 410n675, 428	50:2 .... 428, 428n698
46:3 395		50:3 .... 331, 428, 466n56
46:3–4 .... 392, 429	48:8 411	50:4 277
46:4 .... 395, 404	48:8–14 411	50:4–13 395
46:5 .... 393, 395	48:8–16 976	50:5 .... 428, 992
46:5–7 395	48:9–11 413	50:6 428
46:6 395	48:10 410	50:7 .... 429n702
46:7 395	48:11 411	50:7–8 429
46:8 .... 396n643	48:12 .... 271, 431	50:7–14 429
46:8–15 396	48:13 411	50:8 .... 429, 429n702
46:8–25 395–396	48:13–20 .... 246n354, 743	50:9 429
46:8–27 .... 466n55	48:14 .... 413, 1272	50:10 .... 331, 429, 705
46:11 .... 1088, 1099	48:15 .... 411, 423	50:12–13 .... 429, 992
46:12 396	48:15–16 411–412	50:15 429

50:15–21 429–430
50:15–26 322
50:17 430
50:18 430
50:19 430
50:20 .... 25, 32, 159, 274, 322, 326, 333, 348, 385, 430, 432, 1248
50:21 .... 304n462, 430
50:22 .... 403, 430
50:22–23 .... 1082n19
50:22–26 430–432
50:23 .... 271, 431
50:24 431
50:24–25 .... 429n704, 465
50:24–26 .... 25, 40
50:25 .... 413, 431, 556, 1229
50:26 .... 431, 717

Exodus
Book of 437–463
1 .... 389, 405, 437, 441n3, 446, 464–469, 470, 473
1–2 .... 466n58
1–11 .... 457n39, 463–464
1–15 .... 698, 812, 813
1–17 .... 585, 587
1–19 .... 451, 458, 568
1:1 .... 440, 465n54
1:1–4 465
1:1–5 .... 465–466, 569, 674n543, 693n574, 705, 720, 744, 808n823, 810n827
1:1–6 432
1:1–7 465
1:1–2:22 .... 461, 463
1:1–11:10 ...... 460, 461
1:1–15:21 ...... 437, 461, 461n51
1:5 .... 219, 466n55
1:5a 466
1:5b 466
1:6 466
1:6–7 466
1:7 .... 449, 466, 466n57, 468, 546
1:8 .... 430, 466
1:8–14 .... 465, 466–467
1:9–10 466
1:9–11 468
1:9–14 .... 499n134
1:10 466
1:11 .... 403n659, 458, 466, 466n60, 468, 472
1:11–12 669
1:12 .... 467, 468
1:13–14 .... 467, 468
1:14 543
1:15 .... 152, 467
1:15–16 929
1:15–19 468
1:15–21 467
1:15–22 .... 465, 468
1:16 467
1:17 .... 467, 467n66, 468, 638n462
1:17–21 473
1:19 .... 467, 468
1:19–32 584
1:20 .... 467, 468
1:20–21 .... 467n66
1:21 467
1:22 .... 467–468, 470, 492, 492n127, 519, 563

2 .... 438, 446, 447, 465, 470, 471, 473, 476, 486, 549, 1158
2:1 470
2:1–4 .... 470–471, 473
2:1–10 .... 26, 441n3, 470
2:1–22 469–474
2:2 .... 470, 473
2:3 .... 96, 471, 1312
2:4 .... 471, 1226
2:5 .... 519, 523
2:5–9 471
2:7 471
2:7–8 .... 473, 1226
2:8 471
2:9 471
2:10 .... 470, 471–472, 471n73, 472n77, 502n154, 746
2:11 .... 472, 472n74, 489n117, 492n127
2:11–12 473
2:11–15 .... 470, 472, 473
2:11–25 441
2:12 472
2:13 .... 472, 473
2:14 .... 472, 1183
2:15 .... 219, 489, 588, 1158, 1159
2:15–22 .... 587, 587n320
2:15a 472
2:15b 472
2:16 .... 472, 584, 598, 1158
2:16–19 .... 261n380
2:16–22 .... 470, 472, 588
2:17 473
2:17a 472
2:17–18 .... 261n380
2:18 .... 472, 1158
2:19 .... 472, 588n322
2:21 .... 261n380, 1158, 1172
2:21–22 493
2:22 .... 72, 472, 668
2:23 477
2:23–24 477
2:23–25 .... 438, 476, 477, 536, 549
2:23–4:17 ...... 461, 464, 474–487, 488, 674
2:24 .... 105, 449, 478, 595, 610n381, 737, 1156
2:24–25 .... 477, 479, 485
2:25 775
3 .... 480n91, 486, 501, 687
3–4 .... 438, 447, 477, 486, 580
3–14 389
3–19 441
3:1 .... 207, 478, 1158, 1159, 1309, 1314
3:1–3 .... 478, 577, 587n320, 588, 687
3:1–5 476
3:1–4:13 580
3:1–4:17 476
3:2 .... 478, 558, 559, 878, 1248
3:2–4 .... 412, 478n85
3:3 478
3:4 .... 395, 441, 478, 559, 1020
3:4–6 .... 478–479, 485, 697, 780

3:5 .... 256, 478, 894
3:6 .... 27, 476, 478, 638n462, 718n634, 899
3:7 .... 166, 365, 476, 478n85, 479, 485n115, 486, 534, 775
3:7–8 .... 479, 483
3:7–9 494
3:7–10 .... 479, 485, 536, 549, 549n258, 688
3:8 .... 140, 449, 476, 479, 509, 559, 584, 846, 1255, 1330
3:9 .... 362n597, 476, 479, 534, 669, 775
3:10 .... 479, 775
3:10–11 486
3:10–12 1172
3:11 .... 477, 479, 487
3:11–12 .... 479–480, 487, 491, 524, 525, 526, 529, 532, 688n569
3:12 .... 451, 476, 487, 1159
3:12a 479
3:12b 479
3:13 .... 477, 479, 480, 487, 501
3:13–14 .... 295n450
3:13–15 .... 480–483, 482, 485, 500, 501, 521n190, 526n205, 782n779, 874
3:14 .... 455, 480, 481, 481n99, 486, 487, 1132
3:14b 481n101, 482
3:14–15 .... 476, 1021
3:15 .... 441, 480, 501
3:15a 482
3:15b 482
3:16 .... 432, 476, 483n102, 494, 1167
3:16–17 .... 483, 485, 536
3:16–22 .... 483, 488, 494, 545, 556n267
3:17 .... 449, 476, 479
3:18 .... 205n305, 278n410, 483, 530, 1314
3:18–19 483
3:19 .... 483n103, 500n140, 535, 559
3:19–20 .... 476, 486, 518
3:20 .... 483, 500n140, 1170
3:21–22 .... 483, 534
3:22 .... 545, 774
4:1 .... 477, 479, 483, 487, 1172
4:1–5 .... 516, 560
4:1–9 .... 476, 480, 483–484, 494, 518, 565
4:2–9 .... 483, 487
4:3 .... 483, 516n172
4:4 484
4:5 .... 484, 596
4:6 484
4:7 484
4:7–8 .... 490n119
4:8 484
4:9 484
4:10 .... 477, 479, 484, 506, 1172
4:10–12 .... 484, 506
4:11 .... 476, 484

4:11–12	484, 487	
4:12	476, 484, 485, 487	
4:13	477, 479, 486, 487	
4:13–17	484–485, 489	
4:14	485, 485n113, 487, 1088, 1174	
4:14–17	477, 580	
4:15	476, 487	
4:15–16	494	
4:15b	485	
4:16	485	
4:17	485, 519, 558	
4:18	489, 1158	
4:18–20	488, 489, 577, 582, 583, 587	
4:18–31	461, 464, 488–496	
4:19	489, 1159	
4:20	519, 558, 588, 1313	
4:20a	489	
4:20b	489	
4:21	490, 495, 516	
4:21–23	449, 452, 488, 494, 495, 507, 508, 525, 529, 533, 534, 536, 537, 545, 557n271	
4:22	450, 452, 502n152, 1030, 1103, 1319	
4:22–23	450, 491, 493, 506	
4:23	452, 485n113, 491, 491n125, 548, 551, 1039, 1167, 1188	
4:23b	491n125	
4:24	493	
4:24–26	488, 493–494, 495	
4:25	493, 588n324, 926, 1158n76	
4:25–26	493	
4:26	494	
4:27	478, 485n113, 588, 1159, 1210, 1313	
4:27–28	489, 494	
4:27a	494	
4:27b	494	
4:28	494	
4:29	1313	
4:29–30	494	
4:29–31	489, 494, 497, 498	
4:30–31	518, 560	
4:31	483, 486, 489, 536, 545, 694, 775	
4:31a	494	
4:31b	494	
5	482	
5–12	446, 482	
5:1	166, 451, 479n89, 491, 498, 506, 520, 523, 688n569, 775, 1039n301	
5:1–2	490, 497	
5:1–4	483, 483n103	
5:1–9	498–499, 502, 518, 521, 523, 526, 530, 532	
5:1–6:9	461, 464, 496–504, 505, 508n165	
5:1–15:21	438	
5:2	497, 498, 501, 502, 508, 519, 521, 535	
5:2–9	490n119	
5:3	451, 479n89, 491, 498, 520, 523, 688n569, 1039n301, 1314	
5:3–18	497	
5:4	499, 501	
5:5	499	
5:6–18	502	
5:6–19	1168	
5:8a	499	
5:8b	499	
5:9	499, 502	
5:10–11	499	
5:10–14	492n127, 499	
5:12	499	
5:13	499	
5:14a	499	
5:14b	499	
5:15–16	499	
5:15–18	499	
5:15–21	499n136	
5:17	499	
5:18	499	
5:19–21	497, 499, 502	
5:20–21	497	
5:21	499, 499n137, 844	
5:22	499	
5:22–23	497, 499, 503	
5:23	499, 502	
6	501	
6–7	364	
6:1	441, 483n103, 497, 500, 518, 535	
6:1–8	500–502, 528n210, 745	
6:1–9	503, 508	
6:2	497, 1132	
6:2–3	165n254	
6:2–5	500	
6:3	77n88, 500, 501	
6:3–8a	497	
6:4	500, 501, 503, 1322	
6:4–5	501, 595	
6:4–8	1092	
6:5	105, 486n116, 500, 610n381	
6:5–8	536	
6:5b	503	
6:6	412, 497, 500, 501, 503	
6:6a	501	
6:6–7	449	
6:6–8	501, 518, 846	
6:7	170, 501, 572, 746, 775, 1041	
6:7a	503	
6:7b	503	
6:8	449, 497, 501, 503	
6:8b	501	
6:9	497, 498, 502	
6:10	441	
6:10–12	484, 505, 506, 507	
6:10–7:7	461, 464, 503n156, 504–509	
6:11	506	
6:12	506	
6:13	506, 507	
6:13–27	505, 506–507	
6:14	506n160, 1084	
6:14–16	508	
6:14–25	506	
6:14b–15	506	
6:16	508, 1088, 1099	
6:16–19	506	
6:16–25	506	
6:18	508, 1210	
6:18–21	1200	
6:19	1088	
6:20	470, 508, 561, 897, 1100, 1210	
6:20–25	507	
6:22	506n159	
6:23	507n161, 508, 693, 908, 1084	
6:24	1273	
6:25	506n160, 508, 1088	
6:26–27	506, 507	
6:28–30	507	
6:28–7:7	505, 507	
6:30	506	
7	520	
7–9	360	
7–12	407, 449	
7–14	449, 490	
7:1	441, 1172	
7:1a	507	
7:1b	507	
7:1–2	485, 893	
7:1–5	449	
7:1–7	516	
7:1–12:32	483	
7:2a	507	
7:2b	507	
7:3	490, 495, 517	
7:3a	507	
7:3b	507	
7:3–4a	490n118	
7:3–4	534n231	
7:3–5	503, 507, 508	
7:4	775	
7:4a	507	
7:4b	507	
7:4–5	500, 500n140	
7:5	501, 507, 572, 1021	
7:6	97, 507, 508	
7:7	472, 485, 507, 1083, 1100, 1226, 1230	
7:8	441	
7:8–9	518	
7:8–10	516	
7:8–13	449, 515, 515n170, 516, 518, 522, 535n232, 543	
7:8–11:10	448n28, 461, 464, 505, 509–537, 557	
7:9	516	
7:9–10	494	
7:10	97	
7:10–12	516	
7:11	516n172	
7:11–12a	516, 520	
7:12	516	
7:13	490, 490n118, 491, 516, 534n231	
7:13–14	525	
7:14	441, 490, 490n118, 491, 519	
7:14–19	449, 519–520, 535, 535n232, 543	
7:14–25	518–519	
7:14–10:29	515	
7:14–11:10	514, 515, 517–518, 577n310	
7:14–13:16	503	
7:15	519, 523, 533n223	
7:16	451, 479n89, 520, 688n569, 775, 1039n301	
7:16–18	518	
7:17	482, 485n113, 517n176, 518, 519, 521, 572, 589	
7:17–18	519	
7:18	573	

7:19 .... 494, 519, 520, 521, 522, 558	8:26–27 523	9:32 .... 528, 530
7:20 .... 97, 517n176, 577	8:27 1314	9:33 529
7:20–21 520	8:28 .... 490, 495, 523	9:33–34 .... 598n348
7:20–22a 519	8:28–29 524	9:33–35 .... 526, 529
7:20–23 520	8:29 .... 523n197	9:34 .... 490, 495, 526, 528n208, 536
7:21 .... 519, 521, 573	8:30 .... 528n210	9:34–35 529
7:22 .... 490, 491, 520, 525, 534n231	8:30–31 .... 523, 529	9:35 .... 490, 491
7:22–23 519	8:30–32 524	10:1 .... 441, 490, 529, 533, 533n223
7:22a 520	8:32 .... 490, 519, 523, 525, 529, 536	10:1–2 .... 529, 572
7:22b–23 519	9:1 .... 451, 524, 533n223	10:1–20 529
7:23 520	9:1–4 524	10:1a 529
7:24 .... 519, 519n180, 520	9:1–5 524	10:2 .... 482, 518, 529, 589
7:24–25 .... 519, 520	9:1–7 524	10:2b 529
7:25 .... 517n176, 520, 520n188	9:3 .... 524, 1302	10:3 .... 451, 529, 530, 536, 574
8:1 .... 451, 520, 533n223	9:4 .... 518, 521n189, 523, 524, 527	10:3–6 529–530
8:1–5 520–521	9:5 .... 523n197, 524	10:3b 529
8:1–15 520	9:6 .... 523, 524, 527, 1139	10:4 .... 523n197
8:2 .... 517n176, 521, 572	9:6–7 .... 524–525, 527	10:4–6 529
8:2–4 518	9:6–7a 524	10:5 528
8:3 521	9:7 .... 490, 491, 519, 524, 525	10:6 530
8:3–4 .... 521n189	9:7b 524	10:7 .... 451, 479n89, 529, 530, 537, 545, 688n569
8:5 .... 441, 521, 558	9:8 525	
8:5–6 494	9:8–9 .... 525, 531	10:8 .... 451, 479n89, 530, 688n569
8:6 .... 520, 521, 523, 525, 527	9:8–12 525	
8:7 520	9:9 .... 524, 525	10:8–11 .... 529, 530, 532
8:7–11 .... 521, 535n232, 543	9:10–11 .... 521, 525, 535n232, 543	10:9 .... 491, 498, 530, 1139
8:8 .... 520, 521, 523	9:11 525	10:9–11 .... 429n703
8:9 521	9:11b 525	10:10 530
8:9–10 .... 521n191	9:12 .... 490, 525, 529, 531, 533, 534n231, 537	10:10–11 530
8:10 .... 482, 486, 518, 520, 589		10:12 .... 528, 530
8:10a 521	9:13 .... 451, 526, 533n223	10:12–15 .... 529, 530–531, 532
8:10b 521	9:13–14 .... 526, 535n232, 543	10:13 .... 485, 530, 532, 558, 1228
8:11 .... 490, 495	9:13–19 525	
8:12 .... 521, 528n210	9:13–30 449	10:14–15 .... 530, 572
8:12–13 .... 520, 529	9:13–35 525–526	10:15 .... 524, 527, 528, 531
8:12–14 521–522	9:14 .... 482, 486, 517n176, 521n193, 525, 526, 527, 536, 537, 537n236, 1254	10:16 .... 531, 536, 868n63
8:13 .... 521, 524		10:16–17 .... 529, 531
8:14 .... 521, 573		10:17 .... 527, 531
8:15 .... 490, 491, 519, 520, 522, 523, 524, 525, 529, 534n231, 536		10:18 .... 528n210
	9:14–16 .... 518, 529	10:18–19 531
	9:14–19 526	10:18–20 529
8:16 .... 517n176, 522, 531, 558	9:14b 526n205	10:19 .... 531n219, 559, 559n282
	9:15–16 .... 526–527, 536	
8:16–17 522	9:16 .... 482, 509, 536, 591, 1021, 1254	10:20 .... 490, 531
8:16–19 522		10:21 .... 449, 531–532, 535, 535n232, 543
8:18 522	9:17–18 527	
8:18–19 522	9:17–19 527	10:21–23 531
8:19 .... 490, 518, 519, 522, 525, 534n231, 545	9:18 .... 523n197, 571	10:21–29 531
	9:19 .... 524, 527	10:22–23 532
8:19b 522	9:20 .... 528, 537, 545	10:23 .... 521n189, 523, 527, 531, 532
8:20 .... 451, 533n223	9:20–21 .... 526, 527	
8:20–23 .... 523, 524, 527, 529, 535n232, 543	9:21 .... 527, 537	10:24 .... 429n703, 531, 532, 704n603
	9:22 527	
8:20–24 523	9:22–25 .... 527, 530, 558	10:24–26 .... 451, 479n89, 491, 688n569
8:20–32 522–523	9:23 .... 101, 485, 527, 558, 598n348	
8:20a 523		10:25–29 532–533
8:21 523	9:23–25 .... 526, 527	10:26 .... 398, 532, 532n222
8:21–22 518	9:25 .... 524, 537	10:27 .... 490, 531, 533
8:21–23 .... 518, 524	9:26 .... 518, 521n189, 523, 526, 527	10:27–28 490
8:21b–22 523		10:28 .... 531, 533, 697n587
8:22 .... 482, 518, 523, 572, 589, 1311	9:27 .... 527, 528n208, 531, 536, 868n63	10:28–29 .... 545n248
		10:29 .... 531, 533, 533n226, 534
8:22–23 .... 521n189, 527	9:27–28 .... 526, 527–528, 529, 531n218	
8:23 .... 523, 995		10:29b 533n223
8:24 523	9:28–29 .... 598n348	11 .... 515, 517n176
8:25 .... 523, 523n198	9:29 .... 482, 528	11:1 .... 517n176, 518, 533, 533n227, 545, 1259
8:25–27 .... 498, 523–524	9:29–30 .... 526, 527, 528, 535n232, 543	
8:25–28 532		11:1–2 533
8:25–29 523	9:30 528	11:1–3 .... 533–534, 533n226, 545n248
8:26 501	9:31 528	
	9:31–32 528	

11:1–8 533	12:23 ....542, 779, 1204	13:8 549
11:1–10 ....515, 533	12:24–27a 541, 544	13:8–10 ....541, 548
11:2 ....147n229, 534, 615	12:24–27 ....495, 1013	13:9 ....500n140, 548n257, 549
11:3 534	12:25 1303	
11:4–5 543	12:26–27 ....548, 550, 551, 612, 623	13:11–13 1103
11:4–8a 534, 545		13:11–15 ....992, 1052
11:4–8 ....518, 533, 533n226	12:27 ....694, 779	13:11–16 ....495, 548, 673
11:5 ....491n125, 534	12:27b 545	13:12 ....548, 739
11:6 534	12:27b–28 545	13:12–13 1215
11:7 ....518, 521n189, 523, 527, 534	12:28 ....545, 1150	13:13 ....548, 548n255, 1048, 1052
	12:29 ....545, 1081	
11:8 533	12:29–33 ....518, 545	13:13b–15 ....542n239
11:8a 534	12:29–36 571	13:14 ....549, 623
11:8b 534	12:29–42 ....538, 541, 549	13:14–15 548
11:9 ....534, 534n231	12:30 545	13:14–16 ....492, 541, 548, 551
11:9–10 ....533, 534, 557n271	12:31 ....533n223, 549	13:15 548
11:10 ....490, 534	12:31–42 555	13:16 ....548n257
12 ....208, 460, 533	12:31b–32a 545	13:17 ....239, 556, 689n571, 785n786, 1309n252, 1313n270, 1314
12–13 447	12:32 530	
12–14 94	12:32b 545	
12:1–2 ....542, 549, 682, 809	12:33 ....545, 550	13:17–18 555
12:1–28 ....538, 541, 550	12:33–34 550	13:17–22 ....538, 555–556, 562, 567, 812
12:1–13:16 ....462, 515, 538–552	12:33–36 483	
12:1–15:21 ....460, 462, 538	12:33–19:2 1309	13:17–15:21 ....462, 538, 552–565, 611n383, 667, 672n538, 689n572, 778n769
12:2 ....542, 1013, 1313	12:34 ....543, 544, 545, 546	
12:2–6 571	12:34–36 545	
12:2–27 1149	12:35 545	
12:3 ....534n229, 542, 546, 1149	12:35–36 ....707, 808	13:18 ....556, 1304
	12:36 ....545, 1141	13:19 ....413, 429n704, 432, 556, 1229
12:3–4 547	12:37 ....397, 403n659, 459, 546, 556, 1168, 1309n247	
12:3–13 ....449, 542–543, 546, 682, 684		13:20 ....556, 1309n247
		13:21 ....160, 478, 556, 558, 687, 1151
12:4 542	12:37–42 ....541, 546	
12:5 ....842n22, 1191	12:38 ....541, 546, 546n250, 967n206, 987, 1080, 1139, 1158, 1165, 1302, 1314	13:22 556
12:6 ....534n229, 1013, 1149		14 ....27, 446, 447, 449, 457n39, 687
12:6a 542		14–15 429
12:6b 542	12:39 ....500, 543, 544, 545, 546, 550, 1013	14:1 1312
12:7 542		14:1–2 ....1309n247
12:8 ....544n246, 1150	12:40 ....159, 466n58	14:1–4 ....447, 555, 556–557, 564
12:8–9 547	12:40–41 ....546, 1081	
12:8a 542	12:41 1149	14:1–10 562
12:8b 542	12:42 546	14:1–28 555
12:9 ....542n242	12:43 ....547, 1193	14:1–31 538
12:9a 542	12:43–50 ....544n247, 546–547, 611n384, 669, 677n549, 681	14:2 ....556, 1169
12:9b 542		14:3 ....556, 1312
12:10 ....543, 547, 684n566, 744, 1150		14:4 ....490, 501, 557, 557n272, 558, 559, 559n281, 564, 572
	12:43–51 ....546, 1149	
12:11 543	12:43–13:16 ....538, 541, 550	
12:11–16 ....547–548, 787	12:44 ....547, 1034	14:4a 557
12:11a 543	12:45 ....547, 1151	14:4b 557
12:12 ....449, 482, 492, 517n176, 518, 535, 543, 550, 1141, 1254	12:46 ....455, 542n242, 547, 1150	14:5 557
		14:5–8 557
	12:48 ....547n254, 967n206, 1151	14:6 1238
12:12–13 1103		14:6–7 557
12:13 ....517n176, 542, 544, 753, 1170	12:48–49 ....541, 544n247, 547, 547n254, 988, 1151	14:8 ....490, 557, 562, 1195
		14:9 557
12:14 ....726, 739	12:51 ....546, 547, 1081, 1156	14:9–14 ....557–558, 563
12:14–20 ....543–544, 548, 682, 756	12:51–13:2 ....547–548, 673, 787	14:10 ....521, 557, 558n278, 1165
	13 557	
12:15 ....544, 887n93, 888	13:1–2 ....548, 1103	14:10–12 ....555, 556, 567
12:15–16 549	13:1–16 571	14:11 ....777, 1227
12:16 ....544, 1013	13:2 ....548, 1008n252, 1052	14:11–12 ....557, 1185n100, 1233, 1235
12:17 ....544, 546, 1156		
12:18 ....544n246	13:3 549	14:12 ....1166, 1183
12:18–20 544	13:3–4 548	14:13 ....558n277, 577n308
12:19 ....547n254, 887n93, 888, 988	13:3–10 ....495, 541, 548–549, 548n257	14:13–14 ....555, 557, 558n278, 559
	13:4 ....542, 1149	14:13–29 562
12:19–20 549	13:5 ....479, 543, 549, 584	14:13–31 ....567, 571
12:21 ....206n308, 544, 862	13:5–9 549	14:14 562
12:21–23 ....541, 544, 964	13:6 705	14:15 ....558, 558n278
12:21–27 546	13:6–7 549	14:15–18 ....558, 564
12:21–27a 544, 549	13:7–8 548	14:15–15:21 1312
12:22 542	13:7–9 551	14:16 ....485, 558
12:22–23 942		

14:17............490	15:20b............562	16:20............573, 574, 777, 1185n100
14:17–18........555, 557n272	15:21............562	
14:18............558, 564, 572	15:21b............562	16:21............573
14:19............558, 1160, 1161, 1248	15:22............567, 1157, 1226, 1309n247, 1312	16:22............574, 674
		16:22–26........571, 573–574
14:19–22........558–559	15:22–23........566, 577	16:23............481, 573, 574, 580, 804n811
14:20............531	15:22–24........1164	
14:21............105n143, 517, 532, 558, 562	15:22–26........567–568, 609, 618n415, 629n436, 688, 691, 1166	16:24............574, 1031
		16:25–26........574
14:21–29........555		16:25–30........570
14:22............559	15:22–27........565, 566–569, 571	16:26............1166
14:23............524, 559	15:22–17:7....438, 462, 582, 1164	16:26–27........572
14:23–28........531n219, 559	15:22–17:16...437, 460, 461, 461n51, 462, 565–566, 570, 576	16:27............574, 1185n100
14:24............556, 558, 559, 563, 687		16:27–30........574
		16:28............574
14:25............559, 563	15:23............565, 567	16:29............574
14:26–27........559	15:23–24........1183	16:29–30........611
14:26–29........567	15:24............557, 565, 566, 567, 579, 777, 1185n100, 1235	16:30............565, 574
14:27............559, 1183		16:31............573, 575, 1166
14:28............531, 559		16:31–36........571, 574–575, 576, 763, 776, 807
14:28–29........561	15:24–25a......567	
14:29............1183	15:25............204, 565, 567, 567n294, 568, 580, 618n415	16:32............575
14:29–30........559		16:33............575
14:29–31........555, 559–560		16:34............575, 726
14:30............558n277, 559, 1185n100	15:25–26........565, 571, 577	16:34–35........574
	15:25–27........577	16:35............445, 575, 1166, 1322
14:30–31........563	15:25b–26......567	16:36............445, 573n302, 575
14:30–15:21....562	15:26............567, 568, 629n436	17................200, 441, 594
14:31............518, 559, 560, 562, 564, 596	15:27............565, 567, 568–569, 580, 1312	17:1............565, 577, 1226, 1227, 1309n247, 1313
15................438, 447, 563	16................569–575	
15–17............578	16–17............446	17:1–3..........557
15:1............562, 563	16–19............457n39	17:1–7..........565, 566, 569, 575, 577–578, 576–581, 1166, 1227, 1233
15:1–5............560	16:1............571, 1156, 1157, 1313, 1314	
15:1–18............560n285		
15:1–19..........447n25, 449, 453, 560–561, 562	16:1–3..........557	17:2............565, 576, 577, 579, 1227
	16:1–18........1166	
15:1–21..........555, 560, 562, 563n289	16:1–36..........565	17:2–3..........1235
	16:2............565, 579, 777, 1183	17:2a............577
15:1–22..........538	16:2–3..........567, 570, 571, 577	17:3............567, 577, 1158, 1183, 1227, 1233
15:1b............560	16:3............565, 1169, 1183, 1185n100, 1233, 1235	
15:2–12..........1080		17:4............521, 577
15:2a............560		17:5............577, 579, 1228
15:2b............560	16:4............101, 455, 568, 570, 573, 574, 577, 618n415, 1188, 1236	17:5–6..........565, 577, 580
15:3............560, 1088		17:6............577, 578, 1227, 1314
15:4............557, 560		17:6–7..........1313
15:5............560, 1151		17:7............145, 565, 576, 577, 578, 579, 1227
15:6............561	16:4–5..........565, 571, 572	
15:6–12..........560	16:4a............571	17:8............582, 1261
15:7............561	16:4b............571	17:8–16..........438, 462, 566–585
15:8............561	16:5............571, 574, 1031	17:9............489, 582, 585, 704, 1278
15:9............561, 1041	16:6–7..........572	
15:10............561	16:6–8..........571–572, 782	17:9–10..........1169
15:11............521n193, 526n205, 537n236, 561	16:7............567	17:9–13..........781
	16:7–8..........571, 577, 579	17:10............582
15:12............561	16:8............572, 1183	17:10–13........582–583, 585, 704, 761
15:13............412, 561, 562, 1255	16:9............572	
15:13–14........546	16:9–12..........572, 782	17:10a............582
15:13–17..........560	16:10............572, 572n296, 704n602, 781, 811	17:10b–12........582
15:13–18..........1080		17:11............583
15:14–16a......560n285		17:11–13........566
15:14a............561	16:11............1183	17:12............591
15:14b............561	16:12............572	17:12–13........583
15:15–16........509	16:13............572	17:13............582
15:15a............561	16:13–15........565, 570, 572–573, 575, 580	17:14............441, 582, 583, 821n3, 1233, 1237
15:15b............561		
15:15c............561	16:13b–15......572	
15:16............551, 561	16:14............572	17:14–16........583–584
15:16b............560n285	16:14–18........1164	17:15............582, 583
15:17............561, 979, 1030	16:15............572, 573	17:16............582, 583, 584
15:18............438, 448, 560, 561	16:16............444, 573, 579, 1081	17:20............579
15:19............561	16:16–21........570, 573, 575	17:23............579
15:20............561, 1172, 1173	16:17............573	17:25–26........579
15:20–21........453, 561–562, 924, 1226	16:17–18........565, 573, 573n303	17:27–29........579
	16:19............573, 579	18................438, 585, 586–592, 594
	16:19–21........570	

18–19 585
18:1 .... 509, 587–588, 1158
18:1–12 .... 585, 587
18:1–27 462
18:1–19:25 ..... 438, 460, 462
18:1–24:11 ..... 437, 461
18:2 .... 587, 588n324, 1172
18:2–4 588
18:2–5 .... 472, 588, 588n322, 594
18:3–4 588
18:5 .... 207, 478, 588, 594, 1159
18:5–6 1313
18:5–8 587
18:6 .... 588, 588n324, 1172
18:6–7 588
18:7 .... 494, 588
18:8 .... 588, 591, 694
18:8–10 587
18:8–12 509
18:9 .... 588, 1330
18:9–12 .... 588–589, 695
18:10 .... 589, 648n483, 1158
18:10–11 587
18:10–12 472
18:11 .... 449, 589, 589n327, 638n462
18:12 .... 587, 589, 1158
18:13 589
18:13–23 .... 589–590, 591, 677
18:13–26 632
18:13–27 .... 438, 585, 587
18:14 .... 577n308, 589
18:15–16 .... 587, 589, 780
18:17–18 589
18:17–23 587
18:18 591
18:19–20 590
18:21 .... 587, 592, 677
18:21–22 590
18:23 590
18:24–26 .... 590, 678n550, 704
18:26 979
18:27 .... 590, 1159
18:27–30 979
19 .... 585, 592–601, 603, 692
19–23 694
19–24 .... 27, 588n325, 604, 692, 772n752
19–40 587
19–Num. 10 822
19:1 .... 594n339, 1156, 1159
19:1–Lev. 27:34 .. 1076
19:1–2 .... 588n325, 594, 809, 1314
19:1–8 585
19:1–15 438
19:1–25 .... 462, 696n584, 697, 698
19:2 .... 1080, 1157, 1309n247
19:2–3 705
19:3 .... 595, 840, 1159, 1315
19:3–6 .... 452, 595–596, 600, 692, 698
19:4 .... 595, 599, 605
19:4–6 .... 605, 692
19:5 .... 452, 523, 595, 600, 698, 739, 746, 781
19:5–6 .... 468, 595, 840, 1039
19:5–8 602
19:5a 595
19:5b 595
19:6 .... 32, 180, 439, 455, 596, 631, 632, 781, 819, 839, 852, 895, 944, 1196, 1200, 1280
19:7 596
19:7–8 .... 594, 862
19:7–8a 596
19:8 .... 692, 1191
19:8a 596
19:8b 596
19:8b–13 .... 596–597, 747
19:9 .... 560, 596, 598, 619n420, 705, 789n795, 1315
19:9–13 596
19:9–15 594
19:9–25 .... 585, 594
19:9a 596
19:9b 596
19:10 .... 598, 893, 951, 979
19:10–11 597
19:11 .... 705n605, 772n752
19:12 .... 61n51, 597, 598, 693, 694, 704, 1080
19:12–13 .... 256, 783
19:12–13a 597
19:12–23 .... 772n752
19:13 597
19:14 1315
19:14–15 .... 597, 598
19:14–19 597–598
19:15 .... 597n347, 951, 1145
19:16 .... 598, 598n348, 619, 709, 1029
19:16–17 597
19:16–19 .... 594, 603
19:16–25 439
19:17 .... 598, 618, 1315
19:18 .... 160, 478, 598, 709, 907
19:19 .... 598, 598n348, 709, 1029, 1315
19:20 .... 595, 598, 662n520, 693, 704, 705, 772n752, 1173, 1315
19:20–25 .... 479, 594, 596, 598–599, 782
19:21 .... 377n619, 598, 1080
19:21–24 .... 618n415
19:22 598
19:23 .... 377n619, 598
19:24 .... 598, 599, 783
19:24–25 .... 693n575
19:25 .... 599, 1315
20 .... 605, 626
20–23 .... 441, 447, 457n39, 458, 568, 585, 602, 605, 692, 695
20–24 .... 449, 451, 602
20–31 766
20:1 694
20:1–2 .... 603, 605–606
20:1–17 .... 35, 462, 603, 631, 694, 704, 762, 772n752
20:1–21 .... 447n24, 447n25, 448n31, 458n43, 600, 602–626, 630, 632, 633, 633n449, 634n450, 645, 646, 661, 665, 667, 701n597, 763
20:1–23:33 ...... 460, 631
20:1–24:1 438
20:1–24:11 ...... 462, 602
20:1–Num. 10:10 .. 1154
20:2 .... 458, 605, 619, 973, 988, 1062
20:2–17 .... 788, 788n793
20:3 .... 606, 618n417, 774, 991
20:3–4 666
20:3–5 311
20:3–6 .... 790, 790n797
20:3–11 603
20:3–17 458
20:4 47
20:4–5a 606
20:4–5 774
20:4–6 .... 606–609, 785, 787
20:5 .... 607, 608n367, 609, 784, 1082, 1123, 1184
20:5–6 613
20:5b–6 607
20:6 .... 608, 609, 784, 785, 1193
20:7 .... 609–610, 610n378, 613, 615, 875, 1022
20:8 1012
20:8–11 .... 574, 610–612, 612n389, 622, 681, 762, 765, 765n749, 787, 1028
20:9–10 611
20:10 .... 547n254, 611, 612n390, 615n403, 635, 962n200, 983
20:11 .... 611, 762, 983
20:12 .... 56, 114, 115, 612–613, 643, 644, 646n481, 673n539, 983
20:12–17 603
20:13 .... 613–614, 642, 657
20:14 .... 56, 612, 614, 623, 663n521, 977, 1120
20:15 614–615
20:16 .... 615, 676, 678n551
20:16–18 615
20:17 .... 606, 615–617, 788
20:18 .... 598n348, 617, 618, 696, 709, 905, 1029
20:18–19 598
20:18–21 .... 462, 603, 617–619, 625, 704
20:19 .... 605, 618
20:20 .... 204, 439, 452, 618, 1043, 1188
20:21 .... 618, 627
20:22–23 .... 452, 627
20:22–25 694
20:22–26 .... 462, 627–630, 682, 691, 741
20:22–23:33 630
20:23 .... 630, 774, 790n797
20:24 .... 627, 628, 629, 695
20:24–26 627
20:25 628
20:26 .... 628, 724, 844, 904n108
21 .... 636n458
21–22 636
21–23 .... 603, 605, 631n445, 632, 633n449
21:1 .... 634, 694
21:1–6 640

SCRIPTURE INDEX 1352

21:1–11 633–641
21:1–32 655
21:1–23:19 . . . . .458n43, 462, 627, 630–633, 633n449, 640, 686, 694
21:2 . . . . .634n451, 635, 636, 636n458, 637, 639, 653, 657, 704
21:2–6 . . . . .456, 634–638, 640, 657, 658n514, 663
21:2–11 . . . . .456, 634
21:2–23:19 634
21:3 636
21:3–5 1126
21:3–6 . . . . .634n451, 636
21:4 . . . . .637, 792
21:5 637
21:5–6 . . . . .635, 637
21:6 637
21:7 . . . . .634n451, 639, 639n465
21:7–11 . . . . .634, 638–640, 1126
21:8 . . . . .638, 639, 639n466, 1236
21:8–11 . . . . .634n451, 639
21:9 . . . . .639, 1236
21:10 . . . . .639, 1236
21:11 . . . . .639, 640, 1236
21:12 . . . . .613, 614, 642, 644, 645, 665
21:12–14 . . . . .630, 642–643, 644n477, 1023
21:12–17 . . . . .642–646, 653
21:13 . . . . .643, 651, 652n507
21:14 . . . . .589n327, 643, 645
21:14–17 665
21:15 . . . . .611n383, 613, 613n394, 642, 643–644, 644n477, 645, 646, 778n769
21:15–17 . . . . .644n477
21:16 . . . . .353n573, 635, 642, 644, 1183
21:17 . . . . .613, 613n394, 622, 623, 630, 642, 644–645, 644n477, 646, 672, 673n539
21:18 . . . . .577, 648
21:18–19 . . . . .648, 651
21:18–27 647
21:18–32 . . . . .647–654, 660, 678
21:19 . . . . .648, 654
21:20 . . . . .648, 648n486, 649
21:20–21 648–649
21:21 . . . . .648, 649
21:22 . . . . .526n203, 649, 649n488, 650, 652n506
21:22–23 649
21:22–25 . . . . .649–652, 660
21:22a 649
21:23 . . . . .647, 653, 968
21:23–24 651
21:23–25 . . . . .633, 649, 650, 651, 1023
21:24 1329
21:24–25 654
21:26–27 . . . . .635, 649, 651, 652, 654
21:26–28 649
21:28 . . . . .112, 634, 652, 653, 656
21:28–29 653
21:28–30 653

21:28–32 . . . . .647, 652–653, 753, 994
21:29 . . . . .623, 647, 652, 653
21:29–31 653
21:30 . . . . .652, 653, 1299
21:30–32 650
21:31 . . . . .634, 653
21:32 653
21:33 656
21:33–34 . . . . .655, 656, 660, 1023
21:33–36 656
21:33–22:15 654–661
21:34 656
21:35 . . . . .655, 656, 660
21:35–36 656
21:36 . . . . .655, 660
22:1 . . . . .614, 630, 655, 656, 657, 660, 661, 875, 1119
22:1–4 . . . . .656–657, 661, 1119
22:2 657
22:3 660
22:2–3a 657
22:3–4 630
22:3a 657
22:3b 657
22:4 . . . . .655, 657, 657n511, 658, 660, 661, 875, 1119
22:5 . . . . .657, 658
22:5–6 . . . . .655, 656, 657–658, 660
22:6 658
22:7 . . . . .614, 655, 660, 661
22:7–8 874
22:7–9 . . . . .658–659, 1118
22:7–15 . . . . .656, 658
22:7a 658
22:7b 658
22:8 . . . . .658, 658n515
22:8–9 . . . . .638, 658
22:9 . . . . .655, 658, 658n514, 659, 660
22:10 . . . . .659, 660
22:10–11 . . . . .655, 658
22:10–13 . . . . .659, 1118
22:11 . . . . .609n373, 658, 658n515, 659, 874, 1290
22:12 . . . . .655, 658, 658n515, 659, 660
22:13 . . . . .655, 658, 658n515, 659, 660
22:14 . . . . .658, 659
22:14–15 659
22:15a 659
22:15b 659
22:16 . . . . .662, 663, 664, 1123
22:16–17 . . . . .306, 636n459, 662–665, 664n526
22:17 . . . . .662, 663, 663n523, 664
22:18 . . . . .665–666, 667
22:18–20 665–667
22:19 . . . . .665, 666, 667, 673, 1053
22:20 . . . . .630, 665, 667, 1120
22:21 . . . . .668, 669
22:21–22 670
22:21–24 . . . . .653, 668–669, 670, 677, 678
22:21–27 668–671
22:22 . . . . .669, 1126
22:22–24 668

22:23–24 . . . . .669, 669n533, 670, 679
22:25 . . . . .668, 669, 671, 1033
22:25–27 . . . . .669–670, 671, 875
22:26–27 . . . . .668, 670, 984
22:27 . . . . .671, 679
22:28 . . . . .672–673, 674, 1022
22:28–31 672–675
22:29 . . . . .675, 1217
22:29–30 . . . . .672, 673–674, 681n557, 684, 1008n252, 1215
22:29–31 674
22:29a 673
22:29b 673
22:29b–30 673
22:30 . . . . .466n56, 548, 645, 673, 898, 986, 1008
22:31 . . . . .672, 674, 675, 969n211
23 687
23:1 . . . . .610, 610n377, 610n378, 623
23:1–2 615
23:1–3 . . . . .630, 676–677, 678
23:1–9 676–680
23:1a 676
23:1b 677
23:2a 677
23:2b 677
23:2b–31 690
23:3 . . . . .615, 677, 678
23:4–5 . . . . .676, 677, 679
23:4a 677
23:4b 677
23:5 . . . . .645, 673, 677, 1008
23:6 . . . . .624, 677, 678
23:6–9 . . . . .676, 677–678
23:7 . . . . .630, 679
23:7a 677
23:7b 677
23:8 . . . . .625, 677
23:9 . . . . .547n254, 669, 677, 678, 679
23:10 681
23:10–11 681
23:10–12 . . . . .630, 681, 1008
23:10–19 680–685
23:11 . . . . .623, 681n556, 1029
23:11–12 685
23:11–12a 645, 673
23:11c 681
23:12 . . . . .611, 622, 668–669, 681, 765n747, 787, 994
23:12–33 786
23:13 . . . . .628n432, 681–682, 1305
23:13b 682
23:14 . . . . .682, 682n561
23:14–17 . . . . .682–684, 787, 1011n255
23:14–18 1280
23:14–19 681
23:15 . . . . .682, 1129
23:15–16 . . . . .528n212
23:16 . . . . .673, 682n564, 1014, 1016, 1282, 1286, 1287
23:16b 682, 682n564
23:17 682
23:18 . . . . .684, 788
23:18–19 684
23:18b 684n566

23:19............687, 788, 1214
23:19a............684
23:19b............684
23:20–22.......687–688, 690
23:20–23.......449, 779, 1160, 1161
23:20–33.......447n24, 462, 605n354, 630, 686–691, 694, 763
23:21.............687, 1185
23:21–22.......478n83
23:21a............452
23:21b............452
23:22.............478n83, 687, 688, 689, 696n585, 979
23:22–23.......698
23:22–30.......584
23:23–24.......686, 688, 689, 786, 787n791
23:23–25.......452
23:24.............688n568, 689
23:25–31.......686, 688–689, 691
23:27.............786n788
23:27–30.......698, 786
23:28.............1319
23:30.............459
23:31.............556n264
23:32–33.......452, 686, 689, 787n791
23:33.............689n572, 1319
24................457n39, 602, 707, 811
24:1..............466n56, 694
24:1–2...........597, 692, 693–694, 704, 811, 908
24:1–8...........627
24:1–11.........460, 462, 691–698, 699, 775
24:1a.............693
24:1b–2.........693
24:2..............705
24:3..............692, 694, 695, 697, 1191
24:3–7...........706
24:3–8...........589, 629, 688n568, 692, 694–696, 697, 743, 774
24:3–11.........596n344, 631
24:4..............441, 694, 696, 703, 788, 821n3
24:4–5...........583
24:4–8...........776
24:5..............695, 841, 852
24:5–9...........719n640
24:6..............697, 843
24:6–8...........692, 863, 964
24:6–11.........897
24:6a.............695
24:6b.............695
24:7..............441, 631, 695, 697, 821n3, 1191
24:8..............455, 695, 696, 697, 824, 843, 942
24:9..............696, 1167, 1169, 1315
24:9–11.........589, 629, 692, 695, 696–697, 698, 703, 728, 743, 774, 852, 862, 1021, 1167
24:10............692, 696, 697, 698
24:11............180, 692, 697, 698, 908, 1191
24:12............699, 701, 703, 759
24:12–14.......703–704, 763, 788n793

24:12–18.......462, 699, 702
24:12–25:9....701n598, 702–712, 741, 754n722, 811, 813, 814n836
24:12–31:18....437, 460, 461, 462, 699–701, 716
24:12–40:38....461
24:13............478, 702, 704, 776, 1159, 1169
24:14............583, 703, 704, 761, 777
24:15............704, 1151, 1159
24:15–16.......704
24:15–18.......704–705, 788, 811
24:16............811, 840
24:16–17.......572n296, 718, 782
24:16b...........704
24:17............478, 704, 705, 709, 904
24:18............100, 704, 704n603, 705, 772n752, 773, 1315
24:18a...........705
25................719, 751
25–31...........441, 447, 448, 451, 461n52, 760, 761, 779, 794, 806n814, 813, 892
25:1..............762, 1264
25:1–2...........705–706, 804, 805
25:1–8...........779
25:1–9...........462, 702, 710, 1264–1266
25:1–30:38....699
25:2..............702, 705, 706, 712, 720, 805, 813, 853n42
25:2–3...........706
25:3..............706, 1141
25:3–4...........736
25:3–7...........700, 703, 706–707, 712, 722, 804
25:4..............706, 710, 721, 737
25:4–5a..........706n608
25:5..............717n625, 1110
25:5a.............706
25:5b.............707
25:6a.............707
25:6b.............707
25:7..............707
25:8..............701, 702, 707, 708, 710, 711, 716
25:8–9...........453, 703, 707–709, 719n636
25:9..............708, 711, 717, 720, 725, 761, 1143
25:9–27:21.....708
25:10............707, 717
25:10–11.......706, 710
25:10–16.......716–718, 719, 720, 728, 738, 805, 807, 810
25:10–22.......716
25:10–39.......806n814
25:10–40.......716
25:10–26:37....710
25:10–27:21....462, 712–731, 734
25:11............716, 717, 736
25:11–16.......729
25:12............717, 718n632
25:13............707
25:14............1111
25:15............717, 1110
25:15–25.......720

25:16............575, 699, 708n614, 716, 717, 719, 763
25:17............716, 718
25:17–22.......448, 718–719, 720, 723, 729, 730, 752, 805, 807, 810, 956
25:18............721
25:18–19.......718, 727
25:18–20.......718
25:20............718, 1140n65
25:21............575, 719
25:21–22.......710, 719, 752, 1140
25:22............701, 708, 717, 718, 719, 728, 794n805, 811n833, 957, 1080, 1206
25:23............719
25:23–30.......716, 719, 805, 807, 810
25:24............716, 717
25:24–28.......719
25:25............719, 719n637
25:26–27.......719
25:27............719n637
25:29............717, 719, 1111, 1281
25:30............719, 727, 880, 1020, 1110
25:31............716, 717, 718n632, 720
25:31–40.......716, 720, 805, 807, 810, 1020, 1143
25:32............1111
25:32–33.......1088
25:32–35.......720
25:33............717
25:34............720n643
25:35............720n643
25:36............717, 718n632, 720, 1020
25:37............707, 720, 728, 1020, 1111, 1143
25:38............720
25:38–39.......717
25:39............720, 725, 1138
25:40............455, 720, 725, 761, 1143
25:44–46.......635n452
26–29...........992
26:1..............706, 721, 723, 736, 737
26:1–6...........708, 720–721, 723, 737, 805, 806, 1104
26:1–14.........716, 810
26:1–37.........806n814
26:3..............721
26:4–6...........721
26:6..............710, 722n648, 723
26:7..............706, 708, 721, 1298
26:7–8...........722
26:7–10.........1104
26:7–13.........721–722, 805, 806
26:7–14.........708
26:8–11.........722
26:9..............722, 723
26:10............1236
26:11............706
26:12............722
26:13............721n647, 722
26:14............706, 722, 805, 805n812, 1104
26:15............707
26:15–30.......708, 710, 716, 721n647, 722–723, 806, 810

SCRIPTURE INDEX

26:16............725
26:18–21 722
26:19............721n647, 722
26:22–25 722
26:24............722
26:26............707, 794
26:26–29 723
26:28............723, 723n650
26:29............725
26:30............723, 725
26:31............706, 721, 723, 737, 986, 1110
26:31–33 ....710, 1110
26:31–35 ....723, 727, 729, 805, 806, 810
26:31–37 716
26:32............725
26:32–33 723
26:33............710, 721n647, 723n651, 1001, 1109
26:33–35 ....794n805
26:33b–34......723
26:34............1213
26:34–35 979
26:35............723
26:36............706, 725, 737
26:36–37 ....721, 723–724, 805, 807, 810
26:37............706, 807n815
26:40............723
27:1 ....724, 904n108
27:1–2 ....706, 710
27:1–8 ....628, 716, 724, 727, 745, 752, 805, 807
27:2 ....724, 752
27:3 ....724, 843, 1111
27:4–7 724
27:7b............724
27:8 761
27:8a............724
27:8b............725
27:9 879
27:9–19 ....444, 716, 725–726, 805, 807, 808n821, 811
27:10............725, 725n656
27:10–17 725
27:11............725n656
27:13............844
27:14............806, 1196
27:16............725
27:19............722, 725, 726
27:20............707
27:20–21 ....716, 720, 726, 727, 745n699, 805
27:21............575, 752n709, 1228
28................710, 716, 746, 747, 879, 894, 957
28–29 ....731–749, 815n840
28:1 ....598, 735, 736, 1100
28:1–4 ....735–736, 740, 747
28:1–5 706
28:1–43..........462, 735, 805
28:1–29:42.....734
28:2 ....736, 741, 747, 879, 909, 1230
28:3 ....736, 741, 746, 805
28:4 736
28:5 736
28:5–6 736
28:5–14..........736–737, 746, 754, 808
28:5–39..........735, 742

28:6 ....737, 738, 986
28:6–14..........894
28:8 737
28:9–11..........737
28:9–12..........707
28:10............738n676
28:12............610n379, 737, 738, 746
28:13–14 737
28:14............717n627, 738
28:15............738, 986
28:15–30 ....738–739, 746, 808, 894
28:16............738
28:17–21 ....707, 738
28:20............53
28:21............738
28:22............717n627
28:22–28 738
28:28............738
28:29............575, 738, 746, 862
28:29–30 ....738, 738n679, 880
28:30............232, 575, 1278
28:31–32 739
28:31–35 ....739, 808, 894
28:33............824
28:33–34 739
28:35............575, 739
28:36............717n627, 739, 824, 895
28:36–37 736
28:36–38 ....739–740, 748, 808
28:37............739
28:38............740, 842, 860, 880, 912n118
28:39............739, 740, 742n689, 808
28:40............735, 736, 740, 741, 742n689, 747, 808
28:40–43 741
28:41............740–741, 1100
28:42............894
28:42–43 ....628n433, 736, 741, 808, 879
28:43............710, 711, 1210
29................736, 741, 741n687, 743n694, 754, 1081
29:1 ....746, 1143
29:1–3 ....735, 741
29:1–9 809
29:1–35..........462, 735
29:1–46..........809
29:1a............741
29:1b–3..........741
29:2 744
29:4 741
29:4–9 ....735, 741–742
29:5–6 742
29:6 ....739, 1128
29:7 ....739, 742, 743, 756, 909, 1128
29:8–9 ....742, 879
29:9 ....742, 742n689, 897, 1201
29:10............742
29:10–14........742–743, 753, 753n713, 757
29:10–35........735
29:11–12........742
29:12............526n204, 743, 751
29:13............542n242, 744
29:14............742
29:15–18........742, 743, 744, 752
29:18............752, 844
29:19–21 ....696, 743, 809n825

29:19–28 ....742, 743, 744
29:20............724, 743
29:21............743, 756, 879, 1100, 1111
29:22–24 1213
29:22–25 ....744, 805n813
29:24............1214
29:25............743, 744, 752
29:26............744, 1330
29:26–28 ....743, 744
29:27............1213
29:27–28 ....706, 744
29:29............894
29:29–30 744
29:31–32 744
29:31–33 743
29:31–34 744
29:33............744, 756
29:34............743, 744
29:35............466n56, 705, 744
29:35–37 860
29:36............744, 744n696, 1068, 1194, 1236
29:36–37 751
29:36–42 ....462, 735, 744–745, 747, 752, 810
29:37............745, 863, 895, 1001, 1213, 1221
29:37b 745n697
29:38–42 ....724, 745, 750, 751, 752, 841, 842n22, 880, 896, 1192, 1280
29:40............810n830, 827, 846n28, 1014
29:40–41 ....881, 910
29:41............752
29:42............745, 751, 905, 1206
29:42–43 ....780, 863
29:42–46 708
29:43............745, 811n831
29:43–46 ....453, 462, 734, 735, 745–746
29:44............745, 746
29:44–45 893
29:45............440, 745, 748, 748n704, 815, 815n843
29:45–46 ....450, 707, 708, 748
29:46............439, 701, 746, 767, 779, 803, 811, 812
30................749–758, 759
30:1–3 ....706, 752
30:1–5 ....750, 752, 807, 810
30:1–6 755
30:1–9 719
30:1–10..........710, 716, 723, 727, 750, 751, 805
30:1–38..........462
30:3 717,
30:4–5 752
30:6 ....723, 751, 752, 756, 1080
30:6–10..........750, 752–753, 757, 810
30:7 ....752n711, 1020
30:7–8 ....727, 752, 752n709, 756, 958, 1101, 1111, 1143, 1202
30:7–9 880
30:8 751
30:9 ....724, 909, 1101, 1281
30:9a............752
30:9b............752

30:10............750, 751, 757, 1194	31:7–9..........1102, 1104	32:15b–16......776
30:10a...........753	31:7–11.........761	32:17............702, 704, 775, 776
30:10b 753	31:8 1111	32:18............776
30:11............762	31:11............761, 806	32:18–19 775
30:11–16 ....753–754, 757, 808, 808n819, 873, 1082	31:12............762	32:18–20 439
30:12............751, 753	31:12–17 ....463, 699, 760, 762, 763, 765, 787, 802, 804, 1280	32:19............534, 573, 777, 782
30:12–16 1299	31:13............699, 762, 765, 823, 1012, 1028, 1040	32:20............774n755, 777, 1122
30:13............753, 808n819, 873n69, 1052	31:13–17 685	32:21............194, 777
30:14............753	31:14............756, 762, 887n92, 888n96, 1195	32:21–24 777
30:15............754	31:14–15 762	32:21–25 767
30:15–16 751	31:14–17 1028	32:21–29 440
30:16............750, 751, 754, 1082	31:15............739, 762, 1281	32:22–23 1171–1172
30:17............762	31:16–17 ....699, 762	32:23............777, 777n768
30:17–21 ....751, 754–755, 758, 805, 807, 811, 893	31:17............705	32:24............777
30:18............754	31:18............441, 463, 575, 605n354, 699, 704n600, 708n614, 717n631, 718, 760, 763, 776, 958, 1168–1169	32:25............775, 777, 1121
30:18–20 950		32:25–29 ....452, 453, 777–778
30:18–21 478		32:26............778, 778n769, 1088
30:19–20 754		32:26–27 1146
30:20–21 754		32:26–28 772
30:22............762	32................709, 772, 780, 802, 813, 814, 1264, 1316	32:26–29 ....419, 893
30:22–24 707		32:27............772, 778, 1067
30:22–25 ....707, 726, 755		32:28............778, 1088
30:22–33 ....745n697, 751, 755–756, 805, 807, 809, 809n824	32–34 ....53, 439, 441, 446, 447, 451, 457n39, 461n52, 699, 766–793, 803, 813, 832	32:29............778, 1100, 1266
		32:30............294, 778
30:23–24 895		32:30–31 1315
30:23–25 742		32:30–32 1204
30:25............755n728, 1137	32:1 ....705, 771, 774, 774n753, 777, 1185n100	32:30–35 778–779
30:25–29 ....755, 1111		32:30–33:6 463
30:25–30 742	32:1–6 ....704, 771, 773–775, 774n757, 777n768, 790n797	32:30–34:35....440
30:26–29 ....745, 809, 885		32:31............499n138
30:26–30 758		32:31–32a......778
30:28............724	32:1–14..........463	32:32............1316
30:29............755n730, 756n730, 809n824	32:1–18..........439	32:32–33 ....778n771
	32:1–34:35 .....437, 460, 461, 463, 607, 621, 628, 699	32:32b............778
30:30............756, 756n730, 758, 885, 1200		32:33............779, 1021
	32:2 ....774, 805	32:34............767
30:30–32 1330	32:2–3 ....312, 780	32:34–35 ....607n364
30:31............1111, 1137	32:2–5 767	32:34a...........779
30:31–33 ....756, 758	32:3 777	32:34b 779
30:32............895	32:4 ....774, 774n753, 777, 787	32:35............452, 772, 777
30:33............751, 887n92, 888n96		32:35a...........779
	32:4–5 621	32:26............1088
30:34............726n659, 762	32:5..............523n197, 774	32:28............1088
30:34–35 ....707, 756, 958	32:5–6 ....498, 530	32:29............1266
30:34–37 909	32:6 ....240n348, 695, 774, 775, 1145, 1265	33................1132
30:34–38 ....751, 752, 755, 756–757, 805, 807, 810		33:1 ....412, 779
	32:7 ....775, 776	33:1–2 779
30:35............756	32:7–8 780	33:1–6 ....772, 779–780
30:36............752, 756, 1080	32:7–10..........452, 772, 775, 777, 779	33:1–7 ....461n52
30:36–38 958		33:3 ....767, 779, 781, 781n777
30:37............752	32:8 ....774, 774n753, 787	33:4 ....767, 779
30:37–38 ....756, 758	32:9 785	33:4–6 772
30:38............751, 887n92, 888n96	32:9–10..........775	33:5 ....767, 779, 780, 781, 781n777
	32:10............775, 776, 1184, 1202	
31................759–766, 772n752		33:7 ....754n723, 780
31:1 762	32:11............776	33:7–8 780
31:1–5 759	32:11–13 772	33:7–11..........780–781, 1168
31:1–11.........463, 699, 721, 736, 759, 760–761, 763, 764, 805, 806, 807	32:11–14 775–776	33:7–17 463
	32:11b............776	33:8 ....478n85
31:2 ....583, 760, 761	32:12a...........776	33:8–10..........780
31:3 ....721, 760, 761, 1258, 1278	32:12b...........776	33:11............177, 582, 780, 1131, 1169
	32:13............776, 779, 1255	33:12............781
31:3–5 764	32:14............776, 778	33:12–13 ....767, 772, 781
31:4 721	32:15............763, 788, 1315	33:12–16 1165
31:4–5 761	32:15–19 699	33:12–17 ....461n52, 781
31:6 ....759, 760, 761, 761n738, 805, 806	32:15–20 ....774n755, 776–777	33:14............781, 781n777, 1160
	32:15–29 463	33:15–16 ....767, 772, 781, 1039
31:6–11..........760	32:15a...........776	33:16............905
31:7 1111		33:17............781, 792
		33:18............772, 781, 793, 909
		33:18–23 ....463, 781–782
		33:18–34:7 789

33:19	235, 606n358, 782n779, 783, 1132	
33:19–20	1132	
33:20	696, 780, 782, 958	
33:21	782	
33:21–23	783	
33:22–23	782	
33:23	1132	
33:42	1236	
33:45	1236	
33:49	1264	
34	772, 772n752, 788	
34:1	783, 785, 786, 788, 788n793	
34:1–8	450, 463, 608n369, 609, 782–785, 792	
34:1–28	699	
34:2	521n192, 772n752, 782, 783, 789	
34:3	772n752, 783, 789, 1080, 1166, 1314	
34:4	783, 1315	
34:5	772n752, 789, 1173	
34:5–7	450	
34:5a	783	
34:5b	783	
34:6	406, 438, 483, 487, 566, 590n333, 608n367, 783, 784, 789	
34:6–7a	440, 450, 688, 772	
34:6–7	31, 91, 453, 562, 609, 772, 776, 782n779, 783, 784, 785n783, 792, 803, 909, 996, 1021	
34:7	417, 424, 607n364, 608n367, 608n369, 784, 785, 960, 1082, 1184	
34:7b	440, 450, 452, 688, 772	
34:8	789	
34:9	767, 772, 785–786, 785n785, 791	
34:9–28	463	
34:10	772, 786	
34:10–12	781n777	
34:10–28	772n752	
34:11	786n788	
34:11–16	688, 786–787	
34:11–17	452	
34:11–26	441, 788, 788n793	
34:11a	786	
34:11b	786	
34:11b–17	786	
34:11b–26	786	
34:12–16	689	
34:13	688n568	
34:14	787, 1123	
34:14–17	967	
34:15	1191, 1265	
34:15–16	1069, 1120, 1196, 1266, 1267	
34:16	787n791	
34:17	787	
34:18	787	
34:18–20	787	
34:18–26	786, 787, 1011n255	
34:19–20	787, 1048, 1215	
34:20	548n255, 1129	
34:21	611, 787	
34:22	682, 682n564, 1014, 1016, 1214, 1283, 1287	
34:22–23	787–788	
34:22–24	787	
34:24	616, 788	
34:25	684, 684n566, 787, 788	
34:26	788, 1214	
34:26a	787	
34:26b	787	
34:27	788, 821n3	
34:27–28	441	
34:28	703, 763, 788, 788n793	
34:29	788, 789n794, 1315	
34:29–32	455	
34:29–35	453, 463, 772, 788–790	
34:30	789	
34:31	674, 789	
34:32	789, 804	
34:33	455, 789	
34:34–35	789, 1168	
34:35	455	
35–39	794, 806n814, 813, 892	
35–40	441, 448, 451, 457n39, 461n52, 699, 780, 794–815	
35:1	441, 463, 804	
35:1–3	699, 772n752, 802	
35:1–40:33	440	
35:1–40:38	437, 448n29, 460, 461, 463, 699, 720n645, 748n702, 806, 813, 815n841	
35:2	1195, 1281	
35:2–3	463, 804	
35:3	611, 804, 1195	
35:4	441, 802, 813	
35:4–9	804	
35:4–36:7	463, 802	
35:5	706, 805, 1141, 1193	
35:10	736, 802, 805	
35:10–19	761, 805, 809	
35:11	805	
35:11–19	805	
35:12	805	
35:13	1020, 1110	
35:13–15	805	
35:18	725, 805	
35:19	805	
35:20	805	
35:20–22	813	
35:20–29	805–806, 808n820, 813	
35:20–36:7	440	
35:21	706, 805, 853n42	
35:21–22	706	
35:22	805, 806, 808n820, 889n99	
35:22–28	805	
35:23	707, 805	
35:24	460n49, 706, 808, 1213	
35:24a	805	
35:24b	805	
35:25–26	707, 761, 761n738, 805, 806, 813	
35:26	706, 764, 805	
35:27	805, 813	
35:27–28	806	
35:28	805	
35:29	802, 805, 806, 853n42	
35:30	441	
35:30–34	760	
35:30–36:1	806	
35:34	761	
36:1	802	
36:2	813	
36:2–3a	806	
36:2–7	806, 808	
36:3	706	
36:3–7	707, 806	
36:4	806	
36:5	802, 806, 813	
36:5–7	813	
36:6	706	
36:6–7	806	
36:7	707, 806	
36:8	806	
36:8–13	806	
36:8–38	806n814	
36:8–38:31	808	
36:8–39:43	463, 802, 806	
36:14	1080, 1104	
36:14–19	806	
36:19	805n812, 1080, 1104	
36:20–34	806	
36:31	794	
36:35–36	806	
36:35–38	794n805	
36:37–38	807	
36:38	807n815	
37:1–9	794n805, 807, 810n826	
37:1–28	806n814	
37:5	810n828, 1111	
37:10–16	807	
37:16	1111	
37:17–24	807	
37:23	1111	
37:25–28	807	
37:29	755, 807	
38	460	
38:1	724	
38:1–7	807	
38:8	754, 807, 808n822, 924, 1129, 1265	
38:9–20	807	
38:10	807n815	
38:17	725	
38:21	807, 1088	
38:21–23	760, 807–808	
38:21b	807	
38:22	440, 452	
38:23	761	
38:24	808	
38:24–29	1315	
38:25	808, 1213	
38:25–26	460n49, 753, 808n819	
38:25–28	754	
38:26	459, 460n49, 808, 1082, 1213	
38:27	722	
38:30	724	
39–40	814	
39:1	440, 452, 802	
39:1–7	808	
39:1–31	808, 810	
39:3	737, 737n669, 894	
39:5	440, 452, 802	
39:7	440, 452, 802	
39:8–21	808	
39:21	802	
39:22–26	808	
39:25	717	
39:26	802	

39:27	740n684	
39:27–29	808	
39:29	740, 802	
39:30	739	
39:30–31	808	
39:31	802	
39:32	802, 809, 814, 1109	
39:32–41	761	
39:32–43	809	
39:33–41	809	
39:34	805n812	
39:36	1020, 1110	
39:39	724	
39:40	725	
39:41	741	
39:42	440, 452, 802	
39:42–43	809	
39:43	802, 809, 814, 901	
40	446, 596n344, 693, 745, 794, 810n830, 811	
40:1	441	
40:1–8	809	
40:1–11	809n825	
40:1–15	809	
40:1–33	463, 802	
40:2	809, 1081, 1143, 1151	
40:2–3	728	
40:2b	809	
40:3–5	809	
40:6	724	
40:6–8	809	
40:9–10	1137	
40:9–11	809	
40:9–15	809, 811	
40:10	809n824	
40:12–15	809, 809n825	
40:12–16	892	
40:13–15	1143	
40:15	1137, 1201, 1266, 1271	
40:16	452, 802, 810, 1083	
40:16–33	809, 810	
40:17	809, 821, 822, 839n16, 1136, 1137, 1143, 1151, 1156	
40:17–33	808n823, 810	
40:18	810	
40:18–19	810	
40:18–27	806n814	
40:19	802, 805n812, 810, 1080, 1104	
40:20	810n828	
40:20–21	810	
40:21	802, 958	
40:22	1143	
40:22–23	810	
40:22–26	1080	
40:23	802	
40:24	1020, 1143	
40:24–25	810	
40:25	802	
40:26–27	810	
40:27	802, 810	
40:28	717n630	
40:28–29	810	
40:29	708, 802, 810, 810n830, 1216	
40:30	811	
40:31–32	811	
40:32	803	
40:33	810, 811, 1109	
40:33b	814	
40:34	444, 811, 1151	
40:34–35	455, 572n296, 704n602, 711, 745, 812	
40:34–38	440, 453, 463, 699, 708, 719, 803, 810, 811, 1148, 1151	
40:35	811, 839, 1081, 1278	
40:36	1152, 1155	
40:36–38	812	
40:38	556, 812, 907, 1001, 1151, 1152	

Leviticus
Book of	437n1, 819–838	
1	838–845, 857, 1048	
1–3	839, 857	
1–5	841, 916	
1–7	811, 819, 832, 902, 909, 955, 980, 1020	
1–10	1081	
1–15	820	
1–16	821, 974	
1–25	1044	
1:1	811, 811n833, 822n7, 1027, 1047	
1:1–2	812, 839	
1:1–2a	840	
1:1–9	589	
1:1–17	754n720, 879	
1:2	847, 877, 1145	
1:2–17	896	
1:2b	840–841, 860n55, 924n142	
1:3	95, 711, 727, 841–842, 863, 887, 1006, 1192	
1:3–9	743	
1:3–7:38	839	
1:4	107, 589, 629, 742, 743, 745, 824, 842, 860n55, 896, 960, 1006, 1144	
1:5	112, 711n618, 724, 842–843, 861, 965, 1144, 1216	
1:5–9	1192	
1:6	330n515	
1:6–7	843	
1:8–9a	843	
1:9	752, 843n26, 848, 888	
1:9b	843–844	
1:10	841	
1:10–11	844	
1:10–13	903	
1:11	844, 863, 881, 1144	
1:12–13	844	
1:13	843n26	
1:14	841	
1:15–17	844	
1:16	844, 861	
1:17	158, 843n26	
2	845–850	
2:1	847	
2:1–16	1192	
2:2	843n26, 844, 848, 850, 869, 1021	
2:2–3	880	
2:3	848, 849, 873, 880, 881, 886, 1002n248	
2:4	666, 848	
2:4–7	848–849, 886	
2:5–6	848	
2:6	874	
2:7	848, 849	
2:8	1145	
2:8–10	849	
2:9	843n26, 848	
2:10	880, 1002n248	
2:11	73, 741n688, 1020n271	
2:11–12	849	
2:12	843n26, 849, 1214	
2:13	756, 849–850, 1215	
2:14–15	848n34	
2:14–16	850	
3	851–856, 886	
3:1	727, 842n22, 852–853, 1006	
3:1–5	589	
3:1–17	897	
3:2	206n308, 743, 853, 861, 893, 965	
3:3–4	853–854, 855, 1192	
3:3–5	743, 861	
3:5	752, 843n26, 844, 848, 854, 1191	
3:6	842n22, 853	
3:6–8	854	
3:9–10	854	
3:11	844n27, 854	
3:12–16	855	
3:16	843n26, 844n27	
3:16–17	542n242, 742	
3:17	684n566, 855, 888, 965, 966n203, 968	
4	823, 856–865, 866, 885, 916, 1221	
4–5	869, 959	
4:1–2	859	
4:1–5:13	858	
4:1–6:7	840, 857	
4:2	847n30, 866, 1193	
4:3	842n22, 858, 859, 895, 902n104, 1000, 1006, 1068, 1144	
4:3–4	859–860, 928	
4:3–12	742, 896, 903, 912	
4:4	727, 863	
4:5	859	
4:5–6	860–861, 1080	
4:5–7	742, 903n107	
4:6	466n56, 1068, 1221	
4:6–7	965, 1145	
4:7	843, 861, 965, 1068, 1101, 1144	
4:8	858	
4:8–9	862	
4:8–10	861, 961	
4:11	1221	
4:11–12	861, 881, 882, 961	
4:12	865, 1221	
4:13	1068, 1084, 1144, 1167, 1193, 1194	
4:13–14	861–862, 867, 1144	
4:13–21	860, 1193	
4:14	842n22, 858, 860, 1068, 1194	
4:14–15	863	
4:15	862, 864, 1068, 1084, 1144, 1167, 1193	
4:16	859	
4:16–18	862	
4:17	1221	
4:18	1068	
4:19	862	

4:20 .... 858, 862–863, 864, 868, 882, 911	6:8–9 879	7:24 923
4:20–21 861	6:8–13 745	7:25 .... 887n92
4:21 .... 858, 863, 882	6:8–30 .... 876–883, 884	7:25–26 855
4:22 1068	6:8–7:10 .... 820n2	7:25–27 888
4:22–23 .... 842n22, 863	6:8–7:36 889	7:26–27 .... 888, 920, 923, 965, 966n203, 968
4:23 .... 858, 1194	6:9 .... 822, 877, 880, 905	7:27 .... 847n30, 887n92, 961, 961n195
4:24 .... 858, 863, 874	6:10–11 .... 724, 879	7:28–30 .... 888–889, 1014n260
4:25 .... 858, 882, 968, 1068, 1145	6:11 .... 861, 1111, 1221	7:28–34 589
4:25–26 863	6:12 .... 854, 880, 905, 1192	7:28–36 .... 744, 853, 888
4:26 .... 863, 868, 882	6:12–13 .... 879, 880	7:29 877
4:27 .... 1068, 1193	6:13 .... 880, 905, 909	7:29–30 744
4:27–28 .... 864, 868	6:14 822	7:29–32 1215
4:27–31 .... 778n771	6:14–15 880	7:29–34 743
4:28 .... 842n22, 858, 1194	6:14–16 .... 744n695	7:30–34 854
4:29 858	6:14–17 1213	7:31 .... 744, 889, 897
4:29–31 864	6:15 .... 843n26, 1121	7:31–34 .... 1002n248
4:30 .... 1068, 1145	6:16 1281	7:31–36 897
4:31 .... 752, 843n26, 848, 863, 868, 882, 1192n108	6:16–18 .... 848, 880–881	7:32 .... 706, 744, 1213
	6:17 .... 1002n248	7:32–33 .... 744n695, 889, 897
	6:17–18 1213	7:33 1213
4:32 .... 858, 868	6:18 1130	7:34 .... 706, 1213, 1215
4:32–35 864	6:19–21 881	7:34–35 881
4:33 858	6:20 880	7:34–36 .... 744, 889
4:34 .... 858, 1145	6:21 .... 843n26	7:37–38 889
4:35 .... 858, 863, 868, 882	6:22–23 881	7:38 .... 822n7, 1080
5:1 .... 624, 625, 847n30, 866, 867, 868, 1022	6:24–26 881–882	8 .... 741, 741n687, 743n694, 810, 811, 811n831, 841, 843, 889, 891–899, 927n148
	6:24–30 743	
5:1–4 859	6:25 .... 822, 873, 877, 882, 1002n248, 1143	
5:1–13 865–870	6:25–26 1213	
5:2 867	6:26 .... 863, 864	8–9 907
5:2–4 862	6:27 961	8–10 .... 819, 907, 956
5:3 .... 867, 950	6:27–28 .... 882, 950	8:1–5 893
5:4 .... 867, 868, 1292n221	6:28 542	8:1–10:20 822
5:5 .... 868, 960, 1119	6:28–29 684	8:2 .... 893, 973
5:5–6 .... 867, 868–869	6:29 .... 863, 873, 1002n248	8:3 893
5:6 871	6:29–30 882	8:4 .... 898n103, 907n112, 973
5:7 .... 821, 869, 1049	6:30 .... 861, 911	
5:7–13 .... 754n720, 945	7 .... 853, 883–890, 983	8:5 973
5:8–10 869	7:1 .... 822, 873, 885, 1002n248	8:6 893
5:10 .... 863, 868		8:7 .... 740, 894
5:11 .... 821, 869	7:1–2 885	8:7–9 .... 809n825, 894–895
5:12–13 869	7:1–7 872	8:8 .... 894, 1278
5:13 .... 863, 868	7:2 .... 861, 965	8:9 .... 895, 898n103, 907n112
5:14 872	7:3–5 885	
5:14–16 1006	7:6 .... 848, 873, 885, 1002n248	8:10 .... 840n19, 904
5:14–6:7 .... 870–876, 902		8:10–12 .... 809n825, 860, 895, 933, 1000
5:15 .... 871, 872–873, 944, 1006, 1052	7:6–7 885	
	7:8 .... 843, 885–886, 1210	8:10–13 .... 809n825
5:15–16 872	7:9–10 886	8:11 .... 895, 960
5:15–19 872	7:11 .... 822, 886	8:12 .... 711, 711n619, 724, 895, 898, 910, 944, 1143
5:16 .... 868, 871, 873, 1050	7:11–12 1192	
5:17 .... 867, 871, 873–874, 944, 960	7:11–14 1192	
	7:11–18 853	8:13 .... 740, 896, 898n103, 907n112
5:17–19 872	7:12 .... 853, 1288	
5:18 .... 868, 871, 874	7:12–14 886	8:14 .... 742, 928n152
5:19 874	7:13 .... 854n46	8:14–17 .... 858, 896
6–7 .... 840, 852, 877, 890, 916	7:15 .... 543, 886–887	8:15 .... 724, 861, 896, 960, 964, 968, 1119, 1194
	7:15–16 .... 1139, 1192	
6:1–3 874–875	7:15–18 .... 589, 743, 1215	
6:1–5 .... 614, 657n511	7:15–21 743	8:17 .... 898n103, 907n111, 907n112
6:1–7 .... 610n380, 859n50, 872, 1118	7:16 .... 853, 1050	
	7:16–17 .... 886n88	8:18 .... 742, 928n152
6:2 1118	7:16–18 .... 887, 984	8:18–21 896–897
6:2–3 .... 984, 1118	7:18 .... 842n24	8:21 .... 843n26, 898n103, 907n112
6:3 609	7:19–21 .... 887–888, 994, 1016n263	
6:4 .... 871, 1118		8:22–28 897
6:4–5 875	7:20 .... 823n9, 887n92, 965	8:23 898
6:5 .... 609, 1118	7:20–21 .... 888, 890, 926, 950, 1005	8:23–24 .... 724, 824, 897, 944, 964, 1000
6:5–7 868		
6:6 .... 1118, 1119	7:21 .... 887n92	8:24 942
6:6–7 875	7:22–25 888	8:25–27 .... 889n99
6:7 .... 868, 871, 1118, 1119	7:22–27 888	8:26 897
	7:22–36 888	
	7:23 .... 877, 966	

8:26–27 1100	10:14 .... 886n88, 924n143, 1000, 1192, 1213, 1215	12:5 .... 887n90, 927, 977, 995
8:28 .... 843n26		12:6 .... 711, 840, 858, 893
8:29 .... 897–898, 898n103, 907n112, 1213	10:14–15 706	12:6–7 .... 927–928, 944
	10:16–18 911–912	12:6–8 .... 858, 1221
8:30 .... 711, 711n619, 889, 898, 910, 942, 944, 964, 973, 1100	10:17 .... 912, 1211n126, 1211	12:7 822
		12:8 .... 754n720, 821, 928, 945, 1049
8:31–35 .... 744, 898, 902	10:19–20 912	
8:32 .... 907n111	10:20 918	13 .... 924, 929–937
8:33 .... 811, 898, 910, 943	11 .... 100, 860n55, 914–923	13–14 .... 932n157
8:34 898		13–15 1116
8:35 .... 898, 1143n66	11–15 .... 819, 823n9, 832, 908, 949n177, 955, 959, 1081	13:1 .... 821, 934, 949
8:36 .... 898, 898n103, 901		13:1–44 1116
9 .... 889, 893, 900–906		13:2 .... 933n159, 934
9:1 .... 898, 902, 1137	11:1 .... 821, 949	13:2–8 934
9:2 961	11:1–2a 918	13:3 .... 887n90
9:2–4 902	11:2 934	13:4 1174
9:3 911	11:2–8 916	13:9–17 934
9:4 .... 902, 961	11:2b–3 918–919	13:10 942
9:5 .... 710, 902	11:4–7 919	13:14 .... 942, 977n223
9:7 .... 901, 903, 907n112, 910, 1129	11:8 .... 919, 1203	13:14–15 934
	11:9 919–920	13:15 942
9:8 .... 742, 958	11:9–12 916	13:16 942
9:8–11 .... 902, 903	11:10 .... 920n134	13:18 .... 933n159
9:9 .... 965, 968	11:10–12 .... 521, 920	13:18–22 525
9:10 .... 901, 907n112	11:11 .... 920n134, 995	13:18–23 934–935
9:11 .... 907n111, 912	11:12 .... 920n134	13:21 935
9:12 .... 742, 903, 965	11:13 .... 920n134, 995	13:24 942
9:12–14 .... 902, 903	11:13–19 920	13:24–28 935
9:15 .... 902, 903, 911	11:13–23 916	13:29–37 935
9:15–21 903	11:14 920	13:30 .... 933n159
9:16 .... 902, 903	11:15 920	13:38 .... 933n159
9:17 .... 902, 903, 911	11:16 920	13:38–39 935
9:18 .... 903, 1192, 1213	11:19 920	13:39 .... 933n159
9:18–21 .... 902, 903	11:19–20 45	13:40 .... 933n159
9:21 .... 888, 901, 911, 1192, 1213	11:20 .... 920n134	13:40–44 935
	11:20–23 920	13:41 .... 933n159
9:22 .... 628, 724, 844, 901, 903–904, 1130, 1137	11:23 .... 920n134	13:42 .... 933n159
	11:24 920	13:45 .... 941, 1121
	11:24–25 .... 521, 867	13:45–46 .... 934, 935–936, 944n172
9:23 .... 901, 902, 904, 909	11:24–26 .... 887n91	
9:23–24 1020	11:24–28 .... 919, 920	13:46 .... 855, 936, 941, 1068
9:24 .... 824, 880, 905, 907, 907n111, 1001, 1024	11:29–30 .... 916, 920	13:47–51 936
	11:31 920	13:47–59 945
	11:31–36 920–921	13:48 1298
10 .... 906–913, 1201	11:32–33 950	13:51 .... 933n159
10:1 .... 724, 752n710, 907, 907n111, 1101, 1273	11:36 656	13:52 936
	11:37–38 921	13:52–58 936
	11:39–40 .... 919, 921, 969n211, 970	13:55 .... 887n90
10:1–2 .... 478, 694n577, 752n712, 908–909, 910n116, 1101		13:56 936
	11:41 .... 920n134	13:57 .... 933n159
	11:41–42 916	13:58 936
10:2 .... 907, 907n111, 957, 994, 1000, 1006, 1164	11:41–45 921–922	13:59 .... 822, 936
	11:42 .... 60, 920n134, 921	14 .... 821n4, 924, 932, 938–946
	11:43 .... 920n134, 921, 995	
10:3 .... 557n272, 909–910, 1228	11:44 .... 830, 928, 1106	14:1 999–1000
	11:44–45 .... 822, 918, 919, 982n228	14:1–2a 941
10:4 .... 506n159, 704n603		14:2 .... 822, 1129
10:4–5 910	11:44a 921	14:2b–3 941
10:6 .... 777, 1000, 1166	11:44b 921	14:3 934
10:6–7 910	11:45 928	14:4 .... 941–942, 1221
10:8 1210	11:45a 921	14:4–7 936
10:8–11 910–911	11:45b 921	14:5 .... 942, 1121
10:9 .... 249, 910, 910n116, 1101, 1210	11:46 .... 922, 923n140	14:5–6 950
	11:47 .... 822, 915, 922	14:5–7 942–943
10:9–10 912	12 .... 832, 867, 923–929	14:6 942
10:10 .... 54, 819, 887, 911, 928, 957, 1066, 1145	12–15 .... 841n20, 924	14:7 .... 940, 942
	12:1–2a 925	14:8 943
	12:2 .... 861n56, 887n90, 926, 934, 977, 977n223, 995, 1221	14:8–9 .... 1127, 1129
10:10–11 .... 453, 824, 879, 911, 915		14:9 .... 741, 940, 943
		14:9–13 1221
10:11 54	12:2–5 951	14:10–11 943
10:12 881	12:2b 925–926	14:11 .... 893, 1101, 1265
10:12–13 880	12:3 .... 926, 927, 1008	14:12 .... 840, 858, 872, 888, 943, 1068, 1128
10:12–15 911	12:4 926–927	

14:12–18 943–944	15:20............887n91, 950	16:18–19 ....753n714, 959–960, 1030n289, 1119, 1145, 1194
14:16............943	15:20–23 ....950, 952	
14:18............943	15:21............950	
14:19 ....840, 858, 1068, 1221	15:21–23 945	16:19............742, 942, 1221
14:19–20 ....840, 841, 857, 944, 1116, 1129	15:22............950	16:19–20 887
	15:23............950	16:20............955n181, 955n182, 960, 961n196
14:20............847, 940, 944, 1144	15:24............943, 952, 995	
14:21............872	15:25............926, 1068, 1117	16:20–21 941
14:21–22 ....945, 1049	15:25–27 952	16:21............868, 944n172, 960, 1217
14:21–32 1116	15:25–30 948	
14:22............1128	15:26............950	16:21–22 ....740, 942, 967
14:23............1029n288	15:27............950	16:22............867n62, 937, 961
14:23–32 945	15:28............943	16:23............955n182
14:24............943	15:28–29 1117	16:23–25 961
14:27............943	15:28–30 952	16:24............955n181, 961n196, 1144
14:29............943	15:29............1029n288	
14:31............858, 943	15:29–30 ....858, 1068	16:26............957n185, 961
14:32............822	15:30............944	16:27............955n181, 955n182, 961, 961n196
14:33............821, 949	15:31............820, 831, 840n19, 867, 949, 955, 1117	
14:33–42 945		16:27–28 961
14:34............945, 1322	15:31–33 952–953	16:29............542n238, 924, 962
14:36............945	15:32............822, 1120	16:29–31 ....961–962, 967n206, 1015
14:37–38 945	15:33............974n216	
14:40............861n57, 945	16................455, 729, 820, 823, 908, 912, 953–963, 1015, 1022, 1044, 1081, 1287	16:30............955n181, 957, 961n196, 962, 1287
14:41............861n57		
14:43–47 945		16:31............762n739, 962
14:44............887n90, 945		16:32............895, 955n181, 961n196
14:45............861n57	16–17 980	
14:48............945	16:1 ....694n577, 956	16:32–34 711
14:48–53 945	16:1–2 ....753n712	16:32–34a 962
14:50............942, 1121	16:2 ....694n577, 711, 728, 729, 753n714, 908, 955n182, 956–957, 958, 1143, 1210	16:33............955n181, 961n196, 1330
14:51............942, 1221		
14:52............942		16:33–34 1140
14:53............945		16:34............729, 807, 955n181, 961n196
14:54............935		
14:54–57 ....822, 946	16:2–3 956	16:34b 962
15................867, 947–953	16:3 ....955n182, 957	17................916, 963–970
15:1 821	16:3–5 957	17–20 830
15:1–2a 949	16:3–11.........842n22	17–22 1081
15:2.............887n90, 934, 991n237, 1068, 1117	16:4 ....68n66	17–26 ....825, 908, 955
	16:5 ....957, 1287	17–27 ....820, 821, 955, 964, 974
15:2b............949	16:6 ....778n771, 860n53, 896, 908, 955n181, 957, 961n196, 1330	
15:3 949–950		17:1–2 965
15:3–15.........948		17:2 ....1130, 1143
15:4 ....887n91, 950	16:6–10.........957	17:3 ....965, 991n237, 1215
15:4–6 950	16:7–8 957–958	17:3–4 965–966
15:5–8 ....741, 754	16:8 ....957n185	17:4 ....840n19, 887n92, 965n202, 966n205, 967, 968, 969
15:5–11.........945	16:8–10..........942	
15:6 950	16:9 959	
15:7 ....950, 1053n323	16:9–10..........957, 958	17:5 ....966, 966n205
15:7–8 950	16:10............941, 955n181, 957n185, 958, 961n196	17:5–6 966–967
15:9–10..........950		17:5–7 965
15:10............950		17:6 ....843n26, 965n202, 966, 966n205, 1215
15:11............950	16:11............778n771, 908, 955n181, 957, 958, 961, 961n196	
15:11–12 ....950, 952		17:7 ....726, 957, 967, 986
15:12............921, 950, 1298		17:8 ....965, 991n237
15:13............705, 861n56, 942, 943, 1127, 1221	16:11–19 ....858, 960	17:8–9 ....893, 916, 1006
	16:12............724, 752n710, 1201	17:9 ....887n92, 966n205, 968
15:13–15 ....950–951, 952, 1117	16:12–13 ....909, 958–959	
15:14............1029n288	16:13............955n182, 958	17:10............547n254, 888, 920, 965, 965n202, 967–968, 986, 991n237
15:14–15 ....858, 869n65, 1068	16:13–15 956	
15:15............944, 1221	16:14............955n182, 959, 1221	
15:16............952, 1071, 1117, 1120	16:14–16 ....718, 1140, 1145	
	16:14–19 ....944, 965, 1044	17:10–13 ....962n201
15:16–17 ....948, 951	16:15............911, 942, 955n182, 957, 959, 1068	17:10–16 923
15:16–18 945		17:11............695n582, 778n771, 828, 842, 917n123, 965n202, 968, 1071n11, 1119
15:17............1120, 1287	16:15–16 908	
15:18............597n347, 948, 951, 952, 1120	16:15–19 1287	
	16:16............742, 753n714, 955n181, 955n182, 959, 961n196, 1217, 1287, 1330	
15:19 ....926n144, 950, 951–952, 1071, 1117		17:11–12 ....855, 965
		17:12............965, 965n202, 967, 968–969
15:19–20 925	16:17............955n181, 955n182, 959, 961n196	
15:19–24 ....287, 948		17:13............965, 965n202, 967, 969, 991n237
15:19–26 925	16:18............955n181, 959, 961n196, 968, 1330	
15:19–33 995		17:13–14 855

17:14 .... 888, 965, 965n202, 969
17:15 .... 674, 921, 923, 965, 967, 1005, 1168
17:15–16 .... 674n545, 969–970
18 .... 825, 826, 971–980, 987, 990, 993n239
18–20 .... 832, 972, 997
18–22 1008
18–25 966
18–26 .... 973n212, 982n228
18:1–2 973
18:1–5 .... 972, 1008
18:2 .... 921n139, 973n212
18:3 .... 568, 974, 1322
18:3–4 973–974
18:4 .... 921n139, 973n212, 974
18:5 .... 371, 568, 821n4, 973n212, 974, 987, 1071, 1071n12, 1130
18:6 .... 973, 973n212, 974–975, 991n237
18:6–16 972
18:6–17 977
18:6–18 972
18:6–23 .... 962n201
18:6–30 923
18:7 .... 114, 974, 975
18:7–16 974
18:8 .... 974, 975, 976, 993
18:9 .... 974, 975, 994
18:10 .... 974, 975–976
18:11 .... 974, 975, 976
18:12 974
18:12–13 976
18:12–14 995
18:13 974
18:14 .... 974, 976
18:15 .... 975, 976, 993
18:15–17 974
18:15–18 974
18:16 .... 975, 995
18:17 .... 973, 975, 976–977, 994
18:17–18 972
18:18 .... 266n386, 975, 977
18:19 .... 925, 952, 973, 975, 977, 995
18:19–23 .... 972, 977
18:20 .... 614, 973, 975n219, 977, 977n223, 979n226, 993, 1120
18:21 .... 823n9, 973n212, 977–978, 984
18:22 .... 614n399, 973, 978, 994
18:23 .... 666, 973, 978, 994
18:24 973
18:24–25 .... 832, 978–979
18:24–30 .... 972, 974, 1008
18:25 973
18:26 .... 973, 978
18:26–28 .... 962n201
18:26–29 961
18:27 .... 973, 978
18:28 .... 955, 973, 1331
18:29 .... 887n92, 973, 978
18:30 .... 823, 921n139, 973, 973n212, 978
19 .... 825, 826, 980–988, 990, 994
19–20 1019
19:1–2 983

19:2 .... 453, 822, 826, 921n139, 928, 982n228
19:3 .... 623, 643, 921n139, 982, 982n228, 984, 987, 988
19:3–4 983
19:4 .... 621, 921n139, 982, 982n228
19:4–8 .... 823n9
19:5 .... 842n24, 1006
19:5–8 983–984
19:5–10 821
19:7 .... 842n24
19:8 .... 867n61, 887n92, 888, 1150
19:9 975
19:9–10 .... 35, 624, 669, 846, 984, 987, 1029n284
19:10 .... 921n139, 982n228, 1006
19:11 .... 982, 988
19:11–12 .... 984, 985n232
19:11–13 615
19:12 .... 609, 609n373, 622, 978, 982, 982n228, 1118, 1289, 1290, 1291
19:13 .... 623, 624, 874, 982, 988
19:13–14 .... 984, 985n232
19:14 .... 982n228, 983
19:15 .... 615, 625, 677
19:15–16 .... 985, 985n232
19:16 .... 623, 982, 982n228
19:17 .... 623, 988
19:17–18 .... 985, 985n232, 1032
19:18 .... 430, 615n403, 648n484, 679, 982n228, 988
19:18a 615, 679
19:18b 615, 679
19:19 .... 44, 985–986, 1145
19:20 .... 974n216
19:20–21 .... 872, 1123
19:20–22 986
19:23–25 986
19:25 .... 921n139, 982n228
19:26 .... 360, 667, 986
19:27–28 .... 824, 987
19:28 .... 982n228
19:29 .... 982, 1264
19:29–30 987
19:30 .... 982, 982n228
19:30–31 .... 823n9
19:31 .... 621, 921n139, 979n226, 982n228, 987, 992, 1247
19:32 .... 982n228, 987
19:33–34 .... 547n254, 669, 987–988, 1006
19:34 .... 615n403, 921n139, 982n228, 985
19:35–36a 988
19:35–36 .... 624, 982
19:36 .... 921n139, 973n212, 982n228, 988
19:36b–37 988
19:37 .... 982n228, 1008
20 .... 825, 972, 980, 989–996
20:1–2a 991
20:1–6 173
20:2 .... 962n201, 978, 990, 991, 992, 993, 1130

20:2–5 .... 823n9, 961
20:2b–3 991–992
20:2b–6 991
20:3 .... 831, 832, 888n96, 961n195, 978, 984, 992, 1120
20:3–5 990
20:4–5 .... 887, 992
20:5 .... 888n96, 961n195, 992
20:6 .... 888n96, 961n195, 990, 992
20:7 .... 822, 921n139, 928, 992, 1196
20:7–8 .... 990, 991, 992, 1008
20:8 .... 823, 893, 926, 973n212, 992, 1196
20:9 .... 613, 821n4, 984, 991, 991n237, 992
20:9–16 .... 992, 994
20:9–18 990
20:9–21 991
20:10 .... 614, 821n4, 977, 991, 992, 993, 1120
20:10–21 993
20:11 .... 974n216, 975, 991
20:11–12 993
20:12 .... 666, 973, 974n216, 976, 991
20:13 .... 56, 187, 974n216, 978, 991, 993–994
20:14 .... 340n545, 973, 977, 994, 1195
20:15 991
20:15–16 .... 978, 993, 994
20:16 .... 991, 1265
20:17 .... 961n195, 975, 994, 1246
20:17–21 992
20:18 .... 887n92, 974n216, 977, 995
20:19 976
20:19–20 995
20:20 .... 867n61, 974n216, 976
20:21 .... 976, 995
20:22 1331
20:22–24 .... 993, 995
20:22–26 .... 991, 1008
20:24 .... 502, 921n139, 922, 973n212, 1145
20:24–25 922
20:24–26 918
20:25–26 995
20:26 .... 453, 485n114, 822, 928, 973, 973n212, 990
20:27 .... 823n9, 991, 992, 995, 1195
21 996–1003
21–22 997
21:1 .... 739, 998
21:1–4 .... 1005, 1116
21:1–15 .... 997, 998, 1005
21:1–23 453
21:1–22:16 ..... 820n2, 1019
21:2 .... 910, 998–999
21:3 .... 663n523, 739, 975, 999
21:4 .... 739, 999
21:5 824
21:5–6 999–1000
21:6 .... 822, 844n27, 846, 854n46, 984, 997n241, 1005

SCRIPTURE INDEX

21:7 . . . . 1000, 1001, 1005
21:8 . . . . 822, 844n27, 854n46, 893, 997n241, 1000
21:9 . . . . 340n545, 994, 1000, 1195, 1264
21:10 . . . . 739, 742, 777, 895, 897, 909, 1128, 1330
21:10–12 1000–1001
21:11 . . . . 910, 943, 1001, 1128, 1230, 1296
21:11–12 831
21:12 . . . . 1001, 1005, 1128
21:13–15 1001
21:15 . . . . 893, 973n212
21:16–23 . . . . 997, 998, 1001–1002, 1005
21:17 . . . . 844n27, 854n46, 997n241, 1001, 1102, 1143
21:17–18 1023
21:17–20 . . . . 933n159
21:18 . . . . 997n241, 1001
21:18–20 1007
21:21 . . . . 598, 844n27, 854n46, 997n241, 1001
21:22 . . . . 844n27, 854n46, 1005
21:23 . . . . 973n212, 1001, 1023, 1210
21:24 1002
22 . . . . 916, 1003–1009
22:1–2 1005
22:1–16 1005
22:2 . . . . 984, 1143
22:3 . . . . 887, 887n95, 888
22:3–7 . . . . 950, 1005
22:4 . . . . 881, 1212
22:4a 1005
22:4b–7 1005
22:6 881
22:6–7 1212
22:8 1005
22:8–9 969
22:9 . . . . 867n61, 893, 909, 973n212, 1006
22:10 744
22:10–11 1006
22:10–16 873
22:12 706
22:12–13 1006
22:14 1050
22:14–16 1006
22:16 . . . . 973n212, 1006
22:17–19 896
22:17–20 1006
22:17–28 1005
22:17–33 1019
22:18 . . . . 840, 841, 857, 967, 991n237, 1130, 1143
22:18–19 1050
22:18–20 . . . . 740, 740n682, 745
22:18–25 854
22:19 1006
22:19–25 . . . . 917n123
22:20 1006
22:20–21 1023
22:20–25 966
22:21 . . . . 840, 842n24, 857, 1006, 1050, 1130, 1192, 1287
22:21–23 1007
22:22–24 . . . . 841, 933n159
22:22–25 1001
22:23 . . . . 853n44, 1006
22:24–25 1007–1008
22:25 . . . . 844n27, 854n46, 1006, 1023
22:26–28 1008
22:27 . . . . 673, 674, 898, 966, 1006
22:27–28 821
22:28 . . . . 673, 994, 1215
22:29 . . . . 842n24, 1006
22:29–30 . . . . 886, 1005, 1008
22:31–33 . . . . 825, 1008
22:32 . . . . 875, 893, 973n212, 984, 1005
22:32–33 . . . . 973n212
23 . . . . 821, 1009–1018, 1019, 1280
23–25 1081
23:1–2 1012
23:1–3 1012
23:2 45
23:3 . . . . 574, 611, 683, 762n739, 855, 1012–1013, 1287
23:3–4 . . . . 823, 823n9
23:4 . . . . 1013, 1150
23:4–8 . . . . 1012, 1149
23:4–38 1156
23:5 . . . . 574, 611, 683, 1013, 1029, 1282
23:5–8 . . . . 544n246
23:6 . . . . 574, 611
23:6–8 . . . . 683, 1013
23:7 . . . . 1013n258
23:7–8 . . . . 762n739
23:8 544
23:9 . . . . 1013n259
23:9–11 1013–1014
23:9–14 . . . . 673, 683
23:9–22 1012
23:10 . . . . 528n212, 1280
23:10–11 . . . . 682n564, 1214
23:10–14 986
23:11 . . . . 888, 889n99, 1006, 1014n260
23:12 888
23:12–13 . . . . 1014, 1214
23:13 . . . . 843n26, 846n28
23:14 1014
23:15 . . . . 682n564
23:15–16 1283
23:15–16a 1014
23:15–22 . . . . 682, 683
23:16 682
23:16b–17 1014–1015
23:17 . . . . 684, 855, 889n99, 1193
23:18 . . . . 843n26
23:18–21 1015
23:19 1288
23:19–20 1282
23:20 849
23:22 . . . . 921n139, 1011, 1015
23:23–25 . . . . 683, 1012, 1015
23:24 1154
23:24–43 105
23:26–28 1015
23:26–32 . . . . 683, 1012
23:27 1287
23:29 . . . . 887n92, 888, 962
23:29–30 . . . . 1016, 1087
23:30 962
23:31–32 1016
23:32 . . . . 762n739, 1287
23:33–36 . . . . 683, 1016
23:33–43 . . . . 684, 1012
23:34 . . . . 543, 574, 611, 684, 1287
23:36 . . . . 683, 1287
23:37 . . . . 589n329, 1016
23:37–38 . . . . 1016, 1050
23:38 . . . . 1016, 1287
23:39 1016
23:39–41 . . . . 691, 1016
23:39–43 683
23:41 . . . . 543, 574, 611
23:42–43 . . . . 172, 1016–1017
23:43 . . . . 921n139, 1011
23:44 1017
24 . . . . 632, 719, 1018–1025
24:1–4 . . . . 720, 880, 1020
24:1–9 1019
24:2 . . . . 720n644, 810n829, 1111, 1281, 1281n213
24:2–4 1143
24:3 . . . . 727, 1080
24:5 1020
24:5–6 1020–1021
24:5–8 728
24:5–9 . . . . 719, 1111
24:7 . . . . 719, 728, 1021
24:8 . . . . 728, 1143
24:8–9 1021
24:9 . . . . 844, 881, 1002n248, 1210
24:10–11 1021–1022
24:10–16 . . . . 609, 1150
24:10–23 . . . . 590, 822, 1019
24:11 . . . . 984, 1024, 1195
24:12 . . . . 1022, 1195
24:13–16 1022
24:14 632
24:14–15 . . . . 867n61
24:15 . . . . 991n237
24:15–16 . . . . 632, 672
24:15b–16a 812
24:16 . . . . 547n254, 992, 1022, 1023, 1195
24:16b 1022, 1023
24:17 . . . . 613, 614, 812, 1023
24:17–22 1022–1023
24:18 . . . . 968, 1023
24:18a 812
24:19–20 . . . . 651, 1023
24:19–21 1023
24:20 1329
24:21a 1023
24:21b 1023
24:21c–d 651
24:22 . . . . 615n403, 921n139, 962, 1022, 1023–1024
24:23 1024
25 . . . . 636n458, 825, 985, 1025–1035, 1040, 1047, 1051
25–27 . . . . 1027, 1047
25:1 . . . . 822n7, 1028, 1029, 1037, 1042
25:1–2a 812
25:1–7 681
25:1–26:46 1027
25:2 . . . . 574, 611, 1028
25:3–4 1028
25:4–5 . . . . 681, 681n556
25:5 1127
25:5–7 1028–1029

25:6–7 .... 681, 846, 994	26:9 974	27:20–21 1051
25:7 1028	26:9–10 1041	27:21 .... 739, 895, 1051, 1052
25:8 1044	26:11 .... 840n19, 1040, 1043, 1267	27:22 1126
25:8–9 1029–1030	26:11–12 .... 630, 691, 711, 814, 828, 956, 974, 1027, 1041, 1117	27:22–24 1052
25:8–10 .... 636n458		27:23 1215
25:10 .... 1030, 1051, 1333		27:25 .... 1049, 1052
25:10–13 1030	26:12 .... 440, 711n621, 748, 748n704, 814n838, 815, 815n843, 819, 1040, 1041n306	27:26 .... 1103, 1215
25:14 .... 669n532, 1031, 1032n293		27:26–27 .... 1052, 1215
		27:26–33 1047
25:14–17 1030–1031		27:27 .... 548n255, 1215
25:15–16 1051	26:13 .... 921n139, 973n212, 987, 1041, 1043	27:28 .... 666, 1052, 1214, 1215, 1291n220, 1299
25:17 .... 921n139, 1031		
25:18–22 ...... 681, 1031	26:13–39 .... 1039n302	
25:23 .... 984, 1028, 1029, 1033, 1177	26:14 1042	27:28–29 .... 1051, 1052–1053
	26:14–15 1041–1042	27:29 .... 1052, 1291n220
25:23–24 1031	26:14–39 .... 690, 874	27:30 .... 895, 1216, 1217
25:23–25 974	26:15 1041	27:30–31 673
25:24–28 1333	26:16 1042	27:30–33 .... 673n542, 1053
25:25 .... 1032n293, 1051, 1215, 1329	26:16–17 1042	27:32 .... 483n106, 1328
	26:17 .... 526n203, 1244	27:34 .... 822n7, 1027, 1042, 1053
25:25–28 1032	26:18 .... 466n56, 690, 861n56, 1042, 1044	
25:28 1051		
25:29 .... 73n74, 855	26:19 .... 44n19	*Numbers*
25:29–31 1032	26:19–20 1042	Book of 437n1, 1057–1076
25:31 1328	26:21 1044	1 .... 459, 460, 753n719, 1057, 1063, 1064, 1065, 1076, 1077–1090, 1092, 1094, 1129, 1138, 1154, 1155, 1321, 1333
25:32–34 1032–1033	26:21–22 1042–1043	
25:34 1328	26:22 .... 688n570	
25:35 .... 1032n293, 1033	26:23 690	
25:35–38 ...... 669n534	26:23–24 1043	
25:36 .... 1032n293	26:23–26 1043	
25:36–37 1033	26:24 1044	
25:38 .... 921n139, 973n212, 1033, 1092, 1322	26:25 648	1–2 1096
	26:26 847	1–4 1136
25:39 .... 1032n293	26:27–28 .... 690, 1244	1–6 .... 1081, 1136, 1143, 1148, 1154
25:39–40 669	26:27–29 1043	
25:39–41 1033–1034	26:28 1044	1–10 .... 1059, 1065, 1065n8, 1076–1077, 1154, 1161, 1268
25:39–43 635	26:30 .... 1041, 1127, 1186	
25:39–46 ...... 635n452	26:30–35 1043	
25:41 .... 636n458, 637	26:31 844	
25:42 1029	26:31–33 1244	1–25 .... 1064, 1065, 1065n8
25:42–43 1034	26:33 956	1:1 .... 839n16, 1057, 1058, 1079, 1080, 1083, 1154, 1156
25:44 1298	26:34–35 1028	
25:44–46 ...... 1006, 1034	26:36–39 1043	
25:46 .... 1032n293	26:38 1331	1:1–3 1079
25:47 .... 1032n293	26:40 .... 608n368, 868, 1120	1:1–19 .... 1072, 1079–1085, 1083n21, 1093, 1094, 1103, 1109, 1112, 1114, 1155, 1156, 1203, 1272, 1316
25:47–49 639	26:40–42 869	
25:47–54 1034	26:40–43 1043–1044	
25:47–55 ...... 502n152, 635, 974, 979n227	26:41 506	
	26:42–45 1015	
25:48 .... 1032n293, 1329	26:43 1041	
25:54–55 450	26:44 .... 921n139, 1041	1:1–46 1086
25:55 .... 921n139, 1034, 1038, 1041	26:44–45 .... 1044, 1045	1:1–54 1072
	26:45 .... 486n116, 848	1:1–4:49 1116
26 .... 605, 629, 690, 691, 926, 1036–1045, 1081, 1130	26:46 .... 822, 822n7, 982, 1042, 1044, 1053, 1080	1:1–10:10 ...... 1059, 1064, 1076, 1081
		1:1–10:36 1072
26:1 .... 256, 621, 628, 921n139	27 .... 873, 1007, 1027, 1045–1054, 1289, 1290, 1292	1:2 .... 1081, 1082, 1084, 1086, 1105, 1112, 1155, 1271, 1272, 1298
26:1–2 .... 1038, 1039–1040, 1043		
	27:1–2a 1047	
26:1–4 846	27:2 .... 1291n220	
26:2 987	27:2b–7 1048–1049	1:2–5a 1086
26:3 1040	27:2b–25 .... 1047, 1048	1:2–46 1092
26:3–10 691	27:5 .... 331n520	1:3 .... 753, 1070, 1082, 1083, 1083n21, 1085, 1086, 1089, 1103, 1109, 1114, 1186, 1203, 1271, 1311
26:3–12 568	27:6 1105	
26:3–13 689	27:8 1049	
26:3–39 687	27:9 1289	
26:4 1244	27:9–10 .... 1050, 1053	
26:4–5 .... 1040, 1042	27:10 .... 1130, 1216	1:4 .... 1082, 1084, 1086
26:4–12 629	27:11–13 .... 873, 1050	1:4–16 1083
26:5 .... 1042, 1127	27:14 .... 739, 895	1:5 .... 1084, 1264
26:6 .... 853, 1040, 1043, 1244	27:14–15 1050	1:5–15 .... 314, 1085, 1093, 1094, 1177
	27:16–18 1052	
26:7–8 .... 1040–1041, 1042	27:16–19 1050–1051	1:5–16 1137
26:8 .... 1088, 1160		

SCRIPTURE INDEX

1:6..............1084	2:1–2............1073, 1090, 1092–1093	3:6–10..........1101
1:7..............507n161, 1084	2:1–34..........1066, 1073	3:6b.............1089n39
1:9..............1084	2:1–3:38.........1154	3:7..............53n36, 1099, 1102, 1146
1:10.............1085	2:2..............780, 1092, 1093	3:7a.............1089n39
1:12.............1084	2:3..............507n161, 1085, 1092, 1093, 1095, 1096, 1184, 1310	3:8..............1099, 1102, 1146
1:12–13..........1105		3:9..............1083, 1102, 1211
1:13.............1082		3:10.............1067, 1069, 1071, 1083, 1102, 1103, 1201, 1203, 1204, 1210, 1212, 1266, 1278
1:16.............863, 1084, 1160, 1265, 1276, 1290	2:3–4............1155	
	2:3–9............1073, 1093, 1155, 1184	
1:17.............1084	2:3–31...........314	
1:17–19..........1084	2:4..............1085, 1093	
1:18.............1082, 1083, 1084, 1084n22, 1105	2:5..............1093	3:11.............1099
	2:6..............1093	3:11–13..........1101, 1103
1:19.............1079, 1084	2:7..............1093	3:12.............1087n32, 1103
1:20.............1081, 1082, 1084, 1085, 1094, 1272	2:8..............1093	3:12–13..........1048
	2:9..............1065, 1085, 1092, 1310	3:12–15..........1103
1:20–43..........1085		3:13.............1067, 1103
1:20–46..........1072, 1081, 1082, 1084, 1085–1088, 1105	2:10.............1092, 1093, 1094, 1095, 1302	3:14.............1099
		3:14–16..........1103
	2:10–11..........1155	3:14–20..........807
1:21.............459, 1085, 1272	2:10–14..........1202	3:15.............1086, 1099, 1103
1:22.............1084	2:10–16..........1073, 1094, 1155	3:16.............1103, 1273
1:23.............1085, 1266, 1272	2:14.............1302	3:17.............1103, 1108
1:24.............1094	2:16.............1065, 1092, 1094, 1304	3:17–19..........1130
1:25.............1088		3:17–37..........1100
1:28.............1130	2:17.............1065, 1073, 1089, 1094–1095, 1099, 1100, 1146, 1157	3:18.............1103
1:32.............1085, 1272		3:19.............1103, 1200
1:33.............1272		3:20.............1082, 1103
1:34.............1272	2:18.............1092, 1093, 1095	3:21.............1103
1:35.............1272	2:18–24..........1073, 1094, 1095, 1155	3:21–24..........506n160
1:37.............459		3:21–37..........1104
1:42.............1272	2:20.............1095	3:22.............1104
1:43.............1087n32, 1272	2:22.............1095	3:23.............1066, 1095, 1099, 1104, 1324, 1327
1:44.............1086, 1112, 1137	2:24.............1065, 1092, 1094, 1095	
1:44–46..........1086, 1113		3:24.............1103, 1104
1:45.............1086, 1271	2:25.............1092, 1093, 1095, 1323	3:25.............1080, 1099, 1104
1:46.............459, 460n49, 753, 1082, 1085, 1086, 1092, 1105, 1226, 1272		3:25–26..........1102, 1104
	2:25–31..........1073, 1095, 1155	3:26.............1093n40, 1104, 1151
	2:27.............1095	3:27.............1103
	2:29.............1095	3:27–39..........1273
1:47.............459, 1089, 1099, 1105	2:31.............1065, 1092, 1095	3:28.............1099, 1104, 1105, 1273
	2:32.............1086, 1088, 1092	
1:47–50..........1096	2:32–33a.........1092, 1096	3:29.............1066, 1099, 1104, 1324, 1327
1:47–53..........1099, 1100	2:32–34..........1073, 1096, 1113	
1:47–54..........1072, 1085, 1088–1090, 1150, 1159, 1211	2:33.............1096, 1099, 1100	3:29–31..........1209
	2:33–34..........1096	3:30.............506n159, 1104
	2:33b–34.........1092, 1096	3:31.............1099, 1102, 1104, 1109, 1111, 1142, 1151, 1212, 1296
1:48.............1105	2:34.............1080, 1092, 1093, 1095, 1152, 1161	
1:49.............1089, 1099		
1:50.............807n817, 1069, 1083, 1089, 1102, 1111, 1159, 1169, 1203, 1211, 1216, 1278, 1327	3................1057, 1097–1106, 1108, 1316	3:32.............1089, 1099, 1101, 1104, 1146, 1266
		3:33.............1103
	3–4..............506, 767, 1059, 1099	3:34.............1104
1:50–53..........1209		3:35.............1066, 1099, 1104, 1324, 1327
1:51.............1067, 1071, 1089, 1090, 1101, 1102, 1150, 1204	3:1..............51, 1080, 1099, 1100, 1281, 1313	
		3:36.............1083, 1099, 1104, 1112
	3:1–4............1073, 1099–1101	
1:52.............1066, 1083, 1090, 1092, 1093	3:1–51...........1073	3:36–37..........807, 1102, 1104
	3:2..............1100	3:37.............725
1:53.............807n817, 1066, 1067, 1069, 1089n39, 1090, 1099, 1131, 1146, 1152, 1216, 1298, 1324, 1327	3:2–3............1100	3:38.............597, 1066, 1067, 1071, 1099, 1105, 1324, 1327
	3:3..............1100	
	3:4..............1067, 1070, 1101, 1164, 1210, 1217, 1230, 1273	
		3:38–39..........1104
	3:5..............1099	3:39.............1088, 1099, 1104, 1105, 1113, 1273
1:54.............1079, 1080, 1090, 1152, 1161, 1259	3:5–7............1086	
	3:5–10...........1209	3:40.............1081, 1099, 1105
2................410n674, 1065, 1077, 1083, 1090, 1091–1096, 1099, 1138, 1154, 1157, 1311, 1321, 1333, 1334	3:5–39...........1073, 1082, 1101–1105, 1112	3:40–41..........1067
		3:40–43..........1105
	3:5–4:49.........736, 1146	3:40–50..........1273
	3:6..............1101, 1102, 1103, 1121, 1143, 1146, 1169	3:40–51..........1073, 1103, 1105–1106
		3:41.............1080, 1103, 1105, 1215, 1314, 1328
2–4..............1125	3:6–9............1201	

3:41–51.........1099
3:42.............1105
3:43.............1087, 1105
3:44.............1099
3:44–51.........1105
3:45.............1080, 1103, 1215, 1314
3:47.............873n69, 1052
3:47–48.........548
3:47–51.........1215
3:49.............1105, 1215
3:50.............1105
3:51.............1099, 1105
4.................1057, 1099, 1106–1114, 1129, 1138, 1146, 1316
4:1...............1112
4:1–20..........806n814, 1073, 1109–1112, 1114
4:1–49..........1073
4:2...............1103, 1108, 1109, 1298
4:2–4............1209
4:3...............1082, 1086, 1089, 1109, 1110, 1114, 1146, 1295
4:4...............1109, 1110, 1113, 1138, 1201, 1213
4:4–33..........1209
4:5...............1104, 1109, 1110, 1159, 1206
4:5–6............717, 1138
4:5–14..........717n629
4:5–15..........1110
4:6...............717n630
4:7...............1020n272, 1110
4:7–8............1138
4:8...............1111
4:9...............1111, 1142
4:10.............1111, 1179
4:11.............1111, 1138
4:12.............1111, 1179, 1211
4:13.............1111
4:14.............903, 1111, 1138, 1210, 1211
4:15.............597, 1067, 1069, 1069n10, 1080, 1089, 1094, 1103, 1104, 1109, 1110, 1112, 1138, 1143, 1157, 1159, 1201, 1209
4:16.............506n159, 880, 1101, 1104, 1108, 1111, 1121, 1146, 1220
4:17.............1112
4:17–20.........1210
4:18.............1067, 1112
4:18–20.........1212
4:19.............1069, 1069n10, 1108, 1109, 1112, 1213
4:19–20.........1067
4:20.............1069, 1069n10, 1080, 1103, 1110, 1112, 1143
4:21–28.........1073, 1112
4:21–33.........717n629
4:22.............1103, 1108, 1112
4:23.............755, 1109, 1112, 1113, 1146
4:24.............1108
4:24–26.........1089
4:24–27.........1138

4:25–26.........1112, 1137n62
4:27.............1108
4:28.............506n159, 807, 1089, 1101, 1108, 1112, 1138, 1146, 1211, 1212
4:29.............1103, 1108
4:29–33.........1073, 1112–1113
4:30.............1102, 1109, 1112, 1113
4:31.............1108, 1112
4:31–32.........1113, 1138
4:31–33.........1089
4:32.............1108, 1112
4:33.............506n159, 807, 1101, 1108, 1112, 1138, 1146, 1211
4:34.............1302
4:34–35a........1113
4:34–37.........1073, 1109–1112, 1113, 1114
4:35.............1109, 1113
4:36.............1113
4:36–37a........1113
4:37.............1109
4:37a............1113
4:37b............1113
4:38–41.........1112, 1113
4:39.............1109
4:40.............1113
4:41.............1109
4:42–45.........1073, 1112–1113
4:43.............1109
4:44.............1112, 1113
4:45.............1109
4:46.............1113
4:46–49.........1073, 1113–1114
4:47.............1108, 1109, 1113
4:48.............1113, 1146
4:49.............1108, 1113
5.................1114–1124, 1126, 1195
5–6...............1125, 1131, 1136
5:1–2............1116
5:1–4............1069, 1073, 1116–1117
5:1–31...........1073
5:2...............1069, 1071, 1116, 1117, 1126, 1131, 1174, 1219, 1322
5:2–3............935, 1068, 1071, 1126, 1150, 1173
5:3...............1065, 1066, 1089, 1116, 1117, 1118, 1126, 1174, 1195, 1220, 1324, 1327
5:3–4............1066
5:4...............1067, 1117, 1150, 1220
5:5–6............1116
5:5–7............1070
5:5–10...........1070, 1073, 1118–1119, 1120, 1126, 1212, 1266, 1290
5:6...............1070, 1116, 1118, 1120, 1126, 1131
5:6–31...........871
5:7...............875, 1118, 1119
5:8...............1118, 1119, 1126, 1210, 1329
5:8–10...........1119
5:9...............706, 1101, 1119, 1212
5:11–12.........1116

5:11–28.........777, 1122
5:11–31.........993, 1070, 1073, 1120–1123, 1266, 1290
5:12.............1070, 1116, 1120, 1121, 1126, 1131, 1266
5:12–30.........1070
5:13.............1120
5:14.............1120, 1121, 1122
5:15.............848n33, 1121, 1126
5:16.............1101, 1121
5:17.............1117, 1121, 1122
5:18.............1121, 1122, 1128
5:19.............1120, 1122, 1123, 1290, 1304
5:19–22.........1290
5:20.............1120, 1123
5:20–21.........1122
5:21.............1122, 1137n62
5:22.............1122, 1137n62, 1222n141
5:23.............1121
5:23–24.........1122
5:24.............1122, 1222n141
5:25.............1145, 1212, 1214
5:25–26.........1122
5:27.............1070, 1120, 1121, 1122, 1126, 1128, 1137n62, 1266, 1277, 1290
5:27–28.........1130
5:28.............1119, 1120, 1121, 1122, 1123, 1126, 1304
5:29.............1120, 1123
5:29–30.........1123
5:29–31.........1122
5:30.............1120, 1121, 1123
5:31.............1121, 1123, 1304
6.................1116, 1124–1132, 1290
6:1...............1126
6:1–2............1116
6:1–11..........1129
6:1–12..........1069, 1073, 1117, 1126–1128, 1266
6:1–21..........1116, 1288
6:1–27..........1073
6:2...............924, 1118, 1126, 1127, 1130, 1131
6:2–3............952
6:2–8............1048
6:3...............1127, 1281, 1290
6:3–7............1126
6:4...............1127
6:5...............1127, 1127n57, 1128, 1158n77
6:6...............1069, 1117, 1119, 1127
6:6–7............1127
6:6–8............1126
6:7...............1127
6:7–12...........872
6:8...............1119, 1126, 1127
6:9...............361n591, 1069, 1127, 1128, 1129, 1173
6:9–11...........1068
6:9–12...........944, 1068, 1126, 1127, 1219, 1230
6:10.............1128, 1129
6:11.............858, 944, 1068, 1126, 1127, 1128
6:12.............1126, 1127, 1128

SCRIPTURE INDEX

6:13 .... 1127, 1129, 1265
6:13–17 1288
6:13–20 745
6:13–21 .... 1068, 1073, 1126, 1128–1130, 1282
6:14 .... 1129, 1145
6:14–15 1194
6:15 .... 1129, 1130
6:16 .... 1129, 1282
6:16–17 1288
6:17 .... 1129, 1130, 1288
6:18 .... 361n591, 943, 1127, 1129, 1215
6:18–20 1129
6:19 .... 1127, 1129, 1130, 1214
6:19–20 .... 1130, 1212
6:20 .... 706, 1127, 1130, 1212, 1215
6:21 .... 1119, 1127, 1130, 1289, 1290
6:22–23 1130
6:22–27 .... 360, 629, 1073, 1116, 1126, 1130–1132
6:23 .... 1126, 1130, 1131, 1132, 1143
6:23–27 .... 809, 1092
6:24 .... 1130, 1246, 1258
6:24–26 .... 47, 853, 904, 992
6:25 .... 728, 783, 904, 1130
6:25–26 1131
6:26 1130
6:27 .... 824, 987, 1022, 1132
7 .... 794, 1057, 1081, 1133–1141, 1142, 1143, 1154, 1296, 1321
7:1 .... 1058, 1081, 1083, 1136, 1138, 1143, 1266
7:1–9 .... 1073, 1136–1138, 1143
7:1–88 863
7:1–89 1073
7:1–8:4 1136
7:1–10:10 .... 1058, 1154
7:1–10:36 1136
7:2 .... 1084, 1137, 1155, 1265, 1276, 1290, 1319, 1324
7:2–3 1137
7:2–88 1081
7:3 .... 1137, 1137n62, 1315
7:3–9 808
7:5 .... 1102, 1137
7:6 .... 1137, 1137n62
7:7 .... 1112, 1137, 1137n62
7:7–8 .... 1089, 1138, 1157, 1314n275
7:7–9 .... 717n629
7:8 .... 1101, 1113, 1137, 1137n62, 1138
7:9 .... 717, 1109, 1111, 1112, 1138, 1157
7:10 .... 1138, 1276
7:10–88 .... 1073, 1136, 1138–1139, 1138n63
7:11 .... 1138, 1139
7:11–17 1138
7:12 1138
7:12–83 1177

7:14 .... 719n639
7:15 1139
7:15–16 1194
7:16 1139
7:17 .... 1138, 1139
7:64–88 1139
7:84 .... 1138, 1276
7:85 1139
7:86 .... 1138, 1139
7:87 1139
7:87–88 .... 1080, 1314
7:88 1139
7:89 .... 811n833, 1068, 1073, 1080, 1081, 1139–1140, 1140n64, 1143, 1159, 1160, 1206
8 1141–1147
8:1–4 .... 728, 1069, 1073, 1110, 1111, 1142, 1143
8:1–26 1073
8:2 .... 728, 1111, 1143
8:2–3 727
8:3 1143
8:4 .... 1143, 1155
8:5–13 1143
8:5–22 .... 1073, 1084, 1143–1146, 1201, 1213, 1299
8:5–26 .... 1136, 1142
8:6 1145
8:7 .... 943, 1144, 1236
8:8 .... 858, 1144
8:9–13 1144
8:10 .... 842, 1144
8:11 .... 1102, 1144, 1212
8:11–12 1103
8:12 .... 858, 1068, 1143, 1144, 1299
8:13 .... 1101, 1144, 1212
8:14 .... 1145, 1201
8:14–22 1143
8:15 .... 1144, 1212, 1213, 1214
8:15–16 744
8:15–19 1211
8:16 .... 842, 1102
8:16–19 .... 1048, 1145
8:18–19 848
8:19 .... 1067, 1068, 1102, 1144, 1145, 1146n68, 1194, 1204, 1217
8:20 1146
8:21 .... 1068, 1084, 1144, 1211, 1212, 1222
8:21–22a 1146
8:22 .... 1146, 1150
8:22b 1146
8:23–26 .... 1073, 1082, 1089, 1146–1147, 1211, 1216
8:24 .... 755, 1146
8:25 .... 1082, 1146, 1295
8:25–26 1129
8:26 .... 704, 1089, 1146, 1216
9 1147–1152
9:1 .... 1058, 1136, 1149
9:1–5 .... 1081, 1148, 1149
9:1–14 .... 1073, 1136, 1149–1151, 1150, 1281
9:2 .... 1081, 1149

9:3 .... 1149, 1281
9:5 .... 1136, 1149
9:6 .... 1117, 1150
9:6–8 1150
9:6–14 .... 590, 1069, 1149
9:7 .... 1150, 1299
9:8 1150
9:9–13 1150
9:9–14 .... 1119, 1148, 1150
9:10 .... 1068, 1069, 1117, 1150
9:11 .... 1149, 1150
9:11–12 .... 1149, 1150
9:12 1151
9:13 .... 887n92, 888n96, 1067, 1150, 1170, 1299
9:14 .... 547, 568, 1151
9:15 .... 556, 708n614, 807n817, 1058, 1136, 1148, 1151, 1160
9:15–23 .... 812, 1073, 1148, 1151–1152
9:15–10:10 1136
9:16 .... 1148, 1151
9:16–17 1160
9:17 .... 1160, 1183
9:17–18 1311
9:18 .... 1151, 1152, 1311
9:19 1151
9:20 .... 1152, 1311
9:21 1151
9:22 1151
9:23 .... 1152, 1161
9:31 1060
10 .... 593, 1065, 1077, 1092, 1152–1161, 1321, 1333
10:1–10 .... 1070, 1073, 1084, 1154–1156, 1296
10:1–36 .... 1066, 1073
10:2 .... 1154, 1155
10:3 1155
10:3–8 1015
10:4 .... 1155, 1160, 1265, 1290
10:5 1155
10:5–6 .... 1093, 1152, 1156, 1157, 1311
10:5–7 1155
10:6 1277
10:7 .... 1084, 1155
10:8 1221
10:9 .... 1070, 1082, 1155, 1156, 1176, 1267, 1296, 1320
10:10 .... 737n675, 1015, 1065n8, 1136, 1149, 1156, 1286, 1299
10:10–16 1157
10:11 .... 807n817, 822, 1058, 1065n8, 1076, 1081, 1089, 1136, 1149, 1154, 1156, 1158, 1159, 1178, 1226n144, 1309
10:11–12 .... 1065, 1156, 1157
10:11–13 1093
10:11–28 .... 1073, 1094, 1155, 1156–1157, 1184, 1311
10:11–36 1136

10:11–12:16....1309	11:4–6 ....141, 1163	12:7 ....1173, 1174
10:11–14:45....1059	11:4–10.........1074, 1165–1167, 1169, 1172	12:8 ....193, 1083, 1131, 1173
10:11–21:9 1064	11:4–15 1163	12:9 ....1067, 1167, 1174
10:11–22:1 1064	11:5............28, 164, 1163, 1166	12:10............1174
10:12............1057, 1065, 1154, 1156, 1158, 1164, 1309n247, 1313, 1317	11:6 ....1166, 1185n100	12:11............1174
	11:7 53	12:11–16 ....1074, 1174
	11:7–8 ....573n299	12:12............649, 933, 935, 941, 1071, 1174
10:13............1065, 1156, 1157, 1311	11:7–9 ....1061, 1166	
	11:8 573	12:13............936, 1165, 1174
10:13–28 ....1154, 1157	11:9 1164	12:14............936, 1174, 1220, 1221
10:14............1065, 1156, 1157, 1184	11:10............1066, 1067, 1167, 1174, 1265	
		12:15............1174, 1220, 1221, 1230
10:15–16 1157	11:10–15 778	
10:17............1065, 1089, 1095, 1108, 1146, 1157	11:11............1167, 1303	12:15–16 1178
	11:11–15 ....1074, 1167	12:16............1156, 1164, 1174, 1226, 1310, 1315, 1315n284, 1317
10:18............1065, 1094, 1156, 1161	11:12............1167, 1176, 1177, 1191, 1303, 1319	
		13................90, 1059, 1175–1180, 1182, 1244, 1321
10:18–20 1157	11:13............1066, 1167	
10:18–24 1157	11:14............592, 1167, 1172	
10:21............1065, 1095, 1102, 1105, 1108, 1138, 1146, 1156, 1157	11:14–17 1083	13–14 ....1176, 1190, 1199, 1220, 1225, 1233, 1274, 1316
	11:15............1167, 1303	
	11:16............1155, 1168, 1169, 1172	
10:21–22 1094		13:1–20.........1074, 1176–1178, 1314
10:21a...........1089	11:16–25 ....592, 862	
10:21b 1089, 1102	11:16–30 ....1074, 1167–1169, 1203	13:1–33.........1074
10:22............1065		13:1–36:13 1176
10:22–24 1157	11:17............1167, 1168, 1258, 1278	13:2 ....1092, 1176, 1177, 1196, 1319, 1322
10:25............1065, 1089, 1095, 1157		
	11:18............1163, 1168, 1259	13:3 ....1165, 1177, 1178, 1265, 1273, 1303, 1311, 1317
10:25–27 1157	11:18–20 1176	
10:28............1065, 1157	11:20............1163, 1168, 1170, 1178, 1227	
10:29............1158, 1159, 1177, 1191, 1245, 1246, 1258, 1295, 1319		13:4–16..........1177
	11:21............1168	13:6 1177
	11:22............1139, 1158, 1164, 1302	13:8 1177
10:29–32 ....1073, 1154, 1158–1159		13:11............1093
	11:23............1168	13:16............582, 1177, 1278
10:29–12:16....1157	11:24............1169	13:17............1080, 1156, 1174, 1177, 1322
10:30............1158, 1159, 1313	11:25............1083, 1168, 1169, 1173, 1258	
10:31............1158, 1172		13:17–18 ....1101n44
10:32............1159, 1258	11:25–26 1278	13:18............1168
10:33............207, 278n410, 1065, 1158, 1159, 1160, 1161, 1164, 1177	11:26............1168, 1169, 1258	13:18–20 ....1176, 1177
	11:28............582, 704, 1083, 1146, 1169, 1278	13:19............1305
		13:20............1177, 1314
	11:29............486, 1066, 1172	13:21............1057, 1177, 1178, 1322
10:33–36 ....1073, 1154, 1159–1160	11:30............1168	
	11:31............1169	13:21–22 1178
10:34............1065, 1151, 1156, 1160	11:31–33 1163	13:21–24 ....1074, 1178–1179, 1277, 1323
	11:31–35 ....1074, 1169–1170	
10:35............1065, 1156, 1160, 1161, 1187, 1319	11:32............1169	13:22............1178, 1322
	11:33............1066, 1067, 1167, 1170, 1176	13:23............1111, 1170, 1177, 1179
10:35–36 ....1087, 1088, 1295		
10:36............1160	11:33–34 ....566, 580	13:24............1179
11................1065, 1161, 1162–1170, 1171, 1172, 1225, 1264	11:34............1156, 1164, 1170, 1204	13:25............100, 705, 1177, 1179
	11:34–35 1315	13:25–33 ....1074, 1179–1180, 1191, 1316
11–12 1190	11:34b 481n99	
11–25 ....1059, 1065, 1065n8, 1161, 1264	11:35............1164, 1169, 1310	13:25–14:4 1058
	12................767, 1170–1175, 1199, 1225, 1226	13:25–14:38....1334
11:1 ....557, 1066, 1067, 1164, 1165, 1167, 1172, 1248		13:26............1059, 1065, 1160, 1164, 1174, 1178, 1179, 1185n100, 1187, 1225, 1226, 1303, 1309, 1310, 1315, 1316, 1317
	12–13 1206	
	12:1 ....1171, 1172	
11:1–3 ....478, 566, 580, 1074, 1163, 1164–1165, 1170	12:1–3 ....1074, 1171–1173	
	12:1–9 486	
	12:1–16..........1074	
11:1–6 1183	12:2 ....1172, 1258	
11:1–35.........1074	12:3 ....1058, 1172, 1173, 1174	13:27............1179, 1180
11:1–25:18 1074		13:27–29 1176
11:2 ....1165, 1174, 1188, 1233, 1236	12:4 1173	13:27–14:4 1060
	12:4–10 ....1074, 1173–1174	13:28............1179
11:3 ....1066, 1164	12:5 ....1151, 1173	13:29............479, 582, 1179, 1186, 1238, 1261
11:4 ....145, 546, 546n250, 1066, 1164, 1165, 1166, 1169, 1185n100	12:6 ....193, 1173, 1228, 1259, 1262	
		13:30............1176, 1179, 1274
	12:6–8 780	13:31............1180
		13:31–33 1176

13:32	323, 1177, 1179, 1180	
13:32–33	1180	
13:32–35	1060	
13:33	90, 1178	
13:37	1191	
14	608, 785n783, 1180–1188	
14:1	1182	
14:1–2	1165	
14:1–3	557	
14:1–4	1163	
14:1–10	1074, 1182–1184	
14:1–45	1074	
14:1–17:13	1164	
14:2	567, 1183, 1184, 1186	
14:2–4	1163, 1233	
14:3	28, 1070, 1183, 1259	
14:4	1183, 1186	
14:5	1183, 1202	
14:6	1183	
14:6–9	1274	
14:9	1183, 1254	
14:10	1183, 1184, 1185, 1202	
14:10–12	1227	
14:11	1184, 1185	
14:11–19	1074, 1182, 1184–1185	
14:12	1184, 1188	
14:13	1184	
14:13–19	1062, 1165, 1184, 1188	
14:14	556, 781, 1151, 1160, 1184	
14:15	1184	
14:15–16	776n762	
14:16	1167, 1184, 1191, 1303	
14:17	1184	
14:18	783n781, 785n783, 1082, 1184, 1186, 1190, 1193, 1203, 1211n126	
14:18–19	453, 784	
14:18b	1184	
14:19	785n783, 1184, 1274, 1316	
14:20	1185, 1188, 1190	
14:20–23	580	
14:20–25	1074, 1185–1186, 1203, 1204, 1234, 1310	
14:20–38	1182	
14:21	1185	
14:21–23	785n783	
14:22	204, 572n296, 1185, 1188, 1316	
14:22–23	577, 579	
14:23	1167, 1184, 1191, 1303, 1319	
14:24	639, 1173, 1185, 1186	
14:25	1186, 1310, 1312	
14:26–35	779n772	
14:26–37	580	
14:26–38	1074, 1185, 1186–1187	
14:27	567, 1201	
14:28	1185, 1259	
14:28–29	1186	
14:28–30	785n783	
14:29	567, 1064, 1082, 1186, 1191, 1221, 1222, 1274	
14:30	1186, 1274	
14:31	1060, 1064, 1168, 1186, 1191	
14:32	785n783, 1067, 1070, 1186, 1227	
14:33	524n200, 608, 608n369, 785n783, 1158, 1187, 1207	
14:33–34	575, 1316	
14:33–35	1309	
14:34	1152, 1179, 1187, 1316, 1318	
14:34–35	1061, 1226	
14:35	1067, 1070, 1071, 1186, 1187, 1207	
14:36	1201, 1303	
14:36–38	779n772	
14:37	779, 1067, 1187, 1221	
14:38	1069n10	
14:39	779n772, 1187	
14:39–45	1070, 1074, 1182, 1187–1188, 1233, 1234	
14:40	1187, 1188, 1233, 1236	
14:41	1187	
14:44	1159, 1187, 1188	
14:44–45	1233	
14:45	1186, 1188	
15	1059, 1189–1197, 1280	
15–19	1225	
15:1–16	1280	
15:1–21	1074, 1130, 1191–1193, 1213, 1217, 1281, 1283	
15:1–41	1074	
15:2	1060, 1092, 1190, 1191, 1192, 1193, 1199, 1280, 1319	
15:2–5	886n86	
15:3	589n329, 1130, 1191, 1192, 1281, 1283, 1284, 1287	
15:3–4	1190	
15:3–5	1191	
15:3–16	1191	
15:4	1101, 1192	
15:4–5	1191, 1192	
15:5	1191, 1281, 1284	
15:6	1191	
15:7	1192	
15:8	1130, 1137, 1191, 1192, 1288	
15:8–10	1192	
15:10	844, 1121, 1192, 1281	
15:11	1191, 1192	
15:11–12	1192	
15:13–16	1193	
15:14	967, 1192	
15:15	1060, 1190, 1221	
15:18	1191, 1192, 1193, 1280, 1329	
15:19	1193	
15:19–20	1212	
15:19–21	1191, 1193	
15:20	1193, 1213, 1217, 1284, 1298, 1299	
15:20–21	1068, 1119, 1214	
15:21	1191, 1193	
15:22	1193, 1194	
15:22–29	1194	
15:22–31	1074, 1193–1195, 1211, 1267, 1282	
15:23	1060, 1191, 1193, 1194	
15:24	1192, 1194, 1282	
15:25	1068, 1194, 1211	
15:26	1068, 1329	
15:27	1193, 1194, 1329	
15:27–29	1119	
15:28	1068, 1329	
15:29	1329	
15:30	557n273, 859, 887n92, 1195, 1311	
15:30–31	1067, 1070, 1119, 1121, 1150, 1194	
15:31	859, 1022, 1184, 1195, 1292	
15:32	1195, 1281	
15:32–36	590, 611, 804n810, 992, 1022n277, 1067, 1074, 1150, 1195	
15:33	1195	
15:33–35	1150	
15:34	1195, 1195n116	
15:34–35	1304	
15:35	1066, 1067, 1071, 1195, 1220	
15:36	1220, 1221	
15:37–41	1069, 1074, 1195–1196	
15:38	824, 1191, 1195, 1196	
15:39	1015, 1069, 1196	
15:40	1196, 1200	
15:41	1196	
16	842, 1061, 1085, 1103, 1197–1205, 1206, 1209, 1211, 1217, 1220, 1233, 1274	
16–17	1059, 1199	
16–18	1220, 1225	
16:1	1200, 1210, 1273	
16:1–2	1276	
16:1–19	1074, 1082, 1084, 1199–1202, 1204, 1207	
16:1–33	506n159, 1058	
16:1–50	1074	
16:1–18:32	1199	
16:2	1200, 1203, 1302	
16:3	774, 1084, 1200, 1201, 1226, 1227	
16:4	1200, 1202, 1204	
16:5	523n197, 1200	
16:6	1201	
16:6–7	752n710	
16:7	1201, 1202	
16:8	1201, 1204, 1228	
16:9	1101, 1102, 1146, 1201, 1202	
16:10	1200, 1201	
16:10–11	1200	
16:11	1172, 1201, 1204, 1228	
16:12	1201, 1203	
16:12–13	1200	
16:13	1201, 1203	
16:13–14	1201	
16:14	1201, 1203	

16:15............1202	17:10............575n307, 1069n10, 1070, 1207, 1228	18:21–32........1210
16:16............1058, 1202	17:12............1205, 1207	18:22............960, 1069n10, 1070, 1209, 1211, 1216, 1217
16:17............1202	17:12–13........1067, 1206, 1209	
16:17–18........752n710	17:13............1067, 1070, 1071, 1150, 1207, 1230	18:23............1060, 1211n126, 1216, 1217, 1217n136
16:18............1202, 1203		
16:19............1184, 1185, 1202, 1204	18................1059, 1069, 1206, 1208–1218, 1220, 1274	
16:19–21........1227		18:23–24........1216, 1327
16:20–22........1165	18–19............1059, 1081, 1280	18:24............1033, 1213, 1216
16:20–35........1074, 1201, 1202–1203	18:1..............1105, 1210, 1211n126, 1212, 1217, 1266	18:24–29........1212
		18:25............1217
16:21............1090, 1201, 1202	18:1–7..........729, 1074, 1209, 1210–1212	18:25–32........1216
16:21–24........1266		18:26............1002n248, 1213, 1217
16:22............1183, 1200, 1202, 1277	18:1–32..........1074	
	18:2..............485n112, 708n614, 807n817, 1101, 1146, 1206, 1211	18:26–28........1068
16:24............1202, 1203		18:26–29........706
16:25............1203		18:26–32........1217
16:26............1203		18:27............1214, 1215, 1217
16:27............1203	18:2–3..........1102	18:29............1213, 1217, 1217n138
16:27–35........1060	18:2a............1089n39	
16:28–30........1172, 1203	18:3..............1067, 1069, 1069n10, 1070, 1104, 1111, 1211, 1296	18:30............1215, 1216, 1217
16:29............1058, 1203		18:30–31........1068
16:30............1203		18:31............1216, 1217, 1217n138
16:31............1058, 1203, 1266		
16:32............1112, 1202, 1203, 1221, 1245, 1273	18:3a............1089n39	18:32............1069, 1069n10, 1070, 1217
	18:4..............1211, 1327	
16:32–35........1067	18:5..............1067, 1069, 1090, 1131, 1209, 1211	19................1116, 1199, 1218–1223, 1225
16:33............1070, 1203		
16:35............909n113, 1067, 1164, 1203, 1221, 1227, 1273	18:6..............1083, 1102, 1211	19:1–10..........1074, 1220–1221, 1222, 1316
	18:7..............1067, 1069, 1071, 1201, 1212	
16:36–50........1074, 1128, 1203–1204, 1209, 1267, 1299		19:1–13..........936
	18:8..............1151, 1210, 1212, 1213n128, 1214, 1216	19:1–22..........1074
		19:2..............942n168, 1070, 1220, 1298, 1330
16:37............1201, 1203, 1204, 1266, 1296	18:8–10..........1119, 1210, 1212	
	18:8–19..........740, 1074, 1102, 1122, 1212–1216, 1217, 1283	19:2–10..........1144, 1221
16:37–39........1220		19:3..............1220, 1316
16:38............1202, 1204, 1207		19:4..............1220, 1221
16:38–39........752n710		19:5..............1220, 1221
16:40............744, 756, 1202, 1204, 1210, 1299	18:8–32..........1209	19:6..............941, 1220, 1221
	18:9..............1213, 1214, 1215, 1217n138	19:7..............1221
16:41............567, 1204, 1205		19:8..............1221
16:41–50........1163	18:9–10..........1111	19:9..............1066, 1068, 1111, 1128, 1220, 1221, 1222, 1236, 1298
16:42............774, 1184, 1185, 1204, 1227	18:10............1102, 1213, 1281	
	18:11............1068, 1122, 1212, 1213, 1214, 1215, 1216	
16:45............1202, 1204, 1213, 1227		19:10............547n254, 1221, 1222
	18:11–18........1210	
16:46............1067, 1090, 1101, 1128, 1145, 1204, 1267, 1299	18:11–19........1006, 1213	19:11............887n91, 910, 998, 1150, 1221
	18:12............491, 673, 1214, 1217, 1282	
		19:11–12........1298
16:46–49........753	18:12–13........673, 849, 1215	19:11–13........1068, 1150, 1221
16:48............1069, 1204	18:12–18........873	19:11–21........1221
16:48–49........779	18:12–19........1002n248, 1212	19:11–22........1070, 1074, 1117, 1221–1223, 1316
16:49............1204, 1209, 1221, 1227	18:13............1214	
	18:14............1214, 1234	19:12............998, 1067, 1127, 1221, 1222, 1298
17................339, 352, 1205–1207, 1209, 1220	18:15............1103, 1215	
	18:15–16........873, 1048, 1052	19:13............858, 887n93, 1067, 1070, 1117, 1150, 1219, 1222, 1324
17:1–7..........1074, 1206–1207	18:15–18........1215	
17:1–13..........1074	18:16............548, 1049n315, 1215	
17:1–15..........1203n121		19:14............943, 998, 999, 1221
17:2..............483, 1205, 1206, 1211	18:17............1053, 1215	19:14–15........1222
	18:17–18........1215	19:14–16........1222
17:2–3..........506n160, 1103	18:18............1119, 1212, 1215	19:16............1070, 1194, 1221, 1222
17:3..............1206	18:18–19........706	
17:4..............1206	18:19............743, 756, 849, 889, 1210, 1212, 1214, 1216	19:17............942, 1222, 1222n141
17:5..............1084, 1204, 1205, 1206, 1286		
		19:17–20........1222
17:6..............1205, 1206	18:20............880, 1210, 1212, 1216, 1273, 1327	19:17–22........267
17:7..............708n614, 807n817, 1127n56		19:18............942, 1222
	18:20–21........1210	19:19............1067, 1221, 1222
17:8..............708n614, 807n817, 1207	18:20–32........1074, 1216–1217	19:20............887n94, 1067, 1069, 1117, 1150, 1219, 1222, 1324
	18:21............405, 1216	
17:8–13..........1074, 1150, 1206, 1207, 1212	18:21–24........706, 1053	
	18:21–29........673	19:21............1220, 1221, 1222, 1223
17:9..............1205, 1206, 1228		19:21–22........1223

19:22	1067, 1223	
20	1064, 1188, 1224–1230, 1235, 1271n209	
20–21	1233	
20–25	1059	
20:1	1059, 1070, 1075, 1084, 1174, 1178, 1179, 1188, 1221, 1225, 1226, 1226n144, 1227, 1233, 1235, 1309, 1309n247, 1310, 1310n257, 1317	
20:1–2	1225	
20:1–29	1075	
20:2	774, 1226, 1230	
20:2–5	1163	
20:2–13	767, 1075, 1226–1228, 1233, 1313	
20:3	1207, 1227, 1228, 1230, 1277	
20:4	1139, 1166, 1227, 1302	
20:4–5	1163, 1227	
20:5	1227, 1259	
20:6	1183, 1184, 1185, 1202, 1227	
20:8	1139, 1158, 1227, 1228, 1302	
20:8–13	1058	
20:9	1228	
20:10	1227, 1228	
20:10–11	1228	
20:10–13	1230	
20:11	1222n141, 1227, 1228, 1302	
20:11–13	1071	
20:12	1225, 1227, 1228, 1229, 1230, 1271, 1277	
20:12–22:1	1309	
20:13	1225, 1228	
20:14	1179, 1225, 1228, 1316	
20:14–19	1238	
20:14–21	1075, 1188, 1228–1229	
20:16	1179, 1225, 1228, 1229, 1234, 1235	
20:17	1229, 1238	
20:18	1229	
20:19	1227, 1229, 1238, 1302	
20:20	1229	
20:21	1229	
20:22	1059, 1064, 1169, 1178, 1179, 1187, 1188, 1225, 1226, 1235, 1309n247, 1316, 1317	
20:22–29	1075, 1225, 1229–1230, 1234, 1277	
20:22–22:1	1064	
20:23	1229, 1271, 1318	
20:24	315, 1228, 1229, 1277	
20:25–26	894	
20:26	1067, 1071, 1229	
20:28	506n159, 1070, 1101, 1187, 1220, 1221, 1229, 1230, 1266, 1273, 1309, 1317	
20:28–29	1277	
20:29	910, 1166, 1183, 1207, 1229, 1230, 1244, 1318	
21	1065, 1231–1241, 1263	
21–25	1065	
21:1	1178, 1186, 1188, 1229, 1233, 1234, 1235, 1254, 1317	
21:1–3	1048, 1070, 1075, 1186, 1233, 1233–1234, 1240, 1317	
21:1–9	1267	
21:1–35	1075	
21:2	666, 1052, 1234, 1290	
21:2–3	1291n220	
21:3	1172, 1186, 1233, 1234	
21:4	502n155, 1080, 1234, 1235, 1235n159, 1261, 1312, 1318	
21:4–9	1061, 1163, 1233, 1271	
21:4–11	1075, 1186, 1234–1236, 1318	
21:5	1183, 1227, 1233, 1235	
21:5–9	1318	
21:6	1070, 1221, 1236, 1247	
21:7	1165, 1188, 1233, 1236, 1247	
21:8	1069n10, 1070, 1071, 1204, 1233, 1236	
21:9	1061, 1064, 1069n10, 1247	
21:10	1064, 1318	
21:10–11	1309n247	
21:10–12	1317	
21:10–20	546, 1233	
21:10–36:13	1064	
21:11	1318	
21:12	1235, 1237	
21:12–13	1238	
21:12–20	1075, 1237–1238, 1301, 1318	
21:13	122, 1235, 1317	
21:14	1082, 1233, 1235, 1237	
21:15	1237, 1239	
21:16	1238, 1317	
21:16–18	560, 1238	
21:18	1235, 1238	
21:18–20	1317	
21:19	1238, 1249, 1318	
21:20	1238, 1238n174, 1255, 1277, 1318	
21:21	1238	
21:21–35	1058, 1070, 1075, 1088, 1233, 1238–1240, 1267, 1301, 1305, 1317	
21:22	1229, 1238, 1317	
21:23	1057, 1238, 1239	
21:24	1238, 1239, 1322	
21:24–25	1237	
21:25	1239	
21:26	1239	
21:27	1239	
21:28	1237, 1238, 1239	
21:29	1239, 1249, 1319	
21:30	1238, 1239, 1302, 1305, 1318	
21:31–35	613, 1276	
21:32	1239, 1302, 1305, 1319	
21:33	1082, 1240	
21:34	1240	
21:35	1221, 1240	
22	1059, 1241–1250, 1252	
22–24	360, 1058, 1061, 1070, 1130, 1263	
22:1	1060, 1064, 1240, 1243, 1244, 1272, 1309n247	
22:1–21	1075, 1244–1248, 1249, 1253, 1258, 1267, 1316, 1324	
22:1–41	1075	
22:1–24:25	1243	
22:2	1245	
22:2–36:13	1064	
22:3	1245	
22:4	1245, 1254, 1267	
22:4–7	227	
22:5	531n216, 1245, 1246, 1253, 1260	
22:6	1243, 1246, 1247, 1316	
22:7	1245, 1247, 1258	
22:8	1247, 1249	
22:10	638n462	
22:11	531n216, 1243, 1246, 1247	
22:12	1243, 1246, 1247, 1248, 1249, 1254	
22:13–14	1247	
22:15	612, 1247	
22:17	1243, 1246, 1247, 1247n192, 1249	
22:18	1247, 1260	
22:19	1247, 1249	
22:20	1243, 1247, 1248, 1249, 1253	
22:22	1248, 1249	
22:22–41	1075, 1246n188, 1248–1249, 1265, 1316	
22:23	1248, 1250	
22:23–30	1248	
22:24	1248	
22:24–25	1240	
22:25	1246n188	
22:26	1243, 1248	
22:27	1248	
22:28	1248, 1253	
22:29	529n213	
22:31	1200, 1248, 1250, 1253	
22:32	1248	
22:33	1069n10	
22:34	868n63, 1249	
22:34–35	1240	
22:35	1243, 1248, 1249, 1253	
22:36	1249	
22:37	1247, 1249	
22:38	1243, 1248, 1249	
22:41	1238, 1248, 1249, 1258	
23	1243, 1250–1256, 1258, 1259	

23–24 ....417, 1243, 1251, 1252	24:9 ....249, 1092, 1246, 1247, 1252, 1255, 1258, 1260	25:14.............1272
23:1 ....1249, 1253		25:14–15 1265
23:1–2 1251		25:15.............1296
23:1–12 ....1075, 1246, 1253–1254, 1261n200	24:10.............1246, 1248, 1252, 1260	25:16–18 ......1075, 1267, 1295
		25:17.............1267, 1320
	24:11.............736n668, 1247, 1260	25:18.............1066, 1067, 1267
23:1–30.........1075		25:32.............1100
23:3 ....1248, 1253	24:13.............1253, 1260	25:33.............1100
23:5 ....1247, 1249, 1252, 1253, 1254, 1255	24:14.............418, 1246, 1260, 1261, 1262	26.................1064, 1065, 1070, 1268–1274, 1275, 1276, 1321, 1333
	24:14–19 1260	
23:6 ....782, 1247, 1253	24:15.............1251, 1253, 1258, 1259	
23:7 ....610n377, 1246, 1251, 1252, 1253, 1261n200		26–36 ....1059, 1064, 1065, 1077, 1154, 1268, 1271n208, 1333
	24:15–16 1260	
	24:15–19 ......1251, 1252	
	24:15–25 ......1075, 1253n195, 1260–1262	26:1 ....1067, 1271
23:7–10.........1251		26:1–51.........1075, 1244, 1271–
23:7–11.........1252		26:1–65.........1075
23:8 ....1246, 1252, 1253	24:15b–16a 1258	26:1–27:11 1059
23:9 ....782, 1248, 1253	24:16.............697n586, 1245, 1247, 1248, 1258, 1259, 1260	26:1–36:13 1075
23:10.............1070, 1083n21, 1252, 1253		26:2 ....506n160, 1070, 1082, 1086, 1264, 1271
	24:17.............1158, 1252, 1260, 1260n198, 1261, 1262	
23:11.............1246, 1252, 1254		26:2–3 ....1270, 1273
23:12.............1247, 1249, 1253, 1254, 1255		26:3 ....1060, 1334
	24:17–25 1088	26:4 1082
23:13.............1246, 1252, 1254, 1255, 1258	24:18.............1252, 1260	26:4–9 1246
	24:19.............1260	26:5 ....506n160, 1272
23:13–14 1302	24:20.............1251, 1252, 1261	26:7 ....1305n241
23:13–30 ....1075, 1254–1255	24:20–24 ......1252, 1258	26:10.............1067, 1070, 1233, 1245, 1272, 1273
23:14.............1238, 1238n174, 1248, 1249, 1254	24:21.............1251, 1261	
	24:21–22 ......1252, 1261	26:10–11 1203
23:15.............1253	24:22.............227, 1253n195, 1261, 1262	26:11.............1069n10, 1070, 1272, 1273, 1274
23:16.............1247, 1249, 1252, 1254, 1255		
	24:23.............1069n10, 1251	26:13.............1272
23:17.............1253, 1254	24:23–24 ......1252, 1261	26:14.............1266
23:18.............1251	24:24.............1261, 1262	26:16–33 1246
23:18–24 ....1251, 1252	24:25.............1246, 1262	26:18.............1305n241
23:19–21 249	25.................767, 832, 1161, 1260, 1262, 1263–1268	26:19.............1070, 1272, 1322
23:20.............1088, 1252, 1254		26:28–33 1333
23:21.............1252, 1254, 1259		26:28–34 1276
23:22.............1254, 1255, 1256, 1259	25:1 ....1196, 1264, 1265, 1318	26:29.............1272, 1305
		26:33.............1275
23:23.............1247, 1255	25:1–2 1267	26:33–34 1332
23:24.............1088, 1183, 1255, 1260, 1286	25:1–3 ....790n797, 1058, 1271	26:34.............1272, 1305n241
		26:35.............1272
23:25.............1246, 1252, 1255	25:1–5 1065	26:37.............1272
23:26.............1253, 1254, 1255	25:1–9 ....689, 1061, 1075, 1244, 1267	26:48.............1272
23:27.............1246, 1252, 1255		26:50.............1272
23:28.............1238, 1248, 1255, 1265	25:1–13.........1060	26:51.............1086, 1272, 1296, 1305n241
	25:1–18.........1075	
23:29.............1249	25:2 1265	26:51–53 1319
24..................1256–1262	25:3 ....1167, 1174, 1255, 1265	26:52–56 ......1030, 1272, 1275
24:1 ....1057, 1246, 1247, 1249, 1252, 1258, 1259		26:52–62 ......1075, 1272–1273, 1319
	25:3–4 1067	
24:1–14.........1075, 1084, 1252, 1258–1260	25:4 ....1167, 1195, 1265	26:53.............1216, 1270, 1272, 1324
	25:5 ....1264, 1265	
24:1–25.........1075	25:6 ....1265, 1267, 1276	26:53–56 1271
24:2 ....1244, 1255, 1258, 1259, 1278	25:6–7 1266	26:54.............1272, 1319
	25:6–13.........506n159	26:55.............1216, 1272, 1319
24:3 ....1251, 1252, 1253, 1258, 1259	25:7 ....1101, 1265, 1266	26:56.............1216, 1272, 1319, 1324
	25:7–8 1089	
24:3–4 1260	25:8 ....1066, 1265	26:57.............1103
24:3–9 ....1251, 1252	25:8–9 ....779, 1067	26:57–62 ......1272, 1273
24:3b–4a 1258	25:9 ....1065, 1066, 1067, 1221, 1245, 1264, 1265, 1266, 1271, 1272, 1295	26:58.............1103, 1272, 1273
24:4 ....256, 697n586, 1245, 1247, 1248, 1252, 1258, 1259		26:59.............506n158, 561, 1100, 1103, 1273
		26:61.............1070, 1164, 1272, 1273
	25:10–15 ......1075, 1266–1267	
24:5 ....1258, 1259	25:11.............1067, 1069, 1090, 1101, 1123, 1204, 1265, 1266	26:62.............1273, 1327
24:5–7 1244		26:63.............1271, 1273
24:6 ....1252, 1259		26:63–65 ......1075, 1273–1274
24:7 ....1222n141, 1252, 1259	25:11–13 893	26:64.............1271, 1272, 1273
	25:12.............1216, 1266	26:64–65 ......1061, 1065, 1273
24:8 ....1247, 1252, 1255, 1259	25:13.............743, 1201, 1204, 1266, 1267, 1271	26:65.............1067, 1070, 1071, 1271, 1274, 1275
24:8–9 1088		

SCRIPTURE INDEX

27 . . . . 632, 1065, 1070, 1126, 1268, 1272, 1274–1279, 1280, 1332, 1333, 1334
27–36 . . . . 1334n336
27:1 . . . . 1237, 1273, 1276, 1305, 1333
27:1–11 . . . . 590, 1075, 1275, 1276–1277, 1332
27:1–23 1075
27:2 . . . . 1275, 1276
27:2–3 1265
27:3 . . . . 1070, 1276
27:3–4 632
27:4 . . . . 1273, 1276
27:5 . . . . 1278, 1304
27:5–11 632
27:6 1277
27:7 . . . . 548, 1150, 1275, 1277, 1334
27:8 . . . . 548, 1275
27:8–9a 1277
27:8–11 1277
27:9b–11 1277
27:11 . . . . 568, 1277, 1330
27:12 . . . . 1275, 1277, 1318
27:12–23 . . . . 1059, 1075, 1275, 1277–1279
27:13 . . . . 1273, 1277
27:14 . . . . 1071, 1178, 1179, 1196, 1225, 1277
27:15 1277
27:15–23 1058
27:16 . . . . 1202, 1203, 1277, 1278
27:17 1278
27:18 1278
27:18–23 1169
27:19 1275
27:20 1278
27:21 . . . . 659, 738, 1278, 1319
27:22 . . . . 1084, 1275
28 . . . . 1279–1284, 1286, 1288
28–29 . . . . 841, 896, 1011n255, 1057, 1109, 1111, 1268, 1280, 1281, 1288, 1289, 1290
28–30 1059
28:1 . . . . 1100, 1280, 1288
28:1–8 . . . . 1075, 1281
28:1–15 1280
28:1–31 1075
28:1–29:40 1156
28:2 . . . . 1282, 1284, 1322
28:3 . . . . 1281, 1283
28:3–4 1281
28:3–8 . . . . 719n640
28:5 . . . . 745n698, 1281, 1282
28:6 . . . . 1080, 1100, 1280, 1281, 1282, 1313
28:7 . . . . 1281, 1284
28:8 1281
28:9 1281
28:9–10 . . . . 1068, 1075, 1281–1282
28:10 . . . . 1281, 1282
28:11 . . . . 1282, 1286
28:11–15 . . . . 1075, 1282, 1286
28:12 1282
28:13 1282
28:14 . . . . 1281, 1282
28:15 . . . . 1282, 1286
28:16–25 . . . . 544n246, 1075, 1109, 1149, 1282–1283
28:16–29:40 1280
28:18 . . . . 1109, 1150, 1155, 1286, 1287
28:19 . . . . 1282, 1286
28:19–24 . . . . 682n562
28:22 . . . . 1068, 1280, 1282
28:25 1155
28:26 . . . . 1155, 1283
28:26–31 . . . . 1075, 1214, 1283
28:27 . . . . 1282, 1286
28:28 1283
28:30 . . . . 1068, 1282
28:31 1283
29 1284–1288
29:1 . . . . 1154, 1155, 1286, 1287
29:1–6 . . . . 1075, 1286, 1287
29:1–40 1075
29:2 . . . . 1280, 1282, 1284, 1286, 1287
29:2–4 1286
29:5 . . . . 1068, 1280, 1282, 1286
29:6 . . . . 1284, 1286
29:7 . . . . 1155, 1286, 1287, 1291
29:7–11 . . . . 1075, 1286, 1287
29:8 . . . . 1286, 1287
29:8–10 1287
29:11 . . . . 1068, 1282, 1287, 1288
29:12 . . . . 1155, 1286, 1287
29:12–34 . . . . 842n22
29:12–38 . . . . 1075, 1286, 1287
29:13 1287
29:16 1282
29:18 1286
29:19 1282
29:21 1286
29:22 1282
29:24 1286
29:25 1282
29:27 1286
29:28 1282
29:30 1286
29:31 1282
29:32 1287
29:33 1286
29:34 1282
29:35 1287
29:36 . . . . 1286, 1287
29:37 . . . . 1286, 1287
29:38 1282
29:39 . . . . 1130, 1192, 1287, 1289
29:39–40 . . . . 1075, 1287–1288
29:40 . . . . 1280, 1288
30 1288–1293
30:1 . . . . 1290, 1292
30:1–2 . . . . 1076, 1289, 1290–1291
30:1–16 1076
30:2 . . . . 1048, 1130, 1289, 1290, 1291, 1292, 1304
30:3 . . . . 1290, 1291
30:3–5 . . . . 1050, 1291
30:3–8 1048
30:3–15 924
30:3–16 . . . . 1076, 1290, 1291–1292
30:4 . . . . 1291, 1292
30:5 . . . . 1291, 1292, 1303
30:6 . . . . 1291, 1292
30:6–8 1291
30:7 . . . . 1291, 1292
30:8 . . . . 1291, 1292, 1303
30:9 . . . . 1291, 1292
30:10 1292
30:10–15 1291
30:11 . . . . 1291, 1292, 1303
30:12 . . . . 1291, 1292
30:13 . . . . 1290, 1291, 1292
30:14 . . . . 1291, 1292
30:15 . . . . 1123, 1291, 1292
30:16 1291
31 . . . . 1057, 1116, 1267, 1293–1299, 1301
31:1–8 1070
31:1–11 . . . . 1076, 1295–1297, 1305
31:1–12 613
31:1–54 1076
31:1–33:49 1059
31:2 . . . . 648, 1295
31:3 . . . . 1146, 1295, 1304, 1305
31:4 1295
31:5 . . . . 319, 1086, 1295, 1296, 1296n226
31:6 . . . . 1082, 1101, 1104, 1254, 1295, 1296
31:7 . . . . 1146, 1221, 1296
31:8 . . . . 1070, 1245, 1246, 1248, 1260, 1262, 1267, 1296
31:9 . . . . 1234, 1296, 1302
31:11 1298
31:12 1271
31:12–18 . . . . 1076, 1296, 1298
31:12–24 1295
31:13 . . . . 1066, 1220, 1302
31:14 . . . . 1082, 1295
31:14–16 573
31:15 . . . . 1069n10
31:16 . . . . 1067, 1071, 1120, 1245, 1277, 1295, 1296
31:17 1123
31:18 . . . . 1069n10, 1265
31:19 . . . . 1066, 1067, 1068, 1070, 1150, 1195, 1220, 1221, 1298
31:19–24 . . . . 312, 1076, 1298
31:20 . . . . 921, 1298
31:21 . . . . 1082, 1220, 1298
31:22 . . . . 1127n56, 1298
31:22–23 1068
31:23 . . . . 1295, 1298, 1299
31:23–24 1296
31:24 . . . . 1067, 1068, 1298
31:25–47 . . . . 1076, 1295, 1298
31:26 . . . . 1081, 1298
31:27 . . . . 1082, 1146, 1298
31:28 . . . . 1082, 1298
31:29 . . . . 1193, 1212, 1298
31:29–30 1210
31:30 . . . . 1298, 1299, 1328
31:32 1302
31:32–35 1088
31:32–41 . . . . 1213, 1298
31:37 1298
31:38 1298
31:39 1298
31:40 . . . . 1187, 1298
31:41 . . . . 1193, 1212, 1298

31:47............1298, 1299	32:37............1305	33:38............1058, 1064, 1070,
31:48............1265	32:38............1265, 1302, 1305	1183, 1187, 1225,
31:48–54 ....1076, 1295,	32:39............1305, 1319	1226, 1244, 1277,
1298–1299	32:39–42 ....1272, 1301, 1305	1309, 1318
31:49............1070, 1082, 1298	32:41............1305	33:38–39 1311
31:50............1082, 1137n62,	32:41–42 1305	33:39............1230
1145, 1299	33................1063, 1080,	33:40............1186, 1229, 1311,
31:51............1299	1100, 1152,	1317, 1322
31:52............1193, 1212, 1213,	1156, 1178n92,	33:41............1318
1298, 1299	1307–1320, 1321	33:41b–47a 1309
31:52–54 1296	33–34............1268	33:42............1318
31:54............1234, 1286, 1298,	33:1.............1311	33:43............1235, 1318
1299	33:1–2..........1308, 1311	33:44............1239, 1318
32................1237, 1268,	33:1–15.........1076, 1080, 1100,	33:44–47 1317
1300–1306, 1308,	1156, 1178n92,	33:45............1318
1321, 1327	1311–1315	33:46............1318
32:1 ....422, 1139, 1239,	33:1–49.........1321	33:47............1318
1302, 1306	33:1–56.........1076	33:47–48 1277
32:1–5 1301	33:2 ....441, 1057, 1311,	33:48............1244, 1271, 1318
32:1–15.........1076, 1302–1303	1322	33:48–49 1317
32:1–42.........1076	33:3 ....557n273, 1195,	33:49............1093, 1238, 1244,
32:2 ....1302, 1303	1309	1318
32:3 ....1302, 1305, 1318	33:3–4 1311	33:50............1271, 1319
32:4 ....1167, 1303	33:3–49.........546, 1308, 1309	33:50–56 ....1070, 1076, 1308,
32:5 1303	33:4 ....1303, 1319	1319–1320, 1321
32:6 1303	33:5–7 1311	33:50–36:13....1059
32:6–15.........1301, 1334	33:5–49.........1311	33:51............1319, 1322, 1329
32:7 1303	33:6 1311	33:52............1234, 1319
32:8 ....1156, 1164, 1174,	33:7 ....1311, 1312	33:52–53 1319
1177, 1179, 1226,	33:8 ....278n410, 567,	33:53............1179, 1319
1316, 1317, 1322	1057, 1311, 1312,	33:54............1272, 1273, 1319,
32:8–9 1303	1314	1319n301, 1325,
32:8–13.........1303	33:8–15.........1313	1328
32:9 1303	33:8–35.........1309n248	33:55............1179, 1319, 1320
32:10............1167, 1174	33:9 ....1311, 1312	33:55–56 1319
32:11............1082	33:10............556n264, 1312	33:56............1320
32:12............161n247, 1174,	33:10–11 1080	34................1059, 1316,
1303	33:11............556n264, 1057,	1320–1325, 1327
32:13............1152, 1164, 1167,	1313	34:1 1322
1207, 1248, 1265,	33:12–14 ....577, 1313	34:1–12..........1321
1309, 1318	33:14............1311	34:1–15.........1076, 1316, 1317,
32:14............1065, 1067, 1167,	33:14–15 1313	1321, 1322–1324
1271, 1303	33:15............1080, 1100, 1156,	34:1–29..........1076
32:15............1303	1178n92, 1312,	34:2 ....1316, 1322, 1324,
32:16–19 ....1301, 1304	1313	1325, 1329
32:16–32 ....1076, 1295,	33:16............1165, 1313	34:2–12..........121
1303–1304	33:16–17 1315	34:3 ....1156, 1178, 1226,
32:17............1304	33:16–18a......1076, 1312,	1234, 1244n184,
32:19............1324	1315–1316	1260, 1310, 1317,
32:20............1295, 1304	33:16–36 ....1309n247,	1322, 1323, 1324,
32:20–25 1301	1316n288	1327
32:21............1304	33:18............1310, 1315, 1317	34:4 ....1179, 1235, 1317,
32:22............1304	33:18a...........1310	1317n290, 1322,
32:23............679, 1304	33:18b–30a 1309	1323
32:24............1304	33:18b–36......1076, 1179,	34:5 ....160, 1322, 1323
32:25–27 1304	1316–1317, 1323	34:6 ....1322, 1323, 1327
32:26............1302	33:18b–36a 1310, 1316	34:7 ....1323, 1327
32:27............1304	33:19–35 1309	34:8 1323
32:28............1265, 1310	33:19–36 ....1310n257	34:9 ....1323, 1324
32:28–29 ....1058, 1304	33:29............1317, 1323	34:10............1324, 1327
32:28–30 1301	33:31............1317	34:11............1244n184, 1323,
32:30............1304, 1322	33:33............1317	1324
32:31............1304	33:35............1317	34:12............1244n184, 1322,
32:31–32 ....1301, 1304	33:36............1178, 1179, 1310,	1324, 1327, 1329
32:32............1304, 1322	1310n257, 1311,	34:13............1273, 1321, 1322,
32:33............1303, 1304	1316, 1317, 1322,	1324
32:33–38 1301	1323	34:13–15 1324
32:33–42 ....1076, 1238,	33:36a..........1316	34:14............1273, 1304, 1324
1304–1306	33:36b 1310, 1316	34:14–15 1321
32:34............1302, 1305, 1306,	33:37............1179, 1188, 1226,	34:15............1304, 1324
1318	1229, 1311, 1316,	34:16–29 ....1076, 1321,
32:34–38 ....1302, 1305	1317, 1318, 1323	1324–1325
32:34–39 1058	33:37–39 1317	34:17............1319, 1324
32:35............1305	33:37–49 ....1076, 1093, 1236,	34:18............1324
32:36............1302, 1305	1244, 1317–1318	34:19............1321

34:19–20 1324
34:19–28 1324
34:29 .... 1322, 1324, 1325
35. .... 1268, 1325–1331
35:1 1271
35:1–8 .... 1076, 1093, 1327–1328
35:1–34 1076
35:2 .... 1322, 1327
35:2–5 .... 848n35
35:2–8 1216
35:3 .... 1327, 1328
35:4 .... 1327, 1328
35:4–5 .... 1093, 1328, 1328n325
35:5 .... 1327, 1328
35:6 1328
35:7 .... 1032, 1328
35:8 1328
35:9–29 643
35:9–33 1327
35:9–34 .... 1058, 1076, 1117, 1298, 1328, 1329–1331
35:10 .... 1322, 1329
35:11 .... 1023, 1329
35:12 .... 1069n10, 1328, 1329
35:14 .... 1322, 1329
35:15 .... 988, 1023, 1329
35:16 .... 1071, 1195
35:16–18 1329
35:16–23 1329
35:16–25 643
35:16–34 1070
35:17 .... 1067, 1071
35:18 1071
35:19 .... 648, 648n486, 1329, 1330
35:20–21 1329
35:21 .... 1071, 1330
35:22 312
35:22–23 1330
35:22–25 .... 112n151
35:23 677
35:24 .... 1329, 1330
35:25 .... 643, 912n118, 1070, 1100, 1104, 1329, 1330
35:27 1330
35:28 .... 1070, 1329, 1330
35:29 .... 1060, 1191, 1277, 1298, 1330, 1331
35:30 .... 642, 1071, 1331
35:30–31 .... 1070, 1331
35:30–34 .... 753, 1067
35:31 .... 112n151, 1071, 1331
35:31–32 1299
35:31–34 .... 643, 1049
35:33 .... 1330, 1331
35:33–34 .... 979n226, 1327, 1331
35:34 .... 1065, 1066, 1089, 1116, 1117, 1174, 1324, 1327, 1329, 1331
36. .... 1065, 1070, 1126, 1268, 1272, 1332–1335
36:1 .... 1265, 1276, 1333
36:1–3 1333
36:1–4 .... 1076, 1333–1334
36:1–9 590
36:1–13 1076
36:2 1333

36:3 .... 1150, 1276, 1333
36:4 .... 1150, 1333
36:5–6 1334
36:5–9 1333
36:5–13 .... 1076, 1334
36:6 1334
36:7 1334
36:8 1334
36:8–9 1334
36:9 1334
36:10–12 1333
36:11 .... 502n154, 746, 1058
36:12 .... 1058, 1334
36:13 .... 819, 1060, 1240, 1244, 1271, 1334

Deuteronomy
1 1188
1:1 1244
1:1–3:29 .... 1058, 1061
1:2 .... 1160, 1177, 1178n92, 1309, 1309n252, 1310, 1314
1:3 .... 1058, 1226
1:3–5 1244
1:6 1159
1:7 .... 1179, 1186
1:9 .... 588n325
1:9–18 590
1:16 .... 547n254, 677n549
1:17 625
1:19 .... 1159, 1310
1:21–23 1176
1:22 1177
1:31 494
1:33 1160
1:37 1058
1:38 902
1:40 .... 556n264, 1186
1:41–44 1188
1:43 .... 589n327
1:44 .... 1188, 1234, 1235, 1310
1:46 .... 481, 1188
2:1 .... 1186, 1226, 1235
2:3 1235
2:4 .... 528, 1235
2:5 .... 1235, 1238, 1319
2:7 .... 575, 1152
2:8 .... 1235, 1236, 1317
2:9 .... 1228, 1237, 1238, 1245
2:12 320
2:12b 445
2:13 1235
2:13–14 1318
2:14 .... 1065, 1187, 1226, 1310, 1316
2:19 .... 1082, 1238
2:21 1240
2:23 120
2:25 1245
2:26 1238
2:36 1238
2:37 1238
3:8 .... 1237, 1238
3:10 1239
3:12 .... 1237, 1305
3:13–16 1306
3:14 .... 575, 1305
3:16 1305
3:17 .... 1238, 1244, 1258
3:27 1238
3:28 1058

4:1 568
4:3 .... 1058, 1061, 1267
4:5–8 494
4:7–8 .... 987, 1022, 1253
4:9–10 976
4:10 25
4:11 1151
4:12 .... 606, 1315
4:12–13 605
4:13 606
4:15 606
4:15–18 .... 621, 696
4:16–18 .... 607n361
4:18 .... 607n361
4:19 .... 451, 479n89, 688n569
4:20 .... 746, 786n787
4:21 1058
4:24 .... 535, 607
4:25 337
4:26 .... 1038n299
4:29 780
4:34 .... 502, 502n153, 517
4:34–35 482
4:35 .... 482, 521n193, 543, 638n462
4:39 .... 521n193
4:41–43 643
4:45–49 1061
4:47 1238
4:49 1238
5:4 .... 780n774, 1131
5:4–24 .... 605, 617n412
5:5 528
5:6 973
5:8–9 .... 451, 479n89, 688n569
5:9 .... 607, 1082
5:11 610
5:12 610
5:14 .... 622, 669, 962n200, 1302
5:14–15 611
5:15 .... 502n153
5:16 613
5:18 977
5:20 610
5:21 .... 616n406
5:22 619
5:22–24 .... 605, 617n412
5:22–33 618
5:23 1140
5:25 1140
5:26 .... 1140, 1174
5:29 .... 528, 559, 618, 626
5:30 619
5:31–33 568
5:33 974
6:1–2 .... 612, 622, 623
6:1–9 667
6:2 .... 468, 528, 559, 626
6:4 52
6:5 621
6:6–7 .... 612, 622, 623
6:6–9 549
6:7 496
6:7–9 632
6:10 1234
6:10–11 1319
6:13 .... 609n373
6:14 .... 790n797
6:16 .... 204, 454, 577, 578, 579
6:22 517
6:24 626

7:1 .... 479, 1087	12:5 628	16:22 256
7:1–3 985	12:5–6 967	17:1 1220
7:2–5 1234	12:6 .... 1130, 1288	17:3 1195
7:3 .... 1158n76	12:9 1160	17:5 1195
7:3–4 .... 1266, 1267	12:10 781	17:6 .... 340, 1120
7:5 .... 688n568, 694	12:10–12 .... 682n559, 886	17:6–7 991
7:6 .... 746, 786n787	12:10–14 967	17:7 1022
7:7 .... 459, 1041, 1087	12:11 1130	17:8 .... 533n227
7:8 1290	12:11–12 852	17:8–13 911
7:9 .... 784, 1193	12:11–14 967	17:10 966
7:9–10 .... 608n367	12:12 .... 924, 1016	17:12 1101
7:11–16 568	12:15–16 .... 916n121	17:12–13 .... 589n327
7:12 784	12:16 .... 112, 968	17:16 .... 404n661
7:12–15 689	12:17 .... 611n384, 1050, 1130, 1217, 1288	17:17 .... 977n222
7:13 .... 846n28, 1127, 1191, 1214	12:18 .... 682n559	17:18 .... 885n85
7:15 568	12:20 1165	18:1 1216
7:16 1319	12:21 966	18:1–2 1033
7:18 528	12:23 968	18:1–5 848
7:19 .... 502, 517	12:24 969	18:2 1216
7:22 .... 459, 688n570, 1087	12:26 1050	18:3 1266
7:25 616	12:31 .... 548, 978n224	18:4 1214
8:2 .... 568, 578	13:1–2 1173	18:9–12 .... 978n224
8:2–3 .... 578, 1058, 1061	13:1–15 .... 978n224	18:10 .... 385, 666, 667, 1247
8:3 .... 578, 1166	13:3 .... 204, 568, 578	18:10–11 360
8:4 1152	13:3–4 626	18:14 1247
8:6 626	13:4 .... 468, 559, 590, 626	18:15 1227
8:7–8 846	13:6–11 615	18:16 .... 251, 1140
8:7–10 .... 479, 850	13:13–15 1053	18:19 687–688
8:8 .... 849n36, 1214n133	13:13–16 666	18:22 1173
8:15–16 1061	14:1 .... 987, 999	19:1–13 .... 643, 1058, 1329
8:16 .... 565, 577, 578	14:2 .... 786n787	19:4–5 .... 643n471
8:19 .... 790n797	14:5 .... 918, 969	19:5 1330
9–10 .... 766n750	14:21 .... 611n384	19:6 .... 1267, 1329
9:2 1178	14:22–27 .... 673n542	19:8 1255
9:10 .... 25, 251, 1169	14:22–29 .... 257n374	19:12 .... 1329, 1330
9:16 1304	14:23 .... 1050, 1216, 1217	19:14 1273
9:20 774	14:24–26 873	19:15 615
9:21 .... 777, 1314	14:26 .... 1016, 1165	19:15–21 677
9:22–24 1061	14:27 .... 611n384	19:16–19 661
9:23 .... 1058, 1228, 1277, 1303, 1310	14:27–29 1033	19:16–21 .... 651, 659, 659n516
9:23–24 1165	14:28–29 .... 624, 646, 653, 673, 673n542, 678	19:18–21 615
9:25 .... 481, 1183n97	14:29 638	19:20 .... 615, 661, 1168
9:27 412	15:7–11 670	19:21 .... 968, 1023, 1329
9:28 .... 776n762	15:9 181	20:1 528
9:29 .... 502n153	15:12 .... 485n111, 636n458, 639	20:1–18 613
10:1–5 .... 717n631	15:12–13 637	20:5 .... 76, 1168
10:3 .... 807n816	15:12–15 635	20:10 1238
10:4 .... 251, 703, 763, 788n793	15:13–14 277	20:10–14 1123
10:6 1317	15:16 637	20:12 1234
10:7 1317	15:16–17 635	21:3 1220
10:8 903	15:18 637	21:5 .... 533n227
10:9 1216	15:19–23 1215	21:6–7 862
10:12 .... 468, 528, 559, 590, 626, 688	15:22 966	21:6–9 .... 1022n278
10:12–13 .... 451, 479n89	16 .... 682n563	21:7–9 968
10:16 1196	16:1 1149	21:10–14 1034
10:18 .... 638, 669, 670	16:1–8 .... 682n561, 1149	21:11 1265
10:18–19 669	16:1–17 .... 951, 1011n255, 1156	21:12 943
10:20 .... 609n373, 626	16:3 544	21:15–17 1085
11:6 .... 1058, 1061, 1203	16:6 .... 628, 1149	21:16 .... 606n358
11:9 1319	16:8 1287	21:17 .... 491, 1095
11:10–11 1179	16:9 1283	21:18–20 622
11:10–12 850	16:10 .... 1014, 1283	21:18–21 .... 862, 993
11:10–14 .... 1040n304	16:11 .... 638, 682n559	21:18–22 613
11:13 .... 451, 479n89, 688	16:11–12 635	21:22 1195
11:13–14 846	16:13–15 1006	21:22–23 354
11:14 .... 852, 1179	16:16 .... 682n561, 682n563, 960n193, 1129, 1282, 1287	21:23 .... 979n226
11:16 .... 663n522		22:1–3 874
11:17 101		22:1–4 677
11:24 .... 1095, 1323	16:17 .... 682n563	22:5 .... 978n224
11:31 1322	16:19 .... 590, 625, 1202	22:6–7 .... 645, 673, 674, 1008
12:3 .... 688n568, 694	16:21 .... 786n790	22:8 623
		22:9 .... 986, 986n234, 1217
		22:12 1195
		22:14–19 .... 663n523
		22:15–19 .... 678n550

22:16	663n523	
22:18–19	993	
22:21	305n465, 1195	
22:22	1120	
22:22–24	977	
22:23–24	663, 986	
22:24	347, 640, 993	
22:25–27	993	
22:27	347	
22:28	1123	
22:28–29	304	
22:29	306, 640	
23:1	1007	
23:2	977	
23:2–3	190	
23:3–5	1061	
23:4	219n326, 644, 1245	
23:4–5	1058	
23:5	1130, 1131, 1245, 1248	
23:7	318	
23:14	83, 523, 1295	
23:15–16	635	
23:17	987	
23:19–20	1033n295	
23:20	669n535	
23:21	622, 1289	
23:21–23	1061, 1130	
23:23	1050, 1127	
24:1	993n239	
24:1–4	1124, 1172	
24:2	639	
24:4	979n226	
24:6	670, 874	
24:7	353n573	
24:8	934	
24:8–9	935	
24:9	1061	
24:10–13	670, 874	
24:12–13	671, 984	
24:14–15	624, 874	
24:16	607	
24:17	669, 670, 677n549	
24:19	653, 669, 678	
24:19–20	623	
24:19–22	1029n284	
25:1	528n209	
25:4	1218	
25:5–10	337, 974, 976	
25:9	1174	
25:13–15	624	
25:17–18	584, 1157	
25:19	781, 1261	
26:1	1280	
26:1–10	673	
26:2	628	
26:5	398, 1031	
26:8	47, 502	
26:8–10	1014	
26:12–15	673n542	
26:13	1217	
26:14	911	
26:16–19	568	
26:18	746	
26:19	736n668	
27:7	853	
27:9–28:68	687	
27:15	978n224	
27:16	612	
27:19	677n549	
27:25	625	
28	605, 1038, 1039n302, 1130, 1287	
28:1–14	588n326, 689, 903	
28:2	1246	
28:2–13	1246	
28:7	1160	
28:12	1258	
28:15	1246	
28:15–68	1246	
28:26	998, 1127, 1186	
28:29	531n220	
28:30	1127	
28:35	525	
28:58	821n3	
28:59	1127	
29:1	1264	
29:5	1152, 1226	
29:7	1058, 1061	
29:11	669	
29:13	1041	
29:20	1266	
29:23	189	
30:3	783	
30:3–4	1044	
30:6	1196	
30:6–7	1186	
30:10	821n3	
30:11–14	1024	
30:15	1246	
30:16	568	
30:18	1319	
30:19	979, 1070, 1130, 1246	
31:2	1061, 1278	
31:7	1255	
31:9	1057, 1104, 1159	
31:9–13	885n85	
31:10–13	911, 924, 1017	
31:11	695n583	
31:14	1278	
31:15	1151, 1278	
31:16	967, 1069	
31:18	1131	
31:22	1057	
31:22–23	1278	
31:23	479n88	
31:24	1057	
31:25	1104, 1159	
31:26–28	1038n299	
31:27	775, 1271	
31:29	418, 1260, 1262	
32:1–43	1260	
32:4	875	
32:8	87, 87n102, 88n108, 1260	
32:10	41, 600, 701, 1238	
32:10–11	42	
32:10–12	49	
32:11	494n130, 595n341	
32:13	378n620	
32:16	607	
32:18	1167	
32:21–22	787n792	
32:25	663n523	
32:26–27	776n762	
32:27	557n273	
32:30	1041, 1088, 1160	
32:35	430, 1172	
32:39	567	
32:41	1172	
32:42	520, 1183	
32:43	648, 1262	
32:49	1238, 1277, 1318, 1322	
32:49–52	1061	
32:50	315, 1229, 1295	
32:51	1071, 1118, 1225, 1227, 1228, 1277	
33:1	1246	
33:2	1310	
33:2–29	1260	
33:5	1177	
33:8	895, 1083, 1266	
33:8–9	778, 992	
33:8–11	893, 1137	
33:10	1083, 1147, 1266	
33:13	249	
33:15	1253	
33:16	1217	
33:17	1088	
33:18	421n688	
33:20	1255	
33:24	422	
33:26–29	972	
33:27	640	
33:29	1253, 1261	
34:1	1238, 1244, 1277	
34:5–6	1277	
34:5–8	1058	
34:5–12	445	
34:7	403	
34:7–8	1226	
34:8	1166, 1229	
34:9	1061, 1278	
34:10	780, 1083, 1173	
34:10–12	27	

Joshua

1–11	27
1–12	32
1:1	1169, 1244
1:1–2	1226
1:8	621
1:11	354n577, 546
1:12–15	1061, 1304
1:13	27, 1160
2	306
2:1	1244, 1264
2:2	1177
2:9	1244
2:9–11	688
2:12	784, 1304
2:12–13	1082
2:12–17	1290
2:14	784, 1304
2:17	1304
2:18	1082
3:1	1244, 1264
3:4	1093, 1159
3:5	786, 1295
3:10	121
4:9	575
4:12	1086n28, 1305n241
4:13	1086, 1244, 1305n241
5:1	1179, 1303
5:5	1151
5:10	1151, 1319
5:12	445, 572, 575, 1164, 1166, 1236
5:15	894
6:4	1155, 1295
6:5	1155, 1179, 1254
6:6	1104
6:9	1157
6:9–10	1264
6:12	1159
6:17	1052n322
6:18–19	1234
6:19	1052n322, 1118, 1141, 1299
6:20	786
6:22	1177

6:23 1082	15–19 1325	24:18 1319
6:24 . . . . 872, 1052n322, 1141, 1234	15:1 . . . . 1178, 1226, 1234, 1272, 1310, 1319, 1322	24:19 . . . . 688, 1185
6:25 1082	15:2 . . . . 1312n264	24:20 688
6:26 . . . . 1052n322	15:3 . . . . 1322, 1323	24:21 528
7 1194	15:4 . . . . 1317n290	24:26 312
7:1 . . . . 1118, 1228, 1303	15:19 1276	24:27 . . . . 694n578
7:6 . . . . 998, 1183	15:20 1319	24:31 786
7:11 . . . . 1118, 1120, 1194	15:21–32 1177	24:32 . . . . 556n267, 1229
7:11–12 . . . . 1052n322	15:27 1317	
7:12 1303	15:30 1234	*Judges*
7:13 1168	15:32 1328	1 145
7:14 . . . . 1082, 1273	15:36 1328	1:16 . . . . 161n247, 1158, 1159, 1188, 1234, 1261
7:15 . . . . 305n465	17:1 1306	
7:16–18 1082	17:5 1273	1:17 1188
7:18 . . . . 1082n19	17:14 1216	1:19 1186
7:20 1194	17:15 1203	1:20 1178
7:21 1118	17:16 1186	1:23–26 . . . . 256, 313
7:25 992	17:18 1203	1:31 . . . . 422, 1178
8:3 1086	18:2–6 1273	1:36 . . . . 1234, 1322
8:18–26 583	18:5 1216	2:1 . . . . 1160, 1161, 1248
8:26 1234	18:6 1273	2:2 . . . . 1234, 1265, 1266
8:26–27 1234	18:7 1324	2:3 1319
8:28 575	18:8 1273	2:10–13 . . . . 790n797
8:29 1265	18:9 1216	2:21–22 578
8:34–35 . . . . 695n583	18:10 1273	2:22 568
9:1 1179	19:10–16 421	3:1–4 578
9:3–17 1290	18:11 1273	3:3 1178
9:10 1239	18:19 . . . . 1312n264	3:4 568
9:18 1289	19:1 . . . . 1273, 1324	3:6 . . . . 1234, 1266
9:19–21 1048	19:10 1273	3:8 . . . . 219n326
9:20 1290	19:17 1273	3:9 . . . . 477, 1165
9:27 1298	19:24 1273	3:10 1278
10:10 559	19:32 1273	3:11 . . . . 705n606
10:12–13 786	19:40 1273	3:15 . . . . 424, 477
10:21 1264	19:40–47 1324	3:15–17 847
10:26 . . . . 1195, 1265	19:51 . . . . 1265, 1273	4 560
10:40 1087	20 643	4:4 1226
11:3 1179	20–21 1327	4:9 . . . . 736n668
11:12 1234	20:1–9 1329	4:11 . . . . 1158, 1158n76, 1261
11:13 1234	20:4 . . . . 1329, 1330	4:19 1298
11:14 1234	21:1–42 1032	5 560
11:19 1234	21:2 1328	5:8 638
11:20 1234	21:11 1178	5:11 1239
11:21 1177	21:13–19 1216	5:15–16 419
11:21–22 1178	22:4 320	5:16 . . . . 421n690
12:2 1238	22:9 1237	5:30 1265
12:2–3 . . . . 1238, 1240	22:13 . . . . 1237, 1274	5:31 . . . . 705n606
12:14 1188	22:14 124	6 227
13–21 . . . . 410n674	22:15 1237	6–8 1298
13:2 1087	22:20 1118	6:1 1306
13:4 121	22:21 1160	6:3 . . . . 1245, 1261
13:6 1322	22:26 . . . . 589n329	6:5 . . . . 142n222
13:8 1324	22:28 708	6:11 1245
13:9 1239	22:30 1160	6:14–24 479
13:13 575	22:31 1298	6:15 1082
13:14 . . . . 848, 1033	22:32 1237	6:17–21 180
13:15 1272	22:33 . . . . 499n137, 1183n97	6:22 478
13:16–17 1306	23:7 . . . . 628n432	6:24 . . . . 207n311
13:17 . . . . 1249, 1302	23:10 1088	6:25 . . . . 786n790
13:20 1318	23:12–13 1267	6:32 . . . . 295n451, 1158
13:22 . . . . 1245, 1247	23:13 1319	6:36–40 220
13:24 1272	23:15 1246	6:39 . . . . 528n208
13:25 1239	24:2 . . . . 131, 133, 134, 221, 241, 288, 1245	7 152
13:25–27 1306		7:2 259
13:27 . . . . 300, 1305	24:7 . . . . 563n289	7:20 1155
13:29 1272	24:9 . . . . 644, 1306	8:5–6 1238
13:30 . . . . 1237n167, 1305	24:9–10 . . . . 1244, 1245	8:10 259
13:31 1237	24:10 1131	8:11 1305
13:33 . . . . 848, 1032	24:13 1234	8:19 658
14:1 . . . . 1274, 1319	24:14 . . . . 221, 1205	8:22–24 . . . . 330n516
14:4 1328	24:14–20 528	8:26–27 312
14:7 . . . . 1303, 1310, 1316	24:14–22 . . . . 781n778	8:28 . . . . 705n606, 1168
14:14 1186	24:14–24 405	8:30 219
14:15 1178		8:35 1158

9:4..............307n473
9:6..............312
9:9..............617
9:11.............617
9:28.............498n133
9:43.............1238
10:10............868n63
11...............422
11:1–3...........977
11:10............1304
11:12–13........1239
11:13............1238
11:17............1226
11:18............1233, 1236
11:19–27........1240
11:21–28........1239
11:22............1238
11:24............1239
11:26............1322
11:27............1306
11:30–31........1048
11:31............1290
11:34............562
11:35............1130
11:39............974n217
12:15............1261
13...............422
13:1.............705n606
13:2.............133
13:3–5...........925
13:4–5...........1048
13:9.............1248
13:15–23........924
13:16............589n330, 1248
13:22............478
13:24............72
14...............336n527
14–16............422
14:1–2...........221n329
14:1–4...........1248
14:8.............378n620, 1082
14:15............663n522
16:2.............558
16:5.............663n522
16:25............775
17:2.............867
17:3.............1050
17:10............1049
18:2.............1177
18:11............1264
18:22............1264
18:27............1157
18:28............1178
18:29............152n234
19–21............424
19:19–21........178
19:23–24........305n465
19:24............640
20:2.............1088, 1295
20:6.............305n465
20:10............305n465
20:18............1273
20:26............788
21:12............974n217

Ruth
1:1–2............1226
1:4..............264
1:6..............198n294
1:9..............976
1:16–17..........211n312, 284, 406
1:20.............567
2................1051
2:2..............984
2:4..............1132

2:10.............1303
2:12.............157n240, 1140n65
2:13.............1132n61
2:17.............847, 869
2:20.............974, 1329
2:23.............846, 850
3:2..............847
3:13.............370
3:16.............248n360
4................132n206
4:1..............1276
4:1–2............987
4:1–4............186
4:1–6............974
4:1–9............212
4:3–6............1277
4:4–6............1329
4:5..............1276
4:10–11..........1276
4:11.............137
4:13.............925
4:13–22..........190
4:15.............273
4:16.............271n392
4:16–22..........1096
4:18.............51, 341, 341n547, 396, 1100n42
4:18–22..........341
4:19–22..........507n161

1 Samuel
1................977
1:2..............133
1:3..............1288
1:3–5............924
1:5..............889n100
1:10.............232, 929
1:10–11..........853, 925
1:10–16..........924
1:11.............1048, 1127, 1288, 1290
1:19.............1156
1:20.............72
1:21.............1048, 1288
1:21–22..........1288
1:21–24..........924
1:22–28..........1048
1:24.............1298
1:24–25..........924
1:24–28..........853
2:2..............482
2:6..............1203
2:8..............736n668
2:11.............1102, 1146
2:12.............498
2:13.............542, 684
2:13–14..........724
2:13–17..........747
2:15.............742n692
2:15–17..........885
2:21.............198n294, 1203
2:22.............747, 754, 754n723, 924
2:25.............638, 1150
2:27–36..........747
2:28.............628, 724, 1101, 1202
2:29.............1203
2:29–34..........888
2:30.............726
2:34.............1101
3:1..............1259
3:1–2............247
3:3..............1020
3:4–8............204

3:10.............206
3:13.............1101
3:20.............1173
4:4..............710, 1140
4:5..............1155, 1295
4:10.............546, 1168
4:11.............1101, 1150
4:20.............314
5:2..............1141
6:7..............1220, 1290
6:8–9............1248
6:10.............1215
6:19.............1112
7:9..............629, 745
7:10.............559
7:12.............423
8:3..............336, 590
8:7..............673
8:9..............377n619
8:15–17..........1053
9:22–24..........889
9:24.............744
10:1.............742, 895
10:2.............1239
10:6.............1168
10:10............1258
10:10–13........1168
10:27............73
11...............424
11:2.............743
12:3.............1202
12:23............1165
13:4.............844
13:8–12..........629, 745
13:12............775, 1118
14:6.............152
14:11............319
14:24............589n330, 1290
14:25............378n620
14:28............1290
14:39............658
14:41............1278
14:41–42........738
14:42............1279
14:45............1299
14:47............1305
15:6.............161n247, 1261
15:7.............1186, 1312
15:9.............1053
15:22–23........1118, 1185, 1228
15:23............285, 1247
15:27............1196
15:30............612, 868n63
15:33............1259
16:6–12..........508
16:12............233n341
16:13............895
16:22............577n309
17...............348
17:4.............738
17:16............100
17:17............1083
17:18............1160, 1160n79
17:22............1086
17:26............498
17:34–35........970
17:42............233n341
17:43............644
18:6.............562
18:7.............1088, 1160
18:8.............1160
18:18............1158n76
18:25............636n459, 662n520
19:13............285n422
19:20............1258

Reference	Page(s)
20:9	501
20:41	484n109
21:2–7	951n179
21:5	1264, 1295, 1296
21:6	1111
21:8–9	1296
21:11–15	239n346
22:2	293
22:6	782
23:13	481, 1086
24:8	478, 694
25:1–2	1174
25:10	498n133
25:13	1086
25:15	83
26:1	1238
26:3	1238
26:12	55
27:8	1261
27:10	1159
27:12	844
28:6	232, 987, 1278
28:7–8	1247
30:1	1261
30:6	1183
30:9–10	1086
30:24	1086
30:25	568
31:4	529n213
31:7	1319
31:8	545

2 Samuel

Reference	Page(s)
1:10	739
1:11	739
1:11–12	998
1:12	998
1:21	1295
1:23	595
1:24	706
2:28	1155
3:14	636n459, 662n520
3:18	1174
3:21	1165
3:25	663n522
3:31	998
4:12	1195
5:1	974, 999n244
5:19	1179
5:21	1141
6:2	718, 1140
6:6–7	1112, 1113
6:18	1192
7:1	1296
7:7	1265
7:14	502n154, 746
7:22	482
7:23	1141
7:23–24	746
7:24	1041
8:4	546
8:6	847
8:10–11	1141
8:11–12	1261, 1299
8:12	1261
8:17	1266
9	698
9:7	885
10:6	844
11	141
11:1	1319
11:3	336n529
11:4	952
11:11	1295
12:13	868n63
12:16	788
12:22	783
12:24–25	1158
13:12	305n465, 994
13:14–15	304
13:17	704
13:18	324
13:20	346, 975, 999
13:33	527
14:2	741, 779
14:7	1276
14:24	697n587, 1131
14:26	73n74, 753, 873
14:33	478
15:2–6	990
15:6	285
15:10	1030
15:24	1159
16:6–7	644
16:13	644
16:14	765n747
16:21	314, 844
16:21–22	975
17:9	526n203
18:16	1155
18:20	1315n280
19:12–13	999n244
19:20	527
20:2	1202
20:20	1202
21:1	780
21:1–2	1290
21:6	1265
21:8–14	974
21:9	1265
21:13	1229
21:16	1183n97
21:17	1086
22:1	560
22:7	477
22:14	1183
22:34	422
23:2	1259
23:5	1216
23:9	1202
23:10	545
24:1	1299
24:2	1083n21, 1238
24:9	1088, 1238
24:15	1299
24:15–16	544
24:18–25	212
24:24	869

1 Kings

Reference	Page(s)
1:16	694n577, 785
1:23	694n577
1:28	710
1:39	895, 1030
1:42	1315n280
1:50	863
1:50–53	643
1:52	590n332
2:3	27
2:28–34	643
2:42	377n619
3:7	1278
3:8	1083n21
3:16	710
3:28	991
4:5	241n350
4:13	1237n167, 1305
4:21	689n571, 847
4:23	969
4:24	1261
4:28	1121
5:3	1261
5:4	1248
5:5	1183n97
5:11	726
6:1	458, 821, 1058, 1081
6:2	807n816, 810n826
6:7	126
6:18	126
6:20	828
6:22	752n707
7:31	1137n62
7:40	903
7:48	1111
7:51	1141, 1299
8:1	1290
8:2	1286
8:4	1104, 1296
8:6	1109
8:9	575n307
8:12	1110
8:22	528, 583
8:23	482
8:31	863
8:31–32	528n209, 658
8:39	1277
8:41–43	1006
8:46	869
8:47	868n63
8:50	378
8:63	76
8:65	1178
9:7	1150
9:26	1312, 1317
9:28	123
10:2	755, 847
10:5	710
10:8	902
10:10	755, 847
10:25	378
10:26	1296
11:2	1267
11:5	1245n185
11:17–18	1157
11:18	1159, 1309
11:21	276
11:26	557n273
11:33	1239, 1249
11:37	1165
12:8	199n296
12:18	1183
12:19	959
12:25–13:2	966
13:6	775
13:33	897
14:19	1169
14:23	786n790
15:15	1234, 1299
16:23	1276
16:34	1052n322
17:1	577n309
17:1–16	1035n298
17:12–13	847
17:22–24	483
18	24
18:36–37	521n193
18:38	73, 905n109
19	105n144
19:4	1167
19:8	207
19:10	105n144
19:14	105n144
19:16	1100
19:19	1265
19:21	1169

20:22............1319
20:28............1186
20:29............1168, 1264
21................212
21:1–13.........617
21:1–16.........1276
21:4.............1131
21:8–11.........990
21:13............677
21:26............116
22:11............1255
22:17............1278
22:19............718
22:20–22.......663n522
22:22–23........1247
22:24............1168

2 Kings
2:11–12..........80, 83n92
2:21.............567n294
2:24.............644
3:4..............1053, 1302, 1305
4:1..............635
4:29.............543
4:33.............1165
4:43.............704
5:1–14...........1035n298
5:13–14..........943
5:15.............936
5:27.............936
6:4–5............1244
6:13–17..........329
6:15.............1169
6:15–17..........292
6:18.............187n281
7:1..............1121
7:16.............1121
7:18.............1121
8:20.............959
8:27.............1158n76
9:7..............1295
9:13.............1030
10:33............1306
11:5–9...........48n26
11:10............1296
11:12............739
12:9.............717
12:9–15..........807
12:13............1296
12:16............873
13:20............1319
13:23............412
15:29............1261, 1306
16:7.............439
16:13............847
16:13–14.........1281
16:15............847
17:7–16..........790n797
17:17............986, 1247
17:23–24.........1261
17:25–27.........1043
17:26............1311
17:36............502n153
18:4.............1061, 1236
18:19–25.........478
19:11............1234
20:1–7...........525
20:2–6...........936
20:3.............737n675
20:7.............932, 934
21:6.............986
22:14............1226
23:10............992
23:15............777n766
23:24............285

23:26............608
23:33............1324
23:34............43, 171, 173
24:3.............608
25:8.............332
25:27............352

1 Chronicles
Book of.........825
1–9..............124
1:6..............120
1:7..............120
1:12.............1262
1:13.............1303
1:32.............226
1:42.............1317
1:43.............1254
1:46.............1267
2:3..............336n529
2:3–5............583
2:7..............1118, 1228
2:18–19..........583
2:20.............761
2:21–22..........1305
4:42–43..........1261
5:1..............975
5:1–2............410
5:25.............1306
5:25–26..........875
5:26.............1305
6:3..............1100
6:22–26..........1273
6:49.............177
6:50–53..........1266
6:78.............1080
9:1..............875, 1228
9:2..............1048, 1102
9:17–33..........1147n70
9:19.............1273, 1274
9:20.............1266
9:26.............1147n70
9:32.............1111
10:13............1118, 1228
11:13–14.........1245
12:6.............1274
12:8–14..........422
12:32............1084
15:15............717, 1138
16:18............1216
17:6.............1265
18:8.............1141
18:10–11.........1141
19:6.............219n326
19:19............1238
21:11–13.........1043n309
21:16............502n153
21:21–27.........1008
21:23............847
22:1.............1043n309
23:2–32..........1147n70
23:4.............1168
23:6.............1146
23:13............1100, 1132, 1158
23:14............1100
23:29............1216
24...............886
26:1.............1273
26:19............1273
26:20............1147n70
26:26............1296, 1299
26:26–27.........1141
27:30............142n222
28:2.............1140
28:11–12.........708
28:18............718

29:3.............595, 600, 698
29:9.............706
29:11............850
29:14............850
29:15............1031
29:25............1278
29:29............1245

2 Chronicles
Book of.........825
1:10.............1278
2:16.............1083n21
3:1..............204, 205, 208, 845, 1159
5:10.............575n307
5:12.............1155
6:41.............1160
7:1..............73, 905n109
7:9..............1287
7:13.............1180
8:13.............1282
8:14.............1147n70
11:14............1327
11:15............967
12:2.............875
13:12............1155, 1156, 1254
13:14............1155, 1156
14:11............78
16:14............1204
19:8–10..........1327, 1329
19:11............1168
20...............153
20:1.............1253n195
20:1–3...........905
20:2.............151, 153, 1253n195
20:7.............177
20:10............1253n195
20:19............1274
20:22............1253n195
23:1–7...........1327
23:7.............1147n70
23:9.............1296, 1327
23:18............1147n70
24:6.............708n614, 807n817
24:24............502, 507, 543n243
25:5.............1082
26:11............1168
26:16............752n710, 875
26:16–21.........936
26:18............1202
26:19............752n710
26:19–20.........1173
26:23............936n164
28:13............1183n97
28:19............875, 1121
28:22–25.........875
29:24............1194
29:29............905
29:34............1102n45, 1147n70, 1211
30:1–3...........1150
30:2.............1061
30:15............1211
30:16............1147n70
30:17............1211
30:27............903
31:3–7...........1213
31:5.............849, 1214
31:5–6...........1216
31:6.............1213
31:12............1147n70
31:19............1327
32:1.............1183n97
32:28............466n60
33:6.............666, 667

34:9 .... 1147n70
34:13 .... 1147n70, 1168
35:6 .... 206n308
35:11 .... 1211, 1216
35:12–13 .... 1147n70
35:13 542
36:14–16 875
36:21 825

Ezra
1:6 .... 853n42
2:43 1048
2:62–63 1213
2:63 1213
3:8 1081
4:14 .... 849, 1216
5:14 1141
6:9 1215
6:22 674
7:9 .... 1246, 1246n188
7:27 674
8:15–23 1083
8:20 .... 1084, 1102
8:23 788
8:31 .... 1246n188
9:2 1266
9:7 .... 608n368
9:12 1266
10:8 1276
10:10–11 1119
10:16 124
10:18 1102

Nehemiah
1:11 .... 351, 378
2:1–8 674
5:1–12 624
5:4–5 635
5:5 639
5:9 1033
5:12 1304
5:15 .... 618n418, 1033
6:14 1226
7:64 1102
7:64–65 1210
7:65 1213
7:70 .... 68n66
8:1 1017
8:1–3 924
8:5–8 869
8:7 1147
8:8 1195
8:9 1147
8:9–12 1016
8:18 1287
9 .... 454, 870n67
9:1–3 869
9:2 .... 608n368
9:7 132
9:7–8 .... 170n258
9:9–11 .... 563n289
9:10 .... 517, 589n327
9:11 559
9:12 1151
9:15 580
9:16 .... 589n327
9:16–17 775
9:17 .... 453, 783n781, 1274
9:19 1274
9:20 1168
9:30 1259
9:31 1061
10:14 1265
10:28–39 869
10:33 .... 1020n272
10:35 1214
10:37 1214
10:38 1214
10:39 1217
12:24–25 ..... 1147n70
12:44 1214
13:2 .... 1061, 1252
13:5 1217
13:10–11 1210
13:10–12 1053
13:10–13 848
13:12 1217
13:14 .... 737n675
13:15–21 ..... 48n26
13:16 920
13:23–27 1234
13:25 1289
13:25–27 1266
13:29 .... 1102, 1266

Esther
1:1 .... 847n32
1:6 706
1:14 1131
2:9 885
2:12 .... 847n32
3:7 542
3:10 .... 363n601
3:12 .... 363n601
3:15 .... 557n269
4:3 962
4:11 .... 694n577
4:14 558
4:16 378
6:1 1121
8:4 710

Job
1:1 .... 123n183
1:3 259
1:6 87
1:12 1247
1:20 998
1–2 60
2:7 934
2:7–8 525
2:9 217
2:10 1246
2:12 998
2:13 910
4:7 .... 613n395
6:4 1259
7:17 78
8:4 .... 613n395
8:20 .... 613n395
9:33 .... 192n287
11:13–20 ..... 613n395
11:15 74
11:19 775
12:12 987
12:25 .... 531n220
15:5 .... 60n48
15:12 .... 1200n119
16:14 .... 606n358
17:6 1174
18:13 935
19:3 .... 1185, 1248
19:7 95
21:4 .... 502n155
21:10 1215
21:20 1259
22:4–11 .... 613n395
23:17 1131
24:2 1273
27:1 .... 610n377
28:16 .... 717n627
29:5 1259
31:1 .... 614n398, 624
31:15 650
31:16–23 624
34:11 .... 874n73
34:28 181
34:37 1260
36:6 .... 874n73
37:18 44
38:7 87
41 45
41:23 .... 755n728
42:1–6 785
42:7 .... 613n395
42:11 312
42:14 264
42:15 1276
42:16 .... 431n708, 1082

Psalms
1:1 .... 271n395
1:1–6 667
1:2 621
1:3 .... 423, 589
2 148
2:3 250
2:4 127
2:8–9 139
2:10–12 202
3–7 .... 503, 579, 667
3:3 157
3:6 528
4:6 1131
4:8 249
6:1–5 936
6:4 1184
7:17 622
8:1 1278
8:3 522
8:3–8 645
8:4 .... 483n102
9–10 579
9:7 875
9:12 181
10:1–11 .... 613n395
10:4 621
10:18 670
12:2 610
13 .... 503, 579
13:1–4 468
13:5–6 468
14:1 621
14:4 1183
15:1–5 670
15:4 641
16:2 691
16:4 .... 610n376
16:6 .... 1273, 1319
17:1–15 .... 613n395
17:7 1184
18:2 157
18:9 1110
18:10 718
18:49 591
19:1 709
19:1–4 30
19:1–6 45
19:6 1151
19:7–14 667
19:13 1187
20:1–5 .... 629, 745
20:2–6 745
20:7 .... 628n432
22 .... 503, 579

SCRIPTURE INDEX

22:1 .... 468, 504	50:10–15 .... 844, 884	78:15–16 580
22:1–21 .... 853n43	50:12–13 1191	78:17–20 579
22:22 .... 526n206, 853	50:13 .... 727, 743n693	78:20 580
22:22–31 .... 853n43	50:14 887	78:23–25 580
22:25 .... 853, 1048	50:14–15 1048	78:24 1236
22:25–26 ...... 853n43	50:16 610	78:25 1166
22:27 823	51:1 .... 784, 1195	78:26 1169
23 .... 414, 423	51:2 1217	78:38 1204
23:1 411–412	51:3–4 1119	78:40–41 579
23:4 .... 479n88, 483n106, 487	51:4 .... 864, 1195	78:41 577
23:5 1191	51:5 1217	78:43 1178
23:6 348	51:7 .... 942, 1119, 1221	78:43–53 .... 529n214
24 316	51:10 .... 41, 41n16, 625	78:44–51 454
24:1 .... 527, 528, 536	51:16–17 .... 740, 1195	78:45 .... 523n195
24:3–4 893	53:5 1229	78:49–50 1204
24:3–6 315	55:3 223	78:51 .... 491, 492,
24:4 .... 315, 609	55:15 1203	78:56 579
25 579	56:12 853	78:57 639
27–28 579	56:12–13 .... 887, 1048	79:7 1183
27:1 194	57:4 423	80:1 .... 412, 718
27:4 625	57:9 591	80:1–2 .... 1061, 1095
27:8 1131	58:8 1122	80:3 1131
27:9 1131	58:10 .... 420, 520	80:7 1131
28:2 904	58:11 .... 157n240	80:10 .... 212n314
28:9 412	59:5 639	80:19 1131
29 44	60:1 .... 219n326	81:6–10 454
29:3–9 .... 617n412	60:10 1187	81:11–12 .... 490, 1247
29:10 .... 96n127	61:4 .... 1140n65	81:13–16 454
30:5 .... 740, 1241	63:4 904	83:6–7 .... 1261n200
31 503	64:2 223	83:8 .... 227, 1261n200
31:5 .... 468, 504	65:4 625	83:8–9 227
31:7 .... 479n87, 486	65:9–11 850	84 1274
31:9–10 783–784	65:12 1080	84:10 .... 621, 625, 936
31:19 782	66:1–4 622	85 1274
32:1 1151	66:6 .... 563n289	85:2 960
32:3–5 1119	66:13 629	86:8 482
32:5 .... 960, 1119, 1217	66:13–14 .... 1048, 1290	86:9–10 823
33:5 .... 180, 875	66:13–15 853	86:15 .... 453, 783n781
33:12 .... 173, 320, 786n787	66:13–16 745	87 1274
33:20 55	66:13–20 743	87:6 1085
34 .... 193, 239n346, 1259	66:14 1127	88 1274
34:7 292	66:15 629	89:10 1160
34:8 852	66:15–20 589	89:14 .... 180, 1030, 1331
34:19 .... 613n395	67:4 591	89:15 1131
35:13 .... 962, 962n198, 1287	68:1 .... 1160, 1161	89:17–18 1255
36:1 .... 618n418	68:5 875	89:20 .... 1100, 1330
36:8 889	68:6 670	89:35 1331
37:9 1172	68:8–9 1314	89:35–37 1173
37:10 .... 82n92	68:16 .... 616n408	90 82
37:11 .... 412n680, 1172	68:17 1160	90:3–10 82
37:18 1172	68:23 420	90:7–8 1248
37:22 .... 1150, 1172	68:30 1082	90:10 82
37:26 670	69 78	90:12 .... 1083n21
37:28 1150	69:9 .... 78, 1266	91:7 .... 1088, 1160
37:29 1172	69:23 .... 531n216	91:13 1241
38:1 1119	71:15 622	94:9 47
38:18 1119	72 420	95 .... 457n40
40:1–2 477	72:9 65	95:1–6 .... 457n40
40:9–10 591	73:1–14 .... 613n395	95:3 1160
40:10 1184	73:2–14 102	95:7 .... 860, 916
40:16 780	73:25 .... 157n240	95:7–11 .... 454, 457, 457n40, 579, 1061
41:4 784	74:12 523	95:8 578
41:6 610	74:13 .... 563n289	95:8–11 1061
41:13 875	74:14 45	95:9 577
42 1274	76:2 .... 153n235	95:10 1060
42:6 .... 410n675	76:11 622	95:11 1160
44 503	77 454	96:3–4 591
44–49 1274	77:11–20 .... 529n214	96:10 591
44:1 1260	78:1–8 .... 454, 529n214	98:3 1156
44:3 1131	78:5–7 974	99:1 .... 710, 718n633, 718, 956
45:6 1261	78:7 544	99:6 .... 1105, 1227
45:8 .... 847n32	78:12 1178	99:8 .... 1061, 1230
48:2 1323	78:12–16 454	100:1–5 .... 860, 916
50:5 .... 695n580	78:13 .... 563n289	
	78:14–41 1061	

101:5............623	119:1–176......667	5:15–23.........614n398
102:4–8.........1061	119:10..........859	5:16.............339
102:21..........526n206	119:11..........867	5:18–19.........624
103:1–2.........588n326	119:21..........1194	5:19.............422
103:3–14.......588n326	119:41..........1184	6:20.............623, 646
103:8............453, 783n781	119:105.........35, 729	6:20–35.........646
103:14..........52	119:113.........193n290	6:25.............1200n119
104:10–15......791	119:118.........1194	6:26.............1200n119
104:10–18......681	121:4–8.........1061, 1131	6:32–35.........787n792, 1120
104:14–15......691	122:1............621	7.................623
104:14a.........674	127:3............157n240	7:1–27..........624, 646
104:16..........1259	127:3–4.........111	7:25.............1120
104:29..........89	127:3–5.........81, 929	9:10.............62
104:34..........223	127:5............1259	10:18............323
105:1–3.........984	128:6............411	11:1.............624
105:1–4.........454	129:8............1132	11:3.............639
105:8–10.......1216	132...............423	11:26............365, 624
105:9............1290	132:7–8.........1140	12:10............645, 673, 1008
105:11..........1216	132:8............1160	12:23............60n48
105:15..........1100	132:9............896	13:12............167, 198, 270, 1165
105:24–45......454	132:17..........1255	13:13............527, 537
105:26–38......529n214	133:1............1211	13:19............1165
105:27..........517	133:2............895n102, 1000	14:21............623
105:34–35......531n217	133:3............1130	14:29............502n155
105:36..........491, 492, 1214	134:1............880	14:31............623
105:39..........1151	134:1–3.........1132	15:23............623
105:40..........1166, 1169, 1236	135:8............492	16:6.............618n418, 1185
105:40–41......580	135:8–9.........454, 529n214	16:7.............201
105:42..........1156	135:11..........1061	16:11............624
106...............868n63, 1060	136...............454, 562n288	16:14............1204
106:6–12.......454	136:10..........492	16:14–15.......1131
106:7............1183, 1185n100	136:10–15......454, 529n214	16:20............1258
106:7–12.......529n214	136:11..........1255	16:28............623
106:8–11.......563n289	136:13–14......563n289	16:33............738n679, 957, 1273, 1319
106:13–15......579	136:20..........1061	18:22............55
106:14..........577, 1166	136:25..........589n330	19:6.............775
106:15..........1170, 1176	139:13..........925	19:17............670
106:16–17......1199, 1200	139:13–15......650	19:26............612n391, 622, 646
106:17..........1203	139:16..........778n770	20:19............114
106:17–18......1060	139:20..........610	20:20............623, 673n539
106:19–23......454	139:21–22......995	20:25............1050, 1130
106:20..........775	141:1–2.........752	21:1.............378, 674
106:23..........792, 1185	143:6............528, 583	21:3.............180
106:24–26......1060	143:7............1131	22:6.............76n85
106:24–33......1061	144:3............479n87, 486	22:17............520n187
106:28..........1267	144:8............610	22:22–23.......624, 677
106:28–31......1060	144:11..........610	23:22............612n391, 622, 646
106:31..........1266	144:15..........629	24:25............1258
106:33..........1230	145:7............782	24:32............520n187
106:34–39......689	145:8............453, 783n781	25:15............663n522
106:36–39......1120	145:14–15......884	25:18............423
106:44–47......454	145:15–16......691, 844, 849	26:3.............648n487
106:45..........1015, 1156	146:4............89	26:28............248
106:47..........984	146:9............670	27:4.............1120
107:4............1238	147:9............674	27:23............520n187
107:19–22......887	147:14..........742n692, 854	27:23–27.......791
107:22..........853	147:19–20......1253	28:8.............623, 624
107:27..........617	148:7............45	28:13............1119
107:32..........862		28:24............646
109:18..........1122	*Proverbs*	29:19............648n487
110:1............314	1:1...............1253	29:24............867
110:2............1206	1:8...............623	30:1–9..........592
110:4............154	1:8–9...........646	30:7–9..........625
113:1–3.........984	1:22.............616n408	30:8.............610
113:3............591	1:31.............1248	30:9.............621, 1118
113:9............929	2:9...............180	30:11............646
114:1–3.........529n214	2:17.............1120, 1123	30:17............646
114:8............580	3:6...............498	31:2.............1048
115:5............1079	3:9–10..........1014	31:8–9..........625
115:12..........1156	3:34.............1173	31:10–31.......220, 224
116:4............984	4:15.............1120	31:13............706n610
116:14..........1048	5.................791	31:22............706
116:17..........887	5:1–23..........646	31:30............224, 261
116:17–18......853	5:3...............248	
119...............458	5:8...............624	

Ecclesiastes
1:2 72
1:5–10 130
2:8 .... 595, 600, 698
4:9–12 791
5:4 1289
8:11 308
12:11 412

Song of Solomon
1:7 339
3:4 1266
3:7 717
4:11 224
4:12 224
5:1 224
5:10 233
7:10 66
7:13–14 .... 272n396
8:6 1120
8:8–9 987

Isaiah
1:1 .... 697n586
1:4 1184
1:13 .... 1155, 1287
1:15 .... 528, 583
1:15–17 622
1:17 .... 653, 678
1:24 1259
1:29 .... 616n408
2:1 .... 697n586, 1259
2:1–4 826
2:2 418
2:2–4 .... 126n190
2:3 .... 207, 1159
3:14 669
4:1 1132
4:2 .... 736n668
4:5 .... 41n16, 1151, 1155
4:5–6 454
5:2 1217
5:8 1031
5:16 875
5:24 1184
5:30 530
6 .... 1166, 1185
6:1–2 .... 710, 718
6:1–3 696
6:2 .... 718n634, 1236
6:3 .... 484n109
6:4 904
6:5 .... 478, 479, 899
6:6 .... 720, 1204
6:6–7 1299
6:8 204
7 413
7:13 1228
7:14 1254
7:20 .... 493n129
8:3 1226
8:8 1254
8:10 1254
8:19 987
9:2 49
9:6 .... 201, 1267
9:13 528
10:1–2 669
11:2 1278
11:3–4 .... 985n231
11:6–9 .... 111, 972
11:14 1306
11:15 1312
11:16 454
13:1 .... 697n586
13:3 1295
14:4 1253
14:5 1206
14:12 1261
14:13 1323
14:22 1150
14:26 .... 502n153
15:1 1237
15:2 .... 1127, 1305
16:2 .... 1237n171
16:8–9 1302
16:10 1217
16:12 .... 1217n138
19:19 256
19:21–23 119
21:5 1295
21:17 200
22:5 .... 557n269
22:18 739
23:1 1261
23:12 1261
24:4–5 979
24:5 .... 850, 1124
24:5–6 1331
24:7 1127
24:16 639
25:6 854
25:6–9 922
26:10 522
26:19 937
26:21 968
28:16 1304
29:6 .... 198n294
29:14 1127
29:15 96
30:6 .... 1204, 1314
30:17 1088
30:18–19 1132
30:22 .... 777n765
30:29 1159
30:30 1278
31:5 .... 543n244
34:4 589
34:6 1192
34:11 41
34:17 1273
35:4–5 984
37:4 1165
37:6 1165
37:16 956
40:11 .... 412, 494n130, 928
40:12 738
40:14 46
40:19 .... 44, 777n765
40:28 .... 765n747
41:8 177
41:8–9 137
41:18–20 1259
41:22 527
42:1 1174
42:14 1167
43:2 108
43:5–7 1034
43:14–15 1080
43:23 756
44:6 .... 412, 1080
44:6–8 362
44:9 287
44:9–20 286
44:23 905
45:7 43
45:20 418
45:20–22 986
46:1 1305
46:3 .... 494n130
46:8 .... 738n680
46:9–10 206
46:10 1042
47:3 .... 628n435, 741n686, 975n218
47:9 .... 666n528
47:12 .... 666n528
48:1 609
48:9 1185
48:14 418
48:21 580
49:6 137
49:8–9 1035
49:8–12 1034
49:13 783
49:15 1167
49:15–16 737
49:18 1185
49:26 520
50:6 1174
51:2 .... 33, 137, 139
51:10 .... 563n289
51:10–11 454
52:11 1203
52:12 1157
53:1–12 .... 778n771
53:4 .... 407, 937
53:4–6 208
53:5 1217
53:5–12 .... 550n259
53:6 .... 864, 1217
53:7 .... 208, 329
53:8 961
53:10 876
53:11 .... 960, 1174, 1217
53:12 .... 867n62, 1217
54:5–6 1123
54:8 783
54:10 .... 783, 1184, 1266, 1267
55:1–3 366
55:7 783
55:11 1254
55:12 1259
56:4–5 .... 1007n251
56:6 270
56:7 842
57:15 57
57:17 1131
58:3 .... 962n198, 1287
58:5 .... 962, 962n198
58:5–10 624
58:6 .... 1035n298
58:6–8 962
58:8 1157
58:10 1287
59:2 1131
59:4 610
59:21 1186
60:1–5 826
60:3–4 1137
60:6 756
61:1 .... 895, 1035n298
61:1–2 .... 474, 1035
61:1–3 1035
61:3 944
61:6–7 825
61:8 850
63 425
63:1–7 425
63:3 1261
63:11–14 .... 563n289
65:4 .... 887n89
65:6–7 .... 608n368
65:8 1127

65:11..........271n394
65:16..........1290
65:17..........738n680, 937
65:25..........47
66:1............1140
66:13..........1167
66:19–20......115, 119
66:19–21......1137
66:20..........1137
66:21..........1137

Jeremiah
1:2............156
1:5............650, 925
1:6–7.........1169
1:8............1259
1:11...........1207
1:12...........1207
1:18...........212n316
2:2............967
2:10...........1261
2:13...........791
2:16...........1127
2:30...........528
3:1–2.........967
3:2............1187, 1196
3:6–10.......967
3:8............639
3:9............1120, 1187, 1196
3:11...........639
3:16...........738n680
3:20...........614, 639
4:2............1290
4:19...........1254
4:23...........41
4:23–26......961
5:2............609
5:21...........1228
6:4............1295
6:10...........506
6:20...........756
6:26...........998
7:9............609
7:18...........849
7:20...........524n200
7:29...........610
8:1............1229
9:3............423
9:10...........610n377, 1080
11:20..........843
12:4...........524n200
13:6...........73n74
13:23..........1172
13:26..........628n435, 741n686
13:26–27......1120
14:10–12.....740
14:14..........1247
14:20..........608n368
16:6...........1127
16:11–12.....608n368
16:18..........979n226
17:10..........843
17:14..........936
17:27..........1195
18:4...........100
18:6...........52
18:17..........1132
20:11..........765n747
21:5–6........502n153
21:14..........1248
22:3...........653, 669n532, 678
22:13..........623
22:23..........477
23:2...........1278
23:7–8........454

25:23..........227
24:7...........1041
25:27..........380
27:15..........1203
29:23..........305n465
30:11..........785n782
31:1...........1041, 1117
31:9...........491n122, 502n154, 746, 1272
31:12..........846n28, 1191, 1214
31:19..........1260
31:20..........491n122, 783
31:30..........1184
31:32..........1120
31:33..........1117, 1267
32..............974
32:6–25......213n321
32:7...........1032
32:17..........158
32:27..........1277
32:35..........992
32:40..........850, 1216
32:42..........1246
33:13..........1053
33:21..........743, 1266
33:26..........412
34:8–22......637
34:18..........888, 926n146
37:3...........1165
38:19..........529n213
39:16–18.....1246
40:3...........1304
42:2–4........1165
42:5...........1304
42:6...........1260
42:9...........1165
42:12..........378
43:12..........1141
43:12–13.....1254
44:8...........1195
44:15–19.....1048
44:23..........1304
44:27..........1246
46:4...........1290
46:9...........120
46:28..........785n782
47:4...........120
48:1...........1305
48:15..........1140
48:22..........1305
48:23..........1302
48:32..........1302
48:33..........1248
48:37..........1127
48:45–46.....1239
48:46..........1239
49:2...........1254
49:3...........1141
49:8...........227
49:12–13.....1121
49:16..........595
49:19..........1244
50:15..........1295
50:44..........1244
51:28..........1295
51:63..........1165
51:64..........1165
52:33–34.....885

Lamentations
2:7............1183
2:15...........1260
2:20...........1043
3:22–23......355

3:25–26......355
4:10...........1043
5:18...........1043

Ezekiel
1:1............696n585
1:5............69
1:5–6.........718
1:5–11........718, 986
1:22...........44
1:26–28......696, 904
1:26–28a.....696n585
1:28...........113
1:28b..........696n585
2:1–2.........127n198
3:24...........1278
3:26...........192, 192n287
4:3............849
4:14...........887n89
5:1............1128
5:1–2.........1129
5:1–4.........1127
5:5............1040
5:9–10........502, 507
6:5............1229
7:15...........1180
8:3–11........621
8:11...........752n710
10:8...........708
10:15..........69
10:20–22.....718
11:20..........1041
11:24..........1258
12:22..........1253
12:23..........1253
12:25..........481, 782n779
12:27..........697n586
13:7...........1259
13:8...........610
14:12–23.....182
14:13–23.....177
14:14..........95
16..............967
16:3...........1179
16:4–5........354n578
16:8...........1120, 1123, 1290, 1292
16:10..........706, 1110n46
16:13..........706
16:15..........1187
16:32..........1120
16:36..........975n218
16:37..........975n218
16:42..........1266
16:44..........1253
16:49..........181
16:59..........1292
17:3–6........1259
17:5...........423
17:13..........1292
17:18–19.....1292
18:2...........1253
18:3...........1253
18:28..........369, 369n607
19..............420
19:10..........1259
19:12..........774n754
20:1...........232
20:7–8........1164
20:8–9........1205
20:12–13.....762
20:13–24.....1061
20:18..........1271
20:20–21.....762
20:21..........1271

20:33–34 ......502n153	43:19............909	6:2...............940
20:34–35 1204	43:20............1068, 1119, 1194, 1267	6:10............1069, 1187, 1196
20:37............1053	43:22............1236	7:12.............724
20:41............743, 844	43:24............849n38, 1215	8:6...............777n765
21:6...............477	43:26............1267	8:13.............740
21:14............1260	44:11............1216	9:10............1061
21:17............1260	44:15............1101	10:4.............1292
21:21............1247	44:15–16......1266	11:1.............491n122, 494
21:26............739	44:18............896	12:3.............233
21:27............420	44:19............879, 1211	12:12...........636n459, 662n520, 1158
22:10............975n218	44:23............1066	12:13............1227
22:12............624	44:28–30......889	13:14............1203
22:13............1260	44:29............1215	
22:26............825, 911, 1145	45:1...............1193	*Joel*
22:30............1185	45:4...............1216	1:14.............862, 1287
23..................967	45:11............573n302	1:18.............557n269
23:6...............706	45:12............873n69, 1052	2:1–11..........530n215
23:10............975n218	45:18–20......1194	2:10.............530
23:18............975n218	46:4...............1061	2:12–13........962
23:29............975n218	46:11–15......1192	2:13.............454, 783n781
23:47............1203	46:13............1061	2:15.............1287
24:15–24......999	46:15............1061	2:23.............1179
24:17............910	47..................960	2:24.............1217
27:6...............1261–1262	47:1–12........828	2:28.............193
27:7...............706	47:12............589	2:31.............520
27:31............1127	47:14............1322	3:5...............1141
28:11–13......738n677	47:15–20......121	3:9...............1295
28:13............53, 1084	47:17............1323	3:13.............1261
28:13–14......53	47:18............1322	
28:14............207	48:35............825	*Amos*
28:16............207		1:15.............1127
28:22............557n272	*Daniel*	2:6–7...........621
28:22–23......502, 507	1:2...............126, 1141	2:10.............1061
29:18............1127	1:5...............885, 902	2:12.............1061
30:5...............120	2:14.............332	3:2...............72n70
30:21–25......502n153	2:16–19........352	3:4...............1183
30:24............477	3..................412n678	3:7...............93, 180
31–32...........331	3:25.............412n678	4:7...............101
32:8...............530	3:28.............412n678	5:1...............610n377
33:3...............1155	4:31.............1245n185	5:11–12........669
33:11............994	5:14.............363n598	5:15.............784
33:14–16......994	5:23.............872	5:25.............1061
33:24............33n11	5:29.............1111	6:14.............1178
33:26............1123	5:30.............872	7:2...............1184
34:6...............859, 1193	6:8...............1291	9:4...............1265
34:23............1267	6:12.............1291	9:5...............1165
34:25............1266, 1267	6:16.............1291	9:7...............120
34:27–28......1267	7:13.............127n198	
34:30............1041	8:6–7...........1255	*Obadiah*
34:31............916	9:16.............608n368	4..................595
35..................250	10:3.............1287	
35–36...........318	10:12...........1287	*Jonah*
36:20............1118	11:8.............1141	1..................336n527
36:22–32......825	11:30............1262	1:7...............1279, 1322
36:23............1331		1:9...............122
36:28............1117	*Hosea*	2:5...............1312
37:1...............126n190	1:2...............1120	2:9...............853, 1048
37:10............89	2..................993	3..................189
37:23............1041	2:2...............967, 1120, 1123	3:3...............205n305, 212n314
37:26............850, 1266, 1267	2:5...............706n610, 967	3:4...............189n283, 775n760
37:27............1041, 1267	2:9...............249, 706n610	3:9...............362
38..................118n163	2:10.............974n217	4:2...............454, 783n781
38:6...............119	2:13.............779	4:8...............1167
38:16............418	2:14.............663n522	4:11.............501
38:19............1266	2:16.............1123	
39:23............1118	2:21–22........1040	*Micah*
39:23–24......1131	2:23.............1041	1:1...............1259
40..................53	3:1...............849	2:2...............1031
40:2...............126	4:1–3...........524n200	2:4...............610n377, 1216
40:39............843	4:14.............614n398, 987	2:5...............1273
40:46............1266	4:15.............1264	3:3...............547
42:13............881, 1213	5:4...............967	3:8...............1168, 1278
42:17–18......1213	5:8...............1155	4:2...............1159
42:20............1216	5:10.............1273	5:2...............1260
43:7...............825		

6:4 1226
6:5 . . . . 1061, 1245
6:7 . . . . 491, 876
7:4 . . . . 557n269
7:14 . . . . 483n106, 1302
7:14–15 1061
7:17 . . . . 65, 1122
7:18 960

Nahum
3:5 . . . . 628n435, 741n686

Habakkuk
1:3 1183
1:13 864
2:6 . . . . 610n377
3:2 783
3:3 1310
3:4 . . . . 788n794
3:7 1172
3:10 1183
3:19 422

Zephaniah
1:12 1246
1:18 1266

Haggai
1:13 . . . . 165n253
2:13 887
2:17 528

Zechariah
2:8 600
3 . . . . 68, 312
3:1–7 825
4:2 1111
5:2–4 875
5:3–4 1290
5:4 . . . . 609, 1289, 1290
5:5–11 126
7:12 . . . . 1168, 1259
8:2 1266
8:3 . . . . 207, 1159
8:5 199
8:8 1041
8:16–17 875
9:9–10 420
11 260
11:16 . . . . 774n754
12:1 1202
12:10 . . . . 355, 491
12:13 1061
14:6–7 43
14:16–21 1017
14:20–21 825
14:21 684

Malachi
1:1–5 . . . . 233, 236
1:2–5 . . . . 318, 320
1:6 612
1:7 1191
1:7–8 1007
1:8 . . . . 542, 821
1:12–14 1050
1:14 . . . . 1007, 1290
2:1–9 825
2:4 . . . . 743, 1123
2:4–8 1266
2:7 . . . . 165n253, 911
2:13 844
2:14 . . . . 614, 1120
2:14–16 639
2:17 102

3:6 457
3:9–10 1218
3:10 101
4:2 1002
4:4 1173

Matthew
1:1–17 335
1:3–5 1096
1:17 . . . . 84n96
1:19 993
1:21 . . . . 224, 274, 374, 425, 1254
1:23 1254
2 473
2:2 . . . . 1261, 1262
2:11 847
2:16–18 929
3:4 920
3:8 875
3:13 1278
3:13–17 899
3:16 1278
3:17 . . . . 92, 1188
4 348
4:1 . . . . 961, 1278
4:2 788
4:4 1166
4:7 . . . . 577, 579
4:8–9 148
4:10 148
4:19 689
5:1 730
5:3–10 622
5:5 . . . . 412n680, 1172
5:13 996
5:16 . . . . 495, 730
5:17 622
5:20 661
5:21–22 623
5:21–30 661
5:22 . . . . 309, 620
5:23–24 . . . . 622, 875
5:27–28 . . . . 623, 977
5:27–30 624
5:29 495
5:29–30 . . . . 688, 690
5:30 495
5:35 . . . . 970, 1160
5:37 . . . . 622, 641
5:38–42 . . . . 651n503
5:38–45 623
5:43 . . . . 679, 988n235
5:43–45 988
5:44–45 679
5:45 564
6:6 621
6:9 622
6:10 1188
6:11 . . . . 629, 691
6:12 876
6:19–21 . . . . 621, 625
6:25–33 630
6:25–34 . . . . 629, 691
6:26 674
6:28–30 68
6:33 . . . . 57, 621
7:11 . . . . 494n130
8:1–3 730
8:1–4 1117
8:11 . . . . 412, 923
8:17 937
8:20 214
8:22 689
9:9 689

9:20 . . . . 1069, 1195
9:27–30 730
9:29 1002
9:32–33 551
9:35–36 937
9:36 . . . . 654, 1278
10:10 1218
10:14–15 188
10:16 469
10:28 1202
10:29 . . . . 204, 681
10:37 778
11:5 . . . . 937, 1002
11:5–6 984
11:28 . . . . 1017, 1160
11:28–29 766
11:28–30 . . . . 85, 503, 549, 630, 691
12:5 . . . . 1068, 1281
12:8–13 1017
12:18 . . . . 913, 1174
12:22 551
12:34 1186
12:43 961
12:48 1000
13:24–30 181
14:7 1290
14:36 . . . . 1069, 1195
15:8–9 621
15:11 1207
15:18 . . . . 1186, 1207
15:18–19 1166
15:19 1291
15:36 625
16:24 689
17:1 789
17:1–13 1159
17:2 455
17:5 . . . . 208, 789
17:24 . . . . 873n70
18:1–34 389
18:21–22 77
18:21–35 . . . . 671, 680
18:23–35 876
19:4–6 1124
19:5–6 56
19:8 1124
19:11 56
19:13–15 928
19:14 111
19:19 . . . . 988n235
20:30–34 247
20:34 . . . . 654, 1002
21:1–8 421
21:12 873
21:31–32 342
21:33–41 333
22:20–21 47
22:30 88
22:32 83
22:37–40 . . . . 603n352, 762, 825, 988
22:39 . . . . 830, 988n235
23:5 1195
23:19 . . . . 1204, 1213
23:27 1229
23:37 928
24:36–39 102
24:37–41 . . . . 564n292
24:44 103
25:25 157
25:31–33 564
26:2 455
26:26–29 922
26:28 . . . . 970, 1191

26:36–46 208	2:49 928	1:20 748
26:39 . . . . 296, 1267	2:51 646	1:29 . . . . 32, 108, 203, 208,
26:41 1267	3:17 564	550n259, 865, 870,
26:42 1267	3:33 1084	1149, 1256, 1287
26:45 1267	3:38 . . . . 81n91, 88, 1188	1:33 1278
27:6 . . . . 1048n312	4:1 1188	1:36 1149
27:30 1174	4:1–13 1267	1:51 . . . . 129, 257
27:33 . . . . 208, 970	4:2 100	2:6 . . . . 420, 950
27:45–46 1149	4:18–19 474	2:9 420
27:46 . . . . 296, 468, 504	4:18–21 829	2:17 . . . . 78, 1266
27:50 1149	5:8 899	2:19 . . . . 78, 1140
27:50–51 730	5:14 . . . . 821n4	2:21 1140
27:57–59 252	6:19 953	3:5 1122
28:16 1159	6:27–31 430	3:14–15 1240
28:18–20 1159	6:28 1132	3:14–16 1061
28:19 1161	6:34 670	3:16 . . . . 374, 1240
28:20 . . . . 479n88, 487, 730	6:44 562	3:36 1090
28:20b 1024	7:14 1002	4:5 267
	7:22 937	4:6–7 219
Mark	8:1–3 1141	4:13–14 267
1:1 . . . . 41n15	8:43–48 953	4:17–18 267
1:11 845	9:59–60 1002	4:24 . . . . 267, 782
1:13 111	9:60 910	5 1002
1:40–42 . . . . 653, 937	10:1 . . . . 118n162	5:19 913
2:15–17 922	10:18 551	5:30 . . . . 985n231
2:27 . . . . 611, 612	10:27 . . . . 988n235	5:46 . . . . 473n79
3:7–10 953	10:28 1130	6 1017
3:22–30 . . . . 1024n283	10:29 988	6:1–13 580
3:28–30 1024	10:29–37 679	6:27 581
5:1 919	10:37 . . . . 679, 988	6:30–31 580
5:1–13 551	12:16–21 621	6:31 . . . . 1166, 1236
5:13 919	14:12–14 886	6:31–35 455
5:25–34 1117	14:13 474	6:35 . . . . 580, 850
5:41 1117	14:26 . . . . 56, 778	6:38 . . . . 913, 985n231
5:41–42 1002	15:20 . . . . 143, 299	6:40 1241
6:17–18 995	16:31 1184	6:41 1164
7:1–4 950	17:12 946	6:41–58 1166
7:10 . . . . 821n4	17:13 946	6:48–50 1061
7:10–13 . . . . 612, 622	17:14 946	6:49–51 581
7:11 . . . . 1048n312	17:28–30 190	6:50–55 922
7:19 . . . . 747, 917	19:8 657	6:51 850
7:20–22 826	19:8–10 875	6:56 970
7:32–33 1002	19:9–10 1119	6:61–66 1164
8:22–25 . . . . 54n38	22:1–23 . . . . 455, 550	7:23 1068
9:7 1140	22:14–20 1017	8:3–11 993
9:24 182	22:19–20 . . . . 855, 890	8:5 . . . . 821n4
9:35 293	22:20 . . . . 455, 457, 698	8:29 913
9:42 1230	22:42 183	8:36 1041
10:8 1124	22:44 970	8:39 . . . . 33n11
10:11 . . . . 614n398	22:51 1002	8:44 . . . . 31, 66
10:13–16 730	23:34 970	8:56 . . . . 70, 203, 208
10:45 . . . . 757, 778n771, 845,	23:46 . . . . 468, 504	8:58 . . . . 455, 486, 1132,
970, 1017	24:26 32	1140
11:20–21 1130	24:27 1061	9:2 . . . . 874n73
11:21 1246	24:30–31 922	10:10 1256
11:25 . . . . 613n394	24:46–47 32	10:12 424
12:31 . . . . 988n235	24:50–51 906	10:12–13 260
12:33 . . . . 988n235		10:18 970
12:34 . . . . 119, 133, 226	John	10:22 . . . . 919n131
14:3 937	1:1 . . . . 41n15, 1140	10:28 280
14:24 . . . . 778n771	1:1–14 46	11:25 946
15:17–18 252	1:12–13 202	11:40–44 . . . . 572n296
15:38 963	1:14 . . . . 440, 455, 711, 730,	11:50–51 1259
15:42 . . . . 1149n71	748, 748n703,	12:31 551
	749n705,	12:37 1184
Luke	815, 815n842,	12:49–50 1130
1:1–4 . . . . 445n21	815n844,	13:8 899
1:7 133	974n215, 1117,	13:34 680
1:8–9 886	1140, 1185, 1255	14:1–4 1002
1:27 1226	1:14–18 793	14:3 1161
1:32 1261	1:14a 793	14:6 . . . . 621, 814, 906
2:24 . . . . 928, 929	1:14b 793	14:9 793
2:29–32 397	1:16 793	14:15 728
2:29–38 929	1:17 . . . . 793, 1185, 1255	14:16 730
2:41 928	1:18 . . . . 696, 793	14:17 1024

14:18............1024	7:44.............1143	6:16–23.........473
14:21............568, 728	7:54–60.........1022n279	6:23.............68, 85, 91, 309, 355,
14:23............728, 814	8................870n67	1223
14:26............730	9:4..............206	7................69
14:27............906, 1045	10...............870n67	7:10.............1130
15:2.............1127	10:10–16.......923	7:12.............35
15:10............568	10:12............923n140	7:13.............1166
15:14............709	10:28............923	8:3..............1240
15:14–15........183	10:38............1278	8:11.............214, 1161
16:7.............730	11:18............923	8:14.............92
16:11............551	11:29–30.......1325	8:15.............494n130
16:13............1024	12:25............1325	8:18.............333, 355
17:1–26.........913	13:2.............1109, 1144	8:18–22........865
17:2.............181	13:3.............1144	8:19–21.........92, 1029, 1035
17:5.............181	13:9.............1278	8:20–23.........69
17:15–16.......973	14:23............1167	8:21.............937
17:17............1196	15:8–9..........923	8:23.............937, 1283
17:19............899, 913	15:17............318, 1132	8:28.............61–62, 69, 262, 280,
17:21............258	15:19–20.......830	333, 355, 1096,
17:26............1025	16:15............173	1248
18:36............1207	17:16–31.......621	8:28–30.........214
19:2–3..........1111	18:9–10.........487	8:29.............407
19:14............547, 1149n71	18:18............622	8:31–32.........1045
19:20............865	19:35............1168	8:32.............209, 581, 845
19:26–27.......646	20:3–5..........826	8:35.............581
19:33–36.......547, 550n259	20:7.............906	8:37–39.........581
19:34............970	20:19............1172	8:38–39.........236, 486
19:36............455, 1150	21:24............1129	9–11.............619, 712
20:27............182, 366	23:1–5..........674	9:4..............1319
	23:5.............674	9:7–9............171
Acts	26:18............1161	9:11.............1260
1:6..............1035	27:9.............1287	9:14–16.........231, 233
1:8..............32, 129, 138	28:25............1168, 1259	9:15.............235
1:9..............1161		9:15–16.........782n779
1:26.............1273	*Romans*	9:17.............526n206
2................870n67	1:1..............1034	9:19.............490n121
2:1..............682, 1014, 1283	1:5..............1228	9:20.............52
2:1–4...........1024	1:18.............1299	9:20–21.........490n121
2:3..............906	1:19–32.........584	9:22–29.........490n121
2:7–11..........129	1:21.............1165	10:5.............821n4
2:17.............229	1:24.............1248	10:9–10.........869n64
2:23.............333, 1248	1:24–27.........993	10:10............1186
2:23–24........390, 433	1:24–32.........827	10:17............1184
2:38–39.........229	1:26.............978	11:16............1284
2:39.............98, 224, 414, 1186,	1:26–27.........1248	11:22............1061
1216	1:28.............1248	11:29............311
2:42.............621, 855	1:28–32.........490	11:33–36........490n121
3:25.............124	2:4..............373	12:1.............206, 619, 629, 675,
3:25–26.........138	2:15.............584	712, 827, 845, 1147,
4................870n67	2:16.............584	1283
4:12.............274, 320	3:20.............867	12:1–2..........258, 1144
4:27.............243	3:23.............320, 876, 908, 963	12:3–8..........1141
4:27–28.........243	3:24–25.........963	12:4–7..........1147
4:36–37.........1054	3:25.............718, 730	12:6–8..........1141
5:1–4...........1214	4................40	12:9.............995
5:1–11..........622	4:5..............231	12:13............624
5:5..............1150	4:6..............1132	12:14............1132
5:10.............1150	4:11.............113	12:15............333, 625
5:11.............626	4:11–12.........171, 258	12:17–18........243
5:21.............1167	4:15.............1166	12:18............382
5:29.............469	4:16.............124	12:19............430, 1172, 1299
6................746	4:16–17.........137, 433	13...............309
6:1–3...........1325	4:19–21.........173	13:1.............1293
6:3..............1278	5:1..............320, 374, 853	13:1–7..........673, 674
6:4..............746	5:3–5............355	13:4.............1331
6:6..............1101	5:8..............600	13:4–5..........1265
6:7..............946	5:9..............1090	13:7.............624
6:14.............1262	5:10.............824, 1161	13:8.............876, 985
7:14.............396n647, 466n55	5:12.............31	13:9.............603n352, 613, 830,
7:22.............471n73	5:19.............65	988n235
7:30.............1080, 1159, 1314	5:20.............425, 1184, 1274	13:14............899, 1196
7:32.............412	6:1..............784	15:16............827
7:35.............1177	6:9..............1161	15:8–12.........1137
7:39.............774	6:12.............74, 1304	15:9–12.........1161
7:42.............1247	6:14.............31	15:10............1262

15:16............1196	15:22............59, 69, 427	5:16–17.........1196
15:25–28.......671	15:23............1283	5:22–23.........1172
16:1–2..........1141	15:24............551	6:1–2............867
16:20............1241	15:24–28......563	6:6............848, 890
	15:26............1241	6:10............624
1 Corinthians	15:35–49......52	6:16............296, 414
1:3..............1132	15:51............85	
1:21–24........970	15:54–56......913	*Ephesians*
1:26–29........508	15:55–56......1241	1:2..............1132
1:27–29........473, 486	16:1–3..........1325	1:3..............262, 630, 1130, 1132
1:29.............486		
2:1–5............912	*2 Corinthians*	1:3–12..........139
3:16.............1141	1:3–4............998	1:3–14..........32, 433
4:7..............850	2:15–16.........1284	1:4..............180
5:5..............1150, 1246	2:16............899	1:14............229
5:6..............1303	3................789	1:16............746
5:6–8............1017	3:3–11..........789	1:21............551
5:7..............455, 550, 1283	3:7–11..........789	2:1–3............92
6:9..............614, 614n399, 994	3:10............455	2:6..............1161
6:9–11..........183, 187	3:18............455, 790	2:8–10..........158, 162, 301
6:11.............994	4:6..............49, 455, 790, 793	2:14–16.........855
6:16............56, 1124	4:18............1180	2:16............381
6:18............689, 1122	5:7..............1180	2:21............1141
6:19............953	5:17............32, 69, 92, 980	3:5..............1259
6:19–20.........1002	5:18............824	3:17–19.........1045
6:20............1106	5:19............865	3:18–19.........630
7:1..............56	5:21............162, 207, 267, 342, 864, 865, 1241, 1287	3:20............139
7:2..............1291		4:2..............1172
7:3–5............624, 791, 977	6:14............92, 1265	4:7–12..........1141
7:4–5............1291	6:14–18.........243	4:8..............1161
7:8..............56	6:16............440, 748, 815, 1117, 1267	4:11–16.........1141
7:29–35.........56		4:15............271, 985
7:39............1334	6:16–18.........758	4:24............312, 899
8:1–13..........923	6:18............494n130, 1259	4:25............622
9:9..............1218	7:1..............758, 1071, 1320	4:26–27.........623
9:12............1218	7:9–10..........1187	4:28............624
9:13–14.........890	7:10............962, 1119	4:29............623
9:14............848, 1218	8:1–5............624	4:30............1024
10:1–13.........454	8:1–15..........671	4:32............613n394, 623, 671
10:4............580, 1061, 1256	8:5..............1214	5:1–2............826
10:6............1061	8:8–15..........691	5:2..............680, 845
10:6–11.........34	8:9..............671	5:5–6............1299
10:7–8..........1061	8:13–15.........624	5:6..............1090
10:8–9..........1268	8:15............573n303	5:21............1293
10:9............1061, 1256	8:20–21.........1325	5:22–24.........1293
10:11............29, 1061, 1262	9:1–15..........671	5:22–33.........624
10:11–12........1268	9:6–7............1016	5:24............58
10:13............1268	9:7..............706, 806	5:25............1124
10:14............689	11:2–3..........89n109	5:25–27.........58, 1009
10:17............855	11:8–9..........1141	5:26............1196
10:18–22.......923	11:14............89n109	5:27............1003
10:24............1306	12:7–10.........578	5:28............1124
11:12............66	12:9............78, 296, 1174	5:31............1124
11:17–30.......758	13:11............382	5:32............58
11:20–21.......890		6:1..............1293
11:20–22.......1191	*Galatians*	6:1–3............612, 613n395
11:23–26.......495	1:3..............1132	6:2..............673n539
11:24–25.......355	1:7–8............1246	6:3..............1319
11:25............698n589	1:10............1034	6:4..............496
11:26............355, 855	2:20............826	6:9..............641
11:27............690	3................160, 161	6:10–11.........620
11:27–30.......1150	3:12............1130	6:13............1114
11:27–32.......890	3:13............1045, 1106, 1195, 1241	
11:30............690, 1150		*Philippians*
11:32............690	3:14............1045, 1130, 1132, 1216, 1241	1:1..............1034
12:1–29.........1141		1:3–5............746
12:4–26.........625	3:16............171	1:6..............35, 70
12:25–27.......625	3:28............124	2:1..............494
13:8............1168	4:4..............1017	2:3..............1172
13:9............229	4:19............1167	2:4..............890
14:12............1278	4:21–31.........201	2:5–8............827, 845
15................432	4:29............199	2:5–11..........390, 407
15:9............1274	4:30............174	2:6–8............963
15:19............32, 148	5:14............830, 988n235	2:9–10..........139, 601
15:20............429, 1017, 1283	5:16............1114	2:9–11..........366, 537, 622

2:10 . . . . 78, 425	4:13 621	4:1 1060
2:10–11 469	4:16 621	4:1–2 1165
2:15 1003	5:3–4 . . . . 612n392, 623	4:1–3 1185
2:17 . . . . 827, 1283, 1284	5:3–16 646	4:1–9 1256
2:30 1110	5:4 644	4:1–11 1160
3:10–11 296	5:8 . . . . 612n392, 622	4:1–13 49
3:20 899	5:16 . . . . 612n392, 623	4:9 766
4:6–7 667	5:17 . . . . 673n539, 741, 747	4:9–10 1017
4:7 1045	5:17–18 1218	4:13 . . . . 96, 844
4:11–13 625	5:18 . . . . 890, 1218	4:14 . . . . 457, 1063
4:13 . . . . 585, 620	5:20 1230	4:15 . . . . 864, 1188, 1196, 1267
4:16–17 1141	6:1 641	4:16 . . . . 698, 827
4:18 . . . . 844, 1284	6:6–8 625	5:1–3 . . . . 730, 742
4:19 . . . . 629, 630, 691	6:11 621	5:3 908
	6:16 696	6:5 1185
Colossians		6:6 1185
1:3–4 746	*2 Timothy*	6:7 1130
1:9 746	1:5 1334	6:13 . . . . 776n763
1:13 . . . . 35, 486	2:3 1114	6:13–14 207
1:15 963	2:4 1114	6:13–17 1290
1:19–20 855	2:12 1161	6:17 1290
1:20 963	2:13 . . . . 139, 1044n310	6:20 . . . . 154, 1267
1:29 585	2:22 . . . . 621, 689	7:1–3 1267
2:11–12 175	3:12 243	7:3 154
2:15 1141	3:16 441	7:4–7 154
2:16 49	3:16–17 . . . . 667, 831	7:7 401
3:5 . . . . 621, 625	4:4 . . . . 29n5, 1303	7:9–10 155
3:5–6 1299	4:6 . . . . 827, 1281, 1284	7:11–28 1267
3:10 899		7:16 827
3:18 1293	*Titus*	7:23–27 730
3:20 . . . . 622, 623, 1293	1:1 1034	7:23–8:2 748
3:21 496	1:2 1256	7:24–25 827
4:1 641	1:5 1167	7:25 . . . . 946, 1063
	1:5–9 592	7:26–27 913
1 Thessalonians	1:6 1124	7:26–28 864
1:2 746	1:7 1218	7:27 154
1:10 550	1:14 1303	8:1 827
2:7 1167	1:15 . . . . 1166, 1186	8:1–7 455
4:3 . . . . 1124, 1299	2:4 1334	8:5 . . . . 708n615, 1143
4:3–7 980	2:9–10 641	8:6–13 . . . . 457, 726
4:6 1299	2:11–12 . . . . 1063, 1196	8:10 1267
4:7 . . . . 1071, 1124	2:14 758	9:1–14 455
4:7–8 1299	3:7 1256	9:1–10:18 1140
5:9 . . . . 1090, 1299		9:2 . . . . 752n707
5:12 . . . . 673n539, 747	*Philemon*	9:4 . . . . 575n307, 752n707
5:27 . . . . 1289, 1290	16–21 1034	9:5 . . . . 1140n64, 1140n65
		9:11 899
2 Thessalonians	*Hebrews*	9:11–12 . . . . 748, 827, 864, 963, 970
1:11–12 1025	1:2 . . . . 827, 1262	9:11–14 1287
2:6–7 1204	1:3 . . . . 601, 789, 827, 963, 1184	9:13–14 . . . . 829, 1223
2:13 . . . . 1196, 1283	1:8 . . . . 1140, 1261, 1262	9:14 . . . . 757, 913, 1008
3:10–11 624	2:4 1168	9:15–28 . . . . 455, 698
	2:10–11 899	9:19 1221
1 Timothy	2:14 . . . . 551, 974n215	9:22 . . . . 73, 864, 1069, 1128
1:3 621	2:14–15 563	9:23–24 959
1:10 . . . . 614n399, 994	2:17 748	9:24 1140
1:15 1274	2:18 . . . . 1188, 1196	9:24–26 730
1:15–16 909	3 457	9:25–28 748
1:17 1267	3–4 1061	9:26 1262
1:18 1114	3:1 . . . . 457, 748, 899	10:4–10 107
2:1–2 674	3:1–6 788	10:5 827
2:5 748	3:2 1174	10:5–7 1003
2:8 904	3:5 . . . . 1096, 1173	10:10 748
2:12–15 70	3:6 . . . . 1096, 1174	10:11–14 963
3:1 1111	3:7–11 . . . . 454, 457	10:12 827
3:1–13 . . . . 590, 592, 747, 1207	3:7–12 579	10:14 748
3:2 1124	3:7–19 . . . . 34, 189	10:19 709
3:6–7 1325	3:8 578	10:19–22 . . . . 698, 731, 827, 963
3:8 1218	3:8–9 1188	10:22 . . . . 757, 899
3:12 1124	3:12 . . . . 457, 1165	10:24–25 . . . . 611, 621
3:15 . . . . 1174, 1175	3:15–19 1165	10:26–27 859
3:16 1161	3:16 1228	10:27 1205
4:3–4 . . . . 691, 791	3:18 1160	10:29 899
4:5 1196	3:18–19 . . . . 1184, 1228	
4:7–8 621		

10:30............1172	1:19.............1008	1:10–11.........828
11:4.............74	2:9.............453, 455, 468, 600,	1:12–18.........601
11:5.............82n92, 85	698, 826, 1132	2:10.............89n109
11:6.............1024	2:11.............213, 1031, 1196,	2:14.............1061, 1062, 1245
11:7.............95	1320	2:17.............43
11:10.............32, 76, 148, 161, 172	2:16.............549	3:20.............916, 1191
11:10–16.......316	2:17.............673, 674	4:1–11..........696
11:13............1277, 1279	2:21–23.........468	4–5..............376, 399
11:13–16.......398	2:25.............1111	5:5..............420, 1255
11:19.............205	3:5..............1293	5:6..............828
11:20............252	3:5–6............199	5:8..............752n708
11:21............406, 409n670, 413	3:7..............57	5:9..............129
11:22............431	3:8..............623	5:9–10...........828, 830
11:23............473	3:15.............407	5:10.............129
11:24–26.......473n79	3:18.............845	5:12.............1256
11:26............473n79	3:19–20..........88	6:6..............1121
11:28............1204	3:20.............101, 119	6:9..............828
12:1–2............407	4:1..............1196	6:9–10............968
12:2..............148, 225, 399, 578	4:9–11...........1141	7:9–10............138
12:4–11..........578	5:2..............1218	7:14.............421, 425, 899
12:5–11..........785	5:4..............1218	8:3–4............752n708
12:9..............1202	5:5..............1172, 1293	8:7..............527n207
12:14–15.........985	5:8..............74, 89n109, 1170	9:1–12...........530
12:16............235		9:16.............1160
12:17............301, 1187	*2 Peter*	9:22–25..........530
12:18–29.......626	1:3–4............1045	12:5.............1161
12:24............78, 98, 748, 970	1:4..............1063, 1196	12:9.............31, 65, 89n109,
12:28............626	1:16.............24, 29n5	1241
12:28–29.......709, 913	1:21.............1168, 1259	12:11.............828
12:29............75, 626, 712, 1205	2:5..............95, 103	13:8.............1256
13:2..............179n267	2:7..............34, 147n228,	14:1.............1132
13:4..............614, 614n399, 972,	181n270	14:4.............1283
1120, 1124	2:7–8............186	14:20............420
13:5..............625	2:9..............103	15:3.............1267
13:8..............457, 1140	2:15.............1061, 1245, 1249	16:21............527n207
13:12............748, 865	3:5–13...........96	18:2–3...........129
13:12–15.........79	3:7..............113	18:21–22........129
13:15............1284	3:12–13..........108	19:2.............89n109
13:17............673n539, 747, 1293	3:13.............32, 103	19:9.............366, 856, 883,
	3:14.............1003	1191
James		19:10............1168
1:2–4............134, 389, 578, 625	*1 John*	19:11–16.......601
1:8..............193n290	1:7..............730, 1128, 1140,	19:13............420
1:17.............457	1223	20:2.............1241
1:18.............1283	1:7–8............867	20:6.............1161
1:27.............646, 653, 678	1:9..............179, 665, 730, 757,	20:10............994
2:1–9............653, 678	870, 1140	20:15............564
2:1–13...........474	1:10.............868	21...............42, 76
2:8..............830, 988n235	2:2..............108	21:1.............42
2:13.............1274	2:3..............537	21:1–8..........509
2:14–26.........728	2:16.............1196	21:2–5..........108
2:21–23.........161	2:25.............1130	21:3.............749n705,
2:22–23.........174	3:6..............1114	815n844, 828,
2:26.............1202	3:8..............1114, 1241	1041, 1045, 1267
3:1..............1230	3:9..............1114	21:3–4a.........440
3:8–9............645	3:15.............623	21:3–4..........229, 712,
3:9..............47, 613	3:19–21.........1223	748–749, 767,
4:1..............1196	3:23.............1277	815, 937
4:2..............92	4:11.............680	21:4.............366, 425
4:5..............1196	4:19–21.........985	21:7.............494n130, 1041
4:7..............1114, 1293	4:20–21.........876	21:10............53
4:11–12.........985	5:4..............296	21:16............828
4:12.............1202	5:5..............1114	21:19–20.......738n677
5:15–16.........1188	5:18.............1114	21:25............42
5:16.............870		21:26............78
5:17.............792	*Jude*	21:27............828
5:19–20.........867	5................1061, 1187, 1256	22...............25, 433
	6–7..............88	22:1.............828, 1256
1 Peter	11...............1061, 1245	22:1–2..........53
1:3–5............407		22:3.............1045
1:14–16.........830	*Revelation*	22:4.............828, 1132
1:16.............1106	1:4..............1132	22:14............198
1:18–19.........551, 757, 845, 864,	1:5..............486	22:15............993
876, 1106	1:10.............906	22:16............1261, 1262